DO NOT REMOVE
THIS BOOK FROM
THE LIBRARY

TWENTIETH-CENTURY WESTERN WRITERS

Twentieth-Century Writers Series

Twentieth-Century Children's Writers

Twentieth-Century Crime and Mystery Writers

Twentieth-Century Science-Fiction Writers

Twentieth-Century Romance and Historical Writers

Twentieth-Century Western Writers

TWENTIETH-CENTURY WESTERN WRITERS

SECOND EDITION

PREFACE TO THE FIRST EDITION
C. L. SONNICHSEN

PREFACE TO THE SECOND EDITION
CHRISTINE BOLD

EDITOR
GEOFF SADLER

St J
St James Press
Chicago and London

© 1991 by St. James Press

For information, write:
ST. JAMES PRESS
233 East Ontario Street
Chicago, Illinois 60611
U.S.A.

or

2–6 Boundary Row
London SE1 8HP
England.

All rights reserved.

British Library Cataloguing in Publication Data
Twentieth-century western writers.—2nd ed.
I. Sadler, Geoff, *1943–*
823.914

ISBN 0912289988
Library of Congress Catalog Card Number: 91 61857

First edition published 1982.

Lit Crit
PS
271
.T84
1991

CONTENTS

3-4-96 Gale LRO JM 136.65

EDITOR'S FOREWORD

The selection of writers included in this book is based upon the recommendations of the advisers listed on page xv.

The entry for each writer in the main part of the book consists of a biography, a bibliography, and a signed critical essay. Living authors were invited to add a comment on their work. The bibliographies list writings according to the categories of western fiction and other publications. In addition, western writing is further subdivided into lists of works published under pseudonyms. Series characters are indicated for novels and short story collections. Original British and United States editions of all books have been listed; other editions are listed only if they are the first editions. As a rule all uncollected western short stories published since the entrant's last collection have been listed; in those cases where a story has been published in a magazine and later in an anthology, the anthology has usually been listed.

Entries include notations of available bibliographies, manuscript collections, and book-length critical studies. Other critical materials appear in the Reading List of secondary works on the genre.

* * *

Some months ago, in the course of a conversation with my friend and fellow western writer B.J. Holmes, he happened to remark on the trouble he'd had in trying to place his work in the United States. Being a fair-minded soul, he allowed that one couldn't reasonably expect anything else—after all, the American West was "their" territory, not ours. As he put it in his role as devil's advocate: "How would we like it if they came over here and started writing about Robin Hood?"

As one who lives no more than a 15-minute drive from Sherwood Forest myself, I could understand his point. The Atlantic Ocean is quite a gulf to bridge when you're writing about something you've never actually seen with your own eyes. Then again, Kevin Costner has just followed a successful western film (*Dances with Wolves*) with tales of Robin Hood (*Prince of Thieves*), and has been over here to shoot it. Add to this the fact that I'm writing from the village where J.T. Edson went to school, and the imagined gulf suddenly becomes much smaller. That it can be bridged has been more than confirmed in the production of this edition, where Americans, British, Canadians, and a lone German have all played their parts, each making a vital contribution to the finished work.

Twentieth-Century Western Writers is intended to include works of western fiction by writers who are, or have been, alive and active during this century. Thus Karl May, Mark Twain, and James Fenimore Cooper, despite being major influences in the field of western writing, are excluded from consideration. The fiction stipulation, while not stated in the title, is nevertheless clear. Western poets, dramatists, and authors of nonfiction are not to be found in these pages unless they have also written fiction which is felt to merit inclusion. Whether this line can be maintained indefinitely, particularly when taking into account the acknowledged significance of "private writing" by western women authors, is open to question—indeed, there has been some latitude as regards Elinore Pruitt Stewart, included here—but for the moment, it will have to serve.

"Western" is, of course, an infinitely variable term, and one which is capable of being stretched to fit any number of definitions. The working definition adopted here is intended to cover novels and stories set in or relating to the American frontier experience of the last century, or works that embody that experience in a modern setting. This meaning embraces classic and formula Westerns, together with modern treatments of the western theme—e.g., McMurtry's *Horseman, Pass By*, or Abbey's *The Brave Cowboy*. It also includes those fictional accounts of domestic life on the frontier which present the female viewpoint of the western experience, as exemplified by the writings of Laura Ingalls Wilder, Mary Hallock Foote, Honoré Willsie Morrow, and, in a more contemporary vein, Tillie Olsen's *Yonnondio*.

At some point a line must be drawn, and the view from this desk is that contemporary novels which happen to be located in the western states, but have no other obvious connection with western writing than their geography, should not be included. Works of fiction that are essentially something other than western—hardboiled detective novels (Chandler, Cain), or picaresque social commentary and satire (Kerouac, Robbins, Brautigan)—are not to be found here, and the reader will search in vain for the writings of Ken Kesey, Douglas Woolf, and Bernard Malamud. It is not enough, in my view, that an author's works explore the theme of rugged individualism versus the corporation, as is the case with the novels of Kesey, for example. If this rule were followed, a large amount of crime and science-fiction writing would qualify, as would most of the legends of the aforementioned Robin Hood. As one who has read the work of most of the above writers with interest and enthusiasm, I can honestly say that their novels never at any time struck me as western literature in even its broadest sense. Rather, these are contemporary novelists, on whom one might reasonably expect to find entries in other reference works. This may seem an unnecessarily narrow interpretation to some, but I suspect that most interested readers opening a book devoted to western writers would not normally expect to find them there. To include a large number of these authors would, I feel, have the effect of stretching the "western" definition to virtual dislocation, and thereby undermining the credibility of the book.

There will doubtless be some anomalies, and at times the line drawn may appear to be somewhat arbitrary. The attempt has been made in this edition to give greater emphasis to the writings of authors from the various ethnic groups—notably Native American, Afro-American, and Hispanic—whose contribution is an essential part of the story of the West. Equally important is the role of the western woman, an aspect justly elaborated by Christine Bold in her preface to this edition, which complements the extensive exploration of the western genre undertaken by the late C.L. Sonnichsen for the first edition 10 years ago. The female viewpoint on the West, so often disregarded in the past, is, I hope, allowed greater expression this time around. In this, as with the other categories already mentioned, I am following the example of Jim Vinson, who in the previous edition examined these wider areas of the western field. No doubt there are some who will regard the changes made as insufficient, but they must be seen as a step in the right direction.

The variety of authors and types of literature covered in this volume—which includes both literary giants, and the writers of routine shoot-'em-ups—is considerable, and is to me one of the book's greatest assets. As a so-called "formula" western writer myself, I feel that this particular sub-genre is needlessly vilified, in a way that detective novels and science fiction are not. The "formula Western," in my view, is just as capable of imaginative treatment, and this edition holds a host of excellent examples. Whatever the literary significance of these practitioners, they and their writings constitute a valid and substantial proportion of the western field, and are represented accordingly. Indeed, in the case of some lesser-known figures, this may be the only place where information on them can be found. Throughout, an effort has been made to retain a balance between extremes and to allow for a broad interpretation embracing several different kinds of western writing.

There are a handful of writers I wished to include, who have for various reasons—lack of author response, difficulty in obtaining the relevant texts, or, less frequently, the lack of an essayist—failed to make this edition. To them I apologise, but can fairly claim to have done my best.

As for the work itself, it's been a tough, demanding task which has occupied me over most of the past 12 months. It's also been a uniquely fascinating, absorbing experience, and one which I feel honoured to have been chosen to undertake. I've had the privilege of working with a team of gifted and enthusiastic advisers and contributors, and had the chance to correspond with many authors whose work I have admired for years. The research has also introduced me to writers previously unfamiliar, but whose work I intended to get to know much better. No matter how heavy the workload has proved at times, it's been a wonderful experience, and one I wouldn't have missed for anything.

Time to express my thanks to the many people whose assistance has been so vital to the success of this project. Sadly, the first person to whom thanks are due is no longer here to receive them. Jim Vinson, who died in late 1990, first introduced me to St. James Press and its publications, and was kind enough to commission my essays for his first edition of *Western Writers* in 1981. It's thanks to him, I feel, that I find myself in the privileged position of editor of this work 10 years later. Although I never had the pleasure of meeting him in person, I often had cause to be grateful for his help and encouragement, and during our correspondence and conversations of the past 10 years felt I had come to know him as a friend. I know he is missed by his colleagues at St. James Press, and I shall certainly never forget him. Thanks for everything, Jim.

Thanks, in large measure, must also go: to Daniel Kirkpatrick, Tracy Chevalier, and Lesley Henderson at St. James Press, who provided advice, friendship, and support at all times.

To David Whitehead and Mike Stotter, whose herculean take-up and execution of critical essays (90 in all), together with their help in other areas, contributed so greatly to the success of this edition.

To Jon Tuska, who has been a tower of strength throughout the past year, and who with his wife Vicki Piekarski provided some first-class essays.

Thanks of a similar kind to Marian Blue and Wayne Ude, whose work ensured the inclusion of some interesting new names.

To Christine Bold, for her magnificent preface, her contributions, and suggestions.

To Susan J. Rosowski, who contributed not only a superb Willa Cather essay, but also a list of expert essay writers for other names.

To Peter Messent, for essays and advice, and for organizing a substantial input to this edition from his colleagues in the American Studies Department at the University of Nottingham.

To Richard W. Etulain, Thomas J. Lyon, R. Jeff Banks, Leslie A. Fiedler, Mike Linaker, and Alan R. Velie, whose encouragement and assistance have been invaluable.

To the late C.L. Sonnichsen, who sadly died just before this edition was published.

To Robert E. Briney, Bill Pronzini (who has acted as an adviser in all but name), Philip J. Harbottle, and Fred Nolan, for services above and beyond the call of duty.

To all the contributors who have helped to make this edition possible. Whether undertaking several essays—as George Kelley, Marcia G. Fuchs, or Dale L. Walker—or a single timely name—as Joseph A. Young, Ann L. Putnam, Ann Romines, and Bernd C. Peyer—each one of them has made a valuable addition to the work, and I thank them accordingly.

To the authors and publishers who have cooperated with us on this project, with special thanks to Claire Scott at Robert Hale.

For use of study facilities, and assistance with research, thanks to: Ed Mollon and his colleagues in Bibliographical Services, County H.Q., Derbyshire Library Service, Matlock; Department of American and Canadian Studies, and University Library, University of Nottingham; University Library, University of Sheffield; Central Reference Library, Sheffield City Libraries, Surrey Street, Sheffield; Mrs. Anna Salkeld and the staff of Wakefield Public Library, Wakefield, Yorkshire; Central Reference Library, Manchester City Library, St. Peter's Square, Manchester; Chesterfield Library, New Beetwell Street, Chesterfield, Derbyshire.

Thanks to B.J. Holmes for his wit and wisdom, which has kept me smiling over the past 12 months.

Last, and by no means least, my thanks to my wife Jennifer, who through all this time proved an invaluable research assistant, and whose help with bibliographical checking, envelope stuffing, telephone calls, postage, and accounts deserves an award of its own.

GEOFF SADLER

PREFACE
to the first edition

Professor George Woodberry of Columbia University once noted in a famous essay that the language and literature of the Western World rest on three main supports: the Bible, the Arthurian legends, and the Norse sagas. They enrich even casual conversation. In the last hundred years, however, a new mythology has come to rival the first three in familiarity and influence—the mythology of the American West—the West That Never Was. Western movies and western books have penetrated to regions where the Norse tales, the legends of King Arthur, and even the Bible are unfamiliar. Western films not only are seen all over Europe; they are manufactured there. Novels about the American West are written in England, Germany, Norway, Sweden, and Italy; cowboy clubs and Indian clubs flourish in Germany and France; Westerners societies are active in England and on the continent. At a news-stand in Switzerland I have seen paperback Westerns in four languages offered for sale, and blue jeans are standard equipment for youths in most European countries, including Czechoslovakia—perhaps even Russia. The lore of the mythical West is part of European culture. The West belongs to everybody.

Fiction about the West, mythical or real, has been with us for a long time, has provided diversion and escape for millions of people all over the world, and is as good a barometer as we have for measuring the impact of the western idea on readers everywhere. It has been an object of interest to historians of culture, so much so that books and articles about it appear with almost frightening frequency. Well over 20 books in at least three languages have discussed the western motion picture, and the western novel has received almost as much attention. The time is ripe for an encyclopedic work telling what can still be learned about earlier writers and their books and assembling the essential facts about those who are now producing.

This sort of information is by no means easy to find and verify, but other major problems arise at the beginning. First, the West has to be defined. Are the Dakotas, Nebraska, and Kansas part of the West? Should the northwestern states be included? Is California, like New York, a separate country attached to the United States? Is Los Angeles culture, as John Milton describes it in *The Novel of the American West* (1980) "a phenomenon of its own, or perhaps a vulgarization of the East"? Does the western novel include fiction about northern Mexico—about Canada—about Alaska—about the westernmost state, Hawaii? The Rocky Mountain states are the core of the area, but where are the outer limits?

Next, the western novel has to be defined. Here one finds himself in even deeper water, for attitudes toward the West and its myth have changed radically over the years and western fiction has changed with them. Furthermore, as the West has become urbanized, fiction has tended to leave the cattle range and the small western town and gravitate toward the big cities. As Larry McMurtry observes in a controversial article in the *Texas Observer* (23 October 1981), "Granting certain grand but eccentric exceptions, virtually the whole of modern literature has been a city literature." The "Western or cowboy myth" has "served its time and lost its potency," and writers, including McMurtry, have left the range. Is there, then, such a thing as the western city novel? Probably not, since big cities are said to be pretty much alike. Is a detective story set in San Francisco (Elizabeth Atwood Taylor, *The Cable Car Murder*, 1981) truly a western novel—or a three-generation chronicle of a dynasty of Dallas merchants (Warren Leslie, *The Starrs of Texas*, 1978)—an international espionage story centered on the atomic activities at Los Alamos (A.E. Maxwell, *Steal the Sun*, 1982)—a novel with supernatural overtones about a little colony of outsiders in the Colorado Rockies (Marilyn Harris, *The Portent*, 1980)—the rape of a Mexican-American community in northern New Mexico by developers, cultists, and fast-food emporiums (John Nichols, *The Nirvana Blues*, 1981, last volume of a trilogy)—a novel of Texas low life set mostly in a Fort Worth cafe (Dan Jenkins, *Baja Oklahoma*, 1981)?

Does a western setting make a western novel? The answer must be a tentative no, but anyone who wants to discuss the subject must first decide where the fences are.

Furthermore, the western novel is not what it was. The years between 1940 and 1980 have seen an almost complete reversal of attitudes toward the West, its history and its meaning. The romanticized view, the view of the western myth, is no longer taken for granted. Mention "the winning of the West" and someone will inquire acidly, "Do you mean the raping of the West?" The loss of faith, general in the world, includes loss of faith in the American pioneers, the developers, and the army units who brought "civilization" to the West. Realism, disillusion, and cynicism darken the prevailing mood. Compare Owen Wister's Virginian with Ben Baker, the repulsive, tobacco-chewing cowboy husband of Melissa in Marguerite Noble's Arizona novel *Filaree* (1979). The gulf between them is as deep as the Grand Canyon. Many critics have observed that there are no heroes any more. They were never as common in western fiction as in western movies, and close study reveals that unheroic, even comic, leading men have always been acceptable in western novels. Since the 1950's, however, viewpoint characters have become more and more flawed, defeated, and even repulsive. A good example is Curly Roy in Bobby Jack Nelson's Texas novel *Brothers* (1975)—self-centered, given to homicidal rages, lawless, savage, a rebel who "could outfight any man, bed down any girl, and tear apart anyone or anything that tried to fence him in." Curly is what the western hero has become.

The image of the West has darkened over the years, but the picture has changed radically in other ways. Division and subdivision, development and decline have been at work, making generalization difficult. When some authority, usually an academic person, asserts that the western novel is thus and so, one has the right to ask, "Which western novel?" They come in all sizes, shapes, and colors.

In the beginning there was some uniformity. Bret Harte introduced the American public to California with "The Luck of Roaring Camp" in 1868 and popularized the upside-down morality which became a characteristic of the genre, including the figure of the good-bad man and the prostitute with the heart of gold. Helen Hunt Jackson (*Ramona*, 1885) and Adolph F. Bandelier (*The Delight Makers*, 1890) talked about the western Indian. Alfred Henry Lewis (*Wolfville*, 1897) used Tombstone, Arizona, scenes and characters, accepted Harte's skewed morality and invented the dialect which became more or less standard in later novels. At the same time the dime novel was turning to western characters, beginning with Buffalo Bill Cody, and making Buck Taylor, an actor in Cody's Wild West Show, the first cowboy hero. The western story, as an international audience came to know it, was waiting to be born.

Owen Wister acted as midwife in 1902 with the publication of *The Virginian*. The peculiar ethical system known as the Code of the West was a motivating force in Wister's story, and the West itself, as a maker of men, was played up. The first walkdown (confrontation with pistols) on the streets of a western town closed the action. Cowboy character was crystallized in the persons of Jeff, the Virginian, and his friend Lin McLean. Important also were Wister's background and education. A Harvard graduate, he wrote like the gentleman he was and is said to have brought the Western "up to *Atlantic Monthly* standards." Thanks, at least in part, to him, the western novel after 1902 followed two divergent paths—the high road of well-written and well-plotted stories, often appearing in leading American magazines, and the low road of standard, formula, or commercial fiction exemplified in thousands of pulp-magazine stories and popular novels. The bulk of western fiction published during the first half of the century kept to the low road, but between high and low there were many intermediate types. Zane Grey, for example, published his first novel, *The Heritage of the Desert*, in 1910, and dozens of skillful writers—Ernest Haycox, Luke Short, Alan LeMay, and Will Henry/Clay Fisher, for example—traveled in his footsteps.

The specifications for high-road, middle-road, and low-road novels included, often enough to be thought of as a rule, a hero with a flaw or major fault, a "morally ambiguous character," as John Cawelti describes him (*Focus on the Western*, edited by Jack Nachbar, 1974); a sweet, pure, and unspoiled heroine; and a vicious villain whose destruction brings matters back into equilibrium. The plot begins with confrontation and ends in a violent showdown, but the violence is necessary for good to triumph over evil and is regarded as a cleansing of the temple. For this reason *Time* magazine in 1960 in a much-quoted article called "The Western: The American Morality Play" noted that the good guys always win; the bad guys always lose.

A morality play, of course, is symbolic of reality—does not strive for realism—and although the mythical West resembled the real West, the elements were selected and recombined to create a region that was really out of time and space. Writers of "Westerns" have always been proud to point out that their stories were "authentic"—accurate in detail. Louis L'Amour and Will Henry think of themselves as historical novelists, and their novels are indeed well researched, but the stories are so firmly rooted in the conventions of the Western that they come closer to epic or romance than to realism. It is significant that a writer of Westerns need never have been in the United States. Karl May did very well in 19th-century Germany without ever seeing the Pecos country of which he wrote. A century later J.T. Edson sits in his study at Melton Mowbray, Leicestershire, England, and chronicles the adventures of the Floating Outfit in the Texas Panhandle. When he began his writing career in 1961, he had never been to the United States. He crosses the Atlantic every year now to attend the annual meetings of the Western Writers of America, but he does not visit the range of the Floating Outfit. He doesn't have to. He couldn't if he wanted to. It is all in his head. Likewise, the Englishman Terry Harknett, the creator of Edge, finds the mythical West in his imagination. He doesn't even come to meetings.

Why do Americans and others keep the mythical West going when the reality is close at hand? The answer is, they need it. The West that Never Was offers more than amusement for an idle hour. As Jack Nachbar phrases it, the Western "defined for all Americans their traditional ethics, values, and sources of national pride" (*Focus on the Western*, 1974). This is a function of myth the world over, and for half a century the Western did it for

Americans, and for all others interested. The frontier which the myth defined or distorted lasted only about 25 years (1865 to 1890), but it provided something Americans desperately needed—a heroic age. Every nation or ethnic group wants to look back to the deeds of mighty ancestors, and the frontier West was all the Americans had to serve the purpose, so they made the best of it. When the reality was not satisfactory, as in the case of Wyatt Earp, they changed the facts to fit the specifications.

The foundations of the Western were laid between 1900 and 1918, but after World War I building styles began to change. New and better writers appeared. "Slick" magazines, like the *Saturday Evening Post*, featured serialized Westerns. Harvey Fergusson (*Wolf Song*, 1927), Eugene Manlove Rhodes (*Pasó por Aquí*, 1926), and Conrad Richter (*The Sea of Grass*, 1937) were at work on the high road. The top middle-road professionals—William MacLeod Raine, Eugene Cunningham, Max Brand, Charles Alden Seltzer, W.C. Tuttle, B.M. Bower, and a dozen more—were in full production, and the pulp magazines flourished and prospered. Range novels were still popular but the field was expanding to include a wide variety of backgrounds and character types: miners, peace officers, railroad builders, mountain men, army officers, Indian leaders, Pinkerton detectives, bandits, gamblers, and even, as time went on, preachers, editors, and traveling salesmen. Often a vein of humor came to the surface, and a surprising number of characters were created for laughs.

Before the century was half over, however, the old days and ways were coming to a close. Since the 1890's disillusion had been growing in the United States, a legacy from earlier European thinkers and writers. The pioneers and frontiersmen were no longer heroes or bringers of civilization; they were thieves and exploiters with grimy hands. The Indians were no longer bloodthirsty savages; they were noble human beings, wronged and outraged by the greedy white man. The westward movement was a piratical enterprise which deprived Indians and Mexicans of their birthright.

The Indians found defenders first. Harold Bell Wright gave the Apaches a voice as early as 1923 in *The Mine with the Iron Door*. Edgar Rice Burroughs idealized Geronimo in *The War Chief* (1927); Oliver La Farge searched the soul of a young Navajo in *Laughing Boy* (1929); Will Levington Comfort did the same for Apache Chief Mangus Colorado in *Apache* (1931); Mary Austin gave the Papagos credit for a sense of humor in *One-Smoke Stories* (1934); and Elliott Arnold in *Blood Brother* (1947) presented Cochise as a great and noble leader, a statesman, a poet, and a philosopher, a proud and sensitive man much superior to his white antagonists. By 1962 when Jane Barry published *A Time in the Sun*, few Americans doubted that the Indians were right and the white man was wrong, and the way was prepared for N. Scott Momaday's Pulitzer-Prize-winning *House Made of Dawn* (1968) and for Forrest Carter's *Watch for Me on the Mountain* (1978), which portrays Geronimo as a heaven-sent leader with supernatural powers, in a class with Beowulf, Siegfried, and the Cid. National guilt feelings were not strong enough to suggest giving the country back to the Indians, but they did lead to the payment of many millions of conscience money to these natives and to new directions in western writing.

A similar transformation was waiting for the Mexican, downgraded in American fiction since 1846. Harvey Fergusson had written sympathetically about New Mexican Latinos in *The Blood of the Conquerors* in 1921, but he had seen their plight as hopeless. Robert Herrick in *Waste* (1924) mourned the decay of village honesty and simplicity and the triumph of American materialism. Thanks to writers like Raymond Otis (*Little Valley*, 1937) and Frank Applegate (*Native Tales of New Mexico*, 1934), the Mexican-American began to be a person in the 1930's, but he had to wait until the 1960's to become an important person. José Antonio Villareal (*Pocho*, 1959) is credited with being the first Chicano novelist, but a number of important writers have seized his torch, among them Richard Vasquez (*Chicano*, 1970), Raymond Barrio (*The Plum Plum Pickers*, 1971), and Rudolfo A. Anaya (*Bless Me, Ultima*, 1972). These men are certainly western novelists but not by the earlier definitions.

The role of blacks in the westward movement has also had an increasing amount of attention, but their appearance as focal characters in western fiction has been limited. Black sharecroppers were occasionally featured (John W. Wilson, *High John the Conqueror*, 1934), but the first appearance of a black soldier as a principal in a Western came with James Warner Bellah's *Sergeant Rutledge* in 1960. Fictional and documentary studies of black pioneers in the West multiplied after the publication in 1965 of *The Negro Cowboys* by Philip Durham and Everett L. Jones. Clay Fisher published his novel *Black Apache* in 1976.

As these new voices became stronger, some of the older ones grew weaker. The pulp magazines declined in the 1950's and almost disappeared. Production of conventional Westerns was severely curtailed, though a hard core of seasoned veterans—Louis L'Amour, Wayne D. Overholser, Lewis B. Patten, Nelson Nye, Frank O'Rourke, to name a few—continued to produce, and energetic new writers appeared. The traditional Western never died—never came anywhere near dying—but it did suffer shrinkage and had to make concessions to popular taste, including the demand for sex and violence. It was a sign of the times, of a craving for what the older authors offered, that popular novels of the 1930's, 1940's, and 1950's were revived and reprinted in quantities and made up a substantial part of the paperback offerings in the 1970's.

A sign of the times also was the rise of satirical, burlesque, or humorous Westerns—proof that the traditional Western was under fire. *The Ballad of Cat Ballou*, by Roy Chanslor (1956) was an early example. For two decades after that, mocking the Western seemed to many authors and movie producers a good way to go. Titles included such satires as Thomas Berger's *Little Big Man* (1964), Charles Portis's *True Grit* (1968), Bill Gulick's *Liveliest Town in the West* (1969), John Templeton's *Charlie Eagletooth's War* (1969), and *Blazing Saddles* (1974) by Andrew Bergman.

The conventional Western was not only spoofed and ridiculed and parodied; it was elbowed aside by new developments, beginning with a series of pessimistic treatments of the cowboy and his work. Edward Abbey in *The Brave Cowboy* (1956) demonstrated that there was no place in the 20th century for the old-time, independent product of the great open spaces. In 1961 Larry McMurtry in *Horseman, Pass By* (*Hud* in the movie version) concentrated on a young Texan without soul or morals who raped the black cook in the presence of the teenage narrator and killed his stepfather in order to take over the ranch. Nobody called him to account.

Just a year earlier Max Evans published *The Rounders*, on the surface a hilarious story about two cowboys at a lonely line camp and in town, actually a close look at two ineffectual human beings who can't get ahead. J.P.S. Brown's *Jim Kane* (1970) followed the fortunes of a conscientious cattle buyer in northern Mexico who got his livestock to Chihuahua but was cheated out of his profits by his crooked employers. William Decker in *To Be a Man* (1967) showed that the values of the honest cowhand were archaic in the 20th-century West. Robert Flynn's *North to Yesterday* (1967) focused on a cattle-country Don Quixote who tried in vain to duplicate the cattle drives of the 1880's. Only Elmer Kelton (*The Time It Never Rained*, 1973) found the men and mores of the early-day cattle kingdom still alive here and there in Texas.

The final transformation—perversion might be a better word—of the Western was the birth of the adult Western, known to the publishing industry as the "wicked" or "porno" Western. *Time* magazine had noted the existence of the type and called it by name in 1959 ("The American Morality Play," 30 March), but it really began to flourish in the 1970's. Its elements were brutality for its own sake and explicit sex in large quantities. The paperback editors discovered that there was a tremendous appetite for these commodities and began producing them for the mass market. Most of the books came in series named for the central character, and a house name was used for the author. Since titles in a given series appeared as often as once a month, a battery of writers was needed to turn them out. For money, established craftsmen toiled anonymously to give bloodthirsty or sex-starved readers what they wanted. One of them regrouped and started a series of his own (Foxx) when he found out where his interests lay.

Excessive violence appeared early in novels about the Apache campaigns as writers described in detail the tortures inflicted on captives, and series novels (Fargo, Sundance) featuring violence appeared in the early 1970's. A new day dawned, however, in 1971 with the publication of the first Edge novel—*Edge: The Loner*. Captain Joshua Hedges, home from the Civil War, finds the men of his former command have evened scores with him by murdering his crippled younger brother. He tracks them down one by one and kills them as painfully as possible. Edge was conceived by Terry Harknett, an Englishman writing under the name of George G. Gilman. His publishers warned, "Here is mean, bone-chilling, raw stuff . . . not for the faint-hearted reader." British readers were not faint-hearted. They organized a George G. Gilman fan club and praised the Edge books as "a real breakthrough." The water never ran low in Harknett's well. Number 34 in the Edge series was published in 1980, with worldwide sales of 4,000,000 copies. He kept on writing and started two new series. J.T. Edson's violent Westerns, written in England, became almost as popular as Harknett's.

British readers apparently wanted their violence straight, with no time wasted on heavy sex. American readers, on the other hand, seemed to prefer raw sex with only a seasoning of violence. The Captain Gringo series, with the house name Ramsey Thorne on the cover, is credited with pioneering the wicked Western in the United States in 1975. Publishers immediately saw a golden opportunity, and new series publications sprang up in rapid succession. The John Slocum series bore the name of Jake Logan; Shelter, of Paul Leder; Raider, of J.D. Hardin; Lashtrow, of Roe Richmond; Trailsman, of Jon Sharpe; The Executioner, of Don Pendleton; Faro Blake, of Zeke Masters; Longarm, of Tabor Evans. The list was still growing in the early 1980's. Bedroom scenes were frequent and detailed. Older readers shook their heads in amazement as they contemplated what had happened to the once-righteous Western.

They had reason to be astonished at other developments in the field. One was the appearance of "faction" (a combination of fiction and fact) in such novels as Ron Hansen's *The Desperadoes* (1979) and Robert Houston's *Bisbee 17* (1979). Tremendously popular were western romances by a long list of authors, mostly women, with Janet Dailey (*This Calder Sky*, 1981) and Jeanne Williams (*The Valient Women*, 1980) in the lead, with sales in the millions. Detective stories (Tony Hillerman, *People of Darkness*, 1980) were popular and "thrillers" (stories of suspense, catastrophe, ordeal, international intrigue, the supernatural) published in the late 1970's and early

1980's filled an eight-foot shelf. Ingenious plot devices abounded, for example, an invasion of vampire bats from Mexico carrying bubonic plague to the Navajo Reservation in Arizona in Martin Cruz Smith's *Nightwing* (1977), and the maneuvers of secret agents at the Los Alamos nuclear laboratory in A.E. Maxwell's *Steal the Sun* (1982). The list would include three-generation family chronicles, caravans moving west to California and Oregon, drug smuggling on the Mexican border, Indians trying to adjust to the white man's world, Texas politics, homosexuals in the cities, college athletics, the oil business, the Mexican Revolution. These and many more western themes were exploited by good writers in the 1960's, 1970's, and 1980's. There was even a vein of true humor in such novels as Bonner McMillion's *So Long at the Fair* (1964), Gary Jennings's *The Terrible Teague Branch* (1975), Darby Foote's *Baby Love and Casey Blue* (1975), John Reese's *Omar, Fats, and Trixie* (1976), and William Brinkley's *Peeper* (1981).

Apart from all these, and perhaps above them, stand a group of superior novelists, beloved by the academic communities, whose works are Westerns only in the fact that the western environment is a shaping force in human character and destiny. William P. Bloodworth ("The Literary Extensions of the Formula Western," *Western American Literature*, Winter 1980) describes some of them as "Literary Westerns" and includes Walter Van Tilburg Clark's *The Ox-Bow Incident* (1940), Frederick Manfred's *Riders of Judgment* (1957), Max Evans's *The Rounders* (1960), Larry McMurtry's *Horseman, Pass By* (1961), Thomas Berger's *Little Big Man* (1964), Charles Portis's *True Grit* (1968), and R.G. Vliet's *Rockspring* (1974).

John Milton (*The Novel of the American West*, 1980) takes a different approach to the superior group. He discusses 14 western novelists who, in his view, can claim "high seriousness and literary quality," among them Willa Cather, Oliver La Farge, Conrad Richter, Vardis Fisher, Frank Waters, Paul Horgan, and A.B. Guthrie, Jr.

To these lists might be added the names of important west coast writers like H.L. Davis and Gertrude Atherton, and others from the Rocky Mountain region and the Southwest: Dorothy M. Johnson, William Eastlake, George Sessions Perry, William Humphrey, Glendon Swarthout, Benjamin Capps, James Gilmore Rushing, Douglas C. Jones, Oakley Hall, and Richard Martin Stern. New writers with reputations still to be solidified would include Norman Zollinger, Neal Claremon, Alan Harrington, Bruce McGinnis, Earl Shorris, and 50 more.

Without doubt western fiction has come a long way in a century and has moved far from its roots. It has gone from illusion to disillusion, from a few types to many, from the country to the city, from easy imitation to literary competence. It is not easy to define or to locate, and its moods and ramifications continue to multiply. In the midst of all the change and confusion, however, the novel of the West continues to be written and read. Even the traditional Western, changed sometimes beyond recognition, is alive and apparently sound at heart. It remains to be seen whether it will be choked and destroyed by excrescenses like the porno Western, or will win free of them, keeping the western myth relatively unchanged. It seems safe to predict, however, that the world will want to keep the West That Is, the West That Was, and the West That Never Was for the foreseeable future.

C.L. SONNICHSEN

PREFACE
to the second edition

Sunday, August 3 [1862] . . . We passed by the train I have just spoken of. They had just buried the babe of the woman who died days ago, and were just digging a grave for another woman that was run over by the cattle and wagons when they stampeded yesterday. She lived twenty-four hours, she gave birth to a child a short time before she died. The child was buried with her. She leaves a little two year old girl and a husband. They say he is nearly crazy with sorrow . . .

—Jane Gould Tortillot,
"Touring from Mitchell, Iowa, to California, 1862"

She was the Walking Woman, and no one knew her name . . . she was a woman, not old, who had gone about alone in a country where the number of women is as one in fifteen. She had eaten and slept at the herder's camps, and laid by for days at one-man stations whose masters had no other touch of human kind than the passing of chance prospectors, or the halting of the tri-weekly stage. She had been set on her way by teamsters who lifted her out of white, hot desertness and put her down at the crossing of unnamed ways, days distant from anywhere. And through all this she passed unarmed and unoffended. I had the best testimony to this, the witness of the men themselves. I think they talked of it because they were so much surprised at it. It was not, on the whole, what they expected of themselves.

—Mary Austin,
"The Walking Woman" (1909)

One other person whom I knew at this time stands out unforgettably—Little Wolf, the Cheyenne chief. This Little Wolf had been a great leader, and his name is in a dozen history books—though his squaw did our washing.

—Nannie T. Alderson and Helena Huntington Smith,
A Bride Goes West (1942)

These are voices of the American West, though they do not tell the stories made most familiar by books, cinema, and television. The first author is a woman travelling west on a wagon train, the second a professional writer of fiction, and the third a ranching wife telling her autobiography to her editor. Each of them looks at the West from the perspective of female experience which, in the first and third cases, is rooted in the familial, domestic context. They are typical of women writing about the West, not all telling the same story by any means, but consistently challenging received images of the wild West as the site of shoot-outs, rustling, lynching, and manly bravery. In the most widely known body of western fiction, women conventionally figure as objects or passive beings: characters to be saved from capture or some other wilderness danger, to be wooed by the hero, to be protected from the frontier environment for which they are unfitted by their gentility and fragility. Or, in more displaced form, the female presence emerges in the metaphor of the land as woman (what Annette Kolodny calls "the central metaphor of American pastoral experience"). Yet, since the earliest days of white settlement in America, women have been writing in English about their experiences of the frontier, as it moved westward from New England to California and back to the Rocky Mountains, expressing their subjectivity as authors, their powers as creators of fiction and nonfiction, and their agency as human beings. All that remains readily available and widely known from this rich and diverse output are a few names: Willa Cather comes most readily to mind; sometimes Mari Sandoz and Mary Austin are recalled. The result is that a formative myth of American culture—the myth of the frontier—excludes the female point of view and displaces female figures to the margins of national mythology.

Tracking the causes of the invisibility of women's western writings leads to intensely complicated matters of the educational, political, legal, and cultural positioning of women in various periods of U.S. history. Until recent times, patriarchal institutions discouraged women from seeking public status for their writings, insisting on the domestic limitations of the female sphere, in contrast to the professional, public, and propertied authority of men. The more the book and mass media industries propagated male versions of the frontier, the more that model became the dominant paradigm shaping expectation and popular demand. Women could and did tell stories of western adventure, but without encouragement from the dominant culture, many of these writings remained unpublished, or they were published but did not palpably influence the genre, or they achieved bestselling status and literary attention in their day but were subsequently erased from literary history. The differences between the women's and the men's perspectives which emerge from these, still only partially recovered, writings can be accounted for by gender differences in cultural conditioning; another school of thought would argue from biological determinism, that women's forms of expression are intrinsically different from men's.

Whatever larger frameworks of explanation seem convincing, one apparatus crucial to the formation and reception of literary history is the reference work which classifies, defines, and selectively preserves writings. "Every archive is an ideology," said the French theorist Michel Foucault, recognizing that the acts of inclusion and exclusion involved in the creation of institutional memory are politically interested. On the one hand, archival priorities are shaped by social power structures; on the other, they influence the development of those structures. In the case of the reference work, some authors are empowered with visibility and others rendered extinct. The archive, the encyclopedia, the compendium, the reference work are repositories of information which shape the stories we tell ourselves about our past and present cultures; the more inclusive these works are, the more richly diverse is our narrative of literary production.

What cultural work does *Twentieth-Century Western Writers* effect, then, for the Western? The very appearance of the first edition in 1982 increased the legitimacy of the genre, partly by signalling the quantity of output and partly by implying—by their very conjoining—some relationship between the popular, formulaic fictions and works of a more individualistic cast. The emphasis on diversity, through time and across types of production, was signalled most clearly by C.L. Sonnichsen's preface to the first edition. Roaming over a vast territory of names, works, and periods, Sonnichsen shapes the inchoate contents of the book into a narrative of 19th-century development and 20th-century diversity. There are two main plots of Sonnichsen's story: the lamentable increase in cynicism, violence, and sexual titillation which befell the mass-produced Western after World War II, and the more complex and productive interrogations of the 19th-century Anglo-Saxon myth of the frontier by Native American, Mexican-American, and African-American writers in the 20th-century. Yet for all the range and diversity of Sonnichsen's account, there is one notable omission: the story of women's contribution to western letters. The preface mentions individual women writers, but it does not recognize them as a distinct category, except for the very brief notice given western romances of recent times. That edition's entries echo this pattern of emphasis and omission: less than 10% of the entries deal with women.

There is another way of telling the story of women's western writings, and in several respects this second edition of *Twentieth-Century Western Writers* encourages such a revisionist narrative. One of the explicit projects of this edition was to give increased attention to women's western contributions in the 20th century. In order to appreciate some of the significance of this expanded material, we have to move beyond the periodization of this reference work and resituate 20th-century developments within a larger chronology. The incomplete narrative which results at least questions the dominant construction of the Western's literary history.

Until very recently, the generally accredited account of western adventure fiction began with the Leatherstocking Tales (1823–41) of James Fenimore Cooper, traced their influence on the mass-produced dime novels of 1860–1900—especially as transmitted through one of the earliest dime novels, Edward S. Ellis's *Seth Jones; or, The Captives of the Frontier* (1860)—and climaxed with Owen Wister's *The Virginian* (1902), the novel most often represented as the dawn of the modern Western. This account appears, in considerably greater detail than this, in such authoritative—and still immensely valuable—readings of the West as Henry Nash Smith's *Virgin Land* (1950) and John Cawelti's *Adventure, Mystery, and Romance* (1976). From this literary history, the Western's formulaic pattern is posited as a clash between wilderness and civilization on the frontier, mediated and ultimately resolved by a hero who is able in both spheres. Driving this action is a political imperative to harmonize the oppositions of West and East, with some of the turns and twists in the formula's development emerging from different efforts at resolution. Also complicating the literary historical account are various popular authors' rebellions against the constraints of formulaic production, as they worked to insert their own personal and ideological agendas into the adventure form. Ultimately, however, these subversive efforts are contained by the dominant paradigm of capture, flight, and pursuit which encodes a celebration of male heroism.

In contrast to the limited rebellions of male authors, women's western adventure fiction challenges the dominant formula in more decisive ways. Indeed, many women authors represented the fundamental East-West relationship very differently from their more famous male counterparts. Consider, for example, Catharine Maria Sedgwick's *Hope Leslie* (1827), one of the earliest frontier novels by an American woman, set in Puritan Massachusetts. There are melodrama, undigestible coincidence, and romantic entanglement enough to situate this novel within the category of adventure Westerns. In one regard, however, it is unconventional: it explicitly contrasts itself with James Fenimore Cooper's *The Last of the Mohicans* (1826), the second of the Leatherstocking Tales. While Cooper constructs a scenario of white civilization versus Native savagery mediated by Natty Bumppo, the white man with Native gifts, Sedgwick exposes the levels of savagery in white society, the complicated codes, traditions, and resentments affecting Native relations, and positions between them a noble Pequod maiden, Magawisca, who has been partly raised by Whites but maintains her allegiance to her father's decimated tribe. In stark contrast to Natty Bumppo, Magawisca is torn apart—literally and metaphorically—by her frontier position: at the symbolic and melodramatic climax of the novel, her arm is severed accidentally by her father, as she intervenes to save the life of the beloved white hero. Although this novel was a bestseller in its day, it did not enjoy the influence of Cooper's vision and dropped from sight early in the 20th century, to be recovered recently by Rutgers University Press in its American Women Writers series. Encrusted as the novel is with 19th-century literary conventions, many of its messages about frontier violence, race relations, and gender roles seem modern; only in the later 20th century does this emphasis on the loss and damage undergirding conquest of the wilderness become insistent.

Although it would be difficult to argue identifiable influence, a similar vision is articulated in Ann S. Stephens's *Malaeska, the Indian Wife of the White Hunter*, originally serialized in 1839 but most famous in its republished format of 1860, as number one of *Beadle's Dime Novels*, the series which initiated cheap, massmarket novels in America. There is another tale of unfulfilled possibilities embedded in this story. *Malaeska* tells, again in melodramatic tones, of a Native American woman who has been married, secretly, by a white hunter whose origins turn out to be aristocratic New York. When he is killed in battle—by Native antagonists—Malaeska flees to New York City in search of sustenance for herself and her baby boy. The results are cataclysmic: the boy is abducted by the white grandparents who conceal from him the truth of his parentage, Malaeska flees to the wilderness for her life, and when, many years later, the son—now a young man—discovers his maternity, he jumps to his death before her eyes. The final scenes of the novel record Malaeska's death on her son's grave and his fiancée's retreat from the world to religious chastity. Implicit messages of both racial and gender impotence are suggested in the comment on Malaeska's self-sacrifice: "It was her woman's destiny, not the more certain because of her savage origin. Civilization does not always reverse this mournful picture of womanly self-abnegation." Again, this model had few imitators. On the heels of Stephens's work in the Beadle series came Edward S. Ellis's *Seth Jones*; itself a simplified adaptation of James Fenimore Cooper, its narrative of battle, captivity, rescue, and triumphal marriage set the tone for the popular Western over the decades.

These two examples are symptomatic of a little noted strain within 20th-century western adventure fiction: the adaptations and subversions of women writers. Not all contemporary women writers interrogate the conventions of the formulaic Western; but entries in this volume repeatedly demonstrate that even women who write in the recognizable accents of melodrama and sentimentalism inflect their narratives in unconventional ways. B.M. Bower emphasizes humour, community, and female adventure over the heroic individualism of male characters; similarly, Katharine Burt centres on women's responses to the frontier, Loula Grace Erdman stresses family experiences, and Jean Stafford focuses on children's perceptions of the West. Ann Ahlswede challenges the harmonious closure of the formulaic Western, Jane Barry eschews stereotypes to invoke multicultural issues, and Mary Hallock Foote accents her ostensibly happy endings with loss and regret. Most striking of all is Frances McElrath, who deconstructs Wister's model of western harmony to expose the disastrous clash between eastern woman and western man on the frontier. Although all these writings are ultimately contained within formulaic dimensions, none of them supports the imperialist story of America, as a civilization triumphantly conquering a savage wilderness, in the way that the fictions of Owen Wister, Zane Grey, and Louis L'Amour can be understood to do. Not having a clear political, nationalistic usefulness may well have contributed to the relative invisibilty of such female authors.

Not that all women authors (nor all men, of course) wrote within the formulaic action of adventure stories. Another strain of women's writings portrays the frontier West in less melodramatic, more meditative accents. A distinctive characteristic of this realist project is the central positioning of women within the frontier scene, with all the attendant emphases of that orientation. In 1839, for example, Caroline Kirkland published *A New Home—Who'll Follow?*, a fictionalized account of her experiences in frontier Michigan. Her account is an avowed corrective to the fanciful portraits of popular male writers such as James Hall:

> When I first "penetrated the interior," (to use an indigenous phrase) all I knew of the wilds was from Hoffman's tour or Captain Hall's "graphic" delineations: I had some floating idea of "driving a barouche-and-four anywhere through the oak-openings"—and seeing "the murdered Banquos of the forest" haunting the scenes of their departed strength and beauty. But I confess, these pictures, touched by the glowing pencil of fancy, gave me but incorrect notions of a real journey through Michigan.

The "real Michigan" turns out to be a place measured by and focused on domestic pursuits. Kirkland's most mischievous humour and most artful portraiture are spent on her housekeeping calamities and on the women settlers' efforts at constructing female community through "the Montacute Female Beneficent [*sic*] Society." Even when she inserts conventional romances of young and unrequited love into her account, she dwells on these Easterners' inadequate attempts at frontier homemaking. From this work's perspective, the frontier scene is not the polar opposite of the domestic scene, as so many stories of range and wilderness insist. Rather, drama, interest, and suspense derive from the yoking together of wilderness and domesticity, isolation and community, the hardships and the bonding undergone by women in the undeveloped West. This domestic orientation issues in one further act of community: Kirkland is explicitly passing on utilitarian tips to potential emigrants while entertaining them.

Kirkland's 19th-century feminization of the frontier is refracted in and developed by diverse voices in the 20th century. One of the most distinctive is Mary Austin's, whose short stories create a continuum between the female and the desert West in subtle and harmonious ways. Female presence is embodied either by narrators who observe more than they act; or—as in "The Walking Woman," quoted above—by silent figures who develop a symbiotic, healing relationship with the landscape through which they move; or by the landscape itself. As in Georgia O'Keeffe's paintings, hills fold in womanly curves, earth announcing the maternal principle in its very shapes. Austin's desert is not the site of titanic struggles between man and an alien, life-threatening environment (as recorded by Frank Norris, Eugene Manlove Rhodes, and Zane Grey, among others). There is drama and suspense in her scene, but scaled down to the patterns of climate, plant life, animals, and insects. Only those who are watchful and respectful of the desert's conditions—Native people and women, according to Austin's vision—can appreciate the fascinating shifts and fortunes of desert life. Only those who have been marginalized and rendered invisible are sensitive to the drama of the overlooked.

The most famous western woman's voice of the 20th century is Willa Cather, celebrant of womanly heroism in the farming West. A recent sign of Cather's eminence is her inclusion, as one of a handful of women authors, in the 60 volumes of the new "Great Books" series, a project that purports to select the finest literature of all ages and all cultures. What seem to account for Cather's reputation are the lyricism of her prose, the breadth of her epic vision, and the vigour of her female portraits, from the heroic farmer Alexandra of *O Pioneers!* (1913) to the defiantly unconventional Ántonia of *My Ántonia* (1918). Cather's West is strongly matriarchal, in the agricultural and economic power seized by women, in the feminizing of the fruitful landscape, and in the matrilineal inheritance created by these two forces together, as exemplified by the ending of *O Pioneers!*: "Fortunate country, that is one day to receive hearts like Alexandra's into its bosom, to give them out again in the yellow wheat, in the rustling corn, in the shining eyes of youth!"

In the wake of Cather's achievements, as women have found more strength and confidence in the field of literary production, some writers have challenged the received mythologies of the West more fundamentally than Cather. Her celebrations of the frontier can be read as simple inversion of the dominant model, with women occupying the strong, individualistic, heroic role conventionally reserved for men. To that extent, her work can be understood to negotiate with the dominent tradition of western narratives, rather than to break with it. A more radical rewriting of the West is conducted by Meridel Le Sueur. A radical feminist, Le Sueur portrays both the natural fecundity of the rural West and the political action of the urban West as quintessentially dependent on female communities. Moreover, the narrative strategies with which she articulates this vision defy the plots and patterns of the conventional novel: a patriarchal construct, in Le Sueur's formulation. Native writers such as Leslie Marmon Silko and Louise Erdrich take this search for new narrative forms further. Working with their triple inheritance of indigenous cultural beliefs, experience as women, and intimate knowledge of the western environment, they create works which defy categorization. Their stories are narrated by a community of voices which erase artificial barriers between the secular and the spiritual or the physical and the supernatural. Although the distance from Kirkland in the early 19th century to these Native prose-poets of the late 20th century is immense, their work can be appreciated as the fulfilment of her project, to defy received wisdom and easy fictions about the West.

Of a different order again from either formulaic or literary Westerns are those private writings by women most profoundly complicated by silence. These are the journals, diaries, letters, autobiographies, reminiscences, and oral narratives, often generalized under the term "life writing," many of which are only now being published for the first time. These various forms of expression should not be conflated: letter-writing is a semi-public activity involving a kind of social contract not necessarily in operation in diary-keeping; the memoir or reminiscence is spoken or penned after a lapse of time, in contrast to the immediacy of the daily journal. What all women's life writings have in common, however, is their privileging of the first-person female voice and its personal, quotidian, domestic orbit. This focus constitutes a profound shift in a genre conventionally defined by its investment in men's outdoor adventures. (Men wrote personal narratives of the West, too, but their significance is different: they occupied a smaller role in the array of outlets available to male writers; moreover, accounts such as Andy Adams's *The Log of a Cowboy* of 1903 do not break so completely with the dominant western pattern, in that they centre a male figure outdoors, involved in the male companionship of ranch work.)

The angle of vision in women's personal narratives is similar to that in women's western fiction—indeed, much of that fiction grew out of private writings. Diaries, letters, and autobiographies delineate the frontier in terms of family life, the economic interdependence of neighbours, and the material culture resulting from individual and group initiatives; from this perspective, individualism, outdoor trials, and unexpected adventures are negative qualities. The first epigraph to this preface exemplifies such a revisioning of the frontier scene. A stampede, classic occasion for high drama in western fiction and film, figures in Jane Gould Tortillot's account as a tragic accident which fragments the family, turns birth into death, and causes unbearable sorrow. More generally, these life writings support Annette Kolodny's argument that the relationship between the female speaking subject and the land is conceived not in terms of the psycho-sexual fantasies of rape and conquest familiar from male-ordered works, but in terms of fertility, sustenance, and nurture—or the absence of these qualities. This perspective is evident in Elinore Pruitt Stewart's letters from

Wyoming to the woman who was her former employer, published as *Letters of a Woman Homesteader* (1914). Stewart advocates strongly that women should empower themselves by homesteading their own land, as she did even after her happy marriage to a western rancher. Stewart's vision is almost a westernized version of Virginia Woolf's "a room of one's own": if women tend the land, it will supply the means and space for independence and privacy. Finally, the personal orientation of these life writings issues not in a limited apoliticism but in a rewriting of political events and public history as filtered through personal experience, woven into the day-to-day fabric of living. Nannie Alderson, for example—as the opening quotation from her autobiography suggests—formed her impressions of the Cheyenne not from experience or reports of combat with them, but from their impingement on her daily tasks. Her Native figures are neither noble savages nor howling beasts; they are sometimes pitiful, sometimes tragic and occasionally glorious human beings.

Most revealing of all, perhaps, is what these life writings leave out. Even in these relatively unmediated reflections, unconstrained by the expectations of genre, public reception, or aesthetic standards, writers repeatedly conform to the same taboos, euphemisms, and silences. Most striking is the silence surrounding the experience of pregnancy. Again and again, in the overland diaries collected by Lillian Schlissel in *Women's Diaries of the Westward Journey* (1982), for example, births are reported without preamble or allusion to the immense physical discomforts these pregnant trekkers must have suffered. For all the obsessive detail attending the work, sights, and accidents of western travel, there is no expression of the biological realities of these writers' experiences. Silence is difficult to read, but these lacunae suggest, at the very least, that the frontier did not endow these women with a new freedom from the constraints of civilization; their very articulation is still shaped by eastern society's notions of propriety. Moreover, the lack of commentary on pregnancy and birth can be contrasted with the voluminous attention paid to death: almost every page notes the gravesites of earlier travellers or the sickness and death of some companion, often in quite gruesome detail. This tension between the expansive possibilities of the western vision and the stifled responses of women writers emerges in a different way in Elinore Pruitt Stewart's letters. For several months, she keeps secret from her correspondent the news of her second marriage, finally confessing "I was afraid you would think I did n't [*sic*] need your friendship and might desert me." She is similarly circumspect about the birth and untimely death of the first-born child of this union, initially alluding to these events as if they had happened to a western acquaintance. What again seems to be encoded in this most "artless" of genres is a radical displacement of personal experience. The lack of fit between the western environment and women's sense of themselves not only drives underground the urge to literary creation, it causes a hiatus at the very heart of female expression.

Ultimately, this absence may be the major difference between the private and published utterances by women about the West. The example of Mari Sandoz's *Old Jules* (1935) is instructive. Ostensibly a biography of her father, this work is as much about the youth and early womanhood of the author herself, referred to in the third person as "Marie." This objectification of herself is situated within a number of portraits of women settlers, most of whom have come west reluctantly and are destroyed—physically, mentally, and emotionally—by the environment. Tellingly, destruction is wreaked not so much by the harshness of the natural environment as by the brutality of social conventions which sanction violence against women. Sandoz documents, in the automatic reflexes of her own father and other patriarchs of the settlement, not the romanticized, sanitized violence of *The Virginian* (for example) but the daily, debasing, unrelenting violence of husband against wife and children. Marie is one of the few female characters to hit back, literally against physical blows and symbolically by donning the authority of the author. But Sandoz's refusal to identify herself explicitly with Marie—her representation of herself as other—hints at the fissure of identity experienced by even powerful women in the West. In place of the silence and absence which we encounter in private life writings, *Old Jules* demonstrates the strategies of indirection necessary to the articulation of women's complex western stories. When Sandoz later produced her innovative history of another radically displaced and oppressed group, the Native Americans sensitively individualized in *Cheyenne Autumn* (1953), she articulated explicitly the tension between the language available to her and her western subject-matter, alluding to "much that is difficult to say in white-man words."

The alternative story of western writing which I have been constructing here is not offered as a definitive or full account, nor as an attempt to shape women's western voices into one monolithic utterance. The incomplete material currently available suggests quite the opposite, a diversity of multiple perspectives which share only a fundamental challenge to the dominant fiction of western literary history. These works also share the condition described by Tillie Olsen as "*the unnatural thwarting of what struggles to come into being, but cannot*"; they are struggling to speak the unspoken and perhaps unspeakable experience of women in the West. To advocate paying attention to women's versions of the West is not to imply a counter-erasure of men's writings. The two strains need to be read together, as correctives and qualifications of each other, as well as in the context of the multiple races, ethnic groups, and classes which have voiced their versions of the West. But for writers to be read and for silenced narratives to be interpreted, they first need to be brought to visibility, rescued from oblivion. This second edition of *Twentieth-Century Western Writers* makes a major contribution to this urgent recovery.

CHRISTINE BOLD

[I gratefully acknowledge the enthusiasm and acuity of the graduate students with whom I explored and enjoyed these alternative voices, in the "Women and the West" seminar at the University of Guelph, Fall 1990.]

READING LIST

Adams, Ramon, *Burs Under the Saddle: A Second Look at Books and Histories of the West.* Norman, University of Oklahoma Press, 1964.

Adams, Ramon, *The Rampaging Herd: A Bibliography of Books and Pamphlets on Men and Events in the Cattle Industry.* Norman, University of Oklahoma Press, 1959.

Adams, Ramon, *Six-Guns and Saddle Leather: A Bibliography of Books and Pamphlets on Western Outlaws and Gunmen.* Norman, University of Oklahoma Press, 1954.

Alkofer, Daniel, and others, editors, *Interpretive Approaches to Western American Literature.* Pocatello, Idaho State University Press, 1972.

Allen, Paula Gunn, editor, *Studies in American Indian Literature: Critical Essays and Course Designs.* New York, Modern Language Association, 1983.

Armitage, Susan, and Elizabeth Jameson, *The Women's West.* Norman, University of Oklahoma Press, 1987.

Arnesen, Finn, "Why Norwegians Love Westerns," in *The Roundup* (Sheridan, Wyoming), October 1976.

Ashliman, D.L., "The American West in Twentieth-Century German Literature," in *Journal of Popular Culture* (Bowling Green, Ohio), Summer 1968.

Athearn, Robert G., *The Mythic West in Twentieth-Century America.* Lawrence, University Press of Kansas, 1986.

Attebury, Louie W., "The American West and the Archetypal Orphan," in *Western American Literature* (Logan, Utah), Fall 1970.

Banes, Ruth A., "Autobiography and the Western Woman," in *Turn-of-the-Century Women* (Charlottesville, Virginia), Summer 1984.

Bataille, Gretchen M., and Kathleen Muller Sands, editors, *American Indian Women: Telling Their Lives.* Lincoln, University of Nebraska Press, 1984.

Beitz, Lee, "Heyday of the Pulp Westerns," in *True West* (Austin, Texas), February 1967.

Billington, Ray Allen, *Land of Savagery, Land of Promise: The European Image of the American Frontier.* New York, Norton, 1981.

Blacker, Irving R., *The Old West in Fiction.* New York, Obolensky, 1961.

Bloodworth, William, "The Literary Extensions of the Formula Western," in *Western American Literature* (Logan, Utah), Winter 1980.

Boatright, Mody C., "The Beginnings of Cowboy Fiction," in *Southwest Review* (Dallas), Winter 1966.

Boatright, Mody C., "The Formula in Cowboy Fiction and Drama," in *Western Folklore* (Berkeley, California), April 1969.

Boatright, Mody C., "The Western Bad Man as Hero," in *Publications of the Texas Folklore Society* (Nacogdoches), 27, 1957.

Bold, Christine, *Selling the Wild West: Popular Western Fiction, 1860 to 1960.* Bloomington, Indiana University Press, 1987.

Branch, E. Douglas, *The Cowboy and His Interpreters.* New York, Appleton, 1926.

Brauer, Ralph, and Donna Brauer, *The Horse, the Gun and the Piece of Property: Changing Images of the TV Western.* Bowling Green, Ohio, Bowling Green State University Press, 1975.

Bucco, Martin, *Western American Literary Criticism.* Boise, Idaho, Boise State University Press, 1987.

Bunkers, Suzanne L., "Midwestern Diaries and Journals: What Women Were (Not) Saying in the Late 1800s," in *Studies in Autobiography*, edited by James Olney, Oxford, Oxford University Press, 1988.

Calder, Jenni, *There Must Be a Lone Ranger.* London, Hamish Hamilton, 1974; New York, Taplinger, 1975.

Cancellari, Mike, *Checklist of Western and Northern Fiction.* New York, Cancellari, 1986.

Carr, Nick, editor, *The Western Pulp Hero.* Mercer Island, Washington, Starmont House, 1989.

Cawelti, John G., *Adventure, Mystery and Romance: Formula Stories as Art and Popular Culture.* Chicago, University of Chicago Press, 1976.

Cawelti, John G., "Cowboys, Indians, and Outlaws: The West in Myth and Fantasy," in *American West* (Cupertino, California), Spring 1964.

Cawelti, John G., "The Gunfighter and Society," in *American West* (Cupertino, California), March 1968.

Cawelti, John G., *The Six-Gun Mystique.* Bowling Green, Ohio, Bowling Green State University Press, 1975.

Clough, Wilson, "The Cult of the Bad Man of the West," in *Texas Quarterly*, Autumn 1962.

Collins, James L., editor, *The Western Writer's Handbook.* Boulder, Colorado, Johnson, 1987.

Dary, David, *Cowboy Culture: A Saga of Five Centuries.* New York, Knopf, 1981.

Dinan, John A., *The Pulp Western: A Popular History of the Western Fiction Magazine in America.* San Bernardino, California, Borgo Press, 1983.

Drew, Bernard A., with Martin H. Greenberg and Charles G. Waugh, editors, *Western Series and Sequels: A Reference Guide.* New York, Garland, 1986.

Durham, Philip, and Everett L. Jones, editors, *The Western Story: Fact, Fiction, and Myth.* New York, Harcourt Brace, 1975.

Erisman, Fred, and Richard W. Etulain, editors, *Fifty Western Writers: A Bio- Bibliographical Sourcebook.* Westport, Connecticut, Greenwood Press, 1982.

Erisman, Fred, "Western Fiction as an Ecological Parable," in *Environmental Review* (Denver), Spring 1978.

Etulain, Richard W., *The American Literary West.* Manhattan, Kansas, Sunflower University Press, 1980.

Etulain, Richard W., "The American Literary West and Its Interpreters: The Rise of a New Historiography," in *Pacific Historical Review 45* (Berkeley, California), August 1976.

Etulain, Richard W., "The Basques in Western American Literature," in *Anglo-American Contributions to Basque Studies: Essays in Honor of Jon Bilbao*, edited by Etulain, William A. Douglass, and William H. Jacobden, Jr., Reno, Nevada, Desert Research Institute Publications on the Social Sciences, 1977.

Etulain, Richard W., *A Bibliographic Guide to the Study of Western American Literature.* Lincoln, University of Nebraska Press, 1982.

Etulain, Richard W., "Changing Images: The Cowboy in Western Films," in *Colorado Heritage* (Denver), 1, 1981.

Etulain, Richard W., and Michael T. Marsden, editors, *The Popular Western: Essays Towards a Definition.* Bowling Green, Ohio, Bowling Green State University Press, 1974.

Etulain, Richard W., "The Western," in *Handbook of American Popular Culture 1*, edited by M. Thomas Inge, Westport, Connecticut, Greenwood Press, 1979.

Etulain, Richard W., *Western American Literature: A Bibliography of Interpretive Books and Articles.* Vermillion, University of South Dakota Press, 1972.

Fairbanks, Carol, *Prairie Women: Images in American and Canadian Fiction.* New Haven, Connecticut, Yale University Press, 1986.

Faulkner, Virginia, and Frederick Luebke, editors, *Vision and Refuge: Essays on the Literature of the Great Plains.* Lincoln, University of Nebraska Press, 1982.

Fender, Stephen, *Plotting the Golden West: American Literature and the Rhetoric of the California Trail.* Cambridge, Cambridge University Press, 1981.

Fiedler, Leslie A., *The Return of the Vanishing American.* New York, Stein and Day, and London, Cape, 1968.

Fishwick, Marshall, "The Cowboy: America's Contribution to the World's Mythology," in *Western Folklore* (Los Angeles), April 1952.

Folsom, James K., *The American Western Novel.* New Haven, Connecticut, Yale University Press, 1966.

Folsom, James K., "English Westerns," in *Western American Literature* (Logan, Utah), Spring 1967.

Folsom, James K., editor, *The Western: A Collection of Critical Essays.* Englewood Cliffs, New Jersey, Prentice Hall, 1979.

Frantz, Joe B., and Julian E. Choate, Jr., *The American Cowboy: The Myth and the Reality.* Norman, University of Oklahoma Press, 1955; London, Thames and Hudson, 1956.

Fryer, Judith, "The Anti-Mythical Journey: Westering Women's Diaries and Letters: A Review Essay," in *The Old Northwest* (Oxford, Ohio), Spring 1983.

Fussell, Edwin, *Frontier: American Literature and the American West.* Princeton, New Jersey, Princeton University Press, 1965.

Gaston, Edwin W., Jr., *The Early Novel of the Southwest.* Albuquerque, University of New Mexico Press, 1961.

Gibson, Michael D., "The Western: A Selective Bibliography," in *The Popular Western*, edited by Richard W. Etulain and Michael T. Marsden, Bowling Green, Ohio, Bowling Green State University Press, 1974.

Goetzmann, William H., and William T. Goetzmann, *The West of the Imagination.* New York, Norton, 1986.

Goulart, Ron, *Cheap Thrills: An Informal History of the Pulp Magazines.* New Rochelle, New York, Arlington House, 1972.

Graham, Don, "Old and New Cowboy Classics," in *Southwest Review* (Dallas), Summer 1980.

Graham, Don, with James W. Lee and William T. Pilkington, editors, *The Texas Literary Tradition: Fiction, Folklore, History.* Austin, College of Liberal Arts of the University of Texas, and Texas State Historical Association, 1983.

Graulich, Melody, "Violence Against Women in Literature of the Western Family," in *Frontiers* (Boulder, Colorado), 1984.

Gurian, Jay, "The Unwritten West," in *American West* (Cupertino, California), Winter 1965.

Gurian, Jay, *Western American Writing: Tradition and Promise.* Deland, Florida, Everett Edwards, 1975.

Hamilton, Cynthia, *Western and Hardboiled Detective Fiction in America: From High Noon to Midnight.* London, Macmillan, 1987.

Hampsten, Elizabeth, *Read This Only to Yourself: The Private Writings of Midwestern Women, 1880–1910.* Bloomington, Indiana University Press, 1982.

Harris, Charles W., and Buck Rainey, editors, *The Cowboy: Six-Shooters, Songs, and Sex.* Norman, University of Oklahoma Press, 1976.

Harrison, Dick, "Across the Medicine Line: Problems in Comparing Canadian and American Western Fiction," in *The Westering Experience in American Literature*, edited by Merrill Lewis and L.L. Lee, Bellingham, Western Washington University Press, 1977.

Haslam, Gerald W., "The Light That Fills the World: Native American Literature," in *South Dakota Review* (Vermillion), Spring 1973.

Haslam, Gerald W., "Literature of the People: Native American Voices," in *C.L.A. Journal*, December 1971.

Haslam, Gerald W., "The Other Literary West," in *Arizona Quarterly* (Tucson), Autumn 1982.

Haslam, Gerald W., "Por La Causa: Mexican-American Literature," in *College English* (Urbana, Illinois), May 1970.

Haslam, Gerald W., *Western American Writers* (taped lectures). Deland, Florida, Everett Edwards, 1974.

Haslam, Gerald W., editor, *Western Writing.* Albuquerque, University of New Mexico Press, 1974.

Homan, Peter, "The Uses and Limits of Psychobiography as an Approach to Popular Culture: The Case of the Western," in *The Biographic Process*, edited by Frank E. Reynolds and Donald Capps, The Hague, Mouton, 1976.

Huseboe, A.R., and W. Geyer, editors, *Where the West Begins: Essays on the Middle Border and Siouxland Writing.* Sioux Falls, South Dakota, Center for Western Studies Press, 1978.

Hutchinson, W.H., "Grassfire on the Great Plains: The Story of a Literary Battle," in *Southwest Review* (Dallas), Spring 1956.

Hutchinson, W.H., "Virgins, Villains, and Varmints," in *The Rhodes Reader*, by Eugene Manlove Rhodes, edited by Hutchinson, Norman, University of Oklahoma Press, 1957.

Hutchinson, W.H., "The Western Story as Literature," in *Western Humanities Review* (Salt Lake City), January 1949.

Johannsen, Albert, *The House of Beadle and Adams and Its Dime and Nickel Novels*. Norman, University of Oklahoma Press, 3 vols., 1950.

Jones, Daryl, "Clenched Teeth and Curses: Revenge and the Dime Novel Outlaw Hero," in *Journal of Popular Culture* (Bowling Green, Ohio), Winter 1973.

Jones, Daryl, *The Dime Novel Western*. Bowling Green, Ohio, Bowling Green State University Press, 1978.

Jones, Margaret Ann, "Cowboys and Ranching in Magazine Fiction, 1901–1910," in *Studies in the Literature of the West*, (Laramie, Wyoming), 20.

Karolides, Nicholas J., *The Pioneer in the American Novel 1900–1950*. Norman, University of Oklahoma Press, 1967.

Katz, William Loren, *The Black West*. New York, Anchor Doubleday, 1973.

Kitses, Jim, *Horizon West: Anthony Mann, Budd Boetticher, Sam Peckinpah: Studies of Authorship Within the Western*. Bloomington, Indiana University Press, 1969.

Kolodny, Annette, *The Land Before Her: Fantasy and Experience of the American Frontier, 1630–1860*. Chapel Hill, University of North Carolina Press, 1984.

Kolodny, Annette, *The Lay of the Land: Metaphor as Experience and History in American Life and Letters*. Chapel Hill, University of North Carolina Press, 1975.

Kroes, Robert, editor, *The American West as Seen by Europeans and Americans*. Amsterdam, Free University Press, 1989.

Lamar, Howard R., editor, *The Reader's Encyclopaedia of the American West*. New York, Crowell, 1977.

Lander, Dawn, "Eve Among the Indians," in *The Authority of Experience: Essays in Feminist Criticism*, edited by Arlyn Diamond and Lee Edwards, Dorchester, University of Massachusetts Press, 1988.

Larson, Charles R., *American Indian Fiction*. Albuquerque, University of New Mexico Press, 1978.

Lavender, David, "The Petrified West and the Writer," in *American Scholar* (Washington, D.C.), Spring 1968.

Lee, Hector, "Tales and Legends in Western American Literature," in *Western American Literature* (Logan, Utah), February 1975.

Lee, L.L., and Merrill Lewis, editors, *Women, Women Writers, and the West*. Troy, New York, Whitston, 1979.

Lee, Lawrence B., *Reclaiming the American West: Historiography and Guide*. Santa Barbara, California, ABC Clio, 1980.

Lee, Robert Edson, *From West to East: Studies in the Literature of the American West*. Urbana, University of Illinois Press, 1966.

Leithead, J. Edward, "The Outlaws Rode Hard in Dime Novel Days," in *American Book Collector* (Ossining, New York), December 1968.

Lenihan, John H., *Showdown: Confronting Modern America in the Western Film*. Urbana, University of Illinois Press, 1980.

Lewis, Merrill, and L.L. Lee, editors, *The Westering Experience in American Literature: Bicentennial Essays*. Bellingham, Bureau for Faculty Research, Western Washington State University, 1977.

Lyon, Peter, *The Wild, Wild West*. New York, Funk and Wagnall, 1969.

Malone, Michael P., and Richard W. Etulain, *The American West: A Twentieth-Century History*. Lincoln, University of Nebraska Press, 1989.

Marovitz, Sanford E., "Myth and Realism in Recent Criticism of the American Literary West," in *Journal of American Studies* (Cambridge, England), April 1981.

Marsden, Michael T., "Iconology of the Western Romance," in *Icons of America*, edited by Ray B. Browne and Marshall Fishwick, Bowling Green, Ohio, Bowling Green State University Press, 1978.

Marsden, Michael T., "The Modern Western," in *Journal of the West* (Manhattan, Kansas), January 1980.

Martinez, Julio A., *Chicano, Scholars and Writers: A Bio-Bibliographical Directory*. Metuchen, New Jersey, Scarecrow Press, 1989.

McCourt, Edward, *The Canadian West in Fiction*. Toronto, Ryerson, 1949.

Mead, S. Jean, *Maverick Writers: Candid Comments from Fifty-Two of the Best*. Caldwell, Idaho, Caxton, 1989.

Meldrum, Barbara Howard, *Under the Sun: Myth and Realism in Western American Literature*. Troy, New York, Whitston, 1985.

Messent, Peter, *New Readings of the American Novel*. London, Macmillan, 1990.

Meyer, Roy W., *The Middle Western Farm Novel in the Twentieth Century*. Lincoln, University of Nebraska Press, 1965.

Milton, John R., *The Novel of the American West*. Lincoln, University of Nebraska Press, 1980.

Milton, John R., editor, special western issue of *South Dakota Review* (Vermillion), Autumn 1973.

Mogen, David, with Mark Busby and Paul T. Bryant, editors, *The Frontier Experience and the American Dream*. College Station, Texas A and M University Press, 1989.

Mogen, David, *Wilderness Visions: Science Fiction Westerns 1*. San Bernardino, California, Borgo Press, 1982.

Mottram, Eric, "'The Persuasive Lips': Men and Guns in America, the West," in *Blood on the Nash Ambassador*, London, Century Hutchinson, 1988.

Myres, Sandra, editor, *Ho for California!: Women's Overland Diaries from the Huntington Library*. San Marino, California, Huntington Library, 1980.

Nachbar, Jack, *Focus on the Western*. Englewood Cliffs, New Jersey, Prentice Hall, 1974.

Nachbar, John G., editor, *Western Films: An Annotated Critical Bibliography*. New York, Garland, 1975.

Nemanic, Gerald, editor, *A Bibliographical Guide to Midwestern Literature*. Iowa City, University of Iowa Press, 1981.

Norwood, Vera, and Janice Monk, editors, *The Desert Is No Lady: Southwestern Landscapes in Women's Writing and Art*. New Haven, Connecticut, Yale University Press, 1987.

Nussbaum, Martin, "Psychological Symbolism in the Adult Western," in *Social Forces* (Chapel Hill, North Carolina), October 1960.

Nye, Russel B., *New Dimensions in Popular Culture*. Bowling Green, Ohio, Bowling Green State University Press, 1972.

Ortiz, Simon J., editor, *Earth Power Coming: Short Fiction in Native American Literature*. Tsiale, Arizona, Navajo Community College Press, 1983.

Paredes, Raymund A., "The Evolution of Chicano Literature," in *Three American Literatures*, edited by Houston A. Baker, New York, Modern Language Association, 1982.

Paredes, Raymund A., "Exclusion and Invisibility: Chicano Literature Not in Text Books," in *Arizona English Bulletin* (Flagstaff), 17, 1975.

Paredes, Raymund A., "The Promise of Chicano Literature," in *Minority Language and Literature*, edited by Dexter Fisher, New York, Modern Language Association, 1977.

Pattee, Fred Lewis, *The New American Literature, 1890–1930*. New York, Century, 1930.

Patterson-Black, Sheryll, and Gene Patterson-Black, *Western Women: In History and Literature*. Crawford, Nebraska, Cottonwood Press, 1978.

Paul, Rodman W., and Richard W. Etulain, *The Frontier and American West.* Arlington Heights, Illinois, AHM, 1977.

Pettit, Arthur G., *Images of the Mexican-American in Fiction and Film.* College Station, Texas A and M University Press, 1980.

Phillips, James E., "Arcadia on the Range," in *Themes and Directions in American Literature*, edited by Ray B. Browne and Donald Pizer, West Lafayette, Indiana, Purdue University Press, 1969.

Pilkington, William T., editor, *Critical Essays on the Western American Novel.* Boston, Hall, 1980.

Pilkington, William T., and Don Graham, editors, *Western Movies.* Albuquerque, University of New Mexico Press, 1979.

Powell, Lawrence Clark, *Southwestern Classics: The Creative Literature of the Arid Lands.* Pasadena, California, Ward Ritchie, 1974.

Special issue on western American literature in *Rendezvous* (Pocatello, Idaho), Winter 1972.

Reynolds, Quentin, *The Fiction Factory.* New York, Random House, 1955.

Rivera, Tomas, "Chicano Literature: Festival of the Living," in *Books Abroad* (Norman, Oklahoma), 1949.

Robinson, Cecil, *With the Ears of Strangers: The Mexican in American Literature.* Tucson, University of Arizona Press, 1963.

Rosa, Joseph G., *The Gunfighter: Man or Myth?* Norman, University of Oklahoma Press, 1969.

Savage, William Sherman, *Blacks in the West.* Westport, Connecticut, Greenwood Press, 1976.

Savage, William W., Jr., *The Cowboy Hero: His Image in American History and Culture.* Norman, University of Oklahoma Press, 1979.

Schein, Harry, "The Olympian Cowboy," in *American Scholar* (Washington, D.C.), Summer 1955.

Schlissel, Lillian, *Women's Diaries of the Westward Journey.* New York, Schocken, 1982.

Slotkin, Richard, *The Fatal Environment: The Myth of the Frontier in the Age of Industrialization, 1800–1890.* New York, Atheneum, 1985.

Slotkin, Richard, *Regeneration Through Violence: The Mythology of the American Frontier, 1600–1860.* Middletown, Connecticut, Wesleyan University Press, 1973.

Smith, Henry Nash, *Virgin Land: The American West as Symbol and Myth.* Cambridge, Massachusetts, Harvard University Press, 1950.

Smith, Herbert F., *The Popular American Novel, 1865–1920.* Boston, Twayne, 1980.

Sonnichsen, C.L., *From Hopalong to Hud: Thoughts on Western Fiction.* College Station, Texas A and M University Press, 1978.

Sonnichsen, C.L., "The Wyatt Earp Syndrome," in *American West* (Tucson, Arizona), May 1970.

Stauffer, Helen W., and Susan J. Rosowski, editors, *Women and Western American Literature.* Troy, New York, Whitston, 1982.

Steckmesser, Karl Ladd, "Robin Hood and the American Outlaw: A Note on History and Folklore," in *Journal of American Folklore* (Washington, D.C.), June 1966.

Steckmesser, Kent Ladd, *The Western Hero in History and Legend.* Norman, University of Oklahoma Press, 1965.

Steffen, Jerome O., editor, *American West: New Perspectives, New Dimensions.* Norman, University of Oklahoma Press, 1979.

Tatum, Charles M., *Chicano Literature.* Boston, Twayne, 1982.

Taylor, J. Golden, Thomas J. Lyon, and others, editors, *A Literary History of the American West.* Fort Worth, Texas Christian University Press, 1987.

Topping, Dennis, *'Somebody Fetch the Marshal!': An Englishman's Eye-View of the Modern American West.* Orpington, Kent, No-No, 1985.

Topping, Gary, "The Rise of the Western," in *Journal of the West* (Manhattan, Kansas), January 1980.

Tuska, Jon, and Vicki Piekarski, editors, *The American West in Fiction: An Anthology.* New York, New American Library, 1982.

Tuska, Jon, *The American West in Film: Critical Approaches to the Western.* Westport, Connecticut, Greenwood Press, 1985.

Tuska, Jon, and Vicki Piekarski, editors, *Encyclopedia of Frontier and Western Fiction.* New York, McGraw Hill, 1983.

Tuska, Jon, *The Filming of the West.* New York, Doubleday, 1976.

Tuska, Jon, and Vicki Piekarski, editors, *The Frontier Experience: A Reader's Guide to the Life and Literature of the American West.* Jefferson, North Carolina, McFarland, 1984.

Tuska, Jon, *A Variable Harvest: Essays and Reviews of Film and Literature.* Jefferson, North Carolina, McFarland, 1990.

VanDerhoff, Jack, *A Bibliography of Novels Related to American Frontier and Colonial History.* Troy, New York, Whitston, 1971.

Walker, Don D., "Criticism of the Cowboy Novel: Retrospect and Reflections," in *Western American Literature* (Logan, Utah), Winter 1977.

Walker, Don D., "The Mountain Man as Literary Hero," in *Western American Literature* (Logan, Utah), Spring 1966.

Webster, Duncan, *Looka Yonder! The Imaginary America of Popular Culture.* London, Routledge, 1988.

Westbrook, Max, "The Authentic Western," in *Western American Literature* (Logan, Utah), Fall 1978.

Westbrook, Max, "Conservative, Liberal, and Western: Three Modes of Realism," in *South Dakota Review* (Vermillion), Summer 1966.

Westbrook, Max, "The Practical Spirit: Sacrality and the American West," in *Western American Literature* (Logan, Utah), Fall 1968.

Westbrook, Max, "The Western Novel: A Symposium," in *South Dakota Review* (Vermillion), Autumn 1964.

White, G. Edward, *The Eastern Establishment and the Western Experience: The West of Frederic Remington, Theodore Roosevelt, and Owen Wister.* New Haven, Connecticut, Yale University Press, 1968.

Wiebe, Rudy, "Western Canadian Fiction: Past and Future," in *Western American Literature* (Logan, Utah), 6, 1971.

Williams, John, "The 'Western': Definition of the Myth," in *The Nation* (New York), 18 November 1961.

Wright, Will, *Sixguns and Society: A Structural Study of the Western.* Berkeley, University of California Press, 1975.

Wylder, Delbert, "Recent Western Fiction," in *Journal of the West* (Manhattan, Kansas), January 1980.

ADVISERS

R. Jeff Banks
Christine Bold
Richard W. Etulain
Leslie A. Fiedler
James K. Folsom
B.J. Holmes
Mike Linaker
Thomas J. Lyon
Peter Messent
C.L. Sonnichsen
Mike Stotter
Jon Tuska
Alan R. Velie
David Whitehead

CONTRIBUTORS

Kerry Ahearn
Bert Almon
Steven Almond
Judy Alter
Lucile F. Aly
Wade Austin
R. Jeff Banks
Robert J. Barnes
William Bloodworth
Marian Blue
Christine Bold
R.E. Briney
Ellie Brown
Paul T. Bryant
Martin Bucco
Mark Busby
Tracy Chevalier
Michael Cleary
J. Fraser Cocks, III
Katharine Weston Cohen
Bill Crider
Richard W. Etulain
Cassandra Fedrick
John H. Ferres
John D. Flanagan
Joseph M. Flora
James K. Folsom
Cheryl J. Foote
Marcia G. Fuchs
Robert L. Gale
Robert F. Gish
G. Dale Gleason
Dorys C. Grover
Philip J. Harbottle
John Harvey
Linda M. Hasselstrom
Sam H. Henderson
Jerry A. Herndon
David Marion Holman
B.J. Holmes
William V. Holtz
Jo M. Hudman
W.H. Hutchinson
Joe Jackson
Daryl Jones
Frances W. Kaye
George Kelley
Larry N. Landrum
Joe R. Lansdale
Robert Lawson-Peebles
James W. Lee
L.L. Lee
Mike Linaker
Ellis Lucia
Andrew Macdonald
Gina Macdonald
David W. Madden
James H. Maguire
Charlotte S. McClure
Douglas J. McReynolds
Barbara Howard Meldrum
P.R. Meldrum
Ray Merlock
Peter Messent
Leon C. Metz
David Mogen
Daryl Morrison
David Murray
Clarence Naylor
Nancy Owen Nelson
John D. Nesbitt
Francis M. Nevins, Jr.
Fred Nolan
Kristoffer F. Paulson
Carol Miles Petersen
Bernd C. Peyer
Simon Philo
Vicki Piekarski
William T. Pilkington
Bill Pronzini
Ann L. Putnam
Ann Romines
Susan J. Rosowski
Earl Rovit
Jeff Sadler
John Scheckter
Lee Schultz
Patricia Roth Schwartz
Kathryn Lee Seidel
Walter Shaw
Herbert F. Smith
C.L. Sonnichsen
Ernest B. Speck
Helen Stauffer
Jon C. Stott
Mike Stotter
Don R. Swadley
Martha Scott Trimble
Jon Tuska
Wayne Ude
Owen Ulph
Alan R. Velie
Dale L. Walker
George Walsh
John O. West
David Whitehead
Peter Wild
John L. Wolfe
Joseph J. Wydeven
Delbert E. Wylder
Joseph A. Young

TWENTIETH-CENTURY WESTERN WRITERS

Edward Abbey
Andy Adams
Chuck Adams
Clifton Adams
Frank Ramsay Adams
Ann Ahlswede
Marvin H. Albert
Bess Streeter Aldrich
Luke Allan
Chester Allen
Henry Wilson Allen
Paula Gunn Allen
T.D. Allen
Clay Allison
Rudolfo A. Anaya
Patrick E. Andrews
Elliott Arnold
Burt Arthur
Verne Athanas
Gertrude Atherton
Mary Austin

Gordon C. Baldwin
Willis Todhunter Ballard
Denver Bardwell
S. Omar Barker
J.O. Barnwell
Geoffrey John Barrett
Jane Barry
Wayne Barton
Rex Beach
Amelia Bean
Frederick R. Bechdolt
P.A. Bechko
Ralph Beer
Robert Vaughn Bell
James Warner Bellah
Thomas Berger
Don Berry
Jack M. Bickham
Harold Bindloss
David Ernest Bingley
Hoffman Birney
Samuel P. Bishop
Forrester Blake
Frank Bonham
Michael Bonner
Edwin Booth
Jack Borg
Hal Borland
Allan R. Bosworth
J.L. Bouma
Jim Bowden
B.M. Bower
Terrell L. Bowers
Richard Bradford
W.F. Bragg
Max Brand
Russ Brannigan
Matt Braun
Myron Brinig
Carol Ryrie Brink
Gwen Bristow
Robert W. Broomall
Dee Brown
J.P.S. Brown
Will C. Brown

Bill Burchardt
W.R. Burnett
Walter Noble Burns
Edgar Rice Burroughs
Katharine Burt
Niven Busch

Lou Cameron
Benjamin Capps
Forrest Carter
Raymond Carver
Robert Ormond Case
Willa Cather
Joseph Chadwick
Tim Champlin
Borden Chase
Giff Cheshire
A.M. Chisholm
Matt Chisholm
Frederick H. Christian
Walter Van Tilburg Clark
Walt Coburn
Don Coldsmith
Will Levington Comfort
Robert J. Conley
Ralph Connor
Merle Constiner
Will Cook
William Wallace Cook
Dane Coolidge
Courtney Ryley Cooper
Barry Cord
Edwin Corle
Van Cort
William R. Cox
Bill Crider
James Crumley
Ridgewell Cullum
John H. Culp
Jack Cummings
Chet Cunningham
Eugene Cunningham
Peggy Simson Curry
Tom Curry
James Oliver Curwood
Dan Cushman

Janet Dailey
Pete Danvers
H.L. Davis
Peter Dawson
Robert P. Day
Dudley Dean
Celeste De Blasis
William Decker
Rick DeMarinis
H.A. De Rosso
Bernard De Voto
Al Dewlen
Ross Dexter
Joan Didion
E.L. Doctorow
Emerson Dodge
Ivan Doig
Mark Donovan
Cyril Donson
Michael Dorris

James R. Dowler
Harry Sinclair Drago
Davis Dresser
Marilyn Durham
Paul Durst

William Eastlake
Robert Easton
Allan K. Echols
J.T. Edson
Gretel Ehrlich
Jack Ehrlich
Allan Vaughan Elston
Loula Grace Erdman
Louise Erdrich
Leslie Ernenwein
Susan Ertz
Saran Essex
Loren D. Estleman
Max Evans
Wick Evans
Hal G. Evarts, Sr.
Hal G. Evarts, Jr.
Robert Eynon

Mark Falcon
Cliff Farrell
Howard Fast
John Russell Fearn
Edna Ferber
Harvey Fergusson
William Fieldhouse
Frank Fields
Vardis Fisher
Christopher Flood
Lee Floren
Robert Flynn
T.T. Flynn
Mary Hallock Foote
L.L. Foreman
W. Bert Foster
Kenneth A. Fowler
Norman A. Fox
Steve Frazee
Oscar Friend

Walter Gann
Dorothy Gardiner
Jerome Gardner
Brian Garfield
George Garland
Hamlin Garland
Ray Gaulden
Jack Giles
George G. Gilman
Fred Gipson
Susan Glaspell
Arthur Henry Gooden
Ed Gorman
John Graves
Jackson Gregory
Lee F. Gregson
Zane Grey
Leonard Gribble
Fred Grove
Frederick Philip Grove
Marshall Grover

Frank Gruber
Bill Gulick
A.B. Guthrie, Jr.

Ben Haas
Roderick Haig-Brown
Oakley Hall
E.E. Halleran
Donald Hamilton
Kirk Hamilton
Ron Hansen
Vic J. Hanson
C. William Harrison
Jim Harrison
John Harvey
Gerald Haslam
Ernest Haycox
Charles N. Heckelmann
James B. Hendryx
O. Henry
William Heuman
Jim Heynen
Tony Hillerman
Edward Hoagland
Donald Bayne Hobart
Lee Hoffman
Linda Hogan
Ray Hogan
B.J. Holmes
L.P. Holmes
William Hopson
Paul Horgan
Emerson Hough
Tex Houston
Robert E. Howard
Lois Phillips Hudson
Clair Huffaker
William Humphrey

John Jakes
Laurence James
Will James
H. Paul Jeffers
Will F. Jenkins
George C. Jenks
Richard Jessup
Dorothy M. Johnson
Pauline Johnson
Terry C. Johnston
Douglas C. Jones
Nard Jones
Hal Jons
Archie Joscelyn

MacKinlay Kantor
Leo P. Kelley
Elmer Kelton
Philip Ketchum
J.D. Kincaid
Albert King
General Charles King
Maxine Hong Kingston
William Kittredge
H.H. Knibbs
Will C. Knott
Herbert Krause
Steven M. Krauzer
Peter B. Kyne

Oliver La Farge
Louis L'Amour
Rose Wilder Lane
John Langley
Joe R. Lansdale
Margaret Laurence
Steven C. Lawrence
Norman Lazenby
Tom Lea
Wayne C. Lee
Paul Evan Lehman
Alan LeMay
Elmore Leonard
Meridel Le Sueur
Alfred Henry Lewis
Janet Lewis
Mike Linaker
David Lindsey
Dee Linford
Charles O. Locke
Caroline Lockhart
Jack London
Elliot Long
Noel M. Loomis
Milton Lott
Giles A. Lutz

William Colt MacDonald
Johnny Mack Bride
Alistair MacLean
Norman Maclean
Robert MacLeod
Mason Macrae
Holt Madison
Frederick Manfred
E.B. Mann
Chuck Martin
John Joseph Mathews
Paul McAfee
Robert McCaig
Cormac McCarthy
Gary McCarthy
Johnston McCulley
Peter McCurtin
Frances McElrath
Thomas McGuane
Larry McMurtry
Charles L. McNichols
D'Arcy McNickle
Oscar Micheaux
James A. Michener
George Milburn
Joseph Millard
Jim Miller
N. Scott Momaday
Rutherford Montgomery
Amos Moore
Wright Morris
Honoré Willsie Morrow
William Byron Mowery
Clarence E. Mulford
John Myers Myers

John G. Neihardt
David Nevin
D.B. Newton
Mike Newton
John Nichols
Arthur Nickson
Frederick Niven
Frank Norris
V.G.C. Norwood
Nelson Nye

Bob Obets
Jack O'Connor
Mary O'Hara
T.V. Olsen
Tillie Olsen
Frank O'Rourke
Simon J. Ortiz
Martha Ostenso
Wayne D. Overholser

Lauran Paine
Bernard Palmer
Dan Parkinson
Lewis B. Patten
George Pattullo
Gary Paulsen
Samuel Anthony Peeples
Hugh Pendexter
T.C.H. Pendower
George Sessions Perry
Roger Pocock
Katherine Anne Porter
Charles Portis
James Powell
John Prebble
John Prescott
Ron Pritchett
Bill Pronzini
Herbert Purdum

William MacLeod Raine
Robert J. Randisi
St. George Rathborne
William Rayner
James M. Reasoner
Ishmael Reed
John Reese
Frederic S. Remington
Ed Earl Repp
Bret Rey
Clay Reynolds
Eugene Manlove Rhodes
Gladwell Richardson
Roe Richmond
Conrad Richter
Shepard Rifkin
Howard Rigsby
Tomas Rivera
Tom Roan
Elizabeth Madox Roberts
Frank C. Robertson
Lucia St. Clair Robson
Frank Roderus
Shirlaw Johnston Rodgers
O.E. Rølvaag
Robert Roripaugh
Sinclair Ross
W.E.D. Ross
Zola Ross
M.M. Rowan

Donald S. Rowland
Jane Gilmore Rushing
Charles M. Russell
Marah Ellis Ryan

Amy Sadler
Jeff Sadler
Charles W. Sanders
Mari Sandoz
Ross Santee
Les Savage, Jr.
Thomas Savage
Dorothy Scarborough
Jack Schaefer
John Seelye
Charles Alden Seltzer
Jon Sharpe
Cornelius Shea
John L. Shelley
Gordon D. Shirreffs
Luke Short
Edwin Shrake
Leslie Marmon Silko
Mike Skinner
Agnes Smedley
Charles H. Snow
Virginia Sorensen
Frank H. Spearman
Jean Stafford
Robert J.C. Stead
Harwood E. Steele
William O. Steele
Robert J. Steelman
Wallace Stegner
John Steinbeck
James Stevens
Elinore Pruitt Stewart
Hart Stilwell
E.G. Stokoe
Mike Stotter
Michael Straight
Oliver Strange
Charles S. Strong
C.M. Sublette
Ruth Suckow
Stack Sutton
Glendon Swarthout

Robert Lewis Taylor
L.D. Tetlow
James Alexander Thom
John W. Thomason
C. Hall Thompson
Thomas Thompson
Giles Tippette
Frank X. Tolbert
Walker A. Tompkins
Robert E. Trevathan
Louis Trimble
E.C. Tubb
William O. Turner
W.C. Tuttle

Wayne Ude

William E. Vance
Gerald Vizenor

David Wagoner
Anna Lee Waldo
Dale Waldo
Jonas Ward
Charles Marquis Warren
L.J. Washburn
Frank Waters
James Welch
Paul I. Wellman
Angus Wells
Jessamyn West
Kingsley West
Tom West
Richard S. Wheeler
Stewart Edward White
David Whitehead
John H. Whitson
Harry Whittington
Laura Ingalls Wilder
Jeanne Williams
John Williams
Barbara Wilson
Harry Leon Wilson
Logan Winters
Sophus K. Winther
G. Clifton Wisler
Owen Wister
Bryan Woolley
Richard Wormser
Harold Bell Wright

Carter Travis Young
Gordon Young

Edward R. Zietlow

ABBEY, Edward. American. Born in Home, Pennsylvania, 29 January 1927. Educated at the University of New Mexico, Albuquerque, B.A. 1951, M.A. 1956; University of Edinburgh, (Fulbright Fellow, 1951–52). Served in the United States Army, 1945–47. Married Judith Pepper in 1965 (died 1970); two sons and one daughter. United States Park Service ranger, 1956–68, and Forest Service fire lookout, 1969–80, in the southwest. Recipient: Guggenheim fellowship, 1973. *Died March 1989.*

WESTERN PUBLICATIONS

Novels

The Brave Cowboy. New York, Dodd Mead, 1956; London, Eyre and Spottiswoode, 1957.
Fire on the Mountain. New York, Dial Press, 1962; London, Eyre and Spottiswoode, 1963.
Black Sun. New York, Simon and Schuster, 1971; as *Sunset Canyon,* London, Talmy, 1972.
The Monkey Wrench Gang. Philadelphia, Lippincott, 1975; Edinburgh, Canongate, 1978.
Good News. New York, Dutton, 1980.
Confessions of the Barbarian. Santa Barbara, California, Capra, 1981.
The Fool's Progress. New York, Holt, 1988; London, Bodley Head, 1989.
Hayduke Lives! Boston, Little Brown, 1990.

OTHER PUBLICATIONS

Novel

Jonathan Troy. New York, Dodd Mead, 1954.

Other

Desert Solitaire: A Season in the Wilderness. New York, McGraw Hill, 1968.
Appalachian Wilderness: The Great Smoky Mountains, photographs by Eliot Porter. New York, Dutton, 1970.
Slickrock: The Canyon Country of Southeast Utah, with Philip Hyde. San Francisco, Sierra Club, 1971.
Cactus Country, with the editors of Time-Life Books. New York, Time Life, 1973.
The Hidden Canyon: A River Journey, photographs by John Blaustein. New York, Viking Press, 1977.
The Journey Home: Some Words in Defense of the American West. New York, Dutton, 1977.
Desert Images: An American Landscape, photographs by David Muench. New York, Chanticleer Press, 1978.
Back Roads of Arizona, photographs by Earl Thollander. Flagstaff, Arizona, Northland Press, 1978.
Abbey's Road: Take the Other. New York, Dutton, 1979.
Down the River. New York, Dutton, 1982.
Beyond the Wall. New York, Holt Rinehart, 1984.
Slumgullion Stew: An Edward Abbey Reader. New York, Dutton, 1984.
One Life at a Time, Please. New York, Holt Rinehart, 1988.
The Best of Edward Abbey. San Francisco, Sierra, 1988.
A Voice Crying in the Wilderness: Essays from a Secret Journal. New York, St. Martin's Press, 1990.

*

Manuscript Collection: University of Arizona, Tucson.

Critical Studies: *Edward Abbey* by Garth McCann, Boise, Idaho, Boise State University Press, 1977; *The New West of Edward Abbey* by Ann Ronald, Albuquerque, University of New Mexico Press, 1982; *Resist Much, Obey Little: Some Notes on Edward Abbey* edited by James Hepworth and Gregory McNamee, Salt Lake City, Utah, Dream Garden Press, 1985.

Edward Abbey commented (1982):

I am an enemy of the modern military-industrial state; all of my books, fiction and non-fiction, are written in defense of human liberty and for the greater glory of the natural world.

* * *

To overly urbanized readers, Edward Abbey's main characters offer immediate succor. They are mavericks misplaced in the present, individualistic rebels, and in thumbing their noses at time clocks and assembly lines they catch a glint of the glory of what certainly was a more rural America—one, it is frequently believed, more amenable to personal fulfillment. Typically, Abbey's misfits make their break for freedom by attempting to escape into the surviving remnants of the past, the patches of wilderness still left in the Western United States.

But Abbey is not creating wilderness idylls in the manner of earlier novelists like Zane Grey. Though a romantic himself, Abbey knows that the world and its problems have changed too much since industrialization, and he is too much the sophisticated thinker to settle for that. Taking a cue from his jaded times, he thrives on a Whitmanesque casualness toward inconsistencies. Combining cynicism with hope, fantasy with reality, Abbey refuses to be pinned down. In one breath he can rail against society's abuses to nature and in the next cavalierly toss his empty beer can out of the car window. Which is to say that the former farmboy with a master's degree in philosophy wants things both ways, and his espousal of the urge appeals to the rebel in us all.

Abbey's deservedly popular *The Monkey Wrench Gang* embodies a good deal of this ambivalence. Here a foursome consisting of a medical doctor beginning to feel his years, his girlfriend, a former Green Beret sergeant, and a wily river guide make up a merry band of anarchists. They're determined not so much to escape into the wilds of the desert Southwest as to save them. Confronting the behemoth, a civilization addicted to growth and technology, they're bent on blowing up the highways, bridges, and road-construction equipment invading the outback. It sounds serious, but for the most part Abbey's treatment is humorous, ranging from lighthearted sneers to the revolutionary's laughter in the face of death. *The Monkey Wrench Gang* piques both the wish fulfillment of wilderness protectors and the common itch to tweak the noses of authority figures as Abbey's quipping vagabonds pursue their picaresque antics, pursued in turn by the law in pyrotechnic chases. Yet as a realist, Abbey has the dynamite-toting rebels caught in the end—all but one, that is. The fantasist in Abbey engineers the near miraculous escape of Hayduke, the former Green Beret sergeant, thus providing hope that the Robin Hood-like struggle will continue. It's a tongue-in-cheek romp with appropriately zany touches, one vicariously, if somewhat adolescently, entertaining.

However, Abbey's novels don't always satisfy. Sometimes they manage to careen into ditches of absurdity, then, overcorrecting, plunge into bathos on the other side. His early *The Brave Cowboy* features a rough-hewn desert rat. Jack Burns wants to flee civilization's strictures by riding his horse into the wilderness and living off the land in frontier fashion. Eventually, a truck kills him as he attempts to cross a highway, the machine squashing the naive antimodernist. Burns has his nostalgic appeal, but in the end we're left wondering if the out-of-sync man isn't more of a child than an idealist. With a later novel sardonically titled *Good News*, Abbey deals with the future. After civilization has self-destructed due to its misuse of resources, we watch a revivified Burns trying to outwit a monomaniacal despot whose army has built a fortress in the ruins of a Southwestern city. Again, the forces of evil prevail, but as in *The Monkey Wrench Gang*, Abbey provides a trapdoor for hope through an improbable twist. But the performance is strained, the events and characters unlikely, forced to do Abbey's bidding, for there's little of the devil-take-the-hindmost humor that gives *The Monkey Wrench Gang* its literary license.

The problem is that, for all his many bright passages, Abbey's characters can be flat, his plots tenuous, and his themes inconsistent. On the other hand, his forte lies in his descriptive powers. In short, Abbey is far more the essayist than the novelist, as *Desert Solitaire* illustrates along with his other volumes of non-fiction. In its pages, the irascible, intellectually fun-loving Abbey puts on his most felicitous performance. Within the traditional framework of books describing extended periods of withdrawal into nature, he writes at his literary ease, yet in full control, playing over the range of his best talents. Drawing on three seasons spent in southeastern Utah as a park ranger at Arches National Monument, he recounts his experience of the wilds and the dunderheaded gaffes of tourists. Beyond that, he scolds convincingly over the huckstering claptrap of highways, motels, and neon that seems bent on blighting every square inch of the nature he loves. As in *The Monkey Wrench Gang*, the writer has his chuckles, chiding comfort-addicted travelers to abandon their automobiles, to "get out of those motorized wheelchairs" and dare to "WALK upon our sweet and blessed land!" At turns acid and numinous, *Desert Solitaire* is both a revelation and a defense of the good earth.

Abbey jarred Western American letters. His popularity brought nature writing, always something of a stepchild, further into the literary mainstream. In political terms, as an activist, Abbey gave more than courage to environmentalists, always woefully outnumbered and outspent; he injected panache into their ranks. For blending both literature and politics, Abbey, as an environmental Thomas Paine, gave permission to be outlandish and bitter, flippant and deep-souled at once. If we are doomed, goes the message on his banner, we nonetheless will save ourselves by going down full of heart. It's an old message, of course, one used by prophets and rebels through the ages, but it's also one that has taken fire in the tinder of an ennui-ridden, post-industrial society ready for the excitement of a romantic cause.

—Peter Wild

ADAMS, Andy. American. Born in Whitley County, Indiana, 3 May 1859. Worked in an Arkansas lumber camp, 1881; drover for Smith and Redmon, livestock brokers, San Antonio, 1882–89; in feed and seed business, Rockport, Texas, 1889–93; prospector, Cripple Creek goldfields, 1893; lived in Colorado Springs from 1894, except for periods in Goldfield, Nevada, 1907–09, and Frenchburg, Kentucky, 1919–21. *Died 26 September 1935.*

WESTERN PUBLICATIONS

Novels

The Log of a Cowboy. Boston, Houghton Mifflin, and London, Constable, 1903.
A Texas Matchmaker. Boston, Houghton Mifflin, and London, Gay and Bird, 1904.
The Outlet. Boston, Houghton Mifflin, and London, Constable, 1905.
Reed Anthony, Cowman: An Autobiography. Boston, Houghton Mifflin, and London, Constable, 1907.
Wells Brothers, The Young Cattle Kings. Boston, Houghton Mifflin, and London, Constable, 1911.
The Ranch of the Beaver. Boston, Houghton Mifflin, 1927.

Short Stories

Cattle Brands A Collection of Western Camp-Fire Stories. Boston, Houghton Mifflin, and London, Constable, 1906.
Why the Chisholm Trail Fords and Other Tales of the Cattle Country, edited by Wilson M. Hudson. Austin, University of Texas Press, 1956; as *Andy Adams' Campfire Tales*, Lincoln, University of Nebraska Press, 1976.

*

Manuscript Collection: State Historical Society of Colorado, Denver.

Critical Study: *Andy Adams, Storyteller and Novelist of the Great Plains* by Wilson M. Hudson, Austin, Texas, Steck Vaughn, 1967.

* * *

Andy Adams is famous for one book, *The Log of a Cowboy*, the first and one of the best neo-realist westerns. Most of the criticism of *The Log of a Cowboy* has concerned itself with the "truth" of the narration. That is rather like criticizing *Oedipus Rex* for stretching it a little. Adams's *Log* is mythic creation posing as autobiography no less than Sophocles's great play is myth as drama. The fact that Adams gave a name to his *persona*—Thomas Moore Quirk—has not fooled any of the commentators into believing that the narrator is anyone other than Andy Adams, whose experiences of trail drives exactly correspond to those of *The Log of a Cowboy*. What choice does any author have for his creation but to develop what he knows to be true, whether it be the truth of the imagination or the truth of realism, through an empathic character who is always the author himself? Adams individualized his characters, but they remain archetypes, romantic versions of what such revisionist histories as Frantz and Choate's *American Cowboy Myth and the Reality* (1955) have shown to be entirely the creation of nostalgic and romantic imaginations. Nevertheless, James K. Folsom, for example, in *The American Western Novel* (1966), concludes that the "impersonal quality" of the characterization of *The Log of a Cowboy* serves Adams's "historical" purpose, "a report of the facts of a way of life which has vanished." J. Frank Dobie, on the other hand, in a comment which in context praises Adams's historical accuracy, cited the parallel of Melville: "If all literature on whales and whalers were destroyed with the exception of *Moby-Dick*, we could still get from that novel a just conception of whaling" (in "A Salute to Gene Rhodes," in *The Best Novels and Stories of Eugene Manlove Rhodes*, 1949).

Tom Quirk is no more Andy Adams than Ishmael is Herman Melville—which is to say, of course, that he is something more. Through Tom, through the other characters in the *Log* and the stories they tell around the campfires, myths, not history, come into being. The *Log* is filled with details about a specific trail drive from the Mexican border through Texas and the plains to Montana—but so is Faulkner's *The Bear* about the hunt for a specific animal in Yoknapatawpha County. The *Log* records faithfully virtually every kind of event possible on such a drive—river crossings, stampedes, debauches in towns along the trail, information about the handling of cattle specific enough to generate a textbook on the subject—but so does *Moby-Dick* on whaling. When all the details and trifles are added together with the epic setting and underplayed but heroic style, it becomes clear that the purpose of the *Log* is not to detail a historical phenomenon but to generate a continuing myth. Instead of a stuffed carcass in a museum, Adams gives us live wings for our imagination.

—Herbert F. Smith

ADAMS, Bart. *See* **BINGLEY, David Ernest.**

ADAMS, Chuck. British.

WESTERN PUBLICATIONS

Novels

The Kid from Cripple Creek. London, John Spencer, 1952.
Border Feud. London, John Spencer, 1953.
Border Justice. London, John Spencer, 1954.
Frontier Colts. London, John Spencer, 1954.
Guns of the Ghost Town. London, John Spencer, 1954.
Gunsmoke Heritage. London, John Spencer, 1954.
Outlaw Territory. London, John Spencer, 1954.
The Rustlers of Yellow River. London, John Spencer, 1954.
Spawn of the Badlands. London, John Spencer, 1954.
Trailblazers. London, John Spencer, 1956.
The Savage Country. London, John Spencer, 1957.
The Tall Hellion. London, John Spencer, 1959.
Massacre Trail. London, John Spencer, 1960.
The Fugitive. London, John Spencer, 1961.
The Gunhawk. London, John Spencer, 1961.
The Hired Gun. London, John Spencer, 1961.
The Last Outlaw. London, John Spencer, 1961.
The Man from Abilene. London, John Spencer, 1961.
Warsmoke. London, John Spencer, 1961.
Ambush. London, John Spencer, 1962.
Colt Law. London, John Spencer, 1962.
The Fighting Fury. London, John Spencer, 1962.
Hang the Hellion High. London, John Spencer, 1962.
The Hunted. London, John Spencer, 1962.
The Lawless Ones. London, John Spencer, 1962.
Renegade. London, John Spencer, 1962.
The Savage Gun. London, John Spencer, 1962.
Showdown in Sierra. London, John Spencer, 1962.
Stranger with a Gun. London, John Spencer, 1962.
The Texan. London, John Spencer, 1962.
Thunder in the Dust. London, John Spencer, 1962.
Trouble Shooter. London, John Spencer, 1962.
The Wild Ones. London, John Spencer, 1962.
Brand of the Hunter. London, John Spencer, 1963.
The Drifter. London, John Spencer, 1963.
Frontier Marshal. London, John Spencer, 1963.
The Gunsmoke Breed. London, John Spencer, 1963.
Gunsmoke Heritage. London, John Spencer, 1963.
Hangnoose Justice. London, John Spencer, 1963.
Heller Brand. London, John Spencer, 1963.
Kansas Fury. London, John Spencer, 1963.
The Last Gun. London, John Spencer, 1963.
Law of the Gun. London, John Spencer, 1963.
Lynch Law. London, John Spencer, 1963.
Range Vengeance. London, John Spencer, 1963.
Rawhide Range. London, John Spencer, 1963.
The Rimriders. London, John Spencer, 1963.
Riverboat Renegade. London, John Spencer, 1963.
Two-Gun Judgement. London, John Spencer, 1963.
The Violent Breed. London, John Spencer, 1963.
Badlands Feud. London, John Spencer, 1964.
Danger Trail. London, John Spencer, 1964.
Day of Violence. London, John Spencer, 1964.
Feud. London, John Spencer, 1964.
Gun Range. London, John Spencer, 1964.
The Landbreakers. London, John Spencer, 1964.
The Lone Gun. London, John Spencer, 1964.
Night of the Gunhawk. London, John Spencer, 1964.
Showdown. London, John Spencer, 1964.
Sierra Marshal. London, John Spencer, 1964.
Thunder at Abilene. London, John Spencer, 1964.
The Trailblazers. London, John Spencer, 1964.
Bitter Breed. London, John Spencer, 1965.
Dakota Manhunt. London, John Spencer, 1965.
Day of Vengeance. London, John Spencer, 1965.
The Hostile Country. London, John Spencer, 1965.
Time of the Lawman. London, John Spencer, 1965.
Guns of Rimrock. London, John Spencer, 1966.
High Vengeance. London, John Spencer, 1966.
The Loner. London, John Spencer, 1966.
The Rawhide Ones. London, John Spencer, 1966.
Time of the Gunman. London, John Spencer, 1966.
Gunhawks Westward. London, John Spencer, 1967.
Showdown at Yuma. London, John Spencer, 1967.
The Wild Gun. London, John Spencer, 1967.
The Bounty Riders. London, John Spencer, 1971.

* * *

For more than a decade, from the mid 1950's to the mid 1960's, the London-based publisher John Spencer & Co. churned out hundreds of paperbacks under their Badger Books imprint. Spencer specialised solely in mass-market categories fiction—horror stories, romances, science fiction, thrillers, war, and so on—and of their nearly 140 western titles (which appeared in two numbered series, as either "Blazing Westerns" or "Lariat Westerns"), more than half were produced by the indefatigable Chuck Adams.

The vast majority of Adams's Westerns are fairly formulaic actioners. Little time is spared on extensive characterisation, and as a consequence both hero and villain are nearly always clearly defined. The stories tend to unfold against familiar western locales; ranches, cow-towns, deserts, and so forth, and there is often an element of romance to lift his sometimes rushed but always upbeat endings.

Specifically, Adams appears to have favoured the gun-fast lawman-hero, who crops up again and again in his work, usually sporting a tough and fitting name. Wade O'Mara, the United States Marshal in *The Tall Hellion*, is a good case in point. Assigned to locate and break the notorious Carson gang, O'Mara begins his search in the border town of Senica, joins a wagon train heading west when his investigation reveals that his quarry has already left town, and eventually poses as an outlaw himself in order to infiltrate the gang.

A common recurring theme in Adams's novels is the establishment of justice in a hitherto lawless environment. *Stranger with a Gun*, *Sierra Marshal*, and *The Trailblazers* are just three of many variations on the plot. Often these lawman-heroes have been hardened by circumstances or embittered by some devastating tragedy in their past. Temple Holliday, the marshal brought in to tame a wild town in *Thunder at Abilene*, for example, is still soured by the death of his father and brother at the hands of outlaws some time ago, while in *Dakota Manhunt*, Clint McCorg, hired to clean up the hell-town of Vendado, is soon forced to face up to his past (namely the black sheep of the family, his outlaw brother the Matagorda Kid) when three men are abducted from their hotel and found tied up and shot dead the following day.

Although Adams set many of his stories in that vaguely-defined and somewhat timeless period so beloved of the 1950's B-grade western movie, the years—or sometimes months—following the Civil War featured prominently. In *The Man from Abilene*, for example, Bart Nolan, another U.S. Marshal, is assigned to clean out the Confederate guerillas who have established a string of lawless border towns in post-Civil War Texas, while the men who rode with Quantrell's Raiders are the villains of *Trouble Shooter*, in which Clem Vance's own personal outlaw hunt is interrupted by a spate of cattle rustling which eventually proves to be just a front masking a far more sinister operation.

Similarly, Adams frequently used historical fact as the basis for his stories. The adventure which comes out of *Two-Gun Judgement*, for example, is in part also the story of the Wells Fargo stage-line, and recounts the attempts of troubleshooter Dave Lambert to stamp out a rash of robberies which eventually lead him to a meeting, and subsequent friendship, with real-life badman Sam Bass. (This book is actually one of Adams's better efforts, exhibiting as it does a vivid period feel, an adequate sense of pace, and fairly credible characters.) Other semi-historical entries include *Badlands Feud*, which follows the development of the Winchester repeating rifle, and the steam-boating story *The Landbreakers*, which recounts the history of the Natchez Trace.

Unfortunately, the majority of Adams's Westerns are fairly routine affairs, which tend to rely heavily on previously established themes. Even the most hackneyed of plots is sometimes enlivened by some twist or variation, however. In picking up a discarded newspaper, Steve Noland, the cowboy hero of *The Fugitive*, discovers that he is, in fact, heir to his late uncle's stage-line. Before he can even begin to claim his inheritance, however, he finds himself locking horns with a mysterious gang of killers who seem to be intent on making sure he never reaches his destination. After being falsely accused of the murder of a U.S. Marshal in *Heller Brand*, gun-swift drifter Lex McLean is saved from a lynch party by a hidden rifleman, whose bullets part the hangrope. When gunsmith Gabe Parker discovers that he can't outrun his somewhat shady past in *The Violent Breed*, he is forced to forsake the peaceful life of a devoted husband and father and buckle on his guns for one final showdown.

Most recommended of all Adams's books is *Warsmoke*, the thoughtful and compelling story of a group of Confederates whose trek across Arizona (where they have just collected a fortune in gold bullion to bolster the South's flagging economy) is interrupted by a band of Apaches led by a madman named Quino. While holing up at a fortified *tinaja*, the Southerners are soon joined by a Union patrol, with whom they combine forces to repel their attackers. When it is revealed that the War has recently ended, however, each of the men begins to get ideas about the gold, and to whom it should now rightfully belong . . .

Adams's style constantly adapted to suit his changing readership. His earliest books reveal a tendency towards the melodramatic, a kind of crude, "head-'em-off-at-the-pass" style, whilst the latter is tighter, more interesting, and far more controlled. His dialogue tended to be broad, too, full of "yuhs" and "tuhs" and "git goin'"s, but in general he always struck a good balance between speech and prose. Occasionally, as with *Warsmoke*, he revealed a solid understanding of American history, and when the opportunity arose, could wax quite lyrical in battle scenes or at times of introspection.

In conclusion, it is probably fair to say that, while the majority of his work is largely unremarkable, it is nevertheless well worth reading, if only for the joy of discovering the odd but exceptional gems with which it is littered.

—David Whitehead

ADAMS, Clifton. Also wrote as Jonathan Gant; Matt Kinkaid; Clay Randall. American. Born in Comanche, Oklahoma, 1 December 1919. Attended the University of Oklahoma, Norman. Served in the United States Army, 1942–45: Sergeant; five battle stars. Married Gerry Griffeth in 1948. Professional jazz drummer, then freelance writer. Recipient: Western Writers of America Spur award, 1970. 1971. *Died 7 October 1971.*

WESTERN PUBLICATIONS

Novels

The Desperado. New York, Fawcett, 1950; London, Fawcett, 1953.

A Noose for the Desperado. New York, Fawcett, 1951; London, Fawcett, 1953.

The Colonel's Lady. New York, Fawcett, 1952; London, Miller, 1955.

Two-Gun Law. New York, Fawcett, 1954; London, Fawcett, 1955.

Gambling Man. New York, Fawcett, 1955; London, Fawcett, 1956.
Law of the Trigger. New York, Fawcett, 1956; London, Fawcett, 1957.
Outlaw's Son. New York, Fawcett, 1957.
Killer in Town. New York, Dell, 1959.
Stranger in Town. New York, Doubleday, 1960; London, Hale, 1962.
The Legend of Lonnie Hall. New York, Berkley, 1960; London, Hale, 1963.
Day of the Gun. New York, Ballantine, 1962; Bath, Chivers, 1984.
Reckless Men. New York, Doubleday, 1962; London, Hale, 1963.
The Moonlight War. New York, Fawcett, and London, Muller, 1963.
Hogan's Way. New York, Berkley, 1963; London, Collins, 1964.
The Dangerous Days of Kiowa Jones. New York, Doubleday, 1963; London, Collins, 1964.
Doomsday Creek. New York, Doubleday, 1964; London, Collins, 1965.
The Hottest Fourth of July in the History of Hangtree County New York, Doubleday, 1964; as *The Hottest Fourth of July,* London, Collins, 1965.
The Grabhorn Bounty. New York, Doubleday, 1965; London, Collins, 1966.
Shorty. New York, Doubleday, and London, Collins, 1966.
A Partnership with Death. London, Collins, 1967; New York, Ace, 1968.
The Most Dangerous Profession. New York, Doubleday, 1967; London, Collins, 1973.
Dude Sheriff. New York, Doubleday, 1969; London, Hale, 1970.
Tragg's Choice. New York, Doubleday, 1969.
The Last Days of Wolf Garnett. New York, Doubleday, 1970; as *Outlaw Destiny,* London, Hale, 1972.
Biscuit-Shooter. New York, Doubleday, 1971.
Rogue Cowboy. New York, Doubleday, 1971; London, Hale, 1972.
The Badge and Harry Cole. New York, Doubleday, 1972; as *Lawman's Badge,* London, Hale, 1973.
Concannon. New York, Doubleday, 1972; London, Hale, 1974.
Hard Times and Arnie Smith. New York, Doubleday, 1972; London, Hale, 1974.
Once an Outlaw. New York, Ace, 1973.
The Hard Time Bunch. New York, Doubleday, 1973; London, Hale, 1974.
Hassle and the Medicine Man. New York, Doubleday, 1973; London, Hale, 1975.

Novels as Clay Randall (series: Amos Flagg)

Six-Gun Boss. New York, Random House, 1952; London, Corgi, 1954.
When Oil Ran Red. New York, Random House, 1953.
Boomer. New York, Permabooks, 1957.
The Oceola Kid. New York, Fawcett, 1963; London, Muller, 1964.
Hardcase for Hire. New York, Fawcett, 1963; London, Muller, 1964.
Amos Flagg—Lawman. New York, Fawcett, 1964; London, Coronet, 1966.
Amos Flagg—High Gun. New York, Fawcett, 1965; London, Coronet, 1966.
Amos Flagg—Bushwhacked. New York, Fawcett, and London, Coronet, 1967.
Amos Flagg Rides Out. New York, Fawcett, and London, Coronet, 1967.
The Killing of Billy Jowett. New York, Fawcett, 1968; Bath, Chivers, 1986.
Amos Flagg Has His Day. New York, Fawcett, 1968; London, Coronet, 1969.
Amos Flagg—Showdown. New York, Fawcett, 1969; London, Coronet, 1970.

Uncollected Short Stories

"Empire of Broken Gunmen," in *Star Western* (Chicago), January 1948.
"Ghost Range," in *Mammoth Western* (Chicago), September 1949.
"High Road to Hell," in *Mammoth Western* (Chicago), December 1949.
"Night Ride to Boothill," in *Mammoth Western* (Chicago), April 1950.
"Here's Your Rustler," in *Exciting Western* (London), October 1951.
"The First of May," in *Texas Rangers* (London), October 1952.
"A Dead Man Was Boss," in *Exciting Western* (London), September 1955.
"There's Doom in His Holsters," in *Blazing Guns* (Holyoke, Massachusetts), October 1956.
"Girl Gun-Guard for the Devil," in *Western Story* (London), January 1958.
"Who'll Die for the Double-Cross Queen?," in *Western Story* (London), August 1958.
"Stand-Off at Hell's End," in *Western Story* (London), February 1959.
"A Man to March in Front," in *Western Story* (London), March 1959.
"Hell Command," in *A Western Bonanza*, edited by Todhunter Ballard. New York, Doubleday, 1969.

OTHER PUBLICATIONS

Novels

Whom Gods Destroy. New York, Fawcett, 1953; London, Miller, 1958.
Hardcase (as Matt Kinkaid). New York, Avon, 1953; London, Hale, 1955.
Death's Sweet Song. New York, Fawcett, 1955.
The Race of Giants (as Matt Kinkaid). New York, Dell, 1956.
Never Say No to a Killer (as Jonathan Gant). New York, Ace, 1956.
The Very Wicked. New York, Berkley, 1960.
The Long Vendetta (as Jonathan Gant). New York, Avalon, 1963.

* * *

Clifton Adams was one of the most talented of the contemporary writers of formulary westerns. His best known works are probably *Tragg's Choice* and *The Last Days of Wolf Garnett*, books for which he won Spur awards in 1970 and 1971. A man of obvious sensitivity and intelligence, Adams was also a diligent student of western Americana.

His novels are usually set in the arid High Plains of Texas, Oklahoma, and Colorado during the 1870's and 1880's. Its bleak, harsh prairie landscape dominates his stories, creating men like Morrasey, the ruined sodbuster of *Tragg's Choice*, with his "rawboned, leathery face, washed-out eyes and small down-turned mouth . . . the face of poverty and ignorance and failure." The parched and barren earth withers, in time, even the fresh bloom of young womanhood. Rose Barker, in the same story, is "a classic model of a High Plains woman—dry, colorless, the juice of life long since worked out of her . . . Her face was lined and rough enough to strike matches on." Adams has an admirable compassion for such people and for all those who live on the fringes of respectability. His towns are typically sparse agglomerations of random, burned-out humanity. Strangers are met with sullen disinterest, or are cheated, or beaten—or all three by turns. Frank Gault, in *The Last Days of Wolf Garnett*, is grossly overcharged for a rental horse in the scroungy burg of New Boston, then goes to a local café for breakfast. A sour-looking counterman brings him his order. "He slammed it down in front of him and gimped back to his stove. Gault gazed leerily at the leathery flapjacks, the watery sugar syrup, the slabs of fat side meat, the puddles of grease already congealing in the cold platter. The eggs, also coated in congealing grease, were cooked to a peculiar bluish color, the whites curled, as if in pain, the yolks as hard as grapeshot." Adams delights in this kind of local color that edges onto the universal.

These depressing islands of broken humanity are often in the grip of some ruthless man, like Sheriff Grady Olsen, in *The Last Days of Wolf Garnett*, or Jeremy Hooker, in the comic *Biscuit-Shooter*. The protagonists Adams tortures in these hellholes are remarkable for their human frailty. They are flawed and vulnerable men, usually past their prime and burdened with a weathered sensibility long stripped of youth's happy illusions. Owen Tragg, for example, is an aging ex-Marshal who has suffered in conscience for 10 years for having killed a famous badman. Frank Shade, in *The Grabhorn Bounty*, is haunted by a childhood spent in end-of-track shanty towns.

The most unusual figures in Adams's novels, however, are almost always the women. Whereas his men are riven creatures of conscience and memory, the women are fierce and cold-blooded beneath their masks of innocence. Bess Durell, the naively beautiful daughter of a sodbuster in *The Grabhorn Bounty*, is later revealed to be the daring and elusive masked bandit "Shotgun Brown." In *Tragg's Choice* Rose Barker, the widow of the gunman that Tragg had killed 10 years before, has worked as a scullery maid and cook in order to save every dollar Tragg sent her as compensation for killing her husband—all so that she could use his own money to have him shot. It is women like these who are at the secret heart of Adams's stories. They have the frightening simplicity of a beast of prey. In hope of winning them, men will work, steal, and kill.

Adams infuses his central male characters with a delicate and sometimes complex psychology which is at odds with both their own instinctual drives and the violent, crude world around them. Their impulse for power and survival is offset by their sense of justice and a deepening awareness of life's ultimate futility. It is this psychological and moral tension that gives Adams's fast-paced, gritty stories their capacity to both thrill the nerves and satisfy the intelligence.

—John D. Flanagan

ADAMS, Frank Ramsay. American. Born in Morrison, Illinois, 7 July 1883. Educated at Hyde Park High School, Chicago; University of Chicago, 1900–04, Ph.B. 1904. Served in the United States Army, with Coast Artillery, and in France, 1916–19; 1st lieutenant; French Service Medal. Married 1) Hazel Leslie Judd in 1907 (died); 2) Lorna D. Margrave in 1931; one daughter. Wrote musical comedies with Will M. Hough while in college, producing 13 plays which were performed at Chicago theatres. Reporter, City Press, Chicago, Chicago *Tribune*, and Chicago *Herald Examiner*, 1903–04; manager, Playhouse Theater, Whitehall, Michigan, 1916–32; president, Sylvan Beach Resort Company, Whitehall; owner-operator, Carlson-Adams Garage, Whitehall, 1923–51. From 1913 full-time writer. Stories published in *Smart Set*, *Cosmopolitan*, *Black Cat*, and *Illustrated Detective*; also wrote plays, musical comedies, film scripts, and lyrics for popular songs, including "I Wonder Who's Kissing Her Now." *Died 8 October 1963.*

Western Publications

Novels

Gunsight Ranch. New York, Doubleday, 1939.
Arizona Feud. New York, Doubleday, 1941; London, Harrap, 1944.

Other Publications

Novels

The Secret Attic. London, Paul, 1930.
The Long Night. London, Paul, 1932.
For Valor. London, Paul, 1933.
Pleasure Island. London, Paul, 1935.
Men on Foot. London, Newnes, 1937.

Plays

His Highness the Bey: A Musical Satire in Two Acts, with Will M. Hough, music by Joseph E. Howard (produced Chicago, 1905).
The Isle of Bong-Bong: A Musical Comedy in Two Acts, with Will M. Hough, music by Joseph E. Howard (produced Chicago, 1905).
The Land of Nod: A Musical Extravaganza with a Prologue and Two Acts, with Will M. Hough, music by Joseph E. Howard (produced Chicago, 1905).
The Time, the Place and the Girl: A Three-Act Comedy with Music, with Will M. Hough, music by Joseph E. Howard (produced Chicago, 1906).
Five Fridays. Boston, Small Maynard, 1915.
Molly and I, or the Silver Ring. Boston, Small Maynard, 1915.
Stage Struck. New York, Jacobsen Hodgkinson, 1925.
Almost a Lady. New York, Jacobsen Hodgkinson, 1927.
Help Yourself to Happiness. New York, Macaulay, and London, Newnes, 1929.
King's Crew. New York, Long and Smith, and London, Constable, 1932.

Screenplays: *The Cowboy and the Lady*; *Peg O' My Heart*; *Trade-Winds*; *The Virginia Judge*; *She Made Her Bed*; *The Super Sex*; *Scandal Street.*

Other

When I Come Back. New York, McBride, 1944.
The Impossible Dream: a Report. Camarillo, California, F. Adams, 1976.

* * *

Frank Ramsay Adams is best known as a writer of plays, musical comedies, motion picture scripts, and lyrics for popular songs. He began his writing career composing musical comedies in collaboration with Will M. Hough when both were students at the University of Chicago from 1900 to 1904. Adams wrote the words and Hough the music for a song, "I Wonder Who's Kissing Her Now," that became part of Chicago folklore. Originally composed for one of their student musicals, "A Prince of Tonight," the song gave the title to a 1947 film musical produced by George Jessel and became a national hit.

Adams specialized in romantic adventure and mystery fiction featuring bright, sophisticated, articulate people engaged in witty repartee and light-hearted love affairs. Near the end of his writing career, he wrote two novels that were set in the contemporary American west, *Gunsight Ranch* and *Arizona Feud*.

The nameless narrator in *Gunsight Ranch* on the lam after having taken the rap for fraud in his family's Chicago bank so as to preserve his father's reputation, begins his story while sitting on a bench in a Chicago railroad station. A man next to him begins to have a heart attack and turns to the narrator, thrusting his billfold and a claim check into his hands. Would he please reclaim the striken man's bag and get the medicine in it? He dies before the narrator can return. The narrator now has a new identity as the heir to a ranch in Clovis, New Mexico and a predictable story unfolds from that point.

Arizona Feud is a Hatfield and McCoy story of the murderous rivalry between the Dovers and the Seeleys. The plot centers around the multiple marriages and forlorn love affairs of Phoebe Dover whose popular romantic novels provide the support for her family ranch which, if it were not for her efforts, would quickly go bankrupt. At the inquest inquiring into Phoebe's violent death which concludes the book, all is explained in popular psychological terms and the way cleared for a healing marriage between a Dover daughter and a Seeley son.

Adams's "westerns" draw their inspiration from genre traditions different from that supporting the western story. Both are lightly satirical of the conventions of the western but show little real knowledge of the landscape, the society, or historical context of the frontier. They are, rather, romantic mysteries peopled with Adams's usual cast of urbane sophisticates dressed in western garb acting out their roles on a western stage set.

—J. Fraser Cocks, III

ADAMS, Harrison. *See* **RATHBORNE, St. George.**

AHLSWEDE, Ann. American. Born in California, 29 February 1928. Married John W. Ahlswede in 1948 (divorced 1982); two daughters and one son. Artist: works exhibited in England and the United States. Address: 4616 Rancho Reposo, Del Mar, California 92014, U.S.A.

WESTERN PUBLICATIONS

Novels

Day of the Hunter. New York, Ballantine, 1960.
Hunting Wolf. New York, Ballantine, 1960.
The Savage Land. New York, Ballantine, 1962.

Uncollected Short Story

"The Promise of the Fruit," in *She Won the West: An Anthology of Western and Frontier Stories by Women*, edited by Marcia Muller and Bill Pronzini. New York, Morrow, 1985.

*

Ann Ahlswede comments:

I wanted to say something about human nature, about time, continuity; about an awesome, often cruel land and the workings of human histories in an environment where the ultimate confrontation was with one's self.

For me, the American west speaks insistently to the dream of freedom, and to one last cherished sense of wilderness.

* * *

Ann Ahlswede established her reputation in the early 1960's with the publication of three novels and a short story. *Day of the Hunter*, her first novel, is a formulary Western with a clearly identifiable hero, heroine, and three villains. It embodies the justice/revenge theme plot structure. Johnny Raider, a mixed-blood, was adopted and raised by the white Raider family. When the family is murdered, the women raped in the bargain, the Anglo-American neighbors accuse Johnny of having done it because of his racial background and want to string him up. Johnny eludes capture and, himself a fugitive, goes in search of the real culprits. In his pursuit, he encounters Mrs. Gribbs and her daughter, Angie. Although a stereotypical heroine, Angie is well characterized. The novel ends with a shoot-out in which two of the villains are slain and a third is left alive to confess to the crimes. Dr. Cicero Smith, a mountebank of questionable motivation, makes his appearance in *Day of the Hunter* and is a recurring character in the subsequent novels; he serves as a sounding board for the protagonists when they reach the inevitable confrontation with themselves and their reasons for living, a scene which in Ahlswede's fiction precedes the *anagnorisis*, or recognition, at the end.

Hunting Wolf is a reworking of the same revenge theme plot, but with an interesting variation. Wolfe is a mixed-blood. His pregnant Navajo wife is kidnapped by four villains, and Wolfe, left with his right hand nailed to a tree, frees himself and sets out in pursuit. On the way he enounters Betsy Spear, with whom (after he learns his wife is dead) he falls in love, and Tenner Bice, a 16-year-old drifter who is also attracted to Betsy. Wolfe confronts only one of the villains in a gunfight; the others die, but in ways that have nothing to do with Wolfe. Wolfe, Betsy, and Tenner in their travels meet Dr. Cicero Smith and his character is somewhat more fully developed than in *Day of the Hunter*.

Ahlswede was seriously experimenting with the structure of the formulary Western in these two novels. This tendency reached its apotheosis in *The Savage Land* which is a historical reconstruction, i.e., it is faithful to the place, the period, and the people of a California mining community in 1873. Tully James Davis is the protagonist. He is framed for a bank robbery engineered by Frank Ewell, the banker's son, and Ewell and Tully have a terrific fight. Ewell leads the pursuit of Tully and on the way Ewell picks up Dr. Cicero Smith to attend to his battered face, a result of the fight. Ewell and his men overtake Tully at an old prospector's shack and the old prospector is killed. His young wife, their child, Tully, and Dr. Cicero Smith constitute the forces for good, Ewell and his gang the forces for evil. Searching for water in the desert, Ewell and his men die during a sand storm, a scene reminiscent in its ominous portrayal of the natural elements of Frank Norris's novel *McTeague* (1899). Tully is able to lead his group back to civilization where he is put on trial for robbery and murder and is convicted on the basis of circumstantial evidence. He is hanged. *The Savage Land*, in the telling, becomes an indictment of the greed and crazed power which came to California with Anglo-Americans and their concept of "law and order." Like Max Evans's *The Hi Lo Country* (1962), it is a novel which reverses the traditional harmony of the formulary western by showing how innocent and good men can be destroyed by those very forces which the formulary western prescribes as virtuous and worthy of imitation.

"The Promise of the Fruit" is the only short story Ahlswede has written to date. Although the urgent need to affix guilt—such a central concern in Ahlswede's longer fictions—can be found, the story goes beyond it to probe the underside of what American politicians are always selling, the American dream, the belief that change, while inevitable, is invariably for the better.

Few women have been able to write effectively in the formulary mode of western fiction, and even those who have—B.M. Bower, P.A. Bechko, Lee Hoffman come to mind—did not choose to reverse the structure in mid-stream as did Ahlswede; and even in her formulary books her characters are suddenly forced to examine their reasons for existing and behaving. Hers is a unique talent, and her fiction, all of it, has a singularly gripping quality.

—Jon Tuska

ALBERT, Marvin H. Also writes as Al Conroy; Albert Conroy; Ian Macalister; Nick Quarry; Anthony Rome. American. Born in Philadelphia, Pennsylvania. Served as radio officer on Liberty ships during World War II. Married 1) Vivian Coleman; 2) Xenia Klar. Journalist: copyman for Philadelphia *Record*; researcher for *Look* magazine; then freelance writer. Recipient: Mystery Writers of America award. Address: c/o Arbor House, 235 East 45th Street, New York, New York, 10017, U.S.A.

WESTERN PUBLICATIONS

Novels (series: Clayburn)

The Law and Jake Wade. New York, Fawcett, 1956; London, Fawcett, 1957.
Apache Rising. New York, Fawcett, 1957; London, Fawcett, 1959; as *Duel at Diablo*, London, Coronet, 1966.
The Bounty Killer. New York, Fawcett, 1958; London, Fawcett, 1959.
Renegade Posse. New York, Fawcett, 1958; London, Muller, 1960.
Rider from Wind River. New York, Fawcett, 1959; London, Muller, 1960.
The Reformed Gun. New York, Fawcett, 1959; London, Muller, 1960.
Last Train to Bannock (Clayburn, as Al Conroy). New York, Della, 1963; as Marvin Albert, New York, Fawcett, 1989.
Posse at High Pass. New York, Fawcett, 1964.
Clayburn. New York, Dell, 1979.
Three Rode North. (Clayburn) New York, Fawcett, 1989.
The Man in Black. New York, Fawcett, 1990.

OTHER PUBLICATIONS

Novels

Lie Down with Lions. New York, Fawcett, 1955; London, Red Seal, 1957.
Party Girl (novelization of screenplay). New York, Fawcett, 1958; London, Fawcett, 1959.
That Jane from Maine. New York, Fawcett, 1959; London, Muller, 1960.
Pillow Talk (novelization of screenplay). New York, Fawcett, 1959; London, Muller, 1960.
All the Young Men (novelization of screenplay). New York, Pocket Books, 1960.
Lover Come Back (novelization of screenplay). New York, Fawcett, 1962.
The VIPs (novelization of screenplay). New York, Dell, 1963.
Move Over, Darling (novelization of screenplay). New York, Dell, 1963.
Palm Springs Week-end. New York, Dell, 1963.
Under the Yum Yum Tree. New York, Dell, 1963.
The Outrage (novelization of screenplay). New York, Pocket Books, 1964.
Goodbye Charlie. New York, Dell, 1964.
The Pink Panther (novelization of screenplay). New York, Bantam, 1964.
Honeymoon Hotel. New York, Dell, 1964.
What's New, Pussycat? (novelization of screenplay). New York, Dell, and London, Mayflower, 1965.
Strange Bedfellows (novelization of screenplay). New York, Pyramid, 1965.
Do Not Disturb. New York, Dell, 1965.
The Great Race. New York, Dell, 1965.
A Very Special Flavor (novelization of screenplay). New York, Dell, 1965.
Come September. New York, Dell, 1971.
Crazy Joe (novelization of screenplay, as Mike Barone). New York, Bantam, 1974.
The Gargoyle Conspiracy. New York, Doubleday, and London, Deutsch, 1975.
The Dark Goddess. New York, Doubleday, and London, Deutsch, 1978.
Hidden Lives. New York, Delacorte Press, 1981.
The Medusa Complex. New York, Arbor House, 1982.
Operation Lila. New York, Arbor House, 1983.
Nightmare in Dreamland. New York, Arbor House, 1985.
The Golden Circle. Bethesda, Maryland, Beach, 1985.
Back in the Real World. New York, Ballantine, 1986; London, Macmillan, 1987.
The Stone Angel. New York, Fawcett, 1986; London, Macmillan, 1987.
Get Off at Babylon. New York, Fawcett, 1987; London, Macmillan, 1988.
The Last Smile. New York, Fawcett, 1988; London, Macmillan, 1989.
The Untouchables (novelization of screenplay). London, Severn House, 1988.

The Midnight Sister. New York, Fawcett, and London, Macmillan, 1989.

Novels as Nick Quarry

The Hoods Come Calling. New York, Fawcett, 1958; London, Fawcett, 1959.
Trail of a Tramp. New York, Fawcett, 1958; London, Muller, 1960.
The Girl with No Place to Hide. New York, Fawcett, 1959; London, Muller, 1961.
No Chance in Hell. New York, Fawcett, 1960; London, Muller, 1962.
Till It Hurts. New York, Fawcett, 1960; London, Muller, 1963.
Some Die Hard. New York, Fawcett, 1961; London, Muller, 1963.
The Don Is Dead. New York, Fawcett, and London, Coronet, 1972.
The Vendetta. New York, Fawcett, 1973.

Novels as Anthony Rome

Miami Mayhem. London, Hale, 1961; as *Tony Rome*, New York, Dell, 1967.
The Lady in Cement. London, Hale, 1962.
My Kind of Game. New York, Dell, 1962.

Novels as Albert Conroy

The Road's End. New York, Fawcett, 1952; London, Fawcett, 1960.
The Chiselers. New York, Fawcett, 1953.
Nice Guys Finish Dead. New York, Fawcett, 1957; London, Fawcett, 1958.
Murder in Room 13. New York, Fawcett, 1958; London, Fawcett, 1960.
The Mob Says Murder. New York, Fawcett, 1958; London, Fawcett, 1960.
Mr. Lucky (novelization of screenplay). New York, Dell, 1960.
Devil in Dungarees. New York, Crest, 1960.
The Looters. New York, Crest, 1961.

Novels as Al Conroy

Death Grip. New York, Lancer, 1972.
Soldato! New York, Lancer, 1972.
Blood Run! New York, Lancer, 1973.
Murder Mission! New York, Lancer, 1973.
Strangle Hold! New York, Lancer, 1973.

Novels as Ian MacAlister

Driscoll's Diamonds. New York, Fawcett, 1973; London, Coronet, 1974.
Skylark Mission. New York, Fawcett, 1973; London, Coronet, 1974.
Strike Force 7. New York, Fawcett, 1974; London, Coronet, 1975.
Valley of the Assassins. New York, Fawcett, 1975; London, Coronet, 1976.

Plays

Screenplays: *Duel at Diablo*, with Michel Grilikhes, 1966; *Rough Night in Jericho*, with Sydney Boehm, 1967; *Lady in Cement*, with Jack Guss, 1968; *A Twist of Sand*, 1969.

Other

Becoming a Mother, with Theodore R. Seidman. New York, McKay, 1956; revised edition, New York, Fawcett, 1966, 1978.
Broadsides and Boarders. New York, Appleton Century Crofts, 1957; London, Harrap, 1958.
The Long White Road: Ernest Shackleton's Antarctic Adventures (for children). New York, McKay, 1957; London, Lutterworth Press, 1960.
The Divorce. New York, Simon and Schuster, 1965; London, Harrap, 1966.

* * *

Marvin H. Albert is a prolific writer of westerns, mysteries, suspense thrillers, and novelizations of screenplays as well as miscellaneous non-fiction. A solid professional, his work displays craftsmanship and high-quality writing.

Apache Rising is the story of Jess Remsberg's vengeance after the scalping and slaughter of his young wife by Apaches. The action is intense and violent. *Apache Rising* was filmed as *Duel at Diablo* starring James Garner and Sidney Poitier.

In *The Bounty Killer*, Albert creates the character of Luke Chilson, a bounty hunter whose reputation causes fear in the lawless territories. Chilson is not a killing machine; he's a man of principle and honor, but the nature of his trade forces him to deal in violence and death. Albert carefully shows the true nature of this man's work, without the glamor and exaggeration too often associated with bounty hunters.

Renegade Posse is another example of Albert's unconventional plotting. Logan Keliher finds himself leading a rag-tag group of men after bank robber, Sam Ward. The twist Albert adds is that the posse, with the exception of Keliher, intend to kill Ward and split the money he stole among themselves. Gradually, Keliher begins to realize his honesty is his death warrant. *Renegade Posse* was later made into the movie, *Bullet for a Badman*, starring Audie Murphy and Darren McGavin.

Rider from Wind River begins with Joe Lang being robbed of his horses by a man who closely resembles him. Later, a posse rides into Lang's campsite and wants to hang him for the murder of a miner and the theft of his gold. Lang manages to escape the posse and hanging, but knows he has to find the real killer to clear his name. Although the plot is conventional, Albert's solid characterizations provide compelling storytelling.

Under the pseudonym of "Al Conroy" Albert wrote the Clayburn series of original paperbacks. These books lack the attention to detail and the crisp characterizations of Albert's other western novels.

The first book in the series, *Clayburn*, is a standard revenge novel where Clayburn rides into a little town named Flathead to find the killer of his best friend, Mike Owens, and avenge Mike's brutal murder. Clayburn finds the killer and much more. In *Last Train to Bannock* Clayburn leads a wagon train through badlands infested with Apaches, outlaws, and killing blizzards. *The Man in Black* returns to the theme of vengeance. In *Three Rode North* Clayburn takes on an outlaw gang.

While most of Albert's westerns were out-of-print for decades, recently they have been reprinted—including the "Al

Conroy" books in the Clayburn series—so a new generation of readers can enjoy some of his best writing.

—George Kelley

ALBION, Ken. *See* **KING, Albert.**

ALDRICH, Bess Streeter. Also wrote as Margaret Dean Stevens. American. Born in Cedar Falls, Iowa, 17 February 1881. Educated at Iowa State Teachers College, Cedar Falls, graduated 1901. Married Charles S. Aldrich in 1907 (died 1925); one daughter and three sons. Teacher in public schools in Iowa and Salt Lake City, Utah, five years; assistant supervisor of primary training, Iowa State Teachers College, one year. Contributed short stories to many magazines; also wrote for Paramount Studios, Hollywood. Recipient: *Ladies Home Journal* prize, 1911; O. Henry award, for short stories, 1931. D.Litt: University of Nebraska, 1931. *Died 3 August 1954.*

WESTERN PUBLICATIONS

Novels

The Rim of the Prairie. New York and London, Appleton, 1925.
A Lantern in Her Hand. New York and London, Appleton, 1928.
A White Bird Flying. New York and London, Appleton, 1931.
Spring Came On Forever. New York and London, Appleton Century Crofts, 1935.
Song of Years. New York and London, Appleton Century, 1939.
The Lieutenant's Lady. New York and London, Appleton Century, 1942.

OTHER PUBLICATIONS

Novels

Mother Mason. New York and London, Appleton, 1924.
The Cutters. New York, Burt, 1926.
Miss Bishop. New York and London, Appleton Century, 1933.
The Drum Goes Dead. New York and London, Appleton Century, 1941.
Across the Smiling Meadow. New York, Mattituck/American House, 1984.
Romance in G Minor. New York, Mattituck/American House, 1984.

Short Stories

The Man Who Dreaded to Go Home: A Contest Selection, edited by Olive White Fortenbacher, Boston, Baker, 1928.
The Man Who Caught the Weather, and Other Stories. New York and London, Appleton Century, 1936.
Journey into Christmas, and Other Stories. New York and London, Appleton Century Crofts, 1949.
The Homecoming, and Other Stories. New York, Mattituck/American House, 1984.

Other

A Bess Streeter Aldrich Treasury. New York, Appleton Century Crofts, 1959.

* * *

Bess Streeter Aldrich was born and reared in Cedar Falls, Iowa, a small northeastern Iowa city. Both her father and mother had come pioneering into the area as young adults with their parents and families in the late 1850's. The Streeters had moved westward from New York to Illinois then Iowa; the Andersons, Mrs. Streeter's family, had moved from Frazerburgh, Scotland, to Quebec, to Illinois, then to Iowa. Because Aldrich had grown up listening to tales of westward migration and the mingled trials and pleasures of such undertakings, she developed insights into pioneers' lives in new territories. All of her western books are historically accurate, have been used, and continue to be used as texts in history, social studies, and English classes; all carry a romance mingled with historic facts; and all have been published in England and translated into other languages. Many of her 160 short stories appeared in magazines in England from the 1920's through the 1940's.

The Rim of the Prairie was the first of Aldrich's novels with a pioneering theme as well as her first real novel. Aldrich intended to describe the experiences of Nancy Moore and Warner Field, a young, modern couple, and have as subsidiary characters old Uncle Jud and Aunt Biny Moore. When reviews began to come in, Aldrich realized that she was so steeped in the lore of early settlement that the old couple almost took over her book. Their memories of a half century earlier and their attachment to the land proved of major interest. This work provides insights into the early days and contrasts "the old days" and "progress."

Three years later, *A Lantern in Her Hand*, her most famous novel, was published. Aldrich wrote on this particular theme of the woman pioneer partly because, using as references her mother, grandmothers, and her father's seven lively sisters, she knew that pioneer women were not like the usually portrayed drab and forlorn creatures either going quietly mad through loneliness or perpetually yearning to return to the East. Aldrich had told her pioneering mother that she was sorry that her mother's life had been so hard, while her own and her sisters' had been so much easier. Her mother had looked at her with "an odd little expression" and told her to save her pity, for "'we had the best time in the world!'" This comment began the process of considering the woman pioneer. Many of *Lantern*'s incidents were sent to Aldrich by early settlers in Nebraska or their families after she had asked on the radio (in 1927) for real examples from the pioneering era.

Lantern is the story of Abbie Mackenzie who, as a child, moves with her widowed mother, brothers, and sisters to Iowa. She grows up, meets, and marries Will Deal; three years later, in 1868, they immigrate to eastern Nebraska. Details abound of the move and of the life in a land where trees grow only along creeks and streams and there is little to stop the eye. Abbie Deal and her husband pioneer to the Elmwood, Nebraska, area, raise their family, and take part in the changes that turn open prairie into a settlement and then a town surrounded by handsome farms. Life is not easy for Abbie, who lives some 80 years, yet it is in many ways rewarding. Abbie's has been called an "epic" story.

A White Bird Flying is a sequel to *A Lantern in Her Hand* in that it carries Abbie's family into later generations. Abbie's granddaughter, Laura, prepares to leave for the East coast and a writing career because she feels there is nothing left in the Midwest about which to write. She finds she is wrong. Aldrich stresses in all of her writing that "wherever there are people who live and work and love and die, there is the stuff of which stories are made." In maturing, Laura finds that to write one doesn't need more than a sympathetic understanding of other people. This historically accurate book was in the top three in sales in America for 1931, with Pearl Buck and Willa Cather authoring the other two top sellers.

The story of the German–Lutheran movement into southeast Nebraska is told in *Spring Came On Forever*. This work covers more than 60 years of Amalia Holmsdorfer's life. Here is the universality of a woman's love and pain for her son, grandson, and great grandson. Here, too, is her dismay at disruptive changes in the German way of life, for she sees language, family life, and church break away from the settler's original concepts; the settlers' children become Americanized, speak English, and marry out of the faith. Further, the cycle of "shirtsleeves to shirtsleeves in three generations" is reenacted. The overriding concern throughout the work is the importance of the land.

The history of northeast Iowa in the Cedar Falls vicinity is recounted in *Song of Years*. The story begins in 1854 with the arrival there of a young man, Wayne Lockwood, and concludes shortly after the end of the Civil War. There is great detail of pioneering times along with the romance between Wayne and Suzanne Martin. Included is the coming of the railroad, politics, political fighting between towns, social activities, and even such details as the importance to the community of the first school bell. In many ways it is the story of Aldrich's own family settling in Iowa. The incidents are factual, for Aldrich used events that had been recorded in newspapers and letters.

The Lieutenant's Lady originated from a pair of diaries sent to Aldrich by the niece of the couple who wrote them. The story begins in 1867 in Omaha and follows Linnie Colsworth Stafford and her husband Norman, an army lieutenant, to forts up the Missouri River, beyond the Yellowstone River and into Montana territory. Aldrich retained the writers' styles; thus the book has the sense of having come from the pen of a Victorian woman, for it is told from Linnie's point of view. There are very few, if any, similar histories of the early day forts along the western river system. This work, which Aldrich wrote the year after World War II began for Americans, is her tribute to the soldiers who served in three wars and to the women who went with their men when they could or remained at home as support when they could not.

—Carol Miles Petersen

ALLAN, Luke. Pseudonym for William Lacey Amy. Journalist: editor and proprietor, *Medicine Hat Times*, Alberta, three years. *Died in 1962.*

WESTERN PUBLICATIONS

Novels (series: Blue Pete)

The Blue Wolf: A Tale of the Cypress Hills. London, Hodder and Stoughton, 1913.
Blue Pete, Half Breed: A Story of the Cowboy West. London, Jenkins, 1920; New York, McCann, 1921.
The Lone Trail. London, Jenkins, 1921.
The Return of Blue Pete. London, Jenkins, and New York, Doran, 1922.
The Westerner. London, Jenkins, 1923.
Blue Pete, Detective. London, Jenkins, 1928.
The End of the Trail. Bristol, Arrowsmith, 1931.
Blue Pete, Horsethief. London, Jenkins, 1938.
The Tenderfoot. London, Jenkins, 1939.
The Vengeance of Blue Pete. London, Jenkins, 1939.
Blue Pete, Rebel. London, Jenkins, 1940.
Blue Pete Pays a Debt. London, Jenkins, 1942.
Blue Pete Breaks the Rules. London, Jenkins, 1943.
Blue Pete, Outlaw. London, Jenkins, 1944.
Blue Pete's Dilemma. London, Jenkins, 1945.
Blue Pete to the Rescue. London, Jenkins, 1947.
Blue Pete's Vendetta. London, Jenkins, 1947.
Blue Pete and the Pinto. London, Jenkins, 1948.
Blue Pete Works Alone. London, Jenkins, 1948.
Blue Pete, Unofficially. London, Jenkins, 1949.
Blue Pete, Indian Scout. London, Jenkins, 1950.
Blue Pete at Bay. London, Jenkins, 1952.
Blue Pete and the Kid. London, Jenkins, 1953.
Blue Pete Rides the Foothills. London, Jenkins, 1953.
Blue Pete in the Badlands. London, Jenkins, 1954.

OTHER PUBLICATIONS

Novels

The Beast. London, Cape, 1924; Boston, Small Maynard, 1926.
The Pace. London, Hutchinson, 1926.
The Sire. London, Hutchinson, 1927.
The Masked Stranger. Bristol, Arrowsmith, 1930.
Murder at Midnight. Bristol, Arrowsmith, 1930.
Jungle Crime. Bristol, Arrowsmith, 1931.
The Dark Spot. Bristol, Arrowsmith, 1932.
The Fourth Dagger. Bristol, Arrowsmith, 1932.
The Traitor. Bristol, Arrowsmith, 1933.
Murder at the Club. Bristol, Arrowsmith, 1933.
Five for One. Bristol, Arrowsmith, 1934.
Behind the Wire Fence. Bristol, Arrowsmith, 1935.
The Black Opal. Bristol, Arrowsmith, 1935.
The Case of the Open Drawer. Bristol, Arrowsmith, 1936.
Scotland Yard Takes a Holiday. Bristol, Arrowsmith, 1937.
The Man on the Twenty-Fourth Floor. London, Jenkins, 1937.
The Ghost Murder. London, Jenkins, 1937.
Beyond the Locked Door. London, Jenkins, 1938.

Other (as Lacey Amy)

The White Camel. London, Jarrolds, 1926.
The Many-Coloured Thread. London, Jenkins, 1932.

* * *

W.L. Amy wrote most of his novels under the pseudonym Luke Allan. An Englishman who lived in Canada, his special field was the Canadian western. In literary terms this type of novel owes more to English literature than to the conventional American Western. Amy did, however, have a long career as a writer from 1913 to 1954 and his Westerns show some change over this period.

His first novel, *The Blue Wolf*, was a mystery story set in the Canadian Rockies and is rather typical of English adventure stories of the time with a gentleman as hero. By 1921 Amy had discovered a formula in the shape of Blue Pete, a cowboy character who was to provide the basis of most of his books. The settings in Canada were, however, more important than characterisation. In *The Lone Trail* we do not have Blue Pete, but we do have a return of North West Mounted Policemen. This book shows the elements of Amy's formula for westerns: there is plenty of local colour of the west of Canada, and there is the North West Mounted Police who have a very special romance of their own. They police their territory in a much tighter and effective way than the typical United States Sheriff, and so there is only a limited scope for crime. Into this setting is injected basically a murder mystery with a bit of cowboy detail.

In Blue Pete Amy had found a profitable literary vein. He supplied the cowboy element to Mountie novels without dominating the plot or the action. Blue Pete is a sort of backwoodsman, but Amy is able to avoid too much personality and to allow him to develop in later novels. Thus by 1928 Blue Pete has developed from a half breed into a detective in *Blue Pete, Detective*, which is a cross between a mystery and a western but set in British Columbia. (In the 1920's and 1930's Amy wrote many detective stories and melodramatic thrillers such as *Murder at Midnight* and *Beyond the Locked Door*. The latter is ostensibly set in Toronto but there is so little sense of setting that it could be a detective story from any large city.)

It is, however, the popularity of the Mountie novel which led Amy to write most of his books about the North West Territories of Canada. In the Canadian books Amy sometimes mentions tourists visiting the developing frontier town of Medicine Hat with its rodeos. The English reader would be a literary tourist finding in Amy's books attractive scenery but also the very reassuring presence of the Mounties. The interesting feature of Amy's works is that this Canadianness decreases in time. His novels of the 1950's are more like conventional genre westerns than Mountie stories. In his last western, *Blue Pete in the Badlands*, there is cattle rustling in which the criminals exploit the more lawless conditions on the United States side of the border that the Mounties cannot cross. There is also more violence and western speech in the later novels. Amy's prose developed into a more conventional clipped, tight style. As in most westerns this style suited characters who were economical with words.

—P.R. Meldrum

ALLEN, Chester. Pseudonym for Henry Lloyd Ingham. British.

WESTERN PUBLICATIONS

Novels

Vengeance Trail. London, Herbert Jenkins, 1952.
Marshal of Gunsmoke. London, Herbert Jenkins, 1953.
Badlands Showdown. London, Herbert Jenkins, 1953.
Gallows West. London, Herbert Jenkins, 1954.
Spectre Range. London, Herbert Jenkins, 1954.
Blizzard Range. London, Herbert Jenkins, 1955.
Colt Heritage. London, Herbert Jenkins, 1956.
Bullet Bounty. London, Herbert Jenkins, 1957.

* * *

Chester Allen created the characters of Justice Colt and Pee Wee Detwaller in the early 1950's. This was a time when the Western vogue was at its height and the need for "quality" writing was perhaps less apparent than it was in later decades. The public were content with reading familiar storylines from any author, and during the five-year period that Allen produced his eight books, he satisfied himself with tried and trusted formulae.

The series begins with *Vengeance Trail*, where we are introduced to the hero Justice Colt, a ranch owner operating his spread somewhere between Fort Stockton and Langley. He and his forebears pioneered the settlement of Texas, and helped to create Independence Creek—a typical frontier town. When the stage on its regular run rolls into town, Colt's world is turned upside down. Not only has it been held up by six bandits and the guard wounded, but his sister, Dimtry Colt, has suffered fatal injuries. On her death, Justice decides to take the law into his own hands. Buckling on his brace of Frontier Colts, he sets off on the trail of the murderers. Allen unnecessarily convolutes what should have been a simple "track down and kill" novel by involving Colt in a range war, and introduces myriad characters who seem superfluous to the plot. At the start of the book he helps an old wrangler, Pee Wee Detwaller, who is being picked on by a rival crew, and this fateful meeting has such a profound effect on the oldster that he hitches up with Colt for all his further adventures.

Allen tries to create a mystery element in all of his plots, using Colt and Detwaller as unknown outside forces brought in to solve the problems. Of the two, Detwaller is the more interesting character. He is more outgoing, older and wiser, and tends to voice his opinions whether asked or not. Colt, on the other hand, is a loner, content with his own company, and comes across as rather hard-hearted and stiff in characterization. As with all heroes, he is ready to fight dirty and blow away the bad men with his trusty and unerring Colts.

The books inevitably include a female with whom Colt develops an uneasy liaison. These woman are usually stereotypes being either hopeless or feisty, but always vulnerable, requiring a man's help to solve their problems. Their feelings towards Colt are not returned, as he tends to wear his loner's tag for all to see.

The plotting is predictable, although the settings range from Texas to Kansas, and from Arizona to Colorado. These latter should have provided Allen with enough scope to develop interesting storylines, but all too often he relies on the range war theme. This is evident in *Badlands Showdown*, when land-hungry Bat Hagerman has rival rancher Buck Ames killed in order to take over his land. But Ames's surviving daughter, Honesty, is not prepared to give up without a fight. By a handy coincidence, Ames was a friend of Detwaller, and he and Colt come to the maiden's rescue. *Spectre Range* uses much the same plot, a seemingly helpless female being forced to sell her ranch to a unscrupulous trader backed by his hired gunhands. Our heroes, trading horses nearby, hear about Carnell Quincy's troubles and side with her. In *Gallows West*, the duo are involved in a fight over valley grazing rights. The villain this time is Rock Gilman and his hired guns. In *Blizzard Range*, the range war plot is running thin, so Allen introduces a secondary theme of cattle rustling. Operating as a U.S. marshal, Colt is asked to conduct an inquiry into the disappearance of three investigators from the Stockman's Association.

In *Marshal of Gunsmoke* the partners ride into the cattle town of Ellsworth to find it in the grip of a powerful cattle baron who is forcing his will on others, and abusing his authority. When Dunlap has the marshal killed Colt feels that he has overstepped the mark, and pins on the badge to take on the villain.

Colt Heritage marks a departure from the normal plot, with the intrepid duo returning home to Independence Creek, only to find that Colt's spread is in the hands of a crooked banker. Colt eventually finds himself facing a trumped-up murder charge, but this fails to prevent Detwaller and himself recovering the ranch in their own inimitable way. Characters from *Vengeance Trail* reappear, and their combined strength saves the day, with Colt acting as the catalyst.

Bullet Bounty, Allen's last book, was set in Colorado, and this time he gives the plot the full mystery treatment. U.S. Marshal Colt and Deputy Detwaller are called upon by an ostensibly "good citizen" to arrest a suspected jailbreaker, and to put him back behind bars. It is a routine task, but Colt soon discovers that the small mining town of Lodestone holds a nest of deceivers who are using him for their own ends.

On the surface, Allen often resembles a thwarted mystery writer. Although content to bring his talent to bear in the western genre, it was unfortunate that he was unable to bring any freshness to the Justice Colt series. The reader is rarely asked to extend his or her imagination with any of the plots. The villains are too overtly stereotyped to be of any great effect. In every town they visit, Colt and Detwaller are warned off by the local lawman in much the same way that a gangster would threaten newcomers against operating on his patch. In short, the books are easy to read, no-nonsense adventures with the accent on simplicity.

—John L. Wolfe

ALLEN, Clay. *See* **PAINE, Lauran.**

ALLEN, Henry Wilson. Writes as Clay Fisher; Will Henry. American. Born in Kansas City, Missouri, 29 September 1912. Educated at Kansas City Junior College (now University), 1929–30. Married Amy Geneva Watson in 1937; one daughter and one son. Worked as a used car caravanner, gold miner in Colorado, Indian reservation trading post clerk, mine blacksmith, hot walker and pony exercise rider in Hollywood, house mover, service station attendant, sugar mill crushing operator, industrial shop swamper, veterinary hospital assistant, newspaper columnist, licensed dog show judge, assembly line worker; writer for *Dog World* and *Shepherd Dog Review*; contract writer of short subjects for MGM; then freelance writer. Recipient: Western Writers of America Spur award, for novel, 1961, 1963, 1973, and for short story, 1963, 1966; Western Heritage Center Wrangler award, 1973. Agent: Ray Peekner Literacy Agency, Inc., 3121 Portage Road, Bethlehem, Pennsylvania 18017, U.S.A.

WESTERN PUBLICATIONS

Novels as Will Henry

No Survivors. New York, Random House, 1950; London, Corgi, 1952.
To Follow a Flag. New York, Random House, 1953; London, Corgi, 1955; as *Pillars of the Sky*. New York, Bantam, 1956.
Death of a Legend. New York, Random House, 1954; as *The Raiders*, New York, Bantam, 1956; as *Jesse James*, London, Corgi, 1957.
The Fourth Horseman. New York, Random House, 1954; London, Corgi, 1958.
Who Rides with Wyatt. New York, Random House, 1955; London, Corgi, 1958.
The North Star. New York, Random House, 1956.
Reckoning at Yankee Flat. New York, Random House, 1958.
The Seven Men at Mimbres Springs. New York, Random House, 1958; London, Corgi, 1960.
From Where the Sun Now Stands. New York, Random House, 1960; London, Hammond, 1962.
Journey to Shiloh. New York, Random House, 1960; London, Hammond, 1963.
The Feleen Brand. New York, Bantam, and London, Mills and Boon, 1962.
San Juan Hill. New York, Random House, 1962.
The Gates of the Mountains. New York, Random House, 1963; London, Hammond, 1966; as Henry Wilson Allen, Boston, Gregg, 1980.
Mackenna's Gold. New York, Random House, 1963; London, Hammond, 1964.
The Last Warpath. New York, Random House, 1966.
Custer's Last Stand. Philadelphia, Chilton, 1966.
One More River to Cross. New York, Random House, 1967; London, Jenkins, 1968.
Alias Butch Cassidy. New York, Random House, 1968; London, Hammond, 1969.
Maheo's Children. Philadelphia, Chilton, 1968; as *The Squaw Killers*, New York, Bantam, 1971.
The Day Fort Larking Fell. Philadelphia, Chilton, 1968.
Chiricahua. Philadelphia, Lippincott, 1972.
The Bear Paw Horses. Philadelphia, Lippincott, 1973; London, Corgi, 1974.
I, Tom Horn. Philadelphia, Lippincott, 1975; London, Corgi, 1976.
Summer of the Gun. Philadelphia, Lippincott, 1978; London, Corgi, 1980.

Novels as Clay Fisher

Red Blizzard. New York, Simon and Schuster, 1951; London, Boardman, 1952.
Santa Fe Passage. Boston, Houghton Mifflin, 1952; London, Corgi, 1954.
War Bonnet. Boston, Houghton Mifflin, 1953; Kingswood, Surrey, World's Work, 1955.
Yellow Hair. Boston, Houghton Mifflin, 1953; Kingswood, Surrey, World's Work, 1956.
The Tall Men. Boston, Houghton Mifflin, 1954; Kingswood, Surrey, World's Work, 1956.
The Brass Command. Boston, Houghton Mifflin, 1955; as *Dull Knife*, London, Corgi, 1958.
The Big Pasture. Boston, Houghton Mifflin, 1955; Kingswood, Surrey, World's Work, 1957.
The Blue Mustang. Boston, Houghton Mifflin, 1956; London, Corgi, 1958; as *Starbuck* (as Will Henry), London, Barrie and Jenkins, 1972.
Yellowstone Kelly. Boston, Houghton Mifflin, 1957; London, Corgi, 1959; as Will Henry, New York, Bantam, 1989.
The Crossing. Boston, Houghton Mifflin, 1958; as *River of Decision*, London, Corgi, 1960.
Nino: The Legend of Apache Kid. New York, Morrow, 1961; as *The Legend of Apache Kid*, London, Mills and Boon, 1964; as *The Apache Kid*, New York, Bantam, 1973.
The Return of the Tall Man. New York, Pocket Books, 1961; as Will Henry, New York, Bantam, 1988.
The Pitchfork Patrol. New York, Macmillan, 1962; London, Mills and Boon, 1965.

Outcasts of Canyon Creek. New York, Bantam, 1972.
Apache Ransom. New York and London, Bantam, 1974.
Black Apache. New York and London, Bantam, 1976.

Short Stories as Clay Fisher

The Oldest Maiden Lady in New Mexico and Other Stories. New York, Macmillan, 1962.
Songs of the Western Frontier (as Will Henry). Philadelphia, Chilton, 1966; London, Jenkins, 1968; as *Red Brother and White* and *Outlaws and Legends,* New York, Bantam, 2 vols., 1969.
Nine Lives West. New York, Bantam, 1978.
Seven Card Stud. New York, Bantam, 1981.

Short Stories as Will Henry

Will Henry's West: Short Stories and Essays, edited by Dale C. Walker. El Paso, Texas Western Press, 1984.

Uncollected Short Stories

"The Trap" (as Clay Fisher), in *The Arbor House Treasury of Great Western Stories*, edited by Bill Pronzini and Martin H. Greenberg. New York, Arbor House, 1982.
"Isley's Stranger" (as Clay Fisher), in *The Western Hall of Fame: An Anthology of Classic Western Stories*, edited by Bill Pronzini and Martin H. Greenberg. New York, Morrow, 1984.
"A Mighty Big Bandit" (as Clay Fisher), in *The Outlaws*, edited by Bill Pronzini and Martin H. Greenberg. New York, Fawcett, 1984.
"Lapwai Winter" (as Will Henry), and "The Tallest Indian in Toltepec" (as Clay Fisher), in *The Warriors*, edited by Bill Pronzini and Martin H. Greenberg. New York, Fawcett, 1985.
"For Want of a Horse" (as Clay Fisher), in *The Railroaders*, edited by Bill Pronzini and Martin H. Greenberg. New York, Fawcett, 1986.
"The White Man's Road" (as Clay Fisher), in *The Horse Soldiers*, edited by Bill Pronzini and Martin H. Greenberg. New York, Fawcett, 1987.
"The Streets of Laredo" (as Clay Fisher), in *The Gunfighters*, edited by Bill Pronzini and Martin H. Greenberg. New York, Fawcett, 1987.
"King Fisher's Road" (as Clay Fisher), in *The Texans*, edited by Bill Pronzini and Martin H. Greenberg. New York, Fawcett, 1988.
"Comanche Passport" (as Will Henry), in *More Wild Westerns*, edited by Bill Pronzini. New York, Walker, 1989.
"The Hunting of Tom Horn" (as Clay Fisher), in *The Arizonans*, edited by Bill Pronzini and Martin H. Greenberg. New York, Fawcett, 1989.

OTHER PUBLICATIONS

Novels

Genesis Five. New York, Morrow, 1968.
Tayopa! New York, Pocket Books, 1970.
See How They Run. New York, Pocket Books, 1970.

Plays as Clay Fisher

Television Plays: *The Hunting of Tom Horn*, 1959; *A Mighty Big Bandit*, 1959; *Sundown Smith*, 1959; and others.

Other as Will Henry

Wolf-Eye, The Bad One (for children). New York, Messner, 1951.
The Texas Rangers (for children). New York, Random House, 1957.
Orphan of the North (for children). New York, Random House, 1958.
San Juan Hill. New York, Random House, 1962.
Valley of the Bear (for children; as Clay Fisher). Boston, Houghton Mifflin, 1964.
In the Land of the Mandans (for children). Philadelphia, Chilton, 1965.

Editor, *14 Spurs.* New York, Bantam, 1968.

*

Henry Wilson Allen comments:

A loner, a watcher of others, a skulker about the edges of the main herd, an avoider of the flock, a "shadow rider," like Tom Horn. A man born into the wrong century. Idea of heaven to die and go where they work cattle and ride horses by daylight and dark—where the smell of mown prairie hay and raindrops in dry dust and the wind coming in ahead of the mountain storm all mingle in a man's mind and make fragrant his memories for all of his days on this earth. Greater prizes than these come hard to mind. The American West of this century's turn, if he has seen it and smelled it and ridden over it and crossed its mountains and rivers, is prize enough for any human being who thinks bowed legs and Texas stovepipe boots and a four-xxxx Stetson Hat and a walk that rolls like a man of the prairie sea, ah! that this be Paradise enow.

* * *

Henry Wilson Allen is somewhat of an anomaly in that in his career he has written formulary westerns, i.e., stories with stereotyped heroes, heroines, and villains, romantic historical reconstructions, i.e., stories which treat historical events as if they were romance, and historical reconstructions, i.e., stories which are historically accurate and faithful to the place, the period, and the people. His first novel was *No Survivors.* It is a romantic historical reconstruction insofar as it has an identifiable hero for its central character, John Buell Clayton, and Clayton's fate is ideologically necessary given his values in contrast to those of the majority of other characters. "I cursed an endless chain of Army stupidity, white greed, race pride, and prejudice," Clayton remarks in this supposedly first-hand account. "There was no justice in this crazy hatred of Indians. No logic in a great nation hurling armed forces against a people who never at any time could put more than a couple of thousand troops in the field. Oh, yes, there was some logic. Power Logic. White logic." The romantic historical reconstruction has an option with regard to the hero that the formulary western does not: the hero can die for his principles. This is what happens in *No Survivors.*

Allen published the novel under the pseudonym Will Henry because he was working at the time in the short subjects department at MGM and feared the studio might object to his writing novels on the side. He learned later that the studio would have been pleased with him, only by then he was no longer an employee. Allen's second western novel was *Red Blizzard*, and when it was rejected by Random House Allen created a second pen name, Clay Fisher. In a sense this has subsequently proved to be a false and confusing dichotomy. What distinguished the early Will Henry novels was that Random House accepted them; those Random House rejected became Clay Fisher novels. For example, Allen's next Will Henry novel was *To Follow a Flag*. While Allen wrote in an Author's Note that the book was about "the dark-faced, unsmiling Nez Perce chief, whose steadfast following of a foreign flag has been repaid with the peculiar coin of oblivion reserved by white history for its red-skinned heroes," no attempt was made to characterize that Nez Perce chief, and most of the story is as much a straight action narrative as is the very next Clay Fisher title, *Santa Fe Passage*.

A number of Allen's novels under both names, despite their solid historical content, are romantic historical reconstructions because of his stubborn insistence on having a hero. His heroines, at the same time and almost without exception, are male erotic fantasies. They are invariably women of extraordinary physical beauty and receive minimal characterization. Occasionally, too, Allen could be intimidated by historical sources, merely adding a dramatized floss to an historical account, such as his reworking of James D. Horan's version of Jesse James (*Desperate Men*, 1949) in the Will Henry novel *Death of a Legend*. In the Will Henry novel *Reckoning at Yankee Flat* Allen provided a fictional account of the Henry Plummer gang. Since Professor Thomas J. Dimsdale wrote *The Vigilantes of Montana* in 1866, the story has intrigued novelists. Among the more notable fictional adaptations are Zane Grey's *The Border Legion* (1916), Clarence E. Mulford's *Cottonwood Gulch* (1925), and Ernest Haycox's *Alder Gulch* (1941). Allen was more accurate in his use of the actual historical events than any of these precursors, but he could not succeed in bringing Plummer himself to life; instead he relied on quotations from sources written by people who knew or had seen Plummer. Yet, curiously, in a more recent novel, *Summer of the Gun*, a Will Henry formulary western, Allen was able to create a vivid character in the gang leader Fragg with a fictional personality closely resembling that of the historical Henry Plummer. Perhaps the most successful instance of a Will Henry fictional biography is *I, Tom Horn*.

Allen's best Will Henry titles appear to be *From Where the Sun Now Stands*, *The Last Warpath*, *Maheo's Children*, *Chiricahua*, and *The Bear Paw Horses*—novels which deal with various Indian nations in conflict with the Anglo-Americans. Among the better Clay Fisher titles are *Yellowstone Kelly* and *Red Blizzard*, although his best fiction under this name may well be the two novels featuring a Franciscan friar, Father Nunez, *Apache Ransom* and *Black Apache*. Ben Allison makes an appearance in *Black Apache*; he is a continuing character in the Clay Fisher family saga of the Allisons which begins with *The Tall Men*.

If one of Allen's Will Henry titles were to be cited as required reading, it would be *From Where the Sun Now Stands*. The subject of the novel is the war against the Nez Perce in 1877 and their decimation. The Nez Perce was a tribe with a long tradition of peace and friendliness with the whites, and in their terrible passage from Idaho through Montana to reach Canada, in which attempt they failed, they did not harm a single white woman or child because, in the words of the Indian narrator of the novel, "we had lived too long as brothers of the white man. Even in our last hours, we could not kill and mutilate his loved ones."

In *Mackenna's Gold* (Will Henry) Allen equally was able to characterize frontier buffalo soldiers as having "the hot blood of their savage African ancestors running wild in them," to have a group of Indians and mixed-bloods in "a moment of doubt" turn "to the brain and training of the white man," and to tell the reader, after the heroine buries "the glittering blade in the brain of the giant Mimbreño "died like an Apache"—whatever quality that is supposed to connote!

The American West meant perhaps too many things to Allen during his career; he lacked a sustained historical vision to inform all his novels and stories; he wrote in too many varied moods and attempted too many literary experiments to be ever all of a piece; he had such a personal and internal struggle with heroes and anti-heroes that it is now fundamentally impossible to give him a single label. Readers who admire him for his fine historical fiction find his formulary and romantic writing a source of dismay; while those who prefer formulary and romantic writing are disturbed when they encounter the bleak vision which haunts some of the Will Henry novels no less than some of those by Clay Fisher.

—Jon Tuska

ALLEN, Hugh. *See* **RATHBORNE, St. George.**

ALLEN, Paula Gunn. American, of Laguna, Sioux, and Lebanese descent. Born in Cubero, New Mexico, in 1939. Holder of B.A., M.F.A., and Ph.D. degrees. Lecturer, San Francisco State University, California; University of New Mexico, Albuquerque, and Fort Lewis College, Durango, California; lecturer in Native American studies, University of California, Berkeley. Recipient: National Endowment for the Arts award; Ford Foundation grant. Address: c/o Beacon Press, 25 Beacon Street, Boston, Massachusetts 02108, U.S.A.

WESTERN PUBLICATIONS

Novel

The Woman Who Owned the Shadows. San Francisco, Spinsters Aunt/Lute, 1983.

Verse

The Blind Lion. Berkeley, California, Thorp Springs Press, 1974.

Coyote's Daylight Trip. Albuquerque, New Mexico, La Confluencia, 1978.

A Cannon Between My Knees. New York, Strawberry Hill Press, 1981.

Star Child. Marvin, South Dakota, Blue Cloud Quarterly, 1981.

Shadow Country. Los Angeles, University of California American Indian Studies Center, 1982.

Skins and Bones. Albuquerque, New Mexico, West End, 1988.

Other

Sipapu: A Cultural Perspective. Albuquerque, University of New Mexico Press, 1975.

The Sacred Hoop: Recovering the Feminine in American Indian Traditions. Boston, Beacon Press, 1986.

Editor, *From the Center: A Folio: Native American Art and Poetry.* New York, Strawberry Hill Press, 1981.
Editor, *Studies in American Indian Literature: Critical Essays and Course Designs.* New York, Modern Language Association, 1983.
Editor, *Spider Woman's Granddaughters: Traditional Tales and Contemporary Writing by Native American Women.* New York, Fawcett, 1990.

*

Critical Study: interview in *Winged Words: American Indian Writers Speak* by Laura Coltelli, Lincoln, University of Nebraska Press, 1990.

* * *

Paula Gunn Allen is a wonderful combination of Laguna and Sioux Indian, German Jew and Lebanese, editor, critic, poet and novelist, mother and militant feminist. In her life and her writing thus far, she has focused on her heritage as an American Indian woman.

In the introduction to her landmark work of Native American cultural analysis and literary criticism, *The Sacred Hoop: Recovering the Feminine in American Indian Traditions*, Allen observed that "structural and thematic elements from the oral tradition, usually from the writer's own tribe, always show up in contemporary works by American Indians." Allen's single novel to date, *The Woman Who Owned the Shadows*, is pure Indian in theme and structure.

Dream, memory and legend, shaking, singing and chanting, shadows and spiders, spirits, spiderwomen and sacred twins—traditional Indian motifs and particularly female ones—form the thematic base of this contemporary novel, which, according to the author, centres on "woman lore and the relationship it bears to the events in the life of an individual." The individual here is Ephanie Atencio, who is struggling to find psychic balance amid nearly overwhelming circumstances.

After suffering a mental breakdown when her husband deserts her, Ephanie develops various relationships with friends, lovers, children, finding support but also pain in these liaisons. Finally she turns inward, and backwards, to study her family history and heritage, in order to discover the source of her personal pain and isolation. In the novel's epiphanic conclusion, the spider/Spiderwoman (the spirit who in Laguna and other legends brought the light of intelligence and experience to the people) enlightens Ephanie and helps her to enter the shadows of her psyche and to own them, to dream her own dreams and to own them.

The structure of the novel, too, is distinctly Indian: non-linear, achronological; a brilliant and rhythmic, almost circular, interweaving of dream and reality, past and present, legend and prophecy, spirit-life and earth-life.

"A thirteen-year conversation . . . what I think and what I teach and what I do and who I see and what I feel and who I become . . . my whole life": this is how Allen described *The Woman Who Owned the Shadows* to Laura Coltelli in an interview for Coltelli's recent book *Winged Words: American Indian Writers Speak.* It is a conversation worth listening to.

—Marcia G. Fuchs

ALLEN, T.D. Pseudonym for Terry D. Allen and Don B. Allen. **ALLEN, Terry D.:** American. Born Terril Diener in Douglas, Oklahoma, 13 August 1908. Educated at Phillips University, Enid, Oklahoma, B.A. 1929; Yale University, New Haven, Connecticut, B.A. (cum laude) 1935; University of Oklahoma, Norman, 1940–41; Columbia University, New York, 1941–42; Maren Elwood College, 1945–47; New York University, 1958–59; University of California, Los Angeles, 1965. Married Don B. Allen in 1941 (died 1966). Editor, Presbyterian Board of Christian Education, 1935–39, and Westminster Press, 1936–39, both Philadelphia, and Young Readers' Press, New York, 1942–44; director of communications arts, Bureau of Indian Affairs, 1968–74; lecturer and staff specialist on American Indians, University of California, Santa Cruz, 1969–74; teacher at Institute of American Indian Arts, Santa Fe, New Mexico. Recipient: Phillips University Distinguished Alumna award, 1970. Address: P.O. Box 2775, Carmel-by-the-Sea, California 93921, U.S.A.

WESTERN PUBLICATIONS

Novels

Doctor in Buckskin. New York, Harper, 1951.
Troubled Border. New York, Harper, 1954.
Ambush at Buffalo Wallow. New York, Fawcett, 1956.

OTHER PUBLICATIONS

Plays

Miss Alice and the Cunning Comanche (as Don and Terry Allen). New York, Friendship Press, 1960.

Screenplay: *Ambush at Buffalo Wallow*, 1960.

Other

Prisoners of the Polar Ice (for children). Philadelphia, Westminister Press, 1962.
Tall as Great Standing Rock (for children). Philadelphia, Westminster Press, 1963.
Navahos Have Five Fingers. Norman, University of Oklahoma Press, 1963.
Doctor, Lawyer, Merchant, Chief (for children). Philadelphia, Westminster Press, 1965.
Miracle Hill: The Story of a Navaho Boy, with Emerson B. Mitchell. Norman, University of Oklahoma Press, 1967.
They Can Say It in English. Norman, University of Oklahoma Press, 1981.
The Color-Coded Allergy Cookbook (as Gloria Diener Autry). Indianapolis, Indiana, Bobbs Merrill, 1983.

Editor, *Arrow 1–6*, (children's writing). Washington, D.C., Bureau of Indian Affairs, 6 vols., 1969–74.
Editor (as Terry Allen), *The Whispering Wind: Poetry by Young American Indians.* New York, Doubleday, 1972.

* * *

The novels written by the Allens together are mostly historical romances, based on the experiences of pioneers like Marcus Whitman and John McLoughlin. The historical context and character outlines are accurate and there is an insistence on details of place and date. At the same time, fictionalized events are added and the conventions of romance affect character portrayal and the description of climactic scenes: thus, villains and heroes are absolute opposites and the Whitmans die wrapped in each other's arms, with time for final words of love and comfort. Obviously, the goal is to bring alive historical characters by fictive means. The fidelity to history presents the storyteller with problems of suspense, especially in a book like *Doctor in Buckskin* whose plot—the Whitman's journey to Oregon and their eventual massacre by the Cayuse Indians they try to educate—has an ending which is very widely known. The Allens deal with this sensibly, using their readers' foreknowledge to underline their theme. Instead of ignoring or twisting the ending, they stress its inevitability, working it into the general atmosphere of manifest destiny. Even when Marcus foresees his own murder, he feels he could have chosen no other way; McLoughlin displays a similar sense of determinism when he writes to Narcissa Whitman's sister about the massacre, "You see, that 29th November had to be. Your sister and the doctor were in no way suited by temperament to the position they chose to occupy." In the end, the deaths are seen as necessary evils, helping to hasten the creation of Oregon Territory in 1848.

The commitment to accuracy is upheld in *Navahos Have Five Fingers*, an account of the Allens' stay on an Indian reservation, and it is carried one stage further in *Miracle Hill*, an autobiography by a Navaho boy which Terry Allen edited after her husband's death. In her preface, she explains that she has left undisturbed linguistic irregularities in tense, verb construction, and numbering, for she feels that this grammar translates the Navaho's sensory experience directly. Although her own writing is wholly conventional, she understands the value of a more innovative style, especially in relation to modernism.

The Allens seem more interested in writing harmonious histories than in exposing paradoxes and injustices, but their purpose is serious and their research always conscientious.

—Christine Bold

ALLISON, Clay. Pseudonym for Henry John Keevill; also wrote as Burt Alvord; Bill Bonney; Alison Clay; Virgil Earp; Wes Harding; Frank McLowery; Burt Mossman; Mark Reno; Johnny Ringo; Will Travis. British. Born in Leicester, 5 October 1914. Educated at schools in Aylestone and Leicester. Served in the Coldstream Guards, 1934–37, 1939–45: Sergeant. Married Gladys May Simpson in 1940; two daughters. Dispatch clerk and driver, 1931–33; accounts clerk, British Air Ministry, 1937–39; worked in local government, 1945–60; clerical officer, civil service, London, 1960–78. *Died 31 January 1978.*

WESTERN PUBLICATIONS

Novels

No Rest for Lawmen. London, Ward Lock, 1955.
Branded. London, Ward Lock, 1956.
Brand of a Cowboy. London, Brown Watson, 1960.
The Drifting Gun. London, Brown Watson, 1961.
The Bounty Hunter. London, Wright and Brown, 1961.
He Rode Alone. London, Hale, 1963.
Outlaw Trail. London, Hale, 1963.
Gunsmoke over Wyoming. London, Hale, 1964.
Guns Across the Rio Grande. London, Hale, 1964.
Six Guns for Water. London, Hale, 1964.
Colorado Gunsmoke (as Bill Bonney). London, Hale, 1964.
Hatchet Rides High (as Virgil Earp). London, Hale, 1964; New York, Arcadia House, 1969.
Guns on Eagle Creek (as Burt Mossman). London, Hale, 1964.
Stagecoach to Fremont (as Mark Reno). London, Gresham, 1965.
Gun Gold of the West. London, Brown Watson, 1965.
Gunfighter Breed (as Burt Alvord). London, Hale, 1965.
Six Guns in Sundance. London, Hale, 1966.
The Wandering Gun. London, Hale, 1966.
Lawman Without a Badge (as Will Travis). London, Wright and Brown, 1968.
The Hangrope Trail (as Will Travis). London, Wright and Brown, 1969.
North from Texas. London, Hale, 1969.
Trail of the Iron Horse. London, Hale, 1971.

Novels as Johnny Ringo

Lonely Gun. London, Mills and Boon, 1954.
Action in Abilene. London, Mills and Boon, 1966.
A Gun for Vengeance. London, Mills and Boon, 1966.

Novels as Frank McLowery

Missouri Man. London, Macdonald, 1955.
Herds North. London, Macdonald, 1956.
Guns for the Sioux. London, Brown Watson, 1961.

Novels as Wes Harding

Trail from Yuma. London, Harker, 1956.
Trouble at Gunsight Pass. London, Hale, 1963.
Gun Law in Toledo. London, Hale, 1964.
Cattle Country. London, Hale, 1965.

Uncollected Short Stories

"Too Much for Granted" (as Alison Clay), in *Woman's Realm* (London), 17 February 1968.
"Journey to Nebraska," in *Woman's Story Magazine* (London), December 1972.

* * *

Clay Allison was a formulaic writer who never developed into a great craftsman, but who obviously entered enthusiastically into the Western myth. All his pseudonyms are figures from the second half of the 19th century whose legendary careers epitomize the highest codes of honour and chivalry. (Each of them also has a more accurate reputation for ugly violence.) Although Allison did not make more of these historical personalities, they do web together into a system: in Frank McLowery's *Herds North*, the hero is Clay Allison; Virgil Earp and Frank McLowery appear in Will Travis's *The Hangrope Trail*. The cross-references reinforce the sense of an enclosed world, where the hero always has a fast draw and a faithful partner and where women come in twos—one honest and one duplicitous. The scene is constant, too: ranches, cattle drives, and cattle towns in which there is more adventure than work.

The Clay Allison novels most often portray a range war between big and small ranchers in the late 19th century. The hero arrives on the scene from another part of the west and is persuaded to join the nesters, organizing them into an effective defence. He resolves the difficulties, usually discovering that the conflict has been manufactured by a crooked townsman who plots to capture the land for himself. Once he is exterminated, the cattlemen can co-exist. Allison always provided place and date, along with technical details like the calibre, make, and model of the hero's gun (usually a .44 Navy Colt). But it is not until about 1964 that he began to include historical events, simultaneously reducing his use of formulaic scenes. For example, *Gunsmoke over Wyoming* tells the usual story of a range war, but now it is the Johnston County War in a fictionalized but recognizable form, with historical figures like Chapman and Rae, the rustlers. The main character types never change, and they remain fictional, but the later novels concentrate more on the hero's maturation than on his role as mediator between two sides. Indeed, *North from Texas* tells of a hero who eschews that role during the Civil War: "For Anse there was no right to either side and even less reason for men to fight. To him the AB ranch was more important and that fact held him there in Texas against all the scorn and pointing fingers."

The novels under the other pseudonyms develop in a similar fashion, with those by McLowery and Ringo paying more attention to Indians: the hero is captured by Indians and sometimes takes an indian wife temporarily. A late novel like *The Hangrope Trail* is more risqué than the earlier writings. The hero is seen in bed with various women and it is implied that the female villain is a nymphomaniac. That does not, however, disturb the romantic plot or the final resolution.

—Christine Bold

ALLISON, Sam. *See* **LOOMIS, Noel M.**

ALVORD, Burt. *See*. **ALLISON, Clay.**

ANAYA, Rudolfo A(lfonso). American. Born in Pastura, New Mexico, 30 October 1937. Educated at Albuquerque High School, graduated 1956; Browning Business School, Albuquerque, 1956–58; University of New Mexico, Albuquerque, B.A. in literature 1963, M.A. in literature 1968, M.A. in guidance and counseling 1972. Married Patricia Lawless in 1966. Teacher, Albuquerque public schools, 1963–70. Director of counseling, 1971–73, University of Albuquerque. Associate Professor, 1974–88, and since 1988 Professor of English, University of New Mexico. Lecturer, Universidad Anahuac, Mexico City, Summer 1974; teacher, New Mexico Writers Workshop, Albuquerque, summers 1977–79; guest lecturer, Quebec Writers Exchange, Trois Rivières, 1982, Brazil International Seminar, 1984, University of Haifa, Israel, 1986, University of Bordeaux, 1986, and Southwest Regional Conference of English Language Arts, Albuquerque, University of New Mexico Scholars Exchange Program with Trujillo, Spain, St. John's College, Santa Fe, New Mexico, Fort Lewis College, Durango, Colorado, University of Colorado, Fort Collins, Colorado College, Colorado Springs, and Pike's Peak Community College, Colorado Springs, all 1988, and Clark County Community College, Las Vegas, Nevada, California State University, Los Angeles, Texas A & M University, College Station, and Chico State University, California, all 1989; writer-in-residence, The Loft, Minneapolis, Minnesota, 1989. Associate editor, *American Book Review*, New York; member of Personnel and Policy Committee, 1987–88, and editor, 1988, *Blue Mesa Review*, University of New Mexico. Vice-president, Coordinating Council of Literary Magazines, 1974–80. Recipient: Quinto Sol prize, 1971; University of New Mexico Mesa Chicana award, 1977; City of Los Angeles award, 1977; New Mexico Governor's award, 1978, 1980; National Chicano Council on Higher Education fellowship, 1978; National Endowment for the Arts fellowship, 1979; Before Columbus Foundation award, 1979; Corporation for Public Broadcasting Script Development award, 1982; Kellogg Foundation fellowship, 1983; New Mexico Eminent Scholar, 1989. D.H.L.: University of Albuquerque, 1981; Marycrest College, Davenport, Iowa, 1984. Address: 5324 Canada Vista N.W., Albuquerque, New Mexico 87120, U.S.A.

WESTERN PUBLICATIONS

Novels

Bless Me, Ultima. Berkeley, California, Quinto Sol, 1972.
Heart of Aztlán. Berkeley, California, Justa, 1976.
Tortuga. Berkeley, California, Justa, 1979.
The Legend of La Llorona. Berkeley, California, Tonatiuh-Quinto Sol, 1984.
Lord of the Dawn, The Legend of Quetzalcoatl. Albuquerque, University of New Mexico Press, 1987.

Short Stories

The Silence of the Llano. Berkeley, California, Tonatiuh-Quinto Sol, 1982.

Uncollected Short Stories

"The Place of the Swallows," in *Voices from the Rio Grande.* Albuquerque, New Mexico, Rio Grande Writers Association, 1976.
"Requiem for a Lowrider," in *La Confluencia.* (Albuquerque, New Mexico), vol.2 no. 2–3, 1978.
"A Story," in *Grito del Sol* (Berkeley, California), 1979.
"The Gift," in *2 Plus 2, A Collection of International Writing*, edited by James Gill. Lausanne, Mylabris Press, n.d.
"B. Traven Is Alive and Well in Cuernavaca," in *Escolios*, May–November 1979.
"The Road to Platero," in *Rocky Mountain Magazine*, April 1982.
"The Captain," in *A Decade of Hispanic Literature*, Houston, Texas, Revista Chicano-Riqueña Press, 1982.
"The Village Which the Gods Painted Yellow," in *Nuestro*, January/February 1983.
"In Search of Epifano," in *Wind Row* (Pullman, Washington), Spring 1987.
"Children of the Desert," published as "Figli del Deserto," in *L'Umana Avventura.* Milan, Editoriale Jaca, 1989.

Uncollected Short Stories (for children)

"The Farolitos of Christmas," in *New Mexico Magazine* (Santa Fe), 1987.

Plays

The Season of La Llorona: One-Act Play (produced 1979).
The Farolitos of Christmas (produced Albuquerque, New Mexico, 1987).

Who Killed Don Jose? (produced Albuquerque, New Mexico, 1987). Published in *New Mexico Plays*, edited by David Richard Jones, Albuquerque, University of New Mexico Press, 1989.

Verse

The Adventures of Juan Chicaspatas. Houston, Texas, Arte Publico Press, 1985.

OTHER PUBLICATIONS

Play

Screenplay: *Bilingualism: Promise for Tomorrow*, 1976.

Other

A Chicano in China. Albuquerque, University of New Mexico Press, 1986.

Editor, *Voices from the Rio Grande.* Albuquerque, New Mexico, Rio Grande Writers Association, 1976.
Editor, with Simon J. Ortiz, *A Ceremony of Brotherhood, 1680–1980.* Albuquerque, New Mexico, Academia, 1981.
Editor, with Antonio Márquez, *Cuentos Chicanos—A Short Story Anthology.* Albuquerque, University of New Mexico Press, 1984.
Editor, *VOCES: An Anthology of Nuevo Mexicano Writers.* Albuquerque, New Mexico, El Norte Publications/Academia, 1987.
Editor, with Francisco Lomeli, *Atzlán: Essays on the Chicano Homeland.* Albuquerque, New Mexico, El Norte Publications/Academia, 1989.
Editor, *Tierra: Contemporary Short Fiction of New Mexico.* El Paso, Texas, Cinco Puntos Press, 1989.

Translator, *Cuentos: Tales from the Hispanic Southwest.* Santa Fe, Museum of New Mexico Press, 1980.

*

Manuscript Collection: Zimmerman Library, University of New Mexico, Albuquerque.

Critical Studies: "Extensive/Intensive Dimensionality in Anaya's *Bless Me, Ultima*" by Daniel Testa, in *Latin American Literary Review* (Pittsburgh), Spring–Summer 1977; "Degradacion y Regeneracion en *Bless Me, Ultima*" by Roberto Cantu, in *The Identification and Analysis of Chicano Literature* edited by Francisco Jimenez, New York, Bilingual Press, 1979; *The Magic of Words: Rudolfo A. Anaya and His Writings* (includes bibliography by Teresa Marquez) edited by Paul Vassallo, Albuquerque, University of New Mexico Press, 1982; *Rudolfo Anaya: Focus on Criticism* edited by Cesar A. Gonzalez, La Jolla, California, Lalo Press, 1990.

Rudolfo A. Anaya comments:

I was born and raised in the eastern Ilano, plains country, of New Mexico. I spent my first 14 years in Santa Rosa, New Mexico, a town bisected by the Pecos River and Highway 66. My ancestors were the men and women of the Rio Grande Valley of the Albuquerque area who went east to settle the Ilano.

The Ilano was important for grazing sheep, and yet there were along the Peco River little farming communities. My mother's family comes from such a small Hispanic village, Puerto de Luna. The most important elements of my childhood are the people of those villages and the wide open plains, and the landscape.

In my first novel, *Bless Me, Ultima*, I used the people and the environment of my childhood as elements of the story. Like my protagonist, Antonio, my first language was Spanish. I was shaped by the traditions and culture of the free-wheeling cow punchers and sheep herders of the Ilano, a lifestyle my father knew well, and was also initiated into the deeply religious, Catholic settled life of the farmers of Puerto de Luna, my mother's side of the family.

The oral tradition played an important role in my life. I learned about story from the cuentistas, the oral storytellers. It is a tradition one often loses when one moves into print, but its elements are strong and as valuable today as they have been historically. I want my literature to be accessible to my community, and I want it to reflect the strands of history which define us.

Because the Mexican American community has existed within the larger Anglo-American society since the 19th century, and legally since 1848, our place in the history of this country is unique. We have a long history in the Southwest, in the Western United States. That history is generally not well known. Cultural identity is important to us as a way to keep the values and traditions of our forefathers intact.

In the 1960's the Mexican Americans created a social, political and artistic movement known as the Chicano Movement. As a writer, I was an active participant in that movement. My second novel, *Heart of Aztlán*, deals with themes in the Chicano Movement. The novel explores a return to Mexican mythology. Chicano artists and writers like me returned to Mexican legends, mythology, and symbolism to create part of our Chicano expression.

When I was 16 I hurt my back and stayed a summer in a hospital. In *Tortuga*, I explored some of the consequences of that stay. The hero of the story is a young man who must find some redemption in suffering. The mythopoetic forces which had influenced my first two novels also are at work in the healing process which the protagonist must undergo.

Western writers reflect their landscape. We cannot escape the bond we have to our environment, the elements, especially water. As a Chicano writer I am part of a community which for the first time in our contemporary era produced enough literary works to create a literary movement. Prior to the 1960's western literature was written about us, but seldom by us. Now the world has a truer insight into our world; the view is now from within as more and more Chicano and Chicana writers explore their reality.

* * *

Of all the Chicano writers who began their careers as part of the Civil Rights movement in the late 1960's and early 1970's, Rudolfo A. Anaya has proved the most enduring—and endearing—for both the Chicano and the non-Chicano reader. Anaya has, in effect, achieved as close to what might be called canonization in the mainstream tradition of American authors as any Chicano writer worthy of the name. As contradictory as Anglo-American, Euro-American "establishment" acceptance of Chicano assumptions and agendas might have seemed at one time, Anaya has, over the past two decades (at least among designated "minority" writers), reached something of the status of Chicano *cacique* or *adelantero*—the equivalent of a Chicano William Dean Howells (to pose a somewhat fanciful comparison).

And Anaya is decidedly a Chicano author. More than a Latino author, a Hispanic author, a Mexican-American author,

Anaya is Chicano. He has Indian and Mexican blood ties. He speaks on behalf of the downtrodden, the poor, the deprived, the people of the barrio, *la raza*, those working-class individuals who, like Anaya and his own parents scraping out a living by farming in eastern New Mexico in the 1940's, share kinship and heartfelt affinity with the land, with the rivers and mesas, the mountains and plains, *valle y llano* of the American Southwest. It is a West of mind, spirit, and myth which Chicanos regard as *Aztlán*, their lost but reclaimed homeland which transcends geographical borders between the United States and Mexico and extends far and away into the *carne y hueso*, the blood and bone and psyche of *la familia, la gente*, and their cause: *la lucha*.

Anaya's first novel (and still, in its Chicano and universal appeal his best novel), *Bless Me, Ultima*, came out of an apprenticeship of much labor and love—or as he avows, *"hasta que te lleva la madre, y las almorranas."* That love and labor, that devotion to the writer's craft and the people's cause has provided him with his great theme and has continued through two other novels, *Heart of Aztlán*, and *Tortuga*, which present a kind of New Mexico or Aztlán trilogy which will probably never be surpassed for its authenticity of 20th-century Chicano ambiance, spirit of place, and overall cultural authenticity. His volume of short stories, *The Silence of the Llano*, continues that allegiance to the lives and landscapes of contemporary New Mexico, the larger Southwestern United States and the ghost echoes of *Nueva Granada*, and behind that, of the mythic ancestral center and home, Aztlán.

These echoes or laminations of cultures and racial/ethnic memories of the past and of the future yet to be rediscovered and restored are carried out in more explicit recountings of Chicano heritage and myth in two fascinating narratives: *The Legend of La Llorona*, an empathetic account of the ubiquitous, seductive, ever-searching weeping or wailing woman so frequently and so fearfully encountered in Anaya's fiction and in Chicano culture, but here dramatized as Malinche, the mistress of Cortez; and *Lord of the Dawn*, a retelling of the legend of Quetzalcoatl and that god's role in the exodus from and promised return to Aztlán. In *A Chicano in China*, an account in diary or travelog form of a trip Anaya and his wife took to China in 1984, he achieves one of his most unique and provocative thematic and structural fusions of the ancient and the modern—ancestral gleanings which jump continents and generations and do indeed merge East and West.

In his numerous essays which, one hopes, will soon be collected—e.g., "The Writer's Landscape: Epiphany in Landscape," "One Million Volumes," and "An American Chicano in King Arthur's Court"—Anaya hits again and again on the crucial significance and efficacy of words and language (Spanish, English, and Spanglish) and the role of the writer as cultural creator, preserver, and conduit for the music and message of the earth, the land.

It is a theme seen dramatically in his fictive counterparts, his heroes and heroines of occasion: Antonio Marez, the young poet-priest who thrills to the sounds and sights and their blessings of *la sagrada tierra, la tierra del alma*, the sacred and soulful earth; the old/young curandera, Ultima la Grande, and Cico, the priest of the golden carp, who together lead Antonio safely beyond the evils of Tenorio Trementina and his witchy, conjuring daughters into his epiphany with landscape and with those who people it in goodness; Crispin, the singer and blind/seer, the prophet and strummer of the mythic and mystic "blue guitar" who ushers Clemente Chavez past the soul-threatening temptations of the "bruja de las piedras mala" onto the mountain-top apotheosis and discovery of Aztlán in his own heart; Solomon, the telepathic invalid, the earth-mother Ismelda, and the Turtle-boy himself, Tortuga, who inherits the will, the inspiration, the healing power and messages of Turtle Mountain and the blue guitar which together set him back on the road of forgiveness and love, as epic hero and prophet to his lost people, even those who had crippled him.

Thus through his effulgence of tone and technique, through his aesthetic and his propaganda, Anaya leads Chicano and non-Chicano alike back to old, earth-felt, heart-felt beginnings: to how language reaffirms our humanity, to how our human destiny is inextricably linked to *la tierra*, the sacred earth which blesses us with her goodness if we are only willing to realize it; to how myth and story afford not only our identity but our salvation.

—Robert F. Gish

ANDERS, Rex. *See* **BARRETT, Geoffrey John.**

ANDREWS, A.A. *See* **PAINE, Lauran.**

ANDREWS, Patrick E. Also writes as John Lansing; Patrick Lee. American. Born in Muskogee, Oklahoma, 14 January 1936. Educated at public school in Wichita, Kansas. Served in the United States Army and Army Reserves for 23 years. Married Julie Andrews in 1981; one son. Agent: Diamant Literary Agency, 310 Madison Avenue, New York, New York 10017. Address: 4553 Chelsea Court, Carlsbad, California 92008, U.S.A.

Western Publications

Novels

Kiowa Flats Raiders. New York, Manor, 1979.
The Mestizo. New York, Manor, 1979.
Proud Guidons. New York, Manor, 1980.
The Bent Star. New York, Tower, 1982; London, Hale, 1983.
Apache Gold, with Mark K. Roberts. New York, Zebra, 1986.
Oklahoma Showdown. New York, Zebra, 1986.
Desperado Run. New York, Zebra, 1987.
Lighthorse Creek. New York, Zebra, 1987.
Sabers West. New York, Zebra, 1988.
Blood of Apache Mesa. New York, Zebra, 1988.
Colorado Crossfire. New York, Zebra, 1989.
Gunsmoke at Powder River. New York, Zebra, 1990.
Texas Drawdown. New York, Zebra, 1990.
Texican Vengeance. New York, Zebra, 1991.
Ranger Showdown. New York, Zebra, 1991.

OTHER PUBLICATIONS

Novels

The Ghost Dancers. Toronto, Gold Eagle, n.d
Jihad. Toronto, Gold Eagle, n.d.
Amazon Gold. Toronto, Gold Eagle, n.d.

Novels as John Lansing

Hanoi Hellground. New York, Zebra, 1983; London, Sphere, 1985.
Mekong Massacre. New York, Zebra, 1983; London, Sphere, 1985.
Saigon Slaughter. New York, Zebra, 1984.
Nightmare in Laos. New York, Zebra, 1984.
Pungi Patrol. New York, Zebra, 1984.
AK-47 Firefight. New York, Zebra, 1985.
Beyond the DMZ. New York, Zebra, 1985.
Boocoo Death. New York, Zebra, 1985.
Bad Scene at Bong Son. New York, Zebra, 1986.
Cambodia Kill-Zone. New York, Zebra, 1986.
Duel on the Song Cai. New York, Zebra, 1987.
Encore at Dien Bien Phu. New York, Zebra, 1987.
Firestorm at Dong Nam. New York, Zebra, 1988.
Ho's Hellhounds. New York, Zebra, 1988.
Monsoon Hellhole. New York, Zebra, 1988.
Mau Len Death Zone. New York, Zebra, 1988.
Durong Warrior. New York, Zebra, 1989.
Hoa-Tien Kill. New York, Zebra, 1989.
Bo-Binh Command. New York, Zebra, 1990.
Nguy Hiem War. New York, Zebra, 1990.

*

Patrick E. Andrews comments:

My interest in the American West goes back to my own family and boyhood environment. I am descended from both Union and Confederate Army veterans of the American Civil War, who went west after that conflict. Through my own family, who pioneered in Texas, Oklahoma, and Kansas, I heard first-hand accounts of the people, events, and places, during that time. My novels and the characters in them are based on those impressions. They are gruff, profane, honorable or dishonorable according to circumstances, and possess an unyielding sense of individuality and pride, no matter what side (or sides) of the law they happen to be on.

* * *

Patrick E. Andrews is a very vigorous western writer. His plots tend to unfold in a series of short but telling scenes, and are usually told from multiple viewpoints. More often than not he tells fairly traditional stories in a modern way, and always manages to inject some new twist or variation to ring the changes, although his books remain true to their origins by containing little sex or explicit violence. His westerns might not always boast extensive or detailed characterisation or entirely credible plots, but their shortcomings are ably compensated for by the author's undoubted enthusiasm for the genre.

The best of Andrews's westerns is quite possibly *The Bent Star*, the neatly paced, well-characterised, and frequently atmospheric story of Charlie Martell, once a great lawman but, when the book opens, little more than a crippled drunk. Though sickened by his mean existence, however, Charlie forgets all about his decision to commit suicide when he receives word that his old partner, Nolan Edgewater, has been gunned down during the attempted arrest of an outlaw named Dandy Kilgallen. Suddenly finding something to live for, Charlie straps on his guns and heads for Indian Territory (a favourite Andrews location) with the intention of finding the trio of hard-cases responsible. From that point on, Charlie's life changes dramatically; he meets and falls in love with a widow named Matty Koch, overcomes some of his disabilities (caused by wounds sustained during his time as a lawman), and eventually becomes a marshal under Judge Isaac C. Parker.

The hunt for one or more outlaws often forms the basis for Andrews's westerns, and an interesting variation on the theme can be found in *Oklahoma Showdown*, in which lawman Dace Halston has to track down his best friend, who not only took his girlfriend away from him, but later turned outlaw. Although it suffers from an obviously rushed ending, however, *Oklahoma Showdown* is certainly entertaining enough, and made all the more so by "guest appearances" from no fewer than 12 historical figures, including Heck Thomas (who also features in *The Bent Star*) and Bittercreek Newcombe. Other variations on the outlaw-hunting theme include *Colorado Crossfire*, in which Andrews's good-natured heroes, Lefty McNally and the Kiowa Kid, are hired by a Pinkerton agent to track down a dozen train robbers, and the recommended *Desperado Run*, which is set in 1901 and tells the story of outlaw Ben Cullen's race to reach the relative safety of Indian Territory before a posse of tenacious lawmen can catch him.

Andrews, himself a former U.S. serviceman of 23 years, obviously enjoys writing about the military. His Vietnam series, the "Black Eagles," is one of the most popular of its type currently available in America, and sometimes his westerns also share the soldiering theme. *Apache Gold*, *Blood of Apache Mesa*, and *Sabers West* are all cavalry stories dedicated to the armed forces. Andrews's overworked and underpaid captains, burly Irish NCOs and wet-behind-the-ears young lieutenants, plus a droll sense of humour which permeates this section of his work, clearly reflect his admiration of John Ford's now classic cavalry trilogy.

Most disappointing of his cavalry books, however, is *Apache Gold*, written in collaboration with Mark K. Roberts. A rather overlong story which lacks a definite focus, this book relates the adventures (or possibly, *mis*adventures) of Terry O'Callan, a red-headed Irish NCO posted to a rather mean fort in Arizona. These include fighting off a band of Apaches in order to collect the regimental mail, organising the Annual Regimental Troopers' Christmas Ball (and enlisting all the local prostitutes to ensure that the men have enough women to dance with), and protecting a group of scientists while they carry out their experiments in the middle of the Apache-infested desert. Though frequently amusing, peopled with agreeable enough characters and interspersed with regular bursts of action, however, the book is nevertheless a rambling read which demands great patience.

Although it is distinguished by an exciting "chase" ending, *Blood of Apache Mesa* also tends to unfold in a rather leisurely manner, following the exploits of Lieutenant Wildon Boothe, a West Pointer of wealthy New York stock, during his first tour of duty on the Arizona frontier. *Sabers West*, meanwhile, is possibly the most successful of Andrews's cavalry stories, telling as it does the story of Guy DuBose, an unreconstructed Rebel who joins the U.S. Army at the end of the Civil War, only to tangle first with the Confederate-hating commander of his post, and then with a band of marauding Comanche Indians.

In addition to his unconnected westerns—which also include the recent *Lighthorse Creek*, the stirring and above-average story of the fight to establish a newspaper in the town of the title—Andrews was also one of the three writers behind the

"Six-Gun Samurai" series published under the pseudonym "Patrick Lee" and described in greater detail in the entry for William Fieldhouse. Since the cancellation of that series, Andrews's work in the room has appeared solely under his own name, and while it has not been exceptional, it has most certainly maintained a constant level of quality. Andrews has a reasonable sense of pace, a good ear for period dialogue, and the ability to draw adequate characters within a few sentences. His plots are frequently intriguing and his heroes tough and unglamorous. Although his work sometimes holds an unfortunate "rushed" quality, it is nearly always entertaining, and at the time of this writing, shows little sign of being anything else for some considerable time to come.

—David Whitehead

ARCHER, Dennis. *See* **PAINE, Lauran.**

ARD, William. *See* **WARD, Jonas.**

ARMOUR, John. *See* **PAINE, Lauran.**

ARNOLD, Elliott. American. Born in New York City, 13 September 1912. Educated at New York University, graduated 1934. Served in the United States Army Air Force, 1942–45: Captain; Bronze Star. Married 1) Helen Emmons (divorced 1957), one son and one daughter; 2) Julie Kennedy in 1958 (divorced 1961); 3) Jacqueline Harris Stephens in 1961 (divorced 1963); 4) the actress Glynis Johns in 1964 (divorced 1973); 5) Jeanne Schwam in 1979. Newspaperman, New York *World-Telegram*, 1934–42; member of the editorial staff, *American Indian* from 1948. Recipient: National Conference of Christians and Jews Brotherhood award, 1968. *Died 13 May 1980.*

WESTERN PUBLICATIONS

Novels

Blood Brother. New York, Duell, 1947; London, Corgi, 1953.
Time of the Gringo. New York, Knopf, 1953; London, Corgi, 1956.
The Camp Grant Massacre. New York, Simon and Schuster, 1976.

OTHER PUBLICATIONS

Novels

Two Loves. New York, Greenberg, 1934.
Personal Combat. New York, Greystone Press, 1936; London, Constable, 1937.
Only the Young. New York, Holt, 1939.
The Commandos. New York, Duell, 1942; London, Rich and Cowan, 1944; as *First Comes Courage*, New York, Triangle, 1943.
Tomorrow Will Sing. New York Duell, 1945; London, Rich and Cowan, 1946.
Everybody Slept Here. New York, Duell, 1948.
Walk with the Devil. New York, Knopf, 1950; London, Constable, 1951.
Flight from Ashiya. New York, Knopf, and London, Muller, 1959.
A Night of Watching. New York, Scribner, and London, Longman, 1967.
Code of Conduct. New York, Scribner, and London, Longman, 1970.
Forests of the Night. New York, Scribner, 1971; London, Longman, 1972.
Proving Ground. New York, Scribner, 1973; London, Weidenfeld and Nicolson, 1974.
Quicksand. New York, Simon and Schuster, 1977.

Plays

Screenplays: *Kings of the Sun*, with James R. Webb, 1963; *Flight from Ashiya*, with Waldo Salt, 1964.

Other

Finlandia: The Story of Sibelius. New York, Holt, 1941.
Nose for News: The Way of Life of a Reporter. Evanston, Illinois, Row Peterson, 1941.
Mediterranean Sweep: Air Stories from El Alamein to Rome, with Richard Thruelsen. New York, Duell, 1944.
Big Distance, with Donald Hough. New York, Duell, 1945.
Deep in My Heart: A Story Based on the Life of Sigmund Romberg. New York, Duell, 1949.
Broken Arrow (for children). New York, Duell, 1954; London, Muller, 1956.
White Falcon (for children). New York, Knopf, 1955; London, Muller, 1956.
Rescue! (for children). New York, Duell, 1956; London, Gollancz, 1957.
Brave Jimmy Stone (for children). New York, Knopf, 1962.
A Kind of Secret Weapon (for children). New York, Scribner, 1969; London, Longman, 1970.
The Spirit of Cochise (for children). New York, Scribner, 1972; London, Hamish Hamilton, 1973.

* * *

Elliott Arnold, a writer of historical novels, often avowed his devotion to historical truth in his novels, while pointing out that conversations and incidental details were his creation—with the major exception of several important speeches recorded in *Blood Brother*, speeches he extracted from memoirs and interviews of the historical "pacification" of the Apaches in Arizona. On occasion what he writes comes across as dry-as-dust history, but his main strength is in bringing history to life with his imagination and dramatic skill. In *Time of the Gringo*, the story of the United States takeover of the Mexican Territory of New Mexico, Arnold's imagination is often fed by legend and minority views rather than the "standard" views of scholarly historians. This excess—according to some—marked him as one more interested in fictional atmosphere than in the historian's devotion to historical truth. Yet his skill at creating that atmosphere makes his work worth reading. Had he written only *Blood Brother* he would deserve recognition as an outstanding contributor to the writings on the west. He was the first novelist to break away successfully from the stereotypical view, long a mainstay of western fiction, that all Indians are evil, bloodthirsty, untrustworthy, dirty, and worse. In *Blood Brother* (as well as in the motion picture version, *Broken Arrow*, and the subsequent television series of that name) the red man is seen as a human being, with all the good and bad mixture to be found in any other race. If the Apache chief Cochise comes out larger, more noble than life, perhaps any excess is just compensation for the decades of the reverse. And by 1976, when *The Camp Grant Massacre* came out, critics would say that Arnold had avoided the temptation to over-sentimentalize the Indian while damning the hard-hearted white man. Sometime journalist as well as biographer of artists, Arnold had the journalist's ability to build upon a core of fact. The Camp Grant story, for example, occupied a page and a third in *Blood Brother*—and over 400 pages in the fuller account. In short, he made a historical event live by personalizing it, by making the reader see and know—perhaps love or hate—the participants. And while his sympathy was plainly with the Indians, he took the trouble to account for the whites' hatred of them. Even when he restored to stereotypes, as he did in *The Spirit of Cochise*, with its manipulating Indian agents, greedy storekeepers, and dripplingly sentimental eastern visitors to the reservation, his Indians come through like people—good, bad, indifferent—but believable. Although he wrote some short stories, he was not comfortable with them. "I get cramped when I have to write to size," he once said. And it is on the broad canvases of western history that he was at his best, where he had room to let his creative imagination and narrative skill flow.

—John O. West

ARTHUR, Burt. Pseudonym for Herbert Arthur Shappiro; also wrote as Herbert Arthur; Arthur Herbert. American. Born in Texas c. 1899. Married Hortene Shappiro; had children, including the writer Budd Arthur. Worked as a newspaperman and editor, for an advertising agency, and as playwright and screenplay writer. *Died in 1975.*

WESTERN PUBLICATIONS

Novels

Lead-Hungry Lobos. New York, Phoenix Press, 1945.
Nevada. New York, Doubleday, 1949; London, Boardman, 1951; as *Trigger Man*, New York, New American Library, 1950.
Stirrups in the Dust. New York, Doubleday, 1950; London, Boardman, 1951.
Trouble Town. New York, Doubleday, 1950; London, Clarke and Cockeran, 1951.
Thunder Valley. New York, Doubleday, 1951.
The Killer (as Herbert Arthur). New York, Doubleday, 1952; as Burt Arthur, London, Boardman, 1953.
Gunplay at the X-Bar-X. New York, Avon, 1952.
No Other Love. London, Dennis, 1952.
Killers' Moon. Kingswood, Surrey, World's Work, 1953.
Killer's Crossing. New York, Lion, 1953; Bath, Chivers, 1987.
Action at Spanish Flat. London, W.H. Allen, 1953.
Two-Gun Texas. New York, Lion, 1954.
The Drifter. New York, Ace, 1955; Bath, Chivers, 1986.
Texas Sheriff. New York, Avalon, 1956.
Return of the Texan. New York, New American Library, 1956; Crewe, Cheshire, Ulverscroft, 1985.
Gunsmoke in Nevada. New York, New American Library, 1957; London, Wright and Brown, 1959.
Ride Out for Revenge. New York, Avon, 1957; London, Consul, 1964.
Outlaw Fury. New York, Avon, 1957.
The Stranger, with Budd Arthur. New York, Doubleday, 1959; London, Consul, 1960.
Duel on the Range. New York, Berkley, 1959.
Swiftly to Evil. London, Consul, 1961.
Quemado. London, Wright and Brown, 1961.
Three Guns North, with Budd Arthur. London, Hale, 1962; New York, Macfadden, 1964.
Big Red, with Budd Arthur. New York, New American Library, 1962; London, New English Library, 1963.
Shadow Valley. London, Wright and Brown, 1962.
Empty Saddles. New York, Macfadden, 1962; London, Gold Lion, 1974.
Flaming Guns. New York, Paperback Library, 1964; Bath, Chivers, 1988.
Ride a Crooked Trail, with Budd Arthur. New York, Avon, 1964.
Requiem for a Gun, with Budd Arthur. New York, Avon, 1964.
Sing a Song of Six Guns. New York, Macfadden, 1964.
Two Gun Outlaws. New York, Paperback Library, 1964; London, Gold Lion, 1973.
Gun-Law on the Range. New York, Paperback Library, 1964.
Walk Tall, Ride Tall, with Budd Arthur. New York, New American Library, 1965.
Gunsmoke in Paradise. New York, Macfadden, 1965.
Ride a Crooked Mile, with Budd Arthur. New York, Avon, 1966.
Action at Truxton, with Budd Arthur. New York, Avon, 1966.
The Free Lands. New York, New American Library, 1967.
Action at Ambush Flat. New York, Paperback Library, 1967.
Deadman's Gulch. New York, Belmont, 1967.
The Saga of Denny McCune, with Budd Arthur. New York, Belmont, 1979.
Westward the Wagons, with Budd Arthur. New York, Belmont, 1979.
Canavan's Trail, with Budd Arthur. New York, Nordon, 1980; Bath, Chivers, 1988.
Brothers of the Range, with Budd Arthur. London, Hale, 1982.

Novels as Herbert Shappiro (series: Mustang Marshal)

The Black Rider (Marshal). New York, Arcadia House, 1941; as Burt Arthur, Bath, Chivers, 1985.
The Valley of Death (Marshal). New York, Arcadia House, 1941.
Chenango Pass (Marshal). New York, Arcadia House, 1942.
Mustang Marshal. New York, Phoenix Press, 1943.
Trouble at Moon Pass. New York, Phoenix Press, 1943; Bath, Chivers, 1987.
Silver City Rangers. New York, Phoenix Press, 1944; as Burt Arthur, London, Gold Lion, 1974.
Gunsmoke over Utah. New York, Phoenix Press, 1945.
Woman in the White House. New York, Tech, 1945.
High Pockets. New York, McBride, 1946; as Burt Arthur, New York, Macfadden, 1968.
The Texan. New York, McBride, 1946; as Burt Arthur, Bath, Chivers, 1985.
The Buckaroo. New York, Arcadia House, 1947; as Burt Arthur, London, Gold Lion, 1973.

Boss of the Far West. New York, Phoenix Press, 1948; as Burt Arthur, London, Wright and Brown, 1953.
Sheriff of Lonesome. New York, Phoenix Press, 1948; as Burt Arthur, London, Wright and Brown, 1953.
The Long West Trail. New York, Phoenix Press, 1948.

Novels as Arthur Herbert

Bugles in the Night. New York, Rinehart, 1950; as Burt Arthur, London, Consul, 1961.
The Gunslinger. New York, Rinehart, 1951; as Burt Arthur, London, Consul, 1965.
Freedom Run. New York, Rinehart, 1951; as Burt Arthur, London, Consul, 1965.

* * *

Burt Arthur's books are rather typical pulp Westerns, less violent than the popularly held stereotype of the form but with memorable acting scenes when violence does occur. Major flaws include an apparent unfamiliarity with rural life, a tendency to tell the reader too little and too late about what is going on, and repetitious use of plot ingredients. On the positive side is a tendency for sympathetic characters to show up more than once, though only rarely do heroes such as Texas Ranger Johnny Canavan get encore appearances. Some of the writer's stylistics are much more interesting than in run-of-the-mill Westerns.

Lack of background knowledge is signalled by such mistakes as an old rancher's reminiscence about his early hardships that includes identifying his foundation herd as six *steers* (*Nevada*). Several books, including *The Buckaroo* and *Sheriff of Lonesome*, are hybrid mystery-westerns in which tedious denouements are to be expected, but several others lacking mystery elements have similar expositions of material much of which should have been supplied to the reader earlier. Plot similarities—for instance, the "protection rackets" of villains in *The Texan*, *Gunsmoke in Nevada*, and in part of the episodic collaboration with Budd Arthur, *Requiem for a Gun*, as well as the planned migrations to California of the heroes of the latter two and other Arthur books—might not be too unsettling to readers who do not encounter the works in too rapid sequence.

The Dan Lovetts of *The Free Lands* and *Nevada* are likable minor characters shown at different enough stages of life that they may not even be the same persons. The reader may even hope they are not, as that would mean that the younger Dan's well-deserved and apparently promised happiness had soured rather thoroughly. Other pairs of characters with identical names grace other books.

These minor characters are often drawn at least as carefully and engagingly as Arthur's heroes. Frequently even the character of horses, often the source of humor along with the more predictable bunkhouse bickering, is developed. Sometimes short scenes are effectively done from the point of view of particular horses. Another trait of style that will please some readers and offend others is the striving for phonetic dialogue. This makes some exchanges of conversation, especially in the earlier books, practically forests of apostrophes.

Arthur can best be appreciated in small, infrequent doses, but he should certainly not be neglected altogether.

—R. Jeff Banks

ARTHUR, Herbert. *See* **ARTHUR, Burt.**

ASHBY, Carter. *See* **PAINE, Lauran.**

ATHANAS, (William) Verne. Also wrote as Ike Boone; Bill Colson; Anson Slaughter. American. Born in Cleft, Idaho, 13 August 1917. Married Alice M. Spencer in 1936; two sons. Worked as a logger, farmer, mechanic, and book salesman; then freelance writer. *Died 21 June 1962.*

WESTERN PUBLICATIONS

Novels

The Proud Ones. New York, Simon and Schuster, 1952; London, Rich and Cowan, 1953.
Rogue Valley. New York, Simon and Schuster, 1953; London, Rich and Cowan, 1954.
Maverick. New York, Dell, 1956; London, Viking Press, 1957.

Uncollected Short Stories

"Gasoline Goats on the Logging Pike," in *Railroad Magazine*, April 1948.
"Dynamite Kelly," in *Railroad Magazine*, December 1948.
"Wildcat by the Tail," in *Mammoth Western* (Chicago), September 1949.
"Lobo into Law Dog," in *Action Stories*, Fall 1949.
"This Land Is Mine," in *Short Stories* (New York), March 1950.
"Marshal of Wheel Gap," in *Action Stories*, Spring 1950.
"Farmer," in *Country Gentlemen* (Philadelphia), April 1950.
"Bull of the Big Timber," in *Dime Western* (New York), August 1950.
"Badlands Bargain," in *Western Short Stories*, September 1950.
"Big John's Colt Gun Courtship," in *Star Western* (Chicago), September 1950.
"Lije Had a Bear," in *Blue Book*, September 1950.
"Brand of the Red Warrior" (as Ike Boone), in *Indian Stories*, Fall 1950.
"Death to the White Sioux" (as Anson Slaughter), in *Indian Stories*, Fall 1950.
"Red Arrow Ambush," in *Indian Stories*, Fall 1950.
"That Mule-Drivin' Man!," in *Dime Western* (New York), October 1950.
"Wild Ones," in *Argosy* (New York), November 1950.
"Conestoga Bells," in *Country Gentleman* (Philadelphia), June 1951.
"Richest Vein," in *Collier's* (Springfield, Ohio), 28 July 1951.
"Chinaman's Chance," in *Dime Western* (New York), September 1951.
"Headline Bullet," in *Frontier Stories*, Winter 1951.
"Up Comes McGinty," in *New Western*, January 1952.
"Pursuit," in *Collier's* (Springfield, Ohio), 8 March 1952.
"Hot Lead Homecoming," in *Frontier Stories*, March–May 1952.
"Trader," in *Frontier Stories*, Spring 1952.

"Ointment for Mangas," in *Zane Grey's Western* (New York), April 1952.
"Down Went McGinty," in *.44 Western*, May 1952.
"High-Climber," in *Saturday Evening Post* (Philadelphia), 17 May 1952.
"Fight on the Mountain," in *Adventure*, September 1952.
"Sheriff," in *Frontier Stories*, September–November 1952.
"Buckskin Brat," in *Frontier Stories*, December–February 1952–53.
"My Brother, Smile," in *Fifteen Western Tales*, July 1953.
"Maulers," in *Saturday Evening Post* (Philadelphia), 5 September 1953.
"Hunter," in *Country Gentleman* (Philadelphia), November 1953.
"Rebel's Brand," in *Frontier Stories*, Winter 1953.
"Red Fury," in *Saturday Evening Post* (Philadelphia), 8 May 1954.
"The Pioneers," in *Frontier*, edited by Luke Short. New York, Bantam, 1955.
"Killer's Dark," in *The Killers*, edited by Peter Dawson. New York, Bantam, 1955.
"Maverick in the Bunkhouse," in *Cattle, Guns, and Men*. New York, Bantam, 1955.
"Wild Fury," in *Red Book*, March 1955.
"Man Against Lion," in *Saturday Evening Post* (Philadelphia), 6 July 1957.
"Boothill Brand," in *Adventure*, August 1957.
"Bridge Crossing," in *Hoof Trails and Wagon Tracks*, edited by Don Ward. New York, Dodd Mead, 1958.
"Bush-League Bandits," in *Saturday Evening Post* (Philadelphia), 15 February 1958.
"The Spirit of Katyann," in *Frontiers West*, edited by S. Omar Barker. New York, Doubleday, 1959.
"Timberbeast," in *Saturday Evening Post* (Philadelphia), 23 May and 30 May 1959.
"Wild Geese," in *Short Stories for Men*, June 1959.
"Off-Duty Affair," in *Saturday Evening Post* (Philadelphia), 3 October 1959.
"Hard Man," in *Saturday Evening Post* (Philadelphia), 14 November 1959.
"Night Marshal," in *Saturday Evening Post* (Philadelphia), 2 July 1960.
"Masterpiece," in *Trails of Adventure*, edited by E. D. Mygatt. New York, Dodd Mead, 1961.
"Bomb by the Jailhouse Wall," in *Saturday Evening Post* (Philadelphia), 2 September 1961.
"The Clown," in *Search for the Hidden Places*, edited by E.D. Mygatt. New York, McKay, 1963.
"Royal Elk," in *This Land Around Us*, edited by Ellis Lucia. New York, Doubleday, 1969.

Uncollected Short Stories as Bill Colson

"Seven-Foot Sanders Baits a Trap," in *.44 Western*, June 1950.
"White Bear Medicine," in *Indian Stories*, Summer 1950.
"Long Look—Short Drop," in *Big Book Western*, August 1950.
"Seven-Foot Sanders, Prince of Pizen," in *.44 Western*, August 1950.
"Seven-Foot Sanders, Gun Doc," in *New Western*, October 1950.
"Seven-Foot Sanders, Bullwhip Samaritan," in *Big Book Western*, October 1950.
"Seven-Foot Sanders' Private War," in *New Western*, November 1951.
"More Rope for Shorty," in *Frontier Stories*, Spring 1953.

*

Manuscript Collection: University of Oregon Library, Eugene.

* * *

Verne Athanas was a professional writer only the last 14 years of his life. It was a career he came to choose from necessity rather than design. At 11 he had been stricken by rheumatic fever which led to chronic heart disease in his adult life. Although he had once scoffed at writers, when he could no longer engage in physical labor of any kind, he turned to writing for a living. Much of his early fiction was published in a variety of western pulp magazines and the western story, with its setting and time-frame, was an area in which Athanas felt most comfortable. By the early 1950's, Athanas had broken into the slick markets, writing for *Country Gentleman*, *Collier's*, and *Saturday Evening Post* while also maintaining his production for pulp magazines which were enjoying their final twilight.

If there was a predominant theme in Athanas's short fiction it was the spectre of relentless determination which was required of a man if he were to win through in his life struggle with the land and the hostile human environment of the American West. He also seems to have been especially inclined to variations of the initiation story. In "Bridge Crossing" young Jonny Free hires on with a small wagon train because he wants to go West. He proves his mettle in a confrontation at a wooden bridge over what is known as Murderer's Creek because he is smarter and tougher than those who have staked it out to hold up wagons needing it to cross. The same sort of spirit inflames young Jim Smith in "Maverick in the Bunkhouse," who hires on at the CR ranch. One of the hands picks a fight with Jim only to become terrified when he realizes that the only thing that will stop Jim is killing him. "Killer's Dark" has a slight alteration. The protagonist is a bank robber who unthinkingly kills a lawman's son when making his getaway. Jess Lucey knows that "Abel Bane would follow him until he fell; and when he was fallen, he would crawl, for that was the mold in which Abel Bane was cast."

"The Pioneers" is one of Athanas's most compact and dramatic stories. It tells of Byron Martin's pursuit of renegade rogue Indians who left him for dead and stole his wife and young son. He persists even after he has found his son's body with its neck broken until he has rescued his wife and killed her captors. The experience, however traumatic, builds character in both Martin and his wife who return to their land because they are past fear. In "The Spirit of Katyann," however, Athanas evoked the supernatural, something rare in Western fiction, although there have been other instances of it, such as Clay Fisher's "The Trap." In Athanas's story, Katyann is a burro who, after she is killed, returns as a spirit to save her master from certain death at the hands of the villian who shot her.

Athanas produced only three novels in his brief career. In all of them, with greater or lesser success, he sought to expand the conventions of the formulary Western and in one instance, with his second novel *Rogue Valley*, he created an historical reconstruction truthful to the people, the land, and the times. *The Proud Ones* came first and, although in broad terms a formulary Western using the town marshal plot, Athanas managed to introduce themes unusual in the genre, included unexpected scenes, and achieved some vivid characterizations. Cass Silver is marshal of the trail town of Red Bone and ostensibly the hero. Thad Oglevie, a young wrangler just in town, saves Silver's life during a shoot-out although he is wounded in a leg and henceforth must walk with a limp that prevents him from ever again straddling a horse. Cass takes Thad under his wing, training him in his profession, eventually making him his deputy. Cass sleeps with Nancy Kane, a madam in a brothel, who loves him, but he will not live with her. Thad, in the meantime, vies with Doyle Flanagan, for the attention of the heroine, Dorothy Markham, a storekeeper's daughter. There is an awareness of sexuality in this story quite novel for this period. Cass, of course, is pitted against a powerful saloon boss who eventually succeeds in having him killed. Cass was a man of relentless determination, and so it Thad, as he sets about bringing the saloon boss and his gang to their just deserts. However, Dorothy wants a different kind of man than Thad has become and to win her love he gives up his badge. Twentieth Century-Fox purchased screen rights outright from Athanas and so he was powerless when the *Gunsmoke* series began on television with a town marshal who is intimate with a saloon lady and who has a deputy who limps.

Athanas dedicated *Rogue Valley* to his wife, Alice, "for all the wonderful years we have had" and even included Alice's grandfather by name, Aden Spencer, in one scene for a bit of dialogue. The novel is set in the Jacksonville district in Oregon after the Civil War and the protagonist is Jed Teppard who, with his brother Toby, returns after fighting for the Confederacy. Oregon as it was then is depicted accurately, with its taxes on "Greasers" and Chinamen so they would not beat out the whites, the distrust of the Rogues (even though the war with them and their removal was over), and the prejudice against Southern sympathizers. The characterizations are specially well-etched and the nemesis for Jed and Toby is a man who is psychologically disturbed, a happenstance also found in novels of the time by T.T. Flynn and Alan LeMay. The background is particularly rich with its scenes of mining claims and a small pox epidemic which lays siege to Jacksonville. Bonnie Claire, whom Jed falls in love with, is perhaps Athanas's most memorable female character.

Maverick was Athanas's last novel, a 1951 slick magazine serial expanded for publication as a Dell Books original Western. It is essentially a cattle drive story that does not benefit from the expansion since much of the vital tension of what is a formulary ranch romance is somewhat lost through unnecessary scenes and extended descriptions. Clay Lanahan is the ramrod and ends up with the heroine at the conclusion; but the more interesting character is Tennessee, a truly daring and capable man who saves Clay's life once on the trail and, even though it means his death, prevents Clay from being killed by the villain at the end. As in *The Proud Ones*, Clay has been through an initiation experience, finding himself as a result neither as brutal as the villain nor as tough as Tennessee.

Athanas was master of ceremonies at the Western Writers of America annual meeting in Boise, Idaho in 1962. After introducing the new president and returning to his table, he died of a fatal heart attack. The best of his short fiction deserves to be collected and reissued and, *Rogue Valley* is a novel that belongs in any basic library of the finest western novels from the decade in which it was published.

—Jon Tuska

ATHERTON, Gertrude (Franklin, neé Horn). Also wrote as Frank Lin. American. Born in San Francisco, California, 30 October 1857. Educated in private schools in California and Kentucky. Married George H. Bowen Atherton in 1876 (died 1887). After 1887 travelled extensively and lived in Europe; in later life returned to San Francisco. Trustee, San Francisco Public Library; member, San Francisco Art Commission. President, American National Academy of Literature, 1934; chair of letters, League of American Pen Women, 1939; president, Northern California Section of P.E.N. Recipient: International Academy of Letters and Sciences of Italy Gold Medal. D.Litt: Mills College, Oakland, California, 1935; LL.D.: University of California, Berkeley, 1937. Chevalier, Legion of Honor, 1925; honorary member, Institut Littéraire et Artistique de France. *Died 14 June 1948.*

Western Publications

Novels

Los Cerritos: A Romance of the Modern Times. New York, Lovell, 1890; London, Heinemann, 1891.
The Doomswoman. New York, Tait, 1893; London, Hutchinson, 1895.
A Whirl Asunder. New York, Stokes, and London, Cassell, 1895.
Patience Sparhawk and Her Times. London and New York, Lane, 1897.
American Wives and English Husbands. New York, Dodd Mead, and London, Service and Paton, 1898; revised edition, as *Transplanted*, Dodd Mead, 1919.
The Californians. London and New York, Lane, 1898.
The Valiant Runaways. New York, Dodd Mead, 1898; London, Nisbet, 1899.
A Daughter of the Vine. New York, Lane, and London, Service and Paton, 1899.
Rezánov. New York, Authors and Newspapers Association, and London, Murray, 1906.
Ancestors. New York, Harper, and London, Murray, 1907.
Perch of the Devil. New York, Stokes, and London, Murray, 1914.
The Avalanche: A Mystery Story. New York, Stokes, and London, Murray, 1919.
The Sisters-in-Law: A Novel of Our Time. New York, Stokes, and London, Murray, 1921.
Sleeping Fires. New York, Stokes, 1922; as *Dormant Fires*, London, Murray, 1922.
Rezánov and Doña Concha. New York, Stokes, 1937.
The House of Lee. New York, Appleton Century, 1940; London, Eyre and Spottiswoode, 1942.
The Horn of Life. New York, Appleton Century, 1942.

Short Stories

Before the Gringo Came. New York, Tait, 1894; revised edition, as *The Splendid Idle Forties: Stories of Old California*, New York and London, Macmillan, 1902.

Uncollected Short Stories

"The Vengeance of Padre Arroyo," in *The Arbor House Treasury of Great Western Stories*, edited by Bill Pronzini and Martin H. Greenberg. New York, Arbor House, 1982.
"The Conquest of Dona Jacoba," in *She Won the West: An Anthology of Western and Frontier Stories by Women*, edited by Marcia Muller and Bill Pronzini. New York, Morrow, 1985.
"The Ears of Twenty Americans," in *The Californians*, edited by Bill Pronzini and Martin H. Greenberg. New York, Fawcett, 1989.

OTHER PUBLICATIONS

Novels

What Dreams May Come (as Frank Lin). Chicago, Belford Clarke, 1888; as Gertrude Atherton, London, Routledge, 1889.
Hermia Suydam. New York, Current Literature, 1889; as *Hermia, An American Woman*, London, Routledge, 1889.
A Question of Time (includes *Mrs. Pendleton's Four-in-Hand*). New York, Lovell, 1891; London, Gay and Bird, 1902.
His Fortunate Grace. New York, Appleton, and London, Bliss Sands, 1897.
Senator North. New York and London, Lane, 1900.
The Aristocrats, Being the Impressions of Lady Helen Pole During Her Sojourn in the Great North Woods. New York and London, Lane, 1901.
The Conqueror, Being the True and Romantic Story of Alexander Hamilton. New York and London, Macmillan, 1902.
Heart of Hyacinth. New York, Harper, 1903.
Rulers of Kings. New York, Harper, and London, Macmillan, 1904.
The Travelling Thirds. New York and London, Harper, 1905.
The Gorgeous Isle: A Romance: Scene, Nevis, B.W.I., 1842. New York, Doubleday, and London, Murray, 1908.
Tower of Ivory. New York, Macmillan, and London, Murray, 1910.
Julia France and Her Times. New York, Macmillan, and London, Murray, 1912.
Mrs. Balfame. New York, Stokes, and London, Murray, 1916.
The White Morning: A Novel of the Power of the German Women in Wartime. New York, Stokes, 1918.
Black Oxen. New York, Boni and Liveright, and London, Murray, 1923.
The Crystal Cup. New York, Boni and Liveright, and London, Murray, 1925.
The Immortal Marriage. New York, Boni and Liveright, and London, Murray, 1927.
The Jealous Gods: A Processional Novel of the Fifth Century B.C. (Concerning One Alcibiades). New York, Liveright, 1928; as *Vengeful Gods*, London, Murray, 1928.
Dido, Queen of Hearts. London, Chapman and Hall, 1929.
The Sophisticates. New York, Liveright, and London, Chapman and Hall, 1931.
Golden Peacock. Boston, Houghton Mifflin, 1936; London, Butterworth, 1937.

Short Stories

The Bell in the Fog and Other Stories. New York, Harper, and London, Macmillan, 1905.
The Foghorn: Stories. Boston, Houghton Mifflin, 1934; London, Jarrolds, 1935.

Play

Screenplay: *Don't Neglect Your Wife*, with Louis Sherwin, 1921.

Other

California: An Intimate History. New York, Harper, 1914; revised edition, New York, Boni and Liveright, 1927.
Life in the War Zone. New York, System Printing, 1916.
The Living Present (essays). New York, Stokes, and London, Murray, 1917.
Adventures of a Novelist. New York, Liveright, and London, Cape, 1932.
Can Women Be Gentlemen? Boston, Houghton Mifflin, 1938.
Golden Gate Country. New York, Duell, 1945.
My San Francisco: A Wayward Biography. Indianapolis, Bobbs Merrill, 1946.

Editor, *A Few of Hamilton's Letters, Including His Description of the Great West Indian Hurricane of 1772*. New York, Macmillan, 1903.

*

Bibliography: "A Checklist of the Writings of and about Gertrude Atherton" by Charlotte S. McClure, in *American Literary Realism 1870–1910*, Spring 1976.

Critical Studies: *Gertrude Atherton* by Joseph Henry Jackson, New York, Appleton Century, 1940; *Gertrude Atherton*, Boise, Idaho, Boise State University, 1976, and *Gertrude Atherton*, Boston, Twayne, 1979—both by Charlotte S. McClure.

* * *

In her 60-year-long writing career, Gertrude Atherton focused on western historical and social themes in nearly half of her 50 volumes of fiction and nonfiction works. Not a writer of westerns that feature miners and cowboys, Atherton dramatized a different character, a new American woman, and a new urban western setting that comprised her imaginative paradigm for the progress of western civilization. In numerous short stories and 18 novels, she traced the social history of California, especially that of San Francisco and the Bay area, from the splendid idle 1840's of the Spanish aristocracy to the pre-World-War-II era of the 1930's. In this story-chronicle, both Atherton's western heroine, sensuous, willful, and intellectual in contrast to the demure eastern domestic heroine of James, Wharton, and Howells, and California, paradoxically stimulating and edenic in contrast to the settled East, reflect the author's particular imaginative and historical view of the United States as the "West" of European civilization.

Atherton strove to be a "correct historian" of her own times as a novelist writing "a memoir of contemporary life in fiction." Her short stories and novellas portraying early California heroines and family life celebrated her nostalgia for the arcadian and aristocratic Spanish-Mexican era. Yet in her later California novels, as Kevin Starr in *Americans and the California Dream* declares, she ambivalently sides with the Spanish aristocrats and blames their indolence for hindering the progress of California. Nonetheless, in the 17 novels her heroine stands not only for the progress of California and San Francisco from an arcadian and frequently violent state to a jewel-like city of the present but also for the evolution of a western woman from a dependency on an aristocratic birth as the basis for self-identity to an independent, self-knowing confidence that allows her to contribute responsibly to civilization.

To portray her own times correctly in fiction from the perspective of a California woman, Atherton had to free her heroine from submersion in Victorian mores to a wider recognition and development of her own needs and talents. She chose a romantic-realistic mode of storytelling. In her critically acclaimed *The Californians*, Madeline Yorba struggles against the patriarchal, restrictive Spanish tradition. In *Ancestors*, a Jamesian novel, Isabel Otis, financially independent, explores through friendship with a titled Englishman living in California how to assimilate English aristocratic and American democratic values in a new nation and how to develop a new relationship with a man not based only on romantic affinity but on a sharing of common interests in their private and public lives. A new ideal in Atherton's evolving woman is Ida Hook in *Perch of the Devil*, set in Montana as "a new romantic subdivision of the United States." She exemplifies Atherton's recognition of a middle-class woman who matures individually and socially to achieve a status as significant as that of an old-world aristocratic lady.

In three post-World-War-I novels set in San Francisco, Atherton again told stories of conflict between corrupt power-mongers and democratic and socialist idealists and of rebellion against outmoded social codes that kept women victims of vanity and sex instinct. Not critically successful, these novels, nonetheless, made the San Francisco heroines a fictional paradigm for a discourse on the causes and effects of a changing western civilization. 20 years later, two novels and two memoirs of the San Francisco area brought Atherton's story of California up to date. *The House of Lee* relates the fortune of three generations of aristocratic Californian women whose diminishing economic and social circumstances force them to reassess and change their life purposes. They and Lynn Randolph of *The Horn of Life* epitomize Atherton's fictional proposal of financial and emotional self-reliance for women in the hope that they would help to mold a civilization where work would be available to all, regardless of gender, class, and age, and in which the choice of a mate would rest on desire based on self-knowledge and compatibility rather than on economic dependence.

Though Atherton's works fall short of distinctive artistic merit, her 60-year adaptation of California material to reflect social and economic changes in California, the nation, and the western world imply significance for study by the literary critic and the social historian.

—Charlotte S. McClure

AUSTIN, Brett. *See* **FLOREN, Lee.**

AUSTIN, Frank. *See* **BRAND, Max.**

AUSTIN, Mary (neé Hunter). Also wrote as Gordon Stairs. American. Born in Carlinville, Illinois, 9 September 1868. Educated at Carlinville public schools; Blackburn College, Carlinville, 1884–88, B.S. 1888; State Normal School, Bloomington, Illinois, 1885. Married Stafford Wallace Austin in 1891 (divorced 1914); one daughter. Homesteaded with her family in Joaquin Valley, California, 1888; schoolteacher, Mountain View, California, 1889, Methodist Academy, Bishop, California, 1895–97, Lone Pine school, 1897, and Normal School, Los Angeles, 1899. Lived in Carmel, California, 1904–11, New York City, 1912–24, and Santa Fe after 1924. D.Litt.: University of New Mexico, Albuquerque, 1933. *Died 13 August 1934.*

WESTERN PUBLICATIONS

Novels

Isidro. Boston, Houghton Mifflin, and London, Constable, 1905.
Santa Lucia: A Common Story. New York, Harper, 1908.
Outland (as Gordon Stairs). London, Murray, 1910; as Mary Austin, New York, Boni and Liveright, 1919.
The Lovely Lady. New York, Doubleday, 1913.
The Ford. Boston, Houghton Mifflin, 1917.
Starry Adventure. Boston, Houghton Mifflin, 1931.
Cactus Thorn (novella). Reno, University of Nevada Press, 1988.

Short Stories

Lost Borders. New York, Harper, 1909.
One-Smoke Stories. Boston, Houghton Mifflin, 1934.
Mother of Felipe and Other Early Stories, edited by Franklin Walker. San Francisco, Book Club of California, 1950.
Western Trails: A Collection of Short Stories, edited by Melody Graulich. Reno, University of Nevada Press, 1987.

Uncollected Short Story

"The Walking Woman," in *She Won the West: An Anthology of Western and Frontier Stories by Women*, edited by Marcia Muller and Bill Pronzini. New York, Morrow, 1985.

OTHER PUBLICATIONS

Novels

A Woman of Genius. New York, Doubleday, 1912.
No. 26 Jayne Street. Boston, Houghton Mifflin, 1920.

Short Story

The Green Bough: A Tale of the Resurrection. New York, Doubleday, 1913.

Plays

The Arrow-Maker (produced New York, 1911). New York, Duffield, 1911; revised version, Boston, Houghton Mifflin, 1915.
Fire (produced Carmel, California, 1912).
The Man Who Didn't Believe in Christmas (for children; as *Merry Christmas, Daddy!*, produced New York, 1916). Published in *St. Nicholas Magazine* (New York), December 1917.

Verse

The Children Sing in the Far West. Boston, Houghton Mifflin, 1928.
When I Am Dead. Privately printed, 1935.

Other

The Land of Little Rain. Boston, Houghton Mifflin, 1903.
The Basket Woman: A Book of Fanciful Tales for Children. Boston, Houghton Mifflin, 1904.
The Flock. Boston, Houghton Mifflin, and London, Constable, 1906.

Christ in Italy, Being the Adventures of a Maverick among Masterpieces. New York, Duffield, 1912.
California, The Land of the Sun. New York, Macmillan, and London, A. and C. Black, 1914; as *The Lands of the Sun*, Boston, Houghton Mifflin, 1927.
Suffrage and Government . . . with Special Reference to Nevada and Other Western States, with Anne Martin. New York, National American Woman Suffrage Association, 1914.
Love and the Soul Maker. New York, Appleton, 1914.
The Man Jesus, Being a Brief Account of the Life and Teaching of the Prophet of Nazareth. New York, Harper, 1915; as *A Small Town Man*, 1925.
What the Mexican Conference Really Means. New York, Latin-American News Association, 1915 (?).
The Trail Book (for children). Boston, Houghton Mifflin, 1918.
The Young Woman Citizen. New York, Woman's Press, 1918.
The American Rhythm. New York, Harcourt Brace, 1923; revised edition, Boston, Houghton Mifflin, 1930.
The Land of Journey's Ending. New York, Century, 1924; London, Allen and Unwin, 1925.
Everyman's Genius. Indianapolis, Bobbs Merrill, 1925.
Taos Pueblo, photographs by Ansel Adams. San Francisco, Grabhorn Press, 1930.
Experiences Facing Death. Indianapolis, Bobbs Merrill, and London, Rider, 1931.
Earth Horizon (autobiography). Boston, Houghton Mifflin, 1932.
Can Prayer Be Answered? New York, Farrar and Rinehart, 1934.
Indian Pottery of the Rio Grande. Pasadena, California, Esto, 1934.
Mary Austin on the Art of Writing: A Letter to Henry James Forman. Los Angeles, Friends of the UCLA Library, 1961.
One Hundred Miles on Horseback. Los Angeles, Dawson's Book Shop, 1963.
Literary America 1903–1934: The Mary Austin Letters, edited by T. M. Pearce. Westport, Connecticut, Greenwood Press, 1979.

*

Manuscript Collection: Huntington Library, San Marino, California.

Critical Studies: *Mary Austin, Woman of Genius* by Helen MacKnight Doyle, New York, Gotham House, 1939; *Mary Hunter Austin* by T. M. Pearce, New York, Twayne, 1965; *Mary Austin: The Southwest Works* by Jo W. Lyday, Austin, Texas, Steck Vaughn, 1968; I – *Mary: A Biography of Mary Austin* by Augusta Fink, Tucson, University of Arizona Press, 1983; *Mary Austin: Song of a Maverick* by Esther Lonigan Stineman, New Haven, Connecticut, Yale University Press, 1989.

* * *

Mary Austin is now best known for her short stories and sketches of the desert southwest, but during her long literary career she published in almost every literary form: novels, poetry, essays, short stories, plays, literary theory and criticism, social commentary. Her first publication was a short story in 1892, and she was still publishing actively in 1934, the year she died. In all of this range, however, her most successful and enduring works are those short pieces that set men and women—Indians and whites—in a direct relationship with the untamed western landscape. These works include *The Land of Little Rain, The Flock, Lost Borders, The Land of Journey's Ending*, and *One-Smoke Stories.* These five collections of short stories and sketches, which establish her both as a nature writer and as a writer of the American West, are her finest literary achievement.

Austin's novels range from the historical (*Isidro*, her first) through allegory (*Outland*) to various social and political concerns. In general, they are not successful, although they contain passages of interest. Most often the difficulty is with the excessive contrivance of the plots. *Isidro* contains enough coincidence, masquerade, and mistaken identity for a Shakespearean comedy, but these devices are not easily taken seriously in a novel. The allegorical fantasy of *Outland* might be of passing interest to students of Tolkien. The more socially oriented novels will be of interest to students of social history, most particularly feminists, as the imaginative response of a talented and independent woman in a male-dominated society that too often undervalued or ignored such women.

Of her three plays, two (*The Arrow-Maker* and *Fire*) use folk materials of the American Indian, specifically the Paiutes of California. Although *The Arrow-Maker* was performed in New York, neither play became popular.

Her third play (*The Man Who Didn't Believe in Christmas*), a volume of short stories (*The Basket Woman*), and a volume of poems (*The Children Sing in the Far West*) are for children. The stories and poems use both Indian and frontier white experiences in the West, factual observation of nature, and often the fantasy of personification of natural objects. Frequently they have a moralistic conclusion as a lesson to the child-reader.

Austin's *One-Smoke Stories* are a mixture of Indian legend, folk tale, anecdote, and short, short story. Most are set in the Southwest. Their time, when it is not indeterminate, is late 19th or early 20th century. An introduction to the volume establishes them as a sub-genre of campfire tale developed by western Indians: a narrative that can be told in the time it takes to smoke one hand-rolled cigarette. Thus each tale is brief, direct, presenting a single effect and a single point. They are spare, unembellished, and often wryly humorous, dealing usually in a cryptic way with the foibles of human nature.

It is within the tight discipline of such a closely circumscribed form that Austin's narrative gift shows at its best. Without the intricacies and embellishment of her longer works, this short form displays Austin's insight into human nature with clarity and humor. With equal facility and authority she writes sometimes from the point of view of an Indian, sometimes from that of a white, sometimes that of a man or of a woman. By the same token she can shift from realism to mysticism to whimsy with ease. The result is a series of tales that give the reader a sense of a people in a particular landscape, but at the same time provide insight into universal human nature.

This sense of people coming into harmony with a vivid, particular landscape—the landscape of the desert southwest of New Mexico, Arizona, and southern California—characterizes her finest and most enduring work. As a child in Illinois she already wanted to become a writer, and in her youth she had a mystical experience of oneness with nature, yet in college she concentrated on the study of science rather than of literature or philosophy. Thus in her writing about the southwest, Austin could bring to her work both the resources of art and the human spirit as well as an understanding of the objective, physical world. These are the ideal attributes of the true nature writer, who presents the literal, material world of natural phenomena as well as the subjective response of the human spirit to the perception of that world.

These characteristics are most highly developed in *The Land of Little Rain*, Austin's best-known work. In a series of 14 sketches she presents the deserts and desert mountains of southern California as they were seen through the eyes of the Indians of the region, the frontier whites (in particular the miners), and the trained naturalist delighting in wilderness as yet little touched by technological civilization. It is as a nature writer that her sense of the landscape as a significant element in human affairs is realized most clearly. In her nature writing Austin's description is most evocative, her narrative skill most direct and fully developed. As a nature writer she does not become involved either in the artificial literary devices or the espousal of social causes that complicate and too often weaken her other work. She presents directly what she sees and feels of the landscape.

The Flock is a sequel to *The Land of Little Rain.* It presents also the lower San Joaquin Valley and the Tehachapi Mountains. *Lost Borders* again presents deserts and desert dwellers, both animal and human. These three books of sketches were written during the first decade of this century. Then in 1924 Mary Austin published *The Land of Journey's Ending*, sketches of New Mexico and Arizona in the same vein as her earlier works on southern California. These volumes, with *One-Smoke Stories*, constitute the primary body of her work as a western nature writer and her best literary achievement.

—Paul T. Bryant

AVERILL, H.C. *See* **SNOW, Charles H.**

B

BALDWIN, Gordo. *See* **BALDWIN, Gordon C.**

BALDWIN, Gordon C(ortis). Also writes as Gordo Baldwin; Lew Gordon. American. Born in Portland, Oregon, 5 June 1908. Educated at the University of Arizona, Tucson, 1928–34, A.B. 1933, M.A. 1934; University of Southern California, Los Angeles, 1939–40, Ph.D. 1941. Married Pauline Farriss in 1935; two daughters. Instructor in dendrochronology, 1934–36, and in archaeology, 1936–37, University of Arizona; assistant curator, Arizona State Museum, Tucson, 1937–40; archaeologist in Boulder City, Nevada, 1940–48, and in Omaha, Nebraska, 1948–53, National Park Service; Instructor in anthropology, University of Omaha, 1953–54. Freelance writer, 1954–74. President, 1968–69, and editor of *The Roundup*, 1962–65, Western Writers of America Agent: William Reiss, Paul R. Reynolds Inc., 12 East 41st Street, New York, New York 10017. Address: 426 Poppy Place, Mountain View, California 94043, U.S.A.

WESTERN PUBLICATIONS

Novels

Trouble Range. London, Hale, 1956; New York, Arcadia House, 1959.
Trail North. London, Hale, 1956; New York, Arcadia House, 1957.
Range War at Sundown. London, Hale, 1957; as *Sundown Country*, New York, Arcadia House, 1959.
Powdersmoke Justice. London, Hale, 1957; as Lew Gordon, New York, Avalon, 1961.
Roundup at Wagonmound. New York, Arcadia House, and London, Hale, 1960.
Ambush Basin (as Gordo Baldwin). New York, Avalon, 1960; as Lew Gordon, London, Hale, 1965.
Brand of Yuma. New York, Avalon, 1960; London, Hale, 1966.
Wyoming Rawhide (as Gordo Baldwin). New York, Avalon, 1961; as Gordon C. Baldwin, London, Hale, 1965.

Uncollected Short Story

"Double Barrelled Jackpot," in *Western Roundup*, edited by Nelson Nye. New York, Macmillan, 1961.

OTHER PUBLICATIONS

Other (for children)

America's Buried Past: The Story of North American Archaeology. New York, Putnam, 1962.
The Ancient Ones: Basketmakers and Cliff Dwellers of the Southwest. New York, Norton, 1963.
The World of Prehistory: The Story of Man's Beginnings. New York, Putnam, 1963.
Stone Age Peoples Today. New York, Norton, 1964.
The Riddle of the Past: How Archaeological Detectives Solve Prehistoric Riddles. New York, Norton, 1965.
The Warrior Apaches: A Story of the Chiricahua and Western Apache (for adults). Tucson, Arizona, Dale Stuart King, 1965.
Race Against Time: The Story of Salvage Archaeology. New York, Putnam, 1966.
Strange Peoples and Stranger Customs. New York, Norton, 1967.
Calendars to the Past: How Science Dates Archaeological Ruins. New York, Norton, 1967.
How Indians Really Lived. New York, Putnam, 1967.
Games of the American Indian. New York, Norton, 1969.
Indians of the Southwest. New York, Putnam, 1970.
Talking Drums to Written Word: How Early Man Learned to Communicate. New York, Norton, 1970.
Schemers, Dreamers, and Medicine Men: Witchcraft and Magic among Primitive People. New York, Four Winds Press, 1971.
Pyramids of the New World. New York, Putnam, 1971.
Inventors and Inventions of the Ancient Worlds. New York, Four Winds Press, 1973.
The Apache Indians, Raiders of the Southwest. New York, Four Winds Press, 1978.

*

Manuscript Collection: Special Collections, University of Arizona Library, Tucson.

Gordon C. Baldwin comments (1982):

Since my high school days I had been interested in writing, particularly western writing, probably influenced by avid reading of Zane Grey and pulp magazines, along with anything else I could get my hands on. When I moved to Arizona in 1928, I became even more interested and began gathering information and taking photos of cattle and cattle ranches, cowboys and Indians. During the next 20-odd years my archeological field trips took me all through the back country of Arizona, New Mexico, Colorado, Utah, and Nevada, and later through the northern Rocky Mountain states of Idaho, Montana, Wyoming, and the Dakotas, giving me numerous opportunities to continue collecting information on the West. At the same time I hadn't neglected my reading—Haycox, Short, Dawson, Nye, Holmes, Elston, Case, Fox, Thompson, Ernenwein, Drago, Croy, Evarts, and a host of other old-time western writers.

By 1954, we had had enough of Nebraska's cold winters and humid summers and returned to Tucson, where my wife resumed her teaching at the high school while I tried my hand at writing Westerns. Two years later, my first western, *Trouble Range*, was published as a four-part serial in *Ranch Romances*. In 1961, my agent discovered that I had a Ph.D. in anthropology and suggested that we could make more money writing juvenile non-fiction books on archaeology and Indians. *America's Buried Past* proved to be the first of 17 such books.

After a heart attack in 1974, my doctor advised me to give up writing. I enjoyed writing but I think I enjoy retirement even more. I have always liked to read and now I can read whenever I want to. Both my wife and I do volunteer work at least three afternoons a week at the Mountain View Library and have a wide variety of books from which to choose.

* * *

Gordon C. Baldwin has had an academic career in archaeology and anthropology. He has written articles on these subjects, and most of his non-fiction output is concerned with early American history such as *America's Buried Past*; his more recent major work, *The Apache Indians, Raiders of the Southwest*, was a carefully researched and scientific approach to American history. He traced the prehistoric origins of the Indians in Asia and Apache history down to the Apache Wars with the white man in the 1880's. Baldwin makes a useful contribution to American history by discrediting images of Apache cruelty and investigating their economic system. This book was well-received critically and considered suitable for schools.

Baldwin has also written a number of conventional Westerns. These novels do not show any special historical approach. They come neatly within the bounds of the genre although the dates of the settings, 1880's and 1890's, are rather later than those of most westerns. In *Powdersmoke Justice* the setting is Wyoming in 1882 and the theme domination of a big rancher in the country. Ben Taggart has money and also power over the sheriff. He also has a hold over the girl the small rancher is in love with. While the small rancher wins in a shoot-out in the Main Street of town, rather against expectations he does not get the girl. The book contains familiar themes in addition to that of a range-war resulting from the extension of a ranch's boundary. There is a strong romantic interest and also a useful reminder of the weak political position of the sheriff in the west. Baldwin shows some good descriptive powers in this book, not just with regard to the usual fights but also concerning emotions such as the animosity encountered across a saloon table.

In *Roundup at Wagonmound* Baldwin again creates a good plot around a mystery bad man who has forged a mortgage and forced somebody to claim ownership of a ranch. Although the story is set in New Mexico in 1889 there is not much local colour or description of the country. There is also little technical vocabulary, but plenty of details of bloody violence.

Baldwin likes to use good plots at the centre of his books and build up credible stories around them leading up to a climax such as a shoot-out in *Brand of Yuma*. He does not, however, use very much dialogue and what there is is rather plain by western standards. Baldwin's strong point is description, and his descriptive style is somewhat wasted in the rather clean modern western novel.

—P.R. Meldrum

BALLARD, Willis Todhunter. Also wrote as Brian Agar; P.D. Ballard; Parker Bonner; Sam Bowie; Walt Bruce; Nick Carter; Hunter D'Allard; Brian Fox; John Grange; Harrison Hunt; John Hunter; Willard Kilgore; Neil MacNeil; Clint Reno; John Shepherd; Jack Slade; Clay Turner. American. Born in Cleveland, Ohio, 13 December 1903. Educated at Westtown Preparatory School; Wilmington College, Ohio, B.S. 1926. Married Phoebe Dwiggin in 1936; one son. Recipient: Western Writers of America Spur award, 1956. *Died 27 December 1980.*

WESTERN PUBLICATIONS

Novels

Two-Edged Vengeance. New York, Macmillan, 1951; as *The Circle C Feud*, London, Sampson Low, 1952.
Incident at Sun Mountain. Boston, Houghton Mifflin, 1952; London, Rich and Cowan, 1954.
West of Quarantine. Boston, Houghton Mifflin, 1953; London, Rich and Cowan, 1954.
High Iron. Boston, Houghton Mifflin, 1953; London, Rich and Cowan, 1955.
Showdown, with James C. Lynch. New York, Popular Library, 1953.
Rawhide Gunman. New York, Popular Library, 1954.
Trigger Trail. New York, Popular Library, 1955.
Blizzard Range. New York, Popular Library, 1955.
The Package Deal. New York, Appleton Century Crofts, 1956; London, Corgi, 1959.
Gunman from Texas. New York, Popular Library, 1956.
Guns of the Lawless. New York, Popular Library, 1956.
Roundup. New York, Popular Library, 1957.
Trail Town Marshal. New York, Popular Library, 1957.
Saddle Tramp. New York, Popular Library, 1958.
Fury in the Heart. Derby, Connecticut, Monarch, 1959.
Trouble on the Massacre. New York, Popular Library, 1959.
The Long Trail Back. New York, Doubleday, 1960; London, Jenkins, 1961.
The Night Riders. New York, Doubleday, 1961; London, Jenkins, 1962.
The Long Sword (as Hunter D'Allard). New York, Avon, 1962.
Gopher Gold. New York, Doubleday, 1962; as *Gold Fever in Gopher*, London, Jenkins, 1962.
Westward the Monitors Roar. New York, Doubleday, and London, Jenkins, 1963; as *Fight or Die*, New York, Belmont, 1977.
Desperation Valley. New York, Macmillan, 1964.
Gold in California! New York, Doubleday, 1965.
The Californian. New York, Doubleday, 1971.
Nowhere Left to Run. New York, Doubleday, 1972.
Loco and the Wolf. New York, Doubleday, 1973.
Sierra Massacre (as Clint Reno). New York, Fawcett, 1974.
Home to Texas. New York, Doubleday, 1974; London, Hale, 1977.
Sun Mountain Slaughter (as Clint Reno). New York, Fawcett, 1974.
Trails of Rage. New York, Doubleday, 1975; London, Prior, 1976.
The Sheriff of Tombstone. New York, Doubleday, 1977; London, Prior, 1978.

Novels as John Hunter

West of Justice. Boston, Houghton Mifflin, 1954.
Ride the Wind South. New York, Permabooks, 1957.
The Marshal from Deadwood. New York, Permabooks, 1958.
Badlands Buccaneer. New York, Pocket Books, 1959; London, Ward Lock, 1961.
Duke. New York, Popular Library, 1965.

The Man from Yuma. New York, Berkley, 1965.
A Canyon Called Death. New York, Berkley, 1968.
Death in the Mountain. New York, Ballantine, 1969.
Lost Valley. New York, Ballantine, 1971.
Hell Hole. New York, Ballantine, 1972.
The Burning Land. New York, Ballantine, 1973; London, Gold Lion, 1975.
Gambler's Gun. New York, Ballantine, 1973; London, White Lion, 1976.
The Higraders. New York, Ballantine, 1974.
Manhunt. New York, Ballantine, 1975.
This Range Is Mine. New York, Ballantine, 1975; London, Hale, 1977.

Novels as Parker Bonner

Superstition Range. New York, Popular Library, 1953.
Outlaw Brand. New York, Popular Library, 1954.
Tough in the Saddle. Derby, Connecticut, Monarch, 1964.
Applegate's Gold. New York, Avon, 1967.
Plunder Canyon. New York, Paperback Library, 1968.
The Town Tamer. New York, Paperback Library, 1968.
Borders to Cross. New York, Paperback Library, 1969.
Look to Your Guns. New York, Paperback Library, 1969.

Novels as Brian Fox

A Dollar to Die For. New York, Award, 1968.
The Wild Bunch. New York, Award, 1969.
Outlaw Trail. New York, Award, 1969; London, Tandem, 1973.
Unholy Angel. New York, Award, 1969.
Sabata. New York, Award, 1970.
Dead Ringer. New York, Award, 1971.
Apache Gold. New York, Award, 1971.
Dragooned. New York, Award, 1971.
Return of Sabata. New York, Award, 1972.
Bearcats! New York, Award, 1973.

Novels as Sam Bowie

Thunderhead Range. Derby, Connecticut, Monarch, 1959.
Gunlock. New York, Award, and London, Tandem, 1968.
Canyon War. New York, Ace, 1969.
Chisum. New York, Ace, 1970.
The Train Robbers. New York, Ace, 1973.

Novels as Jack Slade

Lassiter. New York, Tower, 1967.
Bandido. New York, Tower, 1968.
The Man from Cheyenne. New York, Tower, 1968.

Novels as Clay Turner

Give a Man a Gun. New York, Paperback Library, 1971.
Gold Goes to the Mountain. New York, Paperback Library, 1974.
Go West, Ben Gold! New York, Paperback Library, 1974.

Uncollected Short Stories

"The Bandit Chief," in *Cowboy Stories* (New York), May 1936.
"Dark Kill," in *Western* (New York), October 1956.
"The Mayor of Strawberry Hill," in *Iron Men and Silver Spurs*, edited by Donald Hamilton. New York, Fawcett, 1967.
"Run Out of Town," in *Western Romances*, edited by Peggy Simson Curry. New York, Fawcett, 1969.
"The Builder of Murderer's Bar," in *Western Writers of America Silver Anniversary Anthology*, edited by August Lenniger. New York, Ace, 1977.
"The Saga of Toby Riddle," in *The Californians*, edited by Bill Pronzini and Martin H. Greenberg. New York, Fawcett, 1989.

OTHER PUBLICATIONS

Novels

Say Yes to Murder. New York, Putnam, 1942; as *The Demise of a Louse* (as John Shepherd), New York, Belmont, 1962.
Murder Can't Stop. Philadelphia, McKay, 1946.
Murder Picks the Jury (as Harrison Hunt, with Norbert Davis). New York, Curl, 1947.
Dealing Out Death. Philadelphia, McKay, 1948.
Walk in Fear. New York, Fawcett, 1952; London, Red Seal, 1957.
Chance Elson. New York, Pocket Books, 1958.
Lights, Camera, Murder (as John Shepherd). New York, Belmont, 1960.
Pretty Miss Murder. New York, Permabooks, 1961.
Have Love, Will Share (as Brian Agar). Derby, Connecticut, Monarch, 1961.
The Seven Sisters. New York, Permabooks, 1962.
Three for the Money. New York, Permabooks, 1963.
Murder Las Vegas Style. New York, Tower, 1967.
The Sex Web (as Brian Agar). N.p., Soft Cover Library, 1967.
The Kremlin File (as Nick Carter). New York, Award, 1973; London, Tandem, 1976.

Novels as Neil MacNeil

Death Takes an Option. New York, Fawcett, 1958; London, Fawcett, 1960.
Third on a Seesaw. New York, Fawcett, 1959; London, Muller, 1961.
Two Guns for Hire. New York, Fawcett, 1959; London, Muller, 1960.
Hot Dam. New York, Fawcett, and London, Muller, 1960.
The Death Ride. New York, Fawcett, 1960; London, Muller, 1962.
Mexican Slay Ride. New York, Fawcett, 1962; London, Muller, 1963.
The Spy Catchers. New York, Fawcett, 1966.

Novels as P.D. Ballard

End of a Millionaire. New York, Fawcett, 1964.
Brothers in Blood. New York, Fawcett, 1972.
Angel of Death. New York, Fawcett, 1973.
The Death Brokers. New York, Fawcett, 1973.

Other

The Man Who Stole a University (for children), with Phoebe Ballard. New York, Doubleday, 1967.
How to Defend Yourself, Your Family, and Your Home. New York, McKay, 1967.

Editor, *A Western Bonanza*. New York, Doubleday, 1969.

*

Manuscript Collection: University of Oregon Library, Eugene.

Critical Studies: interview with Stephen Mertz, in *Armchair Detective* (White Bear Lake, Minnesota), 1979; *Hollywood Troubleshooter: W.T. Ballard's Bill Lennox* edited by James L. Traylor, Bowling Green, Ohio, Popular Press, 1984.

* * *

A successful writer of mystery stories and novels in the 1930's before publishing his first Western, *Two-Edged Vengeance*, Willis Todhunter Ballard explained in 1951 that the western genre appealed more to him than crime stories "because westerns get out of date very slowly." The elements that gave the western its longevity, he felt, were "good clean living, repeated dashes of excitement and a substantial love interest." These ingredients are invariably present in Ballard's westerns. However, his best writing occurs when he places them in a narrative that expresses his fundamental belief that law and order and moral community will triumph over the near anarchy that was the frontier.

Ballard often thoroughly researched an era and placed his stories securely in it. His best known work is an episodic historical novel, *Gold in California!* Ostensibly told by a young boy, it celebrates the civilizing impulse within the pioneering instinct, and identifies the newspaper editor as the chief carrier of that impulse. The novel starts strongly, describing how the wagon trains organized themselves for the trip across the plains and identifying the social organization best suited to ensure the survival of the travellers. However, the narrative trails off midway, and declines into a series of semi-comic episodes centered in various mining camps and towns in California. A stronger, less-known historical novel is Ballard's second Western, *Incident at Sun Mountain*. This is the well-researched story of the Golden Circle, a group of Southern sympathizers, who planned to seize the silver mines in Sun Mountain, Utah and use the wealth to finance the Rebellion. Ballard effectively interweaves the political intrigue accompanying the formation of Lincoln's first adminstration into the narrative to give the story a convincing historical context. The Cherokees who migrated to Oklahoma and settled in the Cherokee Strip in the 1840's split into pro- and anti-slavery factions during the Civil War. Showing a remarkable sympathy for the native Americans, *Desperation Valley* recounts the murderous difficulties the split caused in the tribe after the war had ended. *Trails of Rage*, published at the end of Ballard's career, recounts the attempt by a band of Confederate guerrillas disguised as Union men to take Denver, cut the West in two, and stir up enough Indian trouble to occupy significant numbers of Union forces. Thinly plotted and peopled with paste-board characters, the novel is a predictable chase sequence conducted through a winter landscape.

Trained as an engineer, Ballard was interested in the mechanics of 19th-century gold and silver mining. He brought this arcane knowledge to bear in some of his work. *Trigger Trail* traces the disputed ownership of a silver mine to ambiguities in the original Spanish land grant titles. Ballard bases the principal action of the story on a detailed description of the mine, its operations, and eventual destruction. (Another, more exotic story pertaining to the building of a wholly implausible millrace occupies a chapter in *Gold in California!*) Ballard used the mine locale as the background nine years later for *Westward the Monitors Roar*. Here, however, he is not as successful in integrating the activities of the mine and the narrative. Ballard, perhaps reflecting contemporary social concerns, emphasizes how the main character, "Ghost" Merrill, denies his real feelings and turns his grief over the loss of his wife into a ruthless pursuit of justice. Merrill recovers his feelings during a long hunt and chase sequence, a denouement that occupies the last half of the book.

Ballard often used the railroad as the setting for his stories. Two of the more successful are *High Iron* and *Badlands Buccaneer*. *High Iron* concerns the highjacking of an express-freight train travelling from west to east and carrying a million-dollar load of silk. The robbers successfully waylay the train, off-load the silk, and store it in a deserted mine shaft. The action of the story concerns the recovery of the silk. *Badlands Buccaneer* describes the interactions between a pathological train robber, his sister, and a Pacific Northern Railroad detective posing as a whiskey salesman who has gone under-cover in the robber's band. The sister and the detective fall in love, and she finally has to kill her brother to keep him from shooting her lover.

Ballard's staple subject was the conflict engendered by disputes over land and cattle. These stories contain his best plots and most believable characters. Their subtext is the gradual replacement of the rule of force by that of law and order. The notion of justice, like the love that flowers at the end of each novel to symbolize the triumph of law and community, arises spontaneously from within the best men and women and generates communal harmony.

Ballard's first Western, *Two-Edged Vengeance*, limns these recurrent themes. Jetthorn Cosgrave returns home from five years of unfairly imposed exile intending to recover the ranch that has been wrongfully taken from him by his uncle. Gathering about him a band of riders as unsavory as those supporting his uncle, Jet forges an unlikely alliance with dispossessed hill people (he eventually marries the rifle-wielding daughter of one of them) and, by using force tempered by his innate sense of justice, retakes the ranch and all the stock. The law, in the person of the local sheriff, is tacitly on Jet's side throughout the conflict, but only after Jet has won without his direct help does the sheriff assert his authority over the now peaceful landscape. *West of Quarantine* shows the difficulties that result when the local marshal uses his position for personal gain. A 19th-century Cincinnatus, former Confederate major Bruce Powell, must overcome his personal distaste and ally with the venal marshal to save the town from depredation by cattlemen. In *Trail Town Marshal* an honest sheriff is assassinated and framed after his death. His friend, former cowhand Joe Condon, puts on the star and goes to work to root out the corrupt businessmen who control the town and manipulate a company of Texas cattlemen who are intent on wreaking a separate vengeance on the town. The spirited daughter of one of gulled businessmen commits herself to a badly wounded Joe as he wins the final gunfight against the criminals. The last two lines of the book link love and law. "[Joe] knew he could not afford to die. He had too much to live for."

Trouble on the Massacre repeats the theme of how unbridled greed perverts the growth of a true community. Here an honest and courageous judge gives timely help to the one man strong enough to control his own seamy allies and to stand against a brutal and domineering rancher. In the end love seals the bargain between order and peace against chaos and lust. Written near the end of his career, *The Burning Land*, a weaker book that relies too much on an extended chase sequence, reiterates these themes in a story about the struggle over water rights. One curious exception to the general thrust of Ballard's beliefs is *Loco and the Wolf*. Two escaped convicts, Loco and Wolf, acquire a map drawn by a deceased train robber which purports to show the way to buried stolen loot. In company with the unsuspecting daughter of the robber who is unaware of her father's profession and an undercover lawman also looking for the money, the four set out across desert badlands in search of the cache. Completely out of his element, the lawman is wholly dependent for his survival on the wilderness skills of the two bandits. The cache is found empty, Loco and Wolf ride off on their own further adventures, and the lawman decides to give up the law to marry the robber's daughter.

Ballard wrote his best Westerns between 1951 and the early 1960's. All his books are distinguished by his ability to evoke the natural landscape and climate. The dialogue carries the narrative smoothly and easily. By the mid-1960's, however, Ballard began to substitute landscape description for character development. His plots became thinner and thinner and the dialogue less and less significant. Compensating for these attenuated elements, Ballard substituted extended chase sequences marked by improbable escapes. The clean living and the love interest are still there, but the excitement and interest generated by believable characters engaged in the hazardous enterprise of building a just and orderly civilization is missing.

—J. Fraser Cocks, III

BALLEW, Charles. *See* **SNOW, Charles H.**

BANTON, Coy. *See* **NORWOOD, V.G.C.**

BARDWELL, Denver. Pseudonym for James Denson Sayers; also wrote as Dan James. *Died.*

WESTERN PUBLICATIONS

Novels

Gun-Smoke in Sunset Valley. New York, Godwin, and London, Wright and Brown, 1935; as *Bullet Valley*, London, Hale, 1971.
Killers on the Diamond A. New York, Godwin, 1935; London, Wright and Brown, 1936.
Beyond Midnight Chasm. New York, Godwin, 1936; London, Hale, 1937.
Rancho Bonita. New York, Godwin, 1936; London, Hale, 1937.
The Exile Returns West. London, Hale, 1937.
Rivers Westward. New York, Curl, and London, Hale, 1939.
Coyote Hunter. New York, Doubleday, and London, Hale, 1940.
Prairie Fire. New York, Doubleday, 1940; London, Hale, 1942.
Eagle Trail. New York, Avalon, 1951.
Calamity at Devil's Crossing. Kingswood, Surrey, World's Work, 1951; New York, Avalon, 1952.
Owl-Hoot Pay-Off. Kingswood, Surrey, World's Work, 1952.
Where the Sun Sets. Kingswood, Surrey, World's Work, 1952.
Gunsmoke Mesa. Kingswood, Surrey, World's Work, 1954; as Dan James, New York, Avalon, 1955.

Novels as Dan James

Gun Thunder on the Rio. New York, Godwin, 1935; London, Wright and Brown, 1936.
Rustlers on the Smoky Trail. New York, Godwin, 1936; London, Hale, 1937.
Stranger at Storm Ranch. New York, Godwin, 1936; as *Storm Ranch* (as Denver Bardwell), London, Hale, 1937.
West of the Sunset. London, Sampson Low, 1937; New York, Curl, 1939.
Range War in Squaw Valley. London, Sampson Low, 1938.
Trouble at Choctaw Bend. New York, Avalon, and London, Hale, 1952.
Shadow Guns. New York, Avalon, 1953.

OTHER PUBLICATIONS

Other

Can the White Race Survive? (as James Denson Sayers). Washington, D.C., Independent, 1929.

* * *

The majority of Denver Bardwell's heroes are young men with a strong sense of justice, who happen to be passing by when they become involved in one sort of trouble or another. Although they are portrayed as youngsters, he fails to give them a young person's outlook on life, and endows them with knowledge and character far beyond their years. This method of characterization creates a two-dimensional figure who is rarely strong enough to carry a story along on his own. David Stanley, in *Where the Sun Sets*, is in his early twenties, but has already been schooled by Kit Carson. He therefore finds it only natural that he should be the leader of an emigrant train bound for Portland, rather than the elected boss, Thomenson. There is obvious rivalry between the two, and they lock horns in this slow-moving story.

Bardwell uses another young, strong-willed central character in *Calamity at Devil's Crossing*, where he has an ex-member of Colonel Roosevelt's Rough Riders—Denklin Purcell—visiting an old friend and his daughter, who are troubled by a land grabbing syndicate. But he is too late to rescue the recently lynched Fell, and decides to help the girl fight off the land-grabber, Sloan. With the assistance of fellow Rough Riders and Sloan's insane wife, justice is served.

All of Bardwell's books proceed at a leisurely pace, where he takes great pains to describe the harshness of the land as well as the people in his stories. Westerners have always had to battle against the elements as much as human enemies, and Bardwell succeeds admirably in getting this point across. Unfortunately, in so doing he fails to allow himself the space to fully develop his characters, and his plotting appears to be rushed towards each book's conclusion. This said, he is a successful writer with the ability to deliver different, though predictable, storylines.

One of his earliest books, *Killers on the Diamond A*, tells of the early years of the Cattleman's Association, when a dying man's confession sets a young range detective to investigate cattle rustling in a wealthy valley. The detective, Bart Madison, is from the same mould as all Bardwell's heroes—young, quick-witted, sure-shooting and courageous. Such heroes are courteous to women, tough-talking to the villains and never, never shirk from a fight be it with fists, knife or gun. To counterbalance their virtues, Bardwell also endows his villains with great quantities of evil and they are often only scant inches away from the top-hatted and cloaked villain of *Perils of Pauline*. Typical of Bardwell's lone hero figure is Bill Radkin in *Coyote Hunter*. He roams the country with his trusted dog, Caeser, who is half-wolf, half-mastiff, looking for work by killing coyotes and making a living from selling their pelts. Fate rears its head when he falls for a young girl, and as in *Killers on the Diamond A*, agrees to help her against an enemy—this time a banker who wants the rich coal deposits on her father's land. Radkin sets himself up as the knight errant, and helps the maiden in distress.

To prove that all Westerns of that time weren't about rustling and land grabs, Bardwell came up with a new twist on the revenge topic. In *Gunsmoke Mesa* the main protagonist is an outlaw, who has plotted a double revenge while imprisoned in the Kansas Penitentiary. Not only is he going to kill the two men responsible for putting him there, but he intends to kill their sons. Talkie Hines and his fellow prisoner Red Batten escape and kidnap the three year-old babies, bringing them up until they are old enough to participate in the outlaws' nefarious activities. It is Hines's plan to have them hung as desperadoes, but his plot is not realized when the boys find out their true identities, and bring down the outlaw band in a savage ending to the novel.

Although the subject matter here is different, Bardwell's treatment of his characters remains the same. Apart from the leader, the outlaws are cast as dim-witted, and the boys transformed from innocents to trail-wearied and experienced outlaws within a few pages. This is very jarring to the eye and brain, for we know that Bardwell could write better, and his later works were much more capably produced as he got into his stride. Perhaps in his simple approach to characters and plots he attempted to lighten the tone of the pulp Westerns, but much of his work fails to satisfy the reader of today. 50 or 60 years ago they were fine for undiscerning readers, but nowadays they seem outdated pieces of work.

—Mike Stotter

BARKER, S(quire) Omar. Also wrote as Dan Scott. American. Born in Beulah, New Mexico, 16 June 1894. Educated at New Mexico Highlands University, Las Vegas, B.A. 1924. Served in the United States Army Engineers, 1917–19: Sergeant. Married Elsa McCormick (i.e., the writer E.M. Barker) in 1927. High school English and Spanish teacher, Tularose, New Mexico, 1913–14; high school teacher and principal, Santa Rosa, New Mexico, 1914–16; English instructor, New Mexico Highlands University, 1921–22; member of the New Mexico legislature, 1925–26; U.S. forest rangers, Los Olgos, New Mexico, 1929–56; worked in Cowboys' Reunion Rodeo; trombonist, Doc Patterson's Cowboy Band. President, Western Writers of America, 1958–59. Recipient: Western Writers of America Spur award, for short story, 1956 for non-fiction, 1958, for poetry, 1967, Justin Golden Boot award, 1961, and Levi Strauss Golden Saddleman award, 1967. Litt.D.: New Mexico Highlands University, 1960. Honorary Chief of the Kiowa Tribe, Anadarko, Oklahoma, 1959. *Died in 1985.*

WESTERN PUBLICATIONS

Novel

Little World Apart. New York, Doubleday, 1966.

Short Stories

Born to Battle. Albuquerque, University of New Mexico Press, 1951.

Uncollected Short Stories

"The Grudge Hound," in *Adventure* (New York), 20 May 1924.
"Cap'n Jenks," in *Adventure* (New York), 10 September 1924.
"The Makin's of a Man," with Dick Halliday, in *Cowboy Story* (London), November 1926.
"The Double Cross," with Dick Halliday, in *Cowboy Story* (London), December 1926.
"Mountain Mercy," in *North-West Stories* (London), Early March 1927.
"Fingers on the Trigger," in *West* (New York), 6 August 1927.
"A 'Bear' Escape," in *Western Story* (New York), 6 August 1927.
"The Mountains Were His Brothers," in *Western Story* (New York), 2 June 1928.
"Buckaroo Ballots," in *Western Story* (New York), 8 September 1928.
"So This Is the West!," in *Western Story* (New York), 10 November 1928.
"Hammered Home," in *Adventure* (New York), 1 July 1929.
"The Tophand Kid," in *West* (New York), 21 August 1929.
"Hard Feelin's," in *West* (New York), 6 July 1932.
"Like Twin Pups," in *West* (New York), 20 July 1932.
"Where the Water Runs," in *Adventure* (New York), 15 September 1932.
"The Courtin' of Bashful Bill," in *West* (New York), December 1932.
"Trail Sign," in *West* (New York), February 1933.
"The Ace of Spuds," in *West* (New York), October 1933.
"The Will to Wind," in *West* (New York), November 1933.
"Smeared," in *Cowboy Stories* (New York), November 1933.
"Trick Tracks," in *Cowboy Stories* (New York), December 1933.
"Caruso, Chuck-Line Runt," in *All Western* (New York), January 1934.
"The Milky Way," in *West* (New York), January 1934.
"Judgement of the Storm," in *Western Story* (New York), 20 January 1934.
"A Man to Kill," in *Western Story* (New York), 3 February 1934.
"Hat Hate," in *All Western* (New York), May 1934.
"The Battle of the Bulls," in *West* (New York), May 1934.
"Burro Bonus," in *Cowboy Stories* (New York), June 1934.
"Quick, Watson! The Needle!," in *All Western* (New York), June 1934.
"Say It with Skunk-Weed," in *Western Story* (New York), 18 June 1934.
"Fence Defense," in *Cowboy Stories* (New York), July 1934.
"Hosstail Has Him a Ruckus," in *All Western* (New York), July 1934.
"The Augurin' Match," in *West* (New York), August 1934.
"The 89¢ Sheriff," in *All Western* (New York), October 1934.
"Tax Tactics," in *Cowboy Stories* (New York), October 1934.
"The Stranger Kid," in *Western Story* (New York), 6 October 1934.
"Gentle Dynamite," in *Western Story* (New York), 20 October 1934.

"El Senor Coyote Rides Again," in *Cowboy Stories* (New York), November 1934.
"Yellow Clues," in *Cowboy Stories* (New York), December 1934.
"Doughbelly Perkins, Coosie," in *All Western* (New York), December 1934.
"Scrub of the Breed," in *West* (New York), December 1934.
"Balloting Billy-Goat," in *All Western* (New York), January 1935.
"4 of a Kind," in *Cowboy Stories* (New York), January 1935.
"Needle Evidence," in *West* (New York), February 1935.
"A Feller Like That," in *West* (New York), March 1935.
"Second Fiddle," in *Cowboy Stories* (New York), March 1935.
"The Beeg Bad Wolf," in *Cowboy Stories* (New York), April 1935.
"Wild and Woolly Willie," in *West* (New York), July 1935.
"Traps on the Trail," in *Cowboy Stories* (New York), November 1935.
"The Son of Jury Joe," in *West* (New York), January 1936.
"The Tale of a Tail," in *West* (New York), February 1936.
"Mister Yooly," in *All Western* (New York), April 1936.
"Hot Water at Horse Tail," in *West* (New York), May 1936.
"Who Shooting the Bool?," in *West* (New York), June 1936.
"El Senor Coyote's Reward," in *Cowboy Stories* (New York), June 1936.
"The Claws of Chispa Charley," in *All Western* (New York), June 1936.
"Bristle Chest Chester," in *All Western* (New York), July 1936.
"All Ears," in *All Western* (New York), August 1936.
"Two Tough Trails," in *All Western* (New York), October 1936.
"Stranger No More," in *Ranch Romances* (New York), 3 November 1936.
"The Big Wet," in *All Western* (New York), January 1937.
"Buggy Buckaroos," in *Cowboy Stories* (New York), February 1937.
"Boosty's Billy," in *All Western* (New York), February 1937.
"Lady Horse Thief," in *Ranch Romances* (New York), 2 February 1937.
"The West Ain't None Too Good," in *Cowboy Stories* (New York), March 1937.
"The Jaws of the Wolf," in *West* (New York), April 1937.
"Cupid the Hareless," in *Ranch Romances* (New York), 2 April 1937.
"Vertebravery," in *All Western* (New York), May 1937.
"The Maverick Code," in *Ranch Romances* (New York), 1 May 1937.
"Renegade's Reckoning," in *West* (New York), June 1937.
"Heads Up," in *Ranch Romances* (New York), 1 June 1937.
"The Dust Buster," in *All Western* (New York), October 1937.
"The Horse-Whipped Kid," in *Cowboy Stories* (New York), November 1937.
"Bill Standifer's Luck," in *Cowboy Stories* (New York), December 1937.
"Peckleberry's Pussy," in *All Western* (New York), December 1937.
"The Empty Bunk," in *All Western* (New York), February 1938.
"Boosty's Bones," in *All Western* (New York), March 1938.
"Boosty's Romance," in *All Western* (New York), May 1938.
"Steer Belles Soup," in *All Western* (New York), June 1938.
"A Gal for Gilhooley," in *Western Story* (New York), 22 October 1938.
"Swaller-Fork," in *Western Story* (New York), 25 March 1939.
"Tack Tracks," in *Western Story* (New York), 20 May 1939.
"Coyote Wranglers," in *Western Story* (New York), 1 July 1939.
"Pack Rat Pardner," in *Western Story* (New York), 12 August 1939.
"A Bear for Cowboying," in *Wild West* (New York), 18 May 1940.
"Tiger by the Tail," in *Wild West* (New York), 15 June 1940.
"Mucho Moneys for Dreamy Dorkin," in *Wild West* (New York), 29 June 1940.
"Mule-Headed Hombre," in *Western Story* (London), July 1940.
"Milk 'em, Cowboy!," in *Wild West* (New York), 20 July 1940.
"Empty Chaps," in *Wild West* (New York), 14 September 1940.
"Too Many Oncles," in *Wild West* (New York), 26 October 1940.
"Bunkhouse Buscadero," in *Wild West* (New York), 21 December 1940.
"The Gent from Australia," in *West* (Kingswood, Surrey), July 1941.
"Porcupine Plague," in *Western Story* (London), June 1943.
"Smoking Showdown," in *Western Story* (London), December 1943.
"Chicken House Champ," in *Western Story* (London), April 1945.
"Porcupine Payoff," in *Western Story* (London), January 1946.
"Ride 'em, Cowgirl!," in *Western Story* (London), May 1946.
"The Sheriff's Hunch Mill," in *West* (Kingswood, Surrey), November 1946.
"Tongue-Waggin' Waddy," in *Western Story* (London), December 1946.
"Nosed Out," in *West* (Kingswood, Surrey), December 1946.
"Bean Patch Buscadero," in *West* (Kingswood, Surrey), March 1947.
"Cibolero's Keepsake," in *Zane Grey's Western* (New York), September 1947.
"Dog Deputy," in *West* (Kingswood, Surrey), February 1948.
"Battle of the Bulls," in *West* (Kingswood, Surrey), March 1948.
"Sons of the Wind," in *West* (Kingswood, Surrey), April 1948.
"Cowgal on the Peck," in *Zane Grey's Western* (New York), June 1948.
"Buscadero Crossing," in *West* (Kingswood, Surrey), July 1948.
"Hairy Side Out," in *West* (Kingswood, Surrey), August 1948.
"Corazón Means Heart," in *Zane Grey's Western* (New York), September 1948.
"Dust on the Big Hat," in *Zane Grey's Western* (New York), October 1948.
"Boolsfight Beezness," in *West* (Kingswood, Surrey), December 1948.
"They've Shot Jud Murphy," in *Western Stories*, edited by William MacLeod Raine. New York, Dell, 1949.
"Between a Rock and a Hard Place," in *Gun Smoke Yarns*, edited by Gene Autry. New York, Dell, 1949.
"Wolf's Nest at Corazon," in *Zane Grey's Western* (New York), February 1949.
"My Guns Talk for Me," in *Saturday Evening Post* (Philadelphia), 9 April 1949.
"Last Cibolero," in *West* (Kingswood, Surrey), May 1949.
"If Hunches Were Horses," in *West* (Kingswood, Surrey), August 1949.
"Oh, Ride the Dry River," in *All Western* (New York), April–June 1950.
"Figgerin' Sheriff," in *Zane Grey's Western* (New York), July 1950.
"Hunch-Drunk Sheriffin," in *West* (Kingswood, Surrey), August 1950.

"Tricky Triplets," in *All Western* (New York), December 1950–January 1951.
"The Girl Who Busted Broncos," in *Saturday Evening Post* (Philadelphia), 16 December 1950.
"Dust on the Big Hat," in *Zane Grey Western Award Stories*, edited by Don Ward. New York, Dell, 1951.
"The Claimer and the Cowboy," in *Zane Grey's Western* (New York), January 1951.
"Delayed in Transit," in *Thrilling Ranch Stories* (London), December 1951.
"Cattymount Cowboys," in *Zane Grey's Western* (New York), February 1952.
"Rowdy Romance," in *Texas Rangers* (London), February 1952.
"Ramshackle Ranch," in *Zane Grey's Western* (New York), June 1952.
"Jaybird Johnny," in *Zane Grey's Western* (New York), July 1952.
"El Coyote Plays Panny-Weenkle," in *Western Story* (London), September 1952.
"Bribed Ballots," in *Thrilling Ranch Stories* (London), October 1952.
"A Wolf in the Hand," in *Zane Grey's Western* (New York), November 1952.
"Stray Man," in *Zane Grey's Western 7* (London).
"Cactus Casanova," in *Zane Grey's Western 18* (London).
"Danger Trail," in *Saturday Evening Post* (Philadelphia), 3 January 1953.
"Don't Pull That Knife," in *Saturday Evening Post* (Philadelphia), 8 August 1953.
"Help for the Sheriff," in *West* (Kingswood, Surrey), September 1953.
"Horse-Thief Trail," in *Zane Grey's Western* (New York), October 1953.
"The Road to Nowhere," in *West* (Kingswood, Surrey), November 1953.
"Man in the Hard Hat," in *Holsters and Heroes*, edited by Noel M. Loomis. New York, Macmillan, 1954.
"Ice on the Trail," in *Zane Grey's Western* (New York), January 1954.
"Notch-Crazy," in *The Fall Roundup*, edited by H.E. Maule. New York, Random House, 1955.
"Trail Fever," in *Branded West*, edited by Don Ward. Boston, Houghton Mifflin, 1956.
"Granger's Girl," in *Thrilling Western* (London), March 1957.
"Macho," in *Wild Horse Roundup*, edited by Jim Kjelgaard. New York, Dodd Mead, 1958.
"Pup and the Bad Man," in *Hound Dogs and Others*, edited by Jim Kjelgaard. New York, Dodd Mead, 1958.
"Outlaw Trail," in *Saturday Evening Post Reader of Western Stories*, edited by E.N. Brandt. New York, Doubleday, 1960.
"Bad Company," in *Spurs West*, edited by S. Omar Barker. New York, Doubleday, 1960.
"Cub on the Prod," in *Trails of Adventure*, edited by E.D. Mygatt. New York, Dodd Mead, 1961.
"A Deal with a Lady," in *They Won Their Spurs*, edited by Nelson Nye. New York, Avon, 1962.
"Saddle or Nothing," in *Rawhide Men*, edited by Kenneth Fowler. New York, Doubleday, 1965.
"Back Before the Moon," in *Great Ghost Stories of the Old West*, edited by Betty Baker. New York, Four Winds Press, 1968.
"Champs at the Chuckabug," in *Great Stories of the West*, edited by Ned Collier. New York, Doubleday, 1971.
"Prisoners of the Snow," in *Western Romances*, edited by Peggy Simson Curry. New York, Fawcett, 1973.
"Tall Men Riding," in *Western Writers of America Silver Anniversary Anthology*, edited by August Lenniger. New York, Ace, 1977.
"Tom Smith of Abilene" (verse), in *The Lawmen*, edited by Bill Pronzini and Martin H. Greenberg. New York, Fawcett, 1984.
"Charlie Bowdre" (verse), in *The Outlaws*, edited by Bill Pronzini and Martin H. Greenberg. New York, Fawcett, 1984.
"Old-Time Cowboys" (verse), and "Trail Fever," in *The Cowboys*, edited by Bill Pronzini and Martin H. Greenberg. New York, Fawcett, 1985.
"Some Call Him Brave" (verse), in *The Horse Soldiers*, edited by Bill Pronzini and Martin H. Greenberg. New York, Fawcett, 1987.
"Three Yuletide Poems: Draggin' in the Tree; Bunkhouse Christmas; A Cowboy's Christmas" (verse), in *Christmas Out West*, edited by Bill Pronzini and Martin H. Greenberg, New York, Doubleday, 1990.

OTHER PUBLICATIONS

Verse

Vientos de las Sierras, Winds of the Mountains. Privately printed, 1922.
Buckaroo Ballads. Privately printed, 1928.
Songs of the Saddlemen. Denver, Sage, 1954.
Sunlight Through the Trees. Las Vegas, New Mexico Highlands University Press, 1954.
Rawhide Rhymes: Singing Poems of the Old West. New York, Doubleday, 1968.

Other (for children) as Dan Scott

The Mystery of Ghost Canyon. New York, Grosset and Dunlap, 1960.
The Secret of Hermit's Peak. New York, Grosset and Dunlap, 1960.
The Range Rodeo Mystery. New York, Grosset and Dunlap, 1960.
The Mystery of Rawhide Gap. New York, Grosset and Dunlap, 1960.
The Secret of Fort Pioneer. New York, Grosset and Dunlap, 1961.
The Mystery at Blizzard Mesa. New York, Grosset and Dunlap, 1961.
The Mystery of the Comanche Caves. New York, Grosset and Dunlap, 1962.
The Phantom of Wolf Creek. New York, Grosset and Dunlap, 1963.
The Mystery of Bandit Gulch. New York, Grosset and Dunlap, 1964.

Other

The Cattleman's Steak Book: Best Beef Recipes, with Carol Truax. New York, Grosset and Dunlap 1967.

Editor, *Frontiers West, By Members of the Western Writers of America.* New York, Doubleday, 1959.
Editor, *Spurs West, By Members of the Western Writers of America.* New York, Doubleday, 1960.
Editor, *Legends and Tales of the Old West, By Members of the Western Writers of America.* New York, Doubleday, 1962.

* * *

S. Omar Barker wrote well within a number of genres in western literature: he is the author of a novel, *Little World Apart*, numerous books for children, and a cookbook (of cattlemen's favorite steak recipes), and the editor of three important anthologies of writings by members of the Western Writers of America. Rather unusually, he also published poetry—and poetry about the West is no more likely to be popular than poetry on any other subject—but Barker published five volumes of "cowboy verse"; he could be said to have popularized the genre. Yet, despite so varied and prolific an output, Barker's greatest excellence may well be in his short stories.

His uncollected short stories are mostly anecdotes of adults—western "characters"—learning a lesson about life as the result of some fortuitous or unexpected occurrence. "Champs at the Chuckabug" concerns two rodeo partners who are accused of a theft and then need rescuing by an old "Grandpaw." "Notch-Crazy" is an interesting story of a young cowboy shamed into submission by a fugitive, then, in effect, shamed (by his own conscience) into standing up to him. "Bad Company" is a charming story of a young 16-year-old, Willy, longing to be a man, who ingratiates himself with a group of high-spirited cowboys (therefore, to him, potential heroes) who are about to leave for Wyoming. Of course, he admires and emulates them; just as certainly they turn out to be rascals who plan to steal his uncle's horses. Willy foils them by stealing them back, and in the process learns something about adults and adulthood.

The stories collected in *Born to Battle* (as well as some of the uncollected stories) are animal stories—stories of animals in the New Mexico wilderness, their relations to man, to the environment, and to each other—again (like the adults) learning some lesson about life as a result of a chance experience or a longing for adventure. "Born to Battle," the title story, is about a renegade bull who becomes feral, a menace to the neighborhood ranchers—but he learns heroism in his fight against other bulls and, finally, a grizzly. In "Valiant Lady" a mule deer, evading a killer coyote, finally through fear and surprise actually kills her enemy. In "King of the Coyotes" a one-eyed coyote who can't really compete in the wild world of the wilderness is roped and belled by a high-spirited cowboy. The bell scares off other coyotes, warning them, and the one-eyed coyote becomes a hero. Even after he loses the bell, his confidence is now such as to allow him to fight and succeed in the wilderness.

Such a description makes both kinds of stories sound of a piece, morally ponderous, and likely to be more appealing to children than to the mature reader. That this is not the case is a tribute to Barker's talents as a writer. With few exceptions, he manages to avoid the "cute" or any imitations of Disney. He varies his style with great dexterity from story to story, and he is a master at establishing that tone that best suits the needs of his narrative. Most importantly, Barker is a humorist in the best western, Mark Twain, sense of the word: as is his poetry, his stories are light, pungent, and amusing, the skill of which is both so subtle and complete as to delight the serious reader of western literature.

—George Walsh

BARNWELL, J.O. Pseudonym for Joseph Caruso. American. Left art school at 17 to travel the West as a hobo for two years. Served in the United States Army, 1941–45: Bronze Star. Married; three children. Visited Missouri, the Mojave Desert, and Wyoming. Since 1955 writer and painter of murals.

WESTERN PUBLICATIONS

Novels

Death Rider. New York, Macmillan, 1955.
Trail of a Gunfighter. London, W.H. Allen, 1962.

OTHER PUBLICATIONS

Novel as Joseph Caruso

The Priest. London, World, 1960.

* * *

It is a pity that Joseph Caruso's output of western fiction was limited to just two novels as by J.O. Barnwell. His vision was true and unique, his skills considerable if in need of honing, and had he continued to write westerns he might well have become a major voice in the genre.

Both *Death Rider* and *Trail of a Gunfighter* are narrated, wholly or in large part, by outlaws of the 1870's—violent but educated and disillusioned men who are seeking redemption for past sins, the meaning of life in general and their own lives in particular. Clay Buell, at the beginning of the former title, is broken by his experiences as a member of the James gang and at the bloody Northfield, Minnesota raid; as the latter title opens, Shelby Scott, a former mercenary soldier in Mexico and self-styled Texas "border scum" bandit, is undone by the mortal wounding of his friend Sam Bass during an abortive holdup. Conscience-stricken, soul-sick, these men set out on different and yet fundamentally similar odysseys. Buell's quest leads him into Dakota Territory, then to Wyoming's Platte River country where he takes a job as a deputy U.S. marshall and becomes embroiled in bitter conflict with vigilantes and ruthless cattle bosses. Scott, keeping a promise to the dying Sam Bass to care for Bass's illegitimate daughter, travels from Texas to Indiana and then, with the young girl in his charge, to Kansas, Arkansas, and finally back to Texas; in the blackland country near the Red River, he accepts a position as schoolmaster and undertakes violent defense of local hard-scrabble ranchers and victimized *Tejanos*. Both men fall in love with good women; both men find at least some of the purpose and meaning that has eluded them all their lives; and yet both men, because of their pasts, of who and what they are, are doomed to ultimately lose their personal Armageddons.

Despite their titles, and despite such trappings as fistfights and gun duels, *Death Rider* and *Trail of a Gunfighter* are literary westerns—episodic mood pieces filled with quotes from and references to Shakespeare, Dickens, Cervantes; with passages from folk songs and such operas as *Il Trovatore*; with obscure but pointed Spanish axioms. They are also historical westerns enriched by an authentic flavor of life on the frontier, of the "rawness of this bleak, full-blown, fat, lean world called America." Actual historical figures march through their pages and figure prominently in their plots: Frank and Jesse James, Cole Younger, Clay Allison, Sam Bass, Bill Tilghman, Charlie Siringo, Bat Masterson, Texas Jack Omohundro. Actual places and historical events also figure prominently in each book.

Caruso's prose is sometimes clumsy, occasionally (and oddly) anachronistic; but its power is undeniable. The narratives of Buell and Scott (and of Sam Bass's daughter, Sarah Ann, which makes up about a third of *Trail of a Gunfighter*) read like factual reminiscences. Scenes in both novels linger in the memory long after reading: Shelby Scott's description of a public hanging in Fort Smith, Arkansas, for instance, in which the onlookers burst into nervous, demented laughter at the "goose floppin' and flappin'" of the strangling man, "as if the faculty of laughter was an audible expression of self-hate, an ostensible mark of despair."

—Bill Pronzini

BARRETT, Geoffrey John. Also writes as Rex Anders; Jeff Blaine; Richard Cole; Sam Gort; Jack Greer; Matt Kilbourn; Edward Leighton; Carn Macey; Cole Rickard; Dan Royal; Brett Sanders; Max Stern; D.B. Summers; Dennis Summers; Bill Wade; James Wallace. British. Born near Norwich, Norfolk, 23 September 1928. Educated at local elementary school; left at the age of 14. Worked in the plastics and brewing industries, as a driver, and in a variety of labouring jobs. Address: 25 Cyprus Road, Attleborough, Norfolk NR17 2DY, England.

WESTERN PUBLICATIONS

Novels as Dan Royal

A Rope at Sun-Up. London, Hale, 1965.
Riders to High Gap. London, Hale, 1966.
The Gallows Breed. London, Hale, 1969.
The Devil Rock. London, Hale, 1969.
Valley of Dispute. London, Hale, 1969.
Gun Booty. London, Hale, 1970.
Lord of the High Lonesome. London, Hale, 1970.
A Hole on Boot Hill. London, Hale, 1970.
Rogue's Justice. London, Hale, 1972.
The Avenger from Fire Mountain. London, Hale, 1972.
Murder in Blaze Canyon. London, Hale, 1973.
Storm Trail to Black Canyon. London, Hale, 1973.
The Hard Men. London, Hale, 1973.
Sixgun Samaritan. London, Hale, 1974.
The Saga of Fire Mountain. London, Hale, 1974.
Come Hell and Sam Hikeman. London, Hale, 1974.
Red Queen of the Crater Range. London, Hale, 1985.
Fight for Grimm Valley. London, Hale, 1986.
The Border Breed. London, Hale, 1986.
The Ghost Horseman. London, Hale, 1987.
Spearman's Grass. London, Hale, 1988.
Dead Man Riding. London, Hale, 1988.
Sixgun Guardian. London, Hale, 1991.
He Died with His Boots Off. London, Hale, 1991.

Novels as Cole Rickard

The Crumpled Star. London, Hale, 1964.
Ride Lonesome. London, Hale, 1964.
Payment in Lead. London, Hale, 1966.
Rider at Dawn. London, Hale, 1967.
Hangmen at Thunderhead. London, Hale, 1968.
Guns of the Brothers Pike. London, Hale, 1970.
Blood on the Golden Spur. London, Hale, 1970.
The Badman of Black Gulch. London, Hale, 1972.
Bones under Buzzard Rock. London, Hale, 1972.
The Kid from Elderville. London, Hale, 1972.
Last Man at Lobo Heights. London, Hale, 1972.
King of Graftersville. London, Hale, 1974.
Funeral at Ferryville. London, Hale, 1976.
The Judas Loot. London, Hale, 1976.
The Grave at San Pedro. London, Hale, 1985.
Dealer Take All. London, Hale, 1986.
Night of the Hangmen. London, Hale, 1987.
A Gun Against Midnight. London, Hale, 1987.
Die, Cowboy—Die! London, Hale, 1988.
Firewater. London, Hale, 1988.
Kidnap in Hunt Valley. London, Hale, 1990.
Riders of the White Hell. London, Hale, 1991.

Novels as Bill Wade

The Brand of Destiny. London, Hale, 1965.
Four Graves to Tomahawk. London, Hale, 1966.
Guns of the Damned. London, Hale, 1966.
Trail to Blood Canyon. London, Hale, 1967.
Gunned Down. London, Hale, 1969.
Killing at Black Notch. London, Hale, 1969.
A Bullet Sped. London, Hale, 1970.
Gun Wolves. London, Hale, 1970.
The Gun from Prison Hill. London, Hale, 1971.
Ride for Revenge. London, Hale, 1971.
The Stage to Friday. London, Hale, 1971.
Massacre at Mission Point. London, Hale, 1972.
The Raiders of Glory River. London, Hale, 1972.
Terror at Black Rock. London, Hale, 1972.
Gunman's Courage. London, Hale, 1972.
The Dastardly Rum Keg Jones. London, Hale, 1973.
The Last Town West. London, Hale, 1973.
The Strong Range. London, Hale, 1973.
Tombstone Tuck. London, Hale, 1973.
The Haunted Prairie. London, Hale, 1974.
John Scar and the Sacre Range. London, Hale, 1974.
Canyon of Gold. London, Hale, 1974.
Flare-up at Battle Creek. London, Hale, 1975.
Revenge for Kid Billy. London, Hale, 1976.
Horsemen at Black Pass. London, Hale, 1983.
West by Boot Hill. London, Hale, 1984.
The Last Round Up. London, Hale, 1985.
The Rancho Blood. London, Hale, 1985.
Blood on the Tomahawk. London, Hale, 1986.
Return to Spanish Hill. London, Hale, 1986.
Cade's Gold. London, Hale, 1987.
Guns in Quiet Valley. London, Hale, 1987.
The Last Rebel. London, Hale, 1988.
Gallows Bend. London, Hale, 1989.
Dead Come Sundown. London, Hale, 1990.

Novels as D.B. Summers

Promised Lead. London, Hale, 1965.
Die by the Gun. London, Hale, 1966.
Escape to Oregon. London, Hale, 1968.
The Little Killer. London, Hale, 1970.
The Killers of Cain River. London, Hale, 1971.
The Gunhawks of Gaunt Range. London, Hale, 1971.
Gun Trail for Gus Hoffman. London, Hale, 1971.
Killers at Kyle Crossing. London, Hale, 1972.
Lament for a Lawman. London, Hale, 1972.
Law into Loudberg. London, Hale, 1972.
Mustang M'Gee. London, Hale, 1972.
They Hanged Jake Kilrain. London, Hale, 1984.
A Ranger Died. London, Hale, 1985.
Hang the Kid High. London, Hale, 1986.
Hideout at Skull Rock. London, Hale, 1986.
The Dead at Hob's Climb. London, Hale, 1988.
Ranch of the Dead. London, Hale, 1989.

Novels as Brett Sanders

Desert Gold. London, Gresham, 1964.
Gem Quest. London, Gresham, 1964.
Forgotten Trails. London, Gresham, 1965.
The Tunstock Range. London, Gresham, 1966.

Novels as Matt Kilbourn

Three Guns from Midnight. London, Hale, 1965.
Face the Quick Gun. London, Hale, 1966.

Novels as Jeff Blaine

Tully's Return. London, Gresham, 1962.
Long Ride to Vengeance. London, Gresham, 1963.
Inherit by Gunsmoke. London, Gresham, 1964.
Destination—Boothill. London, Gresham, 1965.
Vengeance Riders. London, Brown and Watson, 1965.
The Rangebreakers. London, Gresham, 1966.
Valley of the Lawless. London, Hale, 1966.
Sons of the Saddle. London, Hale, 1967.
Wild Man at Smoke Creek. London, Hale, 1972.
Mankiller. London, Hale, 1973.
The Distant Gun. London, Hale, 1974.
Rage at Bedrock. London, Hale, 1974.
He Died on Main Street. London, Hale, 1988.

Novels as Rex Anders

Rider from the Dead. London, Gresham, 1963.
Saddle the Lightning. London, Gresham, 1964.
Troubled Range. London, Gresham, 1964.
The Trail to Hell. London, Gresham, 1965.
The Killers of Iron Bluffs. London, Gresham, 1966.

Novels as Carn Macey

Hired Gun. London, Gresham, 1964.
Marshals West. London, Gresham, 1964.
Guns to Babel. London, Gresham, 1964.
Guns of Dispute. London, Gresham, 1965.

Novels as Sam Gort

Gunn Came Back. London, Hale, 1988.
The Fastest Gun. London, Hale, 1989.

Novels as Jack Greer

Find Pecos Joe. London, Hale, 1988.
The Secret of Lost Butte. London, Hale, 1988.
Ride to Storm Town. London, Hale, 1989.
Riders in Rebel Grey. London, Hale, 1991.

Novels as Max Stern

Hatchet Ridge. London, Hale, 1989.
The Wind River Kid. London, Hale, 1989.
The Guns of Jack Kilroy. London, Hale, 1990.
Shoot Me a Sidewinder. London, Hale, 1991.

OTHER PUBLICATIONS

Novels

Danger in Diamonds. London, Hale, 1968.
The Evil Ones. London, Hale, 1968.
He Died Twice. London, Hale, 1968.
Guilty Be Damned! London, Hale, 1968.
A Hearse for McNally. London, Hale, 1969.
Lonely Is the Grave. London, Hale, 1969.
Concerto of Death. London, Hale, 1969.
His Own Funeral. London, Hale, 1972.
The Brain of Graphicon. London, Hale, 1973.
The Lost Fleet of Astranides. London, Hale, 1974.
The Tomorrow Stairs. London, Hale, 1974.
Overself. London, Hale, 1975.
The Paradise Zone. London, Hale, 1975.
City of the First Time. London, Hale, 1975.
Slaver from the Stars. London, Hale, 1975.
Timeship to Thebes. London, Hale, 1976.
The Night of the Deathship. London, Hale, 1976.
The Bodysnatchers of Lethe. London, Hale, 1976.
The Halls of the Evolvulus. London, Hale, 1977.
The Other Side of Red. London, Hale, 1977.
Robotoria. London, Hale, 1977.
Earthwatch. London, Hale, 1978.

Novels as Edward Leighton

Out of Earth's Deep. London, Hale, 1977.
A Light from Tomorrow. London, Hale, 1977.
Lord of the Lightning. London, Hale, 1977.

Novels as Dennis Summers

A Madness from Mars. London, Hale, 1976.
Stalker of the Worlds. London, Hale, 1976.
Robot in the Glass. London, Hale, 1977.

Novels as James Wallace

A Man for Tomorrow. London, Hale, 1976.
The Plague of the Golden Rat. London, Hale, 1976.

* * *

One of the more accomplished exponents of the light Western currently working in Britain, Geoffrey John Barrett has had long experience with the form. He has been writing Westerns since the 1960's, and although the majority—40, in fact—have appeared under the pseudonym "Bill Wade," his other pen-names enjoy near equal popularity in the marketplace.

A typical Barrett Western almost always combines a good, strong frontier story with elements of mystery and intrigue. He usually tells his stories in 10 or so chapters, ending each one on a cliff-hanger, or at some pivotal point in the plot: just in the moment that a new twist is introduced into the story, say, or the instant before the hero, goaded into a gunfight, reaches for his Colt. Barrett is very good at mixing these components together, and has produced some genuinely puzzling mysteries over the years.

One of the best of these is *The Grave at San Pedro* (as Cole Rickard). Dispatched to locate a young Philadelphian named Rex Althorpe, who came west after an argument with his family (who now want to make amends), Pinkerton operative John Craig soon discovers that Althorpe—of whom he can find no trace—was not a very popular man. A lawyer, he drew up contracts between ranchers impoverished by a recent drought and the local dignitary, Hannibal Winfield; contracts which have since enabled Winfield to take complete control of the ranches. Craig's suspicions tell him that Althorpe is dead. But did he die of natural causes, or was he murdered? Part of the answer lies in the lonely grave of the book's title—but *only* part.

It is another questionable grave—that belonging to his outlaw half-brother—that makes Dave Rowan determined to uncover the truth of another mystery in the earlier (but technically less successful) Bill Wade novel *West by Boot Hill*, in which Barrett's hero once again runs into all manner of obstructions before finally reaching the denoument. Much better is *Blood on the Tomahawk*, in which buffalo hunter Josh Royd rescues a comatose young girl from the aftermath of what appears to be a Comanche attack, only to uncover a conspiracy of much wider implications. This book—which begins with a surprisingly "green" message pertaining to the slaughter of the buffalo—is further enlivened by a wonderful sequence midway through (in which Royd enters into a gunfight with the three nefarious LeBeau brothers) which displays Barrett's talent for sharp, incisive dialogue as well as his ability to choreograph his seldom-explicit—and indeed, relatively infrequent—bursts of action. It should be said, however, that sometimes the author's more complex plots sail dangerously close to utter confusion, though fortunately he is very good at explaining the actions and motives of his characters, thus allaying much potential misunderstanding.

Barrett's heroes are never portrayed as supermen. More inclined to solve problems with their brains than their guns (until events conspire to give them no other choice, of course), virtually all of Barrett's protagonists consequently possess a rounded, plausible quality that makes them at once both heroic and human. This "humanity" also comes through quite clearly in his supporting characters, and adds a sense of credibility to his perception of the West. The author writes about women quite well, and sometimes breaks convention by casting them as the principal villains of his books. When Mark Ralston comes home after the Civil War in Bill Wade's *Return to Spanish Hill*, for example, he learns that his children have died in a fire and his wife has been kidnapped by a former friend (the aptly-named Judas Lack). Returning to Wyoming after a spell in the California gold-fields in *A Gun Against Midnight* (written as Cole Rickard), Tom Beck discovers that his girl has been killed in a disagreement with another local man, Jack Midnight. In both cases, however, the heroes' subsequent actions turn into voyages of discovery which reveal that their women were far less than perfect. Even Sybil Blaze, the *Red Queen of the Crater Range* (written as Dan Royal), though portrayed as a lady of undoubted quality and courage, is nevertheless shown to be something of a man-eater, "unable to resist a predatory dip into the generation behind her."

Barrett's earlier work is perhaps his most interesting, and includes some particularly fine novels. *Tombstone Tuck* (as Bill Wade) remains one of his best. Finding a body out in the desert, outlaw Tuck discovers a letter identifying the corpse as a bank manager en route to take up a new job in a nearby town. Deciding to pose as the manager himself and thus rob the bank "legally," Tuck ends up recovering the money from another band of outlaws and becomes the town hero. Cole Rickard's *Guns of the Brothers Pike*, the story of two brothers who appear to be killing off a band of Rebel sympathisers in order to avenge their ill-treatment in Andersonville prisoner-of-war camp, is another far-from-predictable Western which serves as a good, if overlong, example of Barrett's ability to bring new twists to the Old West.

Although he tends to write to a specific formula (always telling his stories from his hero's point of view, almost never "jump-cutting" ahead, employing multiple view-points and so on), Barrett is nevertheless an intelligent, erudite, and entertaining western writer whose stories seldom adhere to expectation, but can always be relied upon to surprise.

—David Whitehead

BARRY, Jane (née Powell). American. Born in New Baltimore, New York, 25 August 1925. Married John David Barry in 1953; one son. Reporter, 1946–48, and editor of centennial edition, 1950–51, Coxsackie *Union News*, New York; editor, *Greene County News*. Agent: Harold Matson Company Inc., 22 East 40th Street, New York, New York 10016. Address: R.D.3, Lotus Point, Catskill, New York 12414, U.S.A.

WESTERN PUBLICATIONS

Novels

A Time in the Sun. New York, Doubleday, 1962.
A Shadow of Eagles. New York, Doubleday, 1964.
Maximilian's Gold. New York, Doubleday, 1966; London, Gollancz, 1967.

OTHER PUBLICATIONS

Novels

The Long March. New York, Appleton Century Crofts, 1955.
The Carolinians. New York, Doubleday, 1959.
Grass Roots. New York, Doubleday, 1968.
The Cavendish Face. London, Collins, 1983.
The Conscience of the King. London, Joseph, 1987.
Grand Illusions. New York, Avon, 1988.

*

Manuscript Collection: Boston University Library.

Jane Barry comments:

In my writing, I have attempted to portray the country as I know it and the people as I know them, both through research and, in later work, through personal contact. I am, personally, fondest of my western work because of my love for the country and the people, and while I have done my best to separate fact from legend, there are times when legend seems more truthful than fact and I have so used it while at the same time making the necessary distinctions. Having lived in the American west and having worked with Native Americans, I continue to hope that my work bears an authenticity which, while it may now and then be judged a bit romantic, will stand by itself as historically valid.

* * *

Jane Barry began her writing career as a journalist in her native state, New York. Her first novel—not a western—was published in 1955. In the 1960's she followed it with three fine, but little recognized, historical novels about the American

Southwest. The first, *A Time in the Sun*, deals with the sensitive issue of inter-marriage between Indians and whites. The principal characters are Anna Stillman, who is captured by Apaches while on her way to Tucson to marry her soldier fiancé, and Joaquin, an Apache with Mexican blood. Anna and Joaquin fall in love and marry. Although it was not the first novel about inter-marriage between an Indian and a white woman, this was the first time in a fictional work that a white woman, by choice, married an Indian and survived the ceremony. However, the pro-Apache/anti-white story does end tragically as all novels about inter-marriage traditionally do, i.e., with the death of one of the partners. Joaquin is killed by whites. In *From Hopalong to Hud* C.L. Sonnichsen wrote of Barry that she "is unwilling to let her lovers continue their housekeeping, but in other ways she is completely defiant of the old stereotypes." *A Time in the Sun* is a perceptive historical reconstruction, true to the land, the period, and the people; it rejects the idea of white supremacy and questions white values. Set in Arizona Territory in the 1870's, its main focus is on the struggles of the Apaches to retain their freedom and remain independent of the white man's reservations.

Stereotypes were again eschewed by Barry in *A Shadow of Eagles*, although it is the weakest novel in what might be called her southwestern trilogy. The story centers around the Tres Reyes ranch owned by the Ramon Dominquez family who represent the dying traditions of the Spanish aristocracy in Texas. The novel attempts to depict the differences in lifestyles and customs between the Spanish of the Old World and the New World and between the Spanish and Mexican inhabitants of Texas and the Anglo-American inhabitants. Cayetana Dominquez, Ramon's daughter, embodies the cultural conflict by having an Anglo mother and a Spanish-Mexican father. The cultural questions raised are obscured, however, and never clearly addressed because much of the story is given over to a trail drive to Montana and the drama of the drive. Yet, notwithstanding this structural incongruity, life both on the trail and on Tres Reyes ranch are vividly described, and the book demonstrates Barry's ability to recreate adeptly the historical past.

Man's greed for gold and the devastating effects of the Civil War are studied in *Maximilian's Gold*, a book often compared to B. Traven's *The Treasure of the Sierra Madre* (1934). The story, about a cache of gold buried in Texas following the execution of Maximilian, was suggested by a legend contained in J. Frank Dobie's *Coronado's Children* (1930). The six gold-seekers who travel from war-torn Missouri to Texas with the intention of crossing the border into Mexico are individually, and collectively, among Barry's finer literary portraits.

A unique and sensitive author, Barry presents a balanced view of the southwest in her fiction, one without sentimentality. Her concern is not with heroes triumphing over villains, but rather with what happens when peoples of diverse cultures, traditions, and backgrounds collide. Her meticulously constructed stories are gripping and her characters are almost always credible.

—Vicki Piekarski

BARTON, Jack. *See* **CHADWICK, Joseph.**

BARTON, (Samuel) Wayne. American. Born in Odessa, Texas, 23 May 1944. Educated at Texas Tech University, Lubbock, B.S. 1967; Midland College, Texas, 1972; Casper Community College, Wyoming, 1974. Senior engineer, Arco Oil and Gas Company, Midland, Texas. Membership Chair, and member of the board of directors, Western Writers of America, 1985–87; columnist, "Bookmarks for Westerns," *Roundup* magazine, 1985–88; editorial associate, Writer's Digest Schools, 1987–90. Recipient: Western Writers of America Spur award, for story; 1980; Medicine Pipe Bearer's award, 1981. Address: 2509 Emerson, Midland, Texas 79705, U.S.A.

WESTERN PUBLICATIONS

Novels

Ride Down the Wind. New York, Doubleday, 1981; London, Hale, 1982.
Return to Phantom Hill. New York, Doubleday, 1983; London, Hale, 1984.
Warhorse, with Stan Williams. New York, Pocket, 1988; Bath, Chivers, 1989.
Live by the Gun, with Stan Williams. New York, Pocket, 1989.

Uncollected Short Stories

"The Wild One," in *Western Fiction*, 1973.
"Stranger in Town," in *Far West*, August 1978.
"Wind River Survey," in *Far West*, February 1979.
"Rafferty and the Demon Rum," in *Far West*, Spring 1980.
"One Man's Code," in *Far West*, 1980.
"The Tombstone Trade," with Stan Williams, in *Far West*, Winter 1981.
"The Wait By the River," in *Roundup*, edited by Stephen Overholser. New York, Doubleday, 1982.
"Man With Two Lives," in *Roundup*, edited by Stephen Overholser. New York, Doubleday, 1982.
"The Beast and Sergeant Gilhooley," in *The Texans*, edited by Bill Pronzini and Martin H. Greenberg. New York, Fawcett, 1988.

*

Wayne Barton comments:

Some of my earliest memories are of listening to my parents tell of their early lives in central Texas. My father left school after the eighth grade to follow the oil booms of the 1920's. Although I didn't know it at the time, his tales of farm life and of his years in the boomtowns did a lot to awaken my interest in the past, and also to show me what a story ought to look like.

I was a reader, too—comic books and mystery stories, science fiction, and fine short stories from the old *Saturday Evening Post* and *Collier's*. By the time I was 12 years old, I knew I wanted to write stories like that; but I had no idea that somebody from the wilds of West Texas could really become a writer. Some abortive tries at writing while still in my teens left me discouraged, and I ended up in engineering school.

Graduation, marriage, and an engineer's position with a major oil company never quite killed the urge to write, and finally I learned enough to do something about it. After a few false starts, I finished a Western short story about an old Apache returning to New Mexico's Mimbres Valley to die. It sold, and earned a nomination for the Western Writers of America Spur award for best short Western fiction in the year it was published. Since then, I've sold many more stories and articles, to markets as diverse as *Far West, Analog Science Fiction*, and *Fate*.

I've also had four western novels published, two of them in collaboration with Stan Williams. Our most recent novel, *Live by the Gun*, was a finalist in the 1989 Spur award competition.

Years after that first nomination, a short story of mine finally won a Spur, and my initial novel was chosen for the first annual Medicine Bearer's Pipe award for best first Western novel. I'm a member of the Western Writers of America, still a part-time writer, but getting along on the thing I've always wanted most to do.

* * *

It is indicative of the quality of Wayne Barton's work that the most common complaint levelled against him is simply that he has not produced enough to satisfy his many admirers. In more than 10 years he has only written four western novels, two of them in collaboration with his fellow Texan Stan Williams. But in Barton's case, it is most certainly an example of quality rather than quantity, as evidenced by the Western Writers of America Spur award he won for Best Short Story of 1980 ("One Man's Code") and the Medicine Pipe Bearer's award for Best First Novel (*Ride Down the Wind*) in 1981. His writings have also earned him a prestigious WWA Golden Spur.

A chemical engineer by profession, Barton sees his writing mainly as a hobby or diversion. But so far his Westerns have been characterised by strong plots, well-realised characters, and intelligent storytelling. Although humour has little place in his generally sober novels, he is also quite adept at writing lighter material, as his 1979 short story "The Beast and Sergeant Gilhooley" (about the introduction of camels into the U.S. Cavalry) amply testifies.

Essentially, both *Ride Down the Wind* and *Return to Phantom Hill* are concerned with relationships, and how they can be altered by the passage of time. In the former book, the protagonists are two army scouts, Jess Faver, a white man raised by Indians, and his Apache blood-brother, Nantahe. When Nantahe is imprisoned by the army and subsequently kills a guard in his escape, it falls to Faver to bring him in. For Faver, however, the ensuing manhunt soon turns into a voyage of discovery, and as the chase moves from the Texas badlands to the heart of Mexico, he is forced to realise that, though he and the Apache are still bound to each other by memories of happier, less complicated times, the years spent living in a harsh and complex environment have changed them both, so that now they might just as well be strangers.

Barton introduces many of his recurring themes and trademarks in this book: his use of solitary, introspective men as heroes; strong, intelligent women who guide or enlighten them; an atmosphere of suspicion, where few men can be trusted or relied upon until the last shot has been fired; and a solid understanding of how ordinary people react to extraordinary situations.

In *Return to Phantom Hill*, Barton deals with the relationship between two friends, Steve Marritt and Clint Davidson who, separated by the Civil War, resolve to meet up again at the end of hostilities to build a ranch close to a spot called Phantom Hill. When Merritt finally arrives, however, he finds Davidson missing and their spread in the hands of Davidson's distraught wife, Laurie.

As the story develops, Merritt and Laurie (who join forces to keep the ranch going) inevitably find themselves growing closer. Before long, Merritt begins to dread the time when his old friend will return from wherever it is he has disappeared to. But the story concerns itself with much more than the eternal triangle; there is the hostility Merritt must face as a Yankee in post-War Texas; the uncertainty of not knowing the identity of his enemies; the mystery surrounding Davidson's strange absence; and finally, Merritt's own changing attitude to the man he once considered to be his closest friend.

Again Barton deftly fits a strong, human story into a fast-moving, traditional western format, overcoming a relative lack of physical action through a combination of skilful plotting, vivid scene-setting, and assured characterisation—a mixture also evident in the books co-authored with Stan Williams.

Both *Warhorse* and *Live by the Gun* have their origins in traditional western themes. The former tells the story of an ageing gunfighter named Tom Sturdivant, who is forced by fate to finally lock horns with the man who stole his fiancée away from him years before. Set relatively late for a western (towards the close of the 19th century), the action is confined almost solely to a sleepy little Texas town called Lodestone, where resentment and ill-feeling over the local banker's apparently "sharp practices" is growing steadily more violent. The banker, Robert Baze, employs Sturdivant to "resolve" the matter, expecting him to use his gun at any and every opportunity. But Sturdivant, who has grown tired after years of killing, attempts to settle the problem by more peaceful means until, at last, he is left with no choice but to enter into one last showdown.

The real strength of the story, however, lies in the characters with which Barton and Williams people their town. With perhaps one exception, the truly evil Hap Hapgood, there are no clear-cut villains, just as there are no totally clear-cut heroes; they are just ordinary folks caught up in an unfortunate situation, each of them frequently doing all-too-human things which, far from solving the problem, only exacerbate it.

This idea of being caught up in circumstances from which there appears to be no escape also runs through *Live by the Gun*, where a young farmer named Bud Tilden (who also tells the story) is hailed as a celebrity after accidentally killing a rustler who has just murdered his deputy friend in an unusually graphic way. Initially, Bud is quite taken by the notion of being a hero, but as time wears on and he is forced to kill again and again in order to defend his reputation, he begins to wish he could just quit the whole thing and go back to farming.

Although the story is well-plotted and neatly-resolved, *Live by the Gun* is probably the weakest of Barton's books, if only because the first-person narrative tends to get a little too wordy a little too often. However, typically strong characters and a good ear for central Texas dialogue make up for an admittedly minor shortcoming.

Successful Westerns that do not have to rely on non-stop action and virtually super-human heroes are rare, but Barton has an enviably good understanding of the form—especially when writing in tandem with Stan Williams.

—David Whitehead

BASS, Frank. *See* **PEEPLES, Samuel Anthony.**

BASSETT, Jack. *See* **ROWLAND, Donald S.**

BATCHELOR, Reg. *See* **PAINE, Lauran.**

BAXTER, George Owen. *See* **BRAND, Max.**

BAXTER, Shane V. *See* **NORWOOD, V.G.C.**

BEACH, Rex (Ellingwood). American. Born in Atwood, Michigan, 1 September 1877. Educated at Rollins Preparatory School; Rollins College, Winter Park, Florida, 1891–96; Chicago College of Law, 1896; Kent College of Law, 1899–1900. Married Edith Crater in 1907 (died 1947). Professional football player and swimmer; joined the Klondike gold rush, 1900; zinc miner in Missouri; then freelance writer. President, Author's League of America, 1917–21. *Died 7 December 1949.*

WESTERN PUBLICATIONS

Novels

The Spoilers. New York, Harper, 1906; London, Hodder and Stoughton, 1912.
The Barrier. New York, Harper, 1908; London, Hodder and Stoughton, 1912.
The Silver Horde. New York, Harper, 1909; London, Hodder and Stoughton, 1912.
The Iron Trail: An Alaskan Romance. New York, Harper, and London, Hodder and Stoughton, 1913.
Heart of the Sunset. New York, Harper, and London, Hodder and Stoughton, 1915.
The Winds of Chance. New York, Harper, and London, Hodder and Stoughton, 1918.
Flowing Gold. New York, Harper, and London, Hodder and Stoughton, 1922.
Alaskan Adventures (omnibus). New York, Burt, 1935.
Wild Pastures. New York, Farrar and Rinehart, and London, Hutchinson, 1935.
Valley of Thunder. New York, Farrar and Rinehart, 1939; London, Hutchinson, 1940.

Short Stories

Pardners. New York, McClure, 1905; London, Hodder and Stoughton, 1912.

Uncollected Short Stories

"The Weight of Obligation," in *The Arbor House Treasury of Great Western Stories*, edited by Bill Pronzini and Martin H. Greenberg. New York, Arbor House, 1982.
"The Colonel and the Horse Thief," in *The Cowboys*, edited by Bill Pronzini and Martin H. Greenberg. New York, Fawcett, 1985.
"The Stampede," in *The Northerners*, edited by Bill Pronzini and Martin H. Greenberg. New York, Fawcett, 1990.

OTHER PUBLICATIONS

Novels

Going Some: A Romance of Strenuous Affection (novelization of play). New York, Harper, 1910; London, Hodder and Stoughton, 1914.
The Ne'er-Do-Well. New York, Harper, and London, Hodder and Stoughton, 1911.
The Net. New York, Harper, and London, Hodder and Stoughton, 1912.
The Auction Block: A Novel of New York Life. New York, Harper, and London, Hodder and Stoughton, 1914.
Rainbow's End. New York, Harper, and London, Hodder and Stoughton, 1916.
Too Fat to Fight. New York, Harper, 1919.
Padlocked. New York, Harper, 1926; London, Hutchinson, 1927.
The Mating Call. New York, Harper, 1927; London, Hutchinson, 1928.
Son of the Gods. New York, Harper, 1929; London, Hutchinson, 1930.
Money Mad. New York, Cosmopolitan, and London, Hutchinson, 1931.
Beyond Control. New York, Farrar and Rinehart, 1932; London, Hutchinson, 1933.
Jungle Gold. New York, Farrar and Rinehart, 1935.
The World in His Arms. New York, Putnam, 1946; London, Hutchinson, 1948.
Woman in Ambush. New York, Putnam, 1951; London, Hale, 1952.

Short Stories

The Crimson Gardenia and Other Tales of Adventure. New York, Harper, and London, Hodder and Stoughton, 1916.
Laughing Bill Hyde and Other Stories. New York, Harper, 1917; London, Hodder and Stoughton, 1918.
Big Brother and Other Stories. New York, Harper, 1923; London, Hodder and Stoughton, 1924.
North of Fifty-Three. New York, Garden City Publishing Company, 1924.
The Goose Woman and Other Stories. New York, Harper, and London, Hodder and Stoughton, 1924.
Don Careless, and Birds of Prey. New York, Harper, 1928; London, Hutchinson, 1929.
Men of the Outer Islands. New York, Farrar and Rinehart, and London Hutchinson, 1932.
Masked Women. New York, Farrar and Rinehart, and London, Hutchinson, 1934.
The Tower of Flame; An Oil Fields Story; Jaragu of the Lost Islands: A High Seas Story. Los Angeles, Bantam, 1940.

Plays

The Spoilers, with James MacArthur, adaptation of the novel by Beach (produced New York, 1907).
Going Some, with Paul Armstrong (produced New York, 1909). New York, French, 1923.

Screenplay: *Flaming Gold*, with Kenneth Gamet, 1940.

Other

Oh, Shoot! Confessions of an Agitated Sportsman. New York, Harper, 1921; London, Hodder and Stoughton, 1922; as *Confessions of a Sportsman*, New York, Garden City Publishing Company, 1927.

The Miracle of Coral Gables. Privately printed, 1926.
The Hands of Dr. Locke. New York, Farrar and Rinehart, 1934.
Personal Exposures. New York, Harper, 1941; London, Hutchinson, 1942.

* * *

Rex Beach has an eye for descriptive detail that creates a strong sense of character and place, an ear for dialect and accents (particularly French, Russian, and Yukon western), a heart attuned to the complexities of human nature, and a mind intrigued by turns of fate, proofs of maturation, and love/hate relationships. His plots are complex, involve a number of key characters, and extend over a number of years. Though his Yukon tales are his most famous, his stories and novels range along the western frontier from New Orleans to San Francisco to Nome, Alaska.

His books often broach the theme of man's destruction of nature—the massacre of seal, otter, beaver, and buffalo, and the transformation of virgin forest to muddy boomtowns. His heroes are men who learn to take what they need to survive and make their living in harmony with nature's cycles, preserving the best of the new land for future residents. His oldtimers are men who recognize their limitations amid the bitter cold of Yukon winters, yet who strive against snow and ice, raging rivers, and the haunting loneliness of empty spaces. The psychological adjustments necessary for combatting and enduring such wilderness and the eccentricities they inevitably produce form a major part of each work. Sensible men go berserk, drinking too much, gambling too heavily, fighting irrationally for the favors of beautiful but deadly female predators. Cantankerous partners saw boats in half and split tents in their irritation with each other, then share a muddy bed in times of need. Refined Easterners from well-bred families feel the grip of strong passions born in this land, but learn to control the violence and submerge the bestial to win their true-love's approval.

Often Beach contrasts the acts of old-timers—braving ice floes to rescue strangers or enemies, helping newcomers shoot dangerous rapids, leaving dry kindling in a cabin where they have passed the night—with the more selfish, grasping manners of gold-hungry tenderfeet. His is a land where stealing "grub" or jumping a claim is a lynching offense, where mob violence and street shootouts are regular events, where character is tested in the most harrowing of ways, and loyalty to partners is more respected than loyalty to the law. Life might depend on a handful of fresh potatoes or a fellow traveller willing to struggle ahead and bring help to a half-frozen acquaintance. Those unwilling to abide by the code of "help and help alike" find themselves ostracized from the community and ultimately in need of the type of aid they themselves failed to give. Beach is particularly graphic in describing the gradual process of frostbite, snowblindness, and freezing.

Amid such daily struggles for survival the humor is broad and the pranks potentially dangerous. In "Cave Stuff" oldtimers teach a French "gentleman's gentleman" about good-natured, dog-sized bears that dance, until he proves worthy of respect by single-handedly killing three large bears.

The best of his Yukon characters is summed up in the strong, self-sacrificing character of Poleon Doret who, in *The Barrier*, helps a "half-breed" discover her true origins, win a gold claim, escape kidnappers, and win the love of a pompous young Easterner; in *The Winds of Chance* he guides newcomers through treacherous waters, rescues a gambler's daughter from rapids and falls, then endures a grueling sledchase to save the man he thinks she loves. Large, gentle, reticent, at home in the wild, respectful of others and attentive to their needs, Doret nonetheless shows no mercy when men prove truly bad, leaving one villain to be eaten alive by giant mosquitoes and terrorizing another into confession and surrender.

Beach's women are a strange mixture of gentleness and toughness, of beauty and strength; they are able to endure the rigors of wilderness life, yet are feminine and yielding to the right man. While the whore and the lady dealer may seem rough and ready, ready to use and abuse men, occasionally they prove to have unexpected resources that help them break character and expectation in a good cause, even sacrificing their own best interest to help a loved one. On the other hand, genuine ladies show masculine determination and a disregard of proprieties to protect family and beloved or to see justice done; such actions make men at first misjudge their value and then spend the rest of their lives trying to right actions based on such misjudgements. Beach continually makes the point that the frontier both coarsens and refines; it reduces men and women alike to their essential natures. So passions loom large, and violence is always near the surface, ready to break out in grim struggles for land and wealth, for honor and manhood, for life and death.

Since Beach is interested in frontier lawlessness and frontier justice, it is inevitable that one of his favorite themes is the vendetta. A thwarted bride traces her fiancé's murderers from Sicily to the New Orleans of the 1880's to end their reign of terror (*The Net*), a gentle man accused of murder and kidnapping seeks revenge on the true villain (*The Barrier*), a brother seeks to revenge his sister's honor (*The Spoilers*), while various thwarted women try to ruin the men who reject them: a saloon girl in *The Winds of Chance*, the wife of a wealthy politician in *The Ne'er-Do-Well*, a notorious gambling woman in *Woman in Ambush*. In other tales the revenge involves a whole town rising up against the judge and court officers who have jumped their claims (*The Spoilers*) or exposing a partial truth about an enemy to make him look bad in the eyes of those he loves best ("The Michigan Kid").

Another favorite Beach concern is the prodigal son who must make his own way and prove his worth to his rich, successful father. In *The Ne'er-Do-Well* the spoiled son of a railroad magnate, stranded in Panama without money or identification, and subsequently accused of murder and embezzlement, learns that only hard work, ingenuity, and the love of a local beauty can save him. In *Woman in Ambush* a high-spirited young prankster leaves home to make it on his own, learning the successes and dangers of riverboat gambling, working for a circus which he eventually takes over, running for political office in a boomtown, and then, when his past comes back to haunt him, turning to writing, where he finds his forte and exorcises the horrors of his youth. Beach traces the disillusionment and disintegration of young men betrayed by love (*The Mating Call*, *The Winds of Chance*, *The World in His Arms*) or their rescue from depravity and dissolute living by a persistent woman (*The Auction Block*, *Padlocked*, *The Ne'er-Do-Well*). Often his prodigals must live down reputations as gambling men.

Given this interest in the quirks and turns of human nature and the danger of judging by first appearances or hearsay, it is natural that hypocrisy is another favorite Beach concern. *Padlocked*, his most poignant attack on this vice, is a touching story of a good young girl condemned by an obsessive and hypocritical father to battle against suspicion, arrest, and betrayal to prove her worth. *The Mating Call*, an attack on the hypocrisy of small town life, involves the Ku Klux Klan, Florida boomdays, and a Russian countess. *The World in His Arms* turns on the trapper hero's belief in the hypocrisy of his beloved, and only after winning Alaska from the Russians and making his fame and fortune as an explorer, sealer, and landowner does he understand her sacrifice. Occasionally Beach dwells on the nerve-shattering experiences of innocent young women, locked up or abused as "loose" because of the cruel assumptions of frontier life or someone's desire for revenge or leverage.

In sum, Beach, in short stories, novels, and screenplays, provides realistic portraits of frontier emotions from the street of a 1920's Florida boomtown to an 1850's Alaskan wilderness, gripping adventures involving pursuit and treachery over vast spaces, sympathetic and sensitive studies of the confusions of youth, the loneliness of age, the quirks of love. His central characters are restless men and women, spurred to travel and action by a curiosity and a lust for life that cannot be denied.

—Gina Macdonald

BEAN, (Myrtle) Amelia.

Western Publications

Novels

The Fancher Train. New York, Doubleday, 1958; as *The Vengeance Trail*, London, Hamish Hamilton, 1958.
The Feud. New York, Doubleday, 1960; London, Deutsch, 1962.
Time for Outrage. New York, Doubleday, 1967.

Uncollected Short Story

"The Warhorse of Spotted Tail," in *She Won the West: An Anthology of Western and Frontier Stories by Women*, edited by Marcia Muller and Bill Pronzini. New York, Morrow, 1985.

* * *

Amelia Bean's fictionalized accounts of well-known episodes of violence in the American West drew praise for their fast-paced narratives and accurate depictions of frontier life. The historical novels combine a romantic story with a retelling of three western conflicts that eluded peaceful solutions. *The Fancher Train* is the story of the Mountain Meadows massacre of 1857 in Utah; the scene for *The Feud* is the Tonto basin of Arizona, where the Graham-Tewksbury feud periodically erupted in the late 1880's; and *Time for Outrage*, set in southern New Mexico in 1878, chronicles the Lincoln County war.

In these novels, conflict is a major theme. Bean presents a standard view of the frontier as a lawless place where the legal system, if it existed at all, was so weak or corrupt that it was ineffectual. When disputes occurred, they were inevitably settled by violent means. Through an exploration of individual motivations and intentions, Bean portrays the issues in these confrontations as less important than the actions and reactions of the participants. Her skill at conveying the complexity of these events reveals her thorough research into the subjects. Her descriptions of geography and of action scenes, as well as her attention to historical detail, are also noteworthy.

In other aspects of her work, Bean is less successful. She intends dialogue to convey authenticity, but the results are often artificial. At times her language is too flowery and stylized for 20th-century audiences. The love stories, while uncontrived, are quite predictable. Moreover, her characterizations are uneven. Although she presents minor characters convincingly, the heroes and heroines emerge as familiar stereotypes. The men are rugged, virile, experienced creatures designed for action, not contemplation; the women are beautiful, passive, and virginal, waiting for the hero to conquer and subdue their high-spirited nature.

Although her major characters are unoriginal, Bean adeptly uses them to underscore the main theme of conflict. By casting three of the romantic figures (one in each novel) as mixed-bloods who have been the victims of prejudice, Bean reveals racial and cultural tension on the frontier. She is sympathetic in her portrayals of blacks, Indians, and Hispanics. Like her heroes, they possess loyalty, steadfastness, and courage, qualities necessary to survive in a violent land.

—Cheryl J. Foote

BECHDOLT, Frederick R(itchie). American. Born in Mercersburg, Pennsylvania, 27 July 1874. *Died 12 April 1950.*

Western Publications

Novels

The Hard Rock Man. New York, Moffat Yard, 1910.
Mutiny: *An Adventure Story.* New York, Chelsea House, 1927.
Riders of the San Pedro. New York, Doubleday, 1931.
Horse Thief Trail. New York, Doubleday, 1932.
The Tree of Death. New York, Doubleday, 1937.
Bold Raiders of the West. New York, Doubleday, 1940.
Danger on the Border. New York, Doubleday, 1940.
Riot at Red Water. New York, Doubleday, 1941.
Hot Gold. New York, Doubleday, 1941.
The Hills of Fear. New York, Doubleday, 1943.
Drygulch Canyon. New York, Doubleday, 1946.

Short Stories

When the West Was Young. New York, Century, 1922.
Tales of the Old-Timers. New York, Century, 1924.

Uncollected Short Stories

"For the Job's Sake," in *Sunset* (San Francisco), December 1924.
"The Line-Jumper," in *West* (New York), November 1932–February 1933.
"Across the Rio Grande," in *Selected Western Stories*, edited by Leo Marguilies. New York, Popular Library, 1949.

OTHER PUBLICATIONS

Other

9009, with James Hopper. New York, McClure, 1908.
Giants of the Old West. New York, Century, 1930.

* * *

Frederick R. Bechdolt has a singular interest in the pioneers of the Old West, and gives sketches of several, including the events in which they participated, in *When the West Was Young*, *Tales of the Old-Timers*, and *Giants of the Old West*.

In *When the West Was Young* Bechdolt looks back upon the passing of the old order with regret. In *Tales of the Old-Timers* he is concerned with tales about Indian legends of the Pecos and Canadian River areas of Texas, "Adobe Walls" (site of one of the last great Indian battles on the Great Plains), "The Forgotten Expedition to Santa Fe," "The Texans," and "Cassidy and the Wild Bunch." *Giants of the Old West* contains sketches of such notable men as John Colter, Stephen F. Austin, William Becknell, Brigham Young, John Augustus Sutter, Alexander Majors, and Charles Goodnight. Bechdolt's style is suitable for such informal popular history, and he includes legends about his subjects which sometimes appear to make them larger than life.

Most of Bechdolt's novels depend on southwestern scenes within the framework of the historical novel. The Anglo-American Western, *Bold Raiders of the West*, bears on the aftermath of the Civil War.

—Dorys C. Grover

BECHKO, P(eggy) A(nne). Also writes as Bill Haller. American. Born in South Haven, Michigan, 26 August 1950. Educated at Sarasota High School, Florida; Manatee Junior College, Bradenton, Florida, 1968–69. Has worked as an artist's model, legal secretary, delivery person, and gift wrapper. Agent: Anita Diamant, The Writers' Workshop Inc., 51 East 42nd Street, New York, New York 10017. Address: 8324 Midnight Pass Road, Sarasota, Florida 33581, U.S.A.

WESTERN PUBLICATIONS

Novels

Night of the Flaming Guns. New York, Doubleday, 1974.
Gunman's Justice. New York, Doubleday, 1974.
Blown to Hell. New York, Doubleday, 1976; London, Hale, 1978.
Sidewinder's Trail (as Bill Haller). New York, Pinnacle, 1976.
Dead Man's Feud (as Bill Haller). New York, Pinnacle, 1976.
The Winged Warrior. New York, Doubleday, 1977; as *Omaha Jones*, London, Hale, 1979.
Hawke's Indians. New York, Doubleday, 1979.

OTHER PUBLICATIONS

Novels

Dark Side of Love. Sarasota, Florida, Worldwide, 1983.
Harmonie Mexicaine. London and Toronto, Harlequin, 1984.

*

Manuscript Collection: University of Wyoming, Laramie.

P.A. Bechko comments:

Although I still enjoy the standard Western, comedy is more dear to my heart. The last three Westerns published were comedy, and I plan more of the same for the future, even as I diversify into other genres of writing.

* * *

P.A. Bechko's career as a writer of western fiction was launched with the publication of *Night of the Flaming Guns*. It is a clumsily structured novel alternating between first- and third-person narrative. Its story is routine—Apaches and greedy villians menacing the heroine's attempt to save her brother from the Apaches and find her dead father's hidden gold. However, Bechko tried to vary the basic structure of the formulary western by introducing a second hero into the story and by having two sets of villains—the Apaches on one side and the heroine's uncle and the sub-normal Morton clan on the other. The experiment did not work well and the story ends up being merely cluttered with undeveloped characters. The same problem is even more apparent in *Dead Man's Feud*, which has a quaternion hero (four brothers), two heroines (one good and one bad), and four villains as its central characters.

Gunman's Justice is perhaps her best novel. The hero, a gunslinger who wants to lay down his gun and take up ranching, finds himself in the middle of a Wyoming range feud over land and a girl. The second half of the book takes place in the mountains during a snow storm and demonstrates Bechko's ability, when her focus is clear and unimpeded, to create vivid, tension-filled action sequences.

There is a grim tone in her early works, but it was abandoned with *The Winged Warrior*, a preposterous story about a half-breed Sioux, named Omaha Jones, who likes to fly around on homemade leather wings! Omaha's inability to master landings forces him to travel afoot for a time with an unlikely trio of characters pursued by the heroine's Bible-thumping step-brother, who, to express the matter in terms of a benign cliché, is long on brawn and short on brains. (Grizzly Tanner in this novel would appear to be based on the character played by Will Geer in *Jeremiah Johnson*, 1972, illustrating a tendency Bechko has had to base some of her characters and events on motion-picture sources.) *Hawke's Indians* is an equally offbeat story. Set in 1903, it chronicles the adventures of a bumbling gang of train robbers trying to modernize their get-away methods by using motorcycles instead of horses.

Bechko's attempts to break the traditional formulary mode have been for the most part unsuccessful. Her heroes and villians, while they have expanded in multiples, remain stereotypical and unbelievable. Her heroines are a departure from the conventional formulary female characters in what they do, but not in the trouble they cause. They are aggressive, independent, and self-assured, but they ultimately must be saved by the hero. They are not above, or repulsed by, expletives: the heroine in *Hawke's Indians* tells the villian, "I won't ever be all right again until I stick a knife in your liver and twist it until your navel pops, you slimy, self-seeking son-of-a . . . "; or killing: the heroine in *Night of the Flaming Guns* kills two villains; or easy virtue: the heroine in *The Winged Warrior* sleeps with Omaha Jones. These dimensions, while novelties perhaps, do not make the heroines any more realistic than the pure, virginal types formerly populating ranch romances.

Bechko to date is an epigonal writer, teasing the conventions of formulary Westerns, but too often guilty of illogic and begging the reader's credulity.

—Vicki Piekarski

BECK, Harry. *See* **PAINE, Lauran.**

BEDFORD, Kenneth. *See* **PAINE, Lauran.**

BEER, Ralph (Robert). American. Born in Helena, Montana, 16 August 1947. Educated at Montana State University, Bozeman, B.A. 1970; University of Montana, Missoula, M.F.A. 1981. Served in the United States Army, including service in Thailand, 1971–74; Sergeant. Cowboy, Montana and British Columbia, 1965–70; member of Dumpp Family Singers. Since 1974 rancher, Helena. Recipient: University of Montana A.B. Guthrie fiction award, 1985; National Endowment for the Arts fellowship, 1986. Agent: International Creative Management, 40 West 57th Street, New York, New York 10019. Address: 3525 York Road, Helena, Montana, U.S.A.

WESTERN PUBLICATIONS

Novel

The Blind Corral. New York, Viking, 1986.

Uncollected Short Story

"The Harder They Come," in *The Last Best Place: A Montana Anthology*, edited by William Kittredge and Annick Smith. Seattle, University of Washington Press, 1988.

* * *

Ralph Beer's fiction offers a strong if disturbing vision of the American West in what may be the final stages of transition: from a land of towns, small farms, and small ranches to a land of cities surrounded by countryside emptied but for the occasional corporate ranch or farm. That world has not yet arrived—but his characters can see it coming. Perhaps most striking in this fiction is Beer's ability to mix traditional and contemporary western elements, using the contemporary to both illuminate and comment ironically upon the traditional.

In his novel *The Blind Corral*, for example, Beer presents a fight over a waterhole fenced off by a large rancher who wants to become larger by driving out smaller ranchers, something which has become almost a cliché in western fiction. However, in Beer's version the land-greedy rancher wants additional land not for his cattle, but for the housing developments he's planning; he has, in fact, ceased to be primarily a rancher. The fight is won by the small ranchers, who drive off the other's hands, cut the fence, and water their stock. But in the modern West, these riders know that land titles prevent a permanent victory, so they drive their watered cattle away from the waterhole and repair the fence, again cutting off their land. In fact, they've needed to water the stock only as part of a drive to the home ranch, where the cattle will be loaded into trucks and hauled to the stockyard for sale.

The cattle drive itself is detailed in a familiar and convincing manner as several riders on horseback gather cattle out of the hills. Yet even this very traditional cattle drive contains contemporary elements. For one thing, the best "cowperson" among the drivers is a young woman, something which was unlikely in the traditional Western. Further, the drive is disrupted not by rustlers or by gunmen working for the large rancher, but by helicopters carrying cable to a construction site.

Beer's riders, and the ranch families they come from, love the land but face great difficulties in holding it. Some of that difficulty is purely economic: small ranches (the ranchers themselves use the word "ranch" ironically, aware of the differences between their places and the vast ranches of western movies) aren't economical in the last part of the 20th century.

An even greater difficulty comes from the instability of ranch families. Here, Beer turns away from the 20th-century view of ranch families as healthy and tightly-knit to an older western view: this land is hell on women and children—or, in a typical Beer twist, on spouses and children: one of his ranchers is a woman who seems never to have married, though she does have a daughter. In one of Beer's short stories, "The Harder They Come," we see a rancher living alone, his marriage destroyed by his obsession with holding the land for an heir, his wife having drifted away after several miscarriages. In *The Blind Corral*, most families are fragmented, but even a neighbor with a healthy family is considering selling out; his children all have lives in the cities, and none of them wants to inherit.

A further problem is the harshness of ranch life, which isn't made easier by Montana's northern climate. Beer's characters are crippled by this life, but they seem to be equally crippled when they stay away. In *The Blind Corral*, one character spends much of the novel stumping around with a broken leg, gotten when helicopters flew over the trail drive. The young narrator, on the other hand, has been disfigured in an artillery training accident; his Canadian girlfriend is having a hip replacement, presumably as a result of a barrel-racing accident. The rancher in "The Harder They Come" has been crippled psychologically by his insistence on keeping his land for the heir he'll never have.

But even here, Beer is not willing to let traditional elements of the western novel go without contradiction: in *The Blind Corral*, the narrator's grandfather is also crippled, by something like emphysema—but it turns out that he's had the disease since he was a child, in the old country, and his parents emigrated in search of a drier climate. As he says once, he's cheated death out of 83 years, thanks to this harsh land.

This grandfather has been the least isolated of Beer's characters. His wife has been dead for a long time, but she was with him until her death, and his son, the narrator's father, has stayed on the land. Unlike the rancher in "The Harder They Come," the grandfather has remained on good terms with his neighbors (other than the land-hungry large rancher/developer) and his descendents have done the same. There is a sense of community among these people that almost replaces the families which seem no longer to exist.

At first, the harshness of their daily routines—especially in winter—might leave one thinking that Beer's people live in a wild land. Yet we quickly discover that what land isn't fenced and cleared is about to be, and every feature of the landscape has a name. When late in *The Blind Corral* the characters bring back an elk carcass from farther up in the mountains, it's notable that the gulch where the body lies is the first piece of landscape we've seen that isn't named, that might actually be wilderness. The rancher in "The Harder They Come" has not only fenced but padlocked his land.

The struggle in Beer's fiction isn't between wilderness and civilization, but over how tame the land will be. The narrator of *The Blind Corral* thinks of town—the state capital, Helena—and its spreading developments as "the stalking town, which since we'd decided not to live there, seemed now to be coming to us." Intending to leave, the narrator finally stays, resigning himself to a life of labor without much hope, though it costs him the "girl" in Canada: ". . . where would I go? What place would take me in, as this one had?" In contrast, the rancher in "The Harder They Come" seems not to have been taken in by the place, but to have tried to dominate it, to take it in and make it absolutely his.

Beer's vision is bleak; the world he creates is harsh. But in its mixture of traditional and non-traditional elements, his work captures the contemporary West in this moment of transition, and does so effectively, even movingly.

—Wayne Ude

BELL, Robert Vaughn. American. Educated at Golden West College, 1974. Served in the United States Army, 1941–47: Technical Sergeant; Purple Heart, Bronze Star, Asiatic-Pacific Theater Medal with Five Battle Stars and Bronze Arrowhead. Married W. Billie Kostenbader in 1974; two sons and four daughters. Lineman and splicer, Northwestern Bell Telephone Company, Omaha, Nebraska, 1947–48; rancher, Crosby Horse Ranch, Greenwood, Colorado, 1948–49; diver and superintendent, Bautista Undersea Salvage Ltd., Leyte, Philippines, 1950–52; merchant seaman, 1952–54; partner, diver, and tugboat captain, Blue Water Diving and Towing Company, Long Beach, California, 1954–57; owner and diver, Industrial Diving Company, Los Angeles, 1958–59; chief diver, Fierro Metal de Mexico, Acapulco, 1960; contract diver, Elmore Abalone Company, Port Hueneme, California, 1960; diving superintendent, Compania Mexicana de Salvataje, Acapulco, 1961; owner and operator, Gun Corral (sale and repair of antique and modern firearms), Inglewood, California, 1962–71; deputy sheriff, Trinity Country Sheriff's Department, Weaverville, California, 1972–74; partner and captain for Search Inc. diving charter company, 1967–70. Since 1975 owner, Creek Park Ranch, Garden Valley, California. Agent: Lenniger Literary Agency, Inc., 104 East 40th Street, New York, New York 10016. Address: Creek Park Ranch, Garden Valley, California 95633, U.S.A.

WESTERN PUBLICATIONS

Novels (series: McGowan family in all books)

A Valley Called Disappointment. New York, Ballantine, 1982; Leicester, Linford, 1986.
Feud at Devil's River. New York, Ballantine, 1982; Leicester, Linford, 1986.
Stranger in Dodge. New York, Ballantine, 1983.
Platte River Crossing. New York, Ballantine, 1983; Leicester, Linford, 1986.
To the Death. New York, Ballantine, 1984; Leicester, Linford, 1986.
Cold Trail from Fort Smith. New York, Ballantine, 1986.
Trackdown. New York, Ballantine, 1989.

* * *

It wasn't until the age of 58 that Robert Vaughn Bell had his first Western published by Ballantine Books. Much of his childhood was spent in the Nebraska cattle country, and his grandparents were true Westerners. This background, plus his own library of over 25,000 volumes of research material, helps lend authenticity to his stories, the majority of which are told in first-person narrative, much along the same lines as those of Louis L'Amour and Jim Miller. These stories have a "campfire" feel to them, and whoever the main character may be tells his tale to an enraptured audience.

The McGowan family are the the nucleus of all of the novels produced to date. Born of a Choctaw Indian and a white mother, they are Texans by birth and nature, each brother over six feet tall and of muscular build. Using these facts as the basis for each book, Bell then goes on to develop his characters into well-rounded and well-defined heroes.

Each story is developed along the same lines, following a strong central theme which allows for various deviations before returning to the original track to finish the book. Characters and events are normally introduced at a sedate pace, thus allowing Bell to spend time in imparting much of his well-researched information and this tends to detract from the story itself. For example, in *Platte River Crossing*, while being chased by warring Sioux Indians, Rush McGowan takes the time to stop and explain how to tie a "Bridger" or a diamond-hitch knot. This takes two-and-a-half pages to describe, and destroys all the suspense that had been building up. Likewise, a revolver or rifle cannot be passed around without its history, firing capability, and loading procedure being not-so-briefly explained. Undoubtedly some readers enjoy this type of treatment in a story, but Bell went on to prove that he could also write a more traditional type of Western, and still maintain the authentic flavour of the novel, without undue digression.

The McGowan family consists mainly of brothers, who are spread across the country, and pursuing their own particular way of life. Rush McGowan, the eldest, opens the family chronicle in *A Valley Called Disappointment.* Employed as the marshal, in a small Colorado town, he becomes involved in tracking down two gun-happy desperados. As with some of Bell's other stories, McGowan's quest is disrupted by a series of secondary incidents. Thus, we have a pursuing deputy wounded by the gunmen, forcing them back to town; then heavy snow slows McGowan and another deputy down; the latter is attacked by a grizzly bear; an Indian couple are slaughtered by the gunmen leaving McGowan to escort their surviving daughter and his deputy back to safety. Finally, McGowan completes his task with the help of a local rancher and his men.

Bell's second book, *Feud at Devil's River*, continues with Rush as the spokesman, as he and his brothers take a herd of wild longhorn to market in Abilene. There is no doubt that drives such as these have a strong historical basis, and Bell spices his story with factual information. This appears to be central to all his novels, and in his telling of a story, Bell's descriptions of a certain time-period, or weapon, or of the handling of a stagecoach, are exact. The book also delves into the Texan / Mexican conflicts but this is better and more fully covered in *To the Death*. The narrator here is Lysander, or Lightly, McGowan. He is a younger member of the family, but nevertheless, well capable of handling himself in difficult situations. The premise of the story is that a band of renegade "soldiers" from the North have "orders" to occupy the Montoncillo ranch and place the McGowans under arrest, and Lysander happens to be at Don Carlos's ranch visiting his beautiful daughter when the troubles begin. The theme of family is strong in this novel, with both brothers and cousins riding in from all over the country to aid the endangered Lysander and the McGowan ranch.

Bell's later novels are in a more traditional vein, but still involve the McGowans as their main characters. Obviously, out of such a large family, there has to be a black sheep, and Cass McGowan is given that dubious honour. In *Cold Trail from Fort Smith*, he is an outlaw turned lawman working for "Hanging" Judge Parker, but fortunately the expected clichés end there. Although Bell still adheres to his successful formula in this story of captured then escaped prisoners, the need to recapture them becomes the subplot. The true storyline, which involves Parker's nephew and a female reporter, emerges gradually, and all loose ends are neatly tied at the book's conclusion. *Trackdown* concerns a theft by Cass McGowan's former partner, Wes Buck, and McGowan is detailed to bring him in. Interwoven with this plot is murder and bushwhacking, and an original ending involving Comanche and Cheyenne Indians.

All of Bell's heroes could be regarded as stereotypical, being tall, muscular, knowledgeable, tough, and sure shots. But he also writes well on secondary characters, and ably illustrates the way of life of the ordinary working person. A fine example of this is found in *A Valley Called Disappointment*, where Bell takes time out from the main story to create a convincing atmosphere of ordinary ranch hands playing cards; their humour, honesty, and integrity shine through in this and similar passages.

By varying his two styles, Bell can appeal to a wider readership; those interested in his "folksy" stories, and fans of the traditional Western. Bell writes well within both areas of the genre, and undoubtedly will continue to write more of his McGowan family in years to come.

—John L. Wolfe

BELLAH, James Warner. American. Born in New York City, 14 September 1899. Educated at Wesleyan University, Middletown, Connecticut, 1919–22; Columbia University, New York, A.B. 1923; Georgetown University, Washington, D.C., M.A. 1925; University of Pennsylvania, Philadelphia. Served as a pilot in the Royal Air Force, 1917–19: 2nd Lieutenant; served in the United States Army, 1939–45: Colonel; Legion of Merit, Bronze Star, Air Medal, Imperial Russian Order of St. Nicholas. Married Helen Lasater Hopkins in 1942; three sons and one daughter. Advertising copywriter, New York, 1923–26; English Instructor, Columbia University, 1923–26; foreign correspondent, *Aero Digest*, 1927–30; then freelance writer. Vice-president, Lancaster and Chester Railroad. Member of the National Advisory Committee, Civil War Centennial Commission. Recipient: Knopf prize, 1923; *Time* award, for film, 1961; Western Heritage award, for film, 1962; Georgetown University Medal of Honor, 1963. *Died in 1976.*

WESTERN PUBLICATIONS

Novels

Massacre. New York, Lion, 1950.
The Apache. New York, Fawcett, 1951; London, Miller, 1957.
Ordeal at Blood River. New York, Ballantine, 1959.
Sergeant Rutledge. New York, Bantam, and London, Corgi, 1960.
A Thunder of Drums. New York, Bantam, 1961.
The Man Who Shot Liberty Valance. New York, Pocket Books, 1962.

Short Stories

Reveille. New York, Fawcett, 1962.

Uncollected Short Stories

"Massacre," in *The Reel West*, edited by Bill Pronzini and Martin H. Greenberg. New York, Doubleday, 1984.
"Command," and "Big Hunt," in *The Second Reel West*, edited by Bill Pronzini and Martin H. Greenberg. New York, Doubleday, 1985.
"Mission with No Record," in *The Third Reel West*, edited by Bill Pronzini and Martin H. Greenberg. New York, Doubleday, 1986.
"By the Beard of Saint Crispin," in *The Horse Soldiers*, edited by Bill Pronzini and Martin H. Greenberg. New York, Fawcett, 1987.

OTHER PUBLICATIONS

Novels

Sketch Book of a Cadet from Gascony. New York, Knopf, 1923.
These Frantic Years. New York, Appleton, 1927.
The Sons of Cain. New York, Appleton, 1928.
Gods of Yesterday. New York, Appleton, 1928.
Dancing Lady. New York, Farrar and Rinehart, 1932.
White Piracy. New York, Farrar and Rinehart, 1933.
The Brass Gong Tree. New York, Appleton Century, 1936.
This Is the Town. New York, Appleton Century, 1937.
7 Must Die. New York, Appleton Century, 1938.
The Bones of Napoleon. New York, Appleton Century, 1940.
Ward Twenty. New York, Doubleday, 1946.
Rear Guard. New York, Popular Library, 1951.
Divorce. New York, Popular Library, 1952.
The Valiant Virginians. New York, Ballantine, 1953.
The Journal of Colonel De Lancey. Philadelphia, Chilton, 1967.

Short Stories

Fighting Men U.S.A. Evanston, Illinois, Regency, 1963.

Plays

Screenplays: *Ten Tall Men*, with others, 1952; *The Sea Chase*, with John Twist, 1955; *Target Zero*, with Sam Rolfe, 1956;

Sergeant Rutledge, with Willis Goldbeck, 1960; *X-15*, with Tony Lazzarino, 1961; *A Thunder of Drums*, 1961; *The Man Who Shot Liberty Valance*, with Willis Goldbeck, 1962.

Other

South by East a Half East. Privately printed, 1936.
Irregular Gentlemen. New York, Doubleday, 1948.
Soldiers' Battle—Gettysburg. New York, McKay, 1962.

* * *

James Warner Bellah's first novel was *Sketch Book of a Cadet from Gascony*, and it indicated the preoccupation with military subjects and personnel which would inform most of his subsequent fiction. It was not until after World War II, however, that he began writing his stories about Fort Starke during the Indian campaigns for which he is most remembered. Several of these stories, four of which film director John Ford used as the basis of his cavalry trilogy, were later collected into the anthology volume *Reveille*. In these stories the author's attitude toward the cavalry is openly adulatory and, while much time is spent on the atrocities the Indians perpetuate against the whites, no Indian is characterized nor is the Indian point of view ever presented sympathetically. Bellah's opinion of Indians was that they are "child-minded savages." The stories, as most of Bellah's fiction, are in the mode of the romantic historical reconstruction, i.e., history treated as if it were romance and interpreted according to Bellah's distinctive ideology. That ideology was a combination of white supremacy and social Darwinism. In the short story "The Big Hunt," contained in *Reveille*, the reader is told of stampeding buffalo that "the herds turned at the brink, trotted off right and left for a few yards and stood still again in the abysmal stupidity that would kill off seventy-five million of them in a handful of brief years." Separating the slaughter of the buffalo from Bellah's ideological romance, it was not their "abysmal stupidity" that killed off the herds, but rather the insatiable rapacity of the white hunters and, politically, the desire to destroy the Indians' food supply.

Bellah was primarily a magazine writer and only a few of his longer stories were ever reprinted, termed by their publishers "originals." In *The Apache*, a serial that had first run in *The Saturday Evening Post*, Bellah best summed up his attitude toward Native Americans when he wrote of the Apaches that "it can be the phase of the moon that maddens Apaches, or a word from the memory of a medicine chief, or a strange flower by the trailside, or an omen of blood in a stone; because Apaches hate life and they are the enemies of all mankind, even unto each other. That is what Apache means: enemy."

In *Ordeal at Blood River* the conflict is between the cavalry and General Barras, a Mexican revolutionist and bandit who wants to establish a personal empire in the New Mexico Territory. Lieutenant Flintridge Cohill, who frequently functions as Bellah's point-of-view character in his fiction, remarks to the heroine, Athena, that " . . . I would not give a continental for a man who had not been to the wheel and survived his point of breaking—nor for a woman. It's the battles we lose that count. It's the gray jackets we wear in pride to cover our wounds that make us worthy of them." Since most of the female characters in Bellah's fiction do not measure up to this standard, most of them are found undeserving and often, as in *The Apache*, this means capture by the Indians—and, in Bellah's words in "Spanish Man's Grave" (*Reveille*), "you never forget the first white woman you see that the Apaches have worked over."

Following his association with John Ford, Bellah began writing original stories for the screen. *Sergeant Rutledge*, for example, was written especially for Ford. When Rutledge, a black noncom falsely accused of raping and killing a white woman, is first introduced, the reader is told that he would not couple "with Indian blood, because he's come a long way from savagery himself and couldn't go back"; and when the black buffalo soldiers object to the attitude of their white officer, their collective growl rises "like hot bile in their throats. It came free in jungle protest with fury bubbling in it."

A Thunder of Drums was also written especially for the screen, and in it Bellah celebrated male celibacy, misogyny, and devotion to military life. "A woman," the reader is told, "is not a helpless vessel as has been so carefully established for young men to believe. She is a beautifully co-ordinated, predatory animal who goes into the lists deliberately to win . . ." The question is posed if Comanches or Apaches are responsible for raping and killing in the district. Historically, the Apaches did not rape; Bellah ignored this. Instead, the commanding officer discards the Comanche theory because, while the Indian as a species (no matter the tribe or nation) "is lecherous and without honor or mercy, filthy in his ideas and speech and inconceivably dirty in his person and manners," the Comanches do not fancy white women because they "rape their own" instead.

The closest Bellah ever came to imitating General Charles King's Victorian cavalry novels is in *A Thunder of Drums* insofar as there is a mystery—Comanches or Apaches?—and a love triangle. Ernest Haycox also wrote cavalry stories, many of them published in *The Saturday Evening Post*. He dealt not at all with the Indian point of view; it was against *Post* editorial policy to do so; but he did humanize his officers, noncoms, enlisted men, and female characters in a way Bellah never could. Nor could Bellah, even at his best equal Haycox's ability to conjure a striking image. Yet, Bellah wrote a vivid, hard prose and his plots were almost always structured with unusual precision. It was the urgency of his ideology, his greatest flaw, which overwhelmed all that he created; because it limited his humanity, it diminishes his achievement.

—Jon Tuska

BENNETT, Dwight. *See* **NEWTON, D. B.**

BENTEEN, John. *See* **HAAS, Ben.**

BENTON, Will. *See* **PAINE, Lauran.**

BERGER, Thomas (Louis). American. Born in Cincinnati, Ohio, 20 July 1924. Educated at the University of Cincinnati, B.A. 1948; Columbia University, New York, 1950–51. Served in the United States Army, 1943–46. Married Jeanne Redpath in 1950. Libraian, Rand School of Social Science, New York,

1948–51; staff member, *New York Times Index*, 1951–52; associate editor, *Popular Science Monthly*, New York, 1952–54; film critic, *Esquire*, 1972–73; Visiting Professor, University of Kansas, Lawrence, 1974; Distinguished Visiting Professor, Southampton College, New York, 1975–76; Visiting Lecturer, Yale University, New Haven, Connecticut, 1981, 1982; Regent's Lecturer, University of California, Davis, 1982. Recipient: Dial fellowship, 1962; Western Heritage award, 1965; Rosenthal award, 1965; Ohioana Book award, 1982. H.D.L.: Long Island University, Southampton, New York, 1986. Address: c/o Don Congdon Associates, 156 Fifth Avenue, New York, New York 10010, U.S.A.

Western Publications

Novel

Little Big Man. New York, Dial Press, 1964; London, Eyre and Spottiswoode, 1965.

Other Publications

Novels

Crazy in Berlin. New York, Scribner, 1958.
Reinhart in Love. New York, Scribner, 1962; London, Eyre and Spottiswoode, 1963.
Killing Time. New York, Dial Press, 1967; London, Eyre and Spottiswoode, 1968.
Vital Parts. New York, Baron, 1970; London, Eyre and Spottiswoode, 1971.
Regiment of Women. New York, Simon and Schuster, 1973; London, Eyre Methuen, 1974.
Sneaky People. New York, Simon and Schuster, 1975; London, Methuen, 1980.
Who Is Teddy Villanova? New York, Delacorte Press, and London, Eyre Methuen, 1977.
Arthur Rex: A Legendary Novel. New York, Delacorte Press, 1978; London, Methuen, 1979.
Neighbors. New York, Delacorte Press, 1980; London, Methuen, 1981.
Reinhart's Women. New York, Delacorte Press, 1981; London, Methuen, 1982.
The Feud. New York, Delacorte Press, 1983; London, Methuen, 1984.
Nowhere. New York, Delacorte Press 1984; London, Methuen, 1986.
Being Invisible. Boston, Little Brown, 1987; London, Methuen, 1988.
The Houseguest. Boston, Little Brown, 1988; London, Weidenfeld and Nicolson, 1989.
Changing the Past. Boston, Little Brown, 1989; London, Weidenfeld and Nicolson, 1990.
Orrie's Story. Boston, Little Brown, 1990.

Short Stories

Granted Wishes. Northridge, California, Lord John Press, 1984.

Play

Other People (produced Berkshire Theatre Festival, Massachusetts, 1970).

*

Bibliography: in "Thomas Berger Issue" of *Studies in American Humor* (San Marcos, Texas), Spring and Fall 1983.

Manuscript Collection: Boston University Library.

Critical Studies: "Bitter Comedy" by Richard Schickel, in *Commentary* (New York), July 1970; "Thomas Berger's Little Big Man as History" by Leo Oliva, in *Western American Literature* (Fort Collins, Colorado), 8(1–2), 1973; "Thomas Berger's Elan" by Douglas Hughes, in *Confrontation* (New York), Spring–Summer 1976; "The Radical Americanist" by Brooks Landon, and "The Second Decade of Little Big Man" by Frederick Turner, both in *The Nation* (New York), 20 August 1977; "Berger and Barth: The Comedy of Decomposition" by Stanley Trachtenberg, in *Comic Relief*, edited by Sarah Blacker Cohen, Urbana, University of Illinois Press, 1978; "Thomas Berger Issue" of *Studies in American Humor* (San Marcos, Texas), Spring and Fall 1983; "Reinhardt as Hero and Clown" by Gerald Weales, in *Hollins Critic* (Hollins College, Virginia) December 1983; *Thomas Berger* by Brooks Landon, Boston, Twayne, 1989.

* * *

Thomas Berger's *Little Big Man* stands as his only "Western" in a distinguished series of novels which are, in various ways, parodies and more than parodies of a number of popular genres. The single most important influence on *Little Big Man* is doubtless Dee Brown's *Bury My Heart at Wounded Knee*, but Berger did research for his novel in both standard and revisionist histories of the American West. *Little Big Man* is really an examination of the nature of myth, and there are few myths of the West that Berger does not submit to his illuminating but destructive analysis. He truly does "murder to dissect." The most important myth is primitivism vs. civilization, typified in the title character, who oscillates between his white "self" as Jack Crabb, gambler, gunfighter, buffalo-hunter, and all the other western archetypes, and Little Big Man, the Cheyenne demi-god of Odyssean shrewdness. Hardly less important is Lucy Pendrake, the archetypal American woman who, as Jack remarked, "always knowed the *right* thing," but did not let that keep her from lifting her skirts for the local pharmacist. But most important of all is George Armstrong Custer. He is like Lucifer in his majestic representation of all things white in the novel, triumphant in the Sand Creek massacre, dismissed with contempt at Little Big Horn. He sums up all of western philosophy, in the words of Lavendar, a Negro scout, who says of him, "Everything about him says, 'I win, you lose.'"

Opposed to these symbols of white culture are the title character, who achieves his moment at the still point of a turning world the night before the Sand Creek massacre, and, most important, Old Lodge Skins, the epitome of the Indian way of looking at the world as a cosmos of which he, as one of the "human beings"—the Cheyennes—is at the center. *Little Big Man* is probably the best "western" novel that will ever be written.

—Herbert F. Smith

BERRY, Don. American. Born in Redwood Falls, Minnesota, 23 January 1932. Educated at Reed College, Portland, Oregon, 1949–51. Married Wyn Berry in 1957. Freelance writer. Recipient: Western Writers of America Spur award, 1963. Agent: Barthold Fles Literary Agency, 501 Fifth Avenue, New York, New York 10017, U.S.A.

WESTERN PUBLICATIONS

Novels

Trask. New York, Viking Press, and London, Hutchinson, 1960.
Moontrap. New York, Viking Press, 1962.
To Build a Ship. New York, Viking Press, 1963; London, Gollancz, 1964.

Uncollected Short Story

"Across Neahkahnie," in *This Land Around Us*, edited by Ellis Lucia. New York, Doubleday, 1969.

OTHER PUBLICATIONS

Other

A Majority of Scoundrels: An Informal History of the Rocky Mountain Fur Company. New York, Harper, 1961.
Mountain Men: The Trappers of the Great Fur-Trading Era 1822–1843 (for children). New York, Macmillan, 1966.
Women of Hawaii, photographs by Pegge Hopper. Seattle, Winn, 1985.

*

Critical Study: *Don Berry* by Glen A. Love, Boise, Idaho, Boise State University, 1978.

* * *

During the early 1960's Don Berry published three well-received historical novels and a non-fiction work about the tail-end of the fur trade and the difficulties of mountain men attempting to adjust to the social demands of newly founded agricultural communities. Although specialists in the history and literature of the Pacific Northwest have paid the most attention to Berry, he is becoming increasingly noted by other interpreters as a skillful regional and historical writer.

Berry wrote numerous science-fiction stories in the 1950's, but it was his first novel, *Trask*, that attracted critics. The story of Elbridge Trask, a restless mountain man who sets off from Astoria, Oregon, to explore the Tillamook country 60 miles to the south, the novel is also a penetrating account of a man's search to find himself in this new country. Like Berry's later fiction, this novel illustrates the author's interest in using history for fictional purposes and his tendency to create heroes searching for an understanding of themselves and their surroundings. In addition, Berry's descriptions of white–Indian contacts, especially his probings of Indian culture, illustrate his interest in Zen Buddhism and its teachings.

While *Trask* is most often cited as Berry's best novel, others argue that *Moontrap* is the superior work. Not only is *Moontrap* an illuminating depiction of life in Oregon City, Oregon, in the 1840's, it is also a compelling narrative of conflicts between Indian and white values and of men and women caught in the cultural clashes between these two societies. Webster P. Webb, Johnson Monday, and Joe Meek (a historical figure) are former mountain men trying to move from the free, anarchistic life of the mountains to the more settled agricultural life of the far West. In one moving scene, Webb, who has murdered a preacher and is fleeing his pursuers, attempts to trap the reflection of the moon, to freeze time; but, of course, he cannot, and his anti-social actions force Monday and Meek to join the settlers after Webb's scalp. Monday, married to an Indian woman and hoping to adjust to the expectations and demands of Oregon City society, is a particularly well-drawn tragic figure. The treatment of his dilemmas, caught as he is between the old and new, and his tragic ending are finely honed bits of memorable fiction.

Berry's third novel, *To Build a Ship*, is less satisfying, although it too is a penetrating historical account of life on the Oregon Coast in the 1850's. Told through Ben Thaler, an ambitious pioneer who has come to the Tillamook country because he has heard that a man there lives in a tree, this novel also centers on disparities between Indian and white cultures. Thaler relentlessly pushes for progress, symbolized here in the building of a ship to improve trade, at the expense of the Indians and their less materialistic values. By the end of the novel Thatler realizes that his demands for progress have ruined the lives of his friends and opponents; progress has perhaps cost more than it has achieved.

In preparing his three novels, Berry studied the history of the Rocky Mountain fur trade, research that led to the publication of *A Majority of Scoundrels*. Subtitled "An Informal History of the Rocky Mountain Fur Trade," the volume is an informal yet scholarly study that has pleased buffs and professionals alike. Well researched and particularly well written, the book remains a solid and lively account of one of the major Western fur trade firms.

Although Berry's writings are not as widely known as they should be they are smoothly crafted, moving accounts of white-Indian cultural conflicts in the Pacific Northwest in the first half of the 19th century. Moreover, as a serious student of Zen, Berry convincingly portrays the quests, the inner conflicts that power the lives of such characters as Trask, Johnson Monday, and Ben Thaler.

—Richard W. Etulain

BEXAR, Phil. *See* **BORG, Jack.**

BICKHAM, Jack M(iles). Also writes as Jeff Clinton; John Miles; George Shaw. American. Born in Columbus, Ohio, 2 September 1930. Educated at Ohio State University, Columbus, B.A. 1952; University of Oklahoma, Norman, M.A. 1960. Served in the United States Air Force, 1952–54: 1st Lieutenant. Married Janie R. Wallace in 1952; three sons and one daughter. Reporter, Norman *Transcript*, 1956–60; editor, *Daily Oklahoman*, 1960–66, and *Oklahoma Courier*, 1966–69; assistant editor, Oklahoma Publishing Company, from 1960. Part-time teacher of journalism, 1963–66, and since 1969 Professor of journalism, Oklahoma City University. Agent: Andrea Cirillo, Jane Rotrosen Agency, 226 East 32nd Street, New York, New York 10016. Address: 2113 Bois de Arc, Norman, Oklahoma 73071, U.S.A.

WESTERN PUBLICATIONS

Novels

Gunman's Gamble. New York, Ace, 1958; London, Hale, 1959.
Feud Fury. New York, Ace, 1959.
Killer's Paradise. New York, Ace, 1959.
The Useless Gun. New York, Ace, 1960; London, Hale, 1961.
Hangman's Territory. New York, Ace, 1961.
Gunmen Can't Hide. New York, Ace, 1961.
Trip Home to Hell. New York, Berkley, 1965.
The Padre Must Die. New York, Doubleday, 1967.
The War on Charity Ross. New York, Doubleday, 1967.
Target: Charity Ross. New York, Doubleday, 1968.
Decker's Campaign. New York, Doubleday, 1970; as *The Sheriff's Campaign*, London, Hale, 1971.
Fletcher. New York, Berkley, 1971.
Ambush Vengeance. London, Hale, 1971.
Jilly's Canal. New York, Doubleday, 1971; as *Texas Challenge*, London, Hale, 1971.
Dopey Dan. New York, Doubleday, 1972.
Katie, Kelly, and Heck. New York, Doubleday, 1973; London, Hale, 1980.
Baker's Hawk. New York, Doubleday, 1974; London, Hale, 1976.
Hurry Home, Davey Clock. New York, Doubleday, 1975.
A Boat Named Death. New York, Doubleday, 1975.

Novels as Jeff Clinton (series: Wildcat O'Shea)

The Fighting Buckaroo (Wildcat). New York, Berkley, 1961.
Range Killer. New York, Berkley, 1962.
Wildcat's Rampage. New York, Berkley, 1962.
Wildcat Against the House. New York, Berkley, 1963.
Wildcat's Revenge. New York, Berkley, 1964.
Killer's Choice. New York, Berkley, 1965.
Wildcat Takes His Medicine. New York, Berkley, 1966.
Wanted: Wildcat O'Shea. New York, Berkley, 1967.
Wildcat on the Loose. New York, Berkley, 1967.
Wildcat's Witch Hunt. New York, Berkley, 1967.
Watch Out for Wildcat. New York, Berkley, 1968.
Wildcat Meets Miss Melody. New York, Berkley, 1968.
Build a Box for Wildcat. New York, Berkley, 1969.
A Stranger Named O'Shea. New York, Berkley, 1970.
Wildcat's Claim to Fame. New York, Berkley, 1971.
Bounty on Wildcat. New York, Berkley, 1971.
Hang High, O'Shea. New York, Berkley, 1972.
Emerald Canyon. New York, Doubleday, 1974.
Showdown at Emerald Canyon. New York, Doubleday, 1975.

OTHER PUBLICATIONS

Novels

The Shadowed Faith. New York, Doubleday, 1968.
The Invisible Plague. New York, Pyramid, 1975.
Twister. New York, Doubleday, 1976; London, Macmillan, 1977.
The Winemakers. New York, Doubleday, 1977.
The Excalibur Disaster. New York, Doubleday, 1978; London, Macmillan, 1979.
Dinah, Blow Your Horn. New York, Doubleday, 1979; London, Hale, 1980.
Halls of Dishonor. New York, Pocket Books, 1980.
The Regensburg Legacy. New York, Doubleday, 1980; London, Hale, 1981.
All the Days Were Summer. London, Hale, 1982.
I Still Dream About Columbus. New York, St. Martin's Press, 1982.
Ariel. New York, St. Martin's Press, 1984; London, Severn House, 1985.
Miracleworker. New York, St. Martin's Press, 1987.
Day Seven. New York, St. Martin's Press, 1988.
Dropshot. New York, St. Martin's Press, 1990.

Novels as John Miles

Dally with a Deadly Doll. New York, Ace, 1960.
Troubled Trails. New York, Avalon, 1963.
The Night Hunters. Indianapolis, Bobbs Merrill, 1973; London, Hale, 1975.
The Silver Bullet Gang. Indianapolis, Bobbs Merrill, 1974; London, Hale, 1976.
The Blackmailer. Indianapolis, Bobbs Merrill, 1974.
Operation Nightfall, with Tom Morris. Indianapolis, Bobbs Merrill, 1975; London, Souvenir Press, 1976.

Other

The Apple Dumpling Gang (for children). New York, Doubleday, 1971; London, Hale, 1972.
Writing Novels That Sell. New York, Simon and Schuster, 1989.

* * *

Jack M. Bickham has been a newspaper reporter (for the Norman *Transcript* in Oklahoma), magazine writer (for *Time*, *Life*, and *Sports Illustrated*, among others), editor, novelist, and teacher of journalism and creative writing. Since the appearance of his first book in 1958 he has written over 50 novels, of which at least three dozen are westerns. The earliest books, written for mass market paperback publication, are typical formulaic western action tales: standard story lines and characters and "shore do want to thank yuh" dialogue, with somewhat more than the usual amount of brutality and violence. (In Bickham's second novel, *Feud Fury*, there is a graphic scene in which a sadistic gunman shoots a teenage boy almost literally to pieces.) But Bickham quickly tired of clichés in style and subject, and sharpened his storytelling skills while at the same time moving into a new area. With *The Fighting Buckaroo*, published under his Jeff Clinton byline, Bickham embarked on a series of comic westerns about a character called Wildcat O'Shea. O'Shea is a big man with carrot-colored hair, multi-colored attire—a red hat, blue shirt, green trousers, yellow boots with silver spurs, and a purple vest form a typical ensemble—a handy way with dynamite, and an enormous appetite for drink, women, and fighting, preferably in combination. He gets involved with bank robbers, crooked sheriffs, a famous writer of western novels, a lion, a witch, and other complications. The series eventually grew to 14 volumes, the last of which appeared in 1972. These are fast-paced, broad, bawdy tall tales, and enormously enjoyable.

After the first few O'Shea books, Bickham resumed the writing of "straight" western novels. The new books were more thoughtfully conceived and more smoothly written than his earlier books, often with out-of-the-way touches in background or characters. In *Trip Home to Hell* a reporter for Joseph Pulitzer's New York *World* in 1884 returns to his Colorado home town to uncover the story behind the breakup of a large ranch, and finds himself confronting not only present dangers but also echoes from his own past. In *The War on Charity Ross* a young widow fights to preserve her land and build up a ranch in the face of opposition from a greedy and unscrupulous neighbor. A second book about the same character, *Target: Charity Ross*, is a period murder mystery centering around Oklahoma City's underworld and its drug traffic in the 1890's. *The Apple Dumpling Gang* tells how a band of unruly youths helps the local sheriff round up three troublesome outlaw gangs. (This book was filmed by the Walt Disney Studio in 1975.) The title character of *Dopey Dan* is a circus clown in post-Civil War New Mexico who investigates the mysterious death of a friend and mentor. In *Katie, Kelly, and Heck* a proper young woman from the east inherits a bordello in Salvation, Arizona, and tries, against the resistance of the town's rowdy inhabitants, to turn it into a "quality café with a new family policy." In *Emerald Canyon* and *Showdown at Emerald Canyon*, published under the Jeff Clinton byline, an impoverished young farmer in the Arizona of the 1870's organizes a battle against a syndicate of land swindlers.

In addition to his western novels, Bickham wrote a number of suspense novels under the name John Miles. He also wrote *The Shadowed Faith*, a contemporary novel about controversy within the Catholic Church. Bickham has commented that he was not yet ready to handle this theme; the book was not a success. In 1974, spurred by a record-breaking outbreak of tornadoes, Bickham began working on his first "big" novel. *Twister* was published two years later. It is an information-packed chronicle tracing the history of a series of tornadoes and their effects on a large cast of characters spread throughout the eastern half of the United States. This was followed by *The Winemakers*, an even more ambitious novel of family traditions versus corporate infighting in the California wine industry. *Dinah, Blow Your Horn* is a small-scale but vividly recreated piece of Americana in which the young son of a railroading family in rural Pennsylvania in the early years of this century copes with problems of poverty, labor unrest, friendship, and betrayal. These and other novels are the legacy of Bickham's labors in the western field; and the Westerns themselves, particularly those published since 1965, form a solid body of work worth attention in its own right.

—R.E. Briney

BINDLOSS, Harold (Edward). British. Born in Liverpool, Lancashire, in 1866. Spent several years at sea, and in various British colonies; returned to England in 1896, and became freelance writer. *Died 30 December 1945.*

WESTERN PUBLICATIONS

Novels

Alton of Somasco. London, Long, 1905; New York, Stokes, 1906.
The Cattle-Baron's Daughter. London, Long, and New York, Stokes, 1906.
Delilah of the Snows. London, Long, 1907; New York, Stokes, 1908.
Winston of the Prairie. New York, Stokes, 1908.
Lorimer of the Northwest. New York, Stokes, 1909.
The Gold Trail. London, Long, and New York, Stokes, 1910.
The Boy Ranchers of Puget Sound. New York, Stokes, 1910.
Rancher Carteret. London, Long, 1910; as *Sydney Carteret, Rancher*, New York, Stokes, 1911.
Hawtrey's Deputy. London, Ward Lock, 1911; as *Masters of the Wheat-Lands*, New York, Stokes, 1911.
The Pioneer. London, Ward Lock, 1912; as *The Long Portage*, New York, Stokes, 1912.
The Wastrel. London, Ward Lock, 1913; as *Prescott of Saskatchewan*, New York, Stokes, 1913.
Alison's Adventure. London, Long, 1917; as *A Prairie Courtship*, New York, Stokes, 1917.
Partners of the Out-Trail. New York, Stokes, 1919.
The Wilderness Mine. New York, Stokes, 1920.
The Mountaineers. London, Ward Lock, 1922; as *Northwest!*, New York, Stokes, 1922.
The Wilderness Patrol. London, Ward Lock, and New York, Stokes, 1923.
The Keystone Block. London, Ward Lock, 1923.
The Boys of Wildcat Ranch. London, Wells Gardner, and New York, Stokes, 1924.
The Lute Player. London, Ward Lock, 1924; as *Carson of Red River*, New York, Stokes, 1924.
The Broken Net. London, Ward Lock, 1925; as *Prairie Gold*, New York, Stokes, 1925.
Helen the Conqueror. London, Ward Lock, 1926; as *Pine Creek Ranch*, New York, Stokes, 1926.
Footsteps. London, Ward Lock, 1927; as *The Ghost of Hemlock Canyon*, New York, Stokes, 1927.
Frontiersmen. London, Ward Lock, 1929; as *The Frontiersman*, New York, Stokes, 1929.
Harden's Escapade. London, Ward Lock, 1930; as *The Man at Willow Ranch*, New York, Stokes, 1930.
The Lean Years. London, Ward Lock, 1931; as *The Prairie Patrol*, New York, Stokes, 1931.
Carter's Triumph. London, Ward Lock, 1931; as *The Border Trail*, New York, Stokes, 1931.
Sonalta Gold. London, Ward Lock, 1934; as *Valley Gold*, New York, Stokes, 1934.
The Lady of the Plain. London, Ward Lock, 1935; as *Sweetwater Ranch*, New York, Stokes, 1935.
Valeria Goes West. London, Ward Lock, 1939.

OTHER PUBLICATIONS

Novels

Ainslee's Ju-Ju: A Romance of the Hinterland. London, Chatto and Windus, 1900.
A Sower of Wheat. London, Chatto and Windus, 1901.
Sunshine and Snow. London, Partridge, 1902.
The Concession-Hunters. London, Chatto and Windus, 1902.
The Mistress of Bonaventure. London, Chatto and Windus, 1903; New York, Stokes, 1907.
His Master Purpose. London, Long, 1903.
Daventry's Daughter. London, Chatto and Windus, 1904.
The League of the Leopard. London, Long, 1904; New York, Stokes, 1914.
True Grit: The Adventure of Two Lads in Western Africa. London, Partridge, 1904; as *The Young Traders*, New York, Stokes, 1907.
The Imposter. London, White, 1905.
In the Misty Seas: A Story of the Sealers of Behring Strait. London, Partridge, 1905.
Beneath Her Station. London, White, 1906.
A Damaged Reputation. London, White, 1906; New York, Fenno, 1908.
The Dust of Conflict. London, Long, and New York, Stokes, 1907.
His Lady's Pleasure. London, White, 1907.

By Right of Purchase. London, Long, and New York, Stokes, 1908.
Long Odds. Boston, Small Maynard, 1908.
For Jacinta. New York, Stokes, 1908.
Thrice Armed. London, Long, and New York, Stokes, 1908.
The Liberationist. London, Ward Lock, 1908.
The Greater Power. London, Long, and New York, Stokes, 1909.
The Opium Smuggler. London, Unwin, 1910.
Thurston of Orchard Valley. New York, Stokes, 1910.
The Protector. London, Ward Lock, 1911; as *Vane of the Timberlands*, New York, Stokes, 1911.
The Trustee. London, Ward Lock, 1912; as *Ranching for Sylvia*, New York, Stokes, 1913.
The Allinson Honour. London, Ward Lock, 1913; as *For the Allinson Honor*, New York, Stokes, 1913.
Blake's Burden. London, Ward Lock, 1914.
The Secret of the Reef. London, Ward Lock, and New York, Stokes, 1914.
The Intriguers. New York, Stokes, 1914.
A Risky Game. London, Ward Lock, 1915; as *The Coast of Adventure*, New York, Stokes, 1915.

* * *

Harold Bindloss was one of the prototypical writers of adventure stories in the first third of the 20th century. His stories probably appealed to the slightly older readers of G.A. Henty and R.M. Ballantyne in previous generations, but instead of tales written for the adolescent and steeped in "real" history, Bindloss's narratives contain a strong element of romance and center on personal adventure rather than national pride. He was well-known in his own day for his "healthy" and "sane" stories—i.e., there was little psychological complexity or doubt in his characters—and for his vivid descriptive effects. He wrote about northern England and Africa as well as the western North American continent, but his stories about the Canadian Rockies and British Columbia are the ones which most readily reveal his sense of the new and the potential. As his young hero in *The Mountaineers* notes, the look of the "typically western" person is keen and optimistic—and his plots often revolve around a contrast between this "western" characteristic and the sophistication and reliance on social distinction of the English.

Many of the novels use the common themes of rivalry in love, an illegal activity (gold exploitation, dope smuggling), or vengeance for a dead partner or family member. A running motif in almost all the stories is the importance given to work based on a close awareness of the soil, and the hero is usually a rancher, miner, hunter, or settler. Nature may dwarf the individuals who are set against it, but the earth is something to be used, possibly even to define the user. Conquering a mountain pass during a storm is the climax of the plot of *The Mountaineers*; the North West Mounted Police officer must conquer the elements (winter snow, icy rivers, swarms of summer mosquitoes) before he can capture his man (*The Wilderness Patrol*). In both *Sonalta Gold* and *Hawtrey's Deputy* the young heroes must overcome their personal problems before they can become successful ranchers, as if their character faults prevent their proper function as working adults. Usually the theme is more obvious, but even such activities as finding the murderer of a game warden (*The Mountaineers*) or the salmon poacher (*The Boys of Wildcat Ranch*), while serving to validate the manliness of the heroes, and to uphold law and order, also function as the repayment of a debt to the grandeur of the natural world the heroes inhabit.

Bindloss used melodramatic touches in his plots. *Delilah of the Snows* centers on the obvious contrast between a sweet hardworking girl and the haughty, wealthy daughter of an important official. *Hawtrey's Deputy* is a story of rivalry in love reminiscent of "The Courtship of Miles Standish"—where the "deputy" assigned to bring Hawtrey's fiancée back from England eventually wins her for himself. There are opium dens (Chinamen "look much the same"), lost gold mines, and ranching and farming rivalries and feuds. But Bindloss spoke for a massive audience that believed in the spirit of "progress" that is possibly ironic to a modern reader: "So long as Canada calls for pioneers the axe and the saw go first" (*The Keystone Block*).

—George Walsh

BINGLEY, David Ernest. Also wrote as Bart Adams; Adam Bridger; Abe Canuck; Henry Carver; Larry Chatham; Henry Chesham; Will Coltman; Ed Coniston; Luke Dorman; George Fallon; David Horsley; Bat Jefford; Syd Kingston; Eric Lynch; James Martell; Colin North; Ben Plummer; Caleb Prescott; Mark Remington; John Roberts; Steve Romney; Frank Silvester; Henry Starr; Link Tucker; Christopher Wigan; Roger Yorke. British. Born in Leeds, Yorkshire 16 April 1920. Educated at Shenstone Teachers Training College, teacher's certificate 1948. Served in the Royal Navy, 1939–45. Married Vera Pilkington in 1946; one daughter and two sons. Auditor, W.D. Burlinson and Company, Dewsbury, 1938–39; clerk, Vickers-Armstrong Ltd., Barrow-in-Furness, 1939, 1946–47; teacher, Kirkby-Ireleth the Burlington School, Lancashire, 1948–50; housemaster, Horsley's Green School, High Wycombe, 1950–56; teacher, Spring Gardens County Primary School, High Wycombe, 1957–62; committee member, Writers Summer School, 1962–65; teacher, New Romney Primary School, Kent, 1966–80. *Died 9 October 1985.*

WESTERN PUBLICATIONS

Novels

Gunsmoke at Nester Creek. London, Hale, 1964.
Sons of the Diamond V. London, Hale, 1964.
Rustlers' Moon. London, Hale, 1972.
Hellions' Hideaway. London, Hale, 1974.
The Man from Abilene. London, Hale, 1975.

Novels as Christopher Wigan

Mossyhorn Trail. London, Mills and Boon, 1957.
Showdown at Cedar Springs. London, Brown Watson, 1958.
The Man from Casagrande. London, Hale, 1964.
The Trail-Blazer. London, Hale, 1964.
Remuda's Renegades. London, Hale, 1971.
Killer's Canyon. London, Hale, 1973.
Lopez's Loot. London, Hale, 1975.
Buckboard Barber. London, Hale, 1981.
El Yanqui's Woman. London, Hale, 1983.
Triple Canyon. London, Hale, 1985.

Novels as Larry Chatham

The Restless Breed. London, Hale, 1963.
Trails of Destiny. London, Hale, 1963.
Timber Wolves' Trail. London, Hale, 1964.

Trail of Reckoning. London, Hale, 1965.
Two Horse Trail. London, Hale, 1971.
Hangtown Heiress. London, Hale, 1973.
The Judge's Territory. London, Hale, 1973.
Smith's Canyon. London, Hale, 1981.
Tenderfoot Trail Boss. London, Hale, 1983.
Banjo's Brand. London, Hale, 1985.

Novels as Syd Kingston

Railtown Round-Up. London, Hale, 1964.
The Necktie Trail. London, Hale, 1965.
The Kid from Cougar. London, Hale, 1972.
Alias Jack Dollar. London, Hale, 1974.
Hideaway Heist. London, Hale, 1975.
Boot Hill Bandit. London, Hale, 1982.
Renegade Preacher. London, Hale, 1985.

Novels as John Roberts

Showdown at the Lazy T. London, Hale, 1964.
Colorado Gun Law. London, Hale, 1966.
Trailmen's Truce. London, Hale, 1972.

Novels as Dave Carver

The Bar T Brand. London, Hale, 1964.
Gunsmoke Gambler. London, Hale, 1966.
Renegade River. London, Hale, 1973.

Novels as David Horsley

Johnny Pronto. London, Hale, 1964.
The Reluctant Renegade. London, Hale, 1965.
Flying Horseshoe Trail. London, Hale, 1966.
Buckboard Bandit. London, Hale, 1966.
The Diamond Kid. London, Hale, 1972.
Redman Range. London, Hale, 1975.
Sunset Showdown. London, Hale, 1977.
Brigand's Blade. London, Hale, 1978.
The Beauclerc Brand. London, Hale, 1979.
Trouble Shooter on Trial. London, Hale, 1980.
Salt Creek Killing. London, Hale, 1981.
Badlands Bonanza. London, Hale, 1982.
The Long Siesta. London, Hale, 1983.
Stolen Star. London, Hale, 1984.
Wild Bunch Wanton. London, Hale, 1985.

Novels as Ben Plummer

Gunsmoke County. London, Hale, 1964.
The Railroad Renegades. London, Hale, 1965.
Cowtown Killers. London, Hale, 1972.

Novels as Henry Starr

Short Trigger Valley. London, Hale, 1964.
The Border Brigands. London, Hale, 1965.
Lawman's Lament. London, Hale, 1972.

Novels as Adam Bridger

Counterfeit Trail. London, Hale, 1965.
Gunsmoke Gorge. London, Hale, 1966.
Renegade Range. London, Hale, 1969.

Novels as Frank Silvester

Bullhead's Canyon. London, Hale, 1965.
Settlers' Stampede. London, Hale, 1966.
The Palomino Kid. London, Hale, 1969.
Red Bluff Renegades. London, Hale, 1973.
Rogue's Remittance. London, Hale, 1976.
Greenhorn Gorge. London, Hale, 1981.
Renegade Lady. London, Hale, 1984.
Renegade Rancher. London, Hale, 1986.

Novels as Mark Remington

Hellions' Roost. London, Hale, 1965.
Silver City Showdown. London, Hale, 1966.
El Yanqui's Gold. London, Hale, 1969.

Novels as Colin North

The Reluctant Gunman. London, Hale, 1965.
Trail of Tragedy. London, Hale, 1966.
Trailtown Trickster. London, Hale, 1969.

Novels as James Martell

Little Pecos Trail. London, Hale, 1965.
Renegade Trail. London, Hale, 1966.
Salt Creek Showdown. London, Hale, 1970.
Cowtown Kidnap. London, Hale, 1971.

Novels as Roger Yorke

The Iron Trail. London, Hale, 1965.
Guadalupe Bandit. London, Hale, 1966.
Owlhoot Bandits. London, Hale, 1969.

Novels as Luke Dorman

Renegade's Blade. London, Hale, 1965.
Buzzards' Breed. London, Hale, 1966.
Red Rock Renegades. London, Hale, 1970.

Novels as Steve Romney

Gunsmoke Lawyer. London, Hale, 1965.
Sawbones' City. London, Hale, 1967.
Showdown City. London, Hale, 1970.

Novels as Ed Coinston

Bar X Bandit. London, Gresham, 1965.
The Elusive Renegade. London, Gresham, 1967.
Boulder Creek Trail. London, Hale, 1969.

Novels as Link Tucker

Renegade Valley. London, Gresham, 1965.
Circle M Showdown. London, Gresham, 1967.
Hellions at Large. London, Hale, 1969.

Novels as Bart Adams

Owlhoot Raiders. London, Gresham, 1966.
Renegades' Stampede. London, Gresham, 1967.
The Coyote Kids. London, Hale, 1970.

Novels as Will Coltman

The Torrington Trail. London, Gresham, 1966.
Killer's Creek. London, Hale, 1969.
Ghost Town Killer. London, Hale, 1970.

Novels as Caleb Prescott

The Ruthless Renegades. London, Hale, 1966.
Pecos River Posse. London, Hale, 1967.
Six Shooter Junction. London, Hale, 1970.

Novels as Bat Jefford

Creek Town Killer. London, Hale, 1966.
Badman's Bounty. London, Hale, 1968.
Silver Creek Trail. London, Hale, 1970.

Novels as Abe Canuck

The Rioting Renegades. London, Hale, 1966.
Silvertown Trail. London, Hale, 1969.
Hellions' Hostage. London, Hale, 1971.

Novels as Eric Lynch

South Fork Showdown. London, Gresham, 1967.
Murder Mesa. London, Hale, 1968.
Renegades' Retreat. London, Hale, 1971.

OTHER PUBLICATIONS

Novels as David Horsley

Operation Pedestal. London, Brown Watson, 1957.
Tinfish Running! London, Brown Watson, 1958.
The Ocean, Their Grave. London, Brown Watson, 1958.
Torpedoes in the Wake. London, Brown Watson, 1958.
Vinegar Johnnie. London, Brown Watson, 1958.
The Decoys. London, Brown Watson, 1959.
Living Death. London, Brown Watson, 1959.
The Thirty Eight Days. London, Brown Watson, 1959
Don't Compel Me! London, Brown Watson, 1960.
The Time of the Locus: The Terrible Aftermath of the Fall of Singapore. London, Brown Watson, 1960.
Dive, Dive—Dive! London, Brown Watson, 1960.
Elusive Witness (as D.E. Bingley). London, Hale, 1966.
Caribbean Crisis (as D.E. Bingley). London, Hale, 1966.
Rendezvous in Rio (as George Fallon). London, Hale, 1967.

Novels as Henry Chesham

Naples, or Die! London, Hale, 1965.
Skyborne Sapper. London, Hale, 1966.
The Place of the Chins. London, Hale, 1975.
A Surfeit of Soldiers. London, Hale, 1978.
The Angry Atoll. London, Hale, 1981.
A Tide of Chariots. London, Hale, 1983.
Saboteurs fron the Sea. London, Hale, 1985.
Torpedo Tide. London, Hale, 1986.

Other (for children) as David Bingley

Malayan Adventure. London, Blackie, 1962.
Famous Storybook Heroes. London, Odhams Press, 1964.
Study Book of Bridges. London, Bodley Head, 1969.
Adam of Pendle Grange. London, Galliard, 1979.

*

David Ernest Bingley commented (1982):

From my late teens, having read *Complete Writing for Profit* and *The Summing Up* (W.S. Maugham), I wanted to produce fiction. Alas, the saleable stuff did not come quickly. A war, college, and two correspondence courses later I started to sell confession stories in the early 1950's. About one every three months. An article in *The Writer* prompted me to read personal accounts in order to produce novels with a similar appeal. I tried the Foreign Legion first, and managed to place a story of 44,000 words, for which I was paid 12 guineas. After that I exploited my World War II background, writing stories of naval action.

Having studied American history in college, I was drawn towards the western. Cattle drives, range wars, overland stages, railway pioneering, and the shifting frontier provided plenty of scope for this type of action story.

In the 1960's, I temporarily abandoned my second profession (teaching) for a spell of full-time writing. I survived for nearly four years, writing short stories, books and scripts for children, as well as war novels in soft and hard covers, crime novels, and hard-back westerns. However, I missed the teachers' useful holidays, and when some markets dried up I went back to a permanent teaching job. For 14 years my creative output had to slow up a bit, and all I kept doing at all regularly were westerns. It is possible to build into the western background character clashes based on opposing character traits—the very essence of good drama—so I shall keep on writing in this fiction genre indefinitely.

* * *

David Ernest Bingley, who has many pseudonyms, wrote some war and adventure stories but the bulk of his output was Westerns. He published at the rate of two or three books a year from the late 1950's, under the pseudonym of Christopher Wigan and others.

The secret of Bingley's success with his public is that he stayed very much within the conventions of the western novel. His rather spare, economical style suits this formula. He set his books in traditional western areas such as New Mexico and Texas, but was inclined to add Kansas as a location. He did not, however, give us very much detail about the geography or topography of the location, instead using the very familiar small wooden frontier towns in semi-desert areas containing convenient ranges of hills and ridges.

Bingley's heroes tend to be lone men with distinct missions. The hero can be guarding a fortune such as Tex in *The Man from Casagrande* or a private investigator on the trail of murderers in *Killer's Canyon*. The choice of mission can be quite original, such as the task of collecting a coffin, undertaken by the hero of *The Man from Abilene*. An original choice of profession for the hero is that of doctor in *Remuda's Renegades*. Great obstacles often stand in the way of the hero: the coffin is seized by outlaws in *The Man from Abilene;* the brother of an attractive girl in *Killer's Canyon* clashes with the hero. The heroes are, however, more than a match for these obstacles. They are generally lean, good looking, and good with a gun.

Bingley built his plots well by creating suspense at the end of each chapter. (In *Buckboard Barber* there is a murder at the end of chapter one.) Suspense builds up towards the end of his books with a convincing climax, such as the capture of villains, the recovery of gold, or the reuniting of separated cousins as *Lopez's Loot*. There is, however, little romance in Bingley's Westerns, and appearances by women are few. Neither is there the moral interest to be found in older Westerns.

Bingley's prose tends to be overfull of narrative and very short on dialogue. His descriptive abilities are, however, such that this is a virtue. He has a remarkable turn of phrase, and descriptive passages, especially of people, make compelling reading. He became more effective at describing the effects of violence in his later books.

What dialogue there is is very economical and sparse, and is not always sufficient to keep up the interest. He does, however, have a sympathetic ear for the dialogue of Mexicans and makes them sound convincing. Within the rather stark conventions of the modern Western, with its discounting of moral themes, Wigan was a successful practitioner.

—P.R. Meldrum

BIRNEY, (Herman) Hoffman. Also wrote as David Kent. Born in Philadelphia, Pennsylvania, in 1891. Educated at Dickinson College, Carlisle, Pennsylvania. Served in the United States Army Infantry and Aviation Section during World War I: 2nd Lieutenant. Married; one son. Deputy chief of reports and publications, Ballistics Department, Army Ballistic Missile Agency, Huntsville, Alabama; editor, Army rocket research and development department; Western book reviewer, *New York, Times.* Recipient: Western Writers of America spur award, for non-fiction, 1954. *Died 3 June 1958.*

WESTERN PUBLICATIONS

Novels

King of the Mesa. Philadelphia, Penn, 1927; London, Long, 1928.
The Masked Rider. Philadelphia, Penn, 1928; London, Long, 1929.
The Cañon of Lost Waters. Philadelphia, Penn, 1930; as *The Canyon of Lost Waters,* London, Long, 1930.
Barrier Ranch. Philadelphia, Penn, 1933; London, Cassell, 1934.
Grim Journey: The Story of the Adventures of the ... Donner Party ... New York, Minton Balch, 1934.
Forgotten Canõn. Philadelphia, Penn, 1934; London, Long, 1935.
Eagle in the Sun. New York, Putnam, 1935.
A Stranger in Black Butte. Philadelphia, Penn, and London, Long, 1936.
Dead Man's Trail. Philadelphia, Penn, 1937; London, Long, 1938.
Ann Carmeny. New York, Putnam, 1941; London, Nicholson and Watson, 1943.
The Dice of God. New York, Holt, 1956.

OTHER PUBLICATIONS

Novels as David Kent

Jason Burr's First Case. New York, Random House, 1941.
A Knife Is Silent. New York, Random House, 1947.

Other

Steeldust: The Story of a Horse (for children). Philadelphia, Penn, 1928.
Vigilantes. Philadelphia, Penn, 1929.
The Pinto Pony: A Real Horse Story (for children). Philadelphia, Penn, 1930.
Roads to Roam. Philadelphia, Penn, 1930.
Two Little Navajos: A Tale of the Children of the Painted Desert (for children). Philadelphia, Penn, 1931.
Zealots of Zion. Philadelphia, Penn, 1931.
Kudlu, The Eskimo Boy (for children). Philadelphia, Penn, 1932.
Tu'kwi of the Peaceful People (for children). Philadelphia, Penn, 1933.
Holy Murder: The Story of Porter Rockwell, with Charles Kelly. New York, Minton Balch, 1934.
Ay-chee, Son of the Desert (for children). Philadelphia, Penn, 1935.
Mountain Chief: An Indian Legend for Children. Philadelphia, Penn, 1938.
Brothers of Doom: The Story of the Pizarros of Peru. New York, Putnam, 1942.

* * *

Hoffman Birney began his career with conventional adventure stories which are unusual only in the amount of information they provide about the West. All his novels up to 1934 are romantic Westerns, set in the southwest towards the end of the 19th century. One main protagonist is always from the east, come west to inherit a relative's ranch. The tenderfoot learns western ways and defends the ranch against big cattlemen or outlaws. Having won the loyalty of the cowboys, the new rancher marries and settles permanently in the west.

But in 1934 Birney published *Grim Journey*, a precise, unsensational, and convincing account of the Donner party disaster of 1846, written as a fictitious journal by Mr. Eddy of Illinois, a real member of the group. In a postscript, Birney cites his sources, testifying to the accuracy of their identities and major events, and explaining that finer details have been created in accordance with known circumstances. He has a purpose beyond simple accuracy: he also wants to correct the impression of the participants presented by the mid-Victorian writer McGlashan. Birney insists that these people were not heroes or epic pioneers. They were emigrants going west for land and greater prosperity who, through mismanagement and misfortune, met with natural reversals and reacted with normal mixtures of panic, bravery, stoicism, and desperation. Birney shows all this in his novel and, although he does not portray character in any depth, his descriptions of events and reactions seem authentic—he is especially effective in his unmelodramatic treatment of the travellers' notorious resort to cannibalism.

Birney continued to intersperse this more serious work with his adventure stories, which retain the romantic format but become more historically specific and more melodramatic. For example, *Eagle in the Sun* is set within the 1846 war with Mexico and is full of vows of revenge sworn on the Cross, gory killings, and melodramatic duels. Many of the stories make passing references to Mormons, and, again in 1934, Birney produced, with Charles Kelly, a history of Porter Rockwell, the chief of the Danites (the Mormons' secret police force). At the end of his career, he worked some of this material into *Ann Carmeny*, a long historical romance, half of which concerns Ann's experience with Mormons in Salt Lake City and half her involvement in the gold strikes in Montana. It tells a fictional story, conventional in its business of love, intrigue, misunderstanding, and reconciliation. But it also involves accurately drawn figures like Henry Plummer, its characters voice intelligent opinions on the difference between the Mormon faith and some of its evil representatives, and the author tries some stylistic experiments, such as sections of pure dialogue. It is a successful enough romance and combines well Birney's two interests—adventure and history.

—Christine Bold

BISHOP, Martin. *See* **PAINE, Lauran.**

BISHOP, Samuel P. Pseudonym for Shaun Hutson. Also writes as Nick Blake; Mike Dickinson; Clive Harold; Wolf Kruger; Stefan Rostov; Frank Taylor. British. Address: c/o Macdonald & Co., 66–73 Shoe Lane, London EC4P 4AB, England.

WESTERN PUBLICATIONS

Novels

Track. New York, Covered Wagon, 1986.
Partners in Death. New York, Covered Wagon, 1986.
Apache Gold. New York, Covered Wagon, 1988.

OTHER PUBLICATIONS

Novels

Slugs. London, Star, 1982; New York, Dorchester, 1987.
The Skull. Feltham, Hamlyn, 1982; New York, Dorchester, 1989.
Sledgehammer. London, Hale, 1982; as Wolf Kruger, London, W.H. Allen, 1983.
Convoy of Steel. London, Hale, 1982; as Wolf Kruger, London, W.H. Allen, 1984.
Kessler's Raid. London, Hale, 1982; as Wolf Kruger, London, Star, 1984.
Blood and Honour. London, Hale, 1982; as Wolf Kruger, London, W.H. Allen, 1983.
Sabres in the Snow. London, Hale, 1983; as Stefan Rostov, London, W.H. Allen, 1985.
Spawn. London, W.H. Allen, 1983; New York, Dorchester, 1988.
Men of Blood. London, Hale, 1984; as Wolf Kruger, London, W.H. Allen, 1985.
Erebus. London, Star, 1984; New York, Dorchester, 1988.
Chainsaw Massacre (as Nick Blake). London, Star, 1984.
The Terminator (novelization of screenplay). London, W.H. Allen, 1984.
Shadows. London, W.H. Allen, 1985; New York, Dorchester, 1990.
Breeding Ground. London, W.H. Allen, 1985; New York, Dorchester, 1987.
No Survivors. London, Hale, 1985.
Relics. London, W.H. Allen, 1986.
Taken by Force. London, Hale, 1987.
Victims. London, W.H. Allen, 1987.
Deathday. London, Star, 1987.
Swords of Vengeance. London, W.H. Allen, 1988.
Assassin. London, W.H. Allen, 1988.
Nemesis. London, W.H. Allen, 1989.
Renegades. London, Macdonald, 1991.

Novels as Frank Taylor

The Uninvited (as Clive Harold). London, W.H. Allen, 1979.
The Uninvited II: The Visitation. London, W.H. Allen, 1984.
The Uninvited III: The Abduction. London, W.H. Allen, 1985.

Fiction (for children) as Mike Dickinson

My Dad Doesn't Even Notice. London, Deutsch, 1982.
My Brother's Silly. London, Deutsch, 1983.
The Rambling Rat. London, Deutsch, 1985.
Smudge. London, Deutsch, 1987.

* * *

Samuel P. Bishop is a pseudonym of the British writer Shaun Hutson, whose long string of "nasty" horror novels—which include *Slugs*, *Deathday*, *Relics*, and *Breeding Ground*—have, over the last few years, elevated him to cult status on both sides of the Atlantic.

Hutson has written numerous paperback originals, many of them for the now non-existent publisher W.H. Allen, from allegedly "true" accounts of contact with aliens to war stories set very much in the mould of Sven Hassel and Leo Kessler. When W.H. Allen's paperback imprint, Star Books, decided to launch a new western series in 1986, then, Hutson was in many ways the natural choice to write it.

Sadly, however, the series, *Track*, has little to recommend it, and in view of the fact that it only ran for three books (out of a projected six to eight), the British book-buying public evidently seemed to agree.

Track, the central character (one can hardly call him the hero, for reasons which soon become apparent) is a former Union Army lieutenant who was very nearly court-martialled for cold-bloodedly shooting Confederate prisoners-of-war. Wounded in combat, the War leaves him with a badly-scarred right thigh (the legacy of a cannon shell at Gettysburg) that still causes him discomfort.

Track, we are told, did not join the Union Army out of any sense of patriotism, but simply to hone and refine his killing skills. Now, with hostilities at an end, he becomes a bounty hunter, bringing all his prisoners (one might almost call them "victims") in dead whether they resist arrest or not. His armoury includes a pair of Navy Colts, a Spencer carbine, and a wickedly-sharp sabre.

In the first book, called simply *Track*, this particularly murderous anti-hero rides into a town shortly after the local bank has been robbed by a half-breed outlaw called Lone Wolf and his assorted bunch of hardcases. Discovering that, collectively, the gang is worth a considerable bounty, Track sets out after them. Shortly he finds the bodies of the town posse, who have been killed by the outlaws, and dispassionately sets about robbing them of everything of worth. Later, arriving at a ranch that Lone Wolf has recently hit, he discovers a girl the outlaws raped and left for dead. Young Holly Fulton wants to join Track in his hunt, but he shoots her horse to stop her from following him. Of course, the girl finds some way of catching up with him, and eventually, after Track is captured and left to die a lingering death, they manage to dispatch the gang in a bloody shoot-out.

Holly Fulton also appears in the next book, *Partners in Death*, when she, Track, and Track's latest potential target, a gunman named Jim Galton (who may or may not be guilty of murder) have to team up against a wealthy rancher who sends his crew of weapon-heavy cowboys after Track in retaliation for Track having killed his son in an argument over a whore. Somewhere along the line, Galton shows his true colours by betraying Track, and Track eventually exacts a bloody revenge on him.

The final novel, *Apache Gold*, finds Track acting as a bodyguard to a prospector who has found gold in Apache territory. In order to collect the gold and leave Apacheria in one piece, Track decides to break an Apache war-chief named Scala out of the local army post (where he is being held in custody) and use him as a hostage to guarantee safe passage. Things come to a head when Scala escapes, but fortunately the cavalry shows up in time for another violent confrontation.

Written very much in the style of the early Edge books, and clearly influenced by the spaghetti Western, Hutson's *Track* novels present a view of the west that is both harsh and uncompromising, where sudden, violent death is the norm and a double-cross is only to be expected. The plots are slick but quite obviously "manufactured," and supporting characters fit neatly into easily recognisable stereotypes; officious little bank-clerks, nervous, ineffectual townsmen, flamboyant, often perverted outlaws and so on. Track himself is portrayed as a one-dimensional killing machine who only exists to work his way through a series of gruesome set pieces (which are lovingly described in much the same way that Hutson catalogues the no-holds-barred atrocities of his horror and war stories).

It must be said, of course, that poor distribution severely hampered the series' chances of success, but that alone does not account for its particularly short run. In view of the number of similar (though seldom quite so overtly violent) paperback series which were dropped by U.K. publishers in the early 1980's, *Track*, which appeared under the specially-created "Covered Wagon Western" imprint, badly misjudged its market by sticking with an endless procession of gore at the expense of strong, original stories and believeable characters.

—David Whitehead

BLACKSNAKE, George. *See* **RICHARDSON, Gladwell.**

BLAINE, Jeff. *See* **BARRETT, Geoffrey John.**

BLAKE, Forrester (Avery). American. Born in 1912.

WESTERN PUBLICATIONS

Novels

Riding the Mustang Trail. New York, Scribner, 1935.
Johnny Christmas. New York, Morrow, 1948; London, Corgi, 1952.
Wilderness Passage. New York, Random House, 1953.
The Franciscan. New York, Doubleday, 1963.

OTHER PUBLICATIONS

Other

Denver, Rocky Mountain Capital. Denver, Rocky Mountain Pamphlet House, 1945.

Editor, with Levette J. Davidson, *Rocky Mountain Tales.* Norman, University of Oklahoma Press, 1947.

* * *

Forrester Blake's western interests are the mountain men of the southern range and the land itself. While he renders frontiersmen, trappers, hunters, and settlers precise, exact, realistic, interesting, and convincing, his women characters are highly romanticized and unconvincing. He evokes the color, the massiveness, majesty, and grandeur of the western country.

His western works include *Riding the Mustang Trail*, a fictionalized account of a 1932 trail drive from New Mexico to Oklahoma. He relates simply and clearly what happened to the men: from their planning the drive, assembling their "outfits," including a battered 1927 "chev" to serve as chuckwagon, to their last "adios" after the wild mustangs have been delivered to the railroad. These 20th-century cowboys struggle against the same obstacles as the Spanish who had explored the country 400 years earlier: heat, dust, hunger, rattlesnakes, and drought. Amidst this story the narrator expresses a profound nostalgia for the country's past, its color and romance.

Johnny Christmas, one of his best novels and first in a trilogy, portrays a protagonist who is more a representative than actual mountain man. Set against the background of the Mexican-American War, the book contains unrelated sections such as the 30–40 pages at the beginning and the end. The most memorable parts are the vividly stunning descriptions of the deserts and mountains of the Southwest and the detailed realistic portrayals of the men who lived there.

Wilderness Passage tells the story of two mountain men, Johnny Christmas and Tom Gitt, in 1857, 11 years after the time in *Johnny Christmas*. The novel divides into two parts; the first half details the struggle between the United States and the State of Deseret. The second half explores the relationship between Johnny and a Mormon girl, Carey Frietag. Yet as a novel it is more cohesive and unified in action than *Johnny Christmas*. Blake presents a series of contrasts between the old and the new, the unspoiled country and soiled nature, Johnny and Carey, civilization and primitivism, while emphasizing the larger design of nature and its ceaseless changing features rather than minute details.

In *The Franciscan*, third of the trilogy, Blake gives the Old West its most artistic and significant expression in the story of Lorenzo and his struggles as a Franciscan missionary. In spite of the structural problems, the characters are most closely related to the land than in earlier novels.

—G. Dale Gleason

BLUNT, Don. *See* **BOOTH, Edwin.**

BODINE, J.D. *See* **CUNNINGHAM, Chet.**

BOND, Lewis. *See* **PAINE, Lauran.**

BONHAM, Frank. American. Born in Los Angeles, California, 25 February 1914. Educated at Glendale College, California. Served in the United States Army, 1942–43. Married Gloria Bailey in 1938; three sons. Former director, CRASH Inc. (Community Resources and Self-Help). Recipient: George G. Stone Center for Children's Books award, 1967; Southern California Council on Literature for Children and Young People prize, 1980. *Died 17 December 1988.*

WESTERN PUBLICATIONS

Novels

Lost Stage Valley. New York, Simon and Schuster, 1948; Kingswood, Surrey, World's Work, 1950.
Bold Passage. New York, Simon and Schuster, 1950; London, Hodder and Stoughton, 1951.
Blood on the Land. New York, Ballantine, 1952; London, Muller, 1955.
Snaketrack. New York, Simon and Schuster, 1952; as *The Outcast of Crooked River*, London, Hodder and Stoughton, 1953.
Night Raid. New York, Ballantine, 1954.
The Feud at Spanish Ford. New York, Ballantine, 1954.
Rawhide Guns. New York, Popular Library, 1955; as *Border Guns*, London, Muller, 1956.
Defiance Mountain. New York, Popular Library, 1956; London, Consul, 1962.
Hardrock. New York, Ballantine, 1958; London, Muller, 1960.
Tough Country. New York, Dell, and London, Muller, 1958.
Last Stage West. New York, Dell, and London, Muller, 1959.
Sound of Gunfire. New York, Dell, 1959; London, Consul, 1960.
Trago . . . New York, Dell, 1962.
Cast a Long Shadow. New York, Simon and Schuster, 1964; Bath, Chivers, 1983.
Logan's Choice. New York, Fawcett, 1964.
Break for the Border. New York, Berkley, 1980.
Fort Hogan. New York, Berkley, 1980.
The Eye of the Hunter. New York, Evans, 1989.

Short Stories

The Wild Breed. New York, Lion, 1955.
The Best Western Stories of Frank Bonham, edited by Bill Pronzini. Athens, Swallow Press/Ohio University Press, 1989.

Uncollected Short Stories

"River Man," in *Argosy* (New York), 13 December 1941.
"Payoff Pardners," in *Wild West* (New York), 7 February 1942.
"Trial by Trigger," in *Wild West* (New York), 12 September 1942.
"Bonanza Claim in Hell," in *West* (Kingswood, Surrey), October 1943.
"Hell Along the Ox-Bow Route!," in *Dime Western* (New York), 1944.
"Hurry-Call for Hangin' Gus," in *Star Western* (Chicago), August 1944.
"The Gunsight Ghost Fills His Hand," in *Star Western* (Chicago), October 1944.
"Hangin' Hobbs' Hemp Stampede," in *Star Western* (Chicago), November 1944.
"The Secret of Seven Point Mesa," in *Star Western* (Chicago), December 1944.
"Hangin' Hobbs' Thirteenth Knot," in *Star Western* (Chicago), June 1945.
"Beyond the Bear Flag Mutineers," in *Star Western* (Chicago), August 1945.
"The Devil Votes with Lead," in *West* (Kingswood, Surrey), June 1947.
"Outlaws of Butcherknife Ridge," in *Five Novels* (New York), September–October 1947.
"The Devil's Bronc Stomper," in *Star Western* (Chicago), December 1947.
"Gun-Dog of Furnace Flat," in *New Western*, December 1948.
"The Yonder Hills," in *West* (Kingswood, Surrey), August 1949.
"The bloody Bozeman Trail," in *Dime Western* (New York), 1950.
"Rodeo Killers," in *All Western* (New York), December 1950–January 1951.
"Stagecoach West!" and "Dusty Wheels—Bloody Trail!," in *Spurs West!*, edited by Joseph T. Shaw. New York, Permabooks, 1951.
"The Sin of Wiley Brogan," in *West* (Kingswood, Surrey), November 1952.
"Trouble at Temescal," in *They Lived by Their Guns.* New York, New American Library, 1953.
"Under the Gun!," in *Western Story* (London), March 1953.
"Good Loggers Are Dead Loggers," in *Blazing Guns* (Holyoke, Massachusetts), October 1956.
"Loaded," in *Colt's Law*, edited by Luke Short. New York, Bantam, 1957.
"Sons of the Back-Shoot Border," in *Western Story* (London), April 1959.
"Good-By, Mimbres Kid," in *Westerns of the Forties*, edited by Damon Knight. Indianapolis, Bobbs Merrill, 1977.
"Chivaree," in *Wild Westerns: Stories from the Grand Old Pulps*, edited by Bill Pronzini and Martin H. Greenberg. New York, Dalker, 1986.
"The Seventh Desert," in *The Cattlemen*, edited by Bill Pronzini and Martin H. Greenberg. New York, Fawcett, 1986.
"Phinney's Coffin," in *New Frontiers Volume II*, edited by Martin H. Greenberg and Bill Pronzini. New York, Tor, 1990.
"The Bear Flag Mutineers," in *The Californians*, edited by Bill Pronzini and Martin H. Greenberg. New York, Fawcett, 1989.
"Plague Boat," in *More Wild Westerns*, edited by Pill Pronzini. New York, Walker, 1989.

OTHER PUBLICATIONS

Novels

One for Sleep. New York, Fawcett, 1960; London, Muller, 1961.

The Skin Game. New York, Fawcett, 1962; London, Muller, 1963.
By Her Own Hand. Derby, Connecticut, Monarch, 1963.

Fiction (for children)

Burma Rifles: A Story of Merrill's Marauders. New York, Crowell, 1960.
War Beneath the Sea. New York, Crowell, 1962.
Deepwater Challenge. New York, Crowell, 1963.
Honor Bound. New York, Crowell, 1963.
The Loud, Resounding Sea. New York, Crowell, 1963.
Speedway Contender. New York, Crowell, 1964.
Durango Street. New York, Dutton, 1965.
Mystery in Little Tokyo. New York, Dutton, 1966.
Mystery of the Red Tide. New York, Dutton, 1966.
The Ghost Front. New York, Dutton, 1968.
Mystery of the Fat Cat. New York, Dutton, 1968.
The Nitty Gritty. New York, Dutton, 1968.
The Vagabundos. New York, Dutton, 1969.
Viva Chicano. New York, Dutton, 1970.
Chief. New York, Dutton, 1971.
Cool Cat. New York, Dutton, 1971.
The Friends of the Loony Lake Monster. New York, Dutton, 1972.
Hey Big Spender! New York, Dutton, 1972.
A Dream of Ghosts. New York, Dutton, 1973.
The Golden Bees of Tulami. New York, Dutton, 1974.
The Missing Persons League. New York, Dutton, 1976.
The Rascals from Haskell's Gym. New York, Dutton, 1977.
Devilhorn. New York, Dutton, 1978.
The Forever Formula. New York, Dutton, 1979.
Gimme an H, Gimme and E, Gimme an L, Gimme a P. New York, Scribner, 1980.
Premonitions. New York, Holt Rinehart, 1984.

Plays

Television Series: *Wells Fargo*, *Restless Gun*, *Shotgun Slade*, and *Death Valley Days.*

*

Manuscript Collection: Kerlan Collection, University of Minnesota, Minneapolis.

* * *

Frank Bonham is perhaps better known as an author of novels for children, but his early work was in the field of western fiction. During the Depression, Bonham had been trying to write and sell mystery stories when he met veteran western pulp writer Ed Earl Repp. Repp persuaded him to ghost write western stories to be published under Repp's byline and they would split the royalties. This began in 1935 and went on for three years before Bonham declared his independence and made his own way in the pulps writing under his own name. His early models were Ernest Haycox and Luke Short, and not Repp, and one of his early pulp stories from 1944, "Good-By, Mimbres Kid," reprinted in *Westerns of the 40's*, edited by Damon Knight, clearly shows this two-fold indebtedness: its hero, Sam Landers, is introspective about his past (he killed several men while a lawman) as are so many of Haycox's pulp heroes, and the incidents of the plot have the precision and intensity of Luke Short in his best Westerns.

Lost Stage Valley was Bonham's first western novel, and it was turned into a rather dull and disappointing film, *Stage to Tucson*. It is a story which, in Bonham's words in his Foreword, "celebrates the courage and determination of the men who drove the stages, and the passengers who rode them." For all that, it is a formulary Western, with a readily identifiable hero, two heroines between whom the hero must choose (a plot ingredient formulary western writers adapted from its use by Sir Walter Scott), and a master villain whose actual identity remains a mystery until near the end. Bonham in all of the novels he wrote subsequently never attempted to write more than a formulary western. In *Lost Stage Valley* and even more so in a later novel such as *Last Stage West* which is concerned with the last overland stage journey before the outbreak of the Civil War, Bonham might have tried to give as vivid a portrait of stage travel as Mark Twain did in the opening chapters of *Roughing It* (1872); he did not.

Instead, he perfected a narrative structure for his formulae in which a new action episode is introduced every 800 to 1000 words. This structure, in Bonham's best novels, provides an almost breathless sense of pacing.

"I have tried to avoid," Bonham once remarked, "the conventional cowboy story, but I think it was probably a mistake. That is like trying to avoid crime in writing a mystery book. I just happened to be more interested in stagecoaching, mining, railroading, etc." Yet, his opinion notwithstanding, it is precisely the interesting—and, by comparison with the majority of formulary westerns, exotic—backgrounds to Bonham's novels which give them an added dimension. He was obviously knowledgeable in the technical aspects of transportation and communication in the 19th-century West which he introduced into his narratives, and this was combined with a firm grasp of idiomatic (as opposed to textbook) Spanish which many of his characters, being of Mexican origin, naturally tend to speak. Conversely, his view of Native Americans was strictly stereotypical; they are never really characterized; and this deficiency mars an otherwise gripping story such as *Bold Passage*.

Bonham's tendency toward a simplified narrative structure prohibited him, in a novel which deals with the rivalry between two competing stage lines, such as *Cast a Long Shadow*, from ever attaining the more satisfying complexity of incident, sense of community, and richness and characterization which, for example, Peter Dawson attained in treating this same theme in his novel, *The Stagline Feud* (1941). Yet Bonham was innovative in developing his heroes, who are often unconventional. Grif Holbrook in *Lost Stage Valley* is 49, an unusual age for a formulary hero, and Jim Harlan in *Rawhide Guns* is maltreated by one of the villains, hung up by his feet and suspended from a flagpole, and badly beaten at another point—something that would be unthinkable in one of Haycox's formulary efforts where the hero is always the master of the situation.

In 1960 Bonham turned to writing for children. However, in 1979, as part of an arrangement with Berkley Books, whereby all of his vintage western novels were to be systematically reissued, Bonham agreed to write two new Westerns. *Break for the Border*, the first of the two, is notable for its use of a feminist heroine, Lucha Murphy, who is a licensed attorney. The comment is made in an early novel such as *Bold Passage* that "dependency in a woman [is] a fine thing." The majority of Bonham's heroines may be stubborn or wrong-headed throughout his novels, but they finally acquiesce to the hero by the end in the typical ranch romance conclusion. It is not so in *Break for the Border*. True, Lucha is married to a weak and ineffectual man and hopelessly attracted to the hero, but she is still married at the end, and the story does not close with a romantic clinch. Also, unlike the earlier novels, the violence is muted and played down.

Bonham as an author of formulary Westerns never sustained the precision in plotting of which Luke Short or Peter Dawson was capable. Although most of the communities in his stories are imaginary, he could not bring them to life the way, creating such communities, Ernest Haycox could. In his tendency toward a simplified narrative structure and the constant pacing of dramatic event at regular intervals his fiction is reminiscent of that of Louis L'Amour, but here he proves superior; unlike L'Amour, Bonham never betrayed a sloppiness in composition, or a lack of continuity in character and situation. Indeed, these are his strongest qualities as an author of narrative and a reader's attention is seldom permitted to flag; and yet he achieves this end through a novelty of events which are always intimately related and integral to his well-paced, forward-moving, unified plot structures.

Prior to his death in 1988, Bonham returned for a last time to western fiction and in *The Eye of the Hunter* produced what may be his finest work. In terms of its basic structure, it is a ranch romance formulary Western, but in its protagonist, Henry Logan, a gunsmith from Kansas City and a veteran of the Spanish-American War who suffers from debilitating malarial attacks, Bonham provided one of his most interesting characters and one drawn with surprising depth. Gone was the action format he had learned from the pulps and, instead, through an adept use of delayed revelation a murderer is exposed and a hero, Henry's father, debunked, while Frances Parrish, a widow with whom Henry is in love and trained in medicine by her father who was a physician, remains one of Bonham's most engaging and intriguing female creations.

Shortly after his death, two collections of Bonham's earlier pulp fiction appeared, both gathered by Bill Pronzini. *The Best Western Stories of Frank Bonham* consists of 12 stories of varying length and a brief memoir by Bonham of his apprentice years with Ed Earl Repp. Not included is what may be Bonham's finest novelette, "Gun-Dog of Furnace Flat," which was published in the pulp *New Western* in December 1948. This story is set in Death Valley and in its attention to the details of mining is every bit as accurate to the period as the noteworthy historical research which obviously went into his final novel. The relationship between the protagonist and the 74-year-old prospector, Mysterious Smith, and the feisty heroine, Maggie Conway, are vividly brought to life. Especially notable among the *Best Western Stories* are "Trouble in Temescal," a novelette set in southern California after statehood and concerned with the struggle of the native Mexicans to hold their land; and "Chivaree" which involves the means by which Nettie Croft, a *mestiza*, half Cherokee, half Scottish, married to an Anglo-American, goes about winning social acceptance.

Bonham's first western novel, *Lost Stage Valley*, was an expansion of a novelette, "Hell Along the Oxbow Route!," which first appeared in *Dime Western* in 1944. His second novel, *Bold Passage*, was expanded from a pulp novelette featured in *Dime Western* in 1950 under the title "The Bloody Bozeman Trail." That pulp novelette was packaged together with "Stagecoach West!," another pulp novelette from *Dime Western* in 1950, in the second collection of Bonham's early fiction. The former is more desirable in its later expanded version (the pulp version was reprinted still missing a line dropped in the original). An Indian attack is used as a standard prop in it as is also the case in "Stagecoach West!," although the *mestiza* heroine in the former remains intact, indicating that in pulp fiction of that era it was possible to treat a woman of mixed blood sympathetically provided she behaved in every way just as a white person. "Stagecoach West!" is minor Bonham. Yet, the story proves interesting for its background of railroad building, stagelines, and continuous, ever suspenseful action and repays reading as do such hitherto uncollected novelettes as "The Magnificent Gringo" published in *Blue Book* in June 1945, "High Iron" in *Blue Book* in March 1946, "Wanted!" which appeared in *.44 Western* in March 1951, and "One Ride Too Many" collected in the Western Writers of American anthology, *Bad Men and Good*. These stories are strictly in the formulary vein but that was a market Bonham well understood and served more consistently and more adeptly than many of his contemporaries. Notwithstanding, to have tried something entirely different with a Western story, and to have done so well at it as he did in *The Eye of the Hunter*, is a significant literary accomplishment. It is sad that he did not live to complete the sequel he had planned and forge farther ahead in the new direction he had found.

—Jon Tuska

BONNER, Jack. *See* **PAINE, Lauran.**

BONNER, Michael. Pseudonym for Anne Glasscock, née Bonner. American. Born in Dallas, Texas, 19 February 1924. Educated at Stephens College, Columbia, Missouri, 1940–41; Texas Christian University, Fort Worth, 1943; University of Texas, Austin, B.A. 1944 (Phi Beta Kappa); University of Mexico, 1944. Married R. Kerns Glasscock in 1946; one daughter and one son.

WESTERN PUBLICATIONS

Novels (series: Roby MacLane)

Kennedy's Gold. New York, Doubleday, 1960; London, Collins, 1961.
The Iron Noose. (MacLane). New York, Doubleday, and London, Collins, 1961.
Shadow of a Hawk (MacLane). New York, Doubleday, 1963.
The Disturbing Death of Jenkin Delaney (MacLane). New York, Doubleday, 1966; Aylesbury, Buckinghamshire, Milton House, 1975.

* * *

Michael Bonner uses stereotyped characters, scenes, and plots: the able, sometimes violent hero, the domestic heroine, and the sheepish crowd; the duels, ambushes, and Indian attacks; and the maturation of the hero from his personal interest to a more altruistic and legal purpose. However, she treats the formula from an unusual perspective, breaking down illusions about heroic invulnerability. Her first novel tells of Jace Kennedy, who travels on a stagecoach through the desert to steal its gold. From the beginning, his plans go wrong: there are too many passengers, the one woman is too curious about him, and climactically, the coach is attacked by Apaches. Instead of robbing the passengers, Kennedy finds himself trapped in a burned-out stage station with them, pushed into command by his weaker companions. Time and again, they misread Kennedy's actions, not realizing that his courageous deeds are motivated by his overriding desire for the gold on top of the coach. When he finally volunteers to walk across the desert for help, his offer is the result of a secret bargain with the driver that he will be given the gold in return. He eventually reaches a town, after a nightmare journey impeded by Indian attacks, shortages of food and water, and near-fatal injuries. As he recovers, he finds that not only have the passengers escaped to town without any aid (the Indians having unaccountably vanished), but there never was any gold on the coach. Although the hero recognizes the absurdity of his experience, he also realizes that he has gained a new morality, having transcended self-interest in the final stages of his gruesome journey. Where he earlier protested, "I'm no hero," he now accepts the mantle of saga hero endowed on him by the townspeople.

Bonner's next books put less stress on the absurd, but they continue to feature the reluctant hero. She creates a series character, Roby MacLane, who has become a Texas Ranger because his ranch has failed, but would rather be fighting Mexicans and Indians than bringing law and order to frontier communities. In his pursuits of various villains, however, he comes to realize the importance of the law and the ambiguities of personal relationships: while admiring a Mexican rebel, he must arrest him for robbery, and when he finally marries, he knows this will bring no easy peace. These books are more serious, but they involve the same final twist to the plot and they expose similar problems inherent in the hero's role. Bonner's fiction is not radical enough to be classed with Fiedler's "anti-Westerns," but it does fit into the general critical approach to western stereotypes adopted by much 1960's fiction.

—Christine Bold

BONNER, Parker. *See* **BALLARD, Willis Todhunter.**

BONNEY, Bill. *See* **ALLISON, Clay.**

BOONE, Ike. *See* **ATHANAS, Verne.**

BOOTH, Edwin. Also writes as Don Blunt; Jack Hazard. American. Born in Beatrice, Nebraska. Educated at Colorado College, Colorado Springs. Married Irene Sullivan in 1933 (died 1980). Has worked as a post office clerk, guide, grocery store manager, and accountant. Secretary-treasurer, 1963–67, and vice-president, 1970, Western Writers of America. Agent: Paul R. Reynolds Inc., 12 East 41st Street, New York, New York 10017. Address: 5891 Morpeth Street, Oakland, California 94618, U.S.A.

WESTERN PUBLICATIONS

Novels

Showdown at Warbird. New York, Ace, 1957.
Jinx Rider. New York, Ace, 1957.
Boot Heel Range. New York, Avalon, 1958; London, Hale, 1966.
The Man Who Killed Tex. New York, Ace, 1958.
The Trail to Tomahawk. New York, Ace, 1958.
Wyoming Welcome. New York, Ace, 1959.
Danger Trail. New York, Avalon, 1959; as *Danger on the Trail*, London, Hale, 1960.
Lost Valley. New York, Avalon, 1960.
The Broken Window. New York, Arcadia House, 1960.
The Desperate Dude. New York, Ace, 1960; London, White Lion, 1976.
Return to Apache Springs. New York, Avalon, 1960.
Crooked Spur (as Jack Hazard). New York, Arcadia House, 1960.
Reluctant Lawman. New York, Ballantine, 1961.
Outlaw Town. New York, Ballantine, 1961.
The Troublemaker. New York, Ace, 1961.
Short Cut (as Don Blunt). New York, Avalon, 1962.
Sidewinder. New York, Ballantine, 1962.
Valley of Violence. New York, Avalon, 1962; London, Hale, 1966.
Hardcase Hotel. New York, Berkley, 1963.
Dead Giveaway (as Don Blunt). New York, Avalon, 1963.
Devil's Canyon. New York, Avalon, 1964.
The Dry Gulchers. New York, Avalon, 1964.
The Stolen Saddle. New York, Avalon, 1964.
Renegade Guns. New York, Avalon, 1965.
Trouble at Tragedy Springs. New York, Berkley, 1966.
Triple Cross Trail. New York, Berkley, 1967.
Shoot-Out at Twin Buttes. New York, Berkley, 1967.
No Spurs for Johnny Loop. New York, Berkley, 1967.
One Man Posse. New York, Berkley, 1967.
The Man from Dakota. New York, Berkley, 1968.
Stranger in Buffalo Springs. New York, Berkley, 1969.
The Backshooters. New York, Ballantine, 1969.
The Prodigal Gun. New York, Berkley, 1971.
Grudge Killer. New York, Ballantine, 1971.
Hardesty. New York, Ace, 1971.
Stage to San Felipe. New York, Berkley, 1972.
Bushwhack. New York, Ace, 1974.
Small Spread. New York, Ballantine, 1974.
The Colt-Packin' Parson. New York, Avalon, 1975.
Ambush at Adams Crossing. New York, Avalon, 1976.
Crossfire. New York, Ace, 1977.
The Colorado Gun. New York, Belmont, 1980.
Leadville. New York, Belmont, 1980.
Rebel's Return. New York, Belmont, 1980; Bath, Chivers, 1982.

Uncollected Short Stories

"Moonlight Showdown," in *Thrilling Western* (London), April 1954.
"The Guns of Sun Dog," in *Thrilling Western* (London), April 1958.
"Sixgun Showdown," in *Thrilling Western* (London), July 1958.
"The Kid Who Wasn't Wild Bill Hickok," in *Great Western Stories.* New York, Berkley, 1965.

OTHER PUBLICATIONS

Other

John Sutter, Californian. Indianapolis, Bobbs Merrill, 1963.

*

Manuscript Collection: University of Oregon, Eugene.

* * *

There are many western writers of the common man, the angry man, or the unjustly accused, but very few of the reasonable man. Edwin Booth falls into this last, uncommon category. To say that most western heroes seem to think faster with their guns or fists than with their heads is just to point out the obvious. In a typical Booth story, however, the hero tries to think things through before shooting off his mouth—or whatever else is handy.

The western genre is one of action, rough justice, and adventure, however, and so it would seem that creating a character of this sort would be a difficult assignment for any writer, even the most experienced. Reason confronted by the quick tempers and quicker fatality rates so common on western pages would lead a character to confusion, or worse, indecision, and one wonders how long Lord Hamlet would survive soliloquizing across the plains. This problem is most apparent in Booth's early stories. *Boot Heel Range*, a standard initiation story with the young hero Johnny Harper trying to prove he's a man while simultaneously heading off a range war, is unusual only in that Johnny is an early reasonable prototype. Unfortunately, much of the tale is spent in his confused head. A later novel, *Triple Cross Trail*, drops the reasonable motif altogether and opts for a story of revenge; it is straightforward, fast, but not very memorable.

It is in Booth's later writings, however, that he hits his stride. *No Spurs for Johnny Loop*, one of his best-realized works, is a fine example of this theme and style. There's something implicitly humorous about the west when viewed from a distance—something comic, in the literary sense, about a world where men are so ruled by braggadocio and bluster that they'll plug holes in each other just for something to do. It could also be viewed as brutally terrible, but in that case the main character will simply make tracks and leave the scene—in which case you've got no story at all. Johnny Loop, Booth's hero, embodies the first perspective: he's an easterner, very easygoing, given to hearing a man out or even "forgiving him his sins" before blowing off his head. He wears bib overalls and flat-soled shoes, trains horses through patience rather than bronco busting, shoots a single-shot squirrel rifle instead of the standard six-gun, often gets tongue-tied, and generally plays the greenhorn while soaking in the goings-on. Of course, he gets in trouble because of these differences. Johnny's main success, however is his attitude: we stay close to his point of view throughout, and everything from a slap in the face by a pretty girl to a slug in the shoulder by the villain is interpreted through his lightly ironic eye. It is this humor which makes Booth's later writings and characters as human, memorable, and enjoyable as they are.

—Joe Jackson

BORG, Jack (Philip Antony John Borg). Also writes as Phil Bexar; John Q. Pickard.

WESTERN PUBLICATIONS

Novels (series: Hogleg Bailey)

Sheriff of Clinton. London, Jenkins, 1954.
Hellbent Trail. London, Jenkins, 1954.
Big Cherokee. London, Jenkins, 1955.
The Cannon Kid. London, Jenkins, 1955.
Bushwhack Canyon. London, Jenkins, 1956.
Sheriff's Deputy. London, Jenkins, 1956.
Bronco Justice. London, Jenkins, 1957.
Gunsmoke Feud (Bailey). London, Jenkins, 1957.
Kansas Trail (Bailey). London, Jenkins, 1958.
Rawhide Tenderfoot. London, Jenkins, 1958.
Badlands Fury (Bailey). London, Jenkins, 1959.
Rustlers' Range (Bailey). London, Jenkins, 1959.
Range Wolves (Bailey). London, Jenkins, 1960.
Saddle Tramp (Bailey). London, Jenkins, 1960.
Horsethieves Hang High (Bailey). London, Jenkins, 1961.
Kid with a Colt (Bailey). London, Jenkins, 1961.
Guns of the Lawless (Bailey). London, Jenkins, 1962.
Cast a Wide Loop (Bailey). London, Jenkins, 1963.
Texas Wolves (Bailey). London, Jenkins, 1963.
Gun Feud at Sun Creek (Bailey). London, Jenkins, 1964.
Rope for a Rustler (Bailey). London, Jenkins, 1965.
Stagecoach to Concho. London, Jenkins, 1966.
Dry Valley War. London, Jenkins, 1968.
The Owlhooter. London, Jenkins, 1968.
The Long-Ropers. London, Jenkins, 1969.
Tumbleweed Man. London, Hale, 1972.
The Man from San Antonio. London, Hale, 1972.
Badman's Shadow. London, Hale, 1972.
Badman Headed North. London, Hale, 1974.
The Calico Kid. London, Hale, 1974.
Showdown at Sweet Springs. London, Jenkins, 1975.
Trail of Dead Men. London, Jenkins, 1975.

Novels as Phil Bexar

Law of the Six-Gun. London, Jenkins, 1957.
Storm in the Saddle. London, Jenkins, 1957.
Guns over Texas. London, Jenkins, 1958.
Showdown in Gunsmoke. London, Jenkins, 1958.
Outlaw Marshal. London, Jenkins, 1959.
Six-Gun Fury. London, Jenkins, 1959.
The Lone Prairie. London, Jenkins, 1960.
Trail to Slaughter Creek. London, Jenkins, 1961.
Cowtown Fury. London, Jenkins, 1961.
Cowtown Marshal. London, Jenkins, 1962.
Texas Terror. London, Jenkins, 1962.
Maverick Gunfighter. London, Jenkins, 1963.
Rustler Guns. London, Jenkins, 1964.
The Banks of the Sacramento. London, Jenkins, 1968.
Hardcase Prodigal. London, Jenkins, 1969.

Novels as John Q. Pickard

Trail of Fury. London, Ward Lock, 1962.
Medicine Pony. London, Ward Lock, 1962.
Sixgun for Sale. London, Ward Lock, 1963.
Gone to Texas. London, Ward Lock, 1963; New York, Arcadia House, 1965.
Cactus Maverick. London, Ward Lock, 1964.
Black Hawk. London, Ward Lock, 1964.

Whistling Bone Creek. London, Ward Lock, 1965.
The Gringo. London, Ward Lock, 1965.
Pistol Wages. London, Ward Lock, 1966.
Richer Than Tombstone. London, Ward Lock, 1966.
Blood Creek. London, Ward Lock, 1967.
The Horsethieves. London, Ward Lock, 1967.
Buzzard Bait. London, Ward Lock, 1968.
Comanche Crossing. London, Ward Lock, 1968.

OTHER PUBLICATIONS

Other (for children)

The Cherokee Trail. London, Collins, 1958.
The Trail Drivers. London, Collins, 1963.

* * *

Jack Borg is a consummate stylist, whose skill is evident from the initial stages of his career. Most of the characteristics of his writing are found in the early *Hellbent Trail*, where an outlaw on the run redeems himself by thwarting the efforts of a gang of killers to take over a town. Though longer and more descriptive than later works, *Hellbent Trail* moves at a compelling pace, and its tearaway hero and tomboy heroine are familiar Borg characters. The main difference lies in the book's seriousness. One of Borg's most endearing qualities is the dry humour that pervades his fiction, and this quality grows stronger in the novels of his maturity.

Most memorable of Borg's creations is the range detective Charles Proudfoot "Hogleg" Bailey, who for almost 20 years stars as the central figure of a succession of his western novels. Unctuous and soft-spoken in his black preacher's garb, outwardly smooth while packing a .36 Navy Colt in a shoulder holster under his coat, the bearded Bailey is in fact a ruthless gunfighter famed for his speed and skill. Borg manages to invest him with the character of a lovable hypocrite, while at the same time indicating a Satanic streak which emerges when guns are drawn. Though his continual quoting of texts is overdone at times, the general air of sly humour sees him through. His personality transforms the lively action of the novels, most of which conform to a basic pattern, where Bailey not only brings rough justice to the wrongdoers, but usually comes to the aid of a good-natured youngster who finds himself outside the law, and effects a happy ending for him. This is true of *Gunsmoke Feud*, where Bailey sides with the Socorro Kid against outlaws and Apache Indians in a squabble over water rights, and sees him win the heroine in the end. *Saddle Tramp* has a similar theme, Bailey clearing another young man of unjust accusations while the two of them prevent the takeover of a ranch by the Shansey brothers and the land shark Loman. Though the themes are constant, Borg's plots are varied and ingenious. *Horsethieves Hang High* has Bailey investigating the theft of a stud horse, which turns out to be part of an insurance swindle, and *The Man from San Antonio* centres on a gold-smuggling operation over the Texas-Mexican border. In common with all Borg's fiction, the Hogleg Bailey books are marked by dry caustic dialogue and fast gunplay, culminating in glorious last-stand shootouts in the final pages. Borg's fertile imagination crams his works with minor characters, many of whom are blasted down a few pages after their appearance. He is also adept in his creation of grotesques among the villains—Shad Crego, the dissolute sheriff in *Gunsmoke Feud*, is a superb example. Later, he displays a penchant for seedy storekeepers who emerge as the "brains" of the gang—Miles Croome of *Horsethieves Hang High* being one of many. The Bailey novels contain some of Borg's best work, and are a fitting celebration of the genre.

Aside from the Hogleg Bailey books, Borg has written a number of effective stories. *Badman's Shadow* follows the adventures of Thady Corey, reformed gunman, on a trail drive and later in his fight to protect the heroine against rustlers. *The Long-Ropers* has Kane, an ex-convict, bringing a crooked rancher to justice. Among the best books Borg ever did are *Tumbleweed Man* and *Trail of Dead Men*. Fast-paced humorous narratives related in the first person, they have a tough wise-cracking style which lopes through the action with unfaltering ease. The grotesque are deftly drawn, the humour salty and strong, the reader flung in and dragged headlong through the book at a galloping pace. Together with the best Bailey stories, they form a fitting monument to Borg's art.

—Jeff Sadler

BORLAND, Hal (Harold Glen Borland). Also writes as Ward West. American. Born in Sterling, Nebraska, 14 May 1900. Educated at the University of Colorado, Boulder, 1918–20; Columbia University, New York, B. Litt. 1923. Served in the United States Naval Reserve Force, 1918. Married Barbara Ross Dodge in 1945; one stepdaughter and one living son from first marriage. Journalist: reporter, Denver *Post*, 1918; editor, *Flagler News*, 1920–21; worked for King Features and United Press, and for papers in Brooklyn, Salt Lake City, Carson City, Nevada, Fresno, California, San Diego, Marshall, Texas, and Asheville, North Carolina, 1920–24; publicity writer, Ivy Lee, 1925; publicist, Stratton *Press*, Colorado, 1925–26; staff member of Curtis Newspapers, 1926–37: assistant night editor, Philadelphia *Morning Sun*, 1927–28, editorial writer, Philadelphia *Morning Ledger*, 1929–33, and literary editor of morning and evening *Ledger*, 1934–37; staff writer, *New York Times Magazine*, 1937–43. Since 1943 freelance writer: columnist since 1942 for *New York Times*, since 1957 for *Progressive*, and since 1958 for *Berkshire Eagle*, Pittsfield, Massachusetts; contributing editor, *Audubon* magazine, 1967–78. Director of non-fiction section, Rocky Mountain Writers' Conference, University of Colorado, 1955; member of board of supervisors, Bartholomews Cobble Nature Reserve, Ashley Falls, Massachusetts, 1963–78; member, Governor's Commission on Conservation Policy for Connecticut, 1970–71; chair, Berkshire-Litchfield Conversation Council, 1970–78. Recipient: Columbia Univesity School of Journalism award, 1962; John Burroughs Medal, 1968. Litt.D.: University of Colorado, 1944. Address: R.F.D. 1, Salisbury, Connecticut 06068, U.S.A.

WESTERN PUBLICATIONS

Novels

The Amulet. Philadelphia, Lippincott, 1957; London, Heinemann, 1958.
The Seventh Winter. Philadelphia, Lippincott, 1960.
When the Legends Die. Philadelphia, Lippincott, 1963; London, Secker and Warburg, 1964.

Novels as Ward West

Trouble Valley. New York, Greenberg, 1934.
Halfway to Timberline. New York, Greenberg, 1935.
Rustler's Trail. London, Swan, 1948.

Uncollected Short Stories

"Dode," in *Adventure* (New York), 10 December 1925.
"Marguerita," in *Romance* (New York), February 1929.

OTHER PUBLICATIONS

Play

What Is America?, with Philip Dunning. New York, French, 1942.

Verse

Heaps of Gold. Privately printed, 1922.
America Is Americans. London, Harper, 1942.

Other

Rocky Mountain Tipi Tales. New York, Doubleday, and London, Heinemann, 1924.
Valor (for children). New York, Farrar and Rinehart, 1934.
Wapiti Pete (for children). New York, Farrar and Rinehart, 1938; revised edition, as *King of Squaw Mountain*, Philadelphia, Lippincott, 1964.
An American Year: Country Life and Landscapes Through the Seasons. New York, Simon and Schuster, 1946.
How to Write and Sell Non-Fiction. New York, Ronald Press, 1956.
High, Wide, and Lonesome. Philadelphia, Lippincott, 1956.
This Hill, This Valley. New York, Simon and Schuster, 1957.
The Enduring Pattern. New York, Simon and Schuster, 1959.
The Dog Who Came to Stay. Philadelphia, Lippincott, 1961; London, Harrap, 1962.
Beyond Your Doorstep: A Handbook to the Country. New York, Knopf, 1962.
The Youngest Shepherd: A Tale of the Nativity (for children). Philadelphia, Lippincott, 1962.
Sundial of the Seasons: A Selection of Outdoor Editorials from the New York Times. Philadelphia, Lippincott, 1964.
Countryman: A Summary of Belief. Philadelphia, Lippincott, 1965.
Hill Country Harvest. Philadelphia, Lippincott, 1967.
Homeland: A Report from the Country. Philadelphia, Lippincott, 1969.
Plants of Christmas (for children). New York, Golden Press, 1969.
Country Editor's Boy. Philadelphia, Lippincott, 1970.
Borland Country. Philadelphia, Lippincott, 1971.
Penny: The Story of a Free-Soul Basset Hound. Philadelphia, Lippincott, 1972.
Seasons. Philadelphia, Lippincott, 1973.
This World of Wonder (for children). Philadelphia, Lippincott, 1973.
The History of Wildlife in America. Washington, D.C., National Wildlife Federation, 1975.
Hal Borland's Book of Days. New York, Knopf, 1976.
A Place to Begin: The New England Experience. San Francisco, Sierra Club, 1976.
The Golden Circle: A Book of Months (for children). New York, Crowell, 1977.
Hal Borland's Twelve Moons of the Year, edited by Barbara Dodge Borland. New York, Knopf, 1979.
A Countryman's Flowers. New York, Knopf, 1981.
A Countryman's Woods. New York, Knopf, 1983.

Editor, *Our Natural World: The Land and Wildlife of America as Seen and Described by Writers since the Country's Discovery*. New York, Doubleday, 1965.

* * *

The western fiction of Hal Borland is of a piece with the non-fiction writer who often and caringly spoke of experiences with land, country, and changing seasons. For Borland, what really counted in the scale of human affairs was the arrival of the vernal equinox, the blossoming of fruit trees, or one's personal, felt relationship with a particular piece of landscape. His fiction, behind plot and within characterization, often subtly rather than overtly, also upholds the value of natural relationships and continuities. Two of the Westerns that Borland wrote under the name of Ward West in the 1930's (*Trouble Valley* and *Halfway to Timberline*) reflect this value, and his two novels of the late 1950's (*The Amulet* and *The Seventh Winter*) treat it as an explicit theme.

But it is *When the Legends Die* that rightfully represents the Borland's culmination as a western writer. Based in part on his own childhood contact with the southern Colorado Indians, whose lore he presented in his first book, *Rocky Mountain Tipi Tales, When the Legends Die* is a kind of Native American *Bildungsroman*. The pattern of the novel, like most serious novels about American Indians, is alienation and return. Forced to learn "civilized" ways, Tom Black Bull develops a fierce hatred for his own past which he tries to destroy in a violent, punishing career as a rodeo rider: "He was riding a hurt and a hate, deep inside." Borland's hero is brought almost mystically back to traditional ways when he returns, at the end of the novel, to the land of his boyhood. In the final pages "the vengeful demon who rode horses to death" is itself dead and Tom Black Bull, aided by powers of tradition and nature, finds "the truth of his own being."

When the Legends Die lacks the anthropological authenticity of Frank Waters (especially in *The Man Who Killed the Deer*) or Oliver LaFarge (in the much earlier *Laughing Boy*) and the refined artistry of Leslie Silko (in *Ceremony*). In places, as elsewhere in Borland's fiction, there are insufficient safeguards against sentimentality; this is especially true of the unabashed evocation of the Noble Savage concept in Borland's depiction of Tom Black Bull's early life as Bear's Brother. Yet *When the Legends Die* is a deservedly best-selling novel and a good statement about American Indian experience. And like the rest of Borland's writing, it is an imaginative and skillful working out of one man's strong conviction of how life ought to be lived—simply and in touch with what Borland refers to as "the enduring roundness."

—William Bloodworth

BOSWORTH, Allan R(ucker). Also wrote as Alamo Boyd. American. Born in San Angelo, Texas, 29 October 1901. Educated at schools in Ozona, Texas. Married to Charlotte H. Bosworth. Apprentice seaman in the United States Navy,

1922–25; commissioned Ensign in Naval Reserve, 1927; on active duty, 1940–45; recalled, 1948–60: retired as Captain, 1960. Reporter, San Diego *Sun*, 1925–26, and San Diego *Union*, 1926–28; copyreader, Los Angeles *Examiner*, 1928–30; copyreader news editor and managing editors San Francisco *Chronicle*, 1930–36; picture editor, San Francisco *Examiner*, 1937. Worked for United States Naval Intelligence, 1938–39(?). *Died 18 July 1986.*

Western Publications

Novels

Wherever the Grass Grows. New York, Doubleday, 1941; London, Cassell, 1942.
Steel to the Sunset (as Alamo Boyd). New York, Arcadia House, 1941.
Hang and Rattle. New York, Doubleday, 1947; London, Wright and Brown, 1951.
Border Roundup. New York, Bantam, 1947.
Double Deal. New York, Bantam, 1947.
Bury Me Not. New York, Doubleday, 1948; London, Wright and Brown, 1950.
Only the Brave. New York, Popular Library, 1955.
The Drifters. New York, Popular Library, 1956.
The Crows of Edwina Hill. New York, Harper, 1961.

Uncollected Short Stories

"Longhorn," in *North-West Stories* (London), Late December 1927.
"Kidnapping Cupid," in *Western Romances* (New York), December 1930.
"Never Ride a Gift Horse," in *All Western* (New York), June 1933.
"Beartooth Billings," in *All Western* (New York), September 1934.
"The Men Prefer Pants," in *Cowboy Stories* (New York), January 1935.
"Hosses Can't Read," in *Cowboy Stories* (New York), March 1935.
"—And Iron Men," in *Saturday Evening Post* (Philadelphia), 14 October 1939.
"Pull Leather—or Die!," in *Texas Rangers* (London), March 1941.
"Never Sell Your Saddle," in *Western Story* (London), April 1941.
"There Were Bluebonnets Then," in *Ladies' Home Journal* (Philadelphia), May 1942.
"The Girl They Left Behind," in *Ladies' Home Journal* (Philadelphia), June 1944.
"Equitime Point," in *Saturday Evening Post* (Philadelphia), 22 July 1944.
"Old School Tie," in *Saturday Evening Post* (Philadelphia), 10 February 1945.
"Breath of the Devil," in *Saturday Evening Post* (Philadelphia), 12 May 1945.
"Situation Tarfu," in *Saturday Evening Post* (Philadelphia), 9 March 1946.
"Blue Norther," in *Western Triggers*, edited by Arnold Hano. New York, Bantam, 1948.
"And When I find It," in *Thrilling Ranch Stories* (London), February 1948.
"Peaceful Settlement," in *Western Stories* (London), July 1948.
"Texas Man," in *Western Stories* (London), September 1948.
"Christmas Racket," with Jim Bosworth, in *Saturday Evening Post* (Philadelphia), 10 December 1949.
"Impossible Bet," in *Saturday Evening Post* (Philadelphia), 19 May 1951.
"Watch My Smoke," in *American* (Springfield, Ohio), August 1951.
"A Name for the Town," in *Zane Grey's Western 24* (London), 1953.
"Powder, Shot, and Texas Cattle," in *They Lived by Their Guns.* New York, New American Library, 1953.
"Stampede!," in *Frontier*, edited by Luke Short. New York, Bantam, 1955; as "A Rose for Dan Robie," in *Rawhide Man*, edited by Kenneth Fowler, New York, Doubleday, 1965.
"The Windmill Man," in *They Opened the West*, edited by Tom W. Blackburn. New York, Doubleday, 1967.

Other Publications

Novels

Full Crash Dive. New York, Duell, 1942; as *Murder Goes to Sea*, London, Lane, 1948; as *The Submarine Signalled—Murder!*, New York, Select, n.d.
Storm Tide. New York, Harper, 1965.

Other

A Cabin in the Hills. New York, Doubleday, 1947; London, Hammond, 1950.
Sancho of the Long, Long Horns (for children). New York, Doubleday, 1947.
Ladd of the Lone Star (for children). New York, Aladdin, 1952.
Ginza Go, Papa-san. Rutland, Vermont, Tuttle, 1955.
The Lovely World of Richi-san. New York, Harper, and London, Gollancz, 1960.
New Country. New York, Harper, 1962.
Ozona Country. New York, Harper, 1964.
America's Concentration Camps. New York, Norton, 1967.
My Love Affair with the Navy. New York, Norton, 1969.

* * *

Allan R. Bosworth combined his west Texas raising and his naval career to produce some 500 short stories for the pulp magazines and many others for the slick ones, partly sea stories and partly Westerns. Early in his career, he writes (in *Atlantic Monthly*, July 1961), he discovered the "All-purpose Little Jim Dandy opening" to "hook" the editor (and then the reader)—a trick that was "like taking candy from a baby." Such a trick, if it be one, he used in at least two stories in *The Saturday Evening Post:* "Nobody ever found out how Ma Collins managed to locate the camp that night before we threw the herd out on the trail." Thus he began "Stampede!" (reprinted in *Rawhide Men* as "A Rose for Dan Robie"), and anyone who reads Westerns immediately wonders about a lady on a cattle drive (although there were a few women who actually did accompany husbands on the trail). Again, in the six-part novelette "Wherever the Grass Grows" (published, in greatly enlarged form as a novel), he clearly sets the stage: "The little Gulf steamer docked at Indianola with the dawn tide. Ruck [short for Rucker, Bosworth's middle name] Hannan [Hanna in the novel] was all impatience to touch Texas soil again, although he knew there was some risk of putting his neck in a noose . . . " In one of his novels, *Sancho of the Long, Long Horns*, Bosworth takes only a few more words to accomplish his purpose: "That year the spring came early; working its magic along the Alamogordo, awakening a restlessness in all living things. The gnarled mesquites stirred even before rain broke a two-year dry spell, calling upon long-stored moisture from their roots to nourish new, bright-green leaves. Big Dipper cattle left the shelter of box canyons and southern slopes and ranged far across level divide and twisting draw. And the boy Chapo, moved by something more than the season now that he was thirteen, woke at night to listen to the shrill, windy clamor of wild geese against the stars."

Granted that the event of one trail drive north from Texas can be expected to resemble generally those of another one, Bosworth sometimes used plot details quite similar to each other: witness the death of the young Negro cowboy, Dan Robie, who was dragged under by a huge cottonwood tree drifting down the Red River, in "Stampede!" The same detail was used in *Sancho* when Chapo was nearly killed by a huge floating dead tree on the Arkansas River. Another recurring element—one that recalls Elmer Kelton, another writer from the same area of west Texas—involves the historical rivalry between Mexican and Texan.

Like Kelton, generally Bosworth presents the Mexican (and the fair-minded Texan who treats him honorably) as possessing the positive virtues of loyalty, determination, honesty, and the like; but he does not sweepingly generalize: in *Whenever the Grass Grows* the "good guy" has for friends a Mexican family whose kinsman across the Rio Grande is the scourge of border cattlemen, a cold-blooded killer. In *Sancho* Chapo Carroll's best friend—perhaps even *girl* friend when they grow up—is a little Mexican girl, Tomasina. One must note, however, that Ruck Hannan's Mexican girl friend returns to Mexico because of the harassment of her people, leaving the way clear for Ruck to marry a nice Anglo girl. One feels that, given time, the decent folk on both sides will rise above the rivalry—at least in the Bosworth West!

The student of Bosworth's western fiction must feel frustrated indeed over his admission in the *Atlantic Monthly* article that he wrote many stories "under pen names which were owned by Street & Smith: Philip F. Deere, Dean McKinley, Nels Anderson, and Cleve Endicott. I did a series on Judge Roy Bean, Law West of the Pecos, under the Dean McKinley by-line and a series on two cowboys comics named Bugeye and Jeff under the nom de plume of Frank J. Litchfield. I collaborated with myself to produce Circle J. Ranch novelettes under the joint by-line of Cleve Endicott and Dean McKinley; I was both." The task of bringing these materials together for scrutiny borders on the impossible, but doubtless such a project would raise his stature even further as an outstanding, knowledgeable writer of western fiction.

—John O. West

BOSWORTH, Frank. *See* **PAINE, Lauran.**

BOUMA, J(ohanas) L. Also wrote as Steve Shannon. American. Born in Amsterdam, Holland; lived in United States from age of nine. Served in the United States Air Force during World War II; Italian Theater, bomber pilot, 1943. *Died c. 1978.*

WESTERN PUBLICATIONS

Novels

Danger Trail. New York, Popular Library, 1954.
Texas Spurs. New York, Popular Library, 1955; London, Hale, 1982.
Border Vengeance. New York, Popular Library, 1956; Leicester, Linford, 1986.
The Hell-Fire Kid (as Steve Shannon). New York, Fawcett, 1957.
Burning Valley. New York, Popular Library, 1957.
The Avenging Gun. New York, Popular Library, 1958.
Outlaw Frenzy. New York, Hearst, 1967.
Bitter Guns. New York, Dell, 1972.
Slaughter at Crucifix Canyon. Canoga Park, California, Major, 1975; London, Hale, 1981.
Vengeance. New York, Nordon, 1976.
Six-Gun Mule-Skinner. Canoga Park, California, Major, 1976.
Ride to Violence. New York, Nordon, 1978.
Longrider. New York, Nordon, 1978.
Beyond Vengeance. New York, Nordon, 1979.
Hell on Horseback. New York, Dorchester, 1981.

Uncollected Short Stories

"Guns of the Death Raiders," in *Texas Rangers* (London), June 1951.
"Blood of a Badman," in *Best Western*, September 1951.
"Cowman Come Home," in *Zane Grey's Western* (New York), November 1952.
"A Choice to Make," in *Zane Grey's Western 24* (London), 1953.
"Like Son," in *Zane Grey's Western 32* (London), 1953.
"Night in Town," in *Zane Grey's Western* (New York), October 1953.
"Queen for a Maverick," in *Western Story* (London), December 1953.
"Gun Harvest," in *Western Story* (London), May 1954.
"Back Trail to Hell," in *Western Story* (London), January 1955.
"Sudden Six Man," in *Western Story* (London), February 1955.
"Creed of the Ruthless," in *Western Story* (London), May 1955.
"The Raiders," in *Texas Rangers* (London), May 1955.
"Death Deals This Hand," in *Western Story* (London), June 1955.
"Homesteader's Girl," in *Ranch Romances*, September 1955.
"Killer Posse," in *Western* (New York), September 1955.
"Meet Me in Boothill," in *Western* (New York), December 1955.
"Cornered in Hell!," in *Western Story* (London), February 1956.
"Whiskey, Women, and Fighting," in *Best Western*, March 1956.
"The Ruthless One," in *Western* (New York), March 1956.
"Day of Reckoning," in *Texas Rangers* (London), April 1956.
"Lone-Hand Posse," in *Texas Rangers* (London), November 1956.
"Gambler's Gal," in *Western Story* (London), November 1956.
"Return to Carthage," in *Thrilling Western* (London), February 1957.
"Last Waltz with Lefty," in *Western Story* (London), March 1957.
"This Land Called Home," in *Thrilling Western* (London), April 1957.
"Woman on Her Own," in *Thrilling Western* (London), August 1957.

"The Avenging Gun," in *Thrilling Western* (London), September 1957.
"The Stranger," in *Thrilling Western* (London), October 1957.
"Emigrant's Girl," in *Thrilling Western* (London), November 1957.
"The Drifters," in *Thrilling Western* (London), March 1958.

OTHER PUBLICATIONS

Novel

Mediterranean Caper. New York, Nordon, 1981.

* * *

Like so many other writers of popular westerns, J.L. Bouma began his career in the pulp magazines. In the 1940's and 1950's dozens of his stories appeared in such leading Western pulps as *Dime Western*, *Ranch Romances*, and the digest-sized *Zane Grey's Western Magazine*. He also published air-war adventures in *Sky Fighters* and other aviation pulps, and numerous mystery and detective stories.

All of Bouma's early novels are expansions of pulp novelettes and novellas. The best of them is probably *Danger Trail*, a variation on the classic theme of a small rancher fighting back against the ruthless cattle baron who is trying to steal his land. Bouma's later novels are also formulary Westerns; with one exception, they are not as well-crafted as the early books. The exception is *Bitter Guns*, a tense story of a prodigal who returns home to find one of his brothers dead and the other a captive of an outlaw gang, and who, in the words of the back cover blurb, "show(s) the old man he was grown up with the only proof his father would recognize—a pair of blazing guns. . ."

At his best, Bouma wrote smooth, fast-paced "horse operas." If his plots are pure formula, he made up for it with crisp action scenes, good characterization (especially of women), and—unlike many western writers of his day—a sure hand with multiple viewpoints.

—Bill Pronzini

BOWDEN, Jim. Pseudonym for William John Duncan Spence; also writes as Hannah Cooper; Kirk Ford; Floyd Rogers; Bill Spence. British. Born in Middlesbrough, Yorkshire, 20 April 1923. Educated at St. Mary's College, Middlesbrough, 1934–40; St. Mary's College, Strawberry Hill, Middlesex, 1940–42, teacher's certificate 1942. Served in the Royal Air Force Bomber Command, 1942–46. Married Joan Mary Rhoda Ludley in 1944; three daughters and one son. School teacher, Middlesbrough, 1942; stores manager, Ampleforth College, York, 1946–76; then full-time writer. Agent: Laurence Pollinger Ltd., 18 Maddox Street, London W1R OEU. Address: Post Office, Ampleforth College, York YO6 4EZ, England.

WESTERN PUBLICATIONS

Novels (series: Dan McCoy; Cap Millett; Lomax Brothers)

The Return of the Sheriff (McCoy). London, Hale, 1960.
Wayman's Ford (McCoy). London, Hale, 1960.
Two Gun Justice (McCoy). London, Hale, 1961.
Roaring Valley (McCoy). London, Hale, 1962.
Revenge in Red Springs (McCoy). London, Hale, 1962.
Black Water Canyon (McCoy). London, Hale, 1963.
Arizona Gold. London, Hale, 1963.
Trail of Revenge (McCoy). London, Hale, 1964.
Brazo Feud (McCoy). London, Hale, 1965.
Guns Along the Brazo (McCoy). London, Hale, 1967.
Gun Loose (McCoy). London, Hale, 1969.
Valley of Revenge. London, Hale, 1971.
Trail to Texas. London, Hale, 1973.
Thunder in Montana. London, Hale, 1973.
Showdown in Salt Fork. London, Hale, 1975.
Hired Gun. London, Hale, 1976.
Incident at Bison Creek. London, Hale, 1977.
Cap (Cap Millet). London, Hale, 1978.
Dollars of Death (Cap Millett). London, Hale, 1979.
Renegade Riders (Lomax). London, Hale, 1980.
Gunfight at Elm Creek (Lomax). London, Hale, 1980.
The Shadow of Eagle Rock (Cap Millett). London, Hale, 1982.
Pecos Trail. London, Hale, 1983.
Incident at Elm Creek (Cap Millett). London, Hale, 1984.
Hangmen's Trail (Cap Millett). London, Hale, 1986.
Return of the Gunmen. London, Hale, 1988.

Novels as Floyd Rogers

The Man from Cheyenne Wells. London, Hale, 1964.
Revenge Rider. London, Hale, 1964.
The Stage Riders. London, Hale, 1967.
Montana Justice. London, Hale, 1973.
Hangman's Gulch. London, Hale, 1974.
Incident at Elk River. London, Hale, 1979.

Novels as Kirk Ford

Trail to Sedalia. London, Hale, 1967.
Feud Riders. London, Hale, 1974.

OTHER PUBLICATIONS

Novels

Dark Hell (as Duncan Spence). London, Brown Watson, 1959.
Bomber's Moon (as Bill Spence). London, Hale, 1981.
Time Will Not Wait (as Hannah Cooper). London, Hale, 1983.

Other as Bill Spence

Romantic Ryedale, with Joan Spence. York, Ambo, 1977; revised edition, York, Ambo, 1987.
Harpooned: The Story of Whaling. London, Conway Maritime Press, and Los Angeles, Crescent, 1980.
The Medieval Monasteries of Yorkshire, with Joan Spence. York, Ambo, 1981.
Handy Facts: North Yorkshire, with Joan Spence. York, Ambo, 1983.

* * *

Jim Bowden writes in a very modern idiom of the western genre. His novels are set vaguely in the American southwest.

In *Cap* Bowden uses a cattle drive on the Chisholm Trail to Kansas as the setting. There is, however, little attempt to go beyond the western conventions and provide a truly historical setting. In the absence of much history and much identifiable geography, Bowden does create a fictional region of his own, and towns such as Bisbon Creek and Elm Creek and the Hash Knife Ranch reappear in several of his books. There is, however, little linking up of the books or suggestion that a series is being created. The major figure of Cap Millett does, for instance, appear in *Dollars of Death* as well as *Cap*. Other characters reappear but each book owes little to another.

The central characters are either law-abiding figures such as Cap or Sheriff Dan McCoy in *The Return of the Sheriff*, or criminals such as Jim and Gil in *Trail to Texas*. An important theme is the way that good characters suffer injustice and how they attempt to have it righted. The ranch owner Frank McCoy in *Black Water Canyon* has to clear himself on a charge of rustling. The Sheriff of Red Springs in *Guns Along the Brazo* has to protect a suspect from mob violence, and in *Gunfight at Elm Creek* the Deputy who has served a jail sentence has a very difficult time establishing his credibility with the townsfolk.

Some characters are quite interesting, for instance the two brothers in *Trail to Texas* where one is contrasted with the other. The brother who becomes a professional bounty hunter deteriorates very rapidly once he gets the taste for killing. The handling of this character by the author is not, however, as good as it could be given the potential interest this profession has for the western reader. The twists of fate are slightly improbable and brother ends up shooting brother. Most of the narration is taken up with action and the high point is gunplay. Plots in Bowden's novels start well, in fact, but very unexpected overcontrived endings tend to spoil them. Bowden is good at describing mannerisms of strong characters but there are not enough women in his books, especially the strong decent women often found in Westerns.

While staying within the conventions of the western genre, Bowden does economise by leaving out many of the stock types traditionally found in the genre. He does, however, make up for this by adding some modern touches such as violent sex and the presence of a negro. The sparseness of the background detail serves to point up the emotions felt in the characters and the effect of action, sometimes resulting in a rather "cardboard" effect.

—P.R. Meldrum

BOWER, B(ertha, née) M(uzzy). American. Born in Cleveland, Minnesota, 15 November 1871. Educated at public schools, and by private teachers in Montana. Married 1) Clayton J. Bower in 1890, one daughter and two sons; 2) Bertrand W. Sinclair in 1906, one daughter; 3) Robert Ellsworth Cowan. *Died 23 July 1940.*

WESTERN PUBLICATIONS

Novels (series: Flying U)

Chip, Of the Flying U. New York, Dillingham, 1906; London, Nelson, 1920.
Her Prairie Knight, and Rowdy of the "Cross L." New York, Dillingham, 1907; London, Nelson, 1921.
The Lure of the Dim Trails. New York, Dillingham, 1907; London, Nelson, 1921.
The Range Dwellers. New York, Dillingham, and London, Unwin, 1907.
The Lonesome Trail. New York, Dillingham, 1909; London, Nelson, 1920.
The Long Shadow. New York, Dillingham, 1909; London, Nelson, 1921.
The Happy Family. New York, Dillingham, 1910; London, Nelson, 1920.
Good Indian. Boston, Little Brown, 1912; London, Methuen, 1919.
Lonesome Land. Boston, Little Brown, and London, Stanley Paul, 1912.
The Uphill Climb. Boston, Little Brown, 1913; London, Methuen, 1923.
The Gringo. Boston, Little Brown, 1913; London, Methuen, 1923.
Flying U Ranch. New York, Dillingham, 1914; London, Nelson, 1921.
The Ranch at the Wolverine. Boston, Little Brown, 1914; London, Nash, 1916.
The Flying U's Last Stand. Boston, Little Brown, 1915; London, Hodder and Stoughton, 1922.
Jean of the Lazy A. Boston, Little Brown, 1915; London, Methuen, 1918.
The Heritage of the Sioux. Boston, Little Brown, 1916; London, Hodder and Stoughton, 1923.
The Phantom Herd. Boston, Little Brown, 1916; London, Hodder and Stoughton, 1922.
The Lookout Man. Boston, Little Brown, 1917.
Starr, Of the Desert. Boston, Little Brown, 1917; London, Hodder and Stoughton, 1923.
Skyrider. Boston, Little Brown, 1918; London, Methuen, 1920.
Cabin Fever. Boston, Little Brown, 1918.
Rim o' the World. Boston, Little Brown, 1919; London, Hodder and Stoughton, 1922.
The Thunder Bird. Boston, Little Brown, 1919; London, Hodder and Stoughton, 1923.
The Quirt. Boston, Little Brown, 1920.
Cow-Country. Boston, Little Brown, and London, Hodder and Stoughton, 1921.
Casey Ryan. Boston, Little Brown, 1921; London, Hodder and Stoughton, 1922.
Sawtooth Ranch. London, Methuen, 1921.
The Trail of the White Mule. Boston, Little Brown, 1922; London, Hodder and Stoughton, 1923.
The Parowan Bonanza. Boston, Little Brown, 1923; London, Hodder and Stoughton, 1924.
The Voice at Johnnywater. Boston, Little Brown, and London, Hodder and Stoughton, 1923.
The Bellehelen Mine. Boston, Little Brown, 1924; London, Hodder and Stoughton, 1925.
The Eagle's Wing. Boston, Little Brown, and London, Hodder and Stoughton, 1924.
Meadowlark Basin. Boston, Little Brown, 1925; London, Hodder and Stoughton, 1926.
Desert Brew. Boston, Little Brown, and London, Hodder and Stoughton, 1925.
Black Thunder. Boston, Little Brown, and London, Hodder and Stoughton, 1926.
The Adam Chasers. Boston, Little Brown, and London, Hodder and Stoughton, 1927.
Outlaw Paradise. London, Hodder and Stoughton, 1927.
White Wolves. Boston, Little Brown, and London, Hodder and Stoughton, 1927.
Points West. Boston, Little Brown, and London, Hodder and Stoughton, 1928.
Hay-Wire. Boston, Little Brown, and London, Hodder and Stoughton, 1928.
Rodeo. Boston, Little Brown, and London, Hodder and Stoughton, 1929.

The Swallowfork Bulls. Boston, Little Brown, and London, Hodder and Stoughton, 1929.
Fool's Goal. Boston, Little Brown, and London, Hodder and Stoughton, 1930.
Tiger Eye. Boston, Little Brown, and London, Hodder and Stoughton, 1930.
Dark Horse: A Story of the Flying U. Boston, Little Brown, 1931; London, Hodder and Stoughton, 1932.
The Long Loop. Boston, Little Brown, and London, Hodder and Stoughton, 1931.
Laughing Water. Boston, Little Brown, and London, Hodder and Stoughton, 1932.
Rocking Arrow. Boston, Little Brown, and London, Hodder and Stoughton, 1932.
The Whoop-Up Trail. Boston, Little Brown, 1933; London, Hodder and Stoughton, 1934.
Trails Meet. Boston, Little Brown, and London, Hodder and Stoughton, 1933.
Open Land. Boston, Little Brown, and London, Hodder and Stoughton, 1933.
The Flying U Strikes. Boston, Little Brown, and London, Hodder and Stoughton, 1934.
The Haunted Hills. Boston, Little Brown, 1934; London, Hodder and Stoughton, 1935.
The Dry Ridge Gang. Boston, Little Brown, and London, Collins, 1935.
Trouble Rides the Wind. Boston, Little Brown, 1935; London, Collins, 1936.
Five Furies of Leaning Ladder. Boston, Little Brown, 1936; as *The Five Furies,* London, Collins, 1936.
Shadow Mountain. Boston, Little Brown, and London, Collins, 1936.
Van Patten. Boston, Little Brown, 1936.
The North Wind Do Blow. Boston, Little Brown, 1937; as *North Wind,* London, Collins, 1937.
Pirates of the Range. Boston, Little Brown, 1937; London, Collins, 1938.
The Wind Blows West. Boston, Little Brown, 1938; London, Collins, 1939.
A Starry Night. Boston, Little Brown, and London, Collins, 1939.
The Singing Hill. Boston, Little Brown, and London, Collins, 1939.
Man on Horseback. Boston, Little Brown, and London, Collins, 1940.
Spirit of the Range. Boston, Little Brown, and London, Collins, 1940.
Sweet Grass. Boston, Little Brown, and London, Collins, 1940.
Kings of the Prairie. London, Collins, 1941.
The Family Failing. Boston, Little Brown, 1941.
Border Vengeance. New York, Avalon, 1951; London, Wright and Brown, 1954.
Gun Fight at Horsethief Range. New York, Avon, 1951.
Outlaw Moon. New York, Avalon, 1952; London, Wright and Brown, 1954.
Trigger Vengeance. New York, New American Library, 1953.

Uncollected Short Stories.

"Lone Rider," with Buck Connor, in *McClure's* (New York), May 1916.
"Desert Rat," with Buck Connor, in *McClure's* (New York), July 1916.
"Gun-Runners," with Buck Connor, in *McClure's* (New York), October 1916.
"Wolf! Wolf!," in *Western Story* (New York), 1 January 1921.
"Curlew Corliss," in *Western Story* (New York), 22 January 1921.
"The Terror," in *Western Story* (New York), 29 January 1921.
"A Time of Wild Ones," in *Western Story* (New York), 5 January, 26 February 1921.
"The Stayer," in *Western Story* (New York), 12 February 1921.
"A Throne for a Day," in *Western Story* (New York), 12 March 1921.
"The Problem," in *Western Story* (New York), 19 March 1921.
"Three H," in *Western Story* (New York), 16 April 1921.
"For the Love of a Horse," in *Western Story* (New York), 30 April 1921.
"Mounted Music," in *Western Story* (New York), 13 August 1921.
"Flames," in *Western Story* (New York), 27 August 1921.
"When Sleeping Turtle Pays," in *Western Story* (New York), 22 April 1922.
"Music and a Savage Breast," in *Western Story* (New York), 1 June 1922.
"Wolf Bait," in *All Star* (Kingswood, Surrey), October 1932.
"Thirteen Rattles and a Button," in *West* (New York), May 1933.
"Finder Is Keeper," in *West* (New York), July 1933.
"Real Stuff," in *West* (New York), August 1933.
"Law on the Flying U," in *Argosy* (New York), 16 September 1933.
"Man Measure," in *West* (New York), October 1933.
"Chip Rides Alone," in *West* (New York), December 1933.
"Chip and the Wild Bunch," in *West* (New York), March 1934.
"Angel Came Riding," in *American Mercury* (New York), February 1937.
"Proverbs Can Lie," in *Argosy* (New York), 25 June 1938.
"Crater Country," with Roy N. Bower, in *West* (Kingswood, Surrey), January 1954.
"Ananias Green," in *The Arbor House Treasury of Great Western Stories,* edited by Bill Pronzini and Martin H. Greenberg. New York, Arbor House, 1982.
"Bad Penny," in *The Cowboys,* edited by Bill Pronzini and Martin H. Greenberg. New York, Fawcett, 1985.
"The Lamb of the Flying U," in *She Won the West: An Anthology of Western and Frontier Stories Written by Women,* edited by Marcia Muller and Bill Pronzini. New York, Morrow, 1985.

OTHER PUBLICATIONS

Plays

Screenplays: *Chip of the Flying U,* with Lynn Reynolds and Harry Dittmar, 1926; *King of the Rodeo,* with George Morgan and Harold Tarshis, 1929.

* * *

A reviewer in the *Bookman* in 1912, considering both the explosion of popular western fiction since *The Virginian* had appeared a decade earlier and the particular example of such fiction in front of him, wrote that it was refreshing to find a western "in which people are really alive and conduct themselves with human sanity." The author who had produced such a work, and some 70 other Westerns, was B.M. Bower.

The worst of Bower is what one might expect of a writer who published two novels a year and aimed those novels directly at a market of relatively unsophisticated American readers. Much of Bower's work, that is, leans towards the stereotypical and the sentimental. But the best of Bower is simple and direct in style, its sentimentality skewed in the direction of pathos and soft irony, and its characters and situations considerably different from the essentially male tradition in which Bower, a woman, chose to write.

As might be expected of the first woman to make a career out of writing Westerns, Bower's novels deal often with women in the west. In *Chip, Of the Flying U*, her best-known novel, the central character is less the cowboy of the title whose artistic yearnings make him somewhat unsatisfied with his life on the ranch than it is Della Whitmore, the medical doctor who comes west, ultimately to marry the cowboy. In *Lonesome Land*, perhaps the best novel (and the one referred to by the *Bookman* reviewer), the heroine is an eastern woman who goes to Montana to marry her fiancé; there in the raw, ungenteel West she finds herself eventually capable of adaptation while her husband Manley becomes a most unmanly drunkard. In *Jean of the Lazy A* Bower tells of a young woman's successful transition from rancher's daughter to movie star and, at the end of the novel, back to an unglamorous but satisfying life on the ranch. *The Flying U's Last Stand* shows that Bower could also think of women in other than heroic roles, for one of the villains of the novel is a woman land agent out to locate gullible homesteaders on arid land. In other novels, even where women are not given leading roles, Bower deals frequently with themes of community and family (the bunkhouse gang on the Flying U Ranch is "The Happy Family") which suggest that the American west was something other than a proving ground for male individualism.

The importance that Bower assigns to adaptation, especially in her treatment of women, suggests her affirmative view of historical change. Rather than being set in an irrecoverable Old West of epic dimensions, her westerns tend to be contemporaneous with her writing of them. She wrote of a west in process, not one frozen in time. "Progress . . . does not mean decay," opens one novel. Bower often contradicts the backward-looking search for values so prominent in other popular western writers. In other ways, too, Bower's fiction departs from the trail that writers of Westerns increasingly crowded down during the first three decades of the 20th century: it is less violent, more humorous, more attentive to subtle social relationships among people (especially among men and women), more insistent on creating believable rather than mythic characters, and much less obsessed with a need to draw absolute distinctions between good and bad.

None of this makes Bower the Edith Wharton of western fiction. The genre which she practiced, drawing audiences partly from the Street and Smith pulp magazines in which many of her stories first appeared, was hardly rigorous in its artistic demands. Yet given the relative level of achievement in much of Bower's fiction, it is unfortunate that her work did not shape the writing of popular Westerns more than it did.

—William Bloodworth

BOWERS, Terrell L. American. Born in Laporte, Indiana, 9 July 1945. Educated at Mesa College, Grand Junction, Colorado, for two years. Served in the United States National Guard: Sergeant. Married Patricia Jean Calhoun in 1967; two daughters. Clerk, City Market Stores, Delta, Colorado, 1966–70; grocery department manager, Safeway Stores Inc., Glenwood Springs, Colorado, 1970–74; store/station manager, Bold Petroleum, Grand Junction, Colorado, 1975–81; store owner, Desert Gateway, Mack, Colorado, 1981–85. Since 1985 meter setter, Mountain Fuel Supply, Salt Lake City, Utah. Agent: The Belton Agency, P.O. Box 1419, Live Oak, Florida 32060. Address: P.O. Box 651, West Jordan, Utah 84084, U.S.A.

WESTERN PUBLICATIONS

Novels

Noose at Big Iron. New York, Bouregy, 1979.
A Man Called Banker. New York, Bouregy, 1980.
Rio Grande Death Ride. New York, Bouregy, 1980.
Crossfire at Twin Forks. New York, Bouregy, 1980.
Gunfire at Flintlock. New York, Bouregy, 1981.
Frozen Trail. New York, Bouregy, 1981.
Last Stand at Rio Blanco. New York, Bouregy, 1981.
Banyon's War. New York, Bouregy, 1982.
Chase into Mexico. New York, Bouregy, 1982.
Avery's Vengeance. New York, Bouregy, 1982.
Maverick Raid. New York, Bouregy, 1982.
The Fighting Peacemaker. New York, Bouregy, 1983.
Death at Devil's Gap. New York, Bouregy, 1983.
The Fighting McBride. New York, Bouregy, 1983.
The Devil's Badge. New York, Bouregy, 1983.
Gold Trail. New York, Bouregy, 1983.
Dakota Bullets. New York, Bouregy, 1984.
Job for a Gunman. New York, Bouregy, 1984.
Sinclair's Double War. New York, Bouregy, 1984.
Culhane's Code. New York, Bouregy, 1984.
Deadly Bounty. London, Hale, 1985.
Blood Vengeance. London, Hale, 1985.
Banshee Raiders. London, Hale, 1985.
The Masked Cowpoke. New York, Bouregy, 1985.
Skull Mountain Bandit. New York, Bouregy, 1985.
Vendetta. New York, Bouregy, 1985.
The Fighting Lucanes. New York, Bouregy, 1986.
Cheyenne Brothers. New York, Bouregy, 1986.
Trail to Justice. New York, Bouregy, 1986.
The Petticoat War. London, Hale, 1986.
Armageddon at Gold Butte. London, Hale, 1986.
Delryan's Draw. London, Hale, 1986.
Destiny's Trail. New York, Bouregy, 1987.
Lassito's Last War. New York, Bouregy, 1987.
The Railroad War. New York, Bouregy, 1988.
Black Cloud over Gunstock. New York, Bouregy, 1988.
Iron Claw's Revenge. New York, Bouregy, 1988.
The Shadow Killer. New York, Bouregy, 1989.
Justice at Black Water. New York, Bouregy, 1990.
Doctor Totes a Six-Gun. New York, Bouregy, 1990.
Tanner's Last Chance. New York, Bouregy, 1990.

*

Terrell L. Bowers comments:

I write to entertain, not to gain literary notice or fame. My enjoyment is derived from transforming characters and ideas into words that translate into action, adventure, romance, humor, or even grief. The readers of my Westerns are not asked to solve world hunger or fathom the mysteries of the universe (other than understanding the opposite sex). I write simply to entertain.

* * *

Terrell L. Bowers is an accomplished writer with numerous Westerns to his credit. While the quality of his writing might vary from the good to the competent to the downright melodramatic, his books are nearly always distinguished by the freshness of their plots.

A particularly good example of this can be found in *Blood Vengeance*, an entertaining revenge story set in Montana. Returning to Bear County after a 10-year absence, Dave Brenteen has only one aim in mind—to get even with cattle-rancher Henry Striker, who murdered Brenteen's parents in order to gain access to the abundance of water on their spread a decade before. Almost at once, however, he saves the life of Striker's beautiful step-daughter Collette, when she is attacked by a hooded maniac who has been killing young girls in the area for some time. Posing as "Dave Valeron," Bowers's protagonist takes possession of the old Brenteen ranch and cuts off the water to Striker's spread, intending to ruin him before finally killing him.

To his credit, however, Bowers soon begins to add dimension to what is basically a pretty standard tale, and as time wears on, Brenteen begins to question his desire for revenge until it takes second place to the search to find the hooded woman-killer (whose identity isn't really that hard to guess). There is also much more to the murder of Brenteen's parents than meets the eye, which adds originality to the plot.

The Petticoat War, perhaps Bowers's best book, benefits from a much better story. In an effort to out-run a persistent U.S. Marshal who is after him for the murder of a Mormon up in Utah, Marc Kannon crosses the border into Mexico with the intention of joining his brother Steve, who has taken up with a bandit named Paco Basada. It soon becomes obvious that there is little love between the brothers. Steve, we are told, is a "me-myself-and-I-person" whose life is totally dedicated to murder and thievery. Marc, on the other hand, like all of Bowers's heroes, still retains a strong sense of justice (the man he killed in Utah was actually shot in self-defence). Hearing of Basada's intention to cross back over the border and raze the town of Rio Diablo, Marc decides that the least he can do is warn the townsfolk before he quits the area for good. En route, he saves the life of the lovely Darcy Valentine, but upon entering Rio Diablo, he is very nearly hanged, simply because he is a Yankee in post-Civil War Texas. Darcy is able to save him, and eventually he delivers his warning, but the town's male population has been severely thinned by the war, and those few who remain are either too old or too crippled to organise an adequate defence. From that point on, Marc creates an army from the women, eventually settling matters not only with his brother, but also the persistent U.S. Marshal.

Though probably his strangest book, Bowers's *Armageddon at Gold Butte* is, by the same token, potentially his most interesting. Discovering a dead girl clad only in a nightgown out in the desert, freighter Luke Monteen soon finds himself trying to solve a series of puzzling enigmas in nearby Gold Butte. The mining town is owned by an obese Italian nobleman who employs a doctor of questionable qualifications to subjugate beautiful young girls with the use of drugs, and bend them to his will. Cocaine-dependent slaves, the girls willingly sell their bodies in order to increase Count Sal Balducci's already fabulous fortune, and guarantee themselves continued injections of the narcotic. Initially, Monteen is the only man in town to make a stand against this outrage, locking horns as he does with Balducci's henchmen (which include a gunman with the improbable name of Bracken Kolt), but as the plot wears on he attracts a small number of supporters to eventually bring Balducci's nightmare trade to a spectacular end.

Bowers's ability to find new variations on old themes is again displayed in *Delryan's Draw*, where gambler John Delryan wins an Indian girl named Capricho (formerly the "property" of a travelling showman named Faro Lark) in a poker game. Delryan has no desire to keep the girl as a slave, and offers her her freedom, but the girl, who is apparently dumb, is content to remain with him. In reality a white girl abducted by the Apaches years before, Capricho was to be the bride of a war chief named Jutemayo, whom, it is suspected, might well attempt to recapture her. As the story wears on, Lark also attempts to get the girl back, and to further complicate Delryan's life, Bowers introduces another sub-plot about gun-running, which involves Lark's brother.

As with nearly all of Bowers' westerns, *Delryan's Draw* boasts a young, commendable hero (who is usually befriended by or already knows an older, more trail-wise companion), a series of clearly-designated villains, all of whom eventually get their come-uppance, a romance which always works out well, and a happy ending. Bowers further enhances his stories with odd, successful snatches of humour. He has a rather spare style of writing which ensures that his plots fairly gallop along, and a reasonable ability to impart "western"-style speech, though his Indians tend to speak in a rather antiquated, "White-man-speak-with-forked-tongue" manner. When writing about the range, his knowledge of cattle is very good, and his descriptions of the elements—especially harsh winters—are evocative and atmospheric.

For light and reasonably satisfying western action in which old themes are frequently given new treatments, Bowers's books are among the best of their type.

—David Whitehead

BOWIE, Jim. *See* **NORWOOD, V.G.C.**

BOWIE, Sam. *See* **BALLARD, Willis Todhunter.**

BOYD, Alamo. *See* **BOSWORTH, Allan R.**

BOYLES, Clarence Scott, Jr. *See* **BROWN, Will C.**

BRADFORD, Richard (Roark). American. Born in Chicago, Illinois, 1 May 1932. Educated at Tulane University, New Orleans, B.A. 1952. Served in the United States Marine Corps, 1953–56. Married 1) Julie Dollard in 1956 (divorced), one son; 2) Lee Head in 1977. Staff writer, New Mexico State Tourist Bureau, Santa Fe, 1956–59; technical writer and editor, New Orleans Chamber of Commerce, 1959–61, 1967–68; research analyst, Zia Company, Los Alamos, New Mexico, 1963–65, and research analyst, New Mexico Department of Development, in the 1960's; screenwriter, Universal, 1968–71. Litt.D.: New Mexico State University, Las Cruces, 1979. Agent: McIntosh and Otis Inc., 310 Madison Avenue, New York, New York 10017. Address: P.O. Box 1395, Santa Fe, New Mexico 87501, U.S.A.

WESTERN PUBLICATIONS

Novels

Red Sky at Morning. Philadelphia, Lippincott, 1968; London, Hodder and Stoughton, 1969.
So Far from Heaven. Philadelphia, Lippincott, 1973; London, Hodder and Stoughton, 1974.

*

Richard Bradford comments (1982):

I don't consider myself a western writer, in the sense that Zane Grey, Owen Wister, Jack Schaefer, or Louis L'Amour are western writers. The two novels listed were set in the (modern) western United States, but the next one is set in the south, and I'm not a southern writer, either. What I am, I suppose, is a *slow* writer, or perhaps *lazy* writer. I try, and would prefer, to be a humorous writer, but somehow the only passages that turn out to be funny are those involving war or death or pestilence. So much for serious tone. And so much for self-appraisal.

* * *

Richard Bradford has published two novels set in 20th-century New Mexico, *Red Sky at Morning* and *So Far from Heaven.* The first of these is a kind of southwestern *Catcher in the Rye.* It is the story of a young man who moves to Santa Fe as a teenager, and in one eventful year begins to come to terms with such things as sex, family, death, duty, and responsibility. The tale ends with the protagonist leaving his newfound home to serve in the U.S. Navy, where he will presumably grow to full manhood.

So Far from Heaven takes its title from an exclamation allegedly emitted by a 19th-century territorial governor of New Mexico: "Poor New Mexico! So far from heaven, and so close to Texas!" The central character of the novel, David Reed, is a young Texan who is fleeing from the corruption of having spent several years working for an evil Texas billionaire. Reed, rather improbably, joins forces in northern New Mexico with a Chicano family to fight for right and decency. Together they battle political and economic machinations—many of them financed by Texas capital—that threaten to destroy New Mexico's unique culture. Mixed into the brew is a *nativo* insurrection that sounds very much like a fictionalized version of the Reyes Tijerina incident from the late 1960's. Reed's rewards for his good deeds is marriage to the daughter of the family, who turns out to be a liberated lady with degrees from Bryn Mawr and Berkeley.

The best that can be said of Bradford is that he is a professional. His prose style is slick; his plots are neatly stitched together; his reader's attention span is never unduly taxed. What he seems to lack—and not all would agree that this is a flaw—is any shred of Henry James's "high seriousness." Bradford is essentially a romancer. In his fiction event and character are merely pieces of a puzzle to be triumphantly fitted together. Social criticism, of which there is a good deal in the second novel, is administered with the lightest of touches. Though it ends on a solemn note, *Red Sky at Morning* is set to the same brisk, bouncy, wisecracking tempo as *So Far from Heaven.* The author seems good-natured to a fault, as he deals with the traumas of adolescence in the first novel and the wrenching changes that afflict contemporary New Mexico in the second. Still, the books are readable, and they raise, however superficially, important issues to a large reading audience. As popular fiction goes, they are superior examples of their kind.

—William T. Pilkington

BRADFORD, Will. *See* **PAINE, Lauran.**

BRADLEY, Concho. *See* **PAINE, Lauran.**

BRADSHAW, Buck. *See* **PAINE, Lauran.**

BRADY, William S. *See* **HARVEY, John.**

BRAGG, W(illiam) F(rederick). American. Born in Lander, Wyoming, in 1892. Served in World War I. Married Mary Coburn; one son, the writer W.F. Bragg, Jr. Newspaperman in Wyoming, Colorado, and California; radio announcer, KMJ, 1924–26. *Died in 1967.*

WESTERN PUBLICATIONS

Novels

Starr of Wyoming. London, Wright and Brown, 1936.
Smoke Joe. New York, Phoenix Press, 1949; London, Wright and Brown, 1952.
Mountain Maverick. New York, Phoenix Press, 1950; London, Wright and Brown, 1953.
Gun Trouble. New York, Phoenix Press, 1950; London, Wright and Brown, 1954.
Range Camp. New York, Phoenix Press, 1950; London, Wright and Brown, 1953.
Sagebrush Lawman. New York, Phoenix Press, 1951; London, Boardman, 1952.
Texas Fever. New York, Arcadia House, 1953; London, Wright and Brown, 1955.
Bullet Song. New York, Arcadia House, 1953; London, Wright and Brown, 1956.
Stampede Jones. New York, Arcadia House, 1954.
Maverick Showdown. New York, Arcadia House, 1954; Bath, Chivers, 1982.
Guns of Roaring Fork. New York, Arcadia House, 1954; London, Wright and Brown, 1956.
Wildcat Brand. New York, Arcadia House, 1955; London, Wright and Brown, 1957.
Bullet Proof. New York, Arcadia House, 1955.

Ghost Mountain Guns. New York, Arcadia House, 1955; London, Muller, 1957.
Badlands Basin. New York, Arcadia House, 1956; London, Muller, 1957.
Buckskin Rider. New York, Arcadia House, 1956; London, Wright and Brown, 1957.
Buzzard's Roost. New York, Arcadia House, 1956; London, Mills and Boon, 1958.
Ride On, Cowboy! New York, Arcadia House, 1956; London, Wright and Brown, 1958.
Poison Creek Posse. New York, Arcadia House, 1957; London, Mills and Boon, 1958.
Rawhide Roundup. New York, Arcadia House, 1957; London, Wright and Brown, 1958.
Outlaw Moon. New York, Arcadia House, 1958; London, Wright and Brown, 1959.

* * *

Treacherous, greedy cattlemen seeking to expand their herds and ranges; decent cowpokes—tall, silent, and honorable—caught up in duplicitous plots and double-crosses; beautiful, fiery women who don't know their own hearts; loyal friends; reliable horses; noble Indians; and a lot of mean, intolerant cowpunchers out for a fast buck—these are the ingredients that make for fast action and quick thinking in a typical W.F. Bragg Western.

Set on the Wyoming Range near Teton and Shoshoni reservations, Bragg's novels depend on sage breaks, gullies, hidden caves, big rocks, and sudden precipices for the ambushes and escapes that plunge the plot forward. The diction reflects this western environment with folksy metaphors like "jumped like a pronghorn buck" and "horns that snapped like pistol shots," and "cowpoke lingo" like "sabe," "cayuse," "hardpan," "ambuscado," and "faunch."

Usually the plot turns on would-be big-time cattlemen using the Indians and their pale-face sympathizers as scapegoats in a plot to consolidate cattle forces, bring in federal money, and grasp more land. They lie, cheat, and murder to attain their ends, with "shoot'em or lynch'em" their motto, and blackmail, kidnapping, and framing their *modus operandi.* Stolen hats and horses, Indian blankets and moccasins, bank robberies and stampedes are all employed to mislead the law, divide loyalties and eliminate competition and opposition. Ultimately it is the man who talks glibly, womanizes voraciously, and claims altruistic motives that the reader must be most wary of.

In contrast, the Indians are depicted as respected warriors who could give U.S. troops lessons in tactics; simple but noble men; natural orators who speak from the heart and whose code is that of the "stone age ancestors of all men"—the safety and honor of the tribe. They may have been penned up on reservations and reduced to starvation and penury, but the grandeur of their past still ennobles them. Despite numerous attempts to frame them for horse theft and murder or to tempt them to break their treaty, the Indians ultimately perceive the facts and choose the way of the law to which they have sworn, yielding their prisoners to the calvary in *Bullet Proof* and permitting a duel, paleface versus paleface in *Mountain Maverick.*

The typical Bragg hero, a friend of the smaller cattlemen and Indians alike, is alienated from family and community because of his stubborn loyalties, his defense of Indians, and his disagreements with cattle bosses. He is aided by a couple of dedicated friends (also outsiders) who aren't much for talk but who stick to their guns in times of trouble. His straightforward honesty wins respect and his dogged determination to prevent misjustice finally gets results, though he must first endure countless dangers: locoed horses, stampedes, bullets from unseen assailants, near drowning, near lynching, near scalping, etc. Often only a sturdy mustang that can turn on a dime and respond quickly to its rider's needs can save him. In a last-minute effort, he usually prevents an Indian war, vindicates himself, rescues a beautiful girl, exposes the true criminals, and helps free his friends.

—Gina Macdonald

BRAND, Clay. *See* **NORWOOD, V.G.C.**

BRAND, Max. Pseudonym for Frederick Schiller Faust; also wrote as Frank Austin; Lee Bolt; George Owen Baxter; Walter C. Butler; George Challis; Peter Dawson; Martin Dexter; Evan Evans; John Frederick; Frederick Frost; Dennis Lawton; David Manning; Peter Henry Morland; Hugh Owen; Nicholas Silver; Henry Uriel; Peter Ward. American. Born in Seattle, Washington, 29 May 1892. Educated at schools in Modesto, California; University of California, Berkeley, 1911–15. Served in the Canadian Army, 1915–16 (deserted); United States Army, 1918. Married Dorothy Schillig in 1917; two daughters and one son. Freelance writer from 1917; lived in Italy, 1926–38; scriptwriter for MGM, Columbia, and Warner Brothers; war correspondent in Italy for *Harper's*, 1944. *Died 12 May 1944.*

WESTERN PUBLICATIONS

Novels (series: Silvertip)

The Untamed. New York, Putnam, 1919; London, Hodder and Stoughton, 1952.
Trailin'. New York, Putnam, 1920.
The Night Horseman. New York, Putnam, 1920.
The Seventh Man. New York, Putnam, 1921.
Alcatraz. New York, Putnam, 1923.
Dan Barry's Daughter. New York, Putnam, 1924.
Clung. London, Hodder and Stoughton, 1924; New York, Dodd Mead, 1969.
The Guide to Happiness. London, Hodder and Stoughton, 1924.
Gun Gentlemen. London, Hodder and Stoughton, 1924; as *The Gentle Gunman*, New York, Dodd Mead, 1964.
His Third Majesty. London, Hodder and Stoughton, 1925.
Beyond the Outpost (as Peter Henry Morland). New York, Putnam, 1925.
Fire-Brain. New York, Putnam, 1926.
The White Wolf. New York, Putnam, 1926.
Fate's Honeymoon. London, Hodder and Stoughton, 1926.
Luck. London, Hodder and Stoughton, 1926.
Black Jack. London, Hodder and Stoughton, 1926; New York, Dodd Mead, 1970.
Harrigan. London, Hodder and Stoughton, 1926; New York, Dodd Mead, 1971.
The Stranger at the Gate. London, Hodder and Stoughton, 1926.
The Blue Jay. New York, Dodd Mead, and London, Hodder and Stoughton, 1927.

The Garden of Eden. London, Hodder and Stoughton, 1927; New York, Dodd Mead, 1952.
Pride of Tyson. London, Hodder and Stoughton, 1927.
Border Guns. New York, Dodd Mead, 1928; London, Hodder and Stoughton, 1954.
Lost Wolf (as Peter Henry Morland). New York, Vanguard Press, 1928; New York, Dodd Mead, 1986; as Max Brand, London, Hale, 1989.
Pillar Mountain. New York, Dodd Mead, 1928; London, Hodder and Stoughton, 1929.
Pleasant Jim. New York, Dodd Mead, and London, Hodder and Stoughton, 1928.
The Galloping Broncos. New York, Dodd Mead, 1929; London, Hodder and Stoughton, 1953.
The Gun Tamer. New York, Dodd Mead, 1929; London, Hodder and Stoughton, 1951.
Mistral. New York, Dodd Mead, 1929; London, Hodder and Stoughton, 1930.
Destry Rides Again. New York, Dodd Mead, 1930; London, Hodder and Stoughton, 1931.
The Outlaw of Buffalo Flat. New York, Dodd Mead, 1930.
Mystery Ranch. New York, Dodd Mead, 1930; as *Mystery Valley*, London, Hodder and Stoughton, 1930.
The Happy Valley. New York, Dodd Mead, 1931; London, Hodder and Stoughton, 1932.
Smiling Charlie. New York, Dodd Mead, and London, Hodder and Stoughton, 1931.
The Jackson Trail. New York, Dodd Mead, 1932; London, Hodder and Stoughton, 1933.
Twenty Notches. New York, Dodd Mead, and London, Hodder and Stoughton, 1932.
Valley Vultures. New York, Dodd Mead, and London, Hodder and Stoughton, 1932.
The False Rider. New York, Dodd Mead, 1933; London, Hodder and Stoughton, 1950.
The Longhorn Feud. New York, Dodd Mead, and London, Hodder and Stoughton, 1933.
The Outlaw. New York, Dodd Mead, 1933.
Slow Joe. New York, Dodd Mead, and London, Hodder and Stoughton, 1933.
Valley Thieves. New York, Grosset and Dunlap, 1933; London, Hodder and Stoughton, 1949.
Brothers on the Trail. New York, Dodd Mead, 1934; London, Hodder and Stoughton, 1935.
War Party. New York, Dodd Mead, 1934.
Timbal Gulch Trail. New York, Dodd Mead, and London, Hodder and Stoughton, 1934.
Crooked Horn. London, Hodder and Stoughton, 1934.
The Rancher's Revenge. New York, Dodd Mead, 1934; London, Hodder and Stoughton, 1935.
Hunted Riders. New York, Dodd Mead, 1935; London, Hodder and Stoughton, 1936.
Dead Man's Treasure. New York, Dodd Mead, 1935.
Rustlers of Beacon Creek. New York, Dodd Mead, 1935; London, Hodder and Stoughton, 1936.
Frontier Feud. New York, Dodd Mead, 1935.
The Seven of Diamonds. New York, Dodd Mead, and London, Hodder and Stoughton, 1935.
Happy Jack. New York, Dodd Mead, and London, Hodder and Stoughton, 1936.
The King Bird Rides. New York, Dodd Mead, and London, Hodder and Stoughton, 1936.
South of Rio Grande. New York, Dodd Mead, 1936; London, Hodder and Stoughton, 1937.
The Streak. New York, Dodd Mead, and London, Hodder and Stoughton, 1937.
Trouble Trail. New York, Dodd Mead, and London, Hodder and Stoughton, 1937.
Dead or Alive. New York, Dodd Mead, 1938.
The Iron Trail. New York, Dodd Mead, 1938; as *Riding the Iron Trail*, London, Hodder and Stoughton, 1938.
Singing Guns. New York, Dodd Mead, and London, Hodder and Stoughton, 1938.
Fightin' Fool. New York, Dodd Mead, 1939; as *A Fairly Slick Guy*, London, Hodder and Stoughton, 1940.
Gunman's Gold. New York, Dodd Mead, and London, Hodder and Stoughton, 1939.
Marbleface. New York, Dodd Mead, 1939; as *Poker Face*, London, Hodder and Stoughton, 1939.
Lanky for Luck. London, Hodder and Stoughton, 1939.
Danger Trail. New York, Dodd Mead, and London, Hodder and Stoughton, 1940.
The Dude. New York, Dodd Mead, 1940.
Riders of the Plains. New York, Dodd Mead, 1940; London, Hodder and Stoughton, 1941.
Cleaned Out. London, Hodder and Stoughton, 1940.
The Border Kid. New York, Dodd Mead, and London, Hodder and Stoughton, 1941.
The Long Chance. New York, Dodd Mead, 1941.
Vengeance Trail. New York, Dodd Mead, 1941.
Silvertip. New York, Dodd Mead, and London, Hodder and Stoughton, 1942.
The Man from Mustang. New York, Dodd Mead, 1942; London, Hodder and Stoughton, 1943.
Silvertip's Strike. New York, Dodd Mead, 1942; London, Hodder and Stoughton, 1944.
The Safety Killer. London, Hodder and Stoughton, 1942.
Striking Eagle. London, Hodder and Stoughton, 1942.
Silvertip's Roundup. New York, Dodd Mead, 1943; London, Hodder and Stoughton, 1945.
Silvertip's Trap. New York, Dodd Mead, 1943; London, Hodder and Stoughton, 1946.
The Fighting Four. New York, Dodd Mead, 1944; London, Hodder and Stoughton, 1948.
Silvertip's Chase. Philadelphia, Blakiston, 1944; London, Hodder and Stoughton, 1946.
Silvertip's Search. New York, Dodd Mead, 1945; London, Hodder and Stoughton, 1946.
The Stolen Stallion (*Silvertip*). New York, Dodd Mead, 1945; London, Hodder and Stoughton, 1949.
Mountain Riders. New York, Dodd Mead, 1946; London, Hodder and Stoughton, 1949.
Valley of Vanishing Men. New York, Dodd Mead, 1947; London, Hodder and Stoughton, 1949.
Flaming Irons. New York, Dodd Mead, 1948; London, Hodder and Stoughton, 1951.
Hired Hands. New York, Dodd Mead, 1948; London, Hodder and Stoughton, 1951.
The Bandit of the Black Hills. New York, Dodd Mead, and London, Hodder and Stoughton, 1949.
Seven Trails. New York, Dodd Mead, 1949; London, Hodder and Stoughton, 1952.
Single Jack. New York, Dodd Mead, 1950; London, Hodder and Stoughton, 1953.
The Hair-Trigger Kid. New York, Dodd Mead, 1951.
Tragedy Trail. New York, Dodd Mead, 1951; London, Hodder and Stoughton, 1954.
Smiling Desperado. New York, Dodd Mead, 1953; London, Hodder and Stoughton, 1955.
The Tenderfoot. New York, Dodd Mead, 1953; London, Hodder and Stoughton, 1955.

The Gambler. New York, Dodd Mead, 1954; London, Hodder and Stoughton, 1956.
The Invisible Outlaw. New York, Dodd Mead, 1954; London, Hodder and Stoughton, 1956.
Outlaw Breed. New York, Dodd Mead, 1955; London, Hodder and Stoughton, 1957.
Speedy. New York, Dodd Mead, 1955; London, Hodder and Stoughton, 1957.
The Big Trail. New York, Dodd Mead, 1956; London, Hodder and Stoughton, 1958.
Trail Partners. New York, Dodd Mead, 1956; London, Hodder and Stoughton, 1958.
Blood on the Trail. New York, Dodd Mead, 1957; London, Hodder and Stoughton, 1959.
Lucky Larribee. New York, Dodd Mead, 1957; London, Hodder and Stoughton, 1960.
The Long Chase. New York, Dodd Mead, 1960; London, Hodder and Stoughton, 1961.
The White Cheyenne. New York, Dodd Mead, 1960; London, Hodder and Stoughton, 1961.
Mighty Lobo. New York, Dodd Mead, 1962; Bath, Chivers, 1988.
Tamer of the Wild. New York, Dodd Mead, 1962; London, Hodder and Stoughton, 1963.
The Stranger. New York, Dodd Mead, 1963; London, Panther, 1964.
Golden Lightning. New York, Dodd Mead, 1964; London, Hodder and Stoughton, 1965.
The Guns of Dorking Hollow. New York, Dodd Mead, 1965; London, Hodder and Stoughton, 1966.
Torture Trail. New York, Dodd Mead, 1965.
Larramee's Ranch. New York, Dodd Mead, 1966.
Ride the Wild Trail. New York, Dodd Mead, 1966.
Rippon Rides Double. New York, Dodd Mead, 1968.
The Stingaree. New York, Dodd Mead, 1968.
Thunder Moon. New York, Dodd Mead, 1969.
Gunman's Reckoning. New York, Dodd Mead, 1970.
Trouble Kid. New York, Dodd Mead, 1970.
Ambush at Torture Canyon. New York, Dodd Mead, 1971.
Cheyenne Gold. New York, Dodd Mead, 1972.
Drifter's Vengeance. New York, Dodd Mead, 1972.
The Luck of the Spindrift. New York, Dodd Mead, 1972.
Storm on the Range. London, Hale, 1979.
Galloping Danger. New York, Dodd Mead, 1979.
The Man from the Wilderness. New York, Dodd Mead, 1980; London, Hale, 1981.
The Smoking Land. Santa Barbara, California, Capra, 1980.
Wild Freedom. New York, Dodd Mead, 1981; London, Hale, 1982.
Six Gun Country. New York, Dodd Mead, and London, Hale, 1981.
Bull Hunter. New York, Dodd Mead, and London, Hale, 1981.
The Gentle Desperado: Three Westerns. Santa Barbara, California, Capra, 1981; London, Hale, 1988.
Thunder Moon's Challenge. New York, Dodd Mead, 1982.
Thunder Moon Strikes. New York, Dodd Mead, 1982.
The Making of a Gunman. New York, Dodd Mead, 1983.
Lawless Land. New York, Dodd Mead, 1983; London, Hale, 1988.
Rogue Mustang. New York, Dodd Mead, 1984; London, Hale, 1985.
Three on the Trail. New York, Dodd Mead, 1984; London, Hale, 1987.
Trouble in Timberline. New York, Dodd Mead, 1984; London, Hale, 1987.
Riders of the Silences. New York, Dodd Mead, 1986.
Mountain Guns. London, Hale, 1987.
One Man Posse. New York, Dodd Mead, 1987.
The Fastest Draw. New York, Dodd Mead, 1987.
The Nighthawk Trail. New York, Dodd Mead, 1987.
Silvertip's Roundup. New York, Putnam, 1989.

Novels as George Owen Baxter

Free Range Lanning. New York, Chelsea House, 1921; London, Hodder and Stoughton, 1923.
The Gauntlet. London, Lloyd, 1922.
Donnegan. New York, Chelsea House, 1923; London, Hodder and Stoughton, 1924.
The Long, Long Trail. New York, Chelsea House, 1923; London, Hodder and Stoughton, 1924.
The Range-Land Avenger. New York, Chelsea House, 1924; London, Hodder and Stoughton, 1925.
King Charlie. London, Hodder and Stoughton, 1925.
The Shadow of Silver Tip. New York, Chelsea House, 1925; London, Hodder and Stoughton, 1926.
Wooden Guns. New York, Chelsea House, 1925; London, Hodder and Stoughton, 1927.
Train's Trust. New York, Chelsea House, 1926; London, Hodder and Stoughton, 1927; as *Steve Train's Ordeal* (as Max Brand), New York, Dodd Mead, 1967.
The Whispering Outlaw. New York, Chelsea House, 1926; London, Hodder and Stoughton, 1927.
The Trail to San Triste. New York, Chelsea House, 1927; London, Hodder and Stoughton, 1928.
Tiger Man. New York, Macaulay, and London, Hodder and Stoughton, 1929.
The Killers. New York, Macaulay, and London, Hodder and Stoughton, 1931.
Call of the Blood. New York, Macaulay, and London, Hodder and Stoughton, 1934.
Red Devil of the Range. New York, Macaulay, 1934; London, Hodder and Stoughton, 1935.
Brother of the Cheyennes. New York, Macaulay, 1935.
Rusty. London, Hodder and Stoughton, 1937.

Novels as David Manning

Bill Hunter. New York, Chelsea House, 1924.
Bill Hunter's Romance. New York, Chelsea House, 1924; London, Hutchinson, 1926.
Jerry Peyton's Notched Inheritance. New York, Chelsea House, 1925.
Jim Curry's Test. New York, Chelsea House, 1925; London, Hutchinson, 1927.
King Charlie's Riders. New York, Chelsea House, 1925.
The Brute. New York, Chelsea House, 1926.
Blackie and Red. New York, Chelsea House, 1926.
The Black Signal. New York, Chelsea House, 1926; as Max Brand, London, Hale, 1989.
Ronicky Doone. New York, Chelsea House, 1926.
Ronicky Doone's Treasure. New York, Chelsea House, 1926.
Bandit's Honor. New York, Chelsea House, 1927.
On the Trail of Four. New York, Chelsea House, 1927.
The Outlaw Tamer. New York, Chelsea House, 1927.
The Trap at Comanche Bend. New York, Chelsea House, 1927.
The Mountain Fugitive. New York, Chelsea House, 1927.
Western Tommy. New York, Chelsea House, 1927.
The Mustang Herder. New York, Chelsea House, 1928.
Señor Jingle Bells. New York, Chelsea House, 1928.

Novels as Evan Evans

Montana Rides! New York, Harper, 1933; London, Penguin, 1957.
Montana Rides Again. New York, Harper, 1934.
The Song of the Whip. New York, Harper, and London, Cassell, 1936.
The Border Bandit. New York, Harper, 1947.
The Rescue of Broken Arrow. New York, Harper, 1948.
Gunman's Legacy. New York, Harper, 1949; as *Sixgun Legacy*, London, Jenkins, 1950.
Smuggler's Trail. New York, Harper, 1949; as *Smoking Gun Trail*, London, Jenkins, 1951; as *Lone Hand*, New York, Bantam, 1951.
Sawdust and Sixguns. New York, Harper, 1951; London, Jenkins, 1952.
Strange Courage. New York, Harper, 1952; London, Jenkins, 1953.
Outlaw Valley. New York, Harper, 1953; London, Hale, 1954.
Outlaw's Code. New York, Harper, 1953; London, Hale, 1955.

Novels as Frank Austin

The Return of the Rancher. New York, Dodd Mead, 1933; London, Lane, 1934.
The Sheriff Rides. New York, Dodd Mead, 1934; London, Lane, 1935.
King of the Range. New York, Dodd Mead, 1935; London, Lane, 1936.

Short Stories

Wine on the Desert and Other Stories. New York, Dodd Mead, 1940; London, Hodder and Stoughton, 1941.
Max Brand's Best Stories, edited by Robert Easton. New York, Dodd Mead, 1967.
Max Brand's Best Stories, edited by William F. Nolan. New York, Dodd Mead, 3 vols., 1983–87.

Uncollected Short Stories

"A Sagebrush Cinderella," in *All-Story* (New York), 10 July 1920.
"Bullets with Sense," in *Western Story* (New York), 9 July 1921.
"Bull Hunter Feels His Oats," in *Western Story* (New York), 13 August 1921.
"Outlaws All," in *Western Story* (New York), 10 September 1921.
"The Wolf Strain," in *Western Story* (New York), 24 September 1921.
"Sheriff Larrabee's Prisoner" (as Martin Dexter), in *Western Story* (New York), 3 December 1921.
"The Gift," in *Western Story* (New York), 24 December 1921.
"Jim Curry's Compromise," in *Western Story* (New York), 1 April 1922.
"Jim Curry's Scarifice," in *Western Story* (New York), 20 May 1922.
"The Black Muldoon" (as Peter Dawson), in *Western Story* (New York), 30 September 1922.
"Under His Shirt," in *Western Story* (New York), 27 January 1923.
"Hired Guns," in *Western Story* (New York), 10 March-21 April 1923.
"His Name His Fortune," in *Western Story* (New York), 9 June 1923.
"Little Sammy Green, 'Lucky Gent,'" in *Western Story* (New York), 30 June 1923.
"Galloping Danger," in *Western Story* (New York), 14 July-18 August 1923.
"'Safety' McTee," in *Western Story* (New York), 25 August 1923.
"Rodeo Ranch," in *Western Story* (New York), 1 September 1923.
"Wooden Guns," in *Western Story* (New York), 15 September–20 October 1923.
"Timber Line," in *Western Story* (New York), 24 November 1923.
"Uncle Chris Turns North," in *Western Story* (New York), 8 December 1923.
"Master and Man," in *Western Story* (New York), 5 January 1924.
"The Rock of Liever," in *Western Story* (New York), 19 January 1924.
"Cuttle's Hired Man," in *Western Story* (New York), 1 March 1924.
"Lazy Tom Hooks Up with Skinny," in *Western Story* (New York), 22 March 1924.
"The Wedding Quirt," in *Western Story* (New York), 12 April 1924.
"Saddle and Sentiment," in *Western Story* (New York), 19 April–24 May 1924.
"The Gambler," in *Western Story* (New York), 7 June 1924.
"The Red Rider" (as Nicholas Silver), in *Western Story* (New York), 12 July 1924.
"The Love of Danger," in *Western Story* (New York), 2 August–6 September 1924.
"Blackie and Red," in *Western Story* (New York), 13 September 1924.
"When 'Red' Was White," in *Western Story* (New York), 4 October 1924.
"Chick's Fall," in *Western Story* (New York), 15 November 1924.
"The Third Bullet," in *Western Story* (New York), 13 December 1924.
"Fortune's Christmas," in *Western Story* (New York), 20 December 1924.
"Dark Rosaleen," in *Country Gentleman* (Philadelphia), 27 December 1924–24 January 1925.
"The Black Rider," in *Western Story* (New York), 3 January 1925.
"Blackie's Last Stand," in *Western Story* (New York), 7 March 1925.
"Lew and Slim," in *Western Story* (New York), 4 April 1925.
"In the River Bottom's Grip," in *Western Story* (New York), 11 April 1925.
"The Survivor," in *Western Story* (New York), 23 May–27 June 1925.
"Sammy Gregg's Mustang Herd," in *Western Story* (New York), 3 October 1925.
"Gregg's Coach Line," in *Western Story* (New York), 17 October 1925.
"Sammy Gregg and the Posse," in *Western Story* (New York), 31 October 1925.
"Brother of the Beasts," in *Western Story* (New York), 28 November 1925.
"No Man's Friend," in *Western Story* (New York), 26 December 1925.
"The Tyrant" (as George Challis), in *Western Story* (New York), 9 January–13 February 1926.

"Sandy Sweyn Comes Out of the Wilds," in *Western Story* (New York), 16 January 1926.
"A Son of Danger," in *Western Story* (New York), 17 April–22 May 1926.
"Acres of Unrest," in *Western Story* (New York), 12 June–17 July 1926.
"The Fugitive," in *Western Story* (New York), 24 July 1926.
"The Valley of Jewels," in *Western Story* (New York), 21 August 1926.
"The Border Bandit," in *Western Story* (New York), 25 September 1926.
"The Border Bandit's Indian Brother," in *Western Story* (New York), 2 October 1926.
"The Border Bandit's Prize," in *Western Story* (New York), 9 October 1926.
"Comanche," in *Far West* (San Francisco), December 1926.
"Werewolf," in *Western Story* (New York), 18 December 1926.
"The Canyon Coward," in *Western Story* (New York), 15 January 1927.
"Peter Blue, One-Gun Man," in *Far West* (San Francisco), June 1927.
"The Desert Pilot," in *Western Story* (New York), 4 June 1927.
"The City in the Sky," in *Western Story* (New York), 11 June–16 July 1927.
"The Silver Stork," in *Western Story* (New York), 13 August–17 September 1927.
"The Consuming Fire," in *Argosy* (New York), 27 November 1927.
"Weakling of the Wild," in *Western Story* (New York), 14 January–18 February 1928.
"The Path to Plunder," in *Western Story* (New York), 17 March–21 April 1928.
"Three on the Trail," in *Western Story* (New York), 12 May–16 June 1928.
"Gunman's Goal," in *Western Story* (New York), 14 July 1928.
"The Bright Face of Danger," in *Western Story* (New York), 18 August 1928.
"Through Steel and Stone," in *Western Story* (New York), 29 September 1928.
"The House of Gold," in *Western Story* (New York), 13 October 1928.
"Silver Trail," in *Western Story* (New York), 27 October–1 December 1928.
"The Trail to Manhood," in *Western Story* (New York), 13 April–18 May 1929.
"Blood and Iron," in *Munsey's* (New York), May–August 1929.
"The Return of Geraldi," in *Western Story* (New York), 29 June 1929.
"While Bullets Sang," in *Western Story* (New York), 17 August 1929.
"Geraldi in the Haunted Hills," in *Western Story* (New York), 31 August 1929.
"The Duster," in *Western Story* (New York), 2 November 1929.
"Twisted Bars," in *Western Story* (New York), 16 November 1929.
"The Duster's Return," in *Western Story* (New York), 30 November 1929.
"Twelve Peers," in *Western Story* (New York), 1 February–8 March 1930.
"Two Masters," in *Western Story* (New York), 5 April 1930.
"Sixteen in Nome," in *Western Story* (New York), 3 May 1930.
"Battle's End," in *Western Story* (New York), 10 May 1930.
"Rippon Rides Double," in *Western Story* (New York), 18 October–22 November 1930.
"Chip and the Cactus Man," in *Western Story* (New York), 10 January 1931.
"Chip Champions a Lady," in *Western Story* (New York), 24 January 1931.
"Chip Traps a Sheriff," in *Western Story* (New York), 31 January 1931.
"Spot Lester," in *Western Story* (New York), 17 October 1931.
"Nine Lives," in *Western Story* (New York), 31 October 1931.
"Torture Canyon," in *Western Story* (New York), 14 November 1931.
"Tramp Magic," in *Western Story* (New York), 21 November–26 December 1931.
"Dogs of the Captain," in *Western Story* (New York), 2 January–6 February 1932.
"Speedy—Deputy," in *Western Story* (New York), 13 February 1932.
"Outlaw Crew," in *Western Story* (New York), 20 February 1932.
"Seven-Day Lawman," in *Western Story* (New York), 27 February 1932.
"Speedy's Mare," in *Western Story* (New York), 12 March 1932.
"Carcajou's Trail," in *Western Story* (New York), 26 March 1932.
"Speedy's Crystal Game," in *Western Story* (New York), 2 April 1932.
"Red Rock's Secret," in *Western Story* (New York), 16 April 1932.
"Speedy's Bargain," in *Western Story* (New York), 14 May 1932.
"Range Jester," in *Western Story* (New York), 28 May 1932.
"The Geraldi Trail," in *Western Story* (New York), 11 June–2 July 1932.
"The Nighthawk Trail," in *Western Story* (New York), 9 July 1932.
"Outlaws from Afar," in *Western Story* (New York), 20 August 1932.
"Torturous Trek," in *Western Story* (New York), 27 August–17 September 1932.
"The Law Dodger of Windy Creek," in *Western Story* (New York), 24 September 1932.
"Smoking Guns," in *Western Story* (New York), 29 October 1932.
"Cat Hill Fugitive," in *Western Story* (New York), 10–31 December 1932.
"Speedy's Desert Dance," in *Western Story* (New York), 28 January 1933.
"The Stolen Stallion," in *Western Story* (New York), 11 March 1933.
"The Masterman," in *Argosy* (New York), 18 March–22 April 1933.
"The Man from Mustang," in *Western Story* (New York), 15 April 1933.
"Brothers of the West," in *Western Story* (New York), 29 April 1933.
"The Quest," in *West* (New York), May 1933.
"Silver's Strike," in *Western Story* (New York), 20 May 1933.
"Horseshoe Flat's Speedy Stranger," in *Western Story* (New York), 10 June 1933.
"Black Thunder," in *Dime Western* (New York), July 1933.
"Trail of the Eagle," in *West* (New York), July 1933.
"The False Rider," in *Western Story* (New York), 1 July 1933.
"Riding Straight in Danger," in *Western Story* (New York), 22 July 1933.
"Guardian Guns," in *Dime Western* (New York), August 1933.
"The Iron Collar," in *Western Story* (New York), 5 August 1933.
"The Fighting Four," in *Western Story* (New York), 26 August 1933.

"Jingo," in *Western Story* (New York), 9 September 1933.
"Silver's Search," in *Western Story* (New York), 23 September 1923.
"Blue Water Bad Man," in *Western Story* (New York), 16 December 1933–6 January 1934.
"The Rough Tenderfoot," in *Western Story* (New York), 3 February–10 March 1934.
"Gun Gift," in *Western Story* (New York), 24 March–28 April 1934.
"Gunman's Bluff," in *Star Western* (Chicago), April 1934.
"Lawmen's Heart," in *Star Western* (Chicago), May 1934.
"Man Beyond the Law," in *Star Western* (Chicago), June 1934.
"Gallows Gamble," in *Star Western* (Chicago), July 1934.
"Gunless Gunman," in *Star Western* (Chicago), September 1934.
"One Man Posse," in *Mavericks*, September 1934.
"Outcast Breed," in *Star Western* (Chicago), October 1934.
"Sleeper Pays a Debt," in *Mavericks*, October 1934.
"Scourge of the Rio Grande," in *Argosy* (New York), 20 October–24 November 1934.
"Gunman's Rendezvous," in *Star Western* (Chicago), November 1934.
"Satan's Gun Rider," in *Mavericks*, November 1934.
"Man of the West," in *Western Story* (New York), 10 November–15 December 1934.
"Sleeper Turns Horse-Thief," in *Mavericks*, December 1934.
"Rifle Pass," in *Argosy* (New York), 9 February 1935.
"Crazy Rhythm" in *Argosy* (New York), 2 March 1935.
"The Sacred Valley," in *Argosy* (New York), 10 August–14 September 1935.
"Viva! Viva!," in *Argosy* (New York), 2 January 1937.
"Eagles over Crooked Creek," in *Western Story* (New York), 29 January 1938.
"Senor Coyote," in *Argosy* (New York), 18 June–25 June 1938.
"Seven Mile House," in *Argosy* (New York), 4 October–29 November 1941.
"The Laughter of Slim Malone," in *Gunpoint*, edited by Lee Margulies. New York, Pyramid, 1960.
"Dust Storm," in *The Arbor House Treasury of Great Western Stories*, edited by Bill Pronzini and Martin H. Greenberg. New York, Arbor House, 1982.
"Wine on the Desert," in *The Western Hall of Fame: An Anthology of Classic Western Stories*, edited by Bill Pronzini and Martin H. Greenberg. New York, Morrow, 1984.
"The Sun Stood Still," in *Westeryear*, edited by Edward Gorman. New York, Evans, 1988.
"A First Blooding," in *The New Frontier*, edited by Joe R. Lansdale. New York, Doubleday, 1989.

Uncollected Short Stories as John Frederick

"The Man Who Forgot Christmas," in *Western Story* (New York), 25 December 1920.
"The Cure of Silver Canon," in *Western Story* (New York), 15 January 1921.
"His Back Against the Wall," in *Western Story* (New York), 12 March 1921.
"'Jerico's' Garrison Finish," in *Western Story* (New York), 21 May 1921.
"When the Wandering Whip Rode West," in *Western Story* (New York), 18 June 1921
"Riding into Peril," in *Western Story* (New York), 19 November 1921.
"The Emerald Trail," in *Western Story* (New York), 25 February 1922.
"King Charlie—One Year Later," in *Western Story* (New York), 27 May 1922.
"King Charlie's Hosts," in *Western Story* (New York), 24 June 1922.
"Slumber Mountain," in *Western Story* (New York), 8 July 1922.
"The Bill for Banditry," in *Western Story* (New York), 5 August 1922.
"Old Carver Ranch," in *Western Story* (New York), 26 August 1922.
"Without a Penny in the World," in *Western Story* (New York), 21 October 1922.
"The Cabin in the Pines," in *Western Story* (New York), 9 December 1922.
"The Power of Prayer," in *Western Story* (New York), 23 December 1922.
"Winking Lights," in *Western Story* (New York), 6 January 1923.
"Gold King Turns His Back," in *Western Story* (New York), 28 April 1923.
"The Abandoned Outlaw," in *Western Story* (New York), 26 May 1923.
"Slow Bill," in *Western Story* (New York), 13 October 1923.
"The Boy Who Found Christmas," in *Western Story* (New York), 22 December 1923.
"Four Without Fear," in *Western Story* (New York), 8 March–12 April 1924.
"The Girl They Left Behind Them," in *Western Story* (New York), 21 June 1924.
"A Wolf among Dogs," in *Western Story* (New York), 5 July 1924.
"In the Hills of Monterey," in *Western Story* (New York), 4 October–8 November 1924.
"Not the Fastest Horse," in *Western Story* (New York), 7 November 1925.
"The White Wolf," in *Western Story* (New York), 6 March 1925.
"Lightning Lumberjacks," in *Western Story* (New York), 12 March 1927.
"A Lucky Dog," in *Western Story* (New York), 22 October 1927.
"The Magic Gun," in *Western Story* (New York), 7 April 1928.
"The Winged Horse," in *Western Story* (New York), 16 February–23 March 1929.
"Chinook," in *Western Story* (New York), 13 July–17 August 1929.
"Tiger's Den," in *Western Story* (New York), 15 March–19 April 1930.
"The Lightning Runner," in *Western Story* (New York), 9 January–13 February 1932.

Uncollected Short Stories as George Owen Baxter

"Iron Dust," in *Western Story* (New York), 29 January 1921.
"When Iron Turns to Gold," in *Western Story* (New York), 30 July 1921.
"Madcap of the Mountains," in *Western Story* (New York), 13 September 1921.
"The Man Who Followed," in *Western Story* (New York), 10 December 1921.
"The Fugitive's Mission," in *Western Story* (New York), 14 January 1922.
"The One-Way Trail," in *Western Story* (New York), 4 February 1922.
"Three Who Paid," in *Western Story* (New York), 8 April 1922.
"Mountain Madness," in *Western Story* (New York), 26 August 1922.
"Over the Northern Border," in *Western Story* (New York), 16 September 1922.

"Joe White's Brand," in *Western Story* (New York), 14 October 1922.
"Wild Freedom," in *Western Story* (New York), 11 November–16 December 1922.
"Phil, The Fiddler," in *Western Story* (New York), 30 December 1922.
"Two Sixes," in *Western Story* (New York), 17 March 1923.
"'Sunset' Wins," in *Western Story* (New York), 7 April 1923.
"The Bandit of the Black Hills," in *Western Story* (New York), 28 April–2 June 1923.
"Black Sheep," in *Western Story* (New York), 28 July 1923.
"Seven Trails to Romance," in *Western Story* (New York), 1 September–6 October 1923.
"Soft Metal," in *Western Story* (New York), 20 October 1923.
"The Whisperer of the Wilderness," in *Western Story* (New York), 1 December 1923–5 January 1924.
"Train's Trust," in *Western Story* (New York), 26 January–1 March 1924.
"Bared Fangs," in *Western Story* (New York), 10 May 1924.
"Argentine," in *Western Story* (New York), 31 May–5 July 1924.
"The Boy in the Wilderness," in *Western Story* (New York), 19 July 1924.
"The Brute," in *Western Story* (New York), 26 July 1924.
"The Race," in *Western Story* (New York), 9 August 1924.
"Hired by Dad," in *Western Story* (New York), 6 September 1924.
"Billy Angel, Trouble Lover," in *Western Story* (New York), 22 November 1924.
"Mountain Made," in *Western Story* (New York), 13 December 1924–17 January 1925.
"In Dread of the Law," in *Western Story* (New York), 18 April 1925.
"Going Straight," in *Western Story* (New York), 2 May 1925.
"The Battle for Mike," in *Western Story* (New York), 16 May 1925.
"The Outlaw Redeemer," in *Western Story* (New York), 30 May 1925.
"His Fight for a Pardon," in *Western Story* (New York), 27 June 1925.
"Fire Brain," in *Western Story* (New York), 12 September–17 October 1925.
"The Runaways," in *Western Story* (New York), 24 October–28 November 1925.
"The Good Bad-Man," in *Western Story* (New York), 30 January 1926.
"The Man He Couldn't Get," in *Western Story* (New York), 27 February 1926.
"The Vamp's Bandit," in *Western Story* (New York), 20 March 1926.
"Bad Man's Gulch," in *Western Story* (New York), 17 July 1926.
"The Bells of San Felipo," in *Western Story* (New York), 6 November–11 December 1926.
"Flaming Fortune," in *Western Story* (New York), 19 February 1927.
"The Western Double," in *Western Story* (New York), 26 March–30 April 1927.
"The Terrible Tenderfoot," in *Western Story* (New York), 2 July 1927.
"The Gentle Desperado," in *Western Story* (New York), 16 July 1927.
"Tiger, Tiger!," in *Western Story* (New York), 30 July 1927.
"Red Wind and Thunder Moon," in *Western Story* (New York), 27 August 1927.
"Thunder Moon—Paleface," in *Western Story* (New York), 17 September 1927.
"Thunder Moon—Squawman," in *Western Story* (New York), 24 September–22 October 1927.
"Forgotten Treasure," in *Western Story* (New York), 19 November 1927.
"Tragedy Trail," in *Western Story* (New York), 25 February–31 March 1928.
"The Brass Man," in *Western Story* (New York), 23 June–28 July 1928.
"Riders for Fortune," in *Western Story* (New York), 15 September–20 October 1928.
"Thunder Moon Goes White," in *Western Story* (New York), 3 November 1928.
"The Lion's Share," in *Western Story* (New York), 1 December 1928.
"Hunted Hunters," in *Western Story* (New York), 16 February 1929.
"Strength of the Hills," in *Western Story* (New York), 25 May–29 June 1929.
"Happy Valley," in *Western Story* (New York), 24 August–28 September 1929.
"Two Broncos," in *Western Story* (New York), 9 November–14 December 1929.
"Cayenne Charlie," in *Western Story* (New York), 22 February 1930.
"Daring Duval," in *Western Story* (New York), 19 July–23 August 1930.
"Trouble's Messenger," in *Western Story* (New York), 6 September–11 October 1930.
"On Fortune's Back," in *Western Story* (New York), 6 December 1930–11 January 1931.
"Duck Hawk's Master," in *Western Story* (New York), 25 April–30 May 1931.
"Treasure Well," in *Western Story* (New York), 27 June 1931.
"Outlaw's Conscience," in *Western Story* (New York), 11 July 1931.
"Clean Courage," in *Western Story* (New York), 25 July 1931.
"Gun Pearl Trail," in *Western Story* (New York), 12 September–17 October 1931.
"Hawks and Eagles," in *Western Story* (New York), 5 December 1931.
"Black Snake and Gun," in *Western Story* (New York), 19 December 1931.
"Black-Snake Joe," in *Western Story* (New York), 2 January 1932.
"The Three Crosses," in *Western Story* (New York), 23 January 1932.
"White Wolf," in *Western Story* (New York), 13 February–19 March 1932.
"All for One," in *Western Story* (New York), 1–22 October 1932.
"The Two-Handed Man," in *Western Story* (New York), 3 December 1932.
"Señor Billy," in *Western Story* (New York), 7 January 1933.
"The Red Bandanna," in *Western Story* (New York), 4 February 1933.
"The Wolf and the Man," in *Western Story* (New York), 4 March–22 April 1933.
"Kingbird's Pursuit," in *Western Story* (New York), 10 June–29 July 1933.
"The Happy Rider," in *Western Story* (New York), 9 September–28 October 1933.
"Reata," in *Western Story* (New York), 11 November 1933.
"Reata's Danger Trail," in *Western Story* (New York), 25 November 1933.
"Reata's Danger Ride," in *Western Story* (New York), 9 December 1933.

"Reata and the Hidden Gold," in *Western Story* (New York), 23 December 1933.
"Stolen Gold," in *Western Story* (New York), 6 January 1934.
"Reata and the Overland Kid," in *Western Story* (New York), 20 January 1934.
"Reata's Peril Trek," in *Western Story* (New York), 17 March 1934.

Uncollected Short Stories as Peter Henry Morland

"The Squaw Boy," in *Western Story* (New York), 4 July–8 August 1925.
"The Range Finder," in *Western Story* (New York), 14 November 1925.
"Trail of the Stone-That-Shines," in *Western Story* (New York), 29 May–3 July 1926.
"Coward of the Clan," in *Western Story* (New York), 19 May 1928.
"The Man from the Sky," in *Western Story* (New York), 2 June 1928.
"Prairie Pawn," in *Western Story* (New York), 16 June 1928.
"Fugitives' Fire," in *Western Story* (New York), 30 June 1928.
"The Flaming Rider," in *Western Story* (New York), 29 December 1928.
"The Horizon of Danger," in *Western Story* (New York), 21 December 1929–25 January 1930.
"White Water Sam," in *Western Story* (New York), 30 January 1930.
"Rancher's Legacy," in *Western Story* (New York), 20 February–26 March 1932.
"Mountain Raiders," in *Western Story* (New York), 9 April 1932.
"Rawhide Bound," in *Western Story* (New York), 23 April 1932.
"Greaser Trail," in *Western Story* (New York), 21 May 1932.

Uncollected Short Stories as David Manning

"Rustlers' Rock," in *Western Story* (New York), 6 July–10 August 1929.
"The Danger Lover," in *Western Story* (New York), 7 September 1929.
"The Golden Coyote," in *Western Story* (New York), 12 April 1930.
"White Hunger," in *Western Story* (New York), 26 April 1930.
"Mother," in *Western Story* (New York), 17 May 1930.
"Shiver-Nose," in *Western Story* (New York), 24 May 1930.
"Yellow Dog," in *Western Story* (New York), 31 May 1930.
"Back to His Own," in *Western Story* (New York), 7 June 1930.
"The Best Bandit," in *Western Story* (New York), 5 March 1932.
"The Golden Spurs," in *Western Story* (New York), 26 March–30 April 1932.
"Paradise Al," in *Western Story* (New York), 4 June 1932.
"Paradise Al's Confession," in *Western Story* (New York), 16 July 1932.

Uncollected Short Stories as Hugh Owen

"Bad News for Bad Men," in *Western Story* (New York), 8 December 1934.
"The Red Well," in *Western Story* (New York), 29 December 1934.
"The Fighting Coward," in *Western Story* (New York), 26 January 1935.
"Sun and Sand," in *Western Story* (New York), 16 February 1935.

Other Publications

Novels

Children of Night. London, Hodder and Stoughton, 1923.
Cross Over Nine (as Walter C. Butler). New York, Macaulay, 1935.
The Night Flower (as Walter C. Butler). New York, Macaulay, 1936; London, Stanley Paul, 1937.
Six Golden Angels. New York, Dodd Mead, 1937; London, Hodder and Stoughton, 1938.
Calling Dr. Kildare. New York, Dodd Mead, 1940.
The Secret of Dr. Kildare. New York, Dodd Mead, 1940.
Dr. Kildare Takes Charge. New York, Dodd Mead, 1941; London, Hodder and Stoughton, 1942.
Young Dr. Kildare. New York, Dodd Mead, and London, Hodder and Stoughton, 1941.
Dr. Kildare's Crisis. New York, Dodd Mead, 1942; London, Hodder and Stoughton, 1943.
Dr. Kildare's Trial. New York, Dodd Mead, 1942; London, Hodder and Stoughton, 1944.
Dr. Kildare's Search, and Dr. Kildare's Hardest Case. New York, Dodd Mead, 1943; London, Hodder and Stoughton, 1945.
Big Game. New York, Paperback Library, 1973.
The Granduca. New York, Paperback Library, 1973.
The Phantom Spy. New York, Dodd Mead, 1973; London, White Lion, 1975.
Dead Man's Treasure. London, White Lion, 1975.

Novels as John Frederick

Riders of the Silences. New York, H.K. Fly, 1920.
The Bronze Collar. New York, Putnam, 1925.
The Sword Lover. New York, Waterson, 1927.

Novels as George Challis

The Splendid Rascal. Indianapolis, Bobbs Merrill, 1926; London, Cassell, 1927.
Monsieur. Indianapolis, Bobbs Merrill, and London, Cassell, 1926.
The Golden Knight. New York, Greystone Press, 1937; London, Cassell, 1938.
The Naked Blade. New York, Greystone Press, 1938; London, Cassell, 1939.
The Firebrand. New York, Harper, 1950.
The Bait and the Trap. New York, Harper, 1951.

Novels as Frederick Frost

Secret Agent Number One. Philadelphia, Macrae Smith, 1936; London, Harrap, 1937.
Spy Meets Spy. Philadelphia, Macrae Smith, and London, Harrap, 1937.
The Bamboo Whistle. Philadelphia, Macrae Smith, 1937.

Plays

The Gate (oratorio), with Mirza Ahmad Sohrab and Julie Chanler, music by Brand. New York, Associated Music Publishers, 1944.

Screenplays: *Young Doctor Kildare*, with Harry Ruskin and Willis Goldbeck, 1938; *Calling Dr. Kildare*, with Harry Ruskin and Willis Goldbeck, 1939; *Dr. Kildare's Strange Case*, with Ruskin, 1940; *Dr. Kildare Goes Home*, with Ruskin and Goldbeck, 1940; *Dr. Kildare's Crisis*, with Ruskin and

Goldbeck, 1940; *The People vs. Dr. Kildare*, with others, 1941; *The Desperadoes*, with Robert Carson, 1942; *Uncertain Glory*, with Laszlo Ladnay and Joe May, 1944.

Verse as Frederick Faust

The Village Street and Other Poems. New York, Putnam, 1922.
Dionysus in Hades. Oxford, Blackwell, 1931.
The Thunderer. New York, Derrydale Press, 1933.

Other

The Ten Foot Chain; or, Can Love Survive the Shackles?, with others. New York, Reynolds, 1920.
The Notebooks and Poems of Max Brand, edited by John Schoolcraft. New York, Dodd Mead, 1957.

*

Bibliography: *Max Brand: The Man and His Work, Critical Appreciation and Bibliography*, by Darrell C. Richardson, Los Angeles, Fantasy, 1952.

Manuscript Collection: University of California, Berkeley.

Critical Study: *Max Brand, The Big "Westerner"* by Robert Easton, Norman, University of Oklahoma Press, 1970.

* * *

Between 1918 and 1938 Frederick Schiller Faust published over 300 book-length western stories in a variety of pulp magazines under various pseudonyms. He also wrote hundreds of other stories, during the same years, in other genres—adventure, mystery, historical romance, even science fiction—represented in the cheaply printed, widely available medium of the pulps. Late in the 1930's Faust wrote stories also for the so-called "slick" magazines and finished his career writing scripts in Hollywood. All along, through a 52-year life of intense literary and physical activity, driven by romantic, even Faustian urge for extraordinary artistic achievement, Frederick Faust claimed that his first love and most important activity was his slow but unsuccessful creation of traditional poetry.

Some sense of these biographical facts, especially their complexity and irony, is necessary in order to understand that Max Brand—Faust's first and most famous pseudonym, under which virtually all of his work reprinted since his death in 1944 has appeared—is more than just a pen name. For Max Brand represents not only Frederick Faust but also a process, a peculiarly unconscious mode of creation in which Faust, a lover of high art and traditional literature, was able to turn out a complete pulp serial every two or three weeks over a 20-year period. As a "writer" of popular Westerns, Max Brand suggests qualities of imagination quite different from the demands of historical realism sometimes associated with the genre. There is little sense of history or place in Max Brand. Much of Max Brand was written at Faust's Italian villa where he lived in the 1920's and 1930's. Faust himself claimed that the west (he was raised in California) was "disgusting." He took no pride in his pulp stories except for the money they earned him. Yet—not so much in spite of these facts as because of them—the popular Westerns of Max Brand are among the most innovative and imaginative ever produced.

The Untamed, Brand's first Western, appeared six years after Zane Grey had burst to popularity with *Riders of the Purple Sage*. That same year—1918—saw Britain purchase 800,000 copies of Westerns by William Macleod Raine for distribution to its troops in World War I. The genre was well-established. In writing *The Untamed* Faust may have felt that he had to establish a unique style to ensure his own popularity; he certainly seems to have understood, better than any other writer of sagebrush sagas, that the western was mythic rather than realistic. Consequently, the unifying feature of Max Brand Westerns is the almost total absence of any pretentions of dealing with the West of historical record. They are rarely set in specific western places; their plots do not recapitulate historical events; and they make frequent and peculiar use of alien elements, especially characters and events drawn from European mythology and legend. Dozens of western writers have created fiction dealing with the Tonto Basin Feud or the Lincoln County War. Max Brand touched upon neither of these events. But he did adapt Sophocles to western format in *Trailin'*, retell the *Iliad* in *Hired Guns*, and perform similar acts of literary legerdemain on dozens of other occasions.

The story of Dan Barry in *The Untamed*, *The Night Horseman*, and *The Seventh Man* indicates the bizarre, off-trail manner in which Brand established himself as a western writer. This series, which appeared first as pulp serials in *All-Story Weekly* and *Argosy*, creates a western hero out of a mysterious adopted youth who is explicitly named "Pan of the desert" in the first novel, who shows traces of werewolf-like behavior in the second (as he roams in the night with a black horse and black wolf-like dog), and whose atavistic wildness comes to an end in the final novel only when his wife fires a bullet through his heart.

In later stories Brand became somewhat more formulaic, spinning out plots based on the demands of "action, action, action," as Faust himself put it. But in Brand there is always a catch, some leap of Faustian imagination, couched in an economical but still felicitous and resonant style, that urges the story beyond the established borders of the Western and into a vaguer territory of fantasy and universal myth. Many of the traditional concerns of the Western are dropped along the way. Brand shows little interest in the theme of historical and personal regeneration in the West that motivated Zane Grey, in exalted definitions of women, or in supporting the uniquely American myth of frontier development and its attendant virtues. Consequently, racial and sexual stereotyping is less obvious in Brand than elsewhere, and at times his stories even seem to gravitate towards a parody of the popular western and its expectations. The Hollywood treatments of Brand's *Destry Rides Again* may serve as testimony to this last trait.

Yet Max Brand could write appealingly of subjects that matter. His series of novels dealing with a half-Indian, half-white hero whose problems resemble some combination of Oedipus and Natty Bumppo—*War Party*, *Frontier Feud*, and *Cheyenne Gold*—create a surprisingly sympathetic pulp image of Native Americans. His Montana Kid series (1933–36), three novels in which an Anglo drifter performs right-hearted though violent heroics for Mexican peons and bandidos, shows equally surprising sympathy for another ethnic group usually subject to prejudiced treatment in popular Westerns.

The few western stories written for slick magazines display a careful, polished prose. The same kind of prose appears in Brand's pulp work, but in a story like "Wine on the Desert," especially in its economy of characterization and incident, the style approaches the best of Ernest Haycox and Luke Short, two master craftsmen of the Western.

In 1952 *Time* magazine referred to Max Brand as "the gooey residue of boiled pulp," of no more significance than an endless mirage of buffaloes "stamping upside down across the sky." Such a felt need to attack Brand so harshly may suggest better than any other evidence the extent and nature of Brand's appeal. Brand was "King of the Pulps," to be sure, as he has often been described. But for Frederick Faust, as Max Brand, the real medium was neither pulp nor history but imagination and style.

—William Bloodworth

BRANNIGAN, Russ. British?

WESTERN PUBLICATIONS

Novels

Border Feud. London, Muller, 1953.
Rider of the Wastelands. London, Muller, 1953.

* * *

The two western novels that Russ Brannigan wrote in the early 1950's are fairly typical of the lightweight end of the genre during this period, and may even be seen as harking back to a former era, containing as they do the leisurely pace, laboured humour, and high-flown description so often encountered in practitioners of the 1930's and 1940's. Heroes of superhuman strength and determination take on stereotypical villains and bring about their downfall, pausing only to win the hand of a decidedly subordinate—if not submissive—heroine. Brannigan favours descriptive passages at the expense of a dialogue which tends to be stilted and unconvincing. Action scenes, notably the opening of *Border Feud*, where the gunning down of a killer is referred to almost off-handedly in two or three lines, rarely succeed in engaging the reader's attention. The author's abilities are probably best displayed in *Rider of the Wastelands*, which has ex-Texas Ranger Benedict Frail investigating a rancher's murder, and bringing the killer to justice. The unusually named Frail, mounted on his white stallion Blaze, is a hero of Lone Ranger proportions—and about as credible—but the action moves slightly more easily, and the two shoot-outs (Brannigan keeps deaths to a minimum in both his books) are surprisingly effective. When Frail rides into the sunset with the rancher's daughter, we are perhaps not quite so surprised.

Brannigan's penchant for heroes with peculiar names finds its apogee in *Border Feud*, whose central character is the startling Santos Escobar Manuel Patrick O'Toole—"Sempo" to his friends—a giant Irish-Mexican gunfighter and outlaw of predictably superhuman stature and ability. His battle for supremacy as "King of the Outlaws" with his wicked uncle, another Santos, provides most of the threadbare plot, supplemented by the "love interest" of the femme fatale, Carmenella. Sempo settles with the former in a rather stagey sabre duel, while Carmenella—having plotted against our hero for most of the book—reforms somewhat unbelievably at the end in order to effect a dubious "rosy" conclusion. Sempo and his friend Farado display their author's sympathetic view of Mexican characters, which must be noted as being to his credit, although neither man is any more believable as a person than is Frail in the previous novel; one feels that by swapping Sempo for Frail one is leaving the Lone Ranger only to encounter the Cisco Kid!

Brannigan employs formula plots and characters, and presents both at a mundane, uninspired level. Perhaps the most striking aspects of his work are his enlightened view (for his time) of Mexican Westerners, and the outrageous names of his heroes.

—Jeff Sadler

BRANT, Lewis. *See* **ROWLAND, Donald S.**

BRAUN, Matt(hew). American. Born in Oklahoma, 15 November 1932. Served in the United States Army: 1st Lieutenant. Married Bettiane Braun in 1969. Journalist, 1956–69; then freelance writer. Member of the Board of Directors, Western Writers of America. Recipient: Western Writers of America Spur award, 1977 and Stirrup award, 1987, 1988. Agent: Richard Curtis, 171 East 74th Street, New York, New York, 10021 U.S.A.

WESTERN PUBLICATIONS

Novels (series: Luke Starbuck; The Brannocks; Ash Tallman)

Mattie Silks. New York, Popular Library, 1972; London, Coronet, 1974.
Black Fox. New York, Fawcett, 1972; London, Coronet, 1973.
The Savage Land. New York, Popular Library, 1973; London, Coronet, 1974.
El Paso. New York, Fawcett, 1973; London, Coronet, 1974.
Noble Outlaw. New York, Popular Library, 1975; London, Coronet, 1977.
Bloody Hand. New York, Popular Library, 1975.
Cimarron Jordan. New York, Fawcett, 1975; London, Coronet, 1976.
Kinch. New York, Dell, 1975.
Buck Colter. New York, Dell, 1975; London, Coronet, 1976.
The Kincaids. New York, Putnam, 1976.
The Second Coming of Lucas Brokaw. New York, Dell, 1977; London, Magnum, 1978.
Hangman's Creek (Starbuck). New York, Pocket Books, 1979; London, Sphere, 1982.
Lords of the Land. New York, Dell, 1979.
The Stuart Women. New York, Putnam, 1980.
Jury of Six (Starbuck). New York, Pocket Books, 1980; London, Sphere, 1982.
Tombstone (Starbuck). New York, Pocket Books, 1981; London, Sphere, 1982.
The Spoilers (Starbuck). New York, Pocket Books, 1981; London, Sphere, 1982.
The Manhunter (Starbuck). New York, Pocket Books, 1981; London, Sphere, 1982.
Deadwood (Starbuck). New York, Pocket Books, 1981; London, Sphere, 1982.
The Judas Tree (Starbuck). New York, Pocket Books, 1982; London, Sphere, 1983.
The Killing Touch. New York, Charter, 1983.
The Highbinders (Tallman). New York, Avon, 1984.
Crossfire (Tallman). New York, Avon, 1984.
The Wages of Sin (Tallman). New York, Avon, 1984.
Bloodstorm. New York, Pinnacle, 1985; as *Santa Fe*, London, Hale, 1985.

Indian Territory. New York, Pinnacle, 1985.
A Time of Innocence. New York, Walker, 1986.
The Brannocks (Brannocks). New York, New American Library, 1986.
Windward West (Brannocks). New York, New American Library, 1987.
Rio Hondo (Brannocks). New York, New American Library, 1987.
A Distant Land (Brannocks). New York, New American Library, 1988.
Tenbow. New York, New American Library, 1991.

Short Stories

The Road to Hell. New York, Antaeus, 1977.

OTHER PUBLICATIONS

Novel

This Loving Promise. New York, Zebra, 1984.

Other

The Save-Your-Life Defense Handbook. Old Greenwich, Connecticut, Devin Adair, 1977.
How to Write Western Novels. Cincinnati, Ohio, Writers Digest, 1988.
Matt Braun's Western Cooking. Chicago, Contemporary, 1988.

*

Matt Braun comments:

The Old West was the crucible of America. There people from varied cultures came together and were transformed into the plainsmen and pioneers of western folklore. Yet the truly colorful characters of that bygone time were the rogues and the rascals. Nowhere in the pages of history has a greater collection of misfits been brought together. Gunfighters and gamblers, outlaws and drifters, robber barons and corrupt politicians—they formed a roll call unsurpassed for sheer deviltry. Larger than life and immune to the codes that governed common men, these misfits had about them the stuff of legend. They were bold and audacious, they forever dared greatly, and many of our most cherished myths evolved from their shady exploits. Western lore is richer by far because of the rogues and rascals. Their presence lent a certain zest to the deadly business of survival on the frontier.

I write about these rogues and rascals. In my novels, I use real names and actual events, and construct the story around an historical incident. Everything in my novels is heavily researched and documented; the truth of the Old West is far more compelling than the fairy tale. Similarly, the rogues and rascals are far more entertaining than cattle drives and wagon trains. I present them as they were—the true daredevils of the frontier.

* * *

Matt Braun published his first western novel in 1972 and in the next decade followed a course almost in retrograde motion from what one might expect of an author with his considerable talent. He began by writing historical reconstructions, i.e., stories which are historically accurate and faithful to the place, the period, and the people; then he turned to romantic historical reconstructions, i.e., stories which treat historical events as if they were a variety of romance, and formulary Westerns, i.e., stories with stereotyped heroes, heroines, and villains; and, finally, in his Luke Starbuck series he embarked on a group of novels which are interrelated through the continued presence of the series hero and which, but for the inclusion of actual historical personalities, would otherwise be strictly formulary Westerns, with soft-core, pornographic ingredients.

Luke Starbuck was introduced in *Jury of Six*. In this novel Starbuck becomes involved with Pat Garrett and Billy the Kid. Both Garrett and the Kid are stylized so that each is diminished in contrast to Starbuck who emerges a hero embodying what Braun regarded as "heroic" virtues. There is no factual accuracy in the way the Kid is portrayed, and he is drawn as a cold-blooded murderer and thief. Similarly Garrett is shown to be a vain, inexpert, but ambitious self-seeker who intends to kill the Kid for personal gain and political advantage. Starbuck, for his part, wants to see the Kid dead in order to avenge the Kid's murder of his best friend (wholly fictitious). The reader is told that "violence was part of his [Starbuck's] trade. When words failed, he used his fists. Or in the last resort, he used a gun. Certain men, unpersuaded by reason, left him no alternative. Only a fool allowed the other man the first blow." "I'm a manhunter," Starbuck explains to Ellen Nesbeth, one of the two heroines in the novel, the one who is sexually available, "but I don't take bounty." The reader is also told that "over the past four years, Starbuck had grown cold and hard, brutalized by the sight of death." This, then, is the ideological message of the Luke Starbuck series. Neither Garrett nor the Kid, in this novel or in history, demonstrated these qualities as Starbuck does, and so we are supposed to admire his hardness, his isolation, his stoicism, and his ability to kill—not for gain, honest or dishonest—but because it is his job.

Braun's dislike of Wyatt Earp—at least Earp's popular image—first manifests itself as early as *Cimarron Jordan*; and in *Tombstone* Starbuck has a field day finding out how evil Earp is and does his best to kill him. However, given the anti-humanitarian values of Starbuck, when Wyatt blasts a defenseless man with a shotgun, Starbuck is not outraged because "he himself had hung men for lesser crimes [than murder], and an execution, whatever the reason, was still an execution. Some men deserved to die." The only essential difference between Earp, the villain in this novel, and Starbuck, the hero, is that after sexually taking advantage of Mattie Blaylock and tiring of her, Earp deserts her, whereas Starbuck, after sexually taking advantage of Mattie's sister, Alice, and not wanting to settle down, finances her in a millinery business and watches over her until she is "happily" married.

One of Braun's basic weaknesses as a novelist is his inability to draw realistic female characters. Most of the women in his fiction—from his first novel on—are prostitutes or mistresses. They exist primarily to effect detumescence in his macho heroes. In *Kinch*, perhaps Braun's best formulary Western, a character undertakes to "educate" the tubercular, adolescent hero, teaching him how to be a gunfighter and advising Kinch that "a man rules in bed, but the rest of the time it's the woman that calls the tune. They'll make you dance whatever jig they want just for the honor of pumpin' on 'em every now and then." *Buck Colter* is also a formulary western. Its hero, Colter, a mixed-blood, while still a child saw his mother raped and killed by Colonel Covington who supposedly led the massacre at Sand Creek. When, later, as a man, Colter is framed by Covington, who has since become a cattle baron, and Colter's fiancée is killed by Covington's men, Colter goes on the "warpath" with a shotgun.

Noble Outlaw and *El Paso* are both romantic historical reconstructions in a format pioneered by Henry Wilson Allen; that is, these novels are fictionalized floss added to the stories of noted gunmen—John Wesley Hardin in the former, Dallas Stoudenmire in the latter—in which their lives and they themselves are romanticized into heroes; *Noble Outlaw*, for example, concludes with the sentence, "Texas' deadliest outlaw had hung up his guns at last," the implication being that Hardin now will practice law and lead an exemplary life, ignoring Hardin's last years of surly drunkenness, bullying, and his eventual death, being shot in the back by old John Selman.

Braun's *Black Fox* was his second novel and remains his best work, an historical reconstruction in which the Black Fox of the title is Britt Johnson, a freed black from the South. When the Comanches and Kiowas stage a joint raid in 1860 to drive the white-eyes from their sacred lands and take captives, Black Fox, regarded as an "uppity nigger" by the whites, volunteers to negotiate to get the hostages back, not leastwise motivated because his own family is among the captives. Braun deftly characterized Running Dog and Santana among the Kiowas, Little Buffalo among the Comanches, showing at the same time all the minute and quite distinct differences between these two Plains tribes, just as he characterized Black Fox and his relations within his own family and among the whites, the whites among themselves and with members of other races, and the multitude of ways in which various individuals perceive themselves and others. Britt comes to realize that "the strong fight the strong for the right to harness the meek to the plow." His greater inner conflict is induced by Running Dog, his friend among the Kiowas, who cannot understand why Black Fox prefers to live among the whites where he is subjected to the most demeaning treatment when he might live in freedom and dignity among the Kiowas. Each of the central male characters is a fully rounded human being and so, from this perspective, a reader is better able to understand the suffering and personal travail in which each must live and somehow find his own way within the human community and within himself. As in any fine historical reconstruction, we come to recognize our solidarity with these people from the past.

The decade of the 1980's was a fruitful one for Braun, filled with some notable experiments and some equally notable achievements. No doubt somewhat under the influence of Gordon D. Shirreffs who devised the idea of a manhunter and his adventures as an alternative to the traditional ranch romance, Braun had come up with his Luke Starbuck series of violent, soft-porn western novels. With the invention of Cole Braddock in *Bloodstorm*, Braun created a more attractive protagonist as a manhunter. Braddock is a private detective headquartered in Denver who enjoys a national reputation and, therefore, in the best tradition of the dime novels has to resort to disguises when working on a case. He enjoys a stable relationship with Lise Hammond, a top-line hoofer in the Denver area, and in this novel, while trying to break the Santa Fe Ring, Braddock calls on her assistance to work undercover with him. Compared to the vividness with which Shirreffs evoked the regions of the Southwest in his Lee Kershaw, manhunter, series, there is little feeling for New Mexico in Braun's novel, or its multi-layered cultures at the time of the story—1882—and violence, when it occurs, is sudden and terrible, as in the fiction of Noel M. Loomis without, in Braun's case, becoming the focus of the story. One interesting sidelight to Braddock's character is that Starbuck's adventure in *Jury of Six* is attributed to him, including the love affair with Ellen Nesbeth and Starbuck's summary execution of Judge Hough. Perhaps Braun toyed with the idea of revamping the Starbuck series and rewriting it with Cole Braddock as the protagonist. If so, the notion was stillborn since when *Jury of Six* was reissued in 1990 Starbuck was still the protagonist. It is also interesting to find Buck Colter as a major character in *Bloodstorm* who sides Braddock against the Ring and the violent Clay Allison, the only real-life character in the novel.

In *Indian Territory*, Braun did return to the historical reconstruction with a story much in the vein of his fine work in *Blackfox*. John Ryan is a former lawman hired by Colonel Robert Stevens to troubleshoot for the railroad he is building through Indian Territory. While performing this job, Ryan also finds himself sympathetic to and then allied with William Ross, the Cherokee leader who is locked in a fight for the rights of the Five Civilized Tribes and pitted against the bureaucracy in Washington and the rapacity on the frontier. Ross's daughter Elizabeth is the woman with whom Ryan finally falls in love, a strong, complex, attractive female character, as fully developed as Ryan, something that hitherto had been lacking in virtually all of Braun's fiction. By the end, Ryan has found his home among the Cherokees and decides to join their cause.

Braun's tetralogy about the Brannock family which moves west after the war between the states ranks, certainly, as his most ambitious endeavor. In terms of the marketplace, the Brannock saga was obviously intended to attract the same audience as Louis L'Amour did with his multi-book saga about the Sacketts. There is, however, far less romanticism in Braun's saga and his characters are more openly, if not explicitly, sexual than those in L'Amour's novels. The pornographic Starbuck series to one side, Braun's admission in his fiction of the 1980's of sexuality as a drive in men and women alike is another very strong link with the western fiction of Gordon D. Shirreffs. The movement toward more realistic and appealing female characters such as Lise Hammond and Elizabeth Ross is furthered in this saga with Elizabeth Tisdale with whom Virgil Brannock, the eldest of the three Brannock brothers, falls in love in *The Brannocks*, and the coming of age in the third volume of Virgil's and Elizabeth's daughter, Jennifer.

All of these novels repay reading. However, for all of its panorama of the West in the last part of the 19th century, the historical research that went into the saga of the Brannocks tends, in those cases where actual historical personalities are introduced, to be highly fanciful and generally inaccurate. Billy the Kid is introduced as a character in *Rio Hondo* and interviewed at the Mesilla jail by Clint Brannock. The brief sketch Braun provides of the factors and principals involved in the Lincoln County War is a total misrepresentation. Alexander McSween, John Tunstall's attorney, is characterized as "a local storekeeper", and of the Kid, who shot only four men in the most desperate circumstances, it is written that "of the men he'd killed, at least seven had been gunned down with no chance to defend themselves." Yet, these historical fantasies notwithstanding, in terms of Braun's stature as an important western writer, the last hand, happily, was not played in the Starbuck series. In his western fiction in the 1980's he has gone a far way to fulfil the early promise of *Blackfox* in novels of distinguished literary achievement, and to hold out further promise of even better things to come.

—Jon Tuska

BRENNAN, Walt. *See* **KING, Albert.**

BRENNAN, Will. *See* **PAINE, Lauran.**

BRIDGER, Adam. *See* **BINGLEY, David Ernest.**

BRIDGES, Ben. *See* **WHITEHEAD, David.**

BRINIG, Myron. American. Born in Minneapolis, Minnesota, 22 December 1900. Educated at New York University, 1917–19; Columbia University, New York, 1919–21.

WESTERN PUBLICATIONS

Novels

Singermann. New York, Farrar and Rinehart, and London, Cobden Sanderson, 1930.
Wide Open Town. New York, Farrar and Rinehart, 1931.
This Man Is My Brother. New York, Farrar and Rinehart, 1932.
Sons of Singermann. London, Cobden Sanderson, 1932.
The Sun Sets in the West. New York, Farrar and Rinehart, and London, Cobden Sanderson, 1935.
The Sisters. New York, Farrar and Rinehart, and London, Cobden Sanderson, 1937.
The Gambler Takes a Wife. New York, Rinehart, 1943; London, Herbert Jenkins, 1947.
Footsteps on the Stair. New York, Rinehart, 1950.

OTHER PUBLICATIONS

Novels

Madonna Without Child. New York, Doubleday, 1929.
Anthony in the Nude. New York and Toronto, Farrar and Rinehart, 1930.
Copper City. London, Cobden Sanderson, 1931.
The Flutter of an Eyelid. New York and Toronto, Farrar and Rinehart, 1933.
Out of Life. New York and Toronto, Farrar and Rinehart, and London, Cobden Sanderson, 1934.
May Flavin. New York and Toronto, Farrar and Rinehart, and London, Cobden Sanderson, 1938.
Anne Minton's Life. New York and Toronto, Farrar and Rinehart, 1939; London, Heinemann, 1940.
All of Their Lives. New York and Toronto, Farrar and Rinehart, 1941.
The Family Way. New York and Toronto, Farrar and Rinehart, 1942.
You and I. New York and Toronto, Farrar and Rinehart, 1945.
Hour of Nightfall. New York, Rinehart, 1947.
No Marriage in Paradise. New York, Rinehart, 1949.
The Sadness in Lexington Avenue. New York, Rinehart, 1951.
The Street of the Three Friends. New York, Rinehart, 1953.
The Looking Glass Heart. New York, Sagamore Press, 1958.

Uncollected Short Story

"Blissful Interlude," in *The Smart Set Anthology* (New York), 1934.

* * *

Not too many decades ago, a novel about a Jewish immigrant family making its way in a Montana mining town would have seemed somewhat uncharacteristic of western American literature. For a long time, the rosy fog of romanticism lay so heavily over the genre that authors offered a fairly stereotypical cast of cowboys, mountainmen, and Indians. With the slow growth of ethnic awareness, however, Swedes, blacks, and Irish began appearing as valid figures in the West's literature. Several of Myron Brinig's novels helped the shift, though much of his accomplishment lies in his sophistication, in his ability to transcend the sort of stereotypes he is breaking rather than to create new ones. This quality is emphasized in three significant ways. Firstly, by drawing on his knowledge of Montana, he presents the Jewish experience in the West credibly and often powerfully. Secondly, as a sign of his wide talent, he doesn't pigeonhole himself as a voice of the Jewish experience alone, but shows himself capable of revealing the psychological subtlties of the middle-class mainstream. Lastly, his characters are so well-wrought that they take on lives of their own. For Brinig, the West is no mere colorful background, but simply the place where the people he creates happen to live, and he skillfully uses the particularities of his western settings to influence his characters' development. In all this, he implies a larger comment on the region: that it is a place of high expectations often dashed against realities; that it is a lovely and exciting land whose loveliness and excitements may be fleeting; and that it is a place of social changes so rapid that human beings bring ruin upon themselves either if they refuse to change with it, or if they lose their own selfhood by enthusiastically changing too fast. With Brinig the West is a testing ground that can refine character, but perhaps more often overwhelms it. If Brinig's works are overly long and weighted with melodramatic coincidences, if they at times ploddingly haul their characters by the neck toward their ends with a near Dreiseresque fatalism, readers can at least partially forgive the faults, for Brinig reveals a West as complex, as unstable and hence dangerous for individuals unaware of the pitfalls, and he frequently does so with human compassion and, perhaps best, with the touches of poetic description that make such insights memorable.

Two novels, *Singermann* and *The Sisters*, illustrate the above. Both begin around the turn of the century, a period when the West still was a region of burgeoning, if potentially deceptive, opportunities, but also a more peaceful time, for the muscular stage of conquest had just passed. Thus the novelist concentrates not on physicality but on the dynamics of interacting personalities set against the lingering aura of a wild land recently tamed. Both books begin in Silver Bow, the fictionalized copper-mining town of Butte, Montana, the author's boyhood home.

As a context for Brinig's novels, we might recall that 19th-century immigrants flocked westward by the thousands. Their hope was not merely to duplicate their former situations but to achieve in the lands beyond the Mississippi River something closer to their ideals. In this, we often forget, they failed by the tens of thousands. In contrast to their hopes, the West was a rain-poor place; given the arid conditions, the homestead laws allowed much too little land per individual; and the weather could be quirky and severe. In short, the conditions in the West didn't dovetail with settlers' expectations. Unable to grasp the differences, many of the adventurers dragged themselves back across the continent under a forlorn banner: "In God We Trusted, In The West We Busted."

Sharing the buoyant outlook of the pioneers before them, Moses and Rebecca Singermann exchange the poverty and prejudices of their native Romania for the opportunities of Silver Bow. But the Singermanns confront a new and more subtle set of problems than the early pioneers faced. Moses's clothing store in fact prospers, and he looks forward to a stable family raised in the context of the Jewish tradition transported from Romania. However, Montana is a land fostering change, not a place of tightly knit ethnic groups lending individuals their identity. Much to his horror, Moses watches his children fall away from his treasured beliefs. As one of his son's girlfriends, a neoteric Jewish girl turned Christian Scientist, puts it bluntly: "It ain't as if we was living in the Old Country. The trouble with Jews like your father is that they love to roll around in misery." In psychological terms, the children trade the restrictive but comforting folkways and religion for the freedoms and anxieties of secular American life. Yet Brinig's range is wide enough to show that disappointments don't bedevil only conservative immigrants. In *The Sisters*, the happy family of a Silver Bow druggist disintegrates before the onslaught of changing mores. The book follows the bruising experiences of the three Elliott daughters through love and marriage as they attempt to juggle instilled family values with their new roles as independent women. Far more artful and technically ambitious than *Singermann*, the novel creates distinct but complementary figures with the three sisters. Furthermore, it boldly avoids the iron hand of determinism. Despite hundreds of pages of sometimes soap-operaish turmoil, it manages to conclude on an ambiguous but convincing note of hope. If there is sadness in the sisters' hard-won stability years after the novel's beginning, it is one recognized more by the perceptive narrator than by the three grown women.

Granted the stylistic drawbacks mentioned earlier, there are pleasures in reading Brinig beyond observing deftly turned characters moving through sinuous plots. Following Joseph Conrad's charge, Brinig presents common situations as we've never seen them before. Confused at the bustle of a party, the household dog and cat yelped and screamed, then "hid themselves under the table and watched sharply a confusion of lower extremities." Meeting her son's fiancée for the first time, a skeptical mother looks at the girl and smiles "like a horse that finds the bit irksome."

—Peter Wild

BRINK, Carol Ryrie. American. Born in Moscow, Idaho, 28 December 1895. Educated at Portland Academy, 1912–14; University of Idaho, Moscow, 1914–17; University of California, Berkeley, B.A. 1918. Married Raymond Woodard Brink in 1918 (died); one son and one daughter. Recipient: American Library Association Newbery Medal, 1936; University of Minnesota Kerlan award, 1978. D.Litt.: University of Idaho, 1965. *Died 15 August 1981.*

Western Publications

Novels

Buffalo Coat. New York, Macmillan, 1944; London, Cassell, 1949.
Strangers in the Forest. New York, Macmillan, 1959.
Snow in the River. New York, Macmillan, 1964.

Fiction (for children)

Caddie Woodlawn: A Frontier Story. New York, Macmillan, 1935; London, Collier Macmillan, 1963.
All Over Town. New York, Macmillan, 1939.
Magical Melons: More Stories About Caddie Woodlawn. New York, Macmillan, 1944.
Two Are Better Than One. New York, Macmillan, and London, Collier Macmillan, 1968.
Louly. New York, Macmillan, 1974.

Other Publications

Novels

Stopover. New York, Macmillan, 1951.
The Headland. New York, Macmillan, 1955; London, Gollancz, 1956.
Château St. Barnabé. New York, Macmillan, 1963.
The Bellini Look. New York, Bantam, 1976.

Fiction (for children)

Anything Can Happen on the River! New York, Macmillan, 1934.
Mademoiselle Misfortune. New York, Macmillan, 1936.
Baby Island. New York, Macmillan, 1937.
Lad with a Whistle. New York, Macmillan, 1941.
Minty et Compagnie. Paris, Casterman, 1948.
Family Grandstand. New York, Viking Press, 1952.
The Highly Trained Dogs of Professor Petit. New York, Macmillan, 1953.
Family Sabbatical. New York, Viking Press, 1956.
The Pink Motel. New York, Macmillan, 1959; London, Collier Macmillan, 1963.
Andy Buckram's Tin Men. New York, Viking Press, 1966.
Winter Cottage. New York, Macmillan, 1968.
The Bad Times of Irma Baumlein. New York, Macmillan, and London, Collier Macmillan, 1972.

Plays (for children)

The Cupboard Was Bare. Franklin, Ohio, Eldridge, 1928.
The Queen of the Dolls. Franklin, Ohio, Eldridge, 1928.
Caddie Woodlawn, adaptation of her own story (produced Minneapolis, 1957). New York, Macmillan, 1954.
Salute Mr. Washington, in *Plays* (Boston), March 1976.

Other (for children)

Narcissa Whitman: Pioneer to the Oregon Country. Evanston, Illinois, Row Peterson, 1945.
Lafayette. Evanston, Illinois, Row Peterson, 1953.

Editor, *Best Short Stories for Children.* Evanston, Illinois, Row Peterson, 6 vols., 1936–41.

Other

Harps in the Wind: The Story of the Singing Hutchinsons. New York, Macmillan, 1947.
The Twin Cities (on Minneapolis–St. Paul). New York, Macmillan, 1961.
Four Girls on a Homestead (reminiscences). Moscow, Idaho, Latah County Museum Society, 1978.

*

Manuscript Collections: Kerlan Collection, University of Minnesota, Minneapolis; University of Idaho Library, Moscow.

* * *

Best-known as the author of *Caddie Woodlawn* and other books for children, Carol Ryrie Brink was a prolific writer whose works include adult novels, poetry, plays, and short stories. Her western fiction includes several children's books, *Caddie Woodlawn, Magical Melons, All Over Town, Two Are Better Than One*, and *Louly*, as well as three novels, *Buffalo Coat, Strangers in the Forest*, and *Snow in the River*.

Most of these works are set in Idaho, where Brink was born and raised, and to varying degrees reflect her experiences there. In contrast, the setting for *Caddie Woodlawn* and *Magical Melons* is frontier Wisconsin from 1863 to 1866, and these stories are based on the experiences of Brink's maternal grandmother, Caroline Woodhouse. *Caddie Woodlawn*, winner of the Newbery Medal, recounts the adventures of "as wild a little tomboy as ever ran the woods." To Caddie and to others, the frontier offers liberation, where people can break free from the bonds of stuffy, eastern conventions. Yet as Caddie learns, western society is not without its own prejudices, most clearly indicated in attitudes toward Indians. Caddie befriends half-breed children when their Indian mother is driven away, and warns peaceful Indians when settlers plan an attack on their village. 14 additional stories about the Woodlawn family appear in *Magical Melons*. The humorous antics of the seven Woodlawn children and the details of pioneer life related in *Caddie Woodlawn*, have made it a classic in children's literature.

Three of Brink's books for children, *Two Are Better Than One, Louly*, and *All Over Town*, draw on her childhood in Moscow, Idaho. Her memories of those experiences also appear in three adult novels. *Buffalo Coat*, set in the fictional town of Opportunity, Idaho, between 1888 and 1896, is the story of Doc Hawkins, the original town doctor. Symbolic of other western towns, Opportunity has provided Hawkins with the chance to participate in building the town, yet he will resist further progress. An interesting issue raised in the book is that of appropriate roles for women. Despite its name, in Opportunity women are restricted in their participation in society, which partially accounts for an unhappy love affair that ends in tragedy.

A second work that takes place in Opportunity is *Snow in the River*, a semi-autobiographical account of Brink's life in Idaho during the late 1890's and the first decades of the 20th century. The child Kit relates the story of her uncle, Douglas McBain, who comes to Idaho from Scotland and realizes the promise of the frontier—America is indeed the land of opportunity. Yet when he abandons his ideals and marries a woman who is pretentious and shallow, he loses everything, and is forced to begin again. His life mirrors the boom and bust cycle that characterizes much of western life.

The Bitterroot mountains of Idaho's panhandle are the scene for *Strangers in the Forest*, a fictionalized presentation of the efforts of the United States Forest Service to preserve western white pine forests from the depredations of lumber interests in the early 20th century. The predominant theme in this novel is the conflict between conservationists and business interests willing to exploit America's heritage for profit. Other traditional western themes are also present in the work. In his capacity as a botanist for the Forest Service, Bundy Jones encounters an array of homesteaders who have taken up claims within the boundaries of the national forest. Their experience in the wilderness, so marked a contrast with their earlier lives in civilized society, will expose their strengths and weaknesses and test their abilities to grow and adapt. Those who are strong and resourceful survive, while those who are weak and indecisive do not. Several of the homesteaders are women, but character, not gender, determines whether they will succeed or fail.

Brink's novels are rich in descriptions of the landscape of Idaho, and her characterizations are sound; the most memorable protagonist in these three novels is Douglas McBain. Her style is straightforward, and her careful research is evident in the many details that bring her scenes to life. The adult novels, however, do not supplant *Caddie Woodlawn* as Brink's best and best-loved work.

—Cheryl J. Foote

BRISTOW, Gwen. American. Born in Marion, South Carolina, 16 September 1903. Educated at Judson College, A.B. 1924; Columbia School of Journalism, New York, 1924–25; Anderson College, Indiana. Married Bruce Manning in 1929. Reporter, *Times-Picayune*, New Orleans, Louisiana, 1925–34. *Died 16 August 1980.*

WESTERN PUBLICATIONS

Novels

Plantation Trilogy. New York, Crowell, 1962.
Deep Summer. New York, Crowell, and London, Heinemann, 1937.
The Handsome Road. New York, Crowell, and London, Heinemann, 1938.
This Side of Glory. New York, Crowell, and London, Heinemann, 1940.
Tomorrow Is Forever. New York, Crowell, and London, Heinemann, 1944.
Jubilee Trail. New York, Crowell, 1950; London, Eyre and Spottiswoode, 1953.
Celia Garth. New York, Crowell, 1959; London, Eyre and Spottiswoode, 1960.
Calico Palace. New York, Crowell, 1970; London, Eyre and Spottiswoode, 1971.
Golden Dreams. New York, Lippincott and Crowell, 1980.

OTHER PUBLICATIONS

Novels

The Invisible Host, with Bruce Manning. New York, Mystery League, 1930; as *The Ninth Guest*, New York, Popular Library, 1975.

Gutenberg Murders, with Bruce Manning. New York, Mystery League, 1931.
Two and Two Make Twenty-Two, with Bruce Manning. New York, Mystery League, 1932.

* * *

Gwen Bristow is best known as the author of the *Plantation Trilogy*, three novels that trace two Southern families from their arrivals in the Mississippi Valley in the early 19th century through the Civil War and into the era of World War I. Among her other historical novels, two are set in the American West in the 1840's—a crucial decade in which the United States acquired the Mexican territories of California and New Mexico through military conquest.

Jubilee Trail is the story of Garnet Cameron, a young resident of New York City. Properly raised and educated, Garnet longs for adventure, and finds it after her marriage to a Santa Fe trader in 1845. Together they travel the Santa Fe Trail from Missouri to Santa Fe, then continue along the Old Spanish Trail—the Jubilee Trail—to California. Here, Garnet confronts new challenges that test her courage and self-reliance, set against the backdrop of the conquest of New Mexico and California by the U.S. government.

In *Calico Palace*, Kendra Logan arrives in California as news of the discovery of gold at Sutter's Mill sweeps the territory. After a sojourn in the goldfields, Kendra returns to San Francisco and weathers personal tragedies as well as the fires and earthquakes that beset the city between 1848 and 1851. She too finds unexpected strength and abilities that enable her to survive and prosper.

In addition to the protagonists, Bristow's novels include a number of well-drawn characters who exemplify important western themes. For example, each novel includes a second heroine. Florinda of *Jubilee Trail* and Marnie of *Calico Palace* are "fallen" women who have already learned survival skills and self-reliance. In the democratic environment of the frontier, Garnet and Kendra (proper ladies) form enduring friendships with these women of different backgrounds. Florida and Marnie provide emotional support and economic opportunities so that Garnet and Kendra can survive independently.

For the other characters, the West also offers equality of opportunity. Some have come to California hoping to escape their pasts, while others from more prestigious positions assume that they will remain important in the new territory. But the West serves as a proving ground. Family prestige, wealth, and the rules of conventional society count for little compared to character, courage, and stamina.

Other western themes, including the destruction of western lands or native reactions to the American conquest of the territories, receive little attention. Ethnic groups other than the conquering Americans appear only as minor characters or, as in the case of Indians in *Jubilee Trail*, obstacles to be overcome.

These novels may be classed as romantic historical fiction, in part because they feature a conventional "happily ever after" conclusion. Still, Bristow's heroines are strong women equal to the challenges of the frontier, and they demand men who recognize and respect their strength and independence. Bristow's novels also reveal careful research, as the physical settings and historical events are accurately and convincingly portrayed.

—Cheryl J. Foote

BROCK, Stuart. *See* **TRIMBLE, Louis.**

BRONSON, Lee. *See* **KING, Albert.**

BROOKER, Clark. *See* **FOWLER, Kenneth A.**

BROOMALL, Robert W(alter). Also writes as Hank Edwards. American. Born in Baltimore, Maryland, 27 November 1946. Educated at the University of Maryland, College Park, B.A. 1968. Served in the United States Army, 1969–71. Married Frances E. Kenney in 1980; one son and two daughters. Copy editor, Williams and Wilkins publishers, Baltimore, 1968; civilian budget analyst, United States Army Corps of Engineers, Baltimore, 1972–74; property administrator, United States Defense Contracts Supply Agency, Baltimore, 1974–75. Since 1975 freelance writer. Agent: Ethan Ellenberg, 548 Broadway, 5-C, New York, New York 10012. Address 8196 Gray Haven Road, Baltimore, Maryland 21222, U.S.A.

WESTERN PUBLICATIONS

Novels

The Bank Robber. New York, Fawcett, 1985.
Dead Man's Trilogy:
Dead Man's Canyon. New York, Fawcett, 1986.
Dead Man's Crossing. New York, Fawcett, 1987.
Dead Man's Town. New York, Fawcett, 1988.
Texas Kingdoms. New York, Fawcett, 1989.
The Forty-Niners. New York, Fawcett, 1991.
K Company. New York, Fawcett, 1992.

Novels as Hank Edwards (series: The Judge in both books)

Texas Feud. New York, Harper, 1991.
War Clouds. New York, Harper, 1991.

* * *

Each decade seems to spawn new western writers. In the past there have been Zane Grey, Louis L'Amour, and Walt Coburn, all heavyweights in the genre. But they were all working towards the one goal—to entertain. They produced books on the themes of the Old West—fast draws, range-wars, and cattle rustling proliferated between their pages. But today the Western is coming nearer to how the West really was. A handful of rising stars are emerging, and among them is Robert W. Broomall.

His character Jake Moran, created for the Dead Man's Trilogy, is not the normal run-of-the-mill hero one expects; his previous exploits have been exaggerated out of hand by Dime novelists and newspaper reporters. Everyone expects him to be

Colonel Jake Moran—the Legend—but he has a difficult time relating to their expectations, as he alone knows the truth behind that legend.

Dead Man's Canyon is Moran's introduction, and has him helping a brother and sister search for hidden treasure. Moran successfully battles Indians, a gang of outlaws, and even a re-occurring bout of malaria, before the book's suprising ending.

The trials and tribulations of leading a wagon train across Texas is the theme for *Dead Man's Crossing*. Moran continues to expand and develop as a character as he reluctantly takes on the responsibility of wagon master. There is danger from marauding Comanches, an outbreak of cholera, and a power struggle from within the group he is protecting. The book is set in 1854, 12 years before *Dead Man's Canyon*. Curiously enough, the trilogy does not run in chronological order, thus allowing Broomall to skip back and forth through time.

In *Dead Man's Town* the plot moves to 1865, when Moran is persuaded by the elders to try to tame Union City. At this stage of his life, Moran is a virtual alcoholic, turning to the bottle in a period of self-pity and introspection. The book portrays his attempts to come to terms with his failings, and Broomall succeeds in creating a powerful, threatening atmosphere. Moran tries to avoid violence, but is quite capable of dealing out punishment. He is a great sentimentalist, as we are told in *Dead Man's Town*: ". . . now he saw the sordid reality of being a hero, of being a town tamer. He despised himself of having enjoyed it . . ." Broomall tries to show that the Old West did not exist in a vacuum, that it was part of the Victorian Age, and its people were products of that age and its sensibilities.

His first book, *The Bank Robber*, is an exercise in characterization. The theme has been used in previous westerns. Best friend against best friend, one for the law the other "agin it." The dilemma comes when the outlaw Swede finds a girl abandoned in the desert, and must decide whether to leave her to the Indians, or take her with him and almost certainly be overtaken by the posse pursuing him. In Broomall's fiction his character's notions are either confirmed or abandoned in an unrelenting land.

1990 has seen the emergence of the "big" Western in the United States. It is felt that the actual West has not yet been fully explored by western writers, and the favourite period is the 1860's, when the West was still untamed. Broomall set out to create a sweeping saga in *Texas Kingdoms*, a 32-year story of two men, a woman, and a town, set against the background of the cattle industry. The histories of Evans, Cooper, and Faith are fully explored as they face marauding Indians, the Civil War, poverty, and the harshness of nature. But it is their greed and lust that eventually destroys a lifetime's friendship. This different approach from the author makes for an exciting and compelling novel.

The Forty-Niners is written along the same lines as the previous book. Beginning in 1849, the novel has Marlow, Rawson, and Kathy as its three main protagonists who are fatefully thrown together when their travelling party is attacked by river bandits while on their way to the California gold fields. Each has his or her own idea of success, and in pursuing their dreams, they drive themselves to the limits of their endurance. As in both books, the heroine has to decide between the two men in her life. The men appear to be rugged, self-centred, and single-minded. Though they owe their lives to each other, they ultimately destroy the lives of those around them, and eventually one or the other has to die.

Broomall's own interest in history is used to supply material for the topics of his books. Early settlers, the rise of the cattle industry, mining, claim-jumpers, prostitution, and drugs, are some of the themes he explores. He skilfully deals with the complexities of plot and characters, has a convincing style, and the length of the books allows him the space to develop his ideas.

K Company provides an insight into a cavalry company in operation on the Kansas frontier in 1867, and recreates the hardships and degradations forced upon the men. The authenticity of his research is not forced upon the reader, but is used for revealing characters and creating tension. Broomall also allows time for the Indian's chief's point of view, showing how the Indians were driven to war by the land-hungry whites. There are complications arising from clashes of personalities in the barracks, which over-spill onto the battlefield with dire consequences. The Judge series, written as Hank Edwards, has the author returning to formulary writing. The books describe Judge Clay Thorn's search for Melony Hancock, his pre-war fiancée, who disappeared during Sherman's march through the Carolinas. This quest permits the central characters to become involved in fast-paced adventures. *War Clouds* has Thorn appointing himself as arbitrator in a volatile situation which could lead to an Indian war. White developers are keen on aggravating the situation, and Thorn is needed to dispense his own kind of justice.

Texas Feud explores the formula of range-war. Lawlessness abounds when the assigned Federal judge is murdered, and Clay Thorn is appointed his successor. Through his tenacity he brings the villains to justice, and, in living by his own code of honour, actually kills a man who could tell of Melony's whereabouts. He therefore condemns himself to his lonely search.

By using the broad canvas of lives, loves, and hardships, Broomall's novels are progressing from strength to strength. He provides us with different and sometimes unusual viewpoints, and his prose is believable, and characterization credible. He can create the tension of human passions, and his skilful writing enhances the diversity of his works.

—Mike Stotter

BROWN, Dee (Alexander). American. Born in Louisiana, 28 February 1908. Educated at Arkansas State Teachers College; George Washington University, Washington, D.C., B.S. 1937. Served in the United States Army, 1942–45. Married Sara Baird Stroud in 1934; one son and one daughter. Worked as a printer and journalist; library assistant, Department of Agriculture, 1934–42, and technical librarian, War Department, 1945–48; agriculture librarian, University of Illinois, Urbana, 1948–72. Editor, *Agricultural History*, 1956–58; editor, Rural America series, 1973. Address: 7 Overlook Drive, Little Rock, Arkansas 72207, U.S.A.

WESTERN PUBLICATIONS

Novels

Wave High the Banner. Philadelphia, Macrae Smith, 1942.
Yellowhorse. Boston, Houghton Mifflin, 1956.
Cavalry Scout. New York, Permabooks, 1958.
They Went Thataway. New York, Putnam, 1960; as *Pardon My Pandemonium*, Fairbanks, Alaska, August House, 1984.
The Girl from Fort Wicked. New York, Doubleday, 1964.
Action at Beecher Island. New York, Doubleday, 1967.
Creek Mary's Blood. New York, Holt Rinehart, and London, Hutchinson, 1980.

Killdeer Mountain. New York, Holt Rinehart, and London, Hutchinson, 1983.
Conspiracy of Knaves. New York, Holt Rinehart, 1987.

OTHER PUBLICATIONS

Other

Fighting Indians of the West, with Martin F. Schmitt. New York, Scribner, 1948.
Trail Driving Days. New York, Scribner, 1952.
Grierson's Raid. Urbana, University of Illinois Press, 1954.
The Settlers' West, with Martin F. Schmitt. New York, Scribner, 1955.
The Gentle Tamers: Women of the Old Wild West. New York, Putnam, 1958; London, Barrie and Jenkins, 1973; as *Women of the Wild West*, London, Pan, 1975.
The Bold Cavaliers: Morgan's 2nd Kentucky Cavalry Raiders. Philadelphia, Lippincott, 1959.
Fort Phil Kearny: An American Saga. New York, Putnam, 1962; as *The Fetterman Massacre*, London, Barrie and Jenkins, 1972.
The Galvanized Yankees. Urbana, University of Illinois Press, 1963.
Showdown at Little Big Horn. New York, Putnam, 1964.
The Year of the Century: 1876. New York, Scribner, 1966.
Bury My Heart at Wounded Knee. New York, Holt Rinehart, and London, Barrie and Jenkins, 1971; revised edition, as *Wounded Knee* (for children), New York, Holt Rinehart, 1974.
Andrew Jackson and the Battle of New Orleans (for children). New York, Putnam, 1972.
Tales of the Warrior Ants (for children). New York, Putnam, 1973.
The Westerners. New York, Holt Rinehart, and London, Joseph, 1974.
Hear That Lonesome Whistle Blow: Railroads in the West. New York, Holt Rinehart, and London, Chatto and Windus, 1977; revised edition, as *Lonesome Whistle* (for children), Holt Rinehart, 1980.
Teepee Tales of the American Indian. New York, Holt Rinehart, 1979; as *Campfire Tales of the American Indians*, London, Chatto and Windus, 1979.
The American Spa: Hot Springs, Arkansas. Little Rock, Arkansas, Rose, 1982.

Editor, *Pawnee, Blackfoot, and Cheyenne: History and Folklore of the Plains from the Writings of George Bird Grinnell.* New York, Scribner, 1961.

*

Critical Study: *Dee Brown* by Lyman B. Hagen, Boise, Idaho, Boise State University Press, 1990.

Dee Brown comments:

All my western novels except one are based on historical incidents. The exception is *They Went Thataway*, which is a satire on western novels and historical researchers. In most cases, I found it necessary to construct the narratives in fiction form because there was not enough research material available for documented non-fiction, which I prefer. But sometimes there are tales buried in fragmentary records that are too good not to be told. In the novels I have always attempted to keep within the bounds of their historical settings. In the non-fiction I have always attempted to dramatize the true events, using the tools of the novelist (diaries and letters are splendid for inner thoughts and stream of consciousness) but always aiming not to violate the rules of historical writing.

* * *

Dee Brown is a novelist as well as a writer of such respected works of non-fiction as *The Year of the Century: 1876*, *The Galvanized Yankees*, and, especially, *Bury My Heart at Wounded Knee*. Moreover, the strengths of his non-fiction—careful research, usually involving previously unrecognized sources of information, and imaginative presentation—show up in his novels.

Brown's career as a writer began with a 1942 novel based on the life of David Crockett. *Wave High the Banner* departs from both facile patriotism and Davy Crockett tall-telling; instead, it presents a careful, diligently researched (if somewhat unexciting) narrative.

In the 1950's, with Brown serving as a librarian at the University of Illinois, his talent for research produced unspectacular and relatively unnoticed novels about particular western individuals as well as one comic novel (*They Went Thataway*) poking fun at the conventions of the Western. Not until the success of Brown's historical writing, though, has his fiction really come of age, mainly in the form of *Creek Mary's Blood*.

Creek Mary's Blood is Brown's answer to such blockbusters as James Michener's *Centennial* and Ruth Beebe Hill's *Hanta Yo*. It traces five generations of a mixed-blood family from its origins in the southeast to its continued survival, around 1890, on a Minneconjou Sioux reservation in South Dakota. Creek Mary is the matriarch of this family of Indian Americans. Her story, as Brown tells it, is straightforward and effective; it plays no tricks on the reader other than using a white reporter as a frame for the narrative. It lacks mysteries, exotic obscurities, or overly poetic effects. The attitude it takes towards Native Americans is a kind of respectful sentimentality, a shade less accusatory than *Bury My Heart at Wounded Knee*, perhaps, but hardly an invitation to feel proud about Manifest Destiny. The central theme of the novel is its redefinition of America as a Melting Pot. Creek Mary's blood is mixed with that of Creek, Spanish, Cherokee, French, Cheyenne, and Sioux. Of her and her lineage Brown says, "Warriors they all had been, male and female, warrior survivors. What was she, if she was not America?"

Killdeer Mountain explores the familiar terrain of the Indian wars from a fresh and intriguing viewpoint. Brown takes as his starting point the chance encounter of his journalist/narrator and a mysterious stranger aboard a riverboat, and moves smoothly into a complex web of half-revelation and uncertainty. Focusing his reader's attention on a few significant episodes—the mysterious expedition of Major Rawley and his mutinous patrol into Indian country, the apparent failure of nerve which allows the hostiles to escape at Killdeer Mountain, and the subsequent "heroic" abduction of the Sioux chief from his hiding-place in Canada—he proceeds to demonstrate the ambivalent nature of these events by the testimony of several eye-witnesses, whose recollections all too often do not tally with the "official" version of what happened. Concepts of heroism and cowardice are questioned, and found inadequate; even the identity of Rawley, the central character, is far from certain. Which actions are his own, and which those of the embittered soldier Drew Hardesty, the reader is not told. Instead, Brown teaches us that history as the memory of past events must always be partial and suspect, a further evidence of our ability to see what we wish to, rather than what is there.

—William Bloodworth

BROWN, J(oseph) P(aul) S(ummers). American. Born in Nogales, Arizona, 25 August 1930. Educated at St. Michael's High School; Notre Dame University, Indiana, B.A. in journalism 1952. Served in the United States Marine Corps, 1954–58: 1st Lieutenant. Married 1) Barbara Jean Barbour in 1952 (divorced 1956), one son and one daughter; 2) Patricia Louise Burr in 1974, one son. Reporter, El Paso *Herald Post*, Texas, 1953–54; also a boxer, motion picture stuntman and actor, and cattleman. Address: Rt. 8, Box 560, Tucson, Arizona 85710, U.S.A.

WESTERN PUBLICATIONS

Novels

Jim Kane. New York, Dial Press, 1970; as *Pocket Money,* London, Sphere, 1972.
The Outfit: A Cowboy's Primer. New York, Dial Press, 1971.
The Forests of the Night. New York, Dial Press, 1974.
Steeldust New York, Walker, 1986.
Steeldust II: The Flight. New York, Walker, 1987; London, Hale, 1988.

*

J.P.S. Brown comments:

Few novels about cowboys and cattle people have been written by cowboys who made a living working cattle. I write about the cowboy's work from my own experience. I do not write about the cowboy as a detective or the cowboy as a gambler, or the cowboy who goes Boo-hoo, Kiss-Kiss about his life away from the girls. I write as much about the character of cattle and horses and animals who prey on them as I do about the men who husband them. My cowboys are husbandmen and the books are about their lives as they help cattle make a living, not about the drugstore cowboy's evolution to the beer parlor a-lookin' for love.

* * *

Perhaps no western writer deserves more to inherit the mantle of authenticity left by the great Andy Adams than J.P.S. Brown. Like Adams, Brown was a working cowboy. He is still a cattleman in Arizona. Also, like Adams's *The Log of a Cowboy*, Brown's *Jim Kane* was praised for its unerring realistic description of the cowboy and his way of life. Brown's first two works, *Jim Kane* and *The Outfit*, are more narratives than novels. Reviewers of *Jim Kane*, for example, found difficulty in describing the form, and used terms such as "semi-documentary," or "plotless," or "a series of vignettes." It is especially true with *Jim Kane* that there is little plot other than the contemporary cowboy's test of character as he faces the harsh external world, and that the major elements in the book are the cowboys themselves, their lives, their working relationships, and their infrequent sprees. Thus *Jim Kane's* effectiveness depends largely on character development, realistic dialogue, and absolutely authentic descriptions of their everyday lives in what one reviewer called "painful honesty."

However, Brown has developed more toward the novel in each succeeding book without sacrificing his sense of realism. *The Outfit* provides, at least, a satiric undertone, as well as greater tensions between the characters. The outfit for which these cowboys work is owned by a moving-picture company which uses a Nevada ranch as a tax write-off. Although the company makes some attempts to modernize the operation, little is done to improve the human situation; the cowboys are paid little attention, and very little money. Yet Bert Sorrells, the central character, and his outfit take as much pride in their profession as cowboys, and achieve as great a sense of accomplishment (with the exception of a character driven to suicide and used as a counterpoint) as those in *Jim Kane*.

Brown's third book, *The Forests of the Night*, is indeed a novel. It is set in the mountains of western Mexico, and the plot involves a hunter's quest to kill a man-killing jaguar, El Yoco, and the hunter's gradual loss of touch with himself and the world he leaves behind as his obsession grows. The jaguar, the hunter, and the quest itself take on symbolic significance, as in Walter Van Tilburg Clark's *The Track of the Cat*, although without the mystical element. Brown's characterizations of the Mexican mountain people are as clearly and accurately drawn as in Katherine Anne Porter's "Maria Concepcion," and the quest becomes as compulsive as the quest to free the young white girls from the Indians in Alan Le May's *The Searchers*.

Animals again play a central role in the two Steeldust novels, both works taking their name from the prized stallion around whom most of the action revolves. Brown brings the horse alive before the reader's eyes, convincing us of those qualities—the strength, beauty, and intelligence—that make Steeldust what he is. Set in the Texas–Mexico border country in the pre-war years, the novels follow the adventures of the stallion and his owner, the cowhand Bill Shane, whose love interest with the rancher's daughter, and deadly enmity with the murderous Lindano, seem merely to complement the horse's own acts and perceptions. All threads draw together in *Steeldust II: The Flight*, where the stallion is stolen by Lindano, who also kidnaps Mary, drawing Bill in pursuit across the border. The human hero fails against the psychotic and seemingly indestructible Lindano; instead, it is Steeldust, apparently a brutalized victim of the killer, who brings about Lindano's death beneath the hooves of mules and horses in a corral. It is a fitting climax to the Steeldust canon, where the author's skill is confirmed in both human and animal portrayals. Brown has yet to receive proper critical appraisal, but it is clear that he is developing into one of the best of contemporary western novelists.

—Delbert E. Wylder

BROWN, Will C. Pseudonym for Clarence Scott Boyles, Jr. American. Born in Baird, Texas, 1 August 1905. Educated at Howard Payne College, Brownwood, Texas, for three years. Served in United States Marine Corps, 1942–45: Major. Married Ilene Embrey in 1924; one daughter and one son. Editor, *Nolan County News*, Sweetwater, Texas, 1925–34, Lufkin *Daily News*, Texas, 1934–41, Marshall *News-Messenger*, Texas, 1941–42, and Sherman *Daily Democrat*, Texas, 1945–47; owner, Boyles Advertising Agency, Sherman, Texas, 1947–49. Since 1949 freelance writer. Recipient: Dell Books award for Best Western of the Year, 1955; Western Writers of America Spur award, 1960. Address: c/o Dell Publishing, 666 Fifth Avenue, New York, New York 10103, U.S.A.

WESTERN PUBLICATIONS

Novels

Guns Along the Chisholm. New York, Popular Library, 1955.
The Border Jumpers. New York, Dutton, 1955; London, Muller, 1956.
Trouble on the Brazos. New York, Popular Library, 1956.
Laredo Road. New York, Dell, 1959; London, John Long, 1961.
Sam Bass & Co. New York, New American Library, 1960.
The Nameless Breed. New York, Macmillan, 1960; London, Hamilton, 1961.
Think Fast, Ranger! New York, Dell, 1961.
Caprock Rebel. New York, Macmillan, 1962; London, John Long, 1963.
The Kelly Man. New York, Dell, 1964.

Uncollected Short Stories

"Duel in Captive Valley," in *Bar 2 Roundup of Best Western Stories*, edited by Scott Meredith. New York, Dutton, 1953.
"The Marshall and the Mob," in *Branded West*, edited by Don Ward. Boston, Houghton Mifflin, 1955.
"Into the Guns," in *The Killers*, edited by Peter Dawson. New York, Bantam, 1955.
"Trail Man's Bluff," in *Frontier: 150 Years of the West*, edited by Luke Short. New York, Bantam, 1955.
"He's Death on Nesters," in *Cattle, Guns and Men*, edited by Luke Short. New York, Bantam, 1955.
"Cowboy Columbus," in *Hoof Trails and Wagon Tracks*, edited by Don Ward. New York, Dodd Mead, 1957.
"Drive to Glory," in *Colt's Law*, edited by Luke Short. New York, Bantam, 1957.
"First Kill," in *Frontiers West*, edited by S. Omar Barker. New York, Doubleday, 1959.
"Miracle at Circle Seven," in *They Won Their Spurs*, edited by Nelson Nye. New York, Avon, 1962.
"The Big Hat," in *Western Writers of America Presents: Great Western Stories*. New York Berkley, 1965.
"Red Sand," in *The Texans*, edited by Bill Pronzini and Martin H. Greenberg. New York, Fawcett, 1988.

* * *

Descended on both sides from Texas cattle-raising families, Clarence Scott Boyles, Jr. knows the Lone Star state intimately—its history, its geography, its people. This knowledge and his skill at incorporating it into his fiction is what made him an above-average writer of popular Westerns under his Will C. Brown pseudonym. He was particularly adept at depicting the Texas badlands, at making his readers feel the heat, dust, wind, desolation, and deprivation of the Panhandle wastes, the red Caprock land, the southwestern *brasada*, the *Valle de Cuchillos* or Valley of the Knives "where the Spanish dagger brush grows so thick in a mile-long canyon, and the cactus is so dense underfoot, that a man going through it could be bled to death if he let himself get panicky."

Boyles's magnum opus, which was honored by a Western Writers of America Best Novel Spur award, is *The Nameless Breed*. Set in 1844, when the Republic of Texas was on the verge of annexation by the United States, it tells two interwoven stories: first, one of greed and duplicity in which "every third man [in San Antonio, the Republic's capital] is a spy ready to sell out to agents of the United States or Mexico, England or France"; and second, an elemental one of the rescue of rancher Seale McCloud from Comanche captors by his two sons, and of the flight of the McClouds and an English agent named Trakken through savage desert country and the Valley of the Knives, with both the hostile Indians and a vicious soldier named Captain Spide in pursuit. Sharp characterization and unflagging suspense, coupled with Boyles's best outdoor writing, make this a memorable western adventure.

Standouts among the other Brown westerns are *Caprock Rebel*, in which a Confederate army veteran's attempts to reclaim his family homestead are thwarted by a group of ragged and hungry ex-Union Army soldiers bent on stealing a cache of stolen gold double-eagles hidden in the Caprock hills; *Sam Bass & Co.*, which recounts the rise and fall (in Denton County, Texas) of illiterate outlaw and train robber Sam Bass; *Think Fast, Ranger!*, about an undercover man for the Texas Rangers on the trail of an escaped murderer; and *The Border Jumpers*, in which Odessa cattleman and reformed outlaw Lincoln Jones, one of three people stranded after a train holdup by his former gang, is forced to confront the past he has tried to forget. The paperback reprint edition of *The Border Jumpers*, published by Dell Books, received the Dell Book award as the best western novel of 1955.

In addition to his novels, Boyles also published more than 200 western short stories in pulp magazines and in such "slick" magazines as *The Saturday Evening Post* and *Holiday*. Noteworthy among his shorter works is "Red Sand," a moody, suspenseful novelette set in the drought-ridden, wind-tortured Caprock country; its central characters are two outlaws who take refuge in a settler's cabin, and a nester woman who leads one of them into a final choice between good and evil.

—Bill Pronzini

BROWNING, Sterry. *See* **GRIBBLE, Leonard.**

BURCHARDT, Bill (William Robert Burchardt). American. Born in Guthrie, Oklahoma, 16 August 1917. Educated at Central State Teachers' College (now University), Edmond, Oklahoma, B.A. 1938; University of Oklahoma, Norman, M.Mus. Ed. 1947. Served in the United States Navy, 1942–45: Lieutenant. Married to Clara Chaves. High school music director, Seminole and Oklahoma City, 1938–42; music and journalism teacher, Grove and Duncan high schools, Oklahoma, and Northern Oklahoma Junior College, Tonkawa; writer-in-residence, Central State University, 1955–60, 1972–75. Since 1982 Adjunct Professor of history of Mexico, University of Oklahoma, Norman; guest teacher, Hacienda El Cobano, Colima, Mexico. Associate editor, 1957–60, and editor, 1960–80, *Oklahoma Today*, Oklahoma City. President, Western Writers of America, 1960. Recipient: Oklahoma Writers' Federation award, for short story, 1959, for novel, 1979; National Cowboy Hall of Fame Wrangler award, 1975, and Tepee award, 1975. Adopted Kiowa. Address: 127 East Shore Drive, Lake Hiwassee, Arcadia, Oklahoma 73007, U.S.A.

WESTERN PUBLICATIONS

Novels

The Wildcatters. New York, Ace, 1963.
Yankee Longstraw. New York, Doubleday, 1965; London, Hammond, 1966.
Shotgun Bottom. New York, Doubleday, 1966.
The Birth of Logan Station. New York, Doubleday, 1974.
The Mexican. New York, Doubleday, 1977; London, Hale, 1978.
Buck. New York, Doubleday, 1978; London, Hale, 1980.
Medicine Man. New York, Doubleday, and London, Hale, 1980.
The Lighthorsemen. New York, Doubleday, 1981.
Black Marshal. New York, Doubleday, 1981; London, Hale, 1982.

Uncollected Short Stories

"The Devil's Swampers," in *Thrilling Western* (New York), September 1952.
"Incendiary Lady," in *Ranch Romances* (New York), September 1952.
"The Devil's Dry-Gulcher," in *Big Book Western* (New York), January 1953.
"Handy Sandy Andy," in *Ranch Romances* (New York), January 1953.
"Slow Elk Season," in *Texas Western* (New York), March 1953.
"The Crow Eaters," in *Masked Rider Western* (New York), April 1953.
"Blizzard Trail," in *10 Story Western* (New York), April 1953.
"Inside Straight," in *Western Short Stories* (New York), April 1953.
"When Lew Hemp Hit Idaho," in *15 Western Tales* (New York), May 1953.
"The Deputy's Daughter," in *Ranch Romances* (New York), June 1953.
"Cayuse Colors," in *Five Western Novels* (New York), June 1953.
"Mudflat Menace," in *Ranch Romances* (New York), July 1953.
"Girl for Breakfast," in *15 Range Romances* (New York), August 1953.
"A Girl to Tame a Texan," in *15 Range Romances* (New York), October 1953.
"Nesters Ain't Human," in *Ranch Romances* (New York), November 1953.
"Slayer at Skyline Station," in *Ranch Romances* (New York), January 1954.
"Comanche Captive," in *Ranch Romances* (New York), February 1954.
"The Cocklebur Catcher," in *Famous Westerns* (New York), March 1954.
"Suspicion," in *Ranch Romances* (New York), March 1954.
"Ragged Hero," in *Ranch Romances* (New York), June 1954.
"The Marshal and the Family Man," in *Ranch Romances* (New York), November 1954.
"Main Event," in *Western Short Stories* (New York), December 1954.
"Ride the Blood Sign," in *Ranch Romances* (New York), February 1955.
"A Girl to Boot," in *Ranch Romances* (New York), March 1955.
"Man Measure," in *Ranch Romances* (New York), April 1955.
"Cross Timbers Ghoul," in *Ranch Romances* (New York), August 1955.
"Rotten Water," in *Two-Gun Western* (New York), February 1956.
"The Lynching at Six-Killer," in *Ranch Romances* (New York), April 1956.
"Girl from Greasy Creek," in *Ranch Romances* (New York), May 1956.
"Susie's Scotsman," in *Ranch Romances* (New York), August 1956.
"The Long Journey Home," and "Cowtown Cutie," in *Ranch Romances* (New York), October 1956.
"Wine Without Price," in *Spurs West*, edited by S. Omar Barker. New York, Doubleday, 1960.
"The Fort Greer Mules," in *The Pick of the Roundup*, edited by Stephen Payne. New York, Avon, 1963.
"Harley Haug's Reward," in *Great Western Stories.* New York, Berkley, 1965.
"En Pike til Frokost," in *Western* (Oslo), August 1978.
"How Calvin Mullins Became the Caballero of Cowboy Flat," in *Roundup*, edited by Stephen Overholser. New York, Doubleday, 1982.

OTHER PUBLICATIONS

Other

Oklahoma, photographs by David Fitzgerald. Portland, Oregon, Graphic Arts Center, 1979.

*

Manuscript Collections: Western History Collection, University of Oklahoma, Norman; Central State University, Edmond, Oklahoma; University of Wyoming, Laramie.

Bill Burchardt comments:

Early in my career I was fascinated by the untold stories of the Oilrush Wild West. Western literature is filled with writings about the Gold Rush Wild West. The Oil Rush is even more exciting and colorful than the Gold Rush. Any single Oil Rush, Ranger, Burkburnett, Drumright, Seminole, produced more wealth than all the Gold Rushes in the American West combined. So many of my tales, both short stories and novels, are set in the Oil Rush West.

Further, living among the many Indian tribes of Oklahoma, it was inevitable that leaven would rise to produce *Medicine Man*, with its mystical Kiowas setting, and *The Lighthorsemen*, rooted in the heritage of the Cherokee, Creek, Chickasaw, Seminole, and Choctaw Indian police. The turbulent days of Indian Territory also produced the material for *Black Marshal*, which deals with the problems of a negro officer confronted by prejudice.

The American West had its genesis in Mexico. Much of my recent work springs from previously untranslated and untapped sources of this exciting heritage from Mexico. This includes articles for *Oklahoma Today* magazine, my novel *The Mexican*, and a short story, "How Calvin Mullins Became the Caballero of Cowboy Flat." I continue to work with Spanish-American materials in the hope of generating more major work in this area.

* * *

Bill Burchardt's novels are always a good read. His tales are short and snappy, and all seem to take place mainly in or near the Cimarron River valley in Oklahoma.

The Wildcatters, *Yankee Longstraw*, and *Shotgun Bottom* are best described as oil novels. The title reference in *The Wildcatters* is obviously to oil prospectors. Yankee Longstraw is an ex-circus performer who arrives in an Oklahoma boom town and builds a pipeline. Shotgun Bottom is a turn-of-the-century hellhole where cowboys encounter oil roustabouts and where cable-tool drillers fight with rotary-rig crews. *Yankee Longstraw* provides an excellent and accurate picture of early pipeline construction, and *Shotgun Bottom* deals interestingly with some political repercussions of "oil fever."

The Birth of Logan Station features a staple of western fiction, the Oklahoma land-rush. *The Mexican*, however, gives an unusual twist to the stereotypical conflict between those wearing white hats and those wearing black hats. First, the representative of law and order is Justino Guyman, who is half Mexican. Second, he is not fighting rustlers or bank robbers, but rather drug smugglers, bootleggers, and white slaves. In *Buck* Sheriff Buck Mather also has, for a western novel, an uncommon opponent: the local Ku Klux Klan. As the title clearly indicates, Burchardt's latest novel, *Black Marshal*, shows a willingness to graft new possibilities on old formulas.

Probably Burchardt's two best novels are *Medicine Man* and *The Lighthorsemen*. The lighthorsemen are the Indian auxiliaries of the Territorial police who, by virtue of their profession, tread the razor's edge of compromise between the old tribal customs and the laws of the ruling white society. *Medicine Man* is the fascinating story of a young Mexican captured and reared by Indians far from his home south of the Rio Bravo. The familiar theme of Indian captivity is surpassed, however, by the delineation of the central character's attitude toward his medicine-man mentor—an attitude alternately believing and disbelieving. Add to this an incipient conflict between braves over an Indian maiden and an exhausting horseback trek to tropical Mexico. Few readers will be disappointed; it is no wonder Burchardt is an honorary Kiowa.

—Robert J. Barnes

BURNETT, W(illiam) R(iley). Also wrote as John Monahan; James Updyke. American. Born in Springfield, Ohio, 25 November 1899. Educated at Miami Military Institute, German-town, Ohio; Ohio State University, Columbus, 1919–20. Married 1)Marjorie Louise Bartow in 1921; 2)Whitney Forbes Johnston in 1943; two sons. Statistician, State of Ohio, 1921–27; full-time writer from 1927. Recipient: O Henry memorial award, 1930; Mystery Writers of America Edgar Allan Poe award, for screenplay, 1951, and Grand Master award, 1980; Writers Guild of America award, for screenplay, 1963. *Died 25 April 1982.*

Western Publications

Novels

Saint Johnson. New York, Dial Press, 1930; London, Heinemann, 1931.
The Dark Command: A Kansan Iliad. New York, Knopf, and London, Heinemann, 1938.
Adobe Walls. New York, Knopf, 1953; London, Macdonald, 1954.
Pale Moon. New York, Knopf, 1956; London, Macdonald, 1957.
Bitter Ground. New York, Knopf, and London, Macdonald, 1958.
Mi Amigo. New York, Knopf, 1959; London, Macdonald, 1960.
The Goldseekers. New York, Doubleday, 1962; London, Macdonald, 1963.
Sergeants Three (novelization of screenplay). New York, Pocket Books, 1962.
The Abilene Samson. New York, Pocket Books, 1963.

Uncollected Short Story

"Nobody's All Bad," in *Rawhide and Bob-Wire*, edited by Luke Short. New York, Bantam, 1958.

Other Publications

Novels

Little Caesar. New York, Dial Press, and London, Cape, 1929.
Iron Man. New York, Dial Press, and London, Heinemann, 1930.
The Silver Eagle. New York, Dial Press, 1931; London, Heinemann, 1932.
The Giant Swing. New York, Harper, 1932; London, Heinemann, 1933.
Dark Hazard. New York, Harper, 1933; London, Heinemann, 1934.
Goodbye to the Past: Scenes from the Life of William Meadows. New York, Harper, 1934; London, Heinemann, 1935.
The Goodhues of Sinking Creek. New York, Harper, 1934.
King Cole. New York, Harper, 1936; as *Six Days' Grace*, London, Heinemann, 1937.
High Sierra. New York, Knopf, and London, Heinemann, 1940.
The Quick Brown Fox. New York, Knopf, 1942; London, Heinemann, 1943.
Nobody Lives Forever. New York, Knopf, 1943; London, Heinemann, 1944.
Tomorrow's Another Day. New York, Knopf, 1945; London, Heinemann, 1946.
Romelle. New York, Knopf, 1946; London, Heinemann, 1947.
The Asphalt Jungle. New York, Knopf, 1949; London, Macdonald, 1950.
Stretch Dawson. New York, Fawcett, 1950; London, Muller, 1960.
Little Men, Big World. New York, Knopf, 1951; London, Macdonald, 1952.
Vanity Row. New York, Knopf, 1952; London, Macdonald, 1953.
Big Stan (as John Monahan). New York, Fawcett, 1954; London, Fawcett, 1955.
Captain Lightfoot. New York, Knopf, 1954; London, Macdonald, 1955.
It's Always Four O'Clock (as James Updyke). New York, Random House, 1956.
Underdog. New York, Knopf, and London, Macdonald, 1957.
Conant. New York, Popular Library, 1961.
Round the Clock at Volari's. New York, Fawcett, 1961.
The Widow Barony. London, Macdonald, 1962.
The Winning of Mickey Free. New York, Bantam, 1965.
The Cool Man. New York, Fawcett, 1968.

Plays

Screenplays: *The Finger Points*, with John Monk Saunders, 1931; *The Beast of the City*, 1932; *Scarface*, 1935; *The Whole

Town's Talking (*Passport to Fame*), 1936; *Some Blondes Are Dangerous*, with Lester Cole, 1937; *King of the Underworld*, with George Bricker and Vincent Sherman, 1938; *High Sierra*, with John Huston, 1941; *36 Hours to Kill*, 1941; *This Gun for Hire*, with Albert Maltz, 1941; *The Get-Away*, with Wells Root and J. Walter Ruben, 1941; *Wake Island*, with Frank Butler, 1942; *Crash Dive*, with Jo Swerling, 1943; *Action in the North Atlantic*, with others, 1943; *Background to Danger*, 1943; *San Antonio*, with Alan LeMay, 1945; *Nobody Lives Forever*, 1946; *Belle Starr's Daughter*, 1948; *Yellow Sky*, with Lamar Trotti, 1949; *The Iron Man*, with George Zuckerman and Borden Chase, 1951; *Vendetta*, with Peter O'Crotty, 1951; *The Racket*, with William Wister Haines, 1951; *Dangerous Mission*, with others, 1954; *Captain Lightfoot*, with Oscar Brodney, 1955; *Illegal*, with James R. Webb and Frank Collins 1955; *I Died a Thousand Times*, 1955; *Accused of Murder*, with Robert Creighton Williams, 1957; *September Storm*, with Steve Fisher, 1961; *Sergeant 3*, 1962; *The Great Escape*, with James Clavell, 1963.

Other

The Roar of the Crowd (on baseball). New York, Potter, 1965.

*

Bibliography: in *Little Caesar*, Madison, University of Wisconsin Press, 1981.

* * *

W.R. Burnett wrote for eight years without acceptance and then published *Little Caesar*, the novel for which he is perhaps best remembered. His knowledge of the American West—he was born in Ohio and stayed there until he moved to Hollywood in the early 1930's—appears to have been acquired by reading the romantic "histories" of Walter Noble Burns. *Saint Johnson* was Burnett's first western novel, and in it he followed closely the fantasies about Wyatt Earp and the shootout at (actually near) the O.K. Corral in Tombstone, Arizona, set forth a few years previously by Burns in his book *Tombstone*, although Burnett disguised his central characters by giving them different names. What Burnett did retain was Burns's view of the Earps as knights of the Round Table with Wyatt, named Saint Johnson in Burnett's treatment, cast in the role of Sir Galahad. It was not an auspicious beginning in terms of dealing truthfully with his subject, but the novel was brought to the screen, as was *Little Caesar*, and Burnett quickly established himself as a screenwriter.

In writing *The Dark Command* Burnett adapted to the western genre his prototypical plot from *Little Caesar*. He never wrote anything other than formulary western fiction, i.e., a western story with a clearly identifiable hero, heroine, and villain; but his reliance on the *Little Caesar* plot caused him to emphasize the character of his central villain and to portray him somewhat sympathetically for at least the first two-thirds of the story. This tendency on Burnett's part was anticipated as early as his short story, "Nobody's All Bad," which appeared in the 7 June 1930 issue of *Collier's*. In this story, Billy the Kid is the villain but the narrator comes to regard him in a different light—not *only* as a murderer and cattle thief—when together they fight off a band of Mescaleros. "Injuns ain't worth shucks nohow," Burnett had the Kid say; and, apparently, this remained Burnett's own attitude toward Native Americans. In *The Dark Command* the subject is the organization of William Clarke Quantrill's raiders during the Civil War, Quantrill's name changed in the novel to Cantrell. Cantrell is sympathetic until his brigandage turns openly savage and all sympathy is lost.

Burnett did not return to the western genre again in book fiction, as opposed to screenplays, until *Adobe Walls* which in its film version, *Arrowhead* (Paramount, 1953), is probably the most vicious anti-Indian movie ever made—which is saying quite a lot! In the novel Apaches talk in "turkey-gobble" and are termed "enemies of the human race and everything living." Burnett's hero, based on the real-life scout Al Sieber, was called Walter Grein. In a variation of the *Little Caesar* plot, Grein knows from the start that the only way to respond to the renegade Apache leader, Toriano, is to kill him; it takes two-thirds of the novel for the bureaucrats from Washington and the military commanders to realize that Grein is right. For all that, *Adobe Walls* is very thinly plotted and makes for rather dull reading. *Pale Moon*, which followed, was even more thinly plotted.

In *Bitter Ground* Burnett based his central villain on the real-life Doc Holliday, albeit calling him Doc Sprigge and making him a medical doctor instead of a dentist. The reader's sympathy is with Doc until—again—about two-thirds the way through the story when Doc's hired gunmen try to assassinate the hero while he is sleeping. This makes Doc's being gunned down at the end by the hero a "moral" necessity. *El Chavito*—Billy the Kid—is introduced into the narrative in one of Doc's memory flashbacks and when the hero, a man named Brazos, who rode with the Kid, is hiding out after the attempt on his life it is whispered throughout "Mex-town" that he is Billy the Kid. Obviously Burnett's mind was returning again to the Billy the Kid legend, and in his next western novel, *Mi Amigo*, Burnett chose to tell his version of the story, with the Kid called Jamie Wiggan. This notwithstanding, many of the legendary ingredients about the real *El Chivito* are present, that "he killed three men before he was sixteen years old" and he is killed by surprise while staying with a young Mexican girl. The hero is Sergeant John Desportes, known as the "Soldier." In the first two-thirds of the novel he befriends Jamie. When the turning point comes, all that Jamie has done is sleep with two women; he has to be shown, and rather quickly, committing outrages such as shooting a man in the back in order to justify his being hunted down and killed.

Burnett's last westerns were attempts at a comic treatment and are even weaker than his earlier novels. *Sergeants Three* was Burnett's novelization of his screenplay for the motion picture of the same title and was basically a transposition into the American west of the narrative structure of *Gunga Din* (1939), a screen fantasy inspired by Rudyard Kipling's poem. *The Goldseekers* was concerned with the Alaskan gold rush and *The Abilene Samson* was based on the legend of "Wild Bill" Hickok, with the hero's name changed to Link Abilene. Like the historical Hickok, he suffers from incipient blindness, but venereal disease, as was the case with Hickok, was not given by Burnett as the cause.

Burnett was very much a writer of his time. His concern in western fiction, to the extent that he had one, was to make villains interesting, and his heroes are far from "clean-cut." He knew so little of the actuality of the American west that he could (in *Bitter Ground*) have a character remark, "You mean they can lay track that fast? Fifteen miles in five–six months," and not realize the absurdity of the statement. His heroines followed the Hollywood dress code and would change from pants to dresses to please the hero, although they were not always chaste. He lacked the art of invention, and much of his prose—for an author who when he was starting was out praised for his "hard-boiled" style—became flat, even insipid. When he died, Burnett had at least one completed western novel for which he could not find a publisher.

—Jon Tuska

BURNHAM, Charles. *See* **PAINE, Lauran.**

BURNS, Tex. *See* **L'AMOUR, Louis.**

BURNS, Walter Noble. American. Born in Lebanon, Kentucky, 24 October 1872. Educated at schools in Louisville. Served in the 1st Kentucky Infantry during the Spanish-American War, 1898. Journalist: with Louisville *Evening Post*, 1890, St. Louis *Post Dispatch*, Kansas City *Times*, Denver *Republican*, San Francisco *Examiner*, Chicago *Inter-Ocean* (Sunday Editor, 1910–14), Chicago *Examiner*, 1915, and Chicago *Tribune*, 1918. *Died 15 April 1932.*

WESTERN PUBLICATIONS

Novels

The Saga of Billy the Kid. New York, Doubleday, 1926; as *Billy the Kid*, London, Bles, 1926.
Tombstone: An Iliad of the Southwest. New York, Doubleday, 1927; London, Bles, 1928.
The Robin Hood of El Dorado: The Saga of Joaquin Murrieta, Famous Outlaw of California's Age of Gold. New York, Coward McCann, 1932.

OTHER PUBLICATIONS

Other

A Year with a Whaler. New York, Outing, 1913.
The One-Way Ride: The Red Trail of Chicago Gangland from Prohibition to Jake Lingle. New York, Doubleday, and London, Stanley Paul, 1931.

* * *

There is some question as to how Walter Noble Burn's western writing is to be classified. His approach generally looks like that of the historian: he sometimes provides footnotes on matters of curiosity, like the five ways to spell the last name of Joaquin Murieta (he prefers Murrieta); he explains his sources, now and again, in somewhat vague terms, although in *Tombstone* he is more explicit; and the final chapter of his life of Billy the Kid, labeled "Trail's End," is replete with verifiable and generally accurate facts and dates. Yet the very titles and subtitles he employs bespeak a romantic spirit rather than that of the cautious historian: *The Saga of Billy the Kid*; *Tombstone*: *An Iliad of the Southwest*; *The Robin Hood of El Dorado: The Saga of Joaquin Murrieta, Famous Outlaw of California's Age of Gold.* Ramon Adams, dean of western outlaw biographers, says simply that all three works belong in the fiction section of the library!

Generally speaking, Burns writes in the tradition of the romantic novelist—somtimes, even, sounding like the penny-dreadful. Of course, all three of his works deal with times of violence and death, of outlaws and sheriffs. *The Saga of Billy the Kid* combines nearly all the major tales from the manifold legend of this outlaw. The Kid's youthful appearance and the heart-rending story of how he first went wrong by killing (at the age of 12) the ruffian who had insulted his mother are natural lodestones for the reader's sympathy. And the legendary spirit of others in the story of the Lincoln County War gets full treatment; witness the old tale of Mrs. McSween at the piano while her home was under siege:

> She threw herself upon the stool at the keyboard. She still had hope—hope in Billy the Kid and his fighting men. They were battling desperately in their last ditch. A war-song might inspire them to still more heroic courage. It might turn defeat into victory. With one last brave swan-song before the ultimate silence, the piano might yet save the day. At once she plunged into the stirring bars of "The Star-Spangled Banner." Facing death, the men felt the lift and thrill of the old battle hymn. "O say, can you see . . . " The Kid whistled the tune. Tom O'Folliard beat time with his six-shooter. Far through the noise of battle and the swish of flames, the music sounded in half the homes in Lincoln. It rang against cañon walls like a challenge. It carried its message of courage and defiance to the enemy whose bullets thumped like an obbligato against the tottering walls and plunged with sibilant uproar among the smoking embers.

Both these stories are false, but fictional historian Burns seldom bothered to separate fact from legend. And the lengths to which he would go in embroidering the Kid's story can be seen in the passage just before the escape from the Lincoln jail:

> A robin was on her nest in a box-elder tree at the corner of the courthouse, her mate preening his wings on a neighbouring limb. These robins were the Kid's pets. He had seen them arrive from the South, had watched their courtship, their home-building, their start in domesticity. Every day he had saved bread from the meal which Old Man Gross brought in to him and had scattered crumbs along his window-sill for the birds; and the robins had eaten his good-will offerings, cocking their bright eyes at the shackled youth as if to say "We're chums of yours." He wondered vaguely if the little couple would hatch out their nestlings before he dropped through the trapdoor of a gallows.

—John O. West

BURROUGHS, Edgar Rice. Also wrote as John Tyler McCulloch. American. Born in Chicago, Illinois, 1 September 1875. Educated at the Harvard School, Chicago, 1888–91; Phillips Academy, Andover, Massachusetts, 1891–92; Michigan Military Academy, Orchard Lake, 1892–95. Served in the United States 7th Cavalry, 1896–97; Illinois Reserve Militia, 1918–19. Married 1) Emma Centennia Hulbert in 1900 (divorced 1934), two sons and one daughter; 2) Florence Dearholt in 1935 (divorced 1942). Instructor and Assistant Commandant, Michigan Military Academy, 1895–96; owner of a stationery store, Pocatello, Idaho, 1898; worked in his father's American Battery Company, Chicago, 1899–1903; joined his brother's Sweetser-Burroughs Mining Company, Idaho, 1903–04; railroad policeman, Oregon Short Line

Railroad Company, Salt Lake City, 1904; manager of the Stenographic Department, Sears Roebuck and Company, Chicago, 1906–08; partner, Burroughs and Dentzer advertising contractors, Chicago, 1908–09; office manager, Physicians Co-Operative Association, Chicago, 1909; partner, State-Burroughs Company salesmanship firm, Chicago, 1909; worked for Champlain Yardley Company stationers, Chicago, 1910–11; manager, System Service Bureau, Chicago, 1912–13; freelance writer after 1913; formed Edgar Rice Burroughs, Inc. publishers, 1913, Burroughs–Tarzan Enterprises, 1934–39, and Burroughs-Tarzan Pictures, 1934–37; lived in California after 1919; Major of Malibu Beach, 1933; also United Press correspondent in the Pacific during World War II, and columnist ("Laugh It Off"), Honolulu *Advertiser*, 1941–42, 1945. *Died 19 March 1950.*

Western Publications

Novels

The Girl from Hollywood. New York, Macaulay, 1923; London, Methuen, 1924.
The Bandit of Hell's Bend. Chicago, McClurg, 1925; London, Methuen, 1926.
The War Chief. Chicago, McClurg, 1927; London, Methuen, 1928.
Apache Devil. Tarzana, California, Burroughs, 1933.
The Deputy Sheriff of Comanche County. Tarzana, California, Burroughs, 1940.

Other Publications

Novels

Tarzan of the Apes. Chicago, McClurg, 1914; London, Methuen, 1917.
The Return of Tarzan. Chicago, McClurg, 1915; London, Methuen, 1918.
The Beasts of Tarzan. Chicago, McClurg, 1916; London, Methuen, 1918.
The Son of Tarzan. Chicago, McClurg, 1917; London, Methuen, 1919.
A Princess of Mars. Chicago, McClurg, 1917; London, Methuen, 1919.
The Gods of Mars. Chicago, McClurg, 1918; London, Methuen, 1920.
Tarzan and the Jewels of Opar. Chicago, McClurg, 1918; London, Methuen, 1919.
The Warlord of Mars. Chicago, McClurg, 1919; London, Methuen, 1920.
Thuvia, Maid of Mars. Chicago, McClurg, 1920; London, Methuen, 1921.
Tarzan the Terrible. Chicago, McClurg, and London, Methuen, 1921.
The Chessmen of Mars. Chicago, McClurg, 1922; London, Methuen, 1923.
At the Earth's Core. Chicago, McClurg, 1922; London, Methuen, 1923.
Pellucidar. Chicago, McClurg, 1923; London, Methuen, 1924.
Tarzan and the Golden Lion. Chicago, McClurg, 1923; London, Methuen, 1924.
Tarzan and the Ant Men. Chicago, McClurg, 1924; London, Methuen, 1925.
The Outlaw of Torn. Chicago, McClurg, and London, Methuen, 1927.
Tarzan, Lord of the Jungle. Chicago, McClurg, and London, Cassell, 1928.
The Master Mind of Mars. Chicago, McClurg, 1928; London, Methuen, 1939.
The Monster Men. Chicago, McClurg, 1929.
Tarzan and the Lost Empire. New York, Metropolitan, 1929; London, Cassell, 1931.
Tarzan at the Earth's Core. New York, Metropolitan, 1930; London, Methuen, 1938.
Tanar of Pellucidar. New York, Metropolitan, 1930; London, Methuen, 1939.
A Fighting Man of Mars. New York, Metropolitan, 1931; London, Lane, 1932.
Tarzan the Invincible. Tarzana, California, Burroughs, 1931; London, Lane, 1933.
Tarzan Triumphant. Tarzana, California, Burroughs, 1931; London, Lane, 1933.
Jungle Girl. Tarzana, California, Burroughs, 1932; London, Odhams Press, 1933; as *The Land of Hidden Men*, New York, Ace, 1963.
Tarzan and the City of Gold. Tarzana, California, Burroughs, 1933; London, Lane, 1936.
Tarzan and the Lion-Man. Tarzana, California, Burroughs, 1934; London, W.H. Allen, 1950.
Pirates of Venus. Tarzana, California, Burroughs, 1934; London, Lane, 1935.
Lost on Venus. Tarzana, California, Burroughs, 1935; London, Methuen, 1937.
Tarzan and the Leopard Men. Tarzana, California, Burroughs, 1935; London, Lane, 1936.
Tarzan's Quest. Tarzana, California, Burroughs, 1936; London, Methuen, 1938.
Swords of Mars. Tarzana, California, Burroughs, 1936; London, New English Library, 1966.
Back to the Stone Age. Tarzana, California, Burroughs, 1937.
The Oakdale Affair; The Rider. Tarzana, California, Burroughs, 1937.
Tarzan and the Forbidden City. Tarzana, California, Burroughs, 1938; London, W.H. Allen, 1950.
The Lad and the Lion. Tarzana, California, Burroughs, 1938.
Carson of Venus. Tarzana, California, Burroughs, 1939; London, Goulden, 1950.
Synthetic Men of Mars. Tarzana, California, Burroughs, 1940; London, Methuen, 1941.
Land of Terror. Tarzana, California, Burroughs, 1944.
Escape on Venus. Tarzana, California, Burroughs, 1946; London, New English Library, 1966.
Tarzan and the Foreign Legion. Tarzana, California, Burroughs, 1947; London, W.H. Allen, 1949.
Tarzan and the Madman. New York, Canaveral Press, 1964; London, New English Library, 1966.
Beyond the Farthest Star. New York, Ace, 1964.
The Girl from Farris's. Kansas City, Missouri, House of Greystoke, 1965.
The Efficiency Expert. Kansas City, Missouri, House of Greystoke, 1966.
I Am a Barbarian. Tarzana, California, Burroughs, 1967.
Pirate Blood (as John Tyler McCulloch). New York, Ace, 1970.

Short Stories

Jungle Tales of Tarzan. Chicago, McClurg, and London, Methuen, 1919.
Tarzan the Untamed. Chicago, McClurg, and London, Methuen, 1920.

The Mucker. Chicago, McClurg, 1921; as *The Mucker* and *The Man Without a Soul*, London, Methuen, 2 vols., 1921–22.
The Land That Time Forgot. Chicago, McClurg, 1924; London, Methuen, 1925.
The Eternal Lover. Chicago, McClurg, 1925; London, Methuen, 1927; as *The Eternal Savage*, New York, Ace, 1963.
The Cave Girl. Chicago, McClurg, 1925; London, Methuen, 1927.
The Moon Maid. Chicago, McClurg, 1926; London, Stacey, 1972; abridged edition, as *The Moon Men*, New York, Canaveral Press, 1962; augmented edition, London, Tandem, 1975.
The Mad King. Chicago, McClurg, 1926.
Tarzan the Magnificent. Tarzana, California, Burroughs, 1939; London, Methuen, 1940.
Llana of Gathol. Tarzana, California, Burroughs, 1948; London, New English Library, 1967.
Beyond Thirty. Privately printed, 1955; as *The Lost Continent*, New York, Ace, 1963.
The Man-Eater. Privately printed, 1955.
Savage Pellucidar. New York, Canaveral Press, 1963.
Tales of Three Planets. New York, Canaveral Press, 1964.
John Carter of Mars. New York, Canaveral Press, 1964.
Tarzan and the Castaways. New York, Canaveral Press, 1964; London, New English Library, 1966.
The Wizard of Venus. New York, Ace, 1970.

Other

The Tarzan Twins (for children). Joliet, Illinois, Volland, 1927; London, Collins, 1930.
Tarzan and the Tarzan Twins, with Jad-Bal-Ja, The Golden Lion (for children). Racine, Wisconsin, Whitman, 1936.
Official Guide of the Tarzan Clans of America. Privately printed, 1939.

*

Critical Studies: *Edgar Rice Burroughs, Master of Adventure* by Richard A. Lupoff, New York, Canaveral Press, 1965, revised edition, New York, Ace, 1968; *Tarzan Alive: A Definitive Biography of Lord Greystoke* by P.J. Farmer, New York, Doubleday, 1972, London, Panther, 1974; *Edgar Rice Burroughs, The Man Who Created Tarzan* by Irwin Porges, Provo, Utah, Brigham Young University Press, 1975, London, New English Library, 1976 (includes bibliography); *Guide to Barsoom* by John Flint Roy, New York, Ballantine, 1976; *The Burroughs Bestiary: An Encyclopaedia of Monsters and Imaginary Beings Created by Edgar Rice Burroughs* by David Day, London, New English Library, 1981; *Tarzan and Tradition: Classical Myth in Popular Literature* by Erling B. Holtsmark, Westport, Connecticut, Greenwood, 1981; *Burroughs Dictionary: An Alphabetical List of Proper Names, Words, Phrases, and Concepts Contained in the Published Works of Edgar Rice Burroughs* by George T. McWhorter, Lanham, Maryland, University Press of America, 1987.

* * *

Edgar Rice Burroughs is not best-known for his western fiction, yet his novels set in the American West make good reading and are historically noteworthy. They were written between the world wars, well after Tarzan's initial success and all were serialized before appearing in book form. None achieved the astounding popularity of the Tarzan of John Carter stories, yet these western works, in their realism and historical detail, prove Burroughs to have possessed greater depth and broader abilities than are ordinarily acknowledged him.

There are five western novels. The earliest of these, *The Girl from Hollywood*, differs from the others in that its plot is primarily a domestic one. The Pennington family, living comfortably and amiably on its southern California ranch (which is modeled after Burroughs's own Tarzana), is at the center of a plot which contrasts the clean, wholesome life of the ranch with the ghastly, depraved life of the Hollywood drug addict. Of the other four western novels, two focus on the lives of white western ranchers and villagers, and two reflect the viewpoint of native Americans, specifically the Apaches.

The Bandit of Hell's Bend and *The Deputy Sheriff of Comanche County* are of a genre which Burroughs called "Wild West" stories. These lack original plotting, although suspense is certainly the main source of interest in both books. They also contain refreshingly realistic minor characters and ample doses of Burroughs's incisive humor. In the first, sophisticated easterners plot to swindle an innocent Arizona girl out of her ranch inheritance; the leading character, Bull, is a complicated, close-lipped individual around whom the plot moves. The second involves a man falsely accused of murder who adopts a new identity in order to pursue the real killers. In both of these books the contrast between east and west plays a part. It is one of Burroughs's favorite motifs, in which easterners are seen as objects of amusement with their inappropriate clothes and sissified manners. And they are morally objectionable as well with their tendency to cheat and lie to get what they want. In Burroughs's works the city slicker from New York, say, comes west to gain the advantage over those he thinks less clever than himself, but he does not succeed.

The Apache novels contain contrasts of a far deeper nature, and are quite different from Burroughs's more stereotypical Westerns. *The War Chief* and its sequel, *Apache Devil*, form a carefully researched description of the last days of Geronimo's freedom in the mid-1880's. At the same time they comprise the story of the education and maturation of an Apache warrior, Shoz-Dijiji, the Black Bear. In his excellent introduction to the Gregg Press edition (1978) of *Apache Devil*, Robert Morsberger says, "Burroughs' Apache epic is worthy to stand with later treatments of the Southwestern Indian by such novelists as Oliver La Farge, Hal Borland, and Elliott Arnold." One of the reasons for this is that the Apache novels of Burroughs represent the first time the Apache had been seen in literature as anything other than a growling savage. The *New York Times Book Review* noted that *Apache Devil* "has the refreshing quality of sympathy for the Indians." But these Indian novels retain their interest today primarily because Burroughs so consistently balances the viewpoints of Indians and whites without undue sentimentality. At one point, for example, an Indian scouting for the army is about to give the soldiers information which will betray them into an Apache ambush. The narrator remarks, "Shocking! Dishonorable! Disgraceful! Yes, of course; but many a civilized man wears a decoration today for betraying the enemy. It makes a difference who does it—that is all."

Throughout these novels there is a humane recognition of human foible; at the same time Burroughs wryly examines our notions of what it means to be civilized. Burroughs's western fiction is marked by its skillful character portraits, its realistic speech and settings, and its dramatic contrasts between changing, often conflicting cultures. Morsberger rightly assesses Burroughs's accomplishment when he says, "Burroughs' Westerns have an honesty as well as authenticity that makes them a genuine contribution to the genre . . . [and] are valuable for their realism, based upon the author's first hand experience in the West during the final years of the frontier."

—Katharine Weston Cohen

BURT, Katharine (née Newlin). American. Born in 1882. Married to the writer Struthers Burt. Teacher; then freelance writer. *Died in 1977.*

WESTERN PUBLICATIONS

Novels

The Branding Iron. Boston, Houghton Mifflin, and London, Constable, 1919.
Snow-Blind. Boston, Houghton Mifflin, 1921; London, Constable, 1922.
"Q". Boston, Houghton Mifflin, 1922; London, Hutchinson, 1923.
The Tall Ladder. Boston, Houghton Mifflin, 1932.
This Woman and This Man. New York, Scribner, 1934.

Uncollected Short Story

"The Red-Headed Husband," in *Cosmopolitan* (New York), January 1926.

OTHER PUBLICATIONS

Novels

The Red Lady. Boston, Houghton Mifflin, and London, Constable, 1920.
Hidden Creek. Boston, Houghton Mifflin, 1920; London, Constable, 1921.
Quest. Boston, Houghton Mifflin, 1925.
The Grey Parrot. London, Hutchinson, 1926.
Body and Soul. New York, Jacobsen, 1927.
Cock's Feather. Boston, Houghton Mifflin, 1928; London, Heinemann, 1929.
The Men of Moon Mountain. London, Hutchinson, 1930; Philadelphia, Macrae Smith, 1933.
A Man's Own Country. Boston, Houghton Mifflin, 1931.
Beggars All. Boston, Houghton Mifflin, 1933.
Rapture Beyond. New York, Scribner, 1935.
When Beggars Choose. Philadelphia, Macrae Smith, 1937.
Safe Road. Philadelphia, Macrae Smith, 1938; as *A Very Tender Love*, New York, New American Library, 1975.
If Love I Must. Philadelphia, Macrae Smith, 1939.
No Surrender. Philadelphia, Macrae Smith, 1940.
Fatal Gift. Philadelphia, Macrae Smith, 1941.
Captain Millett's Island. Philadelphia, Macrae Smith, 1944.
Lady in the Tower. Philadelphia, Macrae Smith, 1946.
Close Pursuit. New York, Scribner, 1947.
Still Water. Philadelphia, Macrae Smith, 1948; London, Coker, 1951.
Strong Citadel. New York, Scribner, 1949; London, Coker, 1951.
Escape from Paradise. New York, Scribner, 1952.

Plays

Screenplays: *The Man from Lost River*, with Lambert Hillyer and Arthur Statter, 1921; *The Eagle's Feather*, with Winifred Dunn, 1923.

Other (for children)

Smarty. New York, Funk and Wagnalls, 1965.
Girl on a Broomstick. New York, Funk and Wagnalls, 1967.
One Silver Spur. New York, Funk and Wagnalls, 1968.

* * *

Pennsylvania romances and Wyoming Westerns—novelist-husband Struthers Burt grew up in Philadelphia, and later the Burts homesteaded on the Bar BC Ranch—form the body of Katharine Burt's novels. But it is in her literate Westerns that Burt brings the "gentler sex," with its emotional introspection, poetic expression, and aura of romance, to its well-earned home on the range, where, indeed, despite natural disasters, "seldom is heard a discouraging word."

Burt's first novel, *The Branding Iron* (later a 1927 film, *Body and Soul*, starring Lionel Barrymore) might be considered a "Swisstern." Set in the Swiss Alps (the European Rockies), our story is of mad Dr. Leyden (Barrymore), who, taunted by ski-jumper Ruffo for attempting to satisfy a young and pretty wife who might well look elsewhere, is goaded into branding her—literally—his own. In a chilling cinematic scene, Patient Griselde—Hilda—is strung up by her wrists and branded with a white-hot iron. Ever-faithful Hilda is now and forever Dr. Leyden's—"body and soul."

Snow-Blind, set in the Canadian northwest (also filmed, in 1921), is the story of the ugly and deformed Hugh Garth, who stumbles on a girl lost in the snow. Blinded by the white glare, the girl believes the tall tales the unseen Hugh spins. In true romantic fashion, when the girl suddenly sees again, it's love at first sight—but with Hugh's younger brother, Pete. All ends happily, however, for Hugh comes at last to appreciate the devotion of his former nurse, patient Bella, and gives Pete his blessing.

In later Westerns, the Burt heroine matures—becomes stronger, less patient, more courageous and independent-minded, determined to live her own life. Heiress Julia Oliphant (*The Tall Ladder*) flees from New York City, a failed marriage and a not-too-promising engagement to Locksley Greene, her father's ex-partner, to go west. There, in Wyoming, she sets up "a tall ladder against the Western sky," and up that ladder escapes the weight of past, character, and fate, to "make a fresh start, climb into a new life." Chancing upon a cabin in the hills, coincidentally named "The Flying O" (*O*liphant), Julia buys it from the aged frontiersman Seth Gaynor, who needs the money to go to California for an operation. Here, Julia establishes a horse ranch and engages a criminal, "Jefferson Wager," wanted for murder, as foreman, and her own ex-husband, Jasper Clere, as horseman and partner. Romance blooms in the Wyoming wilderness as Julia and Jefferson draw near to each other. But in a spurt of painful insight, Jefferson comments philosophically on their predicament:

> Which of us is free to climb up out of our lives like that? . . . As though God set up an empty ladder agin' his stars! Are you a free woman yourself? You wasn't free when you came riding in your big machine with your face like a kind of hard young angry man's. You had somebody's fate hanging on your woman's neck. I've seen you looking at Jasper Clere—kind of white-lipped

and haunted. It ain't for your happiness you sent back East for him. Since he's been here, you haven't been the same—eager, keen-hearted. You ain't hardly had a happy moment. Free? God A'mighty! Ask for freedom on your knees and listen to the angels laughin'.

This Woman and This Man, also set in the Wyoming mountains, again combines east and west in a love story of an unspoiled and uneducated western girl and a cultured, sophisticated Easterner.

Drawing upon her training as a teacher and her experience with her own children and the boys who came to her Wyoming ranch, Burt wrote novels for young people as well. *Smarty* is a horse with two owners—spunky, 13-year-old Jenny Miller, who renames him "Taffy," trains him, and loves him, and 14-year-old Stormy Mapes, "Smarty's" previous owner. Jenny is confronted with a moral dilemma when her young brother, Funny, has a near-fatal accident just as the Junior Ranch Race is about to begin: should she carry out her family responsibilities, allowing Stormy to ride Smarty/Taffy to glory? Her decision is to follow the mature and maturing course, and another strong and independent-minded Burt heroine is in the making.

Burt's truly feminist viewpoint brings a fresh air to the macho westerns of her precursors and followers.

—Marcia G. Fuchs

BUSCH, Niven. American. Born in New York City, 26 April 1903. Educated at Hoosac School, New York; Princeton University, New Jersey, 1922–24. Married 1) Sonia Frey in 1929; 2) Phyllis Cooper in 1936; 3) the actress Teresa Wright in 1942 (divorced 1952); 4) Carmencita Baker in 1956 (divorced 1969); 5) Suzanne de Sanz in 1973; five sons and two daughters. Associate editor, *Time*, 1924–31; contributing editor, *New Yorker*, 1927–31; writer and producer for Warner Brothers, 20th Century Fox, MGM, Paramount, Universal, and R.K.O., 1931–52; story editor, Sam Goldwyn Productions, 1940–42; independent film producer, 1946–52; operator of fruit and cattle ranch, Hollister, California. Regents Professor, University of California, Irvine, 1970, 1971, 1975, and San Diego, 1972; Guest Lecturer, Princeton University, 1985–86. Agent: Frederick Hill, 1842 Union Street, San Francisco, California 94123, U.S.A.

Western Publications

Novels

Duel in the Sun. New York, Hampton, 1944; London, W.H. Allen, 1947.
The Furies. New York, Dial Press, 1948; London, White Lion, 1974.

Other Publications

Novels

The Carrington Incident. New York, Morrow, 1939; London, Hale, 1942.
They Dream of Home. New York, Appleton Century, 1944.
Day of the Conquerors. New York, Harper, 1946.
The Hate Merchant. New York, Simon and Schuster, and London, W.H. Allen, 1953.
The Actor. New York, Simon and Schuster, and London, Muller, 1955.
Caifornia Street. New York, Simon and Schuster, and London, Cape, 1959.
The San Franciscans. New York, Simon and Schuster, 1962; London, Cape, 1963.
The Gentleman from California. New York, Simon and Schuster, 1965.
The Takeover. New York, Simon and Schuster, 1973; London, W.H. Allen, 1974.
No Place for a Hero. New York, Knight Ridder, 1976.
Continent's Edge. New York, Simon and Schuster, 1980.
The Titan Game. New York, Random House, 1989.

Plays

Screenplays: *The Crowd Roars*, with Kuben Glasmon and John Bright, 1932; *Miss Pinkerton*, with Lillie Hayward, 1932; *College Coach (Football Coach)*, with Manuel Seff, 1933; *The Big Shakedown*, with Rian James, 1934; *The Man with Two Faces*, with Tom Reed, 1934; *Babbitt*, 1934; *In Old Chicago*, with Lamar Trotti and Sonya Levien, 1937; *Off the Record*, with others, 1938; *Angels Wash Their Faces*, with others, 1939; *The Westerner*, with Jo Swerling and Stuart N. Lake, 1940; *Belle Starr*, with Lamar Trotti and Cameron Rogers, 1941; *The Postman Always Rings Twice*, with Harry Ruskin, 1946; *Duel in the Sun*, 1946; *Pursued*, 1947; *Moss Rose*, with Jules Furthman and Tom Reed, 1947; *The Capture*, 1950; *The Furies*, 1950; *Distant Drums*, with Martin Rackin, 1951; *The Man from the Alamo*, with others, 1953; *The Moonlighter*, 1953; *The Treasure of Pancho Villa*, with J. Robert Bren and Gladys Atwater, 1955; *Galveston; California Street*.

Other

Twenty-One Americans, Being Profiles of Some People Famous in Our Time, Together with Silly Pictures of Them Drawn by De Miskey. New York, Doubleday, 1930.

*

Manuscript Collections: University of Wyoming, Laramie; Stanford University, California; University of California, Los Angeles.

Niven Busch comments (1982):

I began writing very young. I was contributing poems and short skits to magazines and newspapers when still in high school. Learning journalism then provided me with a wonderful tool which I've used in researching my novels. Screen writing provided a different but no less valuable workbench technique. The different kinds of fiction I have written have been of dubious advantage in building a literary reputation but I have chosen this course because I become bored if commited to work in a single genre. Hence, I suppose, the variety: my books include "Westerns," sociological novels, political novels, and combinations of these categories. My one requirement of myself is that I do the very best I can, no matter what the nature of the product. My most successful book, due in part to the huge exposure of the film made from it, is *Duel in the Sun*. My best book is, I think, my last, *Continent's Edge*: its canvas is the broadest and best organized and while deeply researched it is enlivened by the fact that I have personally been engaged in most of the activities described—ranching, polo, the oil business, the movies, and the world of corporate business. As I write this, I am hard to work on a suspense–political story centered in part on the space and microprocessor industries of California's "Silicon Valley." I am now more than 78 years old, in quite good health, and able to indulge in golf and other favorite sports. I am married to a lovely woman, my best wife by far after several divorces, I have most of my children living near me. I love them. I love my work. I hope to continue it to the end of the tether. I feel that I have had a happy and successful life, and I am tempted to add—so far . . .

* * *

From journalistic beginnings in New York City on *Time* and *New Yorker* magazines, Niven Busch moved actually and professionally west. Between 1940 and 1955, he wrote 10 western stories or screenplays for motion pictures, two of them adaptations of his western novels *Duel in the Sun* and *The Furies*.

Writing part of the screenplay for *The Westerner*, Busch changed some of the rules of western plotting and characterization. He emphasized the relationship, sometimes an obsessive one, between the legendary Judge Roy Bean and a fictitious cowboy, a relationship predicated upon loneliness. Busch has continued to pursue this theme in his western novels as well as in his western screenplays: sexual obsession in *Duel in the Sun*, psychological obsession with the past coupled with a revenge motif in *Pursued*, and the love–hate relationship between a father and his daughter in *The Furies*. In this way Busch "opened up" the Western for the anti-western and the satirical Western of the 1960's and 1970's.

Because he has been a screenwriter since the early 1930's, it is not surprising that Busch owes more of his concept of the Western to Hollywood than to historical actuality or to the influence of the traditional western writers such as Zane Grey or Owen Wister. He has a technical competence in placing characters in settings and working out the plot which is more cinematic than literary. In addition, he has an economy of style, probably acquired from many years writing for the screen, which is more craftsmanlike than artistic. These attributes are, however, overshadowed by a sensational, almost lurid, treatment. His narrative style and character development show influences of the "hard-boiled" urban thriller writers such as James M. Cain and Raymond Chandler. Pearl Chavez, for instance, heroine of *Duel in the Sun*, would be more at home as a gun moll in the city than she is in a western landscape. In *The Furies* Busch's "hard-hitting" prose style is at odds with the melodrama of a daughter at war with her father. Nonetheless, such prose and atypical western heroines do divert attention from a lack of logic in many of Busch's plots.

Busch has been a prolific and commercial writer for several decades. For better or worse, he did bring something new to the Western—psychological tension. That, a perception of personal relationships, and humor give his work an entertaining quality missing in many traditional western writers.

—Wade Austin

C

CALHOUN, Chad. *See* **CUNNINGHAM, Chet.**

CALHOUN, Wes. *See* **SADLER, Jeff.**

CALLAHAN, John. *See* **CHADWICK, Joseph.**

CAMERON, Lou. Also writes as Justin Adams; L.J. Arnold; Julie Cameron; Tabor Evans (house name); Mary Louise Manning; W.R. Marvin; Ramsay Thorne. American. Born in San Francisco, California, 20 June 1924. Educated at the California School of Fine Arts, San Francisco, 1940–41. Served as an artillery scout and combat instructor in the United States Army, 1941–50; Technical Sergeant; Bronze Star, Purple Heart, 3 battle stars. Married worked as a movie extra, private detective, ranch hand, and trucker. Freelance artist for magazines and comic books, 1950–57, and writer since 1957. Recipient: Thomas Edison award, for comic book, 1956; Western Writers of America Spur award, 1977. Agent: Barbara Lowenstein, 250 West 57th Street, New York, New York 10107, U.S.A.

WESTERN PUBLICATIONS

Novels

Doc Travis. New York, Dell, 1975.
North to Cheyenne. New York, Dell, 1975.
The Guns of Durango. New York, Dell, 1976.
The Spirit Horses. New York, Ballantine, 1976.
How the West Was Won (novelization of screenplay). New York, Ballantine, 1977.
The Wilderness Seekers. New York, Dell, 1980.
The Grass of Goodnight. New York, Fawcett, 1987.
Buntline Special. New York, Fawcett, 1988.
Crooked Lance. New York, Fawcett, 1989.
Yellow Iron. New York, Fawcett, 1990.

Novels (series: Stringer)

Stringer. New York, Berkley, 1987.
Stringer on Dead Man's Range. New York, Berkley, 1987.
Stringer on the Assassin's Trail. New York, Berkley, 1987.
Stringer and the Hangman's Rodeo. New York, Ace, 1988.
Stringer and the Hanging Judge. New York, Berkley, 1988.
Stringer and the Wild Bunch. New York, Berkley, 1988.
Stringer and the Deadly Flood. New York, Ace, 1988.
Stringer in Tombstone. New York, Berkley, 1988.
Stringer and the Oil Well Indians. New York, Berkley, 1989.
Stringer and the Border War. New York, Berkley, 1989.
Stringer on the Mojave. New York, Berkley, 1989.
Stringer on Pike's Peak. New York, Berkley, 1989.
Stringer and the Hell-bound Herd. New York, Berkley, 1989.
Stringer in a Texas Shoot-out. New York, Berkley, 1989.

Novels as Tabor Evans (series: Longarm)

Longarm in Boulder Canyon. New York, Jove, 1982.
Longarm and the Great Train Robbery. New York, Jove, 1982.

OTHER PUBLICATIONS

Novels

Angel's Flight. New York, Fawcett, 1960; London, Muller, 1962.
The Big Red Ball. New York, Fawcett, 1961; London, Muller, 1963.
The Sky Divers. New York, Fawcett, 1962; London, Muller, 1963.
The Empty Quarter. New York, Fawcett, 1962; London, Muller, 1963.
Not Even Your Mother. New York, Fawcett, 1963.
The Bastard's Name Is War. New York, Fawcett, 1963; London, Muller, 1965.
The Black Camp. New York, Fawcett, and London, Muller, 1963.
The Green Fields of Hell. New York, Fawcett, 1964; London, Coronet, 1968.
The Block Busters. New York, McKay, 1964; London, Hale, 1966.
None But the Brave (novelization of screenplay). New York, Fawcett, 1965.
The Dirty War of Sergeant Slade. New York, Fawcett, 1966; London, Coronet, 1967.
Iron Men with Wooden Wings. New York, Belmont, 1967.
The Dragon's Spine. New York, Avon, 1968.
File on a Missing Redhead. New York, Fawcett, 1968; London, Coronet, 1969.
The Good Guy. New York, Lancer, 1968.
The Outsider (novelization of TV series). New York, Popular Library, 1969.
Before It's Too Late. New York, Fawcett, 1970.
The Amphorae Pirates. New York, Random House, 1970; London, Hodder and Stoughton, 1971.
Behind the Scarlet Door. New York, Fawcett, 1971.
Spurhead. New York, Dell, 1971.
Cybernia. New York, Fawcett, 1972; London, Coronet, 1973.
The Girl with the Dynamite Bangs. New York, Lancer, 1973.
The First Blood. New York, Lancer, n.d.
Hannibal Brooks (novelization of screenplay). New York, Lancer, n.d.
Mistress Bayou Labelle. New York, Lancer, n.d.

Mud War. New York, Lancer, n.d.
Tipping Point. New York, Lancer, n.d.
Tunnel War. New York, Lancer, n.d.
California Split (novelization of screenplay). New York, Fawcett, 1974.
Barca. New York, Berkley, and Henley on Thames, Ellis, 1974.
The Closing Circle. New York, Berkley,1974; Henley on Thames, Ellis, 1975.
Devil in the Pines (as Julie Cameron). New York, Berkley, 1975.
The Darklings. New York, Berkley, 1975.
Tancredi. New York, Berkley, 1975; Henley on Thames, Ellis, 1976.
Dekker. New York, Berkley, 1976.
Drop into Hell. New York, Fawcett, 1976; London, Hodder and Stoughton, 1980.
Chains (as Justin Adams). New York, Dell, 1977; London, Hamlyn, 1978.
Code Seven. New York, Berkley, 1977.
The Last Chronicles of Ballyfungus (as Mary Louise Manning). New York, Dell, 1978.
The Big Lonely. New York, Popular Library, 1978.
The Cascade Ghost. New York, Popular Library, 1978.
The Subway Stalker. New York, Dell, 1980.
This Fever in My Blood. New York, Dell, 1980.
The Track Stalker. New York, Dell, 1980.
The Subway Stalker. New York, Dell, 1980.
The Hot Car. New York, Avon, 1981.

Other

Ojibway Warriors' Society in Occupied Anicinabe Park, Kenora, Ontario, August 1974 (as Louis Cameron). Toronto, Better Read Graphics, 1974.

Editor, *Morituri*. New York, McKay, 1965.

* * *

Lou Cameron's Westerns are distinguished by intelligent plots, a good sense of pace, quickly-drawn but nonetheless convincing characters and, above all, a nice line in dry, perceptive humour. Indeed, humour pervades nearly all of Cameron's westerns (with the possible exception of 1989's *Crooked Lance*, and his work on the Renegade series as Ramsay Thorne), and it speaks volumes for his skill as a writer that it generally adds more to his stories than it takes away.

This is especially true of his Longarm novels (written as Tabor Evans) and, more recently, the Stringer sequence, published under his own name. In Cameron's hands, these continuing characters adhere to the popular image of a typical western hero, but seldom take themselves too seriously. They are, in fact, just as likely to make mistakes (as we all do) as they are to gradually link a number of seemingly disparate plot-threads together to bring about an ultimately satisfying denouement, and it is this "human" quality which makes Cameron's work (particularly in the adult western market) stand head and shoulders above many of its competitors.

Although much of his work falls into the thriller category, Cameron nevertheless has a definite knack for devising well-researched Westerns with a strong period flavour. This is nowhere more apparent than in the Stringer books.

To begin with, the Stringer series is something of a departure from the norm in that it is set in the early part of the 20th century. Its hero, Stuart MacKail, is also unconventional. He is a "stringer," or part-time newspaper reporter, who works for the San Francisco *Sun*. A trail-wise pen-pusher, Stringer is invariably dispatched by his editor, the irascible Sam Barca (the series' only other continuing character) to write features or file reports on different aspects of the Old West, a plot-device that cleverly enables him to rub shoulders with actual historical figures, dispel a few myths and create several more.

In the first novel, *Stringer*, MacKail is sent to California to investigate "The Ghost of Sonora," Joaquín Murieta, and gets to spend some time on his uncle's ranch. In *Stringer on the Assassin's Trail*, he meets up with Teddy Roosevelt (whose role in the Spanish-American war he had previously criticised as a war correspondent) and Jack London, finally foiling what he believes to be a plot to kill the president only to discover that *he* is the assassin's target. In *Stringer and the Hangman's Rodeo*, MacKail is sent to Cheyenne to cover Tom Horn's execution, and he finds himself abducted and turned into Kid Curry's unofficial biographer in *Stringer and the Wild Bunch*.

Cameron keeps what could easily become a somewhat deadening formula fresh by constantly shifting location and subject matter. Inevitably, however, some of the novels are little more than variations on a theme, and he overcomes these shortcomings by the strength of his colourful secondary and supporting characters, plus numerous (and sometimes ingenious) twists in the plot. In *Stringer and the Hanging Judge*, Stringer runs afoul of Judge Roy Bean; for *Stringer in Tombstone* the roving reporter starts out to write a routine feature on the Gunfight at the OK Corral and ends up exposing a crooked silver mining scheme. Other historical characters with whom he comes into contact are Chris Madsen and Bill Tilghman (*Stringer and the Oil Well Indians*), and Pancho Villa (*Stringer and the Border War*). Among Cameron's other themes are the discovery of six dead bodies buried in the desert for 50 years (*Stringer on the Mojave*), a miners' strike (*Stringer on Pike's Peak*), and a pack of renegade bounty hunters (*Stringer in a Texas Shoot-out*).

More often than not (and this applies to practically all of his Westerns), Cameron's action—both in and out of the bedroom—flows naturally from the plot, successfully dispensing with the contrived feel of so many other adult Westerns. Similarly, his portrayal of violence is almost never graphic or gratuitous. In general, his Westerns are eminently agreeable.

There are, of course, exceptions, as his work on the Renegade series demonstrates. The continuing adventures of a cashiered U.S. Army officer who travels south of the border to become known as Captain Gringo, the Maxim-wielding renegade of the title, were predominantly sex novels with some action thrown in, the sex growing frequently more outlandish as the series wore on.

Unencumbered by the constraints of the adult or series Western, however, Cameron has written several fine novels of the West. Probably his best known is *The Spirit Horses*, about the introduction of camels into the U.S. Cavalry, which is told in his usual informal, astute manner, and features a number of extremely well-observed characters (particularly the half-crazed camel trainer, Haji Ali). Most recently he has published an interesting (and surprisingly, more sober) novel of friendship between red man and white, George Custer's campaign against the Indians, and a fearsome white buffalo—the aforementioned *Crooked Lance*.

—David Whitehead

CAMPBELL, Cliff. *See* **HECKELMANN, Charles N.**

CANUCK, Abe. *See* **BINGLEY, David Ernest.**

CAPPS, Benjamin (Franklin). American. Born in Dundee, Texas, 11 June 1922. Educated at Olney High School, 1935–37; Archer City High School, 1937–38; Texas Tech College (now University), Lubbock, 1938–39; University of Texas, Austin, 1945–49, B.A. 1948 (Phi Beta Kappa), M.A. 1949. Served in the United States Army Air Force, 1942–45: 1st Lieutenant; 3 battle stars. Married Marie Thompson in 1942; two sons and one daughter. Surveyor, Civilian Conservation Corps, 1940–41, and Corps of Engineers, 1941–42, in Colorado and Texas; Instructor, then Assistant Professor of English and journalism, Northeastern State College, Tahlequah, Oklahoma, 1949–51; tool and die maker, Grand Prairie, Texas, 1951–61; then freelance writer. Writer-in-residence, University of Texas, Arlington, 1976. Honorary lifetime member, Western Literature Association, 1986. Recipient: Levi Strauss Golden Saddleman award, 1964; Western Writers of America Spur award, 1965, 1966, 1970; Agent: A.L. Hart, Fox Chase Agency, 419 East 57th Street, New York, New York 10022. Address: 366 Forrest Hill Lane, Grand Prairie, Texas 75051, U.S.A.

WESTERN PUBLICATIONS

Novels

Hanging at Comanche Wells. New York, Ballantine, 1962.
The Trail to Ogallala. New York, Duell, 1964.
Sam Chance. New York, Duell, 1965; revised edition, Dallas, Texas, Southern Methodist University Press, 1987.
A Woman of the People. New York, Duell, 1966.
The Brothers of Uterica. New York, Meredith Press, 1967.
The White Man's Road. New York, Harper, 1969; London, Tandem, 1975.
The True Memoirs of Charley Blankenship. Philadelphia, Lippincott, 1972.
Woman Chief. New York, Doubleday, 1979.
The Heirs of Franklin Woodstock. Fort Worth, Texas Christian Press, 1989.

Short Stories

Tales of the Southwest. New York, Bantam Doubleday Dell, 1991.

OTHER PUBLICATIONS

Other

The Indians, with the editors of Time Life Books. New York, Time Life, 1973.
The Warren Wagontrain Raid. New York, Dial Press, 1974; revised edition, Dallas, Texas, Southern Methodist University Press, 1989.
The Great Chiefs, with the editors of Time Life Books. New York, Time Life, 1975.

Co-Editor, *Duncan Robinson: Texas Teacher and Humanist.* Arlington, University of Texas at Arlington, 1976.

*

Manuscript Collection: Special Collections, University of Texas at Arlington Library.

Critical Studies: *Benjamin Capps* by Ernest B. Speck, Boise, Idaho, Boise State University Press, 1981; *Benjamin Capps and the South Plains,* Denton, University of North Texas Press, 1990.

Benjamin Capps comments:

It has been my sincere belief that the history of America recapitulates, to a valid extent, the history of the whole world. Here the Human Comedy or Tragedy or Condition or Predicament has been concentrated, and it all happened not long ago. We can know much about it. Things like bookstores, libraries, even great universities, stand today where log cabins, sod shanties, even buffalo-hide tepees, stood only a hundred years ago. Here the mixing, fighting, mingling, changing, of a fantastic variety of people took place.

The West is an era, perhaps beginning in the 15th century, rather than a location. I have written about the United States west of the Mississippi in the 19th century because it is here that my roots lie. But the subject matter which is available to the western writer is as rich for literature as any which has ever existed, as rich as that used by Shakespeare or the Greek creative writers. If western writers do not produce great literature, it is the fault of the writers in their failure to grasp all the implications of their subject matter.

I object to the idea of writing about the "timeless West," as the proposition is often put forward. Change has been a law of the West. It is the universals about human nature which are timeless. Whether I have measured up to the possibilities in western writing is for others to say, now and later, but my intentions have been of the greatest and I have no apologies to make for the material which has been available to me.

* * *

Eight of Benjamin Capps's nine novels are set in the American West of about a century ago. Three of the novels—*A Woman of the People*, *The White Man's Road*, and *Woman Chief*—focus on the Plains Indians who at that time were in the process of being driven from the land by whites moving westward. Capps's other main subject is the life of the white settlers who were responsible for denying the Indian his traditional freedom of the plains. Except for Capps's first novel—*Hanging at Comanche Wells*—his novels about the 19th-century West are serious depictions of the real life on the frontier, which explore serious themes of cultures in confrontation, and recreate the people—both whites and Indians—who lived on the plains a hundred years ago. The one exception is *Hanging at Comanche Wells*, a paperback formula western that is not good enough to be treated seriously, but too good to establish the author as a star of the pulps.

Hanging at Comanche Wells is about life among the white settlers, as are the two novels which followed—*The Trail to Ogallala* and *Sam Chance*. *The Trail to Ogallala* follows the progress of a cattle drive during the last years of the great trail herds. The novel is much superior to Andy Adams's *Log of a Cowboy* (1903), which is always listed as the classic of the trail drive novels. Capps's third novel, *Sam Chance*, is the story of an old-time cattleman who came to the south plains after the Civil War, established a large ranch, and lived to see 20th-century government regulations and population growth restrict the free life of the range.

Sam Chance is followed by Capps's two best novels—*A Woman of the People* and *The White Man's Road*—both about Indian life. In the first a band of Comanches kidnaps two white girls—one 11, the other five—and raises them as members of their tribe. The story is told from the point of view of the older sister, Helen, who resists accepting the new culture and is disturbed at how rapidly her sister adapts to Indian life. It takes years for Helen to realize—suddenly and startlingly—that she too has become an Indian. But she learns of her subtle transformation barely in time to see Indian life give way to the white man's. The novel ends with Helen and her band leaving the plains to go to Ft. Sill so that they can surrender themselves to a life on the reservation. And it is reservation life that informs *The White Man's Road*, Capps's best-known novel. In this book, we can see how the reservation is in the process of destroying the culture of the Indian. Joe Cowbone, the main character, has come to young manhood on the Ft. Sill reservation and longs for one last moment of authentic Indian life before setting out on the white man's road of modern civilization. He and his friends steal a troop of U.S. Cavalry horses, almost get them away to the plains, and, even though the horses are retaken, manage to elude capture. Joe is later forced by a preacher to confess, but the army captain gives him a lecture and lets him go—a final indignity. Capps's other novel of Indian life, *Woman Chief*, is set outside Capps's native Texas. The book tells the story of a Crow woman who becomes a famous war chief in the mid-19th century. The novel is based on a historical figure, but Capps's version is fictionalized. Capps's three Indian novels succeed because the author is sympathetic to the Indians but does not sentimentalize and patronize them. By treating the Indians as humans whose culture is different but not inferior to that of the whites, Capps gives an authentic picture of life among the Plains Indians.

Two of Capps's novels—*The Brothers of Uterica* and *The True Memoirs of Charley Blankenship*— do not have the quality of his best books. The first tells of the establishment and failure of a utopian colony in 19th-century Texas. The book gives a good satiric picture of the squabbles of the colonists and their failure to understand frontier life, but the characters are not as well-drawn as in the best Capps novels. *Memoirs*, one of Capps's weakest novels, is a picaresque full of the usual western adventures that a wandering cowboy might expect to encounter.

Capps's most recent novel—*The Heirs of Franklin Woodstock*—is set in present-day Texas, but the plot turns on the dying frontier. Franklin Woodstock, at age 91, escapes from his nursing home and is the object of lengthy search by his middle-aged heirs, each of whom hopes to gain from Woodstock's estate—a ranch in West Texas. Franklin Woodstock was a pioneer made of stern stuff, but his children, except for middle son George, are spoiled by modern life and never understand what the old man stood for. It takes one of the grandchildren to inherit the true spirit of Franklin Woodstock.

Capps is one of the best writers in America today, and *A Woman of the People* is an American classic. His ability to draw believable characters, his minute rendering of time and place, and his ability to explore a theme in a mature way are his outstanding characteristics. His decision to write serious historical novels has caused him to capture less of the popular audience than some writers about the West have done, and his decision to write about 19th-century Texas has tended to hurt his reputation with serious critics of contemporary fiction.

—James W. Lee

CARDER, Leigh. *See* **CUNNINGHAM, Eugene.**

CARPENTER, John Jo. *See* **REESE, John.**

CARREL, Mark. *See* **PAINE, Lauran.**

CARRINGTON, G. A. *See* **CUNNINGHAM, Chet.**

CARSON, Hank. *See* **FEARN, John Russell.**

CARTER, Forrest. American Indian (Cherokee). Born in Tennessee, in 1925. Married to India Carter. Self-educated; orphaned at five, and a cowboy in the south and southwest from an early age; storyteller in Council to the Cherokee Nation. *Died June 1979.*

WESTERN PUBLICATIONS

Novels

Josey Wales: Two Westerns. Albuquerque, University of New Mexico Press, 1989.
The Rebel Outlaw, Josey Wales. Gantt, Alabama, Whippor-will, 1973; as *Gone to Texas*, New York, Delacorte Press, and London, Weidenfeld and Nicolson, 1975; as *The Outlaw Josey Wales*, New York, Dell, 1976.
The Vengeance Trail of Josey Wales. New York, Delacorte Press, 1976.

Watch for Me on the Mountain. New York, Delacorte Press, 1978; London, Hamish Hamilton, 1979; as *Cry Geronimo*, New York, Dell, 1980.

OTHER PUBLICATIONS

Other

The Education of Little Tree. New York, Delacorte Press, 1976.

* * *

Although Forrest Carter authored four books—three which fall under the label of Westerns—his position as a writer of fine Westerns would have been secure had he written only *The Rebel Outlaw, Josey Wales* (*Gone to Texas*), better known under its movie title *The Outlaw Josey Wales.* Admittedly, it was the movie that made readers aware of the book (it had been mostly overlooked), but the movie—good as it was—fails to capture the epic proportions of Carter's magnificent storytelling and his knowledge of the Old West, both in fact and legend.

Josey Wales surfaces as a blending of reality and myth. He is the super hero, the ultimate pistoleer, the man of unbending honor. Yet he is also vulnerable, ruthless, and blind to change. In short, what Carter created in Wales was a man of mythical proportions, but adorned with enough human sensibilities and weaknesses to make him believable, a very uneasy and difficult trick in the hands of most writers, but one which Carter pulled off superbly, never missing a beat. Where Wales is incredible with his revolvers—no TV or movie pistoleero ever came near his proficiency, let alone any real westerner—his hide is not invulnerable, nor is he insensitive to the loss of a friend or the love of a fair maiden, as evidenced by his romance with Laura Lee whom he saves from a would-be rapist.

The book is a masterpiece of the "epic" variety, and Carter manages to give the reader a feel for the times. He also displays a realism that might be unsettling to some, and the potential reader of this book should be warned of this. Carter does not delight in displaying violent death, but people die realistically and bloodily in this book, and Wales's concern for his victims is hardly sympathetic. This is best demonstrated in a scene where Josey Wales's young comrade remarks: "Wisht we had time to bury them fellas." "'To hell with them fellers,' Josey snarled. He spat a stream of tobacco juice into Abe's upturned face. 'Buzzards got to eat same as worms."'

However, the book is not merely a gory shoot-em-up. It presents action, but is also gives an accurate portrait of the times just after the Civil War, when things were hard and a man could afford very little charity to his enemies, and expected none. The book is one of the very best westerns of modern times, perhaps one of the very best ever. It is natural that it should spawn a sequel.

The Vengeance Trail of Josey Wales, though more slick (perhaps too slick), is a better than average Western, but far below the original. Perhaps it is because Wales, a quiet and mysterious character in the first, is now chatty. The book seems to be nothing better than a good, exciting action story, and very little surprising happens. There is one element, however, that gives it an edge over other Westerns of its type—its knowledge of the Apache Indians. Geronimo is given a sympathetic and realistic portrayal, without noble savage treatment, or ruthless savage treatment. *Vengeance Trail* can be recommended with enthusiasm to any reader seeking good entertainment and action, though after the previous Josey Wales story, it falls a bit flat.

After Carter's examination of Geronimo and the Apaches (the Comanches were treated with respect and knowledge in *The Rebel Outlaw, Josey Wales*), it was only natural that he would turn his talents to a book on the American Indian, a sort of western historical with Geronimo as the principal character. Dee Brown, author of *Bury My Heart at Wounded Knee*, said of this book, *Watch for Me on the Mountain*, "In this dramatic novel, based upon the oral history of the Apaches, Forrest Carter has probably come as close as any writer ever will to recreating the real Geronimo." With this book, Carter returns with all his former glory. The power of his first novel is here, coupled with a passion for historical accuracy and a sincere love for Geronimo and his people. The book is perhaps marred slightly by its overzealous attempt to make the reader aware of just how badly the Apaches were treated. At points, this becomes preaching, not storytelling; one feels Carter's intrusive presence (a rare thing in his novels) standing behind him, striking him over the head with the "point."

Although it is not a true Western, it would be negligent to ignore Carter's *The Education of Little Tree*. It is almost the equal of his westerns, and in it one can find the sources for his western tales. The book is something of a biography of Carter's childhood: his life with his grandparents, growing up in the mountain country of Tennessee, learning the ways of the mountain folks and despairing at the change of those ways as civilization creeps ever onward.

Carter, who died after the publication of only four books, may be the most significant writer of westerns to appear in the 1970's. All of his work is heartily recommended.

—Joe R. Lansdale

CARTER, Nevada. *See* **PAINE, Lauran.**

CARVER, Dave. *See* **BINGLEY, David Ernest.**

CARVER, Raymond. American. Born in Clatskanie, Oregon, 25 May 1938. Educated at Chico State College, California (founding editor, *Selection*), 1958–59; Humboldt State University, Arcata, California, 1960–63, A.B. 1963; University of Iowa, 1963–64, M.F.A. 1966. Married 1) Maryann Burk in 1957 (divorced 1982), one daughter and one son; 2) the writer Tess Gallagher in 1988. Worked in various jobs, including janitor, saw mill worker, delivery man, and salesman, 1957–67; textbook editor, Science Research Associates, Palo Alto, California, 1967–70; Visiting Lecturer, University of California, Santa Cruz, 1970–71, and Santa Barbara, 1975; Visiting Professor of English, University of California, Berkeley 1971–72; Visiting Writer, University of Iowa, 1972–73, Goddard College, Vermont, 1977–78, and University of Texas, El Paso, 1978–79; Professor of English, Syracuse University, New York, 1980–84. Editor, *Quarry*, Santa Cruz, 1971. Recipient: National Endowment for the Arts fellowship, for poetry, 1971, for fiction, 1979; Stanford University Stegner fellowship, 1973; Guggenheim fellowship, 1978; O. Henry award, for short story, 1983; Strauss Living award, 1983. *Died 2 August 1988.*

Western Publications

Short Stories

Put Yourself in My Shoes. Santa Barbara, California, Capra Press, 1974.
Will You Please Be Quiet, Please? New York, McGraw Hill, 1976.
Furious Seasons and Other Stories. Santa Barbara, California, Capra Press, 1977.
What We Talk about When We Talk about Love. New York, Knopf, 1981; London, Collins, 1982.
The Pheasant. Worcester, Massachusetts, Metacom Press, 1982.
Cathedral. New York, Knopf, 1983; London, Collins, 1984.

If It Please You. Northridge, California, Lord John Press, 1984.
The Stories of Raymond Carver. London, Pan, 1985.
Elephant and Other Stories. Fairfax, California, Jungle Garden Press, and London, Collins, 1988.
Where I'm Calling From: New and Selected Stories. New York, Atlantic Monthly Press, 1988.

Uncollected Short Stories

"The Aficionados" (as John Vale), "The Hair," and "Poseidon and Company," all in *Toyon* (Arcata, California), Spring 1963.
"Bright Red Apples," in *Gato* (Los Gatos, California), Spring–Summer 1967.

OTHER PUBLICATIONS

Plays

Carnations (produced Arcata, California, 1962).
Dostoevsky: A Screenplay, with Tess Gallagher; published with *Kind Dog* by Ursula K. LeGuin. Santa Barbara, California, Capra Press, 1985.

Verse

Near Klamath. Sacramento, California, Sacramento State College English Club, 1968.
Winter Insomnia. Santa Cruz, California, Kayak, 1970.
At Night the Salmon Move. Santa Barbara, California, Capra Press, 1976.
Two Poems. Salisbury, Maryland, Scarab Press, 1982.
Where Water Comes Together with Other Water. New York, Random House, 1985.
This Water. Concord, New Hampshire, Ewert, 1985.
Ultramarine. New York, Random House, 1986; with *Where Water Comes Together with Other Water,* as *In a Marine Light,* London, Collins, 1987.
Early for the Dance. Concord, New Hampshire, Ewert, 1986.
A New Path to the Waterfall. New York, Atlantic Monthly Press, and London, Collins, 1989.

Other

Fires: Essays, Poems, Stories. Santa Barbara, California, Capra Press, 1983; London, Collins, 1985.
My Father's Life: A Memoir. Derry, New Hampshire, Babcock and Koontz, 1986.
Bill Burke Portraits, photographs by Bill Burke. New York, Ecco Press, 1987.

Editor, with Tom Jenks, *American Short Story Masterpieces.* New York, Delacorte Press, 1987.

*

Critical Studies: "Voyeurism, Dissociation, and the Art of Raymond Carver" by David Boxer, in *Iowa Review* (Iowa City), Summer 1979; "Raymond Carver: A Chronicler of Blue-Collar Despair" by Bruce Weber, in *New York Times Magazine,* 24 June 1984; "Beyond Hopelessville: Another Side of Raymond Carver," in *Philological Quarterly* (Iowa City), Winter 1985, and article in *Dictionary of Literary Biography Yearbook 1984* edited by Jean W. Ross, Detroit, Gale, 1985, both by William L. Stull; *European Views of Contemporary American Literature* edited by Marc Chénetier, Carbondale, Southern Illinois University Press, 1985.

* * *

Raymond Carver used western locations in his fiction only to deny those associations and images traditionally associated with them. In fact the very idea of place as a point of reference is continually questioned in a fiction in which one part of suburban America is seen as no different from another. Perceived in popular mythology as a panacea for all the frustrations of modern living, we now find in Carver's west not a sense of possibility and seemingly boundless energy but enervation and lethargy. Seen throughout much of recent history as America's backyard Promised Land, the West successfully fulfilled its function as a pressure valve for an entire restless nation. However, in Carver's short stories this image is replaced by an entropic alternative—previous options are exhausted and the symbolic promise of a fresh start the region once held out is denied.

Previously associated with space and freedom, Carver's west is a world of confinement, with much of the action occurring inside cramped homes and trailers. Titles such as "Boxes," "The Compartment," and "Sacks" all suggest limited space, claustrophobia, entrapment. In "Careful" an alcoholic attempts to straighten out his life by locking himself away in an attic bed-sit and controlling his drink intake. The man's physical space is further restricted by the house's sloping roof, which forces him to literally reduce his own size and seems to bear down on him menacingly. The whole story is shot through with an atmosphere of suffocating enclosure, further compounded by the man's temporary deafness which serves to accentuate his hermetically sealed existence. An absence of space implies a character's severely impaired potential for self-improvement, whereas in conventional notions of the west room to move is generally equated with the possibility for personal advancement. Although the story "Sixty Acres" suggests some of this traditional promise, the land alluded to in its title is shown to be slipping through the owner's fingers. Living in a tiny wooden house, sleeping with his wife in the same room as his mother, Lee Waite is tempted to lease his land to a group of local hunters in the hope of buying a way out of his current existence. Yet, gripped by the same mixture of impotence and frustration that afflicts so many of Carver's characters, Lee is unable to take charge of his destiny—the symbolic loss of the land's spatial potential being of greater significance than the money he stands to collect.

Denied the opportunity for new beginnings, the freedom to move, formerly associated with a faith in the future, becomes instead a hollow, knee-jerk reaction to life. In both "Gazebo" and "The Bridle" a couple try to resurrect dying relationships by simply moving. Yet these examples of vain attempts at combining a desire for emotional reunion with the wistfully-held dream of financial success are ultimately doomed to failure. For all of Carver's people, what luck there is always seems to be a little further down the freeway, but when they arrive at the next town it invariably turns out to be a carbon copy of the suburban sprawl recently vacated. The title "What's in Alaska?" illustrates this point in suggesting that the characters who somewhat incredulously ask this question are aware of the desperate logical absurdity of relocation to the furthest westward reach of mainland U.S.A.

Although essentially a fiction of interiors, Carver's field of vision occasionally widens to encompass something of the physical presence of the northwestern states. Yet the psychological and cultural functions popularly attributed to the natural surroundings of this region are almost always denied, as characters remain thwarted in their attempts to mine such potential. Indeed, in most cases, it is apparent that such people, engaged as they are in the daily business of survival, do not have the time or energy to appreciate the backdrop to their struggles.

Those suburbanites who do step outside for a while are invariably "week-enders"—fishermen or hunters—disappearing into the woods for a spot of rest and relaxation. However, even this modest demand for temporary relief proves impossible, as the world they believe they left behind at the city limits effectively follows them, blocking their attempts to escape, closing down all available space. In "The Cabin" Mr. Harrold is one such "week-ender" engaged in an ultimately unsatisfying search for good fishing and spiritual refreshment in the cold, dark Oregon forests. Trying to get away, albeit briefly, from certain unspecified marital problems, the weekend is a total disaster. Last time, we are told, he caught "five nice fish." This time his peace is shattered by a pack of juvenile red-necks who maim a deer, throw rocks at him, and at one point threaten to shoot him. Positioned precariously in the middle of a fast-running river, up to his thighs in icy water, and in danger of slipping on the mossy rocks below, Mr. Harrold is utterly defenseless, and in the ensuing panic loses his fishing rod in the scramble for safety.

As "The Cabin" demonstrates, Carver seldom presents the natural environment as an antidote to contemporary living. It is neither symbolically benign nor capable of inducing some form of emotional rejuvenation. To illustrate this point "Tell the Women We're Going" and "So Much Water so Close to Home" feature the mountains and rivers of Washington state as the stage for a total of three murders and a rape. It is an anti-pastoral world where violent and aggressive human behaviour meets a landscape irreversibly contaminated by society. Indeed, in "Tell the Women We're Going" there is quite literally blood on the landscape, as two young women are bludgeoned to death with a heavy stone picked up at the foot of Picture Rock, a well-known local beauty spot.

In Carver's short fiction the conventional mythological promise of the West is turned inside out. For his characters, not to have "made it" in the very cradle of a culture popularly symbolising personal freedom and success has to hurt. In the land of big dreams and wide horizons, the sawn-off aspirations of Carver's characters contribute to the feeling of life being "a small-change thing . . . chaotic and without much light showing through" (Carver in the essay "Fires").

—Simon Philo

CASE, Robert Ormond. American. Born in Dallas, Texas, 8 October 1895. Educated at the University of Oregon, Eugene, B.A. 1920. Served in the United States Army during World War I. Married. Worked as a logger and farmer; then freelance writer.

WESTERN PUBLICATIONS

Novels

Just Buckaroos. New York, Chelsea House, 1927.
Riders of the Grande Ronde. New York, Doubleday, 1928; London, Jarrolds, 1929.
Dynamite Smith—Cowboy. New York, Chelsea House, 1930; London, Ward Lock, 1934.
The Yukon Drive. New York, Doubleday, 1930.
Whispering Valley. New York, Doubleday, 1932; London, Jarrolds, 1933.
Buckaroo Partners. London, Ward Lock, 1934.
A Pair o' Mavericks. London, Ward Lock, 1934.
Big Timber. Philadelphia, Macrae Smith, 1937; as *Timber Joe*, London, Hodder and Stoughton, 1938.
Wings North. New York, Doubleday, and London, Hodder and Stoughton, 1938.
The Golden Hills. London, Hodder and Stoughton, 1939.
Golden Portage. New York, Doubleday, 1940; London, Jarrolds, 1941.
West of Barter River. New York, Doubleday, 1941; London, Hale, 1950.
White Victory. New York, Doubleday, 1943; London, Hale, 1952.
Buccaneer of the Barrens. London, Hale, 1953.
Cold Gold. London, Hale, 1956.
Bootleg Gold. London, Hale, 1957.

Uncollected Short Stories

"Little Songhee's Big Trouble," in *Western Story* (New York), 20 January 1923.
"Lone Eagle's Squaw," in *Western Story* (New York), 16 June 1923.
"Call of the Kleet," in *Western Story* (New York), 18 August 1923.
"The Prospect Hole," in *Western Story* (New York), 25 August 1923.
"Lone Eagle Against the Field," in *Western Story* (New York), 17 November 1923.
"When Pete Used His Bean," in *Western Story* (New York), 24 November 1923.
"Headed North," in *Western Story* (New York), 19 January 1924.
"'Lonesome' McQuirk and the Amazon," in *Western Story* (New York), 1 March 1924.
"Lonesome Helps the Schoolma'am," in *Western Story* (New York), 5 April 1924.
"Too Good a Horse for a Greaser," in *Western Story* (New York), 19 April 1924.
"Lonesome Drives the Schoolma'am," in *Western Story* (New York), 31 May 1924.
"Lonesome Buys a Horse," in *Western Story* (New York), 7 June 1924.
"Only a Pup," in *Western Story* (New York), 23 August 1924.
"Rung with a Shoe," in *Western Story* (New York), 20 September 1924.
"Lonesome Lays a Ghost," in *Western Story* (New York), 18 October 1924.
"When the Tree Was Lit," in *Western Story* (New York), 20 December 1924.
"When Lightning Helped," in *Western Story* (New York), 7 February 1925.
"Sing Low, Buckaroo!," in *Western Story* (New York), 14 March 1925.
"An Outlaw for a Letter," in *Western Story* (New York), 30 May 1925.
"Lonesome Flees," in *Western Story* (New York), 6 June 1925.
"Lonesome's' Bid for Glory," in *Western Story* (New York), 20 June 1925.
"Busted on the Hip," in *Western Story* (New York), 8 August 1925.
"Dynamite—Handle with Care," in *Western Story* (New York), 12 September 1925.

"Lonesome's Bet," in *Western Story* (New York), 19 September 1925.
" 'Lonesome' Unchains a Wolf," in *Western Story* (New York), 26 September 1925.
"The Rodeo Romeo," in *Western Story* (New York), 24 October 1925.
"Living Dynamite," in *Western Story* (New York), 9 January 1926.
" 'Dynamite' Smith, Buckaroo," in *Western Story* (New York), 23 January 1926.
"The Fence Across the Canyon," in *Western Story* (New York), 13 February 1926.
"Sam and the Thirsty Cowboys," in *Western Story* (New York), 27 February 1926.
"Lonesome's Excuse," in *Western Story* (New York), 3 April 1926.
"King of the Condon Range," in *Western Story* (New York), 29 May 1926.
"Back Home in Arkansas," in *Western Story* (New York), 19 June 1926.
"Windy—Storm Center," in *Western Story* (New York), 14 August 1926.
"The Widow Smiles on Windy," in *Western Story* (New York), 28 August 1926.
"Windy and Lonesome, Driven to Cover," in *Western Story* (New York), 4 September 1926.
"Dig Down, Delong," in *Western Story* (New York), 11 September 1926.
"Timber Beasts and Buckaroos," in *Western Story* (New York), 18 September 1926.
"The Tailor-Made Wrangler," in *Western Story* (New York), 13 November 1926.
"Treasure in White Rock Canyon," in *Western Story* (New York), 4 December 1926.
"Dynamite and the Roaring Kid," in *Western Story* (New York), 18 December 1926.
"Windy Wanders into Wildcat," in *Western Story* (New York), 29 January 1927.
"Windied Bandits," in *Western Story* (New York), 5 March 1927.
"Windy's Hybrid Ace," in *Western Story* (New York), 19 March 1927.
"Nevada Checks Up," in *Western Story* (New York), 16 April 1927.
"The Four-Gun Man," in *Western Story* (New York), 2 July 1927.
"The Golden Husky," in *Western Story* (New York), 13 August 1927.
"Windy Minds the Kids," in *Western Story* (New York), 24 September 1927.
"Dynamite and the Noble Buckaroos," in *Western Story* (New York), 15 October 1927.
"Why Jeb Hung the Jury," in *Western Story* (New York), 14 January 1928.
"When Weapons Failed," in *Western Story* (New York), 24 March 1928.
"Windy's Overgrown Pet," in *Western Story* (New York), 31 March 1928.
"North of Jump-Off," in *Western Story* (New York), 14 April 1928.
"Last River," in *Western Story* (New York), 21 July 1928.
"The Panhandle Wrangler," in *Western Story* (New York), 28 July 1928.
"Windy's Quest for Quiet," in *Western Story* (New York), 8 September 1928.
"Too Rough for His Nibs," in *Western Story* (New York), 15 September 1928.
"The Maverick Gal," in *Western Story* (New York), 6 October 1928.
"Tramp, Tramp!," in *Western Story* (New York), 27 October 1928.
"Buckaroos and Beef," in *Western Story* (New York), 24 November 1928.
"Dynamite Goes Up," in *Western Story* (New York), 22 December 1928.
"Ridin' Luck," in *Western Story* (New York), 26 January 1929.
"Windy's Fowl Play," in *Western Story* (New York), 2 February 1929.
"Tamed by Dynamite," in *Western Story* (New York), 16 February 1929.
"T Bone's Treasure," in *Western Story* (New York), 6 April 1929.
"Partners in the Smiling Hills," in *Western Story* (New York), 11 May–1 June 1929.
"Windy Rides 'em Rough," in *Western Story* (New York), 19 October 1929.
"That Blasting Maverick," in *Western Story* (New York), 4 January 1930.
"King Cole of Hot Rocks," in *Western Story* (New York), 15 February 1930.
"Boomer," in *Western Story* (New York), 22 March 1930.
"Nailed Up," in *Western Story* (New York), 5 April 1930.
"Windy's Wild Cats," in *Western Story* (New York), 17 May 1930.
"Tough as Rawhide," in *Western Story* (New York), 31 May 1930.
"Mushing Out," in *Western Story* (New York), 20 September 1930.
"To the Last Chip," in *Western Story* (New York), 11 October 1930.
"Dynamite's Gentle Ways," in *Western Story* (New York), 1 November 1930.
"Partner's Greed," in *Western Story* (New York), 13 December 1930.
"Partner's Play," in *Western Story* (New York), 20 December 1930.
"Windy Fights Alone," in *Western Story* (New York), 3 January 1931.
"Square Outlaw," in *Western Story* (New York), 14 February 1931.
"One Shell," in *Western Story* (New York), 28 March 1931.
"A Tangled Buckaroo," in *Western Story* (New York), 18 April 1931.
"Sheriff's Choice," in *Western Story* (New York), 9 May 1931.
"The Good Trader," in *Western Story* (New York), 20 June 1931.
"Cassidy's Bluff," in *Argosy* (New York), 9 January 1932.
"Unwanted Men," in *Argosy* (New York), 16 April 1932.
"Blind Canyon," in *Argosy* (New York), 14 May-21 May 1932.
"Exit Star Cross," in *Western Story* (New York), 11 June 1932.
"Knight of the Mesas," in *Western Story* (New York), 2 July–16 July 1932.
"Suicide Trail," in *Western Story* (New York), 30 July 1932.
"Life Watch," in *Collier's* (Springfield, Ohio), 10 September 1932.
"Six-Gun Accounting," in *Argosy* (New York), 24 September 1932.
"Wilson's Dog," in *All Star* (Kingswood, Surrey), November 1932.
"The Silver Concha," in *Western Story* (New York), 26 November 1932.
"Wolf-Hearted Sheep," in *Western Story* (New York), 21 January 1933.
"Maverick Luck," in *Western Story* (New York), 11 February 1933.

"Just Plain Work," in *Western Story* (New York), 25 February 1933.
"And One Loved Dogs," in *Collier's* (Springfield, Ohio), 11 March 1933.
"The Girl from Outside," in *Western Story* (New York), 18 March 1933.
"Outlawed Money," in *Western Story* (New York), 25 March 1933.
"Trail of the Broken Tent," in *Western Story* (New York), 8 July 1933.
"Frozen Fangs," in *Western Story* (New York), 2 September 1933.
"The Snow Burner," in *Western Story* (New York), 7 October 1933.
"Her Hard-Rock Man," in *Western Story* (New York), 14 October 1933.
"Twenty Pokes of Gold," in *Western Story* (New York), 25 November 1933.
"A Ticket Outside," in *Western Story* (New York), 2 December 1933.
"Five-Minute Outlaw," in *Western Story* (New York), 16 December 1933.
"Iron Woman," in *Collier's* (Springfield, Ohio), 24 February 1934.
"Savage Waters," in *Western Story* (New York), 31 March 1934.
"A Four-Eyed Maverick," in *Western Story* (New York), 14 April 1934.
"The Last Trail North," in *Western Story* (New York), 21 April 1934.
"Mortgaged Dogs," in *Western Story* (New York), 5 May 1934.
"The Return of the Wolf," in *Western Story* (New York), 9 June 1934.
"Child of the Wild," in *Western Story* (New York), 4 August 1934.
"Backward Trail," in *Western Story* (New York), 11 August 1934.
"The Last Desert," in *Western Story* (New York), 22 September 1934.
"No-Account Dog," in *Western Story* (New York), 6 October 1934.
"Windy Draws a Hand," in *Western Story* (New York), 24 November 1934.
"Unwilling Outlaw," in *Western Story* (New York), 22 December 1934.
"The Mad Canary," in *Western Story* (New York), 5 January 1935.
"Gambler's Creed," in *Western Story* (New York), 9 February 1935.
"No-Account Dog" (different from above story), in *Western Story* (New York), 23 March 1935.
"Fought and Paid For," in *Western Story* (New York), 27 April–11 May 1935.
"The Waiting Rope," in *Western Story* (New York), 1 June 1935.
"Gambler's Debt," in *Western Story* (New York), 22 June 1935.
"A Flurry in Fuzztails," in *Western Story* (New York), 27 July 1935.
"Outlaw Empire," in *Western Story* (New York), 14 September 1935.
"Lost and Found," in *Collier's* (Springfield, Ohio), 21 September 1935.
"The Hold-Up of Windy," in *Western Story* (New York), 9 November 1935.
"A Bear for Sleep," in *Western Story* (New York), 1 August 1936.
"Gold Blind," in *Western Story* (New York), 26 September 1936.
"Burned Matches," in *American Magazine* (Springfield, Ohio), December 1936.
"Windy Delong—Diplomat," in *Western Story* (New York), 2 January 1937.
"Expert Witness," in *Collier's* (Springfield, Ohio), 13 February 1937.
"Whale of a Bargain," in *American Magazine* (Springfield, Ohio), November 1937.
"Fortitude," in *Collier's* (Springfield, Ohio), 12 November 1938.
"Make Hay in the Moonlight," in *Argosy* (New York), 29 April 1939.
"Not for Millions," in *Saturday Evening Post* (Philadelphia), 28 December 1946.
"Christmas at Whitman's Mission," in *Ladies Home Journal* (Philadelphia), 28 December 1948.
"Golden Trap," in *Saturday Evening Post* (Philadelphia), 3 April–1 May 1954.
"Golden Shadow," in *Saturday Evening Post* (Philadelphia), 2 March–23 March 1957.
"Trouble at Midas Creek," in *Saturday Evening Post* (Philadelphia), 5 October–16 November 1957.
"Secret of Glacier River," in *Saturday Evening Post* (Philadelphia), 10 January–14 February 1959.
"Hard Money," in *This Land Around Us*, edited by Ellis Lucia. New York, Doubleday, 1969.

OTHER PUBLICATIONS

Play

Screenplay: *The Girl from Alaska*, with Edward T. Lowe, 1942.

Other

River of the West: A Story of Opportunity in the Columbia Empire. Portland, Oregon, Northwestern Electricity Company-Pacific Power and Light Company, 1940.
Last Mountains: The Story of the Cascades. New York, Doubleday, 1945.
The Empire Builders. New York, Doubleday, 1947; London, Aldus, 1948; revised edition, Portland, Oregon, Binfords and Mort, 1949.
We Called It Culture: The Story of Chautaugua, with Victoria Case. New York, Doubleday, 1948.

* * *

As one of the leading authors of the Pacific Northwest during the first half of this century, Robert Ormond Case exhibited through his style, impact, and ability an effective way to combine the refreshing and generally little-worked heritage of his homeland with fictional characters of various designs. Case was a friend and contemporary of Ernest Haycox, as were many other Oregon authors of that generation, and Haycox through his continuing successes inspired them all, a group which began at the University of Oregon under Professor W.F.G. Thacher who had a special knack for developing fine professional fiction writers. Case was one of them; and while Thacher's former students inspired each other, they didn't imitate. Each developed his own bent, his own set of interests.

Case worked both sides of the street, so to speak, for he also wrote many non-fiction articles and books, sometimes teaming with his sister, Victoria, who also wrote both fiction and nonfiction, dealing largely with the frontier pioneers. With his strong interest in the immediate past, Case was always reaching out for new territory. He was among the early novelists to use Alaska and northwestern Canada as settings for his books (compare Jack London), and he was forever aware of his rugged individualism that would provoke exciting and rousing stories in unusual surroundings which would hold his readers spellbound. Alaska was a far-off land then, and thus Case found a growing audience. He didn't write formula stories, although like most successful authors of those years, he adhered to wordage and treatment desired by *The Saturday Evening Post*, *Collier's*, and other "slick" magazines. The aim of his stories, like them all, was to entertain, not to project a message or a social stand.

Case was a hard researcher who could transform accurate material, which often tends to be dull, into real people and real life situations that were readily believable. Seldom if ever could Case be caught in error, and this fact alone made him very acceptable in his home territory as well as throughout the world. He wrote of logging, timber, the frozen north and the Old West, made a full-time living at it in a work that satisfied him greatly, and along the way contributed significantly to the literature of the region.

—Ellis Lucia

CASSADY, Claude. *See* **PAINE, Lauran.**

CATHER, Willa (Sibert). American. Born in Wilella, Back Creek Valley, near Winchester, Virginia, 7 December 1873; moved with her family to a farm near Red Cloud, Nebraska, 1883. Educated at Red Cloud High School, graduated 1890; Latin School, Lincoln, Nebraska, 1890–91; University of Nebraska, Lincoln, 1891–95, B.A. 1895. Columnist, *State Journal*, Lincoln, 1893–95; member of the editorial staff, *Home Monthly*, Pittsburgh, 1896–97; telegraph editor and drama critic, Pittsburgh *Daily Leader*, 1897–1901; Latin and English teacher, Central High School, Pittsburgh, 1901–03; English teacher, Allegheny High School, Pittsburgh, 1903–06; staff writer, later managing editor, *McClure's Magazine*, New York, 1906–12; full-time writer from 1912. Recipient: Pulitzer prize, 1923; Howells Medal, 1930; Prix Fémina Américaine, 1932; National Institute of Arts and Letters Gold Medal, 1944. Litt.D.: University of Nebraska, 1917; University of Michigan, Ann Arbor, 1922; Columbia University, New York, 1928; Yale University, New Haven, Connecticut, 1929; Princeton University, New Jersey, 1931; D.L.: Creighton University, Omaha, Nebraska, 1928; University of California, Berkeley, 1931. Member, American Academy of Arts and Letters. *Died 24 April 1947.*

WESTERN PUBLICATIONS

Novels

O Pioneers! Boston, Houghton Mifflin, and London, Heinemann, 1913.
The Song of the Lark. Boston, Houghton Mifflin, 1915; London, Murray, 1916.
My Ántonia. Boston, Houghton Mifflin, 1918; London, Heinemann, 1919.
One of Ours. New York, Knopf, 1922; London, Heinemann, 1923.
A Lost Lady. New York, Knopf, 1923; London, Heinemann, 1924.
The Professor's House. New York, Knopf, and London, Heinemann, 1925.
Death Comes for the Archbishop. New York, Knopf, and London, Heinemann, 1927.

Short Stories

The Troll Garden. New York, McClure Phillips, 1905; variorum edition, edited by James Woodress, Lincoln, University of Nebraska Press, 1983.
Youth and the Bright Medusa. New York, Knopf, 1920; London, Heinemann, 1921.
The Fear That Walks by Noonday. New York, Phoenix Book Shop, 1931.
Obscure Destinies. New York, Knopf, and London, Cassell, 1932.
The Old Beauty and Others. New York, Knopf, 1948; London, Cassell, 1956.
Early Stories of Willa Cather, edited by Mildred R. Bennett. New York, Dodd Mead, 1957.
Collected Short Fiction 1892–1912, edited by Virginia Faulkner. Lincoln, University of Nebraska Press, 1965.
Uncle Valentine and Other Stories: Willa Cather's Uncollected Short Fiction 1915–1929, edited by Bernice Slote. Lincoln, University of Nebraska Press, 1973.
The Short Stories of Willa Cather, edited by Hermione Lee. London, Virago Press, 1989.

OTHER PUBLICATIONS

Novels

Alexander's Bridge. Boston, Houghton Mifflin, and London, Constable, 1912.
My Mortal Enemy. New York, Knopf, 1926; London, Heinemann, 1928.
Shadows on the Rock. New York, Knopf, 1931; London, Cassell, 1932.
Lucy Gayheart. New York, Knopf, and London, Cassell, 1935.
Sapphira and the Slave Girl. New York, Knopf, 1940; London, Cassell, 1941.

Verse

April Twilights. Boston, Badger, 1903.
April Twilights and Other Poems. New York, Knopf, 1923; London, Heinemann, 1924; revised edition, Knopf, 1933; edited by Bernice Slote, Lincoln, University of Nebraska Press, 1962, revised edition, 1968.

Other

My Autobiography, by S.S. McClure. New York, Stokes, 1914 (ghost-written by Cather).
Not Under Forty. New York, Knopf, and London, Cassell, 1936.
On Writing: Critical Studies on Writing as an Art. New York, Knopf, 1949.

Writings from Willa Cather's Campus Years, edited by James R. Shively. Lincoln, University of Nebraska Press, 1950.
Willa Cather in Europe: Her Own Story of the First Journey, edited by George N. Kates. New York, Knopf, 1956.
The Kingdom of Art: Willa Cather's First Principles and Critical Statements 1893–1896, edited by Bernice Slote. Lincoln, University of Nebraska Press, 1967.
The World and the Parish: Willa Cather's Articles and Reviews 1893–1902, edited by William M. Curtin. Lincoln, University of Nebraska Press, 2 vols., 1970.
Willa Cather in Person: Interviews, Speeches, and Letters, edited by L. Brent Bohlke. Lincoln, University of Nebraska Press, 1987.

Editor, *The Life of Mary Baker G. Eddy, and the History of Christian Science*, by Georgine Milmine. New York, Doubleday, 1909.
Editor, *The Best Stories of Sarah Orne Jewett*. Boston, Houghton Mifflin, 2 vols., 1925.

*

Bibliography: *Willa Cather: A Bibliography* by Joan Crane, Lincoln, University of Nebraska Press, 1982.

Critical Studies: *Willa Cather: A Critical Introduction* by David Daiches, Ithaca, New York, Cornell University Press, and London, Oxford University Press, 1951; *Willa Cather: A Critical Biography* by E.K. Brown, completed by Leon Edel, New York, Knopf, and London, McClelland, 1953; *The Landscape and the Looking Glass: Willa Cather's Search for Value* by John H. Randall III, Boston, Houghton Mifflin, 1960; *The World of Willa Cather* by Mildred R. Bennett, Lincoln, University of Nebraska Press, 1961; *Willa Cather's Gift of Sympathy* by Edward A. and Lillian D. Bloom, Carbondale, Southern Illinois University Press, 1962; *Willa Cather* by Dorothy Van Ghent, Minneapolis, University of Minnesota Press, 1964; *Willa Cather and Her Critics* by James Schroeter, Ithaca, New York, Cornell University Press, 1967; *Willa Cather: Her Life and Art* by James Woodress, Lincoln, University of Nebraska Press, 1970; *Willa Cather* by Dorothy Tuck McFarland, New York, Ungar, 1972; *Willa Cather: A Pictorial Memoir* by Bernice Slote, Lincoln, University of Nebraska Press, 1973, and *The Art of Willa Cather* by Slote and Virginia Faulkner, Lincoln, University of Nebraska Press, 1974; *Five Essays on Willa Cather* edited by John J. Murphy, Athens, Ohio University Press, 1974; *Willa Cather's Imagination* by David Stouck, Lincoln, University of Nebraska Press, 1975; *Willa Cather* by Philip L. Gerber, Boston, Twayne, 1975; *Chrysalis: Willa Cather in Pittsburgh, 1896–1906* by Kathleen D. Byrne and Richard C. Snyder, Pittsburgh, Historical Society of Western Pennsylvania, 1980; *Willa: The Life of Willa Cather* by Phyllis C. Robinson, New York, Doubleday, 1983; *Willa Cather's Short Fiction* by Marilyn Arnold, Merrimack College, North Andover, Massachusetts, 1984; *Critical Essays on Willa Cather* edited by John J. Murphy, Athens, Ohio University Press, 1984; *A Certain Slant of Light: Aesthetics of First Person Narration in Gide and Cather* by Jeannée P. Sacken, New York and London, Garland, 1985; *The Voyage Perilous: Willa Cather's Romanticism* by Susan J. Rosowski, Lincoln, University of Nebraska Press, 1986; *Willa Cather: The Emerging Voice* by Sharon O'Brien, New York, Oxford University Press, 1986, London, Oxford University Press, 1987; *Willa Cather: A Literary Life* by James Woodress, Lincoln, University of Nebraska Press, 1987; *Willa Cather in France: In Search of the Lost Language* by Robert J. Nelson, Urbana, University of Illinois Press, 1988; *Willa Cather: Writing at the Frontier* by Jamie Ambrose, Oxford, Berg, 1988; *Willa Cather: A Life Saved Up* by Hermione Lee, London, Virago Press, 1989; *Cather Studies, I* edited by Susan J. Rosowski, Lincoln, University of Nebraska Press, 1990.

* * *

Willa Cather's early life prepared her well to demonstrate that the West provides materials for the most far-reaching themes and the finest art. When she was nine, Cather moved with her family from Virginia to Nebraska, an experience she compared to being "thrown out into a country as bare as a piece of sheet iron." After living for almost 18 months on a ranch in Webster county, the Charles Cathers moved into Red Cloud, the town upon which she would draw throughout her career. After graduating from high school, Cather began the series of moves that enabled her to know the world—knowledge that was necessary, Sarah Orne Jewett later told her, before one could write of the parish. She moved in 1890 to Lincoln, in 1896 to Pittsburgh, and in 1906 to New York. Having moved west as a child, she was well-suited to write of immigrant dislocation; having "had it out" with an alien country, she understood how we may humanize the world with what she called "the gift of sight." And because she was a woman who made her way in roles conventionally reserved for men, she was well suited to explore and challenge gender conventions in literature.

"My first novels [there were two]" Cather was to explain. The earlier, *Alexander's Bridge*, written in a Jamesian mode that she subsequently rejected, tells of the bridge-builder Bartley Alexander's increasingly frenzied quest to reclaim his younger self, lost in the press of getting on in the world. Though set in Boston and London, the novel moves toward Alexander's memory of "a campfire on a sandbar in a Western river" and announces themes Cather was to develop: claiming an original self by the workings of memory, and identifying that original self with the West. With *O Pioneers!*, the first novel in her own voice, Cather gave her artistic allegiance to the West. The country insisted on being the hero of her story and she did not interfere, she wrote to her friend Elizabeth Sergeant. To tell of the country's youth, Cather intertwined two human stories of youthful passion: one of love for the land leading to the success of the immigrant Alexander Bergson as a farmer, the other of romantic love leading to the deaths of the lovers Marie Shabata and Emil Bergson. Here Cather laid out themes she would explore throughout her life: imagination, the ability "to enjoy the idea of things more than the things themselves" is the essential quality of the pioneer; passion is productive in the large endeavors of nature and art, not in romantic love; friendship best undergirds human relationships; with progress come dark questions about power, class, gender, and race.

In *The Song of the Lark*, Cather drew upon her own and the singer Olive Fremstad's lives to tell a woman's story of artistic growth and female development. Thea Kronborg grows up in the small western town of Moonstone, then moves to Chicago, where she studies music, and to Panther Canyon in the Southwest, where she rests in abandoned cliff dwellings; the novel ends with her triumphant performance as Sieglinde. Particularly important are Cather's depictions of an artist's relations to her western community and to the land: Moonstone (so closely based upon Red Cloud that a map drawn from one provides a guide to the other) provides to Thea the education of childhood friends from richly diverse backgrounds, and the land (especially Panther Canyon, called by Ellen Moers "the most thoroughly elaborated female landscape in literature") teaches primitive truths.

By structuring her most famous novel, *My Ántonia*, as a return in memory to possess a personal past, Cather recreated the working of her own artistic imagination. She gave to her middle-aged narrator, Jim Burden, many of her experiences upon arriving in Nebraska, where there "seemed to be nothing to see . . . nothing but land: not a country at all, but the material out of which countries are made." Jim's memories of growing up in a new country center on Ántonia Shimerda, an immigrant family's daughter whom he loves in childhood, then bitterly rejects when he thinks her common, and after 20 years returns to, recognizing that "she lent herself to immemorial human attitudes which we recognize by instinct as universal and true." Again Cather challenges gender conventions, in Jim creating a narrator who imposes standard expectations upon his subject, and in Ántonia creating a woman who defies those conventions.

Drawing upon memories of her cousin killed in action in France before the United States entered World War I, in *One of Ours* Cather told of a young man's attempt to escape from the oppressive provincialism of the Midwest. Writing of Claude Wheeler's search for "something splendid" as an illusory ideal in education, love, and battle, Cather creates an American version of the Arthurian myth, the westering ideal frustrated by modern reality. *One of Ours* was awarded the Pulitzer Prize in 1923.

A Lost Lady is the finest example of Cather's theory of the novel démeublé (by which art is simplified, the stage stripped bare). By the story of Marian Forrester, the young wife of Captain Daniel Forrester who moves with him to the western town of Sweet Water (i.e., Red Cloud), Cather tells of the decline of the great-hearted dreamers "who could conquer but could not hold" and the rise of the "shrewd young man" who would "destroy and cut up [the vast territory] into profitable bits." Cather links Mrs. Forrester to the land, so that upon the death of Captain Forrester both are "at the mercy" of men like Ivy Peters, a snake-like lawyer. Again Cather uses a male narrator to impose conventions society expects of women: Niel Herbert holds it against Mrs. Forrester "that she was not willing to immolate herself, like the widow of all those great men, and die with the pioneer period to which she belonged," and when she insists upon living, he leaves her in "weary contempt." In a coda Cather returns to the idea of the illusory westering dream: years later Niel hears again of "his long lost lady," who had moved further west—to California and then, after remarrying, to her husband's ranch in South America. Finally accepting that he cannot "get the truth out of her," Niel is able to be "very glad that he had known her, and that she had had a hand in breaking him in to life."

Cather continued to explore the depersonalizing consequences of progress in her next two novels. In *The Professor's House* she used a series of western settings to trace Godfrey St. Peter's quest for his original self, lost beneath the public roles he had assumed. St. Peter retreats from his family and professional duties to an attic study, from which Lake Michigan, glimpsed through the window, is a reminder of that which he has lost. To search for his original self, he recalls his former student's discovery of an ancient people who were inhabitants of long-abandoned cliff dwellings in the Southwest; and finally he turns inward, to recover from deep within his memory the boy he "had long ago left behind him in Kansas." California provides the setting for the final scenes of *My Mortal Enemy*, a short novel in which Cather traces the aftermath of romantic love, beginning her story after the young lovers have eloped and then tracing their decline. Significantly, the land figures least in this most grim of Cather's novels.

Re-establishing ties with the primitive truths that she believed lie beneath human experience, Cather returned to the Southwest in *Death Comes for the Archbishop*, her story of two priests, Fathers Latour and Vaillant, sent by Rome to win the area for Catholicism. A narrative without accent in the manner of legend, *Death Comes for the Archbishop* employs a picaresque structure that enables a medley of characters to tell their stories and, by doing so, to demonstrate that miracles rest "not so much upon faces or voices of healing power coming suddenly near to us from afar off, but upon our perceptions being made finer, so that for a moment our eyes can see and our ears can hear what is there about us always."

Though set in Quebec, *Shadows on the Rock* figures in Cather's frontier fiction as the most radically isolated of her landscapes, a colony built on a rock and suspended between annihilating ocean and impenetrable forest. In telling of Cecile Auclair's life the year that she turns 13, Cather explores the role of ritual in bonding together a community otherwise lost in a wilderness. Continuing to write of the importance of ritual in the three stories of *Obscure Destinies*, Cather returned to a Nebraska setting again to outline the tenets fundamental to her writing. In "Neighbour Rosicky," a patriarch, by telling stories to his children, insures that the family will continue after his death; in "Old Mrs. Harris" three generations living within a two-crowded household feel the disruption of change; and in "Two Friends" a narrator recalls the accidental rupture in a friendship as the loss of one of the unalterable realities that "we yet like to think" are there, "somewhere at the bottom of things."

Dark warnings dominate Cather's powerful and important, though critically neglected, late novels. As if retelling *The Song of the Lark*, Cather in *Lucy Gayheart* gave to a talented girl roots in the West (Haverford is yet another version of Red Cloud), then traced her attempts to realize her dream of embracing life; this time, however, she creates characters that lack any "center," and Lucy's story ends inevitably in tragedy. Though the gothic runs through all her writing, only in her last novel did Cather focus directly upon evil, the dark undercurrent beneath civilized facades; significantly, only here does she exclude all reference to the West. For *Sapphira and the Slave Girl*, Cather returned to the Virginia of her earliest memories and told of the aging Sapphira Dodderidge's plot to bring about the rape of her slave girl, Nancy Till. Set immediately before the Civil War, Cather's last novel tells of the corruption possible when one order is dead, another yet to be born. As such, it provides a fitting coda to an oeuvre in which Cather wrote of the new order that the West gave birth to.

—Susan J. Rosowski

CHADWICK, Joseph (L.). Also wrote as Jack Barton; John Callahan; Jim Conroy; John Conway; John Creighton; Jo Anne Creighton; Joselyn Chadwick. American. Born in York, Pennsylvania. Worked in a factory in Pennsylvania; later moved to Tucson, Arizona, where he lived for several years before returning to York. Began writing in 1935, first for magazines and later for novels. Said to have had more than 600 Westerns published. *Died.*

WESTERN PUBLICATIONS

Novels

Texas Fury (as Jack Callahan). New York, Avalon, 1950; Kingswood, Surrey, World's Work, 1952.

Gunsmoke Reckoning. New York, Gold Medal, 1951; London, Foulsham, 1954.

Double Cross. New York, Fawcett, 1952; London, Foulsham, 1954.
Destination Revenge (as Jim Conroy). New York, Doubleday, 1953; London, Barker, 1955.
Rebel Raider. New York, Fawcett, 1954; London, Foulsham, 1955.
Rider from Nowhere. London, Foulsham, 1954.
Devil's Legacy. London, Foulsham, 1954.
Whip Hand. London, Foulsham, 1954.
Come Out Shooting. London, Foulsham, 1955.
Renegade Gun. London, Foulsham, 1955.
The Golden Frame. New York, Fawcett, 1955.
A Town to Tame. New York and London, Fawcett, 1959.
Savage Breed. London, Muller, 1960.
No Land Is Free. New York, Doubleday, 1961; London, Jenkins, 1962.
He Came from Texas. London, Jenkins, 1961.
Edge of the Badlands. London, Jenkins, 1962.
A Gun for a Legacy. London, Jenkins, 1964.
Black Velvet. New York, Coronet, and London, New English Library, 1970.
Sabrina. New York, Paperback Library, 1970; London, New English Library, 1971.
Killer Trail. New York and London, Gold Lion, 1973.
A Bargain in Bullets. New York and London, Gold Lion, 1974.

Novels as Jack Barton

Brand of Fury. New York, Popular Library, 1955.
The Vengeance Rider. New York, Popular Library, 1956.
Texas Rawhider. London, Viking, 1956.

OTHER PUBLICATIONS

Novel

The Golden Frame. New York, Gold Medal, 1955.

Novels as Joselyn Chadwick

The Web of Evil. New York, Avon, 1972.
Evil Is the Night. New York, Avon, 1974.

Novels as John Conway

Hell Is My Destination. New York, Monarch, 1959.
Madigan's Women. New York, Monarch, 1959.
Requiem for a Chaser. New York, Monarch, 1960.
This Dark Desire. New York, Monarch, 1960.
Sin in Time. New York, Monarch, 1961.
Love in Suburbia. New York, Monarch, 1961.

Novels as Jo Anne Creighton

The Mask of Evil. New York, Curtis, 1973.
House of Fury. New York, Curtis, 1973.
Inn of Evil. New York, Popular Library, 1974.
The Dark Side of Paradise. New York, Popular Library, 1976.
The Harlan Legacy. New York, Popular Library, 1977.

Novels as John Creighton

Destroying Angel. New York, Ace, 1956.
Not So Evil as Eve. New York, Ace, 1957.
Trial by Perjury. New York, Ace, 1958.
The Wayward Blonde. New York, Ace, 1958.
Stranglehold. New York, Ace, 1959.
Evil Is the Night. New York, Ace, 1959.
A Half Interest in Murder. New York, Ace, 1960.
The Blonde Cried Murder. New York, Ace, 1961.

Other

The Apache Wars: The Exciting True Saga of the Bloody Conflict Between the White Men and the Apache Indians on the Southwest Frontier (as John Conway). Derby, Connecticut, Monarch, 1961.
The Sioux Indian Wars (as John Conway). Derby, Connecticut, Monarch, 1961.
The Texas Rangers: A Concise History of the Most Colorful Law Enforcement Group in the Frontier West (as John Conway; for children). Derby, Connecticut, Monarch, 1963.
Cowboys and Cattle Drives. New York, Hawthorn, 1967.

* * *

In 1951 the eminent editor and critic, Burton Rascoe, wrote of the first Joseph Chadwick western novel to appear under his own name: "Now that I have finished reading *Gunsmoke Reckoning* I should say that the two best living writers of Westerns are Luke Short and Joseph Chadwick. Yippee for a real Western writer and for his rousing story."

Heady praise, indeed, but unfortunately it says more negative things about Rascoe's critical acumen where Westerns are concerned than positive things about the quality of Chadwick's fiction. *Gunsmoke Reckoning*, like most of Chadwick's work, is a competent and slightly above average traditional Western—nothing more. And while Chadwick was a worthwhile entertainer, even a "real Western writer" when he was at the top of his form, none of his books measures up to Luke Short's, or to those by a number of his and Short's contemporaries.

Chadwick, of course, is not to be blamed for Rascoe's hyperbolic claims; he had no pretensions, in 1951 or at any point in his long career, to be other than a worthwhile entertainer. The fact that he was a successful one is evidenced by his popularity throughout the 1950's and into the 1960's, with aggregate sales of his Westerns reaching several million copies.

Chadwick began writing in 1935, to escape from a 35¢/hour factory job in Pennsylvania, and was soon selling regularly to newspaper syndicates and pulp magazines. His first sales were of romance, detective, and adventure serials; later he switched to Westerns and published more than 600 short stories, novelettes, and novellas. The demise of the pulp markets turned his attention to novels, in particular to the lucrative paperback markets, a medium in which he proved to be equally prolific. From 1950 until the mid-1970's he published scores of paperback originals and a handful of hard-cover novels: Westerns under his own name and as by Jack Barton, John Callahan, Jim Conroy, and John Conway; and mysteries, suspense fiction, "contemporary novels" (i.e., sex-based fiction), Gothics, and books of popular western history (*The Apache Wars, The Sioux Indian Wars, The Texas Rangers*), under a variety of pseudonyms.

Most of Chadwick's Westerns are set in the Southwest—primarily in Arizona, where he lived for a number of years, and Texas. His first-hand knowledge of his settings, and his ability to recreate those settings on paper, are two of the strong points of his work. Other qualities include good characterization, rapid-fire pacing, and an easy-flowing narrative style.

Range wars and other cattle-country intrigues were Chadwick's favorite plot frame. But he was at his best when he used other themes, such as the man out to avenge a wrong done to him or to some member of his family. *Gunsmoke Reckoning*, *Rebel Raider*, and *Killer Trail*, the last two among his most accomplished tales, all deal with a man seeking violent justice for an attack on his sister. *Rebel Raider* is told in the first-person, an uncommon device in Westerns of the 1950's and one which deepens the reader's involvement in narrator Matt Duane's quest; another enhancement is the author's depiction of war-torn Mexico in the years after the Civil War, where much of the action takes place. *Killer Trail*, which may be Chadwick's best novel, is praiseworthy for its villain, a well-developed and non-stereotypical black buffalo hunter; for the intelligent handling of the white-versus-black confrontations; and for an ending that is not at all what the reader might expect.

Other standouts among Chadwick's Westerns are *No Land Is Free*, about an ambitious, land-hungry rancher in the desolate Staked Plains region of Texas; *Renegade Gun*, the story of an ex-Union Cavalry major pitted against renegade soldiers and carpetbaggers in post-Civil War Texas; and *Destination Revenge*, as by Jim Conroy, another tale of vengeance that makes good use of such elements as blackmail, thievery, and the tests of friendship.

—Bill Pronzini

CHAFFIN, James B. *See* **LUTZ, Giles A.**

CHALLIS, George. *See* **BRAND, Max.**

CHAMPLIN, Tim. Pseudonym for John Michael Champlin. American. Born in Fargo, North Dakota, 11 October 1937. Educated at Middle Tennessee State University, Murfreesboro, B.A. in English 1960; Peabody College, Nashville, Tennessee, M.A. 1964. Served in the United States Naval Reserve as radar operator, 1955–63. Married Mary Ellen Hosey in 1967; two sons and one daughter. Youth director, Catholic Youth Organization, Nashville, 1965–67; recreation resource specialist, Bureau of Outdoor Recreation, United States Department of the Interior, Ann Arbor, Michigan, 1967–68; youth director, Stewart Air Force Base, Smyrna, Tennessee, 1968–70. Worker, 1970–77, and since 1977 supervisor of Veterans' Benefits Counsellors, United States Department of Veterans' Affairs, Nashville. Address: 2926 Leatherwood, Nashville, Tennessee 37214, U.S.A.

WESTERN PUBLICATIONS

Novels

Summer of the Sioux. New York, Ballantine, 1982.
Dakota Gold. New York, Ballantine, 1982.
Staghorn. New York, Ballantine, 1984.
Shadow Catcher. New York, Ballantine, 1985.
Great Timber Race. New York, Ballantine, 1986.
Iron Trail. New York, Ballantine, 1987.
Colt Lightning. New York, Ballantine, 1989.
King of the Highbinders. New York, Ballantine, 1989.
Flying Eagle. New York, Evans, 1990.

*

Tim Champlin comments:

Ever since I first learned to read, I have loved exciting adventure stories with plenty of graphic, authentic detail. Now I am writing the types of stories that I always enjoyed reading myself.

Since I was born and reared in the Midwest and Far West, I learned a great deal of the history and geography of the country. This, combined with a desire to write, led me to western historical fiction. I try to concentrate on some of the lesser-known aspects of the westward movement—for example, the lumber schooners that sailed the West Coast, the early-day wet-plate photographers, the young European princes who sought excitement in the American West, the daredevils thrilling crowds with gas balloons and early parachutes, the Tong Wars in San Francisco's Chinatown, the competition to build narrow-gauge railroads into the Rockies, the Basque sheepherders, and The Penitentes of the Southwest.

*   *   *

John Michael Champlin, who writes as Tim Champlin, sees the West "as a huge, everchanging block of space and time in which an individual had more freedom than the average person has today . . . For those brave, and sometimes desperate, souls who ventured west looking for a better life, it must have been an exciting time to be alive. If I can capture even a little of this on paper for current readers I will be satisfied." Champlin's readers are more than satisfied with his intricate, complex, historically accurate narratives.

In *Iron Trail*, one of Champlin's best books, Matt Tierney—Champlin's narrator—describes the boom times in the Colorado Rockies. General Palmer, with his Denver and Rio Grande line, is fighting against the Sante Fe Railroad for control of the Royal Gorge. This plot would seem to be enough for most western writers, but in typical Champlin fashion, Tierney also narrates the story of the Los Hermanos Penitentes—an outlawed sect who celebrate self-flagellation in their religious practices. This totally unconventional sub-plot gives the book a richness rarely found in western novels.

Great Timber Race features the same quirkiness. Tierney describes the battle between the lumber barons and the growing flow of settlers for control of the land. Again, the plot and the historical accuracy is fascinating. But on top of this, Champlin develops an incredible sub-plot: the men who control the timber organize a schooner race with fabulous prizes for the winner. The result is originality rarely found in a genre burdened by too many formula novels.

Flashes of this originality are evident in Champlin's first novel, *Summer of the Sioux*. Champlin introduces Matt Tierney as a youth who works as a reporter for the Chicago *Times-Herald*. Tierney's first big assignment is to accompany General Daniel Buck's expeditionary force to Big Horn and Yellowstone. Along with the story of confrontations with the Indians, Champlin presents the evolution of Matt Tierney from a boy to a man in striking detail and narrative richness.

Dakota Gold and *Staghorn* present the changing of the frontier as the Indians are neutralized and the waves of settlers push unrelentingly west. *Staghorn* possesses the most energy as Matt Tierney rides the great riverboats from New Orleans to the Dakotas. Champlin has great fun with Prince Ferdinand Zarahoff and a cast of unusual characters.

In Matt Tierney, Champlin invents a character who can record the exuberant settlement of the American frontier while holding on to the dreams of youth. And Champlin's technique of complicating his novels with incredible, surprising sub-plots make his original novels even more entertaining to his readership.

—George Kelley

CHARBONNEAU, Louis Henry. *See* **YOUNG, Carter Travis.**

CHASE, Borden. Pseudonym for Frank Fowler. American. Born in Brooklyn, New York, 11 January 1900. Served in the United States Navy during World War I. Married Lee Keith (1st of 3 wives); one daughter. Worked as a shipyard worker, cab driver, carnival high diver, boxer, bootlegger, and tunnel digger on Holland and 8th Avenue subway tunnels in New York; then freelance fiction and screen writer. *Died in 1971.*

WESTERN PUBLICATIONS

Novels

Diamonds of Death. New York, Hart, and London, Popular, 1947.
Blazing Guns on the Chisholm Trail. New York, Random House, 1948; as *Red River*, New York, Bantam, 1948; London, Low, 1949.
Lone Star. New York, Fawcett, 1952.
Viva Gringo! New York, Bantam, 1961.

OTHER PUBLICATIONS

Novels

East River. New York, Crowell, 1935.
Sandhog. Philadelphia, Penn, 1938.

Plays

Screenplays: *Under Pressure*, 1935; *Harrigan's Kid*, with others, 1943; *Destroyer*, with Fread Wead and Lewis Meltzer, 1944; *The Fighting Seabees*, with Aeneas MacKenzie, 1944; *This Man's Navy*, with others, 1945; *Flame of the Barbary Coast*, 1945; *I've Always Loved You*, 1946; *Tycoon*, with John Twist, 1947; *The Man from Colorado*, with Robert D. Andrews and Ben Maddow, 1948; *Red River*, with Charles Schnee, 1948; *Montana*, with others, 1950; *Winchester '73*, with Robert L. Richards, 1950; *The Great Jewel Robbery*, 1950; *The Iron Man*, with George Zuckerman and W.R. Burnett, 1951; *Bend of the River*, 1952; *Lone Star*, with Howard Estabrook, 1952; *The World in His Arms*, with Horace McCoy, 1952; *Sea Devils*, 1953; *Gunfighters of Casa Grande*, with Patricia Chase and Clarke Reynolds, 1953; *His Majesty O'Keeffe*, with James Hill, 1954; *The Far Country*, 1955; *Man Without a Star*, with D.D. Beauchamp, 1955; *Vera Cruz*, with Roland Kibbee and James R. Webb, 1955; *Backlash*, 1956; *Night Passage*, 1957; *Ride a Crooked Trail*, with George Bruce, 1958; *Los Pistoleros de Casa Grande* (Gunfighters of Casa Grande), 1965; *A Man Called Gannon*, with D.D. Beauchamp and Gene Kearney, 1969.

Other

Sandhog: The Way of Life of the Tunnel Builders. Evanston, Illinois, Row Peterson, 1941.

*

Critical Study: interview by Jim Kitses, in *The Hollywood Screenwriter*, edited by Richard Corliss, New York, Avon, 1972.

* * *

A bit of mossy buckaroo advice was, "if some feller gives you a horse, don't never look at its teeth. You'll be lucky if it's got gums." Critics should resist impulses to treat genre fiction as literature despite the occasional appearance of isolated works that achieve this distinction. Borden Chase's smoke-belching melodramas run no risk of being considered a civilized contribution toward culture. In style and content, his works can be summarily described as self-consciously barbaric. All male protagonists and antagonists suffer from *machismo* and their female counterparts from *machisma.* Devlin Burke "was all man." Martha Ronda "was a lot of woman." Blood flows freely and frequently inside his narratives. Outside, they should produce brain hemorrhages among partisans of the movement for Women's Liberation. Possessive males lust after females like excited studs. Smoldering females respond like mares in heat. Nevertheless, the sex which symbiotically accompanies the violence in this brand of Western, must be classified as "pre-porno." The characters do not descend to sub-human levels. They keep their clothes on. "She saw his eyes, blue and cold as they studied her. And suddenly she *felt* naked. Martha *felt* the clothes slip from her body, one garment after another. The ink-stained shirt was gone, unbuttoned and stripped from her shoulders. She *felt* his blue eyes move over the round of her breasts; *felt* her flesh grow warm as her heart sent the blood pulsing through the veins . . . " and so forth. The italics are mine. Subsequently, Martha *actually* becomes unclad, but readers are spared the intimate biological details of acts of copulation and the story stays within the bounds of what once was called "decency."

Chase's plots are saturated with molten situations. Readers are bludgeoned by the Warrior Cult. Although a chivalric component is sometimes crudely present, no evidence indicates that his characters have more than an adolescent comprehension of the nature of honor. Subtlety in either situation or character is not a quality to be sought in the author's novels. For this reason, they made relatively entertaining films for a cinematic era in search of vehicles for the "talents" of Clark Gable and John Wayne. *Lone Star* provided the former with an opportunity to repeat his performance of Rhett Butler in a different costume, and *Blazing Guns on the Chisholm Trail* was turned into a motion picture entitled *Red River*, giving the latter still another chance to play a caricature of himself—if it is possible to caricature what is already a caricature.

Unfortunately, as a book and as a film, *Red River* has achieved an undeserved reputation as a classic on the theme of the trail drive, alongside Emerson Hough's *North of '36.* Andy Adams's *Log of a Cowboy* still possesses the sole vested-right to such a claim. All other explorations of the theme should be used to provide fuel for the energy crises that lie ahead.

Chase's books have gums—a mite bloody from over-use.

—Owen Ulph

CHATHAM, Larry. *See* **BINGLEY, David Ernest.**

CHESHIRE, Giff(ord Paul). Also wrote as Chad Merriman; Ford Pendleton. American. Born in Oregon in 1905. Educated at Oregon State University, Eugene. Served in the United States Navy as medical corpsman; assigned to United States Marines, served in Nicaraguan campaign pre-1934; worked for United States Army Engineers. Married; one son and one daughter. Wrote more than 300 stories and novelettes for Western magazines. *Died.*

WESTERN PUBLICATIONS

Novels

Starlight Basin. New York, Random House, 1954.
River of Gold; Oregon and the Challenge of the Gold Rush, a Tale. New York, Aladdin, 1955.
Year of the Gun. New York, Dell, 1957.
Edge of the Desert. New York, Doubleday, 1958.
The Sudden Guns. New York, Doubleday, 1959; London, Ward Lock, 1961.
Thunder on the Mountain. New York, Doubleday, 1960.
Black List. New York, Doubleday, 1962.
Chance Range. London, Ward Lock, 1963.
Stronghold. New York, Doubleday, 1963; London, Ward Lock, 1964.
Wenatchee Bend. New York, Doubleday, 1966.
Ambush at Bedrock. New York, Doubleday, 1969; London, Arrow, 1971.

Novels as Chad Merriman

Blood on the Sun. Greenwich, Connecticut, Fawcett, 1952.
Fury on the Plains. New York, Fawcett, 1954.
Colorado Gold, with Wayne D. Overholser (as Merriman and Lee Leighton). New York, Ballantine, 1958.
The Avengers. New York, Ballantine, 1959.
Bunch Quitter. New York, Ballantine, 1959.
Night Killer. New York, Ballantine, 1960.
Gunpoint Ransom. London, Ward Lock, 1961.
Ride West for War. New York, Ballantine, 1961.
Rogue River. New York, Ballantine, 1962.
The Harsh Range. New York, Ballantine, 1963.
Snakehead. New York, Ballantine, 1965.
Hard Country. London, Mayflower, 1970.

Novels as Ford Pendleton

Outlaw Justice. Hasbrouck Heights, New Jersey, Graphic, 1954.
Hell Rider. Hasbrouck Heights, New Jersey, Graphic, 1955.
Gunmaster. New York, Graphic, 1956; London, Hale, 1958.
Gun Chance. London, Hale, 1958.
Vengeance Trail. New York, Avalon, 1958.

Uncollected Short Stories

"Six-Gun Slowpoke," in *The Avon Book of New Stories of the Great Wild West.* New York, Avon, 1949.
"Strangers in the Evening," in *Zane Grey Western Award Stories,* edited by Don Ward. New York, Dell, 1951.
"The Bad Year," in *Holsters and Heroes,* edited by Noel Loomis. New York, Macmillan, 1954.
"Whistle on the River," in *They Opened the West,* edited by Tom W. Blackburn. New York, Doubleday, 1967.
"Six-Guns Round the Bend," in *The Northwesterners,* edited by Bill Pronzini and Martin H. Greenberg. Greenwich, Connecticut, Fawcett Gold Medal, 1990.

* * *

Giff Cheshire was born on an Oregon ranch homesteaded by his grandfather in the 1850's, who had crossed the plains by wagon train from Tennessee. He grew up on stories of his family's frontier adventures, which provided impetus for his own fiction. He sold the first short story he wrote for publication, to a pulp magazine in 1934, and over the next 17 years published more than 300 stories and novelettes in such periodicals as *Western Story*, *Dime Western*, *Zane Grey's Western Magazine*, *Blue Book*, and *Adventure*.

He turned to western novels in the early 1950's, as did many of his contemporaries upon the collapse of the pulp-magazine markets. He wrote paperback originals as by Chad Merriman and Ford Pendleton, reserving his own name for several hardcover novels published by Random House and Doubleday. He also collaborated with Wayne D. Overholser on one novel, *Colorado Gold*, which appeared as by Chad Merriman and Lee Leighton (one of Overholser's pseudonyms).

Cheshire specialized in cattle country stories, particularly in cattle country stories, particularly in his novel-length works: cattlemen versus homesteaders (*Starlight Basin*), cattlemen versus sheep ranchers (*Black List*, *Gun Chance*), cattlemen versus rustlers (*Hell Rider*), cattlemen versus an unknown enemy (*Ambush at Bedrock*), cattlemen versus cattlemen in conflict over land and/or water rights or for personal reasons (*Edge of the Desert*, *The Sudden Guns*, *Wenatchee Bend*). For the most part these are set in eastern Oregon, though he also made good use of the Nebraska plains, Wyoming Territory, Washington state, the Owyhee country along the Idaho–Nevada border, and the southern Nevada desert.

In addition to cattle-country yarns, he wrote other Westerns with conventional plotlines—*Gunmaster*, for instance, in which an itinerant gunman is hired to clean up a lawless town. Still others are formulary in design and handling but make use of less standardized elements. *Blood on the Sun* concerns a "buckskin man" and wagon-train guide caught in the midst of a battle between gold-hungry whites and Sioux Indians on the Oregon Trail; *Night Killer* is a western mystery about a gang of robbers operating out of the actual mining town of Silver City, Idaho.

Cheshire's best work is that which is solidly based on historical events in his native Pacific Northwest. *Stronghold* deals effectively with the Modoc Basin Indian War; *Snakehead* recounts the struggle to build a railroad through the Cascade Mountains of Washington state; *Ride West for War* depicts the efforts of Southern sympathizers to exploit Oregon mining interests in the early years of the Civil War. He was at the pinnacle of his abilities when writing about Oregon and Washington rivers—the Columbia, the Rogue, the Willamette, the Umatilla, the John Day—and the men who travelled and worked on them: riverboat owners, captains, pilots, gamblers; freighters, ferrymen, engineers, boat builders, bridge builders. His fascination with the Northwest's waterways and water traffic in both the 19th and 20th centuries resulted in one first-rate novel, *Rogue River*, and dozens of short stories and novelettes.

Despite the formulaic nature of much of his fiction, Cheshire was able to include original plot twists, strong character development, and genuine human emotion in even the most hackneyed of his stories; and his talent for vividly recreating his settings and maintaining a high pitch of suspense throughout his narratives was not inconsiderable. At his best, he was a competent historian and an excellent entertainer.

—Bill Pronzini

CHISHOLM, A(rthur) M(urray). Canadian. Born in Toronto, Ontario, in 1872. Educated at the University of Toronto, B.A. 1895, LL.B. 1896. Practicing lawyer. *Died 24 January 1960.*

WESTERN PUBLICATIONS

Novels

The Boss of Wind River. New York, Doubleday, 1911.
Precious Waters. New York, Doubleday, 1913; London, Gay and Hancock, 1915; as *Desert Conquest*, New York, Grosset and Dunlap, n.d.
The Land of Strong Men. New York, Fly, 1919.
When Stuart Came to Sitkum. New York, Chelsea House, 1924.
The Land of Big Rivers: A Novel of the Northwest. New York, Chelsea House, and London, Hodder and Stoughton, 1924.
Black Powder Dan. London, Hodder and Stoughton, 1925.
The Red-Headed Kids: An Adventure Story. New York, Chelsea House, 1925; as *The Red Heads*, London, Hodder and Stoughton, 1926.
Yellow Horse. London, Hodder and Stoughton, 1926.
Prospectin' Fools: A Western Story. London, Hodder and Stoughton, 1927.
Red. London, Hodder and Stoughton, 1927; as *Red Bill*, New York, Stokes, 1930.

* * *

A.M. Chisholm had some popularity as a writer in the 1920's and 1930's, though not in his native Canada. Chisholm's reputation has not endured because, whatever literary merit his books had, their style and content make them very dated. Chisholm's books bear little resemblance to the conventional Western.

The setting for Chisholm's books is the Northwest, either specified in the title as in *The Land of Big Rivers: A Novel of the Northwest*, or by implication in most of the others. This mountainous area provides an attractive backdrop and is well-described, but we are not given detailed studies of exact localities. This area also provides reasons for stories in some of Chisholm's novels. In his first, *The Boss of Wind River*, a lumber business in the forest provides a plot. The owner's son, a clean-out college boy, has to rescue the business from insolvency. His ultimate success is the climax of a morally uplifting tale for ambitious young men from the cities. Outdoor adventure of this kind gives a briskness to the tale.

A slightly more serious hero is needed in *Precious Waters* when a band of settlers is faced with a struggle with a railway company. Life is hard enough for them in their remote western region, but they are threatened with complete deprivation of their livelihood. *Black Powder Dan* also takes place in the mountainous West but there is not much description, most of the book being taken up with action and fighting Indians. *Prospectin' Fools* is subtitled *A Western Story*; its plot centers on a search for gold in the mountains. *Red* is a rambling adventure story with some gentle romance.

Chisholm's books contain little of the gunfighting and violence which came to be expected in the conventional western. There is not much dialogue in his books, and his prose contains smatterings of French Canadian and Indian as well as rather good English (he even uses Latin phrases). The resilience of Chisholm's style was what made him popular in the United States, where his books were, in their day, well-received. Whatever the merits of the style these adventure stories became quickly outmoded. They still fitted into the pattern of the English colonial western with its optimism and lessons for success. The American Western quickly overtook them and evolved on quite different lines.

—P.R. Meldrum

CHISHOLM, Matt. Pseudonym for Peter Christopher Watts; also wrote as Cy James; Luke Jones; Duncan Mackinlock; Tom Owen; Peter Watts. British. Born in Maida Vale, London, 19 December 1919. Educated at Richmond Hill School; art schools in England. Served in the British Army in North Africa, Syria, and Burma, 1940–46. Married Sonia Chism in 1961; two sons. Civil servant, 1946–80. Founder and secretary, Electro Acupuncture Voluntary Society of Britain and Ireland. *Died 30 November 1983.*

WESTERN PUBLICATIONS

Novels

Half-Breed. London, Panther, 1958.
High Peak. London, Panther, 1958.
Hodge. London, Panther, 1958.
Riders at the Ford. London, Panther, 1958.
Hang a Man High. London, Panther, 1959.
The Saga of Trench Godden. London, Panther, 1959.
Blood on the Land. London, Panther, 1959.
Joe Blade. London, Panther, 1959.
Never Give Ground. London, Panther, 1959.
Wild Mustanger. London, Panther, 1959.
Sutter's Strike. London, Panther, 1959.
The Law of Ben Hodge. London, Panther, 1959.
A Posse of Violent Men. London, Panther, 1960.
Fury at Tombstone. London, Panther, 1960.
Pursuit in the Sun. London, Panther, 1960.
Prayer for a Gunman. London, Panther, 1960.
Hangrope for a Gunman. London, Panther, 1960.
Advance to Death. London, Panther, 1961.
A Rage of Guns. London, Panther, 1961.
Three Canyons to Death (as Luke Jones). London, Consul, 1961.
Brasada (as Luke Jones). London, Consul, 1962.

Bitter Range. London, Panther, 1962.
Three for Vengeance. London, Mayflower, 1963.
The Proud Horseman. London, Mayflower, 1963.
The Last Gun. London, Panther, 1966.
Cash McCord. London, Panther, 1966.
Spur to Death. London, Panther, 1966.
Hunted. London, Panther, 1966.
Gun Marshal. London, Panther, 1967.
Range War. London, Panther, 1967.
Indian Scout. London, Panther, 1967.
Apache Kill. London, Panther, 1967.
Gun Lust. London, Panther, 1968.
A Bullet for Brody. London, Panther, 1968.
Spur. London, Panther, 1968.
The Trail of Fear. London, Panther, 1968.

McAllister Series:

McAllister. London, Mayflower, 1963; New York, Beagle, 1971.
The Hard Men. London, Mayflower, 1963.
Death at Noon. London, Mayflower, 1963.
The Hangman Rides Tall. London, Mayflower, 1963; New York, Beagle, 1971.
Death Trail. London, Panther, 1967.
Kiowa. London, Panther, 1967.
Tough to Kill. London, Panther, 1968.
Rage of McAllister. London, Panther, 1969; New York, Beagle, 1971.
McAllister Strikes. London, Panther, 1969; New York, Beagle, 1971.
Kill McAllister. London, Panther, 1969; New York, Beagle, 1972.
McAllister Rides. London, Panther, 1969; New York, Beagle, 1971.
McAllister Makes War. London, Panther, 1969; New York, Beagle, 1971.
McAllister's Fury. London, Panther, 1969; New York, Beagle, 1971.
McAllister Fights. London, Panther, 1969; New York, Beagle, 1971.
Gunsmoke for McAllister. London, Panther, 1969; New York, Beagle, 1970.
Blood on McAllister. London, Panther, 1969; New York, Beagle, 1970.
McAllister Says No. London, Panther, 1970; New York, Beagle, 1971.
Danger for McAllister. London, Panther, 1970.
McAllister Gambles. London, Panther, 1970; New York, Beagle, 1971.
Hang McAllister. London, Panther, and New York, Beagle, 1970.
Shoot McAllister. London, Panther, 1970; New York, Beagle, 1971.
Trail of McAllister. London, Panther, 1970; New York, Beagle, 1971.
McAllister Runs Wild. London, Mayflower, 1972.
Brand McAllister. London, Mayflower, 1972.
Battle of McAllister. London, Mayflower, 1972.
McAllister Trapped. London, Mayflower, 1973.
Vengeance of McAllister. London, Mayflower, 1973.
McAllister Must Die. London, Mayflower, 1974.
The McAllister Legend. London, Mayflower, 1974.
McAllister Never Surrenders. London, Hamlyn, 1981.
McAllister and Cheyenne Death. London, Hamlyn, 1981.
McAllister and the Spanish Gold. London, Hamlyn, 1981.
McAllister on the Comanche Crossing. London, Hamlyn, 1981.
McAllister and Quarry. London, Hamlyn, 1981.
Die-Hard. London, Hamlyn, 1981.
Wolf-Bait. London, Hamlyn, 1981.
Fire-Brand. London, Hamlyn, 1981.

Storm Series:

Stampede. London, Panther, 1970.
Hard Texas Trail. London, Panther, 1971.
Riders West. London, Mayflower, 1971.
One Notch to Death. London, Mayflower, 1972.
One Man—One Gun. London, Mayflower, 1972.
Thunder in the West. London, Mayflower, 1972.
A Breed of Men. London, Mayflower, 1973.
Battle Fury. London, Mayflower, 1973.
Blood on the Hills. London, Mayflower, 1973.

Blade Series:

The Indian Incident. London, Hamlyn, 1978.
The Tucson Conspiracy. London, Hamlyn, 1978.
The Pecos Manhunt. London, Hamlyn, 1979.
The Laredo Assignment. London, Hamlyn, 1979.
The Colorado Virgins. London, Hamlyn, 1979.
The Mexican Proposition. London, Hamlyn, 1979.
The Nevada Mustang. London, Hamlyn, 1979.
The Arizona Climax. London, Hamlyn, 1980.
The Cheyenne Trap. London, Hamlyn, 1980.
The Montana Deadlock. London, Hamlyn, 1980.
The Navaho Trail. London, Hamlyn, 1981.
The Last Act. London, Hamlyn, 1981.

Novels as Cy James (series: Spur)

The Brasada Guns. London, Panther, 1961.
The Gun Is My Brother. London, Panther, 1961.
The Violent Hills. London, Panther, 1961; revised edition, as *Hell for McAllister* (as Matt Chisholm), 1969.
Death Rides Fast. London, Panther, 1964.
The Battle of Red Rock. London, Panther, 1964.
Ride the Far Country. London, Panther, 1964.
Hellion. London, Panther, 1964.
Hangrope Posse. London, Panther, 1965.
Gun-Rage. London, Panther, 1965.
Blood Creek. London, Panther, 1965.
Gun Hand. London, Panther, 1965.
Savage Horseman. London, Panther, 1966.
Man in the Saddle. London, Panther, 1966.
The Running Gun. London, Panther, 1966.
My Gun Is Justice. London, Panther, 1966; revised edition, as *McAllister Justice* (as Matt Chisholm), 1969.
The Cimmaron Kid (Spur). London, Mayflower, 1969.
Trail West (Spur). London, Mayflower, 1970.
Longhorn (Spur). London, Mayflower, 1970.
Gun (Spur). London, Mayflower, 1971.
The Brave Ride Tall (Spur). London, Mayflower, 1971.
Blood at Sunset (Spur). London, Mayflower, 1971.

Novels (translations to Norwegian, from original English manuscripts)

Blodig Snoe (Bloody Snow). Oslo, Bladkompaniet, 1982.
Doedens Land (Land of the Dead). Oslo, Bladkompaniet, 1982.
Leiemorder (Hired Killer). Oslo, Bladkompaniet, 1983.
En Texaners Doed (Death of a Texan). Oslo, Bladkompaniet, 1983.
Hestetuyne (Horsethieves). Oslo, Bladkompaniet, 1983.

OTHER PUBLICATIONS

Novels as Peter Watts

Out of Yesterday. London, Hodder and Stoughton, 1950.
The Dread and the Glory (as Tom Owen). London, Panther, 1959.
Circus of Horror (novelization of screenplay; as Tom Owen). London, Panther, 1960.
Island of Hell (as Duncan Mackinlock). London, Panther, 1961.
The Long Night Through. London, Corgi, 1962.
Scream and Shout. London, Corgi, 1966.

Other

Indians! (for children). London, Odhams Press, and Chicago, Follett, 1965.
The Corgi Sports Almanac (as Tom Owen). London, Corgi, 1965.
A Dictionary of the Old West 1850–1900 (as Peter Watts). New York, Knopf, 1977.
The True Book of the Wild West. London, Hampton House, 1978.

*

Matt Chisholm commented (1982):

Fictional writing which uses western America as its background, of course, comes in as many forms as there are categories of fictional writing in general. Some of it, often written by native Westerners who know no other locale so intimately, are contributions to the highest standard of American literature. Much of it is written by authors who, though they consider themselves to be writing serious books, create no more than light entertainment. Much of it (in its "pulp" sections) is written by authors from other genres who, with their publishers, think that western fiction is for the illiterate who are indifferent to the poverty of writing offered them. This kind of western sadly lacks any pretentions to historical accuracy and is that part of the genre which tends to keep the standard low.

The majority of western writers aim to contribute a commercial effort which recognises certain honest standards of craftsmanship for a readership which makes up what we may call for convenience sake the lower end of the market. Putting aside the salacious and sado-pornographic (which have used the western as a reluctant host body for the last 10 years or so), the popular western has on the whole claimed only to be light entertainment, simple in plot, strong in action and atmosphere, set against a background of either the legendary or the historic West.

It is my hope that I have succeeded in providing simple entertainment for all classes of reader on several levels, which have not lacked credibility, authentic background, three-dimensional characters, and a gentle irony towards the West's perpetual self-consciousness and awareness of being a living legend. Evidence suggests that, while the majority of my readers are aged between 15 and 25, a substantial porportion ranges through all ages and includes levels of literacy from those who read with moving lips to intellectuals who digest McAllister concealed in the pages of the *Times Literary Supplement*.

A serious novel with a western background has occupied me for some years and I am now halfway through its writing. I am also about the same distance into a long-term production of a bibliographical dictionary of western American literature which should be the companion volume of the *Dictionary*. Another five years should see it done. For four years or so, I have been working on a long novel about the Norse of the 9th century and now have it almost completed.

To sum up one's own work is almost impossible. My western fiction is what the trade calls "pulp," written in an easy-to-read half-dialect style, with an appearance of having been thrown roughly on to the page, but which calls for as much care as polished work. It is not bad, it does no harm, neither does it lift my readers to any great height. However, I hope profoundly that, without their knowing it, some of the younger readers have taken in some of the morality of the tales. I hope that the thoughts, actions, and factual details are accurate to the period 1863–73 about which I usually write. I have never made much money at the game, but it has been a living and a good deal of fun.

* * *

The tragic death of Matt Chisholm robbed the Western of one of its finest modern practitioners. During a lengthy career begun in the 1950's, he gradually honed and perfected his skills to a point where he had few rivals. At its best, the Chisholm Western provides an intriguing plot, with fast action and touches of dry humour, presented in a taut, understated style. Above all it has credible characters, figures who are at once human and heroic.

Character is at the heart of Chisholm's work. Even a relatively routine effort like *Hard Texas Trail*, with its trail-boss hero rescuing an heiress from a fortune-hunting killer, has characters who compel belief. Clay Storm, though hardy, is shown as being capable of making mistakes.

This quality extends to other Chisholm heroes—Ben Hodge, Cash McCord, and particularly Joe Blade and Rem McAllister, the most famous of his creations. Their adventures, in two sequences of novels, form the peak of their author's achievement.

Character is also at the heart of the Storm series of novels, which focus on the Texas family of that name, and their efforts at cattle-ranching in Colorado. In several self-contained but related works, Chisholm recounts the adventures of various members of the Storm clan, shifting the focus in an interesting way from one to the other, while retaining the continuity of the family and its Colorado locale. *One Man—One Gun*, where Jody Storm comes to manhood via a lonely quest through hostile Indian country, and *Battle Fury*, which has the whole clan fighting off a rival rancher, gunmen, and renegade Utes, are typical examples. The Storm novels are notable for their blend of fast-paced action and realism, and for their strongly developed characters. They are perhaps particularly interesting for their balanced but unsentimental portrayal of Native Americans, and for the prominence given to credible and individual female characters. Both traits recur in the author's later fiction.

Aside from novels written under his own name, Chisholm produced some good westerns as Cy James. Of these, *Hellion* and *Ride the Far Country* are perhaps the most striking. Chisholm has also written for younger readers. But it is in the "Blade" and "McAllister" novels that his finest work is to be found.

McAllister is the more obviously "heroic" of the two. A huge man, fast with a gun and tremendously strong, some of his exploits of his exploits appear superhuman. *McAllister Justice* describes his single-handed taming of a Nebraska mining town. In *McAllister* he survives pursuit by the Apaches in a suicide desert mission. *The Hard Men* has him fighting off a greedy cattle-baron, and winning the shoot-out against five killers with only a little help from his friends. All the same, McAllister has his failings. Susceptible to pretty women—he is easily seduced by the villain's daughter in *The Hard Men*—he knows fear at times. This, with his hot-headed obstinacy and his laconic humour, renders him human and likeable. The humorous note is strongest in *McAllister on the Comanche Crossing*, where Chisholm appears as narrator, and he and McAllister exchange insults and challenges on a dangerous trail drive which ends with Chisholm knocking the great man down.

That some readers find Blade more impressive is no reflection on McAllister, but rather a tribute to the man who created them both. Joe Blade, the prematurely greyhaired gunfighter who tours the West offering his services at a price, is for me the best and most endearing of Chisholm's heroes. Tough and resourceful, he gets his way by a combination of sagacity and the luck which every man needs. A skilled gunman, he dislikes and avoids killing whenever he can, and displays a realistic reaction when he is forced into it. His adventures involve some of Chisholm's most imaginative plots. *The Montana Deadlock* has him attempting to trace a missing husband, who turns out to be a horsethief. In *The Mexican Proposition* he prevents the setting up of a Confederate empire in the southwest, and captures their secret weapon, a quick-firing machine gun. In *The Colorado Virgins* he acts as guard to two beautiful—and greedy—women, in a search for hidden gold, while *The Laredo Assignment* shows him defending his Mexican relatives from a rancher and his gunmen. In some of these exploits he is assisted by his girl, the lovely Charity Clayton. Among the best "Blade" stories is *The Nevada Mustang*, where he and his cousin Chavez hunt a wild stallion, also sought by Indians and outlaws. On Chavez's death, Blade, in a gesture of friendship, names the captured horse after him. Blade has scruples, and while aware of the uses of money is never "bought." His decent, rough humanity renders him more credible than the iron-nerved heartless psychopaths in the works of other writers. *The Last Act* presents the striking image of his departure, unarmed and on a mule, to marry Charity and settle down.

The realism of Chisholm's world, its down-to-earth vision, lingers in the mind. The best of his writing takes the reader at a steady lope through the plot, without delay or digression. Action is fast, the humour dry and keen. The humane philosophy, never intrusive, can be felt through the speech and actions of the characters. Men like McAllister and Blade, daring the dangers of their calling to help those in need, are heroes both, yet men. There can be no better tribute to Matt Chisholm, who brought them to life.

—Jeff Sadler

CHRISTIAN, Frederick H. Pseudonym for Frederick Nolan. Also writes as Danielle Rockfern; Donald Severn. British. Born in Liverpool, Lancashire, in 1931. Educated at Aberayron County School, Wales; Liverpool Collegiate. Married Heidi Würmli in 1962; two sons. Editor, Corgi Books, London; sales representative, Penguin Books, London; worked in publicity, Fontana Books, and marketing, Granada Publishing, London, and Ballantine Books, New York; publisher, Warner Communications, London. Agent: Arthur Pine Associates, 1780 Broadway, New York, New York 10019, U.S.A.

WESTERN PUBLICATIONS

Novels (series: Angel; Sudden)

Sudden Strikes Back. London, Corgi, 1966.
Sudden—Troubleshooter. London, Corgi, 1967.
Sudden at Bay. London, Corgi, 1968.
Sudden—Apache Fighter. London, Corgi, 1969.
Sudden—Dead or Alive!. London, Corgi, 1970.
Send Angel. London, Sphere, 1972; New York, Pinnacle, 1974; as *Ride Clear of Daranga*, Los Angeles, Pinnacle, 1979.
Kill Angel. London, Sphere, 1972; New York, Pinnacle, 1974; as *Bad Day at Agua Caliente*, Los Angeles, Pinnacle, 1979.
Find Angel. London, Sphere, 1973; New York, Pinnacle, 1974; as *Ride Out to Vengeance*, Los Angeles, Pinnacle, 1979.
Trap Angel. London, Sphere, 1973; New York, Pinnacle, 1974; as *Ambush in Purgatory*, Los Angeles, Pinnacle, 1979.
Hang Angel. London, Sphere, and New York, Pinnacle, 1975; as *Showdown at Trinidad*, Los Angeles, Pinnacle, 1979.
Frame Angel. New York, Pinnacle, 1974; London, Sphere, 1975; as *Shoot-Out at Silver King*, Los Angeles, Pinnacle, 1980.
Hunt Angel. New York, Pinnacle, and London, Sphere, 1975; as *Massacre in Madison*, Los Angeles, Pinnacle, 1980.
Take Angel. London, Sphere, 1975; as *Warn Angel*, New York, Pinnacle, 1975.
Stop Angel! London, Sphere, and New York, Pinnacle, 1976.

Uncollected Short Stories

"I'll Kiss You Goodnight," in *The Premature Burial*. London, Corgi, 1962.
"The Return of Sudden," in *Western* (London), January 1981.

OTHER PUBLICATIONS as Frederick Nolan

Novels

The Oshawa Project. London, Barker, 1974; as *The Algonquin Project*, New York, Morrow, 1974; as *Brass Target*, New York, Jove, 1979.
NYPD, No Place to Be a Cop. London, Barker, 1974; as *No Place to Be a Cop*, London, Futura, 1975.
The Ritter Double-cross. London, Barker, 1974; New York, Morrow, 1975.
Kill Petrosino! London, Barker, 1975.
The Mittenwald Syndicate. London, Cassell, and New York, Morrow, 1976.
Caver's Kingdom. London, Macmillan, 1978; New York, Warner, 1980.
White Nights, Red Dawn. New York, Macmillan, 1980; London, Hutchinson, 1981.
Wolf Trap. London, Piatkus, 1983; New York, St. Martin's Press, 1984.
A Promise of Glory. London, Arrow, 1983; New York, Bantam, 1984.
Blind Duty. London, Arrow, 1983; New York, Bantam, 1985.
Field of Honour (as Danielle Rockfern). London, Hamlyn, 1985.
Red Centre. London, Grafton, and New York, St. Martin's Press, 1987.
The Garrett Dossier:
Sweet Sister Death. London, Century Hutchinson, 1989; as *A Time to Die* (as Donald Severn), New York, Lynx, 1989.

Alert State Black (as Donald Severn). New York, Lynx, 1989; as Frederick Nolan, London, Century Hutchinson, 1990.
Designated Assassin. London, Century Hutchinson, 1990.
Rat Run. London, Century Hutchinson, 1991.
Maximal Demotion. London, Century Hutchinson, 1991.
Soft Target. London, Century Hutchinson, 1992.

Plays

Television Plays: *Hemingway's. "Fiesta"; New Horizons.* series, 1970; *Westerns* and *Spies and Secret Agents*, both 1980; *Thrillers* and *Bestsellers*, 1981; *A Better Read* series.

Radio Plays: *The Richard Rodgers Story* (six one-hour programmes), 1976.

Other (for children)

Lone Star Western Annual. London, Atlas, 1966.
Jesse James. London, Macdonald, 1973.
Cowboys. London, Macdonald, 1974.
Lewis and Clark. London, Macdonald, 1974.
The Wagon Train. London, Macdonald, 1974.
Geronimo. London, Macdonald, 1975.
The Pilgrim Fathers. London, Macdonald, 1975.
Battle of the Alamo. London, Macdonald, 1978.

Other

The Life and Death of John Henry Tunstall. Albuquerque, University of New Mexico Press, 1965.
Jay J. Armes: Detective. New York, Macmillan, 1976; London, Macdonald, 1977.
Rodgers and Hammerstein: The Sound of Their Music. London, Dent, and New York, Walker, 1978.
The Lincoln County War: A Documentary History. Norman, University of Oklahoma Press, 1991.

Editor (as Frederick H. Christian), *The Authentic Life of Billy the Kid*, by Pat Garrett. London, Sphere, 1973.

Translator, *Lucky Luke* series (*The Stage Coach, Jesse James, Dalton City, Apache Canyon, The Tenderfoot, Western Circus, Curing the Daltons, Ma Dalton, the Dashing White Cowboy*) (for children) by R. Goscinny. Leicester, Brockhampton Press, 9 vols., 1972–74.
Translator, *Gideon [And His Friends, On the Riverbank], Gideon's House* (for children) by Benjamin Rabier. London, Hodder and Stoughton, 4 vols., 1979.
Translator, *The Black Forest Clinic*, by Peter Heim. London, Sphere, 1987.

*

Frederick H. Christian comments:

With regard to the Westerns that I've written, I have no statement to make: the work is the best I can do, or could do at the time it was written. I have always tried (and often, I fear, failed) to make my locations as historically accurate as I could, working from contemporary descriptions and maps. I have tried not to cheapen the genre nor exploit it, and that is all that someone who only writes to entertain can be expected to do. I only wish I could have done more, and better.

* * *

Frederick H. Christian took over the series character Sudden from Oliver Strange, writing episodes which fit into Strange's time scheme at different points. Christian's novels are always formulaic, depending on sets of stereotyped characters and plots. Sudden is the wanderer who enters a conflict, often between ranchers, resolves the difficulty, and then moves on, leaving behind a newly reconciled couple who are about to settle into domestic peace. The early novels seem stilted in their repetitiveness. Not only are events repeated from one novel to the next, but Christian lifts whole scenes out of Strange's writing: for example, in both Strange's *The Range Robbers* and Christian's *Sudden Strikes Back*, the villain tries to buy, then ride the hero's horse, is bucked off, attempts to shoot the animal, and ends by buying drinks for the townspeople who have witnessed the event. But Christian's last Sudden tale, *Sudden—Dead or Alive!*, has a different atmosphere. It is more sophisticated in its use of literary and mythic allusions and it is much more violent. It tells of Sudden setting out to capture a family of vicious outlaws, in the process helping a town to defend itself against their incursions. The wholesale slaughter and the gothic scenes of burning buildings and hanged men seem to owe much to the spaghetti western of the cinema.

This tone is maintained in Christian's next series, which revolves around Frank Angel. In *Find Angel*, Angel's employers are killed by outlaws and he sets out on a revenge quest. He catches two of the murderers and, after torturing one for information, kills them. Subsequently, he is beaten almost to death by the rest of the gang. The Department of Justice in Washington is hunting the same criminals and their Chief Investigator comes west. After he is permanently crippled by the outlaws, he trains Angel, changing him from an amoral nemesis to a highly skilled law enforcer. Angel catches the remaining outlaws and they are hanged. Now he is made a Special Investigator, directly responsible to the Attorney General. The series continues his experiences as a man-hunter. Good characters die violently, Angel kills ruthlessly, and, although the female element is minimal, he often ends the book in bed with a woman, perhaps a rape victim he has earlier helped and whom he is about to leave.

These novels carry a prefatory note about a Frank Angel who is listed in the National Archives in Washington. It ends, "There is no record that any of the events portrayed in this book took place, or that Frank Angel took part in them. Equally, there is no record that he did not." This reflects Christian's interest in western history and legend, which he reveals in his work on Billy the Kid and his translations of western histories, published under his real name. At the same time, he is translating fictional conventions, present from James Fenimore Cooper to Jack Schaefer, into the graphic violence typical of the recent tradition of the western tale.

—Christine Bold

CLARK, Badger. *See* **PAINE, Lauran.**

CLARK, Walter Van Tilburg. American. Born in East Orland, Maine, 3 August 1909. Educated at Reno High School, Nevada, graduated 1926; University of Nevada, Reno, 1926–31, B.A. 1931, M.A. 1932; University of Vermont, Burlington, M.A. 1934. Married Barbara Frances Morse in 1933 (died); one daughter and one son. English teacher and basketball coach, Cazenovia Central School, New York, 1933–45, and a school in Rye, New York, 1945–46; lecturer, 1950–53, and writer-in-residence, 1962–71, University of Nevada; Rockefeller Lecturer, 1953; Associate Professor of English, University of Montana, Missoula, 1953–56; Professor of English and creative writing, San Francisco State College, 1956–62; Fellow in fiction, Center for Advanced Studies, Wesleyan University, Middletown, Connecticut, 1960–61. Recipient: O. Henry award, 1945. Litt.D.: Colgate University, Hamilton, New York, 1958; University of Nevada, 1969. *Died 10 November 1971.*

WESTERN PUBLICATIONS

Novels

The Ox-Bow Incident. New York, Random House, 1940; London, Gollancz, 1941.
The City of Trembling Leaves. New York, Random House, 1945; as *Tim Hazard,* London, Kimber, 1951.
The Track of the Cat. New York, Random House, 1949; London, Gollancz, 1950.

Short Stories

The Watchful Gods and Other Stories. New York, Random House, 1950.

Uncollected Short Stories

"Trial at Arms," in *Saturday Evening Post* (Philadelphia), 25 January 1941.
"Prestige," in *Saturday Evening Post* (Philadelphia), 19 April 1941.
"The Pretender," in *Atlantic* (Boston), April 1942.
"A Letter to the Living," in *The Nation* (New York), 13 June 1942.
"Personal Interview," in *New Yorker,* 12 December 1942.
"The Rise and the Passing of Bar," in *Virginia Quarterly Review* (Charlottesville), Winter 1943.
"The Ascent of Ariel Goodbody," in *Yale Review* (New Haven, Connecticut), Winter 1943.
"Chuangtse and the Prince of the Golden Age," in *Western Review* (Denver), Winter 1949.
"The Indian Well," in *The Western Hall of Fame: An Anthology of Classic Western Stories,* edited by Bill Pronzini and Martin H. Greenberg. New York, Morrow, 1984.

OTHER PUBLICATIONS

Verse

Christmas Comes to Hjalsen, Reno. Reno, Nevada, Reno Publishing House, 1930.
Ten Women in Gale's House and Shorter Poems. Boston, Christopher, 1932.

Other

Editor, *The Journals of Alfred Doten, 1849–1903.* Reno, University of Nevada Press, 3 vols., 1973.

*

Bibliography: "Walter Van Tilburg Clark: A Bibliography" by Richard Etulain, in *South Dakota Review* (Vermillion), Autumn 1965.

Manuscript Collection: Library of Congress, Washington, D.C.

Critical Studies: *Walter Van Tilburg Clark* by Max Westbrook, New York, Twayne, 1969; *Walter Van Tilburg Clark* by L.L. Lee, Boise, Idaho, Boise State College, 1973; *Walter Van Tilburg Clark: Critiques* edited by Charlton Laird, Reno, University of Nevada Press, 1983.

* * *

Walter Van Tilburg Clark is something of an anomaly to the critic of western writing. Probably one of the most widely read—and uniformly widely praised—of contemporary western novelists, criticism of his work is nevertheless curiously thin. The student of Clark's work often gleans the impression that enthusiasm for his remarkable fictional achievement has often clouded critical perception as to its precise nature. This may partly be explained by brief consideration of his first, and most successful, novel *The Ox-Bow Incident,* a study of the behavior of a lynch mob which was widely interpreted in the years following its publication in a quasi-allegorical fashion as a topical study of the rise of Fascism, with particular reference to the growth of political dictatorship in Nazi Germany. This handy reading of the novel has persisted up the present, despite Clark's denial on numerous occasions that the novel had any specific reference to Nazi Germany at all; and it has only been fairly recently that this reading has been seen not as false but as incomplete, and that Clark's concerns have been reinterpreted as ultimately with other matters than political events.

This attractive and pervasive reading of *The Ox-Bow Incident* has nonetheless led to an implicit critical assumption that Clark's real genius as a western author lies in his ability to transform the stock incidents of typical western story from mere blood-and-thunder escapism into something more "relevant" to modern life. While no one would quarrel with the general assessment that Clark has attempted successfully to breathe new life into many a time-worn western cliché, one may well hesitate in applying purely social or political criteria to Clark's endeavor. Indeed, such criteria almost totally ignore *The City of Trembling Leaves,* which is not in any conventional sense a "western" at all, and *The Track of the Cat,* which completely lacks any political reference and which critics often uneasily dismiss as an example of an updated hunting story which supposedly appeals to more sophisticated tastes than does the traditional variety.

A different assessment of Clark's achievement may perhaps be indicated by approaching his work through some of the short stories included in *The Watchful Gods,* which share some common thematic preoccupations even though their specific plots are quite different. The basic concern of many of these stories is the contrast is the contrast between blind—and often hostile—nature and that pattern which mankind wistfully attempts to infer from a universe which is basically without purpose. Somewhat paradoxically, for Clark, life simply *is.* The question of *why* life is? or—better put—of why life is such and such a way, is finally a meaningless question. In Clark's fiction this question finds no answer except as a perhaps comforting illusion in the mind which asks it. Stephen Crane's slight poem in which a character reminds the universe that he exists, only to have the universe retort that this fact does not instill a sense of obligation, might almost stand as a motto for much of Clark's shorter fiction, in which the idea of individual purpose is negated by the nature of life itself.

"Hook," for instance, an often-anthologized story, merely recounts the life history of a hawk. Pushed early out of the nest he nearly perishes before learning to hunt. His wing later broken by the shotgun of a Japanese farmer, Hook manages to hunt on foot. Yet the balance of life has finally turned against him, and in a raid on the farmer's chicken yard he is finally killed by the man's dog. The story concludes simply with the farmer's wife saying "Oh, the brave bird."

The deceptive simplicity of the narration of this story conceals a number of concerns which are basic to Clark's vision. A primary value in this story is the already mentioned indifference of the world to Hook, whose life is a constant progression downwards. Courage, of which the hawk is a perhaps too-obvious symbol, is simply irrelevant to the indifferent world in which Hook is inevitably caught up. Moreover, Hook's "bravery" is, in the story's terms, not a concept the hawk would apply to his own actions. It is, rather, a statement by a human outsider who is attempting to apply some kind of moral sense to a world which is basically an amoral one.

Another variant on much the same theme is found in "The Indian Well." This story begins with a description of a typical day at the Indian Well—a day in which kill or be killed is the routine order of the natural world. This order is disrupted by the arrival of Jim Suttler and his burro Jenny, who set up camp in a ruinous cabin near the well and begin working an old mine nearby. When a cougar kills Jenny, Jim decides to avenge her. He waits throughout the winter for the cougar to return, and when it does he kills it. He then sentimentally completes his moral gesture by skinning the cougar and covering Jenny's carcass with the skin. After he leaves the well, however, the indifferent cycle of nature—upon which he and Jenny have attempted in vain to apply an order—returns. The last scene of the story is a repetition of the first. The world of kill or be killed, profoundly indifferent to man and burro alike, reclaims the Indian Well.

It has escaped sufficient critical notice how the titles themselves of Clark's three novels echo this fundamental contrast between the indifference of nature and the futile pattern which man, in all good faith, attempts to apply to it. *The Ox-Bow Incident*, as clear example, tells symbolically the disastrous "incident" which happens in a pastoral natural setting because of man's attempt to apply a moral order to it. From this perspective a violent and—as it transpires—perverse human order is applied to an indifferent nature in which it has no meaning, nor even much significance. *The City of Trembling Leaves*, Clark's poetic name for Reno, Nevada, is also the title of the symphony which Tim Hazard, the novel's hero, creates during the course of the story. Tim's symbolic feat is to combine the "natural" world with the "urban" world inhabited by man. He does this through the medium of music, an art form which, although it can be conceptualized, cannot be rendered concrete, and which has neither general moral dimension nor specific ethical relevance to the "urban" Reno of which it is a symbolic expression. Tim's ability to create his symphony finally depends upon his almost mystical awareness of how the two cities of trembling leaves do *not* relate. Clark's final novel, *The Track of the Cat*, works with the same basic thematic structure. In this story, the safe world of a Nevada ranch is threatened by the presence of a hostile mountain lion, emblematic of the indifference of nature to the moral order which man attempts to apply to it.

Harvey Fergusson, a western writer contemporary with Clark, was found of quoting the Spanish proverb that only the earth lasts forever. The proverb might well stand as an emblem of Clark's fictional endeavor, in which the permanence of nature is habitually seen in terms of man's tragic attempts mistakenly to assign meaning to it.

—James K. Folsom

CLARKE, Richard. *See* **PAINE, Lauran.**

CLARKSON, Ormand. *See* **RICHARDSON, Gladwell.**

CLAY, Alison. *See* **ALLISON, Clay.**

CLEVELAND, Jim. *See* **KING, Albert.**

CLIFTON, Oliver Lee. *See* **RATHBORNE, St. George.**

CLINTON, Jeff. *See* **BICKHAM, Jack M.**

COBURN, L.J. *See* **HARVEY, John; JAMES, Laurence.**

COBURN, Walt(er J.). American. Born in White Sulphur Springs, Montana Territory, 23 October 1889. Educated at Great Falls High School, Montana, graduated 1908; Manzanita Hall preparatory school, Palo Alto, California, 1909–10. Served in the Air Branch of the Signal Corps during World War I: Sergeant. Married 1) Blake Beck (divorced); 2) Mina Acheson Evans in 1927. Served briefly in Pancho Villa's army; worked as a cowboy and surveyor in Arizona; then freelance writer. *Died 24 May 1971.*

WESTERN PUBLICATIONS

Novels

The Ringtailed Rannyhans. New York, Century, 1927.
Mavericks. New York, Century, 1929.

Barb Wire. New York, Century, 1931.
Walt Coburn's Action Novels (includes *The Four Aces, Cartridges Free, Paths to Glory, The Maverick Legion*). New York, Fiction House, 1931.
Law Rides the Range. New York, Appleton Century, 1935.
Sky-Pilot Cowboy. New York, Appleton Century, 1937; as *The Kansas Killers*, New York, Lancer, 1966.
Pardners of the Dim Trails. Philadelphia, Lippincott, 1951; London, Hammond, 1952; as *Tough Texan*, New York, Lancer, 1966.
The Way of a Texan. New York, Star Guidance, 1953.
Drift Fence. London, Hammond, 1953; New York, Berkley, 1959.
The Burnt Ranch. London, Hammond, 1954; New York, Macfadden, 1970; as *Dark and Bloody Ground*, Bath, Chivers, 1986.
Gun Grudge. London, Hammond, 1954; New York, Lancer, 1963.
Wet Cattle. London, Hammond, 1955; as *Violent Maverick*, New York, Avon, 1956.
The Square Shooter. London, Hammond, 1955; New York, Macfadden, 1970.
The Renegade. Toronto, Harlequin, 1956.
Cayuse. London, Hammond, 1956.
Border Jumper. London, Hammond, 1956; New York, Pyramid, 1961.
Beyond the Wild Missouri. New York, Arcadia House, 1956.
One Step Ahead of the Posse. New York, Ace, 1956.
The Night Branders. New York, Ace, 1957; Bath, Chivers, 1985.
Stirrup High. New York, Messner, 1957.
Fear Branded. London, Hammond, 1957; New York, Avon, 1971.
Buffalo Run. London, Hammond, 1958.
Guns Blaze on Spiderweb Range. New York, Avon, 1958; London, Hammond, 1961.
Free Rangers. London, Hammond, 1959.
Branded. New York, Avon, 1959; Bath, Chivers, 1987.
Fast Gun. New York, Avon, 1959.
Feud Valley, and Sleeper-Marked: Two New Westerns. London, Hammond, 1960; *Feud Valley* published New York, Lancer, 1964.
The Ramrod, and Sons of Gunfighters: Two New Westerns. London, Hammond, 1960.
La Jornada. London, Consul, 1961; New York, Avon, 1971.
Invitation to a Hanging. New York, Avon, 1963; Bath, Atlantic, 1986.
An Avon Triple Western: Renegade Legions; The Lightning Brand; Kilbourne Brothers, Wolf Hunters. New York, Avon, 1965.
Man from Montana. New York, Lancer, 1966.
El Hombre. New York, Belmont, 1967.
Reckless! New York, Belmont, 1968.

Uncollected Short Stories

"The Peace Treaty of the Seven Up," in *Argosy* (New York), 8 July 1922.
"Some Sheep and a Shave," in *Western Story* (New York), 4 November 1922.
"The Man on the Dun," in *Western Story* (New York), 14 April 1923.
"'Silent' Saunders Pays for Two," in *Western Story* (New York), 19 May 1923.
"Sin and Solitude," in *Western Story* (New York), 26 May 1923.
"A Pal to the Last," in *Western Story* (New York), 21 July 1923.
"Shifted Shirts," in *Western Story* (New York), 4 August 1923.
"Triple Cross for Danger," in *Western Story* (New York), 11 August 1923.
"Ride and Tie," in *Western Story* (New York), 15 September 1923.
"Strained Honey," in *Western Story* (New York), 22 September 1923.
"Bill Talks Big," in *Western Story* (New York), 20 October 1923.
"The Back Trail," in *Western Story* (New York), 17 November 1923.
"The Writing on the Rocks," in *Western Story* (New York), 1 December 1923.
"Peaceful Pete's Yuletide Party," in *Western Story* (New York), 22 December 1923.
"Waitin' for the Coffee to Boil," in *Western Story* (New York), 12 January 1924.
"The Branding of a Tenderfoot," in *Western Story* (New York), 26 January 1924.
"Beans for the Wolf," in *Western Story* (New York), 9 February 1924.
"The Shadow's Slave," in *Western Story* (New York), 16 February 1924.
"When the Wild Roses Bloom," in *Western Story* (New York), 1 March 1924.
"A Dog and a Guess," in *Western Story* (New York), 29 March 1929.
"A Sure-Enough 'Paint' Horse," in *Western Story* (New York), 26 April 1924.
"The Survival of Slim," in *Western Story* (New York), 3 May 1924.
"Bert and Sandy Pay," in *Western Story* (New York), 28 June 1924.
"Worked Brands," in *Adventure* (New York), 20 July 1924.
"A Generous Captor," in *Western Story* (New York), 26 July 1924.
"The Secret of Crutcher's Cabin," in *Western Story* (New York), 20 September 1924.
"Chico," in *Western Story* (New York), 7 February 1925.
"Deuce High," in *Adventure* (New York), 20 March 1925.
"Paid Off," in *Adventure* (New York), 10 July 1925.
"Out of the Hole," in *Adventure* (New York), 20 August 1925.
"Freeze-Out," in *Adventure* (New York), 20 September 1925.
"The Glory Hunter," in *Cowboy Story* (London), November 1926.
"'Hunk' Harmony of Texas," in *Cowboy Story* (London), December 1926.
"Six Times One," in *North-West Stories* (London), Early December 1926.
"The Fallacy of 'Faro,'" in *Adventure* (New York), 23 December 1926.
"Fuzzy of the Flying V," in *Cowboy Story* (London), January 1927.
"While the Bannock Cools," in *North-West Stories* (London), Early January 1927.
"The Yellow Streak," in *Cowboy Story* (London), February 1927.
"Ghosts of Fate," in *North-West Stories* (London), Early February 1927.
"The Deadline," in *Cowboy Story* (London), March 1927.
"Cowboy Cole, U.S.," in *Cowboy Story* (London), April 1927.
"Pay Dirt," in *North-West Stories* (London), Early April 1927.
"Hoorawed," in *Cowboy Story* (London), June 1927.
"Ghost Riders," in *Cowboy Story* (London), July 1927.
"Bounty Money," in *North-West Stories* (London), Early July 1927.
"The Yavapai Kid," in *Cowboy Story* (London), August 1927.
"The Killer," in *Adventure* (New York), 15 August 1927.

"The Wild Bunch," in *Cowboy Story* (London), September 1927.
"Don of the Black Serape," in *North-West Stories* (London), Early September 1927.
"Too Much Mex'," in *West* (New York), 21 January 1928.
"Nothing But the Truth," in *West* (New York), 17 March 1928.
"Longhorn Law," in *Western Story* (New York), 5 May 1928.
"El Caballero," in *Adventure* (New York), 1 June 1928.
"The Man Who Hated Himself," in *Adventure* (New York), 1 July 1928.
"Powder," in *Adventure* (New York), 15 August 1928.
"A Notched Gun," in *Adventure* (New York), 15 November 1928.
"Drought," in *Romance* (New York), December 1928.
"Empty Shells," in *Adventure* (New York), 1 December 1928.
"Young Courage," in *Western Story* (New York), 15 June 1929.
"Out of the Dark," in *Western Story* (New York), 20 July 1929.
"Center-Fire Pride," in *Adventure* (New York), 1 September 1929.
"Range Robbers," in *Western Story* (New York), 14 December 1929.
"Salud, Senor!," in *Adventure* (New York), 1 January 1930.
"The Devil's Pitchfork," in *Western Story* (New York), 20 September 1930.
"His Mother's Brand," in *Western Story* (New York), 11 October 1930.
"Wanted Men," in *Western Story* (New York), 30 May 1931.
"Gun Music," in *West* (New York), 27 April 1932.
"The Pot Hook Trail," in *West* (New York), 22 June 1932.
"Hired and Fired," in *Complete Story* (New York), 1 August 1932.
"Stampede," in *West* (New York), 3 August 1932.
"Fightin' Fools," in *Western Story* (New York), 3 September 1932.
"Water Rights," in *West* (New York), November 1932.
"Thumbs Down," in *Western Story* (New York), 12 November 1932.
"The Mister," in *Adventure* (New York), 1 December 1932.
"Sorry Sam, Cowhand," in *Adventure* (New York), 1 January 1933.
"The Fighting Farleys," in *Western Story* (New York), 14 January 1933.
"Bullets in the Black," in *Western Story* (New York), 18 March 1933.
"The Burnt Ranch," in *Western Story* (New York), 1 April 1933.
"Rope Law," in *Western Story* (New York), 13 May 1933.
"The Rough String," in *All Western* (New York), April 1934.
"Fenced Off," in *Argosy* (New York), 2 June 1934.
"The Rawhide Kid," in *All Western* (New York), July 1934.
"The Squarehead," in *Adventure* (Chicago), 1 September 1934.
"Whoop and Holler," in *All Western* (New York), May 1936.
"Bait for Boothill," in *Western Story* (New York), 19 February 1938.
"Killers of Coyote Pass," in *Western Story* (New York), 19 March 1938.
"Gun Lords of Tortilla Range," in *Western Story* (New York), 16 April 1938.
"Pack Rat Killer," in *Western Story* (New York), 21 May 1938.
"Pasear to Sombrero Butte," in *Western Story* (New York), 4 June 1938.
"Quick Trigger Law," in *Western Story* (New York), 9 July 1938.
"The Sidewinder Strikers," in *Western Story* (New York), 23 July 1938.
"Killers of the Carrizo," in *Western Story* (New York), 10 September 1938.
"Rustlers of the Honda," in *Western Story* (New York), 15 October 1938.
"Badlands Buscadero," in *Western Story* (New York), 19 November 1938.
"Traitor's Brand," in *Western Story* (New York), 14 January 1939.
"Range Orphan," in *Western Story* (New York), 11 February 1939.
"Brand Changers of Outlaws' Pass," in *Western Story* (New York), 18 March 1939.
"The Saga of Big Calico," in *Western Story* (New York), 6 May 1939.
"Heir to the Anchor Brand," in *Western Story* (New York), 27 May 1939.
"Satan Was on His Trail," in *Western Story* (New York), 17 June 1939.
"Nesters at Witch Creek," in *Western Story* (New York), 2 September 1939.
"Gun Wolves of the Badlands," in *Western Story* (New York), 11 November 1939.
"Texas Guns Head North," in *Star Western* (Chicago), September 1940.
"Hell Starts at Gringo Doyle's," in *Star Western* (Chicago), October 1940.
"Gun Boss of Powder River," in *Western Story* (New York), February 1941.
"Bronc-Buster Wanted—Dead or Alive!," in *Star Western* (Chicago), March 1941.
"Bullet-Heir to Cottonwood Valley," in *Star Western* (Chicago), June 1941.
"Night Ride," in *Argosy* (New York), 21 June 1941.
"Border-Jumpin' Buscadero," in *Western Story* (London), August 1941.
"Town Marshal," in *Argosy* (New York), 16 August–23 August 1941.
"Hell's Pitchfork Army," in *Star Western* (Chicago), November 1941.
"Gun-Club Law," in *Star Western* (Chicago), January 1942.
"Caballeros of Doom," in *Western Story* (London), February 1942.
"Three Tough Hands," in *Western Story* (London), April 1942.
"Death Buys a Trail Herd," in *Star Western* (Chicago), April 1942.
"Gunsmoke Makes a Man!," in *Star Western* (Chicago), February 1943.
"Missouri River Gun Talley," in *Star Western* (Chicago), April 1943.
"Partners of Massacre Ranch," in *Star Western* (Chicago), June 1943.
"Manhunt!," in *Star Western* (Chicago), July 1943.
"One More Bronc to Ride," in *Star Western* (Chicago), August 1943.
"Hell's Home Ranch," in *Star Western* (Chicago), September 1943.
"Gun-Courage," in *Star Western* (Chicago), October 1943.
"Rodeo Renegades," in *Star Western* (Chicago), November 1943.
"The Son of Horse Thief Britt," in *Star Western* (Chicago), December 1943.
"Kilbourn Bros.—Wolf Wranglers," in *Western Story* (London), December 1943.
"Cotton Top Gets Tough," in *Star Western* (Chicago), January 1944.
"Tenderfoot Jones," in *Star Western* (Chicago), February 1944.
"Coffins for Fence-Cutters," in *Star Western* (Chicago), March 1944.

"Tougher Than a Boot," in *West* (Kingswood, Surrey), March 1944.
"Bushwhacker Wanted," in *Star Western* (Chicago), April 1944.
"Blood-Money Bronc Twister!," in *West* (Kingswood, Surrey), April 1944.
"Texas Guns—Not for Hire!," in *Star Western* (Chicago), May 1944.
"Gun Welcome to Grass Hills," in *Western Story* (London), May 1944.
"The Hunting of Long Jack Maverty," in *Star Western* (Chicago), June 1944.
"Ghost of the Frontier Battalion," in *West* (Kingswood, Surrey), June 1944.
"The Locoed Kid's Private War," in *Star Western* (Chicago), July 1944.
"Ghosts of the Back Trail," in *Western Story* (London), July 1944.
"The 77's Brand-Blot Army," in *Star Western* (Chicago), August 1944.
"Killers of Rustlers' Roost," in *West* (Kingswood, Surrey), August 1944.
"The Bustling of the Bear Paw Pool," in *Star Western* (Chicago), September 1944.
"The Coffeepot Boils Over," in *Western Story* (London), September 1944.
"The Moccasin Track Incastion," in *Star Western* (Chicago), October 1944.
"Outcast of Murder Ranch," in *West* (Kingswood, Surrey), October 1944.
"Hot-Lead Mortgage—Past Due," in *Star Western* (Chicago), November 1944.
"Coffin-Branded!," in *Star Western* (Chicago), December 1944.
"The Gunsmoke Grubstaker," in *Star Western* (Chicago), January 1945.
"Rawson's Well," in *Western Story* (London), January 1945.
"Bring 'er Back Dead!," in *Star Western* (Chicago), February 1945.
"The Running-Iron Rebels," in *Star Western* (Chicago), March 1945.
"Man-Trap Ranch," in *Star Western* (Chicago), April 1945.
"The Jelly Bean Trail," in *Western Story* (London), April 1945.
"The Saga of Curly Ben," in *Star Western* (Chicago), May 1945.
"Cabin-Fever," in *Star Western* (Chicago), June 1945.
"Bible Ben's Rep," in *Western Story* (London), June 1945.
"Ride West of Buzzard Well!," in *Star Western* (Chicago), July 1945.
"Renegade Ramrods," in *Western Story* (London), July 1945.
"Rocky Point's Bullet-Convention," in *Star Western* (Chicago), August 1945.
"For the Bulls of Jagaral," in *Star Western* (Chicago), September 1945.
"The San Pasqual Float," in *Western Story* (London), September 1945.
"Badlands Gun-Buster," in *Star Western* (Chicago), October 1945.
"The Gunman Who Rode Alone," in *Star Western* (Chicago), November 1945.
"Cold-Decked!," in *Star Western* (Chicago), December 1945.
"Your Badge Is a Target," in *Star Western* (Chicago), January 1946.
"The Man from Nowhere," in *Western Story* (London), January 1946.
"Through Hell's Blazing Deadline," in *Star Western* (Chicago), February 1946.
"Here's Lead in Your Eye!," in *Star Western* (Chicago), March 1946.
"The Long S Rep," in *Western Story* (London), March 1946.
"The Ranch That Death Built," in *Star Western* (Chicago), April 1946.
"Black Dice," in *Star Western* (Chicago), May 1946.
"Hank Garretson's Mistake," in *Western Story* (London), May 1946.
"The Big Ramrod," in *Western Story* (London), July 1946.
"Buckshot Payoff," in *Western Story* (London), September 1946.
"Gunsmoke at the House on Stilts," in *West* (Kingswood, Surrey), September 1946.
"Trail Back to Trouble," in *Western Story* (London), March 1947.
"Lobo Gap," in *Western Story* (London), April 1947.
"Laying the Ghosts at Burnt Ranch," in *West* (Kingswood, Surrey), May 1947.
"Reppin' for the Dead," in *Western Story* (London), July 1947.
"Powder River Pilgrim," in *Western Story* (London), August 1947.
"Sheeped-Out," in *Western Story* (London), November 1947.
"Blocking of Buzzard Pass," in *West* (Kingswood, Surrey), November-December 1947.
"The Mocassin Kid," in *Western Story* (London), December 1947.
"Ride Home to the Hang-Tree!," in *Star Western* (Chicago), December 1947.
"The Orneriest Three," in *Popular Book of Western Stories*, edited by Leo Margulies. New York, Popular Library, 1948.
"Wet Cattle in Gringo Pass!," in *Star Western* (Chicago), January 1948.
"Bench Warrants for the Wind River Gang," in *West* (Kingswood, Surrey), January 1948.
"The Devil's Orphan," in *Star Western* (Chicago), March 1948.
"The T Down Ramrod," in *Western Story* (London), March 1948.
"Sky Pilot's Saga," in *Western Story* (London), July 1948.
"Showdown at the Narrows," in *Western Story* (London), September 1948.
"The Lightning Brand," in *Western Story* (London), November 1948.
"The Gotch-Eared Roan," in *Western Story* (London), January 1949.
"Tenderfoot Tough Hand," in *West* (Kingswood, Surrey), January 1949.
"Guns Across the Rio Grande," in *Western Story* (London), March 1949.
"The Windmill Kid," in *Western Story* (London), May 1949.
"Homesteaders' Havoc," in *Western Story* (London), June 1949.
"Emptied Guns," in *West* (Kingswood, Surrey), July 1949.
"Loco Jones," in *Western Story* (London), September 1949.
"Gringo Stand-Off," in *West* (Kingswood, Surrey), September 1949.
"Mister Pell of the Muleshoe Bar," in *Western Story* (London), January 1950.
"3–7–77," in *Western Story* (London), February 1950.
"Guns in San Marcos Pass," in *West* (Kingswood, Surrey), June 1950.
"Blizzard Rider," in *Western Story* (London), July 1950.
"Saddle Test," in *Western Story* (London), September 1950.
"Secret of Painted Rock," in *Western Story* (London), November 1950.
"The Four T Rep," in *West* (Kingswood, Surrey), December 1950.
"Winner Takes All," in *Western Story* (London), January 1951.

"Tinhorn's Trigger Tryst," in *Western Story* (London), March 1951.
"Payoff at Boundary Town," in *Western Story* (London), May 1951.
"Driftin' South to Trouble," in *Western Story* (London), July 1951.
"Tinhorn Rep," in *Western Story* (London), September, 1951.
"The Horse Thief Trap," in *West* (Kingswood, Surrey), November 1951.
"The Tough Teal Brand," in *Western Story* (London), January 1952.
"Gun Seal on Rustlers Range," in *Western Story* (London), March 1952.
"The Wolfer's Whelp," in *West* (Kingswood, Surrey), April 1952.
"Holed Up under the Rim," in *Western Story* (London), May 1952.
"Sleeper Sid's Tally," in *Western Story* (London), July 1952.
"Cottontail," in *Western Story* (London), September 1952.
"Dead Man's Trail Herd," in *West* (Kingswood, Surrey), September 1952.
"The Cibicu Kid," in *Western Story* (London), November 1952.
"A Ticket to Chinook, Montana," in *West* (Kingswood, Surrey), December 1952.
"The Black Maverick," in *Western Story* (London), January 1953.
"Ride the Wild Trail," in *Western Story* (London), September 1955.
"Gun-Cub's Wildcat—Keep Off!," in *Western Story* (London), February 1959.
"Senor Cow-Thief Runs for Sheriff," in *Western Story* (London), August 1959.
"The Devil Sent His Gun-Angels!," in *Western Story* (London), October 1959.
"Draw Your Pay in Hell!," in *Gunpoint*, edited by Leo Margulies. New York, Pyramid, 1960.
"Free Range—If You Fight for It!," in *Western Story* (London), February 1960.
"Joker Law for Coulee County!," in *Western Story* (London), May–June 1960.
"Pud Ackley, Cowboy," in *Great Stories of the West*, edited by Ned Collier. New York, Doubleday, 1971.
"The Line Camp Terror," in *Westerns of the Forties*, edited by Damon Knight. Indianapolis, Bobbs, Merrill, 1977.

OTHER PUBLICATIONS

Plays

Screenplays: *The Black Trail*, with Isadore Bernstein, 1924; *No Man's Land*, with William E. Wing, 1925; *Pals in Peril*, with Frank L. Inghram, 1927; *The Desert of the Lost*, with Frank L. Inghram, 1927; *The Ridin' Rowdy*, with Frank L. Inghram, 1927.

Other

Pioneer Cattleman in Montana: The Story of the Circle C Ranch. Norman, University of Oklahoma Press, 1968.
Walt Coburn, Western Word Wrangler: An Autobiography. Flagstaff, Arizona, Northland Press, 1973.

*

Manuscript Collection: University of Arizona Library, Tucson.

* * *

In the course of his 30-year career as a writer of pulp Westerns, Walt Coburn dashed off over 800 novelettes totaling almost 20 million words. His method was to write four hours each day, six days a week, usually with a bottle of "hooch" beside the typewriter.

"I sort of went at the job of pulp writing like it was a game I got a big kick out of," Coburn once said. "No set plan of work. Nary an idea in my skull. Kind of a cockeyed, haphazard way of putting down words on paper. I like to have a strong dramatic situation sort of pictured in my mind. Like a stage set. The characters on it. I turned them loose. Let them act out their parts, speak their own dialogue. I made no notes. I had no plot to start with. The plot developed as the yarn unfolded."

After his four hours of writing, Coburn neither thought not talked about his story until the next day's work began. He boasted that in all his years of fiction writing he never rewrote a story. Coburn would have to have been endowed with an exceptional talent for this technique to produce anything but rambling, narrow action stories with paper-thin characters. He was not so blessed. As a result, his Westerns are uneven and sometimes remarkably bad. For example, in one of his poorer efforts, *The Night Branders*, a host of foolish "Texicans" are crudely manipulated through a sequence of incredible coincidence.

Nevertheless, Coburn was not without some merit as a western writer. In an era when New York bellhops were hacking out cowboy stories for credulous pulp audiences, Coburn at least knew what he was writing about. He grew up in the West, on his family's 30,000 acre ranch near Zortman, Montana. He worked as a hand on the ranch until it was sold in 1916. After a stint in the army during World War I, Walt wrangled for a time on his brother's new spread near Globe, Arizona, before a knee injury suffered while roping a bull ended his cowpunching days forever. After a year working odd jobs around San Diego, Coburn began writing Westerns based on bunkhouse tales he had heard in Montana and Arizona. However implausible his plots and characterization, these stories do have an authentic middle ground of ranching practice, hardware, and slang.

Coburn's West is an adolescent fantasy landscape of violence where the gun rules and all good women are virgins. No one dies of old age here, but always from the bullet, the knife, or the rope. And the one true measure of a man is the size of his fist. Preacher Sam Magrath in *The Kansas Killers* is a real man because he once whipped half a dozen boozed-up blasphemers. Doc Steele, the physician of Pay Dirt, Montana, in *Law Rides the Range*, is a good decent citizen, but it is his thrashing of the Clanton boys that establishes him as a man worthy of respect. In the view of Spud Dulin in *The Kansas Killers*, Galt Magrath could "kill off all the rustlers on earth and become President of the States and King of Turkey to boot," and still not equal the deed of smashing Sport McAlister's face and ducking him in a water barrel. With Coburn, a man is hammer or anvil—either gives a beating or takes one. The only alternative is cowardice, and cowards die, invariably. According to Lee Jackson in *Invitation to a Hanging*, "Whenever a man loses his guts, that man is better off dead."

If courage is the essential element of manliness in Coburn's West, virginity is the hallmark of womanhood. His heroines usually resemble pre-pubescent girls: they have "boyish" figures and fall in love at first sight. Coburn's formula for handling female characters has a kind of elegant simplicity: she who fornicates, dies. Kit Kavenaugh, the gambler's daughter in *Law Rides the Range*, is chaste and therefore survives the tale. Maria Magdalena, the Mexican bandit's moll in *Invitation to a Hanging*, is not so fortunate. Before she dies, Maria goes blind and insane.

Courage and virtue are always rewarded in Coburn's stories, and vice punished. The author of this hopeful scheme of cosmic justice is God, working in human events through blood fatalism and occasional direct interventions. Such crucial matters as a man's courage and the hour of his death are determined, we are told, the moment he is born. These are in his blood and nothing he can do can change them. There are, consequently, no conversions or reformations in Coburn, only the steady, inevitable grinding out of God's plan. "I'd read in books," says Almanac Jones in *Law Rides the Range*," where men like Wade have been influenced by a good woman. I could tell them writers that they are all wrong. I've done my best to talk killing out of him, but it's in his blood like a disease. He was bound to go like he went today."

This notion of a just God that shaped human destiny was not merely a convenient tool for shoring up failing plots. Coburn believed that God had been at work in his own life. "The Creator of that breed of man called the cowhand, cowboy and cattleman," he wrote at the end of his career, "for some reason known only to the Señor Dios, selected this cowhand-writer among the chosen few to record the history of that hardy breed of pioneer, be it fiction or fact . . . I know that somewhere along the trail the Señor Dios laid a hand on my shoulder and shaped my destiny. Such is my belief and will continue to be until I follow the ghost rider on the pale horse on my last circle into the Shadow Hills."

—John D. Flanagan

COCHRAN, Jeff. *See* **DURST, Paul.**

CODY, Al. *See* **JOSCELYN, Archie.**

CODY, Jess. *See* **CUNNINGHAM, Chet.**

CODY, John. *See* **REPP, Ed Earl.**

CODY, Stetson. *See* **GRIBBLE, Leonard.**

CODY, Walt. *See* **NORWOOD, V.G.C.**

COLDSMITH, Don(ald C.). American. Born in Iola, Kansas, 28 February 1926. Educated at Baker University, Baldwin, Kansas, A.B. 1949; University of Kansas, Lawrence, M.D. 1958. Served in the United States Army, 1944–46. Married 1) Barbara A. Brown in 1949 (divorced 1960); 2) Edna E. Howell in 1960; five children. Congregational minister, gunsmith, and YMCA youth director, Topeka, Kansas 1949–54; grain inspector; Intern, Bethany Hospital, Kansas City, 1958–59, then physician in general practice, Emporia, Kansas, 1959–90; Adjunct Associate Professor of English, Emporia State University, 1981. Also raises cattle and Appaloosa horses. Address: Route 5, Emporia, Kansas 66801, U.S.A.

WESTERN PUBLICATIONS

Novels (series: Spanish Bit in all books)

Trail of the Spanish Bit. New York, Doubleday, 1980.
Buffalo Medicine. New York, Doubleday, 1981.
The Elk-Dog Heritage. New York, Doubleday, 1982.
Follow the Wind. New York, Doubleday, 1983.
Man of the Shadows. New York, Doubleday, 1983.
Daughter of the Eagle. New York, Doubleday, 1984.
Moon of Thunder. New York, Doubleday, 1985.
The Sacred Hills. New York, Doubleday, 1985.
Pale Star. New York, Doubleday, 1986.
River of Swans. New York, Doubleday, 1986.
Return to the River. New York, Doubleday, 1987.
The Medicine Knife. New York, Doubleday, 1988.
The Flower in the Mountains. New York, Doubleday, 1988.
Trail From Taos. New York, Doubleday, 1989.
Song of the Rock. New York, Doubleday, 1989.
Fort De Chastaigne. New York, Doubleday, 1990.
Quest for the White Bull. New York, Doubleday, 1990.
The Changing Wind. New York, Doubleday, 1990.

Novel (series: Rivers West)

The Smoky Hill. New York, Bantam, 1989.

OTHER PUBLICATIONS

Other

Horsin' Around. San Antonio, Naylor, 1975.
Horsin' Around Again. San Antonio, Corona, 1982.

*

Manuscript Collection: Center for Great Plains Studies, Emporia State University, Kansas.

Don Coldsmith comments:

The initial contacts of Spanish exploration in the New World are well-documented. Less well-known are probing expeditions in the middle 1500's, as far north as central Kansas in the Great Plains. *Trail of the Spanish Bit* and my succeeding novels of the Great Plains are based on the supposition of a young Spanish officer, lost from his unit. He is eventually assimilated into the culture of the native buffalo hunters, to whom he introduces the horse.

The native Americans are represented by "the People," a composite of tribes in the area at the time. Cultural and historical material is completely researched for accuracy. The series proceeds to follow succeeding generations of the People and the descendants of the adopted Spaniard.

* * *

Don Coldsmith's Spanish Bit Saga—which has reached 17 books and one "Super Edition"—presents a unique view of the West. The stories are set in the period 1540–1705, when the Spanish and French were claiming the West for their Empires. Much of the stories are told from the Indian perspective—Coldsmith never refers to them as "Indians," they are The People. Coldsmith admits in his introduction to the first book in the series, *Trail of the Spanish Bit*, that there are few historical records of this time period in American history. But clearly, the reintroduction of the horse into the Americas by the Spanish changed the life the People totally.

Coldsmith got his inspiration for the series when he found a Spanish bit—hundreds of years old—in a barrel of junk outside an old store in northern Oklahoma; Coldsmith bought the bit for a $1.00 and compared it to a similar bit he had seen in a Santa Fe museum displaying equipment from Coronado's 1542 expedition to the American Central Plains. They were the same.

How did the Spanish bit get as far north as Oklahoma? Coldsmith asked himself. *Trail of the Spanish Bit* is his answer to his own question and, in turn, generates a whole series of questions about "first contact" between the People and the Spanish—and later, the French.

Trail of the Spanish Bit introduces Juan Garcia, spoiled only son of a powerful Spanish patriarch. Juan, in order to escape punishment after a failed seduction, is offered a position in the New World. He accepts and finds himself part of his commandant's obsession with finding gold. On an expedition far to the north, Juan is thrown from his horse and sustains a head injury. The other Spanish soldiers search for Juan, but failing to find him and disappointed by the lack of gold, head south again.

Juan is watched by Coyote, one of the cleverest characters Coldsmith has created. Where some of the others want to kill Juan, Coyote convinces them to spare him so he can be studied. Almost as interesting as Juan is Juan's horse, which the People called an "elk-dog." Coyote establishes contact with Juan, teaches him hand signals, and begins the learning process. Juan changes from considering the People as "miserable savages" to appreciating their subtle culture and their knowledge of the prairie.

The strength of *Trail of the Spanish Bit* is shown clearly in Chad Oliver's "Afterward" to the paperback edition. Oliver calls *Trail of the Spanish Bit* "a tale of the coming of the horse to North America, but it is more than that. It is a story that introduces us to the human beings who lived here before we did."

Coldsmith's expert knowledge of horses is clear in all the books in the series. His own experiences in World War II in a pack artillery battery at Fort Sill and his series of articles on horses collected in *Horsin' Around* and *Horsin' Around Again* display his vast knowledge and experience. Perhaps the greatest narrative drive in the series is the impact the introduction of the horse has on the way of life of the People. The People change from a passive, sometimes starving band to a powerful force that rules the prairie, the change almost entirely due to their mastery of the horse.

The flaw in the first few books of the Spanish Bit Saga is Coldsmith's pacing: he hurries the changes that must have taken generations into a few years. He overcomes this flaw by *Moon of Thunder* and *The Sacred Hills*. The pace is much more leisurely by this time and the action becomes much more believable. By the time the reader gets to one of the latest book in the series, *Fort De Chastaigne*, the effects of the Spanish and the French on the People are startling.

In *Fort De Chastaigne*, the French, led by Captain LeFever—a young man similar to Juan Garcia in *Trail of the Spanish Bit*—and with the help of medicine man White Fox and his son Red Horse, travel on the Missouri River to set up trade with the Spanish. But a band of *voyageurs* ruin the Captain's mission and force a retreat back to Fort De Chastaigne where even more treachery almost destroys the settlement. The ending, as with most of the books in the series, concludes most of the subplots but leaves a few open for the next book in the series.

Perhaps the finest book Coldsmith has written to date is the "Super Edition" requested by his editor at Bantam Books as a "spin-off novel supplement" to the Spanish Bit Saga. Coldsmith selects White Buffalo, the greatest medicine man the People have ever had—and a critical character in the early books of the series—and places him in the path of *The Changing Wind* which is the transformation of the People by the new technology of the horse. This is truly an epic story of the changing culture of the People and includes some of Coldsmith's best writing.

Coldsmith's versatility can be seen in *The Smoky Hill*, of the Rivers West Series. Coldsmith's description of the Booth family's part in the westward expansion into Kansas and Nebraska features some of his strongest storytelling.

—George Kelley

COLE, Hank. *See* **FEARN, John Russell.**

COLE, Jackson. *See* **CURRY, Tom; HECKELMANN, Charles N.**

COLE, Laramee. *See* **GRIBBLE, Leonard**

COLE, Robert. *See* **SNOW, Charles H.**

COLEMAN, Buck. *See* **RICHARDSON, Gladwell.**

COLSON, Bill. *See* **ATHANAS, Verne.**

COLSON, Laramie. *See* **RICHARDSON, Gladwell.**

COLT, Clem. *See* **NYE, Nelson.**

COLTER, Shayne. *See* **NORWOOD, V.G.C.**

COLTMAN, Will. *See* **BINGLEY, David Ernest.**

COMFORT, Will Levington. American. Born in Kalamazoo, Michigan, 17 January 1878. Served in the United States Cavalry in the Spanish-American War. Married to Adith Duffie-Mulholland; one son and two daughters. Newspaperman, Cincinnati, 1890's; war correspondent in Philippines for Detroit *Journal*, and in Japan and Russia for Pittsburgh *Dispatch*, 1904. *Died 2 November 1932.*

WESTERN PUBLICATIONS

Novels

Routledge Rides Alone. Philadelphia, Lippincott, 1910.
Somewhere South of Sonora. Boston, Houghton Mifflin, 1925.
Apache. New York, Dutton, 1931; as *Magnus Colorado*, London, Stein and Gollancz, 1931.

Short Stories

Trooper Tales: A Series of Sketches of the Real American Private Soldier. New York, Street and Smith, 1899.

Uncollected Short Stories

"Sheriff of Contention," in *Lippincott's* (Philadelphia), March 1906.
"Senor Jim," in *Lippincott's* (Philadelphia), February 1907.
"Old Lights from the Rio Brava," in *Lippincott's* (Philadelphia), August 1907.
"The Tree, The Rope, and the Man," in *Lippincott's* (Philadelphia), March 1909.
"And Away They Galloped Together," in *Lippincott's* (Philadelphia), June 1909.
"A Cabin and a Claim," in *Lippincott's* (Philadelphia), June 1910.
"Mellon Drops a Partner," in *Lippincott's* (Philadelphia), June 1914.
"Outside of a Horse," in *Saturday Evening Post* (Philadelphia), 11 July 1925.
"Hard-Rock Men," in *Adventure* (New York), 10 February 1926.
"The Devil of Eldareb," in *Star* (New York), August 1931.

OTHER PUBLICATIONS

Novels

The Lady of Fallen Star Island. New York, Street and Smith, and London, Shurmer Sibthorp, 1902.
She Buildeth Her House. Philadelphia, Lippincott, 1911.
Fate Knocks at the Door. Philadelphia, Lippincott, 1912.
Down among Men. New York, Doran, 1913; London, Hodder and Stoughton, 1914.
The Road of Living Men. Philadelphia, Lippincott, 1913.
Sport of Kings. Philadelphia, Lippincott, 1913.
Lost and Company. New York, Doran, 1915.
Red Fleece. New York, Doran, 1915; London, Heinemann, 1916.
The Last Ditch. New York, Doran, 1916.
The Shielding Wing. Boston, Small Maynard, 1918.
The Yellow Lord. New York, Doran, 1919.
Magic Hours: A Romance of the East and the Desert. London, Nash, 1920.
Son of Power, with Zamin Ki Dost. New York, Doubleday, 1920; London, Butterworth, 1922.
This Man's World. New York, Doubleday, 1921.
The Public Square. New York, Appleton, 1923.
Samadhi. Boston, Houghton Mifflin, 1927.
The Pilot Comes Aboard. New York, Dutton, 1932; London, Jarrolds, 1933.

Other

Fatherland, with *The Army of the Dead*, by Barry Pain. New York, Doran, 1914.
Midstream: A Chronicle at Halfway. New York, Doran, 1914.
Child and Country: A Book of the Younger Generation. New York, Doran, and London, Hodder and Stoughton, 1916; excerpt, as *A Man Is at His Best*, privately printed, 1953.
The Hive. New York, Doran, 1918.
Nine Great Little Books. Privately printed, 1920.
The Will Levington Comfort Letters. Privately printed, 2 vols., 1920–21.

* * *

Will Levington Comfort was at his best when writing about the frontier life of a cavalryman in the West and Southwest. His *Trooper Tales: A Series of Sketches of the Real American Private Soldier* contains stories about "soldiering" in Army camps from the Rio Grande to San Juan Hill. The tales are of life in the cavalry from the viewpoint of a recruit or private. Comfort mixes facts with fiction to tell his stories, and each, complete in itself, is about black and white recruits in camp and in battle. There is the black trooper in the Black Horse Troop who "could sing like a woman," and who was called "Sadie" by the men. There was Sheridan, a handsome black three-year-old gelding that became one of the best cavalry horses in the service. Sheridan tells part of his story, and the other part is told by the author–recruit who rode him. If one does not know what happens to old cavalry horses, one needs to read the tale "The Story of a Cavalry Horse." Comfort's introduction to the book concerns the black cavalry.

Apache (UK title *Magnus Colorado*) is a historical novel of note. It is a fictional study of one of the first Apaches to come in contact with white men—first with miners, then with the U.S. Army. Comfort's picture is a non-idealized portrait which pictures the great chief Mangus Colorado without any concession to western romanticism, and also without any sociological explanation. The result is a brilliant portrait, and proved Comfort to be a pioneer in his veracity and insight. The *Times Literary Supplement* reviewer found the novel to be in a class with La Farge's *Laughing Boy*. Comfort wrote some 25 other books covering a variety of subjects from ships and shipwrecks (often using a sailor hero) to the education of children.

—Dorys C. Grover

CONISTON, Ed. *See* **BINGLEY, David Ernest.**

CONLEY, Robert J(ackson). American. Born in Cushing, Oklahoma, 29 December 1940. Educated at Midwestern University, Wichita Falls, Texas, B.A. 1966, M.A. 1968. Served in the United States Marine Corps Reserve, 1958–64. Married Evelyn Snell in 1978. Instructor in English, Northern Illinois University, DeKalb, 1968–71, and Southwest Missouri State University, Springfield, 1971–74; coordinator of Indian culture, Eastern Montana College, Billings, 1975–77; assistant programs director, Cherokee Nation of Oklahoma, 1977–78; affiliate, Native American Studies program, Bacone College, Muskogee, Oklahoma, 1978–79. Since 1979 director of Indian Studies, Morningside College, Sioux City, Iowa. Address: P.O. Box 1871, Taclequah, Oklahoma 74465, U.S.A.

WESTERN PUBLICATIONS

Novels

Back to Malachi. New York, Doubleday, 1986.
The Actor. New York, Doubleday, 1987.
Killing Time. New York, Evans, 1988.
The Saga of Henry Starr. New York, Doubleday, 1989.
Colfax. New York, Doubleday, 1989.
Quitting Time. New York, Evans, 1989; London, Hale, 1990.

Short Stories

The Witch of Goingsnake, and Other Stories. Norman, University of Oklahoma Press, 1988.

Verse

Twenty-One Poems. N.p., Aux Ares Press, 1975.
Adawosgi, Swimmer Wesley Snell: A Cherokee Memorial. Marvin, South Dakota, Blue Cloud, 1980.
The Rattlesnake Band and Other Poems. Muskogee, Oklahoma, Indian University Press, 1984.

* * *

When a Cherokee Indian walks onto the page in Robert J. Conley's fiction, the plot takes new twists, the characters experience a deeper irony in their situations, and complex action intensifies. The rich characterization most likely stems from Conley's own Cherokee heritage, which gives him an awareness of the personal problems and attitudes these characters must identify and resolve—or fail to resolve.

The marginal man straddling the line between two conflicting cultures is a typical theme in Conley's work. Cherokee characters wrestle to understand the white and Indian roles within a changing society that is not allowing time for an evolution. Relationships within cultures are also splintered: the post-Confederate era has divided whites on personal and political levels; the Cherokee Nation struggles to achieve harmony between those who would follow traditional paths and those who would travel trails blazed by white people.

In *Back to Malachi*, one of Conley's earlier novels, the characters include full-blooded Cherokees who are refusing to interact with the whites, mixed-bloods who are striving to be white, full-blooded whites, some of whom accept Cherokee rights, most of whom don't and everyone in between. The younger generation is especially trapped between these worlds. Mose Pathkiller, who loves the work of Lord Byron, is driven farther and farther from the white world and rebounds into his own private war to defend Cherokee rights, thus becoming a famous "outlaw." Charlie Blackbird, whose shopkeeper father uses the name Black, struggles for personal identity, white or Indian. He staggers from one extreme—following an outlaw trail—to another-living as a white shopkeeper. It isn't until the end of the book that Blackbird discovers a harmonious solution, one which is not his father's way, nor Pathkiller's way, but within the traditions of Cherokee heritage as taught by Pathkiller's father, Malachi.

In the best of Conley's books, there are no readily identifiable heroes or villians. These are people simply trying to survive an era of transition, struggling to find their own ways. They are sometimes cruel, often angry and frustrated, as well as loving and compassionate.

After characterization, plot is the strongest lure into Conley's West. Rarely do these works follow a monotone plot line typical of some Westerns. In *Quitting Time* there is a basic western plot: the large ranchers confront smaller, incoming groups whom they accuse of rustling; a range war is developing. Yet a secondary plot develops as a detective story when someone begins murdering Shakespearean actors in town for a production of *Titus Andronicus.* Colfax—the ethical hired gun who is also a Shakespeare fan—must discover the murderer at the same time he investigates the rustling. Meanwhile a love story develops as Colfax falls for one of the actresses.

Conley obviously enjoys detective fiction—rarely are murders street gunfights. In *Go-Ahead Rider*, the marginal man, recent Harvard graduate George Tanner, returns to the Cherokee Nation, unsure what to do with his life. Local events plunge him into the role of deputy to Go-Ahead Rider. Together they investigate the trail of a murderer who has killed a councilman opposed to bringing the railroad to town, then tried to frame a local man.

The issue of right and wrong blurs in these western tales. With the exception of Colfax's friend, Sheriff Luton, most white sheriffs tend to be dumb or cruel; Cherokee lawmen make mistakes and misjudge people but strive to be fair and honest. And in *Killing Time* Luton is almost too good, a hero whose virtue actually inspires Colfax, a hired killer, not to shoot him; this is plausible only because the author establishes that Colfax is a killer who must convince himself over and over that humans are basically evil and therefore deserve death. In this novel Colfax turns detective to try to find Luton's "fatal flaw."

Humor generally arises out of the juxtaposition of contradictory situations or people, such as the Harvard graduate trying to become a Cherokee law officer in *Go-Ahead Rider.* Within the short story collection, *The Witch of Goingsnake, and Other Stories*, the humor often becomes more rambunctious and is frequently enhanced by magic. In one story the title character, Wili Woyi, leads white lawmen on an endless search through his protective magic which is funny and harmless; since Wili Woyi is not guilty of anything deserving hanging, the reader must laugh when the desperate deputies declare an unidentified body Wili Woyi's just so they can stop hunting him. Generally the 17 stories in this collection are more literary than the novels, which are well within the genre of action western.

Conley's work is unlike that of many Native American authors in that a sense of place is often lost; we know our geographic location only because we are told. Mountains exist without regard to surrounding elevations affecting flora or fauna. Characters wander through brush or stickers or across rocks or creeks but there is little sense that anyone knows scrub oak from willow or granite from shale. Ironically, the most detailed landscape appears in the mostly-white Colfax novels: *Killing Time*, *Quitting Time*, and *Colfax*. This may be both because the characters travel and note landscape out of railroad car windows and because Colfax must determine how to stalk characters across different landscapes.

Readers will also miss the presence of indepth female characters. Women tend to be "good women" who are family-oriented, or whores and witches with bad attitudes. Particularly in *The Witch of Goingsnake, and Other Stories*, witches who are healers or contributors to society tend to be male; female Cherokee witches do more damage than good. The notable exception is in *Colfax*; Luton's romantic connection, Emily, is present and active often enough to develop as a character.

Any of Conley's work offers a "good read" with intriguing plots, plenty of action, and characters worth remembering. It's interesting to note that all of his book length fiction has been published since 1986; this argues that we can look forward to an impressive compilation of western fiction by this author.

—Marian Blue

CONNOR, Ralph. Pseudonym for Charles William Gordon. Canadian. Born in Indian Lands, Glengarry County, Ontario, 13 September 1860. Educated at St. Mary's High School, Ontario; University of Toronto, B.A. 1883; Knox College, Toronto, B.D. 1887; New College, Edinburgh, 1893–94. Served as a Major (Senior Chaplain) in the Canadian Army and British Expeditionary Force, 1915–18: mentioned in despatches, 1916. Married Helen Skinner King in 1899; one son and six daughters. High school teacher, Chatham, Ontario, 1884–86; teacher, Upper Canadian College, Toronto, 1886–87; ordained Presbyterian Minister, 1890; missionary, Northwest Territories, 1890–93; Minister, St. Stephen's Church, Winnipeg, 1894–1937. Chair, Joint Council of Industry, Province of Manitoba, 1920–24; moderator, Presbyterian Church of Canada, 1921–22. D.D.: Knox College, Kingston, Ontario, 1906. Fellow, Royal Society of Canada, 1904; Companion of the Order of St. Michael and St. George, 1935. *Died 31 October 1937.*

WESTERN PUBLICATIONS

Novels

Gwen's Canyon. Toronto, Westminster, 1898.
Beyond the Marshes. Toronto, Westminster, 1898; Chicago, Revell, 1900.
Black Rock: A Tale of the Selkirks. Toronto, Westminster, New York, Crowell, and London, Hodder and Stoughton, 1898.
The Sky Pilot: A Tale of the Foothills. Toronto, Westminster, Chicago, Revell, and London, Hodder and Stoughton, 1899.
Michael McGrath, Postmaster. London, Sharpe, 1900.
The Prospector: A Tale of Crow's Nest Pass. Toronto, Westminster, 1901; Chicago, Revell, and London, Hodder and Stoughton, 1904.
The Man from Glengarry. Toronto, Westminster, and Chicago, Revell, 1901.
Glengarry School Days: A Story of Early Days in Glengarry (for children). Toronto, Westminster, and Chicago, Revell, 1902; as *Glengarry Days*, London, Hodder and Stoughton, 1902.
The Swan Creek Blizzard. Chicago, Revell, 1904.
Gwen: An Idyll of the Canyon. Chicago, Revell, and London, Hodder and Stoughton, 1904.
Breaking the Record. New York, Revell, 1904.
The Doctor: A Tale of the Rockies. Toronto, Westminster, and Chicago, Revell, 1906; as *The Doctor of Crow's Nest*, London, Hodder and Stoughton, 1906.
The Settler: A Tale of Saskatchewan. New York and London, Hodder and Stoughton, 1906; as *The Foreigner: A Tale of Saskatchewan*, Toronto, Westminster, New York, Doran, and London, Hodder and Stoughton, 1909.
Corporal Cameron: A Tale of the North-West Mounted Police. Toronto, Westminster, and New York, Hodder and Stoughton, 1909.
The Patrol of the Sun Dance Trail. New York, Doran, and London, Hodder and Stoughton, 1914.
The Major. Toronto and New York, McClelland and Stewart, and London, Hodder and Stoughton, 1917.
To Him That Hath. New York, Doran, 1921; London, Hodder and Stoughton, 1922; Toronto, McClelland and Stewart, 1928.
The Gaspards of Pine Croft: A Romance of the Windermere. Toronto, McClelland and Stewart, New York, Doran, and London, Hodder and Stoughton, 1923.
Treading the Winepress. Toronto, McClelland and Stewart, New York, Doran, and London, Hodder and Stoughton, 1925.
The Runner: A Romance of the Niagaras. Toronto and New York, Doubleday, 1929; London, Hodder and Stoughton, 1930.
The Rock and the River: A Romance of Quebec. Toronto, McClelland and Stewart, and New York, Dodd Mead, 1931; London, Lane, 1932.
The Arm of Gold—le Bras d'or. Toronto, McClelland and Stewart, and New York, Dodd Mead, 1932; London, Lane, 1933.
The Girl from Glengarry. Toronto, McClelland and Stewart, and New York, Dodd Mead, 1933; as *The Glengarry Girl*, London, Lane, 1934.
Torches Through the Bush: A Tale of Glengarry. Toronto, McClelland and Stewart, and New York, Dodd Mead, 1934; London, Lane, 1935.
The Rebel Loyalist. Toronto, McClelland and Stewart, and New York, Dodd Mead, 1935; London, Lane, 1936.
He Dwelt Among Us. Toronto, McClelland and Stewart, New York, Revell, and London, Hodder and Stoughton, 1936.
The Gay Crusader: A Romance of Quebec. Toronto, McClelland and Stewart, and New York, Dodd Mead, 1936.

Short Stories

The Pilot at Swan Creek. London, Hodder and Stoughton, 1905.
The Friendly Four and Other Stories. New York, Doran, 1926; London, Hodder and Stoughton, 1927.

OTHER PUBLICATIONS

Other

The Life of James Robertson, Missionary Superintendent in the Northwest Territories (as Charles William Gordon). Toronto, Westminster, Chicago, Revell, and London, Hodder and Stoughton, 1908.
The Angel and the Star. Toronto, Westminster, Chicago, Revell, and London, Hodder and Stoughton, 1908.
The Dawn by Galilee: A Story of the Christ. Toronto, Westminster, and New York and London, Hodder and Stoughton, 1909.
The Recall of Love: A Message of Hope. Toronto, Westminster, and New York and London, Hodder and Stoughton, 1910.
Christian Hope. London, Hodder and Stoughton, 1912.
A Fight for Freedom. Toronto, McClelland and Stewart, 1917.
Postscript to Adventure: The Autobiography of Ralph Connor—Charles W. Gordon, edited by J. King Gordon. New York, Farrar and Rinehart, and London, Hodder and Stoughton, 1938.

*

Critical Study: *Charles William Gordon* by Keith Wilson, Winnipeg, Manitoba, Peguis, 1981.

* * *

Ralph Connor's novels seem to be the quintessence of corniness today, as dated as Dudley Doright. Even his best novels of the lumbering and mining camps of the Canadian Northwest such as *Black Rock: A Tale of the Selkirks*, *The Sky Pilot*, and *The Man from Glengarry*, in which muscular Christians and saintly women triumph melodramatically over moral backsliders, seem implausible and formulaic today, while the alternation in tone between didacticism and sentimentality seems overtly manipulative. Similarly, his heroes' sexual abnegation in the name of religious morality seems unreal, their enthusiasm for violence in the name of the Prince of Peace quite unpersuasive, and their Scots-Canadian ethnocentricity, with its overtones of manifest destiny and cultural imperialism, xenophobic to the contemporary sensibility. Perhaps only the truly great writer can escape the literary conventions of his day to write for the ages, but the qualities that once made Connor Canada's most popular author with sales of five million are precisely those that alienate the modern reader, whose view is likely to be that, apart from a certain skill in narrative and local color description, Connor is mainly of sociological interest as a writer of western idylls offering temporary escape to eastern readers worried by social problems of the new industrial age.

Clearly, though, Connor satisfied several different needs of his readers. Not only could they share vicariously in a life of adventure, but they could glean information helpful in deciding whether to emigrate to the newly developing West. If Connor's enthusiastic descriptions sound more like advertising copy for the Canadian Pacific Railroad than practical guides for emigrants, he nonetheless reinforced the post-Confederation desire to believe that the future of the new young nation was bright. In that less cynical and simpler age, the appeal of Connor's heroes lay in their dedication to hard work and upright Christianity, their clear-eyed and confident moral judgments, and their belief that the Protestant ethic of honesty and justice could solve every problem. Not only was Connor representative of the Canadian sensibility of his time, but he interpreted the western experience in a manner congenial to it.

Connor's imaginative legacy lies in his articulation of the Canadian version of the myth of the West. His millennialistic vision of a morally redeemed empire in the West now seems naive and quaint, but it was inspired by a not ignoble quest for transcendent meaning in the drama of the Canadian West. It is this search for transcendence that gives Connor's fiction whatever residual power it possesses today. Connor believed that western development would provide the best means for deployment of the energies of the new nation and help resolve social conflict stemming from ethnic, class, and religious differences. The "elect" who would lead the new kingdom of God in the West, and provide a necessary cultural link with the east, were Connor's exemplary men from Glengarry, a Highlanders' enclave of Calvinism and true pioneer grit on the Ottawa River in Ontario. As set forth in *The Man from Glengarry* and *Glengarry School Days*, Connor's myth of Glengarry as a transportable Calvinist Camelot—a microcosm of institutions, values, and ways of doing things that would serve as a model for a western empire—typified the eastern view of the West for many decades in Canada. It is not so much that Connor had the wrong myth of the West, but that the myth failed him as it has every westering dreamer from the time of Columbus and indeed from earliest antiquity. That Connor sensed as much but could not admit it to himself or his readers is suggested by the declining vitality of the many books written after the first and best three mentioned above. The once-reliable formula slowly atrophies, the transcendent vision dims, causing the characters to seem more exaggerated, the plots more unbelievable, and the mixture of virtue and violence more meretricious than ever.

—John H. Ferres

CONROY, Al. *See* **ALBERT, Marvin H.**

CONROY, Jim. *See* **CHADWICK, Joseph.**

CONSTINER, Merle. American. Born in Monroe, Ohio, in 1902. Educated at Vanderbilt University, Nashville, Tennessee, M.A. Contributor to action magazines in the 1940's; columnist for *Saturday Evening Post*, *Colliers*, *Adventure*, and *Argosy*. *Died 24 September 1979.*

WESTERN PUBLICATIONS

Novels

Last Stand at Anvil Pass. New York, Fawcett, 1957; London, Fawcett, 1958.
The Fourth Gunman. New York, Ace, 1958.
Short-Trigger Man. New York, Ace, 1964.
Wolf on Horseback. New York, Ace, 1965.
Guns at Q Cross. New York, Ace, 1965.
Outrage at Bearskin Forks. New York, Ace, 1966.
Rain of Fire. New York, Ace, 1966.

Top Gun from the Dakotas. New York, Ace, 1966.
The Action at Redstone Creek. New York, Ace, 1967.
Two Pistols South of Deadwood. New York, Ace, 1967.
Killer's Corral. New York, Ace, 1968.
Steel-Jacket. New York, Ace, 1972; London, Severn House, 1978.
The Four from Gila Bend. New York, Ace, 1974.

Uncollected Short Stories

"Rightful Owner," in *Short Stories*, July 1949.
"The Lady and the Tumblers," in *The Argosy Book of Adventure Stories*, edited by Rogers Terrill. New York, Barnes, 1952.
"Trail Trap," in *Great Westerns from The Saturday Evening Post*, edited by Julie Eisenhower. Indianapolis, Curtis, 1976.
"The Turkey Buzzard Blues," in *The Hard-Boiled Detective*, edited by Herbert Ruhm. New York, Vintage, 1977.

OTHER PUBLICATIONS

Novel

Hearse of a Different Color. New York, Phoenix Press, 1952.

Other (for children)

Meeting at the Merry Fifer. New York, Norton, 1966.
The Rebel Courier and the Redcoats. New York, Meredith Press, 1968.
Sumatra Alley. Camden, New Jersey, Nelson, 1971.

* * *

Merle Constiner learned his craft in the pulp magazines, where for the most part he wrote detective and historical adventure stories throughout the 1940's and early 1950's. With the exceptions of a book-length version of a pulp detective serial (*Hearse of a Different Color*, 1952) and two western novels (*Last Stand at Anvil Pass*, 1957, and *The Fourth Gunman*, 1958), he limited his output to short juvenile fiction and an occasional slick magazine story until the early 1960's, when he turned to the writing of full-length westerns on a regular basis. (The best of his short work is probably "Trail Trap," which originally appeared in *The Saturday Evening Post*—an unusual blend of the traditional western with the detective story, the love story, and the tale of a young man's coming of age.)

Noteworthy among Constiner's novels are his first, *Last Stand at Anvil Pass*, and such later works as *Wolf on Horseback*, *Short-Trigger Man*, and *Steel-Jacket*. The last is a particularly good tale of a tough but soft-hearted drifter who, against his better judgment, agrees to shepherd a young girl through the Oklahoma-Indian Territory in search of her father's stolen gold.

Constiner's work is distinguished by his attention to historical detail (both geographical and social) and a clipped, no-wasted-words style well-spiced with wry humor. Although his characters tend to become involved in more or less conventional situations, they do not act or react quite like any others in western fiction. For these reasons, and for pure entertainment value, Constiner's books are well worth seeking out in secondhand stores.

—Bill Pronzini

CONWAY, John. *See* **CHADWICK, Joseph.**

COOK, Will(iam Everett). Also wrote as Charlie Boomhauer; Wade Everett; James Keene; Frank Peace; Dan Riordan. Born in 1921. Joined the Army Cavalry at age 16; served as a pilot during World War II. Worked as a pilot and deputy sheriff; then freelance writer. *Died in July 1964.*

WESTERN PUBLICATIONS

Novels

Frontier Feud. New York, Popular Library, 1954.
Prairie Guns. New York, Popular Library, 1954.
Fury at Painted Rock. New York, Popular Library, 1955; London, Hale, 1958.
Apache Ambush. New York, Dodd Mead, 1955; London, Corgi, 1958.
Bullet Range. New York, Popular Library, 1955.
Sabrina Kane: A Novel of Frontier Illinois. New York, Dodd Mead, 1956.
The Fighting Texan. New York, Popular Library, 1956.
Trumpets of the West. New York, Popular Library, 1956.
Easy Money (as Frank Peace). New York, Permabooks, 1956.
The Brass Brigade (as Frank Peace). New York, Permabooks, 1956.
Lone Hand from Texas. New York, Popular Library, 1957.
Badman's Holiday. New York, Fawcett, 1958.
Guns of North Texas. New York, Fawcett, 1958; London, Fawcett, 1960.
The Wind River Kid. New York, Fawcett, 1958; London, Gold Lion, 1974.
Elizabeth, By Name. New York, Dodd Mead, 1958.
Outcast of Cripple Creek. New York, Fawcett, 1959.
Killer Behind a Badge. New York, Avon, 1960; London, Corgi, 1961.
The Wranglers. New York, Fawcett, 1960; London, Muller, 1961.
Comanche Captives. New York, Bantam, 1960; as *Two Rode Together*, Bantam, and London, Mills and Boon, 1961.
Ambush at Antler's Spring. New York, Beacon, 1962; London, Tandem, 1965.
The Peacemakers. New York, Bantam, 1961.
The Tough Texan. New York, Bantam, 1963.
The Breakthrough. New York, Macmillan, 1963.
The Speed Merchants. New York, Duell, 1964.
Last Command. New York, Fawcett, 1964.
The Outcasts. New York, Bantam, 1965.
The Apache Fighter. New York, Bantam, 1967.
The Drifter. New York, Bantam, 1969.
Bandit's Trail. New York, Doubleday, 1974.

Novels as James Keene

The Texas Pistol. New York, Random House, 1955; London, Corgi, 1957.
The Brass and the Blue. New York, Random House, 1956; London, Corgi, 1957.
Justice, My Brother! New York, Random House, 1957; London, Corgi, 1958.
Gunman's Harvest. New York, Dell, 1957.
Seven for Vengeance. New York, Random House, 1958.
McCracken in Command. New York, Dell, 1959.

Posse from Gunlock. London, Long, 1959.
Sixgun Wild. New York, Avon, 1960.
Iron Man, Iron Horse. New York, Doubleday, 1960; London, Corgi, 1961.
Gunnison's Empire. New York, Avon, 1963.

Novels as Wade Everett

First Command. New York, Ballantine, 1959; London, Corgi, 1960.
Fort Starke. New York, Ballantine, 1959; London, Corgi, 1960.
Last Scout. New York, Ballantine, 1960; London, Ward Lock, 1963.
Big Man, Big Mountain. New York, Ballantine, 1961; London, Corgi, 1962.
The Big Drive. New York, Ballantine, 1962; London, Collins, 1964.
Killer. New York, Ballantine, 1962; London, Collins, 1963.
Shotgun Marshal. New York, Ballantine, and London, Collins, 1964.
Temporary Duty. New York, Ballantine, and London, Consul, 1964.
Texas Ranger. New York, Ballantine, 1964; London, Collins, 1966.
Top Hand. New York, Ballantine, 1964; London, Collins, 1965.
Cavalry Recruit. New York, Ballantine, 1965; London, Collins, 1967.
Bullets for the Doctor. New York, Ballantine, 1965; London, Collins, 1966.
Texas Yankee. New York, Ballantine, 1966; London, Collins, 1968.
Vengeance. New York, Ballantine, 1966; London, Collins, 1967.
The Warrior. New York, Ballantine, 1967; London, Collins, 1968.
The Horse Trader. New York, Ballantine, 1968.
Broken Gun. New York, Ballantine, 1970.

Uncollected Short Stories

"Half Past Killing Time," in *Max Brand's Western Magazine*, March 1953.
"A Dime's Worth of Rope" (as William Everett Cook), in *15 Western Tales*, May 1953.
"Sixty Miles to Laramie," in *Big-Book Western* (New York), May 1953.
"The Nesters Ride Tonight!," in *Dime Western* (New York), July 1953.
"The Devil's Roundup" (as Frank Peace), in *Dime Western* (New York), July 1953.
"Final Warning" (as Frank Peace), in *Dime Western* (New York), July 1953.
"Night Marshall" (as Frank Peace), in *Western Story* (New York), August 1953.
"Hunt the Man Down!," in *10-Story Western*, August 1953.
"Deadlier than the Male," in *Star Western* (Chicago), August 1953.
"Girl for a Fighting Man," in *Western Story* (London), August 1953.
"The Barb Wire War," in *Western Story* (London), September 1953.
"The Devil's Daughter," in *Western Story* (London), October 1953.
"Drive the Rails Through!," in *10 Story Western*, October 1953.
"Boothill for One," in *Western Ace-High Stories*, October 1953.
"Blood of the Gunborn," in *Max Brand's Western Magazine*, November 1953.
"Born to Hang," in *Dime Western* (New York), November 1953.
"Bullet Quick," in *New Western*, November 1953.
"No Quarter!," in *.44 Western*, November 1953.
"Lawmen Die Sudden!," in *Big-Book Western* (New York), November 1953.
"One Man's Rope," in *Western Story* (London), January 1954.
"The Range That Hell Forgot," in *Dime Western* (New York), January 1954.
"Hang the Man High!," in *Big Book Western* (New York), January 1954.
"Ride Clear of Texas Guns!," in *Dime Western* (New York), January 1954.
"The Failure," in *Star Western* (Chicago), February 1954.
"Blood Sky," in *Western Story* (London), March 1954.
"Brand Her Bad!" (as Frank Peace), in *Star Western* (Chicago), April 1954.
"Rustler's Woman," in *Star Western* (Chicago), April 1954.
"Death Is My Business!," in *Big Book Western* (New York), May 1954.
"A Gun for Satan's Range," in *.44 Western*, May 1954.
"The Big Kill," in *Western Story* (London), May 1954.
"Blood Call," in *Western Story* (London), June 1954.
"The Gunborn Kid" (as Wade Everett), in *New Western*, August 1954.
"Fury at Painted Rock" (novel), in *Ranch Romances* (New York), 24 September 1954.
"Satan's Outpost," in *Western Story* (London), October 1954.
"Wayside Interlude," in *Ranch Romances* (New York), 19 November 1954.
"Bullet Range" (as Dan Riordan), in *Ranch Romances* (New York), 11 February 1955.
"All Trails End at Yuma," in *Western Story* (London), February 1955.
"Boothill for One," in *Western Story* (London), April 1955.
"The Wild Land," in *Western Story* (London), November 1955.
"Lesson in Lead," in *Western Story* (London), December 1955.
"The Contest," in *The Fall Roundup*, edited by H. E. Maule. New York, Random House, 1955.
"The Sheriff's Lady," in *Western Story* (London), October 1956.
"Wildcat on the Prod!," in *Western Story* (London), November 1956.
"The Fight at Renegade Basin," in *3-Book Western* (New York), February 1957.
"Renegade Wipe-Out," in *Western* (New York), October 1957.
"The Gun Job" (as Wade Everett), in *Top Western Stories.* New York, Popular Library, 1964.
"A Gunman Came to Town," in *Great Westerns from the Saturday Evening Post*, edited by Julie Eisenhower. Indianapolis, Curtis, 1976.

OTHER PUBLICATIONS

Novels as Frank Peace

We Burn Like Fire. Derby, Connecticut, Monarch, 1959.
The Speed Merchants (for children). New York, Duell Sloan and Pierce, 1964.

* * *

A youthful fascination with the Cavalry led Will Cook to run away from home at age 16 to join that branch of the Army. With the outbreak of World War II he switched from horses to airplanes and served as a pilot in the South Pacific. After the war he worked as a bush pilot in Alaska, and later took a job as a deputy sheriff in Northern California. He began writing in 1951. During the next few years he produced over 100 short stories, mostly for western pulp magazines such as *Dime Western Magazine*, *.44 Western Magazine*, and *Fifteen Western Tales*. Two stories from *Big-Book Western Magazine* in 1953 are typical. In "Sixty Miles to Laramie" (May) two cavalrymen—a mutinous veteran and an inexperienced Lieutenant—and a young woman are hunted across the Wyoming grasslands by a band of Cheyenne Dog-soldiers. "Lawmen Die Sudden!" (November) presents the dilemma of a sheriff who knows that the town banker has committed a murder, but also knows that an arrest would trigger a run on the bank which might have disastrous results for the local ranchers.

Cook's first two books were published in 1954, heading the list of more than 50 novels under four names that would appear over the next 15 years. 10 of these books appeared first as hardcovers, five of them under the name James Keene; the rest were published only in paperback form in the U.S. (At least a dozen of these paperbacks later appeared in hardcover editions in the United Kingdom.) Most of the books deal with traditional western themes—reformed outlaws, range wars, Indian fighting—but there are also romantic novels such as *Sabrina Kane* (set on the southern Illinois frontier in 1811) and *Elizabeth, By Name* (the Texas plains in the 1870's). Occasionally the prose shows signs of haste and an over-reliance on stock phrases; Cook had a particular fondness for the image "he pawed his mouth out of shape," and in one book used it so many times that it became an active distraction. In spite of this, the general level of quality is high. Locales and historical details are accurately and economically set forth. The books are strongly plotted and peopled with credible characters, depicted with sympathy and insight.

Many of Cook's novels deal with the U.S. Cavalry and its encounters with various Indian tribes. Among his most important works are three related novels: *Comanche Captives* (filmed by John Ford in 1961 under the title *Two Rode Together*) deals with the rescue of white captives from the Indians; *The Peacemakers* concern attempts to establish peace with Chief Quanah Parker's Kiowa/Cheyenne coalition; and *The Outcasts* deals with the reintegration of former captives into an often hostile white society. The books are tied together both thematically and through the presence of continuing characters. Other Cavalry novels include *McCracken in Command*, published under the James Keene byline, and several of the books published as by Wade Everett, notably *First Command* and *Fort Starke*.

Cook sometimes linked otherwise independent books together through the use of recurring characters. Charlie Boomhauer, a very young and inexperienced Federal marshall in the pulp story "Lawmen Die Sudden!," turns up, older and wiser, in the books *Badman's Holiday* and *The Wind River Kid*. Guthrie McCabe, from *The Peacemakers* and *The Outcasts*, also appears in *The Tough Texan*, the story of a Texas Ranger campaign against Mexican border bandits in 1905. And Finley Burkhauser, the Army Lieutenant who woos the title character of *Elizabeth, By Name*, is a grizzled Texas Ranger in Cook's last book, *Bandit's Trail*.

In 1959 Cook adopted the penname Wade Everett for a series of paperbacks for Ballantine Books. Most of these books have been reprinted several times, and some are still in print more than 25 years after their first publication. Aside from the Cavalry novels, one of the best is *Last Scout*, whose title character is an unregenerate hell-raiser named Wind-River Page who comes to Deadwood to live with his daughter's family. The old man resents being treated as a has-been, and rebels by helping his 17-year-old grandson track down the culprit in a series of gold robberies.

Cook died of a heart attack in 1964, at the age of 42. Several books were published posthumously, the last one nearly 10 years after the author's death. At least one of the posthumous Wade Everett books was not written by Cook: *The Whiskey Traders*, published in 1968, has been acknowledged as the work of Giles A. Lutz.

—R. E. Briney

COOK, William Wallace. American. Born in Marshall, Michigan, 11 April 1867. Educated at schools in Ottawa, Kansas, Lafayette, Indiana, and Cleveland; Bryant and Stretton's Business College, Chicago. Married 1) Anne Gertrude Slater in 1891 (died 1913); 2) Mary Ackley in 1926. Stenographer; reporter, Chicago *Morning News;* then freelance writer. *Died 20 July 1933.*

WESTERN PUBLICATIONS

Novels

The Desert Argonaut. New York, Street and Smith, n.d.; London, Wright and Brown, 1938.
The Goal of a Million; or, Fighting for a Fortune. New York, Street and Smith, n.d.
The Gold Gleaners. New York, Street and Smith, n.d.
Innocent Outlaw. New York, Street and Smith, n.d.
Jim Dexter, Cattleman. New York, Street and Smith, n.d.; London, Wright and Brown, 1938.
Montana. New York, Street and Smith, n.d.
Frisbie of San Antone. New York, Street and Smith, n.d.
Trailing of Josephine. New York, Street and Smith, n.d.
The Sheriff of Broken Bow. London, Wright and Brown, 1939.
Buffalo Bill among the Blackfeet; or, The Wizard of the Wind River Mountains. New York, Street and Smith, n.d.

OTHER PUBLICATIONS

Novels

His Friend the Enemy. New York, Dillingham, 1903.
Castaway at the Pole. New York, Street and Smith, 1904.
Adrift in the Unknown. New York, Street and Smith, 1905.
A Quarter to Four. New York, Dillingham, 1909.
At Daggers Drawn. New York, Street and Smith, n.d.
Back from Bedlam. New York, Street and Smith, n.d.
Billionaire pro Tem and the Trail of the Billy Doo. New York, Street and Smith, n.d.
Catspaw. New York, Street and Smith, n.d.
Cotton Bag. New York, Street and Smith, n.d.
A Deep Sea Game. New York, Street and Smith, n.d.
Eighth Wonder. New York, Street and Smith, n.d.
Fateful Seventh. New York, Street and Smith, n.d.
His Audacious Highness. New York, Street and Smith, n.d.
In the Wake of the Scimitar. New York, Street and Smith, n.d.
In the Web. New York, Street and Smith, n.d.
Juggling with Liberty. New York, Street and Smith, n.d.

Little Miss Vassar. New York, Street and Smith, n.d.
Marooned in 1492. New York, Street and Smith, n.d.
The Mysterious Mission. New York, Street and Smith, n.d.
Paymaster's Special. New York, Street and Smith, n.d.
River Tangle. New York, Street and Smith, n.d.
Rogers of Butte. New York, Street and Smith, n.d.
A Round Trip to the Year 2000. New York, Street and Smith, n.d.
Running the Signal. New York, Street and Smith, n.d.
The Spur of Necessity. New York, Street and Smith, n.d.
Testing of Noyes. New York, Street and Smith, n.d.
Thorndyke of the Bonita. New York, Street and Smith, n.d.; London, Wright and Brown, 1939.
Dare of Darling & Co. New York, Street and Smith, n.d.
The Deserter. New York, Street and Smith, n.d.; London, Wright and Brown, 1939.
Fools for Luck. New York, Street and Smith, n.d.
Wanted: A Highwayman. New York, Street and Smith, n.d.

Plays

Screenplays: *Gold Grabbers*, 1922; *The Sunshine Trail*, with Bradley King, 1923; *The Man Who Played Square*, with John Stone, 1924; *The Speed Spook*, with Raymond S. Harris and Ralph Spence, 1924; *The Prairie King*, with Frank Howard Clark, 1927.

Other

Plotto: A New Method of Plot Suggestion for Writers of Creative Fiction. Battle Creek, Michigan, Ellis, 1928.

*

Bibliography: in *Dime Novel Round-up*, 15 May 1970 and 15 July 1972.

* * *

A versatile and prolific contributor to dime novel series and pulp magazines, William Wallace Cook made up in vigor what he lacked in talent. In all, perhaps half of Cook's hundreds of stories are nominally westerns, though little save their sketchy western settings distinguishes them from the science fiction, circus stories, mysteries, sea stories, or rags-to-riches success stories which he penned with equal facility. Characteristic of Cook's western protagonists is Marcus Leonard, the tenderfoot hero of Cook's cloth-bound novel *The Goal of a Million: or, Fighting for a Fortune*. In this story Marcus goes to Montana to make his fortune in mining, but despite his contact with an assortment of Westerners he acquires neither wilderness skills nor the moral insight they customarily signify. He is thrown off his horse, and later his pocket is picked by a scurrilous Indian. Marcus is "not a good judge of horseflesh." In fact, he is "no horseman" and "not much of a marksman." When offered a job on a ranch, Marcus responds: "If he had anything to do with cattle ... he hoped it would be on the bull side of a stock-market—mining stocks preferably."

Authentic western flavor is similarly lacking in *The Gold Gleaners*, another of Cook's cloth-bound westerns. Though set in the Arizona desert and incorporating such traditional elements of the western as a stagecoach, road-agents, a sheriff, and a lynch-mob, the novel focusses on events in and around a cyaniding plant and an abandoned mine. The hero, Whipple, is a soft-spoken, cigarette-rolling detective from Denver who spends his time settling labor disputes with the plant's Mexican laborers and solving a company robbery. Chagrined when he discovers that the robber is his sweetheart's brother, Tom Travis, Whipple experiences a conflict "between Desire and Duty." Whipple however, proceeds to capture Travis, and later attempts to protect him from an angry lynch-mob. But just as the dilemma reaches crisis proportions, Travis, in a singularly redeeming and wholly unbelievable act, swallows a tumbler of cyanide, killing himself in order that Whipple will not also risk death at the hands of the mob. With such fortuitous coincidences, all too frequently crowded into a single closing paragraph, Cook's stories commonly end.

More often than not, Cook's westerns also reveal a penchant for the fantastic. Replete with lost tribes and ancient cities, ghosts and haunted houses, mad scientists and futuristic inventions, the tales rely on brisk action and convoluted plots. Typical of more than 100 stories which Cook penned for Street & Smith's Buffalo Bill Stories is *Buffalo Bill among the Blackfeet: or, The Wizard of the Wind River Mountains.* In this tale a girl arrives in the West and enlists the aid of Bufalo Bill to search for her father, missing and reportedly killed by Indians. Through the efforts of Buffalo Bill and the Wizard, an eccentric inventor who distracts the incredulous Indians with his electrical inventions, the girl and her father are happily reunited. Variations of this plot recur frequently in Cook's fiction, often with an additional complication. Either the missing father or the master villain who holds him captive is mad, a circumstance which prompts sensational action while obviating the need for clear character development and convincing motivation. Although Cook occasionally made effective use of western settings, characters, and incidents, particularly in the Ted Strong stories which he wrote for Street & Smith's Rough Rider Weekly, his contribution to western fiction must be measured in terms of quantity rather than quality.

—Daryl Jones

COOLIDGE, Dane. American. Born in Natick, Massachusetts, 24 March 1873. Educated at Stanford University, California, A.N. 1898; Harvard University, Cambridge, Massachusetts, 1898–99. Married Mary E.B. Roberts in 1906. Naturalist: animal field collector for Stanford University in Nevada, 1895, for the British Museum in California, 1896, for the U.S. Biological Survey in California, 1897, for the U.S. National Zoo in California, 1898, for the New York Zoo in Arizona and California, 1899, and for the U.S. National Museum in Italy and France, 1900. *Died 8 August 1940.*

WESTERN PUBLICATIONS

Novels

Hidden Water. Chicago, McClurg, 1910.
The Texican. Chicago, McClurg, 1911.
Bat Wing Bowles. New York, Stokes, 1914.
The Desert Trail. New York, Watt, 1915; London, Methuen, 1917.
Rimrock Jones. New York, Watt, 1917; London, Methuen, 1920.
The Fighting Fool. New York, Dutton, 1918.
Silver and Gold. New York, Dutton, 1919.
Shadow Mountain. New York, Watt, 1919; London, Methuen, 1921.
Wunpost. New York, Dutton, 1920; London, Hodder and Stoughton, 1921.

The Man-Killers. New York, Dutton, 1921.
Lost Wagons. New York, Dutton, 1923; London, Skeffington, 1935.
The Scalp-Lock. New York, Dutton, and London, Hodder and Stoughton, 1924.
Lorenzo the Magnificent (*The Riders from Texas*). New York, Dutton, 1925.
Not-Afraid. New York, Dutton, 1926.
Under the Sun. New York, Dutton, 1926.
Gun-Smoke. New York, Dutton, 1928; London, Skeffington, 1929.
War Paint. New York, Dutton, and London, Skeffington, 1929.
Horse-Ketchum. New York, Dutton, and London, Skeffington, 1930.
Other Men's Cattle. London, Skeffington, 1931.
Maverick Makers. New York, Dutton, 1931.
Sheriff Killer. New York, Dutton, and London, Skeffington, 1932.
Jess Roundtree, Texas Ranger. New York, Dutton, 1933; as *The Texas Ranger,* London, Skeffington, 1933.
The Fighting Danites. New York, Dutton, and London, Skeffington, 1934.
Silver Hat. New York, Dutton, 1934.
Long Rope. New York, Dutton, and London, Skeffington, 1935.
Wolf's Candle. New York, Dutton, 1935; London, Skeffington, 1936.
Rawhide Johnny. New York, Dutton, and London, Skeffington, 1936.
Snake Bit Jones. New York, Dutton, 1936; London, Skeffington, 1937.
Ranger Two-Rifles. New York, Dutton, 1937.
The Trail of Gold. New York, Dutton, and London, Skeffington, 1937.
Hell's Hip Pocket. New York, Dutton, 1938; London, Hale, 1939.
Comanche Chaser. New York, Dutton, 1938; as *Redskin Trail,* London, Skeffington, 1938.
Wally Laughs-Easy. New York, Dutton, 1939.
Gringo Gold. New York, Dutton, 1939.
Bloody Head. New York, Dutton, 1940.
Yaqui Drums. New York, Dutton, 1940.
Bear Paw. New York, Dutton, 1941.

Uncollected Short Stories

"The Coyote of Tres Palmas," in *Western Story* (New York), 19 March 1921.
"Elder Brother," in *Western Story* (New York), 9 September 1922.
"The Shadow of the Tortugas," in *West* (New York), 5 October 1926.
"The Law West of Queen Creek," in *West* (New York), 20 October 1926.
"Sam from Texas," in *Western Story* (New York), 27 August 1932.

OTHER PUBLICATIONS

Other

The Navajo Indian, with Mary Roberts Coolidge. Boston, Houghton Mifflin, 1930.
Fighting Men of the West. New York, Dutton, 1932; London, Corgi, 1954.
Navajo Rugs, with Mary Roberts Coolidge. Pasadena, California, Esto, 1933.
Texas Cowboys. New York, Dutton, 1937.
Death Valley Prospectors. New York, Dutton, 1937.
Arizona Cowboys. New York, Dutton, 1938.
Old California Cowboys. New York, Dutton, 1939.
The Last of the Seris, with Mary Roberts Coolidge. New York, Dutton, 1939.

* * *

If the formulary Western is defined as one which possesses a hero, a heroine, and a villain, and in which the physical landscape and the events of western history are irrelevant, then the majority of Dane Coolidge's western novels are formulary. Yet, trained as a naturalist, Coolidge was well-versed in the flora and fauna of the western regions and he could name regional examples of both in English, Latin, and Spanish. His heroes are seldom cowboys, but rather middle-aged ranchmen as Lorenzo de Vega in *Lorenzo the Magnificent* and Charley Barr in *Bear Paw*; or they might be prospectors as John Calhoun in *Wunpost* or John Ware in *The Trail of Gold*, salesmen as Juan Fox in *Wolf's Candle*, mustangers as Johnny Lightfoot in *Horse-Ketchum*, or train robbers as Sycamore Brown in *The Fighting Fool*. Coolidge generally eschewed violence in his heroes, and they rarely engage in physical heroics of any kind. For them, competition with the villains is mostly a game. There are occasional exceptions to this, such as Bill Enright in *Gun-Smoke*; but even here it is a matter of degree and the hero kills three men only when absolutely forced to do so—which itself became a formulary convention: violence forced upon a hero following provocation after provocation.

Coolidge established a dress code for females in his fiction. His heroines are generally strong only when they are wearing men's clothing, and this strength is conceived as being definitely masculine in character. However, as in B.M. Bower's novels, Coolidge's heroines tend to become petty or contrary shortly after they appear and thus are able to remain emotionally aloof or estranged from the hero until the inevitable reconciliation at the end. With Bower, the romance was always central. This was true for Coolidge, as for Clarence E. Mulford, only about half the time. He could as easily write a novel as *Sheriff Killer* where the romance is strictly secondary to his retelling a fictionalized account based on Captain Burton Mossman's organization of the Arizona Rangers and capture of the Mexican bandit, Chacon, one of Coolidge's few attempts at a romantic historical reconstruction, i.e., history told in the form of romance. But this is not to say that (with the exception of *Gringo Gold*, a romantic retelling of the Joaquín Murieta legend) Coolidge's novels do not end with an amorous clinch, because they surely do. What is more, for every strong heroine Coolidge might draw in a particular book, he could turn right around and create a Johnsie Blood as he did in *Gun-Smoke* who, when the hero mangles two fingers in a shoot-out, ultimately crippling him for life, responds, "Just think what you did for me! Is that too much—for a finger?" Or then there is Salome Lockhardt in *Bear Paw* who, while still married to the villain, declares that for hero Mark Trumbell who wants to steal her away from her husband, "All I dream of now is a little home, with him, and I'll work my fingers to the bone." Some of Coolidge's heroes—and Mark Trumbell is decidedly one of them—are not as puritanical as most of the heroic male characters in formulary Westerns by a number of his contemporaries, Coolidge being more of a throw-back to Owen Wister whose Virginian is not beyond having sexual relations with a woman toward whom he has no matrimonial aspirations.

Coolidge's wife wrote a book on southwestern Indians and with her Coolidge co-authored *The Navajo Indian*. Yet, despite this, when Coolidge included Native Americans in his fiction, he portrayed them as villains and savages, or condemned them for their laziness. In *Texas Cowboys*, a non-fiction work, Coolidge did not find it in the least remarkable that the Cherrycow Company should be permitted to graze their cattle on the San Carlos reserve and pay rental to government bureaucrats intended for the Apaches which they never received, and he sympathized with the opprobium with which the Company regarded the Apaches for stealing a steer when they needed meat. Notwithstanding, while Coolidge might not grant Native Americans the integrity of having separate and unique cultures, his Anglo-American parochialism did not apply to Spanish-American. He was always wont to balance every portrait of a cruel Mexican with another character of Mexican or Spanish origin who possessed admirable qualities.

As a stylist, Coolidge wrote a straightforward, unencumbered prose. His plots are filled with continuous, at times even hectic, action. He did not physically stereotype his villains the way his contemporaries Mulford and Charles Alden Seltzer tended to do; but, as theirs, his villains are often businessmen whose capital sin is greed and only rarely lust which figures so predominantly in Zane Grey's fiction. His intention, it would seem, was to entertain consistently, and most of the time he achieved his objective. If there is a lack of characterization in his novels, this is not much different from what continues to be the case in most contemporary formulary westerns. The essential difference is the lack of violence and this, to many contemporary readers of formulary Westerns, *is* a flaw.

—Jon Tuska

COOPER, Courtney Ryley. American. Born in Kansas City, Missouri, 31 October 1886. Educated at public schools in Kansas City. Served in the United States Marines during World War I: 2nd Lieutenant. Married Genevieve R. Furey in 1916. Clown for Cook-Barret circus, then circus publicity agent for Sell-Floto Circus, 1914–15, and Ringling Brothers and Barnum and Bailey Circus, 1940; newspaperman: staff member of Kansas City *Star*, 1910–12, New York *World*, 1913, Chicago *Tribune*, 1913, Denver *Post*, 1913; later associated with the *Saturday Evening Post*; also a film director. *Died 29 September 1940.*

WESTERN PUBLICATIONS

Novels

The Cross-Cut. Boston, Little Brown, 1921; London, Collins, 1922.
The White Desert. Boston, Little Brown, 1922.
The Last Frontier. Boston, Little Brown, 1923; as *The The Far Frontier*, London, Hurst and Blackett, 1923.
Oklahoma. Boston, Little Brown, 1926.
The Drowned Bonanza. London, Hurst and Blackett, 1927.
The Mystery of the Four Abreast. London, Collins, 1929.
Ghost Country. London, Collins, 1929.
Trigger Finger. London, Collins, 1930.
Pike's Peak. London, Collins, 1931.
Poor Man's Gold. Boston, Little Brown, and London, Collins, 1936.
The Pioneers. Boston, Little Brown, and London, Collins, 1938.

Uncollected Short Stories

"Christmas Eve at Pilot Butte," in *Redbook* (Dayton, Ohio), January 1921.
"White Riders of the Range," in *Western Story* (New York), 18 June–9 July 1921.
"The Land of the Lost," in *Western Story* (New York), 1 October–22 October 1921.
"Bar O Bar," in *Western Story* (New York), 29 July–12 August 1922.
"The Glacier Cache," in *Western Story* (New York), 23 December 1922–6 January 1923.
"Bears and Bystanders," in *Western Story* (New York), 23 December 1922.
"Around the Dog Wagon," in *Saturday Evening Post* (Philadelphia), 10 May 1924.
"Object: Adventure," in *Western Story* (New York), 18 July–16 August 1924.
"High Country," in *Saturday Evening Post* (Philadelphia), 27 September 1924.
"Son of the Vanquished," in *American Magazine* (Springfield, Ohio), March 1926.
"Weary River," in *Collier's* (Springfield, Ohio), 11 August 1928.
"A Dog's Bad Name," in *Western Story* (New York), 24 January 1931.

OTHER PUBLICATIONS

Novels

The Eagle's Eye: A True Story of the Imperial German Government's Spies and Intrigues in America. New York, Prospect Press, 1918.
The Avalanche. London, Hurst and Blackett, 1925.
Builders of Cities. London, Hurst and Blackett, 1927.
The Golden Bubble. Boston, Little Brown, 1928.
The Challenge of the Bush. Boston, Little Brown, 1929; London, Collins, 1930.
Caged. Boston, Little Brown, 1930.
End of Steel. New York, Farrar and Rinehart, and London, Collins, 1931.
Action in Diamonds. Philadelphia, Penn, 1942.

Short Stories

The Jungle Behind Bars. London, Jenkins, 1923.

Plays

Screenplays: *Sawdust*, with Doris Schroeder and Harvey Gates, 1923; *Weary River*, with Bradley King and Tom J. Geraghty, 1929.

Verse

Us Kids: Verses. Kansas City, Kellogg Baxter, 1910.

Other

The Quick Lunch Cabaret: A Versical Omelette in One Scramble for Male Quartette. Chicago, Denison, 1918.
Memories of Buffalo Bill, with Mrs. Louisa Frederici Cody. New York, Appleton, 1919.

Under the Big Top. Boston, Little Brown, 1923.
Lions 'n' Tigers 'n' Everything. Boston, Little Brown, 1924; London, Cape, 1925.
High Country: The Rockies Yesterday and To-day. Boston, Little Brown, 1926.
With the Circus. Boston, Little Brown, 1927.
Annie Oakley, Woman at Arms. New York, Duffield, 1927; London, Hurst and Blackett, 1928.
Go North, Young Man! Boston, Little Brown, 1929.
Circus Day. New York, Farrar and Rinehart, 1931.
Boss Elephant. Boston, Little Brown, 1934.
Ten Thousand Public Enemies. Boston, Little Brown, and London, Dickson and Thompson, 1935.
Here's to Crime. Boston, Little Brown, 1937.
Designs in Scarlet. Boston, Little Brown, 1939.

Editor, *Dear Folks at Home*—(servicemen's letters). Boston, Houghton Mifflin, 1919.
Editor, *Sawdust and Solitude*, by Lucia Zora. Boston, Little Brown, 1928.

* * *

Courtney Ryley Cooper is noted for his writings of the pageantry, romance, and tragedy of the circus. He has been called the "historian of the circus" for such works as *Under the Big Top, Lions 'n' Tigers 'n' Everything*, and other works.

His novels about the West and the Southwest are not as important as his other works, though a couple of them merge the circus and the western themes. In *The Drowned Bonanza*, for instance, a miner's daughter, kidnapped by two villains who want her rights in her dead father's mine, is rescued by a young circus owner. *The Cross-Cut* also brings an atmosphere of a cultured and thoughtful eastern upbringing to a conventional story of the new owner of a silver mine going west to claim his inheritance, but the villains, the sheriffs, and the heroine are in the usual western mode. *Pike's Peak* is a more sprawling work, centering on the emergence of Colorado as a state after the initial mining, commercial, and banking work has helped stabilize the territory. In *Ghost Country* there is the possibility of reopening a mine whose lode would be profitable if a railroad could be built to make transport simpler—and there is a secret pass through the mountains whose whereabouts must be made known. *Oklahoma* draws upon the Cherokee Strip land rush of 1889.

Informal historical works include *High Country: the Rockies Yesterday and To-day* and *Go North, Young Man!* The latter concerns Canadian history, fact, and legend from the author's viewpoint. Particularly interesting is his treatment of the expansion of the Hudson Bay Railroad to the edge of the Barren Land, and the account of the Peace River district. Cooper collaborated with Mrs. [William] Louisa Frederici Cody to write *Memories of Buffalo Bill.* A treatise on "bad women in the West" and elsewhere is detailed in a partially fictional and somewhat chauvinistic work entitled *Designs in Scarlet. Annie Oakley, Woman at Arms* appears more objective, but his interest in criminals and crime extended throughout the United States as indicated by the nonfictional *Ten Thousand Public Enemies* and *Here's to Crime.*

—Dorys C. Grover

CORD, Barry. Pseudonym for Peter B. Germano; also wrote as Jack Bertin; Jim Kane. American. Born in New Bedford, Massachusetts, 17 May 1913. Educated at Brown University, Providence, Rhode Island, 1946–50, A.B. 1950; Chapman College, Orange, California, 1956–59; Loyola University, 1968–70, M.A. Served in the United States Marine Corps during the World War II. Married Muriel Garant in 1942; two daughters and two sons. Freelance writer from 1946: wrote under house names of Jack Slade and Jackson Cole, and others. *Died 20 September 1983.*

WESTERN PUBLICATIONS

Novels

Trail Boss from Texas. New York, Phoenix Press, and London, Foulsham, 1948.
The Gunsmoke Trail. New York, Phoenix Press, 1951; London, Foulsham, 1952.
Shadow Valley. New York, Phoenix Press, 1951; London, Foulsham, 1952.
Mesquite Johnny. New York, Arcadia House, 1952; London, Foulsham, 1954.
Trail to Sundown. New York, Arcadia House, 1953; London, Foulsham, 1954.
Cain Basin. New York, Arcadia House, 1954; London, Foulsham, 1956.
The Sagebrush Kid. New York, Arcadia House, 1954; London, Foulsham, 1955.
Boss of Barbed Wire. New York, Arcadia House, 1955; London, Foulsham, 1957.
Dry Range. New York, Arcadia House, 1955; as *The Rustlers of Dry Range*, London, Foulsham, 1956.
The Guns of Hammer. New York, Arcadia House, 1956; London, Mills and Boon, 1957.
The Gunshy Kid. New York, Arcadia House, 1957; London, Muller, 1959.
Sheriff of Big Hat. New York, Arcadia House, 1957; London, Brown Watson, 1960.
Savage Valley. New York, Ace, 1957.
The Prodigal Gun. New York, Ace, 1957.
Concho Valley. New York, Arcadia House, 1958; London, Muller, 1959.
Gun-Proddy Hombre. New York, Arcadia House, 1958; London, Mills and Boon, 1959.
The Iron Trail Killers. New York, Arcadia House, 1959; London, Mills and Boon, 1960.
Starlight Range. New York, Arcadia House, 1959; London, Ward Lock, 1960.
The Third Rider. New York, Arcadia House, 1959; London, Muller, 1960.
Six Bullets Left. New York, Avon, 1959; London, Consul, 1961.
War in Peaceful Valley. New York, Ace, 1959.
Maverick Gun. New York, Curl, 1959.
Last Chance at Devil's Canyon. New York, Ace, 1959; London, Consul, 1961.
Two Guns to Avalon. New York, Arcadia House, 1962; London, Hale, 1964.
The Masked Gun. New York, Ace, 1963.
Last Stage to Gomorrah. New York, Ace, 1966.
A Ranger Called Solitary. New York, Arcadia House, 1966; London, Hale, 1970.
Canyon Showdown. New York, Arcadia House, 1967; London, Hale, 1970.
Gallows Ghost. New York, Ace, 1967.
The Long Wire. New York, Ace, 1968.

Trouble in Peaceful Valley. New York, Arcadia House, 1968; London, Hale, 1971.
The Coffin Fillers. New York, Ace, 1972; London, Severn House, 1978.
Brassado Hill. New York, Lenox Hill Press, 1972.
Desert Knights. New York, Ace, 1973.
The Running Iron Samaritans. New York, Ace, 1973.
Hell in Paradise Valley. New York, Belmont, 1978.
Gun Junction. New York, Nordon, 1979.
Deadly Amigos: Two Graves for a Gunman. New York, Belmont, 1979.

Novels as Jim Kane

Gunman's Choice. New York, Arcadia House, 1960; London, Gresham, 1962.
Renegade Rancher. New York, Arcadia House, 1961; London, Muller, 1963.
Spanish Gold. New York, Arcadia House, 1963; London, Hale, 1964.
Tangled Trails. New York, Arcadia House, 1963.
Lost Canyon. New York, Arcadia House, 1964.
Red River Sheriff. New York, Arcadia House, 1965.
Rendezvous at Bitter Wells. New York, Arcadia House, 1966.
The Doublecross Gun. New York, Lenox Hill Press, 1970; London, Remploy, 1975.
Texas Warrior. New York, Lenox Hill Press, 1971.

Uncollected Short Stories

"Owlhoot Haven," in *Red Seal Western* (Springfield, Massachusetts), December 1938.
"Mustang Vengeance" and "A Rustler's Receipt" (as Peter Germane), in *Sure-Fire Western* (Springfield, Massachusetts), January 1939.
"Cayuse to Glory," in *Wild West* (New York), 24 January 1942.
"The Gun Trail Back," in *Mammoth Western* (Chicago), May 1950.
"Red Creek Showdown," in *Thrilling Western* (London), October 1953.
"Boothill's Boy," in *Western Story* (London), June 1954.
"Two Trails to Glory," in *Western Story* (London), August 1961.
"No Quarter for the Sagebrush Kid," in *Western Story* (London), September 1961.
"The Things Men Die For," in *Western Story* (London), December 1961.

OTHER PUBLICATIONS

Novel

The Interplanetary Adventures (as Jack Bertin). New York, Lenox Hill Press, 1970.

Plays

Television Plays: scripts for *Wanted—Dead or Alive*, *The Zane Grey Theatre*, *Cheyenne*, *Bronco*, *Rawhide*, *The Virginian*, *Guns of Will Sonnet*, *The Iron Horse*, *Tales of Wells Fargo*, *The Myra Marshall Story* (*Wagon Train*), 1963–64, *Bonanza*, *Grizzly Adams*, *Maverick*, *The Rebel*, *The Dakotas*, *The Rifleman*, *The Fugitive*, *The New Breed*, *Tarzan*, *Next Stop Beyond*, *Voyage to the Bottom of the Sea*, *Time Tunnel*, *The Untouchables*, *Greatest Show on Earth*, *Buck Rogers*, *Hondo*; also scripts for animated series *Land of the Dinosaurs*, *Land of the Lost*, and *The Little Prince*.

*

Manuscript Collections: University of Oregon, Eugene; University of Utah, Salt Lake City.

Barry Cord commented (1982):

For a boy born and brought up in New Bedford, Massachusetts, a former whaling port and now a mill town, the American West has always held a great fascination. I came upon the scene too late to be a part of that pioneering era (roughly the entire 19th century) but from the time I was old enough to read I was, in spirit if not physically, one with the men and women who streamed west, across the wide Mississippi, to settle in the empty and often hostile land beyond. They were my heroes as I grew up, the miners and the prospectors, the cowboys and trail herders, the gamblers and the hardy people who braved blizzard and burning desert to settle on lonely farms and ranches which they built themselves. It was not until after World War II that I came and settled in southern California where the Mexican border is only a hop, skip, and jump away, where the High Sierras overlook Death Valley, and where the great Mojave desert melts away into the desolate, jagged mountains of Mexico. The great southwest. . .this is the country, and these are the people that have gripped my imagination . . . and this is what I have been writing about for 40 years. And until I die I shall remain the little New England boy who fell in love with the "West," and as a man had the opportunity to see it and live in it.

* * *

Peter Germano, a native of Massachusetts who wrote Westerns under the pseudonyms of Barry Cord and other names, described the type of western novel he wrote as "melodrama," and said that his first books, *Trail Boss from Texas*, *Shadow Valley*, and *Mesquite Johnny*, owe a great deal in style to Ernest Haycox and Luke Short. "I tend to write sparsely, with attention to character delineation," Germano explained. "I've always written my Western sort of like a screenplay (long before I got into writing screenplays), with just enough narrative description to set the physical background of time and place. Maybe this is why I found the transition to screen and teleplay writing easier than some of my contemporaries."

Always fascinated by the southwestern desert country, Germano's Westerns are commonly set in the Mexican border area and are the "traditional" variety of novel rather than the "historical," he says.

Germano's writing career began in the pulp magazines in the 1930's and the one writer he singles out as influencing him most directly was his uncle, Jack Bertin, who wrote in 1920's and 1930's for such magazines as *Western Magazine*, *Short Stories*, *Black Mask*, *Amazing*, and *Wonder Stories*.

"Westerns were my second love," he said. "Science fiction was my first but the first story I ever told was a Western and I still view the Western as one of the most important areas of my writing."

—Dale L. Walker

CORLE, Edwin. American. Born in Wildwood, New Jersey, 7 May 1906. Educated at schools in Wildwood, Philadelphia, and Hollywood; University of California, Los Angeles, A.B. in English 1928; Yale University, New Haven, Connecticut, 1928–30. Married Jean Armstrong in 1944; one daughter. Radio and screen writer, 1930–32. Recipient: Guggenheim fellowship, 1941. *Died 11 June 1956.*

WESTERN PUBLICATIONS

Novels

Fig Tree John. New York, Liveright, 1935; London, Laurie, 1936.
People on the Earth. New York, Random House, 1937.
Burro Alley. New York, Random House, 1938.
Solitaire. New York, Dutton, 1940; as *Virginia's Double Life—Solitaire*, London, Cape, 1940.
Coarse Gold. New York, Dutton, 1942; London, Cape, 1943.
Three Ways to Mecca. New York, Duell, 1947; London, Cape, 1948.
In Winter Light. New York, Duell, 1949.
Billy the Kid. New York, Duell, 1953; London, Corgi, 1959.

Short Stories

Mojave: A Book of Stories. New York, Liveright, 1934.

Uncollected Short Stories

"Great Manta," in *Short Stories from the New Yorker.* New York, Simon and Schuster, 1940.
"Can You Name the Days of the Week?," in *Prairie Schooner Caravan*, edited by Lowry C. Wimberly. Lincoln, University of Nebraska Press, 1943.
"Agocho Finds His Place," in *Continent's End*, edited by J. H. Jackson. New York, McGraw Hill, 1944.
"If You Don't Get Excited—," in *Zane Grey's Western* (New York), February 1948.
"The Widow," in *Yale Review* (New Haven, Connecticut), December 1949.
"Patron of the Arts," in *American Mercury* (New York), November 1951.

OTHER PUBLICATIONS

Other

Desert Country. New York, Duell, 1941; reprinted in part, as *Death Valley and the Creek Called Furnace*, photographs by Ansel Adams, Los Angeles, Ward Ritchie Press, 1962.
Listen, Bright Angel. New York, Duell, 1946; as *The Story of the Grand Canyon*, London, Sampson Low, 1948.
John Studebaker: An American Dream. New York, Dutton, 1948.
The Royal Highway (El Camino Real). Indianapolis, Bobbs Merrill, 1949.
The Gila, River of the Southwest. New York, Rinehart, 1951.

Editor, *Dance Memoranda*, by Merle Armitage. New York, Duell, 1947.
Editor, *Operations Santa Fé: Atchison, Topeka & Santa Fé Railway System*, by Merle Armitage. New York, Duell, 1948.
Editor, *Igor Stravinsky*, by Merle Armitage. New York, Duell, 1949.

* * *

An adopted son of the American West, Edwin Corle began to study the lore and legendry of the region in the 1930's, as a hobby to break the routine of his job as a radio scriptwriter. Eventually he traveled widely getting to know the people and places of the area as well as their history. His personal and scholarly knowledge of the West is evident in two superlative works of interpretive non-fiction, *Desert Country* and *The Gila: River of the Southwest.* It is also apparent in several works of exceptionally good fiction.

Following *Mojave: A Book of Stories*, an inauspicious debut, Corle published *Fig Tree John*, a book that remains his masterpiece and one of the greatest of western American novels. The title character of *Fig Tree John* is an Apache who in the early years of the 20th century uproots himself from his home in Arizona and resettles in the Salton Sea area of southern California. Isolated from his people, he grows increasingly bitter and vengeful, as first his wife is murdered by a pair of white tramps and then his son is gradually lured from the old ways and into the white man's world. John comes to see the whites as the source of all evil: the inevitable result of such a clash of cultural values is hatred, violence, and ultimately the Indian's destruction. Despite the author's penchant for commenting a bit too obtrusively on the workings of the "primitive mind," *Fig Tree John* is a superbly realistic and powerful novel.

Though he never fulfilled the promise of his first novel, Corle continued to publish creditable fiction for two decades—a total of seven more novels. *People on the Earth* and *In Winter Light* are readable and sensitive fictional studies of the plight of the reservation Navajos immediately before and after World War II, a time when the native American's traditional culture was being systematically eroded by white teachers and missionaries. *Burro Alley* is quite unlike any of the writer's other books; it is genuinely funny, a hilarious—some might say scurrilous—satire of Santa Fe, New Mexico, during the tourist season. *Billy the Kid*, Corle's last published book, is a provocative account of the life of the notorious southwestern gunman. Based on thorough research, the book, according to the author, should be considered fiction; it might, indeed, be called an earlyday "non-fiction novel." Corle, invoking the license of fiction, offers interesting solutions to some of the enduring mysteries surrounding the Kid's life. The one nearly unique aspect of the novel is that the writer seems neither pro-Billy nor anti-Billy; unlike the myriad of interpreters before him, he remains thoroughly neutral in reporting the Kid's behavior.

Corle died at the still young age of 50. Even with a foreshortened career, however, his achievement is impressive—one excellent novel and several very good ones, plus some non-fiction that every serious student of the West should be familiar with. Corle has never been ranked very far up in the hierarchy of western American writers. He should be. He produced more and better work than many western authors whose reputations are greater.

—William T. Pilkington

CORT, Van.

WESTERN PUBLICATIONS

Novels

The Rangers of Bloody Silver. New York, Phoenix Press, 1941; as *Blood on the Moon,* London, Hodder and Stoughton, 1941.
Mail Order Bride. New York, Fawcett, 1964.
Journey of the Gun. New York, Berkley, 1966.

Uncollected Short Stories

"A Man for the Rio Flame," in *Spurs West!,* edited by Joseph T. Shaw. New York, Permabooks, 1951.
"Last Canteen," in *Blazing Guns* (Holyoke, Massachusetts), December 1956.
"Blood Money," in *Colt's Law,* edited by Luke Short. New York, Bantam, 1957.

* * *

There are two small anomalies in Van Cort's work; one is that a writer who adheres to imitative formulae should produce so little fiction; the second, that his adventures of the Wild West should put so much emphasis on the value of domesticity, security, and the home. *Blood on the Moon* (*The Rangers of Bloody Silver* in the American edition) is wholly conventional. It tells of a range war in which four cowboys band together to save a young woman's ranch and silver mine from a megalomaniac judge, who is trying to marry the girl to his crooked son. The action consists of the usual romance, shoot-out, disposal of the villains, and final resolution. The plot proceeds by entirely familiar scenes, like the hero's rescue of the heroine and her friend from a runaway stagecoach or the journey of the two girls west on the train, a scene straight out of a Zane Grey novel like *The Shepherd of Guadaloupe*. Because the ranch owner has just returned from college in the East, the usual debate about eastern and western values occurs (she stands for law and civilized procedures; the leader of the cowboy cavalry champions independent executions of justice). Despite the East-West debate, all (except the villains) are working towards the same end: a tamer, more domestic West. The hero recurrently voices his desire to establish towns in the West and, despite the violence of some of his deeds, much of the action involves him in familial or domestic relationships: he has come north from Texas to reconcile himself with his father, he wants to settle down with the heroine and he fights to defend her home. Cort writes his book of the Wild West almost as a prelude to a novel of the settled West, for the adventures are justifiable, not in themselves, but only because of the security they will bring about. This becomes most obvious in the last few lines of the book. The conventional western usually ends with a sunset and a sense of summation; Cort ends with sunrise and the beginning of another, more desirable kind of life: the hero, content at last, "was seeing the sun breaking out over a new and different land."

—Christine Bold

CORTEEN, Wes. *See* **NORWOOD, V.G.C.**

COX, William R(obert). Also wrote as Mike Frederic; Willard d'Arey; John Parkhill; Joel Reeve; Wayne Robbins; Roger G. Spellman; Jonas Ward. American. Born in Peapack, New Jersey, 14 April 1901. Educated at public schools in New Jersey; extension courses at Rutgers University, New Brunswick, New Jersey, and Princeton University, New Jersey. Married 1) Lee Frederick in 1950, one son; 2) Casey Collins. Worked in the family ice, coal, wood, and fuel oil business in the 1930's; then freelance writer. Past president, Western Writers of America; member of the Credit Committee, and the Television Panel, Writers Guild of America West. *Died 7 August 1988.*

WESTERN PUBLICATIONS

Novels (series: Buchanan; Cemetery Jones)

The Lusty Men. New York, Pyramid, 1957.
Comanche Moon: A Novel of the West. New York, McGraw Hill, 1959; London, Corgi, 1962.
The Duke. New York, New American Library, 1962; London, New English Library, 1963.
The Outlawed. New York, New American Library, 1963; as *Navajo Blood,* 1973.
Bigger than Texas. New York, Fawcett, and London, Muller, 1963.
Tall for a Texan (as Roger G. Spellman). New York, Fawcett, 1965.
The Gunsharp. New York, Fawcett, 1965.
Black Silver. N.p., Profit Press, 1967.
Day of the Gun. New York, Belmont, 1967.
Firecreek (novelization of screenplay). New York, Bantam, 1968.
Moon of Cobre. New York, Bantam, 1969.
Law Comes to Razor Edge. New York, Popular Library, 1970.
Buchanan's War (as Jonas Ward). New York, Fawcett, 1970.
Trap for Buchanan (as Jonas Ward). New York, Fawcett, 1971.
The Sixth Horseman. New York, Ballantine, 1972.
Buchanan's Gamble. New York, Fawcett, 1972.
Jack o' Diamonds. New York, Dell, 1972.
Buchanan's Siege. New York, Fawcett, 1972.
Buchanan on the Run. New York, Fawcett, 1973.
Get Buchanan! New York, Fawcett, 1973.
The Gunsharp. London, Gold Lion, 1973.
The Fourth of July Kid. New York, Tower, 1981.
Buchanan's Black Sheep. New York, Fawcett, 1985.
Cemetery Jones. New York, Ballantine, 1985; Bath, Chivers, 1987.
Buchanan's Stage Line. New York, Fawcett, 1986.
Cemetery Jones and the Maverick Kid. New York, Fawcett, 1986.
Cemetery Jones and the Dancing Guns. New York, Fawcett, 1987.
Cemetery Jones and the Gunslingers. New York, Fawcett, 1988.

Uncollected Short Stories

"When Death's Stage Rolled to Cougartown," in *Star Western* (Chicago), February 1941.
"Texas Law Works Alone," in *Star Western* (Chicago), June 1941.
"Bullets for Boom-Town Votes," in *Star Western* (Chicago), August 1941.
"Colt Heritage," in *Wild West* (New York), 6 September 1941.

"When Hell Hit the Lazy A," in *Star Western* (Chicago), October 1941.
"Aces and Eights," in *Wild West* (New York), 4 October 1941.
"Proud Texas Guns," in *Star Western* (Chicago), November 1941.
"The Trio from Hell," in *Star Western* (Chicago), December 1941.
"Gunfire in the Dark," in *Wild West* (New York), 27 December 1941.
"Legacy of Steel," in *Cowboy Movie Thrillers* (New York), January 1942.
"One Damn Good Fighting Man!," in *Star Western* (Chicago), February 1942.
"Short-Handed in Hell," in *Star Western* (Chicago), April 1942.
"Warriors of the Buckskin Trail," in *Star Western* (Chicago), May 1942.
"Fighting Fugitives of the Wagon Trails," in *Star Western* (Chicago), February 1943.
"Duke Bagley's Gallows Rendezvous," in *Star Western* (Chicago), April 1943.
"Texans, Turn and Fight," in *Star Western* (Chicago), May 1943.
"The Duke Meets the Devil," in *Star Western* (Chicago), June 1943.
"Born to the Buckskin Trail," in *Star Western* (Chicago), July 1943.
"The Bar V Shoves 'em North," in *Star Western* (Chicago), August 1943.
"Duke Bagley's Gunsmoke Home-Coming," in *Star Western* (Chicago), September 1943.
"Long Hair, Long Rifle—and Sudden Death," in *Star Western* (Chicago), October 1943.
"Duke Bagley Deals in Death," in *Star Western* (Chicago), November 1943.
"There's Trouble at Fort Tarry!," in *West* (Kingswood, Surrey), November 1943.
"When Terror Rules in Random," in *Star Western* (Chicago), December 1943.
"White Man's War-Path," in *Star Western* (Chicago), January 1944.
"Red Terror from Texas," in *West* (Kingswood, Surrey), January 1944.
"Duke Bagley—Gunsmoke Godfather," in *Star Western* (Chicago), February 1944.
"The Duke Hangs High," in *Star Western* (Chicago), April 1944.
"Hell-Town's Hangnoose Home-Coming," in *Star Western* (Chicago), May 1944.
"Duke Bagley's Indian Medicine," in *West* (Kingswood, Surrey), May 1944.
"Duke Bagley—Gentlemen of Death!," in *Star Western* (Chicago), July 1944.
"Westward the Fighting Legions Go," in *West* (Kingswood, Surrey), July 1944.
"End of the Red War-Trail," in *Star Western* (Chicago), October 1944.
"The Saga of Dan Duval," in *Five Novels* (New York), October–December 1944.
"The Duke's Bullet Blessing," in *Star Western* (Chicago), November 1944.
"The Parson Buries His Dead," in *West* (Kingswood, Surrey), December 1944.
"Buckskin Never Dies!," in *Star Western* (Chicago), February 1945.
"The Duke's Hangtown Homecoming," in *Star Western* (Chicago), March 1945.
"Duke Bagley's Boothill Ballot," in *Star Western* (Chicago), June 1945.
"A Time and a Place," in *West* (Kingswood, Surrey), July 1945.
"No Range to Ride Alone!," in *Star Western* (Chicago), September 1945.
"Duke Bagley Doubles for Death," in *Star Western* (Chicago), November 1945.
"Last of the Range-Wreck Syndicate," in *Star Western* (Chicago), December 1945.
"Don't Turn Your Back in Bootleg!," in *Star Western* (Chicago), March 1946.
"The Duke Bets on Bullets," in *Star Western* (Chicago), May 1946.
"Hell-Wagons West!," in *Star Western* (Chicago), January 1948.
"King of Killers and the Queen of Hearts," in *Star Western* (Chicago), April 1948.
"Sad Sam's Stake," in *West* (Kingswood, Surrey), November 1949.
"The Pop Gun Kid," in *West* (Kingswood, Surrey), April 1950.
"Decision," in *Frontiers West*, edited by S. Omar Barker. New York, Doubleday, 1959.
"Hired Gun," in *Western Roundup*, edited by Nelson Nye. New York, Macmillan, 1961.
"Mountain Man on a Mule," in *The Pick of the Roundup*, edited by Stephen Payne. New York, Avon, 1963.
"One More River to Cross," in *Rivers to Cross*, edited by William R. Cox. New York, Dodd Mead, 1966.
"Cage the Bird," in *Western Romances*, edited by Peggy Simson Curry. New York, Fawcett, 1969.
"Billy the Button," in *Zane Grey Western* (New York), November 1970.
"Death for a Horseman," in *Zane Grey Western* (New York), January 1971.
"Poker Dell," in *The Steamboaters*, edited by Bill Pronzini and Martin H. Greenberg. New York, Fawcett, 1986.
"Long Guns and Scalp Knives," in *More Wild Westerns*, edited by Bill Pronzini. New York, Walker, 1989.

OTHER PUBLICATIONS

Novels

Make My Coffin Strong. New York, Fawcett, 1954; London, Fawcett, 1955.
The Tycoon and the Tigress. New York, Fawcett, 1958.
Hell to Pay. New York, New American Library, 1958.
Murder in Vegas. New York, New American Library, 1960.
Death Comes Early. New York, Dell, 1961.
Death on Location. New York, New American Library, 1962.
Way to Go, Doll Baby! New York, Avon, 1966.
Hot Times. New York, Fawcett, 1973.

Fiction (for children)

Five Were Chosen: A Basketball Story. New York, Dodd Mead, 1956.
Gridiron Duel. New York, Dodd Mead, 1959.
The Wild Pitch. New York, Dodd Mead, 1963.
Tall on the Court. New York, Dodd Mead, 1964.
Third and Eight to Go. New York, Dodd Mead, 1964.
Big League Rookie. New York, Dodd Mead, 1965.
Trouble at Second Base. New York, Dodd Mead, 1966.
The Valley Eleven. New York, Dodd Mead, 1966.
Goal Ahead (as Joel Reeve). New York, Phillips, 1967.
Jump Shot Joe. New York, Dodd Mead, 1968.
Rookie in the Backcourt. New York, Dodd Mead, 1970.

Big League Sandlotters. New York, Dodd Mead, 1971.
Third and Goal. New York, Dodd Mead, 1971.
Playoff. New York, Bantam, 1972.
Gunner on the Court. New York, Dodd Mead, 1972.
The Running Back. New York, Bantam, 1972.
Chicano Cruz. New York, Bantam, 1972.
The Backyard Five. New York, Dodd Mead, 1973.
Game, Set, and Match. New York, Dodd Mead, 1973.
The Unbeatable Five. New York, Dodd Mead, 1974.
Battery Mates. New York, Dodd Mead, 1978.
Home Court Is Where You Find It. New York, Dodd Mead, 1980.

Fiction (for children) as Mike Frederic

Frank Merriwell, Freshman Quarterback. New York, Award, 1965.
Frank Merriwell, Freshman Pitcher. New York, Award, 1965.
Frank Merriwell, Sports Car Racer. New York, Award, 1965.

Plays

Screenplays: *The Veils of Bagdad*, 1953; *Tanganyika*, with William Sackheim and Alan Simmons, 1954.

Television Plays: 100 scripts for *Fireside Theatre*, *Broken Arrow*, 1956–57, *Zane Grey Theatre*, 1956–60, *Bonanza*, 1959–71, *Journey to Ninevah*, 1960–63, *The Virginian*, 1962–69, *The Grey Ghost*, *Alcoa Theatre*, *Wells Fargo*, *Route 66*, and other series.

Other

Luke Short and His Era. New York, Doubleday, 1961; as *Luke Short, Famous Gambler of the Old West*, London, Foulsham, 1962.
The Mets Will Win the Pennant. New York, Putnam, 1964.

Editor, *Rivers to Cross.* New York, Dodd Mead, 1966.

*

Manuscript Collections: University of Oregon, Eugene; University of Wyoming, Laramie.

Critical Study: interview with James L. Traylor, in *Armchair Detective* (White Bear Lake, Minnesota), 1982.

William R. Cox commented (1982):

I believe a writer cannot truly be made. I was writing when I was 10. Had it not been for family pressure to aid in the business I would never have quit newsmongering. The short story form was blissful until there were no markets. I then came west, to television, movies, thence back to prose in 1954. 75 published works since then has been most rewarding. A professional makes no excuses, he tells the story. He is the modern minstrel. I draw the line at "adult Westerns" but otherwise I run the open field. I believe in sex but not pornography. I've retired from WGAW but belong to P.E.N. and Western Writers of America (was twice president); of course I love writers as I love writing. At 80 I am content that I have indeed told the story and am still telling it.

What more can a man ask?

* * *

After a writing career of over 60 years, 75 books, and perhaps 1,000 short stories, plus numerous motion picture and television screenplays, a writer might be expected to slow down. Cox, however, at 80, had the appearance of a man who could still keep up with the 600,000 published words a year he averaged for 14 years during the pulps era. And, as his close friend Brian Garfield (another outstanding western author) said: "Bill Cox is writing better than ever."

Cox had nearly two decades of professional writing behind him before turning to the Western. "To be honest, my work in Westerns started in the pulp magazines in 1939 or 1940," he said. "And I began writing Westerns because I had glutted the market with sports, crime, and adventure stories." It is characteristic of this indefatigable professional that once he turned to the Western, he devoted his entire writing attention to it. Other western fiction writers, he claimed, did not "inspire" him, and the history and romance of the West found in his novels are the result of reading sound history and seeing locales first-hand.

But Cox's Westerns do not depend upon, nor contain, extensive historical backgrounds; he writes the "traditional" western—built around a strong central character of heroic proportions (though not necessarily of heroic virtues), taking revenge or righting a wrong. His novels are noted for their "page-turner" pace, realistic dialogue, and frequent Colt-and-Winchester gunplay. The Series of novels built around the strong West Texas character Tom Buchanan, are very typical Cox Westerns.

—Dale L. Walker

CRANE, Robert. *See* **ROBERTSON, Frank C.**

CREED, Joel. *See* **KING, Albert.**

CRIDER, (Allen) Bill(y). Also writes as Nick Carter. American. Born in Mexia, Texas, 28 July 1941. Educated at the University of Texas, Austin, B.A. 1963, Ph.D. 1972; North Texas State University, Denton, M.A. 1967. Married Judy Stutts in 1965; one daughter and one son. Teacher, Corsicana High School, Texas, 1963–65; Associate Professor, 1971–76, and Professor and Chair of English Department, 1977–83, Howard Payne University, Brownwood, Texas. Since 1984 Chair of English Department, Alvin Community College, Texas. Recipient: Anthony award, 1986. Address: 1606 South Hill, Alvin, Texas 77511, U.S.A.

WESTERN PUBLICATIONS

Novels

Ryan Rides Back. New York, Evans, 1988.
Galveston Gunman. New York, Evans, 1988.
A Time for Hanging. New York, Evans, 1989.
Medicine Show. New York, Evans, 1990.

Uncollected Short Story

"Wolf Night," in *Westeryear*, edited by Ed Gorman. New York, Evans, 1988.

OTHER PUBLICATIONS

Novels

Too Late to Die. New York, Walker, 1986.
Shotgun Saturday Night. New York, Walker, 1987.
Cursed to Death. New York, Walker, 1988.
One Dead Dean. New York, Walker, 1988.
Death on the Move. New York, Walker, 1989.
Dying Voices. New York, St. Martin's Press, 1989.
Evil at the Root. New York, St. Martin's Press, 1990.

Novels as Jack MacLane

Keepers of the Beast. New York, Zebra, 1988.
Goodnight Momm. New York, Zebra, 1989.
Blood Dream. New York, Zebra, 1989.
Rest in Peace. New York, Zebra, 1990.
Just Before Dark. New York, Zebra, 1990.

Other

A Vampire Named Fred (for children). Uffkin, Texas, Temple, 1990.

Editor, *Mass Market American Publishing*. New York, Hall, 1982.

*

Bill Crider comments:

My interests in western fiction are combined in my novels, which have been characterized as "cross genre" books. I'm not trying to confuse anyone; I'm just trying to write Westerns like the ones I've enjoyed, by writers like Harry Whittington, Donald Hamilton, and Elmore Leonard. While I'm probably falling short of that goal, I'm having a fine time.

* * *

In *A Time for Hanging*, Bill Crider displays his expertise in writing mysteries in his story of a poor Mexican boy, Paco Morales, accused of murdering the daughter of the preacher in Dry Springs. Crider captures the bleakness of a small western town and the small-mindedness of its citizens as they decide to by-pass the law because it's "a time for hanging."

Just as skillfully as he portrays the all too human frailties of his contemporary Texas sheriff Dan Rhodes, Crider creates a compelling character in Sheriff Ward Vincent. Sheriff Vincent is a quiet man, slow to anger, a compromiser rather than a confronter. Vincent knows the violence growing in his town is poison but he doubts he has the strength to resist the will of the mob's rush to hang Paco Morales. But by conclusion of *A Time for Hanging*, Vincent not only finds wellsprings of strength he never knew he had, he also identifies the real murderer. The hallmark of Crider's novels in his care to create memorable, complex, human characters. The murdered girl is the daughter of a preacher. Crider goes against the stereotype and adds a dimension to the character: the preacher is a former gunfighter. And with the death of his daughter, the gunfighter part of the man—the deadly part of himself the preacher thought he'd buried long ago—takes hold and extracts vengeance. This type of characterization adds richness and fullness to the novels. Blending the elements of mob justice and a murder mystery makes *A Time for Hanging* Crider's most entertaining western novel.

This attention to careful characterization is also present in Crider's first western novel, *Ryan Rides Back*. Crider takes the familiar plot of the western vengeance novel and makes it interesting because of the characters he creates. Returning to avenge the murder of his sister, Sally, Ryan discovers that Billy Kane, who is about the hang for the crime, is the wrong man. Ryan discovers the real truth about his sister's death. Crider's characters come alive in these pages and transcend the usual clichés of the genre.

Galveston Gunman was Crider's attempt to write a novel more historically based. Crider sets in motion a political plot whose victim is to be President Ulysses S. Grant. The power behind this plot is Colonel Benson who hates blacks and Yankees, who secretly continues to fight his own private Civil War. The characters in *Galveston Gunman* are less compelling than the characters in Crider's other Westerns because the action flows from the plot rather than from the characters.

In Crider's latest book, *Medicine Show*, Ray Storey's brother is an innocent by-stander who's killed during a bank robbery. Ray vows to avenge his brother's death, sells the farm, and joins COLONEL A. J. AHAFFEY'S AUTHENTIC INDIAN MEDICINE SHOW. As "Kit Carson," Ray puts on a marksmanship show. Ray believes Sam Hawkins was the man who killed his brother and by traveling with the medicine show, he hunts for Hawkins in every small East Texas town the medicine show makes a stop.

But again, Crider goes against the stereotype: we find out Ray reads *Hamlet*. Already we're warned that this is not going to be a simple story of revenge. When Sam Hawkins and his brother Ben attack the medicine show, robbing the night receipts and shooting down two of men in the audience while Ray never pulls his guns, the story moves into Ray's discovery he isn't a killer. *Medicine Show* is a story of characters' self-discovery and the ways they change: the preacher and his wife have to resolve their sexual differences, the doctor who has retreated into alcoholism has to decide whether to use his surgical skills to save a man's life, and Ray Storey has to confront his own lack of a killer instinct. The resolution of these human conflicts makes *Medicine Show* Crider's most satisfying western novel.

—George Kelley

CROSS, Polton. *See* **FEARN, John Russell.**

CRUMLEY, James. American. Born in Three Rivers, Texas, 12 October 1939. Educated at Georgia Institute of Technology, Atlanta, 1957–58; Texas A. and I. University, Kingsville, Texas, B.A. 1964; University of Iowa, Iowa City, M.F.A. 1966. Served in the United States Army, 1958–61. Married 1) Judith Ann Ramey in 1975 (divorced); 2) Bronwyn Pugh in 1979 (divorced); two daughters and three sons. Instructor in English, University of Montana, Missoula, 1966–69; Assistant Professor of English, University of Arkansas, Fayetteville, 1969–70, and Colorado State University, Fort Collins, 1971–74; freelance writer, 1974–76; Visiting Associate Professor of creative writing, Reed College, Portland, Oregon, 1976–77; Visiting Writer, Carnegie-Mellon University, Pittsburgh, Pennsylvania, 1979–80; Assistant Professor of English, University of Texas, El Paso, 1981–84. Since 1985 screenplay writer. Agent: Owen Laster, William Morris Agency, 1350 Avenue of the Americas, New York, New York 10019. Address: P.O. Box 9278, Missoula, Montana 59807, U.S.A.

WESTERN PUBLICATIONS

Novels

The Wrong Case. New York, Random House, 1975; London, Hart Davis McGibbon, 1976.
The Last Good Kiss. New York, Random House, 1978; London, Granada, 1979.
Dancing Bear. New York, Random House, 1983; London, Penguin, 1987.

OTHER PUBLICATIONS

Novel

One to Count Cadence. New York, Random House, 1969.

* * *

James Crumley's first novel, *One to Count Cadence*, is a tough, gritty story of American troops in Southeast Asia early in the Vietnam War, and the disillusionment back home over the war. *One to Count Cadence* is a hardbitten novel that gives a realistic picture of the dispirited Americans of the Vietnam era. Crumley's writing is first-class, and his ability to express the feel of disillusionment makes the novel memorable.

After *One to Count Cadence*, Crumley has not returned to the mainstream novel, preferring to stick to detective fiction set for the most part in the western United States. He has almost always written such good crime novels that reviewers and critics have accorded him a leading place in the genre. His second novel, *The Wrong Case*, introduces a hardbitten Montana private eye, Stag Milo Milodragovitch, who is from a pioneer Montana family that has fallen on evil days. His grandfather was a rich early settler, but his father drank himself to death on the streets of Meriwether, where Milo now operates as a seedy divorce detective when he is sober enough. *The Wrong Case* opens when Milo is approached by an attractive young woman from Iowa who is looking for her missing brother. The brother, who was a homosexual involved in a drug scam, is found dead, ostensibly of an overdose. The more Milo digs into this case, the more it turns out to be shrouded by lies—Helen Duffey's, her brother's, and those of half the people Milo encounters in this "wrong" case. There is an air of depression hanging over the novel, the town, the state of Montana, and the world. Milo, who lives his life drunk, stoned, or hung-over, is an extreme version of the dispirited private eye who has populated American detective fiction since the days of Dashiell Hammett. Milo's life is symptomatic of a dying world, a world which Crumley reveals clearly in all his works.

The Last Good Kiss introduces another of Crumley's hardcase private detectives. This one is named C.W. Sughrue, but he is clearly one of Milo Milodragovitch's brothers under the skin.

Sughrue is hired to find and babysit a well-known poet who tends to get drunk and drift from bar to bar. Abraham Trahearne, whose works have made him famous, has a wife, an ex-wife, and a mother who try to keep tabs on him to no avail. Sughrue finds him, but gets sidetracked on a missing persons case while Trahearne is laid up in the hospital after a bar room fight. Sughrue then mixes his search for Betty Sue Flowers with his "handling" of Trahearne. Things are not what they seem—they never are in Crumley's world—and the missing person is no longer Betty Sue, but is involved in the other half of Sughrue's case. *The Last Good Kiss* takes Sughrue from Montana to California to Colorado to Oregon to Idaho and back to several of those places. It is very much a "road" novel that gives a strong sense of America's constant shifting and unrelieved mobility.

Dancing Bear, Crumley's third private-eye novel takes us back to Milo Milodragovitch, almost indistinguishable from Sughrue except in name. Milo, who is marking time as a glorified night watchman until he turns 52 and comes into his father's estate, is hired by an family friend to find out why two apparently illicit lovers are meeting on the street in front of her house. This is a silly thing to worry about, but since Sarah Weddington is an old woman—with a beautiful niece—Milo agrees to look into the non-case.

Of course things are not at all what they seem, and the "lovers" lead Milo all over the Northwest tracking environmental activists, heavyweight polluters, and killers. Milo, who is living almost entirely on a diet of cocaine and peppermint schnapps, is barely able to function as he drives all over the western states. But he does manage to get out of his haze from time to time. He even wins a violent shootout with the polluters and solves the case. At the end Milo returns a wilderness area—"Camas Meadows . . . where the bears used to dance"—to the Indians, who suffer most at the hands of polluters. *Dancing Bear* was well received critically because it dealt with so many modern problems—pollution, drugs, rootlessness—but it is marred by a streak of sentimentality that surfaces despite the tough-guy facade of the action plot.

Crumley is a talented writer who has not quite found his niche. It remains to be seen whether the mystery genre allows him the leeway he needs to develop fully his flawed, disturbed characters in the flawed, disturbed world that Crumley sees all about us.

—James W. Lee

CULLUM, Ridgewell. British. Born in London, 13 August 1867. Married Agnes Winifred Mutz in 1898. Traveller and adventurer from age 17: joined the gold rush in the Transvaal, worked in diamond mines, and traded, in Africa, fought in the Kaffir wars, hunter and trapper in Alaska and the Yukon, rancher in Montana, fought in the Sioux Indian uprisings on Pine Ridge and Rosebud reservations; retired to England as a freelance writer, 1904. *Died 3 November 1943.*

WESTERN PUBLICATIONS

Novels

The Devil's Keg. London, Chapman and Hall, 1903; as *The Story of the Foss River Ranch*, Boston, Page, 1903; as *Foss River Ranch*, London, Newnes, 1927.
The Hound from the North. London, Chapman and Hall, and Boston, Page, 1904.
The Brooding Wild. London, Chapman and Hall, 1905; as *In the Brooding Wild*, Boston, Page, 1905.
The Night-Riders: A Romance of Western Canada. London, Chapman and Hall, 1906; as *The Night-Riders: A Romance of Early Montana*, Philadelphia, Jacobs, 1913.
The Watchers of the Plains. London, Chapman and Hall, 1908; Philadelphia, Jacobs, 1909.
The Sheriff of Dyke Hole. London, Chapman and Hall, and Philadelphia, Jacobs, 1909.
The Trail of the Axe. London, Chapman and Hall, and Philadelphia, Jacobs, 1910.

The One-Way Trail. London, Chapman and Hall, and Philadelphia, Jacobs, 1911.
The Twins of Suffering Creek. London, Chapman and Hall, and Philadelphia, Jacobs, 1912.
The Golden Woman. London, Chapman and Hall, and Philadelphia, Jacobs, 1913.
The Law-Breakers. London, Chapman and Hall, and Philadelphia, Jacobs, 1914.
The Way of the Strong. London, Chapman and Hall, and Philadelphia, Jacobs, 1914.
The Son of His Father. London, Chapman and Hall, and Philadelphia, Jacobs, 1915.
The Men Who Wrought. London, Chapman and Hall, and Philadelphia, Jacobs, 1916.
The Triumph of John Kars. London, Chapman and Hall, and Philadelphia, Jacobs, 1917.
The Purchase Price. London, Chapman and Hall, 1917; as *The Forfeit*, Philadelphia, Jacobs, 1917.
The Law of the Gun. London, Chapman and Hall, and Philadelphia, Jacobs, 1918.
The Heart of Unaga. London, Chapman and Hall, and New York, Putnam, 1920.
The Man in the Twilight. London, Palmer, and New York, Putnam, 1922.
The Luck of the Kid. London, Palmer, and New York, Putnam, 1923.
The Saint of the Speedway. London, Palmer, and New York, Doran, 1924; as *The Man from Lias River*, London, Brown Watson, 1950.
The Riddle of Three-Way Creek. London, Palmer and New York, Doran, 1925.
The Candy Man. London, Palmer, 1926; as *Child of the North*, New York, Doran, 1926.
The Wolf Pack. London, Palmer, and Philadelphia, Lippincott, 1927.
The Mystery of the Barren Lands. London, Cassell, and Philadelphia, Lippincott, 1928.
The Tiger of Cloud River. London, Cassell, and Philadelphia, Lippincott, 1929.
The Treasure of Big Waters. London, Cassell, and Philadelphia, Lippincott, 1930.
The Bull Moose. London, Chapman and Hall, and Philadelphia, Lippincott, 1931.
Sheets in the Wind. London, Chapman and Hall, and Philadelphia, Lippincott, 1932.
The Flaming Wildness. London, Chapman and Hall, and Philadelphia, Lippincott, 1934.
One Who Kills. London, Chapman and Hall, and Philadelphia, Lippincott, 1938.

OTHER PUBLICATIONS

Novels

The Compact. London, Chapman and Hall, and New York, Doran, 1909.
The Vampire of N'Gobi. London, Chapman and Hall, 1935; Philadelphia, Lippincott, 1936.

* * *

Ridgewell Cullum's books runneth over. Cullum combines seemingly discordant and inharmonious events into a cohesive unit with a touch of humor and a sense of ease. Despite the fact that his western fiction centers around his own experiences in western Canada and Montana as a trapper, trader, and sometime Indian fighter, his books are less true adventure and more the stories on which legends are founded.

In *The Sheriff of Dyke Hole*, one of his earliest novels, Cullum demonstrates his ability to pull together some unlikely threads. In *Dyke Hole* he entwines a search for a lost woman and her daughter, a race for a $2 million silver mine, a kidnapping, and a cricket game in Dyke Hole with Joe Tombstone in a light-hearted East-meets-West commentary.

Cullum's characters are more fully developped in his later novels. Still, Joe Tombstone—the sheriff of Dyke Hole—stands out as a meaty scrappy character in this early work. A fighter who is easily moved to action, Tombstone is feared and respected by the town, and usually gets what he wants. He is a simple, direct character who has no illusions about himself. Cullum's men are typically tough, pragmatic individualists. Tombstone said, "Life is one durned long bluff." Consequently, Cullum's characters grab all they can from life. Even his women possess a sphere of power and influence all their own in his novels. In *The Triumph of John Kars* Cullum surprises the reader with ironic twists in his characters. In this and other later Yukon adventure tales, Cullum displays a much surer grip on character development than he does in his Montana fiction (*Dyke Hole*, *The Golden Woman*).

Cullum uses dialectic speech for many of his characters. His Montanans speak tersely, perfunctorily—with the exception of Joe Tomstone. Tombstone's dialogue reminds me of the 1950's television series *Gunsmoke* character Old Festus. Festus used to sidewind a bit before he'd make his point. Cullum sidewinds a bit himself, getting so caught up in the creation of dialect that he sometimes loses the reader. This makes what should be easy reading cumbersome at times. In *The Triumph of John Kars* and *The Luck of the Kid* Cullum's Indians talk about making "heap big pow-wow" and "kill 'em all dead, bang, bang" which is almost a laughing matter for many contemporary readers. Cullum's leaning toward the melodramatic make his books anything but serious reading.

Cullum's descriptions are beautiful but sometimes esoteric. Describing the Yukon as "a world apart," he helps the reader to enter that world and see it through his eyes. Yet his descriptions of the northwest pine woods goes too far when he talks about "conifers" and "lichens." He begins to lose the simple beauty he is trying to portray.

Cullum offers mystery and adventure in each of his novels. His writing is passionately dramatic for his time. His earlier books are a whirlwind of activity. Yet, in later novels, Cullum settles down to practice character development and more simplistic plots. Like Joe Tombstone, Cullum has no illusions about himself and offers no more than imaginative legendary tales about fortune hunting in the pioneer days of the Northwest.

—Cassandra Fedrick

CULP, John H(ewett, Jr.). American. Born in Meridian, Mississippi, 31 August 1907. Educated at the University of Oklahoma, Norman, A.B. 1934 (Phi Beta Kappa). Served in the United States Army Air Force, 1943–45: Sergeant. Married Elizabeth Price in 1934 (died). School teacher, Norman, 1934–41; owner of music store, Ardmore, Oklahoma, 1941–42, and Shawnee, Oklahoma, 1946–48; then full-time writer. Address: 1805 North Louisa, Shawnee, Oklahoma 74801, U.S.A.

WESTERN PUBLICATIONS

Novels

Born of the Sun. New York, Sloane, 1959; London, Deutsch, 1963.
The Men of Gonzales. New York, Sloane, 1960.
The Restless Land. New York, Sloane, 1962.
The Bright Feathers. New York, Holt Rinehart, 1965.
A Whistle in the Wind. New York, Holt Rinehart, 1968.
Timothy Baines. New York, Holt Rinehart, 1969.
The Treasure of the Chisos. New York, Holt Rinehart, 1971.
Oh, Valley Green! New York, Holt Rinehart, 1972.

* * *

John H. Culp began writing late in life, after a career that included service in the Air Corps in World War II, seven years as a public school teacher in Norman, Oklahoma, and many years as owner and operator of a music store. As a youth he had absorbed the tales of frontier life told by his grandfather, who had joined the Frontier Battalion of the Texas Rangers in 1874 and served under Ledbetter, Maltby, and Seay. Culp grew up in Fort Smith, on the Arkansas–Oklahoma border, and worked on ranches in Oklahoma and Texas. This background, combined with a serious study of the history of the Southwest, formed a solid foundation for his novels. But far more then just factual knowledge is involved in these books. Culp breathes life into an era, and creates characters who can recapture a reader's mind and heart. Writing in the *New York Times* about Culp's fourth novel, *The Bright Feathers*, Orville Prescott said, "Mr. Culp is a natural born teller of tales, a man who can spin a yarn with effortless ease. He is a student of Western Americana who delights in the lore of the past and in rescuing from oblivion forgotten episodes and historical tragedies."

Culp's first novel, *Born of the Sun*, was greeted with unanimous praise by reviewers: "true Americana, filled with the exuberance and hardy spirit of the pioneers," "one of the most vivid and refreshing novels of the Southwest to come along in recent years." It is the tale of an epic trail drive from the Tail End Ranch in Texas to Abilene, Kansas, led by a young boy and a crew of wild Texas cowhands. The story is continued in *The Restless Land*, again narrated by 15-year-old Martin Cameron, nicknamed the Kid. The books tell of the Kid's painful and adventurous passage to maturity against the background of post-Civil War Texas. *The Bright Feathers* is another story in the same mode, recounting the picaresque adventures of three teenaged cowhands making their way from Kansas to Texas in the fall of 1871. The background here is the struggle of the Five Civilized Tribes to adapt to the ways of white society.

An earlier phase in the history of the Five Civilized Tribes forms the framework for *Timothy Baines*. This is the story of the intertwined lives of three people: Dorch McIntyre, a part-Chicasaw doctor haunted by the accidental killing of his young sweetheart; the driven and vengeful Denna Cart; and the hunchback, Timothy Baines, "who had been thrown into a garbage can in an alley at birth, and had been named for the gentleman in whose can he was found, and had been brought up in the streets and alleys of New Orleans." Vine Deloria, Jr., in the Boston *Herald Traveler*, wrote, "The beauty of this book is that John Culp knows his subject well. He does not romanticize nor does he favor either white or Indian in his interpretation of his major theme. The book comes straight at the reader as a classic view of what life was like on the old Indian reserves of the Five Civilized Tribes."

A Whistle in the Wind is the story of a Comanchero camp in Texas from before the Civil War until the defeat of the Comanches and the arrival of the homesteaders, as told through events in the life of a remarkable woman, Cesre Chafin. In *The Treasure of the Chisos*, young Colin O'Reiley journeys from St. Louis to southwest Texas in search of his heritage. *Oh, Valley Green!* tells the story of patriarch Jacob Key, who moves his family from the Shenandoah westward over the Santa Fe Trail in 1842, charged with the mission of setting up an undercover network in the New Mexico Territory to help pave the way for the U.S. Government's annexation of Texas and California. As in all of Culp's novels, it is the human story in the foreground that holds the attention and stirs the emotions. Culp's novels are mixtures of myth-making and history, marked by a scrupulous fidelity to the nature of the people, the times, and the country about which he writes.

—R.E. Briney

CUMMINGS, Jack. American. Born in Los Angeles, California, 20 June 1925. Educated at Alhambra High School; Pasadena City College. Served in the United States Army in Iran, 1945, and Italy, 1946. Married to Florence Gualano; one son and one daughter. Light-heavyweight boxer, Pasadena City College; has also worked as a telephone lineman along the U.S.–Mexican border, flight instructor, actor, carpenter, and building contractor. Since 1980 full-time writer. Agent: Ray Peekner Literary Agency, 3121 Portage Road, Bethlehem, Pennsylvania 18017, U.S.A.

WESTERN PUBLICATIONS

Novels

Dead Man's Medal. New York, Walker, 1984; London, Hale, 1985.
Sergeant Gringo. New York, Walker, 1984; London, Hale, 1987.
Lynch's Revenge. New York, Walker, 1985; London, Hale, 1988.
Tiger Butte. New York, Walker, 1986; London, Hale, 1987.
Rebels West. New York, Walker, 1987; London, Hale, 1988.
Once a Legend. New York, Walker, 1988; London, Hale, 1989.
The Rough Rider. New York, Walker, 1988; London, Hale, 1990.
The Surrogate Gun. New York, Walker, 1990.
Escape from Yuma. New York, Walker, 1990.

*

Theatrical Activity:
Actor: **Film**—*La Cronaca Nera*, 1946.

Jack Cummings comments:

I don't think I have been influenced by any particular books or authors. But of all western writers I am most fond of Ernest Haycox. He had a prose style that, to me, ranks with anything in literature, and an uncanny ability to evoke the atmosphere of his western locales.

Perhaps my own novels differ from those of some western writers in that, though I strive for authenticity of background, my primary concern is to present a strong drama, and to resolve it suspensefully against the western setting.

I consider *The Rough Rider* a good example of this, although I also favor *Once a Legend*.

Despite my early dabbling in the humorous field, I do not find humor compatible with the way I see the Old West. I see it as grim, and I see it realistically, with average people put to ultimate tests in a harsh environment. I do *not* see it with mythical supermen who knock a thrown dime out of the air with a .45 slug from a sixgun.

And I am encouraged by a seeming trend in today's Westerns away from such myths and toward more realism.

* * *

Although Jack Cummings was writing fiction as a high school student (and remembers his first rejection coming from the old *Liberty Magazine*), and wrote a variety of off-beat short fiction in the 1960's while working as a carpenter and building contractor, he began his career as western novelist at the age of 55, in 1980, after placing second in the "Best First Western Novel" contest sponsored by Bantam Books and 20th-Century Fox Films. That contest produced over 1,000 entries, of which four—including Cummings's novel titled *Cholo*—were sent to the film studio for final judging. W.W. Southard, a New Mexico newspaper-man, won the $25,000 first prize; Cummings was runner-up.

But *Cholo* was published in 1984 as *Dead Man's Medal*, and Cummings has published eight other novels in the succeeding six years.

Cummings believes his knack for the off-trail setting and plot came from his 1960's discovery, after reading Scott Meredith's book, *Writing to Sell*, of a then relatively new market, the "sophisticated men's magazine."

"It was a fun-to-write market," the author says. "The stories ran about 2,500 words and the magazines paid $150–$250. The best asset, besides writing ability, you needed for this market was an *antic imagination* to produce a far-out premise."

Cummings recalls one short-short story, titled "When Scud Manley Went South," he wrote and sold that concerned an ex-paratrooper with a nagging wife, who took up skydiving as a hobby. "He gets into a plane," Cummings recalls, "goes aloft and makes his jump just as a flock of geese passes beneath him. He never comes down."

He adds, "After those stories in the men's magazines, I did not write again until 1980, but the idea of first hitting on an intriguing *premise* stuck with me, and I use it today in my Westerns. When I get that premise, I can feel it in my gut, and then the characters who will be caught up in it appear and begin to act, and the plot begins to evolve. From then on it is a matter of striking the keyboard."

Examples of Cummings's premise-to-character-to-plot approach to novel writing can be seen in such recent of his books as *The Rough Rider*, *Once a Legend*, *The Surrogate Gun*, and *Escape from Yuma*.

In *The Rough Rider*, the premise has to do with cattle baron Lew Axford, an ambitious schemer and "false hero" of the Spanish-American War who uses his "heroism" and Medal of Honor for political gain but falls afoul of an honest cowhand, Jess Gault, who knows the truth.

Once a Legend concerns a once-celebrated lawman, Drew Hardin, now fallen on bad times and reduced to drawing crowds and cadging drinks in Arizona saloons, and young hero-worshipper, Frank Ladd, who tracks him down. The story is set in 1915 and has to do with the release from prison of Tolbert, a hard-case killer who Hardin had originally apprehended, and the old lawman's determination to recapture the man and some of his past glory.

In *The Surrogate Gun*, Cummings has a New Mexico newspaperman and dime-novel writer named Bret Holt who takes a local saddle tramp and saloon swamper, Will Savage, and transforms him into a fictional hero. When Holt is shot up by a local hired gun, he turns to the man he has "created" for help.

Cummings's newest Walker Western is *Escape from Fort Yuma*. It takes place in Arizona Territory in 1888 and of it the author says, "On the face of it, it is not an unusual story but my escapee is a woman. I based the story, very loosely, on Pearl Hart, about the last of the road agents who was sent to prison for robbing a stagecoach. Hart's crime took place in Globe, Arizona, in 1899."

Cummings says "Of all western writers, I am most fond of Ernest Haycox. He had a prose style that, to me, ranks with any in literature, and an uncanny ability to evoke the atmosphere of his western locales."

—Dale L. Walker

CUNNINGHAM, Chet. Also writes as J.D. Bodine; Chad Calhoun; G.A. Carrington; Jess Cody; Cathy Cunningham; Kit Dalton; Lionel Derrick; Dirk Fletcher. American. Born in Shelby, Nebraska, 9 December 1928. Educated at Pacific University, Forest Grove, Oregon, B.A. 1950; Columbia University, New York, M.S. 1954. Served in the United States Army, 1950–52: Sergeant. Married Rose Marie Wilhoit in 1953; two sons and one daughter. City editor, Forest Grove *News-Times*, 1954–55; writer, Jam Handy, Detroit, 1955–59; columnist, "Truck Talk," 1956–79, and "Your Car," from 1959. Motion picture writer, Convair, San Diego, 1959–60. Publisher and writer, Cunningham Press, San Diego, California. Since 1962 chair, San Diego Writers Workshop. Agent: Don Sheperd, 18645 Sherman Way, Suite 210, Reseda, California 91335. Address: 8431 Beaver Lake Drive, San Diego, California 92119, U.S.A.

WESTERN PUBLICATIONS

Novels (under own name, and as Chad Calhoun; series: Chisholm; Outlaws; Pony Soldiers; Brad Spear; Jim Steel, the "Gold Man")

Bushwhackers at Circle K. New York, Avalon, 1969.
Killer's Range. New York, Avalon, 1970.
The Gold Wagon. New York, Pinnacle, 1972; as Jess Cody, Crewe, Cheshire, Ulcerscroft, 1989.
Die of Gold. New York, Pinnacle, 1973; as Jess Cody, New York, Dorchester, 1986; Crewe, Cheshire, Ulverscroft, 1989.
Bloody Gold. New York, Pinnacle, 1975; as Jess Cody, New York, Dorchester 1986; Bath, Chivers, 1989.
The Patriots. New York, Belmont, 1976.
The Gold and the Glory. New York, Nordon, 1977.
The Power and the Price. New York, Nordon, 1977.
Seeds of Rebellion. New York, Belmont, 1977.
The Poker Club. Westport, Connecticut, Condor, 1978.
Beloved Rebel. New York, Nordon, 1978.
Rainbow Saga. New York, Nordon, 1979.
This Splendid Land. New York, Nordon, 1979.
Apache Ambush (Chisholm). New York, Carousel, 1979; Bath, Chivers, 1988.
Arizona Gunfire (Chisholm). New York, Carousel, 1980; Bath, Chivers, 1988.
Man in Two Camps (Chisholm). New York, Carousel, 1980.

Devil's Gold. New York, Tower, 1980; as Jess Cody, New York, Dorchester, 1987.
Cheyenne Payoff. New York, Dell, 1981.
Gold Train. New York, Tower, 1981; as Jess Cody, New York, Dorchester, 1987; Bath, Chivers, 1990.
The Silver Mistress (Spear). New York, Dell, 1981.
Tuscon Temptress (Spear). New York, Dell, 1981.
Remember the Alamo. New York, Dell, 1981.
Aztec Gold. London, Hale, 1982; as Jess Cody, New York, Dorchester, 1987.
Deepwater Showdown. New York, Dell, 1983.
Pony Soldiers series:
  Slaughter at Buffalo Creek. New York, Dorchester, 1987.
  Comanche Massacre. New York, Dorchester, 1987.
  Comanche Moon. New York, Dorchester, 1988.
  Cheyenne Blood Storm. New York, Dorchester, 1988.
  Sioux Showdown. New York, Dorchester, 1988.
  Sioux Slaughter. New York, Dorchester, 1988.
  Boots and Saddles. New York, Dorchester, 1988.
  Renegade Army. New York, Dorchester, 1988.
  Battle Cry. New York, Dorchester, 1989.
  Fort Blood. New York, Dorchester, 1989.
Outlaws series:
  Ride Tall or Hang High. New York, Dorchester, 1989.
  Six Guns. New York, Dorchester, 1989.
  Dead Man's Hand. New York, Dorchester, 1989.
  Avengers. New York, Dorchester, 1990.

Novels as Dirk Fletcher (series: Spur McCoy in all books)

High Plains Temptress. New York, Dorchester, 1981.
Arizona Fancy Lady. New York, Dorchester, 1981.
St. Louis Jezebel. New York, Dorchester, 1982.
Rocky Mountain Vamp. New York, Dorchester, 1982.
Cathouse Kitten. New York, Dorchester, 1983.
Indian Maid. New York, Dorchester, 1983.
San Francisco Strumpet. New York, Dorchester, 1983.
Wyoming Wench. New York, Dorchester, 1983.
Texas Tart. New York, Dorchester, 1983.
Montana Minx. New York, Dorchester, 1983.
Santa Fe Floozy. New York, Dorchester, 1984.
Nevada Hussy. New York, Dorchester, 1984.
New Mexico Sisters. New York, Dorchester, 1985.
Hang Spur McCoy. New York, Dorchester, 1985.
Rawhider's Woman. New York, Dorchester, 1985.
Saloon Girl. New York, Dorchester, 1985.
Bald Knobber's Woman. New York, Dorchester, 1986.
San Diego Sirens. New York, Dorchester, 1987.
Frisco Foxes. New York, Dorchester, 1988.
Portland Pussycat. New York, Dorchester, 1989.
Boise Belle. New York, Dorchester, 1989.
Bounty Hunter's Moon. New York, Dorchester, 1989.
Tall Timber Trollop. New York, Dorchester, 1989.

Novels as Kit Dalton (series: Buckskin in all books)

Gunpoint. New York, Dorchester, 1986; Bath, Chivers, 1987.
Lever Action. New York, Dorchester, 1986.
Scattergun. New York, Dorchester, 1987.
Winchester Valley. New York, Dorchester, 1987.
Gunsmoke Gorge. New York, Dorchester, 1987.
Remington Ridge. New York, Dorchester, 1987.
Shotgun Station. New York, Dorchester, 1987.
Pistol Grip. New York, Dorchester, 1987.
Peacemaker Pass. New York, Dorchester, 1988.
Silver City Carbine. New York, Dorchester, 1988.
California Crossfire. New York, Dorchester, 1988.
Hangfire Hill and *Crossfire.* New York, Dorchester, 1988.
Gunpoint and *Lever Action.* New York, Dorchester, 1989.
Colt Crossing. New York, Dorchester, 1989.
Powder Charge. New York, Dorchester, 1989.
Laramie Showdown. New York, Dorchester, 1989.
Double Action. New York, Dorchester, 1989.
Dead Man's Moon. New York, Dorchester, 1989.
Apache Rifles. New York, Dorchester, 1990.
Return Fire. New York, Dorchester, 1990.

Novel as J.D. Bondie (series: Quinn's Raiders)

Red Bluff Revenge. New York, Lynx, 1989.

Novel as G.A. Carrington (series: Arrow and Saber)

The Templeton Massacre. New York, Dell, 1990.

OTHER PUBLICATIONS

Novels

The Chacom Affair. New York, Powell, 1969.
Nick Carter: Night of the Avenger. New York, Award, 1971.
Moscow at High Noon Is the Target. New York, Award, 1972.
Fatal Friday. N.p., Venice, 1973.
The Dinner Murder Mystery. San Diego, California, Sandlight, n.d.
Mansion of Dreams. New York, Carousel, 1979.
Silent Murder. New York, Carousel, 1980.
The Deadly Connection. New York, Carousel, 1980.
The Avenger. New York, Warner, 1987.
The Avenger: 2. New York, Warner, 1988.
Colombia Crackdown. New York, Warner, 1988.
Manhattan Massacre. New York, Warner, 1988.

Novels as Cathy Cunningham

The Demons of Highpoint House. New York, Popular Library, 1973.
Lost Love Found. N.p., Pioneer Communications, 1986.
Love's Confession. N.p., Pioneer Communications, 1986.
Young Lovers. N.p., Pioneer Communications, 1986.
Love's Denial. N.p., Pioneer Communications, 1986.

Novels as Don Pendleton

Crude Kill. Toronto, Gold Eagle, 1982.
Hellbinder. Toronto, Gold Eagle, 1983.
Orbiting Omega. Toronto, Gold Eagle, 1983.
Skysweeper. Toronto, Gold Eagle, 1983.
Resurrection Day. Toronto, Gold Eagle, 1984.
Baltimore Trackdown. Toronto, Gold Eagle, 1984.
Nothing Personal. Toronto, Gold Eagle, 1984.
Kill Trap. Toronto, Gold Eagle, 1984.
Motor City Mayhem. Toronto, Gold Eagle, 1985.

Novels as Lionel Derrick

Blood on the Strip, with Mark Roberts. New York, Pinnacle, 1973.
Hijacking Manhattan, with Mark Roberts. New York, Pinnacle, 1974.
Tokyo Purple, with Mark Roberts. New York, Pinnacle, 1974.
Northwest Contract, with Mark Roberts. New York, Pinnacle, 1974.

The Hellbomb Flight, with Mark Roberts. New York, Pinnacle, 1975.
Bloody Boston, with Mark Roberts. New York, Pinnacle, 1975.
Mankill Sport, with Mark Roberts. New York, Pinnacle, 1975.
Deepsea Shootout, with Mark Roberts. New York, Pinnacle, 1976.
Countdown to Terror, with Mark Roberts. New York, Pinnacle, 1976.
The Radiation Hit, with Mark Roberts. New York, Pinnacle, 1976.
High Disaster, with Mark Roberts. New York, Pinnacle, 1977.
Cryogenic Nightmare, with Mark Roberts. New York, Pinnacle, 1977.
Mexican Brown Death, with Mark Roberts. New York, Pinnacle, 1978.
The Skyhigh Betrayers, with Mark Roberts. New York, Pinnacle, 1979.
Computer Kill, with Mark Roberts. New York, Pinnacle, 1979.
Showbiz Wipeout, with Mark Roberts. New York, Pinnacle, 1979.
Death Ray Terror, with Mark Roberts. New York, Pinnacle, 1980.
Deadly Silence, with Mark Roberts. New York, Pinnacle, 1980.
Hawaiian Trackdown, with Mark Roberts. New York, Pinnacle, 1980.
Assassination Factor, with Mark Roberts. New York, Pinnacle, 1980.
Deadly Gold Hijackers, with Mark Roberts. New York, Pinnacle, 1981.
Deep Cover Cataclysm, with Mark Roberts. New York, Pinnacle, 1981.

Fiction (for children)

Dead Start Scramble. New York, Scholastic, 1973.
You Are Expelled. Post Mills, Vermont, Fitzhenry and Whiteside, 1974.
Nare One Going Down. New York, Scholastic 1975.
The Locked Storeroom Mystery. New York, Scholastic, 1977.
Apprentice to a Rip-Off. New York, Scholastic 1978.

Other

Your Wheels: How to Keep Your Car Running. New York, Putnam, 1973.
Baja Bike. New York, Putnam, 1974.
Your Bike: How to Keep Your Motorcycle Running. New York, Putnam, 1975.
Police Tactics. St. Paul, Minnesota, West Publishing, 1975.
Your First Car. New York, Putnam, 1976.
222 Ways to Save Gas and Get the Best Possible Mileage. Englewood Cliffs, New Jersey, Prentice Hall, 1981.

* * *

Although Chet Cunningham has been writing Westerns since 1969, and many other types of book since 1973, his output rose quite dramatically in the late 1980's and continues to show little sign of slowing down. Today his work falls almost exclusively in the "adult" genre, primarily for Leisure Books, and, as may be expected from a man contributing to at least five ongoing western series, the quality of his writing, while workmanlike, is also frequently uneven.

Cunningham made his entry into the series field with the Jim Steel adventures, initially published under his own name but recently reissued as by Jess Cody. Steel is an ex-lawman with a love of (if not a mania for) gold. Indeed, gold is the only currency in which he will trade, and to underline his obsession, the word "gold" features in all the titles. Typical of the series is 1973's *Die of Gold*, in which Steel rides shotgun on a shipment of government dies en route to the U.S. Mint, only to be double-crossed at the eleventh hour.

After another short-lived sequence of Westerns, the Chisholm books, Cunningham penned the adult western series Brad Spear for Dell Books, recounting the somewhat overlong adventures of a Pinkerton agent, first under his own name and then as Chad Calhoun.

In 1987, he began possibly his best, though by no means perfect, series of Westerns, known collectively as the Pony Soldiers. In the opening title, *Slaughter at Buffalo Creek*, a supply column with which Captain Colt Harding's wife and two children are travelling is attacked by Comanches. Harding's wife and son are killed; his four year-old daughter Sadie is "adopted" by the war chief White Eagle. His subsequent search to find his daughter finally makes Harding put into practice a long-cherished dream, the creation of a so-called "Lightning Troop"—soldiers who can fight like the Indians themselves, who are expert horsemen capable of travelling light and living off the land. The third book, *Comanche Moon*, is a pivotal title in the series, for not only does Harding manage to rescue Sadie, marry another white captive, and adopt a young boy named Danny; he also undertakes a commission from General Sheridan himself to set up as many Lightning Troops across the West as he can.

A wealth of Indian and Army lore (which, if not always totally accurate, is certainly authoritative) adds credibility to the adventures of Harding's guerilla company. Cunningham's skill at creating three-dimensional supporting characters is also used to good advantage. In comparison, his companion series Outlaws (clearly inspired by the film *Young Guns*), is something of a disappointment, relying as it does on hefty doses of gratuitous violence and a somewhat sketchy style of storytelling.

The Outlaws series tells of the exploits of a gang of young offenders led by the notorious Willy Boy Lambier. Escaping from the jail of a small Texas town in *Ride Tall or Hang High*, the half-dozen hardcases make a pact to stick together for a year and help each other to do something they have never been able to achieve alone. In the first book, Willy Boy attempts to exact revenge on the bounty hunter who killed his father. In *Six Guns* the gang helps Eagle, its full-blooded Comanche member, to track down the soldiers who slaughtered his family many years before. The gambler/gunman Johnny Joe Williams is next, getting into a card game with a man who cheated him when he was still largely inexperienced. Johnny wins the game this time round, only to die for his troubles (*Dead Man's Hand* and for *Avengers* the Professor, a larcenous college boy, finally manages to pull off a bank robbery that previously nearly cost him his life.

A very busy writer, Cunningham has also recently taken over the reins of two more exceptionally pornographic western series, Buckskin and Spur, written as Kit Dalton and Dirk Fletcher respectively. The former chronicles the adventures of Lee Morgan, the illegitimate son of "Buckskin" Frank Leslie, who was the protagonist of the first five books. Like his father, Morgan is deadly with a gun, but he also carries a rather lethal bullwhip. In Cunningham's hands, Morgan has been as far north as Alaska and as far south as Argentina. In *Colt Crossing* he is hired by the Union Pacific to find hundreds of missing land grants. *Apache Rifles* finds him down on his luck and agreeing to scout for the Army against a band of marauding Chiricahua.

The "Spur" of the latter series is Spur McCoy, an over-sexed U.S. Secret Service agent who works as a trouble-shooter primarily for the Treasury Department. Consequently, Spur's missions frequently revolve around counterfeiters or gangs out to undermine the American economy; *San Diego Sirens*, *Frisco Foxes*, and *Portland Pussycat*, for example, all share this theme, while in *Boise Belle* he is called upon to protect the Governor of Idaho against a masked gang calling itself the Citizen's Vigilance Committee. Cunningham has also contributed giant special editions to both these series.

It is quite possible that this seemingly inexhaustible writer has contributed to other series; unfortunately, copyright lines do not always make clear the identity of the scribe behind the house-name. Cunningham has definitely written at least one book in the Quinn's Raiders series for Lynx (*Red Bluff Revenge*) and another for Dell's Arrow and Saber sequence (*The Templeton Massacre*)—and there is no reason to doubt that he has, in fact, written much more besides.

—David Whitehead

CUNNINGHAM, Eugene. Also wrote as Leigh Carder. American. Born in Helena, Arkansas, 29 November 1896. Educated at public schools in Dallas and Fort Worth, and privately. Served in the United States Navy, 1914–19, and reservist until 1923; served in Naval Intelligence, 1941. Married Mary Emilstein in 1921; two daughters and one son. Journalist: correspondent in Central America for *World Wide* magazine, London, and other magazines, 1919; then freelance writer. *Died 18 October 1957.*

WESTERN PUBLICATIONS

Novels

The Trail to Apacaz. New York, Dodd Mead, and London, Unwin, 1924.
Riders of the Night. Boston, Houghton Mifflin, 1932; London, Selwyn and Blount, 1933.
Buckaroo. Boston, Houghton Mifflin, 1933; London, Hodder and Stoughton, 1934.
Diamond River Man. Boston, Houghton Mifflin, and London, Hodder and Stoughton, 1934; as *Diamond River Range*, New York, Popular Library, 1949.
Texas Sheriff. Boston, Houghton Mifflin, 1934; London, Hodder and Stoughton, 1935.
Quick Triggers. Boston, Houghton Mifflin, 1935; London, Hodder and Stoughton, 1936.
Trail of the Macaw. Boston, Houghton Mifflin, and London, Hodder and Stoughton, 1935.
Pistol Passport. Boston, Houghton Mifflin, 1936.
Whistling Lead. Boston, Houghton Mifflin, 1936; London, Hodder and Stoughton, 1937.
The Ranger Way. Boston, Houghton Mifflin, 1937; London, Collins, 1939.
Texas Triggers. Boston, Houghton Mifflin, 1938; London, Collins, 1939.
The Trail from the River. London, Collins, 1939.
Gun Bulldogger. Boston, Houghton Mifflin, 1939.
Red Range. Boston, Houghton Mifflin, 1939; London, Collins, 1940.
Spiderweb Trail. Boston, Houghton Mifflin, 1940; London, Collins, 1941.
Mesquite Maverick. New York, Popular Library, 1955.
Riding Gun. Boston, Houghton Mifflin, 1956.

Novels as Leigh Carder

Border Guns. New York, Covici Friede, 1935; London, Collins, 1936.
Bravo Trail. New York, Covici Friede, 1935; London, Collins, 1936.
Outlaw Justice. New York, Covici Friede, 1935; London, Collins, 1936.

Short Stories

The Regulation Guy. New York, Cornhill, 1922.

Uncollected Short Stories

"Hartley's Luck," in *Adventure* (New York), 10 October 1922.
"The Scar," in *Adventure* (New York), 10 November 1923.
"Yellow and Red," in *Sunset* (San Francisco), April 1926.
"The Penasco Kid Comes Ridin'," in *The Frontier* (New York), April 1926.
"Two Nights in Abilene," in *The Frontier* (New York), August 1926.
"Once a Ranger Always a Ranger," in *The Frontier* (New York), November 1926.
"Cows in the Dark," in *The Frontier* (New York), December 1926.
"Bill-Anna Swings a Rope," in *The Frontier* (New York), January 1927.
"The Hermit of Tigerhead Butte," in *The Frontier* (New York), March 1927.
"Wanted—?," in *The Frontier* (New York), May 1927.
"The Hammar-Thumb," in *The Frontier* (New York), June 1927.
"Burned Brands," in *Cowboy Story* (London), June–October 1927.
"The Trail of a Fool," in *The Frontier* (New York), July 1927.
"Blotting the Triangle," in *The Frontier* (New York), September 1927.
"Ware Calls It a Day," in *The Frontier* (New York), October 1927.
"The Fortieth Thief," in *The Frontier* (New York), November 1927.
"The House of Whispering Shadows," in *The Frontier* (New York), February 1928.
"Murder at Three Orphans," in *The Frontier* (New York), March 1928.
"The Frame-Up," in *The Frontier* (New York), April 1928.
"Shelley Rides a Killer's Trail," in *The Frontier* (New York), May 1928.
"The Border Patrol," in *The Frontier* (New York), August 1928.
"Shootin' Shelley Shoots to Kill," in *The Frontier* (New York), September 1928.
"Lord of Liarsburg," in *Argosy* (New York), 6 October 1928.
"Chigaroo!," in *Argosy* (New York), 30 March 1929.
"High Line Riders," in *Argosy* (New York), 1 June 1929.
"The Red River Kid," in *Western Romances* (New York), November 1929.
"The Icicle Kid," in *Western Romances* (New York), August 1930.
"Six Gun Love," in *Western Romances* (New York), September 1930.
"Trigger Balance," in *Argosy* (New York), 31 October 1931.
"Gun Bluff," in *Western Romances* (New York), January 1932.

"Man-Style," in *Argosy* (New York), 28 May 1932.
"Banty Grows Spurs," in *All Western* (New York), July 1932.
"Sheriff Trouble," in *All Western* (New York), September 1932.
"Gamblin' Man," in *All Western* (New York), January 1933.
"The Star Hunter," in *All Western* (New York), March 1933.
"Guns of His Father," in *All Western* (New York), June 1933.
"Gun Smoke Country," in *All Western* (New York), July 1933.
"Gun Fighters Beware," in *All Western* (New York), September 1933.
"Soft Rope," in *All Western* (New York), October 1933.
"Buscadero Trail," in *All Western* (New York), December 1933.
"Killer's Country," in *All Western* (New York), February 1934.
"Trouble-Shooter," in *All Western* (New York), May 1934.
"Long Rider," in *All Western* (New York), September 1934.
"Six-Shooter Symphony," in *All Western* (New York), December 1934.
"Concho Guns," in *All Western* (New York), June 1935.
"Lobo Law," in *All Western* (New York), March 1936.
"Texas Jackpot," in *All Western* (New York), June 1936.
"Bravo Code," in *All Western* (New York), September 1936.
"Bar-Nothing's Happy Birthday," in *America West*, edited by William Targ. Cleveland, World, 1946.
"Ranger Luck," in *Gun Smoke Yarns*, edited by Gene Autry. New York, Dell, 1948.
"Hoolihan," in *Zane Grey's Western* (New York), December 1948.
"Grove Girl," in *Western Stories*, edited by William Macleod Raine. New York, Dell, 1949.
"The Two-Day Deputy," in *Selected Western Stories*, edited by Leo Margulies. New York, Popular Library, 1949.
"Sheriff Trouble," in *All Western* (New York), April–June 1950.
"Bar-Nothing Red," in *Zane Grey's Western* (New York), June 1952.
"Bar-Nothing, Feud-Breaker," in *Zane Grey's Western* (New York), August 1952.
"Bar Nothing Troubles Trouble," in *Zane Grey's Western 30* (London), 1953.
"Bar-Nothing Calls the Play," in *Gunpoint*, edited by Leo Margulies. New York, Pyramid, 1960.

OTHER PUBLICATIONS

Other

Gypsying Through Central America. New York, Dutton, and London, Unwin, 1922.
Famous in the West (on criminals). El Paso, Texas, Hicks Hayward, 1926.
Triggernometry: A Gallery of Gunfighters. New York, Press of the Pioneers, 1934; London, Corgi, 1957.
Redshirts of Destiny. New York, Empire, 1935.

Editor, *Buckboard Days*, by Sophie Poe. Caldwell, Idaho, Caxton, 1936.
Editor, *Apache Days and After*, by Thomas Cruse. Caldwell, Idaho, Caxton, 1941.

* * *

Eugene Cunningham shared several personal characteristics with his friend, Eugene Manlove Rhodes: a prickly independence and a you-be-damned integrity. His fiction was far removed from that of Rhodes, for Cunningham was as fine a lapidary as ever polished an action Western for the market place. He was, as well, a volume producer, who could look back at more than nine millions of words *sold* when his last book, *Riding Gun*, appeared in 1956.

It will be noted, it is hoped, that he is described as a writer of "action" Westerns, which were not necessarily straight formula Westerns. Cunningham had "seen it through the smoke," including a stint as a soldier-of-fortune in Central America after World War I. Hence his psychology of the gunsmoke breed and his use of it in his fiction stem from what began as a means of survival and was honed thereafter as an intellectual exercise. In this regard he antedates Ernest Haycox's use of psychological suspense, although Cunningham never let clots of psychology interfere with his action-packed narrative. His non-fiction *Triggernometry: A Gallery of Gunfighters* has had some of its factual details corrected down the years but not the psychology of the various *pistoleros* it presents.

Complaints have been voiced that the body counts in his fiction rival those allegedly scored against the North Vietnamese by the United States. Another complaint voiced by tender-hearted moderns is simply that his heroes and villains alike hold human life pretty cheap. There is valid historical reason for both these aspects of his fiction. As noted above, Cunningham was familiar personally with powdersmoke; furthermore, he was inheritor of the Texas tradition that had 60 years of fighting Comanche and Mexican irregulars in its making. His frame of historical reference was that hectic period when the Texas frontier burst westward—"Beyond the Nuceces, no law; beyond the Pecos, no God"—and direct and forceful action was required to subdue armed anarchy and establish order that the rules of law then might develop. His exemplars were certain paladins of the Texas Rangers; his time frame was roughly 1880–1900, and his chosen locale was the No Man's Land of the West Texas–New Mexico–Old Mexico boundaries. His *Diamond River Man*, for example, is based upon the rise and fall of Pat Coghlan, one time "King of Tularosa" who bought the cattle that Billy the Kid and his friends stole elsewhere; similarly, his *Spiderweb Trail* contains his version of what happened to Colonel Albert Jennings Fountain and his small son in the White Sands of New Mexico.

His novels were crammed with characters involved in an intricately plotted contest between good and evil that used the peak-and-valley technique of keeping the hero in constant trouble before the inexorable climax in gunfire. His geography was straight, as were his flora and fauna. His idioms were true to those who used them and his women, generally two or more competing for the hero's hormones, certainly did not creak when they moved. All this, plus his subtleties and nuances of shading, lifts his action yarns out of the ruck of the genre.

—W.H. Hutchinson

CURRY, Peggy Simson. British. Born in Dunure, Ayrshire, Scotland, 30 December 1911. Educated at the University of Wyoming, Laramie, 1932–36, B.A. 1936. Married William Seeright Curry in 1937; one son. Instructor in creative writing, Casper College, Wyoming 1951–87. Poet-in-Residence, Wyoming Arts Council, 1970–87. Poet Laureate of Wyoming, 1981. Recipient: Western Writers of America Spur award, for story, 1958, 1971. *Died 20 January 1987.*

WESTERN PUBLICATIONS

Novels

So Far from Spring. New York, Viking Press, 1956; London, Muller, 1957.
The Oil Patch. New York, McGraw Hill, 1959.

Uncollected Short Stories

"Night of Champions," in *Saturday Evening Post* (Philadelphia), 31 December 1949.
"Secret of Bogie Bill," in *Saturday Evening Post* (Philadelphia), 22 July 1950.
"Green Willow Growing," in *Collier's* (Springfield, Ohio), 22 March 1952.
"Lady Loved a Jailbird," in *Saturday Evening Post* (Philadelphia), 18 October 1952.
"The Osage Girl," in *Twenty-Two Stories about Horses and Men*, edited by Jack B. Creamer. New York, Coward McCann, 1953.
"Life of Our Own," in *Collier's* (Springfield, Ohio), 19 February 1954.
"Bitter Sunday," in *American Magazine* (Springfield, Ohio), April 1955.
"McCreery and the Colonel's Shirt," in *Colt's Law*, edited by Luke Short. New York, Bantam, 1957.
"Geranium House," in *Frontiers West*, edited by S. Omar Barker. New York, Doubleday, 1959.
"The Brushoff," in *Spurs West*, edited by S. Omar Barker. New York, Doubleday, 1960.
"The Bride Wore Spurs," in *Western Romances*, edited by Peggy Simson Curry. New York, Fawcett, 1973.

Verse

Red Wind of Wyoming. Denver, Sage, 1955; revised edition, Fairbanks, Alaska, Spirit Mount, 1975.
Summer Range. Story, Wyoming, Dooryard, 1981.

OTHER PUBLICATIONS

Novel

Fire in the Water. New York, McGraw Hill, 1951; London, Muller, 1952.

Other

Creating Fiction from Experience. Boston, The Writer, 1964.
A Shield of Clover (for children). New York, McKay, 1970.

Editor, *Western Romances.* New York, Fawcett, 1973.

*

Manuscript Collection: University of Wyoming Library, Laramie.

Peggy Simson Curry commented (1982):

The west, particularly Colorado ranch country where I grew up and Wyoming where I live, dominate most of my poetry, articles, and fiction. It is the persuasion of "place"—the place that dominates memory, present-time living, imagination—history, people, weather, whatever stimulates the senses and the creative impulse. Whether one is in home territory, visiting or traveling, the detail of "place" offers the realism that supports plot, characterization, theme. In cultivation of awareness of "place"—locale—the writer may discover poems, fiction, and articles for local, regional, national, and international markets.

* * *

Peggy Simson Curry's two volumes of modest lyrics accurately reflect the natural background of her adopted western homeland. In poems such as "The Hunt," "Remote Sheep Ranch," "Lupine Ridge," and "Jack Patton," Curry exhibits the talent that earned her the honor of Wyoming's first poet laureate. An interesting exception to the lyrical mode is "Red Wind," a dramatic retelling of the Johnson County cattle war, using both fictional and historical characters, based on Asa Shinn Mercer's *The Banditti of the Plains.*

The characters of her short stories are somewhat stereotyped, appealing principally to consumers of popular magazines. Yet locale is always sharply rendered and the plots are tightly controlled. In such stories as "Geranium House," Curry approaches the realism of Hamlin Garland.

Following her own dictates to her creative writing students, Curry emphasizes setting and realistic detail in her novels, too. *Fire in the Water*, about the fishing industry of her native Scotland, establishes her ability to create recognizable characters as well.

So Far from Spring, her best novel, tells two stories: that of Kelsey Cameron who came from Scotland to the American West to make his fortune; and that of Kelsey's daughter, Heather, whom we see growing up and maturing emotionally and intellectually. But what is most impressive here is the realistic detail about the cattle industry, obviously drawn from personal experience. Curry tells us how it feels to muck a stable, ride a cow pony, dig a ditch or a post hole, and feed, breed, and brand cattle. She knows about grass, about droving, and about natural hazards: wind, drought, blizzards. It is a first-class performance.

Curry is almost as successful with another Wyoming novel, *The Oil Patch.* The setting this time is a dry, dusty oil-company camp in the 1930's. Liz Malloch, newly married to Price Malloch, is the central character, but there are other important roles. Price is hired as a lowly roustabout on a pipeline crew, where his rising ambition leads to social climbing in the company structure and to disagreements about values with his wife. Price eventually espouses "right" and "good," and in a somewhat vapid ending gets a promotion and saves his marriage. Curry is at her best, once more, in depicting the workaday world of the oil field and the pipeline, the dreary company houses, the rules and the impersonality of the oil company. In the latter respect, the novel is reminiscent of Alice Tisdale Hobart's *Oil for the Lamps of China.*

A novel for children, *A Shield of Clover*, is also worthy of mention. The short narrative presents one summer in the life of a young midwestern runaway who learns basic lesson about life while cutting hay on a Wyoming ranch. Once again, Curry competently evokes the presence of the vibrant, brooding land, and the necessity of honest endeavor.

—Robert J. Barnes

CURRY, Tom (Thomas Albert Curry). Also wrote as Jackson Cole; Romer Zane Grey. American. Born in 1900. Educated at Columbia University, New York, B. Sc. Married to Louise Curry: two sons and one daughter. Reporter, New York

American, during early 1920's; engineer with Door-Oliver Inc., 1955–67. From 1925 writer and contributor to pulp magazines. *Died 7 October 1976.*

WESTERN PUBLICATIONS

Novels (series: Captain Mesquite)

Hate Along the Rio. New York, Dodge, and London, Cassell, 1938.
Round-Up Guns. New York, Gateway, 1939; London, Cassell, 1940.
Chaparral Marauders. New York, Gateway, 1939.
Texas Terror. London, Cassell, 1939.
Captain Mesquite. New York, Arcadia House, 1941.
The Buffalo Hunters. New York, Arcadia House, 1941; London, Mills and Boon, 1953.
The Comstock Lode (Mesquite). New York, Arcadia House, 1941; London, Boardman, 1950.
The Mormon Trail (Mesquite). New York, Gateway, 1942; London, Cassell, 1947.
Guns of the Sioux. New York, Arcadia House, 1945; London, Hutchinson, 1948.
Marshal of Wichita. New York, Arcadia House, 1946; London, Wright and Brown, 1949.
Blood on the Plains (Mesquite). New York, Arcadia House, 1947; London, Hutchinson, 1949.
Riding for Custer (Mesquite). New York, Arcadia House, 1947; London, Wright and Brown, 1950
Santa Fe Trail (by Walker A. Tompkins). New York, Popular Library, 1948. (Note: This novel, which appeared under the name of Walker A. Tompkins both at the time of first publication, and in a subsequent printing by Popular Library in 1976, was in fact wrongly attributed to Walker A. Tompkins due to a publisher's error. The book was actually written by Tom Curry, although his name does not appear in it, and it is not copyrighted to him.)

Uncollected Short Stories (series: Rio Kid; Masked Rider)

"Six-Gun Valley," in *Range Rider Western* (New York), April 1939.
"Chaparral Marauders," in *Masked Rider Western* (New York), September 1939.
"Frontier Guns," in *Rio Kid Western* (New York), December 1939.
"The Trail Blazers," in *Rio Kid Western* (New York), Winter 1940.
"The Buffalo Hunters," in *Rio Kid Western* (New York), Spring 1940.
"The Rio Kid Rides Again," in *Rio Kid Western* (New York), June 1940.
"The Comstock Lode," in *Rio Kid Western* (New York), October 1940.
"Guns of the Sioux," in *Rio Kid Western* (New York), December 1940.
"The Mormon Trail," in *Rio Kid Western* (New York), February 1941.
"Kansas Marshal," in *Rio Kid Western* (New York), April 1941.
"Riding for Custer," in *Rio Kid Western* (New York), August 1941.
"Arizona Gunsmoke," in *Masked Rider Western* (New York), September 1941.
"Pards of Buffalo Bill," in *Rio Kid Western* (New York), October 1941.
"The Montana Vigilantes," in *Rio Kid Western* (New York), December 1941.
"Six-Gun Island," in *Range Rider Western* (New York), Winter 1942.
"Arizona Blood," in *Rio Kid Western* (New York), April 1942.
"Guns of Dodge City," in *Rio Kid Western* (New York), August 1942.
"Kit Carson's Way," in *Rio Kid Western* (New York), October 1942.
"Blood on the Plains," in *Rio Kid Western* (New York), December 1942.
"Leadville Avengers," in *Rio Kid Western* (New York), February 1943.
"Riders of Steel," in *Rio Kid Western* (New York), Summer 1943.
"Colorado Blood," in *Range Rider Western* (New York), Summer 1943.
"Indian Outpost," in *Rio Kid Western* (New York), Spring 1944.
"Sierra Gold," in *Rio Kid Western* (New York), Fall 1944.
"Wagons to California," in *Rio Kid Western* (New York), Winter 1945.
"Chaparral Courage," in *Range Rider Western* (New York), Winter 1945.
"Colorado River Gold," in *Rio Kid Western* (New York), Spring 1945.
"Border Patrol," in *Rio Kid Western* (New York), Summer 1945.
"Highway to Boot Hill," in *Rio Kid Western* (New York), September 1945.
"Raiders of New Mexico," in *Rio Kid Western* (New York), November 1945.
"Carpetbagger Guns," in *Rio Kid Western* (New York), January 1946.
"On to Cheyenne," in *Rio Kid Western* (New York), May 1946.
"Guns Along the Brazos," in *Range Rider Western* (New York), June 1946.
"Raiders of the Valley," in *Rio Kid Western* (New York), October 1946.
"Idaho Raiders," in *Rio Kid Western* (New York), February 1947.
"Gun Boss of San Antone," in *Rio Kid Western* (New York), December 1947.
"Santa Fe Trail," in *Rio Kid Western* (New York), April 1948.
"Sign of the Vigilantes," in *Rio Kid Western* (New York), April 1949.
"The Renegade Senator," in *Rio Kid Western* (New York), December 1949.
"Guns of Fort Benton," in *Rio Kid Western* (New York), July 1950.
"Outlaws of Arizona," in *Rio Kid Western* (New York), November 1950.
"Raiders of Deadwood," in *Rio Kid Western* (New York), March 1951.
"Riders of the Central Hills," in *Masked Rider Western* (New York), March 1951.

Uncollected Short Stories as Jackson Cole (series: Jim Hatfield)

"Death Rides the Rio," in *Texas Rangers* (New York), August 1937.
"Guns Along the Pecos," in *Texas Rangers* (New York), November 1937.
"Mesquite Marauders," in *Texas Rangers* (New York), February 1938.
"Red Runs the Rio," in *Texas Rangers* (New York), April 1938.

"Panhandle Bandits," in *Texas Rangers* (New York), October 1938.
"Gunsmoke Empire," in *Texas Rangers* (New York), February 1939.
"Vaquero Guns," in *Texas Rangers* (New York), April 1939.
"Peril Rides the Pecos," in *Texas Rangers* (New York), August 1939.
"Red Raiders of the Rio," in *Texas Rangers* (New York), April 1940.
"Six Gun Fury," in *Texas Rangers* (New York), June 1940.
"Apache Guns," in *Texas Rangers* (New York), October 1940.
"Emperor of the Pecos," in *Texas Rangers* (New York), February 1941.
"Rustler Range," in *Texas Rangers* (New York), April 1941.
"Outlaw Valley," in *Texas Rangers* (New York), August 1941.
"Wild Horses," in *Texas Rangers* (New York), December 1941.
"Six Gun Hills," in *Texas Rangers* (New York), April 1942.
"Free Range," in *Texas Rangers* (New York), August 1942.
"The Black Hat Murders," in *Texas Rangers* (New York), December 1942.
"Haunted Range," in *Texas Rangers* (New York), June 1943.
"Pecos Poison," in *Texas Rangers* (New York), August 1943.
"Panhandle Guns," in *Texas Rangers* (New York), December 1943.
"The Red Marauders," in *Texas Rangers* (New York), August 1944.
"Six Gun Survey," in *Texas Rangers* (New York), December 1944.
"Hell in Paradise," in *Texas Rangers* (New York), April 1945.
"Gun Governor," in *Texas Rangers* (New York), June 1945.
"Pirates on Horseback," in *Texas Rangers* (New York), August 1945.
"Outlaws of the Frontier," in *Texas Rangers* (New York), January 1946.
"Bad Medicine for Buckaroos," in *Texas Rangers* (New York), May 1946.
"The Crimson Flower," in *Texas Rangers* (New York), June 1946.
"Range Pirates," in *Texas Rangers* (New York), October 1946.
"The Nestors' Feud," in *Texas Rangers* (New York), December 1946.
"Six Gun Syndicate," in *Texas Rangers* (New York), March 1947.
"Gulf Guns," in *Texas Rangers* (New York), April 1947.
"Rodeo Raiders," in *Texas Rangers* (New York), August 1947.
"Law on the Winter Range," in *Texas Rangers* (New York), September 1947.
"Guns of the Yellow Hills," in *Texas Rangers* (New York), November 1947.
"Keep Off This Range," in *Texas Rangers* (New York), February 1948.
"Galveston Raiders," in *Texas Rangers* (New York), May 1948.
"Red River Rule," in *Texas Rangers* (New York), June 1948.
"King of the Brazos," in *Texas Rangers* (New York), August 1948.
"Trouble on the Trinity," in *Texas Rangers* (New York), November 1948.
"The Gun Boosters," in *Texas Rangers* (New York), December 1948.
"Raiders of the Forest," in *Texas Rangers* (New York), January 1949.
"Secret of the Central Hills," in *Texas Rangers* (New York), April 1949.
"The Austin Marauders," in *Texas Rangers* (New York), June 1949.
"Rustlers of Black Range," in *Texas Rangers* (New York), August 1949.
"The Riders of Rusk," in *Texas Rangers* (New York), October 1949.
"Guns of Fort Griffen," in *Texas Rangers* (New York), November 1949.
"Bayou Guns," in *Texas Rangers* (New York), December 1949.
"The Land Pirates," in *Texas Rangers* (New York), May 1950.
"The Skeleton Riders," in *Texas Rangers* (New York), August 1950.
"Secret of the Saddlebrand," in *Texas Rangers* (New York), October 1950.
"Gun Paradise," in *Texas Rangers* (New York), January 1951.
"Golden Guns," in *Texas Rangers* (New York), March 1951.
"Riders of the Storm," in *Texas Rangers* (New York), October 1951.

*

Manuscript Collection: University of Oregon, Eugene.

* * *

Tom Curry's primary contributions to 20th-century western fiction consist in the many notable super-hero novelettes he wrote for various pulp magazines. His father and mother both wrote and sold theatrical plays and his father even wrote a western story which was awarded the O. Henry prize in 1922. Curry's first western story was sold to *People's Magazine* when he was 20 and still a student at Columbia University. He graduated the next year with a degree in chemical engineering. At 23 he was hired as a reporter by the New York *American* covering the crime beat in the city's "Tenderloin" district. By 1925 Curry was taking advantage of his experiences and stories he heard from police detectives by writing a series of stories about Mac, a tough New York police investigator, which appeared in *The Black Mask*, then edited by Phil Cody. When Captain Joseph T. Shaw took over as editor, he made Curry one of the inner circle invited to literary drinking parties along with Carroll John Daly, Frederick Nebel, and Dashiell Hammett. In the 1930's Curry also became a regular contributor to *Detective Fiction Weekly*. However, the most propitious contact he was to make in the pulp market was with Leo Margulies, editorial director for N.L. Pines's Standard Magazines which included the Thrilling Group from Better Publications. Margulies encouraged him to write western stories and his first ones were short and humorous.

In 1936, to mark the 100th anniversary of the founding of the Texas Rangers, Margulies launched a new magazine titled *Texas Rangers*. The first issue, which appeared in October of that year, had a 45,000 word "novel" about Texas Ranger Jim Hatfield written by Curry but published under the house name Jackson Cole. He continued to contribute Jim Hatfield "novels" to this magazine along with Leslie Scott and Walker A. Tompkins, as well as others, until it ceased publication in 1958. However, his most significant creation came in 1939 when Margulies asked him to devise a new super-hero for a new magazine and he came up with Bob Pryor, the Rio Kid. *The Rio Kid Western* was launched in October 1939 as a quarterly and Margulies wrote a letter to Curry in which he confided: "We were very much pleased with the way you handled the first Rio Kid story. I honestly think it's one of the best novels you've turned out." For this novel and the second one in the Rio Kid series Curry was paid $250. By the mid 1940's he was being paid $450 for a 45,000-word novel. He had married and lived in a Colonial farm house 175 years old outside Norwalk, Connecticut, a mill town with a population around 50,000. He would divide his time between Connecticut in the summer and Florida in the winter. Also in the 1940's he began turning his pulp novels into book-length novels, most of them published by Samuel Curl's Arcadia House. Davis Dresser and C. William Harrison had soon joined him in writing Rio Kid novels. Dresser at the time was also contributing entries to Morrow's Western series, novels mostly about a trio of characters living in Powder Valley published under the house name Peter Field. Davis received $500 for each one he wrote, no royalties. He got a reversion of rights from Margulies for the four Rio Kid novels he wrote for the magazine and expanded these into 60,000-word book-lengths which Morrow published under the name Don Davis. Although Dresser retained the name Rio Kid for his super-hero in these novels, he was not Bob Pryor and none of the other house characters was used. Dresser was paid a similar sum for these novels and even wrote five more Westerns under his own name for Morrow before concentrating on detective fiction. Curry was not so fortunate at Arcadia House. It would take him a week or two to expand a 45,000-word pulp novel for which he was paid between $200 and $250 and a year later perhaps another $100 when British rights were sold. However, Arcadia House was not a trade publisher. Its market was lending libraries and, while there was a royalty agreement attached to its contracts, royalties were seldom paid above the advance since its press run was limited to 2500 copies which lending libraries at the time would rent out at 5 cents for three days. In 1946 alone, Curry published three book-length novels, all expansions of Rio Kid stories, with all the character names changed, *Guns of the Sioux*, *Marshal of Wichita*, and *Blood on the Plains*.

Curry's best work came during the decade of the 1940's, especially in his original Rio Kid pulp novels and not in his later expansions of them. He had designed the stories to be set around historical characters from the years 1866–76 and these characters and the settings gave them a sense of verisimilitude not found in many super-hero western pulp novels. "Colorado River Gold," for example, one of Curry's finest which appeared in the Spring 1945 issue has for its background Major John Wesley Powell's exploratory expedition on the Colorado River and Curry called on his knowledge of geology and engineering in the story's details. The magazine would supplement the novel by including vignettes and artists' drawings of the historical characters featured. In the late 1940's *The Rio Kid Western* was published bi-monthly and by 1950 it had become a monthly. Much of this popularity can be attributed to Curry's contributions to it, although others also wrote notable entries, including Walker A. Tompkins, Roe Richmond, Joseph Chadwick, D.B. Newton, and Dudley Dean McGaughey under his *nom de plume* Dean Owen. In addition to his Jim Hatfield novels, Curry wrote three lead novels for *The Masked Rider* and a few for *Range Riders*, also *Thrilling* publications. However, by 1955 the pulp magazine market had virtually vanished and Curry made a career change as well, going to work as an engineer for Door-Oliver, Inc., where he stayed for 14 years. In 1967 he turned over all his papers and manuscripts to the archive at the University of Oregon and was essentially retired. It was then that Leo Margulies came once more on the scene. In October 1969, Margulies would begin publishing a new digest-sized pulp magazine, *Zane Grey Western Magazine*, an entirely different publication from Dell's *Zane Grey's Western Magazine* from 1946–54. It was Margulies's idea to have a number of Grey's best-known characters brought back to life in a series of novelettes and Leo wanted Curry to start it rolling with a new Buck Duane, Texas Ranger story for the first issue. Although Curry wrote the Buck Duane novelettes, they were all signed as by Romer Zane Grey, Grey's elder son and one of the advisory editors. To this roster in subsequent issues were added novelettes featuring Arizona Ames as by Romer Zane Grey but actually written by Jeff Wallman and Bill Pronzini and Laramie Nelson novelettes written by Clayton Matthews. The last issue of this magazine appeared in September 1974. Not long thereafter, in 1976, Curry died of an embolism at the age of 75 at his home in Norwalk. Yet, after 15 years of engineering, Leo Margulies had given him a chance once again to write western fiction, just as he had encouraged him in the early days. However, although he might permit a reversion of rights on his pulp novels so Curry could expand them, Standard Magazines also retained the copyrights in the original stories. Some of the Rio Kid Westerns were reprinted as original paperbacks by Popular Library, also owned by N.L. Pines, in the 1940's and by a publisher's oversight one of Curry's best Rio Kid novels, "Santa Fe Trail," which appeared in the April 1948 issue of the magazine was reprinted as a paperback later that year with Walker A. Tompkins credited as its author. It did not matter greatly, perhaps, since neither Curry nor Tompkins received any payment for these reprints nor for the series of paperback reprints of Rio Kid novels issued by Curtis Books in the late 1960's and early 1970's. In Tompkins's words to his wife, Barbara, upon seeing one of these Curtis reprints on the newsstand: "There's somebody else making money on my early pulp writing. I guess I never was much of a businessman."

—Jon Tuska

CURTIS, Tom. *See* **PENDOWER, T. C. H.**

CURWOOD, James Oliver. American. Born in Owosso, Michigan, 12 June 1878. Educated at the University of Michigan, Ann Arbor, 1898–1900. Married to Ethel Greenwood Curwood (2nd wife). Reporter, later editor, Denver *News-Tribune*, 1900–07; writer for the Canadian government, for two years. *Died 13 August 1927.*

WESTERN PUBLICATIONS

Novels

The Courage of Captain Plum. Indianapolis, Bobbs Merrill, 1908; London, Hodder and Stoughton, 1924.

The Wolf Hunters: A Tale of Adventure in the Wilderness. Indianapolis, Bobbs Merrill, 1908; London, Cassell, 1917.

The Gold Hunters: A Story of Life and Adventure in the Hudson Bay Wilds. Indianapolis, Bobbs Merrill, 1909; as *The Treasure Hunters*, London, Cassell, 1917.

The Danger Trail. Indianapolis, Bobbs Merrill, 1910; London, Hodder and Stoughton, 1924.

Philip Steele of the Royal Northwest Mounted Police. Indianapolis, Bobbs Merrill, 1911; London, Everett, 1912; as *Steele of the Royal Mounted*, New York, Pocket Books, 1946.

The Honor of the Big Snows. Indianapolis, Bobbs Merrill, 1911; London, Hodder and Stoughton, 1924.

Flower of the North: A Modern Romance. New York, Harper, 1912; London, Hodder and Stoughton, 1920.

Isobel: A Romance of the Northern Trail. New York, Harper, 1913.
Kazan. Indianapolis, Bobbs Merrill, 1914; as *Kazan, The Wolf-Dog*, London, Cassell, 1914.
Ice-Bound Hearts. London, Everett, 1915.
God's Country—and the Woman. New York, Doubleday, and London, Cassell, 1915.
The Valley of Gold. London, Cassell, 1916.
The Grizzly King: A Romance of the Wild. New York, Doubleday, 1916; as *The Grizzly*, London, Cassell, 1916.
The Hunted Woman. New York, Doubleday, 1916.
Baree, Son of Kazan. New York, Doubleday, 1917; as *Son of Kazan*, London, Cassell, 1917.
The Girl Beyond the Trail. London, Cassell, 1917.
The Courage of Marge O'Doone. New York, Doubleday, 1918.
The Golden Snare. London, Cassell, 1918; New York, Grosset and Dunlap, 1921.
Nomads of the North: A Story of Romance and Adventure under the Open Stars. New York, Doubleday, and London, Hodder and Stoughton, 1919.
The River's End: A New Story of God's Country. New York, Cosmopolitan, 1919; London, Hodder and Stoughton, 1920.
The Valley of Silent Men: A Story of the Three River Country. New York, Cosmopolitan, 1920; London, Hodder and Stoughton, 1921.
Swift Lightning: A Story of Wild-Life Adventure in the Frozen North. London, Hodder and Stoughton, 1920; New York, Cosmopolitan, 1926.
The Flaming Forest: A Novel of the Canadian Northwest. New York, Cosmopolitan, and London, Hodder and Stoughton, 1921.
The Country Beyond: A Romance of the Wilderness. New York, Cosmopolitan, and London, Hodder and Stoughton, 1922.
The Last Frontier. London, Hodder and Stoughton, 1923.
The Alaskan: A Novel of the North. New York, Cosmopolitan, 1923.
A Gentleman of Courage: A Novel of the Wilderness. New York, Cosmopolitan, and London, Hodder and Stoughton, 1924.
The Ancient Highway: A Novel of High Hearts and Open Roads. New York, Cosmopolitan, and London, Hodder and Stoughton, 1925.
The Black Hunter: A Novel of Old Quebec. New York, Cosmopolitan, and London, Hodder and Stoughton, 1926.
The Crippled Lady of Peribonkz. London, Hodder and Stoughton, 1927; New York, Doubleday, 1929.
The Plains of Abraham. New York, Doubleday, and London, Hodder and Stoughton, 1928.
Green Timber, completed by Dorothea A. Bryant. New York, Doubleday, 1930.

Short Stories

The Beloved Murderer. New York, Winthrop Press, 1914.
Back to God's Country and Other Stories. New York, Grosset and Dunlap, 1920.
Falkner of the Inland Sea, edited by Dorothea A. Bryant. Indianapolis, Bobbs Merrill, 1931; as *Son of a Hero*, London, Jarrolds, 1931.

Uncollected Short Stories

"Back to God's Country," in *The Second Reel West*, edited by Bill Pronzini and Martin H. Greenberg. New York, Doubleday, 1985.
"The Yellow-back," in *The Northerners*, edited by Bill Pronzini and Martin H. Greenberg. New York, Fawcett, 1990.

Other Publications

Plays

Screenplays: *The Girl from Porcupine*, 1921; *The Golden Snare*, with David M. Hartford, 1921; *A Captain's Courage*, with George Pyper, 1926; *The Slaver*, with Mabel Z. Carroll, 1927; *The Old Code*, with E.C. Maxwell, 1928; *The Yellowback*, with John Twist and Randolph Bartlett, 1929; *River's End*, with Charles Kenyon, 1930.

Other

The Great Lakes, The Vessels That Plough Them, Their Owners, Their Sailors, and Their Cargoes, Together with a Brief History of Our Inland Seas. New York, Putnam, 1909.
God's Country: The Trail to Happiness. London, Duckworth, 1921.
The Glory of Living: The Autobiography of an Adventurous Boy Who Grew into a Writer and a Lover of Life. London, Hodder and Stoughton, 1928.
Son of the Forests: An Autobiography, completed by Dorothea A. Bryant. New York, Doubleday, 1939.

*

Critical Study: *James Oliver Curwood, Disciple of the Wilds: A Biography* by Hobart D. Swiggett, New York, Paebar, 1943.

* * *

James Oliver Curwood is not seriously read or studied today and it is a rare public library which will have more than two or three of his novels available—generally *Kazan*, *Baree*, *Son of Kazan*, and *Steele of the Royal Mounted*. Few American writers, however, are more deserving of re-evaluation than this engaging conservationist whose ruling passion was the vast wilderness of the Peace River country, the solitary arctic plains, and the uninhabited forests of the Hudson Bay.

Curwood, like Jack London (whose work he admired and, at times, emulated), was a self-taught writer. In his sketchy but valuable (and long out-of-print) autobiography, *Son of the Forests*, Curwood summed up this career struggle by stating, "Such successes as I have achieved has been pounded out with naked fists through many years of hard work." But he learned his craft well and throughout his professional career was a meticulous wordsmith, averaging 500 words a day and often spending half a day on a single paragraph of a dozen lines. The result of this dedication is that he is, on occasion, an evocative, even poetic writer, though he never scaled the heights of a Jack London. One need only contrast *Kazan*, Curwood's wolf-dog novel and his most famous book, with *The Call of the Wild*, London's dog-wolf novel and *his* most famous book. Curwood's is a pleasant, exciting, and well-told story; London's is literature.

Curwood chose to place the burden of this "failure" on his critics, saying, "I sought to win a place for my book like that held by Jack London's *White Fang* and *Call of the Wild*. The critics generally denied me this, but conceded that *Kazan* was a narrative of such interest as to prompt its complete perusal at one sitting."

Still, in such novels as *God's Country—and the Woman*, *The River's End*, and *The Valley of Silent Men* (the latter a tale of the wild crews which took flotillas of scows down the Saskatchewan, Athabaska, and Mackenzie rivers), and even in such stories for young readers as *The Wolf Hunters*, Curwood established his own voice in fiction—and one that was very popular in the years before and after World War I. His strengths in these books and in many others he wrote is his powerful *sense* of God's Country (derived from his many trips into the Canadian wilderness, his wintering with Eskimos, his crossing of the Great Barrens and explorations of the then-unknown regions of British Columbia and the Yukon), his deep reverence for and awe of the wilderness, and his passion to describe it to those who would never see it.

Outside his writing life, his conservation work—tree plantings, game preservation, and waterway cleaning campaigns—was remarkable and, for its time, heroic.

Curwood's principal faults, viewed at this distance from his productive life, are those of many novelists of his day (including Zane Grey): he failed to create dimensional characters—especially female ones—and insisted too much and too unconvincingly on virtue and too little on flaws; and while he created good entertainment for his time, his work does not wear well. He was content to create heroes and heroines and put them to work against the backdrop of "that glorious land whose far frontiers had been a part of my dreams."

—Dale L. Walker

CUSHMAN, Dan. American. Born in Osceola County, Michigan, 9 June 1909. Educated at the University of Montana, B.S. 1934. Married Elizabeth Louise Loudon in 1939; one daughter and three sons. Worked in mining as a prospector, assayer, and geologist, then journalist, and free-lance writer. Founder, stay Away Joe Publishers, Great Falls, Montana. Recipient: Western Writers of American Spur award, 1958. Agent: Scott Meredith, 845 Third Ave, New York, New York 10022; or Drama and Film, H.N. Swanson, Inc., 8523 Sunset Blvd, Los Angles, California, 90069. Address: P.O. Box 2054, Great Falls, Montana 59403; or 1500 4th Avenue North, Great Falls, Montana 59401, U.S.A.

Western Publications

Novels

Montana, Here I Be! New York, Macmillan, 1950; London, Laurie, 1953.
Badlands Justice. New York, Macmillan, 1951.
The Ripper from Rawhide. New York, Macmillan, 1952; London, Laurie, 1953.
Stay Away, Joe. New York, Viking Press, 1953; London, Gollancz, 1954.
The Fastest Gun. New York, Dell, 1955.
The Old Copper Collar. New York, Ballantine, 1957.
The Silver Mountain. New York, Appleton Century Crofts, 1957; London, Hodder and Stoughton, 1958.
Tall Wyoming. New York, Dell, 1957.
Goodbye, Old Dry. New York, Doubleday, and London, Hodder and Stoughton, 1959; as *The Con Man*, New York, Fawcett, 1960.
The Half-Caste. London, Digit, 1960.
Brothers in Kickapoo. New York, McGraw Hill, 1962; as *Boomtown*, London, Barker, 1962; as *On the Make*, New York, Popular Library, 1963.
4 for Texas (novelization of screenplay). New York, Bantam, 1963.
The Grand and the Glorious. New York, McGraw Hill, 1963.
North Fork to Hell. New York, Fawcett, 1964.
The Long Riders. New York, Fawcett, 1967.
Rusty Irons. New York, Walker, 1984.

Uncollected Short Stories

"In Killer's Country," in *Texas Rangers* (London), May 1945.
"Windigo Pass," in *Spur Western Novels* (New York), February-April 1951.
"The Feminine Touch," in *Zane Grey's Western* (New York), October 1952.
"Land of the I-de-ho!," in *Zane Grey's Western 29* (London), 1953.
"Killer's Country," in *Colt's Law*, edited by Luke Short. New York, Bantam, 1957.
"I.O.U.—One Bullet," in *Wild Westerns: Stories from the Grand Old Pulps*, edited by Bill Pronzini. New York, Walker, 1986.
"Bonanza," in *More Wild Westerns*, edited by Bill Pronzini. New York, Walker, 1989.
"Mistress of the Midnight Sun," in *The Northerners*, edited by Bill Pronzini and Martin M. Greenberg. New York, Fawcett, 1990.

Other Publications

Novels

Naked Ebony. New York, Fawcett, 1951; London, Fawcett, 1953.
Jewel of the Java Sea. New York, Fawcett, 1951; London, Miller, 1957.
Savage Interlude. New York, Fawcett, 1952; London, Fawcett, 1953.
Timberjack. New York, Fawcett, 1953; London, Fawcett, 1955.
Jungle She. New York, Fawcett, 1953; London, Fawcett, 1954.
The Fabulous Finn. New York, Fawcett, 1954; London, Fawcett, 1955.
Tongking! New York, Ace, 1954.
Port Orient. New York, Fawcett, 1955.
The Forbidden Land. New York, Fawcett, 1958; London, Fawcett, 1959.
Opium Flower. New York, Bantam, 1963; London, Hammond, 1964.
Adventure in Laos. New York, Bantam, 1963.

Play

Whoop-Up, adaptation of his own novel *Stay Away, Joe* (produced New York, 1958).

Other

The Great North Trail: America's Route of the Ages. New York, McGraw Hill, 1966.
Cow Country Cook Book. Great Falls, Montana, Stay Away, Joe, 1967.
Montana: The Gold Frontier. Great Falls, Montana, Stay Away, Joe, 1973.

Plenty of Room and Air. Great Falls, Montana, Stay Away, Joe, 1975.
The Muskrat Farm. Great Falls, Montana, Stay Away, Joe, 1977.

*

Manuscript Collections: University of Wyoming, Laramie; University of Montana, Missoula.

Dan Cushman comments:

Although I have made half a dozen book clubs, including the largest, and won a couple of minor literary prizes, in the U.S. and Canada I am known if at all for my *Stay Away, Joe*, a humorous account of Métis (French-Indians) living on a reservation in Montana. Although this faded and went out of print after a short cup of coffee on the bestseller lists, it was in time discovered by the Indians, who liked it. Most white people, including especially Indian experts and partisans, felt the book denigrated the Red Man, but the Indians liked it just fine. The reasons for that have been taken up in many articles, and even a speech delivered before the International Congress of Anthropology. Vine Deloria, Jr. said in his *Custer Died for Your Sins* that it was the favorite of the Indian people, and it turned up as required reading at various graduate seminars in the mid-1960's.

* * *

In his "Indian Manifesto" *Custer Died for Your Sins* (1969), Vine Deloria, Jr., cites only three novels which he feels can give "a good idea of what Indians are all about": Hal Borland's *When the Legends Die*, Thomas Berger's *Little Big Man*, and Dan Cushman's *Stay Away, Joe*. Deloria offers especially high praise for Cushman's novel, which, he says, "is the favorite of Indian people."

The appeal of *Stay Away, Joe*, certainly its appeal for Indian readers, is neither sentimental nor serious; the novel does not bemoan in any explicit way the passing of traditional Indian culture nor does it recreate the Noble Savage. Instead, it is a *funny* novel, the humor of which derives partly from the mixture of traditional and white influences on Cushman's contemporary Indian characters. Such humor may suggest a greater respect for Indians than one might find in novels that are more intentionally respectful.

Humor shows up in all of Cushman's novels. At times his efforts at humor appear to crowd other elements, like plot and theme, out of the book. But there is no doubt that Cushman is a kind of original—and indigenous—western wit. *Montana, Here I Be!*, his first novel, about the rollicking adventures of a Montana road agent, set the pace. *The Old Copper Collar*, dealing in turn-of-the-century copper barons, continued the trend. *Goodbye, Old Dry*, perhaps Cushman's funniest novel, subjects a small Montana town to the effects of a con man *cum* promoter. The same situation, in which a small town must cope with pressure from the outside, this time in the form of a multi-million dollar movie production, is the source of humor in *Brothers in Kickapoo*.

In *The Silver Mountain* (Spur award) Cushman showed what he could do in a more "serious" novel, one drawing broadly not only on the characters and landscapes of Montana silver mining in the 1890's but also on the national politics of silver in the age of William Jennings Bryan.

Rusty Irons displays the familiar blend of wit and humour found in Cushman's earlier novels, together with a darker vision which has more in common with *The Silver Mountain*. This story of individual love and conflict, set against the background of a Montana range war, has as its leading character the rakish Rusty Irons, the roguish but appealing eldest son of a family of small ranchers who come up against a powerful landowner with the law at his back. Viewed through the eyes of his staid, conventional brother Henry, Rusty emerges as the kind of daredevil individualist once so common in the West, one who accepts the "every man for himself" philosophy that governs the actions of those about him, and takes what he can by fair means or foul. Whether illegal rustling, or illicit love with the landowner's under-age daughter, Rusty clearly regards his actions as both natural and inevitable, and is free of any spark of conscience. With Henry, the reader watches uneasily as Rusty's bending of the law, and the big rancher's employment of it for personal vengeance, escalate gradually to violence and catastrophe. Cushman, however, refuses to labour the real and harrowing tragedy in his novel, describing events in the matter-of-fact style of the bewildered Henry, whose experiences are constantly leavened with humour. In the end, he endures the fearful aftermath of the range war, and by a supreme irony gets the girl, while Rusty mysteriously disappears. A memorable story, compellingly told, *Rusty Irons* serves as a worthy addition to the work of its author.

Cushman's visibility as a western writer, however, is low. *Stay Away, Joe* became a Broadway production and then an Elvis Presley movie (suggesting the autobiographical basis of *Brothers in Kickapoo*). But Cushman's literary talents, incorporating as they do a frequently bawdy comic sense as well as a deep appreciation for his native Montana, are seldom noted in discussions of western American literature. One would suspect that Cushman has suffered, perhaps unfairly, from the usual expectations of western writing, which ordinarily do not include his brand of humor.

—William Bloodworth

CUSTER, Clint. *See* **PAINE, Lauran.**

CUTTER, Tom. *See* **RANDISI, Robert J.**

D

DAILEY, Janet. American. Born in Storm Lake, Iowa, 21 May 1944. Educated at Independence High School, Iowa, graduated 1962. Married to William Dailey; two stepchildren. Secretary, Omaha, Nebraska, 1963–74. Since 1974 full-time writer. Founder, with William Dailey, Janbill Inc., Wildwood theme park and resort, Branson, Missouri. Recipient: Romance Writers of America Golden Heart award, 1981. Agent: Janbill Ltd., Star Route 4, Box 2197, Branson, Missouri 65616, U.S.A.

WESTERN PUBLICATIONS

Novels (series: Calder)

Big Sky Country. London, Mills and Boon, and Toronto, Harlequin, 1978.
Lord of the High Lonesome. London, Mills and Boon, and Toronto, Harlequin, 1980.
The Rogue. New York, Pocket Books, and London, Fontana, 1980.
Calder:
This Calder Sky. New York, Pocket Books, 1981; London, Futura, 1982.
This Calder Range. New York, Pocket Books, 1982; London, Hodder and Stoughton, 1983.
Stands a Calder Man. New York, Pocket Books, 1982; London, Hodder and Stoughton, 1983.
Calder Born, Calder Bred. New York, Pocket Books, 1983; London, Hodder and Stoughton, 1984.

OTHER PUBLICATIONS

Novels

No Quarter Asked. London, Mills and Boon, 1974; Toronto, Harlequin, 1976.
Savage Land. London, Mills and Boon, 1974; Toronto, Harlequin, 1976.
Something Extra. London, Mills and Boon, 1975; Toronto, Harlequin, 1978.
Fire and Ice. London, Mills and Boon, 1975; Toronto, Harlequin, 1976.
Boss Man from Ogallala. London, Mills and Boon, 1975; Toronto, Harlequin, 1976.
After the Storm. London, Mills and Boon, 1975; Toronto, Harlequin, 1976.
Land of Enchantment. London, Mills and Boon, 1975; Toronto, Harlequin, 1976.
Sweet Promise. London, Mills and Boon, 1976; Toronto, Harlequin, 1979.
The Homeplace. London, Mills and Boon, and Toronto, Harlequin, 1976.
Dangerous Masquerade. London, Mills and Boon, 1976; Toronto, Harlequin, 1977.
Show Me. London, Mills and Boon, 1976; Toronto, Harlequin, 1977.
Valley of the Vapours. London, Mills and Boon, 1976; Toronto, Harlequin, 1977.
The Night of the Cotillion. London, Mills and Boon, 1976; Toronto, Harlequin, 1977.
Fiesta San Antonio. London, Mills and Boon, and Toronto, Harlequin, 1977.
Bluegrass King. London, Mills and Boon, and Toronto, Harlequin, 1977.
A Lyon's Share. London, Mills and Boon, and Toronto, Harlequin, 1977.
The Widow and the Wastrel. London, Mills and Boon, and Toronto, Harlequin, 1977.
The Ivory Cane. London, Mills and Boon, 1977; Toronto, Harlequin, 1978.
Six White Horses. London, Mills and Boon, 1977; Toronto, Harlequin, 1979.
To Tell the Truth. London, Mills and Boon, 1977; Toronto, Harlequin, 1978.
The Master Fiddler. London, Mills and Boon, 1977; Toronto, Harlequin, 1978.
Giant of Medabi. London, Mills and Boon, and Toronto, Harlequin, 1978.
Beware of the Stranger. London, Mills and Boon, and Toronto, Harlequin, 1978.
Darling Jenny. London, Mills and Boon, and Toronto, Harlequin, 1978.
The Indy Man. London, Mills and Boon, and Toronto, Harlequin, 1978.
Reilly's Woman. London, Mills and Boon, and Toronto, Harlequin, 1978.
For Bitter or Worse. London, Mills and Boon, 1978; Toronto, Harlequin, 1979.
Tidewater Lover. London, Mills and Boon, 1978; Toronto, Harlequin, 1979.
The Bride of the Delta Queen. London, Mills and Boon, 1978; Toronto, Harlequin, 1979.
Green Mountain Man. London, Mills and Boon, 1978; Toronto, Harlequin, 1979.
Sonora Sundown. London, Mills and Boon, and Toronto, Harlequin, 1978.
Summer Mahogany. London, Mills and Boon, 1978; Toronto, Harlequin, 1979.
The Matchmakers. London, Mills and Boon, and Toronto, Harlequin, 1978.
Low Country Liar. London, Mills and Boon, and Toronto, Harlequin, 1979.
Strange Bedfellow. London, Mills and Boon, and Toronto, Harlequin, 1979.
For Mike's Sake. London, Mills and Boon, and Toronto, Harlequin, 1979.
Sentimental Journey. London, Mills and Boon, and Toronto, Harlequin, 1979.
Sweet Promise. London, Mills and Boon, and Toronto, Harlequin, 1979.
Bed of Grass. London, Mills and Boon, 1979; Toronto, Harlequin, 1980.
That Boston Man. London, Mills and Boon, 1979; Toronto, Harlequin, 1980.

Kona Winds. London, Mills and Boon, 1979; Toronto, Harlequin, 1980.
A Land Called Deseret. London, Mills and Boon, and Toronto, Harlequin, 1979.
Touch the Wind. New York, Pocket Books, 1979; London, Fontana, 1980.
Difficult Decision. London, Mills and Boon, and Toronto, Harlequin, 1980.
Enemy in Camp. London, Mills and Boon, and Toronto, Harlequin, 1980.
Heart of Stone. London, Mills and Boon, and Toronto, Harlequin, 1980.
The Mating Season. London, Mills and Boon, and Toronto, Harlequin, 1980.
Southern Nights. London, Mills and Boon, and Toronto, Harlequin, 1980.
The Thawing of Mara. London, Mills and Boon, and Toronto, Harlequin, 1980.
One of the Boys. London, Mills and Boon, and Toronto, Harlequin, 1980.
Wild and Wonderful. London, Mills and Boon, 1980; Toronto, Harlequin, 1981.
Ride the Thunder. New York, Pocket Books, and London, Fontana, 1981.
The Travelling Kind. London, Mills and Boon, and Toronto, Harlequin, 1981.
Dakota Dreamin'. London, Mills and Boon, and Toronto, Harlequin, 1981.
The Hostage Bride. New York, Silhouette, 1981.
With a Little Luck. London, Mills and Boon, and Toronto, Harlequin, 1981.
That Carolina Summer. London, Mills and Boon, and Toronto, Harlequin, 1981.
Night Way. New York, Pocket Books, and London, Futura, 1981.
The Lancaster Men. New York, Silhouette, 1981; London, Hodder and Stoughton, 1982.
For the Love of God. New York, Silhouette, 1981; London, Hodder and Stoughton, 1982.
A Tradition of Pride. London, Mills and Boon, and Toronto, Harlequin, 1982.
Northern Magic. London, Mills and Boon, and Toronto, Harlequin, 1982.
Terms of Surrender. New York, Silhouette, and London, Hodder and Stoughton, 1982.
Wildcatter's Woman. New York, Silhouette, and London, Hodder and Stoughton, 1982.
Foxfire Light. New York, Silhouette, 1982; Bath, Firecrest, 1985.
The Second Time. New York, Silhouette, 1982; London, Hodder and Stoughton, 1983.
Mistletoe and Holly. New York, Silhouette, 1982; London, Hodder and Stoughton, 1983.
Separate Cabins. New York, Silhouette, 1983; Bath, Chivers, 1984.
Western Man. New York, Silhouette, and London, Hodder and Stoughton, 1983.
The Best Way to Lose. New York, Silhouette, 1983; London, Hodder and Stoughton, 1984.
Leftover Love. New York, Silhouette, and London, Hodder and Stoughton, 1984.
Silver Wings, Santiago Blue. New York, Poseidon Press, 1984.
The Pride of Hannah Wade. New York, Pocket Books, and London, Hodder and Stoughton, 1985.
The Glory Game. New York, Poseidon Press, 1985; London, Joseph, 1986.
The Great Alone. New York, Poseidon Press, and London, Joseph, 1986.
Heiress. Boston, Little Brown, and London, Joseph, 1987.
Rivals. Boston, Little Brown, and London, Joseph, 1989.

Play

Screenplay: *Foxfire Light*, 1983.

* * *

While Janet Dailey is well-known for careful, accurate incorporation of setting in her romantic fiction, her western settings provide more than a simple backdrop for a romantic tale. Dailey has used setting skillfully to introduce the history and culture of the western United States to give her characters roots and color.

In *The Rogue* Dailey symbolizes the free-spirited adventure and dangerous lure of the Old West in the powerful wild, white mustang. In *This Calder Sky* Dailey blends the old west codes of honor and morality into unyielding men and women who build and hold the Calder Ranch Empire. Dailey's women are bold, independent females who step neatly into a contemporary role rather than a shadowy, silent, "stand-by-your-man" role of the past. Dailey's women not only stand by their men but often stand with them or oppose them as equals.

Dailey's skillful blending of past and present allows the reader to roam freely without bumping into unsettling inconsistencies. As Dailey reincarnates the Old West under Montana Skies, she does not let the reader entirely forget the story's time frame. Her gentle tugs back to the present are subtly woven into the novel. Past and present—horseback and helicopters—never clash in an obtrusive way.

The Calder Empire stretches as far as the eye can see. While this represents bold, hard, even corruptive power, Dailey reminds us this is not a world of bygone days where justice was born by the power of a gun or a hangman's noose. Dailey's powerful characters overcome the crumbling remnants of the old Empire and move forward into the future holding on to what was good in their past and molding a new world under Calder skies.

The Rogue and *This Calder Sky* incorporate an expansive western setting and theme as an integral part of the novel. Dailey writes smoothly, grabbing the reader quickly and holding him right up to the classic formulaic happy ending. Despite Dailey's failure to break away from a formulaic style, she offers clear simple writing, simple plots, and powerful characters—a blend that means good light reading, pure escapism into another world where one can be assured of a happy ending. Formula notwithstanding.

—Cassandra Fedrick

DALGLEISH, James C. *See* **KINCAID, J.D.**

DALTON, Kit. *See* **CUNNINGHAM, Chet.**

DANA, Richard. *See* **PAINE, Lauran.**

DANCER, J.B. *See* **HARVEY, John; WELLS, Angus.**

DANGERFIELD, Clint. *See* **NORWOOD, V.G.C.**

DANIELS, John S. *See* **OVERHOLSER, Wayne D.**

DANVERS, Pete. Pseudonym for James Maddock Henderson. Also wrote as Bryn Jordan.

WESTERN PUBLICATIONS

Novels

Lone Wolf Trail. London, Hammond, 1950.
Rancher's Gold. London, Hammond, 1952.
Sheriff Hater. London, Hammond, 1953.
Border Wolves. London, Hammond, 1954.
The Amateur Sheriff. London, Barker, 1954.
Saddle Fever. London, Ward Lock, 1954.

Novels as Bryn Jordan

Cowboys Three. London, J. Coker, 1950.
Rustler's Roost. London, J. Coker, 1950.
The Drunk of Buzzard Creek. London, J. Coker, 1951.
Nighthawk Trail. London, Gryphon, 1951.
Border Bandit. London, Fiction House, 1951.
Colt Comfort. London, J. Coker, 1952.
The Gentle Outlaw. London, Gryphon, 1952.
Guns Flame in Arcady. London, J. Coker, 1952.
No Peace in Sleepy Valley. London, J. Coker, 1952.
Rimfire Creek. London, Gryphon, 1953.
Arizona Outcast. London, J. Coker, 1953.
Outlaw Sheriff. London, Gryphon, 1954.
Renegade Guns. Kingswood, Surrey, World's Work, 1954.
The War at Muffled Hoof. London, W.H. Allen, 1954.
The Westering Kid. London, W.H. Allen, 1954.
The Burning of the Bar-K-Bar. Kingswood, Surrey, World's Work, 1954.
Border Luck. London, Gryphon, 1955.
Coyote Springs. London, Gryphon, 1956.
Crisis in Cataract. London, Gryphon, 1956.
Lost Mountain. London, Gryphon, 1957.
Wolf Corner. London, Barker, 1957.
Dark Valley. London, Gryphon, 1958.

* * *

Whether he wrote as Pete Danvers or Bryn Jordan, James Henderson's books contained all the elements required for the conventional Western. The settings invariably take place on the ranch where range wars, murders, and duplicity abound. He wrote prolifically in a short 10-year period in the 1950's, and each book abided by the popular formula of the time.

Henderson's fondness for setting up his characters to solve a mystery, or come to the aid of less fortunate souls, was his trademark. Usually, during this time they would undoubtedly prove their worthiness, either through action or thought. In *The Amateur Sheriff*, the protagonist is Dan Preedy; rejected by his fiancée, he sells his ranch and is on the brink of slipping into melancholy, and prepared to become a saddletramp. Drifting into the town of Medusa, and for some reason better known to himself, he takes up the job of sheriff, recently vacated through the death of its previous occupant. Together with the deputy, he brings in the lawman's killers and exposes a rancher's double life.

The theme of hunting down a sheriff's killer is repeated in *Border Wolves*, when two deputies are sent in to investigate the murder. They arrive too late to stave off a lynching, but become embroiled in a range war where the big land owner is facing down the smaller ranchers.

Although the range war theme is a constant anthem throughout his works, Henderson always provided his readers with a subplot to flesh out the story. For example, in *Renegade Guns* the historical fact that cattle ranchers were bitterly opposed to the sheep farmers is used as the main plot, while the subplot concerns Lance Harder's attempts to fuel the range war for his own ill-gotten gains. He discovers that an immense coal deposit runs across both ranches, but his plans are foiled when range detective Dale Leander is called in, and manages to succeed in uniting the warring ranchers against the common enemy, the Sioux. This united force finally brings down Harder and all he stands for.

As in all of his works, Henderson depicts the clear line of good and evil, and the former always wins. Villains are forever power-crazed, land-hungry, and powerful men, but always fall to the hand of the heroes. The little men, united by a strong central character or characters, have a habit of coming out on top, either through sheer tenacity or twists of fate. For example, in *Arizona Outcast* two friends Tom Kennedy and Ken Loder make enemies of Mason Steed and Bull Harnett, owners of the Double Loop and Rolling Y ranches, when they interfere in a fight with a member of a rival ranch. The Lazy S is owned by Ruth Deacon who, along with Maud Rixson is kidnapped, and Kennedy and Loder are determined to bring justice to the territory by preventing Steed and Harnett taking charge.

The same theme of a woman rancher in trouble is used in *Rancher's Gold*. The hero, again a total stranger, comes to her rescue and all comes good in the end. This is a flaw in Henderson's writing; not content in creating an original story, he then bastardises his plots to eke out another yarn along the same lines. It is a method much used and abused, but becomes obvious when one book follows the next using the same techniques.

A change of direction is *Lone Wolf Trail*, the story of Rand Hardstaff, who finds himself fallen among thieves. Not content with the life, his opportunity to escape comes when most of the gang is wiped out in a disastrous bank raid. Hardstaff is befriended by a rancher and his daughters. His chance to show his new colours comes when one of the daughters is captured by rustlers, and he sets out to save her and redeem himself.

In *Sheriff Hater*, Henderson explores the bitterness felt by young Bud Holliday against his stepfather, Sheriff Brett. Brett knows the truth behind Bud's father's death. There is no love lost between the men and on his mother's death, Bud leaves home. He is unfortunate to fall in with Duke Atterval, an outlaw with the answers to Bud's questions. His hatred for Brett is heightened when he learns the truth and joins the outlaws. Here the books falls into an adventure story of bank robberies, range wars, and rustlers, and the token love interest is thrown in for good measure.

In the main, Henderson's central characters are of the straight-talking, straight-shooting mould, determined to right wrongs even if the original fight is not theirs, and over-zealous in laying their life on the line for their belief. Henderson believed in the mythical western hero, and his characterizations are flawed because of that conviction. His plots reflect his interpretation of the West and its way of life, and ultimately what the readers of the 1950's expected to see in print. Compared to today's standards his prose is laboured, and the language in places, esoteric. Rarely are the reader's imagination or attention overtaxed.

—Mike Stotter

DAVIS, Don. *See* **DRESSER, Davis.**

DAVIS, H(arold) L(enoir). American. Born at Rone's Mill, near Nonpareil, Oregon, 18 October 1894. Educated at public schools. Served in the United States Army during World War I: Corporal. Married 1) Marion Lay in 1928 (divorced); 2) Elizabeth M. Tonkin in 1953. Worked as a typesetter, sheep and cattle herder, surveyor, deputy county assessor and sheriff; editor, *Antelope Herald*. Recipient: Levinson prize (*Poetry*, Chicago), 1919; Guggenheim fellowship, 1932; Harper Novel prize, 1935; Pulitzer prize, 1936. Member, American Academy. *Died 31 October 1960.*

WESTERN PUBLICATIONS

Novels

Honey in the Horn. New York, Harper, and London, Lovat Dickson and Thompson, 1935.
Harp of a Thousand Strings. New York, Morrow, 1947; London, Cassell, 1949.
Beulah Land. New York, Morrow, 1949; London, Cassell, 1950.
Winds of Morning. New York, Morrow, and London, Cassell, 1952.
The Distant Music. New York, Morrow, 1957; London, Gollancz, 1958.

Short Stories

Team Bells Woke Me and Other Stories. New York, Morrow, 1953.
Kettle of Fire (story and sketches). New York, Morrow, 1959.

Uncollected Short Story

"Flying Switch," in *The Railroaders*, edited by Bill Pronzini and Martin H. Greenberg. New York, Fawcett, 1986.

OTHER PUBLICATIONS

Verse

Proud Rider and Other Poems. New York, Harper, 1942.
The Selected Poems of H.L. Davis, edited by Orvis C. Burmaster. Boise, Idaho, Ahsahta Press, 1978.

*

Critical Study: *H.L. Davis* by Paul T. Bryant, Boston, Twayne, 1978.

* * *

H.L. Davis's fiction was first praised for lively humor and deft use of western vernacular. Recently, readers have recognized more serious patterns beneath the colorful surface. These patterns link the experience of settlers, cowboys, sheepherders, and laborers in the West with universal human experience.

Davis's earliest writing, from 1919 to 1928, was poetry that dealt primarily with the western landscape and the people who lived there. Although this was praised by Harriet Monroe, Carl Sandburg, Robinson Jeffers, and others, he turned in 1928 to prose and wrote relatively little poetry thereafter. His first novel, *Honey in the Horn*, won the Harper Novel prize and the Pulitzer prize. For the remainder of his career, most of his energy went into writing novels. In all, he published five and was at work on a sixth, tentatively titled *Exit Pursued by a Bear*, when he died.

Most of Davis's short stories and sketches are set in the Pacific Northwest, primarily Oregon, although some are set in the southwest. Most of the short stories are about life in Oregon in the first three decades of this century, drawing on Davis's experiences in childhood and as a young man. Later sketches deal with more modern times, but all the short prose draws upon his memories of the last days of homesteading and open-range ranching.

The best of Davis's short stories were published in *Team Bells Woke Me*, a collection of stories and sketches. The title sketch presents a colorful picture of the early teamsters who drove freight wagons in eastern Oregon in the late 19th and early 20th centuries. Among the stories is "Old Man Isbell's Wife," a humorous but sympathetic picture of a pioneer grown old and senile but still retaining an essential dignity from the dangers he had surmounted in his youth. Another, "Homestead Orchard," explores the Eden theme in the experience of western settlers. Others, such as "Open Winter" and "The Stubborn Spearmen," are stories of a boy's initiation into manhood through western trial and adventure.

Davis's best sketches, and his last short story, were collected in *Kettle of Fire*. The story is his most overly symbolic fiction. The sketches present, for the most part, the Oregon landscape. Written late in Davis's life, these are a recapitulation of the sense of the western landscape that runs through most of Davis's work. Nostalgia is not a strong element but there is a sense of ripeness, of a full realization of a well-known country.

Although *Honey in the Horn* is set entirely in Oregon, Davis ventured onto a broader stage in his next two novels. *Harp of a Thousand Strings* ranges from revolutionary France to Oklahoma Territory, weaving together the stories of four men and a woman and making the point that the history of the American West is not isolated, but rather is part of the history of civilization. *Beulah Land* stays closer to home, beginning in the old Cherokee Nation and ending, finally, in Oregon.

For his fourth, and perhaps best, novel, David returned to Oregon and the 20th century. *Winds of Morning* develops more fully a pattern Davis used earlier in his short story, "Open Winter." Through a series of adventures a boy comes to terms with himself and with society and becomes a man. At the same time, an old man, an early settler disappointed with what both he and the west have become, is reconciled with his own past and the modern west. In effect, the old Wild West and the modern "civilized" west acknowledge their close relationship and thus reconciled are able to move toward a hopeful future.

Davis's last published novel, *The Distant Music*, is again concerned with homesteading in Oregon, but unlike his earlier work this novel moves only through time and not through space. It focusses on successive generations of a single family as they live out their lives on the family land along the Columbia River.

The west of Davis's fiction is presented with adventure, humor, colorful language, a rich sense of the landscape, and a sometimes cynical, deromanticized realism that shows the harshness, folly, and tragedy that were so often a part of western settlement. At the same time, it insists that the western experience was not an isolated, special event but rather a closely connected element of the whole of human history. The picture that merges has humor and much of the excitement commonly associated with western literature, but it has greater depth and complexity than is usually associated with popular treatments of the West.

—Paul T. Bryant

DAWSON, Peter. Pseudonym for Jonathan Hurff Glidden. American. Born in Kewanee, Illinois, in 1907; brother of Frederick D. Glidden (i.e., Luke Short, *q.v.*). Educated at the University of Illinois, Urbana, graduated 1929. Served as an Officer in the United States Army Air Force Intelligence during World War II. Married; two sons. Worked as a salesman during 1930's; won $2000 Writing Contest by Dodd Mead publishers, 1940; later lived in Pojoaque Valley, New Mexico. *Died 22 July 1957.*

WESTERN PUBLICATIONS

Novels

The Crimson Horseshoe. New York, Dodd Mead, and London, Collins, 1941.
The Stagline Feud. New York, Dodd Mead, 1941; London, Collins, 1942.
Gunsmoke Graze. New York, Dodd Mead, 1942; as *Time to Ride,* London, Collins, 1949.
Long Ride. New York, Dodd Mead, 1942; London, Collins, 1944.
Trail Boss. New York, Dodd Mead, 1943; London, Collins, 1944.
High Country. New York, Dodd Mead, and London, Collins, 1947; as *Canyon Hell,* New York, Lion, 1949.
Royal Gorge. New York, Dodd Mead, 1948; as *Battle Royal,* London, Collins, 1949; as *Guns on the Santa Fe,* New York, Lion, 1950.
Renegade Canyon. New York, Dodd Mead, 1949; London, Collins, 1951.
The Stirrup Boss. New York, Dodd Mead, 1949; London, Collins, 1950.
The Outlaw of Longbow. New York, Dodd Mead, 1950; as *High Lonesome,* London, Collins, 1951.
Ruler of the Range. New York, Dodd Mead, 1951; London, Collins, 1952.
The Wild Bunch. New York, Lion, 1953; as *Leashed Guns,* New York, Lion, 1955.
Dead Man Pass. New York, Dodd Mead, 1954; London, Collins, 1955.
Leashed Guns. New York, Lion, 1955.
The Big Outfit. New York, Dodd Mead, and London, Collins, 1955.
Man on the Buckskin. New York, Dodd Mead, and London, Collins, 1957.
Treachery at Rock Point. New York, Dell, 1957; London, Collins, 1958.
The Blizzard. New York, Bantam, 1968.

(The following "Peter Dawson" novels were written by Otis Graylord, with the cooperation of Jonathan Glidden's Estate.)
The Savages. New York, Bantam, 1959.
Yancey. New York, Bantam, 1960.
The Texas Slicks. New York, Bantam, 1961.
The Half-Breed. New York, Bantam, 1962.
Bloody Gold. New York, Bantam, 1963.
The Showdown. New York, Bantam, 1964.
A Pride of Men. New York, Bantam, 1966.

Uncollected Short Stories

"Gun Smoke Pledge," in *Complete Story* (New York), May 1936.
"Lawman of Latigo Wells," in *Cowboy Stories* (New York), September 1936.
"The Sweetest Draw," in *Cowboy Stories* (New York), January 1937.
"A Lone Wolf Returns to the Gun-Pack," in *Star Western* (Chicago), June 1937.
"A Button Sides a Sawbones," in *Ace-High Magazine*, June 1937.
"The Cowman They Couldn't Kill," in *Star Western* (Chicago), August 1937.
"Stone Walls Make a Town-Tamer," in *Dime Western* (New York), September 1937.
"Yuma Sends Back a Man!," in *Dime Western* (New York), August 1937.
"Bondage of the Dark Trails," in *Star Western* (Chicago), October 1937.
"Dark Riders of Doom," in *Star Western* (Chicago), 1937.
"Back-Trail Betrayal," in *Western Story* (New York), 26 March 1938.
"Bushwhack Heritage," in *Western Story* (New York), 2 April 1938.
"A Tinhorn Takes a Tank Town," in *Western Story* (New York), 9 April 1938.
"An Ex-Marshall Ramrods the Malpais," in *Complete Western Book Magazine*, May 1938.
"Bullets Starve a Fever," in *Western Story* (New York), 28 May 1938.
"Ghost-Badge for a Tinhorn," in *Complete Western Book Magazine*, June 1938.
"Owlhoot Nemesis," in *Western Story* (New York), 30 July 1938.
"Posse Guns," in *Popular Western*, July 1938.
"Owlhoot Outcast," in *Complete Western Book Magazine*, August 1938.
"Owlhoot Reckoning," in *Western Story* (New York), 20 August 1938.

"Vengeance in Shadow Canyon," in *Western Story* (New York), 8 October 1938.
"Hell for Homesteaders," in *Western Story* (New York), 5 November 1938.
"Longriding Lawman," in *Western Fiction*, November 1938.
"Tinhorn's Gunsmoke Crusade," in *Star Western* (Chicago), November 1938.
"Boothill Challenge," in *Western Story* (New York), 24 December 1938.
"Manhunt in Malpais," in *Western Story* (New York), 4 February 1939.
"Lone Raiders from Texas," in *Western Story* (New York), 11 March March 1939.
"Ghost-Guards Ride the Sunset Stage," in *Western Short Stories*, March 1939.
"A Gun-Boss for Eternal Range," in *Complete Western Book Magazine*, May 1939.
"Dealer's Double Cross," in *Western Story* (New York), 29 July 1939.
"Charge of the Cowtown Brigade," in *10 Story Western*, August 1939.
"Gun-Pledge," in *Western Story* (New York), 16 September 1939.
"A Ghost-Gun Works a Cure," in *Western Short Stories*, October 1939.
"Gun Purge at Tentrock," in *Western Story* (New York), 28 October 1939.
"Gun Destiny of the Branded," in *Complete Western Book Magazine*, 1939.
"A Gun-Champion for Hell's Half-Acre," in *Best Western*, 1939.
"The Wolf-Pack Sends a Witness," in *Western Fiction*, 1939.
"Hard Boot Claims a Maverick," in *Western Short Stories*, February 1940.
"Hellion, Fan That Hammer!," in *Best Western*, February 1940.
"Even Money He Dies at Noon!," in *Star Western* (Chicago), May 1940.
"Turn-Key Justice," in *Western Story* (New York), 24 August 1940.
"When Gun-Battles Brand a Man's Backtrail," in *Western Short Stories*, September 1940; as "When Blood and Guns Brand a Man's Backtrail," in *Western Novel and Short Stories*, February 1941.
"Gun-Swift Awakening," in *Western Story* (New York), September 1940.
"Half-Owner of Hell's Last Herd," in *Western Novel and Short Stories*, 1940.
"The Wild Bunch Gun-Wages Couldn't Buy," in *Complete Western Book Magazine*, November 1940.
"The Man Who Hired His Own Guns," in *Western Novel and Short Stories*, November 1940.
"Hot-Lead Alibi," in *Western Short Stories*, 1940.
"Trail-Blazer Wanted for Drive Through Hell," in *Complete Western Book Magazine*, 1940.
"Hole-in-the-Wall Heritage," in *Complete Western Book Magazine*, January/February 1941.
"The Gunfighter the Whole Southwest Feared," in *Western Short Stories*, February 1941.
"A Killer Needs a Target," in *Western Story* (New York), 22 February 1941.
"Ballots for Boothill," in *Western Story* (New York), February 1941.
"Land-Grabber, I'll Be Back with Guns!," in *Complete Western Book Magazine*, March 1941.
"Lost Homestead" (novella), in *Western Story* (New York), 5 April 1941.
"Gold Baits a Death Trap," in *Western Story* (New York), 3 May 1941.
"Lucky Lawman, or Gun-King?," in *Complete Western Book Magazine*, May 1941.
"The Raider from the Roost," in *Western Short Stories*, May 1941.
"Treachery in Broken Wheel," in *Western Story* (New York), 12 July 1941.
"When a Land-Grabber Comes Law-Backed," in *Complete Western Book Magazine*, July 1941.
"When a Man Lives By His Guns," in *Western Short Stories*, July 1941.
"Fence-Posts and Wire for Wanted Men," in *Best Western*, July 1941.
"Renegade Retribution," in *Western Story* (New York), 23 August 1941.
"A Texan Chooses Bushwhack Bullets," in *Western Novel and Short Stories*, September 1941.
"The Long-Eared Smoke Pole," in *Western Story* (London), September 1941.
"Paroled to Purgatory," in *Best Western*, 1941.
"Retirement Day," in *15 Western Tales*, February 1942.
"Wanted—Alive!," in *15 Western Tales*, April 1942.
"The Gunfighter who Hated Gunfighters," in *Western Short Stories*, May 1942.
"Pardner, Get Your Gun!," in *Western Story* (New York), 18 July 1942.
"Matching Colts," in *Complete Western Book Magazine*, October 1942.
"Lead Shy," in *15 Western Tales*, February 1947.
"Bullets Are My Destiny!," in *15 Western Tales*, August 1947.
"A Man from Hell's Canyon," in *15 Western Tales*, November 1947.
"The Devil's Night-Hawk," in *New Western*, November 1947.
"Dead Man's Draw," in *15 Western Tales*, February 1948.
"Hell's Free for Nesters!," in *Dime Western* (New York), April 1948.
"Gunhand for Hire," in *15 Western Tales*, July 1948.
"Branded for Bounty," in *Western Story* (New York), August 1948.
"It's Your Town—Die in It!," in *Dime Western* (New York), September 1948.
"Boss of Back-Shoot Claim," in *New Western*, November 1948.
"Back Trail Harvest," in *Western Triggers*, edited by Arnold Hano. New York, Bantam, 1948.
"Colt-Cure for Woolly Fever," in *Big Book Western* (New York), February 1949.
"Retribution River," in *Western Story* (London), March 1949.
"The Homestead," in *Zane Grey's Western Magazine* (New York), May 1950.
"Long Gone," in *Zane Grey's Western Magazine* (New York), 1950.
"Willow Basin Outcast," in *Western Story* (London), January 1953.
"Lead-Law Election," in *Two-Gun Western*, May 1953.
"The Montana Kid Calls on a Killer," in *Complete Western Book Magazine*, June 1955.

OTHER PUBLICATIONS

Other

Editor, *The Killers*. New York, Bantam, 1955.

* * *

Jonathan Glidden, who wrote western fiction under the pseudonym Peter Dawson, was the older brother of Frederick Glidden who wrote western fiction as Luke Short. Although he had written for the pulps prior to 1935, Fred Glidden began to write under the Luke Short name that year and Jonathan followed him into the world of the pulps in 1936 writing as Peter Dawson. Both men had the same New York literary agent, Marguerite E. Harper. Although Fred would produce his first western novel in 1936, Jonathan took longer, continuing to write exclusively for the pulps, both short stories and novelettes, with *Western Story* being one of his mainstays. When Dodd Mead publishers announced a $2000 contest for the best book-length western manuscript, Jonathan submitted *The Crimson Horseshoe* and won. That same year, 1941, one of Jonathan's best Western novelettes appeared in *Western Story* in the 5 April 1941 issue, "Lost Homestead."

While the narrative structure is as old as Homer, Ernest Haycox can be credited for developing and adapting it to western fiction. Retaining the usual ingredients of the formulary Western, i.e., an identifiable hero, a heroine, and a villain or villains, Haycox in such novels as *Trail Smoke* in 1936 broke the structure down into the point-of-view perspectives of various characters. Fred Glidden was profoundly influenced by Haycox in his own fiction and Jonathan was no less profoundly influenced by his brother. Indeed, for some time the brothers lived across the street from each other in Santa Fe, New Mexico. This plot structure is at its most effective when two parallel threads of a plot can be so interwoven that first one of the threads will come to a climax or cliff-hanger at which point the narrative is transferred to the other thread until another climax or cliff-hanger is reached only to be transferred back again, and so on, until at the end the two threads are seen to coalesce. In *Trail Smoke* Haycox added to this structure a murder mystery. And this is the basic structure of Peter Dawson's *The Crimson Horseshoe*, with the further addition of a second mystery: not only does the reader want to know who killed Judge Locheim but also why is Hugh Allard so intent on instigating a range war? In his second novel, *The Stagline Feud*, a story of two rival stagelines, Dawson again resorted to the plot of parallel action but with only one mystery: who kidnapped Belle LeSoeur, obviously the same party who is holding up stagecoaches and yet independent from the principal villain (owner of the rival line) and his gang.

One of Luke Short's most effective plots in his early days was to isolate his hero amid a number of armed camps, fighting completely alone against incredible odds so that, despite the formulary structure, a reader might really wonder how it would all come out. Dawson added this ingredient to the parallel plot structure and mystery killer element in *Gunsmoke Graze* as well as the theme of the two heroines which formulary western writers took over from Sir Walter Scott (which of the two is the "right" one for the hero?) and the theme from Owen Wister's *The Virginian* where the hero's best friend is a villain although not the principal villain. With so much going on, perhaps Dawson can be forgiven a slip: Pecos, one of the bad guys, is somehow lost in the shuffle at the end during the general round-up; although captured at one point, he is later missing without explanation. In *Long Ride*, in addition to an intricate plot and a cleverly concealed mystery, Dawson in his hero, Streak Mathiot, created a character more typical of Luke Short than of himself, a truly hard-boiled man who forces a cigar down a fat sheriff's throat at one point because he does not like the way he was treated when in jail. The complex interplay here between appearance and reality is also strongly reminiscent of Luke Short's *Savage Range*. *Trail Boss* concerns an ambitious local rancher, a crooked Indian agent, and a man who is a bad guy at the beginning but who is won over to doing the right thing through his love for a woman, a romance parallel with that between the hero and the woman who inherits the ranch for which he has been ramrod.

During World War II Glidden served as an officer in the U.S. Air Force Intelligence and so did no writing. When he returned to civilian status, he took up his writing career where he had left off, writing for the pulps and again publishing hardbound novels which were readily reprinted in paperback editions. *High Country*, the first Peter Dawson novel in the post-war group, still employs the theme of the two heroines; there is an interesting background of horse racing and a riverboat; but the plot is more streamlined and less complicated than in the pre-war novels, albeit Dawson did retain at least here the parallel plot structure which had served him so well from the beginning. Although he would continue to write for the pulps to the end of the decade, four of Jonathan's novels would appear as serials in the *Saturday Evening Post* prior to book publication. One of his best short stories, "Long Gone" (1950), would serve as the basis for the only film adapted from his work, *Face of a Fugitive* (Columbia, 1959), which was issued posthumously.

There was always a certain proclivity toward carelessness in Jonathan's early pulp fiction, principally that which did not appear in *Western Story*, and this is quite evident in *The Wild Bunch*, issued as an original paperback in 1953 but actually a pulp novelette from 1940 which had appeared first in *Complete Western Book Magazine*. Even in his *Post* serials he could occasionally write himself into a corner as in *The Outlaw of Longbow* where the hero is framed, sent to prison only to escape, and then finds himself unable to prove his innocence because all the witnesses to the crime are dead. This dilemma, once the end comes, is merely brushed aside and the hero embraces the heroine without anything having been really resolved.

When a rustler is killed in a stampede in *Trail Boss*, another rustler remarks: "'He was a good man and he went sudden, which is as it should be with all of us.'" It happened that way for Jonathan who died suddenly and unexpectedly of a heart attack in 1957. It was Marguerite E. Harper who came up with the notion that the Peter Dawson name was worth money and, with the cooperation of Jonathan's widow, contracted with Otis Gaylord to ghost what became the last eight Peter Dawson titles, all published by Bantam and none of them as fine as Jonathan's own work. Glidden's achievement, especially in the novels of his pre-war group and in his work for *Western Story*, ranks with the best formulary efforts of Ernest Haycox, Luke Short, and Norman A. Fox, stories which are suspenseful, remarkable for their precision and complexity of narrative structures, and yet—to the extent that a distinction can be made between plot and story—engaging for their interaction between various characters and their perceptive use of group psychology within an imaginary western community.

—Jon Tuska

DAWSON, Peter. *See* **BRAND, Max.**

DAY, Robert P. American. Born in 1941. Address: P.O. Box 178, Lynch, Indiana 21646, U.S.A.

WESTERN PUBLICATIONS

Novel

The Last Cattle Drive. New York, Putnam, and London, Secker and Warburg, 1977.

Short Stories

Speaking French in Kansas, and Other Stories. Lawrence, Kansas, Cottonwood, 1989.

OTHER PUBLICATIONS

Verse

The Four Wheel Drive Quartet. Baltimore, Maryland, Galileo, 1986.

Other

In My Stead. Lawrence, Kansas, Cottonwood, 1981.

* * *

Robert P. Day's first book, *The Last Cattle Drive*, is a good novel; and it is a good western story, for it succeeds in making us take the American West seriously, and in making us see it in a slightly different light than we had been accustomed to. If the mainstream of American literature has tended to dramatize the failure of the father, Day makes a case here for connecting the failure of the American spirit with the failure of the son.

And it is an effective case that he makes. The novel's characters—Spangler Tuckle, a contemporary Kansas rancher who has determined to drive his steers to market in Kansas City rather than truck them; Harold, his effete son; Jed Adams, who has been all-around hand to the Tuckle family since, significantly, well before Spangler's own time; and Leo Murdock, the temporary hand who narrates the three-week saga from Hays to Kansas City—participate in a series of relationships, each of which consists of someone secure in his own value system and the congenitally defective creature he voluntarily assumes responsibility for. Spangler and Harold form one of these pairs, but Spangler and Jed form another; so Spangler is in the unique position of being at both ends of some manifestation of the odd bonding. He knows he can do nothing for his son, so he takes it upon himself to demonstrate that he, at least, is capable of action on his spiritual guardian's terms. If Jed Adams is a cowboy from the days when there *were* cowboys, Spangler Tuckle will drive his steers to Kansas City.

It would be easy, of course, to translate Jed into "Old West," Harold into "New West," Spangler into the man in the middle, and so on. It would also be a gross misreading of the characters. Nevertheless, we do sense a fundamental if inarticulate incompatibility between systems. And oddly, what establishes the incongruity is a small tragedy which does not concern any of the principal characters; it is an anecdote recounted in a tavern, and it quickly becomes the moral center of *The Last Cattle Drive*. It concerns a neighboring rancher who had shot and killed his emotionally unbalanced son some 20 years previously. The story is told by a hand of Jed's generation, and the rancher involved had committed suicide three years before the telling. The story is powerful and moving. It represents Day's best writing and it crystalizes the significances in that series of relationships upon which the book is based.

What meaning impels *The Last Cattle Drive*, then, is bound up in those relationships and in their resolutions. None can be taken as Day's allegory for the decline of pioneer hardiness or rugged invididualism or whatever courage it took to people the American west; yet together they must be seen as illustrative of the decay of some epic possibility.

—Douglas J. McReynolds

DEAN, Dudley (Dudley Dean McGaughy). Also writes as Dean Owen; Brian Wynne. American. Born in Rialto, California. Radio and television editor of a Hollywood trade paper; radio writer.

WESTERN PUBLICATIONS

Novels

Ambush at Rincon. New York, Fawcett, 1953; London, Miller, 1957.
The Man from Riondo. New York, Fawcett, 1954; London, Fawcett, 1956.
The Broken Spur. New York, Fawcett, 1955; London, Fawcett, 1956.
Tough Hombre. New York, Fawcett, 1956; London, Fawcett, 1957.
Song of the Gun. London, Fawcett, 1956; New York, Fawcett, 1957.
Six-Gun Vengeance. New York, Fawcett, 1956; London, Fawcett, 1958.
The Diehards. New York, Fawcett, 1956; London, Fawcett, 1957.
Border Renegade. New York, Fawcett, 1957; London, Fawcett, 1958.
Gun in the Valley. New York, Fawcett, 1957; London, Fawcett, 1958.
Lawless Guns. New York, Fawcett, 1959; London, Muller, 1960.
Gun Shy, with Les Savage. New York, Fawcett, 1959; London, Muller, 1960.
Lila My Lovely. New York, Fawcett, 1960; London, Muller, 1962.
Cross of Rope. New York, Berkley, 1963.
Trail of the Hunter. New York, Berkley, 1963.
Gun the Man Down. New York, Fawcett, 1971; Leicester, Linford, 1989.
Gunslick Territory (as Brian Wynne). New York, Ace, 1973.

Novels as Dean Owen

Guns to the Sunset. New York, Phoenix Press, 1948; London, Wright and Brown, 1950.
Point of a Gun. New York, Popular Library, 1953; London, Viking Press, 1957.
The Man from Boot Hill. New York, Ace, 1953.
Rifle Pass. New York, Popular Library, 1954.
Brush Rider. New York, Popular Library, 1955.
The Gunpointer. New York, Popular Library, 1956.
Last-Chance Range. New York, Popular Library, 1957.
Rawhider from Texas. Derby, Connecticut, Monarch, 1958.
This Range Is Mine. New York, Avon, 1959; London, Ward Lock, 1961.
Rebel Ramrod. New York, Curl, 1960.
A Killer's Bargain. London, Wright and Brown, 1961.

The Sam Houston Story. Derby, Connecticut, Monarch, 1961.
Lone Star Roundup. New York, Ace, 1972.

OTHER PUBLICATIONS

Other

History and Genealogy of the Bangs Family in America: Tracing the Descendants, Male and Female, from the Pilgrim Ancestor, Edward Bangs of Plymouth and Eastham. Salem, Massachusetts, Higginson, 1988.

* * *

Set somewhere in cattle country near a large Mexican population, Dudley Dean's Westerns derive their force from the nature of their central character. Dean's heroes are men forced by circumstances into a stance they would rather have avoided—that of notorious gunfighter. Proving fast on the draw disrupts their lives and forces them to be constantly on guard, to mistrust false flattery and fear sudden betrayal. These are tough, just, lonely men, with hard-steely eyes, strong bodies, and a deep sense of loyalty. They are driven and haunted by events from the past—sometimes a regretable act of their own, sometimes the violence and betrayal of another. Though silent and reflective, cynical and world-weary, they remain emotionally vulnerable. Having seen their friends and sweethearts betray them, they are wary of new alliances, but are nonetheless compelled to love and loyalty. In *The Man from Riondo* Brack Ventress cannot bring himself to kill his childhood idol, even though the man betrays him again and again. A typical Dean hero, Brack restores money to injured parties, helps ladies in distress (even when their honor has been besmirched), and tries to rectify the wrongs of a lifetime—resorting to an orgy of killing only when there is no other way. In *Gun the Man Down* it is again the hero's goodheartedness that is the root of his problem. Because he cannot believe a young man he has watched grow up could turn bad, Clete lets down his guard and finally must kill the youth to save himself—an act that leads to a price on his head, accusations of theft and wife-stealing, and a series of self-perpetuating high noon duels.

The plots move from gunfight to gunfight, from betrayal to betrayal. The characters are violent and raw, but in the main adhere to a tough code of fair fights, honorable treatment of women, payment of obligations. They may condone robbery, landgrabbing, and murder, but those who break the Westerners' code and are found out are shunned as pariahs.

Protective of women and children, anxious to avoid a gunfighter image, torn by a love they cannot admit even to themselves, Dean's heroes do not want to kill, but are forced to do so to protect themselves and their own. They befriend outsiders (Mexicans, Chinese, small-time ranchers), value honest townfolk, and prefer minding their own business. They have difficulty giving voice to their affections, but are always ready to act when needed. Ultimately, they must come to terms with their future by coming to terms with their past. One must discover the worth of his father (an infamous gunfighter) and unravel the secrets of a half-breed sister, a distant gold mine, and an avaricious bully before he can find the peace he seeks. Another must endure taunts and suspicions until the facts so convincingly confirm his acts that even his sternest opponents must admit his honesty and rectitude. Such heroes embody the positive values of self-effacing love, loyalty, integrity, and tough-mindedness that Dean believes truly won the West.

—Gina Macdonald

DE BLASIS, Celeste (Ninette). American. Born in Santa Monica, California, 8 May 1946. Educated at Wellesley College, Massachusetts, 1964–65; Oregon State University, Corvallis, 1965–66; Pomona College, Claremont, California, B.A. (cum laude) in English 1968. Lives in California. Agent: Jane Rotrosen Agency, 318 East 51st Street, New York, New York 10022, U.S.A.

WESTERN PUBLICATIONS

Novels (series: Swan)

The Night Child. New York, Coward McCann, and London, Millington, 1975.
Suffer a Sea Change. New York, Coward McCann, 1976.
The Proud Breed. New York, Coward McCann, 1978; London, Arrow, 1979.
The Tiger's Woman. New York, Delacorte Press, 1981; London, Granada, 1982.
Wild Swan. New York, Bantam, 1984.
Swan's Chance. New York, Bantam, 1985; London, Bantam, 1987.
A Season of Swans. New York, Bantam, 1989.

OTHER PUBLICATIONS

Other

Peaches. New York, St. Martin's Press, 1991.

* * *

Celeste De Blasis was born in southern California, so it is understandable that one of her first historical novels, *The Proud Breed*, would contain a strong sense of California's history. She admits to extensively researching the backgrounds to her novels and she excels in interweaving actual and fictional historical events. De Blasis creates realistic characters who bring all of her carefully prepared storylines into perspective.

As with all of her novels, the heroine is predominant in the story; she is often pitted against what is usually considered to be a male dominated area such as business and ranching. The heroines are often isolated either on an island (as in *The Night Child* and *The Tiger's Woman*) or on a ranch (*The Proud Breed* and the Swan books). But wherever the novel may be set, one overwhelming pattern emerges: love and destiny.

The Proud Breed tells the story of Tessa MacLeod, the heroine, her cowboy husband, Gavin Ramsay, and their fight to overcome physical and emotional obstacles to see their dream of a family dynasty flourish in California of the mid 1800's. Tessa is an exceptional woman, not only beautiful and intelligent, but with a great love for the land, an important quality according to De Blasis. ". . . Characters often judge their own well being by that of the particular piece of land they occupy," she once said. Besides a strong love story, *The Proud Breed* also depicts cynical attitudes of the secondary characters and their effects on both Tessa and Ramsay.

The Tiger's Woman treads a fine line between western and historical genres, with a strong leaning toward the latter. A chance meeting in a San Francisco dance hall between Mary Smith and Jason Darke is the catalyst to future events. Mary is forced to remember her mysterious past in seeing Darke. To escape him she flees to the sea port of Seattle, but unfortunately for her Darke has business there. Knowing that there is no escape from "the Tiger," as Darke is known in gambling circles, she strikes a bargain in which Darke would protect her from her murderous past, and she would become his mistress. Darke agrees but soon is drawn into solving the mystery of "Mary Smith." The love story again is the central theme, as the personal desires of men and women are the overriding factors from which all other events take root.

The remainder of De Blasis's output has concentrated on her trilogy of novels concerning the Thaine/Falconer family and their Maryland horse ranch, Wild Swan. These books are far more ambitious than any of her previous writings. The authentic background research is present once again in *Wild Swan*, from England's west country during the Napoleonic wars where smuggling is the order of the day, to the lush Maryland horse country which is overshadowed by the slavery issue. *Wild Swan* attempts to portray the political and physical conditions in which its characters lived. In extending *Wild Swan* into a trilogy (at this time of writing), De Blasis uses to excellent effect the technique of having the Falconer family parallel their country's turbulent growth. *Swan's Chance*, continues with the heroine Alexandria Falconer protecting her race horses and ranch, while her husband Rane battles to save his shipbuilding empire.

The Swan books are De Blasis's best works to date and it would be wrong to class them as formulary Westerns. They contain no stampedes, no cattle drives, no marauding Indians, no gratuitous violence or six-gun wizards. She depicts an era that did exist far away from the rugged frontier of the rolling prairies. Here she creates real people in a world where the readers with a snobbish attitude towards the Western can be excited for a few hours with much the same stories that L'Amour, Schaeffer, and Steinbeck have created.

Because her storylines emphasize the romantic point of view, many hardline western readers may dismiss De Blasis's writing out of hand. But these books should be evaluated differently from the "horse operas," and because of their historical content should remain of interest.

—John L. Wolfe

DECKER, William. American. Born in Richmond, Virginia, in 1926. Educated at Stanford University, California, graduated 1950. Served in the United States Army Air Corps during World War II. Married to Anne Decker. Worked on cattle ranches in Arizona, California, Nevada, and Oregon; horse trainer and professional polo player; editor for New York publishers, 20 years; taught at New York University. Recipient: Western Writers of America Spur award, 1980. Address: c/o Little Brown, 34 Beacon Street, Boston, Massachusetts 02106, U.S.A.

WESTERN PUBLICATIONS

Novels

To Be a Man. Boston, Little Brown, 1967.
The Holdouts. Boston, Little Brown, 1979.

* * *

William Decker is a western writer of fiction whose credentials as a cowboy and rancher in his earlier years tie him directly to the subjects he writes about. Moreover, Decker's development, away from the rural West and into the world of publishing and editing, appears to have provided him with a keen sense of transition and change.

His two novels, *To Be a Man* and *The Holdouts*, take change as their central themes. *To Be a Man* resembles oral history at least as much as it does fiction in the way it allows Roscoe Banks, the protagonist, to relate the events of his long life. Decker's narrative begins with Banks's childhood in the 1880's; moves through Banks's various experiences as a homesteader, wild horse hunter, and rodeo performer; and closes with his death in 1950. The novel is especially faithful to the smells and sounds of ranch work and rodeoing. In its poignant focus on a way of life doomed to oblivion by the very progress to which it contributes, though without the same sure-handed artistry, Decker's novel resembles Jack Schaefer's *Monte Walsh*.

The Holdouts is much less panoramic and much better controlled. What Decker does is to draw elements from the detective tradition into a contemporary story of cattle rustling in northern Arizona. But the novel's strength derives less from suspense than it does from Decker's sense of time, place, and character. His novel renders dialogue with simple accuracy and shows the effects of change within characters as well as in the external world where Decker's detailed knowledge of the cattle industry makes itself felt.

In both of his novels Decker deals heavily with traditional western subjects, particularly with men who have grown up with the expectation of always being a part of ranch life. The sense of men among men is obvious: "Over a last smoke or chew for the day, they swapped yarns and reminisced while bugs bumped against the hissing of a Coleman lantern" (*The Holdouts*). Decker's handling of women is less effective, and both of his novels suggest an essential but understandable nostalgia for the way things were.

—William Bloodworth

DELANEY, John. *See* **ROWLAND, Donald S.**

DeMARINIS, Rick. American. Born in New York City, 3 May 1934. Educated at San Diego State College (now University), California, 1952–54; University of Montana, Missoula, B.A. 1961, M.A. 1967. Served in United States Air Force, 1954–58. Married to Carole Joyce Bubash; one son and two daughters. Instructor in English, University of Montana, Missoula, 1967–69; Assistant Professor of English, San Diego State University, 1969–76. Since 1988 Associate Professor of English, University of Texas, El Paso. Visiting writer, Arizona

State University, Tempe, 1980–81; Distinguished writer-in-residence, Wichita State University, Kansas, 1986, Recipient: Drue Heinz literature prize, 1986; American Academy and Institute of Arts and Letters award, 1990. Agent: Candida Donadio and Associates, 231 West 22nd Street, New York, New York 10011. Address: Department of English, University of Texas at El Paso, El Paso, Texas 79968, U.S.A.

WESTERN PUBLICATIONS

Novel

The Burning Women of Far Cry. New York, Arbor House, 1986.

Short Stories

Under the Wheat. Pittsburgh, Pennsylvania, University of Pittsburgh Press, 1986.

Uncollected Short Stories

"The Jade Marie," in *CutBank*, Fall/Winter 1983.
"Weeds," in *Writers of the Purple Sage.* New York, Viking, 1984.
"Billy Ducks Among the Pharaohs," in *CutBank*, Spring/Summer 1986.
"Gent," in *The Last Best Place*, Montana Historical Society, 1988.
"Desert Places," in *Best of the West.* Salt Lake City, Utah, Peregrine Smith, 1990.

OTHER PUBLICATIONS

Novels

A Lovely Monster: The Adventures of Claude Rains and Dr. Tellenbeck. New York, Simon and Schuster, 1976.
Scimitar. New York, Dutton, 1977.
Cinder. New York, Farrar Straus, 1978.
The Year of the Zinc Penny. New York, Viking, 1989.

Short Stories

Jack and Jill: Two Novellas and a Short Story. New York, Dutton, 1979.
The Coming Triumph of the Free World. New York, Viking, 1988.
The Voice of America. New York, Norton, 1991.

* * *

In no conventional manner is Rick DeMarinis a "western" writer. Born in New York City and raised in San Diego, he tends to set his darkly comic fiction in urban or suburban locales that—on the surface—seem untied to any region. But beneath the jagged contours of his plot and characterization, several DeMarinis works reveal deeply disturbing visions of the West. These have virtually nothing to do with the hoary, shoot-'em-up landscape most commonly sketched. For DeMarinis the West is a fallen frontier—a great, sprawling wasteland poisoned and trampled beneath the march of technology. In the land's oft-commemorated surrender to eastern pioneers, he finds only a harbinger of the destruction that ensues when their subjugating spirit meets the scientific age. This is most powerfully illustrated in the short story "Weeds." The first paragraph tells us all:

> A black helicopter flapped out of the morning sun and dumped its sweet orange mist on our land instead of the Parley farm where it was intended. It was weedkiller, something strong enough to wipe out leafy sponge, knapweek and Canadian thistle, but it made us sick.

Here, the maniacal desire to control the land, and wring money from it, wreaks fitting destruction. This wonder chemical, in fact, helps kill the narrator's father—not to mention his farm animals—drive his mother insane, and renders him unable to carry out even the most quotidian tasks. DeMarinis makes the motivation obvious. "The thirteen-year locusts were back and raising a whirl," he writes. "I expected more helicopters to come flapping over with special sprays meant just for them, even though they would be around for only a few weeks and the damage they would do is not much more than measurable. But anything that looks like it might have an appetite for a money crop brings down the spraying choppers." As the pesticide withers fertile land, so too it implants a sense of hopelessness in the young farmer. "The farm struck me as a pointless wonder," he muses, "and I found the idea depressing and fearsome. Pointless bugs lay waiting in the fields for the pointless drops and the pointless days and seasons ran on and on into the pointless forever."

Eventually the protagonist trades his last surviving animal for a bunch of seeds that, once planted, produce mutant weeds. In this twisted fairytale, the weeds answer those who aspire to rule nature with a set of manmade poisons by reclaiming the land with apocalyptic vengeance.

> They were weeds. The worst kind of weed I had ever seen. Thick, spiny weeds, with broad green leaves tough as leather. ... They were attacked by squadrons of helicopters which drenched them in poisons, the best poisons chemical science knew how to brew. But the poisons only seemed to make the weeds grow faster, tougher, thornier, and more determined than ever to dominate the land. Some of the weeds sent up long woody stalks with seedpods. The day the pods cracked, a heavy wind came up. The wind raised black clouds of seed in grainy spirals that reached the top of the sky, then scattered them, far and wide, across the entire nation.

With the story "Under the Wheat" DeMarinis again explores the modern Westerner's alienation from the land. In this case, he exposes the way in which man has subverted—and perverted—the once amber waves of grain by carving nuclear missile silos under the wheat. "I've seen the wheat go down," he writes, "acres and acres of useless straw." His troubled protagonist is, like the other characters scattered across the North Dakota plains, totally out of touch with the land and its nurturing qualities. Where once prosperous farmers lived, there is now an abandoned ghost town, a rotting monument to a dam-building project. The story is also reflective of DeMarinis's conviction that powerbrokers in the urban East are essentially unconcerned about the West's once pristine naturalism. "They see the West as a great place to dump nuclear waste and not much else," he observed, in a recent interview.

In his bleak—and bleakly precise—vision the rugged West has been tamed and tainted by its human tenants. In his novel *The Burning Women of Far Cry* DeMarinis describes in chillingly plain terms how the nature's elements are bent to human wants: "The river ... cut the town into a two-piece jigsaw puzzle. Clean white smoke rose from the tall stacks of the lumber mills and a haze covered most of the low-lying areas, dulling sharp colors and diluting colors." Such a vision of the West may pale next to the bright hues of remembrance, but it marks DeMarinis as one of the most probing—albeit subtle—western writers of his time.

—Steven Almond

DEMING, Kirk. *See* **DRAGO, Harry Sinclair.**

DENVER, Drake C. *See* **NYE, Nelson.**

DENVER, Lee. *See* **GRIBBLE, Leonard.**

DENVER, Rod. *See* **EDSON, J.T.**

DE ROSSO, H(enry) A(ndrew). American. Born in Carey, Wisconsin, 15 July 1917. Wrote more than 200 short stories, novelettes, and novellas for western pulp magazines, over 15 years. *Died 14 October 1960.*

WESTERN PUBLICATIONS

Novels

Tracks in the Sand. New York, Reader's Choice Library, 1951.
.44. New York, Lion, 1953; London, Mills and Boon, 1957; as *Killer's Brand*, New York, Lancer, 1968.
The Gun Trail. New York, Lion, 1953; as *The Man from Texas*, New York, Lion, 1957.
End of the Gun. New York, Permabooks, 1955; London, Mills and Boon, 1957.
The Dark Brand. New York, Avalon, 1963; London, Mills and Boon, 1965.

Fiction (for children)

The Rebel. Racine, Wisconsin, Whitman, 1961.

Uncollected Short Stories

"The Way of Lead," in *Wild West* (New York), 1 August 1942.
"Last Manhunt," in *Western Triggers*, edited by Arnold Hano. New York, Bantam, 1948.
"Slow Draw—Sudden Grave," in *Western Roundup*, edited by Arnold Hano. New York, Bantam, 1948.
"Boomer, Roam No More!," in *Western Story* (London), May 1948.
"Bloody Valley!," in *.44 Western*, January 1949.
"Only the Gun Swift," in *Texas Rangers* (London), May 1949.
"The Long Sleep," in *Mammoth Western* (Chicago), May 1949.
"Flight from the Desert," in *Mammoth Western* (Chicago), September 1949.
"One Kiss . . . One Grave," in *Mammoth Western* (Chicago), March 1950.
"A Tinhorn Can't Take It," in *Best Western*, June 1951.
"Fear in the Saddle," in *Zane Grey's Western* (New York), September 1952.
"I Ride Alone," in *Texas Rangers* (London), December 1952.
"Hired Gun," in *Complete Western Book*, December 1952.
"For Love or Money," in *Texas Rangers* (London), February 1953.
"Under the Burning Sky," in *Collier's* (Springfield, Ohio), 6 June 1953.
"Killer," in *Gunsmoke* (New York), August 1953.
"Rope Enough," in *Western Story* (London), August 1953.
"The Bitter Trail," in *Bar 3*, edited by Scott Meredith. New York, Dutton, 1954.
"Song of Death," in *Texas Rangers* (London), February 1954.
"Ride Alone—Die Alone," in *Western Story* (London), November 1954.
"My Brother: Killer," in *Western Short Stories*, December 1954.
"I Will Kill Even You . . . ," in *Western Novel and Short Stories*, January 1956.
"An Old Cold Trail," in *Exciting Western* (London), June-July 1956.
"Back Track," in *Bar 6*, edited by Scott Meredith. New York, Dutton, 1957.
"Black Kill in the Desalados," in *3-Book Western* (New York), May 1957.
"Cattle Queen's Hired Killer," in *Western Story* (London), November 1957.
"The Killing Samaritan," in *Western Story* (London), July 1959.
"Fear in the Saddle," in *The Cowboys*, edited by Bill Pronzini and Martin H. Greenberg. New York, Fawcett, 1985.
"Vigilante," in *Wild Westerns: Stories from the Grand Old Pulps*, edited by Bill Pronzini and Martin H. Greenberg. New York, Walker, 1986.
"The Mesteños," in *More Wild Westerns*, edited by Bill Pronzini. New York, Walker, 1989.

* * *

H.A. De Rosso began writing while in high school in 1935, but it was not until 1941, after 79 rejected stories, that he made his first professional sale to *Street & Smith's Western Story Magazine*—something of a monument to perseverance. From 1941 until the mid-1960's, he published well over 200 short stories and five western novels. Most of the stories were westerns as well, with the balance divided between mysteries and science fiction, and most appeared in pulp magazines; his only major magazine publication was a serial, "Under the Burning Sky," in *Collier's* in 1953.

The most accomplished of De Rosso's novels is *.44*, a stark and powerful portrait of a professional gunfighter. Almost as good is *End of the Gun*, the tale of an ex-convict who is forced to break his vow never to use a gun again when one of his friends is murdered and the life of his girlfriend is threatened.

Although De Rosso's plots tended to be formula, his handling of them was uncommon in popular western fiction of the 1940's and 1950's. Nearly all of his work is unrelentingly grim, portraying the seamier side of western life without softening or apology. The motives of his heroes are usually mixed and their victories, if indeed they do triumph (a good many do not even survive), are almost always bittersweet. These unusual qualities are clearly in evidence in the best of his fiction—the novel *.44* and such stories as "Killer," "The Bitter Trail," and "Back Track."

—Bill Pronzini

DESTRY, Vince. *See* **NORWOOD, V.G.C.**

DE VOTO, Bernard (Augustine). Also wrote as John August; Cady Hewes. American. Born in Ogden, Utah, 11 January 1897. Educated at Ogden High School, 1914; University of Utah, Salt Lake City, 1914–15; Harvard University, Cambridge, Massachusetts, 1915–17, 1919–20, A.B. 1920 (Phi Beta Kappa). Served in the United States Army infantry, 1917–19: Lieutenant. Married Helen Avis MacVicar in 1923; two sons. History teacher, Ogden Junior High School, 1921; Instructor, then Assistant Professor of English, Northwestern University, Evanston, Illinois, 1922–27; Instructor and tutor, 1929–34, and Lecturer, 1934–36, Harvard University. Editor, Americana Deserta series, Knopf, 1930–32; editor, *Harvard Graduates' Magazine*, 1930–32; columnist ("Easy Chair"), *Harper's*, 1935–55; editor, *Saturday Review of Literature*, 1936–37; member of the editorial board, *New England Quarterly*, 1942; editor, *America in Books*, 1947–48. Curator, Mark Twain Papers, 1938–46; staff member, Bread Loaf Writers Conference; Member of the Advisory Board on the National Parks, 1949–55. Recipient: Pulitzer prize, for non-fiction, 1948; Bancroft prize, for non-fiction, 1948; National Book award, for non-fiction, 1953. Litt.D.: Middlebury College, Vermont, 1937; Kenyon College, Gambier, Ohio, 1942; University of Colorado, Boulder, 1948; Northeastern University, Boston 1948. Member, American Academy. *Died 13 November 1955.*

WESTERN PUBLICATIONS

Novels

The Crooked Mile. New York, Minton Balch, 1924.
The Chariot of Fire. New York, Macmillan, 1926.
The House of Sun-Goes-Down. New York and London, Macmillan, 1928.
Mountain Time. Boston, Little Brown, 1947; London, Hammond, 1949.

OTHER PUBLICATIONS

Novel

We Accept with Pleasure. Boston, Little Brown, 1934.

Novels as John August

Troubled Star. Boston, Little Brown, 1939.
Rain Before Seven. Boston, Little Brown, 1940.
Advance Agent. Boston, Little Brown, 1942; London, Selwyn and Blount, 1943.
The Woman in the Picture. Boston, Little Brown, and London, Selwyn and Blount, 1944.

Other

The Writer's Handbook: A Manual of English Composition, with W.F. Bryan and Arthur H. Nethercot. New York, Macmillan, 1928.
Mark Twain's America. Boston, Little Brown, 1932.
Forays and Rebuttals. Boston, Little Brown, 1936.
Minority Report. Boston, Little Brown, 1940.
Mark Twain at Work. Cambridge, Massachusetts, Harvard University Press, 1942.
The Year of Decision 1846. Boston, Little Brown, 1943; London, Eyre and Spottiswoode, 1957.
The Literary Fallacy. Boston, Little Brown, 1944.
Across the Wide Missouri. Boston, Houghton Mifflin, 1947; London, Eyre and Spottiswoode, 1948.
The World of Fiction. Boston, Houghton Mifflin, 1950.
The Course of Empire. Boston, Houghton Mifflin, 1952; as *Westward the Course of Empire*, London, Eyre and Spottiswoode, 1953.
The Easy Chair. Boston, Houghton Mifflin, 1955.
Women and Children First (as Cady Hewes). Boston, Houghton Mifflin, 1956.
The Letters of Bernard De Voto, edited by Wallace Stegner. New York, Doubleday, 1975.

Editor, *Mark Twain in Eruption: Hitherto Unpublished Pages about Men and Events.* New York, Harper, 1940.
Editor, *The Portable Mark Twain.* New York, Viking Press, 1946; London, Penguin, 1979.
Editor, *The Journals of Lewis and Clark.* Boston, Houghton Mifflin, 1952; London, Eyre and Spottiswoode, 1954.

*

Manuscript Collection: Stanford University, California.

Critical Studies: *Four Portraits and One Subject: Bernard De Voto* by Catherine Drinker Bowen and others, Boston, Houghton Mifflin, 1963 (includes bibliography by Julius P. Barclay); *Bernard De Voto* by Orlan Sawey, New York, Twayne, 1969.

* * *

Bernard De Voto is best known for his histories of the American West and as a writer of the "Easy Chair" essays for *Harper's Magazine* from 1933 to 1955. He won the Pulitzer prize in history in 1948 for his study of the Rocky Mountain fur trade, *Across the Wide Missouri*, and throughout his controversial career was alternately praised and blamed for his biting commentary on American culture.

A native of Ogden, Utah, De Voto established himself among the East Coast intelligentsia as a sort of trans-mountain intellectual-at-large charged with interpreting American history and culture from a "western" point of view. He began with a series of novels and witty essays stingingly critical of his home city and state. "Ogden: The Underwriters of Salvation" and "Utah" aroused such a furor among the Mormon community that he was repeatedly warned not to step foot in Utah again. His first three novels—all Westerns—did nothing to improve his reputation in the West. *The Crooked Mile* and *The House of Sun-Goes-Down* chronicle the rise and fall of the Abbey family in Utah. Scions of southern gentry, the Abbeys are eventually ruined by the cliquishness and greed of their neighbors, whom De Voto characterizes as scoundrels, liars, and fools. Neither of these books treated the explosive religious issue of Mormons and Gentiles in Utah, but focused instead on related issues of freedom, individualism, and capitalism in the West. It is his novel *The Chariot of Fire* that ridicules and condemns the Pentacostalism that gave birth to the Mormon faith. It traces the development of a lunatic sect of Boggsites from backwoods Elam, Illinois—and it takes little imagination to see the early Mormons in these stupid, credulous farmers who call themselves "saints" and await the "last days." The Boggsites are defeated by a militia of outraged citizenry and are last seen "hurrying westward" to a promised land.

But De Voto does much more than simply twist Mormon tails. He was a thorough student of western history, and presents, in the Abbey family saga, his understanding of the frontier experience and its influence on American civilization. De Voto drew heavily from the journal of his maternal grandfather, Samuel Dye, in creating the character of Jim Abbey. However, whereas Sam Dye had been a Mormon from England, De Voto makes Jim Abbey a Southern aristocrat, a refugee from the corrupt and humiliating conditions of Reconstruction. Like thousands of other Americans, Abbey joins the trek westward in search of a land where men can live in freedom and dignity. His attachment to the soil and unremitting labor make his fortune, but his ambitious attempt to fuse his southern heritage with the promise of the west—by transforming the barren Grouse Creek Basin into a family estate—ultimately ruins him. Jim's son Pemberton is made by De Voto into an archetype of western genius: he is an "uncouth colossus who never slept, who never tired, who was all things in all places at one time . . . Power of the earth, power of the tides—he was one with them, a conduit for them, the copper core along which the world's current ran." By means of daring ruthlessness and brutality Pemberton becomes a mining tycoon, only to be finally destroyed by a monopolistic financial capitalism spreading from the East like a cancer over the West. Gordon Abbey, the "third generation," comes eventually to agree with the historian John Gale that there had never really been a frontier of freedom, opportunity, and virtue, but only "an advancing fringe of dubious civilization where men repeated the unchanging cycle of their race . . . The frontier, the boundary of freedom and manhood, was a mirage, something born of sun and silence, a chimera of the brain." (The original title of *The Crooked Mile* had been *Mirage*.) In the Abbey novels, De Voto challenges Turner's vision of the West as a place of freedom, individualism, and primitive democracy. It was not. Rather, it was collective effort, discipline, and unremitting labor that made the West. In De Voto's words, "the true individualist on the frontier is to be found at one end of a rope whose other end is in the hands of a group of vigilantes." Instead of freedom, De Voto's immigrants find a slavery in the West. They are chained to the land, to the mines, to finance capitalism, religious community, and family tradition.

De Voto is particularly good in his descriptions of the western landscape, for which he seems to have had true feeling. To wrest a living from this land poisoned by alkali and choked by mesquite shrubs requires men of strength and tenacity of will. These are De Voto's heroes—not free men, but farmers chained to the wheel of survival in a barren land. They are the ones who transform the desert into a garden of plenty, whereas ranchers, miners, and lumberman would strip it bare with an "economy of liquidation."

De Voto's books are not formulary Westerns. There are no sheriffs here, no gunslingers or saloon girls. He does not indulge in saddle or spur fetishism. Whatever their defects—and there are many—his novels have the unmistakable feel of reality in them. This is a West that did exist, not an island of the imagination. He consciously refused to reduce the West to formulary clichés. "If as a critic of historical writing," he said in a letter to a friend, "I have challenged the simplicities of certain historians about the American frontier, it is because I know of my own experiences that frontier life was infinitely complex and not reducible to formula." He recalled from his own childhood that he had "played with the sons and grandsons of Hawaiian princes, Scandinavian murderers, German geologists with duelling scars, Irish poets, Spanish mathematicians, French gamblers, Virginian slaveholders, Yankee metaphysicians—of men who came from everywhere, who had every conceivable tradition, education and canon of taste and behavior." His "scientific" method of writing was such as to preclude a formulary approach to the novel. "The only canons which a writer of fiction can accept are precisely the ones that govern the laboratory scientist," he wrote to Hans Zinsser. "A novelist is faithful to human behavior, to human emotion, to human experience—and to the art of communicating them to others. He is faithful to character, to the truth as [he] sees it . . . and to nothing else."

Unfortunately, De Voto was not a great novelist. In his memoirs, Norman Cousins regrets that he ever allowed Sinclair Lewis's brutal attack on De Voto, "Fools, Liars, and Mr. De Voto," to be published in the *Saturday Review*, what with its scurrilous references to De Voto's "frog-like face" and hack work novels. What probably plagued Cousin's conscience most was that Lewis had been right, and to have printed his essay, cruel. For those, like myself, who admire his histories, literary criticism, and cultural commentary, De Voto's fiction is an unpleasant experience. Its style is stilted, exaggerated, and self-conscious, and there is an arrogant didacticism running through it that is certain to grate the sensibilities of all but his most fervant fans. However real their background, De Voto's characters remain cardboard puppets acting out "lessons" in history. Gordon Abbey and Hope Gale in *The Crooked Mile*, for example, are insufferable snobs who despise everything around them and declaim superficial Nietzscheanisms like: "I don't care what life means to any but a dozen people in the world." When you finally realize that these are not foils for a late-entering hero, but the protagonists themselves, you quickly lose interest. It is impossible to care what happens to such people. In his critical study of De Voto, Orlan Sawey argues that his novels have been unjustly ignored, but this is hardly true. If they are read at all, it will be by those who have come to them by way of De Voto's histories and criticism, and so will probably remain a continuing disappointment.

—John D. Flanagan

DEWLEN, Al. American. Born in Memphis, Texas, 30 November 1921. Educated at Memphis public schools, 1927–38; Hillsboro College, Texas, 1939–41; Baylor University, Waco, Texas, 1941–42; University of Oklahoma, Norman, 1952–55. Served in the United States Marine Corps, 1942–45: Technical Sergeant. Married Jean Lamb in 1942; one son (killed in action, Vietnam, 1968). Reporter, Amarillo *Daily News*, Texas, 1946–47; city editor, Amarillo *Times*, 1947–51; night editor, United Press, Dallas, 1951–52; reporter, Oklahoma City, Oklahoma, 1952–54. Since 1952 freelance writer and lecturer. Guest lecturer, University of Oklahoma, Norman; Baylor University, Waco, Texas; West Texas State College (now University), Canyon; Amarillo College, Texas. Recipient: McGraw-Hill fiction award, 1961; Oklahoma award for Literary Excellence, 1971. Agent: Paul R. Reynolds and Son, 12 East 41st Street, New York, New York 10017. Address: 4904 Ponte, Lily Avenue, Berca, Johannesberg, South Africa.

WESTERN PUBLICATIONS

Novels

The Night of the Tiger. New York, McGraw Hill, 1956; London, Longman, 1957; as *Ride Beyond Vengeance*, New York, New American Library, 1966.
The Bone Pickers. New York, McGraw Hill, 1958; as *The Golden Touch*, New York, Popular Library, 1959.
Twilight of Honor. New York, McGraw Hill, 1961; London, Longman, 1962.
Servants of Corruption. New York, Doubleday, 1971.
Next of Kin. New York, Doubleday, 1977.
The Session. New York, Doubleday, 1981.

Uncollected Short Story

"Showdown at San Sabe," in *Saturday Evening Post* (Philadelphia), 18 September 1954.

*

Manuscript Collections: Baylor University, Waco, Texas; University of Wyoming, Laramie; University of Texas, Austin; University of Oklahoma, Norman.

Critical Study: in *New York Times Book Review*, 31 July 1977.

Al Dewlen comments:

The aim of my fiction has been the intimate examination of human happiness—whether achieved, or sought, or merely yearned for; whether gained, or lost, or mistakenly imagined, or not conceived of at all.

My books use entirely dissimilar subject matter and materials. Each is presented in its own idiom and style, so that none bears any readily apparent kinship with the others. The hope is to avoid repetition, and to escape the authorship trap of making a career out of a single idea. But there is a common element. All my stories deal with the pursuit of happiness. They probe at identifying those magnificent fires which, once kindled in the spirit, impel a man to become more than his circumstances indicated he might be, and thus, lend him happiness; or, they inquire into those forces that cause a man to fall short of his expectations of himself, and thus, afflict him with misery.

These two directions account for all the parables I've made and the people I have created and the ideas I have articulated.

* * *

Five of Al Dewlen's six novels are set in or near the city of Amarillo in the Texas panhandle. Only his more recent novel, *The Session*, goes outside the area, and it tells the story of a legislator from that region who goes to the state capital to speak for northwest Texas. Despite Dewlen's close fictional ties to the Amarillo area, there is little that is regional in his works. He seems to have little interest in conveying a sense of place by depicting carefully the physical characteristics, the language, the customs, or the folklore of the region. His main interest seems to be in setting himself a thematic problem and exploring it—often in the manner of the journalistic investigative series.

Dewlen's only novel which is not similar to investigative reporting is his first one, *The Night of the Tiger*. The novel is a "western" that attempts to be more than the standard pulp and yet fails as a serious work. It is Dewlen's only period piece; the rest are concerned with contemporary problems in contemporary settings. *The Bone Pickers* shows the effect of wealth on a Texas family; the novel is one of those familiar stories of the rise and decline of the family dynasty. *Twilight of Honor*, usually thought of as Dewlen's best, is an analysis of justice and injustice in the law courts. The novel follows the progress of a sensational murder trial and shows its effects on a series of participants. *Servants of Corruption*, a little-noticed novel which is, in my opinion, his best work, is an exposé of the John Birch Society's attempt to take over a large Campbellite church in an unnamed panhandle city. *Next of Kin* is an account of a Texas newsman's personal and violent reaction to anti-Vietnam war protestors. The main character's son has been killed in the war, and the father sets out to find and punish the protestor who wrote a letter to the newspaper approving of the son's death and applauding the Viet Cong who killed this foreign aggressor. *The Session* is a timely satire on the corruption found in the Texas Legislature—a body with 150 lawmakers and over 6000 lobbyists.

Dewlen's strength as a novelist is his ability to tell a coherent story, his ability to satirize people and institutions, and his total mastery of whatever problem he is concerned with. Trained as a newspaperman, Dewlen shows the good journalist's talent for getting his facts down clearly and concisely and for immersing himself in the details of his story. But, as is often the case with the newsman-turned-novelist, Dewlen is deficient as a stylist. His prose is serviceable and workmanlike, but little thought is given to its variety or to searching for the perfect word. Dewlen's worst defect as a novelist is his inability to make the characters come to life. He is very good at the caricatures he satirizes, but his real people do not "surprise us with their human complexity," as E.M. Forster says they must.

—James W. Lee

DEXTER, Martin. *See* **BRAND, Max.**

DEXTER, Ross.

WESTERN PUBLICATIONS

Novels

Loot of the Lone Wolf. London, Hale, 1971.
The Black Duke. London, Hale, 1977.
The Killing at Buffalo Crossing. London, Hale, 1978.
The Rainbow Kid. London, Hale, 1978.

* * *

E.G. Stokoe used the pseudonym "Ross Dexter" on one occasion back in the 1950's, when he wrote the western novel *Carson's Killer*. The name has since been utilized by another, unknown writer, who has subsequently produced four Westerns of his own during the period 1971–78. The novels of this latterday Ross Dexter are notable chiefly for their leading characters, Duke Lawson and the decidedly anti-heroic Rainbow Kid.

Lawson, a tall, black-garbed gunfighter who answers to the sobriquet of "The Black Duke," is the more conventional hero-figure of the two. A former United States marshal who has parted with his badge, but remains devoted to the upholding of law and order, he travels the untamed areas of the West as a lone avenging angel, bringing justice to all evil-doers. In novels like *The Black Duke* and *The Killing at Buffalo Crossing*, Lawson is portrayed as an almost superhuman being, adept with both fist and gun, whose invincibility in combat is matched only by his superior knowledge in every given situation. At once a courteous prairie knight and a ruthless exterminator of villains, his role leaves him stranded awkwardly in a no-man's-land somewhere between the Lone Ranger and Clint Eastwood, and effectively deprives him of credibility. All too often he is shown as the only man capable of intelligent thought in a universe otherwise peopled with conniving villains and well-meaning imbeciles, the latter unable to grasp a truth immediately obvious both to the Black Duke and the average reader. This is nowhere better illustrated than in *The Killing at Buffalo Crossing*, where Lawson—arriving in town to find his friend, the sheriff, has been murdered—quickly discovers that the two warring factions in Buffalo Crossing are being set at odds by a third party, but is unable to convince anyone until the closing section of the book. In fact, the identity of the "mysterious" killer of the sheriff should be obvious to anyone long before the halfway stage, and his final unmasking is more of an anti-climax than a surprise. The Lone Ranger, alas, casts a long shadow over the dialogue in many places—the painfully stilted speech of the characters in general, and Lawson in particular, seems to derive from the kind of formal, wooden delivery made famous by Clayton Moore in the old T.V. series. Indeed, the Black Duke's tendency to raise unconversational matters and discuss them in sentences of suspicious grammatical precision infects those about him, as when a female character remarks nonchalantly over the supper-table that "there is something different" about him, and that he "has the look of a United States marshal." Such contrived efforts tend to undermine the interest in Lawson and his exploits, and judged on his performance in *The Black Duke* and *The Killing at Buffalo Crossing*, Dexter would have to be placed some distance behind many of his American and British contemporaries.

Altogether more impressive is *The Rainbow Kid*, the last and by far the best novel of the four. The commonplace title and its opening chapters appear to mark the book as a standard "oater," as the mysterious gunman rides into town and is revealed to the townsfolk as Septimus Phoenix Rainbow, the notorious Rainbow Kid. The fact that he brutally shoots down a child's pet dog that yaps at his heels seems only to confirm the stereotyped nature of the story. However, subsequent developments suggest that these clichés have been deliberately manipulated, for soon afterwards the book breaks away from its expected standard format to become an interesting variation on the well-worn theme, and the result lies somewhere between the Pied Piper and *High Plains Drifter*. Recriminations develop between the townspeople when they realize the gunman is employed by a Syndicate which owns the town, and has been sent to punish them for short-changing their "employer." Although hardly anything happens during the first third of the book, the tension building up among the residents is excellently depicted, with an easy assurance that ensures the reader's interest. One by one the stranger guns down the victims on his list—but this is a Western with no heroes. No upright, fast-drawing benefactor in a white hat is to emerge to face the Rainbow Kid in a Main Street shoot-out. Instead, when the gunman traps himself in the cellar of the fortified cabin of one of his victims, the townsfolk turn into a mob. They burn the Kid to death, but their elation quickly dissipates when they realize that their action has not solved the problem, and that the Syndicate will merely send a replacement. The novel's morality play structure is underlined in its final section, when the mine—the original source of the town's prosperity, but now over-exploited—collapses and explodes, closing the book with a final retribution.

Though *The Rainbow Kid* is not without its faults, and makes frequent use of clichés, it approaches its tired theme in an imaginative way, and demands a more significant appraisal of Dexter's abilities than is suggested by his previous novels.

—B.J. Holmes and Jeff Sadler

DEXTER, Ross. *See* **STOKOE, E.G.**

DIDION, Joan. American. Born in Sacramento, California, 5 December 1934. Educated at California Junior High School and McClatchy Senior High School, both Sacramento; University of California, Berkeley, 1952–56, B.A. in English 1956. Married the writer John Gregory Dunne in 1964; one adopted daughter. Associate feature editor, *Vogue*, New York, 1956–63; moved to Los Angeles, 1964; columnist ("Points West"), with John Gregory Dunne, *Saturday Evening Post*, Philadelphia, 1967–69, and "The Coast," *Esquire*, New York, 1976–77; contributing editor, *National Review*, New York. Visiting Regents' Lecturer, University of California, Berkeley, 1975. Recipient: *Vogue* Paris prize, 1956; Bread Loaf Writers Conference fellowship, 1963; American Academy Morton Dauwen Zabel award, 1979. Agent: Wallace and Sheil, 177 East 70th Street, New York, New York 10021, U.S.A.

Western Publications

Novels

Run River. New York, Obolensky, 1963; London, Cape, 1964.
Play It As It Lays. New York, Farrar Straus, 1970; London, Weidenfeld and Nicolson, 1971.
A Book of Common Prayer. New York, Simon and Schuster, and London, Weidenfeld and Nicolson, 1977.
Democracy. New York, Simon and Schuster, and London, Chatto and Windus, 1984.

Other Publications

Novel

Miami. New York, Simon and Schuster, 1987; London, Weidenfeld and Nicolson, 1988.

Plays

Screenplays: *Panic in Needle Park*, with John Gregory Dunne, 1971; *Play It As It Lays*, with John Gregory Dunne, 1972; *A Star Is Born*, with John Gregory Dunne and Frank Pierson, 1976; *True Confessions*, with John Gregory Dunne, 1981.

Other

Slouching Towards Bethlehem (essays). New York, Farrar Straus, 1968; London, Deutsch, 1969.
Telling Stories. Berkeley, California, Bancroft Library, 1978.
The White Album. New York, Simon and Schuster, and London, Weidenfeld and Nicolson, 1979.
Salvador. New York, Simon and Schuster, and London, Chatto and Windus, 1983.
Essays and Interviews, edited by Ellen G. Friedman, Princeton, New Jersey, Ontario Review Press, 1984.

Recording: *Writing as a Means of Seeing Ourselves*, National Council of Teachers of English.

*

Critical Studies: "Joan Didion: Portrait of a Professional" by Alfred Kazin, in *Harper's Magazine* (New York), December 1971; "A Visit with Joan Didion" by Sara Davidson, in *New York Times Book Review*, 3 April 1977; *Joan Didion* by Mark Royden, Boston, Twayne, 1980; *Joan Didion* by Katherine Usher Henderson, New York, Ungar, 1981.

* * *

The territory that Joan Didion has explored in so much of her writing is her home state of California. The history and the myth of the West informs both her fiction and her non-fiction. In her early and brilliant collection of essays, *Slouching Towards Bethlehem*, she speaks of the attractiveness both for her and an American audience of the figure of John Wayne: "in a world we understood early to be characterized by venality and doubt and paralyzing ambiguities, he suggested another world . . . a place where a man could move free, could make his own code and live by it; a world in which, if a man did what he had to do, he could one day take the girl and go riding through the draw and find himself home free . . . there at the bend in the bright river, the cottonwoods shimmering in the early morning sun." It is Didion's awareness of the gaps and overlaps between the reality of the history of the westward movement, the constructed mythic version of what the West and its heroes can be seen to mean, and contemporary Californian lifestyles, that makes her work so powerful. In it the sense of promise associated with the West has lost all contact with the social and familial codes and bondings so crucial to the original experience and to later representations of it. Didion situates herself between a vision of that wagon train experience and morality which was to reach its positive conclusion in California ("*Eureka*—'I Have Found It'—as the state motto has it") and the sense of cultural dislocation, anomie, and violence that marks the modern-day version of going west. This she sums up in "Some Dreamers of the Golden Dream" when she speaks of those to whom "the future always looks good in the golden land, because no one remembers the past . . . Here is the last stop for all those who come from somewhere else . . . Here is where they are trying to find a new life style, trying to find it in the only places they know to look: the movies and the newspapers."

It is not the John Wayne movies to which such people primarily look for their models, according to Didion (though her questioning of "the primacy of personal conscience" might be usefully related back to the Wayne persona), but those based on the novels of James M. Cain. For Didion "social hemorrhaging" has become the order of new western day and the violence, anomie, drift, and social and familial dislocations of the Cain texts point in exactly such a direction. Moreover, this hemorrhaging seems to Didion particularly appropriate to the physical geography and conditions of the far west where rattlesnakes speak of death and dread, where the Santa Ana wind dries nerves (in Los Angeles) "to the flash point," where brush fires have a season and where literally so much of human existence is built on sand. The image in *Play It As It Lays* of a woman sweeping her concrete clean in a desert area of Nevada with new sand blowing in as she sweeps is revealing both of such a sense of geographical place and of the futility and pointlessness which pervades Didion's work generally.

One of the distinctive qualities of Didion's non-fiction lies in the way she positions her own persona between the sense of dread and moral comprehension as she examines her Californian world. Hers is a type of "waiting for the end" literature. Her first novel, *Run River*, a family melodrama set in the Central Valley of California, very much shows Didion in the process of trying to find her individual fictional voice. By the time of writing her second novel, *Play It As It Lays*, she has found it, with her use of a very spare and flat narrative voice and a very fragmented prose style and structure that reflects the dislocated nature of both the sensibility of her protagonist, Maria, and of the Hollywood world she represents. Hollywood in this novel is a place that operates around false and superficial images and where depthlessness is a permanent condition. Didion's critique of the contemporary far western landscape finds its most appropriate setting here, and the anti-epiphany of the book, if you can call it that, occurs when—at the junction of Sunset and La Brea—it seems to Maria that she is watching "the dead still center of the world, the quintessential intersection of nothing." This is Didion's bleakest novel, and presents a world being drained of energy and meaning as we read.

Where energy does exist, in the second major non-fiction collection, *The White Album*, it is of the most destructive type. The collection hangs around the Manson murders, and again images of disorder, casualty, and collapse, both personal and cultural (as Didion again pulls together her own life with the times she describes), shatter any notion of California Dreaming. Here is an apocalyptic version of where the frontier myth has come to an end, with the murders metaphorically marking the collapse of the sixties and its Californian equation of "freedom" with a drug culture and a belief in "Universal Love." Didion notes on hearing the news of what had happened at the Cielo Drive house: "*I remember no one was surprised.*"

Didion also works as a scriptwriter with her husband John Gregory Dunne. Her strongest work, however, centering on themes of the American West, and the particular Californian variant of those themes, was produced in the 1960's and 1970's. Since then her journalism and fiction have become more politically oriented and she has turned her attention particularly to American involvement in South America in what has been her continuing moral explorations of her country.

—Peter Messent

DILLARD, James. *See* **SNOW, Charles H.**

DOAN, Reece. *See* **KING, Albert.**

DOCTOROW, E(dgar) L(awrence). American. Born in New York City, 6 January 1931. Educated at the Bronx High School of Science; Kenyon College, Gambier, Ohio, A.B. (honors) in philosophy 1952; Columbia University, New York, 1952–53. Served in the United States Army, 1953–55. Married Helen Setzer in 1954; two daughters and one son. Editor, New American Library, New York, 1960–64; editor-in-chief, 1964–69, and publisher, 1969, Dial Press, New York; member of the faculty, Sarah Lawrence College, Bronxville, New York, 1971–78. Since 1982 Glucksman Professor of American and English Letters, New York University. Writer-in-residence, University of California, Irvine, 1969–70; creative writing fellow, Yale School of Drama, New Haven, Connecticut, 1974–75; Visiting Professor, University of Utah, Salt Lake City, 1975; Visiting senior fellow, Princeton University, New Jersey, 1980–81. Director, Authors Guild of America, and American PEN. Recipient: Guggenheim fellowship, 1972; Creative Artists Public Service grant, 1973; National Book Critics Circle award, 1976, 1990; American Academy award, 1976; American Book award, 1986; PEN/Faulkner award, 1990; American Academy Howells Medal, 1990; L.H.D.: Kenyon College, 1976; Litt.D.: Hobart and William Smith Colleges, Geneva, New York, 1979; Brandeis University, 1989. Member, American Academy, 1984. Lives in New Rochelle, New York. Agent: International Creative Management, 40 West 57th Street, New York, New York 10019. Address: c/o Random House Inc., 201 East 50th Street, New York, New York 10022, U.S.A.

WESTERN PUBLICATIONS

Novel

Welcome to Hard Times. New York, Simon and Schuster, 1960; as *Bad Man from Bodie*, London, Deutsch, 1961.

OTHER PUBLICATIONS

Novels

Big as Life. New York, Simon and Schuster, 1966.
The Book of Daniel. New York, Random House, 1971; London, Macmillan, 1972.
Ragtime. New York, Random House, and London, Macmillan, 1975.
Loon Lake. New York, Random House, and London, Macmillan, 1980.
World's Fair. New York, Random House, 1985; London, Joseph, 1986.
Billy Bathgate. New York, Random House, and London, Macmillan, 1989.

Short Stories

Lives of the Poets: Six Stories and a Novella. New York, Random House, 1984; London, Joseph, 1985.

Plays

Drinks Before Dinner (produced New York, 1978). New York, Random House, 1979; London, Macmillan, 1980.

Screenplay: *Daniel*, 1983.

Other

Images of Labor: Discussion Guide. New York, Pilgrim Press, 1981.
American Anthem, photographs by Jean-Claude Suarès. New York, Stewart Tabori and Chang, 1982.

*

Bibliography: *E.L. Doctorow: An Annotated Bibliography* by Michelle M. Tokarezyk, New York, Garland, 1988.

Critical Studies: *E.L. Doctorow: Essays and Conversations*, edited by Richard Trenner, Princeton, New Jersey, Ontario Review Press, 1983; *E.L. Doctorow* (includes bibliography) by Paul Levine, London, Methuen, 1985.

* * *

The freshness and originality of *Welcome to Hard Times*, E.L. Doctorow's first novel, were clear signs of a major talent in the making. Although Doctorow has not written a Western since, his innovations in narrative voice, theme, and tone began with *Hard Times*, a Western which sets out to redefine the stereotype of "Western," while still remaining faithful to the social history of the period. It is a gripping story graced with individual characters, complete personalities whose reality persuades us that this was the way that life on the frontier was actually lived, even though this perception clashes with our expectations and perhaps our wishes.

When described prosaically, the situation and plot seem wholly unpromising. The narrator is a drifter named Blue, 49 years old at the beginning of the story but definitely past his prime. He feels his life has been consumed by the glittering promises of the western states: "Like the West, like my life: the color dazzles us, but when it's too late we see what a fraud it is, what a poor pinched-out claim." Blue has decided to settle finally in Hard Times, a tiny settlement in the Dakota Territory which has grown up to serve the weekend carnal needs of miners in the nearby hills. Blue is the self-appointed "mayor" of Hard Times, a position for which he is qualified by literacy and an obsession with recording the few events that take place in this tiny place where "people naturally come together" in the emptiness of the Dakota flats.

This settled existence comes to a sudden end in the "First Ledger"—we are reading Blue's record of Hard Times's history—when a "Bad Man from Bodie" singlehandedly destroys the town. Only Blue, a prostitute named Molly, and a young boy survive, along with a deaf-and-dumb Indian who serves as a silent witness throughout the story. Blue gathers together this parody of the cleancut frontier family and begins to rebuild the town, alone at first, then with the help of other drifters persuaded by his vision of a prospering community straddling a projected new road to the mines. Zar, a Russian with an entourage of prostitutes that includes a Chinese girl, is the first of the mixed bag of hustlers and ne'er-do-wells to accept Blue's fantasy; around this nucleus others gather, convincing each other and themselves that the presence of human beings in this wasteland betokens future prosperity.

The reader is assured but unsettled at first; as with Doctorow's *Ragtime* there is the disturbing feeling that this is not the way this kind of tale has been told before. But gradually Blue's behavior fits a recognizable modern pattern, one crucial to the settling of the West: Blue is the land promoter, a man consumed with the prospect of creating civilization in an empty and totally unsuitable desert. We are treated to a canny description of the economics of hopes and dreams, the way in which self-interest can be bent to serve the interests of growth—we learn how western towns must have grown.

The inevitable return of the Bad Man from Bodie shatters Blue's vision, just as Molly has warned. Blue's illusory family disintegrates along with his envisioned town. The Bad Man, Doctorow makes clear, is ultimately the force of chaos and anarchy that is nature, ready to undo in minutes the work and dreams of years. Blue's nobility lies in his refusal to accede to this force: he strives for order even while aware of its temporality. Thus we see in *Hard Times* a pattern not only of the demythologized Old West, but also of our own civilization and our own lives, for a Bad Man from Bodie awaits all our best efforts, and must triumph in the end.

If *Hard Times* is a *High Noon* without Gary Cooper, it may also hearken back to a far more ancient tradition. It may well belong, as Mildred Louise Culp argues, to "a Jewish literary tradition," with its focus "on the radicality of evil and the inexplicable cruelty of the alien aggressor toward an insulated community." (One thinks of the tradition of the Golem.) Whether the analogues are old world or new, the determination to experiment with form and shake the reader's faith in conventional pieties is pure Doctorow, as his subsequent works have attested. *The Book of Daniel*, a novel about the McCarthy era and the execution of the Rosenbergs, ends with the narrator's certainty shredded. *Ragtime* is like *Hard Times* in its counter-nostalgic look at a period usually considered a golden age. *Loon Lake, Lives of the Poets* (a collection of short stories), *World's Fair*, and *Billy Bathgate*, though all written in genres other than the Western, continue the central preoccupations first explored in *Hard Times*: the perspective created by an unusual narrative voice and the overlapping of genres; the ethnic variety of American culture; the problem of evil and our responses to it.

—Andrew Macdonald

DODGE, Emerson. Australian.

WESTERN PUBLICATIONS

Novels

All Banner's Brothers. Sydney, Cleveland, n.d.
Killen: U.S. Marshal. Sydney, Cleveland, n.d.
Last Stage to Limbo. Sydney, Cleveland, n.d.
One Man, Two Graves. Sydney, Cleveland, n.d.
The Target Is a Star. Sydney, Cleveland, n.d.
When Gun Kings Die. Sydney, Cleveland, n.d.
Where Gunhawks Roost. Sydney, Cleveland, n.d.

* * *

By its own admission, the Cleveland Publishing Proprietary Limited always tried to offer its readers "thrilling novels of western adventure written in authentic rangeland style by foremost authors of popular fiction," and generally it succeeded. Even 30 years on, Marshall Grover's hundreds of Westerns continue to entertain, as does the work of Cleveland's lesser-known luminaries: Scott McClure, Gunn Halliday, Lee Chandler, E. Jefferson Clay, and so on. One of the most accomplished writers to make good on Cleveland's pledge, however, is the woefully underrated Emerson Dodge.

Rather like his contemporaries, Emerson Dodge appears to have been heavily influenced by the B-grade western movies of the 1950's. His heroes are always tall, tough, and dependable. His villains are avaricious schemers. His plots are traditional and fairly gallop towards their happy endings, and the author never employs even the mildest of profanities to colour his reasonably good dialogue. A particular gift for weaving plot with subplot give Dodge's Westerns a substance and depth not always found in those of his competitors, however, and it is this added dimension which makes his contribution to the genre especially worthy of comment.

One Man, Two Graves (wrongly credited to "Brett McKinley" on its typically lurid cover) is a good example of Dodge's earliest work, opening as it does with an atmospheric duel on the outskirts of an east Texas cattle town (Dodge's Westerns are always set in popular genre locales such as Texas range country or Kansas cow-towns) and ending with a classic showdown on Main Street. Following his victory over the arrogant Floyd Stillman in the opening chapter, however, and his subsequent flight to avoid the wrath of the dead man's powerful father, Grett Kingston falls in with a notorious outlaw named Nat Claybank, and though there is an instant mutual distrust between Grett and Claybank's right-hand man, Faro Pell, the gang's luck certainly improves once Grett begins to plan their crimes. Dodge's protagonist soon comes to realise that he is not cut out to be an outlaw, of course, and eventually manages to bring his new-found comrades to justice, settling matters not only with Floyd Stillman's grieving father, but also with the man who engineered the duel specifically to get rid of him.

When Gun Kings Die, a surprisingly thoughtful and bitter-sweet western, also reveals Dodge's greater use of italicised thoughts and recollections and more overt violence (one bespectacled character having his eyes shot out, for example, and references to, among other things, "scattered intestines"). *When Gun Kings Die* tells the story of two gun-fast adventurers, the erudite Ethan Shelby and young Mace Nolan, the son of Shelby's late partner Travis. Before being falsely imprisoned, Mace was little more than a storekeeper. Under Shelby's tutelage, however, he soon finds himself following in his father's footsteps. During the course of the story he and Shelby guard gold shipments across the Cherokee Badlands, tame helltowns and eventually come to have their exploits recounted by a dime novelist. Mace is never fully comfortable with the high life, however, and soon comes under pressure from his girlfriend Cassie to hang up his gun. How Mace manages to do exactly that takes up the remainder of the book, and despite a predictably happy ending, Dodge also manages to make his two heroes' parting unexpectedly touching.

An especially unusual and interesting example of Dodge's ability to mix plot with sub-plot can be found in *The Target Is a Star*, which in some respects anticipates Clint Eastwood's 1972 movie *High Plains Drifter*. Reaching the end of a manhunt in a lawless cow-town called Adobe and besting his quarry, the outlaw Coley Tarketon, in a gunfight, town-tamer Wes McQueen accepts an offer to become Adobe's new marshal. Almost at once the author opens up his story to introduce numerous subplots: a rancher named Bogan Stedman and his sensual, sluttish wife Carina, who both appear to be strangely nervous and expectant; the lynching of a man wrongly accused of the murder of Stedman's foreman some time earlier, which the citizens of Adobe would sooner forget; the release from prison of a killer named Sam Whiskey, who claims that Stedman framed him five years before; and the arrival in town of McQueen's old love, Gloria. As the plot wears on, it soon becomes obvious that McQueen himself is not without his secrets, either. In fact, he has pinned on the marshal's badge not so much to protect the town as to *destroy* it . . .

Dodge usually tells his stories over 10 titled chapters. He employs multiple viewpoints and generally keeps to a fast but assured pace. Although his supporting characters—storekeepers, turnkeys, Easterners, local dignitaries—tend to be stereotypical, they serve their purpose adequately. Dodge does handle female characters very well, however, and seldom relegates them to type. Neither does he use humour very much in his predominantly grim tales, although when he does (as in the opening sequence of *All Banner's Brothers*, for example, where his lawman hero attempts to arrest a particularly awkward—not to mention excessively inebriated—bad man before he wrecks the hotel at which he is staying), the results are reasonably successful.

Of course, the author is not without his faults. The names of his characters always tend to reflect their natures; the heroes have tough, strong names, their women neat or attractive ones, the villains harsh and sharp ones. Sometimes, though admittedly not often, there is a tendency to rush endings. But even fairly standard revenge stories like *Last Stage to Limbo* are usually enlivened by some twist or variation which rings the changes, however slightly.

It is certainly true that, in its time, Cleveland Publishing issued "thrilling novels of western adventure," but more importantly, it was craftsmen like Dodge who actually *wrote* them.

—David Whitehead

DOIG, Ivan. American. Born in White Sulphur Springs, Montana, 27 June 1939. Educated at Northwestern University, Evanston, Illinois, B.S. 1961; M.S. 1962; University of Washington, Seattle, Ph.D. 1969. Served in the United States Air Force Reserve: Sergeant. Married Carol Muller in 1965. Editorial writer, Lindsay-Schaub Newspapers, Decatur, Illinois, 1963–64; assistant editor, *The Rotarian*, Evanston, Illinois, 1964–66. Since 1969 full-time writer. Address: 17021 10th Avenue N.W., Seattle, Washington 98177, U.S.A.

WESTERN PUBLICATIONS

Novels

The Sea Runners. New York, Atheneum, 1982.
The McCaskill Family Trilogy:
English Creek. New York, Atheneum, 1984.
Dancing at the Rascal Fair. New York, Atheneum, 1987.
Ride with Me, Mariah Montana. New York, Atheneum, 1990.

Other

This House of Sky: Landscapes of a Western Mind. New York, Harcourt Brace, 1978.
Winter Brothers: A Season at the Edge of America. New York, Harcourt Brace, 1980.
Inside This House of Sky, with Duncan Kelso. New York, Atheneum, 1983.

OTHER PUBLICATIONS

Other

News: A Consumer's Guide, with Carol M. Doig. Englewood Cliffs, New Jersey, Prentice Hall, 1972.
The Streets We Have Come Down. Rochelle Park, New Jersey, Hayden, 1975.
Utopian America: Dreams and Realities. Rochelle Park, New Jersey, Hayden, 1976.
Early Forestry Research. New York, United States Forestry Service, 1976.

* * *

With the publication of his first book *This House of Sky*, a memoir, Ivan Doig gained immediate recognition as an important new voice of the American West. The book was nominated for the National Book award. In it, Doig delved deep into his family and Montana roots in an effort to put his past into words. The book spans the time from the death of his mother, when Doig was six, through the deaths some 20 years later of his father and later his maternal grandmother. It is filled with loving portraits of people who influenced Doig, and demonstrates how we are linked to our past, the people and the place, which is one of the most prominent themes in Doig's works.

For his second book, Doig made unusual use of the unpublished journals of James Gilchrist Swan, a "westcomer and stayer" from Boston who, in the 1850's, settled in the Pacific Northwest where Doig made his home. *Winters Brothers* is a sort of journal duet—Doig spent a winter retracing Swan's travels along the Northwest coastline while maintaining his own journal. The two are woven together, past and present, to reveal what Doig calls "a community of time."

Doig remained on the Pacific coastline for the setting of his first novel, *The Sea Runners*, albeit far into its north reaches of Alaska. With a Ph.D in history, Doig admits his imagination is mostly fueled by facts. The idea for the story of *The Sea Runners* came from a letter in an old newspaper. Doig's fictional account chronicles the daring escape of four disparate men from lives of indentureship in Archangel, Alaska, and of their harrowing journey by canoe down the coastline to Astoria in Oregon Territory. Doig constantly surprises and even shocks the reader by what he has in store for these unsavory yet admirable characters. The book contains many magnificent and haunting images as they battle against the sea, weather, starvation, fear, Indians, and each other.

For the setting of his trilogy about the Scottish McCaskill family, Doig returned to his home state, Montana. The story is set in the fictional Two Medicine country. The time period covered over the course of the three novels is from 1889, the year Montana Territory became a state, to 1989, Montana's centennial. The trilogy actually begins mid-story with *English Creek*. It tells of 14-year-old Jick McCaskill's coming of age in the summer of 1939. Jick's world is turned upside down when "a fracture in the family" occurs as his older brother announces his intention to forego college in favor of cowboying and marriage. Jick tries to sort out the world around him as he undergoes a series of unanticipated life experiences. The arrival in Montana of the first McCaskill, Angus, along with his friend Rob Barclay from Scotland, is the focus of *Dancing at the Rascal Fair*. Time is a larger commodity in this book, which covers a 30-year period. The scale is also grander—establishing homes, towns, schools, sheep ranches, national forests, lives, and families. In *Ride with Me, Mariah Montana*, Jick McCaskill is 65. He still puzzles out the past, with more past to puzzle. The Mariah of the story is his daughter, a newspaper photographer. Jick finds himself traveling around the state in a motorhome with Mariah and her ex-husband, a newspaper columnist, on assignment honoring Montana's centennial year. The trilogy is a *tour-de-force* imbued with richly detailed scenes about daily life in the West, many of which are not often found in western fiction—sheepherding, shearing, and counting, outhouse digging, Fourth of July picnics, forest fire fighting, dances rodeos, and fire camp cooking. Doig's deep interest in language is evident, and each entry in the trilogy has its own distinct voice, fashioned to the times and the characters.

Doig's books about the American West are a refutation of many popular western books, "Wisterns" as Doig prefers to label them. Doig's concern has been to recreate a western world challenged and changed by epidemics, wars, economically hard times and good times, a world populated by sheepherders, farmers, teachers, forest service workers, wives who can the summer's harvest during the hottest days of August, and children equally anxious and afraid to grow up. His themes are universal, and reach far beyond the boundaries of the settings of Montana and the Pacific Northwest. His writing is driven by a desire to decipher the past: how history, geography, family, friends, and chance acquaintances interact and play a role in shaping lives and character. Doig's view of the West is not one steeped in legend, but one based on being true to the land and to those who settled its majestic landscapes in the previous century, and their ancestors, as well as to the complexities of the land and those who live upon it.

—Vicki Piekarski

DONALDS, Gordon. *See* **SHIRREFFS, Gordon D.**

DONOVAN, Mark. British.

WESTERN PUBLICATIONS

Novels

The Killer of K-Bar. New York and London, Boardman, 1952.
Ticket to Remington. New York and London, Boardman, 1953.
Cactus Hurts My Toes. Kingswood, Surrey, World's Work, 1953.
Bet Heavy, Gents. Kingswood, Surrey, World's Work, 1954.
Drop Them Colts. London, Jenkins, 1954.
Gunsmoke in Crosbie. London, Mills and Boon, 1954.
Gift Ranch. Kingswood, Surrey, World's Work, 1954.
Loot of the L & E. London, Jenkins, 1954.
Silver Ranch. Kingswood, Surrey, World's Work, 1955.
Gunshots in Hambone. London, Mills and Boon, 1956.
Gunsmoke Range. London, Jenkins, 1956.
Hot Iron. London, Jenkins, 1956.
Jail Break. London, Mills and Boon, 1956.
Sheriff of Aldersville. Kingswood, Surrey, World's Work, 1956.
Turn Your Wolf Loose. Kingswood, Surrey, World's Work, 1956.
Battle at Bitter Creek. Kingswood, Surrey, World's Work, 1957.
Loaded Colt. London, Hale, 1960.
Rawhide Storm. London, Hale, 1960.
Wide and High. London, Hale, 1960.
Wagon Train to Webster. London, Hale, 1980.
Rancho Alamito. London, Hale, 1983.
The Sixth Shot. London, Hale, 1984.
Arrows in the Sun. London, Hale, 1985.
Range Railroad. London, Hale, 1986.
Wet Mountain Gold. London, Hale, 1986.
A Colt for a Railroad. London, Hale, 1987.
Tainted Range. London, Hale, 1987.
Death Range. London, Hale, 1988.
Five Bank Range. London, Hale, 1988.
Lamp Lit Range. London, Hale, 1989.
Swift Jim Haywood. London, Hale, 1990.
Rattlesnake Railroad. London, Hale, 1990.
Third Man's Range. London, Hale, 1991.
Howdy Sheriff. London, Hale, 1991.

OTHER PUBLICATIONS

Novel

The Flying Submarine. London, Nicholson and Watson, 1948.

* * *

Mark Donovan writes lightweight, largely formulaic Westerns primarily for the U.K. library trade. His stories frequently revolve around land disputes concerning ranches and railroads, and this is often reflected in his choice of titles—*Gunsmoke Range*, *Tainted Range*, *Range Railroad*, *Rattlesnake Railroad*.

In the main, Donovan writes in long, rambling paragraphs broken up by semi-colons and dashes. Particularly in his earlier work, four- and seven- line sentences were commonplace. His archaic, heavily-elided dialogue can sometimes make for awkward reading (never more so than in his humorous 1986 novel *Wet Mountain Gold*, which is told in a much clipped first-person narrative) and owes much in style to the pulp westerns of the 1920's and 1930's.

Generally, his stories take place in the years following the Civil War, and are nearly always set in the southwestern states. His heroes (usually easy-going drifters until riled) are more often than not quick on the draw (or expert riflemen) capable of impressive displays of trick shooting. Beyond that, however, characterisation—of both central and supporting characters—is kept to a minimum, as is physical description.

Conspiracy plays a large part in Donovan's westerns, usually between land-hungry ranchers (who already have the local law in their pockets) and corruptible bank managers (who have access to titles, deeds, and letters of credit). When Donovan's heroes first ride into town, it is fairly safe to assume that everyone will be against them until they prove their worth by standing up to the local tyrant. From that point on until they finally triumph, they can usually count on a modicum of support form a few likeable—but seldom entirely credible—secondary characters.

Donovan's protagonists are usually ambushed at least once during the course of a story, but invariably survive unscathed. The author also has a tendency to take the action into a courtroom at some stage of the proceedings.

This is particularly true of *The Sixth Shot* and *Arrows in the Sun*, which both follow Donovan's usual scenario fairly faithfully. In the former, cattleman Karl Brockman inherits two ranches from a man whose life he attempts in vain to save in the opening chapter. Arriving in Arizona to take possession of his properties, he discovers that the local despot, Frank Warner, is out to acquire as much land as he can, figuring to buy cheap and later (having learned that the railroad may soon be coming through the territory) sell dear. Neither is Warner especially particular about his methods; during the course of the story, Brockman is ambushed, double-crossed, and framed for a murder he didn't commit. To make the matter worse, he also falls in love with one of Warner's two daughters, the demure Constance.

At the beginning of *Arrows in the Sun*, Cavalry Sergeant Maris inherits his family's ranch when his mother, father, and kid sister are murdered, presumably by the local Ottoway Indians. (It should be pointed out that Maris shows hardly any reaction at all to this stunning news; indeed, his dead family might just as well be total strangers for all the grief or anger he displays at the manner of their passing). Returning home with orders to investigate the truth of the situation (after further reinforcing his total lack of sorrow by attending a party in the Sergeants' Mess), Maris and his half-Polish sidekick, Jerzy Ambroziak, uncover a plot to remove the Indians from their land so that a band of unscrupulous profiteers can move in and mine a fortune in minerals from the terrain.

Both books share a number of similarities, quite apart from the obvious. Each has a clearly-defined villain motivated solely by greed and an ineffective lawman whose actions are dictated by self-interest. Both stories feature supposedly educated men (Lawyer Williams and Banker Aspinall respectively) who, though they initially appear quite well-spoken and refined, quickly lapse into Donovan's standard "backwoodsy" dialogue for no apparent reason. And finally, both books end in court. In the first, the villain goes berserk when Brockman is acquitted of murder, and is subsequently shot dead; in the second, the malefactor suffers a rather convenient heart attack upon being found guilty of conspiracy, and dies on the witness stand. The credibility of *The Sixth Shot* is further hampered by inaccurate references to bullet-proof vests (approximately 30 years before they were invented) and mortar bombs.

Though technically a better Western, *Rancho Alamito* follows along much the same lines. Here, the hero Link Murlee buys into a troubled ranch when its owner, an old friend from the Civil War, is murdered. In between being ambushed and framed for murder (as well as locking horns with the usual crooked banker), he uncovers a web of deceit and blackmail that is tied into a nearby den of thieves known simply as Mike's place, where a pitched battle forms the climax of the story.

Despite its weak ending (a common flaw in Donovan's westerns), *Lamp Lit Range* shows a long-awaited maturity in the author's work—so much so that it bears hardly any resemblance to his earlier books at all. On the surface, it is just another tale of range wars and feuds between half-brothers, but Donovan tells the story in a remarkably tight and fluid fashion. He also introduces sex into the plot (hardly graphic, but with a surprising snatch of flagellation), and succeeds admirably in creating not only a nice sense of atmosphere, but also a cast of characters whose speech and actions are eminently credible, auguring well for his future work in the western field.

—David Whitehead

DONSON, Cyril. Also wrote as Lonny Cordis; Vin Hartford; Russ Kidd; Russell Kidd; Anita Mackin; Chuck Pinder. British. Born in Mexborough, Yorkshire, 26 May 1919. Educated at Bristol College; Loughborough College, teacher's certificate in psychology and education 1950; University of Nottingham. Served in the Royal Air Force, 1936–40. Married Dorothy Denham in 1942; one daughter. Journalist, 1941–43; school master, 1944–62; public relations officer, 1964. *Died in 1986.*

WESTERN PUBLICATIONS

Novels

Brannan of the Bar B. London, Ward Lock, 1964.
Thunder at Bushwhack. London, Ward Lock, 1965.
Jinx Ranch. London, Ward Lock, 1966.
Gun-Law at Concho Creek. London, Ward Lock, 1966.
Ghost Town Marshall. London, Hale, 1982.
Unsmiling Gun. London, Hale, 1985.
Dollars in the Dust. London, Hale, 1986.
Dakota Feud. London, Hale, 1986.

Novels as Russ Kidd

Fight for Circle C. London, Ward Lock, 1967.
The Man from Wyoming. London, Hale, 1982.
Vengeance Ride to Mesa. London, Hale, 1983.
Town Tamer from Texas. London, Hale, 1983.
Trouble Brand. London, Hale, 1984.
The Merciless Marshal. London, Hale, 1984.
Borrowed Badge. London, Hale, 1985.
Gunsmoke at Slade. London, Hale, 1985.
Six-Shooter Sod-Buster. London, Hale, 1986.
Wyoming's Debt to a Dead Man. London, Hale, 1986.
Six for Mexico. London, Hale, 1986.

Novels as Russell Kidd

Throw a Tall Shadow. London, Hale, 1967.
Battle for Bear Head Creek. London, Hale, 1982.
Banner's Back from Boothill. London, Hale, 1983.

OTHER PUBLICATIONS

Novels

Tritonastra—Planet of the Gargantua. London, Hale, 1969.
The Perspective Process. London, Hale, 1969.
Draco the Dragonman. London, New English Library, 1974.

Other

Lonely-land: A Panorama of Loneliness, from Childhood to the "Sun-set Years," and Including Bedsitter-land: One-Room Living; A Contribution Towards a Greater Understanding of the Loneliness Scene and the Problems of the Lonely with Armand Georges. Bala, Wales, A.J. Chapple, 1967.
Make Your Own Wooden Toys. Bristol, Arrow, 1975.
Guide to Authors. Melksham, Wiltshire, Venton, 1976.

* * *

In his lifetime, Cyril Donson wrote science fiction, romance, horror, and verse, as well as compiling crossword books, documentaries, and even a "how to" book on making wooden toys. The majority of his Westerns were published under the byline Russ Kidd, although a few also appeared under his own name and that of Chuck Pinder. Generally they were fairly standard "oaters" with tall, broad-shouldered heroes and scheming, avaricious villains. Similarly, their titles frequently reflected the author's taste for alliteration. Whether writing under a pseudonym or his own name, however, Donson's Westerns all share a sameness of plot and characterisation which must almost certainly impart a sense of *déjà vu* in all but the most casual reader of his work.

Initially the Russ Kidd stories revolved mainly around traditional western motifs, but in later years the spaghetti Western began to influence his work, and he came to reveal a predilection for the lone hero who rides into town and changes lives and situations irrevocably before moving on into the sunset. As its title might suggest, *Dollars in the Dust* is probably the most obvious example of the influence of this Italian cinematic sub-genre. Fury, a somewhat mercenary drifter, rides into Virginia City following a hunch that there is money to be made in the vicinity. Almost at once he finds himself caught between two warring factions, one gang loyal to Tom Fletcher, the other in the employ of Bull Pilson. In his first encounter with the local toughs, Fury's horse, Storm, kills one of their number at his command. Before long, however, Fury is doing his own killing, usually dispatching his opponents with well-aimed bullets between the eyes (Donson's villains often get shot in the face). Soon Fury is approached by both villains, who want to recruit him, but initially he is not interested. Only when the gangs move on to a Mormon settlement named Little Jordan, where a fortune in gold dust has been secreted, does Fury begin to heed his instincts and follow them, eventually playing both ends against the middle until the dust is his alone for the taking.

Not that all of Donson's protagonists are anti-heroes. Frequently they represent one law-enforcement agency or another; Texas Rangers in Russ Kidd's *Town Tamer from Texas* and Donson's own *Unsmiling Gun*; a Rebel spy recruited by Allan Pinkerton himself in *Six for Mexico*; a sheriff-turned-farmer in *Six-Shooter Sod-Buster*; and U.S. Marshals in *Banner's Back from Boot Hill* and *Gunsmoke at Slade*. Even Donson's only continuing character, the typically gun-fast Wyoming, though not a lawman of any description, possesses an altruistic streak which establishes him firmly as one of the good guys.

Wyoming, in fact, exemplifies the usual Donson hero, conforming as he does to all the conventions of the genre, as the author himself makes plain when first introducing his rather sober protagonist: "He knew, even though he was reluctant to admit it to himself, that there had been moments . . . that he had longed to be free to abandon his endless life of wandering and settle down. Equally, he knew there could be no such future for him. He was doomed now to ride endless trails to places he could never call home, to use his gun, to ride on again to the next, until somebody faster than he put him on some lonely, anonymous Boot Hill."

Wyoming (in his mid- to late-twenties, like most of the author's main characters) makes his first appearance in *The Man from Wyoming*. Working as a bounty hunter with a not entirely trustworthy accomplice named Spade Tiller, Wyoming's life takes a new direction when Tiller double-crosses him, leaving him stranded and stealing their $10,000 bank-roll. Spade's trail eventually leads Wyoming back to his hometown, where he has previously been branded an outlaw for killing the crooked lawman who murdered his father. Now Wyoming decides to settle matters with Spade and swiftly ride on, but since Spade's brother is trying hard to wrest control of the town from Wyoming's mother's new husband, he gradually finds himself being drawn deeper into the inevitable showdown. *Wyoming's Debt to a Dead Man* begins eight months after the conclusion of the first book. Here Wyoming meets a young man named Tex Willard on the trail to a town called Silver Spur, to which he has been summoned by a worried father, but their plan to ride at least part of the way together is spoiled when Willard is mortally wounded by three gunmen the following morning. Feeling a debt to the dying man (who saved his life during the gunfight), Wyoming decides to ride on to Silver Spur alone, and eventually uncovers a conspiracy concerning a played-out gold mine. Interestingly, Wyoming is once again reunited with Spade Tiller during the ensuing adventure.

Overall, Donson's westerns tend to suffer from scant characterisation and somewhat complicated plots, and the Wyoming stories are no exception. There is a strong western influence in his dialogue, but this is also sprinkled with words and phrases peculiar to his native England. Furthermore, there is a tendency to impart background or historical detail rather clumsily through speech, perhaps most conspicuously in the infamous "Tom Smith" sequence at the beginning of *Wyoming's Debt to a Dead Man*. Women perform to a limited degree in Donson's westerns, but usually adhere to type. In the author's favour, however, are his thorough physical descriptions of characters and locations, and a good working knowledge of the flora and fauna of the regions in which his stories take place (most often Texas or Arizona). Likewise, Donson is always very precise about the locations of his stories and the periods in which they occur—nearly always the mid to late 1870's.

Though he must be judged a western writer of somewhat limited capability, Donson's frontier stories move along swiftly enough, and offer competent if rather basic western entertainment.

—David Whitehead

DORMAN, Luke. *See* **BINGLEY, David Ernest.**

DORRIS, Michael (Anthony). American. Born in Louisville, Kentucky, 30 January 1945. Educated at Georgetown University, Washington, D.C., B.A. 1967; Yale University, New Haven, Connecticut, M.Phil. 1970. Married Louise Erdrich, *q.v.*, in 1981; two sons and four daughters. Assistant Professor, Johnston College, University of Redlands, California, 1970; and Franconia College, New Hampshire, 1971–72. Instructor, 1972–76, Assistant Professor, 1976–79, Associate Professor, 1979, Professor of anthropology, 1979–88, since 1979 Chair of Native American Studies Department, and since 1988 Adjunct Professor, Dartmouth College, Hanover, New Hampshire. Visiting Assistant Professor, University of Auckland, 1980. Editor, *Viewspoint*, 1967; since 1974 member of editorial board, *American Indian Culture and Research Journal*; member of editorial advisory board, *MELUS*, 1977–79. Recipient: Woodrow Wilson fellowship, 1967, 1980; National Institute of Mental Health research grant, 1971; Spaulding-Potter Program grant, 1973; Dartmouth College faculty fellowship, 1977; Guggenheim fellowship, 1978; Rockefeller fellowship, 1985; Indian Achievement award, 1985; National Endowment for the Arts fellowship, 1988; National Book Critics Circle award, for non-fiction, 1989. Address: Erdrich/Dorris, Box 70, Cornish Flat, New Hampshire 03746, U.S.A.

WESTERN PUBLICATIONS

Novels

A Yellow Raft in Blue Water. New York, Holt, 1987; London, Hamilton, 1988.

Crown of Columbus, with Louise Erdrich. New York and London, Harper Collins, 1991.

Other

Native Americans: Five Hundred Years After. New York, Crowell, 1975.
Guide to Research on North American Indians, with Arlene B. Hirschfelder and Mary Gloyne Byler. Chicago, American Library Association, 1983.
The Broken Cord. New York, Harper, 1987; London, Harper Collins, 1990.

* * *

Michael Dorris and his wife Louise Erdrich have a rather unique and unusual auctorial technique. In a recent interview with Laura Coltelli for her book *Winged Words: American Indian Writers Speak*, Dorris explains: "We go over every word and achieve consensus on every word; basically we agree on every word when it's finally finished." Further, they use their names interchangeably: books published under the name "Michael Dorris" are equally the work of Louise Erdrich, and the books published under Erdrich's name are equally Dorris's work. Since Erdrich and her *Love Medicine* quartet are treated separately in this volume, this essay deals with the one novel conceived by Dorris and published under his name, *A Yellow Raft in Blue Water*.

Dorris's West is Montana, mostly, his time is contemporary time, and his characters are not cowboys but Indians. *A Yellow Raft* ends with grandmother Ida braiding her long hair to "the rhythm of three strands, the whispers of coming and going, of twisting and tying and blending, of catching and of letting go," and the novel itself is a twisting and tying and blending, a catching and a letting go of three braided lives: 15 year-old Rayona, her mother Christine, and her grandmother Ida. All three women are as strong, as rugged, and as self-reliant as any cowboy you'll ever run into.

Rayona, named after the "rayon" label on her mother's nightgown, is the heroine/narrator the first third of the novel. She is visiting her mother in a Seattle hospital. Christine is dying—Rayona thinks she's faking it—but she doesn't want to go this way, all helpless, so she talks Rayona into helping her with a madcap escape back to her mother on the reservation in Montana, and off they go in Christine's beat-up Volaré. Christine wants to find a home for Rayona, and hopes that her mother will take her in. Rayona describes the reunion with "Aunt Ida," whom she and her mother have not seen in nearly seven years. Ida is "pushing an old lawn mower back and forth across a plot of scrub grass," a black bouffant wig tacked to her head by bobby pins that "shone in the sunlight," the speakers of her Walkman plugged into her ears:

> "I came home, Aunt Ida." Mom stands in the yellow field, her hair blowing across her face like dark string. . . . She's nervous . . . I have a sudden, sure sense that for Mom this is an important moment, a beginning or an end of something, and she's scared to find out which. I have the idea to walk over to her, punch her on the arm, and tell her to lighten up . . .
>
> The music leaking out of Aunt Ida's earphones is tinny and low, but it fills the air around us and we listen . . . while we wait for what Aunt Ida will say. She's taking her time, giving Mom a chance to put in another word if she wants.
>
> "Give me three good reasons why I should be glad to see you." Aunt Ida's forehead bends into a frown. She pulls a red kerchief from her hip pocket and wipes her mouth.
>
> Mom doesn't move. She doesn't even relax her scared smile. She tenses as though she's thought of an answer but she's not quite sure it's right. Then she gives it a try anyway, as if this is a quiz show and she's out to stump the stars.
>
> "One, Mother, I'm your daughter, your only living child."
>
> Aunt Ida doesn't like to hear this. Her face twists as if Mom had punched her below the belt or whacked her from behind when she wasn't looking.
>
> "Two, I need someplace to stay."
>
> Aunt Ida's expression changed fast. She has hit upon some good comeback, something that will start with "ha!" and not quit until "I told you so" is thrown in.
>
> "Three . . ." Mom hesitates. She has been watching Aunt Ida too and knows that the minute she finishes her answer, no matter what it is, Aunt Ida's going to let go with something mean . . . Nobody breathes.
>
> "Three," Mom says, looking up straight at Aunt Ida. "Three, go f—— yourself anyway."
>
> Mom picks up the bags in her fist and turns away, walking, and then, off balance, doing a jerky run toward the car.

This scene is retold later—in two variations—by Christine and once again by Ida. "Aunt Ida" does take Rayona in and Rayona adjusts to life on the reservation until Father Tom, one of the reservation's white Catholic priests, seduces her at Bearpaw Lake, *en route* to a teen retreat. She runs away and ends up back at the Bearpaw Lake State Park working as a maintenance worker. She soon returns to the reservation, though, to check on her sick mother and put her grandmother's mind at ease. Rayona's wild and wonderful moment of glory comes when she goes to the Indian rodeo in search of her mother, and, taking the place of her scornful and too drunk cousin Foxy, rides in the bronco busting contest. She is thrown three times, but leaves the arena walking and wins a silver "hard-luck" buckle for being "the roughest, toughest, *clumsiest* cowboy we've ever seen around here in many a moon."

The roughest, toughest, *clumsiest* cowboy *we've* seen in a long time: that phrase accurately describes Christine and Ida as well, who narrate the following two-thirds of the book.

As its title suggests, *A Yellow Raft in Blue Water* is a painterly novel, full of memorable visual, auditory, and emotional images, from the painted yellow raft in the blue water of Bearpaw Lake to the Stephen King-inspired bumper sticker on Christine's Volaré—"I am Christine. I am pure evil"—from the reunion scene described above to Christine and Rayona's final scene together.

Dorris is a member of the Modoc tribe on his father's side and has taught in the Native American studies department at Dartmouth College, and while *A Yellow Raft* presents a disturbingly accurate picture of American Indian life today—alcoholism, lack of adequate health care, economic, cultural, and spiritual poverty—the reader comes to believe that the Indian, as embodied in these three remarkable women, *will* endure.

—Marcia G. Fuchs

DOUGLAS, Thorne. *See* **HAAS, Ben.**

DOWER, Penn. *See* **PENDOWER, T. C. H.**

DOWLER, James R(oss). American. Born in Royal, Illinois, 19 April 1925. Educated at the University of Illinois, Urbana, B.A. 1949; M.S. 1950. Served in the United States Army Air Force, 1943–45: 2nd Lieutenant; United States Air Force, 1951–53: 1st Lieutenant; Reserves, 1953–68: Major (retired). Married Helen Jean Ernst in 1950; one son. Reporter, Champaign *News-Gazette*, Illinois, 1949–50; publisher, *Adams Republican*, Brighton, Colorado, 1950–51. Advertising manager, New York, 1954–70, and Atlanta, 1970–75, advertising and promotion manager, San Ramon, California, 1975–77, and since 1977, Houston, Shell Chemical Company. Agent: Lenniger Literary Agency, 104 East 40th Street, New York, New York 10016. Address: Shell Chemical Company, 1 Shell Place, Houston, Texas 77001, U.S.A.

WESTERN PUBLICATIONS

Novels

Partner's Choice. New York, Arcadia House, 1958; London, Muller, 1960.
Fiddlefoot Fugitive. New York, Crown, 1970.
Laredo Lawman. New York, Lenox Hill Press, 1970; London, Hale, 1972.
The Copperhead Colonel. New York, Crown, 1972.

* * *

James R. Dowler writes conventional adventure stories about revenge, pursuit, and retribution. He deals in stereotyped characters, set scenes, and predictable outcomes, and his many references to "game" and "code" reveal the well-worn ritualism of his fiction. His first novel, *Partner's Choice*, however, has an interesting social theme. It tells of two cowboys who establish a ranch in Colorado, in defiance of the cattle syndicate which is working to monopolize the rangeland. One of the partners is murdered by the syndicate and the hero sets out on a revenge quest. Eventually, he realizes that the law is more important than personal retribution and he tries to bring the head of the syndicate to jail. When the villain escapes, the hero kills him in self-defense. He retains his ranch, which he will now share with his new wife. In the end, little is made of the incompatibility of the corporation and the individual. All battles—whether it is the hero against his enemies or the heroine fighting her syndicate kidnapper—are translated into individual terms. If any further dimension is implied, it is the philosophical rather than the social: the hero decides, "His existence now depended upon the basic law—survival of the fittest."

The Darwinian theme is enlarged on in later fiction like *Laredo Lawman*, which again concerns revenge. The hero pursues an outlaw who has raped and killed his lover. In the course of his chase, the hero ponders on the atavism of his purpose and, although there is nothing as complex as a character study, he struggles to sublimate his animalistic instincts to legal justice and the cause of western patriotism. This story has more of a historical context, since it occurs within the cattle drives from Texas and features a Missouri herd cutter as villain and a hero who makes possible the first drive to Abilene. Despite the history and the philosophizing, the action is more implausible than in the earlier novels, for it revolves around foolproof traps, melodramatic escapes, impossible shooting tricks, and death by quicksand. Whatever gestures Dowler makes towards larger purposes, his stories remain stereotyped formulas.

—Christine Bold

DRAGO, Harry Sinclair. Also wrote as Stewart Cross; Kirk Deming; Will Ermine; Peter Field; Bliss Lomax; J. Wesley Putnam; Grant Sinclair. American. Born in Toledo, Ohio, 20 March 1888. Journalist: staff member, Toledo *Bee*; Then freelance writer and screen writer. Recipient: Western Heritage award, 1971. *Died 25 October 1979.*

WESTERN PUBLICATIONS

Novels

Suzanna: A Romance of Early California. New York, Macaulay, 1922; London, Hutchinson, 1924.
Whispering Sage, with Joseph Noel. New York, Century, 1922; London, Hutchinson, 1923.
Smoke of the .45. New York, Macaulay, 1923; London, Hutchinson, 1924.
Out of the Silent North. New York, Macaulay, 1923; London, Hutchinson, 1924.
Following the Grass. New York, Macaulay, 1924; London, Hutchinson, 1925.
The Snow Patrol. New York, Macaulay, 1925; London, Hutchinson, 1926.
The Desert Hawk. New York, Macaulay, 1927; London, Nelson, 1929.
Where the Loon Calls. New York, Macaulay, and London, Hutchinson, 1928.
Guardian of the Sage. New York, Macaulay, 1932; as *Top Hand with a Gun*, New York, Fawcett, 1955.
Desert Water. New York, Macaulay, 1933; London, Hurst and Blackett, 1934.
The Wild Bunch. New York, Burt, 1934.
Montana Road. New York, Morrow, 1935; London, Hurst and Blackett, 1936.
Trigger Gospel. New York, Macaulay, and London, Hurst and Blackett, 1935.
Colt Lightning (as Kirk Deming). New York, Macaulay, 1938; London, Ward Lock, 1935.
Grass Means Fight (as Kirk Deming). New York, Macaulay, 1938; London, Ward Lock, 1940.
Buckskin Empire. New York, Doubleday, 1942; Kingswood, Surrey, World's Work, 1949.
Stagecoach Kingdom. New York, Doubleday, 1943; London, Muller, 1944.
River of Gold. New York, Dodd Mead, 1945.
Pay-off at Black Hawk. New York, Permabooks, 1956.
Decision at Broken Butte. New York, Permabooks, 1957.
Wild Grass. New York, Permabooks, 1957.
Buckskin Affair. New York, Doubleday, 1958.
Showdown at Sunset. New York, Permabooks, 1958.
Fenced Off. New York, Doubleday, 1959; London, Hale, 1961.
Rebel Basin. New York, Pocket Books, 1959.
A Gun for Cantrell. New York, Belmont, 1961.
The Long Trail North. New York, Pocket Books, 1961.
The Trail of Johnny Dice. New York, Belmont, 1961.

Sun in Their Eyes. New York, Pocket Books, 1962.
Wild, Woolly, and Wicked. New York, Pocket Books, 1962.
Buckskin Meadows. New York, Pocket Books, 1962.

Novels as Will Ermine

Longhorn Empire. New York, Doubleday, 1933; London, Mills and Boon, 1954.
Laramie Rides Alone. New York, Morrow, and London, Nicholson and Watson, 1934.
Rustlers Ranch. London, Nicholson and Watson, 1935.
Lobo Law. New York, Morrow, 1935.
Plundered Range. New York, Morrow, and London, Nicholson and Watson, 1936.
Prairie Smoke. New York, Green Circle, 1936; London, Harrap, 1937; as *Avenger from Texas*, New York, Fawcett, 1964.
Wind River Outlaw. New York, Green Circle, 1936; London, Harrap, 1938.
Barbed Wire Empire. New York, Green Circle, 1937; London, Rich and Cowan, 1938.
Lawless Legion. New York, Macaulay, and London, Rich and Cowan, 1938.
Trail Trouble. New York, Green Circle, 1938.
Singing Lariat. New York, Morrow, 1939; London, Collins, 1940.
Rustlers' Moon. New York, Morrow, and London, Nicholson and Watson, 1939.
Cowboy, Say Your Prayers. New York, Morrow, 1939; London, Collins, 1940.
Boss of the Plains. New York, Morrow, 1940; London, Collins, 1941.
Rider of the Midnight Range. New York, Morrow, and London, Collins, 1940.
Watchdog of Thunder River. New York, Morrow, 1941; London, Collins, 1942.
My Gun Is My Law. New York, Morrow, 1942; London, Collins, 1943; as *My Gun is Law*, London, Swan, 1947.
Brave in the Saddle. New York, Morrow, 1943; London, Collins, 1944.
Busted Range. New York, Books Inc., and London, Collins, 1944.
The Iron Bronc. New York, Jefferson House, 1944; London, Collins, 1945.
Boss of the Badlands. London, Swan, 1944.
Buckskin Marshal. New York, Jefferson House, 1945; London, Collins, 1946.
War on the Saddle Rock. New York, Jefferson House, 1945; London, Collins, 1946.
Outlaw on Horseback. New York, Doubleday, 1946; London, Sampson Low, 1948.
The Drifting Kid. New York, Doubleday, 1947; London, Sampson Low, 1948.
Last of the Longhorns. New York, Doubleday, 1948; London, Sampson Low, 1949.
Laramie Rides Again. New York, New American Library, 1948.
Rustlers' Bend. New York, Doubleday, 1949; London, Sampson Low, 1950.
Apache Crossing. New York, Doubleday, 1950.
The Silver Star. New York, Doubleday, 1951; London, Sampson Low, 1953.
Arizona Gunsmoke. London, Sampson Low, 1951.
Frenchman's River. New York, Permabooks, 1955.
Guns in the Night. London, Ward Lock, 1957.

Novels as Bliss Lomax

Closed Range. New York, Macaulay, 1936; London, Harrap, 1937.
Canyon of Golden Skulls. New York, Macaulay, 1937.
The Law Bringers. New York, Macaulay, 1937; London, Harrap, 1938.
Mavericks of the Plains. New York, Greenberg, 1938; London, Wright and Brown, 1939.
Colt Comrades. New York, Doubleday, 1939; London, Muller, 1942.
The Leather Burners. New York, Doubleday, 1940; London, Muller, 1941; as *Ambush at Coffin Canyon*, New York, Ace, 1954.
Gringo Gunfire. New York, Doubleday, 1940; London, Ward Lock, 1949.
Secret of the Wastelands. New York, Doubleday, 1940; London, Muller, 1950.
Pardners of the Badlands. New York, Doubleday, 1942; London, Muller, 1944.
Horsethief Creek. New York, Doubleday, 1944; London, Muller, 1947.
Rusty Guns. New York, Dodd Mead, 1944; Redhill, Surrey, Wells Gardner Darton, 1948.
Saddle Hawks. New York, Dodd Mead, 1944; London, Ward Lock, 1949.
Outlaw River. New York, Dodd Mead, 1945; Redhill, Surrey, Wells Gardner Darton, 1949.
The Phantom Corral. New York, Dodd, Mead, 1946; Redhill, Surrey, Wells Gardner Darton, 1950.
Trail Dust. New York, Dodd, Mead, 1947; Redhill, Surrey, Wells Gardner Darton, 1950.
Shadow Mountain. New York, Dodd, Mead, 1948.
The Lost Buckaroo. New York, Dodd, Mead, 1949; Kingswood, Surrey, World's Work, 1950.
Sage Brush Bandit. New York, Dodd, Mead, 1949; Kingswood, Surrey, World's Work, 1950.
Gunsmoke and Trail Dust. New York, Dell, 1949.
The Fight for the Sweetwater. New York, Dodd, Mead, 1950; London, Collins, 1951.
The Law Busters. New York, Dodd, Mead, 1950; London, Collins, 1951.
Guns along the Yellowstone. New York, Dodd, Mead, and London, Collins, 1952.
Riders of the Buffalo Grass. New York, Dodd, Mead, 1952; London, Collins, 1953.
Honky-Tonk Woman. New York, Permabooks, 1955.
The Loner. New York, Dell, 1956; as *Lone Stranger*, London, Collins, 1956.
Stranger with a Gun. New York, Dodd, Mead, 1957; London, Collins, 1958.
Last Call for a Gunfighter. New York, Dodd, Mead, 1958; as *Call for a Gunfight*, London, Collins, 1959.
Appointment on the Yellowstone. New York, Dodd, Mead, 1959; London, Collins, 1960; as *The Lawless Guns*, New York, Curl, 1960.
It Happened at Thunder River. New York, Avon, 1959.

Novels as Peter Field

Doctor Two-Guns. New York, Morrow, 1939; London, Ward Lock, 1940.
The Tenderfoot Kid. New York, Morrow, 1939; London, Faber, 1940.
Law Badge. New York, Morrow, and London, Cassell, 1940.

The Man from Thief River. New York, Morrow, 1940; London, Cassell, 1941.

Short Stories

Their Guns Were Fast. New York, Dodd Mead, 1955.

Uncollected Short Stories

"Square-Shotting Lyda," in *Western Story* (New York), 6 May 1922.
"Desert Law," in *Argosy* (New York), 3 June 1922.
"Good Men and Bad," in *Munsey's* (New York), December 1926.
"Fighting Back," in *Munsey's* (New York), June 1927.
"More Precious Than Gold," in *Munsey's* (New York), November 1927.
"Wanted!," in *Munsey's* (New York), December 1927.
"Ahead of the Law," in *West* (New York), 17 February 1932.
"Squaw Valley War," in *West* (New York), 8 June 1932.
"Trigger Law," in *Western Thrillers*, edited by Leo Margulies. New York, Speller, 1935.
"Nemesis of the North," in *Western Story* (New York), 3 June 1939.
"Talking Kits of Desperation Mountain," in *Western Story* (New York), 16 September 1939.
"Too Tough to Kill," in *Western Story* (New York), 18 November 1939.
"Fool's Gold," in *Western Story* (New York), 25 November 1939.
"Treachery at Thunder Butte," in *Western Story* (London), December 1940.
"The Sheriff Learns His Business," in *West* (Kingswood, Surrey), January 1941.
"A Man Learns Fast," in *West* (Kingswood, Surrey), June 1941.
"Timberline Showdown," in *Western Story* (London), June 1941.
"No Quarter for Killers," in *Western Story* (London), August 1941.
"Redheads Don't Quit," in *Five Novels* (New York), March 1943.
"Sheriff Busters," in *Western Story* (London), August 1943.
"Watchdog of Lonesome Creek," in *Western Stories*, edited by Gene Autry. New York, Dell, 1947.
"The Wrong Side of the Fence," in *Western Stories*, edited by William MacLeod Raine. New York, Dell, 1949.
"Raw Land," in *All Western* (New York), April–June 1950.
"Sunrise on the Cimarron," in *All Western* (New York), December 1950–January 1951.
"Sagebrush Champions," in *Wild Horse Roundup*, edited by Jim Kjelgaard. New York, Dodd Mead, 1958.
"When the Trail Divides," with E.D. Mygatt, in *A Saddlebag of Tales*, edited by Rutherford Montgomery. New York, Dodd Mead, 1959.
"Wide Open for Trouble," in *Gunpoint*, edited by Leo Margulies. New York, Pyramid, 1960.

OTHER PUBLICATIONS

Novels

The Woman Thou Art (as Grant Sinclair). New York, Macaulay, 1925.
Wild Fruit (as Grant Sinclair). New York, Watt, 1926.
Where East Is East (novelization of screenplay), with Tod Browning. New York, Jacobsen, 1929.
Rio Rita (novelization of screenplay). New York, Burt, 1929; London, Readers, Library, 1930.
The Trespasser (novelization of screenplay). New York, Burt, 1929; London, Readers Library, 1930.
The Singer of Seville (novelization of screenplay). New York, Burt, 1930.
Madam Satan (novelization of screenplay), with Jeanie MacPherson. New York, Burt, 1930.
Divorce Trap. New York, Macaulay, 1930.
Women to Love. New York, Amour Press, 1931; London, Melrose, 1932.
The Champ (novelization of screenplay). New York, Burt, and London, Readers Library, 1932.
This Way to Hell (as Stewart Cross). New York, Macaulay, 1933.
Love Toy. New York, Diversey, 1949.

Novels as J. Wesley Putnam

Whoso Findeth a Wife. New York, Macaulay, 1914.
The Hidden Things. New York, Macaulay, 1915.
Playthings of Desire. New York, Macaulay, 1924.
Borrowed Reputations. New York, Macaulay, 1928.

Plays

Screenplays: *Out of the Silent North*, with others, 1922; *Silver Valley*, with Harold B. Lipsitz and Malcolm Stuart Boylan, 1927; *The Cowboy Kid*, with others, 1928; *A Horseman of the Plains*, with Fred Myton, 1928; *Painted Post*, with Buckleigh F. Oxford and Delos Sutherland, 1928; *Hello Cheyenne*, with Fred Myton and Dudley Early, 1928; *The Desert Rider*, with others, 1929; *Sioux Blood*, with others, 1929; *Overland Telegraph*, with others, 1929; *Where East Is East*, with others, 1929; *Lotus Lady*, 1930.

Other

Wild, Woolly, and Wicked: The History of the Kansas Cow Towns and the Texas Cattle Trade. New York, Potter, 1960.
Red River Valley: The Mainstream of Frontier History from the Louisiana Bayous to the Texas Panhandle. New York, Potter, 1962.
Outlaws on Horseback. New York, Dodd Mead, 1964; London, Long, 1965.
Great American Cattle Trails: The Story of the Old Cow Paths of the East and the Longhorn Highways of the Plains. New York, Dodd Mead, 1965.
Lost Bonanzas: Tales of the Legendary Lost Mines of the American West. New York, Dodd Mead, 1966.
Many Beavers (for children). New York, Dodd Mead, 1967.
The Steamboaters: From the Early Side-Wheelers to the Big Packets. New York, Dodd Mead, 1967.
Roads to Empire: The Dramatic Conquest of the American West. New York, Dodd Mead, 1968.
Notorious Ladies of the Frontier. New York, Dodd Mead, 1969.
The Great Range Wars: Violence on the Grasslands. New York, Dodd Mead, 1970.
Canal Days in America. New York, Potter, 1972.
Road Agents and Train Robbers: Half a Century of Western Banditry. New York, Dodd Mead, 1973.
The Legend Makers: Tales of the Old Time Peace Officers and Desperadoes of the Frontier. New York, Dodd Mead, 1975.

* * *

Harry Sinclair Drago wrote over 80 western novels, under a variety of pseudonyms, as well as some dozen non-western novels, screenplays, and non-fiction works on the American West.

Drago's immense output meant that he covered many of the usual themes of the traditional Western. His wide (if unoriginal) research on the West's past made him an expert on cattle trails and Kansas towns, mining and early California, bandits and loose women, range wars and outlaws. *River of Gold*, for instance, is a love and adventure story with a conventional plot, but it is set on the Sacramento River years after the end of the Gold Rush. *Suzanna*, his first novel, is set in 1835 in California, and has a very complicated plot. But it is a real attempt at a historical novel, even though the mystery of the parentage of the two rival girls undercuts the accuracy of the hacienda-based rivalry for the two families. A novel like the *Desert Hawk* uses the sheep vs. cattle theme, with the female interest, as so often, of the sheepish persuasion. *Barbed Wire Empire* is another colorful sheep-cattle novel. Drago's most interesting novels on this theme are *Following the Grass* and *Whispering Sage*, and both employ Basque sheepherders as characters. *Whispering Sage* is a novel about disputed water rights. *Following the Grass* is more interesting, both for its background of the settling of northern Nevada by the Basques, and for its deliberate attempt to suggest something of the boring, unrelieved life of the great basin in the mid-19th century (the novel is set during the great drought of 1862). Other novels also play down the romance and violence of the west. *Brave in the Saddle* features an "ordinary" sheriff, and *Montana Road* is a valuable historical reconstruction of the settling of the Dakota Territory in the 1870's.

The most emphatic of Drago's interests is transportation—wagon freighting and Pony Express, steamboat and canal, and of course the railroad. *Buckskin Empire* is a story of the railroads inching across the Southwest to challenge the supremacy of the freight wagons, the natural clash of interest leading to arson, bribery, and bloodshed. *Boss of the Plains* is set earlier—at the time (the 1850's) of the growth of the wagon freighting business and the Pony Express. Against such historical characters as Brigham Young, General Fremont, and Major Rufus Ingalls, Drago traces the career of a small-scale driver, Ben Holladay. It is an ambitious and successful book.

Drago had to compete with the tail end of the Dime Novel tradition as well as with the rise of the slick magazine writers (like Max Brand), but he managed to carve out a distinct niche for himself. The fact that his non-fiction books on the West all appeared after he had retired from novel writing shows that he retained his interest in the West almost until his death.

—George Walsh

DRESSER, Davis. Also wrote as Asa Baker; Matthew Blood; Kathryn Culver; Don Davis; Hal Debrett; Peter Field; Brett Halliday; Anthony Scott; Anderson Wayne. American. Born in Chicago, Illinois, 31 July 1904. Raised in Texas; joined the United States Army Cavalry at 14; returned to Texas to finish high school; educated at Tri-State College, Angola, Indiana, Certificate in Civil Engineering. Married 1) the writer Helen McCloy in 1946 (divorced, 1961), one daughter; 2) Kathleen Rollins; 3) Mary Savage. Writer from 1927, contributing stories under many pseudonyms to mystery, western, and adventure pulps; novels bylined Brett Halliday after 1958 were ghost, written by others; co-founder, with Helen McCloy, Torquil Publishing Company, and Halliday and McCloy Literary Agency, 1953–64; founding editor, *Mike Shayne Magazine*, 1956 (magazine still carries works bylined Brett Halliday). Recipient: Mystery Writers of America Edgar Allan Poe award, for criticism, 1953. *Died 4 February 1977.*

WESTERN PUBLICATIONS

Novels (series: Twister Malone in all books except *Gunsmoke on the Mesa*)

Death Rides the Pecos. New York, Morrow, and London, Ward Lock, 1940.
The Hangmen of Sleepy Valley. New York, Morrow, 1940; as *The Masked Riders of Sleepy Valley*, London, Ward Lock, 1941.
Gunsmoke on the Mesa. New York, Carlton, and London, Ward Lock, 1941.
Lynch-Rope Law. New York, Morrow, 1941; London, Ward Lock, 1942.
Murder on the Mesa. London, Ward Lock, 1953.

Novels as Don Davis (series: Rio Kid)

Return of the Rio Kid. New York, Morrow, 1940; London, Ward Lock, 1950.
Death on Treasure Trail. London, Hutchinson, 1940; New York, Morrow, 1941.
Rio Kid Justice. New York, Morrow, 1941.
Two-Gun Rio Kid. New York, Morrow, 1941.

Novels as Peter Field (series: Powder Valley in all books)

Guns from Powder Valley. New York, Morrow, 1941; London, Quality Press, 1948.
Powder Valley Pay-off. New York, Morrow, 1941.
Trail South from Powder Valley. New York, Morrow, 1942.
Fight for Powder Valley! New York, Morrow, 1942.
Law Man of Powder Valley. New York, Morrow, 1942; Harmondsworth, Penguin, 1961.
Powder Valley Vengeance. New York, Morrow, 1943; London, Cassell, 1952.
Sheriff on the Spot. New York, Jefferson House, 1943; London, Cassell, 1947.
Death Rides the Night. New York, Jefferson House, 1944; London, Quality Press, 1946.
The Smoking Iron. New York, Books, Inc., 1944.
Midnight Round-up. New York, Jefferson House, 1944; London, Ward Lock, 1946.
The Road to Laramie. New York, Jefferson House, 1945; London, Ward Lock, 1947.
The End of the Trail. New York, Jefferson House, 1945; London, Quality Press, 1947.
Powder Valley Showdown. New York, Jefferson House, 1946.

OTHER PUBLICATIONS

Novels

Let's Laugh at Love. New York, Curl, 1937.
Romance for Julie. New York, Curl, 1938.
Mum's the Word for Murder (as Asa Baker). New York, Stokes, 1938; London, Gollancz, 1939.
The Kissed Corpse (as Asa Baker). New York, Carlyle, 1939.
Before I Wake (as Hal Debrett, with Kathleen Rollins). New York, Dodd Mead, 1949; London, Jarrolds, 1953.

A Lonely Way to Die (as Hal Debrett, with Kathleen Rollins). New York, Dodd, Mead, 1950; London, Jarrolds, 1954.
Charlie Dell (as Anderson Wayne). New York, Coward McCann, 1952; London, Hale, 1953; as *A Time to Remember*, New York, Popular Library, 1959.
The Avenger (as Matthew Blood, with Ryerson Johnson). New York, Fawcett, 1952.
Death Is a Lovely Dame (as Matthew Blood, with Ryerson Johnson). New York, Fawcett, 1954.

Novels as Anthony Scott

Mardi Gras Madness. New York, Godwin, 1934.
Test of Virtue. New York, Godwin, 1934
Ten Toes Up. New York, Godwin, 1935.
Virgin's Holiday. New York, Godwin, 1935.
Stolen Sins. New York, Godwin, 1936.
Ladies of Chance. New York, Godwin, 1936.
Satan Rules the Night. New York, Godwin, 1938.
Temptation. New York, Godwin, 1938.

Novels as Brett Halliday

Dividend on Death. New York, Holt, 1939; London, Jarrolds, 1941.
The Private Practice of Michael Shayne. New York, Holt, 1940; London, Jarrolds, 1941.
The Uncomplaining Corpses. New York, Holt, 1940; London, Jarrolds, 1942.
Tickets for Death. New York, Holt, 1941; London, Jarrolds, 1942.
Bodies Are Where You Find Them. New York, Holt, 1941; in *Michael Shayne Investigates*, 1943.
Michael Shayne Takes Over (omnibus). New York, Holt, 1941.
The Corpse Came Calling. New York, Dodd Mead, 1942; in *Michael Shayne Investigates*, 1943; as *The Case of the Walking Corpse*, Kingston, New York, Quin, 1943.
Murder Wears a Mummer's Mask. New York, Dodd Mead, 1943; in *Michael Shayne Takes a Hand*, 1944; as *In a Deadly Vein*, New York, Dell, 1956.
Blood on the Black Market. New York, Dodd Mead, 1943; in *Michael Shayne Takes a Hand*, 1944; revised edition, as *Heads You Lose*, New York, Dell, 1958.
Michael Shayne Investigates (omnibus). London, Jarrolds, 1943.
Michael Shayne Takes a Hand (omnibus). London, Jarrolds, 1944.
Michael Shayne's Long Chance. New York, Dodd Mead, 1944; London, Jarrolds, 1945.
Murder and the Married Virgin. New York, Dodd Mead, 1944; London, Jarrolds, 1946.
Murder Is My Business. New York, Dodd Mead, and London, Jarrolds, 1945.
Marked for Murder. New York, Dodd Mead, 1945; London, Jarrolds, 1950.
Dead Man's Diary, and Dinner at Dupre's. New York, Dell, 1945.
Blood on Biscayne Bay. Chicago, Ziff Davis, 1946; London, Jarrolds, 1950.
Counterfeit Wife. Chicago, Ziff Davis, 1947; London, Jarrolds, 1950.
Blood on the Stars. New York, Dodd Mead, 1948; as *Murder Is a Habit*, London, Jarrolds, 1951.
Michael Shayne's Triple Mystery (*Dead Man's Diary, A Taste for Cognac, Dinner at Dupre's*). New York, Ziff Davis, 1948.
A Taste for Violence. New York, Dodd Mead, 1949; London, Jarrolds, 1952.
Call for Michael Shayne. New York, Dodd Mead, 1949; London, Jarrolds, 1951.
This Is It, Michael Shayne. New York, Dodd Mead, 1950; London, Jarrolds, 1952.
Framed in Blood. New York, Dodd Mead, 1951; London, Jarrolds, 1953.
When Dorinda Dances. New York, Dodd Mead, 1951; London, Jarrolds, 1953.
What Really Happened. New York, Dodd Mead, 1952; London, Jarrolds, 1953.
One Night with Nora. New York, Torquil, 1953; as *The Lady Came by Night*, London, Jarrolds, 1954.
She Woke to Darkness. New York, Torquil, 1954; London, Jarrolds, 1955.
Death Has Three Lives. New York, Torquil, and London, Jarrolds, 1955.
Stranger in Town. New York, Torquil, 1955; London, Jarrolds, 1956.
The Blonde Cried Murder. New York, Torquil, 1956; London, Jarrolds, 1957.
Weep for a Blonde. New York, Torquil, 1957; London, Long, 1958.
Shoot the Works. New York, Torquil, 1957; London, Long, 1958.
Murder and the Wanton Bride. New York, Torquil, 1958; London, Long, 1959.

Novels as Kathryn Culver

Love Is a Masquerade. New York, Phoenix Press, 1935.
Too Smart for Love. New York, Curl, 1937.
Million Dollar Madness. New York, Curl, 1937.
Green Path to the Moon. New York, Curl, 1938.
Once to Every Woman. New York, Godwin, 1938.
Girl Alone. New York, Grammercy, 1939.

Other

Editor, with Helen McCloy, *20 Great Tales of Murder*. New York, Random House, 1951; London, Hammond, 1952.
Editor, *Dangerous Dames*. New York, Dell, 1955.
Editor, *Big Time Mysteries*. New York, Dodd Mead, 1958.
Editor, *Murder in Miami*. New York, Dodd Mead, 1959.
Editor, *Best Detective Stories of the Year* (*16th* [and *17th*] Annual Collection). New York, Dutton, 2 vols., 1961–62.

* * *

Davis Dresser wrote most of his Westerns before he became famous (as Brett Halliday) for creating Mike Shayne, and continuing his saga in a long series of detective novels. He had written other novels even before then, but his Westerns, written under his own name and as Don Davis, possibly served as a simultaneous "check" on the origins of Mike Shayne.

Dresser's narrative sense, in fact, is the most noticeable feature of his Westerns. All the Twister Malone novels begin with a neutral opening in which Malone and his sidekick, Chuckaluck Thompson, are heading for a friend's hacienda in Old Mexico when they are suddenly drawn into a "plot." As outsiders, they are at first confused by what is happening, but the pieces are gradually put together by the quick intelligence of Malone (aided by the more lugubrious cleverness of Chuckaluck)—and the reader too is drawn into the story almost without realizing it. This "flat" plotting allows any number of stories to be spun off the same threads, but Dresser stopped after a few, obviously finding some satisfaction in continuing the Shayne books.

Malone is a character type who emerges more fully developed in Mike Shayne. But they both probably reflect the closing frontier generation in which Dresser himself grew up—in west Texas, the locale of all the Westerns. Malone is a loner: even though he is accompanied by the rotund and musical Chuckaluck, he does not think aloud, but keeps his own counsel, always rides back into the melee instead of away from it, and thoughtfully shoots or thinks his way out of trouble. More importantly, he also manages to solve someone else's problem—and there is usually a young woman whose romance is in jeopardy until the mystery has been cleared up—before riding on.

There is always a mystery in the Westerns, even though the mystery is sometimes a bit creaky. Most involve matters appropriate to the ranchers and miners of the Davis Mountains and Big Bend country: a lost mine claim in *Lynch-Rope Law*, brand switching in *The Masked Riders of Sleepy Valley*, dubious water rights in *Death Rides the Pecos*, a peculiar will in *Murder on the Mesa*. (The non-series novel *Gunsmoke on the Mesa* has a complicated plot entering on a death which has caused one character to exile himself to Mexico and another to be blackmailed. This novel involves bringing Kentucky thoroughbreds to the unsuitable west Texas ranges.) But because of the adroit narrative handling, and the unforced and pervasive humor (centering on Chuckaluck), the reader rarely realizes the simplicity of the themes, but merely reads on.

—George Walsh

DRISCOLL, Eli. *See* **KING, Albert.**

DRYDEN, John. *See* **ROWLAND, Donald S.**

DUNCAN, Duke. *See* **RATHBORNE, St. George.**

DURHAM, John. *See* **PAINE, Lauran.**

DURHAM, Marilyn (née Wall). American. Born in Evansville, Indiana, 8 September 1930. Educated at Evansville College (now University), 1949–50. Married Kilburn Durham in 1950; two daughters. Agent: Ann Elmo Agency, 60 East 42nd Street, New York, New York 10017. Address: 1508 Howard Street, Evansville, Indiana 47713, U.S.A.

WESTERN PUBLICATIONS

Novels

The Man Who Loved Cat Dancing. New York, Harcourt Brace, and London, Macmillan, 1972.
Dutch Uncle. New York, Harcourt Brace, and London, Macmillan, 1973.

OTHER PUBLICATIONS

Novel

Flambard's Confession. New York, Harcourt Brace, 1982.

*

Manuscript Collection: Indiana State University, Evansville.

Marilyn Durham comments (1982):

There is little to tell of me. I am that caricature figure well-known to critics, the housewife–novelist who hit the bestseller list on her first attempt at writing a novel. My education consists of a lifetime spent reading other people's books. I am a history buff of a very low order, also interested in Italian opera, good actors, bad movies, people who like to talk about something besides themselves. I smoke and eat too much. A cat has consented to live with me. My opinion of my own work is that I do it as well as I'm able. I write stories about people, rather than issues, problems, or archetypes. My latest book is longer than *War and Peace*, though not half so good. There exists a vast underground of people who have never heard of me, but I am not dismayed. I've never heard of them, either.

* * *

In 1972 Marilyn Durham's first novel, *The Man Who Loved Cat Dancing*, became a national bestseller and was eventually translated into 12 languages. Superlative praise about this new author ("a natural born story-teller") gushed from the pens of reviewers in all major American newspapers and magazines. The story of *Cat Dancing* centers around Catherine Crocker, a woman attempting to get out of a stifling, loveless marriage she entered to escape her tyranical, hard-drinking father, and Jay Grobart, a man haunted by the past and bent on collecting his two mixed-blood children from the Shoshones, the tribe of their mother, Cat Dancing, whom he killed. Catherine happens upon a train robbery perpetrated by Grobart and his cohorts and is kidnapped in the first chapter. The remainder of the book is turned over to the pursuit of Catherine and Grobart headed by her husband and Harvey Lapchance, an express agent. The standard love-hate relationship with a few unusual twists develops between Catherine and Grobart. Durham focused on her characters, adeptly exploring their inner workings and psychological subtleties. The popularity of the book may have stemmed from the fact that Catherine is essentially a 20th-century heroine espousing contemporary views about women in a 19th-century setting.

Dutch Uncle also generated high praise from the critics. The story, set in New Mexico, focuses on Jake Hollander, an aging gunslinger turned professional gambler who is afraid to make commitments. Through a series of unusual circumstances he is saddled with the care of two Mexican children—perhaps Durham's finest creations—and the job of town marshal in a small mining community. The town is inhabited by lonely male miners who have invested their savings in a mail-order bride plan, a newspaperman and his spinster sister, a Mexican cantina owner and his family, and a flock of soiled doves. Like *Cat Dancing*, *Dutch Uncle* is a tragi-comedy, but, unlike the first novel, it ends happily for the majority of characters.

Durham's two novels are well-plotted stories with plenty of action and suspense as well as delightful characters. They are basically main-stream novels, concerned with the dynamics of human relationships, which happen to be set in the west. Neither book evokes a feeling of the West of the period—both are set in the 1880's—nor is the western landscape an integral part of the story-line.

—Vicki Piekarski

DURST, Paul. Also writers as Peter Bannon; John Chelton; Jeff Cochran; John Shane. American. Born in Archbald, Pennsylvania, 23 April 1921. Educated at St. Francis Xavier and Christian Brothers schools, St. Joseph, Missouri, 1926–38; Colorado State College (now University), Greeley, 1938–40; Northwest Missouri Teachers College (now University), Maryville, 1940–41. Served as an aviator in the United States Naval Reserve, 1941–46: Lt. Commander. Married 1) June Rockliffe in 1942 (died 1972), one son and one daughter; 2) Doris L. Lamb in 1973. Chief editorial writer and newscaster, St. Joseph *News-Press*, 1946–48; advertising supervisor, Southwestern Bell Telephone Company, Kansas City and St. Louis, 1948–50; advertising manager, Crofts Engineering, Bradford, 1958–60, and J.G. Graves, mail order firm, Sheffield, 1960–62. Agent: Gerald Pollinger, 18 Maddox Street, London WIR OEU, England. Address: The Keep, West Wall, Presteigne, Powys LD8 2BY, Wales.

WESTERN PUBLICATIONS

Novels

Die, Damn You! New York, Lion, 1952; London, Mills and Boon, 1955.
Bloody River. New York, Lion, 1953; Kingswood, Surrey, World's Work, 1955.
Trail Herd North. New York, Avon, 1953.
Guns of Circle 8 (as Jeff Cochran). New York, Avon, 1954; London, Mills and Boon, 1955.
Showdown. London, Mills and Boon, 1955.
Justice. New York, Ace, 1956.
Kid from Canadian. Kingswood, Surrey, World's Work, 1956.
Prairie Reckoning. New York, Fawcett, 1956; London, Fawcett, 1957.
John Law, Keep Out. New York, Ace, 1957.
Ambush at North Platte. London, Long, 1957.
The River Flows West. London, Long, 1957.
Kansas Guns. New York, Avalon, 1958.
Dead Man's Range. London, Hale, 1958.
The Gun Doctor. New York, Avalon, 1959.
Johnny Nation. London, Mills and Boon, 1960.

Novels as John Shane

Along the Yermo Rim. London, Mills and Boon, 1954.
Sundown in Sundance. London, Mills and Boon, 1956.
Six-Gun Thursday. London, Mills and Boon, 1956.
Gunsmoke Dawn. London, Mills and Boon, 1957.

OTHER PUBLICATIONS

Novels

My Deadly Angel (as John Chelton). New York, Fawcett, 1955; London, Fawcett, 1956
Backlash. London, Cassell, 1967.
Badge of Infamy. London, Cassell, 1968.
The Florentine Table. New York, Scribner, 1980.
Paradiso County. London, Hale, 1986.

Novels as Peter Bannon

They Want Me Dead. London, Jenkins, 1958.
If I Should Die. London, Jenkins, 1958.
Whisper Murder Softly. London, Jenkins, 1963.

Play

Screenplay: *The Informers* (*Underground Informers*), with Alun Falconer, 1963.

Other

Intended Treason: What Really Happened in the Gunpowder Plot. London, W.H. Allen, 1970; South Brunswick, New Jersey, A.S. Barnes, 1971.
A Roomful of Shadows (autobiography). London, Dobson, 1975.

* * *

All of Paul Durst's western novels were written in the decade after 1952 (his last was published in 1960), but he maintained a high standard in all of them, often with a wider angle of objectivity than other popular writers achieve. Though his plots tend to be conventional, Durst often attempts to bring an outside element into play. Some of his other novels are mysteries, and in many of the Westerns there is a mystery element as well (is there an alibi? a forged document? a hidden secret?); past relationships are sometimes not clear, and people travel under assumed names. His novels also tend to have a large cast of characters, giving a sense of social density often missing in this sort of work. Moreover, there is often a genuine conflict that goes beyond merely personal antagonism or rivalry for land or water rights. In two of the novels written as John Shane, for instance, there is a strong post-Civil War theme: can the wounds of the war be healed, and can a newspaperman (*not* a gunman or a rancher) help heal them (*Gunsmoke Dawn*)? In *Sundown in Sundance* the young man who left the small Texas town after killing his father's murderer returns as a school teacher prepared to forget the past; this is such an unlikely role for a young Texas hero that it is greeted with disbelief by almost all the characters, though in terms of the novel's theme it is an effective stroke.

Many of Durst's Westerns *do* use standard plots and conflicts: the ranchers versus the nesters (*Prairie Reckoning*, *Johnny Nation*), corrupt law officials (*Six-Gun Thursday*, *Dead Man's Range*). And there are the usual run-ins and plot devices (often seemingly based on or with an eye toward the movies). But *Kid from Canadian* is a fine first-person narrative of a young tearaway, Ross Riverhide, who murders his father's killer in the courtroom after he has been (wrongly) acquitted for the crime, makes a run for it, becomes a gambler, gets involved in other killings, and is finally waiting to "take my medicine" in his jail cell. *Johnny Nation* is probably the most typical (and best) Durst novel. Johnny comes back to his native rangeland years after he and his mother went south following his father's death. There is a complicated plot, centering on the top hand (and gunman) of the biggest rancher in the area who has been trying to drive out the small farmers who are beginning to settle. Johnny's claim to his own range is firm, and he slowly convinces the rancher's daughter, and then the rancher himself, that there is room for both ranching and farming in the west. This novel has a strong lawman (the brother of the gunman), and Johnny himself functions as a force for law and order ("a man has to take a stand")—and the novel's conclusion is more satisfying than most novels using this theme.

—George Walsh

E

EARLY, Tom. *See* **KELTON, Elmer.**

EARP, Virgil. *See* **ALLISON, Clay.**

EASTLAKE, William (Derry). American. Born in New York City, 14 July 1917. Educated at Bonnie Brae School; Caldwell High School, New Jersey; Alliance Française, Paris, 1948–50. Served in the United States Army in World War II: Bronze Star. Married Martha Simpson in 1943 (divorced 1971). Writer-in-residence, Knox College, Galesburg, Illinois, 1967, University of New Mexico, Albuquerque, 1967–68, University of Southern California, Los Angeles, 1968–69, University of Arizona, Tucson, 1969–71, and United States Military Academy, West Point, 1975. Correspondent for *Nation* in Vietnam, 1968. Recipient: Ford grant, 1964; Rockefeller grant, 1966, 1967. D. Litt.: University of Albuquerque, 1970. Address: 15 Coy Road, Bisbee, Arizona 85603, U.S.A.

Western Publications

Novels

Go in Beauty. New York, Harper, 1956; London, Secker and Warburg, 1957.
The Bronc People. New York, Harcourt Brace, 1958; London, Deutsch, 1963.
Portrait of an Artist with Twenty-Six Horses. New York, Simon and Schuster, 1963; London, Joseph, 1965.
Dancers in the Scalp House. New York, Viking Press, 1975.

Uncollected Short Stories

"Ishimoto's Land," in *Essai* (Geneva, Switzerland), Summer 1952.
"Two Gentlemen from America," in *Hudson Review* (New York), Fall 1954.
"Homecoming," in *Quarto* (New York), Fall 1954.
"The Barfly and the Navajo," in *Nation* (New York), 12 September 1959.
"A Long Day's Dying," in *The Best American Short Stories 1964*, edited by Martha Foley and David Burnett. Boston, Houghton Mifflin, 1964.
"Little Joe," in *The Best American Short Stories 1965*, edited by Martha Foley and David Burnett. Boston, Houghton Mifflin, 1965.
"Something Big Is Happening to Me," in *New American Story*, edited by Robert Creeley and Donald Allen. New York, Grove Press, 1965.
"What Nice Hands Held," in *Gallery of Modern Fiction*, edited by Robie Macauley. New York, Salem Press, 1966.
"Three Heroes and a Clown," in *Evergreen Review Reader 1957–1967*, edited by Barney Rosset. New York, Grove Press, 1968.
"Now Lucifer Is Not Dead," in *Evergreen Review* (New York), November 1968.
"The Message," in *New Mexico Quarterly* (Albuquerque), Winter 1968.
"The Hanging at Prettyfields," in *Evergreen Review* (New York), February 1969.
"The Biggest Thing since Custer," in *Prize Stories 1970: The O. Henry Awards*, edited by William Abrahams. New York, Doubleday, 1970.
"The Death of Sun," in *The Best American Short Stories 1973*, edited by Martha Foley. Boston, Houghton Mifflin, 1973.
"Mrs. Gage in Her Bed of Pain with a Nice Cup of Gin," in *Ms.* (New York), March 1977.
"Don't Be Afraid, The Clown's Afraid Too," in *South Shore* (Au Train, Michigan), 1 (2), 1978.
"Inside the Belly of the Whale," in *Bisbee Times* (Bisbee, Arizona), March 1982.

Other Publications

Novels

Castle Keep. New York, Simon and Schuster, 1965; London, Joseph, 1966.
The Bamboo Bed. New York, Simon and Schuster, 1969; London, Joseph, 1970.
The Long Naked Descent into Boston: A Tricentennial Novel. New York, Viking Press, 1977.
Prettyfields: A Work in Progress, with *The Man Who Cultivated Fire* by Gerald Haslam. Santa Barbara, Capra, 1987.

Short Stories

Jack Armstrong in Tangier, And Other Escapes. Flint, Michigan, Bamberger, 1984.

Verse

A Child's Garden of Verses for the Revolution (includes essays). New York, Grove Press, 1971.

*

Critical Studies: "The Novels of William Eastlake" by Delbert W. Wylder, in *New Mexico Quarterly* (Albuquerque), 1965; "Of Cowboys, Indians and the Modern West" by Peter M. Kenyon, in *Sage* (Las Vegas, Nevada), Winter 1969; *Covering Ground: Essays for Now* by Donald Phelps, New York, Croton Press, 1969; *William Eastlake* by Gerald Haslam, Austin, Texas, Steck Vaughn, 1970; "William Eastlake Issue" of *Review of Contemporary Fiction* (Elmwood Park, Illinois), Spring 1983.

* * *

William Eastlake, in a comment in *Contemporary Novelists*, quotes himself:

> Below at the post, the exact center and the capital of the world for The People, two Indians crouched at the massive stone root of the petrified-wood house where it made its way into the ground.
>
> "This crack," the Indian said, tracing it with his brown finger.
>
> "They can fix it," Rabbit Stocking said.
>
> "No. And perhaps even The People cannot stop something coming apart and beginning here at the center of the world."

He continues: "The artist's job is to hold the world together. What the politicians cannot do with reality the artist does with magic. . . ." For Eastlake, the small section of northwest New Mexico where four of his novels are set can be seen as a representative section of human geography. And if his comment sounds a bit over-earnest, the novels themselves are anything but that. In fact, Eastlake's most notable characteristic as a writer is possibly his complete lack of presuppositions about the way people think or act, and this attitude is presented in a tone of voice that, involving as it does irony, illogic, ellipses, is often difficult to make out. But what emerges in the books is something human, humorous, lively, moving, and possibly magical.

Each of the first three New Mexico novels novels deals with various members of the Bowman family, and they are all variations on a theme of life in the West. Each centers on a contrast between brothers or friends, one an artist or a searcher after experience, the other a person who can find something like happiness among the ranchers and Indians of the world he inhabits. The first, *Go in Beauty*, is an almost paradigmatic fable of two brothers, Alexander and George Bowman. Alexander is a writer who lives a peripatetic life in search of experience, while George finds contentment living among the Indians. *The Bronc People* centers on two young men arriving at manhood. One is Sant Bowman who wants to live the life of the country he's been reared in. The other is Alexander Benjamin, a black boy reared with Sant (and the son of a man who had been killed by Sant's father); he has artistic ambitions, and at the end of the book leaves New Mexico for school, and another life.

The pattern of contrast is most richly seen in the beautiful book *Portrait of an Artist with Twenty-Six Horses*. The narrative pattern—perhaps too explicit in the first novel, too indeterminate in the second—is here given momentum by a series of seeming flashbacks called up by one of the young heroes, Rick Bowman, as he is lying in quicksand after being thrown by his horse, fearful of death. His background of life in and around Coyote, New Mexico, is brilliantly presented. Much of the material centers on Twenty-Six Horses, a young Navajo artist trying to find sanity in his life outside (or even back inside) the reservation. There is a refreshing picture of his mother, The Queen of Coyote, who has set up a restaurant in Coyote, and apes the white man's ways. She does not see the irony of her repeated remark, "I'm trying to make a buck." One of the many signs in the restaurant reads, "Real Live White People in Their Native Costumes Doing Native White Dances." Since no one will buy his pictures, Twenty-Six Horses has painted the cliff walls in vivid scenes. His attempts to find the spirit of his ancestors have failed—though when he hears Rick's cries for help from the quicksand he at first mistakes them for a spirit voice. The fourth New Mexico book, *Dancers in the Scalp House*, is a lighter work, a satire of a group of Navajos and their teacher fighting against the construction of a dam which will drown their land.

Eastlake's satiric and whimsical tone shouldn't blind us to his obviously strong concern with American values in general (he has also written novels about World War II and the Vietnam War). His pictures of Indians and rodeo stars, rich tourists and bemused middle-aged women searching through the textbooks for a religion are not meant to be a regional portrait of a limited part of New Mexico, but an overview of a world in which honor, self-fulfillment, and justice are difficult to define. If the irony and fantasy are sometimes a bit inexplicit, the facts of life, distilled through the mind of the artist, are also present.

—George Walsh

EASTON, Robert (Olney). American. Born in San Francisco, California, 4 July 1915. Educated at Santa Barbara High School, California, 1929–32; Phillips Academy, Andover, Massachusetts, 1932–33; Stanford University, California, 1933–34, 1938–39; Harvard University, Cambridge, Massachusetts, 1935–38, S.B. 1938. Served in the United States Army, 1942–46: Private to 1st Lieutenant. Married Jane Faust in 1940: four daughters. Cattle ranch hand; engineering firm field supervisor; associate editor, *Coast Magazine*, San Francisco, 1939–40; co-publisher and editor, Lampasas *Dispatch*, 1946–50, and co-owner and manager, Radio Station KHIT, 1948–50, Lampasas, Texas; Professor of English, Santa Barbara City College, California, 1960–66; consultant, Naval Civil Engineering Laboratory, Port Hueneme, California, 1963–69. Co-founder, Sisquoc Sanctuary for the California condor, 1937, and of the first wilderness area established under National Wilderness Act, Los Padres National Forest, California, 1968. Agent: Sandra Dijkstra Literary Agency, 1237 Camino Del Mar, Suite 515C, Del Mar, California 92014. Address: 2222 Las Canoas Road, Santa Barbara, California 93105, U.S.A.

WESTERN PUBLICATIONS

Novels (series: Saga of California)

The Happy Man. New York, Viking Press, 1943.
This Promised Land (Saga of California). Santa Barbara, California, Capra Press, 1982.
Power and Glory (Saga of California). Santa Barbara, California, Capra Press, 1989.

Uncollected Short Stories

"To Find a Place," in *Great Tales of the American West*, edited by Henry E. Maule. New York, Modern Library, 1944.
"Bonaparte McPhail," in *Collier's* (Springfield, Ohio), 26 August 1944.
"Banker Clayton's Interest," in *Collier's* (Springfield, Ohio), 9 December 1950.
"Wild Challenge," in *Argosy* (New York), February 1952.
"Death in October," in *Out West*, edited by Jack Schaefer. Boston, Houghton Mifflin, 1955.
"The Legend of Storm," in *Esquire* (New York), September 1956.
"First Dawning," in *The New Frontier*, edited by Joe R. Lansdale. New York, Doubleday, 1989.

OTHER PUBLICATIONS

Other

Lord of Beasts: The Saga of Buffalo Jones, with Mackenzie Brown. Tucson, University of Arizona Press, 1961; London, Deutsch, 1964.
The Book of the American West, with others. New York, Messner, 1963.
California Condor: Vanishing American, with Dick Smith. Charlotte, North Carolina, McNally and Loftin, 1964.
Max Brand, The Big Westerner. Norman, University of Oklahoma Press, 1970.
Black Tide: The Santa Barbara Oil Spill and Its Consequences. New York, Delacorte Press, 1972.
Guns, Gold, and Caravans: The Extraordinary Life of Fred Meyer Schroder. Santa Barbara, California, Capra Press, 1978.
China Caravans: An American Adventurer in Old China. Santa Barbara, California, Capra Press, 1982.
Life and Work: Autobiography, with David Russell. Santa Barbara, University of California Press, 1990.
Love and War: Pearl Harbor Through V–J Day, with Jane Easton. Norman, University of Oklahoma Press, 1991.

Editor, *Max Brand's Best Stories*. New York, Dodd Mead, 1967; London, White Lion, 1976.
Editor, with Mackenzie Brown, *Bullying the Moqui*, by Charles F. Lummis. Prescott, Arizona, Prescott college Press, 1968.

*

Manuscript Collections: University of Wyoming, Laramie; University of California, Santa Barbara.

Robert Easton comments:

Whether fiction or nonfiction, my work has always come from what has moved me most. Thus it has included history, natural history, and the environment, as well as biography and imaginative writing. Since I have lived mostly in the American West, much of my work is set in and deals with the West, and has a strong sense of place. It seems to me that what concerns a writer most, wherever he or she may be, is the living word—the one that captures the essential truth of what he is trying to say—and that is what I have tried to put down.

* * *

Despite its bland title and loose, episodic structure, Robert Easton's *The Happy Man* is a minor western classic, and one of the best books ever written about modern feed-lot ranching. It grew out of Easton's experiences as a ranch hand with A.B. Miller's B.B. Cattle Company on the Sacramento River Delta, and for the McCreery Ranch in the Coast Range near Hollister, California, during 1940–41. Although it was first published by Viking Press in 1943, four chapters—including the title piece—had already appeared in *The Atlantic Monthly* in 1942.

The Happy Man is a series of beautifully written, well-crafted vignettes about the men of T.S. Ordway's El Dorado Investment Company near San Francisco, a large-scale stock feeding enterprise where beef was "turned into dollars as fast as Henry Ford turned cars off the assembly line." The time is the 1930's. The men are, for the most part, Dust Bowl refugees: Okies, Arkansawyers, Texans, and Missourian. Men with names like Uncle Arky Billy, Jaydee, Cherokee, Dynamite, and Happy Jack Patee. Men who have been busted and scarred, who have lost much and earned little. But there is a grandeur among this human dross and a heroism in their labor. Easton is at his very best when describing them at work. His accounts of cattle trucks unloading at night, of turning a wind-spooked herd, of stemming a flood with "Jim Magee's sand," and vaccinating cattle against Anthrax, are unforgettable. Easton has captured the romance and strange beauty of these men struggling at the very heart of life. His highly praised vernacular prose is too polished and poetic to be natural, but is a triumph of style nevertheless.

—John D. Flanagan

ECHOLS, Allan K.

WESTERN PUBLICATIONS

Novels

Keep Off My Ranch. London, Foulsham, 1949.
The Stranger from Texas. London, Foulsham, 1949; New York, Macfadden Bartell, 1970.
Red River Road. London, Foulsham, 1950.
Dead Man's Range. London, Foulsham, 1950.
The Saddle Wolves. London, Foulsham, 1950.
Wildhorse Range. London, Foulsham, 1950.
The Renegade Hills. London, Foulsham, 1952.
Vengeance Valley. New York, Eton, 1953; London, Gold Lion, 1973.
Killers Two. New York, Macfadden Bartell, 1963; London, Gold Lion, 1973.

* * *

The works of Allan K. Echols are consistent with most other Westerns produced in the late 1940's and 1950's. He writes traditional Westerns set in or around Texas and peopled with various stock characters. Themes are repeated as well—in 1948 he wrote *Red River Road*, only to repeat the story of an absent ranch owner returning home to claim his ranch in a better version written as *The Saddle Wolves*. The familiarity of the main plot is (matched by the repetetive) female interest, an ex-fiancée or loved one lost years before, who by the end of the book is reunited with the hero. Then there is the omnipresent land-mad cattle baron, claiming the absentee's ranch as opened brand.

But for all that, Echols's characters are interesting. He portrays his hero as single-willed, upright, honest, and prepared to allow the other man to draw first—all true to western tradition. He uses the main character as the pivot for all the secondary characters, letting them swirl about him, and in their contact discovers that things and people aren't always what they seem to be on the surface. Echols excels in picturing the little man. Tush Hog Terry in *The Saddle Wolves*, spurred on by the hero's words, finds himself at the dentist and changing his appearance. Along the way he discovers a new dignity within himself and returns to Jim Wister's side an altered character, helping him to fight against those who would double-cross, cheat, and steal from his friend.

In *The Stranger from Texas*, young Merle Roberson rides into the small town of Staghorn looking for his father. He's 10 days too late—Cord Roberson has been killed and his killer is still on the loose. Roberson takes it on himself to find the killer, but is also drawn into the fight between the valley ranchers and the two big operators who would take their land from them. Echols's heroes always have a decision foisted upon them, and the outcome of this personal conflict is that they inevitably take the fight to the bad guys—regardless of their reputation or physical size.

Echols usually treats his readers to a long drawn-out fight that can last for anything up to eight pages. It is an annoying and overdone ploy, and these knockdowns and drag outs do nothing to enhance the storyline, which could have easily been told in one or two pages. It is fair enough to want to show that the hero is a tough man, with stamina and courage but there are better ways of doing this, and this is one of Echols's failings.

In portraying women characters, another area in which Echols fails, his characterisations can be broken down into three categories. Either she has loved or is in love with the hero; or she is as scheming and devious as her male counterparts—the evil rancher's daughter usually appears in this role, or finally, she is the strong-willed wife who cares for the hero who has come to the aid of her husband and family.

A change of direction is *The Renegade Hills*, which is written as a mystery. Jim Webster is hired by a rancher and his female partner to discover who has been stealing cattle from them and their neighbours. Interwoven with this is a subplot of stolen gold, which was in Webster's charge at the time, and the finger of suspicion points at him. Needless to say, Webster has to clear his name, find the thieves, and get the girl. Basic plotting and characters do nothing to make this one of Echols's better works.

On the other hand, *Dead Man's Range*, although it is a conventional range-war Western, has very good character studies woven into the plot. Here Echols explores that area which Elmore Leonard does so well, the little man pushed too far. Heddon, the little man, uses the land-baron and the protagonist, Jim Weldon, for his own gains, and lifts the story out of its well-trodden path. *Vengeance Valley* and *Wildhorse Range* follow the same themes of Echols's earlier works. The characters are ever the same—villains who are greedy and operate outside the law to achieve their aims. The first novel tells of a ruthless gang prepared to put the settlers' valley to the torch, with Jim Ballinger and his friends out to stop them. The second covers much the same ground, reworking it a little by adding a love interest with the leading character losing his girl to the antagonist, who also wants Jim Birdsong's land. *Keep Off My Ranch* or *Killers Two* makes for different and better reading as Echols makes a rare change in his approach to his formulae Westerns. Rancher Jim Woodbine is sent by the law to capture two cold-blooded rustlers, with the odds against him coming back alive. But like all Echols's heroes, Woodbine comes out on top.

It must be noted that although the mainstay of Echols's Westerns are standard and formula plots, his ability to draw idiosyncratic characters makes for good reading.

—Mike Stotter

EDSON, J(ohn) T(homas). Also wrote as Rod Denver; Chuck Nolan. British. Born in Workshop, Nottinghamshire, 17 February 1928. Educated at Hodthorpe Primary School, 1933–39; Shirebrook Selective Central School, 1939–43. Served with the Rifle Brigade, 1946–48; Royal Army Veterinary Corps, in Europe, Africa, and the Far East, 1948–59. Married Dorothy Mary Thompson in 1957; two sons and one daughter. Worked as a haulage hand in stone quarry, Steetley. Story, serial and series writer for Rover, Hotspur and Victor comic books. Army dog trainer, 1946–58; owner, fish and chip shop, Melton Mowbray, Leicestershire, 1958–62; production hand, Petfoods Industries 1962–65; postman 1965–68. Since 1968 freelance writer. Hon. Admiral, Texas Navy; Hon. Commodore, Powder River Navy, Wyoming; Hon. Deputy Sheriff, Travis County, Texas, Thurston County, Washington, and Natrona County, Wyoming. Agent: Joanna Marston, Rosica Colin Ltd., 4 Hereford Square, London SW7 4TU. Address: 1, Cottesmore Avenue, Melton Mowbray, Leicestershire LE13 0HY, England.

WESTERN PUBLICATIONS

Novels (series: Floating Outfit in all books)

Trail Boss. London, Brown and Watson, 1961; New York, Berkley, 1980.
The Hard Riders. London, Brown and Watson, 1962.
The Texan. London, Brown and Watson, 1962.
Rio Guns. London, Brown and Watson, 1962.
The Ysabel Kid. London, Brown and Watson, 1962; New York, Berkley, 1978.
Quiet Town (as Chuck Nolan). London, Brown and Watson, 1962; as J.T. Edson, New York, Berkley, 1980.
Waco's Debt. London, Brown and Watson, 1962.
The Rio Hondo Kid. London, Brown and Watson, 1963.
Apache Rampage. London, Brown and Watson, 1963.
The Half Breed. London, Brown and Watson, 1963.
Gun Wizard. London, Brown and Watson, 1963.
Gunsmoke Thunder. London, Brown and Watson, 1963.
Wagons to Backsight. London, Brown and Watson, 1964; New York, Berkley, 1980.
The Rushers. London, Brown and Watson, 1964.
The Rio Hondo War. London, Brown and Watson, 1964.
Trigger Fast. London, Brown and Watson, 1964.
The Wildcats. London, Brown and Watson, 1965.
The Peacemakers. London, Brown and Watson, 1965.
Troubled Range. London, Brown and Watson, 1965; New York, Berkley, 1979.
The Fortune Hunters. London, Brown and Watson, 1965.
The Man from Texas. London, Brown and Watson, 1965.
The Trouble Busters. London, Brown and Watson, 1965.
Guns in the Night. London, Brown and Watson, 1966.
A Town Called Yellowdog. London, Brown and Watson, 1966.
The Law of the Gun. London, Brown and Watson, 1966.
Return to Backsight. London, Brown and Watson, 1966.
The Fast Gun. London, Brown and Watson, 1967.
Terror Valley. London, Brown and Watson, 1967.
Sidewinder. London, Brown and Watson, 1967; New York, Berkley, 1979.
The Floating Outfit. London, Corgi, 1967.
The Bad Bunch. London, Corgi, 1968; New York, Berkley, 1979.
The Hooded Riders. London, Corgi, 1968; New York, Berkley, 1980.
Rangeland Hercules. London, Corgi, 1968.
McGraw's Inheritance. London, Corgi, 1968; New York, Berkley, 1979.
The Making of a Lawman. London, Corgi, 1968; New York, Bantam, 1971.
The Town Tamers. London, Corgi, 1969; New York, Bantam, 1973.
The Small Texan. London, Corgi, 1969; New York, Bantam, 1974.
Cuchilo. London, Corgi, 1969.
Goodnight's Dream. London, Corgi, 1969; as *The Floating Outfit*, New York, Bantam, 1974.

From Hide and Horn. London, Corgi, 1969; New York, Bantam, 1974.
44 Calibre Man. London, Corgi, 1969; New York, Bantam, 1974.
A Horse Called Mogollon. London, Corgi, 1971; New York, Berkley, 1980.
Hell in the Palo Duro. London, Corgi, 1971; New York, Berkley, 1979.
Go Back to Hell. London, Corgi, 1972; New York, Berkley, 1979.
The South Will Rise Again. London, Corgi, 1972; New York, Berkley, 1980.
To Arms, To Arms, in Dixie. London, Corgi, 1972; New York, Berkley, 1980.
Set Texas Back on Her Feet. London, Corgi, 1973; New York, Berkley, 1980.
The Hide and Tallow Man. London, Corgi, 1974; New York, Berkley, 1978.
The Quest for Bowie's Blade. London, Corgi, 1974.
Set A-Foot. London, Corgi, 1978.
Beguinage. London, Corgi, 1978; as *The Texas Assassin*, New York, Berkley, 1986.
Beguinage Is Dead! London, Corgi, 1978.
Renegade. New York, Berkley, 1978.
Viridian's Trail. New York, Berkley, 1978.
The Gentle Giant. London, Corgi, 1979.
Master of Triggernometry. London, Corgi, 1981; as *Trigger Master*, New York, Berkley, 1986.
White Indian. London, Corgi, 1981.
Old Mocassins on the Trail. London, Corgi, 1981.
Ole Devil's Hands and Feet. London, Severn House, 1984.
Buffalo Are Coming. London, Severn House, 1985.
Decision for Dusty Fog. London, Hale, 1987.
Diamonds, Emeralds, Cards and Colts. London, Hale, 1988.
The Code of Dusty Fog. London, Hale, 1989.
Mark Counter's Kin. London, Corgi, 1990.

Novels (series: Waco in all books)

Sagebrush Sleuth. London, Brown and Watson, 1962.
Arizona Ranger (as Rod Denver). London, Brown and Watson, 1962.
The Drifter. London, Brown and Watson, 1963.
Waco Rides In. London, Brown and Watson, 1964.
Hound Dog Man. London, Brown and Watson, 1967.
Doc Leroy, M.D. London, Corgi, 1977; as *The Night Hawk*, New York, Berkley, 1990.
Waco's Badge. London, Corgi, 1981.

Novels (series: Civil War in all books)

The Fastest Gun in Texas. London, Brown and Watson, 1963.
The Devil Gun. London, Brown and Watson, 1966; New York, Bantam, 1969.
The Colt and the Sabre. London, Brown and Watson, 1967.
Comanche. London, Brown and Watson, 1967; New York, Berkley, 1978.
The Rebel Spy. London, Corgi, 1968.
The Bloody Border. London, Corgi, 1969; New York, Berkley, 1978.
Under the Stars and Bars. London, Corgi, 1970.
Kill Dusty Fog! London, Corgi, 1970.
Back to the Bloody Border. London, Corgi, 1970.
You're In Command Now, Mr. Fog. London, Corgi, 1973; as *Rebel Vengeance*, New York, Berkley, 1987.
The Big Gun. London, Corgi, 1973.
A Matter of Honour. London, Corgi, 1981.

Novels (series: Calamity Jane in all books)

Trouble Trail. London, Brown and Watson, 1965.
The Cow Thieves. London, Brown and Watson, 1965.
The Bull Whip Breed. London, Brown and Watson, 1965; New York, Bantam, 1969.
The Big Hunt. London, Brown and Watson, 1967.
Calamity Spells Trouble. London, Corgi, 1968.
Cold Deck, Hot Lead. London, Corgi, 1969.
White Stallion, Red Mare. London, Corgi, 1970.
The Remittance Kid. London, Corgi, 1978.
The Whip and the War Lance. London, Corgi, 1979.
Cut One, They All Bleed. London, Corgi, 1983.
Hide and Horn Saloon. London, Severn House, 1984.
Calamity, Mark and Belle. London, Hale, 1986; as *Texas Trio*, New York, Berkley, 1989.
Wanted! Belle Starr. London, Severn House, 1986.

Novels (series: Rockabye County in all books)

The Professional Killers. London, Corgi, 1968.
The 1/4-Second Draw. London, Corgi, 1969.
Point of Contact. London, Corgi, 1970.
The Owlhoot. London, Corgi, 1970.
Run for the Border. London, Corgi, 1971.
Bad Hombre. London, Corgi, 1971.
Sixteen-Dollar Shooter. London, Corgi, 1974.
The Deputies. London, Severn House, 1988.
Sheriff of Rockabye County. London, Severn House, 1988.
The Lawmen of Rockabye County. London, Severn House, 1989.

Novels (series: Ole Devil Hardin in all books)

Young Ole Devil. London, Corgi, 1975.
Get Urrea. London, Corgi, 1975.
Ole Devil and the Caplocks. London, Corgi, 1976.
Ole Devil and the Mule Train. London, Corgi, 1976.
Ole Devil at San Jacinto. London, Corgi, 1977.

Novels (series: Cap Fog in all books)

Cap Fog, Meet Mr. J.G. Reeder. London, Corgi, 1977.
You're a Texas Ranger, Alvin Fog. London, Corgi, 1979.
Rapido Clint. London, Corgi, 1980.
The Justice of Company "Z." London, Corgi, 1981.
The Return of Rapido Clint and Mr. J.G. Reeder. London, Corgi, 1984.
Rapido Clint Strikes Back. London, Corgi, 1990.

Novel (series: Waxahachie Smith)

No Finger on the Trigger. London, Hale, 1987.

Novels (out of series titles)

Slaughter's Way. London, Brown and Watson, 1965; New York, Bantam, 1974.
Slip Gun. London, Corgi, 1971.
Two Miles to the Border. London, Corgi, 1972.
J.T.'s Hundredth. London, Corgi, 1979.
J.T.'s Ladies. London, Corgi, 1980.
Is-a-Man. London, Corgi, 1984.

More J.T.'s Ladies. London, Corgi, 1987.
J.T.'s Ladies Ride Again. London, Corgi, 1989.

OTHER PUBLICATIONS

Novels

Blonde Genius, with Peter Clawson. London, Corgi, 1973.
Bunduki. London, Corgi, 1975; New York, Daw, 1976.
Bunduki and Dawn. London, Corgi, 1976.
Sacrifice for the Quagga God. London, Corgi, 1976.
Fearless Master of the Jungle. London, Corgi, 1980.

*

J.T. Edson comments:

I write action-escapism-adventure fiction for a living, therefore go into paperback publication first—where the money is—having my titles re-issued in hard cover at a later date. Although my first publishers, Brown Watson, Ltd., first published *Quiet Town* and *Arizona Ranger* under the pseudonyms Chuck Nolan and Rod Denver, this was done without consulting me, and subsequently they re-issued each title in my own name. As I do not consider writing westerns in any way beneath my dignity, I insist upon using my own name and not a pseudonym.

* * *

Like the majority of successful western writers, J.T. Edson is not a native-born Westerner. Indeed, he was born in England, lives presently in Melton Mowbray, Leicestershire, worked in a stone quarry, served for 12 years in the British Army, and devised many of his plots while making his rounds as a postman. With over 100 novels to his credit (one was written in 11 days; most entail 6 weeks), Edson, now retired from the postal service, is England's best-known western writer.

His books—some of which are complete novels, some of which consist of several novellas or short stories—involve the Floating Outfit, Dusty Fog, the Ysabel Kid, and Mark Counter, who roam the Southwest looking out for the interests of "Ole Devil" Hardin's O.D. Connected Ranch. Mark Counter is a herculean cowboy, well-dressed to the point of dandyism, at ease with the ladies (in *Troubled Range* Belle Starr and Calamity Jane fight over him). The Ysabel Kid (Lancey Dalton Ysabel) is a quarter-breed, reformed smuggler, who, after the murder of his father in *The Ysabel Kid*, joined Dusty. Dressed in black, riding a white stallion named "Nigger," Ysabel is a skilled tracker (a result of his Indian blood) and an expert with a knife and rifle. Dusty Fog is Edson's particular favorite, a character modeled after Audie Murphy. Dusty, known as the Rio Hondo Gun Wizard, is Ole Devil Hardin's nephew and the leader of the Floating Outfit. A Confederate guerilla captain at 17, Fog is a smallish man, but—when the situation calls for it or when others underestimate him—he is a natural leader, unbeatable in a fight either with or without guns. He learned ju-jitsu and karate from an Oriental servant on his uncle's ranch, and his crossdraw is legendary. Edson's stories usually involve one, two, or all three of these characters.

Edson's strength as a western writer is that he loves his main characters. His prose, as one critic said, is "circa 1930," sometimes verging on the unfortunate: "Twisting around towards the man, she drove her right knee up to where it would do the most good, or harm depending upon which end of the knee one was at" (*Troubled Range*). Edson's own estimate is that he "unshamedly writes for money, producing a commercial product that will be enjoyed by readers." All his work is action/escapism/adventure motivated, and an important influence is said to be the fictionist genealogy style of writing perfected by Philip José Farmer. Edson has a disdain for middle-class, "liberal" snobbery and affirms his Westerns have no message, no ethnic butt-licking, and do not glorify losers and anti-heroes.

Readers interested in Edson's work might begin with *The Ysabel Kid*. Although not his first Floating Outfit novel, this is the story of how Dusty Fog, The Ysabel Kid, and Mark Counter meet. Edson also enjoys having actual Western personages (Jesse James, Belle Starr, Calamity Jane, Cattle Annie, and Little Britches) appear in his stories, either as walk-ons, or, in the case of the ladies, as love interests for Mark Counter. Although his Westerns average 12 killings per novel, and some of the Mark Counter stories involve sensual dalliance, there is little emphasis on gore or sexual detail. His villains are stereotyped, his plots usually familiar, but his emphasis on his three, rather pleasant leading characters is the basis for his understandable popularity.

—Ray Merlock

EDWARDS, Hank. *See* **BROOMALL, Robert W.**

EHRLICH, Gretel. Born in California. Educated at Bennington College, Bennington, Vermont; University of California at Los Angeles Film School; New School for Social Research, New York. Worked as a ranch hand and sheep herder, documentary film maker in Wyoming. Since 1979 full-time writer. Address: c/o Viking Books, Penguin USA, 375 Hudson Street, New York, New York 10014, U.S.A.

WESTERN PUBLICATIONS

Novel

Heart Mountain. New York, Viking, 1988; London, Heinemann, 1989.

Short Stories

Wyoming Stories, with *City Tales* by Edward Hoagland. Santa Barbara, California, Capra Press, 1986.

OTHER PUBLICATIONS

Verse

Geode/Rock Body. Santa Barbara, California, Capricorn Press, 1970.
To Touch the Water. Boise, Idaho, Ahsata Press, 1981.

Other

The Solace of Open Spaces. New York, Viking, 1985.

* * *

For a startling perspective on World War II in America, Gretel Ehrlich brings the world to eastern Wyoming. In her only novel, *Heart Mountain*, a Japanese settlement camp is established near Luster, Wyoming. Here 10,000 Japanese who have been ripped from their homes suffer the indignity of living under guard in primitive living conditions. They have come to an alien landscape populated by people who hate them.

Ehrlich follows the lives of the people within and without the camp as they try to maintain their dignity and sanity. Different characters narrate individual chapters; their perspectives often provide opposing views. Rarely do characters within the camp communicate with Wyoming natives. However, two main characters serve as a link: Mariko, a Japanese camp resident, and McKay, a local young rancher, fall in love. The relationship is exhausting for both of them, partly because both already suffer splintered lives.

Mariko, of course, has suffered the forced move to the camp, where she is emotionally trapped in an unhappy relationship with a long-term lover. McKay, although living at home, is no less disoriented. Because of an earlier injury, he is exempt from the draft, and he suffers guilt that he is not going to war. His already tense relationship with one of his two brothers, Champ, deteriorates when Champ leaves for war. The relationship suffers again when Champ discovers McKay's interest in Mariko. McKay's life is further complicated because he had impulsively renewed an old love affair with a woman whose husband is a prisoner of war. Again the relationship is more debilitating than healing.

Such disharmony and disruption within characters and relationships is a continuing theme of the book. McKay's cook and housekeeper, Bobby Korematsu, has been with the family for decades. Now he is torn by the fact that the children he helped raise are at war with his people. In an attempt to make connections with his Japanese heritage, he visits the settlement camp. He discovers his own people are alien; he can't understand the language. He belongs nowhere.

Even within the camp, families are divided. Some young Japanese rebel against the camp as a violation of their democratic rights as U.S. citizens; others prefer unquestioning support of the government, even to the point of joining the military. Others, especially the older generation, merely want to quietly get through the indignity and return to their lives.

Ehrlich's imagery suits the theme of disruption. Unlike many western novels, the local landscape is not necessarily at harmony with itself; even Heart Mountain seems not to belong:

> Nothing about it resembled a heart. It was, instead, a broken horn or a Cubist breast, as McKay's mother had once remarked. . .Forty million years ago Heart Mountain broke off from the Rockies and skidded twenty-five miles on a detachment fault to its present site. There was no other limestone in the area like it. . .

To this torn landscape Ehrlich brings her California background as sea imagery, certainly unusual for a Wyoming ranching novel. McKay's parents have drowned, his mother's hair floating like seagrass. Pinky, McKay's cowhand, walks through grass as though swimming. A feeding wagon leaves a line of hay that looks like a boat's wake.

Ehrlich's awareness of loss and disorientation within the Wyoming landscape may well come from within. She discovered the Wyoming people and environment when she was enduring her own personal tragedy. Her recovery is discussed in her book of essays, *The Solace of Open Spaces*, published in 1985. The novel grew slowly during her time of adjustment and recuperation. She began her fiction with a series of short stories, published as *Wyoming Stories* in a back-to-back book with Edward Hoagland. The stories are actually densely packed character studies which served as anchors for the novel, *Heart Mountain*. Many of these characters echo people described in her essays. In *The Solace of Open Spaces*, Ehrlich mentions the retarded boy sometimes hired around the ranches; this character becomes Willard in her fiction. Interestingly, this retarded mute character is one of the few people in the novel able to find connections, a sort of harmony, between his environment and the activities around him.

The short stories, which appear almost intact within the novel, provide an intriguing look at how Ehrlich may work to develop a character. Without the surrounding dressing of the novel's themes and plot, her use of landscape and detail particularly shines. Similar links between her essays and fiction also provide interesting resonances within the body of her work.

Yet it is within her novel that Ehrlich's writing is most startling, partly because of the subject matter within the setting. Rarely has World War II literature successfully reached into the rural West and created a microcosm; Ehrlich has done so. She brings the world chaos into focus; by the conclusion, we understand that there are no winners of a war, but only survivors left in various stages of healing. The Japanese leave the camp to return to homes which may no longer exist. Husbands and brothers, wounded physicallly or emotionally, return to Wyoming from overseas and try to renew lives. McKay, going through his own healing processes, takes a ride:

> The errant bomb had gone, the hard carapace, the shrapnel—all behind him. What lay ahead?
>
> He came on a deadfall, a ruin of pines and spruce lying across each other, midsections broken, torn roots lifted into air, and the slender lighter limbs crosshatched in a rotting canopy over his head. He and the horse threaded a way through, picked up the tracks, and followed them to a clearing.

Such a clearing provides space for the eyes to refocus, reinterpret familiar surroundings. Ehrlich has successfully provided such a vision for the reader of *Heart Mountain*.

—Marian Blue

EHRLICH, Jack (John Gunther Ehrlich). American. Born 6 April 1930. Educated at Colorado State College, 1948; Denver University, 1949; Syracuse University, New York, A.B. 1952; Brooklyn Law School, LL.B. 1962. Served in the United States Air Force Reserve, 1952–54: Captain. Married Rickie Vernon (divorced); one son and one daughter. Reporter, *Newsday*, New York, 1955–60, and New York *Herald Tribune*. Lawyer: Chief Prosecutor-Investigator District Attorney, Suffolk County, New York. Recipient: National Association of Home Builders News Reporting prize. Agent: Theron Raines, Raines and Raines, 475 Fifth Avenue, New York, New York 10017. Address: 145 Oakside Drive, Smithtown, New York 11787, U.S.A.

WESTERN PUBLICATIONS

Novels

The Fastest Gun in the Pulpit. New York, Pocket Books, 1972; London, Hale, 1974.

The Laramie River Crossing. New York, Pocket Books, 1973.

The Chatham Killing. New York, Pocket Books, 1976.
Rebellion at Cripple Creek. New York, Pocket Books, 1979.

OTHER PUBLICATIONS

Novels

Revenge. New York, Dell, 1958.
Court-Martial. New York, Pyramid, 1959.
Parole. New York, Dell, 1960.
Slow Burn. New York, Dell, 1961.
Cry, Baby. New York, Dell, 1962.
The Girl Cage. New York, Dell, 1967.
Close Combat. New York, Pocket Books, 1969.
The Drowning. New York, Pocket Books, 1970; London, Hale, 1972.
Bloody Vengeance. New York, Pocket Books, 1973.

*

Jack Ehrlich comments:

Introduce my westerns . . . I've tried to do two things in these books. One, accuracy instead of myth as to the people, the horses, the way of life, and the land itself. Horses are dumb critters, so dumb they make jackasses brilliant by comparison. And a lot of the heroes were much the same. I believe that without the courage that comes from a bottle, the Indians would still reign supreme and the OK Corral would not have made it big. The Old West had no deodorants and precious little perfume, and 60 years after the frontier was officially closed, we still used coleman lanterns and kerosene and bathed Saturday nights in an old tub in the kitchen. The rest of the week was odoriferous. I try to show things as they were, warts and all, but the physical descriptions are accurate. I've ridden and hunted the land and I can tell you that the Grand Tetons *are* snow-covered in August. But the snow is too dirty to eat or boil down for coffee, and I've tried to paint these things as they are.

* * *

Jack Ehrlich has written only a few Westerns, but each of his books is entertaining and unique. In *The Fastest Gun in the Pulpit* a wanted outlaw, Ernie Parsons, takes on the identity of a murdered preacher and becomes not only an effective minister for the town of Castle Rock, Colorado, but its savior as well. He is not entirely comfortable in his role, and the book derives a good bit of humor from the contrast between Parson's spicy speech and his position as a man of God. Even more humorous is *Rebellion at Cripple Creek.* This book is essentially a tall tale in the Paul Bunyan vein. Denny O'Toole organizes the best gang of Irishmen ever assembled in Colorado in order to protect a silver strike, marries a girl who has whipped him with a cat-o'-nine-tails, and fights Gentleman Jim Corbett for the heavyweight championship of the world in a fight which is described round by round. All of this comes in a coherent plot, to boot. *The Laramie River Crossing,* too, has its share of humor, though of a more deadly sort. The gang of amoral outlaws assembled here has its own "code," which is broken by its leader, a man not above lying to men he has hired to make the range safe for his sheep. Trying to stir up a range war, the leader makes the mistake of underestimating the intelligence and overestimating the loyalty of his men. He soon finds himself in serious trouble and makes even more disastrous errors of judgment; various double-and triple-crosses soon lead to his demise. Perhaps Ehrlich's best book is *The Chatham Killing,* in which a town marshal tries to discover who raped and killed a young girl, no matter what the consequences to himself or his town. The book contains some fine scenes between the marshal and the judge who hears the trial and raises some interesting questions about the relationship between the Law and Justice, implying clearly that the two are not always compatible.

—Bill Crider

ELSTON, Allan Vaughan. American. Born in Kansas City, Missouri, 28 July 1887. Educated at the University of Missouri, Columbia, B.S. in civil engineering 1909. Served in the United States Army Corps of Engineers, 1917–18: Captain; in the Tank Destroyers, 1942–45: Lt. Colonel. Married Kathleen Chastain in 1919; two sons and one daughter. Railroad transitman, 1909–13; engineer, Chile Copper Company, Chuquicamata, 1913–15; cattle rancher, Barela, Colorado, 1915–17; consulting engineer, Wood Elston and Witten, Tulsa, Oklahoma, 1918–19, and Elston Axon and Russell, Springfield, Missouri, 1920–24; then freelance writer. *Died 21 October 1976.*

WESTERN PUBLICATIONS

Novels

Come Out and Fight! New York, Doubleday, 1941; Kingswood, Surrey, World's Work, 1948.
Guns on the Cimarron. Philadelphia, Macrae Smith, 1943; London, Ward Lock, 1945.
Eagle's Eye. Kingswood, Surrey, World's Work, 1943.
Hit the Saddle. Philadelphia, Macrae Smith, 1947; London, Ward Lock, 1948.
The Sheriff of San Miguel. Philadelphia, Lippincott, 1949; London, Ward Lock, 1952.
Ranch of the Roses. London, Ward Lock, 1949.
Deadline at Durango. Philadelphia, Lippincott, 1950; London, Ward Lock, 1951.
Grass and Gold. Philadelphia, Lippincott, 1951; London, Ward Lock, 1952.
Roundup on the Picketwire. Philadelphia, Lippincott, 1952; London, Ward Lock, 1953.
Saddle Up for Sunlight. Philadelphia, Lippincott, 1952; London, Ward Lock, 1953.
Stage Road to Denver. Philadelphia, Lippincott, 1953; London, Ward Lock, 1954.
Colorado Showdown. New York, Dell, 1953.
Gold Brick Range. New York, Dell, 1953.
Wagon Wheel Gap. Philadelphia, Lippincott, 1954; London, Ward Lock, 1955.
Long Lope to Lander. Philadelphia, Lippincott, 1954; London, Ward Lock, 1955.
Forbidden Valley. Philadelphia, Lippincott, 1955; London, Ward Lock, 1956.
The Wyoming Bubble. Philadelphia, Lippincott, 1955; London, Ward Lock, 1956.
The Marked Men. Philadelphia, Lippincott, 1956; London, Ward Lock, 1957.
Last Stage to Aspen. Philadelphia, Lippincott, 1956; London, Ward Lock, 1957.
Showdown. New York, Pocket Books, 1956.
Grand Mesa. Philadelphia, Lippincott, 1957; London, Ward Lock, 1958.
Rio Grande Deadline. Philadelphia, Lippincott, 1957; London, Ward Lock, 1958.

Wyoming Manhunt. Philadelphia, Lippincott, 1958; London, Ward Lock, 1959.
Gun Law at Laramie. Philadelphia, Lippincott, 1959; London, Ward Lock, 1960.
Beyond the Bitterroots. Philadelphia, Lippincott, and London, Ward Lock, 1960.
Sagebrush Serenade. Philadelphia, Lippincott, 1960; London, Ward Lock, 1961.
Timberline Bonanza. Philadelphia, Lippincott, 1961; London, Ward Lock, 1962.
Treasure Coach from Deadwood. Philadelphia, Lippincott, 1962; London, Ward Lock, 1963.
Roundup on the Yellowstone. Philadelphia, Lippincott, 1962; London, Ward Lock, 1963.
The Seven Silver Mountain. New York, Berkley, 1964; London, Ward Lock, 1965.
The Landseekers. Philadelphia, Lippincott, and London, Ward Lock, 1964.
The Lawless Border. New York, Berkley, 1966.
Montana Passage. New York, Berkley, 1967; London, Ward Lock, 1968.
Montana Manhunt. New York, Berkley, 1967; London, Hale, 1974.
Arizona Skyline. New York, Berkley, 1969; London, Hale, 1971.
Paradise Prairie. New York, Berkley, 1971; London, Hale, 1973.
The Big Pasture. London, Hale, 1972; New York, Berkley, 1976.
Saddle Up for Steamboat. New York, Curtis, 1973.

Uncollected Short Stories

"Peepsight Shoots High," in *The Frontier* (New York), June 1925.
"Triggers in Leash," in *The Frontier* (New York), July 1925.
"The Cup of the Mesas," in *The Frontier* (New York), August 1925.
"Relinquishments," in *Argosy* (New York), 29 August 1925.
"The Bullet on the Hearth," in *The Frontier* (New York), September 1925.
"The Mettle of the Range," in *The Frontier* (New York), October 1925.
"The Gray-Green Hill," in *The Frontier* (New York), July 1926.
"The Jack-Pot," in *The Frontier* (New York), August 1926.
"On the Volcano's Rim," in *The Frontier* (New York), September 1926.
"Pirates of the Pampa," in *The Frontier* (New York), October 1926.
"The Heel of Achilles," in *The Frontier* (New York), January 1927.
"The Drylanders," in *The Frontier* (New York), February 1927.
"The Challenge of the Range," in *The Frontier* (New York), March 1927.
"Down Around Wagon Mound," in *The Frontier* (New York), April 1927.
"Down on the Picketwire," in *The Frontier* (New York), August 1927.
"The Perfect Witness," in *West* (New York), 8 October 1927.
"Blood on the Butcherblock," in *The Frontier* (New York), December 1927.
"Red for Rogues," in *Adventure* (New York), 15 January 1928.
"Squad One," in *The Frontier* (New York), March 1928.
"Muley Blacks," in *West* (New York), 7 April 1928.
"The E-Town Stampede," in *The Frontier* (New York), May 1928.
"The Vanishing Vandal," in *Adventure* (New York), 1 June 1928.
"The Spoon Trail," in *West* (New York), 8 September 1928.
"Table Stakes," in *Adventure* (New York), 1 November 1928.
"All on One Show-Down," in *Complete Story* (New York), 2 November 1928.
"A Night in Gyp Buttes," in *Adventure* (New York), 1 January 1929.
"Four Miles an Hour," in *Romance* (New York), February 1929.
"The Road to Sandoval," in *Adventure* (New York), 1 February 1929.
"A Matter of Courage," in *Complete Story* (New York), 2 February 1929.
"Champion's Choice," in *West* (New York), 29 May 1929.
"The Ranch on Red River," in *Adventure* (New York), 1 July 1929.
"Justice of the Range," in *Adventure* (New York), 1 September 1929.
"No Holds Barred," in *Adventure* (New York), 1 October 1929.
"Mystery Lake," in *Adventure* (New York), 15 December 1929.
"Mystery Mountain," in *Adventure* (New York), 1 February 1930.
"The Show-Down at Fyffe's," in *Argosy* (New York), 26 July 1930.
"Bait for Bullets," in *Complete Story* (New York), 15 November 1931.
"Treed Treasure," in *Adventure* (New York), 1 March 1932.
"The Thief of Taos," in *Argosy* (New York), 19 March 1932.
"The Strayman," in *Complete Story* (New York), 1 May 1932.
"Rogue's Parade," in *Argosy* (New York), 30 July 1932.
"The Crystal Ball," in *Complete Story* (New York), 1 August 1932.
"The Grapevine Telegraph," in *Adventure* (New York), 15 March 1933.
"The Magic Brush," in *West* (New York), June 1933.
"Black Mesa," in *Complete Story* (New York), 15 August 1933.
"Mystery Camp," in *Argosy* (New York), 25 November 1933.
"Fool's Fire," in *Complete Story* (New York), 1 March 1934.
"Badge of Honor," in *Argosy* (New York), 16 February 1935.
"The Lavender Lamp," in *Argosy* (New York), 30 March 1935.
"Half-Million Murder," in *Argosy* (New York), 28 September–5 October 1935.
"North Star," in *Argosy* (New York), 28 December 1935.
"The Pathfinders," in *Argosy* (New York), 6 June 1936.
"On Patrol," in *Argosy* (New York), 22 August 1936.
"The Howling Wilderness," in *Argosy* (New York), 17 October 1936.
"Two and Two Is Four," in *Argosy* (New York), 5 February 1938.
"Campaign Promise," in *Argosy* (New York), 4 June 1938.
"Death Due North," in *Argosy* (New York), 21 January 1939.
"Mutiny on the Box Cross," in *Western Story* (London), August 1940.
"The Silver Spoon," in *West* (Kingswood, Surrey), January 1948.
"This Water Is Mine," in *Thrilling Ranch Stories* (London), October 1948.
"Sheriff's Wife," in *American Magazine* (Springfield, Ohio), May 1950.
"The Lost Arrow," in *West* (Kingswood, Surrey), June 1953.
"Ghost Town," in *Wild Streets*, edited by Don Ward. Boston, Houghton Mifflin, 1956.
"Message Delayed," in *Branded Men*, edited by Don Ward. Boston, Houghton Miflin, 1956.
"Dark Trail," in *Hound Dogs and Others*, edited by Jim Kjelgaard. New York, Dodd Mead, 1958.

"Caballero Alegre," in *Rawhide Men*, edited by Kenneth Fowler. New York, Double-day, 1965.
"Dead Man's Alegre," in *Great Western Stories*. New York, Berkley, 1965.
"The Trailsman," in *A Quintet of Sixes*, edited by Donald Wollheim. New York, Ace, 1969.

OTHER PUBLICATIONS

Novels

Pacific Passage. London, Wells Gardner, 1942.
Lost Harbours. Kingswood, Surrey, World's Work, 1947.

* * *

Authenticity is the key to the work of Allan Vaughan Elston, whose background settings are often culled from newspaper cuttings and other contemporary accounts of western history. Invariably a precise date is given to the action, and a sense of place established in many of his titles—*Guns on the Cimarron*, *Deadline at Durango*, and *Last Stage to Aspen* are three examples among many. At its best, as in his description of the 1886–87 "big freeze" in *Montana Manhunt*, this factual background gives a definite conviction to his novels, which are further strengthened by some skilful plots. *Treasure Coach from Deadwood*, based on an actual robbery in 1878, involves an intricate system of codes and mirror-readings which the criminals use to pass "inside information," and makes for a compelling read. The murder mystery element surfaces often in his writing, sometimes with one crime setting another in motion. In *Roundup on the Yellowstone* a crooked rancher murders his blackmailer, while in *Montana Manhunt* a dying outlaw's loot drives a respectable lawyer to murder. *Paradise Prairie* centres on a kidnapping by criminals who use their captives to blackmail another murderer, again a lawyer.

Plot and authenticity are Elston's strengths. His style tends to be flat and unremarkable, and most of his characters lack the actuality of their setting. He also has a disconcerting habit of fixing the reader's attention on the villian in the opening chapter, prior to his crime—as is the case in both *Yellowstone* and *Montana Manhunt*—and abruptly switching to the hero, who makes a delayed entrance. The success of his work is varied. *Gun Law at Laramie*, for instance, falls into two halves which do not quite interlock. The adventures of Dan Logan as a boy in Laramie in 1868, and as a man 10 years later, are in effect two separate stories. Among his most convincing efforts are *Paradise Prairie* and *Montana Manhunt*. In the former, Elston ably follows his hero Kent Durwin in his discovery of a faked "Indian massacre" in Oregon, and his subsequent kidnapping and escape from white renegades. The latter, where lawyer Emmett Thorpe kills a rancher to secure stolen money, only to be brought to justice by the man's heir, is memorable mainly for the superb description of the bitter Montana winter. *Treasure Coach from Deadwood*, which combines a complex plot with some brisk, sustained action, is another worthy contender.

—Jeff Sadler

ERDMAN, Loula Grace. American. Born in Missouri. Educated at Central Missouri State College, B.A. 1931; Columbia University, New York, M.A. 1941; University of Wisconsin, Madison; University of California, Los Angeles; West Texas State College, (later University), Canyon. English school teacher, Amarillo, Texas; Assistant Professor, then Associate Professor of English, 1945–65, and novelist-in-residence, 1963–76, West Texas State University. Recipient: Dodd Mead-*Redbook* award, 1946; *American Girl*-Dodd Mead award, 1952. *Died 20 June 1976.*

WESTERN PUBLICATIONS

Novels

The Years of the Locust. New York, Dodd Mead, 1947; London, Hodder and Stoughton, 1948.
Lonely Passage. New York, Dodd Mead, 1948; London, Hodder and Stoughton, 1950.
The Edge of Time. New York, Dodd Mead, 1950; London, Hodder and Stoughton, 1951.
My Sky Is Blue. New York, Longman, 1953.
Three at the Wedding. New York, Dodd Mead, 1953; London, Hodder and Stoughton, 1954.
The Far Journey. New York, Dodd Mead, 1955; London, Hodder and Stoughton, 1956.
The Short Summer. New York, Dodd Mead, 1958; London, Hodder and Stoughton, 1959.
Many a Voyage. New York, Dodd Mead, 1960; London, Hodder and Stoughton, 1962.
Another Spring. New York, Dodd Mead, 1966.

Short Stories

The Man Who Told the Truth. New York, Dodd Mead, 1962.
A Wonderful Thing and Other Stories. New York, Dodd Mead, 1964.

OTHER PUBLICATIONS

Other

Separate Star (for children). New York, Longman, 1944.
Fair Is the Morning (for children). New York, Longman, 1945.
The Wind Blows Free (for children). New York, Dodd Mead, 1952; London, Hodder and Stoughton, 1955.
The Wide Horizon (for children). New York, Dodd Mead, 1956; London, Hodder and Stoughton, 1957.
The Good Land (for children). New York, Dodd Mead, 1959; London, Hodder and Stoughton, 1960.
Room to Grow (for children). New York, Dodd Mead, 1962.
Life Was Simpler Then. New York, Dodd Mead, 1963; London, Hodder and Stoughton, 1964.
A Time to Write. New York, Dodd Mead, 1969.
A Bluebird (for children). New York, Dodd Mead, 1973.
Save Weeping for Night (for children). New York, Dodd Mead, 1975.

*

Critical Study: *Loula Grace Erdman* by Ernestine P. Sewell, Austin, Texas, Steck Vaughn, 1970.

* * *

The decade of the 1980's has seen severe reduction in the number of books by Loula Grace Erdman in print, from seven in 1982 to only one in 1990. Her output is widely available in libraries, however, especially school libraries, primarily because Erdman has been truly a popular writer but also because of the suitability of her works to young people. Several of the novels were directed specifically toward such an audience. Any reader, however, who wants a realistic presentation of the permanent settlement and development of Erdman's part of the West will find much that is satisfying in the steady concentration on daily life in a harsh, unformed land, a depiction that accurately reflects what the lives of the early settlers must have been. Erdman's philosophy was similar to that of William Dean Howells, who held that realism in writing consists more in truthful presentation of the common, the usual, the more "smiling aspects" of life than in the bizarre and unusual. This is not to say that Erdman's characters never experience violence, injustice, thwarting of hopes, for they do: the range of human emotions is complete. Absent, however, is the sensational, bizarre action which frequently dominates Westerns and raises corresponding action and feeling in the characters.

Erdman's novels, set as they are in the Texas Panhandle during the settlement and early development of the region, focus upon the characters' struggles with the hardships of existing in and bringing a measure of civilization into an inhospitable land. There are no bad men from Bodie. The enemies are less sensational but fully as formidable in their own fashion: drought, loneliness, boredom with too few means of release, blizzards, prairie fires—in short, what Erdman's research showed her were the chief hardships of pioneer daily life in her part of the West. The hardships were tempered by hopes and aspirations, of course, and frequently by their attainment. The ultimate achievement of happiness and comfort overshadows the occasional failure.

The center of consciousness in the novels, with rare exceptions, is a woman. As a result the novels lean toward action and events that might be called domestic in that the thoughts and feelings of women predominate. There is much on the routine of daily life: making a home in a cramped half-dugout; the dangers and hardships of a woman's travelling alone cross-country in a wagon; cooking and eating with its necessary make-do; nursing the sick with inadequate knowledge, time, and medicine; helping fight prairie fires which threaten everything in their path; outfacing evil-intentioned male intruders through sheer moral courage. The two chief concerns of the women are family and community, with unremitting struggle toward making them both better and stronger. Erdman viewed the prospering, established home, the school, and the church as the fruits of the battle to conquer the plains.

Previous to the publication of *Lonely Passage* Erdman had written from her own experiences. About that time she turned to wholehearted and thorough research on the history of her adopted region with the intention of treating it fictionally. The result was a series of novels on the settlement and gradual development of the Panhandle region. The first was her best, *The Edge of Time*. The action covers a one-year span in a couple's life as homesteaders in the Panhandle during the early 1880's. The center of consciousness is, of course, the wife Bethany. The novel is significantly titled; Erdman's part of the West was on the edge of one "time" which was to give way to a new one featuring the march of civilization. Only a few years earlier the land had been the domain of nomadic Indians and buffalo; shortly after the time of the novel the railroads came with their concomitant flood of settlers. But for Bethany and Wade, transplanted into this strange new world from the Midwest, everything was new.

They have horses and a plow for farming, a few cows for breed stock and one for milking, bare housekeeping utensils for their dugout, a rose bush rooting brought by Bethany, and immense confidence in themselves and in the future. Readers have confidence along with them, but the harsh surroundings and living conditions make even this valorous pair falter at times. Three other women figure in the novel as foils to Bethany and as symbols of the lives and fate of many of the pioneers. One waits passively for the next move West that she knows her husband will insist upon; one sickens and dies as a victim of the land; one cannot accept the conditions of settlement and finally persuades her husband to move them back East—but Bethany and Wade stay on.

Following *The Edge of Time* came a series of three related novels treating Panhandle life during the two decades surrounding the turn of the century: *The Wind Blows Free*, *The Wide Horizon*, and *The Good Land*. Western aficionados will find these less satisfying than *The Edge of Time* because of the adolescent central character in each, the growing urbanization of the region, and the use of events, details, and motifs already used in other Erdman novels.

The Far Journey as a Western ranks above the trilogy but short of *The Edge of Time*. It tells of a young woman reared as a southern belle who marries a "common" Midwesterner. Worse yet, he hears the siren song of the West and wants to answer it. The wife, Catherine, tries to hold him to storekeeping, but when he goes anyway she decides to follow him—in a wagon, with only an alcoholic uncle for guidance and protection. When the uncle gets killed by runaway horses the ignorant but resourceful Catherine finds herself alone on the prairie with a decision: whether to push on or to return home. Because she is a true Erdman heroine she struggles on through myriad adversities to her goal—the Texas Panhandle town of Mobeetie, where she will be united with her husband.

Bare summaries make Erdman's novels sound trite and repetitious. They are neither. Her Westerns provide authentic pictures of the time and place depicted without either undue sensationalism or treacly sentimentality. Erdman set out to write the truth about the settlement of her region—and she did it.

—Don R. Swadley

ERDRICH, Louise. American (part Chippewa Indian). Born in Little Falls, Minnesota, 7 June 1954. Educated at Dartmouth College, Hanover, New Hampshire, B.A. 1976; Johns Hopkins University, Baltimore, Maryland, M.A. 1977. Married Michael Dorris, *q.v.*, in 1981; three sons and three daughters. Recipient: Nelson Algren award, for story, 1982; National Book Critics Circle award, 1984; Virginia Sully prize, 1984; Sue Kaufman award, 1984; Los Angeles Times book award, 1985. Address: c/o Harper and Row, 10 East 53rd Street, New York, New York 10022, U.S.A.

WESTERN PUBLICATIONS

Novels

Love Medicine. New York, Holt, 1984; London, Deutsch, 1985.

The Beet Queen. New York, Holt, 1986; London, Hamilton, 1987.

Tracks. New York, Holt, and London, Hamilton, 1988.

Crown of Columbus, with Michael Dorris. New York and London, Harper Collins, 1991.

OTHER PUBLICATIONS

Verse

Jacklight. New York, Holt, 1984; London, Sphere, 1990.
Baptism of Desire. New York, Harper, 1991.

* * *

Louise Erdrich has written four related novels (*Love Medicine*, *The Beet Queen*, *Tracks*, and *American Horse* which has yet to appear), which have a common setting and interrelated families. She and her husband Michael Dorris (author of *A Yellow Raft in Blue Water*), who also has American Indian ancestry, always work collaboratively, although usually only one author is credited.

Erdrich's novels, with the exception of *The Beet Queen*, which uses her German-American origins, all draw on her Chippewa Indian ancestry. Based on the North Dakota Indian reservations and small towns of her childhood, her settings are bleak and poverty-stricken, but her characters' inner lives and secret compulsions are vivid and absorbing. She uses an interlocking set of families, the Pillagers, Morrisseys, and Kashpaws, over several generations, so that each novel throws more light on the past, and on her characters' motivations, in the manner of William Faulkner's treatment of the families of Yoknapatawpha County. The political and economic exploitation of the Chippewa or Ojibway Indians is a constant backdrop to the personal dramas, as Indian land is steadily sold off. Allotment policy, in the early years of this century, meant that tribal land was split up and divided among the members of the tribe. Poverty and debt led to mortgages, foreclosures, and the loss of the Indians' land base, and the increasing difficulty of continuing to live in traditional ways. The steady increase of the urban Indian population is also reflected in her characters' trips to the "Twin Cities" of Minneapolis and St. Paul.

Erdrich's characters are driven by memories and visions rather than surface rationality, and the past, expressing itself through family relationships is something that we, and they, have to reconstruct and come to terms with. Fleur Pillager, in *Tracks*, for instance is described as not knowing which world she lived in, "this place of reservation surveys [and white control] or the other place, boundless, where the dead sit talking." In presenting such characters Erdrich is at pains to situate us in the same mythic world, so that we have to accept that Fleur drowned twice and is still alive. Her style has been called postmodern, because of its rejection of realist certainties and normal time-sequences, but it is perhaps more relevant to see her work as an attempt to blend the oral storytelling traditions of the Indians—in which myth and history merge into each other—with the Modernist novelistic conventions of Faulkner. This corresponds to her political aims, of showing the complexity and validity of Indian communities without either idealising or demeaning them.

In *Love Medicine*, the best way into her themes, she takes two twin brothers of the Kashpaw family, and uses the different directions of their lives to explore the diversity and difficulty of ways of being Indian in the 20th century. Nector Kashpaw is taken away to a government boarding school, while Eli is kept hidden in a cellar by his mother, who in this way, as she says, has a son "on either side of the line." Nector literally plays the Indian for whites, even working in Hollywood, but discovers that "Death was the extent of Indian acting in the movie theater." Because of the traditional importance of the Kashpaw family he becomes a tribal chairman, but this involves endless compromises with land-hungry whites and government officials. The contradictions of his life come to a head when as chairman he has to evict from her land his mistress Lulu, so that a factory can be built to make tourist items such as tomahawks. In her unconventional and life-embracing ways Lulu represents many of the traditional (to whites "backward") aspects of the Indians, in contrast to his wife, Marie, who wants respectability. His brother Eli also offers a contrast, living in the woods as a hunter and trapper. The younger generation have to steer their own path between these extremes, and one of Erdrich's recurrent themes is the extent of the continuing usefulness of traditional spiritual values. Nector's grandson Lipsha, for instance, tries to create a "love medicine" to keep his grandfather from straying from his wife, but, unable to get the heart of a wild goose, is reduced to using frozen turkey heart from the supermarket. This comic scene, though, which seems to suggest that past ways are irretrievable, has to be set against the tenacity with which such beliefs hold on, if only in reaction to the dismal and racist version of Christianity on offer from Catholic nuns. Lipsha comes to the conclusion that "Since the Old Testament, God's been deafening up on us." The many Indian Gods "aren't perfect, is what I'm saying, but at least they come around . . . if you ask them right." Lipsha's ability to bridge past and present is characteristic of Erdrich's fictional enterprise. In a scene which recurs throughout modern Indian fiction he finds his own identity by finding out whom his relatives are. In this case he identifies his father, who has become an Indian activist, on the run from the police, and the book reflects, in this final merging of the politically radical and culturally conservative, the paradoxes of American Indian politics.

—David Murray

ERMINE, Will. *See* **DRAGO, Harry Sinclair.**

ERNENWEIN, Leslie. American. Born in Oneida, New York, c.1900. Married; one daughter. Worked as telegraph operator with Postal Telegraph; telegraph editor for a New York daily; painter and member of Art Students' League, New York City; cowhand in various parts of United States; managing editor, Schenectady *Sun*; writer, Tucson *Daily Citizen*. Settled in Tucson, Arizona, 1938. Editor, Western Writers of America *Round-up*, 1954–61. Recipient: Western Writers of America Spur award, 1956. *Died 19 December 1961.*

WESTERN PUBLICATIONS

Novels

Gunsmoke Galoot. New York, Phoenix Press, 1941; London, Partridge, 1946.
Kinkaid of Red Butte. New York, Phoenix Press, 1942; London, Pictorial Art, 1946; as *Kinkaid*, New York, Belmont, 1975.
Boss of Panamint. New York, Phoenix Press, 1942; London, Ward Lock, 1944.
The Faro Kid. New York, Phoenix Press, 1944; London, Quality Press, 1946.
Bullet Breed. New York, McBride, 1946; London, Ward Lock, 1948.

Rio Renegade. New York, McBride, 1946; London, Ward Lock, 1947.
Rebels Ride Proudly. New York, Dutton, 1947; London, Foulsham, 1950; as *Trigger Justice*, New York, New American Library, 1949.
Rebel Yell. New York, Dutton, 1948; London, Foulsham, 1949.
Horseshoe Combine. New York, Dutton, 1949; London, Foulsham, 1950.
Ambush at Jubilo Junction. New York, Dutton, 1950; London, Foulsham, 1951.
Renegade Ramrod. Kingston, New York, Quinn, 1950; London, Kelly, 1953; as *Big T Ramrod*, New York, Arcadia House, 1955.
Gunfighter's Return. New York, Fawcett, 1950; London, Fawcett, 1954.
Gunsmoke. New York, New American Library, 1950.
Gunhawk Harvest. New York, Dutton, 1951; London, Foulsham, 1952; as *Gun Hawk*, New York, Graphic, 1952.
The Texas Gun. New York, Fawcett, 1951; London, Fawcett, 1954.
Hell for Leather. New York, New American Library, 1951.
Savage Justice. Toronto, Harlequin, 1952.
Give a Man a Gun. New York, Fawcett, 1952; London, Fawcett, 1953.
Mystery Rider. New York, Fawcett, 1953; London, Fawcett, 1954.
Rampage. New York, Fawcett, 1954; London, Fawcett, 1955.
Bullet Barricade. New York, Fawcett, 1955; London, Fawcett, 1956.
Hell-Town in Texas. New York, Avon, 1955.
Texas Guns. New York, Graphic, 1956.
High Gun. New York, Fawcett, 1956; London, Fawcett, 1958.
The Gun-Hung Men. New York, Lion, 1957.
Ramrod from Hell. New York, Popular Library, 1958; London, Corgi, 1959.
Warrior Basin. New York, Doubleday, 1959.
Rampage West. Derby, Connecticut, Monarch, 1963.
The Way They Died. New York, Belmont, 1978.

Uncollected Short Stories

"Buzzard Bait for Broken Bow," in *Star Western* (Chicago), March 1941.
"Killer's Code," in *Wild West* (New York), 19 April 1941.
"Gallows Ghost," in *Wild West* (New York), 22 August 1942.
"A Gun-Ghost's Rebel Fights in Hell!," in *Star Western* (Chicago), September 1944.
"Bullet Miracle at the Circle S," in *Star Western* (Chicago), July 1945.
"Border Breed," in *Thrilling Western* (London), Autumn 1946.
"Lawman's Last Chore," in *Exciting Western* (London), June 1951.
"No Peace for Prodigal," in *Exciting Western* (London), February 1952.
"Pistol Pride," in *Texas Rangers* (London), February 1952.
"Comical on a Clown," in *Texas Rangers* (London), April 1952.
"Renegade Romeo," in *Texas Rangers* (London), May 1952.
"Trail Hand," in *Bad Men and Good*, edited by Luke Short. New York, Dodd Mead, 1953.
"Tinhorn Hero," in *Texas Rangers* (London), May 1954.
"Boomtown Babe," in *Western Story* (London), May 1958.
"Too Hot for Blondes!," in *Western Story* (London), March–April 1960.
"Shiftless Slow," in *Western Roundup*, edited by Nelson Nye. New York, Macmillan, 1961.
"Storm Rope," in *They Won Their Spurs*, edited by Nelson Nye. New York, Avon, 1962.

* * *

There is an Old West of the mind where Evil is absolute, society has no power, and Good is held dear by only an embattled few; a Manichean landscape of blindest night and blinding day, where there is no temperate climate but only a season of extremes. This is the land where gunfighters reign supreme, where women hold all wisdom hidden in their eyes, where the language is that of "galoots" and "six-gun smokeroos," where once-brave men are shackled rather than protected by the law. This is the Mythic West: the American version of the medieval morality play.

This is also the Old West of Leslie Ernenwein, one of the wandering minstrels of this mythic land. A reader can have no doubt as to which West he is visiting when, in an early novel, *Boss of Panamint*, Ernenwein begins, "They were a strange trio, these three who halted dust-peppered broncs on the rimrock above Apache Tank. They were entirely dissimilar in face and form, yet they were marked by one common brand—the renegade brand of the gunsmoke breed," nor when, years later, the lead line in the novel *Bullet Barricade* states, "This was Sonora, with moon's shadowless sun scorching the high-walled slot of the Barranca Prieta, where one man crouched behind a scabrous rock reef while another man lay groaning on the ground." Ernenwein's characters seem blown by the winds of chance, pawns for the Fates, or as one protagonist, Clay Quantrelle of *Renegade Ramrod*, states it: "What good was if for a man to strive against the strong tide of circumstance? Dame Fortune had stacked the cards at the start and a man had to play them the way they were dealt. Or so it seemed." In such a fatalistic world, the purpose for the strong is to challenge Evil and hopefully beat the house odds. For the weak there is no other choice but getting thrown from the game.

Ernenwein's stories, then, are allegories—light against dark, good against evil—with a single bullet-weary everyman striving to stamp out injustice before it does the same to him. Because of this allegorical focus, however, Ernenwein's early stories often suffer. The plots are too similar, the characters flat, the images repeated and the style itself—due to that mythical urgency—clichéd and unfortunately ludicrous at times (one example being the constant use and reuse of the phrase "thrusting need" to describe the hero's attraction for the heroine). In his later works, however, Ernenwein has learned: the characters show more depth, and, more important to his roots, the plots often resonate with the issues he invokes. *Bullet Barricade*, for example, begins at the climax of one story, takes us through a second, and implies at the end the beginning of a third. This is what Ernenwein is shooting for stylistically: a celebration of the wide open spaces, and an affirmation that men's lives are not encapsulated within cruel tales of Fate over which they have no control.

—Joe Jackson

ERTZ, Susan. British. Born in Walton-on-Thames, Surrey, in 1894. Educated privately in England, 1901–06, and in California, 1906–12. Married John Ronald McCrindle in 1932 (died 1977). Undertook war work in England and France during World War I. Fellow, Royal Society of Literature. *Died 11 April 1985.*

WESTERN PUBLICATIONS

Novel

The Proselyte. London, Hodder and Stoughton, and New York, Appleton Century, 1933.

OTHER PUBLICATIONS

Novels

Madame Claire. London, Unwin, and New York, Appleton, 1923.
Nina. London, Unwin, and New York, Appleton, 1924.
After Noon. London, Unwin, and New York, Appleton, 1926.
Now East, Now West. London, Benn, and New York, Appleton, 1927.
The Galaxy. London, Hodder and Stoughton, and New York, Appleton, 1929.
Julian Probert. London, Hodder and Stoughton, 1931; as *The Story of Julian*, New York, Appleton, 1931.
Now We Set Out. London, Hodder and Stoughton, 1934; New York, Appleton Century, 1935.
Woman Alive. London, Hodder and Stoughton, 1935; New York, Appleton Century, 1936.
No Hearts to Break. London, Hodder and Stoughton, and New York, Appleton Century, 1937.
One Fight More. New York, Appleton Century, 1939; London, Hodder and Stoughton, 1940.
Anger in the Sky. London, Hodder and Stoughton, and New York, Harper, 1943.
Two Names under the Shore. London, Hodder and Stoughton, 1947; as *Mary Hallam*, New York, Harper, 1947.
The Prodigal Heart. London, Hodder and Stoughton, and New York, Harper, 1950.
The Undefended Gate. London, Hodder and Stoughton, 1953; as *Invitation to Folly*, New York, Harper, 1953.
Charmed Circle. London, Collins, and New York, Harper, 1956.
In the Cool of the Day. New York, Harper, 1960; London, Collins, 1961.
Devices and Desires. London, Collins, 1972; as *Summer's Lease*, New York, Harper, 1972.
The Philosopher's Daughter. London, Collins, and New York, Harper, 1976.

Short Stories

And Then Face to Face and Other Stories. London, Unwin, 1927; as *The Wind of Complication*, New York, Appleton, 1927.
Big Frogs and Little Frogs. London, Hodder and Stoughton, 1938; New York, Harper, 1939.

Other

Black, White and Caroline (for children). London, Hodder and Stoughton, and New York, Appleton Century, 1938.

* * *

It is instructive in considering Susan Ertz as a "Western" writer also to consider the protean nature of western writing, taken as a whole; for Ertz would never be considered primarily as a writer of Westerns, at least in any conventional sense. Those who love to categorize might (if they felt condescending) pass over her work as "sentimental"; more sympathetic observers would place her writing generally in the tradition of the "novel of manners," more specifically within the sub-category of "stories of country life." Literary critics of a feminist bent might point out that her fiction has a curious relevance today: for her basic plots reiterate, in different fictional guises, a common thematic structure. Put in general terms, her stories normally deal with the plight of a young woman who is thrust out on her own from a sheltered environment into a vaguely hostile external world with which she is initially unprepared to cope. Her coming to terms with this hostile world provides the fictional interest of Ertz's novels. Significantly, "endurance" (much in the sense in which William Faulkner used the term) is the quality required for success in Ertz's imaginative world.

The adaptability of western writing is nowhere more evident than in the one major novel, *The Proselyte*, in which Ertz translates her basic concerns into a purely western idiom. The proselyte of the title, a young English girl named Zillah Purdy, is converted to Mormonism and ultimately, on the promise of "marching to Zion," taken to America and finally to Salt Lake City. The novel chronicles Zillah's successive disillusionments with the journey to Zion (which, in complete contrast to her initial expectations, is fraught with hardship and peril), with Zion itself (Salt Lake City is not in reality at all what her dreams of Zion had led her to anticipate), and with the hard tenets of Mormonism. A less sure author would have used this framework as a frame for a sentimental statement of how the cruel world heartlessly destroys the happiness of a sweet and innocent young heroine. Ertz is made of sterner stuff. As she tells the story, Zillah's increasing awareness of the hardships of *this* world lead her to a greater understanding of the promises of the *next*. Salt Lake City becomes, by the novel's conclusion, not Zion itself but only an imperfect representation of that heavenly Zion for which, unbeknownst to her, Zillah has always really yearned.

The Proselyte, then, is in many ways directly within the main tradition of western writing. From Cooper's Natty Bumppo on, the west has traditionally represented some ultimate reality beyond its concrete representations; often the "way west" has been conceived as a journey best described in terms of deprivation; and to the tough minded, the flaws of the present have forcefully implied the perfection of the future.

—James K. Folsom

ESSEX, Saran. British. Born in West Bromwich, West Midlands, 31 December 1948. Educated at Crew Road School, Old Park Road School, and Kings Hill School, all Wednesbury, West Midlands. Married Colin Raymond Aldridge in 1983. Office worker, GKN Sankey, Bilston, West Midlands, 1965–68, and Walsh Graham, Wednesbury, 1968–70; V.D.U. operator, Wednesbury, 1970–83; receptionist, 1987–88, and office worker, 1989, G. Eliot Hospital, Nuneaton, Warwickshire. Since 1990 receptionist, Dr. Shirazi, Nuneaton. Address: c/o Robert Hale Ltd., Clerkenwell House, 45–47 Clerkenwell Green, London EC1R OHT, England.

WESTERN PUBLICATIONS

Novels

Trail to Vengeance. London, Hale, 1988.
Treacherous Gun. London, Hale, 1990.

*

Saran Essex comments:

I wrote my first story when I was nine years old, and it was a Western, but it was not published. I like Westerns because I grew up with them; all my heroes were of course cowboys. There were so many western series on the television—*Rawhide*, *Maverick*, etc. I also loved actual western heroes as well as the fictional ones. Butch Cassidy and the Sundance Kid fascinated me, their whole life story is fascinating, and they are the main characters in my stories, although I try not to make them look like the good guys, and I try to show that robbery is not right. I write my stories because I like writing them, and I hope to bring pleasure to western readers.

* * *

The stars of Saran Essex's Westerns are Butch Cassidy and the Sundance Kid. In the first book, *Trail to Vengeance*, they are described as being in their late twenties; in the sequel, *Treacherous Gun*, they appear several years younger. In both books they are said to have been partners for six years.

Essex's view of Cassidy and Sundance is very much an idealised one. Butch, "the happy-go-lucky leader of the most wanted outlaw gang in the West," is painted as a rather over-sensitive, somewhat naive young man who does not enjoy doing wrong, but inside of whom lives "a free, adventurous spirit that delighted in rustling and robbing." The Sundance Kid, on the other hand, comes across as a slightly more credible outlaw character—stubborn, determined, quick-tempered, and vaguely sadistic.

Although the books have a little historical detail to set the scene, the author's view of outlaws and outlaw life is largely romanticised. There is also a tendency to overplay the relationship between the two young badmen.

In the first book, Butch is captured by a bounty hunter while sleeping off an uncharacteristically heavy bout of drinking, and used as bait to lure Sundance into a trap. During the course of the story he is whipped, beaten, and staked out beneath a merciless sun, just so that Sundance's fictitious sister Samanna can get revenge on her brother for having brought shame on the family name. *Treacherous Gun* follows much the same pattern, in that Butch again has to undergo an assortment of degradations before being used as bait to lure his partner into an ambush. This time the villain of the piece is Butch's real-life cohort, Mike Cassidy, who, having been overshadowed by his young protege, decides to turn him in to the authorities for a $15,000 bounty.

Essex favours long chapters (no more than five per book), which are generally broken up into several short scenes. Prose and plot lean towards the melodramatic, and supporting characters tend to be a little flat. The author clearly enjoys writing about the two main characters, however, and in some respects this is where the problem with the books ultimately lies.

Although the fictional Butch and Sundance are described very much like Paul Newman and Robert Redford, the two actors who played them in the famous film, there the similarity most definitely ends. Because, particularly in *Treacherous Gun*, the outlaws are depicted not so much as partners, but as *lovers*. This is obviously unintentional, since we are told at the outset that Butch has a wife, Amy, and three children, while "Sundie" (to call the Kid by Butch's rather familiar nickname) has a whole string of pretty girlfriends scattered across Wyoming. The situation is compounded, however, by a number of ill-advised scenes and some rather clumsy phrasing.

By the author's own admission, Butch and Sundance share "a bond that was stronger than that of most married couples." Whenever Sundance is endangered, Butch grows "frantic with worry." As soon as the Kid extricates himself from trouble, Butch is so relieved that he has to take "several deep breaths to steady himself."

Taken alone, of course, these examples mean little. It is quite probable that, in trying to express the youth, inexperience, and mutual admiration of the duo, Essex has created an unfortunate and totally erroneous impression. But when Butch rejects Mike Cassidy's suggestion that they go back into partnership together, he does so in the following, curiously feminine, way: "It's not that I don't care about you any more . . . You meant so much to me at one time, you even came before Amy . . . If you had not walked out on me, I would have gone on being your partner for always. But you did walk out, and things are different now; Sundance is my partner, he's my family and there ain't no-one in this world who can take his place in my life—not even you—"

Butch (and, to a lesser degree, Sundance as well) tends to shake, weep, and whimper at the slightest provocation. When Butch is told that Sundance has been murdered, for example, his first reaction is not to strap on iron and find the miscreant responsible (which, though a little hackneyed, would certainly have made for a more satisfying Western); he simply loses the will to live. Upon discovering that Sundance is still alive, he once again displays emotion: "Having Sundance beside him alive and well, and hearing the concern in his voice was suddenly all too much for Butch to handle, and a fresh flood of tears came to his eyes, almost blinding him. His breath started coming in compulsive gasps. He tried to fight it, but could not, and gave way to low, weak sobbing."

After a while, these constant displays of sentiment begin to grow a little tiring, and the end result of so much unintentional ambiguity, where supposedly tough young men sob and swoon like belles at a ball, will inevitably leave the serious Western reader with a feeling of confusion and disbelief.

—David Whitehead

ESTLEMAN, Loren D. American. Born in Ann Arbor, Michigan, 15 September 1952. Educated at Dexter community schools, Michigan, 1957–70; Eastern Michigan University, Ypsilanti, 1970–74, B.A. in English and journalism 1974. Married Carole Ann Ashley in 1987. Reporter, Ypsilanti *Press*, 1973; editor, *Community Foto-News*, Pinckney, Michigan, 1975–76; special writer, Ann Arbor *News*, 1976–77; staff writer, Dexter *Leader*, 1977–80. Recipient: Western Writers of America Spur award, 1982, 1987; Stirrup award, 1983; Michigan Arts Foundation award, 1986. Agent: Ray Peekner Literary Agency, 3121 Portage Road, Bethlehem, Pennsylvania 18017. Address: 5552 Walsh Road, Whitmore Lake, Michigan 48189, U.S.A.

WESTERN PUBLICATIONS

Novels (series: Page Murdock)

The Hider. New York, Doubleday, 1978.
The High Rocks (Murdock). New York, Doubleday, 1979; London, Hale, 1983.
Stamping Ground (Murdock). New York, Doubleday, 1980.
Aces and Eights. New York, Doubleday, 1981; London, Hale, 1983.
The Wolfer. New York, Pocket Books, 1981; London, Hale, 1983.
Murdock's Law. New York, Doubleday, 1982; London, Hale, 1983.
Mister St. John. New York, Doubleday, 1983; London, Hale, 1985.
This Old Bill. New York, Doubleday, 1984.
Bloody Season. New York, Bantam, 1988.

Short Stories

The Best Western Stories of Loren D. Estleman, edited by Bill Pronzini and Martin H. Greenberg. Athens, Ohio, Ohio University Press/Swallow Press, 1989.

Uncollected Short Stories

"Rossiter's Stand," in *Pulpsmith*, September 1981.
"The Bandit," in *The Best of the West*, edited by Joe R. Lansdale. New York, Doubleday, 1986.
"Mago's Bride," in *Westeryear*, edited by Edward Gorman. New York, Evans, 1988.
"Hell on the Draw," in *The New Frontier*, edited by Joe R. Lansdale. New York, Doubleday, 1989.
"The Angel of Santa Sofia," in *The Arizonans*, edited by Bill Pronzini and Martin H. Greenberg. New York, Fawcett, 1989.
"The Pilgrim," in *The Northwesterners*, edited by Bill Pronzini and Martin H. Greenberg. New York, Fawcett, 1990.
"The Death of Dutch Creel," in *Christmas Out West*, edited by Bill Pronzini and Greenberg. New York, Doubleday, 1990.

OTHER PUBLICATIONS

Novels

The Oklahoma Punk. Canoga Park, California, Major, 1976.
Sherlock Holmes Versus Dracula; or, The Adventure of the Sanguinary Count. New York, Doubleday, and London, New English Library, 1978.
Dr. Jekyll and Mr. Holmes. New York, Doubleday, 1979; London, Penguin, 1980.
Motor City Blue. Boston, Houghton Mifflin, 1980; London, Hale, 1982.
Angel Eyes. Boston, Houghton Mifflin, 1981.
The Midnight Man. Boston, Houghton Mifflin, 1982.
The Glass Highway. Boston, Houghton Mifflin, 1983; London, Hale, 1984.
Kill Zone. Boston, Houghton Mifflin, 1984; London, Macmillan, 1986.
Roses Are Dead. New York, Mysterious Press, 1985; London, Century, 1987.
Gun Man. New York, Doubleday, 1985.
Sugartown. Boston, Houghton Mifflin, 1985; London, Macmillan, 1986.
Every Brilliant Eye. Boston, Houghton Mifflin, and London, Macmillan, 1986.
Lady Yesterday. Boston, Houghton Mifflin, and London, Macmillan, 1987.
The Stranglers. New York, Doubleday, 1987; London, Hale, 1988.
Any Man's Death. New York, Mysterious Press, 1987; London, Century, 1989.
Downriver. Boston, Houghton Mifflin, and London, Macmillan, 1988.
Silent Thunder. Boston, Houghton Mifflin, and London, Macmillan, 1989.
Whiskey River. New York, Bantam, 1990.

Short Stories

General Murders: 10 Amos Walker Mysteries. Boston, Houghton Mifflin, 1988; London, Macmillan, 1989.

Other

The Wister Trace: Classic Novels of the American Frontier. Ottawa, Illinois, 1987.

*

Loren D. Estleman comments:

At its best, my style is highly visual, and depends upon exterior description to elicit a subjective opinion from the reader. Whether a character is to be thought of as wicked or heroic or comical or otherwise is up to my audience to decide based upon what I have shown them of his appearance or behavior. Nowhere in my work will you find a passage wherein the narrator turns face forward and says, "He was an evil man." If that fact isn't evident on the face of things, I've failed. Needless to say, this reticence on my part to present my own opinions upon a given subject or character has led to some involved and not always civil discussion with editors. I expect this and bear them no ill will because of it. Amiable concurrence does not good art make. Nevertheless, the tightrope between subtlety and incomprehensibility is one I prefer to walk rather than plunge into the ephemeral depths of the obvious.

* * *

Although perhaps best known for his mystery novels, Loren D. Estleman is also an accomplished writer of western fiction. His career in this field began with *The Hider*, the story of an old man and a boy who go on a hunt for the last surviving buffalo, in the year 1898. The account of the boy's initiation is fast-moving and spiced with action, including encounters with such antagonists as a mad dog and malevolent Indians. The boy, Jeff Curry, recounts his experience after many years have passed, and his perspective on the events adds to the meaning they have for both him and the reader. A similar theme appears in *The Wolfer*, in which an Eastern writer accompanies Asa North, a near-legendary wolf hunter, on the trail of Black Jack, a wolf of almost supernatural capacities. Much of the material in this book is based on research into what Estleman refers to as a "massive campaign to exterminate the Great Plains wolf," a campaign which appears to have been overlooked by most historians, but one which Estleman brings to life in his novel.

Estleman has also written a series of books featuring Page Murdock, a United States Marshal who does not exactly conform to the conventional image of the good-guy hero. Murdock will take whatever advantage he can, yet he remains an amiable character. In *The High Rocks* he encounters Bear Anderson, a character loosely based on Liver Eating Johnson. Anderson, a childhood friend of Murdock's, is causing a great deal of unrest with his depredations among the Flathead Indians. It becomes Murdock's job to stop him and bring him in, a feat easier to assign than to accomplish. In *Stamping Ground* Murdock must capture Ghost Shirt, a powerful Cheyenne chief, and bring him back for a public hanging, much as he did Anderson in *The High Rocks*. His job is certainly no easier this time, though he eventually accomplishes it.

While Estleman began his western-writing career with a number of entertaining books, he has continued to develop as a writer. He has published several excellent novels based on well-known characters and events, and succeeded in throwing new light on both people and circumstances. These books include *Aces and Eights*, about the death of Wild Bill Hickok; *This Old Bill*, which fictionalizes the life of Buffalo Bill Cody; and *Bloody Season*, perhaps the best of the group, which retells the story of the Earps, the Clantons, and the OK Corral. These books show a high regard for both historical fact and the storyteller's art, and are well worth seeking out.

—Bill Crider

EVAN, Paul. *See* **LEHMAN, Paul Evan.**

EVANS, Evan. *See* **BRAND, Max.**

EVANS, Max. American. Born in Ropes, Texas, 29 August 1925. Educated at Andrews High School, Texas; private art study with Ida Strawn Baker, Woody Crumbo, and Dal Holcomb. Served in the United States Army infantry during World War II. Married Pat James in 1950; twin daughters. Worked as a cowboy, rancher, trapper, prospector, and mining promoter. Vice-president, Taos Minerals, Inc., 1955–58, and president, Solar Metals Inc., 1957–59, both in Taos, New Mexico. Painter: individual shows in Taos and elsewhere. Recipient: Commendation from City of Los Angeles. Hon. member, board of chancellors, University of Texas, El Paso. Agent: Russell and Volkening, Inc., 551 Fifth Avenue, New York, New York 10017. Address: 1111 Ridgecrest Drive S.E., Albuquerque, New Mexico 87108, U.S.A.

WESTERN PUBLICATIONS

Novels

The Rounders. New York, Macmillan, 1960; London, Corgi, 1965.
The Hi Lo Country. New York, Macmillan, 1961; London, Davies, 1962.
The Mountain of Gold. Dunwoody, Georgia, Berg, 1965.
Shadow of Thunder. Chicago, Swallow Press, 1969.
Bobby Jack Smith, You Dirty Coward! Los Angeles, Nash, 1974.
The White Shadow. San Diego, Joyce Press, 1977.
Rounders Three. New York, Doubleday, 1990.

Short Stories

Southwest Wind. San Antonio, Texas, Naylor, 1958.
Three Short Novels: The Great Wedding, The One-Eyed Sky, My Pardner. Boston, Houghton Mifflin, 1963; *My Pardner* published separately, 1972.
Xavier's Folly and Other Stories. Castlerock, Colorado, Zia, 1984.

Uncollected Short Stories

"The Far Cry," in *The Pick of the Roundup*, edited by Stephen Payne. New York, Avon, 1963.
"Big Shad's Bridge," in *Rivers to Cross*, edited by William R. Cox. New York, Dodd Mead, 1966.
"Xavier's Folly," in *South Dakota Review* (Vermillion), Summer 1972.
"Candles in the Bottom of the Pool," in *South Dakota Review* (Vermillion), 1973.
"The Ultimate Giver," in *The Far Side of the Storm.* Cerrillos, New Mexico, San Marcos Press, 1975.
"The Wild one," in *The New Frontier*, edited by Joe R. Lansdale. New York, Doubleday, 1989.

OTHER PUBLICATIONS

Other

Long John Dunn of Taos. Los Angeles, Westernlore Press, 1959.
Three West: Conversations with Vardis Fisher, Max Evans, Michael Straight, by John R. Milton. Vermillion, University of South Dakota, 1970.
Sam Peckinpah, Master of Violence. Vermillion, Dakota Press, 1972.
Super Bull and Other True Escapades. Albuquerque, University of New Mexico Press, 1989.

*

Manuscript Collection: University of Texas, El Paso.

Max Evans comments:

Having spent my entire life in the Southwest working as a cowboy, rancher, miner, painter, writer of this vast land, I have tried to put down the humor, tragedy, loneliness, and adventure as I lived and loved it during my lifetime.

* * *

A long and checkered career in the School of Experience brought Max Evans to his calling as a writer and provided him with his best material. Born on a ranch in Texas near the New Mexico line, he began as a cowboy but spent many years as a rodeo performer, miner, salesman, fortune teller, and painter. He had almost enough talent to make a career of painting, but writing was always on his mind and he read extensively, mostly the 19th-century novelists. The volume to which he gave his closest attention, however, was the Book of Earth, which taught him about the land and the creatures who inhabit it. His chosen terrain was the cattle country of New Mexico south and east of Taos, and he is at his best in describing that rocky, wind-swept landscape and the rugged beings who survive on it—Anglos, Mexicans, a few Indians, horses, coyotes, and rattlesnakes. In such an environment it is not difficult to study "man's relationship to the earth and what that relationship does to him." Evans is a philosopher and teacher as well as a keen observer and this is the lesson he wants to teach: the dependence of every living thing on the earth from which it came, and the interdependence of all the lives involved. He says he never wrote a story without a coyote in it. Man is not alone, and neither is he independent.

Southwest Wind, his first published book, is a series of vignettes almost too short and unstructured to be called short stories, which probe the dark corners of this little universe. In an interview with John Milton published in *Three West*, Evans described these first gropings for a style and a mood as "pretty horrible," but they are, in fact, full of life and human feeling and insight, a good introduction to the work which was to follow. His second book, *Long John Dunn of Taos*, explored the territory a little further. Long John was a salty character, in some ways resembling Evans, who had lived an adventurous life and survived in an often hostile environment. The third book, *The Rounders*, brought him to full development and was something of a triumph. It went through several editions, and was made into a highly successful motion picture, Glenn Ford and Henry Fonda taking the leads.

The book and the movie made Evans famous, but it seems now, in the light of hindsight, that even his most enthusiastic admirers were shortsighted and did not give him all the credit he deserved. They praised him for being a first-class funny man and for portraying the New Mexican cowboy with understanding and accuracy, but they did not really take him seriously. "Leave it be said at the very outset," wrote Red Fenwick in the Denver *Post* for 28 August 1960, "that *The Rounders* is undoubtedly one of the funniest cowpoke yarns to come off the presses in many a fall roundup." John Barkham of the New York *World-Telegram* took the other tack on 9 August: "*The Rounders* is a little gem of a book—brief, salty, Mark Twainish in its vernacular, and as authentic as a western saddle." When the moving picture appeared, *Time* magazine called it "an amiable knuckle-headed Western" written in a vein of "high dry comedy."

There was more to it than these reviewers saw, as Evans himself was well aware. He declared himself in the Milton interview: "*The Rounders*, though it is known as a comedy, is really tragi-comedy. These men are trapped in their environment and are trying to break out." They never make it. Dusty Rhodes and Wrangler Lewis, his two cowboy leads, can't get away from their employer and exploiter Jim Ed Love. They are Dead Enders; they can't win. It is easy to miss this point because they are so funny, but our laughter is at cracked ribs, broken teeth, the frustrations of bachelor life in a lonely line camp, wicked horses hoping to kill their riders, wild debauches when the lonely men come to town. Evans's home country is full of danger, pain, and violence, and that country, as he sees it, is a metaphor for the world. "Nobody can be satisfied," comments Big Boy, the central figure in *The Hi Lo Country*, "because everything in this goddam world is in competition with everything else. Every blade of grass is in competition with the one next to it . . . and every vulture is hoping to find more dead." This lethal competition is the theme of "The One-Eyed Sky," regarded by some as Evans's finest story, in which an old mother cow gives her all to protect her calf from a coyote which must kill the cow if her pups are to survive.

Evans returns to his vein of bawdy country humor in *My Pardner* and *Bobby Jack Smith, You Dirty Coward!*, but his work after 1963 is increasingly symbolic, violent, and tragic. In *The Mountain of Gold* Benito Anaya finds a gold nugget on his mountain and spends the rest of his life in a fruitless search for the mother lode. In *Shadow of Thunder* a latter-day incarnation of Pan or Dionysos evangelizes a rural community with a gospel of carnal love, literally losing his head in a violent ending. A connection might be established between such scenes and Evans's non-fiction study, *Sam Peckinpah, Master of Violence*. *The White Shadow*, the story of a white doe which actually survived for 13 years close to a San Diego freeway, is a gentler story, but Evans says it is "as much parable as novel."

More recent works, still to be published, are *Silver City Millie* (the story of a famous southwestern madam) and *The King of Taos*, set in his old Hi Lo country, which he hopes will be his masterpiece. If it lives up to his expectations, the reviewers will be able to say of it, as they did of *The One-Eyed Sky*, that in it Evans "sees the world in a sandy arroyo."

—C.L. Sonnichsen

EVANS, Tabor. *See* **CAMERON, Lou; KNOTT, Will C.; WHITTINGTON, Harry.**

EVANS, Wick.

Western Publications

Novels

Steamboat West. New York, Arcadia House, 1959; London, Mills and Boon, 1961.
Twin Guns. New York, Arcadia House, 1960; London, Mills and Boon, 1962.

* * *

Although Wick Evans has only written two Westerns to date, they are both worth mentioning in this edition. His first, curiously entitled *Steamboat West*, begins with the book's hero, Clay Durand, physically interfering when he sees a stranger horsewhipping his mare. After beating the man, Durand becomes concerned for his life when he discovers that the stranger was a noted quick draw artist named Jack Wells. Putting Wells's death threat behind him, Durand visits his new neighbours, and here he meets the book's obligatory love interest, but also falls foul of Wells. The latter kills the rancher and has Durand framed for the murder. Now the plots twists and turns as Durand has to fight to clear his name and an earlier introduced character named Wyoming comes to his aid, wanting to kill Wells because he suffered an earlier degradation at the man's hand and is doomed to go blind in one eye. Together they set out to recapture the outlaw, and are destined to succeed. Characterization is rather staid. With predictable heroes and villain, but Evans uses their strengths and shortcomings to enhance the plot, which is well-paced and neatly written. Not given to delving into excessive Westernisms, it creates an air of authenticity in its settings and description of the surrounding country. The only drawback is that one would expect the book, written in the early 1960's to move away from its predictable "boy gets girl" ending that was prevalent in the previous decade, and to arrive at a more satisfactory conclusion.

Twin Guns, however, is a much better book and sadly Evans's last. It is the story of identical twins who are torn apart by their personal differences. Kirby and Bill Street have never liked each other since the death of their parents, for whose death Kirby blames Bill. But before his death their father, Muddy Street, divides the Wagon Spoke ranch between the boys. Bill moves away, sets up the Lazy B ranch, and changes from being a careless, unthinking individual to a ruthless, power-crazed rancher. Inevitably, they both love the same girl, so Evans weaves this in as a sub-plot, but she in turn rejects both their advances until they can sort out their own problems. Kirby refuses to sell his ranch to Bill, and sets to wondering where the money is coming from. He is surprised to learn that his brother is a rustler, which Bill denies, but when Kirby's cattle is found on Bill's land, there can be no denying the fact. Once again Evans provides us with a turn in events, and we learn that a gunman named Dawes has a hold over Bill, has been using him for his own ends, and is actually the thief. Now Bill needs to clear his own name (echoes of Clay Durand) and in doing so exposes the real villains and dies at their hands. The ending is the same as in *Steamboat West*, with the hero getting his girl and all the loose ends tied up.

Evans's style is simple in its approach but is enlivened by his ability to develop male characters. Unfortunately he is unable to treat his women in the same way. They are mere ciphers to add to his story to make for happy endings. His descriptions of ranch life, albeit fairly brief, in *Twin Guns* are accurate and a welcome change from some of the misconceived ideas written at the time. These books have appeal to both the younger reader and the more ardent fan of the genre.

—Mike Stotter

EVARTS, Hal G(eorge), Sr. American. Born in Topeka, Kansas, 24 August 1887. Educated at Topeka high school. Served in the Officer Training Corps, 1918–19: Lieutenant. Married Sylvia Abraham in 1912; one son, Hal, *q.v.* Surveyor in the Indian Territory, rancher, trapper, guide in Wyoming; raised fur-bearing animals; outdoor editor, *Saturday Evening Post*, and freelance writer. *Died 18 October 1934.*

WESTERN PUBLICATIONS

Novels

The Cross-Pull. New York, Knopf, and London, Hodder and Stoughton, 1920.
The Passing of the Old West. Boston, Little Brown, 1921.
The Yellow Horde. Boston, Little Brown, and London, Hodder and Stoughton, 1921.
The Settling of the Sage. Boston, Little Brown, and London, Hodder and Stoughton, 1922.
Tumbleweeds. Boston, Little Brown, 1923.
Tomahawk Rights. Boston, Little Brown, 1925; London, Skeffington, 1936.
Spanish Acres. Boston, Little Brown, 1925; London, Hodder and Stoughton, 1926.
The Painted Stallion. Boston, Little Brown, and London, Hodder and Stoughton, 1926.
The Moccasin Telegraph. Boston, Little Brown, 1927; London, Skeffington, 1935.
Fur Brigade. Boston, Little Brown, 1928; London, Skeffington, 1936.
The Shaggy Legion. Boston, Little Brown, 1930; London, Skeffington, 1937.
Shortgrass. Boston, Little Brown, and London, Skeffington, 1932.
Wolf Dog. New York, Doubleday, and London, Skeffington, 1935.

Short Stories

The Bald Face and Other Animal Stories. New York, Knopf, 1921; London, Hodder and Stoughton, 1922.

OTHER PUBLICATIONS

Plays

Screenplays: *Tumbleweeds*, with C. Gardner Sullivan, 1925; *The Big Trail*, with others, 1930.

Fiction (for children)

Fur Sign. Boston, Little Brown, 1922.
Jerbo, The Jumper. Racine, Wisconsin, Whitman, 1930.
Kobi of the Sea. Racine, Wisconsin, Whitman, 1930.
Phantom, The White Mink. Racine, Wisconsin, Whitman, 1930.
Swift, The Kit Fox. Racine, Wisconsin, Whitman, 1930.

*

Critical Study: *From Skunk Ranch to Hollywood: The West of Author Hal G. Evarts* by Hal G. Evarts, Jr., Santa Barbara, California, Capra, 1989.

* * *

Hal G. Evarts's writing career was a logical extension of his occupational preoccupation in his early years with the out-of-doors west and the wildlife it held. His first major offerings were articles on wild animals and on natural resources conservation appearing in *The Country Gentleman*. He continued writing such articles long after he backed into fiction, as it were, and they entitle him to recognition as forerunner of today's overweening concern with the natural environment.

Evarts's contributions to the "western" genre, *Tumbleweeds* for example, belong in that category established by no better authority than this writer as the "epic" western. This epic phase began with the 1922 serialization of Emerson Hogh's *The Covered Wagon* in *Saturday Evening Post*, and the epic western remained a staple in the *Post's* pages so long as George Horace Lorimer, the five-button mandarin who dominated the fortunes of that great magazine, remained alive. It was, of course, imitated or adopted, as you prefer, by the other mass circulation "slicks." There was a plot line in these epic westerns and a romantic interest as well, but these were almost subordinate to the vast canvas of the west that contained the epic event, virtually a pageant in itself, that was never static but filled with life and movement.

It was to this sub-genre, or perhaps the climatic phase, of the "Western," that Evarts applied his knowledge of and affection for the wildlife of the West; for the vast land in which it and all things moved by the grace of their gods, and for the real people who he knew lived and often died by the natural resources they conserved or exploited as their natures or their needs demanded. He brought to the task of portraying all these things correctly a solid, driving, straight-line narrative, free of cursive tricks of light and shadow but redolent of prairie and sky, that was most effective in grabbing the reader's attention and holding it. He deserves more attention than he has received from students of the literature of the American West.

—W.H. Hutchinson

EVARTS, Hal G(eorge, Jr.). American. Born in Hutchinson, Kansas, 8 February 1915; son of Hal G. Evarts, Sr., *q.v.* Educated at Stanford University, Californa, B.A. 1936. Served in the 89th Infantry Division of the United States Army during World War II. Married Dorothea Van Dusen Abbott in 1942; one daughter and two sons. Toured world, 1936–37. Screenwriter and reporter; staff member, Paris edition of New York *Herald Tribune*, 1939–40; then full-time writer. Vice-president, Western Writers of America, 1959–60. *Died 26 August 1989.*

WESTERN PUBLICATIONS

Novels

Renegade of Rainbow Basin. New York, Popular Library, 1953.
Highgrader. New York, Popular Library, 1954.
Apache Agent. New York, Popular Library, 1955.
Ambush Rider. New York, Popular Library, 1956; London, Hale, 1957.
The Night Raiders. New York, Popular Library, 1956.
Man Without a Gun. New York, Popular Library, 1957.
The Man from Yuma. New York, Popular Library, 1958.
The Long Rope. New York, Dell, 1959.
The Blazing Land. New York, Dell, 1960; London, Panther, 1961.
Turncoat. New York, Fawcett, 1960; London, Muller, 1962.
The Silver Concubine. New York, Dell, 1962.
Massacre Creek. New York, Fawcett, 1962.
Colorado Crossing. New York, Dell, 1963.
The Branded Man. New York, Fawcett, 1965; London, Gold Lion, 1974.
The Sundown Kid. New York, Fawcett, 1969; London, Gold Lion, 1974.

Short Stories

Fugitive's Canyon. New York, Popular Library, 1955.

Uncollected Short Stories

"Waterhole," in *Western Roundup*, edited by Arnold Hano. New York, Bantam, 1948.
"Killer in the Pass," in *Collier's* (Springfield, Ohio), 1 December 1951.
"Branded Woman," in *Saturday Evening Post* (Philadelphia), 26 January 1952.
"Legend in the Dust," in *Branded West*, edited by Don Ward. Boston, Houghton Mifflin, 1956.
"The Lady and the Lash," in *Bar 5*, edited by Scott Meredith. New York, Dutton, 1956.
"Horse for the Colonel," in *Wild Horse Roundup*, edited by Jim Kjelgaard. New York, Dodd Mead, 1957.
"Herd Law," in *Frontiers West*, edited by S. Omar Barker. New York, Doubleday, 1959.
"To Lhasa," in *A Saddlebag of Tales*, edited by Rutherford Montgomery. New York, Dodd Mead, 1959.
"One Night in the Red Dog Saloon," in *Spurs West*, edited by S. Omar Barker. New York, Doubleday, 1960.
"Gorge of Death," in *Saturday Evening Post* (Philadelphia), 13 February 1960.
"Pioneers of Lonely Canyon," in *Saturday Evening Post* (Philadelphia), 14 May 1960.
"Portrait of a Gunfighter," in *Western Roundup*, edited by Nelson Nye. New York, Dodd Mead, 1961.
"Saturday Matinee," in *Search for the Hidden Places*, edited by E.D. Mygatt. New York, McKay, 1963.
"Pursuit," in *Great Western Stories.* New York, Berkley, 1965.
"Woman Trader," in *Western Romances*, edited by Peggy Simson Curry. New York, Fawcett, 1969.

OTHER PUBLICATIONS

Fiction (for children)

Jedediah Smith, Trail Blazer of the West. New York, Putnam, 1959.
Jim Clyman. New York, Putnam, 1959.
The Secret of the Himalayas. New York, Scribner, 1962.
Treasure River. New York, Scribner, 1964.
The Talking Mountain. New York, Scribner, 1966.
Smugglers' Road. New York, Scribner, 1968.
Mission to Tibet. New York, Scribner, 1970.
The Pegleg Mystery. New York, Scribner, 1972.
Big Foot. New York, Scribner, 1973.
The Purple Eagle Mystery. New York, Scribner, 1976.
Jay-Jay and the Peking Monster. New York, Scribner, 1978.

Other

Rolling Ahead (combat history). Paris, USFET Headquarters, 1945.
From Skunk Ranch to Hollywood: The West of Author Hal G. Evarts. Santa Barbara, Capra Press, 1989.

*

Manuscript Collection: University of Oregon Library, Eugene.

Hal G. Evarts commented (1982):

I wrote the following (slightly paraphrased) for Scribner's years ago: "My primary function as a writer is to entertain, striving for realism, telling it like it is.' My greatest challenge is to write a book that readers find so enjoyable and meaningful they want to come back for more. I enjoy the reassurance of knowing that 'someone out there' is reading my work and derive the greatest satisfication when I receive letters from readers."

* * *

Hal G. Evarts's fiction is the most difficult kind to describe—conventional tales of adventure undistinguished by any peculiarities, good or bad. Perhaps the author's only idiosyncracy is his habit of literary allusion in the midst of violent action—for example in *Ambush Rider* the foreman makes an explicit reference to Poe's "The Purloined Letter." Evarts is a competent storyteller who writes about misunderstood heroes whom the reader watches working quietly in the interests of good and who are finally recognized in their true colours by the other characters.

A typical novel is *The Blazing Land*, which tells how a Texan, loyal to the Union, endangers himself to save his rebel brother from imprisonment. He guides his brother and his brother's fiancée from Los Angeles across the Mojave Desert, pursued by Union soldiers and bounty hunters. They survive, only to be attacked by Apaches, who kill the brother. In the end, the hero returns to scout for the Union army and it is implied that he will marry the fiancée. The stories have none of the gore or debauchery of many modern westerns. In this case, the violence is not excessive (the hero kills no white men) and it is made clear that the woman, although she is a faro dealer, is virtuous.

Evarts has written Westerns for children as well, and both types of writing are similar, in that they resolve around god-fearing, unusually literate heroes who are nation-builders. (Jim Clyman, Jedediah Smith, and Will Colladay of *The Blazing Land* all fit this description). In all of them, too, there is s strong sense of security, since none of the wrong people die. In the later novels, the action becomes more nearly tragic: in *The Sundown Kid*, for instance, a man's five-year quest for an outlaw is set in motion by the murder of his eight-year-old son, which is the first event the reader encounters.

Although Evarts writes of range wars in the 1880's or struggles between whites and Indians during and after the Civil War, his tales are not centrally concerned with any western code or issue. With a change in scene and period, they could easily belong to any adventure genre.

—Christine Bold

EVERETT, Wade. *See* **COOK, Will; LUTZ, Giles A.**

EYNON, Robert. British. Born in Tynewydd, Rhondda, Wales, 20 March 1941. Educated at Dunraven Primary School, Rhondda, 1944–52; Porth County Grammar School, Rhondda, 1952–59; King's College, University of London, 1959–63, B.A. (hons.) in Spanish 1962, B.A. (hons.) in French 1969. Language teacher, The High School, Bedford, 1963–65; teacher of English, Lycée Foch, Rodez, France, 1965–66, and Ecole de La Salle, Lille, France, 1966–67; language teacher, Peter Symond's School, Winchester, Hampshire, 1967–69, and Girls' Grammar School, Pontypridd, Glamorgan, 1969–72; Lecturer in education, University College, Cardiff, Glamorgan, 1972–84; Visiting lecturer, Ibadan University, Nigeria, 1975; Parks labourer, Rhondda Borough Council, 1985–86. Since 1987 full-time writer. Address: 5 Troedyrhiw Terrace, Treorchy, Mid-Glamorgan CF42 6PG, Wales.

WESTERN PUBLICATIONS

Novels

Bitter Waters. London, Hale, 1988.
Texas Honour. London, Hale, 1988.
Johnny One-Arm. London, Hale, 1989.
Y Gwr o Phoenix. Cardiff, Glamorgan, Bob Eynon/Gwas Y Dref Wen, 1989.
Gunfight at Simeon's Ridge. London, Hale, 1991.

OTHER PUBLICATIONS

Novels (in Welsh)

Perygl yn Sbaen. Cardiff, Glamorgan, Bob Eynon/Gwas Y Dref Wen, 1987.
Y Giangster Coll. Cardiff, Glamorgan, Bob Eynon/Gwas Y Dref Wen, 1988.
Marwolaeth Heb Ddagrav. Cardiff, Glamorgan, Bob Eynon/Gwas Y Dref Wen, 1989.
Arian Am Ddim. Cardiff, Glamorgan, Bob Eynon/Gwas Y Dref Wen, 1990.

Short Stories

Anturiaethau Cei Cadno. Cowbridge, Glamorgan, Bob Eynon/Brown and Sons, 1981.

*

Robert Eynon comments:

My writing is influenced by the western books and films that gave me so much enjoyment in my teens, some 30 years ago. I am not interested in writing about gratuitous sex and violence. My characters clash violently because of differences of personality and ambition. Build-up of personality and complexity of plot are therefore of prime importance to me. Both heroes and villains must be rounded characters, otherwise the hostility and animosity which so frequently erupt into violence in my books would not stir the reader's emotions. I am particularly interested in the psychology of the gang leader, who strives by fear or guile to forge his individualistic and wayward gunslingers into a coherent unit. My heroes, too, have their problems, caused either by external relationships or internal conflict. These heroes are often enigmatic and elusive, and are only stirred to action when the forces of evil threaten them, or those they care for.

* * *

Robert Eynon is a western writer from Wales, who utilises the standard plots and conventions of the genre in his writing, while at the same time approaching them in an individual manner which renders his narratives less predictable than they might at first appear. This is nowhere better illustrated than in his first novel, *Bitter Waters*, where the land-hungry villain is opposed not by a single heroic figure, but by three quite distinct central characters—a rancher, a lawman, and a gambler—who together manage to defeat their more powerful adversary. While much of the characterisation is of a surface nature, and the actual theme less than unusual, Eynon shows considerable skill in sustaining the pace of his novel, ensuring that the sequence of events moves smoothly to the inevitable shoot-out at the Silver Horn saloon. He also succeeds in maintaining the difficult balance between his three main characters, so that no single individual "takes over" the book.

Subsequent novels by Eynon tend to confirm the promise implicit in *Bitter Waters*, but are perhaps less imaginative. *Texas Honour* follows the fortunes of a Texan cowhand who becomes involved with a band of robbers led by an ex-Confederate major and his psychotic killer son. In the course of the book the reader is treated to some interesting set-pieces, with Cordell—the cowhand—taking part in contests of shooting and horsemanship, as well as the inevitable fist-fight. Pat Garrett puts in a cameo appearance, and a more important role is played by the Mexican horse-dealer Gonzalez, who is sympathetically portrayed by the author as a resourceful, intelligent man, and who eventually helps Cordell to bring the outlaw gang to justice. Major Carr and his minions are defeated in the final gun-battle, and Cordell wins the marshal's daughter, but although the novel ends on a familiar note, Eynon has shown us enough in the preceding pages to indicate that he has more to offer than the hoary theme might suggest. *Johnny One-Arm* is chiefly memorable for the portrayal of its one-armed hero, who is convincingly presented as a fully-rounded personality with a credible outlook on life, rather than the grotesque monster—so familiar in a number of "adult westerns"—he might so easily have become. Johnny's humanity, and his eventual success against the odds, reflect Eynon's feeling for his creations. While it would be wrong to regard him as an innovator, it can truthfully be said that this Welsh author has succeeded in bringing his own individual vision to bear on the formula Western.

—Jeff Sadler

F

FALCON, Mark. Pseudonym for Eileen Marion Pickering. British. Born in Bedford, 24 July 1940. Married; one son. Publisher, *Writers' Own Magazine* and other limited editions on a subsidy basis. Address: 121 Highbury Grove, Clapham, Bedford, MK41 6DU, England.

WESTERN PUBLICATIONS

Novels

Reluctant Outlaw. London, Hale, 1979.
The Yellow Bandanna. London, Hale, 1979.
Lightning Hits Glory Town. London, Hale, 1980.

*

Mark Falcon comments:
I think the western genre will always be popular, although sadly it is looked down upon by many who consider it to be for the less literate. I think the modern Western is probably better than it used to be.

* * *

Unlike most 10-year-old girls, the young Eileen Pickering was already writing Westerns as a pastime. At the age of 14 she started sending her manuscripts to various publishers, without success. Her 39th birthday was understandably brightened, however, when her first novel, *Reluctant Outlaw*, was published, under the pseudonym Mark Falcon.

In *Reluctant Outlaw* (originally written just after the birth of her son in 1965), we are introduced to the notorious Hay Bassett gang, which has outwitted the law for several years. When Denver Branch and his two riders throw in with Bassett, however, a red-headed youth also tags along. Trouble starts when Bassett discovers that the red-head is in fact a girl, who will inevitably cause problems in a town inhabited solely by men. But, predictably, the beautiful Kelly Branch turns out to be more than Bassett has bargained for. Indeed, as Falcon states, "she had the heart of a lion and more guts than most men he had ever met."

The product of five rewrites, *Reluctant Outlaw* is, like all the Falcon books, a largely traditional Western, but this is no criticism. The Falcon style is tight and orderly, and the plots are usually laced with enough twists to confound expectations.

Falcon followed her first novel with *The Yellow Bandanna*, a gun-fast tale of revenge. The central character here is farmer Dan Rylands, who returns home to find his parents murdered. Dan's only clue to the identity of the killer is a yellow bandanna. His vengeance hunt eventually leads him to Dodge City and the Chisholm Trail, where he tangles with a pretty young schoolteacher who provides the romantic interest, and a get-rich-quick bounty hunter named Max Vargas.

In many respects, *The Yellow Bandanna* is a much more accomplished Western, with a more ambitious plot and better-drawn characters. But Falcon showed an even greater improvement in her third, and to date final Western, *Lightning Hits Glory Town*.

This book, which was originally written on journeys to and from school in Luton, concerns a nameless gunslinger known only as Lightning. When he falls from his horse during a fight with Comanches, Lightning receives a blow to his head that results in temporary blindness and total loss of memory. In his subsequent quest to discover his identity, he has to find a young runaway before the cryptic Leonora Billington will agree to answer at least *some* of his questions.

Although Pickering has two more Westerns in various stages of completion, her time in recent years has been taken up with her many publishing activities. She has been producing *Writers' Own Magazine* since 1982, and publishes a number of interesting, though non-Western, limited editions.

—David Whitehead

FARGO, Doone. *See* **NORWOOD, V.G.C.**

FARRELL, Cliff. American. Born in Zanesville, Ohio, 20 November 1899. Educated at public schools in Zanesville. Married Mildred K. Raddon in 1927; one son and one daughter. Telegraph editor, night news editor, and sports news editor, Los Angeles *Examiner*, 1925–36; then full-time writer. Recipient: Western Writers of America Spur award, 1970. *Died 5 November 1977.*

WESTERN PUBLICATIONS

Novels

Follow the New Grass. New York, Random House, 1954; London, Ward Lock, 1958.
West with the Missouri. New York, Random House, 1955; as *Rawhide River*, New York, Popular Library, 1956.
California Passage. New York, Popular Library, 1957.
Sante Fe Wagon Boss. New York, Doubleday, 1958; London, Ward Lock, 1959.
Gun Hand. New York, Popular Library, 1958.
Ride the Wild Trail. New York, Doubleday, 1959; London, Ward Lock, 1960.
The Lean Rider. New York, Doubleday, 1960.
Fort Deception. New York, Doubleday, 1960; London, Ward Lock, 1961.
Trail of the Tattered Star. New York, Doubleday, 1961; London, Ward Lock, 1963.
The Walking Hills. New York, Doubleday, 1962; London, Ward Lock, 1963.

Ride the Wild Country. New York, Doubleday, 1963; as *The Wild Country*, London, Ward Lock, 1964.
Return of the Long Riders. New York, Doubleday, 1964; London, Ward Lock, 1965.
Cross-Fire. New York, Doubleday, 1965; London, Ward Lock, 1967.
Bucko. New York, Doubleday, 1965; London, Ward Lock, 1966.
Comanch'. New York, Doubleday, 1966; London, Ward Lock, 1967.
The Guns of Judgment Day. New York, Doubleday, 1967.
Death Trap on the Platte. New York, Doubleday, 1968; London, Gold Lion, 1973.
Treachery Trail. New York, Doubleday, 1969.
The Renegade. New York, Doubleday, 1970; London, Gold Lion, 1972.
Owlhoot Trail. New York, Doubleday, 1971.
Patchsaddle Drive. New York, Doubleday, 1972.
Shoot-Out at Sioux Wells. New York, Doubleday, 1973.
Gambler's Long Chance. London, Hale, 1974.
Terror in Eagle Basin. New York, Doubleday, 1974.
The Devil's Playground. New York, Doubleday, 1976.

Uncollected Short Stories

"Bullets of Fate," in *West* (New York), 13 October 1928.
"Once a Killer," in *West* (New York), 6 March 1929.
"Wrecker's Roundup," in *West* (New York), 10 June 1931.
"The Trouble Dodger," in *West* (New York), 8 July 1931.
"Cold Deck," in *West* (New York), 22 July 1931.
"High Explosion," in *West* (New York), 23 December 1931.
"In the Middle," in *West* (New York), 16 March 1932.
"Killers of the Ice," in *Argosy* (New York), 16 April 1932.
"Drum Ice," in *West* (New York), 27 April 1932.
"Blind Speed," in *Frontier Stories* (London), May 1932.
"Old Lightning," in *All Star* (Kingswood, Surrey), October 1932.
"Big River," in *All Star* (Kingswood, Surrey), December 1932.
"Yellow Bait," in *All Star* (Kingswood, Surrey), May 1933.
"Thread of Life," in *Argosy* (New York), 17 June 1933.
"The Right to Live," in *Argosy* (New York), 29 July 1933.
"Discipline," in *Argosy* (New York), 16 December 1933.
"Mule's Luck," in *Argosy* (New York), 20 January 1934.
"Arctic Cargo," in *Argosy* (New York), 3 February 1934.
"The Great Name of McNish," in *Complete Story* (New York), 1 March 1934.
"Troopers Three," in *Complete Story* (New York), 1 April 1934.
"Big Guns," in *Argosy* (New York), 25 August 1934.
"Satan Drives the Deadwood Stage," in *Western Story* (New York), 1 April 1939.
"Ticket to Boothill," in *Western Story* (New York), 15 April 1939.
"Deputy for the Damned," in *Star Western* (Chicago), March 1940.
"When Hell-on-Wheels Went Mad," in *Star Western* (Chicago), September 1940.
"From Rail-Head to Ruin," in *Star Western* (Chicago), October 1940.
"Stolen Guns, Heading South!," in *Star Western* (Chicago), November 1940.
"The Last Outpost This Side of Hell," in *Star Western* (Chicago), December 1940.
"Guardian of the Graveyard Gold-Strike," in *Star Western* (Chicago), March 1941.
"That Gringo Buckskin Devil," in *Star Western* (Chicago), April 1941.
"The Black Sheep Prodigal Wears a Badge," in *Star Western* (Chicago), May 1941.
"Red Scarlet Rides the Graveyard Trick," in *Star Western* (Chicago), July 1941.
"Hell's Last Legion Rides to War," in *Star Western* (Chicago), August 1941.
"The Devil Sends His Ploughman," in *Star Western* (Chicago), September 1941.
"Master of Hell's Acre," in *West* (Kingswood, Surrey), September 1941.
"Trail Drive of the Damned," in *Star Western* (Chicago), December 1941.
"War-Cry of Death's Legionnaires," in *Star Western* (Chicago), January 1942.
"Wagon Wheels, Rolling to Hell!," in *Star Western* (Chicago), February 1944.
"Blind Man's Gun-Bluff," in *Star Western* (Chicago), March 1944.
"Frost on the Orange Blossom," in *Saturday Evening Post* (Philadelphia), 18 March 1944.
"Gray Wool and Cowman's Blood," in *Star Western* (Chicago), June 1944.
"Gun-Master of Robber's Roost," in *Star Western* (Chicago), July 1944.
"Back to the Beach," in *Saturday Evening Post* (Philadelphia), 2 September 1944.
"Roll'er Through to Fort Bridger!," in *Star Western* (Chicago), October 1944.
"I'm Going to California," in *Saturday Evening Post* (Philadelphia), 21 October 1944.
"Hell's High-Graders," in *Star Western* (Chicago), June 1945.
"Scoop Boat," in *Saturday Evening Post* (Philadelphia), 18 August 1945.
"Thorns for Johnny Spring," in *Saturday Evening Post* (Philadelphia), 15 September 1945.
"Long Gone from Kentucky," in *Saturday Evening Post* (Philadelphia), 30 November 1946.
"Glory Is a Dream," in *Five Novels* (New York), May–June 1947.
"Woman Who Cracked the Whip," in *Saturday Evening Post* (Philadelphia), 29 July 1950.
"He Knew All about Women," in *Saturday Evening Post* (Philadelphia), 7 June 1952.
"The Pitchfork Boss," in *Zane Grey's Western* (New York), August 1953.
"Petticoat Pitfall," in *American Magazine* (Springfield, Ohio), July 1954.
"Prairie Treasure," in *Western* (New York), June 1955.
"River Ambush," in *Western Story* (London), July 1955.
"Lady Was a Dude," in *Saturday Evening Post* (Philadelphia), 22 October 1955.
"Deal with the Devil," in *Western Story* (London), January 1957.
"Head-Money Hideout," in *Western Story* (London), March 1957.
"Last of the Wild McVeys," in *Western Story* (London), April 1957.
"Beware Miss Boothill!," in *Western Story* (London), August 1957.
"Cruel Decision," in *Saturday Evening Post* (Philadelphia), 5 April 1958.
"Fiddle-Footed," in *Saturday Evening Post Reader of Western Stories*, edited by E.N. Brandt. New York, Doubleday, 1960.
"Rigged Race," in *Saturday Evening Post* (Philadelphia), 16 January 1960.

"Desperate Journey," in *Great Western Stories*. New York, Berkley, 1965.
"Deadline," in *Rawhide Men*, edited by Kenneth Fowler. New York, Doubleday, 1965.
"High-Water Highway," in *They Opened the West*, edited by Tom W. Blackburn. New York, Doubleday, 1967.
"Westward—To Blood and Glory," in *A Western Bonanza*, edited by Todhunter Ballard. New York, Doubleday, 1969.
"Boss of Buckskin Empire," in *Westerns of the Forties*, edited by Damon Knight. Indianapolis, Bobbs Merrill, 1977.

OTHER PUBLICATIONS

Other

The Mighty Land. New York, Doubleday, 1975.

* * *

From a job as a newspaper office boy in his home town of Zanesville, Ohio, Cliff Farrell gradually worked his way westward from one newspaper job to another. He joined the staff of the Los Angeles *Examiner* in 1925 and remained with that paper for 31 years, serving as telegraph editor, night news editor, and sports news editor. When he retired from the newspaper to become a full-time writer in 1956, he had already been writing for 30 years, and had sold more than 600 stories to the pulp magazines and to slicks such as *Liberty*, *Collier's*, and the *Saturday Evening Post*. One of his long magazine stories, "Westward—to Blood and Glory," from *Pioneer Western Magazine* in 1937, was reprinted in 1969 and received the Spur award from the Western Writers of America as best short fiction of the year.

The falsely accused loner is a frequently occurring figure in Farrell's books, often in combination with the theme of a misunderstanding between two major characters, each believing the other guilty of some ignoble act until the villainous third party is unmasked in the final pages. A variant of this device is used in one of Farrell's most satisfying books, *Return of the Long Riders*. The Long Riders were a band of border raiders in Arizona, preying solely on the Camden ranch, whose owner, Walsh Camden, had once been a friend of the Riders' leader, Dave Kittredge, but had inexplicably turned against him and driven him into outlawry. Several years after Kittredge's death from an assassin's bullet, his son Del returns to the home range on a strange mission: to take a herd of horses into Mexico to ransom Walsh Camden from the Mexican bandit who holds him prisoner. The Long Riders gather once more, and in company with Camden's arrogant children set out on the perilous mission, with present dangers augmented by enmities out of the past.

The action of *West with the Missouri* takes place on and around the great paddlewheel steamers plying the Missouri River from St. Louis to Montana during the Sioux uprising of the early 1870's. River pilot Britt Cahill's attempts to clear his name and settle the score with the man whose false testimony has sent him into hiding are recounted with color and excitement. In *The Lean Rider* a sheltered young woman from Chicago travels to southwest Texas as a "picture bride" and becomes involved with the wild Barbee clan and their desperate cattle drive through Apache territory. In *Cross-Fire*, hatreds spawned by the Civil War are carried westward into the railroad camps and trail towns of Nebraska. And in *Patchsaddle Drive* a crew of ragged, aging ranchers embark on a cattle drive from south Texas to Missouri, their last chance to recoup their fortunes in the aftermath of the Civil War.

Farrell's books are varied in setting and, whatever the theme, are carefully plotted, briskly paced, and smoothly written. The books continue to be reprinted in paperback editions, for which the author's consistent quality and entertaining style have built a large audience.

—R.E. Briney

FAST, Howard (Melvin). Also writes as E.V. Cunningham; Walter Ericson. American. Born in New York City, 11 November 1914. Educated at George Washington High School, New York, graduated 1931; National Academy of Design, New York. Served with the Office of War Information, 1942–43, and the Army Film Project, 1944. Married Bette Cohen in 1937; one daughter and one son, the writer Jonathan Fast. Correspondent, United States Signal Corps, and war correspondent, 1944–45; foreign correspondent, *Esquire* and *Coronet* magazines, 1945; teacher at Indiana University, Bloomington, Summer 1947; imprisoned for contempt of Congress, 1950; owner, Blue Heron Press, 1952–57. Founder, World Peace Movement, and member, World Peace Council, 1950–55; currently, member of the Fellowship for Reconciliation. Since 1989 weekly columnist, New York *Observer*. American-Labor Party candidate for Congress for the 23rd District of New York, 1952. Recipient: Bread Loaf Writers Conference award, 1933; Schomburg Race Relations award, 1944; Newspaper Guild award, 1947; Jewish Book Council of America award, 1948; Soviet International Peace prize, 1954; Screenwriters award, 1960; National Association of Independent Schools award, 1962; American Library Association Emmy award, for television play, 1976. Agent: Sterling Lord Literistic, Inc., 1 Madison Avenue, New York, New York, 10010, U.S.A.

WESTERN PUBLICATIONS

Novels

The Last Frontier. New York, Duell, 1941; London, Lane, 1948.
The Immigrants. Boston, Houghton Mifflin, 1977; London, Hodder and Stoughton, 1978.
Second Generation. Boston, Houghton Mifflin, and London, Hodder and Stoughton, 1978.
The Establishment. Boston, Houghton Mifflin, 1979; London, Hodder and Stoughton, 1980.

OTHER PUBLICATIONS

Novels

Two Valleys. New York, Dial Press, 1933; London, Dickson, 1934.
Strange Yesterday. New York, Dodd Mead, 1934.
Place in the City. New York, Harcourt Brace, 1937.
The Call of Fife and Drum: Three Novels of the Revolution. Secausus, New Jersey, Citadel Press, 1987.
  Conceived in Liberty: A Novel of Valley Forge. New York, Simon and Schuster, and London, Joseph, 1939.
  The Unvanquished. New York, Duell, 1942; London, Lane, 1947.

The Proud and the Free. Boston, Little Brown, 1950; London, Lane, 1952.
The Tall Hunter. New York, Harper, 1942.
Citizen Tom Paine. New York, Duell, 1943; London, Lane, 1945.
Freedom Road. New York, Duell, 1944; London, Lane, 1946.
The American: A Middle Western Legend. New York, Duell, 1946; London, Lane, 1949.
The Children. New York, Duell, 1947.
Clarkton. New York, Duell, 1947.
My Glorious Brothers. Boston, Little Brown, 1948; London, Lane, 1950.
Spartacus. Privately printed, 1951; London, Lane, 1952.
Fallen Angel (as Walter Ericson). Boston, Little Brown, 1952; as *The Darkness Within*, New York, Ace, 1953; as *Mirage*, as Howard Fast, New York, Fawcett, 1965.
Silas Timberman. New York, Blue Heron Press, 1954; London, Lane, 1955.
The Story of Lola Gregg. New York, Blue Heron Press, 1956; London, Lane, 1957.
Moses, Prince of Egypt. New York, Crown, 1958; London, Methuen, 1959.
The Winston Affair. New York, Crown, 1959; London, Methuen, 1960.
The Golden River, in *The Howard Fast Reader*. New York, Crown, 1960.
April Morning. New York, Crown, and London, Methuen, 1961.
Power. New York, Doubleday, 1962; London, Methuen, 1963.
Agrippa's Daughter. New York, Doubleday, 1964; London, Methuen, 1965.
Torquemada. New York, Doubleday, 1966; London, Methuen, 1967.
The Hunter and the Trap. New York, Dial Press, 1967.
The Crossing. New York, Morrow, 1971; London, Eyre Methuen, 1972.
The Hessian. New York, Morrow, 1972; London, Hodder and Stoughton, 1973.
The Legacy. Boston, Houghton Mifflin, 1981.
Max. Boston, Houghton Mifflin, 1982; London, Hodder and Stoughton, 1983.
The Outsider. Boston, Houghton Mifflin, 1984; London, Hodder and Stoughton, 1985.
The Immigrant's Daughter. Boston, Houghton Mifflin, 1985; London, Hodder and Stoughton, 1986.
The Dinner Party. Boston, Houghton Mifflin, and London, Hodder and Stoughton, 1987.
The Pledge. Boston, Houghton Mifflin, 1988; London, Hodder and Stoughton, 1989.
The Confession of Joe Cullen. Boston, Houghton Mifflin, and London, Hodder and Stoughton, 1989.

Novels as E.V. Cunningham

Sylvia. New York, Doubleday, 1960; London, Deutsch, 1962.
Phyllis. New York, Doubleday, and London, Deutsch, 1962.
Alice. New York, Doubleday, 1963; London, Deutsch, 1965.
Lydia. New York, Doubleday, 1964; London, Deutsch, 1965.
Shirley. New York, Doubleday, and London, Deutsch, 1964.
Penelope. New York, Doubleday, 1965; London, Deutsch, 1966.
Helen. New York, Doubleday, 1966; London, Deutsch, 1967.
Margie. New York, Morrow, 1966; London, Deutsch, 1968.
Sally. New York, Morrow, and London, Deutsch, 1967.
Samantha. New York, Morrow, 1967; London, Deutsch, 1968; as *The Case of the Angry Actress*, New York, Dell, 1984.
Cynthia. New York, Morrow, 1968; London, Deutsch, 1969.
The Assassin Who Gave Up His Gun. New York, Morrow, 1969; London, Deutsch, 1970.
Millie. New York, Morrow, 1973; London, Deutsch, 1975.
The Case of the One-Penny Orange. New York, Holt Rinehart, 1977; London, Deutsch, 1978.
The Case of the Russian Diplomat. New York, Holt Rinehart, 1978; London, Deutsch, 1979.
The Case of the Poisoned Eclairs. New York, Holt Rinehart, 1979; London, Deutsch, 1980.
The Case of the Sliding Pool. New York, Delacorte Press, 1981; London, Gollancz, 1982.
The Case of the Kidnapped Angel. New York, Delacorte Press, 1982; London, Gollancz, 1983.
The Case of the Murdered Mackenzie. New York, Delacorte Press, 1984; London, Gollancz, 1985.
The Wabash Factor. New York, Delacorte Press, 1986; London, Gollancz, 1987.

Short Stories

Patrick Henry and the Frigate's Keel and Other Stories of a Young Nation. New York, Duell, 1945.
Departures and Other Stories. Boston, Little Brown, 1949.
The Last Supper and Other Stories. New York, Blue Heron Press, 1955; London, Lane, 1956.
The Edge of Tomorrow. New York, Bantam, 1961; London, Corgi, 1962.
The General Zapped an Angel. New York, Morrow, 1970.
A Touch of Infinity. New York, Morrow, 1973; London, Hodder and Stoughton, 1975.
Time and the Riddle: Thirty-One Zen Stories. Pasadena, California, Ward Ritchie Press, 1975.

Plays

The Hammer (produced New York, 1950).
Thirty Pieces of Silver (produced Melbourne, 1951). New York, Blue Heron Press, and London, Lane, 1954.
General Washington and the Water Witch. London, Lane, 1956.
The Crossing (produced Dallas, 1962).
The Hill (screenplay). New York, Doubleday, 1964.
David and Paula (produced New York, 1982).
Citizen Tom Paine, adaptation of his own novel (produced Williamstown, Massachusetts, 1985).
The Novelist (produced Williamstown, Massachusetts, 1987).
The Second Coming (produced Greenwich, Connecticut, 1991).

Screenplays: *Spartacus* (with Dalton Trumbo), 1965; *The Hessian*, 1971.

Television Plays: *What's a Nice Girl Like You . . . ?*, 1971; *The Ambassador* (*Benjamin Franklin* series), 1974; *21 Hours at Munich*, with Edward Hume, 1976.

Verse

Never to Forget the Battle of the Warsaw Ghetto, with William Gropper. New York, Jewish Peoples Fraternal Order, 1946.
Korean Lullaby. New York, American Peace Crusade, n.d.

Other

The Romance of a People (for children). New York, Hebrew Publishing Company, 1941.

Lord Baden-Powell of the Boy Scouts. New York, Messner, 1941.
Haym Salomon, Son of Liberty. New York, Messner, 1941.
The Picture-Book History of the Jews, with Bette Fast. New York, Hebrew Publishing Company, 1942.
Goethals and the Panama Canal. New York, Messner, 1942.
The Incredible Tito. New York, Magazine House, 1964.
Intellectuals in the Fight for Peace. New York, Masses and Mainstream, 1949.
Tito and His People. Winnipeg, Contemporary Publishers, 1950.
Literature and Reality. New York, International Publishers, 1950.
Peekskill, U.S.A.: A Personal Experience. New York, Civil Rights Congress, and London, International Publishing Company, 1951.
Tony and the Wonderful Door (for children). New York, Blue Heron Press, 1952; as *The Magic Door*, Culver City, California, Peace, Press, 1979.
Spain and Peace. New York, Joint Anti-Fascist Refugee Committee, 1952.
The Passion of Sacco and Vanzetti: A New England Legend. New York, Blue Heron Press, 1953; London, Lane, 1954.
The Naked God: The Writer and the Communist Party. New York, Praeger, 1957; London, Bodley Head, 1958.
The Howard Fast Reader. New York, Crown, 1960.
The Jews: Story of a People. New York, Dial Press, 1968; London, Cassell, 1970.
The Art of Zen Meditation. Culver City, California, Peace Press, 1977.
Being Red (autobiography). Boston, Houghton Mifflin, 1990.

Editor, *The Selected Work of Tom Paine*. New York, Modern Library, 1946; London, Lane, 1948.
Editor, *The Best Short Stories of Theodore Dreiser*. Cleveland, World, 1947.

*

Manuscript Collections: University of Pennsylvania, Philadelphia; University of Wisconsin, Madison.

Critical Studies: *History and Conscience: The Case of Howard Fast* by Hershel D. Meyer, Princeton, New Jersey, Anvil Atlas, 1958; *Counterpoint* by Roy Newquist, New York, Rand McNally, 1964.

* * *

It is difficult to place Howard Fast as a western novelist although his 1942 novel, *The Last Frontier*, and his recent popular trilogy, *The Immigrants*, *Second Generation*, and *The Establishment*, take place in the west. Playwright, historian, and mystery writer (under the pseudonym E.V. Cunningham), Fast is best known as an historical novelist. After *The Immigrants* and its successful screen adaptation, Fast's best-known work is *Spartacus*.

Fast has long been associated with left-wing causes in America, and has served a federal prison sentence in 1950 for his refusal to answer questions before the House Committee on Un-American Activities. While this concern with radical politics finds its most complete expression in *The Passion of Sacco and Vanzetti*, Fast's theme of the violation of human rights by government and business underlies his only true western novel, *The Last Frontier*. *The Last Frontier*, a fictional account of an actual event, is the story of the 1878 rebellion of a tribe of northern Cheyenne Indians against the conditions forced upon them on the Oklahoma Indian Territory Reservation. Starved and denuded of pride, the small group of 300 men, women, and children illegally leave the reservation to return to their ancestoral homeland. After eluding the U.S. cavalry for weeks and escaping from numerous armed encounters, part of the tribe is eventually captured. As a result of their unwavering determination not to return to the Oklahoma reservation, the imprisoned Indians suffer from starvation and exposure, and are eventually massacred when they attempt a desperate escape. As a result of their tragedy, the rest of the tribe is granted freedom by the Secretary of the Interior. Throughout the novel, Fast impresses upon the reader the inherent racism of American settlers' treatment of the Indian and points out the irony of double standards of freedom in a democracy. J.H. Jackson has called *The Last Frontier* "a model which may easily become a classic example of what to put in and what to leave out in the writing of an historical novel."

The Immigrants trilogy chronicles an Italian-French family who immigrate to America in 1889. Though essentially labor and political novels, these works depict San Francisco as it moves into the 20th century. The portraits drawn of the fishing industry, the labor strikes of 1934, the growth and rebuilding of San Francisco, and the intricate political maneuverings of California politics will be of interest to the student of western literature. With the exception of several stories, of which "Where Are Your Guns?" is a notable example, this trilogy and *The Last Frontier* constitute the bulk of Fast's claim to the title of western writer.

—David Marion Holman

FEARN, John (Francis) Russell. Also wrote as Geoffrey Armstrong; Thornton Ayre; Hugo Blayn; Gene Bentley; Maria Cappelin; Hank Carson; Dennis Clive; Hank Cole; John Cotton; Polton Cross; Poulton Cross; Astron Del Martia; Mark Denholm; Spike Gordon; Volsted Gridban; Griff; Conrad G. Holt; Frank Jones; Nat Karta; Clem Larson; Paul Lorraine; Jed McCloud; Mick McCoy; Jeb McNab; Dom Passante; Lawrence F. Rose; Frank Russell; John Russell; Elizabeth Rutland; Tex Ryan; Bryan Shaw; John Slate; Vargo Statten; K. Thomas; Earl Titan; John Wernheim; Ephriam Winiki. British. Born in Worsley, Lancashire, 5 June 1908. Married Carrie Worth in 1956. Worked as a cotton salesman on leaving school, and briefly as a cinema projectionist during World War II. Full-time writer, 1933–60. Editor, as Vargo Statten, *British Science Fiction Magazine*, Luton, Bedfordshire, 1954–56. *Died 18 September 1960.*

WESTERN PUBLICATIONS

Novels (series: Merridrew)

The Flying Horseman. Glasgow, Western, 1947.
The Avenging Ranger. Llandudno, Caernarvonshire, Kaner, 1948.
Rustlers Canyon. Llandudno, Caernarvonshire, Kaner, 1948.
Thunder Valley. Redhill, Surrey, Wells Gardner Darton, 1948.
Yellow Gulch Law. Llandudno, Caernarvonshire, Kaner, 1948.
Dead Man's Shoes. London, Paget, 1949.
Outlaw's Legacy (as Clem Larson). London, Paget, 1949.
Six-Gun Prodigal (as Hank Cole). London, Paget, 1949.

Six-Guns Shoot to Kill (as Hank Carson). Glasgow, Muir Watson, 1949.
Gunsmoke Valley. Glasgow, Muir Watson, 1949.
Stockwhip Sheriff (as Poulton Cross). Glasgow, Muir Watson, 1949.
Lawless Range (as Tex Ryan). Glasgow, Muir Watson, 1949.
Valley of the Doomed (Merridrew). Kingswood, Surrey, World's Work, 1949.
Tornado Trail. Glasgow, Muir Watson, 1949.
Arizona Love. London, Rich and Cowan, 1950.
Aztec Gold. London, Scion, 1950.
Ghost Canyon. London, Scion, 1950.
Merridrew Rides Again. Kingswood, Surrey, World's Work, 1950.
Rattlesnake. London, Scion, 1950.
Skeleton Pass. London, Scion, 1950.
Bonanza. London, Scion, 1950.
Firewater. London, Scion, 1950.
Hell's Acres (as Mick McCoy). London, Scion, 1950.
Lead Law. London, Scion, 1950.
Merridrew Marches On. Kingswood, Surrey, World's Work, 1951.
The Hanging 9. London, Scion, 1951.
Guntoter from Kansas (as Jeb McNab). London, Hamilton, 1951.
Golden Canyon. London, Partridge, 1951.
Killer's Legacy. London, Rich and Cowan, 1952.
Merridrew Fights Again. Kingswood, Surrey, World's Work, 1952.
Merridrew Follows the Trail. Kingswood, Surrey, World's Work, 1953.
Accident Trail (as Jed McCloud). London, Dragon, 1955.
Feather-Fist Jones (as Jed McCloud). London, Dragon, 1955.
Sheriff of Deadman's Bend (as Jed McCloud). London, Brown Watson, 1956.
Phantom Avenger (as Jed McCloud). London, Brown Watson, 1956.
Navajo Vengeance. London, Rich and Cowan, 1956.

Uncollected Short Stories

"Third Time Does It" (as Poulton Cross), in *Hands Up* (Glasgow), 1, 1946.
"Stranger in Town," in *Hands Up* (Glasgow), 1, 1946.
"Rope Enough," in *Hands Up Annual* (Glasgow), 1947.
"Winner Takes All," in *Hands Up Annual* (Glasgow), 1947.

OTHER PUBLICATIONS

Novels

The Intelligence Gigantic. Kingswood, Surrey, World's Work, 1943.
The Golden Amazon. Kingswood, Surrey, World's Work, 1944.
Other Eyes Watching (as Polton Cross). London, Pendulum, 1946.
The Test of Love (published anonymously). London, Popular Fiction, 1947.
Liners of Time. Kingswood, Surrey, World's Work, 1947.
Slaves of Ijax. Llandudno, Caernarvonshire, Kaner, 1948.
The Golden Amazon Returns. Kingswood, Surrey, World's Work, 1948; as *The Deathless Amazon*, Toronto, Harlequin, 1955.
Account Settled (as John Russell). London, Paget, 1949.
Murder's a Must. Glasgow, Muir Watson, 1949.
The Trembling World (as Astron Del Maria). London, Frances, 1949.
Emperor of Mars. London, Hamilton, 1950.
Warrior of Mars. London, Hamilton, 1950.
Red Men of Mars. London, Hamilton, 1950.
Goddess of Mars. London, Hamilton, 1950.
Operation Venus. London, Scion, 1950.
The Golden Amazon's Triumph. Kingswood, Surrey, World's Work, 1950.
Shattering Glass (as Frank Russell). London, Brown Watson, 1953.
Dark Boundaries (as Paul Lorraine). London, Warren, 1953.
The Hell Fruit (as Lawrence F. Rose). London, Pearson, 1953.
Formations (as Bryan Shaw). London Warren, 1953.
The Amazon's Diamond Quest. Kingswood, Surrey, World's Work, 1953.
Liquid Death (as Griff). London, Modern Fiction, 1953.
Cosmic Exodus (as Conrad G. Holt). London, Pearson, 1953.
For Sale (as Maria Cappelin). London, Brown Watson, 1953.
The Amazon Strikes Again. Kingswood, Surrey, World's Work, 1954.
Conquest of the Amazon. London, Futura, 1976.
No Grave Need I. Wallsend, Harbottle, 1984.
The Slitherers. Wallsend, Harbottle, 1984.
Climate Incorporated. Wallsend, Harbottle, 1985.
Land's End—Labrador. Wallsend, Harbottle, 1991.

Novels as Vargo Statten

Annihilation. London, Scion, 1950.
The Micro Men. London, Scion, 1950.
Wanderer of Space. London, Scion, 1950.
2000 Years On. London, Scion, 1950.
Inferno. London, Scion, 1950.
The Cosmic Flame. London, Scion, 1950.
Nebula X. London, Scion, 1950.
The Sun Makers. London, Scion, 1950.
The Avenging Martian. London, Scion, 1951.
Cataclysm. London, Scion, 1951.
The Red Insects. London, Scion, 1951.
Deadline to Pluto. London, Scion, 1951.
The Petrified Planet. London, Scion, 1951.
Born of Luna. London, Scion, 1951.
The Devouring Fire. London, Scion, 1951.
The Renegade Star. London, Scion, 1951.
The New Satellite. London, Scion, 1951.
The Catalyst. London, Scion, 1951.
The Inner Cosmos. London, Scion, 1952.
The Space Warp. London, Scion, 1952.
The Eclipse Express. London, Scion, 1952.
The Time Bridge. London, Scion, 1952.
The Man from Tomorrow. London, Scion, 1952.
The G-Bomb. London, Scion, 1952.
Laughter in Space. London, Scion, 1952.
Across the Ages. London, Scion, 1952.
The Last Martian. London, Scion, 1952.
Worlds to Conquer. London, Scion, 1952.
Decreation. London, Scion, 1952.
The Time Trap. London, Scion, 1952.
Science Metropolis. London, Scion, 1952.
To the Ultimate. London, Scion, 1952.
Ultra Spectrum. London, Scion, 1953.
The Dust Destroyer. London, Scion, 1953.
Black-Wing of Mars. London, Scion, 1953.
Man in Duplicate. London, Scion, 1953.
Zero Hour. London, Scion, 1953.
The Black Avengers. London, Scion, 1953.

Odyssey of Nine. London, Scion, 1953.
Pioneer 1990. London, Scion, 1953.
The Interloper. London, Scion, 1953.
Man of Two Worlds. London, Scion, 1953.
The Lie Destroyer. London, Scion, 1953.
Black Bargain. London, Scion, 1953.
The Grand Illusion. London, Scion, 1953.
Wealth of the Void. London, Scion, 1954.
A Time Appointed. London, Scion, 1954.
I Spy. . . . London, Scion, 1954.
The Multi-Man. London, Scion, 1954.
Creature from the Black Lagoon (novelization of screenplay). London, Dragon, 1954.
1,000-Year Voyage. London, Dragon, 1954.
Earth 2. London, Dragon, 1955.

Novels as Volsted Gridban

Moons for Sale. London, Scion, 1953.
The Dyno-Depressant. London, Scion, 1953.
Magnetic Brain. London, Scion, 1953.
Scourge of the Atom. London, Scion, 1953.
A Thing of the Past (Brooks). London, Scion, 1953.
Exit Life. London, Scion, 1953.
The Master Must Die (Quirke). London, Scion, 1953.
The Purple Wizard. London, Scion, 1953.
The Genial Dinosaur (Brooks). London, Scion, 1954.
The Frozen Limit. London, Scion, 1954.
I Came, I Saw, I Wondered. London, Scion, 1954.
The Lonely Astronomer (Quirke). London, Scion, 1954.

Novels as Gene Bentley

Loves of Lydia. London, Scion, 1954.
Bitter Harvest. London, Dragon, 1955.
En Route to Romance. London, Dragon, 1955.
Glamour in the Morning. London, Dragon, 1955.
No Rain for Maria. London, Dragon, 1955.

Novels as Elizabeth Rutland

Cherie. London, Dragon, 1954.
Hearts Can Heal. London, Dragon, 1955.
Moon Magic. London, Dragon, 1955.
Heedless Heart. London, Dragon, 1955.
Night Nurse. London, Scion, 1955.
Devil's Daughter. London, Brown Watson, 1956.
Summer Fires. London, Brown Watson, 1956.

Novels as John Slate

Black Maria, M.A. London, Rich and Cowan, 1944.
Maria Marches On. London, Rich and Cowan, 1945.
One Remained Seated. London, Rich and Cowan, 1946.
Thy Arm Alone. London, Rich and Cowan, 1947.
Framed in Guilt. London, Rich and Cowan, 1948.
Death in Silhouette. London, Rich and Cowan, 1950.

Novels as Hugo Blayn

Except for One Thing. London, Stanley Paul, 1947.
The Five Matchboxes. London, Stanley Paul, 1948.
Flashpoint. London, Stanley Paul, 1950.
What Happened to Hammond? London, Stanley Paul, 1951.
Vision Sinster (as Nat Karta). London, Dragon, 1954.
The Silvered Cage. London, Dragon, 1955.

Novels as Earl Titan

The Gold of Akada. London, Scion, 1951.
Anjani the Mighty. London, Scion, 1951.

Novels as Spike Gordon

Don't Touch Me. London, Modern Fiction, 1953.
You Take the Rap. London, Modern Fiction, 1953.

Novels as Dennis Clive

Valley of Pretenders. New York, Columbia, 1942.
The Voice Commands. New York, Columbia, 1942.

*

Critical Study: *The Multi-Man: A Biographic and Bibliographic Study of John Russell Fearn* (includes bibliography) by Philip Harbottle, privately printed, 1968.

* * *

John Russell Fearn, an English writer born at the beginning of this century, was successful in breaking the American stranglehold on science-fiction publishing, and then flooded the British market under a variety of pseudonyms. He had the ability to produce works with a great speed and reliability that upset many of his fellow writers, who frowned upon this skill. But he remained unrepentant, and went on to produce Westerns when his SF book sales faltered. In 1947 he wrote four short stories which he sold to Western Book Distributors, then produced six Westerns in 1948. It was this genre that Fearn now began to exploit and it paid him enough for him to consider ". . . the Western is my bread and butter, leaving me time to concentrate on my science-fiction works."

The Westerns that Fearn did produce seem to be based on the many films he had seen as a young man. In believing that a view of the lighter side to the West was called for, he brought a fresh twist to the usual series-type formula, and created the Merridrew series. Jenkinson Talbot Merridrew, a former English butler and playboy, works as the man-servant to fellow expatriate Bradley Wood and his wife. Merridrew is middle-aged, weighs 18 or more stone, wears a bowler hat, and has decidedly sadistic tendencies.

Valley of the Doomed was the first novel in the series, and introduces these naive Englishmen to the seemingly sleepy, one-horse town of Double Peak, Arizona. They find the American way of life quite unlike the life style they were expecting, but they quickly learn to adapt, and find themselves embroiled in their first adventure. *Merridrew Rides Again* continues with these characters when they face up to Steve Barrington and his gang of outlaws who, having killed the sheriff, declare themselves the law of Double Peak. Indignant that someone should have the temerity to tell Englishmen what to do, Merridew and Wood take on the cut-throats. In this book Merridrew is voted in as the Mayor, and Wood as sheriff, a fine way for this Laurel-and-Hardy partnership to continue in *Merridrew Marches On*. The author packs his stories full of action and vivid characterization. As the series progressed, so these characters became more outrageous. The Reverend Walter Prendergast, the high priest of the All Sinners Gospel, is the main adversary in *Merridrew Marches On*, and when "Hardware" Saunders arrives on the scene the stage is set for Merridrew and Wood to launch themselves into another of their typical adventures. *Merridrew Fights Again* is a more formulaic piece of work, and involves a stranger buying the town, on behalf of the railroad, for one million dollars. The gold is delivered but—not so surprisingly—it is stolen right back some time afterwards. It is up to our two intrepid heroes to bring the men involved to justice. *Merridrew Follows the Trail*, the final book in the series, is a hodgepodge of a story, with the supporting characters not so convincing as in previous works. A female singer, a saddletramp, and six hardened gunmen are thrown into this cocktail, with Merridrew finding himself on trial for murder.

Fearn set out to baffle simultaneously his critics and his readers with *Navajo Vengeance*. Starting in the traditional manner, this otherwise unpromising book contains a bizarre twist that takes it to the border of fantasy. Carl Rutter is convicted by the boss of an up-and-coming cattle town for a murder he didn't commit. He escapes being lynched by the timely intervention of Connie McBride, a young girl secretly in love with him. He and "Smoky" Jones leave the town and take to wandering the country. Almost too conveniently they find an ancient Navajo temple, and upon exploring the catacombs discover a hoard of gold. Rutter figures on using his new-found wealth to buy out Whittacker Brice. He asks the help of a Navajo medicine man to alter his features and voice, thus creating a new persona. He now becomes a dangerous enemy to Brice, and events develop into a race for supremacy between the two men.

The Avenging Ranger also explores familiar ground, with a wealthy land owner wanting more to feed his megalomanic appetites. Here, Fearn makes him an oilman, who has discovered that a rich field spreads across four ranches. One man stands in Emerton Martin's way, and Jeff Ward is summarily executed, leaving his son to take up the gauntlet as his avenger. There is nothing to recommend this book as being any different from the hundreds of revenge-motivated plots which were better written examples of their genre.

Fearn's western works are significant because of their numbers rather than their content. He set out to show that a basic formula could be adapted to any particular genre. His science-fiction works have been republished since his death, and possibly his more obscure Westerns may see the light of day again.

—Mike Stotter

FEIKEMA, Feike. *See* **MANFRED, Frederick.**

FERBER, Edna. American. Born in Kalamazoo, Michigan, 15 August 1885. Educated at Ryan High School, Appleton, Wisconsin, graduated 1902. Reporter, Appleton *Daily Crescent*, 1902–04, Milwaukee *Journal*, 1905–08, and Chicago *Tribune*; full-time writer from 1910; lived in New York after 1912; served with the Writers War Board and as a war correspondent with the United States Army Air Force during World War II. Recipient: Pulitzer prize, 1924. Litt.D.: Columbia University, New York; Adelphi College, Garden City, New York. Member, American Academy. *Died 16 April 1968.*

WESTERN PUBLICATIONS

Novels

So Big. New York, Doubleday, and London, Heinemann, 1924.
Cimarron. New York, Doubleday, and London, Heinemann, 1930.
Giant. New York, Doubleday, and London, Gollancz, 1952.
Ice Palace. New York, Doubleday, and London, Gollancz, 1958.

OTHER PUBLICATIONS

Novels

Dawn O'Hara, The Girl Who Laughed. New York, Stokes, 1911; London, Methuen, 1925.
Fanny Herself. New York, Stokes, 1917; London, Methuen, 1923.
The Girls. New York, Doubleday, 1921; London, Heinemann, 1922.
Show Boat. New York, Doubleday, and London, Heinemann, 1926.
American Beauty. New York, Doubleday, and London, Heinemann, 1931.
Come and Get It. New York, Doubleday, and London, Heinemann, 1935.
Nobody's in Town (includes *Trees Die at the Top*). New York, Doubleday, and London, Heinemann, 1938.
Saratoga Trunk. New York, Doubleday, 1941; London, Heinemann, 1942.
Great Son. New York, Doubleday, and London, Heinemann, 1945.

Short Stories

Buttered Side Down. New York, Stokes, 1912; London, Methuen, 1926.
Roast Beef, Medium: The Business Adventures of Emma McChesney and Her Son, Jock. New York, Stokes, 1913; London, Methuen, 1920.
Personality Plus: Some Experiences of Emma McChesney and Her Son, Jock. New York, Stokes, 1914.
Emma McChesney & Co. New York, Stokes, 1915.
Cheerful, By Request. New York, Doubleday, 1918; London, Methuen, 1919.
Half Portions. New York, Doubleday, 1920.
Gigolo. New York, Doubleday, and London, 1920; as *Among Those Present*, London, Nash and Grayson, 1923.
Mother Knows Best. New York, Doubleday, and London, Heinemann, 1927.
They Brought Their Women. New York, Doubleday, and London, Heinemann, 1933.
No Room at the Inn. New York, Doubleday, 1941.
One Basket: Thirty-One Stories. New York, Simon and Schuster, 1947.

Plays

Our Mrs. McChesney, with George V. Hobart (produced New York, 1915).
$1200 a Year, with Newman Levy. New York, Doubleday, 1920.
Minick, with George S. Kaufman, adaptation of the story "Old Man Minick" by Ferber (produced New York, 1924). Published as *Old Man Minick: A Short Story . . . Minick: A*

Play, New York, Doubleday, 1924; London, Heinemann, 1925.

The Eldest: A Drama of American Life. New York, Appleton, 1925.

The Royal Family, with George S. Kaufman (produced New York, 1927). New York, Doubleday, 1928; as *Theatre Royal* (produced London, 1935), London, French, 1936.

Dinner at Eight, with George S. Kaufman (produced New York, 1932; London, 1933). New York, Doubleday, 1932; London, Heinemann, 1933.

Stage Door, with George S. Kaufman (produced New York, 1936; London, 1946). New York, Doubleday, 1936; London, Heinemann, 1937.

The Land Is Bright, with George S. Kaufman (produced New York, 1941). New York, Doubleday, 1941.

Bravo!, with George S. Kaufman (produced New York, 1948). New York, Dramatists Play Service, 1949.

Screenplay: *A Gay Old Dog*, 1919.

Other

A Peculiar Treasure (autobiography). New York, Doubleday, and London, Heinemann, 1939.

A Kind of Magic (autobiography). New York, Doubleday, and London, Gollancz, 1963.

*

Critical Studies: *Women and Success in American Society in the Works of Edna Ferber* by Mary Rose Shaughnessy, New York, Gordon Press, 1977; *Edna Ferber: A Biography* by Julie Goldsmith Gilbert, New York, Doubleday, 1978.

* * *

Novelist, short story writer, dramatist, Edna Ferber is a facile, competent author whose work is too often spoiled by superficiality and an excess of sentimentality. Ferber was extremely popular, particularly in the 1920's and 1930's; but critical success, then and now, has largely eluded her.

Probably the literary qualities of her work have, to some extent, been underestimated. Certainly Ferber has a good reportorial ear for dialogue. She is capable of creating the occasionally memorable character, most often a woman. Her plots are usually well-constructed with a minimum of coincidence. On the other hand, writing primarily for entertainment, Ferber introduces very few weighty ideas, message, or themes.

Typically, Ferber's fiction focusses on a young American woman who is suddenly thrust into a new, unusual role, often in a world where she must compete with men. Thus, Selina Peake Dejong, in *So Big* (winner of a 1924 Pulitzer prize), is left penniless when her father dies, but is ultimately victorious in her struggle to survive amid much hardship and privation, first as a school teacher, then as the wife of a truck-gardener.

Along with *So Big*, Ferber's best novels are probably *Cimarron* and *Giant*. Both novels reflect extensive research into the history and customs of the American Southwest; a certain raw authenticity is the result. *Cimarron* is a reduplication of life in pioneer Oklahoma from 1889 to about 1923. The heroine, Sabra Cravat, and her weak, drifter husband, Yancey, survive the vicissitudes of Territorial days, making the land-run, starting a newspaper, and rearing two children. The novel ends during the oil-boom, presenting, incidentally, one of the first fictional treatments of the impact of oil money on the Osage Indians.

In *Giant* Leslie Lynnton from Virginia marries Jordan Benedict, who manages a family ranch, Reata, in south Texas. Reata is huge: over two million acres and obviously patterned after the King ranch. Although *Giant* covers some 25 years beginning in the early 1920's, over half the novel is devoted to the first few weeks of the Benedict marriage to show the cultural shock of the newcomer and her determination to face up to Texas and Texans. Leslie Benedict faints at her first barbecue, but when she vows, "I'm never going to faint again," the reader is ready to cheer her spirit and character. The broader picture of Texas sketched in *Giant* is a caricature, albeit an entertaining one. It gives Ferber ample opportunity to describe what she describes best—various kinds of food and the consumption thereof.

Brief mention should be made of *Ice Palace*, set in modern Alaska, a novel which can claim some credit for fostering eventual admission to statehood of the former territory. Ferber should be remembered also for having written *Show Boat*, the adaptation of which has been highly successful on both stage and screen.

—Robert J. Barnes

FERGUSSON, Harvey. American. Born in Albuquerque, New Mexico, 28 January 1890. Educated at New Mexico Military Institute, Roswell, 1906; Washington and Lee University, Lexington, Virginia, 1907–11, B.A. 1911. Married 1) Polly Pretty in 1919 (divorced); 2) Rebecca McCann in 1927 (died 1927). Ranger, Kit Carson National Forest, New Mexico, 1911; reporter, Washington, D.C. *Herald*, 1912, Savannah *Morning News*, Georgia, 1912 and Richmond *Times-Dispatch*, Virginia, 1912; with Washington bureau, Chicago *Record-Herald*, 1914–15; assistant to columnist Frederic H. Haskin, for several years; freelance writer from 1923: screenwriter, 1931–42. *Died 27 August 1971.*

WESTERN PUBLICATIONS

Novels

Followers of the Sun: A Trilogy of the Santa Fe Trail. New York, Knopf, 1936; as *The Santa Fe Omnibus*, New York, Grosset and Dunlap, 1938.

The Blood of the Conquerors. New York, Knopf, 1921; London, Chapman and Hall, 1922.

Wolf Song. New York, Knopf, 1927.

In Those Days. New York, Knopf, 1929; London, Corgi, 1956.

Grant of Kingdom. New York, Morrow, 1950; London, Cassell, 1951.

The Conquest of Don Pedro. New York, Morrow, 1954; London, Cassell, 1955.

OTHER PUBLICATIONS

Novels

Capitol Hill. New York, Knopf, 1923; London, Lane, 1924.

Women and Wives. New York, Knopf, and London, Lane, 1924.

Hot Saturday. New York, Knopf, 1926.

Footloose McGarnigal. New York, Knopf, 1930.

The Life of Riley. New York, Knopf, 1937; as *Riley*, London, Constable, 1938; as *What a Man Wants*, New York, Bantam, 1952.

Plays

Screenplays: *It Happened in Hollywood*, with others, 1937; *Stand Up and Fight*, with others, 1939.

Other

Rio Grande. New York, Knopf, 1933.
Modern Man: His Belief and Behavior. New York, Knopf, 1936.
Home in the West: An Inquiry into My Origins. New York, Duell, 1945.
People and Power: A Study of Political Behavior in America. New York, Morrow, 1947.

Editor, *The Last Rustler: The Autobiography of Lee Sage*. Boston, Little Brown, 1930.

*

Critical Studies: *Harvey Fergusson* by James K. Folsom, Austin, Texas, Steck Vaughn, 1969; *Harvey Fergusson* by William T. Pilkington, Boston, Twayne, 1975; *Frontier's End: The Life and Literature of Harvey Fergusson* by Robert F. Gish, Lincoln, University of Nebraska Press, 1988.

* * *

Harvey Fergusson was born in Albuquerque, New Mexico, but, like Eugene Manlove Rhodes, left the territory as a young man to go east and returned only for brief visits. Of the 14 books Fergusson wrote, critics have singled out five of them for special commendation. The first three, chronologically, are *The Blood of the Conquerors*, *Wolf Song*, and *In Those Days*, which Fergusson brought together in his trilogy *Followers of the Sun*. They are, as the later two novels with a southwestern setting, romantic historical reconstructions. This is to say, in all five of these novels Fergusson preserved the classic structure of romance: there is an *agon*, or conflict, that requires a clearly defined hero to resolve it during the *pathos*, or passion portion of the story, resulting in a final *anagnorisis*, or recognition. Fergusson articulated the recognition to be found in all five of his southwestern novels in his Foreword to *Followers of the Sun* when he observed that "the pioneering past has now been diligently debunked, but as surely as the flavor of reality has been recaptured the quality of the heroic has been lost. I sought to unite them because it seemed to me the heroism of the pioneer life was genuine and had lost its value."

In terms of the internal chronology of the trilogy, *Wolf Song* comes first. It is a mountain-man story, and its hero, Sam Lash, was based loosely on Fergusson's impression of Kit Carson. The story concerns Sam Lash's impassioned love affair with Lola Salazar, a beautiful *rico* maiden, and his life and death battle, a *sparagmos*, or mangling, also an ingredient of classical romance, with a savage Cheyenne warrior. The Cheyenne is vanquished, of course, and Lash is united with Lola at the end. But such a bald statement of Fergusson's plot does not convey the remarkable lyricism of his style, an almost tactile sensuosity, or his gift for vividly characterizing the land in its many moods. In his Foreword to the trilogy Fergusson also insisted that "what ails the huge and infantile body of our conventional Western romance, from Beadle's dime novels on down, is not that its stories are melodramatic but that its heroes and heroines are lifeless." This is a significant statement. Fergusson tried to bring his heroes and heroines to life, but not in such a way that they cease being types: they are still heroes and heroines. The same year *Wolf Song* was published Fergusson married for a second time, and *Wolf Song* is dedicated to Rebecca McCann who, tragically, died before the year ended, having contracted pneumonia. John R. Milton in *The Novel of the American West* (1980) remarked that the sensitively drawn female characters in all of Fergusson's later novels may well be a tribute to Rebecca. As fine and perceptive a critic as Milton has been upon occasion, before too much stock is placed in this statement it must be tempered with an acknowledgment that for Milton—as he wrote in an essay titled "The Western Novel: Whence or What?" (1972)—the west is primarily a masculine experience, in part because the landscape "West of the Mississippi [is] masculine—hard, big, open, often dangerous, often harsh."

After a fashion Fergusson drew thoroughly characterized stereotypes and there is no doubt that he was, philosophically, a believer in white supremacy. This has often led his critical advocates to appear in the guise of apologists. William T. Pilkington commented in his Introduction to *Grant of Kingdom* that "although readers today may see traces of racial or ethnic stereotyping in an occasional phrase or characterizaton, it must be remembered that such instances represent the feelings only of characters in the novel; in reprinting *Grant of Kingdom* the present publisher intends no endorsement of any such cultural prejudice, nor should prejudice be attributed to Harvey Fergusson, all of whose writings are marked by a deeply humanistic spirit." The key words in what Pilkington wrote are "such instances represent the feelings only of characters in the novel . . ." "Arnold Blore," Fergusson remarked in *Grant of Kingdom*, "learned from childhood how to be faultlessly polite to the men he dealt with and also how to despise them. Although he did not know it, he had toward these people the same attitude the Negroes had toward the whites—an attitude subtly compounded of hypocrisy, cunning, envy, and contempt." If Blore did not know it, and Blore is the character being discussed, then whose feelings are being represented? At another point in the novel Fergusson reflected that "an Indian who had not been ruined by contact with dishonest white men was always a good friend in two days. He would never forget you, any more than a dog or horse will forget you, and he would keep his word."

"Some of these Mexican girls took a powerful hold upon his flesh," the reader is told about Jean Ballard, the hero of *Grant of Kingdom*. "Many of them were pretty and they had a soft and voluptuous quality, a completeness of submission and response that made them wholly different from the shrill and nervous women, laborious and full of malaria, he had known in Indiana." Perhaps we might shrug our shoulders and say, well, all the Mexican women Ballard met *were really* this way, to say nothing of the "shrill and nervous" women back in Indiana. However, every character in this novel agrees with Ballard's experience. "Waverly [Buncombe] believed not at all in the value of chastity and very little in its existence," the reader is told. "Moreover, it had small place in the customs of a country which abounded in willing brown women and had a long tradition of erotic license." Milton's comment about Fergusson's female characters and his belief in the West as a masculine experience can now be put into the proper context by reflecting that Fergusson's "heroines" are Mexican women displaying all the traits observed by Ballard, Buncombe, and other characters in the other novels, and the novels are so structured that it is evident that these traits are prescribed as being virtues. In *The Blood of the Conquerors* the hero, Ramon Delcasar, falls in love with a blonde-haired Anglo-American, but by the time of the recognition he has forgotten her and is living happily with Catalina, a Mexican woman.

Fergusson, it would appear, was closer to his maternal grandfather, Franz Huning, who arrived in Santa Fe in 1850 and became a successful merchant in Albuquerque in the years after 1857, and then a representative to Washington, D.C., once New Mexico became a state. Huning left behind him a memoir and Fergusson, to an extent, based on it both *In Those Days* and the fifth and perhaps finest novel of his southwestern group, *The Conquest of Don Pedro*. Robert Jayson is the hero of *In Those Days*, a man who comes to New Mexico, becomes a prosperous merchant, only to wind up a victim of change. This is essentially the same plot as that of *The Conquest of Don Pedro* in which Leo Mendes, a Jewish peddlar, comes to New Mexico, becomes a successful merchant, and, finally, loses everything, including his young and beautiful Hispanic wife who is attracted to and won by an Anglo-American, although for Leo, "a man's destiny is a thing he discovers, a mystery that unfolds," and the end of the novel can be interpreted as a new beginning.

Robert Jayson is a victim, as almost every sympathetic character is in these five novels, to the encroaching Anglo-American invasion. Ideologically he fails because he must fail because he is a victim; and he is a victim because the "historical" aspect of the romance declares that he must be a victim in order to make poignantly evident the moral message concerning the spiritual emptiness of Anglo-American materialism. Leo Mendes, on the other hand, is not so completely a victim because, while Leo may be "wholly unable to deal with the world that was creeping up on him, a world in which men were always counting their dollars and their minutes," he is left with an option, namely to pull out and leave. "The West," James K. Folsom wrote in *Harvey Fergusson*, "in [Fergusson's] fiction is constantly a good place *to be from* rather than a desirable place to *return to*." The italics are Folsom's, and this perspective is most visible in *The Conquest of Don Pedro* which makes it the least romantic of Fergusson's romantic historical reconstructions, but it is still only a matter of degree. The most compelling imagery in Fergusson's southwestern fiction is his whole-hearted questioning of Anglo-American values; the problem critics who like his fiction have with Fergusson is that they want to applaud his imagery and do not know what to conclude about the plot contrivances and stereotypical characterizations Fergusson employed in ideologically dramatizing it.

—Jon Tuska

FIELD, Charles. *See* **ROWLAND, Donald S.**

FIELD, Frank Chester. *See* **ROBERTSON, Frank C.**

FIELD, Peter. *See* **DRAGO, Harry Sinclair; DRESSER, Davis; MANN, E.B.**

FIELDHOUSE, W. L. *See* **FIELDHOUSE, William.**

FIELDHOUSE, William. Also writes as W. L. Fieldhouse; Patrick Lee. Address: c/o Pinnacle Books, P.O. Box 737, Liberty, Missouri 64068, U.S.A.

WESTERN PUBLICATIONS

Novels (series: Klaw)

Klaw. New York, Tower, 1980.
Town of Blood (Klaw). New York, Tower, 1981.
The Rattler Gang (Klaw). New York, Tower, 1981.
Gun Lust (as W. L. Fieldhouse). New York, Tower, 1982.

Novels as Patrick Lee (series: Six-Gun Samurai in both books)

Gundown at Golden Gate. New York, Pinnacle, 1981.
Bushido Lawman. New York, Pinnacle, 1982.

* * *

Before turning his attention to the action/adventure genre (and becoming the main contributor to the Phoenix Force series), William Fieldhouse wrote a number of fast-paced formula westerns for the U.S. paperback market. The first of these was the *Klaw* series, written very much in the ultra-violent, hero-with-a-gimmick style that proliferated in the late 1970's and early 1980's.

The fairly predictable "origin" story begins just after the Civil War, when the hero, John Klawson, returns home to discover that his parents have been murdered (presumably by a band of drunken Shoshone, who have since been hanged for the crime) and their ranch in the hands of the local bank. Suspecting that there is more to the business than meets the eye, Klawson decides to investigate, but before he can discover the truth, he is ambushed. In a particularly bloody fray his gun-hand is sliced off by a machete, and he is shot in the stomach and left for dead.

Friends manage to nurse him back to life, however, and the local doctor designs two types of hook to replace his lost hand. With the help of the local blacksmith, they also devise a way for Klawson (or Klaw, as he soon becomes known) to fit his Colt or sabre to the stump.

As soon as Klaw is back on the trail, he discovers that his home town has actually been chosen as the base of operations for a group calling itself the Euro-American Financial Alliance, whose plan is to take over America. After successfully putting a stop to that, he then decides to track down the men who ambushed him, and when his search takes him to Mexico (where the last of his enemies now lead a bandit gang some 20 men strong), he manages to get inside their fortress and turn their own weapons against them in a far-fetched, but nevertheless rousing, climax.

Two further Klaw adventures followed before the series was cancelled, both of them fairly routine stories that deviated little from the dictates of this particular sub-genre. In *Town of Blood* Klaw reluctantly becomes the sheriff of a small Texas town under threat from a former Rebel officer and his army of killers, who are searching for a fortune in Confederate gold hidden somewhere in the town. In *The Rattler Gang*, Klaw's plans to head for California with $10,000 in his saddlebags are spoilt when a gang of masked raiders robs him. Klaw tracks them through Apache country in order to retrieve the stolen cash, and along the way also tangles with two deadly killers who have been hired by the aforementioned Euro-American Financial Alliance to eliminate him for having ruined their plans for the domination of America (a plot-thread which is ultimately left unresolved).

With Patrick Andrews and Mark K. Roberts, Fieldhouse created another equally improbable but nonetheless serviceable western series, Six-Gun Samurai, for Pinnacle Books, under the pseudonym Patrick Lee. When ninja warriors attack an American mission in Japan in 1854, a 12-year-old former midshipman named Tommy Fletcher, who survives the raid, is forced to fend for himself on the streets of a teeming, alien metropolis. Fortunately, his Cherokee ancestry helps him pass for an *Ainu* (barbaric white Japanese). After some weeks, Tommy meets a samurai warrior named Tanaka Nobunara who, impressed by the boy's courage, takes him in and eventually adopts him. 20 years later, Tommy (who has now learned all the warrior tricks his adopted father can teach him) discovers that his natural family has been murdered, and their Georgia plantation razed to the ground by a renegade Union colonel named Edward Hollister. What follows is a fairly standard revenge series in which "Tanaka" Tom tracks down Hollister and his men and dispatches them with a variety of swords, knives, and throwing stars, as well as the odd display of martial arts. Fieldhouse wrote two books in the sequence, the third and the sixth, entitled *Gundown at Golden Gate* and *Bushido Lawman* respectively.

To date, Fieldhouse has only written one non-series Western under his own name, *Gun Lust*, and a surprisingly above-average offering it is, too, showing just what the author can do when the restraints of writing popular series Westerns no longer apply. When a veteran bounty hunter (and one-time Confederate officer) named Cougar meets up with Alexander Shaddrock, a former Union officer new to bounty hunting, and discovers that they are both after the same outlaw, they decide to team up. Before long, however, they find themselves involved in a plan to restart the Confederacy and some very suspect railroad dealings. As the title might imply, there is more sex than usual for a Fieldhouse western, and it is quite graphically described, but to a certain extent this is offset by a fair amount of humour, much of which comes from the failure of most of the cast to pronounce Shaddrock's name correctly. The growing sense of camaraderie between Cougar and Shaddrock is also very well handled.

Although much of his work in the western field has been fairly predictable, there is no denying that Fieldhouse does have a knack for creating pacy stories with plenty of action, aimed directly at the modern paperback market. Since he appears to have abandoned the field, however, we can only conclude that his passing has most definitely been the action/adventure genre's gain.

—David Whitehead

FIELDS, Frank. Address: c/o Robert Hale Ltd., Clerkenwell House, 45–47 Clerkenwell Green, London EC1R 0HT, England.

Western Publications

Novels (series: Ellis Stack)

Dirt Farmers. London, Hale, 1988.
The Revenge of Ellis Stack. London, Hale, 1989.
Stack's Law. London, Hale, 1989.

* * *

The antecedents of Frank Fields's three western novels would seem to be as much cinematic as literary. The Eastwood vogue of spaghetti Westerns, with their cold-eyed psychopathic gunmen and sweating victims, appears to have been a major influence on his work, allied perhaps with the adult westerns of the late 1970's and early 1980's. Certainly the graphically described violence, melodramatic sex, and frequent outbursts of gratuitous profanity evoke such cinematic comparisons. *Dirt Farmers*, Fields's debut novel, centres on the struggle of ex-soldier Gort Bailey to keep his farm and family out of the clutches of the land-grabbing Victor Calhoun. In the course of his efforts, Bailey undergoes a savage beating by Calhoun's men in his own farmhouse—his wife, not too surprisingly, is giving birth at the time—and the reader is regaled with details of his vomiting over himself in the process. Later, displaying a truly Eastwoodish touch of sadism, Bailey retaliates by cornering a gunman and shooting off the tips of his ears at close range. These repellent aspects of the novel, together with the liberal use of industrial language—characters are frequently instructed to "go shit," for example—tend to detract from the more individual contributions of the author. Calhoun, interestingly, reforms his ways in the latter part of the book, and saves Bailey's life, an unusual twist of which more might perhaps have been made. Fields also introduces a detective element at one stage, with Bailey showing unexpected sophistication in his use of a plaster cast to identify a footprint. These virtues, however, are overshadowed by the grim pseudo-realism that pervades the rest of the story. The preponderance of dialogue at the expense of true description is perhaps also further evidence of movie influence.

The two Ellis Stack novels which were written after *Dirt Farmers* both testify to Fields' storytelling abilities, although at times showing a lack of factual knowledge in matters of detail. The amount of salt required for the salting of beef is badly underestimated, for instance, and the admixture of Hereford cattle with cross-breeds would be immediately visible to an experienced eye. More significantly, when Ellis is on trial, no mention is made of the note he has seen pinned to the door of the sheriff's office, a note which proves his innocence. These aside, Fields maintains a brisk, dramatic pace in both works, opening *The Revenge of Ellis Stack* with a crisis which emphasizes the conflict between the Stacks and their land-hungry adversary, and maintaining the action with Ellis standing trial on a trumped-up rustling charge. Unfortunately, once he finds himself in prison, the story degenerates into further porno-violence, with graphic descriptions of bestiality, buggery, and under-age sex performed by various inmates. This section, I feel, undermines *The Revenge of Ellis Stack* as a successful Western, and is compounded by a somewhat anti-climactic ending. The result, while confirming the author's narrative skill, is a flawed, uneven work of fiction.

Stack's Law is more impressive, with a strong storyline in which Ellis, posing as another ex-convict, enters a town controlled by two unscrupulous and powerful men. The reader's attention is engaged throughout the novel, and there are some useful character studies, notably the figure of Tom Blake and his story of rags to riches and back to rags again in three generations. This is not to say that the novel is without its faults—this time there is an excess of description in places, with frequent repetition of the same word within a few sentences, while in the dialogue between Esther and Ellis we are several times treated to a mention of the lady's "sexy arse," comment which is both tedious and unnecessary. It could also be argued that the novel is too long, and could have been more effectively ended at the point where Ellis talks things over with Doc, and heads for the bar. This said, *Stack's Law* comes over as a capable, well-executed western novel, and the best of its author's work so far.

Fields's writing shows obvious limitations, and is—in this writer's view, at least—rather too indebted to the ethos of the spaghetti Western. On the other hand, it is clear that he has definite ability as a storyteller, and both Ellis and other characters like Tom Blake have the potential for further development in future western novels.

—Clarence Naylor

FISHER, Clay. *See* **ALLEN, Henry Wilson.**

FISHER, Vardis (Alvero). American. Born in Annis, Idaho, 31 March 1895. Educated at Rigby High School, Idaho, graduated 1915; University of Utah, Salt Lake City, B.A. 1920; University of Chicago, A.M. 1922, Ph.D. (magna cum laude) 1925. Served in the United States Army Artillery Corps, 1918: Corporal. Married 1) Leona McMurtrey in 1917 (died 1924), two sons; 2) Margaret Trusler in 1928 (divorced 1939), one son; 3) Opal Laurel Holmes in 1940. Assistant Professor of English, University of Utah, 1925–28, and New York University, 1928–31; full-time writer from 1931: teacher at Montana State University, Bozeman, Summer 1932, 1933; director, Idaho Writers' Project and Historical Records Project (Works Progress Administration), 1935–39; syndicated columnist ("Vardis Fisher Says") in Idaho newspapers, 1941–68. Recipient: Western Writers of America Spur award, for novel, 1966, for non-fiction, 1969. *Died 9 July 1968.*

WESTERN PUBLICATIONS

Novels

Toilers of the Hills. Boston, Houghton Mifflin, 1928; London, Gollancz, 1929.
Dark Bridwell. Boston, Houghton Mifflin, and London, Gollancz, 1931; as *The Wild One*, New York, Pyramid, 1952.
Vridar Hunter tetralogy:
In Tragic Life. Caldwell, Idaho, Caxton, 1932; as *I See No Sin*, London, Boriswood, 1934.
Passions Spin the Plot. New York, Doubleday, 1934; London, Boriswood, 1935.
We Are Betrayed. New York, Doubleday, 1935; London, Boriswood, 1936.
No Villain Need Be. New York, Doubleday, 1936.
April: A Fable of Love. New York, Doubleday, 1937; London, Methuen, 1939.
Children of God. New York, Harper, 1939; London, Methuen, 1940.
City of Illusion. Caldwell, Idaho, Caxton, and London, Methuen, 1941.
The Mothers. New York, Vanguard Press, 1943; London, Methuen, 1945.
Pemmican: A Novel of the Old Hudson Bay Territory. New York, Doubleday, 1956; London, Hale, 1958.
Tale of Valor: A Novel of the Lewis and Clark Expedition. New York, Doubleday, 1958.
Orphans in Gethsemane. Denver, Swallow, 1960; as *For Passion, For Heaven* and *The Great Confession*, New York, Pyramid, 2 vols., 1962.
Mountain Man. New York, Morrow, 1965.

Short Stories

Odyssey of a Hero. Philadelphia, Rittenhouse, 1937.
Love and Death: The Complete Stories of Vardis Fisher. New York, Doubleday, 1959.

OTHER PUBLICATIONS

Novels

Forgive Us Our Virtues: A Comedy of Evasions. Caldwell, Idaho, Caxton, and London, Methuen, 1938.
Darkness and the Deep. New York, Vanguard Press, 1943; London, Methuen, 1944.
The Golden Rooms. New York, Vanguard Press, 1944; London, Methuen, 1947.
Intimations of Eve. New York, Vanguard Press, 1946; London, Methuen, 1947.
Adam and the Serpent. New York, Vanguard Press, 1947.
The Divine Passion. New York, Vanguard Press, 1948.
The Valley of Vision. New York, Abelard Press, 1951.
The Island of the Innocent. New York, Abelard Press, 1952.
Jesus Came Again: A Parable. Denver, Swallow, 1956.
A Goat for Azazel. Denver, Swallow, 1956.
Peace Like a River. Denver, Swallow, 1957; as *The Passion Within*, New York, Pyramid, 1960.
My Holy Satan: A Novel of Christian Twilight. Denver, Swallow, 1958.

Verse

Sonnets to an Imaginary Madonna. New York, Vinal, 1927.

Other

The Neurotic Nightingale (essays). Milwaukee, Casanova Press, 1935.
The Caxton Printers in Idaho: A Short History. Cincinnati, Society of Bibliographers, 1944.
God or Caesar? The Writing of Fiction for Beginners. Caldwell, Idaho, Caxton, 1953.
Suicide or Murder? The Strange Death of Governor Meriwether Lewis. Denver, Swallow, 1962.
Thomas Wolfe as I Knew Him and Other Essays. Denver, Swallow, 1963.
Gold Rushes and Mining Camps of the Early American West, with Opal Laurel Holmes. Caldwell, Idaho, Caxton, 1968.
Three West: Conversations with Vardis Fisher, Max Evans, Michael Straight, by John R. Milton. Vermillion, University of South Dakota, 1970.

Editor, *Idaho: A Guide in Word and Picture.* Caldwell, Idaho, Caxton, 1937.
Editor, *The Idaho Encyclopedia.* Caldwell, Idaho, Caxton, 1938.
Editor, *Idaho Lore.* Caldwell, Idaho, Caxton, 1939.

*

Bibliography: "Vardis Fisher: A Bibliography" by George Kellogg, in *Western American Literature* (Fort Collins, Colorado), Spring 1970.

Manuscript Collections: University of Idaho, Moscow; Boise State College, Idaho.

Critical Studies: "Vardis Fisher Issue" of *American Book Collector* (Chicago), September 1963; *Vardis Fisher* by Joseph M. Flora, New York, Twayne, 1965; *Vardis Fisher: The Frontier and Regional Works* by Wayne Chatterton, Boise, Idaho, Boise State College, 1972; *Vardis Fisher: The Novelist as Poet* and *A Solitary Voice: Vardis Fisher*, both by Dorys C. Grover, New York, Revisionist Press, 1973; *The Epic of Evolution: Its Ideology and Art: A Study of Vardis Fisher's "Testament of Man"* by Alfred K. Thomas, New York, Revisionist Press, 1973; *The Past in the Present: Two Essays on History and Myth in Fisher's Testament of Man* by Lester Strong, New York, Revisionist Press, 1979.

* * *

Vardis Fisher is something of a paradox: he is a western writer who does not write Westerns—that is, if *Western* means tales of cowboys and Indians, rustlers and bad sheriffs, nesters and sheepmen. He writes about *people*—people who happen to live in or pass through the part of the United States we call the West. These are people in a continuing state of conflict: male against female, man (and woman) against nature, the flesh against the spirit. He often resisted being labeled a regionalist, and for good reason: the marks and brands of the country, its wildness and its challenges, often provide simply a canvas upon which his characters are made to work out their destinies. The ruggedness of nature, in many of his novels, simply provides a bolder, fiercer, more unfeeling set of barriers for these characters. Wayne Chatterton notes that the short stories published in *Love and Death* often revolve around characters like Vridar Hunter (properly identified as a thinly disguised Vardis Fisher) and others from the Antelope Hills novels. But here again, the locale is not required for the success of the story. One example should suffice: in "Joe Burt's Wife," an "Antelope country variation of the 'mail-order marriage' motif," to quote Chatterton, the setting could be any frontier area where women available for marriage are few. The situation is a painfully comic one; it could fit without alteration into Hamlin Garland's *Main-Travelled Roads* or even William Faulkner's rural Mississippi settings. Others of the short stories are equally non-western. Even historical novels like *The Mothers*, based upon the Donner party of emigrants who were reduced to cannibalism to keep their spark of life glimmering, could have been set in the snowy parts of Russia or China or Alaska with no strain of credibility. The main loss (excepting for a few incidental details) would have been to historicity. And *Mountain Man*, Fisher's powerful novel suggested by the life of a real man, Liver-Eating (or, Crow-Killer) Johnston, is a moving account of man's will to survive, to master the wilderness and its inhabitants, whatever the latitude and longitude of the setting.

Having said all this, one must point out the consummate skill with which Fisher makes that western wilderness setting serve his literary purposes. His biography certifies that he knew his terrain, as surely as Faulkner, for example, knew his created county of Yoknapatawpha. Many of the perils faced by his characters Fisher had himself faced, and in the same area—the Antelope Hills, the Snake river, the rugged, lonely wilderness areas of Utah and Idaho. In fact, many of his novels are, as Chatterton and Joseph Flora have pointed out, strongly autobiographical; hence it is natural that he uses the western setting of his own painful childhood and groping maturation.

Fisher does some unusual things in his writing—witness the musical patterning of *Mountain Man* noted by Flora—indeed, making the central character of that novel educated in music, capable of playing complex serious music on his mouth organ in celebration of the beauty of the wilderness, the power of the rising sun, the immensity of his love for his Flathead bride, Lotus. And while his hero, Sam Minard, is the epitome of the mountain man, he has the elusive mystical quality of a romantic seer, an eastern philosopher, in addition to a terribly vengeful spirit. He seems in many respects to be not just the figure suggested by the Crow-Killer, but perhaps the essence of what the "Fisher hero" was never able to reach in his development in many of Fisher's novels.

The language Fisher uses in his western writing is memorable, distinct, accurate. Repeatedly the way folks mumble their words, run them together, and altogether mispronounce them in Fisher's fiction is the best job of capturing vernacular speech since Mark Twain wrote *Huckleberry Finn.* The realism of dialogue in Fisher's writings brings to mind what the Boston *Transcript* had to say about his picture of the West (8 August 1931), calling it "the most living of all the Wests because it is sordid as well as epic, his men have more guts than good manners ... more sex than chivalry, more hauntingly real personalities than conventional charm ... " Such is high praise for a man whose University of Chicago teacher told him he'd never write a novel worth opening! Yet, allowing for the vast amount of blunt truth to be found in his fiction, Fisher cannot really be classed as a naturalistic writer. In *The Mothers* he has scoundrels, mountain men who promise to carry starving children to safety in California, but drop them off in another camp of death; but there are contrasts—strong persevering children; selfless men who die trying to save others; abject cowards; but above all the strong, indomitable mothers: not all of them survive, but hardly a one of them lacks nobility and determination and strength of will to keep the children alive. The book is truly titled, yet when the mothers' work is ended, and rescuers are at hand to literally carry the children to safety across the Sierras, the story just quits, leaving the reader frustrated as to the loose ends left untied—indeed, one must look elsewhere even for the head count of survivors! One other point must be made on the evaluation of Fisher as naturalist or realist: On hearing the phrase "The Donner Party," one thinks immediately of cannibalism; yet Fisher doesn't even use the word, much less drag his reader through the details of how eating their fellows helped some of the party to survive. He spent far more space describing the preparation for consumption of the hides of oxen, and the nauseating, glue-like soup the people lived on for days. One would swear that Fisher had himself experienced freezing cold and near starvation for weeks on end, so believable is his prose. That his work is not as popular as it should be is another part of the paradox: his "truth" is not sufficiently romanticized for the readers who want to see the West as it really was!

—John O. West

FISHER, Wade. *See* **NORWOOD, V.G.C.**

FLETCHER, Dirk. *See* **CUNNINGHAM, Chet.**

FLOOD, Christopher (Jr). American. Born in Brockton, Massachusetts, 6 August 1936. Educated at Whitman Grammar Schools, Massachusetts, 1942–51; Whitman-Hanson Regional High School, 1951–55. Served in the United States Army National Guard, 1955–63. Married Theresa M. Harshani in 1960; one daughter and one son (deceased). Stock clerk, Bostonian Shoe Company, Whitman, 1956–65; heat treater, USM-Emhart Corporation, Whitman, 1965–87; Caretaker-/farmhand, Krispi Ranch for thoroughbred horses, Plympton, Massachusetts, 1969–70. Since 1988 custodian, Upper Cape Regional Vocational–Technical High School, Bourne, Massachusetts. Recipient: Emhart Safety Person of the Year, 1986. Address: 50 Prospect Road, Plympton, Massachusetts 02367, U.S.A.

WESTERN PUBLICATIONS

Novel

Plenty Wagon, No Horse. London, Hale, 1988.

Uncollected Short Stories

"The Final Time," in *Delaware Today Magazine* (Wilmington), September 1979; reprinted as "Circus Finale," in *Right Here Magazine* (Huntington, Indiana), May–June 1986, and in *Mirror Northern Report* (High Prairie, Alberta), September 1988.

* * *

Christopher Flood's sole western novel to date, *Plenty Wagon No Horse* offers a crowded canvas and a fairly involved plot, which centres on the robbery of the locomotive known as the Iron Trailhorse, from which the title is derived. Flood's narrative tracks his government official hero, Cass Taeger, in his pursuit of the criminals, and through a number of not entirely related adventures. Secondary characters abound—most of them outlaws—and at times it is difficult to keep up with the different gangs and individuals as they plot and murder to gain their unholy ends. Taeger emerges as a strong, credible figure, and lesser pen-portraits of the villains Link Bradford and Doc De Vree are fair, but on occasion the author seems to cram the page with minor villains who are shot down almost as they appear. Flood's writing is strongest in its descriptive passages—there is, for instance, a memorable pursuit sequence where Taeger trails his quarry through a violent thunderstorm—and he frequently succeeds in lending conviction to the story with evocative images of the desert landscape. Dialogue has rather less assurance, however, and at times the action wanders into secondary themes, some of which appear to be unnecessary additions to the story. Action itself is constant, with the author occasionally showing a welcome touch of gallows humour. There is irony, too, in the final scene, where two Apache Indians study the whites and the train from a distance, commenting with puzzled amusement on the "plenty wagon, no horse" which has invaded their homeland. Although the novel has several flaws, it is to be regretted that Flood has not followed it with any subsequent western fiction. *Plenty Wagon, No Horse* displays some refreshingly inventive touches, and was a worthwhile effort on the part of its author. It also repays a careful reading.

—Jeff Sadler

FLOREN, Lee. Also writes as Brett Austin; R.V. Donald; Lisa Fanchon; Claudia Hall; Wade Hamilton; Matt Harding; Matthew Whitman Harding; Felix Lee Horton; Stuart Jason; Mark Kirby; Grace Lang; Marguerite Nelson; Lew Smith; Maria Sandra Sterling; Sandra Sterling; Lee Thomas; Len Turner; Will Watson; Dave Wilson. American. Born in Hinsdale, Montana, 22 March 1910. Educated at the University of Montana, Missoula; Santa Barbara State College (now University of California), B.A.; Occidental College, Los Angeles, teacher's certificate; Texas Western College (now University of Texas at El Paso), M.A. 1964. Divorced: one daughter and one son. Teacher of woodwork and science, California, 1942–45; teacher of creative writing, San Bernardino College, California. Since 1945 full-time writer. Recipient: Colt .44 award. Address: Apartado 31-419, Guadalajara 5, Jalisco, Mexico.

WESTERN PUBLICATIONS

Novels

Cottonwood Pards. New York, Phoenix Press, 1944.
The Gun-Slammer. New York, Phoenix Press, 1945; London, Wright and Brown, 1947.
The Long S. New York, Phoenix Press, 1945; London, Wright and Brown, 1948.
Riders of Death. London, Wright and Brown, 1946.
Bonanza at Wishbone. New York, Phoenix Press, 1946; London, Wright and Brown, 1949.
Gunsmoke Holiday. New York, Phoenix Press, 1947; London, Quality Press, 1949.
Hangman's Range. New York, Phoenix Press, 1947; London, Wright and Brown, 1949.
Guns of Powder River. New York, Phoenix Press, 1947; London, Wright and Brown, 1950.
Broken Creek. Stoke-on-Trent, Staffordshire, Archer Press, 1948; as Lee Thomas, New York, Arcadia House, 1952.
Puma Pistoleers. Hanley, Staffordshire, Archer Press, 1948; as Dave Wilson, New York, Arcadia House, 1951.
Riders in the Night. Stoke-on-Trent, Staffordshire, Archer Press, 1948; New York, Phoenix Press, 1950.
Guns of Post-Hole Valley. London, Swan, 1949.
Boothill Buckaroo. London, Swan, 1949.
Whispering Butte. London, Quality Press, 1949.
Sonora Stage. Stoke-on-Trent, Staffordshire, Archer Press, 1949; New York, Arcadia House, 1953.
Milk River Range. New York, Phoenix Press, 1949; London, Quality Press, 1951; as *Shoot-Out at Milk River*, Leicester, Linford, 1987.
The Trail North. London, Foulsham, 1950.
This Grass Is Mine. London, Quality Press, 1950.
Guns of Wyoming. London, Partridge, 1950; New York, Arcadia House, 1952.

Pinon Mesa. New York, Arcadia House, 1951.
Pioneer Printer. London, Boardman, 1951.
Rifles on the Rimrock. New York, Arcadia House, 1952; as *Rifle Law*, Bath, Chivers, 1989.
Renegade Riders. London, Ward Lock, 1952.
Troubled Grass: A Story of the Old Southwest. New York, Abelard, 1952; London, Ward Lock, 1954.
Four Texans North. London, W.H. Allen, 1953; New York, Ace, 1955.
Freight for the Little Snowies. Kingswood, Surrey, World's Work, 1953.
Hell's Homestead. Kingswood, Surrey, World's Work, 1953.
Shadow of My Gun. New York, Arcadia House, 1953.
Wild Border Guns. New York, Arcadia House, 1953.
Wyoming Rustlers. London, Foulsham, 1953.
Blackleg Bullets. New York, Arcadia House, 1954.
Border Gold. New York, Arcadia House, 1954.
Broken Horn. London, Quality Press, 1954.
Law of the West. London, W.H. Allen, 1954; New York, Tower, 1977.
Pistol Partners. London, W.H. Allen, 1954.
Rifles on the Rattlesnake. New York, Arcadia House, 1954; London, Hale, 1956.
Guns Along the Pecos. Kingswood, Surrey, World's Work, 1955.
Hot Gun Holiday. Kingswood, Surrey, World's Work, 1955.
Riders in the Storm. New York, Arcadia House, 1955; London, W.H. Allen, 1956.
Winchester Wages. New York, Arcadia House, 1955; London, Ward Lock, 1956.
The Way of the Gun. London, Hale, 1955.
Gunsmoke Range. London, Hale, 1956.
Bitter Is the Land. Kingswood, Surrey, World's Work, 1956.
Gunsmoke Lawyer. London, Wright and Brown, 1957.
Guns Along the Arrowhead. London, Wright and Brown, 1957.
Cow-Thief Trail. London, Wright and Brown, 1958.
Thunder in the Gunsmoke. London, Wright and Brown, 1958.
Hard Riders. London, Hale, 1958.
Winchester War. London, Wright and Brown, 1960.
Renegade Gambler. London, Hale, 1961.
Guns on Circle S. London, Hale, 1962.
High Thunder. London, Hale, 1962.
Montana Maverick. London, Hale, 1962.
The Last Freighter. London, Wright and Brown, 1962.
John Wesley Hardin, Texas Gunfighter. New York, Macfadden, 1962.
Two Guns North. New York, Avon, 1963; as *Two Riders North*, London, Hale, 1963.
Rifles for Fort Hall. London, Consul, 1963.
Rifles on the Range. New York, Macfadden, 1964; Leicester, Ulverscroft, 1988.
Fighting Ramrod. New York, Macfadden-Bartell, 1964; London, Hale, 1986.
Mad River Guns. New York, Macfadden, 1965.
Wyoming Gun Law. New York, Lancer, 1965; London, Hale, 1986.
West of Barbwire. New York, Bouregy, 1967; London, Hale, 1985.
The Tall Texan. New York, Bouregy, 1967; London, Hale, 1987.
Black Gunsmoke. New York, Paperback Library, 1968.
Rustler's Trail. New York, Paperback Library, 1968; Leicester, Ulverscroft, 1988.
Rustlers of Cyclone Pass. New York, Avalon, 1968.
Wyoming Justice. New York, Avalon, 1969.
Trail to Latigo. New York, Avalon, 1970.
Riders of Rifle Range. New York, Bouregy, 1970.
Legacy of the Lost. New York, Lancer, 1970.
Ben Thompson: Gambler with a Gun. New York, Lancer, 1970; as *Gambler with a Gun*, London, Hale, 1985.
Frontier Lawman. New York, Lancer, 1970; London, Prior, 1981.
Wyoming Showdown. New York, Lancer, 1970.
The Last Gun. New York, Lancer, 1971.
Bloody Rifles. New York, Lancer, 1971.
Female Feud. New York, Associated Press, 1971.
Muskets on the Mississippi (as Matthew Whitman Harding). New York, Popular Library, 1972.
With Long Knife and Musket (as Felix Lee Horton). New York, Popular Library, 1972.
Callahan Rides Alone. New York, Tower, 1977; Bath, Chivers, 1983.
The Saddle Tramps. New York, Tower, 1977.
Gunlords of Stirrup Basin. New York, Manor, 1978; Bath, Chivers, 1988.
Gun to Gun. New York, Manor, 1978.
Wyoming Saddles. New York, Manor, 1978.
This Grass, This Gun. New York, Manor, 1978.
Rails West to Glory. New York, Manor, 1978.
Gun Wolves of Lobo Basin. New York, Manor, 1978; Bath, Chivers, 1988.
Gunpowder Grass. New York, Manor, 1978.
Powdersmoke Lawyer. New York, Manor, 1979; London, Hale, 1981.
Renegade Rancher. New York, Manor, 1979; Bath, Chivers, 1989.
High Trail to Rawhide. New York, Manor, 1979.
The Bushwhackers. New York, Manor, 1979; Bath, Chivers, 1987.
Gunpowder Mesa. New York, Tower, 1979.
Edge of Gunsmoke (as Matt Harding). New York, Manor, 1979.
Scattergun Grass. New York, Manor, 1980.
This Trail to Gunsmoke. New York, Tower, 1980.
The Rawhide Men. New York, Manor, 1980.
High Border Riders. New York, Manor, 1980; London, Hale, 1981.
The High Gun. New York, Manor, 1980.
North to Powder River. New York, Manor, 1980.
Cowthief Clanton. London, Hale, 1983.
Buckskin Challenge. London, Hale, 1983.
Renegade Rifles. London, Hale, 1983.
Trail to High Pine. London, Hale, 1984.
Bring Bullets, Texan. London, Hale, 1986.

Novels as Brett Austin

Rawhide Summons. New York, Phoenix Press, 1947; London, Wright and Brown, 1950.
Gambler's Gun Luck. London, Wright and Brown, 1949.
Gun-Doc of the Ambush Trail. London, Wright and Brown, 1949.
Black Boulder Ranch. New York, Phoenix Press, 1950; as *Black Boulder*, London, Wright Brown, 1950.
Burnt Wagon Ranch. New York, Phoenix Press, 1950; London, Wright and Brown, 1952; as Lee Floren, Bath, Chivers, 1986.
Rolling River Range. New York, Phoenix Press, 1950.
Lobo Valley. New York, Arcadia House, 1951; London, Wright and Brown, 1956; as Lee Floren, Bath, Chivers, 1986.
Broomtail Basin. New York, Arcadia House, 1952.
Guns of Montana. New York, Arcadia House, 1952.
When a Renegade Rides. New York, Arcadia House, 1952.

Coyotes of Willow Brook. New York, Arcadia House, 1952.
Wind River Range. New York, Arcadia House, 1953.
Call to Montana. Kingswood, Surrey, World's Work, 1953.
Rimrock Rifles. London, W.H. Allen, 1954.
Arizona Saddles. New York, Arcadia House, 1954.
Circle M Triggers. New York, Arcadia House, 1954; London, Wright and Brown, 1955.
Hammerhead Range. New York, Arcadia House, 1955.
Roll the Wagons. New York, Arcadia House, and London, Wright and Brown, 1956; as Lee Floren, New York, Lancer, 1970.
Two Sons of Satan. London, Ward Lock, 1956.
Texans Ride North. New York, Avalon, 1968.
Sagebrush Saga. New York, Avalon, 1969.

Novels as Lew Smith

Raiders of White Pine. London, Boardman, 1951; New York, Arcadia House, 1953; as *Night Riders* (as Lee Floren), Bath, Chivers, 1988.
Smoky River. New York, Arcadia House, 1953; as Lee Floren, Boston, Hall, 1979.
Rimrock Raiders. London, Gryphon, 1953; New York, Arcadia House, 1954.
Boothill Court. New York, Arcadia House, 1954.
Powdersmoke Canyon. New York, Arcadia House, 1954.
Riders of Rifle Range. Kingswood, Surrey, World's Work, 1954.
Dusty Wheels. New York, Arcadia House, 1955.
Ramrod. London, Ward Lock, 1955.
Gun Quick. London, Hale, 1984.

Novels as Wade Hamilton

Cougar River Range. London, Modern Publishing, 1950.
Sagebrush. London, Modern Publishing, 1950; New York, Arcadia House, 1952.
Rimrock Renegades. New York, Phoenix Press, 1951; London, Foulsham, 1952.
Gun Lobos. New York, Arcadia House, 1952.
The Longhorn Brand. New York, Arcadia House, 1952.
Cougar Basin. New York, Arcadia House, 1953.
Muddy Wheels. New York, Arcadia House, 1953; as Lee Floren, Kingswood, Surrey, World's Work, 1954.
Gun Luck. New York, Arcadia House, 1954; as Lee Floren, Bath, Chivers, 1990.
Trail's End. New York, Arcadia House, 1954.
Saddle Wolves. London, Ward Lock, 1956.
They Ride with Rifles. London, Ward Lock, 1956.
Trail to High Pine. New York, Arcadia House, 1956; London, Hale, 1984.
Saddles North. New York, Avalon, 1968; London, Hale, 1985.
Gunsmoke Law. New York, Avalon, 1969.
Ride the Wild Country. New York, Tower, 1977; as Lee Floren, Boston, Hall, 1989.
Gunsmoke. New York, Tower, 1977.
Ride Against the Rifles. New York, Manor, 1979.

Novels as Lee Thomas

Texas Talbert. New York, Phoenix Press, 1945.
The Circle W. New York, Phoenix Press, 1945.
Smokestack Iron. New York, Phoenix Press, 1947; as *The Smokestack Iron* (as Lee Floren), London, Swan, 1948.
Texas Cowman. New York, Phoenix Press, 1947.
Dusty Boots. New York, Phoenix Press, 1950; London, Hale, 1985.
Broken Creek. New York, Arcadia House, 1952.
The Ambush Trail. New York, Arcadia House, 1952.
Gambler's Guns. New York, Arcadia House, 1953.
Wolf Dog Town. New York, Arcadia House, 1953.
The Gringo. London, Hale, 1985.

Novels as Will Watson

Wolf Dog Range. New York, Phoenix Press, 1946; Redhill, Surrey, Wells Gardner Darton, 1949; as Lee Floren, New York, Macfadden, 1967; Leicester, Ulverscroft, 1988.
Saddle Pals. New York, Phoenix Press, 1947.
Double Cross Ranch. New York, Phoenix Press, 1950; as Lee Floren, London, Coker, 1950.
War on Alkali Creek. New York, Phoenix Press, 1951; as Lee Floren, Bath, Chivers, 1988.
North to Wyoming. Kingswood, Surrey, World's Work, 1953.
Boothill Brand. London, Hale, 1984.

Novels as Len Turner

Texas Medico. New York, Arcadia House, 1954; London, Ward Lock, 1955.
Winter Kill. New York, Arcadia House, 1954; London, Wright and Brown, 1956.

OTHER PUBLICATIONS

Novels

Wait for the Day (as Claudia Hall). New York, Arcadia House, 1955.
War Drum (as Maria Sandra Sterling). New York, Popular Library, 1972.
College for Sex (as Mark Kirby). London, Softcover Library, 1972.

Novels as Marguerite Nelson

Forever This Love. New York, Avalon, 1957.
Jill's Hollywood Assignment. New York, Avalon, 1958.
Nancy's Dude Ranch. New York, Avalon, 1958.
Air Stewardess. New York, Bouregy, 1961.
Far Are the Hills. New York, Bouregy, 1961.
Hollywood Nurse. New York, Arcadia House, 1963.
High Pines Singing. New York, Avalon, 1969.
Doctor Wilson's Dilemma. New York, Avalon, 1969.
Tropic Nurse. New York, Avalon, 1969.
Mercy Nurse. New York, Manor, 1979.

Novels as Lisa Fanchon

Girls Wanted. New York, Universal, 1964; as *Embrace*, London, Softcover Library, 1973.
Migrant Girl. New York, Universal, 1964; as *She Knew What He Wanted*, London, Softcover Library, 1973.
The Kidnapped Virgin. N.p., P.E.C., 1968.
Sex Club of Don Pedro. N.p., Lastimas, 1969.
The Gay Girls. N.p., Lastimas, 1969.
Palace of Sin. N.p., Greenleaf Classics, 1969.
Palace of Lust. N.p., Greenleaf Classics, 1969.
Naked When I Fled. N.p., Lastimas, 1969.
Scandalous Confessions of an English Traveller. N.p., Lastimas, 1970.

All Woman. New York, Macfadden, 1971.
Man Trap. New York, Macfadden, 1971.

Novels as Matt Harding

The Sex Bums. New York, Universal, 1965; as *Wild Passion*, London, Softcover Library, 1973.
The Dancing Diva. N.p., Lastimas, 1968.
Plundered Virgin. N.p., Greenleaf Classics, 1968.
Women of Lust. N.p., Lastimas, 1968.
I, Margo. N.p., Lastimas, 1968.
Rap Softly, Lover. N.p., Lastimas, 1969.
Boys and Women. N.p., Lastimas, 1969.
Las Vegas Madame. N.p., Lancer, 1970.
I, Jonathon Richardson. N.p., Lastimas, 1970.
They Couldn't Say No. New York, Mcfadden, 1970.
The Office Game. New York, Lancer, 1972.

Novels as Sandra Sterling

Strickland's Women. N.p., Lastimas, 1968.
Love Cult. N.p., Lastimas, 1968.
The Tortured Virgin. N.p., Lastimas, 1969.

Novels as R.V. Donald

The Arab Captors. N.p., Lastimas, 1968.
I, Coxswain. N.p., Lastimas, 1970.

Novels as Stuart Jason

Kingblood. New York, Paperback Library, 1969; London, New English Library, 1974.
Black Prince. New York, Lancer, 1970; London, New English Library, 1972.
Black Lord. New York, Lancer, 1970; London, New English Library, 1971.
Valley of Death. New York, Pinnacle, 1973.
The Deadly Doctor. New York, Pinnacle, 1973.

Novels as Grace Lang

Love a Hostage. New York, Avalon, 1969.
The Singing Pines. New York, Avalon, 1969.

Other

The American Dream (as Lew Smith). Glenview, Illinois, Scott Foreman, 1980.

* * *

Lee Floren's hundreds of undemanding and largely traditional Westerns have established him as a prolific writer of some proficiency. Conflict lies at the heart of his work, although he displays little time for involved characterisation, evidently preferring to keep the pace up and punctuate his plots with regular bursts of action. His heroes are usually young and principled, his villains cold and calculating. Often they will have a habit or characteristic which sets them apart from others of their type. There is usually an element of romance in the books, and generally they always work towards a satisfying and happy resolution.

Any prolonged exposure to Floren's work must inevitably produce a sense of *déjà vu*, however, for there is an unfortunate tendency towards repetition. The same key words crop up again and again in his titles—"Guns," "Riders," "Rimrock," "Rawhide," "Gambler," and so on. Sometimes titles are repeated in their entirety. The range war is an especially popular theme (*Trail to High Pine*, *Rustler's Trail*, *Fighting Ramrod*, *The Bushwhackers*, and so on), most notably between cattlemen and newly arrived farmers (*The Hell Raisers*, *War on Alkali Creek*, *Guns of Wyoming*, *Wolf Dog Town*, *Puma Pistoleers*, *Saddles North* and *Bring Bullets, Texan!* being just a few examples which feature this premise). Floren's own native Montana is a particularly favourite location, with Wyoming and Texas running a close second.

This does not mean that Floren is a bad writer. In fact, he displays an enviable gift for expression, although his style can sometimes veer dangerously towards the melodramatic ("Ucross's dull eyes probed him like sharp Bowie knives"), and his main characters, while frequently appearing somewhat hastily drawn, seldom perform in a less than adequate fashion. But *The Hard Riders*, say, and *Sagebrush* (published under the pseudonym Wade Hamilton) amply demonstrate just a few of the similarities which recur all too often in his work. (In the first book, storekeeper Jim Carlson meets increasing opposition when he invites a bunch of farmers onto the range around the town of Mad Horse, while in the second, lawyer Ed Haverty faces the same kind of antagonism when he settles a band of homesteaders in Sagebrush Basin). One of the best variations on the ranchers vs. farmers theme can be found in *Gambler's Gun Luck* (written as Brett Austin), an early title which shows the fine characterisation of which Floren is occasionally capable.

Floren is more than just a "one-trick pony," however. *Rifles on the Rimrock* and *Riders in the Storm*, for example, are both murder mysteries. *Dusty Boots* (written as Lee Thomas) is an entertaining western which charts the adventures of two itinerant journalists who run into all sorts of trouble when they take over the *Linda Vista View*, mainly from ranchers angry at the arrival of the railroad, who are sponsoring the newspaper. Although the book once again goes over familiar Floren territory (if the rails come to Linda Vista, they will almost certainly bring farmers onto hitherto open cattle range), it is distinguished by a nice line in humour—a relatively rare commodity in Floren's Westerns—and the neatly drawn relationship between its two protagonists, Kirk Roper and his one-handed illiterate proofreader, the aptly named Iron Hand.

The addition of humour also lifts the Buckshot McKee and Tortilla Joe sequence, which recounts the exploits of a pair of amiable drifters. In *Milk River Range* the duo become involved in a range war. In *High Border Riders* they lock horns with a band of outlaws smuggling Mexican beef into Texas. They break up another rustling operation in *Rope the Wild Wind*, foil a land-grabbing scheme in *Powdersmoke Lawyer* and in a particularly enjoyable volume, *North to Powder River*, they drive a herd of Brahma bulls from Texas to Wyoming. As with all of Floren's work, the pace is constant and there is just enough geographical and historical detail to set the scene accurately. Another duo who have appeared in more than one book (Floren's heroes often come in pairs) are Tobacco Jones and Judge Lemanuel Bates, an unlikely but engaging pair of characters who are based in the Wyoming town of Cowtrail (where Jones is also the postmaster). Now men of means, they are "at the stage of life where good health and good companionship meant more to either of them than did money." In *Double Cross Ranch* they tangle with a rival jurist who is out to add one of their many spreads to his already considerable empire. Sitting in for a colleague in *Broomtail Basin*, the judge and Jones have to deal with another mob of ranchers angered by the coming of the railroad.

As entertaining and well-presented as his work can be, however (his 1979 novel *The Rawhide Men* is a Colt .44 award-winner), there is a sameness to Floren's Westerns which soon proves tiresome. This is probably why *Gambler with a Gun*, his semi-fictional biography of Ben Thompson, comes as such a welcome surprise. Orderly and unsensational, the book is an absorbing and exceptionally well-crafted life story, even if it does come to some rather illogical conclusions: "From his English parents he'd inherited glistening black hair and sharp blue eyes, the darkness of his hair contrasting with the light blue of his eyes, which, when their owner was angry, became slate-grey and deadly, for Ben was destined to be a gunman—a town tamer—and, like almost all western gunslingers, his eyes were light blue." A much recommended volume, *Gambler with a Gun* once again shows the heights to which his work can rise.

Since the mid-1980's, Floren has forsaken writing to concentrate on selling reprint rights in his considerable backlist, an endeavour in which he has enjoyed singular success. Today many of his earliest (and best) books are widely available in a variety of editions—but for maximum enjoyment of a most accomplished writer, his work is best taken in small and infrequent doses.

—David Whitehead

FLYNN, George. *See* **PAINE, Lauran.**

FLYNN, Jackson. *See* **SHIRREFFS, Gordon D.**

FLYNN, Robert (Lopez). American. Born in Chillicothe, Texas, 12 April 1932. Educated at Baylor University, Waco, Texas, B.A. 1954, M.A. 1956; Southwestern Baptist Theological Seminary. Served in the United States Marine Corps, 1950–52. Married Jean Sorrels in 1953; two daughters (one deceased). Instructor, Gardner-Webb College, Boiling Springs, North Carolina, 1957–59; Assistant Professor, Baylor University, 1959–63. Since 1963 Professor and novelist-in-residence, Trinity University, San Antonio. President, Texas Institute of Letters, 1990–91. Recipient: Western Heritage award, 1968. Agent: Maryanne Colas, 229 East 79th Street, New York, New York, U.S.A.

WESTERN PUBLICATIONS

Novels

North to Yesterday. New York, Knopf, and London, Hutchinson, 1967.
Wanderer Springs. Fort Worth, Texas Christian Press, 1987.

Short Stories

Seasonal Rain and Other Stories. San Antonio, Texas, Corona Press, 1986.

Uncollected Short Stories

"Stampede!," in *Saturday Evening Post* (Philadelphia), 25 March 1967.
"Babe in the Wilderness," in *Saturday Evening Post* (Philadelphia), 22 April 1967.
"Boy from Chillicothe," in *Yale Review* (New Haven, Connecticut).
"The Bad Time," in *Descant* (Fort Worth, Texas).

Other Publications

Novels

In the House of the Lord. New York, Knopf, and London, Hutchinson, 1967.
The Sounds of Rescue, The Signs of Hope. New York, Knopf, 1970.
And Holy Is His Name. Denville, New Jersey, Dimension, 1983.

Plays

Journey to Jefferson, adaptation of the novel *As I Lay Dying* by William Faulkner (produced Dallas, 1964).

Television Plays: *A Cowboy Legacy*, 1964.

Other

A Personal War in Vietnam. College Station, Texas A & M University Press, 1989.

*

Robert Flynn comments:

I am in the broadest sense of the work a religious writer. I want to record, clarify, and celebrate man's efforts to understand, endure, and ultimately survive his world. Because my formative years were spent on a farm I have always felt close to nature. Perhaps that is more readily apparent than literary influences in my work.

* * *

Until the mid 1980's Robert Flynn's modest reputation as a western writer rested on a little-known novel titled *North to Yesterday* published in 1967. Although he had won the Western Heritage award, in the 1970's Flynn seemed to stop publishing, and *North to Yesterday* went out-of-print. But the novel's supporters continued to praise it, Flynn began to publish again in the mid-1980's, and he is now one of the most important writers in Texas, elected president of the Texas Institute of Letters for 1990–91.

North to Yesterday has begun to find its proper place in western American literature, because it is a small masterpiece for several reasons. Firstly, it is beautifully written, full of excellent description and incisive characterization. Secondly, it demonstrates a comic genius not ofend found previously in literature about the West. Thirdly, its ambivalence toward the passing of the older western values connects it with some of the best post-World War II works about the West, books William Bloodworth calls "Literary" or "Off-Trail Westerns," such as Larry McMurtry's *Horseman, Pass By* and Edward Abbey's *The Brave Cowboy*, as well as the "New Westerns" of the 1960's like Thomas Berger's *Little Big Man* and E.L. Doctorow's *Welcome to Hard Times*. Finally its combined use of a journey, a regional setting, individual characters' obsessions, and a comic treatment of human folly becoming heroic suggests its imaginative connection with William Faulkner's *As I Lay Dying*. Flynn, in fact, won a Special Jury award, Theater of Nations, for his 1964 adaptation of Faulkner's *As I Lay Dying* called *Journey to Jefferson*.

Each characater in *North to Yesterday* has a special reason for making this journey. Lampassas, the former storkeeper who organizes the drive from Texas to Trails End in Kansas 15 years after the end of trail drives, wishes to fulfill his youthful dreams sidetracked by a demanding wife. His son, the Kid, goes so he can become a railroad engineer. Pretty Shadow, an aging Lothario, hopes to see Diamond Annie, a saloon girl he had met at Trails End 25 years earlier. The Preacher goes because the Lord has spoken to him, telling him to build His church in "Ninevah" which the Preacher translates as Trails End. Gattis, a big-footed Georgia farm stableboy, is escaping an unwanted marriage and the sodbuster's weary life. June, an east Texas stablehand, wants to become a gun-toting hero. And Covina, an 18-year-old girl with an illegitimate baby they pick up along the way, believes she will get rich working the saloons in Trails End.

These dreams prove to be illusions. Their horses are stolen, Pretty Shadow is gored to death, Gattis drowns, June gets shot, the Kid cuts the railroad's weeds instead of guiding its locomotive. As the novel ends, the Preacher and Lampassas head back, tired but undaunted: "Well, maybe we ain't where we aimed to be, but we ain't where we was, neither." The quest is fruitless, but like Samuel Beckett's Didi and Gogo in *Waiting for Godot* and Albert Camus's Sisyphus, they continue, and by doing so, they define themselves.

North to Yesterday was named one the the Best Books of the Year by the *New York Times*, and Flynn went on to publish two more quick novels without a western background or settings: *In the House of the Lord* and *The Sounds of Rescue, The Signs of Hope*. Neither of these books had the reception of his first one. His wife's illness and a daughter's death in 1971, coupled with Flynn's concern with the Vietnam War and a change in editors at this publisher, Alfred A. Knopf, caused him to fall silent for the rest of the 1970's.

But like his characters in *North to Yesterday*, Flynn endured and in 1986 he published a collection of stories entitled *Seasonal Rain*, many of which are centered around a mythical west Texas town, Wanderer Springs, based on Flynn's home of Chillicothe. These stories trace the small, sometimes tragic, sometimes comic, always appealing narratives of the various settlers of Wanderer Springs from the 19th century to the present with compassion and humor.

And in 1988 Flynn returned to his mythical town as the subject for a novel, *Wanderer Springs*. Again like his strong influence Faulkner, who returned again and again to the families that populate his created "postage stamp of soil"—Yoknapatawpha County, Mississippi—Flynn expands and extends the characters and events of his fictional but recognizable towns of Wanderer Springs and Center Point, Texas. Through the central character of Will Callahan, described as "one of the great howevers, who spent his entire life trying to become a human being," Flynn consolidates the past into the present by telling the stories of the farmers, ranchers, townspeople, "those without known family," and the outsiders of his memory and imagination.

Callahan works for the Texas Institute for Cultural Research in San Antonio, but he must return to Wanderer Springs for the funeral of an old girlfriend. The physical journey leads into a journey through the history of the area and through Will's memories of dropping the pass in the championship football game, getting his chewing gum stuck in his girlfriend's hair, watching his father's painful decline, and others. These stories, told with sensitivity and humor, celebrate the tragicomedy of humanity which, Faulkner concluded, reveals that mankind will not only endure but prevail.

—Mark Busby

FLYNN, T(homas) T(heodore). American. Born in 1902. Raised in Indianapolis, Indiana. Married; two sons. Worked as a seaman, salesman, taxi-driver, and factory hand in a steel mill. Writer of Western and other stories for *Saturday Evening Post* and other magazines. Subsequently lived in Washington, D.C., and New Mexico.

WESTERN PUBLICATIONS

Novels

Two Faces West. New York, Dell, 1954; London, Ward Lock, 1956.
The Man from Laramie. New York, Dell, 1954; London, Ward Lock, 1955.
The Angry Man. New York, Dell, 1956; London, Ward Lock, 1957.
The Man from Nowhere. New York, Dell, 1958; as *Wrong Man at Soledad*, London, Ward Lock, 1958.
Riding High. New York, Dell, 1961; London, Ward Lock, 1962.

OTHER PUBLICATIONS

Novels

It's Murder! London, Kelly, 1950.
Murder Caravan. London, Kelly, 1950.

* * *

T.T. Flynn wrote only a few Westerns, but they were typical of the sort of novel being published in the 1950's, with complicated plots, sometimes involving mistaken identity, and often with an under-the-surface neuroticism replacing the usual thoughtless villainy.

Several themes turn up over and over in these novels: selling rifles to the Indians in an effort to keep an area at arms; the use of a foreman or top hand to serve as the villain instead of the usual rancher; an older, often salty, female character to give a bit of social cohesion to the cast of characters. But mistaken identity is the most emphatic device Flynn uses, and it adds an additional ironic level to the novels.

The entire plot of *The Man from Nowhere* centers on the device of Roger Travis's name and identity (as well as his money) being taken over by a vaguely neurotic young man who actually believes Travis has been killed in the Guatemala jungles. Travis, of course, isn't dead, and manages to trace the imposter to the ranch of his friend, Kilgore, where he has endeared himself to the Kilgores and joined in the family feud with the Markhams. When the real Travis arrives on the scene, the imposter views him almost as his own alter ego, but he is killed in the general mêlée, and cedes his girlfriend to the real Travis. The San Francisco cabman Travis has taken up with en route adds a bit of humor to an otherwise very serious novel. *Two Faces West* goes even further in the mistaken identity scheme by having twin brothers as hero and (supposed) villain.

Riding High and *The Angry Man* are more conventional in plot, using the traditional devices of the complicated ownership of a silver mine in New Mexico in the first, and a villain who has arranged Indian raids in order to buy up the cattle from the dispirited ranchers in the second. The involved plot of *Riding High* centers on the impressive figure of Con McCloud, the partner-foreman of the supposed owner of the mine who feels he has been betrayed when it is willed to the niece. (Another sinister villain is the bounty hunter, Wiswald, in *Two Faces West*.)

The Man from Laramie combines most of these motifs in a very elaborate (and rather slow-moving) story. Will Lockhart, a cavalry officer searching for the opportunist trader who has sold illegal rifles to the Indians and thus indirectly caused the death of his brother, comes incognito as a teamster to work the salt flats while trying to trace a shipment of rifles he thinks is destined for the Indians. The niece of the owner of the biggest ranch in the area is engaged to a suspicious merchant; Will has a run-in with the massive foreman of the ranch, Hansbro, and goes to work for the pepperish Kate Canaday, who owns the adjoining ranch. To cement his authority on the ranch, the power-mad Hansbro attempts to kill the owner, but Will, by now having worked out an understanding with the niece, manages to overcome him, and Will's sidekick, a half-Indian sergeant who has accompanied him on his mission, gets proof which links the merchant with the illegal rifles. The initial fist-fight between Will and Hansbro is a superb passage, and the other scenes of violence (including one of the slaughter of over 20 pack mules) are worked well into the theme of the novel.

—George Walsh

FOOTE, Mary Hallock. American. Born in New York in 1847. Married in 1876. Spent latter part of life in Colorado, Idaho, and California. *Died in 1938.*

WESTERN PUBLICATIONS

Novels

The Led-Horse Claim: A Romance of a Mining Camp. Boston, Osgood, and London, Warne, 1883.
John Bodewin's Testimony: A Mining Romance. Boston, Ticknor, 1886; London, Warne, 1887.
The Chosen Valley. Boston, Houghton Mifflin, 1892; London, Osgood and McIlvaine, 1892.
Coeur d'Alene. Boston, Houghton Mifflin, 1894.
The Prodigal. Boston, Houghton Mifflin, 1900.
The Desert and the Sown. Boston, Houghton Mifflin, 1902.
Edith Bonham. Boston, Houghton Mifflin, 1917.

Short Stories

The Idaho Stories and Far West Illustrations of Mary Hallock Foote, edited by Barbara Cragg, Dennis M. Walsh, and Mary Ellen Walsh. Pocotello, Idaho, Idaho State University Press, 1988.

Uncollected Short Stories

"New Alameda, or A California Mining Camp," in *Scribners Monthly Magazine* (New York), February 1878.

OTHER PUBLICATIONS

Novels

The Last Assembly Ball, and The Fate of a Voice. Boston, Houghton Mifflin, 1889.
The Royal Americans. Boston, Houghton Mifflin, 1910.
A Picked Company. Boston, Houghton Mifflin, 1912.
The Valley Road. Boston, Houghton Mifflin, 1915.
The Ground-Swell. Boston and New York, Houghton Mifflin, 1919.

Short Stories

In Exile, and Other Stories. Boston, Houghton Mifflin, 1894.
The Cup of Trembling, and Other Stories. Boston, Houghton Mifflin, 1895; London, Gay and Bird, 1896.
The Little Fig Tree. Boston, Houghton Mifflin, 1899.
A Touch of Sun, and Other Stories. Boston, Houghton Mifflin, 1903.

Other

A Victorian Gentlewoman in the Far West: The Reminiscences of Mary Hallock Foote, edited by Rodman W. Paul. San Marino, California, Huntington Library, 1972.

*

Critical Study: *Mary Hallock Foote* by James H. Maguire and Wayne Chatterton, Boise, Idaho, Boise State University Press, 1972.

* * *

Mary Hallock Foote's western art and letters were widely admired by her peers from her very first essay on the West: "A California Mining Camp," in 1878, which she both authored and illustrated. Her work merits recovery for a contemporary audience, as part of the largely forgotten story of women's responses to the West, specifically because the subtleties and ambivalences in her vision adumbrate some of the stronger criticisms of modern western women writers. Her 20th-century output is most fruitfully read in the knowledge of her 19th-century work, given the changes which occurred over time both in her depiction of the meaning of the West (especially for women) and in her literary style.

Thematically, the note which dominates the early narratives is loss. Foote's first novel, *The Led-Horse Claim*, is the tangled love story of an eastern woman, Cecil Conrath, who comes to Colorado to join her ne'er-do-well brother, and of the mine superintendent, Hilgard (also from the East), with whom she falls in love. A range of East–West tensions are conveyed, in Cecil's repulsion by the coarseness of her new environment and by the Eastern capitalists' negligence of their western workers. Underlining these schisms is the conventional device of the family feud: Cecil's brother manages a rival mine which is poaching on Led-Horse territory. Eventually, Conrath is killed in a battle between the two mines' workers, very possibly by Hilgard's hand. Many complications and coincidences lead Cecil and Hilgard to eventual reunion and marriage, but the reconciliation is strongly undermined both by Cecil's relatives' undying opposition to the match and by the novel's ending, which stresses death and loss. Harry Conrath, damaged morally and physically by his western experiences, is transported east to be buried next to his long-departed mother: "One might fancy the mother, in her sleep, reaching out unconsciously and covering her child." The West emerges as a place of degeneration and death. Stylistically, this early work is melodramatic and romantic in its action, and relies heavily on stereotyped characters. Setting is handled realistically, however, in the many details of mining work and terrain. That stylistic mixture and thematic emphasis characterizes most of Foote's work of the 19th century. In both "The Exile" and "The Fate of a Voice", for example, woman's journey to the West amounts to exile from the culture of the East. In the latter story, a conventionally happy ending—the heroine's marriage to a western mining engineer—is undercut by her necessary renunciation of her own singing career.

Foote's 20th-century portrayal of the West is kinder. In *The Prodigal*, going west has a morally uplifting effect on the eastern hero, while the eastern heroine of *Edith Bonham* voluntarily and happily makes a permanent move west. Stylistically, Foote's writing became more realist, and her attention to political and social issues more pronounced. *The Desert and the Sown* demonstrates the interweaving of these three characteristics. The narrative traces the marriage of Adam Bogardus, a hired hand of eastern landowners, to the daughter of the family, Emily. The two elope to the West, only for the privileged Emily to receive a rude shock at her primitive surroundings. When her husband disappears mysteriously into the wilderness, she returns east with her children to live a life of refined widowhood. Many years later, Emily's son, Paul, unwittingly hires Adam as guide for a western hunting trip. When the two men almost die together in the wilderness, their relationship is revealed. Spurned by Emily, Adam once more disappears west, but eventually turns up on her estate, there dying a cruel death which reunites husband and wife and leads Emily to make the relationship public. The West, here, teaches Paul valuable lessons: he discovers and accepts responsibility for his heritage in the western wilderness, by coming to terms with the reality of his father. Emily, too, comes to appreciate and tries to embrace the western qualities which Adam embodies. Woven into the geographical pattern are class questions, too: it is clear that Adam's status as an uneducated working man is also a thorn to be grasped by the Easterners, and the characters conduct many earnest political discussions on the question of "The Poor Man." Issues of generation and gender are also raised. Paul's new wife, for example, accuses him of denying his mother the right of self-determination: "You, as a man and a husband, resent what she, as a woman and a wife, has dared to do. And I, as another woman and a wife, I say she could do nothing else and be true." While the narrative does depend on melodrama to a degree, it also involves much more reflection and more realistic characterization than Foote's earlier work. The dominant impression here is that the West is a positive force which can be integrated with the East to good purpose; but the role of death in facilitating integration sustains the hint of loss and irreconcilable tension.

Owen Wister heralded Foote's achievement: "At last a voice was lifted to honor the cattle country and not to libel it," and it is undeniable that both her illustration and her writing pay homage to the sweep and grandeur of the West. But her fictional portrayal of the West is also less single-mindedly celebratory, more ambiguous than Wister's remark suggests. This equivocal response seems related to Foote's gender in at least two ways. Specifically, her own relationship with the West, as an Easterner reluctantly following her mining engineer husband west, was fraught for a long time, as can be understood from her powerful autobiography, published as *A Victorian Gentlewoman in the Far West*, as well as from Wallace Stegner's fictionalization of her life, *Angle of Repose*. More generally, her work qualifies the heroic narrative of the West by inscribing female perspectives which value nurture and reconciliation over violent adventure.

—Christine Bold

FORBES, Aleck. *See* **RATHBORNE, St. George.**

FORD, Kirk. *See* **BOWDEN, Jim.**

FORD, Lewis. *See* **PATTEN, Lewis B.**

FORD, Wallace. *See* **KING, Albert.**

FOREMAN, L(eonard) L(ondon). British. Born in London, 23 June 1901. Served in the British Army during World War I. Settled in the United States; worked at "various inconsiderable pursuits" prior to becoming a freelance writer. *Died.*

WESTERN PUBLICATIONS

Novels

Don Desperado. New York, Dutton, 1941; London, Cassel, 1942; as *Desperado's Gold*, New York, Pocket Books, 1950.
The Renegade. New York, Dutton, 1942.
The Road to San Jacinto. New York, Dutton, 1943.
Gunning for Trouble. New York, Dutton, 1953; London Lane, 1954.
Arrow in the Dust. New York, Dell, 1954.
Gunfire Men. New York, Dell, 1955.
Woman of the Avalon. New York, Dell, 1955.
Lone Hand. New York, Dell, 1956.
Return of the Texan. New York, Ballantine, 1958.
Gunsmoke Men. New York, New American Library, 1958.
Desperation Trail. New York, Doubleday, 1959.
Longrider. New York, Doubleday, 1961.
Spanish Grant. New York, Doubleday, 1962.
Gringo. New York, Fawcett, 1964.
Farewell to Texas. New York, Doubleday, 1964.
Rawhiders of the Brasada. New York, Ace, 1965.
The Mustang Trail. New York, Doubleday, 1965.
The Jayhawkers. New York, New American Library, 1965.
Lobo Gray. London, New English Library, 1965.
The Silver Flame. New York, Doubleday, 1966.
The Plundering Gun. New York, Ace, 1967; London, Gold Lion, 1975.
Rogue's Legacy. New York, Doubleday, 1968.

Triple Cross at Trinidad. New York, Doubleday, 1971.
Powdersmoke Partners. New York, Ace, 1973.
Last Stand Mesa. New York, Ace, 1974.
The Quiet Man. New York, Belmont, 1977.

Uncollected Short Stories

"Senor Renegado," in *All Western* (New York), August 1937.
"Ghosts of Owlhoot Trail," in *All Western* (New York), August 1937.
"Mr. Smith Passes," in *All Western* (New York), January 1938.
"Renegade's Ransom," in *All Western* (New York), February 1938.
"Gun-Ghost's Return," in *Western Story* (New York), 26 February 1938.
"Solitary Stray," in *All Western* (New York), March 1938.
"Raiders of Rainbow Rock," in *Western Story* (New York), 5 March 1938.
"Dead Men Rest Easy," in *Western Story* (New York), 16 April 1938.
"Renegade's Revenge," in *Western Story* (New York), 28 May 1938.
"Bounty Rider," in *Western Story* (New York), 18 June 1938.
"Up the Long Trail," in *Western Story* (New York), 2 July 1938.
"Saddle for Satan," in *Western Story* (New York), 9 July 1938.
"Guns Mean Trouble," in *Western Story* (New York), 13 August 1938.
"Day of Gun Judgment," in *Western Story* (New York), 1 October 1938.
"Cowmen Can't Quit," in *Western Story* (New York), 29 October 1938.
"Gunman's Gospel," in *Western Story* (New York), 12 November 1938.
"Vaquero Code," in *Western Story* (New York), 17 December 1938.
"Cattleman's Pass," in *Western Story* (New York), 14 January 1939.
"Gun-Powder Pact," in *Western Story* (New York), 18 March 1939.
"Raiders of Puerco Ridge," in *Western Story* (New York), 1 April 1939.
"Gun Maverick," in *Western Story* (New York), 1 July 1939.
"Bullet Blockade," in *Western Story* (New York), 19 August 1939.
"Pinto," in *Western Story* (New York), 2 September 1939.
"Dead Men Can't Deliver," in *Western Story* (New York), 25 November 1939.
"Contrabando," in *Western Story* (London), April 1940.
"Mavericks Don't Wear Brands," in *Western Story* (London), July 1940.
"Heir to Hell's Honkytonk," in *Star Western* (Chicago), September 1940.
"Satan Calls a Showdown," in *Western Story* (London), October 1940.
"Raiders of the Scarlet Feather," in *Star Western* (Chicago), March 1941.
"Warriors of the Salt Creek Strip," in *Star Western* (Chicago) July 1941.
"Powdersmoke Pilgrims," in *Western Story* (London), May 1946.
"Gun-Aces Wild," in *Western Story* (London), July 1946.
"Renegades Reveille," in *Western Story* (London), December 1946.
"Long-Rider Legacy," in *Western Story* (London), March 1948.
"Lone Star of Texas," in *Western Story* (London), June 1949.
"Trigger Traitor," in *Western Story* (London), September 1949.
"Colt Caballeros," in *Western Story* (London), November 1949.
"Powdersmoke Paymasters," in *Western Story* (London), July 1950.
"Sinc, Desert Wind," in *Zane Grey's Western* (New York), October 1951.
"Triggerman Tarry," in *Zane Grey's Western* (New York), May 1951.
"Powdersmoke Partnership," in *Western Story* (London), September 1951.
"And Then There Were Five," in *Western Story* (London), November 1951.
"Powdersmoke Empire," in *Zanes Grey's Western* (New York), November 1951.
"Gunsmoke Gamboleers," in *Western Story* (London), January 1952.
"Bullet Bankers," in *Western Story* (London), March 1952.
"Vagabond Vaquero," in *Zane Grey's Western* (New York), March 1952.
"Powdersmoke Promoters," in *Western Story* (London), May 1952.
"Call Me Solo," in *Zane Grey's Western* (New York), July 1952.
"Six-Gun Stopover," in *Western Story* (London), September 1952.
"Platte River Gamble," in *Zane Grey's Western 32* (London), 1953.
"The Cave," in *Western Story* (London), March 1953.
"Red Is the Blade," in *Western Story* (London), May 1953.
"Gunman," in *The Killers*, edited by Peter Dawson. New York, Bantam, 1955.
"Deadline in Barrio," in *Western* (New York), September 1955.
"Longrider Jones," in *Riders West*. New York, Dell, 1956.
"Trail of Angry Men," in *Western* (New York), March 1956.
"Gunslinger of the Cibola," in *Western* (New York, October 1956.
"Wagon-Tongue North," in *Hoof Trails and Wagon Tracks*, edited by Don Ward. New York, Dodd Mead, 1957.
"Exile of the Valiant," in *Western* (New York), January 1957.
"Tramp Gunfighter," in *Western* (New York), April 1957.
"The Sixgun Sins of Smoke Joe," in *3-Book Western* (New York), May 1957.
"A Lady Boss Means Trouble," in *Western Story* (London), October 1957.
"Tall, Tough, and Texan," in *Western* (New York), October 1957.
"Showdown at Saber Pass," in *Western* (New York), February 1958.

OTHER PUBLICATIONS

Plays

Screenplays: *The Lone Gun*, with Don Martin and Richard Schayer, 1955; *The Gambler Wore a Gun*, with Owen Harris, 1961.

* * *

L.L. Foreman had a busy career as a pulp and a popular western writer, beginning with stories in the American pulp magazines in the 1930's and publishing copiously until the early 1970's. He also wrote non-western stories, though all his novels are in the western mode.

Foreman's stories and novels reflect an interest in plot and dialogue at the expense of action and atmosphere. His books are not centered on a confrontation between good and evil, but rather on developing the changing nature of his characters, often influenced by a past mistake or circumstance which makes their actions confusing to the other characters, or even to the reader until he realizes the background. He is also interested in women as characters in their own right, and not merely as rewards or plot complications.

By choosing his initial situations clearly, Foreman is able to suggest the importance of the story he is telling—since it will illustrate, for instance, dangers of a cattle drive (*The Jayhawkers*), the historical impact of a small town in a newly developed area of the country as it proceeds to turn into a small city (*Lobo Gray*), a similar small city seeking to keep a reputation for law and order even though all the leading citizens have been compromised by their past actions (Tucson in *The Plundering Gun*). *Gringo* is actually based on the diary of William Watts Hart Davis, the United States Attorney to the Territory of New Mexico from 1835 to 1856—and the book is dedicated to him. Foreman is at ease in dealing with Mexicans and Indians, and his novels have a sense of authority because he does not deal in simple characters or simple answers.

—George Walsh

FOREMAN, Lee. *See* **KING, Albert.**

FORREST, Allen. *See* **SNOW, Charles H.**

FOSTER, Evan. *See* **KING, Albert.**

FOSTER, Harry. *See* **PAINE, Lauran.**

FOSTER, Jeanne. *See* **WILLIAMS, Jeanne.**

FOSTER, W(alter) Bert(ram). American. Born in Providence, Rhode Island, 3 November 1869. Married Clara Louise Read in 1893. *Died 26 April 1929.*

WESTERN PUBLICATIONS

Fiction (for children)

The Lost Galleon of Doubloon Island. Philadelphia, Penn, 1901.
With Washington at Valley Forge. Philadelphia, Penn, 1902.
With Ethan Allen at Ticonderoga. Philadelphia, Penn, 1903.
In Alaskan Waters. Philadelphia, Penn, 1903.
The Eve of War. Philadelphia, Penn, 1904.
The Lost Expedition. Philadelphia, Penn, 1905.
The Quest of the Silver Swan. New York, Chatterton Peck, 1907.
The Frozen Ship. Chicago, Donohue, 1913.
From Sea to Sea. Chicago, Donohue, 1914.
From Six to Six. New York, Clode, 1927.
Sea Express. Chicago, Donohue, n.d.
Swept Out to Sea. Chicago, Donohue, n.d.

Plays

Screenplays: *Cactus Trails*, with Harry P. Crist and George Merrick, 1927; *Galloping Thunder*, with George Morgan, 1927.

*

Bibliography: in *Dime Novel Round-up*, 15 May 1970 and 15 July 1972.

* * *

Prolific author of railroad stories, rags-to-riches stories, girls' books and historical novels, W. Bert Foster is perhaps best remembered for the fast-paced and carefully constructed Westerns which he penned between 1906 and 1911 for Street & Smith's Buffalo Bill Stories. In fact, Foster wrote more Buffalo Bill dime novels than any other author, a total of 136 titles. Despite the haste with which he wrote, drafting his stories in longhand on a drawing board while wearing a green eyeshade, Foster's westerns exhibit surprising craftsmanship. As the Buffalo Bill authority Don Russell has noted, the stories "have closely knit plots, they use modern short-story techniques, and their characters occasionally come to life."

The Buffalo Bill who emerges in Foster's fiction is a knight-errant who roams the countryside redressing wrongs and enforcing the law. Among the companions who assist him in his quest are an Indian friend known as "Little Cayuse of the Piutes," Wild Bill Hickok, Cody's real-life business partner Pawnee Bill, and a fictional scout named Nick Nomad, whose frontier dialect serves to inject comic relief. Another comic character who appears prominently in the stories is a stock German, Baron Villum von Schnitzenhauser. A good-natured bungler, the Baron nevertheless manages, on occasion, to be of genuine assistance, as he is when rounding up bandits in "Buffalo Bill's O.K.; or, Pawnee Bill's Warning." Even more diverse than Buffalo Bill's sidekicks are the villains he faces; they range from Apaches to riverboat gamblers to Mormons to, in two instances at least, Russians. But no matter the antagonists, the Action in Foster's Buffalo Bill stories is invariably brisk and suspensful.

Not one to abandon a successful formula, Foster employed similar characters and plots in his other Westerns, including the considerable number of stories he published in Diamond Dick Jr. Weekly. In stories such as "Diamond Dick and the Barilla Apaches" and "Diamond Dick's Trail to Nome," Diamond Dick roams the frontier from the Southwest to the Klondike, accompanied by his faithful companion Handsome Harry. Together they right wrongs and defend the down-trodden. The same formula prevails in some 20 Ted Strong stories which Foster contributed to Rough Rider Weekly, stories chiefly distinguishable from other authors' efforts by the extent to which they feature Ted Strong's female partner Stella Fosdick. Always, though, the pattern of hero and partner remained a constant in Foster's westerns. Among the more memorable twosomes he created were saddlemates "Two Gun" Homer Stillson, a poet and minstrel, and his poker-playing sidekick "Poke" Fellows, cowboy characters featured in a run of stories published over a span of years in *Ace-High* magazine.

—Daryl Jones

FOWLER, Kenneth A(brams). Also wrote as Clark Brooker. American. Born in New York City, 8 October 1900. Educated at New York University, Bachelor of Commercial Science 1922. Served in the United States Army Air Force Intelligence during World War II. Married Martha Schamack in 1944. Reporter, Yonkers *Herald*, 1923–26, head of copy desk staff, Yonkers *Statesman*, 1926–28, and reporter and columnist, Yonkers *Herald-Statesman*, 1928–37, all New York; associate editor, *Western Story Magazine*, 1937–38; on public relations staff, Todd Shipyards, New York, 1942–44; editor, *Dime Western* and *Star Western*, 1944–46; then freelance writer: editor, Western Writers of America magazine *The Roundup*, 1972–78; also book reviewer, New York *Herald Tribune* and New York *World Telegram*. *Died 24 March 1987.*

WESTERN PUBLICATIONS

Novels

Outcast of Murder Mesa. New York, Fawcett, 1954; London, Fawcett, 1956.
The Range Bum. New York, Avon, 1955.
Lone Gun (as Clark Brooker). New York, Ballantine, 1955.
Fight at Sun Mountain (as Clark Brooker). New York, Ballantine, 1957.
Summons to Silverhorn. New York, Fawcett, 1957; London, Fawcett, 1958.
Ride with a Dark Moon. New York, Avon, 1962.
Juggernaut of Horns. London, Ward Lock, 1962.
Dead Reckoning. New York, Belmont, 1968.
Jackals' Gold. New York, Doubleday, 1980.

Uncollected Short Stories

"Dead Man's Freight for Kearney Post," in *Star Western* (Chicago), October 1940.
"The Marshal Who Had No Heart," in *Dime Western* (New York), October 1940.
"Doc Hornett's Owlhoot Assistant," in *Dime Western* (New York), January 1941.
"Blood-Barrier for Starvation Caravan," in *Star Western* (Chicago), May 1941.
"The Fight for Purgatory Ann," in *Big Book Western*, August 1941.
"Johnny Get Your Gunman," in *10-Story Western*, October 1941.
"Mistress at the JR," in *Romantic Range*, October 1941.
"Gunsmoke Buys a Ranch," in *Dime Western* (New York), 1942.
"Rebellion at Arnall's Creek," in *10-Story Western*, 1942.
"The Cowboy Who Wouldn't Be Tamed," in *Rangeland Romances*, February 1942.
"Moonlight on the Bar BQ," in *Romantic Range*, April 1942.
"Cattle Kingdom for Two," in *10-Story Western*, September 1942.
"Gypsy Feet," in *Romantic Range*, September 1942.
"Rodeo at Alamosa," in *Romantic Range*, February 1943.
"Crazy over Horses," in *Romantic Range*, May 1945.
"Cinderella of Circle D," in *Rangeland Romances*, November 1945.
"Rough, Tough, and Glamorous," in *Rangeland Romances*, January 1946.
"Spitfire of the Circle S," in *Romantic Range*, April 1946.
"Never Jilt a Saucy Jill," in *Rangeland Romances*, July 1946.
"Boomers, Ride!," in *Dime Western* (New York), July 1946.
"Dude from Silver Dollar," in *15 Western Tales*, November 1946.
"Two Trails to Boothill," in *15 Western Tales*, February 1947.
"The Long Trail Back," in *Dime Western* (New York), March 1947.
"Texas Is a Long Way Back," in *Dime Western* (New York), April 1947.
"A Star for Peaceful Perry," in *15 Western Tales*, April 1947.
"When the Storm Gods Laughed," in *New Western*, April 1947.
"The Man from Massacre Ridge," in *New Western*, June 1947.
"Where the Gun Trails Split," in *Dime Western* (New York), July 1947.
"Tease Queen of Hearts," in *Rangeland Romances*, July 1947.
"Dead Man's Deputy," in *15 Western Tales*, August 1947.
"Sunset Trail," in *15 Western Tales*, September 1947.
"Return of the One-Shot Kid," in *15 Western Tales*, October 1947.
"Gun Ghost Wanted," in *New Western*, December 1947.
"The No-Surrender Rebels," in *Star Western* (Chicago), January 1948.
"Slow Draw," in *New Western*, January 1948.
"The Ninth Notch," in *15 Western Tales*, January 1948.
"That Bullet-Dodging Gringo," in *New Western*, February 1948.
"Death Is My Brother," in *15 Western Tales*, April 1948.
"Death Rides the High Trail," in *15 Western Tales*, June 1948.
"Honor the Blood Badge," in *15 Western Tales*, July 1948.
"Brothers of the Bugle," in *Dime Western* (New York), August 1948.
"No Badge, No Shoot!," in *New Western*, November 1948.
"Grubstaked in Gunsmoke," in *New Western*, December 1948.
"Boothill Bell," in *10-Story Western*, 1949.
"Yellow Stripes, Red Blood," in *Star Western* (Chicago), September 1949.
"The Black Badge of Quemadero," in *Mammoth Western* (Chicago), July 1950.
"No Man to Mourn Him," in *Zane Grey's Western* (New York), March 1952.
"Deaf Man's Draw," in *Thrilling Western* (London), May 1953.
"Three on a Bullet," in *Western Story* (London), August 1955.
"The Law and the Gun," in *Branded West*, edited by Don Ward. Boston, Houghton Mifflin, 1956.
"Army Wife," in *Spurs West*, edited by S. Omar Barker. New York, Doubleday, 1960.
"Jackass Judgment," in *Western Roundup*, edited by Nelson Nye. New York, Macmillan, 1961.
"Goliad Goes to War," in *Rivers to Cross*, edited by William R. Cox. New York, Dodd Mead, 1966.
"Peaceful John," in *They Opened the West*, edited by Tom W. Blackburn. New York, Doubleday, 1967.
"Wilderness Gamble," in *Western Romances*, edited by Peggy Simson Curry. New York, Fawcett, 1969.
"Brothers of the Bugle," in *With Guidons Flying*, edited by Charles N. Heckelmann. New York, Doubleday, 1970.

OTHER PUBLICATIONS

Other

Editor, *Rawhide Men*. New York, Doubleday, 1965.

*

Manuscript Collection: Western History Research Center, University of Wyoming, Laramie.

* * *

Kenneth A. Fowler has written many short stories for magazines, edited and provided an introduction for an anthology *Rawhide Men*, and done much research into western history.

A strong historical basis, in fact, is evident in Fowler's Westerns. This comes through particularly well in the case of *Juggernaut of Horns*. We are given the reasons for the general failure of the Shawnee Trail from Texas to Kansas. The book is set on the trail, and closely built around real events. There is also a revealing insight in this book into the post-Civil War bitterness prevalent in the south, and the types of people the war brought in its wake. There is also much good technical detail about cattle handling and a very rich vocabulary of Americana.

Fowler has improved his formula over the years and has been able to produce a more authentic sounding background. This is, however, achieved at the expense of plot: *Juggernaut of Horns* is somewhat overloaded with events and characters by comparison with *Outcast of Murder Mesa* and has a less convincing ending. Fowler also seems to have toned down the romance and love interest in more recent books. It is a pity that fewer women appear in his books, since Fowler's grasp of female psychology is unusually acute. There is a good description of Belle and her emotions in *Outcast of Murder Mesa*. There is also in this book an unusually extended account of a western brothel. Fowler is also good at recreating the inner thoughts of a western drifter and he gives a sympathetic view of the Indian. Fowler has a good turn of phrase, though his writing is over-rich by the standards of the modern formula Western.

—P.R. Meldrum

FOX, Norman A(rnold). Also wrote as Mark Sabin. American. Born in Sault Ste. Marie, Michigan, 26 May 1911. Educated at schools in Great Falls, Montana. Married Rosalea Spaulding in 1949. Bookkeeper and accountant, 1929–38; then freelance writer. *Died 24 March 1960*.

WESTERN PUBLICATIONS

Novels

Gun-Handy. New York, Phoenix Press, 1941; London, Wright and Brown, 1942.
The Gunsight Kid. New York, Phoenix Press, 1941; London, Wright and Brown, 1942.
The Six-Gun Syndicate. New York, Phoenix Press, 1942; London, Wright and Brown, 1943.
The Stampede Kid. New York, Phoenix Press, 1942; London, Wright and Brown, 1944.
Lord Six-Gun. New York, Phoenix Press, 1943; London, Wright and Brown, 1948.
The Thundering Trail. New York, Dodd Mead, 1944; London, Wright and Brown, 1946.
Thorson of Thunder Gulch. New York, Dodd Mead, 1945; London, Wright and Brown, 1947.
Silent in the Saddle. New York, Dodd Mead, 1945; London, Collins, 1946.
Dead End Trail. New York, Dodd Mead, 1946; London, Collins, 1947.
The Valley of Vanishing Riders. New York, Dodd Mead, 1946; as *Riders in the Rain*, London, Collins, 1947.
The Rider from Yonder. New York, Dodd Mead, 1947; London, Collins, 1948.
Cactus Cavalier. New York, Dodd Mead, 1947; London, Collins, 1948.
The Devil's Saddle. New York, Dodd Mead, 1948; London, Collins, 1949.
The Feathered Sombrero. New York, Dodd Mead, 1948; London, Collins, 1949.
Shadow on the Range. New York, Dodd Mead, 1949; London, Collins, 1950.
The Thirsty Land. New York, Dodd Mead, 1949; London, Collins, 1950.
The Phantom Spur. New York, Dodd Mead, 1950; London, Collins, 1951.
Stormy in the West. New York, Dodd Mead, 1950; London, Collins, 1951.
The Longhorn Legion. New York, Dell, 1951.
Roughshod. New York, Dodd Mead, 1951; London, Collins, 1952.
Tall Man Riding. New York, Dodd Mead, 1951; London, Collins, 1952.
Winchester Cut (as Mark Sabin). New York, Fawcett, 1951; revised edition, as *Stranger from Arizona* (as Norman A. Fox), New York, Dodd Mead, 1956; as *Arizona Stranger*, London, Collins, 1957.
Ghostly Hoofbeats. New York, Dodd Mead, 1952; London, Collins, 1953.
Long Lightning. New York, Dodd Mead, and London, Collins, 1953.
The Rawhide Years. New York, Dodd Mead, 1953; London, Collins, 1954.
Broken Wagon. New York, Ballantine, and London, Collins, 1954.
Night Passage. New York, Dodd Mead, and London, Collins, 1956.
War on the Range. New York, Fawcett, 1956.
The Badlands Beyond. New York, Dodd Mead, and London, Collins, 1957.
Rope the Wind. New York, Dodd Mead, 1958; London, Collins, 1959.
Reckoning at Rimbow. New York, Dodd Mead, 1959; London, Collins, 1960.
The Hard Pursued. New York, Dodd Mead, 1960; as *Showdown at Signal*, London, Collins, 1961.
The Trembling Hills. New York, Dodd Mead, 1961; London, Collins, 1962.

Short Stories

The Valiant Ones. New York, Dodd Mead, 1957.
They Rode the Shining Hills. New York, Dodd Mead, 1968.

Uncollected Short Stories

"House-Breaker from Purgatory," in *Western Story* (New York), 9 September 1939.
"Kin to the Untamed," in *Western Story* (New York), 4 November 1939.
"Hogtied to Trouble," in *Western Story* (New York), 30 September 1939.
"Hot Lead with Printer's Ink," in *Western Story* (London), July 1940.
"Doomed Cargo," in *Western Story* (London), February 1941.
"Ghost-Town Gunsmoke," in *Western Story* (London), May 1941.
"Six-Shootin' Schoolmaster," in *Western Story* (London), September 1941.
"Whang-Leather Loyalty," in *Western Story* (London), April 1942.
"The Bushwhacker," in *Western Story* (London), January 1943.
"Trouble-Shootin' Music Maker," in *Western Story* (London), May 1944.
"Doc Comanche's Gun-Smoke Debt," in *Western Story* (London), July 1944.
"Gun Law for Hungry Gulch," in *Western Story* (London), September 1944.
"Trigger Call for a Free Trapper," in *Western Story* (London), January 1945.
"Colts Ring Down the Curtain," in *Western Story* (London), July 1947.
"Doc Comanche's Perilous Pitch," in *Western Story* (London), November 1948.
"The Makings," in *Western Stories*, edited by William MacLeod Raine. New York, Dell, 1949.
"The Man Who Rode Back," in *Zane Grey Western Award Stories*, edited by Don Ward. New York, Dell, 1951.
"Wild Leather," in *Spurs West!*, edited by Joseph T. Shaw. New York, Permabooks, 1951.
"The Mystery of Lost Creek," in *Western Story* (London), July 1952.
"Man and a Half," in *Western Story* (London), September 1952.
"Bet the Wild Queen!," in *Bad Men and Good*, edited by Luke Short. New York, Dodd Mead, 1953.
"The Marshal of Trailtown," in *Gunpoint*, edited by Leo Margulies. New York, Pyramid, 1956.
"Weep No More, My Lady!," in *Hoof Trails and Wagon Tracks*, edited by Don Ward. New York, Dodd Mead, 1957.
"Another Man's Boots," in *Frontiers West*, edited by S. Omar Barker. New York, Doubleday, 1959.
"Way of the Valiant," in *A Saddlebag of Tales*, edited by Rutherford Montogomery. New York, Dodd Mead, 1959.
"Coffins for Tomahawk Town," in *Western Story* (London), October 1961.
"Only the Dead Ride Proudly," in *The Steamboaters*, edited by Bill Pronzini and Martin H. Greenberg. New York, Fawcett, 1986.
"The Longhorn Legion," in *The Cattlemen*, edited by Bill Pronzini and Martin H. Greenberg. New York, Fawcett, 1986.

* * *

Norman A. Fox was born in Michigan, but grew up in Montana. Nearly all of his 33 western novels are set in his adopted state. The early books are rough products, in which an inventive incident or moment of insightful characterization occasionally surfaces amid the cliché of the pulp Western. In *Lord Six-Gun* a gambler-turned-actor becomes involved with multiple impersonations and a genuine castle, complete with ghost and secret passage, in the Montana badlands. The best of the early group is probably *The Six-Gun Syndicate*, a story of a young man's quest for vengeance against his father's killers. The book provides a foretaste of the vigor and emotional power which characterize Fox's later work.

The mountains, valleys, and badlands of Montana and their changing seasons form an almost palpable presence in Fox's novels. Drought pushes the Purgatory Range into a war in *The Thirsty Land*. In *Stormy in the West* the great Montana blizzard of 1886 is an important story element, and in the posthumously published novel *The Trembling Hills* the Montana earthquake of August 1959 has been transposed 50 years into the past to provide the climax for the story. Against backgrounds such as these, Fox's people are often caught in a conscious or unconscious search for self-knowledge: having to come to terms with a desire for revenge for past wrongs, like Larry Madden in *Tall Man Riding* or Terry Mullane in *Rope the Wind*; or driven by a need to uncover the truth about the past, like the orphaned Steve Reardon in *The Six-Gun Syndicate* or Will Yeoman in *The Rawhide Years*; or simply yearning for something fixed and permanent in a rootless life, like gunfighter Reb Kittredge in *Roughshod*. These characters grow and change, and the changes are not grafted on but are an essential part of the story.

A different type of story is told in *Reckoning at Rimbow*. Ross Kingman returns with his wife and teen-aged children to the town he had left in anger 17 years earlier. His struggle to overcome the antagonism of townsmen and ranchers, and to make a secure home for his family without being pushed into violence, makes a strong and satisfying book.

All but two of Fox's novels were written for hardcover publication. The first exception, and Fox's only pseudonymous book, was *Winchester Cut*, published in the Gold Medal line of original paperbacks in 1951 under the byline Mark Sabin (the name of the leading character in *Stormy in the West* from the previous year). Fox later reworked this novel and published it in hardcover form as *Stranger from Arizona*, under his own name. The other book written for paperback publication was *Broken Wagon*.

Four of Fox's novels from the 1950's were turned into films. *Gunsmoke* was based on *Roughshod*, and featured Audie Murphy. Randolph Scott and Dorothy Malone had the leading roles in *Tall Man Riding*; Tony Curtis was featured in *The Rawhide Years*, and James Stewart and Audie Murphy in *Night Passage*. Other stories by Fox were adapted for radio or television presentation.

In addition to his novels, Fox wrote more than 400 short stories and novelettes for magazines. 11 of these were collected in book form under the title *The Valiant Ones*. While Fox's novels seldom dealt with actual persons or events in western history, the stories gathered here are, as Fox wrote in his Foreward to the book, "as authentic as research and my personal knowledge of the West could make [them]; and in several of the selections the fiction is interwoven with actual historical happenings so that men of history walk side by side with men and women of my invention." Alexander Majors, General Jack Casement, Kid Curry, and other figures from the annals of the West play significant roles in these well-wrought tales, all chosen to illustrate the varieties of courage possessed by those who settled and tamed the land.

In both novels and short stories, Fox dealt with the standard ingredients of the western tale, but treated these ingredients with skill and respect. The best of his work—*Tall Man Riding*, *The Badlands Beyond*, *Reckoning at Rimbow*, *The Hard Pursued*,

The Valiant Ones—is worthy of a permanent place in any library of western fiction.

—R.E. Briney

FRAZEE, (Charles) Steve. Also writes as Dean Jennings. American. Born in Salida, Colorado, 28 September 1909. Educated at Western State College, Gunnison, Colorado, A.B. 1937. Married Patricia Thomass in 1937; one son and one daughter. Worked in heavy construction and mining, 1926–36, 1941–43; journalism teacher, La Junta High School, Colorado, 1937–41. Since 1946, freelance writer. Building inspector, City of Salida, 1950–63; director, Salida Building and Loan Association. Since 1959, member of advisory council, San Isabel National Forest. President, 1954, and vice-president, 1962, Western Writers of America. Recipient: *Ellery Queen's Mystery Magazine* prize, 1953; Western Heritage award, 1961; Cowboy Hall of Fame, 1961. Agent: Scott Meredith Literary Agency, 845 Third Avenue, New York, New York 10022. Address: Box 534, Salida, Colorado, 81201, U.S.A.

WESTERN PUBLICATIONS

Novels

Range Trouble (as Dean Jennings) New York, Phoenix Press, 1951.
Shining Mountains. New York, Rinehart, 1951; London, Muller, 1953.
Pistolman. New York, Lion, 1952; London, Panther, 1967.
Utah Hell Guns. New York, Lion, 1952; London, Panther, 1968.
The Sky Block. New York, Rinehart, 1953; London, Lane, 1955.
Lawman's Feud. New York, Lion, 1953;
Sharp the Bugle Calls. New York, Lion, 1953; as *Gold at Kansas Gulch*, New York, Fawcett, 1958; London, Red Seal, 1959.
Cry Coyote. New York, Macmillan, 1955; London, Lane, 1956.
Many Rivers to Cross. New York and London, Fawcett, 1955.
Spur to the Smoke. New York, Permabooks, 1955.
Tumbling Range Woman. New York, Pocket Books, 1956.
He Rode Alone. New York, Fawcett, 1956; London, Fawcett, 1958.
High Cage. New York, Macmillan, 1957.
Running Target. New York, Fawcett, 1957; London, Fawcett, 1958.
Desert Guns. New York, Dell, 1957; as *Gold of the Seven Saints*, London, Consul, 1961.
Rendezvous. New York, Macmillan, 1958.
High Hell. New York, Fawcett, 1958.
Smoke in the Valley. New York, Fawcett, 1959; London, Muller, 1960.
A Day to Die. New York, Avon, 1960.
Hellsgrin. New York, Rinehart, 1960.
The Alamo. New York, Avon, 1960.
More Damn Tourists. New York, Macmillan, 1960.
Bragg's Fancy Woman. New York, Ballantine, 1966; as *A Gun for Bragg's Woman*, London, Panther, 1967.
Outcasts. New York, Popular Library, 1967.
Flight 409. New York, Avon, 1969.
Fire in the Valley. New York, Lancer, 1972.

Short Stories

The Gun-Throwers. New York, Lion, 1954.
The Best Western Stories of Steve Frazee, edited by Bill Pronzini and Martin H. Greenberg. Carbondale, Illinois, Southern Illinois University Press, 1984.

Uncollected Short Stories

"Where the Gunhawks Gather," in *Best Western*, June 1951.
"Four Graves West," in *Western Story Roundup* (New York), June 1951.
"Look Behind Every Hill," in *Complete Western Book* (New York), December 1952.
"The Man at Gantt's Place," "The Fire Killer," "Great Medicine," "The Bretnall Feud," "The Bounty Killers," and "Payroll of the Dead," in *Bar 1–6*, edited by Scott Meredith. New York, Dutton, 6 vols., 1952–57.
"Learn the Hard Way," in *The Killers*, edited by Peter Dawson. New York, Bantam, 1955.
"Legacy of Violence," in *Gunfight at the OK Corral and Other Western Adventures.* New York, Avon, 1957.
"Due Process," in *Western Roundup*, edited by Nelson Nye. New York, Macmillan, 1961.
"My Brother Down There," in *The Reel West*, edited by Bill Pronzini and Martin H. Greenberg. New York, Doubleday, 1984.
"The Bounty Killers," in *The Lawman*, edited by Bill Pronzini and Martin H. Greenberg. New York, Fawcett, 1984.
"The Singing Sands," in *The Second Reel West*, edited by Bill Pronzini and Martin H. Greenberg. New York, Doubleday, 1985.
"Great Medicine," in *The Warriors*, edited by Bill Pronzini and Martin H. Greenberg. New York, Fawcett, 1986.
"The Big Die Up," in *The Cattlemen*, edited by Bill Pronzini and Martin H. Greenberg. New York, Fawcett, 1986.

OTHER PUBLICATIONS

Play

Screenplay: *Running Target*, with others, 1957.

Other (for children)

Walt Disney's Zorro (novelization of TV play). Racine, Wisconsin, Whitman, 1958; London, Daily Mirror, 1959.
First Through the Grand Canyon. Philadelphia, Winston, 1960.
Year of the Big Snow. New York, Holt Rinehart, 1962.
Killer Lion. Racine, Wisconsin, Whitman, 1966.
Lassie: The Mystery of the Bristlecone Pine. Racine, Wisconsin, Whitman, 1967.
Where Are You? All about Maps. New York, Meredith Press, 1968.
Lassie: Lost in the Snow [*The Secret of the Smuggler's Cave*, *Trouble at Panter's Lake*]. New York, Golden Press, 3 vols., 1979; last vol. published, London, W.M. Allen, 1982.

*

Manuscript Collections: University of Wyoming, Laramie; University of Kentucky, Lexington.

* * *

During the 1950's, no one wrote better popular western novels and stories than Steve Frazee. Testimony to this fact is a highly impressive record of 18 published novels; first prize in an annual contest conducted by *Ellery Queen's Mystery Magazine* for a modern western story, "My Brother Down There," later anthologized in Martha Foley's *Best American Short Stories of the Year*; several other anthology appearances; one collection; and such film adaptations as *Many Rivers to Cross, Running Target*, and *The Alamo*—all between 1951 and 1960.

"My Brother Down There," the tense, savage tale of a manhunt in the wilds of Colorado, in which both the hunters and the hunted are dominated by the primitive elements in man's personality, is easily the finest of Frazee's short work. (It was later expanded into the novel *Running Target*, which then became the film of the same title.) Of his traditional western stories, the best are probably "Great Medicine," the story of a Crow Indian named Little Belly, who believed he could defeat the white man if he could only steal the white man's "medicine"; "The Man at Gantt's Place," which deals with a young man's coming of age on the frontier; and "Due Process," the delightfully good-humored account of the shooting of a bully and the efforts of a bunch of well-meaning cowhands to disburse his "estate."

In the novel form, Frazee is at his best when writing about wilderness areas in general and the Colorado Rockies in particular. *High Cage*, for instance, is a superior tale of five miners and one woman snowbound at an isolated gold mine high atop Bulmer Peak, in which the twin themes of the lust for gold and man's struggle to survive against the savagery of both the elements and his fellow man are beautifully interplayed. Almost as good are *Shining Mountains, Hellsgrin*, and *The Sky Block*—the last a present-day chase/adventure story in the mode of Geoffrey Household and John Buchan, set in a remote section of the Rockies and involving a plot to alter meteorological conditions through the use of cosmic rays.

Frazee is also adept at the historical western. *Rendezvous* has been called the best novel on the mountain man since A.B. Guthrie, Jr.'s *The Big Sky*; and *The Alamo*, a dramatization of the famous clash between a handful of American soldiers and the Mexican army, the movie version of which starred John Wayne.

Since 1960, Frazee has published only a few western novels; the only one of comparable quality to his earlier efforts is *A Gun for Bragg's Woman*, the saga of a free-spirited lady named Casey and how she tames a family of thieves and toughs. The balance of Frazee's output in the 1960's and 1970's is comprised of suspense novels such as *Flight 409* and a number of books for children, among them the excellent *Year of the Big Snow*.

It may safely be said that few contemporary writers can match Frazee for evocative, lyrical descriptions of wide-open spaces and of the awesome power of nature. Other of his attributes include flawless characterization, particularly when it involves the clash of human passions; believable dialogue; and the ability to create and sustain damp-palmed suspense. His work deserves more critical attention than it has thus far received, and it is to be hoped that this neglect will one day be rectified.

—Bill Pronzini

FREDERICK, John. *See* **BRAND, Max.**

FRIEND, Oscar (J). Also wrote as Owen Fox Jerome; Ford Smith. American. Born in 1897. Magazine editor, later literary agent. *Died in 1963.*

WESTERN PUBLICATIONS

Novels

The Round-Up: A Story of Ranchmen, Cowboys, Rustlers and Bad-Men, Happening in the Days when the Great South West Was Being Won for Civilization. Chicago, McClurg, 1924.
The Bullet Eater. Chicago, McClurg, 1925; London, Kemsley Newspapers, 1953; abridged edition, London, Hammond, 1949.
Click of Triangle T. Chicago, McClurg, and London, Fisher Unwin, 1925.
The Wolf of Wildcat Mountain. Chicago, McClurg, 1926; as *Wolf of Wildcat*, London, Brown Watson, 1950.
Gun Harvest. Chicago, McClurg, 1927; London, Nelson, 1929.
Bloody Ground. Chicago, McClurg, 1928.
The Mississippi Hawk. Chicago, McClurg, 1929; London, Hammond, 1950.
Half-Moon Ranch. New York, Watt, 1931; London, Wright and Brown, 1932.
The Range Maverick. New York, Watt, 1931; London, Wright and Brown, 1933.
The Long Noose. New York, Gateway, 1942; London, Ward Lock, 1943.
Guns of Powder River. New York, Bond-Charteris, 1945; London, Quality Press, 1950.
Trouble at Lazy-S. London, Hammond, 1951.
Buzzard Meat Range. London, Hammond, 1953.
Deputies of Death. London, Hammond, 1954.
Lobo Brand. New York, Avalon, 1954; London, Hammond, 1955.
Montana Ermine. New York, Avalon, 1955.
The Gun-Runner. London, Hammond, 1956.

Novels as Ford Smith

The Range Doctor. London, Ward Lock, 1948; New York, Avalon, 1958.
Buzzards' Roost. New York, Avalon, 1961.

OTHER PUBLICATIONS

Novels as Owen Fox Jerome

The Hand of Horror. New York, Clode, 1927.
The Red Kite Clue. New York, Clode, 1928.
The Golf Club Murder. New York, Clode, 1929.
The Domes of Silence. London, Stanley Paul, 1929.
The Murder at Avalon Arms. New York, Clode, 1931.
Murder—As Usual. New York, Gateway, 1942.
The Corpse Awaits. New York, Mystery House, 1946.

The Kid from Mars. New York, Fell, 1949; London, Kemsley Newspapers, 1951.
Barricade (as Oscar J. Friend). New York, Quinn, 1950.

Other

Editor, *My Best Science Fiction Story, as Selected by 25 Outstanding Authors*, with Leo Margulies. New York, Merlin, 1949.
Editor, *The Giant Anthology of Science Fiction: 10 Complete Short Novels*, with Leo Margulies. New York, Merlin, 1954.

* * *

Oscar Friend was 28 when his first Western was published, and although he continued to write Westerns for a while, his main love was science fiction and murder mysteries. He became the editor of *Thrilling Wonder Stories*, *Starling Stories*, and *Captain Future* in the early 1940's, finally becoming the head of a literary agency. Though he died in 1963, ending those final few years with sci-fi writings, his western works were numerous from 1924 up to 1956.

Friend wrote in an uncluttered prose, with the accent on high adventure, and extolling human nature for better or for worse, with each novel containing all the elements essential for standard-plotted Westerns. In *The Bullet Eater*, Jack Montague, the eponymous hero, destroys a gang of rustlers called the Nightbirds, but is unable to capture their leaders. However, he is determined to bring down their chief, Sandy McGregor. When the antagonist realizes that Montague is set on capturing him, he kidnaps Jack's fiancée and holds her hostage to force Jack to give up. But like every good western hero, Jack accomplishes his mission in the finale at a border hotel—McGregor's Inn. This book is by no means one of Friend's best, and is far outshone by *Bloody Hand* (or *Trouble at Lazy S*). This novel approaches the Western from a different angle, and provides an unusual viewpoint to a chain of events sparked off by the accidental meeting of a daughter and son of rival families. Their seemingly innocent kiss is the catalyst for the bloodshed that follows. After the initial chapter the book virtually becomes a collection of short stories recounting the power struggle between the Eustace and Mellor households. Men are killed, thieves unmasked, there is a suicide, but eventually right, personified by Sophia Eustace and her sweetheart, triumphs over the Mellors and forces them to sell out.

Friend proved that one can successfully transfer a hard-boiled thriller story into a Western, given the right treatment. His story *The Gun-Runner* is a prime example of this achievement. The premise for the plot is simple—Simon Carter, Chief of the Cattleman's Protective Association, is called in to investigate the theft of a prize Hereford bull, and the disappearance of one of his deputies he'd assigned to trace the animal. On arriving in the town of Cactus, Arizona, Carter is run out of town and ambushed. He escapes with his life and seeks refuge at the hacienda of Don Ramon Feliz. Carter sends for Curly Preston and Stogie Alton, who take over the investigation. They come up against antagonism between ranch owners—McNamara and Feliz—the lust for gold, and duplicity when they finally unmask the gun-runner. The book is well balanced in adventure and suspense. The characters are a little over-the-top, but this adds to Friend's style of writing.

In *Lobo Brand*, the three main characters of *The Gun-Runner* reappear when they are called upon to investigate claims from ranchers that their land and stock are being poisoned. Carter is outraged that the victims are innocents, and he swears to capture the man using the strange signature of the wolf, left wherever he strikes. This is not so suspenseful as *The Gun-Runner*, as it is only a mystery to Carter and his men, because the reader is already aware who the murderer is from the outset.

Friend continued to write about Simon Carter in *Deputies of Death* and *Buzzard Meat Range*, both stories concerning cattle rustling. Not one to be set in his ways, Friend also wrote on other western subjects. His *Wolf of Wildcat* is an off-key Western complete with automobiles, radios, and electric lights. A native New Yorker, Rufus Rundell, has his head full of dreams of the Wild West, but finds his illusions shattered in his sojourn to the Southwest. It makes for a different read, with the whole tone of the book very light-hearted. Its characters are that little bit larger-than-life, to compensate for Rundell's own dime-novelistic view.

Friend's *The Mississippi Hawk* is a more traditional Western, with a look at the old South when Negroes were still slaves, and handicapped with names such as Tangle-Eye and Uncle Nebbo. Friend states that much of the feel for the book came from his great-uncle, a general who fought for the Confederacy, and that is probably his excuse for using such incredible dialogue for the Negroes in passages such as: ". . . 'Pears to me like as heah 'em comin' down de road. Lawdy! Lawdy! What we gwine do? . . . " Apart from this hiccup, the story is one that has been used before. A spoilt young man is forced to run after he apparently kills a judge. Campbell escapes downriver and meets a look-alike named Mississippi Hawk. When Hawk dies Campbell takes his place, figuring on escaping any punishment from the judge's men, but finds himself in a whole new world, of deceit, treachery, and villainy.

Even though Friend's first love was science fiction, he still put the same amount of detailed attention into his western works. He showed that he had the ability to produce first-rate stories which covered a variety of ground, and the skill to bring to life the characters that peopled his books.

—Mike Stotter

FROST, Frederick. *See* **BRAND, Max.**

FROST, Ryker. *See* **GILES, Jack.**

G

GANN, Walter. American. Born in Texas. Cowboy on the Concho and Pecos rivers in Texas, in Montana, summers 1908–09, and in West Kansas.

WESTERN PUBLICATIONS

Novel

The Trail Boss. Boston, Houghton Mifflin, 1937; as *Montana Trail*, London, Cassell, 1938.

OTHER PUBLICATIONS

Other

Tread of the Longhorns. San Antonio, Naylor, 1949.

* * *

The work of Walter Gann is almost entirely unknown today, and its obscurity emphasizes an interesting anomaly in the general interpretation of western fiction. For Gann comes to the craft of western writing with all the proper biographical credentials. In his Introduction to Gann's short history of the cattle industry, *Tread of the Longhorns*, William MacLeod Raine enthusiastically supports Gann's qualifications. A Texan, Gann was also a cowboy, and these two facts, when properly evaluated, assure us—Raine proclaims—not only of the book's authenticity but of its existence.

Yet Gann himself, in the first chapter of this work, unwittingly introduces an unsettling qualification to Raine's praise. His history of the cattle industry, he says, will not only be a recitation of the facts of the cattle industry, but will have a polemic purpose. For although the present-day cattle industry "is being conducted in a modern, business-like manner," and although admittedly "a much better grade of beef is being produced than ever before," nevertheless "the romance is dead."

This offhand remark sharply emphasizes the basic problem in Gann's fiction: how best to unite the facts of western history with the presumed romance of the western past. The solution Gann attempts is one common to many other western writers, and in his case—as in theirs—not totally successful. This is to combine the prosaic facts of the cattle business with a romantic story which presumably will supply a wider fictional interest than would a mere recitation of statistics.

However theoretically viable, this solution is fraught with practical difficulties, the most obvious of which is that the romantic elements of the story may deteriorate into sensationalism or mere silliness. Such is in fact the basic flaw in Gann's best-known western piece, *The Trail Boss*, a tale which attempts to arouse interest in the plight of the trail boss Bill Sanders by involving the reader in a blood-and-thunder plot concerning a gang of outlaws led by one Ben Harte; in a sweet love story involving one Virginia Lowe, a visitor from the East; and in a sentimental animal story concerning a one-horned steer named Sancho, Sander's unlikely friend whose cruel and untimely death at the hands of Ben Harte provides the novel's breathtaking finale. By this time, most readers could not care less, and this is something of a pity: for the prosaic elements of *The Trail Boss* which Gann attempted to camouflage beneath a he-man adventure story are actually quite interesting, and well told. Gann is at his best with the arcana of range life, at his worst when he panders to the tastes of what he considers a sophisticated "literary" audience. He remains a minor writer precisely because he does not tell his audience the truth, but what he believes they want to hear.

—James K. Folsom

GANT, Jonathan. *See* **ADAMS, Clifton.**

GARDINER, Dorothy. American. Born in Naples, Italy, 5 November 1894. Educated at the University of Colorado, Boulder. Executive secretary, Mystery Writers of America, 1950–57. *Died 4 December 1979.*

WESTERN PUBLICATIONS

Novels (series: Sheriff Moss Magill)

The Golden Lady. New York, Doubleday, and London, Hurst and Blackett, 1936.
Snow-Water. New York, Doubleday, and London, Hurst and Blackett, 1939.
The Great Betrayal. New York, Doubleday, 1949; London, Hammond, 1956.
What Crime Is It? (Magill). New York, Doubleday, 1956; as *The Case of the Hula Clock*, London, Hammond, 1957.
The Seventh Mourner (Magill). New York, Doubleday, 1958; London, Hammond, 1960.
Lion in Wait (Magill). New York, Doubleday, 1963; as *Lion? or Murder?*, London, Hammond, 1964.

OTHER PUBLICATIONS

Novels

The Transatlantic Ghost. New York, Doubleday, and London, Harrap, 1933.
A Drink for Mr. Cherry. New York, Doubleday, 1934; as *Mr. Watson Intervenes*, London, Hurst and Blackett, 1935.

Beer for Psyche. New York, Doubleday, 1946; London, Hurst and Blackett, 1948.

Other

West of the River. New York, Crowell, 1941.

Editor, *For Love or Money*. New York, Doubleday, 1957; London, Macdonald, 1959.
Editor, with Katherine Sorley Walker, *Raymond Chandler Speaking*. Boston, Houghton Mifflin, and London, Hamish Hamilton, 1962.

* * *

In addition to mystery stories, Dorothy Gardiner wrote three remarkable, and unjustly forgotten, historical novels set in Colorado. In each work Gardiner created a world marked by extraordinary verisimilitude, be it the mining frontier (*The Golden Lady*), the agricultural frontier (*Snow-Water*), or the military frontier (*The Great Betrayal*). The first two are noteworthy contributions to western fiction because of their sensitive and realistic portraits of Colorado settlers struggling against odds and nature to attain their visions and dreams for a new life, the third for its vivid recreation of a controversial episode in Anglo-American military history.

The Golden Lady is one of the best novels ever written about the mining frontier of the American West. It is perhaps ideally compared with Frank Waters's *Pike's Peak*, which is also set in the same general area. Gardiner's book, however, much more adeptly depicts the boom and bust cycles of a mining community. In tracing the life of Evantha Aurelia Swenk, the daughter of a former prostitute and a gambler, Gardiner managed successfully to evoke the illusory quality of the search for gold contrasted with the significance of searching in and of itself. Evantha confuses the pursuit of happiness with the pursuit of wealth, and even after she marries the richest man in Duke's Gulch and moves to Greencliff, she finds her life empty and wanting. The novel is made infinitely richer by virtue of the fascinating community of characters populating Duke's Gulch and Greencliff, who fill out and thereby add different perspectives and dimensions to the story.

Snow-Water has an unusual plotline in that it is concerned with irrigating the high farming land of Colorado. The story chronicles 66 years in the life of Daniel Bartor who founds Bartorville with the hope of creating an agrarian utopia in a land that both blisters and blossoms. Celie, Daniel's wife, is an intriguing character whom the reader despises when she is first introduced because of her snobbish airs and New England hauteur and because of her unfaithfulness to Daniel early in their marriage. However, by the end of the story, Celie has accepted life in the West and has developed an inner strength and a loyalty to Daniel and to her family which incline a reader to reverse this former harsh judgment of her—so that it almost becomes admiration. The final chapters contain comical scenes and interchanges between Daniel and Celie which are actually the high point of the novel.

The Great Betrayal is a meticulously researched rendering of the events leading up to, during and after the Sand Creek Massacre told from the white point of view but nonetheless cognizant of the perspective of the Cheyennes who, at the time, were at peace with the United States and protected by a treaty. Colonel Chivington comes closest perhaps to a villain in any Gardiner novel. He is shown to have been a power-hungry man who would do anything to gain political advantage. His philosophy toward the Indian is reiterated throughout the book in his motto "nits make lice." This is a truly moving story in which real and fictional characters and events are complexly intertwined to dramatize the ways in which a number of Indian nations were manipulated and exploited by certain of the white invaders.

These three novels deserve much more critical recognition and a wider readership than they have so far been accorded. Gardiner was a truly masterful storyteller who paid the strictest attention to historical detail—her Cavalrymen march in groups of four in contrast to movies where they march in twos; rarely elsewhere, with the possible exception of Bret Harte, is the weather shown so poignantly to be the decisive, life-and-death force it surely was on the frontier. She skillfully wove the elements of her stories together to form a vibrant and honest reconstruction of the past.

—Vicki Piekarski

GARDNER, Jerome. Also writes as Jeremy Gardner; John Gilchrist; Paul Tully. British. Born in Surrey in 1932. Educated at Kings College School, Wimbledon. Married Audrey Blanshard in 1957. Address: c/o Robert Hale Ltd., Clerkenwell House, 45–47 Clerkenwell Green, London EC1R OHT, England.

WESTERN PUBLICATIONS

Novels

Trail out of Leavenworth. London, Hale, 1970.
Pistolero. London, Hale, 1971.
Frenchman's Brand. London, Hale, 1972.
Heist at Apache Pass. London, Hale, 1972.
The Mossyhorns. London, Hale, 1972.
Lucky Cowpoke. London, Hale, 1973.
Wagon to Hangtown. London, Hale, 1973.
Huntsville Break. London, Hale, 1973.
Travelling Judge. London, Hale, 1974.
The All-Show Sheriff. London, Hale, 1974.
Wilderness Saloon. London, Hale, 1974.
Two-Bit Town. London, Hale, 1977.
The Bounty Scalper. London, Hale, 1983.
Medicine Show Doc. London, Hale, 1983.
Judgement in the Territory. London, Hale, 1983.

Novels (series: Dripspring in all books)

Gunman's Holiday. London, Hale, 1975.
Dilemma at Dripspring. London, Hale, 1976.
The Underhand Mail. London, Hale, 1976.
The Oldtimers. London, Hale, 1979.
Confession at Dripspring. London, Hale, 1982.
The Jayhawk Legacy. London, Hale, 1983.
The Pitchman Healer. London, Hale, 1985.
The Rawhide Redeemer. London, Hale, 1986.
The Owlhoot Convention. London, Hale, 1988.
Wide Open Town. London, Hale, 1990.

Novels (series: Hanging Judge in all books)

The Hangman and the Ladies' League. London, Hale, 1984.
The Blood-Tie. London, Hale, 1984.
The Hangman's Apprentice. London, Hale, 1985.
The Tumbleweed Twosome. London, Hale, 1986.
Get Maledon! London, Hale, 1986.

The Parker Ransom. London, Hale, 1987.
The Hanging Week. London, Hale, 1987.
Double on Death Row. London, Hale, 1988.
Date with a Noose. London, Hale, 1990.
Maledon Calls the Shots. London, Hale, 1990.

Novels as Paul Tully

The Horsing Blacksmith. London, Hale, 1985.
The Jehovahs' Jailbreak. London, Hale, 1987.
The Bond Jumper. London, Hale, 1987.
The Strychnine Stand-Off. London, Hale, 1988.
A Tale of Three Bullets. London, Hale, 1990.

OTHER PUBLICATIONS

Novels as John Gilchrist

Birdbrain. London, Hale, 1975.
Out North. London, Hale, 1975.
Lifeline. London, Hale, 1976.
The English Corridor. London, Hale, 1976.
The Engendering. London, Hale, 1978.

Novel as Jeremy Gardner

Summer Palace. London, Faber, 1960.

*

Jerome Gardner comments:

Much of the work published under my own name has reflected my lasting fascination with the Federal District Court at Fort Smith, during the time when Isaac C. Parker was its complex and formidable presiding judge (1875–96). The extraordinary relationship that existed between Parker and his apparently so different—yet essentially similar—executioner, George Maledon, struck me as an absolute gift for purposes of fiction. I was also attracted by the late frontier period whose values Parker was attempting, valiantly and hopelessly, to preserve into the dawning new century.

The first-person tales written under my Paul Tully pseudonym are an attempt to continue the tall story tradition which I see as an important element of the western ethos. I find these books rather hard to do, in that my narrator has to be simultaneously the world's worst writer from a technical standpoint while still being able to get the tales across.

I was first enthused to write Westerns by the work of the late Clifton Adams—which though well-known is still much underrated, I think. His free use of western imagery conveyed an "indepth" effect that was quite unique. I have also been influenced by the lighter and more humorous style of W.C. Tuttle.

* * *

After flirting briefly with science fiction in the mid-1970's, Jerome Gardner turned his attention to the Old West, and has been producing entertaining (and frequently amusing) Westerns for the British hardcover market ever since. Today he is probably best-known for his Hangman books, which recount the fictional exploits of the real-life jurist "Hanging Judge" Isaac C. Parker of Fort Smith, Arkansas, and his principal neck-stretcher, George Maledon.

In tone, these books differ little in style from Gardner's many unconnected Westerns; they are largely undemanding, usually fast-paced, often gently humorous and seldom overly violent. Gardner portrays Parker as "a Methodist zealot concerned with keeping his pet hangman forever busy," and indeed, his desire to make the guilty pay for their crimes does border on the fanatical. As a character, however, he always retains an undeniably likeable streak. Maledon, on the other hand, is more of a caricature. In Gardner's hands, this "Prince of Hangmen" displays a near ghoulish passion for his work; so much so, in fact, that his workshop walls are littered with daguerreotypes of all the men he has hanged, beneath which are suspended the very coils of hemp used to dispatch them. In addition to these dubious pillars of justice, the author maintains an interesting and varied cast of supporting characters; U.S. Marshals, turnkeys and so on.

It should be said that Gardner's plots often stretch credibility. In *The Hangman and the Ladies' League*, for example, Maledon runs into trouble when he travels to another town to give a demonstration of his particular skill, while in *The Hangman's Apprentice* the good judge keeps his 12-trap gallows so busy that Maledon hires extra help in the shape of a young Pennsylvanian whose interest in the art of hanging soon takes a sinister turn. In one of the weakest novels, *The Tumbleweed Twosome*, Parker has problems with a whiskey-runner named Julius Kratoch who uses his head as a stepping stone to reach a window that offers freedom before he can even so much as bang his gavel. *Get Maledon!* finds the hangman being haunted by one of his previous victims, while in *The Hanging Week* he starts giving tuition in the business of gallows management in order to make some extra cash to pay for his daughter's wedding.

Parker and Maledon are not always the central characters, however. In probably the best book of the sequence, *Double on Death Row*, Maledon in particular is little more than a supporting character, while the action centres on an escaped doxy-killer and the ill-matched trio of unofficial law-men—an inexperienced kid, a vengeance-hungry cripple and a city jailer—Parker dispatches to track him down.

Women seldom feature to any great degree in Gardner's westerns. If they do, they are more often than not portrayed as either dizzy wives or cynical saloon-girls. Gardner's men are also frequently presented as stereotypes, but his grasp of plot and pace are particularly strong, and a good ear for period dialogue adds a neat touch of frontier America to his prose.

Gardner has penned numerous single Westerns, among them *The Bounty Scalper*, which charts the rather less than inspiring adventures of a cowhand-turned-bounty hunter, and *Medicine Show Doc*, where two cowboys turn to bank robbery only to find themselves being tracked down by a bank detective and a Dutch lawman (Gardner's West is littered with emigrants, whose accents are reflected in their dialogue). The latter novel even boasts an appearance by a remarkably erudite Quanah Parker. But again, these westerns have been overshadowed by another series.

The Dripspring stories centre around a border town in Chanatte County, West Texas, and while there are a number of amiable enough characters who carry over from one book to the next (the crusty Scotsman, Doc Meadows; Frank Holly, the daydreaming barber; saloon-owner and mortician, Art Capel and so on), the main protagonists are the marshal, a one-time cowboy named Charlie Pearce, and his guileless deputy, William Hart, whose relationship Gardner sustains well.

As may be assumed, the Dripspring stories are somewhat lighter in tone than Gardner's Hangman novels, but the added humour can just as easily break an already improbable story as make it. Considering the self-imposed confines of the series, however, the author has, over the years, managed to keep the books remarkably fresh. In *Confession at Dripspring*, the Chanatte County coroner makes a deathbed confession that produces some surprising results. If you overlook the fallacious reference to plastic surgery in *The Rawhide Redeemer*, you may well believe that an outlaw with the face of Jesus really could unite the citizens of two border towns and turn them into an unstoppable army of looters. In *The Owlhoot Convention*, Pearce and Hart have their hands full when Frank Holly inherits a fortune, and in *Wide Open Town*, the trouble-prone lawmen have to stop a notorious bandit from using Chanatte County as his new base of operations.

As Paul Tully, Gardner has taken his use of humour one step further for the intentionally farfetched reminiscences of one Deputy U.S. Marshal Hooky Gibbs, whom he introduces in *The Horsing Blacksmith*. Set in the town of Weaver's Bend, Oklahoma Territory, the series is a sincere, though not always entirely successful, attempt to sustain the traditional western tall story, and to his credit, Gardner adds so many small but amusing touches to his farcical plots that one cannot help but smile, no matter how outlandish those stories become. Humour is, of course, no easy thing to write, but fortunately the author succeeds more often than he fails. Even so, these amiable enough "memoirs" do tend to test the patience of their readers on occasion. Of particular note, however, is 1990's *A Tale of Three Bullets*, in which the author appears most comfortable with the first-person narrative he has adopted for the sequence. In this book, the one-handed Gibbs has to deal with (among other things) a cowboy who confesses to a murder for which another man has already been sentenced to hang, a lady sharpshooter—and a rather uncooperative typewriter.

—David Whitehead

GARFIELD, Brian (Francis Wynne). Also writes as Bennett Garland: Alex Hawk; John Ives; Drew Mallory; Frank O'Brian; Jonas Ward; Brian Wynne; Frank Wynne. American. Born in New York City, 26 January 1939. Educated at Southern Arizona School, Tucson, graduated 1955; University of Arizona, Tucson, B.A. 1959, M.A. 1963. Served in the United States Army and Army Reserve, 1957–65. Married 1) Virve Sein in 1962 (divorced 1965); 2) Shan Willson Botley in 1969 (divorced 1982); 3) Bina Grossblat in 1985. Musician and bandleader, "The Casuals," 1958–59, and "The Palisades," 1959–63; teaching assistant in English, University of Arizona, 1962–63. Since 1963 self-employed writer. Since 1974 president, Shan Productions Company. Advertising manager director, and vice-president, 1965–69, and president, 1967–68, Western Writers of America; director, Mystery Writers of America, 1974–78; co-organizer, Second International Congress of Crime Writers, New York, 1978. Recipient: Mystery Writers of America Edgar Allan Poe award, 1976. Agent: John Cushman, JCA Agency, 242 West 27th Street, New York, New York 10001. Address: 3660 Glenridge Drive, Sherman Oaks, California 91423, U.S.A.

WESTERN PUBLICATIONS

Novels

Range Justice. New York, Bouregy, 1960; as *Justice at Spanish Flat*, New York, Ace, 1961.
The Arizonans. New York, Bouregy, 1961.
The Lawbringers. New York, Macmillan, 1962; London, Long, 1963.
Trail Drive. New York, Bouregy, 1962.
Vultures in the Sun. New York, Macmillan, 1963; London, Long, 1964.
Apache Canyon. New York, Bouregy, 1963.
The Vanquished. New York, Doubleday, 1964.
Buchanan's Gun (as Jonas Ward). New York, Fawcett, and London, Hodder and Stoughton, 1968.
Savage Guns (as Alex Hawk). New York, Paperback Library, 1968.
Valley of the Shadow. New York, Doubleday, 1970; London, White Lion, 1973.
Sliphammer. New York, Dell, 1970.
Gun Down. New York, Dell, 1971; as *The Last Hard Men* (as Frank Wynne), London, Hodder and Stoughton, 1974.
Sweeney's Honor. New York, Dell, 1971; as Frank Wynne, London, Hodder and Stoughton, 1974.
Relentless. Cleveland, World, 1972; London, Hodder and Stoughton, 1973.
Gangway!, with Donald E. Westlake. New York, Evans, 1973; London, Barker, 1975.
Tripwire. New York, McKay, 1973; London, Coronet, 1976.
The Threepersons Hunt. New York, Evans, 1974; London, Coronet, 1975.
Wild Times. New York, Simon and Schuster, 1978; London, Macmillan, 1979.

Novels as Bennett Garland

Seven Brave Men. Derby, Connecticut, Monarch, 1962; as Brian Garfield, New York, Lancer, 1969.
High Storm, with Theodore V. Olsen. Derby, Connecticut, Monarch, 1963; as Brian Garfield, New York, Lancer, 1970.
The Last Outlaw. Derby, Connecticut, Monarch, 1964.
Rio Chama. New York, Award, 1968.

Novels as Frank O'Brian

The Rimfire Murders. New York, Bouregy, 1962.
Bugle and Spur. New York, Ballantine, 1966; as Brian Garfield, London, Sphere, 1968.
Arizona. New York, Ballantine, 1969.
Act of Piracy. New York, Dell, 1975.

Novels as Brian Wynne (series: Marshal Jeremy Six)

Mr. Sixgun. New York, Ace, 1964.
The Night It Rained Bullets. New York, Ace, 1965.
The Bravos. New York, Ace, 1966.
The Proud Riders. New York, Ace, 1967.
A Badge for a Badman. New York, Ace, 1967.
Brand of the Gun. New York, Ace, 1968.
Gundown. New York, Ace, 1969.
Big Country, Big Men. New York, Ace, 1969.

Novels as Frank Wynne

Massacre Basin. New York, Bouregy, 1961.
The Big Snow. New York, Bouregy, 1962.
Arizona Rider. New York, Bouregy, 1962.
Dragoon Pass. New York, Bouregy, 1963.
Rio Concho. New York, Bouregy, 1964.
Rails West. New York, Bouregy, 1964.
Lynch Law Canyon. New York, Ace, 1965.
The Wolf Pack. New York, Ace, 1966.
Call Me Hazard. New York, Ace, 1966.

The Lusty Breed. New York, Bouregy, 1966; London, Hale, 1974.
Letter to a Gunfighter. Derby, Connecticut, Monarch, 1966.

Uncollected Short Stories

"The Toll at Yaeger's Ferry," in *Rivers to Cross*, edited by William R. Cox. New York, Dodd Mead, 1966.
"Riverboat Fighter," in *They Opened the West*, edited by Thomas W. Blackburn. New York, Doubleday, 1967.
"Peace Officer," in *Iron Men and Silver Stars*, edited by Donald Hamilton. New York, Fawcett, 1967.
"Hunting Accident," in *Ellery Queen's Mystery Magazine* (New York), June 1977.
"The Glory Hunter," in *Ellery Queen's Mystery Magazine* (New York), September 1977.
"Jode's Last Hunt," in *Best Detective Stories of 1978*, edited by Edward D. Hoch. New York, Dutton, 1978.
"Two-Way Street" (as John Ives), in *Ellery Queen's Mystery Magazine* (New York), August 1978.
"The Glory Riders," in *The Horse Soldiers*, edited by Bill Pronzini and Martin H. Greenberg. New York, Fawcett, 1987.
"At Yuma Crossing," in *The Gunfighters*, edited by Bill Pronzini and Martin H. Greenberg. New York, Fawcett, 1987.

OTHER PUBLICATIONS

Novels

The Last Bridge. New York, McKay, 1966.
The Villiers Touch. New York, Delacorte Press, 1970.
The Hit. New York, Macmillan, 1970.
What of Terry Coniston? Cleveland, World, 1971; London, Hodder and Stoughton, 1976.
Deep Cover. New York, Delacorte Press, 1971; London, Hodder and Stoughton, 1972.
Line of Succession. New York, Delacorte Press, 1972; London, Hodder and Stoughton, 1974.
Death Wish. New York, McKay, 1972; London, Hodder and Stoughton, 1973.
Tripwire. New York, McKay, 1973; London, Hodder and Stoughton, 1976.
Kolchak's Gold. New York, McKay, and London, Macmillan, 1974.
The Romanov Succession. New York, Evans, and London, Macmillan, 1974.
Hopscotch. New York, Evans, and London, Macmillan, 1975.
Target Manhattan (as Drew Mallory). New York, Putnam, 1975.
Death Sentence. New York, Evans, 1975; London, Macmillan, 1976.
Recoil. New York, Morrow, and London, Macmillan, 1977.
Fear in a Handful of Dust (as John Ives). New York, Dutton, 1977; as *Fear*, London, Macmillan, 1978.
The Marchand Woman (as John Ives). New York, Dutton, 1979; London, Macmillan, 1980.
The Paladin, with Christopher Creighton. New York, Simon and Schuster, and London, Macmillan, 1980.
Necessity. New York, St. Martin's Press, and London, Macmillan, 1984.
Manifest Destiny. New York, Penzler, 1989.

Short Stories

Checkpoint Charlie. Yonkers, New York, Mysterious Press, 1981.

Play

Screenplay: *Hopscotch*, with Bryan Forbes, 1981.

Other

The Thousand-Mile War: World War II in Alaska and the Aleutians. New York, Doubleday, 1969.
Western Films: A Complete Guide. New York, Rawson Associates, 1982.

Editor, *War Whoop and Battle Cry*. New York, Scholastic, 1968.
Editor, *I, Witness: True Personal Encounters with Crime by Members of the Mystery Writers of America*. New York, Times Books, 1978.
Editor, *The Crime of My Life*. New York, Walker, 1984; London, Severn House, 1986.

*

Manuscript Collection: University of Oregon Library, Eugene.

Brian Garfield comments:

I grew up in the southwest desert and spent some of my childhood summers on working cattle ranches at a time, not so very long ago, when there was still unfenced open range in Arizona (a prerequisite to semi-annual roundups). It seemed natural, when I began writing, to attempt to write westerns—partly because I knew the background, partly because our family friends included such established western writers as Nelson Nye, Elliott Arnold—and especially Fred Glidden (aka "Luke Short"), who generously read and criticized the short stories I wrote starting at the age of 12.

My first published novel, written when I was 18 and published three years later in 1960, was a Western; a 10-year apprenticeship followed, during which I wrote about 30 novels, most of them written directly for paperback under a half dozen pseudonyms. I've reverted and retired most of those books; they represented the growing pains of on-the-job training and I don't mean to publish them again. Largely they were derivative work, formulaic. I'm not ashamed of them but neither do they represent the kind of work to which I aspire.

Now and then, at intervals, I'd write a book more from the heart than from formula, and am still rather pleased with the way a few of them turned out. The Westerns I try to keep in print are (chronologically) *The Vanquished*, *Bugle and Spur*, *Arizona* from the 1960's; and from the 1970's *Sliphammer*, *The Last Hard Men* (we filmed this one, with Charlton Heston as the good guy and James Coburn as the bad guy; that was fun), *Sweeney's Honor*, *Tripwire*, and finally two lengthy labor-of-love books: the novel into which I put everything I knew and felt about the west, *Wild Times* (we filmed this one too, and it was fun too), and the nonfiction book into which I put everything I knew and felt about the Western, *Western Films: A Complete Guide*.

Between them, those two books say everything I know how to say about the subject, so I won't clutter these pages with further pontifications.

* * *

Brian Garfield is probably the most critically and commercially successful writer producing fiction in several fields who makes the western a regular and important part of his fictional output. Probably best known for the very violent *Death Wish* and its sequel or the tour-deforce non-violent *Hopscotch*, both of which were highly visible (if, in ways, inadequate) in motion picture adaptations, he began writing with westerns and has continued turning out better than competent ones throughout his career.

Most of his early work was westerns published under pen names that have since been abandoned. These, including the Marshal Jeremy Six series, are generally interesting reading somewhere above the level of the pulp action story, but hardly comparable to the western fiction written under his own name.

Wild Times, the huge pseudo-autobiography of a Buffalo Bill sort of Wild West showman, is epic in subject matter as well as length. Although its highpoints may include some of Garfield's best work (and that is very good indeed) its infrequent lows betray an author as subject to occasional sleepiness as Homer.

Sliphammer, with its real historical gunmen (the Earps and Doc Hollady) presented in an unflatteringly realistic light, achieves its principal brilliance by managing to be a traditionally romantic Western for all the gloss of its realism. The hero, a sheriff's deputy sent to arrest Wyatt Earp after the O.K. Corral shootout, succeeds more because of his wit than the considerable skill at "fanning" his pistol that gained him the nickname Sliphammer.

Garfield's most frequent heroes in Westerns under his own name are Army men, not always officers or gentlemen or even cavalrymen for all that usually at least one of these expected labels applies. Lt. Miles Cultrane of *Valley of the Shadow* is an engineer with an unusual assignment; he is returned to his mountain home with the job of keeping peace between the farmers and the industrial-stage miners who are ready to ruin the local environment. He is not entirely successful—is anyone on the really big challenges of life?—but his struggles make fascinating reading. In *Tripwire* Sgt. Boag, late of Crook's Buffalo Soldiers, mustered out in Arizona and apparently damned by his black skin to insignificance in the 1880's, experiences an almost unending run of bad luck. This begins with his being recruited while on a county-prisoner road gang to help with an audacious gold robbery. After that is successful, his employers try to kill him and come very near succeeding more than once. He devotes himself to a seemingly hopeless revenge, and the rest of the saga (reminiscent of *The Rebel Outlaw, Josey Wales* for its scope and episodic construction) recounts his constantly worsening situation until finally he succeeds. In *Sweeney's Honor* the setting is cavalry and the problem, at least partly, is Indians, but this is fictionized history about the maintaining of an outpost—against odds as seemingly impossible as those which Boag faced in *Tripwire*—of a Colorado river crossing at Yuma in the early 1850's. This was at the proximate site, a few decades later, of the Arizona Territorial Prison which was located there because the area was not judged fit for human habitation, and much of the writer's skill is expended on making the reader feel the hellish hardships provided the troops by nature.

The two Sam Watchman books provide an obvious connecting link between Garfield's Westerns and his modern suspense novels. Less obviously, the suspense novels are connected by frequently being at least partially set in the contemporary west (*Line of Succession* and, not quite incongruously, *Death Wish*), by characters such as the prominent western movie character actor and the "modernday gunslinger" private eye (both of *Recoil*) and some interesting stylistic similarities. *Relentless* introduces Watchman, the Indian policeman whose "wide loop" includes lots of desert and reservation country, and provides excellent suspense pitting his peace officer plus traditional Indian skills against a trio of Green Berets gone rogue. This was made into a television film, as was *Wild Times*, and is altogether the most satisfactory film treatment of a Garfield novel. In the sequel, *The Threepersons Hunt*, Watchman's quarry is another Indian, but suspense and character development are as interesting as in the hero's first case.

—R. Jeff Banks

GARLAND, Bennett. *See* **GARFIELD, Brian.**

GARLAND, George. Pseudonym for Garland Roark. American. Born in Groesbeck, Texas, 26 July 1904. Educated at West Texas State Normal College (now State University), Canyon, 1920. Married Leola Elizabeth Burke in 1939; two daughters. Advertising staff, Skillern Drug Stores, Dallas, 1924–28, Courthouse Pharmacies, Houston, 1929, Walgreen Drugstores, Chicago, 1929, Sommers Drugstores, San Antonio, 1930–33, Henke and Pillot supermarket, Houston, 1933–39, and Gordon Jewelry Stores, Houston, 1941–46; then freelance writer: columnist, Houston *Chronicle*, 1960–63. Also painter: oil paintings part of permanent collection, Sam Houston Room, Nacogdoches, Texas. Recipient: Western Writers of America Spur award, 1967. *Died 9 February 1985.*

WESTERN PUBLICATIONS

Novels

Doubtful Valley. Boston, Houghton Mifflin, 1951.
The Big Dry. Boston, Houghton Mifflin, 1953; London, Barker, 1954.
Star in the Rigging (as Garland Roark). New York, Doubleday, 1954; London, Hodder and Stoughton, 1955.
Apache Warpath. New York, New American Library, 1959; London, Mills and Boon, 1961.
Bugles and Brass. New York, Doubleday, 1964.
Hellfire Jackson (as Garland Roark), with Charles Thomas. New York, Doubleday, 1966.
The Eye of the Needle. New York, Doubleday, 1970.
Slow Wind in the West. New York, Doubleday, 1973.

OTHER PUBLICATIONS as Garland Roark

Novels

Wake of the Red Witch. Boston, Little Brown, 1946.
Fair Wind to Java. New York, Doubleday, 1948; London, Falcon Press, 1951.
Rainbow in the Royals. New York, Doubleday, 1950.

Slant of the Wild Wind. New York, Doubleday, 1952.
The Wreck of the Running Gale. New York, Doubleday, 1953; London, Hodder and Stoughton, 1954.
The Outlawed Banner. New York, Doubleday, and London, Hodder and Stoughton, 1956.
The Cruel Cocks. New York, Doubleday, and London, Hodder and Stoughton, 1957.
Tales of the Caribbean. New York, Doubleday, 1959.
Should the Wind Be Fair. New York, Doubleday, 1960.
The Witch of Magna Reva. New York, Doubleday, 1962; London, Redman, 1964.
Bay of Traitors. New York, Doubleday, 1966.
Angels in Exile. New York, Doubleday, 1967; as *Sinner in the Sun*, London, Cassell, 1968.

Other

Captain Thomas Fenlon, Master Mariner. New York, Messner, 1958.
The Coin of Contraband: The True Story of United States Customs Investigator Al Scharff. New York, Doubleday, 1964.

Editor, with Ronald Michell, *The Diamond Six*, by William Fielding Smith. New York, Doubleday, 1958; as *The Chronicle of the Diamond Six*, London, Hammond, 1960.

* * *

George Garland is the pseudonym of Garland Roark, and under the Roark name he was quite well known in the heyday of the sea adventure. In the 1950's his reputation was firmly established with the publication of his first book, *Wake of the Red Witch*. This fame was greater heightened when a movie was made of the book and John Wayne starred as the central character. It is interesting to note that Wayne's movie company, Batjac productions, bears the same name as a company in Roark's novel. This is in no small way due to the fact that many of Roark's main characters display the proud independence that was Wayne's trademark, as well as the trademark of the western hero. Taking that into consideration, it is not surprising that Garland Roark turned to westerns, producing six of them under the George Garland byline.

Although these Westerns broke no new ground in the field, they are all well written, if not exactly inspired, and evidence of historical research is obvious throughout. Perhaps the best of these is *Slow Wind in the West*. As in most of the Garland Westerns, the hero is a military man, and something of a lovable rogue. The story is tight and moves at a pleasant clip, and the author causes you to care about Knox Lavender—the hero of the book—and wish him the best. Perhaps the second best of Garland's Westerns is *Apache Warpath*, and it can favorably be compared to middle-of-the-road James Warner Bellah.

Perhaps had Roark written these Westerns under his own name, and had his sea stories not been the great success they were, he would have further developed his Westerns and given them more writing flair. Certainly this ability is evidenced by his non-western books.

—Joe R. Lansdale

GARLAND, (Hannibal) Hamlin. American. Born near West Salem, Wisconsin, 14 September 1860. Educated at Cedar Valley Seminary, Osage, Iowa, 1876–81. Married Zulime Taft in 1899; two daughters. Taught at a country school, Grundy County, Ohio, 1882–83; homesteader in McPherson County, Dakota Territory, 1883–84; student, then teacher, Boston School of Oratory, 1884–91; full-time writer from 1891: lived in Chicago, 1893–1916, New York, 1916–30, and Los Angeles, 1930–40. Founding president, Cliff Dwellers, Chicago, 1907. Recipient: Pulitzer prize, for biography, 1922; Roosevelt Memorial Association Gold Medal, 1931. D.Litt: University of Wisconsin, Madison, 1926; Northwestern University, Evanston, Illinois, 1933; University of Southern California, Los Angeles, 1937. Member, 1918, and director, 1920, American Academy. *Died 5 March 1940.*

WESTERN PUBLICATIONS

Novels

Jason Edwards, An Average Man. Boston, Arena, 1892; with *A Little Norsk*, London, Thacker, 1898.
A Little Norsk; or, Ol'Pap's Flaxen. New York, Appleton, and London, Unwin, 1892.
Rose of Dutcher's Coolly. Chicago, Stone and Kimball, 1895; London, Beeman, 1896; edited by Donald Pizer, Lincoln, University of Nebraska Press, 1969.
The Spirit of Sweetwater. New York, Doubleday, and London, Service and Paton, 1898; revised edition, as *Witch's Gold*, Doubleday, and London, Harper, 1906.
The Eagle's Heart. New York, Appleton, and London, Heinemann, 1900.
Her Mountain Lover. New York, Century, and London, Heinemann, 1901.
The Captain of the Gray-Horse Troop. New York, Harper, and London, Richards, 1902.
Hesper. New York and London, Harper, 1903.
Money Magic. New York and London, Harper, 1907; as *Mart Haney's Mate*, New York, Harper, 1922.
Moccasin Ranch. New York and London, Harper, 1909.
Cavanagh, Forest Ranger. New York and London, Harper, 1910.
The Forester's Daughter. New York and London, Harper, 1914.

Short Stories

Main-Travelled Roads: Six Mississippi Valley Stories. Boston, Arena, 1891; London, Unwin, 1893; revised edition, New York, Macmillan, 1899; New York, Harper, 1920, 1930.
Prairie Folks. Chicago, Shulte, and London, Sampson Low, 1893.
Wayside Courtships. New York, Appleton, and London, Beeman, 1897.
Other Main-Travelled Roads (includes *Prairie Folks* and *Wayside Courtships*). New York, and London, Harper, 1910.
They of the High Trails. New York and London, Harper, 1916.
The Book of the American Indian. New York and London, Harper, 1923.

Uncollected Short Stories

"Lone Wolf's Old Guard," in *The Warriors*, edited Bill Pronzini and Martin H. Greenberg. New York, Fawcett, 1985.
"The Return of a Private," in *Westeryear*, edited by Edward Gorman. New York, Evans, 1988.

OTHER PUBLICATIONS

Novels

A Member of the Third House. Chicago, Shulte, 1892.
A Spoil of Office. Boston, Arena, and London, Brentano, 1892.
The Light of the Star. New York and London, Harper, 1904.
The Tyranny of the Dark. New York and London, Harper, 1905.
Victor Ollnee's Discipline. New York and London, Harper, 1911.

Play

Under the Wheel. Boston, Barta Press, 1890.

Verse

Prairie Songs. Cambridge, Massachusetts, and Chicago, Stone and Kimball, 1893.
Iowa, O Iowa! Iowa City, Clio Press, 1935.

Other

Crumbling Idols: Twelve Essays on Art. Chicago, Stone and Kimball, 1894.
Ulysses S. Grant: His Life and Character. New York, Doubleday, 1898.
The Trail of the Goldseekers: A Record of Travel in Prose and Verse. New York and London, Macmillan, 1899.
Boy Life on the Prairie. New York and London, Macmillan, 1899; revised edition, New York, Macmillan, 1908.
The Long Trail (for children). New York and London, Harper, 1907.
The Shadow World. New York and London, Harper, 1908.
A Son of the Middle Border. New York, Macmillan, and London, Lane, 1917.
A Daughter of the Middle Border. New York, Macmillan, and London, Lane, 1921.
A Pioneer Mother. Chicago, Bookfellows, 1922.
Commemorative Tribute to James Whitcombe Riley. New York, American Academy of Arts and Letters, 1922.
Trail-Makers of the Middle Border. New York, Macmillan, and London, Lane, 1926.
The Westward March of American Settlement. Chicago, American Library Association, 1927.
Back-Trailers from the Middle Border. New York, Macmillan, 1928.
Prairie Song and Western Story (miscellany). Boston, Allyn and Bacon, 1928.
Roadside Meetings. New York, Macmillan, 1930; London, Lane, 1931.
Companions on the Trail: A Literary Chronicle. New York, Macmillan, 1931.
My Friendly Contemporaries: A Literary Log. New York, Macmillan, 1934.
Afternoon Neighbors: Further Excerpts from a Literary Log. New York, Macmillan, 1934.
Joys of the Trail. Chicago, Bookfellows, 1935.
Forty Years of Psychic Research: A Plain Narrative of Fact. New York, Macmillan, 1936.
The Mysteries of the Buried Crosses: A Narrative of Psychic Exploration. New York, Dutton, 1939.
Diaries, edited by Donald Pizer. San Marino, California, Huntington Library, 1968.
Observations on the American Indian 1895–1905, edited by Lonnie E. Underhill and Daniel F. Littlefield, Jr. Tucson, University of Arizona Press, 1976.

*

Bibliography: *Hamlin Garland and the Critics: An Annotated Bibliography* by Jackson R. Bryer and Eugene Harding, Troy, New York, Whitson, 1973; *Henry Blake Fuller and Hamlin Garland: A Reference Guide* by Charles L.P. Silet, Boston, Hall, 1977.

Manuscript Collection: Doheny Library, University of California, Los Angeles.

Critical Studies: *Hamlin Garland: A Biography* by Jean Holloway, Austin, University of Texas Press, 1960; *Hamlin Garland's Early Work and Career* by Donald Pizer, Berkeley, University of California Press, 1960; *Hamlin Garland: L'Homme et l'Oeuvre* by Robert Mane, Paris, Didier, 1968; *Hamlin Garland: The Far West* by Robert Gish, Boise, Idaho, Boise State University Press, 1976; *Hamlin Garland* by Joseph B. McCullough, Boston, Twayne, 1978; *Critical Essays on Hamlin Garland* edited by James Nagel, Boston, G.K. Hall, 1982; *The Critical Reception of Garland 1891–1978* edited by Charles L.P. Silet and Robert E. Welch, New York, Whitston Press, 1985.

* * *

Andy Adams's famous denigration (in "Western Interpreters") of Hamlin Garland's achievements as a "western" writer is probably just, and it is amiably put in the context of Garland's success as a writer of the "middle border"—the area of Iowa, Wisconsin, and the Dakotas. Garland's importance—and contemporary fame—as a writer stems from his style of realism, which might seem most appropriate when applied to an urban setting. Garland, in fact, did use large cities as the setting of several of his books, but his most famous works—*Main-Travelled Roads, A Son of the Middle Border*, and *A Daughter of the Middle Border*—are set firmly in rural farming areas.

Garland's brand of realism was one he called "veritism": "The realist or veritist is really an optimist, a dreamer. He sees life in terms of what it might be, as well as in terms of what it is, but he writes of what is, and, at his best, suggests what is to be by contrast." Farm conditions in the 1880's were appalling, but even at best farm life in the late 19th century was compounded of privations, toil and squalor, with the attendant hopelessness and despair, and these conditions are strongly described. His mastery of the details of farm life, based on his own early life, make his descriptions of dress, eating, and the weather, as well as the loss of spirit of many of the characters, effective and moving. Several of the works also suggest a naturalistic element in the economic forces at play (Garland was a "single-tax" convert). But Garland's lightening of the usual negative tone of absolute naturalism give the stories a less than pessimistic flavor: perhaps because he had escaped the world he had been reared in, he always retained a strong sense of the possibilities of change. One of his best novels is *Rose of Dutcher's Coolly*, in which a farm girl, made ambitious by schooling, goes to Chicago to become a writer, a pattern paralleling Garland's own life.

Another motif used in the middle-border stories, and also in the more clearly western works, is that of the return of a young man to his childhood home. This tends to add a reflective note, as if the recognition of his past influences helps clearly define himself. Yet this very awareness prompts a reaction against the conventional and prosaic Midwest.

The sense of possibility in the states further West was appealing, and Garland, especially after moving to Chicago from Boston, visited the West frequently. Of his western fiction, the conventional mining and forest ranger romances are probably the least interesting. The romantic elements dominate the plots, even though a novel like *Hesper* deals with the Bull Hill Miner's War. Feminist and economic themes are often important in the plots. The Easterner Ann Rupert, for instance, gradually becomes "Hesper," a daughter of the evening, as she feels herself become a Westerner. *The Eagle's Heart* is a more interesting book. It is an episodic novel which shows how a Midwesterner, Harold Excell, during a long series of typically western occupations—sheepherder, miner, finally Indian agent—loses the conventional community spirit and replaces it with the individual aspiration associated with an eagle. The strong sense of elation and freedom of Harold Excell is matched in the stories of The Saddle Tramp in *They of the High Trails*. Ed Kelley refuses to make commitments or settle down, and wanders the West; in fact, he turns up as a minor character in several of the other western books. Though *They of the High Trails* is a collection of stories, the titles—The Grub-Staker, The Cow-Boss, The Remittance Man, The Lonesome Man, The Trail Tramp, The Prospector, The Outlaw, The Leaser, The Ranger, The Tourist, The Fugitive—suggest a deliberate attempt to categorize the interesting and picturesque types found in the West.

The Book of the American Indian (published in 1923, but mostly written much earlier) consists of fictional stories, despite the title. Garland's sympathetic view of the Indians, based on extensive visits and tours of reservations, is strong and genuine: "I am going to tell of the red man . . . as a man of the polished stone age trying to adapt himself to steam and electricity." This humanitarian interest, possibly a bit naive to the modern reader, was advanced for its time. Garland ignores the condescending "simple" savage as well as the "wily redskin" stereotypes. Most of the stories involve forceful missionaries (often the villains), Indian agents, or teachers demanding or encouraging change to accommodate the world of the white man. Garland's indignation at reservation treatment is clear, and he is fact compares their lot with poor white farmers, thus strengthening his personal response. And he is aware that change, even though necessary, is not necessarily equal to a positive sense of "progress." One of Garland's more sentimental responses to the white man-Indian conflict is seen in the novel *The Captain of the Gray-Horse Troop*, in which Senator Brisbane (Indians are "a greasy lot of vermin") sides with the cattlemen who are trying to expel Indians from land they want. Because of the killing of an Indian, a community reaction sets in, and Brisbane loses his next election fight, thus guaranteeing the reservation for the Indians.

Garland's best work is that in which he was personally involved (as Andy Adams suggested). His Indian stories, and the works involving the wandering Excell and Kelley, seem to have elicited his strongest response, though these works are less impressive than his middle-border stories. Garland's stature as a renowned writer no doubt helped to encourage other writers to deal with western themes in romance and adventure fiction.

—George Walsh

GARRETT, Charles C. *See* **JAMES, Laurence; WELLS, Angus.**

GAULDEN, Ray. Also wrote as Wesley Ray. American. Born in Fort Worth, Texas, 27 June 1914. Married Thelma Fells in 1940; one daughter. Worked as a sign painter, hospital admittance clerk, expediter in a munitions factory during World War II, and hotel clerk; then freelance writer. Vice-president, Western Writers of America, 1969. Recipient: Colorado Authors' League Top-Hand award, for story (twice). *Died.*

WESTERN PUBLICATIONS

Novels

The Rough and Lonely Land. London, Arrow, 1957.
Shadow of the Rope. New York, Permabooks, 1957; London, Hale, 1962.
The Vengeful Men. New York, Permabooks, 1957; London, Hale, 1963.
Damaron's Gun (as Wesley Ray). New York, New American Library, 1958; London, New English Library, 1963.
Rita. New York, Zenith, 1959; as *A Good Place to Die*, London, Hale, 1965.
High Country Showdown. Derby, Connecticut, Monarch, 1961.
Action at Alameda. New York, Avalon, 1962.
The Devil's Deputy. New York, Avalon, 1963; London, Hale, 1966.
McVey's Valley. New York, Doubleday, 1965.
Long Day in Latigo (as Wesley Ray). New York, Paperback Library, 1965; London, Mayflower, 1969.
Glory Gulch. New York, Berkley, 1967; as *Five Card Stud*, 1968.
The Lawless Land. New York, Berkley, 1967.
A Time to Ride. New York, Ballantine, 1969.
Shoot to Kill. New York, Ballantine, 1970; London, Hale, 1973.
Rage at Red Butte. New York, Berkley, 1971.
The Wicked Women of Lobo Wells. New York, Belmont, 1971.
Deputy Sheriff. New York, Ballantine, 1972; London, Remploy, 1973.
A Man Called Murdo, and Rough Road to Denver. New York, Zebra, 1981.

Uncollected Short Stories

"Lawman's Last Chore," in *10 Story Western*, January 1945.
"Star for the Doomed," in *10 Story Western*, March 1945.
"Fodder for the Owlhoot," in *10 Story Western*, April 1945.
"The Redemption of Whiskey Jones," in *Big Book Western*, June 1945.
"Last of the Wild Ones," in *.44 Western*, July 1945.
"Powdersmoke Pawn," in *10 Story Western*, August 1945.
"Vamoose, Little Nester," in *10 Story Western*, September 1945.
"Jailbird's First Bluff," in *10 Story Western*, November 1945.
"A Good Range to Die For," in *Ace High Western*, 1945.
"The Devil and Pinto Larkin," in *Ace High Western*, November 1945.
"Shine Your Badge with Blood," in *Ace High Western*, November 1945.

"Gambler's Creed," in *Western Story* (New York), February 1946.
"While the Hangman Waits," in *10 Story Western*, January 1946.
"Taming of Dusty Dallas," in *Ace High Western*, July 1946.
"The Button Goes to War," in *10 Story Western*, August 1946.
"Killer, Cut Loose Your Wolf," in *New Western*, September 1946.
"Nobody Loves a Lawman," in *Real Western*, 1946.
"Blood, Water, and Whiskers," in *10 Story Western*, October 1946.
"The Devil Is a Trapper," in *Western Story* (New York), January 1947.
"The Devil's Gun Double," in *Lariat*, 1947.
"Gunsmoke Miracle," in *Lariat*, July 1947.
"Button's Long Quest," in *10 Story Western*, April 1947.
"Adios, Owlhoot," in *10 Story Western*, September 1947.
"Lawman's Last Gamble," in *Western Story* (New York), December 1947.
"Gun Ghosts Never Die," in *Fifteen Western Tales*, December 1947.
"Tin Badge Hater," in *Western Story* (New York), February 1948.
"Debt to a Badman," in *10 Story Western*, April 1948.
"Bound by His Badge," in *Western Aces*, 1948.
"Bake Your Bread in Boothill," in *Fifteen Western Tales*, May 1948.
"Give Us a Man to Hang," in *Western Trails*, August 1948.
"Nobody Loves a Sodbuster," in *Fifteen Western Tales*, December 1948.
"Fiddle a Gunsmoke Tune," in *Fifteen Western Tales*, April 1949.
"Derelict's Redemption," in *10 Story Western*, April 1949.
"Ride That Horse!," in *Mammoth Western* (Chicago), May 1949.
"No Love for a Bronc Buster," in *Jubilee*, June 1949.
"My Friend, The Killer," in *10 Story Western*, June 1949.
"Death Deal," in *Fifteen Western Tales*, July 1949.
"Who'll Die for Sage City?," in *Lariat*, November 1949.
"Once a Bronc Buster," in *Western Love Romances*, 1950.
"Violence Builds a Stage Line," in *Mammoth Western* (Chicago), June 1950.
"Pelted With Lead," in *10 Story Western*, June 1950.
"Night of the Long Knives," in *44 Western*, August 1950.
"Blind Bullet," in *Fifteen Western Tales*, August 1950.
"The Colorado Code," in *Complete Western Book*, February 1951.
"Sing a Song of Six Guns," in *Ranch Romances*, 25 May 1951.
"No Time for Trouble," in *Ranch Romances*, 20 July 1951.
"The Son of Mike McQuade," in *Texas Rangers* (London), October 1951.
"Kid with the Lobo Look," in *Best Western*, December 1951.
"The Devil Wears Boots," in *Thrilling Ranch Stories*, August 1952.
"Brother of the Groom," in *Ranch Romances*, 4 January 1952.
"Down from the Hills," in *Ranch Romances*, 15 February 1952.
"Taming of Wild Bill," in *Western Short Stories*, March 1952.
"Gunman," in *Western Novels and Short Stories*, May 1952.
"Boom Town Trouble-Shooter," in *Thrilling Western* (London), May 1952.
"Badman's Bride," in *Ranch Romances*, 6 June 1952.
"Ride a Crooked Trail," in *Ranch Romances*, 20 June 1952.
"No Range for a Drifter," in *Ranch Romances*, 18 July 1952.
"The Killer Behind the Badge," in *Western Novels and Short Stories*, August 1952.
"Farmers Keep Out," in *Ranch Romances*, 12 September 1952.
"Bet a Killing," in *Fifteen Western Tales*, September 1952.
"The Woman on Willow Creek," in *Ranch Romances*, 10 October 1952.
"Bronc-Buster—Heart-Buster," in *Rangeland Love Stories*, June 1953.
"Gunmen in the Streets," in *Best Western*, 1953.
"Trail to San Juan," in *Texas Rangers*, August 1953.
"I Ride with Death," in *West* (New York), Fall 1953.
"The Rider from Nowhere," in *Thrilling Western* (London), September 1953.
"Wrong Side of the River," in *Ranch Romances*, 4 December 1953.
"They Called Me Killer," in *5 Western Novels*, Winter 1954.
"The Man from the Brazos," in *Ranch Romances*, 20 May 1955.
"My Brother Wears a Badge," in *Ranch Romances*, 3 June 1955.
"Girl on the Tomahawk," in *Ranch Romances*, 1 July 1955.
"Part Time Hero," in *Ranch Romances*, 1955.
"Valley of Violence," in *Ranch Romances*, 2 December 1955.
"One Night at Sadie Hogan's," in *Top Western Fiction Annual*, 1955.
"A Bullet for Brenda," in *Ranch Romances*, 3 November 1956.
"Woman at Wagonwheel," in *Ranch Romances*, 28 December 1956.
"Man Without a Gun," in *Ranch Romances*, 20 September 1957.
"My Sister and the Gunman," in *Spurs West*, edited by S. Omar Barker. New York, Doubleday, 1960.
"My Friend, The Gunman," in *Texas Rangers* (London), August 1961.
"The Taming of Jim Shannon," in *Roundup*. New York, Doubleday, 1982.

*

Manuscript Collection: University of Wyoming, Laramie.

* * *

Ray Gaulden has written a small number of Westerns since the 1950's. He writes tightly constructed stories set generally in small towns. There is no special sense of geographical location although Denver, as an early mining town, is the setting for *Shoot to Kill*, and Gaulden shows a general preference for using Colorado as a locale for his works.

Gaulden tends to use his town in an allegorical way: the town is a little world in itself and all the necessary elements of life are to be found there. Justice is represented by public opinion in the town. Law and order is demanded by taxpayers who pay the sheriff to protect them from lawless elements. There are many representatives of lawlessness, such as horsethieves, and social failure in the town, such as drunken hotel-keepers, broken down rodeo hands, spongers, and card sharps. The more respectable elements are often hard to find in Gaulden's books.

Gaulden's favourite type of character is the sheriff. In most of his books the hero is the sheriff and we see the stock western town through his eyes. Gaulden is very good at portraying the mentality of the type of man who becomes sheriff. In *Shadow of the Rope*, for instance, Frank had been a tough drifting cowhand before becoming a sheriff. He has a "clean hardness," but has settled down. He is foremost loyal, and tries to save an innocent old friend from hanging. In *Long Day in Latigo* the whole of the story is seen through the eyes of the Sheriff Owen Dallas who has to steer an impartial course between the demands of the more vocal citizens. He is often in conflict with the wishes of the richest rancher in town, who did in fact put him in the job. Gaulden, unlike many western writers, stresses the difficulties of a sheriff's life. In *Shoot to Kill* the sheriff confesses, "Packing a star is not what it is cracked up to be. I would rather be back in the mine." In *Long Day in Latigo* life is made even harder for the sheriff who tells us that "few had made a go at anything once they had worn a badge." Cattlemen had put this sheriff in office, and the appointment is often seen as an almost accidental occurence. In *Damaron's Gun* a professional gunfighter is asked to sign on as a deputy to bring peace to a lawless town. Once in office, however, the sheriffs are often idolized by the young. They are, however, aware of the importance of the job, and not necessarily corrupted by leading citizens. Sheriffs are, however, attracted by pretty women, such as Beth in *Long Day at Latigo*, but are not generally successful in love, being rather solitary self-contained characters. There are many minor characters that pass through Gaulden's books. In some cases, such as the Benbow family in *Long Day at Latigo*, they are well-drawn portraits of rough mountain people. In most cases, however, they are rather improbable, such as Miss Matilda or the overdressed banker in the same book.

Gaulden's plots are often rather contrived, such as that of *Shadow of the Rope*: too much mystery is made to depend on a horse with a white star. Plots tend to be predictable from the beginning: it always seems likely that the sheriff will get his man or save his brother from the rope. Gaulden's style, like his characters, is lean. Sentences are often very short and his prose has a clipped quality that suits the characters it describes. It does, however, sometimes descend into a corny sentimentality as in *Shoot to Kill*, told in the first person singular. Gaulden does produce some memorable western lines such as "There are other towns; a man can always start over."

Gaulden has performed a valuable service in his concentration on the sheriff in the Western. He gives us some uncommon viewpoints, and lets moral forces revolve around the sheriff in a suggestive, almost allegorical, manner.

—P.R. Meldrum

GIFFORD, Matt. *See* **KING, Albert.**

GILES, Jack. Pseudonym for Raymond Keith Foster. Also writes as Ryker Frost. British. Born in Finchley, London, 29 September 1945. Educated at Orpington County Secondary School for Boys, Kent, 1955–60. Married Sandra Letitia Giles in 1970; four daughters and one son. Clerk, Judge and Priestley solicitors, Bromley, Kent, 1961, William F. Prior and Co. solicitors, Sidcup, Kent, 1962, Coward Chance solicitors, City of London, 1963, and Payne Hicks Beach and Co. solicitors, Lincoln's Inn, London, 1964; conveyancing clerk, Crofts and Ingram and Wyatt and Co. solicitors, London, 1964–76, Okell and Stewart solicitors, Ross-on-Wye, Herefordshire, 1976–80, Crofts and Ingram and Wyatt and Co., London, 1980–86, and Latter and Willett solicitors, Bromley, Kent, 1987–89. Since 1990 freelance writer. Address: 16 Foxglove Crescent, Walderslade, Kent ME5 OSH, England.

WESTERN PUBLICATIONS

Novels

Poseidon Smith: Vengeance Is Mine. London, Hale, 1984.
Leather Face. London, Hale, 1984.
Rebel Run. London, Hale, 1985.
The Man from Labasque. London, Hale, 1985.
Ten Thousand Dollar Bounty. London, Hale, 1986.
Duggan. London, Hale, 1987.
Coalmine. London, Hale, 1987.

Novels as Ryker Frost

A Fortune for War. London, Hale, 1988.
The Battle of Sun Valley. London, Hale, 1989.

*

Jack Giles comments:

If it had not been for my two eldest daughters, I would not have written a Western. For Christmas 1976 they gave me the first two books in the Edge series by George G. Gilman. A few weeks later I found out he was British. I had always thought that Westerns were written by Americans, so now that I knew Gilman was British, I thought I would have a go.

I like a good Western both in book and film form, so I try to write in a visual form in the hope that the reader's imagination is stimulated. I try to get away from stereotypes and once in a while attempt a little role reversal, e.g. *Ten Thousand Dollar Bounty*, where the bad guy turns out to be the good guy and vice versa.

I do read my own books after publication and I like what I have written. They may not become classics like the works of Zane Grey or Jack Schaefer, but as long as they bring enjoyment to others, then I am content. I know that there is a man in Melbourne, Australia, who has read all my books and has liked every one. For me—that is enough.

* * *

Jack Giles is an above-average western writer from Kent, England, whose style initially owed much to that of his better-known contemporary, George G. Gilman. This is nowhere more apparent than in Giles's Civil War adventure *Rebel Run*, in which an ill-matched group of Confederate prisoners-of-war escape from an island stockade to cut a bloody swathe back to their own lines. The leading character, a Dutch artilleryman named Van Essen, shares a number of similarities with Gilman's enduring paperback anti-hero Edge. Both are mainly concerned with their own survival, capable of killing with very little compunction, and have a tendency to make the most appalling puns which, in Giles's case, generally detract from an otherwise first-rate story. Indeed, at one point in the book, Van Essen is described as "a man alone . . . always looking for the edge," a line that is too similar to the slogan used on the Edge books ("Edge is a man alone") to be dismissed as mere coincidence.

Despite this literary "tip of the hat," however, Giles does not portray Van Essen as just another wise-cracking killer. Instead he imbues the character with humanity and depth, giving him a history and values not always present in other western heroes. Even the supporting characters, some of whom may only appear for a page or two before dropping out of sight, are surprisingly well-drawn.

Conflict plays a large part in Giles's Westerns, and he handles it well, usually presenting both sides of any given argument, and then expressing the frustrations experienced by each character as he tries to impress his point upon the others. He seldom describes violence as graphically as Gilman, but he has a similar tendency to chop one sentence down into two or three, a gimmick which sometimes makes for a very staccato read. Neither do women feature prominently in his mainly male representation of the West, though when they *do* appear, they are invariably characterised as strong, resourceful, and sometimes scheming.

Giles again uses an artilleryman as the central character of *Duggan* in which the hero—once a respected army officer and now the town drunk—regains some of his lost dignity when he has to organise the defence of the town against attack by hostile Apaches.

Giles's view of the Indian Wars is a fashionably cynical one, and as the story unfolds, we learn that it is memories of the needless slaughter of a band of Apaches by a power-hungry colonel several years earlier that turned Duggan into a drunk and cost him his career. Sobered up by an old friend from his cavalry days, and talked into acting as a scout to ensure the safe transportation of three cannons from one fort to another, Duggan is subsequently called upon to fight the Apaches again, only to confirm his original conclusion: that war produces no winners, just losers. Despite this rather grim pronouncement, the book boasts a satisfyingly optimistic ending (as indeed do all of Giles's Westerns), and once again the author acknowledges a fellow western writer—this time Louis L'Amour himself—by setting the opening chapter in Bendigo's Saloon, in the town of Shafter (*Bendigo Shafter* being the title of one of L'Amour's books).

This idea of the underdog eventually making good is also carried over into *Coalmine* a sometimes convoluted but well-researched story of miners and unions set in the coalfields of Colorado. The underdog here is a former mining engineer who, having lost the use of his right arm in a cave-in some years earlier (which effectively ended his career), now ekes out a living by shooting fresh game for the local restaurant. Known only as "The Hunter," he is summoned to Colorado by a mysterious telegram, and soon becomes involved in a web of death and deceit until, in a well-crafted and totally-unforeseen twist ending, he manages to bring about an ultimately happy conclusion.

While Giles generally manages to avoid most—but by no means *all*—western clichés, his plots can sometimes stretch credibility pretty thin. This problem he usually manages to overcome by the originality and plausibility of his characters. A particularly good example of this can be found in an early title, *The Man from Labasque*, in which a vengeful young woman hires a gang of hardcases to wipe out the town her late father founded—simply because, in her view, the townsfolk did not show enough respect at his passing. Only one man is allowed to survive the orgy of violence that follows, a family friend named Pad Maghee. This, of course, proves to be the killers' undoing, because in true western tradition, Maghee promptly embarks upon a venegeance hunt of his own, armed only with a revolutionary type of rifle he himself has invented.

No matter how close Giles comes to shattering his own improbable illusion (and in this book that is pretty close indeed), the strength of his characters is such that disbelief is successfully suspended right until the very last line—a considerable feat given the unlikely nature of the plot.

Giles's work has also appeared under the pseudonym Ryker Frost, and *A Fortune for War* and *The Battle of Sun Valley*, echo aspects of his previous westerns. The first book is set in a silver mining town and tells the story of a conspiracy to siphon ore back East to bolster flagging Confederate funds. The second deals with the Confederate defence of a bridge in the valley of the book's title, which the Union army must take at all costs. In style these novels differ little from the work Giles has produced under his own name.

More recently, Giles has been conspicuous on the western scene largely by his absence. In view of the intelligence of most of his plots and the skill of his characterisation, we can only hope that this "literary silence" is a temporary one.

—David Whitehead

GILMAN, George G. Pseudonym for Terry Williams Harknett; also writes as Frank Chandler; David Ford; Jane Harman; Joseph Hedges; William M. James; Charles R. Pike; William Pine; James Russell; Thomas H. Stone; William Terry. British. Born in Rainham, Essex, 14 December 1936. Educated at Rainham Secondary Modern school. Served with the Royal Air Force, 1955–57. Married Jane Harman in 1960. Copy boy, Reuters, 1951–52, clerk, Newspaper Features Ltd., 1952–55, typist, Reuters Comtelburo, 1956–57, publicity assistant, 20th-Century Fox, 1957–58, editor, Newspaper Features Ltd., 1958–61, and reporter and features editor, *National Newsagent*, 1961–72, all London; then freelance writer. Address: Spring Acre, Springhead Road, Uplyme, Lyme Regis, Dorset DT7 3RJ, England.

WESTERN PUBLICATIONS

Novels (series: Edge)

1. *The Loner*. London, New English Library, and New York, Pinnacle, 1972.
2. *Ten Thousand Dollars, American*. London, New English Library, 1972; as *Ten Grand*, New York, Pinnacle, 1972.
3. *Apache Death*. London, New English Library, and New York, Pinnacle, 1972.
4. *Killer's Breed*. London, New English Library, and New York, Pinnacle, 1972.
5. *Blood on Silver*. London, New English Library, 1972; New York, Pinnacle, 1973.
6. *The Blue, The Grey, and The Red*. London, New English Library, 1973; as *Red River*, New York, Pinnacle, 1973.
7. *California Killing*. London, New English Library, 1973; as *California Kill*, New York, Pinnacle, 1974.
8. *Seven out of Hell*. London, New English Library, 1973; as *Hell's Seven*, New York, Pinnacle, 1973.
9. *Bloody Summer*. London, New English Library, 1973; New York, Pinnacle, 1974.
10. *Vengeance Is Black*. London, New English Library, 1973; as *Black Vengeance*, New York, Pinnacle, 1974.
11. *Sioux Uprising*. London, New English Library, and New York, Pinnacle, 1974.
12. *The Biggest Bounty*. London, New English Library, 1974; as *Death's Bounty*, New York, Pinnacle, 1974.
13. *A Town Called Hate*. London, New English Library, 1974; as *The Hated*, New York, Pinnacle, 1975.
14. *The Big Gold*. London, New English Library, 1974; as *Tiger's Gold*, New York, Pinnacle, 1975.
15. *Blood Run*. London, New English Library, 1975; as *Paradise Loses*, New York, Pinnacle, 1975.
16. *The Final Shot*. London, New English Library, and New York, Pinnacle, 1975.
17. *Vengeance Valley*. London, New English Library, 1975; New York, Pinnacle, 1976.
18. *Ten Tombstones to Texas*. London, New English Library, 1975; as *Ten Tombstones*, New York, Pinnacle, 1976.
19. *Ashes and Dust*. London, New English Library, and New York, Pinnacle, 1976.

20. *Sullivan's Law*. London, New English Library, and Los Angeles, Pinnacle, 1976.
21. *Rhapsody in Red*. London, New English Library, 1976; Los Angeles, Pinnacle, 1977.
22. *Slaughter Road*. London, New English Library, and Los Angeles, Pinnacle, 1977.
23. *Echoes of War*. London, New English Library, and Los Angeles, Pinnacle, 1977.
24. *The Day Democracy Died*. London, New English Library, 1977; as *Slaughterday*, Los Angeles, Pinnacle, 1978.
25. *Violence Trail*. London, New English Library, and Los Angeles, Pinnacle, 1978.
26. *Savage Dawn*. London, New English Library, and Los Angeles, Pinnacle, 1978.
28. *Eve of Evil*. London, New English Library, and Los Angeles, Pinnacle, 1978.
29. *The Living, The Dying, and the Dead*. London, New English Library, 1978; Los Angeles, Pinnacle, 1979.
30. *Waiting for a Train*. London, New English Library, 1979; as *Towering Nightmare*, Los Angeles, Pinnacle, 1979.
31. *The Guilty Ones*. London, New English Library, and Los Angeles, Pinnacle, 1979.
32. *The Frightened Gun*. London, New English Library, and Los Angeles, Pinnacle, 1979.
33. *The Hated*. London, New English Library, 1979; as *Red Fury*, New York, Pinnacle, 1980.
34. *A Ride in the Sun*. London, New English Library, and New York, Pinnacle, 1980.
35. *Death Deal*. London, New English Library, and New York, Pinnacle, 1980.

Two of a Kind: Edge Meets Steele. London, New English Library, and New York, Pinnacle, 1980.

36. *Town on Trial*. London, New English Library, and New York, Pinnacle, 1981.
37. *Vengeance at Ventura*. London, New English Library, and New York, Pinnacle, 1981.
38. *Massacre Mission*. London, New English Library, and New York, Pinnacle, 1981.
39. *The Prisoners*. London, New English Library, 1981; New York, Pinnacle, 1982.
40. *Montana Melodrama*. London, New English Library, and New York, Pinnacle, 1982.

Matching Pair: Edge Meets Adam Steele. London, New English Library, and New York, Pinnacle, 1982.

41. *The Killing Claim*. London, New English Library, 1982.
42. *Bloody Sunrise*. London, New English Library, 1982; New York, Pinnacle, 1983.
43. *Arapaho Revenge*. London, New English Library, and New York, Pinnacle, 1983.
44. *The Blind Side*. London, New English Library, 1983; New York, Pinnacle, 1984.
45. *House on the Range*. London, New English Library, 1983; New York, Pinnacle, 1984.
46. *The Godforsaken*. London, New English Library, and New York, Pinnacle, 1984.
47. *The Moving Cage*. London, New English Library, and New York, Pinnacle, 1984.

Edge Meets Steele No.3: Double Action. London, New English Library, 1984.

48. *School for Slaughter*. London, New English Library, and New York, Pinnacle, 1985.
49. *Revenge Ride*. London, New English Library, and New York, Pinnacle, 1985.
50. *Shadow of the Gallows*. London, New English Library, 1985.
51. *A Time for Killing*. London, New English Library, 1986.
52. *The Brutal Border*. London, New English Library, 1986.
53. *Hitting Paydirt*. London, New English Library, 1986.
54. *Backshot*. London, New English Library, 1987.
55. *Uneasy Riders*. London, New English Library, 1987.
56. *Doom Town*. London, New English Library, 1987.
57. *Dying Is Forever*. London, New English Library, 1987.
58. *The Desperadoes*. London, New English Library, 1988.
59. *Terror Town*. London, New English Library, 1988.
60. *The Breed Woman*. London, New English Library, 1989.
61. *The Rifle*. London, New English Library, 1989.

Novels (series: Adam Steele)

1. *The Violent Peace*. London, New English Library, 1974; as *Rebels and Assassins Die Hard*, New York, Pinnacle, 1975.
2. *The Bounty Hunter*. London, New English Library, 1974; New York, Pinnacle, 1975.
3. *Hell's Junction*. London, New English Library, 1974; New York, Pinnacle, 1976.
4. *Valley of Blood*. London, New English Library, 1975; New York, Pinnacle, 1976.
5. *Gun Run*. London, New English Library, 1975; New York, Pinnacle, 1976.
6. *The Killing Art*. London, New English Library, 1975; Los Angeles, Pinnacle, 1976.
7. *Cross-Fire*. London, New English Library, 1975; Los Angeles, Pinnacle, 1977.
8. *Comanche Carnage*. London, New English Library, 1976; Los Angeles, Pinnacle, 1977.
9. *Badge in the Dust*. London, New English Library, 1976; Los Angeles, Pinnacle, 1977.
10. *The Losers*. London, New English Library, 1976; Los Angeles, Pinnacle, 1978.
11. *Lynch Town*. London, New English Library, 1976; Los Angeles, Pinnacle, 1978.
12. *Death Trail*. London, New English Library, 1977; Los Angeles, Pinnacle, 1978.
13. *Bloody Border*. London, New English Library, 1977; Los Angeles, Pinnacle, 1979.
14. *Delta Duel*. London, New English Library, 1977; Los Angeles, Pinnacle, 1979.
15. *River of Death*. London, New English Library, 1977; New York, Pinnacle, 1980.
16. *Nightmare at Noon*. London, New English Library, 1978; New York, Pinnacle, 1980.
17. *Satan's Daughters*. London, New English Library, 1978; New York, Pinnacle, 1980.
18. *The Hard Way*. London, New English Library, 1978; New York, Pinnacle, 1980.
19. *The Tarnished Star*. London, New English Library, 1979; New York, Pinnacle, 1981.
20. *Wanted for Murder*. London, New English Library, 1979; New York, Pinnacle, 1982.
21. *Wagons East*. London, New English Library, 1979; New York, Pinnacle, 1982.
22. *The Big Game*. London, New English Library, 1979.
23. *Fort Despair*. London, New English Library, 1979.
24. *Manhunt*. London, New English Library, 1980.

Two of a Kind: Edge Meets Steele. London, New English Library, and New York, Pinnacle, 1980.

Steele's War:

25. *The Woman*. London, New English Library, 1980.
26. *The Preacher*. London, New English Library, 1981.
27. *The Storekeeper*. London, New English Library, 1981.
28. *The Stranger*. London, New English Library, 1981.
29. *The Big Prize*. London, New English Library, 1981.

30. *The Killer Mountains.* London, New English Library, 1982.
Matching Pair: Edge Meets Adam Steele. London, New English Library, 1982.
31. *The Cheaters.* London, New English Library, 1982.
32. *The Wrong Man.* London, New English Library, 1982.
33. *The Valley of the Shadow.* London, New English Library, 1983.
34. *The Runaway.* London, New English Library, 1983.
35. *Stranger in a Strange Town.* London, New English Library, 1983.
36. *The Hellraisers.* London, New English Library, 1984.
Edge Meets Steele 3: Double Action. London, New English Library, 1984.
37. *Canyon of Death.* London, New English Library, 1985.
38. *High Stakes.* London, New English Library, 1985.
39. *Rough Justice.* London, New English Library, 1985.
40. *The Sunset Ride.* London, New English Library, 1986.
41. *The Killing Strain.* London, New English Library, 1986.
42. *The Big Gunfight.* London, New English Library, 1987.
43. *The Hunted.* London, New English Library, 1987.
44. *Code of the West.* London, New English Library, 1987.
45. *The Outcasts.* London, New English Library, 1987.
46. *The Return.* London, New English Library, 1988.
47. *Trouble in Paradise.* London, New English Library, 1988.
48. *Going Back.* London, New English Library, 1989.
49. *The Long Shadow.* London, New English Library, 1989.

Novels (series: The Undertaker)

1. *Black as Death.* London, New English Library, 1981; New York, Pinnacle, 1985.
2. *Destined to Die.* London, New English Library, 1981.
3. *Funeral by the Sea.* London, New English Library, 1982.
4. *Three Graves to a Showdown.* London, New English Library, 1982.
5. *Back from the Dead.* London, New English Library, 1982.

Novels as William Terry

A Town Called Bastard (novelization of screenplay). London, New English Library, 1971.
Hannie Caulder (novelization of screenplay). London, New English Library, 1971; New York, Pinnacle, 1972.
Red Sun (novelization of screenplay). London, New English Library, 1972.
A Fistful of Dollars (novelization of screenplay; as Frank Chandler). London, Tandem, 1972.

Novels as Charles R. Pike (series: Jubal Cade)

1. *The Killing Trail.* London, Mayflower, 1974; New York, Chelsea House, 1980.
2. *Double Cross.* London, Mayflower, 1974; New York, Chelsea House, 1980.
3. *The Hungry Gun.* London, Mayflower, 1975; New York, Chelsea House, 1980.

Novels as William M. James (series: Apache)

1. *The First Death.* New York, Pinnacle, 1974; London, Sphere, 1975.
3. *Duel to the Death.* New York, Pinnacle, 1974; London, Sphere, 1975.
5. *Fort Treachery.* New York, Pinnacle, and London, Paramount, 1975.
6. *Sonora Slaughter.* New York, Pinnacle, 1976; London, New English Library, 1979.
8. *Blood on the Tracks.* Los Angeles, Pinnacle, 1977; London, New English Library, 1979.
10. *All Blood Is Red.* Los Angeles, Pinnacle, 1977; London, New English Library, 1980.
13. *The Best Man.* Los Angeles, Pinnacle, 1979.

Uncollected Short Stories

"Guns at the Silver Horseshoe" (as Terry Harknett), in *Reveille* (London), 1955.
"Raw Edge," in *Club International* (London), 1973.
"Edge: The Quiet Gun," in *Western* (London), October 1980.
"Steele: Bad Business at Newville," in *Western* (London), January 1981.
"Edge: The Vengeance Guns," in *Short Stories* (London), February 1981.

OTHER PUBLICATIONS

Novels as Terry Harknett

The Benevolent Blackmailer. London, Hale, 1962.
The Scratch on the Surface. London, Hale, 1962.
Invitation to a Funeral. London, Hale, 1963.
Dead Little Rich Girl. London, Hale, 1963.
The Evil Money. London, Hale, 1964.
The Man Who Did Not Die. London, Hale, 1964.
Once A Copper (as William Terry). London, Hammond, 1965.
Death of an Aunt. London, Hammond, 1967.
The Two-Way Frame. London, Hammond, 1967.
The Protectors (as William Pine). London, Constable, 1967.
The Softcover Kill. London, Hale, 1971.
W.I.T.C.H. (as Jane Harman). London, New English Library, 1971.
Promotion Tour. London, New English Library, 1972.
The Weekend Game (as William Terry). London, New English Library, 1972.
The Upmarket Affair. London, Hale, 1973.
Crown series:
The Sweet and Sour Kill. London, Futura, and New York, Pinnacle, 1974.
Macao Mayhem. London, Futura, 1974.
Bamboo Shoot-Out. London, Futura, 1975.

Novels as Thomas H. Stone

Dead Set. London, New English Library, 1972.
One Horse Race. London, New English Library, 1972.
Stopover for Murder. London, New English Library, 1973.
Black Death. London, New English Library, 1973.
Squeeze Play. London, New English Library, 1973.

Novels as Joseph Hedges

Funeral Rites. London, Sphere, 1973; New York, Pyramid, 1974.
Arms for Oblivion. London, Sphere, 1973; New York, Pyramid, 1975.
The Chinese Coffin. London, Sphere, 1974; New York, Pyramid, 1975.
The Gold-Plated Hearse. London, Sphere, 1974; New York, Pyramid, 1975.
Rainbow-Coloured Shroud. London, Sphere, 1974; New York, Pyramid, 1975.
Corpse on Ice. London, Sphere, and New York, Pyramid, 1975.

The Mile-Deep Grave. London, Sphere, 1975.
Mexican Mourning. London, Sphere, 1975.
The Stainless Steel Wreath. London, Sphere, 1975.
The Chauffeur-Driven Pyre. London, Sphere, 1976.

Other

The Caribbean (as Terry Harknett). London, New English Library, 1972.
The Balearic Islands (as James Russell). London, New English Library, 1972.
Cyprus (as David Ford). London, New English Library, 1973.

Ghostwriter of the following books: *The Hero* by Peter Haining, 1973; *The Savage* and *Doomsday Island*, both by Alex Peters, 1979.

* * *

From the moment Edge pulled out a straight razor and sliced open a Mexican's throat, the Western was never going to recover. The Edge series, written by George G. Gilman, was the prototype of modern Westerns that were produced from the early 1970's onwards. Its influence on the adult Western is inescapable. Gone was the image of the old kind of western hero, in came a six-foot three killing machine. Gilman created a notable character in Edge, who throughout the series lapses into periods of introspection and self-doubt, thus stopping short of making him a psychopathic killer or a mere cipher, rather than the larger-than-life, three-dimensional, victim-of-circumstance anti-hero he is intended to be.

To compensate for the violence in the books, Gilman injects graveyard humour throughout. This balance of mayhem and jokes proved popular with readers, and it is the humour which sticks in the mind rather than the violence. *California Killing*, with its masses of Hollywood references, is a fine example. The majority of Edge books are "non-message" stories—something that annoys the critics. They are, at their best, entertaining reading from a self-confessed commercial writer who found a gap in the original market and exploited it for all it was worth. It is interesting to note that although the series finished in 1989 with 61 books to its credit, Gilman saw off all his competitors.

It was his publishers who asked Gilman to create another Gilman hero. Adam Steele was born out of a rejected screenplay, and it was easy to make his character different from Edge. Steele is short whereas Edge was tall, grey-haired as opposed to Edge's black colouring. Steele fought for the South while Edge was for the Union. These are obvious devices to use, but apart from these differences Edge and Steele are alike in that they are both loners and losers. If either of them kept their women or money it would make them different characters; instead, their similar destinies force them to kill, and they gain nothing from what they have done. When Steele or Edge try, there's always someone with a long memory who knows about their dark pasts, putting a stop to any chance of a normal life for either man.

The two heroes' Civil War experience has much to do in moulding their characters, so this was retold in detail with books written specifically to deal with that time. Edge appeared in *Killer's Breed*, *The Blue, The Grey, and the Red*, *Seven out of Hell*, *Vengeance Is Black*, *The Biggest Bounty*, and *The Final Shot*. *Steele's War* contained *The Woman*, *The Preacher*, *The Storekeeper*, and *The Stranger*. Inevitably, both characters have a common theme—revenge. In *The Loner*, Edge returns home from the war to his Iowa farm only to find that his brother has died at the hands of his former subordinates. The similarities between the characters of Josiah Hedges and Forrest Carter's Josey Wales are inescapable. Did Carter write *The Rebel Outlaw, Josey Wales* after reading *The Loner* but made subtle changes? In *The Violent Peace*, Steele is similarly bereaved when his father is lynched by drunkards at the end of the War. Steele is forced to kill a lawman and is therefore destined to become a drifter, and one step ahead of the law.

It was inevitable that two strong characters would cross paths. In their appearances in *Two Of A Kind: Edge Meets Steele* and *Matching Pair*, Gilman handles the crossover extremely well and allows them to take centre stage in alternate chapters. In *The Rifle*, the final Edge book, they meet up again, with Steele's unique rifle drawing Edge to find the Virginian. Steele is on his way to face trial for a former murder after attempting to settle down and Edge resolves the situation, forcing them together once again—their destinies unknown.

It is in the final chapter of *The Rifle* that Gilman's third, and least successful, character gets a mention. Barnaby Gold from The Undertaker series was, from the outset, a cold killer. There were no feelings of remorse after his violent acts, and from the moment he shoots and kills Channon for murdering his wayward wife, Gold is forced to flee. He is young and inexperienced in killing, but a tough New York upbringing has hardened him. He has much to learn about life, and he goes about it systematically, learning to use his weapons in an effective, deadly way. No doubt it was this character's difference to Edge and Steele which did not appeal to Gilman's avid readers. And appearing at the time when the English western paperback market was in a recession decreed its fateful short run.

Just over two-thirds of Gilman's books have been Westerns. Between 1971 and 1972 he started off writing novelizations of western screenplays. These were to establish his name with his publisher, and at their suggestion he blocked out two Edge proposals, and the rest, as they say, is history. In 1974 he and Laurence James began the Apache series, for the American publisher Pinnacle. Cuchillo Oro, Golden Knife, takes on the mantle of avenger, seeking to destroy Cyrus Pinner, the cavalry officer responsible for outrages on Oro and his kin. The plots are rather clichéd, but by using a wronged Indian and building the series around him, the authors provide a different viewpoint.

During the same period Gilman embarked on the Jubal Cade series for yet another publisher. But pressure from the success of Edge and Steele forced him to bow out after three books, handing it over to a fellow English writer, Angus Wells. Again, as in many western series, it has its origins in revenge. On this occasion Cade, a doctor, seeks out a new life with his bride in the West. Obviously he is not destined to succeed, and she is killed by a band of outlaws, which results in Cade embarking on *The Killing Trail*.

In all of Gilman's characters we find suffering and the loss of innocence. Edge simply wanted to return to his brother and restart his farming life; Steele wanted to make amends with his father; Gold, shunned by townsfolk for his callousness, is forced into a new life; Cade was looking for happiness in a new land and Oro, his happiness taken from him and physically violated, has no choice but to retaliate. Each has to adapt to a new life foisted upon him by fate. There is violence, humour, and sympathy to be found in these works, alongside excellent portrayals of credible characters. All of these elements combine to produce exciting reading which undoubtedly will stand the test of time.

—Mike Stotter

GIPSON, Fred(erick Benjamin). American. Born in Mason, Texas, 7 February 1908. Educated at Mason High School, graduated 1926; University of Texas, Austin, 1933–37. Married Tommie Eloise Wynn in 1940 (divorced 1964); two sons. Worked as farm and ranch hand, and as clerk, 1926–33; reporter and columnist, Corpus Christi *Caller-Times*, San Angelo *Standard-Times*, and Paris *News*, all in Texas, 1938–40; associate editor, *True West* magazine, Austin, 1953–59; editorial director, *Frontier Times*, Bandera, Texas, 1958–59. President, Texas Institute of Letters, 1960. *Died 14 August 1973.*

WESTERN PUBLICATIONS

Novels

Hound-Dog Man. New York, Harper, 1949.
The Home Place. New York, Harper, 1950; London, Joseph, 1951; abridged edition, as *Return of the Texan*, Edinburgh, Oliver and Boyd, 1962.
Recollection Creek. New York, Harper, 1955; revised edition, for children, 1959.

Uncollected Short Stories

"They Grow 'em Tough on the Llano!," in *Star Western* (Chicago), August 1943.
"Snakebite Mean and Blackjack Tough!," in *Star Western* (Chicago), September 1943.
"The Toughest Man in Texas," in *West* (Kingswood, Surrey), October 1943.
"Last of the Fighting McCauleys," in *Star Western* (Chicago), October 1943.
"Pistol Passport for Llano Invaders," in *Star Western* (Chicago), November 1943.
"The Circle A Invasion," in *West* (Kingswood, Surrey), May 1944.
"Hog-Wild in Hell!," in *West* (Kingswood, Surrey), June 1944.
"Gun-Lord of Platte River," in *West* (Kingswood, Surrey), September 1944.
"Comanche's Whisky-Bottle War," in *Star Western* (Chicago), February 1945.
"Cowman, Guard Your Sheep!," in *West* (Kingswood, Surrey), April 1945.

OTHER PUBLICATIONS

Fiction (for children)

The Trail-Driving Rooster. New York, Harper, 1955.
Old Yeller. New York, Harper, 1956; London, Hodder and Stoughton, 1957.
Savage Sam. New York, Harper, and London, Hodder and Stoughton, 1962.
Little Arliss. New York, Harper, 1978.
Curly and the Wild Boar. New York, Harper, 1979.

Plays

Screenplays: *Old Yeller*, with William Tunberg, 1957; *Hound Dog Man*, with Winston Miller, 1959; *Savage Sam*, with William Tunberg, 1962.

Television Play: *Brush Roper.*

Other

Fabulous Empire: Colonel Zack Miller's Story. Boston, Houghton Mifflin, 1946; as *Circles Round the Wagon*, London, Joseph, 1949.
Big Bend, with J. Oscar Langford. Austin, University of Texas Press, 1952.
Cowhand: The Story of a Working Cowboy. New York, Harper, 1953; London, Transworld, 1957.
The Cow Killers: With the Aftosa Commission in Mexico. Austin, University of Texas Press, 1956.
An Acceptance Speech. New York, Harper, 1960.

*

Critical Studies: *Fred Gipson* by Sam H. Henderson, Austin, Texas, Steck Vaughn, 1967; *Fred Gipson, Texas Storyteller* by Mike Cox, Austin, Texas, Shoal Creek, 1980.

* * *

Fred Gipson's tales of the Texas "hill country" have charmed young and old, in print and in film, for more than three decades now. Several of Gipson's stories were made into motion pictures by the Disney company, and these perennially popular movies have no doubt done more to keep the author's name alive than the books—though the books continue to be read, particularly by young people. Gipson had the ability—not to be sneered at, since few writers seem to have inherited or acquired it—to appeal simultaneously to many different levels of awareness; pre-teen children and sophisticated literary critics can read his novels apparently with equal pleasure and appreciation.

Gipson's two best novels, by far, are *Hound-Dog Man* and *Old Yeller*. Both are narratives of the Texas frontier, and both are initiation stories; the first is narrated by a 12-year-old named Cotton, the second by a 14-year-old, Travis. *Hound-Dog Man* is structured around a three-day raccoon hunt during which Cotton is initiated into the ritual of the hunt and into some of the mysteries of adult life by Blackie Scantling, the "hound-dog man" of the title. The novel is notable for presenting a character with one of the memorable names in American fiction: Hog Waller, a mean-spirited farmer who appears in the story from time to time.

Old Yeller, which spawned the best known of the movies made from Gipson's works, is again a story of growing up. Young Travis assumes an adult role when his father leaves on a months-long cattle drive to Kansas. With the aid of his beloved dog Old Yeller, Travis successfully battles the elements and a threatened plague of hydrophobia to keep family and farm intact until his father's return. Gipson's remaining fiction—*The Home Place*, *Recollection Creek*, *Savage Sam*, and two books that were cobbled together posthumously, *Little Arliss* and *Curly and the Wild Boar*—do not come close to matching the high quality of the two best novels.

Some critics have professed to see latent "literary greatness" in Gipson's work. This seems, however, to claim too much. Gipson was a top-notch storyteller. He had a good ear for dialect and a light hand in transcribing it. He handled well, if not very originally, that most familiar theme in American fiction: initiation. He was conscientious and honorable as a craftsman, and he will be read when writers with flashier reputations have disappeared without a ripple. To say that greatness eluded him is not to say that he failed.

—William T. Pilkington

GIRTY, Simon. *See* **KING, Albert.**

GLASPELL, Susan (Keating). American. Born in Davenport, Iowa, 1 July 1882 (possibly 1876). Educated at schools in Davenport; Drake University, Des Moines, Iowa, Ph.D. 1899; University of Chicago, 1902. Married 1) the writer George Cram Cook in 1913 (died 1924); 2) the writer Norman Matson in 1925 (divorced 1932). Reporter, Des Moines *Daily News* and *Capital*, 1899–1901; freelance writer in Davenport, 1901–11; founder, with George Cram Cook, Provincetown Players, 1915, and wrote for the company in Provincetown, Massachusetts, and New York, 1915–22; lived in Greece, 1922–24; director, Midwest Play Bureau of the Federal Theater Project, Chicago, 1936–38. Recipient: Pulitzer prize, 1931. *Died 27 July 1948.*

WESTERN PUBLICATIONS

Short Story

A Jury of Her Peers. London, Benn, 1927.

Plays

Trifles (produced Provincetown, Massachusetts, 1916). Boston, Baker, 1924; London, French, 1932.
Inheritors (produced New York, 1921). Boston, Small Maynard, 1921; London, Benn, 1924.

OTHER PUBLICATIONS

Novels

The Glory of the Conquered: The Story of a Great Love. New York, Stokes, and London, Putnam, 1909.
The Visioning. New York, Stokes, 1911; London, Murray, 1912.
According to His Lights. New York, Winthrop Press, 1914.
Fidelity. Boston, Small Maynard, 1915; London, Jarrolds, 1924.
Brook Evans. New York, Stokes, and London, Gollancz, 1928.
Fugitive's Return. New York, Stokes, and London, Gollancz, 1929.
Ambrose Holt and Family. New York, Stokes, and London, Gollancz, 1931.
The Right to Love. London, Reader's Library, 1932.
The Morning Is Near Us. New York, Stokes, and London, Gollancz, 1940.
Norma Ashe. Philadelphia, Lippincott, 1942; London, Gollancz, 1943.
Judd Rankin's Daughter. Philadelphia, Lippincott, 1945; as *Prodigal Giver*, London, Gollancz, 1946.

Short Stories

Lifted Masks. New York, Stokes, 1912.
Cherished and Shared of Old: A Christmas Story. New York, Messner, 1940.

Plays

Suppressed Desires, with George Cram Cook (produced Provincetown, Massachusetts, 1915). Boston, Baker, and London, French, 1924.
The Provincetown Plays. New York, Shay, 1916.
The People (produced New York, 1917). New York, Shay, 1918.
Close the Book (produced New York, 1917).
The Outside (produced New York, 1917). Published in *Sea Plays*, edited by C.C. Clements, Boston, Small Maynard, 1952.
Woman's Honor (produced New York, 1918).
Tickless Time, with George Cram Cook (produced New York, 1918). Boston, Baker, 1925.
Bernice (produced New York, 1919). Boston, Small Maynard, 1922; London, Benn, 1924.
Plays. Boston, Small Maynard, 1920; revised edition, edited by C.W.E. Bigsby, Cambridge, Cambridge University Press, 1987.
The Verge (produced New York, 1921). Boston, Small Maynard, 1922; London, Benn, 1924.
Chains of Dew (produced New York, 1922).
The Comic Artist, with Norman Matson (produced London, 1928). New York, Strokes, and London, Benn, 1927.
Alison's House (produced New York, 1930). New York, and London, French, 1930.

Other

The Road to the Temple: A Biography of George Cram Cook. London, Benn, 1926; New York, Stokes, 1927.
Looking After Clara: A Contest Selection, edited by Lilian Holmes Strack. Boston, Baker, 1928.
Whom Mince Pie Hath Joined Together: A Contest Selection, edited by Lilian Holmes Strack. Boston, Baker, 1928.

*

Critical Studies: *Susan Glaspell* by Arthur E. Waterman, New York, Twayne, 1966; *Susan Glaspell und die Provincetown Players: die Anfunge des modernen amerikanischen Dramas und Theaters* by Gerhard Bach, Frankfurt and Cirencester, Lang, 1979; "Reading About Reading: 'A Jury of Her Peers', 'The Murders in the Rue Morgue', and 'The Yellow Wallpaper,'" in *Gender and Reading*, edited by Elizabeth A. Flynn and Patrocinio P. Schweickart, Baltimore, Maryland, Johns Hopkins University Press, 1986; "A Map for Reading and the Interpretation of Literary Texts" by Annette Kolodny, in *The New Feminist Criticism*, edited by Elaine Showalter, London, Virago Press, 1986.

* * *

Jack Schaefer's *Shane* is typical of the classic Western in its celebration of American ideological values. The sanctity of the family, private property, and democracy are all endorsed in the novel. The Starretts form an ideal family unit, with mom literally baking apple pie in the kitchen as Shane and Joe combine in their outdoor male sphere to shift the root of the tree that prevents the cultivation of the land.

The text written by Susan Glaspell which has aroused most critical comment is her short story "A Jury of Her Peers," adapted from her play *Trifles*. Set in a small midwestern community, the story uses this setting to examine the internal mechanics of male-female relationships. In doing so, it undercuts any notion of the united family as wellspring of American value; as that solid, valuable, and secure edifice on which the whole social and institutional structure of the nation depends. In traditional westens the central tension is often that between community and outside threat. In Glaspell's narrative it is domestic space and the relations within it which are foregrounded, as she examines the reductive and oppressive nature of masculine thought, and the feminine response to this.

Male effacement of the female is a recurrent concern of the story. Twice on the first page Mrs. Peters is referred to as the "sheriff's wife," her identity swallowed by her male partner's social role. The fact that the sheriff is "a heavy man with a big voice" leads others to look for an appropriate match in his marital partner. Thus, the county attorney misdirects his remarks to Mrs. Hale, the "big farmer woman" whose appearance betters suits his expectations of how a sheriff's wife should look. The fragility of female identity in such a social world is clear. And the theme of misrecognition is central to the narrative, connecting up with the larger one of reading and misreading. The women of the narrative can read the signs in what Annette Kolodny calls "the male . . . realm of meaning and activity" and indeed have to be able to do so to function effectively in a social situation where their status is subordinate. The opposite is not the case, however. The sheriff and attorney do not see the clues to John Wright's murder which are to be found in the woman's sphere, the kitchen. They consider kitchen matters "trifles" and search for information about the murder elsewhere. Mrs. Hale and Mrs. Peters can, however, reconstruct what has occurred there. They see and find what the men do not: the half-done work, the "crazy sewing" for the quilt, the damaged bird cage, the canary with a broken neck. As a result they can both "solve" the mystery and sympathize with the "criminal."

Two ways of seeing are in complete opposition here. John Wright is a "good man" in conventional social terms: one who is honest, sober, and who pays his debts. The men look to punish his murder and expect their wives—"a sheriff's wife is" after all "married to the law"—to identify with their activity. The women, however, in the course of the story stop reading the situation in the way that their menfolk would like. They find parts of themselves long buried, and realize that the phrase "a good man" is one which puts to one side the cruel, damaging, and heartless way Wright has treated his wife. The women end up hiding the evidence of Minnie Foster's crime (Wright's wife is so called, by her maiden name, throughout; the women remember her thus as that lively girl she was before Wright metaphorically squeezed the life from her) from the representatives of the "official" male world. Judith Fetterley sums up the story as "nothing less than [that] of men's systematic, institutionalized, and culturally approved violence toward women, and of women's potential for retaliatory violence toward men." Glaspell uses the midwestern rural setting both to point to the potential for loneliness for the women who lived there and to explode any notion of domestic harmony and shared interest as that which welds society valuably together at its base.

Glaspell wrote a great deal during her career, and her present lack of literary status is undeserved. She was best-known as a playwright and her early plays have been described as being "as challenging and original as those with which [Eugene] O'Neill made his debut." She also wrote 10 novels and a large number of short stories. Of her other work dealing with western themes, perhaps the most interesting is the play *Inheritors*. Set in the Midwest both of the pioneer generation and of Glaspell's own time, it illustrates the idealism and generosity of some of the early settlers, represented at their best by Silas Morton. He gives the hill he owns above the town to "plant a college . . . [to] wake things in [the] minds [of the local youth]—so ploughing's more than ploughing." Silas believes in the American democratic experiment (though his sympathy with the Indian is a recognition of at least one of its costs and failings) and in the power and beneficial nature of both education and aspiration. His values are contrasted with those of a later America where the business ethic is paramount, and xenophobia and fear of radicalism characterize the members of that college he founded. This sense of the best of the old pioneer ideals being lost is only modified by the actions of Madeline, Silas's grandaughter, who prefers to become alien from society rather than to give up the values her grandfather practiced. The feminist impulse behind so much of Glaspell's work is evident in her use of Madeline as the heroine who can thus bridge the gulf between past and present. Here however the author's movement away from sexual politics as her major theme means that the idea of the West and the positive aspects of its settling can emerge with more force.

—Peter Messent

GLASTON, W.B. *See* **LAZENBY, Norman.**

GLENDENNING, Don. *See* **PAINE, Lauran.**

GLENN, James. *See* **PAINE, Lauran.**

GLIDDEN, Frederick Dilley. *See* **SHORT, Luke.**

GLIDDEN, Jonathan. *See* **DAWSON, Peter.**

GOODEN, Arthur Henry. Also wrote as Brett Rider. British. Immigrated to the United States at age nine, raised on ranch in San Joaquín Valley, California. Worked as a cowhand, promoted to top hand, before becoming script writer in Hollywood, where he spent 16 years writing for serials, shorts, and features.

WESTERN PUBLICATIONS

Novels

Cross Knife Ranch. London, Harrap, 1933; New York, Phoenix Press, 1939.
Wayne of the Flying W. New York, Kinsey, and London, Harrap, 1934.
Valley of the Kings. New York, Kinsey, 1935.
Brant from Cimarron. London, Harrap, 1936.
Smoke Tree Range. New York, Kinsey, and London, Harrap, 1936.
Donovan Rides. New York, Macaulay, and London, Harrap, 1937.
Boss of the Circle B. London, Harrap, 1938.
Tenderfoot Boss. London, Harrap, 1939.
The Trail of Vengeance. New York, Phoenix Press, 1939.
The Range Hawk. New York, Carlton House, and London, Harrap, 1940.
Painted Buttes. New York, Carlton House, 1941; London, Harrap, 1944.
Roaring River Range. Boston, Houghton Mifflin, 1942; London, Harrap, 1946.
Guns on the High Mesa. Boston, Houghton Mifflin, 1943.
The Valley of Dry Bones. Boston, Houghton Mifflin, 1945; London, Harrap, 1949.
The Shadowed Trail. Boston, Houghton Mifflin, 1946; London, Harrap, 1948.
Trouble in the Saddle. Boston, Houghton Mifflin, 1948; London, Harrap, 1950.
High Mesa. London, Harrap, 1948.
The Boss of Santa Ysabel. London, Harrap, 1949.
The Amateur Outlaw. London, Harrap, 1950.
Diamond D for Danger. London, Harrap, 1951.
Call of the Range. Philadelphia, Macrae Smith, 1951.
The Long Trail. New York, Dutton, and London, Hodder and Stoughton, 1952.
Ride for Hell Pass. London, Hodder and Stoughton, 1956.
Death Rides the Range. London, Hale, 1961.
Trails into Danger. London, Hale, 1962.

Novels as Brett Rider

Boss of the OK. New York, Phoenix Press, 1940.
Circle C Moves In. Philadelphia, Macrae Smith, 1944; as Arthur Henry Gooden, London, Harrap, 1946.
Death Stalks the Range. Philadelphia, Macrae Smith, 1945; as Arthur Henry Gooden, London, Harrap, 1949.
Circle C Carries On. Philadelphia, Macrae Smith, 1948; as Arthur Henry Gooden, London, Harrap, 1950.
No Benefit of Law. Philadelphia, Macrae Smith, 1949.
Law of the Gun. Philadelphia, Macrae Smith, 1950.

OTHER PUBLICATIONS

Plays

Screenplays: *Below the Deadline*, 1921; *The Verdict of the Desert*, 1925.

* * *

Arthur Henry Gooden had considerable popularity as a western writer and his books were reprinted long after first publication. His books consistently received critical acclaim and were regarded as exceptionally good Westerns. He wrote screenplays for western films in America before turning to novel writing.

Gooden's early Western, *Wayne of the Flying W*, attracted favourable reviews as it was clear that the writer knew the life of the range and could write about it in good English. In *Cross Knife Ranch*, too, there are all the elements expected of a good Western: a mysterious archrustler with a suitable name, King Buzzard, a Spanish beauty named Anita Callahan, a cowboy hero quick with a gun, and a happy end to the story. Gooden's mastery shows in the finishing touches he adds to parts of the book: evocative chapter titles such as "In Lobo Pass," corny western dialogue, a bit of Spanish colonial history, and of course the suggestive names given to people and places. Gooden was not tempted into using overly detailed descriptions or portraying too much violence. The expert touches of Gooden, however, did not disguise flimsy plots, but polished off the solid core of a good story.

In *Guns on the High Mesa* the heart of the plot is the essential need of a cattle ranch for a mountain watershed. The young owner has to fight a timber company as well as rustlers. An escaped convict with a grudge is hired as a gunmen to murder him. The story is sufficiently credible and is well written. A stronger love interest is apparent in *Roaring River Range* where an affair grows between the young attractive hero and the boss's daughter. If the basis of the plot—a 20-year mystery unsolved, and the boss's daughter not being his daughter at all—strains our credibility somewhat, it does provide for great surprise and a conclusive end. What is lacking in the story is made up for in the telling with its keen psychology, Mexican and Chinese comic moments, and the pathos of the lame cowboy. In *The Shadowed Trail* there is very good scene setting: we get the real feel of western country. Gooden also makes us conscious of the presence of animals, adding a fight between two bulls on the range. In *Trouble in the Saddle* authentic observations on farming and ranching add to the believability of the plot. There is in this book considerable detail, especially in descriptions of women, but it is handled well and doesn't dominate. Gooden can still add a romantic whimsical last line: "... sunset faded into twilight. This was trail's end." In addition to the other attributes of his books Gooden adds very lively dialogue. There is rather more in his later books, but unlike the dialogue in many Westerns it doesn't appear ridiculous on the printed page.

The easiness with which one can read Gooden's prose perhaps disguises the amount of craftsmanship in his work. Gooden's words were chosen with care and worked into sentences of just the right length. Sentimentality, comedy, and the occasional mock-serious finishing line are all put together in the right proportions. Gooden had obviously mastered the art of writing in the western genre.

—P.R. Meldrum

GORDON, Bill. *See* **ATHANAS, Verne.**

GORDON, Lew. *See* **BALDWIN, Gordon C.**

GORDON, Stewart. *See* **SHIRREFFS, Gordon D.**

GORMAN, Ed(ward). American. Born in Cedar Rapids, Iowa, 29 November 1941. Educated at Coe College, Iowa, 1962–65. Married Carol Gorman in 1982; one son and one stepson. Worked in advertising as a writer and freelance writer, 20 years. Since 1989 full-time writer. Co-founder and editor, *Mystery Scene* magazine. Recipient: Private Eye Writers of America Shamus award. Agent: Dominick Abel, 146 West 82nd Street, New York, New York 10024. Address: 3840 Clark Road South East, Cedar Rapids, Iowa 52403, U.S.A.

WESTERN PUBLICATIONS

Novels (series: Guild)

Guild. New York, Evans, 1987; Bath, Chivers, 1989.
Death Ground (Guild). New York, Evans, 1988; Bath, Chivers, 1990.
Blood Game (Guild). New York, Evans, 1989; Bath, Chivers, 1991.
Graves Retreat. New York, Doubleday, 1989.
Night of Shadows. New York, Doubleday, 1990.
Dark Trail. New York, Evans, 1991.

Uncollected Short Story

"Guild and the Indian Woman," in *Westeryear*, edited by Edward Gorman. New York, Evans, 1988.

OTHER PUBLICATIONS

Novels

Rough Cut. New York, St. Martin's Press, 1985; London, Hale, 1987.
New, Improved Murder. New York, St. Martin's Press, 1986.
Murder Straight Up. New York, St. Martin's Press, 1986.
Murder in the Wings. New York, St. Martin's Press, 1986.
Murder on the Aisle. New York, St. Martin's Press, 1987.
The Autumn Dead. New York, St. Martin's Press, 1987; London, Allison and Busby, 1989.
Several Deaths Later. New York, St. Martin's Press, 1988.
A Cry of Shadows. New York, St. Martin's Press, 1990.
Night Kills. New York, Ballantine, 1990.

Other

Editor, *Westeryear.* New York, Evans, 1988.
Editor, *Black Lizard Anthology of Crime Fiction.* New York, Black Lizard, 1989.
Editor, *Under the Gun.* New York, New American Library, 1990.

*

Ed Gorman comments:

I hope I'm writing the sort of books I like to read—stronger on character than plot twists, and historically accurate but not tediously so.

* * *

Ed Gorman has written successfully within other genres apart from his contribution to Westerns. He is well-known for his Jack Dwyer mysteries, while under the byline Daniel Ransom he has delved into horror, and has also contributed to short story anthologies. And until 1989 he worked as a full time advertising executive, and found the time to be the co-founder and editor of *Mystery Scene* magazine.

He established a memorable character in Leo Guild, a bounty hunter in his twilight years, operating as the 19th century is drawing to a close. He is a complex character who strives to come to terms with his torment over an accident when he shot and killed an eight-year-old girl. This incident becomes a recurring nightmare to him, and serves as a central theme running through the books.

The appeal of the Guild books is that the leading character is neither oversentimental nor given to extreme violence, as other loners are depicted in rival series. His casual brushes with the opposite sex are plentiful, touching the whole spectrum from whores to well-connected women. Women are as important in Gorman's works as their counterparts, and he uses them for social balance. Moreover, the genuine conflict that runs through the books is likely to be influenced by a woman, for instance Annie in *Guild*, the granny woman in *Death Ground*, or Clarise Watson in *Blood Game*.

Gorman doesn't confine his women to mere support roles—*Night of Shadows* deals with the first uniformed policewoman in Cedar Rapids, Iowa, in 1895. Anna Tolan is given the job of shepherding a noted gunslinger in and out of town, a job that her superiors feel is all that she is capable of. But when a murder occurs and the finger of suspicion points to Stephen Fuller, the gunslinger, she sets out to impress her bosses by using up-to-the-minute methods of detection to prove Fuller's innocence. Anna is successful in locating the real psychopath, and unwittingly unearths the town's dark secret. *Night of Shadows* is a well-written book which exemplifies the lean style Gorman developed for his mysteries, and that is exactly how he treats the storyline—as a murder mystery.

Develop a theme along the trusted formula of a megalomanic banker whose greed has blinded him to law and order, add a revenge element, and the mixture becomes *Guild*. An ex-lawman turned bounty hunter, Leo Guild is pleased when he brings in his prisoner, although a short time afterwards he becomes involved in helping a young girl avenge her companion's death. Gorman probes into a variety of personal problems which do not necessarily sustain the novel's drama. It is peopled with a handful of characters, each fighting for center stage to put their feelings on show, but it is a book which is not devoid of honest emotions: "He looked over at Annie sleeping next to him. It had been long years since he'd felt the things her frightened little body had given him. He had clung to her there in the darkness. Clung."

Death Ground was praised as "a Western for grown-ups," and "a Western for those who don't like reading Westerns." Again it is the hard-boiled style which stands out. Indeed, there is a "police procedural" feel to the book together with echoes of Ed McBain's skeletal dialogue: "The priest said, 'They're going to vote.' 'Who is?' 'The people of the settlement.' 'On what?' 'On you.' 'Me?'" and so it continues. *Death Ground* not only covers a standard plot, but is interwoven with love and revenge, bare-faced lies and corrupt lawmen. Guild sets himself up as a figure for the law when he discovers he cannot trust those elected to the job, but his reasoning behind it is fragile: "he owed Rig a death. Maybe he even owed the Tolliver kid a death." The outlaw, Kriker, with whom Guild finds he has much in common, is a strong character, but I personally feel that he is too sentimental for a man who has survived for so long among his kind.

The art of pugilism is the background topic to the third book concerning Leo Guild. In *Blood Game* he accepts the job of finding a missing bare-knuckle prize fighter. He succeeds and then accepts a further assignment to protect the takings for the big fight. There is an instant dislike between Guild and John Stoddard, his employer, whom he finds detestable in his narrow-minded pursuit of wealth. Stoddard even ignores his own son's pitiful attempts for fatherly affection, and the young man turns to Guild for advice. As in all of the books, the bounty hunter is the center pin and his strength of character is called upon rather than his ability with a handgun. Guild draws all secondary characters into the story frame like a magnet, and once there the plot swirls around them. Although *Blood Game* is very thin on plot, its strength lies in Gorman's ability to draw out sympathy for his characters.

It wasn't long before publishers realized that Gorman's name could be used to front anthologies, and he was the editor for *Westeryear*, followed by *The Silver Spur Anthology of Western Fiction*. Undoubtedly Gorman will continue to produce Westerns of high quality for many years to come and will become an established name in the genre.

—Mike Stotter

GORT, Sam. *See* **BARRETT, Geoffrey John.**

GRAHAM, Harry. *See* **JONS, Hal.**

GRANT, Landon. *See* **GRIBBLE, Leonard.**

GRAVES, John. American. Born in Fort Worth, Texas, 6 August 1920. Educated at Rice University, Houston, B.A. 1942; Columbia University, M.A. 1948. Served in the United States Marine Corps, 1942–46: captain; Purple Heart. Married Jane Marshall Cole in 1958; two daughters. Instructor in English, University of Texas, Austin, 1948–50; Adjunct Professor of English, Texas Christian University, Fort Worth, 1957–65; consultant/writer, United States Department of the Interior, Washington, D.C., 1965–68. During 1950's travelled abroad, living in New York, Mexico, and Spain. Since 1968 freelance writer. Distinguished Alumnus, Rice University, 1983; president, 1984, and fellow, 1985, Texas Institute of Letters. Recipient: Texas Institute of Letters Carr P. Collins award, for nonfiction, 1960; Guggenheim fellowship, 1963; Rockefeller fellowship grant, 1972; Texas Institute of Letters Barbara McCombs/Lon Tinkle Memorial award, 1983. D.Litt.: Texas Christian University, 1983. Address: P.O. Box 667, Glen Rose, Texas 76043, U.S.A.

WESTERN PUBLICATIONS

Uncollected Short Stories

"The Last Running," in *The Best American Short Stories 1960*. Boston, Houghton Mifflin, 1960; published separately, Austin, Encino Press, 1974.
"The Dreamers," in *Readers and Writers*, May–June 1966.

Other

Home Place: A Background Sketch in Support of a Proposed Restoration of Pioneer Building in Fort Worth, Texas. Fort Worth, Pioneer Texas Heritage Committee, 1958.
Brazos Trilogy:
Goodbye to a River: A Narrative. New York, Knopf, 1960.
Hard Scrabble: Observations on a Patch of Land. New York, Knopf, 1974.
From a Limestone Ledge: Some Essays and Other Ruminations About Country Life in Texas. New York, Knopf, 1980.
The Creek and the City: Urban Pressures on a Natural Stream, Rock Creek Park and Metropolitan Washington. Washington, D.C., Department of the Interior, 1967.
The Nation's River. Washington, D.C., G.P.O., 1968.
The Water Hustlers, with R. Boyle and T.H. Watkins. San Francisco, Sierra Club, 1971.
Texas Heartland: A Hill Country Year, photographs by Jim Bones. College Station, Texas A & M University Press, 1975.
Blue and Some Other Dogs. Austin, Encino Press, 1981.
Of Birds and Texas. Fort Worth, Gentling Editions, 1986.

Editor, *Mall* by Gail W. Starr. N.p., Envision Commission, 1980.

*

Manuscript Collections: Humanities Research Center, University of Texas, Austin; Southwest Texas State University, San Marcos, Texas.

Critical Study: *John Graves* by Dorys Crow Grover. Boise, Idaho, Boise State University, 1989.

John Graves comments:

Fiction has been a minor part of my work, and all of it that I have published has been short in length. Primarily I seem to be an essayist, even when the essays turn out to be books. I suppose that I am a legitimate Westerner, my Texas heritage having often influenced and flavored my writing, and the Southwest being the region where I feel most at home, despite much wandering elsewhere in former years.

* * *

John Graves is the author of many essays and articles on the natural world of Texas, and has some seven books relating to Texas history, fiction, and folklore, including three exceptional nonfiction classics called the Brazos Trilogy: *Goodbye to a River*; *Hard Scrabble: Observations on a Patch of Land*, and *From a Limestone Ledge: Some Essays and Other Ruminations About Country Life in Texas*.

At the beginning of his writing career Graves was publishing short stories in magazines such as *Atlantic* and the *Texas Monthly* magazine. Three of his stories have received special recognition: "The Green Fly," "The Aztec Dog," and "The Last Running." His first published story, "Quarry," went to the *New Yorker* in 1947. The first of his Brazos Trilogy, *Goodbye to a River*, concerns a canoe trip he took in the autumn of 1957, after he learned that a stretch of the river, which winds across a number of counties west of Fort Worth, was to be dammed by the federal government. The Brazos is the largest river between the Rio Grande and the Red River, and third in size of all rivers flowing in Texas. The largest reservoir on the Brazos is Lake Whitney; another is Lake Possum Kingdom, and the stretch of the river between these two lakes is the major concern of Graves in his river book. The book is an autobiographical account of a man with his dog and what he sees as he drifts along on the river.

Goodbye to a River was the result of material left over from a magazine article Graves had contracted to write for *Holiday Magazine*. He said he found he had so much additional material that he just decided to write a book. Leaving the river, in *Hard Scrabble*, he writes about the ungentle use of the land. It is not an "account of a triumphant return to the land, a rustic success story, but mainly a rumination over what a certain restricted and unmagnificent patch of the earth's surface has meant to me, and occasionally over what it may mean in wider terms." The third of the Brazos books is *From a Limestone Ledge*, in which he continues to ruminate about the land and what it has meant to him. The Brazos Trilogy has brought Graves recognition as a true naturalist and the title of Dean of Texas Letters. The three works on country living in north central Texas give an intimate portrait of a landscape and culture as perceived and lived in by the author.

Graves's works have recurrent themes which center on Texas and the Southwest. The region is distinctive, and lends itself to strong interpretation, not only because the landscape is so various and beautiful, but also because its people are so disparate, with Poles, Germans, Mexicans, Swedes, and others providing a kaleidoscope of cultural themes—not only for writers, but also for music, dance, and the other arts. Like other artists, nature writers too see the world in a special way, for they are engaged in a search for a rhythm in which they can perceive the natural world, and Graves says, "it's a neverending fight to find it."

In addition to the Brazos Trilogy, and recognition for the three prize-winning stories, Graves has received special commendation for an especially fine essay titled "Blue and Some Other Dogs," which first appeared as "Ol' Blue," in *Texas Monthly*. The essay is about one of his favorite dogs, Blue, and appears in *From a Limestone Ledge*, although it has been republished several times and is presently in a hardcover edition by The Encino Press, Austin. In 1990 Lyons & Burford Publishers issued *The Last Running* in a beautiful hardcover edition with drawings by John Groth. "The Last Running" is a story about a last buffalo hunt on the plains of west Texas. "The Aztec Dog" is set in Mexico and concerns an elderly aristocratic man and a rather worthless American youth. The Aztec dog named Vidal has meaning in the lives of both. "The Green Fly" is a tragic story about a young man who learns the rewards of companionship with a learned old doctor. Set in Mexico, the story ends on a note of hope with the doctor as hero.

Graves has a number of other short stories, but his strength lies in the writing of essays, and he has a special interest in writing about nature. He is a superb writer—a stylist. His essays are clear and beautifully crafted. He is able to relate his experiences to the reader with the hope that they may understand some of nature's secrets, but admits he encounters problems he cannot solve. He brings to his prose a subtle wit, understated and provocative.

Although he complains about the destruction of the natural wild and seems to have little hope for better management of the natural resources, he meditates and speculates and would like to see humankind take better care of the earth. The strength of his work lies in his knowledge of nature, history, and folklore, and the development of these themes into interesting and readable material. He is widely read in literature and often humorously expands a problem he encounters through literary allusion.

—Dorys Grover

GREER, Jack. *See* **BARRETT, Geoffrey John.**

GREGORY, Jackson. American. Born in Salinas, California, 12 March 1882. Educated at the University of California, Berkeley, B.L. 1906. Married Lotus McGlashan in 1910; two sons. Teacher and principal of several California high schools, then reporter and journalist. *Died 12 June 1943.*

WESTERN PUBLICATIONS

Novels

The Outlaw. New York, Dodd Mead, 1916; as *The Splendid Outlaw*, London, Melrose, 1918.
The Short Cut. New York, Dodd Mead, 1916; London, Melrose, 1917.
Wolf Breed. New York, Dodd Mead, 1917; London, Melrose, 1918.
The Joyous Trouble Maker. New York, Dodd Mead, and London, Melrose, 1918.
Six Feet Four. New York, Dodd Mead, 1918; London, Melrose, 1919.
Judith of Blue Lake Ranch. New York, Scribner, and London, Melrose, 1919.
The Bells of San Juan. New York, Scribner, 1919; London, Melrose, 1920.
Man to Man. New York, Scribner, 1920; London, Hodder and Stoughton, 1921.
The Desert Valley. New York, Scribner, and London, Hodder and Stoughton, 1921.
Daughter of the Sun. New York, Scribner, 1921; London, Hodder and Stoughton, 1923.
The Everlasting Whisper: A Tale of the California Wilderness. New York, Scribner, and London, Hodder and Stoughton, 1922.
The Wilderness Trail. London, Hodder and Stoughton, 1923.
Timber-Wolf. New York, Scribner, 1923.
The Maid of the Mountain: A Romance of the California Wilderness. New York, Scribner, 1925; as *Babs of the Backwoods*, London, Hodder and Stoughton, 1925.
The Desert Thoroughbred: A Romance of the California Desert Country. New York, Scribner, and London, Hodder and Stoughton, 1926.
Emerald Trails. New York, Scribner, and London, Hodder and Stoughton, 1928.
Redwood and Gold. New York, Dodd Mead, and London, Hodder and Stoughton, 1928.
Sentinel of the Desert. New York, Dodd Mead, and London, Hodder and Stoughton, 1929.

Mystery at Spanish Hacienda. New York, Dodd Mead, 1929; as *Rapidan*, London, Hodder and Stoughton, 1929.
The Trail to Paradise. New York, Dodd Mead, and London, Hodder and Stoughton, 1930.
The Silver Star. New York, Dodd Mead, and London, Hodder and Stoughton, 1931.
Riders Across the Border. New York, Dodd Mead, and London, Hodder and Stoughton, 1932.
The Shadow on the Mesa. New York, Dodd Mead, 1933.
Red Rivals. London, Hodder and Stoughton, 1933.
High Courage. New York, Dodd Mead, and London, Hodder and Stoughton, 1934.
Valley of Adventure. New York, Dodd Mead, 1935; as *White Water Valley*, London, Hodder and Stoughton, 1935.
Into the Sunset. New York, Dodd Mead, and London, Hodder and Stoughton, 1936.
Mountain Men. New York, Dodd Mead, and London, Hodder and Stoughton, 1936.
Dark Valley. New York, Dodd Mead, and London, Hodder and Stoughton, 1937.
Sudden Bill Dorn. New York, Dodd Mead, 1937.
Marshal of Sundown. New York, Dodd Mead, and London, Hodder and Stoughton, 1938.
Mysterious Rancho. New York, Dodd Mead, 1938; London, Hodder and Stoughton, 1939.
Powder Smoke on Wandering River. New York, Dodd Mead, 1938; as *Powder Smoke*, London, Hodder and Stoughton, 1938.
Mad O'Hara of Wild River. New York, Dodd Mead, 1939; London, Hodder and Stoughton, 1940.
Rocky Bend. New York, Dodd Mead, 1939; as *High hand at Rocky Bend*, London, Hodder and Stoughton, 1939.
Secret Valley. New York, Dodd Mead, 1939; as *The Secret of Secret Valley*, London, Hodder and Stoughton, 1940.
The Girl at the Crossroads. New York, Dodd Mead, 1940.
I Must Ride Alone. New York, Dodd Mead, and London, Hodder and Stoughton, 1940.
The Far Call. New York, Dodd Mead, and London, Hodder and Stoughton, 1940.
The Red Law. New York, Dodd Mead, 1941; London, Hodder and Stoughton, 1942.
Guardians of the Trail. New York, Dodd Mead, and London, Hodder and Stoughton, 1941.
Ace in the Hole. New York, Dodd Mead, 1941; London, Hodder and Stoughton, 1942.
The Man from Texas. New York, Dodd Mead, 1942.
Two in the Wilderness. New York, Dodd Mead, 1942; London, Collins, 1948.
Border Line. New York, Dodd Mead, 1942; London, Collins, 1948.
Lonely Trail. New York, Dodd Mead, 1943; London, Collins, 1947.
The Man from Painted Rock. New York, Dodd Mead, 1943; London, Collins, 1949.
Aces High at Golden Eagle. Philadelphia, Blakiston, 1944; London, Hodder and Stoughton, 1947.
The Hermit of Thunder King. New York, Dodd Mead, 1945; London, Collins, 1949.
The Silver River. London, Collins, 1950.
The Lone Rider. New York, Popular Library, 1950.
Hardcase Range. New York, Popular Library, 1958.

Uncollected Short Stories

"Beyond the Law," in *Adventure* (New York), October 1915.
"If the Shoe Fits—," in *McBride's* (New York), April 1916.
"Yahoya," in *Adventure* (New York), August 1916.
"Silver Slippers," in *Adventure* (New York), November 1916.
"Beyond San Juan," in *Western Story* (New York), 14 October–18 November 1920.
"Treasure in the Hills," in *Western Story* (New York), 11 December 1920–22 January 1921.
"The Secret of Black Mountain," in *Western Story* (New York), 25 June 1921.
"The Diamond Trail," in *Western Story* (New York), 29 October–3 December 1927.
"Greasewood Gold," with Hal Waldo, in *Western Story* (New York), 11 August 1928.
"The Island in the Desert," in *Western Story* (New York), 22 September–3 November 1928.
"The Stone Safe," in *Western Story* (New York), 7 November 1931.
"Scared Deputy," in *Western Story* (New York), 14 January 1933.
"Gold in the Blue Smokes," in *Western Story* (New York), 12 December 1936–16 January 1937.
"Gun Thunder in Ghost Town," in *Western Story* (New York), 14 August–11 September 1937.
"Aces Come High," in *Western Story* (New York), 4 February–4 March 1939.
"Crossing the Gorge," in *Selected Western Stories*, edited by Leo Margulies. New York, Popular Library, 1949.
"The Light on Rainbow Mountain," in *West* (Kingswood, Surrey), October 1953.
"You Never Can Tell," in *West* (Kingswood, Surrey), November 1953.

OTHER PUBLICATIONS

Novels

Under Handicap. New York, Harper, 1914.
Ladyfingers. New York, Scribner, 1920; London, Melrose, 1921.
Captain Cavalier. New York, Scribner, and London, Hodder and Stoughton, 1927.
The Island of Allure: A Romance of the South Seas. London, Hodder and Stoughton, 1931; New York, Dodd Mead, 1934.
The House of the Opal. New York, Scribner, 1932; as *The First Case of Mr. Paul Savoy*, London, Hodder and Stoughton, 1933.
A Case for Mr. Paul Savoy. New York, Scribner, 1933; as *The Second Case of Mr. Paul Savoy*, London, Hodder and Stoughton, 1933.
Ru, The Conqueror. New York, Scribner, 1933.
The Emerald Murder Trap. New York, Scribner, 1934; as *The Third Case of Mr. Paul Savoy*, London, Hodder and Stoughton, 1934.
Lords of the Coast. New York, Dodd Mead, and London, Hodder and Stoughton, 1935.

Play

Screenplay: *Billy Jim*, with Frank Howard Clark, 1922.

* * *

Among the better-known writers of popular books of the range during the first half of the 20th century was Jackson Gregory, who wrote approximately 50 western novels. Beginning with *The Outlaw* (1916), he published two and sometimes three novels a year until his death.

Many of his Westerns are set on the California–Mexico border, and several involve a mystery. The *Times Literary*

Supplement refers to his reputation "as an adventure-novelist of anywhere in the West where raw passions in fighting and in love may be suitable." Certainly his heroes are usually dominant men who treat the heroines (and the villains) with something approaching brutality. Even a three-day beard gives one hero merely "greater vitality" (*The Everlasting Whisper*). There is a wide range of literary conventions embodied in Gregory's novels, from an untamed frontier girl educated by a sedate settler (*The Maid of the Mountain*), rivals for a young girl's inheritance (*Redwood and Gold*), villainous sheriffs, corrupt towns, gold fever, piracy in the 1820's along the California coast, eastern or even English visitors to the wild West. (Gregory wrote in other popular genres as well, including a group of mystery novels and a South Seas romance.)

Usually written in the formula western style, Gregory's stories are among the literary ancestors of today's popular western fiction. It is a kind of literature which has been continuously popular for nearly one hundred years, beginning with the Dime Novels of the late 1800's. From the literary point of view, nine-tenths of the popular range romances are negligible because of their stereotyped style, unconvincing characters, and exaggerated plots. But it is a mistake to consider all fictional stories of the cowboy and life on the cattle frontier as poor literature. There are many good western novels by excellent craftsmen.

—Dorys C. Grover

GREGORY, Lester. *See* **GRIBBLE, Leonard.**

GREGSON, Lee F. New Zealander. Address: c/o Robert Hale Ltd., Clerkenwell House, 45–47 Clerkenwell Green, London EC1R QHT, England.

WESTERN PUBLICATIONS

Novels

The Killings at Sligo. London, Hale, 1989.
The Ballad of the Stalking Man. London, Hale, 1989.
A Posse from Stratton Forks. London, Hale, 1990.
The Pistol and the Rose. London, Hale, 1990.
The Man Out There. London, Hale, 1990.
The Gunman from the Grave. London, Hale, 1991.
Hanging Day. London, Hale, 1991.

* * *

Every so often a new writer will come, apparently from nowhere, to push the confines of his chosen genre that much wider. He or she may decide to shake up a few old themes and present them in a new way, or add that extra, elusive *something* to his characters to make them behave less like stereotypes and more like real people. Maybe they will enhance the quality of their writing by using familiar words in a new or clever way.

One such writer is New Zealander Lee F. Gregson, who made his first appearance on the British western scene with 1989's *The Killings at Sligo*, a flawed but nonetheless interesting introductory novel which, despite being probably the weakest of his stories to date, still hints strongly at the originality of the work to come. The book tells the story of what happens following a bank robbery in the town of the title, during which several innocent bystanders are slain. One man, who calls himself Jack Gray, comes out of the hills to track down the outlaws responsible, and the revelation of his true identity, as well as his motive for embarking upon such a manhunt, are two of the key ingredients which set the story apart from others of its type; a knack for creating three-dimensional characters, and an apparently genuine enthusiasm for documenting their often less than perfect lives on the frontier, are two more.

Gregson also rings the changes in his range story *The Ballad of the Stalking Man* and another variation on the manhunting theme, *A Posse from Stratton Forks*, mainly by odd little touches—an unexpected slant here or the creation of a particularly fresh character there.

Quite probably the best of his novels so far—and certainly one which confirms his preference for mixing elements of the mystic or inexplicable with the Western—is *The Pistol and the Rose*, in which a wounded, nameless stranger staggers into a sleepy border town called Delpano and is taken in by one of the local prostitutes, Rosa, who nurses him back to life. During the stranger's convalescence, however, the two men from whom he has evidently been fleeing ride into town and embark upon a campaign of terror in the hopes that someone will betray the whereabouts of the wounded man. Only three people know that information, however: Rosa (from whose point of view the story is told), the local priest, and an inoffensive cripple named Carlos. As the tension mounts, Rosa (an excellently drawn character) struggles to keep her nerve. But when Poland and Gault begin to systematically set fire to the town, the nameless stranger realises that he can afford to recuperate no longer, and finally goes out to meet his pursuers . . .

A most unusual, haunting and vaguely supernatural western, *The Pistol and the Rose* raises more questions than it answers. Who is the nameless man? Why was he being hunted? That he is no stranger to death and violence becomes obvious in one moment of bed-ridden introspection which neatly showcases Gregson's way with words; "It was something with which he was already acquainted, and now in his mind could see again, in other places, the soundless enactments of death in ramshackle streets; flashes of fire, mouths opening in screams that were forever soundless; sombre, slow processions wending to burial grounds that were shrouded in dust, footfalls of dark mourners, without sound; desert lands clawed with brush, shifting with driven sand, where there were the soundless screams of dying horses, a land of mummers with the skull's heads of the long dead." Even though there are few, if any, satisfactory explanations for what happens in Gregson's dusty, scared little town, the book remains exactly that—satisfactory. The author also adopts a gentle but formal style of writing, deliberately Spanish in intonation, to emphasise the story's Mexican location, and describes firearms as huge, heavy objects to further reinforce Rosa's hitherto total unfamiliarity with guns and gunmen.

Gregson again blends the western with the vaguely mysterious in *The Man Out There*, constantly describing his main villain, a gun-fast killer-for-hire named Kyle, as "the dark man" to underline the character's almost uncanny skill with weapons. The hero of the book is Tom Hallet, a peacekeeper of some repute whose devotion to duty, as well as to a town which doesn't especially like him, caused his wife to walk out on him some unspecified time before. Now, as Hallet grows older, he begins to understand what his one true friend, Kemble, means about there always being a "man out there" looking to challenge him and, by besting him in a gunfight, adding something to his own reputation. Before he can get out of the badge-packing life and stop living each day as a potential target, however, Kyle, an old enemy from his past, comes to town . . .

Gregson is a writer of great skill and imagination. He creates interesting stories and tells them in a quiet but effective manner, often employing multiple viewpoints and italicised flashbacks. A tendency towards clipped and rather old-fashioned dialogue sometimes lets him down, but in the main he strikes a good balance between speech and description. Similarly, the pace of his westerns can sometimes fluctuate, and quite often they appear to lack a definite focus, but generally they are fast-moving and ultimately carry a strong, though never preachy, moral. Insightful characterisation of men and women is another of Gregson's strengths, as also is his ability to depict convincing and sometimes bittersweet romance without resorting to sentimentality. Quite apart from all this, however, his books are worth reading for the sheer pleasure of seeing words used well—and in Gregson's case, that means very well indeed.

—David Whitehead

GREY, Romer Zane. *See* **CURRY, Tom.**

GREY, Zane. American. Born Pearl Zane Gray in Zanesville, Ohio, 31 January 1872. Educated at Moore High School, Zanesville; University of Pennsylvania, Philadelphia, D.D.S. 1896. Married Lina Elise Roth in 1905; two sons and one daughter. Practised dentistry in New York City, 1896–1904; thereafter a full-time writer; traveled in the West, 1907–18; settled in California, 1918. *Died 23 October 1939.*

WESTERN PUBLICATIONS

Novels

Betty Zane. New York, Charles Francis Press, 1903; London, Hodder and Stoughton, 1920.
The Spirit of the Border. New York, Burt, 1906; London, Laurie, 1920.
The Last of the Plainsmen. New York, Outing, and London, Hodder and Stoughton, 1908.
The Last Trail. New York, Burt, 1909; London, Laurie, 1920.
The Heritage of the Desert. New York, Harper, 1910; London, Nelson, 1918.
Riders of the Purple Sage. New York, Harper, 1912; London, Nelson, 1919.
Desert Gold. New York, Harper, 1913; London, Nelson, 1919.
The Light of Western Stars. New York, Harper, 1914; London, Nelson, 1919.
The Rustlers of Pecos County. New York, Munsey, 1914; Hornchurch, Essex, Henry, 1980.
The Lone Star Ranger. New York, Harper, 1915; London, Nelson, 1919.
The Rainbow Trail. New York, Harper, 1915; London, Nelson, 1919.
The Border Legion. New York, Harper, 1916; London, Nelson, 1919.
Wildfire. New York, Harper, 1917; London, Nelson, 1920.
The U.P. Trail. New York, Harper, 1918; as *The Roaring U.P. Trail*, London, Hodder and Stoughton, 1918.
The Desert of Wheat. New York, Harper, and London, Hodder and Stoughton, 1919.
The Man of the Forest. New York, Harper, and London, Hodder and Stoughton, 1920.
The Mysterious Rider. New York, Harper, and London, Hodder and Stoughton, 1921.
To the Last Man. New York, Harper, and London, Hodder and Stoughton, 1922.
Wanderer of the Wasteland. New York, Harper, and London, Hodder and Stoughton, 1923.
The Call of the Canyon. New York, Harper, and London, Hodder and Stoughton, 1924.
The Thundering Herds. New York, Harper, and London, Hodder and Stoughton, 1925.
The Vanishing American. New York, Harper, 1925; as *The Vanishing Indian*, London, Hodder and Stoughton, 1926.
Under the Tonto Rim. New York, Harper, 1926; London, Hodder and Stoughton, 1927.
Forlorn River. New York, Harper, 1927; London, Hodder and Stoughton, 1928.
Nevada. New York, Harper, and London, Hodder and Stoughton, 1928.
Wild Horse Mesa. New York, Harper, 1928; London, Hodder and Stoughton, 1929.
Fighting Caravans. New York, Harper, 1929; London, Hodder and Stoughton, 1930.
The Shepherd of Guadaloupe. New York, Harper, and London, Hodder and Stoughton, 1930.
Sunset Pass. New York, Harper, and London, Hodder and Stoughton, 1931.
Arizona Ames. New York, Harper, and London, Hodder and Stoughton, 1932.
Robbers' Roost. New York, Harper, and London, Hodder and Stoughton, 1932.
The Drift Fence. New York, Harper, and London, Hodder and Stoughton, 1933.
The Hash Knife Outfit. New York, Harper, and London, Hodder and Stoughton, 1933.
Code of the West. New York, Harper, and London, Hodder and Stoughton, 1934.
Thunder Mountain. New York, Harper, and London, Hodder and Stoughton, 1935.
The Trail Driver. New York, Harper, and London, Hodder and Stoughton, 1936.
The Lost Wagon Train. New York, Harper, and London, Hodder and Stoughton, 1936.
West of the Pecos. New York, Harper, and London, Hodder and Stoughton, 1937.
Majesty's Rancho. New York, Harper, 1938; London, Hodder and Stoughton, 1942.
Raiders of Spanish Peaks. New York, Harper, and London, Hodder and Stoughton, 1938.
Western Union. New York, Harper, and London, Hodder and Stoughton, 1939.
Knights of the Range. New York, Harper, and London, Hodder and Stoughton, 1939.
30,000 on the Hoof. New York, Harper, and London, Hodder and Stoughton, 1940.
Twin Sombreros. New York, Harper, and London, Hodder and Stoughton, 1941.
Stairs of Sand. New York, Harper, and London, Hodder and Stoughton, 1943.
Shadow on the Trail. New York, Harper, and London, Hodder and Stoughton, 1946.

Valley of Wild Horses. New York, Harper, and London, Hodder and Stoughton, 1947.
Rogue River Feud. New York, Harper, 1948; London, Hodder and Stoughton, 1949.
The Deer Stalker. New York, Harper, and London, Hodder and Stoughton, 1949.
The Maverick Queen. New York, Harper, and London, Hodder and Stoughton, 1950.
The Dude Ranger. New York, Harper, 1951; London, Hodder and Stoughton, 1952.
Captives of the Desert. New York, Harper, 1952; London, Hodder and Stoughton, 1953.
Wyoming. New York, Harper, 1953; London, Hodder and Stoughton, 1954.
Lost Pueblo. New York, Harper, 1954; London, Hodder and Stoughton, 1955.
Black Mesa. New York, Harper, 1955; London, Hodder and Stoughton, 1956.
Stranger from the Tonto. New York, Harper, 1956; London, Hodder and Stoughton, 1957.
The Fugitive Trail. New York, Harper, 1957; London, Hodder and Stoughton, 1958.
The Arizona Clan. New York, Harper, 1958; London, Hodder and Stoughton, 1959.
Horse Heaven Hill. New York, Harper, 1959; London, Hodder and Stoughton, 1960.
Boulder Dam. New York, Harper, 1963; London, Hodder and Stoughton, 1965.
The Reef Girl. New York, Harper, 1977.
The Buffalo Hunter, edited by Loren Grey. New York, Belmont, 1977; Hornchurch, Essex, Henry, 1979.
The Westerner, edited by Loren Grey. New York, Belmont, 1977.
Tenderfoot and *The Secret of Quaking Asp Cabin.* New York, Belmont, 1977; Hornchurch, Essex, Henry, 1982.
Lost in the Never Never and Silvermane. New York, Belmont, 1977; Hornchurch, Essex, Henry, 1982.

Short Stories

Zane Grey, Outdoorsman: Zane Grey's Best Hunting and Fishing Tales, edited by George Reiger. Englewood Cliffs, New Jersey, Prentice Hall, 1972.
Zane Grey's Greatest Western [Indian, Animal] Stories, edited by Loren Grey. New York, Belmont, 3 vols., 1975; *Western [and Indian] Stories* published Hornchurch, Essex, Henry, 2 vols., 1979–80.
The Big Land, edited by Loren Grey. New York, Belmont, 1976.
Yaqui and Other Great Indian Stories, edited by Loren Grey. New York, Belmont, 1976.
Shark! Zane Grey's Tales of Man-Eating Sharks, edited by Loren Grey. New York, Belmont, 1976.
Savage Kingdom. Hornchurch, Essex, Henry, 1979.

Uncollected Short Stories

"From Missouri," in *The Arbor House Treasury of Great Western Stories*, edited by Bill Pronzini and Martin H. Greenberg. New York, Arbor House, 1982.
"Tappan's Burro," in *The Western Hall of Fame*, edited by Bill Pronzini and Martin H. Greenberg. New York, Morrow, 1984.
"The Ranger," in *The Texans*, edited by Bill Pronzini and Martin H. Greenberg. New York, Fawcett, 1988.

Other Publications

Novels

The Day of the Beast. New York, Harper, 1922.
Wilderness Trek. New York, Harper, 1944; London, Hodder and Stoughton, 1945.

Plays

Screenplays: *The Vanishing Pioneer*, with others, 1928; *Rangle River*, with Charles and Elsa Chauvel, 1936.

Other (for children)

The Short-Stop. Chicago, McClurg, 1909.
The Young Forester. New York, Harper, 1910; London, Nelson, 1922.
The Young Pitcher. New York, Harper, 1911; London, Lloyds, 1919.
The Young Lion Hunter. New York, Harper, 1911; London, Nelson, 1919.
Ken Ward in the Jungle. New York, Harper, 1912; London, Nelson, 1919.
The Red-Headed Outfield and Other Baseball Stories. New York, Grosset and Dunlap, 1920.
Tappan's Burro and Other Stories. New York, Harper, and London, Hodder and Stoughton, 1923.
Don: The Story of a Lion Dog. New York, Harper, 1928.
The Wolf Trackers. New York, Harper, 1930.
Book of Camps and Trails. New York, Harper, 1931.
King of the Royal Mounted [and the Northern Treasure, in the Far North, Gets His Man, Policing the Far North, and the Great Jewel Mystery, and the Ghost Guns of Roaring River]. Racine, Wisconsin, Whitman, 7 vols., 1936–46.
The Ranger and Other Stories. New York, Harper, and London, Hodder and Stoughton, 1960.
Blue Feather and Other Stories. New York, Harper, 1961; London, Hodder and Stoughton, 1962.

Other

Nassau, Cuba, Yucatan, Mexico: A Personal Note of Appreciation of These Nearby Foreign Lands. New York, New York and Cuba Mail, 1909.
Tales of Fishes [Lonely Trails, Southern Rivers, Fishing Virgin Seas, the Angler's Eldorado—New Zealand, Swordfish and Tuna, Fresh Water Fishing, Tahitian Waters]. New York, Harper, 8 vols., and London, Hodder and Stoughton, 8 vols., 1919–31; augmented edition of *Tales of the Angler's El Dorado*, as *Angler's El Dorado: Grey in New Zealand*, 1982.
An American Angler in Australia. London, Hodder and Stoughton, 1936; New York, Harper, 1937.
Adventures in Fishing, edited by Ed Zern. New York, Harper, 1952.
The Undiscovered Zane Grey Fishing Stories, edited by George Reiger. Piscataway, New Jersey, New Century, 1983.
Zane Grey: A Photographic Odyssey (photographs), text by Loren Grey. Dallas, Taylor, 1985.

*

Bibliography: *Zane Grey, Born to the West: A Reference Guide* by Kenneth W. Scott, Boston, Hall, 1979.

Critical Studies: *Zane Grey: A Biography* by Frank Gruber, New York, World, 1970; *Zane Grey* by Carlton Jackson, New York, Twayne, 1973; *Zane Grey* by Ann Ronald, Boise, Idaho,

Boise State University Press, 1975; *Zane Grey: Story Teller* by Carol Gay, Columbus, State Library of Ohio, 1979; *Zane Grey's Arizona* by Candace C. Kant, Flagstaff, Arizona, Northland Press, 1984; *Zane Grey, A Documented Portrait: The Man, The Bibliography, The Filmography* by G.M. Farley, Tuscaloosa, Alabama, Portals Press, 1985.

* * *

During his prolific 30-year career as a western writer, Zane Grey wrote on just about every aspect of the American West—the railroad, the telegraph, the cattle drive, the mountains, the range, the canyons, the desert, cowboys, outlaws, gunmen, Indians, Mexicans, Mormons, buffaloes, wild horses, range wars between cattlemen, and the timeless feud between cattlemen and sheepherders. Much of his knowledge was gained first-hand through trips in the regions he wrote about; in addition, he performed diligent historical research (*The U.P. Trail* and *Western Union*, notably) and collected extensive background material through personal inquiry and interview (*To the Last Man* and *Robbers' Roost*).

Although he came by much of his material originally, his literary method was derivative. He was heavily influenced by books he read in his youth—*Robinson Crusoe*, *The Last of the Mohicans*, and Harry Castlemon's *Frank in the Mountains* and *Frank at Don Carlos' Rancho*—and the indebtedness (especially to Cooper) is frequently evident in Grey's work. He is often and justly criticized for his use of the language (the leading western fiction magazine of the late 1970's and early 1980's decrees, in its guidelines, "Try not to write like Zane Grey"), for he adopted the idiom of 19th-century romance without rejuvenating it.

The mass audience, nevertheless, has continued to read his books. Of Grey's extensive list of productions, some works have prevailed as perennially more readable than others. *The Man of the Forest* and *Wanderer of the Wasteland*, explorations of the relationship between man and nature, were popular in their day but have not remained so. Those novels most widely read today are *Riders of the Purple Sage*, *The U.P. Trail*, and *The Vanishing American*.

Riders of the Purple Sage has been his best-known novel. Like all Grey novels, it is distinguished by an urgent evocation of the landscape; it generates a *Robinson Crusoe* type of appeal from its romantic seclusion in an Edenic enclave. It succeeds as entertainment fiction through strong suspense and mystery, application of moral relativity rather than absolute law, and vicarious wish-fulfillment through definite problem-solving and domestic happiness. Simultaneously, it is marred by frequent overly lavish landscape descriptions, archaic diction, stilted dialogue, unrefined bigotry in its anti-Mormon sentiment, and an uncertain and sometimes puerile depiction of erotic attraction.

The U.P. Trail has earned its fame by virtue of its sound historical detail about the building of the transcontinental railroad. As historical edification it is gratifying, but Grey has chosen to undergird the historical exposition with a worn-out melodramatic plot (hero, abducted heroine, ogre villains) and a continuous explication of Grey's second-hand naturalism. This novel also presents a seeming contradiction in that it celebrates the march of the railroad as a great achievement of man, and then it closes by suggesting that the railroad will help defeat and displace the American Indian, for whom Grey had sympathies.

The Vanishing American was the novel that Grey wished to be remembered by, and it displays his strengths and weaknesses. In its day it constituted heated social commentary on the treatment of American Indians on the reservation. It successfully elicits sympathy for the Indians' mistreatment at the hands of government administrators, but it often degenerates into a bombastic panegyric to the noble and dispossessed savage. It exposes corrupt missionaries and Indian gents, but it reduces their seriousness by casting them in the roles of typically overbearing villains spurred on by cupidity and lust. The novel displays the beauty of the Arizona desert and it makes metaphoric use of the famous Zane Grey sunsets; it explicates (although somewhat tediously) the affinity between man and his natural environment. Grey further analyzes (explicitly and at great length) the spiritual consequences of being caught between two cultures: Nophaie, the Indian hero, was educated by the whites but is elementally rooted in the natural world of his people. Complicating this conflict, Grey dares to place, at the center of his novel, the love between a red man and a white woman; but, in adhering to the precedent set down in Cooper's *The Last of the Mohicans*, he does not dare to end the novel with an interracial marriage.

A few of Grey's other novels deserve passing comment by merit of their characteristic features. *The Lone Star Ranger* has been praised for its insight into the psychological composition of a gunman, and for its portrayal of the difficulties one faces in trying to escape a sordid past. The subject of the novel is original to Grey (and he deserves praise for varying his theme from one work to the next, at least through the 1920's), and with his characteristic prolixity he explores his topic fully. *To the Last Man* integrates the sheepherder-cattlemen feud with a Romeo-Juliet Plot, and it features a half-Indian hero and a nature-girl heroine; Grey's characterization of the heroine is relatively daring (bared bosoms also occur in *Riders of the Purple Sage* and *The U.P. Trail*). *Knights of the Range*, set at a place called Don Carlos' Rancho, has been praised for its depiction of the black cowboy, a figure often overlooked in western fiction. The characterization of Ride-'Em Jackson, however, is hardly flattering, nor is Grey's commentary on Mexican women in this novel. His characterization is stereotyped throughout his work, and his rendering of dialect is frequently exaggerated; in this novel, these weaknesses become flaws that offset some of the virtues of Grey's more sympathetic treatment of non-whites.

Grey's novels have enjoyed perpetual popularity because, like the most popular Westerns by any author, they articulate problems clearly (albeit simply and often verbosely) for the common reader, and they provide safe, comfortable, reassuring answers. His novels affirm the reader's faith in love between man and woman, in the benefits of progress, in the dependability of law and justice, and in the benevolent power of nature. In an obituary notice in the *Saturday Review*, Burton Rascoe (one of Grey's less favorable critics) predicted that Grey would fade into obscurity because "each generation produces its own Zane Greys." Although Grey has suffered at the hands of literary scholars, he has continued to find new readers in successive generations. Only in recent years has he been surpassed (by Louis L'Amour) as the all-time best-selling western writer; and judging from his continuing popularity, one expects that Zane Grey's novels will continue to find new readers in generations to come.

—John D. Nesbitt

GRIBBLE, Leonard (Reginald). Also wrote as Sterry Browning; Stetson Cody; Lee Denver; James Gannet; Landon Grant; Lester Gregory; Leo Grex; Louis Grey; Chuck Kelso; Cole Laramee; Peirs Marlow; Dexter Muir; Bruce Sanders; Steve Shane. British. Born in London, 1 February 1908.

Educated at schools in England. Served in the Press and Censorship Division of the Ministry of Information, London, 1940–45. Married Nancy Mason in 1932; one daughter. Worked as literary advisor to several publishers; started Empire Bookshelf series, B.B.C. Radio, London. Founding member, Crime Writers Association, 1953. *Died.*

Western Publications

Novels as Lee Denver (series: Cheyenne Jones)

Cheyenne Swings a Wide Loop. London, Mayflower, 1971.
Cheyenne Jones, Maverick Marshal. London, Hale, 1977.
Cheyenne's Sixgun Justice. London, Hale, 1980.
Cheyenne's Trail to Perdition. London, Hale, 1982.
Cheyenne's Two-Gun Shoot-Out. London, Hale, 1983.
Cheyenne at Dull Knife Pass. London, Hale, 1984.
Close Call for Cheyenne. Bath, Chivers, 1988.

Novels as Stetson Cody (series: Jim "Cactus" Clancy)

Cactus Clancy Rides. London, W.H. Allen, 1949.
The Range Hawk. London, W.H. Allen, 1950.
Texas Triggers. London, W.H. Allen, 1951.
Wolf Trail. London, W.H. Allen, 1952.
Cactus Justice. London, W.H. Allen, 1952.
Overland Guns. London, W.H. Allen, 1953.
Vengeance Rider. London, W.H. Allen, 1954.
Rawhide Range. London, W.H. Allen, 1955.
Branding Bullets. London, W.H. Allen, 1956.
Gunsmoke at Necktie. London, W.H. Allen, 1957.
Moon River Outlaw. London, W.H. Allen, 1957.
Double X Ranch. London, W.H. Allen, 1958.
Renegade Triggers. London, W.H. Allen, 1959.
Sagebrush Bandit. London, W.H. Allen, 1959.
Colt Fever. London, W.H. Allen, 1960.
Hair-Trigger Justice. London, W.H. Allen, 1961.
The Violent Breed. London, W.H. Allen, 1962.
The Fast Gun. London, W.H. Allen, 1963.
Trouble Shooter. London, W.H. Allen, 1964.
The Wide Loop. London, W.H. Allen, 1964.
Lawdog's Bite (Clancy). London, W.H. Allen, 1965.
The Gunslick Code (Clancy). London, W.H. Allen, 1965.
Sinister Valley. London, Jenkins, 1967.
Guns along the Ruthless (Clancy). London, Hale, 1973.

Novels as Landon Grant

Rustlers' Gulch. London, Rich and Cowan, 1935.
Wyoming Deadline. London, Rich and Cowan, 1939.
Texas Buckaroo. London, Sampson Low, 1948.
Ramrod of the Bar X. London, Sampson Low, 1949.
Scar Valley Bandit. London, Sampson Low, 1951.
The Rawhide Kid. London, Burke, 1951.
Gunsmoke Canyon. London, Sampson Low, 1952.
Outlaws of Silver Spur. London, Stanley Paul, 1953.
Marshal of Mustang. London, Macdonald, 1954.
Thunder Valley Deadline. London, Stanley Paul, 1956.

Novels as Chuck Kelso

Trigger Hawks of the Bar Y. London, Muller, 1952.
Rimrock Rustlers. London, Muller, 1953.
Montana Lawdog. London, Muller, 1954.
Canyon of No Return. London, Muller, 1961.
Breed of the Pecos. London, Muller, 1962.
Dead Man's Range. London, Muller, 1964.
Doom Trail. London, Muller, 1965.

Novels as Steve Shane

Lone Star Kid. London, Muller, 1955.
Trigger Trail. London, Muller, 1959.
Guns of Sunset Mesa. London, Muller, 1963.
The Shadow Riders. London, Muller, 1965.

Other Publications

Novels

The Case of the Marsden Rubies. London, Harrap, 1929; New York, Doubleday, 1930.
The Gillespie Suicide Mystery. London, Harrap, 1929; as *The Terrace Suicide Mystery*, New York, Doubleday, 1929.
The Grand Modena Murder. London, Harrap, 1930; New York, Doubleday, 1931.
Is This Revenge? London, Harrap, 1931; as *The Serpentine Murder*, New York, Dodd Mead, 1932.
The Stolen Home Secretary. London, Harrap, 1932; as *The Stolen Statesman*, New York, Dodd Mead, 1932.
The Secret of Tangles. London, Harrap, 1933; Philadelphia, Lippincott, 1934.
The Yellow Bungalow Mystery. London, Harrap, 1933.
The Death Chime. London, Harrap, 1934.
The Riddle of the Ravens. London, Harrap, 1934.
The Signet of Death (as Louis Grey). London, Nicholson and Watson, 1934.
Mystery at Tudor Arches. London, Harrap, 1935.
The Case of the Malverne Diamonds. London, Harrap, 1936; New York, Greenberg, 1937.
Riley of the Special Branch. London, Harrap, 1936.
Who Killed Oliver Cromwell? London, Harrap, 1937; New York, Greenberg, 1938.
Tragedy in E Flat. London, Harrap, 1938; New York, Curl, 1939.
The Arsenal Stadium Mystery. London, Harrap, 1939; revised edition, London, Jenkins, 1950.
Coastal Commandoes (as Sterry Browning). London, Nicholson and Watson, 1946.
Atomic Murder. London, Harrap, and Chicago, Ziff Davis, 1947.
Hangman's Moon. London, W.H. Allen, 1950.
They Kidnapped Stanley Matthew. London, Jenkins, 1950.
The Frightened Chameleon. London, Jenkins, 1951; New York, Roy, 1957.
Mystery Manor. London, Goulden, 1951.
Crime at Cape Folly (as Sterry Browning). London, Clerke and Cockeran, 1951.
Santa Fe Gunslick (as Sterry Browning). London, Clerke and Cockeran, 1951.
The Glass Alibi. London, Jenkins, 1952; New York, Roy, 1956.
Murder Out of Season. London, Jenkins, 1952.
She Died Laughing. London, Jenkins, 1953.
Murder Mistaken, with Janet Green. London, W.H. Allen, 1953.
Sex Marks the Spot (as Sterry Browning). London, Long, 1954.
The Inverted Crime. London, Jenkins, 1954.
Sally of Scotland Yard, with Geraldine Laws. London, W.H. Allen, 1954.
Death Pays the Piper. London, Jenkins, 1956; New York, Roy, 1958.

Stand-In for Murder. London, Jenkins, 1957; New York, Roy, 1958.
Dangerous Mission. London, Brown and Watson, 1957.
Don't Argue with Death. London, Jenkins, and New York, Roy, 1959.
Wantons Die Hard. London, Jenkins, 1961; New York, Roy, 1962.
Heads You Die. London, Jenkins, 1964.
The Violent Dark. London, Jenkins, 1965.
Strip-Tease Macabre. London, Jenkins, 1967.
A Diplomat Dies. London, Jenkins, 1969.
Alias the Victim. London, Hale, 1971.
Programmed for Death. London, Hale, 1973.
You Can't Die Tomorrow. London, Hale, 1975.
Midsummer Slay Ride. London, Hale, 1976.
Crime on Her Hands. London, Hale, 1977.
Death Needs No Alibi. London, Hale, 1979.
Dead End in Mayfair. London, Hale, 1981.
The Dead Don't Scream. London, Hale, 1983.
Violent Midnight. London, Hale, 1986.

Novels as Bruce Sanders

Kiss for a Killer. New York, Roy, 1956.
Madame Bluebeard: A Case for Anatole Fox. New York, Roy, 1957.
Secret Dragnet. New York, Roy, 1957.
To Catch a Spy. New York, Roy, 1958.
Murder Behind the Bright Lights. London, Jenkins, 1958.
Murder in Lonely Places. London, Jenkins, 1960.
They Couldn't Lose the Body. London, Jenkins, 1966; as *The Telltale Corpus Delecti*, South Brunswick, New Jersey, Barnes, 1968.

Novels as Leo Grex

The Tragedy at Draythorpe. London, Hutchinson, 1931.
The Nightborn. London, Hutchinson, 1931.
The Lonely Inn Mystery. London, Hutchinson, 1933.
The Madison Murder. London, Hutchinson, 1933.
The Man from Manhattan. London, Hutchinson, 1934; New York, Doubleday, 1935.
Murder in the Sanctuary. London, Hutchinson, 1934.
Crooner's Swan Song. London, Hutchinson, 1935.
Stolen Death. London, Hutchinson, 1936.
Transatlantic Trouble. London, Hutchinson, 1937.
The Carlent Manor Crime. London, Hutchinson, 1939.
The Black-Out Murders. London, Harrap, 1940.
The Stalag Mites. London, Harrap, 1947.
King Spiv. London, Harrap, 1948.
Crooked Sixpence. London, Harrap, 1949.
Ace of Danger. London, Hutchinson, 1952.
Thanks for the Felony. London, Long, 1958.
Larceny in Her Heart. London, Long, 1959.
Terror Wears a Smile. London, Long, 1962.
The Brass Knuckle. London, Long, 1964.
Violent Keepsake. London, Long, 1967.
The Hard Kill. London, Long, 1969.
Kill Now—Pay Later. London, Long, 1971.
Die—as in Murder. London, Hale, 1976.
Death Throws No Shadow. London, Hale, 1976.
Mix Me a Murder. London, Hale, 1978.
Hot Ice. London, Hale, 1983.

Novels as Dexter Muir

The Pilgrims Meet Murder. London, Jenkins, 1948.
The Speckled Swan. London, Jenkins, 1949.
Rosemary for Death. London, Jenkins, 1953.

Short Stories

The Case-Book of Anthony Slade. London, Quality Press, 1937.
The Velvet Mask and Other Stories. London, W.H. Allen, 1952.
Superintendent Slade Investigates. London, Jenkins, 1956; New York, Roy, 1957.

Play

Screenplay: *Death by Design*, 1943.

Verse

Toy Folk and Nursery People. London, Jenkins, 1945.

Other

Queens of Crime. London, Hurst and Blackett, 1932.
Famous Feats of Detection and Deduction. London, Harrap, 1933; New York, Doubleday, 1934.
All the Year Round Stories, with Nancy Gribble. London, Hutchinson, 1935.
Heroes of the Fighting R.A.F. London, Harrap, 1941.
Epics of the Fighting R.A.F. London, Harrap, 1943.
Heroes of the Merchant Navy. London, Harrap, 1944.
Battle Stories of the R.A.F. London, Burke, 1945.
Great Detective Feats. London, Burke, 1946.
Murder First Class. London, Burke, 1946.
On Secret Service. London, Burke, 1946.
Famous Manhunts: A Century of Crime. London, Long, 1953; New York, Roy, 1955.
Adventures in Murder Undertaken by Some Notorious Killers in Love. London, Long, 1954; New York, Roy, 1955.
Triumphs of Scotland Yard: A Century of Detection. London, Long, 1955.
Famous Judges and Their Trials: A Century of Justice. London, Long, 1957.
Great Detective Exploits. London, Long, 1958.
Murders Most Strange. London, Long, 1959.
The True Book about the Old Bailey. London, Muller, 1959; New Rochelle, New York, Sportshelf, 1960.
Hands of Terror: Notable Assassinations of the Twentieth Century. London, Muller, 1960.
The True Book about the Mounties. London, Muller, 1960; New Rochelle, New York, Sportshelf, 1961.
Clues That Spelled Guilty. London, Long, 1961.
The True Book about Great Escapes. London, Muller, 1962.
When Killers Err. London, Long, 1962.
Stories of Famous Detectives. London, Barker, and New York, Hill and Wang, 1963.
They Challenged the Yard. London, Long, 1963.
The True Book about Smugglers and Smuggling. London, Muller, 1963.
The True Book about the Spanish Main. London, Muller, 1963.
Stories of Famous Spies. London, Barker, 1964.
Such Women Are Deadly. London, Long, 1965; New York, Arco, 1969.
Great Manhunters of the Yard. London, Long, and New York, Roy, 1966.

Stories of Famous Explorers. London, Barker, 1966.
They Had a Way with Women. London, Long, 1967; New York, Roy, 1968.
Stories of Famous Conspirators. London, Barker, 1968.
Famous Stories of Police and Crime. London, Barker, 1968.
Famous Historical Mysteries. London, Muller, 1969.
Famous Stories of Scientific Detection. London, Barker, 1969.
Stories of Famous Modern Trials. London, Barker, 1970; as *Justice?*, New York, Abelard Schuman, 1971.
Strange Crimes of Passion. London, Long, 1970.
Famous Detective Feats. London, Barker, 1971.
They Got Away with Murder. London, Long, 1971.
More Famous Historical Mysteries. London, Muller, 1972.
Sisters of Cain. London, Long, 1972.
Famous Feats of Espionage. London, Barker, 1972.
The Hallmark of Horror. London, Long, 1973.
Stories of Famous Master Criminals. London, Barker, 1973.
Such Was Their Guilt. London, Long, 1974.
Famous Stories of the Murder Squad. London, Barker, 1974.
They Conspired to Kill. London, Long, 1975.
Murder Stranger than Fiction (as Leo Grex). London, Hale, 1975.
Famous Mysteries of Detection. London, Barker, 1976.
Famous Mysteries of Modern Times. London, Muller, 1976.
The Cardinal's Diamonds. London, Hale, 1976.
The Deadly Professionals. London, Long, 1976.
Compelled to Kill. London, Long, 1977.
Detection Stranger than Fiction (as Leo Grex). London, Hale, 1977.
They Came to Kill. London, Long, 1979.
Mystery Stranger Than Fiction (as Leo Grex). New York, St. Martin's Press, and London, Hale, 1979.
These Crimes Made Headlines (as Leo Grex). London, Hale, 1980.
Crime Stranger Than Fiction. London, Hale, 1981.
Notorious Killers in the Night. London, Hale, 1983.
Mysteries Behind Notorious Crimes. London, Hale, 1984.
Notorious Crimes. London, Hale, 1985.
Such Lethal Ladies. London, Hale, 1985.
They Shot to Slay. London, Hale, 1986.

Editor, *A Christmas Treasury in Prose and Verse*. London, SPCK, and New York, Macmillan, 1929.
Editor, *The Jesus of the Poets: An Anthology*. London, Student Christian Movement Press, and New York, R.R. Smith, 1930.
Editor, *Best Children's Stories of the Year*. London, Burke, 4 vols., 1946–49.
Editor, *Fifty Famous Stories for Boys*. London, Burke, 1948.
Editor, *Fifty Famous Stories for Girls*. London, Burke, 1949.
Editor, *Fifty Famous Animal Stories* (for children). London, Burke, 1949.
Editor, *The Story Trove: A Collection of the Best Stories of Today for Boys and Girls*. London, Burke, 1950.
Editor, *Stories for Boys*. London, Spring Books, 1961.
Editor, *Stories for Girls*. London, Spring Books, 1961.
Editor, *Famous Stories of High Adventure* (for children). London, Barker, 1962; New York, Hill and Wang, 1964.
Editor, *Famous Stories of the Sea and Ships* (for children). London, Barker, 1962; New York, Hill and Wang, 1964.
Editor, *Great War Adventures*. London, Barker, 1966.

Other (for children)

The Secret of the Red Mill. London, Burke, 1948.
The Missing Speed Ace. London, Burke, 1950.
The Riddle of the Blue Moon. London, Bruke, 1950.
Speed Dermot, Junior Reporter. London, Bruke, 1951.
The True Book About Scotland Yard. London, Muller, 1957.
Famous Stories of the Wild West. London, Barker, 1967.

*   *   *

Leonard Gribble was a prolific British wordsmith who produced more than 200 full-length novels and anthologies in a career which spanned over half a century. Although his best-known work appears in the crime and thriller categories, however (particularly the long-running Inspector Anthony Slade sequence, published under his own name), he also penned several dozen traditional Westerns.

Most of these—which appeared under a string of suitable aliases such as Landon Grant, Sterry Browning, Cole Laramee, and so on—are straightforward and largely unremarkable "oaters" reflective of the formula Westerns of the 1940's and 1950's, when most of them were first published. The principal characters are usually young cattlemen, and the often unnecessarily complicated plots unfold against backdrops of ranches and small but troubled towns. Many of them revolve around rustling and murder (Gribble introduced elements of mystery into his Westerns on more than one occasion), but every so often he also reworked other, marginally less familiar themes, perhaps the best example being that of the admittedly well-worn story of the reluctant young outlaw who finally proves his worth by helping to stop a crime instead of committing it.

Of all his western pseudonyms, Stetson Cody proved to be one of Gribble's most enduring, and an interesting if flawed series of occasional novels featuring a range detective-turned-Deputy U.S. Marshal appeared under the name, beginning with *Cactus Clancy Rides* in 1949. Gribble's style changed little from one pen-name to the next, however, and the observations and comments one might make about Chuck Kelso, say, or Steve Shane, could apply equally well to the aforementioned Landon Grant and Cole Laramee.

This does not mean to say that Gribble's style did not *develop* over the years. Indeed, the differences between his earliest work in the genre and that published toward the end of his life are many and varied. For their time, his first few westerns were surprisingly violent, and though he toned this aspect of his work down in later years, he could still be fairly graphic ("The steel-shod hooves smashed the man's skull like an egg. Cheyenne winced at the sound of a human head being pulped into an oozy liquid of blood and brains") when he chose to be. In the earlier books he often cushioned some of the impact of the more gratuitous violence with a rather broad line in humour, but whether by accident or design, this became virtually non-existent in more recent titles. As a writer, Gribble seldom displayed much time for romance or any great degree of female involvement in his stories, and overall his women tended to get a rather raw deal at his hands, although to his credit he did appear to redress this somewhat in his last few books. His plots, too, underwent a metamorphosis of sorts, almost Daedalian in the earlier books but more streamlined—though by no means less meandering—in the later ones.

The most durable of all Gribble's western heroes is Cheyenne Jones, who features in many of the books published under the Lee Denver byline. Jones, like Cactus Jim Clancy before him, is a Deputy U.S. Marshal. Based in Wyoming, this tough but amiable peacekeeper first appeared in paperback with *Cheyenne Swings a Wide Loop* in 1971, but soon graduated to hardcover, in which form the bulk of his dozen adventures were published.

A fairly standard series in many respects, the Cheyenne stories (which always feature the hero's name in their titles) are nevertheless enlivened by surprisingly strong continuity and a number of recurring characters and locations (The Elk Horn Saloon being the most popular), which add a nice sense of "family" and reader involvement to the proceedings. Cheyenne himself is answerable to Marshal Sam Travis, a crusty old law-dog from whom he normally receives his assignments, and it is a neatly drawn relationship which predates that of Deputy Marshal Custis Long and his boss, the irascible Billy Vail, in the better-known Longarm Westerns. Cheyenne also has a junior deputy in the youthfully enthusiastic Matt Rossmer.

The stories echo most of the usual familiar themes, but are distinguished by some good plot twists and occasionally insightful characterisation. In *Cheyenne's Trail to Perdition*, for example, Jones, dispatched to find a rancher's daughter who has apparently run off to find her missing boyfriend, ends up smashing a rustling operation. In *Cheyenne's Two-Gun Shoot-Out*, Cheyenne sides with a young Quaker girl and her brother when they come under pressure from their trigger-happy neighbours. In *Cheyenne at Dull Knife Pass*, the Wyoming-based lawman is sent to bring in a bank robber and sheriff-killer named Spade Gambell, while the last book of the sequence, *Close Call for Cheyenne*, is another range war story which boasts an exceptionally good beginning. As with nearly all of Gribble's work, however, characterisation is, in the main, kept to a minimum, and historical and geographical detail is rather loose.

A sometimes tedious writer, Gribble's Westerns are frequently made all the more tiring by the steady stream of colloquialisms which proliferate both his speech ("Clay Jaggers and his Slash Circle outfit have been causing more smoke trouble. His crew are too damned ready to be proddy and grab iron. I think . . . you should take in Warbonnet Pass and cool those rannies. They are too durned trigger-itchy. Cool them, and nothing does that more effectively than tossing some lead around. It freezes an *hombre* quicker than ice in January") and prose ("Cheyenne . . . forked leather and checked his irons"), and far from adding colour or period feel to the text, this constant overuse of such slang tends to paint a picture of the author as a greenhorn. Misuse of such vernacular can also create some truly puzzling sentences, such as the scene in *Close Call for Cheyenne* where the hero "sprang into the kak and forked his mount"—in effect, climbing aboard his horse *twice*.

Now considered a somewhat dated writer, Gribble's Westerns can nevertheless still be relied upon to conjure up a whole string of proficient if largely uninspired set pieces in stories which adhere very much to expectation and tradition.

—David Whitehead

GRIFFIN, Andrew. *See* **HECKELMANN, Charles N.**

GROVE, Fred(erick Herridge). American. Born in Hominy, Oklahoma, 4 July 1913. Educated at the University of Oklahoma, Norman (studied under the Western author Foster Harris, the historian Walter Stanley Campbell, and the teacher and science-fiction writer Dwight V. Swain), B.A. in journalism 1937. Married Lucile Elizabeth Riley in 1938; one son. Reporter and sports editor, Cushing *Daily Citizen*, Oklahoma, 1937–39; reporter, Shawnee *Morning News*, Oklahoma, 1940–42; sports editor, Harlingen *Star*, Texas, 1942; reporter, 1943–44, and managing editor, 1944–45, Shawnee *Morning News and Star;* on copy desk, Oklahoma City *Times* and *Daily Oklahoman*, 1946–47; senior assistant, University of Oklahoma Public Relations office, 1947–53; part-time instructor of journalism, University of Oklahoma, 1964–68; director of public information, Oklahoma Educational Television Authority, Norman, 1969–74. Recipient: National Cowboy Hall of Fame Wrangler award, for story, 1961, for novel, 1968; Western Writers of America Spur award, for novel, 1962, 1977, 1982, for story, 1963, 1969. Agent: Oscar Collier, 2000 Flat Run Road, Seaman, Ohio 45679, U.S.A.

WESTERN PUBLICATIONS

Novels

Flame of the Osage. New York, Pyramid, 1958.
Sun Dance. New York, Ballantine, 1958; London, Corgi, 1960.
No Bugles, No Glory. New York, Ballantine, 1959.
Comanche Captives. New York, Ballantine, 1961.
The Land Seekers. New York, Ballantine, 1963.
Buffalo Spring. New York, Doubleday, 1967.
The Buffalo Runners. New York, Doubleday, 1968.
War Journey. New York, Doubleday, 1971.
The Child Stealers. New York, Doubleday, 1973.
Warrior Road. New York, Doubleday, 1974.
Drums Without Warriors. New York, Doubleday, 1976.
The Great Horse Race. New York, Doubleday, 1977.
Bush Track. New York, Doubleday, 1978; London, Hale, 1979.
The Running Horses. New York, Doubleday, 1980.
Phantom Warrior. New York, Doubleday, 1981.
Match Race. New York, Doubleday, 1982.
A Far Trumpet. New York, Doubleday, 1985.
Search for the Breed. New York, Doubleday, 1986.
Deception Trail. New York, Doubleday, 1988.
Bitter Trumpet. New York, Doubleday, 1989.

Uncollected Short Stories

"Hostage Trail," in *Spurs West*, edited by S. Omar Barker. New York, Doubleday, 1960.
"The Marshal of Indian Rock," in *Western Roundup*, edited by Nelson Nye. New York, Macmillan, 1961.
"Comanche Woman," in *The Pick of the Roundup*, edited by Stephen Payne. New York, Avon, 1963.
"The Homeseekers," in *They Opened the West*, edited by Tom W. Blackburn. New York, Doubleday, 1967.
"Be Brave, My Son," in *Searchlights*. New York, Harper, 1969.
"War Path," in *With Guidons Flying*, edited by Charles N. Heckelmann. New York, Doubleday, 1970.

*

Manuscript Collections: University of Wyoming, Laramie; Texas Tech University, Lubbock.

Fred Grove comments:

My writing interests have focused mainly on the changing American frontier from the Civil War on—the U.S. government's policy of forcing Indian tribes onto reservations and their resistance from one way of life to another, the near extermination of the great buffalo herds, pioneer families in a new land; much later, the exploitation of the oil-rich Osage Indians of Oklahoma during the so-called Roaring Twenties. Thanks to my father, who was a trail driver and rancher, and to my mother, who was of Osage and Sioux Indian blood, I feel fortunate that I can write about the American Indian and white man from a middle viewpoint, each in his own fair perspective—at least try.

As a writer grows in understanding, and time must pass for us to change, he often finds himself shifting back to his beginnings with clearer insights. As a boy, I was always interested in horses. Thus, in late years, it is refreshing to be writing about match races on the frontier, and also about modern Quarter Horse racing. Perhaps this is a sign of hoped-for maturity.

* * *

Fred Grove was born, lives, and works in the West that he writes about. His father was an oldtime cowman and his mother was of Osage and Sioux descent. His earlier novels, among them *Sun Dance*, *Comanche Captives*, *Buffalo Spring*, and *The Buffalo Runners*, focus on the vanishing frontier and also demonstrate the author's use of thematic emphasis. His characters grow and change in their understanding of the so-called uncivilized American Indian.

Another of Grove's story traits is his sympathy for women of the frontier. Although they are often plain of face and make do with little, they have their own beauty and sensuality, though Grove avoids strong sexual themes. One of his best examples is Serena Hubbard, a white girl in *The Land Seekers*. She gave birth to an Indian son while being held in Indian captivity, and yet this is a novel without losers.

Again in *War Journey* the continuing theme of change and development persists within the lead character as he lives among Indians. Paul Latimer Benedict, a sensitive young eastern artist, comes west just to paint Indians. Before long he is participating in raids, although he finally returns to the white world.

In *Warrior Road* the plot steps up to the early 1920's. In this case the viewpoint character is half Osage and half white, a racetrack driver who investigates the mysterious death of an Indian friend. With different variations the same happens in *Drums Without Warriors*. A World War I veteran enters the Osage reservation as an undercover FBI agent determined to solve a string of Indian murders. Recently the author has shifted his plots to quarter horse match racing, examples being *The Great Horse Race* (which won a Spur award), and *Bush Track*. There are threats of violence in these horse yarns, but no one gets shot—a departure from the author's earlier works. Grove's most modern western has been *The Running Horses*. In this novel he shifts to several viewpoints, and the result is an alternating tempo.

While the thrill of match racing is the core of the most popular tales, the author returned at least temporarily to his earlier themes in *Phantom Warrior*. Lt. Mackay plays the familiar role as the white man who grew to understand the warlike Apaches. His relationship with his Army scouts, the fierce Tontos, is good because he shares their dangers, lives as they do, and never lies to them.

Grove's characterizations are real and sympathetic. His plots are never complex, and he is an excellent storyteller. Nobody ever goes to sleep with a Fred Grove book in his hand.

—Leon C. Metz

GROVE, Frederick Philip. Canadian. Born Felix Paul Berthold Friedrich Greve, in Radomno, Prussia–Poland, 14 February 1879; naturalized citizen, 1921. Educated at St. Pauli school, Hamburg, 1886–95; Gymnasium des Johanneums, Hamburg, 1895–98; University of Bonn, 1898–1900; Maximiliens University, Munich, 1901–02; University of Manitoba, Winnipeg, B.A. 1921. Married Catherine Wiens in 1914; one daughter and one son. Writer and translator in Germany, 1902–09; imprisoned for fraud, 1903–04; emigrated to Canada c. 1909; settled in Manitoba: taught in Haskett, 1913, Winkler, 1913–15, Virdin, 1915–16, Gladstone, 1916–17, Ferguson, 1918, Eden, 1919–22, and Rapid City, 1922–24; editor, Graphic Press, Ottawa, 1929–31, and associate editor, *Canadian Nation*, 1929; manager of a farm in Simcoe, Ontario, 1931–38, and lived on the farm after his retirement. Recipient: Lorne Pierce Gold Medal, 1934; Canadian Writers' Federation pension, 1944; Governor-General's award, for nonfiction, 1947. D.Litt.: University of Manitoba, 1945, Fellow, Royal Society of Canada, 1941. *Died 19 August 1948.*

Western Publications

Novels

Settlers of the Marsh. Toronto, Ryerson Press, and New York, Doran, 1925.

Our Daily Bread. Toronto and New York, Macmillan, 1928; London, Cape, 1929.

The Yoke of Life. Toronto, Macmillan, and New York, R.R. Smith, 1930.

Fruits of the Earth. Toronto and London, Dent, 1933.

Short Stories

Tales from the Margin: The Selected Short Stories of Frederick Philip Grove, edited by Desmond Pacey. Toronto, McGraw Hill Ryerson, 1971.

Other Publications

Novels

Fanny Essler (in German). Stuttgart, Juncker, 1905.

Maurermeister Ihles Haus. Berlin, Schnabel, 1906; translated by Paul P. Gubbins, as *The Master Mason's House*, edited by Douglas O. Spettigue and A.W. Riley, Ottawa, Oberon Press, 1976.

A Search for America. Ottawa, Graphic, 1927; New York, Carrier, 1928.

Two Generations: A Story of Present-Day Ontario. Toronto, Ryerson Press, 1939.

The Master of the Mill. Toronto, Macmillan, 1944.
Consider Her Ways. Toronto, Macmillan, 1947.

Verse

Wanderungen. Privately printed, 1902.
Helena und Damon (verse drama). Privately printed, 1902.

Other

Oscar Wilde (in German). Berlin, Gose and Tetzlaff, 1903.
Randarabesken zu Oscar Wilde. Minden, Germany, Bruns, 1903.
Over Prairie Trails. Toronto, McClelland and Stewart, 1922.
The Turn of the Year. Toronto, McClelland and Stewart, 1923.
It Needs to Be Said. . . . Toronto and New York, Macmillan, 1929.
In Search of Myself. Toronto, Macmillan, 1946.
The Letters of Frederick Philip Grove, edited by Desmond Pacey. Toronto, University of Toronto Press, 1976.
An Edition of Selected Unpublished Essays and Lectures by Frederick Philip Grove Bearing On His Theory of Art, edited by Henry Makow. Ottawa, National Library of Canada, 1984.

Translator of works by Balzac, Robert and Elizabeth Barrett Browning, Cervantes, Ernest Dowson, Dumas, Flaubert, Gide, Le Sage, Meredith, Henri Murger, Pater, Wells, and Wilde into German, 1903–09.

*

Critical Studies: *Frederick Philip Grove*, Toronto, Copp Clark, 1969, and *FPG: The European Years* (includes bibliography), Ottawa, Oberon Press, 1973, both by Douglas O. Spettigue; *Frederick Philip Grove* by Ronald Sutherland, Toronto, McClelland and Stewart, 1969; *Frederick Philip Grove* edited by Desmond Pacey, Toronto, Ryerson Press, 1970; *Frederick Philip Grove* by Margaret R. Scobie, New York, Twayne, 1973; *Frederick Philip Grove*, Winnipeg, Manitoba. Department of Cultural Affairs and Historical Resources, 1981.

* * *

Both in quality and quantity, Frederick Philip Grove is now recognized as the most important writer of western Canadian fiction. A German immigrant, Grove in effect created a new Canadian identity for himself through his prairie novels and short stories set in rural Manitoba, where he taught school in the 1910's and 1920's. Grove's familiarity with late 19th-century European literature, and friendship with some of its authors, helped enrich and universalize his interpretation of the pioneering, homesteading experience to a degree unmatched by other prairie writers.

The conflicts in Grove's four prairie novels—*Settlers of the Marsh*, *Our Daily Bread*, *The Yoke of Life*, and *Fruits of the Earth*—pit his characters against the unremitting hardships of prairie homesteading, their own self-destructive natures, and the destructiveness of time. *Our Daily Bread* shows both the heroic determination and the futility of the homesteaders' attempts to build permanence and continuity across the generations, while *The Yoke of Life* is equally dour in treating the wasted life and death of a younger settler neurotically obsessed with the wrong woman, and quite incapable of mounting any assault on impermanence. More autobiographical is the struggle of the artist and cosmopolite to lead a fulfilling life in a wilderness of spiritual and cultural deprivation. Material progress, as represented by the cosmopolis, is not the answer; and the challenge of Abe Spalding and Niels Lundstedt in *Fruits of the Earth* and *Settlers of the Marsh*, respectively, is to preserve the old pastoral values, which are the best protection against eastern materialism's invasion of the western eden. In all four books, the vagaries of economics in a capitalist society or the psychology of the characters themselves mocks any effort to influence lives and events in time.

The inevitable, uncomprehending failure of these stoic, enduring heroes in the struggle against circumstances and an indifferent, if not hostile, environment marks Grove as a literary naturalist, and in fact he has many of the strengths and weaknesses of other writers in the European-American naturalist tradition: on the one hand, a massive solidity, a precision in rendering natural and social detail, and a straightforwardness of prose style and characterization; on the other, a dearth of wit, elegance, or innovation, and a penchant for melodrama, implausible narrative twists, and unwieldy structure. If early readers were loath to accept his grim view of the settling of the prairies, however, the full light of current critical and biographical scrutiny is revealing a complexity of thought, a strength of moral vision, and a contemporaneity in Grove's writings that not only make him the most durable of Canada's prairie writers, but a seminal figure in 20th-century Canadian literature as well.

—John H. Ferres

GROVER, Marshall. Pseudonym for Leonard Frank Meares. Also writes as Grant Barlow; Ward Brennan; Shad Denver; Frank Everton; Lester Malloy; Marshall McCoy; Glenn Murrell; Johnny Nelson; Robert E. Rand; Shane E. Sharpe; Clyde B. Shawn; Val Sterling; Lee Thorpe; Brett Waring. Australian. Born 13 February 1921. Stationed in Merauke, New Guinea with the Royal Australian Air Force Mobile Fighter Control Unit during World War II. Married in 1958; two daughters. Worked as a salesman, and as a clerk with the Australian Department of Immigration; mail sorter, Australian Post Office, eight years. Full-time writer. Address: c/o Horwitz Grahame Pty. Ltd., 506 Miller Road, Cammeray, New South Wales 2062, Australia.

WESTERN PUBLICATIONS

Novels

Trouble Town (as Johnny Nelson). Sydney, Cleveland, 1955.
Ghost Canyon Showdown. Sydney, Cleveland, 1955.
Wagon Boss. Sydney, Cleveland, 1955.
Savage Sundown (as Robert E. Rand). Sydney, Cleveland, 1955.
Ride or Die. Sydney, Cleveland, 1956.
Dollar Buys My Gun. Sydney, Cleveland, 1956.
Ramrod Rebel. Sydney, Cleveland, 1956.
The Violent Dawn. Sydney, Cleveland, 1956.
Whiplash. Sydney, Cleveland, 1956.
Proud Day at Packer's Creek. Sydney, Cleveland, 1956.
The Blue Hawk. Sydney, Cleveland, 1956.
Bullets Back East. Sydney, Cleveland, 1956.
Adios, Ben Strong. Sydney, Cleveland, 1956.
Kid Faro. Sydney, Cleveland, 1956.
Yaller! Sydney, Cleveland, 1956.
Stacked Deck (as Shad Denver). Sydney, Cleveland, 1956.

Johnny Ringo. Sydney, Cleveland, 1957.
The Enforcer. Sydney, Cleveland, 1957.
The Devil's Claw. Sydney, Cleveland, 1957.
Captive Canyon. Sydney, Cleveland, 1957.
Gun for a Marshal. Sydney, Cleveland, 1957.
Kid Fury. Sydney, Cleveland, 1957.
The Last Gunfight. Sydney, Cleveland, 1957.
Fast Shell. Sydney, Cleveland, 1957.
Busted Flush. Sydney, Cleveland, 1957.
The Lonely Gun. Sydney, Cleveland, 1957.
Siege at Round Rock. Sydney, Cleveland, 1957.
Long Trail North. Sydney, Cleveland, 1957.
Bullet Scar. Sydney, Cleveland, 1957.
Gun Wise. Sydney, Cleveland, 1957.
Lonesome Lightning. Sydney, Cleveland, 1957.
Outcast Trail. Sydney, Cleveland, 1957.
Along Came Jake. Sydney, Cleveland, 1958.
Gun Town. Sydney, Cleveland, 1958.
Pardon My Gun. Sydney, Cleveland, 1958.
The Survivors. Sydney, Cleveland, 1958.
Legacy of Hate. Sydney, Cleveland, 1958.
How Tall the Man. Sydney, Cleveland, 1958.
Gunsmoke Reunion. Sydney, Cleveland, 1958.
Wear the Star Proudly. Sydney, Cleveland, 1958.
The Wolf Pack. Sydney, Cleveland, 1958.
Vengeance Is a Bullet. Sydney, Cleveland, 1958.
Fury of a Mob. Sydney, Cleveland, 1958.
The Defender. Sydney, Cleveland, 1959.
Where the Guns Rode. Sydney, Cleveland, 1959.
My Kind of Law. Sydney, Cleveland, 1959.
Dawn Stage South. Sydney, Cleveland, 1959.
Dead Man Riding. Sydney, Cleveland, 1959.
Satan's Six-Gun. Sydney, Cleveland, 1959.
Blood Trail. Sydney, Cleveland, 1959.
Hang-Town. Sydney, Cleveland, 1959.
The Tin Badge. Sydney, Cleveland, 1959.
Wyoming Bound. Sydney, Cleveland, 1959.
The Showdowner. Sydney, Cleveland, 1959.
Shadow of a Lawman. Sydney, Cleveland, 1959.
Gunfighter's Dawn. Sydney, Cleveland, 1959.
Always a Lawman. Sydney, Cleveland, 1959.
The Lone Shadow. Sydney, Cleveland, 1959.
Back Down Fast. Sydney, Cleveland, 1959.
Violent Gun (as Brett Waring). Sydney, Cleveland, 1959.
Border Crisis. Sydney, Cleveland, 1959.
Get Out Alive! Sydney, Cleveland, 1959.
No Back Trail. Sydney, Cleveland, 1959.
Heat of Noon. Sydney, Cleveland, 1960.
Colt Conflict. Sydney, Cleveland, 1960.
Gunsmoke Challenge. Sydney, Cleveland, 1960.
Men of the Canyon. Sydney, Cleveland, 1960.
Posse Boss. Sydney, Cleveland, 1960.
Sound of Gunfire. Sydney, Cleveland, 1960.
Escort for a Badman. Sydney, Cleveland, 1960.
Gallows Cheater. Sydney, Cleveland, 1960.
Carbine. Sydney, Cleveland, 1960.
Johnny Law. Sydney, Cleveland, 1960.
The Last Gun. Sydney, Cleveland, 1960.
Every Violent Mile. Sydney, Cleveland, 1960.
Draw Down. Sydney, Cleveland, 1960.
Siege at Jethro. Sydney, Cleveland, 1960.
Day of Doom. Sydney, Cleveland, 1961.
Pursuit Trail. Sydney, Cleveland, 1961.
Best Gun Wins. Sydney, Cleveland, 1961.
Ambush at Forty-Mile. Sydney, Cleveland, 1961.
Call Me Trouble. Sydney, Cleveland, 1961.
Rope Scar. Sydney, Cleveland, 1961.
Five Desperate Men. Sydney, Cleveland, 1961.
Tall Shadow. Sydney, Cleveland, 1961.
Ghost Town Guns. Sydney, Cleveland, 1961.
Remember Buck Roarke. Sydney, Cleveland, 1961.
Wanted in Texas. Sydney, Cleveland, 1961.
Inherit My Gun. Sydney, Cleveland, 1961.
Johnny on the Prod. Sydney, Cleveland, 1961.
Vengeance Is a Tall Man. Sydney, Cleveland, 1961.
Kid Lawless. Sydney, Cleveland, 1961.
Voice of the Gun. Sydney, Cleveland, 1961.
Battle Valley. Sydney, Cleveland, 1961.
Widow Maker. Sydney, Cleveland, 1962.
Death Devil. Sydney, Cleveland, 1962.
Rampage. Sydney, Cleveland, 1962.
Bullets Won't Wait. Sydney, Cleveland, 1962.
Left for Dead. Sydney, Cleveland, 1962.
The Noose. Sydney, Cleveland, 1962.
Big Jim. Sydney, Cleveland, 1962.
.45 Calibre Trap. Sydney, Cleveland, 1962.
Boot Hill for Lawmen. Sydney, Cleveland, 1962.
Don't Call Me Hero. Sydney, Cleveland, 1962.
Trouble Along the Trail. Sydney, Cleveland, 1963.
Judgement at Bandera. Sydney, Cleveland, 1963.
Trouble Is a Long Rope. Sydney, Cleveland, 1963.
24 Hours at Anvil Rock. Sydney, Cleveland, 1963.
Brock Canyon Crisis. Sydney, Cleveland, 1963.
Trail's End Showdown. Sydney, Cleveland, 1963.
Three for Durango. Sydney, Cleveland, 1963.
Chad. Sydney, Cleveland, 1963.
Sixty Miles to Sundance. Sydney, Cleveland, 1964.
Saturday Night in San Ramon. Sydney, Cleveland, 1964.
The Two Lives of Luke Gault. Sydney, Cleveland, 1964.
Wes Blade. Sydney, Cleveland, 1964.
Kid Solitary. Sydney, Cleveland, 1964.
Shoot and Run. Sydney, Cleveland, 1964.
Kincaid. Sydney, Cleveland, 1964.
.44 Fury. Sydney, Cleveland, 1964.
Man from Denver. Sydney, Cleveland, 1964.
Eagle over Sonora. Sydney, Cleveland, 1964.
Jago. Sydney, Cleveland, 1964.
Aces Wild. Sydney, Cleveland, 1964.
Town to Tame (as Shane E. Sharpe). Sydney, Cleveland, 1964.
Ride with the Law. Sydney, Cleveland, 1965.
On the Run. Sydney, Cleveland, 1965.
Wanted. Sydney, Cleveland, 1965.
Too Late for Law. Sydney, Cleveland, 1966.
Trail Terror. Sydney, Cleveland, 1966.
Bounty Gun. Sydney, Cleveland, 1966.
Holster Heritage. Sydney, Cleveland, 1966.
Polka-Dot Kid. Sydney, Cleveland, 1966.
Whiplash. Sydney, Cleveland, 1966.
Born to Ramble. Sydney, Horwitz, 1970.
Colorado Runaround (as Leonard F Meares. London, Hale, 1991.

Novels (series: Larry and Stretch/Larry and Streak in all books)

Drift! Sydney, Cleveland, 1956.
Arizona Wildcat. Sydney, Cleveland, 1957.
Texans Are Trouble. Sydney, Cleveland, 1957.
Trigger Trap. Sydney, Cleveland, 1957.
Tall Riders. Sydney, Cleveland, 1957.
Trail Dust. Sydney, Cleveland, 1958.
Rawhide River Ambush. Sydney, Cleveland, 1958.
Bend of the River. Sydney, Cleveland, 1958.
Half-Cold Trail. Sydney, Cleveland, 1958.

Hell Raisers. Sydney, Cleveland, 1958.
Seventeen Guns. Sydney, Cleveland, 1958.
Ride Out, Texans. Sydney, Cleveland, 1958.
Tall, Tough And Texan. Sydney, Cleveland, 1959.
Texas Drifters. Sydney, Cleveland, 1959.
Ride Reckless. Sydney, Cleveland, n.d.
Day of the Posse. Sydney, Cleveland, 1959.
Decoys from Hell. Sydney, Horwitz, n.d.
North of Texas. Sydney, Cleveland, 1960.
Back in Texas. Sydney, Cleveland, 1960.
Texans Die Hard. Sydney, Cleveland, 1960.
Lone Star Hellions. Sydney, Cleveland, 1960.
Start Shooting, Texans. Sydney, Cleveland, 1961.
Where Danger Rides. Sydney, Cleveland, 1961.
Texans Never Quit. Sydney, Cleveland, 1961.
Lone Star Bodyguards. Sydney, Cleveland, 1961.
Texans Hit Hard. Sydney, Cleveland, 1961.
Saludos, Texans. Sydney, Cleveland, 1962.
Lone Star Lucky. Sydney, Cleveland, 1962.
Kid Wichita. Sydney, Cleveland, 1962.
Texans Ride Tall. Sydney, Cleveland, 1962.
Double Trouble. Sydney, Cleveland, 1962.
We're from Texas. Sydney, Cleveland, 1962.
The Lawless Miles. Sydney, Cleveland, 1962.
Bravados from Texas. Sydney, Cleveland, 1962.
Nomads from Texas. Sydney, Cleveland, 1962.
Ride Wild to Glory. Sydney, Cleveland, 1963.
Ride Out Shooting. Sydney, Cleveland, 1963.
Texans Walk Proud. Sydney, Cleveland, 1963.
Draw, Aim and Fire. Sydney, Cleveland, 1963.
Never Prod a Texan. Sydney, Cleveland, 1963.
Close in for Showdown. Sydney, Cleveland, 1963.
Texas Gun-Ghost. Sydney, Cleveland, 1963.
Lone Star Valiant (includes *Hellions, Reckoning, Fury, Reckless, Vengeance, Firebrands, Bodyguards, Lucky*). Sydney, Cleveland, 1963.
The Fast Right Hand. Sydney, Cleveland, 1963.
Follow the Texans. Sydney, Cleveland, 1963.
Lone Star Fury. Sydney, Cleveland, 1964.
Colorado Pursuit. Sydney, Cleveland, 1964.
Don't Count the Odds. Sydney, Cleveland, 1964.
Face the Gun. Sydney, Cleveland, 1964.
Find Kell Wade. Sydney, Cleveland, 1964.
A Texan in My Sights. Sydney, Cleveland, 1964.
Ride Slow, Ride Wary. Sydney, Cleveland, 1964.
Feud at Mendoza. Sydney, Cleveland, 1964.
Born to Drift. Sydney, Cleveland, 1964.
The Eyes of Texas. Sydney, Cleveland, 1964.
Nobody Wants Riley. Sydney, Cleveland, 1964.
Rob a Bank in Kansas. Sydney, Cleveland, 1964.
Now, Texan! Sydney, Cleveland, 1964.
Lone Star Vengeance. Sydney, Cleveland, 1965.
This Range Is Mine! Sydney, Cleveland, 1965.
The Emerson Challenge. Sydney, Cleveland, 1965.
Texas Rampage. Sydney, Cleveland, 1965.
Turn and Fire. Sydney, Cleveland, 1965.
All the Tall Men. Sydney, Cleveland, 1965.
Trouble Is Our Shadow. Sydney, Cleveland, 1965.
The Freebooters. Sydney, Cleveland, 1965.
The Big Dinero. Sydney, Cleveland, 1965.
Crisis in Babylon. Sydney, Cleveland, 1965.
Noon Stage to Denver. Sydney, Cleveland, 1965.
Lone Star Reckless. Sydney, Cleveland, 1965.
The Defiant Texans. Sydney, Cleveland, 1965.
Decoys from Texas. Sydney, Cleveland, 1966.
Border Storm. Sydney, Cleveland, 1966.
Diary of a Desperado. Sydney, Cleveland, 1966.
Lone Star Firebrands. Sydney, Cleveland, 1966.
Noon Train to Breslow. Sydney, Cleveland, 1966.
Cold Trail to Kirby. Sydney, Cleveland, 1966.
Too Many Texans. Sydney, Cleveland, 1966.
Wild Trail to Denver. Sydney, Cleveland, 1966.
Rouge Calibre. Sydney, Cleveland, 1966.
The Wayward Kind. Sydney, Cleveland, 1966.
Lone Star Reckoning. Sydney, Cleveland, 1966.
Gun Glory for Texans (as Marshall McCoy). New York, Bantam, 1966.
Trouble Trail Yonder (as Marshall McCoy). New York, Bantam, 1966.
Many a Wild Mile. Sydney, Horwitz, 1967.
Two Tall Strangers. Sydney, Horwitz, 1967.
Lone Star Rowdy. Sydney, Horwitz, 1967.
High Spade (as Marshall McCoy). New York, Bantam, 1967.
Tombstone for a Fugitive. Sydney, Horwitz, 1967.
The Texans Came Shooting. Sydney, Horwitz, 1967.
Boom Town Bravados. Sydney, Horwitz, 1967.
Too Rough for San Remo (as Marshall McCoy). New York, Bantam, 1967.
The Legend of Bell Canyon. Sydney, Cleveland, 1967; as Marshall McCoy, New York, Bantam, 1967.
The Bar G Bunch (as Marshall McCoy). New York, Bantam, 1968.
Wyoming Thunder (as Marshall McCoy). New York, Bantam, 1968.
Kin to the Wild Wind (as Marshall McCoy). New York, Bantam, 1968.
Big Day at Blue Creek (as Marshall McCoy) New York, Bantam, 1968.
Amarillo Ridge (as Marshall McCoy). New York, Bantam, 1968.
The Glory Wagon. Sydney, Horwitz, 1968.
Hour of Jeopardy. Sydney, Horwitz, 1968.
Calaboose Canyon. Sydney, Horwitz, 1968.
Guns Across the Rockies. Sydney, Horwitz, 1968.
Our Kind of Law. Sydney, Horwitz, 1968.
The Garrard Heritage (as Marshall McCoy). New York, Bantam, 1969.
Wheels Out of Jericho(as Marshall McCoy). New York, Bantam, 1969.
Hot Sky over Paraiso(as Marshall McCoy). New York, Bantam, 1969.
Three Trails to Modoc. Sydney, Horwitz, 1969; as Marshall McCoy, New York, Bantam, 1969.
Saturday Night in Candle Rock. Sydney, Horwitz, 1969.
Two for the Gallows. Sydney, Horwitz, 1969.
Gun Fury at Sun-up. Sydney, Horwitz, 1969.
Sundance Creek. Sydney, Horwitz, 1969.
The Noose-Cheaters. Sydney, Horwitz, 1969.
They Won't Forget Sweeney. Sydney, Horwitz, 1969.
Savage Sunday. Sydney, Horwitz, 1969.
Rampage at Rico Bend. Sydney, Horwitz, 1969.
San Saba Blockade. Sydney, Horwitz, 1970.
Fast, Free and Texan. Sydney, Horwitz, 1971.
The Feuders. Sydney, Horwitz, 1971.
The 4 O'Clock Fracas. Sydney, Horwitz, 1971.
Seven for Banner Pass. Sydney, Horwitz, 1971; Leicester, Thorpe, 1987.
Here Lies Andy McGraw. Sydney, Horwitz, 1971.
Montana Runaway. Sydney, Horwitz, 1971.
The Hellion Breed. Sydney, Horwitz, 1971; Leicester, Thorpe, 1987.
Hangrope for Beaumont. Sydney, Horwitz, 1971.
The Last Ambush. Sydney, Horwitz, 1971.
Gunsmoke in Utopia. Sydney, Horwitz, 1971.

War Dance at Red Canyon. Sydney, Horwitz, 1971.
Pursuit Trail. Sydney, Horwitz, 1973.
Mexican Jackpot. Sydney, Horwitz, 1973.
McCracken's Marauders. Sydney, Horwitz, 1973.
Red Bandana. Sydney, Horwitz, 1973.
Get Goin', Greeley. Sydney, Horwitz, 1973.
Guns for the Ladies. Sydney, Horwitz, 1973.
Cold-Eye Cordell. Sydney, Horwitz, 1973.
The Desperate Hours. Sydney, Horwitz, 1973.
Madigan's Day. Sydney, Horwitz, 1973.
Who Killed Rico? Sydney, Horwitz, 1973.
Dakota Red. Sydney, Horwitz, 1973.
The Predators. Sydney, Horwitz, 1973.
Hijacker's Moon. Sydney, Horwitz, 1973.
The Odds Against O'Shay. Sydney, Horwitz, 1973.
High Country Shootout. Sydney, Horwitz, 1973.
Man on Pulpit Rock. Sydney, Horwitz, 1973.
Saddletramp Justice. Sydney, Horwitz, 1974.
Doom Trail. Sydney, Horwitz, 1974.
Tin Stars for Tall Texans. Sydney, Horwitz, 1974.
Too Many Enemies. Sydney, Horwitz, 1974.
First Kill. Sydney, Horwitz, 1974.
They'll Hang Billy for Sure. Sydney, Horwitz, 1974.
Devil's Dinero. Sydney, Horwitz, 1974; Leicester, Thorpe, 1988.
Two Jacks and the Joker. Sydney, Horwitz, 1974.
Rescue Party. Sydney, Horwitz, 1974; Leicester, Thorpe, 1987.
Damn' Outlaws. Sydney, Horwitz, 1974.
The Last Challenge. Sydney, Horwitz, 1974.
Delaney and the Drifters. Sydney, Horwitz, 1974.
Dollar Trail to Ramirez. Sydney, Horwitz, 1974.
Winners and Losers. Sydney, Horwitz, 1975.
Dawson Died Twice. Sydney, Horwitz, 1975.
Follow That Train. Sydney, Horwitz, 1975.
Day of the Tornado. Sydney, Horwitz, 1975.
Kiss the Loot Goodbye. Sydney, Horwitz, 1975.
Baxter's Last Laugh. Sydney, Horwitz, 1975.
27 Rifles. Sydney, Horwitz, 1975.
Outcasts of Sabado Creek. Sydney, Horwitz, 1975.
Colorado Belle. Sydney, Horwitz, 1975.
The Calaboose Gang. Sydney, Horwitz, 1975.
The Battle of Blunder Ridge. Sydney, Horwitz, 1975.
Suddenly a Hero. Sydney, Horwitz, 1975.
The Bandit Trap. Sydney, Horwitz, 1975.
Prelude to a Showdown. Sydney, Horwitz, 1975.
The Sundown Seven. Sydney, Horwitz, 1976.
Raid a Painted Wagon. Sydney, Horwitz, 1976.
Guns of the Valiant. Sydney, Horwitz, 1976.
Track of the Lawless. Sydney, Horwitz, 1976.
Before He Kills Again. Sydney, Horwitz, 1976.
Bullion Route. Sydney, Horwitz, 1976.
Left-Hand Luke. Sydney, Horwitz, 1976.
Dealer Takes Three. Sydney, Horwitz, 1976.
After the Payoff. Sydney, Horwitz, 1976.
Jokers Wild. Sydney, Horwitz, 1976.
Lone Star Godfathers. Sydney, Horwitz, 1976.
8.10 from Verdugo. Sydney, Horwitz, 1976.
Royal Target. Sydney, Horwitz, 1976.
Everything Happens to Holley. Sydney, Horwitz, 1976.
Midnight Marauders. Sydney, Horwitz, 1976.
Kansas Hex. Sydney, Horwitz, 1976.
Three Days in Davisburg. Sydney, Horwitz, 1977.
The Only Bank in Town. Sydney, Horwitz, 1977.
California Runaround. Sydney, Horwitz, 1977.
Ghost of a Chance. Sydney, Horwitz, 1977.
Eight Defiant Men. Sydney, Horwitz, 1977.
Troubleshooters Die Hard. Sydney, Horwitz, 1977.
Beecher's Quest. Sydney, Horwitz, 1977.
In Memory of Marty Malone. Sydney, Horwitz, 1977.
Nebraska Trackdown. Sydney, Horwitz, 1977.
Double Shuffle. Sydney, Horwitz, 1977.
Guns, Gold and the Girl. Sydney, Horwitz, 1977.
Hammer's Horde. Sydney, Horwitz, 1977; Leicester, Thorpe, 1990.
Mark of the Star. Sydney, Horwitz, 1977.
Dinero Fever. Sydney, Horwitz, 1977.
Calaboose Express. Sydney, Horwitz, 1978; Leicester, Thorpe, 1989.
Bullet for a Widow. Sydney, Horwitz, 1978; Leicester, Thorpe, 1989.
The Killing of Kirby. Sydney, Horwitz, 1978.
Last Stage to Delarno. Sydney, Horwitz, 1978.
The Rescuers Rode West. Sydney, Horwitz, 1978.
Fogarty's War. Sydney, Horwitz, 1978.
Wyoming Longshot. Sydney, Horwitz, 1978.
Phantom of Fortuna. Sydney, Horwitz, 1978.
The Doomed of Mesa Rico. Sydney, Horwitz, 1978.
Baker City Breakout. Sydney, Horwitz, 1978.
The Women of Whitlock. Sydney, Horwitz, 1978.
High Stakeout. Sydney, Horwitz, 1978.
Run from the Buzzards. Sydney, Horwitz, 1978.
Dead Man's Share. Sydney, Horwitz, 1978.
Keep Allison Alive. Sydney, Horwitz, 1979.
Pearson County Raiders. Sydney, Horwitz, 1979.
Both Sides of Battle Creek. Sydney, Horwitz, 1979.
Turn the Key on Emerson. Sydney, Horwitz, 1979.
Fort Dillon. Sydney, Horwitz, 1979; Leicester, Thorpe, 1990.
Wrong Name on a Tombstone. Sydney, Horwitz, 1979.
They Came to Jurado. Sydney, Horwitz, 1979.
The Seventh Guilty Man. Sydney, Horwitz, 1979; Leicester, Thorpe, 1989.
In Pursuit of Quincey Budd. Sydney, Horwitz, 1979; Leicester, Thorpe, 1990.
Posse Plus Two. Sydney, Horwitz, 1979.
Brady's Back in Town. Sydney, Horwitz, 1979.
Siege of Jericho. Sydney, Horwitz, 1979.
Wait for the Judge. Sydney, Horwitz, 1979.
El Capitan's Enemies. Sydney, Horwitz, 1979.
Four Aces and the Knave. Sydney, Horwitz, 1979.
One More Showdown. Sydney, Horwitz, 1979.
Day of the Killers. Sydney, Horwitz, 1979.
Going Straight in Frisbee. Sydney, Horwitz, 1980.
Prey of the Rogue Riders. Sydney, Horwitz, 1980.
Rough Night for the Guilty. Sydney, Horwitz, 1980.
Hackett's Gold. Sydney, Horwitz, 1980.
Vengeance in Spades. Sydney, Horwitz, 1980.
Death Quest. Sydney, Horwitz, 1980.
Ride Boldly in Dakota. Sydney, Horwitz, 1980.
Kid Lightfingers. Sydney, Horwitz, 1980.
Doc Rance of Rambeau. Sydney, Horwitz, 1980.
"He's Valentine, I'm Emerson." Sydney, Horwitz, 1980.
The Lady Is a Target. Sydney, Horwitz, 1980.
Gun Reckoning at Grundy's Grave. Sydney, Horwitz, 1980.
The Twenty-Year Man. Sydney, Horwitz, 1980.
Lone Star Survivors. Sydney, Horwitz, 1980.
The Deadly Dollars. Sydney, Horwitz, 1981.
We Ride for Circle 6. Sydney, Horwitz, 1981.
Load Every Rifle. Sydney, Horwitz, 1981.
Five Bullets for Judge Blake. Sydney, Horwitz, 1981.
Ride out of Paradise. Sydney, Horwitz, 1981.
Lone Hand Emerson. Sydney, Horwitz, 1981.
Greel County Outcasts. Sydney, Horwitz, 1981.
Miss Lou and the Tall Men. Sydney, Horwitz, 1981.

Little Town, Big Trouble. Sydney, Horwitz, 1981.
Tin Star Shadow. Sydney, Horwitz, 1981.
Bravados of Bandera. Sydney, Horwitz, 1981.
Wild Widow of Wolf Creek. Sydney, Horwitz, 1981.
For the Hell of It. Sydney, Horwitz, 1981.
Ride Strong, Ride Free. Sydney, Horwitz, 1981.
Human Target. Sydney, Horwitz, 1981.
We Call Him Tex. Sydney, Horwitz, 1981.
Spanish Gold and Texas Guns. Sydney, Horwitz, 1981.
The Law Always Wins. Sydney, Horwitz, 1981.
Pursuit Party. Sydney, Horwitz, 1981.
Hide in Fear. Sydney, Horwitz, 1982.
Lucky Jake. Sydney, Horwitz, 1982.
Cormack Came Back. Sydney, Horwitz, 1982; Leicester, Thorpe, 1987.
Cedro County Crisis. Sydney, Horwitz, 1982.
Latimer's Loot. Sydney, Horwitz, 1982.
Tame a Wild Town. Sydney, Horwitz, 1982.
Forgotten Enemy. Sydney, Horwitz, 1982.
The Last Witness. Sydney, Horwitz, 1982.
McEvoy's Mountain. Sydney, Horwitz, 1982.
Emerson's Hex. Sydney, Horwitz, 1982.
The Bullet in Mason's Back. Sydney, Horwitz, 1982.
Six-Gun Wedding. Sydney, Horwitz, 1982.
Colorado Woman. Sydney, Horwitz, 1982.
Young Bucks from Texas. Sydney, Horwitz, 1982.
Castle on Claw Creek. Sydney, Horwitz, 1982.
Pledge to a Doomed Man. Sydney, Horwitz, 1982.
Greenback Trail. Sydney, Horwitz, 1982.
The After-Midnight Gang. Sydney, Horwitz, 1982.
Bon Chance, Texans! Sydney, Horwitz, 1982.
Two-Time Winner. Sydney, Horwitz, 1982.
The Cobb Creek Bunch. Sydney, Horwitz, 1982.
Howdy, Ladies. Sydney, Horwitz, 1983.
Debt to a Tin Star. Sydney, Horwitz, 1983.
Miracle at Dry Fork. Sydney, Horwitz, 1983.
Lady Luck and F J Beck. Sydney, Horwitz, 1983.
Peligro's Last Hour. Sydney, Horwitz, 1983.
Beauty and the Brigands. Sydney, Horwitz, 1983.
Wagon Number Three. Sydney, Horwitz, 1983.
Wrong Side of Glory Mountain. Sydney, Horwitz, 1983.
Claw Creek Crisis. Sydney, Horwitz, 1983.
The Piketown Flood. Sydney, Horwitz, 1983.
Calamity Is a Woman. Sydney, Horwitz, 1983.
Tanglefoot. Sydney, Horwitz, 1983.
Duffy's Dollars. Sydney, Horwitz, 1983.
The Saga of Sam Burdew. Sydney, Horwitz, 1983.
Texas Born, Chicago Bound. Sydney, Horwitz, 1983.
Shotgun Sharkey. Sydney, Horwitz, 1983; Leicester, Thorpe, 1988.
Reunion in Slade City. Sydney, Horwitz, 1983.
Save a Bullet for Keehoe. Sydney, Horwitz, 1983; Leicester, Thorpe, 1987.
Walking Tall, Striking Fear. Sydney, Horwitz, 1983.
Stakeout at Council Creek. Sydney, Horwitz, 1983.
The Dude Must Die. Sydney, Horwitz, 1983.
Terror Trail to Tortosa. Sydney, Horwitz, 1984.
Ventura Pass. Sydney, Horwitz, 1984.
The Tinhorn Murder Case. Sydney, Horwitz, 1984.
The Devil's Dozen. Sydney, Horwitz, 1984; Leicester, Thorpe, 1986.
Emerson's Hideout. Sydney, Horwitz, 1984; Leicester, Thorpe, 1986.
Heroes and Hellers. Sydney, Horwitz, 1984; Leicester, Thorpe, 1986.
The Dinero Train. Sydney, Horwitz, 1984.
Day of the Plunderers. Sydney, Horwitz, 1984.
Ghost-Woman of Castillo. Sydney, Horwitz, 1984; Leicester, Thorpe, 1986.
Kincaid's Last Ride. Sydney, Horwitz, 1984; Leicester, Thorpe, 1987.
Defend Beacon Spring. Sydney, Horwitz, 1984.
Reunion in San Jose. Sydney, Horwitz, 1984; Leicester, Thorpe, 1987.
The Only Way Is Up. Sydney, Horwitz, 1984.
Bandit Bait. Sydney, Horwitz, 1984; Leicester, Thorpe, 1986.
Meet the McEgans. Sydney, Horwitz, 1984.
Wyoming Gun-Trap. Sydney, Horwitz, 1984.
Tandy's Legacy. Sydney, Horwitz, 1984.
Stay Away, Slade! Sydney, Horwitz, 1984.
Destination Fort Ross. Sydney, Horwitz, 1985.
The Sound of Seeger's Guns. Sydney, Horwitz, 1985.
Montana Mail. Sydney, Horwitz, 1985.
The Best and the Worst. Sydney, Horwitz, 1985.
Five for the Shootout. Sydney, Horwitz, 1985.
Wild Night in Widow's Peak. Sydney, Horwitz, 1985.
The Domino Man. Sydney, Horwitz, 1985.
The Cannon Mound Gang. Sydney, Horwitz, 1985.
Billy Hull, R.I.P. Sydney, Horwitz, 1985.
Sonora Wildcat. Sydney, Horwitz, 1985.
Trigger-Fast. Sydney, Horwitz, 1985.
Who's Gunning for Braid? Sydney, Horwitz, 1985.
Night of the Guns. Sydney, Horwitz, 1985.
Gollan County Gallows. Sydney, Horwitz, 1985.
Run with the Loot. Sydney, Horwitz, 1985.
The President's Segundo. Sydney, Horwitz, 1985.
The Truth About Snake Ridge. Sydney, Horwitz, 1985; Leicester, Thorpe, 1988.
Two Weeks in Wyoming. Sydney, Horwitz, 1985.
Greenback Fever. Sydney, Horwitz, 1985.
Whiskey Gulch. Sydney, Horwitz, 1985; Leicester, Thorpe, 1990.
Terror's Long Memory. Sydney, Horwitz, 1985.
The Logantown Looters. Sydney, Horwitz, 1986; Leicester, Thorpe, 1989.
Two Gentlemen from Texas. Sydney, Horwitz, 1986.
The Alibi Trail. Sydney, Horwitz, 1986; Leicester, Thorpe, 1990.
Rough Route to Rodd County. Sydney, Horwitz, 1986.
Six Guilty Men. Sydney, Horwitz, 1986; Leicester, Thorpe, 1990.
The Badge and Tully McGlynn. Sydney, Horwitz, 1986.
The Last Big Deal. Sydney, Horwitz, 1986.
The Trial of Slow Wolf. Sydney, Horwitz, 1986.
The Jubilo Stage. Sydney, Horwitz, 1986.
Plummer's Last Posse. Sydney, Horwitz, 1986.
Two Graves Waiting. Sydney, Horwitz, 1987.
Bandido Hunters. Sydney, Horwitz, 1987.
Fontaine's Sidekicks. Sydney, Horwitz, 1987.
Never Cheat a Texan. Sydney, Horwitz, 1987.
The Late Yuma Smith. Sydney, Horwitz, 1987.
One Mean Town. Sydney, Horwitz, 1987.
It Had to Be Ortega. Sydney, Horwitz, 1987.
Harrigan's Star. Sydney, Horwitz, 1987.
One Ticket to Sun Rock. Sydney, Horwitz, 1987.
Galatea McGee. Sydney, Horwitz, 1987.
Seven Killers East. Sydney, Horwitz, 1987.
Dynamite Demon. Sydney, Horwitz, 1988.
The Jonah Rock. Sydney, Horwitz, 1988.
McAllister's Victims. Sydney, Horwitz, 1988.
Queen of Spades. Sydney, Horwitz, 1988.
The Bridegroom's Bodyguards. Sydney, Horwitz, 1988.
Where the Money's Buried. Sydney, Horwitz, 1988.
Wyoming War-Fever. Sydney, Horwitz, 1988.

Four-Wheeled Target. Sydney, Horwitz, 1988.
Waiting for Wilkie's Wagon. Sydney, Horwitz, 1988.
Go West, Joe Best. Sydney, Horwitz, 1988.
Battle of Hogan's Hole. Sydney, Horwitz, 1988.
Feud-Breakers. Sydney, Horwitz, 1988.
Is Glennon Guilty? Sydney, Horwitz, 1988.
Legend of Coyote Ford. Sydney, Horwitz, 1988.
Widow From Nowhere. Sydney, Horwitz, 1989.
The Second Chance Man. Sydney, Horwitz, 1989.
Hostage Hunters. Sydney, Horwitz, 1989.
Alias Ed Dacey. Sydney, Horwitz, 1989.
The Doomsday Gun. Sydney, Horwitz, 1989.
Beeby's Big Night. Sydney, Horwitz, 1989.
The Langan Legacy. Sydney, Horwitz, 1989.
Hackett's Bluff. Sydney, Horwitz, 1989.
Backtracking Little Red. Sydney, Horwitz, 1989.
The Selina Crisis. Sydney, Horwitz, 1989.
Wells Fargo Decoys. Sydney, Horwitz, 1989.
Wolf Creek or Bust. Sydney, Horwitz, 1989.
Friends of Barney Gregg. Sydney, Horwitz, 1989.
Runaway Ramsey. Sydney, Horwitz, 1989.
Battle Alley. Sydney, Horwitz, 1989.
High Card Killer. Sydney, Horwitz, 1989.
Revenge Is the Spur. Sydney, Horwitz, 1989.
The No Name Gang. Sydney, Horwitz, 1989.
Challenge the Legend. Sydney, Horwitz, 1989.
Slow Wolf and Dan Fox. Sydney, Horwitz, 1989.
The Lawman Wore Black. Sydney, Horwitz, 1989.
Uneasy Money. Sydney, Horwitz, 1989.
Terror for Sale. Sydney, Horwitz, 1989.
Rescue a Tall Texan. Sydney, Hale, 1989.
Spencer Started Something. Sydney, Horwitz, 1989.
Dakota Death-Trap. Sydney, Horwitz, 1989.
Whatever Became of Johnny Duke? Sydney, Horwitz, 1989.
Once Upon a Gallows. Sydney, Horwitz, 1989.
The Gold Movers. Sydney, Horwitz, 1989.
Fortune Fever. Sydney, Horwitz, 1990.
Never Say Quit. Sydney, Horwitz, 1990.
In Cahoots. Sydney, Horwitz, 1990.
Banished from Bodie. Sydney, Horwitz, 1990.
Hold 'Em Back! Sydney, Horwitz, 1990.
One Hell of a Showdown. Sydney, Horwitz, 1990.
South to Sabine. Sydney, Horwitz, 1991.
Rough, Ready and Texan. Sydney, Horwitz, 1991.
Ruckus at Gila Wells. Sydney, Horwitz, 1991.
The Woman Hunt. Sydney, Horwitz, 1991.
The Wrong Victim. Sydney, Horwitz, 1991.
Bunko Trail. Sydney, Horwitz, 1991.
Bequest to a Texan. Sydney, Horwitz, 1991.
Right Royal Hassle. Sydney, Horwitz, 1991.
Moonlight and Gunsmoke. Sydney, Horwitz, 1991.
Wrangle Creek. Sydney, Horwitz, 1991.
Strangers Riding By. Sydney, Horwitz, 1991.
Conways Chronicle. Sydney, Horwitz, 1991.
Vigil on Sundown Ridge. Sydney, Horwitz, 1992.
Eyes of a Killer. Sydney, Horwitz, 1992.
The Wildcat Run. Sydney, Horwitz, 1992.

Novels (series: Big Jim Rand/Nevada Jim in all books)

The Night McLennan Died. Sydney, Cleveland, 1964.
Gun-Trapped. Sydney, Cleveland, 1964.
Meet Me in Moredo. Sydney, Cleveland, 1965.
Gun Sinister. Sydney, Cleveland, 1965.
Killer's Noon. Sydney, Cleveland, 1965.
One Man Jury. Sydney, Cleveland, 1965.
Devil's Legend. Sydney, Cleveland, 1965.
No Escape Trail. Sydney, Cleveland, 1965.
League of the Lawless. Sydney, Cleveland, 1965.
The Valiant Die Fast. Sydney, Cleveland, 1965.
One Thousand Dollar Target. Sydney, Cleveland, 1965.
The Hour Before Disaster. Sydney, Cleveland, 1965.
Main Street, Gallego. Sydney, Cleveland, 1965.
Saturday Wild. Sydney, Cleveland, 1966.
Wear Black for Johnny. Sydney, Cleveland, 1966.
The Man Who Hunts Jenner. Sydney, Cleveland, 1966.
Canyon Vigil. Sydney, Cleveland, 1966.
Shadow of a Colt .45. Sydney, Cleveland, 1966.
They Came to Plunder. Sydney, Cleveland, 1966.
Tall Man's Challenge. Sydney, Cleveland, 1966.
A Bullet Is Faster. Sydney, Cleveland, 1966.
Die Lonesome. Sydney, Cleveland, 1966.
Thirty Raiders South. Sydney, Cleveland, 1966.
Satan Pulled the Trigger. Sydney, Cleveland, 1966.
Diablo's Shadow. Sydney, Horwitz, 1966.
Kid Daybreak. Sydney, Horwitz, 1966.
Vengeance Rides a Black Horse. Sydney, Horwitz, 1966.
A Man Called Drago (as Marshall McCoy). New York, Bantam, 1967.
Six Rogues Riding. Sydney, Horwitz, 1967.
Fury at Broken Wheel. Sydney, Horwitz, 1967.
Big Lobo (as Marshall McCoy). New York, Bantam, 1967.
Challenge the Guilty. Sydney, Horwitz, 1967.
Driscoll. Sydney, Horwitz, 1967.
Limbo Pass (as Marshall McCoy). New York, Bantam, 1967.
Seven Westbound (as Marshall McCoy). New York, Bantam, 1967.
Justice for Jenner (as Marshall McCoy). New York, Bantam, 1967.
Bury the Guilty. Sydney, Horwitz, 1967; as Marshall McCoy, New York, Bantam, 1967.
Crisis at Cornerstone (as Marshall McCoy). New York, Bantam, 1967.
No Gun Is Neutral (as Marshall McCoy). New York, Bantam, 1967.
Die Brave (as Marshall McCoy). New York, Bantam, 1967.
The Killers Came at Noon (as Marshall McCoy). New York, Bantam, 1967.
Guns of Greed (as Marshall McCoy). New York, Bantam, 1968.
Gun Flash (as Marshall McCoy). New York, Bantam, 1968.
Killer Bait (as Marshall McCoy). New York, Bantam, 1968.
Hangrope Fever. Sydney, Horwitz, 1968.
Spur Route. Sydney, Horwitz, 1968.
Behind a Black Mask. Sydney, Horwitz, 1968; as Marshall McCoy, New York, Bantam, 1968.
Requiem for Sam Wade. Sydney, Horwitz, 1968.
Dead Man's Bluff. Sydney, Horwitz, 1968.
Satan's Back-Trail. Sydney, Horwitz, 1968; as Marshall McCoy, New York, Bantam, 1968.
Bounty on Wes Durand. Sydney, Horwitz, 1968; as Marshall McCoy, New York, Bantam, 1968.
The Willing Target. Sydney, Horwitz, 1969.
Stand Alone. Sydney, Horwitz, 1969.
Rogue Trail. Sydney, Horwitz, 1969.
Danger Rode Drag. Sydney, Horwitz, 1969; Leicester, Thorpe, 1987.
Day of Vengeance. Sydney, Horwitz, 1969.
Carson's Bonanza. Sydney, Horwitz, 1969.
Savage Sunday. Sydney, Horwitz, 1969.
The Name on the Bullet. Sydney, Horwitz, 1969.
Ransom on a Redhead. Sydney, Horwitz, 1969.
Fort Ricks. Sydney, Horwitz, 1970.
Sundance Creek. Sydney, Horwitz, 1970.

No Tomorrow for Tobin. Sydney, Horwitz, 1970.
The Killers Wore Black. Sydney, Horwitz, 1971; Leicester, Thorpe, 1987.
Hartigan. Sydney, Horwitz, 1971; Leicester, Thorpe, 1988.
Gunfight at Doone's Well. Sydney, Horwitz, 1971.
Hell in High County. Sydney, Horwitz, 1984; Leicester, Thorpe, 1986.
Ten Fast Horses. Sydney, Horwitz, 1984; Leicester, Thorpe, 1986.

Novels (series: Bleak Creek in all books)

Bleak Creek. Sydney, Cleveland, 1960.
Peaceable Man. Sydney, Cleveland, 1960.
Hit the Leather. Sydney, Cleveland, 1960.
The Tyler Cache. Sydney, Cleveland, 1960.
No Safe Trail. Sydney, Cleveland, 1960.
Ride the Wild River. Sydney, Cleveland, 1961.
Wanted in Texas. Sydney, Cleveland, 1961.
Gun Against Gun. Sydney, Cleveland, 1961.
Try Me! Sydney, Cleveland, 1962.
Colt Hostages. Sydney, Cleveland, 1962.
Devil's Trail. Sydney, Cleveland, 1962.

Novels as Grant Barlow

Gun Wrangler. Sydney, Cleveland, 1957.
Top Gun Kid. Sydney, Cleveland, 1966.

Novels as Ward Brennan

Face the .45. Sydney, Cleveland, 1961.
Holster Heat. Sydney, Cleveland, 1961.
Trail of Courage. Sydney, Cleveland, 1961.
Stay Alive. Sydney, Cleveland, 1961.
Running Target. Sydney, Cleveland, 1962.
3.10 from Red Rock. Sydney, Cleveland, 1962.
Barstow Deputy. Sydney, Cleveland, 1962.
Fast as they Come. Sydney, Cleveland, 1962.
Come Gunnin'. Sydney, Cleveland, 1962.
Act of Defiance. Sydney, Cleveland, 1962.
Luke Blane. Sydney, Cleveland, 1962.
Hang-rope at Sundown. Sydney, Cleveland, 1962.
Shotgun Deegan. Sydney, Cleveland, 1962.
Clint Ryker. Sydney, Cleveland, 1963.
No Mercy in a Bullet. Sydney, Cleveland, 1963.
Adios Bandido. Sydney, Cleveland, 1963.
Now or Never. Sydney, Cleveland, 1963.
Legend of Rio McGill. Sydney, Cleveland, 1963.
Steel of the Hardings. Sydney, Cleveland, 1963.
Satan's Partner. Sydney, Cleveland, 1963.
Odds Against the Gallows. Sydney, Cleveland, 1964.
The Waiting Gun. Sydney, Cleveland, 1964.

Novels as Glenn Murrell

One Man Law. Sydney, Cleveland, 1956.
Three Acres of Hell. Sydney, Cleveland, 1957.
Under Cover Marshal. Sydney, Cleveland, 1957.
Gun Fever. Sydney, Cleveland, 1957.
Preacher with a Gun. Sydney, Cleveland, 1957.
Gun Hazard. Sydney, Cleveland, 1957.
Hidden Guns. Sydney, Cleveland, 1957.
Ride Wary, Stranger. Sydney, Cleveland, 1958.
Tribute to a Gun. Sydney, Cleveland, 1958.
Buzzards Hover. Sydney, Cleveland, 1958.
Lynch Fever. Sydney, Cleveland, 1958.
Raiders at Noon. Sydney, Cleveland, 1958.
The Scar. Sydney, Cleveland, 1958.
Suddenly a Gun. Sydney, Cleveland, 1958.
Vigil on Boot Hill. Sydney, Cleveland, 1958.
Six Feet Tall. Sydney, Cleveland, 1959.
The First Marshal. Sydney, Cleveland, 1959.
Half-way to Hell. Sydney, Cleveland, 1959.
Reb Conroy. Sydney, Cleveland, 1959.
Call the Tune. Sydney, Cleveland, 1959.
Trail Three South. Sydney, Cleveland, 1960.
Diablo Rock. Sydney, Cleveland, 1960.
The Bowden Brand. Sydney, Cleveland, 1960.
Cimarron Trail. Sydney, Cleveland, 1960.
Run for the Border. Sydney, Cleveland, 1960.
Unknown Gun. Sydney, Cleveland, 1960.
Five for Boot Hill. Sydney, Cleveland, 1960.
Gallows Bait. Sydney, Cleveland, 1960.
Guns of the Guilty. Sydney, Cleveland, 1960.
Trigger Trap. Sydney, Cleveland, 1961.
Handful of Hell. Sydney, Cleveland, 1961.
Fill a Saddle Fast. Sydney, Cleveland, 1961.

Novels as Clyde B. Shawn

Judas Gun. Sydney, Cleveland, 1956.
Bullet Breed. Sydney, Cleveland, 1956.

Novels as Lee Thorpe

Draw Cards! Sydney, Cleveland, 1957.
The Naked Gun. Sydney, Cleveland, 1966.

OTHER PUBLICATIONS

Novels

I'll Come Back and Haunt You (as Leonard Meares). Sydney, Horwitz, 1979.
Jo Jo and the Private Eye (as Lester Malloy). London, Hale, 1981.
The Happiest Ghost in Town (as Lester Malloy). London, Hale, 1981.
The Future and Philomena (as Val Sterling). London, Hale, 1982.
So Help Me Hannah (as Lester Malloy). London, Hale, 1982.
Beware the Yellow Packard (as Lester Malloy). London, Hale, 1982.
The Battle of Jericho Street (as Frank Everton). London, Hale, 1984.
Dead Man Smiling (as Leonard Meares). London, Hale, 1986.

*

Marshall Grover comments:

From my earliest years—and I go way back to Mix, McCoy, Maynard, Buck Jones, et al.—the western movie won my youthful enthusiasm. Naturally I also became a reader of Westerns, and found myself analyzing Zane Grey, Norman Fox, Luke Short, but especially Jack Schaefer, whose great talent for characterization fired my imagination.

From the time I wrote my first Western in 1955 to the present day, my output now exceeding 700 titles, I have held to the theory that the characters of the Old West were more significant to those eventful years between the end of the Civil War and the turn of the century than the grandeur and variation of the land in which they lived, worked, and built a future for themselves; the people matter most.

And, through research, I came to understand that they weren't all dour pioneers lacking imagination nor bereft of a sense of humor. Not all saloonkeepers and gamblers were sardonic opportunists, nor were all wranglers and cowhands as taciturn as some western writers depict them.

This is why, in a Marshall Grover Western, off-beat characters, a wide assortment of eccentrics and dogged individualists are very much to the fore. I enjoy my work, but it is more important to me that the book-buyers, those who read and collect my work, get their due of entertainment and value for money.

I still don't regard Larry and Stretch as conventional western heroes and, over half a lifetime of putting words on paper, I have made it a point to keep those wanderers in touch with a cross-section of out-of-the-rut frontier characters. Doc Beaumont is well to the fore of these, as is Cathcart P. Slow Wolf, that most unusual of all half-breeds. During the Nevada Jim series, the comically unsavory Benito Espina was used to, I hope, good effect. And I shamelessly admit to deriving considerable pleasure from the bombastic ranting of Hoolahan the Pinkerton and his secretly sceptical aides, Agents Casey and Zimmerman.

Humor *should* be as valid to the western genre as the depredations of the lawless, the shootouts, stampedes, and life-threatening climatic conditions.

It is also true that the women of the West were a mixed bunch. As well as the saloon bawds and traditional "helpless heroines," there were hardy townswomen and ranch-wives, schoolteachers dedicated to the task of ensuring the small fry would be better educated than their sometimes semi-illiterate parents, and actually *hundreds* who, in the absence of qualified physicians, midwifed expectant mothers. If they were tough ladies, it was because they had to be in those rugged times.

Finally, were I able to do it all over again, I would. My only regret is that I didn't abandon amateur theatricals, my civil service job, and the dozen and one dead-end careers I pursued long before 1955; I wish I'd begun writing earlier.

* * *

The incredibly prolific Leonard Meares bought his first typewriter in 1954 with the intention of writing for radio and films, but when this proved to be harder to achieve than originally thought, he was urged by a friend to write a novel. Checking around, he discovered that a great many Westerns were published locally, and while recovering from flu, he devised and wrote his first book, *Trouble Town*, in 1955, which was purchased by the Cleveland Publishing Pty Ltd for £52.50 (approximately $90). Thereafter he began turning out largely traditional "oaters" one after another, all of them published by Cleveland, initially in staple-bound form and later in paperback.

Meares's most enduring series has been that featuring his two nomadic Texans, Larry and Stretch. The "Lone Star Hellions" made their first appearance in *Drift!* 1956 and are still being published today, nearly four decades later.

The Larry and Stretch series always combines action with humour, the humour frequently bordering on slapstick. Although the books generally end with a shoot-out in which the bad guys bite the dust, the plots can be surprisingly intricate. Often they revolve around bank or train robberies, the abduction of wealthy land-owners' relatives and so on. In their time, Meares's altruistic Texans have ridden shotgun for Wells Fargo, pinned on badges to bring law to disorderly towns (although they are anathema to most lawmen, who see them as interfering busybodies), and foiled attempts to break incarcerated gang-bosses out of jail. At one time or another, both Larry (the brains of the partnership) and Stretch (whose guileless smile and jug-handle ears should, by rights, relegate him to the role of stooge, but never do) have both loved and lost, suffered amnesia and somehow come back from the dead after receiving near-fatal bullet wounds. Although they invariably tangle with whole gangs of outlaws in each book, they remain constantly optimistic that one day they will find Utopia.

The Larry and Stretch stories are always told in a light, largely comical style. Background and historical detail is kept to a minimum and speech is broadly "western" ("Wal, chop off my legs an' call me 'Shorty'," and so on). The author has a penchant for creating oddball supporting characters who frequently upstage his protagonists, and though he avoids lengthy descriptions of violence when connected to gunplay, he can get quite graphic when describing a fist-fight.

A companion series featuring an ex-cavalry sergeant called Big Jim Rand ran for more than 70 stories. These adventures were more serious than the Larry and Stretch Westerns, but usually followed the same action-orientated pattern. In the earlier titles, Jim wanders the West in search of the man who killed his brother. Later on, when Jim settles down to run a horse-ranch outside the town of Cornerstone, and a number of regular supporting characters are introduced, the series becomes even more engaging.

Since mid-1967, Meares has been published by the Horwitz Grahame Pty. Ltd. In the late 1960's, 32 of his Larry and Stretch/Big Jim stories were published by Bantam Books in the United States, giving Meares the distinction of being the only Australian author ever to sell Westerns to America, the home of the genre. For contractual reasons, however, "Marshall Grover" became "Marshall McCoy," and his heroes became "Larry and Streak" and "Nevada Jim."

These characters always team up whenever Meares notches up another century. So far these team-ups include *San Saba Blockade* (1970, written to commemorate his 400th western), *Last Stage to Delarno* (1978, his 500th), *Reunion in Slade City* (1983, his 600th) and *One Hell of a Showdown* (1991, his 700th). A non-anniversary team-up can be found in *Four Aces and the Knave* (1979).

Inevitably, some of Meares's books are better than others. *Reunion in San José*, in which Larry and Stretch have to track down the offspring of an apparently dying man who wants to make amends for his wayward past, relies a little too heavily on coincidence to be wholly satisfactory. Larry's love interest in *First Kill* fails to convince. But Meares succeeds more often than he fails. *Hartigan*, a Big Jim story in which a wounded gunslinger rides into Corner-stone to die peacefully is genuinely moving, as is the scene in which two deadbeats finally rediscover their lost dignity in one of the very best Larry and Stretch stories, *Going Straight in Frisbee*.

In more recent times, Meares has started to produce the odd, interesting "flashback" story, in which Larry and Stretch (usually portrayed as 30-plus in years) appear in their teens. *Young Bucks from Texas* and *Texas Born, Chicago Bound*, set against the backdrop of Chicago's great fire of 1871 are well worth seeking out.

Meares can usually complete a 45–50,000-word manuscript in three weeks. Although he appears to have slowed down a little in the past few years, this is mainly due to a falling demand for the Western. He is still a very active wordsmith, however, and in recent years has also published a ghost story, a romance, and several detective novels.

—David Whitehead

GRUBER, Frank. Also wrote as Stephen Acre; Charles K. Boston; John K. Vedder. American. Born in Elmer, Minnesota, 2 February 1904. Served in the United States Army, 1920–21. Married Lois Mahood in 1931; one son. Editor of trade journals; teacher in correspondence schools; self-employed writer from 1934. *Died 9 December 1969.*

WESTERN PUBLICATIONS

Novels

Peace Marshal. New York, Morrow, 1939; London, Barker, 1957.
Outlaw. New York, Farrar and Rinehart, 1941; London, Wright and Brown, 1942.
Gunsight. New York, Dodd Mead, 1942; London, Wright and Brown, 1943.
Fighting Man. New York, Rinehart, 1948; London, Wright and Brown, 1951.
Broken Lance. New York, Rinehart, 1949; London, Wright and Brown, 1952.
Smoky Road. New York, Rinehart, 1949; London, Wright and Brown, 1952; as *The Lone Gunhawk*, New York, Lion, 1953.
Fort Starvation. New York, Rinehart, 1953.
Quantrell's Raiders. New York, Ace, 1954.
Bitter Sage. New York, Rinehart, 1954; London, Wright and Brown, 1955.
Bugles West. New York, Rinehart, 1954; London, Barker, 1956.
Johnny Vengeance. New York, Rinehart, 1954; London, Wright and Brown, 1956.
Rebel Road. New York, Ace, 1954.
The Highwayman. New York, Rinehart, 1955; London, Barker, 1957; as *Ride to Hell*, New York, New American Library, 1955.
The Man from Missouri. New York, Popular Library, 1956.
Buffalo Grass. New York, Rinehart, 1956; London, Barker, 1957.
The Big Land. New York, Bantam, 1957.
Lonesome River. New York, Rinehart, 1957; London, Barker, 1958.
The Marshal. New York, Rinehart, 1958; London, Barker, 1959.
Town Tamer. New York, Rinehart, and London, Barker, 1958.
The Bushwhackers. New York, Rinehart, 1959; London, New English Library, 1960.
This Gun Is Still. New York, Bantam, 1967.
The Dawn Riders. New York, Bantam, 1968.
The Curly Wolf. New York, Bantam, 1969; London, Bantam, 1979.
Wanted! New York, Bantam, 1971; London, Bantam, 1979.

Short Stories

Tales of Wells Fargo. New York, Bantam, and London, Corgi, 1958.

Uncollected Short Stories

"This Outlaw Business," in *Argosy* (New York), 12 March 1938.
"Young Sam Began to Roam" in *West* (Kingswood, Surrey), March 1941.
"The Marshal of Broken Lance," in *Western Stories*, edited by Gene Autry. New York, Dell, 1947.
"Ride No More," in *Zane Grey's Western* (New York), November 1950.
"The Road to Nowhere," in *Rawhide and Bob-Wire*, edited by Luke Short. New York, Bantam, 1958.
"The Store," in *Zane Grey Western* (New York), October 1969.
"Town Tamer," in *The Reel West*, edited by Bill Pronzini and Martin H. Greenberg. New York, Doubleday, 1984.
"Assassin," in *The Outlaws*, edited by Bill Pronzini and Martin H. Greenberg. New York, Fawcett, 1984.

OTHER PUBLICATIONS

Novels

The French Key. New York, Farrar and Rinehart, 1940; London, Hale, 1941; as *The French Key Mystery*, New York, Avon, 1946; as *Once Over Deadly*, New York, Spivak, 1956.
The Laughing Fox. New York, Farrar and Rinehart, 1940; London, Nicholson and Watson, 1942.
The Hungry Dog. New York, Farrar and Rinehart, 1941; London, Nicholson and Watson, 1950; as *The Hungry Dog Murders*, New York, Avon, 1943; as *Die Like a Dog*, New York, Spivak, 1957.
The Navy Colt. New York, Farrar and Rinehart, 1941; London, Nicholson and Watson, 1942.
Simon Lash, Private Detective. New York, Farrar and Rinehart, 1941; as *Simon Lash, Detective*, London, Nicholson and Watson, 1943.
The Silver Jackass (as Charles K. Boston). New York, Reynal, 1941; London, Cherry Tree, 1952.
The Talking Clock. New York, Farrar and Rinehart, 1941; London, Nicholson and Watson, 1942.
The Last Doorbell (as John K. Vedder). New York, Holt, 1941; as *Kiss the Boss Goodbye* (as Frank Gruber), New York, Spivak, 1954.
The Buffalo Box. New York, Farrar and Rinehart, 1942; London, Nicholson and Watson, 1944.
The Gift Horse. New York, Farrar and Rinehart, 1942; London, Nicholson and Watson, 1943.
The Yellow Overcoat (as Stephen Acre). New York, Dodd Mead, 1942; London, Boardman, 1945; as *Fall Guy for a Killer* (as Frank Gruber), New York, Spivak, 1955.
The Mighty Blockhead. New York, Farrar and Rinehart, 1942; London, Nicholson and Watson, 1948; as *The Corpse Moved Upstairs*, New York, Belmont, 1964.
The Silver Tombstone. New York, Farrar and Rinehart, 1945; London, Nicholson and Watson, 1949; as *The Silver Tombstone Mystery*, New York, New American Library, 1959.
Beagle Scented Murder. New York, Rinehart, 1946; as *Market for Murder*, New York, New American Library, 1947.
The Fourth Letter. New York, Rinehart, 1947.
The Honest Dealer. New York, Rinehart, 1947.
The Whispering Master. New York, Rinehart, 1947.
The Lock and the Key. New York, Rinehart, 1948; Kingswood, Surrey, World's Work, 1950; as *Too Tough to Die*, New York, Spivak, 1954; as *Run Thief Run*, New York, Fawcett, 1955.
Murder '97. New York, Rinehart, 1948; London, Barker, 1956; as *The Long Arm of Murder*, New York, Spivak, 1956.
The Scarlet Feather. New York, Rinehart, 1948; London, Cherry Tree, 1951; as *The Gamecock Murders*, New York, New American Library, 1949.

The Leather Duke. New York, Rinehart, 1949; Manchester, Pemberton, 1950; as *A Job of Murder*, New York, New American Library, 1950.
The Limping Goose. New York, Rinehart, 1954; London, Barker, 1955; as *Murder One*, New York, Belmont, 1973.
The Lonesome Badger. New York, Rinehart, 1954; as *Mood for Murder*, Hasbrouck Heights, New Jersey, Graphic, 1956.
Twenty Plus Two. New York, Dutton, and London, Boardman, 1961.
Brothers of Silence. New York, Dutton, and London, Boardman, 1962.
Bridge of Sand. New York, Dutton, 1963; London, Boardman, 1964.
The Greek Affair. New York, Dutton, 1964; London, Boardman, 1965.
Swing Low Swing Dead. New York, Belmont, 1964.
Little Hercules. New York, Dutton, 1965; London, Boardman, 1966.
Run, Fool, Run. New York, Dutton, 1966; London, Hale, 1967.
The Twilight Man. New York, Dutton, and London, Hale, 1967.
The Gold Gap. New York, Dutton, and London, Hale, 1968.
The Etruscan Bull. New York, Dutton, 1969; London, Hale, 1970.
The Spanish Prisoner. New York, Dutton, 1969; London, Hale, 1970.

Short Stories

Brass Knuckles. Los Angeles, Sherbourne Press, 1966.

Plays

Screenplays: *Northern Pursuit*, with Alvah Bessie, 1943; *Mask of Dimitrios*, 1944; *Johnny Angel*, with Steve Fisher, 1945; *The French Key*, 1946; *Terror by Night*, 1946; *Accomplice*, with Irving Elman, 1946; *In Old Sacramento*, with Frances Hyland and Jerome Odlum, 1946; *Dressed to Kill*, with Leonard Lee, 1946; *Bulldog Drummond at Bay*, 1947; *The Challenge*, with Irving Elman, 1948; *Fighting Man of the Plains*, 1949; *The Cariboo Trail*, with John Rhodes Sturdy, 1950; *Dakota Lil*, with Maurice Geraghty, 1950; *The Texas Rangers*, with Richard Schayer, 1950; *The Great Missouri Raid*, 1951; *Warpath*, 1951; *Silver City*, 1951; *Flaming Feather*, with Gerald Drayson Adams, 1952; *The Denver and Rio Grande*, 1952; *Hurricane Smith*, 1952; *Pony Express*, with Charles Marquis Warren, 1953; *Rage at Dawn*, with Horace McCoy, 1955; *Twenty Plus Two*, 1961; *Town Tamer*, 1965; *Arizona Raiders*, with others, 1965.

Television Plays: creator of *Tales of Wells Fargo*, *The Texan*, and *Shotgun Slade* series; author of some 200 scripts.

Other

Horatio Alger, Jr.: A Biography and Bibliography. Privately printed, 1961.
The Pulp Jungle (autobiography). Los Angeles, Sherbourne Press, 1967.
Zane Grey: A Biography. Cleveland, World, 1970.

* * *

Frank Gruber made a study of the western novel and developed a formula of seven basic categories. All westerns have one or more of the following elements: railroad, ranch, cattle, empire (the ranch story enlarged), revenge, cavalry versus Indian, outlaw, and marshal or law and order. Gruber wrote some 60 novels, 25 or more of which were popular westerns. His first westerns were *Peace Marshal* (filmed as *The Kansan*), and *Outlaw*. He hit his stride with *Fighting Man*, *Quantrell's Raiders*, *Tales of Wells Fargo*, and *The Dawn Riders*.

An examination of a Gruber western will give an idea of how he follows his formula. In *Fighting Man* Gruber includes variations of his formula—the railroad, ranch (here it is land developed for wheat in Kansas), revenge, cavalry (without Indians), outlaw and marshal categories. The major action takes place immediately after the Civil War, but the story opens as the hero, Captain Jim Dancer, rides with the Confederate guerrilla raider, William Clarke Quantrell (1837–65), into Kansas in 1863. Nine years later Dancer is a captive of a Pleasanton Detective Agent who has been searching for years for the notorious Dancer who had committed crimes while riding with Quantrell. Dancer escapes, becomes marshal of the small railroad town of Lanyard, Kansas, and struggles to become an honest lawman. In his attempts to bring law and order to the town, he is thwarted by powerful, greedy landowners, and by the railroad builders. Surrounded by bad as well as good men, he does succeed in his struggle. He shows moral courage and displays a sense of true justice in his dealing with the outlaws, dishonest politicians, and landowners.

Gruber relies on the apparatus of the popular western, such as card games (usually poker), Indian trouble, tall tales, six-shooters, outlaws, dudes, horses, cattle, silent men, and dramatic gun battles. Women are scarce, and when they appear they are stereotypes and male dominated.

Most of Gruber's settings are in Texas, Oklahoma, Kansas, and the Great Plains, and his characters are officers who served in the Civil War, people or families who have moved from the south to make a new life, or outlaws. His novels rely on the Horatio Alger theme of "good men and true." Gruber transplanted the code of the south to the west (an idea he may have gotten from Emerson Hough). Gruber was a self-taught historian of the Civil War, and much of the realism in his westerns comes from his use of Civil War history. *Quantrell's Raiders* is set during the Civil War, and *The Dawn Riders, Fort Starvation, Bugles West*, and *This Gun Is Still* make reference to or have characters who were participants in the Civil War.

In his autobiography, *The Pulp Jungle*, Gruber gives considerable background on his writing life. *Zane Grey, A Biography* appeared posthumously.

—Dorys C. Grover

GULICK, Bill (Grover C. Gulick). American. Born in Kansas City, Missouri, 22 February 1916. Educated at the University of Oklahoma, Norman, 1935–37, 1939–41 (studied under Walter S. Campbell and Foster Harris). Married Marcella Jeanne Abbott in 1946. Freelance writer. President, Western Writers of America, 1955–56. Recipient: Western Writers of America Spur award, for story, 1959, 1961; University of Oklahoma School of Professional Writing award, 1965; Cowboy Hall of Fame Western Heritage award, 1966; Washington State Arts Commission Governor's award, 1967, 1972; Pacific Northwest Booksellers award, 1971; Levi Strauss Co. and Western Writers of America Golden Saddleman award, 1983. Agent: Carl Brandt, Brandt and Brandt, 1501 Broadway, New York, New York 10036. Address: Route 3, Box 319, Walla Walla, Washington 99362, U.S.A.

WESTERN PUBLICATIONS

Novels

Bend of the Snake. Boston, Houghton Mifflin, 1950; London, Museum Press, 1952.
A Drum Calls West. Boston, Houghton Mifflin, 1952; London, Museum Press, 1953.
A Thousand for the Cariboo. Boston, Houghton Mifflin, 1954; London, Hale, 1955; as *Trail Drive*, New York, Popular Library, 1955.
The Land Beyond. Boston, Houghton Mifflin, 1958.
Showdown in the Sun. New York, Popular Library, 1958.
The Moon-Eyed Appaloosa. New York, Doubleday, 1962.
The Hallelujah Train. New York, Doubleday, 1963; London, Deutsch, 1964; as *The Hallelujah Trail*, Doubleday, 1965.
They Came to a Valley. New York, Doubleday, 1966.
Liveliest Town in the West. New York, Doubleday, 1969.
The Country Club Caper. New York, Doubleday, 1971.
Treasure in Hell's Canyon. New York, Doubleday, 1979.
Northwest destiny: A Trilogy:
Distant Trails 1805–1836. New York, Doubleday, 1988; London, Hale, 1990.
Gathering Storm 1837–1868. New York, Doubleday, 1988; London, Hale, 1990.
Lost Wallowa 1869–1879. New York, Doubleday, 1988.

Short Stories

White Men, Red Men, and Mountain Men. Boston, Houghton Mifflin, 1955; as *The Mountain Men*, New York, Popular Library, 1956.
The Shaming of Broken Horn and Other Stories. New York, Doubleday, 1961.

Uncollected Short Stories

"No Chance for Honest Cowmen," in *Star Western* (Chicago), December 1944.
"Death in the Mountains," in *West* (Kingswood, Surrey), February 1950.
"Fair Trade," in *Zane Grey's Western* (New York), February 1950.
"Cascades Crossing," in *All Western* (New York), December 1950–January 1951.
"Rendezvous Romance," in *Bad Men and Good*. New York, Dodd Mead, 1953; as "Indian Trap," in *Frontier*, edited by Luke Short, New York, Bantam, 1955.
"Two-Faced Promise," in *Bar 1*, edited by Scott Meredith. New York, Dutton, 1953.
"The Courting Feud," in *Gunsmoke* (New York), August 1953.
"Waters of Manitou," in *Holsters and Heroes*, edited by Noel M. Loomis. New York, Macmillan, 1954.
"That's a Good Trick, Professor," in *Thrilling Western* (London), July 1954.
"The Kid That Rode with Death," in *Wild Horse Roundup*, edited by Jim Kjelgaard. New York, Dodd Mead, 1957.
"New Saddle," in *A Saddlebag of Tales*, edited by Rutherford Montgomery. New York, Dodd Mead, 1959.
"Trial by Jury," in *Frontiers West*, edited by S. Omar Barker. New York, Doubleday, 1959.
"The Marriage of Moon Wind," in *The Saturday Evening Post Reader of Western Stories*, edited by E.N. Brandt. New York, Doubleday, 1960.
"Thief in Camp," in *Spurs West*, edited by S. Omar Barker. New York, Doubleday, 1960.
"Killer Blood," in *Trails of Adventure*, edited by E.D. Mygatt. New York, Dodd Mead, 1961.
"Night Run," in *They Won Their Spurs*, edited by Nelson Nye. New York, Avon, 1962.
"Big Olaf Paints for War," in *Rawhide Men*, edited by Kenneth Fowler. New York, Doubleday, 1965.
"Something in the Air," in *This Land Around Us*, edited by Ellis Lucia. New York, Doubleday, 1969.
"Tear Up the Orders," in *With Guidons Flying*, edited by Charles N. Heckelmann. New York, Doubleday, 1970.
"Border Incident," in *The Northwesterners*, edited by Bill Pronzini and Martin H. Greenberg. New York, Fawcett, 1990.
"Where the Wind Blows Free," in *The Northwesterners*, edited by Bill Pronzini and Martin H. Greenberg. New York, Fawcett, 1990.

OTHER PUBLICATIONS

Plays

The Magic Musket (produced Walla Walla, Washington, 1953).
Pe-wa-oo-yit: The First Treaty Council (produced Walla Walla, Washington, 1955).
Trails West (produced Walla Walla, Washington, 1976).

Screenplays: *Bend of the River*, 1951; *The Road to Denver*, 1955; *Hallelujah Trail*, 1965.

Other

Cowboy, Fisherman, Hunter, with Larry Mersfelder. Kansas City, Brown White Lowell Press, 1942.
Abilene or Bust (for children), with Thomas Rothrock. New York, Cupples and Leon, 1946.
Desolation Trail (for children), with Thomas Rothrock. New York, Cupples and Leon, 1946.
Snake River Country, photographs by Earl Roberge. Caldwell, Idaho, Caxton, 1971.
Chief Joseph Country: Land of the Nez Percé. Caldwell, Idaho, Caxton, 1981.
Roadside History of Oregon. Missoula, Montana, Mountain Press, 1990.

*

Manuscript Collections: University of Oregon Library, Eugene; University of Wyoming Library, Laramie; Idaho Historical Society, Boise.

Bill Gulick comments:

I have never considered myself a writer of Westerns. I am simply a writer who lives in the West, knows its past and present very well, and is concerned for its future. I write books that are set in the West—not Westerns.

* * *

It was while attending the University of Oklahoma in 1940 that Bill Gulick first became interested in writing fiction. His early efforts were sports stories, and some of these were incorporated into his first book, a collaboration with Larry Mersfelder titled *Cowboy Fisherman, Hunter*. Gulick was already writing fiction for the pulps when he went to live in Greenwich Village for nine months during 1943–1944 and he again collaborated, this time with Thomas Rothrock, in writing two novels for children, both with a western setting. This experience convinced Gulick that his true *métier* was western fiction. He continued to turn out short stories for pulp magazines until, by the end of the decade, he became a regular contributor to the *Saturday Evening Post*. The two Spur awards he was to win from the Western Writers of America were for short stories which first appeared in the *Post*, "Thief in Camp" in 1958 and "The Shaming of Broken Horn" in 1960. His first effort at longer fiction was also published by the *Post*, "The Man from Texas," a three-part serial which was eventually brought to the screen as *The Man from Denver*. His first novel was *Bend of the Snake* which was also filmed, retitled *Bend of the River*.

"The Man from Texas" is a good, if rather conventional, ranch romance formulary Western which sets forth a theme explored later at greater length in *Bend of the Snake*: two men united against all odds. In the serial, the twosome consists of two brothers, one a hard worker and reliable, the other more flamboyant and willing to ally himself for a time with the lawless element. In *Bend of the Snake*, the twosome consists of old friends joined together in the area around Walla Walla, Washington, operating a stageline and freighting business. The plot of the novel makes use of two hoops, a strategy Gulick would employ in a number of his novels. The first hoop has to do with the contest between the twosome and their dishonest adversaries. The second hoop comes about when the hero, Scott Burton, discovers that his partner resorted to murder and theft and must take off after him.

Bend of the Snake—although the river where the showdown takes place is the Columbia—remains an elaborate formulary Western very much in the later Ernest Haycox tradition. Gulick's next three novels were also formulary efforts, each one better, more complicated, with stronger characterizations and more unusual elements and themes than the last. *A Drum Calls West* is set in a mining town but as a sub-theme replays the torments in several characters engendered by the Civil War. *A Thousand for the Cariboo* is a cattle drive story which begins at The Dalles in Oregon and pushes up into British Columbia. Although he moved around the country for a time following his marriage, Gulick soon settled on a small ranch outside Walla Walla where he continued to live. Among the places he resided briefly were Arizona and Mexico and these locations provide the settings for *Showdown in the Sun*, perhaps the finest formulary Western he wrote. Each of these novels employs the two-hoop strategy. *Showdown in the Sun*, for example, has much of its early action centered in Sunslope, Arizona Territory, before the story moves to San Cristobal in northern Mexico and a pitched battle between a renegade local militia and *peon* miners fighting on the side of the hero. Nothing in these early novels is predictable, however, despite the broad formulary conventions, so that it is Popo and his band of Apaches who come to the rescue of the imperiled miners by attacking the militia at the rear!

Gulick's most impressive work from these years is to be found in his shorter fiction. A *Post* editor once told him, "What I like about your stories is that they're not Westerns," and, truthfully, there is little that is formulary in Gulick's short stories, much that is humorous, characters that are ornery and constantly interesting, with a background of historical detail that is vividly evoked. His mountain man stories are especially noteworthy, some of which he included in his collection *White Men, Red Men, and Mountain Men*; foremost among them, surely, is "Conquest," a long short story about a group of mountain men who decide to sojourn in peaceful southern California. The variety of setting, characters, circumstances, always leavened with humor, are no less impressive in the stories he included in *The Shaming of Broken Horn and Other Stories*.

The Hallelujah Trail—originally titled *The Hallelujah Train* prior to its motion picture incarnation—along with *The Moon-Eyed Appaloosa, Liveliest Town in the West*, and *The Country Club Caper* constitute notable efforts at writing comic novels with a western setting. In the first, a shipment of spirits is the prize sought by a number of groups, a determined suffragette, and the Indians among them. The second involves Army horses, the Cavalry, the Indians, and a group of jittery settlers bound for Oregon. *The Country Club Caper* is a contemporary story with a golf course abutting an Indian reservation. The least successful is *Liveliest Town in the West*, a spoof on the whole world of dime novels and the iconography of the Wild West shows. Here the second hoop of the plot does not sustain as much interest as the first, a problem which also affects a serious novel, *Treasure in Hell's Canyon*, which is utterly gripping in its first hoop concerned with the Chinese community in Portland and the miscegenation rampant in Oregon, while the second hoop, with the formulary ingredient of villains preying upon Chinese miners in Idaho, tends to have a diffusive effect.

As fine as many of Gulick's efforts have been in other directions, his best work is found in his historical novels, *The Land Beyond, They Came to a Valley*, and the saga of Tall Bird and John Crane which he titled *Northwest Destiny* and which encompasses the period 1805–1879. Through a disastrous blunder in publishing, this last book was issued in three volumes as Double D Westerns by Doubleday, so that the first volume was out of print before the final volume appeared. *The Land Beyond* is a mountain man novel which is readily as fine as those produced by Guthrie, Fisher, or Harvey Fergusson. *They Came to a Valley* is an even more graphic portrayal of the passage westward than *Honey in the Horn* by H.L. Davis or *The Way West* by A.B. Guthrie, Jr. Gulick's "trilogy," which one day must be united into one book, is a powerful, moving, panoramic vision of life in the Pacific Northwest, as honest and fair in its presentation of the dilemma of the Indians as of the settlers. The region explored in these books, as in most of Gulick's fiction, is one which he knew intimately. His historical novels deserve a permanent place among the finest American literature from any period and it is to be hoped that Bill Gulick will come, in time, to be accorded the recognition and stature which these books surely warrant and will ultimately make secure.

—Jon Tuska

GUTHRIE, A(lfred) B(ertram), Jr. American. Born in Bedford, Indiana, 13 January 1901. Educated at schools in Choteau, Montana; University of Washington, Seattle, 1919–20; University of Montana, Missoula, A.B. in journalism 1923. Married 1) Harriet Larson in 1931 (divorced 1963), one son and one daughter; 2) Carol B. Luthin in 1969. Worked for the Choteau *Acantha*, 1915–19; reporter, 1926–29, city editor and editorial writer, 1929–45, and executive editor, 1945–47, Lexington *Leader*, Kentucky. Fellow, and Lecturer, Bread Loaf Writers Conference, Vermont, 1945–47. Professor of Creative Writing, University of Kentucky, Lexington, 1947–52. Recipient: Nieman fellowship, 1944; Pulitzer prize, 1950; Boys' Clubs of America Junior Book award, 1951; Academy award, for screenplay, 1952; National Association of Independent Schools award, 1961; National Cowboy Hall of Fame Wrangler award, 1970; Western Literature Association award, 1972; Western Writers of America Golden Saddleman award, 1978; State of Indiana Distinguished Contribution award, 1979; Commonwealth of Kentucky commemorative award, 1979; Montana Governor's award, 1982. Litt.D.: University of

Montana, 1949; Montana State University, Bozeman, 1977; L.H.D.: Indiana State University, Terre Haute, 1975. *Died 26 April 1991.*

PUBLICATIONS

Novels (series: Chick Charleston and Jason Beard)

Murders at Moon Dance. New York, Dutton, 1943; as *Trouble at Moon Dance*, New York, Popular Library, 1951; London, Long, 1961.
The Big Sky. New York, Sloane, and London, Boardman, 1947.
The Way West. New York, Sloane, 1949; London, Boardman, 1950.
These Thousand Hills. Boston, Houghton Mifflin, 1956; London, Hutchinson, 1957.
Arfive. Boston, Houghton Mifflin, 1971; London, Eyre Methuen, 1972.
Wild Pitch (Charleston/Beard). Boston, Houghton Mifflin, 1973; London, David Bruce and Watson, 1974.
The Last Valley. Boston, Houghton Mifflin, 1975.
No Second Wind (Charleston/Beard). Boston, Houghton Mifflin, 1980.
The Genuine Article (Charleston/Beard). Boston, Houghton Mifflin, 1981.
Fair Land, Fair Land. Boston, Houghton Mifflin, 1982.
Playing Catch-Up (Charleston/Beard). Boston, Houghton Mifflin, 1985.

Short Stories

The Big It and Other Stories. Boston, Houghton Mifflin, 1960; London, Hutchinson, 1961; as *Mountain Medicine*, New York, Pocket Books, 1961.

Uncollected Short Stories

"Newcomer," in *Gunsmoke* (New York), June 1953.
"Loco," in *Esquire* (New York), November 1967.
"Posse on the March," in *Saturday Evening Post* (Philadelphia), September 1976.
"First Principal," in *The Arbor House Treasury of Great Western Stories*, edited by Bill Pronzini and Martin H. Greenberg. New York, Arbor House, 1982.
"The Therefore Hog," in *The Cowboys*, edited by Bill Pronzini and Martin H. Greenberg. New York, Fawcett, 1985.

OTHER PUBLICATIONS

Novel

Murder in the Cotswolds. Boston, Houghton Mifflin, 1989.

Plays

Screenplays: *Shane*, with Jack Sher, 1951; *The Kentuckian*, 1955.

Other

The Blue Hen's Chick (autobiography). New York, McGraw Hill, 1965.
Once upon a Pond (for children). Missoula, Montana, Mountain Press, 1973.
Four Miles from Ear Mountain. Missoula, Montana, Kutenai Press, 1987.
Images from the Great West. Flintridge, California, Chaco Press, 1990.

*

Bibliography: in *Western American Literature* (Fort Collins, Colorado), Summer 1969.

Manuscript Collection: University of Kentucky, Lexington.

Critical Studies: *A.B. Guthrie, Jr.*, Austin, Texas, Steck Vaughn, 1968, and *A.B. Guthrie, Jr.*, Boston, Twayne, 1981, both by Thomas W. Ford.

* * *

After more than 20 years as a journalist, A.B. Guthrie, Jr., turned to fiction writing. Although he was not remarkably prolific in the succeeding 45 years, his productions have been of high quality. Aside from *Murders at Moon Dance*, an early work which the author himself belittles, Guthrie produced *The Big It*, a collection of short stories; *Once upon a Pond*, a collection of animal fables for children; *Wild Pitch*, *The Genuine Article*, *No Second Wind*, and *Playing Catch-Up*, murder mysteries set in the contemporary West; *The Big Sky*, *The Way West*, *These Thousand Hills*, *Arfive*, and *The Last Valley*, a five-novel series chronicling the development of the American West; and *Fair Land, Fair Land*, a novel that fits in, chronologically, between *The Way West* and *These Thousand Hills*.

The series of murder mysteries is set in a small modern-day Montana town. Each novel is narrated by Jason Beard, a younger friend and later the deputy of Sheriff Chick Charleston. In the first novel, Jason is a 17-year-old kid who pitches on the local baseball team; through the series he develops into a college kid home on vacation, and then a college graduate preparing to get married and follow a career in law enforcement. While many other town characters remain consistent from one novel to the next, Jason matures, as does the subject matter he narrates. Stylistically, the narrative voice is nicely done, and it is an effective medium for observations of the landscape, small town life, and human nature.

The short stories, animal stories, and mystery stories are respectable but not exceptional in their own genres, and Guthrie scholars agree that his major achievement, upon which his literary reputation will be based, is the five-novel series and its later inclusion that spans the development of the west from 1830 to 1946 and that also spans Guthrie's fiction-writing career. These novels have in common the best features of Guthrie's fiction: well-researched and artistically employed historical detail, a convincing feeling for the land and the power it works upon character, and a serious examination of the blessings and evils brought on by progress and civilization.

The Big Sky, commonly regarded as Guthrie's masterpiece, chronicles the era of the mountain men, or fur trappers and hunters. Set in the era 1830–43, it recreates the vastness and freedom that the early exploiters felt under the big sky. While it presents moving portraits of the landscape, the rivers, the weather, and the details of the trade (hunting, trapping, skinning), the novel gains its full power by developing a sense of what this exploitation of the pristine land amounts to. The tragic paradox realized in the conclusion of the novel is that in pursuing the life that he loved, the mountain man helped destroy the very thing that he loved. What is left to him is the vocation of guide, to help others journey across the land and despoil it further.

An additional merit of this book, and one that continues through all five of the major novels, is Guthrie's treatment of characters and their relationships. In *The Big Sky*, as in later works, the main character is interesting but not attractive in a heroic sense. Boone Caudill is surly, brooding, impulsive; his actions demonstrate that adult relations have far-reaching consequences, and they generate tensions that are not easily resolved, especially by physical violence.

The Way West, which won a Pulitzer prize in 1950, continues with the next phase of America's westering—the wagon train emigration. Once again the narrative is enriched by historical and geographical detail, so that the reader is liberally educated about the danger and ennui of the transcontinental trek. An impressive achievement in this novel is Guthrie's success at subordinating the research material to his narrative and characterization. The "authentic" material is not thrust in gratuitously, for its own sake, but for the sake of bringing out character or tension between characters. The artist's eye is always on the complex of motives underlying action; realistic, pragmatic concerns such as the merits of mules as opposed to horses, the amount of provisions required, or the burning of *bois de vache* on the treeless prairies provide occasions to portray avarice, vindictiveness, prudery, and other human traits. This novel, like its predecessor, demonstrates that relationships do not have neat endings or tidy resolutions, just as the march of civilization is not neatly affirmative or negative.

Just as *The Big Sky* and *The Way West* are linked by a character, Dick Summers, who appears in both novels, there is a character link between *The Way West* and *These Thousand Hills*. Lat Evans, the protagonist of the latter novel, is the grandson of Lije Evans, the main character of the former. The Evans family has settled in Oregon after the trek, and now the grandson is restless to move on. He seeks his fortune in Montana, and through following his fortunes the reader learns of the next phase of westward settlement—the establishment of the cattle industry. Lat's experiences include driving cattle, breaking and racing horses, hunting wolves, visiting brothels, establishing a ranch, punishing rustlers, and accepting civic responsibility. But despite the abundance of colorful material in this novel, there is not much sustained drama, not much ado or issue to give the novel continuity. Again Guthrie probes into the problem of civilization encroaching upon the wild free land, with the conclusion that the good and the bad are mixed, but this issue does not forcefully undergird the novel.

These Thousand Hills has been the least popular of Guthrie's novels, perhaps because it follows the two novels that have rightfully gained him distinction. *These Thousand Hills* is not a bad novel; it simply doesn't have the force of the earlier two.

Arfive, the next in the series, takes place in the early years of the 20th century. It focuses mainly upon the personal and public problems encountered by Benton Collingsworth, a high school principal who brings education, a moral conscience, and a Victorian prudishness to a small western town. As Guthrie's novels progress in history, his dramatic conflicts draw less upon civilization vs. savagery and man vs. environment, and more upon problems within civilization, such as attitudes towards prostitution, homosexuality, venereal disease, sexual drive, bodily functions, technology, and capitalistic competition. There is still the central problem of change, but it becomes redefined as civilization takes a greater hold on the country. Thus the interpersonal conflicts become more subdued, with outdoor adventure giving way to social drama.

The Last Valley is a sequel to *Arfive*, taking place a few years later in the same town of Arfive, and therefore containing many of the same characters. Like Collingsworth in the earlier novel, Ben Tate is drawn by the openness and beauty of the country, and he comes to Arfive to take over the town newspaper. Also like Collingsworth, he has a profession that is emblematic of civilization. In this last novel Guthrie examines the process of later growth, from shortly after World War I to shortly after World War II, showing once again, in dialogue and in the incidents of the plot, that progress and change bring mixed blessings. This novel expresses, even more clearly than the earlier novels, the conclusion that in human relations as well as in social progress, there are paradoxes and contradictions, and no "clean choices."

The end effect is neither an affirmation nor a rejection of the march of civilization; Guthrie sees change as inevitable, as something that one must confront with an informed conscience and with the expectation that seemingly good choices may turn out to be mistakes. From a reading of the five-novel set, one is impressed with the conclusion that man has a responsibility to the land he has settled and developed, just as he has a responsibility to the people he is linked to through community or family. Man's reward is the fulfillment he gains through his relationships with the land and with others. For Guthrie those relationships change with history, but they persist.

Having produced these five novels in chronological order, Guthrie returned to the period 1845–70 for *Fair Land, Fair Land*, which, as the author's note tells us, is meant to bridge the gap between *The Way West* and *These Thousand Hills*. The principal character is Dick Summers, brought back from *The Big Sky* and *The Way West;* he keeps company with Teal Eye (*The Big Sky*) and Higgins (*The Way West*) as he settles in that part of Montana where Guthrie lived much of his life. Although the novel fits in with the characters and chronology of the other novels, it does not fit thematically. The plot turns a little more heavily on coincidence and improbability, and the ending has a more definitive resolution of conflicts. Thus the novel delivers a more pronounced judgment on civilization and the changes brought by time, and there is less moral negotiation than in the other novels. *Fair Land, Fair Land* presents beautiful evocations of the landscape and a rich sense of a life lived there, but its heavy elegiac tone and concluding bitterness will trouble some readers who try to fit it into the continuity of the five novels written earlier.

Readers are bound to like some novels better than others, but *The Big Sky* and *The Way West* will probably prevail as Guthrie's two best. All of his novels are worth reading, however, and the body of his work is thought-provoking to consider in its totality.

—John D. Nesbitt

H

HAAS, Ben(jamin Leopold). Also wrote as John Benteen; Thorne Douglas; John Michael Elliott; Richard Meade. American. Born in Charlotte, North Carolina, 21 July 1926. Educated at schools in Charlotte. Served in the United States Army for two years: Sergeant. Married Douglas Thornton Taylor in 1950; three sons. Proofreader, Charlotte *News*, 1947; clerk, American Oil Company, Charlotte, 1947–52; steel estimator, Southern Engineering Company, Charlotte, 1953–56; estimator and assistant sales manager, B.L. Montague Co., Sumter, South Carolina, 1956–59; manager, Raleigh Metal Products, North Carolina, 1959–61; then full-time writer. *Died 27 October 1977.*

WESTERN PUBLICATIONS

Novels as John Benteen (series: Fargo in all books)

Panama Gold. New York, Belmont Tower, 1969; Leicester, Thorpe, 1985.
Alaska Steel. New York, Belmont Tower, 1969.
Massacre River. New York, Belmont Tower, 1969; Leicester, Thorpe, 1986.
The Wildcatters. New York, Belmont Tower, 1970; Leicester, Thorpe, 1985.
Apache Raiders. New York, Belmont Tower, 1970.
The Sharpshooters. New York, Belmont Tower, 1970; Leicester, Thorpe, 1986.
Valley of Skulls. New York, Belmont Tower, 1970.
Wolf's Head. New York, Belmont Tower, 1970.
The Black Bulls. New York, Belmont Tower, 1971.
Fargo. New York, Belmont Tower, 1971.
Killing Spree. New York, Belmont Tower, 1972.
The Phantom Gunman. New York, Belmont Tower, 1972.
Shotgun Man. New York, Belmont Tower, 1973.
Bandolero. New York, Tower, 1973.
The Border Jumpers. New York, Tower, 1976.
Death Valley Gold. New York, Tower, 1976.
Hell on Wheels. New York, Tower, 1976.
Killer's Moon. New York, Belmont Tower, 1976.
Fargo and the Texas Rangers. New York, Belmont Tower, 1977.
Dakota Badlands. New York, Belmont Tower, 1977.

Novels as John Benteen (series: Sundance in all books)

Overkill. New York, Dorchester, 1971; Leicester, Thorpe, 1985.
Death in the Lava. New York, Dorchester, 1971; Leicester, Thorpe, 1985.
Dead Man's Canyon. New York, Dorchester, 1972; Leicester, Thorpe, 1984.
Dakota Territory. New York, Dorchester, 1972.
The Pistoleros. New York, Dorchester, 1972.
Ride the Man Down. New York, Dorchester, 1973.
The Bronco Trail. New York, Dorchester, 1973.
The Wild Stallions. New York, Dorchester, 1973.
Bring Me His Scalp. New York, Dorchester, 1973; Leicester, Thorpe, 1984.
Taps at Little Big Horn. New York, Dorchester, 1973.
War Party. New York, Dorchester, 1974.
The Ghost Dancers. New York, Dorchester, 1975.
Run for Cover. New York, Dorchester, 1976; Leicester, Thorpe, 1990.
Blood on the Prairie. New York, Dorchester, 1976.
War Trail. New York, Dorchester, 1976.
Manhunt. New York, Dorchester, 1976.
Silent Enemy. New York, Dorchester, 1977; Leicester, Thorpe, 1986.
Riding Shotgun. New York, Dorchester, 1977.
Gunbelt. New York, Dorchester, 1977.

Novels as John Benteen (series: John Cutler in both books)

Wolf Pack. New York, Tower, 1972.
The Gunhawks. New York, Tower, 1972.

Novels as Thorne Douglas (series: Rancho Bravo in all books)

Calhoon. New York, Fawcett, 1973.
The Big Drive. New York, Fawcett, 1973; London, Coronet, 1974.
Killraine. New York, Fawcett, 1975; London, Coronet, 1977.
The Night Riders. New York, Fawcett, 1975; London, Coronet, 1979.
The Mustang Men. New York, Fawcett, 1977; London, Coronet, 1979.

Novels as Richard Meade

Cimarron Strip. New York, Popular Library, 1967.
Rough Night in Jericho (novelization of screenplay). New York, Fawcett, 1967.
Big Bend. New York, Doubleday, 1968; London, Mayflower, 1969.
Cartridge Creek. New York, Doubleday, 1973.
Gaylord's Badge. New York, Doubleday, 1975; London, Prior, 1976.

OTHER PUBLICATIONS

Novels

The Foragers. New York, Simon and Schuster, 1962; London, Davies, 1963.
Look Away, Look Away. New York, Simon and Schuster, 1964.
The Last Valley. New York, Simon and Schuster, and London, Davies, 1966.
The Troubled Summer. Indianapolis, Bobbs Merrill, 1966.
The Chandler Heritage. New York, Simon and Schuster, and London, Davies, 1972.
Daisy Canfield. New York, Simon and Schuster, and London, Davies, 1973.

The House of Christina. New York, Simon and Schuster, and London, Davies, 1977.

Novels as Richard Meade

Two Surgeons. New York, Dell, and London, Mayflower, 1964.
Summer Always Ends. New York, Dell, 1966.
Beyond the Danube. London, Davies, 1967; as *The Danube Runs Red*, New York, Random House, 1968; as *The Gun Runner*, London, New English Library, 1969.
The Sword of Morningstar. New York, Signet, 1968.
A Score of Arms. London, Davies, 1969; as *The Last Fraulein*, New York, Random House, 1970.
Exile's Quest. New York, Signet, 1970.
The Belle From Catscratch, with Jay Rutledge. New York, Fawcett, 1972.

Other

KKK: A Study of the Ku Klux Klan. Evanston, Illinois, Regency, 1963.

* * *

Ben Haas is at once one of the most influential—and underrated—western writers of recent times. Although little of his work remains in print today, the hard-hitting adventures of his two most famous characters, freelance fighting man Neal Fargo and half-breed soldier of fortune Jim Sundance, were largely responsible for creating the western series market virtually singlehanded.

Haas always looked upon himself as a serious novelist. He made no secret of the fact that the dozens of paperback novels he published during the 1960's and 1970's were written solely to support him during the writing of his more 'important' work. He never penned a single Western that he considered to be a major novel, but his interest in the history and lore of the Old West, plus a deep and detailed knowledge of the American Indian, constantly ensured the authenticity of his western characters, plots and backgrounds.

Born into a family of avid readers, Haas and his two brothers grew up in the lonely country just outside Charlotte, North Carolina. Recalling those days for a biographical sketch in *Contemporary Authors*, Haas noted, "We hunted, fished, trapped, collected Indian relics . . . We back-packed into the Smoky Mountains long before progress had erased the old-time mountaineers, and, in our very early youth, knew Confederate veterans and ex-slaves."

Haas decided that he wanted to be a writer at the age of 14, and sold his first short story to a western pulp magazine four years later. Back in civilian life after two years in the army, he continued to write part-time, penning his first novel, a Civil War story entitled *The Foragers*, in 1961. Shortly thereafter he turned to writing full-time.

His earliest Westerns were published under the pseudonym Richard Meade, a pen-name which also appeared on some of his suspense and fantasy novels. The Meade Westerns are largely traditional, with gun-fast heroes and black-hatted villains, but, as with all his work, Haas's skill in characterisation and dialogue is such that even these stereotypes become credible.

During the late 1960's and throughout the 1970's, Haas created and continued three western series under the pseudonym John Benteen, and it is this work which has proved to be his most popular and enduring. The aforementioned Fargo and Sundance are both professional fighting men who hire themselves out for money. In Fargo's case, the money is quickly spent on month-long binges of high city living. Sundance, on the other hand, is a half-English, half-Cheyenne warrior; he sends his fees back East to help finance the fight against the notorious Indian Ring.

Both of these characters have friends in high places. In Fargo's case it is President Teddy Roosevelt; in Sundance's, General George Crook. Quite often, Fargo's adventures take place in exotic locations; the Philippines, Panama, Alaska. Many more, and virtually all of the Sundance titles, are set in some of America's most inhospitable terrain.

In the Benteen books, women are often portrayed as strong, shrewd, and ambitious. Rarely do Haas' tough-as-leather men succeed in dominating them. An arch-villain appears in each book, usually sporting a suitable name—Austin Shell, Tulso Dart, Cleve Bruckner. Without exception, these villains are always dispatched by the hero at the climax of the book.

Generally, Haas used a tight, hardboiled style of writing to tell his stories, and it worked to particularly good effect in the Fargo books. It is difficult to know exactly why the third continuing character he created under the Benteen name never became as successful as his predecessors, however.

John Cutler is a marshal turned man- and animal-tracker. Slightly crazed by the death of his wife, he now roams the West in search of the rogue grizzly who killed her. Most of the time he rides a wagon drawn by two sleek black mules called Kate and Emma, but he also boasts a bay gelding named Apache and a gigantic Red Setter known, aptly enough, as Red. As with nearly all the Benteen stories, the lead character seldom involves himself in other folks' troubles unless hired to do so, usually for a substantial monetary reward.

Haas only penned the first two books in the Cutler series. It was continued much later (and for four books only) by H.V. Elkin. (Incidentally, the Sundance series was later taken over by Jack Slade, another very popular Leisure Books author, and then Peter McCurtin.) Although Haas wrote the majority of the Fargo stories, at least three of them—*Dynamite Fever*, *Sierra Silver*, and *Gringo Guns*—are the work of other authors.

The violence of the Benteen books was toned down considerably for the more traditional Rancho Bravo sequence, which Haas wrote as Thorne Douglas, although it should be said that this superb five-book saga (concerning the formation of a cattle spread just after the Civil War) always boasted more than its share of action. Characterisation was one of the strongest themes here, as a Confederate, a Yankee, an unreconstructed Texan, and a Negro join forces to tame the Lone Star wilderness and shape it to their will.

Haas was a compulsive writer, but, since he saw little point in listing all of his paperback originals, preferring to be remembered for his admittedly fine "serious" novels, it is quite likely that some of his other work in the western field will never now come to light. While attending a dinner in New York, at which he was one of several authors being honored by an American book club, he suffered a heart attack and died on 27 October 1977. He was 51 years old.

—David Whitehead

HAIG-BROWN, Roderick (Langmere). Canadian. Born in Lancing, Sussex, England, 21 February 1908; emigrated to Canada, 1926. Educated at Charterhouse, Godalming, Surrey. Served in the Canadian Army, 1939–45: Major. Married Ann Elmore in 1934; one son and three daughters. Worked as a logger, trapper, fisherman, and guide, Washington, U.S.A., 1926, and British Columbia, 1927–29; provincial magistrate and judge, Campbell River Children's and Family Court, British Columbia, 1942–75. Frequent broadcaster and moderator of television programs. Chancellor, University of Victoria, British Columbia, 1970–73. Recipient: Canadian Library Association Book of the Year Medal, 1947, 1964; Governor-General's citation, 1948; Crandell Conservation Trophy, 1955; Vicky Metcalf award, 1966. LL.D.: University of British Columbia, Vancouver, 1952. *Died 9 October 1976.*

WESTERN PUBLICATIONS

Novels

Pool and Rapid: The Story of a River. Toronto, McClelland and Stewart, and London, A. and C. Black, 1932.
Timber: A Novel of Pacific Coast Loggers. New York, Morrow, 1942; as *The Tall Trees Fall*, London, Collins, 1943.
On the Highest Hill. Toronto, Collins, and New York, Morrow, 1949; London, Collins, 1950.

Short Stories

Woods and River Tales, edited by Valerie Haig-Brown. Toronto, McClelland and Stewart, 1980.

Fiction (for children)

Silver: The Life of an Atlantic Salmon. London, A. and C. Black, 1931.
Ki-yu: A Story of Panthers. Boston, Houghton Mifflin, 1934; as *Panther*, London, Cape, 1934.
Starbuck Valley Winter. New York, Morrow, 1943; London, Collins, 1944.
Saltwater Summer. Toronto, Collins, and New York, Morrow, 1948; London, Collins, 1949.
Mounted Police Patrol. London, Collins, and New York, Morrow, 1954.
Fur and Gold. Toronto, Longman, 1962.
The Whale People. London, Collins, 1962; New York, Morrow, 1963.
Alison's Fishing Birds. Vancouver, Colophon, 1980.

Other (for children)

Captain of the Discovery: The Story of Captain George Vancouver. Toronto and London, Macmillan, 1956.
The Farthest Shores. Toronto, Longman, 1960.

Other

The Western Angler: An Account of Pacific Salmon and Western Trout in British Columbia. New York, Derrydale Press, 1939.
Return to the River: A Story of the Chinook Run. New York, Morrow, 1941; London, Collins, 1942.
A River Never Sleeps. Toronto, Collins, and New York, Morrow, 1946; London, Collins, 1948.
Measure of the Year. Toronto, Collins, and New York, Morrow, 1950.
Fisherman's Spring. Toronto, Collins, and New York, Morrow, 1951.
Spring Congregation Address 1952: Power and People. Vancouver, University of British Columbia, 1952.
Fisherman's Winter. New York, Morrow, 1954.
Divine Discontent: An Address to the Annual Assembly of Victoria College. Victoria, British Columbia, Victoria Daily Times, 1954.
The Case for the Preservation of Strathcona Park. Victoria, British Columbia, Daily Colonist, 1955.
Fabulous Fishing in Latin America. New York, Pan American World Airways, 1956.
The Face of Canada, with others. Toronto, Clarke Irwin, 1959; London, Harrap, 1960.
Fisherman's Summer: Toronto, Collins, and New York, Morrow, 1959.
The Living Land: An Account of the Natural Resources of British Columbia. Toronto, Macmillan, and New York, Morrow, 1961.
The Pacific Northwest, with Stewart Holbrook and Nard Jones, edited by Anthony Netboy. New York, Doubleday, 1963.
A Primer of Fly Fishing. Toronto, Collins, and New York, Morrow, 1964.
Fisherman's Fall. Toronto, Collins, and New York, Morrow, 1964.
Canada's Pacific Salmon, revised edition. Ottawa, Queen's Printer, 1967.
The Canadians 1867–1967. Toronto, Macmillan, 1967.
The Salmon. Ottawa, Queen's Printer, 1974.
Bright Waters, Bright Fish: An Examination of Angling in Canada. Vancouver, Douglas and McIntyre, and Portland, Oregon, Timber Press, 1980.
The Master and His Fish, edited by Valerie Haig-Brown. Toronto, McClelland and Stewart, and Seattle, University of Washington Press, 1981.
Writings and Reflections: From the World of Roderick Haig-Brown, edited by Valerie Haig-Brown. Toronto, McClelland and Stewart, and Seattle, University of Washington Press, 1982.

*

Manuscript Collection: University of British Columbia Library, Vancouver.

Theatrical Activities:
Actor: **Films**—*Out of the North*, 1952; *Rural Magistrate*.

* * *

Before the "boom period" of the last two decades, Roderick Haig-Brown was an undisputed giant of Canadian children's literature. The two-time winner of the Canadian Library Association Medal had distinguished himself as a writer of animal stories, boys' adventures, history, biography, and a *Bildungsroman* of pre-contact Native life. His works combined well-established genres, especially the animal and adventure story, with his deep knowledge and appreciation of the Canadian landscape and his respect for what he called "quiet heroes." His work as logger, fisherman, trapper, and guide sharpened his knowledge of nature and deepened his understanding of human nature; his lifelong love of nature provided inspiration and guides for his writing.

Four works illustrate his achievements in the different genres. *Ki-yu: A Story of Panthers* draws on detailed study of panthers; but, in the manner of the realistic animal story, he elevates his presentation of details to the level of symbol. Ki-yu, the most noble animal of the area, engages in heroic confrontation with the most dedicated hunter, one who respects and understands his prey. *Captain of the Discovery* combines historical facts with sensitive understanding of the challenges and responsibilities of leadership to present the life of George Vancouver, the 18th-century explorer who showed respect for his own men as well as the lands and people he encountered.

Foremost among the Haig-Brown titles that might justifiably be regarded as western are *Starbuck Valley Winter* and *The Whale People*. The first of these novels describes the coming of age of teenager Don Morgan, who spends a winter trapping to earn money for a new fishing boat. While Haig-Brown draws on ideas of manly virtue found in boys' adventure novels, his presentations of Don's inner life and of his struggles and achievements in the rugged West Coast landscape are convincing and authentic, drawn as they are on the author's own experience and knowledge. *The Whale People* is also an initiation novel, this time about a Nootka Indian teenager who assumes the role of chief after the death of his father. As in his other books, Haig-Brown's research is impeccable. More significant, he succeeds in recreating the inner life of someone of another culture and time, capturing the hero's response to his physical, social, and, perhaps most important, spiritual environments.

Although some critics consider Haig-Brown's writing old-fashioned, using 19th- and early 20th-century forms and focussing mainly on heroic male figures, his books are important treatments of a significant aspect of the Canadian experience: the human encounter with the grandeur and danger of the natural environment.

—Jon C. Stott

HAINES, John. *See* **RICHARDSON, Gladwell.**

HALL, Evan. *See* **HALLERAN, E. E.**

HALL, Oakley (Maxwell). Also writes as Jason Manor. American. Born in San Diego, California, 1 July 1920. Educated at the University of California, Berkeley, B.A. 1943; University of Iowa, Iowa City, M.F.A. 1950. Served in the United States Marine Corps, 1939–45. Married Barbara Edinger in 1945; four children. Teacher, University of Iowa Writers' Workshop, Iowa City, 1950–52; writer in-residence, 1967–69, Professor of English and Director of the Programs in Writing, 1969–1990, and Emeritus professor, 1990, University of California at Irvine. Founding director, 1970, and since 1986 executive director, Squaw Valley Community of Writers. Recipient: National Endowment for the arts grant, 1975, 1979; Western Writers of America Spur award, for short fiction, 1982; Western Heritage Wrangler award, for article, 1989. Agent: Don Congdon, Harold Matson Co., 276 Fifth Avenue, New York 10001. Address: P.O. Box 2101, Olympic Valley, California 95730, U.S.A.

WESTERN PUBLICATIONS

Novels (series: Legends West)

Warlock (Legends West). New York, Viking Press, 1958; London, Bodley Head, 1959.
The Adelita. New York, Doubleday, 1975.
The Bad Lands (Legends West). New York, Atheneum, 1978.
The Children of the Sun. New York, Macmillan, 1983.
The Coming of the Kid. New York, Harper, 1985.
Apaches (Legends West). New York, Simon and Schuster, 1986.

Uncollected Short Stories

"How to Make Jimsonweed Beer," in *Tri-Quarterly* (Evanston, Illinois), Winter 1976.
"The Flame Ceremony," in *Hawaii Review* (Honolulu), Fall 1978.
"The Kid," in *Tri-Quarterly* (Evanston, Illinois), Winter 1979.
"Henry Plummer," in *Tri-Quarterly* (Evanston, Illinois), Winter 1980.
"Casus Belli," in *Tri-Quarterly* (Evanston, Illinois), Spring 1980.
"Horseman," in *Antioch Review* (Yellow Springs, Ohio), Fall 1982.

OTHER PUBLICATIONS

Novels

Murder City (as O.M. Hall). New York, Farrar Straus, 1949.
So Many Doors. New York, Random House, and London, Barker, 1950.
Corpus of Joe Bailey. New York, Viking Press, and London, Reinhardt, 1953.
Mardios Beach. New York, Viking Press, and London, Reinhardt, 1955.
The Downhill Racers. New York, Viking Press, and London, Bodley Head, 1963.
The Pleasure Garden. New York, Viking Press, 1966.
A Game for Eagles. New York, Morrow, 1970.
Report from Beau Harbor. New York, Morrow, 1971.
Lullaby. New York, Atheneum, 1982.

Novels as Jason Manor

Too Dead to Run. New York, Viking Press, 1953; London, Secker and Warburg, 1954.
The Red Jaguar. New York, Viking Press, 1954; London, Secker and Warburg, 1955; as *The Girl in the Red Jaguar*, New York, Popular Library, 1955.
The Pawns of Fear. New York, Viking Press, and London, Secker and Warburg, 1955; as *No Halo for Me*, New York, Popular Library, 1956.
The Tramplers. New York, Viking Press, and London, Secker and Warburg, 1956.

Play

Angle of Repose, music by Andrew Imbrie, adaptation of the novel by Wallace Stegner (produced San Francisco, 1976). Water Gap, Delaware, Shawnee Press, 1976.

*

Manuscript Collection: Bancroft Library, University of California, Berkeley.

Oakley Hall comments:

My purpose in my western historical novels has been to gather up the three grand myths of the American West into a trilogy of novels. The first of these, *Warlock*, was based upon the frontier marshals such as Wyatt Earp, who brought civilization to the wild frontier towns. The second, *The Bad Lands*, is concerned with the range wars; big cattlemen vs. little, and cattlemen vs. settlers—based in particular upon the Johnson County War of Wyoming in 1892. The third novel, *Apaches*, is a fictionalization of the Lincoln County War and Victorio's War, combining the Billy the Kid legend and that of the Apaches, as the enemies of the congealing civilization of the New Mexico Frontier. *The Coming of the Kid* is serio-comic, a treatment of a connected bundle of western myths. *The Adelita* and *The Children of the Sun* are two volumes of a projected trilogy laid in Mexican history. *Children* is concerned with the Conquest of Mexico to the Coronado Expedition, *Adelita* with the Revolution of 1910–20. The central novel, *Independencia!* has still to be written.

* * *

Oakley Hall is an author of great invention. What mars his writing is that he involves too many characters in overly complicated plots in most of his novels. Seemingly, he attaches too much importance to his material and, thus, overwrites. Let it be said quickly, however, that he can create and analyze character well, that he is a genius at establishing a narrative milieu, and that he almost always writes with flair and grace.

Warlock was nominated for a Pulitzer Prize in 1958. It is probably still Hall's best-known work. Together with *The Bad Lands* and *Apaches*, it forms what is known as the Legends West trilogy. Warlock is a dusty western town resembling Tombstone, Arizona. Its citizens are forced to hire a marshal-savior, named Clay Blaisedell, as a weapon against trouble makers, led by cowboy-rustler Abe McQuown. Johnny Gannon is the deputy sheriff and the man-in-the-middle. The reader also meets gambler Tom Morgan, Morgan's ex-girlfriend, hordes of striking miners, an insane General, a drunken judge, and Apaches and Mexicans galore. The intermittent interruption of the story by the journal entries of a Warlock storekeeper provides an aura of historic truth, but the novel simply sprawls too much.

The same fault may be found in *The Bad Lands* and *Apaches*. *The Bad Lands* focuses on Andrew Levingston, an easterner who falls in love with the Dakota territory in the 1880's. Levingston is a thinly disguised Theodore Roosevelt, and other characters resemble the Marquis de Morès, real ranchers, and assorted plainsmen. Despite the Golden Spur award won by *The Bad Lands*, *Apaches* is a better novel. It is the story of Lt. Pat Cutler, a cavalry officer who cares more for his small group of Apache scouts than he does for his fellow officers or the Army chain-of-command. As long as Hall sticks with Cutler and his Indians, the novel is an excellent account of the Apache wars. But to merge this successful plot line with others, such as that of Johnny Angel (read Billy the Kid) and the Lincoln County range wars, is once more to overcrowd the canvas.

Too many plots and characters also spoil *The Adelita* and *The Coming of the Kid*. *The Adelita* covers the years 1904–70, mostly in Mexico, where Robert McBean prospects for oil until he is forced to join the rebels in the Mexican Revolution. *The Coming of the Kid* is Hall's attempt to become a fabulist by creating grotesque, one-dimensional characters (a dwarf herbalist, a blind Army officer, a man who can talk to horses, a Chinese cook, a decrepit general, and a bear called Duke of Cumberland). These creatures, once again, are based upon the participants in the Lincoln County wars.

While *The Children of the Sun* also has many characters on a panoramic scale, the plot is more tightly controlled. Four soldiers, sole survivors of an ill-fated Spanish expedition are shipwrecked on the Texas coast. One of them is Cabeza de Vaca and another is Andrés Dorantes, the novel's hero. They are called the children of the sun because they always walk westward in an attempt to rejoin their comrades in New Spain, 1600 miles away. The year-long journey (1535–36) ends in Mexico City, but then, via flashback, we learn of Dorantes's role in the loss and reconquest of Tenochtitlán (1520–36). Returning to a chronological sequence, Hall describes the experiences of Dorantes in Mexico City (1536–39) and his reluctant return, with the expedition of Coronado, to the lands of his earlier journey (1539–41). This book is rewarding for its historical sweep and accuracy, for its wealth of important detail, and its astute understanding of native practices and beliefs. It deserves to be better known. If only Hall had more narrative discipline—as he does in his excellent short stories.

—Robert J. Barnes

HALLER, Bill. *See* **BECHKO, P. A.**

HALLERAN, E(ugene) E(dward). Also writes as Evan Hall. American. Born in Wildwood, New Jersey, 28 February 1905. Educated at Bucknell University, Lewisburg, Pennsylvania, A.B. 1927; Temple University Law School, Philadelphia; Rutgers University, New Brunswick, New Jersey, Ed.M. 1938; University of Pennsylvania, Philadelphia. Married Edna Muriel Whittington in 1929 (died 1986); one son. Social studies teacher, Ocean City High School, New Jersey, 1928–49. Recipient: Western Writers of America Spur award, 1965. Address: 14448 Golf Club Drive, Indiantown, Florida 33495, U.S.A.

WESTERN PUBLICATIONS

Novels

No Range Is Free. Philadelphia, Macrae Smith, 1944.
Prairie Guns. Philadelphia, Macrae Smith, 1944; London, Quality Press, 1948.
Outposts of Vengeance. Philadelphia, Macrae Smith, 1945; London, Quality Press, 1949.
Shadow of the Badlands. Philadelphia, Macrae Smith, 1946; London, Quality Press, 1949.
Double Cross Trail. Philadelphia, Macrae Smith, 1946; London, Quality Press, 1949.
Outlaw Guns. Philadelphia, Macrae Smith, 1947; London, Hammond, 1949.
Rustlers' Canyon. Philadelphia, Macrae Smith, 1948; London, Hammond, 1950.
Outlaw Trail. Philadelphia, Macrae Smith, 1949; as *The Outlaw*, London, Hammond, 1952.
High Prairie. Philadelphia, Macrae Smith, 1950; London, Hammond, 1953.
Smoky Range. Philadelphia, Lippincott, 1951; London, Hammond, 1953.
Gunsmoke Valley. London, Hammond, 1952.
Straw Boss. Philadelphia, Lippincott, 1952; London, Hammond, 1954.
Colorado Creek. New York, Lion, 1953; London, Hammond, 1955; as *Logan* (as Evan Hall), Lion, 1956.
Winter Ambush. Philadelphia, Macrae Smith, 1954; London, Hammond, 1957.

Blazing Border. Philadelphia, Macrae Smith, 1955; London, Hammond, 1956.
Devil's Canyon. New York, Ballantine, 1956; London, Hammond, 1958.
Wagon Captain. New York, Ballantine, 1956; London, Hammond, 1958.
The Hostile Hills. New York, Ballantine, 1957; London, Hammond, 1959.
Spanish Ridge. New York, Ballantine, 1957; London, Hammond, 1959.
Shadow of the Big Horn. New York, Ballantine, 1960; London, Hammond, 1961.
The Dark Raiders. New York, Fawcett, 1960; London, Muller, 1961.
Warbonnet Creek. New York, Ballantine, 1960; London, Hammond, 1962.
Blood Brand. London, Hammond, 1961; as *Gringo Gun*, New York, Lancer, 1961.
Boot Hill Silver. New York, Avon, 1962.
Crimson Desert. New York, Ballantine, 1962; London, Hammond, 1964.
The Far Land. New York, Ballantine, 1963.
Indian Fighter. New York, Ballantine, and London, Hammond, 1964.
Summer of the Sioux. London, Hammond, 1965.
High Iron. New York, Ballantine, 1965.
Red River Country. New York, Ballantine, 1966.
The Pistoleros. New York, Belmont, 1967.
Outlaws of Empty Poke. New York, Ballantine, 1969; London, Hale, 1971.
Cimarron Thunder. New York, Ballantine, 1970.

Uncollected Short Stories

"Apache Style," in *Wild West* (New York), 30 May 1942.
"Battle Sights," in *Wild West* (New York), 10 April 1943.
"Two Gun Giveaway," in *Texas Rangers* (London), February 1945.
"Lawman's Chance," in *Texas Rangers* (London), August 1945.

OTHER PUBLICATIONS

Novels

Thirteen Toy Pistols. Philadelphia, McKay, 1945.
Convention Queen. New York, Ace, 1960.

*

E.E. Halleran comments:

I became a writer of "Westerns" by accident. As a teacher of U.S. history I had certain background historical information and it seemed that I might break into the fiction business by using it. I never liked Westerns. I did not read them and did not attend western movies. No one was more surprised than I was when I made my first sale. After 15 novels and many magazine Westerns had been published, I made my first trip west of the Mississippi River. To quote someone (?), "There is a special Providence that takes care of drunks and idiots—and me."

I have written nothing for about 24 years. I take my retirement quite seriously—if not quietly. Golf remains my main hobby, and while I no longer play to the 10 handicap I once had, I can still enjoy making life miserable for younger colleagues.

* * *

If most Westerns can be said to exist in that never-never land of time and place commonly known as the Old West, then the works of E.E. Halleran could be considered an exception to the rule. Ranging in period from the Leatherstocking days of General Mad Anthony Wayne's defeat of the Miami Indians to the post-Civil War feuding between the cattle drovers and sodbusters along the Chisolm Trail, Halleran's novels are well-researched pieces of history as well as classical Westerns to boot. In fact, it is probably his obsession with the minutiae of each period that sets Halleran apart from most writers of his genre and continues his success.

Two common factors uniting historical fiction are larger-than-life characters and details of the time: Halleran gives the reader both. In *Prairie Guns*, an early novel, we meet Wild Bill Hickok while still a U.S. Marshal and the Indian chieftain Roman Nose; *Outposts of Vengeance*, his next work, parades Mad Anthony Wayne, William Henry Harrison, and Daniel Boone across the page. Halleran will often place his characters—both fictional and historical—in the midst of the documented events they actually lived through, and though the results may not be so freewheeling as in the standard shoot-em-ups, the effects are more believable. One such example is a later book, *Winter Ambush*, a tale of cautious vengeance set in the frustrating, abortive expedition by the U.S. Army to quell a Mormon "uprising" in pre-Civil War days.

Halleran's novels are fast-paced and fun. Although his plots tend to be formulaic—beginning with boy-meets-girl, proceeding onto boy-loses-girl, and ending with boy-gets-girl-back—it is the action sequences intrinsic to this structure which keep the reader involved. Halleran possesses a descriptive gift for movement, especially mass movement, and the more frenetic or violent this movement the better he succeeds. A fine example of this is the mad rush by the Indian chief Roman Nose's braves upon the outnumbered soldiers near the end of *Prairie Guns*. This descriptive talent sweeps the reader up and carries him past the parts where action might bog down.

Another trick of Halleran's is a subplot of suspense. In *Prairie Guns*, who is behind the attacks on the cattle drovers if not the sodbusters (whom we soon find it is not)? In *Outposts of Vengeance*, what happened to the hero's fiancée in an Indian raid, and will he find her among the Miami tribes? In *Winter Ambush*, how was the hero's military career slandered, and will he be able to set it right? This subplot is often more effective than the romantic formula, and takes the reader quickly to the end.

And so the list continues. In such works as *Double Cross Trail, Rustlers' Canyon, Outlaw Trail, High Prairie*, and others Halleran maintains the suspense. He functions both as a writer and a teacher, practicing the craft of his fiction while simultaneously informing his readers of the esoterica of his western world.

—Joe Jackson

HAMILTON, Donald (Bengtsson). American. Born in Uppsala, Sweden, 24 March 1916; emigrated to the United States in 1924. Educated at the University of Chicago, B.S. 1938. Served in the United States Naval Reserve: Lieutenant. Married Kathleen Stick in 1941 (died 1990); two daughters and two sons. Since 1946 self-employed writer and photographer. Recipient: Western Writers of America Spur award, for story, 1967. Agent: Flora Roberts Inc., 65 East 55th Street, New York, New York 10022. Address: P.O. Box 1045, Santa Fe, New Mexico 87504, U.S.A.

WESTERN PUBLICATIONS

Novels

Smoky Valley. New York, Dell, 1954.
Mad River. New York, Dell, 1956; London, Wingate, 1957.
The Big Country. New York, Dell, 1957; London, Panther, 1958.
The Man from Santa Clara. New York, Dell, 1960; as *The Two-Shoot Gun*, New York, Fawcett, 1971.
Texas Fever. New York, Fawcett, 1960; London, Muller, 1961.

Uncollected Short Stories

"The Guns of William Longley," in *Iron Men and Silver Spurs*, edited by Donald Hamilton. New York, Fawcett, 1967.
"The Last Gunman," in *The Gunfighters*, edited by Bill Pronzini and Martin H. Greenberg. New York, Fawcett, 1987.

OTHER PUBLICATIONS

Novels

Date with Darkness. New York, Rinehart, 1947; London, Wingate, 1951.
The Steel Mirror. New York, Rinehart, 1948; London, Wingate, 1950.
Murder Twice Told. New York, Rinehart, 1950; London, Wingate, 1952.
Night Walker. New York, Dell, 1954; as *Rough Company*, London, Wingate, 1954.
Line of Fire. New York, Dell, 1955; London, Wingate, 1956.
Assignment: Murder. New York, Dell, 1956; as *Assassins Have Starry Eyes*, New York, Fawcett, 1966.
Death of a Citizen. New York, Fawcett, and London, Muller, 1960.
The Wrecking Crew. New York, Fawcett, 1960; London, Muller, 1961.
The Removers. New York, Fawcett, 1961; London, Muller, 1962.
Murderer's Row. New York, Fawcett, 1962; London, Muller, 1963.
The Silencers. New York, Fawcett, 1962; London, Hodder and Stoughton, 1966.
The Ambushers. New York, Fawcett, 1963; London, Hodder and Stoughton, 1967.
The Ravagers. New York, Fawcett, 1964.
The Shadowers. New York, Fawcett, and London, Muller, 1964.
The Devastators. New York, Fawcett, 1965; London, Hodder and Stoughton, 1967.
The Betrayers. New York, Fawcett, 1966; London, Hodder and Stoughton, 1968.
The Menacers. New York, Fawcett, and London, Hodder and Stoughton, 1968.
The Interlopers. New York, Fawcett, and London, Hodder and Stoughton, 1969.
The Poisoners. New York, Fawcett, and London, Hodder and Stoughton, 1971.
The Intriguers. New York, Fawcett, and London, Hodder and Stoughton, 1972.
The Intimidators. New York, Fawcett, and London, Hodder and Stoughton, 1974.
The Terminators. New York, Fawcett, 1975; London, Hodder and Stoughton, 1976.
The Retaliators. New York, Fawcett, 1976; London, Coronet, 1979.
The Terrorizers. New York, Fawcett, 1977.
The Mona Intercept. New York, Fawcett, 1980.
The Revengers. New York, Fawcett, 1982.
The Annihilators. New York, Fawcett, 1983.
The Infiltrators. New York, Fawcett, 1984.
The Detonators. New York, Fawcett, 1985.
The Vanishers. New York, Fawcett, Fawcett, 1986.
The Demolishers. New York, Fawcett, 1987.
The Frighteners. New York, Fawcett, 1989.

Play

Screenplay: *Five Steps to Danger*, with Henry S. Kessler and Turnley Walker, 1957.

Other

On Guns and Hunting. New York, Fawcett, 1970.
Cruises with Kathleen. New York, McKay, 1980.

Editor, *Iron Men and Silver Spurs*. New York, Fawcett, 1967.

*

Critical Study: "Donald Hamilton," in *Conversations, Vol. IV* by Ray Newquist, New York, Rand McNally, 1967.

* * *

Donald Hamilton has been a freelance writer and photographer since 1946, when he completed his wartime service in the Naval Reserve. He has written numerous magazine articles on hunting, yachting, and photography. A collection of his articles from *Outdoor Life* and other sources was published in 1970 as *Donald Hamilton on Guns and Hunting*. His first fiction appeared in *Collier's* magazine in 1946, and his first novel was published in the following year. *Date with Darkness* is a well-crafted story of counter-espionage; it set an enviable level of quality which has been maintained through nearly two dozen subsequent novels of crime and secret agents. The best known of these are the books about counterspy Matt Helm. Of this series, critic Anthony Boucher wrote in the *New York Times*: "Donald Hamilton has brought to the spy novel the authentic hard realism of Hammett; and his stories are as compelling, and probably as close to the sordid truth of espionage, as any now being told."

Hamilton is also the author of five western novels which display all the same virtues as his suspense fiction. They are tough-minded and unsentimental, though not by any means devoid of honest emotion. The hero of the first of these novels, *Smoky Valley*, is the quintessential Hamilton protagonist: a quiet, self-contained, capable man with a clear knowledge of both his abilities and his faults, avoiding violence until it is forced upon him, but then willing to take whatever action is necessary and accept responsibility for the consequences. The protagonist of *The Big Country* is a similar figure. He is a Maryland sea-captain who comes to Texas in 1886 to marry the daughter of a local cattleman. He finds himself in the midst of a relentless feud, and his eastern ways earn him the derision of the cattleman's trouble-making foreman. Both *Smoky Valley* and *The Big Country* were made into memorable films, the former under the title *The Violent Men*. *The Man from Santa Clara* (later reprinted as *The Two-Shoot Gun*) is arguably the best of Hamilton's Westerns. It is a tale of tangled emotions and bitter vengeance, centered around the title character, a deceptively quiet stranger whom an antagonist describes as "a walking shot-gun looking for a target."

Texas Fever was first published in 1960. This was also the year in which the first two of the Matt Helm books appeared. Hamilton has devoted himself principally to this series ever since. (A non-series suspense novel, *The Mona Intercept*, was published in 1980.) He returned to the western field briefly in 1967 to edit that year's Western Writers of America anthology *Iron Men and Silver Stars*. The short story which he wrote for that volume won the WWA Spur award as best Western short story of the year. Hamilton's preface to the book, reprinted from the WWA journal *The Roundup*, sets forth his attitude towards his westerns: "If I can write one book that gives some reader the wonderful hot-and-cold feeling down the spine that I got upon reading Zane Grey's *Riders of the Purple Sage* at the age of 14 (and still get, thinking about it! I wouldn't dream of spoiling it by reading the book again today), I'll be a proud and satisfied author, even if the critics pan the yarn and historians pick holes in it." Hamilton has certainly achieved this objective, and his western novels will continue to be read and reread for many years.

—R.E. Briney

HAMILTON, Kirk. Australian.

WESTERN PUBLICATIONS

Novels (series: Bannerman the Enforcer in all books)

The Enforcer. Sydney, Cleveland, n.d.
Ride the Lawless Land. Sydney, Cleveland, n.d.
Guns of Texas. Sydney, Cleveland, n.d.
A Gun for the Governor. Sydney, Cleveland, n.d.
Rogue Gun. Sydney, Cleveland, n.d.
Trail Wolves. Sydney, Cleveland, n.d.
Dead Shot. Sydney, Cleveland, n.d.
A Man Called Sundance. Sydney, Cleveland, n.d.
Mad Dog Hallam. Sydney, Cleveland, n.d.
Shadow Mesa. Sydney, Cleveland, n.d.
Day of the Wolf. Sydney, Cleveland, n.d.
Tejano. Sydney, Cleveland, n.d.
The Guilty Guns. Sydney, Cleveland, n.d.
The Toughest Man in Texas. Sydney, Cleveland, n.d.
Manstopper. Sydney, Cleveland, n.d.
The Guns That Never Were. Sydney, Cleveland, n.d.
Tall Man's Mission. Sydney, Cleveland, n.d.
Day of the Lawless. Sydney, Cleveland, n.d.
Gauntlet. Sydney, Cleveland, n.d.
Vengeance Rides Tall. Sydney, Cleveland, n.d.
Backtrack. Sydney, Cleveland, n.d.
Barbary Guns. Sydney, Cleveland, n.d.
The Bannerman Way. Sydney, Cleveland, n.d.
Yesterday's Guns. Sydney, Cleveland, n.d.
Viking with a Gun. Sydney, Cleveland, n.d.
Deathwatch. Sydney, Cleveland, n.d.
Rio Renegade. Sydney, Cleveland, n.d.
Bullet for Bannerman. Sydney, Cleveland, n.d.
Trail to Purgatory. Sydney, Cleveland, n.d.
The Lash. Sydney, Cleveland, n.d.
Gun Mission. Sydney, Cleveland, n.d.
Hellfire. Sydney, Cleveland, n.d.
Seven Guns to Moonlight. Sydney, Cleveland, n.d.
The 12:10 from San Antone. Sydney, Cleveland, n.d.
Only the Swift. Sydney, Cleveland, n.d.
Die for Texas. Sydney, Cleveland, n.d.
Dealer in Death. Sydney, Cleveland, n.d.
Long Trail to Texas. Sydney, Cleveland, n.d.
The Rawhiders. Sydney, Cleveland, n.d.
Brace Yargo. Sydney, Cleveland, n.d.
The Buckskinners. Sydney, Cleveland, n.d.
Tame the Tall Hombre. Sydney, Cleveland, n.d.
Texas Empire. Sydney, Cleveland, n.d.
Death Rides Tall. Sydney, Cleveland, n.d.
King Iron. Sydney, Cleveland, n.d.
Call Me Texas. Sydney, Cleveland, n.d.
Hire a Gun. Sydney, Cleveland, n.d.
The Lobo Line. Sydney, Cleveland, n.d.

Novels

Johnny Stark. Sydney, Cleveland, n.d.
Day of Courage. Sydney, Cleveland, n.d.
West of Fury. Sydney, Cleveland, n.d.
Brand of the Border. Sydney, Cleveland, n.d.
One Desperate Gun. Sydney, Cleveland, n.d.
One More Notch. Sydney, Cleveland, n.d.
Kid Fargo. Sydney, Cleveland, 1970?.
Notch Twelve. Sydney, Cleveland, n.d.
String of Notches. Sydney, Cleveland, n.d.
The Devil Rode In. Sydney, Cleveland, n.d.
Ridin' Lonesome. Sydney, Cleveland, n.d.
Dead by Noon. Sydney, Cleveland, n.d.
One Savage Gun. Sydney, Cleveland, n.d.
Code of a Texan. Sydney, Cleveland, n.d.
Saddled for Showdown. Sydney, Cleveland, n.d.

* * *

From the mid-1950's to the mid-1960's, the Australian western market was dominated by the Sydney-based Cleveland Publishing Proprietary Ltd., a small company which spent the decade issuing hundreds of largely traditional—and often instantly forgettable—"oaters," romances, and detective stories. In many ways these 40–45,000-word books resembled the American pulp magazines of the 1930's; they usually appeared in staple-bound form, had titled chapters, were printed on rather grainy paper and always sported lurid covers. Generally they were numbered and promoted as Santa Fe Westerns, Bison Westerns, Peacemaker Westerns, and so on.

It was in this uninspiring format that the 48 novels which comprise Kirk Hamilton's Bannerman the Enforcer series first appeared. (In 1980, four of the books were reprinted in paperback by Leisure Books in New York).

On the surface, these books appear little different from any of their contemporaries. Indeed, Hamilton churned out several formulaic non-series Westerns himself while recounting the Bannerman adventures. But a number of factors make this particular series worthy of comment, not the least of which are its scope, characters, and plots, all of which remained consistently high throughout its lengthy run.

The premise of the series is simple; because the crime rate in post-Civil War Texas is so great, the ailing Governor Dukes creates a special corps of "Enforcers" (culled from the *crème de la crème* of other law-enforcement agencies) to handle the most sensitive, or important, assignments to reach his desk. To become an Enforcer, each hopeful candidate must pass a number of physical and mental tests. As the series wears on, a special assault course and training ground is established expressly for this purpose.

Yancey Bannerman is one of the first Enforcers to make the grade. His sidekick, the often bloodthirsty Johnny Cato, is not far behind.

From this point on, the series develops into a string of different cases with which the two men have to deal. For the most part, they involve fairly traditional western motifs: plots to assassinate the Governor or resurrect the Confederacy, gun-running, cattle-rustling, bank and train robberies. What stops the series from degenerating into basic, pulp-style shoot-'em-ups, however, is Hamilton's cleverly drawn characters and an unusually strong thread of continuity which runs through the entire saga.

Bannerman himself conforms to the rules of the genre in that he has a strong sense of right and wrong, is quick on the draw and pretty handy with his fists. But Hamilton adds depth to the character by making him the black sheep of a wealthy family of industrialists from back East. In several books, meetings with Bannerman's surprisingly ruthless father end in arguments which the Enforcer does not always win. Bannerman's wayward younger brother also crops up in a number of stories, either mixed up in the shady deal Bannerman is currently investigating, or using his knowledge of the underworld to help Bannerman bring his present case to a speedy and satisfying conclusion.

The regular supporting cast—which includes the Governor, his beautiful daughter (who provides the love interest for Bannerman, and often becomes involved in his missions), and Johnny Cato—are equally well-drawn. Cato is particularly interesting in that he sports a lethal six-shot gun onto which has been grafted an extra barrel capable of firing a surprise seventh shot. (With a ghoulishness he retains throughout the series, Cato refers to the gun as his "Manstopper".)

Unfortunately, Hamilton's supporting characters tend to be somewhat stereotypical. Outlaw gang-bosses are invariably portrayed as grudge-toting homicidal maniacs. The brains behind landgrabbing schemes are usually urbane politicians. Hamilton also tends to overuse Governor Dukes's ill-health as a plot device (on average the poor old politician suffers at least one heart attack in each book). For all that, however, the series remains engaging and, at times (as with the two-part story *Rio Renegade* and *Bullet for Bannerman*), even riveting.

Hamilton's writing style is clear and terse. His settings tend to be vague but his gun detail is exceptional. He sprinkles his dialogue with westernisms, not all of them authentic, and tends to break up his stories with contrived gun and fist fights to keep the action coming. He builds up a credible relationship between Bannerman and Cato and, with the exception of perhaps the last five or so books, constantly manages to push the scope of the series just that little bit further. Of special note are *Trail Wolves* (which ends with a dramatic and well-written battle aboard a burning riverboat), *Manstopper*, *Barbary Guns*, and *The 12:10 from San Antone*.

The western genre is distinguished by few Australian practitioners. Marshall Grover is probably the best, but Kirk Hamilton is a very close second.

—David Whitehead

HAMILTON, Wade. *See* **FLOREN, Lee.**

HAMMOND, Brad. *See* **KING, Albert.**

HANSEN, Ron. American. Born in Omaha, Nebraska, 8 December 1947. Educated at Creighton University, Omaha, B.A., 1970; University of Iowa, Iowa City, M.F.A. 1974; Stanford University, California, 1977–78. Jones Lecturer in creative writing, Stanford University, 1978–81; Affiliate, Michigan Society of Fellows, University of Michigan, Ann Arbor, 1981–84; Affiliate, The Writers Workshop, University of Iowa, Iowa City, 1985. Member of staff, 1985–86, and since 1986 Professor of English, Cornell University, Ithaca, New York, Agent: Liz Darhansoff, 1220 Park Avenue, New York, N.Y. 10128. Address: Department of English, Cornell University, Ithaca, New York, N.Y. 14853, U.S.A.

WESTERN PUBLICATIONS

Novels

Desperadoes. New York, Knopf, 1979; London, Souvenir Press, 1980.
The Assassination of Jesse James by the Coward Robert Ford. New York, Knopf, 1983; London, Souvenir Press, 1984.

Short Stories

Nebraska Stories. New York, Atlantic Monthly Press, 1989.

OTHER PUBLICATIONS

Novels

The Shadowmaker. New York, Harper, 1986.
You Don't Know What Love Is. Princeton, Ontario, Review Press, 1987.

* * *

Ron Hansen's first novel, *Desperadoes*, is the story of the infamous Dalton gang who were legends during the last years of the 19th century. Hansen uses the unusual technique of having the story narrated retrospectively by the lone surviving member of the Dalton gang, Emmett Dalton. The tone throughout the book is ironic: the Daltons began their careers as lawmen in the Indian Territories, but the combination of low wages and the high risk of catching a bullet led them to the conclusion of "if we can't beat them, let's join them." So the Daltons turned to cattle rustling. This proved so successful that they branched out into other lines of criminal activity: bank robbing, train robbing, and raiding Wells Fargo shipments.

Based on fact and the historical records of the Daltons, Hansen captures the world of the outlaw superbly. Some critics condemned the book's irony, but when Emmett Dalton states he is an outlaw no longer but a "real-estate broker, a building contractor, a scriptwriter for western movies; a church man, a Rotarian, a member of Moose Lodge 29" it's clear Hansen's perspective of the Dalton gang and the world of outlaws is beyond the simple-minded stereotypes so often used to present "authentic" portrayals of Western badmen.

Hansen's best book is *The Assassination of Jesse James by the Coward Robert Ford*. The book is a curious blend of biography and fiction. Hansen presents the story of Jesse James as a tragedy: he begins the novel with James already a legend at 34. But James's world is crumbling. Although the people think of Jesse James as a western version of Robin Hood—he steals from wealthy institutions and gives some of booty to the poor—Missouri's Governor Crittenden offers a $50,000 reward for the capture and conviction of the James gang and additional moneys for anyone who can bring in Frank or Jesse James.

19-year-old Bob Ford becomes Jesse's friend, but both men are seriously unstable. Bob Ford doesn't want to be like Jesse James, he wants to be Jesse James. And when he realizes he can never be his hero, he murders Jesse. Ironically, Bob Ford achieves his own fame as the "dirty little coward who laid poor Jesse in his grave." *The Assassination of Jesse James by the Coward Robert Ford* is a brilliant novel with richness and depth of characterization seldom found in the Western genre. Hansen carefully develops characters that remain memorable long after his books are read.

—George Kelley

HANSON, V. Joseph. *See* **HANSON, Vic J.**

HANSON, Vern. *See* **HANSON, Vic J.**

HANSON, Vic(tor) J(oseph). Also writes as Vern Hansen; V. Joseph Hanson; Vern Hanson; Jay Hill Potter. British. Educated in schools in Staffordshire. Worked for firm of church magazine publishers and printers, later sales representative, bookshop manager, and jazz club owner. Address: c/o Robert Hale Ltd., Clerkenwell House, 45–47 Clerkenwell Green, London EC1R 0HT, England.

WESTERN PUBLICATIONS

Novels

Colt Harvest (as Vern Hanson). Leicester, Fiction House, 1956.
Savage Sunrise. London, Hale, 1979.
Muldare. London, Hale, 1980.
Men on a Dusty Street. London, Hale, 1981.
Hannibal's Jump. London, Hale, 1991.

Novels (series: Amos Crowle in all books)

Black Heart Crowle. London, Hale, 1978.
Bells in an Empty Town. London, Hale, 1979.
Guns of Black Heart. London, Hale, 1980.
The Hands of Amos Crowle. London, Hale, 1981.
Black Heart's Bunch. London, Hale, 1982.
Hardneck and Amos. London, Hale, 1982.
The Greenhorn Days. London, Hale, 1983.
The Law of Amos C. London, Hale, 1985.
Amos Lives. London, Hale, 1989.
The Legend of Amos. London, Hale, 1991.

Novels as Jay Hill Potter

The Long Guns. London, Hale, 1979.
Black-Horse Moon. London, Hale, 1979.
Killer's Journey. London, Hale, 1980.
The Bitter Trail. London, Hale, 1981.
Jasper and Hack. London, Hale, 1981.
Turkey Shoot. London, Hale, 1986.

Novels as Jay Hill Potter (series: Pilgrim in all books)

Call Me Pilgrim. London, Hale, 1981.
Pilgrim's Blood. London, Hale, 1982.
Pilgrim's Trail. London, Hale, 1982.
Young Joe Pilgrim. London, Hale, 1982.
The Pilgrim Raid. London, Hale, 1983.
Bounty for Pilgrim. London, Hale, 1983.
A Coffin for Pilgrim. London, Hale, 1986.
Pilgrim's Revenge. London, Hale, 1990.
Hills of the Dead. London, Hale, 1991.

Novels as V. Joseph Hanson

Blue Lightnin'. London, Scion, 1950.
Bushwhacker! London, Scion, 1950.
Gunsmoke Saga. London, Fiction House, 1950.
Lead Bites Deep. London, Scion, 1950.
Spawn of the Badlands. London, Scion, 1950.
Lawless River. London, Scion, 1951.

OTHER PUBLICATIONS

Novels

The Morgue Has Guests: Diary of a Killer (as V. Joseph Hanson). London, Scion, 1950.
The End of the Kill. London, Hale, 1980.

Novels as Vern Hansen

Death and Little Girl Blue. London, Fleetway, 1962.
Murder with Menaces. London, Brown Watson, 1962.
The Whisper of Death. London, Brown Watson, 1963.
The Twisters. London, Brown Watson, 1963.
Creatures of the Mist. London, Brown Watson, 1963.
Claws of the Night. London, Brown Watson, 1963.
The Grip of Fear. London, Brown Watson, 1964.

* * *

Vic J. Hanson has been a keen western fan all his life. Indeed, his first short story, published in the magazine of the Staffordshire school he attended, was a tale of the Old West. Before long, he was also contributing other types of fiction to a wide range of magazines, annuals, and anthologies on a regular basis.

Leaving school and going to work for a company which published church magazines, he continued to write as often as possible. His first Westerns were published in the 1950's under the name of V. Joseph Hanson, but in the following decade he turned to writing thrillers—this time as Vern Hansen—and it was not until 1978 that he returned to his "first love"—the Western—with a sometimes chaotic but undoubtedly enthusiastic novel entitled *Black Heart Crowle*. Crowle, who has continued to appear regularly ever since, is a town-tamer and bounty hunter with a reputation for being "cruel, ruthless, amoral, but . . . with strange loyalties."

The Black Heart books (which have changed their name to "Black Amos" in the last few years) invariably recount Crowle's attempts to bring order back to a whole string of beleaguered towns. In the first book he goes up against a villain named Big Sam Naylor in order to tame a community called Wolvers Creek. In *Guns of Black Heart*, he wrests control of a town called Widows' Hole from another "kingpin of the hardcases" named Dakota Phil. In both *The Greenhorn Days* and *The Law of Amos C*, he dispenses his own kind of Dragoon Colt justice on the streets of Lackaday Springs. In *The Hands of Amos Crowle*, Hanson's protagonist (who, contrary to his description, rarely performs as the "anti-hero" the author would have us believe) has his hands crushed by a one-time friend named "Boss" Bleaker, but still manages to triumph in the final shoot-out, and in a neat crossover, the aptly named villain Hardneck (so called because of the leather collar he wears), who appears in an early non-series Western, *Muldare*, later turns up in *Hardneck and Amos* to give Crowle a run for his money.

In general, Hanson writes fast, incident filled westerns in a spare, modern style. He favours short scenes and multiple viewpoints, and sprinkles his dialogue with just enough westernisms to give an adequate "period" flavour to his speech. Most of his books are split into about 20 short chapters. He has a tendency to italicise odd words for no apparent reason, and occasionally throws in an exclamation mark for effect. During the course of a story, he makes frequent references to events described in previous books, and reinforces this sense of continuity by adding brief footnotes for his readers' benefit. In the main, characterisation is kept to a minimum, and description can be so thin that, as with *The Law of Amos C*, we are not even told that Crowle has a moustache until the very last page! Hanson usually writes in short, direct sentences, and has a habit of using informal words peculiar to England which sometimes seem out of place in a Western.

Under the pseudonym Jay Hill Potter, his best-known work is probably the Pilgrim series, which has run intermittently now for more than a decade. In the first novel, *Call Me Pilgrim*, Old Marshal Joe, the Pilgrim patriarch, retires from a long and distinguished career as a federal lawman to establish a ranch down along the Pecos River. Joining him are his fiery daughter Rebbie and her husband, Cal Youngman.

The main character of the series, however, is Pilgrim's "completely ruthless" son, known for obvious reasons as Young Joe, who periodically quits badge-packing and bounty hunting to come home and recharge his batteries. Young Joe is not a particularly laudable character, as Hanson, writing as Potter, makes plain in *The Pilgrim Raid*, describing him as "dark and hard-bitten and with a notorious *killing* temper when roused." Unfortunately, events arouse the temper of this "gunfighter extraordinary" in every book, thus ensuring that each story always includes a regular procession of fast and violent set pieces.

Frequently the ranch acts as a magnet for trouble. In *The Pilgrim Raid* the spread is attacked by a border gang led by the notorious Leon the Fox. In *A Coffin for Pilgrim*, Rebbie is kidnapped by yet another bunch of marauders. In *Young Joe Pilgrim*, a killer by the name of Loco Wendell heads for the ranch solely to get even with Old Marshal Joe, who arrested and sent him to prison several years before.

To ring the changes, however, Hanson periodically shifts the action away from the ranch, but nearly always to send his characters on some kind of manhunt. In *Bounty for Pilgrim*, for example, Young Joe teams up with a lady sharp-shooter and a broken-down old rodeo rider to track down Solo Lincroft, a bounty hunter gone bad. *Pilgrim's Blood* and *Pilgrim's Revenge* are two more variations on the theme.

As with the Black Heart books, Hanson links the series with a strong, though not quite so pronounced, thread of continuity. Despite Young Joe's somewhat homicidal temperament, Hanson always succeeds in portraying him as a rather charismatic, if single-minded, young man. He also handles Old Marshal Joe's tenacity well, and Rebbie (described as "a dark shapely *dancing* sort of girl, with dark curly hair and a big-eyed elfin face") conforms to the beautiful, spirited tomboy stereotype so beloved of westerns published in the 1950's and 1960's.

Under both his own name and the Potter alias, Hanson has written several single westerns. In style they differ little from his series. Of particular note, however, are *Jasper and Hack* and *Turkey Shoot*. In the first, Hanson reveals his ability to combine the western with light comedy; in the second, he adds depth to his main character, Pelligree, by making him a bounty hunter who only plies his violent trade in order to earn money to help his ailing wife.

—David Whitehead

HARDIN, Clement. *See* **NEWTON, D.B.**

HARDIN, Dave. *See* **HOLMES, L. P.**

HARDING, Matt. *See* **FLOREN, Lee.**

HARDING, Matthew Whitman. *See* **FLOREN, Lee.**

HARDING, Wes. *See* **ALLISON, Clay.**

HARDY, Russ. *See* **SNOW, Charles H.**

HARKNETT, Terry. *See* **GILMAN, George G.**

HARLAN, Ross. *See* **KING, Albert.**

HARLOW, John. *See* **SNOW, Charles H.**

HARRISON, C(hester) William. Also wrote as Coe Williams; Will Hickok. American. Born in Indiana. Raised in Illinois, later moved to California. Married; one son, one daughter. Worked as a portrait photographer, builder of house trailers. Wrote up to 1200 novels and stories for pulp magazines, and other publications.

WESTERN PUBLICATIONS

Novels

Boothill Trail. New York, Phoenix Press, 1940.
Puncher Pards. New York, Phoenix Press, 1942.
The Missouri Maiden. New York, Lion Books, 1952.
Barbed Wire Kingdom. New York, Jason, 1955.
Go for Your Gun (as Coe Williams). New York, Popular Library, 1955.
Border Fever. New York, Permabooks, 1956.
The Guns of Fort Petticoat. New York and London, Fawcett, 1957.
Unarmed Killer. New York, Permabooks, 1957; London, Transworld, 1959.
Winter Kill (as William Harrison). New York, Belmont Tower, 1972.

Novels as Will Hickock

Web of Gunsmoke. New York, New American Library, 1955.
The Restless Gun. London, World, 1959.
Trail of the Gun. London, World, 1960.

OTHER PUBLICATIONS

Other (for children)

Forest Fire Fighters and What They Do. New York, Watts, 1962.

* * *

Another of the legion of writers who began their careers in the pulps, C. William Harrison sold his first piece of fiction in 1936 and was remarkably prolific thereafter, publishing some 1200 short stories, novelettes, novellas, and serials over the next 20-plus years. His primary output was of Westerns, but he also wrote detective, sports, science fiction, even love stories. Most of his sales were to pulp magazines, though he contributed to such slick-paper periodicals as *Collier's* and *Redbook* as well.

When the pulps foundered in 1950, Harrison gravitated, as did many of his contemporaries, into the novel markets. (His two novels published in the early 1940's, *Boothill Trail* and *Puncher Pards*, were conceived for and first published in pulp magazines.) With one exception, his books written during the 1950's are paperback originals; most appeared under his own name, the rest under the pseudonym Coe Williams.

Harrison's most accomplished novels are *Barbed Wire Kingdom* and *The Guns of Fort Petticoat.* The former is built around the introduction of barbed wire to the West in the late 1870's, portraying the violent resistance of free-range Texas cattlemen to the efforts of ex-felon turned drummer Ross Kennett to sell the hated wire. A nicely handled love story and some fine descriptive passages enhance the narrative. The latter title first appeared as a two-part serial in *Collier's* and later became a film with Audie Murphy, thanks to its unorthodox premise. Frank Hewitt, fighting for the Union during the Civil War, deserts his post in the Texas *llano* rather than participate in the bloody Chivington raid, and is then forced by circumstances to join an isolated group of 22 soldiers' wives and to organize and lead them into a desperate battle for survival against marauding Comanches.

Winter Kill is an elemental tale of a trouble-hardened man pursued by hired killers, who is trapped on an icy Wyoming ridge by a sudden blizzard; Harrison's descriptions of the storm's fury and Emmett Clelling's struggle for survival against both man and nature are effectively done. Also good, though it is marred by a truncated and somewhat unsatisfying ending, is *Unarmed Killer*, which concerns a remorseful manslayer turned pacifist, who is prodded into the midst of a range war; the novel's highlight is its depiction of Quaker characters and attitudes. *Outlaw of the Natchez Trace*, although packaged as a novel, is in fact an interesting and well-researched biography of John Murrell, the cold-blooded megalomaniac who in the 1830's envisioned a takeover of all the territory east of the Mississippi River and south of the Ohio River—the famed Natchez Trace—with an "army" consisting of wilderness outlaws and rebellious slaves.

While Harrison's books show evidence of his pulp origins, particularly in action scenes that tend toward stock fistfights and pitched gun battles, they are nonetheless well-written, entertaining, and worth reading.

—Bill Pronzini

HARRISON, Fred. *See* **PAINE, Lauran.**

HARRISON, Jim (James Thomas Harrison). American. Born in Grayling, Michigan, 11 December 1937. Educated at Michigan State University, East Lansing, B.A. in comparative literature 1960, M.A. in comparative literature 1964. Married Linda King in 1960; two daughters. Assistant Professor of English, State University of New York, Stony Brook, 1965–66. Screenplay writer for Warner Brothers, and other film companies. Now lives on a farm in Michigan. Recipient: National Endowment for the Arts grant, 1967, 1968, 1969; Guggenheim fellowship, 1969. Agent: Robert Datilla, 233 East 8th Street, New York, New York 10028. Address: c/o Houghton Mifflin Company, One Beacon Street, Boston, Massachusetts 02108, U.S.A.

WESTERN PUBLICATIONS

Novels

Wolf: A False Memoir. New York, Simon and Schuster, 1971.
A Good Day to Die. New York, Simon and Schuster, 1973; London, W.H. Allen, 1975.
Farmer. New York, Viking Press, 1976.
Legends of the Fall (novellas; includes *Revenge*; *The Man Who Gave Up His Name*; *Legends of the Fall.* New York, Delacorte Press, 1979; London, Collins, 1980.
Warlock. New York, Delacorte Press, and London, Collins, 1981.
Sundog. New York, Dutton, 1984; London, Heinemann, 1985.
Dalva. New York, Dutton, 1988; London, Cape, 1989.
The Woman Lit by Fireflies. Boston, Houghton Mifflin, 1990; London, Weidenfeld and Nicolson, 1991.
Sunset Limited (three novellas). Boston, Houghton Mifflin, 1990.

OTHER PUBLICATIONS

Verse

Plain Song (as James Harrison). New York, Norton, 1965.
Locations. New York, Norton, 1968.
Walking. Cambridge, Massachusetts, Pym Randall Press, 1969.
Outlyer and Ghazals. New York, Simon and Schuster, 1971.
Letters to Yesenin. Fremont, Michigan, Sumac Press, 1973.
Returning to Earth. Ithaca, New York, Ithaca House, 1977.
Selected and New Poems 1961–1981. New York, Delacorte Press, 1982.
The Theory and Practice of Rivers. Seattle, Winn, 1986.
The Theory and Practice of Rivers and New Poems. Livingston, Montana, Clark City Press, 1989.

Other

Natural World, with Diana Guest. Barrytown, New York, Open Book, 1983.

* * *

I first became aware of Jim Harrison's writing during a visit to California in 1981. A friend, thinking, no doubt, that my own efforts would benefit from some stiffening of style and elevation of purpose, presented me with the Delta paperback edition of Harrison's *Legends of the Fall* and having, as it were, lit the touchpaper, tactfully withdrew. I read the three novellas in the book with greed and widening amazement, part on a Greyhound bound from Sacramento to San Francisco, more in a cabin south of Point Lobos, within earshot of Big Sur. When I'd finished them through once and my companion had done the same, I read them again. When the British hardcover edition was, sadly, remaindered in conspicuous quantities, I bought enough to give to most of my friends and not a few of my enemies.

Rereading *Legends of the Fall* before writing this piece, my reactions to the first story, "Revenge," and the last, the title story, were scarcely less effusive. What is audacious is Harrison's ambition—there is no getting around either the narrative scope here, nor its extreme seriousness and emotional intensity—and the control of material and style, which never seems to desert him. Apparently, Harrison was told by a regretful publisher that if only he'd written "Legends of the Fall" to around 600 pages instead of a mere 80, the *New York Times* Best Sellers List would have been theirs for the taking. He was right, of course—it's all there: generation, war, unforgetting love and unforgiveable lust, insanity, individuality, honour and betrayal. But at that length it would have been another fat epic, better than most. As it stands it's as close to perfect as you can get without falling off the edge.

This is how it begins:

> Late in October in 1914 three brothers rode from Chocteau, Montana, to Calgary in Alberta to enlist in the Great War (the U.S. did not enter until 1917). An old Cheyenne named One Stab rode with them to return with the horses in tow because the horses were blooded and their father did not think it fitting for his sons to ride off to war on nags. One Stab knew all the shortcuts in the northern Rockies so their ride traversed wild country, much of it far from roads and settlements. They left before dawn with their father holding an oil lamp in the stable dressed in his buffalo robe, all of them silent, and the farewell breath he embraced them with rose in a small white cloud to the rafters.

Much of the style and the substance of Harrison's writing is contained in that opening paragraph. The language is direct, the world is primarily a masculine one with its own rituals and codes, and that ritual quality is achieved through the language and structure. The influence, I would guess, is Hemingway, but there's a weightier, almost a biblical cadence here that is Harrison's own. The land—specifically the land of the mid- and north-west—and the journeys from that land to take part in foreign wars, are integral to much of his work, as is the relationship between the descendants of white European settlers and the surviving Native Americans. The graceful muscularity of the prose and the normally unsentimental presentations of the natural world enable Harrison (in my contention) to get away with the final description of the father's farewell breath here, allowing it to take on a metaphoric, almost mythic quality, rather than subsiding towards bathos and sentimentality.

There are links between Harrison and an informal Montana-Key West group which includes fellow-writer Thomas McGuane, the painter Russell Chatham, singer Jimmy Buffet and actors such as Peter Fonda and Harry Dean Stanton. All of the U.S. editions of his books have reproductions on their jackets of Chatham's work—two of them with the permission of their current owner, Stanton. It was McGuane who gave Harrison an important, early push and the two have collaborated together on at least one original screenplay, *Cold Feet.* Harrison, it seems, writes screenplays to keep his head above financial water while concentrating most of his creative energies on poetry and fiction.

What he will think of being included in an encyclopedia of Western Writers, I can't be sure. (No more than it would be wise to lay bets on the reaction of his friend McGuane, similarly included.) In a *Paris Review* interview he shrugged off the term "midwestern writer" as not particularly useful; if its regionalism is the only thing that makes literature worth noting, it probably isn't literature anyway. But Harrison, again and again, takes on the west, pushing away at its history, its mythologies: he worries at the shameful legacy of the treatment of the American Indians as if it were a cancer that must be his country's undoing—"Our doom as a nation will be unveiled in the way we have treated the blacks and Indians, the entire Third World. Washington is a flunked Passion Play."

This theme is at the heart of Harrison's last-but-one novel, and the one which seems to have brought him the most critical attention in the U.S., *Dalva*. Though a unified novel, *Dalva* makes use of the three-part form Harrison seems to feel at ease with: the narration is shared between Dalva herself, a woman searching for her lost son and haunted by her past, and Michael, a professor for whom the past is the raw material of his scholarship. Aside from these two, there is a third voice which shares the narrative—that of Dalva's great-grandfather, a missionary who lived among the Sioux and became increasingly eccentric as the destruction of that people at the hands of the army drew inexorably closer. Dalva's family comes from Anglo-Saxon and Indian stock: the Indian wars lie as heavily upon her as the Korean War which killed her father, the Vietnam war which killed Duane Stone Horse, her husband-for-a-day and father of her missing child.

Dalva has drawn attention through its use of a central female character, supposedly remarkable in a male writer of supposedly macho sensibilities. More significant and worthy of comment is the manner in which Harrison has brought his themes together within a complex, but never difficult narrative, allowing them to reverberate against one another to achieve historical and mythic depth, at the same time as he has foregrounded characters who are convincing in their consistencies as well as their ambiguities and about whom we are brought to care deeply.

Harrison's work is a world away from the self-regarding ironists so fashionable in New York literary circles. In that sense, he *is* a regional, a Western writer. As he said in an interview in *Publishers Weekly*: "I like grit, I like love and death, I'm tired of irony. . . I would rather give full vent to all human loves and disappointments, and take a chance on being corny, than die a smartass."

—John Harvey

HARMON, Gil. *See* **KING, Albert.**

HARVEY, John. Also writes as Jon Barton; William S. Brady; L.J. Coburn; J.B. Dancer; Jon Hart; William M. James; Terry Lennox; James Mann; John J. McLaglen; Thom Ryder; J.D. Sandon; Jonathan White. British. Born in London, 21 December 1938. Educated at Goldsmiths' College, University of London, 1960–63, teaching certificate; Hatfield Poly, 1970–74, B.A. in English 1974; Nottingham University, 1978–79, M.A. in American studies, and further graduate work. Has two children. English and drama teacher in London, Heanor, Derbyshire, Andover, Hampshire, and Stevenage, Hertfordshire, 1963–74. Part-time film and literature teacher, Nottingham University, 1979–86. Film reviewer, Nottingham *News* and *Trader*, since 1981; occasional film and book reviewer, *Time Out*. Agent: Blake Friedmann, 37–41 Gower Street, London WC1E 6HH. Address: 58 Rutland Road, West Bridgford, Nottingham NG2 5DG, England.

WESTERN PUBLICATIONS

Novels (series: Hart the Regulator)

1. *Cherokee Outlet*. London, Pan, 1980.
2. *Blood Trail*. London, Pan, 1980.
3. *Tago*. London, Pan, 1980.
4. *The Silver Lie*. London, Pan, 1980.
5. *Blood on the Border*. London, Pan, 1981.
6. *Ride the Wide Country*. London, Pan, 1981.
7. *Arkansas Breakout*. London, Pan, 1982.
8. *John Wesley Hardin*. London, Pan, 1982.
9. *California Bloodlines*. London, Pan, 1982.
10. *The Skinning Place*. London, Pan, 1982.

Novels as John J. McLaglen (series: Herne the Hunter)

2. *River of Blood*. London, Corgi, 1976.
4. *Shadow of the Vulture*. London, Corgi, 1977.
Death in Gold. London, Corgi, 1977.
8. *Cross-Draw*. London, Corgi, 1978.
10. *Vigilante!* London, Corgi, 1979.
12. *Sun Dance*. London, Corgi, 1980.
13. *Billy the Kid*. London, Corgi, 1980.
15. *Till Death. . . .* London, Corgi, 1980.
Dying Ways. London, Corgi, 1982.
Hearts of Gold. London, Corgi, 1982.
Wild Blood. London, Corgi, 1983.

Novels as J.B. Dancer (series: Lawmen)

1. *Evil Breed*. London, Coronet, 1977.
3. *Judgement Day*. London, Coronet, 1978.
5. *The Hanged Man*. London, Coronet, 1979.

Novels as L.J. Coburn (series: Caleb Thorn)

2. *The Raiders*. London, Sphere, 1977.
4. *Bloody Shiloh*. London, Sphere, 1978.

Novels as William S. Brady (series: Hawk)

2. *Blood Money*. London, Fontana, 1979.
4. *Killing Time*. London, Fontana, 1980.
6. *Blood Kin*. London, Fontana, 1980.
8. *Desperadoes*. London, Fontana, 1981.
10. *Dead Man's Hand*. London, Fontana, 1981.
11. *Sierra Gold*. London, Fontana, 1981.
Death and Jack Shade. London, Fontana, 1982.
Border War. London, Fontana, 1983.
Killer! London, Fontana, 1983.

Novels as William S. Brady (series: Peacemaker in all books)

Whiplash. London, Fontana, 1981.
War Party. London, Fontana, 1983.
One Thousand Dollar Death. London, Fontana, 1983.

Novels as William M. James (series: Apache)

15. *Blood Rising*. Los Angeles, Pinnacle, 1979.
17. *Blood Brother*. Los Angeles, Pinnacle, 1980.
20. *Death Dragon*. New York, Pinnacle, 1981.
Death Ride. New York, Pinnacle, 1983.
The Hanging. New York, Pinnacle, 1983.

Novels as J.D. Sandon (series: Gringos)

2. *Cannons in the Rain*. London, Granada, 1979.
4. *Border Affair*. London, Granada, 1979.
6. *Mazatlan*. London, Granada, 1980.

8. *Wheels of Thunder*. London, Granada, 1981.
9. *Durango*. London, Granada, 1982.

Uncollected Short Story

"Riding Track" (Hart the Regulator), in *Western* (London), January 1981.

OTHER PUBLICATIONS

Novels

Avenging Angel (as Thom Ryder). London, New English Library, 1975.
Angel Alone (as Thom Ryder). London, New English Library, 1975.
Amphetamines and Pearls. London, Sphere, 1976.
The Geranium Kiss. London, Sphere, 1976.
One of Our Dinosaurs Is Missing (novelization of screenplay). London, New English Library, 1976.
Junkyard Angel. London, Sphere, 1977.
Neon Madman. London, Sphere, 1977.
Herbie Rides Again (novelization of screenplay). London, New English Library, 1977.
Herbie Goes to Monte Carlo (novelization of screenplay). London, New English Library, 1978.
Frame. London, Magnum, 1979.
Blind. London, Magnum, 1981.
Endgame (as James Mann, with Laurence James). London, New English Library, 1982.
Dancer Draws a Wild Card (as Terry Lennox). London, Hale, 1985.
Duty Free (novelization of TV series). Horsham, West Sussex, Ravette, 1985.
More Duty Free (novelization of TV series). Horsham, West Sussex, Ravette, 1986.
Lonely Hearts: A Resnick Novel. London, Viking, and New York, Holt, 1989.
Rough Treatment: A Resnick Novel. London, Viking, and New York, Holt, 1990.
Cutting Edge. London, Viking, 1991.

Novels as Jon Barton

Kill Hitler. London, Corgi, 1976.
Forest of Death. London, Corgi, 1977.
Lightning Strikes. London, Corgi, 1977.

Novels as Jon Hart

Black Blood. London, Granada, 1977.
High Slaughter. London, Granada, 1977.
Triangle of Death. London, Granada, 1977.
Guerilla Attack! London, Granada, 1977.
Death Raid. London, Granada, 1978.

Fiction (for children)

What About It, Sharon. London, Penguin, 1979.
Kidnap! London, Beaver, 1987.
Daylight Robbery! London, Beaver, 1987.
Hot Property! London, Beaver, 1987.
Terror Trap! London, Beaver, 1988.
Downeast to Danger. London, Beaver, 1988.
Runner! London, Beaver, 1988.

Plays

Radio Plays: *Ivy Who?*, 1987; *Shipbuilding*, 1989.

Television Plays: *Just Another Little Blues Song*, 1984; *Anna of the Five Towns*, 1985; *Sophia and Constance*, 1987; *Hard Cases* series, 1987–88; *Dance, Girls, Dance* (in *Spender* series), 1991.

Verse

Provence. Berkhamstead, Hertfordshire, Priapus Press, 1978.
The Old Postcard Trick. Nottingham, Slow Dancer Press, 1985.
Neil Sedaka Lied. Huddersfield, Yorkshire, Smith/Doorstop, 1987.
Taking the Long Road Home. Nottingham, Slow Dancer Press, 1988.
The Downeast Poems. Huddersfield, Yorkshire, Smith/Doorstop, 1989.
Sometime Other Than Now, with Sue Dymoke. Nottingham, Slow Dancer Press, 1989.

*

John Harvey comments:

The qualities I admire most in prose are an uncluttered and spare style and clarity and pace of narrative: hopefully the more successful of my own writing comes close to achieving these things. In the Western I'm interested in finding a balance between the myth of the West (as it comes through American literature and film) and the historical reality. Increasingly, I'm concerned to attempt to make a stronger place for women in the Western, which is traditionally a refuge of masculinity and male fantasy.

I suppose my strongest inspirations come from western movies—my father took me to see almost every Western released when I was a kid and I've kept to the habit ever since. One thing I'm doing when I write is making western movies in my head: I don't suppose I'll ever achieve anything as fine as Peckinpah's *Pat Garrett and Billy the Kid*, William Fraker's *Monte Walsh*, or Arthur Penn's *The Missouri Breaks*, but I'll keep trying.

I read few writers of orthodox western fiction, though there are some fine writers now working in the States who make excellent use of a "western" setting—Larry McMurtry, Thomas McGuane, Jim Harrison, Michael Dorris, and Louise Erdrich, for examples. Elmore Leonard, a writer of Westerns who found extra scope and freedom in crime novels, is a constant source of inspiration, as is the late Raymond Carver. Those English writers of Westerns I have worked with—Laurence James, Angus Wells, and Terry Harknett—have been unstinting in their guidance and friendship.

* * *

John Harvey, a former English and drama school teacher, began his writing career in 1975 with various non-westerns. These early works were conventional adventure and private-eye stories. In an attempt by his publishers to satisfy the public's demand for the "new wave" violent westerns started by George G. Gilman's Edge series, Harvey co-devised the Herne the Hunter series with Laurence James. Harvey's personal interest in the western film influences his writing, and this cinematic style dominates these books, rather than the more violent prose of his co-writer. Harvey was responsible for the even numbers of the Herne series up until 12, then switched to the odd numbers. He once said, "One thing I'm doing when I write is making western movies in my head." Thus the pseudonym of John J. McLaglen for the Herne books, an amalgam of John Ford and Victor McLaglen. Harvey's first western was *River of Blood*, where he presents the central character of Jed Herne, an ex-gunfighter brought out of idyllic retirement by the suicide of his raped wife. Herne is forced to take along a 15-year-old girl, Becky, until she undermines the plotting of the books and exits in *Shadow of the Vulture*. Harvey's imagery of women in the western supports his own belief that the West was not populated solely by kind-hearted soiled doves or matriarchal characters. His stories attempt to defuse sexual stereotypes, and this can be seen in *Till Death* . . . which contains a flash-back of his first meeting with his wife, and his hanging up of the .45, recaptured in tender prose. Unfortunately he lapses back into the sexist trap with *Hearts of Gold*, a story involving the ever present "soiled-doves." The contrast between his style and that of Laurence James can clearly be seen within the series, but nevertheless they went on to work on the Caleb Thorn series.

Changing pace and setting we are introduced to Thorn, a rich and spoilt Union soldier bent on a personal mission against the Confederates, using the backdrop of the Civil War to wreak his revenge. Both *The Raiders* and *Bloody Shiloh* are formulae westerns created specifically for the 1970's-and Caleb Thorn's exploits are brutal, bloody, and far from heroic.

As J.B. Dancer, Harvey co-created the short-lived Lawmen series. This time he worked with Angus Wells, but the series faltered after only five books. Lawmen's characters are no more than two-dimensional, and the series covers much the same ground as a routine detective story.

At the beginning of 1980, Harvey had his first solo western series published, namely Hart the Regulator. With this series Harvey aimed to present the stereotyped "gun for hire" from a different point of view. Keeping to the code that the hero has to be tall, world-weary, and fast with a Colt .45, Hart is, nonetheless, a credible character, who possesses both humour and a sudden violent temper. The latter quality is shown in *Cherokee Outlet*, where he has spent the first quarter of the book chasing a horse-thief; finally catching up with him, and disgusted that the thief should also lie to him, Hart shoots the back of his head away. *The Silver Lie* reveals the more human side of Hart's character, as he fights for his life after failing to stop a young girl, entrusted into his care, from being kidnapped. Harvey shows that Hart can fail, as most of us frequently do, and in order to regain his standing in the community he must don the mantel of a killer and recapture her. Elsewhere, using the actual gunfighter John Wesley Hardin in the book of the same name, Harvey again excels in bringing his fictional hero into contact with the famous outlaw in a battle of wits, a device he had already used in the Herne series with Billy the Kid. We all know Hardin's fate, but Harvey's development of his characters within the story-frame is outstanding.

Having firmly established himself as a western writer and despite the success of solo writing, Harvey went on to co-create a series that broke new ground, writing the Gringos Series with Angus Wells. Set during the Mexican Revolution, plots are taken from historical events and given a new twist by introducing the four fictional *gringos* of the title. These are gun-runners from different walks of life, who find themselves fighting for a cause in which they have no belief, since money is their god. The traditional western themes in Harvey's works are there: train robbery (*Cannons in the Rain*), bank hold-up (*Mazatlan*), and gun-running (*Border Affair*).

It was an ambitious move by Fontana to release two series under the pseudonym of William S. Brady, i.e., Harvey and Wells. Jared Hawk and John T. McLain, the heroes of Hawk and Peacemaker series respectively, are total opposites. Hawk is more in the tradition of the hard, modern western, its "hero" an unpleasant young man with a penchant for killing: "Hawk had a simple code: kill first and ask questions later. If there was anyone left alive to ask." Bounding across the action-packed pages, Hawk hardly pauses for breath before gunning down another victim in gory technicolor. From range wars to riding herd on prisoners, from appointed marshal of some border town to avenging Wild Bill Hickok, Harvey maintains the violence and excitement.

With Peacemaker the reader encounters another side of Brady's writing, violent in places but showing rather more originality. Harvey brings to life a border town at its genesis, populated by all manner of varied characters, and into which comes McLain, forced out of Missouri and Gone To Texas to start a new life. It was nothing new for the men of that time, but hadn't been done on the British paperback scene. Bloody realism abounds, but with it Harvey displays a feeling for not only the central character, but those lesser figures about him, with whom the reader grows to identify himself. McLain is the hero, but also a man with all the human frailties.

Harvey's last foray into Westerns was his contribution to the Apache series. Unfortunately, the stories were in the familiar mould of blood, guts, mutilations, and rapes required by the adult western market, and are mere extensions of the series. Sadly, these were the last western works he produced.

Harvey can write appealingly on the more formulaic Western, stretching out the plots and characters to appeal to the public demand. He is able to flesh out not only his heroes, but their supporting cast as well, and there have been some memorable villains crossing his pages. But with the demise of the western pulps by the mid 1980's, he turned his hand to a former love—the detective thriller. Recently he has received rave reviews on both sides of the Atlantic for his Resnick novels, *Rough Treatment* and *Lonely Hearts*. He has also delved into the world of radio and TV, bringing him greater audience appreciation. After 10 years of cutting his teeth on westerns, Harvey is now finding the critical success which eluded him before.

—Mike Stotter

HASLAM, Gerald (Williams). American. Born in Bakersfield, California, 18 March 1937. Educated at San Francisco State College, California, B.A. 1963, M.A. 1965; Union Graduate School, Cincinnati, Ohio, Ph.D. 1980. Served in the United States Army, 1958–60. Married Janice E. Pettichord in 1961; two daughters and three sons. Instructor in English, San Francisco State College, 1966–67. Assistant Professor, 1967–70, and Associate Professor, 1970–74, and since 1974 Professor of English, Sonoma State College, Rohnert Park, California. Since 1984 Adjunct Professor, Union Graduate School, Cincinnati, Ohio, and The National Faculty, Atlanta, Georgia. Vice-president, 1982, and president-elect, 1983–84. Recipient: California Arts Council Creative Writing fellowship, 1989. Western Literature Association. Sonoma State University Summer Writing Stipend, 1990. Agent: Sandra Dijkstra Agency, 1237 Camino del Mar No. 515c, Del Mar, California 92014. Address: P.O. Box 969, Penngrove, California 94251, U.S.A.

WESTERN PUBLICATIONS

Novel

Masks. Penngrove, California, Old Adobe Press, 1976.

Short Stories

Okies: Selected Stories. San Rafael, California, New West, 1973.
The Wages of Sin. Fallon, Nevada, Duck Down Press/Windriver, 1980.
Hawk Flights: Visions of the West. Big Timber, Montana, Seven Buffaloes Press, 1983.
Snapshots: Glimpses of the Other California. Walnut Creek, California, Devil Mountain, 1985.
The Man Who Cultivated Fire, and Other Stories. Santa Barbara, California, Capra Press, 1987.
That Constant Coyote: California Stories. Reno, University of Nevada Press, 1990.

Other

William Eastlake. Austin, Texas, Steck Vaughn, 1970.
The Language of the Oil Fields: Examination of an Industrial Argot. Penngrove, California, Old Adobe Press, 1972.
Jack Schaefer. Boise, Idaho, Boise State University Press, 1976.
Voices of a Place. Walnut Creek, California, Devil Mountain, 1987.
Coming of Age in California. Walnut Creek, California, Devil Mountain, 1990.
The Other California. Santa Barbara, California, Capra Press, 1990.

Editor, *Forgotten Pages of American Literature.* Boston, Houghton Mifflin, 1970.
Editor, *Western Writing.* Albuquerque, University of New Mexico Press, 1974.
Editor, with James D. Houston, *California Heartland.* Santa Barbara, California, Capra Press, 1978.
Editor, with J. Golden Taylor and others, *Literary History of the American West.* Fort Worth, Texas Christian University Press, 1987.

*

Critical Study: *Gerald Haslam* by Gerald Locklin, Boise, Idaho, Boise State University, 1987.

Gerald Haslam comments:

I write about a California that is still western—that 70% of the state that remains small town or rural: ranches, farms, vast wilderness tracts. My stories and essays work against the California stereotype—no glitzy blondes, just hard-working people of all colors, who struggle to survive on a harsh landscape.

Here can be found all the great dramas, all the passions, and people as complex as any. It is the quintessential California, as vital as blood and bones.

* * *

Gerald Haslam's six collections of short stories, three collections of essays, and one novel all deal with what he calls "The Other California." Bounded by mountains and larger than some states, the Great Central Valley is 430 miles long and 75 miles wide, an arid country containing the richest farming region in the world as well as one of the country's most productive oilfields; recently, the Great Central Valley has also become California's third largest population area.

A sense of place figures strongly in all of Haslam's work. Though some of his characters leave the valley—the college professor in his novel *Masks,* for example—they return frequently; even when they do not return, the valley goes with them. As Haslam has said, "Home is the place you cannot leave, no matter where you go."

Place first means landscape; Haslam follows his characters along the rivers and into the mountains, though more often they move across the wide plain of the Central Valley, onto the farms and among the oilrigs, into the towns. Haslam's sense of place can't be separated from people, especially from family, as in "Crossing the Valley," in which a young man's account of the death of his grandfather is mixed with the grandfather's memories.

The representation of an uneasy ethnic diversity is another strength in Haslam's stories. He presents the West as it really was and is, populated not only by several social classes of whites (with, always, the first-comers constituting themselves as an upperclass, regardless of their actual social origins), but also by Mexicans, Indians, Japanese, Chinese, Filipinos, and blacks. The resulting mixture is one in which individuals from the various races may become friends while the races as groups walk warily around and past one another. For this vision of the American West, the Great Central Valley offers an ideal stage, and Haslam, himself descended on one side from dust-bowl-era migrants—the "Okies" whose lives are recreated in his 1973 collection of the same name—and Spanish-American on the other, makes good use of his materials.

Important as are place and people in Haslam's work, perhaps his greatest subject is time and change. Yet, paradoxically, what is most important persists through and despite time, not only in memory but sometimes in actual fact or in transcendence which overcomes time.

The most obvious changes, those in landscape, occur in such stories, as "Someone Else's Life," in which the river where the narrator and his mentor once fished is flooded out by a dam which has created "a water-skier's lake now, oily, with supermarkets and trailer parks and honky tonks growing around it, and neon lights to guide lost travelers in from the threatening dark." Other changes occur in "Missing in Action," narrated by a young man, home for a visit with his father, who learns that the Japanese woman he remembers as "the old woman, shuffling through alleys mostly, picking up stale produce from grocery store garbage cans" had owned, with her husband, a small truck farm. When the Japanese were placed in relocation camps, she and her husband lost their land; just as shocking for the young man is the revelation of his father's part in burning her family's home after they were taken away.

Other stories create changes in individual lives which are partly transcended by the persistence of memory, as in "The Hearse Across the Street," which reminds an old man of the single afternoon he spent with the dead woman. Memory becomes reality in "Snapshots," as persons from the past speak to an old woman leafing through her photo album, enabling her to re-enter that past. Still other characters simply pick up their past lives despite years which have intervened, as in "Lives Touching," in which an old love affair isn't rekindled so much as continued.

This continuation of the past takes a more concrete form in such stories as "Joaquin," in which a movie star on location meets an older man who may be Joaquin Murieta himself. She becomes, for a while, the former lover she will play in the film. In "That Constant Coyote," a rancher, dying from cancer, comes to accept his end and celebrate his life after a visit from his father and grandfather, both dead before he was born. Another variant on this theme involves a young black man in "Rider," a city kid who disbelieves his grandfather's rodeo career as a bull-rider until he reads of it in a book on black cowboys. Finally he attends a rodeo where he enters and wins novice bull-riding, his grandfather's talent persisting in him.

Not all of Haslam's characters are able to accommodate themselves to or make use of the past; in *Masks*, for example, the narrator finally flees his home town, taking with him not only his memories and angers but also his unworthy dead brother's widow, a young woman whose past—not least that inflicted upon her by the brother—may have damaged her beyond recovery. The Chicano farmer in "Earthquake Summer" first disbelieves the Indian *Bruja* who warns him not to plow the field where her ancestors are buried; finally, he gives up his lease on that ground, entirely. In "Trophies," a doctor on a visit to his hometown is so crippled by a former classmate's revelations—which may be false—about the doctor's wife that he's unable to intervene to save the man's life. Some pasts no American can accommodate to, as in "Home to America," a powerful evocation of the Japanese-American internment during World War II. The story's closing line, in which a little Japanese-American girl asks her mother, "When are we going home to America?" is especially hunting.

The diversity of Valley life offers Haslam appropriate material for his range of styles, which include good-old-boy tall tales, lyrical pieces built around language and image, stories in the magical realist vein in which time, space, and identity are mysteriously transcended, and meticulously realistic stories in which time, space, and identity are inescapable. Haslam's vision is as varied and complex as is the Great Central Valley itself.

—Wayne Ude

HAWK, Alex. *See* **KELTON, Elmer; LUTZ, Giles A.**

HAYCOX, Ernest. American. Born in Portland, Oregon, 1 October 1899. Educated at Reed College, Portland, 1919–20; University of Oregon, Eugene, B.A. 1923. Military service from 1915; served with the 3rd Oregon National Guard on the Mexican border, 1916; served in France, 1917–19: Chair of the Selective Service Board, Multnomah County, Oregon. Married Jill Marie Chord in 1925; one daughter and one son. Police court reporter, Portland *Oregonian*, 1923; then freelance writer. Litt.D.: Lewis and Clark College, Portland, 1946. *Died 13 October 1950.*

WESTERN PUBLICATIONS

Novels

Free Grass. New York, Doubleday, 1929; London, Corgi, 1958.

Chaffee of Roaring Horse. New York, Doubleday, and London, Stanley Paul, 1930; as *Roaring Horse*, London, Corgi, 1959.

Whispering Range. New York, Doubleday, 1930; London, Stanley Paul, 1931.

All Trails Cross. London, Stanley Paul, 1931.

Starlight Rider. New York, Doubleday, 1933; London, Stanley Paul, 1934.

Riders West. New York, Doubleday, 1934.

Rough Air. New York, Doubleday, 1934; as *Smoky Pass*, London, Stanley Paul, 1934.

The Silver Desert. New York, Doubleday, 1935; London, Stanley Paul, 1936.

Trail Smoke. New York, Doubleday, and London, Stanley Paul, 1936.

Deep West. Boston, Little Brown, and London, Stanley Paul, 1937.

Trouble Shooter. Boston, Little Brown, and London, Stanley Paul, 1937; as *Frank Peace, Trouble Shooter*, New York, Paperback Library, 1963.

Man in the Saddle. Boston, Little Brown, 1938; London, Stanley Paul, 1939.

Sundown Jim. Boston, Little Brown, and London, Stanley Paul, 1938.

The Border Trumpet. Boston, Little Brown, 1939; London, Hodder and Stoughton, 1940.

Rim of the Desert. Boston, Little Brown, 1940; London, Hodder and Stoughton, 1941.

Saddle and Ride. Boston, Little Brown, and London, Hodder and Stoughton, 1940.

Trail Town. Boston, Little Brown, and London, Hodder and Stoughton, 1941.

Alder Gulch. Boston, Little Brown, 1942; as *No Law and Order*, London, Hodder and Stoughton, 1942.

Action by Night. Boston, Little Brown, and London, Hodder and Stoughton, 1943.

The Wild Bunch. Boston, Little Brown, 1943; London, Hodder and Stoughton, 1944.

Bugles in the Afternoon. Boston, Little Brown, and London, Hodder and Stoughton, 1944.

Canyon Passage. Boston, Little Brown, and London, Hodder and Stoughton, 1945.

Long Storm. Boston, Little Brown, 1946; London, Hodder and Stoughton, 1947.

The Earth Breakers. Boston, Little Brown, 1952; London, Corgi, 1960.

Pioneer Loves. Boston, Little Brown, 1952.

Return of a Fighter. New York, Dell, 1952; London, Corgi, 1956.

Head of the Mountain. New York, Popular Library, 1952; London, Prior, 1978.

The Grim Canyon: Three Short Novels. New York, Popular Library, 1953.

Guns Up, and The Hour of Fury. New York, Popular Library, 1954; *The Hour of Fury*, as *Guns of Fury*, with *Night Raid*, New York, Belmont Tower, 1972.

The Adventurers. Boston, Little Brown, 1954.

Secret River, and The Trail of the Barefoot Pony. New York, Popular Library, 1955.

Vengeance Trail, and Invitation by Bullet. New York, Popular Library, 1955.

A Rider of the High Mesa. New York, Popular Library, 1956.

Dead Man Range. New York, Popular Library, 1957; as *Clint*, New York, Paperback Library, 1973.

On the Prod. New York, Popular Library, 1957.

Brand Fires on the Ridge includes *Night Raid.* Derby, Connecticut, Monarch, 1959; as *Wipe Out the Brierlys*, New York, Belmont, 1975.

Lone Rider. New York, Popular Library, 1959.

Guns of the Tom Dee, and Valley of the Rogue. New York, Popular Library, 1959.
The Feudists. New York, New American Library, 1960; London, New English Library, 1963.
Outlaw Guns: Three Short Novels. New York, Pyramid, 1964.
Sixgun Duo: Two Short Novels. New York, Ace, 1965.
Trigger Trio: Three Short Novels. New York, Ace, 1966.
Starlight and Gunflame: Three Short Novels. New York, Ace, 1973.

Short Stories

Rough Justice. Boston, Little Brown, 1950.
By Rope and Lead. Boston, Little Brown, 1951; London, Hodder and Stoughton, 1952.
Murder on the Frontier. Boston, Little Brown, 1952.
Rawhide Range. New York, Popular Library, 1952.
Outlaw. Boston, Little Brown, 1953.
Prairie Guns. Boston, Little Brown, 1954.
Gun Talk and Other Stories. New York, Popular Library, 1956.
The Last Rodeo. Boston, Little Brown, 1956.
The Best Western Stories of Ernest Haycox. New York, Bantam, 1960.
The Man from Montana. New York, Dell, 1964.
Powder Smoke and Other Stories. New York, Avon, 1966.
Frontier Blood. New York, Ace, 1974.

Uncollected Short Stories

"High Wind," in *The Arbor House Treasury of Great Western Stories*, edited by Bill Pronzini and Martin H. Greenberg. New York, Arbor House, 1982.
"A Day in Town" and "Stage to Lordsburg," in *The Western Hall of Fame*, edited by Bill Pronzini and Martin H. Greenberg. New York, Morrow, 1984.
"McQuestion Rides," in *The Lawmen*, edited by Bill Pronzini and Martin H. Greenberg. New York, Fawcett, 1984.
"A Night on Don Jaime Street," in *The Outlaws*, edited by Bill Pronzini and Martin H. Greenberg. New York, Fawcett, 1984.

OTHER PUBLICATIONS

Novel

Wind of Rebellion. New York, Criterion, 1954.

Plays

Screenplays: *Apache Trail*, with Maurice Geraghty and Gordon Kahn, 1942; *Heaven Only Knows*, with others, 1947; *Montana*, with others, 1950.

Other

American Character. Eugene, Oregon State Board of Higher Education, 1943.

*

Critical Study: *Ernest Haycox* by Richard W. Etulain, Boise, Idaho, Boise State University Press, 1988.

* * *

More than any other early 20th-century writer, Ernest Haycox changed the formulaic western novel into one featuring complex heroes, contrasting heroines, and varied themes. He began in pulps, moved to slicks, and tried to branch into Hugo-like panoramic historical novels. His plots usually concern range rivalries, revenge, and fights against Indians. Many perceptive readers prefer his short stories to any novels but his best. His tales are notable for crispness and variety.

The typical Haycox hero embodies the Code of the West: fight fair, admit no hurts, be courteous but firm with women. Though born in the West, Haycox lived in the east a while; therefore, his preference for western ways resulted from experience. He regarded the east as past its prime, enervated, fancy, feminine, bookish; opposite in all respects, his West is vibrant, captivating, plain and rough, masculine, with grass-roots culture. Haycox often portrays eastern villains coming west for a second chance but failing to measure up. Hence, instead of being an arena for the touted second chance, Haycox's West is a catalyst triggering everyone's most elemental responses to raw life.

Haycox dramatizes tentative answers to this question: How should one live? His good men are loyal to those close to them, demand loyalty of those they help, are patient, are ferocious when aroused. Heroic leaders among Haycox's males inspire their crews, are stoical and long-suffering, and oddly combine self-reliance with an almost monotonous fatalism. The metaphor which Haycox employs most frequently is "the book of fate." Curiously, the hero of Haycox's best novel, *Bugles in the Afternoon*, rationalizes the defeat of Colonel George Armstrong Custer as something "written in the book" and adds that "The hand that writes in the book is one over which we have no control." Further, Haycox too airily rationalizes America's shameful treatment of the Indian as justifiably managed in the name of Manifest Destiny. Related is Haycox's reiterated comparison of life to a poker game: we get one hand, cannot turn it in for a better one, must play it well—bluffing at times—should guard our chips, must never complain. Another fate image is the weary trail of life. Mostly one is doomed to follow it where it leads; but occasionally he can quit drifting, settle down, stay put, put down roots.

Since Haycox's world is a man's world, his males are active. They do the choosing in love relationships—or seem to. Women should be passive, responsive, decent, and certainly feminine rather than aggressive or initiatory. Haycox often dramatizes a given hero's protracted loyalty to the wrong woman prematurely chosen. The result is unrealistic but unfailingly suspenseful. The currently outmoded double standard pervades Haycox's fiction. His most anti-feminist line occurs when a frustrated woman lacklogically advises the heroine in *Rim of the Desert* to accompany her man anywhere: "If he's not worth following then you're not worth having."

Haycox loved western variety, plenitude, vastness, and solitude. Man seems especially puny in the west and, compared to slow western time, is demonstrably ephemeral. Human transitoriness is Haycox's major philosophical theme. His favorite sense was that of hearing; his favorite sound, silence. The word "silence" appears with remarkable frequency in his writing; often near it in a given passage is the word "time." In Haycox's west, when all sounds die away eternity seems uniquely near.

Haycox was an even writer; so it is hard to single out his best works. But the following novels are especially durable: *Free Grass* (rivalry on Dakota grazing lands); *Trouble Shooter* (building the Union Pacific Railroad, 1868–69); *The Border Trumpet* (army life in Arizona, early 1870's); *Alder Gulch* (Montana Vigilantes, 1863–64); *Bugles in the Afternoon* (Custer's defeat, 1876); *Canyon Passage* (Oregon freighters vs. Rogue Indians, 1850's); *Long Storm* (Oregon Copperhead activities); and *The Earth Breakers* (early Oregon settlers). His best novella is surely "On the Prod" (fighting to keep an inherited ranch from rustlers). His best short stories concern individualistic lawmen ("McQuestion Rides," "When You Carry the Star," "Wild Jack Rhett"), resolute soldiers ("Officer's Choice," "Weight of Command," "Dispatch to the General," "Tactical Maneuver"), frontier-town mores ("On Texas Street," "Deadline," "A Day in Town," "Night on Don Jaime Street"), and above all Oregon homesteading ("Quarter Section on Dullknife Creek," "Cry Deep, Cry Still," "Call This Land Home"). Haycox's best-known story is probably "Stage to Lordsburg"; it is popular, however, not because of any special merit but because it became the 1939 movie *Stagecoach*, directed by John Ford and starring John Wayne.

—Robert L. Gale

HAYDEN, Jay. *See* **PAINE, Lauran.**

HAYES, Timothy. *See* **MACRAE, Mason.**

HAZARD, Jack. *See* **BOOTH, Edwin.**

HECKELMANN, Charles N(ewman). Also wrote as Cliff Campbell; Jackson Cole; Andrew Griffin; Charles Lawton; Charles Mann; Chuck Mann; Mat Rand; James Rourke; Charles Smith; Reeve Walker. American. Born in Brooklyn, New York, 24 October 1913. Educated at Hempstead High School, New York, graduated 1929; University of Notre Dame, Indiana, B.A. (maxima cum laude) 1934. Married Anne Marie Auer in 1937; one daughter and one son. Sports writer, Brooklyn *Eagle*, 1934–37; editor-in-chief, Cupples and Leon, New York, 1937–41; editor-in-chief, 1941–58, and vice-president, 1953–58, Popular Library, New York; editor-in-chief, and president, Monarch Books, New York, 1958–65; managing editor, David McKay, New York, 1965–68; senior editor, Cowles Book Company, New York, 1968–71; senior editor, 1971–72, and editor-in-chief and vice-president, 1972–75, Hawthorn Books, New York; book editor, *National Enquirer*, 1975–78; editorial consultant, Valueback Publishing, Palm Beach Gardens, Florida, 1981–83. President, Catholic Writers Guild of America, 1949–52; vice-president, 1955–57, and president, 1964–65, Western Writers of America; life member, National Cowboy Hall of Fame and Western Heritage Center. Agent: Scott Meredith Literary Agency, 845 Third Avenue, New York, New York 10022. Address: 10634 Green Trail Drive South, Boynton Beach, Florida 33436, U.S.A.

WESTERN PUBLICATIONS

Novels

Vengeance Trail. New York, Arcadia House, 1944.
Lawless Range. New York, Arcadia House, 1945; London, Quality Press, 1947.
Six-Gun Outcast. New York, Arcadia House, 1946; London, Quality Press, 1948.
Deputy Marshal. New York, Arcadia House, 1947.
Guns of Arizona. New York, Doubleday, 1949; Kingswood, Surrey, World's Work, 1951.
Outlaw Valley. New York, Cupples and Leon, 1950.
Danger Rides the Range. New York, Cupples and Leon, 1950.
Two-Bit Rancher. New York, Doubleday, 1950; Kingswood, Surrey, World's Work, 1951.
Let the Guns Roar! New York, Doubleday, 1950; Kingswood, Surrey, World's Work, 1951.
Fighting Ramrod. New York, Doubleday, 1951; Kingswood, Surrey, World's Work, 1952.
Hell in His Holsters. New York, Doubleday, 1952; Kingswood, Surrey, World's Work, 1953.
The Rawhider. New York, Holt, 1952; London, Hodder and Stoughton, 1953.
Hard Man with a Gun. Boston, Little Brown, 1954; London, Hale, 1955.
Bullet Law. Boston, Little Brown, 1955; London, Hale, 1957.
Trumpets in the Dawn. New York, Doubleday, 1958.
The Big Valley. Racine, Wisconsin, Whitman, 1966.
The Glory Riders. New York, Avon, 1967.
Stranger from Durango. New York, Lancer, 1971.
Return to Arapahoe. New York, Popular Library, 1980.
Wagons to Wind River. New York, Popular Library, 1982.

Uncollected Short Stories

"The Desert Devil," in *Western Trails*, August 1937.
"Law Comes to Saddle City," in *Thrilling Western*, May 1939.
"A Jailbird Robs Red Gap," in *Range Riders*, June 1939.
"The Waddy Takes Over," in *Popular Western*, September 1939.
"Colt Claws of the Vulture Brood," in *Blue Ribbon Western*, September 1939.
"Range of the Man-Breaker," in *Western Action*, February 1940.
"Gunsmoke on the Range," in *Popular Western*, March 1940.
"The Land That Law Forgot" (as Mat Rand), and "Canyon of Wanted Men," in *Western Action*, June 1940.
"Man-Breaker's Blood Dinero," in *Blue Ribbon Western*, September 1940.
"Gun Wolf of Silver Bow," in *Cowboy Short Stories*, September 1940.
"Marshal Law for Gun-Slicks," in *Western Action*, October 1940.
"Sidewinder Breed," in *All American Western*, December 1940.
"Waterhole Roundup," in *Wild West* (New York), 21 December 1940.
"Man-Trap Rancho," in *Greater Western Action Novels*, January 1941.
"Gun Devil's Death Trap," in *All American Western*, February 1941.
"Death's Head Killer" (as Mat Rand), in *Real Western*, May 1941.
"The Fastest Gun Is the Law" (as James Rourke) and "Red Hell on Wheels," in *Western Yarns*, June 1941.
"Gun Guard for the Purgatory Legion," in *Big Book Western*, June 1941.

"The Last Outpost in Hell," in *.44 Western*, July 1941.
"Colt Damned as a Back-Shooter," in *Real Western*, August 1941.
"Built for Trouble," in *Thrilling Western*, September 1941.
"Town Tamer of Hell's Acre," in *Famous Western*, Fall 1941.
"River Packets to Boothill," in *Wild West* (New York), 25 October 1941.
"Guns for Boothill," in *Wild West* (New York), 22 November 1941.
"Man-Bait for Night Raiders," in *Big Book Western*, December 1941.
"Escape to Boothill" (as Andrew Griffin), in *Wild West* (New York), 6 December 1941.
"Valley of Doom," in *Famous Western*, Winter 1942.
"Boom-Town Buckaro," in *Western Adventures*, February 1942.
"Six-Gun Reprieve," in *Complete Cowboy Wild Western Stories*, February 1942.
"Noose-Dodger's Payoff," in *Western Trails*, March 1942.
"Open Road to Boothill," in *Wild West* (New York), 14 March 1942.
"Six-Gun Ticket to Hades" (as Andrew Griffin), in *Wild West* (New York), 21 March 1942.
"Red Hell in His Holsters," in *Wild West* (New York), 11 April 1942.
"Trouble at Storm River," in *Wild West* (New York), 2 May 1942.
"Devil's Diggings," in *Wild West* (New York), 20 June 1942.
"The Bullet Trail," in *Exciting Western*, Summer 1942.
"Six-Gun Send-off," in *Western Yarns*, Summer 1942.
"The Gunsmoke Masquerade," in *Thrilling Western*, July 1942.
"Range Beyond the Law," in *Masked Rider Western*, July 1942.
"Reunion in Hell," in *Double Action Western*, July 1942.
"Snare for a Polecat," in *Western Aces*, August 1942.
"Colt Call to Disaster," in *Popular Western*, September 1942.
"Lawman's Gunsmoke Crusade" (as Cliff Campbell), in *Complete Cowboy Wild Western Stories*, September 1942.
"The Black Stallion" (as Charles Smith), in *Exciting Western*, Fall 1942.
"Hoodoo Caravan," in *Frontier Stories*, Fall 1942.
"Range of Doomed Men" (as Mat Rand), in *Western Yarns*, Fall 1942.
"Steel Rails to Boothill," in *Wild West* (New York), 26 September 1942.
"Six-Gun Storm in Deadwood," in *Thrilling Western*, November 1942.
"Range of Hate," in *Masked Rider Western*, November 1942.
"Hot Lead for a Range Hog" (as Cliff Campbell), in *Complete Cowboy Wild Western Stories*, November 1942.
"Outcast from a Lawless Town," in *Famous Western*, January 1943.
"Showdown at Silver Creek," in *Thrilling Western*, January 1943.
"Fugitive from Hell," in *Western Yarns*, January 1943.
"Ride the Owlhoot to Hell," in *Complete Cowboy Stories*, January 1943.
"Desert Road to Ruin," in *Wild West* (New York), 16 January 1943.
"Bounty Hunter" (as Chuck Mann), in *Texas Rangers* (New York), February 1943.
"Gateway to Doom" (as Jackson Cole), in *Thrilling Adventures*, February 1943.
"The Brahma Herd" (as Chuck Mann), in *Rodeo Romances*, Spring 1943.
"The Fighting Parson," in *Famous Western*, Spring 1943.
"Bullet Passport to Purgatory," in *Wild West* (New York), 22 May 1943.
"Bullet Harvest for Renegades," in *Masked Rider Western*, June 1943.
"Prescription for Killers," in *Range Riders Western*, Summer 1943.
"Texas Manhunt," in *Famous Western*, Summer 1943.
"Rodeo Clown" (as Tex Mumford), in *Rodeo Romances*, Summer 1943.
"Suicide Ranch," in *Wild West* (New York), 3 July 1943.
"Red Hell Waits for a Lawman," in *Wild West* (New York), 31 July 1943.
"Riding for Love" (as Charles Mann), in *Rodeo Romances*, Fall 1943.
"Lone Wolf Lawman," in *Famous Western*, Fall 1943.
"The Cheyenne Trail" (as Reeve Walker), in *Exciting Western*, October 1943.
"Raiders of the Wilderness" (as Reeve Walker), in *Exciting Western*, December 1943.
"Steel Rails to Peril," in *Masked Rider Western*, March 1944.
"Heir to Hell's Home Ranch," in *Big-Book Western*, April 1944.
"The Texas Roper," in *Rodeo Romances*, Summer 1944.
"Death Valley Showdown," in *Thrilling Western*, July 1944.
"Mutineers of the Big Muddy," in *Big-Book Western*, August 1944.
"Cheyenne Death-Trap" (as Reeve Walker), in *Exciting Western*, October 1944.
"Pilgrim Ramrod for Hell's Range," in *Big-Book Western*, October 1944.
"Journey to Doom," in *Rio Kid Western*, November 1944.
"Rails of Doom," in *Western Story* (New York), November 1944.
"Outlaw Range," in *Thrilling Western*, January 1945.
"The Trail to Purgatory," in *Range Riders Western*, Spring 1945.
"Arena Showdown," in *Rodeo Romances*, Spring 1945.
"War in Massacre Basin," in *Masked Rider Western*, September 1945.
"Partners' Luck," in *The Fall Roundup*, edited by Harry E. Maule. New York, Random House, 1955.
"Death Trap for an Iron Horse," in *Western Bonanza*, edited by Todhunter Ballard. New York, Doubleday, 1969.

OTHER PUBLICATIONS

Novel

Jungle Menace (novelization of screenplay). New York, Cupples and Leon, 1937.

Novels (for children) as Charles Lawton

Clarkville's Battery; or, Baseball Versus Gangsters. New York, Cupples and Leon, 1937.
Ros Hackney, Halfback; or, How Clarkville's Captain Made Good. New York, Cupples and Leon, 1937.
The Winning Forward Pass; or, Onward to the Orange Bowl Game. New York, Cupples and Leon, 1940.
Home Run Hennessey; or, Winning the All-Star Game. New York, Cupples and Leon, 1941.
Touchdown to Victory; or, The Touchdown Express Makes Good. New York, Cupples and Leon, 1942.

Other

Writing Fiction for Profit. New York, Coward McCann, 1968.

Editor, *With Guidons Flying: Tales of the U.S. Cavalry in the Old West by Members of the Western Writers of America.* New York, Doubleday, 1970.

*

Manuscript Collection: Western History Research Center, University of Wyoming, Laramie.

Charles N. Heckelmann comments:

Fiction writing fascinated me very early in life and I can remember writing little stories and squibs when I was eight or nine years old. They were terrible, of course, but they whetted my appetite for more. At the University of Notre Dame I began getting some of my fiction published in college quarterlies.

Since I had always been fascinated by the frontier West and had read many western novels and stories, I decided to try my hand at a western story (this was in the heyday of pulp magazines). That first story, "The Desert Devil," was accepted by and published in *Western Trails* magazine in August 1937, just a few months after I married my wife, Anne. And that sale started me on my way. From then on I spent much of my spare time writing western stories that I tried to sell to pulp magazines and I soon enjoyed considerable success in that milieu. I was helped by experience I gained as a pulp magazine editor on westerns, mysteries, and adventure stories for Better Publications and Thrilling Magazines in New York City. And from that post I went to editor-in-chief of Popular Library, one of the early publishers of pocket-size paperbacks. So I was purchasing and editing western stories and novels on the one hand and writing my own western fiction on the other hand. In 1944 I began to concentrate on full-length novels as the popularity of pulp magazines began to wane with the influx of paperback books into the marketplace.

Always Westerns have been my first love. I've traveled a great deal in the West, have an extensive library of research volumes and always strive to make my books as authentic as possible. My basic idea is to provide good reading entertainment. I try to concentrate on making my characters likable and believable, to give my stories good pace and excitement and to provide proper and logical motivation for the events that take place. I usually work from a carefully prepared and detailed chapter outline (I'm the kind of writer who has to know just where his story is going before he positions himself at the typewriter). I write fairly fast but with considerable care so that I am usually faced with a minimum of revisions and pride myself on trying to provide my publishers with "clean" manuscripts (scripts that require very little in the way of copyediting).

My short stories and my novels cover a wide range of subjects and locales in the West and that is precisely according to plan. I've run the gamut from stories involving range hogs, range wars, rustling, town taming, trailing beef, ranching, timber cutting, riverboating, railroading, mining, cavalry and Indian wars. If I have any favorite novel it is *Trumpets in the Dawn*, a novel about the Custer Massacre (it was something I had always wanted to write about). I spent six months of my spare time doing research before I wrote a line of the book. It has many historical characters and a number of fictional characters. Though I took some editorial liberties and the first half of the novel is largely fictional, I expended a great deal of effort to stick to actual history in describing the movements of the U.S. Cavalry in the days that led up to the climactic battle on the Little Big Horn, while providing color and excitement and suspense through the actions and emotions of my key fictional characters.

In conclusion, I can happily say that it's all been a great deal of fun. I still get a kick out of writing westerns. I still enjoy seeing each new book come out and I look forward to writing western novels as long as I can sit at my typewriter.

* * *

Charles N. Heckelmann was one of the solid practitioners of the pulp western era. His shorts, such as "Outlaw Range," were not the sort to appear in the prestigious anthologies of yesterday nor the more recent academic ones, but did appear and compare favorably with other work in various collections of pulp stories. When his work appeared in a pulp magazine his name was featured on the cover with a frequency approaching regularity.

His novels, most predating the period of wide paperback interest in the Western, have also not been as popular as those of more acclaimed writers. Yet these longer stories were always a fast-paced read, generally involving a *Ranch Romances* sort of love story that was integral to the plot, and often providing more items of additional interest than the well-constructed story, hero, and background.

In the important area of titles, he was again not as fortunate as he might have been. While they never left doubt that the books behind them were Westerns, truth in packaging was seldom one of their virtues. His most ambitious work, *The Rawhider*, has as its supposed title character a riverboat pilot during the Civil War. The hero of *Hard Man with a Gun*, again surely the title character as well, might be better described as "brave" or even "lucky" man, for he is presented as considerably less "hard" than several of the ruthless enemies he overcomes.

A favorite Heckelmann device, the hero sneaking up on (or through) the Indians, would have been more effective as a reversal of what the western reader has been taught to expect had it been used more sparingly. Reading Heckelmann's books in close succession might be likely to foster the idea that the Indians were "babes in the wood" in the field of stealth. This is especially true of *Guns of Arizona* where the hero performs his feat more than once, and with companions equally successful though not invested with his quality of herohood and so not entitled to quite so much suspension of disbelief.

—R. Jeff Banks

HENDERSON, James Maddock. *See* **DANVERS, Pete.**

HENDRYX, James B(eardsley). American. Born in Sauk Center, Minnesota, 9 December 1880. Educated at Sauk Center public schools; University of Minnesota, Minneapolis, 2 years. Married Hermione Flagler in 1915. Newspaperman in Springfield, Ohio, 1905–10; special writer, Cincinnati

Enquirer, 1915–20; salesman, tan bark buyer, cowboy in Montana, insurance man, and construction foreman. *Died 1 March 1963.*

WESTERN PUBLICATIONS

Novels (series: Corporal Downey)

The Promise: A Tale of the Great Northwest. New York, Putnam, 1915.
The Gun-Brand: A Feud of the Frozen North. New York, Putnam, 1917; London, Jarrolds, 1921.
The Texan: A Story of the Cattle Country. New York, Putnam, 1918; London, Jarrolds, 1922.
The Gold Girl. New York, Putnam, 1920.
Prairie Flowers. New York, Putnam, 1920; London, Jarrolds, 1923.
Snowdrift: A Story of the Land of the Strong Cold. New York, Putnam, 1922.
North. New York, Putnam, 1923.
Marquard the Silent. New York, Garden City Publishing Company, 1924.
At the Foot of the Rainbow. New York, Putnam, 1924.
Beyond the Outposts. London, Hutchinson, 1924.
Without Gloves. New York, Putnam, and London, Hutchinson, 1924.
The Challenge of the North. New York, Garden City Publishing Company, 1925.
Oak and Iron: Of These Be the Breed of the North. New York, Putnam, and London, Hutchinson, 1925.
Downey of the Mounted. New York, Putnam, and London, Hutchinson, 1926.
Frozen Inlet Post. New York, Doubleday, and London, Hutchinson, 1927.
Gold—and the Mounted. New York, Doubleday, and London, Hutchinson, 1928.
Man of the North. New York, Doubleday, 1929; London, Hutchinson, 1930.
Blood on the Yukon Trail (Downey). New York, Doubleday, 1930; as *In the Days of Gold*, London, Jarrolds, 1930; as *Devil's Gold*, Jarrolds, 1940.
Corporal Downey Takes the Trail. New York, Doubleday, 1931; London, Hutchinson, 1932.
Raw Gold. New York, Doubleday, and London, Jarrolds, 1933.
The Yukon Kid (Downey). New York, Doubleday, and London, Jarrolds, 1934.
Grubstake Gold. New York, Doubleday, 1936; London, Jarrolds, 1937; as *Death Heads North*, n.p., Adventure Novel Classics, n.d.
Blood of the North. New York, Doubleday, and London, Jarrolds, 1938.
Edge of Beyond. New York, Doubleday, 1939.
Hard Rock Man. New York, Carlton House, 1940; London, Hale, 1941.
Gambler's Chance. New York, Carlton House, 1941; London, Museum Press, 1943.
New Rivers Calling. New York, Doubleday, 1943; London, Hale, 1953.
The Way of the North. New York, Doubleday, 1945; London, Edwards, 1946.
Courage of the North. New York, Doubleday, 1946; London, Hammond, 1954.
On the Rim of the Arctic. New York, Doubleday, 1948; London, Museum Press, 1952.
Murder in the Outlands. New York, Doubleday, 1949; London, Museum Press, 1953.
The Stampeders. New York, Doubleday, 1951; London, Hammond, 1956.
Sourdough Gold. New York, Doubleday, 1952; London, Hammond, 1957.
The Long Chase. New York, Dell, 1952.
Gold Is Where You Find It. New York, Doubleday, 1953; London, Hammond, 1957.
Good Men and Bad. New York, Doubleday, 1954; London, Hammond, 1958.

Short Stories (series: Halfaday Creek)

Outlaws of Halfaday Creek. New York, Doubleday, and London, Jarrolds, 1935.
Black John of Halfaday Creek. New York, Doubleday, and London, Jarrolds, 1939.
The Czar of Halfaday Creek. New York, Doubleday, 1940; London, Jarrolds, 1955.
Law and Order on Halfaday Creek. New York, Carlton House, 1941; London, Jarrolds, 1954.
Gold and Guns on Halfaday Creek. New York, Carlton House, 1943; London, Hale, 1953.
Strange Doings on Halfaday Creek. New York, Doubleday, 1943; London, Hale, 1952.
It Happened on Halfaday Creek. New York, Doubleday, 1944.
Skullduggery on Halfaday Creek. New York, Doubleday, 1946; London, Hammond, 1953.
The Saga of Halfaday Creek. New York, Doubleday, 1947; London, Hammond, 1954.
Justice on Halfaday Creek. New York, Doubleday, 1949; London, Museum Press, 1954.
Badmen on Halfaday Creek. New York, Doubleday, 1950; London, Hammond, 1956.
Murder on Halfaday Creek. New York, Doubleday, 1951.
Intrigue on Halfaday Creek. New York, Doubleday, 1953.
Terror on Halfaday Creek. London, Consul, 1963.

Uncollected Short Stories

"Black John Gives a Tip," in *The Northerners*, edited by Bill Pronzini and Martin H. Greenberg. New York, Fawcett, 1990.

OTHER PUBLICATIONS

Fiction (for children)

Connie Morgan in Alaska. New York, Putnam, 1916; London, Jarrolds, 1919.
Connie Morgan in the Lumber Camps. New York, Putnam, 1919; London, Jarrolds, 1928.
Connie Morgan in the Fur Country. New York, Putnam, 1921; London, Jarrolds, 1928.
Connie Morgan in the Cattle Country. New York, Putnam, 1923; London, Jarrolds, 1927.
Connie Morgan with the Mounted. London, Jarrolds, 1924; New York, Putnam, 1928.
Connie Morgan with the Forest Rangers. New York, Putnam, 1925; London, Jarrolds, 1926.
Connie Morgan Hits the Trail. New York, Doubleday, 1929.
Connie Morgan, Prospector. London, Jarrolds, 1930.
Connie Morgan in the Barren Lands. London, Jarrolds, 1934.
Connie Morgan in the Arctic. New York, Putnam, and London, Jarrolds, 1936.

Play

Screenplay: *Snowdrift*, 1923.

* * *

James Hendryx had an unusually long career lasting from 1915 until the 1960's. He wrote many Westerns in several series of books including the Corporal Downey series, Connie Morgan series for juvenile readers, and the Halfaday Creek series. Hendryx was born in Minnesota but his special contribution could be said to be the successful development and maintenance of the Canadian Western, a sub-species of the western genre. While he is not alone in this achievement, his novels maintained their popularity, while the mainstream U.S. Western has developed along different lines.

The setting of Hendryx's novels is the Northwest, either in Canada or in Alaska or Montana. Indeed Hendryx makes a point of the fact that Montana is much more lawless than Canada and that criminals can cross over the border to the United States to find a safe haven there. Hendryx is very good at setting his novels in a convincing place and time. He produces an affectionate picture of the Montana Hills in *The Texan*, but an even more affectionate picture of the Canadian "land of the strong cold" occurs in *Gambler's Chance*. In *The Promise* there are references to the then current temperance viewpoints.

A comparison of *The Promise* with later novels shows the considerable development of Hendryx as a writer. *The Promise* is a rather juvenile book with an immature style and a plot which is slow to develop. In a way it is more like an English colonial western, in which the northwest of America is seen as a land of opportunity for the spoiled young man of the cities to make good in. Hendryx improves on this shaky start and gives his brand of Canadian western a genuine identity in the 1920's. In *The Gold Girl* there is plenty of local colour with distinctively Canadian dialogue. There are good descriptions of the "frontier" town of Regina, but more importantly Hendryx does succeed in creating a credible character in the shape of Corporal Downey of the North West Mounted Police. Corporal Downey was to become a favourite character and he appears in many more books. He is, of course, quite a different type to the formula western sheriff. While he is knowledgeable about the outdoors and good with a gun, he upholds the reputation of the Mounted Police in Canada. In *Gambler's Chance* Hendryx succeeds very effectively in portraying another Canada in addition to the northwest. It is basically a well contrived French Canadian crime thriller about Montreal, although it ends in the northwest.

Latterly Hendryx created another series of books, the Halfaday Creek series set on the Yukon-Alaska border. Although Corporal Downey appears in *Terror on Halfaday Creek* he was given only a token appearance. The principal character in this series is a rather idiosyncratic figure called Black John. His methods are more in line with those of some characters in mainstream American western novels: "breaking the law in the interests of justice" is his favourite pastime. In his ardent pursuit of justice he adds yet a few more headstones to the Halfaday Creek cemetery. There is, however, much less violence than is to be found in the American western of this period.

Hendryx's books had an appeal to the English reader in that, as well as providing authentic local colour, he was able to give Canada a distinct identity in the West. It is a Canada which has reliable police, assize courts on English lines, and a healthy confidence that law does rule in remote wild territory. It is this optimistic view which contrasts strongly with the cynical views to be found in the U.S. Western. This optimism makes the Canadian Western a type of old fashioned English western, and it is surprising that Hendryx was able to maintain his type of Western over such a long period of time in such a narrow field.

—P.R. Meldrum

HENRY, O. Pseudonym for William Sydney, or Sidney, Porter. American. Born in Greensboro, North Carolina, 11 September 1862. Educated at his aunt's private school in Greensboro to age 7; apprentice pharmacist in Greensboro, 1878–81; licensed by the North Carolina Pharmaceutical Association, 1881. Married 1) Athol Estes Roach in 1887 (died 1897), one son and one daughter; 2) Sara Lindsay Coleman in 1907. Moved to Texas, 1882, and worked on a ranch in LaSalle County, 1882–84; bookkeeper in Austin, 1884–86; contributed to Detroit *Free Press*, 1887; draftsman, Texas Land office, Austin, 1887–91; teller, First National Bank, Austin, 1891–94; founding editor, *Iconoclast*, later *Rolling Stone* magazine, Houston, 1894–95; columnist ("Tales of the Town," later "Some Postscripts"), Houston *Post*, 1895–96; accused of embezzling funds from his previous employers, First National Bank, Austin, 1895; fled to Honduras to avoid trial, 1896–97; returned to Austin because of wife's illness, 1897; jailed for embezzling in the Federal Penitentiary, Columbus, Ohio, 1898–1901 (5-year sentence reduced to 3): while in prison began publishing stories as O. Henry; moved to Pittsburgh, 1901, and New York, 1902; thereafter a full-time writer; regular contributor, New York *Sunday World*, 1903–05. O. Henry Memorial Award established by the Society of Arts and Sciences, 1918. *Died 5 June 1910.*

WESTERN PUBLICATIONS

Short Stories

Heart of the West. New York, McClure, 1907; London, Nash, 1912.

O. Henry Westerns, edited by Patrick Thornhill. London, Methuen, 1961.

Uncollected Short Stories

"The Reformation of Calliope," in *The Arbor House Treasury of Great Western Stories*, edited by Bill Pronzini and Martin H. Greenberg. New York, Arbor House, 1982.

"A Double-Dyed Deceiver," in *The Reel West*, edited by Bill Pronzini and Martin H. Greenberg. New York, Doubleday, 1984.

"An Afternoon Miracle," in *The Western Hall of Fame*, edited by Bill Pronzini and Martin H. Greenberg. New York, Morrow, 1984.

"The Caballero's Way," in *The Outlaws*, edited by Bill Pronzini and Martin H. Greenberg. New York, Fawcett, 1984.

"The Passing of Black Eagle," in *The Second Reel West*, edited by Bill Pronzini and Martin H. Greenberg. New York, Doubleday, 1985.

"The Lonesome Road," in *Westeryear*, edited by Ed Gorman. New York, Evans, 1988.

"The Higher Abdication," in *The Texans*, edited by Bill Pronzini and Martin H. Greenberg. New York, Fawcett, 1988.

"Christmas by Injunction," in *Christmas Out West*, edited by Bill Pronzini and Martin H. Greenberg. New York, Doubleday, 1990.

OTHER PUBLICATIONS

Short Stories

Cabbages and Kings. New York, McClure, 1904; London, Nash, 1912.
The Four Million. New York, McClure, 1906; London, Hodder and Stoughton, 1916.
The Trimmed Lamp. New York, McClure, 1907; London, Hodder and Stoughton, 1915.
The Voice of the City. New York, McClure, 1908; London, Hodder and Stoughton, 1916.
The Gentle Grafter. New York, McClure, 1908.
Roads of Destiny. New York, Doubleday, 1909; London, Nash, 1913.
Options. New York, Harper, 1909; London, Hodder and Stoughton, 1916.
Strictly Business: More Stories of the Four Million. New York, Doubleday, 1910.
Whirligigs. New York, Doubleday, 1910; London, Hodder and Stoughton, 1916.
Let Me Feel Your Pulse. New York, Doubleday, 1910; London, Elek, 1960.
The Two Women. Boston, Small Maynard, 1910.
Sixes and Sevens. New York, Doubleday, 1911; London, Hodder and Stoughton, 1916.
Rolling Stones. New York, Doubleday, 1912; London, Hodder and Stoughton, 1916.
Waifs and Strays. New York, Doubleday, 1917; London, Hodder and Stoughton, 1920.
Selected Stories, edited by C. Alphonse Smith. New York, Doubleday, 1922.
The Best of O. Henry. London, Hodder and Stoughton, 1929.
More O. Henry. London, Hodder and Stoughton, 1933.
The Best Short Stories of O. Henry, edited by Bennett Cerf and Van H. Cartmell. New York, Modern Library, 1945.
The Pocket Book of O. Henry, edited by Harry Hansen. New York, Pocket Books, 1948.
Cops and Robbers, edited by Ellery Queen. New York, Spivak, 1948.
The Stories of O. Henry, edited by Harry Hansen. New York, Limited Editions Club, 1965.

Play

Lo, with Franklin P. Adams, music by A. Baldwin Sloane (produced Aurora, Illinois, 1909).

Other

The Complete Writings of O. Henry. New York, Doubleday, 14 vols., 1918.
O. Henryana: Seven Odds and Ends: Poetry and Short Stories. New York, Doubleday, 1920.
Letters to Lithopolis from O. Henry to Mabel Wagnalls. New York, Doubleday, and London, Heinemann, 1922.
Postscripts (from Houston *Post*), edited by Florence Stratton. New York, Harper, 1923.
O. Henry Encore: Stories and Illustrations (from Houston *Post*), edited by Mary Sunlocks Harrell. Dallas, Upshaw, 1936; London, Hodder and Stoughton, 1939.

*

Bibliography: *A Bibliography of William Sydney Porter (O. Henry)* by Paul S. Clarkson, Caldwell, Idaho, Caxton Press, 1938; *William Sidney Porter (O. Henry): A Reference Guide* by Richard C. Harris, Boston, Hall, 1980.

Critical Studies: *O. Henry Biography* by C. Alphonse Smith, New York, Doubleday, 1916; *The Caliph of Bagdad* by Robert H. Davis and Arthur B. Maurice, New York, Appleton, 1931; *O. Henry: The Man and His Work*, Philadelphia, University of Pennsylvania Press, 1949, and *O. Henry, American Regionalist*, Austin, Texas, Steck Vaughn, 1969, both by Eugene Hudson Long; *The Heart of O. Henry* by Dale Kramer, New York, Rinehart, 1954; *Alias O. Henry: A Biography of William S. Porter* by Gerald Langford, New York, Macmillan, 1957; *O. Henry from Polecat Creek* by Ethel Stephens Arnett, Greensboro, North Carolina, Straughans Book Shop, 1962; *O. Henry* by Eugene Current-Garcia, New York, Twayne, 1965; *O. Henry: The Legendary Life of William S. Porter* by Richard O'Connor, New York, Doubleday, 1970; *From Alamo Plaza to Jack Harris's Saloon: O. Henry and the Southwest He Knew* by Joseph Gallegly, The Hague, Mouton, 1970; *O. Henry: A Biography of William Sydney Porter* by David Stuart, Chelsea House, Scarborough House, 1987.

* * *

William Sidney Porter, better known by his pen name O. Henry, was a southerner by birth—a North Carolinian, to be specific—and later an adopted son of New York, a city he portrayed memorably in some of his most famous stories. As a young man, however, Porter spent two years on an isolated ranch in southwest Texas near the U.S.–Mexican border, working in a desultory way as a cowboy and a sheepherder. He later lived in the cities of Austin, San Antonio, and Houston. When Porter became O. Henry, he naturally began to draw on his experiences and observations as the stuff of his fiction, to transmute those experiences into literary gold. Not surprisingly then, the Texas years form the backdrop for a sizable number of his tales.

Most of O. Henry's western stories were collected in *Heart of the West*. Their depiction of south Texas ranch life at a time when the west was still at least semi-wild is as accurate as the author's powers of observation and absorption could make them. Among the more notable tales in the collection are "The Higher Abdication," "The Princess and the Puma," "The Hiding of Black Bill," "Hygeia at the Solito," and "The Last of the Troubadours." Of the final work named, no less an authority than J. Frank Dobie called it—in his *Guide to Life and Literature of the Southwest*—"the best range story in American fiction." While that seems an overstatement, "The Last of the Troubadours" is unquestionably an interesting and authentic narrative of Texas ranch life in the late 19th century. In terms of lasting influence, one of O. Henry's most remarkable stories is "The Caballero's Way," which features as a character the Cisco Kid, who has appeared and reappeared throughout the 20th century in film, radio, and television. In praising "The Caballero's Way" in his *Guide*, Dobie focuses on the author's knowledgeable use of background detail; "nobody," Dobie says, "has written a better description of a prickly pear flat."

Despite his enormous popularity during his lifetime, O. Henry's critical reputation has plummeted as years have passed. Most of the technical and aesthetic weaknesses that recent critics have found in the writer's works overall are present in the western stories. A sometimes facile, flowery style, for instance, grates on the modern reader's sense of aesthetic rightness. Here is a brief passage from "A Call Loan": "In those days the cattlemen were the anointed. They were the grandees of the grass, kings of the kine, lords of the lea, barons of beef and bone." From "Hygeia at the Solito": "They sped upon velvet wheels across an exhilarant savanna. The pair of Spanish ponies struck a nimble, tireless trot, which gait they occasionally relieved by a wild untrammelled gallop."

At the height of his celebrity O. Henry worked with astonishing speed, turning out more than a story per week. Such haste could not possibly contribute to the attainment of high literary quality. To satisfy the demands of his many readers, the author inevitably slipped into the use of the melodramatic, the sentimental, the plot formula, the cheap, pat surprise ending. All of these criticisms apply in some measure to the western tales. For example, the formula device of the greenhorn's initiation is invoked, with slight variations, in several of the stories. Still, O. Henry was a born storyteller whose words have pleased millions of readers down through the years. In a sense the tales are "realistic" in that he ordinarily wrote only about things of which he had some firsthand knowledge. Though they are perhaps too glib and cheery to be realistic in the deeper sense, O. Henry's western stories and sketches are valuable portraits of the cattle kingdom at the end of an era—the age of the open range.

—William T. Pilkington

HENRY, Will. *See* **ALLEN, Henry Wilson.**

HERBERT, Arthur. *See* **ARTHUR, Burt.**

HEUMAN, William. Also wrote George Kramer. American. Born in Brooklyn, New York, 11 February 1912. Educated at local high school. Married Esther Read in 1942; one son and one daughter. Clerk, National Supply Corporation, New York, for 12 years; freelance writer 1950–71; also taught private classes in writing. *Died 21 August 1971.*

Western Publications

Novels (series: Mulvane)

Guns at Broken Bow. New York, Fawcett, 1950; London, Miller, 1957.
Hunt the Man Down. New York, Fawcett, 1951; London, Fawcett, 1954.
Roll the Wagons. New York, Fawcett, 1951; London, Miller, 1957.
Red Runs the River. New York, Fawcett, 1951; London, Fawcett, 1954.
Maverick with a Star. New York, Ace, 1952.
Secret of Death Valley. New York, Fawcett, 1952; London, Fawcett, 1954.
South to Santa Fe. New York, Ace, 1952.
Keelboats North. New York, Fawcett, 1953; London, Fawcett, 1954.
On to Santa Fe. New York, Fawcett, 1953; London, Fawcett, 1957.
Captain McRae: A Novel of the Northwest Frontier. New York, Morrow, 1954.
The Range Buster. New York, Fawcett, 1954; London, Fawcett, 1956.
Ride for Texas. New York, Fawcett, 1954; London, Fawcett, 1956.
Gunhand from Texas. New York, Avon, 1954.
Bonanza on the Big Muddy. New York, Arcadia House, 1955.
The Girl from Frisco. New York, Morrow, 1955.
Night Stage. New York, Arcadia House, 1955.
Rimrock Town. New York, Arcadia House, 1955.
Wagon Train West. New York, Fawcett, 1955; London, Muller, 1960.
Man in Blue. New York, Ace, 1956.
Stagecoach West. New York, Fawcett, 1957; London, Fawcett, 1959.
Violence Valley. New York, Fawcett, 1957; London, Fawcett, 1958.
Heller from Texas. New York, Fawcett, 1957; London, Fawcett, 1958.
Guns of Hell Valley. New York, Arcadia House, 1958.
Rustlers' Range. New York, Arcadia House, 1958; London, Muller, 1959.
Sabers in the Sun. New York, Arcadia House, 1958.
Wagon Wheel Drifter. New York, Arcadia House, 1958; London, Wright and Brown, 1960.
My Brother, The Gunman. New York, Ace, 1959.
Then Came Mulvane. New York, Avon, 1959.
Rimrock City. New York, Arcadia House, 1959.
Bullets for Mulvane. New York, Avon, 1960.
Pistoleers on Patrol. New York, Arcadia House, 1960; London, Wright and Brown, 1962.
Mulvane's War. New York, Avon, 1960.
Last Chance Valley. New York, Arcadia House, 1962; London, Wright and Brown, 1963.
Mulvane on the Prod. New York, Avon, 1962.
Guns along the Big Muddy. New York, Arcadia House, 1962; London, Wright and Brown, 1963.
Tall in the Saddle. London, Jenkins, 1963.
Hardcase Halloran. New York, Ace, 1964.
Crossfire Creek. New York, Arcadia House, 1964; London, Wright and Brown, 1965.

Uncollected Short Stories

"Gun-Doctor for a Dying Range," in *Star Western* (Chicago), May 1944.
"There's Hell on the Silver Frontier," in *West* (Kingswood, Surrey), December 1944.
"Last Call for the Frisco Kid," in *Star Western* (Chicago), September 1945.
"Basin of Doom," in *Western Story* (London), September 1945.
"Ride Out and Die!," in *Star Western* (Chicago), December 1945.
"Troopers of Hell's Outpost," in *Big-Book Western*, 1946.
"Gambler's Guns," in *Western Story* (London), September 1946.
"Death on the Mesa," in *Western Story* (London), August 1947.
"Fast Stage to Hell," in *Fifteen Western Tales*, 1947.
"There's Blood on His Star!," in *Star Western* (Chicago), February 1948.
"The Sudden Silence," in *Zane Grey's Western* (New York), December 1953.
"Hell Rides the River," in *Triple Western*, 1953.
"The Bouncer," in *Texas Rangers* (London), December 1953.
"Gambler's Choice," in *Western Story* (London), May 1955.
"Outlaw's Girl," in *Western* (New York), June 1955.
"Fight or Drag," in *Western* (New York), March 1956.

"Tenderfoot's Girl," in *Western Story* (London), October 1956.
"Shotgun Messenger," in *Thrilling Western* (London), April 1958.
"The Testing of Francis Mulvane," in *Thrilling Western* (London), June 1958.
"The Last Stage Out," in *Western Story* (London), October 1959.
"Big Muddy Freeze-Out," in *Western Story* (London), December 1959.
"Ride the Night Wind," in *Zane Grey Western* (New York), June 1970.
"Return of the Prodigal," in *Zane Grey Western* (New York), August 1970.
"Pony Express Rider," in *Zane Grey Western* (New York), October 1970.

OTHER PUBLICATIONS (for children)

Fiction

Fighting Five. New York, Morrow, 1950.
Wonder Boy. New York, Morrow, 1951.
Junior Quarterback. New York, Morrow, 1952.
Little League Champs. Philadelphia, Lippincott, 1953.
Strictly from Brooklyn. New York, Morrow, 1956.
Rocky Malone. Austin, Texas, Steck, 1957.
Left End Luisetti. Austin, Texas, Steck, 1958.
Second String Hero. Austin, Texas, Steck, 1959.
Missouri River Boy. New York, Dodd Mead, 1959.
Back Court Man. New York, Dodd Mead, 1960.
King of the West Side. Grand Rapids, Michigan, Eerdmans, 1961.
The Wonder Five. New York, Dodd Mead, 1962.
Rookie Backstop. New York, Dodd Mead, 1962.
Powerhouse Five. New York, Dodd Mead, 1963.
City High Five. New York, Dodd Mead, 1964.
The Horse That Played the Outfield. New York, Dodd Mead, 1964.
The Left Hander (as George Kramer). New York, Putnam, 1964.
The Indians of Carlisle. New York, Putnam, 1965.
Horace Higby and the Field Goal Formula [and the Scientific Pitch, and the Gentle Fullback, Coxwain of the Crew]. New York, Dodd Mead, 4 vols., 1965–71.
Hillbilly Hurler. New York, Dodd Mead, 1966.
Tall Team. New York, Dodd Mead, 1966.
Scrambling Quarterback. New York, Dodd Mead, 1967.
Kid Battery (as George Kramer). New York, Putnam, 1968.
Backup Quarterback. Austin, Texas, Steck Vaughn, 1968.
The Goofer Pitch. New York, Dodd Mead, 1969.
Buffalo Soldier. New York, Dodd Mead, 1969.
City High Champions. New York, Dodd Mead, 1969.
Gridiron Stranger. Philadelphia, Lippincott, 1970.
Home Run Henry. New York, Dodd Mead, 1970.
Fastbreak Rebel. New York, Dodd Mead, 1971.
Little League Hotshots. New York, Dodd Mead, 1972.

Other

Famous American Athletes. New York, Dodd Mead, 1963.
Famous Pro Football [and *Basketball*] *Stars*. New York, Dodd Mead, 2 vols., 1967–70.
Famous Coaches. New York, Dodd Mead, 1968.
Custer, Man and Legend. New York, Dodd Mead, 1968.
The "Go Ye" Men: The Life Story of Elmer Kile. Joplin, Missouri, College Press, 1968.
The Mountain Mission: The Story of Sam R. Hurley. Joplin, Missouri, College Press, 1968.
Famous American Indians. New York, Dodd Mead, 1972.

* * *

William Heuman went to work as a clerk with the National Supply Corporation in 1938, and over the next 12 years went about establishing himself as an author of western fiction for the pulp magazines. All that he would write was strictly in the formulary mode of a clearly identifiable hero, heroine, and villain. Yet what is most notable about even his early stories is Heuman's subtlety in plotting. If the outcome to a particular tale was never in doubt, Heuman could generate quite a lot of tension as to just how that outcome would be reached, and he was usually able to include a surprise twist at the end. Heuman also employed a wide variety of different settings for his plots. In "Troopers of Hell's Outpost," published in *Big-Book Western*, the location is Fort Henderson and the town of Otalie across the river, and the plot concerns who is responsible for successful holdups of Army paymasters on their way to the fort. Initially, Sergeant Neil Carlson crosses over to Otalie intending to fight Sam Buckline, a saloon tough who has been winning fights with enlisted men. In the course of the story, Neil recognizes Buckline as his brother, whom he regards as a waster but who turns out to be a trooper from Fort McLain working under cover to solve the payroll thefts; he also solves the question of who is behind the thefts, thus exposing a gambler who has been hitherto a sympathetic character. In "Fast Stage to Hell," which appeared in *Fifteen Western Tales*, Ed Harrigan's stageline was brought to ruin and he was left for dead after having been shot in the back by his former partner, George Lamonte, who now owns a successful stageline himself and has married the woman with whom Harrigan was in love. Thanks to the alcoholic physician who treated his gunshot wound and who has inherited money, Harrigan is able to start up a new stageline and effectively compete with Lamonte, who is accidentally killed in an attempt to murder Harrigan. The heroine, now Beth Lamonte, is able to slip Harrigan a Derringer before he is taken for what is supposed to be his final stagecoach ride by Lamonte and two of his hirelings.

By 1950, when Heuman published his first original paperback novel, *Guns at Broken Bow*, he was generating sufficient income from his Western fiction for pulp markets to retire from his job as a clerk and to devote himself exclusively to working as a freelance writer. In this first novel, Merritt Kane is a former lawman who rides into Broken Bow seeking peace and a place to take up cattle ranching. What he finds is a sly villain named Stephen West, a land speculator who has set up an elaborate scheme whereby the citizens of the district are convinced that the railroad will be building a spur to their town when, in fact, it is all a fraud perpetrated to inflate real estate values. West is engaged to marry the heroine, Sabine Bell, who is running her own ranch. The secondary characters really help to carry the story, as had long been the case in Heuman's shorter fiction; in this case a former pugilist and barroom bouncer named Sam McGee, who sides Kane, Roxy Bell, Sabine's younger sister, and the man with whom she is in love, Jonathan West, Stephen's gentle and highly talented pianist brother. There is also use made of the theme of the two heroines.

Heuman continued throughout the decade of the 1950s' to produce yearly two, three, or even four original paperback novels while simultaneously continuing his production of longer stories and novelettes for the pulps. *Roll the Wagons* has a background of rival freighting companies while *Hunt the Man*

Down combines the rather conventional vengeance/pursuit theme of the hero searching for his brother's murderer with running into problems generated by the whisper of gold amidst a land-grabbing scheme. While a good many of Heuman's novels employ the basic ranch romance plot structure—*The Range Buster* and *Heller from Texas* being among the best of these—Heuman also could and did introduce more exotic elements, keelboating in *Keelboats North*, a Tennessee mountain man in New Mexico in *On to Santa Fe*, fighting Sioux Indians and winter weather in *Wagon Train West*, riverboating in *Ride for Texas*, stagecoach robberies in *Stagecoach West*. He could also come up with a most unusual plot as he did for "Hell Rides the River," a novelette which appeared in *Triple Western*, a pulp magazine, and neither reprinted nor expanded: here the villains are more ambiguous than usual, a detachment of Confederates who are disguised as Union soldiers scheming to rob miners from the Montana gold fields as they are returning to their homes aboard a riverboat on the Missouri. Heuman's most ambitious book of the decade, *Captain McRae*, an historical romance and his first hardbound novel, possesses a similar setting of riverboating on the Missouri with an added Cavalry versus Indians plot complication.

Heuman's hero in *Stagecoach West* is a man named Grady Mulvane. Around the time this novel appeared he published a short story titled "The Testing of Francis Mulvane," the tale of a frontier schoolteacher who has to fight for the hand of an eighteen year-old female student, and one which has the distinction of having been reprinted in one of the last issues of *Ranch Romances* in November 1971. Heuman must have liked the name Mulvane, since that is the appellation he also gave to Cass Mulvane, the one series character he created and who made his debut in *Then Came Mulvane*. Although Mulvane is primarily a hired gun working in the interests of large ranchers against incoming droves of nesters, he goes on to battle hardcases and toughs, including an ex-Prussian officer who has come to Wyoming intent upon realizing pseudo-Nietzschean notions about founding a race of supermen, in subsequent novels in this series.

Heuman can be described as a consistently competent author of formulary Westerns whose plots always manage to keep a reader's interest. One among his many ranch romances, *Gunhand from Texas*, is particularly satisfying due to its setting on the Wyoming ranges during a bitter winter, and for the adept variation he was able to devise on the theme of the two heroines with the hero making finally anything but what at the beginning seemed the obvious choice. He lacked the intensity, complexity, and colorful plots of more able formulary authors, Ernest Haycox, Luke Short, Peter Dawson, and Norman A. Fox among them, but for what he may have lacked of these qualities he made up for in subtlety of subplots and interesting secondary characters. His heroines are often often very strong characters, women who manage their own ranches and occasionally a stageline, who are never helpless in the face of adversity, and who frequently provide essential assistance to the hero without which he would be lost. Heuman may never have questioned the premises of the formulary Western, from the faceless roles assigned to the Indians to the sympathy generally shown ranchers over nesters, but he could always be counted upon to provide an entertaining and interesting story.

—Jon Tuska

HEYNEN, Jim (James Heynen). American. Born near Sioux Center, Sioux County, Iowa, 14 July 1940. Educated at Calvin College, Grand Rapids, Michigan, B.A. 1960; University of Iowa, Iowa City, M.A. 1965; University of Oregon, Eugene, M.F.A. 1972. Married 1) De Laine Bliek in 1960 (divorced 1967); 2) Carol Jane Bangs in 1973; one daughter. Worked on farm to age 18; lived in South Dakota, where studied Sioux language; Lecturer in English, University of Michigan, Ann Arbor, 1967–68; Instructor in English, Calvin College, Grand Rapids, 1969–70; Visiting Instructor in English, University of Oregon, Eugene, Summer 1975; program director, arts administration, Idaho Commission on the Arts; 1975–76; Since 1976 program director, Centrum Fort Worden State Park, Port Townsend, Washington. Recipient: National Endowment for the Arts fellowship, 1974; U.S. State Department Bicentennial Fellowship award, 1977. Address: Centrum Fort Worden State Park, Port Townsend, Washington 98368, U.S.A.

Western Publications

Short Stories

The Boys: Prose Fables. Port Townsend, Washington, Graywolf Press, 1978.
The Man Who Kept Cigars in His Cap. Port Townsend, Washington, Graywolf Press, 1979.
You Know What Is Right. San Francisco, North Point Press, 1985.

Verse

The Funeral Parlor. Port Townsend, Washington, Graywolf Press, 1976.
Notes from Custer. Ann Arbor, Michigan, Bear Claw Press, 1976.
How the Sow Became a Goddess. Lewisburg, Idaho, Confluence Press, 1977.
A Suitable Church. Port Townsend, Washington, Copper Canyon Press, 1981.

Other Publications

Other

Editor, *Somewhere Down the Road: An Anthology of Washington High School Student Poetry and Fiction*. Port Townsend, Washington, Centrum, 1983.
Editor, *One Hundred over 100: Moments with a Hundred North American Centenarians*. Golden, Colorado, Fulcrum Press, 1990.

* * *

Jim Heynen's fiction blends folktale structure with his own farming background to capture early 20th century rural America. Within two collections of fiction, *The Man Who Kept Cigars in His Cap* and *You Know What Is Right*. Heynen's narrator might well be leaning on a shovel handle while he relates the story of "The Goose Lady," or "Bloating and Its Remedies." The reader is sometimes welcomed into these stories with direct address such as " . . . you have wondered where the story got started."

In spite of casual narration, Heynen's language is tight, leading the stories into the area of prose poetry. In some cases stories echo specific poems: "Sometimes a Sow" from his poetry collection *A Suitable Church*, becomes a story, or "The Boys Learn to Use Wire," in *The Man Who Kept Cigars in His Cap*.

Heynen's stories are typical of both folktale and prose poetry in length: short, usually 200–300 words each. *The Man Who Kept Cigars in His Cap* includes 41 stories; *You Know What Is Right* tallies 80. Within each collection the stories connect, through style, setting, and characters, to build a complete vision of the time and people; Heynen's collections have been compared to Sherwood Anderson's *Winesburg, Ohio*.

Unlike Anderson's more conventional fiction, Heynen's characters acquire individuality through circumstance rather than description. Instead of names, they are known as "The Neighbor," "The Undertaker," or the title character of his first book of fiction: *The Man Who Kept Cigars in His Cap*. These titles are acquired, in the tradition of folktale and rural life, through local knowledge of an event or occupation.

Generally these characters do not reappear outside their own stories. The primary exception in both books is "the boys" who often serve as the eyes and ears around the farm and in town. These children are known as "the youngest," "the poorest at baseball," "the slowest runner." As a result "the boys" become archetypal and, as a group, represent all stages of childhood within each moment. Through them we see the realities of farm life in all its complexities of innocence, brutality, and magic. No one character, especially an adult, could as successfully build such a complete perception.

In town, "the boys" are on alien turf and their own discomfort allows for some startling views. In the title story of *You Know What Is Right*, "the boys" discover coins in a town urinal. Their ultimate decision to each add a few coins, then urinate over the growing money pile, satisfies them as the "right thing to do," something they hadn't successfully identified in other town situations.

One character with a name who reappears, only in Section III of *You Know What Is Right*, is Uncle Jack. In these five stories he sings and rhymes in a magical world others dismiss as dimwitted delusion. Meanwhile this trickster/noodle tale character delights in outwitting "the boys" and others. In "Uncle Jack and the Beautiful Schoolteacher" we discover a world of shadow figures which becomes beautifully substantial through some of Heynen's most captivating and lyrical language.

Magic, in the sense of magical realism, is important, especially within *The Man Who Kept Cigars in His Cap*. Magic may appear as a peculiar oddity, as with the man who builds a shed full of sheds, smaller and smaller; when all the doors open "the boys" see a never-ending rainbow. Magic may simply exist, as when "the boys" in their room smell first a young girl, then an elusive lady, then finally an old woman; they ultimately discover the scent is carried on the dust of the earth itself outside their window.

Magic is enhanced by modernization typical during the early part of the century. Chamber pots and outhouses are common, though people are discovering indoor bathrooms, a startling concept. In *The Man Who Kept Cigars in His Cap*, tractors are replacing horses so the man who used to walk "The Breeding Circuit" with a stallion for hire now walks alone. This story takes a humorous twist: the man has taken over the stallion's role by now paying visits to farm wives, a fact husbands fail to recognize. Many of Heynen's stories present such surprise endings in the best O. Henry tradition of the short-short story.

Although magic is a vital part of his work, Heynen successfully presents harsh realities of the farm world, including animal castration, birth, mating, and death. However, he dresses reality in shifting awareness and perceptions which make it new. In "Dehorning" from *You Know What Is Right*, "the boys" leave the site where cattle are dehorned and turn the event into a gruesome game, taking turns playing the part of the cow, even to the point of using water to simulate blood running into their eyes. Discovery results: "They learned that the animal can see the horns sticking out from its head, hard pieces of its own body that turned whichever way its head turned, that could be used to keep other animals away or to rip hay loose from a bale. The boys learned what it felt like to see one horn fall to the ground and then see the dehorner move with his saw to the other side for the one that was left . . . Playing the dehorning game didn't make watching dehorning any easier. But it did make the chores of feeding the cattle and pitching their manure, even in cold weather, much easier."

The Man Who Kept Cigars in His Cap generally focuses less often on the harsh physical world and more often on the peculiar: the woman who uses her dentures to perfectly crimp pie crust; the minister's wife who lightens guests' coffee with her breast milk. This collection also includes several beautiful illustrations by Tom Pohrt.

Both of Heynen's story collections are satisfying to read. He presents work which is harmonious in tone and mood; his unique style is created through his lyrical language and whimsy which combine ideally with the folktale structure appropriate to both the rural setting and the early 1900's time period.

—Marian Blue

HICKOCK, Will. *See* **HARRISON, C. William.**

HILL, Roger. *See* **PAINE, Lauran.**

HILLERMAN, Tony. American. Born in Sacred Heart, Oklahoma, 27 May 1925. Raised among Pottawatomie and Seminole Indians; educated at Indian boarding school for eight years; Oklahoma State University, Stillwater; University of Oklahoma, Norman, B.A. in journalism 1948; University of New Mexico, Albuquerque, M.A. in English 1965. Served in the United States Army Infantry, 1943–45: Silver Star, Bronze Star, Purple Heart. Married Marie E. Unzner in 1948; three daughters and three sons. Reporter, *News Herald*, Borger, Texas, 1948; news editor, *Morning Press*, 1949, and city editor, *Constitution*, 1950, Lawton, Oklahoma; political reporter, United Press, Oklahoma City, 1952; bureau manager, United Press, Santa Fe, New Mexico, 1953; executive editor, *The New Mexican*, Santa Fe, 1954–62. Assistant to the President, 1962–64, 1976–81, Associate Professor 1965–66, and Professor of Journalism and Chair of Department, 1966–85, University of New Mexico. Recipient: Burrows award, for journalism; Shaffer award, for reporting, 1952; Mystery Writers of America Edgar Allan Poe award, 1974; French Grand Prix, for novel in translation; Navajo Special Friend award. D.H.L.: University of New Mexico. Agent: Curtis Brown Ltd., 10 Astor Place, New York, New York 10003. Address: 2729 Texas N.E., Albuquerque, New Mexico 87110, U.S.A.

WESTERN PUBLICATIONS

Novels (series: Sergeant Jim Chee; Lieutenant Joe Leaphorn)

The Blessing Way (Leaphorn). New York, Harper, and London, Macmillan, 1970.
The Fly on the Wall. New York, Harper, 1971.
Dance Hall of the Dead (Leaphorn). New York, Harper, 1973.
Listening Woman (Leaphorn). New York, Harper, 1978; London, Macmillan, 1979.
People of Darkness (Chee). New York, Harper, 1980; London, Gollancz, 1982.
The Dark Wind (Chee). New York, Harper, 1982; London, Gollancz, 1983.
The Ghostway (Chee). New York, Harper, and London, Gollancz, 1985.
Skinwalkers (Chee and Leaphorn). New York, Harper, 1987; London, Joseph, 1988.
A Thief of Time (Chee and Leaphorn). New York, Harper, 1988; London, Joseph, 1989.
Talking God (Chee and Leaphorn). New York, Harper, 1989; London, Joseph, 1990.
The Joe Leaphorn Mysteries (omnibus). New York, Harper, 1989.
Coyote Waits (Chee and Leaphorn). New York, Harper, 1990; London, Joseph, 1991.

OTHER PUBLICATIONS

Other

The Boy Who Made Dragonfly: A Zuni Myth (for children). New York, Harper, 1972.
The Great Taos Bank Robbery and Other Indian Country Affairs. Albuquerque, University of New Mexico Press, 1973.
New Mexico, photographs by David Muench. Portland, Oregon, Belding, 1974.
Rio Grande, photographs by Robert Reynolds. Portland, Oregon, Graphic Arts Center, 1975.
Indian Country: America's Sacred Land, photographs by Béla Kalman. Flagstaff, Arizona, Northland Press, 1987.

Editor, *The Spell of New Mexico.* Albuquerque, University of New Mexico Press, 1977.

*

Manuscript Collection: Zimmerman Library, University of New Mexico.

Critical Study: *Tony Hillerman: Blessing Way to Talking God*, by Louis A. Heib, n.p., Press of the Gigantic Hound, 1990.

* * *

The Tony Hillerman books are unlike most Westerns. They're thrillers . . . Western Thrillers.

The author concentrates on the Indian aspect. His main character in several books is a Navajo Indian, Jim Chee, a Sergeant in the Tribal Police of New Mexico. While the Navajo reservation is in Northeastern Arizona, the Hillerman "home on the range" is as wide and as vast as the United States itself, extending from Washington D.C. to Los Angeles.

Steeds, mustangs, and Indian ponies are replaced by Mercedes, Datsuns, Plymouths, trans-continental express trains and planes. Hillerman's Navajos are part of modern America, largely integrated with the white man, yet retaining their individuality. They wear denims, jeans, even tuxedos, rather than the expected feathered head-dress or gaudy paint . . . except when ancient tribal rituals demand they should.

Hillerman weaves a fascinating, authentic picture of Indian customs and beliefs in his thoroughly absorbing thrillers. He takes his reader back to a dark, mysterious past without leaving the present. Sorcery, witchcraft, and mummery is harnessed to modern police work and techniques without ridicule to either.

Born in Oklahoma, Hillerman received some of his early education among Indian children. They must have made an impression on him, for in later life he became an authority on Indian culture and religion. A fine ethnologist, his books are used in American schools to assist in teaching the subject, and promoting a growing tolerance and understanding of the "First Americans."

Sergeant Jim Chee and Lieutenant Joe Leaphorn appear in most of his novels. Although Chee is outranked by Leaphorn, his is the leading role. He tracks his way through mystery, murder, and intrigue, with the added ingredient of the Navajo and Hopi ancestral rituals.

The opening chapter of *People of Darkness* is intriguing. The story starts in the Cancer Research and Treatment Centre on the North Campus of the University of New Mexico. A female bacteriologist, confined to a wheelchair while waiting for cultures to grow, toxins to develop, anti-bodies to form, and reagents to react, habitually rolls her wheelchair to the window and looks down on the car park through binoculars. A routine for no specific purpose—other than to avoid boredom. She sees a package being transferred from a car to the back of a dirty green pickup which has been illegally parked. Local meter maids are pretty keen, and she expects the vehicle to be towed away after a few minutes. Later, having determined that the life form reproduced in her petri dish is harmless, she writes a report and returns to the window; she's in time to see the pickup being hooked to a tow-truck. It's being winched, and as the rear of the vehicle rises, there's a violent explosion:

> Abruptly, all vision was lost in a dazzle of light. The sound came a second later—a cannon-shot boom. The glass on the bacteriologist's window was pressed inwards to its tolerance and just beyond; it cracked, then flexed violently outwards, where its shards joined those of a hundred other windows raining down on the empty sidewalks below.

This conjures a thousand queries (at least for me). There's a need to read on. What happens next? I won't satisfy your curiosity and spoil the reading of an excellent book.

In *The Dark Wind*, Hillerman fascinates with descriptions of a secret Indian initiation ceremony, and cultures little known to white men.

The Ghostway shows its author's versatility. Hillerman is equally at home giving a graphic description of the wild, savage Navajo countryside, or the squalor of a backwater Los Angeles underworld. Through Jim Chee he again attains the combination of an ancient and a modern world, a trait which continues from book to book without becoming boring. In fact it adds interest, and encourages one to learn more about Navajo customs and beliefs.

Skinwalkers, another Jim Chee/Joe Leaphorn success, was voted the best U.S.A. mystery of 1987. Hillerman's description of the land takes in deep canyons, mesas, and the emptiness of Southwest America.

Here and there the author resorts to the use of Indian language, using phrases the reader might have difficulty in understanding. However he usually finds an unobtrusive way to translate without deviating from the action. Of course there's the odd irritation. Words like "belagaana," "hataalii," "yei," "pahos," are used, without explanation. These detract from the action, but are a minor flaw when measured against the many strengths of his work. I shall continue to read Hillerman's novels with interest, and I know that many other Western aficionadoes will be doing the same.

—Walter Shaw

HOAGLAND, Edward. American. Born in New York City, 21 December 1932. Educated at Harvard University, Cambridge, Massachusetts, A.B. 1954. Served in the United States Army, 1955–57. Married 1) Amy J. Ferrara in 1960 (divorced); 2) Marion Magid in 1968; one daughter. Lived in New York, Europe, San Francisco, and British Columbia, 1957–63; Instructor in creative writing, New School for Social Research, New York, 1963–64; teacher in Europe, 1965; Instructor in creative writing, Rutgers University, New Brunswick, New Jersey, 1966; Sarah Lawrence College, Bronxville, New York, 1967; and City University, New York, 1967–68; lived in New York and Africa, 1972–77; Instructor in literature and creative writing, Writers Workshop, University of Iowa, Iowa City, 1978, 1982, Columbia University, New York, 1980, 1981, Bennington College, Vermont, 1987–89, Brown University, Providence, Rhode Island, 1988, and University of California, Davis, 1990. General editor, Penguin Nature Library. Recipient: Houghton Mifflin Literary fellow, 1954; Longview Foundation award, 1961; Prix de Rome, 1964; Guggenheim fellowship, 1965, 1975; New York State Arts Council grant, 1972; Brandeis University Citation in Literature, 1972; American Academy Harold Vursell award, 1981; National Endowment for the Arts grant, 1982; New York Public Library Literary Lion, 1988; National Magazine award, 1989. Agent: Robert Lescher, 155 East 71st Street, New York, New York 10021. Address: 463 West Street, New York, New York 10014, U.S.A.

Western Publications

Novel

Seven Rivers West. New York, Summit, 1986; London, Penguin, 1987.

Other Publications

Novels

Cat Man. Boston, Houghton Mifflin, 1955.
The Circle Home. New York, Crowell, 1960.
The Peacock's Tail. New York, McGraw Hill, 1965.

Short Stories

City Tales. Santa Barbara, California, Capra Press, 1986.

Other

Notes from the Century Before: A Journal from British Columbia. New York, Random House, 1969.
The Courage of Turtles: 15 Essays About Compassion, Pain, and Love. New York, Random House, 1970.
Walking the Dead Diamond River. New York, Random House, 1973.
The Moose on the Wall: Field Notes from the Vermont Wilderness. London, Barrie and Jenkins, 1974.
Red Wolves and Black Bears. New York, Random House, 1976.
African Calliope: A Journey to the Sudan. New York, Random House, 1979.
The Edward Hoagland Reader, edited by Geoffrey Wolff. New York, Random House, 1979.
The Tugman's Passage. New York, Random House, 1982.
Heart's Desire. New York, Summit, 1988; London, Collins, 1990.

* * *

Edward Hoagland reads like a writer with the wilderness in his blood. In his personal essays, almost any topic can lead him (physically and meditatively) to the woods, from the forests of Vermont and Maine to the Rocky Mountains and the rugged terrain of British Columbia. Hoagland's wilderness is a necessary antidote to the pace and materialism of contemporary life, a place which fosters freedom, individuality, and thoughtfulness, where people can "live more intensely." It is also, however, imminently vanishing: as he says in "Of Cows and Cambodia" "Against the sense of exuberant release I felt on long walks in the woods was the knowledge that this in fact was just a hermetic patch of wilderness with highways on all sides, scarcely larger than a park: it was a ship in a bottle, and I was only hiding out." The dwindling area harbours an evanescent spirit, always just out of the narrator's reach. This spirit is symbolized most vividly in "Hailing the Elusory Mountain Lion" by the big cat which all hunters seek, of which an occasional traveller catches a "cryptic glimpse," but whose existence is never substantively proven.

That vision of the wilderness animates Hoagland's great novel of the West, *Seven Rivers West.* The novel tells the familiar manly rite-of-passage narrative, but with several radical twists which undermine the Western's conventional affirmation of masculinity. Set in 1887, mainly in the Rocky Mountains around the Canadian-U.S. border, the novel creates a topography and native peoples who are partly factual, partly fictional, and partly fantastical. Into this landscape rides Cecil Roop, a bear-tamer from New England, who has abandoned his nagging wife and children to search for a grizzly to tame and take back east as a circus attraction. As his quest unfolds, it becomes more quixotic: hearing of the mythical Bigfoot (also known as *Sasquatch* and *Nakina*), he determines to use his communicative skills with animals to attract and capture one of them. His main companion is Sutton, a gold-seeker whose equally idiosyncratic characteristics cut across the stereotype. Sutton's speciality is diving from 40 feet into one foot of water; he explains his repeated performance of this desperately dangerous act: "It's what I do that's different from anybody else in the world." Providing the "love interest" are two middle-aged native women, the one plump and grey-haired, the other scrawny from starvation and mistreatment by an enemy tribe.

What these eccentric characters share is human tenderness and, ultimately, this is the quality which Hoagland's frontier seems to validate. At various times, Cecil plans to take part of the wilderness back east with him: in the shape of the grizzly, the Bigfoot, and his Indian woman. In the event, none of these proves to be transportable. When he encounters several Bigfoots, Cecil is unsure what he has found and what form of communication he is experiencing with the mysterious beings, and the encounter causes first Sutton's death and then the Sikink woman's return to her tribe. The implication is that the West cannot be carved up for eastern titillation. The frontier is not a trophy for display, nor a resource for commercial exploitation: "Cecil, just in gazing, wondered whether even finding gold or successfully netting a Bigfoot in one of those myriad crevices wouldn't be like picking up a sea shell at the beach—a pleasant matter that in this giant setting lost its meaning." What survives the stripping away of illusion is human love and the recognition of interdependency. When Cecil and Sutton's surviving Kluatantan lover struggle out of the dangerous wilderness together, they make love: "They did this not in spite of but in tribute to the lovers they had left behind and because they would now probably die together if either of them was unable to survive."

Hoagland's vision, with his central equation of heroism and tenderness, his blend of fantasy and history, and his richly comic characters, seems far distant from the conventional story of shoot-outs and conquests. Essentially, he reviews the Western's traditional motifs of flight, individualism, and male bonding by accenting them with multicultural, cross-gender messages about collectivism and caring. The very wilderness itself is cherished, in the novel's many loving descriptions of the landscape: "They got above the rainbows and the clouds and watched the fog unfold and separate and stream below them like a narrative being dramatized." The depth and gentleness of this huge, important novel can be read as example and warning, as is made explicit in another of Hoagland's essays: "The swan song sounded by the wilderness grows fainter, ever more constricted, until only sharp ears can catch it at all. It fades to a nearly inaudible level, and yet there never is going to be any one time when we can say right *now* it is gone."

—Christine Bold

HOBART, Donald Bayne.

Western Publications

Novels

The Whistling Waddy: A Western Story. New York, Chelsea House, 1928.
The Adventure Trail. London, Nelson, 1929.
The Horseshoe Trail. New York, Arcadia House, 1952; as *Trail of the Twisted Horseshoes*, London, Wright and Brown, 1954.
Ruthless Range. London, Wright and Brown, 1957; New York, Arcadia House, 1959.
Dark Trail. New York, Arcadia House, 1959.
Hardcase Guns. New York, Arcadia House, 1959; London, Mills and Boon, 1962.
Arizona Outlaw. New York, Arcadia House, 1961; London, Muller, 1963.
Six-Gun Empire. New York, Curtis, 1965.
Iron Horse Gunsmoke. New York, Curtis, 1965.
Vulture Valley. New York, Curtis, 1966.
Guns of the Big Hills. New York, Curtis, 1966.
Gallows Gold. New York, Curtis, 1966.
The Longhorn Trail. New York, Curtis, 1967.
Red River Guns. New York, Curtis, 1967.
Black Stallion Mesa. New York, Curtis, 1967.
Gunsmoke Country. New York, Curtis, 1967.
Guns along the River. New York, Curtis, 1968.
Warrior Range. New York, Curtis, 1968.
Sinister Ranch. New York, Arcadia House, 1968.

Other Publications

Novels

Double Shuffle. New York, Clode, 1928.
Hunchback House. Racine, Wisconsin, Whitman, 1929.
The Clue of the Leather Noose. Racine, Wisconsin, Whitman, 1930.
The Cell Murder Mystery. New York, Fiction League, 1931.
Homicide Honeymoon. New York, Arcadia House, 1959.

* * *

Donald Bayne Hobart's Westerns are tales of the Masked Rider and his silent Yaqui companion, Blue Hawk, whose "dog-like devotion" saves the Rider time and again. Though Hobart did not create the series, or its leading characters, it is they who dominate the content of his published novels. His background mysterious, the Masked Rider roams the west seeking wrongs to right atop his magnificent steed, Midnight. Though bad men have committed crimes in his guise, his own acts have won him the affectionate nickname, Robin Hood of the West. Wherever there are people in trouble, he is on the spot with a fast draw, "his heavy Colts roaring their song of leaden death." His diction is stilted, presumably because of his lonely life; he occasionally mutters aloud to himself, "That's interestin'!," as he tackles another conspiracy.

The standard Hobart plot involves the Masked Rider and Blue Hawk riding into a confusing, anarchical situation where two or more opposing groups are being played off against each other for profit and advantage of a third group, wild outlaws headed by a secret leader who is accepted by both opposing parties as a decent citizen. The outlaws, their faces hidden by bandannas, masks, or clay, attack both sides, leaving clues to suggest acts by the opposition. They rustle cattle, rob banks, steal gold shipments, dynamite river boats, burn down ranches, start landslides, execute honest citizens, and in general create as much chaos and havoc as possible. They even try to incriminate the Masked Rider. But before total war breaks out the Masked Rider proves the existence of the third faction, calls for cooler heads and calmer thought, befriends important leaders, kills dozens of outlaws, discovers the outlaws' cache of stolen cattle, supplies, gold, etc., rescues a kidnapped maiden, and ferrets out the motive behind the violent acts. There is a great deal of drygulching (bushwacking), bullets flying, good men dying, villains calling for lynch law and riot.

The hero is aided in his acts by various disguises (cowpoke, ranger, gunslinger, riverboat gambler) that enable him to move between factions, gather facts and rumors, and study character, until he can finally uncover who is doing what and why. He quickly realizes that the bullies picking fights are clearly in on the plots, but has more difficulty dealing with smooth-talking peace-makers who often prove most villainous. Ultimately the Masked Rider must kill off his assumed disguise (usually as cowpoke Morgan) to protect his identity, but by that time he and Blue have solved the mystery and are ready to face new dangers, "battling valiantly for those who need their aid," "twin forces in the cause of justice," helping those "living in the shadow of some unfathomed dread."

In *Iron Horse Gunsmoke* outlaws precipitate a battle between cattlemen and railroad men to further the interests of a rival railway company. In *Gallows Gold* a town endures a reign of terror and miners feud with cattlemen—all because of a secret gold mine. In *Guns along the River* a scheme to buy up land along a railroad route results in stolen riverboats, rustled cattle, and bloody executions. And the pattern continues in tales of range wars (*Six-Gun Empire*), Indian Wars (*Warrior Range*), renegades (*Red River Guns*), and gold fever (*Vulture Valley*). In *Gunsmoke Country* the Masked Rider faces a deadly foe, an outlaw with a charmed life who is out to destroy him and the justice he represents. Slow talking, fast acting, the Masked Rider and his Yaqui compadre face the greed that Hobart feels made the west so violent and dangerous a place for the innocent of heart.

—Gina Macdonald

HODSON, Arthur. *See* **NICKSON, Arthur.**

HOFFMAN, Art. *See* **KING, Albert.**

HOFFMAN, Lee. Also writes as Georgia York. American. Born in Chicago, Illinois, 14 August 1932. Educated at Armstrong Junior College, Savannah, Georgia, A.A. 1951. Married Larry T. Shaw (divorced). Printer's devil, Savannah Vocational School; staff member, Hoffman Radio-TV Service; assistant editor, *Infinity*, 1956–58, and *Science Fiction Adventures*, 1956–58; staff member, MD Publications; claim handler, Hoffman Motors; in printing production, Arrow Press, Allied Typographers, and George Morris Press: has also worked as teacher in Writers Workshop. Since 1965 free lance writer. Recipient: Western Writers of America Spur award, 1967. Address: 401 Sunrise Trail N.W., Port Charlotte, Florida 33952, U.S.A.

WESTERN PUBLICATIONS

Novels

Gunfight at Laramie. New York, Ace, 1966; London, Gold Lion, 1975.
The Legend of Blackjack Sam. New York, Ace, 1966.
Bred to Kill. New York, Ballantine, 1967.
The Valdez Horses. New York, Doubleday, 1967; London, Tandem, 1972.
Dead Man's Gold. New York, Ace, 1968.
The Yarborough Brand. New York, Avon, 1968; London, Hale, 1981.
Wild Riders. New York, New American Library, 1969; London, Hale, 1979.
Loco. New York, Doubleday, 1969; London, Tandem, 1973.
Return to Broken Crossing. New York, Ace, 1969; London, Hale, 1982.
West of Cheyenne. New York, Doubleday, 1969; London, Tandem, 1973.
Wiley's Move. New York, Dell, 1973; London, Hale, 1980.
The Truth about the Cannonball Kid. New York, Dell, 1975; London, Hale, 1980.
Fox. New York, Doubleday, 1976; London, Hale, 1980.
Nothing But a Drifter. New York, Doubleday, 1976; London, Hale, 1980.
Trouble Valley. New York, Ballantine, 1976; London, Hale, 1982.
Sheriff of Jack Hollow. New York, Dell 1977; London, Hale, 1979.
The Land Killer. New York, Doubleday, 1978; London, Hale, 1981.

OTHER PUBLICATIONS

Novels

Telepower. New York, Belmont, 1967.
The Caves of Karst. New York, Ballantine, 1969; London, Dobson, 1970.
Always the Black Knight. New York, Avon, 1970.
Change Song. New York, Doubleday, 1972.
Savage Key (as Georgia York). New York, Fawcett, 1979.
Savannah Grey (as Georgia York). New York, Fawcett, 1981.
Savage Conquest (as Georgia York). New York, Fawcett, 1983.

*

Manuscript Collection: University of Wyoming, Laramie.

* * *

Lee Hoffman made a quite entrance upon the western book scene in 1966 with the publication by Ace Books of *Gunfight at Laramie*. Although it has a rather unremarkable storyline, it demonstrates Hoffman's ability to create interesting, credible, and sympathetic characters. In the course of her career, the heroes of her novels have remained particularly engaging because of their very human qualities—guilt, fear, and upon occasion stupidity—which are rarely traits to be found in western heroes. Without exception, Hoffman's heroes share the problem of an inability to understand a situation easily and in turn are constantly misunderstood. These mutual misunderstandings contribute in large measure to the intricate plottings of the stories—misunderstanding between the hero and his adversary or adversaries, between the hero and his friends, or between the hero and the heroine. Readjustment is often a problem for the Hoffman hero: to civilian life after having fought in the Civil War (*West of Cheyenne*, *Wild Riders*, and *Trouble Valley*,) to changes within the family (*The Yarborough Brand*), to changing times (*Sheriff of Jack Hollow*). In the best of Hoffman's books motivation works hand in hand with characterization to build an exciting story.

Unlike B.M. Bower, another female western writer with a sufficiently ambiguous name to attract male readers, Hoffman writes formulary western which focus on the exploits of a male hero. Her heroines, while generally mature, practical, and surprisingly aggressive, are primarily in the story for romantic interest and tend to cause a lot of trouble for the hero. Also, unlike Bower, Hoffman is not reticent to write about fist fights, gun battles, lynchings, and elaborate chase scenes; in fact, her books never want for fast-paced, suspenseful action sequences.

Her villains are usually men of property with positions of power or men bent on securing wealth and power by dishonest or illegal means. Her plots often involve the hero coming into conflict with a man whose position is threatened.

The Legend of Blackjack Sam, "Being an Absolutely Accurate Account (More or Less) of the Violent Events Leading up to the Notorious Showdown at the O'Shea Corral," was the first of Hoffman's attempts at a comic western. This group, which also includes *The Truth about the Cannonball Kid*, are among her most weakly structured stories and depend on outlandish plot ingredients. *Wiley's Move* is perhaps the best written and most amusing of them, with its outrageous cast of characters, especially the Wiley clan of Texas headed by Deke who has returned from a cattle-buying trip in the form of a buzzard, a laudanum-drinking mother who gives her eldest daughter her kitchen as a birthday present, and a charming albeit extremely precious youngest daughter.

Hoffman's finest novel, *The Valdez Horses* (Spur award) is a carefully structured, evocative story about a Mexican horse breeder named Chino. The reader becomes attached to the vividly drawn horses, especially Banner, a young colt who lives for a time in the house with Chino. It is a perfect blending of plot, characterization, and mood; its only weakness is its frivolous heroine. The story also includes one of Hoffman's few characterizations of Indians—Arapahoes—and her depiction of them as a people is characterized by a sympathetic understanding. Hoffman ingeniously reversed the potentially tragic ending of the story in the last line of the book.

Like Ann Ahlswede and P.A. Bechko, Hoffman proved capably that the action-packed formulary western story people with heroes, villains, and heroines is not limited to the domain of male writers. In fact, she has illustrated that a woman can add a human dimension and depth to such conventional fiction.

The Land Killer was the last Western Hoofman wrote. She followed it with three historical romances set in the South and published under the pseudonym Georgia York. Although rather different, particularly in their treatment of female characters, they are as enjoyable to read as her Westerns.

—Vicki Piekarski

HOGAN, Linda. American Indian. Born in Denver, Colorado, 16 July 1947. Educated at University of Colorado, Boulder, B.A. 1973, M.A. 1978. Married Pat Hogan (divorced); two daughters. Worked as a nurse's aide, dental assistant, waitress, home-maker, secretary, administrator, teacher's aide, library clerk, freelance writer and researcher; Instructor in creative writing, fiction, and Native American literature, University of Colorado, Boulder, 1977–79; Instructor in creative writing and English, Colorado Women's College, Colorado Springs, 1979; associate, Rocky Mountain Women's Institute, University of Denver, Colorado, 1979–80; writer-in-residence, Colorado State Arts Council, 1980–84, and Oklahoma State Arts Council, 1982–83; facilitator, Creative Writing and Creativity, Arvada Center for the Performing Arts Womanschool Network, 1982–84; Assistant Professor of English, TRIBES Program, Colorado College Institutes, Colorado Springs, 1982–84; Associate Professor of American studies/American Indian studies, University of Minnesota, Minneapolis, 1984–89. Since 1989 Associate Professor of English, University of Colorado, Boulder. Member, Board of Directors of Denver Native Americans United, Denver, Colorado, 1979; Chair, Western States Women Studies Association, 1981; member of National Council of Teachers of English Minority Literature Panel, 1983, 1984, and Task Force on Racism and Bias, 1983–86; Organizer, Colorado Cultural Congress, 1984. Recipient: Five Civilized Tribes Museum Playwriting award, 1980; Newberry Library D'Arcy McNickle Tribal Historian fellowship, 1981; Yaddo Invitation award, 1982; *Stand* Magazine award, for story, 1983; Colorado Council on the Arts Independent Writer's fellowship, 1984; University of Minnesota, Before Columbus Foundation American Book award, for poetry, 1986; National Endowment for the Arts award, 1986; Minnesota State Arts Board grant, for poetry, 1986; Pushcart Prize, 1986; Best American Short Stories award, 1989. Address: P.O. Box 141, Idledale, Colorado 80453, U.S.A.

WESTERN PUBLICATIONS

Novel

Mean Spirit. New York, Atheneum, 1990.

Short Stories

That Horse. Acoma, New Mexico, Pueblo of Acoma Press, 1985.
The Big Woman. New York, Firebrand Press, 1987.

Plays

A Piece of Moon (produced Stillwater, Oklahoma, 1981).

Screenplays: *Mean Spirit*, 1986; *Aunt Moon*, 1986.

Television Play: *Keeper*, 1986.

Verse

Calling Myself Home. New York, Greenfield Review Press, 1979.
Daughters, I Love You. Denver, Colorado, Loretto Heights, 1981.
Eclipse. Los Angeles, University of California Press, 1984.
Seeing Through the Sun. Amherst, Massachusetts, University of Massachusetts Press, 1985.
Savings. Minneapolis, Minnesota, Coffee House Press, 1988.

Other

Editor, with Carol Buechal and Judith McDaniel, *The Stories We Hold Secret.* New York, Greenfield Review Press, 1985.

* * *

Linda Hogan's long-awaited first novel, *Mean Spirit*, establishes this Chickasaw writer as an important voice in American Indian fiction, fulfilling the promise of early stories like "New Shoes" and "Amen." The book, set in oil-boom Oklahoma of the 1920's, has elements of the historical novel and the crime thriller, while transcending the limitations of such genres. Oklahoma in 1922 had many Indians whose sudden oil wealth made them targets for exploitation and even murder. Hogan has used extensive research into printed sources and—more important—oral traditions to form her work. She probes into a conspiracy to cheat and murder rich Osage Indians, and at the same time reveals the dire effects of prejudice and misguided paternalistic policies on the Indian population as a whole. Economic persecution was only one aspect of the oppression: entire peoples were robbed of their cultures by the forced education of their children in boarding schools.

But the novel goes beyond social commentary by exploring the values of a race whose world view was essentially animistic and reverent toward nature. Nature is almost a character in the book. Readers will be fascinated with the recurrent images of bats, bees, and horses, beings which are treated as entities worthy of respect as partners in the economy of life. Traditional religious views of Native Americans are shown as waning but capable of renewal. Hogan has fascinating depictions of ceremonies that provide an alternative to the acquisitive, environment-wrecking spirit of the dominant culture. She notes the appeal of traditional Indian values by depicting white characters who "go Indian." She also shows acculturated Indians reverting to ancient values. The events of the novel often approach magic realism without quite sliding into fantasy. The aim is to assert the continued value of an outlook that accepts the primacy of the natural world, and Sorrow Cave, with its bats (beautifully evoked) and its ancient artifacts, is the symbolic core of the novel. "Bat medicine" and fragments of a primordial way of life are asserted as more valuable than the status tokens of the white way of life, like cars and crystal chandeliers; Indians who have the money to buy such toys are not made happy by them. The continuity of Indian culture is symbolized by the sacred fire that Michael Horse watches over, a fire that has been kept burning since ancient times. The Hill Indians who have kept the ancient ways have a wholeness denied both to the rich Indians and those who live in Tar Town, the shantytown of the dispossessed.

The novel is not flawless. The threads of the highly episodic plot are woven very loosely, and crucial events are sometimes passed over too quickly. Details of the conspiracy are kept murky for the sake of suspense, which seems reasonable enough, but they are not illuminated very well in the denouement. The complications of the conclusion aren't adequately prepared for, and the nature of the plot seems at times too familiar from the Western movies, a tale of land-grabbing with a sinister villain, John Hale, whose character remains shadowy. It could be said that Hogan needs a pasteboard villain, a man dehumanized by greed. Several other characters aren't developed very well: especially Nola, the young heiress, whose feelings aren't imagined from inside, and whose relationship with her white husband isn't explored convincingly. However, several others, like Michael Horse, the old visionary who wants to add a few chapters to the white man's Bible, and John Stink, who emerges from premature burial to be treated as a ghost by the Indian community, are superbly drawn. John Tate, the voyeuristic one-eyed photographer, seems more symbol than character, and his role in the plot, especially at the climax, is never clear. But *Mean Spirit* is a major effort. Indian spirituality is often symbolized by the term "medicine," and the book is meant to be medicinal in the widest sense. It offers a healing vision as well as a painful description of a wounded people.

Hogan's reputation was built on her fine poetry. In her first collection, *Calling Myself Home*, she examined her Oklahoma rural roots in a series of quiet but moving lyrics written in the short lines that are her stylistic hallmark. In *Eclipse*, she dealt with the beauty of the physical world and with threats—ecological and thermonuclear—to it. As in *Mean Spirit*, she means to represent animals and birds unable to speak for themselves. Her third major collection, *Seeing Through the Sun*, which received an American Book Award from the Before Columbus Foundation, showed a mature lyrical and meditative talent. Her most recent collection, *Savings*, has a darker social vision and shows a concern for urban lives (often women's) of quiet desperation. Her concerns are not theoretical but deeply felt and therefore completely convincing.

—Bert Almon

HOGAN, (Robert) Ray. Also writes as Clay Ringold. American. Born in Willow Springs, Missouri, 15 December 1908. Educated at schools in Albuquerque, New Mexico; Hoosier Institute of Journalism, 2 years. Married Lois Easterday Clayton in 1927; one daughter and one son. Freelance writer: editor, *New Mexico Sportsman*, 1956–57; sports columnist, Albuquerque *Tribune*, 4 years. Address: 700 Stagecoach Road S.E., Albuquerque, New Mexico 87123, U.S.A.

WESTERN PUBLICATIONS

Novels (series: Doomsday; Marshal; John Mosby; Civil War Raider; Shawn Starbuck; Fortuna West)

Ex-Marshal. New York, Ace, 1956; London, Miller, 1959.
The Friendless One. New York, Ace, 1957.
Walk a Lonely Trail. New York, Ace, 1957.
Land of the Strangers. New York, Ace, 1957; London, Miller, 1959.
Longhorn Law. New York, Ace, 1957.
Marked Man. New York, Ace, 1958.
Hangman's Valley. New York, Ace, 1959; Bath, Chivers, 1989.
Wanted: Alive! New York, Ace, 1959.
Marshal Without a Badge. New York, Fawcett, 1959; London, Muller, 1960.
Outlaw Marshal. New York, Fawcett, 1959; London, Muller, 1960.
Guns Against the Sun. New York, Avon, 1960.
Lead Reckoning. New York, Avon, 1960; London, Hale, 1989.
The Ghost Raider (Mosby). New York, Pyramid, 1960.
The Shotgunner. New York, Avon, 1960.
The Hasty Hangman. New York, Ace, 1960; London, New English Library, 1977.
Raider's Revenge (Mosby). New York, Pyramid, 1960.
Rebel Raid (Mosby). New York, Berkley, 1961; Bath, Chivers, 1988.
The Life and Death of Clay Allison. New York, New American Library, 1961.
The Ridge-Runner. New York, Ace, 1961.
Ride to the Gun. New York, Avon, 1961; Bath, Chivers, 1988.
Ambush at Riflestock. New York, Ace, 1961.
Track the Man Down. New York, Ace, 1961.
Marshal for Lawless. New York, Ace, 1961.
The Jim Hendren Story. New York, Pyramid, 1962.
Rebel in Yankee Blue (Mosby). New York, Avon, 1962.
Hell to Hallelujah (Mosby). New York, Macfadden, 1962.
New Gun for Kingdom City, and The Shotgunner. New York, Ace, 1962.
Stranger in Apache Basin. New York, Avon, 1963; London, Gold Lion, 1973.
The Outside Gun. New York, Ace, 1963.
The Life and Death of Johnny Ringo. New York, New American Library, 1963; as *Johnny Ringo, Gentleman Outlaw*,

London, Long, 1964; as *Tombstone Outlaw*, London, Arrow, 1966.
Trail of the Fresno Kid. New York, Ace, 1963; London, New English Library, 1976.
Last Gun at Cabresto. New York, Ace, 1963.
Hoodoo Guns. New York, Ace, 1964.
Man from Barranca Negra. New York, Ace, 1964.
The Trackers. New York, New American Library, 1964; London, New English Library, 1965.
Rebel Ghost (Mosby). New York, Macfadden 1964; London, Hale, 1989.
Night Raider (Mosby). New York, Avon, 1964.
Mosby's Last Raid (Mosby). New York, Macfadden, 1966.
Panhandle Pistolero. New York, Ace, 1966; London, Severn House, 1978.
Killer's Gun. New York, Ace, 1966.
Dead Man on a Black Horse. New York, New American Library, 1966.
The Hellsfire Lawman. New York, Ace, 1966; Leicester, Ulverscroft, 1989.
Outlaw Mountain. New York, Ballantine, 1967.
Legacy of the Slash M. New York, Ace, 1967.
Border Bandit. New York, Lancer, 1967.
The Wolver. New York, Ace, 1967.
Devil's Butte. New York, Ace, 1967.
Texas Lawman. New York, Lancer, 1967.
The Moon-Lighters. New York, Avon, 1968.
Trouble at Tenkiller. New York, Ace, 1968.
The Gunmaster. New York, New American Library, 1968.
The Hell Road. New York, New American Library, 1968.
Killer on Warbucket. New York, Ace, 1968.
The Man Who Killed the Marshal. New York, New American Library, 1969.
The Trail to Tucson. New York, New American Library, 1969.
Bloodrock Valley War. New York, Ace, 1969.
Texas Guns. New York, Lancer, 1969; London, Severn House, 1988.
The Rimrocker (Starbuck). New York, New American Library, 1970.
The Searching Guns. New York, New American Library, 1970.
Guns along the Jicarilla. New York, Ace, 1970.
Jackman's Wolf. New York, Doubleday, 1970.
The Outlawed (Starbuck). New York, New American Library, 1970.
Three Cross (Starbuck). New York, New American Library, 1970.
Deputy of Violence (Starbuck). New York, New American Library, 1971.
Duel in Lagrima Valley. New York, Ace, 1971.
A Bullet for Mr. Texas (Starbuck). New York, New American Library, 1971.
Marshal of Babylon (Starbuck). New York, New American Library, 1971.
Brandon's Posse (Starbuck). New York, New American Library, 1971.
A Man Called Ryker. New York, Ace, 1971.
The Devil's Gunhand (Starbuck). New York, New American Library, 1972.
Passage to Dodge City (Starbuck). New York, New American Library, 1972.
The Night Hell's Corner Died. New York, Ace, 1972; as Clay Ringold, London, Severn House, 1978.
The Hangman of San Sabal. New York, New American Library, 1972.
The Hell Merchant (Starbuck). New York, New American Library, 1972.
Lawman for Slaughter Valley (Starbuck). New York, New American Library, 1972; as *Lawman for the Slaughter*, 1980.
Showdown at Texas Flat. New York, Ace, 1972; London, Severn House, 1979.
Conger's Woman. New York, Doubleday, 1973.
The Guns of Stingaree (Starbuck). New York, New American Library, 1973.
Highroller's Man(Starbuck). New York, New American Library, 1973.
Skull Gold (Starbuck). New York, New American Library, 1973.
The Vengeance Gun. New York, Ace, 1973.
Day of Reckoning. New York, New American Library, 1973.
Man Without a Gun. New York, Doubleday, 1974.
The Texas Brigade (Starbuck). New York, New American Library, 1974.
Wolf Lawman. New York, New American Library, 1974.
The Jenner Guns (Starbuck). New York, New American Library, 1974.
The Scorpion Killers (Starbuck). New York, New American Library, 1974.
The Tombstone Trail (Starbuck). New York, New American Library, 1974.
The Doomsday Marshal. New York, Doubleday, 1975; London, Hale, 1976.
Honeymaker's Son. New York, Doubleday, 1975.
The Proving Gun. New York, Doubleday, 1975; London, Prior, 1981.
Betrayal in Tombstone. New York, Popular Library, 1975.
Day of the Hangman (Starbuck). New York, New American Library, 1975.
The Last Comanchero (Starbuck). New York, New American Library, 1975.
Roxie Raker. New York, Ace, 1975; Leicester, Ulverscroft, 1989.
The Vigilante. New York, New American Library, 1975.
The Yesterday Rider.New York, Doubleday, 1976; London, Hale, 1977.
High Green Gun (Starbuck). New York, New American Library, 1976.
The Regulator: Bill Thompson. New York, New American Library, 1976.
The Shotgun Rider (Starbuck). New York, New American Library, 1976.
The Iron Jehu. New York, Doubleday, 1976; London, Hale, 1978.
The Doomsday Posse. New York, Doubleday, 1977.
Omaha Crossing. New York, Ace, 1977; London, Hale, 1978.
Tall Man Riding. New York, New American Library, 1977.
Bounty Hunter's Moon (Starbuck). New York, New American Library, 1977.
A Gun for Silver Rose (Starbuck). New York, New American Library, 1977.
The Peace Keeper. New York, Doubleday, 1978; London, Hale, 1979.
The Glory Trail. New York, Doubleday, 1978.
Adam Gann, Outlaw. New York, New American Library, 1978.
Gun Trap at Arabella. New York, New American Library, 1978; London, Severn House, 1990.
The Raptors. New York, Doubleday, 1979; London, Hale, 1980.
The Doomsday Trail. New York, Doubleday, 1979.
The Hellborn. New York, New American Library, 1979.

Overkill at Saddle Rock. New York, New American Library, 1979.
Brandon's Posse and the Hell Merchant. New York, New American Library, 1979.
Lawman's Choice. New York, Doubleday, 1980.
Pilgrim. New York, Doubleday, 1980.
Ragan's Law. New York, Doubleday, 1980.
The Dead Gun. New York, New American Library, 1980.
The Hell Raiser. New York, New American Library, 1980; London, Severn House, 1990.
Outlaw's Pledge. New York, New American Library, 1981.
The Doomsday Bullet. New York, Doubleday, 1981; London, Hale, 1982.
Decision at Doubtful Canyon. New York, New American Library, 1981.
Renegade Gun. New York, Doubleday, 1982.
The Renegades. New York, New American Library, 1982.
Fortuna West, Lawman. New York, Doubleday, 1983.
The Law and Lynchburg. New York, New American Library, 1983.
The Vengeance of Fortuna West. New York, Doubleday, 1983.
The Copper-Dun Stud. New York, New English Library, 1983.
Agony Ridge. New York, New American Library, 1984.
The Doomsday Canyon. New York, Doubleday, 1984; London, Hale, 1988.
Apache Mountain Justice. New York, New American Library, 1985.
The Rawhiders. New York, Doubleday, 1985.
The Cornudas Guns. New York, New American Library, 1985.
Wyoming Drifter. New York, New American Library, 1986.
Outlaws Empire. New York, Doubleday, 1986.
The Doomsday Marshal; and The Hanging Judge. New York, Doubleday, 1986; Bath, Chivers, 1988.
Guns Along the Mora. New York, New American Library, 1987.
Solitude's Lawman. New York, Double day, 1988.
The Doomsday Marshal and the Comancheros. New York, Doubleday, 1988.
The Crosshatch Men. New York, Doubleday, 1989.
Stampede Outlaw. Bath, Chivers, 1990.
The Whipsaw Trail. New York, Doubleday, 1990.

Novels as Clay Ringold

Return to Rio Fuego. New York, Ace, 1968.
Reckoning in Fire Valley. New York, Ace, 1969.
The Hooded Gun. New York, Ace, 1969.

Uncollected Short Stories

"A Place for Danny Thorpe," in *They Opened the West*, edited by Tom W. Blackburn. New York, Doubleday, 1967.
"A Question of Faith," in *Zane Grey Western* (New York), December 1969.
"Bitter Sunset," with Gwynn Grady, in *With Guidons Flying*, edited by Charles N. Heckelmann. New York, Doubleday, 1970.
"Guns along the Mimbros," in *Zane Grey Western* (New York), April 1970.

*

Manuscript Collections: University of Wyoming Laramie; University of Oregon, Eugene; Texas Tech University, Lublock.

Ray Hogan comments:

I am not a tongue-in-cheek writer of western books and stories. I take my work seriously, bearing in mind the primary need to entertain but adhering to authenticity as much as possible.

I subscribe to the conception of the western hero—a rugged man of integrity who, in magnificent loneliness, meets and overcomes all obstacles despite overwhelming odds.

* * *

Among readers of "classic" Westerns, Ray Hogan has a following every bit as loyal, if not quite as notorious, as Max Brand and the late Louis L'Amour. In grouping Hogan with this kind of paperback and popularized writer of the formulaic, "shoot 'em up" narrative of pursuit and capture, escape and revenge, one should avoid invidious comparisons with altogether different western writers such as Harvey Fergusson, Wallace Stegner, or most especially Paul Horgan—a western writer who has almost nothing in common in terms of sensibilities and style with Hogan, although they are sometimes confused with each other.

This is not to demean in any way Hogan's talents as a popularizer—or to disparage the place of popular literature and the traditional Western. In terms of the kind of novel he writes he is a master. If he is not the consummate artist, he is a skilled craftsman who has perfected both his pattern and his process. Within that pattern there is surprising, seemingly endless room for variation. And it is for his amazing ability to vary internal aspects of his more or less externally fixed formula and architectonic that Hogan must be approached and appreciated.

Hogan is a born son of the West. Starting out in Missouri, the historic gateway to the West, he headed as a boy for Albuquerque, New Mexico, where he grew up and still lives today in the foothills of the Sandia and Manzano mountains. Before becoming a full-time writer, he worked in bakeries, filling stations, hardware stores, and managed a retail store for more than a decade.

He knows the history and the people of the West, and the walls of his study are lined with various firearms, spurs, pictures, books, and memorabilia which he can talk about in dramatic detail. His father was a policeman in the Albuquerque Police Department for many years, and the western lawman is more than a myth for Hogan. What all of this means is that Hogan knows the West first-hand, an important prerequisite for his job since 1956—western writer.

Since his first book, *Ex-Marshal*, Hogan has published over 125 books—most of them novels, except for books on Old West gunfighters Johnny Ringo and Clay Allison. At least half of Hogan's 100-odd books, including many titles appearing in the 1980's, are still in print. Perhaps his most popular works are those which follow the westering journey of Shawn Starbuck, a courageous searcher for a lost brother who, something like his American prototype, Natty Bumppo, has a clear sense of right and wrong and is willing to act on behalf of justice whenever needed.

But Starbuck is only one of a long roster of knowable "white-hatted" heroes and "black-hatted" villains with distinctive names and caricatured features. In keeping with the pleasures of melodrama, Hogan's way with names, good and bad, tells his readers immediately just who is on the right and who is on the wrong side. Jake Royce, John Rye, John Rutledge, lawmen; Adam Raitt, wagon master; John Temple, Luke Brazil . . . the list continues. All are names which sound principled and strong and belong to men who act accordingly.

Although one of his earliest publishers has dropped the Western from its lists, and although Hogan's output has abated somewhat from years when he would deliver seven or eight books annually, he still brings new interest to the popular, pulp Western. Ironically, much of that interest comes today from outside the United States, particularly Germany and Spain. With sustaining interest in titles like *The High Green Gun, The Crosshatch Men, The Doomsday Marshal*, and *The Hanging Judge*, Hogan appeals to a new Europe nostalgic for, desperately wanting—against more cynical certainties—clear demarcations of right and wrong as ostensibly was the case in the Old West. Like his characters, his is a name synonymous with a unique American culture hero of days gone by: the man who through grit and common sense and, if necessary, violence stood solo for order over chaos.

—Robert F. Gish

HOLLAND, Tom. *See* **KING, Albert.**

HOLMES, B(ryan) J(ohn). British. Born in Birmingham, Warwickshire, in 1939. Educated at Wednesbury Boys' High School, Wednesbury, West Midlands, 1950–56, University of Keele, Staffordshire, B.Sc. (hons.) in economics and psychology 1968. Divorced; two sons. Worked in industrial advertising, 1956–63; Lecturer, North Staffordshire Polytechnic, Stafford, and Derbyshire Business School, Derbyshire College of Higher Education, Derby. Has published many papers on economics and its teaching methodology. Address: 34 Saxton Avenue, Heanor, Derbyshire DE7 7PZ, England.

WESTERN PUBLICATIONS

Novels (series: The Reaper)

The Avenging Four. London, Hale, 1978.
Hazard. London, Hale, 1979.
Blood, Sweat and Gold. London, Hale, 1980.
Gunfall. London, Hale, 1980.
A Noose for Yanqui. London, Hale, 1981.
Shard. London, Hale, 1982.
Bad Times at Backwheel. London, Hale, 1982.
On the Spin of a Dollar. London, Hale, 1983.
Guns of the Reaper. London, Hale, 1983.
Another Day, Another Dollar. London, Hale, 1984.
Dark Rider. London, Hale, 1987.
I Rode with Wyatt. London, Hale, 1989.
A Legend Called Shatterhand. London, Hale, 1990.
Dollars for the Reaper. London, Hale, 1990.

Uncollected Short Stories

"Dry Run," published as "Menneske Jakt" (Manhunt) in *Western Magazine* (Oslo), 1979.
"A Hanging at Constitution," published as "I Morgan Skal Du Do" (Tomorrow You Shall Die), in *Western Magazine* (Oslo), 1979.

* * *

B.J. Holmes made his entry into the western genre with *The Avenging Four*, a familiar tale of a group of strangers who by force of circumstance are bound together in the quest to bring to justice the outlaws who robbed them. Although the theme is well worn and the characters recognisable—the green Easterner, the smooth gambler, a Negro, all welded together into a fighting unit by the ex-military man—the story follows traditional western lines and tells a pleasing tale of retribution against strong odds. As a debut it heralded the emergence of a writer who was to develop his own style over the following years with a string of novels that added to his stature as a western storyteller.

In *Another Day, Another Dollar* Holmes returns to the theme that has dominated a number of his novels, the ageing hero. Not the usual steely-eyed, lean and hard Westerner who dominates the genre, Jed Davitt is no youngster. He's grey haired and haggard, an alcoholic on the way down, with little to look forward to except a bleak, empty future—until he rides into a town called Hades. Here he faces his future and despite his weaknesses, fights his way back to self-esteem against the the opposition.

Before this novel, Holmes introduced readers to a character who appeared in two books. Jonathan Grimm, a greying, middle aged bounty hunter first appeared in *Guns of the Reaper*. Grimm is a no-nonsense character who follows his calling with true dedication. Aware of his own mortality he is plagued in the first book by bouts of dizziness, bad eyesight, and relentless headaches that turn out to be migraines. This touch of normality in a hero renders him more sympathetic. The Old West of fiction is populated by granite-faced individuals who carry their invulnerability like great shields; it makes a refreshing change to have a lead character with human frailties, and who is not eternally 25 years old. With Jonathan Grimm, one can hear the bones creak in time to his saddle leather—not that this places any restraint on his capabilities as a bounty hunter. With age comes wisdom and an understanding of human nature. Grimm uses both, and is no slouch when it comes to using the guns he carries. Grimm's return in a later book *Dollars for the Reaper* finds him eventually on the trail of Jesse James, and in the final confrontation it is Grimm who backshoots the outlaw in the legendary showdown in James's home. This twist to the tale is neatly and convincingly portrayed—in Holmes's version the outlaw has a hideaway gun behind the picture on the wall, which is why Grimm shoots him. As an extra fillip the bounty hunter passes the glory over to Bob Ford—who under a different name had saved Grimm's life at the beginning of the book. Holmes's novel takes the Jesse James myth and presents and unusual—but not incredible—version of the story.

Holmes's novels step back from the standard Western and paint familiar landscapes with different brush strokes. His books are in the genre, but he has taken the time to deliver variations on a theme, with pleasing results.

Dark Rider, on the face of it, is a revenge Western, one man on the trail of outlaws who have robbed and killed his friend. In this instance the dead man is a British Army officer. The man on the trail is his second in command, a Corporal of the British Indian Army. Thousands of miles from his beloved country, Corporal Singh, in the proud tradition of his forebears, refuses to return home until he has avenged his Colonel. Crossing the American wilderness, Singh confronts many hazards and handles them with typically mystic coolness. The novel portrays the meeting of West and East with deft touches. Singh handles both physical and spiritual confrontations with common sense and a deep awareness. He learns to shoot the American way, yet puts across his argument on religion with equal skill. He even outbrags a loudmouth Texan with a tall tale about "gophers so big that men ride on their backs," and their ability to carry away uprooted trees with their noses. The climax of the book has Singh a captive of the Apaches, facing death by snakebite. Here, in another Holmes surprise ending, the soldier uses the rhythmic chant and body sway of the Indian snake charmers to calm the reptile. His survival not only astounds his Apache captors, but gains his freedom and the respect of the native Americans. With the killers of his Colonel dead, Singh is able to return home with honour.

The starting point for *A Legend Called Shatterhand* was the series of books, written by German author Karl May, many years ago. Holmes took up the story of Shatterhand's life years on from the original novels—again returning to his aged hero theme. But in this case the main character is more than a hero. In his fictional world Shatterhand is a legend. Revered by the Indians, with whom he has a close affinity, Shatterhand prefers their nomadic life. He is more of a wanderer of the wilderness than an archetypal hero, philosophical and steeped in the lore of the land. The characterisation of Shatterhand is carefully crafted, the book staying close to the Karl May style without becoming too heavy. Holmes develops a lyrical tone to his writing, easing it away from the conventions of the mundane Western. It lends the novel an air of authenticity and brings with it the true feel of classic adventure.

Holmes has contributed a number of well constructed and original novels—in the sense that they are looking at the West through the eyes of a writer not content with turning out standard Westerns. He has expanded the genre, without losing the true stuff of the Western. When the gunfire rolls it does so with conviction and in the unashamed dictum of the genre when his men do what a man has to do—they do it well.

—Mike Linaker

HOLMES, L(lewellyn) P(erry). Also wrote as Dave Hardin; Matt Stuart; Perry Westwood. American. Born in Breckenridge, Colorado, 4 January 1895. Educated at local grammar and high schools. Married Lydia Marie Hillman in 1920 (died 1977); one son. Worked as a draughtsman in naval shipyard; oil company truck driver; cattle rancher. Full-time writer, 1923–88. Wrote 51 novels and 700 stories for pulp magazines. *Died 30 December 1988.*

WESTERN PUBLICATIONS

Novels

Roaring Range. New York, Greenberg, 1935; London, Hurst and Blackett, 1936.
The Law of Kyger Gorge. New York, Greenberg, 1936; London, Hurst and Blackett, 1937.
Destiny Range. New York, Greenberg, 1936; London, Ward Lock, 1937.
Bloody Saddles. New York, Greenberg, 1937; as *Gunman's Greed*, New York, Graphic, 1954.
Outlaws of Boardman's Flat. New York, Phoenix Press, 1941; London, Ward Lock, 1942.
Flame of Sunset. New York, Samuel Curl, 1947; London, Ward Lock, 1948.
Desert Rails. New York, Simon and Schuster, 1949; London, Ward Lock, 1952.
Water, Grass, and Gunsmoke. New York, Doubleday, 1949; Kingswood, Surrey, World's Work, 1950; as *Range Pirate*, New York, Bantam, 1950.
Black Sage. New York, Doubleday, 1950; Kingswood, Surrey, World's Work, 1951.
Summer Range. New York, Doubleday, 1951; London, Transworld, 1953.
Dead Man's Saddle. New York, Doubleday, 1951; Kingswood, Surrey, World's Work, 1952.
Apache Desert. New York, Doubleday, 1952; London, Transworld, 1954.
High Starlight. New York, Doubleday, 1952; London, Transworld, 1954.
Delta Deputy. New York, Doubleday, 1953.
Brandon's Empire (as Dave Hardin). New York, Ballantine, 1953; as L.P. Holmes, New York, Warner, 1986.
Six-Gun Code (as Perry Westwood). New York, Fawcett, 1953; as *Payoff at Pawnee*, as L.P. Holmes, New York, Popular Library, 1981.
Somewhere They Die. Boston, Little Brown, 1955; London, Hale, 1957.
The Plunderers. New York, Dodd Mead, and London, Hale, 1957.
Modoc, The Last Sundown. New York, Dodd Mead, 1957; as *The Last Sundown*, London, Hale, 1958.
Hill Smoke. New York, Dodd Mead, 1959; London, Hale, 1960.
Catch and Saddle. New York, Dodd Mead, 1959; London, Hale, 1961.
Night Marshal. New York, Dodd Mead, 1961; London, Transworld, 1962.
Smoky Pass. New York, Ace, 1962.
Wolf Brand. New York, Ace, 1962.
The Buzzards of Rocky Pass. New York, Ace, 1963.
Side Me at Sundown. New York, Ace, 1963.
The Shackled Gun. New York, Avalon, 1963.
Edge of Sundown. New York, Avalon, 1964.
The Hardest Man in the Sierras. New York, Ace, 1965.
The Savage Hours. New York, Ace, 1966.
The Maverick Star. New York, Ace, 1969.
Showdown on the Jubilee. New York, Bouregy/Avalon, 1970.
Rustler's Moon. New York, Ace, 1971.
Rawhide Creek. New York, Ace, 1975.
Shadow of the Rim. New York, Popular Library, 1982.
The Distant Vengeance. New York, Warner, 1987.

Novels as Matt Stuart

Dusty Wagons. Philadelphia, Lippincott, 1949; as *Savage Guns*, New York, Lancer, n.d.
Bonanza Gulch. Philadelphia, Lippincott, 1950; as *Bloody Bonanza*, New York, Lancer, n.d.
Gun Smoke Showdown. Philadelphia, Lippincott, 1950; as *Saddle-Man*, New York, Bantam, 1951.
Gun Law at Vermillion. Philadelphia, Lippincott, 1951.
The Smoky Trail. Philadelphia, Lippincott, 1951.
Sunset Rider. Philadelphia, Lippincott, 1952; as *The Fugitive Gun*, New York, Lancer, n.d.
Wire in the Wind. Philadelphia, Lippincott, 1952; as *Nevada Rampage*, New York, Lancer, n.d.
Deep Hills. Philadelphia, Lippincott, 1954; as *Ride into Gunsmoke*, New York, Bantam, 1956.
The Lonely Law. New York, Dodd Mead, 1957; London, Hale, 1960.
Wild Summit. New York, Dodd Mead, 1959.
Tough Saddle. New York, Dodd Mead, 1959.
Warrior Creek. New York, Dodd Mead, 1960.

The Hackamore Feud. Derby, Connecticut, New International Library, 1964.
Edge of the Desert. New York, Lancer, 1966.

* * *

According to L.P. Holmes, he was literally born with an urge to write. He began contributing to the pulps in 1925 and could later say with pride: "You name a Western pulp and I was in it at one time or another." His first hardbound novel was *Roaring Range*, one of five books he published between 1935 and 1941. The pacing he learned from the pulps was there but also less attractive elements: characters inadequately drawn, sometimes just named in order to be killed, and a vague sketchiness even about the heroes. When his son was sent to the Pacific theatre by the Navy during World War II, Holmes for a time became involved in shipbuilding. However, he continued to write for the pulps and unless his pulp fiction from this period is read the transformation which occurs with publication of *Flame of Sunset* in 1947 will come as a shock. This novel concerns river boats on the Sacramento. "Hides on the River" published in *Western Story* in August 1945, is clearly a precursor of the later novel (albeit the riverboats in this case are on the Colorado), with Captain Lew Deckard clearly an earlier version of Captain Bill Ballinger in the subsequent novel while the gambler in "Farallone Bounty" in *Western Story* in November 1946 foreshadows the sympathetic gambler in *Flame of Sunset*.

By this time, Holmes had come to reside in Napa, California and he could say on the flyleaf that "I like room to flap my wings . . . When crowds move in, I move out. Skyscrapers are too high for me, but mountains never are. I live now where the shadow of one strikes every morning. I'm a lucky and happy man." What followed were a series of novels which, while strictly formulary in structure, remain among the finest and most polished examples of their kind, all of them produced during Holmes's Golden Age which extended from 1947 until 1957. In that decade most of what he wrote deserves a high place in any basic library of traditional Western fiction. Under his own name after *Flame of Sunset* (the name of a riverboat), he produced an excellent railroad-building story *Desert Rails*, a no less fine freighting story *Apache Desert*, and unusual law man story *Delta Deputy* (in which, for the first time, a Holmes hero is beaten in a first fight), and the type of story at which he was truly adept: the ranch romance. This is the basic plot in *Water, Grass, and Gunsmoke*, *Black Sage*, *Summer Range*, *Dead Man's Saddle*, *High Starlight*, *Somewhere They Die*, and *The Plunderers*. Several of these novels were expanded from condensed pulp versions which appeared before cloth publication and all were reprinted in paperback.

In *Apache Desert*, the Indians are not characterized but the narrative tone is sympathetic: "Their customs, their legends, and they themselves were dying, and their despair was a great and silent cry in the desert night . . ." This sympathy is even more markedly present in *Black Sage* where the hero is intent on protecting the rights of the Mescaleros and in *Modoc, The Last Sundown* Holmes characterized the plight of the Modocs as "just one more phase of the same sad, blood-stained, miserable conflict that had accompanied the white man on his march of conquest all across a continent," not-withstanding the brutality that is shown on both sides of that conflict.

Some aspects of Holmes's western fiction even during his Golden Age were already hackneyed in the formulary Western, the frequent use of the theme of the two heroines (one of whom the hero must choose), the "destiny" theme in which the confrontation between the hero and the villain is fated, the terrific fistfights which Holmes narrated with the kind of intensity also to be found in Luke Short. However, equally basic to Holmes's fiction are his own individual themes: the loyalty which unites one man to another, the pride one must take in work and a job well done, and the innate generosity of most of the people who live in the West. There are generally progressions in these novels, changes through which a number of characters must pass, and the need of some people (even, if not especially, heroines) to learn the hard way. Holmes's heroes are never alone, but bound to others by imperishable ties of friendship and to the communities in which they live. In fact, whether Holmes was writing about actual places, as he did half the time, or imaginary ones, as he did the other half, he could make his Western communities so desirable and populate them with such interesting and well-developed secondary characters that often a reader would prefer to live there. The heroine is frequently kidnapped by the villains, as early as *Bloody Saddles* and as late as *Water, Grass, and Gunsmoke*, but in the latter it serves a higher purpose than melodrama, revealing the true nature of the hero and the villain in a subtle fashion. It remained a basic proposition in Holmes's fiction that some men are reprobates and must be judged harshly while, to others, who are not reprobates but only men misled or who have shown poor judgment (as heroines also do upon occasion), mercy must be granted and once more they are to be accepted back into the community.

During his Golden Age, Holmes produced a number of notable novels under other names as well, principally as Matt Stuart, in freighting stories such as *Dusty Wagons* and *Gun Law at Vermillion*, a telegraph-building story such as *Wire in the Wind*, and ranch romances like *Gun Smoke Showdown*, *The Smoky Trail*, and *Sunset Rider*. The last three, along with *Brandon's Empire* and *Six-Gun Code*, ranch romances published under other names, employ the same basic plot as similar books under his own name: the conflict produced in the hero and the community by a variety of range pirate. Yet each is varied sufficiently, with careful attention paid to secondary characters and to setting, to prove consistently rewarding. There were, also, regrettable failures such as *Bonanza Gulch*, set in a gold rush town in which the goldseekers are nearly as unsavory as the villains preying upon them and motivation is so weak that only the "destiny" theme holds the story together.

A turn for the worse occurred when Holmes acquired a new agent and he began producing potboilers as original paperbacks for Ace Books and hardbound novels for Avalon Books which were never issued in paperback. A similar decline occurred in the Matt Stuart titles culminating in *Edge of the Desert*, a ranch romance unusual for Holmes only in that, as in a B.M. Bower Western from four decades before it the story is told from the heroine's point of view. Holmes wrote his last two books as part of a package deal with Popular Library which entailed reissue of a number of his earlier titles. He published his final novel, *The Distant Vengeance*, in his 92nd year.

Throughout his career, Holmes produced (by his own count) nearly 600 short stories and novelettes, mostly Westerns, and undertook to reprint only a small fraction of these among his expanded novels. This is unfortunate because some of them, such as "The Tomahawk Herd" from 1941, clearly anticipate the fine work from the late 1940's and early 1950's. At his best Holmes's style, his striking images, and his craftsmanship leave a lasting impression.

—Jon Tuska

HOLT, Tex. *See* **JOSCELYN, Archie.**

HOPKINS, Hiram. *See* **SELTZER, Charles Alden.**

HOPSON, William (L). Also wrote as John Sims. American. Born in Texas in 1907. Served in the United States Marine Corps, medical discharge 1926; later served as weapons instructor, Aberdeen Proving Ground, Maryland, during World War II. Worked as a coyote hunter, barnstormer and parachute jumper, welder, and janitor. Writer of short stories and nonfiction for *Saturday Evening Post, Liberty, Popular Aviation*, and Western, Mystery, and pulp magazines.

WESTERN PUBLICATIONS

Novels

Gun-Thrower. New York, Phoenix Press, and London, Eldon Press, 1940.
Cowpoke Justice. New York, Phoenix Press, 1941; London, Ward Lock, 1942.
The Laughing Vaquero. New York, Phoenix Press, 1943; London, Ward Lock, 1945; as *Cattle-War Buckaroo*, New York, Avon, 1950.
Sunset Ranch. New York, Phoenix Press, 1943; as *Killers Five*, New York, Lion, 1951.
Silver Gulch. New York, Phoenix Press, 1944; as *Vegas, Gunman Marshal*, New York, Avon, 1956.
Hell's Horseman. New York, Phoenix Press, 1946; London, Wright and Brown, 1948.
Rambling Top Hand. New York, Phoenix Press, 1946; London, Wright and Brown, 1948.
The Man from Sonora. London, Quality Press, 1946.
Notched Guns. Chicago, Century, 1947; London, Wright and Brown, 1950.
The Gringo Bandit. New York, Phoenix Press, 1947; London, Wright and Brown, 1950.
Straight from Boothill. New York, Phoenix Press, 1947; London, Gold Lion, 1974; as *The Ranch Cat*, New York, Lion, 1951.
Arizona Roundup. New York, Phoenix Press, 1948.
N P Puncher. New York, Phoenix Press, 1948.
The Tombstone Stage. New York, Phoenix Press, 1948; Bath, Chivers, 1985.
The Border Raider. New York, Phoenix Press, 1949; London, Wright and Brown, 1953.
Big Matt McKee. Stoke on Trent, Archer Press, 1949.
Horse Thief Masquerade. New York, Phoenix Press, 1949; London, Wright and Brown, 1951; as *Twin Masquerade*, New York, Berkley, 1959; as *Twin Mavericks*, Bath, Chivers, 1987.
Yucca City Outlaw. New York, Phoenix Press, 1949; London, Wright and Brown, 1952.
A Thousand Head North. Stoke on Trent, Archer Press, 1950.
Desperado of the Range. London, Wright and Brown, 1951.
The Last Apaches. New York, Avalon, 1951; London, Corgi, 1954.
Gunfighter's Pay. New York, Avalon, 1952; Kingswood, Surrey, World's Work, 1954.
High Saddle. New York, Arcadia House, 1952; London, Ward Lock, 1953.
Cow Thief Empire. New York, Arcadia House, 1953; London, Rich and Cowan, 1954.
Cry Viva! New York, Avalon, 1953.
Apache Kill. New York, Avalon, 1954; London, Corgi, 1955.
A Gunman Rode North. New York, Avalon, 1954; London, Corgi, 1955.
Apache Greed. New York, Lion, 1954.
Bullet-Brand Empire. New York, Ace, 1954; Bath, Chivers, 1987.
Trouble Rides Tall. New York, Fawcett, 1955; London, Fawcett, 1956.
Gunfire at Salt Fork. New York, Fawcett, 1956; London, Fawcett, 1957.
Montana Gunslinger. New York, Avon, 1956.
Ramrod Vengeance. New York, Berkley, 1957.
Backlash at Cajon Pass. New York, Ace, 1958; Bath, Chivers, 1989.
Long Ride to Abilene. New York, Avon, 1958.
The Last Shoot-Out. New York, Ace, 1958; London, Gold Lion, 1972.
Six Shooter from Socorro. London, Wright and Brown, 1959.
Killers Five. Princeton, New Jersey, Prestige, 1963; Bath, Chivers, 1986.
Trouble Takes All. New York, Award, 1964.
Guns of the Clan. New York, Curtis, 1967.
Born Savage. New York, Ace, 1970; London, Gold Lion, 1973.
The Guns of MacCameron. New York, Macfadden, 1971.

Novels as John Sims

The New Cowhand. New York, Phoenix Press, 1949; London, Boardman, 1952.
Outlaw of Hidden Valley. New York, Phoenix Press, 1949; London, Barker, 1951.
Desert Campfire. New York, Phoenix Press, 1951; as *Desert Rampage* (as William L. Hopson), New York, Belmont, 1966.
Hangtree Range (as Tex Holt). New York, Arcadia House, 1952; as John Sims, London, Wright and Brown, 1954.

Uncollected Short Stories

"Senor Texas Man," in *West* (New York), September 1939.
"Bobcats Are Bad Hombres," in *West* (New York), January 1941.
"Retribution," in *Saturday Evening Post* (Philadelphia), 30 November 1946.
"Last of the Tinhorns," in *Mammoth Western* (Chicago), April 1948.
"Desperado," in *Mammoth Western* (Chicago), May 1948.
"Man Tracker," in *Mammoth Western* (Chicago), July 1949.
"Get Out by Sundown," in *Mammoth Western* (Chicago), February 1950.
"The Making of a Cowman," in *Exciting Western* (London), April 1952.
"Trail Blazers," in *Thrilling Ranch Stories* (London), February 1953.

Other Publications

Other

Mexico after Dark, with Lois O'Conner. New York, Macfadden, 1964.

* * *

William Hopson wrote a number of books to a rather limited formula that his ingenuity lifted above the level one might expect. His heroes were always unusual—first or second generation outlaws ready to "go straight," captured whites reared as Indians, bounty hunters driven by an obvious death wish, disillusioned lawyers fleeing into the gunfighter life, etc. They typically faced such overwhelming opposition that some of their enemies must eliminate each other, a necessity he did not always manage convincingly. There was always a love triangle involving the hero, frequently two or even more overlapping ones, and these two were often predictably resolved. Finally, the hero did always personally overcome his most dangerous enemy; but, again, this was often too pat and predictable and at times unconvincing.

When the formula elements mixed perfectly, as in *The Last Shoot-Out*, the result was a compelling read, with the breakneck pace smoothing out the few rough spots. When they did not, as in the later and too similar *Born Savage*, the book was likely to show as many seams and be as ineffective as some early failure in Dr. Frankenstein's attempts to create life.

Most such writers attempted at least one epic beginning with the Civil War and running into the wildest parts and days of the west. Generally, the result was dismal. Hopson's attempt, *Cry Viva!*, was highly unusual. Set in Mexico in that country's bloodiest 20th-century civil war, it features a hero who is an apostate Mormon, a United States citizen who had never set foot on U.S. soil, a failed matador turned bull breeder, and a fired major domo to one of the richest old Spanish families. Surprisingly, this is one of the best western epics and one of this author's most compelling novels.

Reading Hopson is rather like panning for gold. The prospector is usually all wet and goes for long periods without discovering anything worthwhile, but when he does there is genuine cause for celebration.

—R. Jeff Banks

HORGAN, Paul. American. Born in Buffalo, New York, 1 August 1903. Educated at Nardin Academy, Buffalo; Albuquerque public schools; New Mexico Military Institute, Roswell, 1920–23. Served in the United States Army as Chief of the Army Information Branch, 1942–46: Lieutenant Colonel; Legion of Merit; recalled to active duty, General Staff, 1952. Member of the production staff, Eastman Theatre, Rochester, New York, 1923–26; librarian, 1926–42, and assistant to the President, 1947–49, New Mexico Military Institute (the Institute library is named for him); Lecturer, University of Iowa, Iowa City, 1946. Senior fellow, 1959–61, and director, 1962–67, Center for Advanced Studies, Adjunct Professor of English and author-in-residence, 1967–71, and since 1971 Professor Emeritus and permanent author-in-residence, Wesleyan University, Middletown, Connecticut. Hoyt fellow, 1965, and since 1967 associate fellow, Saybrook College, Yale University, New Haven, Connecticut. President, Roswell Museum, 1946–52; member of the Board, Roswell Public Library, 1958–62; Chair of the Board, Santa Fe Opera, New Mexico, 1958–62. President, American Catholic Historical Association, 1960. Member, National Council on the Humanities, 1966–71. Scholar-in-residence, 1968, 1970, 1972, 1973, and since 1974 fellow, Aspen Institute, Colorado. Member of the Editorial Board, 1969–72, Book of the Month Club, New York. Recipient: Harper Prize Novel award, 1933; Guggenheim fellowship, 1945, 1958; Pulitzer prize, for history, 1955, 1976; Bancroft prize, for history, 1955; Texas Institute of Letters award, 1955, 1971, 1976; Catholic Book Club Campion award, 1957; Catholic Book award, 1965, 1969; Christopher award, 1976; Western Writers of America Spur award, for non-fiction, 1976; University of Notre Dame Laetare Medal, 1976; Smithsonian Institute Bronze Medal, 1980; National Portrait Gallery Medal, 1982; Wesleyan University Baldwin Medal, 1982; Washington College award, 1985; McConaughy Memorial award, 1986; Los Angeles *Times* Kirsch award, 1987. D. Litt.: Wesleyan University, 1956; Southern Methodist University, Dallas, 1957; University of Notre Dame, Indiana, 1958; Boston College, 1958; New Mexico State University, Las Cruces, 1961; College of the Holy Cross, Worcester, Massachusetts, 1962; University of New Mexico, Albuquerque, 1963; Fairfield University, Connecticut, 1964; D'Youville College, Buffalo, New York, 1965; Pace College, New York, 1968; Loyola College, Baltimore, 1968; Lincoln College, Illinois, 1969; St. Bonaventure University, New York, 1969; LaSalle College, Philadelphia, 1971; Catholic University, Washington, D.C., 1973; St. Mary's College, 1976; Yale University, 1978; University of Hartford, Connecticut, 1987; D.H.L.: Canisius College, Buffalo, 1960; Georgetown University, Washington, D.C., 1963. Member, American Academy, and American Academy of Arts and Sciences. Knight of St. Gregory, 1957. Address: 77 Pearl Street, Middletown, Connecticut 06457, U.S.A.

Western Publications

Novels

No Quarter Given. New York, Harper, and London, Constable, 1935.

Mountain Standard Time (trilogy). New York, Farrar Straus, and London, Macmillan, 1962.

Main Line West. New York, Harper, and London, Constable, 1936.

Far from Cibola. New York, Harper, and London, Constable, 1938.

The Common Heart. New York, Harper, 1942.

A Lamp on the Plains. New York, Harper, and London, Constable, 1937.

The Devil in the Desert: A Legend of Life and Death in the Rio Grande. New York, Longman, 1952.

The Saintmaker's Christmas Eve. New York, Farrar Straus, 1955; London, Macmillan, 1956.

Give Me Possession. New York, Farrar Straus, 1957; London, Macmillan, 1958.

A Distant Trumpet. New York, Farrar Straus, and London, Macmillan, 1960.

Whitewater. New York, Farrar Straus, 1970; London, Bodley Head, 1971.

Mexico Bay. New York, Farrar Straus, and Henley-on-Thames, Oxfordshire, Ellis, 1982.

Short Stories

The Return of the Weed. New York, Harper, 1936; as *Lingering Walls*, London, Constable, 1936.

Figures in a Landscape. New York, Harper, 1940.
Humble Powers: 3 Novelettes. London, Macmillan, 1954; New York, Doubleday, 1956.
The Peach Stone: Stories from Four Decades. New York, Farrar Straus, 1967; London, Bodley Head, 1968.

OTHER PUBLICATIONS

Novels

The Fault of Angels. New York, Harper, 1933; London, Hamish Hamilton, 1934.
The Richard Trilogy. Middletown, Connecticut, Wesleyan University Press, 1990.
Things as They Are. New York, Farrar Straus, 1964; London, Bodley Head, 1965.
Everything to Live For. New York, Farrar Straus, 1968; London, Bodley Head, 1969.
The Thin Mountain Air. New York, Farrar Straus, 1977; London, Bodley Head, 1978.

Short Story

One Red Rose for Christmas (novella). New York, Longman, 1952.

Plays

Yours, A. Lincoln (produced New York, 1942).
A Tree on the Plains: A Music Play for Americans, music by Ernst Bacon (produced Spartanburg, South Carolina). Published in *Southwest Review* (Dallas), Summer 1943.

Verse

Lamb of God. Privately printed, 1927.
Songs after Lincoln. New York, Farrar Straus, 1965.
A Gallery of Clerihews. Middletown, Connecticut, Piratical Primrose Press, 1984.
The Annotated Clerihew. Middletown, Connecticut, Piratical Primrose Press, 1984.
The Clerihews of Paul Horgan. Middletown, Connecticut, Wesleyan University Press, 1985.

Other

Men of Arms (for children). Philadelphia, McKay, 1931.
From the Royal City of the Holy Faith of Saint Francis of Assisi, Being Five Accounts of Life in That Place. Santa Fe, Villagra Bookshop, 1936.
The Habit of Empire. Santa Fe, Rydal Press, and New York, Harper, 1938.
Look at America: The Southwest, with the editors of Look. Boston, Houghton Mifflin, 1947.
Great River: The Rio Grande in North American History. New York, Rinehart, 2 vols., 1954; revised edition, Austin, Texas Monthly Press, 1 vol., 1984.
The Centuries of Santa Fe. New York, Dutton, 1956; London, Macmillan, 1957.
Rome Eternal. New York, Farrar Straus, 1957.
One of the Quietest Things (address). Los Angeles, University of California School of Library Service, 1960.
Citizen of New Salem. New York, Farrar Straus, 1961; as *Abraham Lincoln: Citizen of New Salem*, London, Macmillan, 1961.
Toby and the Nighttime (for children) New York, Farrar Straus, and London, Macmillan, 1963.
Conquistadors in North American History. New York, Farrar Straus, 1963; as *Conquistadors in North America*, London, Macmillan, 1963.
Peter Hurd: A Portrait Sketch from Life. Austin, University of Texas Press, 1965.
Memories of the Future. New York, Farrar Straus, and London, Bodley Head, 1966.
The Heroic Triad: Essays in the Social Energies of Three Southwestern Cultures. New York, Holt Rinehart, 1970; London, Heinemann, 1971.
Encounters with Stravinsky: A Personal Record. New York, Farrar Straus, and London, Bodley Head, 1972; revised edition, Middletown, Connecticut, Wesleyan University Press, 1989.
Approaches to Writing. New York, Farrar Straus, 1973; London, Bodley Head, 1974; revised edition, Middletown, Connecticut, Wesleyan University Press, 1988.
Lamy of Santa Fe: His Life and Times. New York, Farrar Straus, 1975; London, Faber, 1977.
Josiah Gregg and His Vision of the Early West. New York, Farrar Straus, 1979.
On the Climate of Books. Middletown, Connecticut, Wesleyan University Press, 1981.
Henriette Wyeth, with Michael Hurd. Santa Fe, New Mexico, Peters Corporation, 1982.
Of America East and West. New York, Farrar Straus, 1984.
Under the Sangre de Cristo. Santa Fe, New Mexico, Rydal Press, 1985.
A Writer's Eye: Field Notes and Water Colors. New York, Abrams, 1988.
A Certain Climate: Essays and Lectures. Middletown, Connecticut, Wesleyan University Press, 1988.

Editor, *Selected Poems by Witter Bynner.* New York, Knopf, 1936.
Editor, with M.G. Fulton, *New Mexico's Own Chronicle: Three Races in the Writings of Four Hundred Years.* Dallas, Upshaw, 1937.
Editor, *Maurice Baring Restored: Selections from His Work.* New York, Farrar Straus, and London, Heinemann, 1970.

*

Manuscript Collection: Beinecke Library, Yale University, New Haven, Connecticut.

Critical Studies: *Paul Horgan*, Boston, Twayne, 1983, and "The Enduring Value of Paul Horgan" (interview), in *The Bloomsbury Review* (London), January-February 1989, both by Robert Gish.

Paul Horgan comments:

I rest somewhat uneasily under the classification of Western writer, for though much of my work in fiction and history has its setting in the American southwest, almost as much has other parts of the United States for backgrounds. My life has been divided between East and West, and I have found my subjects in both parts of the nation. The "Westernness" of popular romance has played no part in my work, and I fear that for me to be classified as a Western Writer will mislead followers of that genre. The matter is further complicated since in many of my individual novels settings and subject matter are concerned with both East and West under the dictates of a given story, and according to my life experience.

* * *

Paul Horgan has remained prolific throughout his career, with nearly 50 books to his name. And at the age of 87 he is still hard at work, still writing every day. His most recent books, *Of America East and West*, *Under the Sangre de Cristo*, *A Writer's Eye*, and *A Certain Climate* are, largely, reissues of previously published writings. His *The Clerihews of Paul Horgan* make humorously visible his lifelong ability as a satirist and caricaturist—in words and drawings. Similarly, *A Writer's Eye* features in brilliantly colorful and executed watercolors, his method of recording visual "field notes" for his works, particularly the Pulitzer-prize winning *Great River*. *A Certain Climate* collects some of his most intriguing personal and critical essays, with his devotion to Willa Cather, and her influence on him as an author, serving as a centerpiece. Soon to come will be yet another gathering of his short fiction in the masterful tradition of his earlier collections, *Figures in a Landscape* and *The Peach Stone*.

His relatively recent novel, *Mexico Bay*, is his 15th major work of fiction if one includes his *The Richard Trilogy*, and excludes *Mountain Standard Time*, another trilogy of sorts which incorporates three earlier novels, including the poignant *Main Line West* and *The Common Heart* which so consummately exemplify life in New Mexico in northeastern cities like Albuquerque and southeastern towns like Roswell. Horgan has also published many short stories and many splendid works of history and nonfiction (winning as he did the Pulitzer prize for history / biography, as well, for *Lamy of Santa Fe*) to round out a career which in 1990 is in its seventh decade. In addition to being prolific he has been versatile—a true person of letters, rare for these specialized, 20th century times. As *America East and West* proves, he is, moreover, a transcontinental writer, as cosmopolitan as he is regional.

Although he is often regarded as a western writer, a "regionalist" writer, he is more accurately an American author who writes about both New York and New Mexico—America East and West, urban and rural. Much of Horgan's fiction utilizes his dual, transcontinental setting, whether in terms of emigrating west or in backtrailing, if only temporarily, to the ostensibly more "cultured" environs of Washington, D.C., or Dorchester, New York (Horgan's fictive composite of his early homes of Rochester and Buffalo).

Thus, even though it is Horgan's fiction about the American West which is of interest here, it should be acknowledged that Horgan is not a typical "western" writer in the "shoot-'em-up," "wild and woolly," "horse opera" sense of the term. Certainly the people and landscapes of the West—particularly the Southwest—prove a major inspirational force for him. But to think of his fictions as "Western" in some stereotyped way is completely to miss his accomplishment as an artist; not to hear his voice and appreciate his style. If Horgan is a western writer (and he most assuredly is), he is a most refined and sophisticated one.

With the exception of *A Distant Trumpet*, which concerns the U.S. Cavalry and Apache war in Arizona of the 1890's, New Mexico and Texas are the two Southwestern states which provide the settings for most of Horgan's fiction. And aside from some of his earliest novels, namely *No Quarter Given* and *The Common Heart* which have northern New Mexico for their locale, even Horgan's novels about southeastern New Mexico and the Pecos river valley read, not surprisingly, like Texas novels insofar as that part of New Mexico is often identified—in speech patterns, topography, and folkways—as "Little Texas."

Such novels as *Main Line West*, *A Lamp on the Plains*, *Far from Cibola*, and *Whitewater* capture that special ambience associated closely with the wide-open spaces and distances, the paradoxical abundance and austerity of the Southwest, reach the heart's core of Texas. The effect such a place has on the attitudes and actions, the psychology, and even the visage of the people drawn there to "home" is a key ingredient of Horgan's success as a word painter of Southwestern lives and landscapes.

In this respect, *Mexico Bay* is the epitome of his "Texas" west—as geography, idea, and inspiration. Howard Debler, Horgan's historian hero, at home on the Texas plains, in Gulf cities like Brownsville and Corpus Christi, and the society worlds of Washington and upstate New York, realized his professional and personal hopes precisely because of the vision and presence of Mexico Bay (i.e., the Gulf of Mexico) in his life. Debler's completed history of the Mexican War (like Horgan's *Great River* and *Lamy of Santa Fe*) is representative of the special, almost spiritual, affinity he feels with the landscape and the past and present lives and cultures which experience it. And it is this pre-eminence of place, this "certain climate" of the American Southwest, which gives impetus and shape, the "writer's eye," to Horgan's East-West, transcontinental "western" fiction.

—Robert F. Gish

HORSLEY, David. *See* **BINGLEY, David Ernest.**

HORTON, Felix Lee. *See* **FLOREN, Lee.**

HOUGH, Emerson. American. Born in Newton, Iowa, 28 June 1857. Educated at Newton High School; University of Iowa, Iowa City, A.B. 1880. Married Charlotte A. Cheeseborough in 1897. Called to the Bar, and practiced law briefly in White Oaks, New Mexico; then journalist: writer on wildlife topics for papers in Des Moines and Sandusky, Ohio; Chicago office manager, *Field and Stream*; Out-of-Doors Department editor, *Saturday Evening Post*. *Died 30 April 1923.*

WESTERN PUBLICATIONS

Novels

The Girl at the Halfway House: A Story of the Plains. New York, Appleton, 1900; London, Heinemann, 1901.

The Mississippi Bubble. Indianapolis, Bowen Merrill, 1902; London, Methuen, 1903.

Heart's Desire. New York and London, Macmillan, 1905.

The Way of a Man. New York, Outing, 1907; London, Methuen, 1911.

54-40 or Fight. Indianapolis, Bobbs Merrill, 1909; London, Hodder and Stoughton, 1924.

The Purchase Price; or, The Cause of Compromise. Indianapolis, Bobbs Merrill, 1910; London, Hodder and Stoughton, 1925.

The Magnificent Adventure. New York, Appleton, 1916; London, Hodder and Stoughton, 1926.

The Man Next Door. New York and London, Appleton, 1917.

The Sagebrusher. New York and London, Appleton, 1919.
Maw's Vacation: The Story of a Human Being in the Yellowstone. St. Paul, Minnesota, Haynes, 1921.
The Covered Wagon. New York and London, Appleton, 1922.
North of 36. New York and London, Appleton, 1923.
Mother of Gold. New York and London, Appleton, 1924.
The Ship of Souls. New York and London, Appleton, 1925.

Uncollected Short Stories

"President's Forest," in *Saturday Evening Post* (Philadelphia), 14 January and 21 January 1922.
"'Curly' and the Grizzly," in *Western Story* (New York), 30 September 1922.
"The Horse-Thief Society," in *Western Story* (New York), 11 November 1922.
"A Little Old Bear," in *Western Story* (New York), 13 January 1923.
"Secret of Powder Basin," in *Argosy* (New York), 3 March–24 March 1923.
"The Landscape Company, Limited," in *Western Story* (New York), 14 April 1923.
"'Curly' Gets Back on the Soil," in *Western Story* (New York), 21 April 1923.
"Curly and Homer Cayenne," in *Western Story* (New York), 28 April 1923.
"'Curly's' Coon," in *Western Story* (New York), 5 May 1923.
"'Curly' Meets a Real Man," in *Western Story* (New York), 12 May 1923.
"The Late Mr. Jenkins," in *Western Story* (New York), 28 July 1923.
"Tall Men," in *Saturday Evening Post* (Philadelphia), 7 June 1924.
"On His Own," in *Sunset* (San Francisco), October 1924.
"Stolen Bridegroom," in *Golden Book* (New York), May 1926.
"Science at Heart's Desire," in *The Arbor House Treasury of Great Western Stories*, edited by Bill Pronzini and Martin H. Greenberg. New York, Arbor House, 1982.

Other Publications

Novels

The Law of the Land. Indianapolis, Bobbs Merrill, 1904.
John Rawn, Prominent Citizen. Indianapolis, Bobbs Merrill, 1912.
The Lady and the Pirate. Indianapolis, Bobbs Merrill, 1913.
The Broken Gate. New York and London, Appleton, 1917.
The Way Out: A Story of the Cumberlands Today. New York and London, Appleton, 1918.
The Young Alaskans [on the Trail, in the Rockies, in the Far North, on the Missouri] (for children). New York, Harper, 5 vols., 1908–22.
The Sowing: A "Yankee's" View of England's Duty to Herself and to Canada. Chicago, Vanderhoof Gum, 1909.
Getting a Wrong Start: A Truthful Autobiography. New York, Macmillan, 1915.
Out of Doors. New York, Appleton, 1915; London, Appleton, 1916.
Let Us Go Afield. New York, Appleton, 1916.
The Firefly's Light. New York, Trow Press, 1916.
The Indefinite American Attitude Toward the War and When Shall It Change? New York, American Defense Society, 1918.
The Passing of the Frontier: A Chronicle of the Old West. New Haven, Connecticut, Yale University Press, 1918.
The Web. Chicago, Reilly and Lee, 1919.
The American Rifle. Albuquerque, New Mexico, Vinegar Tom Press, 1970.

Play

Madre d'Oro: A Four-Act Spectacular Drama. Chicago, Hough, 1889.

Other

The Singing Mouse Stories (for children). New York, Forest and Stream, 1895; revised edition, Indianapolis, Bobbs Merrill, 1910.
The Story of the Cowboy. New York, Appleton, and London, Gay and Bird, 1897; as *The Cowboy*, New York, Brampton Society, 2 vols., 1908.
The Way to the West and the Lives of Three Early Americans: Boone, Crockett, Carson. Indianapolis, Bobbs Merrill, 1903; London, Hodder and Stoughton, 1925.
The King of Gee-Whiz (for children), lyrics by Wilbur D. Nesbit. Indianapolis, Bobbs Merrill, 1906.
The Story of the Outlaw: A Study of the Western Desperado. New York, Outing, 1907; London, Hodder and Stoughton, 1925.

*

Bibliography: in *Bibliography of American Literature 4*, edited by Jacob Blanck, New Haven, Connecticut, Yale University Press, 1963.

Critical Study: *Emerson Hough* by Delbert E. Wylder, Boston, Hall, 1981 (includes bibliography).

* * *

In his late thirties, Emerson Hough had almost despaired of being a successful writer, but the reception of his early book, *The Story of the Cowboy*, particularly a congratulatory letter from Theodore Roosevelt, provided him with the impetus to continue. In his next 26 years he produced an amazing number of short stories, articles, novels, and books primarily about the American West and became one of the most prolific and well-known of the many writers who wrote for the popular magazines.

As a journalist, Hough was known as a conservationist, as well as an expert in hunting and fishing. His short stories, especially those stories which dealt with the humorous exploits of his cowboy character "Curly," were usually about the west that he had known from his short stay in White Oaks, New Mexico, and later in Kansas. Although he wrote novels about the South and the Midwest, most of his novels are set in the West. Two historical novels, *The Mississippi Bubble* and *54–40 or Fight*, brought him his greatest financial success until, late in his life, he wrote *The Covered Wagon*. The early historical novels are all marred by Hough's penchant for melodrama, his bad habit of philosophizing, and his insistence on archaic language. Although many of his novels were financially unrewarding, Hough continued to make a good living from his journalistic writing.

In his last years, Hough's interest once more returned to the West he had known as a young man, and he wrote of it in *The Covered Wagon* and *North of 36*. The first of these is a novel depicting the movement of a wagon train across the Oregon trail. It was an extremely popular novel and was made into one of the first epic films of the American West by the director James Cruze. Although the novel unfortunately includes a rather ridiculous love affair, it does introduce many of the scenes that have become standard fare in wagon train novels and films, including river-crossings, Indian attacks, and arguments about leadership. *North of 36*, the result of a good deal of research, is the story of the first trail drive from Texas to the head of the railroad at Abilene. It was being serialized in *The Saturday Evening Post* when Hough died in 1923. It also was made into a popular film, and it, too, is unfortunate in having a love affair that is not only ineptly handled but which intrudes into the action of the novel. Although women may have, at one time or another, accompanied men on the trail drive, none of them would have acted as ridiculously as Hough's heroine, Taisie Lockhart. Two novels were in manuscript at Hough's death and were published posthumously—*Mother of Gold* and *The Ship of Souls*.

Early in his career, Hough had hopes of producing a novel that would challenge Owen Wister's *The Virginian* in its influence on western literature. With a good deal of help from Herbert P. Williams at Macmillan, and another popular writer, Harris Dickson, Hough put together a number of his "Curly" stories into a novel about the coming of "civilization" to a tiny bachelor town in New Mexico. Civilization, in this case, comes in the form of both a railroad and a woman, and these two elements tend to disrupt the peace and tranquility of this Edenic western garden. The theme concerns the human paradox that, as the narrator puts it, " . . . your Anglo Saxon, craving ever savagery, has no sooner found it than he seeks to civilize it; there being for him in his aeon of the world no real content or peace." Based on the humorous Curly stories, the novel treats this serious subject as a mock-heroic drama. The tone is consistently maintained, allowing Hough to make what Eugene Manlove Rhodes called "a great magic" with this novel, *Heart's Desire*. It is considered one of the classics of southwestern American literature. Unfortunately, it was a financial failure, and Hough turned once again to historical novels.

Hough did not expect to be remembered. However, *The Covered Wagon* and *North of 36*, thanks to the film industry, have found their way into film history, and *Heart's Desire*, the novel Hough thought of as a failure, has been revived by scholars of western American literature.

—Delbert E. Wylder

HOUSTON, Tex.

WESTERN PUBLICATIONS

Novels

The Sheriff of Hammer County. London, Mills and Boon, 1956.
Gunman Deputy. London, Mills and Boon, 1957.
Gunslinger. London, Mills and Boon, 1959.

* * *

In the small number of books which Tex Houston wrote in the 1950's, his preference was for writing about sheriffs. In *The Sheriff of Hammer County* his hero is a sort of superman figure who has "a man's face, a fighting face," strength as well as tremendous bravery. This sheriff has to bring law to a town whose citizens are at the mercy of those with guns. The town is on the very fringe of civilised territory, and the sheriff is another type of pioneer. The book contains a very good picture of mob rule and, a rarity in the western, a preacher who is a major figure. The preacher is, however, not a force for good, and in the end receives his just deserts. The book has very little plot and tends to drift along, with too much action and gunfighting, and therefore little sense of climax. The language used is very rich, full of colourful phrases and long sentences.

Houston's later books, more conventional, are in some ways less interesting. *Gunman Deputy* and *Gunslinger* both have a more conclusive climax and a more visible plot. In *Gunslinger* the sheriff very decisively puts down the disruptive influence of mountain folk and is undoubtedly the best lawman the town ever had. In these two books dialogue is much reduced and much less colourful. It is a pity that, while handling some interesting ideas about areas of the west which were completely lawless, Houston has presented them in a less colourful way. His books have become less rich in western language and more concerned with some very basic ideas of law and order.

—P.R. Meldrum

HOUSTON, Will. *See* **PAINE, Lauran.**

HOWARD, Robert E(rvin). American. Born in Peaster, Texas, 22 January 1906. Educated at schools in Bagwell, Cross Cut, Burkett, Cross Plains, and Brownwood, Texas; Howard Payne College, Brownwood. *Died 12 June 1936.*

WESTERN PUBLICATIONS

Short Stories

A Gent from Bear Creek. London, Jenkins, 1937; West Kingston, Rhode Island, Grant, 1965; selection, as *The Pride of Bear Creek*, Grant, 1966.
The Vultures; *Showdown at Hell's Canyon*. Lakemont, Georgia, Fictioneer, 1973.
Vultures of Whapeton. New York, Zebra, 1976.
The Last Ride. New York, Berkley, 1978.

Uncollected Short Stories

"A Man-Thinking Jeopard," in *Cowboy Stories* (New York), June 1936.
"A Gent from the Pecos," in *Argosy* (New York), 3 October 1936.
"Gents on the Lynch," in *Argosy* (New York), 17 October 1936.
"The Riot at Bucksnort," in *Argosy* (New York), 31 October 1936.
"Vultures' Sanctuary," in *Argosy* (New York), 28 November 1936.
"Knife-River Prodigal," in *Cowboy Stories* (New York), July 1937.
"Extermination of Yellow Donory," in *Zane Grey Western* (New York), June 1970.

OTHER PUBLICATIONS

Novels

Conan the Conqueror. New York, Gnome Press, 1950; with *Sword of Rhiannon*, London, Boardman, 1954.
Almuric. New York, Ace, 1964; London, New English Library, 1971.

Short Stories

Skull-Face and Others. Sauk City, Wisconsin, Arkham House, 1946; London, Spearman, 1974; as *Skull-Face Omnibus*, Spearman, 3 vols., 1976.
The Sword of Conan. New York, Gnome Press, 1952.
King Conan. New York, Gnome Press, 1953.
The Coming of Conan. New York, Gnome Press, 1953.
Conan the Barbarian. New York, Gnome Press, 1954.
Tales of Conan, with L. Sprague de Camp. New York, Gnome Press, 1955.
The Dark Man and Others. Sauk City, Wisconsin, Arkham Press, 1963; London, Panther, 1978.
Conan the Adventurer, with L. Sprague de Camp. New York, Lancer, 1966; London, Sphere, 1973.
Conan, with L. Sprague de Camp and Lin Carter. New York, Lancer, 1967; London, Sphere, 1974.
Conan the Warrior, with L. Sprague de Camp. New York, Lancer, 1967.
Conan the Usurper, with L. Sprague de Camp. New York, Lancer, 1967; London, Sphere, 1974.
King Kull, with Lin Carter. New York, Lancer, 1967; London, Sphere, 1974.
Wolfshead. New York, Lancer, 1968.
Conan the Freebooter, with L. Sprague de Camp. New York, Lancer, 1968; London, Sphere, 1974.
Conan the Wanderer, with L. Sprague de Camp and Lin Carter. New York, Lancer, 1968; London, Sphere, 1974.
Red Shadows. West Kingston, Rhode Island, Grant, 1968.
Conan of Cimmeria, with L. Sprague de Camp and Lin Carter. New York, Lancer, 1969; London, Sphere, 1974.
Red Blades of Black Cathay, with Tevis Clyde Smith. West Kingston, Rhode Island, Grant, 1971.
Marchers of Valhalla. West Kingston, Rhode Island, Grant, 1972; London, Sphere, 1977.
The Sowers of the Thunder. West Kingston, Rhode Island, Grant, 1973; London, Sphere, 1977.
The Incredible Adventures of Dennis Dorgan. West Linn, Oregon, Fax, 1974.
The Lost Valley of Iskander. West Linn, Oregon, Fax, 1974; London, Futura, 1976.
The People of the Black Circle. West Kingston, Rhode Island, Grant, 1974.
Tigers of the Sea. West Kingston, Rhode Island, Grant, 1974.
Worms of the Earth. West Kingston, Rhode Island, Grant, 1974; London, Futura, 1976.
A Witch Shall Be Born. West Kingston, Rhode Island, Grant, 1975.
Red Nails. West Kingston, Rhode Island, Grant, 1975.
Swords of Shahrazar. West Linn, Oregon, Fax, and London, Futura, 1976.
Black Vulmea's Vengeance and Other Tales of Pirates. West Kingston, Rhode Island, Grant, 1976.
The Devil in Iron. New York, Grosset and Dunlap, 1976.
Son of the White Wolf. West Linn, Oregon, Fax, 1977.
The Hour of the Dragon. New York, Putnam, 1977.
The People of the Black Circle. New York, Berkley, 1977.
The Road of Azrael. West Kingston, Rhode Island, Grant, 1979.

Verse

Always Comes Evening: The Collected Poems of Robert E. Howard. Sauk City, Wisconsin, Arkham House, 1958.
Etchings in Ivory. Pasadena, California, Glenn Lord, 1968.
Singers in the Shadows. West Kingston, Rhode Island, Grant, 1970.
Echoes from an Iron Harp. West Kingston, Rhode Island, Grant, 1972.
A Song of the Naked Lands. N.p., Squires, 1973.
The Gold and the Grey. N.p., Squires, 1974.

* * *

Robert E. Howard, a well-known name to readers of lusty fantasy adventure, is less-known to readers of western literature. This is due in no small part to his relatively minimal production in the field, and the fact that most of his western stories are rather dreary. Where Howard's star shone brightly in the heavens of fantasy, he has little glow at all within the cosmos of western fiction. In that Howard had considerable interests in the Old West, and was proud of his Texas heritage, this is somewhat surprising.

L. Sprague DeCamp, the famous fantasist and critic, has said that Howard would have turned to the western and regional novel in time, and that it would have become his forte. But there is little of Howard's western writing that would indicate this possibility, and much of his writing in this field would have been best left buried in the vaults of pulpdom.

One recent collection of his work, *The Last Ride*, is only readable. The stories in the book are dull and clichéd, even for their time. Many of the stories, in fact, were not reprinted while Howard lived, and one might think that the author intended them to remain lost within his files. However, the boom in all things Howard caused life to be forced into them, and like the tired old clumsy Frankenstein monster, they shuffle lackluster-ly across the page.

Howard's other western work is not quite so dismal, and the Breckenridge Elkins stories—which have been turned into chapters and cobbled together into a book titled *A Gent from Bear Creek*—are often humorous and action packed. Unfortunately, the Pecos Bill-type humor these stories employ is sometimes forced and the yarns grow tiresome quickly if not read in small doses.

It is interesting to note that a number of Howard's stories, though not strictly Westerns, contained western themes, and in these he came closer to capturing the spirit, the verve, and the color of the Old West. Most notable of these stories is perhaps "People of the Black Circle." Though it takes place outside the realms of reality, its structure is very much like that of a frontier adventure, and it takes more than the swords and magic employed by Howard to disguise this fact. Had the story been written as a straight Western it would not have broken new ground, but it would have been an exciting pulp Western. As it stands, it is an unusual and highly recommended fantasy, probably the second best of all of Howard's Conan stories (the best in my opinion is "The Tower of the Elephant").

Howard also wrote a number of stories that took place in western times, but once again the element of the fantastic was interjected. The most notable of these stories is "The Horror from the Mound." And as I have said earlier, it was in these that Howard came closest to capturing the spirit of the Western.

In this we have a stalwart western hero who pits a strong back and a "never say die" attitude against an accidentally uncovered vampire from the days of the Spanish Conquistadores. The story is exciting and, though it abounds with pulp convention, will stay with the reader long after being laid aside. Howard's writing makes it near impossible for us to forget that horrible, red-eyed thing that has escaped the mound. Another of his stories in this area is worth mentioning. "The Man on the Ground" is a western spectre story that displays clear, colorful writing and a strong understanding of the western character.

Though Howard's western work is of little interest to the western fan, his work borderlining the field is of more than passing interest to both western and fantasy readers.

—Joe R. Lansdale

HOWARD, Troy. *See* **PAINE, Lauran.**

HOWARD, Vechel. *See* **RIGSBY, Howard.**

HOYT, Nelson. *See* **KING, Albert.**

HUDSON, Lois Phillips. American. Born in Jamestown, North Dakota, 24 August 1927. Educated at the University of Puget Sound, Tacoma, Washington, B.A. 1949; University of Washington, Seattle, 1949; Cornell University, Ithaca, New York, M.A. 1951. Married Randolph Hudson in 1950 (divorced); two daughters. Teacher at junior high school, Shelton, Washington, 1949–50; and high school, Ithaca, New York, 1951–55. Assistant Professor, 1969–75, and since 1975 Associate Professor of English, University of Washington, Seattle. Since 1952 full-time writer. Recipient: Friends of American Writers award, 1962. Address: Department of English, GN-30, University of Washington, Seattle, Washington 98195, U.S.A.

WESTERN PUBLICATIONS

Novel

The Bones of Plenty. Boston, Little Brown, 1962; London, Heinemann,1963.

Short Stories

Reapers of the Dust: A Prairie Chronicle. Boston, Little Brown, 1965.

* * *

Lois Phillips Hudson's reputation is secured chiefly by two works, a novel of the Great Drought and Depression published in 1962, *The Bones of Plenty*, followed by a collection of short stories, *Reapers of the Dust* in 1964. Although both of these works were reviewed widely at the time of publication, and almost universally praised, Hudson has acquired only a modest critical reputation. Part of the reason is that both books went out of print rather quickly and remained so for almost 20 years. But with the paperback re-issue of both books in 1984, her work has become accessible to a whole new generation of readers. In the interim years Hudson has written many stories and essays which as yet remain uncollected, although a number of her stories have been widely anthologized. Her principal effort during these intervening years has gone toward a new novel, a manuscript of some 2000 pages, titled *The Kindly Fruits of the Earth.*

Both *The Bones of Plenty* and *Reapers of the Dust* have frequently been compared to *The Grapes of Wrath*, a comparison Hudson herself dislikes. Although the comparison is perhaps inevitable, as the books recount the same historical disasters, Hudson's conceptualization seems grittier, without a trace of sentimentality or cosy romanticizing of prairie life, though no less eloquent or impassioned than Steinbeck's work. Katherine Anne Porter praised Hudson for just this sense of authenticity: "[Hudson has created] an answer in pure human speech to the sub-human characters in *Grapes of Wrath* . . . Maybe this is because she is within her scene, a living part of it, and not a tourist with a note-book."

In her essay, "On Saving History from the Historians," Hudson writes that in order to truly understand the irreconcilable *fact* of any wholescale disaster, one must begin with "feeling one rape, one death," of experiencing the "'small desolations' that have added up to that incomprehensibly vast desolation." In *The Bones of Plenty* Hudson evokes the whole "desolation" of the Dust Bowl through her rendering of the "small desolations" one family experiences in their last year as "reapers of the dust" of the North Dakota plains.

To this end Hudson invests her narrative with nothing short of a tragic sense by juxtaposing the urgency of time with the human desire for timelessness, symbolized in the idea of *roots*. Her narrative strategy is to isolate a moment in time by choosing a day and telling the story of that day. The first chapter is titled simply, "Friday, February 16, 1933," the last, "Saturday, May 16, [1934]." Yet within each specific moment, Hudson employs another technique which gives a sense of the simultaneity of time and the tragic connection of events. Mighty events are placed against little ones. World events are juxtaposed to the "small desolations" of prairie life, creating a tragic montage of events with workings of its own. Thus she succeeds in creating a nonlinear structure, which is framed by the linear structure of chronology—the tiny "desolations" are set within the larger context of a world in turmoil. Banks may be failing all across the country, but we feel the closing of the Eureka town bank because the characters we have come to know have put their money there.

Take the chapter titled, "Saturday, November 11." It is turkey slaughtering day, the final harvest of the year. But across the plains, form strikes disrupt this final harvest. In New York, a "cloud of dust . . . from the prairies [darkens] the sky . . . as it pass[es] over on its way to sink into the Atlantic." And across the Atlantic, the German Reich withdraws from the League of Nations.

If *time* is the relentless pursuer, then *space* is that spot in the universe where humankind endeavors to hold still, to create places which speak his name. What the book establishes is the terrible cost of putting down *roots*—those connections of culture, craft, and habit which tell us who we are.

The book, to be sure, is full of social protest. Hudson mercilessly exposes the economic system which has betrayed the farmer out of existence, and shows the western myth of rugged individualism to be fatally flawed, a myth that has become as used up as the land itself. The pioneer virtues extolled by the central character George Custer are in marked contrast to the realism of his father-in-law, Will Shepard, who knows that the days of the small farmer are over. Sheer will and strength, even cleverness, are no match for the economic and natural forces unleashed upon the world in 1933. But Hudson's work goes beyond a critique of the economic and political debacle that sent the world into chaos. Her ultimate concern is to affirm the determination of the human spirit to endure the impermanence of existence.

Reapers of the Dust begins where *Bones* leaves off. It is comprised of a series of 12 interlocking stories which trace the family's last months on the prairie and their journey to the Washington coast, where they begin a nomadic life in search of the roots they have lost. The child Lucy, through whose eyes many of the events in *Bones* are shown, becomes the grown narrator of the stories in *Reapers of the Dust*. The stories are bound together by the themes of displacement and loss, and by the redemption the discovery of love provides. Again and again her characters seek out the "landmarks" which will tell them who they are. They search for a configuration of footprints in the snow, a pattern in the prairie sky, the "fresh and green fields" of their innocence, and they look into the faces of their children for intimations of their own immortality.

Both *Reapers* and *Bones* depict the betrayal of good people by a harsh and indifferent universe, the rootlessness and dislocation which follow, and the courage and pride with which they bear their sorrows. Though both *Bones* and *Reapers* chronicle the last grim years of the prairie former, ultimately, Hudson writes not of defeat but of hope. Both works, and the stories of the intervening 20 years, are bound together by a single narrative thread: the search for permanence in a world that has become tragically impermanent.

The Kindly Fruits of the Earth bears mention not only because it has occupied so much of Hudson's life, but because it is a fictional reflection of her years of work as an environmental and human rights activist. The book connects the Abolitionist movement on the East coast with the settlement of California during the tumultuous decade that preceded the Civil War. It describes the devastation to the land as well as the outright genocide of the Native American people of California.

Hudson is a consummate writer who possesses a wondering, remembering eye for the tiniest detail, a keen ear for the rhythms of human speech, and a comic sense that redeems her work from bitterness, a writer whose time has clearly come.

—Ann Putnam

HUFFAKER, Clair. American. Born in Magna, Utah, in 1928. Educated at Princeton University, New Jersey; Columbia University, New York, B.A.; the Sorbonne, Paris. Served in United States Navy during World War II; gunner's mate on aircraft carrier "Ranger." Married: one son. Assistant editor, *Time*, Chicago, Illinois; editor, *Action* magazine; writer and screenwriter, head of production company, 1969–90. *Died in 1990.*

WESTERN PUBLICATIONS

Novels

Badge for a Gunfighter. New York and London, Fawcett, 1957.
Rider from Thunder Mountain. New York, Fawcett, 1957; London, Fawcett, 1959.
Cowboy (novelization of screenplay). New York and London, Fawcett, 1958.
Guns of Rio Conchos. New York, Fawcett, 1958; London, Fawcett, 1959; as *Rio Conchos*, London, Futura, 1975.
Posse from Hell. New York, Fawcett, 1958; London, Fawcett, 1959.
Badman. New York and London, Fawcett, 1958; as *The War Wagon*, London, Gold Lion, 1974.
Flaming Lance. New York, Simon and Schuster, 1958.
Seven Ways from Sundown. New York, Fawcett, 1960; London, Futura, 1974.
Nobody Loves a Drunken Indian. New York, McKay, 1967.
The Cowboy and the Cossack. New York, Trident Press, 1973.
Guns from Thunder Mountain. New York, Pocket Books, 1975.

OTHER PUBLICATIONS

Novel

Good Lord, You're Upside Down! New York, Cornerstone Library, 1963; London, Muller, 1964.

Plays

Screenplays: *Seven Ways from Sundown*, 1960; *Flaming Star*, with Nunnally Johnson, 1960; *Posse from Hell*, 1961; *Comancheros*, with James Edward Grant, 1961; *The Second Time Around*, 1962; *Rio Conchos*, with Joseph Landon, 1964; *Tarzan and the Valley of Gold*, 1966; *The War Wagon*, 1967; *100 Rifles*, with Tom Gries, 1969; *Hellfighters*, 1970; *Flap* (*The Last Warrior*), 1970; *The Deserter* (as Cecil D. Hanse), 1971.

Other

One Time, I Saw Morning Come Home: A Remembrance. New York, Simon and Schuster, 1974.
Clair Huffaker's Profiles of the American West (for children). New York, Pocket Books, 1976.

* * *

With the production of the movie *Flap* in 1970, Clair Huffaker gained national recognition. Huffaker's early western novels had been fairly typical formula westerns (some adapted from film scripts), although his service as a script writer had given him particular effectiveness with plot situation and dialogue. However, *Flap*, which had originally been published as a novel under the title *Nobody Loves a Drunken Indian*, immediately became a popular movie, and the paperback reprints ran through a number of editions. Huffaker had hit the temper of the times, for the novel dealt with the civil rights of the American Indian and, for good measure, the white man's destruction of the natural environment. The novel even begins with Flapping Eagle's (or Flap's) battle against a bulldozer. Most of all, however, Huffaker introduced a protagonist of romantically heroic proportions who could out-drink, out-fight, and out-maneuver his antagonists. Flap is not dissimilar to Kazantzakis's Zorba the Greek. Interestingly enough, in the film version of Huffaker's novel, Anthony Quinn, who had played Zorba on the screen, was given the role of Flap. This bigger-than-life hero charges both the film and the novel with tension and vitality, as well as dialogue, that seemed perfectly appropriate for his satire on "progress" in the American west, and upon American society in general.

Huffaker's other most important novel is *The Cowboy and the Cossack*, which details the delivery of a herd of cattle by a group of freedom-loving American cowboys to a town peopled by anti-Czarist freedom-loving Russians somewhere in the frontiers of Russia. The novel was conceived as a "kind of emotional and spiritual bridge between the American and Russian peoples," and, despite the Russian setting, the novel is replete with all the characteristics of a typical western epic of the trail drive. There is not only a river crossing, there is also a cattle-drive from a ship through the ocean to the shores of Russia. Tartars replace the Indians as the savage forces that must be overcome before the cattle can be delivered, and the Imperial Cossacks serve as the "official" rustlers who must also be overcome by the combined efforts of the cowboys and their counterparts, the small group of freedom-loving independent Cossacks. Of major importance is the gradual respect gained by the cowboys and their Cossack friends as they overcome the superficial differences of language, dress, and traditions by working together in a common endeavor.

Huffaker's best writing is characterized by strong formulaic plots with slightly unusual twists, and a marvelous recreation of western speech. He has a tendency to use certain western tricks (such as a friend shooting a friend to keep him from being tortured, as in both *The Cowboy and the Cossack* and *Rider from Thunder Mountain*) that call attention to themselves, but he manages usually to turn the formula western into exciting and fast-moving novels that stress the masculine values of the Old West.

—Delbert E. Wylder

HUMPHREY, William. American. Born in Clarksville, Texas, 18 June 1924. Educated at Southern Methodist University, Dallas; University of Texas, Austin. Married. Recipient: American Academy award, 1962. Lives in Lexington, Virginia. Address: c/o Delacorte Press, 1 Dag Hammarskjold Plaza, New York, New York 10017, U.S.A.

WESTERN PUBLICATIONS

Novels

Home from the Hill. New York, Knopf, and London, Chatto and Windus, 1958.
The Ordways. New York, Knopf, and London, Chatto and Windus, 1965.
Proud Flesh. New York, Knopf, and London, Chatto and Windus, 1973.
No Resting Place. New York, Delacorte Press, and London, Secker and Warburg, 1989.

Short Stories

The Last Husband and Other Stories. New York, Morrow, and London, Chatto and Windus, 1953.
A Time and a Place: Stories. New York, Knopf, 1968; as *A Time and a Place: Stories of the Red River Country*, London, Chatto and Windus, 1969.
The Collected Stories of William Humphrey. New York, Delacorte Press/Seymour Lawrence, 1985; London, Secker and Warburg, 1986.

Uncollected Short Story

"Mrs. Shumlin's Cow Trixie," in *Esquire* (New York), December 1969.

OTHER PUBLICATIONS

Novel

Hostages to Fortune. New York, Delacorte Press, 1984; London, Secker and Warburg, 1985.

Other

The Spawning Run: A Fable. New York, Knopf, and London, Chatto and Windus, 1970.
Ah, Wilderness! The Frontier in American Literature. El Paso, Texas Western Press, 1977.
Farther Off from Heaven. New York, Knopf, and London, Chatto and Windus, 1977.
My Moby Dick. New York, Doubleday, 1978; London, Chatto and Windus, 1979.
Open Season: Sporting Adventures. New York, Delacorte Press, 1986.

*

Critical Study: *William Humphrey* by James W. Lee, Austin, Texas, Steck Vaughn, 1967.

* * *

Until recent years, most of William Humphrey's literary output was limited to Red River County, Texas. Three novels, two volumes of stories, and an autobiographical volume are set in the rural northeast Texas county that he was born in. It is a region of small farmers and their workworn wives, small businessmen and their families, and large landowners and their retainers, all of whom are pictured in acute detail. And nobody writing about the southwest has ever been better than Humphrey at rendering the speech patterns and the landscape of the region.

Humphrey's ability to capture the essence of east Texas in the 1930's is largely responsible for the nationwide success of his first novel, *Home from the Hill*. The plot of the novel is the familiar American story of the coming to awareness of a young man. Theron Hunnicutt grows up torn between a masculine, powerful father and a prim, frigid, but equally powerful mother. He tries to live down his father's infidelities, but live up to his prowess as hunter, woodsman, and patron of the country. When Captain Wade Hunnicutt is killed by the father of the girl made pregnant by Theron, the young man tracks his father's murderer down, kills him, and disappears into the river bottoms, where, the reader assumes, he dies. The plot of the novel, though well handled through three quarters of the book, is ordinary and perhaps a little too melodramatic. What saves the work, and makes it a Texas classic, is Humphrey's ability to make the folklore, the customs, and the speech of the people of Red River County, Texas seem totally real to the reader.

Home from the Hill is Humphrey's best piece of fiction, but *The Ordways* and *Proud Flesh*, his other two Red River County novels, received good reviews and enjoyed good sales. *The Ordways* traces four generations from the Civil War to the 1920's. The region is, once again, captured by Humphrey's camera eye, and what the novel lacks in unity is made up for by the richness of its setting. For one of the few times in Humphrey's early fiction, the reader is taken out of northeast Texas and shown other parts of the state when Sam Ordway spends a large part of the novel searching for his kidnapped son. The search is standard picaresque, but some of the Red River County scenes are among Humphrey's best.

Proud Flesh treats Humphrey's persistent theme of the effects of place and family upon people, but there is not much new on the subject in his third novel. The region is carefully rendered, the language of the characters is accurate in every detail, and the style is up to Humphrey's usual high standard. But the Renshaw clan is not as interesting a family as the Hunnicutts or the Ordways.

The two volumes of short stories are not especially distinguished, though each has a story or two that would merit discussion in a longer essay. The first volume, *The Last Husband and Other Stories*, appeared five years before Humphrey's first novel and is a good apprentice collection. In it, one can see the beginnings of his interest in the impact of place upon people. The second volume, *A Time and a Place*, was published some 15 years and two novels after his first fiction. But the bits and pieces are well written. A reader cannot complain about style and setting in either collection of stories, but neither volume constitutes Humphrey's best work.

The best writing—perhaps the best work in all respects—is to be found in Humphrey's 1977 autobiographical volume entitled *Farther Off from Heaven*. The events narrated in the book are true, but the story is told in the best tradition of fiction. That is, Humphrey does not merely retail facts but manipulates time, creates character, and makes Clarksville, Texas of the 1930's come to life for the reader.

In the 1980's Humphrey abandoned Red River County for other parts of the country. *Hostages to Fortune* is set in upstate New York, where Humphrey has lived for 40 years. The novel is about the effects of a young man's suicide on his family. The subject is, needless to say, sad, but Humphrey's treatment of the family's suffering is not well sustained throughout the novel. Also missing are the effects of place that made Humphrey's early novels critical successes.

No Resting Place is a novel about the Cherokees of the 1830's who were uprooted from their homeland in North Carolina, Tennessee, and North Georgia and herded west to the less desirable lands of Texas and Oklahoma. The novel follows one group of Indians who are driven like cattle by the Army and made to settle in Texas. Then they are driven from that state and put on a reservation in Oklahoma, then called the Indian Nations. Humphrey's picture of the dispossession of the Indians by white-trash southerners is poignant, as is his description of life on the "trail of tears." But the novel reads more like a historical narrative than a work of fiction.

—James W. Lee

HUNT, John. *See* **PAINE, Lauran.**

HUNTER, John. *See* **BALLARD, Willis Todhunter.**

HUNTER, Neil. *See* **LINAKER, Mike.**

HUTSON, Shaun. *See* **BISHOP, Samuel P.**

INGRAM, Hunter. *See* **LUTZ, Giles A.**

J

JAKES, John (William). Also writes as John Lee Gray; Alan Payne; Rachel Ann Payne; Jay Scotland. American. Born in Chicago, Illinois, 31 March 1932. Educated at DePauw University, Greencastle, Indiana, A.B. 1953; Ohio State University, Columbus, M.A. 1954. Married Rachel Ann Payne in 1951; three daughters and one son. Copywriter, then promotion manager, Abbott Laboratories, North Chicago, 1954–60; copywriter, Rumrill Company, Rochester, New York, 1960–61; freelance writer, 1961–65; copywriter, Kircher Helton and Collett, Dayton, Ohio, 1965–68; copy chief, then vice-president, Oppenheim Herminghausen and Clarke, Dayton, 1968–70; creative director, Dancer Fitzgerald Sample, Dayton, 1970–71. Since 1971 freelance writer. Writer-in-residence, DePauw University, Fall 1979; research fellow, University of South Carolina, Columbia, 1989. Recipient: Porgie award, 1977; Ohio Governor's award, 1977. L.L.D.: Wright State University, Dayton, Ohio, 1976; Litt. D.: DePauw University, 1977. Address: P.O. Box 2287, Hilton Head, South Carolina 29925, U.S.A.

WESTERN PUBLICATIONS

Novels (Series: Kent Family Chronicles)

Wear a Fast Gun. New York, Arcadia House, 1956; London, Ward Lock, 1957.
Six-Gun Planet. New York, Paperback Library, 1970; London, New English Library, 1978.
American Bicentennial Series [Kent Family Chronicles]:
- *The Bastard.* New York, Pyramid, 1974; as *Fortune's Whirlwind* and *To an unknown Shore*, London, Corgi, 2 vols., 1975.
- *The Rebels.* New York, Pyramid, 1975; London, Corgi, 1979.
- *The Seekers.* New York, Pyramid, 1975; London, Corgi, 1979.
- *The Furies.* New York, Pyramid, 1976; London, Corgi, 1979.
- *The Titans.* New York, Pyramid, 1976; London, Corgi, 1979.
- *The Patriots* (includes *The Bastard* and *The Rebels*). Dayton, Ohio, Landfall Press, 1976.
- *The Pioneers* (includes *The Seekers* and *The Furies*). Dayton, Ohio, Landfall Press, 1976.
- *The Warriors.* New York, Pyramid, 1977; London, Corgi, 1979.
- *The Lawless.* New York, Jove, 1978; London, Corgi, 1979.
- *The Americans.* New York, Jove, 1980.

California Gold. New York, Random House, 1989; London, Collins, 1990.

Short Stories

The Best Western Stories of John Jakes, edited by Bill Pronzini. Athens, Ohio University Press/Swallow Press, 1991.

Uncollected Short Stories

"The Woman at Apache Wells," in *The Arbor House Treasury of Great Western Stories*, edited by Bill Pronzini and Martin H. Greenberg. New York, Arbor House, 1982.
"Hell on the High Iron," in *The Railroaders*, edited by Bill Pronzini and Martin H. Greenberg. New York, Fawcett, 1986.
"The Tinhorn Fills His Hand," in *The Steamboaters*, edited by Bill Pronzini and Martin H. Greenberg. New York, Fawcett, 1986.
"The Naked Gun," in *More Wild Westerns*, edited by Bill Pronzini. New York, Walker, 1989.
"Little Phil and the Daughter of Joy" (as John Lee Gray), in *New Frontiers Vol.I*, edited by Martin H. Greenberg and Bill Pronzini. New York, Tor, 1990.
"Snakehead" (as John Lee Gray), in *New Frontiers Vol.II*, edited by Martin H. Greenberg and Bill Pronzini. New York, Tor, 1990.

OTHER PUBLICATIONS

Novels

Gonzaga's Woman. New York, Universal, 1953.
A Night for Treason. New York, Bouregy, 1956.
The Devil Has Four Faces. New York, Bouregy, 1958.
Murder He Says (as Alan Payne). New York, Ace, 1958.
This'll Slay You (as Alan Payne). New York, Ace, 1958.
The Impostor. New York, Bouregy, 1959.
Johnny Havoc. New York, Belmont, 1960.
Johnny Havoc Meets Zelda. New York, Belmont, 1962.
Johnny Havoc and the Doll Who Had "It." New York, Belmont, 1963.
G.I. Girls. Derby, Connecticut, Monarch, 1963.
Ghostwind (as Rachel Ann Payne). New York, Paperback Library, 1966.
When the Star Kings Die. New York, Ace, 1967.
Making It Big. New York, Belmont, 1968.
The Asylum World. New York, Paperback Library, 1969; London, New English Library, 1978.
Brak Versus the Mark of the Demons. New York, Paperback Library, 1969; as *Brak the Barbarian—The Mark of the Demons*, London, Tandem, 1970.
Brak the Barbarian Versus the Sorceress. New York, Paperback Library, 1969; as *Brak the Barbarian—The Sorceress*, London, Tandem, 1970.
The Hybrid. New York, Paperback Library, 1969.
The Last Magicians. New York, New American Library, 1969.
The Planet Wizard. New York, Ace, 1969.
Tonight We Steal the Stars. New York, Ace, 1969.
Black in Time. New York, Paperback Library, 1970.
Mask of Chaos. New York, Ace, 1970.
Master of the Dark Gate. New York, Lancer, 1970.
Monte Cristo 99. New York, Curtis, 1970.

Mention My Name in Atlantis. New York, DAW, 1972.
Witch of the Dark Gate. New York, Lancer, 1972.
Conquest of the Planet of the Apes (novelization of screenplay). New York, Award, 1972.
On Wheels. New York, Paperback Library, 1973.
Brak: When the Idols Walked. New York, Pocket Books, 1978.
Excalibur!, with Gil Kane. New York, Dell, 1980.
North and South Trilogy:
North and South. New York, Harcourt Brace, and London, Collins, 1982.
Love and War. San Diego, California, Harcourt Brace, 1984; London, Collins, 1985.
Heaven and Hell. San Diego, California, Harcourt Brace, and London, Collins, 1987.

Novels as Jay Scotland

The Seventh Man. New York, Bouregy, 1958.
I, Barbarian. New York, Avon, 1959; revised edition, as John Jakes, New York, Pinnacle, 1976.
Strike the Black Flag. New York, Ace, 1961.
Sir Scoundrel. New York, Ace, 1962; revised edition, as *King's Crusader*, New York, Pyramid, 1977.
The Veils of Salome. New York, Avon, 1962.
Arena. New York, Ace, 1963.
Traitors' Legion. New York, Ace, 1963; revised edition, as *The Man from Cannae*, New York, Pyramid, 1977.

Short Stories

Brak the Barbarian. New York, Avon, 1968; London, Tandem, 1970.
The Best of John Jakes, edited by Martin H. Greenberg and Joseph D. Olander. New York, DAW, 1977.
Fortunes of Brak. New York, Dell, 1980.

Plays

Dracula, Baby (lyrics only). Chicago, Dramatic Publishing Company, 1970.
Wind in the Willows. Elgin, Illinois, Performance, 1972.
A Spell of Evil. Chicago, Dramatic Publishing Company, 1972.
Violence. Elgin, Illinois, Performance, 1972.
Stranger with Roses, adaptation of his own story. Chicago, Dramatic Publishing Company, 1972.
For I Am a Jealous People, adaptation of a story by Lester del Rey. Elgin, Illinois, Performance, 1972.
Gaslight Girl. Chicago, Dramatic Publishing Company, 1973.
Pardon Me, Is This Planet Taken? Chicago, Dramatic Publishing Company, 1973.
Doctor, Doctor! music by Gilbert M. Martin, adaptation of a play by Molière. New York, McAfee Music, 1973.
Shepherd Song. New York, McAfee Music, 1974.
A Christmas Carol, adapted from the novel by Charles Dickens, (produced Alabama, 1989).

Other

The Texans Ride North (for children). Philadelphia, Winston, 1952.
Tiros: Weather Eye in Space. New York, Messner, 1966.
Famous Firsts in Sports. New York, Putnam, 1967.
Great War Correspondents. New York, Putnam, 1968.
Great Women Reporters. New York, Putnam, 1969.
Secrets of Stardeep (for children). Philadelphia, Westminster Press, 1969.
Mohawk: The Life of Joseph Brant. New York, Crowell, 1969.
Time Gate (for children). Philadelphia, Westminster Press, 1972.
The Bastard Photostory. New York, Jove, 1980.
Susanna at the Alamo: A True Story (for children). San Diego, Harcourt Brace, 1986.

*

Manuscript Collections: DePauw University, Greencastle, Indiana; University of Wyoming, Laramie.

* * *

John Jakes started his writing career in the 1950's specializing in short fiction—Westerns, spy thrillers, adventure stories, science fiction, and fantasy—yet achieved international success in the 1970's for his American Bicentennial Series that traced American history through the use of the family saga.

Jakes's early books were Westerns: *The Texans Ride North* was a children's novel with a shallow plot and cardboard characters. Jakes's next western was a more mature effort, *Wear a Fast Gun*, which began a relationship with Ace Books that continued into the 1960's when Ace published four of Jakes's historical novels under the pseudonym of Jay Scotland and three science-fiction novels under his own name.

Wear a Fast Gun features Reb Fallon, gunfighter, who becomes sheriff of Longhorn to rid the town of a wild band of nightriders who are terrorizing the ranchers and rustling their herds. Fallon falls in love, unmasks the nightriders, and fights his way to a savage conclusion. The strength of the book is Jakes's care in developing the characters within a clichéd plot.

Although Jakes abandoned westerns until he was writing the American Bicentennial Series. In the mid-1970's, he did publish a pastiche of the western genre in science-fiction terms with *Six-Gun Planet*, where the human colony on the planet Missouri duplicated the Old West right down to robot pintos.

Jakes's best writing, and best treatment of the West, is in the American Bicentennial Series. In Volume 3, *The Seekers*, the Tennessee and Ohio homesteads endure Indian attacks as Abraham Kent becomes part of the drive westward. Volume 4, *The Furies*, has the Kent Family at the siege of the Alamo and later in the Californian Gold Rush. Volume 5, *The Titans*, presents the tragedy of the Civil War. Volume 6, *The Warriors*, shows the Civil War coming to an end while the Union Pacific Railroad moves westward and Indian attacks become worse. Volume 7, *The Lawless*, comes closest to the traditional western with its cattle booms and the settling of the United States from coast to coast. Even Wild Bill Hickok is on hand to keep things stirred up in Abilene and Deadwood.

After the success of that series, Jakes turned to the period of American history that fascinated him most: the Civil War. In three mammoth volumes—*North and South, Love and War, Heaven and Hell*—Jakes traces the fate of two families, one from the North, one from the South, through the beginning of the Civil War, the famous battles, and the dismal aftermath of Reconstruction. Although successful, these books lacked the freshness of the American Bicentennial Series.

Jakes's latest effort, *California Gold*, is one of his weakest books as he chronicles the life of James Macklin Chance, a poor youth from Pennsylvania, who goes to California to seek his fortune at the beginning of the 20th century and finds himself in a soap opera plot right out of *Dallas* and *Dynasty*. Although this is a fascinating historical period featuring greats like Teddy Roosevelt and William Randolph Hearst, Jakes's clichéd plot of Chance's climb to the top overwhelms the history.

Jakes has emerged as one of the world's best-selling authors. But before the fame, Jakes produced solid western writing that later found its way into his famous American Bicentennial Series, particularly in the volumes presenting the history of the settling of the Old West.

—George Kelley

JAMES, Cary. *See* **RICHARDSON, Gladwell.**

JAMES, Cy. *See* **CHISHOLM, Matt.**

JAMES, Dan. *See* **BARDWELL, Denver.**

JAMES, Laurence. Also writes as James Axler; L.J. Coburn; James Darke; Charles C. Garrett; Mary Fraser; Arthur Frazier; Thomas Goane; Richard Haigh; William M. James; Neil Langholm; Jonathan May; James W. Marvin; John J. McLaglen; James Mcphee; Klaus Netzen; Mick Norman; Andrew Quiller. British. Born in West Bromwich, Staffordshire, in 1942. Educated at King Edward's School, Edgbaston, West Midlands; Goldsmith's College, London. Married Elizabeth Laurence in 1965; one daughter and two sons. Bookseller for Foyles and Harrods; editor, Leslie Frewin, publishers, 1968; editor, New English Library, 1970–73. Full-time writer. Address: c/o Sphere Books Ltd., Orbit House, 1 New Fetter Lane, London EC4P 4EE, England.

WESTERN PUBLICATIONS

Novels as James W. Marvin (series: Crow)

1. *The Red Hills.* London, Corgi, 1979.
2. *Worse Than Death.* London, Corgi, 1979.
3. *Tears of Blood.* London, Corgi, 1980.
4. *The Black Trail.* London, Corgi, 1980.
5. *Body Guard.* London, Corgi, 1981.
6. *The Sisters.* London, Corgi, 1981.
7. *One-Eyed Death.* London, Corgi, 1982.
8. *A Good Day.* London, Corgi, 1982.

Novels as Charles C. Garrett (series: Gunslinger)

1. *The Massacre Trail.* London, Sphere, 1977.
3. *White Apache.* London, Sphere, 1978.
5. *Arizona Bloodline.* London, Sphere, 1979.
7. *Death Canyon.* London, Sphere, 1979.
10. *Blood Target.* London, Sphere, 1981.

Novels as L.J. Coburn (series: Caleb Thorn)

1. *The First Shot.* London, Sphere, 1977.
3. *Brotherly Death.* London, Sphere, 1978.
5. *Death River.* London, Sphere, 1978.

Novels as John J. MacLaglen (series: Herne the Hunter)

1. *White Death.* London, Corgi, 1976.
3. *The Black Widow.* London, Corgi, 1977.
5. *Apache Squaw.* London, Corgi, 1977.
7. *Death Rites.* London, Corgi, 1978.
9. *Massacre!* London, Corgi, 1978.
11. *Silver Threads.* London, Corgi, 1979.
14. *Death School.* London, Corgi, 1980.
16. *Geronimo.* London, Corgi, 1981.
17. *The Hanging.* London, Corgi, 1981.
19. *Bloodline.* London, Corgi, 1982.
21. *Pony Express.* London, Corgi, 1983.
23. *Texas Massacre.* London, Corgi, 1984.
24. *The Last Hurrah!* London, Corgi, 1984.

Novels as William M. James (series: Apache)

2. *Knife in the Night.* London, Sphere, and New York, Pinnacle, 1974.
4. *Death Train.* London, Sphere, and New York, Pinnacle, 1975.
7. *Blood Line.* London, Sphere, and New York, Pinnacle, 1976.
9. *The Naked and the Savage.* London, New English Library, and New York, Pinnacle, 1977.
11. *The Cruel Trail.* London, New English Library, 1978.
12. *Fool's Gold.* New York, Pinnacle, 1978; London, New English Library, 1979.
14. *Born to Die.* New York, Pinnacle, 1979.
16. *Texas Killing.* New York, Pinnacle, 1980.
18. *Slow Dying.* New York, Pinnacle, 1980.
19. *Fast Living.* New York, Pinnacle, 1981.
21. *Blood Wedding.* New York, Pinnacle, 1981.
22. *Border Killing.* New York, Pinnacle, 1982.
23. *Death Valley.* New York, Pinnacle, 1983.
25. *Times Past.* New York, Pinnacle, 1983.

Uncollected Short Story

"New Blood," in *Western Magazine*, 1979.

OTHER PUBLICATIONS

Novels

Earth Lies Sleeping. London, Sphere, and New York, Zebra, 1974.

Starcross. London, Sphere, 1974; as *War on Aleph*, New York, Zebra, 1974.

Backflash. London, Sphere, and New York, Zebra, 1975.
Planet of the Blind. London, Sphere, and New York, Zebra, 1975.
New Life for Old. London, Sphere, 1975.
Endgame (as James Mann), with John Harvey. London, New English Library, 1982.
The Road. London, New English Library, 1983.
Paradise Lost. London, New English Library, 1984.

Novels as Klaus Netzen

To Win and To Lose. St. Albans, Hertfordshire, Mayflower, 1974.
The Winston Churchill Murder. St. Albans, Hertfordshire, Mayflower, 1974.
Night and Fog. St. Albans, Hertfordshire, Mayflower, 1974.
The Fatal Friends. St. Albans, Hertfordshire, Mayflower, 1975.
Pearl of Blood. St. Albans, Hertfordshire, Mayflower, 1975.
Death Village. St. Albans, Hertfordshire, Mayflower, 1976.
The Silent Enemy. St. Albans, Hertfordshire, Mayflower, 1976.

Novels as Andrew Quiller

The Hill of the Dead. St. Albans, Hertfordshire, Mayflower, 1976.
Blood on the Sand. St. Albans, Hertfordshire, Mayflower, 1977.

Novels as Thomas Goane

Journal of a Young Rake. London, Hodder and Stoughton, 1977.
Journal of a Navvy. London, Hodder and Stoughton, 1977.
Journal of a Prize-Fighter. London, Hodder and Stoughton, 1977.
Journal of a Jailbird. London, Hodder and Stoughton, 1978.
Journal of a Cavalry Officer. London, Hodder and Stoughton, 1978.
Journal of a Slaver. London, Hodder and Stoughton, 1978.

Novels as Richard Haigh

The Farm. London, Grafton, 1984.
The City. London, Grafton, 1986.

Novels as Jonathan May

Confessions of a Shop Assistant. London, Sphere, 1974.
Confessions of a Travel Courier. London, Sphere, 1975.
Confessions from the Beat. London, Sphere, 1975.
Confessions of a Games Master. London, Sphere, 1975.
Confessions from a Strip Club. London, Sphere, 1976.
Confessions of a Housewife. London, Sphere, 1976.
Confessions from a Sex Clinic. London, Sphere, 1977.
Confessions of a Stuntman. London, Sphere, 1977.
Confessions of a Gasman. London, Sphere, 1977.
Confessions of an Astronaut. London, Sphere, 1978.
Confessions from a Stud Farm. London, Sphere, 1978.
Confessions from the Olympics. London, Sphere, 1980.

Novels as Arthur Frazier

A Light in the West. London, New English Library, 1974.
Viking Slaughter. London, New English Library, 1974.

Novels as Mary Fraser

The First Summer. London, Sphere, 1979.
The Long Winter. London, Sphere, 1979.
Time of Change. London, Sphere, 1980.

Novels as Neil Langholm

Blood Sacrifices. London, Sphere, and New York, Pinnacle, 1975.
The Sun in the Night. London, Sphere, and New York, Pinnacle, 1976.

Novels as James Axler

Red Holocaust. Toronto, Gold Eagle/Harlequin, 1987.
Neutron Solstice. Toronto, Gold Eagle/Harlequin, 1987.
Crater Lake. Toronto, Gold Eagle/Harlequin, 1987.
Homeward Bound. Toronto, Harlequin, 1988.
Pony Soldiers. Toronto, Harlequin, 1988.
Deccra Chain. Toronto, Gold Eagle/Harlequin, 1988.
Ice and Fire. Toronto, Gold Eagle/Harlequin, 1988.
Red Equinox. Toronto, Gold Eagle/Harlequin, 1989.
Northstar Rising. Toronto, Harlequin, 1989.
Time Nomads. Toronto, Harlequin, 1990.
Latitude Zero. Toronto, Harlequin, 1990.
Seedling. Toronto, Harlequin, 1991.
Beyond Time. Toronto, Harlequin, 1991.

Novels as Mick Norman

Angels from Hell. London, New English Library, 1973.
Angel Challenge. London, New English Library, 1973.
Guardian Angels. London, New English Library, 1974.
Angels on My Mind. London, New English Library, 1974.

Novels as James Darke

The Prisoner. London, Sphere, 1983.
The Trial. London, Sphere, 1983.
The Torture. London, Sphere, 1983.
The Escape. London, Sphere, 1984.
The Meeting. London, Sphere, 1985.
The Killing. London, Sphere, 1985.
The Feud. London, Sphere, 1986.
The Plague. London, Sphere, 1986.

Novels as James McPhee

Blood Quest. Toronto, Gold Eagle, 1991.
Renegade War. Toronto, Gold Eagle, 1991.
Frozen Fire. Toronto, Gold Eagle, 1991.

Fiction (for children)

First and Ten, with Matthew James. London, Methuen, 1987.
Second and Five, with Matthew James. London, Methuen, 1987.
Touchdown! with Matthew James. London, Methuen, 1987.
Third and Goal, with Matthew James. London, Blackie, 1988.

Home Run, with Matthew James. London, Methuen, 1988.
Grand Slam, with Matthew James. London, Methuen, 1988.
Running Back, with Matthew James. London, Methuen, 1988.
End Zone, with Matthew James. London, Methuen, 1989.
Outside Shot, with Matthew James. London, Mammoth, 1989.
Tunnel Vision. London, Blackie, 1989.
The Past's Present. London, Blackie, 1989.
The Revengers. London, Transworld, 1991.
Beyond the Grave. London, Transworld, 1992.
Horned God. London, Transworld, 1992.
The Gift. London, Transworld, 1993.

Other

Dracula (comic annual and monthly magazine; English text). London, New English Library, 1973.

Editor, *Electric Underground: A City Lights Reader*. London, New English Library, 1973.

* * *

While the name of Laurence James is not synonymous with Westerns, those of John J. McLaglen, William M. James, and James W. Marvin, to name but a few, are. The bulk of James's western career has been shared with several other English authors. His work is distinguished by realistic violence and period detail—based on many visits to the United States—and with a leavening of dark humour. The series of books on Herne the Hunter, written under the name of John J. McLaglen, are among his best work. Jedediah Herne, the hero of the series, an old retired gunfighter, who straps on his Colt .45 to exact vengeance on his wife's killers. In all James wrote 13 books in the series, and helped to create a memorable central character. Taking Herne through the mechanics of the modern Western, the storylines hit their stride with some varied plots. Kidnapping appears in both *Apache Squaw* and *Death Rites;* a flashback to Herne's days with the Quantrill Raiders at Lawrence, Kansas in *Massacre!* Herne pitting his wits against two seemingly harmless sisters and their brood, who run a town and are actively concerned in embezzling the local silver mine, in *Silver Threads*. In *The Hanging*, he is involved in a case of mistaken identity, and becomes both the hunted and the hunter. It is rare in a western series that the hero actually meets his death, but in *The Last Hurrah!* Jed Herne does. Throughout this series Herne is portrayed as a flawed hero. He is essentially a loser, never actually obtaining anything positive, but generally leaves things better than they were before he moves on.

The Caleb Thorn series, James's only foray into the Civil War, was not the success he had hoped for. *The First Shot*, *Brotherly Death*, and *Death River* were his contributions to the series, and all are action-packed books, with Thorn and his Raiders riding through some pretty bloodthirsty adventures. Again, the series uses revenge as its initial catalyst. James believes that there must be such a catalyst to make a man take the law into his own hands, and the revenge motive is the most powerful motive there is. Thorn misuses his position to direct his hatred against the Confederate Army, who killed his family.

James's involvement with the Apache books, under the William M. James byline, saw his biggest output in one series, writing 14 novels in all. He and Terry Harknett (and later John Harvey), took as their theme the American Indian as "noble savage," putting Cuchillo Oro, ("Golden Knife"), centre-stage as the principal character of the series. In doing so, they ran counter to many other western writers, who tend to present the Indian solely as an antagonist. Throughout the stories, Cuchillo Oro has mixed loyalties; does he serve the Indian people, or the whites? The Apache is spurred on through his adventures in his desire to get his revenge on a cavalry officer, who mutilated his right hand. He does so, but only in a much later book. The novels are often bloody and violent, and the victims cannot rely on their gender to save them. Scores of deaths, mutilations, and rapes pepper the whole series, but the unusual angle of the books' outlook makes for an intriguing read.

In Crow, the only series that James wrote on his own, he created a character who is virtually psychopathic. Dressed from head to toe in black, save for the yellow cavalry bandana at his throat, Crow is the epitome of evil. Whether shotgunning a wayward dog or stomping on a lizard, his outrages go against the grain of James's previous belief that a man doesn't kill for fun. During the series the tall killer clashes with Indians and Cavalry alike, using both sides to satisfy his blood-lust. James's trademark is his use of graphic dialogue and vivid descriptions of death and dying. He feels strongly that violence, when shown, should be explicit, and should be shown as painful. In *Tears of Blood* Crow is forced to face a mouthy would-be killer. Using his sawn-down Purdey, he dispatches the kid thus . . . "The shot took away most of his belly, cutting under the floating ribs, into the welded mass of soft intestines, driving through with a fearful impact, some of the buckshot angling upwards to burst the boy's heart into tatters of torn muscles and blood." The series goes on in similar vein with Crow competing for the Marquis de Sade's crown.

With the Gunslinger series, co-written with Angus Wells, the approach to the format was entirely different from anything James had written before. He made the central character, John Ryker, a gunsmith, gave him a seemingly inexhaustible supply of different weapons, and created the series around them. *The Massacre Trail* concerns a Derringer that he sold to John Wilkes Booth, and the result eventually leads Ryker to become a killer himself. *White Apache* has the Gatling-gun as the centrepiece, and warring Mescalero Apaches doing their best to make life difficult for Ryker. *Arizona Bloodline* has Ryker helping an old enemy to recapture his kidnapped daughter, with a 12-gauge English shotgun for company. *Death Canyon* pits Ryker and his Winchester .73 against Quartermain, an English hunter out to kill the gunsmith. *Blood Target* was the last in the series and concerned a prized Schuetzen rifle. The series managed to combine a well-paced story incorporating some heavy technical sections on weaponry.

James's heroes, whether Jed Herne, Cuchillo Oro, or Crow, are like a blunt instrument moving through the West. They never actually achieve riches, and none becomes happy. As James says, "There's no such thing as a happy western hero. Never. They can't be. They've got to be men alone. They've got to be heroes."

—Mike Stotter

JAMES, Livia. *See* **REASONER, James M.; WASHBURN, L. J.**

JAMES, Will(iam Roderick). Pseudonym for Joseph Ernest Nephtali Dufault. Canadian. Born in St. Nazaire de Acton, Quebec, 6 June 1892. Educated at a Catholic primary school, Montreal; California School of Fine Arts, San Francisco, 1919;

Yale University School of Fine Art, New Haven, Connecticut, 1921. Served in the United States Army, 1918–19. Married Alice Conradt in 1920 (separated 1935). Worked as cowhand, rodeo rider, stuntman for Thomas Ince Studio, Hollywood. Served a prison sentence for cattle rustling, 1915. Recipient: American Library Association Newbery Medal, 1927. *Died 3 September 1942.*

WESTERN PUBLICATIONS

Novels

The Three Mustangeers. New York and London, Scribner, 1933.
Home Ranch. New York and London, Scribner, 1935.
Flint Spears, Cowboy Rodeo Contestant. New York, Scribner, 1938.
The American Cowboy. New York, Scribner, 1942.

Short Stories

Book of Cowboy Stories. New York, Scribner, 1951; London, Phoenix House, 1952.

OTHER PUBLICATIONS

Fiction (for children)

Smoky the Cowhorse. New York and London, Scribner, 1926.
Sand. New York and London, Scribner, 1929.
Sun Up: Tales of the Cow Camps. New York and London, Scribner, 1931.
Big Enough. New York and London, Scribner, 1931.
Uncle Bill: A Tale of Two Kinds of Cowboy. New York and London, Scribner, 1932.
In the Saddle with Uncle Bill. New York and London, Scribner, 1935.
Young Cowboy. New York, Scribner, 1935.
Scorpion, A Good Bad Horse. New York and London, Scribner, 1936.
Look-See with Uncle Bill. New York and London, Scribner, 1939.
The Dark Horse. New York and London, Scribner, 1939.
My First Horse. New York, Scribner, 1940.
Horses I've Known. New York, Scribner, 1940.

Other

Cowboys North and South (for children). New York and London, Scribner, 1924.
Drifting Cowboy (for children). New York and London, Scribner, 1925.
Cow Country (for children). New York and London, Scribner, 1927.
Lone Cowboy: My Life Story (for children). New York and London, Scribner, 1930.
All in a Day's Riding. New York and London, Scribner, 1933.
Cowboy in the Making (for children). New York and London, Scribner, 1937.
The Will James Cowboy Book (for children), edited by Alice Dalgliesh. New York, Scribner, 1938.

Illustrator: *Wild Animal Homesteads* by Enos A. Mills, 1923; *Tombstone: An Iliad of the Southwest* by Walter Noble Burns, 1933.

*

Critical Studies: *Will James, The Gilt Edged Cowboy* by Anthony A. Amaral, Los Angeles, Westernlore Press, 1967; revised edition, as *Will James: The Last Cowboy Legend*, Reno, University of Nevada Press, 1980; *Will James: The Life and Work of a Lone Cowboy* by William Gardner Bell, Flagstaff, Arizona, Northland Press, 1987.

* * *

Even at his death in 1942 Will James's once relatively bright literary reputation was in eclipse. By that time the spokesman for the West who had once been enthusiastically hailed as an authentic voice of the American cowboy had been consigned to imaginative limbo as a children's author and then, perhaps mercifully, forgotten. No one today will quarrel with this assessment of James's place in the western literary pantheon. Anthony Amaral, his most perceptive critic and biographer, notes a steady decline in James's work beginning soon after publication of his greatest success, *Smoky the Cowhorse*, in 1926. Amaral suggests that this decline is most obviously indicated by James's retreat into the conventions of pulp western fiction, and again few would disagree. Nevertheless, the question remains open as to the reasons behind James's retreat from western fact into cliché, and the answer becomes even more difficult when one reflects that James had lived much of his life as an authentic cowboy and, from the beginning to the end of his literary career, wrote very largely out of his own personal experience with ranch life.

A partial explanation may be found by contemplating the fact—only recently discovered by Amaral—that almost all of James's autobiography, *Lone Cowboy* (1930), is a complete fabrication. Even if one admits that no autobiography can legitimately be held up to the canon of unsparing objectivity, nonetheless the kind of fabrication James undertakes in *Lone Cowboy* is instructive. For this fictional fantasy about his own life conforms not only to the clichés of western pulp fiction, but even more strongly to the clichés of children's adventure stories. The fantasy is peculiarly regressive: young James, orphaned at an early age, is raised by a trapper he calls Bopy (his childish misunderstanding of the French "Beaupré") who guides him through a western American version of the pre-adolescent world of *The Purple Island*, *Swiss Family Robinson*, and other such books. It is a world filled with adventures which have no serious consequences, with romantic deserted ghost towns, with friendly cowboys, and with an ever-present opportunity for young Will's escape should present surroundings prove too hard to handle—his own horse. The ambience of *Lone Cowboy*, in short, is one where perils are both external and unreal, where all strangers are friendly and no big animals ever bite. For all its apparent excitement and danger, the world of *Lone Cowboy* is finally a snug and comfortable one in which, as in the world of childhood fantasy, perils only *look* serious.

Much the same pattern is evident in James's avowedly fictional works, not all of which were ostensibly written only for children. Though things may seem grave for Smoky, we know that his loving master Clint will somehow rescue him from the perils that surround him, as in fact happens; in *Sand* we are always comfortably aware that the relationship between the hero and his ornery horse will ultimately turn into one of mutual trust and respect, and even in *The Three Mustangeers* we know that no harm can come to the just boy—at least to the just boy who is lucky enough to have three noble-hearted bad men for tutors in the art of horsemanship and in gentlemanly manners toward his Ma.

That James's fiction is incurably optimistic is of course no good reason for the adult reader not to read it. That his optimism depends entirely upon the values of a child's world, to which one cannot return because it never in fact existed, is.

—James K. Folsom

JAMES, William M. *See* **GILMAN, George G.; HARVEY, John; JAMES, Laurence.**

JEFFERS, H. Paul. American. Address: c/o Zebra Books, 475 Park Avenue South, New York, New York 10016, U.S.A.

WESTERN PUBLICATIONS

Novels (series: Morgan in all titles)

Morgan. New York, Zebra, 1989.
Blood on the Nueces. New York, Zebra, 1989.
Texas Bounty. New York, Zebra, 1989.

OTHER PUBLICATIONS

Novels

Rubout at the Onyx. New Haven, Connecticut, Ticknor and Fields, 1981.
Murder Most Irregular. New York, St. Martin's Press, 1983; London, Hale, 1984.
Murder on Mike. New York, St. Martin's Press, 1984.
A Portrait in Murder and Gay Colours. Stamford, Connecticut, Knights Press, 1985.
The Rag Doll Murder. New York, Ballantine, 1987.
Gods and Lovers. Stamford, Connecticut, Knights Press, 1989.
Secret Orders. New York, Zebra, 1989.

Other

Gallant Women, with Margaret Chase Smith. New York, McGraw Hill, 1968.
How the U.S. Senate Works: The ABM Debate. New York, McGraw Hill, 1970.
The C.I.A.: A Close Look at the Central Intelligence Agency. New York, Lion Press, 1970.
See Parris and Die: Brutality in the U.S. Marines, with Dick Levitan. New York, Hawthorn, 1971.
Wanted by the F.B.I. New York, Hawthorn, 1972.
Sex in the Executive Suite, with Dick Levitan. Chicago, Playboy Press, 1972.
Murder Along the Way: A Prosecutor's Personal Account of Fighting Violent Crime in the Suburbs. New York, Pharos, 1989.

Editor, with Everett McKinley Dirksen, *Gallant Men: Stories of American Adventures.* New York, McGraw Hill, 1967.
Editor, *The Adventure of the Stalwart Companions.* New York, Harper, 1978; London, Cassell, 1979.

* * *

It is strange when you stop to consider the number of thriller or detective writers who have turned their hand to western writing—Ed Gorman, Terry Harknett, Loren D. Estleman, Alistair MacLean, and Elmore Leonard to name but a few. Now H. Paul Jeffers has joined that ever-growing list. His works in the mystery field have given Jeffers the ability to create characters and strong plots, which are easily transposed to the western genre.

Morgan is the first in a trilogy of books based on the exploits of Hugh Morgan. In this book we are introduced to a young, innocent, barefooted kid caught up in the opening of the Civil War. This cliché-ridden opening has Ward Kimball, an influential character, telling Morgan after the youngster had killed his first man, "What counts isn't who shoots first, what counts is who shoots true." Unfortunately, Morgan's character becomes a caricature, based upon Jeffers's own concept of what makes a hero.

It would be harsh to judge the series from this point, because the books do actually improve. Even though he is 15 years old, Morgan discovers that he enjoys killing, and despite advice from Hank Kidder, a war correspondent who befriends the farmboy, he goes on to join up with George Custer's Seventh Cavalry. Suddenly, sick of the senseless killing going on all around him, Morgan decides that he should leave Custer to his fate and head for Kansas.

Now we enter a different phase of Morgan's growing into manhood. We have already seen that he is an impressionable youngster, quick-on-the-draw, and ready to protect his honour and those who he considers friends. One particular character, California Joe, treats him like a son, and by that token is a substitute father figure for Morgan, who loses his family early on in the book. The rest of *Morgan* is the story of his rise to fame as a gunslinger in Abilene.

The following books, *Blood on the Nueces* and *Texas Bounty*, continue the saga of Morgan's development. The plots for the series remain traditional. *Blood on the Nueces* centres on Morgan's search for retribution when his cattle boss, and friend, is killed by Mexican bandits. In the remainder of the book he becomes romantically entangled with Rebecca Colter, the dead boss's daughter, and becomes her trail-boss and lover.

Texas Bounty sees the two marry, and here's where the series seems to go awry. This books contains huge chunks of previously written passages acting as padding for the story, which in itself is rather thinly plotted. It is by far the worst written of the series, as Jeffers tends to concentrate on Rebecca as the central character. It is not until 200 pages into the book that the reader is reunited with Morgan—the true central character of the book.

The Morgan series could be best described as a rambling adventure story with some romance thrown in for good measure. Of Hugh Morgan, we are told a great deal; from farmboy with a fondness of quoting Shakespeare and other classic writers to a hardened gunfighter, with no man to match him. On the one hand he is a steroetyped character but on the other, by giving him an unusual upbringing Jeffers attempts to bring a different quality to his protagonist.

Throughout the trilogy, Jeffers treats his readers to history lessons; albeit overbearing at times, this makes for interesting reading. Firstly, it's the Civil War, then Custer's Indian Campaign, and then the rise and eventual fall of Abilene as a cow-town. We are told details of the cattle drive, the hardships which the cowboys had to endure and the mettle needed to run an outfit. In every instance, Hugh Morgan is able to conquer anything or anyone opposing him, a superman in the true sense of the word. Only at the end of *Texas Bounty* do we actually see a glimmer of humanity in an older Morgan. This is where his sons are gunned down in cold blood by an unsavoury character first introduced in *Morgan*. No longer with a reason to carry on the Morgan empire he had built for himself, he hands it over to his *segundo* and rides away.

What Jeffers is good at is giving the reader an assortment of rich characters who breathe life into his books. From the whole spectrum of human beings who appear in the stories—barkeepers, prostitutes, colonels, ranchers, segundo and ranch-hands—Jeffers can, and does, create believable characters.

—Mike Stotter

JEFFORD, Bat. *See* **BINGLEY, David Ernest.**

JENKINS, Will(iam) F(itzgerald). Also wrote as Murray Leinster. American. Born in Norfolk, Virginia, 16 June 1896. Educated in public and private schools in Norfolk. Served with the committee of Public Information, and in the United States Army, 1917–18; served in the Office of War Information during World War II. Married Mary Mandola in 1921; three daughters and one son. Freelance writer from 1918. Recipient: *Liberty* award, 1937; Hugo award, 1956. Guest of Honor, 21st World Science Fiction Convention, 1963. *Died 8 June 1975.*

WESTERN PUBLICATIONS

Novels

The Gamblin' Kid. New York, King, 1933; London, Eldon Press, 1934.
Mexican Trail. New York, King, 1933; London, Eldon Press, 1935.
Fighting Horse Valley. New York, King, 1934; London, Eldon Press, 1935.
Outlaw Sheriff. New York, King, 1934; as *Rustlin' Sheriff*, London, Eldon Press, 1934.
The Kid Deputy. New York, King, and London, Eldon Press, 1935.
Outlaw Guns (as Murray Leinster). New York, Star, n.d.; as *Wanted—Dead or Alive!*, London, Wright and Brown, 1951.
Texas Gun Slinger (as Murray Leinster). New York, Star, n.d.
Dallas (novelization of screenplay). New York, Fawcett, 1950; London, Muller, 1961.
Son of the Flying "Y." New York, Fawcett, 1951; London, Muller, 1957.
Cattle Rustlers. London, Ward Lock, 1952.

OTHER PUBLICATIONS

Novels

Sword of Kings. London, Long, 1933.
Murder Will Out. London, John Hamilton, 1932.
Murder in the Family. London, John Hamilton, 1935.
No Clues. London, Wright and Brown, 1935.
Black Sheep. New York, Messer, and London, Eldon Press, 1936.
Guns for Achin. London, Wright and Brown, 1936.
The Man who Feared. New York, Gateway, 1942.
The Murder of the U.S.A. New York, Crown, 1946; as *Destroy the U.S.A.*, New York, Newsstand, 1950.

Novels as Murray Leinster

Scalps. New York, Brewer and Warren, 1930; as *Wings of Chance*, London, John Hamilton, 1935.
Murder Mystery. New York, Harcourt Brace, 1930.
Murder Madness. New York, Brewer and Warren, 1931.
The Last Space Ship. New York, Fell, 1949; London, Cherry Tree, 1952.
Fight for Life. New York, Crestwood, n.d.
Gateway to Elsewhere. New York, Ace, 1954.
The Forgotten Planet. New York, Gnome Press, 1954.
The Brain-Stealers. New York, Ace, 1954; London, Badger, 1960.
Operation: Outer Space. Reading, Pennsylvania, Fantasy Press, 1954; London, Grayson, 1957.
The Black Galaxy. New York, Galaxy, 1954.
The Other Side of Here. New York, Ace, 1955.
Colonial Survey. New York, Gnome Press, 1957; as *The Planet Explorer*, New York, Avon, 1957.
War with the Gizmos. New York, Fawcett, 1958; London, Muller, 1959.
The Monster from Earth's End. New York, Fawcett, 1959; London, Muller, 1960.
The Mutant Weapon. New York, Ace, 1959.
The Pirates of Zan. New York, Ace, 1959.
Four from Planet 5. New York, fawcet, 1959; London, White Lion, 1974.
The Wailing Asteroid. New York, Avon, 1960.
Creatures of the Abyss. New York, Berkley, 1961; as *The Listeners*, London, Sidgwick and Jackson, 1969.
This World Is Taboo. New York, Ace, 1961.
Talents, Incorporated. New York, Avon, 1962.
Operation Terror. New York, Berkley, 1962; London, Tandem, 1968.
The Duplicators. New York, Ace, 1964.
The Other Side of Nowhere. New York, Berkley, 1964.
Time Tunnel. New York, Pyramid, 1964.
The Greks Bring Gifts. New York, Macfadden, 1964.
Invaders of Space. New York, Berkley, 1964; London, Tandem, 1968.
Space Captain. New York, Ace, 1966.
Checkpoint Lambda. New York, Berkley, 1966; in *A Murray Leinster Omnibus*, London, Sidgwick and Jackson, 1968.
The Time Tunnel (novelization of TV series). New York, Pyramid, 1967; London, Sidewick and Jackson, 1971.
Miners in the Sky. New York, Avon, 1967.
Space Gypsies. New York, Avon, 1967.
Timeslip! (novelization of TV series). New York, Pyramid, 1967.
Land of the Giants (novelization of TV play). New York, Pyramid, 1968.
The Hot Spot (Novelization of TV play). New York, Pyramid, 1969.
Unknown Danger (Novelization of TV play). New York, Pyramid, 1969.

Short Stories

Sidewise in Time. Chicago, Shasta, 1950.
Out of This World. New York, Avalon, 1958.
Monsters and Such. New York, Avon, 1959.
Twists in Time. New York, Avon, 1960.

Men into Space (novelization of TV series). New York, Berkley, 1960.
The Aliens. New York, Berkley, 1960.
Doctor to the Stars. New York, Pyramid, 1964.
Get Off My World! New York, Belmont, 1966.
S.O.S. from Three Worlds. New York, Ace, 1967.
The Best of Murray Leinster, edited by Brian Davis. London, Corgi, 1976; New York, Ballantine, 1978.

Play

Screenplay: *Torchy in Chinatown*, with George Bricker, 1938.

Other

Space Platform (for children). Chicago, Shasta, 1953.
Space Tug (for children). Chicago, Shasta, 1953.
City on the Moon (for children). New York, Avalon, 1957.
Tunnel Through Time (for children). Philadelphia, Westminster Press, 1966.

Editor, *Great Stories of Science Fiction*. New York, Random House, 1951; London, Cassell, 1953.

* * *

Will F. Jenkins spent the early years of his writing career producing career producing pulp magazine fiction in mystery, science-fiction, and western genres. However, using the Murray Leinster Pseudonym, Jenkins went on to establish a major legacy in science fiction by writing such classic SF stories as "First Contact" and his Hugo Award-winning "Exploration Team." Jenkins's early western pulp fiction has been largely forgotten but the western novels he published in the 1930's, 1940's, and early 1950's before he abandoned the western field to write science fiction almost exclusively are solid efforts. *Mexican Trail* blends western action with elements of mystery as Pete Gray of the Border Patrol handles love and gunplay in a entertaining page-turner. *The Gamblin' Kid* is even more fun as the Kid shows up at the Blue streak Mine and is instantly plunged into a frantic series of kidnappings, stage coach holdups, and gunfights. The final scene, with the Kid putting everything on the line with the turn of a card, is a classic gambling showdown. *Outlaw Sheriff* features a complicated plot as a self-outlawed young rancher becomes a sheriff in an area plagued by rustlers. Fortunately, the pages turn so quickly the plot inconsistencies don't mar the action.

In *Outlaw Guns* (also published as *Wanted—Dead or Alive!*) Jenkins introduces a more contemporary western setting complete with gangsters and hitmen. Slim Galway returns to his Lazy Branch after his brother Buck is murdered. Slim suddenly sparks a flurry of violence as he hunts for his brother's murderer and the rustlers who threaten everyone in Las Almas valley. This was one of the few westerns Jenkins published under the Murray Leinster pseudonym; the other was *Texas Gun Slinger*, both published by Star Books in digest format.

Jenkin's best western novel was one of the last he published: *Son of the Flying "Y"*, a paperback original that lacks much of the silliness of Jenkin's other Westerns. *Son of the Flying "Y"* is the story of the rite of passage from spoiled rich kid to mature young adult of Bud Hornaby, son of the fabuluously wealthy rancher King Hornaby. When Bud's Uncle Paul is gunned down in a showdown, Bud swears revenge and launches himself into an odyssey that features a Jenkins variation of the prince and pauper plot with Bud exchanging identities with another cowhand. The explosive climax features the best of Jenkin's plotting and romance, and makes *Son of the Flying "Y"* superior western entertainment.

Although Jenkins's western fiction remains out-of-print and largely forgotten, he did produce a series of popular western novels that were action-packed and fun to read.

—George Kelley

JENKS, George C(harles). Also wrote as W.B. Lawson. British. Born in London, 13 April 1850; immigrated to the United States in 1872. Worked as a journalist in Pittsburgh, then in New York City, where became drama critic. Wrote dime novels for Street and Smith as "W.B. Lawson." *Died 13 September 1929.*

WESTERN PUBLICATIONS

Novels

The Climax. New York, Fly, 1909.
The Deserters, with Anna Alice Chapin. New York, Fly, 1912.
Stop Thief!, with Carlyle Moore. New York, Fly, 1913.

Short Stories

Double Curve Dan, The Pitcher Detective. New York, Beadle and Adams, 1883.
The Demon Doctor; or, Deadhold the "Kid" Detective. New York, Beadle and Adams, 1887.
The Giant Horseman; or, Tracking the Red Cross Gang. New York, Beadle and Adams, 1887.

Play

Screenplay: *The Desperate Game*, 1926.

* * *

George C. Jenks has been credited as the originator of Diamond Dick. In fact, he was far from original: he was merely a hack writer who was paid to copy material long in use, whose writing was virtually indistinguishable from his fellow dime novelists' and who, in 177 stories, created only two new, peripheral characters. He was one of the later authors in a line of seven who were hired by Street and Smith to write about Diamond Dick under the house name "W.B. Lawson." Diamond Dick first appeared 1878, in imitation of Beadle and Adams's successful Deadwood Dick, and by 1896 he was starring in *Diamond Dick Jr., The Boys' Best Weekly*. Jenks wrote 177 of the 762 episodes, between 1905 and 1909.

It was in the nature of the task that Jenks's writing should be routine, for Street and Smith were paying him to be anonymous, to fashion his fiction to the usual blend of pageant and melodrama. The firm controlled their authors' output closely, concealing the multi-authorship from their audience. Little sense of Jenks as author survives, but there remain vestigial differences between his stories and those of the other contributors to the series.

Jenks never wrote about Diamond Dick proper (that is, Richard Wade) but concentrated on his son, Bertie, who was introduced a few issues after the father. He first appears as a 10-year-old who kills his father's ex-lover. Both father and son operate as violent enforcers of justice, roaming around mining and railroad settlements, decked out in bejewelled Mexican costumes. Under Jenks, young Diamond Dick appears in a much more sober cowboy costume. He functions as scout, cowboy, and U.S. Marshal—a law-bringer fully authorized by the state—usually on the ranch and range of cattleland. The emphasis is on neatness and self-control: typically, Jenks describes Dick, "All in all, he was the beau ideal of a youthful American athlete at the zenith of his powers." This new emphasis on youth and morality was in keeping both with the quieter tone of century dime series (enforced by the Postmaster General's censorship) and with Street and Smith's newest series—*Rough Rider Weekly* whose hero, Ted Strong, also wears a neat uniform and acts as a marshal. It is impossible to know if only the firm, and not the author, desired this tamer atmosphere. It is interesting, however, that Jenks's two creations seem to strain towards a higher melodrama: Belle Bellair, the dark-haired beauty, and Jack Sinn, the knife-slinging gambler. When Jenks's contribution ended, these characters disappeared and the stories became increasingly lifeless, until the series died in 1911.

Jenks wrote some dime novels for Beadle and Adams in the 19th century and he published a little outside the dime firms, but it is typical of the dime novelist that his most important western output is now identifiable only by the bibliographical expert, an indistinguishable fraction of the mass of fiction which made Diamond Dick a household name.

—Christine Bold

JENNINGS, Dean. *See* **FRAZEE, Steve.**

JESSUP, Richard. Also wrote as Richard Telfair. American. Born in 1925. Worked as a merchant seaman for 11 years. Full-time writer, 1948–82. *Died 22 October 1982.*

WESTERN PUBLICATIONS

Novels

Cheyenne Saturday. New York, Fawcett, 1957; London, Fawcett, 1958.
Comanche Vengeance. New York, Fawcett, 1957; London, Fawcett, 1959.
Long Ride West. New York, Fawcett, 1957; London, Fawcett, 1958.
Texas Outlaw. New York, Fawcett, 1958; London, Fawcett, 1959.
Sabadilla. New York, Fawcett, 1960; London, Muller, 1961.
Chuka. New York, Fawcett, 1961; London, Muller, 1962.

Novels as Richard Telfair (series: Wyoming Jones)

Wyoming Jones. New York, Fawcett, 1958; London, Fawcett, 1959.
Day of the Gun. New York, Fawcett, 1958; London, Fawcett, 1960.
The Secret of Apache Canyon. New York, Fawcett, 1959; London, Muller, 1960.
Wyoming Jones for Hire. New York, Fawcett, 1959; London, Muller, 1960.
Sundance. New York, Fawcett, 1960; London, Muller, 1961.

OTHER PUBLICATIONS

Novels

The Cunning and the Haunted. New York, Fawcett, 1954.
A Rage to Die. New York, Fawcett, 1955.
Cry Passion. New York, Dell, 1956.
Night Boat to Paris. New York, Dell, 1956; London, Consul, 1960.
The Young Don't Cry. New York, Fawcett, 1957; London, Miller, 1959.
The Man in Charge. London, Secker and Warburg, 1957.
Lowdown. New York, Dell, and London, Secker and Warburg, 1958.
The Deadly Duo. New York, Dell, 1959; London, Boardman, 1961.
Port Angelique. New York, Fawcett, 1961.
Wolf Cop. New York, Fawcett, 1961; London, Muller, 1963.
The Cincinnati Kid. Boston, Little Brown, 1963; London, Gollancz, 1964.
The Recreation Hall. Boston, Little Brown, 1967.
Sailor. Boston, Little Brown, 1969.
A Quiet Voyage Home. Boston, Little Brown, and London, Hutchinson, 1970.
Foxway. Boston, Little Brown, 1971.
The Hot Blue Sea. New York, Doubleday, 1974; London, W.H. Allen, 1975.
Threat. New York, Viking Press, 1981.

Novels as Richard Telfair

The Bloody Medallion. New York, Fawcett, 1959; London, Muller, 1960.
The Corpse That Talked. New York, Fawcett, 1959; London, Muller, 1960.
Scream Bloody Murder. New York, Fawcett, 1960; London, Muller, 1961.
Good Luck, Sucker. New York, Fawcett, 1961; London, Muller, 1962.
The Slavers. New York, Fawcett, 1961; London, Muller, 1962.
Target for Tonight (novelization of TV series). New York, Dell, 1962.

Plays

Screenplays: *The Young Don't Cry*, 1957; *Chuka*, 1967.

Television Plays: *Come Out, Come Out Wherever You Are*, with Stirling Silliphant and Anthony Basta, 1960–63.

* * *

Best-known for the story of a professional gambler, *The Cincinnati Kid*—later made into a feature film starring Steve McQueen—and contemporary thrillers like *Threat*, Richard Jessup wrote a series of remarkable western paperback originals for Gold Medal in the late 1950's and early 1960's before abandoning the field.

Jessup went to sea as a young man, serving 10 years in the merchant marine. He got started as a writer in a unique fashion: he copied *War and Peace* on a typewriter at sea, corrected all errors, then threw the pages over the side. Leaving the merchant marine, Jessup wrote mysteries and westerns before striking it big with *The Cincinnati Kid*.

The best of the Gold Medal westerns is *Texas Outlaw* where Sheriff Shim Fowler finds his sleepy town of Fury, Texas ravaged by an Indian attack, which a gang of outlaws uses as a diversion for their robbery of the town's bank. The book also presents one of the coldest killers in the genre: Babe Long, with a lightning draw and "eyes that were black and moist looking, as if there might be frost on them."

Also outstanding is *Comanche Vengeance* where a lone woman rides to avenge her slaughtered family. When a band of Comanche led by Chief One Nest murders Sara Phelps's husband, rapes and kills her young daughter, and butchers her little boy, Sarah straps on a gun and goes hunting for the Indian leader. The book is unique for its early treatment of a female in the lead role in a male-dominated genre. Love interest is supplied by Sarah's guardian angel with a fast gun, Gibson Duke. Together they spend over a year on the trail of the Comanche band before the final showdown; Jessup portrays that time in a adult, realistic fashion too often missing from westerns writing during that era.

Sabadilla is unconventional because the hero is Mexican. The story of Juan Cortez trying to survive in white Texas is unusually sympathetic. *Chuka* presents some of Jessup's best characterizations as a varied group of people—a whore, a Spanish-Mexican lady of quality, and a gunman named Chuka—are trapped at besieged Fort Clendennon, Colorado, during a series of Indian raids. The interplay of personalities is skillfully drawn by Jessup.

Under the pseudonym of "Richard Telfair" Jessup wrote five novels in the Wyoming Jones series. When Indians kill his adoptive father in the first chapter, Wyoming Jones vows revenge. The rest of *Wyoming Jones* is the tale of that vengeance. The best book in the Wyoming Jones series is *The Secret of Apache Canyon*. Not only does it generate considerable suspense, it also features one of Jessup's more intriguing characters: Boston businessman Sidney Rogett. Sidney starts out as the classic Eastern greenhorn, but Jessup goes against the stereotype and shows how education is more than an equalizer. Sidney triumphs over gun-fighters and Indians by shrewdly applying his unconventional skills; to everyone's surprise—even his own—Sidney even gets the girl! The Wyoming Jones series offers solid writing and Jessup's unique approach of turning the genre's stereotypes on their heads.

Although Jessup abandoned the western genre after the early 1960's to write for television and motion pictures, his Westerns are still highly regarded for their craftsmanship and high quality writing.

—George Kelley

JOHNSON, Dorothy M(arie). American. Born in McGregor, Iowa, 19 December 1905. Educated at the University of Montana, Missoula, B.A. 1928. Magazine editor, Gregg Publishing Company, 1935–44, and Farrell Publishing Corporation, 1944–50; news editor, Whitefish *Pilot*, Montana, 1950–53; secretary-manager, Montana Press Association, 1953–67; Assistant Professor of journalism, University of Montana, 1954–67. Honorary member of the Blackfeet tribe in Montana. Recipient: Western Writers of America Spur award, for story, 1957. University of Montana Alumni Association Distinguished Service award, 1961; Levi Strauss Golden Saddleman award, 1976; Western Heritage Wrangler award, 1978; Western Literature Association Distinguished Achievement award, 1981; H.G. Merriam award, 1982. D. Litt.: University of Montana, Missonla, 1973. *Died 11 November 1984.*

Western Publications

Novels

Buffalo Woman. New York, Dodd Mead, 1977.
All the Buffalo Returning. New York, Dodd Mead, 1979.

Short Stories

Beulah Bunny Tells All. New York, Morrow, 1942; as *Miss Bunny Intervenes,* London, Chapman and Hall, 1948.
Indian Country. New York, Ballantine, 1953; London, Deutsch, 1960; as *A Man Called Horse*, Ballantine, 1970.
The Hanging Tree. New York, Ballantine, 1957; London, Deutsch, 1959.
The Man Who Knew the Buckskin Kid. London, Corgi, 1976.

Uncollected Short Stories

"I Woke Up Wicked," in *The Arbor House Treasury of Great Western Stories*, edited by Bill Pronzini and Martin H. Greenberg. New York, Arbor House, 1982.
"The Man Who Shot Liberty Valance," in *The Reel West*, edited by Bill Pronzini and Martin H. Greenberg. New York, Doubleday, 1984.
"Lost Sister," in *The Western Hall of Fame*, edited by Bill Pronzini and Martin H. Greenberg. New York, Morrow, 1984.
"A Man Called Horse," in *The Western Hall of Fame*, edited by Bill Pronzini and Martin H. Greenberg. New York, Morrow, 1984.
"The Hanging Tree," in *She Won the West*, edited by Marcia Muller and Bill Pronzini. New York, Morrow, 1985.
"The Unbeliever," in *The Horse Soldiers*, edited by Bill Pronzini and Martin H. Greenberg. New York, Fawcett, 1987.

Other Publications

Other (for children)

Famous Lawmen of the Old West. New York, Dodd Mead, 1963.
Greece, Wonderland of the Past and Present. New York, Dodd Mead, 1964.
Farewell to Troy. Boston, Houghton Mifflin, 1964.
Some Went West. New York, Dodd Mead, 1965.
Witch Princess. Boston, Houghton Mifflin, 1967.
Flame on the Frontier: Short Stories of Pioneer Women. New York, Dodd Mead, 1967.
Warrior for a Lost Nation: A Biography of Sitting Bull. Philadelphia, Westminster Press, 1969.
Western Badmen. New York, Dodd Mead, 1970.
The Bloody Bozeman: The Perilous Trail to Montana's Gold. New York, McGraw Hill, 1971.
Montana. New York, Coward McCann, 1971.
The Bedside Book of Bastards (for adults), with R.T. Turner. New York, McGraw Hill, 1973.
When You and I Were Young. Whitefish, Montana, Mountain Press, 1982.

*

Manuscript Collections: Princeton University, New Jersey; State University of Iowa, Iowa City; University of Wyoming, Laramie; University of Montana, Missoula.

Critical Study: *Dorothy Johnson* by Judy Alter, Boise, Idaho, Boise State University Press, 1980.

* * *

Dorothy M. Johnson was the author of 16 books and numerous short stories and articles ranging from history and biography to personal experience. She wrote both for adults and young adults. Her literary reputation, however, deservedly rests on the western short stories which are characterized by a spare but powerful style in which the prose rhythm of carefully chosen language serves to hold the reader: "When it came time for them to die, Pete Gossard cursed and Knife Hilton cried, but Wolfer Joe Kennedy yawned in the face of the hangman" ("The Last Boast"). Johnson complements this economy of treatment with an incisive way of giving the whole idea in the first paragraph, then spinning it out. In "A Man Called Horse" she tells the reader of an easterner who went west in search of his equals. "On a day in June, he learned what it was to have no status at all. He became a captive of a small raiding party of Crow Indians." Such foreshadowing effectively heightens rather than diminishes the tension of the story.

"A Man Called Horse" also illustrates Johnson's basic technique for constructing stories. She uses what she called "the switch" or "iffing," a way of turning a situation around and looking at it from a different angle. After much research on the Crow Indians, she felt she knew enough to survive if she had ever found herself in a Crow camp. (Because extensive research is characteristic of her work, her stories are rich with accurate details of frontier life.) Then she wondered what would happen to someone totally ignorant of Crow ways in the same predicament. The result is one of her most powerful stories. Its theme of clash between cultures, however, is found in much of her work.

Johnson's characters are real people tested by the circumstances of life in the West. The hero of "A Man Called Horse" not only survives but grows in self-confidence, responsibility, and maturity during his captivity so that he emerges a far different man. Johnson said that she believed in such old-fashioned virtues as courage, strength, honor, and integrity and had no time for weaklings. She brought these values to life in her characters, so that her stories are a positive affirmation of man's ability to prevail. She also believed in the importance of bonds between individuals that go beyond the celebrated western self-reliance, and her stories frequently indicate the importance of romantic love, family, responsibility, obligation, all the things that tie people together.

Although the wider range of her work makes Johnson difficult to pigeonhole, she does belong to the slim but strong tradition of women who have written about the American West. Her use of the women's point of view was a rare contribution to the Western, yet she was equally able to write from the masculine approach. And if her stories are marked by a hardcore realism about life on the frontier, they are also spiced with an ironic humor that cuts through the pretensions and misconceptions of people and softens the blows of fate. Frequently, in essays and articles, Johnson turned that same humor on herself with devastating effect.

Her other western works include a history of the Bozeman trail, two powerful novels presenting the dilemma of the displaced Indian in a white man's world, both written from the Indian point of view, and an early collection of vignettes about a mountain school teacher. The books for young adults present heroes and women of the West in realistic yet positive tones and show outlaws in what Johnson considered their true and unflattering light. Like the short stories, these works are characterized by conciseness of prose style and accuracy of detail. They also present clearly Johnson's strong affection for western life and her admiration for people of the frontier.

—Judy Alter

JOHNSON, (Emily) Pauline. Also known as Tekahionwake. Canadian, Mohawk Indian. Born at Chiefswood, Six Nations Reservation, Brantford, Ontario, 10 May 1861 (some sources say 1862 or 1863). Educated at Central Collegiate, Brantford, Ontario, 1877–79; clerk, Indian Office, Brantford, 1884–92; performance poet, touring Canada, United States, and Britain, 1892–1909; settled in Vancouver, British Columbia, Canada, in 1909. *Died 7 March 1913.*

WESTERN PUBLICATIONS

Short Stories

Legends of Vancouver. Toronto, Sunset, 1911.
The Shagganappi. Toronto, W. Briggs, 1913.
The Moccasin Maker. Toronto, Ryerson Press, 1913; Tucson, University of Arizona Press, 1987.

Verse

The White Wampum. London, Lane, 1895; Boston, Lansson Wolffe, 1895.
In the Shadows. New York, Adirondack Press, 1898.
Canadian Born. Toronto, Morang, 1903.
When George Was King, and Other Poems. Brockville, Ontario, Brockville Times, 1908.
Ojistoh: Illustrated Indian Woman Monologue. New York, Werner, 1911.
Flint and Feather: Complete Poems. Toronto, Musson, 1912.
And He Said, Fight On. Toronto, Musson, 1913.

*

Critical Studies: *Canadian Poets* by John Garvin, Toronto, McClelland and Stewart, 1916; *Candid Chronicles* by Hector Charlesworth, Toronto, Macmillan, 1925; *The Mohawk Princess* by Garland Foster, Vancouver, British Columbia, Lion's Gate, 1931; *Pauline Johnson and Her Friends* by Walter McRaye, Toronto, Ryerson, 1947; *Pauline Johnson, Her Life and Work* by Marcus Van Steen, Toronto, Musson, 1965; *Pauline: A Biography of Pauline Johnson* by Betty Keller, Vancouver, British Columbia, Douglas and McIntyre, 1981; introduction by Lavanne Brown Ruoff to *The Moccasin Maker*, Tucson, University of Arizona Press, 1987.

* * *

Pauline Johnson's place in the early chapters of the history of Canadian literature is secure, but it has not been left unchallenged. Her fame as a poet, and status as one of the foremost exponents of the Canadian literary renaissance at the turn of this century, have proven to be more resilient in the public mind than the frequent dismissal of her work among literary critics under the rubric of melodramatic romanticism.

As may be expected, her significance lies somewhere between these two rather extreme points of view.

Whether positive or negative, reception and evaluation of Johnson's work has primarily revolved around her poetry. In fact, it is in this particular genre that she earned sufficient recognition at the outset of her career to ensure her future as a Canadian literary figure. Her first collection of poems, *The White Wampum*, was published in London in 1895 by the prestigious press of John Lane (formerly of Bodley Head), and it received substantial acclaim from contemporary English critics. Several of her early poems, such as "The Song My Paddle Sings" or "Cry from an Indian Wife," became immensely popular in Canada, and were later reprinted in a number of anthologies representing that country's foremost poets. Even though her second collection, *Canadian Born*, proved to be a much less fortunate choice of her work and did much to tarnish her reputation among literary critics, her popularity in Canada never diminished. *Flint and Feather*, a compilation of almost all of her poems, has turned out to be one of the best-selling books ever put out by a Canadian poet.

Johnson's special contribution to Canadian poetry is her early use of Pacific Coast material, particularly this region's grand natural settings and the unique people living there. She has rightly been referred to as the "Apostle of Canadianism." However, even her staunchest supporters have admitted that her reputation as a poet had much to do with the fact that she was one of the most successful stage performers of her time. Captivating her audiences with a vibrant personality and an exotic appearance—she was usually billed as the "Mohawk Princess"—Johnson delivered hundreds of dramatic presentations of her poetry all over Canada, in parts of the United States and even as far away as England. Thus her special place in Canadian cultural history is in the field of dramatic arts, as a leading recitalist of the early 20th century.

The regionalist character of Johnson's literary work, her "Canadianism," is particularly evident in her prose writings. Together with her contemporary in the United States, Gertrude Bonnin (Zitkala Sa), she is not only one of the earliest writers of Indian descent, but also one of the first North American authors to write extensively about Indian women. Though she was more a Mohawk by virtue of Canadian law than by her direct participation in traditional Iroquois life, she nevertheless took upon herself the task of bringing Indian culture to the general public. She wrote many ethnographic articles on the Iroquois and other Indian groups for major magazines like *Harper's Weekly*, *Saturday Night*, and *Canadian Magazine*, as well as for newspapers like the Toronto *Sunday Globe* and London *Daily Express*.

Unable to make a living as a poet, Johnson turned more and more to the short story after 1904, to supplement her income from her stage performances. Between 1906 and 1912 she wrote numerous short stories for *Mothers' Magazine* and *Boys' World*, some of which belong to her very best work. The stories are, almost without exception, quite simplistic and often very sentimental. But it should be remembered in this context, that they appeared at a time in which the short story was a medium of popular entertainment, directed primarily at middle-class housewives and children, and was not yet really accepted as a *bona fide* genre of literature. Her merit here is the attempt to counteract the negative stereotypes generally affixed to persons of mixed Indian-white ancestry and so frequently propounded in popular literature. In several of her stories a protagonist of mixed ancestry confronts the racial prejudice of Anglo society with a fervent (and sometimes overdone) pride in his/her Indian background. Even though her rendition of the "half-breed" remains rather flat, perhaps reflecting Johnson's own uncertain feeling about her racial background, she nevertheless introduces the theme of biculturalism from an Indian point of view into fiction—a theme which has since become a central element of contemporary Candian and American Indian literature. Most of her short stories were published collectively in 1913 under the titles *The Moccasin Maker* (containing her better Indian material and reprinted as recently as 1987) and *The Shagganappi* (with her stories for *Boys' World*).

Johnson also made use of Squamish oral tradition, as told to her by Joe Capilano, a Squamish leader whom she had met and befriended during one of her tours to England, to produce a series of imaginative legendary stories for the Vancouver *Province* between 1910 and 1911. Each begins with a conversation between herself and Capilano, and then relates a tale about some prominent natural phenomenon in the environs of Vancouver. Published collectively in 1911 as *Legends of Vancouver* (and reprinted several times), it has since become a kind of literary hallmark of the Canadian Pacific Northwest.

The centennial of Johnson's birthday was duly celebrated in Canada and her image was printed on a postage stamp. But an editorial in the Vancouver *Sun* titled "Our Pride in Pauline" complains bitterly about academic attacks made on her literary reputation on this occasion, showing that the rift between popular and scholarly views of her work is still very much present. Johnson is, in essence, a Canadian people's poet, whose prominence as a public figure has made it difficult for her literary work to find the proper critical distance. Her distinction as an author is more subtle, but nonetheless quite remarkable: Canada's first lady of Indian literature.

—Bernd C. Peyer

JOHNSTON, Terry C(onrad). American. Born in Arkansas City, Kansas, 1 January 1947. Educated at Central State University, Edmond, Oklahoma, B.S. 1969. Married Doris A. Howard in 1974 (divorced 1982); one son. Worked at a variety of jobs, including pipeline laborer, heavy equipment operator, dog catcher, oil-field roughneck, truck driver, cook, paramedic, ambulance driver, teacher, electronics firm production manager, roustabout, and auto leasing manager. Member, Western Writers of America. Recipient: Western Writers of America Medicine Pipe Bearers award, for novel, 1983. Address: P.O. Box 111, Lafayette, Colorado, U.S.A.

WESTERN PUBLICATIONS

Novels (series: Titus Bass; General Custer; The Plainsmen)

Carry the Wind (Bass). Aurora, Illinois, Green Hill/Caroline House, 1982.
Borderlords (Bass). Aurora, Illinois, Caroline House, 1984.
One-Eyed Dream (Bass). Ottawa, Illinois, Jameson, 1988.
Sioux Dawn (Plainsmen). New York, St. Martin's Press, 1990.
Red Cloud's Revenge (Plainsmen). New York, St. Martin's Press, 1990.
Long Winter Gone (Custer). New York, Bantam, 1990.
Seize the Sky (Custer). New York, Bantam, 1991.
Whisper of the Wolf (Custer). New York, Bantam, 1991.
Black Sun (Plainsmen). New York, St. Martin's Press, 1991.

Devil's Backbone (Plainsmen). New York, St. Martin's Press, 1991.
Shadow Riders (Plainsmen). New York, St. Martin's Press, 1991.

* * *

Exhaustive research, a keen sense of pace, and a good understanding of human nature characterize the work of Terry C. Johnston, whose first novel, *Carry the Wind*, was nominated for two WWA Golden Spurs before finally going on to win the coveted Medicine Pipe Bearer's award.

A weighty tome, *Carry the Wind* (which opens Johnston's Titus Bass trilogy) is not an easy book to precise, for to do more than skim the surface would certainly drown any attempted synopsis in its vast wealth of detail. Briefly, however, it is the story of Josiah Paddock, who meets up with a mountain man known as "Scratch" Bass after a nightmarish escape from St. Louis, where he killed the son of a powerful French merchant in a duel. Bass befriends the young Easterner and before long a strong bond develops between them.

Trouble comes when one of Bass's cronies, the Bible-quoting Asa McAfferty, shows up at the Crow village where the two partners are wintering, and crazed with grief following the death of his pregnant wife, kills an old Crow woman before disappearing back into the wilds. Bass and Paddock set out in pursuit, and the remainder of the book chronicles their manhunt, which eventually builds to a satisfying and well-choreographed climax.

As the saga continues, Johnston expands many of the subplots introduced in the first book. In *Borderlords*, for example, the story reaches a rousing finale when assassins hired by the LeClerc family (whose son Paddock killed in the aforementioned duel) launch an all-out attack on the trappers during their rendezvous, while in *One-Eyed Dream*, the partners (who by now have both taken Indian wives) decide to visit St. Louis in an effort to settle matters with the LeClercs before rejoining their families in Taos for an ultimately cheering conclusion.

This is, of course, a considerable oversimplification of three long, immensely powerful historical novels, but many of the observations drawn from them can also apply to Johnston's subsequent titles.

Although he is no mean hand as a writer, Johnston's greatest strength is his eye for historical detail. Particularly in the Titus Bass trilogy, he combines a roaring good tale with fascinating insights into the lives and times of his principal characters, generally managing to employ his extensive knowledge to *enhance* a story rather than intrude upon it. Similarly, his characters are at once both larger than life and all too human. Johnston's heroes are not afraid to show affection for their companions, male *or* female. They laugh, hug, weep, and grow angry. In short, they are as real as their creator can make them. Despite all their foibles, however, these heroes always remain exactly that—heroic.

Women seem to fare slightly less well. While they are frequently depicted as strong, intelligent, independent, and beautiful, they generally perform in ways that *support* the story rather than direct it. For better or worse, Johnston's view of the West is very much that of a man's world; gritty, realistic, and violent. He also has a penchant for the interplay between the young and old—that is, the wise, gruff oldsters who, over a period of time, impart their wisdom to the younger and less experienced, teaching them all about the mountains, the West—and life itself.

Not that the above is meant to imply that Johnston's work is without fault. Sometimes he displays a tendency toward what Edgar Rice Burroughs critics refer to as the "small jungle" syndrome (in this case, the "small west" syndrome); at times a story or plot will turn on a coincidence, especially the coincidence of people running into one another out in the vast wilderness of the American west. On very rare occasions, loose ends may also be left unexplained. But these are minor criticisms when compared to the overall strength of the end product.

Johnston's wealth of historical detail is less of a factor in his projected 15-book saga of the Indian Wars, *The Plainsmen*. Here the author seems to have trimmed his material in order to pick up the pace of the novels and propel them along at a greater clip. Although they are more geared toward the commercial market, Johnston's twin trademarks of factual minutiae and accuracy are still very apparent, particularly in *Sioux Dawn*, which introduces the series' hero, Seamus Donegan, and relates the events that led to the Fetterman Massacre of 1866. The second book, *Red Cloud's Revenge*, picks up the story several months later and takes us through the summer of 1867, with stories of the Hayfield and Wagon Box fights.

Johnston's most recent trilogy revolves around General Custer. The first volume, *Long Winter Gone*, is among many other things the little-known story of Custer's love affair with a 17-year-old Cheyenne squaw named Monaseetah. *Seize the Sky* is a "completely different" account of the Battle of the Little Big Horn, and *Whisper of the Wolf* is an entirely fictionalised account of the life of Custer's half-breed son, "Yellow Bird." Among his future plans is another trilogy, this time concerning the "galvanised Yankees"—the Confederate prisoners-of-war who agreed to fight Indians during the War years rather than rot in prison.

—David Whitehead

JONES, Calico. *See* **RICHARDSON, Gladwell.**

JONES, Douglas C(lyde). American. Born in Winslow, Arkansas, 6 December 1924. Educated at the University of Arkansas, Fayetteville, B.A. 1949; Army Command and General Staff College, 1961; University of Wisconsin, Madison, M.S. 1963. Served in the United States Army, in Pacific Theater, 1943–45. Married Mary Arnold in 1949; three daughters and one son. Career officer in the United States Army, 1943–68: commander of infantry rifle companies in Europe and Korea; information officer, Philadelphia Army Air Defense Command; Chief of Armed Forces Press Branch, Department of Defense, Washington: Commendation Medal (3 times), Legion of Merit. Faculty member, School of Journalism, 1968–74, and since 1974 visiting lecturer, University of Wisconsin. Artist: individual exhibitions in Washington, 1967, and Fayetteville, 1968. Recipient: Western Writers of America Spur award, 1977, 1984, 1986. Agent: George Wieser, Wieser and Wieser, Inc., Box 608, Millwood, New York, New York 10546. Address: 1987 Greenview Drive, Fayetteville, Arkansas 72710, U.S.A.

WESTERN PUBLICATIONS

Novels

The Court-Martial of George Armstrong Custer. New York, Scribner, 1976; London, W.H. Allen, 1977.
Arrest Sitting Bull. New York, Scribner, 1977; London, Prior, 1978.
A Creek Called Wounded Knee. New York, Scribner, 1978.
Winding Stair. New York, Holt Rinehart, 1979; as *The Winding Stair Massacre*, London, Allen and Unwin, 1980.
Elkhorn Tavern. New York, Holt Rinehart, 1980.
Weedy Rough. New York, Holt Rinehart, 1981.
The Barefoot Brigade. New York, Holt Rinehart, 1982.
Season of Yellow Leaf. New York, Holt Rinehart, 1983.
Gone the Dreams and Dancing. New York, Holt Rinehart, 1984.
Roman. New York, Holt Rinehart, 1986.
Come Winter. New York, Holt Rinehart, 1989.

Short Stories

Hickory Cured. New York, Holt Rinehart, 1987.

OTHER PUBLICATIONS

Novel

Remember Santiago. New York, Holt Rinehart, 1988.

Other

The Treaty of Medicine Lodge: The Story of the Great Treaty Council as Told by Eyewitnesses. Norman, University of Oklahoma Press, 1966.

*

Critical Study: *Douglas C. Jones*, by Lyman B. Hagen, Jonesboro, Arkansas, Craighead County and Jonesboro Public Library, 1982.

* * *

Douglas C. Jones, retired Chief of the Armed Forces Press Branch, is acclaimed as an artist and as an author. His paintings, three of his novels, and his non-fiction study *The Treaty of Medicine Lodge* focus upon the American Indian.

The major theme in Jones's first three novels is Indian–white relations following the Civil War. In *The Court-Martial of George Armstrong Custer* Jones conjectures that had Custer survived the Battle of the Little Bighorn in 1876, he would have been court-martialed. Via the testimony of witnesses in Custer's trial, Jones skillfully depicts the massacre and the confusion about it and, more particularly, about Custer, that has persisted since the incident. *Arrest Sitting Bull* examines the events surrounding the attempted arrest of the famous Sioux leader in December 1890, which resulted in his death. A few weeks later, the Wounded Knee Massacre took place, as Jones relates in *A Creek Called Wounded Knee*. A second theme is the effect or presumed effect that the press had on the events Jones narrates. He portrays the animosity that often existed between the military and reporters.

Jones's characters are real and fictional. Women are not merely romantic foils or sex objects in these novels. They are well-drawn and portray elements essential to the story. The developing relationship between a white teacher and an Indian policeman in *Arrest Sitting Bull* is more a revelation of intercultural conflict and tension between the two races than a love story. Elizabeth Custer emerges as a fascinating, enigmatic partner of the immature and deranged Custer. She juggles the emerging truth about her husband with the myth of Custer as hero that she seeks to maintain.

Jones displays sympathy for whites and Indians but never slips into a maudlin sentimentality. The villains of his novels are not the people caught up in the events but a government that repeatedly dealt with Indian-white conflict ineptly and insensitively. The novels are written in the present tense, with flashback episodes, to convey a sense of immediacy. The understated, succinct narratives move the reader inexorably toward tragedy.

More recently, Jones has turned to a different type of fiction. The locale has shifted from the West to the area in northwestern Arkansas where he was born. *Winding Stair*, *Elkhorn Tavern*, and *Weedy Rough* trace the four generations of a family from the Civil War to the 1930's. Family loyalty and solidarity are major themes in these novels. The characters are affected by times of stress and social change. In *Elkhorn Tavern* the Confederate heroine marries a Union officer; their son, in *Winding Stair*, defies local opinion to marry an Indian girl. The fourth generation representative in *Weedy Rough* is accused of murder, and draws strength and support from his family.

The saga of the Hasford family of northwestern Arkansas continues in *The Barefoot Brigade*, *Roman*, and *Come Winter*, and several of the characters also appear in Jones's novels about the west. *The Barefoot Brigade*, a novel about the Civil War experiences of the Third Arkansas Infantry regiment, introduces Liverpool Morgan, who narrates *Gone the Dreams and Dancing*. Following the war, the protagonist of *Roman* leaves the family farm to explore the West before settling in Arkansas in *Come Winter*. Arkansas is also the scene of 10 stories set in the 1930's that are collected in *Hickory Cured*.

In *Roman*, *Season of Yellow Leaf*, and *Gone the Dreams and Dancing*, Jones returns to the setting and the themes of his early novels. The advance of the American frontier brings white Americans into contact with American Indians who are struggling to preserve their heritage. *Roman* depicts the conflict between the Cheyenne and the army of Phil Sheridan and George Armstrong Custer. *Season of Yellow Leaf* and *Gone the Dreams and Dancing* are based on the experience of Cynthia Ann Parker, captured as a child by the Comanches, and her son Quanah Parker, one of the last great leaders of the Comanche nation. *Season of Yellow Leaf*, which takes place between 1838 and 1854, portrays Comanche life before increasing westward expansion curtails their freedom on the plains. *Gone the Dreams and Dancing* returns to the Comanches at the end of an era, as they come to terms with life on the reservation after 1870.

In these works, Jones displays the sensitivity and artistry for which he has become renowned. His appreciation for the culture and tradition of the Comanches is apparent, and he does not diminish his subjects by romanticizing them. His balanced treatment of whites reflects that they too are caught in processes of change that they cannot control. Jones's characters are complex and memorable. His descriptions of the western landscape reflect his artist's eye for color and form, and his careful research recreates settings that disappeared long ago. His novels are important contributions to western literature.

—Cheryl J. Foote

JONES, Harry Austin. *See* **JONS, Hal.**

JONES, Luke. *See* **CHISHOLM, Matt.**

JONES, Nard (Maynard Benedict Jones). American. Born in Seattle, Washington, 12 April 1904. Educated at Whitman College, Walla Walla, Washington, graduated 1926. Served as a public relations officer for the 13th Naval District and Northwest Sea Frontier during World War II. Married 1) Elizabeth Dunphy in 1928 (died 1940), one son; 2) Anne Marie Mynar in 1942, one daughter. Journalist: reporter, Walla Walla *Daily Bulletin*; editor, *Pacific Motor Boat* magazine; manager of the New York office of Miller Freeman publishers, after World War II. *Died 3 September 1972.*

WESTERN PUBLICATIONS

Novels

Oregon Detour. New York, Payson and Clarke, 1930.
The Petlands. New York, Brewer Warren and Putnam, 1931.
Wheat Women. New York, Duffield and Green, 1933.
All Six Were Lovers. New York, Dodd Mead, 1934.
Swift Flows the River. New York, Dodd Mead, and London, Hamish Hamilton, 1940.
Scarlet Petticoat. New York, Dodd Mead, 1941; London, Hamish Hamilton, 1942.
Still to the West. New York, Dodd Mead, 1946; London, Martin, 1947.
The Island. New York, Sloane, 1948.

OTHER PUBLICATIONS

Novels

The Case of the Hanging Lady. New York, Dodd Mead, 1938.
I'll Take What's Mine. New York, Fawcett, 1954; London, Fawcett, 1955.
Ride the Dark Storm. New York, Fawcett, 1955; London, Fawcett, 1956.

Other

Pulp, Paper, and People. Privately printed, n.d.
West, Young Man! (for children), with J. Gordon Gose. Portland, Oregon, Metropolitan Press, 1937.
Evergreen Land: A Portrait of the State of Washington. New York, Dodd Mead, 1947.
The Great Command: The Story of Marcus and Narcissa Whitman and the Oregon Country Pioneers. Boston, Little Brown, 1959.
Rediscovering Washington State. Olympia, Washington State Department of Commerce and Economic Development, 1960.
The Pacific Northwest, with Roderick Haig-Brown and Stewart Holbrook, edited by Anthony Netboy. New York, Doubleday, 1963.
Seattle. New York, Doubleday, 1972.

* * *

The works of the late Nard Jones spanned a broad range of years and subject matter, from the very early frontier to Seattle and Alaska during World War II. Jones's novels reflect his vast knowledge and love for the Pacific Northwest, and several are hopefully of lasting life as part of the region's literature.

Jones was a lifetime professional writer and craftsman of the first caliber, who also for many years was chief editorial writer for a major Seattle daily newspaper. He was one of the best historical novelists the Pacific northwest has produced to date. *Swift Flows the River* is without doubt the finest fictional work on the Columbia River steamboating years that is on the shelves. While parts of the story and some of the characters are generally fictional, it is at times difficult to tell where the fiction leaves off and fact takes over, even among those familiar with the heritage of the old Oregon country. Jones did his homework and made few changes in this saga which led to a tough, greedy monopoly on the great river and its tributaries by the powerful Oregon Steam Navigation Company. It is an excellent portrayal which has stood the test of the years and is still worth an occasional rereading. His prose flows like the river itself, and the reader feels he has learned from the book without becoming bored.

An eye for the bizarre and unusual often characterize Jones's novels. Among his early works is *Scarlet Petticoat*, built around the true story of a British barmaid and adventuress who became the first white woman on the northwest coast as paramour of the administrator of Fort Astoria, renamed Fort George by British fur traders. Jane Barnes is a dandy character, the kind of stuff that bestsellers and musical shows are made from. But somehow Jones fails to bring it off in retelling, so that the novel winds up as one of his poorest. Jones can't be classified as a "western writer," but rather a writer about the West. His novels weren't formula stories, nor were his characters stock and trade.

He was truly an historical novelist, and at times a social critic, of which few emerged in the Northwest during his generation. His wide interests may have stemmed from his newspaper work. Another early book, *Wheat Women*, falls in this social category. This novel upset his home town of Walla Walla, Washington, by cutting too close to reality with easily identified real people and events, as did H.L. Davis's *Honey in the Horn*. Both authors were forced to move elsewhere as a result. For Jones, history was only yesterday; his *The Island* was a graphic contemporary portrayal of wartime Seattle in the conflict with the Japanese and the invasion of the Aleutians, in which Jones was a participant. Yet save for *Swift Flows the River*, Jones failed to gain lasting national or even regional stature. His work is deserving of more.

—Ellis Lucia

JONS, Hal. Pseudonym for Harry Austin Jones. Also wrote as Harry Graham.

WESTERN PUBLICATIONS

Novels

Montana Nemesis. London, Muller, 1960.
Cattleman's Gold. London, Muller, 1961.
The Llano Kid. London, Muller, 1962.
Saddle Tramps. London, Muller, 1963.
Mochita Stage. London, Muller, 1964.

Ghost Gunman. London, Muller, 1964.
Rogue Ramrods. London, Muller, 1965.
Alamosa Guns. London, Muller, 1965.
Guns of Justice. London, Hale, 1980.
Gringo Gold. London, Hale, 1981.
Assassin Trail. London, Hale, 1981.
Mustang Valley. London, Hale, 1982.
Travis, U.S. Marshal. London, Hale, 1982.
Guns at Chinooga Peak. London, Hale, 1983.
Cheyenne Medicine. London, Hale, 1983.

* * *

Under the pseudonym Hal Jons, Harry Austin Jones wrote several largely traditional Westerns for the U.K. library market, and although most of them were unconnected, Jones did create a continuing character, U.S. Marshal Carl Travis, towards the end of his career.

As a rule, Jones's heroes are always tall, athletic, pistol-quick, and handsome (in *Cheyenne Medicine*, in fact, his protagonist is *so* handsome that one dazzling smile is enough to render two young women speechless). For the most part, characterisation is rather perfunctory and his plots somewhat routine, but it must be said that a Jons western always delivers exactly what it promises: a competently written horse opera in which good men and bad are always clearly defined, intrigue is never far from the surface, and the hero always gets the girl in a satisfying if predictable conclusion. Possibly Jones's best book is the early *Montana Nemesis*, the story of an unscrupulous speculator who specialises in selling land to settlers and later "persuading" them to sell back cheap with the help of a pack of hired gunmen. The speculator, Red Hanson, meets his match, however, when two such settlers, Nick and Letty Randall, refuse to sell, no matter what . . .

Although Jons wrote to a fairly standard formula and tended to employ easily identifiable stereotypes to carry his sometimes contrived stories along, he did at least constantly endeavour to vary his themes. After helping to foil a stagecoach robbery in the aforementioned *Cheyenne Medicine*, for example, Mark Holden, a doctor on his way to St. Louis, befriends the old man who runs the line, Dave Lomas, and Lomas's headstrong young daughter Kate. Almost at once Holden finds himself siding with them against a mining company intent on taking over the local town, eventually bringing into play all the tricks learned during his childhood among the Cheyenne to fight off the gunmen the book's avaricious mine owner, Henry Bowden, sends his way. In *Assassin Trail*, another personal favourite, Steve Grant returns home to Texas after the War to resume his old life as a cattleman, but within days he joins three friends on a personal quest to track down a notorious band of Yankee guerillas who slaughtered and raped their way through the South during the war years. When stagecoach robber Ed Wallis is released from prison in *Mustang Valley*, U.S. Marshal Dave Hallett is dispatched to follow him in the hope that Wallis will lead him to the hitherto unrecovered proceeds of the robbery—a fortune in bullion and currency. What should be a fairly routine mission is soon complicated by the arrival of two other recently released convicts, Carter and Dyer, who force Wallis to leave town with them, presumably with the same idea in mind. As usual, Jons's hero stirs up the rest of the cast in one way or another before finally completing his mission. And in the first of his Carl Travis adventures, *Travis, U.S. Marshal*, the robbery of the Pierre town bank (and subsequent killing of seven townspeople) brings Travis, a softspoken but typically gun-swift young man, to town to investigate the crime. Most of the people he questions are sure that the robbery is the work of a well-known badman named Abe Lovatt, but when asked why, they admit that they are only repeating rumours started by persons unknown. Travis himself keeps an open mind, and naturally is proved right by the time the book reaches a typically romantic finale.

Jons did have a predilection for "framed-for-murder" stories, however, and it was a plot device he used several times in the course of his career, most notably in *Guns of Justice*, in which young Des Willard, accused of the double killing of his brother and the local sheriff, loses even the scant support of a few loyal friends when the town banker is also found murdered, and is only able to prove his innocence with the help of Sal Dormer, the spunky daughter of a visiting horse trader; *Guns at Chinooga Peak*, in which U.S. Marshal Travis and his deputy Joe Wallace, playing a hunch, decide on impulse to investigate the murder of a rancher, hoping to catch the runaway suspect (a hitherto well-liked and trustworthy member of the community) before a merciless bounty hunter named Moss Hanney can shoot him on sight; and in *Gringo Gold*, the leader of an immigrant wagon train is framed for murder so that a gang of outlaws can catch up with the column and steal the solid gold cross the immigrants are carrying with them.

Jons's books reveal a good balance between prose and speech, and his dialogue, which is liberally sprinkled with western words and phrases, reinforces their traditional, pulp-style feel. Jons's characters rarely have names, for example, although they do have "monikers," just as they seldom ride horses although they will frequently "fork a cayuse." Most curious of all, however, is his constant habit of substituting the word "salivate" for "kill" or "murder," a tendency which can sometimes produce some very odd sentences. Likewise, violence, while present, is generally glossed over, although the author can on occasion allude to "throats exploding in red gouts of blood."

Although by no means an inspired writer, Jons usually managed to produce an entertaining if flawed product, and while the extent of his contribution to the genre is debatable, there is little doubt that his books will be read for many years to come.

—David Whitehead

JORDAN, Bryn. *See* **DANVERS, Pete.**

JORDAN, Matt. *See* **LINAKER, Mike.**

JOSCELYN, Archie (Lynn). Also writes as A.A. Archer; Al Cody; Tex Holt; Evelyn McKenna; Lynn Westland. American. Born in Great Falls, Montana, 25 July 1899. Educated at International Union College, 1921–24. Married Hazel Peterson in 1926; two sons and one daughter. Grew up on a ranch in Montana; freelance writer from age 19. President, Montana Institute of the Arts. Agent: Donald Mac Campbell, Inc., 12 East 41st Street, New York, New York. Address: 227 Connell, Apt. 3, Missoula, Montana 598 01, U.S.A.

WESTERN PUBLICATIONS

Novels

The Golden Bowl. Cleveland, World, 1931.
Black Horse Rider. New York, Phoenix Press, and London, Cassell, 1935.
Six-Gun Sovereignty. New York, Phoenix Press, 1935; as *Gun Sovereignty*, London, Cassell, 1935.
The Law Man of Lonesome River. New York, Phoenix Press, 1935; London, Cassell, 1936.
The King of Thunder Valley. New York, Phoenix Press, and London, Cassell, 1936.
Ranch of the Two Thumbs. New York, Phoenix Press, and London, Cassell, 1937.
The Riding Devils. New York, Phoenix Press, and London, Cassell, 1937.
Cottonwood Canyon. New York, Phoenix Press, 1938; London, Cassell, 1939.
Hoot Owl Canyon. New York, Phoenix Press, 1938; London, Cassell, 1939.
The Heart E Horsemen. New York, Phoenix Press, 1939; London, Cassell, 1941.
Tenderfoot Bill. New York, Phoenix Press, 1939; London, Ward Lock, 1940.
Guns of Lost Valley. New York, Phoenix Press, 1940.
Double Diamond Brand. New York, Phoenix Press, 1940; London, Ward Lock, 1941.
Dead Man's Range. New York, Phoenix Press, 1941; London, Ward Lock, 1942.
The Sawbones of Desolate Range. New York, Phoenix Press, 1941; London, Ward Lock, 1942.
Yates of Red Dog. New York, Phoenix Press, 1942; London, Ward Lock, 1943.
Double Cross Tangles. Kingswood, Surrey, World's Work, 1942.
Satan's Range. New York, Phoenix Press, 1942; London, Ward Lock, 1944.
Trail to Bang-Up. New York, Phoenix Press, 1943; London, Ward Lock, 1944.
Valley Ranch. New York, Phoenix Press, 1943; London, Wright and Brown, 1950.
Troublesome Cowhand. New York, Phoenix Press, 1944; London, Wright and Brown, 1947.
Blue River Riders. New York, Phoenix Press, 1944; London, Ward Lock, 1945.
Boss of the Northern Star. New York, Phoenix Press, 1944; London, Wright and Brown, 1946.
Rusty Mallory. New York, Phoenix Press, 1945; London, Wright and Brown, 1948.
Sign of the Gun. New York, Phoenix Press, 1945; London, Wright and Brown, 1946.
Death in the Saddle. New York, Arcadia House, 1946; London, Sampson Low, 1947.
Judge Colt. New York, Arcadia House, 1946; London, Sampson Low, 1948.
Thunder of Hooves. London, Swan, 1948.
Smoky in the West. New York, Curl, 1948; as Al Cody, London, Sampson Low, 1950.
Border Wolves. New York, Star, 1950.
Death's Bright Angel. Kingswood, Surrey, World's Work, 1950.
Shannahan's Feud. Kingston, New York, Quinn, 1950; Bath, Chivers, 1987; as *The Claim Jumpers*, London, Foulsham, 1953.
Texas Outlaw. New York, Star, 1950; London, W.H. Allen, 1953.
Stardance Post. Kingswood, Surrey, World's Work, 1950.
Star Toter. London, United Anglo-American Book Company, 1950; as Al Cody, New York, Arcadia House, 1962.
Doomrock. New York, Avalon, 1950; as *Doomrock Range* (as Al Cody), London, Sampson Low, 1951.
Maverick Range. Kingswood, Surrey, World's Work, 1951.
Vengeance Trail. New York, Star, 1951; as *The Kempsey Outfit*, London, Foulsham, 1954; as *Ambush of Satan's Hill*, New York, Paperback Library, 1963.
Outlaw's Holiday. New York, Star, 1951.
Gun Thunder Valley. New York, Fawcett, 1951; London, Gold Lion, 1973.
Hell for Leather. New York, Novel Selections, 1951.
Wagons West. New York, Avalon, 1951.
The Golden Stagecoach. London, Foulsham, 1952.
Hostage. New York, Avalon, 1952; Kingswood, Surrey, World's Work, 1953.
The Texan's Revenge. New York, Star, 1952.
Valley of the Sun. Kingswood, Surrey, World's Work, 1952; Toronto, Harlequin, 1956.
Two Gun Vengeance. New York, Star, 1953.
Texas Showdown. Toronto, Harlequin, 1953; New York, Paperback Library, 1962.
Gunman. New York, Avalon, 1953.
Canyon Man Hunt. London, Foulsham, 1953.
Outlaw Holiday. London, Foulsham, 1954.
Trappers' Rendezvous. New York, Avalon, 1954; as *Wyoming Rendezvous*, London, Foulsham, 1956.
Renegade Scout. New York, Avalon, 1954; Kingston, Surrey, World's Work, 1956.
Cheyenne Justice. New York, Avalon, and London, Ward Lock, 1955.
The Silver Saddle. London, Muller, 1955.
The Sundowners. New York, Avalon, 1956; London, Ward Lock, 1959; as *Gunhand's Pay*, New York, Pyramid, 1957.
Hired Gun. New York, Avon, 1956.
Six-Gun Sawbones. New York, Avon, 1957.
Texas Revenge. New York, Avon, 1957.
The Man from Salt Creek. New York, Avalon, 1957; London, Ward Lock, 1961.
Cheyenne Kid. New York, Avon, 1958.
Fighting Kid from Texas. New York, Avon, 1958; Bath, Chivers, 1987.
High Prairie. New York, Avalon, 1958.
River of the Sunset. New York, Ace, 1958.
Dead Man's Trail. New York, Avon, 1959.
Gunsmoke at Gila Gulch. New York, Avalon, 1959; as *Gunsmoke on the Gila*, London, Ward Lock, 1960.
Marshal of Broken Wheel. New York, Arcadia House, and London, Wright and Brown, 1960.
Massacre Creek. New York, Arcadia House, 1962.
Sheriff of Red Wolf. New York, Arcadia House, 1963.
The Man Behind the Star. New York, Avon, 1963.
A Sky Pilot for Powderhorn. New York, Arcadia House, 1963; Bath, Chivers, 1988.
Rim of the Range. New York, Arcadia House, 1963; Bath, Chivers, 1984.
Gun in Hand. London, Consul, 1964.
King of Silverhill. New York, Avalon, 1964; Bath, Chivers, 1986.
Duel at Killman Creek. New York, Paperback Library, 1964.
Logan. New York, Paperback Library, 1964.
West from Deadwood. New York, Arcadia House, 1964.
Storm along the Rattlesnake. New York, Arcadia House, 1964.
Rimrock Vengeance. New York, Arcadia House, 1965; as Al Cody, Bath, Chivers, 1984.

The Sheriff of Singing River. New York, Arcadia House, 1965.
The Golden River. New York, Arcadia House, 1966; London, Hale, 1971.
The Gunhand. New York, Avalon, 1966.
Fort Fear. New York, Arcadia House, 1967; as Lynn Westland, Bath, Chivers, 1987.
Trail North. New York, Avalon, 1967.
Trouble at Sudden Creek. New York, Avalon, 1967; Bath, Chivers, 1986.
The Guns of Yesterday. New York, Arcadia House, 1968; London, Hale, 1970.
The Forbidden Frontier. New York, Arcadia House, 1968.
Bushwhack Range. New York, Avalon, 1968.
Freeze-Out Creek. New York, Arcadia House, 1969; London, Hale, 1970.
Montana's Golden Gamble. New York, Lenox Hill Press, 1971.
The Coming of the Gunman. New York, Bouregy, 1971.
Cheyenne Country. New York, Lenox Hill Press, 1974.
East to Montana. New York, Lenox Hill Press, 1974.
Empty Holsters. New York, Avalon, 1974.
Restless Spurs. New York, Lenox Hill Press, 1974; Bath, Chivers, 1987.
Guns for Fort Garryowen. New York, Bouregy, 1975.
Gunsmoke Holiday. New York, Lenox Hill Press, 1975.
The Trail to Dismal River. New York, Avalon, 1975.
Lost River Canyon. New York, Avalon, 1976.
Kiowa Pass. New York, Avalon, 1976.
The Trail to Lost Horse Ranch. New York, Avalon, 1977.
The Lost Herd. New York, Avalon, 1978.
The Hooded Falcon. New York, Manor, 1978.

Novels as Lynn Westland

Son of the Saddle. New York, Phoenix Press, 1936; London, Nicholson and Watson, 1937.
Powdersmoke Pass. New York, Phoenix Press, and London, Nicholson and Watson, 1937.
Dakota Marshal. New York, Phoenix Press, 1937; London, Nicholson and Watson, 1938; as *Lone Tree Renegade* (as Archie Joscelyn), New York, Belmont, 1968.
Maverick Molloy. New York, Phoenix Press, 1938.
Quick on the Draw. London, Nicholson and Watson, 1938.
King Cayuse. New York, Phoenix Press, 1939.
The Range of No Return. New York, Phoenix Press, 1939; London, Wright and Brown, 1940.
Born to the Saddle. New York, Phoenix Press, and London, Wright and Brown, 1940.
The Nightmare Riders. New York, Phoenix Press, 1940; London, Wright and Brown, 1952.
King of the Rodeo. New York, Phoenix Press, 1941; London, Ward Lock, 1942.
Shooting Valley. New York, Phoenix Press, 1941; Brighton, Global, 1949.
Saddle River Spread. New York, Phoenix Press, 1942; London, Ward Lock, 1943.
Shootin' Iron. New York, Phoenix Press, and London, Ward Lock, 1942.
Trail to Montana. New York, Phoenix Press, 1943; London, Partridge, 1945.
Prentiss of the Box H. New York, Phoenix Press, 1943; London, Ward Lock, 1944.
Gunsight Ranch. New York, Phoenix Press, 1943; London, Ward Lock, 1944.
Prairie Pinto. New York, Phoenix Press, 1944; London, Wright and Brown, 1952.
Wagon Train Westward. New York, Phoenix Press, 1944.
Over the Frontier Trail. New York, Phoenix Press, 1945; London, Wright and Brown, 1952.
Prairie Pioneers. New York, Phoenix Press, 1945; London, Wright and Brown, 1951.
Return to the Range. New York, Phoenix Press, 1945; London, Partridge, 1946.
Long Loop Raiders. New York, Phoenix Press, 1946; London, Wright and Brown, 1949.
The Lone Pine Ranch. New York, Phoenix Press, 1947.
The Silver Cayuse. New York, Phoenix Press, 1947; London, Wright and Brown, 1949.
Black River Ranch. New York, Phoenix Press, 1948; London, Foulsham, 1949.
Home Range. New York, Phoenix Press, 1948; London, Foulsham, 1949.
North from Montana. New York, Phoenix Press, and London, Foulsham, 1948.
Silvertip Ranch. New York, Phoenix Press, 1949; London, Foulsham, 1950.
Texas Red. New York, Phoenix Press, 1950; London, Foulsham, 1951.
Trail Rider. Kingston, New York, Quinn, 1951.
Tough Sheriff Jameson. London, Foulsham, 1953.
Outlaw. London, Wright and Brown, 1953; as Archie Joscelyn, New York, Avon, 1958.
Ride to Blizzard. New York, Avalon, 1953; London, Foulsham, 1954.
Legion of the Lawless. Toronto, Harlequin, 1953.
The Dead Ride Hard. London, Foulsham, 1954; New York, Avon, 1958.
Gun Ranch. New York, Arcadia House, 1962.
The Heart of Texas. New York, Arcadia House, 1963; as Al Cody, Bath, Chivers, 1984.
Powdersmoke Payoff. New York, Arcadia House, 1963; as Al Cody, Bath, Chivers, 1985.
Deadman's Gold. New York, Arcadia House, 1964.
Thunder to the West. New York, Arcadia House, 1964; as Al Cody, Bath, Chivers, 1984.
Smoke Against the Sky. New York, Arcadia House, 1965; London, Wright and Brown, 1966.
The Red Gun. New York, Arcadia House, 1965.
Heritage in Powdersmoke. New York, Arcadia House, 1967; London, Hale, 1971.
Rogue's Range. New York, Arcadia House, 1968; London, Hale, 1970.
Dragoon Pass. London, Hale, 1970.
Iron Trail to Stirrup. New York, Bouregy, 1975.

Novels as Al Cody

Empty Saddles. New York, Dodd Mead, 1946; London, Nimmo, 1947.
West of the Law. New York, Dodd Mead, 1947; London, Nimmo, 1949.
Bitter Creek. New York, Dodd Mead, and London, Quality Press, 1947.
Disaster Trail. New York, Dodd Mead, 1948; London, Sampson Low, 1950.
Outpost Trail. New York, Dodd Mead, 1948; London, Sampson Low, 1950.
The Marshal of Deer Creek. New York, Dodd Mead, 1949; London, Sampson Low, 1950.
The Big Corral. New York, Dodd Mead, 1949; London, Macdonald, 1954.
Sundown. New York, Dodd Mead, 1950.
Reservation Range. London, Sampson Low, 1950.
Hangman's Coulee. New York, Dodd Mead, 1951.

Forlorn Valley. London, Sampson Low, 1951.
Red Man's Range. London, Sampson Low, 1951; New York, Berkley, 1957.
Thunder River Trail. London, Sampson Low, 1951.
Forbidden River. New York, Avalon, 1952.
The Thundering Hills. New York, Avalon, 1952; London, Muller, 1954.
Outlaw Justice at Hangman's Coulee. New York, Avon, 1952.
Guns Blaze at Sundown. New York, Avon, 1952.
Outlaw Valley. Toronto, Harlequin, 1952.
Bad Man's Town. London, Sampson Low, 1952.
Riders of Stormhold. London, Sampson Low, 1953; as *Montana Helltown*, New York, Avon, 1958.
Powder Burns. New York, Avalon, 1953; London, Muller, 1955.
Brand of Iron. New York, Star, and London, Muller, 1954.
Lost Valley. Toronto, Harlequin, 1954.
Guns on the Bitterroot. New York, Avalon, 1955.
Whiplash War. New York, Avon, 1956.
Bloody Wyoming. New York, Avon, 1958; Bath, Chivers, 1986.
Wyoming Ambush. New York, Avon, 1959.
Winter Range. New York, Avalon, 1959.
Long Night at Lodge Pole. New York, Ace, 1961.
Gunsmoke Hill. New York, Arcadia House, 1961.
Homestead Range. New York, Arcadia House, 1962.
Wyoming Outlaw. New York, Paperback Library, 1962.
The Golden Saddle. New York, Arcadia House, 1963.
Squatter Sovereignty. New York, Arcadia House, 1964.
Trail of the Innocents. New York, Arcadia House, 1964.
The Renegade. New York, Avalon, 1966.
Montana Fury. New York, Bouregy, 1967; Bath, Chivers, 1986.
Montana's Territory. New York, Lenox Hill Press, 1970.
The Ranch at Powder River. New York, Lenox Hill Press, 1972.
Gunsong at Twilight. New York, Manor, 1974.
Return to Fort Yavapa. New York, Avalon, 1975.
Broken Wheels. New York, Manor, 1976; Bath, Chivers, 1988.
Iron Horse Country. New York, Manor, 1976.
Triple Cross Trail. New York, Manor, 1977.
Flame in the Forest. New York, Manor, 1977.
The Fort at the Dry. New York, Avalon, 1977.
Once a Sheriff. New York, Manor, 1977.
The Three McMahons. New York, Manor, 1977.
High Lonesome. New York, Manor, 1978; Bath, Chivers, 1986.
The Mine at Lost Mountain. New York, Manor, 1978.
Return to Texas. New York, Manor, 1978.
West from Abilene. New York, Manor, 1978.
West of Sundown. New York, Manor, 1978; Bath, Chivers, 1988.

Novels as Tex Holt

Thunder of Hoofs. New York, Arcadia House, 1946.
Dark Canyon. New York, Phoenix Press, 1948; as Al Cody, London, Quality Press, 1949.
Point West. New York, Phoenix Press, 1949.
Cactus on the Range. New York, Phoenix Press, 1950.
This Land Is Mine. New York, Arcadia House, 1963.
The Silent Guns. New York, Arcadia House, 1963.
There Were Giants. New York, Lenox Hill Press, 1970.

Uncollected Short Stories

"The Last o' the Tarnwells," in *Wild West* (New York), 22 October 1927.
"One Tough Tenderfoot," with Guy Rader, in *Wild West* (New York), 5 November 1927.
"Loop of the Law," with Guy Rader, in *West* (New York), 14 January 1928.
"Law of the Lawless," in *West* (New York), 12 May 1928.
"Buzzards Roost," in *Wild West* (New York), 7 July 1928.
"Fer Foolin' the Sheriff," with Hazel Joscelyn, in *Wild West* (New York), 28 July 1928.
"Double Cross Ranch," in *Wild West* (New York), 11 August 1928.
"Wide Loopin'," in *Wild West* (New York), 8 September 1928.
"The Samaritan of Double JH," in *Wild West* (New York), 15 September 1928.
"Rattlesnake's Fangs," in *Wild West* (New York), 13 October 1928.
"The Whistlin' Kid's Lullaby," in *Wild West* (New York), 3 November 1928.
"One Hard-Boiled Hombre," in *Wild West* (New York), 8 December 1928.
"Trail Drivin' from HK," in *Wild West* (New York), 12 January 1929.
"Cold-Nerve Moran," in *Wild West* (New York), 27 April 1929.
"Scourge of the Snowies," in *Wild West* (New York), 13 July 1929.
"A Joke on the Sheriff," in *Wild West* (New York), 27 July 1929.
"Swede Mulligan's Way," in *Wild West* (New York), 10 August 1929.
"$500 Reward," in *Wild West* (New York), 24 August 1929.
"The Tenderfoot from Yale," in *Wild West* (New York), 21 September 1929.
"Riders of Devil's Ranch," in *Wild West* (New York), 8 March 1930.
"Crooked Brands," in *Wild West* (New York), 29 March 1930.
"Coyote Bait," in *Riders of the Range* (Springfield, Massachusetts), April–May 1931.
"Satan's Shuffle," in *Cowboy Stories* (New York), November 1934.
"Death Code," in *Cowboy Stories* (New York), January 1935.
"Jell on the Hoof," in *Cowboy Stories* (New York), April 1935.
"Gunman's Gamble," in *Cowboy Stories* (New York), September 1935.
"Backed Up," in *Cowboy Stories* (New York), October 1935.
"Devil's Herd," in *Cowboy Stories* (New York), November 1935.
"Kestry Trails a Killer," in *Cowboy Stories* (New York), February 1936.
"Branding Iron," in *Cowboy Stories* (New York), June 1936.
"The Court of No Appeal," in *Cowboy Stories* (New York), October 1936.
"The Red One," in *Cowboy Stories* (New York), May 1937.
"The Range of No Return," in *West* (New York), September 1938.
"Coyote's Corral," in *Wild West* (New York), 21 June 1941.
"Blood Code," in *Wild West* (New York), 19 July 1941.
"Satan's Stagecoach," in *Wild West* (New York), 23 August 1941.
"Cloudy in the West," in *Wild West* (New York), 4 October 1941.
"Renegade of the Rio," in *Wild West* (New York), 22 November 1941.

"Ranch of No Return," in *Wild West* (New York), 6 December 1941.
"Revenge of the River," in *Wild West* (New York), 20 December 1941.
"Bear Trap for Lobos," in *Wild West* (New York), 10 January 1942.
"Hell Rolls on Wheels," in *Wild West* (New York), 7 February 1942.
"Powder-Smoke Pasear," in *Wild West* (New York), 23 May 1942.
"Sidewinder Season," in *Wild West* (New York), 20 June 1942.
"Port of Missing Packets," in *Wild West* (New York), 1 August 1942.
"Set-Up for Sidewinders," in *Wild West* (New York), 22 August 1942.
"Death Wears a Diamond Horseshoe," in *Wild West* (New York), 12 September 1942.
"Death on the Mountain," in *Wild West* (New York), 3 October 1942.
"Bill for Bushwhack," in *Wild West* (New York), 28 November 1942.
"Revenge Rides by Night," in *Wild West* (New York), 19 December 1942.
"Gunsmith's Gamble," in *Wild West* (New York), 13 March 1943.
"Spooked Spurs," in *Wild West* (New York), 24 April 1943.
"Double-Cross Decision," in *Wild West* (New York), 3 July 1943.
"Trail of the Golden Boulder," in *Wild West* (New York), 14 August 1943.
"Guns or Grain for Arizona," in *Wild West* (New York), November 1943.
"River Hog's Showdown," in *Western Story* (London), May 1944.
"Mantrap Trail," in *Texas Rangers* (London), April 1961.

OTHER PUBLICATIONS

Novels

Eric Hearle, Detective. Cleveland, World, 1934.
Three Men Murdered (as A.A. Archer). New York, Phoenix Press, 1936.
The Week-End Murders (as A.A. Archer). New York, Phoenix Press, 1938.
The Thief. Rock Island, Illinois, Augustana Press, 1958.
The Crown. Rock Island, Illinois, Augustana Press, 1960.
The Beast of Babylon. Minneapolis, Augsburg, 1963.

Novels as Evelyn McKenna

Fire in My Heart. New York, Phoenix Press, 1936.
One Romantic Summer. New York, Phoenix Press, 1936.
The Enchanted Park. New York, Grammercy, 1937.
Castle Midnight. New York, Arcadia House, 1966.
Castle Light. New York, Bouregy, 1976.

Other

Prisoner's Valley (for children). Cleveland, World, 1935.

* * *

In such a huge output, Archie Joscelyn obviously tells a number of different stories, but it is not difficult to identify his favourite devices, which form the scaffolding for practically all the tales, whatever name is signed to them. Routine novels about range war figure a hero who usually has been both cowboy and student, earning a degree in law or engineering in the east. He returns to his homeland, to claim his inheritance or to help the smaller side in a feud. He has many obstacles to overcome: he has to clear his name of a false reputation for rustling or murder; very often he is mistaken for some more notorious figure, an identity he has to maintain for chivalrous reasons; he may even have lost his memory and be unable to recall his true identity; or an evil double or twin brother may be operating in the neighbourhood. His main opponent is a suave easterner, evil behind his civilized façade and desperate for both the land and the woman claimed by the hero. The battle is conducted through a series of melodramatic scenes, told with perfunctory haste.

Joscelyn likes enclosed valleys, prairie fires, and rivers with whirlpools or quicksands, the latter usually serving to dispose of the villain at the end. A typically fantastic quicksand occurs in a Cody story, *Forlorn Valley*. A rancher has built his house on stilts over a marsh, in which he disposes of enemies. The hero is thrown into the quicksand and, in escaping, so loosens the foundations that the whole building is sucked under ("like the fall of the house of Usher"), taking with it the hero's outlaw brother, who chooses to die thus rather than see the woman he loves married to the hero. Joscelyn tends to need some ingenious finale for, at least in the early novels, he never lets the hero kill anyone. He always encrusts his narrative with Biblical, mythic, or literary allusions, and his earliest novels are particularly cliché-riddled. For example, the opening pages of *Black Horse Rider* pack in a cowboy who "dies with his boots on," a hero "riding the revenge trail," and two factions "pouring lead" at each other. Although the language becomes less stilted in time, motives, complications, and consequences remain implausible.

Some social issues seem to arise, but they never come to fruition. In *Blue River Riders* the hero, battling against an undeserved infamy, tries to save his valley, which is being ruined by the Slaghorn Copper Company. It turns out that only the superintendent is evil having framed the hero, stolen his ranch, courted his cousin, and failed to inform the company of the ranchers' complaints. The company itself is very benign, eager to clear up the sulphurous smoke and return the hero's land to him.

Joscelyn's debt is clearly to the dime novel. He writes like a latter-day Beadle and Adams author, with his symbolic names, his disguises, mistaken identities and familial complications, his perfunctory melodrama, and his irrelevant, incredible fantasies.

—Christine Bold

K

KANE, Jim. *See* **CORD, Barry.**

KANTOR, MacKinlay. American. Born in Webster City, Iowa, 4 February 1904. Educated at Webster City High School. Married Florence Irene Layne in 1926; two sons. Reporter, Webster City *Daily News*, 1921–24; advertiser in Chicago, 1925–26; reporter, Cedar Rapids *Republican*, Iowa, 1927; columnist, Des Moines *Tribune*, Iowa, 1930–31; scenario writer for Hollywood studios; war correspondent for United States and British air forces, 1943, 1950, and technical consultant to the United States Air Force, 1951–53; member of the uniformed division, New York City Police, 1948–50. Member of the National Council, Boy Scouts of America; trustee, Lincoln College, Illinois; 1960–68. Recipient: Pulitzer prize, 1956, National Association of Independent Schools award, 1956; Medal of Freedom. D.Litt.: Grinnell College, Iowa, 1957; Drake University, Des Moines, 1958; Lincoln College, 1959; Ripon College, Wisconsin, 1961; LL.D.: Iowa Wesleyan College, Mount Pleasant, 1961. Fellow, Society of American Historians. *Died 11 October 1977.*

WESTERN PUBLICATIONS

Novels

The Voice of Bugle Ann. New York, Coward McCann, and London, Selwyn and Blount, 1935.
Gentle Annie: A Western Novel. New York, Coward McCann, 1942; London, Hale, 1951; as *The Goss Boys*, London, Corgi, 1958.
Warwhoop: Two Short Novels of the Frontier: Behold the Brown-Faced Man and *Missouri Moon.* New York, Random House, 1952.
The Daughter of Bugle Ann. New York, Random House, 1953.
Spirit Lake. Cleveland, World, 1961; London, W.H. Allen, 1962.

Short Stories

Author's Choice: 40 Stories. New York, Coward McCann, 1944.
Frontier: Tales of the American Adventure. New York, New American Library, 1959.
The Gun-Toter and Other Stories of the Missouri Hills. New York, New American Library, 1963.

Uncollected Short Story

"The Last Bullet," in *The Outlaws*, edited by Bill Pronzini and Martin H. Greenberg. New York, Fawcett, 1984.

OTHER PUBLICATIONS

Novels

Diversey. New York, Coward McCann, 1928.
El Goes South. New York, Coward McCann, 1930.
The Jaybird. New York, Coward McCann, 1932.
Long Remember. New York, Coward McCann, and London, Selwyn and Blount, 1934.
Arouse and Beware. New York, Coward McCann, 1936; London, Gollancz, 1937.
The Romance of Rosy Ridge. New York, Coward McCann, 1937.
The Noise of Their Wings. New York, Coward McCann, 1938; London, Hale, 1939.
Valedictory. New York, Coward McCann, 1939.
Cuba Libre. New York, Coward McCann, 1940.
Happy Land. New York, Coward McCann, 1943.
Glory for Me (in verse). New York, Coward McCann, 1945.
Midnight Lace. New York, Random House, 1948; London, Falcon Press, 1949.
Wicked Water: An American Primitive. New York, Random House, 1949; London, Falcon Press, 1950.
The Good Family. New York, Coward McCann, 1949.
One Wild Oat. New York, Fawcett, 1950; London, W.H. Allen, 1952.
Signal Thirty-Two. New York, Random House, 1950.
Don't Touch Me. New York, Random House, 1951; London, W.H. Allen, 1952.
God and My Country. Cleveland, World, 1954.
Andersonville. Cleveland, World, 1955; London, W.H. Allen, 1956.
The Work of St. Francis. Cleveland, World, 1958; as *The Unseen Witness*, London, W.H. Allen, 1959.
Beauty Beast. New York, Putnam, 1968.
I Love You, Irene. New York, Doubleday, 1972; London, W.H. Allen, 1973.
The Children Sing. New York, Hawthorn Books, 1973; London, Hale, 1974.
Valley Forge. New York, Evans, 1975.

Short Stories

The Boy in the Dark. Webster Groves, Missouri, International Mark Twain Society, 1937.
Silent Grow the Guns and Other Tales of the American Civil War. New York, New American Library, 1958.
Again the Bugle. New York, American Weekly, 1958.
It's about Crime. New York, New American Library, 1960.
Story Teller. New York, Doubleday, 1967.

Plays

Screenplays: *Gun Crazy* (*Deadly Is the Female*), with Millard Kaufman, 1950; *Hannah Lee*, with Rip Von Ronkel, 1953.

Verse

Turkey in the Straw: A Book of American Ballads and Primitive Verse. New York, Coward McCann, 1935.

Other

Angleworms on Toast (for children). New York, Coward McCann, 1942.
But Look, the Morn: The Story of a Childhood (reminiscences). New York, Coward McCann, 1947; London, Falcon Press, 1951.
Lee and Grant at Appomattox (for children). New York, Random House, 1950.
Gettysburg (for children). New York, Random House, 1952.
Lobo (reminiscences). Cleveland, World, 1957; London, W.H. Allen, 1958.
If the South Had Won the Civil War. New York, Bantam, 1961.
Mission with LeMay: My Story, with General Curtis LeMay. New York, Doubleday, 1965.
The Historical Novelist's Obligation to History (lecture). Macon, Georgia, Wesley College, 1967.
The Day I Met a Lion. New York, Doubleday, 1968.
Missouri Bittersweet (reminiscences). New York, Doubleday, 1969; London, Hale, 1970.
Hamilton County, photographs by Tim Kantor. New York, Macmillan, 1970.

*

Manuscript Collections: Library of Congress, Washington, D.C.; University of Iowa, Iowa City.

Critical Study: *My Father's Voice: MacKinlay Kantor Long Remembered* by Tim Kantor, New York, McGraw Hill, 1988.

* * *

When MacKinlay Kantor's western novel *Gentle Annie* was published in 1942, reviewers praised it for taking liberties with the conventional western formula. Wrote one in *The New Yorker*, "Because MacKinlay Kantor is a better novelist than most writers of Westerns, this is a better Western."

Kantor, who freely admitted that he wrote "to sell, because I needed money," had a consuming interest in the Civil War but apparently little sense of commitment to the American West as a source of regional literature. For example, "The Doll with a Busted Leg," a short story about a kind-hearted gunman, was originally set in the Midwest, based on a true incident. When it didn't sell, Kantor revised it, allowing the gunman to survive the final shootout, and set it in the Wild West. Another story, "The Horse Looked at Him," is a classic tale of death in the desert, but Anderson once confessed that the story idea came from a friend.

Writing to create popular and entertaining works that would sell, Kantor broke away from some of the Western's basic traditions. With his considerable narrative skills, he was able to take the ingredients of the western formula and create surprisingly new works. They reveal the streak of sentimentality which, he said once, infected him throughout the years. That American paradox, the good, clean, wholesome boy who is an outlaw, is often pivotal in the stories. Like most Westerns, these are morality plays, exploring the problems of the relationship between good and evil. But in spite of his sentimentality Kantor rarely sees sharp distinctions, clearcut answers. His heroes are sometimes on the receiving end of the action rather than always in charge, and they are not always strong, sure, and convinced of their own right. There are few satisfactory endings, because Kantor rarely ties up all the loose ends as neatly as many traditional western authors. As a result, some of the works seem enigmatic.

Slim as they are, Kantor's western works are significant because they illustrate that the western formula can be used with skill and originality by talented authors neither born in the West nor dedicated to it. *Gentle Annie*, for instance, rises above the classification of a pulp to rest on a level with the sentimental and chaste western novels of Mary Hallock Foote or Emerson Hough.

—Judy Alter

KEENE, James. *See* **COOK, Will.**

KEENE, Lt. *See* **RATHBORNE, St. George.**

KELLEY, Leo P(atrick). American. Born in Wilkes Barre, Pennsylvania, 10 September 1928. Educated at the New School for Social Research, New York, B.A. in English 1957. Advertising copywriter and manager, McGraw-Hill Book Company, New York, 1959–69. Since 1969 freelance writer. Address: 702 Lincoln Boulevard, Long Beach, New York 11561, U.S.A.

WESTERN PUBLICATIONS

Novels (series: Cimarron; Luke Sutton)

Luke Sutton: Outlaw. New York, Doubleday, and London, Hale, 1981.
Luke Sutton: Gunfighter. New York, Doubleday, and London, Hale, 1982.
Luke Sutton: Indian Fighter. New York, Doubleday, 1982; London, Hale, 1983.
Luke Sutton: Avenger. New York, Doubleday, and London, Hale, 1983.
Cimarron in the Cherokee Strip. New York, New American Library, 1983.
Cimarron and the Border Bandits. New York, New American Library, 1983.
Cimarron and the Bounty Hunters. New York, New American Library, 1983.
Cimarron and the Elk Soldiers. New York, New American Library, 1983.
Cimarron and the Hanging Judge. New York, New American Library, 1983.

Cimarron Rides the Outlaw Trail. New York, New American Library, 1983.
Cimarron in No Man's Land. New York, New American Library, 1984.
Cimarron on Hell's Highway. New York, New American Library, 1984.
Cimarron and the High Rider. New York, New American Library, 1984.
Cimarron and the Medicine Wolves. New York, New American Library, 1984.
Cimarron and the Vigilantes. New York, New American Library, 1984.
Cimarron and the War Women. New York, New American Library, 1984.
Cimarron and the Bootleggers. New York, New American Library, 1984.
Luke Sutton: Outrider. New York, Doubleday, 1984; London, Hale, 1986.
Luke Sutton: Bounty Hunter. New York, Doubleday, 1985; London, Hale, 1991.
Cimarron and the Gun Hawks' Gold. New York, New American Library, 1985.
Cimarron and the Prophet's People. New York, New American Library, 1985.
Cimarron and the Scalp Hunters. New York, New American Library, 1985.
Cimarron and the Hired Guns. New York, New American Library, 1986.
Cimarron and the Red Earth People. New York, New American Library, 1986.
Cimarron and the Manhunters. New York, New American Library, 1986.
Cimarron on the High Plains. New York, New American Library, 1986.
Morgan. New York, Doubleday, 1986.
A Man Named Dundee. New York, Doubleday, 1988.
Thunder Gods' Gold. New York, Evans, 1988.
The Last Cowboy. Belmont, California, Lake, 1988.
Luke Sutton: Hired Gun. New York, Doubleday, 1987; London, Hale, 1991.
Luke Sutton: Lawman. New York, Doubleday, 1989.

OTHER PUBLICATIONS

Novels

The Counterfeits. New York, Belmont, 1967.
Odyssey to Earthdeath. New York, Belmont, 1968.
The Accidental Earth. New York, Belmont, 1968.
Time Rogue. New York, Lancer, 1970.
Brother John (novelization of screenplay). New York, Avon, 1971; London, Pan, 1971.
The Coins of Murph. New York, Berkley, 1971; London, Coronet, 1974.
Mindmix. New York, Fawcett, 1972; London, Coronet, 1973.
Time: 110100. New York, Walker, 1972; as *The Man from Maybe*, London, Coronet, 1974.
Deadlocked. New York, Fawcett, 1973.
Mythmaster. New York, Dell, 1973; London, Coronet, 1974.
The Earth Tripper. New York, Fawcett, 1973; London, Coronet, 1974.

Fiction (for children)

The Time Trap: Pacesetters. Belmont, California, Pitman, 1977; London, Murray, 1979.
Night of Fire and Blood. Belmont, California, Pitman, and London, Murray, 1979.
Star Gold. Belmont, California, Pitman, and London, Murray, 1979.
Dead Moon. Belmont, California, Pitman, 1979; London, Murray, 1980.
Goodbye to Earth. Belmont, California, Pitman, 1979; London, Murray, 1980.
King of the Stars. Belmont, California, Pitman, 1979; London, Murray, 1980.
On the Red World. Belmont, California, Pitman, 1979; London, Murray, 1980.
Vacation in Space. Belmont, California, Pitman, 1979; London, Murray, 1980.
Where No Sun Shines. Belmont, California, Pitman, 1979; London, Murray, 1980.
Backward in Time. Belmont, California, Pitman, 1979; London, Hutchinson, 1980.
Death Sentence. Belmont, California, Pitman, 1979; London, Hutchinson, 1980.
Earth Two. Belmont, California, Pitman, 1979; London, Hutchinson, 1980.
Prison Satellite. Belmont, California, Pitman, 1979; London, Hutchinson, 1980.
Sunworld. Belmont, California, Pitman, 1979; London, Hutchinson, 1980.
Worlds Apart. Belmont, California, Pitman, 1979; London, Hutchinson, 1980.
Johnny Tall Dog. Belmont, California, Pitman, 1981.

Other

Editor, *Themes in Science Fiction: A Journey into Wonder.* New York, McGraw Hill, 1972.
Editor, *The Supernatural in Fiction.* New York, McGraw Hill, 1973.
Editor, *Fantasy: The Literature of the Marvelous.* New York, McGraw Hill, 1974.

* * *

Though initially best-known for his many adult and juvenile science-fiction novels, Leo P. Kelley has also been writing Westerns since 1981, and can now lay claim to a string of frontier stories that are distinguished by their fast pace and wealth of wilderness lore.

Kelley's first western, *Luke Sutton: Outlaw* is, like all the volumes that comprise this sequence, a mixture of the traditional and modern. Through the eyes of his protagonist (who wanders the West initially in search of the four men who killed his brother to obtain a map pinpointing "the fabled silver mine of San Saba"), Kelley explores different aspects of the Old West in each volume. Consequently, the stories sometimes have a rather episodic feel to them, as if we are really only witnessing a series of interesting but often pointless incidents in Sutton's life.

Luke Sutton: Indian Fighter is a good case in point, being a strong, well-told story encumbered by too many needless asides. Having already located and dispatched two of his brother's killers (one in the first book, the second in 1982's *Luke Sutton: Gunfighter*), Sutton's search takes him to the Black Hills. After losing all his possessions in a buffalo stampede, Sutton fashions a raft and rides the river deep into the hills. Meeting up with an old mule skinner whom he offers to help, he heads for a mining town called Dustville, but soon the mule skinner is injured in a fall, fortunately managing to sign over all his stock to Sutton before he dies. Solvent once again, Sutton meets an old friend in Dustville and discovers that one of the men he is seeking, a half-breed named Johnny Loud Thunder, is acting as a scout for General Custer, who is just launching his latest campaign to exterminate the Indians.

Setting out after his quarry straight away, Sutton is momentarily sidetracked by a chance meeting with a lost paleontologist. The very next morning two men appear at their campsite, kill the paleontologist and force Sutton to join a whole army of slaves in working their remote gold mine. Here Sutton meets a Negro who, upon being judged unfit for work, is callously shot dead. Finally making his escape (and leaving a potentially interesting, if incredible, subplot entirely unresolved), Sutton eventually reaches Custer's column and takes part in the Battle of the Little Big Horn (which the author depicts very well) before ultimately killing Loud Thunder when the latter, in an attempt to humiliate him, tries to force him to scalp the dead Custer.

Kelley is by no means a poor writer, and his largely unadorned dialogue is equally as good as his prose. Particularly in the early books, however, he tended to impart facts in a rather obvious or contrived fashion, although this has since improved. Sutton is also presented as something of a superman. There appears to be nothing of which he is incapable. He is quick on the draw, handy with his fists, attractive to women, and adept at living off the land. No amount of punishment can break his spirit or force him to voice his pain. In short, he is almost too good to be true. For all of that, however, the series is undeniably appealing, and improves dramatically once Sutton is no longer saddled with his vengeance quest. (A particularly noteworthy title is 1984's *Luke Sutton: Outrider*, in which Sutton is hired to find a man who was captured by the Apaches two decades earlier).

Kelley's second western series, Cimarron (originally announced as "Bronc"), was launched in 1983, adding sex to the author's already familiar blend of historical detail, western lore, and often bloody action. Cimarron's adventures often lack the credibility of the Luke Sutton stories, however, most probably because of the unreal, fantasy-based nature of the adult western, where even the most desperate of manhunts will stop for the requisite number of ever-inventive bedroom scenes.

The central character, whose real name is never revealed, carries a crescent-shaped scar on his face as a reminder of the time when his strict disciplinarian father burned him with a branding iron. Leaving home at an early age, Cimarron (who takes his name from the Spanish word for wild or unruly) takes to the outlaw trail. A turning point comes years later when he shoots down the marshal of a small town whose bank he has just robbed, only to discover that the marshal is actually his father (who had also gone on the drift). Vowing that he will never kill lawlessly again, Cimarron eventually rides into Fort Smith, Arkansas, and in the tradition of countless other western heroes, allows himself to be persuaded to work for the celebrated real-life dispenser of justice, Judge Isaac C. Parker (as told in *Cimarron and the Hanging Judge*). From the moment Cimarron pins on his badge, he is continually dispatched to find and bring in outlaws hiding out in the Indian Nations. In *Cimarron Rides the Outlaw Trail*, for example, the scar-faced deputy goes undercover to infiltrate an outlaw gang led by Belle Starr herself, while in one of the best of an admittedly routine series of adventures, *Cimarron and the Prophet's People*, Cimarron locks horns with a sermon-spouting religious leader whose cult of fanatics actually masks something much more sinister. (It is also worth noting that towards the end of its quite lengthy run, Kelley's Cimarron stories were supplemented by frequently better contributions by writer Lew Baines).

Today Kelley intersperses further Luke Sutton novels with single, unrelated Westerns, among them *Morgan*, *A Man Named Dundee*, and *Thunder Gods' Gold*.

—David Whitehead

KELLEY, Ray. *See* **PAINE, Lauran.**

KELSO, Chuck. *See* **GRIBBLE, Leonard.**

KELTON, Elmer. Also writes as Tom Early; Alex Hawk; Lee McElroy. American. Born in Andrews County, Texas, 29 April 1926. Educated at the University of Texas, Austin, 1942–44, 1946–48, B.A. in journalism 1948. Served in the United States Army Infantry, 1944–46. Married Anna Lipp in 1947; two sons and one daughter. Agricultural editor, San Angelo *Standard Times*, Texas, 1943–63; editor, *The Ranch Magazine*, San Angelo, 1963–68; associate editor, *Livestock Weekly*, San Angelo, 1968–90. Recipient: Western Writers of America Spur award, 1956, 1971, 1973, 1981; Cowboy Hall of Fame Western Heritage award, 1973, 1978, 1987; Texas Institute of Letters Barbara McCombs/Lon Tinkle memorial award, 1986; Western American Literature Distinguished Achievement award, 1990. Agent: Nat Sobel, Sobel Weber Associates, Inc., 146 East 19th Street, New York, New York 10003-2404. Address: 2460 Oxford, San Angelo, Texas, 76904, U.S.A.

Western Publications

Novels

Hot Iron. New York, Ballantine, 1956.
Buffalo Wagons. New York, Ballantine, 1957; London, Four Square, 1960.
Barbed Wire. New York, Ballantine, 1958; London, Four Square, 1961.
Shadow of a Star. New York, Ballantine, 1959.
The Texas Rifles. New York, Ballantine, and London, Four Square, 1960.
Donovan. New York, Ballantine, 1961; London, New English Library, 1962.
Bitter Trail. New York, Ballantine, 1962.
Horsehead Crossing. New York, Ballantine, 1963.
Massacre at Goliad. New York, Ballantine, 1965; London, New English Library, 1967.
Llano River. New York, Ballantine, 1966; London, Panther, 1968.
After the Bugles. New York, Ballantine, 1967.
Captain's Rangers. New York, Ballantine, 1969; London, Arrow, 1971.
Shotgun Settlement (as Alex Hawk). New York, Paperback Library, 1969.
Hanging Judge. New York, Ballantine, 1969.

The Day the Cowboys Quit. New York, Doubleday, 1971.
Bowie's Mine. New York, Ballantine, 1971.
Wagontongue. New York, Ballantine, 1972.
The Time It Never Rained. New York, Doubleday, 1973.
Manhunters. New York, Ballantine, 1974.
The Good Old Boys. New York, Doubleday, 1978.
The Wolf and the Buffalo. New York, Doubleday, 1980.
Stand Proud. New York, Doubleday, 1984; Bath, Chivers, 1988.
Dark Thicket. New York, Doubleday, 1985.
The Man Who Rode Midnight. New York, Doubleday, 1987.
Honor at Daybreak. New York, Doubleday, 1991.

Novels as Tom Early

Sons of Texas:
The Danger, the Daring. New York, Berkley, 1989.
The Raiders. New York, Berkley, 1989.
The Rebels. New York, Berkley, 1990.

Novels as Lee McElroy

Joe Pepper. New York, Doubleday, 1975.
Long Way to Texas. New York, Doubleday, 1976.
The Eyes of the Hawk. New York, Doubleday, 1981; Bath, Chivers, 1987.

Short Stories

The Big Brand. New York, Bantam, 1986.
There's Always Another Chance, and Other Stories. San Angelo, Texas, Fort Concho Museum Press, 1986.

Uncollected Short Stories

"Duster," in *Farm Journal* (Philadelphia), April 1956.
"Yellow Devil," in *Hound Dogs and Others*, edited by Jim Kjelgaard. New York, Dodd Mead, 1958.
"Coward," in *Wild Streets*, edited by Don Ward. New York, Doubleday, 1958.
"The Debt of Harely Buckelew," in *Frontiers West*, edited by S. Omar Barker. New York, Doubleday, 1959.
"The 7X Bull," in *Western Roundup*, edited by Nelson Nye. New York, Macmillan, 1961.
"Man on the Wagon Tongue," in *They Won Their Spurs*, edited by Nelson Nye. New York, Avon, 1962.
"Uncle Jeff and the Gunfighters," in *The Pick of the Roundup*, edited by Stephen Payne. New York, Avon, 1963.
"In the Line of Duty," in *Iron Men and Silver Spurs*, edited by Donald Hamilton. New York, Fawcett, 1967.
"The Last Indian Fight in Kerr County," in *The Roundup*, edited by Stephen Overholser. New York, Doubleday, 1982.
"A Bad Cow Market," in *The Best of the West*, edited by Joe Lansdale. New York, Doubleday, 1986.
"Desert Command," in *The Horse Soldiers*, edited by Bill Pronzini and Martin H. Greenberg. New York, Fawcett, 1987.

OTHER PUBLICATIONS

Other

Looking Back West: Selections from the Pioneer News-Observer. San Angelo, Texas, Talley Press, 1972.
Frank C. McCarthy: The Old West. Greenwich, Connecticut, Greenwich Press, 1981.
Permian, A Continuing Saga, paintings by Tom Lovell. Midland, Texas, Permian Basin Petroleum Museum, 1986.
Living and Writing in West Texas. Abilene, Texas, Hardin-Simmons University Press, 1988.
Writing the Western Novel (audiocassette). Austin, Texas, Davenport Writers Audio Shop, 1989.

Editor, *Yesteryear in Ozona and Crockett County*, by V. I. Pierce. Ozona, Texas, Crockett County Historical Society, 1980.

*

Manuscript Collection: Southwest Collection, Texas Tech University, Lubbock.

Critical Study: *Elmer Kelton* by Lawrence Clayton, Boise, Idaho, Boise State University Press, 1986.

Elmer Kelton comments:

A majority of my fictional works are based strongly in history, mostly Texas history, my own personal niche. I have chosen various periods of change or of stress in which an old order is being pushed aside by the new, and through the fictional characters try to give the reader some understanding of the human reasons for and effects of these changes. The challenge of meeting changing times is one thing each generation faces in common with all those which have gone before and all those yet to come. I strongly believe history remains highly relevant to us today, for what we are—our customs, our attitudes, our reactions to events at home and around the world—is the sum product of all that has gone before us. The better we understand history the more likely we are to understand the present and to be able to cope with the future.

* * *

Elmer Kelton was born and reared in west Texas, and his western novels are realistic studies of the land, animals, and men and women who gradually settled the Llano Estacado and other parts of Texas. Kelton is the author of more than 30 western historical novels, including five exceptional works issued by Doubleday: *The Day the Cowboys Quit*, *The Time It Never Rained*, *The Good Old Boys*, *The Wolf and the Buffalo*, and *The Man Who Rode Midnight.*

At the beginning of his writing career he was publishing short stories in magazines such as *Ranch Romances.* His first novel, *Hot Iron*, deals with Texas in the days of the great cattle empires when a ranch was the size of Massachusetts and Connecticut. Next came *Buffalo Wagons* (Spur award), about the bison hunters in Comanche territory in 1873. By 1974 Ballantine had issued paperback editions of 16 of his novels, including the Buckalew tetralogy, *Massacre at Goliad*, *After the Bugles*, *Bowie's Mine*, and *Long Way to Texas*, which follows members of the Buckalew family through the various eras of Texas history. *Shotgun Settlement*, published under a house pseudonym, Alex Hawk, is about the conflict between Blair Bishop, a proud cow rancher, and a cattle rustler named Macy Modock.

Barbed Wire is about a feud between settlers and a cattle baron, Captain Andrew Rinehart, whose R. Cross Ranch sprawls haphazardly across land known as Kiowa County. *Shadow of a Star* tells of the vicissitudes of a deputy sheriff, Jim-Bob McClain of Coldridge County, who is trying to establish law and order in western Texas. In *The Texas Rifles* Captain

Aaron Barcroft leads a company of Texas Mounted Rifles made up of Union and Confederate sympathizers who are apparently less afraid of the Comanches than of staying home and fighting in the Civil War.

Clabe Donovan (*Donovan*) was an outlaw who rode both sides of the United States–Mexican border, and became a legend in his time. His brother, Morg, seeks revenge for Clabe's death by terrorizing and murdering people in order to keep his brother's legend alive. *Bitter Trail* deals with Union activities along the Mexican border in 1863. Kelton recounts from history the last battle of the Civil War, fought at Palmito Hill 12 miles downriver from Brownsville on 13 May 1865. Ironically the battle was won by the Confederacy which had already lost the war.

Moving to the cattle frontier of the 1880's, and to southwest Texas in *Horsehead Crossing*, Kelton takes his hero Johnny Fristo along the San Antonio-El Paso Road to Sonora where he is involved in murder not of his own doing. *Llano River* is set in the 1870's in the brush country of south Texas where the main character, Dundee, goes to work for John Titus, a self-made rancher who is losing cattle to rustlers in the Llano River country. *Captain's Rangers* concerns Captain L.H. McNelly's Rangers and their problems along the Nueces Strip, a stretch of coastal prairie and desert wasteland lying between the Nueces and the Rio Grande and belonging to Texas. Trouble erupts in the spring of 1875 when *gringo* land grabbers and the Mexicans meet on the Strip. It takes the Texas Rangers to bring law and order to the region.

Far and wide Judge Isaac C. Parker is known as the "hanging judge," and hanging day always draws a crowd to Fort Smith. In *Hanging Judge* Marshal Sam Dark must find a way to stop the whiskey runner Harvey Oates so that there can be a hanging sentence from the less than respectable Judge Parker, who is a pious fraud. *Wagontongue* is the story of Isaac Jefford who has been a slave belonging to Major Estel Lytton and who has gone west with him after the Civil War. Although the title is symbolic of frontier justice when a criminal was hanged from a wagontongue, the only kind of tree on the treeless staked plains, the title concerns Isaac's dilemma. It is the wagontongue of the chuckwagon on which Isaac sits when he eats, away from the men because he is African-American.

Manhunters is based loosely on the true story of Gregorio Cortez, who killed a sheriff in Karnes County, Texas, soon after the turn of the 20th century. The murder sparked one of the biggest manhunts in Texas history. Kelton's fictional Chacho Fernandez, who is running from the law, is in many ways an admirable and resourceful man, and one marvels at the stamina and heart of the magnificent saddle mare he rides and loves.

Kelton's works have recurrent themes which center on the courage and integrity of the cow rancher, cowboy, and settler; the ordeals, losses, and successes of his people; the authenticity of his locales; the effect of change upon people and how they meet the challenge of change. His recent novels have more fully developed characters, men like Charlie Flagg in *The Time It Never Rained*, a proud and strong man with a determination to stay on the land during the terrible drought years of the 1950's. Hugh Hitchcock in *The Day the Cowboys Quit* is an honest cowboy, and the leader of the men during the Canadian River cowboy strike of 1883, a bitter, little-known episode in the history of the West. Cowboys and ranchers were opposed on issues of land ownership and wages, and the outcome has great consequences for the Old West. Hewey Calloway in *The Good Old Boys* is one of the last of his breed, and a true drifter of his time. He cannot adjust to the changing west. *The Wolf and the Buffalo* is a departure from Kelton's other westerns. The story is about the black cavalry in Comanche Indian territory on the Texas high plains shortly after the Civil War and concerns Gray Horse Running and Gideon Ledbetter, whose lives and destinies cross during the late 1870's. Not many western writers have given so warm and human a portrayal of Negroes, Indians, and Mexicans as has Kelton in his novels.

The Eyes of the Hawk deals with Thomas Canfield's people who were among the earliest settlers around Stonehill, Texas. Canfield's conflict with Branch Isom, a newcomer to the state, provides the action in the carting trade and land ownership story. Canfield may be land poor, but he is honest—unlike his rival. *Stand Proud* is a powerful story of the Old West. Centering on the taciturn and cantankerous Frank Claymore, the story takes an unexpected twist, justifying this honorable man. With flashback technique, Kelton contrasts Claymore's youth with the now arthritic, proud old rancher.

Kelton's hero, Owen Danforth, in *Dark Thicket*, has been wounded in the War Between the States, and has come home to find his uncle and the father from whom he is estranged in danger from home patrols because they are part of a resistance group. A Confederate soldier, Danforth is a skilfully drawn character who has an inner conflict, a trait not generally found in formula heroes. In *The Man Who Rode Midnight*, the hero, old Wes Hendrix, is a man much like Charlie Flagg. No matter what, he is going to stay on his land, and in the end he persuades his grandson to stay there too; although Jim Ed may have had a little extra persuasion from the attractive Glory B. who lives with her grandmother on an adjoining ranch. The novel is set in the present time. Ranching becomes a bookkeeping business for Jim Ed.

The Sons of Texas is a series of three historical novels charting the arrival in 1816 of the Lewis family to Texas: their survival and growth, and the roles they play in the history of the Lone Star State. Each novel centers on one of the Lewis brothers. Michael arrives from Tennessee in book one; Andrew is prominent in book two which opens in 1825 with the Lewis family and their neighbors in conflict with the Plains Indians and the Mexican government. Stephen F. Austin has settled his first colony in Texas in 1821, the year Mexico gained independence from Spain. The third book ends with the Battle of San Jacinto and the winning of Texas independence from Mexico in 1836, and centers on James Lewis.

Honor at Daybreak is Kelton's oil-boom novel. The two major characters are Anglo; one a young cowboy whose ranch job falls through so that he has to go to work in the oilfield, the other the county sheriff who finds himself almost overwhelmed by the pressures of the population explosion in what had been a quiet little town. Two minority characters, an Hispanic cowboy and a Choctaw Indian work as roustabouts on a drilling rig. Kelton again places his characters in situations that reveal a changing way of life from the old cattle country of Charlie Flagg and Wes Hendrix.

The five best novels in Kelton's long list are *The Time It Never Rained*, *The Day the Cowboys Quit*, *The Wolf and the Buffalo*, *The Good Old Boys*, and *The Man Who Rode Midnight*. All of his work is realistic and filled with action. The strength of his fiction lies in the historical background, the folklore, and the development of his characters. He is especially good with dialogue and he certainly knows Texas history.

—Dorys C. Grover

KENNEDY, Cody. *See* **REESE, John.**

KENT, Pete. *See* **RICHARDSON, Gladwell.**

KETCHUM, Cliff. *See* **PAINE, Lauran.**

KETCHUM, Frank. *See* **PAINE, Lauran.**

KETCHUM, Jack. *See* **PAINE, Lauran.**

KETCHUM, Philip (L). Also wrote as Miriam Leslie; Mack Saunders. American. Born in Trinidad, Colorado, 19 October 1902. Educated at Denver University; Long Beach State College, California; New York University. Married Miriam P. Sylvester (second wife) in 1965; one daughter and one son. Social worker: with Denver Bureau of Charity, 2 years; worked in Tucson; with Omaha Federation and Community Chest; organized United Seamen's Service during World War II; freelance writer from 1936. *Died 13 December 1969.*

WESTERN PUBLICATIONS

Novels (series: Cabot)

Texan on the Prod. New York, Popular Library, 1952; London, Consul, 1956.
Decision at Piute Wells. New York, Popular Library, 1953.
Guns of the Barricade Bunch. New York, Popular Library, 1953; London, Consul, 1956.
The Saddle Bum. New York, Popular Library, 1954; London, Consul, 1956.
The Texas Gun. New York, Popular Library, 1954.
Gun Law. New York, Popular Library, 1954.
Desperation Valley. New York, Popular Library, 1955.
Rider from Texas. New York, Popular Library, 1955; London, Hale, 1956.
The Gunslinger. New York, Lion, 1955; London, Banner, 1957.
Longhorn Stampede. New York, Popular Library, 1956; London, Hale, 1957.
The Night of the Coyotes. New York, Ballantine, 1956.
The Big Gun. New York, Popular Library, 1956.
The Elkhorn Feud. New York, Popular Library, 1956.
Gun Trail (as Mack Saunders). New York, Graphic, 1956.
Dead Man's Trail. New York, Popular Library, 1957.
Six-Gun Maverick. New York, Popular Library, 1957.
Feud at Forked River. New York, Fawcett, 1958; London, Fawcett, 1960.
The Dead-Shot Kid. New York, New American Library, 1959; London, New English Library, 1966.
Gun Code. New York, New American Library, 1959.
Gunfire Man. New York, Popular Library, 1959.
The Hard Man. New York, Avon, 1959.
Apache Dawn. New York, Avon, 1960.
Gunsmoke Territory. New York, Curl, 1960.
The Buzzard Guns. New York, Avon, 1960.
The Stalkers. New York, Berkley, 1961.
Harsh Reckoning. New York, Ballantine, 1962; Leicester, Ulverscroft, 1988.
Renegade Range. Derby, Connecticut, Monarch, 1962.
Traitor Guns. New York, Avon, 1962.
The Night Riders. New York, Lancer, 1966.
Wyoming. New York, Ballantine, 1967.
The Man from Granite. New York, Ballantine, 1967.
The Man Who Tamed Dodge (Cabot). New York, Lancer, 1967.
The Man Who Turned Outlaw (Cabot). New York, Lancer, 1967.
The Man Who Sold Leadville (Cabot). New York, Lancer, 1968.
The Men of Moncada. New York, Avon, 1968.
Cabot. New York, Lancer, 1969.
Mad Morgan's Hoard. New York, Ace, 1969.
Support Your Local Sheriff (novelization of screenplay). New York, Popular Library, 1969.
Halfbreed. New York, Ballantine, 1969.
Gila Crossing. New York, Ballantine, 1969.
The Cougar Basin War. New York, Ace, 1970.
Rattlesnake. New York, Ballantine, 1970.
Buzzard Ridge. New York, Ballantine, 1970.
Judgment Trail. New York, Ballantine, 1971.

Uncollected Short Stories

"The Devil's Agent," in *Cowboy Stories* (New York), July 1934.
"Wrong Number," in *Cowboy Stories* (New York), November 1934.
"Two Through the Heart," in *Cowboy Stories* (New York), May 1937.
"The Traitor in Sage Creek Valley," in *Cowboy Stories* (New York), November 1937.
"Main Line West," in *Argosy* (New York), 6 November 1937.
"Ribbon of Steel," in *Argosy* (New York), 25 December 1937.
"Trigger Trio," in *Western Story* (New York), 12 February 1938.
"A Kerry Comes Home," in *Argosy* (New York), 12 February 1938.
"Quick-Trigger Tenderfoot," in *Western Story* (New York), 5 March 1938.
"Powder Smoke Justice," in *Western Story* (New York), 12 March 1938.
"Guns Across the Range," in *Western Story* (New York), 19 March 1938.
"Indians Coming," in *Argosy* (New York), 9 April 1938.
"Not by Gun-Play," in *Western Story* (New York), 16 April 1938.
"Gun Law Justice," in *Western Story* (New York), 30 April 1938.
"Deputy for a Day," in *Western Story* (New York), 7 May 1938.
"Dead Men Don't Pay Off," in *Western Story* (New York), 21 May 1938.
"Trial by Lead," in *Western Story* (New York), 28 May 1938.
"Make Way for the Longhorns," in *Western Story* (New York), 13 August 1938.
"Six-Gun Rendezvous," in *Western Story* (New York), 31 December 1938.
"West of Water," in *Argosy* (New York), 3 June 1939.
"Where Vengeance Rides," in *Five Novels* (New York), November 1940.

"Prison Champion for a Lost Range," in *Star Western* (Chicago), December 1940.
"Valley of Vengeance," in *Five Novels* (New York), January 1941.
"Three Took the Trail," in *Five Novels* (New York), March 1941.
"Caravan to Hell," in *Five Novels* (New York), July 1941.
"A Rebel Moves West," in *Western Story* (London), July 1941.
"Ghost of the Rimrocks," in *Wild West* (New York), 12 July 1941.
"Trouble-Buster Bill," in *Five Novels* (New York), September 1941.
"Water for Mesa," in *Western Story* (London), November 1941.
"Wolf-Pack Welcome," in *Wild West* (New York), 7 February 1942.
"Justice in Gunsmoke," in *Five Novels* (New York), June 1942.
"The Devil Builds a Bridge," in *Five Novels* (New York), August 1942.
"The Mad Gringo," in *Wild West* (New York), 15 August 1942.
"Homesteader for Hire," in *Five Novels* (New York), January 1943.
"Judge Colt Rules Again," in *Wild West* (New York), 13 March 1943.
"An Outcast Rides the Boothill Watch," in *Star Western* (Chicago), August 1943.
"The Gold-Camp Terror Strikes Tonight," in *West* (Kingswood, Surrey), August 1944.
"Squatters' Rights Are Gun-Rights!," in *Star Western* (Chicago), November 1944.
"Trail to Yesterday," in *West* (Kingswood, Surrey), May 1947.
"The Iron Road," in *West* (Kingswood, Surrey), July 1947.
"The Saga of Jingo Carter," in *West* (Kingswood, Surrey), June 1949.
"Deadline," in *Zane Grey's Western* (New York), August 1949.
"The Murderer's Brand," in *Mammoth Western* (Chicago), February 1950.
"The Shadow Trail," in *Zane Grey's Western* (New York), July 1950.
"Tonto, The Unwanted," in *Texas Rangers* (London), October 1950.
"The Gray Ghost of Camarillo," in *Zane Grey's Western* (New York), January 1951.
"The Gun Doctor," in *Thrilling Western* (London), March 1952.
"No Badge for a Gun-Hawk," in *Western Story* (London), September 1952.
"The Runaway," in *Thrilling Ranch Stories* (London), April 1953.
"The Lady Takes a Walk," *Exciting Western* (London), June 1953.
"Friends from Texas," *Exciting Western* (London), August 1953.
"His Brother's Gunhand," in *Western* (New York), June 1955.
"Hang the Man High," in *Western Story* (London), October 1955.
"Votan, the Proud," in *Thrilling Western* (London), January 1956.
"Tezca," *Exciting Western* (London), January 1956.
"Land of Violence," in *Western* (New York), July 1956.
"Hell Is Full of Heroes," *Western* (New York), April 1957.
"The Rider from Hangman's Valley," in *Western* (New York), July 1957.
"The Forty Dollar Bride," in *Thrilling Western* (London), October 1957.
"Night Ride," *Thrilling Western* (London), January 1958.
"Spring Blizzard," in *Texas Rangers* (London), February 1958.

Other Publications

Novels

Death in the Library. New York, Crowell, 1937.
Death at Dusk. New York, Phoenix Press, 1938; as *Kill at Dusk*, New York, Red Dagger, 1946.
Death in the Night. New York, Phoenix Press, 1939; as *Good Night for Murder*, New York, Red Dagger, 1946(?).
The Great Axe Bretwalda. Boston, Little Brown, 1955.
Quartet in White. N.p., Medical Fiction, 1963.
Cavanaugh Keep (as Miriam Leslie). New York, Lancer, 1968.

* * *

Philip Ketchum became a prolific contributor to the pulp magazines during the 1930's, and over the next 20 years wrote nearly a thousand stories for the adventure, detective and western pulps. In the 1960's he was a steady contributor to the *Saint Detective Magazine* and *Alfred Hitchcock's Mystery Magazine*. An interesting series of novelettes in *Argosy* magazine in 1939 traced the history of a magic axe called Bretwalda and its influence on several generations of an aristocratic British family. The book version of this story, *The Great Axe Bretwalda* was one of only four Ketchum books to be published in hardcover form. Ketchum's first books were detective novels, starting with *Death in the Library* in 1937.

In 1952 Ketchum turned to the writing of western novels. Some of his early books were expanded from stories that had appeared in *Ranch Romances* and other pulp magazines. These are traditional western adventures, built out of standard ingredients: Indian attacks (*Apache Dawn*), greedy land-barons (*Desperation Valley*), stolen trail herds (*Gun Law*), unjustly accused loners (*The Saddle Bum*). But if the plot elements are familiar, they are handled with skill and assurance. The characters are frequently off-beat and always interesting, and the action well-paced.

In the late 1950's a note of cynicism and grimness entered Ketchum's novels, replacing the easy plot resolutions of the traditional action western with a more realistic treatment. The extremes of the transition can be seen in two books published during the same year, 1959. *Gun Code* and *The Hard Man* open with the same situation: a young man returning to the town where his father had been killed and uncovering secrets that the town had thought safely buried. In *Gun Code* the young man finds friends on every side, and wins through to safety and fortune with only nominal discomfort. In *The Hard Man*, on the other hand, the searcher finds that virtually the entire town bears some degree of culpability in his father's death. The guilty ultimately fail in their efforts to keep the secret from being exposed, but the hero's victory is not without its emotional cost.

In *The Stalkers* an undercover agent for the Army attempts to recover $50,000 in stolen gold, aided by a former outlaw, his half-Indian daughter, and a group of supposedly law-abiding people being warped by the stresses of greed and jealousy.

In the mid-1960's Ketchum wrote a series of four books about a character called Cabot, the scion of a wealthy New England shipping family who seeks his fortune in the west after a bitter quarrel with his father. Cabot becomes known as *The Man Who Tamed Dodge* (and *Turned Outlaw* and *Sold Leadville*). He is obsessed with the need to accumulate money, and this single-mindedness gives the books a cold and unsympathetic aura.

At the same time that he was producing the formulaic Cabot series, Ketchum was doing some of the best work of his career for another publisher. The half dozen books which he wrote for Ballantine Books in 1967–71 are superior examples of western storytelling. The orphan Dante who became *The Man from Granite* and the half-Apache Red Pardee in *Halfbreed* are fully rounded characters whose passages to maturity make compelling reading. Two of the best books in this group are *Wyoming* and *Buzzard Ridge*, in both of which a strong, self-reliant woman plays a central role.

—R.E. Briney

KIDD, Russ(ell). *See* **DONSON, Cyril.**

KILBOURN, Matt. *See* **BARRETT, Geoffrey John.**

KILDARE, Maurice. *See* **RICHARDSON, Gladwell.**

KILGORE, John. *See* **PAINE, Lauran.**

KIMBALL, Frank. *See* **PAINE, Lauran.**

KIMBALL, Ralph. *See* **PAINE, Lauran.**

KIMBER, Lee. *See* **KING, Albert.**

KINCAID, J.D. Pseudonym for James Corteen Dalgleish. Scottish. Born in Galashiels, Selkirk, Scotland, 20 April 1936. Educated at Corstorphine Primary and Boroughmuir Senior Secondary Schools, Galashiels, 1941–53. Served in the British Army, 1955–57. Married Pamela Kincaid in 1966. Clerical officer, Civil Service, 1953–87. Since 1988 Library assistant, Cambridgeshire Libraries and Information Service, Huntingdon. Address: 10 Kings Ripton Road, Sapley, Huntingdon, Cambridgeshire PE17 2NU, England.

WESTERN PUBLICATIONS

Novels (series: Jack Stone in all books)

Corrigan's Revenge. London, Hale, 1989.
The Fourth of July. London, Hale, 1990.
Showdown at Medicine Creek. London, Hale, 1990.
The Sheriff of Fletcher County. London, Hale, 1990.
Coyote Winter. London, Hale, 1990.

OTHER PUBLICATIONS

Novels as James Dalgleish

The Black Eagle of Badenoch. London, Hale, 1974.
The Plunderers. London, Hale, 1975.
A Jacobite Dream. London, Hale, 1976.
The Duke's Right Hand. London, Hale, 1977.
The Golden Spider. London, Hale, 1979.

*

J.D. Kincaid comments:

My western novels are all written with the simple intention of giving the reader an entertaining and exciting story to read. Although each novel is complete in itself, all form part of a series of western adventures featuring a fictional Kentuckian gunfighter named Jack Stone. He is a man who does his best to avoid trouble, yet seems to attract it as a magnet attracts metal. A lone figure, Stone travels the West, forever being drawn into wild and dangerous situations. He has a strong sense of right and wrong and, with singleminded ruthlessness, sets about wreaking death and destruction among the ungodly. Consequently, the Jack Stone novels, while undoubtedly both violent and bloodthirsty, are nevertheless moral tales in which good invariably triumphs over evil.

* * *

Although his historical adventure novels are influenced by the likes of Robert Louis Stevenson, Alexandre Dumas, and Rafael Sabatini, James Dalgleish's Westerns, written as J.D. Kincaid, clearly take their inspiration from the cinema, and in particular, the "oaters" of the 1940's and 1950's.

Kincaid's continuing character, Jack Stone, reflects this influence admirably. A six-foot-two-inch Kentuckian, Stone is the archetypal western hero: a legendary gunfighter and town-tamer who is "destined forever to be a wanderer." Once married and now a widower, Stone is a Civil War veteran and former U.S. Marshal. His prowess with knuckles and six-guns is well-known, and his trademarks include a distinctive knee-length buck-skin jacket. Though he is portrayed as somewhat reticent and content to mind his own business, however, there is an altruistic streak within him which always guarantees his involvement in each new adventure. Having said that, it should also be pointed out that implied sex and regular, often explosive bursts of action also give Kincaid's westerns a distinctly modern feel.

When Stone makes his debut in *Corrigan's Revenge*, he is working as a bouncer in a sleepy Californian town named Mallam Springs. Into his life comes the newly widowed Beth Corrigan and her son Danny. Beth wants to hire Stone to kill Ben Harper, the outlaw who murdered her rancher husband. At first Stone refuses to help. He killed Harper's brother Cole during his time as a marshal, but has no argument with Ben. All that changes, however, when Harper, hearing of Beth's intention, rides into town, kidnaps her son in order to lead Stone into an ambush, and kills his lover, saloon owner Lucy Quarrell, in the process. Stone eventually sets out after Harper with Beth, dressed as a man and calling herself the "Colorado Kid," in tow, finally engineering an explosive finale.

The Fourth of July finds Stone in Arizona, killing time with a prostitute before moving on to celebrate Independence Day in

Phoenix. Helping to foil a bank robbery (and winging the outlaw leader Rick Claypole along the way), Stone soon decides to share part of the journey with two inveterate gamblers who are headed for a high stakes poker game in the town of Dempster. Before long, Kincaid begins to introduce a string of subplots, which include a scheming young couple intent on winning enough money to set themselves up in the real estate business back East, and a plan to rob the well-heeled poker players on the night of the big game. Like all of Kincaid's books, the final showdown is fast and bloody, with the villains getting their long-awaited comeuppance and the hero winning through with customary ease.

Showdown at Medicine Creek opens with a violent confrontation between four outlaws and a bounty hunter, then moves swiftly on to the massacre of a pioneer family out in the wilds of Indian Territory. Only Jack Stone's timely intervention scares off the marauders (a band of Comanches led by a notorious renegade named Running Wolf) before they can also kill the raid's sole survivor, 11-year-old Billy McKenzie. Taking Billy under his wing, Stone delivers him to relatives in the nearest town, but although this should be the end of the story, it really only signifies the beginning. For some reason that Stone soon becomes determined to uncover, Billy's uncle, a Civil War veteran turned unscrupulous businessman named Glenn Rogers, wants the boy dead. To make the matter worse, Running Wolf's Comanches return to ensure another violent finale at the way-station that gives the book its title.

The fourth of Kincaid's Jack Stone adventures is possibly the most curious, if only because Stone is "off-screen" during most of the action, and with the exception of the climax, is relegated to the role of supporting player. Following the murder of an outspoken newspaperman whose editorials lay the blame for a series of brutal and intimidatory attacks at the doorstep of the local land-hungry rancher, P.W. Brewster, in *The Sheriff of Fletcher County*, young Julie Hobhouse decides to take the law into her own hands—quite literally. Because he is on Brewster's payroll, Sheriff Lloyd Duffen is of little help, so when Duffen's term of office draws to an end, Julie proposes another candidate for the post—herself. It is into this increasingly explosive situation that Stone rides, and though he rejects Julie's invitation to act as her deputy, he does get drawn deeper into the feud between the lady sheriff and the rancher, finally taking a hand in time to effect a frantic but action-packed conclusion.

Kincaid's books are good, traditional Westerns, but they are not without their faults. Historical detail is conspicuous by its paucity, and with the exception of Stone's character, which is quite well-drawn, characterisation and background description are, at best, perfunctory. However, while certain sequences or aspects of Kincaid's plots may tend to stretch credibility, there can be little denying that, overall, the author delivers fast-paced westerns which mix action and intrigue in equally generous proportions. His violence is graphic and, in keeping with the undemanding nature of his work, his heroes and villains are clearly defined. He uses an uncluttered style of writing, and his westernisms frequently spill over from his dialogue into his prose.

After completing his fifth Western, *Coyote Winter*, Kincaid intends to take a break from the frontier in order to explore other genres, but like all the best western heroes, Stone will doubtless be back in the saddle again before too long.

—David Whitehead

KING, Albert. Also writes as Ken Albion; Mark Bannon; Walt Brennan; Catherine Brent; Wade Bronson; Jim Cleveland; Paul Conrad; Craig Cooper; Joel Creed; Steve Dallas; Reece Doan; Eli Driscoll; Wallace Ford; Lee Foreman; Evan Foster; Floyd Gibson; Matt Gifford; Simon Girty; Brad Hammond; Ross Harlan; Gil Harmon; Art Hoffman; Tom Holland; Scott Howell; Nelson Hoyt; Mark Kane; Janice Kelsey; Lee Kimber; Ames King; Berta King; Christopher King; Carl Mason; Paul Muller; Clint Ogden; Ray Owen; Bart Prender; Alvin Ripley; Walt Santee; Grover Scott; Cole Shelby; Dean Taggart; Ellis Tyler; Simon Waldron; Agnes Wallace; Lewis Wetzel; Steve Yarbo. British. Born in Portadown, County Armagh, Northern Ireland, 16 March 1924. Married Dorothy Hilda King in 1986; two daughters and one son from earlier marriages. Journalist, Morton Newspapers, Lurgan, County Armagh, prior to 1964; also wrote scripts for boys' comic papers, and stories for annuals. Full-time writer, 1964–74. Reporter, feature writer, columnist, and since 1974 sub-editor, *News Letter*, Century Newspapers, Belfast. Address: 3 Judes Crescent, Rosehill, Newtonards, County Down, Eire.

WESTERN PUBLICATIONS

Novels

Guns of Cougar Range (as Joel Creed). London, Hale, 1975.
Law of the Gun-Wolves (as Matt Gifford). London, Hale, 1975.
Gunsmoke in Elkhorn (as Bart Prender). London, Hale, 1975.
Catamount Valley (as Ellis Taylor). London, Hale, 1975.

Novels as Lee Foreman

Gun Fury on Rainbow River. London, Hale, 1964.
Shoot-out in Harmony. London, Hale, 1965.
Pay-off at Thunder Pass. London, Hale, 1966.
Ride Back to Fury. London, Hale, 1967.
Bandits of Buzzard Flat. London, Hale, 1967.
Gunman's Shadow. London, Hale, 1967.
Hang-Rope Trail. London, Hale, 1967.
Maggarty. London, Hale, 1968.

Novels as Ames King

Gunsmoke Showdown. London, Brown, Watson, 1958.
Rider from Yesterday. London, Hale, 1961.
Tangled Trails. London, Hale, 1961.
Stranger in Alamos. London, Hale, 1962.
Outlaw Breed. London, Hale, 1962.
Ride the Wind. London, Hale, 1963.
Bullet Harvest. London, Hale, 1963.
Desperado. London, Hale, 1963.
Pistol Justice. London, Hale, 1964.
Hamerick. London, Hale, 1965.
Shasta City Showdown. London, Hale, 1966.
High Valley Massacre. London, Hale, 1967.
Man from Kettle Ridge. London, Hale, 1967.
Guns of Wrath. London, Hale, 1969.
Gun Wolves at Rondo. London, Hale, 1979.
Showdown at Twin Fork. London, Hale, 1980.
Man-Hunter in Town. London, Hale, 1981.
Powdersmoke Trail. London, Hale, 1983.
Nester Fury. London, Hale, 1989.
Death Rides the Thunderhead. London, Hale, 1990.

Novels as Brad Hammond

Raiders of Storm River. London, Hale, 1972.
Killer in Town. London, Hale, 1973.
Riders of Owl Canyon. London, Hale, 1974.
Colt Feud. London, Hale, 1974.
Ride to Vengeance. London, Hale, 1988.
Trouble Town. London, Hale, 1989.

Novels as Gil Harmon

The Wild Guns. London, Hale, 1972.
Gunsmoke on the Wind. London, Hale, 1973.
Law Trail to Tylerstown. London, Hale, 1974.
The Vengeance Gun. London, Hale, 1974.
The Way of the Kid. London, Hale, 1976.
Owlhoot Trail. London, Hale, 1989.
The Tarnished Star. London, Hale, 1990.

Novels as Nelson Hoyt

Colt Showdown. London, Hale, 1962.
Town Tamer. London, Hale, 1962.
Guns of Paradise Valley. London, Hale, 1963.
Renegade Rider. London, Hale, 1963.
Return of Haven. London, Hale, 1964.
Kintell. London, Hale, 1965.
Killer Sheriff. London, Hale, 1967.
Tracks to Treachery. London, Hale, 1967.
Colt Trail to Clovis. London, Hale, 1968.
Guns of Justice. London, Hale, 1968.

Novels as Dean Taggart

Vigilante Terror. London, Hale, 1972.
Rage at Roaring Fork. London, Hale, 1973.
Law of the Bullet. London, Hale, 1974.
Riders of Eagle Valley. London, Hale, 1976.
Bushwhack Pay-off. London, Hale, 1989.
Outlaw Heritage. London, Hale, 1990.

Novels as Lewis Wetzel

Bushwhacker Range. London, Hale, 1962.
The Judas Gun. London, Hale, 1962.
Gunsmoke Heritage. London, Hale, 1963.
Six-Gun Fugitive. London, Hale, 1963.
Owlhoot Rendezvous. London, Hale, 1964.
Stage to Yuba Basin. London, Hale, 1964.
Grass of Spanish Run. London, Hale, 1967.

Novels as Wade Bronson

Powdersmoke Pay-off. London, Hale, 1973.
Fighting Ramrod. London, Hale, 1974.

Novels as Jim Cleveland

Six-Gun Hellions. London, Hale, 1973.
Trail of the Gun Hawks. London, Hale, 1973.
Colt Thunder. London, Hale, 1989.
Rambo's Treasure. London, Hale, 1990.

Novels as Reece Doan

Lawman Riding. London, Hale, 1973.
Sidewinder Breed. London, Hale, 1973.

Novels as Eli Driscoll

Gun Law in Willow Basin. London, Hale, 1973.
Pistol Breed. London, Hale, 1974.

Novels as Wallace Ford

Colt Paymaster. London, Gresham, 1966.
Bullet Roundup. London, Gresham, 1967.
Rogue Brand. London, Gresham, 1967.
Showdown in High Valley. London, Hale, 1989.
Colt Justice. London, Hale, 1990.

Novels as Evan Foster

Bar O Justice. London, Hale, 1975.
Fence War. London, Hale, 1989.

Novels as Simon Girty

Lawless Brand. London, Gresham, 1966.
Raiders' Range. London, Gresham, 1966.

Novels as Ross Harlan

Boss of Storm Valley. London, Gresham, 1966.
Wire. London, Gresham, 1966.
Savage Sundown. London, Gresham, 1967.

Novels as Art Hoffman

Stormy Range. London, Hale, 1967.
Wolfpack Renegade. London, Hale, 1987.

Novels as Tom Holland

Desperado Trail. London, Hale, 1973.
Rustler Range. London, Hale, 1989.
Fugitive Trail. London, Hale, 1990.

Novels as Lee Kimber

Renegade Lawman. London, Hale, 1973.
Outlaw Shoot-out. London, Hale, 1973.

Novels as Carl Mason

Trail Branded. London, Hale, 1973.
Trail of the Lawless. London, Hale, 1973.
Guns of Broken Valley. London, Hale, 1974.
Gunslinger's Way. London, Hale, 1974.

Novels as Clint Ogden

Gunsmoke Vendetta. London, Gresham, 1966.
Smoke on the Trail. London, Gresham, 1967.
Wolf River Rampage. London, Gresham, 1967.
Stranger in San Simon. London, Hale, 1989.

Novels as Alvin Ripley

Bushwhack Country. London, Hale, 1972.
The Hostile Land. London, Hale, 1973.

Colt Rendezvous. London, Hale, 1974.
Hill Thunder. London, Hale, 1974.
Texas Pay-Off. London, Hale, 1986.
Ranger Justice. London, Hale, 1989.

Novels as Walt Santee

Powdersmoke Pass. London, Hale, 1964.
Trail South to Danger. London, Hale, 1964.
The Range Hawks. London, Hale, 1989.

Novels as Grover Scott

Outlaw Haven. London, Gresham, 1966.
Gun Talk at Red Mesa. London, Gresham, 1967.
Smoke-out on Sabre. London, Gresham, 1967.
Renegade Showdown. London, Hale, 1988.
Culver of the Lazy M. London, Hale, 1989.

Novels as Cole Shelby

Destiny's Saddle. London, Gresham, 1966.
A Colt for Texas. London, Gresham, 1966.
Trail Pards. London, Hale, 1989.
Thunder Valley. London, Hale, 1990.

Novels as Steve Yarbo

Hardcase. London, Hale, 1973.
Back-Trail Shadows. London, Hale, 1974.
Shoot-out in Sundown. London, Hale, 1974.

Novels as Steve Dallas

Six-Gun Reckoning. London, Hale, 1990.
Rogue Rancher. London, Hale, 1991.

OTHER PUBLICATIONS

Novel

Stage Two. London, Hale, 1974.

Novels as Mark Bannon

The Wayward Robot. London, Hale, 1974.
The Assimilator. London, Hale, 1974.
The Tomorrow Station. London, Hale, 1975.

Novels as Catherine Brent

Shadow of Summer. London, Hale, 1969.
Turn Back to Love. London, Hale, 1969.
Once upon a Springtime. London, Hale, 1970.
Beyond the River Bend. London, Hale, 1971.
The Seeking Heart. London, Hale, 1975.
Girl with Two Faces. London, Hale, 1979.
Deceive Me Never. London, Hale, 1985.

Novels as Paul Conrad

Ex Minus. London, Hale, 1974.
The Slave Bug. London, Hale, 1975.
Last Man on Kluth V. London, Hale, 1975.

Novels as Craig Cooper

Blackmail Is Murder. London, Hale, 1968.
Catch and Squeeze. London, Hale, 1968.
You'll Die Laughing. London, Hale, 1968.
No Haloes for Hoods. London, Hale, 1969.
Snatch the Lady. London, Hale, 1970.
Run with the Fox. London, Hale, 1971.
Running Scared. London, Hale, 1972.
Value for Murder. London, Hale, 1972.

Novels as Floyd Gibson

A Slip in Time. London, Hale, 1974.
The Manufactured People. London, Hale, 1975.
Shadow of Gastor. London, Hale, 1975.

Novels as Scott Howell

Menace from Magor. London, Hale, 1974.
Passage to Oblivion. London, Hale, 1975.

Novels as Mark Kane

Reluctant Transgressor. London, Hale, 1967.
Walk of the Devil. London, Hale, 1968.
Fit to Kill. London, Hale, 1972.

Novels as Janice Kelsey

Snare of Deception. London, Hale, 1969.
Dangerous Legacy. London, Hale, 1969.
Three Loves Had Freda. London, Hale, 1970.
Reluctant to Love. London, Hale, 1971.
Two Weeks in Summer. London, Hale, 1973.

Novels as Berta King

Fateful Holiday. London, Hale, 1967.
Uncertain Journey. London, Hale, 1967.
Dear Imposter. London, Hale, 1967.
Dangerous Quest. London, Hale, 1969.
The Unsure Heart. London, Hale, 1969.
Yesterday's Sweetheart. London, Hale, 1970.
Out of the Shadows. London, Hale, 1976.

Novels as Christopher King

Operation Mora. London, Hale, 1974.
The World of Jonah Klee. London, Hale, 1976.

Novels as Paul Muller

You Kill Me! London, Hale, 1967.
Make Mine Mayhem. London, Hale, 1967.
The Lady Is Lethal. London, Hale, and New York, Roy, 1968.
Slay Time. London, Hale, and New York, Roy, 1968.
The Hasty Heiress. London, Hale, 1968.
Some Dames Don't. London, Hale, 1970.
Don't Push Your Luck. London, Hale, 1970.
This Is Murder. London, Hale, 1971.
The Wistful Wanton. London, Hale, 1971.
The Friendly Fiends. London, Hale, 1972.
The Man from Ger. London, Hale, 1974.
A Viper in Her Bosom. London, Hale, 1975.

Novels as Ray Owen

Find Tracey George. London, Hale, 1968.
Who Cries for a Loser? London, Hale, 1968.
The Fall Guy. London, Hale, 1969.
Flight from Fear. London, Hale, 1969.

Seek and Destroy. London, Hale, 1970.
Date with Doom. London, Hale, 1971.
So Deadly a Web. London, Hale, 1971.
Mask of Shadows. London, Hale, 1972.
End of the Road. London, Hale, 1972.

Novels as Simon Waldron

Caught in the Middle. London, Hale, 1972.
The Grayson Affair. London, Hale, 1975.

Novels as Agnes Wallace

Hearts in Conflict. London, Hale, 1970.
Never Let Me Go. London, Hale, 1971.
Dear Doctor. London, Hale, 1973.

*

Albert King comments:

I have been writing seriously since 1960, and have published perhaps 250 to 300 novels—western, romance, sci-fi, and crime thrillers. I have also worked at scripts for boys' comics and stories for annuals. These were written for Amalgamated Press, as it was then, in the late 1950's and early 1960's. I have published a few poems which were of little consequence, several short stories, and numerous articles, features, and news stories in my capacity as a newspaperman.

My list of pseudonyms would be much too long to inflict on you, as would the complete list of my titles. My novels have been published in the United States, Portugal, Norway, Sweden, Denmark, France, Italy, Holland, Germany, and Yugoslavia, and have also gone into various paperback and large print editions. My tough, Gothic-type thrillers went down pretty well in Germany in the 1970's, and my private eye series as Paul Muller did well in France and Italy. Despite all this, I have never made enough money to buy a villa in Spain, or even a cabin in the mountains. I suppose I have written too much too fast for that to happen. However, I am working on a novel at the moment which might change all that.

I think that quite a few of my Westerns are not too bad, and I really do enjoy writing these—in order to find my own escape hatch, I suppose. But I would never pretend that I am anything but a storyteller. I am not lumbered with pretension, and I have no great message to convey to the world. I don't mind how critics react to my yarns, or indeed if they bother to react at all. The fact is that my Westerns and romances are read by—here I hesitate for about 10 seconds, but I think in all truth I am correct—millions of people. I have thousands of readers of Westerns who have never saddled a horse, or hunted down an outlaw, or smelled rain on sagebrush, but who can get close to these sensations by reading my stories, even though they are too old or too ill.

I didn't have much of a formal education, but I cannot say that I missed it much. All I recall ever wanting to do was write, tell stories, entertain. I want my readers to sweat with me in the heat, feel those saddle-sores, freeze with me in the snow, feel hungry enough to eat the horse my hero is riding, and relish all those other sensations and experiences that God deemed appropriate to send my way, as much as I do.

* * *

Albert King is another prolific British writer whose work has appeared under a multitude of pen-names, and as may be expected given the volume of his output, the quality of his westerns can vary considerably—from, say, the excellent *Trail Pards* to the rather poor *Texas Pay-Off*. More often than not, however, King's work is remarkably good, offering as it does plausible characters caught up in strong and interesting situations.

King tends to base his Westerns on traditional themes—rustling and range disputes (*Thunder Valley*), the establishment of justice in a hitherto lawless environment (*Renegade Showdown*), revenge (*The Tarnished Star*), and outlawry (*Rambo's Treasure*). In the main, his heroes adhere to expectation by being young, handsome, gun-fast, and tenacious, and justice almost always triumphs in the end, although it should be said that a King ending can never really be predicted.

Many of his stories are set on ranches, and the range dispute, or outbreak of cattle rustling, appears to be a favourite theme, because it recurs so often in his work—*Death Rides the Thunderhead*, *Nester Fury*, *Six-Gun Reckoning*, *Fence War*, and *Fugitive Trail* being just a small proportion of the titles which spring to mind. *Ranger Justice* is an interesting if somewhat convoluted variation on the theme, in which Texas Ranger Ellis Tyler (actually one of King's pseudonyms) is sent to infiltrate and break up a gang of rustlers after the first Ranger to be dispatched turns up back at headquarters with his throat cut. Much more successful is *The Range Hawks*, in which Russ Corby returns to the family ranch after an absence of five years only to discover that his weak-willed brother Burt (who married the girl with whom Russ himself was in love) has turned into an alcoholic and, worse, also fallen in with a band of rustlers. Corby's initial reaction is to say nothing of his suspicions for fear of upsetting Myra, his lost love. But when one of Burt's rustling trips ends in murder, he must decide whether or not to tell the truth about his brother—and thus bring even greater misery to Myra's already miserable existence—or ignore his conscience and remain silent.

This idea of returning home to find that everything has changed—usually for the worse—underlines the wistfulness apparent in so many of King's protagonists. Frequently they recall lost loves or happier times, and wonder how things might have been "if only . . . " This sense of longing for "the old days" is a common feature in King's books, though its main function is usually to add depth to the author's characters by giving them some sort of history, and rarely encroaches upon the main plot.

One man who would sooner forget his past, however, is Mark Price, the hero of another recommended western, *Outlaw Heritage*. But Price, once an outlaw and now a respected rancher, is forced to face up to his erstwhile misdeeds when a wounded bank robber rides into his secluded valley one night in search of treatment, bringing with him a whole pack of other outlaws, among whom is Price's brother, Al. From this point on, King skillfully turns Price's idyllic home into an open prison, from which the hero and his pregnant wife can only escape by outwitting their captors.

As good as *Outlaw Heritage* may be, however, probably King's best work to date is the aforementioned *Trail Pards*, which neatly encapsulates his enviable sense of plot, pace, dialogue, and characterisation. Having been released after four years in prison, Trev Foster heads for a reunion with his old partner and the remnants of their gang. En route he meets up with a veritable giant named Squat Bratton, whom he befriends and takes along to the gang's hideaway. As may be expected from King's other work, Foster soon discovers that much has changed over the previous few years: his old partner, Bill Vale, is with a woman named Retha; two of his other friends have died; and of their replacements, a man named Ben Snide takes an instant dislike to him. Things soon go from bad to worse when the gang's robberies begin to go wrong, and a couple of the men turn up stabbed to death. Soon the book takes an unexpectedly sinister turn as paranoia sets in—for the reader as well as the characters—until an ironic but nonetheless satisfying denouement brings this very unusual western to a close.

In the main, King strikes a good balance between speech (which contains just enough westernisms to set the tone of the books) and prose (which is informal and uncluttered). He is adept at creating atmosphere, and frequently reveals a thoughtful streak which successfully elevates his westerns above those of most of his competitors. His plots involve plenty of gunplay and fist-fights, though their results are seldom described in detail, and while there is nearly always a hint of romance, there is no explicit sex.

King offers competent western action, primarily for an undemanding audience, and although his phrasing can sometimes sound rather melodramatic or clichéd, he undoubtedly possesses the happy knack of being able to imbue even the most hackneyed plot or character with some degree of originality.

—David Whitehead

KING, Ames. *See* **KING, Albert.**

KING, General Charles. American. Born in Albany, New York, 12 October 1844. Educated at the United States Military Academy, West Point, New York, graduated 1866. Married Adelaide Yorke in 1872; three daughters and one son. Career army officer: served in New Orleans from 1866 with the First Artillery; with the Fifth Cavalry, 1870: fought in the Apache Wars in Arizona, wounded 1874; regimental adjutant in the Sioux campaign, 1876–78; retired as Captain, 1879; inspector and instructor, Wisconsin National Guard, 1882–89; Colonel, 1890; Adjutant General, 1895; Brigadier General of Volunteers, 1898–99, on active duty in Hawaii and the Philippines during the Spanish-American War. Professor of military history, University of Wisconsin, Madison; Superintendent, Michigan Military Academy, 1901. *Died 18 March 1933.*

WESTERN PUBLICATIONS

Novels

The Colonel's Daughter; or, Winning His Spurs. Philadelphia, Lippincott, 1883.
The Deserter, and From the Ranks: Two Novels. Philadelphia, Lippincott, 1888.
Dunraven Ranch. London, Warne, 1889.
Laramie; or, The Queen of Bedlam. Philadelphia, Lippincott, 1889; as *The Queen of Bedlam*, London, Warne, 1889.
Sunset Pass; or Running the Gauntlet Through Apache Land. New York, Lovell, 1890; London, Gay and Bird, 1892.
Two Soldiers, and Dunraven Ranch: Two Novels. Philadelphia, Lippincott, 1891.
Captain Blake. Philadelphia, Lippincott, 1891.
Foes in Ambush. Philadelphia, Lippincott, 1893.
Sergeant Croesus. Philadelphia, Lippincott, 1893.
A Soldier's Secret, ... An Army Portia: Two Novels. Philadelphia, Lippincott, 1893.
Captain Close and Sergeant Croesus: Two Novels. Philadelphia, Lippincott, 1895.
The Story of Fort Frayne. New York, Neely, and London, Ward Lock, 1895; as *Fort Frayne,* New York, Hobart, 1901.
Under Fire. Philadelphia, Lippincott, and London, Warne, 1895.
A Garrison Triangle. New York, Neely, 1896.
An Army Wife. Chicago, Neely, 1896.
Trooper Ross and Signal Butte. Philadelphia, Lippincott, 1896.
Trumpeter Fred. Chicago, Neely, 1896.
Warrior Gap. New York, Neely, 1897.
A Wounded Name. New York, Neely, 1898.
A Trooper Galahad. Philadelphia, Lippincott, 1899.
The Way of the West. Chicago, Rand McNally, 1902.
An Apache Princess. New York, Hobart, 1903.
A Daughter of the Sioux. New York, Hobart, 1903.
A Soldier's Trial: An Episode of the Canteen Crusade. New York, Hobart, 1905.
Lieutenant Sandy Ray. New York, Fenno, 1906.
The Further Story of Lieutenant Sandy Ray. New York, Fenno, 1906.
Tonio, Son of the Sierras. New York, Dillingham, and London, Unwin, 1906.
Lanier of the Cavalry; or, A Week's Arrest. Philadelphia, Lippincott, 1909.

Short Stories

Starlight Ranch and Other Stories of Army Life on the Frontier. Philadelphia, Lippincott, 1890.

OTHER PUBLICATIONS

Novels

Kitty's Conquest. Philadelphia, Lippincott, 1884.
Marion's Faith. Philadelphia, Lippincott, 1886.
A War-Time Wooing. New York, Harper, 1888.
Between the Lines. New York, Harper, 1889.
Waring's Peril. Philadelphia, Lippincott, 1894.
Cadet Days. New York, Harper, 1894.
A Tame Surrender. Philadelphia, Lippincott, 1896.
The General's Double. Philadelphia, Lippincott, 1898.
Ray's Recruit. Philadelphia, Lippincott, 1898.
Found in the Philippines. New York, Hobart, 1901.
In Spite of Foes; or, Ten Years' Trial. Philadelphia, Lippincott, 1901.
Norman Holt. New York, Dillingham, 1901.
Ray's Daughter: A Story of Manila Life. Philadelphia, Lippincott, 1901.
The Iron Brigade. New York, Dillingham, 1902.
Comrades in Arms. New York, Hobart, 1904.
A Knight of Columbia. New York, Hobart, 1904.
A Broken Sword. New York, Hobart, 1905.
The Rock of Chickamauga. New York, Dillingham, and London, Unwin, 1907.
To the Front. New York, Harper, 1908.

Short Stories

The Conquering Corps Badge and Other Stories of the Philippines. Milwaukee, Rhoades, 1902.

Play

Screenplay: *The Indian Wars Refought*, 1914.

Other

Campaigning with Crook. Milwaukee, Sentinel, 1880; augmented edition, as *Campaigning with Crook and Stories of Army Life*, New York, Harper, 1890; revised edition, 1891.
Famous and Decisive Battles of the World. Philadelphia, McCurdy, 1884.
Major General George Crook, United States Army. Privately printed, 1890.
Trials of a Staff Officer. Philadelphia, Hamersly, 1891.
From School to Battlefield (juvenile). Philadelphia, Lippincott, 1899.
The True Ulysses S. Grant. Philadelphia, Lippincott, 1914.

Editor, *The Colonel's Christmas Dinner*. Philadelphia, Hamersly, 1890; augmented edition, as *The Colonel's Christmas Dinner and Other Stories*, Philadelphia, Lippincott, 1892.
Editor, *By Land and Sea*. Philadelphia, Hamersly, 1891.
Editor, *An Initial Experience and Other Stories*. Philadelphia, Lippincott, 1894.
Editor, *Captain Dreams and Other Stories*. Philadelphia, Lippincott, 1895.

Translator, with Ann Williston Ward, *Noble Blood: A Prussian Cadet Story*, by Ernst von Wildenbruch. New York, Neely, 1896.

*

Bibliography: *Charles King, American Novelist: A Bibliography from the Collection of the National Library of Australia, Canberra* by C.E. Dornbusch, Cornwallville, New York, Hope Farm Press, 1963.

Critical Study: *Campaigning with King: Charles King, Chronicles of the Old Army* by Don Russell, Lincoln, University of Nebraska Press, 1991.

* * *

Charles King was not promoted to the rank of general in the U.S. Army until he was placed in charge of the Military Department of Hawaii during the Spanish-American War. His rank was then changed on the spines of his novels from Captain King to General King. His first book—which is the only one still in print—was originally a pamphlet published in a limited edition titled *Campaigning with Crook*; it contains a series of newspaper sketches he had earlier written for publication in his father's newspaper, the Milwaukee *Sentinel*. King followed this volume of memoirs—which is also, incidentally, a spirited defense of Crook's military policies—with a romance set against the Indian campaigns in the West, *The Colonel's Daughter; or, Winning His Spurs. The Colonel's Daughter* established the literary formulae King would tend to use in his many subsequent fictions: a romantic intrigue, a carefully concealed secret, and a gossip-obsessed frontier fort amid an Indian campaign. There is no question that King's adulation for General Crook and for the military point of view influenced several of Owen Wister's early short stories in his collection *Red Men and White* (1895); but at his best, King could not muster even the modicum of realism Frederic Remington injected into his "Cavalry" novel, *John Ermine of the Yellowstone* (1902). King proved an exceedingly prolific author, investing in an Ediphone dictating machine in 1890 and using both it and a stenographer to "manufacture" his books more quickly. It may be coincidental that the novels he wrote before 1890 are better-plotted and structured—relatively—than his later ones, but more likely it is not.

A Soldier's Secret bears an inscription to Elizabeth Bacon Custer and introduces the King formulae into the massacre of Indians at Wounded Knee. Early in the novel, King mounted his defense of U.S. Indian Policy in the field while condemning any attempt to view Native Americans as anything other than vicious savages. "Outbreak has followed outbreak, campaign has succeeded campaign, each marked by bitter losses in many a regiment, each swelling the list of the widowed and the fatherless, each terminated by the final surrender of hostile bands satiated with the summer's slaughter and shrewd enough to know that they have only to wave the white rag of submission to be restored to public confidence and double rations." The dedication to Colonel Custer's widow was only the first move in stacking the deck. After further preparing his reader through example after example of Indian brutality, King at last could treat Wounded Knee: "Indian tactics, stooping to anything, stopping at nothing, are too much for men trained to fight only as soldiers and gentlemen. Already squaws are rushing forward, knife and revolver in hand. Already the hidden savages are firing from under tent and *travois*. Already a score of the best and bravest of the Twelfth have bit the dust."

The tense change was deliberate. Until after the turn of the century when dealing with an action sequence, King would switch from the perfect to the historical present, presumably to make the events seem more immediate. King consistently glorified the officers and even the enlisted men in the U.S. Army and he would customarily invoke Latin authors, his obvious favorite (based on a count of citations) being Horace, especially "*Dulce et decorum est pro patria mori.*" Nor did King's attitude toward Native Americans soften as the Indian wars passed into history. Indeed, in *An Apache Princess*, an Apache maiden is attracted to Neil Blakely, a lieutenant of the Cavalry (King's heroes are usually first or second lieutenants), and she commits several vicious and violent acts in her romantic pursuit of him before Blakely finally succeeds in convincing her that, he, being white, and she, being "red," she will be better off marrying one of her own people.

King's novels are all romantic historical reconstructions, which is to say that in them he treated historical settings and events as if they were romance. He had no more use for Mexicans, Jews, or foreigners (other than the British) than he had for Indians, and this exclusionist policy was part of the historical romance. In *An Army Portia* King observed that "all through the North . . . we have an immense foreign population that has fled the Old World to escape military duty. They hate the very sight of a soldier." The principal villain in the novel is Schönberg, a man with "the unmistakable cut of the German Jew. Any one could 'place' him, even had he maintained silence, while, on the other hand, his coarse tones would in the blackest darkness have proclaimed his class." *A Wounded Name* opens in Arizona where, in King's words, "perhaps five thousand souls were counted within its borders . . . not counting the soulless Apaches," and in *An Army Wife* the reader is told that "Greasers [are] natural horse thieves" and that the Mexicans in New Mexico are "unnatural naturalized voters and citizens . . ." His heroines, almost invariably, are of one type, in the words he used in *Two Soldiers*: a "gentle, modest, domestic little woman who will make his [the hero's] home a restful, peaceful refuge always"—what is now termed "the angel in the parlour."

Given these perspectives and this tone, can there be any possible reason for reading General King's books? The answer can be only tentatively in the affirmative. Some of his novels have nothing to do with the Indian wars. *Dunraven Ranch* would be a good example of such a novel, combining a vivid description of a west Texas setting with an interesting portrait of English upper-class immigrants. His verisimilitude in recreating fort life on the frontier, because his knowledge was firsthand, remains superior to many later attempts to do so by Ernest Haycox, James Warner Bellah, and Luke Short. Also, compared to a writer like Bellah, whose *Sergeant Rutledge* centers on a court-martial, King knew how courts-martial were conducted in the American West in the 19th century, as Bellah did not, and novels as *An Army Portia* and *A Wounded Name* might be recommended on this basis if no other. He had the wrong number of the American military dead at the Custer battle of the Little Big Horn in *A Daughter of the Sioux*, but he could occasionally generate genuine suspense with his convoluted plots. He was an avid spokesman for the outlook, attitudes, and conditions of many Anglo-Americans on the military frontier in the previous century and perhaps in this, ultimately, his significance can be said to consist.

—Jon Tuska

KINGSTON, Syd. *See* **BINGLEY, David Ernest.**

KINGSTON, Maxine (Ting Hing) Hong. American. Born in Stockton, California, 27 October 1940. Educated at the University of California, Berkeley, A.B. 1962; teaching certificate 1965. Married Earll Kingston in 1962; one son. Teacher of English and mathematics, Sunset High School, Hayward, California, 1965–67; teacher of English, Kahuku High School, Hawaii, 1967; teacher, Kahaluu Drop-In School, 1968; teacher of English as a second language, Honolulu Business College, Hawaii, 1969; teacher of language arts, Kailua High School, Hawaii, 1969; and Mid-Pacific Institute, Honolulu, 1970–77; from 1977 Visiting Associate Professor of English, University of Hawaii, Honolulu. Recipient: National Book Critics Circle award, for nonfiction, 1976; *Mademoiselle* Magazine award, 1977; Anisfield-Wolf Race Relations award, 1978; National Education Association writing fellowship, 1980; American Book award, for nonfiction, 1981; Arts Commission award, 1981. Address: c/o Alfred A. Knopf Inc., 201 East 50th Street, New York, New York 10022, U.S.A.

Western Publications

Other

China Men. New York, Knopf, 1980; London, Pan, 1981.

Other Publications

Novels

The Woman Warrior: Memoirs of a Girlhood Among Ghosts. New York, Knopf, 1976; London, Allen Lane, 1977.
Tripmaster Monkey. New York, Knopf, 1989.

Other

The Making of More Americans. Honolulu, Hawaii, InterArts, 1980.
Through the Black Curtain. Berkeley, University of California, 1987.

*

Critical Study: *Die Schnaucht nach den anderen: eine Studie zum Verhaltnis von Subjekt und Gesellschaft in den Autobiographien von Lillian Hellman, Maya Angelou und Maxine Hong Kingston*, Frankfurt, Lang, 1986.

* * *

Maxine Hong Kingston, as a Chinese-American, brings a perspective to her novels/biographies that is lacking in most views of the American experience. Kingston has written three books to date. Her work is considered surrealistic and is a blend of memoirs. She is seen as a major American author whose importance resides not only in her works, but also in her ability to provide a fresh cultural perspective to the American experience. Her stories combine a Chinese family history, the history of the Chinese immigration to America, and a mixture of folklore, fairytale, and ghost story, all blended with the reality of her life and that of her family. Kingston refers to herself as a story-talker, like her mother.

In her book *The Woman Warrior: Memoirs of a Girlhood Among Ghosts* the mother exasperates and dazzles her daughter with bewildering stories from China. Kingston recollects a rogue's gallery of family members, and describes her family as more imaginative and brave than most people, who have travelled half-way round the world to find a new life.

Each chapter is a different story, and the contrast between the Chinese and Chinese-American woman is evident. Kingston's aunt, for instance, is erased from the family memory because of a pregnancy caused by rape in her Chinese village. Yet her mother also tells her a story of a warrior woman who led her husband and soldiers into battle. The author's mother, Brave Orchid, is an infuriating, awe-inspiring, unforgettable character. Throughout the book Kingston battles with her mother, trying to decipher her deliberately ambiguous stories, and struggling to assert her own identity. Kingston states, "She said I would grow up a wife and a slave, but she taught me the song of the warrior woman."

In the chapter "Shaman," Kingston's mother is left behind by her husband who leaves for the "Gold Mountain" (America). She studies as a midwife in a school in China in order to gain skills to bring to her husband. Tricking the other girls in the school to believe she has beaten a ghost, one sees the cleverness of the Chinese woman mixed with her superstitions and a world of prescribed right and wrong.

The self-hatred of the Chinese-American against the Chinese who are "just-off-the-boat" is painful and bitter. In one instance, Kingston physically attacks another child who will not speak, for she is angry that this girl stands out as different. The proudness of Chinese and Chinese-Americans in their native culture is in constant conflict with the need to assimilate. But assimilation is impossible when the Chinese-American faces society with an Asian face.

China Men opens with the story of Kingston's father's experiences in China. We learn how the Chinese work around the legal visa system to be able to get Chinese men into the U.S. to work. Kingston tells two stories of her father's journeys to America, one as a stowaway to San Francisco, and the other his arrival in New York. Both the father's and mother's immigrations are arduous and include trick questions to be answered to immigration officials.

The Chinese called Hawaii "Sandalwood Mountain," and some Chinese married Hawaiians and stayed, while others, like

Kingston's great grandfather, later returned to China. In the story of the "Great Grandfather of the Sandalwood Mountains," Kingston describes her ancestor's time in Hawaii cutting cane. The working conditions were brutal, and the white bosses forbade the laborers to talk while they were in the fields. In one of the most powerful scenes in *China Men*, Kingston imagines her ancestor, Bak Goong, leading a rebellion against the enforced silence. The men dig a hole in the ground and shout in their secrets, while the frightened white foremen hide.

"The Grandfather of the Sierra Nevada Mountains" is the story of the Chinese working on the Trans-Continental Railroad, digging through granite with rock-pounding, muscle-pounding work. When dynamite is discovered it is the Chinese that are often endangered by hanging over ledges to place the fuse—the dynamite caused more accidents and deaths. When the bosses try to instigate a longer work day for minimal pay, it is the Chinese who try to protest with a strike. The whites do not stand with them, and the Chinese workers are attacked by the army, but in the end their strike succeeds—the bosses give up and return to the eight-hour day. After the building of the railroad, while the demons (whites) posed for photographs, the Chinese dispersed—it was dangerous to stay. The driving out had begun, and the Chinese left to build railroads across the country. They were soon to be attacked and driven out of mining, too. The author stops to include a chapter listing the Chinese Exclusion Laws and other racist legislation, like the San Francisco ordinance banning the use of poles to carry laundry baskets. Amazingly, it was not until 1968 that quotas based on race were not allowed, and it took until 1978 when there was not a division of quotas by hemispheres.

China Men is a powerful book, and a history lesson. If *Woman Warrior* is primarily a feminist vision, *China Men* is an indictment of racism, and an homage to the tough, resourceful Chinese men who came to American and conquered it with their labor and their lives.

Kingston's *Tripmaster Monkey* is completely different from her first two books. She speaks through a male-ego that one would have trouble believing a woman could present so convincingly. The book at first makes difficult reading for one not in the "Chinese-American, Berkeley-graduate, San Francisco-dwelling-clan." The story refers to many "inside" locations, names, and activities, that take the uninitiated time to understand, but is well worth the effort.

The novel's character, Wittman Ah Sing, is a young Chinese-American, who as poet, playwright, and storyteller, cannot take on the role of pushing sales in a department store, and quits. He struggles against the stereotypes of being Chinese-American, seeing himself as the warrior, master monkey. The reader follows him through tripping parties, the bureaucratic idiocies of the unemployment line, his efforts to romance women, and the play he develops and produces within the story. The play within the story is pure Chinese, and involves battles, beautiful maidens, flying horses, and culminates in an explosion of fireworks.

Kingston's books have been embraced by college teachers for their courses in American literature, women's studies, and ethnic studies. Her work provides new insight into the lives and history of Chinese-Americans.

—Daryl Morrison

KINGSTON, Syd. *See* **BINGLEY, David Ernest.**

KINKAID, Matt. *See* **ADAMS, Clifton.**

KIRK, Matthew. *See* **WELLS, Angus.**

KITTREDGE, William. Also writes as Owen Rountree. American. Born in Portland, Oregon, 24 August 1932. Educated at Oregon State University, Corvallis, Oregon, B.S. in agriculture 1953; University of Oregon, Eugene, 1968; University of Iowa, Iowa City, M.F.A. in English 1969. Served in the United States Air Force, 1954–57. Has one daughter and one son. Ranch manager, McRanch, Adel, Oregon, 1958–67. Assistant Professor, 1969–74, Associate Professor, 1974–79, and since 1979 Professor of English, University of Montana, Missoula, Montana. Stegner fellow, Stanford University, California, 1973–74. Assistant editor and consulting editor, *Northwest Review*, Eugene, Oregon, 1968–70; consulting editor, *Rocky Mountain Magazine*, 1979–83, *Pacific Northwest Magazine*, 1979–86, and *Outside*; advisory board member, *Puerto Del Sol*; publication board member, *Montana: Magazine of Western History*. Recipient: University of Oregon Ernest Haycox Fiction prize, 1968; National Endowment for the Arts award, 1974; 1981; University of Montana summer grant, 1970, 1976, 1982, and Innovative Summer Program Grant, 1977, 1978; Montana Committee for the Humanities grant, 1979; PEN/NEA Syndicated Fiction Project award, 1983, 1988, and Fiction award, 1984; Neil Simon award, for script, 1984; Montana Governor's Award for Literature, 1985; H.G. Merriam award, 1988. Agent: Amanda Urban, International Creative Management, 40 West 57th Street, New York, New York, 10019, U.S.A.

WESTERN PUBLICATIONS

Novels as Owen Rountree, with Steven M. Krauzer (series: Cord)

Cord. New York, Ballantine, 1982.
Cord: The Nevada War. New York, Ballantine, 1982.
Cord: Black Hills Duel. New York, Ballantine, 1983.
Cord: Gunman Winter. New York, Ballantine, 1983.
Cord: Hunt the Man Down. New York, Ballantine, 1984.
Cord: King of Colorado. New York, Ballantine, 1984.
Cord: Gunsmoke River. New York, Ballantine, 1985.
Cord: Paradise Valley. New York, Ballantine, 1986.
Cord: Brimstone Basin. New York, Ballantine, 1986.

Short Stories

The Van Gogh Field and Other Stories. Columbia, University of Missouri Press, 1978.

We Are Not in This Together. Port Townsend, Washington, Graywolf Press, 1984.
Phantom Silver. Missoula, Montana, Kutenai Press, 1987.

Uncollected Short Stories

"Society of Eros," in *Northwest Review* (Eugene, Oregon), 1965–66.
"The Waterfowl Tree," in *Northwest Review* (Eugene, Oregon), 1966–67.
"The Voice of Water," in *Minnesota Review*, 1967.
"The Cove," in *Descant*, 1968.
"Native Cutthroat," in *Northwest Review* (Eugene, Oregon), 1970.
"The Red Room," in *December*, 1970.
"Autumn on Steens Mountain," in *Bullfrog Information Service*, 1971.
"Images of Spiritual Childhood," in *Sumac*, 1971.
"The Waterfowl Tree," in *Stories That Count*, edited by William Roecker. New York, Holt Rinehart, 1971.
"Silver and Gold," in *North American Review* (Cedar Falls, Iowa), 1972.
"Sometimes There's Nothing There," in *Falcon*, Winter 1972.
"Sunday Love," in *Fiction*, 1(3), 1972.
"Breaker of Horses," in *Antioch Review* (Yellow Springs, Ohio), 32(4).
"The Stone Corral," in *TriQuarterly* (Evanston, Illinois), 29.
"Horses in Heaven," in *Ark River Review*, 1973.
"Blue Stone," in *Ohio Journal*, 1973.
"Unnecessary Beasts," in *Sequoia*, 1974.
"The Man Who Loved Buzzards," in *Carolina Quarterly*, 1974.
"The Vineland Lullaby," in *Tales*, 1974.
"The Vineland Lullaby," *Ploughshares* (Cambridge, Massachusetts), 2(3), 1975.
"Medusa," in *Spectrum* (Paxton, Massachusetts), 1975.
"Kookooskia," in *Chariton Review* (Kirksville, Missouri), 1(2), 1975.
"The Mercy of the Elements," in *TriQuarterly* (Evanston, Illinois), 1976.
"Good Boys," in *Slackwater Review*, 1979.
"Momentum Is Always the Weapon," in *Portland Review*, 25, 1979.
"Breaking of Glass," in *Scratchgravel Hills*, 1979.
"One More Time," in *Portland Review*, 25, 1979.
"Performing Arts," in *TriQuarterly* (Evanston, Illinois), May 1980.
"No More Money," in *Western Star*, December 1980.
"Stoneboat," in *Montana Eagle*, April 1981.
"34 Seasons of Winter," in *Matters of Life and Death: New American Stories*, edited by Tobias Wolff. N.p., Wampeta Press, 1982.
"We Are Not in This Together," in *Writers of the Purple Sage*, edited by Russell Martin. New York, Viking, 1984.
"Stone Boat," in *The Available Press/PEN Short Story Collection*, edited by Anne Tyler. New York, Ballantine, 1985.
"Agriculture," in *The Pushcart Prize I: Best of the Small Presses, 1985/86*, edited by Bill Henderson. New York, Pushcart Press, 1985.
"Be Careful What You Want," in *Paris Review*, Fall 1985.
"Revenge," in *Northern Lights*, August 1985.
"Warfare," in *Cream City Review*.
"Balancing Water," in *Paris Review*, Fall 1987.
"Cities in the Sky," in *Epoch 36.3* (Ithaca, New York), 1988.
"Rich," in *Cutbank*, Spring 1988.
"Phantom Silver," in *Graywolf Annual Four: Stories by Men*. Port Townsend, Washington, Graywolf Press, 1988.
"The Underground River," in *The Best of the West*. Layton, Utah, Peregrine Smith, 1988.

OTHER PUBLICATIONS

Other

Owning It All: Essays. Port Townsend, Washington, Graywolf Press, 1987.

Editor, with Steven M. Krauzer, *Great Action Stories*. New York, New American Library, 1977.
Editor, with Steven M. Krauzer, *The Great American Detective*. New York, New American Library, and London, New English Library, 1978.
Editor, with Steven M. Krauzer, *Fiction into Film*. New York, Harper and Row, 1979.
Editor, with Steven M. Krauzer, *Contemporary Western Fiction TriQuarterly*, special edition, May 1980.
Editor, *Montana Spaces: Essays and Photographs in Celebration of Montana*. New York, Nick Lyons, 1988.
Editor, with Annick Smith, *The Last Best Place: A Montana Anthology*. Helena, Montana Historical Society, 1988.

* * *

Readers may at first puzzle over the violence in William Kittredge's stories, most of them set in Montana and nearby states. Coming unhinged from anger mixed with alcohol, men fight in bars and with their women. Farmhands are crushed by their machinery, and a grizzly bear disembowels a backpacking girl. Granting the continuing influence of the region's stormy history and considering the author's focus on ordinary people gnashing their teeth in welters of frustration, one might conclude that Kittredge is imposing the tenets of late 19th-century naturalism on the American West.

Other pieces hint, however, that Kittredge intends much more than this, that he is in fact probing beyond the portrayal of broken noses and squashed desires to test a more complex and delicate psychic fabric. Sometimes he achieves in his fiction the loveliness that he yearns for in his personal life. By such nurturing amid contrary reality, Kittredge illuminates the possibility of hope amid difficulties, once they are defined, and offers promise for a restless and unsure society in the midst of confusion and change.

The title piece of his short story collection, *The Van Gogh Field*, contains a death and certainly its share of alienation, but in its delicate construction the story devolves toward an ending that prefigures healing. While young Robert Onnter wanders to Chicago and has an affair with a married woman, he struggles within himself to find the roots so often sliced off by a mobile society. That by story's end Robert seems determined to return to the family's wheat farm in eastern Oregon and live among its comforting agricultural cycles is not a failure of the young man's nerve to face the larger world. Nor is it the writer's easy escape into the sentimental nimbus of the agrarian ideal. Instead it reveals a complex process, effecting a realization in the man of what might be valuable and enduring in his life, whether or not he can achieve it. It is, too, a process ongoing both in many Westerners and demonstrably in Kittredge himself.

For in contrast to many of his fellow writers, Kittredge represents an increasingly rare phenomenon in western American literature, the writer who has known the rural West from childhood. That he grew up on a ranch in eastern Oregon and went on to become an English professor at the University of Montana does not automatically give him more cachet to write about the West than anyone else has, yet it does equip him to see the region from a rough-hewn perspective overlain with a wider and more intellectual view. Kittredge's ability to draw on this background lends his work depth and authority.

It also means that with Kittredge's particular concerns for his material we have a much closer link than usual between an author's work and his autobiographical details. Kittredge's characters aren't necessarily versions of himself, but in the larger view the problems they contend with often are those Kittredge has struggled with, and in part resolved, over much of his life. This shakes down basically to one question: how should we live in the American West? The answer is not simple. Kittredge, in common with Robert Onnter of his story, would like to return to the circumstances of his boyhood. He'd like to live close to the fructifying earth, so isolated from the wrangles of the world that even news of war does not disturb. Yet having sold the ranch that he inherited and loved, Kittredge admits that modern agriculture, overpopulation, and the inroads of technology make the old dream impossible. Putting a sardonic twist on Huck Finn's words, he says in his series of collected essays, *Owning It All:* "There is no more running away to territory." The seemingly senseless violence in many of his stories, then, arises from people deluding themselves by yearning for the rural ideal. Not understanding its impossibility, they bash themselves and others against an unyielding reality. Much of Kittredge's writing saws back and forth between hope and despair, with emphasis on the latter.

Yet though the image of the West as a "great good place" is fast fading, there still may be some cause for optimism. The region may no longer be the paradise for personal fulfillment that aggressive settlers, trying to hammer it into the shape of their dreams, imagined, but there may be another way: "We have no choice but to live in community," one that "teaches us to abhor our old romance with conquest and possession." Just what that gentler community life should be, given the counter tides of modern circumstances, Kittredge does not define, though it would seem that if he has abandoned the muscular heroism of the old romance of the West he has replaced it with the attractions of an equally elusive and delusory ideal, as the last, wish-fulfilling chapter of *Owning It All* describes. Here the West is once again a natural paradise, and now, somehow, small bands of concerned individuals live at one with it, much as, Kittredge assumes, the traditional Indians did. Their lives in wild nature are physically satisfying and rich with mystery. In that "somehow" and in that willful assumption lies much of the tension, and, perhaps, much of the whimsical sadness, of Kittredge's writing.

—Peter Wild

KNIBBS, H(enry) H(erbert). Also wrote as Henry K. Herbert. American. Born in Clifton, Ontario, Canada, 24 October 1874. Educated at Woodstock College, Ontario; Bishop Ridley College, St. Catherines, Ontario; Harvard University, Cambridge, Massachusetts. Married Ida Julia Pfeiffer in 1899. Worked as wholesale coal salesman, clerk, Lehigh Valley Railroad, and stenographer, B.R.& P. Railway; then freelance writer. *Died 17 May 1945.*

Western Publications

Novels

Lost Farm Camp. Boston, Houghton Mifflin, and London, Constable, 1912.
Stephen March's Way. Boston, Houghton Mifflin, 1913.
Overland Red. Boston, Houghton Mifflin, 1914; London, Hodder and Stoughton, 1925.
Sundown Slim. Boston, Houghton Mifflin, 1915; London, Hodder and Stoughton, 1917.
Tang of Life. Boston, Houghton Mifflin, 1918; London, Melrose, 1922; as *Jim Waring of Sonora Town*, New York, Grosset and Dunlap, n.d.
The Ridin' Kid from Powder River. Boston, Houghton Mifflin, 1919; London, Hodder and Stoughton, 1921.
Partners of Chance. Boston, Houghton Mifflin, 1921; London, Hutchinson, 1922.
Wild Horses. Boston, Houghton Mifflin, and London, Hutchinson, 1924.
Temescal. Boston, Houghton Mifflin, and London, Hutchinson, 1925.
The Sungazers. Boston, Houghton Mifflin, and London, Hutchinson, 1926.
Sunny Mateel. Boston, Houghton Mifflin, and London, Hutchinson, 1927.
The Tonto Kid. Boston, Houghton Mifflin, 1936; London, Hutchinson, 1937.

Uncollected Short Stories

"Rancho in the Rain," in *Red Cross Magazine* (New York), July 1920.
"Broncho Shod with Wings," in *Current Opinion* (New York), December 1922.
"Lee of Rimrock," in *Adventure* (New York), 1 April 1928.
"An Old Fashioned Sheriff," in *Adventure* (New York), 15 April 1928.
"Tonto Charley," in *Adventure* (New York), 15 August 1929.
"Head Money," in *West* (New York), 25 November 1931.
"Crow Bait," in *Western Story* (London), March 1932.
"Three Swinging Shadows," in *West* (New York), 30 March 1932.
"Three of a Kind," in *West* (New York), 31 August 1932.
"Why, Pericles!," in *Saturday Evening Post* (Philadelphia), 1 April 1933.
"That Colt Pericles," in *Horses, Dogs, and Men*, edited by C.W. Gray. New York, Holt, 1935.
"Pericles' Honeymoon," in *Gallant Horses*, edited by F.E. Clarke. New York, Macmillan, 1938.
"Shot in the Dark," in *Great Tales of the American West*, edited by H.E. Maule. New York, Modern Library, 1945.
"Mebbyso a Thousand Dollars," in *West* (Kingswood, Surrey), August 1946.
"The Rats' Nest," in *Gun Smoke Yarns*, edited by Gene Autry. New York, Dell, 1948.
"Road Runner," in *Western Stories*, edited by William MacLeod Raine. New York, Dell, 1949.
"Young Pete Pays a Bill," in *Selected Western Stories*, edited by Leo Margulies. New York, Popular Library, 1949.
"Thunder Mountain," in *Zane Grey's Western* (New York), February 1949.
"Apuni Oyis," in *The Warriors*, edited by Bill Pronzini and Martin H. Greenberg. New York, Fawcett, 1985.
"The Killer," in *The Gunfighters*, edited by Martin H. Greenberg. New York, Fawcett, 1986.

"Voyageurs," in *The Steamboaters*, edited by Bill Pronzini and Martin H. Greenberg. New York, Fawcett, 1986.

Verse

First Poems (as Henry K. Herbert). Rochester, New York, Genesee Press, 1908.
Songs of the Outlands: Ballads of the Hoboes and Other Verse. Boston, Houghton Mifflin, 1914.
Riders of the Stars: A Book of Western Verse. Boston, Houghton Mifflin, 1916.
Songs of the Trail. Boston, Houghton Mifflin, 1920.
Saddle Songs and Other Verse. Boston, Houghton Mifflin, 1922.
Songs of the Lost Frontier. Boston, Houghton Mifflin, 1930.

OTHER PUBLICATIONS

Novel

Gentlemen, Hush!, with Turbese Lummis. Boston, Houghton Mifflin, 1939.

Play

Screenplay: *Tony Runs Wild*, with Edfrid Bingham and Robert Lord, 1926.

* * *

H.H. Knibbs first met the western author Eugene Manlove Rhodes while Knibbs was still working for the B.R.& P. Railroad in the East. As a result of their association and Knibbs's own burning desire to write western fiction, Knibbs migrated to California in 1910 and for 11 months went on an extended camping trip to give himself a feeling for the land before he settled in Los Angeles to write his first novel, *Lost Farm Camp*. This novel, like Knibbs's subsequent *Overland Red*, owed more than a little, in terms of its picaresque structure and its slow pacing interspersed with occasional shoot-outs, to Clarence E. Mulford. These novels also established a truth about Knibbs's fiction: he was an epigonal writer; his talent was strictly derivative, never original. This epigonal quality even extended to much of the "philosophy" he would incorporate into his novels, as, for example his imitation of Zane Grey in attributing to the western regions not only physically, but morally, regenerative qualities. In his early novels, he depended too greatly on contrivance and elaborate coincidence, and this amid a distressing tendency toward plots that are often too diffuse and episodic to hold a contemporary reader's attention.

Knibbs, however, also demonstrated one outstanding ability: he could draw sympathetic portraits of young male adolescents. Collie in *Overland Red* comes to mind, whom the reader sees grow into responsible maturity, and also Pete Annersley in *The Ridin' Kid from Powder River*, Little Jim in *Partners of Chance*, and Young Pete in *The Tonto Kid*. Knibbs thought little of Mexicans, and in *The Ridin' Kid from Powder River*, he has his hero remark that "Mexicans is mostly figurin' out to-day what they're goin' to do to-morrow, and they never git through figurin. I dunno who my father and mother was, but I know one thing—they wa'n't Mexicans." Knibbs, referred to cordially by Rhodes as "His Knibbs," based his character of the Spider, an outlaw leader in *The Ridin' Kid from Powder River*, on Rhodes, and Rhodes was not pleased by the portrayal, feeling that Knibbs had taken too many liberties. For a time it endangered their friendship. Knibbs tried to make up for it by basing his hero, Cheyenne Hastings, in *Partners of Chance*, on Rhodes. Using the sobriquet of movie cowboy Harry Carey's screen character, Cheyenne Harry (both Rhodes and Knibbs were friends of Carey and Carey purchased several of Rhodes's stories for screen adaptation), Knibbs drew Hastings as a cheerful wanderer of the plains and deserts, a man always with a song on his breath, and a man who, like Rhodes, eschewed violence. What Rhodes remembered most of the West of his youth was its kindness and generosity, and so Knibbs was being true to his source when he remarked that "in direct and effectual kindliness, without obviously expressed sympathy, the Westerner is peculiarly supreme."

Like Owen Wister in *Lin McLean* (1897), Knibbs showed his hero in *Partners of Chance* involved in a foolish marriage; and as in Wister's *The Virginian* (1902), B.M. Bower's *The Lure of the Dim Trails* (1907), and Charles Alden Seltzer's *The Two Gun Man* (1911), Knibbs's narrator in the same novel, John Bartley, is an eastern writer who comes west and decides to stay in order to write stories about it. Cheyenne Hastings is reconciled with his wife at the end, and Bartley falls in love, a double ranch romance ending with an appropriate final chapter titled "Two Trails Home."

In *Riders of the Night* (1932) Eugene Cunningham adapted Dashiell Hammett's *"Blut und Boden"* plot from *Red Harvest* (1929), in which there is so much killing that the characters, in Hammett's words, become "blood simple," to a western setting, and 50 villains are killed in the course of his novel. This plot became almost a sub-genre in formulary western fiction—it was still being practised in the 1970's by Terry Harknett, J.T. Edson, and Gordon D. Shirreffs—and Knibbs tried his hand at it in *The Tonto Kid* in which he had 47 people killed off.

In *Temescal* Knibbs attempted to set a novel in revolutionary Mexico, a plot handled more adeptly by Dane Coolidge and others; moreover, lacking Coolidge's grasp of idiomatic Spanish, Knibbs made numerous linguistic errors, such as a Mexican saying "*Bueno suerte*" when he means "*Buena suerte*."

After Rhodes died, Knibbs wrote a lengthy Introduction to Rhodes's last novel, *The Proud Sheriff* (1935); and, in turn, the best portrait we have so far of Knibbs is to be found in May Davison Rhodes's *The Hired Man on Horseback: My Story of Eugene Manlove Rhodes* (1938), a book Rhodes's widow dedicated to Knibbs and Turbesë Lummis. One quality which Knibbs definitely shared with Rhodes was his ability to describe unusual and interesting characters; and in the case of both authors it can sometimes compensate a reader sufficiently that one might overlook the structure and predictability of their plots. One thing more: neither could draw believable female characters, but in Rhodes's favor it can be said he attempted to do so less frequently than did Knibbs.

—Jon Tuska

KNOTT, Bill. *See* **KNOTT, Will C.**

KNOTT, Will(iam) C(ecil, Jr.). Also writes as Bill Carol: Tabor Evans (house name); Bill Knott; Laura Layne; Jake Logan; Hank Mitchum; Jon Sharpe; Bryan Swift. American. Born in Boston, Massachusetts, 7 August 1927. Educated at Boston University, Associate in Arts 1949, B.S. 1951; State University of New York College, Oswego, M.A. 1966. Served in the

United States Air Force, 1946–47. Married 1) Elizabeth Ann Knott in 1950 (divorced), two daughters and one son; 2) Constance Seifert in 1971 (divorced); one daughter; 3) Mary Agnes Lee in 1986. Junior high school teacher, Old Lyme, Connecticut, 1951–52, Lesage, West Virginia, 1952–53, Plainfield, New Jersey, 1953–57, and Hannibal, New York, 1957–63; English teacher, Baldwinsville Academy Central School, New York, 1963–67; Assistant Professor, later Associate Professor of English, State University of New York College, Potsdam, 1967–83. Agent: Jim Trupin, Jet Literary Associates, 124 East 84th Street, New York, New York 10028. Address: R.D. 1, Cottage Road, Colton, New York 13625, U.S.A.

WESTERN PUBLICATIONS

Novels

Caulder's Badge. New York, Ace, 1977.
Killer's Canyon. New York, Doubleday, 1977.
Kiowa Blood. New York, Berkley, 1977.
Stampede. New York, Berkley, 1978.
Red Skies over Wyoming. New York, Berkley, 1980.
The Golden Mountain. New York, Berkley, 1980.
Lyncher's Moon. New York, Berkley, 1980; Bath, Chivers, 1990.
The Return of Zach Stewart. New York, Berkley, 1980.

Novels (series: Golden Hawk in all books)

1. *The Golden Hawk.* New York, New American Library, 1986.
2. *Blood Hunt.* New York, New American Library, 1986.
3. *Grizzly Pass.* New York, New American Library, 1987.
4. *Hell's Children.* New York, New American Library, 1987.
5. *Kill Hawk.* New York, New American Library, 1987.
6. *Scalper's Trail.* New York, New American Library, 1987.
7. *The Eyes of the Cat.* New York, New American Library, 1988.
8. *Captive's Trail.* New York, New American Library, 1988.
9. *The Searchers.* New York, New American Library, 1988.

Novels (series: Vengeance Seeker)

1. *The Vengeance Seeker Number One.* New York, Ace, 1975.
2. *The Vengeance Seeker Number Two.* New York, Ace, 1975.
3. *The Vengeance Seeker Number Three.* New York, Ace, 1976.

Novels as Hank Mitchum (series: Stagecoach Station in all books)

Cheyenne. New York, Bantam, 1983.
Seattle. New York, Bantam, 1983.
Sonora. New York, Bantam, 1983.
Abilene. New York, Bantam, 1984.
Cimarron. New York, Bantam, 1984.

Novels as Jake Logan (series: Slocum)

Slocum and the Cattle Queen. New York, Berkley, 1983.
Slocum and the Lost Dutchman Mine. New York, Berkley, 1983.

Novels as Tabor Evans (series: Longarm)

Longarm and the Avenging Angels. New York, Jove, 1978.
Longarm and the Loggers. New York, Jove, 1979.
Longarm and the Hatchet Men. New York, Jove, 1979.
Longarm in Lincoln County. New York, Jove, 1979.
Longarm and the Dragon Hunters. New York, Jove, 1980.
Longarm in Northfield. New York, Jove, 1981.
Longarm and the Boot Hillers. New York, Jove, 1981.
Longarm and the Devil's Railroad. New York, Jove, 1981.
Longarm and the Moonshiners. New York, Jove, 1982.
Longarm and the Great Train Robbery. New York, Jove, 1982.
Longarm in the Big Bend. New York, Jove, 1982.
Longarm and the Calico Kid. New York, Jove, 1983.
Longarm and the Big Outfit. New York, Jove, 1984.
Longarm and the Desert Duchess. New York, Jove, 1984.

Novels as Jon Sharpe (series: Trailsman in all books)

Hostage Trail. New York, New American Library, 1984.
White Savage. New York, New American Library, 1984.
Apache Gold. New York, New American Library, 1984.
Sharps Justice. New York, New American Library, 1984.
The Badge. New York, New American Library, 1984.
The Lost Patrol. New York, New American Library, 1985.
The Grizzly Man. New York, New American Library, 1985.
The Renegade Command. New York, New American Library, 1985.
Scorpion Trail. New York, New American Library, 1985.
Hell Town. New York, New American Library, 1985.
Blood Oath. New York, New American Library, 1985.
Posse from Hell. New York, New American Library, 1986.
Killer Clan. New York, New American Library, 1986.

OTHER PUBLICATIONS

Novels

Journey Across the Third Planet. Philadelphia, Chilton, 1969.
Nurse June's Dilemma (as Laura Layne). New York, Ace, 1977.

Novels as Bill Knott

Junk Pitcher. Chicago, Follett, 1963.
Night Pursuit (for children). Austin, Texas, Steck Vaughn, 1966.
They Work and Serve. Austin, Texas, Steck Vaughn, 1967.
The Dwarf on Black Mountain (for children). Austin, Texas, Steck Vaughn, 1967.
Danger at Half-Moon Lake (for children). Austin, Texas, Steck Vaughn, 1968.
The Secret of the Old Brownstone (for children). Austin, Texas, Steck Vaughn, 1969.
The Taylor Street Irregulars (for children). Austin, Texas, Steck Vaughn, 1970.
The Serpent of Pirate Cove (for children). Austin, Texas, Steck Vaughn, 1971.

Novels as Bryan Swift

King's Pawn. New York, Jove, 1981.
Minotaur. New York, Jove, 1981.
Springboard. New York, Jove, 1982.

Fiction (for children) as Bill Carol

Circus Catch. Austin, Texas, Steck Vaughn, 1963.
Backboard Scrambler. Austin, Texas, Steck Vaughn, 1963.
Clutch Single. Austin, Texas, Steck Vaughn, 1964.
Scatback. Austin, Texas, Steck Vaughn, 1964.

Hit Away! Austin, Texas, Steck Vaughn, 1965.
Full-Court Pirate. Austin, Texas, Steck Vaughn, 1965.
Hard Smash to Third. Austin, Texas, Steck Vaughn, 1966.
Long Pass. Austin, Texas, Steck Vaughn, 1966.
Long Throw from Center. Austin, Texas, Steck Vaughn, 1967.
Lefty's Long Throw. Austin, Texas, Steck Vaughn, 1967.
Inside the Ten. Austin, Texas, Steck Vaughn, 1967.
Touchdown Duo. Austin, Texas, Steck Vaughn, 1968.
Lefty Finds a Catcher. Austin, Texas, Steck Vaughn, 1968.
Lefty Plays First. Austin, Texas, Steck Vaughn, 1969.
Crazylegs Merrill. Austin, Texas, Steck Vaughn, 1969.
Sandy Plays Third. Austin, Texas, Steck Vaughn, 1970.
Stop That Pass! Austin, Texas, Steck Vaughn, 1970.
Squeeze Play. Austin, Texas, Steck Vaughn, 1971.
Linebacker Blitz. Austin, Texas, Steck Vaughn, 1971.
High Fly to Center. Austin, Texas, Steck Vaughn, 1972.
Fullback Fury. Austin, Texas, Steck Vaughn, 1972.
Double-Play Ball. Austin, Texas, Steck Vaughn, 1973.
Flare Pass. Austin, Texas, Steck Vaughn, 1973.
Single to Center. Austin, Texas, Steck Vaughn, 1974.
Blocking Back. Austin, Texas, Steck Vaughn, 1974.

Other

The Craft of Fiction. Englewood Cliffs, New Jersey, Reston, 1973; as *How to Write and Publish Your Novel*, Englewood Cliffs, Prentice Hall, 1983.
The Craft of Nonfiction. Englewood Cliffs, New Jersey, Reston, 1974.

* * *

A veritable chameleon of a writer, whose contributions to several series (including Longarm, Slocum, and Stagecoach Station) blend seamlessly with those of his fellow scribes, Will C. Knott's work is, however, distinguished by its clarity of expression, the intelligence of the author's plots, and the credibility he brings to his characters and situations. That he has a firm understanding of the requirements of the single and series western become obvious after even a cursory examination of his novels; indeed, his 1986 Trailsman story *Killer Clan* continues to remain in all likelihood the best book of that series' particularly lengthy run.

Conflict, confrontation, and revenge lie at the heart of Knott's westerns. In *Killer's Canyon*, Kyle Robinson comes to the aid of an old friend named Juan Ramirez, who, though found innocent of murdering the son of powerful rancher Carl Beecher, still remains in very real danger of being lynched by the dead man's bereaved and vengeance-hungry clan. Robinson arrives just in time to witness the murder of Juan's wife during a siege of his property, and following Juan's death from wounds sustained during the shootout, Robinson decides to deal with the despotic Beechers himself. As with all of Knott's work, however, there is more to the story that follows than simply revenge, and events seldom work out as expected. (It is also interesting to note that Knott later republished the book, almost word for word, as *Longarm and the Big Outfit*, under the pseudonym Tabor Evans).

Confrontation also plays a key role in other single westerns, such as the unusually violent *Red Skies over Wyoming*, which revolves around the antagonism between cattlemen and railroaders, and *Lyncher's Moon*, the story of one particular rancher's hatred of nesters.

An accomplished exponent of the series western, Knott has published two series under his own name. Generally, however, this segment of his work forsakes the indepth characterisation at which he is so good in favour of action—the "action," in this instance, usually being confused with "violence." Knott's picture of the West in these books is consequently a much tougher, more cruel and blood thirsty one.

The principal character in his first series was Wolf Caulder, a.k.a. "The Vengeance Seeker." When he was 12 years old, Caulder watched five outlaws ride into his father's ranch and gun down his parents. When he tried to go to their aid, the outlaws shot him, too; so badly that he lost one eye and sustained a hideous scar which now gives his face a lopsided, caved-in aspect. Nursed back to life by Diego Sanchez, his father's foreman, Caulder is taught to fight with guns and fists. Sanchez also nurtures the boy's desire for revenge.

It will come as little surprise to learn that Caulder eventually catches up with the men who turned him into an orphan, and dispatches each with a distinctive flourish. Later he appoints himself as judge, jury, and executioner by dispensing his own particular brand of justice when the law itself appears to fall short, as in 1976's *The Vengeance Seeker Number 3* (the books were initially published without specific sub-titles), in which Caulder tracks down a gang of train robbers who were acquitted of the infamous Tipton Train Massacre, which Caulder himself actually watched them commit.

Knott's other relatively short-lived series, Golden Hawk, adds regular bouts of sex to the familiar mix of violence and retribution, although, being set in the 1850's, the stories take place much earlier than most of Knott's adventures. Captured by the Comanches when he was 12 years old, young Jed Thompson (later called Golden Hawk by the Indians because of his shoulder-length blond hair) eventually decides to escape from a life of virtual slavery in order to find his sister Annabelle, who was also taken captive, and from whom he was later separated. Killing an important chief and several braves during his escape, Golden Hawk spends his subsequent adventures as a hunted man. His search for Annabelle is the main theme which runs through the first few novels, although his quest is constantly interrupted for the requisite number of sexual encounters, as well as numerous other distractions, which include a clash with pirates. When Golden Hawk finally manages to rescue her, Annabelle marries and goes back East, leaving Knott's protagonist to become a mountain man.

It is in the traditional western format, where there is no need to punctuate an otherwise good, solid story with explicit sex and violence, that Knott's best work can often be found, as his contributions to the Stagecoach Station series prove. One of the best of these, *Abilene*, is an especially satisfying blend of (not always entirely accurate) fact and fiction which chronicles Wild Bill Hickok's tenure as city marshal of Abilene, Kansas, a saga continued in an equally enjoyable companion volume, *Deadwood*, written by D.B. Newton. Not quite so convincing, but a very good example of Knott's abilities nonetheless, is *Cimarron*, a tale of robbery, abduction, love, and determination set in a particularly well-drawn Rocky Mountain mining town.

A proficient and adaptable writer, Knott has a gift for creating male and female characters who are at once both memorable and likely (one of the most impressive of these is the mentally disturbed Apache girl in 1980's *The Golden Mountain*). Added to this is a skill with words which, if not always entirely stunning or original, is certainly assured and concise. Together they form a combination which makes for some of the most professional western writing around.

—David Whitehead

KOEHLER, Frank. *See* **PAINE, Lauran.**

KOZLOW, Mark. *See* **NEWTON, Mike.**

KRAUSE, Herbert (Arthur). American. Born in Fergus Falls, Minnesota, 25 May 1905. Educated at St. Olaf College, Northfield, Minnesota, B.A. 1933; University of Iowa, Iowa City, M.A. 1935. Instructor, University of Iowa, 1937–38; member of the English Department from 1938, Chair of the Department, 1939–45, and 1945–76, and Director of the Center for Western Studies, 1970–76, Augustana College, Sioux Falls, Iowa. Fulbright Lecturer, University of the Witwatersrand and the University of Natal, South Africa, 1961; National Audubon Society lecturer, 1963; Rockefeller lecturer, University of the Philippines, 1966–69. Regional editor, National Audubon Society *Field Notes*, 1958–60. President, South Dakota Ornithologists Union, 1958–59; Member of the Executive Council, Western Literature Association, 1971–74. Recipient: Bread Loaf fellowship, 1937; American Association for the Advancement of Science grant, 1958. Litt.D.: Augustana College, 1970. *Died 22 September 1976.*

WESTERN PUBLICATIONS

Novels

Wind Without Rain. Indianapolis, Bobbs Merrill, 1939.
The Thresher. Indianapolis, Bobbs Merrill, 1946.
The Oxcart Trail. Indianapolis, Bobbs Merrill, 1954.

Uncollected Short Stories

"Horning in the Fall," in *Eve's Stepchildren*, edited by Lealon N. Jones. Caldwell, Idaho, Caxton, 1942.
"The Oak Tree," in *Prairie Prose*, Winter 1943.

OTHER PUBLICATIONS

Plays

Bondsmen to the Hills (produced Cape Girardeau, Missouri, 1936).

Television Documentary: *The Big Four* (on conservation), 1962.

Verse

Neighbor Boy. Iowa City, Midland House, 1939.

Other

Myth and Reality on the High Plains (address). Northfield, Minnesota, St. Olaf College, 1962.
The McCown's Longspur: A Life History. Manila, MDB, 1968.

Editor, *Fiction 151–1: Short Stories.* Manila, MDB, 1968.
Editor, with Gary D. Olson, *Prelude to Glory: A Newspaper Accounting of Custer's 1874 Expedition to the Black Hills.* Sioux Falls, Iowa, Brevet Press, 1974.

*

Manuscript Collection: Center for Western Studies, Augustana College, Sioux Falls, Iowa.

Critical Study: *Herbert Krause* by A.R. Huseboe, Boise, Idaho, Boise State University Press, 1985.

* * *

Herbert Krause wrote three novels, *Wind Without Rain*, *The Thresher*, and *The Oxcart Trail*. The first two are set in "P ockerbrush country," a term original with Krause to describe the area along the Dakota–Minnesota border where the Dakota prairie pushes a series of jagged fingers into those horseback ridges, "knotty with oak clumps," of west-central Minnesota. These two novels render a magnificent description of the brutality and, to a much lesser extent, the beauty of farm life at the turn of the 20th century. The third novel is a disappointing historical romance.

Wind Without Rain is a study of unfulfilled dream. Franz Vildvogel is the sensitive and artistic youngest son of a brutal father and a fear-ridden mother. Temperamentally unfit for the back-breaking, soul-destroying work of the hill farm, he grows up with the burdens coming from a closed family, a confining German-American community, and an overwhelmingly dark Lutheranism. He attempts to find beauty through love and the music of the fiddle, but circumstance and his own sensitivity defeat him. The two women to whom he is drawn are opposites: the solid, fun-loving, garrulous Tinkla—his friend—and the shallow, fickle, exquisitely beautiful Liliem, a tease with golden hair—his desire and his dream. Tinkla becomes pregnant by Franz and he is forced to marry her, but he continues to idealize his desire for Liliem until discovering her in bed with a rival destroys the dream. The fiddle, his major outlet for expressing joy and beauty, he puts away in guilt after accidentally causing the death of his daughter. The simile which explains the book, Franz and the reader learn early: beauty and pain are two that go together, "balancing on the pivot of experience, like two buckets pulling at the ends of the wooden yoke Mother put on her shoulders when she carried water from the pasture spring." Inevitably the bucket of pain becomes heavier and heavier, as the beauty runs out, faster and faster from the leaking bucket until it hangs empty and dry. The novel ends: Liliem lost, Tinkla estranged, his daughter dead, the fiddle silent, and his future empty.

The Thresher, an even better novel, is a study of power. Johnny Black, orphaned at seven, raised by his aunt and uncle, grows up even harder than the harsh land in which he loves. The drive for power which the western novel so frequently romanticizes is in *The Thresher* open, raw, and real. Johnny Black's character is established the first time he runs his uncle's threshing rig: ". . . his legs spread commandingly over the wheeling iron . . . Power—power which spun iron and lifted shakers, which ripped the coffined life of the wheat from the husk and poured grain from the spout . . . Power—and it lay under his hand, at the touch of a whip, in a bark from his throat." Later, in his rise to power, he crushes all opposition, rival threshers and farmers alike. Lilice, his wife, rather than sharing in the joys of triumph and subjugation, cringes at the hardening ruthlessness accompanying his conquests. In her increasing derangement she visualizes the threshing machine as "a monster with open jaws to swallow all she loved." Power, of course, corrupts; given Johnny Black's pride, exultation, and triumph, the reversal, the fall, and the catastrophe of tragedy are inevitable. Johnny dies in a threshing fire, unreconciled with his wife, his community, or his ambitions. When his men drag him from the flames, one fist is still clenched tight, grasping "a scattering of wheat, golden, unseared by flame."

Even in death Johnny Black does not willingly relinquish his grasp upon the wheat, or, symbolically, on his power.

Krause's third and last novel, *The Oxcart Trail*, was written too fast and is really an unfinished historical romance set in the Minnesota Territory of the 1840's when the pack trains of Red River Oxcarts travelled between St. Paul and the settlements along the Red River three hundred miles to the northwest. Although historically fascinating, *The Oxcart Trail* is structurally faulty and thematically uncertain. It does not have the plot, the characters, or the power of the earlier "Pockerbrush" novels.

Krause's reputation as a writer rests on these two earlier novels. Both present a dark vision of America, a tragedy of dreams, whether unfulfilled or destructively realized. In these novels Krause is a poet of dark reality and "shadow-haunted" beauty. From these novels his reputation as a writer will continue to grow.

—Kristoffer F. Paulson

KRAUZER, Steven M(ark). Also writes as J.W. Baron; Terry Nelson Bonner; Adam Lassiter; Don Pendleton; Owen Rountree. American. Born in Jersey City, New Jersey, 9 June 1948. Educated at Yale University, New Haven, Connecticut, B.A. 1970; University of New Hampshire, Durham, M.A. 1974. Agent: Ginger Barber, Virginia Barber Literary Agency, Inc., 353 West 21st Street, New York, New York 10011, U.S.A.

WESTERN PUBLICATIONS

Novels

Blaze (as J.W. Baron). New York, Pinnacle, 1983.
The Diggers (as Terry Nelson Bonner). New York, Dell/Emerald, 1983.

Novels as Owen Rountree, with William Kittredge (series: Cord)

Cord. New York, Ballantine, 1982.
The Nevada War. New York, Ballantine, 1982.
The Black Hills Duel. New York, Ballantine, 1983.
Gunman Winter. New York, Ballantine, 1983.
Hunt the Man Down. New York, Ballantine, 1984.
King of Colorado. New York, Ballantine, 1984.
Gunsmoke River. New York, Ballantine, 1985.
Paradise Valley. New York, Ballantine, 1986.
Brimstone Basin. New York, Ballantine, 1986.

Uncollected Short Stories

"Code of the West," in *Cavalier*, December 1977.
"Me and Buck" (as Cole Harding), in *Far West*, December 1978.
"Streets of Gold," in *TriQuarterly*, Spring 1980.

OTHER PUBLICATIONS

Novels

Frame Work. New York, Bantam, 1989.
Brainstorm. New York, Bantam, 1991.

Novels as Adam Lassiter

Dennison's War. New York, Bantam, 1984.
Conte's Run. New York, Bantam, 1985.
Hell on Wheels. New York, Bantam, 1985.
King of the Mountain. New York, Bantam, 1985.
Triangle. New York, Bantam, 1985.
Snowball In Hell. New York, Bantam, 1986.

Novels as Don Pendleton

Double Crossfire. New York, Gold Eagle, 1982.
Terrorist Summit. New York, Gold Eagle, 1982.
Renegade Agent. New York, Gold Eagle, 1982.
Brothers in Blood. New York, Gold Eagle, 1983.

Other

Editor, with William Kittredge, *Great Action Stories*. New York, New American Library, 1977.
Editor, with William Kittredge, *The Great American Detective*. New York, New American Library, and London, New English Library, 1978.
Editor, with William Kittredge, *Fiction into Film*. New York, Harper and Row, 1979.
Editor, with William Kittredge, *Contemporary Western Fiction TriQuarterly*, special edition, May 1980.

* * *

It is not rare nowadays for two writers to produce a western series, using a joint pseudonym. Under the byline of Owen Rountree, Steven M. Krauzer and William Kittridge combined their writing skills to produce the Cord series in the early 1980's. Their hero, Cord, is basically an outlaw, who rides with a partner. Nothing new in this one might say, except that in this case the partner is a woman. By pairing up these opposites, Krauzer has a fine time letting them both ponder the sexual nature of their partnership. They realize that to bed each other would bring nothing but personal and emotional disaster, and to give vent to their frustrations, they regularly seek out "one night stands." Descriptions of these lustful encounters tend to concentrate on Cord rather than the Mexican female, Chi, enabling Krauzer to emphasize the macho qualities of his hero.

Cord and Chi do not enjoy the happiest of careers, and their partnership suffers from the success of their work. In *The Nevada War*, Chi is ready to turn her back on Cord after a botched bank robbery, but the intervention of Cord's brother brings them back together again. As with all the books in the series, there is an afterword, with an explanation of what the book is setting out to achieve. This approach is rather pretentious, failing to credit the reader with sufficient intelligence to realize that any novel set in the West is based on fact to some extent. In this particular book, Krauzer explores the range war theme, citing the Montana Range War of 1884, and the Johnson County War of 1892, as examples. Here, though, it is Jim Cord who faces up to the powerful land baron and Cord and Chi back him with their guns. Their actions force the other smaller land owners to face up to McQuire, the foreman for the absent owner, and to come to terms with themselves for being so cowardly in the past, and letting McQuire have his own way for so long.

Krauzer's view of the western frontier is that of a timeless plateau, where arguments are settled with guns, knives, and fists. Women, with the exception of Chi, are there as sex objects, or to bake sourdoughs. Krauzer is at his best when describing scenes of emotional conflict, when his writing pulls what is fundamentally a formulaic series out of its rut, and his abilities in this area are probably underrated.

What Krauzer is very good at is male characterization. Whether his creations are a full-blown villain, or a humble barkeep, their vitality seems to spring from the page. On the debit side, he does tend to pigeon-hole his villains as either rich or ruthless men, who will stop at nothing to achieve their desires. Added to this is Cord's own contradictory personal outlook—here is a man who walks on the knife's edge of corruption, an outlaw who spends much of his time helping others—a latter-day Robin Hood. A paradoxical character, indeed, and the problem seems to be that the series suffers from an identity crisis as much as Cord himself, both alike unable to find their niche.

Perhaps the reason why the Cord series makes such entertaining reading is that the characters have depth, and are presented as normal human beings, complete with emotional flaws, as evidenced by Cord's own constant battle with his drinking problem. So it cannot be said that action alone is the determining factor which keeps the reader turning the pages. The character of Cord is the centre of attention throughout the series, and his life emerges in carefully ordered flashbacks, avoiding any convolution of the storyline.

Krauzer's western writings are worth seeking out in order to savour his, and William Kittridge's differing view of traditional Westerns. The fact that the series ran over a period of years indicates its popularity with the western reader.

—John L. Wolfe

KROLL, Burt. *See* **ROWLAND, Donald S.**

KYNE, Peter B(ernard). American. Born in San Francisco, California, 12 October 1880. Educated at public schools, and at business college. Served in the 14th United States Army Infantry in the Philippines, 1898; in the 144th Field Artillery during World War I: Captain. Married Helen Catherine Johnston in 1910. Worked as a clerk in a general store, and in the wholesale lumber and shipping business, and as a haberdasher, lumber broker, and newspaperman. *Died 25 November 1957.*

Western Publications

Novels

The Three Godfathers. New York, Doran, 1913; London, Hodder and Stoughton, 1914.
The Long Chance. New York, Fly, 1914; London, Hodder and Stoughton, 1919.
Webster—Man's Man. New York, Doubleday, 1917; London, Hodder and Stoughton, 1919.
The Valley of the Giants. New York, Doubleday, 1918; London, Hodder and Stoughton, 1919.
Kindred of the Dust. New York, Cosmopolitan, and London, Hodder and Stoughton, 1920.
The Go-Getter. New York, Cosmopolitan, and London, Hodder and Stoughton, 1921.
The Pride of Palomar. New York, Cosmopolitan, and London, Hodder and Stoughton, 1921.
Never the Twain Shall Meet. New York, Cosmopolitan, and London, Hodder and Stoughton, 1923.
The Enchanted Hill. New York, Cosmopolitan, and London, Hodder and Stoughton, 1924.
The Understanding Heart. New York, Cosmopolitan, and London, Hodder and Stoughton, 1926.
Made of Money. London, Hodder and Stoughton, 1927; as *Money to Burn*, New York, Grosset and Dunlap, 1928.
Tide of Empire. New York, Cosmopolitan, and London, Hodder and Stoughton, 1928.
The Silent Comrade. New York, Cosmopolitan, and London, Hodder and Stoughton, 1929.
Jim the Conqueror. New York, Cosmopolitan, and London, Hodder and Stoughton, 1929.
The Thunder of God. New York, Grosset and Dunlap, 1930.
Outlaws of Eden. New York, Cosmopolitan, 1930; London, Hodder and Stoughton, 1932.
Golden Dawn. New York, Cosmopolitan, and London, Hodder and Stoughton, 1930.
The Gringo Privateer, and Island of Desire. New York, Cosmopolitan, 1931; London, Hodder and Stoughton, 1932.
Lord of Lonely Valley. New York, Kinsey, and London, Hodder and Stoughton, 1932.
Two Make a World. New York, Kinsey, 1932; London, Hodder and Stoughton, 1933.
Comrades of the Storm. New York, Kinsey, and London, Hodder and Stoughton, 1933.
The Golden West: Three Novels (omnibus). New York, Farrar and Rinehart, 1935.
Dude Woman. New York, Kinsey, and London, Hodder and Stoughton, 1940.

Short Stories (series: Cappy Ricks)

Cappy Ricks; or, The Subjugation of Matt Peasley. New York, Fly, 1916; London, Hodder and Stoughton, 1919.
Cappy Ricks Retires. New York, Cosmopolitan, and London, Hodder and Stoughton, 1922.
The Parson of Panamint and Other Stories. New York, Cosmopolitan, and London, Hodder and Stoughton, 1929.
Cappy Ricks Comes Back. New York, Kinsey, and London, Hodder and Stoughton, 1934.
The Cappy Ricks Special. New York, Kinsey, 1935; London, Hodder and Stoughton, 1936.
Soldiers, Sailors and Dogs. New York, Kinsey, 1936.

Uncollected Short Stories

"The Parson of Panamint," in *The Third Reel West*, edited by Bill Pronzini and Martin H. Greenberg. New York, Doubleday, 1986.

Other Publications

Novels

Ireland uber Alles: A Tale of the Sea. London, Nash, 1917; as *The Stolen Ship*, London, Hodder and Stoughton, 1919.
The Green-Pea Pirates. New York, Doubleday, 1919; as *Captain Scraggs*, New York, Grosset and Dunlap, n.d.
They Also Serve. New York, Cosmopolitan, 1927.

Plays

Screenplays: *The Beautiful Gambler*, with Hope Loring, 1921; *The Innocent Cheat*, with J. Grubb Alexander, 1921; *Brothers under the Skin*, with Grant Alexander, 1922; *Home-ward Bound*, with Jack Cunningham and Paul Sloane, 1923; *Never the Twain Shall Meet*, with Eugene Mullin, 1925; *War Paint*, with Charles Maigne and Joe Farnham, 1926; *The Shamrock Handicap*, with John Stone and Elizabeth Pickett, 1926; *California*, with others, 1927; *Freedom of the Press*, with others, 1928; *The Rawhide Kid*, with others, 1928; *Born to Fight*, with Sascha Baraniev, 1936; *Gallant Defender*, with Ford Beebe, 1936; *The Mysterious Avenger*, with Ford Beebe, 1936; *Put on the Spot*, with Al Martin, 1936; *Secret Patrol*, with Robert Watson and J.P. McGowan, 1936; *Stampede*, with Robert Watson, 1936; *Code of the Range*, with Ford Beebe, 1937; *Rio Grande Romance*, with Al Martin, 1937; *Tough to Handle*, with Sherman Lowe and Jack Neville, 1937; *Headline Cracher*, with Sherman Lowe and Harry O. Hoyt, 1937; *Racing Blood*, with Sam Roeca, 1938; *Ride, Kelly, Ride*, with Irving Cummings, Jr., and William Conselman, Jr., 1940; *Belle le Grand*, with D.D. Beauchamp, 1951; *Bronco Buster*, with Horace McCoy and Lillie Hayward, 1952.

Other

The French Wounded Emergency Book. San Francisco, Nash, 1917.
Peter B. Kyne. New York, International Magazine, 1919.
The Book I Never Wrote. Privately printed, 1942.

*

Manuscript Collection: University of Oregon Library, Eugene.

* * *

Among the most beloved authors of the West along the Pacific Slope—and also one of the most colorful—was Peter B. Kyne, better known in many circles as the indomitable and indefatigable Cappy Ricks. In Cappy Ricks, Kyne created a wonderful personality, a wheeler-dealer who sparked the imaginations of two generations of readers who found it difficult to believe that Cappy hadn't actually lived to walk the streets of San Francisco, Portland, Seattle, and Aberdeen.

Kyne was a lumber company bookkeeper of rare talent and lively imagination which spawned great skill as a storyteller. It was no wonder he became bored with his paper work at Grays Harbor (Aberdeen-Hoquiam) and began writing stories for relaxation. Everything around him in Grays Harbor's boom years was grist for his mill, a tonic or a mixed drink that Kyne couldn't let alone. He created Cappy in the image of his boss at the lumber company, and Ricks's adversary and utterly impossible son-in-law, Matt Peasley, from the skipper of one of the tall lumber ships that called there during Aberdeen's wildest years. Many of the anecdotes and happenings Kyne drew from the logging and lumbering waterfront life around him, and later in the San Francisco Bay area to which Kyne migrated, becoming so successful through his stories that he was a local celebrity, pointed out as "Cappy Ricks." Most everyone read and loved the Cappy Ricks stories.

The Ricks stories were lapped up eagerly whenever they appeared in *The Saturday Evening Post* and then in hardcover book form; and despite their rough and tumble settings and situations, parents allowed their youngsters to read them, for they were written on a high level of entertainment. As a youngster I read many of them, and well remember the adventures of Cappy and Matt.

Kyne began with *Cappy Ricks; or, The Subjugation of Matt Peasley*, which he boldly dedicated to a list of Aberdeen lumbermen. Where today such things might well instigate a lawsuit, the timber people were highly amused by it, and especially to their liking was the image of Matt Peasley. For many years Peasley lived the role, wheeling and dealing in free for-all showmanship fashion as he slipped the sleek schooner *Vigilant* in and out of Grays Harbor to Pacific ports of call. He was indeed Kyne's and Cappy's foremost promoter, even long after Kyne's death. The Cappy Ricks stories are as good as they ever were, and in their time of high popularity would undoubtedly have provoked a television series, for Cappy was indeed among the most popular fiction personalities of his years. The stories, with their lively telling, situations, anecdotes, manipulations, and dialogue, can still be enjoyed, and I can only regret that they just don't make storytellers like Peter B. Kyne anymore.

—Ellis Lucia

L

LA FARGE, Oliver (Hazard Perry). American. Born in New York City, 19 December 1901. Educated at the Groton Academy, Cowell, Massachusetts, graduated 1920; Harvard University, Cambridge, Massachusetts (editor, *Harvard Lampoon*; president, *Advocate*; Class Poet), 1920–24, B.A. 1924, then did graduate work in anthropology (Hemenway Fellow), M.A. 1929. Served in the United States Army, 1942–46: Lieutenant-Colonel; Legion of Merit, 1946. Married 1) Wanden E. Mathews in 1929 (divorced 1937), one son and one daughter; 2) Consuelo Otille C. de Baca in 1939, one son. Anthropologist: involved in expeditions for the Peabody Museum, Harvard, in Arizona, 1921, 1922, 1924; assistant in ethnology, Department of Middle American Research, Tulane University, New Orleans, 1925–26; involved in research expeditions to Mexico and Guatemala, 1926–28; research associate in ethnology, Columbia University, New York, 1931; director of the Columbia University expedition to Guatemala, 1932; thereafter a full-time writer and historian: columnist, Santa Fe *New Mexican*, 1950–63. President, Association on American Indian Affairs, 1932–41, 1948. Recipient: Pulitzer prize, 1930; O. Henry award, 1931; Guggenheim fellowship, 1941. A.M.: Brown University, Providence, Rhode Island, 1932. Fellow, American Association for the Advancement of Science, 1938, American Anthropological Association, 1947, and American Academy of Arts and Sciences, 1953. Member, American Academy, 1957. *Died 2 August 1963.*

WESTERN PUBLICATIONS

Novels

Laughing Boy. Boston, Houghton Mifflin, 1929; London, Constable, 1930.
Sparks Fly Upward. Boston, Houghton Mifflin, 1931; London Lane, 1932.
The Enemy Gods. Boston, Houghton Mifflin, 1937.

Short Stories

All the Young Men. Boston, Houghton Mifflin, 1935.
A Pause in the Desert: A Collection of Short Stories. Boston, Houghton Mifflin, 1957.
The Door in the Wall. Boston, Houghton Mifflin, 1965; London, Gollancz, 1966.
Yellow Sun, Bright Sky: The Indian Country Stories of Oliver La Farge, edited by David L. Cuffey. Albuquerque, University of New Mexico Press, 1988.

Uncollected Short Stories

"The Young Warrior" in *The Warriors*, edited by Bill Pronzini and Martin H. Greenberg. New York, Fawcett, 1985.

OTHER PUBLICATIONS

Novels

Long Pennant. Boston, Houghton Mifflin, 1933.
The Copper Pot. Boston, Houghton Mifflin, 1942.

Play

Screenplay: *Behold My Wife*, with William R. Lipman, 1934.

Other

Tribes and Temples: A Record of the Expedition to Middle America Conducted by the Tulane University of Louisiana in 1925, with Frans Blom. New Orleans, Tulane University, 2 vols., 1926–27.
The Year Bearer's People, with Douglas Byers. New Orleans, Tulane University, 1931.
An Alphabet for Writing the Navajo Language, with J.P. Harrington. Washington D.C., United States Indian Service, 1936.
As Long as the Grass Shall Grow, photographs by Helen M. Post. New York, Longman, 1940.
War below Zero: The Battle for Greenland, with Bernt Balchen and Corey Ford. Boston, Houghton Mifflin, 1944.
Raw Material (autobiography). Boston, Houghton Mifflin, 1945; London, Gollancz, 1946.
Santa Eulalia: The Religion of a Cuchumatán Indian Town. Chicago, University of Chicago Press, 1947.
The Eagle in the Egg. Boston, Houghton Mifflin, 1949.
Cochise of Arizona: The Pipe of Peace Is Broken (for children). New York, Aladdin, 1953; London, Transworld, 1956.
The Mother Ditch (for children). Boston, Houghton Mifflin, 1954.
A Pictorial History of the American Indian. New York Crown, 1956; London, Deutsch, 1958; edition for children, as *The American Indian*, New York, Golden Press, 1960.
Behind the Mountains. Boston, Houghton Mifflin, 1956.
Sante Fe: The Autobiography of a Southwestern Town, with Arthur N. Morgan. Norman, University of Oklahoma Press, 1959.
The Man with the Calabash Pipe: Some Observations, edited by Winfield Townley Scott. Boston, Houghton Mifflin, 1966.

Editor, *Introduction to American Indian Art*. New York, Exposition of Indian Tribal Arts, 1931.
Editor, with Jay Bryan Nash, *The New Day for the Indians: A Survey of the Working of the Indian Reorganization Act of 1934*. New York, Academy Press, 1938.
Editor, *The Changing Indian*. Norman, University of Oklahoma Press, 1940.

Translator, *A Man's Place*, by Ramón Sender. New York, Duell, 1940; London, Cape, 1941.

*

Manuscript Collection: University of Texas, Austin.

Critical Studies: *Oliver La Farge* by Everett A. Gillis, Austin, Texas, Steck Vaughn, 1967; *Indian Man: A Life of Oliver La Farge* by D'Arcy McNickle, Bloomington, Indiana University Press, 1971: *Oliver La Farge* by T.M. Pearce, New York, Twayne, 1972.

* * *

Oliver La Farge was an easterner who went west, and his role as a western writer fits into a classic American pattern. For more than three centuries the West was more a place to go than to be from. And from the time of the earliest explorers, western writing has been an encounter with life lived under different terms than elsewhere. In La Farge, whose first encounter with the West was a student of anthropology and whose chief contributions to American literature are novels and stories about aboriginal American cultures, the classic pattern has one of its final and best expressions.

La Farge also wrote fiction about other subjects: about his student days, about New Orleans (where he lived in the 1920's) and about life in Rhode Island. His primary western works are two novels about Navajos, *Laughing Boy* and *The Enemy Gods*. Some of his short stories, collected in two volumes during his life and one after his death in 1963, also deal with Indians or with anthropologists who have established close relationships with Indian cultures (like the central character of "Haunted Ground"). Some other works, especially the novel *Sparks Fly Upward*, set in 19th-century Guatemala (where La Farge had done anthropological field studies), are only marginally western. In 1953 La Farge also wrote a fictional narrative, essentially a book for juvenile readers about the Apache leader Cochise.

La Farge's place in American literature is partly dependent on his various identities: as a member of an elite eastern family (his grandfather John La Farge was a painter and a muralist, his father an architect), as a scientist, as president of the Association of Indian Affairs, and as a Santa Fe journalist for the last 13 years of his life. But *Laughing Boy* and *The Enemy Gods* stand out above all his other achievements. And of these two Navajo novels, the first—and La Farge's first novel—is the more significant, partly because it attracted more attention when it appeared, winning the Pulitzer prize in 1930, and partly because in it La Farge was more willing to give rein to his romantic impulses.

In a scientific report La Farge once said of Indians in Guatemala that they reveal "an unconscious clinging to the remnants of something that once was glamorous." In *Laughing Boy* the glamorous something is the traditional Navajo way, the trail of beauty, of *hozoji*, to which the title character still belongs. Laughing Boy is a symbol of what La Farge felt Navajos were fast losing under the pressures of progress and assimilation. The novel dramatizes the problem through a romance plot in which Laughing Boy falls in love with corrupted Navajo girl, Slim Girl, who desires reunion with her people's traditions but whose contact with white missionaries and prostitutes dooms her quest for cultural regeneration. Thus in the two central characters of the novel La Farge symbolizes both a romantic view of the glorious Navajo past and a tragic view of the Navajo present. The novel is most successful in its poetic evocation of the trail of beauty, down to the details of Laughing Boy's jewelry-making and Slim Girl's blanket-weaving. The manner in which La Farge's anthropological sympathy for Navajos and Navajo land (he had spent a number of summers doing field work on the reservation prior to writing the novel) sometimes slips into sentimentalism is occasionally a problem for readers.

In *The Enemy Gods* La Farge approached the same subject with different means. The novel embodies cultural conflict in its male hero (Myron Begay), a Navajo youth taken to away-school in early childhood, and assigns to a female character (Juniper) the values of traditional Indian culture. *The Enemy Gods* also differs from *Laughing Boy* in its more discursive structure; it thus gains in authenticity but sacrifices the romantic qualities of the earlier work.

Behind all of La Farge's fiction, and rather explicitly so in his short stories, is a careful attention to matters of diction and style. La Farge, even in his scientific identities, was always a writer first.

—William Bloodworth

L'AMOUR, Louis (Dearborn). Also wrote as Tex Burns; Jim Mayo. American. Born Louis Dearborn LaMoore in Jamestown, North Dakota, in 1908. Served in the United States Army, 1942–46: Lieutenant. Married Katherine Elizabeth Adams in 1956; one son and one daughter. Worked in a variety of jobs, including prizefighter, tugboat deckhand, lumberjack, gold prospector, deputy sheriff, longshoreman, miner, elephant handler, flume builder, and fruit picker. Recipient: Western Writers of America Spur award, 1969; Theodore Roosevelt Rough Rider award, 1972; American Book award, 1980, 1981; Buffalo Bill award, 1981; Distinguished Newsboy award, 1981; National Genealogical Society award, 1981; Congressional Gold Medal, 1983; Presidential Medal of Freedom, 1984. LL.D.: Jamestown College, 1972; North Dakota State University, 1981; University of Laverne, 1981; Pepperdine University, 1984. *Died 10 June 1988.*

WESTERN PUBLICATIONS

Novels

Westward the Tide. Kingswood, Surrey, World's Work, 1950; New York, Bantam, 1977.

Hondo (novelization of screenplay, originally adapted from story "The Gift of Cochise"). New York, Fawcett, 1953; London, Fawcett, 1954.

Showdown at Yellow Butte (as Jim Mayo). New York, Ace, 1953; as Louis L'Amour, London, Tandem, 1972.

Crossfire Trail. New York, Ace, 1954; London, Tandem, 1972.

Utah Blaine (as Jim Mayo). New York, Ace, 1954; as Louis L'Amour, Tandem, 1972.

Kilkenny. New York, Ace, 1954; London, Tandem, 1972.

Heller with a Gun. New York, Fawcett, 1955; London, Fawcett, 1956.

To Tame a Land. New York, Fawcett, 1955; London, Fawcett, 1956.

Guns of the Timberlands. New York, Jason Press, 1955; London, Corgi, 1957.

The Burning Hills. New York, Jason Press, 1956; London, Corgi, 1957.

Silver Canyon. New York, Avalon, 1956; London, Corgi, 1958.

Last Stand at Papago Wells. New York, Fawcett, 1957; London, Fawcett, 1958.

The Tall Stranger. New York, Fawcett, 1957; London, Fawcett, 1959.

Sitka. New York, Appleton Century Crofts, 1957; London, Corgi, 1973.

Radigan. New York, Bantam, 1958; London, Corgi, 1959.
The First Fast Draw. New York, Bantam, and London, Corgi, 1959.
Taggart. New York, Bantam, and London, Corgi, 1959.
Flint. New York, Bantam, 1960; London, Corgi, 1961.
Shalako. New York, Bantam, and London, Corgi, 1962.
Killoe. New York, Bantam, and London, Corgi, 1962.
High Lonesome. New York, Bantam, 1962; London, Corgi, 1963.
How the West Was Won (novelization of screenplay). New York, Bantam, and London, Corgi, 1963.
Fallon. New York, Bantam, and London, Corgi, 1963.
Catlow. New York, Bantam, and London, Corgi, 1963.
Dark Canyon. New York, Bantam, 1963; London, Corgi, 1964.
Hanging Woman Creek. New York, Bantam, and London, Corgi, 1964.
Kiowa Trail. New York, Bantam, and London, Corgi, 1964.
The High Graders. New York, Bantam, and London, Corgi, 1965.
The Key-Lock Man. New York, Bantam, 1965; London, Corgi, 1966.
Kid Rodelo. New York, Bantam, 1966; London, Hale, 1978.
Kilrone. New York, Bantam, and London, Corgi, 1966.
The Broken Gun. New York, Bantam, and London, Corgi, 1966.
Matagorda. New York, Bantam, 1967; London, Corgi, 1968.
Brionne. New York, Bantam, and London, Corgi, 1968.
Chancy. New York, Bantam, and London, Corgi, 1968.
Down the Long Hills. New York, Bantam, and London, Corgi, 1968.
The Empty Land. New York, Bantam, and London, Corgi, 1969.
Conagher. New York, Bantam, and London, Corgi, 1969.
The Man Called Noon. New York, Bantam, and London, Corgi, 1970.
Reilly's Luck. New York, Bantam, 1970; London, Corgi, 1971.
Under the Sweetwater Rim. New York, Bantam, and London, Corgi, 1971.
Tucker. New York, Bantam, 1971; London, Corgi, 1972.
Callaghen. New York, Bantam, and London, Corgi, 1972.
The Man from Skibbereen. New York, Bantam, and London, Corgi, 1973.
The Quick and the Dead. New York, Bantam, 1973; London, Corgi, 1974.
The Californios. New York, Saturday Review Press, and London, Corgi, 1974.
Where the Long Grass Blows. New York, Bantam, 1976; London, Corgi, 1977.
The Rider of Lost Creek. New York, Bantam, and London, Corgi, 1976.
The Mountain Valley War. London, Corgi, 1978.
Bendigo Shafter. New York, Dutton, and London, Corgi, 1979.
The Iron Marshal. New York, Bantam, and London, Corgi, 1979.
The Proving Trail. New York, Bantam, and London, Corgi, 1979.
Lonely on the Mountain. New York, Bantam, 1980; London, Century, 1986.
Comstock Lode. New York, Bantam, 1981.
The Cherokee Trail. New York, Bantam, 1982.
The Shadow Riders. New York, Bantam, 1982; London, Severn House, 1984.
The Lonesome Gods. New York, Bantam, and London, Corgi, 1983.
Son of a Wanted Man. New York, Bantam, 1984; London, Century, 1985.
Passin' Through. New York, and London, Bantam, 1985.
The Haunted Mesa. New York, and London, Bantam, 1987.

Novels (series: The Sacketts in all books)

The Daybreakers. London, Tandem, 1960; London, Hammond, 1964.
Sackett. New York, Bantam, 1961; London, Hammond, 1964.
Lando. New York, Bantam, 1962; London, Corgi, 1963.
Mojave Crossing. New York, Bantam, and London, Corgi, 1964.
The Sackett Brand. New York, Bantam, and London, Corgi, 1965.
Mustang Man. New York, Bantam, and London, Corgi, 1966.
The Sky-Liners. New York, Bantam, and London, Corgi, 1967.
The Lonely Men. New York, Bantam, 1969; London, Corgi, 1971.
Galloway. New York, Bantam, and London, Corgi, 1970.
Ride the Dark Trail. New York, Bantam, and London, Corgi, 1972.
Treasure Mountain. New York, Bantam, 1972; London, Corgi, 1973.
Sackett's Land. New York, Saturday Review Press, 1974; London, Corgi, 1975.
To the Far Blue Mountains. New York, Saturday Review Press, 1976; London, Corgi, 1977.
The Warrior's Path. New York, Bantam, 1980; London, Corgi, 1981.
Ride the River. New York, Bantam, 1983; London, Corgi, 1985.
Jubal Sackett. New York, Bantam, 1985; London, Bantam Press, 1986.

Novels (series: The Chantrys in all books)

North to the Rails. New York, Bantam, and London, Corgi, 1971.
The Ferguson Rifle. New York, Bantam, and London, Corgi, 1973.
Over on the Dry Side. New York, Saturday Review Press, 1975; London, Corgi, 1976.
Borden Chantry. London, Corgi, 1978.
Fair Blows the Wind. New York, Dutton, 1978; London, Corgi, 1979.

Novels (series: The Talons in all books)

The Man from the Broken Hills. New York, Bantam, 1975; London, Corgi, 1976.
Rivers West. New York, Saturday Review Press, and London, Corgi, 1975.
Milo Talon. New York, Bantam, 1981.

Novels as Tex Burns (series: Hopalong Cassidy in all books)

Hopalong Cassidy and the Riders of High Rock. New York, Doubleday, 1951; London, Hodder and Stoughton, 1952.
Hopalong Cassidy and the Rustlers of West Fork. New York, Doubleday, and London, Hodder and Stoughton, 1951.
Hopalong Cassidy and the Trail to Seven Pines. New York, Doubleday, 1951; London, Hodder and Stoughton, 1952.

Hopalong Cassidy, Trouble Shooter. New York, Doubleday, 1952; London, Hodder and Stoughton, 1953.

Short Stories

War Party. New York, Bantam, and London, Corgi, 1975.
The Strong Shall Live. London, Corgi, 1980.
Buckskin Run. New York, Bantam, 1981; London, Severn House, 1982.
Bowdrie. New York, Bantam, 1983.
Law of the Desert Born. New York, Bantam, 1983.
Bowdrie's Law. New York, Bantam, 1984.
Dutchman's Flat. New York, Bantam, 1986.
Riding for the Brand. New York, Bantam, 1986.
The Trail to Crazy Man. New York, Bantam, 1986.
The Rider of the Ruby Hills. New York, Bantam, 1986.
Lonigan. New York, Bantam, 1988.
Long Ride Home. New York, Bantam, 1989.
The Outlaws of Mesquite. New York, Bantam, 1990.

Uncollected Short Stories

"The Gift of Cochise," in *The Arbor House Treasury of Great Western Stories*, edited by Bill Pronzini and Martin H. Greenberg. New York, Arbor House, 1982.

OTHER PUBLICATIONS

Novels

The Walking Drum. New York, Bantam, 1984; London, Bantam, 1985.
Last of the Breed. New York, and London, Bantam, 1986.

Short Stories

Yondering. New York, Bantam, and London, Corgi, 1980.
The Hills of Homicide. New York, Bantam, 1983; London, Corgi, 1985.
Night over the Solomons. New York, Bantam, 1986; London, Century, 1988.
West from Singapore. New York, Bantam, 1987.

Plays

Screenplays: *East of Sumatra*, with Frank J. Gill, Jr., and Jack Natteford, 1953; *Four Guns to the Border*, with George Van Marter and Franklin Coen, 1954; *Treasure of the Ruby Hills*, with Tom Hubbard and Fred Eggers, 1955; *Stranger on Horseback*, with Herb Meadow and Don Martin, 1955; *Kid Rodelo*, with Jack Natteford, 1966.

Verse

Smoke from This Altar. Oklahoma City, Lusk, 1939.

Other

Frontier (essays), photographs by David Muench. New York, Bantam, 1984.
A Trail of Memories: The Quotations of Louis L'Amour, edited by Angelique L'Amour. New York, Bantam, 1988.
The Sackett Companion: A Personal Guide to the Sackett Novels. New York, Bantam, 1988.
Education of a Wandering Man (autobiography). New York, Bantam, 1989.

* * *

Louis L'Amour is far and away the best-selling western writer who ever lived. Some 225,000,000 copies of his 108 books, including 87 novels and 17 collections of short stories—mostly on western subjects—are in print worldwide. During the height of his popularity, his books sold at the rate of 15,000–20,000 copies a day, seven days a week, for years on end. Along with many other conservative western writers, L'Amour helped preserve the western novel as a living art form, against the inroads of the sleazy "adult western," and hence has had a beneficial effect on the middle-of-the-road American imagination.

L'Amour held a variety of rough jobs on land and at sea during what he called his "knockabout" years. In the late 1930's and early 1940's, he published scores of slap-dash short stories, about sailors and soldiers as well as cowboys. These action yarns are generally undistinguished; but writing them fast, minimizing characterization, sketching natural settings with topographical accuracy, and stressing melodramatic plots honed his ability as the kind of campfire troubadour he later described himself as being.

His first novel, *Westward the Tide*, was published in England in 1950, and went unnoticed, but is rousing and suspenseful, and introduces many of the ingredients of his later work: war-hardened hero, pioneers both brave and inept, energetic but naive and obedient heroine, villains of various stripes, action on the trail involving Indians and gunfights, and accurate historical touches, including mention of a few real-life notables.

Then with *Hondo* L'Amour achieved immediate fame. In this novel (adapted from the screenplay, which itself was based on his original story, "The Gift of Cochise"), Hondo Lane, the laconic, John Wayne-like hero, rides for but does not greatly admire the U.S. Army in the Southwest in 1874, vies with Apaches, befriends an endangered white woman, and is later forced to kill her degenerate husband. Footloose Hondo is torn between his arid independence and an emerging desire to settle down; but can he hope for love from the woman he made a widow?

15 action novels swiftly followed before the end of the 1950's. Especially notable are *Sitka*, an unusually well-structured historical novel with a sailor for hero, and the Alaska Purchase as background, and *The First Fast Draw*, based loosely on Cullen Baker, post-Civil War Texas gunfighter. Then came *The Daybreakers*, about pioneering brothers who leave their Tennessee home in 1866 in a cloud of gunsmoke, to make new lives for themselves in New Mexico Territory. This novel is the first of 17 books concerned with the Sackett family, whose members migrate from Elizabethan England to the Carolinas, and over several generations move on for action in Tennessee, the Southwest, California, and even Mexico and Canada, and into the very late 1870's. L'Amour ambitiously planned to write many Talon- and Chantry-family sagas as well, and even to have occasional Talons, who were of French background and who would be builders, and Irish Chantrys, more scholarly and statesman-like, interact with certain gunslinging, trailblazing Sacketts, as all three family groups moved west. In his preface to *Sackett's Land*, L'Amour promised that "[w]hen the journeys are ended and the 40-odd books are completed, the reader should have a fairly true sense of what happened on the American frontier." But death cut short these family sagas at 25 volumes, counting the five completed Chantrys and three completed Talons.

Such an accomplishment by itself would be enough for most novelists. But L'Amour interspersed among these mini-epics a few dozen standard Westerns—the best being *Flint*, *Shalako*, *Down the Long Hills*, *Bendigo Shafter*, *Comstock Lode*, and *The Cherokee Trail*—and also several novels indicating his ambition to diversify. For example, *The Broken Gun* represents his first effort to cast a novel in the 20th century. Being a combat veteran turned writer, its hero is partly autobiographical. Still, the action is that of a typical western, with the telephone instead of smoke signals and jeeps for horses. *The Californios* was another effort at innovation. In it, as in the later bestseller *The Lonesome Gods*, L'Amour makes stronger a thread of mysticism which he had prepared his readers to expect when, earlier, he characterized certain Sackett wives as having the gift of prophecy. In *The Californios*, non-material Indians help the Irish-Mexican hero, not only by silently crossing desert sands, but also by slipping through time barriers neatly symbolized by desert heat waves. Displaying L'Amour's continued versatility in his final years is *Last of the Breed*, another bestseller, which may be called an eastern Siberian western since it features a Sioux-Cheyenne U.S. Air Force pilot forced down over Siberia in the 1960's. He calls on his immemorial Indian skills to help him escape the KGB and live off the frozen tundra. Finally, *The Haunted Mesa*, L'Amour's last novel, combines into a veritable L'Amour anthology autobiographical hero, mystical time warps, Indians, and contemporary setting. In it, a well-traveled scholar-author investigates the Anasazi tribe of the old Southwest, whose survivors, good and bad, dramatically break the time barrier between their 13th century and our present one.

L'Amour's main subjects are male-dominated pioneering and pioneer-family life, frontier women often traditionally obedient but sometimes fiercely courageous, American Indians neither noble nor bestial, and praise of old-fashioned American love of the land, self-reliance, stoicism, realistic but not sentimental racial tolerance, and never-say-die patriotism. L'Amour's stylistic weaknesses include grammatical and syntactical errors, careless handling of details, narrative point-of-view violations, occasional jerry-built structures, and shallow characterization of minor figures. His strengths, however, outweigh his lapses, and include an oral-narration sort of unrehearsed excitement, breathless action, and devotion to America's Western past in all its goriness and glory.

—Robert L. Gale

LANE, Rose Wilder. American. Born in De Smet, South Dakota, 5 December 1886; daughter of Laura Ingalls Wilder, *q.v.* Moved to Ozark Mountains, Missouri, in 1894. Educated at high schools in Missouri and Louisiana. Married Gillette Lane in 1909 (divorced 1918). Telegrapher, Western Union, Kansas City, c. 1903–10—took part in first Western Union walkout in 1903, and advocated women's suffrage; real estate agent in California 1910–13; reporter, San Francisco *Bulletin*, 1915–18; campaigned on behalf of Californian agricultural workers; worked for Red Cross and Near East Relief in Europe, 1918–23; returned to parents' Rocky Ridge Farm in Mansfield, Missouri, 1923; freelance writer and journalist, 1923–68; travelled to Albania, 1926–27; editor of *Review of Books*, National Economic Council, 1943–45; war correspondent, *Woman's Day*, 1965. Recipient: O. Henry award, for short story, 1922. *Died 30 October 1968.*

WESTERN PUBLICATIONS

Novels

Diverging Roads. New York, Century, 1919.
Hill-Billy. New York, Harper, 1926; as *A Man of the Hills*, London, Thornton Butterworth, 1926.
Cindy: A Romance of the Ozarks. New York and London, Harper and Brothers, 1928.
Let the Hurricane Roar. New York and London, Longmans Green, 1933; as *The Young Pioneers*, New York, McGraw Hill, and London, Bantam, 1976.
Free Land. New York and London, Longmans Green, 1938; sound recording, American Forces Radio and Television Service, 1973.

Short Stories

Old Home Town. New York, Longmans Green 1935; London, Longmans Green, 1936.

OTHER PUBLICATIONS

Other

Life and Jack London (serial). N.p., Sunset, c. 1914–18.
Art Smith's Story: The Autobiography of the Boy Aviator. San Francisco, Bulletin, 1915.
Charlie Chaplin's Own Story, as Told to Rose Wilder Lane (serial). San Francisco, Bulletin, c. 1915.
Henry Ford's Own Story, as Told to Rose Wilder Lane: How a Farm Boy Rose to the Power That Goes with Millions, Yet Never Lost Touch with Humanity. Forest Hills, New York, Jones, 1917.
The Making of Herbert Hoover. New York, Century, 1920.
The Peaks of Shala: Being a Record of Certain Wanderings Among the Hill-Tribes of Albania. London, Chapman and Dodd, 1922; New York, Harper, 1923.
He Was a Man. New York and London, Harper, 1925; as *Gordon Blake*, London, Thornton Butterworth, 1925.
An Autobiographical Sketch. New York and London, Longmans Green, 1935.
Give Me Liberty. New York and London, Longmans Green, 1936; revised edition, Caldwell, Idaho, Caxton, 1954.
The Discovery of Freedom: Man's Struggle Against Authority. New York, John Day, 1943.
What Is This, the Gestapo? New York, National Economic Council, 1943.
The Woman's Day Book of American Needlework. New York, Simon and Schuster, 1963.
The Lady and the Tycoon: The Letters of Rose Wilder Lane and Jasper Crane, edited by Roger Lea MacBride. Caldwell, Idaho, Caxton, 1973.
Rose Wilder Lane: Her Story, with Roger Lea MacBride. New York, Stein and Day, 1977.
Travels With Zenobia: Paris to Albania by Model T Ford: A Journal, with Helen Dore Boylston. Columbia, University of Missouri Press, 1983.
A Little House Sampler, with Laura Ingalls Wilder, edited by William T. Anderson. Lincoln, University of Nebraska Press, 1988.

Editor, *On the Way Home: The Diary of a Trip from South Dakota to Mansfield, Missouri, in 1894*, by Laura Ingalls Wilder. New York, Harper and Row, 1962.

* * *

The writing career of Rose Wilder Lane began in 1915, when a friend, the women's editor of the San Francisco *Bulletin*, began using excerpts from Lane's letters as a feature of the page. Soon Lane found herself working as an editorial assistant, and shortly began a career as a feature writer. Her early writing consisted of romantic serials designed to keep readers buying the paper daily. She also wrote serialized biographies with the same aim; these were based on interviews with people much in the public eye, such as Charlie Chaplin and Henry Ford. Later she became a roving California reporter for the *Bulletin*, covering such issues as the building of the Hetch-Hetchy Reservoir and the problems of farmers in the California valleys. During this time she also expanded her market to *Sunset Magazine*, for whom she wrote serial lives of Jack London and Herbert Hoover, and her first serious fiction, *Diverging Roads*. This novel tells of a naive young California women who mistakenly marries a dashing salesman, but who is propelled by his failures to take charge of her own life as a working woman. The magazine version returns the heroine to an earlier love from her home town; but for book publication Lane composed another ending in which the heroine rejects such a relapse for a life as a freelance writer among a group of similarly liberated women.

In 1918 Lane went to Europe, writing a travel column for the *Bulletin* and working as a publicity writer for the American Red Cross and the Near East Relief. She traveled Europe and the Near East until 1923, writing stories of her adventures for magazines as well. Her experiences in Albania are engagingly told in *The Peaks of Shala*, which was largely composed from her newspaper columns. In this period she also wrote her best short story, "Innocence" which won second prize in the O. Henry competition for 1922. She returned to the U.S. for two years to live with her parents in the Missouri Ozarks, during which time she began to write short stories for *Country Gentleman* to finance a return to Albania. Many of these stories, replete with Ozark dialect, told of the exploits of a shrewd country lawyer; they were collected as *Hill-Billy*; and *Cindy*, serialized in the same magazine, is a romance in a similar setting. Driven by a need for money, Lane often described herself as a hack writer; but at her best she was capable of subtle and complex effects, and her style was always vibrant and controlled, as in the occasional story she would publish in *Harper's*, such as "Autumn," "The Blue Bead," and "Harvest."

After a year in Albania Lane returned to the U.S. in 1927, when she settled again on her parents' farm. She began to write for the *Saturday Evening Post* and *Ladies' Home Journal*, composing a series of stories about small-town life at the turn of the century as seen through the eyes of an adolescent girl. All of these stories suffer in plot and theme from the requirements of the slick-paper family magazine; but when Lane published them as collection as *Old Home Town*, she added a preface in which she tried to evoke a moral resonance for the collection that was not apparent in the stories individually. "It was a hard, narrow, relentless life. It was not comfortable. Nothing was made easy for us . . . This may be an old-fashioned, middle-class, small-town point of view. All that can be said for it is that it created America."

This preface marks a watershed in Lane's writing career, as her scattered energies began to focus on the theme that would dominate the rest of her life. She had lost her tiny fortune in the Depression, and as she contemplated her own diligent effort to work toward solvency, her parents' earlier lives as self-sufficient pioneers, and the unprecedented expansion of governmental programs under the New Deal, her instinctive values became formalized in a doctrine of individualism. In a short novel, *Let the Hurricane Roar* (reprinted as *Young Pioneers*) and in the longer and more complex *Free Land*, Lane embodied in stories of pioneer homesteading life on the Dakota prairies the values of individual responsibility and heroic struggle that she had absorbed from her parents. The title of *Free Land* was intended as ironic, a response to the Depression-era complaint that life would be easier if there were still free land to settle: her point was that the land was never free, but could be won only by unremitting toil. These titles represent her best work and were her most popular: *Let the Hurricane Roar* has been continuously in print and *Free Land* was a bestseller.

This period also saw the most significant of Lane's work in a mode that can only be called ghost-writing. During her newspaper career she had written a number of pieces ostensibly by figures of some renown or notoriety, and in 1919 she had contracted to do a wholesale revision of the manuscript of Frederick O'Brien's *White Shadows on the South Seas*, which became a bestseller. In the 1930's she ghosted several books for Lowell Thomas, and also began the same service for her mother, Laura Ingalls Wilder, whose subsequent fame outshone her daughter's, and whose *Little House* books later became the basis of a popular television series. All of her mother's books passed through Lane's typewriter before they reached the publisher, and a study of the manuscripts reveals that their literary grace is a result of Lane's professional skill in bringing to life awkward and amateurish efforts.

After *Free Land* Lane ceased to write fiction, as her sensibility was increasingly consumed with her political concerns. Already in the 1930's she had published several political essays in the *Saturday Evening Post*, and her only books after *Free Land* were a treatise on political theory, *The Discovery of Freedom*, and *The Woman's Day Book of American Needlework*, which described innovative American needlework as analogues of American political freedom. In 1965, Lane went to Vietnam as a correspondent for *Woman's Day*. Her report, "August in Vietnam," (*Woman's Day*, December 1965) revealed a talent for vivid and moving narrative still vital at age 78.

—William V. Holtz

LANGLEY, John.

WESTERN PUBLICATIONS

Novels (series: Walt Warren in all "Six-Gun" books)

Rustler's Brand. London, Lane, 1954.
Riders of Red Range. London, Lane, 1955.
Six-Gun Trial. London, Hale, 1958.
Six-Gun Feud. London, Hale, 1959.
Kit of Slash K. London, Brown Watson, 1960.
Heir to Bar 60. London, Brown Watson, 1960.
Six-Gun Law. London, Hale, 1960.
Six-Gun War. London, Hale, 1960.
Six-Gun Justice. London, Hale, 1961.
Six-Gun Gamble. London, Hale, 1963.
Six-Gun Strife. London, Hale, 1963.
Six-Gun Champion. London, Hale, 1964.
Six-Gun Citadel. London, Hale, 1964.
Six-Gun Smoke. London, Hale, 1965.
Six-Gun Cavalier. London, Hale, 1965.
Six-Gun Vengeance. London, Hale, 1966.

Six-Gun Salute. London, Gresham, 1967.
The Badlands Gang (Warren). London, Hale, 1970.

* * *

Though probably best known for his "Six-Gun" series of novels, John Langley has in fact produced a varied number of works in the genre. Earlier stories such as *Riders of Red Range* and *Rustler's Brand* display his ability to stick to the basic essentials of the plot, and sustain the course of the action. *Rustler's Brand* in particular impresses, showing qualities of depth and solidity denied to later works. Despite an awkward shift in focus—the main villain, Buck Sieber, dies rather too early on in the book—the reader's interest is held throughout. Will Pearce, the cowhand out to clear his brother of false accusations of rustling, emerges as an effective but human hero, and there are some compelling scenes.

With Walt Warren, the gun-toting attorney who stars in the "Six-Gun" books, human frailty is notable for its absence. An ex-marshal and paragon of all the virtues, Walt combines the qualities of a skilled gunfighter with those of a 19th-century Perry Mason, dominating the many courtroom scenes in which he appears. His long-standing courtship and quarrelling with the fiery but loving Marion Owens provide a leitmotif to the novels, which usually contain a detective element. *Six-Gun Vengeance* has Walt solving an attempt to murder a Confederate veteran, the origins of which go back to the Civil War. In *Six-Gun Feud* he saves the cattlemen of his native Quanah County from the machinations of the crooked railroad boss Chester Harden. *The Badlands Gang* sees his combined legal skill and dexterity with a gun thwart the efforts of a lawyer and a ranch foreman to cheat the pretty Helen Fowler of her inheritance, though not without antagonizing Marion in the process. Langley's plots are thin, and the characters two-dimensional. Walt's endless courting of Marion and their frequent tiffs become tedious after a while, and attention fixes on him to such an extent that villains and secondary characters barely find space to breath. Still, Langley makes a virtue of his skeleton plots, keeping the action moving while ably utilising the mystery aspect of his writing to provide the occasional surprise. Not one of the great names of the western, Langley nevertheless has made his niche.

—Jeff Sadler

LANSDALE, Joe R(ichard). American. Born in Gladewater, Texas, 28 October 1951. Educated at Tyler Junior College, 1970–71; University of Texas, Austin, 1971–72; Stephen F. Austin State University, Nacogdoches, 1973, 1975, 1976. Married 1) Cassie Ellis in 1970 (divorced 1971); 2) Karen Ann Morton in 1973, one son and one daughter. Truck crop farmer; transportation manager, Goodwill Industries, 1973–76; custodian, Stephen F. Austin State University, Nacogdoches, 1976–80. Since 1981 full-time writer. Vice-president, Horror Writers of America, 1987–88. Recipient: Horror Writers of America award, for story, 1989, for novella, 1990. Agent: Barbara Puechner, Peekner Literary Agency, 3121 Portage Road, Bethlehem, Pennsylvania 18017. Address: 113 Timber Ridge, Nacogdoches, Texas 75961, U.S.A.

WESTERN PUBLICATIONS

Novel

The Magic Wagon. New York, Doubleday, 1986; Bath, Chivers, 1988.

Short Stories

By Bizarre Hands. Shingletown, California, Ziesing, 1989.

Uncollected Short Stories

"Waziah," in *Creature!*, edited by Bill Pronzini. New York, Arbor House, 1981.
"Man with Two Lives," in *Roundup*, edited by Stephen Overholser. New York, Doubleday, 1982.

OTHER PUBLICATIONS

Novels

Act of Love. New York, Zebra, 1981; London, Kinnel, 1989.
Dead in the West. New York, Space and Time, 1986; London, Kinnel, 1990.
The Nightrunners. Niles, Illinois, Dark Harvest, 1987.
The Drive-In: A B-Movie with Blood and Popcorn. New York, Bantam, 1988; Harrow, Middlesex, Kinnell, 1990.
Cold in July. New York, Bantam, 1989.
The Drive-In 2: Not Just One of Them Sequels. New York, Bantam, and Harrow, Middlesex, Kinnell, 1990.
Savage Season. New York, Bantam, 1990.

Short Stories

Stories by Mama Lansdale's Youngest Boy. N.p., Pulphouse, 1991.

Plays

Drive-In Date (produced New York, 1991).
By Bizarre Hands (produced New York, 1991).

Other

Editor, *Best of the West*. New York, Doubleday, 1986.
Editor, *The New Frontier: The Best of the West Two*. New York, Doubleday, 1989.
Editor, with Pat LoBrutto, *Razored Saddles*. Niles, Illinois, Dark Harvest, 1989.

*

Joe R. Lansdale comments:

I merely write the best I can, and try to write a story I care about, a story I'd write if I were paid or not—though payment doesn't hurt my feelings one bit.

* * *

Joe R. Lansdale is a horror, mainstream, fantasy, mystery, genre writer who writes Westerns. His self-taught eclecticism made his early dealings with editors and agents a rebellion against the "pigeon-hole" marketing tendencies of the publishing establishment. Born in Gladewater, "East" Texas in 1951, Lansdale was at age nine writing, "doing all that I ever really wanted to do." Ironically, the young author has farmed, janitored, and mopped blood in the emergency room of an East Texas Hospital as ways to support himself and family. He took several courses at Stephen F. Austin University in Nacogdoches, where he served as a janitor, but opted not to finish a degree for two reasons: full-time education wouldn't allow him the time necessary for writing, and a degree might have allowed an alternate means of support when writing was not paying his bills.

The early stories have a fantasy or gothic bite, often containing a high degree of the macabre grotesque. One of his most recent, "On the Far Side of the Cadillac Desert with Dead Folks" (in *By Bizarre Hands*) uses a graphic visceral backdrop wherein an escaped virus has begun to resuscitate corpses. The protagonist, a bounty hunter, captures his prey in a "Tonk," where denizens of the night pay to dance and fornicate with female resuscitates whom the "Meat Boys" had made safe: "cut off the hands so they couldn't grab, ran screws through their jaws to fasten on wire muzzles so they couldn't bite, sold them to the honky-tonks about time the germ started stirring." The action culminates in the Cadillac Desert where the Chevy-Cadillac wars had taken place.

Such fare, though winning him two Bram Stoker Awards, has served to inhibit western readers because of the non-traditional backdrops, the geographical-phantasmagorical aura of the pieces, and also because of the extremely graphical nature of the gothic and the grotesque. As editor, Lansdale has waged war against the stereotypical idea of the Western. While agreeing that the term "Cowpunk" is a joke, he continues that there is an "unnamed movement in the air, and it's one that combines genres, both those commonly considered, and the genres of the literary and the mainstream . . . So if we're part of any movement, it's one that wants to see more unique stories. Stories that do not feel bound and gagged to any tradition, and the best way to do this is to assault a tradition (introduction to *Razored Saddles*). Thus the Doubleday anthologies edited by Lansdale, *Best of the West* and *The New Frontier*, may be an oblique way to sample the writer's own western purview. Although there are several traditional stories in each collection, most "stretch" the term Western. Readers must be prepared for pyrotechnics in language and in situation. Four letter phonemes are not off-limits.

Some stories such as "Man with Two Lives" begin with traditional underpinnings. In a sensitive revisionist treatment, Wild Bill Hickok is brought to life as a loving old grandfather reminiscing the real truth and the real facts of his life and contrived death. The gimmick is fleshed out in a very human characterization of the survivor. So it is with "Trains Not Taken," a story ignored by a number of markets until published in a literary review (*RE Arts & Letters, III*, later anthologized in *By Bizarre Hands*). The story is an alternate time-line piece wherein Hickok and Cody meet on a train travelling the Great Cherry Roads, a Japanese construction across the transcontinental during the time the Japanese and the whites have joined forces against the Red. Cody announces that Crazy Horse has wiped out Custer and Japanese General Miyamoto Yoshi "to the man, U.S. Cavalry and Samurai alike." Intensely imagistic with sensuous descriptions of the scenery and the travellers, the story portrays the two men who have an inkling that alternate universes and choices *do* exist. In this case, Hickok is reconsidering his fading marriage to Mary Jane while Lansdale weaves a baroque display of "might have beens" and "might be yets" in suggestive imagism, calling to Hickok of possibilities to come. Lansdale shows his knowledge of the times—reading, history, customs, geography—but does not overdo it. Young Casey Jones has a cameo appearance. Dialogue is accurate and "sounds" well.

In "Trains," as in his more delicately wrought stories such as "Fish Night," "Letter from the South, Two Moons West of Nacogdoches," and "The Windstorm Passes" (reprinted in *By Bizarre Hands*; "Windstorm" is excerpted with few changes from *The Magic Wagon*) Lansdale encodes social commentary, parody of rich and poor, high and low ironic tragedy with an eclectic array of techniques: imagistic description, accurate dialogue partaking of low-life and poverty-stricken vernacular, and settings that in many cases vie with the characters for the narrative stage. In "Fish Night," two down-and-out salesmen come to grips with the primal desert in a surreal portrayal where the undersea desert becomes a psychic landscape. The poetic descriptions of the desert and the convincing colloquial dialogue between the old and the young salesmen make it a favorite at Lansdale's readings. "Letter from the South," an epistolary presentation, is another alternate time piece wherein the opinionated Native American letter-writer pronounces on foibles and narrow-mindedness of Southern Baptists while letting loose racist diatribes on whites and blacks. The alternative solutions to the race problem, though ironic and satirical, are not for the faint-hearted.

Criticism of Lansdale's gothic grotesques and the academic impatience with his "adolescent desire to shock for the sake of display," has been blunted by the appearance of *The Magic Wagon*, the author's *magnum opus* to date. In the short novel, well-received by reviewers, Lansdale's eclecticism reaches a critical mass in which everything seems to work. Set in East Texas in 1909, the picaresque novel is narrated by 17-year-old orphaned-by-tornado Buster Fogg, who catalogues his travels with Billy Bob Daniels, proprietor of the Magic Wagon. Daniels, believing he is the son of Wild Bill Hickok, is travelling with what he believes to be the corpse of his own father. The retinue includes Albert, the black wagon driver, and Rot Toe, a wrestling chimpanzee. The story appears as a type of Huckleberry Finn rewritten by Ray Bradbury (one of Lansdale's favorites). Indeed, several critics compare the writing to Twain's, suggesting the novel is "about greed and vanity and violence, and [Lansdale] uncovers it with perfect timing and clarity . . . There aren't any easy answers" (Lewis Shiner, *The Austin Chronicle*, 13 March 1987).

Lansdale is a developing talent. What appears distasteful in his writing to the traditionalists—his eclecticism, his penchant for the gothic, the grotesque, and the shocking or surprising—are indictments leveled at cutting-edge writers of every age. However, these traits in a young fiction writer and editor at the close of the 20th century are certainly those which keep western writing alive and well.

—Lee Schultz

LANT, Harvey. *See* **ROWLAND, Donald S.**

LARSON, Clem. *See* **FEARN, John Russell.**

LAURENCE, (Jean) Margaret (née Wemyss). Canadian. Born in Neepawa, Manitoba, 18 July 1926. Educated at the University of Manitoba, Winnipeg, B.A. 1947. Married John

F. Laurence in 1947 (divorced 1969); one son and one daughter. Lived in Somali and Ghana, 1950–57, and in England; writer-in-residence, University of Toronto, 1969–70, University of Western Ontario, London, 1973, and Trent University, Peterborough, Ontario, 1974. Chancellor, Trent University, 1981–83. Recipient: Beta Sigma Phi award, 1961; University of Western Ontario President's Medal, 1961, 1962, 1964; Governor-General's award, 1967, 1975; Canada Council senior fellowship, 1967, 1971; Molson prize, 1975; B'nai B'rith award, 1976; Periodical Distributors award, 1977; City of Toronto award, 1978; Canadian Booksellers Association Writer of the Year award, 1981; Banff Centre award, 1983. Honorary Fellow, United College, University of Winnipeg, 1967. D.Litt.: McMaster University, Hamilton, Ontario, 1970; University of Toronto, 1972; Carleton University, Ottawa, 1974; Brandon University, Manitoba, 1975; Mount Allison University, Sackville, New Brunswick, 1975; University of Western Ontario, 1975; Simon Fraser University, Burnaby, British Columbia, 1977; LL.D.: Dalhousie University, Halifax, Nova Scotia, 1972; Trent University, 1972; Queen's University, Kingston, Ontario, 1975. Companion, Order of Canada, 1971; Fellow, Royal Society of Canada, 1977. *Died 5 January 1987.*

WESTERN PUBLICATIONS

Novels

This Side Jordan. Toronto, McClelland and Stewart, London, Macmillan, and New York, St. Martin's Press, 1960.
The Stone Angel. Toronto, McClelland and Stewart, London, Macmillan, and New York, Knopf, 1964.
A Jest of God. Toronto, McClelland and Stewart, London, Macmillan, and New York, Knopf, 1966; as *Rachel, Rachel*, New York, Popular Library, 1968; as *Now I Lay Me Down*, London, Panther, 1968.
The Fire-Dwellers. Toronto, McClelland and Stewart, London, Macmillan, and New York, Knopf, 1969.
The Diviners. Toronto, McClelland and Stewart, London, Macmillan, and New York, Knopf, 1974.

Short Stories

The Tomorrow-Tamer. Toronto, McClelland and Stewart, and London, Macmillan, 1963; New York, Knopf, 1964.
A Bird in the House. Toronto, McClelland and Stewart, London, Macmillan, and New York, Knopf, 1970.

Other

The Prophet's Camel Bell (travel). Toronto, McClelland and Stewart, and London, Macmillan, 1963; as *New Wind in a Dry Land*, New York, Knopf, 1964.
Long Drums and Cannons: Nigerian Novelists and Dramatists 1952–1966. London, Macmillan, and New York, Praeger, 1968.
Jason's Quest (for children). Toronto, McClelland and Stewart, London, Macmillan, and New York, Knopf, 1970.
Heart of a Stranger (essays). Toronto, McClelland and Stewart, 1976; Philadelphia, Lippincott, 1977.
Six Darn Cows (for children). Toronto, McClelland and Stewart, 1979.
The Christmas Birthday Story (for children). New York, Knopf, 1980.
A Place to Stand On. Edmonton, Alberta, NeWest Press, 1983.
Dance on the Earth. Toronto, McClelland and Stewart, 1989.

Editor and Translator, *A Tree of Poverty: Somali Poetry and Prose.* Nairobi, Eagle Press, 1954.

*

Bibliography: by Susan J. Warwick, in *The Annotated Bibliography of Canada's Major Authors 1*, edited by Robert Lecker and Jack David, Downsview, Ontario, ECW Press, 1979.

Manuscript Collections: McMaster University, Hamilton, Ontario; York University, Toronto.

Critical Studies: "The Maze of Life" by S.E. Read, in *Canadian Literature* (Vancouver), Winter 1966; "Geographer of Human Identities" by Walter Swayze, in A.C.U.T.E. (Ottawa), 1967; *Margaret Laurence*, Toronto, McClelland and Stewart, 1969, and *The Manawaka World of Margaret Laurence*, McClelland and Stewart, 1975, both by Clara Thomas; "Ten Years' Sentences," in *Canadian Literature* (Vancouver), Summer 1969, and "Sources," in *Mosaic* (Winnipeg), April 1970, both by Laurence; *Three Voices: The Lives of Margaret Laurence, Gabrielle Roy, and Frederick Phillip Grove* by Joan Hind-Smith, Toronto, Clarke Irwin, 1975; *Margaret Laurence: The Writer and Her Critics* edited by W.H. New, Toronto, McGraw Hill Ryerson, 1977; "Margaret Laurence Issue" of *Journal of Canadian Studies* (Peterborough, Ontario), vol.13 no.3, 1978, and *Journal of Canadian Fiction* (Montreal), no.27, 1980; *Margaret Laurence* by Patricia Morley, Boston, Twayne, 1981; *A Place to Stand On: Essays by and About Margaret Laurence* edited by George Woodcock, Edmonton, Alberta, NeWest Press, 1983.

* * *

Margaret Laurence's West is primarily the fictional town of Manawaka, in southwest Manitoba, the central site of her five linked Manawaka books, *The Stone Angel*, *A Jest of God*, *The Fire-Dwellers*, *A Bird in the House*, and *The Diviners*. It is secondarily Vancouver and the former West of central Ontario, the frontier of the 1820's and 1830's. Her book of essays, *Heart of a Stranger*, and her posthumous memoir, *Dance on the Earth*, provide some specific insights into those Wests in the contexts both of her life in those places, and the connections she saw between the North American frontier and the global conflicts between technological and tribal peoples. All her work, including her four African books, her children's books, her journalism, and her other writings, deals with what she saw as the major human question of our time, how to recognize and celebrate both the common humanity and the cultural diversity of all the globe's peoples. Having realized from the beginning of her career, when she spearheaded the first publication of oral Somali poetry (*A Tree of Poverty*), that the oppressed peoples of the world with whom she so deeply empathized had their own voices, and did not need her or anyone else to speak for them, she returned to her Manitoba roots to write the stories she felt she had the right to tell in her own voice.

A hallmark of Laurence's best writing is her interweaving of the past and the present. In *The Stone Angel*, the first of the Manawaka novels, the present is the days approaching the death of Hagar Currie Shipley, a woman of 90 who is "rampant with memory." Without willing it, Hagar struggles to set her mind in order. Like her pioneer storekeeper father, she has allowed pride and fear to deny her humanity to herself and to those she loves. A matriarchy can be as cruel and destructive as a patriarchy. Hagar is a difficult character to love, but the reader is drawn to understand and to sympathize. (The book has been taught in geriatric nursing classes to give students a glimpse into the world of the very old.) Finally the same strength that has caused Hagar to be destructive all her life gives her the spirit for two free acts, not important for themselves but for Hagar's acceptance of her own humanity. In defiance of a lifetime's nagging, she praises her son, and in defiance of rules she gets up to get a bedpan for her young hospital roommate. As is often the case with Laurence, these victories are seemingly paltry, but represent humanity's capacity to change and to bless rather than to curse.

A Jest of God and *The Fire-Dwellers* are literally sister novels, detailing the same summer in the life of Rachel Cameron, unmarried school teacher in Manawaka (*A Jest of God*), and her sister, Stacey Cameron MacAindra, married mother of four in Vancouver (*The Fire-Dwellers*). Each woman envies her sister's life, talks to a god in whom she less than half believes, and has an affair that serves as a catalyst for her to take responsibility for her own life. Rachel's life is isolated and austere, a claustrophobic existence in an apartment above the funeral parlor, dominated by a whining and manipulative mother. Stacey is overwhelmed by the demands of her children, her husband, and her neighbors, at the same time as she is bombarded by images of the war in Vietnam, possible nuclear holocaust, and the everyday fears of motherhood: children hit by cars or drowning. At the end of each novel each heroine acknowledges that she is strong, that she has, in fact, no option but to be strong. Again, the victory is small but its resonance immense.

A Bird in the House is a short-story cycle portraying the artist as a young woman, Vanessa MacLeod, growing up in Manawaka during the Depression. While clearly fictional, it is the closest of the Manawaka books to literal autobiography. Vanessa fears and even hates her craggy pioneer grandfather at the same time that she recognizes how much she is like him. She learns through her doctor father's example, and through the dislocation of the family following his early death, her fundamental human identity with the "wretched of the earth," as well as the chasm imposed by her relative comfort and security.

The last of the Manawaka books, *The Diviners*, rounds out the series quite literally. The treasured Scots plaid pin, lost in *The Stone Angel*, is found again and retreasured in another family, an emblem of how one adopts the ancestors of one's formative years, regardless of bloodlines. *The Diviners* focuses on Morag Gunn, the adopted daughter of Christie Logan, the town "scavenger" or garbage collector. Morag has fled both the wrong side of the tracks in Manawaka and a stiflingly proper marriage to become a successful author. After living in Vancouver and London, she has made her home in an old log cabin in Ontario, beside the "River of Now and Then," a river that seems to flow both ways and becomes emblematic of the constantly changing dynamic of past and present. Morag is the mother of Pique Gunn Tonnerre, her daughter by Jules (Skinner) Tonnerre, a "halfbreed" and fellow outcast of Manawaka, who has achieved some success as a folk and country-western singer.

The Diviners, which Laurence considered her spiritual autobiography, makes explicit the themes that she was most concerned with throughout her life. Morag and Skinner are artists, but so is Christie, who "told" the garbage, and Morag's landlady, an exotic dancer with a live snake as a prop. Art is a way of getting outside the community, with the possibility that the artist may see it more clearly and embrace it. Morag's distant yet loving relationship with Skinner brings together the two pioneer ethnic strains of the Canadian West, the Métis and the Scots. Pique, the youthful inheritor of both traditions, will live up to them because she has no choice and because she chooses to. Finally *The Diviners* deals with the difficulty of knowing the past. Like *The Stone Angel*, *The Diviners* is structured in two parallel chronologies, the past of Morag's life and the summer present of the novel. Morag mediates between an objective past and the subjective present that changes the past, not only through the vagaries of memory but through the insistence of living every day.

Laurence's West is that of the small agrarian town in the 20th century. There are neither cowboys nor mountain men, and the Indians are neither Noble Savages nor Beautiful Losers but rather the Tonnerre family, dispossessed, marginalized, and alienated in a century that has excelled in such dispossession. There are no clear cut bad guys and good guys. All the protagonists, and most of the major characters, are women. There is no breath-taking and soul-restoring scenery except for a small and modest vacation lake in the north, near a Cree reserve. The small town is hypocritical and destructive, but also sheltering. Artists and prophets, mostly unrecognized, flourish. These books set the conquest of the North American West in the context of a worldwide technological revolution that displaced tribal peoples from Scotland to North Africa to Manitoba. They are about, on the largest level, forging an understanding of the past that goes beyond conqueror and conquered to construct a livable myth of ancestors.

—Frances W. Kaye

LAWRENCE, Steven C. Pseudonym for Lawrence Agustus Murphy; also writes as C.L. Murphy. American. Born in Brockton, Massachusetts, 17 May 1924. Educated at Massachusetts Maritime Academy, B.S. 1944; Boston University, B.S. in journalism 1950, M.A. 1951. Served in the United States Naval Reserve, 1942–44; Maritime Service, 1944–46; Lieutenant Sr. Grade; United States Navy, 1946–47. Married Charlotte A. Heuser in 1950; one son. English teacher, South Junior High School, Brockton, 1951–81; instructor in creative writing, Stonehill College, North Easton, Massachusetts, 1967. Recipient: Western Writers of America Scroll award, 1967; Knights of Columbus Certificate of Merit, 1980. Agent: Paul R. Reynolds Inc., 12 East 41st Street, New York, New York 10017. Address: 30 Mercedes Road, Brockton, Massachusetts, 02401, U.S.A.

WESTERN PUBLICATIONS

Novels (series: Slattery)

The Naked Range. New York, Ace, 1956.
Saddle Justice. New York, Fawcett, 1957; London, Fawcett, 1958.
Brand of a Texan. New York, Fawcett, 1958; London, Fawcett, 1960.
The Iron Marshal. New York, Avon, 1960; London, Panther, 1961.
Night of the Gunmen. New York, Avon, 1960; London, Gold Lion, 1974.
Gun Fury. New York, Avon, 1961.
With Blood in Their Eyes. New York, Ace, 1961.
Slattery; *Bullet Welcome for Slattery*. New York, Ace, 1961; *Slattery* published separately as *The Lynchers*, New York, Nordon, 1975.
Walk a Narrow Trail (Slattery); *A Noose for Slattery*. New York, Ace, 1962.

Longhorns North (Slattery); *Slattery's Gun Says No.* New York, Ace, 1962.
A Texan Comes Riding. New York, Fawcett, 1966; Bath, Chivers, 1986.
That Man from Texas. Indianapolis, Curtis, 1972; Bath, Chivers, 1986.
Edge of the Land. New York, Ace, 1974.
Six-Gun Junction. New York, Curtis, 1974.
North to Montana (Slattery). New York, Nordon, 1975.
Slattery Stands Alone. New York, Nordon, 1976.
Trial for Tennihan. New York, Ace, 1976.
Day of the Comancheros (Slattery). New York, Nordon, 1977.
Gun Blast. New York, Belmont, 1977.

OTHER PUBLICATIONS

Novel

A Northern Saga: The Account of the North Atlantic-Murmansk, Russia, Convoys. Chicago, Playboy Press, 1976.

Other

Buffalo Grass (for children, as C.L. Murphy), with Charlotte Murphy. New York, Dial Press, 1966.

* * *

Steven C. Lawrence—mistakenly by-lined "Steven G. Lawrence" on the first Ace Book editions of his best-known Westerns, the Tom Slattery series—specializes in fast, furious acton set in painstakingly researched situations.

In *Slattery*—later reprinted as *The Lynchers* in the Leisure Books series—Tom Slattery returns from five years in a federal prison after being framed for a crime he didn't commit. Slattery avenges himself and moves on to *Bullet Welcome for Slattery* where he gets involved with smuggling over the Texas-Mexico border. In *Walk a Narrow Trail* Lawrence writes in his introduction that the history behind the action at Estancia used in the story is based on facts about the leader of a Texas trail drive delivering a criminal to the Indians. The Indians skinned the man alive alongside a river, which has since been called the Rawhide. *Longhorns North* uses incidents with Indians and buffalo hunters in the history of Llano Estacado when the Indians made their last effort to hold their land and defeat the whites.

When Leisure Books reprinted the Slattery series in the mid-1970's, Lawrence wrote some new volumes. The best of these are *North to Montana*, where Slattery faces treachery in Calligan Valley at the end of a 1200-mile trail drive, and *Day of the Comancheros*, a story of Slattery's vengeance when he finds a woman raped, beaten, and left to die in the desert. Slattery takes on the outlaw army in one of his most violent adventures.

Of the non-Slattery Westerns, the best is *Saddle Justice*. Will Roderick investigates why a town would lynch his younger brother. The portrait of a corrupt town is convincing and the character of Will Roderick is memorable.

Lawrence writes thrilling western adventures based on historical fact and solid plotting.

—George Kelley

LAWTON, Charles. *See* **HECKELMANN, Charles N.**

LAZENBY, Nat. *See* **LAZENBY, Norman.**

LAZENBY, Norman (Austin). Also writes as Kay Bayes; John Blaze; Ace Capelli; Allan Carson; Mike T. Dallas; Earl Ellison; Max Gordon; Don Hugo; Nat Karta; Rex Kleiner; Ramon Lacroix; Arnold Lane; Nat Lazenby; Duke Linton; Benny Logan; Clark Macey; Colt Mahone; Bengo Mistral; Glenn Morton; Nesta Norman; Cal Scott; Peter Standish; Jed Storme; Brett Vane; Hans Vogel; Peter Webb; Wes Yancey; Hyman Zore. British. Born in Gateshead, Tyneside, 4 January 1914. Married in 1942. Worked for local electrical engineering firm as apprentice before World War II. Since 1945 full-time writer. Address: 24 Clitheroe Road, St. Anne's, Lancashire, England.

WESTERN PUBLICATIONS

Novels

Singing Lead (as Nat Lazenby). London, Grant Hughes, 1949.
Colt Fever (as Glen Morton). London, Hamilton, 1950.
The Sheriff of Green Coulee (as Colt Mahone). London, Scion, 1950.
Fighting Guns. London, Curtis Warren, 1950.
A Fightin' Hombre. London, Coker, 1951.
Texan Frontier (as Cal Scott). London, Curtis Warren, 1951.
The Buckaroo. London, Coker, 1951.
Gunplay over Laredo. London, Coker, 1952.
Apache Country (as Allan Carson). London, Curtis Warren, 1952.
Double-X Ranch (as W.B. Glaston). London, Brown Watson, 1956.

Novels as Wes Yancey

Kill That Deputy! Sydney, Cleveland, 1971.
The Hard Faces. Sydney, Cleveland, 1971.
Lander's Kingdom. Sydney, Cleveland, 1972.
Easy Gold. Sydney, Cleveland, 1972.
Shadow of the Hangnoose. Sydney, Cleveland, 1973.
Sixgun Lawyer. Sydney, Cleveland, 1973.
The Killer Stamp. Sydney, Cleveland, 1973.
The Death Dealer. Sydney, Cleveland, 1974.
Gold of the Padres. Sydney, Cleveland, 1974.
Three To Die. Sydney, Cleveland, 1974.
Red Hide. Sydney, Cleveland, 1974.
Smash That Bounty-Man. Sydney, Cleveland, 1974.

Novels as John Blaze

Lawless Hideout. London, Hale, 1990.
Desert Trails. London, Hale, 1990.
Hell-Bent Gents. London, Hale, 1990.
Colt Flame. London, Hale, 1991.
Kiowa Blood. London, Hale, 1991.
The Killers. London, Hale, 1991.

OTHER PUBLICATIONS

Novels

You Can't Escape Love. London, Swan, 1942.
Death in the Stars. London, Scion, 1950.

Dead Sinners. London, Curtis Warren, 1950.
Always a Dame (as Brett Vane). London, Curtis Warren, 1950.
Rosalind Runs Wild (as Earl Ellison). London, John Spencer, 1950.
At Night I Live (as Hans Vogel). Glasgow, Muir Watson, 1950.
Bad Women (as Hans Vogel). Glasgow, Muir Watson, 1950.
Main Drag (as Hans Vogel). Glasgow, Muir Watson, 1950.
Man Trap (as Hans Vogel). Glasgow, Muir Watson, 1950.
Passion's Not for Noon (as Hyman Zore). Glasgow, Muir Watson, 1950.
Love from Las Vegas (as Hans Vogel). Glasgow, Muir Watson, 1951.
Mind My Innocence (as Hans Vogel). Glasgow, Muir Watson, 1951.
Dancing with Danger (as Peter Webb). London, Paget, 1951.
I Never Killed (as Max Gordon). London, Curtis Warren, 1952.
Mitzi-State Enemy (as Peter Standish). London, Curtis Warren, 1952.
Unwilling Guest (as Earl Ellison). London, John Spencer, 1952.
A Guy Named Judas (as Nat Karta). Glasgow, Muir Watson, 1952.
Reckless Lovers (as Roman Lacroix). London, Modern Fiction, 1952.
Give Me the Lowdown (as Duke Linton). London, Scion, 1952.
Play It Your Way (as Ace Capelli). London, Kaye, 1953.
Ya Don't Say (as Benny Logan). London, Gannet, 1953.
Baby, You're Grief! (as Clark Macey). London, Hollyfield, 1953.
We, the Condemned (as Nat Karta). London, Scion, 1953.
The Brains of Helle (as Bengo Mistral). London, Gannet, 1953.
Death Wears Nylon (as Mike T. Dallas). London, Gannet, 1954.
Midnight Rendezvous (as Rex Kleiner/Jed Storme). London, Modern Fiction, 1955.

Short Stories

Terror Trap. Mansfield, Shenstone, 1949.

*

Norman Lazenby comments (1991):

In all honesty, I write stories for the possible monetary gain. Of course, I could do better work if there was a basic assurance that the product of my labour would not be returned, and the outcome really valued. As the fiction market was never like that—and is still a precarious field—the person who paddles in this ditch really needs wellies!

But like actors, once the itch to write—or act—is germinated, the growth will survive, and here I am, in my seventh decade, still writing. Of course, there are some really old characters in the game, like Catherine Cookson, still working at 84, and Barbara Cartland, who has written her 507th novel in the romance genre at the age of 89!

Yes, *Red Hide* is about the standard for these efforts of mine, and *Green Coulee* relates to the old bang-bang stuff of the 1950's. Of course, if Hale raised their rate somewhat, a better standard of prose could be obtained.

My western novels are about people, and how they react to each other and the wilderness and frontier that was the land they adopted. Story values in a confession yarn are just as basic as those in a western novel, with the reservation that the Western is really a historical story, and the modern confession portrays life as it is today.

These days, my writing is just a hobby. I only write when I can, and when the house is full of prams, nappies, and paper bags, work is impossible. I have two daughters, five grand-kids and now two great-grand-kids, and they all demand time from me at various intervals. There are other things in life besides sitting behind a typewriter. Maybe I should feel lucky!

* * *

Norman Lazenby is the consummate professional writer. He started writing at the age of 16, while apprenticed to a big local firm of electrical engineers. His first success came in 1941, when he sold short stories to Gerald G. Swan, and quickly followed with his first novel, a romance entitled *You Can't Escape Love*. Lazenby was in a reserved occupation during the war, and continued with his writing. Like many of his contemporaries at that time, he wrote all kinds of fiction, endeavouring to give publishers what they wanted, and to ensure saleability. Times were hard, and compromises had to be struck. Lazenby wrote and sold hundreds of stories and dozens of novels, and his work ranged from fairy stories to crime, from Westerns to sexy confessions, from adult gangster yarns to schoolboy stories. After the war he became a full-time writer, often working up to 12 hours a day to fulfil commissions from rapacious publishers. In 1969, he moved with his wife and family to St. Annes, just outside Blackpool, where he still resides. Lazenby's career has spanned more than 50 years, during which time the publishing market has undergone many vicissitudes and sea changes. In the late 1940's and early 1950's Lazenby specialised in tough, sexy gangster stories, becoming one of the highest paid (for the period!) authors in this peculiar genre. Since 1970, following the contraction of the popular fiction market, he has concentrated on lurid "confessions". However, throughout his career he has written Westerns, and in recent years has tended to specialise in this field.

Lazenby's style has been shaped and moulded over the years by the markets for which he had to work. Having to be prolific, he quickly adopted a lean, economical style, shorn of any flowery adjectives and purple prose. His endless writing of "confessions" called for a stark simplicity of language, but every line also had to have an emotional charge, albeit on a simple level. "Confessions" are actually one of the hardest types of fiction to produce, because the author has to write from a personal viewpoint, and to convey human emotions in simple, economical terms. Thus, Lazenby's western novels are extremely interesting and effective, comparing favourably with his contemporaries. The field of western writing is notorious for hack authors, and cliched, padded writing. This was particularly the case in the late 1940's and early 1950's, when numerous small "backyard" publishers flourished during a period of paper shortages, when practically anything would sell. Few of them strove for quality, and most of the western authors had little acquaintance with the history of the real West. Their stories seem to have been based on Hollywood "B" Westerns, and all of the characters were made to speak in a sub-literate form of "Gabby Hayes-ese." "To" became "tuh," "of" became "uv," "you" became "yuh," and so forth. Lazenby's early western novels were written in this idiom, in the fashion of the day, a typical example being *The Sheriff of Green Coulee*. But even here, there were signs that Lazenby had the talent to to rise above the constraints of the formula plot, which centred around an honest rancher being framed for cattle rustling, so that an unscrupulous "Mr. Big" could buy up his spread, on which there were unsuspected gold deposits. Lazenby's experience in writing in other genres, particularly crime stories, enabled him to disguise the hoary western standard plot forms by making them initially mysterious. And his characters, however one-dimensional, were made to seem vivid and alive, through his "confession" skills. Thus, when Ezra, one of his characters—ironically a "Gabby Hayes" stereotype old prospector—is murdered, one feels a sense of loss and can readily identify with the hero: "He stared grimly at the canyon walls, an unspoken curse in his heart against the unknown men who had killed Ezra. He jumped to his feet and his hands fell to his gun butts. He crouched, wishing some enemy would appear so that he could could kill him!"

Lazenby soon began to shed the stylistic trappings of the pulp publishers, and to drop the "padding" of cliched phraseology. He realised that it was perfectly possible to write a Western in which the characters spoke a recognisable English (or rather, American), and to convey their lack of culture in more subtle ways. He reached his peak in a series of paperback Westerns written for the Australian publishers, Cleveland, under the pseudonym of Wes Yancey. Published in the early 1970's, these short novels are striking for their emotional impact and vivid characterisation. The heroes (and heroines) are not plaster saints: they have their faults and human frailties. The villains are given a plausible motivation for their villainy.

In *Red Hide*, perhaps the best of the series, Mick Bayner, the hero's younger brother, and a prominent subsidiary character, is a racist with a bigoted dislike of Indians. His sister Rosa attracts the romantic attentions of Johnny Eagle, a half-breed Kiowan Indian. Rosa herself is strangely attracted to the Indian, but she already has suppressed romantic feelings towards her elder brother, Jed, striking a disquieting incestuous undertone. Rosa's widowed mother Kate is portrayed as a woman with a secret, and a note of eerie mystery is introduced when the Bayner family is subjected to periodic visits from a strange, one-eyed lunatic, Simon Greer. The madman rides around their home at night, yelling cryptic verbal abuse, half of it in Kiowan Indian dialect: "Curse you, bitch! A-yaka a-gumba!" The family also attracts the enmity of Downey Hollister, another racist and sadistic Indian killer, who is embittered because Indians caused him to lose the use of one arm. When Hollister and Greer form an unholy partnership, aided by hired gunmen, the Bayner family is in mortal danger. Events move quickly as, with power and economy, Lazenby unravels all the strands of his complex plot. Rosa is revealed to be a pure bred Indian, secretly brought up as Kate's own daughter (who had died as a baby). Rosa had been unaware of her ancestry, as had Mick, although Jed had shared the secret with his mother. Into this maelstrom of emotional turmoil, Lazenby weaves a tight plot of heart-stopping action, tragedy and death, all of which is eventually resolved in a surprising and satisfactory manner.

In 1988, now in semi-retirement, Lazenby created the pen name of John Blaze to launch a new series of intriguing westerns; as in the Yancey series, these rely on the interplay of human emotions, rather than the paraphernalia of western lore. With 50 years of experience behind him, Lazenby still has much to offer.

—Philip J. Harbottle

LEA, Tom. American. Born in El Paso, Texas, 11 July 1907. Educated at El Paso High School, graduated 1924; Art Institute, Chicago, 1924–26. Married Sarah Catherine Dighton in 1938; one son. Artist and art teacher, Chicago, 1926–33; worked in an anthropology laboratory, Santa Fe, New Mexico, 1933–36. Since 1936 freelance artist and illustrator, and since 1947 freelance writer; artist and correspondent for *Life* magazine, 1941–46. Has executed murals for many public buildings; has collection in Dallas Museum of Fine Arts, El Paso Museum of Art, University of Texas, Austin, and the Pentagon, Arlington, Virginia. Litt.D.: Baylor University, Waco, Texas, 1967; L.H.D.: Southern Methodist University, Dallas, 1970. Address: 2401 Savannah Street, El Paso, Texas 79930, U.S.A.

Western Publications

Novels

The Brave Bulls. Boston, Little Brown, 1949; London, Heinemann, 1950.
The Wonderful Country. Boston, Little Brown, 1952; London, Heinemann, 1953.
The Primal Yoke. Boston, Little Brown, 1960; London, Macmillan, 1961.
The Hands of Cantú. Boston, Little Brown, and London, Hammond, 1964.

Short Stories

A Grizzly from the Coral Sea. El Paso, Texas, Hertzog, 1944; as *Battle Stations*, Dallas, Still Point Press, 1988.

Uncollected Short Story

"Quite a Beach," in *Atlantic* (Boston), September 1949.

Other Publications

Other

John W. Norton, American Painter 1876–1934, with Thomas E. Tallmadge. Chicago, Lakeside Press, 1935.
George Catlin Westward Bound a Hundred Years Ago. El Paso, Texas, Hertzog, 1939.
Randado. El Paso, Texas, Hertzog, 1941.
Peleliu Landing. El Paso, Texas, Hertzog, 1945.
A Calendar of Twelve Travelers Through the Pass of the North. El Paso, Texas, Hertzog, 1946.
Bullfight Manual for Spectators. El Paso, Texas, Hertzog, 1949.
Western Beef Cattle: A Series of Eleven Paintings. Dallas, Museum of Fine Arts, 1950.
Tom Lea: A Portfolio of Six Paintings. Austin, University of Texas Press, 1953.
The Stained Glass Designs in the McKee Chapel, Church of Saint Clement, El Paso, Texas. El Paso, Texas, Guynes, 1953.
The King Ranch. Boston, Little Brown, 1957.
Maud Durlin Sullivan 1872–1944: Pioneer Southwestern Librarian: A Tribute. Los Angeles, University of California School of Library Service, 1962.
A Picture Gallery. Boston, Little Brown, 1968.
In the Crucible of the Sun. Kingsville, Texas, King Ranch, 1974.
The Art of Tom Lea: Paintings, compiled by Kathleen G. Hjerter. College Station, Texas A and M University Press, 1989.

*

Critical Studies: *Tom Lea, Artist in Two Mediums* by John O. West, Austin, Texas, Steck Vaughn, 1967; *Tom Lea, His Life and Work* by Evan Haywood Antone, El Paso, Texas Western Press, 1988.

* * *

Tom Lea, a product of the desert Southwest and its rich mixture of cultures, ranges geographically in his fiction from the Mexico of *The Brave Bulls* and *The Hands of Cantú* to the Wyoming mountains of *The Primal Yoke*, with a powerful survey of his home area in *The Wonderful Country* in between. In time he moves from the 16th century of New Spain to the story of a Marine returning home from World War II. He creates nostalgia for a bygone day, but he can also grasp and write about the problems of the present. And in approach, while he is basically a realist in the tradition of Robert Frost, he can almost be sentimentally romantic as well as bluntly naturalistic. Lea's home country, centered in El Paso, Texas, is thoroughly mixed culturally. English and Spanish intermingle in conversation and business dealings. Texans eat Mexican foods, drink Mexican drinks, use Spanish words aplenty, and even have a tendency toward the easygoing *mañana* attitude from South of the Border—tomorrow is soon enough for most matters of business; let's enjoy today!

It is thus quite natural that Lea's first novel grows out of the Mexican culture and the bullfight. *The Brave Bulls*, first published serially in *Atlantic*, began with Lea's study of the cattle industry for a set of oil paintings to illustrate a proposed *Life* magazine presentation. The *Life* publication (which never materialized) brought Lea face to face with the national sport of Mexico. And Lea researched it well. His friend Carl Hertzog tells of one experience in the 23 April 1949 *Saturday Review*: "When Tom was learning about the bulls, I waited two hours in a cold wind while he talked low Spanish to the *peon* truck driver who delivered the bulls to the Plaza de Toros. The *peon* had ideas which might be deeper than those of the *hacendado* who was supposed to know all about the bulls. Tom's eyes sparkled with enthusiasm as he interviewed this unexpected aficionado. Here was a new angle—more know-how—the inside dope. No bits of knowledge are too small. No compromise with half facts. He had to know everything, regardless of the hours of energy it took." Lea, like many *norteamericanos*, had seen a number of bullfights. His novel, however, goes much deeper than the stirring music, the colorful garb of the *torero*, the excitement of the crowd. He gets inside the bullfighter, Luis Bello, and examines his hopes and fears, lusts and irritations. We are also shown the leeches—family and business associates alike—who cling to him for life. The fear of the horns is a constant, of course, for the bullfight novel. Ernest Hemingway taught us that. But Lea deals with the human rather than the symbolic; his *torero* fights in a real world, not the guilt-ridden one of shadows that Hemingway shows us. There is romance, assuredly, in the *fiesta brava*—but Lea also gives us realistic detail. The resulting novel has gone through dozens of printings, and has been translated into at least eight languages. Such success says much for his method. And when *The Brave Bulls* became a movie starring Mel Ferrer, the director filmed Lea's book, not the script extracted from it by Hollywood screenwriters!

The second of Lea's novels, *The Wonderful Country*, deals with the mingling of cultures and ways of life to be found on the southwestern border in El Paso—called El Puerto in the novel—in the period of time just before the coming of the railroads to the Pass of the North. Knowledgeable about the history of the area, Lea did not write that history but built on it: the impact of desert and violence and a raw, new, wonderful country upon a varied cast of characters. As in *The Brave Bulls*, romanticism comes through, and lurks behind each picturesque cactus or hillock of sand crested with mesquite. El Puerto is filled with the heroes of the past that Lea loves to paint, but an army wife is driven near to madness by the sand and the harsh wind; an army captain dies valiantly—but still he dies—in the unfriendly, waterless mountains; and the realism of heartless, bloodthirsty southwestern man is present, in pistol-whippings, ambushes, street gunfights, and scalpings. But the essence of the story—man in search of his home—is perhaps more universal, more real, than all the realism of bloodshed and violence.

Dropping below the border (indeed, going back to a time when there was no border), Lea recreates the world of Nueva Viscaya—desert outpost of New Spain—in *The Hands of Cantú*. The hands are those that gentle horses rather than break them, hands that hold the destiny of the Spanish conquerors and settlers who vie with the Indians for control of that part of the world. Don Vito Cantú is beautifully drawn in words as a man one would follow—for love and respect—through the gates of Hell; and, unusually for Lea, he is also beautifully drawn in the author's illustrations—magnificent paintings that have the quality of the finest steel engravings. Don Vito meets and conquers the worst of man and desert that can be thrown at him, and with an equanimity that is almost too good to be true. But the fierceness of this mountain-desert land is absolutely realistic in Lea's depiction.

The Primal Yoke leaves the Southwest for the Wind River Mountains of Wyoming (renamed the Cloudrocks in the novel), but it moves even farther in theme and atmosphere. It focuses upon Haven Spurlock, a United States Marine just back from the war in the Pacific, where he had fought in such battles as Peleliu, which Lea had covered as a *Life* artist-correspondent. The yoke is one that ties him to the land he loves. He also loves a headstrong rich girl who proves to be his downfall in a story that has the inevitability of Greek tragedy built into it. Lea's realism-mingled-with-romance has turned to naturalism, and nature (both capitalized and lower case) crushed the protagonist.

Lea continues to paint, both in pastels (which is an exciting change for him) and oils. A recent oil painting about the fabulous Big Bend area gave him opportunity to revel in the "light of West Texas"—which as an artist and as a man he loves. Hearing him talk of that light recalls *The Hands of Cantú*, a book that came straight from the heart. He has given up on his projected story of Juan Sanchez and the Mexican Revolution that simmered so long in his mind, and the resulting loss to the world of literature is real and deep. The book would doubtless have reinforced the view of his friend Frank Dobie that "Tom Lea would starve rather than lie in paint or words for any amount of money" (*Tom Lea: A Portfolio of Six Paintings*). Given that honesty, the story of the simple *peon* caught up in the Mexican Revolution would have been worth waiting for.

—John O. West

LEE, Patrick. *See* **ANDREWS, Patrick E.**

LEE, Ranger. *See* **SNOW, Charles H.**

LEE, Wayne C(yril). Also writes as Lee Sheldon. American. Born in Lamar, Nebraska, 2 July 1917. Graduated from high school, 1935; attended the University of Nebraska, Lincoln. Served in the United States Army Signal Corps during World War II. Married Pearl M. Sheldon in 1948; two sons. Farmer, 1935–51; mailman, U.S. Postal Service, 1951–77. Teacher and board member, Disciples of Christ Church. President, Western Writers of America, 1970–71, and Nebraska Writers Guild, 1974–76. Since 1977 member of the board, Nebraska Historical Society Foundation, Lincoln. Recipient: High Plains Preservation of History Communion Historian of the Year award, 1981. Address: Box 907, Imperial, Nebraska 69033, U.S.A.

WESTERN PUBLICATIONS

Novels

Prairie Vengeance. New York, Arcadia House, 1954; London, Barker, 1955.
Broken Wheel Ranch. New York, Arcadia House, 1956; London, W.H. Allen, 1958.
His Brother's Guns. New York, Arcadia House, 1958; London, Jenkins, 1959.
Killer's Range. New York, Arcadia House, 1958; London, W.H. Allen, 1959.
Gun Brand. New York, Arcadia House, 1961; London, Jenkins, 1962.
Blood on the Prairie. New York, Arcadia House, 1962; London, Consul, 1965.
A Stranger in Stirrup. New York, Arcadia House, 1962; London, Jenkins, 1963.
The Gun Tamer. New York, Arcadia House, 1963; London, Hale, 1964.
Devil Wire. New York, Arcadia House, 1963; London, Hale, 1965.
The Hostile Land. New York, Arcadia House, 1964; London, Hale, 1965.
Gun in His Hand. New York, Arcadia House, 1964; London, Hale, 1966.
Warpath West. New York, Ace, 1965.
The Fast Gun. New York, Avalon, 1965.
The Brand of a Man. New York, Avalon, 1966.
Trail of the Skulls. New York, Avalon, 1966.
Showdown at Julesburg Station. New York, Avalon, 1967.
Return to Gunpoint. New York, Ace, 1967.
Only the Brave. New York, Avalon, 1967.
Sudden Guns. New York, Avalon, 1968.
Trouble at the Flying H. New York, Avalon, 1969.
Stage to Lonesome Butte. New York, Avalon, 1969.
Showdown at Sunrise. New York, Avalon, 1971.
The Buffalo Hunters. New York, Avalon, 1972; London, Hale, 1974.
Suicide Trail. New York, Lenox Hill Press, 1972; London, Hale, 1974.
Wind over Rimfire. New York, Lenox Hill Press, 1973.
Son of a Gunman. New York, Ace, 1973.
Law of the Prairie. New York, Lenox Hill Press, 1974; London, Remploy, 1975.
Die-Hard. New York, Ace, 1975.
Law of the Lawless. New York, Ace, 1977.
Skirmish at Fort Phil Kearny. New York, Avalon, 1977.
Gun Country. New York, Ace, 1978.
Petticoat Wagon Train. New York, Ace, 1978.
The Violent Man. New York, Ace, 1978.
Ghost of a Gunfighter. New York, Zebra, 1979.
McQuaid's Gun. New York, Avalon, 1980.
Shadow of a Gun. New York, Zebra, 1981.
Guns at Genesis. New York, Nordon, 1981.
Putnam's Ranch War. New York, Avalon, 1982.
Barbed Wire War. New York, Avalon, 1983.
The Violent Trail. New York, Avalon, 1984.
White Butte Guns. New York, Avalon, 1984.
War at Nugget Creek. New York, Avalon, 1985.
Massacre Creek. New York, Avalon, 1985.
The Waiting Gun. New York, Avalon, 1986.
Hawks of Autumn. New York, Avalon, 1986.
The Empty Land. New York, Doubleday, 1991.

Uncollected Short Stories

"Sail Buggy," in *Trails of Adventure*, edited by E.D. Mygatt. New York, Dodd Mead, 1961.
"Inkspot," in *Search for the Hidden Places*, edited by E.D. Mygatt. New York, McKay, 1963.

OTHER PUBLICATIONS

Novel as Lee Sheldon

Doomed Planet. New York, Avalon, 1967.

Plays

Bachelor Bait. Franklin, Ohio, Eldridge, 1951.
Lightly Turn Toward Love. St. Paul, Minnesota, Schubert, 1952.
Poor Willie. Minneapolis, Denison, 1954.
Deadwood. Minneapolis, Denison, 1955.
Hold the Phone. Minneapolis, Denison, 1955.
Big News. Minneapolis, Denison, 1957.
For Evans Sake. Minneapolis, Denison, 1957.

Other

Slugging Backstop (for children). New York, Dodd Mead, 1957.
Bat Masterson (for children). Racine, Wisconsin, Whitman, 1960.
Thunder in the Backfield (for children). New York, Watts, 1962.
Mystery at Scorpion Creek (for children). New York, Abingdon Press, 1966.
Scotty Philip: The Man Who Saved the Buffalo. Caldwell, Idaho, Caxton Press, 1975.
Trails of the Smoky Hill. Caldwell, Idaho, Caxton Press, 1980.
Wild Towns of Nebraska. Caldwell, Idaho, Caxton Press, 1988.

*

Manuscript Collection: University of Wyoming Library, Laramie.

Wayne C. Lee comments:

The bulk of my writing is intended for entertainment reading only, though many of my books do have a historical background. My plays are comedies or farces. Many of my short stories were written for religious magazines. My non-fiction books are intended for the history buff and the researcher.

* * *

For those who like fast-action novels, Wayne C. Lee has written over 60 of them. Formula Westerns, Lee's stories satisfy those who like gunplay, spunky heroines, vile villains, and staunch heroes. Lee's West is that of the romanticized 1800's: six-shooters, rifles, horses, wagon trains, cattle rustling, well poisoning, fist fights in saloons, mean hombres ready for a show-down in a ghost town, occasional rapine, and plenty of robbery and murder. The hero wins, often by solving a little mystery, sometimes with the help of a clever girl, whom he eventually marries.

Although Lee has lived in western Nebraska all his life and has an active interest in the area, his geography of the locale is peculiarly unidentifiable. He names places and occasionally alludes to historical events, but the reader has little feeling that they are based on actuality. The names of Julesburg, Fort Kearny, St. Joseph, Wood River, or Ash Hollow might just as well have been invented in most cases. Nor, in most instances, does he recreate a specific moment in history. *Suicide Trail* must take place early in the 1850's, since Tom Brent is taking a herd of horses via the Oregon Trail to California, to be used for stage coach service, greatly increased by the gold rush. *The Violent Man* deals with the return of Dane Banning to the ranch after the Civil War, but descriptions of land, weather, sky, or other details of nature or historically accurate scenes do not appear.

Lee's forte is action—old fashioned but still popular. His heroes are usually uncomplicated, the plot moves quickly and easily, there is a touch of romance—two women vie for one man or vice versa—and plenty of physical activity. Obviously this writing fulfills a place in popular fiction, sometime appealing, as John Cawelti points out in *The Six-Gun Mystique*, to wishes for violence and action that the reader's conscious mind may not be prepared to admit.

Lee's short stories, on the other hand, seem to depend more heavily on development of human relationship to the land.

—Helen Stauffer

LEHMAN, Paul Evan. Also wrote as Paul Evan.

WESTERN PUBLICATIONS

Novels

Idaho. New York, Macaulay, 1933; as *Cowboy Idaho*, London, Ward Lock, 1933.
Blood of the West. New York, Macaulay, and London, Ward Lock, 1934.
Son of a Cowthief. New York, Macaulay, and London, Ward Lock, 1935.
The Cougar of Canyon Caballo. New York, Green Circle, and London, Ward Lock, 1936.
Texas Men. New York, Curl, 1936; London, Ward Lock, 1937.
Valley of the Hunted Men. New York, Green Circle, 1937; London, Ward Lock, 1938.
Wolves of the Chaparral. New York, Green Circle, and London, Ward Lock, 1938.
Calamity Range. New York, Macaulay, and London, Ward Lock, 1939.
Vultures of Paradise Valley. London, Ward Lock, 1940; New York, Graphic, 1951.
Brand of the Outlaw. New York, Hillman, 1942.
Trail of the Outlaw. New York, Arcadia House, 1942; London, Ward Lock, 1943.
Cow Kingdom. London, Ward Lock, 1943; New York, Curl, 1945; as *Cowhand Justice*, New York, Belmont, 1968; as *Blood on the Range*, South Yarmonth, Massachusetts, Curley, 1989.
West of the Wolverine. London, Ward Lock, 1945; New York, Curl, 1946.
Only the Brave. New York, Curl, and London, Long, 1947.
The Cold Trail. Kingston, New York, Quinn, 1949; London, Kelly, 1951.
The Devil's Doorstep. New York, Dutton, and London, Streamline, 1949; as *Helltown*, Bath, Chivers, 1988.
Montana Man. New York, Dutton, 1949; London, Ward Lock, 1951.
Passion in the Dust. New York, Lion, 1949; as *Hot Triggers*, New York, Macfadden, 1968; London, Gold Lion, 1974.
Brother of the Kid. New York, Dutton, 1950; London, Ward Lock, 1951.
The Siren of Silver Valley. Kingston, New York, Quinn, 1950; London, Kelly, 1951.
Vengeance Valley. Kingston, New York, Quinn, 1950; London, Kelly, 1951.
The Man from the Badlands. New York, Dutton, 1951.
Range Justice. Toronto, Harlequin, 1951; London, W.H. Allen, 1953.
Law of the .45. Toronto, Harlequin, 1951; London, Hennel Locke, 1953.
Redrock Gold. London, Hennel Locke, 1951; as *Outlaw Loot*, New York, Avon, 1956.
Gun Law. Toronto, Harlequin, 1952.
The Doves of War. New York, Dutton, 1952.
Faces in the Dust. New York, Graphic, and London, Hennel Locke, 1952.
Fightin' Sons of Texas. New York, Dutton, 1953.
Pistols on the Pecos. New York, Avon, 1953; London, Gold Lion, 1972.
By Means of a Gun. London, Kelly, 1953.
Stagecoach to Hellfire Pass. New York, Eton, 1953.
Vultures on Horseback. New York, Ace, 1953.
Bullets Don't Bluff. New York, Ace, 1954.
Texas Vengeance. London, Hennel Locke, 1954; New York, Berkley, 1957.
Fighting Buckaroo. Toronto, Harlequin, 1954.
Trojans from Texas. Kingswood, Surrey, World's Work, 1955.
The Fighting Texan. New York, Avon, 1955.
Bandit in Black. London, Hennel Locke, 1956; New York, Avon, 1958.
The Gunhand. New York, Pyramid, 1956.
Pistol Law. New York, Berkley, 1956; Leicester, Linford, 1985.
The Vengeance Trail. New York, Avon, 1956.
Rustlers of the Rio Grande. New York, Berkley, 1957; as *Law of the Six-Gun*, New York, Paperback Library, 1962.
Law in the Saddle. Toronto, Harlequin, 1957.
Gun-Whipped. New York, Avon, 1958; London, Gold Lion, 1974.
The Tough Texan. New York, Avon, 1958; London, Gold Lion, 1973.
The Young Texan. New York, Pyramid, 1958.
Renegade Marshal. New York, Avon, 1958.
Thunderbolt Range. New York, Avon, 1958.
Troubled Range. New York, Avalon, 1959; London, Ward Lock, 1960.
Gunsmoke at Buffalo Basin. New York, Avon, 1959.
The Manhunter. New York, Avon, 1959.
Poverty Range. New York, Arcadia House, 1960; London, Ward Lock, 1961.
Colt '60. New York, Hillman, 1961.

Outlaw's Revenge. New York, Pyramid, 1965.
Range War at Keno. New York, Pyramid, 1965.
Hot Triggers. New York, Dorchester, 1979.

Novels as Paul Evan

The Twisted Trail. New York, Avalon, 1952; Kingswood, Surrey, World's Work, 1956.
This Range Is Mine. New York, Avalon, 1953; as *This Is My Range* (as Paul Evan Lehman), London, Boardman, 1953.
Gunsmoke Kingdom. New York, Ace, 1953.
Outlaws of Lost River. New York, Avalon, 1954; as Paul Evan Lehman, London, Gold Lion, 1973.
Call of the West. New York, Avalon, 1955.
Gunsmoke over Sabado. New York, Avalon, 1955; London, Consul, 1962.
Lynch Law. New York, Pyramid, 1956.
Thunder Creek Range. New York, Avalon, 1957; London, Consul, 1962.
West of the Pecos. New York, Avalon, 1957; London, Consul, 1962.
Law of the Gun. New York, Avalon, 1958; London, Consul, 1962.
Action at the Bitterroot. New York, Avalon, 1959.

Uncollected Short Stories

"The Night Rider of Gopher Flats," in *Wild West* (New York), 19 January 1929.
"Hell on Wheels McGorgan," in *West* (New York), 20 August 1930.
"Ox Gunther Kicks Off," in *Argosy* (New York), 23 August 1930.
"Gunsmoke on the Guadalupe," in *West* (New York), 29 April 1931.
"The Man from Montana," in *Western Romances* (New York), September 1931.
"Powder-Smoke Pass," in *All Western* (New York), March 1932.
"Wings of Lead," in *Western Story* (New York), 28 July 1934.
"The Wagon Wheel," in *Western Story* (New York), 1 September 1934.
"Bullets and Bobwire," in *All Western* (New York), April 1935.
"Son of a Cow Thief," in *Western Story* (New York), 11 May–8 June 1935.
"The Ringtail Snorter," in *All Western* (New York), August 1935.
"Bad Man from Texas," in *Western Story* (New York), 30 November 1935.
"Something Big in Arizona," in *Western Story* (New York), 16 January 1937.
"Border Bad Man," in *Western Story* (New York), 17 April 1937.
"Valley of Hunted Men," in *Ranch Romances* (New York), 1 June–3 July 1937.
"West of the Saddlefork," in *Western Story* (New York), 4 September 1937.
"Buckaroo Sheriff," in *Western Story* (New York), 25 June 1938.
"Vultures of Paradise Valley," in *West* (New York), September 1940.
"The Pale Stranger," in *Thrilling Ranch Stories* (London), May 1946.
"Heartbreak Ranch," in *Thrilling Ranch Stories* (London), October 1949.
"Heart of the Range," in *Thrilling Ranch Stories* (London), January 1950.
"Tenderfoot Treasure," in *Thrilling Ranch Stories* (London), February 1952.

* * *

Paul Evan Lehman's early work in the 1930's was typically amateurish and ambitious. Any beginning novelist might have done it. A strong plot thread, which continued a characteristic through his long career, was the Tender Foot's discovery of the West. His good people were more squeaky clean and nice than White Hatters in a B Western movie. His top villains wore a mask of affability and goodness that would have fooled no one save the incredible innocents upon whom they preyed, and the heroes for awhile.

In his middle period, strongly punctuated by the well-researched Billy the Kid yarn, *Pistols on the Pecos*, his work was smooth and slick but lacked substance. Reading it is somewhat like listening to a musician you might suspect of being competent running endless scales and performing similar elementary exercises. Many of the clichés from the early period are still there, but handled with sure-handed artistry. All the ambition seems to have fled.

From the mid-1950's on, Lehman is in concert. The work is still smoothly professional, but much of the freshness which saved his earliest efforts from being totally unsatisfactory seems to have been somehow recaptured. He is still not producing great literature, but he is immensely better than he promised to be. *Bandit in Black* is a mature story of switched identities and hairbreadth escapes. *Poverty Range*, a western mystery, narrowly misses as a mystery, but hits a near perfect note as a Western. *Troubled Range* tells a *Shane*-like story, adding compatible complications expertly culled from Lehman's middle-period works.

—R. Jeff Banks

LEIGHTON, Lee. *See* **OVERHOLSER, Wayne D.**

LEIGHTON, Len. *See* **PATTEN, Lewis B.**

LEINSTER, Murray. *See* **JENKINS, Will F.**

LeMAY, Alan. American. Born in Indianapolis, Indiana, 3 June 1899. Educated at Stetson University, De Land, Florida, 1916 University of Chicago, Ph.B. 1922. Served in the U.S. Army, 1918: 2nd Lieutenant; Illinois National Guard, 1923–24: 1st Lieutenant. Married 1) Esther Skinner in 1922 (divorced 1938), one daughter and one son; 2) Arlene Hoffman in 1939, one daughter and one son. Film producer, 1950–51, and director. *Died 27 April 1964.*

WESTERN PUBLICATIONS

Novels

Painted Ponies. New York, Doran and London, Cassell, 1927.
Old Father of Waters. New York, Doubleday, 1928.
Pelican Coast. New York, Doubleday, 1929.
Bug Eye. New York, Farrar and Rinehart, 1931.
Gunsight Trail. New York, Farrar and Rinehart, and London, Collins, 1931.
Winter Range. New York, Farrar and Rinehart, and London, Collins, 1932.
Cattle Kingdom. New York, Farrar and Rinehart, and London, Collins, 1933.
Thunder in the Dust. New York, Farrar and Rinehart, and London, Collins, 1934.
The Smoky Years. New York, Farrar and Rinehart, and London, Collins, 1935.
Deep Water Island. New York, Farrar and Rinehart, and London, Collins, 1936.
Empire for a Lady. New York, Farrar and Rinehart, 1937; London, Collins, 1938.
Useless Cowboy. New York, Farrar and Rinehart, 1943; London, Collins, 1944.
Hell for Breakfast. New York, Bantam, 1947.
Wild Justice. New York, Bantam, 1948.
The Searchers. New York, Harper, 1954; London, Collins, 1955.
The Unforgiven. New York, Harper, 1957; London, Collins, 1958; as *The Siege at Dancing Bird*, London, Fontana, 1959.
By Dim and Flaring Lamps. New York, Harper, 1962; London, Collins, 1963.

Uncollected Short Stories

"Needin' Help Bad," in *Western Story* (New York), 20 September 1924.
"Mustang Breed," in *Adventure* (New York), 10 March 1925.
"Terlegaphy and the Bronc," in *Adventure* (New York), 30 June 1925.
"Top Horse from Hogjaw," in *Adventure* (New York), 30 July 1925.
"The Legacy Mule," in *Adventure* (New York), 10 October 1925.
"Whack Ear's Pup," in *Adventure* (New York), 30 October 1925.
"The Contest Man," in *Adventure* (New York), 20 November 1925.
"Strange Fellers," in *Adventure's Best Stories 1926*, edited by Arthur S. Hoffman. New York, Doran, 1926.
"Long Bob from 'Rapahoe,'" in *Adventure* (New York), 20 February 1926.
"The Fourth Man," in *Adventure* (New York), 8 April 1926.
"Two Old Men," in *Adventure* (New York), 23 December 1926.
"The Bells of San Juan," in *Adventure* (New York), 15 November 1927.
"Loan of a Gun," in *Collier's* (Springfield, Ohio), 23 February 1929.
"Wolf Hunter," in *Collier's* (Springfield, Ohio), 18 May 1929.
"Young Rush In," in *Collier's* (Springfield, Ohio), 1 June 1929.
"Sentenced to Swing," in *Collier's* (Springfield, Ohio), 7 December 1929.
"Shot in the Dark," in *Collier's* (Springfield, Ohio), 14 December 1929.
"Just a Horse of Mine," in *Collier's* (Springfield, Ohio), 22 February 1930.
"Old Thunder Pumper," in *Collier's* (Springfield, Ohio), 22 March 1930.
"Battle of Gunsmoke Lode," in *Collier's* (Springfield, Ohio), 26 April 1930.
"The Creeping Cloud," in *Complete Story* (New York), 1 May 1930.
"Tombstone's Daughter," in *Collier's* (Springfield, Ohio), 31 May 1930.
"One Charge of Powder," in *Collier's* (Springfield, Ohio), 26 July 1930.
"To Save a Girl," in *Collier's* (Springfield, Ohio), 27 September 1930.
"Kindly Kick Out Bearer," in *Collier's* (Springfield, Ohio), 18 October 1930.
"Horse Laugh," in *Collier's* (Springfield, Ohio), 8 November 1930.
"Braver Thing," in *Collier's* (Springfield, Ohio), 31 January 1931.
"Biscuit Shooter," in *Collier's* (Springfield, Ohio), 6 June 1931.
"Mules," in *Collier's* (Springfield, Ohio), 27 June 1931.
"Horse for Sale," in *Collier's* (Springfield, Ohio), 1 August 1931.
"Saddle Bum," in *Collier's* (Springfield, Ohio), 22 August 1931.
"Delayed Action," in *Collier's* (Springfield, Ohio), 19 September 1931.
"Six-Gun Graduate," in *Collier's* (Springfield, Ohio), 24 October 1931.
"Neat, Quick Case," in *Collier's* (Springfield, Ohio), 7 November 1931.
"Have One on Me," in *Complete Story* (New York), 15 February 1932.
"Eyes of Doom," with L.L. Bryson, in *Collier's* (Springfield, Ohio), 9 April 1932.
"Thanks to a Girl in Love," in *Collier's* (Springfield, Ohio), 16 April 1932.
"Bronc Fighter's Girl," in *Collier's* (Springfield, Ohio), 14 May 1932.
"Girl Is Like a Colt," in *Collier's* (Springfield, Ohio), 18 June 1932.
"The Killer in the Chute," in *Adventure* (New York), 1 July 1932.
"Pardon Me, Lady," in *Collier's* (Springfield, Ohio), 15 October 1932.
"Spanish Crossing," in *Collier's* (Springfield, Ohio), 28 January 1933.
"Nester's Girl," in *Collier's* (Springfield, Ohio), 11 February 1933.
"Cold Trails," in *Collier's* (Springfield, Ohio), 4 March–6 May 1933.
"The Fiddle in the Storm," in *Nash's* (London), November 1933.
"They Sometimes Come Back," in *Collier's* (Springfield, Ohio), 18 November 1933.
"Out of the Whirlpool," in *Collier's* (Springfield, Ohio), 24 February 1934.
"Gun Fight at Burnt Corral," in *Nash's* (London), May 1934.
"After the Hounds," in *Collier's* (Springfield, Ohio), 20 October 1934.
"Revolt of a Cowgirl," in *Collier's* (Springfield, Ohio), 26 June 1937.
"Man with a Future," in *Collier's* (Springfield, Ohio), 3 July 1937.
"Night by a Wagon Train," in *Collier's* (Springfield, Ohio), 7 August 1937.
"Pinto York," in *Collier's* (Springfield, Ohio), 26 February 1938.
"Little Kid," in *Collier's* (Springfield, Ohio), 9 July 1938.

"Sundown Corral," in *Collier's* (Springfield, Ohio), 16 July 1938.
"Impersonation," in *Collier's* (Springfield, Ohio), 20 August 1938.
"Uncertain Wings," in *Collier's* (Springfield, Ohio), 26 November 1938.
"West of Nowhere," in *Collier's* (Springfield, Ohio), 29 July 1939.
"Aces in His Hair," in *Collier's* (Springfield, Ohio), 2 September 1939.
"Feud Fight," in *Collier's* (Springfield, Ohio), 23 March 1940.
"Baldy at the Brink," in *Western Stories*, edited by Gene Autry. New York, Dell, 1947.
"And Him Long Gone," in *Western Triggers*, edited by Arnold Hano. New York, Bantam, 1948.
"Trail Driver's Luck," in *Western Roundup*, edited by Arnold Hano. New York, Bantam, 1948; in *The Cowboys*, edited by Bill Pronzini and Martin H. Greenberg. New York, Fawcett, 1985.
"Fight at Painted Rock," in *Popular Book of Western Stories*, edited by Leo Margulies. New York, Popular Library, 1948.
"The Contest Man," in *Selected Western Stories*, edited by Leo Margulies. New York, Popular Library, 1949.
"Ghost at His Shoulder," in *Dealer's Choice*, edited by Jerry D. Lewis. New York, A.S. Barnes, 1957.
"Under Fire," in *Rawhide and Bob-Wire*, edited by Luke Short. New York, Bantam, 1958.

OTHER PUBLICATIONS

Novel

One of Us Is a Murderer. New York, Doubleday, and London, Jarrolds, 1930.

Plays

Screenplays: *North West Mounted Police*, with Jesse Lasky, Jr., and C. Gardner Sullivan, 1940; *Reap the Wild Wind*, with others, 1941; *The Adventures of Mark Twain*, 1944; *The Story of Dr. Wassell*, with Charles Bennett and Jeanie Macpherson, 1944; *San Antonio*, with W.R. Burnett, 1945; *Cheyenne*, with Thames Williamson and Paul I. Wellman, 1947; *Gunfighters*, 1947; *Tap Roots*, 1948; *The Walking Hills*, with Virginia Roddick, 1949; *Rocky Mountain*, with Winston Miller, 1950; *High Lonesome*, 1950; *The Sundowners*, 1950; *Quebec*, 1951; *I Dream of Jeannie*, 1952; *Blackbeard the Pirate*, with De Vallon Scott, 1952; *Flight Nurse*, 1953; *The Vanishing American*, 1955.

*

Theatrical Activities:
Director: **Film**—*High Lonesome*, 1950.

* * *

Alan LeMay was a writer of formula Westerns who created one excellent book—*The Searchers*—that artistically and literarily soars far beyond anything else he ever published. *The Searchers* is no doubt best-known as the basis for John Ford's motion picture of the same title—certainly one of the great western movies of all time. The novel, however, possesses its own considerable virtues and ought to be better appreciated, more so than it is, for the high level of quality it attains.

Before *The Searchers* about the only spark to emanate from LeMay's works came from a novel called *Useless Cowboy*, a satirical story about a self-styled "useless cowboy" who becomes a swaggering cowboy when he is temporarily mistaken for a notorious outlaw. The book is mildly humorous and entertaining; beyond that, it serves to demonstrate the author's sense of fun and sense of irony—qualities notably absent from his other stories.

The Searchers concerns the quest for a girl who has been captured by Comanches during a raid on settlers in the Texas Panhandle. The central character of the novel is Amos Edwards (whose name is changed, interestingly, to Ethan Edwards in the movie). Edwards is an "Indian hater," a character type common enough on the western frontier. In his hatred Edwards is as relentless and savage as his adversaries, and he plans to kill the captive girl, his niece Debbie, when he finds her because she has been "contaminated" by the Indians. Eventually Debbie is recaptured, and her life is spared—but only after enormous inner conflict within the protagonist. Tautly and economically told, *The Searchers* is a subtle and powerful tale. The psychosexual implications of the characters' behavior are not insisted upon, but are provocative nonetheless. The theme of the work—the disintegrative impact of Indians and their culture upon frontier whites—is still very much relevant, even alarming, in a world in which individual and collective "hearts of darkness" lurk ubiquitously.

Following *The Searchers*, LeMay brought out *The Unforgiven* which was also made into a well-known motion picture. Again set in the Texas Panhandle during the Indian wars of the 19th century, *The Unforgiven* explores essentially the same ideas as those developed in *The Searchers*. Unfortunately, the later novel is much less impressive than its predecessor. LeMay appears to be an example of a not-unusual kind of writer who toils unobtrusively at his craft for years, and is finally rewarded at the close of a long career with one superb book. That is enough; we, as readers, should be grateful.

—William T. Pilkington

LEONARD, Elmore. American. Born in New Orleans, Louisiana, 11 October 1925. Educated at the University of Detroit, 1946–50, Ph.B. in English 1950. Served in the United States Naval Reserve, 1943–46. Married 1) Beverly Claire Cline in 1949 (divorced 1977); 2) Joan Leanne Lancaster in 1979; two daughters and three sons. Copywriter, Campbell Ewald advertising agency, Detroit, 1950–61; writer of industrial and educational films, 1961–63; director, Elmore Leonard Advertising Company, 1963–66. Since 1967 full-time writer. Recipient: Western Writers of America award, 1977; Mystery Writers of America Edgar Allan Poe award, 1984; Michigan Foundation for the Arts award for literature, 1985. Agent: H. N. Swanson, 8523 Sunset Boulevard, Los Angeles, California 90069, U.S.A.

WESTERN PUBLICATIONS

Novels

The Bounty Hunters. Boston, Houghton Mifflin, 1953; London, Hale, 1956.
The Law at Randado. Boston, Houghton Mifflin, 1955; London, Hale, 1957.
Escape from Five Shadows. Boston, Houghton Mifflin, 1956; London, Hale, 1957.

Last Stand at Saber River. New York, Dell, 1959; as *Lawless River*, London, Hale, 1959; as *Stand on the Saber*, London, Corgi, 1960.
Hombre. New York, Ballantine, and London, Hale, 1961.
Valdez Is Coming. London, Hale, 1969; New York, Fawcett, 1970.
Forty Lashes Less One. New York, Bantam, 1972.
Gunsights. New York, Bantam, 1979.

Uncollected Short Stories

"Trail of the Apache," in *Argosy* (New York), December 1951.
"Red Hell Hits Canyon Diablo," in *Ten Story Western*, 1952.
"Apache Medicine," in *Dime Western*, May 1952.
"You Never See Apaches," in *Dime Western*, September 1952.
"Cavalry Boots," in *Zane Grey's Western* (New York), December 1952.
"Long Night," in *Zane Grey's Western 18* (London).
"The Rustlers," in *Zane Grey's Western 29* (London), 1953.
"Under the Friar's Ledge," in *Dime Western*, January 1953.
"The Last Shot," in *Fifteen Western Tales*, September 1953.
"Trouble at Rindo's Station," in *Argosy* (New York), October 1953.
"Blood Money," in *Western Story* (London), February 1954.
"Saint with a Six-Gun," in *Frontier*, edited by Luke Short. New York, Bantam, 1955.
"No Man's Gun," in *Western Story* (London), May 1956.
"Moment of Vengeance," in *Colt's Law*, edited by Luke Short. New York, Bantam, 1957.
"The Tall T," in *The Tall T and Other Western Adventures*. New York, Avon, 1957.
"Only Good Ones," in *Western Roundup*, edited by Nelson Nye. New York, Macmillan, 1961.
"The Boy Who Smiled," in *The Arbor House Treasury of Great Western Stories*, edited by Bill Pronzini and Martin H. Greenberg. New York, Arbor House, 1982.
"3:10 to Yuma," in *The Reel West*, edited by Bill Pronzini and Martin H. Greenberg. New York, Doubleday, 1984.
"The Nagual," in *The Cowboys*, edited by Bill Pronzini and Martin H. Greenberg. New York, Fawcett, 1985.
"The Captive," in *The Second Reel West*, edited by Bill Pronzini and Martin H. Greenberg. New York, Doubleday, 1985.
"Law of the Hunted Ones," in *Wild Westerns*, edited by Bill Pronzini and Martin H. Greenberg. New York, Walker, 1986.
"The Rancher's Lady," in *The Cattlemen*, edited by Bill Pronzini and Martin H. Greenberg. New York, Fawcett, 1986.
"The Colonel's Lady," in *The Horse Soldiers*, edited by Bill Pronzini and Martin H. Greenberg. New York, Fawcett, 1987.
"Jugged," in *The Gunfighters*, edited by Bill Pronzini and Martin H. Greenberg. New York, Fawcett, 1987.
"The Hard Way," in *Westeryear*, edited by Edward Gorman. New York, Evans, 1988.
"The Tonto Woman," in *The Arizonans*, edited by Bill Pronzini and Martin H. Greenberg. New York, Fawcett, 1989.
"The Big Hunt," in *More Wild Westerns*, edited by Bill Pronzini. New York, Walker, 1989.

Play

Television Play: *High Noon Part II: The Return of Will Kane*, 1980.

OTHER PUBLICATIONS

Novels

The Big Bounce. New York, Fawcett, and London, Hale, 1969.
The Moonshine War. New York, Doubleday, 1969; London, Hale, 1970.
Mr. Majestyk (novelization of screenplay). New York, Dell, 1974.
Fifty-Two Pickup. New York, Delacorte Press, and London, Secker and Warburg, 1974.
Swag. New York, Delacorte Press, 1976; London, Penguin, 1986; as *Ryan's Rules*, New York, Dell, 1976.
The Hunted. New York, Delacorte Press, 1977; London, Secker and Warburg, 1978.
Unknown Man No. 89. New York, Delacorte Press, and London, Secker and Warburg, 1977.
The Switch. New York, Bantam, 1978; London, Secker and Warburg, 1979.
City Primeval. New York, Arbor House, 1980; London, W.H. Allen, 1981.
Gold Coast. New York, Bantam, 1980; London, W.H. Allen, 1982.
Split Images. New York, Arbor House, 1982; London, W.H. Allen, 1984.
Cat Chaser. New York, Arbor House, 1982; London, Viking, 1986.
Stick. New York, Arbor House, 1983; London, Allen Lane, 1984.
La Brava. New York, Arbor House, 1983; London, Viking, 1984.
Glitz. New York, Arbor House, and London, Viking, 1985.
Bandits. New York, Arbor House, and London, Viking, 1987.
Touch. New York, Arbor House, 1987; London, Viking, 1988.
Freaky Deaky. New York, Arbor House, and London, Viking, 1988.
Killshot. New York, Morrow, and London, Viking, 1989.
Get Shorty. New York, Delacorte Press, and London, Viking, 1990.
Notebooks. Northridge, California, Lord John Press, 1990.
Maximum Bob. New York, Delacorte Press, and London, Viking, 1991.

Plays

Screenplays: *The Moonshine War*, 1970; *Joe Kidd*, 1972; *Mr. Majestyk*, 1974; *Stick*, with Joseph C. Stinson, 1985.

*

Manuscript Collection: University of Detroit Library.

Critical Study: *Elmore Leonard* by David Geherin, New York, Ungar/Continuum, 1989.

* * *

Elmore Leonard is not only an accomplished writer of novels, short stories, and screenplays about the Old West; he has carried western themes and attitudes into his non-western writing as well. Such a traditional situation as "the good man pushed too far" has cropped up in his work often, including his modern novel *Fifty-Two Pickup* and his modern screenplay *Mr. Majestyk*. In these, as in a number of Leonard's Westerns, the soft-appearing prey is often in actuality quite leathery and more than willing to exhibit, and put to use, its cunning as well as extend its claws and bare its fangs. This particular posture is best taken in what may be Leonard's finest western novel, *Valdez Is Coming*. Herein, Bob Valdez, a seemingly insignificant lawman, is forced to dig out the hardboiled man buried beneath the flesh and bring him into play against a ruthless land baron. Valdez's transformation is handled slowly and with great skill by Leonard, and one almost finds himself cheering near the end of the novel. (The movie version is a near-perfect adaptation in tone and mood.)

Hombre, Leonard's most famous novel, and the one often thought to be his masterwork (the Western Writers of America named it one of the 25 best Westerns ever written), once again deals with a simple western theme—the loner. But in *Hombre* the loner is not (at least on the surface) a knight righting wrongs. In fact, he is quite willing to let others do as they please—and some please to do some very rough things in the book—as long as it does not bother him. This attitude is mellowed somewhat by the end of the novel, but John Russell, known as Hombre, remains fiercely independent, proud, and unbreakable throughout. The book's only flaw seems to lie in Leonard's attempt at de-dramatizing it toward the end. He allows the narrator to tell us what happens to Hombre before he tells us how it happened. This unfortunately distracts from the book's suspense—which at this point is considerable—and leaves us with a somewhat exasperated feeling. It is a minor, and perhaps the only, flaw in an otherwise masterful book.

This simplicity of theme is the key to Leonard's work, as it was the key to Hemingway's work. It disguises, at least on the surface, a deeper intent on the part of the author and makes for novels that can be read at more than one level. These novels and stories stay with you long after they are read.

Another example of "the good man pushed too far" is evident in *Last Stand at Saber River* where Paul Cable, a former Rebel soldier, returns from the war to find his home teeming with Yankee sympathizers. Once again, we have the fox turning on the hounds in true Leonard fashion. A slightly different novel by Leonard, at least in tone, is his humorous and exciting *Gunsights*. How can one resist a novel that opens: "The gentleman from *Harper's Weekly*, who didn't know mesquite beans from goat shit, looked up from his reference collection of back issues and said, 'I've got it!'"

Before leaving this discussion of Leonard, credit must also be given him for one of the three or four finest western short stories ever written, "3:10 to Yuma," a suspenseful tale of two honorable men at odds. The ending is satisfying and surprising, and, once again, there is more depth to the tale than first meets the eye.

Elmore Leonard is undoubtedly the best stylist working in the western field today, and his work can not be recommended too highly.

—Joe R. Lansdale

Le SUEUR, Meridel. American. Born in Murray, Iowa, 22 February 1900. Educated at Fort Scott High School, Kansas; American Academy of Dramatic Art. Married Yasha Rabonoff in 1927 (died); two daughters. Worked as journalist and labor reporter; actress during 1920's, appearing in "The Last of the Mohicans" and "The Perils of Pauline"; instructor, Writing Courses, University of Minnesota, Minneapolis. Recipient: Works Progress Administration Writing Contest prize; *California Quarterly* annual award. Address: 1653 Victoria South, Saint Paul, Minnesota 55118, U.S.A.

WESTERN PUBLICATIONS

Novel

The Girl. Cambridge, Massachusetts, West End Press, 1978; expanded edition, Minneapolis, West End Press, 1990.

Short Stories

Salute to Spring, and Other Stories. New York, International Publishers, 1940.
Corn Village: A Selection. Sauk City, Wisconsin, Stanton and Lee, 1970; also as *Village Corn: A Selection,* Sauk City, Wisconsin, Stanton and Lee, 1970.
Harvest: Collected Stories. Minneapolis, West End Press, 1977.
Song for My Time: Stories of the Period of Repression. Minneapolis, West End Press, 1977.
I Hear Men Talking, and Other Stories. Minneapolis, West End Press, 1984.
Ripening: Selected Work. New York, Feminist Press, 1990.

Verse

Annunciation. Los Angeles, California, Platen Press, 1935.
Rites of Ancient Ripening. Minneapolis, Vanilla Press, 1975.

Other (for children)

Little Brother of the Wilderness: The Story of Johnny Appleseed. New York, Knopf, 1947.
Nancy Hanks of Wilderness Road: A Story of Abraham Lincoln's Mother. New York, Knopf, 1949.
Sparrow Hawk: The Story of an Indian Boy. New York, Knopf, 1950.
Chanticleer of Wilderness Road: A Story of Davy Crockett. New York, Knopf, 1951.
The River Road: A Story of Abraham Lincoln. New York, Knopf, 1954.
Conquistadores. New York, Franklin Watts, 1973.
The Mound Builders. New York, Franklin Watts, 1974.

OTHER PUBLICATIONS

Other

North Star Country. New York, Duell Sloane and Pearce, 1945.
Crusaders. New York, Blue Heron, 1955.
Women On the Breadlines. Minneapolis, West End Press, 1977.
Worker Writers, with John Crawford. Minneapolis, West End Press, 1978.
Word Is Movement: Journal Notes from Atlanta to Tulsa to Wounded Knee. Tulsa, Oklahoma, Cardinal Press, 1984.

*

Bibliography: by Mary K. Smith, in Le Sueur's *Conquistadores,* New York, Franklin Watts, 1973.

* * *

Meridel Le Sueur's distinctive contribution to western writing lies in the intersection of her three major concerns: her native Midwest, woman's condition, and radical politics. From her short stories of the 1920's, through her reportage and documentary fiction of the 1930's, to her recent experiments in prose poetry, these three themes have remained constant.

Her feminization of the western landscape both borrows from and critiques traditional fictions. One demonstration of her approach is her handling of the Demeter-Persephone myth, which tells of Pluto abducting the corn goddess's daughter to the underworld, and of the drought which consequently afflicts the land. Le Sueur first revisioned the Greek myth in her story "Persephone," which transports the action to the Kansas farmlands of the modern era, focusing on the mysterious young woman whose disabling sadness is reproduced in the dying countryside. What has shattered both this woman's bond with her mother and the tranquil fecundity of the farmlands is an aggressive masculinity represented by a dark man and his bulls, come out of the West. The lesson is of death: "She among us all had known that living was a kind of dying." When the mythic reference reappears in more recent work, such as the poem "Rites of Ancient Ripening," the emphasis has shifted to Demeter, the ancient mother whose perspective is less elegiac in that she sees life repeatedly emerging from death; "I am luminous with age / In my lap I hold the valley." That equation of land and female sexuality echoes throughout Le Sueur's work, in, for example, her short story "The Girl," which tells of a prim schoolmistress on a lonely drive through the Tehachapi mountains of California. When the protagonist reluctantly gives a lift to a farmboy, who becomes threatened not just by his literal sexual advances, but by the symbolic sexual aura of the land through which she is passing: "She saw his wrists, his giant breast, his knees, and behind him the tawny form and heat of the great earth woman, basking yellow and plump in the sun, her cliffs, her joints gleaming yellow rock, her ribs, her sides warm and full."

This representation of the West as sexual agent is even threaded through Le Sueur's proletarian writings of the 1930's, her best-known work. *The Girl* (written in 1939, but not published until 1978, and a different work from her short story of the same title) is quintessentially urban in its orientation. It deals with the fate of a nameless young woman who comes to St. Paul, Minnesota, only to be buffetted by the Depression, abused sexually and emotionally by various men, and ultimately saved by a community of homeless women whose affiliation is explicitly Communist. Crucial to an understanding of the narrator's responses are her origins in the rural Midwest, specifically her traumatic experiences in a farming family cowed by patriarchal violence and repeated economic failure. A similarly harsh, moving exploration of western conditions appears in reportage such as "Cows and Horses Are Hungry," which itemizes the droughts and dust storms of the Depression years and paints a picture of both human and animal suffering: "Starvation stands up in the blazing sun naked at last." Le Sueur can be read as celebrating the western landscape for its formative impact on American culture, but not in any easy or pretty sense.

She also articulates a distinctively feminist revisioning of what she has labelled, in characteristic terms, "the womb of history." In her 1978 afterword to *The Girl*, she wrote: "we as woman contained the real and only seed, and were the granary of the people." This emphasis on memory, particularly as passed down from mother to daughter, and on an organic notion of historiography shapes her narrative of the West most centrally in *North Star Country*. This is an innovative history of the Midwest which weaves together personal memory, folklore, and recorded history in an effort to make visible the human struggles acted out on "this violent, remembering earth." Expanding received histories of the West in another direction is her interest in Native American women, which has been expressed increasingly emphatically in recent times. Both as narrative voices and as actors in history, Natives serve in Le Sueur's work to remind the reader of ancient beliefs and practices central to the culture of the West. Since the early 1980's, Le Sueur has been sewing together the strands of memory, female sexuality, indigenous civilization, and prairie lands into a cycle of highly experimental historical novels, which attempt to escape "from the linear narrative form so highly developed by the male scientific aggressive orientation of the past." The logic of her literary inventions has led her from rewriting the West to reorienting narrative expression itself.

Clearly, then, Le Sueur's construction of the topography and history of the Midwest is vivid, individualistic, and committedly feminist. She can be accused of sentimental politics and, in her emphasis on female sexuality and reproduction, of biological determinism. But she is an undeniably vigorous and important figure within western letters, creating a subtle, original West which is centred both within feminist poetics and within stylistic experimentation of the contemporary era. Hers is a voice demanding to be heard.

—Christine Bold

LEWIS, Alfred Henry. Also wrote as Quin. American. Born in Cleveland, Ohio, 20 January 1857. Educated in Cleveland schools, and studied law: admitted to the Ohio bar, 1876. Married to Alice Ewing. Practiced law in Cleveland: City Prosecuting Attorney by 1880; spent several years as a cowboy in Kansas, Texas, and Arizona during the 1880's; then journalist and newspaperman, Kansas City *Star*; head of bureau, New York *Journal*; head of Washington bureau of Chicago *Times* for 3 years, then joined Hearst organization; editor, *The Verdict*, New York, 1898–1900, and *Human Life*, Boston, 1905–11. *Died 23 December 1914.*

WESTERN PUBLICATIONS

Novels

The Sunset Trail. New York, A.S. Barnes, 1905; London, Brown Langham, 1906.
The Throwback: A Romance of the Southwest. New York, Outing, 1906; London, Cassell, 1907.

Short Stories (series: Wolfville in all books)

Wolfville. New York, Stokes, and London, Lawrence and Bullen, 1897.
Sandburrs. New York, Stokes, 1900.
Wolfville Days. New York, Stokes, and London, Isbister, 1902.
Wolfville Nights. New York, Stokes, 1902; London, Nelson, 1924.
The Black Lion Inn. New York, Russell, 1903.
Wolfville Folks. New York, Appleton, 1908.
Faro Nell and Her Friends: Wolfville Stories. New York, Dillingham, 1913.
Old Wolfville: Chapters from the Fiction of Alfred Henry Lewis, edited by Louis Filler. Yellow Springs, Ohio, Antioch Press, 1968.
Wolfville Yarns (selection), edited by Rolfe Humphries. Kent, Ohio, Kent State University Press, 1968.

OTHER PUBLICATIONS

Novels

The Old Plantation Home: A Story of Southern Life Just After the War (as Quin). Nashville, Gospel Advocate, 1899.
Peggy O'Neal. Philadelphia, Biddle, 1903.
The Boss, and How He Came to Rule New York. New York, A.S. Barnes, 1903.
The President. New York, A.S. Barnes, 1904.
The Story of Paul Jones: An Historical Romance. New York, Dillingham, and London, Unwin, 1906.

Short Stories

Confessions of a Detective. New York, A.S. Barnes, 1906.
The Apaches of New York. New York, Dillingham, 1912.

Other

Richard Croker. New York, Life, 1901.
When Men Grew Tall; or, The Story of Andrew Jackson. New York, Appleton, 1907.
An American Patrician; or, The Story of Aaron Burr. New York, Appleton, 1908.
Nation-Famous New York Murders. New York, Dillingham, 1914.

Editor, *A Compilation of the Messages and Speeches of Theodore Roosevelt 1901–1905.* Washington, D.C., Bureau of National Literature and Art, 1906.

*

Bibliography: in *Bibliography of American Literature 5* by Jacob Blanck, New Haven, Connecticut, Yale University Press, 1969.

Critical Study: *Alfred Henry Lewis*, by Abe C. Ravitz, Boise, Idaho, Boise State University, 1978.

* * *

As a young man Alfred Henry Lewis practiced law; he was City Prosecuting Attorney of Cleveland by the age of 23. At 32 he was speculating in real estate in Kansas City. Then he became a journalist and writer of fiction, eventually moving on from Kansas City back east to Washington and New York. For the next 25 years he lived by his pen, and his writings were fashionable. In the early part of this century, as now, there was a taste for historical romance set during the period of the Civil War, and Lewis produced two novels, *The Old Plantation Home* and *Peggy O'Neal*, that met the demand. It was also the age of the muckraker, and Lewis responded to that challenge with the novel *The Boss, and How He Came to Rule New York* and the short stories *The Apaches of New York*, both exposés of New York gangland, and a novel, *The President*, in which he examines the intrigues and corruption of national politics. Lewis also rose to the occasion of American patriotism with such non-fiction works as *When Men Grew Tall; or, The Story of Andrew Jackson* and *An American Patrician; or, The Story of Aaron Burr*.

This is not to denigrate these books. The romances are discountable, but the exposés and histories are seriously researched and obviously heart-felt. Lewis was contemptuous of the eastern city, of "civilization," of the corruption of the American dream—and his books about the East are imbued with this concern. But though these books are of a piece, as literary efforts they are merely competent, their moment has passed, and it is unlikely that Lewis would be remembered as a writer today on the strength of these novels, histories, and short stories. But between the young Cleveland lawyer and the middle-aged New York journalist there was another Lewis: in the 1880's, in his mid- and late-20's, Lewis gave up his law practice, headed west, and worked for several years as a cowboy in Kansas, Texas, and Arizon—and the experience colored his life thereafter and became the inspiration for the stories about Wolfville for which he is still remembered.

Wolfville is, more or less, Tombstone, Arizona, in the 1880's, the time of Lewis's residence in the West and a time that he came to regard (with other chroniclers) as a kind of Golden Age. Though narrated by a third person—Don Quin—the stories are actually told (within the story) by the "Old Cattleman," an irascible commentator on life's vagaries (his anecdotes and homilies are offered in his own peculiar language, rendered phonetically) who is surely the progenitor of the wizened, philosophical side-kick "old-timer" beloved of later western novelists and screenwriters.

Lewis's western novels are poor performances: *The Sunset Trail* involves an improbable romance about Bat Masterson; *The Throwback* is a story about that familiar figure, the ineffectual eastern dude who learns how to become the scourge of the Panhandle. But in *Wolfville* and its successors Lewis had found his time, his place, his characters. The stories are of life in the town, and that life is an exemplum of what Zane Grey called the "Code of the West"—patriotism, swift justice, courage, fair play, eastern decadence versus western vitality, the veneration of children and old folks, white supremacy, the triumph of the forces of good over those of evil. This is not the Wild West, not the world of covered wagons and first settlements. There are sidewalks in Wolfville, an opera house, several churches, a saloon, and a hotel-restaurant: it is a real town; it has its main street, its downtown. And, as with all such towns, it has its ethos—in Wolfville, an exalted one: it is the town of the Earps, Doc Holliday, and Bat Masterson. There is, as well, a cast of characters: Doc Peets, the "wisest sharp in Arizona"; Cherokee Hall, a card dealer; Jack Moore, leader of the Vigilantes; Old Monte, the Wells Fargo driver; and ladies of both dubious and flawless reputation. If it all sounds a bit like *Gunsmoke*—of course it is, but Wolfville is the source, not the copy.

Lewis regarded his years in the West as the great event of his life—and his feelings may well be responsible for certain characteristics of the Wolfville stories: they are more skillful as literature, more secure, even more passionate, than his other work; some of the stories are not unworthy, as literary exercises, of comparison with Twain or Bret Harte. They evoke and sustain themes—of spirituality, integrity, love of land and of one's fellow men—more successfully than do his novels or his non-fiction. They create atmosphere; they provide detail, often contradictory and sometimes incoherent, that has fascinated readers since their publication. The characters are memorable—so much so that they have recurred, in behavior, even in speech patterns, in the works of later western writers. The stories are the stuff of dreams. For, despite his eastern savvy, Lewis romanticized his great event, made it a personal and, because he wrote it down, a public mythology.

He published seven volumes of Wolfville stories—yet there is no progression one volume to the next. The town, in effect, never grows, the characters never age; it is always the 1880's, a particular time and place in the history of America and the West. That was the appeal of the stories when they were published; it remains their appeal today. The stories may objectify what we have come to call the Code of the West, and they may offer details of time and place which have been a veritable well for later writers, but their greatest interest is that they are themselves nostalgia, the myth of the West. It is a myth that in some particulars—its prejudices, its violence, its reliance on Biblical justice, its valuation of human life—offends the modern sensibility. But is is also the myth of the frontier, of the second chance, of man living in harmony with himself and nature, of the possibility of the just and golden city—a myth that both explains and sustains the most noble aspirations of America. Wolfville endures, unchanging.

—George Walsh

LEWIS, Janet. American. Born in Chicago, Illinois, 17 August 1899. Educated at the Lewis Institute, Chicago, A.A. 1918; University of Chicago, Ph.B. 1920. Married the writer Yvor Winters in 1926 (died 1968); one daughter and one son. Passport Bureau clerk, American Consulate, Paris, 1920; proofreader, *Redbook* magazine, Chicago, 1921; English teacher, Lewis Institute, 1921–22; editor, with Howard Baker and Yvor Winters, *Gyroscope*, Palo Alto, California, 1929–30; Lecturer, Writers Workshop, University of Missouri, Columbia, 1952, and University of Denver, 1956; Visiting Lecturer, then Lecturer in English, Stanford University, California, 1960, 1966, 1969, 1970. Recipient: Friends of American Literature award, 1932; Shelley Memorial award, for poetry, 1948; Guggenheim fellowship, 1950; Los Angeles *Times* Kirsch award, 1985. Address: 143 West Portola Avenue, Los Altos, California 94022, U.S.A.

WESTERN PUBLICATIONS

Novels

The Invasion: A Narrative of Events Concerning the Johnston Family of St. Mary's. New York, Harcourt Brace, 1932.
Against a Darkening Sky. New York, Doubleday, 1943.

Short Stories

Goodbye, Son, and Other Stories. New York, Doubleday, 1946.

Verse

The Indians in the Woods. Bonn, Germany, Monroe Wheeler, 1922; Palo Alto, California, Matrix Press, 1980.
Poems 1924–1944. Denver, Swallow, 1950.
The Ancient Ones. Portola Valley, California, No Dead Lines, 1979.
Poems Old and New 1918–1978. Athens, Ohio University Press-Swallow Press, 1981.

OTHER PUBLICATIONS

Novels

The Wife of Martin Guerre. San Francisco, Colt Press, 1941; London, Rapp and Carroll, 1967.
The Trial of Sören Qvist. New York, Doubleday, 1947; London, Gollancz, 1967.
The Ghost of Monsieur Scarron. New York, Doubleday, and London, Gollancz, 1959.

Plays (opera libretti)

The Wife of Martin Guerre, music by William Bergsma, adaptation of the novel by Lewis (produced New York, 1956). Denver, Swallow, 1958.
The Last of the Mohicans, adaptation of the novel by Cooper, music by Alva Henderson (produced Wilmington, Delaware, 1976).
A Birthday of the Infanta, adaptation of the story by Wilde, music by Malcolm Seagrave (produced Carmel, California, 1977). Los Angeles, Symposium Press, 1979.
Mulberry Street, music by Alva Henderson. Onset, Massachusetts, Dermont, 1981.
The Swans. Santa Barbara, California, Daniel, 1986.

Verse

The Wheel in Midsummer. Lynn, Massachusetts, Lone Gull Press, 1927.
The Earth-Bound 1924–1944. Aurora, New York, Wells College, 1946.
The Hangar at Sunnyvale 1937. San Francisco, Book Club of California, 1947.

Other

The Friendly Adventure of Ollie Ostrich (for children). New York, Doubleday, 1923.
Keiko's Bubble (for children). New York, Doubleday, 1961; Kingswood, Surrey, World's Work, 1963.
The U.S. and Canada, with others. Green Bay, University of Wisconsin Press, 1970.

*

Manuscript Collection: Stanford University Library, California.

Critical Studies: "The Historical Novels of Janet Lewis" by Donald Davie, in *Southern Review* (Baton Rouge, Louisiana), January 1966; *Janet Lewis* by Charles L. Crow, Boise, Idaho, Boise State University, 1980.

* * *

In her 70-year ongoing writing career, Janet Lewis has imaginatively captured the frontier-like landscapes and people of California, the Southwest, and early 20th-century northern Michigan. Among her western writings, two novels, *The Invasion* and *Against a Darkening Sky*, are concerned with familiar themes of American history—the mixing of settlers and Indians on a frontier, and the California version of the American Dream respectively. In her three historical novels with European settings, for which she is better known, Lewis deals with the nature of authority, political and domestic, in which milieu she characterizes a usurper who is more able, more agreeable (but not always more successful) than the rightful ruler he would displace. The usurper as critic of the civilized status quo appears in other guises in her work, especially in the role of a strong woman.

Lewis's collection of poems, *The Indians in the Woods*, began her career, and her most recent book of verse, *The Ancient Ones*, rediscovers the landscape and the Indians of northern Arizona.

In her single collection of short stories, *Good-bye, Son, and Other Stories*, Lewis unites her regions and characters in stories of the Old Northwest, Chicago, and California, the title story being a novella that also combines the major themes of her short fiction—nature, death, and the sympathy and friendship of women.

In all of her fiction and poetry, the reader notes Lewis's transparent style—seeing what is being told without getting too involved with how it is being told. Although Lewis fashioned *The Invasion* as half-documentary and half-fiction, avoiding the usual dramatic masculine epic approach, its essential shape, and her imagining of the inner life of her characters, is fiction. It is a novel of settlement in which white people invade the Ojibway territory in the Sault region of northern Michigan. In the characterization and marriage of real-life John Johnston, the Irish fur trader, and Neengay the Ojibway, Lewis narrates the constantly changing social order from 1791 to 1928, during which time the Ojibway mystic vision gives way to American pragmatism. Neengay, one of Lewis's strong women characters, symbolizing discipline, order, and decency in images of well-run households, understands the historical forces that eventually obliterate her people. *Against a Darkening Sky* captures the landscape and the decline of the western American Dream in California. Mary Perrault sees the decline in the encroaching mechanization of the folkways of her generation. The Perrault family life in an "urban homestead" in edenic California, observed and told through the eyes and thoughts of Mary, wife of Aristide and mother of four, represents a "steady lighthouse" in a storm of local and national violence. The violence occurs, the author intimates, when abstractions such as social justice and responsibility fail to hold the community together.

Lewis's short stories, thematically interconnected though never reprinted, have earned comparison with James Joyce's *Dubliners* and Ernest Hemingway's *In Our Time*. Under the controlling image of "Proserpina," the title story suggesting death as part of the cycle of nature, the stories portray strong women at all stages of their lives; they value friendship and grow psychologically in their facing of life's joys and death. "People Don't Want Us" is probably one of the first stories to treat the circumstances of Japanese-Americans during World War II, while the long "Good-bye, Son" unites Lewis's three regions in the ghostly return of a dead son to his mother's imagination over two decades.

Images of nature as panoramic landscape and home of teeming life abound in Lewis's poetry as in her fiction. Her first published poem in Harriet Munroe's *Poetry* in 1920, titled "Cold Hills," employs a geologic image of a fossil and man's invention of a daguerrotype to portray earth's creation and the continuing but constrained human life on it. In *Poetry*'s 75th anniversary issue in 1987, Lewis published a poem titled "Sunday Morning at the Artist's Home," in which as artist she tries to invent herself in a world where a cat and redwood trees provide images of surviving natural creatures despite man's mechanical domestication of them. If man's activities, portrayed in an "old rusted boiler" among the 100-year-old redwood tree stumps, are those of decay, how can a poet invent a lasting thing? Between these two poems, Lewis collected her poetry in two volumes, *Poems 1924–1944* and *Poems Old and New 1918–1978*, in which readers can observe her direct and original approach to her major poetic preoccupations: birth, perception of good and evil, the battle against passion, change and choice, love and death as well as the American Indian consciousness. This last thematic emphasis is concentrated in her first and most recent books of poems. The two different regions of Indian life—the woods and the desert—evoke images of the trickster as "the variant principle of life" in the first volume and of water (or its absence) as a Navajo "shape-changer" in the latter. As in her fiction, Lewis draws the reader into the inner world of an individual, revealing empathy with others, as in her meditation on the life in harmony "with this spare, stony land" of an ancient mummy in "The Anasazi Woman." In one of her best poems, "Helen Grown Old" in *Poems 1924–1944*, Lewis invents a deeper insight into Helen of Troy's "tempestuous years, by passion bound," calling for a poem that brings "A tale of quiet love." A complete edition of Lewis's poetry could open a wider acceptance of her verse and its complementary relationship to her fiction.

—Charlotte S. McClure

LIGGETT, Hunter. *See* **PAINE, Lauran.**

LINAKER, Mike. Also writes as John Benteen; Frederick H. Christian; Neil Hunter; Matt Jordan; Dan Stewart; Gar Wilson; Richard Wyler. British. Born in Lancashire, 7 February 1940. Educated at English and Army schools, including two and a half years at an Anglo-Chinese school in Malaya, now Malaysia; graduated with Arts Certificate. Married Marlene Ward in 1967; two daughters and three sons. Since 1979 trouble-shooter in Technical Advisory Department, Joseph Mason paint manufacturing company, Derby, Derbyshire. Address: 7 Swanwick Road, Leabrooks, Derbyshire DE55 1LJ, England.

WESTERN PUBLICATIONS

Novels (series: Sundance)

Bounty Killer (Sundance; as John Benteen). New York, Nordon, 1975.
Savage Gun (as Dan Stewart). London, Herbert Jenkins, 1976.
Talman's War (as Dan Stewart). London, Herbert Jenkins, 1976.
Brigham's Way (as Matt Jordan). London, Herbert Jenkins, 1976.
Jacob's Road (as Matt Jordan). London, Herbert Jenkins, 1976.

Novels as Richard Wyler

Savage Journey. New York, Avon, 1967.
Incident at Butler's Station. New York, Avon, 1967.
Travis. London, Hale, 1985.

Novels as Neil Hunter

Brand series:
1. *Gun For Hire*. Oslo, Bladkompaniet As, 1978.
2. *Hardcase*. Oslo, Bladkompaniet As, 1978.
3. *Lobo*. Oslo, Bladkompaniet As, 1978.
4. *Kill*. Oslo, Bladkompaniet As, 1978.
5. *Day of the Gun*. Oslo, Bladkompaniet As, 1978.
6. *Brotherhood of Evil*. Oslo, Bladkompaniet As, 1978.
7. *Legacy of Evil*. Oslo, Bladkompaniet As, 1978.

8. *Devil's Gold.* Oslo, Bladkompaniet As, 1978.
9. *Gunloose.* Oslo, Bladkompaniet As, 1978.

Bodie the Stalker series:

1. *Trackdown.* London, Star, 1979.
2. *Bloody Bounty.* London, Star, 1979.
3. *High Hell.* London, Star, 1979.
4. *Killing Trail.* London, Star, 1979.
5. *Hangtown.* London, Star, 1979.
6. *Day of the Savage.* London, Star, 1979.

Novels as Frederick H. Christian

Angel series:

1. *Hell's Angel.* London, Sphere, and New York, Pinnacle, 1978.
2. *Wild Angel.* London, Sphere, and New York, Pinnacle, 1978.
3. *Angel's Law.* London, Sphere, and New York, Pinnacle, 1978.
4. *Angel's Way.* London, Sphere, and New York, Pinnacle, 1978.
5. *Long Ride to Hell.* London, Sphere, and New York, Pinnacle, 1978.

OTHER PUBLICATIONS

Novels

Scorpion. London, New English Library, 1980.
Touch of Hell. London, New English Library, 1981.
Scorpion—Second Generation. London, New English Library, 1982.

Novels as Gar Wilson

Missile Menace. Toronto, Gold Eagle, 1988.
Amazon Strike. Toronto, Gold Eagle, 1989.
Search and Destroy. Toronto, Gold Eagle, 1989.
Main Offensive. Toronto, Gold Eagle, 1989.
Barracuda Run. Toronto, Gold Eagle, 1990.

*

Mike Linaker comments:

From the moment I decided to write seriously I knew my subject would be the Western. I had cut my teeth on anything and everything western (films, TV, books), so I had my grounding. And I had a genuine feel for the genre, which I have always *tried* to put into my work. I still enjoy the Western—when it's done properly—and some of *my* most fulfilling pieces of writing have been Westerns. The western novel can have many levels, each with its own moments of satisfaction. The single novel; the series. I've done both, and I'm satisfied with the results. Others may disagree, but criticism comes from a separate viewpoint. It cannot take away an author's pride in *his* own creation—because it is his personal work. Of my work, I'm in no doubt that *Brigham's Way* is my favourite single novel, and the Jason Brand series the one I'm most proud of.

* * *

A western fan since childhood, Mike Linaker published his own first frontier novel while still in his mid-20's. *Incident at Butler's Station* is a variation on the "group of people under siege" theme, in this case a cavalryman, a group of outlaws en route to jail and an independent female (who eventually falls in love with the hero), all of them trapped in a Wells Fargo way-station surrounded by hostile Apaches.

Now considered somewhat clichéd the book is nevertheless a competent effort which establishes many of its author's subsequent "trademarks," particularly his use of hard action (Linaker is an advocate of realism in writing, and as a consequence his violence is always explicit, though seldom just for effect), relatively complex plots, and economic but assured characterisation.

Essentially a pursuit story, *Savage Journey* reflects Linaker's penchent for creating heroes who are "ordinary," unremarkable men until pushed too far. The hero in this case is Luke Kennick, a rancher when the book opens but formerly an army officer whose last patrol was ambushed by Comanches some years earlier. When the Indian chief who led the ambush is finally captured, Kennick's old commanding officer requests that he escort the prisoner across country for trial. Three men are pursuing Kennick, however, among them the brother of one of the men who died in the ambush, while the love interest is provided by a young woman Kennick rescues from the desert.

A writer of some considerable skill, Linaker's next book is probably his most disappointing, although it should be stressed that this is no fault of the author's. Although *High Kill* was purchased by Leisure Books in 1975, it has only ever appeared in a severely truncated form as *Bounty Killer.* The result is a somewhat confusing and often incoherent story which can also make for schizophrenic read, with the hero being referred to as "Sam" on one page and "Sundance" on the next. (Incidentally, a less complex, and infinitely preferable, reworking of the story appeared 10 years later as *Travis.*

More indicative of Linaker's ability to handle plot, pace, atmosphere, and accurate, though seldom intrusive, historical detail, are the four hardcover titles he published in the U.K. in 1976. *Talman's War,* in which an established rancher finds himself in conflict with a greedy neighbour primarily over water rights, is, admittedly, a fairly standard tale. *Savage Gun,* however, is far more interesting, and employs another of the author's recurring themes, that of the maverick lawman. This introductory novel for a series which never materialised features a hero named Cord, who goes too far in the name of justice and is sentenced to a term of imprisonment in Yuma Penitentiary. In return for his freedom Cord is asked by the Government to undertake a special mission—to track down and deal with a gang of outlaws who have been kidnapping women. Along the way, Cord also finds himself a typically tough lady-friend.

The "maverick lawman" also turns up in the Jason Brand series which, to date, has only ever appeared in Norway. This is a great pity as the adventures of this former U.S. Marshal-turned-soldier of fortune include some of Linaker's most intriguing and experimental work, particularly *Devil's Gold,* where a trail of Confederate bullion leads Brand to Jamaica, there to lock horns with a fiendish Chinese renegade and join forces with a British secret agent.

The Matt Jordan books quite possibly represent the author's best work. The first, *Brigham's Way,* introduces the three Tyler brothers, who came to the United States from Lancashire in an attempt to improve their lot, and settled in a Colorado boom town called Hope. Brigham Tyler (who tells the story) becomes a cattleman, making an epic drive across virtually impassable mountains. Seth becomes the town marshal and Jacob, the youngest and most restless brother, moves on at the end of the novel to make a life for himself elsewhere. Jacob's adventures are continued in *Jacob's Road,* in which he falls foul of the law, and is only able to clear his name with the help of his brother Seth.

The Tyler books are distinguished by plenty of action and gunplay. The characters and exploits of the three brothers are also handled especially well, which makes it doubly unfortunate that the third and final book in the trilogy, *Seth's Law*, was never published.

Linaker is probably most at home in the series format. Indeed, this is how the bulk of his work, including five Angel Westerns ghost-written for Frederick H. Christian, has appeared. The relatively brief but ultra-violent novels which make up his Bodie the Stalker sequence reinforce his tough and uncompromising picture of the West, but it is a picture painted so vividly here that the line between the graphic and the gratuitous often becomes blurred.

The title character is a bounty hunter. In a deliberate attempt to set him apart from his fictional rivals, Linaker makes it plain that there was no traumatic event in Bodie's life which set him on his violent path, and consequently there is no almost obligatory "origin" story. Bodie is simply what he is. The stories, like the character, also reflect the influence of the "spaghetti" Western. They are fast, violent, intense, and boast a hero only marginally less ruthless than the villain. The West of Linaker's human killing machine is a place of dust, sweat, blood, and revenge, and though death may come suddenly, it is always described at great and detailed length.

Although he is by no means a perfect writer, it is difficult to find fault with Linaker since his shortcomings are so slight. Humour in his Westerns is conspicuous by its absence, although it is used to good effect in the action/adventure novels which have occupied his time since 1988. In all other respects he is a workmanlike entertainer; he has a good sense of pace, a keen ear for dialogue, and he rarely uses his female characters solely for decoration.

—David Whitehead

LINDSEY, David (L). American. Born in Kingsville, Texas, 6 November 1944. Educated at North Texas State University, Denton, B.A. 1969. Married Joyce Grace in 1965; one son and one daughter. Book editor for various regional publishers, 1970–80; founder, Heidelberg Publishers, 1972–76. Address: c/o Doubleday, 666 Fifth Avenue, New York, New York 10103, U.S.A.

WESTERN PUBLICATIONS

Novels (series: Stuart Haydon)

Black Gold, Red Death. New York, Fawcett, 1983.
A Cold Mind. (Haydon). New York, Harper, 1983.
Heat from Another Sun (Haydon). New York, Harper, 1984.
Spiral. (Haydon). New York, Atheneum, 1986.
In the Lake of the Moon (Haydon). New York, Atheneum, 1988.
Mercy. New York, Doubleday, 1990.

* * *

David Lindsey's first novel, a paperback original entitled *Black Gold, Red Death*, is pure formula fiction. Lindsey, who had been an editor and publisher in Austin, Texas, for 15 years when the novel came out, says he read a great many adventure-crime novels until he figured out the formula. Then he took his main character, set him in motion, and kept him running until the end of the novel. Martin Gallagher, a San Antonio newspaperman, has a sister who is deeply involved in Mexican politics and who persuades him to deliver a message to a revolutionary organization in Mexico called El Gato—the cat. The rest of the novel has Gallagher eluding the CIA and the Mexican Federales as he carries the message across Texas and deep into Mexico where the story ends in fiery violence.

Lindsey's second novel, *A Cold Mind*, a hardback that Harper and Row launched with a great deal of fanfare, bore little resemblance to Lindsey's short, formulaic first novel. Elegant in style and much more highly developed than *Black Gold, Red Death, A Cold Mind* was chosen by the Literary Guild, was optioned for a TV movie, and received excellent reviews in a number of major newspapers. Set in Houston, the novel is about a policeman's search for a rich Brazilian medical student who is infecting prostitutes with a deadly rabies virus. The central character is Stuart Haydon, a homicide detective, whose attempts first to find and then to punish Rafael Guimaraes become very personal. Haydon is rich, drives a Jaguar, lives in a posh section of town, and is married to a fashionable interior designer. Subject to bouts of extreme depression that cause him to disappear periodically for orgies of drunkenness and dissolution, Haydon is, nevertheless, Houston's finest detective and the only person on the force who can track down and destroy the deranged killer. *A Cold Mind* tells an excellent but unpleasant story about life in one of America's largest cities. Lindsey is especially good at capturing the nightmarish quality of Houston—with its oppressive climate, its pollution, and its cosmopolitan criminal element.

Heat from Another Sun has Stuart Haydon tracking down Josef Roeg, a rich executive who lives in a world of vicarious violence. Roeg has special temperature-controlled vaults to store films of torture, pain, violence, and murder. When his library of masochism, sadism, war, and pillage is not enough, he stages live performances that end in death. The bloody scenes are graphically described, lending a decadent air to the whole novel. Strong points are the descriptions of hot, fetid Houston, the sickness of Roeg and his coterie, and well-described lifestyle of Haydon and his wife Nina.

Lindsey's third novel featuring Stuart Haydon is *Spiral*, an excellent work about a war that expatriate Mexicans are waging on the streets of Houston. The novel takes place just after a change of administrations in Mexico. A number of ranking officials of the Lopez Portillo government have gathered up their stolen loot and fled Mexico for the United States. They are pursued by death squads, who want them killed and the money returned to the people of Mexico. Haydon's job is to stop the violence on the streets and bring the killers of Ed Mooney—his partner who got killed in a Mexican crossfire—to justice. *Spiral* is the best Lindsey novel so far. Its plot is fast-moving and tight, and Lindsey's considerable knowledge of Mexican politics makes the events seem real and immediate.

In the Lake of the Moon takes Stuart Haydon to Mexico to delve into his father's past. The story begins when Haydon starts getting yellowed photographs of his late father and a beautiful woman—photographs made when Webster Haydon was working for an oil company in Mexico in the 1920's. The final photo in the series shows Stuart Haydon with a drawing of a bullet going into his brain. Haydon goes to Mexico to find Amaranta, the femme fatale who had an affair with his father years before. He knows he is being lured to Mexico City by someone who plans his death, but he doesn't know that Saturnino Sarmiento, a professor of anthropology at the National University, is his deadly adversary. Sarmiento worships strange gods and plans revenge against the son of the man he presumed to be his father. The novel is filled with the violence that we have come to expect from Lindsey, as well as the acute descriptions of place that many readers have admired.

In *Mercy*, Lindsey drops Stuart Haydon, but keeps the Houston police scene and the depravity of his earlier novels. The main character of Lindsey's sixth novel is Carmen Palma, a rising star in the homicide division of Houston's police department. The case she is investigating involves gay and bisexual women from Houston's upper crust who are being murdered and mutilated by a serial killer. Carmen Palma is aided on the case by FBI agent Sander Grant, an expert at "criminal personality profiling." His job is to help Carmen "crawl inside the guy's mind." The novel once again takes the reader on a tour through the castes and crannies of Houston, from high-class homes of professionals to torture parlors for the degenerate. Carmen Palma is an interesting character, who is working her way up from the minority community to the mainstream of Houston life. A more believable character than Stuart Haydon, Palma may replace Haydon as Lindsey's main character. She is interesting, reflective, and full of life, and the reader tends to take a greater interest in her personal life than in Haydon's rather hothouse existence.

Lindsey has said that he wants to take detective fiction "to the limits" and make of it literature. His style is sophisticated and his characters are well developed. The only aspect of his work that is frequently criticized is his propensity to take the reader into the depths of human depravity in a graphic—and some say gratuitous—way. But nobody fails to marvel at his handling of place and atmosphere and his ability to bring his world to life.

—James W. Lee

LINFORD, Dee. American. Worked for several years for Wyoming State Fish and Game Department; editor of Department's monthly publication *Wyoming Wildlife*. *Died 20 August 1971.*

WESTERN PUBLICATIONS

Novel

Man Without a Star. New York, Morrow, 1952.

OTHER PUBLICATIONS

Other

Wyoming: A Guide to Its History, Highways and People, with Agnes Wright. New York, Oxford University Press, 1941.
Wyoming Stream Names. Cheyenne, Wyoming Game and Fish Department, 1944.
The Pecos River Commission of New Mexico and Texas: A Report of a Decade of Progress, 1950–1960, with Robert T. Lingle. Carlsbad, New Mexico, Pecos River Commission, 1961.

* * *

Dee Linford is known principally for his novel *Man Without a Star*, a relatively successful attempt at writing a serious (i.e., not popular or formulaic) Western. This novel tells the story of Jeff Jimson from age 17 to 22 as he grows uncertainly into manhood in the range country of territorial Wyoming.

The book is so titled because Jeff does not have a star to guide him, a star to which he can hitch his wagon. The novel is serious fiction because it explores the problem of developing a moral sense in a predominantly indifferent world. Jeff is without a guiding star, and, for most of the book, without a friend.

In the first part of the novel he repeatedly gets into trouble with the law and with his employer for not reporting wrong-doing that he sees, and makes matters worse when his temper flares and his fists fly. He loves the rancher's daughter and he aspires to be a "bullionaire," but finds himself in jail for murder and horse thievery, neither of which he committed. Convinced that the two horse thieves have blabbed, he tells all he knows. As part of the deal offered him, he gets out of jail and goes back to work for the big rancher, to learn later, ironically, that the thieves hadn't talked, and his testimony has helped send them to the territorial prison in Laramie.

The narrative is slow getting under way, but it becomes absorbing as Jeff struggles to determine which side of the law to live on, and whether to side with the big ranchers or the small homesteaders. The novel is more ambitious than the popular western model because it does not portray good and bad as easily defined or identified—there are no easy standards of right and wrong, and no easy guidance to a friendless youth in a rough world.

In part two, Jeff goes back to work for the company, rising from horse wrangler to outrider (a kind of spy informant) to deputy sheriff back in town. Despite the tentative reward of the boss's daughter's hand, he refuses to perjure himself to disenfranchise a nester. By the end of part two, he is on his own again, without the deputy's badge or a guiding star, mistrusted and despised by the system and by the homesteaders who try to buck it.

In part three the plot weakens somewhat into sensationalism, with Jeff giving courtroom speeches, stalking his would-be assassin by moonlight, and offering sanctuary to the defeated rancher and his still winsome daughter. Jeff wrestles with his conscience until the very end, but he will get the ranch and the gal, an ending that is perhaps too reassuring a resolution for the troubles the young man has caused and been caused.

Despite some problems in pacing and plot resolution, Linford's novel is an original, serious Western. It rejects the popular formula and follows its own trail, providing the reader with well-sustained moral dilemmas as well as plenty of close-up detail on life and work in the cattle country. Some of the passages on working cattle and horses are captivating to read, in and for themselves, without digressing from the narrative. Linford makes the reader believe in the world of his novel, and without the literary flourishes of better-known authors.

There have been dozens, perhaps hundreds, of novels written about the range wars in Wyoming. *Man Without a Star* is one of the better ones, not quite in a class with Robert Roripaugh's *Honor Thy Father* or Frederick Manfred's *Riders of Judgment*, but edging up pretty close.

—John D. Nesbitt

LOCKE, Charles O(tis). American. Born c. 1896. Worked as a newspaper reporter in Toledo, Ohio, and New York City during 1920's, and as lyricist and radio script writer in 1930's. Novelist during 1950's. *Died in 1977.*

WESTERN PUBLICATIONS

Novels

The Hell-Bent Kid. New York, Norton, 1957; as *Road to Socorro*, London, Hutchinson, 1958.
Amelia Rankin. New York, Norton, 1959; London, Hutchinson, 1960.
The Taste of Infamy: The Adventures of John Killane. New York, Norton, 1960; London, Hutchinson, 1961.

OTHER PUBLICATIONS

Novels

A Shadow of Our Own. New York, Scribner, 1951.
The Last Princess: A Novel of the Incas. New York, Norton, 1954.

* * *

Charles O. Locke wrote only three Westerns, but his reputation rests on his first western novel, *The Hell-Bent Kid* or *Road to Socorro*. This is a departure form the normal formulaic western story, and is told in diary form.

The Hell-Bent Kid follows the career of Tot Lohman, a youngster placed in the probationary care of a rancher after killing Shorty Boyd. The Boyd family are the local bullies and vow to avenge their kin. This creates a tension on the ranch until Lohman, the Kid, decides it is time to see his father in the New Mexico town of Socorro. He knows that whenever he makes his break form the safety of the ranch the Boyds will be out to kill him. Nevertheless, he begins his journey, and narrowly escapes an ambush on the Staked Plains. The Boyds, fearful of the Kid's ability with a rifle, leave him without horse or water after he has held them at bay.

Fortunately for the Kid, he is befriended by Amos and Nita Bradley, a father and daughter who are on their way home. Nita becomes infatuated with Lohman, and her father encourages the friendship. Seeing the loneliness of the Kid, and realizing the impending danger from the Boyds, Amos does all he can to save him.

It appears that all of Southwest Texas knows of the feud between the Boyds and Lohman, and the former call in the services of an experienced tracker named Carmody. Lohman manages to elude the man, and even wounds him at one point, but he appears to have run out of luck when he is trapped in the cabin of a wolfer and his wife. Curiously, it is the wife who proves the more tenacious ally, and saves Lohman.

The novel reaches a crucial point when Lohman reaches Socorro, only to find that his father is dead, killed by unknown assailants. He is more pleasantly surprised to meet his only remaining brother, and agrees to rendezvous with him once he has settled with the Boyds. Hunter Boyd is ready to face Lohman in Santa Rosa, and the former's journey takes him into contact with Amos and Nita, this time at their home. Their feelings towards each other rekindled, the Kid and Nita plan for the future, but Amos knows that this is an act on Lohman's part.

The Kid leaves the Bradley household early one morning, and is trapped on a mountain face by Hunter Boyd and a whole army of onlookers. The Kid's skill with the rifle keeps his enemies at bay, but he knows that his time is running out. Amos arrives at the scene (one which I find very similar to that in Elmore Leonard's *Valdez Is Coming*) only in time to see Lohman step from behind the protective cover of a boulder to be killed. He remembers Lohman's last words, and is convinced that the youngster has allowed himself to be killed: ". . . can't any people in the world understand that killing a man sickens a man?"

The novel shows such a vivid picture of personal conflict that the images stay with the reader long after the book ends. One senses that the Kid will inevitably meet a violent end, both from the title and from the innate nature of his character. Locke's deliberately understated prose is extremely effective in underlining the Kid's own straightforward outlook on life.

Unfortunately, Locke was unable to surpass or even equal *The Hell-Bent Kid* in his second Western, *Amelia Rankin*. Although his treatment of the subject matter is original, it doesn't have the impact of his previous novel. As one review put it: ". . . it's a long, long gunshot below his best work . . ." *Amelia Rankin* is a more conventional Western, which adheres to formulary material. Locke uses a female in the leading role, and again explores human nature as it is affected by its surroundings. Once more Texas is the setting for the novel, a land for which Amelia Rankin feels an affinity, as did Tot Lohman. A warm, human portrait emerges from this story of the early Southwest, as Locke probes the difficulties of a unrelenting land and the perils of everyday existence.

The emphasis in Locke's novels is on people rather than action, and it is in his portrayal of characters that he truly excels. Although he tends to concentrate on crippled and diseased figures, he counterbalances these by pitting old and young characters against each other. He can whip up sympathy for a character within a paragraph, as when Tot Lohman reflects on the moments after he has killed: "I wanted to throw the rifle away just for a minute. I sat looking at the gun. That gun I knew I could never throw away." Or he can startle the reader by his descriptions of landscape: "the crack was dry as dead skin."

There are no illusions in Locke novel, as his characters know their fate from the outset. All the same, he presents us with strong and believable characters, attempting to overcome emotional and physical handicaps to the best of their ability.

—John L. Wolfe

LOCKHART, Caroline. American. Born in Eagle Point, Illinois, 24 February 1875. Educated at Bethany College, Topeka, Kansas, and Moravian Seminary, Bethlehem, Pennsylvania. Worked as a reporter for Boston *Post*, 1890, and Philadelphia *Bulletin*, 1894–1904. Settled in Cody, Wyoming, 1904; owner and publisher, *Cody Enterprise*, and president of Cody Stampede wild west show; rancher, Dryhead Ranch, Wyoming, 1904–55. *Died 5 July 1962.*

WESTERN PUBLICATIONS

Novels

Me—Smith. Philadelphia, Pennsylvania, and London, Lippincott, 1911.
The Lady Doc. Philadelphia, Pennsylvania, and London, Lippincott, 1912.
The Full of the Moon. Philadelphia, Pennsylvania, and London, Lippincott, 1914.
The Man from the Bitter Roots. Philadelphia, Pennsylvania, and London, Lippincott, 1915.
The Fighting Shepherdess. Boston, Massachusetts, Small Maynard, 1919; London, Hodder and Stoughton, 1925.

Old West—and New. New York, Doubleday, and London, Cassell, 1933.
The Dude Wrangler. London, Allan, 1935.

*

Critical Study: *Caroline Lockhart: Liberated Lady, 1870–1962* by Lucille Patrick Hicks, Cheyenne, Wyoming, Pioneer Printing and Stationery Company, 1984.

* * *

Caroline Lockhart's novels are not widely read today, but they are good examples of entertainment fiction from the early part of the 20th century. For the modern reader, they abound with firsthand observations of the still-open West, and frequent passages of gracefully written humor.

Me—Smith is written in the mode of the contemporary "ranch romance," as practiced by Clarence Mulford, William MacLeod Raine, B.M. Bower, and others. Apparently set in northwest Wyoming, it features the familiar conflict of East vs. West, with many recognizable character types. The novel is graced with vivid scene descriptions, authentic details of ranch life, snappy dialogue, and some literary flourishes that climb to the level of Edith Wharton. Still, this is a melodrama, with the central character as villain and at least a couple of echoes of *Macbeth*. Overall, it is an evenly textured work, with the freshness and originality such as one finds in the fiction of Eugene Manlove Rhodes.

The Lady Doc combines social realism and melodrama, with the title character again in the evil role. This novel, inspired largely by a vendetta Lockhart had against a Cody, Wyoming doctor and her crooked hospital enterprise, is less entertaining than *Me—Smith*, yet it aspires to a serious purpose. And, daring for its day, it depicts a lesbian affair—regrettably, as a way of vilifying the Lady Doc. As in *Me—Smith*, Justice comes inexorably to the depraved, amoral protagonist. Set in a town called Crowheart (the actual town by that name is quite a ways south from Lockhart's adopted home town of Cody), the novel also presents an entertaining satire on small-town developers and frontier boosterism.

The Man from Bitter Roots continues the satire against flash-in-the-pan developers and opportunists, this time in the mining country, apparently in Idaho. The comedy and satire of life in a frontier town remind one of Emerson Hough's *Heart's Desire*, in this novel as in *The Lady Doc*. In Lockhart's novels, villains and scoundrels are respectable members of society, driven by greed and cupidity. In *The Man form the Bitter Roots* the plot is again melodrama, pitting a greedy capitalist against a young enterprising miner, the title character. As always, Lockhart writes from firsthand observation of the mining business, which becomes interesting in her authentic treatment.

In *The Fighting Shepherdess*, the title character is based loosely on Ella Moore (also known as Lucy L. Morrison), the fabled Sheep Queen of Wyoming, whom Lockhart visited in 1917. Again, Lockhart's close-up observation rewards the reader with realistic scenes of sheep-herding and range life. It is to Lockhart's credit that she does not duplicate her subject matter form one novel to the next, but in this novel she does renew her critical portrayal of small-town economic development and petty social stratification. By this novel, the town itself is the antagonist, and Kate Prentice, the shepherdess, fights the town more than she ever fights coyotes or cowpunchers. The town is Prouty, presumably a combination of the names Powell and Cody, neighboring towns in Wyoming, and clearly echoing, ironically, the word "proud." Kate wins her fight in the final scene, and this novel, like *The Lady Doc* and *The Man from Bitter Roots*, ends with the young lovers arm in arm.

With *The Dude Wrangler*, Lockhart eases up on civic criticism to write a bright, sparkling comedy. Much of the novel is set in and around Prouty, but without vindictiveness. Lockhart wrote in her diary that she hoped "to put a grin in every paragraph," and she came close. This is the story of one Wallie Macpherson, a sissy of an eastern lad who lives off his aunt, but who, having been embarrassed in front of a girl from Wyoming, decides to go there and become a man. He tries his hand at homesteading, which occasions some delightful comedy, and then he hits upon the idea of running a dude ranch, at which he succeeds. In addition to seeing contemporary Easterners chasing grasshoppers, the reader is treated to an early-day excursion into Yellowstone Park. By the end of the novel, Wallie has grown into the ways of the country, sold his dude business, become a wool grower, and won the respect (and hand) of the girl from Wyoming.

Lockhart's novels are clearly of their era, but they hold some interest for the modern reader. They depict frontier Wyoming life in a way that cannot be recreated by today's "historical" novelists. They reflect popular literary tastes of the time, yet they speak, occasionally, in the timeless language of sharp literary humor. Of the novels surveyed here, *Me—Smith* and *The Dude Wrangler* are probably the most readable to today's general reader, but all of them would be worthwhile to readers interested in early Wyoming fiction, in women western writers, or in popular literature of the early 20th century.

—John D. Nesbitt

LOGAN, Ford. *See* **NEWTON, D. B.**

LOGAN, Jake. *See* **KNOTT, Will C.**

LOGAN, Matt. *See* **WHITEHEAD, David.**

LOMAX, Bliss. *See* **DRAGO, Harry Sinclair.**

LONDON, Jack (John Griffith London). American. Born in San Francisco, California, 12 January 1876. Educated at a grammar school in Oakland, California; Oakland High School, 1895–96; University of California, Berkeley, 1896–97. Married 1) Bessie Maddern in 1900 (separated 1903; divorced 1905), two daughters; 2) Charmain Kittredge in 1905, one daughter. Worked in a cannery in Oakland, 1889–90; oyster "pirate," then member of the California Fisheries Patrol, 1891–92; sailor on the *Sophia Sutherland*, sailing to Japan and Siberia, 1893;

returned to Oakland, wrote for the local paper, and held various odd jobs, 1893–94; tramped the U.S. and Canada, 1894–96; arrested for vagrancy in Niagara Falls, New York; joined the gold rush to the Klondike, 1897–98, then returned to Oakland and became a full-time writer; visited London, 1902; war correspondent in the Russo-Japanese War for the San Francisco *Examiner*, 1904; moved to a ranch in Sonoma County, California, 1906; attempted to sail round the world on a 45-foot yacht, 1907–09; war correspondent in Mexico, 1914. *Died 22 November 1916.*

WESTERN PUBLICATIONS

Novels

The Cruise of the Dazzler. New York, Century, 1902; London, Hodder and Stoughton, 1906.
A Daughter of the Snows. Philadelphia, Lippincott, 1902; London, Isbister, 1904.
The Call of the Wild. New York, Macmillan, and London, Heinemann, 1903.
White Fang. New York, Macmillan, 1906; London, Methuen, 1907.
Burning Daylight. New York, Macmillan, 1910; London, Heinemann, 1911.

Short Stories

The Son of the Wolf: Tales of the Far North. Boston, Houghton Mifflin, 1900; London, Isbister, 1902; as *An Odyssey of the North*, London, Mills and Boon, 1915.
The God of His Fathers and Other Stories. New York, McClure, 1901; as *The God of His Fathers: Tales of the Klondike*, London, Isbister, 1902.
Children of the Frost. New York, Macmillan, 1902.
The Faith of Men and Other Stories. New York, Macmillan, and London, Heinemann, 1904.
Love of Life and Other Stories. New York, Macmillan, 1907; London, Everett, 1908.
Lost Face. New York, Macmillan, 1910; London, Mills and Boon, 1915.
Smoke Bellew. New York, Century, 1912; London, Mills and Boon, 1913; as *Smoke and Shorty*, Mills and Boon, 1920.
Jack London's Tales of Adventure, edited by Irving Shepard. New York, Hanover House, 1956.
Jack London's Yukon Women. New York, Belmont, 1982.
Young Wolf: The Early Adventure Stories, edited by Howard Lachtman. Santa Barbara, California, Capra Press, 1984.
In a Far Country: Jack London's Western Tales, edited by Dale L. Walker. New York, Jameson, 1986.

OTHER PUBLICATIONS

Novels

The Kempton-Wace Letters (published anonymously), with Anna Strunsky. New York, Macmillan, and London, Isbister, 1903.
The Sea-Wolf. New York, Macmillan, and London, Heinemann, 1904.
The Game. New York, Macmillan, and London, Heinemann, 1905.
Before Adam. New York, Macmillan, 1907; London, Laurie, 1908.
The Iron Heel. New York, Macmillan, and London, Everett, 1908.
Martin Eden. New York, Macmillan, 1909; London, Heinemann, 1910.
Adventure. London, Nelson, and New York, Macmillan, 1911.
The Abysmal Brute. New York, Century, 1913; London, Newnes, 1914.
John Barleycorn. New York, Century, 1913; London, Mills and Boon, 1914.
The Valley of the Moon. New York, Macmillan, and London, Mills and Boon, 1913.
The Mutiny of the Elsinore. New York, Macmillan, 1914; London, Mills and Boon, 1915.
The Scarlet Plague. New York, Macmillan, and London, Mills and Boon, 1915.
The Jacket (*The Star Rover*). London, Mills and Boon, 1915; as *The Star Rover*, New York, Macmillan, 1915.
The Little Lady of the Big House. New York, Macmillan, and London, Mills and Boon, 1916.
Jerry of the Islands. New York, Macmillan, and London, Mills and Boon, 1917.
Michael, Brother of Jerry. New York, Macmillan, 1917; London, Mills and Boon, 1918.
Hearts of Three. London, Mills and Boon, 1918; New York, Macmillan, 1920.
The Assassination Bureau Ltd., completed by Robert L. Fish. New York, McGraw Hill, 1963; London, Deutsch, 1964.

Short Stories

Tales of the Fish Patrol. New York, Macmillan, 1905; London, Heinemann, 1906.
The Apostate. Chicago, Kerr, 1906.
Moon-Face and Other Stories. New York, Macmillan, and London, Heinemann, 1906.
When God Laughs and Other Stories. New York, Macmillan, 1911; London, Mills and Boon, 1912.
South Sea Tales. New York, Macmillan, 1911; London, Mills and Boon, 1912.
The Strength of the Strong (story). Chicago, Kerr, 1911.
The Dream of Debs. Chicago, Kerr, 1912(?).
The House of Pride and Other Tales of Hawaii. New York, Macmillan, 1912; London, Mills and Boon, 1914.
A Son of the Sun. New York, Doubleday, 1912; London, Mills and Boon, 1913; as *The Adventures of Captain Grief*, Cleveland, World, 1954.
The Night Born. . . . New York, Century, 1913; London, Mills and Boon, 1916.
The Strength of the Strong (collection). New York, Macmillan, 1914; London, Mills and Boon, 1917.
The Turtles of Tasman. New York, Macmillan, 1916; London, Mills and Boon, 1917.
The Human Drift. New York, Macmillan, 1917; London, Mills and Boon, 1919.
The Red One. New York, Macmillan, 1918; London, Mills and Boon, 1919.
On the Makaloa Mat. New York, Macmillan, 1919; as *Island Tales*, London, Mills and Boon, 1920.
Dutch Courage and Other Stories. New York, Macmillan, 1922; London, Mills and Boon, 1923.
Short Stories, edited by Maxwell Geismar. New York, Hill and Wang, 1960.
Stories of Hawaii, edited by A. Grove Day. New York, Appleton Century Crofts, 1965.
Great Short Works of Jack London, edited by Earle Labor. New York, Harper, 1965.
Goliah: A Utopian Essay. Berkeley, California, Thorp Springs Press, 1973.

Curious Fragments: Jack London's Tales of Fantasy Fiction, edited by Dale L. Walker. Port Washington, New York, Kennikat Press, 1975.
The Science Fiction of Jack London, edited by Richard Gid Powers. Boston, Gregg Press, 1975.

Plays

The Great Interrogation, with Lee Bascom (produced San Francisco, 1905).
Scorn of Women. New York, Macmillan, 1906; London, Macmillan, 1907.
Theft. New York and London Macmillan, 1910.
The Acorn-Planters: A California Forest Play. . . . New York, Macmillan, and London, Mills and Boon, 1916.
Daughters of the Rich, edited by James E. Sisson. Oakland, California, Holmes, 1971.
Gold, with Herbert Heron, edited by James E. Sisson. Oakland, California, Holmes, 1972.

Other

The People of the Abyss. New York, Macmillan, and London, Isbister, 1903.
The Tramp. New York, Wilshire's Magazine, 1904.
The Scab. Chicago, Kerr, 1904.
Jack London: A Sketch of His Life and Work. London, Macmillan, 1905.
War of the Classes. New York, Macmillan, and London, Heinemann, 1905.
What Life Means to Me. Princeton, New Jersey, Intercollegiate Socialist Society, 1906.
The Road. New York, Macmillan, 1907; London, Mills and Boon, 1914.
Jack London: Who He Is and What He Has Done. New York, Macmillan, 1908(?).
Revolution. Chicago, Kerr, 1909.
Revolution and Other Essays. New York, Macmillan, 1910; London, Mills and Boon, 1920.
The Cruise of the Snark. New York, Macmillan, and London, Mills and Boon, 1911.
Jack London by Himself. New York, Macmillan, and London, Mills and Boon, 1913.
London's Essays of Revolt, edited by Leonard D. Abbott. New York, Vanguard Press, 1926.
Jack London, American Rebel: A Collection of His Social Writings. . ., edited by Philip S. Foner. New York, Citadel Press, 1947.
(*Works*) [Fitzroy Edition], edited by I.O. Evans. London, Arco, and New York, Archer House and Horizon Press, 18 vols., 1962–68.
The Bodley Head Jack London, edited by Arthur Calder-Marshall. London, Bodley Head, 4 vols., 1963–66; as *The Pan Jack London*, London, Pan, 2 vols., 1966–68.
Letters from Jack London, Containing an Unpublished Correspondence Between London and Sinclair Lewis, edited by King Hendricks and Irving Shepard. New York, Odyssey Press, 1965; London, MacGibbon and Kee, 1966.
Jack London Reports: War Correspondence, Sports Articles, and Miscellaneous Writings, edited by King Hendricks and Irving Shepard. New York, Random House, 1970.
Jack London's Articles and Short Stories in the (Oakland) High School Aegis, edited by James E. Sisson. Cedar Springs, Michigan, London Collector, 1971.
No Mentor But Myself: A Collection of Articles, Essays, Reviews, and Letters on Writing and Writers, edited by Dale L. Walker. Port Washington, New York, Kennikat Press, 1979.
Revolution: Stories and Essays, edited by Robert Barltrop. London, Journeyman Press, 1979.
Jack London on the Road: The Tramp Diary and Other Hobo Writings, edited by Richard W. Etulain. Logan, Utah State University Press, 1979.
The Unabridged Jack London, edited by Lawrence E. Nicholls. Philadelphia, Running Press, 1981.
Sporting Blood: Selections from Jack London's Greatest Sports Writing, edited by Howard Lachtman. Novato, California, Presidio Press, 1981.
Novels and Stories and *Novels and Social Writings*, edited by Donald Pizer. New York, Literary Classics of the United States, and London, Cambridge University Press, 2 vols., 1982–84.
Jack London's California: The Golden Poppy and Other Writings, edited by Sal Noto. New York, Beaufort, 1986.
The Letters of Jack London, edited by Earle Labor, Robert C. Leitz III, and I. Milo Shepard. Stanford, California, Stanford University Press, 3 vols., 1988.

*

Bibliography: *Jack London: A Bibliography* by Hensley C. Woodbridge, John London, and George H. Tweney, Georgetown, California, Talisman Press, 1966; supplement by Woodbridge, Milwood, New York, Kraus, 1973; in *Bibliography of American Literature 5* by Jacob Blanck, New Haven, Connecticut, Yale University Press, 1969; *The Fiction of Jack London: A Chronological Bibliography* by Dale L. Walker and James E. Sisson, El Paso, University of Texas, 1972; *Jack London: A Reference Guide* by Joan R. Sherman, Boston, Hall, 1977.

Manuscript Collections: Huntington Library, San Marino, California; Utah State University, Logan.

Critical Studies: *Jack London: A Biography* by Richard O'Connor, Boston, Little Brown, 1964, London, Gollancz, 1965; *Jack London and the Klondike: The Genesis of an American Writer* by Franklin Walker, San Marino, California, Huntington Library Publications, 1966; *The Alien Worlds of Jack London* by Dale L. Walker, Grand Rapids, Michigan, Wolf House, 1973; *Jack London* by Earle Labor, Boston, Twayne, 1974; *Jack London: The Man, The Writer, The Rebel* by Robert Barltrop, London, Pluto Press, 1976; *Jack: A Biography of Jack London* by Andrew Sinclair, New York, Harper, 1977, London, Weidenfeld and Nicolson, 1978; *Jack London: Essays in Criticism* edited by Ray W. Ownbey, Layton, Utah, Peregrine Smith, 1979; *Jack London: An American Myth* by John Perry, Chicago, Nelson Hall, 1981; *Solitary Comrade: Jack London and His Work* by Joan D. Hedrick, Chapel Hill, University of North Carolina Press, 1982; *The Novels of Jack London: A Reappraisal* by Charles N. Watson, Jr., Madison, University of Wisconsin Press, 1983; *Critical Essays on Jack London* edited by Jacqueline Tavernier-Courbin, Boston, Hall, 1983; *Jack London* by Gorman Beauchamp, Mercer Island, Washington, Starmont House, 1984; *Jack London: An American Radical?* by Carolyn Johnston, Westport, Connecticut, Greenwood Press, 1984; *The Tools of My Trade: The Annotated Books in Jack London's Library* by David Mike Hamilton, Seattle, University of Washington Press, 1986; *Jack London* by James Lundquist, New York, Ungar, 1987.

* * *

Although Jack London gained a large following during his lifetime and although he remains one of the most popular American writers throughout the world, his place among major American authors has never been secure. Aficionados of London's writings cite his abilities to depict man-environmental conflicts and also point to his socialistic writings and his literary realism and pathbreaking developments in American literary history. On the other hand, London's detractors note the unevenness of his career, the diminished artistic quality of his later works, and the muddled and sometimes contradictory quality of his ideas. In the last generation, London's supporters have won increasing support for their position, although many critics are reluctant to place London among the highest ranks of the American literary pantheon.

Early in his career London established a reputation as a writer of lively Northland tales. Returning from the Klondike in 1898, he quickly capitalized on his recent experiences and knowledge of the far north in a series of short stories. In such notable tales as "White Silence," Love of Life," and later in "To Build a Fire," London portrayed gripping conflicts between men, animals, and nature in the frozen Northland.

These short stories were finger exercises for London's most significant novel, *The Call of the Wild*, which augmented his growing reputation as a writer of compelling narratives. Set in the frozen reaches of the Klondike, this novel details the story of Buck, a magnificent half St. Bernard, half Scottish shepherd who relinquishes his ties to civilization and succumbs to the "call of the wild." Buck sloughs off his California backgrounds, his attachments to his friend John Thornton, and gives way to the primitive, the primordial that calls him into the woods and away from society. In pitting civilization against wilderness, London was invoking a popular theme in American literature at the beginning of the 20th century. While he would take up the conflict again in *White Fang*, where a dog is "called in" from the Northland wilds to civilization in California, he never again achieved the power characterizing *The Call of the Wild*.

In addition to his interest in wilderness-civilization clashes, London betrayed a strong attachment to class-conflict themes in his earliest writings. Drawing upon his experience as oyster pirate, able-bodied seaman, hobo, and visitor to the slums of London, he produced memorable criticism and fiction about societal struggles in several works. London argued that his tramp trip in 1894 and his imprisonment for one month for vagrancy opened his eyes to the "submerged tenth" of society, and he decided to sell his brains for a living to avoid the social abyss that threatened to swallow so many working men. In the late 1890's he read widely in the writings of Karl Marx and Herbert Spencer, became a socialist, joined the Socialist Labor Party, and eventually ran twice as a socialist for the mayorship of Oakland.

London worked some of his socialist ideas into several essays early in the 20th century. In addition, his experiences in the East End of London in 1902 augmented his misgivings about modern industrial societies, and in *The People of the Abyss* his account of the miseries of the East End, London depicted what happened to work beasts unable to compete with the inexorable forces of an urban-capitalist system coercing them into a pit of despair, degradation, and ruin. While *The People of the Abyss* is far from London's best book—he once listed it as his favorite—it is a notable illustration of his interest in and sympathy for those deep in the chasm of social-economic conflict. *The Road*, a loose collection of essays based on London's hobo experiences and his month in prison for vagrancy, is another testament of his sympathies for underdogs. London claimed his prison days changed his life, although too little of the trauma of his jail experiences or the dangers of his tramping are worked into the essays.

More memorable is London's utopian novel, *The Iron Heel*, ostensibly based on the long-lost manuscript of Avis Everhard, widow of radical leader Ernest Everhard. Ernest had warned Avis and Bishop Morehouse about "The Iron Heel" (a capitalist Oligarchy) and had challenged them to be more humanitarian to laborers. They take up his challenge, though it means the churchman loses his position and Avis is snubbed by her friends. The Oligarchy attacks and destroys the socialists and is searching for the socialist leaders when the manuscript breaks off in mid sentence. Although not a major artistic success, *The Iron Heel* is an important novel of ideas and a revealing document of its times. London calls for the destruction of a capitalistic oligarchy encouraging corrupt and selfish civilization and in its place the building of a society based on brotherhood.

While London illustrated his attraction to socialistic viewpoints in his tramp essays and in *The Iron Heel*, he also seemed intrigued with Nietzscheian ideas of the superman in *The Sea-Wolf* and *Martin Eden*, in which he created notable individualistic heroes who will their ways to momentary success. Wolf Larsen, the protagonist of *The Sea-Wolf* and one of the memorable figures in American literature, dominates the novel; but his gradual physical deterioration and death reflect a perverse individualism destructive of everything it touches. London's Wolf Larsen destroys himself because he is unable to forge any meaningful relationships; his arrogance and selfishness are the reverse of the willingness of Humphrey Van Weyden and Maud Brewster to help one another.

London's criticism of the anti-social tendencies of superman is also evident in *Martin Eden*, perhaps the most autobiographical of his novels. Like his creator, Martin Eden falls in love with a refined upper-class girl and tries to reform his working-class ways to please her and her family. Reading voraciously, attempting to become a writer, and working around the clock, he achieves a good deal, except as a writer, where his first attempts are rejected. Depressed and disillusioned, Martin is ready to give up when the tide suddenly turns and his submissions are accepted and win literary acclaim. He cannot adjust, however, to his sudden success. Taking passage on a ship bound for the South Seas, he commits suicide by climbing through a porthole and dropping into the Pacific Ocean. As Earle Labor points out, Martin "is destroyed ultimately by the delusion that an ideal goal may be attained through material means and that success is synonymous with happiness." In short, Martin discovers that what he has dedicated his life to—success, literary reputation, social acceptance—are hollow achievements.

Many students of London's career argue that his writing suffered artistically in the years after 1910. While it is true that none of his writings after that date are as important as his earliest best work, he did produce significant works in his last years. *John Barleycorn*, an intriguing commentary on alcoholism, also contains a good deal of material about London's life. *The Valley of the Moon* is a revealing novel concerning London's attachment to land and his involvements in scientific farming. Both of these books illustrate London's sometimes careless attitude about form, but in addition they demonstrate his extraordinary talent for suffusing his works with provocative ideas.

If, in the final analysis, London fails to find his place among the best dozen or so American writers, he nonetheless merits praise as an author of remarkable energy, diversity, and innovation. Several of his Northland tales and *The Call of the Wild* are first-rate literary achievements; *The Sea-Wolf*, *Martin Eden*, and *The Iron Heel* are memorable if flawed fictional works; and *The People of the Abyss*, *The Road*, and several of his socialistic essays are still worthy of attention. Altogether,

London is a notable man of ideas, whose many and diverse works are revealing documents of America's vanishing frontier and its early years in the 20th century.

—Richard W. Etulain

LONG, Elliot. Pseudonym for Reginald George Stephen Bennett. British. Born in Burbage, Buxton, Derbyshire, 15 October 1928. Educated at local council schools, left at age 13. Served in the Royal Navy, 1946–47; invalided out due to ill health. Married Pamela Blood in 1954; two daughters and one son. As a child, worked as a drift miner in Dane Valley; apprentice butcher, Co-operative Wholesale Society, Buxton, 1943–46; lorry driver, Thomas Smith, Taddington, Derbyshire, 1947–49; bus driver, Hampshire, and Dorset Transport Company, Bournemouth, and North Western Road Car Company, Buxton, 1949–60; limestone quarryman and cement plant operative, Imperial Chemical Industries, Hindlow and Tunstead, in Buxton area, 1960–88; retired due to ill health, 1988. Address: c/o Robert Hale Ltd., Clerkenwell House, 45-47 Clerkenwell Green, London EC1R 0HT, England.

WESTERN PUBLICATIONS

Novels

The Brothers Gant. London, Hale, 1990.
Savage Land. London, Hale, 1990.
Incident at Ryker's Creek. London, Hale, 1990.
Death on High Mesa. London, Hale, 1991.

*

Elliot Long comments:

These are stories from a man with a lot of snow on his head. They are stories he has decided to write to fill in his declining years with the hope that they entertain those who read them. For, over long years, he has had a great deal of entertainment from similar fiction. Happy reading!

* * *

One of the more talented British western writers to emerge in recent years, Elliot Long has swiftly established himself with a string of frontier stories in which the traditional and modern are neatly combined to form strong, pacy stories filled with action, adventure, romance, and exceptionally strong characterisation.

Although there are few surprises in his first book, *The Brothers Gant*, it is nonetheless a entertaining novel, which introduces a number of recurring trademarks. Basically, as the title implies, it is the story of two brothers, one (Sully) a reluctant outlaw, the other (Chet) an owlhoot to the core. Drawn into the bank-robbing business by their father (who is shot dead by Chet after trying to light out with the proceeds of their most recent crime), the brothers go their separate ways, but when a range war in which Chet hires out his gun to the villainous Tate Carbin threatens to erupt around the very town in which Sully has become a deputy, a final confrontation becomes inevitable.

Long employs another relatively familiar western scenario—that of an outlaw family seeking revenge upon the bounty hunter responsible for killing and claiming the reward on one of their number—in *Savage Land*. Wisely, however, he adds a number of twists and variations (including a bittersweet love affair) in order to breathe new life into the plot, and succeeds in producing another engaging, if light, Western.

Incident at Ryker's Creek, the author's third book, is probably his best, and reveals an enviable ability to dovetail fact with fiction. Having helped to fight off a band of Cheyenne besieging a lone wagon, young Kitt Byatt, who is just coming out of the Black Hills with enough gold-dust to buy some land and start a ranch, finds himself saddled with a woman named Mary Ann Coulton, with whom he eventually falls in love. With the Indians in the area already stirred up by General Custer, Byatt decides to join forces with three trappers and seek refuge in a nearby military outpost called Ryker's Station. The outpost itself, manned only by raw recruits led by an inexperienced Englishman, is under siege, and the remainder of the book recounts the attempts of the trapped whites to overcome their red enemies, culminating in a thought-provoking but ultimately happy ending.

After a startling but effective opening line ("Ryan Tame could see his mother was a running, living torch as she came screaming out of the raging orange flames of the homestead, lurid against the black night") *Death on High Mesa* quickly settles down to become another traditional variation on the vengeance theme. Although they were apparently killed by marauding Indians, the Tame family's land is soon taken over by greedy rancher Merton Pierce, whose own men have been behind the recent "attacks." Pierce has made one mistake in his campaign of terror, in assuming that young Ryan perished alongside the rest of his family during the attack. In fact, Ryan is secretly nursed back to life by an old Hopi Indian, and taught to use a handgun by ageing shootist Macey Fenner. Now badly scarred by the fire that destroyed his parents' home, Ryan decides to get even with Pierce and his men, but this proves to be easier said than done, and before long he is arrested for murder and appears certain to hang for the crime . . .

To the regular reader, Long's trademarks soon become obvious. Each of his books is characterised by a strong, incident-filled plot which has just enough obstacles to ensure that its resolution will be no easy matter, an element of romance and an ultimately up-beat conclusion. His heroes are all young, determined, honorable, and quite handy with firearms. His villains are generally ambitious, greedy land-owners who surround themselves with uncouth, and largely unintelligent, henchmen. To be fair, Long seldom portrays his heroes as anything other than ordinary men struggling against adversity, just as his villains are never really villainous without reason.

Almost without exception, his women have known little but hardship until they meet the hero; Jane Casey's night-watchman father has his throat slit in the first chapter of *The Brothers Gant*; Sally Holmes's father was murdered by the very man bounty hunter Clay Ivers brings in at the start of *Savage Land*; Mary Ann Coulter's father is killed by Cheyenne in the first few pages of *Incident at Ryker's Creek*; and Martha Newsome helps the hero of *Death on High Mesa* primarily because her late husband was swindled out of his land by the villain.

Long's West is a wild but beautiful place, and he is equally at home describing the desert wastes and canyon country of one book as he is showing us the timber-littered dips and swells of Dakota and Wyoming in another. Although there is little humour in his work, his dialogue (filled with "thet" and "git" and so on) is quite good. Sometimes his phraseology is a little awkward ("Ryan stared at Walking Antelope over the saddle of his chestnut mare, that Walking Antelope had brought him into the canyon on from the burnt-out hulk of his father's homestead on High Mesa") but in general the quality of his writing is high. There is no explicit sex in his books, but the effects of violence are often described quite graphically.

Long is, in fact, something of a craftsman, and this is reflected not only in his strengths as a storyteller, but also in the quality of his plots. It is fortunate, then, that although he has expressed a desire to write a novel set in his native Derbyshire, he has no intention of abandoning the western genre for some considerable time to come.

—David Whitehead

LONGLEY, W.B. *See* **RANDISI, Robert J.**

LOOMIS, Noel M(iller). Also wrote as Sam Allison; Frank Miller; Silas Water. American. Born in Wakita, Oklahoma, 3 April 1905. Educated at Clarendon College, 1921; University of Oklahoma, Norman, 1930. Married Dorothy Moore Green in 1945; one son and one daughter. Printer and editor, then newspaperman; freelance writer from 1929; English Instructor, San Diego State College, 1958–69. President and secretary-treasurer, Western Writers of America. Recipient: Western Writers of America Silver Spur award, for novel, 1959, for story, 1960. *Died 7 September 1979.*

WESTERN PUBLICATIONS

Novels

Rim of the Caprock. New York, Macmillan, and London, Collins, 1952; as *Battle for the Caprock*, Collins, 1959.
Tejas Country (as Frank Miller). New York, Avalon, 1953; London, Corgi, 1955.
Trouble on the Crazyman (as Sam Allison). New York, Lion, 1953; London, Hale, 1955; as *Wyoming War*, New York, Lion, 1957.
The Buscadero. New York, Macmillan, 1953; as *Trouble Shooter*, London, Collins, 1953.
West to the Sun. New York, Fawcett, 1955; London, Fawcett, 1957; as *Rifles on the River*, London, Collins, 1957.
The Twilighters. New York, Macmillan, 1955.
North to Texas. New York, Ballantine, 1956; as *Texas Rebel*, London, Corgi, 1956.
Johnny Concho. New York, Fawcett, 1956; London, Fawcett, 1957.
Wild Country. New York, Pyramid, 1956.
Hang the Men High, with Paul Leslie Peil. New York, Fawcett, 1957; London, Fawcett, 1959.
The Maricopa Trail. New York, Fawcett, 1957; London, Fawcett, 1958.
Short Cut to Red River. New York, Macmillan, 1958; as *Connelly's Expedition*, London, Collins, 1959.
The Leaden Cache. London, Collins, 1958; as *Cheyenne War Cry*, New York, Avon, 1959.
Above the Palo Duro. New York, Fawcett, 1959.
A Time for Violence. New York, Macmillan, 1960; London, Collins, 1961.
Have Gun, Will Travel. New York, Dell, 1960.
Bonanza. New York, Popular Library, 1960; London, Jenkins, 1963.
Ferguson's Ferry. New York, Avon, 1962.

Uncollected Short Stories

"Pitchfork Country," in *Exciting Western* (London), February 1952.
"The Coming Home," in *Zane Grey's Western 32* (London), 1953.
"The Man Who Had No Thumbs," in *Gunsmoke* (New York), June 1953.
"A Decent Saddle," in *Zane Grey's Western* (New York), August 1953.
"Bear Bait," in *Texas Rangers* (London), June 1954.
"The St. Louis Salesman," in *Zane Grey Western* (New York), November 1969.
"When the Children Cry for Meat," in *The Texans*, edited by Bill Pronzini and Martin M. Greenberg. New York, Fawcett, 1988.

OTHER PUBLICATIONS

Novels

Murder Goes to Press. New York, Phoenix Press, 1937.
City of Glass. New York, Columbia, 1955.
The Man with Absolute Motion (as Silas Water). London, Rich and Cowan, 1955.

Other

Wells Fargo, Danger Station (for children). Racine, Wisconsin, Whitman, 1958.
The Linecasting Operator-Machinist. Pittsburgh, Stockton, 1958.
The Texan-Santa Fé Pioneers. Norman, University of Oklahoma Press, 1958.
Pedro Vial and the Roads to Santa Fe, with Abraham P. Nasatir. Norman, University of Oklahoma Press, 1967.
Wells Fargo. New York, Clarkson N. Potter, 1968.

Editor, *Holsters and Heroes.* New York, Macmillan, 1954.

* * *

Violence shapes the work of Noel M. Loomis. There is a savage force at work in his novels, evoking the atmosphere of a harsh untamed land. His writing captures the taste and scent of another time, when danger stalked a man with every stride and life hung by a thread. Yet the violence is not all. Against the cruelty of man and nature Loomis sets his heroes, tough, honest men embodying the frontier virtues, strong enough to face the challenge of the land and tame it.

Some of Loomis's early work appears under pseudonyms, such as Sam Allison and Frank Miller, names which served him for the novels *Trouble on the Crazyman* and *Tejas Country*. Nevertheless, his reputation rests—justly—on the handful of novels produced under his own name between 1952 and 1959, when his creative powers were at their peak. Five outstanding works, whose merits indicate their author as the foremost in his field, are *Rim of the Caprock*, *The Twilighters*, *Rifles on the River*, *The Leaden Cache*, and *Connelly's Expedition*. In each of these novels, Loomis selects a precise time and place, and brings then stunningly alive. The "feel" of the period is magnificently caught—in description, in attitudes revealed by the laconic dialogue, most of all in full-blooded action which at times takes the breath away. The sense of barbaric savagery in whites and redskins alike anticipates the Eastwood vogue in the cinema by 10 or 15 years, in works which that cult has never equalled. *The Twilighters*, with its casual stomach-turning violence, is among the most savage books in the genre. It is also a tour de force, a superb picture of wilderness America at the time of the 1802 Louisiana Purchase. And in the honest, hardy Nathan Price it has possibly the finest of Loomis's heroes, a man whose struggle with his conscience renders him more human than most.

Though brutality is part of the world he describes, Loomis does not rely on it for his effects. His plots are authentic and imaginative, often with a strong historical basis. *Rifles on the River* (in the U.S., *West to the Sun*) takes the frontiersman Dan Shankle through Comanche ambushes and imprisonment in Mexico in the 1770's, returning him at last to unmask and kill the gunrunner Meservy prior to the outbreak of the Revolutionary War. Ross Phillips in *Connelly's Expedition* (*Short Cut to Red River* in its American edition) braves attacks by Indians and renegade whites as he leads a trading expedition from Chihuahua to Arkansas. *Rim of the Caprock* shows life among the Comancheros in Texas, while in *The Leaden Cache* (*Cheyenne War Cry* in the U.S.) Stuart Nichols undertakes a dangerous mission to prevent lead and powder from falling into Indian hands. Captured by the Cheyennes, he undergoes horrifying tortures before being rescued. The savagery is present in every book—the scalping and mutilation, the massacres, the vicious frontier fighting with its biting and eye-gouging. Loomis describes this darker side of western life without comment, but at no time is he seen to condone it. Though never "soft" or "liberal" in his sentiments, he shows a refreshing racial tolerance, with Indians and Mexicans often shown in a good, if unromantic, light. Two of his heroes marry Mexican girls, and most of them count them among their friends. The strength of Loomis lies not in his cruelty but in his vigour, and this breathes life equally into villians and men of solid virtues. Usually the latter prevail.

This is true of *The Twilighters*, most violent and convincing of Loomis's works. The plot brings together two related threads, the family of the despotic Mat Foley—run out of Mississippi for the killing of a neighbour's son—and the outlaw bands of Harpe and Mason. Opening with a murder by Harpe and his accomplice Claydon, the plot shifts to the Foleys, and traces the circumstances which lead to the death of the boy, and the family exodus which crosses the path of the outlaws. Nathan Price defies Mat, his father-in-law, and with his wife sets off to begin afresh. He avoids the fate of the others, who are massacred by the Twilighters at a river crossing. A fight to the death between two of the outlaws ends the book. The violence, described in terse prose, is often appalling. Yet at the heart of it, Nathan endures, and it is with him that the reader's sympathies lie. In time, we know, his kind will tame the wilderness.

The work of Loomis is far ahead of its time. No other western writer of the 1950's depicts so honestly the nature of the land and its people, or renders them so alive. Avoiding comment, he concentrates on the atmosphere of time and place. One experiences with him the smell of Indian camps and frontier trading posts, the breathtaking vision of the Caprock, the sudden terror of a surprise attack. Loomis, in his swift character sketches, his striking descriptions, his lithe effective style, brings that world to life before our eyes. In the field he chose, he has yet to be surpassed.

—Jeff Sadler

LOTT, Milton. American. Born in Menan, Idaho, 14 January 1919. Educated at the University of California, Berkeley, A.B. 1940. Served in the United States Navy, 1944–46. Married Vivian Chabier in 1940; four children. Welder in a shipyard, 1940–44; millwright, 1948–54. Recipient: Houghton Mifflin fellowship, 1954; American Academy award, 1955. Address: 1212 Soda Canyon Road, Napa, California 94558, U.S.A.

WESTERN PUBLICATIONS

Novels

The Last Hunt. Boston, Houghton Mifflin, 1954; London, Collins, 1955.
Dance Back the Buffalo. Boston, Houghton Mifflin, 1959.
Backtrack. Boston, Houghton Mifflin, 1965.

* * *

Milton Lott's best-known novel, and the one which won him most literary honours, is *The Last Hunt*. It has been compared to A.B. Guthrie's *The Big Sky* and it is certainly in the same vein: not a formulaic Western, but a serious, authentic novel about the end of one era in the West. It recounts the experiences of four men who live through the final phase of buffalo-hunting, in the early 1880's, reacting differently to the sudden disappearance of the animals after years of easy carnage. Sandy, an experienced buffalo hunter who has always worked alone, joins forces with Charley, a young, hard-hearted killer. They shoot buffalo in thousands and employ Woodfoot, a peg-legged cook, and Jimmy, a half-breed, to skin the carcasses. While the four work they all reminisce silently on their pasts, reviving memories which, again and again concern endings—failures in other enterprises, deaths of relatives and friends, the massacre of Indians. It becomes increasingly clear that the present story, too, is one of ending, as evocative scenes of death accumulate: a newly born buffalo calf struggles after Charley, blood streaming from its throat, which he has just cut; Charley skins an Indian he has killed and then tries, unsuccessfully, to rid himself of the hide. Images like these lead up to the climax, in which Charley kills one of the very few remaining buffalo, then dies, trapped inside its hide, which freezes around him. Not all the endings are as ominous. Woodfoot is killed by Charley, but Sandy and Jimmy manage to adjust to the new West. They both take up work with cattle and, while Sandy settles down with an Indian and her child, Jimmy marries a white girl.

Clearly, Lott does not deal in the easy heroics and programmatic events of the popular Western. Indeed, he openly spurns formulaic imagery: it is a taunt when Charley is called "a real gun-slick from the Wild West," and this West is shown to be no resurrected Eden when a nativity play, made up of a prostitute, a drunkard, and a doll, is violently disrupted by a snake crawling on the the stage.

There have been better novelists of the West, and Lott, to a certain extent, deals in types made recognizable by his predecessors. But, if he lacks unique vision, he does create a sense of chronicle, chanelling series of events through the same geographical area, and he is solidly artistic in his depiction of landscape, atmosphere, and emotion.

—Christine Bold

LUTZ, Giles A(lfred). Also wrote as Zeke Carson; James B. Chaffin; Brad Curtis; Curt Donovan; Wade Everett; Alex Hawk; Hunter Ingram; Sebastian Morales; Reese Sullivan; Gene Thompson. American. Born in Kansas City, Missouri, in 1910. Recipient: Western Writers of America Spur award, 1962. *Died 14 June 1982.*

WESTERN PUBLICATIONS

Novels

Fight or Run. New York, Popular Library, 1954.
The Golden Bawd. New York, Fawcett, 1956; London, Fawcett, 1957.
To Hell—and Texas. New York and London, Fawcett, 1956.
Fury Trail. New York, Fawcett, 1957; London, Fawcett, 1958.
Gun the Man Down. New York, Fawcett, 1957; London, Fawcett, 1959.
Outcast Gun. New York, Fawcett, 1958; London, Fawcett, 1959.
Relentless Gun. New York, Fawcett, 1958; London, Fawcett, 1960.
The Homing Bullet. New York, Fawcett, 1959; London, Fawcett, 1960.
Guns of Abilene (as James B. Chaffin). New York, Popular Library, and London, World Distributors, 1959.
Law of the Trigger. New York, Ace, 1959.
The Challenger. New York, Ace, 1960.
The Honyocker. New York, Doubleday, 1961; as *Range Feud,* London, New English Library, 1963.
The Wild Quarry. New York, Ace, 1961.
The Long Cold Wind. New York, Doubleday, 1962.
Gun Rich. New York, Ace, 1962.
Killer's Trail. New York, Avon, 1963.
Halfway to Hell. New York, Fawcett, 1963; London, Muller, 1964.
The Golden Land. New York, Doubleday, 1963; London, Mayflower, 1965.
The Bleeding Land. New York, Doubleday, 1965; London, New English Library, 1967.
The Hardy Breed. New York, Doubleday, 1966; London, Collins, 1973.
The Magnificent Failure. New York, Doubleday, 1967; London, Gold Lion, 1972.
Wild Runs the River. New York, Doubleday, 1968; London, Gold Lion, 1973.
The Whisky Traders (as Wade Everett). New York, Ballantine, 1968; London, Collins, 1973.
The Wolfer (as James B. Chaffin). New York, Belmont/Tower, 1968.
The Deadly Deputy. New York, Ace, 1969.
Montana Crossing. New York, Lancer, 1970.
The Lonely Ride. New York, Doubleday, 1971; London, Gold Lion, 1973.
The Unbeaten. New York, Doubleday, 1972.
The Outsider. New York, Fawcett, 1973; London, Gold Lion, 1974.
The Black Day. New York, Ace, 1974.
The Grudge. New York, Doubleday, 1974.
The Offenders. New York, Doubleday, 1974.
Blood Feud. New York, Fawcett, 1974.
Stagecoach to Hell. New York, Doubleday, 1975; London, Hale, 1977.
The Stubborn Breed. New York, Doubleday, 1975.
My Brother's Keeper. New York, Ace, 1975.
Man on the Run. New York, Ace, 1976.
Reprisal! New York, Ace, 1976.
The Stranger. New York, Ace, 1976.
A Drifting Man. New York, Manor, 1976.
Night of the Cattlemen. New York, Doubleday, 1976.
The Way Homeward. New York, Doubleday, 1977.
A Time for Vengeance. New York, Ace, 1977.
The Turn Around. New York, Doubleday, 1978; London, Hale, 1980.
The Shoot Out. New York, Doubleday, 1978; as *War on the Range,* London, Hale, 1982.
Lure of the Outlaw Trail. New York, Doubleday, 1979; London, Hale, 1980.
The Echo. New York, Doubleday, 1979; Bath, Chivers, 1986.
The Great Railroad War. New York, Doubleday, 1981; London, Hale, 1982.
Thieves' Brand. New York, Doubleday, 1981; London, Hale, 1983.
The Feud. New York, Doubleday, 1982; London, Hale, 1986.
Smash the Wild Bunch. New York, Walker, 1982.
The Tangled Web. New York, Doubleday, 1983.

Novels as Gene Thompson

Six-Guns Wild. New York, Graphic, 1957.
Range Law. New York, Avalon, 1962.
The Branded One. New York, Berkley, 1964.
Ambush in Abilene. New York, Berkley, 1967.
The Outcast. New York, Berkley, 1968.
Wolf Blood. New York, Berkley, 1971.

Novels as Reese Sullivan

Nemesis of Circle A. New York, Ace, 1965; as Giles A. Lutz, New York, Ace, 1987.
The Blind Trail. New York, Ace, 1965.
The Demanding Land. New York, Ace, 1966.
Deadly Like a .45. New York, Ace, 1966.
The Trouble Borrower. New York, Ace, 1968.
The Vengeance Ghost. New York, Ace, 1968; as Giles A. Lutz, London, Collins, 1977.

Novels as Hunter Ingram

The Trespassers. New York, Ballantine, 1965.
Man Hunt. New York, Ballantine, 1967.
Contested Valley. New York, Ballantine, 1968.
The Long Search. New York, Ballantine, 1969; London, Hale, 1971.
Forked Tongue. New York, Ballantine, 1970.
Border War. New York, Ballantine, 1972.
Fort Apache. New York, Ballantine, 1975.
The Forbidden Land. New York, Ballantine, 1975.

Novels as Alex Hawk

Tough Town. New York, Paperback Library, 1969.
Drifter's Luck. New York, Paperback Library, 1970.

Mexican Standoff. New York, Paperback Library, 1970.
Half Breed. New York, Paperback Library, 1971.

Uncollected Short Stories

"There's Gold in Them Thar Hosses," in *Thrilling Western* (London), Winter 1945.
"Square in the Saddle," in *Western Story* (London), January 1946.
"Vineyards of Vengeance," in *Western Story* (London), December 1947.
"Don't Find Me a Woman," in *Thrilling Ranch Stories* (London), September 1949.
"Silent Guns," in *Mammoth Western* (Chicago), September 1950.
"Pack a Gun or Get Out of Town," in *Western Story* (London), May 1951.
"Guns, Sing My Love Song," in *Thrilling Ranch Stories* (London), August 1951.
"Man's Business," in *Thrilling Western* (London), November 1952.
"Dig the Hole Deep," in *Texas Rangers* (London), April 1953.
"Throw Lead or Die," in *Texas Rangers* (London), May 1953.
"Peace Has Its Price," in *Texas Rangers* (London), January 1954.
"Bullet Ballot," in *Exciting Western* (London), April 1954.
"Fight or Drift," in *Texas Rangers* (London), April 1955.
"No Second Chance," in *Exciting Western* (London), December 1955.
"Traces Cut," in *Exciting Western* (London), April/May 1956.
"Black Kettle," in *Texas Rangers* (London), January 1961.
"Free from Fear," in *Texas Rangers* (London), February 1962.
"Gun Search," in *A Quintet of Sixes*, edited by Donald A. Wollheim. New York, Ace, 1969.
"Westward Rails," in *Western Writers of America Silver Anniversary Anthology*, edited by August Lenniger. New York, Ace, 1977.

OTHER PUBLICATIONS

Novel

Stranger in My Bed. New York, Beacon, 1960.

Novels as Curt Donovan

The Lusting Hours. New York, Beacon, 1961.
Witch with Blue Eyes. New York, Beacon, 1962.
The Wife Game. New York, Beacon, 1963.

Novels as Brad Curtis

Man Trap. New York, Midwood, 1963.
Anatomy of a Mistress. New York, Midwood, 1963.
The Pleasure Game. New York, Midwood, 1963.
For Services Rendered. New York, Midwood, 1964.
Man-Tamer. New York, 1964.
Private Property. New York, Midwood, 1964.
Night Shift. New York, Midwood, 1965.
The Pick-Up. New York, Midwood, 1965.
The Love Goddess. New York, Midwood, 1965.
The Golden Greed. New York, Midwood, 1965.
Live and Let Live. New York, Midwood, 1966.
Too Young, Too Wild. New York, Midwood, n.d.
A Female Female. New York, Midwood, n.d.
Thrill Crazy. New York, Midwood, n.d.

* * *

Giles A. Lutz was for many years a rancher specializing in the breeding of Black Angus cattle. At the same time, he was writing fiction for both pulp and slick magazines. He was the author of over 300 short stories and 60 novelettes, including sports stories and some crime fiction published in *Doc Savage* magazine in the mid-1940s. His novelette "Gun Search," from a 1952 pulp magazine, was reprinted in the 1969 Western Writers of America anthology, *A Quintet of Sixes*.

Outcast Gun is typical of the early Lutz paperbacks. A gunfighter, attempting to break from his past, allies himself with the family of an ex-convict struggling to run a small ranch against the opposition of greedy and arrogant neighbors. These standard ingredients are assembled into a vigorous tale populated with interesting characters.

The first of Lutz's novels to be published in hardcover form was *The Honyocker*. It is the story of Ashel Backus, the youngest son of a hardscrabble homesteading family in Montana in the 1890's. Ashel has to shoulder most of the work and responsibility for keeping his family together, with negligible help from his shiftless father and sly older brothers. When the brothers are caught slaughtering a steer belonging to rancher Milo Vaughan, Ashel indentures himself to Vaughan for a month to pay off the cost of the animal. The other homesteaders, including Ashel's own family, view this as a betrayal, and Ashel finds himself caught in the middle of an escalating conflict. The author focuses firmly on the people involved, treating them with insight and compassion, while not skimping on action and suspense. The book received WWA's Spur award as best western novel of 1961.

Subsequent books maintained the high standard set by *The Honyocker*. *The Long Cold Wind* is also set in Montana. The "wind" of the title is not only the great blizzard of 1886 which climaxes the book, but also the wind of change, as the freewheeling pioneer ways are forced to give ground before the coming of law and the inevitable schemes of men who use the law for their own purposes. *The Golden Land* is a tale of Los Angeles in the mid-19th century, and of the smoldering antagonisms between the old-time Spanish families and the Anglo invaders. *The Bleeding Land* centers around the abolitionist versus pro-slavery battle for control of the Kansas Territory in the 1850's. Each of these books is firmly placed in an authentic historical context, and illuminates its time and place through the medium of a compelling human drama. *The Magnificent Failure* is a historical novel of Louis Riel and the Métis rebellion in Montana and southern Canada in 1885.

In 1965–68 Lutz wrote six paperback Westerns for Ace Books under the byline Reese Sullivan. These are standard action Westerns, smoothly written and fast-paced. The best of the group is *The Trouble Borrower*. Some of the Sullivan books have subsequently been reprinted under Lutz's own name.

Also in 1965 Lutz began using the name Hunter Ingram for a series of novels for Ballantine Books. *The Trespassers* concerns the attempts of Joseph Smith and the Mormons to settle in Missouri after their expulsion from Illinois. *The Long Search* tells of Wiley Anderson's search for the man who had stolen his wife, set against the background of the Mexican War. Col. Aleck Doniphan and his Missouri volunteers play a substantial role, as they do also in *The Trespassers*. *Forked Tongue* is the story of an Army campaign against the Modoc Indians in Oregon, while *Border War* is a tale of Quantrill and Bloody Bill Anderson in post-Civil War Missouri.

Lutz's books have been reprinted frequently in paperback. On the covers of a matched set of ten titles issued by Pocket Books in 1978–79 the publisher could justifiably claim: "Millions of Giles Lutz Westerns in print!" The best of Lutz's books, and those under the Ingram byline, have a solidity and a historical and psychological truth which makes them superior entertainment.

—R.E. Briney

LYNCH, Eric. *See* **BINGLEY, David Ernest.**

LYON, Buck. *See* **PAINE, Lauran.**

M

MacDONALD, (Allan) William Colt. American. Born in Detroit, Michigan, in 1891. Educated at local grammar school, and for three months in high school. Worked as writer and publicist in Detroit area; from 1929 full-time writer; screenplay writer, Columbia and Republic Pictures (including *The Three Mesquiteers* series), 1932–36. *Died.*

WESTERN PUBLICATIONS

Novels (series: Gregory Quist; The Three Mesquiteers)

Restless Guns. New York, Chelsea House, 1929; London, Collins, 1934.
Rustlers' Paradise. New York, Covici Friede, 1932; London, Collins, 1933.
Law of the Forty-Fives. New York, Covici Friede, 1933; London, Collins, 1934; as *Sunrise Guns*, New York, Avon, 1960.
Six-Gun Melody. New York, Covici Friede, and London, Collins, 1933.
The Singing Scorpion. New York, Covici Friede, 1934; London, Collins, 1935; as *Ambush at Scorpion Valley*, New York, Avon, 1943.
Powdersmoke Range. New York, Covici Friede, 1934; London, Collins, 1935.
Riders of the Whistling Skull. New York, Covici Friede, 1934; London, Collins, 1935.
King of Crazy River. London, Collins, 1934; New York, Hillman, 1950(?).
The Man from the Desert. London, Collins, 1934.
Ghost-Town Gold. New York, Covici Friede, 1935; London, Collins, 1936; as *The Town That God Forgot*, New York, Avon, 1959.
Roarin' Lead. New York, Covici Friede, 1935; London, Collins, 1936.
Gun Country. London, Collins, 1935.
The Red Rider of Smoky Range. London, Collins, 1935; New York, Hillman, 1949(?).
Bullets for Buckaroos. New York, Covici Friede, 1936; London, Collins, 1937; as *Bullet Trail*, New York, Avon, 1974.
California Caballero. New York, Covici Friede, and London, Collins, 1936.
Trigger Trail. New York, Covici Friede, 1936.
Spanish Pesos. New York, Covici Friede, and London, Collins, 1937.
Roamin' Holiday. London, Collins, 1937.
Sleepy Horse Range. New York, Covici Friede, and London, Collins, 1938; as *The Fighting Kid from Eldorado*, New York, Avon, 1955.
The Deputy of Carabina. London, Collins, 1938; New York, Hillman, 1949(?).
Punchers of Phantom Pass. London, Collins, 1939.
Six-Shooter Showdown. New York, Doubleday, and London, Collins, 1939.
Renegade Roundup. London, Collins, 1939; New York, Doubleday, 1940.
Black Sombrero. New York, Doubleday, 1940; as *Sombrero*, London, Collins, 1940.
The Phantom Pass. New York, Doubleday, 1940.
The Battle at Three-Cross. New York, Doubleday, and London, Hodder, and Stoughton, 1941.
The Shadow Rider. London, Hodder and Stoughton, 1941; New York, Doubleday, 1942.
Boomtown Buccaneers. New York, Doubleday, 1942.
The Crimson Quirt. New York, Doubleday, 1942; London, Hodder and Stoughton, 1944.
The Riddle of Ramrod Ridge. New York, Doubleday, and London, Hodder and Stoughton, 1942.
Rebel Ranger. New York, Doubleday, 1943; London, Hodder and Stoughton, 1945.
The Vanishing Gun-Slinger. New York, Doubleday, 1943.
Peaceful Jenkins. London, Hodder and Stoughton, 1943.
The Three Mesquiteers. New York, Doubleday, 1944.
Cartridge Carnival. New York, Doubleday, 1945; London, Hodder and Stoughton, 1948.
Thunderbird Trail. New York, Doubleday, 1946.
Wheels in the Dust. New York, Doubleday, 1946.
Bad Man's Return: A Three Mesquiteers Story. New York, Doubleday, 1947; London, Hodder and Stoughton, 1950.
Master of the Mesa. New York, Doubleday, 1947; London, Hodder and Stoughton, 1949.
Dead Man's Gold. New York, Doubleday, 1948; London, Hodder and Stoughton, 1951.
Gunsight Range. New York, Doubleday, 1949; London, Hodder and Stoughton, 1952.
Powdersmoke Justice (Mesquiteers). New York, Doubleday, 1949; London, Hodder and Stoughton, 1951.
The Killer Brand. New York, Doubleday, 1950; London, Hodder and Stoughton, 1953.
Mesquiteer Mavericks. New York, Doubleday, 1950; London, Hodder and Stoughton, 1953.
Stir Up the Dust. London, Hodder and Stoughton, 1950; New York, Avon, 1953.
Blind Cartridges. New York, Doubleday, 1951; London, Hodder and Stoughton, 1954.
Ranger Man. New York, Doubleday, 1951; London, Hodder and Stoughton, 1954.
The Galloping Ghost (Mesquiteers). New York, Doubleday, 1952; London, Hodder and Stoughton, 1955.
Three-Notch Cameron. New York, Doubleday, 1952.
Law and Order, Unlimited (Quist). New York, Doubleday, 1953; London, Hodder and Stoughton, 1955.
Lightning Swift. New York, Doubleday, 1953; London, Hodder and Stoughton, 1956.
Cow Thief. New York, Pyramid, 1953.
Showdown Trail. New York, Pyramid, 1953.
Mascarada Pass (Quist). New York, Doubleday, 1954; London, Hodder and Stoughton, 1957.
Two-Gun Deputy. New York, Pyramid, 1954.
The Comanche Scalp (Quist). Philadelphia, Lippincott, 1955; London, Hodder and Stoughton, 1958.

Destination Danger (Quist). Philadelphia, Lippincott, 1955; London, Hodder and Stoughton, 1957; as *Whiplash*, Leicester, Ulverscroft, 1979.
The Range Kid. New York, Pyramid, 1955; London, Hodder and Stoughton, 1959.
The Devil's Drum (Quist). Philadelphia, Lippincott, 1956; London, Hodder and Stoughton, 1962; as *Hellgate*, New York, Belmont, 1978.
Flaming Lead. New York, Pyramid, 1956; London, Hodder and Stoughton, 1960.
California Gunman. New York, Avon, 1957.
Ridin' Through. New York, Ace, 1957; London, Hodder and Stoughton, 1958.
Action at Arcanum (Quist). Philadelphia, Lippincott, 1958; London, Hodder and Stoughton, 1961.
The Mad Marshal. New York, Pyramid, 1958.
Guns Between Suns. New York, Pyramid, 1959; London, Hodder and Stoughton, 1963.
Blackguard. London, Hodder and Stoughton, 1959.
Tombstone for a Troubleshooter (Quist). Philadelphia, Lippincott, 1960; London, Hodder and Stoughton, 1961; as *Trouble Shooter*, New York, Berkley, 1965.
The Gun Branders. London, Hodder and Stoughton, 1962; New York, Berkley, 1960.
The Gloved Saskia. New York, Avalon, 1964; London, Hodder and Stoughton, 1965.
The Osage Bow (Quist). London, Hodder and Stoughton, 1964.
West of Yesterday. New York, Avalon, 1964; London, Hodder and Stoughton, 1966.
Wildcat Range. New York, Berkley, 1964.
Fugitive from Fear. London, Hodder and Stoughton, 1966.
Shoot Him on Sight! New York, Ace, 1966.
Alias Dix Ryder. New York, Berkley, 1967; London, Hodder and Stoughton, 1969.
Marked Deck at Topango Wells. New York, Ace, 1968.
Incident at Horcado City. New York, Belmont, 1978; Hornchurch, Essex, Henry, 1979.

Uncollected Short Stories

"Gun Justice," in *West* (New York), 18 September–30 October 1929.
"Stage Driver Sam Turns Detective," in *Frontier Stories* (London), February 1930.
"Cowthief Paradise," in *West* (New York), 28 May–9 July 1930.
"Powder Smoke," in *West* (New York), 4 February 1931.
"The Gun Wonder," in *West* (New York), 8 July 1931.
"The Bandit of Brazo Butters," in *West* (New York), 30 September 1931.
"Old King Colt," in *Outlaws of the West* (Springfield, Massachusetts), September–October 1931.
"Long Loop Laramie," in *West* (New York), 11 Nobember 1931.
"Dead Man's Return," in *Outlaws of the West* (Springfield, Massachusetts), January–February 1932.
"The Bullet Trail," in *West* (New York), 17 February–30 March 1932.
"Greedy Ropes," in *West* (New York), 20 July 1932.
"Slow Smoke," in *West* (New York), June 1933.
"Rodeo Racketeers," in *West* (New York), February 1934.
"Lightin' Cowhand," in *West* (New York), June 1934.
"Too Much Beef," in *West* (New York), April 1935.
"The Frosty Kid," in *Western Story* (New York), 21 September 1935.
"Cactus Cavaliers," in *Western Story* (New York), 26 October–30 November 1935.
"Skelton's Gold," in *Western Story* (New York), 6 March 1937.
"Jinglebone Jenkins, Trouble Trailer," in *Western Story* (New York), 4 December 1937–1 January 1938.
"Boots for a Buckaroo," in *Western Story* (New York), 3 September–29 October 1938.
"Ramrod Ridge," in *Argosy* (New York), 15 November 1941–29 January 1942.
"No Shining Armour," in *West* (Kingswood, Surrey), June 1950.

Plays

Screenplays: *Three Mesquiteers* series, 1935–36.

OTHER PUBLICATIONS

Plays

Screenplays: *Daring Danger*, with Michael Trevelyan, 1932; *Man of Action*, 1933.

* * *

William Colt MacDonald specialized in humor that reminds many of the comic relief passages in *The Virginian*, with tales tall as the western mountains to bemuse the "greenhorn" characters and frequent scenes of good-fun "hoorawin'" of the ranch cook or other likely targets. Even his best work, such as *Powder Smoke*, is cluttered with characters nicknamed Gabby because they talk so little or with names such as Hub Wheeler and Smoky Kandle. About the only other place such possibly dated humor is found in such abundance is the B-Movie Western, to which MacDonald was a heavy contributor. He wrote two important series and numerous non-series books, deftly grafting the traditional larger-than-life heroes and romantic plots to his humor.

His Three Mesquiteers series was the source of the "trio" Western so popular through the 1930's and 1940's as the bottom half of double features. As done by MacDonald, the Mesquiteers had a single hero with two comic sidekicks who constantly bickered, while the film presentation offered a pair of co-heroes sharing a single comic sidekick. That change was copied by several imitative "trio" series and probably stemmed from the shortage of comedic ability among run-of-the-mill horse opera actors. In both media the comic Mesquiteers, at least, were more than capable of taking care of themselves in any sort of violent action.

His other series featured detective Gregory Quist of the Texas Northern and Arizona Southern Railroad. Not without their humor, Quist's adventures are also competent, if usually predictable, mysteries. Author and readers found this hero compelling enough to return to for many adventures set around the 1880's.

Many of the non-series books were also mysteries set in the Old West. *Powder Smoke* was more complicated than most and featured a fractioned hero with the title character in what might be most easily capsuled as "the latterday John Wayne role" and a younger colleague with whom young readers might more easily identify being framed for the murder of his older brother. The book was tied neatly to the well-known Quist books by the retailing of a youthful peccadillo shared by the older hero and the older brother, who were contemporaries.

The Roaring Twenties "modern Western Mystery" *The Shadow Rider* is surely the writer's worst book, and he wisely abandoned that special field early to Erle Stanley Gardner and others more adept in it. *Rebel Ranger*, one of the few MacDonalds without appreciable mystery elements, is probably his finest "straight" Western.

—R. Jeff Banks

MACEY, Carn. *See* **BARRETT, Geoffrey John.**

MACK BRIDE, Johnny. Pseudonym for John McGeough. British. Born in Airdrie, Scotland, 18 August 1926. Educated at St. Margaret's Primary School, Airdrie, 1931–38; St. Mary's Secondary School, Coatbridge, Scotland, 1938–40; Edinburgh University, 1966–70, B.Ed. 1970. Served in the British Army, national service in Royal Army Medical Corps, 1945–47, and as a regular soldier in Royal Scots Regiment, 1947–50. Assistant English teacher, Strathclyde Regional Council, Cumbernauld, Scotland, 1970–72, and Lothian Regional Council, Bathgate, Scotland, 1972–73; Assistant Principal Teacher of English, Coatbridge, 1973–75; Principal Teacher of English, Burnbank, Hamilton, Scotland, 1975–83. Address: 3A Clark Street, Airdrie, Lanarkshire ML6 6DH, Scotland.

WESTERN PUBLICATIONS

Novels

Lame Dog Lawman. London, Hale, 1990.
Tenderfoot Veteran. London, Hale, 1990.
Dutch Pensey Can Ride. London, Hale, 1991.
Brand Iron Justice. London, Hale, 1991.

*

Johnny Mack Bride comments:

I left school in disgrace at 14, with no educational qualifications. Worked in a number of awful jobs until rescued by call-up for national service in 1945. Transferred to regular army in 1947 to join army band and spent one year at Royal Military School of Music, Kneller Hall. Became professional musician (saxophone and clarinet) on leaving army. For next 16 years spent nomadic life playing in dance bands, jazz bands, stage bands, etc.

I had always been interested in the American West but had not always found western novels satisfying. Frankly, many seemed to me to be rubbishy and to underestimate their readers. Could I, I wondered, write more realistic novels of the West? "Don't do it!" everyone assured me. "Readers want to be entertained, not educated." I knew that already. I still thought that readers could appreciate more than they were sometimes being offered. People are interested in Life and in Living, I believed, and still believe. They can recognise and appreciate in fiction those human forces—fear, greed, doubt, courage, humour, faith, compassion, etc.—which enmesh them in their own lives.

Could I, I wondered, write a novel which would convey to the reader the feeling of that time and place we call the American West—and at the same time deal with the eternal realities of living?

After years of wondering I decided to give it a try. Now I wonder whether I have had any success.

* * *

Though still a relative newcomer to the western genre, Johnny Mack Bride has swiftly established himself as an author of fast and sometimes violent frontier stories which neatly dovetail the traditional with the modern. A common thread that recurs in his work is that of the underdog finally making good. His heroes are always ordinary men caught up in extraordinary situations.

In *Lame Dog Lawman* the hero is Jim McShane, a cowboy with a game leg and a fondness for drink. Losing his job and promptly drowning his sorrows, McShane eventually stows away aboard a freight wagon and ends up in a lawless hell-town called Tumbledown. There, events conspire to make him take the job of sheriff (which has been vacant for some time), and almost at once he finds himself having to arrest three of the local low-lives for rape.

As Mack Bride's plot unfolds, his "lame-dog" lawman finally begins to regain some of his lost dignity. He meets the girl of his dreams, learns to read and write and beats his craving for alcohol. To keep the pace up, Mack Bride introduces a couple of murders into the proceedings, and ends with a pitched battle against the local cattle-baron, "Ironhand" Gatling, whose boorish son McShane has arrested. In the classic western tradition, the author rounds off his story by quite literally sending his protagonist off into the sunset.

There is, of course, more to it than that. By making a stand against the lawless element, McShane gives some self-respect back to the town (which is optimistically renamed "Resolution"). In a clever variation, Mack Bride keeps gunplay to a minimum, portraying McShane as a man who would rather use his brain than his trigger-finger. On the minus side, however, the author does tend to overemploy profanity (in particular the same two words used again and again) to no particular effect, and depict his supporting characters more as caricatures.

Neither is the plot without its weaknesses. In one scene, the rancher, "Ironhand" Gatling, remarks that he has never heard of a cowboy named Terry Colbrook. Within a few pages, however, Colbrook reveals that he has worked for "Ironhand" all his life. The two murders McShane has to investigate are both solved, conveniently, by confessions. And in the book's single strangest moment (when McShane drops a drunken polecat into a hen-house in order to create a diversion), we are treated to the thoughts of the panicking fowls thus: "'A goddam polecat!' the chickens screamed. 'A polecat for Crissakes! A goddam polecat inside our home! There must be a way out of here for Crissake! Will some bastard open the door!'"

Mack Bride is nothing if not a fast learner, however, and as a consequence *Tenderfoot Veteran* is a much better Western, benefitting from a stronger story and more credible characters. The tenderfoot of the title is Ohio-born Frank Wady, who comes west in an effort to outrun a debilitating nervous disorder brought on by a nightmarish experience during the Civil War, when he was taken for dead and nearly buried alive. Frank is befriended by an old man named Gabriel Weatherby who, seeing something of his late son in the newcomer, eventually sets about helping him overcome his periodic bouts of paralysis.

The valley in which the tenderfoot settles down is not exactly conducive to a speedy recovery, however, and in between dealing with some pilfering Cheyenne Indians, there are also the Bueller brothers (who soon increase their efforts to scare Weatherby, Frank, and their neighbour Jed Hogan off their land in order to have the valley all to themselves) to worry about.

Following the theme developed in *Lame Dog Lawman*, Mack Bride's central character soon finds himself regaining some of his lost nerve. Frank also falls in love with Hogan's daughter Helen, further reinforcing his sense of self-worth. Eventually he is forced to conquer his secret fears in time for a furious and well-executed finale which, following something of a Mack Bride custom, is ultimately both optimistic and encouraging.

Dutch Pensey Can Ride begins when four young cowboys on their way to California are taken prisoner by an outlaw gang led by the notorious badman of the title. In their subsequent escape, Ben, the unofficial leader of the quartet, not only shoots Pensey in the leg, but also steals his prized palomino stallion. What follows is a desperate, and reasonably well-written, chase across inhospitable badlands which, after the massacre of a wagon train and an off-screen attack on a cavalry patrol, culminates in the inevitable climactic confrontation. The manhunt theme is also reprised in *Brand Iron Justice*, when, following the murder of two of his men, cattleman Cal Slade forms an unofficial posse to track the killers down. This proves to be easier said than done, though, and during the course of the hunt, the characters of all the men subtly change and evolve before the splendid final showdown and predictably upbeat ending.

As with all of Mack Bride's books, characterisation and description are kept to a minimum. The story's the thing, and it is told in a spare, fast manner which allows for few frills. Neither does the book have any one particular hero, since all the characters distinguish themselves somewhere along the way. For all that, however, Mack Bride does succeed in making us care about the fate of his characters, and continues to show a gradual strengthening of plot and execution, plus the courage to continually depart from convention, which augurs well for his future in the genre.

—David Whitehead

MacLEAN, Alistair (Stuart). Also wrote as Ian Stuart. British. Born in Daviot, Invernesshire, Scotland, 28 April 1922. Educated at Glasgow University, B.A. (honours) in English. Served in the Royal Navy, 1941–45. Married 1) Gisela MacLean, three sons; 2) Marcelle Georgeus in 1972 (died). Teacher, Gallowfleet Secondary School, near Glasgow in the early 1950's; lived in Geneva, 1957–63; owned Jamaica Inn, Bodmin Moor, Cornwall; ran hotels in England for four years in the 1960's. *Died 2 February 1987.*

WESTERN PUBLICATIONS

Novel

Breakheart Pass. London, Collins, and New York, Doubleday, 1974.

OTHER PUBLICATIONS

Novels

H.M.S. Ulysses. London, Collins, 1955; New York, Doubleday, 1956.

The Guns of Navarone. London, Collins, and New York, Doubleday, 1957.

South by Java Head. London, Collins, and New York, Doubleday, 1958.

The Last Frontier. London, Collins, 1959; as *The Secret Ways*, New York, Doubleday, 1959.

Night Without End. London, Collins, and New York, Doubleday, 1960.

Fear Is the Key. London, Collins, and New York, Doubleday, 1961.

The Dark Crusader (as Ian Stuart). London, Collins, 1961; as *The Black Shrike*, New York, Scribner, 1961; as Alistair MacLean, London, Collins, 1963.

The Satan Bug (as Ian Stuart). London, Collins, and New York, Scribner, 1962; as Alistair MacLean, New York, Fawcett, 1971, London, Collins, 1979.

The Golden Rendezvous. London, Collins, and New York, Doubleday, 1962.

Ice Station Zebra. London, Collins, and New York, Doubleday, 1963.

When Eight Bells Toll. London, Collins, and New York, Doubleday, 1966.

Where Eagles Dare. London, Collins, and New York, Doubleday, 1967.

Force 10 from Navarone. London, Collins, and New York, Doubleday, 1968.

Puppet on a Chain. London, Collins, and New York, Doubleday, 1969.

Caravan to Vaccarès. London, Collins, and New York, Doubleday, 1970.

Bear Island. London, Collins, and New York, Doubleday, 1971.

The Way to Dusty Death. London, Collins, and New York, Doubleday, 1973.

Circus. London, Collins, and New York, Doubleday, 1975.

The Golden Gate. London, Collins, and New York, Doubleday, 1976.

Seawitch. London, Collins, and New York, Doubleday, 1977.

Goodbye California. London, Collins, 1977; New York, Doubleday, 1978.

Athabasca. London, Collins, and New York, Doubleday, 1980.

River of Death. London, Collins, 1981; New York, Doubleday, 1982.

Partisans. London, Collins, 1982; New York, Doubleday, 1983.

Floodgate. London, Collins, 1983; New York, Doubleday, 1984.

San Andreas. London, Collins, 1984; New York, Doubleday, 1985.

Santorini. London, Collins, 1986; New York, Doubleday, 1987.

Death Train. London, Collins, 1989.

Short Stories

The Lonely Sea: Collected Sea Stories. London, Collins, 1985; New York, Doubleday, 1986.

Plays

Screenplays: *Where Eagles Dare*, 1968; *Puppet on a Chain*, with Don Sharp and Paul Wheeler, 1970; *When Eight Bells Toll*, 1971; *Caravan to Vaccarès*, 1974; *Breakheart Pass*, 1975.

Television Play: *Hostage Power*, 1980.

Other

All About Lawrence of Arabia (for children). London, W.H. Allen, 1962; as *Lawrence of Arabia*, New York, Random House, 1962.
Captain Cook. London, Collins, and New York, Doubleday, 1972.

* * *

Scotsman Alistair MacLean, an English teacher turned novelist, is best remembered for his action-packed adventure thrillers. Therein a quietly heroic and competent man of integrity must pit his strength and wit not only against vicious evil men (usually despicably cruel foreigners—Nazis, Japanese, terrorists, drug dealers, outlaws, and Indians), their amoral machinations and terrible machines (whether repeater rifles in western days or the latest in the technology of destruction in more modern ones), but also against harsh terrain (icy mountain passes, deep gulches, impregnable cliffs, treacherous straits, frozen Arctic tundra, desert quicksands) and the destructive force of menacing natural elements (wintry North Atlantic seas, hurricane-force Pacific winds, mountains of ice). His struggle is often inspired or assisted by an empathetic, self-sacrificing woman with keen perceptions and a deep inner strength. MacLean's clearcut delineation of character, his highly dramatic settings, his taut narrative, and the clarity, tension, and fast pace of his plots have made them easily adaptable to the screen, where a number of novel-based films have proven box office hits, including *Where Eagles Dare*, *The Guns of Navarone*, *Ice Station Zebra*, and *Breakheart Pass*. MacLean has an international following, with 18 of his novels having topped a million sales, and with his mysteries under the pseudonym Ian Stuart remaining popular with young adults from Tupelo to Prague.

Whether war story, sea adventure, detective thriller, or Western, a MacLean novel depicts men at the limits of their physical and sometimes mental endurance, limits that exaggerate weaknesses and demonstrate hidden strengths. His heroes are driven men on whose shoulders rest the responsibility for others. Whether representatives of authority or individualists in conflict with it, in order to live up to that responsibility, they must sometimes hide their strength, knowledge, values, and authority and instead feign weakness, indifference, incompetence, cowardice, or treachery—even when it means a loss of public reputation, of friends, and perhaps of love. Often there are spies and traitors in their midst, double and triple agents. For example, in MacLean's one Western, *Breakheart Pass*, federal agent John Deakin poses as a thief, a murderer, and a coward, and tolerates the contempt and rude comments of his fellows and the bad opinion of a young woman he finds attractive (the Governor's niece), in order to disarm the opposition and gain access to information that will expose a conspiracy, thwart a daring robbery of gold bullion, and save innocent lives. His guise helps him expose a Civil War hero, a U.S. Marshal, and the Governor of Nevada, all of whom have betrayed their offices for quick and easy profit. The plot follows a troop train carrying medical supplies to a snowbound Nevada fort supposedly overcome by cholera but actually in the hands of scheming outlaws and the renegade Indians with whom they have formed an uneasy alliance. Disaster accompanies the train's progress as telegraph wires go dead, troop cars uncouple and plunge down ravines, and death follows death.

Amid these events, Deakin (played by Charles Bronson in a 1975 film version) is silent and controlled: a keen observer, a master of understatement, an unpredictable, resilient, quick and deadly adversary. As in most MacLean novels, this protagonist is caught up in pursuits, escapes, and violent encounters, with the opposition always close to gaining its goals. The action hurtles both on top of and through a moving train and then on horseback with Indians puffing in pursuit, as Deakin investigates the disappearance of two Army officers, a murder, a mysterious cargo, and a number of "accidents" that take numerous innocent lives. In the process he wreaks confusion among the conspirators and paves the way for their demise. He is tough, confident, and secretive; his occasional quips (like those of the Clint Eastwood figure, Major Smith in *Where Eagles Dare*) reveal his depth of character, his cynical knowledge, and his calm, offbeat humor in the face of difficult odds. At the end he and the young lady he has so impressed agree that violence must be matched with violence if right is to prevail.

Though set in the American West of the 1870's with wild Indians, a captured fort, gun-toting outlaws, and an occasional Americanism, this "Western" could just as easily be transferred to any of MacLean's more modern settings with only minimal changes. Like *Bear Island* or some of the Ian Stuart novels, MacLean's Western follows the detective novel format of mysterious deaths and a careful investigation by a seeming amateur, with the murderer's identity withheld as long as possible. It also follows an adventure novel focus on a brave man's efforts to get a train unimpeded through a treacherous pass, with villains throwing obstacles in his way at every turn.

By means of sketchy characterization of all but the main figure, MacLean skillfully follows his own advice to "keep the action moving so fast" the reader has no "time to stop and think." Critics may attack MacLean's style as clumsy or his plots as implausible, but all agree with *Guardian* critic Stephen Hugh-Jones that he writes "thoroughly thrilling" thrillers. His books are highly readable, his narrative pace a sprint. He knows his landscapes and has experienced hardship, torture and terror firsthand, so there is a harsh immediacy to his descriptions. His moral vision of good and evil is clear-cut, with the good committed soul and body to combatting the wicked, by whatever means possible. In this sense all his novels are very much in the western spirit of manly heroes battling dastardly villains for the welfare of the community as a whole.

—Gina Macdonald

MACLEAN, Norman. American. Born in Clarinda, Iowa, 23 December 1902. Educated at Dartmouth College, Hanover, New Hampshire, A.B. 1924; University of Chicago, Chicago, Illinois, Ph.D. 1940. Married Jessie Burns in 1931 (died 1968); one daughter and one son. Instructor in English, Dartmouth College, 1924–26; worked in logging camps and United States Forest Service in Montana and Idaho, 1926–28; Instructor, 1930–41; Assistant Professor, 1941–44, Dean of students, 1941–46, Associate Professor, 1944–54, Professor of English, 1954–73, Chair of Committee on General Studies, 1956–64, William Rainey Harper Professor of English, 1963–73, and Professor Emeritus, 1973–90, University of Chicago. Member, Board of Directors, Southeast Chicago Commission. D.Litt.: Montana State University, Missoula, 1980. *Died 2 August 1990.*

WESTERN PUBLICATIONS

Short Stories

A River Runs Through It, and Other Stories. Chicago, University of Chicago Press, 1976.

OTHER PUBLICATIONS

Other

A Manual for Instruction in Military Maps and Aerial Photographs, with Everett C. Olson. New York and London, Harper, 1943.

* * *

Norman Maclean's reputation rests on a single extraordinary collection, *A River Runs Through It, and Other Stories*, written following his retirement from teaching in 1973 when he was past 70, and published in 1976 to immediate acclaim. *A River Runs Through It* consists of the title novella; a short story, "Logging and Pimping and 'Your Pal, Jim'"; and a second novella, "USFS 1919: The Ranger, the Cook, and a Hole in the Sky."

Some reviewers have referred to Maclean's work as memoir rather than fiction; in fact, all three of these pieces exist on the delicate borderline between fiction and nonfiction. Clearly Maclean's writing is strongly autobiographical; the narrator is always a version of Maclean himself, recollected from 1937, 1919, or 1927. Other characters are family members, men he worked with in the woods, or men and women he met in towns between times in the woods or on the river.

Maclean's careful attention to detail seems partly a loving remembrance of his youth, partly the desire to record a part of the Montana past. Indeed, the foreward to *A River Runs Through It* suggests that these pieces began as tales told to his children at bedtime, partly to put them to sleep but mostly to let them know what sort of man their father had been, what his life had been like, and how things were done in a time they could never experience. Those last three impulses continue strongly in the published stories; one suspects that the first purpose was never successful—these stories are too vivid, told with too much pleasure in the telling, to have ever put anyone to sleep.

Taken together, Maclean's stories capture for those of us born too late a good portion of what life in the mountains of Montana must have been like in the first half of this century. The earliest story, "USFS 1919: The Ranger, the Cook, and a Hole in the Sky," is both a coming-of-age story and an interesting account of the United States Forest Service in its early years, when crews travelled on foot or, if they were lucky, on horseback; when the two most important men in the outfit were the cook and the packer—the man who could "build two packs weighing the same and together weighing 150 or 200 pounds when a top pack has been added" and build those packs, working without a scale, for an entire string of horses and mules. "Logging and Pimping and 'Your Pal, Jim'" mixes an account of life as a logger with what at least one logger did in the off-season in 1927. The title story, "A River Runs Through It," set in 1937, moves effectively between town and the rivers where Maclean and his doomed brother fly-fish, avoid talking about the brother's problems, and remember their father (who gets out to the river only once in the novella and then, because of his age, can only fish the easier water).

In Maclean's West, life in the woods or along the river, important though it may be as both the source and the testing of value, is only one part of the story; the small towns of western Montana are at least as strong a presence. Maclean's characters choose not to live permanently in the wilderness; they move in and through and out, making a living or, more importantly, fly-fishing, which seems to be Maclean's vision of man's highest achievement and strongest relationship with nature.

Yet the Maclean who narrates these stories seems not to have examined many of the time's attitudes in the years since. Men are respected insofar as they are fly-fishermen or fighters; women are wives, mothers, sisters, waitresses, or whores. Maclean as a young man measured up in a harsh and lovely world; his pride in that achievement—and it is an achievement—seems unleavened by doubts about whether all of what he measured up to was worthy of his efforts.

As memoir, Maclean's work is valuable for its preservation of a part of the western past; as fiction, it is an intriguing use of autobiographical elements in narratives artfully shaped to appear shapeless, natural, artless. Whether read as memoir or fiction, his prose dances so skilfully along the boundary between memoir and fiction as to obliterate that boundary entirely.

—Wayne Ude

MacLEOD, Robert. Born in 1906. Formerly wrote *Red Ryder* comic strip.

WESTERN PUBLICATIONS

Novels

The Appaloosa. New York, Fawcett, 1966.
The Californio. New York, Fawcett, 1966.
The Muleskinner. New York, Fawcett, 1967.
Apache Tears. New York, Pocket Books, 1974; London, Coronet, 1976.
Feather in the Wind. New York, Pocket Books, 1976.
Ambush at Junction Rock. New York, Fawcett, 1979.
The Running Gun. New York, Fawcett, 1979.
Six Guns South. New York, Fawcett, 1979.

* * *

Two of Robert MacLeod's novels have been made into films, *The Appaloosa*, with Marlon Brando, and *The Californio*, filmed as *100 Rifles* with Jim Brown, Raquel Welch, and Burt Reynolds. He also scripted for a time the *Red Ryder* comic strip.

His Westerns, however, are far removed from comic strips. They are gritty and unsentimental with believable, flawed characters and authentic, grim backgrounds replete with historic accuracy. The setting is likely to be the Southwest or Mexico, and many of his plots involve principal characters who are Mexican or Indian (Apache or Navajo). The main characters in his novels are never standard, always-in-control western heroes. Instead they are uncouth and usually in what might be deemed lowly professions—a buffalo hunter in *The Appaloosa*, a muleskinner in *The Muleskinner*, a hard-bitten scout in *Apache Tears*, and a trading post proprietor in *Ambush at Junction Rock*. MacLeod's heroes survive in their naturalistic world often by mere fortune. Hot-tempered, mean, entrapped often by vengeance, lacking a social conscience, the man is, to an extent, redeemed by the love and attention of a woman who seems to understand, better than he, the workings of the world and the hero's strengths and weaknesses.

Family relationships (for good or ill) and male/female affiliations (sometimes destructive; involvement produces difficulties) are characteristic of MacLeod's Westerns. The unpleasant qualities of the books are responsible for what popularity he has enjoyed and explain, in a sense, why he has not been more widely received. Among other western writers he is perhaps closest in spirit, style, and milieu to Alan LeMay.

—Ray Merlock

MACRAE, Mason. Pseudonym for James Lyon Rubel; also wrote as Timothy Hayes. Born in 1894. *Died.*

WESTERN PUBLICATIONS

Novels

The Sheriff of Elk Ridge. New York, Clode, 1935; London, Nicholson and Watson, 1936.
Two-Gun Troubadour. London, Collins, 1939.
The Outlaw of Clover Creek. London, Collins, 1939.
Limberleg of the Lazy Y. London, Collins, 1939.
Gun Gospel. London, Collins, 1940.
Rawhide. London, Collins, 1943.
The Sheriff of Hangtown. London, Collins, 1943.
The Distant Hills. London, Collins, 1944.
The Doctor of Painted Springs. London, Collins, 1944.
The Scarlet Saddle. London, Collins, 1944.
The Fiddle-Back Brand. London, Collins, 1945.
The Gun-Slammer. London, Collins, 1945.
The Bounty-Hunters. London, Collins, 1946.
Greenhorn. London, Collins, 1949.
Black Sheep. London, Collins, 1950.
Four Frightened Horses. London, Collins, 1950.
Bitter Basin. London, Collins, 1952.
Rocking M Ranch. London, Collins, 1952.
Six-Gun Serenade. London, Collins, 1953.
Coffin Canyon. London, Collins, 1954.
Thunder Valley. London, Collins, 1956.
The Man from Tucson. London, Collins, 1956.
Showdown at Sundance. London, Collins, 1958.
Shoot-Out. London, Collins, 1959.
Death Was Their Business. London, Collins, 1960.

Novels as James L. Rubel (series: The Medico)

The Medico of Painted Springs. New York, Phoenix Press, 1934; London, Mills and Boon, 1935.
The Medico Rides. New York, Phoenix Press, 1935; London, Mills and Boon, 1936.
Thunder over White Horse. New York, Phoenix Press, 1935; London, Ward Lock, 1940.
War on the Range. London, Mills and Boon, 1936.
Prairie Dust. New York, Phoenix Press, 1936; London, Mills and Boon, 1937.
Renegade Guns. New York, Phoenix Press, and London, Mills and Boon, 1936.
Cyclone of the Sage Brush. New York, Phoenix Press, and London, Mills and Boon, 1937.
The Lazy L Brand. New York, Phoenix Press, 1937; London, Ward Lock, 1939.
The Medico on the Trail. New York, Phoenix Press, 1938; London, Ward Lock, 1939.
The Salty Six-Guns of Pinto. London, Ward Lock, 1941.
No Business for a Lady. New York, Fawcett, 1950; London, Fawcett, 1952.
The Fraudulent Broad. London, Digit, 1959.

Novels as Timothy Hayes

The Two-Gun Parson. New York, Phoenix Press, and London, Wright and Brown, 1936.
King of the Mesa. New York, Phoenix Press, 1938; London, Wright and Brown, 1939.
Fighting Sheriff. New York, Phoenix Press, 1939.

* * *

Mason Macrae is one of the established names of western fiction. Author of a large body of work spanning three decades, his output is impressive, with novels and stories under three different names. Given the rate of production, it is perhaps inevitable that his work has its flaws, and that sometimes dross is mingled with the gold. In the end, it is the good writing that counts, and no reader should have trouble finding it.

For the most part Macrae's novels follow the familiar, well-worn themes: return of the hero to a changed homeland, the hunting down of his father's killer, thwarting of rustlers or crooked ranch-bosses, and the like. His style—in common with several authors of the pre-war generation—is leisurely, the action widely spaced in a landscape crammed with superfluous minor characters. At times description tends to become rambling and verbose, wandering into unnecessary subplots so that the main thread is temporarily lost. Sometimes Macrae overcomes this, with shorter, more direct accounts and interesting characters. Elsewhere plots are quite imaginative, but fail due to poor characterization and long-winded style, as in *The Bounty-Hunters*, with its incredible number of villains gunned down. Inconsistency seems to dog Macrae throughout, with good and indifferent works running almost parallel. *Showdown at Sundance*, arguably one of his least convincing efforts, appeared within two years of the excellent *The Man from Tucson*, and much the same is true of his work under other pseudonyms. As James Lyon Rubel he produced some lively action in the "Medico" series of novels—*The Medico on the Trail* and the later *The Medico Rides* are good examples—and *King of the Mesa* provides an interesting instance of his writing as Timothy Hayes.

Singling out particular Macrae titles for praise is no easy task, as good examples abound through the 1940's and 1950's. *The Doctor of Painted Springs*, where Dr. Monroe returns home to prevent a crooked rancher from foreclosing on his nester neighbours, is an interesting early novel, with more direction than the rambling *The Gun-Slammer* of a year later. *Rocking M Ranch* is a fine effort, whose basic theme is enlivened by the assistance of two ageing—and amusing—gunslingers. Though ponderous humour and the urge to ramble are present as always, they are more tightly curbed. *Black Sheep* is one of Macrae's best, where the prodigal son of a rancher comes home to find his father dead and the ranch under new ownership. Later he prevents a range war, and finally unmasks his father's killer. The plot is uncluttered, the action sustained, and in Dave McCabe and the tomboy heroine Eli Fowler Macrae presents two of his most striking characters. Almost equally good, *Bitter Basin* has a similar theme, a lawyer hero disputing possession of the family ranch, foiling a range war, and besting a rustler and a crooked banker. Dorrance, the lawyer, is convincingly presented—not least in his weakness for the lures of the flesh—and the novel compels throughout. *The Man from Tucson*, one of Macrae's last works, is also among his best, with an interesting plot featuring white renegades disguised as Apaches. Such novels represent Macrae at his peak, the faults under firm control, and his natural skills given full expression.

—Jeff Sadler

MADISON, Hank. *See* **ROWLAND, Donald S.**

MADISON, Holt.

WESTERN PUBLICATIONS

Novels (series: Batwing Jones series in all books)

Brush Country Killers. London, Barker, 1952.
Lawless Marshall. London, Barker, 1955.
Killers' Round-up. London, Barker, 1958.

* * *

Each author creates a character who he hopes will be a success with the buying public. From that success he is able to produce more books based on further adventures of the character. In this, Holt Madison is no different from most in creating his unlikely-named hero, Batwing Jones. He penned a trio of formulaic Westerns with this character, his ideas undoubtedly coming from watching American Western B movies, as he saddled Jones with a "straight man" sidekick named Gabby Moss. Working on the assumption that those who enjoyed an hour and half in the cinema being entertained by Roy Rogers, Tex Ritter and the like, Madison believed they would also like to spend two or three hours in the comfort of their own home with a book containing similar characters to take them across imaginary range country. To this end he was successful.

Unfortunately for today's readers, his dialogue was his downfall. He peppered the stories with stifled language, such as: ". . . They swirled their horses to a lunging halt in a cloud of dust and sang out a boisterous welcome. 'Goddam, ef'n you don't look like you been wrastlin' with a rogue steer!' Gabby exclaimed in an anxious voice." If you close your eyes you can see the scene being acted out by a Walter Brennan-type figure. This said, Madison could write eloquently on the harshness of sudden death, as in *Lawless Marshall*: "Four bodies lay in sprawling attitudes a few feet from him. Darkly opalescent pools of blood, still moist, were patterned around the bodies. He did not need to move nearer to see that death had come to each man." Such is this conflicting style that the reader can overlook the sometimes outré dialogue, and be entertained by the story-lines. Each book is told at a well-paced canter through often predictable circumstances.

Brush Country Killers is set in south Texas, where a band of marauding, masked killers are leaving a trail of bodies and burned-out homesteads. The attacks seem senseless and their cause obscure. An old friend of Batwing Jones falls victim to the marauders, his ranch is burned and his cattle driven off. This is a familiar setting from which to introduce Jones and Moss to the readers, and they have to face the anonymous ring leaders. The story unfolds as Jones seeks revenge against a backdrop of greed, gold lust and secret identities.

Madison overexaggerates his gunplay, with Jones shooting pistols out of hands, and hats off heads, and he would have disgraced himself in his treatment of his horse. But he was following the trend set in the mid-1950's of super-human heroes, who could be beaten up, wounded several times, and still get up for more to lick the villains. Any comic relief is provided by Moss, while Jones remains serious and thoughtful.

Lawless Marshall is the best book of the three, as the story is given more consideration and the action taken away from traditional rustling and into the world of counterfeited stock and share certificates, which are being used to undermine a town's commerce. In making Jones an ex-ranger and ex-law officer, Madison gives him a creditable background, from which he can draw on past experiences. With Lawless City allowing Jones to become its marshal, they depend on his ability to solve the mysteries of murder, rustling, extortion, and blackmail, and to force the real power seeker out into the open. The story flows well until its ending, which reads like a Sherlock Holmes adventure, with everyone sitting around like little children and having everything explained to them.

The final book on Batwing Jones is *Killers' Round Up*, whose plot, unfortunately, relies on the theme already explored in *Brush Country Killers*. It is a mixed up story of revenge, greed, and misplaced loyalties, with Jones and Moss going mechanically through their paces to solve yet another "range mystery." Undoubtedly if Madison had given more thought to this book and continued to develop his characters he would have gone on to write more in the series. But being written at the end of the 1950's when people wanted more than just ranch operas, he didn't quite ring the changes, and Jones's fate was sealed.

His cast of characters were the usual stock figures—the big rancher in trouble, fiesty females who give balance to the stories, the villain of the piece who hides behind a mask of respectability, and the whole array of friends on whom Jones could depend to bring him their problems.

—Mike Stotter

MAHONE, Colt. *See* **LAZENBY, Norman.**

MANFRED, Frederick (Feikema). Has also written as Feike Feikema. American. Born near Doon, Rock Township, Iowa, 6 January 1912. Educated at Western Academy, Hull, Iowa; Calvin College, Grand Rapids, Michigan, 1930–34, B.A. 1934; Nettleton Commercial College, Sioux Falls, South Dakota, 1937; correspondence courses, University of Minnesota, Minneapolis, 1941–42. Married Maryanna Shorba in 1942 (divorced 1978); two daughters and one son. As a young man, star basketball player, Calvin College, Michigan. Worked as a filling-station attendant, harvest and factory hand, salesman, etc., 1934–37; reporter, Minneapolis *Journal*, 1937–39; interviewer, Minnesota Opinion Poll, St. Paul, 1939–40; patient in a tuberculosis sanitarium, 1940–42; abstract writer, *Modern Medicine*, Minneapolis, 1942–43; reporter, *East Side Argus*, Minneapolis, 1943–44; writer-in-residence, Macalester College, St. Paul, Minnesota, 1949–52, and University of South Dakota, Vermillion, 1968–82. Since 1983 chair in regional heritage, Augustana College, Sioux Falls, South Dakota. Recipient: Rockefeller fellowship, 1944, 1945; American Academy grant, 1945; Field fellowship, 1948; Andreas fellowship, 1949, 1952; McKnight fellowship, 1958, Huntington Hartford fellowship, 1963, 1964; Hon. Life Member, Western Literature Association, 1967; National Endowment for the Arts grant, 1976, 1983; Iowa's Most Distinguished Contribution to Literature award, 1980; Society for the Study of Midwestern Literature Mark Twain award, 1981; D. Litt.: Augustana College, 1977; D.H.L.: Morningside College, Sioux City, Iowa, 1981; Buena Vista College, Storm Lake, Iowa, 1984. Agent: Curtis Brown, 10 Astor Place, New York, New York 10003. Address: Roundwind, R.R. 3, Luverne, Minnesota 56156, U.S.A.

Western Publications

Novels

Buckskin Man Tales:
- *Lord Grizzly*. New York, McGraw Hill, 1954; London Corgi, 1957.
- *Riders of Judgment*. New York, Random House, 1957.
- *Conquering Horse*. New York, McDowell Obolensky, 1959.
- *Scarlet Plume*. New York, Simon and Schuster, 1964.
- *King of Spades*. New York, Simon and Schuster, 1966.

The Manly-Hearted Woman. New York, Crown, 1976.

Short Stories

Arrow of Love. Denver, Swallow, 1961.
Apples of Paradise and Other Stories. New York, Simon and Schuster, 1968.

Uncollected Short Stories

"Sleeping Dogs," in *Fiction 8* (New York), 1974.
"The Founding of the Rock River Church," in *The Far Side of the Storm*, edited by Gary Elder. Los Cerillos, New Mexico, San Marcos Press, 1975.
"Splinters," in *Dakota Arts Quarterly* (Fargo, North Dakota), Summer 1977.
"Going to Town with Ma," in *Great River Review* (Winona, Minnesota), vol. 5 no. 1, 1984.

Other Publications

Novels

Morning Red: A Romance. Denver, Swallow, 1956.
The Man Who Looked Like the Prince of Wales. New York, Simon and Schuster, 1965; as *The Secret Place*, New York, Pocket Books, 1967.
Eden Prairie. New York, Simon and Schuster, 1968.
Milk of Wolves. Boston, Avenue Victor Hugo, 1976.
Green Earth. New York, Crown, 1977.
Sons of Adam. New York, Crown, 1980.
Flowers of Desire. Salt Lake City, Utah, Dancing Badger, 1989.
No Fun on Sunday. Norman, University of Oklahoma Press, 1990.

Novels as Feike Feikema

The Golden Bowl. St. Paul, Minnesota, Webb, 1944; London, Dobson, 1947; revised edition, as Fredrick Manfred, Vermillion, University of South Dakota Press, 1969.
Boy Almighty. St. Paul, Minnesota, Itasca Press, 1945; London, Dobson, 1950.
This Is the Year. New York, Doubleday, 1947; as Fredrick Manfred, Boston, Gregg Press, 1979.
The Chokecherry Tree. New York, Doubleday, 1948; London, Dobson, 1950; revised edition (as Frederick Manfred), Denver, Swallow, 1961.
World's Wanderer, revised edition (as Frederick Manfred), as *Wanderlust*, Denver, Swallow, 1962.
- *The Primitive*. New York, Doubleday, 1949.
- *The Brother*. New York, Doubleday, 1950.
- *The Giant*. New York, Doubleday, 1951.

Play

Lord Grizzly: The Legend of Hugh Glass (screenplay of his novel). Vermillion, University of South Dakota Libraries, 1972.

Verse

Winter Count: Poems 1934–1965. Minneapolis, Thueson, 1966.
Winter Count II: Poems 1966–1985. Minneapolis, Thueson, 1985.

Other

Writing in the West (recorded lecture). Deland, Florida, Everett/Edwards, 1974.
Conversations with Frederick Manfred, edited by John R. Milton. Salt Lake City, University of Utah Press, 1974.
The Wind Blows Free: A Reminiscence. Sioux Falls, South Dakota, Augustana College Center for Western Studies, 1979.
Dinkytown. Minneapolis, Dinkytown Antiquarian Bookstore, 1984.
Prime Fathers (biographical portraits). Salt Lake City, Howe, 1985.
The Selected Letters of Frederick Manfred, 1932–1954, edited by Arthur R. Huseboe and Nancy Owen Nelson. Lincoln, University of Nebraska Press, 1989.

*

Bibliography: *Frederick Manfred: A Bibliography* by George Kellogg, Denver, Swallow, 1965; *Frederick Manfred: A Bibliography and Publishing History* by Rodney J. Mulder and John H. Timmerman, Sioux Falls, South Dakota, Augustana College Center for Western Studies, 1981.

Manuscript Collection: University of Minnesota, Minneapolis.

Critical Studies: "Writing in the West and Midwest Issue" of *Critique* (Minneapolis), Winter 1959; "The Novel in the American West" by John R. Milton, in *South Dakota Review* (Vermillion), Autumn 1964; "Sinclair Lewis-Frederick Manfred Issue" of *South Dakota Review* (Vermillion), Winter 1969–70; *The Literature of the American West* by J. Golden Taylor, Boston, Houghton Mifflin, 1971; *Frederick Manfred* by Joseph M. Flora, Boise, Idaho, Boise State College, 1973; "An Interview in Minnesota with Frederick Manfred" by James W. Lee, in *Studies in the Novel* (Denton, Texas), Fall 1973; *Frederick Manfred* by Robert C. Wright, Boston, Twayne, 1979.

Frederick Manfred comments (1982):

I got started on the *Buckskin Man Tales* et al. when it dawned on me one day that I really didn't have a true progenitor for my other earlier work, as, say, a Shakespeare might have a Chaucer and a Spenser. I got to wondering who'd lived in Siouxland (a term I invented in 1946 for *This Is the Year*). I went back through my father's time, then grampa's time, then pioneers, trappers and at last into Indian times. I decided to write about those hoary days to educate myself as well as to become my own progenitor. Also, the grand notion of "making" a history (in fiction) of Siouxland from roughly 1800 until the day I died caught my imagination (and my nighttime fantasies) and caused me to write books on the early West. I have 20 more years of writing left, and that will make a full 200 years of living in Siouxland in fiction and poetry.

* * *

For Frederick Manfred, the voice of the "Old Lizard," of man's primate nature, is the creative muse. This voice, unlike the more dogmatic "literary" mode of the east coast writers and critics and the formulaic mode of the conventional western novelists, is Manfred's creative impulse. It has allowed him, as a prolific writer for over 40 years, to produce a canon which represents not only his individual, autobiographical vision of his native Siouxland (encompassing southeastern South Dakota, southwestern Minnesota, and northwestern Iowa), but also a broader, more universal perspective on man's roots, the importance of his relationship to the land.

It is this primal voice which qualifies Manfred as a writer of vision; his materials, while they tend to fall into two broad categories—midwestern "prairie-wilderness" literature and western historical fiction—are unified by this pervasive theme of the search for identity. Unfortunately, much of what Manfred has written has been dismissed by eastern critics as regionally limited, as having neither realism nor broader applications.

Such limiting judgments should have no impact on the reader's response to Manfred's fiction, for in both categories of writing Manfred's strength lies in his storytelling capabilities. In the prairie grouping, Manfred's autobiographical focus is found in his creation of the genre "rume," a writing which is so closely tied to the author's life that it does not qualify as fiction. Thus, much of the material found in his collections of poems *Winter Count* and *Winter Count II*, provide accounts of Manfred's life from 1934 through 1985. Equally autobiographical are the rumes. *Boy Almighty* traces the spiritual and physical struggles of Manfred through two years in a tuberculosis sanitorium. *Eden Prairie* and *The Man Who Looked Like the Prince of Wales* are patterned after relatives of Manfred's, a cousin who looked like the Prince of Wales but led an otherwise blighted life, and a schoolteacher aunt overly concerned with the sins of the flesh. *Green Earth* is Manfred's book about his first 17 years of life, his roots on the land as a farmer's son, his decision to be a writer, and his mother's death. Each of these works has as a central concern the search for identity of characters who grew up with and on the land. In particular, *Green Earth* is Manfred's focus on his own nature as a young and budding artist. The recently published *No Fun on Sunday*, set in 1920's Siouxland, uses many of the characters from *Green Earth*, and focuses on Sherm Engleking's aspirations for national baseball.

In some of Manfred's prairie novels, the protagonists, although they do not return to farm life to find themselves, do acknowledge the importance of their upbringing on the land. Little Elof Lofblom, an ordinary young man searching for personal heroism, finds his destiny not in this quest, but in the return to his home territory and to the Earth Mother figure of Gert; Alan Ross and Red Engleking, spiritual brothers in Manfred's novel *Sons of Adam*, both admit an indebtedness to their rural upbringings; Red returns to work the land with his wife and son. Likewise, Manfred shows the victory of land and country over city life in the recent *Flowers of Desire*, in which he breaks new ground by writing from the point of view of a young woman. Protagonist Carla Simmons discovers her sexual identity while coming to accept her roots in Siouxland.

Others of Manfred's prairie novels are even more directly concerned with the theme of man's identity in or through the land. His early novels *The Golden Bowl* and *This Is the Year* are excellent examinations of this theme. Maury Grant of *The Golden Bowl* faces the conflict between his commitment to the land in its dustbowl poverty, represented by the girl Kirsten, and his rootlessness. His decision to make a commitment to both the desolate land and Kirsten affirms Manfred's belief in the importance of identity through the land. *This Is the Year*, one of Manfred's better novels, treats the issue of man's identity in both his ethnic and agricultural contexts. Pier Frixen, while he rebels against his strong Frisian background represented by his first-generation parents, ignores advice on both the treatment of his land and his wife, and in the end he loses both—Manfred's comment about the folly of ignoring our humanity. Juhl Melander's search for artistic identity in *Milk of Wolves* outlines best Manfred's definition of his own artistic vision as it relates to the wilderness. Juhl's pilgrimage leads him from city to wilderness, from society's values to the values of nature. In the process he discovers, as has Manfred, that his creativity is best realized through natural forms; he sculpts figures out of the boulders on his island, a process which allows his artistry to be natural from conception to completion. Only after all vestiges of his "primitive" life are gone—his Indian wife Flur, his son Wulf, and his friend wolf "Three Legs"—does Juhl return to civilization armed with this new artistic knowledge.

The "civilization" to which Juhl returns, Manfred implies, will have little or no impact on him or on his artistic efforts for the remainder of his life. In these prairie works, as in the western historical fiction, man's cities will offer no particular aid in the protagonists' identity searches. The identity search is completed in the wilderness.

Manfred's historically based western novels have gained him the most exposure. The *Buckskin Man Tales* are five novels written to encompass the time-frame of 1800–92 in the American West, or from pre-whiteman through cattleman times. Although considered uneven in quality, the novels reflect a more than adequate amount of historical research and transcend the conventional western formulae. Each of these Buckskin novels, as well as the later Indian novel *The Manly-Hearted Woman* and others of Manfred's Indian stories, contain some of the conventional motifs of the Western: the mountain man's battle for survival in the wilderness, the conflict between cattle baron and nester, the gunfight and barroom scenes, the Indian-whiteman conflict, and the Indian tribal wars. But Manfred's western fiction goes beyond such conventions to focus on the theme of the identity search in the wilderness. *Lord Grizzly*, one of Manfred's most widely read and popular novels, traces the epic journey of Hugh Glass, a mountain man mauled by a bear and left to die. Hugh crawled over 100 miles to Fort Kiowa; his motivation was his hatred and revenge for those men who deserted him. In Manfred's novel, he learns forgiveness, not only of these men, but of himself for his own personal failings. Earl Ransom of *King of Spades*, victim of amnesia, repeats his father's pattern by sleeping with his mother and finally shooting her. Overcome with grief at the loss of his lovely Erden and at the knowledge of his own identity, Ransom hangs himself. His greatest happiness was when he lived away from civilization with Erden, a white girl raised as a Dakota Indian.

In the two Indian novels of the Buckskin series, Manfred affirms the superiority of the wilderness over civilization. In *Scarlet Plume* Judith Raveling, a white woman, finds her love in the Indian Scarlet Plume, whose people carried out the Sioux uprising and slaughter of white people. After Scarlet Plume's castration and hanging, Judith abandons her white heritage, or "civilization," to return to the Indian society, carrying Scarlet Plume's child. In *Conquering Horse* the plight of the young Yankton Sioux brave No Name is his lack of a vision to declare his manhood. His mission, to conquer the white stallion Dancing Sun, his union with Leaf, and the propagation of both his and the stallion's seed complete the process of his search for identity. The purity of the Indian culture—its communion with nature—suggests again Manfred's affirmation of the theme of man's identity within the wilderness, rather than in civilization.

Despite his prolific and long-lasting publishing career, Manfred continues to write energetically and has stated that he has several novels and short stories waiting to be written. However, Manfred has also revealed his diversity as a writer by producing a book of essays, and an edited collection of his correspondence from 1932 to 1954. In *Prime Fathers*, Manfred collects some of his best published essays related to a 50-year span of his public life, and includes portraits of Sinclair Lewis, Hubert Humphrey, and Manfred's father. Manfred's *Selected Letters* reveal his struggles as a young writer, a newspaper man, a victim of tuberculosis, and a young father. Here Manfred's literary vision is traced and documented.

There is little doubt that Manfred is establishing a place for himself in the annals of American fiction; his work is distinctive for its flavor of the midwestern region which he has named "Siouxland," and for his unique language often consisting of puns and created words. It is also distinctive for the energy of the man himself, not only in the autobiographical "rumes," but just as clearly in the prairie and western fiction. Here we are confronted with Manfred's deep and abiding concern that his canon—his "Book"—will clearly define the importance of man's treatment of and identity in the land.

—Nancy Owen Nelson

MANLY, Marline. *See* **RATHBORNE, St. George.**

MANN, Charles. *See* **HECKELMANN, Charles N.**

MANN, Chuck. *See* **HECKELMANN, Charles N.**

MANN, E(dward) B(everly). Also wrote as Peter Field; Zachary Strong. American. Born in Hollis, Kansas, 31 January 1902. Educated at the University of Florida, Gainesville, 1923–27, A.B. 1927. Married 1) Helen Frazier Cubberly in 1928 (divorced 1939); 2) Elizabeth Goodell Parkhurst in 1942. Staff member, Willard Price advertising agency, New York, 1927–29. Since 1929 freelance writer and editor: editor, *American Rifleman*, Washington, D.C., 1943–45; editor, Military Service Publishing Company, Harrisburg, Pennsylvania, 1945–48; guns editor *Sun Trails*, Tucson, 1946–56; editor, *Guns Magazine*, *Guns Annual*, and *Shooting Industry*, all Skokie, Illinois, 1956–58. Director, University of New Mexico Press, Albuquerque, 1949–56.

WESTERN PUBLICATIONS

Novels (series: Jim Sinclair, The Whistler)

The Man from Texas. New York, Morrow, 1931; London, Hurst and Blackett, 1934.
The Blue-Eyed Kid. New York, Morrow, 1932.
The Valley of Wanted Men. New York, Morrow, 1932; London, Hurst and Blackett, 1933.
Killers' Range. New York, Morrow, 1933; London, Hurst and Blackett, 1934.
The Terror of Tombstone Trail. London, Hurst and Blackett, 1933.
Stampede. New York, Morrow, and London, Hurst and Blackett, 1934.
Gamblin' Man. New York, Morrow, 1934; London, Hurst and Blackett, 1935; as *Brett Randall, Gambler*, Leicester, Linford, 1988.
Rustlers' Round-Up (Whistler). New York, Morrow, 1935; London, Collins, 1936.
Thirsty Range. New York, Morrow, and London, Hurst and Blackett, 1935.
El Sombra (Whistler). New York, Morrow, and London, Collins, 1936.
Boss of the Lazy 9 (as Peter Field). New York, Morrow, 1936; London, Ward Lock, 1937.
Comanche Kid. New York, Morrow, and London, Collins, 1937.
With Spurs. New York, Morrow, 1937; as *Up from Texas*, London, Collins, 1938.
Shootin' Melody. New York, Morrow, and London, Collins, 1938.
Gun Feud. New York, Morrow, and London, Collins, 1939.
The Mesa Gang (as Zachary Strong). New York, Morrow, 1940.
Troubled Range. New York, Morrow, 1940; London, Collins, 1941.
Gunsmoke Trail. New York, Morrow, 1942; London, Collins, 1943.
Outlaws Against the Law-Badge (as Zachary Strong). London, Swan, 1947.
Dead Man's Gorge. New York, Lion, 1950.
Gunslick—By Request!; Luck Rides with the Fastest Gun. New York, Belmont, 1965.
The Buzzards of Apache Gap; Return of the Sun-Cub. New York, Belmont, 1966.
The Avenger; Colt Crusade. New York, Belmont, 1966.

Short Stories

The Whistler: Three Western Novelettes. New York, Greenberg, 1953.

Uncollected Short Stories

"Quick Sixes," in *Western Story* (New York), 12 May 1934.
"A Fool for Land," in *Western Story* (New York), 23 June 1934.
"Gun Clue," in *Cowboy Stories* (New York), March 1936.
"Six-Gun Spurs," in *Western Story* (New York), 10 July–14 August 1937.
"Bullets for a Badman," in *Western Story* (New York), 25 June 1938.
"A Green Hand Hits the Owlhoot," in *Star Western* (Chicago), April 1940.
"Six-Gun Signature," in *Western Story* (London), June 1943.

OTHER PUBLICATIONS

Other

New Mexico, Land of Enchantment, with Fred E. Harvey. East Lansing, Michigan State University Press, 1955.

Editor, *The World of Guns.* Skokie, Illinois, Publishers' Development Corporation, 1964.

* * *

E.B. Mann's *El Sombra* is one of his several "Whistler" novels. U.S. Marshal Jim Sinclair, "The Whistler," is in northern Mexico to sell his ranch, the Hacienda Real, when he becomes aware of the dicatorship being imposed on the local people by an avaricious moneylender, Miguel Cuesta. Sinclair joins forces with an old friend, the young hidalgo Don Guido Moraga to oppose Cuesta's schemes. Sinclair and Moraga, who rallies the peasants as the mysterious masked rider, "El Sombra," expose Cuesta's crime and destroy him after a pitched battle with his men. The style is terse and vigorous, and the Mexican atmosphere is convincingly sketched. Danger, death, hair-breadth escapes, chilling suspense, romance—this fast-paced narrative has them all. But it is Moraga who claims the girl, while Sinclair rides into the sunset, with his eerie whistling trailing behind him.

Two more substantial novels, *Gamblin' Man* and *Comanche Kid*, may be taken as representative of Mann's best work. Like *El Sombra*, these novels show Mann's interest in the heroic legend of the American West. The characters are larger than life. *Gamblin' Man* is about a cool, gray-eyed youngster called Billy the Kid, and his part in the Lincoln County War. Mann fleshes out the narrative with historical details of the conflict, presenting The Kid as a born gambler led to outlawry by the consequences of his loyalty to the losing side. Once branded an outlaw, he becomes one. This novel does not end with the customary execution of The Kid in the darkness of Pete Maxwell's home. Mann opts for the legend, as Pat Garrett shoots a look-alike, and The Kid flees with his sweetheart, Kathie Haskell, to establish a new life under a new name. The hero becomes immortal.

Comanche Kid is not just a Western, but an intriguing and deftly handled detective story. It opens with Dallas Spain riding into Comanche, a gold-mining and cattle town, in search of his father's murderer. He soon befriends the sheriff and leading citizens, but becomes the enemy of a mine operator, Brick Zimmerman. Spain and Zimmerman are rivals for the affections of Paula Doran, a cattleman's daughter, and Spain suspects his enemy of being his father's killer. Spain does track down his father's slayer, and he earns the nickname "Comanche Kid," as the town's boxing champion. He also wins the hand of his sweetheart. As he solves one mystery, he discovers another, and his heroic image is enhanced as he solves this one, too. Unlike the other novels, this one is told by a first-person narrator, Sandy McNair, owner of the Paystreak Saloon. The narrator's involvement *in* the action (and the mystery) he recounts is a fascinating angle not often seen in a straightforward western novel. The technique is handled with aplomb, and it adds a great deal to the novel's effectiveness.

—Jerry A. Herndon

MANNING, David. *See* **BRAND, Max.**

MANNING, Roy. *See* **WEST, Tom.**

MARSHALL, Gary. *See* **SNOW, Charles H.**

MARTELL, James. *See* **BINGLEY, David Ernest.**

MARTIN, Bruce. *See* **PAINE, Lauran.**

MARTIN, Chuck. Pseudonym for Charles Morris Martin. American. Born in Cincinnati, Ohio, 25 December 1891. Worked for the California Land and Cattle Company, c.1910; fought in Mexico as a mercenary soldier on the side of Pancho Villa in 1915; later worked on cattle ranches in California and elsewhere in the West, sold paint products in China and Japan, was a cowboy singer in vaudeville, and worked as a rodeo announcer in such places as New York City's Madison Square Garden and San Francisco's Cow Palace. Wrote 300 gangster stories, and during 1930's wrote under six different pseudonyms. Deputy Chief Air Raid Warden, Oceanside, California, during World War II, Newspaper columnist, ("Freedom of the Press"), *Brewery Gulch Gazette*, Oceanside, California. *Died in 1954.*

Western Publications

Novels

Lefthanded Law. New York, Greenberg, 1936.
Tie-Fast Hombre. New York, Greenberg, 1936.
Stick 'Em Up, Cowboy! London, Nicholson and Watson, 1936.
Range Law. London, Nicholson and Watson, 1936.
Gun Boss Reynolds. London, Nicholson and Watson, 1937.
Arizona Sheriff. London, Nicholson and Watson, 1937.
Lost River Buckaroos. London, Nicholson and Watson, 1937.
The Deuce of Diamonds. London, Nicholson and Watson, 1938.
Gun Bait. London, Nicholson and Watson, 1938.
Gun Law. London, Nicholson and Watson, 1938.
Maverick Money. London, Nicholson and Watson, 1938.
Powder Smoke Blood. London, Nicholson and Watson, 1938.
Double or Nothing. London, Nicholson and Watson, 1939.
Pinto Blood. London, Nicholson and Watson, 1939.
Riders of Purgatory. London, Cassell, 1940.
Rawhide. London, Quality Press, 1946.
Texas Law. London, Webb Gardner, 1948.
Once a Cowboy. New York, Viking Press, 1948.
Bring Me Wild Horses. Redhill, Webb, Gardner, Darton & Co., 1948.
Orphans of the Range. New York, Viking Press, 1950.
Vigilante Law. New York, Phoenix Press, 1950; Bath, Chivers, 1987.
Six Gun Town. New York, Phoenix Press, 1951.
The Lobo Breed. New York, and London, Boardman, 1951.
Box Star Buckaroos. New York, Phoenix Press, 1951.
Repentance at Boot Hill. London, Hammond, 1951; as *Boothill Gospel,* New York, Manor, 1969.
Hell-Bender from Texas. London, Hammond, 1952.
Dapper Donnelly, Six Gun Doctor. London, Hammond, 1952.
Cowboy Charley, 4-H Champ. New York, Viking Press, 1953.
Gunsmoke Bonanza. New York, Tower, 1953; London, Hammond, 1955.
Circle F Cowboy. London, Hammond, 1954.
Texas Pride. Hasbrouck Heights, New Jersey, Graphic, 1954.
Bloody Kansas. New York, Avon, 1955; London, Gold Lion, 1974.
Montana Dead-Shot. New York, Macfadden Bartell, 1958; London, Gold Lion, 1974.
Tall in the Saddle. New York, Macfadden Bartell, 1958; London, Gold Lion, 1974.
The Deputies from Hell. New York, Macfadden Bartell, 1964; London, Gold Lion, 1974.

Other Publications

Other

Monsters of Old Angeles: Prehistoric Animals of the La Brea Tar Pits. New York, Viking Press, 1950.

* * *

Charles M. "Chuck" Martin was one of pulp fiction's legendary million-words-a-year producers in the 1920's and 1930's. He was also one of its genuine characters.

Like many early western writers, Martin was a Westerner born and bred; he had first-hand knowledge of cowboy and ranching life, and claimed to have known Wyatt Earp and the Daltons. He was a brawling, hard-drinking individualist, after the fashion of his fictional heroes: salty, opinionated, violently patriotic. He carried on feuds with editors and other writers, and worked so hard at writing and other pursuits that he suffered at least one nervous breakdown. He believed passionately in the stories he wrote, so passionately that for him his fictional creations were real people and therefore entitled to the same privileges and courtesies. In the back yard of his southern California home he constructed a small private graveyard, complete with hand-made tombstones, in which he solemnly "buried" the characters he killed off in his Westerns.

Martin began writing for the pulps—in particular, for such Clayton and Hersey magazines as *Cowboy Stories*, *Ace-High Western*, and *Ranch Romances*—in the years following the end of World War I, and for more than two decades was one of the half-dozen or so most prolific manufacturers of old-fashioned horse opera. He boasted of an output, on good days, of 10,000 words at a single sitting. In 1929 he earned upwards of $1500 per month from his pulp writing—a princely sum in those days. By 1941 he had published 850 magazine stories (mostly novelettes and novellas) and 29 full-length novels under his own name and the pseudonym Clay Starr.

Few writers can keep up that sort of production pace throughout long careers; Martin was no exception. "The million-word-a-year man," he once wrote, "was sired by low rates, and killed off by his own exertion." Changing market requirements, and his inability to adapt to them, also contributed to Martin's decline from a big-name western pulpster to one who, in the post World War II 1940's and 1950's, was able to sell sporadically, and then only to bottom-of-the-barrel magazines and book publishers.

Even at its best his fiction is so highly colored, so determinedly western, that it approaches self-parody. For instance, this representative passage of dialogue from *Two-Gun Fury*: "Elevate, you mangy old wart-hog! I shot that Bisley Colt from your filly's hand, and never broke the skin. With you it will be different, you long-jointed old pelican. Drop your Winchester and sky them dew-claws before I do you a meanness!" His plots are hackneyed, generally implausible, and contrived to maximize violent action. His heroes and villains are grand-scale stereotypes, the West they inhabit—despite Martin's background—as wholly mythical as they are.

Nevertheless, his stories have great energy and narrative pace, of the sort that can only be created by True Believers, and may be read and enjoyed today as undemanding escape literature, as high camp, and/or as examples of the type of pulp western fiction popular in the 1920's and 1930's.

Notable among Martin's novels are those featuring his many series characters, particularly gunfighter and Wells Fargo troubleshooter Alamo Bowie (*Law for Tombstone*, *Gun Law*); roving cowboys Roaming Reynolds and Texas Joe (*Deuce of Diamonds*, *Double or Nothing*); and "Gospel" Cummings, a drunken, Bible-spouting gun artist and self-appointed caretaker of Boot Hill (*The Lobo Breed*, *Boot Hill Gospel*). Cummings is easily Martin's most interesting creation, "a man with a dual personality. The good man of his nature lived on the left side, where his heart was. In the left tail of his coat, he carried a well-thumbed copy of Holy Writ. The bad man of his nature lived on the right side. It was there he carried a balanced Colt .45 six-shooter [and] a quart of Three Daisies Whiskey, the token of his besetting sin . . ."

—Bill Pronzini

MARTIN, Tom. *See* **PAINE, Lauran.**

MARVIN, W.R. *See* **JAMES, Laurence.**

MASON, Carl. *See* **KING, Albert.**

MASON, Chuck. *See* **ROWLAND, Donald S.**

MATHEWS, John Joseph. American. Born in Pawhuska, Oklahoma, 16 November 1895. Educated at the University of the South, Sewanee, Tennessee, 1915; University of Oklahoma, Norman, B.A. 1920 (Phi Beta Kappa); Oxford University, B.A. 1923; University of Geneva, 1923. Served in the United States Air Force, 1918: Lieutenant. Married Elizabeth Palmour in 1945; one daughter and one son. Realtor in Los Angeles and Pasadena, California, 1926–28. From 1928 rancher and freelance writer. Member of the Osage Tribal Council, 1934–42, and the Oklahoma Board of Education, 1935. Recipient: Guggenheim fellowship, 1939; University of Oklahoma Distinguished Service citation, 1962; American Association of State and Local History award, 1962. *Died.*

WESTERN PUBLICATIONS

Novel

Sundown. New York and London, Longman, 1934.

OTHER PUBLICATIONS

Other

Wah'kon-tah: The Osage and the White Man's Road. Norman, University of Oklahoma Press, 1932.
Talking to the Moon. Chicago, University of Chicago Press, 1945.
Life and Death of an Oilman: The Career of E.W. Marland. Norman, University of Oklahoma Press, 1951.
The Osages, Children of the Middle Waters. Norman, University of Oklahoma Press, 1961.

* * *

John Joseph Mathews wrote only one book that can properly be called a novel; and often that novel, *Sundown*, reads like a social documentary. On the other hand, his nonfiction works often have the vivid thrust of narrative. Certainly this is true of *Wah'kon-tah: The Osage and the White Man's Road.* Universally praised by critics, *Wah'kon-tah* was a Book-of-the-Month Club selection in 1932, a rare occurrence for a university press publication. The book was based on a journal left by Major Laban J. Miles, who became agent to the Osage Indians in 1878 and was their friend until his death in 1931. The journal itself is fortuitously enlivened with tribal feeling and thinking in Mathews's capable hands.

With the exception of *Sundown*, the remainder of Mathews's work is straightforward history and sociology. *Life and Death of an Oilman: The Career of E.W. Marland*, for example, has a sure niche in bibliographies of the Southwest. Mathews has always seemed most comfortable with this kind of prose. Indeed, he has said of his own novel that he was asked to write it, really didn't want to, but did. Authors' statements about their own work are always suspect, but apparently Mathews really does hold *Sundown* in little regard. Though it is not a great novel, it is certainly not to be disregarded.

As the novel opens, in the 1890's, Challenge Windzor is born to a pure-breed Osage mother and a half-breed father. With his name shortened to Chal, the boy grows up on the reservation, graduates from high school, and attends the University of Oklahoma. After serving as an officer pilot in World War I, he drifts back to the reservation. There are no dramatic, memorable incidents in the novel, just a continuous mood of despair as the protagonist encounters Indian values he can no longer accept and white values which deny his heritage. He is truly, in Mathew Arnold's words, "wandering between two worlds, one dead, / The other powerless to be born." In addition to being one of the first novels to treat the problem of cultural assimilation, *Sundown* has another distinction. It is among the earliest and best novels dealing with the impact of oil money on the Osage and how it degrades and weakens him. When Mathews takes his readers to the reservation, he waxes most lyrical. At one point, he contrasts the black, encroaching oil derricks with the native blackjack oak trees. This is a simple but effective device for illustration of his major theme.

—Robert J. Barnes

MAXWELL, Grant. *See* **RICHARDSON, Gladwell.**

MAYO, Jim. *See* **L'AMOUR, Louis.**

McADAMS, Charles. *See* **RICHARDSON, Gladwell.**

McAFEE, Paul (K.). Address: c/o Robert Hale Ltd., Clerkenwell House, 45–47 Clerkenwell Green, London EC1R 0HT, England.

WESTERN PUBLICATIONS

Novels

High Meadows Showdown. London, Hale, 1988.
Gunsmoke Valley. London, Hale, 1989.

Wild Horse Canyon. London, Hale, 1990.
Bonner. London, Hale, 1991.

* * *

Paul McAfee's light and rather unassuming Westerns tend to be traditional affairs which rarely depart from expectation. His heroes are usually young and handsome. His villains are older and almost embarrassingly direct when plotting their evil machinations. Generally McAfee sets his stories in open country, and appears to introduce female characters mainly to provide an element of romance for his heroes. McAfee is obviously a very keen writer, and this comes through in all his books, but sadly his talent doesn't always match his enthusiasm. His development as a novelist can be traced quite clearly through his first three books, and it is a development which augurs well for his future in the genre.

High Meadows Showdown is a fairly standard "oater" which begins, like all of McAfee's books, with the arrival of the hero into the country around which the story is set. In this case, young Guy Lowell has come to the mountains to inherit a sizeable tract of land from his recently deceased father. He soon discovers that he is to share the land with a partner, the beautiful Jo Gunther. Before long, Lowell also encounters cattle-baron Terrance Hubert, who is after their land and not at all fussy as to how he gets it. During the course of the rather familiar plot which follows, Lowell is framed for murder, his cattle are rustled, and Jo is kidnapped. The climax takes the shape of a curious kind of "double" gunfight.

Although by no means a bad Western, *High Meadows Showdown* does tend to suffer from some rather perfunctory characterisation and stilted, largely unabbreviated dialogue. McAfee clearly defines his heroes and villains, leaving no grey areas on either side, and handles the romance between Lowell and Jo in a predictable and somewhat clumsy fashion. He is at least able to sustain plot and character from start to finish, however, and for the less discriminating western reader, the book would doubtless provide adequate entertainment. The author treads much the same ground again in his second range-based novel, *Gunsmoke Valley*, in which his hero, Brad Colton, returns home from the Civil War to find that his father has been murdered and his cattle are being rustled.

Wild Horse Canyon, by contrast, shows a remarkable maturity, and boasts rounder, more credible characters caught up in a more convincing and ultimately better resolved plot. It is, in fact, quite probably McAfee's best work to date, and certainly shows the rousing, albeit still fairly conventional kind of Western he is capable of producing.

Again the story begins with an arrival of sorts, or, to be more accurate, a *return*, since his protagonist Chase Weston, like Brad Colton before him, has just come home following the end of the Civil War. As with many other fictional western heroes, however, Weston soon discovers that much has changed. His parents are both dead, for one thing, and his prize horse, Brutus, is in the hands of two of his less than respectable neighbours, the Glover brothers.

Weston has to kill the Glovers to get his horse back, and with little else to keep him in the area, he rides on to Denver. But even there Weston runs into trouble when the local "nasty," Bart Slocum, takes a fancy to his stallion and, after first attempting to trick him out of the animal, has him beaten up and then simply takes it. While recovering, Weston decides to cut his losses and teams up with a wily old horse-catcher named Crawford and the man's beautiful half-Ute daughter Tanya, and together they set about trapping fresh horses in the canyon of the book's title. Inevitably, of course, Weston tangles with Slocum again, and following much the same formula created in *High Meadows Showdown*, McAfee's young protagonist is framed for murder. Eventually Weston tries to settle the enmity between them by suggesting a horse race (he having caught and trained a new animal called Red Star), the winner to take sole legal possession of Brutus. The race forms the climax of the story.

Despite the presence of another standard text-book villain and some often creaky dialogue ("Tanya, we will soon be done here. But I don't want it to end there. I mean . . . I want to see you more!"), *Wild Horse Canyon* is a most entertaining diversion which clearly displays the author's growing confidence when developing plot and character.

McAfee's work is undemanding and without pretension. His West is the West of the 1940's B-movie. His main characters usually speak without elision although his supporting players communicate more through clipped speech sprinkled with odd westernisms. The author does not favour graphic violence, although when his villains are in their death-throes, their heels invariably "beat a rapid tattoo upon the hardpan." Neither is there much humour in his essentially male-dominated West. A potentially interesting writer, it remains to be seen if his future work in the genre will validate the promise shown in *Wild Horse Canyon.*

—David Whitehead

McCAIG, Robert (Jesse). Also wrote as Edith Engren. American. Born in Seattle, Washington, 8 September 1907. Educated at Great Falls High School, Montana, graduated 1923. Married Edith V. Engren in 1953. Receiving clerk, Paris Dry Goods Store, Great Falls, 1922–25; meter reader and divisional assistant, 1923–63, and divisional chief accountant, 1963–72, Montana Power Company, Great Falls. Director, 1961–62, vice-president, 1974–75, and president, 1975–76, Western of Writers of America. *Died 28 April 1982.*

WESTERN PUBLICATIONS

Novels

Toll Mountain. New York, Dodd Mead, 1953; London, Collins, 1954.
Haywire Town. New York, Dodd Mead, 1954; as *Ghost Town*, London, Collins, 1955.
Danger West! New York, Dodd Mead, 1954; London, Collins, 1955.
Bronc Stomper. New York, Dodd Mead, 1956; as *The Sun and the Dust*, London, Collins, 1957.
Snow on the Prairie. London, Collins, 1958.
The Rangemaster. New York, Ace, 1958; London, Collins, 1960.
Wild Justice. New York, Macmillan, 1959; London, Collins, 1960.
Drowned Man's Lode. New York, Macmillan, 1960; as *Five Dead Men*, London, Collins, 1962.
The Burntwood Men. New York, Macmillan, and London, Collins, 1961.
Crimson Creek. New York, Macmillan, and London, Collins, 1963.
The Gotherson Spread. New York, Berkley, 1966.
The Shadow Maker. New York, Ace, 1970.
The Danger Trail. New York, Doubleday, 1975.

Stoneman's Gap. New York, Ballantine, 1976.
Sweet Deadly Eden. New York, Zebra, 1982.

OTHER PUBLICATIONS

Novel

Marcy Tarrant (as Edith Engren), with Edith McCaig. New York, Fawcett, 1978; London, Coronet, 1979.

Other

That Nester Kid (for children). New York, Scribner, 1961.
Electric Power in America. New York, Putnam, 1970.

*

Manuscript Collection: University of Wyoming, Laramie.

* * *

Robert McCaig fits the mold when it comes to western writing. His books pit the good guy against the bad guy, plenty of action is included, and justice always triumphs. McCaig is traditional. His books reflect the West substantially in three stages: the time of the fur traders, the era of the American cowboy, and the development of the West in the years of World War I and beyond. Regardless of the time, however, McCraig writes of honest, decent people who prevail over those who would cheat and kill. If good does not triumph over evil, then obviously the novel is not about the West that McCaig understands and loves.

In *Snow on the Prairie*, for instance, the hanging of a stranger for horse stealing starts a chain of circumstances that haunts the hero, Dallas Kinross. The reader watches Kinross grow stronger in character as he overcomes the evil that threatens the Montana range. In *Wild Justice* a professional gunman with a maniacal hatred of lawbreakers teaches the tricks of the killer's trade to his young apprentice, Tod Morgan. But Tod learns there is more to life and justice than the path of hatred, when his mentor, John Starr, is treacherously killed and Tod nearly loses the girl he loves. *The Burntwood Men* follows the career of Tam Harris, a peaceable, civil young Easterner thrust into the turmoil of the tough frontier. Tam learns how to cope with a hard country and hard men, as he struggles to foil the machinations of Cleland Strike. How he succeeds makes a story of character development against a background of oppressed people and a vast frontier.

As the basic Western has changed throughout the years, the author has kept pace. Women have a greater role. The books reflect painstaking research as McCaig makes certain that clothes, weapons, speech, habits, politics, customs and mannerisms are true to life. Any Westerner will recognize the landscape and people.

McCaig wrote one book for children. *That Nester Kid* was the story of a youngster growing up on a farm in the West. Although the tale had a fine plot, McCaig obviously did not consider stories for young people to be his forte, for he never wrote another. His one nonfiction book, *Electric Power in America*, broke new ground in terms of American understanding of this vital utility. He also contributed the opening chapter in *Water Trails West*, a project of the Western Writers of America, of which McCaig is a former president.

McCaig writes for the average reader. He doesn't preach, and he doesn't write smut. His books return the reader to a time when life seemed much simpler, when choices were more clear-cut, when one didn't need a score card to recognize the bad guys. That's what the true Western is all about, and that's why McCaig is one of its most successful practictioners.

—Leon C. Metz

McCARTHY, Cormac. American. Born in Providence, Rhode Island, 20 July 1933. Educated at the University of Tennessee. Served in the United States Air Force, 1953–56. Married to Anne de Lisle. Recipient: Ingram Merril Foundation grant, 1960; American Academy of Arts and Letters travel fellowship, 1965–66; William Faulkner Foundation award, for novel, 1965; Rockefeller Foundation grant, 1966; Guggenheim fellowship, 1976.

WESTERN PUBLICATIONS

Novels

Suttree. New York, Random House, 1979; London, Chatto and Windus, 1980.
Blood Meridian, or The Evening Redness in the West. New York, Random House, 1985; London, Picador, 1989.

OTHER PUBLICATIONS

Novels

The Orchard Keeper. New York, Random House, 1965.
Outer Dark. New York, Random House, 1968.
Child of God. New York, Random House, 1974; London, Picador, 1989.

Play

Television Play: *The Gardener's Son*, 1977.

* * *

Cormac McCarthy is often compared with writers such as William Faulkner, Carson McCullers, Flannery O'Connor and William Styron, all Southern-based writers. He is in no way a commercial writer, and many critics liken him to an ancient Greek dramatist. In fact, he won the William Faulkner Foundation award in 1965 for his novel *The Orchard Keeper*. He has only produced four books since then, each of which has received great critical acclaim.

Blood Meridian recounts the adventures of a young man from Tennessee (McCarthy's own hunting ground), who is simply called "the kid," as he drifts away from his drunken father into the Texas of the 1840's. Already there is a violent nature lurking within him, and a perfect outlet arises when he joins a party of crazed and violent Indian scalphunters, led by Judge Holden and John Glanton. Others in the band are perfectly willing to be led across the country collecting their grisly prizes by the two men, whom they hold in awe, along with the ex-priest Tobin. As they journey on they deal out death and destruction to Apaches, Mexicans, and cowboys alike. Their "prey" is given no quarter as the men fight to survive the harshness of the Southwest.

The atmosphere of violence which permeates the novel is intensified by descriptions of the landscape, such as "They struggled all day across a terra damnata of smoking slag," or, "the young corn in the roadside fields had been washed by recent rains and stood white and luminous, bleached almost transparent by the sun." The elements are the men's enemies as well, as they suffer the sun, rain, journeys across arid deserts without horses and water, and occasionally without headgear. McCarthy's vivid description holds the reader, its strange, magnetic prose both unsettling and powerful, demanding attention from the opening passage: "See the child. He is pale and thin, he wears a thin and ragged linen shirt . . . He can neither read nor write and in him broods already a taste for mindless violence. All history present in that visage, the child the father of the man . . ."

McCarthy's dialogue is sparse in places, but credible and to the point. The author manages to grasp the authenticity of the mid-19th century with a feel for rich detail almost casually cast down on the page.

The violence McCarthy depicts so well is darkly disturbing; he simply refuses to glorify the deaths: "The Delaware let drop the reins and took down his warclub from his bag and stepped astraddle of the man and swung the club and crushed his skull with a single blow . . ." Other passages are more violent and vivid: ". . . seizing them up by the hair and passing blades about the skulls of the living and the dead alike and snatching aloft the bloody wigs and hacking and chopping at the naked bodies, ripping off limbs, heads, gutting the strange white torsos and holding up great handfuls of viscera, genitals . . ." A far cry from anything that the Adult Western has to offer.

He manages to break from the "traditional" Western to produce an anti-Western as vivid as any Sam Peckinpah movie. The myth that both pulp novels and celluloid created is shattered in *Blood Meridian.* Gone are specific characters of good and evil; in their places he creates demi-gods, capable of the taking and the giving of life, with the balance of power held almost wantonly. The kid, the judge, and Glanton are the book's central characters: all are instruments of death, whose vagrant way of life moulds their destinies into one. Their exchanges and personal conflicts are the highlights of the book, and even at the end McCarthy shields the kid's and Holden's final meeting in a mystical shroud.

It would be errant not to include *Child of God* in this essay. It is set sometime in the 19th century, not a true Western, but it does deal with social issues which have so far been considered taboo by many. The setting is Faulkner's domain—Tennessee—and within it McCarthy tells the story of Lester Ballard, a solitary backwoodsman who loses everything when he is dispossessed of his property and forced to roam the hill country. The novel is told in a series of short scenes, with rape, incest, murder, and necrophilia brought vividly home to the reader. As in *Blood Meridian*, the underlying theme is of endurance and persistence. Ballard refuses to give in as his world crumbles around him. McCarthy does not dwell too much on Ballard's past nor on what makes him the unbalanced killer that he is—the dissecting is literally left to the end. This may be the book's main flaw—the reader has to accept Ballard at face value, and is never allowed to identify with or pity him. Considering the bestial crimes Ballard commits, McCarthy distances the reader from any sympathetic support by paring his prose down to the bone.

McCarthy is a gifted writer, who excels in novels of human degradation. He is a born storyteller, and his unusually perceptive views of life will undoubtedly continue to intrigue. The power of his narrative is strong, inasmuch as when *Blood Meridian* begins one feels that there is a stanzaic quality to the prose. It draws one deeper into the book, and as with all his works he makes us want to read more.

—Mike Stotter

McCARTHY, Gary. American. Born in South Gate, California, 23 January 1943. Educated at California State Polytechnic College, Pomona, 1964–68, B.S. in agriculture 1968; University of Nevada, Reno, 1968–70, M.S. in agricultural economics 1970. Served as a hospital corpsman in the United States Navy, 1960–64. Married Virginia Kurzweil in 1969; three daughters and one son. Labor economist, State of Nevada, Carson City, 1970–76; economist, Copley International Corporation, La Jolla, California, 1977–79. Since 1979 full-time writer. President, Rotary of Ojai, 1991–92. Agent: Joseph Elder, 150 West 87th Street, Apt. 6.D, New York, New York 10024. Address: 1211 Maricopa Highway, no.265, Ojai, California 93023, U.S.A.

Western Publications

Novels (series: Rivers West)

The First Sheriff. New York, Doubleday, 1979.
The Legend of the Lone Ranger (novelization of screenplay). New York, Ballantine, 1981.
The Last Buffalo Hunt. New York, Doubleday, 1985.
Mando. New York, Bantam, 1986.
The Mustangers. New York, Doubleday, 1987.
Sodbuster. New York, Doubleday, 1988.
Blood Brothers. New York, Doubleday, 1989.
The Colorado River (Rivers West). New York, Bantam, 1990.
Gringo Amigo. New York, Doubleday, 1991.
The Russian River (Rivers West). New York Bantam, 1991.

Novels (series: Derby Man in all books)

The Derby Man. New York, Doubleday, 1976; London, Hale, 1978.
Showdown at Snakegrass Junction. New York, Doubleday, 1978; London, Hale, 1979.
Mustang Fever. New York, Doubleday, 1980; London, Hale, 1981.
The Pony Express War. New York, Bantam, 1980.
Silver Shot. New York, Bantam, 1981.
Explosion at Donner Pass. New York, Bantam, 1981.
North Chase. New York, Bantam, 1982.
Rebel of Bodie. New York, Bantam, 1982.
The Rail Warriors. New York, Bantam, 1982.

Other Publications

Novels

Winds of Gold. New York, Pocket Books, 1980.
Silver Winds. New York, Ballantine, 1983.
Wind River. New York, Ballantine, 1984.
Powder River. New York, Ballantine, 1985.
Transcontinental. New York, Paperjacks, 1987.

*

Gary McCarthy comments:

I most enjoy conveying the drama of Western Americana through fictional characters. The Derby Man series, for example, was a perfect vehicle for this, and allowed me to both entertain and enlighten the reader about such dramatic events as the Pony Express, the building of the transcontinental railroad, and the Comstock Lode. After a nine-year hiatus, I have contracted with Doubleday to do more Derby Man novels, and will continue to have the decidedly offbeat series character, Darby Buckingham, write about his adventures while telling the story of the West.

More and more, my interest seems to be in longer historical novels. Bantam's Rivers West series is an example of how fiction and fact can be blended to tell exciting, informative stories about the exploration of the West's major rivers. Following The Colorado and The Russian River novels, I am now researching The American, which will tell the story of the famed Forty-Niner Gold Rush. The trick for a writer is not deciding which story to tell, but in concluding which not to tell because there are so many magnificent historical events just begging to be developed and peopled with real-life characters.

* * *

Gary McCarthy has been a successful writer of popular genre westerns for 15 years. His novels fall generally into three groups: the Derby Man series, historical novels, and assorted Westerns in the popular mode. His 24 novels so far comprise a substantial production, and his work is well respected among other practitioners of western writing. By virtue of the originality and humor of his tales, plus the solid historical settings, McCarthy promises to be a significant producer of western fiction in the years to come.

McCarthy first secured a reputation with the Derby Man series. After the first two books (*The Derby Man* and *Showdown at Snakegrass Junction*), the Derby Man moves west out of Wyoming into Nevada and California, where his adventures take place in more historically detailed settings. The Derby Man, Darby Buckingham, is an eastern dime novelist, a short, stocky, but powerfully built man who has a flair for becoming embroiled in major historical events—the Pony Express (*The Pony Express War*), the Comstock silver strike (*Silver Shot*), the building of the Central Pacific railroad (*Explosion at Donner Pass*), the building of the Union Pacific railroad (*The Rail Warriors*), and the Alaskan purchase (*North Chase*). *Mustang Fever* is about the mustang trade in Nevada, and *Rebel of Bodie* is set in the high Sierra town of Bodie, which is today a gold-mining ghost town and California state park. The reader may feel a cumulatively strained suspension of disbelief as Darby Buckingham becomes a central participant in shaping historical process, but each book on its own is a pleasant piece of entertainment. The stories are well-plotted, well-paced, and well-researched; the writing is sprightly and frequently witty, and the historical material is usually integrated comfortably into the narrative.

The *Derby Man* series has emerged at a time when western writers have been expected to turn out well-researched, historically sound material, so the historical dimension of these stories is fairly conventional. In the characterization of the title character, however, the series is atypical in conception. The Derby Man is not the usual tall, lean-hipped, broad-shouldered, seasoned tough man of the frontier. Being quite the opposite, he finds himself in more cerebral conflicts and more genial conversations than the typical hero does. (Of course, there is plenty of physical conflict and adventure as well.) The incongruity between the stocky Easterner, who likes elegant cuisine, expensive brandy, and Cuban cigars, and his new environment, which consists of beef, beans, red-eye, and roll-your-owns, adds humor and innovation to the conventionally structured conflicts of the popular Western.

McCarthy's historical novels are not as humorous as the Derby Man stories, but they are more ambitious and more comprehensive. The best of these are *Winds of Gold*, set in the California gold rush; *Wind River*, set in and around Fort Bridger and the Wind River country of Wyoming; and *The Colorado* (part of the Rivers West series, by various writers), set mainly along the Colorado River. McCarthy's historicals are characterized by thoroughly researched historical information, a wide cast of characters (some of them from history), and a continuous flow of action and suspense. McCarthy, who visits the locales he writes about, draws evocative portraits of the gold country, Fort Bridger and the sheep country, and the country along the Colorado. The narrative is best when it is out of doors, which it frequently is.

McCarthy's other Westerns vary in style in content. *The Last Buffalo Hunt* is a not entirely plausible but sometimes humorous tale of a buffalo hunt in Wyoming. *Mando*, set during the battle for Texas independence, is rife with action and killings but speaks sincerely for respecting Spaniards and Mexicans. *Sodbuster*, a personal favorite of McCarthy's, tells the story of a Wyoming homesteader boy and his older sister, who gets seduced by a Texas cowboy; this story is somewhat daring, for the genre, in portraying the boy's awareness of his sister's sexuality, and it also gives serious treatment to the theme of self-determination.

In all of his work, McCarthy adheres to the general rules of entertainment fiction. His characterizations are individualized but recognizable, his conflicts are clearly defined and decisively resolved (frequently by violence), and his thematic content affirms rather than challenges the broadly held values of the popular audience. His prose style and his incorporation of historical material have improved with the years, and his ability to tell a fast-moving story has not slackened. With his announced return to the Derby Man series and his certain continuation in the historical mode, McCarthy promises to bring forth honest, entertaining fiction in the years to come.

—John D. Nesbitt

McCLOUD, Jed. *See* **FEARN, John Russell.**

McCORD, Whip. *See* **NORWOOD, V.G.C.**

McCOY, Marshall. *See* **GROVER, Marshall.**

McCOY, Mich. *See* **FEARN, John Russell.**

McCULLEY, Johnston. American. Born in Ottawa, Illinois, 2 February 1883. Educated by private tutors and in local schools. Married Louise Munsey Powers in 1925; one daughter. Freelance writer: special correspondent for newspapers in the United States and abroad. *Died 23 November 1958.*

WESTERN PUBLICATIONS

Novels (series: Zorro)

The Mark of Zorro. New York, Grosset and Dunlap, 1924; London, Macdonald, 1959.
John Standon of Texas. New York, Chelsea House, 1924; London, Hutchinson, 1926.
The Rangers' Code. New York, Watt, 1924; London, Hutchinson, 1925.
Captain Fly-by-Night. London, Jenkins, 1925; New York, Watt, 1926.
Further Adventures of Zorro. London, Hutchinson, 1926.
A White Man's Chance. New York, Watt, and London, Hutchinson, 1927.
The Blocked Trail. New York, Watt, 1932; London, Hutchinson, 1933.
The Flaming Stallion. New York, Watt, and London, Hutchinson, 1932.
Range Lawyer. New York, Arcadia House, 1932; London, Hutchinson, 1940; as *Bullet Law*, New York, Avon, 1959.
The Range Cavalier. New York, Watt, 1933; London, Hutchinson, 1934.
Rangeland Justice. New York, Watt, and London, Hutchinson, 1934.
The Trusted Outlaw. New York, Watt, and London, Hutchinson, 1934.
Riders Against the Moon. New York, Watt, 1935; London, Hutchinson, 1936.
Canyon of Peril. New York, Watt, and London, Hutchinson, 1935.
Reckless Range. New York, Dodge, and London, Hutchinson, 1937.
Smoky Sarn. London, Hutchinson, 1938.
Holsters in Jeopardy. London, Hutchinson, 1939.
Gold of Smoky Mesa. New York, Gateway, 1942.
South of the Pass. New York, Arcadia House, 1944; London, Hutchinson, 1949.
The Cougar Kid. New York, Arcadia House, 1945; London, Hutchinson, 1950.
Ghost Bullet Range. New York, Arcadia House, 1945; London, Hutchinson, 1948.
Señor Avalanche. New York, Arcadia House, 1946; London, Hutchinson, 1950.
The Caballero. New York, Curl, 1947; London, Hutchinson, 1950.
Iron Horse Town. New York, Arcadia House, 1952.
Texas Showdown. New York, Arcadia House, 1953; London, Mills and Boon, 1954.
The Outlaw Trail. Toronto, Harlequin, 1953.
Black Grandee. London, Hale, 1955.
Gunsight Showdown. New York, Avon, 1956.
Blood on the Saddle. New York, Avon, 1957.
Gunsmoke Vengeance. New York, Avon, 1957.
The Tenderfoot. London, Wright and Brown, 1957.

Uncollected Short Stories (series: Zorro)

"A Trail of Mysteries," in *Argosy* (New York), June 1910.
"The Strength of Small," in *Adventure* (New York), November 1915.
"Little Erolinda," in *Adventure* (New York), February 1916.
"Daughter of the Sun," in *Argosy* (New York), 4 May–18 May 1918.
"The Brute Breaker," in *All-Story* (New York), 10 August 1918.
"The Gentle Stranger," in *Western Story* (New York), 25 November 1920.
"Settled Claims," with William D. Hoffman, in *Western Story* (New York), 11 December 1920.
"The Cactus Fool," with William D. Hoffman, in *Western Story* (New York), 18 December 1920.
"The Christmas Go-Between," in *Western Story* (New York), 25 December 1920.
"Butts First," in *Western Story* (New York), 26 February 1921.
"Code of the Woods," in *Western Story* (New York), 19 March–9 April 1921.
"In the Candelaria Reserve," with William D. Hoffman, in *Western Story* (New York), 23 April 1921.
"Reflected in the Mirage," with William D. Hoffman, in *Western Story* (New York), 30 April 1921.
"To the Satisfaction of Sheriff Tom," with William D. Hoffman, in *Western Story* (New York), 7 May 1921.
"Cowboy Avengement," in *Western Story* (New York), 6 August 1921.
"The Gorgeous Idiot," in *Western Story* (New York), 3 September 1921.
"The Tiny Tamer of Men," in *Western Story* (New York), 29 October 1921.
"'Hurricane' Hale," in *Western Story* (New York), 17 December 1921.
"Blurred Heroism," in *Western Story* (New York), 13 May 1922.
"Bad Man's Bluff," in *Western Story* (New York), 30 September 1922.
"The Strong-Box Trap," in *Western Story* (New York), 14 October 1922.
"Glorious Enemies," in *Western Story* (New York), 10 March 1923.
"Two Softies in Sunland," in *Western Story* (New York), 5 May 1923.
"The King of Cactusville," in *Western Story* (New York), 4 August–25 August 1923.
"Hard-Up Hayes and His Pearl-Handled Gun," in *Western Story* (New York), 10 November 1923.
"Saddle Mates," in *Western Story* (New York), 12 January 1924.
"Old Sidewinder Plays Samaritan," in *Western Story* (New York), 15 March 1924.
"The Red Finger of Dawn," in *Western Story* (New York), 3 May 1924.
"Slaves of the Desert Cup," in *Western Story* (New York), 14 June 1924.
"Ride 'em Cowboy!," in *Western Story* (New York), 2 August 1924.
"Yakima Copeland—Coward," in *Western Story* (New York), 6 December 1924.
"The Village of Wanted Men," in *Western Story* (New York), 8 August 1925.
"Holsters Tied Down," in *Western Story* (New York), 29 August–12 September 1925.
"The Unbranded 30," in *Western Story* (New York), 10 October 1925.
"Avengers Three," in *Western Story* (New York), 5 December 1925.
"Devil's Portage," in *Western Story* (New York), 24 April 1926.
"Twice-Found Gold," in *Argosy* (New York), 26 June 1926.
"Poison for Bad Men," in *Western Story* (New York), 31 July 1926.

"The Answering Flame," in *Western Story* (New York), 30 October 1926.
"New Boots," in *Argosy* (New York), 6 November 1926.
"The Broken Dollar," in *Far West* (New York), January 1927.
"Shootin' Mad," in *Western Story* (New York), 8 January 1927.
"The Trouble Man," in *Western Story* (New York), 23 April 1927.
"The Masked Trailer," in *Western Story* (New York), 21 May 1927.
"Drawn Fangs," in *Western Story* (New York), 8 October 1927.
"Plotters of Gopher Gulch," in *Western Story* (New York), 12 November 1927.
"A Snow-Bound Yuletide," in *Western Story* (New York), 24 December 1927.
"The Bunk House Pest," in *Western Story* (New York), 7 January 1928.
"The Green Sombrero," in *Western Story* (New York), 18 February 1928.
"Burning Feet," in *Western Story* (New York), 3 March 1928.
"Violence Valley," in *Western Story* (New York), 10 March 1928.
"Sixty Miles of Peril," in *Western Story* (New York), 17 March 1928.
"The Trail to Revenge," in *Western Story* (New York), 28 April 1928.
"Hands Down," in *Western Story* (New York), 9 June 1928.
"Ride North!," in *Western Story* (New York), 16 June 1928.
"Baby Beef," in *Western Story* (New York), 7 July 1928.
"At the Pit's Edge," in *Western Story* (New York), 14 July 1928.
"White Mask and Black Heart," in *Western Story* (New York), 28 July 1928.
"The Last Man," in *Western Story* (New York), 4 August 1928.
"Six-Guns and Soap," in *Western Story* (New York), 11 August 1928.
"Bedded Cattle," in *Western Story* (New York), 18 August 1928.
"The Town Tamer," in *Western Story* (New York), 15 September 1928.
"The Trouble Dodger," in *Western Story* (New York), 27 October 1928.
"The Bigwig Bandit," in *Western Story* (New York), 24 November 1928.
"Wild Wolf of Wyoming," in *Western Story* (New York), 15 December 1928.
"Wolf Claws and Santa Claus," in *Western Story* (New York), 22 December 1928.
"Wild William Wilts," in *Western Story* (New York), 5 January 1929.
"Tricky Hardware," in *Western Story* (New York), 12 January 1929.
"Chaps Make the Chap," in *Western Story* (New York), 19 January 1929.
"Traps and Trails," in *Western Story* (New York), 29 November 1930.
"The Bunk House Brute," in *Western Story* (New York), 17 January 1931.
"Zorro Rides Again," in *Argosy* (New York), 3 October–24 October 1931.
"What Price Outlaws?," in *Western Story* (New York), 10 September 1932.
"Taming an Outlaw," in *Western Story* (New York), 17 September 1932.
"Zorro Saves a Friend," in *Argosy* (New York), 12 November 1932.
"Crow Bait," in *Western Story* (New York), 7 January 1933.
"The Panamint Wolf," in *Western Story* (New York), 14 January 1933.
"Terror Town," in *Western Story* (New York), 22 April 1933.
"Zorro Hunts a Jackal," in *Argosy* (New York), 22 April 1933.
"The Trusted Outlaw," in *Western Story* (New York), 19 August 1933.
"The Black Dude," in *Western Story* (New York), 30 September 1933.
"Horgan Rides Alone," in *Western Story* (New York), 13 January 1934.
"The Romance Kid," in *Western Story* (New York), 3 February 1934.
"Zorro Deals with Treason," in *Argosy* (New York), 18 August 1934.
"Sheriffing for a Season," in *Western Story* (New York), 5 January 1935.
"Shooting Stranger," in *Western Story* (New York), 16 February 1935.
"Waste-Land Riders," in *Western Story* (New York), 13 April 1935.
"Señor Scalawag," in *Western Story* (New York), 8 June–29 June 1935.
"Sagebrush Sand," in *Western Story* (New York), 17 August 1935.
"Mysterious Don Miguel" (Zorro), in *Argosy* (New York), 21 September–28 September 1935.
"Weak Brother," in *Western Story* (New York), 28 September 1935.
"Hostile Town," in *Western Story* (New York), 26 October 1935.
"Treasure Trek," in *Western Story* (New York), 23 November 1935.
"Son of the Forest," in *Western Story* (New York), 1 February 1936.
"The Frontier Frame-Up," in *Western Story* (New York), 7 March 1936.
"Cowboy Afoot," in *Western Story* (New York), 18 April 1936.
"High and Mighty," in *Western Story* (New York), 6 June 1936.
"Circus Cowboy," in *Western Story* (New York), 20 August 1936.
"Don Peon," in *Western Story* (New York), 22 August–12 September 1936.
"Barriers of Gold," in *Western Story* (New York), 10 October 1936.
"Wench Caravan," in *Argosy* (New York), 26 December 1936–16 January 1937.
"The Romance Buster," in *Western Story* (New York), 23 January 1937.
"Señor Vulture," in *Argosy* (New York), 12 June–26 June 1937.
"Tumble-Down's Top Hand," in *Western Story* (New York), 19 June 1937.
"Crown Prince of Cattle Land," in *Western Story* (New York), 25 September 1937.
"Tainted Caballero," in *Argosy* (New York), 5 March–12 March 1938.
"Guns of the Cleanup Trail," in *West* (New York), January 1941.
"Dusty Reward," in *Wild West* (New York), 14 February 1942.
"Sue Saves Her Man," in *Thrilling Ranch Stories* (London), September 1944.
"Love in Emerald Valley," in *Thrilling Ranch Stories* (London), February 1945.
"Sons of Satan's Valley," in *Texas Rangers* (London), October 1945.
"Brush Poppers," in *Thrilling Western* (London), Winter 1945.
"Calf Love," in *Thrilling Ranch Stories* (London), March 1946.
"Ranger Out of Bounds," in *Texas Rangers* (London), April 1946.

"Senorita Whirlwind," in *Thrilling Ranch Stories* (London), September 1946.
"Tilda of the Tomboy Spread," in *Thrilling Ranch Stories* (London), December 1946.
"Christmas at Broken Wheel," in *Thrilling Western* (London), Summer 1947.
"New Year's Stranger," in *Thrilling Ranch Stories* (London), June 1949.
"Blister City Sawbones," in *Western Story* (London), May 1949.
"Ranger's Happy New Year," in *Texas Rangers* (London), July 1949.
"Trail to Heart's Desire," in *Thrilling Ranch Stories* (London), February 1951.
"Pilgrim on the Prod," in *Exciting Western* (London), June 1951.
"Trading Post Christmas," in *Thrilling Western* (London), January 1954.
"Undercover Santa Claus," in *Exciting Western* (London), November 1954.
"New Year's at Coyote Creek," in *Exciting Western* (London), January 1955.
"Buckskin Santa Claus," in *Exciting Western* (London), April 1955.
"Gunsmoke's Happy New Year," in *Thrilling Western* (London), May 1955.
"Hunted Man," in *Exciting Western* (London), July 1955.
"Santa Rides a Burro," in *Texas Rangers* (London), May 1956.
"Feast of Flaming Guns," in *Texas Rangers* (London), December 1960.
"Shaggy Pants," in *Texas Rangers* (London), February 1961.
"Singin' Steve Comes Home," in *Texas Rangers* (London), October 1961.
"Zorro Draws His Blade," in *The Californians*, edited by Bill Pronzini and Martin H. Greenberg. New York, Fawcett, 1989.

OTHER PUBLICATIONS

Novels

Broadway Bab. New York, Watt, 1919; London, Hutchinson, 1926.
The Masked Woman. New York, Watt, 1920; London, Jenkins, 1925.
The Black Star. New York, Chelsea House, 1921; London, Hutchinson, 1924.
The Thunderbolt Collects. London, Lloyd, 1921.
Black Star's Campaign. New York, Chelsea House, 1924; London, Hutchinson, 1925.
The Demon. New York, Chelsea House, 1925.
The Scarlet Scourge. New York, Chelsea House, 1925.
The Spider's Den. New York, Chelsea House, 1925.
Black Star's Return. New York, Chelsea House, 1926; London, Hutchinson, 1927.
Alias the Thunderbolt. New York, Chelsea House, 1927; London, Cassell, 1930.
The Avenging Twins. New York, Chelsea House, and London, Hutchinson, 1927.
The Avenging Twins Collect. New York, Chelsea House, 1927.
The Thunderbolt's Jest. New York, Chelsea House, 1927.
The Crimson Clown Again. New York, Chelsea House, and London, Cassell, 1928.
The Spider's Debt. New York, Chelsea House, and London, Hutchinson, 1930.
The Spider's Fury. New York, Chelsea House, 1930; London, Hutchinson, 1931.
Black Star's Revenge. New York, Chelsea House, n.d.; as *Black Star Again*, London, Hutchinson, 1934.
The Rollicking Rogue. London, Hutchinson, 1939; New York, Arcadia House, 1941.
The Devil's Dubloons. London, Hutchinson, 1955.

Short Stories

The Crimson Clown. London, Cassell, 1927; New York, Chelsea House, 1928.

Plays

Screenplays: *Ride for Your Life*, with Raymond L. Schrock and E. Richard Schayer, 1924; *The Beloved Rogue*, with Wells Root, 1936; *The Trusted Outlaw*, with George H. Plympton, 1937; *The Red Rope*, with George H. Plympton, 1937; *Rootin' Tootin' Rhythm*, with Jack Natteford, 1937; *Rose of the Rio Grande*, with Dorothy Reid and Ralph Bettinson, 1938; *Doomed Caravan*, with Ralph Bettinson, 1941; *Overland Mail*, with Paul Huston, 1941; *Raiders of the Border*, with Jess Bowers, 1944; *Mark of the Renegade*, with Robert H. Andrews and Louis Solomon, 1951.

Television Plays: *Zorro* series, 1957–59.

* * *

Johnston McCulley was a hack writer with no pretensions other than to write adventure stories steadily and successfully. He began as a newspaperman, became a playwright, and the author of numerous short stories for the pulp magazine market. His subject matter ranged from the crime thriller to the Western.

Although he lived and worked primarily in New York City, McCulley had an avid interest in the California mission system of the early Spanish settlers. From this evolved an affinity with Old West lore. Drawing from these two areas, McCulley created one of the most popular fictional characters of all time—Zorro, the fox.

Zorro first appeared in the serial "The Curse of Capistrano" published in the pulp magazine *All Story Weekly* in 1919. The character received a very popular reception, so it was not surprising to find Zorro on the motion picture screen in *The Mark of Zorro* (1920), brought to movie life by Douglas Fairbanks. As the popularity of the character grew, McCulley published the original story in book form in 1924, using the title of the Fairbanks film.

A definite similarity exists between Zorro and the Scarlet Pimpernel from the book of the same name published by Baroness Orzy in 1905. The Pimpernel took his name from a flower; Zorro took his from the fox. The Pimpernel protected the French aristocracy; Zorro, more of a democrat, protected the peasants. Conceived by McCulley, he was a masked rider, dressed in black, coming to the aid of an oppressed people, and then leaving behind his symbol, the slashing Z. Zorro has conquered print (selling several million copies in America alone), motion pictures (at least 24 movies have featured the character), and television (82 segments on American television in the 1950's). Zorro books have been translated into several languages, and Zorro has become a popular film character in Spanish-speaking countries.

McCulley contributed little, if anything at all, of artistic value to literature in general or to western literature in particular. In addition to his stories, plays, and novels, he sold story ideas for low-budget western movies such as Gene Autry's

Rootin' Tootin' Rhythm and the Hopalong Cassidy's *Doomed Caravans*. One doesn't look to McCulley for realistic writing on the West or for writing in a straight western tradition. His pedestrian craftsmanship turned out adventure stories with an eye always on commercial possibility. And, of course, Zorro.

—Wade Austin

McCURTIN, Peter. American. Also writes as Gene Curry; Bruno Rossi; Frank Scarpetta.

WESTERN PUBLICATIONS

Novels (series: Carmody in first six books; Sundance in all subsequent books)

Hangtown. New York, Belmont, 1970.
The Slavers. New York, Belmont, 1970.
Tough Bullet. New York, Belmont, 1970.
Screaming on the Wire. New York, Belmont, 1972.
The Killers. New York, Belmont, 1972.
Tall Man Riding. New York, Belmont, 1973.
The Nightriders. New York, Norden, 1979.
Day of the Halfbreeds. New York, Norden, 1979.
Death Dance. New York, Norden, 1979.
The Marauders. New York, Norden, 1980.
The Savage. New York, Norden, 1980.
Los Olvidados. New York, Norden, 1980.
Scorpion. New York, Norden, 1980.
Hangman's Knot. New York, Norden, 1980.
Apache War. New York, Norden, 1980.
Gold Strike. New York, Norden, 1980.
Trail Drive. New York, Norden, 1981.
Iron Men. New York, Norden, 1981.
Drumfire. New York, Norden, 1981.
Buffalo War. New York, Norden, 1981.
The Hunters. New York, Norden, 1981.
The Cage. New York, Norden, 1982.
The Choctaw County War. New York, Norden, 1982.
Texas Empire. New York, Norden, 1982.
Rockwell. New York, Leisure, 1984.

Novels as Gene Curry (series: Jim Saddler in all books)

A Dirty Way to Die. New York, Belmont, 1979.
Wildcat Woman. New York, Belmont, 1979.
Colorado Crossing. New York, Belmont, 1979.
Hot as a Pistol. New York, Belmont, 1980.
Wild, Wild Women. New York, Belmont, 1980.
Ace in the Hole. New York, Belmont, 1981.
Yukon Ride. New York, Belmont, 1981.

OTHER PUBLICATIONS

Novels

Mafioso. New York, Belmont, 1970.
The Sundance Murders. New York, Belmont, 1970.
Cosa Nostra. New York, Belmont, 1971.
Escape from Devil's Island. New York, Belmont, 1972.
Omerta. New York, Belmont, 1972.
The Syndicate. New York, Belmont, 1972.
Death Hunt. New York, Belmont, 1973.
Kill Them All. New York, Belmont, 1973.
Boston Bust-out. New York, Dell, 1973.
Manhattan Massacre. New York, Dell, 1973.
New Orleans Holocaust. New York, Dell, 1973.
Vendetta. New York, Belmont, 1973.
The Pleasure Principle. New York, Belmont, 1973.
The Deadliest Game. New York, Belmont, 1976.
Spoils of War. New York, Belmont, 1976.
The Massacre at Umtali. New York, Belmont, 1976.
Ambush at Derati Wells. New York, Belmont, 1977.
First Blood. New York, Belmont, 1977.
The Guns of Palembang. New York, Belmont, 1977.
Operation Hong Kong. New York, Belmont, 1977.
Body Count. New York, Belmont, 1977.
Battle Pay. New York, Belmont, 1978.
Loanshark. New York, Belmont, 1979.
Minnesota Strip. New York, Belmont, 1979.
Moro. New York, Belmont, 1986.
Golden Triangle. New York, Belmont, 1986.
Death Squad. New York, Belmont, 1986.
Bloodbath. New York, Belmont, 1986.
Somalia Smashout. New York, Belmont, 1986.
Blood Island. New York, Belmont, 1986.

* * *

Given that there are so many odd gaps in Peter McCurtin's bibliography, where he apparently published little or nothing for years at a time, it seems safe to assume that a great deal of his work in both the western and action/adventure genres has appeared under various house names. A prolific and sometimes inspired writer, McCurtin is certainly equally at home writing about the Old West or recounting tales of Mafia hitmen and soldiers of fortune.

McCurtin's first book, a Mystery Writers of America award-winner entitled *Mafioso*, was published in 1970. Other slick Mafia-based novels soon followed, cashing in on the popularity of Mario Puzo's *The Godfather*, and Don Pendleton's *Executioner* series. In between these, McCurtin also found time to write his first, and probably best, western series, Carmody.

Carmody is, on the surface at least, just another trail-wise adventurer. Sometimes he is presented as an outlaw, sometimes as a gun for hire. Whatever his current occupation, however, Carmody's eye is always on the main chance, as McCurtin's tough, spare narrative frequently makes plain.

Carmody's exploits set the tone for most of the Westerns McCurtin was to write over the next two decades. His view of the frontier is harsh and unforgiving, a place where a man with any sense looks to his own safety, and to hell with everyone else. McCurtin's Westerns are fast, violent and chauvinistic, but the violence and sex are seldom overly explicit. McCurtin further distances his protagonist from other stock western anti-heroes by recounting the series in the kind of hard-boiled first-person style normally associated with the private-eye genre, giving us a deeper insight into this rather self-centred drifter, and adding an extra dimension to what could so easily be a somewhat off-putting character.

Now rightly regarded by aficionados as classics of their type, the Carmody stories are, in the main, fairly successful variations on familiar themes, filled with twists and interesting characters which afford them a certain degree of originality. In the first, *Hangtown*, Carmody is employed by a wealthy mine owner whose daughter has been abducted and held to ransom. Complications set in, however, when Carmody discovers that the kidnapper is an old friend. For *The Slavers*, Carmody locks horns with a powerful rancher who treat his Indian employees (who once saved Carmody's life) like slaves. In *Tough Bullet*,

Carmody is living high in New Orleans when his money is stolen and he is framed for murder, while in *Screaming on the Wire*, possibly the best book of the sequence, he tangles with a psychotic killer claiming to be the younger brother of Billy the Kid. In *The Killers*, Carmody pins on a marshal's badge in order to dodge a posse, and finds himself caught between a bunch of outlaws and a clan of hillbilly killers, and one of the weaker novels, *Tall Man Riding*, sees Carmody tracking down the men who attacked him and stole the proceeds of a bank robbery he had recently committed.

After a prolonged spell writing various mercenary and anti-Mafia stories, McCurtin returned to the Western in 1979 to take over the Sundance series created by the late Ben Haas. In McCurtin's hands, however, Sundance—a half-breed Cheyenne who undertakes various missions in order to raise funds to fight the corrupt Indian Ring—became a colder, more impersonal figure, more violent and less credible. Having said that, it should be added that overall, McCurtin nevertheless did a reasonable job of continuing Sundance's exploits, producing some interesting (and, in some cases, truly memorable) action-oriented) Westerns, among them *Day of the Halfbreeds*, in which Sundance is sent to Canada to infiltrate Louis Riel's *Métis* movement and eventually stop a rebellion; *Hangman's Knot*, where Sundance, having killed a man and been sentenced to death in Fort Smith, Arkansas, is forced to bring in an old outlaw friend in return for a pardon; *Iron Men*, which sees Sundance helping the Central Colorado Railroad against the underhand tactics of a much larger competitor; and *The Hunters*, in which an English big game hunter, bored with hunting grizzly bears and mountain lions, decides to try his hand at tracking a much deadlier target—Sundance. (It is also worth mentioning that the 1980 Sundance story *Los Olvidados* is are re-working of the Carmody title *The Slavers*).

Mid-way through his tenure on the Sundance books, McCurtin wrote the "adult" western series Jim Saddler, returning to the gritty, first-person style of narration that made the Carmodys so distinctive. Of the seven books that comprise Saddler's adventures, however, four are little more than straight re-writes of Carmody novels; *A Dirty Way to Die* (*Tough Bullet*), *Wildcat Woman* (*Screaming on the Wire* with Jesse James's daughter replacing Billy the Kid's brother), *Colorado Crossing* (*Hangtown*) and *Hot as a Pistol* (*The Killers*). Of the rest, *Yukon Ride* is particularly notable (Saddler has to transport the body of a dead judge from the Yukon border to San Francisco, with surprising results).

McCurtin's Westerns are distinguished by unusual plots with neatly resolved conclusions, well-drawn secondary characters, regular bursts of action and tight, smooth writing. Though far from perfect, they are nonetheless excellent examples of their type, now much in demand among collectors.

—David Whitehead

McELRATH, Frances. American.

WESTERN PUBLICATIONS

Novel

The Rustler: A Tale of Love and War in Wyoming. New York and London, Funk and Wagnall, 1902.

* * *

In western literary history, the year 1902 is noted for the publication of *The Virginian*, the paradigmatic western novel which stimulated countless imitations and adaptations. The record fails to note that in 1902 also appeared *The Rustler* which, like *The Virginian*, fictionalizes the Johnson County War in Wyoming, pits an eastern lady-turned-schoolma'am against the western foreman of a cattle ranch, and follows the sinuous unfolding of their mutual attraction. So thoroughly has Frances McElrath dropped from sight that it is impossible to tell whether she might have read Owen Wister's earlier stories which were incorporated into *The Virginian*, and there is no evidence that she had access to his manuscript. For the modern reader, however, McElrath's novel reads uncannily like a point-by-point critique of Wister's famous work.

Starting with very similar figures and situations to Wister, McElrath develops her plot in the opposite direction. Hazel Clifford, a genteel eastern lady, comes West to escape Horace, her eastern fiancé, and temporary financial embarrassment. On her cousin's ranch she encounters Jim, the trustworthy foreman. His primitive energy, innate refinement, and initial resistance to Hazel's charms intrigue her, and she sets about winning his attentions, by adapting her dress and manners to western conventions and by playing up her position as governess to a western family, a role she adopts more through curiosity than through need. She succeeds to well, winning Jim's unqualified, inexperienced love. Recognizing the discrepancy between Jim's response and her playful intentions, Hazel tries to extricate herself from the situation, turning her attention back to her fiancé, who has just arrived as the new owner of a vast Wyoming ranch. The results are cataclysmic. Jim turns rustler, harrassing the large ranchers to the extent that he sets off a fictionalized version of the 1892 Johnson County War. Surviving that conflict, he kidnaps Hazel and takes her to his fiefdom of outlaws in the Hole-in-the-Wall. In time, Jim reconverts to honesty, Hazel discovers that her thoughtless self-indulgence has caused his moral decline, and the two reach an understanding on Jim's death-bed: he declares his love, and she dedicates herself to the moral education of rustlers' children.

Paralleling the main plot are the adventures of Horace, the eastern gentleman-turned-stockman, who becomes the fascination of Mavvy (short for Maverick), a beautiful, untutored orphan adopted by rustlers. Mavvy risks her life for Horace during the war between stockmen and rustlers, betraying her own people to protect him; he in turn sends her east to be educated by his mother; and, once Hazel declares her dedication to lifelong, unmarried service, he declares his intention to marry Mavvy.

There are many more suggestive echoes than can be summarized here, but even an unelaborated plot synopsis indicates the distance between McElrath's narrative and Wister's celebration of East-West alliances. *The Rustler* articulates this historical moment—"a transition period on the range, when the old, vigorous, baronial conditions . . . were passing away, and a new, and so to speak more commercial condition of things was coming into play"—in more explicitly problematical accents than *The Virginian*. McElrath is no disciple of the Turner Thesis with its myth of classless democracy: her West is riddled with class barriers which function just as emphatically for the middle-class citizens of Wyoming who look down on Mavvy's adoptive parents as "the Grimes trash," as they do for the eastern "gentlemen lynchers" who cannot appreciate the humanity of the common people whom they shoot down. Hazel's great error—which sets the entire catastrophe in motion—is to pretend an effacement of the class difference which structures this society in destructive and dehumanizing directions.

McElrath's representation of class tension is complicated by her handling of gender. Horace can cross class lines to raise Mavvy up the social hierarchy in a way that Hazel cannot. More sweepingly, the West emerges as an environment forbidding to female sexuality: Mavvy must be sent east to be suited for marriage; Hazel's experience of the West leads her to celibacy and spinsterhood; her desire for the maternal role is sublimated in her nursing of a sick orphan and her presiding over a "Mothers' Club" for rustlers' wives. The contrast with *The Virginian* is instructive, again. After the wedding of Molly and the Virginian, the two retreat to an isolated, Edenic mountain camp. A parallel scene occurs in *The Rustler*, when Jim and Hazel retreat to the mountains encircling the Hole-in-the-Wall, to the "peaceful, chapel-like" Black Gulch. They commune here, "they two alone together," not in the delight of new marriage but in the pause before Jim's imminent death. He is paralyzed from the waist down, and she is the nurse who can comfort but cannot cure him. As the most harmonious meeting of eastern heroine and western hero in the novel, the moment says much about the unbridgeable chasm created by gender, class, and geography. For woman, this West functions primarily as the site of guilt and expiation: Hazel comes to realize that "all this had come about through the most idle of whims ... She had been more than unworthily foolish .... "Jim has brought me here to show me my work and to punish me,' she thought, 'and I'm going to take my punishment as I find it.'".

McElrath's style is considerably less polished than Wister's, and her handling of action and character less assured. But the social vision informing the work seems more complex in its awareness of social and political tensions which defy the easy, heroic transcendence posited by Wister. Her own political sympathies are not explicitly articulated, but they clearly do not lie with the eastern gentry who, as individuals and businessmen, bring such trouble to the West. Where *The Virginian* can be read as a *paean* to the eastern patriarchy with which even the western hero affiliates himself, *The Rustler* tells a less flattering story of the motives which brought eastern men and women to exploit the developing West and suggests a less triumphant vision of the consequences for all. The novel offers a qualification of Wister's master narrative which should, at least, be heard.

—Christine Bold

McELROY, Lee. *See* **KELTON, Elmer.**

McGEOUGH, John. *See* **MACK BRIDE, Johnny.**

McGUANE, Thomas (Francis, III). American. Born in Wyandotte, Michigan, 11 December 1939. Educated at the University of Michigan, Ann Arbor; Olivet College, Michigan; Michigan State University, East Lansing, 1958–62, B.A. 1962; Yale University School of Drama, New Haven, Connecticut, 1962–65, M.F.A. 1965; Stanford University, California (Stegner Fellow), 1966–67. Married 1) Portia Rebecca Crockett in 1962 (divorced 1975), one son; 2) the actress Margot Kidder in 1976 (divorced 1977), one daughter; 3) Laurie Buffet in 1977, two daughters. Since 1968 freelance writer and film director. Recipient: Rosenthal Foundation award, 1972. Agent: Amanda Urban, International Creative Management, 40 West 57th Street, New York, New York 10019, U.S.A.

WESTERN PUBLICATIONS

Novels

The Sporting Club. New York, Simon and Schuster, 1968; London, Deutsch, 1969.
The Bushwhacked Piano. New York, Simon and Schuster, 1971.
Ninety-Two in the Shade. New York, Farrar Straus, 1973; London, Collins, 1974.
Nobody's Angel. New York, Random House, 1982.
Keep the Change. Boston, Houghton Mifflin, 1989; London, Secker and Warburg, 1990.

Short Stories

To Skin a Cat. New York, Dutton, 1986; London, Secker and Warburg, 1987.

Uncollected Short Story

"Another Horse," in *Atlantic* (Boston), October 1974.

OTHER PUBLICATIONS

Novels

Panama. New York, Farrar Straus, 1978.
Something to Be Desired. New York, Random House, 1984; London, Secker and Warburg, 1985.

Plays

The Missouri Breaks (screenplay). New York, Ballantine, 1976.

Screenplays: *The Bushwhacked Piano*, 1970; *Rancho Deluxe*, 1973; *The Missouri Breaks*, 1975; *Ninety-Two in the Shade*, 1975; *Tom Horn*, with Edwin Shrake, 1980; *Cold Feet*, with Jim Harrison; 1989.

Other

An Outside Chance: Essays on Sport. New York, Farrar Straus, 1980; enlarged edition, Boston, Houghton Mifflin, 1990.

*

Manuscript Collections: University of Rochester, New York; Brigham Young University, Provo, Utah.

Critical Study: *The New American Novel of Manners: The Fiction of Richard Yates, Dan Wakefield, and Thomas McGuane* by Jerome Klinkowitz, Athens, University of Georgia Press, 1986.

Theatrical Activities:
Director: **Film**—*Ninety-Two in the Shade*, 1975.

* * *

Thomas McGuane writes about the new Old West, "soon to be a major postcard," in cool, laconic language while populating his surreal situations with bizarre characters.

McGuane's first novel, *The Sporting Club*, explodes the myth of the rugged, macho outdoorsman. The weird group of men who belong to the sporting club are wealthy, wacky, and spoiled by civilization. The centennial celebration of the club's heritage is marred by the discovery that the former club members were perverts. In the final scene, McGuane shows the destruction of the fish and game preserve by the new manager, Earl Olive, by dynamiting it out of revenge on the old guard membership, while the novel's lead character, Vernor Stanton, is insane by the final pages. The grimness of the book is tempered by the wildness of the action as the black humor parallels the destruction of the sporting club with the decline of America.

The Bushwhacked Piano features Nicholas Payne, who displays his insanity at an early age by bushwhacking a neighbor's piano with a rifle. When Nick falls in love with rich, bitchy Ann Fitzgerald, a cross-country adventure begins. Ann's parents hate Nick so they spirit her away to Montana with Nick in hot pursuit. Nick teams up with C.J. Clovis—they build a tower for mosquito-eating bats—before they link up with Ann in Montana; then the three adventurers leave for Key West to build another bat tower. Disaster and disappointment befall Nick in Key West as he plays out his doomed, failed life.

Ninety-Two in the Shade is a novel of confrontation between two men: Tom Skelton, incomplete and bordering on insanity, and Nichol Dance, substantial and dangerous. Tom decides to become a fishing guide after failing to make a career out of marine biology. In Key West, Dance—the best guide in the Keys—tells Tom not to compete with him. But Tom's choice dooms both men in the book's deadly conclusion.

Not to be ignored is the published version of McGuane's fine screenplay, *The Missouri Breaks*, which shows how Arthur Penn completely ruined a promising script and produced a dismal film. *The Missouri Breaks* displays McGuane's finest writing, without the verbal excesses that characterize most of his novels.

Nobody's Angel is McGuane's best novel. The hero, Patrick Fitzpatrick, returns to rescue the old ranch in Deadrock, Montana. Patrick seems like a character out of the horse operas of the pulp magazine era, a hero on the edge of burn-out and alcoholism who has just enough energy and dignity for one more showdown. When Patrick falls in love with Claire, a wealthy married woman, the book takes on an emotional intensity missing from McGuane's previous novels. The writing is controlled, and the characters are carefully drawn.

Something to be Desired and *Panama* reflect the some of the troubles in McGuane's own life with the breakup of his first marriage, his brief second marriage to actress Margot Kidder, and his present marriage to Laurie Buffett, sister of singer Jimmy Buffett. *Panama* received mixed reviews about its first-person narrative of the imploding life of Chester Hunicutt Pomeroy, rock star. The story of a success who is burning out because of a self-destructive, excessive lifestyle was called "self-indulgent" by some critics and "ambitious" by others. *Something to be Desired* is a novel of reconciliation and healing. Lucien Taylor's infidelity causes a separation from his wife and son. Taylor helps his former lover when she's accused of murdering her husband. He lives on her Montana ranch until she jumps bail, leaving Taylor the ranch, then converts it into a health resort and becomes a millionaire. He invites his wife and son up for a visit and when they arrive, Taylor puts his life back together again. Both of these books are deeply personal accounts of wounded men.

McGuane's latest works—*To Skin a Cat*, a collection of edgy short stories—and *Keep the Change*, a novel of a quest for spiritual renewal, both lack the intensity of his earlier work. In *Keep the Change* Joe Starling leaves Montana for Yale University. He becomes a successful artist, but finds he lacks an emotional and spiritual center. He retreats to Montana, hoping to find meaning in restoring a run-down ranch. But Starling's romantic notions of the Old West lose out to the cunning realities of the New West as he's betrayed by his goofy Uncle Smitty and the not-so-innocent Ellen. Although McGuane populates his latest works with losers, he still can write about the Montana wilderness with evocativeness no other contemporary writer comes close to.

Thomas McGuane's fables of the contemporary West are unique, wild, and inventive.

—George Kelley

McHUGH, Stuart. *See* **ROWLAND, Donald S.**

McLAGLEN, John J. *See* **HARVEY, John; JAMES, Laurence.**

McLENNAN, Will. *See* **WISLER, G. Clifton.**

McLOWERY, Frank. *See* **ALLISON, Clay.**

McMURTRY, Larry (Jeff). American. Born in Wichita Falls, Texas, 3 June 1936. Educated at Archer City High School, Texas, graduated 1954; North Texas State College, Denton, B.A. 1958; Rice University, Houston, 1954, 1958–60, M.A. 1960; Standford University, California (Stegner Fellow), 1960–61. Married Josephine Scott in 1959 (divorced 1966); one son. Taught at Texas Christian University, Fort Worth, 1961–62, Rice University, 1963–64 and 1965, George Mason College, Fairfax, Virginia, 1970, and American University, Washington, D.C., 1970–71. Since 1971 owner, Booked Up Inc., antiquarian booksellers, Washington, D.C. Regular reviewer, Houston *Post* in 1960's, and Washington *Post* in 1970's; contributing editor, *American Film*, New York, 1975. President, PEN, 1989. Recipient: Texas Institute of Letters Jesse M. Jones award, 1962; Guggenheim grant, 1964; Academy award, 1972; Pulitzer Prize, 1986. Address: Booked Up Inc., 1209 31st Street N.W., Washington, D.C. 20007, U.S.A.

WESTERN PUBLICATIONS

Novels

Horseman, Pass By. New York, Harper, 1961; as *Hud*, New York, Popular Library, 1963; London, Sphere, 1971.

Leaving Cheyenne. New York, Harper, 1963; London, Sphere, 1972.
The Last Picture Show. New York, Dial Press, 1966; London, Sphere, 1972.
Lonesome Dove. New York, Simon and Schuster, 1985; London, Pan, 1986.
Texasville. New York, Simon and Schuster, and London, Sidgwick and Jackson, 1987.
Anything for Billy. New York, Simon and Schuster, 1988; London, Collins, 1989.
Buffalo Girls. New York, Simon and Schuster, 1990; London, Century, 1991.

Uncollected Short Stories

"The Best Day Since," in *Avesta* (Denton, Texas), Fall 1956.
"Cowman," in *Avesta* (Denton, Texas), Spring 1957.
"Roll, Jordan, Roll," in *Avesta* (Denton, Texas), Fall 1957.
"A Fragment from Scarlet Ribbons," in *Coexistence Review* (Denton, Texas), vol. 1 no. 2, 1958(?).
"There Will Be Peace in Korea," in *Texas Quarterly* (Austin), Winter 1964.

Play

Screenplay: *The Last Picture Show*, with Peter Bogdanovich, 1971.

OTHER PUBLICATIONS

Novels

Moving On. New York, Simon and Schuster, 1970; London, Weidenfeld and Nicolson, 1971.
All My Friends Are Going to Be Strangers. New York, Simon and Schuster, 1972; London, Secker and Warburg, 1973.
Terms of Endearment. New York, Simon and Schuster, 1975; London, W.H. Allen, 1977.
Somebody's Darling. New York, Simon and Schuster, 1978.
Cadillac Jack. New York, Simon and Schuster, 1982.
The Desert Rose. New York, Simon and Schuster, 1983; London, W.H. Allen, 1985.
Some Can Whistle. New York, Simon and Schuster, 1989; London Century, 1990.

Other

In a Narrow Grave: Essays on Texas. Austin, Texas, Encino Press, 1968.
It's Always We Rambled: An Essay on Rodeo. New York, Hallman, 1974.
Larry McMurtry: Unredeemed Dreams, edited by Dorey Schmidt. Edinburg, Texas, Pan American University, 1980.
Film Flam: Essays on Hollywood. New York, Simon and Schuster, 1987.

*

Manuscript Collection: University of Houston Library.

Critical Studies: *Larry McMurtry* by Thomas Landess, Austin, Texas, Steck Vaughn, 1969; *The Ghost Country: A Study of the Novels of Larry McMurtry* by Raymond L. Neinstein, Berkeley, California, Creative Arts, 1976; *Larry McMurtry* by Charles D. Peavy, Boston, Twayne, 1977; *Larry McMurtry's Texas: Evolution of the Myth* by Lera Patrick Tyler Lich, Austin, Eakin Press, 1987; *Taking Stock: A Larry McMurtry Casebook* edited by Clay Reynolds, Dallas, Southern Methodist University Press, 1989.

* * *

Larry McMurtry's career demonstrates the mythical pattern of escape and return. After gaining initial fame writing about the passing Southwest of the cowboy, McMurtry scorned the work the critics praised and praised the work the critics scorned: urban novels cut off from the old Southwest. In the 1980's, however, McMurtry returned to the settings and themes he previously rejected, and the critical acclaim he previously enjoyed came back as well.

McMurtry's highly praised early novels—*Horseman, Pass By, Leaving Cheyenne*, and *The Last Picture Show*—draw their strength from a deep ambivalence produced by grappling with the positive and negative values of the passing southwestern frontier mythos: anti-intellectualism, primitivism, sexism, racism, classism, violence, courage, endurance, straightforwardness, honesty, and others. These early novels depend upon the rural or small-town Southwest for setting, themes, and characters. Generally McMurtry concentrates on youthful characters initiated into the painful knowledge that the old Southwest and its associated values are passing from the earth.

In *Horseman, Pass By* the conflict is between Hud and his stepfather, Homer Bannon, who represents the old way of life. Homer gives way to Hud, whose raw amorality indicates the new way. Lonnie, the youthful narrator whose initiation results from the conflict between Hud and Homer, tries to decide which—if either—character's values to adopt. On the surface McMurtry seems to have him side with Homer and lament the passing of the old: Homer is a courageous, heroic figure in many ways. And yet, the novel reveals an implicit ambivalence toward the old that becomes explicit in McMurtry's later works. Homer's stubbornness, and his insensitivity to Hud's youthful desires, bring about the old man's downfall.

McMurtry's ambivalence toward the possibility of fulfilment in southwestern rural life is more subtly presented in *Leaving Cheyenne*. There, Molly tries to choose between two recognizable southwestern figures: Johnny, the unfettered, forever free cowboy, and Gid the aspiring, settled rancher. The two impulses cannot be reconciled, nor can Molly choose. Rather, she marries a third, Eddie, a brutal oilfield worker. Throughout, she tries loving both Johnny and Gid as the three age and their world, the blood's country, passes on.

Initiation, loneliness, and unfulfilment are central to McMurtry's third novel, too. But *The Last Picture Show* is not a nostalgic lament; it is a biting satire about the small-mindedness of small-town southwestern life. Duane and Sonny try to combat the boredom of growing up in Thalia, Texas, based on McMurtry's hometown of Archer City, through sex, sports, and movies, but living close to the earth in McMurtry's world does not create enlightened human beings. The most admirable character, Sam the Lion, owner of the pool hall and former rancher, dies long before the novel ends.

The satire led to a bitter, goodbye-to-all-that attitude in his first essay collection. Published during Lyndon Johnson's presidency, when being Texan was not chic among intellectuals, *In a Narrow Grave* continues to strike out at many things southwestern such as small towns where "many Texans . . . live and die in woeful ignorance." This antagonism to the rural marked the shift to the second category of McMurtry novels: the urban novels set in Texas; such as *Moving On, All of My Friends are Going to Be Strangers*, and *Terms of Endearment.*

Patsy Carpenter in *Moving On* is an initiate and a searcher. Looking for love in strange place, she marries a wealthy young graduate student, falls in love with a poor one, is attracted to a rodeo clown, and eventually finds her own independence. Danny Deck in *All My Friends are Going to Be Strangers* wanders from Texas to California and back. At the end of the novel he drowns his manuscript in the Rio Grande. And Emma, in *Terms of Endearment*, finds only an early death from cancer after following her graduate student, then college professor husband Flap from Houston to Kearney, Nebraska. Of all the characters in these novels, only Aurora Greenway in *Terms of Endearment* escapes the suffering the others endure. However, her strength does not derive from a surfeit of character, but from a solipsistic and single-minded selfishness that shuts out the rest of the world.

McMurtry then moved beyond the Southwest as the stuff of sentimentalism, and wrote urban novels set outside the Southwest: Hollywood (*Somebody's Darling*), Las Vegas (*The Desert Rose*), and Washington, D.C. (*Cadillac Jack*). Critics generally found these works less satisfying than either the rural or urban Texas novels, calling them formless, unfocused, and boring. The characters in these novels are urban searchers looking for something of value in the chaos of contemporary life.

With *Lonesome Dove*, a novel in which one of the most powerful scenes concerns one Texas Ranger's promise to return his friend and partner's body to Texas for burial, McMurtry came back to Texas and the old Southwest as the subject and setting for his fiction. The novel won the Pulitzer Prize. As Ernestine Sewell points out, the three former Rangers—Augustus McCrae, Woodrow Call, and Jake Spoon—form a composite that embodies the Cowboy God, a mythic figure that McMurtry witnessed passing from the old Southwest.

Since *Lonesome Dove*, McMurtry has alternated between novels with contemporary settings that return to characters from previous works (the Thalia gang in *Texasville*, a sequel to *The Last Picture Show*, and Danny Deck in *Some Can Whistle*) and novels about historical western characters (Billy the Kid in *Anything for Billy*, and Calamity Jane in *Buffalo Girls*). Both types demonstrate one of his predominant themes: the effects of the end of a way of life, a subject McMurtry continues to examine with a complex ambivalence.

Throughout his career McMurtry has enjoyed successful film and television adaptations of his work, such as *Hud* starring Paul Newman, Peter Bogdanovich's films of *The Last Picture Show* and *Texasville*, and especially a *Lonesome Dove* television miniseries starring Robert Duvall in 1989. McMurtry's second nonfiction book, *Film Flam*, collects his essays about movies.

McMurtry works with varying styles and themes. He is particularly fond of varying points of view, especially for using female narrators, and he deals with different levels of realism. He is often concerned with displaced characters searching for something to provide their lives with stability and purpose, especially since the elements that provided direction in the past have disappeared. They long for ways to combine love and work into a satisfying and enduring whole. Although their lives are ultimately fraught with difficulty, pain, and uncertainty, McMurtry demonstrates how these characters take pleasure in moments of creativity, love, or humor.

—Mark Busby

McNAB, Jeb. *See* **FEARN, John Russell.**

McNICHOLS, Charles L(ongstreth). American. Born in Greenfield, Massachusetts, 21 October 1887.

WESTERN PUBLICATIONS

Novel

Crazy Weather. New York, Macmillan, 1944; London, Gollancz, 1945.

OTHER PUBLICATIONS

Other

Japan: Its Resources and Industries, with Clayton D. Carus. New York, Harper, 1944.

* * *

Crazy Weather, Charles L. McNichols's only novel, is as fresh and appealing now as it was when it appeared in 1944. It is a story of growing up, but it is set in the relatively unknown western Arizona area, and its hero is a 14-year-old white boy who lives in a milieu almost completely dominated by Mojave Indians. The boy is the son of a small rancher; both his father and mother are away (his father buying cattle, his mother in California for her health), and during the four-day period of "crazy weather" the boy can do as he likes.

South Boy (his Indian name, given because he was wet-nursed by an Indian who lives down-river; he is given no other name in the book) is at an age and in a situation where his present and future condition is much on his mind. His mother, a religious woman who abhors living in such an isolated part of the world, earnestly desires that he be sent away to a boarding school before he becomes a wild drunkard with a Mexican wife like their foreman; his more easy-going father is perfectly willing for South Boy to stay on the ranch, but only if he takes responsibilities that the hired hands can't be expected to take. South Boy hates both the thought of school *and* the ranch-life responsibilities. He'd prefer to be an Indian, like his friend Havek: a Mojave boy his age goes on an adventure, and from it is able to adopt a name, i.e., provide himself with an identity, a much more sensible way of growing up, he feels, than the sliding into adulthood of the white man.

The opportunity for such a trip comes with the absence of his parents, the beginnings of a nerve-wracking heat wave (the "crazy weather"), and the encouragement of Havek. They trek north to where they hear there is a Piute "war," in the meantime stopping off for various visits: to a gathering of Mojave boys having a "sing," to the Whisperer who will make South Boy a bow for his trip, and to Havek's great-uncle, the old-style warrior Yellow Road, who in Mojave fashion sings (like the boys at the "sing") of the victories and defeats of the Mojave past. The central adventure itself centers not on a war, but on a crazy Piute "witch" who has been wandering around the Mojave territory on a mission only he himself knows. He has managed to wound the Mormonhater, a white man who lives as a trapper and fisherman of frontier days (and who has in the past served as a model for South Boy). Havek finds the Piute and returns to make a war club in order to defeat him in a set battle (a "great thing"). The boys manage to wound the Piute, drive him over the river to Nevada, and burn his teepee with his medicine bag full of witching materials.

They return to find that Yellow Road is dying, and the entire clan has gathered for his death and cremation. A reservation policeman has also arrived to make sure that he is not buried prematurely. South Boy admires the policeman, an Indian who has been away to school, and who has learned both the white man's and the Indian's ways, and seems to have no inner conflicts about it. (*Cohiva-michiva*—one thing one time, another thing another time—is a running motif in the novel.) With Havek joining the clan during the ritual of cremation, South Boy feels alone outside the circle of mourners.

The climax of the story, and the crazy weather, is a terrific wind and rain storm. Almost as if by magic, however, South Boy realizes that the soaking of the mesa by the rain means that his father can pasture a great herd of cattle over the winter, and make a huge profit. He returns to bring the news to the foreman, and they agree that South Boy could form a holding ground for driving the cattle to the mesa, an operation that should last until November (and incidently keep him out of school one more year—and perhaps forever). Havek won't join him, since his adventure with the Piute will have given him an adult name, and he should visit all his relatives and be feasted.

What McNichols manages to do in a relatively short book is quite impressive. The environment of the Colorado River area comes clear; moreover, the various adventures, conversations, Mojave "sings" and legends, and relationships reveal an entire world-view of Mojave life—one that greatly appeals to South Boy, but that is just a bit off-center to his upbringing as a white. The schematic theme of the book is perhaps a trifle obvious, but the naturalness of the narrative, the careful prose, and the sense of revelation all add up to a novel that repays reading.

—George Walsh

McNICKLE, (William) D'Arcy. American. Born in St. Ignatius, Montana, 18 January 1904. Educated at the University of Montana, Missoula, 1921–25; Oxford University, 1925–26; University of Grenoble, 1931. Married Roma Kaufman in 1939; two daughters. Editor in New York, 1926–35; staff writer, Federal Writers Project, Washington, D.C., 1935–36; assistant to the commissioner, then field representative and director of tribal relations, Bureau of Indian Affairs, Washington, D.C., 1936–52; director, American Indian Development Inc., Boulder, Colorado, 1952–77; program director, Center for American Indian History, Newberry Library, Chicago, 1972–77. Former Professor of Anthropology, University of Sasketchewan, Regina. Recipient: Guggenheim fellowship, 1963. Fellow, American Anthropological Association. *Died in December 1977.*

WESTERN PUBLICATIONS

Novels

The Surrounded. New York, Dodd Mead, 1936.
Wind from an Enemy Sky. New York, Harper, 1978.

Uncollected Short Story

"Train Time," in *Scholastic* (Pittsburgh), 24 October 1936.

OTHER PUBLICATIONS

Other

La Política de los Estados Unidos sobre los Gobiernos Tribales y los Empresas Communales de los Indios, with Joseph C. McCaskill. Washington, D.C., Department of the Interior, 1942.
They Came Here First: The Epic of the American Indian. Philadelphia, Lippincott, 1949; revised edition, New York, Harper, 1975.
Runner in the Sun: A Story of Indian Maize (for children). Philadelphia, Winston, 1954.
Indians and Other Americans: Two Ways of Life Meet, with Harold E. Fey. New York, Harper, 1959; revised edition, 1970.
The Indian Tribes of the United States: Ethnic and Cultural Survival. London and New York, Oxford University Press, 1962; revised edition, as *Native American Tribalism*, 1973.
Indian Man: A Life of Oliver La Farge. Bloomington, Indiana University Press, 1971.

*

Critical Study: *D'Arcy McNickle* by Ruppert James, Boise, Idaho, Boise State University, 1988.

* * *

D'Arcy McNickle's first novel, *The Surrounded*, was widely praised. Its theme is now a conventional one—of a young man's desire for a wider life away the reservation, contrasted with the living tradition of his Montana tribe. That Archilde is the son of a Spanish father and an Indian mother emphasizes the conflict within him. The novel is episodic, full of details of Indian life and lore and the Montana landscape, but, as Oliver La Farge said when he reviewed it in the *Saturday Review of Literature*: "Perhaps the most interesting aspect of Mr. McNickle's book is his success in catching the whole in small compass, by the exercise of a thoroughly artistic selection, and writing of such sort that the reader is primarily interested in an excellent story as such, and only secondarily in the background, which he sets in proper balance."

A novel for children, *Runner in the Sun*—about the journey of Saly to Aztec country to procure a hardier grain species than is available in his own tribal area—and several nonfiction works on American Indians followed. But his masterpiece, *Wind from an Enemy Sky*, was published posthumously.

Wind from an Enemy Sky is a wonderfully coherent book that takes as its theme the entire history of the Indian-white man conflict but presents it in one relatively small and compact plot. A dam built on a Little Elk reservation stream "drowns" the water. Bull, the traditionalist "speaker" of the tribe can't believe it can be done: "How can a stream out of the mountains be killed? Will they open the earth and drop us in it? Will they take the sun out of the sky? It was bad for us when they came with guns. Now they will kill us in other ways." At the same time that one of the young Indians shoots and kills a dam worker to avenge the loss of the water, Bull's older brother, Henry Jim, who had accepted white men's ways years ago and lost the respect of the tribe, hears the singing that presages his death, and arrives at Bull's camp to make his peace: he wants to die "in my own tepee" and not in the white man's house. The symbol of the tribe's disintegration is the loss of the medicine bundle, given to the Reservation missionary 25 years before and sent to a museum. The double quest that ensues—the return of the medicine bundle, and the punishment of the killer of the dam employee—results in a tragic conflict, as difficult to reconcile as the white man's and the Indian's sense of justice, based as they are on completely different traditions. As Two Sleeps, an Indian visionary, says when the Indians arrive at Henry Jim's place:

> Tell this man: We are camped here at the old man's place so he will feel our power and not be discouraged. It got so we forgot to do these things, or it didn't seem worthwhile. Maybe this man will think we are childish to believe we can do this. He comes from a big world where his power is in a machine. Or maybe he carried it in his pocket and he can take it out and tell you where the sun is. We live here in this small world and we have only ourselves, the ground where we walk, the big and small animals. But the part that is man is not less because our world is small. When I look out in the coming day and see a bluebird—we call it our mother's sister—I see the whole bluebird, the part that is blue and the part that is yellow, just as this man does. I don't have half an eye because I live in this small world.

The most ironic misunderstanding comes through Adam Pell, the director of the museum that received the medicine bundle, and also the builder of the dam. He is a keen student of Indian cultures, but his role as museum director is fitting, since he fails to see the living nature of what he is dealing with. When he offers a gift of an Inca gold figurine in place of the bundle, his motive is sincere but misguided. Bull's energy and power, neutralized up to now, finally emerges in a violent climax.

The novel is a complex one, with many characters and strands of past and present action. Objectivity is provided by the presence of several characters: Rafferty, the Reservation Superintendent, a sympathetic and caring man learning as the events unfold; Mrs. Cooke, the mother of the dead man, who, when she first sees an Indian (Bull) up close, realizes he is not a savage but a human; and especially by Antoine, Bull's grandson just back from school. The Indian's history is seen from both Indian and white man's point of view, through Henry Jim's awareness of his mistake in abandoning his tribe, and through Pell's search through documents that prove how the Indians have been cheated over the decades. But the final impression the reader has is of Bull's force in speaking and acting for a way of life he has steadfastly refused to abandon, but which eventually causes his death.

—George Walsh

MEADE, Richard. *See* **DOUGLAS, Thorne; HAAS, Ben.**

MERRICK, Mark. *See* **RATHBORNE, St. George.**

MERRIMAN, Chad. *See* **CHESHIRE, Giff.**

MESSMAN, John. *See* **SHARPE, Jon.**

MICHAELS, Kristin. *See* **WILLIAMS, Jeanne.**

MICHEAUX, Oscar. American. Born in Metropolis, Illinois, 2 January 1884. Married Alice Russell in 1929. Worked in a variety of jobs, including car factory worker, coal miner, Pullman porter, farmer in South Dakota, and in Chicago stockyards and a steel mill; founder, Western Book Supply Company, Sioux City, Iowa, 1915, and Micheaux Film and Book Corporation, 1918; filmmaker, 1919–1948. *Died 26 March 1951.*

WESTERN PUBLICATIONS

Novels

The Conquest: The Story of a Negro Pioneer. Lincoln, Nebraska, Woodruff Press, 1913.
The Homesteader. Sioux City, Iowa, Western Book Supply Company, 1917.
The Wind from Nowhere. New York, Book Supply Company, 1941.

OTHER PUBLICATIONS

Novels

The Forged Note: A Romance of the Darker Races. Lincoln, Nebraska, Western Book Supply Company, 1915.
The Case of Mrs. Wingate. New York, Book Supply Company, 1944.
The Story of Dorothy Stanfield, Based on a Great Insurance Swindle, and a Woman! New York, Book Supply Company, 1946.
The Masquerade: An Historical Novel. New York, Book Supply Company, 1947.

Plays

Screenplays: *The Homesteader*, 1919; *Within Our Gates*, 1920; *The Brute*, 1920; *Symbol of the Unconquered*, 1920; *The Gunsaulus Mystery*, 1921; *Deceit, or The House Behind the Cedars*, 1921; *Son of Satan*, 1922; *Uncle Jasper's Will*, 1922; *The Virgin of the Seminole*, 1922; *The Dungeon*, 1922; *Marcus Garland/Body and Soul*, 1925; *Birthright, The Conjure Woman*, 1926; *The Spider's Web*, 1926; *The Broken Violin*, 1927; *The Millionaire*, 1927; *When Men Betray*, 1928; *Easy Street*, 1928; *Thirty Years Later*, 1928; *Wages of Sin*, 1929; *Daughter of the Congo*, 1930; *Darktown Revue*, 1931; *The Exile*, 1931; *Black Magic*, 1932; *Ten Minutes to Live*, 1932; *Veiled Aristocrats*, 1932; *The Girl from Chicago*, 1933; *Ten Minutes to Kill*, 1933;

Harlem After Midnight, 1934; *Lem Hawkin's Confession*, 1935; *Underworld/Temptation*, 1936; *God's Step Children*, 1938; *Swing*, 1938; *Lying Lips*, 1940; *The Notorious Elinor Lee*, 1940; *The Betrayal*, 1948.

*

Critical Studies: *From Sambo to Superspade: The Black Experience in Motion Pictures* by Daniel J. Leab, Boston, Houghton Mifflin, 1975; *Slow Fade to Black: The Negro in American Film, 1900–1942* by Thomas Cripps, London, Oxford University Press, 1977; "Oscar Micheaux, Black Novelist and Film Maker" by Chester Fontenot, Jr., in *Vision and Refuge: Essays on the Literature of the Great Plains*, edited by Virginia Faulkner and Frederick C. Luebke, Lincoln, University of Nebraska Press, 1982; *Black Novelist as White Racist: The Myth of Black Inferiority in the Novels of Oscar Micheaux* by Joseph A. Young, New York, Greenwood Press, 1989.

Theatrical Activities:
Producer and director of many films.

* * *

Oscar Micheaux's fictional chronicles of the South Dakota West present the ideal of an agrarian utopia for a few brave and true African-Americans. That ideal becomes manifest in the western hero of *The Homesteader*, Jean Baptiste, who has the initiative and enterprise to go to the untamed country as a youth to grow up and flourish with it. With Baptiste, Micheaux is able to project his desire to participate in post-bellum America's expansion, by creating a protagonist whose experience is based partly on his own. In an era of what many African-American literary critics would characterize as the Age of Booker T. Washington (the age of accommodation, conciliation, and assimilation), Micheaux's fiction answers the question of what a black American should be: a conservative Negro and black pioneer.

By stepping into the iconography of the white western pioneer tradition, Micheaux illustrates a species of assimilationism. Micheaux's purpose is to offer an alternative mental landscape to that emerging from the black experience in an urban reality. African-Americans had migrated in large numbers to the northern cities partly as a way of fleeing the Atlanta Compromise: Booker T. Washington's 1895 Atlanta speech, in which he assumed the role of national black leader and accepted Jim Crow custom for African-Americans. Assimilationist Micheaux co-opted white stereotypes of blacks and interpolated them into his own personal myth as a way of improving his status in America. Micheaux believed that adopting whites' images of blacks was prescriptive for success. But he also needed to distinguish himself from that pitiful stock of stereotypes he had adopted in order to prove he was worthy of equality. So he rewrote his own life in several fictionalized autobiographies, injecting the traits of the western hero into his protagonist.

Micheaux's western hero, in terms which apply more completely to the dominant culture, is distinctively American in his impoverished conception of African-Americans, a conception which becomes an ubiquitous motif in Micheaux's canon: that the majority of African-Americans are inferior, or at least their moral development has been stunted by urban deprivation. Such an observation reflects the kind of attitude an African-American of that day would be encouraged to sublimate in order to publish or be marginally successful in Jim Crow America, especially the America of the untamed West. But there is, of course, self-deception in Micheaux's assumptions about individualism, blacks, himself, and even whites. Micheaux's belief that his portrayal of a black western hero who competes effectively with nature, villains, and varmints would ensure for him first-class citizenship with attendant privileges was at least a comforting illusion.

Micheaux's other novels either anticipate or nostalgically reflect on the completed vision of his western hero created in *The Homesteader*, his best effort. *The Conquest*, Micheaux's first novel, is a fictional autobiography about Oscar Devereaux who, like his creator, is left unfulfilled by the end of the narrative. Devereaux is unable to bring his utopian dream of growing up with the land to full fruition. Motivated by his disgust for eastern rural and city blacks, whose lack of insight he believes leaves them hopelessly blaming racism and Jim Crow custom for the squalor in their lives, Devereaux purchases a relinquishment on the Little Crow in South Dakota and moves there to homestead. By acting on his own, he intends to expose the moral hypocrisy and ineptitude among blacks, and become a model for them. As he attempts to make good on his land, his vision of an agrarian utopia comes face to face with the details of the harsh facts of rural life. But, unlike many characters in granger stories and novels like those of Hamlin Garland, who are frustrated by a rural life of privation—which hard work, tenacity of will, and patience do not necessarily remedy—Devereaux is able to break out 120 acres of pristine prairie and, in his spare time, freight coal between nearby towns. He is also able to purchase another homestead, extending his landholdings to half a section.

Even though Devereaux becomes enamored with a Scottish woman who moves to the Little Crow, he decides to marry instead an urban black woman, pursuing his original goal of being both a model for his people and, by not breaking the law against miscegenation, a credit to his race. He marries Orlean McCraline, a city woman whose weak disposition and overbearing father inevitably destroy the couples' marriage and foil Devereaux's dream. These intrusions of evil, along with overpowering forces in nature such as drought and pestilence, cause the foreclosure of Devereaux's holdings and force him to abandon his utopian dream of growing up with the land and becoming a successful homesteader.

Preoccupied with setting things right with his failed hero of *The Conquest*, Micheaux published three novels that all have eastern or urban settings: *The Forged Note*, *The Case of Mrs. Wingate*, and *The Story of Dorothy Stanfield*. Micheaux's purpose in *The Forged Note*, as in his other novels with urban settings, is to defend the hero's vision of *The Conquest* and to attack the majority of blacks as being immoral, incompetent, criminal, and mentally lethargic. The Rosebud (renamed from the Little Crow) becomes symbolic of an idyllic past spoiled by the kind of blacks whom Sidney Wyeth, the protagonist, encounters in the cities.

Perhaps the most successful defense of the hero's vision in *The Conquest* is Micheaux's revision of it in both *The Homesteader* and *The Wind from Nowhere*.

The hero in *The Wind from Nowhere*, Martin Eden (fashioned after Jack London's "Martin Eden," who has the aggressive will and determination to survive because he can adapt and prevail), realizes his dream of bringing civilization to the Rosebud Country by making it a black colony.

In *The Homesteader* Micheaux presents a quiet Western, unlike the blood-and-thunder of typical horse epics. He combines elements of the frontiersman and agrarian settler traditions. Jean Baptiste, the protagonist and hero, goes to the not-yet-civilized land of South Dakota as the first black pioneer of the area with the intention of homesteading. The protagonist's name becomes emblematic of his personal character, alluding to Jean Baptiste Point du Sable, the black Frenchman who established a trading post in 1779 that eventually became

Chicago. Jean Baptiste of *The Homesteader* is chaste; and he possesses the acumen that will lead him to success, given the almost boundless opportunities of the West.

Baptiste is also skilled. He experiments with improved farming and homesteading methods by utilizing a deep cut plowing method, and by subsidizing his farming with stock raising. These methods, coupled with his skills in writing—he commences a career in writing after the foreclosure of his lands—enable him to recover lost landholdings.

Baptiste is also solitary. His contempt for the attitudes of eastern and urban blacks, and his resolve to go to the untamed country to make his way alone, his determination to withstand a blizzard as he freights coal from Bonesteel for extra money, and his ability, as a child alone in the woods, to kill a catamount with only a club, bespeak attributes in his character rather than antisocial flaws. Baptiste stands aloof from the hypocrisy and weakness inherent in blacks who find his assumption about them, about the West, and about American culture silly and crude.

The majority of the blacks whom Baptiste encounters become his great antagonists, the villains; they attempt to foil his efforts to successfully grow up with the West. Black hostility to Baptiste reflects the typical western theme that one who has not been exposed to the particularly beneficial aspects of nature, whether in the rural districts of the South or of the West, will experience a lack of metaphysical insight and moral perception that the western hero possesses. The urban black, like the social man or dude of the Western, is weak, hypocritical, unable to see below the surface of things, and therefore unable to take charge of his or her destiny.

Though the ending of *The Conquest* leaves Micheaux's hero a failure, the ending of *The Homesteader* revises the story: the hero wins and is united with his beloved, and his homestead is profitable.

A critical assessment of Micheaux's western novels reveals that he adopted the quintessential assimilationist voice for masking the practical expedient of individual emancipation. His purpose was not didactic; it was to move himself beyond Jim Crow restrictions so that he could join the elite of the white mainstream.

—Joseph A. Young

MICHENER, James A(lbert). American. Born in 1907(?); brought up by foster parents. Educated at Doylestown High School, Pennsylvania; Swarthmore College, Pennsylvania, A.B. (summa cum laude) 1929 (Phi Beta Kappa); University of Northern Colorado, Greeley, A.M. 1935; University of St. Andrews, Scotland. Served in the United States Navy, 1944–45: Lieutenant Commander. Married 1) Patti Koon in 1935 (divorced 1948); 2) Vange Nord in 1948 (divorced 1955); 3) Mari Yoriko Sabusawa in 1955. Master, Hill School, Pottstown, Pennsylvania, 1929–31, and George School, Newtown, Pennsylvania, 1934–36; Professor, University of Northern Colorado, 1936–40; Visiting Professor, Harvard University, Cambridge, Massachusetts, 1940–41; associate editor, Macmillan Company, New York, 1941–49. Since 1949 freelance writer. Member, Advisory Committee on the Arts, United States Department of State, 1957; chair president Kennedy's Food for Peace Program, 1961; secretary, Pennsylvania Constitution Convention, 1967–68; member of the Advisory Committee, United States Information Agency, 1970–76, and NASA, 1980–83. Since 1983 member of the Board, International Broadcasting. Recipient: Lippincott travelling Fellowship, 1930–33; Pultizer prize, 1948; National Association of Independent Schools award, 1954, 1958; Einstein award, 1967; National Medal of Freedom, 1971; Spanish Institute Gold Medal, 1980. D.H.L.: Rider College, Lawrenceville, New Jersey, 1950; Swarthmore College, 1954; LL.D.: Temple University, Philadelphia, 1957; Litt.D.: Washington University, St. Louis, 1967; Yeshiva University, New York, 1974; D.Sc.: Jefferson Medical College, Philadelphia, 1979. Address: c/o Random House Inc., 201 East 50th Street, New York, New York 10022, U.S.A.

Western Publications

Novels

Centennial. New York, Random House, and London, Secker and Warburg, 1974.
Texas. New York, Random House, and London, Secker and Warburg, 1985.

Other Publications

Novels

The Fires of Spring. New York, Random House, 1949; London, Corgi, 1960.
The Bridges at Toko-Ri. New York, Random House, and London, Secker and Warburg, 1953.
Sayonara. New York, Random House, and London, Secker and Warburg, 1954.
The Bridge at Andau. New York, Random House, and London, Secker and Warburg, 1957.
Hawaii. New York, Random House, 1959; London, Secker and Warburg, 1960.
Caravans. New York, Random House, 1963; London, Secker and Warburg, 1964.
The Source. New York, Random House, and London, Secker and Warburg, 1965.
The Drifters. New York, Random House, and London, Secker and Warburg, 1971.
Chesapeake. New York, Random House, and London, Secker and Warburg, 1978; selections published as *The Watermen*, Random House, 1979.
The Covenant. New York, Random House, and London, Secker and Warburg, 1980.
Space. New York, Random House, and London, Secker and Warburg, 1982.
Poland. New York, Random House, and London, Secker and Warburg, 1983.
Legacy. New York, Random House, and London, Secker and Warburg, 1987.
Alaska. New York, Random House, and London, Secker and Warburg, 1988.
Journey. New York, Random House, and London, Secker and Warburg, 1989.
Caribbean. New York, Random House, 1989.

Short Stories

Tales of the South Pacific. New York, Macmillan, 1947; London, Collins, 1951.

Return to Paradise. New York, Random House, and London, Secker and Warburg, 1951.

Other

The Unit in the Social Studies, with Harold M. Long. Cambridge, Massachusetts, Harvard University Graduate School of Education, 1940.
The Voice of Asia. New York, Random House, 1951; as *Voices of Asia*, London, Secker and Warburg, 1952.
The Floating World (on Japanese art). New York, Random House, 1954; London, Secker and Warburg, 1955.
Rascals in Paradise, with A. Grove Day. New York, Random House, and London, Secker and Warburg, 1957.
Selected Writings. New York, Modern Library, 1957.
Japanese Prints from the Early Masters to the Modern. Rutland, Vermont, Tuttle, and London, Paterson, 1959.
Report of the County Chairman. New York, Random House, and London, Secker and Warburg, 1961.
The Modern Japanese Print: An Introduction. Rutland, Vermont, Tuttle, 1962.
Israel: A Nation Too Young to Die. Des Moines, Iowa, Look, 1967.
Iberia: Spanish Travels and Reflections. New York, Random House, and London, Secker and Warburg, 1968.
The Subject Is Israel: A Conversation Between James A. Michener and Dore Schary. New York, Anti-Defamation League of B'nai B'rith, 1968.
Presidential Lottery: The Reckless Gamble in Our Electoral System. New York, Random House, and London, Secker and Warburg, 1969.
The Quality of Life. Philadelphia, Lippincott, 1970; London, Secker and Warburg, 1971.
Facing East: A Study of the Art of Jack Levine. New York, Random House, 1970.
Kent State: What Happened and Why. New York, Random House, and London, Secker and Warburg, 1971.
A Michener Miscellany 1950–1970, edited by Ben Hibbs. New York, Random House, 1973; London, Corgi, 1975.
About "Centennial": Some Notes on the Novel. New York, Random House, 1974.
Sports in America. New York, Random House, 1976; as *Michener on Sport*, London, Secker and Warburg, 1976.
Testimony. Honolulu, White Knight, 1983.
Collectors, Forgers—and a Writer: A Memoir. New York, Targ, 1983.
Six Days in Havana, with John King. Austin, University of Texas Press, 1989.

Editor, *The Future of the Social Studies: Proposals for an Experimental Social-Studies Curriculum*. New York, National Council for the Social Studies, 1939.
Editor, *The Hokusai Sketch Books: Selections from the Manga*. Rutland, Vermont, Tuttle, 1958.
Editor, *Firstfruits: A Harvest of 25 Years of Israeli Writing*. Philadelphia, Jewish Publication Society of America, 1973.

*

Manuscript Collection: Library of Congress, Washington, D.C.

Critical Studies: *James Michener* by A. Grove Day, New York, Twayne, 1964, revised edition, 1977; *James Michener* by George J. Becker, New York, Ungar, 1983; *James A. Michener: A Biography* by John P. Hayes, Indianapolis, Bobbs Merrill, and London, W.H. Allen, 1984; *New American Paintings: A Tribute to James and Mari Michener* by Eric McCready and Becky Duval Reese, Austin, University of Texas Press, 1984.

* * *

James A. Michener is almost an American institution. Since *Tales of the South Pacific* (and the musical play based on it, *South Pacific*) appeared in the 1940's, all his books—fiction and non-fiction—have been widely read and discussed. On the other hand, few might expect his work to be treated in a discussion of western fiction, even after being reminded that *Centennial* is the history of a small western town. Yet *Centennial*, a massive book of 909 pages in its original edition, contains fictional (and factual) material on topics that are the very heart of both popular and the more studied "Western"—Indian life (mainly Arapaho), early trappers and traders, the early settlers, the organization of cattle and sheep ranching and farming, and the modern problems of western identity, conservation, leisure, pollution.

The book is divided into some 14 chapters, most of them discrete, several in fact constituting short novels in themselves. Yet the overall cohesion of the book is generated by its clear focus on the fictional town of Centennial in northeast Colorado, and by its "epitome" character of chapter 14, Paul Garrett, who we realize is a descendant or friend of almost all the major characters from the preceding chapters. But this overall design doesn't seem artificial, and Michener gives himself space (and the reader gladly permits it) to give exhaustive background and digressions—so that we learn of Lancaster, Pennsylvania, the town that produced the farmer-butcher Levi Zendt (whose original settlement of Zendt's Farm became Centennial in 1876), or a traveling stage show in the Opera House in 1889.

Most readers, I suspect, will be happiest with the earlier sections of the novel. "The Many Coups of Lame Beaver," for instance, is a moving account of a heroic life. Lame Beaver, a brave but slightly off-center Arapaho, never becomes a chief, but is an imaginative leader central to his tribe's history. He brings the first horses to the tribe, and achieves many coups (tokens of bravery through touching—not killing—the enemy). He has a happy marriage (his descendants play an important role in Centennial's history), and dies bravely. His most touching moment is when he steals into some strange hunters' tent to look at their guns, and in a moment of frozen intensity finds himself staring into the staring eyes of the white man for the first time. No violence occurs—each recognizes the other as human—yet the "implied treaty" between the two races will eventually be broken.

"The Yellow Apron" celebrates the early mountain men. Michener deals with Pasquinel (the hunter who returned Lame Beaver's stare) and Alexander McKeag. Pasquinel is the roving wild man, never satisfied to settle, with wives in several cities as well as an Indian wife. McKeag is the more interesting character, much concerned with freedom, yet prey to his friendship with Pasquinel and his women. After a particularly hard winter alone in a caved-out snowbank, he attends one of the trappers' rendezvous (1827), and is so exhilarated at the awareness of other trappers all emerging from their mountain lairs that he rejoins civilization, and actually helps found Centennial with Levi Zendt.

The wagon trail and cattle drive sections are more familiar, but interesting nonetheless. As events become more complicated and characters multiply, the reader sees the grid of eastern Colorado fill, peak, diminish, as settlers, blacks, chicanos, and orientals arrive. Michener adds a narrative framework to the book—concerning a Georgia history professor doing research for a special bicentennial issue of a leading magazine—and this in some ways diminishes his achievement. In place of footnotes we have editor's notes, and Michener's didactic and patriotic purpose is rather heavily emphasized. Yet the invented details like Lame Beaver's and Pasquinel's stares, or McKeag's cry of anguish ("Oh God! I am so alone!"), remain in the memory after the factual notes and maps are forgotten.

With *Texas*, Michener tackles an even larger canvas, attempting his own "factional" history of the Lone Star State. Opening his novel with an imaginary conference of eminent historians—meeting, appropriately enough, in San Antonio, home of the famous Alamo—he examines the differing personalities of the academics as they deliberate over how best to produce a definitive history of the state, then moves rapidly into flashback to trace the actual past events through the eyes of their ancestors. Fixing adroitly on representative characters from the many pioneer communities—Hispanic, German, Scottish-Irish, Afro-American—who between them established the modern state, Michener demonstrates the many truths and mythologies of the Texas past, and how they have so often survived in a subtly altered form to the present day. His narrative, which manages somehow to take in the opposed viewpoints of *Tejano* outlaws and Texas Rangers, black cavalry troopers and white Anglo-Saxons, Catholics and Quakers, carries the reader through the crucial developments of the last 150 years without becoming laboured or sermonistic. Michener describes through the eyes of his many participants the early massacres of the native Amerindians, the heroism and the brutality of the Texas War of Independence, the Mexican War, the Civil War. The fratricidal struggle between Anglo and Hispanic, with its many shameful episodes on both sides, is presented sympathetically, but without undue sentiment. By constantly cutting from his historic creations to their modern descendants, and back again, he manages to show the growth of the state as a single continuous process leading to modern times, where the paradoxes of the past become those of today. Texas emerges convincingly in all its intriguing and contradictory aspects—a dangerous, inhospitable terrain peopled by a population noted for its open-handed generosity; a state harbouring extremes of wealth and poverty; outwardly the home of a rigid Anglo-Saxon conservatism, yet at the same time the home of daring ventures and experiments which include the latest developments in medical and space research. It seems an almost impossible task to encapsulate so large a subject in a single work, but—using similar techniques to those in *Centennial*—Michener brings it off. *Texas*, while perhaps less memorable than its predecessor, is more ambitious in scope, and an achievement greatly to its author's credit. It may also be seen as an indication that the western landscape still holds attractions for Michener, and is a setting to which he may yet again return.

—George Walsh

MILBURN, George. American. Born in Coweta, Indian Territory (now Oklahoma), 27 April 1906. Educated at University of Tulsa, Oklahoma, 1923–34; Oklahoma A and M College, Stillwater, 1925; University of Oklahoma, Norman, 1928–30. Married Vivien Custard in 1929. Freelance journalist and writer from 1922. Recipient: Guggenheim fellowship, 1934. *Died 22 September 1966.*

WESTERN PUBLICATIONS

Novels

Catalogue. New York, Harcourt Brace, 1936; as *All over Town,* New York, Dell, 1953.
Flannigan's Folly. New York, McGraw Hill, 1947.
Julie. New York, Lion, 1956; as *Old John's Woman,* New York, Pyramid, 1960.

Short Stories

Oklahoma Town. New York, Harcourt Brace, 1931.
No More Trumpets and Other Stories. New York, Harcourt Brace, 1933.
Sin People. New York, Lion, 1953.
Hoboes and Harlots. New York, Lion, 1954.

OTHER PUBLICATIONS

Other

A Handbook for Amateur Magicians. Girard, Kansas, Haldeman Julius, 1926.
Lives of the U.S. Presidents. Girard, Kansas, Haldeman Julius, 1926.
How to Become a United States Citizen [Prepare Manuscripts, Tie All Kinds of Knots]. Girard, Kansas, Haldeman Julius, 3 vols., 1927.
A Rapid Calculator: How to Make Rapid Arithmetical Calculations. Girard, Kansas, Haldeman Julius, 1928.

Editor, *The Best Jewish [Hobo, Rube, Scotch, Yankee] Jokes.* Girard, Kansas, Haldeman Julius, 5 vols., 1926–27.
Editor, *A Book of Interesting and Amusing Puns [College Humor, Puzzles and Teasers, Popular Recitations, the Best Ford Jokes].* Girard, Kansas, Haldeman Julius, 5 vols., 1926–27.
Editor, *Casey at the Bat and Other Humorous Favorites.* Girard, Kansas, Haldeman Julius, 1926.
Editor, *The Best Jokes about Drunks [Doctors, Preachers, Lawyers].* Girard, Kansas, Haldeman Julius, 4 vols., 1927.
Editor, *Love Tales of the Queen of Navarre.* Girard, Kansas, Haldeman Julius, n.d.
Editor, *Gargantua, Mighty Monster,* by Rabelais. Girard, Kansas, Haldeman Julius, n.d.
Editor, *The Hobo's Hornbook: A Repertory for a Gutter Jongleur.* New York, Washburn, 1930.

* * *

When H.L. Mencken began publishing in his *American Mercury* the stories that were later to appear in George Milburn's *Oklahoma Town,* he was recognizing a highly competent realist who was squarely in the current vogue of short story writing. Following the route pioneered in *Winesburg, Ohio* and *Spoon River Anthology,* Milburn began writing vignettes about the folk in his native Oklahoma. He soon produced pieces with more narrative line and greater character development.

The stories in *No More Trumpets* are Milburn's best work. Several, such as "Heel, Toe, and a 1, 2, 3, 4," "The Apostate," "A Student in Economics," and "A Pretty Cute Little Stunt," were deservedly widely anthologized. Some were not set in Oklahoma, but Milburn only occasionally handled well settings outside his native heath.

Although Milburn continued to publish some stories, his major later efforts were in the novel and scripts for radio shows.

Catalogue was greeted with considerable praise by critics, but it is in part a device for presenting a miscellaneous assortment of small town and rural Oklahoma characters. The impact of the arrival of mail order catalogues one summer causes a variety of traumas. Milburn's deft picturing of assorted folk is the major feature of the book, for the plot is thin. Although the interlocking lives do come to a serio-comic head at the end, the arrival of the catalogues and the attempt of the local merchants to keep trade at home do not provide the focus a central figure would have done.

Flannigan's Folly is a strange concoction of traditional romantic tale, a vaudeville-like comic Irishman, and some unorthodox agricultural theory. Flannigan, filled with blarney, plays suitor to a young widow who owns a fertile farm next to his rocky one. But a newcomer goes to work for her, and, with the usual delays, a romance buds between them. Oddly, Flannigan and the newcomer both practice the theories expounded in Edward A. Faulker's *Plowman Folly*, which condemns the deep plowing then used. It is a strange inspiration for a novel. Milburn's last novel, *Julie*, is even less successful. Based on Chaucer's "Miller's Tale," the story has digressions, and the characters do not have the sharp verisimilitude evident in the earlier works.

One other book Milburn produced deserves mention. *The Hobo's Hornbook* is a substantial collection of hobo songs and rhymes that Milburn collected during his years among the jungles. However, in this day of greater permissiveness in publishing, they seem rather tame to be hobo creations.

It is unfortunate that Milburn could not carry his evident talent farther than he did. His best short stories ranked with any being done in the early 1930's, but he could not go beyond the social realism of the day.

—Ernest B. Speck

MILLARD, Joseph (John). Also writes as Joe Millard. American. Born in Canby, Minnesota, 14 January 1908. Educated at Pioneer School of Business, St. Paul, Minnesota, graduated 1926. Married Amy Leone Lee in 1931; one son. Worked for an advertising agency, St. Paul, 1926, then advertising manager, *Northwest Furniture Digest*, Minneapolis, account executive, Kraff Advertising Agency, Minneapolis, and Industrial Advertising Associates, Chicago, and editor, *How to Sell* and *National Mortician* magazines, Chicago. Since 1936 freelance writer. Address: 9421 Beck Street, Dallas, Texas 75228, U.S.A.

WESTERN PUBLICATIONS

Novels (series: Man with No Name in all "Dollar" books)

The Wickedest Man. New York, Fawcett, 1954; London, Muller, 1960.
The Good, The Bad, and the Ugly (novelization of screenplay; Man with No Name). New York, Award, 1967; London, Tandem, 1968.
For a Few Dollars More (novelization of screenplay). New York, Award, 1967; London, Star, 1980.
The Good Guys and the Bad Guys. New York, Award, and London, Tandem, 1970.
The Last Rebel. New York, Award, 1970.
Macho Callahan. New York, Award, 1970.
Chato's Land. New York, Award, 1971.
The Hunting Party (novelization of screenplay). New York, Award, and London, Tandem, 1971.
Coffin Full of Dollars. New York, Award, 1971; London, Tandem, 1972.
The Devil's Dollar Sign. New York, Award, 1972; London, Tandem, 1973.
Blood for a Dirty Dollar. New York, Award, 1973; London, Tandem, 1974.
Cahill, United States Marshal (novelization of screenplay). New York, Award, 1973.
The Million-Dollar Bloodhunt. New York, Award, 1973; London, Tandem, 1974.
The Hunted (novelization of screenplay). New York, Award, 1974; as *Hec Ramsey—The Hunted*, London, Tandem, 1974.
Thunderbolt and Lightfoot (novelization of screenplay). New York, Award, 1974.
Dollar to Die For. London, Tandem, 1977.

Uncollected Short Story

"Dangerous Type," in *American Magazine* (Springfield, Ohio), March 1949.

OTHER PUBLICATIONS

Novels

Mansion of Evil. New York, Fawcett, 1950.
The Gods Hate Kansas. Derby, Connecticut, Monarch, 1964.

Other

Edgar Cayce: Mystery Man of Miracles. New York, Fawcett, 1956; London, Spearmen, 1961.
True Civil War Stories. New York, Fawcett, 1961.
No Law But Their Own. Evanston, Illinois, Regency, 1963.
The Cheyenne Wars. Derby, Connecticut, Monarch, 1964.
Cut-Hand, The Mountain Man (for children). Philadelphia, Chilton, 1964.
The Incredible Bowles (for children). Philadelphia, Chilton, 1965.

* * *

There is a certain fitting irony in the fact that the first novel by Joseph Millard to appear in England was entitled *The Wickedest Man.* Since that time, its author has gone on to secure himself a deserved reputation as forefather of the psychopathic Western, a much imitated genre embodied in his novelizations of Clint Eastwood films starring the professional killer, The Man with No Name. And they don't come any more wicked than he.

The Good, The Bad, and the Ugly set the pattern for Millard's subsequent work. Based on the popular film, it follows the nameless bounty hunter in search of a hoard of gold which has been buried in a cemetary in New Mexico at the height of the Civil War. Unprincipled and pitiless, The Man with No Name cares for one thing only—money, in any of its forms. To acquire it, he will lie, cheat, and kill without compunction. The wanted men he shoots down en route are seen by him merely as a means of enriching himself. His grim duel with Tuco the bandit and Sentenza the rival gunman is enlivened by touches of gallows humour, and Millard impresses with the cinematic scenes—the driverless ambulance filled with dead soldiers, the shootout in the cemetery—with a style that relies on careful understatement. Unlike most of his imitators, he avoids the gloating sadism of some "adult Westerns," the restraint of his writing serving to sharpen the focus of the brutality he describes.

Millard followed up this first—and best—of his works with a series of novels based either on Eastwood films or on original plots conceived around the leading character. Millard has tried his hand with other themes—*Macho Callahan* and *The Hunted* are both effective examples of his craft—but it is on the adventures of The Man with No Name that his reputation rests. Over the years, the plots have grown increasingly bizarre. *Coffin Full of Dollars* has the bounty hunter starring in a travelling circus, and in *The Million-Dollar Bloodhunt* he takes to a hot-air balloon to hunt down his desperado victims. Some of these later works show attempts to humanize the character—even, in *Coffin*, to the extent of giving money away—but judged beside the nature of the Man with No Name such efforts lack conviction. The character's main asset in the calling he pursues is the lack of feeling for anyone but himself.

The world Millard's characters inhabit is not very appealing: a brutal degraded universe where the dollar is king, and where only the cynical and tough survive at the expense of those weaker than themselves. The other extreme from the sunlit, "singing cowboy" world of earlier writers, Millard's world is no more "real." Psychopathic killers undoubtedly existed in the West, but in Millard's novels one is asked to accept them as the norm, which was never true. For something closer to the reality of that time, Noel Loomis and Matt Chisholm offer more convincing models.

Millard, whose novelizations began a cult of sadistic Westerns, remains unrivalled by virtue of his plain, terse style, where horrors are noted but not unduly dwelt upon. All the same, the perverse nature of the world he presents leaves the reader uneasy. He tells an ugly story, but there is no denying that he tells it well.

—Jeff Sadler

MILLER, Frank. *See* **LOOMIS, Noel M.**

MILLER, Jim.

WESTERN PUBLICATIONS

Novels

Sunsets. New York, Fawcett, 1983; Leicester, Ulverscroft, 1987.
Sonny. New York, Doubleday, 1987; London, Hale, 1989.
Shotgun and Sagebrush. New York, Fawcett, 1989.

Novels (series: Colt Revolver in all books)

Gone to Texas. New York, Fawcett, 1983; Leicester, Linford, 1987.
Comanche Trail, with James Collins. New York, Fawcett, 1984; Leicester, Ulverscroft, 1986.
Riding Shotgun. New York, Fawcett, 1985; London, Severn House, 1988.
Orphans Preferred. New York, Fawcett, 1985; Leicester, Ulverscroft, 1988.
Campaigning. New York, Fawcett, 1985; Leicester, Linford, 1988.

Novels (series: The Long Guns in all books)

Mister Henry. New York, Fawcett, 1986.
The Big Fifty. New York, Fawcett, 1986.
The Brass Boy. New York, Fawcett, 1987.
Spencer's Revenge. New York, Fawcett, 1987.
War Clouds. New York, Fawcett, and Leicester, Ulverscroft, 1987.
That Damn Single Shot. New York, Fawcett, 1988.

Novels (series: The Old-Timers in all books)

The Old-Timers of Gun Shy. New York, Dell, 1987.
The Old-Timers in the Sangrc de Cristos. New York, Dell, 1988.
The Old-Timers on the Open Range. New York, Dell, 1988.

Novels (series: The Ex-Rangers in all books)

Rangers' Revenge. New York, Fawcett, 1990.
The Long Rope. New York, Fawcett, 1990.
Hell With the Hide Off. New York, Fawcett, 1991.

*   *   *

Although Jim Miller decided that he wanted to be a western writer when he was given a Zane Grey book for his 10th birthday, he tells his stories in an amiably "folksy" first-person narrative more reminiscent of that used by Louis L'Amour in the Sackett novels. At no time do Miller's books get so poetic in their colourful use of language that they cease to be fast, event-filled Westerns, however. Indeed, the author's meticulous research (gleaned from a personal library of more than 2,000 volumes), plus a tendency to set his stories against a backdrop of actual historical events, constantly enable him to invoke a remarkably accurate sense of period.

The majority of Miller's Westerns are about families, and in particular the relationships between fathers and sons. He is equally at home writing about the earlier part of the 19th century as he is the post-Civil War years, and with the exception of a couple of single titles and the Old-Timers of Gunshy trilogy, all of his books have so far appeared in series format.

His first series, published as the Colt Revolver novels, recounts the adventures of the Callahan family, and gradually builds into a modest generation-spanning saga that follows the fortunes—and otherwise—of these pistol-packing pioneers. (As the general title would suggest, a different handgun is worked into, or forms part of the basis for, every story). The main character of the first book, *Gone to Texas*, is the eldest son Nate, who, having been forced to flee to the Lone Star State after taking part in a duel, returns home as a hard-bitten Texas Ranger who eventually joins Sam Houston at the Battle of the Alamo. In *Comanche Trail* the youngest son, Finn, proves that, though bookish and the "thinker" of the family, he can still be as tough as his older brother.

During the course of *Riding Shotgun*, the whole family (which by now includes the wives of Nate and Finn, as well as Nate's young son James) moves west from Connecticut, but the

Callahan patriarch dies before his youngest son Sean is born. Sean grows to become the main character in *Orphans Preferred* riding for the Pony Express, while James manages a way station which is eventually attacked by raiders, with devastating consequences. The final novel of the series, *Campaigning* sees Sean riding with Kit Carson and taking part in the First Battle of Adobe Walls.

Miller's companion series, The Long Guns, follows pretty much the same pattern, with the emphasis shifting from handguns to saddle-guns. A tall, bear-like former mountain man named Ezra "Black Jack" Hooker is the central character here, although his two sons, Matthew (known as "Guns") and Jedediah ("Diah") also feature prominently. In *Mister Henry*, the Hookers arrive in Lawrence, Kansas, just before Quantrill's Raiders razed the town in 1863. In *The Big Fifty*, "Guns" starts a trading post for buffalo hunters in the ruins of Adobe Walls, which eventually comes under attack by vengeful Kiowa and Comanche. *The Brass Boy* sees "Black Jack" and his sons running cattle up the Shawnee Trail to Kansas (and coming up against some pretty tough opposition along the way) and in *Spencer's Revenge*, which finds Diah escorting a wagon train through hostile Indian territory, tragedy strikes when his part-Indian girlfriend is lynched by an angry mob following an outbreak of Arapahoe trouble, an event from which Diah never fully recovers.

Miller's most recent series has been The Ex-Rangers, which once again teams a father—in this case, Town Marshal Will Carston—with his two sons, Chance and George Washington (called "Wash"). In the first book, *Rangers' Revenge*, Chance and Wash return home after the Civil War (having both fought on opposing sides) to continue their private feud. All other considerations are set aside, however, when Will tells them that their mother has been killed in a recent Comanchero raid. All three are experienced lawmen, having served together in the Texas Rangers before the War, and after a well-handled period of soul-searching and scene setting, they put that experience to good use by tracking down the killers. The Carston ranch—or at least what's left of it—is attacked again in *The Long Rope*, this time by ex-Confederate desperadoes, and when Will and Wash are captured, Chance has to play a lone hand to save them.

Of course, it can be argued that one of Miller's Westerns reads pretty much like another. Certainly his assorted fathers and sons tend to come from similar moulds, and his constant choice of first-person narrative, though entertaining and certainly ideal for this type of novel, can sometimes be repetitive.

These elements have become Miller's trademarks, however, and in any case, his strengths as a storyteller far outweigh such potential weaknesses. The author has a knack for creating credible, likeable characters who compel belief. By subtly altering his choice of language and phrasing according to the "identity" of the narrator, he adds greater depth to his various clansmen, as well as a certain degree of individuality. Added to this is a good understanding of human nature, an enviable ability to combine historical fact with fictional fancy, and a genuine enthusiasm for his characters that should almost certainly keep Miller's work fresh for quite some time to come.

—David Whitehead

MILLER, Warne. *See* **RATHBORNE, St. George.**

MITCHUM, Hank. *See* **KNOTT, Will C.; NEWTON, D.B.**

MOMADAY, N(avarre) Scott. American. Born in Lawton, Oklahoma, 27 February 1934. Educated at the University of New Mexico, Albuquerque, A.B. 1958; Stanford University, California (Creative Writing Fellow, 1959), A.M. 1960, Ph.D. 1963. Married 1) Gaye Mangold in 1959 (divorced), three daughters; 2) Regina Heitzer in 1978, one daughter. Assistant Professor, 1963–67, and Associate Professor, 1967–69, University of California, Santa Barbara; Professor of English and comparative literature, University of California, Berkeley, 1969–72; Professor of English, Stanford University, 1972–80. Since 1980 Professor of English and comparative literature, University of Arizona, Tucson. Professor, University of California Institute for the Humanities, 1970; Whittall Lecturer, Library of Congress, Washington, D.C., 1971; Visiting Professor, New Mexico State University, Las Cruces, 1972–73, State University of Moscow, Spring 1974, Columbia University, New York, 1979, and Princeton University, New Jersey, 1979; writer-in-residence, Southeastern University, Washington, D.C., 1985, and Aspen Writers' Conference, Colorado, 1986. Artist: has exhibited drawings and paintings. Since 1978 member of the Board of Trustees, Museum of the American Indian, New York. Recipient: Academy of American Poets prize, 1962; Guggenheim grant, 1966; Pulitzer prize, 1969; American Academy award, 1970; Western Heritage award, 1974; Premio Litterario Internazionale Mondello, Italy, 1979; Western Literature Association award, 1983. D.H.L.: Central Michigan University, Mt. Pleasant, 1970; University of Massachusetts, Amherst, 1975; Yale University, New Haven, Connecticut, 1980; Hobart and William Smith Colleges, Geneva, New York, 1980; College of Santa Fe, 1982; D.Litt.: Lawrence University, Appleton, Wisconsin, 1971; University of Wisconsin, Milwaukee, 1976; College of Ganado, 1979; D.F.A.: Morningside College, Sioux City, Iowa, 1980. Address: 1041 Roller Coaster Road, Tucson, Arizona 85704, U.S.A.

WESTERN PUBLICATIONS

Novels

House Made of Dawn. New York, Harper, 1968; London, Gollancz, 1969.
The Ancient Child. New York, Doubleday, 1989.

Play

Screenplay: *The Man Who Killed the Deer*, adaptation of a novel by Frank Waters.

Verse

Angle of Geese and Other Poems. Boston, Godine, 1974.
Before an Old Painting of the Crucifixion, Carmel Mission, June 1960. San Francisco, Valenti Angelo, 1975.
The Gourd Dancer. New York, Harper, 1976.

Other

The Journey of Tai-me (Kiowa Indian tales). Privately printed, 1967; revised edition, as *The Way to Rainy Mountain*, Albuquerque, University of New Mexico Press, 1969.

Colorado: Summer, Fall, Winter, Spring, photographs by David Muench. Chicago, Rand McNally, 1973.
The Names: A Memoir. New York, Harper, 1976.

Editor, *The Complete Poems of Frederick Goddard Tuckerman*. New York, Oxford University Press, 1965.
Editor, *American Indian Authors*. Boston, Houghton Mifflin, 1976.
Editor, *A Coyote in the Garden*, by Ann Painter. Lewiston, Idaho, Confluence Press, 1988.

*

Manuscript Collection: Bancroft Library, University of California, Berkeley.

Critical Studies: *Four American Indian Literary Masters* by Alan R. Velie, Norman, University of Oklahoma Press, 1982; *Ancestral Voice: Conversations with N. Scott Momaday* by Charles L. Woodard, Lincoln, University of Nebraska Press, 1989.

* * *

The renaissance in American Indian literature began with the publication of N. Scott Momaday's *House Made of Dawn* in 1968. Indians have been working in mainstream American genres since the 18th century, but with a few exceptions—e.g., John Joseph Mathews and D'Arcy McNickle—before *House Made of Dawn* their works did not receive much attention. Momaday's novel won the Pulitzer prize in 1969. Encouraged by that, the sense of ethnic pride fostered by the Civil Rights movement, and the interest in minority cultures that developed in the 1960's and 1970's, writers like Vine Deloria, James Welch, and Leslie Silko began publishing, and the Indian Renaissance was in full swing.

House Made of Dawn is the story of a man identified only as Abel, a reference to the archetypal victim of Genesis. Abel is from a pueblo Momaday calls Walatowa, which may be recognized as Jemez, New Mexico, the place where Momaday was raised. The novel portrays Abel's difficulties after returning from World War II in fitting into either tribal life in Walatowa or life among whites in Los Angeles. In Walatowa Abel kills a man who publicly humiliates him, and goes to prison. Upon his release from jail the government relocates him in Los Angeles, but he drinks so much he loses his job, and provokes a fight with a policeman who almost beats him to death.

The plight of an Indian from a pueblo in the Southwest who is willing to die for his country in war but cannot live in it successfully in peacetime evokes memories of Ira Hayes, the Pima who became famous for helping to raise the flag on Iwo Jima, then died drunk in a ditch on the reservation a few years later. Hayes's story, which became symbolic of Indian heroism and victimization, was made into a film, *The Outsider*.

Momaday's novel is far more complex than *The Outsider*, and although Abel is a victim, he is not simply a victim of white injustice. The biblical Abel was killed by his brother, and appropriately two of the people who hurt Abel the worst are Indians, and the third either an a Mexican or an Indian with a Spanish surname.

The man whom Abel kills for humiliating him is a Jemez albino whom Momaday refers to as "the white man." The language of the murder scene is full of double entendres, which suggest that while in a literal sense Abel is killing an Indian albino, in a symbolic sense the white man—i.e., white society—is raping Abel.

In Los Angeles the man who humiliates Abel is John Big Bluff Tosamah, a Kiowa preacher who runs a storefront Native American church. Tosamah, Abel's antagonist—the character who fills the slot of villain in the novel—is a caricature of Momaday himself. Not only does he physically resemble Momaday, and belong to Momaday's tribe, but the biographical memoir he relates is Momaday's life story.

In the end Abel survives his humiliation and beating and returns to Walatowa, where he buries his grandfather in the tradtional Jemez way, and participates in a ritual race for good hunting and harvests. These acts indicate that Abel is making an effort at fitting himself into the life of the tribe.

In his next work Momaday extracts Tosamah's account of his family history from *House Made of Dawn*, amplifies it with additional historical and autobiographical material, and issues it as *The Way to Rainy Mountain*. The book is an account of the Kiowa migration from the Rocky Mountains of Montana and Wyoming to the plains of western Oklahoma. Momaday makes a pilgrimage along the route the Kiowas had taken, ending at his grandmother's grave at Rainy Mountain cemetery outside Mountain View, Oklahoma.

The book has three sections, each dealing with a phase of Kiowa history. Each section is divided into short chapters with three parts, a Kiowa legend or myth, a historical passage, and a personal reminiscence. Alternating three types of cryptic, lyric voices allows Momaday to achieve a densely textured poetic narrative.

Momaday's next work, *The Names*, is a beautiful memoir about his family history and his childhood. Momaday describes the existential decision his mother, whose only Indian forebear is a Cherokee great-grandmother, makes in defining herself as Indian, and going to an Indian boarding school where she meets Momaday's father, a fullblood Kiowa. The book is a valuable source of information on Momaday's life and ideas.

Momaday's most recent work is *The Ancient Child*, the story of a man who changes into a bear. Momaday uses a traditional Kiowa legend as the basis of a realistic novel, giving the novel a mythic dimension.

The hero and heroine of the book, a painter named Locke Setman, and a young girl called Grey, represent two sides of Momaday—the artist who lives in the white world, and the Indian who lives in the world of his tribe. Setman, called Set (the Kiowa word for bear), is Kiowa by birth, but has been raised in San Francisco, and knows extremely little of his Indian heritage. Grey is half Navajo, half Kiowa, and totally Indian in identity. She refers to herself as "mayor of Bote, Oklahoma," *bote* being the word for the quintessential Kiowa dish, the intestines that they love to eat raw.

In the *dramatis personae* Momaday describes Grey as a "dreamer," and in her dreams she rides with the 19th-century New Mexico outlaw Billy the Kid. Years ago Momaday had written a series of newspaper columns in which he was Billy's sidekick, and he reworks the pieces into *The Ancient Child*.

Momaday also describes Grey as a "medicine woman," and it is her medicine that transforms Set into the bear in the surprise climax to the book.

—Alan R. Velie

MONTGOMERY, Rutherford (George). Also wrote as A.A. Avery; Al Avery; Everitt Proctor. American. Born in Straubville, North Dakota, 12 April 1894. Educated at schools in Velva, North Dakota; Colorado Agricultural College, Fort Collins; Western State College, Gunnison, Colorado; University of Nebraska, Lincoln. Served in the United States Army

Air Corps, 1917–18: Sergeant. Married Eunice Opal Kirks in 1930; one son and two daughters. Teacher, Hot Springs Elementary School, Wyoming, 1915–17; teacher and principal, Delta County High Schools, Cedaredge, Colorado, 1921–24, principal Montrose County Junior High School, Colorado, 1924–28; manager, Chamber of Commerce, 1928–32, and judge, Court of Records, 1932–37, Gunnison County, Colorado; state budget and efficiency commissioner, Denver, 1937–39; creative writing teacher, adult education classes, Los Gatos, California, 1955–57; writer, Walt Disney Studios, Burbank, California, 1958–62. Freelance writer, 1939–74; ghost writer for Dick Tracy series, 1941–46. Recipient: New York *Herald Tribune* Festival award, 1956; Boys' Clubs of America award, 1956; Western Writers of America Spur award, for children's book, 1966. *Died 3 July 1985.*

Western Publications

Novels

Call of the West. New York, Grosset and Dunlap, 1933.
Black Powder Empire. Boston, Little Brown, 1955; London, Ward Lock, 1957.
Posted Water. London, Ward Lock, 1959.
Smoky Trail. London, Ward Lock, 1967.

Other Publications

Novels

Anything for a Quiet Life (as A.A. Avery). New York, Farrar and Rinehart, 1942.
Sex Isn't Everything. New York, Torquil, 1961.

Fiction for children

Troopers Three. New York, Doubleday, 1932.
Broken Fang. Chicago, Donohue, 1935.
Carcajou. Caldwell, Idaho, Caxton, 1936; Bristol, Arrowsmith, 1937.
Yellow Eyes. Caldwell, Idaho, Caxton, 1937; London, Blackie, 1939.
Gray Wolf. Boston, Houghton Mifflin, 1938; London, Hutchinson, 1939.
Timberline Tales. Philadelphia, McKay, 1939; London, Hutchinson, 1951.
The Trail of the Buffalo. Boston, Houghton Mifflin, 1939.
Orphans of the Wild. London, Arrowsmith, 1939.
Midnight. New York, Holt, 1940; London, Hutchinson, 1944.
Stan Ball of the Rangers. Philadelphia, McKay, 1941.
Ice Blink. New York, Holt, 1941; London, Hutchinson, 1949.
A Yankee Flier with the R.A.F. [*in the Far East, in North Africa, in the South Pacific, in Italy, over Berlin, in Normandy, on a Rescue Mission, under Secret Orders*] (as Al Avery). New York, Grosset and Dunlap, 9 vols., 1941–46.
Thumbs Up! Philadelphia, McKay, 1942; London, Hutchinson, 1943.
Hurricane Yank. Philadelphia, McKay, 1942; London, Hutchinson, 1943.
Ghost Town Adventure. New York, Holt, 1942.
Husky, Co-Pilot of the Pilgrim. New York, Holt, 1942; London, Ward Lock, 1949.
Spike Kelly of the Commandos. Racine, Wisconsin, Whitman, 1942.
Out of the Sun. Philadelphia, McKay, 1943; London, Wells Gardner Darton, 1947.
War Wings. Philadelphia, McKay, 1943; London, Wells Gardner Darton, 1948.
Trappers' Trail. New York, Holt, 1943; London, Hutchinson, 1948.
Warhawk Patrol. Philadelphia, McKay, 1944; London, Wells Gardner Darton, 1948.
The Last Cruise of the "Jeanette" (as Everitt Proctor). Philadelphia, Westminister Press, 1944.
Big Brownie. New York, Holt, 1944; London, Hutchinson, 1947.
Sea Raiders Ho! Philadelphia, McKay, 1945; London, Wells Gardner Darton, 1947.
Thunderboats Ho! Philadelphia, McKay, 1945; London, Wells Gardner Darton, 1948.
Thar She Blows (as Everitt Proctor). Philadelphia, Westminister Press, 1945; London, Pictorial Art, 1947.
Rough Riders Ho! Philadelphia, McKay, 1946.
Blue Streak and Doctor Medusa. Racine, Wisconsin, Whitman, 1946.
Men Against the Ice (as Everitt Proctor). Philadelphia, Westminster Press, 1946.
The Mystery of the Turquoise Frog. New York, Messner, 1946; London, Hutchinson, 1951.
Kildee House. New York, Doubleday, 1949; London, Faber, 1953.
The Mystery of Crystal Canyon. Philadelphia, Winston, 1951.
Hill Ranch. New York, Doubleday, 1951.
The Capture of the Golden Stallion. Boston, Little Brown, 1951.
Wapiti, The Elk. Boston, Little Brown, 1952.
Mister Jim. London, Faber, 1952; Cleveland, World, 1957.
McGonnigle's Lake. New York, Doubleday, 1953; London, Faber, 1957.
White Mountaineer. Boston, Little Brown, 1953.
The Golden Stallion's Revenge. Boston, Little Brown, 1953; London, Hodder and Stoughton, 1957.
The Golden Stallion to the Rescue. Boston, Little Brown, 1954; London, Hodder and Stoughton, 1956.
Amikuk. Cleveland, World, 1955.
The Golden Stallion's Victory. Boston, Little Brown, 1956; London, Hodder and Stoughton, 1957.
Claim Jumpers of Marble Canyon. New York, Knopf, 1956.
Beaver Water. Cleveland, World, 1956.
Mountain Man. Cleveland, World, 1957.
Jets Away! New York, Dodd Mead, 1957.
Tom Pittman, U.S.A.F. New York, Duell Sloan Pearce, 1957.
White Tail. Cleveland, World, 1958.
In Happy Hollow. New York, Doubleday, 1958.
The Silver Hills. Cleveland, World, 1958.
Kent Barstow, Special Agent. New York, Duell Sloan Pearce, 1958.
The Golden Stallion and the Wolf Dog. Boston, Little Brown, and London, Hodder and Stoughton, 1958.
A Horse for Claudia and Dennis. New York, Duell Sloan Pearce, 1958.
Jet Navigator, Strategic Air Command, with Grover Heiman. New York, Duell Sloan Pearce, 1959.
The Golden Stallion's Adventure at Redstone. Boston, Little Brown, 1959; London, Hodder and Stoughton, 1960.
Tim's Mountain. Cleveland, World, 1959.
Missile Away. New York, Duell Sloan Pearce, 1959.
Mission Intruder. New York, Duell Sloan Pearce, 1960.
The Odyssey of an Otter. New York, Golden Press, 1960; London, Purnell, 1962.
Weecha, The Raccoon. New York, Golden Press, 1960; London, Purnell, 1962.
King of the Castle. Cleveland, World, 1961.

Kent Barstow, Space Man. New York, Duell Sloan Pearce, 1961.
Klepty. New York, Duell Sloan Pearce, 1961.
Cougar. New York, Golden Press, 1961; London, Purnell, 1962.
El Blanco. New York, Golden Press, 1961.
The Capture of West Wind. New York, Duell Sloan Pearce, 1962.
Monte, The Bear Who Became a Celebrity. New York, Duell Sloan Pearce, 1962.
Kent Barstow and the Commando Flight. New York, Duell Sloan Pearce, 1963.
Crazy Kill Range. Cleveland, World, 1963.
The Defiant Heart. New York, Duell Sloan Pearce, 1963.
McNulty's Holiday. New York, Duell Sloan Pearce, 1963.
Kent Barstow on a B-70 Mission. New York, Duell Sloan Pearce, 1964.
Kent Barstow Aboard the Dyna Soar. New York, Duell Sloan Pearce, 1964.
Ghost Town Gold. Cleveland, World, 1965.
The Stubborn One. New York, Duell Sloan Pearce, 1965.
Into the Groove. New York, Dodd Mead, 1966.
Thornbrush Jungle. Cleveland, World, 1966.
A Kinkajou on the Town. Cleveland, World, 1967.
The Golden Stallion and the Mysterious Feud. Boston, Little Brown, 1967; Leicester, Brockhampton Press, 1970.
Corey's Sea Monster. New York, World, 1969.
Pekan, The Shadow. Caldwell, Idaho, Caxton, 1970.
Big Red, A Wild Stallion. Caldwell, Idaho, Caxton, 1971.
Rufus. Caldwell, Idaho, Caxton, 1973.

Plays

Screenplays: *Killers of the High Country*, 1959; *The Hound That Thought He Was a Raccoon*, with Albert Aley, 1960; *Flash, The Teenage Otter*, with Albert Aley, 1961; *Sancho, The Homing Steer*, 1961; *Ida, The Off-Beat Eagle*, 1962; *El Blanco, The Legend of a White Stallion*, 1962.

Other (for children)

High Country (for adults). New York, Derrydale Press, 1938.
See Catch (reader). Boston, Ginn, 1955.
The Golden Stallion Picture Book. New York, Grosset and Dunlap, 1962.
Snowman. New York, Duell Sloan Pearce, 1962.
The Living Wilderness. New York, Torquil, 1964.
Dolphins as They Are. New York, Duell Sloan Pearce, 1966.

Editor, *A Saddlebag of Tales: A Collection of Stories by Members of the Western Writers of America.* New York, Dodd Mead, 1959.

*

Manuscript Collection: University of Oregon Library, Eugene.

* * *

All Rutherford Montgomery's Westerns for adults are about range wars, between timberman and cattlemen in *Call of the West* and between big and small ranchers in *Black Powder Empire, Posted Water*, and *Smoky Trail*. It is interesting that, although the tales of conflict are somewhat repetitive, sympathies are shown towards different factions in each book: in *Posted Water*, right is firmly on the side of the small ranchers, but in *Smoky Trail* nesters are shown to be taking unfair and harmful advantage of the big, open-range rancher. In every case, however, the conflict turns out to have been manufactured by a third party—a crook who wants all the land for himself—and the two sides can always be reconciled in the end. The resolution inevitably involves the marriage of the hero and heroine who, throughout the story, have belonged to opposing factions. Even this conflict is illusory since, although the hero and the heroine's father are leaders of warring groups, it always turns out that both the heroine and her father are innocent of any wrong-doing.

Montgomery wrote many Westerns for children, often about animals or about hunters who make their homes in the wilds and learn to co-exist peacefully with the animals around them. Tales set on ranches, like the Golden Stallion series, revolve around the rancher's son and tend to focus on the misunderstandings which occur in his romance with a western girl or in his interpretation of the mysteries around him. In all these cases, as in the adult stories, the predominant note is one of harmony, broken only temporarily and re-asserted at the end. The ending of *The Mystery of Crystal Canyon* could well stand for the final impression left by all the novels: the heroine "felt warm and good inside. The Lazy Y gang hadn't changed. They were all together as they had been before the trouble."

In the light of this recurrent presentation of a harmonious world, it is revealing that Montgomery dedicates *Smoky Trail* to "the old ranch, the LAZY-Y-BAR-Z where I grew up." He used this ranch name more than once in his earlier fiction, and the association suggests that, despite the danger and violence in his Westerns, they have much to do with his sentiment and nostalgia for his own childhood.

—Christine Bold

MOORE, Amos. Pseudonym for George (Barron) Hubbard. American. Born in Croydon, New Hampshire, 18 November 1884. Educated at Kimball Union Academy, Meriden, New Hampshire; Brown University, Providence, Rhode Island, graduated 1908. Married Marguerite Hall Young in 1919; two daughters. Actor: appeared in *Peter Pan* by Barrie and in plays by William Gillette; retired from the stage, 1916; then freelance writer. *Died 6 July 1958.*

WESTERN PUBLICATIONS

Novels

The Boss of Lightning C. New York, Chelsea House, 1930; London, Hutchinson, 1933.
Lead Law. New York, Macaulay, and London, Harrap, 1934.
Sandy of Skyline. New York, Washburn, 1935; London, Harrap, 1936.
Daredevil Douglass. New York, Macaulay, and London, Harrap, 1935.
Quicksilver. New York, Washburn, 1936; as *Quicksilver Rides.* London, Harrap, 1936.
Quicksilver Justice. London, Harrap, 1936.
Wind over the Range. New York, Washburn, 1936; London, Harrap, 1937.
A Ranger Rides Alone. New York, Washburn, 1936; London, Harrap, 1937.
Gun-Smoke at Clarion. New York, Washburn, and London, Harrap, 1937.
Six-Gun Cyclone. New York, Washburn, 1937; London, Hale, 1939.

The Two-Gun Quacker. New York, Washburn, 1938; London, Hale, 1939.
Border Justice. New York, Washburn, 1938; London, Hale, 1940.
Death Rides the Desert. New York, Washburn, 1939; London, Hale, 1940.
A Ranger's Round-Up. New York, Washburn, 1940.
Ruckus at Roaring Gap. New York, Washburn, 1941.
Devlin's Day Off. New York, Doubleday, 1942; Kingswood, Surrey, World's Work, 1949.
Texas Round-Up. London, Hale, 1942.

OTHER PUBLICATIONS as George Hubbard, with Lilian Bennet-Thompson

Novels

Without Compromise. New York, Century, 1922.
The Golden Ball: A Detective Story. New York, Chelsea House, 1929.
Royce of the Royal Mounted (by Hubbard only) New York, Macaulay, 1932; London, Harrap, 1933.
The Love Doctor. New York, Macaulay, 1932; London, Eldon Press, 1933.
Fruit of Folly. New York, Macaulay, 1934.

Plays

In the Dark. New York, French, 1922.
A Narrow Squeak. New York, French, 1922; as *A Near Squeak*, London, French, 1923.

* * *

Amos Moore wrote conventional formula Westerns and a novel about the Royal Canadian Mounted Police: *Royce of the Royal Mounted.* This Mountie novel set in Canada had a non-western and 20th-century theme, the successful capture of a band of drug runners.

Moore's other books fall neatly within the conventions of average Westerns. *Lead Law*, for instance, is set in a typical southwestern town, Three Buttes, with a bad law-and-order problem. The man with the quickest draw beats the rustlers and earns the thanks of the townsfolk. *A Ranger Rides Alone* concerns a disguised Texas Ranger who infiltrates a gang of train robbers. Some of the robbers themselves are in disguise and work on a respectable ranch owned by the beautiful young heroine. The heroine and the Ranger wipe out the gang after many narrow scrapes. Critics did consider this book above average with its skillfully devised plot. Critics did not consider *Sandy of Skyline* to have a very probable plot, but the clever manipulation of it and the tense excitement which surrounded it more than compensated.

A Texas Ranger is also the hero of *Texas Round-Up*. He has to capture a particularly murderous band of train robbers. He tracks them across country and over rivers to a showdown in a hotel. The Ranger is quick with his gun, for we are told "four of them went down in that first withering of shots," and, like cowards, the rest of the gang fled. In *Ruckus at Roaring Gap* a small cowtown is dominated by a gang of bullies to the extent that the sheriff asks the law-abiding hero to move on. The hero does so, but after finding the gang terrorising a girl at a ranch house he decides to return to town to restore proper order. Cruelty to women and gratuitous violence of a sadistic nature appear in modern westerns, and Moore's books anticipated this trend. A very frightened and desperate girl appears as heroine in *Devlin's Day Off* which also contains a particularly cruel and ruthless gang leader. He is also a tyrant who is able to boss the town before being put down in the final climax.

Moore's books were popular because he was able to write Westerns in a vigorous unselfconscious way. Typical western dialogue is colourful and only used where appropriate, but does not descend into comedy. Moore was especially competent with his descriptive passages. He was able to create the right atmosphere of intense heat in *Texas Round-Up*, or a thudding lively description of a gunfight in *Lead Law*. The gripping quality of Moore's narrative was praised by critics and ensured him a high reputation as a western writer in the 1930's and 1940's.

—P.R. Meldrum

MÖRCK, Paul. *See* **RØLVAAG, O. E.**

MORGAN, Frank. *See* **PAINE, Lauran.**

MORGAN, G. J. *See* **ROWLAND, Donald S.**

MORGAN, John. *See* **PAINE, Lauran.**

MORLAND, Peter Henry. *See* **BRAND, Max.**

MORRIS, Wright (Marion). American. Born in Central City, Nebraska, 6 January 1910. Educated at Lakeview High School, Chicago; Crane College, Chicago 1929; Pomona College, Claremont, California, 1930–33. Married 1) Mary Ellen Finfrock in 1934 (divorced 1961); 2) Josephine Kantor in 1961. Lecturer at Haverford College, Pennsylvania, Sarah Lawrence College, Bronxville, New York, Swarthmore College, Pennsylvania, Princeton University, New Jersey, 1971–72; and University of Nebraska, Lincoln, 1975; Professor of English, California State University, San Francisco, 1962–75. Also a photographer. Recipient: Guggenheim fellowship, 1942, 1946, 1954; National Book award, 1957; American Academy grant, 1960; Rockefeller grant, 1967; National Endowment for the Arts senior fellowship, 1976, award, 1986; Western Literature Association award, 1979; American Book award, 1981; Common Wealth award, 1982; Whiting award, 1985. Honorary degrees: Westminister College, Fulton, Missouri, 1968; University of Nebraska, Lincoln, 1968; Pomona College, 1973. Member, American Academy, 1970. Address: 341 Laurel Way, Mill Valley, California 94941, U.S.A.

Western Publications

Novels

My Uncle Dudley. New York, Harcourt Brace, 1942.
The Man Who Was There. New York, Scribner, 1945.
The World in the Attic. New York, Scribner, 1949.
Man and Boy. New York, Knopf, 1951; London, Gollancz, 1952.
The Works of Love. New York, Knopf, 1952.
The Deep Sleep. New York, Scribner, 1953; London, Eyre and Spottiswoode, 1954.
The Huge Season. New York, Viking Press, 1954; London, Secker and Warburg, 1955.
The Field of Vision. New York, Harcourt Brace, 1956; London, Weidenfeld and Nicolson, 1957.
Love Among the Cannibals. New York, Harcourt Brace, 1957; London, Weidenfeld and Nicolson, 1958.
Ceremony In Lone Tree. New York, Atheneum, 1960; London, Weidenfeld and Nicolson, 1961.
What a Way to Go. New York, Atheneum, 1962.
Cause for Wonder. New York, Atheneum, 1963.
One Day. New York, Atheneum, 1965.
In Orbit. New York, New American Library, 1967.
Fire Sermon. New York, Harper, 1971.
War Games. Los Angeles, Black Sparrow Press, 1972.
A Life. New York, Harper, 1973.
The Fork River Space Project. New York, Harper, 1977.
Plains Song: For Female Voices. New York, Harper, 1980.

Short Stories

Green Grass, Blue Sky, White House. Los Angeles, Black Sparrow Press, 1970.
Here Is Einbaum. Los Angeles, Black Sparrow Press, 1973.
The Cat's Meow. Los Angeles, Black Sparrow Press, 1975.
Real Losses, Imaginary Gains. New York, Harper, 1976.
The Origin of Sadness. Tuscaloosa, University of Alabama/Parallel Editions, 1984.
Collected Stories, 1946–1986. New York, Harper and Row, 1986.

Other Publications

Other

The Inhabitants (photo-text). New York, Scribner, 1946.
The Home Place (photo-text). New York, Scribner, 1948.
The Territory Ahead (essays). New York, Harcourt Brace, 1958; London, Peter Smith, 1964.
A Bill of Rites, A Bill of Wrongs, A Bill of Goods (essays). New York, New American Library, 1968.
God's Country and My People (photo-text). New York, Harper, 1968.
Wright Morris: A Reader. New York, Harper, 1970.
Love Affair: A Venetian Journal (photo-text). New York, Harper, 1972.
About Fiction: Reverent Reflections on the Nature of Fiction with Irreverent Observations on Writers, Readers, and Other Abuses. New York, Harper, 1975.
Structures and Artifacts: Photographs 1933–1954. Lincoln, University of Nebraska Press, 1976.
Conversations with Wright Morris: Critical Views and Responses, edited by Robert E. Knoll. Lincoln, University of Nebraska Press, 1977.
Earthly Delights, Unearthly Adornments: American Writers as Image Makers. New York, Harper, 1978.
Will's Boy: A Memoir. New York, Harper, 1981.
Wright Morris: A Portfolio of Photographs. Roslyn Heights, New York, Witkin Berley, 1981.
Picture America, photographs by Jim Alinder. Boston, New York Graphic Society, 1982.
Wright Morris: Photographs and Words. Carmel, California, Friends of Photography, 1982.
The Writing of My Uncle Dudley (address). Berkeley, California, Bancroft Library, 1982.
Solo: An American Dreamer in Europe: 1933–1934. New York, Harper and Row, 1983; London, Penguin, 1984.
Time Pieces: The Photographs and Words of Wright Morris (exhibition catalogue). Washington, D.C., Corcoran Gallery, 1983.
Time Pieces: Photography, Imagination and Writing. New York, Aperture, 1989.

Editor, *The Mississippi River Reader.* New York, Doubleday, 1962.

*

Manuscript Collection: Bancroft Library, University of California, Berkeley.

Critical Studies: *Wright Morris* by David Madden, New York, Twayne, 1965; *Wright Morris* by Leon Howard, Minneapolis, University of Minnesota Press, 1968; *The Novels of Wright Morris: A Critical Interpretation* (includes bibliography) by G.B. Crump, Lincoln, University of Nebraska Press, 1978; *Wright Morris: Memory and Imagination* by Roy K. Bird, Berne, Switzerland, Lang, 1985.

* * *

Wright Morris's emergence as a writer was slow and studied, and thus it is not surprising that creative potential is the subject of much of his fiction, nor that his works emphasize process over product. This was indicated early by his apparent inability to decide between photography and fiction as his primary medium. From the outset he was seemingly obsessed with clarity of detail in reshaping the past for comprehension, resulting in experiments juxtaposing photographs and prose. The tension between the two media (as in *The Inhabitants*) echoes the polarity of object and action, percept and concept, and was intended to engage the reader-viewer dynamically. Such experimentation, of course, slighted narrative, and the process by which Morris moved beyond it became the dominant theme of his mature work, in which he focuses on the problem of *making* meaning in the modern world.

Certainly the creation of meaning is the central task of Morris's early development as a novelist. Almost all of Morris's work is autobiographical, but none more so than the early novels in which he needed first to recover, then to overcome, the influence of the past. In these novels one observes a writer attempting to "repossess" the past through an exploration of identity determined by *place*—the Nebraska of Morris's childhood and adolescence. The key to these works is what Morris called being "half an orphan"—the loss of a mother who died within days of his birth ("having given her life that I might live")—and the frequent absence of a father who fled to the open road, disappearing from Morris's life for months at a time.

In *The Man Who Was There* the protagonist, Agee Ward (the name is doubly significant), is missing in action, and the novel follows his "recovery" by others through what he has left behind. Ward is revealed (in prose) both through a snapshot album and by his artistic sketches which show conflict between memory and logic—clearly emblematic of Morris's quest to anchor the past to photographed facts. In the next novel, *The Home Place*, Morris focused for the first time on Nebraska, combining photographs with prose and embedding real-life characters and settings in a fictional narrative, thereby raising intriguing questions about the relations between fiction, memory, and photographic images—and anticipating the non-fiction novel. The protagonist, Clyde Muncy, returns with his city wife and children to reconsider country living; in doing so, he encounters Wright Morris's own Aunt Clara and Uncle Harry.

As might be expected, Muncy decides to return to the city, but before doing so, in the next novel, *The World in the Attic*, he visits a childhood friend and discovers that excessive nostalgia is simply "small-town nausea"—an observation characteristic of Morris's sometimes caustic irony, often pointed at his chief characters. That irony is never more trenchant than in the fictional portrayal of Morris's father in *The Works of Love*, an attempt to exorcise the past through a tale which both honors and criticizes Will Brady—perhaps a necessary step to make possible his later work. Nevertheless, his adolescence continued to haunt him, as evidenced later in the memoir *Will's Boy*, which more or less retells *The Works of Love* from the son's perspective.

If the early works are instructive in showing an artist developing perspective on the past, the works of Morris's maturity show him in firm control of a theme: an inquiry into the values of present-day America, including satirical attacks on individuals and institutions which cater to nostalgia at the cost of imaginative thought. In support of his theme, Morris wrote an important critical study, *The Territory Ahead*, to insist that American literature has relied too much on Nature, too little on conscious craft—a perception which helps to explain his own interest in experiment, and his creative use of evolution and vitalism in his novels of the 1950's and 1960's (see, for example, *The Huge Season* and *Love Among the Cannibals*, in relation to *The Field of Vision*).

Morris's two major western works, *The Field of Vision* and *Ceremony in Lone Tree*, combine satire with meditation on human potential. In *The Field of Vision* the satire is aimed at midwestern middle class values brought to a bullfight in Mexico, but the emphasis is on the possibilities of *transformation* of character, what in *The Territory Ahead* Morris calls a "synthesizing act of the imagination." Morris's meditation is centered on the mythic navel of the world at the center of the bullring—deliberately associated with Theseus in the labyrinth, and linked very specifically to the American pioneer myth of Davy Crockett. The problem worked out through a complex interplay of characters is how, from the midst of pervasive consumerism and a corollary loss of traditional values, American *things* may be reinvested with genuine heroic meaning, how a person might *be* a hero.

In the "sequel," *Ceremony in Lone Tree*, Morris is somewhat more gentle, flooding the novel with moonlight. The ceremony is actually a series of rituals which both celebrate the past and put it in its place (by killing it off). The difference in tone is attributable to Charles Starkweather, who in 1958 terrorized Nebraska and murdered 11 people; Morris changed the murderer's name to Munger and placed him into his novel as a precipitant to a kind of cultural examination of conscience. Morris seems to suggest that although midwestern values may be shallow, they are at least decent. In view of violence and carnage, any ceremonies which sustain the archetypally human are valuable.

After *Ceremony in Lone Tree* the novels with western settings tend to be retrospective. In *Fire Sermon* old-timer Floyd Warner backtrails from California to Nebraska, where he mythically confronts the old home place from which he has long been removed: the title refers to the burning down of the house by an irresponsible hippy—representing the mindless, but potentially creative, destruction of the past. The story is continued in *A Life*: Warner, now devoid of earthly responsibility, recognizes that his time has come; in a mythical and mystical conclusion, he is "given" his death by George Blackbird, a Vietnam-era version of an archetypal shaman.

Morris's most recent western novel, much admired by many readers, is *Plains Song: For Female Voices*—a remarkable return to the Nebraska farm setting, now with satire muted and Morris's view of women thoroughly revised (from such earlier works as *Man and Boy* and *The Deep Sleep*). A carefully modulated study of the female response to the frontier through several generations, the novel is a chorus of praise to the female survivors and descendants of the westward trek.

Morris may be considered a western writer not primarily because of his settings but because he confronts the myths which have beset the West, challenging the nostalgia which has so captivated the American (and European) mind. Such a challenge, added to Morris's sometimes difficult irony, has not endeared Morris to readers of popular fiction, who often complain that Morris is too complex for his "regionalism." The upshot is that Morris's work must constantly be rediscovered. Nevertheless, Morris has made his mark on the western landscape, and no doubt he will continue to appeal to selective readers—as well as to viewers of his evocative photographs of western scenes and artifacts.

—Joseph J. Wydeven

MORROW, Honoré Willsie (née McCue). American. Born in Ottumwa, Iowa, in 1880. Educated at the University of Wisconsin, Madison, B.A. Married 1) Henry Elmer Willsie (divorced 1922); 2) the publisher William Morrow in 1923; two sons and one daughter. Editor, *Delineator*, 1914–19; freelance writer, 1919–40. *Died 12 April 1940.*

WESTERN PUBLICATIONS

Novels

The Heart of the Desert. New York, Stokes, 1913.
Still Jim. New York, Stokes, 1915.
Lydia of the Pines. New York, Stokes, 1917.
The Forbidden Trail. New York, Stokes, 1919.
The Enchanted Canyon: A Novel of the Grand Canyon and the Arizona Desert. New York, Grosset and Dunlap, 1921.
Judith of the Godless Valley. New York, Stokes, 1922.
The Exile of the Lariat. New York, Stokes, 1923.
The Devonshers. New York, Stokes, 1924.

We Must March: A Novel of the Winning of Oregon. New York, Stokes, 1925.
Beyond the Blue Sierra. New York, Morrow, 1932.

Uncollected Short Story

"The Lariat: Love and Politics in the West," in *Everybody's Magazine*, July 1923.

Fiction for children

On to Oregon! The Story of a Pioneer Boy. New York, Morrow, 1926; as *The Splendid Journey: The Story of a Pioneer Boy.* London, Heinemann, 1939.

OTHER PUBLICATIONS

Novels

Benefits Forgot: A Story of Lincoln and Mother Love. New York, Stokes, 1917.
The Lost Speech of Abraham Lincoln. New York, Stokes, 1925.
Great Captain, Three Great Lincoln Novels. New York, Morrow, 1930.
Forever Free: A Novel of Abraham Lincoln. New York, Morrow, 1927.
With Malice Toward None. New York, Morrow, 1928.
The Last Full Measure. New York, Morrow, 1930.
Splendour of God. New York, Morrow, 1929; London, Hodder and Stoughton, 1932.
Black Daniel: The Love Story of a Great Man. New York, Morrow, 1931.
The Lincoln Stories of Honore Morrow: Dearer Than All, Benefits Forgot, and The Lost Speech of Abraham Lincoln. New York, Morrow, 1934.
Yonder Sails the Mayflower. New York, Morrow, 1934.
Let the King Beware. New York, Morrow, 1936.
Demon Daughter: The Confession of a Modern Girl and Her Mother. New York, Morrow, 1939.

Other

Honoré Willsie: A Biography. New York, Stokes, 1922.
The Father of Little Women. Boston, Little Brown, 1927.
God in the Darkness. New York, Cosmopolitan Magazine, 1927.
Mary Todd Lincoln: An Appreciation of the Wife of Abraham Lincoln. New York, Morrow, 1928.
Lincoln's Last Day Described in the Letters of His Wife. New York, Hearst's International/Cosmopolitan, 1930.
Tiger! Tiger! The Life Story of John B. Gough. New York, Morrow, 1930.
Argonaut. New York, Morrow, 1933.
Ship's Monkey, with William J. Swartman. New York, Morrow, 1933.
Ship's Parrot, with William J. Swartman. New York, Morrow, 1936.

* * *

If Honoré Willsie Morrow is remembered today it is most likely for her fictional trilogy about Abraham Lincoln known collectively as *The Great Captain* and consisting of *Forever Free*, *With Malice Toward None*, and *The Last Full Measure*. Yet over the span of her 30-year writing career Morrow produced an impressive body of western fiction. Unable to interest editors in her early attempts at writing, a trip to the Southwest proved to be her muse. In 1909, she began contributing stories as well as political articles to such magazines as *Collier's*, *Harper's Weekly*, and *The Delineator*, a woman's magazine for which Morrow served as editor from 1914 to 1919. Her novels with a western setting fall into two groups, contemporary and historical stories.

In her contemporary Westerns, Morrow's uniqueness stems from her offbeat and unconventional treatment of standard storyline material. A good example is *The Heart of the Desert*, which tackles the subject of interracial marriage between a "red" man and a white woman. It is the story of Easterner Rhoda Tuttle, come to the West in an effort to reverse the mental and physical deterioration suffered since the death of her parents, and Kut-Le Cartwell, an Apache/Pueblo/Mohave Indian educated in the East and now an engineer. Kut-Le saves Rhoda's life when she is stung by a scorpion. He falls in love with Rhoda and, confident in his ability to restore her health otherwise, he kidnaps her. Rhoda is both attracted and repelled by Kut-Le's Indianness. Most of the story is concerned with their adventures in the desert while being pursued by Rhoda's ex-fiancé and one of Kut-Le's good white friends. In time, Rhoda recognizes her love for both Kut-Le and the desert, and the two "young people, one of a vanishing and one of a conquering race" are happily united in marriage. The story ends with a kiss before the two ride off into "the desert sunset."

That the two lovers marry and survive the union was a daring ending in light of the fact that, 13 years later, it would be considered unacceptable by the hardback publisher of Zane Grey's *The Vanishing American* for the white heroine to marry the Nopah Indian, Nophaie, and 50 years later, it was still impossible for the interracial marriage created by Jane Barry in *A Time in the Sun* to end happily: the Apache husband is killed.

In *Still Jim*, Morrow's only novel to be serialized, and written in support of the U.S. Reclamation Act—in this case dam projects in the Northwest and Southwest—the idea of the Indian being a vanishing race is taken a step further. Indians and whites of old New England stock are both pronounced dead races. The protagonist, Jim Manning, an engineer, "had learned that many a pauperized and decrepit old Indian ... despised of whites, held locked in his marvelous mind treasures of philosophy, of comment on life and living. Indians and whites, that the world can ill afford to lose, yet never will know." Morrow's treatment of Indians in her contemporary Westerns is here one of generosity. They are a disappearing race and are generally friends to the whites. Yet her condemnation of prejudice, racial or otherwise, in numerous books is contradicted by her harsh, even if occasional, commentary on Mexicans and blacks.

Still Jim is the book in which Morrow introduced what would be a continuing theme, one of public duty. Jim Manning must stop being single-minded in his building of dams and work at courting the farmers in the area in order to prevent them from disavowing the project. Similarly, in *The Exile of the Lariat*, Hugh Stewart, a paleontologist, must choose between abandoning his cache of bones on the Old Sioux Tract to run a bookstore in Wyoming for two years or lose access to the dig forever as stipulated in a will. Circumstances lead to his running for governor and becoming a staunch supporter of the Children's Code, a law which would provide financial assistance to mothers and their children. *Exile*, while an uneven and often times cluttered book of ideas, has one of the more intriguing openings in western fiction. Stewart discovers a perfect specimen of a triceratops in a hidden Indian cave, which also contains piles of ancient Indian bones as well as one lone skeleton—there only in recent years—keeping watch at the entrance.

The romantic plot elements of Morrow's stories also break with tradition in their lack of sentimentality, and their attempt to understand better the complexities of relationships. Whether the story's protagonist is in love with a woman who married someone else (*Still Jim*), is married himself (*Exile of the Lariat*), or even in love with an accused murderer as in *The Devonshers* (a courtroom story unique in that a woman is on trial for perpetrating a grisly murder), Morrow portrayed a successful relationship as being one built on mutual trust and loyalty.

Midpoint in her career and well in advance of the trend of historical novels, Morrow began writing fictional renderings of historical personalities. Her interest in the struggle between the British and the Americans over Oregon was touched on in *The Devonshers*, with the heroine's grandfather having been a traitor to the British. But it was the story of Narcissa Whitman, the wife of Marcus Whitman and the first white woman to cross the Rocky Mountains, that intrigued Morrow. It was only the saga, as she called her historicals, that "could hope to picture the beauty and poignancy of the efforts and sacrifices that made their plain, human souls heroic." In *We Must March*, Morrow attributes the Whitmans, particularly Narcissa, key roles in the winning of Oregon for the United States. While the novel is based a good deal on legends surrounding the two, it is a tightly written story filled with vivid and suspenseful scenes. It ends with the arrival of the first large train of settlers led by Marcus, several years before the massacre at the Whitman mission.

A related story is to be found in Morrow's only children's novel, *On to Oregon*. This morality tale is about John Sager, a 13 year-old, who traveled over 1,000 miles overland with his six younger brothers and sisters. It is is a finely honed overland story, which concludes with the Sager children arriving at the Whitman mission.

Morrow reached farther back in time to 1775 in the writing of *Beyond the Blue Sierra*. It is concerned with the efforts of explorer Don Juan de Anza and the Spanish viceroy, Don Antonio Bucareli, to establish a colony in San Francisco. The story is about the colonizing expedition led by Anza with its political and religious intrigues. It differs from other Morrow books in that Apaches are warriors, though respected by Anza, and that Anza's relationship with his wife takes second place to his friendship with Bucareli and his political and professional aspirations through to the end. All three historicals differ from her contemporary Westerns in that the land is much more of a character, which may be due to her extensive travel to these areas when she was writing them.

Morrow's fiction is ever innovative and is filled with interesting and yet credible characters. Her heroes are ordinary hard-working people trying to get a job done well; her villians are ordinary people driven by avarice and self-aggrandizement. She was prone to use her books as a platform for her ideas on a variety of political and social topics. But for Morrow, at the time she was writing, the West was still a land of possibilities. It was a land that could mold better humans and therefore a better society. She was not concerned so much with the winning of the West as with the shaping of it. Her books demand more attention.

—Vicki Piekarski

MORTON, Glen. *See* **LAZENBY, Norman.**

MOSSMAN, Burt. *See* **ALLISON, Clay.**

MOWERY, William Byron. American. Born in Adelphi, Ohio, 15 August 1899. Educated at Ohio State University, Columbus, 1919–20; University of Illinois, Urbana, A.B. 1921, A.M. 1922. Served in the tank corps during World War I. Married 1) Mildred Mirian Vincel in 1922, three daughters; 2) Dorothy Dunsing in 1935, one daughter. Taught English at the University of Illinois, 1922, University of Texas, Austin, 1924–44, and New York University, 1944–57. *Died 2 April 1957.*

WESTERN PUBLICATIONS

Novels

The Silver Hawk. New York, Doubleday, 1929.
The Girl from God's Mercie. New York, Doubleday, 1929.
Heart of the North. New York, Doubleday, 1930; London, Stanley Paul, 1931.
The Gentle Stranger. London, Stanley Paul, 1930.
The Flaming Mesa. London Stanley Paul, 1931.
Singer of the Wilderness. New York, Doubleday, 1931; London, Methuen, 1932.
Forbidden Valley. New York, Long and Smith, and London, Methuen, 1933.
Challenge of the North. Boston, Little Brown, and London, Methuen, 1934.
Resurrection River. Boston, Little Brown, and London, Methuen, 1935.
The Phantom Canoe. Boston, Little Brown, 1935.
Paradise Trail. Boston, Little Brown, 1936; London, Methuen, 1937.
The Outlaw Trail. London, Methuen, 1936.
Vengeance Trail. London, Methuen, 1937.
The Black Automatic. Boston, Little Brown, 1937.
The Valley Beyond. New York, Doubleday, 1938; London, Methuen, 1939.
Outlaw Breed. New York, Popular Library, 1949.
Guns in the Valley. New York, Popular Library, 1949.

Short Stories

The Long Arm of the Mounted. New York, McGraw Hill, 1948.
Sagas of the Mounted Police. New York, Bouregy, 1953.

Uncollected Short Story

"The Long Shadow," in *The Northerners*, edited by Bill Pronzini and Martin H. Greenberg. New York, Fawcett, 1990.

OTHER PUBLICATIONS

Plays

The Election of the Roulette, in *Poet Lore* (Boston), 1922.

Screenplay: *Red Riders of Canada*, with Oliver Drake and Randolph Bartlett, 1928.

Other

Professional Short-Story Writing. New York, Crowell, 1953.
Tales of the Ozarks. New York, Bouregy, 1954.

Swift in the Night and Other Tales of Field and Wood. New York, Coward McCann, 1956.

* * *

William Byron Mowery was born and educated in the United States and held university posts there teaching English. He had some success as a writer of popular fiction, being known as the Zane Grey of the Canadian Northwest.

Mowery's speciality was adventure stories set in the north and northwest of Canada. He catered for the popular demand for North Westerns which was very keen before World War II. Mowery wrote about little else, preferring to stay within the bounds of a clearly successful formula. The backdrop of the remote, wild, and very cold Canadian sub-arctic region is very strongly drawn in his books. Mowery described this environment with painstaking detail. In *The Gentle Stranger* the hero is a biologist, thus providing an excellent *raison d'être* for much interesting geographical and biological detail. The area is thus given a genuine scientific interest. There is also an appropriate population of Eskimos and Indians. Against this setting a leisurely romance takes place.

In addition to a certain novelty provided by this region Mowery also provides novelty with his means of travel. He makes full use of the aeroplane as transport for his main characters in several books. In *The Flaming Mesa* an ex-Royal Canadian Air Force pilot is the hero, and much of the action would not be possible without the aeroplane. In *The Silver Hawk* a pilot and his plane also form the centre of the action. The aeroplane helps the fast adventurous movement of the tale in *Forbidden Valley*; a fight in the air forms the climax of the book.

Mowery's books were said to breathe the very spirit of the Canadian Northwest. This opinion rested not simply on the basis of the well-selected detail of sub-arctic life, but also on the presence of the North West (later Royal Canadian) Mounted Police. The Mounties are an important ingredient in his books. In *Forbidden Valley* the hero is a Mountie, and against almost insurmountable odds he gets his man. In *Vengeance Trail* a Mountie had even had to leave the force because he had used too much violence against a criminal. In *The Long Arm of the Mounted* Mowery provided four short stories about different aspects of the Mounties. Whatever the literary merits of these stories, the book was well received by critics as being an accurate and well-illustrated picture of the force.

The Mounties have a distinct romantic appeal of which Mowery made full use. Thus the Mountie in *Forbidden Valley* gets his girl as well as his man. All Mowery's novels have a strong romantic element: the heroes are manly and attractive, the heroines pretty and mysterious, and thus romance blossoms. In *Challenge of the North* a hasty marriage blooms into love against the adversity of the climate. While many of Mowery's plots revolve around romances, the more substantial of his books are built on the triumph of a hero or the establishment of his innocence in the eyes of public opinion. Strong features of the hero's characters are therefore brought out.

Mowery's style of writing was much praised. His language involves a rather restricted use of dialogue, often mixed with a Canadian *patois* or a pidgin English which is not always successful. But the dialogue generally is well written and does not intrude on the story or appear too contrived. A *New York Times* critic described Mowery as a "skilled fictionist." This is a shrewd assessment, given Mowery's ability to exploit a very narrow field of popular fiction. If the fiction was narrow, Mowery was highly successful in it. He was successful enough to produce a guide (*Professional Short-Story Writing*) for those who wanted to perfect techniques of short story fiction and sell to popular magazines. Curiously a reviewer described Mowery not as a writer but as an experienced teacher of writing.

—P.R. Meldrum

MUIR, James A. *See* **WELLS, Angus.**

MULFORD, Clarence E(dward). American. Born in Streator, Illinois, 3 February 1883. Educated at schools in Streator and in Utica, New York. Married Eva Emily Wilkinson in 1920 (died 1933). Worked for *Municipal Journal and Engineer*, New York; then a civil servant. *Died 10 May 1956.*

WESTERN PUBLICATIONS

Novels (series: Hopalong Cassidy; Mesquite Jenkins)

The Orphan. New York, Outing, 1908; London, Hodder and Stoughton, 1922.

Hopalong Cassidy. Chicago, McClurg, 1912; London, Hodder and Stoughton, 1920.

Buck Peters, Ranchman (Cassidy), with John Wood Clay. Chicago, McClurg, 1912; London, Hodder and Stoughton, 1921.

The Man from Bar-20: A Story of the Cow-Country. Chicago, McClurg, 1918; London, Hodder and Stoughton, 1921.

Johnny Nelson (Cassidy). Chicago, McClurg, 1920; London, Hodder and Stoughton, 1921.

The Bar-20 Three. Chicago, McClurg, and London, Hodder and Stoughton, 1921; as *Hopalong Cassidy Sees Red*, New York, Grosset and Dunlap, 1950.

Bring Me His Ears. Chicago, McClurg, 1922; as *Beckoning Trails*, London, Hodder and Stoughton, 1923.

Tex (Cassidy). Chicago, McClurg, 1922; as *Tex—of Bar 20*, London, Hodder and Stoughton, 1922.

Black Buttes. New York, Doubleday, 1923; London, Remploy, 1979.

Hopalong Cassidy Returns. New York, Doubleday, and London, Hodder and Stoughton, 1924.

Rustlers' Valley. New York, Doubleday, and London, Hodder and Stoughton, 1924.

Cottonwood Gulch. New York, Doubleday, and London, Hodder and Stoughton, 1925.

The Bar-20 Rides Again. New York, Doubleday, and London, Hodder and Stoughton, 1926; as *Hopalong Cassidy's Bar-20 Rides Again*, New York, Doubleday, 1950.

Hopalong Cassidy's Protégé. New York, Doubleday, and London, Hodder and Stoughton, 1926; as *Hopalong Cassidy's Saddle Mate*, New York, Popular Library, 1949.

Corson of the JC. New York, Doubleday, and London, Hodder and Stoughton, 1927.

Mesquite Jenkins. New York, Doubleday, and London, Hodder and Stoughton, 1928.

Me an' Shorty. New York, Doubleday, and London, Hodder and Stoughton, 1929.

The Deputy Sheriff. New York, Doubleday, and London, Hodder and Stoughton, 1930.

Hopalong Cassidy and the Eagle's Brood. New York, Doubleday, and London, Hodder and Stoughton, 1931.
Mesquite Jenkins, Tumbleweed. New York, Doubled y, and London, Hodder and Stoughton, 1932.
The Round-Up. New York, Doubleday, and London, Hodder and Stoughton, 1933.
Trail Dust. New York, Doubleday, and London, Hodder and Stoughton, 1934; abridged edition, as *Hopalong Cassidy with the Trail Herd*, Doubleday, 1950.
On the Trail of the Tumbling T. New York, Doubleday, and London, Hodder and Stoughton, 1935.
Hopalong Cassidy Takes Cards. New York, Doubleday, 1937; London, Hodder and Stoughton, 1938.
Hopalong Cassidy Serves a Writ. New York, Doubleday, 1941; London, Hodder and Stoughton, 1942.

Short Stories (series: Hopalong Cassidy in all books)

Bar-20. New York, Outing, 1907; London, Hodder and Stoughton, 1914; *as Hopalong Cassidy's Round-Up*, New York, Grosset and Dunlap, 1950.
Bar-20 Days. Chicago, McClurg, 1911; London, Hodder and Stoughton, 1921; as *Hopalong Cassidy's Private War*, New York, Grosset and Dunlap, 1950.
The Coming of Cassidy—and the Others. Chicago, McClurg, 1913; London, Hodder and Stoughton, 1921; as *The Coming of Hopalong Cassidy*, New York, Grosset and Dunlap, n.d.

Uncollected Short Stories

"Ridin' with the Mails," in *The Frontier* (New York), October 1925.
"Frenchy," in *West* (New York), 31 August 1932.
"The Hold-up," in *The Arbor House Treasury of Great Western Stories*, edited by Bill Pronzini and Martin H. Greenberg. New York, Arbor House, 1982.
"Hopalong Sits In," in *Wild Westerns*, edited by Bill Pronzini and Martin H. Greenberg. New York, Walker, 1986.

* * *

Clarence E. Mulford's style is a fairly vivid but stiff and humorless Victorian English. His plots are disunified heaps sprawling every which way over the terrain. His skills with character and relationship were feeble, especially when it came to women. His versions of cowboy and ethnic dialect grate harshly on the ear. But in grasp of historic detail and breadth of vision he was among western writers second to none, and his best action sequences rank with the most exciting in the genre.

The factual data in his enormous library of books and materials on the West were cross-indexed on more than 17,000 file cards. Thanks to these, even though he set foot in the West only once and then was vastly disapponted, he could describe ranch life, cattle drives, trail towns, poker games, roundup lore, firearms trivia, and everything else in the interstices of his novels with meticulous accuracy. But beyond the factual detail in his books was a philosophic vision, the Darwinian view of nature as a violent panorama and of life as a struggle in which each creature tries to become more fit to survive. And the people of Mulford's world aren't at all like workaday cowboys but resemble the brawling larger-than-life heroes of the Greek epics and Arthurian legends and Dumas.

Their spiritual home, the mythical Texas ranch known as Bar-20, is a sort of Camelot West, an idealized government-that-governs-least, the focus of free men's loyalty to the death. Hopalong Cassidy, Buck Peters, Johnny Nelson, Red Connors and the other Bar-20 alumni are good pagans one and all, irreligious like Mulford but full of natural piety, the spiritual sons of Achilles and Lancelot and d'Artagnan, standing together through backbreaking range work and battles with rustlers, relaxing with practical jokes and elaborate insult matches and roughhouse. Like epic heroes they have an infinite capacity for ignoring multiple combat wounds and fighting on, genuine knights of the frontier, Nature's Noblemen to the core.

Besides the accuracy of background detail and the wild energy of his heroic community, Mulford offers the crowning gift of scope. His fictional universe is a vast saga of interlocking novels and stories whose protagonists begin young, go adventuring, marry, procreate, grow old and witness or share the adventures of their now-adult natural or symbolic children. In Mulford's first book, *Bar-20*, Hopalong Cassidy is a tough-mouthed tobacco-spitting redhead of 23, and his first appearance culminates in a bunkhouse food fight that would remind a modern reader of *Animal House*. Decades later Cassidy is described as almost 60, with faded thinning hair, a straggly mustache and corded neck. Eventually he would have had to die, but rather than kill off his hero Mulford stopped writing and spent his last 15 years in retirement.

If Conan Doyle's Sherlock Holmes stories are the first great series in mystery fiction, Mulford's books are the first great series Westerns, yet they are not so much a string of adventures about the same characters as a sort of Galsworthyesque Forsyte Saga set in a less polite and far more violent milieu. Those who remember Hopalong Cassidy are much more likely to be thinking of William Boyd's sanitized portrayal in the excellent-in-their-own-right but hopelessly unhistorical movies of the 1930's and 1940's. But whoever rediscovers the novels and stories of Mulford will enter a universe like nothing else in fiction.

—Francis M. Nevins, Jr.

MUMFORD, Tex. *See* **HECKELMANN, Charles N.**

MYERS, John Myers. American. Born in Northport, Long Island, New York, 11 January 1906. Educated at St. Stephens College; Middlebury College, Vermont; University of New Mexico, Albuquerque. Served in the United States Army during World War II. Married Charlotte Shanahan in 1943; two daughters. Advertising copywriter in New York; newspaperman in New York, Texas, and Arizona; farmer in South Carolina; then freelance writer: lecturer and writers conference director, Arizona State University, Tempe 1948–49; assembled a Western Americana collection for the Arizona State University Library. Agent: Ned Brown, 315 South Beverly Drive, Beverly Hills, California. Address: 6515 East Hermosa Vista Drive, Mesa, Arizona 85205, U.S.A.

WESTERN PUBLICATIONS

Novels

Dead Warrior. Boston, Little Brown, 1956; London, Arrow, 1957.
I, Jack Swilling, Founder of Phoenix, Arizona. New York, Hastings House, 1961.

OTHER PUBLICATIONS

Novels

The Harp and the Blade. New York, Dutton, 1941.
Out on Any Limb. New York, Dutton, 1942.
The Wild Yazoo. New York, Dutton, 1947; London, Macdonald, 1948.
Silverlock. New York, Dutton, 1949.
The Moon's Fire-Eating Daughter, edited by Hank Stine. Virginia Beach, Donning, 1980.

Verse

Maverick Zone. New York, Hastings House, 1961.
The Chaparral Cock, Crow I. Privately printed, 1967.
The Chaparral Cock, Crow II. Privately printed, 1968.

Other

The Alamo. New York, Dutton, 1948.
The Last Chance: Tombstone's Early Years. New York, Dutton, 1950; as *The Tombstone Story*, New York, Grosset and Dunlap, n.d.
Doc Holliday. Boston, Little Brown, 1955; London, Jarrolds, 1957.
The Deaths of the Bravos. Boston, Little Brown, 1962.
Pirate, Pawnee, and Mountain Man: The Saga of Hugh Glass. Boston, Little Brown, 1963; as *The Saga of Hugh Glass*, Lincoln, University of Nebraska Press, 1976.
San Francisco's Reign of Terror. New York, Doubleday, 1966.
Print in a Wild Land. New York, Doubleday, 1967.
The Border Wardens. Englewood Cliffs, New Jersey, Prentice Hall, 1971.

Editor, *Building a State in Apache Land*, by Charles D. Poston. Tempe, Arizona, Aztec Press, 1963.
Editor, *The Westerners: A Roundup of Pioneer Reminiscences.* Englewood Cliffs, New Jersey, Prentice Hall, 1969.

*

Critical Study: *A Silverlock Companion: The Life and Works of John Myers Myers* edited by Fred Lerner, Center Harbor, New Hampshire, Niekas, 1988.

*

John Myers Myers comments:

My works concerning the West have taken the form of histories rather than fiction, though I believe I have succeeded in making them as exciting to read as novels. (My best western "fiction" is the three verse tales in *Maverick Zone.*) I have dealt with a variety of scenes and periods, and not concentrated on the American pioneering period; my chosen medium has frequently been verse rather than prose. As my major effort, indeed, I hoped to compass the frontier in a series of continent-spanning poems. But I commenced with the West—and when I fought for a beginning it became clear that the initial point had to be London, England, and my Atlantic-straddling figure had to be Sir Walter Raleigh. Experiment showed, however, that neither the town nor the man could be crammed into narratives of the modest length established by the already published items of the series. It became clear, in fact, that I must either write a full-fledged epic or forfeit the project; so I invested the necessary dozen years and did what I had to do. Since I am invited to preen my feathers, I shall roundly state that *The Song of Raleigh's Head* (unpublished) is a work of depth, scope, and melody to rank with the greatest epics by whatever predecessors.

* * *

John Myers Myers has worked as a newspaperman, advertising copywriter, farmer, teacher, and freelance writer. In a writing career that has extended, with interruptions, through more than 40 years, he has written historical novels and fantasies, as well as fiction, verse, and nonfiction about the American West. His work is marked by a wide knowledge of history, literature, and folklore, an enthusiasm for his chosen subjects, and an irrepressible humor. All of his novels are enlivened by songs and verse: vigorous, often bawdy and always enjoyable. His nonfiction shows a distinctive blend of scholarly research with an informal and sometimes even irreverent style.

Myers's first book, *The Harp and the Blade*, was a first-person account of the adventures of Finnian, a wandering Irish bard and scholar in 10th-century France. The novel appeared as a serial in *Argosy* magazine in 1940, a year before its publication in book form. The uniformly favorable critical reaction was studded with such terms as "rousing," "zestful," "action-packed," "lusty," and "full-blooded." The second novel, *Out on Any Limb*, set in Elizabethan England, was given an equally approving reception. *The Wild Yazoo*, written after the author's army service in World War II, was laid in Natchez and the frontier country of northern Mississippi in the early 19th century.

Silverlock is Myers's most unusual novel, a picaresque adventure set in a mythical land called the Commonwealth, populated by lightly disguised characters from the folklore, mythology, and literature of all ages. It is a delightful literary puzzle as well as a rousing story, and has attracted a considerable following among enthusiasts of fantasy fiction. A related book, *The Moon's Fire-Eating Daughter*, appeared in 1980.

In 1948 Myers published a nonfiction work, *The Alamo*, the first account in print to attempt to tell the complete story of that structure from its beginnings in the 18th century up through the fateful siege in 1836. *The Last Chance: Tombstone's Early Years* appeared in 1950, and in 1955 a highly regarded biography, *Doc Holliday*. After these nonfiction volumes Myers wrote his first novel to have a strictly western setting. Laid against the background of the Arizona mining camps in the late 1870's, *Dead Warrior* is the story of the founding and violent early years of a boom town, chronicled with authentic spirit and robust humor. The author's only other novel of the West is *I, Jack Swilling*, a fictionalized biography of the founder of Phoenix, Arizona. Three further tales of the West, told in the form of narrative poems, were collected in *Maverick Zone*. After the appearance of these last two books in 1961, Myers turned his attention exclusively to nonfiction.

The Deaths of the Bravos is a panoramic account of the development of the West in the period from 1812 to 1878. *Pirate, Pawnee, and Mountain Man* is a biography of the near-legendary Hugh Glass. *Print in a Wild Land* is a the story of frontier journalism during the opening of the West, incorporating plentiful quotations from original sources. These books, like the author's earlier nonfiction, are works of genuine scholarship, meticulously researched and told in a lively colorful style. This blend of information and entertainment is difficult to match.

—R.E. Briney

N

NEIHARDT, John G(neisenau). American. Born near Sharpsburg, Illinois, 8 January 1881. Educated at Nebraska Normal College, now Nebraska State Teachers College, Wayne, diploma in science 1897. Married Mona Martinsen in 1908 (died 1958); four daughters. Taught in a country school in Nebraska, 1897–98; worked at various jobs, 1899–1901; staff member, Omaha *Daily News*, 1902; worked for an Indian trader in Bancroft, Nebraska, 1902–05, and edited the Bancroft *Blade* for a year; lived among the Omaha Indians and later among the Sioux; literary editor, Minneapolis *Journal*, 1911–20; Professor of poetry, University of Nebraska, Lincoln, 1923; literary editor, St. Louis *Post-Dispatch*, 1926–38; director of information, Chicago, 1943–46, and field representative, 1946–48, Bureau of Indian Affairs; Lecturer in English and poet-in-residence, University of Missouri, Columbia, 1949–65. Editor, *Mark Twain Quarterly*, Kirkwood, Missouri, from 1936. Recipient: Poetry Society of America prize, 1919. Litt. D.: University of Nebraska, 1917; University of Missouri, 1947; Midland Lutheran College, Fremont, Nebraska, 1972; LL.D.: Creighton University, Omaha, 1928. Member, American Academy; Chancellor, Academy of American Poets, 1959–67. *Died 3 November 1973.*

Western Publications

Novels

The Dawn-Builder. New York, Kennerley, 1911.
Life's Lure. New York, Kennerley, 1914.
When the Tree Flowered: An Authentic Tale of the Old Sioux World. New York, Macmillan, 1951; as *Eagle Voice*, London, Melrose, 1953.

Short Stories

The Lonesome Trail. New York and London, Lane, 1907.
Indian Tales and Others. New York, Macmillan, 1925.

Uncollected Short Stories

"When the Snows Drift," in *Overland Monthly* (San Francisco), August 1901.
"The Singing of the Frogs," in *Overland Monthly* (San Francisco), September 1901.
"The Spirit of Crow Butte," in *Overland Monthly* (San Francisco), November 1901.
"The Face in the Balcony," in *All-Story* (New York), September–December 1905.
"Like a Woman," in *All-Story* (New York), May–August 1906.
"The Ancient Memory," in *Smart Set* (New York), June 1907.
"The Discarded Fetish," in *Smart Set* (New York), July 1908.
"The Epic-Minded Scott," in *Outing* (New York), December 1908.

Other Publications

Play

Two Mothers (includes *Eight Hundred Rubles* and *Agrippina*). New York, Macmillan, 1921.

Verse

The Divine Enchantment: A Mystical Poem. New York, White, 1900.
A Bundle of Myrrh. New York, Outing, 1907.
Man-Song. New York, Kennerley, 1909.
The Stranger at the Gate. New York, Kennerley, 1912.
A Cycle of the West. New York, Macmillan, 1949; reprinted as *The Mountain Men* and *The Twilight of the Sioux*, Lincoln, University of Nebraska Press, 2 vols., 1971.
The Song of Hugh Glass. New York, Macmillan, 1915.
The Song of Three Friends. New York, Macmillan, 1919.
The Song of the Indian Wars. New York, Macmillan, 1925.
The Song of the Messiah. New York, Macmillan, 1935.
The Song of Jed Smith. New York, Macmillan, 1941.
The Quest. New York, Macmillan, 1916.
Collected Poems. New York, Macmillan, 1926.
Lyric and Dramatic Poems. Lincoln, University of Nebraska Press, 1965.

Other

The River and I. New York, Putnam, 1910.
The Splendid Wayfaring: The Story of the Exploits and Adventures of Jedediah Smith and His Comrades.... New York, Macmillan, 1920.
Laureate Address of John G. Neihardt upon Official Notification of His Choice as Poet Laureate of Nebraska. Chicago, Bookfellows, 1921.
Poetic Values: Their Reality and Our Need of Them. New York, Macmillan, 1925.
Black Elk Speaks, Being the Life Story of a Holy Man of the Ogalala Sioux. New York, Morrow, 1932; London, Barrie and Jenkins, 1972.
All Is But a Beginning: Youth Remembered 1881–1901. New York, Harcourt Brace, 1972.
Patterns and Coincidences: A Sequel to All Is But a Beginning. Columbia, University of Missouri Press, 1978.
The Sixth Grandfather: Black Elk's Teaching Given to John G. Neihardt, edited by Raymond J. DeMallie. Lincoln, University of Nebraska Press, 1984.

Editor, *The Poet's Pack.* Chicago, Bookfellows, 1921.

*

Bibliography: *Rawhide Laureate: John G. Neihardt: A Selected Annotated Bibliography*, Metuchen, New Jersey, Scarecrow Press, 1983.

Manuscript Collection: Ellis Library, University of Missouri, Columbia.

Critical Studies: *John G. Neihardt, Man and Poet* by Julius T. House, Wayne, Nebraska, Jones, 1920; *Luminous Sanity: Literary Criticism Written by John G. Neihardt* by John Thomas Richards, Cape Girardeau, Missouri, Concord, 1973; *John G. Neihardt* by Blair Whitney, Boston, Twayne, 1976; *John G. Neihardt* by Lucile F. Aly, Boise, Idaho, Boise State University, 1976.

* * *

The American West as a symbol of hope for humanity in a new, unspoiled world has fired the imagination of a host of writers, among them the Nebraska poet John G. Neihardt. The major part of his work is set in the West and draws its themes from the grandeur of the setting, the hopes for a more enlightened society, and the potentiality for heroism in all people.

Neihardt's first writing on western themes was based on his extensive research in western history, particularly of the fur trade, the westward movement of white men, and the Indian Wars. In early years he supported himself partly with short stories about fur traders, prospectors, and Indians that found a ready market in magazines. Two collections of the stories were published, *The Lonesome Trail* and *Indian Tales and Others*, but some of the best stories were not included in either volume. The fur trade and mining stories describe the exploits of mountain men and develop some of Neihardt's major themes—the ruthlessness and exploitation in the fur trade, the faulty values of adventurers hoping to make a quick fortune, and the brutality of rough men battling with hardship. The Indian stories derived from Neihardt's association with the Omahas on the reservation near Bancroft; he camped there at intervals and developed a rapport with the Longhairs that provided him with authentic material not available to many white men. The stories create charming scenes of Indian life and dramatic scenes of buffalo hunts, battles, sometimes warm human incidents. Some stories deal with the misfit Indian, the dreamer who prefers composing songs to taking the war path, or the crippled lad who cannot cope with the physical demands of tribal life, or the wistful girl who loves the wrong man. In this experimental period Neihardt tried out various techniques of structure, particularly frame formats, and perfected his style. Some of the stories or incidents appear later in his masterwork; in one story he roughed out the plot of *The Song of Three Friends*, the first part of the epic. In several stories, notably "The Epic-Minded Scott," he forecast the last part of the epic about the Messiah movement of the 1880's.

The best of the rugged-west stories is "The Alien," which has been compared with Balzac's "A Passion in the Desert." It concerns a vicious outlaw whose first experience with love comes from nursing a wounded female wolf back to health, only to meet his death when, recovered, she finds a mate and the two wolves attack him. The point of the story is the inability of an abused person to cope with a world unwilling to accept him, and the impossibility, if a man rejects the values of civilization, of transfering them to the savage world, even when his need is crucial. The best of the Indian stories is probably the gently ironic "The Heart of a Woman," about a loving Indian girl driven by jealousy to "murder" her white lover's violin, under the impression that it is the "singing spirit" of a white woman he loves. The story demonstrates the inability of two different cultures really to understand each other.

The two novels of Neihardt's early period, *The Dawn-Builder* and *Life's Lure*, received—and merited—little critical attention. Each was compounded, not too happily, of two or more of the short stories, and particularly in *The Dawn-Builder* the unlikely combination of earthy, ironic realism and romantic fantasy proved the two strands unfusible. The realistic story of Mr. Waters and his self-deprecating love for a kindly widow would have made a good novel on its own. *Life's Lure*, about the uglier side of prospecting in the West, joined more compatible stories of greed, ruthless competition, and the savagery of survival. The novel suffers from Neihardt's lack of experience with black-heartedness, but it contains one excellent scene of the callow greenhorn in his new western togs amusing the old hands with his attempts to sound knowledgeable. The atmosphere of the stories is heavily masculine; white women appear briefly if at all. Neihardt sustained an old-world attitude about nice women; any woman in his writings who shows spirit is Indian, old, a half-breed, or a prostitute.

At the age of 30 Neihardt abandoned lyrics and short stories to devote his talents to larger works with more profound themes, specifically to the major work for which he had been preparing—the five-part *A Cycle of the West*. He defined the purpose of literature as showing people how to "live together decently on this planet," and undertook the epic as an obligation to his daemon, a mystic sense of power that he called "Otherness." He insisted that men are finer than they think themselves, for ordinary people carry the seeds of heroism, and, in a world filled with wonder, are secure in a spirit-infused cosmos, integrated in all its atoms.

The writing of the epic occupied Neihardt for 28 years. He had fallen in love with the Missouri River when he first saw it at the age of five, and his avid research in western materials led him in 1908 to travel down the river from its headwaters to observe the country his trapper heroes had traveled. He visited as much of the West as possible to make his settings authentic, and he read accounts, documents, journals, any materials he could find. He visited Indians and old Indian fighters from the Wars; his description of the death of Crazy Horse is taken from an eye-witness account. He had the further advantage of having tapped oral sources as a small child listening to the stories of old-timers on his grandfather's farm in Kansas.

The epic follows a time-space pattern. It opens in St. Louis in 1822 with the departure of the first Ashley-Henry men up-river to engage in the fur trade, and takes them west across deserts, over mountains, past Salt Lake, and on to the coast. The time sequence runs from 1822 through the years of expansion of the fur trade, the advance of white settlers, the Indian Wars, the Messiah movement, and the massacre at Wounded Knee that marked the end of organized Indian resistance.

One of Neihardt's best works of western fiction is his last novel, *When the Tree Flowered*, based loosely on the life of a Sioux, Eagle Elk, who lived through the last years of Indian resistance. The novel reflects the uneasiness of Indian life in Eagle Elk's childhood and relates events through the eyes of a boy and then young man, including his view of the defeat of Custer and his army. The novel also weaves in legends and folk tales, describes the education of children by the grandparents, and throws light on the ethical system and tribal rituals. It paints warm, human pictures of daily life, sometimes gently ironic, sometimes humorous, often grim, but always illuminating.

Only recently has Neihardt begun to receive the critical attention his work merits. Reviews of his early works were respectful, but major critics accorded him no attention, possibly because American writers who remain in the West seldom catch the notice of establishment critics in New York or Chicago, the publishing centers. Whether he has written the great American epic as he hoped is a problem for posterity to judge, but his fiction makes a valid contribution to western American literature. His best known book is not fictional; it is the biography of an Indian holy man and his power vision, *Black Elk Speaks*.

—Lucile F. Aly

NEVIN, David. American. Born in Washington, D.C., 30 May 1927. Educated at Centenary College, Shreveport, Louisiana, 1946–47; Texas Technological College, Lubbock, Texas, 1948–49; Louisiana State University, Baton Rouge, Louisiana, 1949–50. Served in the United States Navy, in Pacific Theatre, 1944–46; United States Merchant Marine, 1946–47: chief electrician. Married Luciana Colla in 1958; one son. Reporter, *Brownsville Herald*, Texas, 1950–52, *Dallas Times Herald*, Texas, 1952–54, and *San Antonio Light*, Texas, 1954–60; staff writer, *Life* magazine, New York, 1960–70. Since 1970 freelance writer; editor, *Southern Journal*. Recipient: R. F. Kennedy Memorial Journalism Award, for magazine article, 1969. Agent: Eugene Winick, McIntosh and Otis Inc., 310 Madison Avenue, New York, New York 10017, U.S.A.

WESTERN PUBLICATIONS

Novel

Dream West. New York, Putnam, 1983; London, New English Library, 1984.

Other (series: Old West)

The Texans. New York, Morrow, 1968.
The Soldiers. New York, Time-Life, 1973.
The Expressmen. New York, Time-Life, 1973.
The Mexican War. New York, Time-Life, 1978.
The Pathfinders. New York, Time-Life, 1980.
The Road to Shiloh. New York, Time-Life, 1983.
Sherman's March. Alexandria, Virginia, Time-Life, 1986.

OTHER PUBLICATIONS

Other

Muskie of Maine. New York, Random House, 1972.
The Schools That Fear Built: Segregationist Academies in the South, with Robert E. Bills. Washington, D.C., Acropolis, 1976.
The American Touch in Micronesia. New York, Norton, 1977.
Architects of Air Power. New York, Time-Life, 1981.
Left-Handed Fastballers: Scouting and Training America's Grass-Roots Leaders, 1966–77: A Report Based on a Study for the Ford Foundation. New York, The Foundation, 1981.
John Charles Fremont—The Pathfinder. New York, Rockland County History, 1987.

*

David Nevin comments:

In fiction and nonfiction I now concentrate on the initial American century, 1750–1850. I'm currently working on a book of nonfiction, but oriented to stories dealing with aspects of Andrew Jackson's administration. I have a novel in progress dealing with Sam Houston, hero of the Texas Revolution in 1836. I plan further biographical novels around leading figures of the period. While these are novels in the sense that they contain imagined scenes and dialogue, they pay more attention to the historical scene they present than to the usual form of the novel.

In dealing with nonfiction in this period, what interests me is the story sense of the individuals, and the effect of their emotional lives on history. Thus my nonfiction, though entirely accurate and quoting only from sources, nevertheless has novelistic overtones, while my fiction, with its emphasis on history and its meaning, has a nonfictive quality. It's my contention that this produces a unified whole.

* * *

The main output of David Nevin's work has been his contribution to Time-Life's Books Old West series and numerous books on public affairs (for example, *Muskie of Maine*). Texan by birth, he spent much of his life on army outposts with his father, acting as a veterinary officer for the U.S. Army. He has written for *Life* magazine and edits the *Southern Journal*.

Dream West, his first novel, was inspired by his research for the Old West books. To make the book accurate where evidence existed he and his wife Luciana spent four years collating material on John Charles Frémont's life, to turn it into a splendid rich slice of American history.

In his attempt to gain a feel for Frémont's failed expedition of the 1844 Sierra Nevada winter crossing, Nevin, like writers Matt Braun and Terry Johnson personally travelled the Carson Pass in midwinter. This, and other experiences, help to fuel the novel with high adventure, romance, and politics.

Nevin had originally intended to write a hard biography of Frémont and his wife, Jessie, but as he continued his research he was drawn to the broader canvas of the historical novel. He did not see Frémont as the bungling, vain fool he was so often described as, and was determined to set the record straight.

Dream West begins with Frémont as a young lieutenant with the United States Army Corps of Topographical Engineers, who were to map out the American West for the first time. The 1844 expedition already mentioned, was almost the end for the army officer, but his ability as a leader was to prove exceptional, and he successfully rescued the mission. His career faltered in 1847, when he was court-martialled for his part in the Bear Flag revolt—the rebellion that led to California's independence from Mexico. This first brush with political power entranced the young Frémont, drawing him on like a magnet. He pursued this career, and, much to the chagrin of fellow army officers, was successfully elected as senator to California in 1850.

Nevin delves into Frémont's political activities with relish, and his narrative is rich with the detail of his failed attempt at Republican presidential nomination in 1864, when he spoke out on the anti-slavery programme. This issue was to prove a thorn in Frémont's side, for in 1881 he was relieved of his army command for issuing proclamations under his own initiative. It was this arrogance which eventually damaged his political career.

Jessie Frémont is a powerful figure within the book, and it is she who supports her husband when a business deal almost bankrupts them. They became millionaires when gold was discovered on their Californian property, but an unwise investment in a railroad led the Frémonts to lose it in 1870. Frémont was never to fully recover from this failure, but went on to serve as governor of Arizona between 1878 to 1883, dying in poverty in 1890.

Dream West is an admirable piece of work, a thought-provoking study of one of America's great pioneers. Nevin's descriptions of landscape are captivating, and the portrayals of husband and wife excellent. Perhaps the 639 pages make for an overlong read, but nevertheless, it remains a pleasing and enjoyable insight into a side of frontier life not fully explored within the western genre. It had taken Nevin and his wife eight years to create this massive novel, and he is currently working on another historical account of the United States between 1810 and 1860.

—John L. Wolfe

NEWTON, D(wight) B(ennett). Also writes as Dwight Bennett; Jackson Cole; Clement Hardin; Ken Jason; Johnny Lawson; Ford Logan; Hank Mitchum; Dave Sand; Dan Temple. American. Born in Kansas City, Missouri, 14 January 1916. Educated at the University of Missouri, Kansas City, 1937–42, A.B. 1940, M.A. in history and political science 1942. Served in the United States Army Engineers, 1942–46. Married Mary Jane Kregel in 1941; two daughters. Since 1946 freelance writer: story consultant and staff writer for television series *Wagon Train*, 1957, *Death Valley Days*, 1958, and *Tales of Wells Fargo*. Founding member, 1953, and secretary-treasurer, Western Writers of America, 1953–58, and 1967–71. Address: 11 N.W. Kansas Avenue, Bend, Oregon 97701, U.S.A.

WESTERN PUBLICATIONS

Novels (series: Jim Bannister; Johnny Logan)

Guns of the Rimrock. New York, Phoenix Press, 1946; London, Sampson Low, 1947.
The Gunmaster of Saddleback. New York, Phoenix Press, and London, Sampson Low, 1948.
Range Boss. New York, Pocket Books, 1949; as *The Trail Beyond Boothill*, London, Sampson Low, 1949.
Shotgun Guard. Philadelphia, Lippincott, 1950; as *Stagecoach Guard*, London, Sampson Low, 1951.
Six-Gun Gamble. Philadelphia, Lippincott, 1951; London, Macdonald, 1954.
Guns along the Wickiup. New York, Fawcett, 1953; London, Fawcett, 1955.
Rainbow Rider. London, Macdonald, 1954; in *Triple Trouble*, New York, Ace, 1978.
Fire in the Desert (as Ford Logan). New York, Ballantine, 1954.
The Outlaw Breed. New York, Fawcett, 1955; London, Muller, 1956.
Maverick Brand. Derby, Connecticut, Monarch 1962.
On the Dodge (Bannister). New York, Berkley, 1962.
Guns of Warbonnet. New York, Berkley, 1963.
The Savage Hills (Bannister). New York, Berkley, 1964.
Bullets on the Wind (Bannister). New York, Berkley, 1964.
Fury at Three Forks. New York, Berkley, 1964.
The Manhunters (Bannister). New York, Berkley, 1966.
Hideout Valley (Bannister). New York, Berkley, 1967.
The Tabbart Brand. New York, Berkley, 1967.
Shotgun Freighter. New York, Berkley, 1968.
The Wolf Pack (Bannister). New York, Berkley, 1968.
The Judas Horse (Bannister). New York, Berkley, 1969.
Syndicate Gun (Bannister). New York, Berkley, 1972.
Massacre Valley (Logan). New York, Curtis, 1973.
Range Tramp (Bannister). New York, Berkley, 1973.
Trail of the Bear (Logan). New York, Popular Library, 1975.
The Land Grabbers (Logan). New York, Popular Library, 1975.
Bounty on Bannister. New York, Berkley, 1975.
Broken Spur (Bannister). New York, Berkley, 1977.

Novels as Dwight Bennett (series: Eden Grove)

Stormy Range. New York, Doubleday, 1951; as *Range Feud* (as D.B. Newton), London, Sampson Low, 1953.
Lost Wolf River. New York, Doubleday, 1952; London, Corgi, 1954.
Border Graze. New York, Doubleday, 1952.
Top Hand. New York, Permabooks, 1955.
The Avenger. New York, Permabooks, 1956.
Cherokee Outlet. New York, Doubleday, 1961; London, Ward Lock, 1962.
The Oregon Rifles. New York, Doubleday, 1962; London, Ward Lock, 1964.
Rebel Trail. New York, Doubleday, 1963; London, Collins, 1965.
Crooked River Canyon. New York, Doubleday, 1966; London, Gold Lion, 1973.
Legend in the Dust. New York, Doubleday, 1970; London, Gold Lion, 1973.
The Big Land. New York, Doubleday, 1972.
The Guns of Ellsworth. New York, Doubleday, 1973.
Hangman's Knot. New York, Doubleday, 1975.
The Cheyenne Encounter. New York, Doubleday, 1976.
West of Railhead (Eden Grove). New York, Doubleday, 1977; London, Hale, 1979.
The Texans (Eden Grove). New York, Doubleday, 1979.
Disaster Creek. New York, Doubleday, 1981.

Novels as Clement Hardin

Hellbent for a Hangrope. New York, Ace, 1954.
Cross Me in Gunsmoke. New York, Ace, 1957.
The Lurking Gun. New York, Ace, 1961.
The Badge Shooters. New York, Ace, 1962.
Outcast of Ute Bend. New York, Ace, 1965.
The Ruthless Breed. New York, Ace, 1966.
The Paxman Feud. New York, Ace, 1967.
The Oxbow Deed. New York, Ace, 1967.
Ambush Reckoning. New York, Ace, 1968.
Sheriff of Sentinel. New York, Ace, 1969.
Colt Wages. New York, Ace, 1970.
Stage Line to Rincon. New York, Ace, 1971.

Novels as Dan Temple

Outlaw River. New York, Popular Library, 1955.
The Man from Idaho. New York, Popular Library, 1956.
Bullet Lease. New York, Popular Library, 1957.
Gun and Star. Derby, Connecticut, Monarch, 1964.

Novels as Hank Mitchum

Stagecoach series:
Station 1: Dodge City. New York, Bantam, 1982.
Station 2: Laredo. New York, Bantam, 1982.
Station 4: Tombstone. New York, Bantam, 1983.
Station 6: Santa Fe. New York, Bantam, 1983.
Station 11: Deadwood. New York, Bantam, 1984.
Station 13: Carson City. New York, Bantam, 1984.

Station 20: Leadville. New York, Bantam, 1985.
Station 26: Tulsa. New York, Bantam, 1986.

Uncollected Short Stories

"Brand of the Hunted," in *Western Novels and Short Stories*, (New York), July 1938.
"Range Where Men Died Twice," in *Western Short Stories* (New York), December 1938.
"Gunshot Granger," in *Western Short Stories* (New York), May 1939.
"Cowboy, You're Going to Die," in *Western Short Stories* (New York), October 1939.
"Guns in the Dust," in *Complete Western Book* (New York), May 1940.
"Return of the Cutbank Cub," in *Western Novels and Short Stories* (New York), June 1940.
"Deliver, Law-Dog—Dead or Alive!" in *Western Fiction* (New York), October 1940.
"Jump-Rope Justice," in *2-Gun Western Novels* (New York), October 1940.
"Lead Purge for a Hard-Case Town," in *Best Western* (New York), November 1940.
"Hired-On to Rod Hell," in *Complete Western Book* (New York), November 1940.
"Guns Across the Years," in *.44 Western* (New York), December 1940.
"For Hire—the Fastest Gun in Hell!" in *Western Short Stories* (New York), February 1941.
"Doc Grant's Cutbank Colt Cure," in *Western Novels and Short Stories* (New York), February 1941.
"Dead-or-Alive Means Draw and Deliver!" in *Complete Western Book* (New York), March 1941.
"Satan Sides a Tinhorn," in *Big-Book Western* (New York), April 1941.
"A Tinhorn Chooses Hot Lead," in *Western Short Stories* (New York), July 1941.
"The Nester Who Stayed," in *New Western* (New York), July 1941.
"Powdersmoke Reprieve," in *Western Novels and Short Stories* (New York), September 1941.
"Back-Trail Bondage," in *Best Western* (New York), October 1941.
"Doom Guns for Box-S Neighbors," in *Big-Book Western* (New York), October 1941.
"Be Fast, Battle-Cub, or Hire Boothill!," in *Western Short Stories* (New York), February 1942.
"Wanted: Four Kill-Crazy Gunslammers!," in *Western Short Stories* (New York), May 1942.
"Treachery Trail," in *Western Novels and Short Stories* (New York), July 1942.
"Tin-Badge-Backed Bushwhacker," in *Western Short Stories* (New York), August 1942.
"Manhunt Trail to Hell," in *Complete Western Book* (New York), February 1943.
"Three from the Dark Trails" and "Never Too Old To Fight" (as Dave Sand), in *.44 Western* (New York), March 1943.
"Pine Gap Payoff," in *Western Novels and Short Stories* (New York), April 1943.
"Written in Lead," in *Western Short Stories* (New York), May 1943.
"The Kid Who Looked Like a Killer," in *Western Short Stories* (New York), January 1944.
"Peacemaker Means Powdersmoke," in *Best Western Novels* (New York), January 1944.
"Powdersmoke Wisdom," in *10 Story Western* (New York), May 1944.
"A Side Bet for Satan," in *Western Trails* (New York), May 1944.
"Rolling West to Hell!" in *.44 Western* (New York), November 1944.
"Powdersmoke Recruit," in *Western Aces* (New York), January 1945.
"Shackled to the Owlhoot," in *Western Aces* (New York), March 1945.
"Deal 'Em, Lawshark!" in *10 Story Western* (New York), May 1945.
"Guntown of the Dead," in *Western Trails* (New York), June 1945.
"Owlhoot Brotherhood," in *New Western* (New York), September 1945.
"Outcast, Keep on Ridin'!" in *Big-Book Western* (New York), October 1945.
"Colt Craftsman," in *Western Trails* (New York), October 1945.
"The Boss of Boothill," in *Western Novels and Short Stories* (New York), January 1946.
"His Guest, the Killer!," in *Big-Book Western* (New York), February 1946.
"The Devil Sends a Drifter," in *Ace-High Western* (New York), February 1946.
"Bushwhack Bounty," in *Complete Western Book* (New York), March 1946.
"Gun-Ghost of the Big Muddy," in *New Western* (New York), April 1946.
"Boothill's Boy," in *Fifteen Western Tales* (New York), April 1946.
"Reveille for the Damned," in *Big-Book Western* (New York), June 1946.
"Smoke-Pole Rendezvous in Abilene," in *Lariat* (New York), July 1946.
"Born to the Brand," in *Lariat* (New York), September 1946.
"Bullets Before Breakfast," in *Western Trails* (New York), September 1946.
"Boomer Bait," in *Fifteen Western Tales* (New York), September 1946.
"On Treachery Trail," in *Frontier Stories* (New York), Winter 1946.
"Shootout on the Catamount Trail," in *Western Trails* (New York), November 1946.
"One Last Gun-Chore," in *.44 Western* (New York), November 1946.
"Battle-Wise Means Boothill Bound!" in *Western Novels and Short Stories* (New York), November 1946.
"Deputies-on-the-Dodge!" in *Big-Book Western* (New York), November 1946.
"The Hardrock Man-Breaker," in *Ace-High Western* (New York), December 1946.
"Drifters Spell Trouble,' in *Lariat* (New York), January 1947.
"Derelict's Showdown," in *10 Story Western* (New York), January 1947.
"Dry Wells Rebels," in *Ace-High Western* (New York), February 1947.
"Brimstone Bridegroom," in *.44 Western* (New York), March 1947.
"—And Damned If You Don't!" in *.44 Western* (New York), April 1947.
"Last Stand of the Grave-Fillers' Combine," in *Big-Book Western* (New York), April 1947.
"Button's Nightmare," in *10 Story Western* (New York), May 1947.
"Guns of the Empty-Saddle Legion," in *Big-Book Western* (New York), June 1947.

"Bullets Buy Hell's Half-Acre!" in *.44 Western* (New York), June 1947.
"Triggers at Trail's End," in *10 Story Western* (New York) June 1947.
"Black Dunstan's Skullduggery," in *10 Story Western* (New York), July 1946.
"'Reach High, Tophand!'," in *Lariat* (New York), July 1947.
"Gunhawk!" in *Axe-High Western* (New York), July 1947.
"Saddle-Bum's Battle-Call," in *Big-Book Western* (New York), August 1947.
"Texas-on-the-Trail!" in *Ace-High Western* (New York), August 1947.
"Lobo's Den," in *Ranch Romances* (New York), August 1947.
"Tinhorn's Last-Chance Salvation," in *Complete Western Book* (New York), August 1947.
"Saga of the Tombstone Kid," in *Lariat* (New York), September 1947.
"Law West of Sanity," in *Big-Book Western* (New York), September 1947.
"The Boom-Camp Manbreakers," in *Ace-High Western* (New York), September 1947.
"Tinstar Buster," in *Fifteen Western Tales* (New York), October 1947.
"Powdersmoke Reprieve," in *Western Short Stories* (New York), November 1947.
"Bullets for Breakfast," in *Ace-High Western* (New York), November 1947.
"Satan's Town," in *Fifteen Western Tales* (New York), November 1947.
"Powdersmoke over the Panhandle," in *Two-Gun Western Novels* (New York), December 1947.
"Too Many Buzzards," in *New Western* (New York), December 1947.
"Gunhawk's Kid," in *Western Novels and Short Stories* (New York), December 1947.
"The Ranch That Bullets Built," in *.44 Western* (New York), January 1948.
"Death to Fort Defiance," in *Famous Western* (New York), January 1948.
"Head 'Em West of Hell!" in *Ace-High Western* (New York), January 1948.
"Gunsmoke Crossing," in *Western Trails* (New York), February 1948.
"Holster Basin's Last Pistol-Patroit," in *Big-Book Western* (New York), February 1948.
"Parson Dan's Bullet Benediction," in *Ace-High Western* (New York), February 1948.
"The Bullet Barrier," in *Western Novels and Short Stories* (New York), March 1948.
"The Stranger," in *Complete Western Book* (New York), March 1948.
"The Taming of Johnny Peters," in *Ace-High Western* (New York), March 1948.
"To Hell with the Sodbusters' Sheriff!" in *Ace-High Western* (New York), April 1948.
"Gun Doomed!" in *Five Western Novels* (New York), April 1948.
"River Tinhorn's Blood-Bet," in *Ace-High Western* (New York), May 1948.
"Powdersmoke Providence" (as Ken Jason) and "Owlhoot Bait," in *Western Short Stories* (New York), June 1948.
"Nighthawk's Code," in *Rio Kid Western* (New York), June 1948.
"Traitor of Gunsmoke Graze," in *Western Story* (New York), July 1948.
"Satan Rules the River," in *Giant Western* (New York), Summer 1948.
"Feud Firebrands," in *Western Trails* (New York), August 1948.
"Reba Rides Alone," in *Exciting Western* (New York), September 1948.
"Bullet-Boss of Devil's Gulch," in *Three Western Novels* (New York), September 1948.
"Fighting Men from Boothill," in *Ace-High Western* (New York), September 1948.
"Hero . . . Off His Home Range!" in *Western Short Stories* (New York), October 1948.
"The Sixgun Savior," in *Western Novels and Short Stories* (New York), October 1948.
"Six Fast Horses to Hell!" in *.44 Western* (New York), October 1948.
"Riders of Vengeance Trail," in *Frontier Stories* (New York), October 1948.
"Greenhorn's Bullet Baptism," in *Western Story* (New York), October 1948.
"The Kid with the Graveyard Grin," in *Western Novels and Short Stories* (New York), December 1948.
"Monty Stevens' Skunk Trap," in *Big-Book Western* (New York), December 1948.
"Colt Quarantine," in *Avon Book of New Stories of the Great Wild West*. New York, Avon, 1949.
"Faster Guns, Bigger Fists, Tougher!" in *Complete Western Book* (New York), February 1949.
"Gun-Rule Rebel," in *Western Short Stories* (New York), February 1949.
"Swing High, Nester!" in *Lariat* (New York), March 1949.
"Badman on His Backtrail," in *Complete Western Book* (New York), April 1949.
"Cold Trail to Death," in *Western Short Stories* (New York), April 1949.
"Bully Boss of Devil's Landing," in *Western Story* (New York), May 1949.
"White Thunder of the Cherokees," in *Frontier Stories* (New York), Summer 1949.
"Range of No Return," in *Complete Western Book* (New York), June 1949.
"Broomtail Boomerang" and "Way of the Wild" (as Ken Jason), in *Western Short Stories* (New York), June 1949.
"Blood on the Gold," in *Western Novels and Short Stories* (New York), June 1949.
"One Against the Wild Bunch," in *Complete Western Book* (New York), July 1949.
"The Maverick Makers," in *Western Story* (New York), August 1949.
"The Gun-Gambler," in *Complete Western Book* (New York), October 1949.
"Riders of the Shadow Trail," in *Masked Rider Western* (New York), October 1949.
"Land's Free—for Fighters!," in *.44 Western* (New York), October 1949.
"The Gun-Brand Kid," in *Two Western Books* (New York), Winter 1949.
"The Killer Who Took No Chances," in *Western Short Stories* (New York), November 1949.
"'Guns Buy This Grass!'," in *Three Western Novels* (New York), December 1949.
"For a Gun and a Silver Star" (as Johnny Lawson) and "The Tenderfoot Manbreaker," in *Western Short Stories* (New York), January 1950.
"Stranger in Bushwhack Basin," in *Big-Book Western* (New York), April 1950.
"The Kid No Range Would Hire," in *Best Western Novels* (New York), April 1950.

"Texas Beef Means Texas Bullets," in *Complete Western Books* (New York), April 1950.
"Ute Basin Raiders," in *Range Riders Western* (New York), May 1950.
"Medico of Manhunt Hills," in *Big-Book Western* (New York), June 1950.
"Trail Fever," in *Western Short Stories* (New York), September 1950.
"Law of the Strong," in *Western Novels and Short Stories* (New York), September 1950.
"Maverick Is My Brand," in *Two Western Books* (New York), Winter 1950.
"Gunslammers' Valley," in *Big-Book Western* (New York), December 1950.
"Steel Rails for Texas" (as Jackson Cole), in *Texas Rangers* (New York), February 1951.
"Beware a Bullwhacker Babe," in *Rangeland Love Stories* (New York), March 1951.
"The Muleshoe Marauders," in *Range Riders Western* (New York), July 1951.
"Guns for the Golden Lady," in *Masked Rider Western* (New York), August 1951.
"Badman on His Backtrail," in *Complete Western Book* (New York), August 1951.
"Scorpions of Silverado," in *Rio Kid Western* (New York), September 1951.
"Three Gunhawks and a Girl," in *Best Western* (New York), September 1951.
"Trail's End at the Hangtree" (as Dwight Bennett), in *Five Western Novels* (New York), October 1951.
"Rogues' Rendezvous," in *Rio Kid Western* (New York), January 1952.
"Look for Two Texans" and "The Marshal They Laughed At" (as Ken Jason), in *Complete Western Book* (New York), February 1952.
"Panhandle Freight" (as Jackson Cole), in *Texas Rangers* (New York), February 1952.
"Stage Coach West," in *Frontier Stories* (New York), Spring 1952.
"Ten Thousand Killers on His Backtrail," in *Complete Western Book* (New York), May 1952.
"The Slack Rein," in *Western Short Stories* (New York), June 1952.
"The Kid Who Wouldn't Talk," in *Best Western* (New York), July 1952.
"Bride of the Wild Bunch Boss," in *Western Short Stories* (New York), August 1952.
"Who'll Take the Cowgirl?" in *Best Western* (New York), September 1952.
"Longhorn War," in *Rio Kid Western* (New York), November 1952.
"The Kid That Satan Sent," in *Western Novels and Short Stories* (New York), April 1953.
"The Barbed Barrier" (as Jackson Cole), in *Texas Rangers* (New York), July 1953.
"The Bronc Stealers," in *Giant Western* (New York), August 1953.
"Peaker Kid," in *.44 Western* (New York), November 1953.
"Mule Tracks," in *Bad Men and Good*, edited by Luke Short. New York, Dodd Mead, 1953.
"Missouri Passage" (as Dan Temple), *Ranch Romances* (New York), June 1954.
"Lone Gun," in *Blue Book* (New York), May 1956.
"Born to the Brand," in *A Quintet of Sixes*, edited by Donald A. Wollheim. New York, Ace, 1969.
"Chain of Command," in *With Guidons Flying*, edited by Charles N. Heckelmann. New York, Doubleday, 1970.
"The Storm Riders," in *Zane Grey Western* (New York), October 1970.

OTHER PUBLICATIONS

Novel

The Love Goddess. New York, Universal, 1962.

Plays

Television Plays: *Wagon Train*, *Death Valley Days*, *Tales of Wells Fargo*, *Colt .45*, *Cimarron City*, and *Whiplash* series, 1957–60.

*

Manuscript Collection: University of Oregon Library, Eugene.

D.B. Newton comments:

I write (and read) Westerns for the sheer pleasure of watching vividly drawn characters, larger than life and sometimes nearly Homeric, act out strong emotions and situations and conflicts by the most direct and dramatic of means. Add to this a swiftly moving plot, and an evocation of the natural beauty and the extraordinary vitality of the Old West, and it seems no wonder that the western story should have captured the popular imagination of the whole world.

Even if the books I write are, strictly speaking, ephemeral, I work hard and take satisfaction from knowing that every page contains the very best prose of which I was capable at the time. If others happen to have enjoyed reading them, there's very little more I could have asked for.

* * *

D.B. Newton has long been one of the western genre's most accomplished exponents. His work contains all the elements of the most popular frontier stories—a tough, determined hero (usually aged between 25 and 30, a thoroughly despicable villain (complete with assorted henchmen), and a spunky, strong-willed (but rarely stereotypical) heroine. His product is at once convincing, intelligent, pacy, and entertaining, and even a relatively early effort such as *Lost Wolf River* displays the enviable clarity of thought and expression which characterises so much of his later work. His hero, a down-at-heel cowboy named Chick Bronson, is especially well-drawn, as are the circumstances which involve him with a bank robber and land him in the middle of a range war. The credibility of Newton's work is further strengthened by conscientious research and the fact that his own fictional West is made up not just of good men and bad, but rather of *human beings* who are sometimes a little of both. Particularly in the earlier books, there was the occasional lapse into melodrama, but these were few and far between, and in any case were soon phased out.

The land itself is also central to Newton's Westerns, and he describes its tall snowcaps, timbered ridges and sparkling rivers eloquently. Whenever possible he also likes to base his work on solid historical fact, and these two trademarks are especially evident in *Cherokee Outlet*, in which the arrival in 1889 of sodbusters to the hithero "Unassigned Lands" signifies the end of cattleman Lee Stormont's way of life; and *The Big Land*, in which a former soldier named Chad Osborn comes out to post Civil War Oregon (a favourite Newton locale) to finds more trouble than he can handle when his relationship with the tough but dignified Emily Bishop creates a web of tension and jealousy. Added to this is the ever-present threat of Indian attack, which Newton presents exceptionally well, creating a sense of realism further reinforced by the fact that several of the supporting characters—most notably the Wal-papi Snake renegade Chief Paulina and Cincinnatus Hiner "Joaquin" Miller—actually existed. Even in Newton's less ambitious work, the countryside plays a vital role; in his 1975 Johnny Logan adventure *The Land Grabbers*, his Cheyenne Indian hero (who was raised in the white man's way and thus has a foot in both worlds) uncovers a plot to discredit the Indians and take over reservation land.

Newton's plots encompass far more than this one aspect of the West, however, and even the most hackneyed of stories appears to undergo some form of revitalisation at his hands. On the surface, *Legend in the Dust* is little more than a re-working of another familiar theme: that of the young tenderfoot in search of adventure who joins forces with an older, more experienced Westerner and is forever changed by the involvement. The book is distinguished by the superb characterisation of Newton's protagonists, young Rim Adams and the gun-fast Frank Keyhoe, who sign on to tame a lawless town. An ending which is by no means as upbeat as Newton's usual conclusions also ensures that the novel is not easily forgotten.

More recently, Newton's energies have been expended on the Book Creations series Stagecoach Station, now acknowledged to be the most popular western paperback series of all time. Though perhaps not quite as successful as the unconnected Westerns which have appeared under his own name and the pseudonyms Dwight Bennett and Clement Hardin (the very premise of the series, to tell "adventures set in the West's most dramatic towns—filled with the danger, history and romance of the bold men and women who conquered the frontier", lends an unfortunate but inescapably "manufactured" feel to the stories), Newton's contributions are nevertheless typically entertaining and worthy of comment. Furthermore, they also allow him to indulge his preference for setting plots in specific geographical locations and historical timespans. *Dodge City*, for example, features Bat Masterson. Mark Twain appears in *Carson City*. In *Deadwood*, Newton concludes the fictionalised exploits of Wild Bill Hickok started by Will C. Knott in *Abilene*. Set in the famous mining town that gives the book its title, *Leadville* centres on Griff Connor's quest to find the men who committed the crimes for which he has been framed, but is actually played out against the miners' strike of 1880.

Quite possibly the best of these semi-factual books is *Tombstone*, on the surface a straightforward adventure in which the hero, a former Pinkerton man named Dan Stockwell, is hired to stop a rash of stagecoach robberies occurring on the outskirts of "The Town Too Tough To Die." As Newton himself, writing under the house name Hank Mitchum, admits in his introduction, however, the story is also tied into the gunfight at the OK Corral, and "tries to make a plausible guess or two as to what really happened that day, and why." Among his other contributions to the series is *Santa Fe*, a predictable but nonetheless enjoyable tale which chronicles the adventures a group of stagecoach passengers experience when their four-and-a-half day run from Kansas to New Mexico is disrupted by bad weather.

Virtually all of Newton's work carries three specific brands—strong and well-executed plots, a nice line in believable dialogue and character reactions, and a firm but seldom preachy belief in the triumph of good over evil. In the main his longer works tend to make the most satisfying reads, but even his most seemingly insignificant paperback original can usually be relied upon to deliver the very best in western entertainment.

—David Whitehead

NEWTON, Mike. Also writes as Mack Bolan; John Cannon; Mark Kozlow; Paul Malone; Vince Robinson. American. Born in Bakersfield, California, 16 September 1951. Educated at California State University, Bakersfield, B.A. 1973; University of Las Vegas, Nevada. Married Judy Ann Newton in 1976. Public school teacher for eight years in Nevada. Since 1986 full-time writer. Agent: Scott Meredith Agency, 845 3rd Avenue, New York, New York 10022. Address: P. O. Box 1035, Nashville, Indiana 47448, U.S.A.

WESTERN PUBLICATIONS

Novels

Vengeance Ride. Los Angeles, Carousel, 1980.
Massacre Trail. Los Angeles, Carousel, 1980.
Lawman series:
1. *Creed's Vengeance*. Los Angeles, Carousel, 1981.
2. *Creed's Gold*. Los Angeles, Carousel, 1982.
3. *Creed's War*. Los Angeles, Carousel, 1982.
4. *Creed's Kill*. Los Angeles, Carousel, 1982.
5. *Creed's Treasure*. Los Angeles, Carousel, 1982.
6. *Creed's Hell*. Los Angeles, Carousel, 1982.
7. *Creed's Vendetta*. Los Angeles, Carousel, 1982.
8. *Creed's Ransom*. Los Angeles, Carousel, 1982.
9. *Creed's Gauntlet*. Los Angeles, Carousel, 1982.

Novels as Mark Kozlow

Murder in the Gold Hills. Los Angeles, Carousel, 1981.
The Range War Nobody Won. Los Angeles, Carousel, 1981.

OTHER PUBLICATIONS

Novels

The Ripper. Los Angeles, Carousel, 1978.
The Satan Ring. Los Angeles, Carousel, 1978.
Web of Terror (as John Cannon). Los Angeles, Carousel, 1980.
Death Cruise (as John Cannon). Los Angeles, Carousel, 1980.
Terror at Boulder Dam (as Vince Robinson). Los Angeles, Carousel, 1981.
Death at Sea (as Vince Robinson). Los Angeles, Carousel, 1981.
Child of Dust. New York, Bantam, 1988.
Korea Kill. New York, Bantam, 1990.
China White. New York, Bantam, 1991.
Trigger Pull (as Paul Malone). Toronto, Gold Eagle, 1991.
Border War (as Paul Malone). Toronto, Gold Eagle, 1991.
The Undertaker's Wind (as Paul Malone). Toronto, Gold Eagle, 1991.

Novels as Mack Bolan

The Executioner's War Book, with Don Pendleton and Steven Mertz. New York, Pinnacle, 1977.

Command Strike, with Pendleton and Mertz. New York, Pinnacle, 1977.
Cleveland Pipeline, with Pendleton and Mertz. New York, Pinnacle, 1977.
Arizona Ambush, with Pendleton. New York, Pinnacle, 1977.
Tennessee Smash, with Pendleton. New York, Pinnacle, 1977.
Satan's Sabbath, with Pendleton. New York, Pinnacle, 1980.
The Violent Streets. Toronto, Gold Eagle, 1982.
Paramilitary Plot. Toronto, Gold Eagle, 1982.
Doomsday Disciples. Toronto, Gold Eagle, 1983.
Paradine's Gauntlet. Toronto, Gold Eagle, 1983.
Sold for Slaughter. Toronto, Gold Eagle, 1983.
Prairie Fire. Toronto, Gold Eagle, 1984.
Blood Dues. Toronto, Gold Eagle, 1984.
The Bone Yard. Toronto, Gold Eagle, 1985.
Hollywood Hell. Toronto, Gold Eagle, 1985.
Shockwaves. Toronto, Gold Eagle, 1985.
Flight 741. Toronto, Gold Eagle, 1986.
Missouri Deathwatch. Toronto, Gold Eagle, 1985.
Defenders and Believers. Toronto, Gold Eagle, 1986.
The Trial. Toronto, Gold Eagle, 1986.
Rogue Force. Toronto, Gold Eagle, 1987.
Blood Testament. Toronto, Gold Eagle, 1987.
Eternal Triangle. Toronto, Gold Eagle, 1987.
Assault on Rome. Toronto, Gold Eagle, 1987.
Run to Ground. Toronto, Gold Eagle, 1987.
Time to Kill. Toronto, Gold Eagle, 1987.
Flesh and Blood. Toronto, Gold Eagle, 1988.
The Fiery Cross. Toronto, Gold Eagle, 1988.
Cold Judgment. Toronto, Gold Eagle, 1988.
Line of Fire. Toronto, Gold Eagle, 1988.
Night Kill. Toronto, Gold Eagle, 1989.
Haitian Hit. Toronto, Gold Eagle, 1989.
Blood Run. Toronto, Gold Eagle, 1989.
Fatal Error. Toronto, Gold Eagle, 1990.
Assault. Toronto, Gold Eagle, 1990.
Blood Sport. New York, Dell, 1990.
Golden Quad. Toronto, Gold Eagle, 1991.
Slay Ride. New York, Dell, 1991.
The Necro File. New York, Dell, 1991.
Head Games. New York, Dell, 1991.
Road Kills. New York, Dell, 1991.
Black Lace. New York, Dell, 1991.
Wet Work. New York, Dell, 1991.
Jigsaw. New York, Dell, 1991.
Summer Fires. New York, Dell, 1991.

Other as Michael Newton

The King Conspiracy. Los Angeles, Holloway, 1987.
Terrorism in the United States & Europe, 1800–1959: An Annotated Bibliography, with Judy Ann Newton. New York, Garland, 1988.
How to Write Action-Adventure Novels. Cincinnati, Ohio, Writers Digest, 1989.
Armed and Dangerous: A Writer's Guide to Weapons. Cincinnati, Ohio, Writers Digest, 1990.
Hunting Humans: An Encyclopedia of Modern Serial Killers. Port Townsend, Washington, Loompanics, 1990.

Editor, with Judy Ann Newton, *The FBI Most Wanted: An Encyclopedia*. New York, Garland, 1989.

* * *

Like many writers, Mike Newton was born into a family of readers, although his taste in literature—the kind of lurid "men's adventure" stories normally associated with the pulps—did not always meet with his parents' approval. Today, however, Newton is one of the most respected writers working in that self-same genre, having written numerous action/adventure paperback originals, and more of Gold Eagle's Mack Bolan books than Don Pendleton, the man who created the character.

A one-time junior high school teacher (and security guard for the country and western singer Merle Haggard), Newton's now lengthy list of literary credits also include many volumes of nonfiction (among them a critically acclaimed encyclopedia of 20th-century serial killers) and an excellent "how to write" book covering the action/adventure genre. In the early 1980's, Newton also wrote several Westerns for a small California-based company called Carousel Books.

The majority of these novels—eight, in fact—appeared in series form as The Lawman, although after the obligatory "origin" story, *Creed's Vengeance* the hero, Joshua Creed, actually makes his living as a bounty hunter. When the series begins, however, Creed, a Texan who fought for the Confederacy and ended the war in a Union prisoner-of-war camp, is a newly married town marshal.

When four strangers ride into town and rein in outside the local bank, Creed's suspicions are aroused, but before he can check through his wanted posters, a volley of gunshots erupts from the bank, and when he and the rest of the townsfolk come running, the bank robbers are forced to take refuge inside a nearby store. Taking a woman hostage, they offer a simple ultimatum: unless they are allowed to leave town unhindered, and given a two-hour head-start, the woman (Creed's bride of three months, Carrie) will be shot. Reluctantly, then, the robbers are allowed to make their escape, and when the posse finally sets out after them at the agreed time, it is only to find Carrie's body. She has been raped and murdered.

It doesn't really need to be stated that Creed continues after the killers, because that, like the rest of the plot, soon becomes glaringly obvious. Before too long he dispatches the first of his adversaries in a knife fight, escapes from jail after being arrested by the *federales*, kills the second of the four robbers by pushing him into a nest of rattlesnakes, and finally guns down the last two in a sleepy little Mexican town.

As a character, Joshua Creed differs little from the tough western anti-heroes upon whom he is clearly based, and neither do his subsequent adventures break new ground. In *Creed's Gold*, for example, the widow of a dead train robber enlists his help in recovering a fortune in stolen gold so that her son will not find out about his father's criminal past. Newton throws in a subplot about hostile Apaches and a few double-crosses, but these cannot disguise the fact that his story is clearly taken from the 1973 John Wayne movie *The Train Robbers*. In *Creed's Vendetta*, which reads more like something of a dry run for Newton's later action/adventure novels, Creed visits New Orleans and finds himself tangling with the Mafia when he stops a pair of thugs from beating up an attractive lady restauranteur. As the story wears on, the Mafia tries to kill him for daring to defy them, and in retaliation Creed virtually declares war by joining forces with the local vigilance committee and a rival Mafia leader. When Creed's lady-friend is kidnapped by the story's main villain, Don Carlo Vannucci (after a series of confrontations), Creed storms the Don's headquarters in true "Mack Bolan" style, finally leaving the city police to mop up once he has effected the girl's rescue and killed the Don.

It must be said that, though Newton's Westerns are certainly fast-paced, they are also heavily derivative. Both *Creed's Vengeance* and *Creed's Gold*, for example, are virtually straight re-writes of two of the author's earlier books, *Vengeance Ride* and *Massacre Trail*, which first saw publication as The Bounty

Man series. It should also be pointed out that the "origin" story in both cases bears an uncanny resemblance to that used in *Jubal Cade: The Killing Trail* by Charles R. Pike, published some five years earlier.

This is not to denigrate or cast aspersions on Newton's work. His Westerns are functional enough, though hardly inspired. In effect, they are exactly what they purport to be, but no more. On the other hand, he is obviously more comfortable when writing action/adventure novels—and it is in this field that his most satisfying work can be found.

—David Whitehead

NICHOLS, John. American. Born in Berkeley, California, 23 July 1940. Educated at Hamilton College, Clinton, New York, B.A. 1962. Married Ruth Harding in 1965 (marriage dissolved 1975); one son and one daughter. Blues singer; firefighter in Chiricahua Mountain, Arizona; dishwasher, Hartford, Connecticut; partner and artist in "Jest-No" greeting card business, 1962; teacher of English, Barcelona, Spain, for three months. Recipient: New Mexico Governor's award, 1981. Agent: Curtis Brown Ltd., 10 Astor Place, New York, New York 10003. Address: Box 1165, Taos, New Mexico 87571, U.S.A.

WESTERN PUBLICATIONS

Novels

New Mexico trilogy:
- *The Milagro Beanfield War*. New York, Holt Rinehart, 1974.
- *The Magic Journey*. New York, Holt Rinehart, 1978.
- *The Nirvana Blues*. New York, Holt Rinehart, 1981.

A Ghost in the Music. New York, Holt Rinehart, 1979.
American Blood. New York, Holt Rinehart, 1987.

Uncollected Short Stories

"Ask Edgar Cayce," in *The Taos Review* (Taos, New Mexico), 1989.
"The Revolt of Eddie Starner," in *Tierra: Contemporary Short Fiction of New Mexico*, edited by Rudolfo A. Anaya El Paso, Cinco Puntos Press, 1989.
"Garbage," in *The Taos Review* (Taos, New Mexico), 1990.

OTHER PUBLICATIONS

Novels

The Sterile Cuckoo. New York, McKay, 1965.
The Wizard of Loneliness. New York, Putnam, and London, Heinemann, 1966.

Other

If Mountains Die, photographs by William Davis. New York, Knopf, 1979.
The Last Beautiful Days of Autumn, photographs by the author. New York, Holt Rinehart, 1982.
On the Mesa. Salt Lake City, Utah, Peregrine Smith, 1986.
A Fragile Beauty. Salt Lake City, Utah, Peregrine Smith, 1987.
The Sky's the Limit. New York, Norton, 1990.

*

Critical Study: *John Nichols* by Peter Wild, Boise, Idaho, Boise, State University, 1986.

John Nichols comments:

During the 1960's, mostly because of the Vietnam War and my involvement in the anti-war movement, my writing changed radically. I became much more interested in trying to create a literature with a social conscience, a kind of armed creativity. *The Milagro Beanfield War* was the first successful book to come out of this effort, and it was followed up four years later with *The Magic Journey*, which for me focuses most accurately the changes I underwent during the 1960's, and the political, economic, and social beliefs which govern my life today. I understand history from a Marxist perspective, and this colors all my work. I hope also that this gives to my literature universal connections which are often lacking in the cultural works of my country.

*   *   *

The fame of John Nichols's *The Milagro Beanfield War* can distort an understanding of the novelist's other works and, indeed, of the writer's own intentions. Isolated in New Mexico's mountains, Nichols's imaginary community plunges into turmoil when it shakes off its dreamy, nearly medieval torpor. At long last the Hispanic townspeople realize that for decades they've been abused by the larger, predominantly Anglo, society, now bent on the final insult of turning their natural landscape into dollars through real-estate development. Revolt is in the air; bullets fly, and the local authorities reveal their dedication to greed by applying their hells to the necks of the good citizens who are trying to save their way of life. Yet what in outline appears as grim social upheaval Nichols turns into an *opéra bouffe*. Confronted by the rebellion, officials blunder about, a "herd of thundering clowns," while the townfolk appear as a cast of colorful country bumpkins. After hundreds of pages of comedy and a number of cliffhangers, all is forgiven, at least for the nonce, and the village slips back into its old drowsiness. It's all so much fun that the political message may be lost in the laughter.

Such is not nearly the danger, however, with two subsequent novels, *The Magic Journey* and *The Nirvana Blues*, both of them with similar settings and the same themes found in the first book. If anything, the humor is more rollicking and bizarre, but the fun doesn't work as well here. It's contrasted with a stark, irremediable reality: the ages-old, harmonious bond of a traditional people with its land has been steamrollered, replaced by a thoroughly corrupt Anglo society so hopelessly addicted to moneymaking that it is headed for certain destruction.

Increasingly, Nichols has committed himself to a rigid dualism. An apparent devotee of the Devil Theory of History, he divides the world into "good people" and "bad people," with the villains carrying the day. Yet rarely do human affairs conform with so simple an approach. Added to that, Nichols's view ignores historical events. Contrary to what the novelist would have us believe, New Mexico was not an idyllic land before the Anglos' arrival. It saw oppression of the Indians by the Hispanics, ruthless landgrabs among the feuding conquerors, rampant disease, hunger, and political backstabbing. And the bugaboo—not as Nichols, an avowed Marxist, would have us assume—can hardly be capitalism, for throughout history other economic systems, including Marxism, have visited havoc upon people and their environments around the globe. The real issues here, since Nichols proposes to reform humanity through "a literature of social conscience," are twofold: the pervasive orneriness of mankind and the inability of societies everywhere to use technology wisely. It may well be that the roots of such problems lie far beyond politics, in the murky depths of human nature itself. In any event, by the end of his New Mexican trilogy Nichols has created a troublesome situation for himself as a novelist. He's eliminated hope for positive change, replacing it with blind anger, and leaving few places for his future work to go. The circumstance faces many authors in the American West, to the extent that it becomes a central feature of much western American writing. Romantic novelists celebrate the West as a once pristine and spirit-buoying land, but a land now blighted by modern civilization. The handling of the problem largely determines the shape of the writers' books. Some authors escape into historical romance, others hold out the hope of political reform, while still others maintain that the unsullied West still exists in wild nooks and crannies of Montana or Wyoming. Nichols has found his own answer. Convinced of his own rectitude and full of rage that the world is not a place of justice, dreamy woodlands, and Christian charity, he watches with I-told-you-so satisfaction as his nation pitches hellbent toward cataclysm.

The position becomes painfully clear in a recent novel, *American Blood*. It opens as a soldier, Michael Smith, witnesses an atrocity in the Vietnam War, the first of many described. Thereafter, the geography changes, but the violence, especially the sexual violence, multiplies into a novel-long chain of gruesome episodes. Michael returns to the United States haunted by his memories, his civilian life "a chorus of moans from Nam." On top of that, when he attempts escape to rural New Mexico he realizes that the entire nation is a ghoul feeding on its own living corpse. Disembowelment, decapitation, shootings, drug addiction, rape, and often combinations of the foregoing make up the menu here, and the weary reader begins to wonder at the supposedly moralistic writer's fascination with the details of gore. That aside, the cause behind the mayhem, as presented here and in Nichols's other works, is a system that exploits the good-hearted under-dogs to feed the greed of the wealthy. In Michael's simplistic analysis, "Justice beleaguers the innocent . . . but allows the guilty free rein to continue plundering at will."

Nichols can be a master of snappy dialogue; sometimes he hones descriptions of nature to a painful beauty; and on occasion he elevates moments of human tenderness above cliché. Yet admirable as his talents are, he seems to have written himself into a corner in which he stands pouting. No doubt a rational person could brand large aspects of many societies as unsavory, if not mad. One also can suggest this might best be the departure point, rather than the beginning, middle, and end, of novels.

—Peter Wild

NICKSON, Arthur (Thomas). Also wrote as Arthur Hodson; Roy Peters; John Saunders; Matt Winstan. British. Born in Lancashire c. 1902. Married to Hilda Pressley. Worked as an electrician on the Liverpool docks, and was active as a trade union member. Emigrated to Canada during 1920's, and also visited the United States, where gained experience of cattle ranching. Returned to England, lived at various times in Liverpool, Lancashire, East Harling, Norfolk, and Dilham, Norfolk. *Died April 1974.*

WESTERN PUBLICATIONS

Novels (series: Rusty Hines)

Tin Star Sheriff. London, Jenkins, 1956.
Silver Town. London, Jenkins, 1957.
Gold Trail. London, Jenkins, 1957.
No Star for the Deputy (Hines). London, Jenkins, 1958.
Rusty Hines Hits the Trail (Hines). London, Jenkins, 1958.
Rusty Hines—Trouble Shooter (Hines). London, Jenkins, 1959.
Dust Was His Shroud (Hines). London, Jenkins, 1960.
Guns Blaze at Noon. (Hines). London, Jenkins, 1960.
Lone Killer (Hines). London, Jenkins, 1961.
Bounty Hunter's Trail (Hines). London, Jenkins, 1961.
Arizona Gun Feud (Hines). London, Jenkins, 1962.
Gunfight at Nolan's Canyon (Hines). London, Jenkins, 1963.
Two Deputies Came Riding (Hines). London, Jenkins, 1963.
Arizona Hideout (Hines). London, Jenkins, 1964.
Gun Trail (Hines). London, Jenkins, 1964.
Silvercrop (as Arthur Hodson). London, Mills and Boon, 1964.
Range Tramp. London, Jenkins, 1965.
Ride a Crooked Trail. London, Jenkins, 1966.
Sandy Creek Rustlers. London, Jenkins, 1967.

Novels as Matt Winstan (series: Reuben Brown)

The Big Herd. London, Jenkins, 1957.
Gunslick Gambler. London, Jenkins, 1958.
One-Gun Justice. London, Jenkins, 1959.
Vengeance Rode West. London, Jenkins, 1959.
New Trails Blaze West. London, Jenkins, 1960.
Pay Off in Lead. London, Jenkins, 1961.
Gunsmoke on the Iron Trail. London, Jenkins, 1961.
Bandit Trail (Brown). London, Jenkins, 1962.
Trail to Boot Hill (Brown). London, Jenkins, 1962.
Drive to Dodge City. London, Jenkins, 1963.
No Branding Fire (Brown). London, Jenkins, 1963.
Guns at Salt Flats (Brown). London, Jenkins, 1964.
Gold-Lust City. London, Jenkins, 1965.
Gunslick Marshal. London, Jenkins, 1966.
Greenhorn Sheriff. London, Jenkins, 1966.
Colt Justice. London, Jenkins, 1967.
Land Grab. London, Jenkins, 1968.

Novels as John Saunders

Two Gun Marshal. London, Hale, 1959.
A Colt for the Kid. London, Hale, 1960.
Guns in High Summer. London, Hale, 1961.
The Next Stage Out. London, Hale, 1961.
Arizona Feud. London, Hale, 1962.
Lynch Law Justice. London, Hale, 1965.

Novels as Roy Peters

Gunman's Bluff. London, Ward Lock, 1963.
Shootup in Cleaver Valley. London, Ward Lock, 1964.
The Shotgun Marshal. London, Ward Lock, 1964.
Stranger in Oak City. London, Ward Lock, 1964.
Cattle Doctor. London, Ward Lock, 1965.
Rail War. London, Ward Lock, 1965.
Buffalo! London, Ward Lock, 1966.

Vigilante Justice. London, Ward Lock, 1966.
West to Arizona. London, Ward Lock, 1967.
Women Ain't Angels. London, Ward Lock, 1967.
Silver Stampede. London, Ward Lock, 1968.
Alias Sam Smith. London, Ward Lock, 1968.

* * *

A prolific author of more than 50 western novels, and who at times used four different pseudonyms, Arthur Nickson's earliest writings appeared under his own name, and are notable mainly for the Rusty Hines series of books. These feature the nomadic partnership of Hines and his splendidly-named sidekick Spike Jones, who tour the western cattle towns righting wrongs and defeating ruthless villains. Rusty Hines makes his debut in *No Star for the Deputy* as a good-natured hell-raiser, prone to excessive drinking and brawling. Later books reveal a gradual change in his character, the feckless cowhand developing into an efficient trouble-shooter. Nickson's routine plots rarely tax the imagination, and there are regular appearances by villainous landowners and wild, headstrong ranchers' daughters. Racial stereotyping, with "dumb" Swedes and terrified Chinese cooks, is also evident. This said, action is lively and continuous, relieved at times by a humorous dialogue which brings W.C. Tuttle to mind. Occasionally these qualities are matched by an unusual plot, as in *Gun Trail*, where Rusty and Spike fall foul of a travelling evangelist, or *Dust Was His Shroud*, which has two towns battling for the lifeline of an oncoming railroad.

The novels written as John Saunders have no series characters, but are self-contained explorations of basic western themes. *Arizona Feud* depicts the struggle of two brothers to defend their water rights in the war-torn Pleasant Valley. *Guns in High Summer* describes a conflict between two ranchers, which is given added complexity by being an Anglo-Mexican confrontation. Interestingly, Nickson has the Mexican emerge victorious, and he and the other Hispanic characters are sympathetically presented.

The Matt Winstan books, together with those Nickson wrote as Arthur Hodson and Roy Peters, contain the best of his work. All are noted for their sharp, neatly balanced prose style and action which is swift and well sustained. His heroes and heroines with their slightly tarnished reputations are utterly convincing, and they and the secondary characters are among their author's strengths. If "Winstan" can be said to have a weakness, it is perhaps in his seeming inability to create and sustain a single dominating villain to balance the figure of his hero. In most of his novels the focus shifts continually from one adversary to the next, an aspect in keeping with the rapid action of the stories themselves. This, though, is a minor point, and on occasion Winstan overcomes it completely.

Many of Nickson's works as Winstan feature the gunfighting rancher Reuben Brown, and the desert community of Henderson City. In such novels as *No Branding Fire*, *Bandit Trail*, *Guns at Salt Flats*, and *Trail to Boot Hill*, the author follows him in exciting adventures to track down rustlers or bank robbers, often in the company of ably realized secondary characters. The stories are lively and interesting, and Winstan achieves a genuine little universe in Henderson and its inhabitants. On the other hand, Reuben himself is a touch too perfect, and his life with his wife Ruth rather too cosy for actuality.

Better, and more typical, is *Gunslick Marshal*. Its anti-hero, the cynical marshal Womack, becomes involved in a deal by a crooked syndicate to secure farming land in readiness for the coming of the railroad. Torn by his love for a saloon girl and friendship for one of the threatened farmers, Womack discovers a conscience and takes on the syndicate to win through in the end. The result is a first-rate Western, with fast action and striking dialogue, and strong central characters. Womack and his girl, who hold the book together, are characters encountered in many Winstan novels, the hard unidealistic hero, and the heroine "no better than she should be."

Silvercrop (as Arthur Hodson) follows the same pattern. Neil Ramer, young gambler and gunman, finds himself elected marshal of a mining town, in alliance with the saloon owner heroine, Lil Shanus. Ramer tames the local badmen, sides with miners against a crooked boss, and rescues Lil from the mine when it collapses at last, the two of them leaving to start a new life together. The personalities of Neil and Lil, and the continuous spate of action, give vital force to the book, and hold the interest throughout.

Nickson reaches a peak as Roy Peters, with a series of slight but excellent novels. The curt, uncluttered style nears perfection here, and storylines and characters are among his best. Peters's heroes, though tough, are often rendered human by their vulnerability. Steve Marshal, in *Rail War*, is a good example—unhandy with a gun, scared at times, and easily seduced by the saloon girl heroine. *Rail War* also contains fine action scenes, notably a cattle stampede and a showdown gunfight in Dodge City. *Shootup in Cleaver Valley* has buried gold, a crooked marshal, and a tough mining engineer for a hero. *Silver Stampede* describes the struggle between the heir to a fortune and two killers who want him dead. Peters's plots are ingenious, not least in *Cattle Doctor* where a medical student saves a diseased herd and tames a lawless cattle town. Best of all, perhaps, are *Alias Sam Smith* and *Vigilante Justice*, where Peters combines his familiar strengths with two powerful villains. The former, a story of a robber's return from the past and the hunt for his buried loot, puts a middle-aged sheriff against the demented killer Wilson in a balance of strong credible characters. In *Vigilante Justice* young Sven Olsen is caught between love and duty in a struggle over desert water rights. Stevens, the crooked ranch foreman, provides him with a powerful opponent who shares centre stage throughout. Though Sven wins in the end, his defeat in a fist-fight earlier on gives the story added authenticity.

Nickson is a skilled and individual writer. In his novels, especially as Roy Peters, where characters are shown acting from a mixture of motives—not all of them laudable—he creates good examples of western fiction unlike those of anyone else.

—Jeff Sadler

NIVEN, Frederick (John). British. Born in Valparaiso, Chile, 31 March 1878; moved to Scotland, 1883. Educated at Hutchesons Grammar School, Glasgow; Glasgow School of Art. Served in the Ministry of Food and the Ministry of Information during World War I. Married Pauline Thorne-Quelch in 1911. Worked in the cloth business briefly, then a librarian in Glasgow and Edinburgh; worked in construction camps in western Canada; journalist: worked for the Glasgow *Weekly Herald*, papers in Edinburgh and Dundee, and reviewer for *Observer*, *Pall Mall Gazette*, and *Bookman*, all London; after 1920 lived in Nelson and Vancouver, British Columbia. *Died 30 January 1944.*

Western Publications

Novels

The Lost Cabin Mine. London, Lane, 1908; New York, Lane, 1909.
Cinderella of Skookum Creek. London, Nash, 1916.
The Lady of the Crossing: A Novel of the New West. London, Hodder and Stoughton, and New York, Doran, 1919.
The Wolfer. New York, Dodd Mead, 1923.
Treasure Trail. New York, Dodd Mead, 1923.
Queer Fellows. London, Lane, 1927; as *Wild Honey*, New York, Dodd Mead, 1927.
Trilogy:
The Flying Years. London, Collins, 1935.
Mine Inheritance. London, Collins, and New York, Macmillan, 1940.
The Transplanted. London, Collins, 1944.

Short Stories

Sage-Brush Stories. London, Nash, 1917.

Uncollected Short Stories

"Sheriff 'Baby,'" in *Western Story* (New York), 8 July 1922.
"The Queer Place," in *Western Story* (New York), 16 February 1924.
"Five Cents Change," in *Western Story* (New York), 3 May 1924.
"Expiation," in *Argosy* (New York), 15 March 1930.

Other Publications

Novels

The Island Providence. London, Lane, 1910.
A Wilderness of Monkeys. London, Secker, and New York, Lane, 1911.
Dead Men's Bells. London, Secker, 1912.
Hands Up! London, Secker, and New York, Lane, 1913.
Ellen Adair. London, Nash, 1913; New York, Boni and Liveright, 1925.
The Porcelain Lady. London, Secker, 1913.
Justice of the Peace. London, Nash, 1914; New York, Boni and Liveright, 1923.
The S.S. Glory. London, Heinemann, 1915; New York, Doran, 1916.
Two Generations. London, Nash, 1916.
Penny Scot's Treasure. London, Collins, 1918.
A Tale That Is Told. London, Collins, and New York, Doran, 1920.
The Three Marys. London, Collins, 1930.
The Paisley Shawl. London, Collins, and New York, Dodd Mead, 1931.
The Rich Wife. London, Collins, 1932.
Mrs. Barry. London, Collins, and New York, Dutton, 1933.
Triumph. London, Collins, and New York, Dutton, 1934.
Old Soldier. London, Collins, 1936.
The Staff at Simson's. London, Collins, 1937.
The Story of Their Days. London, Collins, 1939.
Brothers in Arms, Being the Account Written by James Niven . . . of Glasgow, in the 18th Century. . . . London, Collins, 1942.
Under Which King. London, Collins, 1943.

Short Stories

Above Your Heads. London, Secker, 1911.

Verse

Maple-Leaf Songs. London, Sidgwick and Jackson, 1917.
A Lover of the Land and Other Poems. New York, Boni and Liveright, 1925.

Other

Go North, Where the World Is Young (on Alaska and the Yukon). Privately printed, n.d.
The Story of Alexander Selkirk. London, Wells Gardner, 1929.
Canada West. London, Dent, 1930.
Colour in the Canadian Rockies, with Walter J. Phillips. Toronto, Nelson, 1937.
Coloured Spectacles. London, Collins, 1938.

* * *

Frederick Niven was born in Chile but educated in Scotland. His life was marked by a good deal of wandering, but his affection for Scotland and Canada was such that he became known as a Scots-Canadian novelist. He was best-known for his novels, but he also wrote poetry, a guide book to Canada for would-be emigrants, as well as travel articles for magazines. He was also one of the talented team of writers doing war work with John Buchan at the Ministry of Information during World War I.

Niven's earlier works can be considered Westerns of the Canadian variety. His youthful wanderings in North America, where he worked in lumber and railway construction camps, are reflected in books such as *The Lost Cabin Mine* which was, by the standards of the day, a real Western. *The S.S. Glory* gives a good picture of the rough and crude life of transatlantic itinerant workers. This type of person is well represented in Niven's work. *Queer Fellows* is one of many "tramp" novels fashionable in the 1920's. This book does, however, give a good picture of labourers in remote parts of British Columbia.

In many ways Niven's later work did not match up to the promise he showed as a western writer in *The Lost Cabin Mine*. The bloodstained combat, the mysterious Apache Kid, and the exciting action in this book were overtaken by Niven's more literary aspirations. Niven's great knowledge of Canada gave his writing a solid factual background, apparent in such books as *Treasure Trail* and *The Wolfer*, which concern prospecting for gold in the far West and trying to hold on to it in the face of crooks. But Niven became less interested in contemporary Canadian Westerns and devoted himself to writing in a sentimental vein. He worked in archives about Scots-Canadian history and produced historical novels such as *The Flying Years* and *The Transplanted*. By the 1930's Niven had quite a high reputation in Britain, being considered by Hugh Walpole (to whom he was compared) one of the finest novelists. Scottish themes, as well as Canadian themes, became more important in the late part of Niven's career. The historical novels such as *Under Which King* (Scotland 1745) and *Mine Inheritance* (Scots-Canadian) were better received by critics than the other Scottish books; *The Paisley Shawl* and *Mrs. Barry* were considered very sentimental and the latter very unsophisticated.

The lack of really convincing plots and action in Niven's books was, to some extent, made up for by his style. He was praised for his fitting descriptions of Canadian scenery but especially for the clean economy of words on which much of his literary reputation rested.

—P.R. Meldrum

NOLAN, Chuck. *See* **EDSON, J. T.**

NORRIS, (Benjamin) Frank(lin, Jr.). American. Born in Chicago, Illinois, 5 March 1870; moved with his family to San Francisco, 1884. Educated at Belmont Academy, California, 1885–87; Boys' High School, San Francisco; studied art at Atelier Julien, Paris, 1887–89; attended University of California, Berkeley, 1890–94, and Harvard University, Cambridge, Massachusetts, 1894–95. Married Jeannette Black in 1900; one daughter. War correspondent for San Francisco *Chronicle* in South Africa during the Uitlander insurrection, 1895–96; editorial staff member, San Francisco *Wave*, 1896–97; Spanish-American War correspondent in Cuba for *McClure's* magazine, New York, 1898; reader for Doubleday publishers, New York, 1899–1902; moved to San Francisco, 1902. *Died 25 October 1902.*

WESTERN PUBLICATIONS

Novels

McTeague: A Story of San Francisco. New York, Doubleday, and London, Richards, 1899.
The Octopus: A Story of California. New York, Doubleday, and London, Richards, 1901.

Short Stories

A Deal in Wheat and Other Stories of the New and Old West. New York, Doubleday, and London, Richards, 1903.

OTHER PUBLICATIONS

Novels

Moran of the Lady Letty: A Story of Adventure off the California Coast. New York, Doubleday, 1898; as *Shanghaied*, London, Richards, 1899.
Blix. New York, Doubleday, 1899; London, Richards, 1900.
A Man's Woman. New York, Doubleday, and London, Richards, 1900.
The Pit: A Story of Chicago. New York, Doubleday, and London, Richards, 1903.
The Joyous Miracle. New York, Doubleday, and London, Harper, 1906.
The Third Circle. New York, and London, Lane, 1909.
Vandover and the Brute, edited by Charles G. Norris. New York, Doubleday, and London, Heinemann, 1914.

Verse

Yvernelle: A Legend of Feudal France. Philadelphia, Lippincott, 1891.

Other

The Responsibilities of the Novelist and Other Literary Essays. New York, Doubleday, and London, Richards, 1903.
(*Complete Works*) (Golden Gate Edition). New York, Doubleday, 7 vols., 1903.
The Surrender of Santiago: An Account of the Historic Surrender of Santiago to General Shafter, July 17, 1898. San Francisco, Elder, 1917.
Collected Writings. New York, Doubleday, 10 vols., 1928.
Two Poems and "Kim" Reviewed. San Francisco, Taylor, 1930.
Frank Norris of "The Wave": Stories and Sketches from the San Francisco Weekly 1893 to 1897, edited by Oscar Lewis. San Francisco, Westgate Press, 1931.
The Letters of Frank Norris, edited by Franklin Walker. San Francisco, Book Club of California, 1956; revised edition, edited by Jesse S. Crisler, San Francisco, Book Club of California, 1986.
The Literary Criticism of Frank Norris, edited by Donald Pizer. Austin, University of Texas Press, 1964.
A Novelist in the Making: A Collection of Student Themes and the Novels Blix and Vandover and the Brute, edited by James D. Hart. Cambridge, Massachusetts, Harvard University Press, 1971.

*

Bibliography: *Frank Norris: A Bibliography* by Kenneth A. Lohf and Eugene P. Sheehy, Los Gatos, California, Talisman Press, 1959; *The Merrill Checklist of Frank Norris* by John S. Hill, Columbus, Ohio, Merrill, 1970; in *Bibliography of American Literature 6* by Jacob Blanck, New Haven, Connecticut, Yale University Press, 1973; *Frank Norris: A Reference Guide* by Jesse S. Crisler and Joseph R. McElrath, Jr., Boston, Hall, 1974.

Critical Studies: *Frank Norris, 1870–1902* by Charles G. Norris, New York, Doubleday, 1914; *Frank Norris: A Biography* by Franklin Walker, New York, Doubleday, 1932; *Frank Norris: A Study* by Eugene Marchard, Stanford, California, Stanford University Press, 1942; *Frank Norris* by Warren French, New York, Twayne, 1962; *The Novels of Frank Norris* by Donald Pizer, Bloomington, Indiana University Press, 1966; *Frank Norris* by Wilbur M. Frohock, Minneapolis, University of Minnesota Press, 1969; *Frank Norris: Instinct and Art* by William D. Dillingham, Lincoln, University of Nebraska Press, 1969; *The Fiction of Frank Norris: The Aesthetic Context* by Don Graham, Columbia, University of Missouri Press, 1978; *Frank Norris: The Critical Reception* edited by Joseph R. McElrath, Jr., New York, Franklin Burt, 1979; *Frank Norris: A Literary Legend* by S.N. Verma, New Delhi, Vikas, 1986.

* * *

Writing in the San Francisco *Wave* in 1897, Frank Norris, citing the wealth of material and opportunities available to writers in turn-of-the-century San Francisco, issued a ringing challenge to his fellow writers. "Give us stories now," he urged, "give us men, strong, brutal men, with red-hot blood in 'em, with unleashed passions rampant in 'em, blood and bones and viscera in 'em, and women, too, that move and have their being, people that love and hate . . . It's the life we want, the vigorous, real thing . . . We don't want literature, we want life." The passage might well stand as Norris's artistic credo, for to a great extent his own fiction would answer the challenge.

Only two years later, Norris published *McTeague*, the first of his works to make serious use of authentic western characters and locale. Written in large part while Norris was a creative writing student at Harvard, and finished in 1897 during a stay at the Big Dipper Mine in Colfax, California, *McTeague* is a powerful story of the atavistic decline of a Polk Street dentist whose finer instincts and aspirations are gradually overpowered by his suppressed brute nature. Possessed of the physical and mental characteristics of the brute, McTeague leads a harmless and contented existence until a chance meeting with the beautiful Trina Sieppe arouses his suppressed sexual instincts. In spite of the efforts of Marcus Schouler, a rival for Trina's affection, McTeague succeeds in marrying Trina, and for a time they live together happily. But again chance intervenes; Trina wins $5000 on a lottery ticket, which prompts the formerly disappointed but now envious Marcus Schouler to expose McTeague's lack of a license to practice dentistry. Deprived of his occupation, McTeague grows mean and surly, as Trina, hoarding her money, grows increasingly miserly. They enter an irreversible spiral into poverty and degradation, a decline motivated and accelerated by greed. Eventually, McTeague steals Trina's money and brutally murders her. Fleeing, he takes a job at the Big Dipper Mine, working there contentedly until a "sixth sense" warns him of the proximity of his pursuers. He then attempts to cross Death Valley, where Schouler, now a deputy, apprehends him. McTeague kills Schouler, only to discover that in the struggle Schouler has managed to handcuff their wrists together, dooming McTeague to die of thirst, locked to the body of his mortal enemy. Despite the melodramatic frame of pursuit and capture in the desert, the Death Valley sequence is authentically rendered and thematically consistent, the bleached and arid western landscape an apt backdrop for man's primitive struggle for survival. A masterpiece of naturalism, rich in symbol and significant detail, *McTeague* cuts through the outer surfaces of "civilization" and penetrates to the heart of "life," revealing man's nature at its most instinctive, fundamental level.

The open space and sheer magnitude of the western landscapes likewise provide an epic backdrop for the conflict of titantic forces in *The Octupus*, the first work in an unfinished trilogy which Norris intended to devote to the raising, marketing, and worldwide distribution of wheat. Convinced that "the big American novel is going to come out of the West," Norris set the narrative in the San Joaquin Valley. The main storyline traces the decline of Magnus Derrick, the master of the Los Muertos ranch, whose economic struggle with S. Behrman and the Pacific and Southwestern Railroad ends in moral and financial bankruptcy. Contributing to the grand scope of the novel are several subplots: the tragic love story of Annixter, a rancher, and milkmaid Hilma Tree; the mystical romance between Vanamee, a shepherd, and the spirit of his dead sweetheart Angèle; the metamorphosis of Dyke from loyal railroad man to political extremist and outlaw; the aesthetic and social education of Presley, whose classicism hardens to socialism, whose projected Homeric epic of the West turns out to be a misunderstood propaganda document. All of these subplots merge in one elemental, impersonal conflict between the Life Force, symbolized by the wheat, "indifferent, gigantic, resistless," and the Machine, symbolized by the railroad, a "soulless force," a "leviathan with tentacles of steel." In the climactic confrontation between ranchers and railroad men at the irrigation ditch, an incident based on the actual Mussel Slough affair of 1880, the railroad appears to triumph. Yet the wheat remains, symbolic of the earth's fecundity, evidence that in the "larger view," "all things surely, inevitably, resistlessly work together for good." Clouded by Norris's metaphysical inconsistency, flawed by its vacillation between mechanistic determinism and mystical theism, *The Octopus* is nonetheless Norris's most ambitious and impressive achievement.

A number of tales in *A Deal in Wheat and Other Stories*, published in 1903, make use of western material, but few are satisfying. "The Wife of Chino" and "A Bargain with Peg-Leg" exploit the atmosphere of mining camps. "The Passing of Cock-Eye Blacklock" is of interest because of its introduction of Bunt McBride, an old cowboy and "one of a fast-disappearing type" who had seen the West pass through successive phases from nomad and hunter to herder to husbandman. McBride reappears in lesser roles in "A Memorandum of Sudden Death," a cavalry and Indian story, and "Two Hearts That Beat As One," a sea story set off the coast of Guatemala. Overall, however, Norris's efforts in *A Deal in Wheat and Other Stories* are thinly developed and anecdotal. Dead of peritonitis at the age of 33, Norris was never to equal his early achievements in *McTeague* and *The Octopus*.

—Daryl Jones

NORTH, Colin. *See* **BINGLEY, David Ernest.**

NORWOOD, V(ictor) G(eorge) C(harles). Also wrote as Coy Banton; Shane V. Baxter; Jim Bowie; Clay Brand; Walt Cody; Shane Colter; Wes Corteen; Clint Dangerfield; Johnny Dark; Vince Destry; Doone Fargo; Wade Fisher; G. Gearing-Thomas; Mark Hampton; Hank Janson; Nat Karta; Whip McCord; Brett Rand; Brad Regan; Shane Russell; Mark Shane; Rhondo Shane; Dillon Strange; Jim Tressidy; Paul Tyrone; Portman Willard. British. Born in Scunthorpe, Lincolnshire, 21 March 1920. Left school at age of 14; later studied by correspondence course to obtain diploma from Bennett's College, Sheffield. Served in the British Merchant Marine, 1939–44, anti-aircraft gunner with Atlantic and Malta convoys, three times mined or torpedoed, wounded 17 times; Special Marine War Medal and Bar, four campaign stars (Italy, Africa, Pacific, and Atlantic.) Married Elizabeth McKie in 1947; two sons. Worked as a bank guard, heavyweight boxer and wrestler, singer, head croupier in gambling establishment, gold and diamond prospector, and private detective. *Died in 1983.*

WESTERN PUBLICATIONS

Novels

Gun Trail to Glory. London, Barker, 1954.
The Hellbender. London, Hale, 1963; as *Rails to Thunderhead*, New York, Arcadia House, 1965.
Ranger Gun Law (as Wade Fisher). London, Hale, 1963.
Hard Hombre (as Jim Tressidy). London, Hale, 1964.
Lawman's Code. London, Hale, 1965.

Crossfire (as Clint Dangerfield). London, Hale, 1965.
Journey of Fear. London, Hale, 1965.
Boothill for Bad Men. London, Hale, 1965.
Killer's Gold. London, Barker, 1966.
Reap the Wild Wind (as Walt Cody). London, Hale, 1966.
Gunsmoke Justice. London, Hale, 1966.
Shadow of a Gunhawk (as Shane V. Baxter). London, Hale, 1966.
Blood on the Sage (as Coy Banton). London, Hale, 1966.
Gunsmoke Justice (as Coy Banton). London, Hale, 1966.
Death Valley (as Doone Fargo). London, Hale, 1966.
Killer's Code (as Doone Fargo). London, Hale, 1966.
Hellfire Range (as Whip McCord). London, Hale, 1966.
Gun Chore (as Wes Corteen). London, Hale, 1966.
Halfway to Hell (as Shayne Colter). London, Hale, 1966.
Code of the Lawless (as Brett Rand). London, Hale, 1967.
The Gun Hellion (as Rhondo Shane). London, Hale, 1967.
The Texan (as Shane V. Baxter). London, Hale, 1967; New York, Lenox Hill, 1974.
Black Day at Eagle Rock (as Walt Cody). London, Hale, 1968.
Hell Town. London, Hale, 1970.

Novels as Jim Bowie

Buffaloed. London, Scion, 1951.
Powdersmoke. London, Scion, 1951.
Apache Kid. London, Scion, 1951.
Gunshot Grief. London, Scion, 1951.
Pay Dirt. London, Scion, 1951.
Dakota Badlands. London, Scion, 1951.
Gun Flash! London, Scion, 1951.
The Drifter. London, Scion, 1951.
Colt Country. London, Scion, 1952.
Raw Deal. London, Scion, 1952.
Scarred Leather. London, Scion, 1952.
Red Hellions. London, Scion, 1952.
Five-Point Law. London, Scion, 1952.
Trigger Music. London, Scion, 1952.
Renegade Ranger. London, Scion, 1952.
Showdown in Lead. London, Scion, 1953.
Boothill Trail. London, Milestone, 1954.

Novels as Mark Shane

Crossfire. London, Barker, 1953.
Chango. London, Barker, 1955.
Vengeance Valley. London, Barker, 1955; as V.G.C. Norwood, 1966.

Novels as Shane Russell

The Bounty Trail. London, Hale, 1963.
Gun Trail and Boot Hill. London, Hale, 1963.
Gun Trail to Boot Hill. London, Hale, 1964.
The Lobo Breed. London, Hale, 1965.

Novels as Clay Brand

Colt Courage. London, Hale, 1965.
Powdersmoke. London, Hale, 1966.
Lattimer's Last Ride. London, Hale, 1967.

Novels as Vince Destry

Trail's End. London, Hale, 1965.
The Glory Trail. London, Hale, 1967.
A Badge and a Gun. London, Hale, 1970; New York, Lenox Hill, 1975.

OTHER PUBLICATIONS

Novels

The Caves of Death. London, Scion, 1951.
The Untamed. London, Scion, 1951.
The Skull of Kanaima. London, Scion, 1951.
Temple of the Dead. London, Scion, 1951.
Island of Creeping Death. London, Scion, 1952.
Brother Rat (as Nat Karta). London, Scion, 1952.
Raw Deal for Dames (as Brad Regan). London, Gannet, 1952.
Killer Take All (as Mark Hampton). London, Barker, 1953.
Drums Along the Amazon. London, Scion, 1953.
Cry of the Beast. London, Scion, 1953.
Hell's Wenches. London, Hale, 1963.
The Long Way Home. London, Hale, 1967.
Valley of the Damned. London, Hale, 1968.
The Loser. N.p., Greenleaf Classics, 1974.
Black Orchids for Ophelia. N.p., Greenleaf Classics, 1974.
The Flame and the Flesh. N.p., Greenleaf Classics, 1974.
River of the Damned. London, Dobson, 1975.
The Terror. London, Dobson, 1975.
The Alien. London, Dobson, 1975.
The Primitives. London, Futura, 1975.
The Professional. London, Barker, 1976.
The Dark Star. London, Millington, 1976.
Venom. N.p., Carmody Press, 1980.

Novels as Hank Janson

Kill for Kicks. London, Moring, 1958.
Don't Scare Easy. London, Moring, n.d.
Murder Magnifique. London, Moring, n.d.
Willpower. London, Moring, n.d.
Drop Dead, Sucker! London, Moring, 1960.
Sensuality. London, Roberts and Vinter, 1963.
Top Ten. London, Roberts and Vinter, n.d.
Playgirl. London, Roberts and Vinter, n.d.
Raw Deal. London, Roberts and Vinter, n.d.
Blood Bath. London, Roberts and Vinter, n.d.
Go With a Jerk. London, Roberts and Vinter, 1965.

Novels as Mark Shane

The Lady Bites the Dust. London, Comyns, 1952.
Borrowed Time. London, Comyns, 1953.
Death at Her Fingers. London, Comyns, 1953.
Honey Ain't So Sweet. London, Comyns, 1953.
Hail and Farewell. London, Comyns, 1953.
Obsession to Kill. London, Comyns, 1953.
They Kill to Live. London, Comyns, 1953.
Borrowed Time. London, Morirz, 1955.

Novels as Johnny Dark

Snake Walk. London, Milestone, 1951.
Dame on the Lam. London, Milestone, 1952.
Fig Leaves for a Lady. London, Milestone, 1953.
Venom. London, Milestone, 1953.

Other

Man Alone. Adventures in the Jungles of British Guiana and Brazil. London, Boardman, 1956.
A Handful of Diamonds. London, Boardman, 1960.
Jungle Life in Guiana. London, Hale, 1964.
The Long Haul. London, Hale, 1967.
Australian Adventure. London, Joseph, 1975.

Jungle Treasure. London, Angus and Robertson, 1975.
Campfire Tales. London, Millington, 1976.
Biography of an Adventurer. London, Millington, 1976.
The Opal "Gougers". Hong Kong, Horwitz, 1977.
Wandering Star. N.p., Farnal, 1977.
Along the Barrier Reef. N.p., Packard, 1978.
The Catacombs of Old Mexico. Norway, Folke Forlaget, 1978.
The Green Stones of Burma. Sweden, Wlimenesson Boker, 1979.
The Sapphire Seekers. Hong Kong, Horwitz, 1979.
A Lifetime of Cheating Death. London, Thomson, 1980.
Miracles of Cardiac Surgery. N.p., Jameson Press, 1980.
Across Australia by Volkswagen. N.p., Quadrant, 1980.

* * *

Like many Westerns produced in the early 1960's, V.G.C. Norwood's works provide his readers with a myriad of standard themes—ranch wars, cattle rustling, and the contest between two fast guns all appear in his books. Norwood himself would have been the first to admit the commercial basis of his work, and at one time produced a book every month for Robert Hale of London, until illness forced him to slow down. He was a much traveled man, and his insight into many different aspects of life has been used to broaden the spectrum of what would normally be considered routine western novels.

Using a plethora of pseudonyms, Norwood wrote over 150 books, many of which were Westerns. As Shane Russell (using his sons' Christian names) he wrote *The Bounty Trail* in 1963. This story has ex-lawman Jode Silver brought out of retirement when Cort Ringo's bunch hit the Big Bend Country. The theme is familiar, but Norwood's treatment of the central character is far better than one would expect. Silver is a stubborn man, who bears a grudge against a world which had treated him badly. He has given up his job for love, but his beloved dies before he can find happiness. When Ringo retaliates at Silver's interference in grouping together the ranchers against him, he dynamites a dam that floods the valley in which Silver's ranch lies. The explosion kills a young man with whom the law officer has formed a friendship, and a dual determination to bring in Ringo and to use the reward money to rebuild his ranch sets Jode Silver on a merciless trail.

Gun Trail to Boot Hill is a study of vengeance seen through the eyes of a young man. Lassiter cares for his sick mother, while his father heads a gang of hellions. When the gang arrives at the Lassiter home, the father has been wounded, a posse traps them, and all are finally captured. Lassiter witnesses his father's hanging, and his mother suffers a fatal heart attack. Imprisonment for four years in Yuma sours Lassiter's outlook on life, and he vows revenge on the gang member who turned informer. Norwood shows skill in creating believable characters in a plausible plot, and even though at times the subject is a familiar one, he does bring a certain twist to events which creates a freshness in the story. Given the fact that he wrote his books within three weeks, this is something of an achievement.

His novels contain some unusual perceptions of character, such as Chard Jardine in *Killer's Code*. The story itself is simple: Jardine is a seasoned killer, lone and remorseless, and after blinding a town marshal he finds himself on the run. In a meeting with an old timer, the man sums up Jardine's character: "Kind of leaves a sour taste, don't it, gunslinger . . . You're just a no account gunslinger, always hankerin' for trouble. So far you've been lucky, but someday you'll come up agin some jasper as'll cut you down to size." To which Jardine replies, "Ain't nobody lives forever. Likely there's a bullet with my name on it. A man gets side-tracked early, shooting comes easy, and life's exciting." All this builds up to a showdown with Billy Bonney—a killer more violent than Jardine.

Norwood's central male characters are stereotyped hero, figures, but this said, they do exude a certain quality of humanity in their make-up. They are always reaching for that certain "something" which always lies beyond the next mountain or across the prairie. Silver in *Bounty Trail* desires only peace, but is rudely brought out of retirement to a fight that he doesn't want. Jardine, in *Killer's Code* leans towards megalomania, needing the glory of killing to assure himself of his own existence. Norwood's "heroes" are always striving to justify themselves.

He continues this theme in *Boothill for Bad Men* with the character of Rhondo Kane. He is a typical loner—hard, bitter, and fearless, given to broody introspection, sombrely dressed, and lightning-fast with his handgun. This drifter hires out his guns to a land grabber, but when he learns the true situation he sides with the valley settlers. There are the usual confrontations between fast guns and tough men in this tale, but it is told at a good pace. The narrative is fine, but there is nothing new to be learned here.

Norwood's works are never heavy reading; they are adventure stories, and are told as such. They can be exciting whether they are set in the desert, prairies, mountains or towns. When you pick up any of his books you instantly know that you are entering a mythical world of hold-ups, bad men, range wars, marauding Indians, and larger-than-life characters. Obviously some of his plots become repetitive and somewhat contrived, but he wasn't writing artistic books. His style was relevant to the time and type of stories he was telling and in that, he cannot be faulted.

—Mike Stotter

NYE, Nelson (Coral). Also writes as Clem Colt; Drake C. Denver; Montague Rockingham. American. Born in Chicago, Illinois, 28 September 1907. Educated at schools in Ohio and Massachusetts, and at Cincinnati Art Academy. Served in the United States Army Field Artillery during World War II. Married Ruth Hilton in 1937; one daughter. Publicity writer and reviewer for Buffalo and Cincinnati newspapers; ranch hand in California and Texas; rancher and breeder of quarter horses in Arizona, 1935–60; since 1935 freelance writer: horse editor, *Texas Live Stock Journal*, San Antonio, Texas, for 4 years; book editor, *Hoofs and Horns*, Tucson, for 21 years; frontier fiction reviewer, *New York Times Book Review*, 1958–62; horse consultant, *World Book Encyclopedia*, for 15 years. Founding member, 1953, and president, 1953 and 1960–61, Western Writers of America. Recipient: Western Writers of America Spur Award, 1954, 1959; Golden Saddleman award, 1968; Quarter Horse Owners of America award, 1972. Agent: Ann Elmo, 60 East 42nd Street, New York, New York 10165. Address: 2290 West Ironwood Ridge Drive, Tucson, Arizona 85745, U.S.A.

WESTERN PUBLICATIONS

Novels (series: Wild Horse Shorty)

Two-Fisted Cowpoke. New York, Greenberg, 1936; London, Nicholson and Watson, 1937; as *The No-Gun Fighter*, New York, Ace, 1956.

The Killer of Cibecue. New York, Greenberg, 1936; as *The Sheriff of Navajo County*, London, Nicholson and Watson, 1937; as *Trouble on the Tonto Rim*, New York, Avon, 1961.
The Leather Slapper. New York, Greenberg, and London, Nicholson and Watson, 1937.
Quick-Fire Hombre. New York, Greenberg, and London, Nicholson and Watson, 1937; as *Gunfighter Brand*, New York, Berkley, 1958.
The Star-Packers. New York, Greenberg, 1937; as Drake C. Denver, London, Wright and Brown, 1938.
The Waddy from Roarin' Fork. London, Nicholson and Watson, 1938; as *Fiddle-Back Ranch* (as Clem Colt), New York, Phoenix Press, 1944; as *Tornado on Horseback*, New York, Ace, 1955; as *Feud at Single Cinch*, London, Hale, 1984.
G Stands for Gun. New York, Greenberg, and London, Nicholson and Watson, 1938.
Prairie Dust. London, Nicholson and Watson, 1938.
The Bandit of Bloody Run. New York, Phoenix Press, 1939.
Smoke-Wagon Kid. London, Nicholson and Watson 1939; as Clem Colt, New York, Phoenix Press, 1943.
Pistols for Hire. New York, Macmillan, 1941; London, Foulsham, 1942; as *The Bullet for Billy the Kid*, New York, Avon, 1950.
Gunfighter Breed. New York, Macmillan, 1942; London, Foulsham, 1944.
Salt River Ranny. New York, Macmillan, 1942; as *Gunshot Trail*, New York, Berkley, 1955.
Come A-Smokin'. London, Wright and Brown, 1943; New York, Dodd Mead, 1953.
Beneath the Belt. London, Wright and Brown, 1943.
Renegade Cowboy. New York, Phoenix, 1944.
Gunslick Mountain. London, Foulsham, 1944; as Clem Colt, New York, Arcadia House, 1945.
Wild Horse Shorty. New York, Macmillan, and London, Foulsham, 1944.
Cartridge-Case Law. New York, Macmillan, 1944; London, Quality Press, 1947.
Blood of Kings (Shorty). New York, Macmillan, 1946; London, Quality Press, 1947.
The Barber of Tubac. New York, Macmillan, 1947; London, Instructive Arts, 1951; as *The Gun-Wolf of Tubac*, New York, Avon, 1949; as *Arizona Dead-Shot*, Avon, 1957; as *The Gun Wolf*, New York, Zebra, 1980.
Gunman, Gunman. Golden, Colorado, Sage, 1949; as Long Rope (as Drake C. Denver), London, Wright and Brown, 1949; as *Plunder Valley*, New York, Ace, 1952.
Riders by Night. New York, Dodd Mead, 1950; as *Rustlers of K.C. Ranch*, London, Partridge, 1950.
Caliban's Colt. New York, Dodd Mead, 1950; London, Wright and Brown, 1953.
Horses Is Fine People. London, Coker,1950.
Thief River. New York, Dodd Mead, 1951; London, Wright and Brown, 1952.
Born to Trouble. New York, Dodd Mead, 1951; London, Wright and Brown, 1953.
Wide Loop. New York, Dodd Mead, 1952; as *The Crazy K*, London, Ward Lock, 1953.
Desert of the Damned. New York, Dodd Mead, 1952; London, Wright and Brown, 1954.
Hired Hand. New York, Dodd Mead, and London, Ward Lock, 1954.
The Red Sombrero. New York, Dodd Mead, 1954; London, Miller, 1959.
The Lonely Grass. New York, Dodd Mead, 1955; as Clem Colt, London, Mills and Boon, 1955.
The Parson of Gunbarrel Basin. New York, Dodd Mead, and London, Mills and Boon, 1955.
Blood Sky. London, Mills and Boon, 1956; as *Horses, Women, and Guns*, New York, Hillman, 1959; as *Arizona Renegade*, New York, Lancer, 1969
Bandido. New York, New American Library, 1957; as *Boss Gun*, New York, Lancer 1969.
South Fork. London, Mills and Boon, 1957; as *Maverick Marshal*, New York, New American Library, 1958.
The Overlanders. New York, New American Library, 1959.
Long Run. New York, Macmillan, 1959; as *River of Horns*, London, Mills and Boon, 1960.
Ride the Wild Plains. London, Mills and Boon, 1959; as *The Last Bullet*, New York, Hillman, 1960; Bath, Chivers, 1983; as *Loco*, New York, Lancer, 1969.
The Wolf That Rode. New York, Macmillan, 1960; as *Johnny Get Your Gun*, London, Muller, 1960.
Gunfight at the OK Corral (novelization of screenplay). New York, Hillman, 1960; London, Hale, 1985.
Not Grass Alone. New York, Macmillan, 1961; London, Collins, 1962.
The Irreverent Scout. London, Mills and Boon, 1961; Fresno, California, Vega, 1964; as *Frontier Scout*, New York, Belmont, 1982.
Rafe. New York, Ace, 1962; as *Man on the Skewbald Mare*, Ace, 1962.
Hideout Mountain. New York, Ace, 1962.
Death Comes Riding. London, Collins, 1962; as *The Seven Six-Gunners*, New York, Ace, 1963.
Death Valley Slim, The Kid from Lincoln County. New York, Ace, and London, Collins, 1963.
Bancroft's Banco. New York, Ace, 1963; as *Wild River*, London, Collins, 1963.
Treasure Trail from Tucson. New York, Ace, 1964; Bath, Chivers, 1987; as *Weeping Widow Mine*, London, Collins, 1964.
Sudden Country. New York, Ace, 1964; London, Hale, 1979.
Gun Feud at Tiedown, Rogue's Rendezvous. New York, Ace, 1964; *Gun Fued at Tiedown* published separately, London, Hale, 1983.
Ambush at Yuma's Chimney. New York, Ace, 1965; London, Hale, 1978.
The Bravo Brand. London, Collins, 1965.
The Marshal of Pioche. New York, Ace, 1966; London, Hale, 1983.
Iron Hand. New York, Ace, 1966.
Single Action. New York, Ace, 1967; London, Hale, 1983.
The Trail of Lost Skulls. New York, Ace, 1967.
Rider on the Roan. New York, Ace, 1967.
A Lost Mine Named Salvation. New York, Ace, 1968; London, Hale, 1983.
The Trouble at Peña Blanca. New York, Avon, 1968; London, Hale, 1983.
Wolftrap. New York, Ace, 1969; London, Hale, 1983.
Gringo. New York, Ace, 1969.
The Texas Gun. New York, Ace, 1970; London, Jenkins, 1976.
Trouble at Quinn's Crossing. New York, Ace, 1971; London, Severn House, 1978.
Hellbound for Ballarat. New York, Ace, 1971; London, Hale, 1984.
Kelly. New York, Dell, 1971; Bath, Chivers, 1983; as *The Palominas Pistolero*, London, Hale, 1980.
The Clifton Contract. New York, Ace, 1972; London, Severn House, 1978.
Horse Thieves. New York, Evans, 1987; Bath, Chivers, 1988.

Deadly Companions. New York, Walker, 1987; London, Hale, 1988.
Mule Man. New York, Doubleday, 1988.
No Place to Hide. Toronto and New York, Paperjacks, 1988; London, Hale, 1989.
The Lost Padre. New York, Jove, 1988.
The Fight at Four Corners. New York, Jove, 1992.

Novels as Clem Colt (series: Pony George).

Gun-Smoke (Pony Goerge). New York, Greenberg, 1938; as Nelson Nye, London, Nicholson and Watson, 1938.
The Shootin' Sheriff. (Pony George). New York, Phoenix Press, 1938; London, Nicholson and Watson, 1939.
The Bar Nothing Brand. New York, Phoenix Press, 1939; as *No Wire Range* (as Drake C. Denver), London, Wright and Brown, 1939.
Center-Fire Smith. New York, Phoenix Press, 1939; London, Wright and Brown, 1940.
Hair-Trigger Realm. New York, Phoenix Press, 1940; London, Wright and Brown, 1941.
Trigger-Finger Law. New York, Phoenix Press, 1940; Bath, Chivers, 1989.
The Five Diamond Brand. New York, Greenberg, 1941; London, Wright and Brown, 1942.
Triggers for Six. New York, Phoenix Press, 1941; London, Wright and Brown, 1943.
The Sure-Fire Kid. New York, Phoenix Press, 1942; London, Wright and Brown, 1943.
Trigger Talk. New York, Phoenix Press, 1942; London, Wright and Brown, 1944.
Rustlers' Roost. New York, Phoenix Press, 1943; London, Wright and Brown, 1944; as *The Texas Tornado* (as Nelson Nye), New York, Ace, 1955.
Guns of Horse Prairie. New York, Phoenix Press, 1943; London, Wright and Brown, 1944.
Maverick Canyon. New York, Phoenix Press, 1944.
Once in the Saddle. New York, Arcadia House, 1946; as *The One-Shot Kid* (as Nelson Nye), New York, Ace, 1954; London, Jenkins, 1976; as *Gun-Hunt for the Sundance Kid* (as Nelson Nye), New York, Belmont, 1962.
Coyote Song. New York, Curl, 1947; as Nelson Nye, London, Quality Press, 1949; as *Ranger's Revenge* (as Nelson Nye), New York, Berkley, 1956.
Saddle Bow Slim. New York, Phoenix Press, 1948; Bath, Chivers, 1986.
Tough Company. New York, Dodd Mead, 1952; London, Wright and Brown, 1953.
Strawberry Roan. New York, Dodd Mead, and London, Ward Lock, 1953; as Nelson Nye, South Yarmouth, Massachusetts, Curley, 1982.
No Tomorrow. London, Mills and Boon, 1953.
Smoke Talk. New York, Dodd Mead, 1954; as Nelson Nye, London, Mills and Boon, 1954; as *Six-Gun Buckaroo*, New York, Popular Library, 1954.
Quick Trigger Country. New York, Dodd Mead, 1955; as Nelson Nye, London, Mills and Boon, 1955.

Novels as Drake C. Denver

Turbulent Guns. London, Wright and Brown, 1940; as *The Renegade Cowboy* (as Clem Colt), New York, Phoenix Press, 1944.
The Feud at Sleepy Cat. New York, Phoenix Press, 1940; as Nelson Nye, New York, Dorchester, 1979.
Tinbadge. New York, Phoenix Press, 1941; London, Wright and Brown, 1942; as *Shotgun Law* (as Nelson Nye), New York, Belmont, 1967.
Wildcats of Tonto Basin. New York, Phoenix Press, 1941; London, Wright and Brown, 1943.
Gun Quick. New York, Phoenix Press, 1942; London, Wright and Brown, 1943.
The Desert Desperadoes. New York, Phoenix Press, 1942.
Lost Water. London, Wright and Brown, 1942.
Breed of the Chaparral. New York, McBride, 1946; as Clem Colt, London, Quality Press, 1949; as *Guns of Arizona* (as Nelson Nye), New York, Berkley, 1958; as *Ramrod Vengeance* (as Nelson Nye), New York, Lancer, 1969.

Uncollected Short Stories

"Death at Rattler's Hollow," in *Sure-Fire Western* (Springfield, Massachusetts), April 1938.
"Rock Bottom," in *Bad Men and Good*, edited by Luke Short. New York, Dodd Mead, 1953.
"Homecoming," in *Holsters and Heroes*, edited by Noel M. Loomis. New York, Macmillan, 1954.
"Caprock," in *Fall Roundup*, edited by Harry E. Maule. New York, Random House, 1955.

OTHER PUBLICATIONS

Other

Outstanding Modern Quarter Horse Sires. New York, Morrow, 1948.
Champions of the Quarter Tracks... New York, Coward McCann, 1950.
Your Western Horse: His Ways and His Rider. New York, A. S. Barnes, 1963.
The Complete Book of the Quarter Horse. New York A.S. Barnes, 1964.
Speed and the Quarter Horse: A Payload of Sprinters. Caldwell, Idaho, Caxton, 1973.
Great Moments in Quarter Racing History. New York, Arco, 1983.

Editor, *Western Roundup.* New York, Macmillan, 1961.
Editor, *They Won Their Spurs.* New York, Avon, 1962.

*

Manuscript Collections: Western History Research Center, University of Wyoming, Laramie; University of Arizona, Tucson.

Nelson Nye comments:

My prime object in writing Westerns has always been to entertain. In early days I foolishly told a reporter I wrote for money—but it did not take me a great while to realize there was no pot of gold in store for a writer in this category. Nevertheless, my books have sold more than 50,000,000 copies.

When I was with Dodd Mead I wrote blurbs and catalog copy before I had even started writing the actual books; naturally the books then had to live up to this promotion. I once wrote three books in 20 days each in order to meet a deadline. In the first three years of my book writing career I wrote six books a year. In later years I did not hit so high an average; several of my books took six months to complete. After selling my first two or three short stories I decided that book-length writers got most of the cover promotion (in the pulps), so I switched to novels. Primarily what I wrote were action (adventure) stories, fast-paced and with much suspense. Some had redeeming elements of humor of the droll, wry variety. There was no pathos: I could never write tear-jerking material. One of our younger writers recently wrote to me: "Your work greatly influenced me whan I was reading Westerns in junior high and high school. They were tough and fast moving, a real difference from Zane Grey and others."

The late Will Cuppy called me "An expert in local color" and remarked that "Nye is doing for Westerns what Dashiell Hammett did for the detective story." Leslie Ernenwein, another worker in this vineyard, said: "Stand back, men. Here's Clem Colt, the baron of blood and thunder, come barging through with a riptide tale that'll scorch your whiskers! Old Clem didn't use a typewriter for this one, he hammered it out an anvil, studding her with historical incident and corral-dust pungency."

* * *

Nelson Nye, a prolific western writer, won the Spur award in 1960 for *Long Run*. *Long Run* embodied several of Nye's favorite themes: a down-and-out former gunfighter, a powerful, rich rancher trying to control everything around him, and a beautiful spunky woman whose independence is the key to the plot.

Although Nye wrote over a hundred Westerns, he stopped writing in 1971. In a revealing interview published in the Zebra Books edition of *The Trouble at Peña Blanca*, Nye claims that after more than 30 years of writing he "just lost the bug." But when Nye was in his prime, he could write three western novels a month and in the 1960's had the same popularity as Louis L'Amour. Because his fluency brought him much money, he refused to have any of his novels made into movies.

One of Nye's best Westerns is *Kelly*, the story of gunfighter-for-hire Happenstance Kelly. Kelly is hired by a Mexican owner to protect Rancho Palominas from the gringos who want his land. Kelly is more than a match for the killers and the Spanish spitfire who seduces him, and the book—one of the last Nye wrote—provides non-stop action and entertainment. Nye's strangest Western is *The Trail of Lost Skulls*—dedicated to editor Donald Wollheim—a philosophical Western about evolution and an archeological dig for the skull of a missing link in the deserts of Arizona.

Nye also published Westerns under the pseudonyms Clem Colt and Drake C. Denver. The best of the Clem Colt Westerns is *Quick Trigger Country* where Turkey Red, an orphan, hooks up with an outlaw gang lead by Curly Bill Graham. When Graham and his gang slaughter a group of unarmed Mexicans, the Turk changes sides and finds his true identity. Another Clem Colt classic is *Smoke-Wagon Kid* where Sheriff Stone Lothrop and the Kid outgun a gang of ruthless rustlers. Also notable is *Strawberry Roan*, the story of a range war featuring one of Nye's most memorable women characters, Joyce Darling. The best of the Drake C. Denver books is *Tinbadge*. Girt Sasabe gets involved in the Mexican border dispute using his guns and wits to survive.

In addition to writing Westerns, Nye is one of the world's foremost authorities on quarter horses, writing the definitive book on the subject, as well as articles on them for encyclopedias. One of the founding members of the Western Writers of America, Nye served as its first president.

—George Kelley

O

OBETS, Bob. American. Born in Texas. Lived in Corpus Christi.

WESTERN PUBLICATIONS

Novels

Blood-Moon Range. New York, Pyramid, 1957.
Rails to the Rio. New York, Avalon, 1965; London, New English Library, 1967.

Uncollected Short Stories

"Ranger Breed," in *Zane Grey's Western* (New York), October 1953.
"Set Your Hat and Grab Your Gun," in *Blazing Guns* (Holyoke, Massachusetts), October 1956.
"The Deserters," in *Rawhide and Bob-Wire*, edited by Luke Short. New York, Bantam, 1958.
"The Girl Who Invaded Texas," in *The Texans*, edited by Bill Pronzini and Martin H. Greenberg. New York, Fawcett, 1988.

* * *

There is very little that is unusual about *Rails to the Rio*, but it is refreshing in its omission of one convention of formulaic western writing. Very many western authors use the action of their tales as occasions for philosophizing about life, usually in a Social Darwinist vein. Neither Obets nor his characters concern themselves with such abstract discourse: the plot consists almost exclusively of vivid action by highly coloured characters. The story concerns the building of the Texas section of the St. Louis, Brownsville & Mexico railroad, after the end of the Spanish-American War. The action consists of the conflict between the forces for and against the new railway. The adherents and opponents to the plan are, generally, only different kinds of businessman, but the dispute is simplified and melodramatized by the depiction of one side as a gang of murderous criminals and the other as a group of far-sighted empire-builders, who wish to transform the Rio Grande Valley into "the market basket to the whole nation." The latter group, of course, includes the hero, a former Rough Rider and now troubleshooter for the railroad, and, in time, the Mexican heroine, a rancher who at first objects to the railroad crossing her land. None of the real problems of a rancher's accommodation to the railway are considered; instead, she is shown as clearly in the wrong because her position causes her to line up with the criminal element. Further weight is given to the railroad's cause by the single piece of oratory in the book. The hero explains to the heroine that, for Texans, the land is more important than any individual, thus great events like the Alamo occur. The railroad builders are fighting a similar fight, he maintains: like Lewis and Clark or Joe McCoy, they are opening up an empire. Although the book could be said to personify this kind of high-minded belief in progress, it must be said that, in the main, the story concerns itself with the series of fistfights between the hero and his enemies, culminating in the final shoot-out in which both hero and heroine participate, side by side.

—Christine Bold

O'BRIAN, Frank. *See* **GARFIELD, Brian.**

O'CONNER, Bert. *See* **PAINE, Lauran.**

O'CONNER, Clint. *See* **PAINE, Lauran.**

O'CONNOR, Jack (John Woolf O'Connor). Born in Nogales, Arizona, 22 January 1902. Educated at Arizona State Teachers College (now University), Tempe, 1921–23; University of Arizona, Tucson, 1923–24; University of Arkansas, Fayetteville, A.B. 1925; University of Missouri, Columbia, M.A. 1927. Served in the United States Army, 158th Infantry, 1917–18. Married Eleanor Bradford Barry in 1927; two sons and two daughters. Newspaper reporter, 1924–26; Associate Professor of English, Sul Ross College (now University), Alpine, Texas, 1927–31; correspondent for Associated Press and for Texas newspapers, 1931–34; Associate Professor of Journalism, University of Arizona, 1934–35; editor, arms and ammunition department, *Outdoor Life*, New York, 1939–72. *Died 20 January 1978.*

WESTERN PUBLICATIONS

Novels

Conquest: A Novel of the Old Southwest. New York, Harper, 1930.
Boom Town: A Novel of the Southwestern Silver Boom. New York, Knopf, and London, Constable, 1938.

OTHER PUBLICATIONS

Other

Game in the Desert. New York, Derrydale Press, 1939; revised edition, as *Hunting in the Southwest*, New York, Knopf, 1946; as *Game in the Desert Revisited*, Clinton, New Jersey, Amwell, 1977.

Hunting in the Rockies. New York, Knopf, 1947.
Sporting Guns. New York, Watts, 1947.
The Rifle Book. New York, Knopf, 1949; revised edition, 1964, 1978.
The Big-Game Rifle. New York, Knopf, 1952.
Sportsman's Arms and Ammunition Manual. New York, Outdoor Life, 1952.
Outdoor Life Shooting Book. New York, Outdoor Life, 1957.
The Complete Book of Rifles and Shotguns. New York, Outdoor Life, 1961; revised edition, 1965.
The Big Game of North America. New York, Dutton, 1962; revised edition, as *The Big Game Animals of North America*, New York, Outdoor Life, 1977.
Big Game Hunts. New York, Outdoor Life, 1963.
The Shotgun Book. New York, Knopf, 1965.
The Art of Hunting Big Game in North America. New York, Outdoor Life, 1967; revised edition, 1977.
Horse and Buggy West: A Boyhood on the Last Frontier. New York, Knopf, 1969.
The Hunting Rifle. New York, Winchester, 1970.
Sheep and Sheep Hunting. New York, Winchester, 1974.
The Last Book: Confessions of a Gun Editor. Clinton, New Jersey, Amwell, 1984.

* * *

Jack O'Connor's *Conquest* is a vigorously written, realistic novel of the conquest of Arizona by the Anglos. Jard Pendleton, a Virginia poor white, winds up in the Southwest after service as a soldier in the Mexican War. Forced to flee the outraged authorities of Sonora when they discover that he is not above selling the scalps of Mexico's citizens as Apache hair, Pendleton lands on his feet in Arizona as foreman for a stage company. He is soon in charge of a stage station on the Salt River, where he begins to irrigate and farm the rich bottom lands.

Pendleton is not without a capacity for friendship, but he is a hard, heroic man who repays savagery with ferocity. He is capable of watching impassively for a whole night as a dying man he has shot through the spine in a fight crawls painfully to the river for water. When Apaches kill his partner, he leads a raiding party which exacts vengeance and shatters Apache power by destroying the largest hostile village, killing men, women, and children without mercy.

By the mid-1870's Pendleton is the kingpin in thriving Pendleton City. He is the biggest landholder in the valley as well as the town's dominant businessman, and chief stockholder in the all-important irrigation company. He is also the owner of a 300-square-mile ranch in the Apache country of northern Arizona. But economic success does not seem to be enough for him. The prostitute he married when he came to Arizona has long since reverted to type and decamped, and the Mexican girl he bought from her drunken father as a replacement has turned to lard. She has also given Pendleton six children, but he casually boots his "greaser" family out when he has a chance to marry the youthful daughter of an ex-Virginia planter down on his luck. The poor white has moved into the aristocracy. When we last see Jard Pendleton, he is complacently attending a fair and rodeo put on in honor of the sterling, stalwart pioneers of Arizona, men like himself, an ironic ending to a bitter story.

In *Boom Town*, a vigorous, convincing sketch of the birth, life, and death of an Arizona silver-mining town, O'Connor attempts to infuse new life into some of the stereotypes of western fiction. But the stereotypes often smother the characterization, and the effect of the vigorous diction is marred by the fact that all of the characters sound alike. Frank O'Reilly is the tough, callous miner whose inner tenderness leads him to take charge of a feckless eastern tenderfoot, Larry Richards, who becomes his partner in his fabulous silver strike, the Lucky Bighorn. In looking out for Richards, O'Reilly has the assistance of a highly cultured consumptive gambler and deadly gunman, and he has to cope with the interference of a happy-go-lucky strumpet who enjoys seducing Richards. After seducing his partner's lovely young wife, O'Reilly dies in a cave-in in the Lucky Bighorn. The town dies with him.

—Jerry A. Herndon

OGDEN, Clint. *See* **KING, Albert.**

O'HARA, Mary (Mary O'Hara Alsop). Also wrote as Mary Sture-Vasa. American. Born in Cape May Point, New Jersey, 10 July 1885. Educated at Packer Institute, Brooklyn, New York; learned languages and music during European travel. Married 1) Kent Kane Parrot in 1905 (divorced 1922); one daughter (deceased) and one son; 2) Helge Sture-Vasa in 1922 (divorced 1947). Worked as screenplay writer in California, and as author/composer in Wyoming before returning East in 1948. *Died 15 October 1980.*

WESTERN PUBLICATIONS

Novels

My Friend Flicka (for children). Philadelphia, Pennsylvania, Lippincott, 1941; London, Eyre and Spottiswoode, 1943.
Thunderhead (for children). Philadelphia, Pennsylvania, Lippincott, 1943; London, Eyre and Spottiswoode, 1945.
Green Grass of Wyoming (for children). Philadelphia, Pennsylvania, Lippincott, 1946; London, Eyre and Spottiswoode, 1947.
The Son of Adam Wingate. New York, McKay, and London, Eyre and Spottiswoode, 1952.
Wyoming Summer. New York, Doubleday, 1963.
The Catch Colt (novelization of her play). London, Methuen, 1979.

OTHER PUBLICATIONS

Plays

The Catch Colt, music by O'Hara (produced Washington D.C.). New York, Dramatists Play Service, 1964.

Screenplays: *The Last Card*, with Molly Parro, 1921; *Life's Darn Funny*, with Arthur Ripley, 1921; *There Are No Villains*, 1921; *Turn to the Right*, with June Mathis, 1922; *The Prisoner of Zenda*, 1922; *Peg O' My Heart*, 1922; *The Age of Desire*, with Lenore Coffee and Dixie Willson, 1923; *Merry-Go-Round*, with Finis Fox and Harvey Gates, 1923; *The Woman on the Jury*, 1924; *Braveheart*, 1925; *The Home Maker*, 1925; *The Honeymoon Express*, 1926; *Frames*, 1927; *Perch of the Devil*, 1927.

Other

Let Us Say Grace (as Mary Sture-Vasa). Boston, Christopher, 1930.

Novel-in-the-Making (autobiography). New York, McKay, 1954.
A Musical in the Making. Chevy Chase, Maryland, Markane Publishing, 1966.
Awakening the Silent Majority: The Changing Role of Women in My Church, Past, Present, Future (study guide), edited by Dorothy C. Bass and David K. McMillan. New York, Auburn Theological Seminary, 1975.
Flicka's Friend: The Autobiography of Mary O'Hara. New York, Putnam, 1982.

* * *

A boy and his horse and the wild, green grass of Wyoming: these are the primary elements of Mary O'Hara's novels and, indeed, the elements that may be said to characterize them as "Westerns."

All three elements appear (the last figuratively) in the very first sentence of O'Hara's first and most famous novel, *My Friend Flicka*: "High up on the long hill they called the Saddle Back, behind the ranch and the country road, the boy sat his horse, facing east, his eyes dazzled by the rising sun." O'Hara has said that she always loved horses and that when she was a little girl she was promised one but never got it. The longing she must have felt for that horse has been touchingly and vividly transferred to the novel's 10-year-old hero—the boy, Ken McLaughlin—who aches with longing for a colt of *his* own: "Dad—if I only had a colt—" he pleads, a "lump choking his throat." His mother Nell, suspecting that her stern husband Rob might not let Ken have his wish this summer because Ken hasn't been promoted at school this term, and he's been dreamy and inattentive to his chores, asks him why he wants a colt when there are other horses on the ranch he can ride. Ken replies, "'Oh, Mother, it isn't just the riding. I want a colt to be friends with me. I want him to be mine—*all my own*, Mother— As she looked down into the upturned face, her heart misgave her at the passion and intensity of his longing . . ." Knowing how important this colt is to Ken, Nell persists in talking Rob into letting him have it this summer. Ken chooses his colt, or rather, as in most real-life animal-human relationships, the filly looks Ken in the eye and chooses him. He names her "Flicka"—Gus the Swedish ranch hand's expression for "little gurl." Although his father and the ranch hands tell him Flicka is "loco"—her grandsire was the wild Albino, after all—by summer's end Ken has not only trained Flicka, he has risked his life for her, she is truly his friend, and he is well on his way to becoming the man his father wants him to be.

In *Thunderhead*, Ken McLaughlin, now 14, is once again a boy with a dream: the dream of raising Flicka's first foal, Thunderhead, into a prize-winning race horse. Thunderhead is strong, and lightning fast. Alas, he is also a throw-back to his great-grandsire the Albino, and when the time comes for him to race the big race and win the big prize that will solve the McLaughlins' financial problems, he bucks his rider and proudly demonstrates to the screaming crowd his glorious wildness. In the end, Ken must decide whether to try to keep Thunderhead on the ranch, or to let him be wild and free. He bravely chooses the one right course and takes another giant step on the road to manhood.

In *Green Grass of Wyoming* Ken is a tall, thin boy of 16 "with a sensitive face and dark blue eyes that moved ceaselessly, sweeping the land—the characteristic far-reaching look of one who has been brought up on the plains," still riding his beloved sorrel mare Flicka. Thunderhead, wild and free, returns finally to win the big race for Ken, but now Ken's sights are set on another prize—the pretty girl, Carey Palmer Marsh—and he wins her too.

Although Ken McLaughlin may be Mary the-girl-who-wanted-a-horse's alter ego, his mother Nell McLaughlin—with her concern for her children's safety, her problems with Rob's stubbornness, her sometime doubts about life on the frontier, her love of music, and her deep religious faith—is the character through whom the grown-up O'Hara speaks.

After *Thunderhead* was published in 1943, the critic Orville Prescott called O'Hara "one of the most enduring novelists now writing in America," and her dramatic, action-filled, and, yes, sentimental novels as well as the films made from them endure to this day.

—Marcia G. Fuchs

OLSEN, T(heodore) V(ictor). Also writes as Joshua Stark; Christopher Storm; Cass Willoughby. American. Born in Rhinelander, Wisconsin, 25 April 1932. Educated at Rhinelander public schools; Stevens Point State College, Wisconsin, 1951–55, B.Sc. 1955. Married Beverly Butler in 1976. Since 1955 freelance writer. Recipient: State Historical Society of Wisconsin award of merit, 1983. Agent: Barbara Puechner, Ray Peekner Literary Agency, P.O. Box 3308, Bethlehem, Pennsylvania 18017-6308. Address: P.O. Box 856, Rhinelander, Wisconsin 54501, U.S.A.

Western Publications

Novels

Haven of the Hunted. New York, Ace 1956.
The Man from Nowhere. New York, Ace, 1959.
McGivern. New York, Fawcett, 1960; London, Muller, 1961
High Lawless. New York, Fawcett, 1960; London, Muller, 1961.
Gunswift. New York, Fawcett, 1960; London, Muller, 1962.
Ramrod Rider. New York, Fawcett, 1961; London, Barker, 1974.
Brand of the Star. New York, Fawcett, 1961; London, Muller, 1963.
Savage Sierra. New York, Fawcett, 1962; London, Muller, 1963.
A Man Called Brazos. New York, Fawcett, 1964.
Canyon of the Gun. New York, Fawcett, 1965; London, Coronet, 1971.
The Stalking Moon. New York, Doubleday, 1965; London, White Lion, 1972.
The Hard Men. New York, Fawcett, 1966; London, Barker, 1974.
Bitter Grass. New York, Doubleday, 1967; London, Sphere, 1971.
Blizzard Pass. New York, Fawcett, 1968; London, Coronet, 1971.
Arrow in the Sun. New York, Doubleday, 1969; as *Soldier Blue*, New York, Dell, 1970; London, Sphere, 1971.
A Man Named Yuma. New York, Fawcett, 1971.
Eye of the Wolf. New York, Doubleday, 1971; London, Sphere, 1973.
Starbuck's Brand. New York, Doubleday, 1973.
Mission to the West. New York, Doubleday, 1973; London, Sphere, 1977.
Run to the Mountain. New York, Fawcett, 1974; London, Coronet, 1975.
Track the Man Down. New York, Doubleday, 1975.

Day of the Buzzard. New York, Fawcett, 1976; London, Coronet, 1977.
Bonner's Stallion. New York, Fawcett, 1977; Leicester, Ulverscroft, 1982.
Rattlesnake. New York, Doubleday, 1979.
Blood of the Breed. New York, Doubleday, 1982; London, Hale, 1986.
Lazlo's Strike. New York, Doubleday, and London, Hale, 1983.
Lonesome Gun. New York, Fawcett, 1985.
Blood Rage. New York, Fawcett, 1987.
A Killer Is Waiting. New York, Fawcett, 1988.
Under the Gun. New York, Fawcett, 1989.
The Burning Sky. New York, Fawcett, 1991.

Novels as Joshua Stark

Break the Young Land. New York, Doubleday, 1964.
The Lockhart Breed. New York, Berkley, 1967.
Keno. New York, Berkley, 1970.

Short Stories

Westward They Rode. New York, Ace, 1976.

Uncollected Short Stories

"Journey of No Return," in *Ranch Romances* (New York), 20 April 1956.
"Gold Madness," in *Ranch Romances* (New York), 18 May 1956.
"Outcast's Chance," in *Ranch Romances* (New York), 15 June 1956.
"A Time to Fight," in *Ranch Romances* (New York), 27 July 1956.
"Stampede," in *Ranch Romances* (New York), 26 December 1956.
"The Man They Didn't Want," in *Ranch Romances* (New York), 11 January 1957.
"Man Without a Past," in *Ranch Romances* (New York), 17 May 1957.
"Trouble from Texas," in *Ranch Romances* (New York), 12 July 1957.
"End of the Trail," in *Ranch Romances* (New York), 26 July 1957.
"Killer's Law," in *Ranch Romances* (New York), 4 October 1957.
"Lone Hand," in *Ranch Romances* (New York), 13 December 1957.
"His Name Is Poison," in *Real Western Romance* (New York), January 1958.
"Bandit Breed," in *Texas Rangers* (New York), February 1958.
"The Man We Called Jones," in *The Gunfighters*, edited by Bill Pronzini and Martin H. Greenberg. New York, Fawcett, 1987.
"Vengeance Station," in *Westeryear*, edited by Edward Gorman. New York, Evans, 1988.

OTHER PUBLICATIONS

Novels

Brothers of the Sword. New York, Berkley, 1962.
Autumn Passion (as Cass Willoughby). New York, Universal, 1966; London, Tandem, 1968.
There Was a Season. New York, Doubleday, 1972.
Summer of the Drums. New York, Doubleday, 1972.
Red Is the River. New York, Fawcett, 1983.

Novels as Christopher Storm

The Young Duke. New York, Universal, 1963; as *Young Duke*, London, Softcover Library, 1970.
The Sex Rebels. New York, Universal, 1964.
Campus Motel. New York, Universal, 1965.

Verse

Allegories for One Man's Moods. Rhinelander, Wisconsin, Pineview, 1979.

Other

Roots of the North (history). Rhinelander, Wisconsin, Pineview, 1979.
Our First Hundred Years. Rhinelander, Wisconsin, Rhinelander Centennial Committee, 1981.
Birth of a City. Rhinelander, Wisconsin, Pineview, 1983.

*

Manuscript Collection: University of Oregon Library, Eugene.

T.V. Olsen comments:

My childhood was unremarkable except for an inordinate preoccupation with Zane Grey and Edgar Rice Burroughs. During my junior high and high school years I planned to become a comic strip artist. Drawing up my own comic books, I found myself becoming more and more absorbed by the story lines. Presently I found myself writing out my adventure epics longhand, featuring several friends as the hardy heroes. In 1950, before going to college, I spent a year battling around a variety of jobs and trying (unsuccessfully) to sell stories, mostly Westerns. During my junior year at college I labored on *Haven of the Hunted*, which sold to Ace Books three months after my graduation.

The next four years were hard ones. These were parlous times for young would-be commercial writers who could no longer depend on the pulp magazines, all but wiped out by spiraling production costs and the electronic cyclops that now occupied Everyman's parlor. My conspicuously few successes included selling another novel to Ace and a number of short stories to *Ranch Romances*, last of the pulps. Finally, at the end of 1959, I made a good novel sale to Fawcett, and they bought three more of my Westerns in 1960. The pinch was off for good. Since than I have made a good living at writing western novels and an occasional historical or contemporary novel for both the hardcover and the paperback markets. I consider my magnum opus to be *There Was a Season*, a biographical novel about Jefferson Davis.

My only purpose in writing is to make a living. All of my work is pure entertainment and nothing more; it is all in the action-adventure vein, mostly oriented toward the American past. As the bulk of my output is Westerns, I suppose I like to write about rugged men striving in rugged conditions—but when women feature in my work, they are just as strong and just as individualistic as the men.

* * *

T.V. Olsen is one of the most prolific and underrated writers in the field of western literature. His work ranges over a 25-year period, and unlike many writers who either start out strong with one good book and follow with numerous mediocre ones, or who get better with each book, Olsen's work has been consistently of high quality throughout his career. Any Olsen book is a guaranteed entertainment and a careful presentation of historical facts in a dramatic form.

Olsen has shown a special interest in the American Indian, especially the Apache, and this interest is reflected in his work by careful research and careful writing. His understanding of Apache culture and the difficulties of their adapting to the white man's ways is expressed with great skill and sympathy in his near modern Western *Rattlesnake*, which is primarily the story of two friends—a white and an Apache—who, due to changing times and growing racial prejudice, are cast on opposite sides of the fence and forced to reconsider their friendship. The contrast of cultures is displayed well, and achieves its intended effect without resorting to gross sentimentality.

His feelings for the Indians are again displayed in his exciting, often humorous, off-beat Western *Arrow in the Sun*. Olsen has said of it: "I wanted to depict a somewhat inverted image of the traditional American Western. Accordingly, I presented the hero not as an typical hard-bitten frontiersman, but as a fairly inept cavalry recruit from the Midwest; while the heroine comes on stage not as a shrinking, calico-clad violet, but rather as a tough, foul-mouthed little bitch from the New York slums." Olsen then elaborates and complicates this idea by stranding these two opposing types on the western plains in the wake of a Cheyenne massacre.

This novel is perhaps better known under its movie title, *Soldier Blue*, which captures much of the character and tone of Olsen's novel, but adds a very violent section from our history known as The Sand Creek Massacre—a true and disgraceful event in which in 1864 a cavalry unit directed by Colonel John M. Chivington, a sometime Methodist minister, attacked a peaceful settlement of Cheyenne and completely wiped it out. Of 900 Cheyenne, a large number of which were women and children, roughly 700 were murdered. Many bodies were mutilated and women were raped by the soldiers.

T.V. Olsen's unquestioned masterpiece, at least in this reader's eye, is his suspenseful *The Stalking Moon*. As in many of his novels, Olsen uses methods of attack that are not generally thought to be the furniture of the western writer—horror and suspense, for example. In many ways, his methods seem to foreshadow the technique of such a successful and serious western writer as Brian Garfield in *Gun Down*, *Relentless*, and *The Three-Persons Hunt*. *The Stalking Moon* concerns Sam Vetch, a retired army scout who takes Sara Carver (a former captive of the Apache) and her son (a half-Apache) under his wing, only to discover the boy's father, Salvaje—otherwise known as The Ghost—is stalking them in an attempt to take his son back. No horror movie has ever outclassed Olsen's unseen, creeping "villain," who is indeed ghostlike throughout most of the book. The final, fateful encounter between Sam and Salvaje is the terrifying highlight of the book, and there are surprises right up to the end. (The movie did an excellent job of transferring Olsen's book to the screen.)

Olsen as of late has been writing some fine novels for Fawcett/Gold Medal. Among them are the superior *Lonesome Gun* and *Red Is the River*. Even in earlier, more basic Westerns like *Ramrod Rider*, *Brand of the Star*, and *High Lawless*, Olsen is an efficient and compelling storyteller who more often than not uses his skill to touch on serious themes. He should be better known outside the immediate Western field, and as I can not help but feel that with the right press Olsen could command the position currently enjoyed by the late Louis L'Amour as America's most popular and foremost author of traditional Western novels.

—Joe R. Lansdale

OLSEN, Tillie (née Lerner). American. Born in Omaha, Nebraska, 14 January 1913. High school education. Married Jack Olsen in 1936; four daughters. Has worked in the service, warehouse, and food processing industries, and as an office typist. Visiting Professor, Amherst College, Massachusetts, 1969–70; Visiting Instructor, Stanford University, California, Spring 1971; writer-in-residence, Massachusetts Institute of Technology, Cambridge, 1973; Visiting Professor, University of Massachusetts, Boston, 1974; Visiting Lecturer, University of California, San Diego, 1978; International Visiting Scholar, Norway, 1980. Creative Writing Fellow, Stanford University, 1956–57; Fellow, Radcliffe Institute for Independent Study, Cambridge, Massachusetts, 1962–64; William James Synoptic Lecturer, Grand Valley College, Michigan, and Cestennial Visitor and Lecturer, Radcliffe College, Cambridge, Massachusetts, both 1980. Recipient: Ford grant, 1959; O. Henry award, 1961; National Endowment for the Arts grant, 1966; American academy award, 1975; Guggenheim fellowship, 1975; Unitarian Women's Federation award, 1980; Nebraska State Convention of Business and Professional Women Outstanding Woman Author award, 1980. Doctor of Arts and Letters: University of Nebraska, Lincoln, 1979; Litt.D.: Knox College, Galesburg, Illinois, 1982. Address: 1435 Laguna, No. 6, San Francisco, California 94115, U.S.A.

WESTERN PUBLICATIONS

Novel

Yonnondio: From the Thirties. New York, Delacorte Press, 1974; London, Faber, 1975.

OTHER PUBLICATIONS

Short Stories

Tell Me a Riddle: A Collection. Philadelphia, Lippincott, 1961; enlarged edition, London, Faber, 1964.

Play

I Stand Here Ironing (produced New York, 1981).

Other

Silences. New York, Delacorte Press, 1978; London, Virago Press, 1980.

Editor, *Mother to Daughter, Daughter to Mother: Mothers on Mothering.* Old Westbury, New York, Feminist Press, 1984; London, Virago Press, 1985.

Editor, *Life in the Iron Mills and Other Stories* by Rebecca Harding Davis. Old Westbury, New York, Feminist Press, 1985.

*

Manuscript Collection: Berg Collection, New York Public Library.

Critical Studies: "The Short Stories of Tillie Olsen" by William Van O'Connor, in *Studies in Short Fiction* (Newberry, South Carolina), Fall 1963; Annie Gottlieb, in *New York Times Book Review*, 31 March 1974; "Fragments of Time Lost" by Jack Salzman, in *Washington Post Book World*, 7 April 1974; "Tillie Olsen: The Weight of Things Unsaid" by Sandy Boucher, in *Ms.* (New York) September 1974; "De-Riddling Tillie Olsen's Writings" by Selma Burkom and Margaret Williams, in *San Jose Studies 2* (California), 1976; "'Limning, or Why Tillie Writes" by Ellen Cronan Rose, in *The Hollins Critic* (Hollins, Virginia), April 1976; "Alternative Responses to Life in Tillie Olsen's Work" by Annette Bennington McElheney, in *Frontiers 2*, Spring 1977; "Tillie Olsen: In Mutuality" by Thomazina Shanahan, in *Heliotrope*, May–June 1977; "Tillie Olsen on the Privilege to Create," in *Radcliffe Centennial News* (Cambridge, Massachusetts), July 1979; "Tillie Olsen: Story Teller of Working America" by Sally Cuneen, in *The Christian Century*, 21 May 1980; "Tillie Not So Unsung" by Sally Vincent, in *The Observer* (London), 5 October 1980; "Surviving Is Not Enough: A Conversation with Tillie Olsen" by Kay Mills, in *Los Angeles Times*, 26 April 1981; "Writer Tillie Olsen: Upbeat on Woman's Future" by Christina Van Horn, in Boston *Sunday Globe*, 31 May 1981; "From the Thirties: Tillie Olsen and the Radical Tradition" by Deborah Resenfelt, in *Feminist Studies*, Fall 1981; "Coming of Age in the Thirties: A Portrait of Tillie Olsen" by Erika Duncan, in *Book Forum*, 6, 1982; *Symposium: Tillie Olsen Week, The Writer and Society, 21–26 March 1983*, St. Ambrose College, Iowa, and others; *Tillie Olsen and a Feminist Spiritual Vision* by Elaine Neil Orr, Jackson, Mississippi, University Press of Mississippi, 1987.

* * *

Tillie Olsen has built a career on failure, or rather, on near-failure. Her remarkable reputation as a writer of fiction is based on a handful of stories and the fragmentary draft of a novel from the 1930's *Yonnondio*, which is set in the American West. She has also written a major study of why writers often fail to write, *Silences*, drawing not only on her own experiences but on the examples of other promising but thwarted talents, many of them women. Her readers lament that she has written so little, while feeling thankful for what there is.

Her most important work is the long story, or novella, "Tell Me a Riddle," the title story of her one collection. It deserves to be ranked with other important examples of this relatively rare form, which Henry James called the blessèd *nouvelle*—Joseph Conrad's "Heart of Darkness," James Joyce's "The Dead," and D. H. Lawrence's "The Virgin and the Gypsy." With remarkable compression, Olsen creates her probing inquiry into fundamental questions of life through the device of a quarrel between Eva and David, Russian Jewish immigrants who have been married for 47 years, and nursing a submerged quarrel for much of that time. As the domestic quarrel reaches a climax, Eva develops cancer (a metaphoric equivalent to the quarrel in this terse, tense story). As the cancer devours her life, the terms of the quarrel shift, revealing its buried origins and raising profound issues about social justice and the fundamental tragedies of life.

The couple, we learn, were revolutionaries filled with hope when they lived in their Russian village, Olshana. The wife had witnessed the murder of a fellow revolutionary and spent time in Siberia. But her courage and idealism did not survive emigration: first the burdens of raising a family in the New World sapped her intellectual strength; then, prosperity itself distracted her and her husband from their ideals. Approaching death revives those ideals, leaving Eva distraught over their betrayal, especially by her husband, who turned out to be a puny David. The Biblical character names are symbolic: Eva has been a mother, not of humankind, but of her seven children. After a while, the quarrel is less with David or social arrangements than with the limitations of life itself. Life is the riddle, and the answer is not clear. The title of the story implies that the riddle of life is not asked but told: it is a narrative, like stories from the Bible—or Olsen's own novella. The presence of Eva's grandaughter, Jeannie, who wants to learn about the revolutionary past, offers some comfort: Eva's life will not simply vanish.

A discussion of theme cannot convey the source of the real power of this work, its extraordinary style. Olsen stretches the language, distorting syntax and normal typography; she jumps about in time, shifts point of view, often turns schematic instead of presenting a smooth narrative texture. This work is not experiment for experiment's sake: Olsen simply brings the full resources of the language to bear on the deepest issues of life. Hence the impact of this short, knotty, and troubling work.

Her other stories are excellent. "I Stand Here Ironing" presents the long monologue of a mother ironing and imagining how she can justify herself to her daughter's teacher, who is concerned about the girl's need to develop her comic talents. The mother tells the story of her own frustrations and deprivations, and acknowledges that her daughter has suffered from the family's hardships. Olsen's central theme is always the loss of human opportunity in the widest sense. In "Hey Sailor, What Ship?" she examines the life of Whitey, a sailor who has worked many years and has few human relationships to draw on. He visits friends in San Francisco, but they cannot help him. "O Yes" looks at the decline of a friendship between a white girl, Carol, and her black friend, Parialee (here, the name symbolism—blacks are "pariahs" in America—seems forced).

After the success of the collection *Tell Me a Riddle*, Olsen discovered fragments of drafts of her lost novel of the Depression, *Yonnondio*. This work is a grim and painfully vivid story of a proletarian family ground down by the capitalist system. The Holbrooks are seen first in a western mining town, where they are exploited by the company; they try farming, but the sharecropping system crushes them; they move to the city, but the construction companies and meat packing houses in Omaha exploit the husband's labor. The story breaks off with a powerful description of a heat wave and its effects on the packing house workers. The work transcends its obvious propagandistic purposes as a "proletarian novel" through the intensity of its style. Like "Tell Me a Riddle," it freely stretches and even distorts the language to gain its effects. The strangeness of the work is heightened by its mutilated form.

In *Silences*, Olsen explores the plight of writers who fall silent or write little because of circumstances that make it difficult for them to work. She observes that there are 12 successful male writers for every woman writer, so her work has a feminist direction which has made it popular with the women's movement. Her chief example of a frustrated woman writer is Rebecca Harding Davis, a prophetic social critic whose work was patronized and finally ignored. Olsen has edited her stories. The prose in *Silences* is neither academic nor journalistic. It is impassioned, experimental, abounding in quotations and interjections. It diagnoses and makes prescriptions. It has appendices quoting from Davis and Baudelaire. This unorthodox book has a long index, which is appropriate for a work that serves as a sourcebook as well as a study. Olsen herself was almost silenced by poverty and familial duties. Her triumph in *Silences* and in her fiction was to make something enduring of her own experience of deprivation.

—Bert Almon

O'RILEY, Warren. *See* **RICHARDSON, Gladwell.**

O'ROURKE, Frank. Also wrote as Kevin Connor; Frank O'Malley; Patrick O'Malley. American. Born in Denver, Colorado, 16 October 1916. Educated at Kemper Military School, Boonville, Missouri, 1934–36. Served in the United States Army during World War II. Married to Edith Carlson O'Rourke. Recipient: Southwestern Library Association award, 1958. *Died in 1989.*

WESTERN PUBLICATIONS

Novels

Action at Three Peaks. New York, Random House, 1948; London, Quality Press, 1953.
Thunder on the Buckhorn. New York, Random House, 1949; London, Boardman, 1951.
Blackwater. New York, Random House, 1950; London, Boardman, 1951.
The Gun. New York, Random House, 1951; London, Boardman, 1952; as *Warbonnet Law*, New York, Bantam, 1952.
Gold under Skull Peak. New York, Random House, 1952; London, Quality Press, 1955.
Gunsmoke over Big Muddy. New York, Random House, 1952; London, Quality Press 1954.
Concannon. New York, Ballantine, 1952; as Frank O'Malley, London, Benn, 1956.
Violence at Sundown. New York, Random House, 1953; London, Pan, 1958.
Latigo. New York, Random House, 1953; London, Panther, 1960.
Gun Hand. New York, Ballantine, 1953; London, Panther, 1961.
Thunder in the Sun. New York, Ballantine, 1954; London, Panther, 1960.
High Vengeance. New York, Ballantine, 1954; London, Panther, 1960.
The Big Fifty. New York, Dell, 1955; Manchester, World Distributors, 1959.
Dakota Rifle. New York, Dell, 1955; London, Panther, 1960.
Battle Royal. New York, Dell, 1956; Manchester, World Distributors, 1959.
The Last Chance. New York, Dell, 1956; London, Harborough, 1957.
Segundo. New York, Dell, 1956; London, Panther, 1960.
The Diamond Hitch. New York, Morrow, 1956; London, Mayflower, 1963.
Legend in the Dust. New York, Ballantine, 1957; London, Pan, 1958.
The Bravados. New York, Dell, 1957; London, Heinemann, 1958.
A Texan Came Riding. New York, New American Library, 1958; London, Panther, 1960.
Ambuscade. New York, New American Library, 1959.
Desperate Rider. New York, New American Library, 1959.
Violent Country. New York, New American Library, 1959; London, Fontana, 1972.
Gunlaw Hill. New York, Ballantine, 1961; London, Mayflower, 1962.
The Great Bank Robbery. New York, Dell, 1961; London, Sphere, 1969.
Bandolier Crossing. New York, Ballantine, 1961; London, Mayflower, 1962.
A Mule for the Marquesa. New York, Morrow, 1964; as *The Professionals*, London, Fontana, 1967.
The Swift Runner. Philadelphia, Lippincott, 1969; London, Fontana, 1971.
The Abduction of Virginia Lee. Philadelphia, Lippincott, 1970.
The Shotgun Man. New York, Bantam, 1976.
Badger. New York, Bantam, 1977.

Short Stories

Ride West. New York, Ballantine, 1953.
Hard Men. New York, Ballantine, 1956.

OTHER PUBLICATIONS

Novels

"E" Company. New York, Simon and Schuster, 1945.
Flashing Spikes. New York, A.S. Barnes, 1948.
The Team. New York, A.S. Barnes, 1949.
The Best Go First (as Frank O'Malley). New York, Random House, 1950; London, Benn, 1955.
Bonus Rookie. New York, A.S. Barnes, 1950.
The Football Gravy Train. New York, A.S. Barnes, 1951.
Never Come Back. New York, A.S. Barnes, 1952.
Nine Good Men. New York, A.S. Barnes, 1952.
The Catcher, and The Manager: Two Baseball Fables. New York, A.S. Barnes, 1953.
High Dive. New York, Random House, 1954.
Car Deal! New York, Ballantine, 1955.
The Last Round. New York, Morrow, 1956.
The Man Who Found His Way. New York, Morrow, 1957; London, Panther, 1960.
The Last Ride. New York, Morrow, 1958; London, Mayflower, 1962.
The Far Mountains. New York, Morrow, 1959.
The Bride Stealer. New York, Morrow, 1960.
Window in the Dark. New York, Morrow, 1960.
The Springtime Fancy. New York, Morrow, 1961.
New Departure (as Kevin Connor). New York, Jefferson House, 1962.
The Bright Morning. New York, Morrow, 1963.
A Private Anger, and Flight and Pursuit. New York, Morrow, 1963.
Instant Gold. New York, Morrow, 1964; London, New English Library, 1966.
The Duchess Says No. New York, Morrow, 1965.
P's Progress. New York, Morrow, 1966.

Novels as Patrick O'Malley

The Affair of the Red Mosaic. New York, Mill, 1961.
The Affair of Swan Lake. New York, Mill, 1962.
The Affair of Jolie Madame. New York, Mill, 1963; London, Hale, 1965.
The Affair of Chief Strongheart. New York, Mill, 1964.
The Affair of John Donne. New York, Mill, 1964.

The Affair of the Blue Pig. New York, Mill, 1965.
The Affair of the Bumbling Briton. New York, Mill, 1965.

Short Stories

The Greatest Victory and Other Baseball Stories. New York, A.S. Barnes, 1950.
The Heavenly World Series and Other Baseball Stories. New York, A.S. Barnes, 1952.

*

Frank O'Rourke commented (1982):
A writer's work, if it speaks at all, speaks for him.

* * *

Frank O'Rourke was an underrated writer who produced nearly 70 books in a 40-year career. He wrote sports novels, mysteries, mainstream fiction, and Westerns. O'Rourke's western novels are clearly his most enduring works. His award-winning *The Far Mountains*—an historical novel set in the early 19th century, about the ill-fated Nolan Expedition—is his most popular novel.

O'Rourke specialized in writing caper novels with western locales. The best of these is *A Mule for the Marquesa* (filmed as *The Professionals*, starring Burt Lancaster and Lee Marvin). A group of Mexican revolutionaries kidnap Angelina Grant, the Mexican wife of Augustus Grant, an American cattle and mining baron. Grant recruits a band of five specialists led by Henry Fardan to cross the desert and rescue his wife. Each man is an expert in an logistics, combat, and cavalry. The caper—five men against a hundred—is ingenious, exciting, with a surprise ending. In a more humorous vein, *The Great Bank Robbery* (also filmed, with Zero Mostel, Kim Novak, and Clint Walker) is a comic caper in the best Donald E. Westlake tradition. *The Abduction of Virginia Lee* is the ingenious story of the hijacking of a very special railroad car.

O'Rourke was also a master of the traditional Western. *Warbonnet Law* contains his best character: John McMahon, a detective on a mission to find the secret behind the range war for the land north and west of Dodge City. O'Rourke's most memorable character is Andres "Shotgun" Arau, hero of *The Shotgun Man.* The time is 1914, and Arau is battling his way north through dangerous Mexico amid its revolution and the presence of Pancho Villa. His companions are a beautiful woman, a .97 shotgun, and a hidden fortune killers are after. O'Rourke's best vengeance novel is *Gunsmoke over Big Muddy*, where Lance Holbrook takes on the town that killed his brother. The action is fast and furious as Lance beats the odds to discover the town's secret.

Some of O'Rourke's best writing is to be found in his more mainstream novels like *The Bride Stealer*, which features the unforgettable Talache Coyote. In *The Diamond Hitch* and *The Last Ride* O'Rourke wrote about his friend, Doughbelly Price, one of the most famous men in the Southwest; *Life* magazine featured Price in one of its 1950 issues. Perhaps O'Rourke's most satisfying novel is *The Swift Runner*, where Doc Neely's unlikely band of misfits steal Barker's Boy—the fastest and most famous stallion around. This story of a gang of wacky horse thieves in the final days of the Old West is both funny and surprisingly moving. O'Rourke was a master writer who could blend unlikely elements and produce top-notch novels of originality and delight.

—George Kelley

ORTIZ, Simon J. American Indian (Acoma Pueblo). Born in Albuquerque, New Mexico, 27 May 1941. Educated at Fort Lewis College, Durango, Colorado, 1962–63; University of New Mexico, Albuquerque, 1966–68; University of Iowa, Iowa City (International Writing Fellow), 1968–69. Served in the United States Army, 1963–66. Married 1) Joy Harjo (divorced 1975); 2) Marlene Foster; three children. Public relations consultant, Rough Rock Demonstration School, Arizona, 1969–70, and National Indian Youth Council, Albuquerque, 1970–73; taught at San Diego State University, California, 1974, Institute of American Arts, Sante Fe, New Mexico, 1974, Navajo Community College, Tsaile, Arizona, summers 1975–77, College of Marin, Kentfield, California, 1976–79, and University of New Mexico, 1979–81. Since 1982 consultant editor, Pueblo of Acoma Press. Editor, *Quetzal*, Chinle, Arizona, 1970–73. Recipient: National Endowment for the Arts grant, 1969, 1982. Address: 308 Sesame S.W., Albuquerque, New Mexico 87105. U.S.A.

WESTERN PUBLICATIONS

Short Stories

Howbah Indians. Tucson, Blue Moon Press, 1978.
Fightin': New and Collected Stories. New York, Thunder's Mouth Press, 1983.

Uncollected Short Stories

"The San Francisco Indians," in *The Man to Send Rain Clouds*, edited by Kenneth Rosen, New York, Viking Press, 1974.
"The Killing of a State Cop," in *The Man to Send Rain Clouds*, edited by Kenneth Rosen, New York, Viking Press, 1974.

Verse

Naked in the Wind. Pembroke, North Carolina, Quetzal Vhio Press, 1970.
Going for the Rain. New York, Harper, 1976.
A Good Journey. Berkeley, California, Turtle Island Press, 1977.
Song, Poetry, Language. Tsaile, Arizona, Navajo Community College Press, 1978.
From Sand Creek: Rising in This Heart Which Is Our America. New York, Thunder's Mouth Press, 1981.
A Poem Is a Journey. Bourbanais, Illinois, Peternandon Press, 1981.

Other

The People Shall Continue (for children). San Francisco, Children's Press, 1977.
Traditional and Hard-to-Find Information Required by Members of American Indian Communities: What to Collect, How to Collect It, and Appropriate Format and Use, with Roxanne Dunbar Ortiz. Washington, D.C., Office of Library and Information Services, 1978.
Fightback: For the Sake of the People, For the Sake of the Land. Albuquerque, University of New Mexico Native American Studies, 1980.
Blue and Red (for children). Acoma, New Mexico, Pueblo of Acoma Press, 1982.
The Importance of Childhood. Acoma, New Mexico, Pueblo of Acoma Press, 1982.

Editor, with Rudolfo A. Anaya, *A Ceremony of Brotherhood 1680–1980.* Albuquerque, Academia, 1981.

Editor, *Earth Power Coming*. Tsiale, Arizona, Navajo Community College Press, 1983.

Editor, *These Hearts, These Poems*. Acoma, New Mexico, Pueblo of Acoma Press, 1984.

*

Critical Studies: "Old Voices of Acoma: Simon Ortiz' Mythic Indigenism" by Willard Gingerich, in *Southwest Review* (Dallas), 64, 1979; "Coyote Ortiz: Canis Latrans Latrans in the Poetry of Simon Ortiz" by Pat Clark Smith, in *Minority Voices*, vol.3 no.1, 1980; "Common Walls: The Poetry of Simon Ortiz" by Kenneth Lincoln, in *The Colphin 9* (Aarhus, Denmark), 1984; "Simon Ortiz Issue" of *SAIL: Studies in American Indian Literature*, vol.8 nos. 3–4, 1984; "The Killing of a New Mexican State Trooper: Ways of Telling an Historical Event" by Larry Evers, in *Wicazo Sa Review*, vol.1 no.1, 1985.

* * *

In the work of Simon J. Ortiz we find two worlds, one uniquely whole, the other deeply fractured. Ortiz is from Acoma Pueblo, west of Albuquerque, New Mexico, the "Sky City" built on a mesa, perhaps the oldest continuously inhabited city in the Americas. He is aware of a tenacious traditional culture which uses language as song, which views all beings as part of the community of life, which illuminates conduct through a mythology that still grows in response to modern conditions. But he is also aware that modern conditions have broken that traditional world through poverty, prejudice and an education that denies its values. His knowledge of both worlds gives his work its complexity and lets him steer between a sentimental view of tradition and simple-minded social protest. He has stories to tell, and he tells them as skillfully in verse as prose.

His first collection of poems, *Going for the Rain*, is remarkably mature. He moves easily among traditional myths, updated myths (hilarious accounts of Coyote), bitter social comment, love poetry, poetry about family: a wealth of perceptions expressed mostly in a short line that serves him equally for narration and lyricism. There is some influence of Gary Snyder here, but it is well assimilated, and Ortiz possesses as a birthright the nature vision that Snyder labored to acquire. His second collection of poems, *A Good Journey*, is less focused than *Going for the Rain*. It mixes prose and poetry: Ortiz likes to blur formal boundaries. His storytelling interests get full play, and sometimes the narratives ramble, lapsing into the prosaic. Clearly Ortiz wants to convey the oral storytelling traditions of his culture, and the discursive nature of many of the poems captures that atmosphere. Coyote, the trickster-clown-creator figure, gets particular attention. A number of poems address his children and seek to make them aware of Indian traditions and the beauty of nature. Near the end of the book, a set of poems from the Veterans' Administration Hospital in Ft. Lyons, Colorado, foreshadows Ortiz's third major collection, *From Sand Creek*.

In 1864, Sand Creek was the site of a notorious and completely unprovoked massacre of Cheyenne and Arapaho people by Colonel Chivington's Colorado Volunteers. It was natural for Ortiz to meditate on Sand Creek during a stay in the VAH Hospital, where he and a number of other Native Americans were being treated for alcoholism. Alcohol has been a scourge of Indians since the days of the whiskey traders on the frontier. In this book Ortiz writes with sorrow and anger, but the book is not a personal confession or a polemic. It is a sustained meditation on America, created through a series of concise and moving poems printed on the right hand pages, with brief prose comments on the left. Details of the hospital routine and details of American history are used to explore what America has been and what it is. There is also hope for what it might become. This is an angry, compassionate, and generous book.

Ortiz has a gift for fiction, though he has not fully developed it. His latest collection, *Fightin'* is subtitled *New and Collected Stories*, but it is by no means complete. Readers will find some of Ortiz's best stories scattered through Kenneth Rosen's anthology, *The Man to Send Rain Clouds*, while others appear in *Howbah Indians*. "The San Francisco Indians," published in Rosen's book, is a fine and understated account of an old Indian searching for his granddaughter in the Haight-Ashbury drug culture. Another story in Rosen, "The Killing of a State Cop," is a powerful account based on a true incident. And a third, "Kaiser and the War," later reprinted in *Fightin'*, is one of Ortiz's best, a tragic but droll tale of cultural conflict: Kaiser runs away from the draft, and evades his bumbling white pursuers in the New Mexico wilderness. Later he decides to join the army, but is sent to prison. He emerges from jail with his free gray suit, which he chooses to wear for the rest of his life. The suit is an emblem of his unsuccessful encounter with white culture. Another of Ortiz's best stories, "Men on the Moon," published in *Howbah Indians* and *Fightin'*, juxtaposes white technology and traditional Indian views of the universe as an old man watches the televised Apollo landing on the moon. Many of the stories in the most recent book, *Fightin'*, are sketches more than sustained narratives. They show wit (as in "You Were Real, the White Radical Said to Me") and pathos (as in the stories about broken families), but Ortiz is capable of more substance. His major theme in the fiction is cultural conflict. A novel would give him scope for dealing with that theme in depth.

Ortiz is a writer of accomplishment and promise. In *Going for the Rain* he established himself as an important American poet, one whose voice could range from lyrics to stories. In *From Sand Creek* he extended his range to create a sustained exploration of a complex of problems. His knowledge of two worlds, one of mythic wholeness, one of alienation and social injustice, offers a diagnosis of the American malaise and some hope for healing it. His stories deal mostly with the malaise. The poems move freely between both conditions.

—Bert Almon

OSTENSO, Martha. American. Born in Bergen, Norway, 17 September 1900; emigrated to the United States in 1902. Educated at Brandon Collegiate School, Manitoba; Kelvin Technical High School, Winnipeg; University of Manitoba, Winnipeg; Columbia University, New York, 1921–22. Married Douglas Durkin in 1945. Schoolteacher in Manitoba, 1918; reporter, Winnipeg *Free Press*; social worker, Bureau of Charities, Brooklyn, New York, 1920–23; freelance writer from 1923. Lived at Gull Lake, Minnesota, 1931–45; Seattle, Washington, 1963. Recipient: *Pictorial Review*-Dodd Mead prize, 1925. M.E.: Wittenberg University, Springfield, Ohio. *Died 24 November 1963.*

WESTERN PUBLICATIONS

Novels

Wild Geese. New York, Dodd Mead, 1925; as *The Passionate Flight*, London, Hodder and Stoughton, 1925.
The Dark Dawn. New York, Dodd Mead, 1926; London, Hodder and Stoughton, 1927.
The Mad Carews. New York, Dodd Mead, 1927; London, Heinemann, 1928.
The Young May Moon. New York, Dodd Mead, 1929; London, Butterworth, 1930.
The Waters under the Earth. New York, Dodd Mead, 1930; London, Butterworth, 1931.
Prologue to Love. New York, Dodd Mead, 1932.
There's Always Another Year. New York, Dodd Mead, 1933.
The White Reef. New York, Dodd Mead, 1934; London, Cassell, 1935.
The Stone Field. New York, Dodd Mead, 1937.
The Mandrake Root. New York, Dodd Mead, 1938.
Love Passed This Way. New York, Dodd Mead, 1942.
O River, Remember! New York, Dodd Mead, 1943; London, Long, 1945.
Milk Route. New York, Dodd Mead, 1948.
The Sunset Tree. New York, Dodd Mead, 1949; London, Long, 1951.
A Man Had Tall Sons. New York, Dodd Mead, 1958.

Uncollected Short Stories

"White Tryst," in *North American Review* (New York), December 1928.
"Strange Woman," in *Delineator* (New York), October 1929.
"Bridge," in *Pictorial Review* (New York), December 1934.
"Last Mad Sky," in *Good Housekeeping* (New York), October 1935.
"Gardenias in Her Hair," in *Pictorial Review* (New York), September 1937.
"Dreamer," in *Collier's* (Springfield, Ohio), 19 March 1938.
"Tumbleweed," in *Woman's Home Companion* (Springfield, Ohio), July 1938.
"Tonka Squaw," in *Good Housekeeping* (New York), September 1938.
"Prairie Romance," in *Woman's Home Companion* (Springfield, Ohio), April 1943.

OTHER PUBLICATIONS

Verse

A Far Land. New York, Seltzer, 1924.

Other

And They Shall Walk: The Life Story of Sister Elizabeth Kenny. New York, Dodd Mead, 1943; London, Hale, 1951.

* * *

The Midwest of Minnesota and South Dakota, the Northwest of Vancouver, and the frontier lake region of Manitoba, Canada, the landscapes for Martha Ostenso's fiction, almost always play a major part in her work. Her characters are often Nordic people similar to those of her own Scandinavian background; many protagonists are strong women, whose physical and psychological problems she handles with frankness and sympathy.

The relationship between the land and the people is always important, but her attitude varies considerably from book to book. Her first novel, *Wild Geese*, is placed in Manitoba, according to her own testimony, yet reviewers could only identify the area as "the Northwest." Although the setting is rural, the story is, as one critic noted, "*about* the soil, but not *of* it." Hamlin Garland's kind of realism influences her depiction of the hard field work, the never-ending chores, the manure and frozen mud in the farm yard. But in later books Ostenso's strong affection for the farms and rural communities, the Northwest and Middlewest, is more apparent. Her descriptions of the sky, the land, the weather, and the fields are among the best features of her work. Throughout most of her novels, the close affiliation of the characters with the land is a major factor, and she handles this aspect of her writing well.

Ostenso's strongest writing indicates her affinity to Scandinavian authors in treatment of both theme and character. One critic mentions Selma Lagerlof and Knut Hamsun. Sigrid Undset's great medieval sagas must also have had a strong effect. The two authors are concerned about religious peace and attempts at self-discovery. However, Ostenso's religious people are often the worst kind of hypocrites. Caleb Gare in *Wild Geese* is perhaps the most vicious, but Magdali Wing in *O River, Remember!* and Matt Welland in *The Waters under the Earth* are also memorable villains. Closer to Undset's heroes is Luke Darr in *A Man Had Tall Sons*, who begins as a religious bigot but eventually feels he finds true faith and understanding of God through personal suffering and through reading a poem of Whitman's that speaks of the "bursting forth" of the soul after death.

Ostenso's plots become repetitious, her people often stock characters, predictable and not very remarkable. It is difficult to separate the plots or people of *The Mad Carews* and *The Stone Field*, for example. The dominating, narrowly religious parent appears in book after book, and Ostenso's consistent habit of telling the story from each character's point of view weakens her work. Nevertheless, her themes of will to power, of rebellion, of self-searching, and, in most of her books, the relationships of humans with the land often result in strong writing. Her works are western in treatment of the importance of nature and its significance to the fate of the people who live there, and her poetic descriptions of the elements. While the farm is a grim place to escape from in *Wild Geese*, in most later books the protagonists are closely allied to nature: if they try to escape, it is usually from other people rather than from the country itself. This is perhaps best illustrated in *O River, Remember!* In this immigrant story of four generations, the bad characters exploit both humans and the land. The good are closely identified with the country they settle in the Red River Valley of the North. Both the good people and the land endure. This is one of Ostenso's major themes.

—Helen Stauffer

OVERHOLSER, Wayne D. Also writes as John S. Daniels: Lee Leighton; Mark Morgan; Wayne Roberts; Dan J. Stevens; Joseph Wayne. American. Born in Pomeroy, Washington, 4 September 1906. Educated at Albany College, 1924–25; Oregon Normal School, Monmouth, 1925–26; University of Montana, Missoula, 1934; University of Oregon, Eugene, B.S. 1934; University of Southern California, Los Angeles, 1939. Married Evaleth Miller in 1934; three sons. Teacher, Tillamook, Oregon, 1926–29, 1930–42; school principal, Mohler, Oregon, 1929–30; teacher, Bend, Oregon, 1942–45. Since 1945 freelance writer. Member of the Board of Directors, Western Writers of America, 1953–54, 1957–58. Recipient: Colorado Authors' League award, 1950, 1960; Western Writers of America Spur award, for novel, 1953, 1954, and for children's book, 1969. Address: 500 Mohawk Drive, Apartment 406, Boulder, Colorado 80303, U.S.A.

WESTERN PUBLICATIONS

Novels

Buckaroo's Code. New York, Macmillan, 1947; Redhill, Surrey, Wells Gardner, 1948.
West of the Rimrock. New York, Macmillan, 1949.
Gun Crazy. New York, Readers Choice Library, 1950.
Draw or Drag. New York, Macmillan, 1950; London, Corgi, 1958.
Steel to the South. New York, Macmillan, 1951; London, Wright and Brown, 1953.
Fabulous Gunman. New York, Macmillan, 1952; London, Ward Lock, 1954.
Fighting Man (as Mark Morgan). New York, Lion, 1953.
Valley of Guns. New York, Macmillan, 1953; London, Ward Lock, 1955.
The Violent Land. New York, Macmillan, 1954; London, Ward Lock, 1956.
Tough Hand. New York, Macmillan, 1954; London, Wright and Brown, 1955.
High Grass Valley, by William MacLeod Raine, completed by Overholser. Boston, Houghton Mifflin, and London, Hodder and Stoughton, 1955.
Cast a Long Shadow. New York, Macmillan, 1955; London, Ward Lock, 1957.
Gunlock. New York, Macmillan, 1956; London, Ward Lock, 1958.
Silent River (as Wayne Roberts, with Robert Greenleaf Athearn). New York, Avalon, 1956.
The Lone Deputy. New York, Macmillan, 1957; London, Ward Lock, 1959.
Desperate Man. New York, Macmillan, 1957; London, Ward Lock, 1958.
Hearn's Valley. New York, Macmillan, 1958; London, Ward Lock, 1959.
War in Sandoval County. New York, Bantam, 1960; London, Ward Lock, 1961.
The Judas Gun. New York, Macmillan, 1960; London, Ward Lock, 1962.
Standoff at the River. New York, Bantam, 1961.
The Killer Marshal. New York, Macmillan, 1961; London, Ward Lock, 1963.
The Bitter Night. New York, Macmillan, 1961; London, Ward Lock, 1962.
The Trial of Billy Peale. New York, Macmillan, 1962; London, Ward Lock, 1963.
A Gun for Johnny Deere. New York, Macmillan, 1963; London, Ward Lock, 1964.
To the Far Mountains. New York, Macmillan, 1963; London, Ward Lock, 1964.
Day of Judgment. New York, Macmillan, 1965; as *Colorado Incident*, London, Ward Lock, 1966.
Brand 99. New York, Dell, 1966; London, Hale, 1974.
Ride into Danger. New York, Bantam, and London, Corgi, 1967.
Summer of the Sioux. New York, Dell, 1967.
North to Deadwood. New York, Dell, 1968.
Buckskin Man. New York, Dell, 1969.
The Meeker Massacre (for children), with Lewis B. Patten. New York, Cowles, 1969.
The Long Trail North. New York, Dell, 1972; London, Hale, 1973.
The Noose. New York, Dell, 1972.
Sun on the Wall. New York, Ballantine, 1973.
Red Snow. New York, Dell, 1976.
The Mason County War. New York, Ace, 1976.
The Dry Gulcher. New York, Dell, 1977; London, Hale, 1989.
The Trouble Kid. New York, Ace, 1978.
The Diablo Ghost. New York, Dale, 1978.
The Cattle Queen Feud. New York, Bantam, 1979.
Nightmare in Broken Bow. New York, Dell, 1980.
Revenge in Crow City. New York, Bantam, 1980.
Danger Patrol. New York, Ballantine, 1982.

Novels as Dan J. Stevens

Oregon Trunk. New York, Avalon, 1950.
Wild Horse Range. New York, Avalon, 1951; London, Wright and Brown, 1954.
Blood Money. New York, Permabooks, 1956.
Hangman's Mesa. Derby, Connecticut, Monarch, 1959.
Gun Trap at Bright Water. New York, Ace, 1963.
Land Beyond the Law. New York, Ace, 1964.
Stage to Durango. New York, Ace, 1966.
Deadline. New York, Belmont, 1966.
The Killers from Owl Creek. New York, Ace, 1967.
Stranger in Rampart. New York, Ace, 1968.
The Dry Fork Incident. New York, Ace, 1969.
Landgrabbers. New York, Belmont, 1969.
Hunter's Moon. New York, Ace, 1973.

Novels as Joseph Wayne

The Sweet and Bitter Land. New York, Dutton, 1950; London, Wright and Brown, 1953; as *Gunplay Valley*, New York, New American Library, 1951.
The Snake Stomper. New York, Dutton, 1951; London, Wright and Brown, 1953.
By Gun and Spur. New York, Dutton, 1952; as *Gun and Spur*, London, Wright and Brown, 1952; as *The Colt Slinger*, Wright and Brown, 1954.
The Long Wind. New York, Dutton, 1953; as *Guns at Lariat*, London, Wright and Brown, 1955.
Bunch Grass. New York, Dutton, 1954; London, Wright and Brown, 1955.
The Return of the Kid. New York, Dutton, 1955; London, Wright and Brown, 1956.
Showdown at Stony Creek, with Lewis B. Patten. New York, Dell, 1957.
Pistol Johnny. New York, Doubleday, 1960; London, Wright and Brown, 1961.
The Gun and the Law, with Lewis B. Patten. New York, Dell, and London, Wright and Brown, 1961.
Land of Promises. New York, Doubleday, 1962.
The Bad Man. New York, Avon, 1962.
Proud Journey. New York, Doubleday, 1963.
Deadman Junction. New York, Avon, 1964.
Red Is the Valley. New York, Doubleday, 1967; London, Gold Lion, 1972.

Novels as John S. Daniels

Gunflame. Philadelphia, Lippincott, 1952.
The Nester. Philadelphia, Lippincott, 1953.
The Land Grabbers. Philadelphia, Lippincott, 1955; London, Wright and Brown, 1960.

The Man from Yesterday. New York, New American Library, 1957.
Smoke of the Gun. New York, New American Library, 1958; London, Ward Lock, 1959.
Ute Country. New York, New American Library, 1959; London, Ward Lock, 1961.
The Gunfighters. London, Wright and Brown, 1961; New York, New American Library, 1962.
The Crossing. New York, New American Library, 1963.
Trail's End. New York, Belmont, 1964; as *The Violent Men*, New York, Tower, 1967.
The Hunted. New York, Belmont, 1965.
War Party. New York, New American Library, 1966.
The Day the Killers Came. New York, Belmont, 1968.
The Three Sons of Adam Jones. New York, Belmont, 1969.

Novels as Lee Leighton

Law Man. New York, Ballantine, 1953; Kingswood, Surrey, World's Work, 1955.
Beyond the Pass. New York, Ballantine, 1956; London, Corgi, 1958.
Tomahawk, with Lewis B. Patten. New York, Ballantine, 1958.
Colorado Gold, with Chad Merriman. New York, Ballantine, 1958.
Fight for the Valley. New York, Ballantine, 1960; London, Panther, 1962.
Gut Shot. New York, Ballantine, 1962; London, Collins, 1977.
Big Ugly. New York, Ballantine, 1966; London, Sphere, 1967.
Hanging at Pulpit Rock. New York, Ballantine, 1967; London, Panther, 1968.
Bitter Journey. New York, Ballantine, 1969; London, Mayflower, 1970.
Killer Guns. New York, Ballantine, 1969.
You'll Never Hang Me. New York, Ballantine, 1971; London, Hale, 1973.
Cassidy. New York, Ballantine, 1973; London, White Lion, 1976.
Greenhorn Marshal. New York, Ballantine, 1974.

Short Stories

The Best Western Stories of Wayne D. Overholser edited by Bill Pronzini and Martin H. Greenberg. Carbondale, Illinois, Southern Illinois University Press, 1984.
The Riders of Carne Cove and *Last Cowman of Lost Squaw Valley* (two novellas). New York, Tor, 1990.

Uncollected Short Stories

"Showdown in Tonapos," in *Western Story* (New York), 26 November 1938.
"Range Hog and Die," in *Wild West* (New York), 18 February 1939.
"Death Rides Double," in *Western Story* (New York), 11 November 1939.
"Gunsmoke Interest," in *Western Story* (London), August 1940.
"Harvest of Fate," in *Western Story* (London), November 1940.
"Powdersmoke Reckoning," in *Western Story* (London), December 1940.
"Holdup Boomerang," in *Wild West* (New York), 5 April 1941.
"Don't Run, Runt!," in *Wild West* (New York), 21 June 1941.
"Winchester Welcome," in *Wild West* (New York), 20 September 1941.
"$10,000 Worth of Bull," in *Western Story* (London), March 1942.
"Bullets or Blackstone," in *Western Story* (London), July 1942.
"Medico Miracle," in *Western Story* (London), September 1942.
"Button Business," in *Wild West* (New York), 19 September 1942.
"Gun-Lucky Kid," in *Wild West* (New York), 10 October 1942.
"Badge Toter for Boothill," in *Wild West* (New York), 31 October 1942.
"Trouble Bound," in *Western Story* (London), November 1942.
"Ten Steps from Tophet," in *Wild West* (New York), 21 November 1942.
"Buckaroo's Choice," in *Wild West* (New York), 26 December 1942.
"Vigilante Brand," in *Wild West* (New York), 23 January 1943.
"Renegade Roost," in *Western Story* (London), February 1943.
"A Rebel Takes His Gun," in *Wild West* (New York), 27 March 1943.
"Rebels of the Stage Trails," in *Ace-High Western*, May 1943.
"Pasear to Death," in *Western Story* (London), June 1943.
"Murder-Trap Boomerang," in *Wild West* (New York), 5 June 1943.
"Ghost of Glory," in *Western Story* (London), September 1945.
"Gun-Song of the Melody Kid," in *Star Western* (Chicago), April 1946.
"Ghost of the Glory Gold," in *Western Story* (London), December 1946.
"Move On, Sawbones," in *Western Story* (London), November 1947.
"Four Guns in Purgatory," in *Thrilling Ranch Stories*, (London), December 1947.
"Debt Cancelled," in *Zane Grey's Western* (New York), February 1948.
"The Petticoat Brigade," in *Zane Grey's Western* (New York), May 1948.
"Fighting Ed Garvey," in *Western Story* (London), November 1948.
"The Long Haul," in *Western Story* (London), March 1949.
"Boss Gunman," in *Western Story* (London), September 1949.
"Jury for Juniper," in *Texas Rangers* (London), September 1951.
"Home to Rafter C," in *Thrilling Ranch Stories*, (London), October 1951.
"Buckskin Man," in *Western Story* (London), November 1951.
"Every Trail Has a Rider," in *Exciting Western* (London), April 1952.
"High-Grade," in *Zane Grey's Western* (New York), September 1952.
"Trail to Sundown," in *Thrilling Ranch Stories*, (London), December 1952.
"Vigilante Valley," in *Exciting Western* (London), December 1952.
"Nester's Nemesis," in *Western Story* (London), January 1953.
"Gun in His Hand," in *Thrilling Ranch Stories*, (London), February 1953.
"Outlaw's Wife," in *Zane Grey's Western* (New York), April 1953.
"Patriarch of Gunsight Flat," in *Holsters and Heroes*, edited by Noel M. Loomis. New York, Macmillan, 1954.
"Judge Guppy's Colt Law," in *Exciting Western* (London), September 1954.
"The Steadfast," in *Fall Roundup*, edited by Harry E. Maule. New York, Random House, 1955.

"The Price of Pride," in *Thrilling Western* (London), February 1955.
"Ride the Red Trail!," in *Western Story* (London), April 1956.
"Ring-Tailed Catamount," in *3-Book Western* (New York), February 1957.
"Broody Rustles a Bride," in *Western Story* (London), December 1957.
"Mean Men Are Big," in *Frontiers West*, edited by S. Omar Barker. New York, Doubleday, 1959.
"Justice for Sidewinders," in *Texas Rangers* (London), October 1960.
"Smart," in *Western Roundup*, edited by Nelson Nye. New York, Macmillan, 1961.
"The Legend of Weminuche," in *Legends and Tales of the Old West*, edited by S. Omar Barker. New York, Doubleday, 1962.
"Rancho of Fear," in *The Killer Breed*. New York, Belmont, 1967.
"The O'Keefe Luck," in *Iron Men and Silver Spurs*, edited by Donald Hamilton. New York, Fawcett, 1967.
"They Hanged Wild Bill Murphy," in *A Quintet of Sixes*, edited by Donald A. Wollheim. New York, Ace, 1969.
"Winchester Wedding," in *Western Romances*, edited by Peggy Simson Curry. New York, Fawcett, 1969.
"Beecher Island," in *With Guidons Flying*, edited by Charles N. Heckelmann. New York, Doubleday, 1970.
"Steel to the West," in *Western Writers of America Silver Anniversary Anthology*, edited by August Lenniger. New York, Ace, 1977.
"Lawyer Two-Fist", in *Wild Westerns*, edited by Bill Pronzini and Martin H. Greenberg. New York, Walker, 1986.

*

Manuscript Collection: University of Wyoming, Laramie.

Wayne D. Overholser comments:

My career as a fiction writer began in 1936 with the sale of my first short story to a magazine. I sold my first book in 1946, and since then I have sold some 100 books, all western or historical fiction. I taught school for 19 years before I began writing full time. I have a strong feeling that the purpose of writing is to communicate and that the best writing is simple. I have tried to be accurate in describing my settings and I consider character more important than action. Sex is a basic part of life and therefore should be included in any work of fiction, but I do not believe it should be used for its own sake as is so common in the so-called adult Westerns of the present time. If a writer can make a point on the material or metaphysical level, or both, he is going a step beyond producing an average piece of fiction. However, above everything else, he has done his job if he truly entertains the reader. When someone tells me he sat up all night to read one of my books because he couldn't put it down, I am pleased and know that I have done my job.

* * *

Danger Patrol, published in May 1982, was billed as Wayne D. Overholser's one hundredth novel. He has been writing western fiction for over 45 years, and is the author of more than 400 shorter works in addition to his novels. His stories have often appeared in Western Writers of America anthologies and other collections of short western fiction. The books bearing either of his two best-known pseudonyms, Lee Leighton and Joseph Wayne, constitute in themselves a body of work of which any writer could be proud. His books have been published in several languages, and have been adapted for both motion pictures and television. The Colorado Authors' League presented him with an award for best novel of the year in 1950, and again in 1960. He received the Western Writers of America Spur award for best novel in the first two years the award was given: in 1954 for *Law Man* (as by Lee Leighton) and in 1955 for *The Violent Land*. He shared a third Spur award with co-author Lewis B. Patten for *The Meeker Massacre*, voted 1969's best western novel for young people. (The habit of winning awards has been carried on by his son Stephen Overholser, who won the Spur for his first novel, *A Hanging in Sweetwater*, in 1975.)

Overholser began writing for the western pulp magazines in 1936. Typical examples of his magazine stories are "Rebels of the Stage Trails," about an attempt to found a Pacific Republic in Oregon during the Civil War, and "They Hanged Wild Bill Murphy," a tale of land fraud centering around the "swamp land" Act of 1870. When Bill Pronzini and Martin H. Greenberg started their series of short-story collections by western writers in 1984 *The Best Western Stories of Wayne D. Overholser* was one of the first two volumes published. "They Hanged Wild Bill Murphy" was the earliest and most traditional of the 16 stories included, and served as a fitting summation of Overholser's early pulp years. The remaining stories are drawn from the latter part of the author's career, and mostly from magazines such as *Blue Book*, *Argosy*, and the quality digest *Zane Grey's Western Magazine* rather than from the standard western pulps. They are more thoughtful stories than the fast-action tales of the earlier years; in many of them the problems are solved by appeals to reason and decency rather than the traditional shoot-out. Nevertheless, they do not lack for excitement, with touches of violence when the story makes it necessary. All are well-crafted and make satisfying reading.

By the mid-1940's Overholser was contributing longer stories to the magazines, and some of these were sources for his early books. His first book, *Buckaroo's Code*, appeared originally in the October 1945 issue of *Western Action Magazine*. A 1946 magazine novel, *Gun Crazy*, was published as a paperbound book in 1950. His third hardcover novel, *Draw or Drag*, was an expansion of a magazine story called "Showdown Valley." Until the magazine fiction markets disappeared in the 1950's, Overholser continued to sell both short fiction and abridged versions of his novels to *Blue Book*, *Ranch Romances*, and similar magazines.

For most of the 1950's and 1960's Overholser produced three or four new novels each year. On two occasions the annual tally climbed as high as seven. In addition to his own name, he kept four other bylines active: Joseph Wayne, Lee Leighton, John S. Daniels, and Dan J. Stevens. (The last two pen-names were constructed from the names of Overholser's three sons.) The books published under the name Joseph Wayne were often concerned with the history of a particular locale. *By Gun and Spur* tells of the founding of an Oregon town much like Bend, where the Overholsers lived during the 1940's. *The Sweet and Bitter Land* is the story of the settling of an Oregon valley, and of the larger-than-life cattlemen whose vision shaped its early history. *The Long Wind* is a story of homesteaders in the valley of the Frenchman River in Nebraska. The books by Lee Leighton, in contrast, were usually built around an interesting central character, often following his fortunes over a span of years. The title character of *Big Ugly* is Bill Shell, who returns to his Nebraska home after several years as a gunfighter and tries to build a life for himself and the woman he loves. *Bitter Journey* is the story of 20 years in the life of Bill Lang, as he changes from gunman to Army scout to deputy sheriff and respectable citizen. All of the Leighton books have been reprinted numerous times, and continue to be popular.

The books published under Overholser's own name are closest to the patterns of the traditional Western. *Steel to the South* tells of an attempt to build a railroad in central Oregon, against the opposition of a self-styled King of the Desert. *Cast a Long Shadow* centers around the tangled claims to ownership of a Spanish land grant. *The Violent Land* is the powerful story of a young man's passage to maturity against the background of a newly settled land. *Sun on the Wall* is a historical novel of the early years of Cheyenne, Wyoming, before the coming of the railroads. These and other books, under whatever name, are founded on a solid knowledge of the American West, particularly the history of Oregon and Colorado. Overholser writes with skill, an uncommon sensitivity, and a consistently accurate and vivid treatment of both land and people.

—R. E. Briney

OWEN, Dean. *See* **DEAN, Dudley.**

OWEN, Hugh. *See* **BRAND, Max.**

P

PAINE, Lauran (Bosworth). Also writes as Ray Ainsbury; Roy Ainsworthy; Clay Allen; Rosa Almonte; A. A. Andrews; Dennis Archer; John Armour; Carter Ashby; Kathleen Bartlett; Reg Batchelor; Harry Beck; Kenneth Bedford; Will Benton; Martin Bishop; Lewis H. Bond; Jack Bonner; Frank Bosworth; Ruth Bovee; Will Bradford; Concho Bradley; Buck Bradshaw; Will Brennan; Charles Burnham; Mark Carrel; Nevada Carter; Claude Cassady; Badger Clark; Richard Clarke; Robert Clarke; Clint Custer; Amber Dana; Richard Dana; Audrey Davis; J. F. Drexler; Antoinette Duchesne; John Durham; Margot Fisher; Betty Fleck; George Flynn; Harry Foster; Joni Frost; Donn Glendenning; James Glenn; Angela Gordon; Beth Gorman; Fred Harrison; Travis Hartley; Jay Hayden; Roger Hill; Helen Holt; Will Houston; Elizabeth Howard; Troy Howard; John Hunt; Jared Ingersol; Ray Kelley; Cliff Ketchum; Frank Ketchum; Jack Ketchum; John Kilgore; Frank Kimball; Ralph Kimball; Frank Koehler; Hunter Liggett; J. K. Lucas; Buck Lyon; Bruce Martin; Tom Martin; Angela Morgan; Arlene Morgan; Frank Morgan; John Morgan; Valerie Morgan; Bert O'Conner; Clint O'Conner; Arthur St.George; Helen Sharp; Jim Slaughter; Buck Standish; Margaret Stuart; Buck Thompson; Russ Thompson; Barbara Thorn; P. F. Undine. American. Born Duluth, Minnesota, 25 February 1916. Educated at Pacific Military Academy, California and St. Alban's Episcopal Academy, Illinois. Married; two sons (one deceased). Trapped wild horses in the U.S. and Mexico, worked on cattle ranches, in a saddle and harness shop, broke and traded horses, and traded cattle. Full-time writer since 1948. Address: Post Office Box 130, Greenview, California, 96037, U.S.A.

WESTERN PUBLICATIONS

Novels (series: Sheridan Township)

All Men Are Strangers. London, Hamilton, n.d.
Buckskin Buccaneer. London, Hamilton, n.d.
Moon Prairie. London, Hamilton, n.d.
The Outcast. London, Hamilton, n.d.
The Renegade. London, Hamilton, n.d.
Adobe Empire. London, Hamilton, 1950.
The Apache Kid. London, Hamilton, 1950.
Geronimo! London, Hamilton, 1950.
The Modoc War. London, Hamilton, 1950.
Timberline. London, Hamilton, 1950.
The Bounty Hunter. London, Hamilton, 1955.
Decade of Deceit. London, Hamilton, 1955; as *Dakota Deathtrap*, Bath, Chivers, 1986.
Californios. London, Hamilton, 1955.
Greed at Gold River. London, Hamilton, 1955.
Kiowa-Apache. London, Hamilton, 1955.
Lawman. London, Hamilton, 1955.
Lord of the South Plains. London, Hamilton, 1955.
Six-Gun Atonement. London, Hamilton, 1955.
The Story of Buckhorn. London, Hamilton, 1955.
Valour in the Land. London, Hamilton, 1955.
Wake of the Moon. London, Hamilton, 1955.
Arrowhead Rider. New York, Arcadia House, 1956.
The Hangrope. London, Hamilton, 1956.
Land Beyond the Law. London, Hamilton, 1956.
The Long Years. London, Corgi, 1956.
Rogue River Cowboy. New York, Arcadia House, 1956.
Trail of the Freighters. New York, Arcadia House, 1956.
Trail of the Sioux. New York, Arcadia House, 1956.
Trail of the Hunter. London, Hamilton, 1956.
Apache Trail. New York, Arcadia House, 1957.
The Farthest Frontier. London, Corgi, 1957.
The Forbidding Land. London, Hamilton, 1957.
Man from Butte City. New York, Arcadia House, 1957.
The Manhunter. London, Hamilton, 1957.
The Past Won't End. London, Hamilton, 1957.
The Rawhiders. London, Hamilton, 1957.
Texas Revenge. London, Foulsham, 1957.
Wilderness Road. London, Ward Lock, 1957.
Man Behind the Gun. New York, Arcadia House, 1958.
Return of the Hunted. London, Hamilton, 1958.
The San Luis Range. London, Ward Lock, 1958.
The Texan Rides Alone. London, Foulsham, 1958.
Vengeance Trail. London, Foulsham, 1958.
Western Vengeance. London, Foulsham, 1958.
The Fifth Horseman. London, Foulsham, 1959.
Range War. London, Foulsham, 1959.
The Long Law Trail. New York, Arcadia House, 1960.
Wyoming Trail. London, Foulsham, 1960.
Outpost. London, Hamilton, 1963.
The Sheepmen. London, Ward Lock, 1963.
Frontier Doctor. London, Hale, 1979.
The Ragheads (as Hunter Liggett). London, Hale, 1980.
Morgan Valley (as Bert O'Conner). London, Hale, 1980.
Saginaw Hills (as Frank Kimball). London, Hale, 1981.
The Hammerhead. London, Hale, 1981.
Punchbowl Range. London, Hale, 1981.
Trouble Valley (as Frank Koehler). London, Hale, 1982.
Scarface. London, Hale, 1982.
Adobe Wells. London, Hale, 1982.
The Lord of Lost Valley. London, Hale, 1982.
Thunder Valley. London, Hale, 1982.
The Trail Drive. London, Hale, 1983.
High Ridge Range. London, Hale, 1983.
The South Desert Trail. London, Hale, 1983.
The Bordermen. London, Hale, 1984.
Skye. New York, Walker, 1984.
Tanner. New York, Walker, 1984; London, Hale, 1986.
The War-Wagon. London, Hale, 1984.
Zuni Country. London, Hale, 1984.
Buffalo Range (as Frank Koehler). London, Hale, 1985.
The Horseman. New York, Walker, 1986.
The Marshal. New York, Walker, 1986.
The Blue Basin Country. New York, Walker, 1987.
The Medicine Bow. London, Hale, 1987.
The New Mexico Heritage. New York, Walker, 1987.
Spirit Meadow. New York, Walker, 1987.
The Trail of the Hawks. London, Hale, 1987.
Custer Meadow. New York, Walker, 1988.

Nightrider's Moon. New York, Walker, 1988.
The Guns of Summer (Sheridan Township). New York Fawcett 1988.
The Sheridan Stage (Sheridan Township). New York, Fawcett, 1989.
The Taurus Gun. New York, Walker, 1989.
The Catch Colt. New York, Fawcett, 1989.
The Young Marauders (Sheridan Township). New York, Fawcett, 1990.
The Open Range Men. New York, Walker, 1990.
The Bandoleros (Sheridan Township). New York, Fawcett, 1990.
Riders of the Trojan Horse. New York, Walker, 1990.
The Squaw Men. New York, Walker, 1990.
Land of the Winter Moon. London, Hale, 1991.
Hangtown. London, Hale, 1991.
The Crow Horse. London, Hale, 1991.
The Left-Hand Gun. London, Hale, 1991.
The Prairietown Raid. New York, Fawcett, 1991.
Thunder Valley. London, Hale, 1991.
The Undertaker. New York, Walker, 1991.
The Guns of Peralta. New York, Walker, 1992.
The Saddlegun Man. London, Hale, 1992.
The Stranger at Buckhorn. London, Hale, 1992.

Novels as Clay Allen

The Tombstone Range. London, Hale, 1965.
The Steeldust Hills. London, Hale, 1966.
The Guns of Bitter Creek. London, Hale, 1966.
The Iron Stirrup. London, Hale, 1966.
Cheyenne Range. London, Hale, 1972.
Apacheria. London, World, 1972.
Sixguns and Saddleguns. London, Hale, 1978.
Range Trouble. London, Hale, 1979.
Cougar Canyon. London, Hale, 1980.
Oxyoke. London, Hale, 1981.
Piute Range. London, Hale, 1981.
The Wagon Road. London, Hale, 1982.
The Outlaw's Trap. London, Hale, 1990.

Novels as A. A. Andrews

Thunderbird Range. London, Gresham, 1963.
Under the Gun. London, Gresham, 1963.
The Six-gun Brand. London, Gresham, 1964.
Gun Country. London, Gresham, 1965.
The Short Guns of Texas. London, Hale, 1965.
Skull Valley. London, Gresham, 1968.
The Bald Hills. London, Gresham, 1969.
The Cannonball Cattle Company. London, Hale, 1973.
The Guns of Lincoln. London, Hale, 1973.
Connall's Valley. London, Hale, 1975.
Land of Barbed Boundaries. London, Hale, 1975.
April's Guns. London, Hale, 1976.
Buffalo Township. London, Hale, 1977.
Four Aces. London, Hale, 1977.
Devil's Meadow. London, Hale, 1980.
Sixkiller. London, Hale, 1983.
Marshal Redleaf. London, Hale, 1988.

Novels as Dennis Archer

Cannon's Law. London, Hale, 1978.
The Vermillion Hills. London, Hale, 1978.
Juniper Range. London, Hale, 1979.
Cloud Prairie. London, Hale, 1987.

Novels as John Armour

The Longland Plain. London, Hale, 1981.
Carter Valley. London, Hale, 1982.
Paloverde. London, Hale, 1983.
The Witness Tree. London, Hale, 1983.
The Sun Devils. London, Hale, 1990.

Novels as Carter Ashby

Pine Ridge. London, Hale, 1980.
The Timber Trail. London, Hale, 1982.
Tenino. London, Hale, 1983.

Novels as Reg Batchelor

Cody Jones. London, Hale, 1979.
Stolen Gold. London, Hale, 1981.
The Nighthawks. London, Hale, 1982.
Guns of the Hunters. London, Hale, 1983.
Crow Range. London, Hale, 1983.

Novels as Harrry Beck

Centre-Fire Country. London, Hale, 1965.
Desert Guns. London, Gresham, 1965.
The Blazed Trail. London, Gresham, 1966.
The Scarlet Hills. London, Gresham, 1967.
Colorado Guns. London, Hale, 1975.
Cain's Trail. London, Hale, 1976.
The Long-Rope Riders. London, Hale, 1976.
Sawgrass Range. London, Hale, 1976.
Casadora. London, Hale, 1977.
The Lawbreaker. London, Hale, 1977.
Utah Summer. London, Hale, 1977.
Colt's Law. London, Hale, 1978.
The Longhorns. London, Hale, 1978.
West of Tucumcari. London, Hale, 1978.
Baylor's Bounty. London, Hale, 1979.

Novels as Kenneth Bedford

Solitaire. London, Hale, 1978.
Saddle Mountain. London, Hale, 1979.
The Hideout. London, Hale, 1980.
The Mexican Treasure. London, Hale, 1981.
The Piegan Range. London, Hale, 1982.
Eagle Valley. London, Hale, 1983.
Cowman's Legacy. London, Hale, 1990.

Novels as Will Benton

The Man Without a Gun. London, Gresham, 1961.
Rainy Valley. London, Gresham, 1962.
The Brush Country. London, Gresham, 1962.
Bushwhacker Vengeance. London, Gresham, 1964.
The Drifter. London, Gresham, 1964.
Bushwhacker's Moon. London, Gresham, 1965.

Cheyenne Pass. London, Gresham, 1965.
The Buckskin Hills. London, Gresham, 1966.
Wild Horse Mesa. London, Gresham, 1967.
The Last Ride. London, Hale, 1972.
Wild Horse Pass. London, Hale, 1973.
Trouble at Lansing Ferry. London, Hale, 1973.
The Outlaw. London, Hale, 1974.
Buffalo Butte. London, Hale, 1975.
Horsethief! London, Hale, 1975.
The Long Sleep. London, Hale, 1975.
Big Mesa. London, Hale, 1976.
The Horsetrader. London, Hale, 1976.
Cayuse Country. London, Hale, 1977.
Indian Summer. London, Hale, 1977.
Logan's Guns. New York, St. Martin's Press, and London, Hale, 1978.
The Lodgepole Trail. London, Hale, 1979.
Vaso Valley. London, Hale, 1980.
Secret Valley. London, Hale, 1982.
Big Meadow Range. London, Hale, 1983.

Novels as Martin Bishop

Evergreen. London, Hale, 1980.
Knight's Meadow. London, Hale, 1982.
Hardin's Valley. London, Hale, 1983.
The Fourth Horseman. London, Hale, 1989.

Novels as Lewis H. Bond

Ohlund's Raiders. London, Hale, 1979.
Black Rock. London, Hale, 1982.

Novels as Jack Bonner

Red Autumn. London, Hale, 1979.
The Lalo Trail. London, Hale, 1980.
Surprise Attack. London, Hale, 1981.
The Trail Riders. London, Hale, 1982.
The Fenwick Stage. London, Hale, 1983.
The Cache Hunter. London, Hale, 1984.
Buffalo Grass. London, Hale, 1986.
The Evening Gun. London, Hale, 1987.
The Trail to Nowhere. London, Hale, 1987.
The Shadow Horseman. London, Hale, 1988.

Novels as Frank Bosworth

Hangtown. London, Hale, 1964.
Trail to Deming. London, Hale, 1965.
The Purple Plain. London, Hale, 1966.
Bags and Saddles. London, Hale, 1967.
The Guns of Big Valley. London, Hale, 1967.
The Loser. London, Hale, 1967.
The Long-Riders. London, Hale, 1971.
Mustang Mesa. London, Hale, 1971.
The Singing Wind Trail. London, Hale, 1971.
Rainy Valley. London, Hale, 1971.
The South Slope. London, Hale, 1972.
Sunday's Guns. London, Hale, 1972.
Bear-Claw Range. London, Hale, 1973.
Riders in the Dusk. London, Hale, 1974.
The Rogue Hills. London, Hale, 1976.
Stranger's Trail. London, Hale, 1978.
Barling's Guns. London, Hale, 1980.
The Bountymen. London, Hale, 1981.
Rawhide. London, Hale, 1982.
The Brand Tree. London, Hale, 1986.
The Oxyoke. London, Hale, 1987.

Novels as Will Bradford

The Time of the Texan. London, Gresham, 1962.
Range of the Winter Moon. London, Gresham, 1964.
Rustler's Moon. London, Hale, 1964.
Ambush Canyon. London, Gresham, 1965.
The Last Gun. London, Gresham, 1965.
The Fast-Draw Men. London, Gresham, 1966.
Avenger's Trail. London, Gresham, 1967.
The Left-Hand Gun. London, Hale, 1972.
Cache Valley Guns. London, Hale, 1973.
Land of Low Hills. London, Hale, 1973.
Squatter's Rights. London, Hale, 1973.
The Dawnrider. London, Hale, 1974.
The Butte Country. London, Hale, 1975.
Gunhill. London, Hale, 1975.
The Legend of Lost Valley. London, Hale, 1975.
Lodgepole Range. London, Hale, 1976.
The Sundowners. London, Hale, 1976.
Lightning Strikes. London, Hale, 1977.
Outlaw Town. London, Hale, 1977.
Buffalo Gun. London, Hale, 1980.
The Hangrope Posse. London, Hale, 1982.
The Prisoner of Lonesome Valley. London, Hale, 1984.
High Lift Trail. London, Hale, 1987.
The Sand Painting. London, Hale, 1987.
The Squaw Blanket. London, Hale, 1987.

Novels as Concho Bradley

Lynch Law. London, Hale, 1964.
Guns of Arizona. London, Hale, 1965.
Johnny Colt. London, Hale, 1966.
Land of Long Rifles. London, Hale, 1966.
The Scattergun Men. London, Hale, 1967.
Winchester Hills. London, Hale, 1967.
The Cactus Country. London, Hale, 1972.
A Gunman's Code. London, Hale, 1974.
The Guns of San Angelo. London, Hale, 1975.
Culpepper County. London, Hale, 1975.
The Killer's Legacy. London, Hale, 1975.
The Blue Hills. London, Hale, 1976.
Carleton's Meadow. London, Hale, 1976.
Raider's Moon. London, Hale, 1976.
The Juniper Shadow. London, Hale, 1977.
Return to the South Desert. London, Hale, 1980.
Wyoming Springtime. London, Hale, 1980.
Copperdust Valley. London, Hale, 1982.
Moon Meadow. London, Hale, 1986.

Novels as Buck Bradshaw

Forbes Prairie. London, Hale, 1984.
Sweetwater. London, Hale, 1984.
Graveyard Meadow. London, Hale, 1985.
Pine Mountain. London, Hale, 1986.
The Tomahawk. London, Hale, 1986.
Trouble at Valverde. London, Hale, 1987.

Novels as Will Brennan

The Flint Hills. London, Gresham, 1963.
The Savage Land. London, Gresham, 1964.
Jubelo Junction. London, Gresham, 1964.
Way of the Outlaw. London, Gresham, 1965.

The Guns of Nevada. London, Gresham, 1966.
Gunman's Moon. London, Gresham, 1967.
Muleshoe Range. London, Hale, 1972.
Black Rock Range. London, Hale, 1973.
Rustler's Law. London, Hale, 1973.
The Gunsight Incident. London, Hale, 1974.
Scarface. London, Hale, 1975.
The Border Pawn. London, Hale, 1977.
The Ghost Rider. London, Hale, 1977.
Quade. London, Hale, 1980.
Cowman's Vengeance. London, Hale, 1982.
Round Rock Range. London, Hale, 1986.
Cheyenne Dawn. London, Hale, 1987.
Wolf Country. London, Hale, 1987.
The Hourglass. London, Hale, 1987.

Novels as Charles Burnham

Montana Moon. London, Hale, 1980.
Blackfeet Country. London, Hale, 1982.
The Mustang. London, Hale, 1987.
Sage City. London, Hale, 1987.

Novels as Mark Carrel

Comanche Trail. London, Hamilton, n.d.
The Hate Trail. London, Hamilton, n.d.
Wagon Train. London, Hamilton, n.d.
Comancheria. London, Hamilton, 1950.
El Vengador! London, Hamilton, 1950.
Land of the Harmattan. London, Hamilton, 1955.
Last of the Balfreys. London, Hamilton, 1955.
The Oldest Treachery. London, Hamilton, 1955.
The Hangrope's Shadow. London, Ward Lock, 1959.
Alamo Jefferson. London, Hale, 1990.

Novels as Nevada Carter

Texan Fast Gun. London, Gresham, 1963.
Perdition Wells. London, Gresham, 1964.
Perdition Range. London, Gresham, 1964.
Frontier Steel. London, Gresham, 1965.
Hangtown Sheriff. London, Gresham, 1966.
The Chaparral Trail. London, Gresham, 1967.
The Outsiders. London, Gresham, 1968.
The Gunsight Range. London, Hale, 1972.
The Green Hills. London, Hale, 1973.
A Man Called Faro. London, Hale, 1974.
The Badlands Trail. London, Hale, 1975.
Fugitive Trail. London, Hale, 1975.
The Lost Trail. London, Hale, 1977.
Buffalo Range. London, Hale, 1980.
The Horse Camp. London, Hale, 1986.

Novels as Claude Cassady

The Prairie Fighter. London, Hale, 1963.
The Law of Langley Valley. London, Hale, 1964.
The Outriders. London, Hale, 1965.
Sunset Guns. London, Hale, 1966.
Sunset Marshal. London, Hale, 1966.
The Man from Cody County. London, Hale, 1966.
Bounty Hunters' Range. London, Hale, 1967.
Monday's Guns. London, Hale, 1967.
The Hideout. London, Hale, 1977.
The Man from Tucson. London, Hale, and New York, St. Martin's Press, 1978.

Novels as Badger Clark

Cow-Country Killer. London, Hale, 1976.
Round Mountain Range. London, Hale, 1976.
Trouble at Fenmore. London, Hale, 1976.
Pawnee Dawn. London, Hale, 1977.
Phantom Canyon. London, Hale, 1977.
Secret Mesa. London, Hale, 1977.
Singleton. London, Hale, 1978.

Novels as Richard Clarke

The Shoshone Trail. London, Hale, 1980.
The Copperdust Hills. New York, Walker, 1983.
Pinon Country. London, Hale, 1983.
The Homesteaders. New York, Walker, 1986.
The Peralta Country. New York, Walker, 1987.
The Arrowhead Cattle Company. New York, Walker, 1988; London, Hale, 1989.
The Arizona Panhandle. New York, Walker, 1989.

Novels as Clint Custer

Apache Wells. London, Gresham, 1964.
Ute Peak Country. London, Gresham, 1964.
Webb County Sheriff. London, Gresham, 1965.
Night of the Gunman. London, Gresham, 1966.
Sixguns and Sam Logan. London, Gresham, 1966.
The Wells of San Saba. London, Hale, 1967.
Gila Bend. London, Hale, 1976.
Matanzas. London, Hale, 1986.

Novels as Richard Dana

The Long Ride. London, Hale, 1980.
Mandan Valley. London, Hale, 1981.
Shadow Valley. London, Hale, 1982.

Novels as John Durham

Shoot-Out. London, Gresham, 1963.
Hate Trail to Idaho. London, Gresham, 1963.
Caprock Vengeance. London, Gresham, 1964.
The Border Guns. London, Gresham, 1965; as *Arizona Drifter*, New York, Arcadia House, 1966.
Catch and Kill! London, Gresham, 1966.
Guns Along the Border. London, Gresham, 1966.
The Killer-Gun. London, Gresham, 1967.
Apache Moon. London, Hale, 1972.
Sundown. London, Hale, 1973.
The Buckaroo. London, Hale, 1974.
The Cowtown Debt. London, Hale, 1974.
Caine's Range. London, Hale, 1975.
The Purple Mesa. London, Hale, 1975.
The Arapaho Trail. London, Hale, 1976.
Circle H Range. London, Hale, 1976.
Nightrider's Moon. London, Hale, 1977.
Signal Rock Range. London, Hale, 1977.
Tomahawk Meadow. London, Hale, 1977.
The Reluctant Partner. London, Hale, and New York, St. Martin's Press, 1978.
Bound Out. London, Hale, 1978.

Cottonwood. London, Hale, 1980.
The Horsebreaker. London, Hale, 1981.
The Tennyson Rifle. London, Hale, 1982.

Novels as George Flynn

Rancheria. London, Hale, and New York, St. Martin's Press, 1979.
Colorado Stage. London, Hale, 1982.
The Titusville Country. London, Hale, 1989.
Six Silver Bullets. London, Hale, 1990.

Novels as Harry Foster

The Gunbearers. London, Hale, 1979.
Canbyville. London, Hale, 1980.
The Mud Wagon. London, Hale, 1981.
The Mexican Gun. London, Hale, 1989.

Novels as Don Glendenning

The Border Country. London, Hale, 1963.
The Hashknife. London, Hale, 1964.
Thunder Pass. London, Hale, 1966.
Salt-Lick Range. London, Hale, 1967.
Shadow Valley. London, Hale, 1976.
High Ridge Country. London, Hale, 1977.
The Hunter of Faro Canyon. London, Hale, 1977.

Novels as James Glenn

The Law Behind the Gun. London, Gresham, 1962.
Last of the Gunmen. London, Gresham, 1963.
Gun Town. London, Gresham, 1964.
Guns of the Hunter. London, Gresham, 1965.
Longhorn Trail. London, Gresham, 1966.
Oregon Guns. London, Gresham, 1966.
The Border Men. London, Gresham, 1967.
The Guns of Autumn. London, Gresham, 1967.
Broken Wheel Range. London, Gresham, 1968.
The Big Sky Trail. London, Hale, 1976.
Stedman's Law. London, Hale, 1977.
The Tumbleweed Stage. London, Hale, 1977.
The Law Trail. London, Hale, 1978.

Novels as Fred Harrison

Horse Mesa. London, Hale, 1980.
Horsethief's Moon. London, Hale, 1980.
The Long Rope. London, Hale, 1982.
The Mars Gun. London, Hale, 1990.

Novels as Travis Hartley

Longland Range. London, Hale, 1980.
Shawnee County. London, Hale, 1980.
The Bronc Buster. London, Hale, 1982.

Novels as Jay Hayden

The Canada Kid. London, Gresham, 1964.
The Ridge Runners. London, Gresham, 1965.
Cimarron Guns. London, Gresham, 1966.
The Long Trail Back. London, Gresham, 1966.
Sonora Pass. London, Gresham, 1967; New York, Lennox Hill Press, 1970.
Pinon Range. London, Hale, 1976.
Wanderer of the Open Range. London, Hale, 1977.

Novels as Roger Hill

Red Rock. London, Hale, 1979.
Navajo Country. London, Hale, 1980.
Redstone. London, Hale, 1981.
Round-Up. London, Hale, 1981.
The Trinity Brand. London, Hale, 1986.

Novels as Will Houston

Iron Marshal. London, Gresham, 1964.
Outlaw Range. London, Hale, 1965.
Sixshooter Trail. London, Gresham, 1965.
Stranger in Canebrake. London, Gresham, 1965.
Night of the Outlaws. London, Gresham, 1966.
The Sixgun Judge. London, Hale, 1972.
Ride to Battle Mountain. London, Hale, 1974.
The Gunman's Grave. London, Hale, 1975.
The Professionals. London, Hale, 1975.
The Shotgun Sheriff. London, Hale, 1976.
Gila Pass. London, Hale, 1977.
Howe. London, Hale, 1977.
Colorado Trail. London, Hale, 1977.
The Loner. London, Hale, 1978.
Death of a Gambler. London, Hale, 1982.
The Springfield Stage. London, Hale, 1984.
Sam's Valley. London, Hale, 1986.

Novels as Troy Howard

Longbow Range. London, Hale, 1978.
Iron Mountain Range. London, Hale, 1980.
Carrigan's Law. London, Hale, 1984.
The Black Colt. London, Hale, 1985.
Buffalo Run. London, Hale, 1986.
Eagle Trail. London, Hale, 1986.
Big Blue Canyon. London, Hale, 1987.
The Big High Desert. London, Hale, 1987.

Novels as John Hunt

Guns of Revenge. London, Gresham, 1963.
The Sagebrush Sea. London, Gresham, 1963.
The Kansas Kid. London, Hale, 1964.
Larkspur Range. London, Gresham, 1964.
Fast Guns of Deadwood. London, Gresham, 1965.
Thunder Guns. London, Gresham, 1966.
Rebel Guns. London, Gresham, 1967.
The Bushwhackers. London, Gresham, 1968.
A Town Called Centrefire. London, Gresham, 1972.
Bitterbrush Range. London, Hale, 1975.
Colt Country. London, Hale, 1975.
Oxbow. London, Hale, 1975.
Outlaw's Moon. London, Hale, 1976.
Roundup. London, Hale, 1976.
Seven Bullets. London, Hale, 1976.
Law Along the Trail. London, Hale, 1977.
The Skyline Trail. London, Hale, 1977.
Cannonball Canyon. London, Hale, and New York, St. Martin's Press, 1978.
Cantrell. London, Hale, 1978.
The Long Autumn. London, Hale, 1978.
Shawnee Valley. London, Hale, 1979.

Shepler's Spring. London, Hale, 1981.
The Pine Cone Ranch. London, Hale, 1985.
Lee's Meadow Country. London, Hale, 1986.
The Guns of Summer. London, Hale, 1987.
A Town Named Meridian. London, Hale, 1987.
The Expedition. London, Hale, 1988.
Charley Choctaw. London, Hale, 1989.
Sam Coyote. London, Hale, 1990.

Novels as Ray Kelley

The Long-Riders. London, Hale, 1964.
The Guns of El Paso. London, Hale, 1965.
High Desert Guns. London, Hale, 1966.
The High Plains. London, Hale, 1966.
The Mankiller. London, Hale, 1967.
Shotgun Rider. London, Hale, 1967.
The Gunsight Affair. London, Hale, 1975.
Cane's Mesa. London, Hale, 1976.
A Gunman's Shadow. London, Hale, 1976.
Justice in New Mexico. London, Hale, 1976.
Bluegrass Range. London, Hale, 1977.
Johnny Centavo. London, Hale, 1977.
Sixgun Assassin. London, Hale, 1977.
Blue Rock Range. London, Hale, and New York, St. Martin's Press, 1978.

Novels as Cliff Ketchum

The Border Men. London, Hale, 1977.
Rustler's Brand. London, Hale, 1978.
Gunnison Valley. London, Hale, 1980.
The Forsythe Stage. London, Hale, 1992.

Novels as Frank Ketchum

Idaho Trail. London, Hale, 1978.
The Kiowa Plains. London, Hale, 1978.
The Guns of Parral. London, Hale, 1984.
Ghost Meadow. London, Hale, 1986.
The Last Ride. London, Hale, 1987.
The Renegade's Moon. London, Hale, 1988.

Novels as Jack Ketchum

The Laramie Plains. London, Hale, 1964.
Winchester Pass. London, Hale, 1965; New York, Arcadia House, 1966.
Dead or Alive. London, Hale, 1966.
The Guns of Amarillo. London, Hale, 1966.
The Guns of Buck Elder. London, Hale, 1967.
The Trail Without End. London, Hale, 1973.
Cactus Country. London, Hale, 1975.
Border Dawn. London, Hale, 1976.
Guns of the South Desert. London, Hale, 1976.
Open Range. London, Hale, 1981.

Novels as John Kilgore

Return of the Fast Gun. London, Hale, 1961.
Sheriff of Cow County. London, Hale, 1962.
The Short-Gun Man. London, Hale, 1962.
The Gunfighter. London, Hale, 1963.
The Man from Secret Valley. London, Hale, 1964.
The Hidden Hills. London, Hale, 1965.
Man from the Cherokee Strip. London, Hale, 1966.
Nightrider's Moon. London, Hale, 1966.
Oklahoma Fiddlefoot. New York, Arcadia House, 1966.
Lynch Town. London, Hale, 1967.
Pawnee Butte. London, Hale, 1975.
The Painted Pony. London, Hale, 1976.
The Partnership. London, Hale, 1976.
Southwest Law. London, Hale, 1976.
Topar Rim. London, Hale, 1979.
The Shadow Gunman. London, Hale, 1986.
The Deadwood Stage. London, Hale, 1987.
The Sun Devils. London, Hale, 1987.
Three Silver Bullets. London, Hale, 1987.

Novels as Ralph Kimball

Buckeye. London, Hale, 1980.
Manning. London, Hale, 1981.
The Bushwhacker. London, Hale, 1989.

Novels as Buck Lyon

Trail of the Hunted. London, Gresham, 1967.
Sundown. London, Hale, 1978.
Sandrock. London, Hale, 1979.
Cow Camp. London, Hale, 1979.
Bear Valley. London, Hale, 1980.
Carver Valley. London, Hale, 1981.
The Rain-Maker. London, Hale, 1983.

Novels as Bruce Martin

The Top Lash. London, Gresham, 1963.
Fighting Marshal. London, Gresham, 1963.
Guns of the Law. London, Mills and Boon, 1963.
Badland Guns. London, Gresham, 1964.
The Texas Twister. London, Gresham, 1965; New York, Arcadia House, 1966.
The Raw Country. London, Gresham, 1966; New York, Arcadia House, 1967.
Arizona Ambush. London, Gresham, 1967; New York, Lennox Hill Press, 1971.
The Pinon Hills. London, Hale, 1978.

Novels as Tom Martin

Land of Long Shadows. London, Gresham, 1963.
Lone Trail to Puma. London, Gresham, 1964.
The Oxbow Range. London, Gresham, 1964.
The Texas Trail. London, Hale, 1964.
Deadwood. London, Gresham, 1965; as *Hangrope Canyon*, London, Hale, 1980.
The Lone Pine Trail. London, Gresham, 1966.
Vengeance in Hangtown. London, Gresham, 1966.
Deadman Canyon. London, Gresham, 1967.
Gunsight Pass. London, Hale, 1967.
Guntown Justice. London, Hale, 1976.
Long Lance. London, Hale, 1977.
The Men from El Paso. London, Hale, 1977.

Novels as Frank Morgan

The Desert Riders. London, Hale, 1978.
Trail Guns. London, Hale, 1980.
Tomahawk Range. London, Hale, 1981.
San Saba Trail. London, Hale, 1982.
Farnham's War. London, Hale, 1987.

Novels as John Morgan

Windriver Hills. London, Hale, 1980.
Harper's Trail. London, Hale, 1981.

Bluegrass Range. London, Hale, 1982.
The Autumn Hunter. London, Hale, 1990.

Novels as Clint O'Conner

The Tall Texans. London, Hale, 1964.
Dead Man's Range. London, Hale, 1965.
Thieves' Trail. London, Hale, 1966.
Cooper's Moon. London, Hale, 1973.
Guns of Black Rock. London, Hale, 1975.
Mule-Train. London, Hale, 1978.
Broken Bow Range. London, Hale, 1982.
The Paloverde Tree. London, Hale, 1984.
White Stone. London, Hale, 1984.

Novels as Leland Rhodes

The Danger Trail. London, Hale, 1981.
Eagle Mountain Range. London, Hale, 1981.
Morning Gun. London, Hale, 1982.

Novels as Jim Slaughter

Gun Country. London, Hale, 1964.
Rustler's Trail. London, Hale, 1965.
The Sonora Plains. London, Hale, 1965.
The Guns of Johnny Dalton. London, Hale, 1966.
The Guns of Fortune. London, Hale, 1967; New York, Arcadia House, 1969.
The Stage to Amarillo. London, Hale, 1967.
Lariat Law. London, Hale, 1974.
The Mustangers. London, Hale, 1974.
Gun Country. London, Hale, 1975.
Gunnison Butte. London, Hale, 1975.
Shadow Range. London, Hale, 1975.
Boone's Law. London, Hale, 1976.
The Gunman's Choice. London, Hale, 1976.
Rendezvous on the South Desert. London, Hale, 1976.
Blue Star Range. London, Hale, 1977.
The Guns of Summer. London, Hale, 1977.
The Hangtree. London, Hale, 1977.
The Legend of Chilili. London, Hale, 1978.
Montana Trail. London, Hale, 1978.
Deuce. London, Hale, and New York, St Martin's Press, 1979.
Mandan Meadow. London, Hale, 1983.
The Bordermen. London, Hale, 1987.
Horse Canyon. London, Hale, 1989.

Novels as Buck Standish

The Durango Kid. London, Gresham, 1963.
Gunsight. London, Gresham, 1963.
Incident at Alturas. London, Hale, 1964.
Prairie Town. London, Hale, 1965.
Brothers of Vengeance. London, Gresham, 1966.
Montana Trail. London, Gresham, 1966.
Eagle Pass. London, Gresham, and New York, Arcadia House, 1967.
Gundown. London, Hale, 1973.
The Guns of High Meadow. London, Hale, 1973.
The Guns of Dawn. London, Hale, 1974.
Custer County. London, Hale, 1974.
Custer Meadow. London, Hale, 1975.
The Jayhawker. London, Hale, 1975.
Shipman's Meadow. London, Hale, 1976.
Squatter's Guns. London, Hale, 1976.
White Mountain Range. London, Hale, 1976.
The Land of Buffalo Grass. London, Hale, 1977.
Riders of the Law. London, Hale, 1977.
The Gunman's Legacy. London, Hale, 1978.
Phantom Trail. London, Hale, 1979.
The Line Riders. London, Hale, 1982.
The Lodgepole Trail. London, Hale, 1983.
Hardin County. London, Hale, 1985.
The Rim Rock Country. London, Hale, 1986.

Novels as Bruce Thomas

Sioux Autumn. London, Hale, and New York, St. Martin's Press, 1979.
Blue Sage Country. London, Hale, 1982.
Mormon Meadow. London, Hale, 1985.
Men for Boot Hill. London, Hale, 1986.
Arrowhead Range. London, Hale, 1987.
The Horse Trap. London, Hale, 1987.
The Moccasin Trail. London, Hale, 1987.

Novels as Buck Thompson

Starfire Range. London, Hale, 1975.
The Juniper Hills. London, Hale, 1976.
Shiloh. London, Hale, 1978.
Harmon Valley. London, Hale, 1979.
Bull Mountain Range. London, Hale, 1981.
The Warbonnet. London, Hale, 1982.
The Yucca Cattle Company. London, Hale, 1984.
The Camp Robbers. London, Hale, 1985.
The Bob-Tailed Horse. London, Hale, 1986.
Stranger to Dogwood. London, Hale, 1986.

Novels as Russ Thompson

Trail Town. London, Hale, 1963; as *West of Sioux Pass*, New York, Arcadia House, 1965.
The Night Riders. London, Hale, 1964.
Riders in the Night. London, Hale, 1964.
Tumbleweed Trail. London, Hale, 1965.
Bitterbrush Basin. New York, Arcadia House, 1966.
Green River Marshal. London, Hale, 1966.
Winchester Plains. London, Hale, 1966.
A Pair of Aces. London, Hale, 1967.
Carson City. London, Hale, 1968; New York, Lennox Hill Press, 1970.
The Copperhead. London, Hale, 1973.
Laramie Stage. London, Hale, 1974.
The Man Called Corbett. London, Hale, 1974.
A Lawman's Choice. London, Hale, 1975.
The Top Whip. London, Hale, 1975.
The Gun Brand. London, Hale, 1976.
Range Law. London, Hale, 1976.
The Iron Mountains. London, Hale, 1977.
Desert Journey. London, Hale, 1978.
The Patterson Stage. London, Hale, 1978.
Gundown. London, Hale, 1979.
Solablo. London, Hale, 1983.
The Last Fugitive. London, Hale, 1987.
Beyond the Law. London, Hale, 1990.
The Copper Bullet. London, Hale, 1992.

OTHER PUBLICATIONS

Novels

When the Moon Ran Wild (as Ray Ainsbury). London, World, 1962.

This Time Tomorrow (as Lauran Paine). London, World, 1963.
Love in the Clouds (as Rosa Almonte). London, Hale, 1967.
Love Has Two Faces (as Elizabeth Howard). London, Hale, 1968.
The Maltese Moon (as Margot Fisher). London, Hale, 1968.
The Merchant of Menace (as Kenneth Bedford). London, Hale, 1968.
The Girl in Blue (as Joni Frost). London, Hale, 1968.
To Face the Sun (as Joni Frost). London, Hale, 1968.
The Ides of Love (as Valerie Morgan). London, Hale, 1968.
April Is Our Time (as Margaret Stuart). London, Hale, 1968.
A Doctor in Exile (as Margaret Stuart). London, Hale, 1968.
The Mathematics of Murder (as Kenneth Bedford). London, Hale, and New York, Roy, 1969.
Haight Is the Killer (as J.K. Lucas). London, Hale, 1969.
Murder Now, Pay Later (as Frank Bosworth). London, Hale, 1969.
Identity of a Lover (as Richard Clarke). London, Hale, 1969.
A Race with Love (as Arthur St. George). London, Hale, 1969.
Some Die Young (as John Kilgore). London, Hale, 1970.
A Fortune for Love (as Frank Morgan). London, Hale, 1971.
Murder to Music (as John Kilgore). London, Hale, 1972.
Focolor (as Roy Ainsworthy). London, Hale, 1973.
Two Loves for Sue (as Angela Morgan). London, Hale, 1974.
The Born Survivor (as J.K. Lucas). London, Hale, 1975.
The Lovers (as Valerie Morgan). London, Hale, 1981.

Novels as John Armour

Run with the Killer. London, Hale, 1969.
The Love of a Banker. London, Hale, 1969.
A Killer's Category. London, Hale, 1973.
Murder in Hawthorn. London, Hale, 1975.
The Saturday Night Massacre. London, Hale, 1976.

Novels as Kathleen Bartlett

Love and a Rusty Moon. London, Hale, 1968.
The Love Match. London, Hale, 1971.
Love of an Heiress. London, Hale, 1971.
Loves Takes Its Choice. London, Hale, 1971.
Love Has a Hard Heart. London, Hale, 1972.
Lovers in Autumn. London, Hale, 1972.
Love in a Glass Suit. London, Hale, 1973.
The Hemstead Women. London, Hale, 1978.

Novels as Reg Batchelor

Blue Sea and Yellow Sun. London, Hale, 1967.
The Time of Assassins. London, Hale, 1969.
Inspector Cole. London, Hale, 1970.
The Murder Game. London, Hale, 1970.
Murderer's Row. London, Hale, 1970.
The Twilight People. London, Hale, 1970.
A Legacy of Shadows. London, Hale, 1972.
The Triangle Murder. London, Hale, 1973.
Achilles' Isle. London, Hale, 1974.

Novels as Ruth Bovee

Angelina. London, Hale, 1967.
Antoinette. London, Hale, 1968.
The Lady and the Moon. London, Hale, 1968.
Love and a Dark Heart. London, Hale, 1971.
A Heart of Shadows. London, Hale, 1974.

Novels as Mark Carrel

The Sinister Horde. London, Hamilton, 1955.
The Case of the Hollow Man. London, Foulsham, 1958.
The Case of the Innocent Witness. London, Foulsham, 1959.
The Case of the Perfect Alibi. London, Foulsham, 1960.
The Blood-Pit. London, Hale, 1967.
The Dark Edge of Violence. London, Hale, 1967.
Shadow of a Hawk. London, Hale, 1967.
A Sword of Silk. London, Hale, 1967.
Tears of Blood. London, Hale, 1967.
The Steel Mask. London, Hale, 1968.
Kill and Be Damned. London, Hale, 1970.
The Emerald Heart. London, Hale, 1971.
A Crack in Time. London, Hale, 1971.
Another View. London, Hale, 1972.
The Undine. London, Hale, 1972.
Counsel for the Killer. London, Hale, 1972.
Bannister's Z-Matter. London, Hale, 1973.
One Last Time. London, Hale, 1973.
Murder Without Motive. London, Hale, 1974.
The Octopus' Shadow. London, Hale, 1974.
Assignment for Trouble. London, Hale, 1974.
The Underground Men. London, Hale, 1975.

Novels as Robert Clarke

The Case of the Gambler's Corpse. London, Hale, 1969.
Murderers Are Silent. London, Hale, 1969.
The Thirteenth Lover. London, Hale, 1970.
Love in New England. London, Hale, 1970.
Death of a Flower Child. London, Hale, 1970.
A Synonym for Murder. London, Hale, 1972.

Novels as Amber Dana

Love and Company. London, Hale, 1969.
Love Is a Red Rose. London, Hale, 1969.
Love Is Forever. London, Hale, 1969.
The Widow Is a Temptress. London, Hale, 1969.
One Love for Summer. London, Hale, 1969.
Helen of Troydon. London, Hale, 1970.
Love Is Triumph. London, Hale, 1970.
A Rich Girl's Love. London, Hale, 1970.
The Queen of Hearts. London, Hale, 1971.
A Rose Without Love. London, Hale, 1973.
A Scarlet Dawn. London, Hale, 1978.
The Kiss of Life. London, Hale, 1980.
The Jade Moon. London, Hale, 1981.

Novels as Richard Dana

Death of a Millionaire. London, Hale, 1969.
Murderer's Moon. London, Hale, 1969.

Murder in Paradise. London, Hale, 1969.
Death Was the Echo. London, Hale, 1975.

Novels as Audrey Davis

Love by Starlight. London, Hale, 1968.
Love in Eden. London, Hale, 1973.
A Favoured Dawn. London, Hale, 1974.
An Autumn to Remember. London, Hale, 1976.

Novels as J. F. Drexler

The Anonymous Assassin. London, Hale, 1968.
The Fire Ant. London, Hale, 1975.
The Unsuspecting Victim. London, Hale, 1976.

Novels as Antoinette Duchesne

Love Is a Triangle. London, Hale, 1967.
Decision to Love. London, Hale, 1968.
Love Is the Enemy. London, Hale, 1968.

Novels as Betty Fleck

Under a Dark Moon. London, Hale, 1967.
A Rose for Love. London, Hale, 1968.
The Love Thief. London, Hale, 1968.
Love and a Winter Moon. London, Hale, 1968.
The Love That Never Was. London, Hale, 1969.
A Different Kind of Marriage. London, Hale, 1970.

Novels as Angela Gordon

Fate of the Lovers. London, Hale, 1968.
Heart of a Widow. London, Hale, 1968.
The Little Goddess. London, Hale, 1968.
Love Has Many Faces. London, Hale, 1969.
Love Is a Tempest. London, Hale, 1969.
Not Without Love. London, Hale, 1969.
A Game Called Love. London, Hale, 1970.
Jacqueline. London, Hale, 1970.
Love in Her Life. London, Hale, 1970.
The Love of Damocles. London, Hale, 1971.
Love on the Moors. London, Hale, 1973.
Stranger in the Shadows. London, Hale, 1974.
The Love Harvest. London, Hale, 1974.
Carlotta. London, Hale, 1976.
Autumn Gold. London, Hale, 1978.
The House on Sorrel Lane. London, Hale, 1978.
Forbidden Autumn. London, Hale, 1979.
A Gentle Spring. London, Hale, 1980.
Misty's Mother. London, Hale, 1980.
April D'Auriac. London, Hale, 1990.

Novels as Beth Gorman

Lanterns of the Night. London, Hale, 1967.
Gentle Lover. London, Hale, 1968.
Love Is a Stranger. London, Hale, 1968.
Love Has a Golden Touch. London, Hale, 1969.
Love Has a Double. London, Hale, 1973.
Lover's Valley. London, Hale, 1974.

Novels as Francis Hart

Moment of Truth. London, Hale, n.d.
Red Autumn. London, Hale, 1967.
Once There Was a Golden Moon. London, Hale, 1968.
Love Is a Secret. London, Hale, 1968.
Doctor Blaydon's Dilemma. London, Hale, 1968.
The Gulls of Autumn. London, Hale, 1974.
Lover's Dilemma. London, Hale, 1974.
Topaz. London, Hale, 1974.

Novels as Helen Holt

Dilemma for the Doctor. London, Hale, 1968.
Only with Love. London, Hale, 1971.
A Troubled Heart. London, Hale, 1973.
June Love. London, Hale, 1973.
One Love Lost. London, Hale, 1973.

Novels as Troy Howard

The Black Light. London, Hale, 1968.
The Harbinger. London, Hale, 1972.
The Kernel of Death. London, Hale, 1973.
The Misplaced Psyche. London, Hale, 1973.

Novels as Jared Ingersol

The Night of the Crisis. London, Hale, 1968.
A Game Called Murder. London, Hale, 1969.
A Rose Can Kill. London, Hale, 1969.
The Beautiful Murder. London, Hale, 1970.
Diamond Fingers. London, Hale, 1970.
The Jade Eye. London, Hale, 1970.
The Steel Garotte. London, Hale, 1970.
The Killer's Conscience. London, Hale, 1971.
The Man Who Stole Heaven. London, Hale, 1971.
The Money Murder. London, Hale, 1971.
The Non-Murder. London, Hale, 1972.
The Man Who Made Roubles. London, Hale, 1972.
The Golden Gloves. London, Hale, 1973.
A Fine Day for Murder. London, Hale, 1974.
The Witchcraft Murder. London, Hale, 1975.

Novels as Hunter Liggett

Murder for Money. London, Hale, 1969.
The Murder Maze. London, Hale, 1969.
The Victim Died Twice. London, Hale, 1969.
The Unknown Murderer. London, Hale, 1975.

Novels as Arlene Morgan

Ten Days to Remember. London, Hale, 1967.
Starfire. London, Hale, 1974.
A Time for Lovers. London, Hale, 1974.

Novels as John Morgan

Death to Comrade X. London, Hale, 1969.
Murderers Don't Smile. London, Hale, 1969.
Spy in the Tunnel. London, Hale, 1969.
To Kill a Hero. London, Hale, 1969.
The Nicest Corpse. London, Hale, 1970.
The Perfect Frame. London, Hale, 1970.
The Midnight Murder. London, Hale, 1971.

The Killer's Manual. London, Hale, 1972.
The Ivory Penguin. London, Hale, 1974.

Novels as Helen Sharp

Ward Nurse. London, Hale, 1968.
Love and Heather. London, Hale, 1969.
The Image of Love. London, Hale, 1970.
Love Came Slowly. London, Hale, 1970.
A Girl Named Gardenia. London, Hale, 1971.
Love and a Half Moon. London, Hale, 1971.
The Love Token. London, Hale, 1971.
Love the Second Time. London, Hale, 1972.
The Huntress. London, Hale, 1973.
Love Is a New World. London, Hale, 1973.
Lover from Another Time. London, Hale, 1973.
The Sunday Lover. London, Hale, 1973.

Novels as Barbara Thorn

Beyond This Valley. New York, Thomas Bouregy, 1964.
From Karen with Love. London, Hale, 1967.
Love is a Crescent Moon. London, Hale, 1967.
Nurse for a Night. London, Hale, 1968.
To Sandy with Love. London, Hale, 1968.
Love Once, Love Twice. London, Hale, 1970.
Midsummer Love. London, Hale, 1970.
One Woman's Heart. London, Hale, 1971.
The Doctors Nelson. London, Hale, 1973.
Love and the Blue Moon. London, Hale, 1973.

Other

The Long War Trail. London, Transworld, 1957.
The Massacre at Mountain Meadows. London, Transworld, 1958.
Northwest Conquest. London, Foulsham, and Hartford, Connecticut, McBride, 1959.
The General Custer Story. London, Foulsham, 1960.
Tom Horn: Man of the West. London, John Long, 1962; New York, Barre, 1963.
Benedict Arnold: Hero and Traitor. London, Hale, 1965.
Viet-Nam. New York, Barre, 1965.
Texas Ben Thompson. Tucson, Arizona, Westernlore, 1966.
Warm Beer and Cold Comfort. London, Hale, 1968.
Bolivar the Liberator. London, Hale, and New York, Barre, 1970.
A Gaggle of Ghosts. London, Hale, 1971.
The Hierarchy of Hell. London, Hale, and New York, Hippocrene, 1972.
Sex in Witchcraft. London, Hale, and New York, Taplinger, 1972.
Witches in Fact and Fantasy. London, Hale, and New York, Taplinger, 1972.
Captain John Smith and the Jamestown Story. London, Hale, 1973.
Gentleman Johnny: The Life of General John Burgoyne. London, Hale, 1973.
Saladin: A Man for All Ages. London, Hale, 1974.
Witchcraft and the Mysteries. London, Hale, and New York, Taplinger, 1975.
The Terrorists. London, Hale, 1975.
The Assassins. London, Hale, 1975; as *The Assassin's World*, New York, Taplinger, 1975.
The Invisible World of Espionage. London, Hale, 1976.
Mathilde Carre: Double Agent. London, Hale, 1976.
The CIA at Work. London, Hale, 1977.
Double Jeopardy. London, Hale, 1978.
The Technology of Espionage. London, Hale, 1978.
Britain's Intelligence Service. London, Hale, 1979.
D-Day. London, Hale, 1981.
The Abwehr (German Military Intelligence in WWII). London, Hale, and Stein and Day, 1984.
America and the Americans. London, Hale, 1984.
Silicon Spies. London, Hale, and New York, St. Martin's Press, 1986.

* * *

The virtual writing-machine that is Lauran Paine describes his entry into western fiction thus: "It began on the XIH ranch in northern Colorado lo, these many years ago when, to my horror, I found a stack of Street and Smith western magazines—the old-time pulps—that were so riddled with errors that I decided to try my own hand." Although events occurred to delay that intent, Paine was finally able to redeem his pledge in 1945.

Today he has no idea how many stories he wrote for the pulps, but the number of his full-length Westerns (written under both his own name and a staggering 59 pseudonyms) is now approaching 700—and *this*, incidentally, in addition to his 200-plus novels in the romance, mystery, SF and action/adventure genres, and 30 volumes of nonfiction, which cover everything from biographies of Tom Horn and George Custer to histories of the British Secret Service and sex in witchcraft!

A former cowboy and rancher, Paine writes mainly from experience. Given the sheer volume of his work, however, there is inevitably some similarity of theme and character. *The Tennyson Rifle*, for example, in which a stranger is locked up on suspicion of murder and/or robbery only to be revealed as an honest citizen fleeing from some kind of domestic dispute back home, bears a remarkable resemblance to *Pine Mountain. Cheyenne Dawn*, in which a half-breed Indian baby is given to a childless white couple who then have to fight the authorities to keep it, is reminiscent of one of Paine's best books, *Spirit Meadow*.

Generally, Paine likes to use older, largely inoffensive men as his protagonists, usually range- or stockmen past their prime or blacksmiths and stable-owners who, never having had to deal with trouble before, somehow manage to overcome their present difficulties and bring order back to their lives and communities. He usually groups such characters together in threes, as with his recent Sheridan Township series.

A large proportion of Paine's stories feature town marshals or "constables." Quite often these lawmen are mild-mannered and easy-going, content to sashay through any given predicament in the hope that it will eventually resolve itself. As a rule they make lousy coffee, are possessed of a laconic sense of humour and have to be nagged by friends or town elders before they will act. Paine has an undeniable knack for characterisation, and his players—men and women whose lives have developed in an environment of hardship, basic convictions and a very simple acceptance of life—are always imbued with a gritty sense of realism.

For the most part, Paine tells his stories in a direct, matter-of-fact style. Sometimes he employs clipped dialogue riddled with Westernisms (mainly for old-timers), but more often than not he leaves speech unadorned. He titles his chapters (which can number anything between 12 and 24) and through the observations of his characters, frequently reveals an understanding of human nature that is shrewd, wry, and always accurate.

Although violence in his books is kept to a minimum and its effects usually described rather vaguely, one of his most popular themes is that of murder and attempted murder. In *The Hidden Hills*, a soldier is found hanging outside a hotel. A young woman is struck down by a sniper's bullet before she can inherit her father's ranch in *The New Mexico Heritage*. A banker is shot to death in mysterious circumstances in *The Sheridan Stage* and so on. This plot device also recurs in *Rainy Valley* and *The Autumn Hunter*, among many others. It must be said that the author usually manages to ring the changes with twists and variations that stop his work from becoming hackneyed, however.

Because he is more interested in telling stories than increasing body-counts, Paine's bursts of action are few and far between. Sometimes, as with *The Paloverde Tree*, there is so *little* action that the villain of the piece is actually killed "off-camera," and reader and hero alike only get to discover the fact through a third party much later in the book. However, this relative lack of violence is by no means a fault; indeed, it usually serves to make the gunplay more powerful when at last it *does* happen.

Although Paine is a Minnesotan now resident in California, only a relatively small proportion of his work has been published in America, but fittingly, this work is usually his best (most probably because of sub-editing, which is seldom performed on Westerns in Britain). Some of his British Westerns, such as *The Springfield Stage* and *A Town Named Meridian*, are little more than expanded short stories, while others—notably *The Lodgepole Trail* and *Matanzas*—are especially worthy of mention.

Paine sets his stories right across the West, but appears to have a predilection for New Mexico, about which he writes very well. In the main, he avoids basing plots on actually historical events (although he has a firm understanding of American history), but nevertheless succeeds in giving his Westerns a neat "period" feel. He is also surprisingly good at writing about women, seldom presenting them as stereotypes, and inclines towards short, punchy titles that guarantee immediate reader identification.

Sometimes the author reveals a tendency to end his stories rather too soon. In several titles—*Guns of the Hunters*, *Tanner*, *The Horse Camp*, and *The Guns of Summer*—the plot comes to a head 30 or 40 pages from the end of the book, a habit which can leave the reader with a sense of anti-climax. On the whole, though, Paine's Westerns are solid and dependable, offering as they do engaging characters in exciting situations, who constantly triumph over evil to bring about an ultimately satisfying finale.

—David Whitehead

PALMER, Bernard. Also writes as John Runyan. American. Born in Central City, Nebraska, November 1914. Educated at Kearney State College, Nebraska, 1933; Hastings College, Nebraska, 1940. Married 1) June Berger in 1934 (died 1939), one son (deceased); 2) the writer Marjorie Matthews in 1940, one son and two daughters. Stonecutter and shop foreman, 1957–67, vice-president, 1962–74, and since 1974 president and chairman of board of directors, Palmer Brothers Monument Company, Holdrege, Nebraska. Since 1963 member of board of directors, Tyndale Foundation. Past president of Nebraska chapter, Gideons International. Since 1967 full-time writer. Address: 1013 14th Avenue, Holdrege, Nebraska 68949, U.S.A.

WESTERN PUBLICATIONS

Novels (series: Breckinridge in all books)

Kid Breckenridge. Wheaton, Illinois, Tyndale, 1984; London, Hale, 1990.
Breck's Choice. Wheaton, Illinois, Tyndale, 1984; London, Hale, 1989.
Hunted Gun. Wheaton, Illinois, Tyndale, 1984; as *Wanted Gun*, London, Hale, 1990.
Shoot-Out at Buffalo Gulch. Wheaton, Illinois, Tyndale, 1985; London, Hale, 1990.

OTHER PUBLICATIONS

Fiction for children

Parson John. Grand Rapids, Michigan, Eerdmans, 1942.
Storm Winds. Grand Rapids, Michigan, Eerdmans, 1942.
Visibility Zero. Grand Rapids, Michigan, Zondervan, 1944.
Dark Are the Shadows. Grand Rapids, Michigan, Zondervan, 1945.
Dangerous Mission. Grand Rapids, Michigan, Zondervan, 1945.
Mission of Mercy. Wheaton, Illinois, Hitchcock, 1946.
Goon Walford Fights Back. N.p., Van Kampen, 1946.
Withering Grass. N.p., Van Kampen, 1949.
Sky Pilot Gang Busters. N.p., Sky Pilot Press, 1955.
Jungle Jim. Chicago, Moody, 1956.
Storm on the Muskeg. Chicago, Moody, 1957.
New Skipper of the Flying Swede, with Marjorie Palmer. Chicago, Moody, 1957.
Miracle of the Prairies. Chicago, Moody, 1958; as *Beacon on the Prairies*, n.p., Briercrest Bible Institute, 1970.
Andy Logan and the Oregon Trail Mystery. Chicago, Moody, 1961.
Mystery of Dungu Re. Chicago, Moody, 1961.
Tattered Loin Cloth. Chicago, Moody, 1962.
Adventure in Tangyanika. Chicago, Moody, 1963.
Yukuma the Brave. Chicago, Moody, 1963.
The Wind Blows Wild. Chicago, Moody, 1963.
Sue Riley and the Mysterious Cargo. Chicago, Moody, 1968.
Across the Deep Valleys. Lincoln, Nebraska Christian Press, 1969.
So Restless, So Lonely. Minneapolis, Bethany Fellowship, 1970.
Seek Not Tomorrow. Chicago, Moody, 1971.
Whisper the Robin. Grand Rapids, Michigan, Zondervan, 1972.
Frosty Roberts and the Golden Jade Mystery. Chicago, Moody, 1975.
The Davis Triplets and the Film Action. Chicago, Moody, 1975.
White Water on the Yukon. Chicago, Moody, 1975.
I'm a Louie, Atsa Phil. Chicago, Moody, 1975.
Yoneko. Lincoln, Nebraska, Back to the Bible, 1976.
McTaggart's Promise. Elgin, Illinois, David Cook, 1978.
Run for the West. Elgin, Illinois, David Cook, 1979.
Ted and the Secret Club. Wheaton, Illinois, Victor, 1980.
Hitched to a Star. Chicago, Moody, 1981.

Fiction for children (series: Bradley in all books)

The Mysterious Letter. Lincoln, Nebraska, Back to the Bible, 1975.
Mystery of the New Sky. Lincoln, Nebraska, Back to the Bible, 1975.

Jon and the Break-In Mystery. Lincoln, Nebraska, Back to the Bible, 1976.
Trena and the Old Diary. Lincoln, Nebraska, Back to the Bible, 1976.
Homesteading in Standing Bear's Territory. Lincoln, Nebraska, Back to the Bible, 1976.
Princess Pat Saves the Day. Lincoln, Nebraska, Back to the Bible, 1977.
Trena's Rodeo Vial. Lincoln, Nebraska, Back to the Bible, 1977.
Mystery of the Missing Fossil. Lincoln, Nebraska, Back to the Bible, 1977.

Fiction for children (series: Brigade Boys in all books)

Brigade Boys and the Flight to Danger. Chicago, Moody, 1960.
Brigade Boys and the Phantom Radio. Chicago, Moody, 1960.
Brigade Boys in the Arctic Wilderness. Chicago, Moody, 1961.
Brigade Boys and the Disappearing Stranger. Chicago, Moody, 1961.
Brigade Boys and the Basketball Mystery. Chicago, Moody, 1963.

Fiction for children (series: Career in all books)

Student Nurse, with Marjorie Palmer. Chicago, Moody, 1960.
Barbara Nichols, Fifth Grade Teacher, with Marjorie Palmer. Chicago, Moody, 1960.
Big Season. Chicago, Moody, 1960.
Mystery of the Musty Ledger. Chicago, Moody, 1960.
Peggy Archer, Missionary Candidate. Chicago, Moody, 1961.
Brad Foster, Engineer. Chicago, Moody, 1962.
Karen Simms, Private Secretary, with Marjorie Palmer. Chicago, Moody, 1963.
Randy Warren, First Term Missionary. Chicago, Moody, 1963.
Cal Henderson, M.D. Chicago, Moody, 1963.
Jim Shelton, Radio Engineer. Chicago, Moody, 1964.
Sandra Emerson, R.N., with Marjorie Palmer. Chicago, Moody, 1966.
Lee Sloan, Missionary Pilot. Chicago, Moody, 1966.
Dennis Harper, Missionary Journalist. Chicago, Moody, 1966.

Fiction for children (series: Danny Orlis in all books)

Danny Orlis and the Point Barrow Mystery. N.p., Good News, 1954.
Danny Orlis and the Angle Inlet Mystery. Chicago, Moody, 1954.
Danny Orlis and the Strange Forest Fires. Chicago, Moody, 1955.
Danny Orlis and the Hunters. Chicago, Moody, 1955.
Danny Orlis Goes to School. Chicago, Moody, 1955.
Danny Orlis and the Rocks That Talk. Chicago, Moody, 1955.
Danny Orlis on Superstition Mountain. Chicago, Moody, 1956.
Danny Orlis Makes the Team. Chicago, Moody, 1956.
Danny Orlis Changes Schools. Chicago, Moody, 1956.
Danny Orlis and the Wrecked Plane. Chicago, Moody, 1956.
Danny Orlis and the Big Indian. Chicago, Moody, 1956.
Danny Orlis and the Sacred Cave. Chicago, Moody, 1957.
Danny Orlis, Star Back. Chicago, Moody, 1957.
Danny Orlis and the Boy Who Would Not Listen. Chicago, Moody, 1957.
Danny Orlis Plays Hockey. Chicago, Moody, 1957.
Danny Orlis and His Big Chance. Chicago, Moody, 1958.
Danny Orlis and the Contrary Mrs. Forester. Chicago, Moody, 1958.
Danny Orlis and the Man from the Past. Chicago, Moody, 1959.
Danny Orlis, Big Brother. Chicago, Moody, 1959.
Danny Orlis on the Valiant. Chicago, Moody, 1959.
Danny Orlis and Marilyn's Great Trial. Chicago, Moody, 1959.
Danny Orlis and the Mystery of the Sunken Ship. Chicago, Moody, 1960.
Danny Orlis and Ron Orlis in the Canadian Wilderness. Chicago, Moody, 1960.
Danny Orlis in the Mysterious Zandeland. Chicago, Moody, 1960.
Danny Orlis and the Time of Testing. Chicago, Moody, 1961.
Danny Orlis, Bush Pilot. Chicago, Moody, 1961.
Danny Orlis and Hal's Great Victory. Chicago, Moody, 1962.
Danny Orlis and the Drug Store Mystery. Chicago, Moody, 1962.
Danny Orlis and Ron's Call to Service. Chicago, Moody, 1963.
Danny Orlis and the Headstrong Linda Penner. Chicago, Moody, 1963.
Danny Orlis and the Ordeal at Camp. Chicago, Moody, 1963.
Danny Orlis and Linda's Struggle. Chicago, Moody, 1964.
Danny Orlis and the Ice Fishing Escapade. Chicago, Moody, 1964.
Danny Orlis and Linda's New Mother. Chicago, Moody, 1965.
Danny Orlis and Ron in the Mexican Jungle Mystery. Chicago, Moody, 1965.
Danny Orlis and the Defiant Kent Gilbert. Chicago, Moody, 1965.
Danny Orlis and Robin's Big Battle. Chicago, Moody, 1965.
Danny Orlis and the Old Mine Mystery. Chicago, Moody, 1966.
Danny Orlis and Kent's Encounter with the Law. Chicago, Moody, 1966.
Danny Orlis and Robin's Rebellion. Chicago, Moody, 1966.
Danny Orlis and Robin's Big Mistake. Chicago, Moody, 1966.
Danny Orlis and Jim's Northern Adventure. Chicago, Moody, 1967.
Danny Orlis and Kent Gilbert's Tragedy. Chicago, Moody, 1967.
Danny Orlis and the Teen-Age Marriage. Chicago, Moody, 1967.
Danny Orlis and the Guatemala Adventure. Chicago, Moody, 1967.
Danny Orlis and Fritz McCloud, High School Star. Chicago, Moody, 1968.
Danny Orlis and the Excitement at the Circle R. Chicago, Moody, 1968.
Danny Orlis and Jim Morgan's Scholarship. Chicago, Moody, 1968.
Danny Orlis and Trouble on the Circle R Ranch. Chicago, Moody, 1968.
Danny Orlis and the Accident That Shook Fairview. Chicago, Moody, 1968.
Danny Orlis: Bid for Victory. Chicago, Moody, 1969.
Danny Orlis and the Dry Gulch Mystery. Chicago, Moody, 1969.
Danny Orlis and Johnny's New Life. Chicago, Moody, 1969.
Danny Orlis and DeeDee's Defiance. Chicago, Moody, 1970.
Danny Orlis and DeeDee's Best Friend. Chicago, Moody, 1970.
Danny Orlis and the Football Feud. Chicago, Moody, 1971.
Danny Orlis and the Crisis at Cedarton. Chicago, Moody, 1971.
Danny Orlis and the Bewildered Runaway. Chicago, Moody, 1971.
Danny Orlis and the Mexican Kidnapping. Chicago, Moody, 1971.

Danny Orlis and the Canadian Caper. Chicago, Moody, 1972.
Danny Orlis and the Alaskan Highway Adventure. Chicago, Moody, 1972.
Danny Orlis: Forced Down. Chicago, Moody, 1972.
Danny Orlis and the Live-in Tragedy. Chicago, Moody, 1972.
Danny Orlis and the Colorado Challenge. Chicago, Moody, 1972.
Danny Orlis and Doug's Big Disappointment. Chicago, Moody, 1973.
Danny Orlis and the Ski Slope Emergency. Chicago, Moody, 1973.
Danny Orlis and the Mystery at Northwest High. Chicago, Moody, 1973.
Danny Orlis and the Girl Who Dared. Chicago, Moody, 1974.
Danny Orlis and the Mysterious Intruder. Chicago, Moody, 1974.
Danny Orlis and the Rock Point Rebel. Chicago, Moody, 1974.
Danny Orlis and the Model Plane Mystery. Chicago, Moody, 1975.

Fiction for children (series: Dell Norton in all books)

The Wild Float Trip. Chicago, Moody, 1958.
The Vanishing Mountain Lion. Chicago, Moody, 1958.
The Echo Mountain Hermit. Chicago, Moody, 1958.
Dell Norton in the Ozarks. Chicago, Moody, 1958.
Dell Norton and the Hidden Cave. Chicago, Moody, 1959.

Fiction for children (series: Felicia Cartwright in all books)

Felicia Cartwright and the Frantic Search. Chicago, Moody, 1958.
Felicia Cartwright and the Missing Sideboard. Chicago, Moody, 1958.
Felicia Cartwright and the Green Medallion. Chicago, Moody, 1958.
Felicia Cartwright and the Uncut Diamond. Chicago, Moody, 1958.
Felicia Cartwright and the Case of the Twisted Key. Chicago, Moody, 1959.
Felicia Cartwright and the Case of the Frightened Students. Chicago, Moody, 1959.
Felicia Cartwright and the Case of the Lonely Teacher. Chicago, Moody, 1960.
Felicia Cartwright and the Case of the Dancing Fire. Chicago, Moody, 1960.
Felicia Cartwright and the Case of the Troubled Rancher. Chicago, Moody, 1961.
Felicia Cartwright and the Case of the Storm-Scarred Mountain. Chicago, Moody, 1961.
Felicia Cartwright and the Case of the Hungry Fiddler. Chicago, Moody, 1962.
Felicia Cartwright and the Case of the Antique Bookmark. Chicago, Moody, 1963.
Felicia Cartwright and the Case of the Lost Puppy. Chicago, Moody, 1965.
Felicia Cartwright and the Case of the Knotted Wire. Chicago, Moody, 1966.
Felicia Cartwright and the Case of the Honorable Traitor. Chicago, Moody, 1967.
Felicia Cartwright and the Case of the Black Phantom. Chicago, Moody, 1968.
Felicia Cartwright and the Case of the Lone Ski Boot. Chicago, Moody, 1969.
Felicia Cartwright and the Case of the Bad-Eyed Girl. Chicago, Moody, 1970.
Felicia Cartwright and the Case of the Pink Poodle. Chicago, Moody, 1970.

Fiction for children (series: Golden Boy in all books)

Golden Boy. N.p., Van Kampen, 1954.
Golden Boy: Outlaw. N.p., Van Kampen, 1954.
Golden Boy and the Counterfeiters. Wheaton, Illinois, Scripture Press, 1958.

Fiction for children (series: Halliway Boys in all books)

The Halliway Boys on Crusade Island. Chicago, Moody, 1957.
The Halliway Boys and the Disappearing Staircase. Chicago, Moody, 1958.
The Halliway Boys and the Secret Expedition. Chicago, Moody, 1958.
The Halliway Boys on a Dangerous Voyage. Chicago, Moody, 1958.
The Halliway Boys and the Mysterious Treasure Map. Chicago, Moody, 1960.
The Halliway Boys and the Missing Film Mystery. Chicago, Moody, 1960.
The Halliway Boys on Forbidden Mountain. Chicago, Moody, 1962.
The Halliway Boys on a Secret African Safari. Chicago, Moody, 1962.

Fiction for children (series: Little Feather in all books)

Little Feather Goes Hunting. Grand Rapids, Michigan, Zondervan, 1946.
Little Feather at Big Bear Lake. Grand Rapids, Michigan, Zondervan, 1947.
Little Feather Rides Herd. Grand Rapids, Michigan, Zondervan, 1947.
Little Feather and the Mystery Mine. Grand Rapids, Michigan, Zondervan, 1948.
Little Feather at Tonak Bay. Grand Rapids, Michigan, Zondervan, 1950.
Little Feather and the Secret Package. Grand Rapids, Michigan, Zondervan, 1951.
Little Feather and the River of Grass. Grand Rapids, Michigan, Zondervan, 1953.

Fiction for children (series: Lori Adams in all books)

Lori Adams and the Old Carter House Mystery. Chicago, Moody, 1969.
Lori Adams and the Adopted Rebel. Chicago, Moody, 1971.
Lori Adams and the River Boat Mystery. Chicago, Moody, 1971.
Lori Adams and the Jungle Search. Chicago, 1974.

Fiction for children (series: Mel Webb in all books)

Mel Webb and the Border Collie. Chicago, Moody, 1964.
Mel Webb on the Danger Trail. Chicago, Moody, 1964.
Mel Webb and the Stolen Dog Mystery. Chicago, Moody, 1964.

Fiction for children (series: Mickey Turner in all books)

The Fire Detectives. Chicago, Moody, 1955.
Trapped on Sugar Loaf Mountain. Chicago, Moody, 1955.

Mickey Turner and the Phantom Dog. Chicago, Moody, 1955.
Mickey Turner, Ranger's Son. Chicago, Moody, 1955.

Fiction for children (series: The Orlis Twins in all books)

The Orlis Twins and the Secret of the Mountain. Chicago, Moody, 1959.
The Orlis Twins and the High School Gang. Chicago, Moody, 1959.
The Orlis Twins Live for Christ. Chicago, Moody, 1959.
The Orlis Twins and the New Coach. Chicago, Moody, 1960.
The Orlis Twins and Mike's Last Chance. Chicago, Moody, 1960.
The Orlis Twins and Ron's Big Problem. Chicago, Moody, 1961.
The Orlis Twins and Jim Morgan's Ordeal. Chicago, Moody, 1962.
The Orlis Twins and Roxie's Triumph. Chicago, Moody, 1963.

Fiction for children (series: Pat Collins; Jim Dunlap)

Pat Collins and the Peculiar Dr. Brockton. Chicago, Moody, 1957; as *Jim Dunlap and the Strange Doctor Brockton*, Chicago, Moody, 1967.
Pat Collins and the Hidden Treasure. Chicago, Moody, 1957.
Pat Collins and the Wingless Plane. Chicago, Moody, 1957; as *Jim Dunlap and the Wingless Plane*, Chicago, Moody, 1968.
Pat Collins and the Captive Scientist. Chicago, Moody, 1958.
Pat Collins and the Mysterious Orbiting Rocket. Chicago, Moody, 1958; as *Jim and the Mysterious Orbiting Rocket*, Chicago, Moody, 1968.
Pat Collins and the Secret Engine. Chicago, Moody, 1967.

Fiction for children, with Marjorie Palmer (series: Pioneer Girls in all books)

Pioneer Girls and the Mystery of Oak Ridge Manor. Chicago, Moody, 1959.
Pioneer Girls and the Mystery of the Missing Cocker. Chicago, Moody, 1959.
Pioneer Girls and the Strange Adventures on Tomahawk Hill. Chicago, Moody, 1959.
Pioneer Girls at Caribou Flats. Chicago, Moody, 1959.
Pioneer Girls and the Secret of the Jungle. Chicago, Moody, 1962.
Pioneer Girls and the Mysterious Bedouin Cave. Chicago, Moody, 1963.
Pioneer Girls and the Dutch Mill Mystery. Chicago, Moody, 1968.

Fiction for children (series: Powell Family in all books)

Rebel of the Lazy H Ranch. Denver, Accent, 1980.
The Case of the Missing Dinosaur. Denver, Accent, 1981.
The Clue of the Old Sea Chest. Denver, Accent, 1981.
The Mystery at Poor Boy's Folly. Denver, Accent, 1981.

Fiction for children (series: Ted and Terri in all books)

Ted and Terri and the Broken Arrow. Chicago, Moody, 1971.
Ted and Terri and the Crooked Trapper. Chicago, Moody, 1971.
Ted and Terri and the Troubled Trumpeter. Chicago, Moody, 1971.
Ted and Terri and the Stubborn Bully. Chicago, Moody, 1971.
Ted and Terri and the Secret Captive. Chicago, Moody, 1971.

Fiction for children as John Runyan (series: Biff Norris in all books)

Biff Norris and the Clue of the Lonely Landing Strip. Chicago, Moody, 1962.
Biff Norris and the Clue of the Worn Saddle. Chicago, Moody, 1962.
Biff Norris and the Clue of the Nervous Stranger. Chicago, Moody, 1962.
Biff Norris and the Clue of the Golden Ram. Chicago, Moody, 1962.
Biff Norris and the Clue of the Midnight Stage. Chicago, Moody, 1963.
Biff Norris and the Clue of the Lavender Mink. Chicago, Moody, 1964.
Biff Norris and the Clue of the Gold Ring. Chicago, Moody, 1965.
Biff Norris and the Clue of the Angry Fisherman. Chicago, Moody, 1966.
Biff Norris and the Clue of the Disappearing Wolf. Chicago, Moody, 1967.
Biff Norris and the Clue of the Mysterious Letter. Chicago, Moody, 1968.
Biff Norris and the Clue of the Half-Burned Book. Chicago, Moody, 1969.

Fiction for children as John Runyan (series: Tom Barnes in all books)

Tom Barnes and the Substitute Second Baseman. Chicago, Moody, 1964.
Tom Barnes, Blocking Back. Chicago, Moody, 1966.
Tom Barnes, Forward. Chicago, Moody, 1968.

Short Stories

Radio Stories. Lincoln, Nebraska, Back to the Bible, 1950.
Radio Stories 3. Lincoln, Nebraska, Back to the Bible, 1952.
Danny Orlis Stories. Lincoln, Nebraska, Back to the Bible, 1953.

Plays

Screenplays: *My Son, My Son*; *Silent Thunder*.

Other

My Son, My Son. Chicago, Moody, 1970.
Journey to a Lonely Land: The Birth and Growth of the NCEM. Prince Albert, Northern Canada Evangelical Mission, 1971.
God Understands. Chicago, Moody, 1973.
The Winds of God Are Blowing, with Marjorie Palmer. Wheaton, Illinois, Tyndale, 1973.
The Wheelbarrow and the Comrade, with Irene Hanson. Chicago, Moody, 1973.
Amsterdam Rebel. Chicago, Moody, 1973.
A Bag Without Holes, with Fred Eggerichs. Minneapolis, Bethany Fellowship, 1975.
Pattern for a Total Church. Wheaton, Illinois, Victor, 1975.
People's Church on the Go. Wheaton, Illinois, Victor, 1976.
How Churches Grow, with Marjorie Palmer. Minneapolis, Bethany Fellowship, 1976.
Who Made? Who Tells? Who Cares? Who Loves? Minneapolis, Bethany Fellowship, 1979.
Nothing Is Impossible. Chicago, Moody, 1979.
What'll You Have to Drink? N.p., Horizon House, 1979.

The Flood, with Marjorie Palmer. Elkhart, Indiana, Bethel, 1982.
Who Helps, with Marjorie Palmer. Elkhart, Indiana, Bethel, 1982.
Who Shows, with Marjorie Palmer. Elkhart, Indiana, Bethel, 1982.
Light a Small Candle. Minneapolis, Free Church, 1983.
While the Sun Is High, with Marjorie Palmer. Minneapolis, Free Church, 1984.

Editor, *Medicine and the Bible*. New York, Attic Press, 1984; London, Paternoster Press, 1986.

* * *

In the mid-1980's, Bernard Palmer began to chronicle the exploits of a fictional gunfighter named John Breckenridge. An inexperienced teenager at the start of the sequence, Breckenridge (who soon drops the last two syllables from his surname to become known simply as "Breck") is later portrayed quite well as an older, more grizzled man, and his life and times are recounted in an orderly and largely unadorned style which fits the tone of the books adequately.

The first of the Breck adventures is *Kid Breckenridge*, a somewhat meandering affair which reads very much like a "young adult" novel, although it is not billed as such in either its British or American editions. The feeling is reinforced, however, by an almost fairytale "good step-brother, bad step-brother" premise, and the fact that the principal character is a naive 16-year-old when the story begins. Neither does the book contain any real or implied sex or sexual attraction, and absolutely no profanity, even from the wildest of characters—which is not necessarily meant as a criticism, but simply an observation of Palmer's approach to the Western.

Following the death of his mother, the friction between young Breckenridge and his stepbrother, Fletcher Ross, builds dramatically. Fletcher is something of a bully, and jealous of John's relationship with his father, Waddy. Following a fight in the family barn, John finds himself believing Fletcher's claim that he is no longer wanted on the ranch, and as soon as he can he steals away to make a new life for himself elsewhere. After a brush with Indians he meets Lee Corbitt, an old friend of his late father's and as a friendship of sorts flourishes between them, Corbitt teaches him how to use a gun. Before long, though, Corbitt is revealed to be an outlaw, and following a bank robbery during which he becomes a reluctant accomplice, John manages to escape from the man's gang.

From this point on the book chronicles John's subsequent adventures, forming a rather convoluted story in which Palmer's young hero signs on with a rancher named Snyder who, soured by a string of bad luck, eventually falls in with Corbitt and turns to rustling. Before the climax, John is wounded in a gunfight and nursed back to health by Rebecca and Matt Norval and their two daughters, Elizabeth and Helen.

The Norvals re-appear in *Breck's Choice*, when John marries Helen and attempts to hang up the gun with which he has become so proficient, in order to return to the more peaceful life of a rancher. His attempt to start over again is thwarted when a neighbour, hungry for both his land and the gold it contains, tries to scare him away—a tactic which results in Helen's murder. No longer restrained by his wife's calming influence, Breck at least makes an effort to get his revenge without further violence. Inevitably, though, he finds little choice but to strap on his gun again.

From this point forward, the Breck stories improve dramatically. The near-labrinthine wanderings of the first novel are replaced by stories of stronger, albeit vaguely familiar, construction, and further enhanced by the presence of an older and more experienced hero.

In *Hunted Gun*, which begins with a superbly atmospheric opening chapter, Palmer's protagonist is summoned by his sister-in-law Elizabeth, whose husband, Charlie Sims (who was also introduced in *Kid Breckenridge*), has just been murdered following his discovery of gold in the hills surrounding the local town of Bison. Now Elizabeth's son David is causing her additional worry, because he is so determined to kill the man he *believes* to have been responsible for his father's death. Her daughter Millie, who has developed boyfriend troubles, is also a source of concern. Within hours of his arrival in Bison, which proves to be a haven for the lawless, the local banker, Harrison Dufield, tells Breck that it would be wiser if he forgot all about trying to solve his brother-in-law's murder. The man is also sceptical about Charlie's alleged gold-strike. But the warning only makes Breck all the more determined to uncover the truth of the situation which, of course, he eventually does.

The fourth, and arguably best, book of the series, *Shoot-Out at Buffalo Gulch*, finds Breck en route to Colorado, where he intends to try his hand at prospecting. After foiling an attempt on the life of a wealthy railroader named Cornelius Devin, Breck and an Easterner named Hunter become involved in the search to find the niece of Devin's partner, who came west to find her uncle (who had disappeared), and then went missing herself. Almost at once an attempt is made on the lives of Breck and his partner, but this only serves to make them all the more set on finding the girl and her uncle, whose vote is crucial if Devin is to maintain control of his railroad.

Palmer's work is, of course, derivative. His protagonist, Breck, is very much the archetypal western hero—a gun-fast man of few words but much dignity, whose share of tragedy has doomed him to the life of a wanderer. The author's stories, too, reflect all that is best in the traditional Western. Although they might appear somewhat trite, however, the books are distinguished by a strong human quality, a firm thread of continuity and a realistic time-span. *Shoot-Out at Buffalo Gulch*, for instance, takes place five years after the events described in *Breck's Choice* not always apparent in rival series of this type.

Despite a relatively short run, the Breck books still make for an entertaining read, with the last few most agreeable and convincing of all.

—David Whitehead

PARKINSON, Dan. American. Born in Liberal, Kansas, 19 March 1935. Educated at the University of Kansas, Lawrence. Married Carol Lindh in 1955; two daughters and two sons. Sportswriter, *Journal-Review*, Crawfordsville, Indiana, 1956–58; reporter and editor, *Southwest Times*, Liberal, Kansas, 1958–60, and *Wichita Eagle-Beacon*, Kansas, 1960–62; department manager, Chamber of Commerce, Wichita, Kansas 1962–64; executive vice-president, Chamber of Commerce, Paola, Kansas, 1964–66, McPherson, Kansas, 1966–67, and Brazosport, Texas, 1967–88. Since 1988 full-time writer. Agent: Scott Siegel, P.O. Box 20340, Dag Hammarskjold Center, New York, New York 10017. Address: 221 Carnation, Lake Jackson, Texas 77566, U.S.A.

WESTERN PUBLICATIONS

Novels

The Texians, with David Larry Hicks. Houston, Larksdale, 1980.
The Slanted Colt. New York, Zebra, 1984.
Gunpowder Glory. New York, Zebra, 1984.
Blood Arrow. New York, Zebra, 1985.
Calamity Trail. New York, Zebra, 1985.
Brother Wolf. New York, Zebra, 1985.
The Sundown Breed. New York, Zebra, 1986.
Thunderland. New York, Zebra, 1987.
Jubilation Gap. New York, Zebra, 1987.
Shadow of the Hawk. New York, Zebra, 1988.
The Way to Wyoming. New York, Zebra, 1988.
Gunpowder Wind. New York, Zebra, 1988.
The Westering. New York, Zebra, 1989.
Summer Land. New York, Zebra, 1989.
A Man Called Wolf. New York, Zebra, 1989.
Ride the Devil's Trail. New York, Zebra, 1990.

OTHER PUBLICATIONS

Novels

Starsong. Wisconsin, TSR, 1988; London, Penguin, 1989.
The Fox and the Faith. New York, Pinnacle, 1989.
The Fox and the Fury. New York, Pinnacle, 1989.
The Fox and the Flag. New York, Pinnacle, 1990.
The Gates of Thorbardin. Wisconsin, TSR, 1990.

*

Dan Parkinson comments:

I write in a variety of ways, about a variety of things, but primarily I write novels about people. These novels become categorized—with my blessing and assistance—because that is how original paperbacks are marketed: as Westerns, or Science Fiction, or Historicals, etc. My books have been well received by readers, and by those reviewers—few though they be—who will consider paperback originals, and I think it is because I write for the pleasure of reading—my own, first, and then that of anyone else who happens to pick up what I have written.

* * *

Growing up as a Great Depression "Dust Bowl kid" in Liberal, Kansas, and the Texas Panhandle, Don Parkinson, getting his "strongest impressions of how the world really is" from the valley of Hackberry Creek in the Texas High Plains, remembers reading *The Call of the Wild*, *Robin Hood*, *King Solomon's Mines*, *The Last of the Mohicans*, *Tarzan*, and *Tom Sawyer*.

"Ask me when I started writing," the former newspaperman and Chamber of Commerce manager says, "and I think it was about then, in those early years. I wanted power! Seriously, if you can make people laugh, or cry, or cheer, if you can reach the mind and the emotions of somebody you don't even know, simply by putting words on paper—if that isn't power, what is?"

His first book, *The Texians*, about the Battle of Velasco in 1832, the first engagement in the Texas War for Independence, was issued by a small Houston publisher in 1980. Four years later, Parkinson's first two novels, *The Slanted Colt* and *Gunpowder Glory* were published as paperback originals by Zebra Books, a house in which (with Zebra's other imprint, Pinnacle Books) Parkinson has found a home for all but two of his 21 novels thus far.

While Parkinson's forte is the action-adventure Western (he also writes some science fiction and recently launched a series of Horatio Hornblower-type novels set in the American Revolutionary War), he is no potboiler writer and has earned a reputation as a thinking author of considerable range, employing fresh and often unusual ideas (his *The Sundown Breed* begins in Texas Kiowa country and ends up in midtown Manhattan; his *The Way to Wyoming* has its hero winding up with over 7,000 head of cattle and only 12 men to drive them), one with a "good ear" for dialogue and a knack for humor—not a typical commodity in western fiction.

"Humour does occur a lot in my work," he says, "and I let it happen because I enjoy it. *Calamity Trail* and *Jubilation Gap* are preponderantly humorous books. *Gunpowder Glory*, *The Sundown Breed*, *Ride the Devil's Trail*, even *The Slanted Colt* contain humor, along with varying themes."

Two other characteristics of a Parkinson Western are that he employs more dialogue than is common, and makes a studied use of pathos in his stories.

"I feel comfortable writing dialogue," the author says. "It comes easily to me, and I find I can give a richness to characters just by what they say and how they say it." He observes that while there is a tendency to paint Old West characters as phlegmatic, stoic, and silent—"and some were, of course"—that most were a "chatty, talky bunch of people—really more so than we are today."

On pathos: "I use it as a characterization device to a greater extent than most writers. It may not be front-stage (although it sometimes is, as at the conclusion of *Shadow of the Hawk* and in several scenes in *The Way to Wyoming*. But, like humor, I find that a flavoring of pathos can give power to a characterization and thus to a story. Beyond pathos, I like a simple tight-throated flavor—poignance, a touch of melancholy, a pinch of glory, human frailty and raw courage. These are powerful ingredients."

Use of foreign words and phrases—Spanish, Russian, German, even Greek (*Shadow of the Hawk* ends with a page of phonetic *Tasalagi*); occasional versifying (*Summer Land*, a view of frontier life in Kentucky during the Revolutionary War, has Parkinson poetry written as folk songs and the book ends with two poems); use of dialect; a willingness to "shade history a bit" for "good effect and to make a story better"—all are standard Parkinson fare.

His credo: "I write novels. I am not trying to teach anybody anything, or make a personal statement about politics or religion or the state of the human race. I write for fun, and for people who read for fun. My ultimate goal, beyond personally enjoying what I write, is that those who pay four dollars or more for a copy of what I write come away satisfied that they have had a damn good read."

—Dale L. Walker

PATTEN, Lewis B(yford). Also wrote as Lewis Ford; Len Leighton; Joseph Wayne. American. Born in Denver, Colorado, 13 January 1915. Educated at the University of Denver, 1940–42. Served in the United States Navy, 1933–37. Married 1) Betsy Lancaster in 1938 (divorced 1962), one daughter and two sons; 2) Catherine Crane in 1963. Senior auditor, Colorado Department of Revenue, Denver; rancher in DeBeque, Colorado, 1943–49; then freelance writer. Recipient: Western Writers of America Spur award, for novel, 1968,

1972, and for children's book, 1969, and Golden Saddleman award, 1979. *Died 22 May 1981.*

WESTERN PUBLICATIONS

Novels

Massacre at White River. New York, Ace, 1952; London, Ward Lock, 1961.
Gunsmoke Empire. New York, Fawcett, 1955; London, Fawcett, 1956.
Back Trail. London, Muller, 1956.
White Warrior. New York, Fawcett, 1956; London, Fawcett, 1957.
Rope Law. New York, Fawcett, 1956; London, Fawcett, 1957.
Guns of the Vengeful. London, Ward Lock, 1957.
The Massacre at San Pablo. New York, Fawcett, 1957; London, Fawcett, 1959.
Pursuit. New York, Permabooks, 1957; London, Ward Lock, 1960.
Showdown at Stony Crest (as Joseph Wayne, with Wayne D. Overholser). New York, Dell, 1957.
Valley of Violent Men. New York, Fawcett, 1957; London, Fawcett, 1959.
Gun Proud. New York, Graphic, 1957.
Home Is the Outlaw. New York, Fawcett, 1958; London, Fawcett, 1959.
Five Rode West. New York, Fawcett, 1958; London, Fawcett, 1959.
Sunblade. London, Abelard Schuman, 1958; as *Fighting Rawhide*, New York, Fawcett, 1959.
Showdown at War Cloud. New York, Fawcett, 1958; London, Muller, 1960.
Tomahawk (as Lee Leighton, with Wayne D. Overholser). New York, Ballantine, 1958.
The Man Who Rode Alone. New York, Avon, 1959.
The Ruthless Men. New York, Fawcett, 1959; London, Muller, 1960.
Savage Star. New York, Avon, 1959; London, Muller, 1960.
Top Man with a Gun. New York, Fawcett, 1959; London, Muller, 1960.
Hangman's Country. New York, Lancer, and London, Abelard Schuman, 1960.
The Gun and the Man (as Joseph Wayne, with Wayne D. Overholser). New York, Dell, 1960.
Savage Town. New York, Avon, 1960.
Range 45. London, Ward Lock, 1960.
Renegade Gun. New York, Avon, 1961.
The Savage Country. London, Ward Lock, 1961.
Law of the Gun. New York, New American Library, 1961; London, New English Library, 1963.
The Angry Horsemen. New York, Hillman, 1961; as Lewis Ford, London, Ward Lock, 1961.
The Gold Magnet. London, Ward Lock, 1962.
Flame in the West. New York, Berkley, 1962; London, Collins, 1964.
Savage Vengeance. London, Ward Lock, 1962.
The Ruthless Range. New York, Berkley, 1963; London, Collins, 1967.
The Tarnished Star. New York, New American Library, 1963.
The Scaffold at Hangman's Creek. New York, Avon, and London, Ward Lock, 1963.
Vengeance Rider. New York, Berkley, 1963; London, Collins, 1965.
Guns at Gray Butte. New York, Doubleday, and London, Collins, 1963.
Wagons East. New York, New American Library, 1964.
Ride for Vengeance. New York, Avon, 1964.
Proudly They Die. New York, Doubleday, and London, Collins, 1964.
Outlaw Canyon. London, Collins, 1964; New York, Berkley, 1965.
Giant on Horseback. New York, Doubleday, 1964; London, Collins, 1966.
The Killer from Yuma. New York, Berkley, 1964; London, Collins, 1965.
The Arrogant Guns. New York, Doubleday, 1965; London, Collins, 1966.
No God in Saguaro. New York, Doubleday, and London, Collins, 1966.
Death Waited at Rialto Creek. New York, Doubleday, 1966; London, Collins, 1967; as *The Trap*, New York, Belmont, 1976.
The Odds Against Circle L. New York, Ace, 1966.
Prodigal Gunfighter. New York, Berkley, 1966.
Deputy from Furnace Creek. New York, Lancer, 1967.
The Star and the Gun. New York, Ace, 1967.
Bones of the Buffalo. New York, Doubleday, 1967; London, Collins, 1974.
Ambush Creek. New York, Berkley, 1967.
Cheyenne Drums. New York, Berkley, 1968.
Death of a Gunfighter. New York, Doubleday, 1968.
The Red Sabbath. New York, Doubleday, 1968; London, Mayflower, 1970.
The Youngerman Guns. New York, Doubleday, 1969; London, Mayflower, 1970.
Posse from Poison Creek. New York, Doubleday, 1969; London, Mayflower, 1970.
Apache Hostage. New York, New American Library, 1970.
A Death in Indian Wells. New York, Doubleday, 1970.
Red Runs the River. New York, Doubleday, 1970.
Six Ways of Dying. New York, Ace, 1970.
Showdown at Mesilla. New York, Doubleday, 1971; London, Hale, 1978.
Ride the Hot Wind. New York, Ace, 1971.
A Killing at Kiowa New York, New American Library, 1972.
The Feud at Chimney Rock. New York, New American Library, 1972.
The Trial of Judas Wiley. New York, Doubleday, 1972.
The Cheyenne Pool. New York, Doubleday, 1972; London, Hale, 1978.
The Hide Hunters. New York, New American Library, 1973.
The Gun of Jesse Hand. New York, Ace, 1973.
The Ordeal of Jason Ord. New York, Doubleday, 1973.
The Tired Gun. New York, Doubleday, 1973; London, Hale, 1978.
Hands of Geronimo. New York, Ace, 1974.
Two for Vengeance. New York, New American Library, 1974; with *Redskin*, 1982.
Bounty Man. New York, Doubleday, 1974; London, Jenkins, 1975.
Death Stalks Yellowhorse. New York, New American Library, 1974.
The Angry Town of Pawnee Bluffs. New York, Doubleday, 1974; London, Jenkins, 1975.
Lynching at Broken Butte. New York, Doubleday, 1974; London, Hale, 1978.
The Orphans of Coyote Creek. New York, New American Library, 1975.
Vow of Vengeance. New York, New American Library, 1975.

The Gallows at Graneros. New York, Doubleday, 1975; London, Hale, 1979.
Ride a Crooked Trail. New York, New American Library, 1976.
The Lawless Breed. New York, New American Library, 1976.
Ambush at Soda Creek. New York, Doubleday, 1976; London, Prior, 1978.
Man Outgunned. New York, Doubleday, 1976; London, Prior, 1979.
Hunt the Man Down. New York, Doubleday, 1977; London, Hale, 1979.
Guilt of a Killer Town, and *Massacre Ridge.* New York, New American Library, 1977.
Villa's Rifles. New York, Doubleday, 1977; London, Hale, 1980.
The Trial at Apache Junction. New York, New American Library, 1977.
The Killings at Coyote Springs. New York, Doubleday, 1977; London, Hale, 1979.
Cheyenne Captives. New York, Doubleday, 1978; London, Hale, 1980.
Death Rides a Black Horse. New York, Doubleday, 1978; London, Hale, 1980.
The Law in Cottonwood. New York, Doubleday, 1978; London, Hale, 1981.
The Trail of the Apache Kid. New York, Doubleday, 1979.
Rifles of Revenge. New York, Zebra, 1979.
Ride a Tall Horse. New York, Doubleday, 1980; London, Hale, 1981.
Track of the Hunter. New York, New American Library, 1981.
Sharpshod and *They Called Him a Killer* (short novels). New York, Torr, 1990.

Novels as Lewis Ford

Gunmen's Grass. New York, Popular Library, 1954; London, Ward Lock, 1961.
Gunfighter from Montana. New York, Popular Library, 1955; London, Muller, 1957.
Maverick Empire. New York, Popular Library, 1957.

Short Stories

The Best Western Stories of Lewis B. Patten, edited by Bill Pronzini and Martin H. Greenberg. Carbondale, Illinois, Southern Illinois University Press, 1989.

Uncollected Short Stories

"Massacre at Cottonwood Springs," in *Mammoth Western* (Chicago), May 1950.
"A Man's Beginnings," in *Mammoth Western* (Chicago), December 1950.
"Nester Kid," in *Zane Grey's Western* (New York), December 1950.
"Payday," in *Zane Grey's Western* (New York), June 1951.
"Flowers for His Bride," in *Thrilling Ranch Stories* (London), December 1951.
"Stable Boy," in *Texas Rangers* (London), September 1952.
"Too Good with a Gun," in *Bad Men and Good,* edited by Luke Short. New York, Dodd Mead, 1953.
"Mama Rides the Norther," in *Thrilling Western* (London), August 1953.
"Rustler's Run," in *Exciting Western* (London), October 1953.
"Winter of His Life," in *Holsters and Heroes,* edited by Noel M. Loomis. New York, Macmillan, 1954.
"Dancehall Gal," in *Exciting Western* (London), February 1954.
"Rope's End," in *Western Story* (London), July 1954.
"Ride the Red Trail," in *Western Story* (London), October 1954.
"Death Fans This Gun," in *Western Story* (London), December 1954.
"Big Black and the Bully," in *Wild Horse Roundup,* edited by Jim Kjelgaard. New York, Dodd Mead, 1957.
"High-Carded," in *Western Roundup,* edited by Nelson Nye. New York, Macmillan, 1961.
"Dobbs Ferry," in *Rivers to Cross,* edited by William R. Cox. New York, Dodd Mead, 1966.

OTHER PUBLICATIONS

Other (for children)

Gene Autry and the Ghost Riders. Racine, Wisconsin, Whitman, 1955.
The Meeker Massacre, with Wayne D. Overholser. New York, Cowles, 1969.

* * *

Lewis B. Patten wrote more than 90 western novels in 30 years, and received recognition of his ability through four Western Writers of America awards.

Patten's books cover a wide range of subjects, almost all traditionally used in popular Westerns. A loner in search of revenge (*Ride a Crooked Trail, Bounty Man*), or a supposed killer on the run from it (*The Tired Gun*); family feuds with a conflict of types of justice (*Hunt the Man Down* with the complication of rape, and *The Trial of Judas Wiley* with the complication of a kidnapping); an avengeful foreman not wanting to be cut out of a family inheritance (*Death Rides a Black Horse*); a cavalry unit tracking down a band of Apaches (*Red Runs the River*); a young runaway faced with decisions he's too old to ignore but too young to make (*The Ordeal of Jason Ord, Death Rides a Black Horse*); a Romeo-and-Juliet love story among rival families (*Showdown at Mesilla*); a killer who has escaped from jail and is now out for revenge (*The Trial of the Apache Kid*—again involving a kidnapping); a Pancho Villa novel, the Mexicans out to get guns, and a group of U.S. outlaws out to get Villa's money (*Villa's Rifles*); a cattle town novel with the sheriff caught between the rumbustious cowhands and the gradually civilizing town (*The Law in Cottonwood*)—these are some of the themes Patten used, though usually with his own refinements and details.

If one theme turns up more than another in Patten's books, it is justice, and particularly as it is seen practiced in small towns on the frontier. *Man Outgunned* concerns a town interrupted during a 4th of July picnic by a gang of robbers and kidnappers; *The Angry Town of Pawnee Bluffs* reveals a town at the mercy of its own lynch-mob mentality due to the attack on two girls; *The Lynching at Broken Butte,* more interestingly, shows a small town *after* two innocent men have been lynched, but so prey to its own guilt that more violence ensues; *Guilt of a Killer Town* is similar, except that the son of the victim returns to confront the members of the jury.

Several of these small-town stories involve violence against Indians. In *A Death in Indian Wells,* for instance, a wounded Cheyenne is displayed in a cage, and when the sheriff's half-breed son takes the body back to the Cheyenne for burial more violence results. In *The Gallows at Graneros* a dead Apache is found hanging from the public gallows, but here the motive is to play on the town's supposed prejudice. In *The Killings at Coyote*

Springs an entire band of Arapaho is massacred, but again the seeming motive—to avenge Custer's death—is not the real one. When these small town's values are analyzed, Patten usually finds them wanting. Conformity is easier than making a stand, but there is usually a man (or a woman) willing to confront the injustice or prejudice.

Patten's books are usually compact and clearly centered on the theme, and sometimes this makes them seem too narrow in scope. His villains are often not clearly characterized (though this is a fault most writers share), and he seems to have a prejudice against Indian fighters or military officers (Custer himself is negatively characterized in *The Red Sabbath* and *Cheyenne Captives* and Colonel Detrick is an Apache-killer in *Ambush at Soda Creek*). But Patten's sheriffs and marshals are usually concerned at what is happening, and are often the active agent in turning the tide. If his books lack humor, it is because his West is not a particularly pleasant place.

—George Walsh

PATTULLO, George. Canadian. Born in Woodstock, Ontario, Canada, 9 October 1879. Worked as a journalist on newspaper in Montreal, London, and Boston, prior to 1908; special correspondent, *Saturday Evening Post*, with American Expeditionary Force in Europe, 1917–18. *Died 30 July 1967.*

WESTERN PUBLICATIONS

Novels

The Sheriff of Badger. New York, Appleton, 1912.
All Our Yesterdays. San Antonio, Texas, Naylor, 1948.
Always New Frontiers. Reno, Nevada, Eldridge, 1951.
Giant Afraid. San Antonio, Texas, Naylor, 1957.
Some Men in Their Time. San Antonio, Texas, Naylor, 1959.

Short Stories

The Untamed: Range Life in the Southwest. New York, Fitzgerald, 1911.
A Good Rooster Crows Everywhere. Privately printed, 1939.

Uncollected Short Story

"Off the Trail," in *Western Stories*, edited by William MacLeod Raine. New York, Dell, 1949.

OTHER PUBLICATIONS

Short Stories

Tight Lines! Privately printed, 1938.
Horrors of Moonlight. Privately printed, 1939.

Play

Screenplay: *Minnie*, with Marshall Neilan and Frances Marion, 1922.

Other

One Man's War: The Diary of a Leatherneck, with J.E. Rendinell. New York, Sears, 1928.
Era of Infamy. San Antonio, Texas, Naylor, 1952.
Morning after Cometh. San Antonio, Texas, Naylor, 1954.
How Silly Can We Get? San Antonio, Texas, Naylor, 1956.

* * *

George Pattullo's western stories have always attracted a small but devoted coterie of readers, mostly Westerners themselves, who have collectively responded sympathetically to Pattullo's attempt at presenting southwestern life in fiction with a strong factual basis. Pattullo began his western writing with a book of short stories, *The Untamed*, and a novel, *The Sheriff of Badger*, both of which take place along the border between the United States and Mexico around the turn of the century. The stories are all at least partly autobiographical, and this explains some of both their strengths and their weaknesses. In their favor it must be said that they are generally both vividly and precisely realized; it must also be admitted that they suffer from the inherent weakness of much autobiographical writing—that they are often anecdotal and trivial. Thus, many of the animal stories in *The Untamed* seem to present-day tastes to have little significance beyond shock value, and *The Sheriff of Badger* can be unsympathetically dismissed as just another western pot-boiler. These criticisms are admittedly not completely fair, but they do emphasize a pervasive weakness in Pattullo's western fiction: that he thinks primarily in terms of individual incidents rather than in terms of plot development. Consequently, Pattullo is more at home in the short-story form than he is in the novel. His novels tend to be episodic, with little unity other than that all the episodes happen to the same protagonist. Scenes shift into one another almost surrealistically, often baffling the reader by their abrupt transitions.

Later in his career, Pattullo expands the scope of his western stories to include the southwestern oil boom of the 1920's. These stories, collected with others in *A Good Rooster Crows Everywhere*, are more successful than his earlier tales. In *Rooster* Pattullo attempts, from the perspective of the Great Depression, an analysis of the course of western history. Many of his fictional characters are the stock figures of general western story—the old cattleman, the rascally nester, and the like—but the burden of the tales is not the predictable lament for the good old days. Pattullo's social philosophy in these stories is implicitly optimistic. The old order changes, it is true, but the new order to which it yields is not necessarily inferior. One of Pattullo's heroes states the case succinctly: "The country ain't going to the dogs because our own stock peters out," he says; "there's others just as good who'll come up to take our places and do the work."

Pattullo's most expanded treatment of the course of western history is to be found in his ambitious novel *All Our Yesterdays*, a sprawling work which attempts to encompass, in terms primarily of the American Southwest, a general social history of 20th-century America from shortly after 1900 until the end of World War II. Pattullo again turns to autobiographical reminiscence, leading his protagonist, "Ex" (for "Xavier") White, from childhood in an upstate New York village through young manhood as a cowboy to adult life as an oil speculator. The novel is prey to Pattullo's usual faults. It is episodic and lacks structural unity. It also contains some of Pattullo's most vivid writing and, especially in its opening sections, gives a remarkable "feel" for an America which is gone. The novel should be better known, if only as a vivid picture of American social history.

—James K. Folsom

PAULSEN, Gary. American. Born in Minneapolis, Minnesota, 17 May 1939. Educated at Bemidji State University, Minnesota, 1957–58; University of Colorado, Boulder, 1976. Served in the United States Army, 1959–62. Married Ruth Ellen Wright in 1971 (second marriage); one son. Has worked as a teacher, electronics field engineer, actor, director, farmer, rancher, truck driver, trapper, professional archer, singer, and sailor. Recipient: Central Missouri award, for children's literature, 1976. Agent: Ray Peekner Literary Agency, 2625 North 36th Street, Milwaukee, Wisconsin 53210. Address: Box 123, Elbert, Colorado 80106, U.S.A.

WESTERN PUBLICATIONS

Novels (series: Al Murphy in all books)

Murphy. New York, Walker, and London, Hale, 1987.
Murphy's Gold. New York, Walker, 1988.
Murphy's Herd. New York, Walker, 1989.
Murphy's War. New York, Walker, 1990.

OTHER PUBLICATIONS

Novels

The Death Specialists. New York, Major, 1976.
The Implosion Effect. New York, Major, 1976.
C.B. Jockey. New York, Major, 1977.
The Sweeper. New York, Raven, 1980.
Meteorite-Track 291. New York, Pinnacle, 1981.
Survival Guide. New York, Pinnacle, 1981.
Compkill. New York, Pinnacle, 1981.
Clutterkill. New York, Raven, 1981.
The Meatgrinder. New York, Raven, 1984.
Night Rituals. New York, Fine, 1989.
The Madonna Stories. Minneapolis, Van Vliet, 1989.

Fiction for children

Mr. Tucket. New York, Funk and Wagnalls, 1969.
The C.B. Radio Caper. Milwaukee, Raintree, 1977.
The Curse of the Cobra. Milwaukee, Raintree, 1977.
The Foxman. Nashville, Nelson, 1977.
The Golden Stick. Milwaukee, Raintree, 1977.
Tiltawhirl John. Nashville, Nelson, 1977.
Winterkill. Nashville, Nelson, and London, Abelard, 1977.
The Green Recruit, with Ray Peekner. Independence, Missouri, Independence Press, 1978.
Hope and a Hatchet. Nashville, Nelson, 1978.
The Night the White Deer Died. Nashville, Nelson, 1978.
The Spitball Gang. New York, Elsevier, 1980.
Dancing Carl. Scarsdale, New York, Bradbury Press, 1983.
Popcorn Days and Buttermilk Nights. New York, Dutton, 1983.
Tracker. New York, Bradbury Press, 1984.
Dogsong. New York, Bradbury Press, 1985.
Sentries. New York, Bradbury Press, 1986.
The Crossing. New York, Orchard, 1987.
Hatchett. New York, Bradbury Press, 1987; as *Hatchet*, London, Macmillan, 1989.
The Island. New York, Orchard, 1988.
The Voyage of the Frog. New York, Orchard, 1989.
The Winter Stories. New York, Orchard, 1989.
The Cookcamp. New York, Orchard, 1991.

Plays

Communications (produced New Mexico, 1974).
Together-Apart (produced Denver, 1976).

Other

The Special War, with Raymond Friday Locke. Los Angeles, Sirkay, 1966.
Some Birds Don't Fly. Chicago, Rand McNally, 1968.
The Building a New, Buying an Old, Remodeling a Used, Comprehensive Home and Shelter How-to-Do-It Book. Englewood Cliffs, New Jersey, Prentice Hall, 1976.
Farm: A History and Celebration of the American Farmer. Englewood Cliffs, New Jersey, Prentice Hall, 1977.
Successful Home Repair. Farmington, Michigan, Structures, 1978.
Money-Saving Home Repair Guide. Milwaukee, Ideals, 1981.

Other (for children)

Dribbling, Shooting, and Scoring Sometimes, photographs by Heinz Kluetmeier. Milwaukee, Raintree, 1976.
The Grass Eaters. Milwaukee, Raintree, 1976.
Martin Luther King, The Man Who Climbed the Mountain, with Dan Theis. Milwaukee, Raintree, 1976.
The Small Ones. Milwaukee, Raintree, 1976.
Careers in an Airport, photographs by Robert Nye. Milwaukee, Raintree, 1977.
Hitting, Pitching, and Running Maybe, photographs by Heinz Kluetmeier. Milwaukee, Raintree, 1977.
Riding, Roping, and Bulldogging—Almost, photographs by Heinz Kluetmeier. Milwaukee, Raintree, 1977.
Tackling, Running, and Kicking—Now and Again, photographs by Heinz Kluetmeier. Milwaukee, Raintree, 1977.
Forehanding and—Backhanding If You're Lucky, photographs by Heinz Kluetmeier. Chicago, Children's Press, 1978; revised edition, with Roger Barrett, as *Tennis*, Milwaukee and London, Macdonald, 1980.
Hiking and Backpacking, with John Morris. New York, Messner, 1978.
Running, Jumping, and Throwing—If You Can, photographs by Heinz Kluetmeier. Chicago, Children's Press, 1978; revised edition, with Roger Barrett, as *Athletics*, Milwaukee and London, Macdonald, 1980.
Canoeing, Kayaking, and Rafting, with John Morris. New York, Messner, 1979.
Downhill, Hotdogging, and Cross-Country—If the Snow Isn't Sticky, photographs by Heinz Kluetmeier and Willis Wood. Milwaukee, Raintree, 1979; revised edition, with Roger Barrett, as *Skiing*, Milwaukee and London, Macdonald, 1980.
Facing Off, Checking, and Goaltending—Perhaps, photographs by Heinz Kluetmeier and Melchior DiGiacomo. Milwaukee, Raintree, 1979; revised edition, with Roger Barrett, Milwaukee and London, Macdonald, 1980.
Going Very Fast in a Circle—If You Don't Run Out of Gas, photographs by Heinz Kluetmeier and Bob D'Olivo. Milwaukee, Raintree, 1979; revised edition, with Roger Barrett, as *Motor Racing*, Milwaukee and London, Macdonald, 1980.
Launching, Floating High, and Landing—If Your Pilot Light Doesn't Go Out, photographs by Heinz Kluetmeier. Milwaukee, Raintree, 1979.

Pummeling, Falling, and Getting Up—Sometimes, photographs by Heinz Kluetmeier and Joe DiMaggio. Milwaukee, Raintree, 1979.
Track, Enduro, and Motocross—Unless You Fall Over, photographs by Heinz Kluetmeier. Milwaukee, Raintree, 1979; revised edition, with Roger Barrett, as *Motor-cycling*, Milwaukee and London, Macdonald, 1980.
TV and Movie Animals, with Art Browne, Jr. New York, Messner, 1980.
Sailing, From Jibs to Jibing. New York, Messner, 1981.

* * *

The hero of Gary Paulsen's Westerns is Al Murphy, a big, battered New Yorker in his early 30s, who came west with the army shortly after the Civil War. According to Paulsen, Murphy deserted after a fight with a mean-tempered corporal (who ended up in a wheelchair with a broken back), and eventually drifted into badge-packing. Although he is a lawman's lawman, whose actions are dictated more by instinct than conscious thought, Murphy soon proves to be more than just another gun-fast hero. In Paulsen's hands, he is as close to human—with all the foibles and contradictions that this entails—as any fictional character is likely to get. In short, Al Murphy is a remarkable creation.

Murphy, Paulsen's first Western, finds the title character keeping the peace in a dying Colorado mining town called Cincherville. When a 12-year-old girl is raped and murdered, Murphy's subsequent hunt for the killer forces him to question not only his own role in the community—which, at best, sees him as a necessary evil—but also his own future and his relationship with Midge, the local café owner.

Murphy has no hard and fast answers to the murder. His hunches invariably peter away to nothing. But this serves only to make his dogged attempts at solving the crime all the more credible. Similarly, the plot, and its eventual resolution, are made more plausible by the careful and clever crafting of well-drawn supporting characters—Midge; the local medic, Doc Hensley; Murphy's new deputy, Milt Hodges, and so on—and by a vivid description of Cincherville, the as-good-as-dead town inhabited by people who have either lost the will or the energy to move on to pastures new.

Murphy is still trying to come to terms with the death of little Sarah Penches at the beginning of *Murphy's Gold*—one good reason why the book should not been read out of sequence, since it reveals a number of facts about the earlier story, including the identity of the child's killer, which would almost certainly spoil any subsequent reading. Indeed, it is only when he receives a summons from a Chinese woman named Tonsun that Murphy is able to involve himself in a new conundrum that chases away some of the haunting memories of the earlier one.

For this sequel (which boasts an uncommonly strong, and very welcome, thread of continuity), Murphy is asked to find the woman's husband, who has been missing for a week, and this he agrees to do. But as soon as he begins to make enquiries around town, he detects an air of conspiracy or intrigue, as if the townsfolk know something he doesn't. And to be honest, Murphy is one step behind everyone (reader included) from start to finish, since the plot is a little obvious, and each new twist or revelation easily foreseen.

In this particular case, however, the plot is really little more than a device around which to expand upon the relationship between Murphy (the lawman who is as reluctant to give up his badge and start over as a rancher or farmer as he is loath to continue upholding the law) and Midge (whose very presence and shrewd understanding of his life and problems exerts a convincingly calming influence over him). And, because Paulsen's single biggest strength is his ability to create seemingly "real" people, the direction this relationship will take next is of infinitely greater interest than the machinations of the missing Chinaman. It should be noted, however, that the book is considerably enlivened by a taut and well-executed climax. Leaving Cincherville, however, proves to be easier than quitting his profession, and *Murphy's War* finds Paulsen's eponymous hero attempting to keep the peace in the town of Fletcher, Wyoming, and locking horns with a power-hungry storekeeper and a wealthy rancher out to avenge the lynching of his son in the process.

Paulsen employs a deceptively simple, straightforward style of writing to tell his stories—a remarkable achievement given the complexity of his characters—and his picture of the West is drawn with uncompromising honesty. His description of the grieving parents in *Murphy*, for example, is excellent, as is the subtle way in which the child-murder affects the man entrusted to investigate it. His grim and unrelenting stories usually unfold from Murphy's point of view, and are sometimes brightened by odd but successful touches of humour. Paulsen's violence is stark but never gratuitous; he simply brings to it the same candour which makes the rest of his work so convincing (finding a dying man out on the trail, for example, Murphy fights the impulse to move him because he has seen "guts in the wound").

"Psychological" Westerns similar in style to the more pretentious Guild sequence by Edward Gorman (which have also been appearing since 1987), Paulsen's work is blunt, artistic, entertaining, original—and much recommended.

—David Whitehead

PEACE, Frank. *See* **COOK, Will.**

PEEPLES, Samuel Anthony. Also wrote as Frank Bass; Brad Ward. American.

WESTERN PUBLICATIONS

Novels

The Dream Ends in Fury: A Novel Based on the Life of Joaquin Murrieta. New York, Harper, 1949; London, Quality Press, 1954.
Broken Rainbow Ranch. London, Hodder and Stoughton, 1951.
Canyon Country. London, Hodder and Stoughton, 1952.
Gun Feud at Stampede Valley. New York, Avon, 1954; London, Hale, 1955.
The Baron of Boot Hill. London, Hodder and Stoughton, 1955.
The Lobo Horseman. London, Hale, 1956.
The Call of the Gun. London, Hale, 1957.
Doc Colt. London, Hale, 1958.
Terror at Tres Alamos. London, Hale, 1958.
The Angry Land (as Frank Bass). New York, Dodd Mead, 1958; London, Ward Lock, 1959.

Novels as Brad Ward

The Spell of the Desert. New York, Dutton, 1951; London, Hodder and Stoughton, 1952.

The Hanging Hills. New York, Dutton, 1952; London, Hodder and Stoughton, 1953.
Johnny Sundance. New York, Dutton, 1952; London, Hodder and Stoughton, 1954.
Marshal of Medicine Bend. New York, Dutton, 1953; London, Hodder and Stoughton, 1954.
Trouble at Tall Pine. New York, Dutton, 1954; London, Hodder and Stoughton, 1955; as *Whiplash*, New York, Bantam, 1956.
Thirty Notches. New York, Macmillan, 1956; London, Hodder and Stoughton, 1958.
Six-Gun Heritage. London, Hodder and Stoughton, 1956.
The Missourian. New York, Macmillan, 1957; London, Hale, 1958.
The Man from Andersonville. New York, Macmillan, 1957; as *Rough Justice*, London, Transworld, 1958.
Frontier Street. New York, Macmillan, 1958; London, Hale, 1959.

OTHER PUBLICATIONS

Novels

The Man Who Died Twice: A Novel About Hollywood's Most Baffling Murder. New York, Putnam, 1976.
Star Trek, Where No Man Has Gone Before (novelization of television series). Toronto and London, Bantam, 1977.

* * *

Whether he wrote under his own name, or as Brad Ward, Samuel Anthony Peeples had a strong sense of character, an awareness of his surroundings, and a feel for the subtleties of human nature. His books do not work on the linear plane of ranch wars, land grabs, or rustling, but rather involve the "knock on effect" of one man's actions, and describe how the resulting consequences influence others around him.

In *Rough Justice*, Hart Craven witnesses the death of his brother at the hands of three prison wardens. He vows vengeance, and, when he is finally freed from Andersonville, searches out the murderers. A chance meeting at a hobo's railroad fire brings him into contact with the first victim, and before killing him Craven learns the vague whereabouts of the remaining men. Fortunately, Peeples stops the book from sliding into the all too familiar revenge/retribution storyline. Craven is a bitter, sombre man, but his one aim in life, to avenge Davey Craven is softened by the people he meets. It is their influence on him that alters his character, and the ending is something of a surprise.

This theme of personal vendetta is repeated in *Doc Colt*. A prison breakout by Cade Tallant sets him on the trail of the two men who framed him to spend five and a half years in Yuma Prison. Upon his harrowing escape, which is well-described with the suspense escalating to fever pitch, Tallant learns that his would-be victims are rich and powerful men who own the town of Boothill, and has to decide the best course of action. *Doc Colt* is not so well-told as *Rough Justice*, with the book's opening remaining its best feature.

My personal favourite is *The Call of the Gun*. Here, Peeples allows his creative writing to shine through, when two seeming opposites are thrown together in the desert: Johnny Trigo, an outlaw, and Davey Kibbard, a youngster unfamiliar with the western way of life. In the beginning Trigo steals Kibbard's horse, but, feeling sorry for the kid with the "gimpy" leg, returns to offer to take Kibbard into town. The opening of the novel hints at unusual future developments, and these in fact ensue, with Kibbard idolizing Trigo and the latter desperately trying to dissuade the youngster from life as an outlaw. But Davey is dogged in pursuing Trigo, and finally the latter capitulates to Kibbard's incessant badgering. Both Trigo and Kibbard are hired by Silman Ventor to rid his range of nesters. Kibbard now has to face up to the facts of life, and bring himself to kill innocent men, women and children. Sickened by the violence and senseless killings, Kibbard exerts pressure on Trigo to turn against Ventor and bring the cattle baron down. *The Call of the Gun* could be classed as a rite of passage novel for Davey Kibbard, from an inexperienced youth to a young adult with a true sense of identity. The climax to the book couldn't have been bettered, and features Peeples at his most dramatic.

Personal conflict is also well-explored in *Six-Gun Heritage*, a well-constructed and convincing story of how a Texas Ranger, known for his cowardice, is found alongside a dead, notorious gunman. But is Wayne Ferris in reality King Cassmead? It is up to Ferris to prove his identity to his doubters, and as the book progresses one is left in some doubt as to who he actually is. Nothing is spelt out in this fast-paced novel, and further elements are added to the plot—a doubting Ranger, land hungry ranchers, a double-crossing judge, evil gunmen, and Ferris's wife's hesitancy to commit herself to the man who had been missing from the second day of their marriage, over four years ago. In all, Peeples gives us a fine story, and its characters are ably drawn, even to the German storekeeper, Herr Meuler—speaking in broken English—who provides the comic relief.

In *The Angry Land*, a one-off novel using the byline of Frank Bass, the story is based on the most famous of all Southwest legends—Billy the Kid and the Lincoln County War. Here Peeples freely admits ". . . liberties have been taken with dates, chronology and distances. Certain historical characters can be easily identified despite their fictional names." Peeples's storyline is simple; English rancher Trumball saves Billy Bascom from being lynched by Ryan's men. They in turn murder Trumball, and Billy kills them all until only Ryan remains. The trouble is that Ryan also owns the law. Such is Peeples's use of prose; he avoids the numerous technical Westernisms that clogged down the works of competing writers. His vision of the West is of that land we have seen on the cinema and TV screens many times. His almost casual description of landscape or weather can convey much more in his truncated style, than the overlong and often boring prose from such authors as Archie Joscelyn.

—Mike Stotter

PENDEXTER, Hugh. American. Born in Pittsfield, Maine, 15 January 1875. Educated at Nicholl's Latin School, Lewiston, Maine, graduated 1896. Married Helen M. Faunce in 1897; two children. Staff member, Rochester *Post Express*, New York, 1900–11; full-time writer, from 1911. Hon. M.A., Bates College, Lewiston, Maine, 1933. *Died 11 June 1940.*

WESTERN PUBLICATIONS

Novels

Tiberius Smith, as Chronicled by His Right-Hand Man, Billy Campbell. New York and London, Harper, 1907.
The Mantle of Red Evans. New York, Winthrop Press, 1914.
Gentlemen from the North. New York, Doubleday, Page, 1920; London, Collins, 1929.

Red Belts. New York, Doubleday, Page, 1920.
Kings of the Missouri. Indianapolis, Bobbs Merrill, 1921.
A Virginia Scout. Indianapolis, Bobbs Merrill, 1922; London, Collins, 1926.
Pay Gravel. Indianapolis, Bobbs Merrill, and London, Collins, 1923.
Old Misery. Indianapolis, Bobbs Merrill, 1924.
In the Black Hills. London, Collins, 1924.
Streak o' Scarlet. London, Collins, 1924.
The Wife-Ship Woman. Indianapolis, Bobbs Merrill, 1925; London, Collins, 1929.
Harry Idaho. Indianapolis, Bobbs Merrill, 1926; London, Collins, 1927.
The Red Road: A Romance of Braddock's Defeat. Indianapolis, Bobbs Merrill, and London, Collins, 1927.
Bird of Freedom. Indianapolis, Bobbs Merrill, and London, Collins, 1928; as *Freedom*, London, Collins, 1934.
The Road to El Dorado. London, Collins, 1929.
The Gate Through the Mountain. Indianapolis, Bobbs Merrill, 1929; London, Collins, 1930.
Red Autumn. London, Collins, 1931.
Wolf Law. London, Collins, 1931.
The Scarlet Years. London, Collins, 1932.
The Border Breed. London, Collins, 1932.
Rifle Rock. London, Collins, 1932.
The Fighting Years. London, Collins, 1933.
Over the Ridge. London, Collins, 1933.
Partners. London, Collins, 1933.
The Bush Lopers: A Wild West Novel. London, Collins, 1933.
The Trail of Pontiac. London, Collins, 1933.
The Flaming Frontier. London, Collins, 1933.
The Blazing West. London, Collins, 1934.
Red Man's Courage. London, Collins, 1934.
Log Cabin Men. London, Collins, 1934.
The Dark Road. London, Collins, 1935.
The Bushfighters. London, Collins, 1935.
The River Frontier. London, Collins, 1935.
White Dawn. London, Collins, 1935.
The Woods Runner. London, Collins, 1935.
Devil's Brew. London, Collins, 1936.
Go-Ahead Davie. London, Collins, 1936.
The Torch-Bearers. London, Collins, 1936.
The Homesteaders. London, Collins, 1937.
The Long Knives. London, Collins, 1937.
Call of the Wilderness. London, Collins, 1938.
Red Traps. London, Collins, 1941.
Tomahawk Law. London, Collins, 1942.
Vigilante of Alder Gulch. New York, Arcadia House, 1955.

OTHER PUBLICATIONS

Fiction for children

The Young Gem-Hunters: or, The Mystery of the Haunted Camp. Boston, Small Maynard, 1911.
The Young Timber-Cruisers: or, Fighting the Spruce Pirates. Boston, Small Maynard, 1911.
The Young Fishermen: or, The King of Smuggler's Island. Boston, Small Maynard, 1912.
The Young Woodsmen: or, Running Down the Squaw-Tooth Gang. Boston, Small Maynard, 1912.
The Young Sea-Merchants: or, After Hidden Treasure. Boston, Small Maynard, 1913.
The Young Trappers: or, The Quest of the Giant Moose. Boston, Small Maynard, 1913.
The Young Loggers: or, The Gray Axeman of Mount Crow. Boston, Small Maynard, 1917.

*

Manuscript Collection: Oshkosh Library, Wisconsin.

* * *

Hugh Pendexter has an impressive list of credits, evidence of his varied interests in the many aspects of western history. Many of his novels are set in the pioneering days, and are based on historical fact. He can combine humour with passion, adventure with escapism, but above all his style inspires the reader to seek out more of his work.

Old Misery is a good adventure story, set in California in the early 1850's. Pendexter takes considerable pains to ensure accuracy of historical background and characters. The latter are thoughtful studies, as in the case of Old Misery himself. This novel is really a series of disconnected short stories, each one linked in some way to the mountain man.

Pendexter continues with varied subplotting within in a single novel in *Over the Ridge*. The "Ridge" is local terminology for the Sierra Nevada, which countless covered wagons had to cross on their way to the California fields. The main protagonist is Washoe, a gentle gambling man, who becomes involved with feisty young Matilda Jaimson, who is searching for her father. The author is not attempting fine writing, but enlivens his work with fine character studies which move the story along at a fine pace. He repeats the "honest gambler" character in *Partners*, another adventure of pioneering days in the Californian gold fields. Frank Ellis, who considers himself to be a failure, teams up with his sister Annie and Nate Gross, the gambler; together they hit the high trail. The book is pleasantly written, although repeating views explored in *Over the Ridge*, but Pendexter doesn't allow his own knowledge of the time to obtrude, and gives an excellent picture of the people and the hardships of the Westerner during this period.

His earliest work, *Tiberius Smith*, is the retelling of the veteran showman's life by Billy Campbell, his right-hand man, and shows Pendexter's good eye and ear for exploring a different view of the West. At his son's request, he also produced a number of works aimed at younger readers. The Camp and Trail series feature the adventures of Stanley Malcolm and Bub Thomas, and are much akin to latter-day Boy's Own Stories, but are filled with knowledge of the various subjects dealt within the books, and show Pendexter's skill in creating the aura of adventure.

Kings of the Missouri brought him firmly back to the western genre, with its story of the American Fur Company, and of Ralph Lander's adventures alongside Jim Bridger and his French mentor, Papa Clair. Pendexter's descriptions of fur trapping, and his authentic picture of St. Louis all add colour to the book, and excitement is provided with constant clashes with Indians along the Missouri. Lander starts out as a day-dreamer, but returns to claim his girl as a more mature character, who can now claim to be a mountain man.

Pendexter carved himself a niche is relating tales of the early American West, and two of his works attest to his own historical interest in this early period. *The Scarlet Years* tells of the time when the French and the English struggled for mastery of Canada. Against this background Pendexter introduces a likeable character named Louis Valtry, every inch the hero, but who is forced to play the part of a spy. *The Scarlet Years* has been likened to the works of Fennimore Cooper, not least in its retelling of the fall of the old Fort Frontenac.

A Virginia Scout continues the exploration of late 18th-century American history. Describing the events through first-person narrative of his main character, Morris, Pendexter relates to the reader the Indian wars and outrages, moving through to Dunmore's War of 1774.

Pendexter's writings cannot be described as "action" Westerns, because at the time he wrote them there was no formula for the genre, and he wrote what he believed would be of interest to readers and to keep the past alive. His earlier books were well received at the time, and many of these early editions carried black and white plates illustrating the story. As time went on Pendexter succumbed to producing more stylised works, although always retaining his sense of adventure, colourful language, and detailed description of landscape. On the whole, Pendexter's works showed greater depth than those of his counterparts, although he was not inclined to delve into more complex human frailties, other than to make the fears and worries of his characters known.

—Mike Stotter

PENDLETON, Ford. *See* **CHESHIRE, Giff.**

PENDOWER, T(homas) C(urtis) H(icks). Also wrote as Kathleen Carstairs; Tom Curtis; Penn Dower; T.C.H. Jacobs; Lex Pender; Marilyn Pender; Jacques Pendower; Anne Penn. British. Born in Plymouth, Devonshire, 30 December 1899. Educated at a grammar school in Plymouth. Served in the British Army, 1918–21: Second Lieutenant. Married Muriel Newbury in 1925; one son. Worked as a revenue investigating officer prior to 1950. Founder member, 1953, and chair, 1960–61, Crime Writers Association. *Died in 1976.*

WESTERN PUBLICATIONS

Novels as Penn Dower

Lone Star Ranger. London, Long, 1952.
Bret Malone, Texas Marshal. London, Long, 1953.
Gunsmoke over Alba. London, Long, 1953.
Texas Stranger. London, Long, 1954.
Indian Moon. London, Long, 1954.
Malone Rides In. London, Long, 1955.
Two-Gun Marshal. London, Long, 1956.
Desperate Venture. London, Long, 1956.
Guns in Vengeance. London, Long, 1957.
Frontier Marshal. London, Long, 1958.
Bandit Brothers. London, New English Library, 1964.

Novels as Tom Curtis

Bandit Gold. London, Stanley Paul, 1953.
Gunman's Glory. London, Stanley Paul, 1954.
Trail End. London, Stanley Paul, 1954.
Frontier Mission. London, Stanley Paul, 1955.
Border Justice. London, Stanley Paul, 1955.
Ride and Seek. London, Stanley Paul, 1957.
Phantom Marshal. London, Long, 1957.
Gun Business. London, Long, 1958.
Lone Star Law. London, Long, 1959.

OTHER PUBLICATIONS

Novels as T.C.H Jacobs

The Terror of Torlands. London, Stanley Paul, 1930.
The Bronkhorst Case. London, Stanley Paul, 1931; as *Documents of Murder*, New York, Macaulay, 1933.
Scorpion's Trail. London, Stanley Paul, 1932; New York, Macaulay, 1934.
The Kestrel House Mystery. London, Stanley Paul, 1932; New York, Macaulay, 1933.
Sinister Quest. London, Stanley Paul, and New York, Macaulay, 1934.
The 13th Chime. London, Stanley Paul, and New York, Macaulay, 1935.
Silent Terror. London, Stanley Paul, 1936; New York, Macaulay, 1937.
Appointment with the Hangman. London, Stanley Paul, and New York, Macaulay, 1936.
The Laughing Men. London, Hodder and Stoughton, 1937.
Identity Unknown. London, Stanley Paul, 1938.
Traitor Spy. London, Stanley Paul, 1939.
Brother Spy. London, Stanley Paul, 1940.
The Broken Knife. London, Stanley Paul, 1941.
The Grensen Murder Case. London, Stanley Paul, 1943.
Reward for Treason. London, Stanley Paul, 1944.
The Black Box. London, Stanley Paul, 1946.
The Curse of Khatra. London, Stanley Paul, 1947.
With What Motive? London, Stanley Paul, 1948.
Dangerous Fortune. London, Stanley Paul, 1949.
The Red Eyes of Kali. London, Stanley Paul, 1950.
Lock the Door, Mademoiselle. London, Stanley Paul, 1951.
Blood and Sun-Tan. London, Stanley Paul, 1952.
Lady, What's Your Game? London, Stanley Paul, 1952.
No Sleep for Elsa. London, Stanley Paul, 1953.
The Woman Who Waited. London, Stanley Paul, 1954.
Good Knight, Sailor. London, Stanley Paul, 1954.
Results of an Accident. London, Stanley Paul, 1955.
Death in the Mews. London, Stanley Paul, 1955.
Cause for Suspicion. London, Stanley Paul, 1956.
Broken Alibi. London, Stanley Paul, and New York, Roy, 1957.
Deadly Race. London, Long, 1958.
Black Trinity. London, Long, 1959.
Women Are Like That. London, Hale, 1960.
Let Him Stay Dead. London, Hale, 1961.
The Tattooed Man. London, Hale, 1961.
Target for Terror. London, Hale, 1961.
The Red Net. London, Hale, 1962.
Murder Market. London, Hale, 1962.
The Secret Power. London, Hale, 1963.
Danger Money. London, Hale, 1963.
The Elusive Monsieur Drago. London, Hale, 1964.
Final Payment. London, Hale, 1965.
Ashes in the Cellar. London, Hale, 1966.
Sweet Poison. London, Hale, 1966.
Death of a Scoundrel. London, Hale, 1967.
Wild Week-End. London, Hale, 1967.

House of Horror. London, Hale, 1969.
The Black Devil. London, Hale, 1969.
Security Risk. London, Hale, 1972.

Novels as Jacques Pendower

The Dark Avenue. London, Ward Lock, 1955.
Hunted Woman. London, Ward Lock, 1955.
Mission in Tunis. London, Hale, 1958; New York, Paperback Library, 1967.
Double Diamond. London, Hale, 1959.
The Long Shadow. London, Hale, 1959.
Anxious Lady. London, Hale, 1960.
The Widow from Spain. London, Hale, 1961; as *Betrayed*, New York, Paperback Library, 1967.
Death on the Moor. London, Hale, 1962.
The Perfect Wife. London, Hale, 1962.
Operation Carlo. London, Hale, 1963.
Sinister Talent. London, Hale, 1964.
Master Spy. London, Hale, 1964.
Spy Business. London, Hale, 1965.
Out of This World. London, Hale, 1966.
Traitor's Island. London, Hale, 1967.
Try Anything Once. London, Hale, 1967.
A Trap for Fools. London, Hale, 1968.
The Golden Statuette. London, Hale, 1969.
Diamonds for Danger. London, Hale, 1970.
She Came By Night. London, Hale, 1971.
Cause for Alarm. London, Hale, 1971.
Date with Fear. London, Hale, 1974.

Novels as Kathleen Carstairs

It Began in Spain. London, Gresham, 1960.
Third Time Lucky. London, Gresham, 1962.
Shadows of Love. London, Gresham, 1966.

Novels as Marilyn Pender

The Devouring Flame. London, Gresham, 1960.
A Question of Loyalty. London, Gresham, 1961.
The Golden Vision. London, Gresham, 1962.
Rebel Nurse. London, Gresham, 1962.
Dangerous Love. London, Gresham, 1966.

Novels as Anne Penn

Dangerous Delusion. London, Gresham, 1960.
Prove Your Love. London, Gresham, 1961.
Mystery Patient. London, Gresham, 1966.

Play

Radio Play: *The Grensen Murder Case*, from his own novel.

Other

Cavalcade of Murder (as Jacques Pendower). London, Stanley Paul, 1955.
Pageant of Murder (as Jacques Pendower). London, Stanley Paul, 1956.
Aspects of Murder (as Jacques Pendower). London, Stanley Paul, 1956.

* * *

Writing under the pseudonyms of Penn Dower and Tom Curtis, the English-born writer T.C.H. Pendower produced around 20 Westerns in one decade. His works falls into the category of the traditional Western, and contains the familiar themes of ranch wars, cattle rustling, kidnapping, and Indian fights.

A constant figure in most of Pendower's western novels is the lawman, always, one of the staples of western literature. As Penn Dower, he wrote a series on Marshal Bret Malone—a colourful character, intelligent, courageous and ruggedly handsome, everything that befits a stereotype.

Bret Malone, Texas Marshal introduces the hero as he is called in to intervene in a range war. With the aid of wily old Judge Rees, he sets about bringing a killer to justice. Tied in with this plot is Malone's attempt to unmask a crooked attorney. Pendower often succumbs to clichés, but these can be overlooked when measured against overall strength of the book, and he manages to maintain suspense to the novel's conclusion. This story contains twists and turns more appropriate to the thriller genre, to which Pendower was no stranger.

There is no doubt of the author's ability to write an exciting and competent Western, and in developing the Malone character he continually pits him against seemingly overwhelming odds. There is an overzealous rancher with delusions of grandeur in *Texas Stranger*, or the rancher who threatens to dominate a whole town in *Gunsmoke Over Alba*. This is an area where Pendower is thoroughly at home, and readers are fully aware as to what to expect from him. Another favourite device of his is to portray the central character as a duplicitous soul. In *Bret Malone, Texas Marshal*, in order to gain certain confidences the hero poses as an outlaw. Wade Markham, in *Border Justice*, is in reality a Pinkerton Agent who follows a 15-year-old trail to find a missing girl, now a woman, while at the same time aiming to avenge the murder of a friend; and marshal Johnny Bray, in *Bandit Gold*, poses as a faro dealer in order to recover previously stolen gold and bring the perpetrators to justice.

But when you least expect it, Pendower comes up with a surprise. I consider *Indian Moon* a personal favourite of this author, where Pendower uses the well-tried formula of gun-running to the Indians. Uncharacteristically, Comanches, Apaches, and Cheyenne, join together to fight the white man. The military call in Bret Malone, but he is torn between his duty and his personal sympathy for the dispossessed Indians. In contrast to the other Malone books, the characters emerge fully-rounded.

Frontier Mission has Pendower combining law and Indian warfare again. Oddly enough, when he wrote as Tom Curtis, his books were a marked improvement on those as Penn Dower. Here we have Marshal Logan searching for Apache war leader Fuerte Toro, but when the wagon train he is riding with is attacked only he, fugitive Johnny Grell, and Mary Austin survive. Attempting to get back to Fort Lobo, Logan is wounded, and Grell decides to redeem his character and—to obtain a pardon—resumes the hunt for Toro. Together with Sutton, an Army scout, he succeeds. From the beginning one wonders where the author is actually leading his reader, but there is a break-off point and, unfortunately, the outcome is all too predictable.

Trail End is a curious book, if only for the simple reason that Pendower veers away from what could have been a disaster, and turns the story around to achieve a spirited Western. This is by no means a profound work, but it is written with the professional ease one expects from such a craftsman. A young man named Seth has one aim in life—to avenge his father's murder. Two happy-go-lucky characters who are fond of the boy take it upon themselves to look after him. With the help of a woman they nurture the boy, turning his aggression from a forceful to a passive nature. It is not such a downbeat story, as the book is peppered with plenty of gunfire, and is set against the backdrop of a range war.

Repetition is a natural feature in language, so it is not unreasonable that an author can repeat successful storylines and get away with it. I was beginning to dismiss Pendower, as the sagas of Bret Malone appeared to be merging into a single blur, with too many similarities in description, dialogue and personal traits jarring the eye and brain. But clearly books such as *Trail End* and *Indian Moon* are exceptions to the rule.

—Mike Stotter

PERRY, George Sessions. American. Born in Rockdale, Texas, 5 May 1910. Educated at Rockdale High School; Allen Academy, Bryan, Texas; Southwestern University, Georgetown, Texas; Purdue University, Lafayette, Indiana; University of Houston. Married Claire E. Hodges in 1933. War correspondent in Africa and Europe for *New Yorker* and *Saturday Evening Post* during World War II. Recipient: National Book award, 1942. *Died 13 December 1956.*

WESTERN PUBLICATIONS

Novels

Walls Rise Up. New York, Doubleday, 1939.
Hold Autumn in Your Hand. New York, Viking Press, 1941.

Short Stories

Hackberry Cavalier. New York, Viking Press, 1944.

Uncollected Short Stories

"Don't Sit under That Family Tree," in *Saturday Evening Post* (Philadelphia), 15 March 1947.
"The Fourflusher," in *21 Texas Short Stories*, edited by W.W. Peery. Austin, University of Texas Press, 1954.
"For the Honor of the Family," in *Country Gentleman* (Philadelphia), September 1954.

OTHER PUBLICATIONS

Novel

30 Days Hath September, with Dorothy Cameron Disney. New York, Random House, 1942; London, Hale, 1950.

Plays

My Granny Van (produced Dallas).

Screenplay: *The Arkansas Traveler*, with Viola Brothers Shore and Jack Cunningham, 1938.

Other

Texas: A World in Itself. New York, McGraw Hill, 1942; revised edition, 1952.
Where Away: A Modern Odyssey, with Isabel Leighton. New York, McGraw Hill, 1944.
Cities of America. New York, McGraw Hill, 1947.
Families of America: Where They Come From and How They Live. New York, McGraw Hill, 1949.
My Granny Van: The Running Battle of Rockdale, Texas. New York, McGraw Hill, 1949.
The Story of Texas A and M. New York, McGraw Hill, 1951.
Tale of a Foolish Farmer. New York, McGraw Hill, 1951.
The Story of Texas (for children). New York, McGraw Hill, 1956.

Editor, *Roundup Time: A Collection of Southwestern Writing.* New York, McGraw Hill, 1943.

*

Critical Study: *George Sessions Perry* by Stanley G. Alexander, Austin, Texas, Steck Vaughn, 1967.

* * *

Walls Rise Up, George Sessions Perry's first novel, begins ambiguously in California when a trio of vagabonds fail to qualify for relief. They embark on the well-traveled picaresque road when Jimmy, the self-appointed leader, says, "I think we better take a little trip." The route takes them, led by the "Higher Powers," to the bucolic bliss of a bridge camp on the Brazos River near the fictional Hackberry, Texas. There, with luck reinforced by picaresque amorality, the friends of the road begin a series of adventures which end only when their camp is flooded. In the course of events, the author reveals his indebtedness to Defoe, Twain, and Steinbeck, among others. It is the freshness and authenticity of the pastoral Texas setting that save the novel from triteness. The characters live in harmony with nature, accepting the bounty of the river and neighboring fields and providing for creature comforts with ingenuity. In keeping with its forebears the novel has little plot continuity. The episodes involve a variety of tricks directed against a miserly store keeper and a tightfisted farmer. Others involve amorous adventures with remarkably receptive, and usually married, females. The only false note in this otherwise entertaining novel is the smuggled Mexican laborer Oof, menial to the others and occasional butt of degrading horseplay.

The derivative trappings of *Walls Rise Up* have disappeared from *Hold Autumn in Your Hand*, Perry's second novel. It is tightly structured, well paced, and achieves a continuity lacking in the first novel. Basically, it is the story of a young Texas sharecropper, Sam Tuckery, who commits himself for a year to a riverbottom farm to provide for his family and fulfill his long-held ambition to work a good piece of land. The underplot develops a rivalry between Tucker and his neighbor. The plots converge near the end when, wiped out by a devastating flood, he bargains away his rights to a legendary catfish to get help from his neighbor. Reader interest derives mainly from close identification with Tucker as he becomes increasingly involved in the near-epic struggle to survive. His closeness to nature, ingenuity in adversity, and stoic resolve make a compelling character. The wife and children are ciphers, the country neighbors too fleeting for much development, and the vivid Granny Tucker too hyperbolic for believability. These deficiencies are offset by the skillful concentration on the main character. The book is enhanced by a strong evocation of the land, as the author binds events to seasonal fluctuations in what Tucker calls his "play pretty" year. It is further enhanced by Perry's ear for regional idioms. Its ultimate success stems from the fact that the novel transcends its regional locale to deal with universals.

The last book of fiction by Perry is *Hackberry Cavalier*. It is a collection of 17 tales, some among his earliest works, mainly published earlier in various periodicals. He has given the work a loose unity by employing a recurring main character, a localized rural setting, and transitional material at the beginning of each tale. But the work is not successful as a sustained piece of fiction, and the hyperbole of the tall-tale becomes tedious. Some of the tales show the idiomatic authenticity and feel for the land that are characteristic of Perry's best work, particularly "Wooden Wedding" and "Love on the Hoof."

—Sam H. Henderson

PETERS, Roy. *See* **NICKSON, Arthur.**

PICKARD, John Q. *See* **BORG, Jack.**

PICKERING, Eileen Marion. *See* **FALCON, Mark.**

PIKE, Charles R. *See* **GILMAN, George G.; WELLS, Angus.**

PINDER, Chuck. *See* **DONSON, Cyril.**

PLUMMER, Ben. *See* **BINGLEY, David Ernest.**

POCOCK, Robert. *See* **POCOCK, Roger.**

POCOCK, (Henry) Roger (Ashwell). Also wrote as Robert Pocock. British. Born in Tenby, Pembrokeshire, Wales, 9 November 1865. Educated on the Wellesley Training Ship; at Ludlow Grammar School; School of Submarine Telegraphy, London; Guelph Agricultural College, Ontario. Served in the Imperial Army: Captain. Had many jobs, including constable in Royal Canadian Mounted Police, seaman and missionary in the Pacific, and cowboy and miner in the western United States. *Died in 1941.*

WESTERN PUBLICATIONS

Novels

The Arctic Night. London, Chapman and Hall, 1896.
Curly: A Tale of the Arizona Desert. London, Gay and Bird, 1904; as Robert Pocock, Boston, Little Brown, 1905.
Jesse of the Cariboo. London, Murray, 1911.
The Wolf Trail. New York, Appleton, and Oxford, Blackwell, 1923.

OTHER PUBLICATIONS

Novels

The Blackguard. London, Beeman, 1896.
The Dragon-Slayer. London, Chapman and Hall, 1896; as *Sword and Dragon*, London Hodder and Stoughton, 1909.
The Chariot of the Sun: A Fantasy. London, Chapman and Hall, 1910.
A Man in the Open. Indianapolis, Bobbs Merrill, 1912.
The Splendid Blackguard. London, Murray, 1915; as *The Cheerful Blackguard*, Indianapolis, Bobbs Merrill, 1915.

Other

Tales of Western Life, Lake Superior, and the Canadian Prairie (as H.R.A. Pocock). Ottawa, Mitchell, 1888.
Rottenness: A Study of America and England. London, Beeman, 1896.
A Frontiersman. London, Methuen, 1903; as *Following the Frontier*, New York, McClure, 1903.
Captains of Adventure. Indianapolis, Bobbs Merrill, 1913.
Canada's Fighting Troops. London, Newnes, 1914.
Horses. London, Murrary, 1917.
Chorus to Adventurers, Being the Later Life of Roger Pocock ("A Frontiersman"). London, Lane, 1931.

Editor, *The Frontiersman's Pocket-Book.* London, Murrary, 1909.
Editor, *Reflections from Shakespeare: A Series of Lectures*, by Lena Ashwell. London, Hutchinson, 1926.

* * *

Roger Pocock was one of the first writers to exploit the western novel as a forum for his ideas on Populism as a social force. Pocock's two concerns were, on the one hand, the epical fortitude and valor of the man on the American frontier and the great historical significance of the opening of the continent, and, on the other, what he identified as the rottenness of political corruption in England and America. In the frontiersman—in his simplicity, his strength, his honesty—Pocock saw the only hope for overcoming the corruption of the centers of civilization in England and America. All of his novels of the frontier present simple, steady characters either at war or at odds with political sophistication and chicanery. But the best of these is probably *Curly: A Tale of the Arizona Desert.* Curly is virtually a Populist tract in its insistence that the large landowners, the banks, and the politicians are leagued against the poor farmer-cowboy, who must turn outlaw in order to survive. Pocock uses the innocent-eye technique to satirize the complex hypocrisies that are practiced upon his frontiersmen. The satire is not subtle, but it is nonetheless effective. Pocock is thus one of the original sources of the American version of the Robin Hood myth that was to lead eventually to such disparate "western" archetypes as the Lone Ranger on the one hand and Bonnie and Clyde on the other.

—Herbert F. Smith

PORTER, Alvin. *See* **ROWLAND, Donald S.**

PORTER, Katherine Anne. American. Born Callie Russell Porter in Indian Creek, Texas, 15 May 1890. Educated at Thomas School, San Antonio, Texas. Married 1) John Henry Koontz in 1906 (separated 1914; divorced 1915); 2) Ernest Stock in 1925; 3) Eugene Dove Pressly in 1933 (divorced 1938); 4) Albert Russell Erskine, Jr., in 1938 (divorced 1942). Journalist and film extra in Chicago, 1911–14; tuberculosis patient, Dallas, San Angelo, Texas, and Carlsbad, New Mexico, 1915–17; worked with tubercular children in Dallas, 1917; staff member, Fort Worth *Critic*, Texas, 1917–18; reporter, 1918, and drama critic, 1919, *Rocky Mountain News*, Denver; lived in New York, 1919, and mainly in Mexico, 1920–31, and Europe in 1930's; copy editor, Macauley and Company publishers, New York, 1928–29; taught at Olivet College, Michigan, 1940; contract writer for M.G.M., Hollywood, 1945–46; Lecturer in writing, Stanford University, California, 1948–49; Guest Lecturer in literature, University of Chicago, Spring 1951; Visiting Lecturer in contemporary poetry, University of Michigan, Ann Arbor, 1953–54; Fulbright Lecturer, University of Liège, Belgium, 1954–55; writer-in-residence, University of Virginia, Charlottesville, Autumn 1958; Glasgow Professor, Washington and Lee University, Lexington, Virginia, Spring 1959; Lecturer in American literature for U.S. Department of State, in Mexico, 1960, 1964; Ewing Lecturer, University of California, Los Angeles, 1960; Regents' Lecturer, University of California, Riverside, 1961. Library of Congress Fellow in Regional American Literature, 1944; U.S. delegate, International Festival of the Arts, Paris, 1952; member, Commission on Presidential Scholars, 1964; consultant in poetry, Library of Congress, 1965–70. Recipient: Guggenheim fellowship, 1931, 1938; New York University Libraries Gold Medal, 1940; Ford Foundation grant, 1959, 1960; O. Henry award, 1962; Emerson-Thoreau Medal, 1962; Pulitzer prize, 1966; National Book award, 1966; American Academy Gold Medal, 1967; Mystery Writers of America Edgar Allan Poe award, 1972. D.Litt.: University of North Carolina Woman's College, Greensboro, 1949; Smith College, Northampton, Massachusetts, 1958; Maryville College, St. Louis, 1968; D.H.L.: University of Michigan, Ann Arbor, 1954; University of Maryland, College Park, 1966; Maryland Institute, 1974; D.F.A.: La Salle College, Philadelphia, 1962. Vice-president, National Institute of Arts and Letters, 1950–52; member, American Academy, 1967. *Died 18 September 1980.*

Western Publications

Short Stories

Flowering Judas. New York, Harcourt Brace, 1930; enlarged edition, as *Flowering Judas and Other Stories*, New York, Harcourt Brace, 1935; London, Cape, 1936.
Hacienda: A Story of Mexico. New York, Harrison of Paris, 1934.
Noon Wine. Detroit, Schuman, 1937.
Pale Horse, Pale Rider: Three Short Novels. New York, Harcourt Brace, and London, Cape, 1939.
Selected Short Stories. New York, Harcourt Brace, 1945.
Collected Short Stories. London, Cape, 1964; New York, Harcourt Brace, 1965; enlarged edition, London, Cape, 1967.

Other Publications

Novel

Ship of Fools. Boston, Little Brown, and London, Secker and Warburg, 1962.

Short Stories

The Leaning Tower and Other Stories. New York, Harcourt Brace, 1944; London, Cape, 1945.
The Old Order: Stories of the South. New York, Harcourt Brace, 1944.
A Christmas Story. New York, Mademoiselle, 1958.

Other

My Chinese Marriage. New York, Duffield, 1921.
Outline of Mexican Popular Arts and Crafts. Los Angeles, Young and McAllister, 1922.
What Price Marriage. 1927.
The Days Before: Collected Essays and Occasional Writings. New York, Harcourt Brace, 1952; London, Secker and Warburg, 1953; enlarged edition, as *The Collected Essays and Occasional Writings*, New York, Delacorte, 1970.
A Defense of Circe. New York, Harcourt Brace, 1955.
The Never-Ending Wrong (on Sacco-Vanzetti case). Boston, Little Brown, 1977.
Works on Paper, 1969–79. San Francisco, Fine Arts Museum, 1980.
Conversations with Porter, Refugee from Indian Creek, with Enrique Hank Lopez. Boston, Little Brown, 1981.
Katherine Anne Porter: Conversations, edited by Joan Givner. Jackson, University of Mississippi, 1987.
Letters, edited by Isabel Bayley. New York, Atlantic Monthly Press, 1990.
This Strange Old World and Other Book Reviews, edited by Darlene Harbour Unrue. Athens, University of Georgia Press, 1991.

Editor, *What Price Marriage*. New York, Sears, 1927.

Translator, *French Song-Book*. Paris, Harrison, 1933.
Translator, *The Itching Parrot*, by Fernandez de Lizardi. New York, Doubleday, 1942.

*

Bibliography: *Katherine Anne Porter: A Critical Bibliography* by Edward Schwartz, New York, New York Public Library, 1953;

A Bibliography of the Works of Katherine Anne Porter and *A Bibliography of the Criticism of the Works of Katherine Anne Porter* by Louise B. Waldrip and Shirley Ann Bauer, Metuchen, New Jersey, Scarecrow Press, 1969; *Katherine Anne Porter and Carson McCullers: A Reference Guide* by Robert F. Kiernan, Boston, Hall, 1976; *Katherine Anne Porter: A Bibliography* by Kathryn Hilt, New York, Garland, 1985.

Critical Studies: *The Fiction and Criticism of Katherine Anne Porter* by Harry John Mooney, Jr., Pittsburgh, University of Pittsburgh Press, 1957, revised edition, 1962; *Katherine Anne Porter* by Ray B. West, Jr., Minneapolis, University of Minnesota Press, 1963; *Katherine Anne Porter and the Art of Rejection* by William L. Nance, Chapel Hill, University of North Carolina Press, 1964; *Katherine Anne Porter* by George Hendrick, New York, Twayne, 1965; *Katherine Anne Porter: The Regional Stories* by Winifred S. Emmons, Austin, Texas, Steck Vaughn, 1967; *Katherine Anne Porter: A Critical Symposium* edited by Lodwick C. Hartley and George Core, Athens, University of Georgia Press, 1969; *Katherine Anne Porter's Fiction* by Myron M. Liberman, Detroit, Wayne State University Press, 1971; *Katherine Anne Porter* by John Edward Hardy, New York, Ungar, 1973; *Katherine Anne Porter: A Collection of Critical Essays* edited by Robert Penn Warren, Englewood Cliffs, New Jersey, and London, Prentice-Hall, 1979; *Katherine Anne Porter: A Life* by Joan Givner, New York, Simon and Schuster, 1982; *Katherine Anne Porter's Women: The Eye of Her Fiction* by Jane Krause DeMouy, Austin, University of Texas Press, 1983; *Truth and Vision in Katherine Anne Porter's Fiction* by Darlene Harbour Unrue, Athens, University of Georgia Press, 1985.

* * *

Katherine Anne Porter, one of America's foremost writers of the long short story, or novella, was a writer less of location than of dis-location. The setting of her writing is predominantly Texas, where she grew up around the turn of the century, but where she lived little during her adult writing life. That distance, of writing from memory, is marked in Porter's depiction of landscape as a foreign, rootless place. The mood is not nostalgic, but rather alienated, as characters drift from others and themselves.

In modern literature the West has often represented freedom, providing a vast, non-judgmental space where pepople can fulfill their dreams. It is the basis of the American Dream, the resource behind the feeling that you can get what you want if you try hard enough. The darker side to this optimism is the West's disinterested, impersonal, and rootless nature. It does not provide a history or social structure to ground people: people are often seen to flee to the West to find that groundless feeling. Porter emphasizes that aspect of the landscape in her writing, particularly with one character, Miranda, who appears in several stories and reaches a crisis of alienation in the beautiful, haunting *Pale Horse, Pale Rider*.

Miranda first appears in "Old Mortality," a long story spanning 27 years about members of her extended family—flirtatious, dissatisfied Aunt Amy, defeated, alcoholic Uncle Gabriel, the strong matriarchal grandmother. This family is fleshed out more in a later series of stories called "The Old Order," but it is in "Old Mortality" that Miranda separates from her family. At a chance encounter on a train with her Cousin Eva, the 18-year-old Miranda hears a different side of old family stories about Amy and Gabriel that throws into question the "truth" about their family. And the seed of rebellion is planted as Eva rages about family in general: ". . . the whole hideous institution should be wiped from the face of the earth. It is the root of all human wrongs." Later Miranda senses her own alienation from her family: "'It is I who have no place . . . Where are my own people and my own time?' She resented, slowly and deeply and in profound silence, the presence of these aliens who lectured and admonished her, who loved her with bitterness and denied her the right to look at the world with her own eyes, who demanded that she accept their version of life and yet could not tell her the truth, not in the smallest thing." Eventually Miranda concludes that she must make her own way without them, and can only trust in herself: "At least I can know the truth about what happens to me, she assured herself silently, making a promise to herself in her hopefulness, her ignorance."

Miranda's alienation widens to take on an existential dimension in *Pale Horse, Pale Rider*. Set during World War I in a nameless western city, it tells the story of Miranda's near death from an outbreak of influenza and of her brief affair with a soldier about to go to war. (The city may be Denver, where Porter herself nearly died from influenza in 1918; she, like Miranda, was working as a reporter at the time.) The ubiquitousness of death, the drifting lives of both characters, their fear of both intimacy and separation are all heightened by the anonymity and indifference of their surroundings. When Miranda realizes she has influenza, which has already killed many people in the city, she searches in her mind for a more welcoming landscape: ". . . I suppose I should ask to be sent home, she thought, it's a respectable old custom to inflict your death on the family if you can manage it. No, I'll stay here, this is my business, but not in this room, I hope . . . I wish I were in the old mountains in the snow, that's what I should like best; and all about her rose the measured ranges of the Rockies wearing their perpetual snow, their majestic blue laurels of cloud, chilling her to the bone with their sharp breath." But this vision provides no comfort and her attempt to visualize the landscape of her past only turns into nightmare.

However, in the height of her illness, close to death, Miranda discovers a wondrous, welcoming landscape in complete contrast to the western one surrounding her. It is a "deep clear landscape of sea and sand, of soft meadow and sky, freshly washed and glistening with transparencies of blue." Miranda finds this place only through her trust in herself, in that "minute fiercely burning particle of being that knew itself alone . . . set itself unaided to resist destruction, to survive and to be in its own madness of being, motiveless and planless beyond that one essential end. Trust me, the hard unwinking angry point of light said. Trust me. I stay."

Once back from that place, herself better but her lover dead from the 'flu, and the war suddenly over, Miranda must try to recreate that vision in her sterile surroundings, in the "noiseless houses with the shades drawn, empty streets, the dead cold light of tomorrow. Now there would be time for everything."

"Noon Wine," another of Porter's best stories, is set on a dairy farm in southern Texas. A stranger appears at Mr. Thompson's farm, asking for work. Mr. Helton is a silent Swedish man from North Dakota who in the nine years he works for Thompson turns a good profit on the farm. He partially tames the hot, oppressive land, keeps to himself, and never spends his money, except occasionally on a new harmonica, on which he plays the same Swedish drinking song every night. An uneasy feeling underlies the story, and it is no surprise when another stranger appears after nine years to reveal Helton's sordid past. The tragedy that ensues is as inevitable as the heat and dryness of the land; again the landscape both reflects and is a cause of the characters' alienation.

Porter was an assured, graceful writer who used the ambivalence of the western landscape to underline her characters' own uncertainties. *Pale Horse, Pale Rider* in particular uses landscape skillfully to reflect internal turmoil.

—Tracy Chevalier

PORTIS, Charles (McColl). American. Born in El Dorado, Arkansas, 28 December 1933. Educated at Hamburg High School, Arkansas, graduated 1951; University of Arkansas, Fayetteville, 1955–58, B.A. in journalism 1958. Served in the United States Marine Corps, 1952–55. Reporter, *Commercial Appeal*, Memphis, 1958, *Arkansas Gazette*, little Rock, 1959–60, and reporter and London correspondent, New York, *Herald-Tribune*, 1960–64. Since 1964 freelance writer. Agent: Lynn Nesbit, Janklow and Nesbit Associates, 598 Madison Avenue, New York, New York 10022. Address: 7417 Kingwood, Little Rock, Arkansas 72207, U.S.A.

WESTERN PUBLICATIONS

Novel

True Grit. New York, Simon and Schuster, 1968; London, Cape, 1969.

OTHER PUBLICATIONS

Novels

Norwood. New York, Simon and Schuster, 1966; London, Cape, 1967.
The Dog of the South. New York, Knopf, 1979.
Masters of Atlantis. New York, Knopf, 1985.
Gringos. New York, Simon and Schuster, 1991.

* * *

Charles Portis is one of the most inventively comic writers of western fiction. With an unerring ear for the rhythms of speech and idiosyncrasies of language, he delivers deadpan humor as his characters strive to come to terms with their own limitations and an increasingly cockeyed world.

True Grit is easily one of the best contemporary Westerns, a curious amalgam of parody, formula, and myth. At first, the novel seems a straight parody. Deputy Marshal Rooster Cogburn, "an old one-eyed jasper," violates almost all of the preconceptions of the western hero. He is an immoderate drinker, a questionable marksman, a hapless gambler. Motivated by greed, not justice, he chooses his cases according to the size of the reward and constantly schemes to cheat the government, his prisoners, and his clients.

Portis overlays realism on the romantic world of the West. Rooster is not burdened by the moral introspection of a Virginian or Shane. He plots to shoot an outlaw in the back, drags another over a fire, and casually kicks another. Through the plain and graceful narration of Mattie Ross (another superior achievement), we are given a new vision of the West that verges on the grotesque. The characters bear the obvious signs of their harsh lives: Rooster has lost an eye, is wounded in the shoulder, has shotgun pellets embedded in his face; Mattie has an arm amputated; outlaws have their fingers chopped off and part of their lips shot away.

Despite its realism and debunking, the novel is not merely a spoof, for its theme and structure fall within the borders of the genre. The pursuit of individual justice is one of the most common plots in western literature, and although Rooster is clearly imperfect, he eventually proves himself to be heroic: unflinchingly brave, enormously skilled, and capable of affection and self-sacrifice.

Portis's accomplishments in *True Grit* are considerable. By introducing fresh elements of parody and realism, he has taken some of the sweetness out of the western formula and made it more palatable. *True Grit* does not mock the western myth, but creates new variations and suggests other possibilities for western writers.

In *Norwood* and *The Dog of the South* Portis turns his attention to the contemporary American West. The novels are a blend of the picaresque and absurd, describing an American character that has changed since the simpler times of the 19th century. Norwood Pratt and Ray Midge are flawed innocents propelled on fool's errands. Norwood journeys from Texas to New York and back to collect a 70 dollar debt; Midge sets out from Arkansas for Mexico and the Honduras to regain the car and credit cards taken by his runaway wife. The stuff of legend that infuses *True Grit* is replaced by a muddled quest that marks Portis's perceptions of 20th-century America. These are common men, a bit naive and weak, lacking Mattie Ross's iron convictions and clear purpose. Yet Portis treats them with compassion and gentle humor, not condescension. The abuses and betrayals that they endure are overcome by gritty determination. The lines between good and evil, right and wrong, are blurred, yet the characters share Mattie's insistence that one may not be wronged with impunity.

Portis effectively uses humor to define and explain an American character comprised of innocence, pluck, and a stubborn insistence on human dignity. They survive with battered integrity, and thus speak profoundly to the American spirit.

—Michael Cleary

POTTER, Jay Hill. *See* **HANSON, Vic J.**

POWELL, James. American. Born in Albuquerque, New Mexico, 25 April 1942. Educated at New Mexico State University, Las Cruces, B.S. in agriculture 1965. Married Pauline Powell in 1963; two sons and two daughters. Conservationist for the Department of Agriculture, in Captain, 1965–67, Deming, 1967–68, Silver City, 1968–72 in Las Cruces, all in New Mexico. Agent: Richard Curtis Associates, 156 East 52nd Street, New York, New York 100022. Address: 1415 Grover Drive, Las Cruces, New Mexico 88005, U.S.A.

WESTERN PUBLICATIONS

Novels

A Man Made for Trouble. Canoga Park, California, Major, 1976; London, Hale, 1981.
Deathwind. New York, Doubleday, 1979; London, Hale, 1980.

Stage to Seven Springs. New York, Ace, and London, Hale, 1979.
Vendetta. New York, Ace, 1980; London, Hale, 1981.
The Malpais Rider. New York, Doubleday, 1981; London, Hale, 1984.
The Hunt. New York, Doubleday, 1982.
Apache Moon. New York, Doubleday, 1983; London, Hale, 1987.
A Summer with Outlaws. New York, Walker, 1984; London, Hale, 1987.
The Mule Thieves. New York, Walker, 1986.
The Last Stronghold. London, Hale, 1987.

*

Manuscript Collection: University of Wyoming, Laramie.

James Powell comments:

Western fiction writing is undergoing a metamorphosis. So many years in the larval stage, the butterfly, I truly hope, is about to emerge.

My first books are mostly just that: first efforts. They are influenced mainly by the western writing of the past; they are a bit larval. I don't mean that to be demeaning. It is simply the way things were, and, to some extent, still are. The perhaps not-so-clear but present danger is that we are being almost overwhelmed just now by not always well-founded talk about the "myth" we have created. My belief is that most myths are created by the contemporaries of the time in question, but are never wholly false. An example in this case were the "dime" novels of the late 19th century. Today, as we try to clean some of this up a bit, we live in a very great danger of creating new and even *lesser* myths. I say this in light of some who would impose today's views and politics and morals on yesterday's very different climate. My hope is that, in my writing, I can remain true to that part of the American western "myth" that really was, while at the same time joining with those who would make an honest move toward greater truth. As I continue to write, I would hope that others can see at least a bit of the metamorphosis going on in me.

* * *

James Powell writes conventional Westerns set in the New Mexico area. The male characters in his novels conform to the western convention of being strong, silent, and infallible, if a little dull.

Powell mentions real towns and writes with extensive knowledge of the area, with a considerable amount of scenic description of the mountains and forests. Mining in this area for gold provides plots: hidden gold dust is the centre of attention in *A Man Made for Trouble*, where the villains' search for it takes place in the mountains. The chief characters know the area well, and there is an extensive tracking episode through the woods. Mining also forms an important influence in *Deathwind* in that the social effects of an influx of miners are well portrayed. The rapid prosperity and its results are shown as disturbing factors in the life of the town of Grafton.

The thinness of the veneer of civilisation in these wild areas is stressed in Powell's novels. The leading figure in Grafton is also the biggest saloon owner, and saloons upset law and order. This figure also ends up as the arch villain of the book. The stock western town in the novel with its Chinese eating house, its hotel, and its newspaperman is a little outpost of civilisation literally fighting to preserve order among rough miners in rough country. The hero, Cal, does, however, see a better future for the area when it goes over to cattle raising and homesteading as opposed to mining. There is a surprise ending in *Deathwind* with a horrific death for the villain which is justified by his misdeeds.

The familiar theme in Westerns of the conflict between civilisation and the wild outdoors appears in *A Man Made for Trouble*. It is personified in the shape of Leah, the heroine, or rather the hero's lover, who is a mixture of Indian and white blood. She has been educated in the East while leaving her soul in the mountains. The beauty of this girl forms an important element in the story. Despite her eastern education, she does not fail us as she rescues the hero Strapp from death at the hand of villains right at the end of the book. There is much woodcraft and tracking in the scenic mountains in *A Man Made for Trouble*. There is also a certain amount of technical gun knowledge in the book, but less violence than one usually expects in a modern Western.

Powell makes up for this by including a rape as well as a murder in *Vendetta*, which essentially concerns the detection of the crime and the possibility of mob hanging for the suspect. Three women, an unusually large number for Powell, appear in *Stage to Seven Springs*, and they are more than a handful for the gunman who has to protect them against Apaches.

The plots in Powell's novels are, as in *Deathwind*, rather contrived with climaxes that come too late and with little comic relief. Powell does succeed in providing a rather serious picture of the edges of civilisation in the 19th-century West.

—P.R. Meldrum

PREBBLE, John (Edward Curtis). British. Born in Edmonton, Middlesex, 23 June 1915. Educated at Sutherland Public School, Saskatchewan; Latymer Upper School, London. Served in the Royal Artillery, 1940–45; reporter, British Army Newspaper Unit, Hamburg, 1945–46. Married Betty Golby in 1936; two sons and one daughter. Reporter and feature writer for several London newspapers and magazines, 1934–40, 1946–60. Recipient: Western Writers of America Spur award, for novel, 1960, and for story, 1962; National Association of Independent Schools award, 1960. Fellow, Royal Society of Literature. Agent: Curtis Brown Ltd, 162–168 Regent Street, London W1R STB. Address: Hill View, The Glade, Kingswood, Surrey, England.

WESTERN PUBLICATIONS

Novels

Spanish Stirrup. New York, Harcourt Brace, 1958.
The Buffalo Soldiers. London, Secker and Warburg, and New York, Harcourt Brace, 1959.

Short Stories

My Great-Aunt Appearing Day and Other Stories. London, Secker and Warburg, 1958; enlarged edition, as *Spanish Stirrup and Other Stories*, Secker and Warburg, and New York, Holt Rinehart, 1973.

OTHER PUBLICATIONS

Novels

Where the Sea Breaks. London, Secker and Warburg, 1944.
The Edge of Darkness. London, Secker and Warburg, 1947; as *The Edge of the Night*, New York, Sloane, 1948.

Age Without Pity. London, Secker and Warburg, and New York, Holt, 1950.
The Mather Story. London, Secker and Warburg, 1954.
The Brute Streets. London, Secker and Warburg, 1954.

Plays

Screenplays: *Mysterious Island*, with Daniel Ullman and Crane Wilbur, 1961; *Zulu*, with Cy Enfield, 1963; *Gypsy Girl* (*Sky West and Crooked*), with Mary Hayley Bell, 1965.

Radio Plays: *Loss of the Birkenhead*, 1977; *The Glencoe Inquiry*, 1977.

Television Plays: *The Creevey Column*, 1963; *Mr. Douglas*, 1964; *Catherine Parr* (*The Six Wives of Henry VIII* series), 1970; *The Enterprise of England* (*Elizabeth R* series), 1971; *Baden Powell*, 1972; *The Artisan* (*The Love School* series), 1975; *The Wallace* (*History of the English Speaking Peoples* series), 1975; *John Macnab*, 1976; *The Three Hostages*, 1977; *The Wonderful Transaction*, 1978; *Bothwell*, 1979; *Mendelssohn in Scotland*, 1980; *The Borgias* series, 1981.

Other

Mongaso, Man Who Is Always Moving: The Story of an African Hunter. London, Kaye, 1956; as *Elephants and Ivory*, New York, Rinehart, 1956.
The High Girders (on Tay Bridge disaster). London, Secker and Warburg, 1956; as *Disaster at Dundee*, New York, Harcourt Brace, 1957.
Culloden. London, Secker and Warburg, 1961; New York, Atheneum, 1962.
The Highland Clearances. London, Secker and Warburg, 1963.
Glencoe: The Story of the Massacre. London, Secker and Warburg, and New York, Holt Rinehart, 1966.
The Darien Disaster. London, Secker and Warburg, 1968; New York, Holt Rinehart, 1969.
The Lion in the North: A Personal View of Scotland's History. London, Secker and Warburg, and New York, Coward McCann, 1971.
The Massacre of Glencoe. London, Jackdaw, 1972; New York, Viking Press, 1973.
Mutiny: Highland Regiments in Revolt 1743–1804. London, Secker and Warburg, 1975.
John Prebble's Scotland. London, Secker and Warburg, 1984.
The King's Jaunt: George IV in Edinburgh. London, Collins, 1988.

*

John Prebble comments:
I write. Whatever the success, I do nothing so well. Thus I write.

* * *

An Englishman noted mainly for his factual works on the history of Scotland, John Prebble has written only a select handful of Westerns. These, while a minor aspect of his own career as a writer, provide an interesting and individual contribution to the genre. All of Prebble's western stories share a quietly effective style and qualities of understatement and restraint that are a hallmark of his writing.

His two longest, most sustained works in the western field are also his best—*The Buffalo Soldiers* and the novella *Spanish Stirrup*. *The Buffalo Soldiers*, his only western novel, describes the experiences of a white officer who sets out to hunt a band of renegade Comanches with his unit of untried Negro cavalry. Prebble portrays the gradual change in the relationship between the officer—a Civil War veteran—and the suspicious troopers, many of them ex-slaves. Faced with the threat of the hostile Comanches, and equally hostile whites, the bond between the soldiers moves from bitter resentment to a grudging respect, and when—at considerable cost—their mission is accomplished, those who remain are united as never before. The story is presented soberly and without undue emphasis, allowing the reader to draw his conclusions from the action, avoiding philosophy or sermons to let the characters speak for themselves.

Its place as Prebble's supreme achievement as a western writer is rivalled only by *Spanish Stirrup*, a story of the Estribo ranch and the long trail drive to bring their Texan cattle north to Kansas, braving Indians and outlaws on the way. A dominant theme is the struggle between Ferguson, the blind patriarchal rancher, and his foreman, the orphaned Adam Carthage, whose efforts at independence are hampered by the responsibility he feels for the rancher's worthless son Johnny. Prebble follows the conflict to final resolution, ably depicting the dangers the cowhands meet along the way, not only from hostile Indians and border ruffians, but threats from the land itself—storms, flooded rivers, and stampedes. *Spanish Stirrup* is an excellent short novel, the age-old western themes rendered the more striking by the author's understated style.

Prebble has written a number of short stories in the western vein which display the same restrained, stark quality as his longer works. Perhaps slightly less significant, they are equally effective. "The Regulator" is a neat, precise work on the familiar theme of the peace-loving man who takes up his gun against a band of killers to regain his self-respect. "Almighty Voice," based on factual events, describes the life and death of a Cree Indian forced by circumstance into a last heroic stand against the Canadian Mounted Police. "My Great-Aunt Appearing Day," which recounts the courting of a Cheyenne girl by the Englishman Josh Tanner during peace talks between Indians and whites, is probably the best of Prebble's shorter pieces. It too has a factual basis, Appearing Day being one of the author's ancestors. A recent story, "The Long Hate," explores the corrupting influence of carefully nursed hatred, which in this case results in the lynching of an innocent man. In common with the longer works, the short stories display Prebble's calm undramatic style. Characters and scenery are evoked with a few deft strokes, violent death recorded but not dwelt upon, the plot of each unfolded in the same spare lean-fleshed prose.

—Jeff Sadler

PRENDER, Bart. *See* **KING, Albert.**

PRESCOTT, Caleb. *See* **BINGLEY, David Ernest.**

PRESCOTT, John (Brewster). American. Born in Menominee, Michigan, 29 July 1919. Educated at Lawrence College (now University), Appleton, Wisconsin, B.A. 1941. Served as a navigator-bombardier in the United States Army Air Force Heavy Bombardment Group, 1941–45: Air Medal, Presidential Unit Citation. Married Jane Louise Zimmermann in 1946; two sons and one daughter. Worked for advertising agency in Milwaukee, Wisconsin, and Phoenix, Arizona. Freelance writer. Member of the Board of Directors, Western Writers of America, 1962–63. Recipient: Western Writers of America Spur award, 1955. Address: c/o Bantam Doubleday Dell, 666 Fifth Avenue, New York, New York 10103, U.S.A.

WESTERN PUBLICATIONS

Novels

The Renegade. New York, Random House, 1954; London, Hale, 1956.
Journey by the River. New York, Random House, 1954.
Guns of Hell Valley. New York, Graphic, 1957.
Wagon Train. New York, Bantam, 1957.
Ordeal. New York, Random House, 1958.
Valley of Wrath. New York, Fawcett, 1961; London, Muller, 1963.
Lion in the Hills. New York, Dodd Mead, 1961; as *Mountain-Lion: A Puma Called Rusty*, London, Deutsch, 1962.
Treasure of the Black Hills. New York, Dell, 1962.

Uncollected Short Stories

"Ribbon for Ginger," in *Hound Dogs and Others*, edited by Jim Kjelgaard. New York, Dodd Mead, 1958.
"Bear-Sign," in *Frontiers West*, edited by S. Omar Barker. New York, Doubleday, 1959.
"Man Afoot," in *Spurs West*, edited by S. Omar Barker. New York, Doubleday, 1960.
"The Runt," in *Trails of Adventure*, edited by E.D. Mygatt. New York, Dodd Mead, 1961.
"Way of the Law in Calico," in *Western Roundup*, edited by Nelson Nye. New York, Macmillan, 1961.
"Winter Harvest," in *Rawhide Men*, edited by Kenneth Fowler. New York, Doubleday, 1965.
"Thirst," in *The Californians*, edited by Bill Pronzini and Martin H. Greenberg. New York, Fawcett, 1989.

OTHER PUBLICATIONS

Other (for children)

The Beautiful Ship: A Story of the Great Lakes. New York, Longman, 1952.
Meeting in the Mountains. New York, Longman, 1953.

* * *

John Prescott has written a small number of Westerns and other novels. He started writing novels about America but not proper Westerns. *The Beautiful Ship* is a story of commercial fishing in Lake Michigan written for older boys. This book was well received by critics who were impressed by the clear character development shown in it. *Meeting in the Mountains* is a story of the early inhabitants of Arizona long before Apache days. It is more than a run-of-the-mill Indian book, and its sensible presentation of early American history caused it to be recommended by librarians for school use.

The Renegade, Prescott's first proper Western, was also distinguished by clear character development. There were, perhaps, too many characters in the book, as well as the standard features of the formula Western, such as an Arizona setting, gunplay, and Mexican characters. The plot was strong and simple: an innocent man has to clear his name. There were, however, too many sub-plots which distracted. *Journey by the River* is an offbeat Western and does not fall into any of the orthodox patterns. It was nevertheless distinguished by realistic characterisation and was well received by critics. Prescott returned to Arizona as a setting for *Valley of Wrath*. It is rather unusual to set a Western during the Civil War itself, rather than afterwards, but at least in Arizona there was a territory less wracked by deep controversy than the eastern states. All sorts of feuds, brawls, and intrigues surface, with many familiar characters such as untrustworthy politicians. The book contains plenty of historical colour as well as action. The hero, a young army lieutenant, stands out and has to face up to danger. He is a hero strong enough to meet the many challenges thrown at him. He is, however, human enough to be involved in romance.

Prescott's style of writing includes very realistic descriptions of the land and exceptionally good treatment of natural features and the weather. Descriptions of people tend to be physical rather than psychological.

Dialogue is extensive but with short effective sentences. Prescott's obvious ability won him a Spur Award for western historical fiction in 1954, but his early promise has not been followed by many full-length western novels.

—P.R. Meldrum

PRITCHETT, Ron(ald). British. Born in Nottingham, 14 May 1929. Married Beryl Pritchett in 1957; two daughters. Office worker, Nottingham *Journal*, 1943–47; reader, *Evening News*, Nottingham, 1947–62; reader/computer operator, *Evening Post*, Nottingham, 1962–73; reader, Thomas Forman, Nottingham, 1973–77, and *Derby Trader*, Heanor, Derbyshire, 1978–86; self-employed reader, Nottinghamshire and Leicestershire, 1988–90. Since 1990 reader, Boots, Nottingham. Recipient: Nottingham Writers Club Writer of the Year award, 1990. Address: c/o Robert Hale Ltd., Clerkenwell House, 45–47 Clerkenwell Green, London EC1R 0HT, England.

WESTERN PUBLICATIONS

Novels

Peaceful Guns. London, Hale, 1988.
Cougar City. London, Hale, 1990.

*

Ron Pritchett comments:

My two western novels so far include the same two characters, who spark off each other to provide (hopefully) a touch of humour. Both contain a mystery which needs solving, much the same as W.C. Tuttle's *Hashknife* series, although I don't presume to have his expertise.

At present I am engaged on a non-fiction book and another Western, this time featuring Texas Rangers. I do hope, however, to write more of my first two heroes. I think I have grown to like 'em!

* * *

The two novels produced by Nottingham-born author Ron Pritchett are set in an established tradition some distance away from the "adult Western". Eschewing gratuitous sex and violence, their leisurely pace and frequent humorous asides between the characters recall the kind of western story popularised in the 1930s and 1940's by such writers as W.C. Tuttle, William Colt Macdonald, and Charles Alden Seltzer, authors for whom Pritchett admits a great admiration. Of the three, it is perhaps Tuttle whose style is most closely approached by the British writer, with his bantering but effective partnership of Buck Lawrence and Zeke Henderson suggesting a certain kinship with Hashknife Hartley and Sleepy Stevens, those other cowhands-turned-detectives who featured in so many adventures in the past. Pritchett shares with Tuttle a mastery of the gradually unfolding narrative which contains an element of mystery, a puzzle which must be solved by shrewd detective work. His penchant for outrageous nicknames for secondary characters, and for wise-cracking humour of a rather hoary kind, suggest further parallels with his mentor. This said, it must not be supposed that Pritchett merely follows in the footsteps of these earlier role models. Within the stylistic parameters he has set himself, he is very much his own man, and the characters he has created bear comparison with the best of the authors who first inspired him.

Buck Lawrence and Zeke Henderson are a pair of drifting ex-cowhands who, through force of circumstance, find themselves acting as detectives to uncover the mysteries at the heart of both Pritchett's novels. Netiher man is a gunfighter—indeed, the gigantic, pipe-smoking Zeke does not even carry a weapon at all—but both are well able to take care of themselves when the need arises. Buck, the brains of the partnership, shows a healthy fear when his life is threatened, and takes practical steps to ensure that he stays alive—his "cheating" use of a swivel holster to outdraw the killer Lightnin' Hogan, a man he knows to be faster than himself, is a case in point. It is the essential ordinariness of Pritchett's heroes, their everyday human qualities, which impress themselves on the reader, and their characters are realized with an apparent ease of utterance that conceals a rare skill on the part of the author. Pritchett shows a real affection for his two creations, and after a while it begins to rub off on the reader, who is readily able to identify with the partners in their relentless search for the truth.

Pritchett's first novel, *Peaceful Guns*, fixes the attention with a burst of gunfire on the opening page, before settling into an ambling, unhurried stride. Buck and Zeke take on the task of clearing the name of a young man wrongly accused of murder, tackling the problem in a no-nonsense, pragmatic fashion to expose the facts beneath the surface. Pritchett reveals a considerable knowledge of Western history, and the inevitable firearms—a .36 Whitney Navy pistol, and a Henry .44 rimfire lever-action rifle both feature in the action—but his main strength is his ability to sustain his easily-paced narrative through to the showdown without betraying any strain or creaking joints in the plot, and his assured skill in holding the interest of the reader without resorting to littering the pages with bodies. There are few deaths in Pritchett's novels, the main action focusing on the gradual process of detection. Needless to say, humour is constantly to the fore, with semi-comic fistfights and dumpings in the horse trough, and plenty of old-fashioned, bantering dialogue. Occasional Anglicisms suggest the nationality of the author, as when one character declares that he is "fed up." On the other hand, Tuttle would surely have been proud to have coined the phrase that Pritchett allots to the hungry Zeke: "I could eat a fried mule, sunnyside up." *Peaceful Guns* is an interesting debut, and shows the storytelling gifts possessed by its author.

Second novels tend to be the most difficult to write, but Pritchett clears this hurdle extremely well, with a story which surpasses *Peaceful Guns*. *Cougar City* has Buck and Zeke called in by a local banker to investigate a stage robbery and murder which, predictably, is not all that it seems. Their search reveals the mysterious secret of the neighbouring silver mine, and implicates some leading citizens, though not before Pritchett has led us through further attempted murders and close calls, as well as introducing some intriguing secondary characters. Of these, the most striking are the mountain man Jed Dean (complete with tame cougar!), the tall-story-telling drunk, Joe Waters, and the immigrant German saloon pianist Jerry Miller, whose own mysterious past provides an effective subplot. The strength of these lesser figures adds a depth to *Cougar City* which improves on its predecessor, and the narrative itself shows a greater degree of skill, with words honed down to a minimum. Pritchett's descriptions are brief, but effective, with situations established by a couple of sentences or so. Treatment of some minor characters is perhaps a little too cursory at times, and the novel has an abrupt and rather unlikely conclusion, but these cavillings apart, there is little else to fault in *Cougar City*. Once more, the author's deceptively simple style carries the reader with Buck and Zeke through a plot whose climaxes and transitions are capably interwoven, and although the body count is again on the low side—four deaths, three of them "offstage"—the interest never flags for a moment. Pritchett's warmth and humour infuse the narrative, and lend an individual voice to the proceedings. *Peaceful Guns* was a good start, but *Cougar City* is better, and bodes well for the future.

Ron Pritchett utilises traditional materials in his own particular manner, and the results so far are encouraging. One awaits his forthcoming work with genuine interest.

—Jeff Sadler

PRONZINI, Bill (William John Pronzini). Also writes as Jack Foxx; Romer Zane Grey; William Jeffrey; Alex Saxon. American. Born in Petaluma, California, 13 April 1943. Educated at a junior college for 2 years. Married 1) Laura Patricia Adolphson in 1965 (divorced 1966); 2) Brunhilde Schier in 1972 (divorced). Has worked as a newsstand clerk, sports reporter, warehouseman, typist, salesman, civilian guard with U.S. Marshall's office. Since 1969 self-employed writer. Traveled extensively in Europe; lived in Majorca and West Germany, 1970–73. Recipient: Private Eye Writers of America award, 1981, 1983, Life Achievement award, 1987. Agent: Clyde Taylor, Curtis Brown Ltd., 10 Astor Place, New York, New York 10003. Address: P.O. Box 1349, Sonoma, California 95476, U.S.A.

Western Publications

Novels

The Gallows Land. New York, Walker, 1983; London, Hale, 1984.
Starvation Camp. New York, Doubleday, 1984; London, Hale, 1985.
Quincannon. New York, Walker, 1985.
Beyond the Grave, with Marcia Muller. New York, Walker, 1986.

The Last Days of Horse-Shy Halloran. New York, Evans, 1987; Bath, Chivers, 1989.
The Hangings. New York, Walker, 1989.
Firewind. New York, Evans, 1989.

Novels as William Jeffrey, with Jeffrey Wallmann

Duel at Gold Buttes. New York, Tower, 1981; London, Hale, 1982.
Border Fever. New York, Leisure, 1983; London, Hale, 1984.

Short Stories

The Best Western Stories of Bill Pronzini, edited by the author and Martin H. Greenberg. Athens, Ohio University Press, Swallow Press, 1990.

Uncollected Short Stories

"Sawtooth Justice," in *Zane Grey Western* (New York), November 1969.
"Danger Rides the Dollar Wagon" (as Romer Zane Grey, with Jeffrey M. Wallmann), in *Zane Grey Western* (New York), March 1970.
"Siege at Forlorn River" (as Romer Zane Grey, with Jeffrey M. Wallmann), in *Zane Grey Western* (New York), May 1970.
"The Maurauders of Gallows Valley" (as Romer Zane Grey, with Jeffrey M. Wallmann), in *Zane Grey Western* (New York), July 1970.
"Thunderstorm," in *Zane Grey Western* (New York), October 1970.
"The Raid at Three Rapids" (as Romer Zane Grey, with Jeffrey M. Wallmann), in *Zane Grey Western* (New York), November 1970.
"Day of the Hanging," in *Zane Grey Western* (New York), August 1971.
"Attack of the Bandito Horde" (as Romer Zane Grey, with Jeffrey M. Wallmann), in *Zane Grey Western* (New York), August 1971.
"Taggart's Gold" (as Jack Foxx), in *Zane Grey Western* (New York), December 1971.
"Moment of Reckoning" (as William Jeffrey, with Jeffrey Wallmann), in *Zane Grey Western* (New York), June 1972.
"Apache Massacre at Puma Junction" (as Romer Zane Grey, with Jeffrey Wallmann), *Zane Grey Western* (New York), August 1972.
"The Coward," in *Zane Grey Western* (New York), October 1972.
"The Gun Fanner," in *Zane Grey Western* (New York), April 1973; as "The Gunny," in *The Gunfighters*, edited by the author and Martin H. Greenberg, New York, Fawcett, 1987.
"The Posse from Paytonville," in *The Outlaws*, edited by the author and Martin H. Greenberg. New York Fawcett, 1984.
"Old Tom," in *The Californians*, edited by the author and Martin H. Greenberg. New York, Fawcett, 1989.

Other

Editor, with Martin H. Greenberg, *The Arbor House Treasury of Great Western Stories.* New York, Arbor House, 1982.
Editor, with Martin H. Greenberg, *The Western Hall of Fame.* New York, Morrow, 1984.
Editor, with Martin H. Greenberg, *The Lawmen.* New York, Fawcett, 1984.
Editor, with Martin H. Greenberg, *The Outlaws.* New York, Fawcett, 1984.
Editor, with Martin H. Greenberg, *The Reel West.* New York, Doubleday, 1984.
Editor, with Martin H. Greenberg, *The Best Western Stories of Steve Frazee.* Carbondale, Southern Illinois University Press, 1984.
Editor, with Martin H. Greenberg, *The Best Western Stories of Wayne D. Overholser.* Carbondale, Southern Illinois University Press, 1984.
Editor, with Marcia Muller, *She Won the West: An Anthology of Western and Frontier Stories by Women.* New York, Morrow, 1985.
Editor, with Martin H. Greenberg, *The Cowboys.* New York, Fawcett, 1985.
Editor, with Martin H. Greenberg, *The Warriors.* New York, Fawcett, 1985.
Editor, with Martin H. Greenberg, *The Second Reel West.* New York, Doubleday, 1985.
Editor, with Martin H. Greenberg, *The Railroaders.* New York, Fawcett, 1986.
Editor, with Martin H. Greenberg, *The Third Reel West.* New York, Doubleday, 1986.
Editor, *Wild Westerns: Stories from the Grand Old Pulps*, New York, Walker, 1986.
Editor, with Martin H. Greenberg, *The Steamboaters.* New York, Fawcett, 1986.
Editor, with Martin H. Greenberg, *The Cattlemen.* New York, Fawcett, 1987.
Editor, with Martin H. Greenberg, *The Horse Soldiers.* New York, Fawcett, 1987.
Editor, with Martin H. Greenberg, *The Best Western Stories of Lewis B. Patten.* Carbondale, Southern Illinois University Press, 1987.
Editor, with Martin H. Greenberg, *The Gunfighters.* New York, Fawcett, 1988.
Editor, with Martin H. Greenberg, *The Texans.* New York, Fawcett, 1988.
Editor, with Martin H. Greenberg, *The Californians.* New York, Fawcett, 1989.
Editor, *More Wild Westerns.* New York, Walker, 1989.
Editor, with Martin H. Greenberg, *The Best Western Stories of Loren D. Estleman.* Athens, Swallow Press/Ohio University Press, 1989.
Editor, with Martin H. Greenberg, *The Arizonans.* New York, Fawcett, 1989.
Editor, with Martin H. Greenberg, *The Best Western Stories of Frank Bonham.* Athens, Swallow Press/Ohio University Press, 1989.
Editor, with Martin H. Greenberg, *New Frontiers, I*, New York, Tor, 1989.
Editor, with Martin H. Greenberg, *New Frontiers II*, New York, Tor, 1990.
Editor, with Martin H. Greenberg, *Christmas Out West.* New York, Doubleday, 1990.
Editor, with Martin H. Greenberg, *The Northerners.* New York, Fawcett, 1990.
Editor, with Martin H. Greenberg, *The Best Western Stories of Ryerson Johnson.* Athens, Swallow Press, Ohio University Press, 1990.
Editor, with Martin H. Greenberg, *The Northwesterners.* New York, Fawcett, 1991.
Editor, with Martin H. Greenberg, *The Montanas.* New York, Fawcett, 1991.
Editor, with Martin H. Greenberg, *The Best Western Stories of John Jakes.* Athens, Swallow Press/Ohio University Press, 1991.

OTHER PUBLICATIONS

Novels

The Stalker. New York, Random House, 1971; London, Hale, 1974.
The Snatch. New York, Random House, 1971; London, Hale, 1974.
Panic! New York, Random House, 1972; London, Hale, 1974.
A Run in Diamonds (as Alex Saxon). New York, Pocket Books, 1973.
The Vanished. New York, Random House, 1973; London, Hale, 1974.
Undercurrent. New York, Random House, 1973; London, Hale, 1975.
Snowbound. New York, Putnam, 1974; London, Weidenfeld and Nicolson, 1975.
Games. New York, Putnam, 1976; London, Hamlyn, 1978.
The Running of Beasts, with Barry N. Malzberg. New York, Putnam, 1976.
Blowback. New York, Random House, 1977; London, Hale, 1978.
Acts of Mercy, with Barry N. Malzberg. New York, Putnam, 1977.
Twospot, with Collin Wilcox. New York, Putnam, 1978.
Night Screams, with Barry N. Malzberg. Chicago, Playboy Press, 1979.
Prose Bowl, with Barry N. Malzberg. New York, St. Martin's Press, 1980.
Labyrinth. New York, St. Martin's Press, 1980; London, Hale, 1981.
The Cambodia File, with Jack Anderson. New York, Doubleday, 1980; London, Sphere, 1983.
Hoodwink. New York, St. Martin's Press, and London, Hale, 1981.
Masques. New York, Arbor House, 1981.
Scattershot. New York, St. Martin's Press, and London, Hale, 1982.
Dragonfire. New York, St. Martin's Press, 1982; London, Hale, 1983.
Bindlestiff. New York, St. Martin's Press, 1983; London, Severn House, 1984.
Day of the Moon (as William Jeffrey, with Jeff Wallmann). London, Hale, 1983.
Quicksilver. New York, St. Martin's Press, 1984; London, Severn House, 1985.
The Eye, with John Lutz. New York, Mysterious Press, 1984.
Nightshades. New York, St. Martin's Press, 1984; London, Severn House, 1986.
Double, with Marcia Muller. New York, St. Martin's Press, 1984.
Bones. New York, St. Martin's Press, 1985.
Quincannon. New York, Walker, 1985.
Deadfall. New York, St. Martin's Press, 1986.
The Lighthouse, with Marcia Muller. New York, St. Martin's Press, 1987; London, Hale, 1988.
Shackles. New York, St. Martin's Press, 1988.
Jackpot. New York, Delacorte Press, 1990; London, Severn House, 1991.
Breakdown. New York, Delacorte Press, 1991.

Novels as Jack Foxx

The Jade Figurine. Indianapolis, Bobbs Merrill, 1972.
Dead Run. Indianapolis, Bobbs Merrill, 1975.
Freebooty. Indianapolis, Bobbs Merrill, 1976.
Wildfire. Indianapolis, Bobbs Merrill, 1978.

Short Stories

A Killing in Xanadu. Richmond, Virginia, Waves Press, 1980.
Casefile: The Best of the "Nameless Detective" Stories. New York, St. Martin's Press, 1983.
Cat's-Paw. Richmond, Virginia, Waves Press, 1983.
Graveyard Plots. New York, St. Martin's Press, 1985.
Small Felonies: Fifty Mystery Short Shorts. New York, St. Martin's Press, 1988.
Stacked Deck. Eugene, Oregon, Pulp House, 1991.

Other

Gun in Cheek. New York, Coward McCann, 1982.
1001 Midnights: The Aficionado's Guide to Mystery and Detective Fiction, with Marcia Muller. New York, Arbor House, 1986.
Son of Gun in Cheek. New York, Mysterious Press, 1987.

Editor, with Joe Gores, *Tricks and Treats.* New York, Doubleday, 1976; as *Mystery Writers Choice,* London, Gollancz, 1977.
Editor, *Midnight Specials.* Indianapolis, Bobbs Merrill, 1977; London, Souvenir Press, 1978.
Editor, with Barry N. Malzberg, *Dark Sins, Dark Dreams.* New York, Doubleday, 1977.
Editor, with Barry N. Malzberg, *The End of Summer: Science Fiction of the Fifties,* New York, Ace, 1979.
Editor, *Werewolf!* New York, Arbor House, 1979.
Editor, with Barry N. Malzberg, *Shared Tomorrows: Collaboration in SF.* New York, St. Martin's Press, 1979.
Editor, with Barry N. Malzberg, *Bug-Eyed Monsters.* New York, Harcourt Brace, 1980.
Editor, *The Edgar Winners.* New York. Random House, 1980.
Editor, *Voodoo!* New York, Arbor House, 1980.
Editor *Mummy!* New York, Arbor House, 1980.
Editor, *Creature!* New York, Arbor House, 1981.
Editor, *The Arbor House Necropolis: Voodoo!, Mummy! Ghoul!* New York, Arbor House, 1981; revised edition as *Tales of the Dead,* New York, Bonanza, 1982.
Editor, with Barry N. Malzberg and Martin H. Greenberg. *The Arbor House Treasure of Horror and the Supernatural [Mystery and Suspense].* New York, Arbor House, 2 vols., 1981.
Editor, *Specter!* New York, Arbor House, 1982.
Editor, *The Arbor House Treasury of Detective and Mystery Stories from the Great Pulps.* New York, Arbor House, 1983.
Editor, with Marcia Muller, *The Web She Weaves: An Anthology of Mysteries and Suspicious Stories by Women.* New York, Morrow, 1983.
Editor, with Charles G. Waugh and Martin H. Greenberg, *The Mystery Hall of Fame.* New York, Morrow, 1984.
Editor, with Marcia Muller, *Child's Ploy.* New York, Macmillan, 1984.
Editor, with Marcia Muller, *Witches' Brew: Horror and Supernatural Stories by Women.* New York, Macmillan, 1984.
Editor, with Marcia Muller, *Chapter and Hearse.* New York, Morrow, 1985.
Editor, with Charles G. Waugh and Martin H. Greenberg, *Murder in the First Reel.* New York, Avon, 1985.
Editor, with Martin H. Greenberg, *13 Short Mystery Novels.* New York, Greenwich House, 1985.

Editor, with Martin H. Greenberg, *13 Short Espionage Novels.* New York, Bonanza, 1985.
Editor, with Marcia Muller, *Dark Lessons: Crime and Detection on Campus.* New York, Macmillan, 1985.
Editor, with Marcia Muller, *Kill or Cure.* New York, Macmillan, 1985.
Editor, with Martin H. Greenberg, *Women Sleuths.* Chicago, Academy, 1985.
Editor, with Martin H. Greenberg, *Police Procedurals,* Chicago, Academy, 1985.
Editor, with Marcia Muller, *The Wickedest Show on Earth: A Carnival of Circus Suspense.* New York, Morrow, 1985.
Editor, with Marcia Muller, *The Deadly Arts: A Collection of Artful Suspense.* New York, Arbor House, 1985.
Editor, with Martin H. Greenberg, *A Treasury of Civil War Stories.* New York, Bonanza, 1985.
Editor, with Martin H. Greenberg, *A Treasury of World War II Stories.* New York, Bonanza, 1985.
Editor, with Martin H. Greenberg, *Great Modern Police Stories.* New York, Walker, 1986; London, Severn House, 1987.
Editor, with Martin H. Greenberg, *101 Mystery Stories.* New York, Avenel, 1986.
Editor, with Martin H. Greenberg, *Locked Room Puzzles.* Chicago, Academy, 1986.
Editor, with Martin H. Greenberg, and Barry N. Malzberg, *Mystery in the Mainstream.* New York, Morrow, 1986.
Editor, with Martin H. Greenberg, *The Mammoth Book of Short Crime Novels.* London, Robinson, 1986.
Editor, with Martin H. Greenberg, *The Mammoth Book of Short Spy Novels.* London, Robinson, 1986.
Editor, with Martin H. Greenberg, *Prime Suspects.* New York, Ivy, 1987; London, Severn House, 1988.
Editor, with Martin H. Greenberg, *Uncollected Crimes.* New York, Walker, 1987.
Editor, with Martin H. Greenberg, *Suspicious Characters.* New York, Ivy, 1987; London, Severn House, 1988.
Editor, with Carol-Lynn Rössel Waugh and Martin H. Greenberg, *Manhattan Mysteries.* New York, Avenel, 1987.
Editor, with Martin H. Greenberg, *Criminal Elements.* New York, Ivy, 1988.
Editor, with Martin H. Greenberg, *13 Short Detective Novels.* New York, Bonanza, 1988.
Editor, with Martin H. Greenberg, *Cloak and Dagger.* New York, Avenel, 1988.
Editor, with Marcia Muller and Martin H. Greenberg, *Lady on the Case.* New York, Bonanza, 1988.
Editor, with Martin H. Greenberg, *The Mammoth Book of Private Eye Stories.* New York, Carroll and Graf, and London, Robinson, 1988.
Editor, with Martin H. Greenberg, *Homicidal Acts.* New York, Ivy, 1989.
Editor, with Martin H. Greenberg, *Felonious Assaults.* New York, Ivy, 1989.

*

Manuscript Collections: University of Wyoming, Laramie; Mugar Memorial Library, Boston University, Boston; California State Library, Sacramento.

* * *

Although he is best know for his "Nameless Detective" novels and has, in his time, written horror, SF, suspense, and the odd "adult" paperback original (frequently in collaboration with other established writers), Bill Pronzini has also authored a fistful of impressive western novels and literally scores of western short stories.

A fan of the old-time pulps, whose knowledge of the genre and its writers is now almost encyclopaedic, Pronzini grew up in a small Californian town on a diet of *Texas Rangers* and *.44 Western* magazines. While working at a variety of jobs (including a spell as a civilian guard in a U.S. Marshal's office), he began to sell short stories to *Zane Grey's Western Magazine*, *Ellery Queen*, and others. In 1969 he turned to writing full-time.

Generally, Pronzini's Westerns are distinguished by a neat sense of pace and regular, though seldom graphic, bursts of action. While they are usually traditional enough to satisfy even the most ardent purist, however, they rarely adhere to convention or expectation for very long.

Pronzini's women are more often than not portrayed as strong, wise and capable. His men are frequently less than perfect. Zachary McQuestion, the Mounted Policeman in *Starvation Camp* and the eponymous hero of *Quincannon* are both lawmen haunted by their own private demons. When we first meet Roy Boone, the young hero of *The Gallows Land*, he is still trying to come to terms with the death of his wife four months earlier, and the stagecoach-robber in *The Last Days of Horse-Shy Halloran* is so afraid of horses that he actually plans to make his escape from the scene of the crime aboard a buggy.

This last example also serves to illustrate Pronzini's ability to write humour as well as drama. *Starvation Camp*, a revenge story which stretches from the Yukon Basin to San Francisco's Barbary Coast is, for the most part, grim and unrelenting. There are few laughs to be had in *Quincannon*, where the hero, a U.S. Secret Service agent haunted by a crime he committed by accident several years earlier, constantly attempts to find comfort in cheap rotgut. But when Pronzini decides that he's going to make us see the funny side of life, he tends to succeed admirably. A particularly good example of this can be found in his adventure/mystery, *Freebooty*, published under the pseudonym Jack Foxx.

Pronzini's largely tough, no-nonsense writing style seems to owe more to the hard-boiled detective story than the old western pulps he so admires. His plots tend to twist, unfold, and then confound in much the same way. He crafts plausible characters mainly through extensive passages of dialogue, at which he is very good, and a rather direct, uncluttered style of narration. He leans toward modern speech without elision, and has a habit of giving his characters unusual names—such as Turnbuckle, Coffin, Quarternight, and Truax—which add a colourful sense of period to his stories.

Pronzini's sequel to *Quincannon*, aptly entitled *Beyond the Grave*, written in collaboration with the crime writer Marcia Muller, is probably one of the most unusual, and truly inventive, Westerns of all time. In it, Quincannon (whose adventures take place in the late 19th century) somehow manages to team up with Elena Oliverez—Marcia Muller's *present-day* historian-cum-sleuth.

At the moment, Pronzini's new Westerns appear to be limited to one a year, but the two most recent, *The Hangings* and *Firewind*, show a strengthening sense of plot and narrative that hint at greater things to come. In *The Hangings* (an expanded version of his 1981 short story "The Hanging Man," which combines the mystery with the Western: a Pronzini trademark), Constable Lincoln Evans has to find a madman who has started hanging his victims from the trees surrounding the town—before the mysterious hangman can find *him*. *Firewind*, on the other hand, is a magnificent race-against-time story in which the inhabitants of a northern California logging town are forced to use an ancient locomotive to try and outrun a forest fire consuming the surrounding valley at an alarming rate.

Together with Martin H. Greenberg, Pronzini has, in the last few years, been responsible for unearthing many classic western stories for Fawcett Books "Best of the West" series. The first nine volumes collected stories with a specific theme—lawmen, outlaws, cowboys and so on. Later volumes have focused more on regions, Texas, California and Arizona being the first three. Pronzini's short fiction can be found in several of these anthologies, and a collection of his short western stories has been published by Ohio University Press.

Most recently, Pronzini and Greenberg have performed an invaluable service to the western genre by creating an important market for fresh, hitherto unpublished material for the "New Frontiers" series from Tor Books.

—David Whitehead

PURDUM, Herbert (R). Recipient: Western Writers of America Spur award, 1967.

WESTERN PUBLICATIONS

Novel

My Brother John. New York, Doubleday, 1966.

OTHER PUBLICATIONS

Novel

A Hero for Henry. New York, Doubleday, 1968.

Plays

Screenplays: *Target Hong Kong*, 1952; *El Alamein*, with George Worthing Yates, 1953; *The Dalton Girls*, with Maurice Tombragel, 1957.

* * *

Herbert Purdum's western work, *My Brother John*, illustrates the interrelationship of moral and statutory law in one's attitude and its effect on one's behavior. John Niles, a circuit rider, lives in "the wildest, toughest part of the whole blamed frontier, where the law came in calibers and God was nothing but a word used to cuss with." John was not happy preaching religion. He had to live it, not only on Sunday but everyday of the week. Not only does John believe in doing what is right and just but in doing it within statutory law. He works to remove, by election, the sheriff who "uses his power for wickedness" at the bidding of the powerful local cattleman, Belknap. When he is told that Belknap is too big and is the law, John replies that the "Law is the will of the people; all of them, not of one man. No man can own the law." Knowing that Belknap and his men will attempt to disrupt the election, John stations children with slingshots in trees on the town's main road. When Belknap and his men ride into town on election day, their horses become confused and dash off in every direction when bombarded by stones from the children's slingshots. Belknap and his men are quickly and easily rounded up. With the help of friends, John, a law-abiding citizen who believes that the higher law dictates not only what one should do but how, within statutory law, has the situation well in hand when two troops of the Sixth Cavalry ride into town with a warrant for Belknap and Overstreet, his henchman.

—G. Dale Gleason

R

RAINE, William MacLeod. American. Born in London, England, 22 June 1871; emigrated to the United States at age 10. Educated at Sarcey College, Arkansas; Oberlin College, Ohio, B.A. 1894. Married 1) Jennie P. Langley in 1905 (died 1922); 2) Florence A. Hollingsworth in 1924, one daughter. Worked on a ranch; school principal, Seattle; reporter for several Denver newspapers, including *Republican*, *Post*, and *Rocky Mountain News*; then freelance writer. Lecturer in Journalism, University of Colorado, Boulder. M.L.: University of Colorado, 1920. *Died 25 July 1954.*

WESTERN PUBLICATIONS

Novels

Wyoming. New York, Dillingham, 1908; London, Hodder and Stoughton, 1921.
Ridgway of Montana. New York, Dillingham, 1909; London, Hodder and Stoughton, 1923.
Bucky O'Connor: A Tale of the Unfenced Border. New York, Dillingham, 1910; London, Hodder and Stoughton, 1920.
A Texas Ranger. New York, Dillingham, 1911; London, Hodder and Stoughton, 1920.
Mavericks. New York, Dillingham, 1912; London, Hodder and Stoughton, 1921.
Brand Blotters. New York, Dillingham, 1912; London, Hodder and Stoughton, 1921.
Crooked Trails and Straight. New York, Dillingham, 1913; London, Hodder and Stoughton, 1920.
The Vision Splendid. New York, Dillingham, 1913; London, Hodder and Stoughton, 1921.
A Daughter of the Dons: A Story of New Mexico Today. New York, Dillingham, 1914; London, Hodder and Stoughton, 1920.
The Highgrader. New York, Dillingham, 1915; London, Hodder and Stoughton, 1923.
Steve Yeager. Boston, Houghton Mifflin, 1915; London, Jarrolds, 1922.
The Yukon Trail. Boston, Houghton Mifflin, 1917; London, Jarrolds, 1919; as *Grip of the Yukon*, New York, Grosset and Dunlap, 1928.
The Sheriff's Son. Boston, Houghton Mifflin, 1918; London, Melrose, 1919.
A Man Four-Square. Boston, Houghton Mifflin, 1919; London, Jarrolds, 1921; as *Arizona Guns*, New York, Popular Library, 1952.
The Big-Town Round-Up. Boston, Houghton Mifflin, 1920; London, Hodder and Stoughton, 1922.
Oh, You Tex! Boston, Houghton Mifflin, 1920; London, Hodder and Stoughton, 1923.
Tangled Trails. Boston, Houghton Mifflin, and London, Hodder and Stoughton, 1921.
Gunsight Pass. Boston, Houghton Mifflin, and London, Hodder and Stoughton, 1921.
Man-Size. Boston, Houghton Mifflin, and London, Hodder and Stoughton, 1922.
The Fighting Edge. Boston, Houghton Mifflin, 1922; London, Hodder and Stoughton, 1923.
Ironheart. Boston, Houghton Mifflin, and London, Hodder and Stoughton, 1923.
The Desert's Price. New York, Doubleday, and London, Hodder and Stoughton, 1924.
Troubled Waters. London, Hodder and Stoughton, 1924; New York, Doubleday, 1925.
Roads of Doubt. New York, Doubleday, and London, Hodder and Stoughton, 1925.
Bonanza: A Story of the Gold Trail. New York, Doubleday, and London, Hodder and Stoughton, 1926.
The Last Shot. New York, Doubleday, and London, Hodder and Stoughton, 1926.
The Return of the Range Rider. London, Hodder and Stoughton, 1926.
Judge Colt. New York, Doubleday, and London, Hodder and Stoughton, 1927.
Colorado. New York, Doubleday, and London, Hodder and Stoughton, 1928.
Texas Man. New York, Doubleday, 1928; London, Hodder and Stoughton, 1929.
Moran Beats Back. London, Hodder and Stoughton, 1928; Boston, Houghton Mifflin, 1939; as *Gunsmoke Trail*, New York, Popular Library, 1948.
Roaring River. London, Hodder and Stoughton, 1928; Boston, Houghton Mifflin, 1934.
The Fighting Tenderfoot. New York, Doubleday, and London, Hodder and Stoughton, 1929.
Rutledge Trails the Ace of Spades. New York, Doubleday, 1930; as *The Knife Through the Ace*, London, Hodder and Stoughton, 1930.
The Valiant. Boston, Houghton Mifflin, and London, Hodder and Stoughton, 1930.
Beyond the Rio Grande. Boston, Houghton Mifflin, 1931.
Bad Man. London, Hodder and Stoughton, 1931.
The Black Tolts. Boston, Houghton Mifflin, and London, Hodder and Stoughton, 1932; as *Pistol Pardners*, New York, Popular Library, 1959.
Under Northern Stars. Boston, Houghton Mifflin, 1932; London, Hodder and Stoughton, 1933; as *Bullet Ambush*, New York, Popular Library, 1958.
The Broad Arrow. Boston, Houghton Mifflin, and London, Hodder and Stoughton, 1933; as *Range Beyond the Law*, New York, Popular Library, 1952.
Banded Stars. London, Hodder and Stoughton, 1933.
The Trail of Danger. Boston, Houghton Mifflin, and London, Hodder and Stoughton, 1934.
Border Breed. Boston, Houghton Mifflin, and London, Hodder and Stoughton, 1935.
Square-Shooter. Boston, Houghton Mifflin, and London, Hodder and Stoughton, 1935.
To Ride the River With. Boston, Houghton Mifflin, 1936; as *Ride the River*, New York, Popular Library, 1973.
Sorreltop. London, Hodder and Stoughton, 1936.
Run of the Brush. Boston, Houghton Mifflin, and London, Hodder and Stoughton, 1936.

Bucky Follows a Cold Trail. Boston, Houghton Mifflin, 1937; as *Cool Customer*, London, Hodder and Stoughton, 1937.
King of the Bush. Boston, Houghton Mifflin, 1937.
Sons of the Saddle. Boston, Houghton Mifflin, and London, Hodder and Stoughton, 1938.
On the Dodge. Boston, Houghton Mifflin, and London, Hodder and Stoughton, 1938.
The River Bend Feud. Boston, Houghton Mifflin, and London, Hodder and Stoughton, 1939.
Riders of Buck River. Boston, Houghton Mifflin, 1940; as *Riders of the Rim Rocks*, London, Hodder and Stoughton, 1940.
Trail's End. Boston, Houghton Mifflin, and London, Hodder and Stoughton, 1940.
They Called Him Blue Blazes. Boston, Houghton Mifflin, 1941; as *Drygulch Trail*, New York, Popular Library, 1960.
Justice Deferred. London, Hodder and Stoughton, 1941; Boston, Houghton Mifflin, 1942.
Gone to Texas. London, Hodder and Stoughton, 1942.
The Damyank. Boston, Houghton Mifflin, 1942.
Hell and High Water. Boston, Houghton Mifflin, and London, Hodder and Stoughton, 1943.
Courage Stout. Boston, Houghton Mifflin, and London, Hodder and Stoughton, 1944; as *Rustlers' Gap*, New York, Popular Library, 1949.
Who Wants to Live Forever? Boston, Houghton Mifflin, and London, Hodder and Stoughton, 1945.
Plantation Guns. London, Hodder and Stoughton, 1945; as *Arkansas Guns*, Boston, Houghton Mifflin, 1954; as *Six-Gun Feud*, New York, Popular Library, 1964.
Clattering Hoofs. Boston, Houghton Mifflin, and London, Hodder and Stoughton, 1946.
This Nettle Danger. Boston, Houghton Mifflin, 1947; as *Top Rider*, London, Hodder and Stoughton, 1948; as *Powder-smoke Feud*, New York, New American Library, 1950; Leicester, Ulverscroft, 1978.
The Outlaw Trail. London, Hodder and Stoughton, 1947; as *The Bandit Trail*, Boston, Houghton Mifflin, 1949.
He Threw a Long Shadow. London, Hodder and Stoughton, 1948; as *Challenge to Danger*, Boston, Houghton Mifflin, 1952.
Saddletramp. London, Hodder and Stoughton, 1949; as *Saddlebum*, Boston, Houghton Mifflin, 1951.
Ranger's Luck. Boston, Houghton Mifflin, and London, Hodder and Stoughton, 1950.
Texas Breed. New York, Popular Library, 1950.
Jingling Spurs. Boston, Houghton Mifflin, 1951; as *His Spurs a-Jingling*, London, Hodder and Stoughton, 1951; as *The Six-Gun Kid*, New York, New American Library, 1952.
Glory Hole. London, Hodder and Stoughton, 1951; Boston, Houghton Mifflin, 1952; as *West of the Law*, New York, Popular Library, 1953.
Justice Comes to Tomahawk. Boston, Houghton Mifflin, 1952; as *Rawhide Justice*, London, Hodder and Stoughton, 1952.
Gun Showdown. New York, Pocket Books, 1952.
The Texas Kid. New York, Popular Library, 1952.
Dry Bones in the Valley. Boston, Houghton Mifflin, and London, Hodder and Stoughton, 1953.
Reluctant Gunman. Boston, Houghton Mifflin, 1954; as *Boldly They Rode*, London, Hodder and Stoughton, 1954; as *A Gun for Tom Fallon*, New York, Popular Library, 1974.
High Grass Valley, completed by Wayne D. Overholser. Boston, Houghton Mifflin, and London, Hodder and Stoughton, 1955.
Whipsaw. New York, Lion, 1955.
The Tough Tenderfoot. New York, Popular Library, 1958.

Uncollected Short Stories

"The Highgrader," in *Adventure* (New York), March 1915.
"Pasqual and the Puncher," in *American Magazine* (Springfield, Ohio), April 1915.
"Seattle Changed Its Mind about Hi Gill," in *American Mercury* (New York), September 1915.
"Men in the Raw," in *Argosy* (New York), November 1915.
"The Man Who Told Where the West Begins," in *American Magazine* (Sprinfield, Ohio), June 1916.
"The Sheriff's Daughter," in *Western Story* (New York), 7 October 1920.
"The Mal Pais Kid," in *Western Story* (New York), 22 January 1921.
"Texas As Was," in *The Frontier* (New York), January 1928.
"Texas Man," in *Adventure* (New York), 1 February–1 April 1928.
"Without Fear or Favor," in *The Frontier* (New York), May 1928.
"Scalisi Claws Leather," in *Western Story* (New York), 16 January 1932.
"Unfinished Business," in *All Star* (Kingswood, Surrey), October 1932.
"A Hell-for-Miler Functions," in *Western Thrillers*, edited by Leo Marguiles. New York, Speller, 1935.
"Judge Pleasants Brings Law to Dewitt County," in *West* (Kingswood, Surrey), January 1941.
"Last Warning," in *Great Tales of the American West*, edited by Henry E. Maule. New York, Modern Library, 1945.
"Notches on His Gun," in *West* (Kingswood, Surrey), August 1946.
"Timid Guy," in *Popular Book of Western Stories*, edited by Leo Marguiles. New York, Popular Library, 1948.
"Fat Man in a Brown Derby," in *Selected Western Stories*, edited by Leo Marguiles. New York, Popular Library, 1949.
"Jack Sibley Comes Home," in *Thrilling Western* (London), Autumn 1949.
"Better Dead," in *West* (Kingswood, Surrey), December 1949.
"New Chum," in *West* (Kingswood, Surrey), March 1951.
"Through Fire and Water," in *West* (Kingswood, Surrey), August 1952.
"Friend of Buck Hollister," in *Bad Men and Good*, edited by Luke Short. New York, Dodd Mead, 1953.
"Last Warning," in *The Arbor House Treasury of Great Western Stories*, edited by Bill Pronzini and Martin H. Greenberg. New York, Arbor House, 1982.
"Doan Whispers," in *Wild Westerns*, edited by Bill Pronzini and Martin H. Greenberg. New York, Walker, 1986.

OTHER PUBLICATIONS

Novels

A Daughter of Raasay: A Tale of the '45. New York, Stokes, 1902; as *For Love and Honour*, London, Isbister, 1904.
The Pirate of Panama. New York, Dillingham, 1914; London, Hodder and Stoughton, 1921.
For Honor and Life. Boston, Houghton Mifflin, 1933.

Cry Murder in the Market Place. London, Hodder and Stoughton, 1941; as *Cry Murder*, New York, Phoenix Press, 1947.

Other

Famous Sheriffs and Western Outlaws. New York, Doubleday, 1929.
Cattle, with Will C. Barnes. New York, Doubleday, 1930; as *Cattle, Cowboys, and Rangers*, New York, Grosset and Dunlap, 1930.
Guns of the Frontier: The Story of How Law Came to the West. Boston, Houghton Mifflin, 1940.
45-Caliber Law: The Way of Life of the Frontier Peace Officer. Evanston, Illinois, Row Peterson, 1941.

Editor, *Western Stories: A Corral of Top-Hand Westerns.* New York, Dell, 1949.

* * *

The fact that William MacLeod Raine wrote 81 westerns in a career that lasted for 50 years—from 1908 to the 1950's—might cause the reader unfamiliar with his work (but knowledgeable about the work of many of his contemporaries) to conclude that Raine is likely to be a hack given to churning out novels to formula. A glance at his bibliography should dispel any such notions. Houghton Mifflin became his publisher in 1915 and remained his publisher until his death in 1954, and Houghton Mifflin, as every serious reader knows, is not given to publishing the second-rate in anything. That Raine could remain a first-rate writer for so long a period in so many books is the result not only of his talent but also of what might be called his attitude, the kinds of goals that he obviously set for himself.

He knew his stuff. Although he worked on a ranch for a time, he was, for most of his career, before he became a full-time writer, a teacher, and a journalist—in other words, an intellectual, and one who had mastered his subject: he published non-fiction works on famous outlaws, the world of the cattle range, the work of the western law officer, and the history of the development of the American legal system in the West. More importantly, despite his huge output, he was one of those writers who is capable of learning and growing with each novel. Throughout his career reviewers were to note that he was "getting better and better," and, though there were some fallings-off along the way, it is clear that, though his knowledge of his subject was profound from first to last, he did improve book by book as a writer of fiction, in his setting of scene, his dramatic presentation, his characterizations, his rendering of the natural world of the American West.

But it is in his attitude, his freshness of approach and his spirit of innovation, that Raine is most interesting—most likely, that is, to be of interest to the modern reader. It is obviously not possible for any writer to write nearly 100 western novels without occasionally drawing on some of the stock situations of the genre—but Raine's particular accomplishment was, as it were, to attempt all possible variants of the western novel and, as well, to introduce to it plots, situations, and characterizations that were uniquely his own. In *Ironheart* he introduced the problems of a morphine addict—a tramp on a Colorado ranch: the ranch-owner's daughter's faith helps him to break the habit. In *The Yukon Trail* he introduces the theme of conservation. In *The Big-Town Round-Up* he transports the themes and characters of western fiction to New York City; in *Bucky Follows a Cold Trail* he attempts the conventions of a "mystery" within the western. In *The Black Tolts* the plot is of outlaw brothers attempting to prevent their youngest brother from following the family profession. *Bonanza* is the story of the law-abiding versus the lawless in a Nevada mining town: the author's knowledge of such towns produces a kind of flawless verisimilitude. *The Desert's Price* imagines *Romeo and Juliet* in the West. *Gunsight Pass* presents oil prospecting as a vehicle of the New West. In *Steve Yeager* the hero, a cowpoke stranded when the Lone Star Cattle Company retreats before the invasion of the farmers, finds a job in the movies: the problems of the west, human problems that are eternal, follow him.

Two novels—*The Fighting Edge* and *The Sheriff's Son*—are particularly compelling in their use of "foreign" elements. Both involve the difficulties of living by the noble moral codes of the West: Raine creates real, frightened, cowardly men up against the almost impossibly god-like standards of behavior that the western novel itself has added to the store of American mythology. With great skill, Raine demonstrates the conflict between men and their illusions.

Raine was a prolific writer of westerns, and thus he is of historical interest. But he was also a writer who continued to grow and develop within his chosen genre, and in the variety of his interests and methods he demonstrated that the western could be infinitely flexible and various—a lesson that many of the best western writers of the past two decades have taken to heart.

—George Walsh

RANDALL, Clay. *See* **ADAMS, Clifton.**

RAND, Brett. *See* **NORWOOD, V.G.C.**

RAND, Mat. *See* **HECKELMANN, Charles N.**

RANDALL, Clay. *See* **ADAMS, Clifton.**

RANDALL, Joshua. *See* **RANDISI, Robert J.**

RANDISI, Robert J(oseph). American. Also writes as Nick Carter; Tom Cutter; W.B. Longley; Joseph Meek, Joshua Randall; J.R. Roberts; Cole Weston. American. Born in Brooklyn, New York, 24 August 1951. Educated at Canarsie High School, New York, graduated 1968. Married Anna Y.

Hom in 1972; two sons. Worked as mailboy, mailroom manager, and collection clerk, 1968–72; administrative aide, New York City Police Department, 1973–81. Since 1982 full-time writer. Founder, Private Eye Writers of America, 1981; president, Private Eye Press; co-founder, *Mystery Scene* magazine, Cedar Rapids, Iowa. Agent: Dominick Abel Literary Agency Inc., 146 West 82nd Street, New York, New York 10024. Address: 1952 Hendrickson Street, Brooklyn, New York 11234, U.S.A.

WESTERN PUBLICATIONS

Novels as J.R. Roberts

The Gunsmith series:
1. *Macklin's Woman.* New York, Ace, 1982.
2. *The Chinese Gunmen.* New York, Ace, 1982.
3. *The Woman Hunt.* New York, Ace, 1982.
4. *The Guns of Abilene.* New York, Ace, 1982.
5. *Three Guns for Glory.* New York, Ace, 1982.
6. *Leadtown.* New York, Ace, 1982.
7. *The Longhorn War.* New York, Ace, 1982.
8. *Quanah's Revenge.* New York, Ace, 1982.
9. *Heavyweight Gun.* New York, Ace, 1982.
10. *New Orleans Five.* New York, Ace, 1982.
11. *One-Handed Gun.* New York, Ace, 1982.
12. *The Canadian Payroll.* New York, Ace, 1983.
13. *Draw to an Inside Death.* New York, Ace, 1983.
14. *Dead Man's Hand.* New York, Ace, 1983.
15. *Bandit Gold.* New York, Ace, 1983.
16. *Buckskins and Sixguns.* New York, Ace, 1983.
17. *Silver War.* New York, Ace, 1983.
18. *High Noon at Lancaster.* New York, Ace, 1983.
19. *Bandido Blood.* New York, Ace, 1983.
20. *The Dodge City Gang.* New York, Ace, 1983.
21. *Sasquatch Hunt.* New York, Ace, 1983.
22. *Bullets and Ballots.* New York, Ace, 1983.
23. *The Riverboat Gang.* New York, Ace, 1983.
24. *Killer Grizzly.* New York, Ace, 1984.
25. *North of the Border.* New York, Ace, 1984.
26. *Eagle's Gap.* New York, Ace, 1984.

Chinatown Hell. New York, Charter, 1984.
The Panhandle Search. New York, Charter, 1984.
Wildcat Roundup. New York, Charter, 1984.
The Ponderosa War. New York, Charter, 1984.
Trouble Rides a Fast Horse. New York, Charter, 1984.
Dynamite Justice. New York, Charter, 1984.
The Posse. New York, Charter, 1984.
Night of the Gila. New York, Charter, 1984.
The Bounty Women. New York, Charter, 1985.
Black Pearl Saloon. New York, Charter, 1985.
Gundown in Paradise. New York, Charter, 1985.
King of the Border. New York, Charter, 1985.
The El Paso Salt War. New York, Charter, 1985.
The Ten Pines Killer. New York, Charter, 1985.
Hell With a Pistol. New York, Charter, 1985.
The Wyoming Cattle Kill. New York, Charter, 1985.
The Golden Horseman. New York, Charter, 1985.
The Scarlet Gun. New York, Charter, 1985.
Navaho Devil. New York, Charter, 1985.
Wild Bill's Ghost. New York, Charter, 1985.
The Miners' Showdown. New York, Charter, 1986.
Archer's Revenge. New York, Charter, 1986.
Showdown in Raton. New York, Charter, 1986.
When Legends Meet. New York, Charter, 1986.
Desert Hell. New York, Charter, 1986.
The Diamond Gun. New York, Charter, 1986.
Denver Duo. New York, Charter, 1986.
Hell on Wheels. New York, Charter, 1986.
The Legend-Maker. New York, Charter, 1986.
Walking Dead Man. New York, Charter, 1986.
Crossfire Mountain. New York, Charter, 1986.
The Deadly Healer. New York, Charter, 1986.
The Trail Drive War. New York, Charter, 1987.
Geronimo's Trail. New York, Charter, 1987.
The Comstock Gold Fraud. New York, Charter, 1987.
Boom Town Killer. New York, Charter, 1987.
Texas Trackdown. New York, Charter, 1987.
The Fast Draw League. New York, Charter, 1987.
Showdown in Rio Malo. New York, Charter, 1987.
Outlaw Trail. New York, Charter, 1987.
Homesteader Guns. New York, Charter, 1987.
Five Card Death. New York, Charter, 1987.
Trail Drive to Montana. New York, Charter, 1987.
Trial by Fire. New York, Charter, 1987.
The Old Whistler Gang. New York, Charter, 1988.
Daughter of Gold. New York, Charter, 1988.
Apache Gold. New York, Charter, 1988.
Plains Murder. New York, Charter, 1988.
Deadly Memories. New York, Charter, 1988.
The Nevada Timber War. New York, Charter, 1988.
New Mexico Showdown. New York, Charter, 1988.
Barbed Wire and Bullets. New York, Charter, 1988.
Death Express. New York, Charter, 1988.
When Legends Die. New York, Charter, 1988.
Six-Gun Justice. New York, Charter, 1988.
Mustang Hunters. New York, Charter, 1988.
Texas Ransom. New York, Charter, 1989.
Vengeance Town. New York, Charter, 1989.
Winner Take All. New York, Charter, 1989.
Message from a Dead Man. New York, Charter, 1989.
Ride for Vengeance. New York, Charter, 1989.
The Takersville Shoot. New York, Charter, 1989.
Blood on the Land. New York, Charter, 1989.
Six-Gun Sideshow. New York, Charter, 1989.
Mississippi Massacre. New York, Charter, 1989.
The Arizona Triangle. New York, Charter, 1989.
Brothers of the Gun. New York, Charter, 1989.
The Stagecoach Thieves. New York, Charter, 1989.
Judgement at Firecreek. New York, Charter, 1990.
Dead Man's Jury. New York, Charter, 1990.
Hands of the Strangler. New York, Charter, 1990.
Nevada Death Trap. New York, Charter, 1990.
Wagon Train to Hell. New York, Charter, 1990.
Ride for Revenge. New York, Charter, 1990.
Dead Ringer. New York, Charter, 1990.
Trail of the Assassin. New York, Charter, 1990.
Shoot Out at Cross Fork. New York, Charter, 1990.
Buckskin's Trail. New York, Charter, 1990.
Helldorado. New York, Charter, 1990.
The Hanging Judge. New York, Charter, 1990.
The Bounty Man. New York, Charter, 1990.

Novels as Cole Weston (series: Ryder in all books)

Badlands Blood. New York, Ballantine, 1987.
Blood on the Staked Plains. New York, Ballantine, 1987.
Buffalo Gal. New York, Ballantine, 1987.
Longhorn Sisters. New York, Ballantine, 1987.

Ryder's Army. New York, Ballantine, 1987.
Showdown. New York, Ballantine, 1987.
The Yellow Lotus Tong. New York, Ballantine, 1987.

Novels as Tom Cutter (series: Tracker in all books)

The Winning Hand. New York, Avon, 1983.
The Blue Cut Job. New York, Avon, 1983.
Lincoln County. New York, Avon, 1983.
Chinatown Chance. New York, Avon, 1983.
The Oklahoma Score. New York, Avon, 1985.
The Barbary Coast Tong. New York, Avon, 1985.
Huntsville Breakout. New York, Avon, 1985.

Novels as W.B. Longley (series: Angel Eyes in all books)

The Miracle of Revenge. New York, Paperjacks, 1985.
Death's Angel. New York, Paperjacks, 1985.
Wolf Pass. New York, Paperjacks, 1985.
Chinatown Justice. New York, Paperjacks, 1985.
Logan's Army. New York, Paperjacks, 1986.
Bullets and Bad Times. New York, Paperjacks, 1986.
Six Gun Angel New York, Paperjacks, 1986.
Avenging Angel. New York, Paperjacks, 1986.
Angel for Hire. New York, Paperjacks, 1987.

Novels as Joshua Randall (series: The Bounty Hunter in all books)

Double the Bounty. New York, Paperjacks, 1987.
Bounty on a Lawman. New York, Paperjacks, 1987.
Beauty and the Bounty. New York, Paperjacks, 1988.
Bounty on a Baron. New York, Paperjacks, 1988.
Broadway Bounty. New York, Paperjacks, 1988.

Novels as Joseph Meek (series: Mountain Jack Pike in all books)

Mountain Jack Pike. New York, Zebra, 1989.
Rocky Mountain Kill. New York, Zebra, 1989.
Crow Bait. New York, Zebra, 1989.
Comanche Come-On. New York, Zebra, 1989.
Green River Hunt. New York, Zebra, 1990.
St. Louis Fire. New York, Zebra, 1990.

OTHER PUBLICATIONS

Novels

The Disappearance of Penny. New York, Ace, 1980.
Dangerous Games, with Warren Murphy. Los Angeles, Pinnacle, 1980.
Midnight Man, with Warren Murphy. Los Angeles, Pinnacle, 1981.
Eye in the Ring. New York, Avon, 1982.
Lucifer's Weekend, with Warren Murphy. New York, Pocket Books, 1982.
The Steinway Collection. New York, Avon, 1983.
Full Contact. New York, St. Martin's Press, 1984; London, Macmillan, 1986.
Total Recall, with Warren Murphy. New York, Pinnacle, 1984.
The Ham Reporter. New York, Doubleday, 1986.
Once Upon a Murder. Lake Geneva, Wisconsin, TSR, 1987.
No Exit from Brooklyn. New York, St. Martin's Press, 1987.
Caribbean Blues, with others. New York, Paperjacks, 1988.
The Black Moon, with others. New York, Lynx, 1989.
Separate Cases. New York, Walker, 1990.

Novels as Nick Carter

Pleasure Island. New York, Ace, 1981.
Chessmaster. New York, Ace, 1982.
The Mendoza Manuscript. New York, Ace, 1982.
The Greek Summit. New York, Ace, 1983.
The Decoy Hit. New York, Ace, 1983.
The Caribbean Coup. New York, Ace, 1984.

Other

Editor, *The Eyes Have It* (anthology). New York, Mysterious Press, 1984; London, Severn House, 1988.
Editor, *Mean Streets* (anthology). New York, Mysterious Press, 1986.
Editor, *An Eye for Justice* (anthology). New York, Mysterious Press, 1988.
Editor, with Ed Gorman, *Under the Gun* (anthology). New York, New American Library, 1990.
Editor, *Justice for Hire* (anthology). New York, Mysterious Press, 1990.

* * *

Robert J. Randisi is probably one of the most prolific western writers working today. A New Yorker all his life, he started writing at the age of 15 and made his first sale to *Mike Shayne's Mystery Magazine* in 1974. By his own admission, Randisi writes "in order to eat." He usually starts work between eight and eleven o'clock each evening, and goes on until four or five the following morning.

Primarily a mystery writer (he co-founded the Private Eye Writers of America with Bill Pronzini in 1981), Randisi made his entry into the western genre in 1982 with the series which has remained his most popular to date, The Gunsmith, written under the pseudonym J.R. Roberts.

Like most of Randisi's subsequent Westerns, The Gunsmith falls into the "adult" category. It is very rare indeed for the principal character, Clint Adams, to bed less than three willing females per book. Adams is a former lawman said to be the fastest gun since Hickok, an old friend whom he once served as a deputy. In his early days as a lawman, he was nicknamed "The Gunsmith" by a newspaperman because of his hobby of mending guns. After retiring as a peacekeeper he wanders the West, and when not driving the wagon that contains the tools of his gunsmithing trade, he rides a black gelding called Duke.

Adams's adventures range from the traditional—fighting off gunmen seeking to make reputations for themselves, hunting down Mexican bandits, becoming involved in range wars and so on—to the downright bizarre; tracking down a killer in foggy London *Hands of the Strangler* taking a vacation in Australia *Six-Gun Justice*, and tangling with a whole bunch of ninja warriors (*The Golden Horseman*, clearly inspired by the film *Red Sun*). Adams has also tracked the legendary Bigfoot (*Sasquatch Hunt*), visited New York to solve the murder of an old girlfriend (*Archer's Revenge*), and locked horns with the Chinese Tongs (*Black Pearl Saloon*).

Despite a perhaps understandable tendency to oversimplify his plots, depict sex in a rather casual manner, and occasionally take up great chunks of story with extraneous dialogue, strong continuity, plus a sense of Randisi's own enthusiasm, make "The Gunsmith" probably the best of the current crop of "adult" Westerns.

Randisi's second series, Tracker, only ran for seven books, but as with all of Randisi's heroes, Tracker's background is meticulously chronicled. When the series begins, he is living in a San Francisco hotel he won in a poker game and working as a "recovery agent," reclaiming items that his clients have either lost or had stolen.

The author's next series, again "adult" in content, was Angel Eyes, and his hero is actually a *heroine* named Liz Archer. In the first book, *The Miracle of Revenge*, Archer's family is murdered and she is left for dead, but when a passing gunsmith named Tate Gilmore rescues her and teaches her how to use a gun, she promptly sets off to find the killers. During the course of a rather improbable plot (which sets the tone for the equally unlikely adventures that follow), Archer poses as a whore to gain entry into the outlaws' camp, and sleeps with one of the killers to gain his confidence before eventually strapping on her guns and getting her revenge. In the final book of the sequence, *Angel for Hire*, Archer and Tate Gilmore undertake to protect a Mexican village from marauding bandits, but unlike *The Magnificent Seven*, from which the book takes its premise, they fail. Wounded and surrounded, Archer and Gilmore attempt to break out, only to discover that more bandits have arrived, and rather like the ending of *Butch Cassidy and the Sundance Kid*, they meet a spectacular, though by no means satisfying, death "off-screen."

The Bounty Hunter, Randisi's fourth series, was written under the pen-name Joshua Randall (the name of Steve McQueen's character in the TV series *Dead or Alive*). The bounty hunter of the title is Decker (no first name is ever given), whose trademark is a hangman's noose wound around his saddlehorn as a reminder of the time a lynch-mob nearly hung him for a crime he didn't commit. During his short, five-book career, Decker faces crooked lawmen, a lady outlaw, and a murderous European nobleman. In *Broadway Bounty* probably the best book of the series, he turns up in New York to track down the killer of a fellow bounty hunter, and the story ends with a novel showdown in Central Park.

Ryder, another "adult" series, chronicles the adventures of a former Confederate officer who returns home from the Civil War to find that his fiancée has been raped and murdered. The novels follow Andrew Ryder's hunt for the killers, but probably the least exciting of Randisi's many series, the books are unusually slow, reasonably violent (one of Ryder's weapons is a cut-down sabre), and have a particularly heavy "adult" content.

Randisi's most recent series is Mountain Jack Pike. Pike is a surprisingly well-educated mountain man, whose adventures are set in the first half of the 19th century. In the first book, he has to play detective while attending a trappers' rendezvous. In *Rocky Mountain Kill* he faces a killer grizzly and conquers one of his deepest fears. In the only story so far not to take place in the wilds (*St. Louis Fire*), Pike and his sidekick, Skins McConnell, have to travel to Missouri when someone attempts to underpay them for their furs.

With his often interchangeable plots, sometimes overly graphic sex and frequently rushed, "first draft" style of writing, it is unlikely that Randisi will be remembered as a great western writer (although his more mainstream work in the genre can be found under the pseudonym Robert Lake), but his always entertaining novels show a flair and imagination that has already established him—quite rightly—as one of the most reliable and accomplished exponents of the modern "light" Western.

—David Whitehead

RATHBORNE, St. George (Henry). Also wrote as Harrison Adams; Hugh Allen; Oliver Lee Clifton; Duke Duncan; Aleck Forbes; Lieutenant Keene; Marline Manly; Mark Merrick; Warne Miller; Harry St. George; Ned Taylor; Col. J.M. Travers. American. Born in Covington, Kentucky, 26 December 1854. Educated at a Cincinnati high school. Married Jessie Fremont Conn in 1879; three sons and one daughter. Editor and freelance writer. *Died 16 December 1938.*

WESTERN PUBLICATIONS

Novels (many of these books are for children)

Battle Smoke; or, The War Correspondent among Guerrillas (as Hugh Allen). New York, Novelist Publishing Company, 1883.

Fredericksburg (as Aleck Forbes). New York, Novelist Publishing Company, 1883.

The Snow-Shoe Trail. New York, Beadle and Adams, 1884.

Paddling in Florida. New York, Dillingham, 1889; as *The Boy Cruisers*, New York, Burt, 1893.

Doctor Jack. New York, Street and Smith, 1890; London, Aldine, 1894.

The Cartaret Affair. Chicago, Laird and Lee, 1891; as *Witch or Wife*, 1895.

The Colonel by Brevet. St. Paul, Minnesota, Price McGill, 1892; London, Aldine, 1895.

The Detective and the Poisoner. Chicago, Laird and Lee, 1892; London, Aldine, 1894.

The Man from Wall Street. Chicago, Morrill Higgins, 1892.

The Color Bearer (as Aleck Forbes). New York, Novelist Publishing Company, 1893.

Baron Sam. New York, American News Company, 1893; London, Aldine, 1894.

Captain Tom. New York, Street and Smith, 1893; London, Aldine, 1894.

Doctor Jack's Wife. New York, Street and Smith, 1893; London, Aldine, 1894.

Major Matterson of Kentucky. St. Paul, Minnesota, Price McGill, 1893.

Miss Caprice. New York, Street and Smith, 1893; London, Aldine, 1894.

Mynheer Joe. New York, Bonner, and London, Henderson, 1893.

The Bachelor of the Midway. New York, Mascot, 1894; London, Aldine, 1896.

Monsieur Bob. St. Paul, Minnesota, Price McGill, and London, Aldine, 1894.

The Fair Maid of Fez. New York, Home, 1895; London, Aldine, 1896.

Mrs. Bob. New York, Street and Smith, 1896.

Her Rescue from the Turks. New York, Neely, and London, Henderson, 1896.

The Great Mogul. New York, Street and Smith, and London, Aldine, 1896.

A Bar-Sinister. New York, Hobart, 1897; as *A Cruel Case*, London, Aldine, 1897.

A Goddess of Africa. Boston, Dickermann, and London, Henderson, 1897.

Masked in Mystery. New York, Hobart, and London, Henderson, 1897.

A Son of Mars. New York, Neely, and London, Henderson, 1897.

Squire John. New York, Neely, 1897.

The Girl from Hong-Kong. New York, Hobart, and London, Henderson, 1898.

Saved by the Sword. New York, Hobart, and London, Henderson, 1898.
The Spider's Web. New York, Street and Smith, 1898.
A Fair Revolutionist. New York, Street and Smith, and London, Henderson, 1898.
A Chase for a Bride. New York, Street and Smith, 1899.
Miss Fairfax of Virginia. New York, Street and Smith, 1899.
A Sailor's Sweetheart. New York, Street and Smith, 1900.
Under Egyptian Skies. New York, Street and Smith, 1900.
Paddling under Palmettos. New York, Street and Smith, and London, Henderson, 1901.
Sunset Ranch. New York, Street and Smith, 1901; London, Shurmer and Sibthorp, 1904.
Chums of the Prairie. New York, Street and Smith, and London, Shurmer and Sibthorp, 1902.
The Gulf Cruisers. New York, Street and Smith, 1902.
Rival Canoe Boys. New York, Street and Smith, 1902.
The Young Range Riders. New York, Street and Smith, and London, Shurmer and Sibthorp, 1902.
Shifting Winds. New York, Street and Smith, 1902.
A Brazilian Free-Lance. London, Shurmer and Sibthorp, 1903.
The Witch from India. New York, Street and Smith, and London, Shurmer and Sibthorp, 1903.
A Filibuster in Tatters. London, Shurmer and Sibthorp, 1903.
For Love and Glory. New York, Street and Smith, and London, Shurmer and Sibthorp, 1903.
A Yankee Consul. London, Shurmer and Sibthorp, 1903.
Kinkaid, from Peking. New York, Street and Smith, and London, Shurmer and Sibthorp, 1903; as *Well Worth Winning*, Street and Smith, 1903.
Dr. Jack's Paradise Mine. New York, Street and Smith, and London, Shurmer and Sibthorp, 1904.
My Florida Sweetheart. New York, Street and Smith, and London, Shurmer and Sibthorp, 1904.
The Red Slippers. New York, Street and Smith, 1904.
For Love of a Duchess. London, Shurmer and Sibthorp, 1904.
The Young Castaways. Akron, Saalfield, 1905.
The Young Voyagers of the Nile. Akron, Saalfield, 1905.
Down in Dixie. New York, Street and Smith, 1905.
Favorite of Fortune. New York, Street and Smith, 1905.
Rival Toreadors. New York, Street and Smith, 1905.
Wizard of the Moors. New York, Street and Smith, 1905.
Adrift on a Junk; or, Boy Sailors of the China Sea. Akron, Saalfield, 1905.
Down the Amazon. Akron, Saalfield, 1905.
Dr. Jack and Company. New York, Street and Smith, 1906.
Dr. Jack's Talisman. New York, Street and Smith, 1906.
An American Monte Cristo. London, Mascot, 1909.
Campmates in Michigan. Chicago, Goldsmith, n.d.
American Nabob. New York, Street and Smith, n.d.
At Swords' Points. New York, Street and Smith, n.d.
Back to Old Kentucky. New York, Street and Smith, n.d.
Canoe and Camp Fire. New York, Street and Smith, n.d.
Captain of the Kaiser. New York, Street and Smith, n.d.
Companions in Arms. New York, Street and Smith, n.d.
Daughter of Russia. New York, Street and Smith, n.d.
Dr. Jack's Widow. New York, Street and Smith, n.d.
Felipe's Pretty Sister. New York, Street and Smith, n.d.
Little Miss Millions. New York, Street and Smith, n.d.
Montezuma's Mines. New York, Street and Smith, n.d.
My Hildegard. New York, Street and Smith, n.d.
Nabob of Singapore. New York, Street and Smith, n.d.
Teddy's Enchantress. New York, Street and Smith, n.d.
Voyagers of Fortune. New York, Street and Smith, n.d.
Warrior Bold. New York, Street and Smith, n.d.
Winning of Isolde. New York, Street and Smith, n.d.
Canoe Mates in Canada. Chicago, Donohue, 1912.
Chums in Dixie. Chicago, Donohue, 1912.
The House Boat Boys. Chicago, Donohue, 1912.
The Young Fur-Traders. Chicago, Donohue, 1912.
Tom Turner's Adventures with the Radio. Racine, Wisconsin, Whitman, 1924.
Carried by Storm. Cleveland, Westbrook, n.d.
Jeff Clayton's Strong Arm. Cleveland, Westbrook, n.d.
Rocky Mountain Boys. Chicago, Donohue, n.d.
Texan Thoroughbred. Cleveland, Westbrook, n.d.
Under Troubled Skies. Cleveland, Westbrook, n.d.
Lend-a-Hand Boys Team-Work [Sanitary Squad, as Wild Game Protectors]. New York, Goldsmith, 3 vols., 1931.

Novels as Marline Manly

Old Shadow. Chicago, Pictorial, 1871.
Crack Skull Bob. New York, Ornum, 1872.
Bouncing Dick. New York, Ornum, 1873(?).
Dave Barton. New York, Ornum, 1873(?).
Gray Wolf. Chicago, Pictorial, 1877.
Howdega. Chicago, Pictorial, 1877.
The Mohawk Rangers. Chicago, Pictorial, 1877.
Old Solitary. Chicago, Pictorial, 1877.
The Young Gold Hunters. Chicago, Pictorial, 1877.
Kit Carson's Last Bullet. Chicago, Pictorial, 1878.
The Marked Moccasin. New York, Tousey, 1878.
The Winding Trail. Chicago, Pictorial, 1878.
The Young Lion Hunters. Chicago, Pictorial, 1878.
Winged Moccasin. Chicago, Pictorial, 1878.
Leadville Luke. Chicago, Pictorial, 1879.
The Money-Maker. Chicago, Pictorial, 1879.
Payne's Trail. Chicago, Pictorial, 1879.
Prairie Coyote. Chicago, Pictorial, 1879.
Mexican Mose. New York, Ornum, n.d.
Kit Carson's Ghost. Chicago, Pictorial, 1880.
Leadville Luke's Last Shot. Chicago, Pictorial, 1880.
Leadville Luke's Luck. Chicago, Pictorial, 1880.
Moccasin Mat. Chicago, Pictorial, 1880.
The Red Sagamore. Chicago, Pictorial, 1880.
Pandy Ellis, The Prairie Ranger. New York, Ornum, n.d.
Little Hurricane. Chicago, Pictorial, 1881.
The Phantom Smuggler. Chicago, Pictorial, 1881.
Prairie Whirlwind. Chicago, Pictorial, 1881.
Rope and Rifle. Chicago, Pictorial, 1881.
Tavern League. Chicago, Pictorial, 1881.
The Girl Spy. Chicago, Pictorial, 1882.
Night Riders. Chicago, Pictorial, 1882.
Blue Blazes. New York, 1887(?).
Killpatrick's Best Bower. New York, Novelist Publishing Company, 1887.
The Young Tiger Hunters. New York, Novelist Publishing Company, 1888.
The Poker King. New York, Street and Smith, 1890.
Rube Burrows' League. New York, Street and Smith, 1891.
The Stranglers of Ohio. New York, Street and Smith, 1895.
Old Specie. New York, Street and Smith, n.d.
Vestibule Limited Company. New York, Street and Smith, n.d.

Novels as Harry St. George

Old Iron Arm. Chicago, Pictorial, 1878.
Traps and Trails. Chicago, Pictorial, 1878.
Old Hickory; or, Pandy Ellis's Scalp. New York, Beadle and Adams, 1878.
Wabash Trailers. Chicago, Pictorial, 1878.
The White Slave. Chicago, Pictorial, 1878.

Skipper Sandy. Chicago, Pictorial, 1878.
Forest Phantom. Chicago, Pictorial, 1878.
The Texan Rifles. Chicago, Pictorial, 1878.
Rattling Rube; or, The Night Hawks of Kentucky. New York, Beadle and Adams, 1878(?).
Daring Davy, The Young Bear Killer; or, The Trail of the Border Wolf. New York, Beadle and Adams, 1879.
Prince of Detectives. Chicago, Pictorial, 1879.
Hickory Harry; or, The Trapper-Brigade's Spy. New York, Beadle and Adams, 1880.
Thunderbolt Tom. New York, Beadle and Adams, 1880.
The White Wampum. Chicago, Pictorial, 1880.
The Fire Witch. Chicago, Pictorial, 1881.
Roaring Ralph Rockwood, The Reckless Ranger. New York, Beadle and Adams, 1884.

Novels as Lieutenant Keene

Little Silver Knife. Chicago, Pictorial, 1878.
The Water Witch. Chicago, Pictorial, 1878.
Silver Bullet. Chicago, Pictorial, 1879.
The Snake Charmer. Chicago, Pictorial, 1879.
Gold Dust. Chicago, Pictorial, 1880.

Novels as Duke Duncan

The Head Hunter. Chicago, Pictorial, 1878.
The Hunted Detective. Chicago, Pictorial, 1880.
Pittsburg Landing. New York, Novelist Publishing Company, 1883.

Novels as Col. J.M. Travers

Charley Charlton. New York, Tousey, 1881.
The Creole Brothers. New York, Tousey, 1881.
The Black Hercules. New York, Tousey, 1882.
Fred Baxter. New York, Tousey, 1882.
The Lost Island. New York, Tousey, 1882.
Custer's Last Shot. New York, Tousey, 1884.
Detective Jack Anderson. New York, Munro, 1884.
Gotham Detectives in New Orleans. New York, Munro, 1884.
Jack Sharp, Keenest Detective in Gotham. New York, Munro, 1884.
A House of Mystery. New York, Munro, 1884.
Old Gold-Eyes, The Miner Detective. New York, Munro, 1884.
The Diamond Detective. New York, Munro, 1885; as *Silas Quirk, The Diamond Detective* (as Warne Miller, M.D.), n.d.
Tom Barker, The Detective from the Bowery. New York, Munro, 1885.
Detective Jack Anderson (not the same as previous title). New York, Munro, 1886.
Old Broadbrim's Double Game. New York, Munro, 1886
Old Saddlebags, The Circuit-Rider Detective. New York, Munro, 1886.
Sombrero Sam, The Cowboy Detective. New York, Munro, 1886.
Tom Throttle, The Engineer Detective. New York, Munro, 1886.
Tracked at Midnight. New York, Munro, 1886.
Jack Sharp in Florida. New York, Munro, 1887.
The Great Travers Case. New York, Street and Smith, 1890.

Novels as Warne Miller, M.D.

Jockey Joe. New York, Munro, 1885.
Old Broadbrim's Latest Trail. New York, Munro, 1885.
Gypsy Jock. New York, Munro, 1886.
Old Revenue, The Niagara Falls Detective. New York, Munro, 1886.
Tracked by the Dead. New York, Munro, 1886.
The Crescent Star. New York, Munro, 1893.
Entangled in Crime. New York, Munro, 1895.

Novels as Harrison Adams

The Pioneer Boys of the Ohio [*Mississippi, on the Great Lakes, Missouri, Yellowstone, Columbia, Colorado, Kansas*]. Boston, Page, 8 vols., 1912–28.

Novels as Oliver Lee Clifton

The Camp Fire Boys at Log Cabin Bend [*in Muskrat Swamp, Canoe Cruise, Tracking Squad*]. New York, Barse and Hopkins, 4 vols., 1923–26.

*

Bibliography: in *Dime Novel Round-up*, 15 May 1970 and 15 July 1972.

* * *

Writing under more than 20 pseudonyms, St. George Rathborne between 1868 and 1935 penned countless adventure novels, boys' books, dime novels, and short stories. Perhaps best known for his swashbuckling historical romances, most notably his "Doctor Jack" books, Rathborne nevertheless made a substantial contribution to the canon of western fiction.

Following the sale of his first story, "Sure Shot, The Hunter Chief," to the *New York Weekly* in 1868, there flowed from Rathborne's pen a series of dime novels devoted to western adventure. *Rattling Rube; or, The Night Hawks of Kentucky*, *Hickory Harry; or, The Trapper-Brigade's Spy*, and *Old Hickory; or, Pandy Ellis's Scalp*, for instance, chronicle the exploits of backwoods hunters or trappers and prairie scouts. Hybridized descendants of Cooper's Leather-stocking and the half-horse half-alligator heroes of the southwestern tradition of American humor, Rathborne's backwoodsmen speak a nearly indecipherable dialect laced with expletives such as "B'ars' claws an' buffler-hoofs!" Roughhewn and elderly, such characters are generally excluded from the tales' love plots, their roles instead confined to adventure plots based on capture and pursuit. An exception to this general rule is *Daring Davy, The Young Bear Killer; or, The Trail of the Border Wolf*, a story which introduces a young and comparatively genteel backwoodsman in the person of Davy Crockett. Here the story's love plot and adventure plot fuse in Davy's ultimately successful quest to rescue his future bride, Rosebud Thornton, from the clutches of a band of border ruffians led by giant Hercules Dan and masterminded by a woman, Barbara Warner, whose unrequited love for Davy has turned to jealous hatred. The love-crazed tigress who finally atones for her treachery was a favorite character of Rathborne's, as evidenced by the female avenger who appears in *Roaring Ralph Rockwood, The Reckless Ranger*. Remarkably similar in character and incident, all of these tales likewise display the florid description and abundance of classical allusions characteristic of Rathborne's early prose.

Experience and the sheer volume of writing he produced probably led to the simplified style apparent in Rathborne's later work, notably in the 50 or so titles which he penned for Street & Smith's Buffalo Bill Stories. In tales such as *Buffalo Bill's Dead Drop; or, Pawnee Bill Betrayed* and *Buffalo Bill's Blindfold Duel; or, Pawnee Bill's Timely Shot* the prose is plain and the action brisk. In these later stories Rathborne also proved adept at writing detective Westerns. Typical of this sub-genre is *Buffalo Bill and the War Hawk; or, Pawnee Bill and the Five Nations*, a story of Indian fighting and outlaws in which Wally Burt, a New York tenderfoot, displays courage in combat and turns out to be a clever gumshoe who gets his man.

Rathborne perhaps made his greatest contribution to western fiction, however, in the 39 stories which he wrote under the pseudonym Ned Taylor for Street & Smith's *Rough Rider Weekly*. Published between 1904 and 1907 and clearly designed to capitalize on the popularity of Teddy Roosevelt as a spokesman for the values of the West, the stories introduce manly cowboy Ted Strong, a youthful veteran of San Juan Hill who has inherited a cattle ranch in the Black Hills. In stories such as "Ted Strong on the Trail; or, The Cattlemen of Salt Licks" and "Ted Strong's Nerve; or, Wild West Sport at Black Mountain", Ted and his quasi-military band of "Young Rough Riders" face the familiar cast of assorted dime novel bad men. Yet the tales are unique in the extent to which they introduce round-ups, cattle drives, rustling, rodeos, and other activities associated with authentic ranch life. Eventually, under different authorship, the stories in *Rough Rider Weekly* wandered from the series' original purpose, and Ted Strong was to be found less often on his ranch than on a baseball diamond or a polo field. Nonetheless, Rathborne's early Ted Strong stories established a precedent and paved the way for the manly cowboy who would ultimately become the dominant type-hero in the modern Western.

—Daryl Jones

RAY, Wesley. *See* **GAULDEN, Ray.**

RAYNER, William. British. Born in Barnsley, Yorkshire, 1 January 1929. Educated at Holgate Grammar School, Barnsley; Wadham College, Oxford, B.A. (hons.) 1952. Married Pamela Ross in 1953; 3 sons. English teacher in England and Central Africa for 16 years. Since 1970 full-time writer. Address: Spurriers Close, West Porlock, Minehead, Somerset TA24 8NL, England.

WESTERN PUBLICATIONS

Novels

The Bloody Affray at Riverside Drive. London, Collins, 1972; as *Seth and Belle and Mr. Quarles and Me.* New York, Simon and Schuster, 1973.
The Trail to Bear Paw Mountain. London, Collins, 1974; New York, Ballantine, 1976.
A Weekend with Captain Jack. London, Collins, 1975; New York, Ballantine, 1977.

OTHER PUBLICATIONS

Novels

The Reapers. London, Faber, 1961.
The Barebones. London, Faber, 1963.
The Last Days. London, Joseph, 1968; New York, Morrow, 1969.
The Knifeman. London, Joseph, 1969; New York, Morrow, 1969.
The World Turned Upside Down. London, Joseph, and New York, Morrow, 1970.
The Day of Chaminuka. London, Collins, 1976; New York, Atheneum, 1977.
Eating the Big Fish. London, Collins, 1977; as *The Interface Assignment*, New York, Atheneum, 1977.
Wheels of Fortune. London, Collins, 1979.
Knave of Swords. London, Collins, 1980.

Other

The Tribe and Its Successors: An Account of African Traditional Life and European Settlement in Southern Rhodesia. London, Faber, 1962; New York, Praeger, 1963.
Chief Joseph (for children). London, Collins, 1976.
Stag Boy (for children). London, Collins, 1972; New York, Harcourt Brace, 1973.
Big Mister (for children). London, Collins, 1974.

* * *

An author of mainstream and historical novels, and of adventure stories for both adults and children, William Rayner's reputation as a western writer rests on three specific titles. These are *The Bloody Affray at Riverside Drive* (published in the United States as *Seth and Belle and Mr. Quarles and Me*), *The Trail to Bear Paw Mountain*, and *A Weekend with Captain Jack*, and together they are more than enough to justify his claim.

In each of these works Rayner forgoes the conventional approach to his material, and in all three cases his treatment reveals considerable imagination and originality. *The Bloody Affray at Riverside Drive* is presented in the form of a letter written by the novel's leading character, Missouri Fynn, as he awaits his execution for an alleged act of murder. Fynn, a well-meaning but naive farmboy lately turned gunfighter, hopes to set the record straight before he dies, and his description of the events which have brought him to the gallows is contrasted throughout the book with the "official" version represented in the Chicago press and generally accepted by the reading public. It soon becomes clear to readers of the novel, however, that Missouri is telling the truth, and that the newspaper version of events is a fiction and a sham, with no real evidence to support it. Viewing the past in flashback through young Fynn's eyes, one encounters the varied group of characters whose acquaintance and influence has led him to killing and the shadow of the hangman's noose—Mister Johnson, the misanthropic English-born gunfighter, the handsome but treacherous Seth Walsh, Quarles the powerful businessman, and the saloon-girl Belle, who later becomes Quarles's wife. Utilising Fynn's direct, untutored western speech as the voice for his novel, Rayner allows the understated style to weave a compelling and utterly credible story around these central characters, at the same time bringing home to us the genuine, unromanticised flavour of frontier life and its many hardships. He also uses Fynn's naive but probing vision to ridicule the official view and the respectable society behind it. Quarles, celebrated in the *Mirror* as a pillar of rectitude, is shown to be a sexual pervert and a fraud, whose investment in western paintings and memorabilia is merely another aspect of his greed, while Belle and Seth emerge as shallow, unfeeling, and unscrupulous, each betraying the youthful Fynn, who loves and trusts them both in vain. Rayner pokes fun at accepted notions of taste, laying bare the poverty and wretchedness that lie beneath the false veneer of polite society. He makes plain to the reader that Missouri's crime is to have called the bluff on which all the power of Quarles and his kind ultimately rests, a challenge which society and its pretensions cannot abide. One of the greatest ironies of the story is that Fynn, who finally kills Seth in retribution and self-defence, is the nearest to an innocent of all the novel's characters, while his victim has already committed murder and abandoned the mother of his child. Rayner's message is serious and thought-provoking, but at no point degenerates into a sermon, and is constantly enlivened with sly touches of humour, the narrative as a whole achieved with a light, deft skill, convincingly expressed through the voice of the condemned Fynn. *The Bloody Affray at Riverside Drive* is an outstanding and highly individual western novel, and firmly establishes its author in the genre.

The Trail to Bear Paw Mountain makes use of the first-person account again, but this time presents two separate viewpoints. Missouri Fynn, released from jail as a result of last-minute testimony by Belle, appears once more, this time to relate the tragic story of Chief Joseph of the Nez Perce, and his doomed resistance to the United States Army. A further imaginative dimension is brought to the novel by Rayner's introduction of another real-life character, the British explorer and student of erotic literature, Captain Richard Burton. His chance meeting with Missouri, and their subsequent adventures with the retreating Nez Perce, are memorably detailed in alternating chapters told by Fynn and Burton in turn. Rayner's mastery of the differing speech patterns—and thought processes—of his two main characters is shown to full advantage here, and once again he is able to present a tragic episode movingly and with conviction, while allowing the humorous side of his writing plenty of room to express itself. The plight of the Nez Perce, forced into war by the theft of their ancestral lands, is sympathetically portrayed, but the author is careful to note the unenviable position of the American soldiers, called in to do the dirty work for unscrupulous commercial interests back East. *The Trail to Bear Paw Mountain*, while perhaps marginally less impressive than its predecessor, definitely breaks new ground, and has a strength and individuality which make it well worth seeking out.

Most striking and unusual of the three western novels is the last, *A Weekend with Captain Jack*. Rayner himself puts in an appearance in this work, which progresses in swiftly alternating and contrasting scenes to depict two parallel narratives—Rayner the writer, struggling to produce an account of the Modoc rebellion and its aftermath as he awaits the result of the 1974 General Election which returns the Labour Party to power; and the actual events of the 19th-century conflict, in which Missouri Fynn once more takes an active role. It is a risky device, and one that might well have spelled disaster in the hands of a lesser writer, but Rayner somehow achieves a superb balance between the centuries, managing not only to bring to life the problems of the Modoc leader—again manoeuvred into war by the greed of others—but also adding a wry, humorous perspective from the "Rayner" of the accompanying storyline. The same qualities of wit and penetrating vision that distinguished the previous novels are present here, together with a clear, incisive prose style. *A Weekend with Captain Jack* must be counted as one of the strangest western novels ever written. It is also one of the most accomplished. On the basis of this work, and his two earlier novels, William Rayner deserves to be ranked with the leading exponents of the genre.

—Jeff Sadler

REASONER, James M(orris). Also writes as William Grant; Livia James; M. R. James; Justin Ladd; R. Mason; Hank Mitchum. American. Born in Fort Worth, Texas, 5 June 1953. Educated at Southwest Texas State University, San Marcos, 1971–72; North Texas State University, Denton, 1972–75, B.A. 1975. Married Livia Jane Washburn in 1976; two daughters. Worked as a bookstore clerk, video store manager, television repair man, and newspaper columnist, all in and around Azle, Texas. Member, Western Writers of America; Private Eye Writers of America. Agent: Barbara Puechner, Peekner Literary Agency, 3121 Portage Road, Bethlehem, Pennsylvania 18017. Address: Route 5, P.O. Box 392, Azle, Texas 76020, U.S.A.

Western Publications

Novels

The Emerald Land (as Livia James, with Livia Jane Washburn). New York, Fawcett, 1983.

Has also written several novels for the Bantam *Stagecoach* series (as Hank Mitchum), the Lynx *Faraday* series (as William Grant), and the Pocket Books *Abilene* series (as Justin Ladd).

Uncollected Short Stories

"Hacendado," in *Westeryear*. New York, Evans, 1988.

Other Publications

Novel

Texas Wind. New York, Manor, 1980.

*

James M. Reasoner comments:

I've always been an avid reader of all types of fiction, and never wanted to be anything else except a writer. My goal in my work is to entertain the reader, and maybe make him or her think a little every now and then. My writing definitely springs from the pulp tradition, and I like to think of myself as being the contemporary equivalent of the pulp writer of the 1930's and 1940's, and the paperback writers of the 1950's and 1960's. Western novels are probably my favourites, both as a writer and a reader, because of their mixture of history and myth. I try to tell a good story in as realistic a background as possible.

* * *

Although best known for his fine mystery novel, *Texas Wind*, James M. Reasoner is a prolific writer of Westerns. Unfortunately, legal obligations prevent revealing the exact titles of the novels he's written. Hopefully, Reasoner's work will be identified in future volumes so he can receive the credit for his excellent writing.

George Engle, head of Book Creations, who packages the series James Reasoner writes for, released this summary of Reason's work: Reasoner has written one novel in the *Faraday* series, he has written seven books in the *Stagecoach* series, and 15 books in the *Abilene* series.

Reasoner is a gifted writer and produces work of the highest professionalism.

—George Kelley

REBEL, Adam. *See* **ROAN, Tom.**

REED, Ishmael (Scott). American. Born in Chattanooga, Tennessee, 22 February 1938. Educated at Buffalo Technical High School; East High School, Buffalo, graduated 1956; University of Buffalo, 1956–60. Married 1) Priscilla Rose in 1960 (separated 1963, divorced 1970), one daughter; 2) Carla Blank-Reed in 1970, one daughter. Staff writer, *Empire Star Weekly*, Buffalo, 1960–62; freelance writer, New York, 1962–67: co-founder, *East Village Other*, New York, and *Advance*, Newark, New Jersey, 1965. Teacher, St. Mark's in the Bowery prose workshop, New York, 1966. Since 1971 chair and president, Yardbird Publishing Company, editor, *Yardbird Reader*, 1972–76, since 1973 director, Reed Cannon and Johnson Communications, and since 1981 founder and editor, with Al Young, *Quilt* magazine, all Berkeley, California. Since 1967 Lecturer, University of California, Berkeley. Lecturer, University of Washington, Seattle, 1969–70, State University of New York, Buffalo, 1975, 1979, Sitka Community Association, summer 1982, University of Arkansas, Fayetteville, 1982, Columbia University, New York, 1983, Harvard University, Cambridge, Massachusetts, 1987, and University of California, Santa Barbara, 1988. Visiting Professor, fall 1979, and since 1983 Associate Fellow of Calhoun House, Yale University, New Haven, Connecticut; Visiting Professor, Dartmouth College, Hanover, New Hampshire, 1980; since 1987 Associate Fellow, Harvard University Signet Society. Since 1976 president, Before Columbus Foundation. Chair, Berkeley Arts Commission, 1980, 1981. Associate editor, *American Book Review*. Recipient: National Endowment for the Arts grant, 1974; Rosenthal Foundation award, 1975; Guggenheim fellowship, 1975; American Academy award, 1975; Michaux award, 1978. Agent: Ellis J. Freedman, 415 Madison Avenue, New York, New York 10017, U.S.A.

WESTERN PUBLICATIONS

Novel

Yellow Back Radio Broke Down. New York, Doubleday, 1969; London, Allison and Busby, 1971.

OTHER PUBLICATIONS

Novels

The Free-Lance Pallbearers. New York, Doubleday, 1967; London, MacGibbon and Kee, 1968.
Mumbo-Jumbo. New York, Doubleday, 1972.
The Last Days of Louisiana Red. New York, Random House, 1974.
Flight to Canada. New York, Random House, 1976.
The Terrible Twos. New York, St. Martin's Press-Marek, 1982; London, Allison and Busby, 1990.
Reckless Eyeballing. New York, St. Martin's Press, 1986.
The Terrible Threes. New York, Atheneum, 1989.

Verse

Catechism of d neoamerican hoodoo church. London, Paul Breman, 1970.
Conjure: Selected Poems 1963–1970. Amherst, University of Massachusetts Press, 1972.
Chattanooga. New York, Random House, 1973.
A Secretary to the Spirits. New York, NOK, 1978.
New and Collected Poems. New York, Atheneum, 1988.

Other

The Rise, Fall and . . .? of Adam Clayton Powell (as Emmett Coleman), with others. New York, Bee-Line, 1967.
Shrovetide in Old New Orleans (essays). New York, Doubleday, 1978.
God Made Alaska for the Indians. New York, Garland, 1982.
Cab Calloway Stands In for the Moon. Flint, Michigan, Bamberger, 1986.

Editor, *19 Necromancers from Now.* New York, Doubleday, 1970.
Editor, *Yardbird Reader* (annual). Berkeley, California, Yardbird, 5 vols., 1971–77.
Editor, with Richard Cherry and Bernard Hirsch, *A Return to Vision.* Boston, Houghton Mifflin, 1971.
Editor, with Richard Cherry, *Poems for Comparison and Contrast.* New York, Macmillan, 1972.
Editor, with Richard Cherry and Bernard Hirsch, *The Shadow Within.* Boston, Houghton Mifflin, 1973.
Editor, with Al Young, *Yardbird Lives!* New York, Grove Press, 1978.
Editor, *Calafia: The California Poetry.* Berkeley, California, Yardbird, 1979.
Editor, with Al Young, *Quilt 2–3.* Berkeley, California, Reed and Young's Quilt, 2 vols., 1981–82.
Editor, *Echoes of Our Being.* Bloomington, Indiana University Press, 1982.
Editor, *Writin' Is Fightin': Thirty-Seven Years of Boxing on Paper.* New York, Atheneum, 1988.

*

Bibliography: "Mapping Out the Gumbo Works: An Ishmael Reed Bibliography" by Joe Weixlmann, Robert Fikes, Jr., and Ishmael Reed, in *Black American Literature Forum* (Terre Haute, Indiana), Spring 1978; *Ishmael Reed: A Primary and Secondary Bibliography* by Elizabeth A. and Thomas A. Settle, Boston, Hall, 1982.

Critical Studies: "Robin the Cock & Doopeyduk Doing the Boogaloo in Harry Sam with Rusty Jethroe and Letterhead America . . ." by Lawrence Lipton, in *Cavalier* (Greenwich, Connecticut), no.70, 1967; review by Tam Fiofori, in *Negro Digest* (Chicago), December 1969; "Blood of the Lamb" by Calvin Hernton, in *Amistad 1*, New York, Knopf, 1970; "Ishmael Reed Issue" of *Review of Contemporary Fiction* (Elmwood Park, Illinois), vol.4 no.2, 1984; *Ishmael Reed and the New Black Aesthetic Critics* by Reginald Martin, New York,

Macmillan, 1988; interview in *Over Here* (Nottingham), Winter 1989.

* * *

Ishmael Reed is one of the most important black writers of the postwar period. Frederic Jameson among others categorizes Reed as a postmodernist, and certainly the former's description of postmodern style (though his immediate subject here is architecture) as "with gusto cannibalis[ing] all the . . . styles of the past and combin[ing] them in overstimulating ensembles" would serve as a direct description of Reed's work. Reed is, though, a member of a minority group, and all of his writing criticizes the exclusionary assumptions of the dominant culture. Early in his career, for example, in *19 Necromancers from Now*, he wrote "In the beginning was the Word and the Word is the domain of the White patriarchy. Beware. Women and natives are not to tamper with the word." Reed's tone has become less immediately confrontational in recent years, but the fact that there is most definitely a political intent behind his writing does give a kind of social and historical dimension to it, which Jameson sees postmodernist writing as generally lacking.

Reed's work ranges widely in subject matter. *Mumbo-Jumbo* is set mainly in 1920's Harlem while *Flight to Canada* is a "slave's-eye-view of the Civil War." The brilliance of Reed's comic writing is perhaps most obviously accessible in his major novel about the American West, *Yellow Back Radio Broke Down*, in which he takes the generic form which is the Western, plays with it, turns it on its head, and finally deconstructs it entirely. The novel is set in the West, but the reader is swiftly destabilised by what one of the cowpokes calls the "weird irrational discontinuous landscape" which the book describes. These discontinuities are suggested when the Indian Chief Showcase rescues the Loop Garoo Kid, the main figure of the narrative, from certain death. He arrives by helicopter and hands out champagne, before launching a complaint against white appropriation of minority group talent which refers in passing to George Gershwin, Mae West, and Martha and the Vandellas. He then details the unequal exchange which occurred between white and Indian in the early days of settlement: "we showed the cat . . . how to plant, woodcraft . . . Taught them to pop corn . . . Man they didn't know from dick . . . You know what we got in return? . . . Liquor smallpox and guns."

We move in the text from Lewis and Clark describing their work for Thomas Jefferson to a papal visit to the western town of Yellow Back Radio, and from references to the 1960's counter culture to feminist separatism. Along with such synchronic effects Reed disrupts linear narrative. Conventional boundaries between high culture and low are also collapsed as Reed mixes various levels of discourse and, in Reginald Martin's words, creates "a kind of contemporary bathetic language, whose principal rules of discourse are taken from the streets, popular music, and television." The novel is highly self-reflexive as the Loop Garoo Kid's argument with Bo Schmo, head of the "neo-social realist gang" suggests: "What's your beef with me Bo Schmo, what if I write circuses? No one says a novel has to be one thing. It can be anything it wants to be, a vaudeville show, the six o'clock news, the mumblings of wild men saddled by demons."

In fact Reed's novelistic playfulness has serious intent. He turns the western genre on its head here in order both to reverse conventional readings of American history and ideology and to suggest alternative modes of (Afro-American) art. The clear links between the western genre and racist ideology are slyly suggested by Reed as he tells us that "Roy Rogers' movie double's name was Whitey Christensen." That "real American personality" which Turner tells us "begins with the frontier" is that represented in this text by the ranchowner Drag Gibson, whose french-kissing of his green mustang suggests the perversions associated with the dominant culture's fixation on property and power. Drag, this culture's representative, is locked in conflict with the "crazy dada nigger," Loop Garoo. Reed however reverses the conventional oppositions and iconography of the Western to make the dominant American social world signify badness and to make the outsider, the black man in the black buckskins, the hero. Allied with Chief Showcase, these members of two minority cultures join forces against Drag, the evil representative of a repressive master culture.

In artistic terms, too, Loop Garoo is associated with alternative forms to the cultural dominant. His "Hoo-Doo" art is a variant of that "neo-hoodooism" of which Reed speaks in *19 Necromancers from Now*. Based on the idea of that religion taken from Africa to the new world by blacks and practiced underground ("an unorganized religion without ego-games or death worship"), it suggests the development of an art both devoted to the depiction of black people and based on the cultural forms distinctive to them. Loop Garoo, and by extension Reed himself, are committed then to an aesthetic practice which can stand alongside that of the dominant culture, and which can draw on the resources of an Afro-American tradition. Reed refers to such a tradition in Loop's own activity: he "seems to be scatting arbitrarily, using forms of this and adding his own. He's blowing like that celebrated musician Charles Yardbird Parker—improvising as he goes along. He's throwing clusters of demon chords at you." Reed celebrates American variation and difference. His own art uses humour to critique an oppressive society. His own distinctive literary mode is based on what he can draw from both those artistic traditions—African and American—available to him. The sense of what Martin calls "performance and style" of a black oral culture, and the kinds of improvisation and lack of rigidity associated with jazz, combine with a surrealistic humour as Reed plays his variation on the western form and transforms it to serve his own needs as black man and artist.

—Peter Messent

REESE, John. Also wrote as John Jo Carpenter; Cody Kennedy, Jr. American. Born in Sweetwater, Nebraska, 18 December 1910. Educated at a high school in Dunbar, Nebraska, graduated 1928. Married 1) Margaret Smith in 1938; 2) Niki Spivack in 1962; seven children. Worked for United States Department of Internal Revenue; reporter, Los Angeles *Examiner*; then freelance writer. Recipient: New York *Herald-Tribune* award, for children's book, 1952. *Died 15 August 1981.*

WESTERN PUBLICATIONS

Novels (series: Jefferson Hewitt)

Signal Guns at Sunup (as John Jo Carpenter). New York, Simon and Schuster, 1950.
The High Passes. Boston, Little Brown, 1954; London, Hale, 1955.
Rich Man's Range. New York, New American Library, 1966.
Sure Shot Shapiro. New York, Doubleday, 1968.

Sunblind Range. New York, Doubleday, 1968; London, Hale, 1970.
Singalee. New York, Doubleday, 1969.
Horses, Honor, and Women. New York, Doubleday, 1970.
Jesus on Horseback: The Mooney County Saga. New York, Doubleday, 1971; as *Angel Range*, *The Blowholers*, and *The Land Baron*, Doubleday, 3 vols., 1973–74; *The Blowholers* reprinted as *Lonesome Cowboy*, New York, Belmont, 1975.
The Wild One. New York, Fawcett, 1972; London, Gold Lion, 1974.
Big Hitch. New York, Doubleday, 1972.
Springfield .45–70. New York, Doubleday, 1972.
They Don't Shoot Cowards. New York, Doubleday, 1973; Aylesbury, Buckinghamshire, Milton House, 1975.
Weapon Heavy (Hewitt). New York, Doubleday, 1973; Aylesbury, Buckinghamshire, Milton House, 1975.
The Sharpshooter (Hewitt). New York, Doubleday, 1974; London, Hale, 1978.
Texas Gold (Hewitt). New York, Doubleday, 1975; London, Hale, 1978.
Wes Hardin's Gun (Hewitt). New York, Doubleday, 1975; London, Hale, 1979.
Hangman's Springs (Hewitt). New York, Doubleday, 1976; London, Hale, 1979.
Blacksnake Man. New York, Doubleday, 1976; London, Hale, 1978.
A Sheriff for All the People. New York, Doubleday, 1976.
Omar, Fats, and Trixie. New York, Fawcett, 1976.
Halter-Broke. New York, Doubleday, 1977; London, Hale, 1980.
The Cherokee Diamondback (Hewitt). New York, Doubleday, 1977.
Sequoia Shootout (Hewitt). New York, Doubleday, 1977; London, Hale, 1979.
A Pair of Deuces (Hewitt). New York, Doubleday, 1978; London, Hale, 1981.
Dead Eye (Hewitt). New York, Doubleday, 1978; London, Hale, 1980.
Legacy of a Land Hog. New York, Doubleday, 1979; London, Hale, 1980.
Two Thieves and a Puma. New York, Doubleday, 1980.
Maximum Range. New York, Doubleday, 1981; London, Hale, 1982.

Novels as Cody Kennedy, Jr.

This Wild Land. New York, Warner, 1979.
The Warrior Flame. New York, Warner, 1980.
The Conquering Clan. New York, Warner, 1980.

Uncollected Short Stories

"The Nester of Coffinrock," in *Ace High*, March 1942.
"Doctor of Frontier Medicine," in *10 Story Western*, April 1942.
"Death Trail's Sixgun Saint," in *Ace High*, May 1942.
"Six-Horse Express to Hell," in *Big Book Western*, June 1942.
"Hell Rides a Roan Horse," in *All Western* (New York), December 1942.
"Suffer the Little Children," in *Prairie Schooner Caravan*, edited by Lowry C. Wimberly. Lincoln, University of Nebraska Press, 1943.
"Hanging's a Family Matter," in *Speed Western*, May 1946.
"Just Middlin' Mean Can Kill," from *Leading Western*, June 1946.
"Gun-Whelps Ain't Welcome," in *10 Story Western* (New York), August 1946.
"Kid from Nowhere," in *10 Story Western* (New York), September 1946.
"Battle Call for the Bushwack War," in *Dime Western*, October 1946.
"Fugitive. Light and Tie," in *Six-Gun Western*, December 1946.
"Heal 'em and Hang 'em," in *New Western*, December 1946.
"Boothill Boomerang," in *15 Western Tales*, January 1947.
"A Little Less Law, Please!," in *10 Story Western* (New York), January 1947.
"One Big Trigger," in *10 Story Western* (New York), February 1947.
"One More Man to Kill," in *Dime Western*, February 1947.
"High, Low, Jack," in *Action Stories*, Spring 1947.
"Lemon-Drop Gunhawk," in *10 Story Western* (New York), March 1947.
"Saddle-Bum's Revolt," in *10 Story Western* (New York), April 1947.
"Cowpuncher's Battle Cry," in *10 Story Western* (New York), May 1947.
"Jail-Bustin' Ace," in *10 Story Western* (New York), July 1947.
"Freighter Blood Is Fighting Blood," in *Big Book Western*, August, 1947.
"Two for a Boothill Honeymoon," in *Ace High*, August 1947.
"Trail to Nowhere," in *10 Story Western* (New York), August 1947.
"A Matter of Killer-Savvy," in *.44 Western*, August 1947.
"Walk Soft—Here Comes the Killer!," in *New Western*, August 1947.
"A Gun Ain't Enough," in *10 Story Western* (New York), August 1947.
"No Bargains on Boothill," in *Lariat*, September 1947.
"The Last Border," in *Dime Western*, September 1947.
"Hit the Trail, Cowpunch," in *Big Book Western*, September 1947.
"Outlaw-Buster," in *New Western*, September 1947.
"No Time to Die," in *10 Story Western* (New York), September 1947.
"Nesters Reap a Red-Hot Harvest," in *10 Story Western* (New York), October 1947.
"Curtains for a Killer," in *West* (New York), October 1947.
"Brand of Majic," in *Speed Western*, October 1947.
"Posse Bait," in *Lariat*, November 1947.
"Drifter's Trail," in *Leading Western*, November 1947.
"Open Season on Neighbors," in *Dime Western*, November 1947.
"Death Camp Gets a Gun Boss," in *10 Story Western* (New York), November 1947.
"Shoot-Out at Black Canyon," in *10 Story Western* (New York), November 1947.
"Gunsmoke Wedding Wreath," in *10 Story Western* (New York), December 1947.
"Hard Cash or Hot Lead," in *Dime Western*, January 1948.
"Hit It Rich," in *Speed Western*, January 1948.
"Badlands Stunt," in *Leading Western*, February 1948.
"Red Chips on His Shoulder," in *10 Story Western* (New York), February 1948.
"Swing Your Pardner High," in *Big Book Western*, March 1948.
"Two-Bit King of Hell's Half Acre," in *Ace High*, April 1948.
"Bullets to the Bridegroom," in *New Western*, April 1948.
"First Kill," in *.44 Western*, April 1948.
"Too Tough to Take," in *10 Story Western* (New York), April 1948.
"The Damned of Salvation Wells," in *Star Western* (Chicago), May 1948.
"Trial by Blood," in *Dime Western*, June 1948.

"Boothill round the Bend," in *Western Trails*, June 1948.
"Rannyhan, Get Your Gun," in *Western Aces*, July 1948.
"Plant Your Own Corpses," in *New Western*, July 1948.
"The Devil's Basin," in *15 Western Tales*, July 1948.
"Go for Your Iron," in *New Western*, August 1948.
"Once an Owlhoot," in *10 Story Western* (New York), August 1948.
"Catamount," in *Action Stories*, Fall 1948.
"Queen of the Five Jacks," in *Star Western* (Chicago), September 1948.
"Graveyard Watch," in *Big Book Western*, September 1948.
"Kill Kinfolk First," in *.44 Western*, September 1948.
"Fighting Son of Rio Hondo," in *10 Story Western*, October 1948.
"Tophands Bluff Hard," in *10 Story Western* (New York), October 1948.
"Where the Trail Divides," in *Star Western* (Chicago), October 1948.
"The Kill," in *Argosy* (New York), October 1948.
"Brown-Eyed and Gunshy," in *Ranch Romances* (New York), 3 October 1948.
"Cold Deck, Hot Gun," in *Dime Western*, November 1948.
"Hangover in Helltown," in *10 Story Western* (New York), November 1948.
"Git His Gringo Scalp," in *Dime Western*, December 1948.
"Dig Your Own Damn' Grave," in *.44 Western*, January 1949.
"Renegade Row," in *10 Story Western* (New York), January 1949.
"Sixty Years of Guts," in *Dime Western*, January 1949.
"Hell-Town Homecoming," in *New Western*, January 1949.
"30-30 Bust-Up," in *Star Western* (Chicago), January 1949.
"Last of the Wild Fayettes," in *Big Book Western*, February 1949.
"Singing Spurs," in *Ranch Romances* (New York), 1 February 1949.
"Rope for a Range Bum," in *Action Stories*, Spring 1949.
"Cull Out Your Weaklings," in *Ranch Romances* (New York), 1 April 1949.
"The Rose of Dead Man's Range," in *Star Western* (Chicago), May 1949.
"Texan, Pick Your Tree!," in *10 Story Western* (New York), May 1949.
"Say Your Gun-Piece," in *Ranch Romances* (New York), 1 June 1949.
"Warrior's Woman," in *Star Western* (Chicago), July 1949.
"Outside the Law," in *Lariat*, September 1949.
"Payoff in Bluff," in *10 Story Western* (New York), October 1949.
"Lawmen Can't Kill Personal," in *10 Story Western*, November 1949.
"Good-for-Nothin Trash and Managin' Woman," in *Ranch Romances* (New York), 2 December 1949.
"Brand Her Senorita Killer," in *Star Western* (Chicago), January 1950.
"Once a Horsethief," in *New Western*, February 1950.
"High Court of Gun Law," in *Rio Kid Western*, February 1950.
"A Ghost Doesn't Need Bullets," in *Big Book Western*, February 1950.
"Bullets for Breakfast," in *Frontier Stories*, Spring 1950.
"The Last of the Terrible Men," in *Argosy* (New York), August 1950.
"Slow-Fuse Vengeance," in *Thrilling Western* (London), January 1951.
"Killer Mule," in *Elks Magazine* (Chicago), October 1951.
"The Temptation of Cactus Slim," in *Saturday Evening Post* (Philadelphia), 7 June 1952.
"Ride the Black Stallion," in *Saturday Evening Post* (Philadelphia), 16 October 1954.
"Frontier Frenzy," in *Bar 5*, edited by Scott Meredith. New York, Dutton, 1956.
"Sudden Hombre," in *.44 Western*, May 1956.
"Saddle Brothers," in *Saturday Evening Post* (Philadelphia), 18 May 1957.
"The Scarlet Brand," in *Western Story* (London), November 1957.
"The Last Bullet," in *Thrilling Western* (London), August 1958.
"Fear Is a Blind Bullet!," in *Lariat*, n.d.
"Last Match," in *Dime Western*, n.d.
"Six-Gun Cupid," in *Golden West Romances*, n.d.
"Hundred Days of Hell," in *10 Story Western* (New York), n.d.
"Horse-Thief Trail," in *10 Story Western* (New York), n.d.
"A Man with Spurs," in *Thrilling Western* (London), n.d.
"Killer, Stay Away from My Girl," in *Star Western* (Chicago), n.d.
"Woman Called Dagger," in *Famous Western*, n.d.
"Mister Feeney and the Jack of Diamonds," in *Fifteen Western Tales*, n.d.
"Signal Guns at Sunup," in *Giant Western*, n.d.

Uncollected Short Stories as John Jo Carpenter

"Bad-Medicine Boomerang," in *Wild West* (New York), 26 September 1942.
"Man Hunt on the Niobrara," in *Star Western* (Chicago), November 1947.
"Gun Down Those Humphrey Twins," in *Mammoth Western* (Chicago), November 1949.
"Dead Men Die Hard," in *Mammoth Western* (Chicago), October 1950.
"Marshal Blow-Hard," in *Western Story* (London), November 1953.
"Showdown on Dead Man's Flat," in *Western Story* (London), November 1954.
"Lynch Him," in *Texas Rangers* (London), April 1956.
"The Reluctant Hangman," in *Texas Rangers* (London), October 1956.
"Rough, Tough—and Kissable," in *Western Story* (London), November 1957.
"The Rose of Dead Man's Range," in *Western Story* (London), April 1958.

OTHER PUBLICATIONS

Novels

Sheehan's Mill. New York, Doubleday, 1943.
The Looters. New York, Random House, 1968; London, Hale, 1969.
Pity Us All. New York, Random House, 1969; London, Hale, 1970.

Other (for children)

Big Mutt. Philadelphia, Westminster, 1952.
The Shouting Duke. Philadelphia, Westminster, 1952.
Three Wild Ones. Philadelphia, Westminster, 1963.
Dinky. New York, McKay, 1964.

*

Manscript Collection: Western History Research Center, University of Wyoming, Laramie.

John Reese commented (1981):

I was the eldest of six children of a very poor couple. My father was a horsebreaker and former cavalryman; my mother was the daughter of a frontier blacksmith and woodworker. I may be the last professional writer who talked to those survivors of the 1880's and 1890's and who grew up in the same environment. It was a specialized education for one job alone, the one I have.

I have never cared what any critic said about my work and still do not. I believe that over the years I have developed two rules. The first derives from Joseph Conrad, who, during a discussion of the writer's "job," declared "It is above all to make you *see*." If you can work toward that sort of story you can't go far wrong.

Second, I have never understood how otherwise responsible writers and editors can talk about "plot" and "character" as though they were two separate elements. Plot grows out of character. Certainly sometimes one starts with a good plot, but unless it can be fleshed out with three-dimensional people it is a wasted plot.

* * *

"I was never an 'author,'" wrote John Reese, "but I was a production professional." His output has indeed been remarkable. He began by selling about 500 Westerns and suspense stories to the pulps, then graduated to the slicks, becoming, in his own words, "the top freelance contributor to the old *Saturday Evening Post*." Doubleday published his first novel, *Sheehan's Mill* in 1943, and by 1980 he had written close to 40 more. His list included many highly original Westerns, especially the *Jesus on Horseback* trilogy, his best work, but he developed in other directions. *Big Mutt* was a best-selling dog story for children, still in print after 30 years. *The Looters* explored the world of organized crime. Nine novels spotlighted frontier private investigator Jefferson Hewitt. Another trilogy beginning with *This Wild Land* chronicled the activities of the powerful and passionate Shepherd family on several frontiers and made concessions to the current appetite for sex and violence.

His production record alone would stamp Reese as a notable western writer, but he had other claims to a high rating. One would be originality. An agent once described him as "incredibly imaginative." Fresh ideas appear in every book. *Sure Shot Shapiro*, his first Western, focused on a Jewish traveling salesman who had heroism forced upon him. The viewpoint character in *Singalee* is an auctioneer with a spellbinding voice and personality who can do everything but stay ahead of a pursuing woman. *Blacksnake Man* features a tenderfoot hero who uses a blacksnake whip instead of a pistol. Rolf Ledger in *Angel Range*, an ex-convict, becomes the spiritual sparkplug of Mooney, Colorado.

These characters, and others as well, are not only new, interesting, and original; they are also funny. Reese was one of the few writers of Westerns who can combine humor with violent adventure. Perhaps his best fun is in *Omar, Fats, and Trixie*, which he called a "modern Western."

There is a strong element of disillusion in Reese's humor. The antics of the human race left him "confused and depressed." After his years in politics and the newspaper business, he suspected that crooks and phonies outnumber the honest men in our world. He thought that many of today's college graduates "ought to be recalled as unsafe at any speed." Observation told him that "the noble red man was a myth" and that "tribal life was hell." At the same time he respected courage and honor and loyalty. The mixture of skepticism and faith adds a special tone to his work.

The flavor is sharpened by a high degree of literacy. His scheduled studies ended with high school but he was formidably self-educated. He once sold a short story in which a young scientist solved a murder mystery by using Boolean algebra. He had considerably fluency in Spanish and called himself "a nut about the English language." He delighted in good prose and was a fine stylist himself.

From all this his principles as a writer emerge. "I always tell ambitious writers-to-be," he said, "that if they haven't read, they can't write." His second dictum: "If they haven't lived, they can't write." He himself drew on an incredible reservoir of experience. His country beginnings taught him rural skills and made him a horseman. He hoboed from Canada to Texas during the Depression, drove a taxi in Omaha, cooked for the crew of a Missouri River steamboat, ran a cement factory in California, headed James Roosevelt's campaign for governor of that state, spent years as a Los Angeles newsman and was at home in Hollywood. Nothing like this happens to the young literati of today. "I drive past 20,000 college students every day," he remarks, "and they don't know I'm alive because they never read. They write."

There is no Reese cult—yet—but Reese fans contend that he was the equal of the better-known practitioners of his craft; that in his own territory he was as good as they come.

—C.L. Sonnichsen

REMINGTON, Frederic S(ackrider). American. Born in Canton, New York, 4 October 1861. Educated at Yale School of Fine Arts, New Haven, Connecticut, 1878–80. Worked as sheep rancher in Kansas, 1880–84; saloon owner, Arizona, 1884–85; gold prospector in Pinal Mountains, Arizona, 1885; war correspondent in Cuba in Spanish-American war, 1898. Painter, sculptor, book illustrator, and later author, on Western frontier subjects; work published by *Harper's* and *Collier's* magazines; paintings and bronze sculptures exhibited in Metropolitan Museum of Art, New York City. *Died 26 December 1909.*

WESTERN PUBLICATIONS

Novels

John Ermine of the Yellowstone. New York and London, Macmillan, 1902.

The Way of an Indian. New York, Fox Duffield, and London, Gay and Bird, 1906.

Short Stories

Pony Tracks. New York, Harper and Brothers, 1895.

Crooked Trails. New York and London, Harper, 1898.

Sundown Leflare (four novelettes). New York and London, Harper, 1899.

Stories of Peace and War. New York and London, Harper, 1899.

Horses of the Plains, and A Scout with the Buffalo Soldiers. Santa Barbara, California, Genn, n.d.

Men with the Bark On. New York and London, Harper, 1900.

The Collected Writings of Frederic Remington, edited by Peggy and Harold Samuel. New York, Doubleday, 1979.
Selected Writings. Secaucus, New Jersey, Castle, 1981.

OTHER PUBLICATIONS

Other

Reproductions of the Work of Frederic Remington. New York, New York Public Library, 1888–1906.
Drawings by Frederic Remington. New York, Russell, and London, Lawrence and Bullen, 1897.
Remington's Frontier Sketches. Chicago and New York, Werner, 1898.
Four Reproductions in Color of Paintings by Frederic Remington. New York, Collier, 1900.
Roosevelt's Rough Riders (eight mounted plates). No publisher given, 1901.
A Bunch of Buckskins: Eight Drawings in Pastel. New York, Russell, 1901.
Done in the Open (drawings). New York, Collier, 1902.
Frederic Remington: Western Life: Colored Plates from Collier's Weekly. New York, Collier, 1903–07.
Six Remington Paintings in Colors. New York, Collier, 1906.
Eight New Remington Paintings. New York, Collier, 1909.
Scrapbook of Clippings and Pictures. New York, New York Public Library, 1927.
101 Frederic Remington Drawings of the Old West (text by Irvin W. Hanson). Willmar, Minnesota, Color Press, 1968.
Drawings by Frederic Remington. New York, Lenox Hill Press, 1971.
73 Drawings and Illustrations. New York, Dover, 1972.
My Dear Wister: The Frederic Remington–Owen Wister Letters, edited by Ben Merchant Vorpahl, Palo Alto, California, American West, 1972.
Buffalo Soldiers, illustrated by the author. Palmer Lake, Colorado, Filter Press, 1974.

Illustrator: *Ranch Life and the Hunting Trail* by Theodore Roosevelt, 1888; *The Song of Hiawatha* by Henry Wadsworth Longfellow, 1891; *The Jonah of Lucky Valley and Other Stories* by Howard Seely, 1892; *The Borderland of Czar and Kaiser* by Poutney Bigelow, 1895; *Personal Recollections and Observations of General N.A. Miles* by Nelson A. Miles, 1896; *Red Men and White* by Owen Wister, 1896; *Wolfville* by Alfred Henry Lewis, 1897; *Cuba in War Time* by Richard Harding Davis, 1897; *The Story of Evangelina Cisneros* by Evangelina Betancourt Cosio y Cisneros, 1898; *The Way to the West and the Lives of Three Early Americans—Boone, Crockett, Carson* by Emerson Hough, 1903; *The Old Santa Fe Trail*, 1916; *The Book of the American Indian* by Hamlin Garland, 1923; *Captain Lee Hall of Texas* by Dora Neill Raymond, 1940; *General Crook in the Indian Country* by John Gregory Bourke, 1974; *How the Law Got into the Chaparral: Conversations with Old Texas Rangers* edited by John H. Jenkins, 1987.

*

Critical Studies: *Frederic Remington, Artist of the Old West*, Philadelphia, Lippincott, 1947; *Frederic Remington's Own West* edited by Harold McCracken, London, Foulsham, 1960; *The Eastern Establishment and the Western Experience: The West of Frederic Remington, Theodore Roosevelt and Owen Wister*, New Haven, Connecticut, Yale University Press, 1968; *The Illustrations of Frederic Remington, with a Commentary by Owen Wister, Edited with a Concise Biography and an Account of Remington's Work and Career* by Martin Jackson, New York, Bounty, 1970; *Frederic Remington and the Spanish-American War* by Douglas Allen, New York, Crown, 1971; *Frederic Remington: Artist on Horseback* by La Verne Anderson, New York, Garrard, 1971; *The Western Art of Frederic Remington* edited by Matthew Baigell, New York, Ballantine, 1976; *Frederic Remington, the American West: An Official Publication of the American Museum of Natural History* edited by Philip R. St. Clair, Kent, Ohio, Volair, 1978; *Frederic Remington and the West: With the Eye of the Mind* by Ben Merchant Vorpahl, Austin, University of Texas Press, 1978; *Frederic Remington: A Biography* by Peggy and Harold Samuels, New York, Doubleday, 1982; *Frederic Remington* by Ernest Lloyd Raboff, New York, Lippincott, 1988.

* * *

Frederic Remington attended the Yale School of the Fine Arts from 1878–1880 before he went to Kansas to take up sheep ranching. Although the area where he settled was definitely not the frontier, the isolation and loneliness, particularly during the harsh winters, gave him many long hours to pursue his drawing and painting. In the spring of 1884, he decided to sell his ranch and became a wanderer. He went first to Kansas City and then proceeded southwest through Indian Territory into Arizona, returning in late summer that year to Kansas City whereupon he went into partnership in a saloon. When his partners cheated him out of his interest, he took up a pistol and wanted to use a little "frontier justice" on them before being talked out of it at the last minute. In the summer of 1885, after his marriage failed due to penury, he went prospecting in the Pinal Range in Arizona Territory. Coincidentally, Geronimo broke loose from his reservation captivity and the Third U.S. Cavalry under General Crook took up the pursuit. Remington sought to use the situation to his advantage by engaging to sketch the pursuit, but he had second thoughts and decided instead to make the theme of his photographs and sketches "Soldiering in the Southwest." General Miles replaced General Crook, and Remington met Miles after Geronimo had surrendered. Miles could see the usefulness of having a champion working for *Harper's Weekly*, and so he proposed to assist Remington in preparing a report on the positive aspects of the campaign. Later, Miles would provide Remington with the opportunity of illustrating the pursuit of Geronimo for his book, *Personal Reminiscences*. The fact that Remington had never come within 200 miles of Geronimo did not faze Easterners when, upon his return, with a full portfolio of Indian portraits and sketches of Army life, he was suddenly in great demand to illustrate stories of the conflict between the Apaches and the Cavalry. Remington's reputation was established.

No less a one than Theodore Roosevelt, who had just begun to publish the sketches which would comprise his book, *Ranch Life and the Hunting Trail*, asked for Remington to be his illustrator. Along with this commission and numerous others, Remington himself turned to writing, often illustrating his own material. In the 1890's he published, first in magazine and then in book form, the stories and sketches contained in *Pony Tracks*, perhaps his best-known book, and *Crooked Trails*. Remington also published additional compilations of his magazine articles and stories, together with his illustrations for them, but it was not until 1986 that Peggy and Harold Samuels, who in 1982 had written the definitive biography of Remington, gathered all 111 of these into one volume appropriately titled *The Collected Writings of Frederic Remington*.

For Remington, the meaning of the western experience was the confrontation between man and a hostile physical environment. He was never quite the romantic that his friend,

Owen Wister, was and whose stories he frequently illustrated. Absent from Remington's fiction is Wister's fondness for idealizing the courtship of eastern women in a western environment. Nor was Remington a believer, as was Roosevelt, in the rugged life for its own sake. He was, however, more highly prejudicial than either, no matter how much Wister shared his innate eastern snobbery, and in a letter he wrote in 1893 he summed up what might be termed his "cowboy philosophy": "Jews, Injuns, Chinamen, Italians, Huns—the rubbish of the Earth I hate—I've got some Winchesters and when the massacring begins, I can get my share of 'em and what's more, I will . . ." Many of his stories were concerned with one aspect or another of the Indian wars and, in common with General Charles King and even with Wister in the latter's *Red Men and White*, the officers and the enlisted men were the ones he singled out for his heroes, while the Indians were characterized by ruthless savagery which could only be dealt with (men and women alike) through victorious combat. It was Remington, even more than General King, who popularized the Indians versus Cavalry story and provided it with such an impetus that it became a commonplace setting for many decades after in fiction by Ernest Haycox, James Warner Bellah, and Gordon D. Shirreffs, among numerous others.

Yet, toward the end of the decade, Remington's personal contradictions came increasingly to the surface. As much as he personally detested wilderness conditions, he felt more and more drawn to them as his hatred for the industrial civilization of the East intensified. *Sundown Leflare*, four novelettes about the title character, found Leflare observing: "'White man mak de wagon un de seelver dollar, un de dam railroad, un he tink dat ees all dair ees een de country.'"

Although Remington regarded himself primarily as an artist and not a writer, publication of Wister's *The Virginian* stirred him to compete with his friend by writing his own western novel. The result, *John Ermine of the Yellowstone*, may well be Remington's finest literary effort. In it, he abandoned, seemingly, all of his earlier prejudices and told a story singularly without romance of a white child raised by the Indians, who eventually joins the U.S. Cavalry as a scout. Through Ermine's eyes the reader sees contrasted the Indian way of life with the "senseless mass of white humanity" always pressing further westward from the East. Ermine is popular with the white soldiers until he has the audacity to fall in love with a white woman, the Major's daughter, after which he is ostracized and, seeking vengeance against her fiancé, he is killed by a Native American scout hoping to impress the white officers. The novel embodies a powerful idea, far ahead of its time; and it was not popular, as was Wister's more romantic view which became a minor "classic" that has never been out of print. Decades later, Edgar Rice Burroughs would make use of the basic elements of this plot in his Apache novels, and Henry Wilson Allen would forge even farther ahead in telling the Indians versus Cavalry plot from the Indians' point-of-view. Yet, by then, Remington's literary endeavors would be all but forgotten, and only his paintings would be treasured.

In "A Few Words from Mr. Remington," published in 1905 in *Collier's*, Remington summed up his disillusionment when he wrote: "I knew the railroad was coming. I saw men already swarming into the land. I knew the derby hat, the smoking chimneys, the cord-binder, and the thirty-day note were upon us in a restless surge. I knew the wild riders and vacant land were about to vanish forever, and the more I considered the subject, the bigger the forever loomed."

"Cowboys!" Remington had cried out when near death. "There are no cowboys any more!" Yet he himself had in his way helped romanticize the West, and because he had such an influential impact when others came to experience the same feeling, what was created to fill the void was the formulary Western and the cinematic cowboy hero, which too, were not the real West and certainly not what Remington decried as having vanished.

—Jon Tuska

REMINGTON, Mark. *See* **BINGLEY, David Ernest.**

RENO, Clint. *See* **BALLARD, Willis Todhunter.**

RENO, Mark. *See* **ALLISON, Clay.**

REPP, Ed(ward) Earl. Also wrote as John Cody; Peter Field. American. Born in Pittsburgh, Pennsylvania, 22 May 1900. Married Margaret Louise Smith in 1925; one son. Newspaperman: reporter and feature writer for Hearst papers and others; screenwriter and publicity director for Warner Brothers, Columbia, and RKO; wrote Westerns using the house name Peter Field. *Died 19 February 1979.*

WESTERN PUBLICATIONS

Novels

Cyclone Jim. New York, Godwin, 1935; London, Wright and Brown, 1936.
Hell on the Pecos. New York, Godwin, 1935; London, Wright and Brown, 1936.
Gun Hawk. New York, Godwin, 1936; London, Wright and Brown, 1937.
Hell in the Saddle. New York, Godwin, and London, Wright and Brown, 1936.
Suicide Ranch. New York, Godwin, 1936; London, Wright and Brown, 1937.
Empty Holsters (as John Cody). New York, Godwin, 1936; London, Wright and Brown, 1937.
Canyon of the Forgotten. London, Wright and Brown, 1950.
Don Hurricane. London, Wright and Brown, 1950.
Hell's Hacienda. London, Wright and Brown, 1951.
Six-Gun Law. London, Wright and Brown, 1951.

Colt Carrier of the Rio. London, Ward Lock, 1952.
Desperado. London, Wright and Brown, 1954.

OTHER PUBLICATIONS

Short Stories

The Radium Pool. Los Angeles, Fantasy, 1949.
Stellar Missiles. Los Angeles, Fantasy, 1949.

Plays

Screenplays: *The Cherokee Strip*, with Joseph K. Watson and Luci Ward, 1937; *The Old Wyoming Trail*, with J. Benton Cheney, 1937; *Prairie Thunder*, 1937; *Devil's Saddle Legion*, 1937; *Cattle Raiders*, with Joseph F. Poland and Folmer Blangsted, 1938; *Outlaws of the Prairie*, 1938; *Call of the Rockies*, 1938; *West of Cheyenne*, 1938; *Rawhide Raiders*, 1941; *The Vigilantes Ride*, 1943; *Saddles and Sagebrush*, 1943; *The Last Horseman*, 1944; *Silver City Raiders*, 1944; *Six Gun Gospel*, with Jess Bowers, 1944; *Trigger Trial*, 1944; *Texas Panhandle*, 1945; *Galloping Thunder*, 1945; *Gunning for Vengeance*, with Louise Rousseau, 1946; *Heading West*, 1946; *Prairie Raiders*, 1946; *Terror Trail*, 1947; *The Lone Hand Texan*, 1947; *The Fighting Frontiersman* (serial), 1947; *The Stranger from Ponca City*, 1947; *Guns of Hate*, with Norman Houston, 1948; *Challenge of the Range*, 1948; *Storm over Wyoming*, 1950; *Rider from Tucson*, 1950; *Saddle Legion*, 1951; *Law of the Badlands*, 1951; *Gunplay*, 1951; *Cyclone Fury*, with Barry Shipman, 1952; *The Kid from Broken Gun*, with Barry Shipman, 1953; and short films.

Television Plays: for *The Lone Ranger*, *Arizona Rangers*, and *Broken Arrow* series.

* * *

Except for the hard-cover format, Ed Earl Repp's writings would qualify perfectly as latter-day dime novels. Telling of range wars manufactured by greedy financiers or the heroic rescue of sweethearts and dependants from captivity, they subscribe to the simplistic morality of dime fiction and they are populated with the same kinds of cardboard characters who die violently by the dozen. There are bloodthirsty heroes, beautiful heroines, incredible physical feats, sensational violence, ritualistic devices, and caricatured dialogue. There is also much unintended comedy.

Repp's first novel, *Cyclone Jim*, tells of a rancher's rescue of a young boy from road agents. The story is full of indiscriminate mythic allusions—a town named Purgatory, a hero referred to as an angel of vengeance—and it firmly adheres to the crudest of stereotypes. The hero is the swiftest man on the draw in 20 states, a long, human wedge with small hands and feet, who always walks with a stiff-legged stride. This is Cyclone Jim: "A man of less intestinal fortitude might have melted and begged for mercy from such an array of enemies that confronted him. But not Cyclone Jim Gale!" He comes from Texas—a good excuse for the author to pepper his speech with exotic *sabe*'s, *pronto*'s and *chiquita*'s. The heroine is a beauty with raven black hair in a white Stetson and the villain a Comanche breed with hairless arms and smelly feet.

Later books do not bring any greater degree of credibility. *Empty Holsters* has a villain, Ace Cain, whose real name seems to be Vulture Vultee and it contains the forgettable challenge by the sheriff, "one uh us is goin' tuh hell because this world ain't big enough fer both." The latest works, *Colt Courier of the Rio* and *Desperado*, constitute a mini-series about a Texas Ranger, Jim Hayfield. They are slightly more artistic and, since they use a hero newly come from college in the east, show some improvement in both the hero's and the author's language. They maintain the same facile level of philosophy, however, as in the dying words of a Mexican to the Ranger: "'I'm not afraid to die now. Funny, isn't it. A man finds himself just when he loses. It's life.' 'One of those things,' agreed Jim soberly."

Repp openly followed production-line techniques, saying that a commercial writer should produce 20 pages of manuscript a day. His novels prove that not only his narrative technique, but his entire authorial procedure, are hangovers from dime novel days. *Hell's Hacienda* is an almost exact copy of his *Hell in the Saddle* from 15 years earlier. The plot, many individual incidents, much of the dialogue, and whole paragraphs are identical. There are only changes in the names and in a few incidental details to justify the later book being sold as a different novel.

Repp introduced no novelty to the genre of the formulaic Western, but he does have a distinctive identity as a curiosity—an unusual, if sometimes unreadable, example of the tenacity of 19th-century dime and pulp methods.

—Christine Bold

REY, Bret. British. Lives in Harwood, Bolton. Address: c/o Robert Hale Ltd., Clerkenwell House, 45-47 Clerkenwell Green, London EC1R 0HT, England.

WESTERN PUBLICATIONS

Novels (series: Ned Butler; Ralph Coates; Will Foreman)

Birth of a Gunman (Coates). London, Hale, 1985.
Stranger in Town (Coates). London, Hale, 1987.
Hold-up (Butler). London, Hale, 1987.
Ned Butler—Bounty Hunter (Butler). London, Hale, 1988.
Railroad Robbers. (Butler), London, Hale, 1988.
Arizona Ambush. London, Hale, 1989.
Trouble Valley. London, Hale, 1989.
The Killing Game. London, Hale, 1990.
Runaway (Foreman). London, Hale, 1990.
Arizona Break-out (Foreman). London, Hale, 1990.
Black Day in Woodville. London, Hale, 1991.
Marshal Without a Badge. London, Hale, 1991.

* * *

Bret Rey's Westerns tend to be brisk and incident-filled, with personable, do-right heroes and black-hearted villains. He handles female characters commendably well, and though his work may not be perfect, he can usually be relied upon to deliver a reasonably well-told and interesting tale. In the main, Rey tells his largely traditional stories in a procession of short sequences, with much unattributed dialogue. He favours brief chapters, rarely depicts sex or violence explicitly (although both often appear by intimation in his work), and apparently prefers to work in a series format, having created three continuing characters in less than a dozen books (although again, he has also written a clutch of unrelated Westerns).

Rey's first novel, the sometimes juvenile but nonetheless interesting *Birth of a Gunman* introduces Ralph Coates, the gun-fast rancher's son, who appears again in 1987's *Stranger in*

Town. *Birth of a Gunman* begins when Ralph finally catches up with the man who raped his sister Jean some months before and, after calling him out, kills him in a gunfight. The matter does not end there, however. Returning home to the family ranch, Ralph finds Jean still as apathetic and fearful of men as she was when he first set out on his vengeance hunt. One possible cure for the girl is a change of scene, so Ralph is given the task of escorting his sister to their aunt's spread in Oregon. The remainder of the book catalogues the adventures they have on the journey (meeting a girl with whom Ralph immediately falls in love, for example, and a brief encounter with a scheming, horse-poor prospector who befriends them, and later tries to make off with their mounts). Neither do these adventures end when they finally reach their destination, for there is still the matter of their uncle's murder to be solved.

Stranger in Town is an equally agreeable tale in which Ralph (now on his way back home to Arizona) befriends an old Mexican rancher named Hidalgo and the man's plain but undeniably sensual daughter Isabelita, who have been experiencing problems with their ranch since refusing to sell out to a neighbouring empire-builder named Brendan Clunie. A number of subplots, including a reconciliation between Hidalgo and his estranged daughter Maria, add some originality to an otherwise well-worn theme, and Rey draws the story to a neat and satisfying conclusion with remarkable confidence.

By the very nature of his profession—bounty hunting—Rey's Ned Butler stories are all variations on the manhunting theme, and as may be expected, this tends to limit both plot and character. When we first meet Butler in *Hold-up*, however, he is a shotgun guard of 12 years' standing. Dismissed following the robbery of 5,000 dollars from his most recent trip from Glenwood to Denver, and consequently unemployed, Butler decides to turn bounty hunter and, if possible, track down the robber who cost him his job. Employing a series of fluid scene shifts, Rey soon begins to introduce the remainder of his cast, which includes Bruce Dawson, the sheriff of Plainsville, Colorado, and the widowed Tabitha Beaumont, a beautiful woman with a dark but not entirely surprising secret. The town and its inhabitants recur in the fairly standard *Ned Butler—Bounty Hunter*, which begins with a bang (as Rey's Westerns usually do) when the Plainsville bank is robbed and Sheriff Dawson is wounded. Recognising the leader of the robbers as a murderer named Charlie Drago, Butler decides to track him down. Before he can leave town, however, he is joined by a local man (who answers to the surprisingly British sobriquet of "Ginger") and the wounded sheriff. What follows is a protracted chase in which a few twists delay the inevitable climax. *Railroad Robbers* is another short story idea stretched out to book-length: this time Butler is after the three outlaws who robbed a train on which he was travelling and killed one of the passengers in the process. Stopping off in a mean little town called Woodline, Butler soon manages to identify the robbers. Before he can set about tracking them down, however, they also arrive in Woodline. He arrests one of them and eventually shoots another, but the third, Elmer Logan, takes the beautiful widow Colleen O'Donnell hostage, and Butler reluctantly has to let him go. How he finally captures the third and final "railroad robber" comprises the rest of a fairly routine adventure.

Technically, Rey is a competent if largely unremarkable writer, although the quality of his work is occasionally lifted by the odd twist of plot or character which suggests a certain degree of preparation before writing begins. Overall, his plots tend to stay well within the previously defined limits of the genre; the hunt for a fortune in stolen greenbacks (*Arizona Ambush*); the mysterious disappearance of some sheepherders (*Trouble Valley*); and an ageing outlaw who wants to put the owlhoot trail behind him (*The Killing Game*) for example. Reminiscent of the Ralph Coates stories (possibly Rey's most entertaining work) are the author's Will Foreman novels, *Runaway*, in which the author's 16-year-old protagonist is forced by circumstances to become a fugitive after killing a man in self-defence, and *Arizona Break-out*, which tells of his attempts to help a young girl whose father has recently been murdered.

—David Whitehead

REYNOLDS, (Richard) Clay. American. Born in Quanah, Texas, in 1949. Educated at the University of Texas, Austin, B.A.; Trinity University, San Antonio, Texas, M.A.; University of Tulsa, Ph.D. Married to Judy Reynolds; one son and one daughter. Lecturer, Lamar University, Beaumont, Texas; Associate Professor of English, and novelist-in-residence, University of North Texas, Denton. Fiction editor, *American Literary Review*, and *New Texas*; associate director, Center for Texas Studies. Address: c/o E.P. Dutton, 375 Hudson Street, New York, New York 10014, U.S.A.

WESTERN PUBLICATIONS

Novels

The Vigil. New York, St. Martin's Press/Marek, 1986.
Agatite. New York, St. Martin's Press, 1986.
Franklin's Crossing. New York, Dutton, 1991.
Texas Augustus. Fort Worth, Texas Christian University Press, 1991.

OTHER PUBLICATIONS

Other

Stage Left: The Development of the American Social Drama in the 1930s (as Richard Clay Reynolds), New York, Whitston Press, 1986.
Taking Stock: A Larry McMurtry Casebook. Dallas, Southern Methodist University Press, 1989.

* * *

Richard Clay Reynolds, whose novels are published under the name Clay Reynolds, began writing fiction after a 10-year career as a professor of English dedicated to producing scholarship and criticism. Reynolds is still a prolific writer of academic papers, articles, and books, but since the middle 1980's he has been mainly thought of as a writer of fiction. His first two novels came out in quick succession, and at least three others are in process of publication as the decade of the 1990's begins.

Like many Texas writers, Reynolds is much concerned with life in the part of Texas he grew up in, and returns to that landscape again and again in his novels and stories. Quanah, Texas, Reynolds's hometown, is named for Quanah Parker, the Comanche chief, whose white mother—Cynthia Ann Parker—was stolen by Indians when she was a small child. Quanah Parker in many ways exemplifies the Texas that Reynolds uses in his fiction. Like Parker, the South Plains of Texas is part savage, part civilized. Hot in summer, bitterly cold in winter, dry when not swept by occasional flash floods. Windy in both summer and winter the South Plains is an unforgiving country, a relentless region.

It is the harshness of the land that informs Reynolds's first two novels—*The Vigil* and *Agatite*—both of which are set in Reynolds's fictionalized Quanah, Texas. In *The Vigil*, a mother and daughter from Georgia are passing through Agatite on the highway that leads from North Texas though the high plains and Panhandle into New Mexico. They stop briefly, and when the daughter goes into the local drug store to buy an ice cream cone, she disappears—never to be seen again.

The mother desperately searches the town for her daughter. The local sheriff looks for the teenage girl until he is sure that she will never be found, and then tries to persuade the mother to accept the fact. But Imogene McBride is stubborn, and from 1948 until the mid 1980's she remains in Agatite, Texas, waiting for the daughter who will never return. Imogene sits on a park bench in front of the courthouse intermittently for the rest of the novel. When her money runs out, she takes a job in a local café, but her leisure time is spent keeping a vigil for the daughter who, we finally learn, is long dead. *The Vigil* is a haunting novel about loneliness and fear and loss, and the refusal of the mother to see reality adds an unsentimental sadness to the novel.

One of the best features of the novel is the sense of place that pervades the work from beginning to end. No matter where the story leads, the reader is never far away from the landscape and the relentless wind and dust that make up so much of west Texas life. The pulsations of life in Hardeman County, Texas, provide the rhythm that underlies the themes of the book.

The same rhythm provides the beat for Reynolds's second novel, *Agatite*. The novel opens in the hottest months of summer, when a corpse is found hanging in an outhouse not far from the town of Agatite. The body of a young woman has been left in the hot and fetid privvy, long enough for wasps to have nested in her mouth.

As in *The Vigil*, the mystery surrounding the crime becomes secondary to the intrigue connecting the characters of the small town as their lives unfold. Roy Breedlove's story provides a counterplot to the investigation of the girl's murder, and links Breedlove's history to the present-day crime and to the 15 or 18 characters involved, both with Breedlove and the lawmen investigating the murder. Breedlove, son of the town drunk, wanders the country for several years before returning to Agatite in the company of desperate men. Back home, he sees all his old schoolmates married and living lives of quiet desperation. The mystery is never solved by the lawmen, though the reader learns who murdered the girl. But the solution of the crime is not a critical factor in the novel, since the crime is simply the hook on which to hang this story of life in a hot west Texas town. Except for an ending that lapses into absurdity when a train blocks main street during a bank robbery, and all the pent-up emotions of the townspeople are unleashed in a free-for-all gunfight, *Agatite* is a very satisfying novel about present-day life on the South Plains.

Reynolds has published a number of short stories about life in Texas among the roughnecks and rednecks, and his novel *Texas Augustus*, is a comic look at a Texan transplanted in New York who suddenly finds that his hometown has disappeared from the map. The loss of his hometown forces him to go back to Texas to find the life he feared was lost.

Another work published in 1991 is *Franklin's Crossing*, a long novel about a wagon train on its way from east Texas to New Mexico. The wagons are being led by Moses Franklin, an ex-slave who is held in contempt by the whites on the wagon train, but who is the only person among them who knows the way West. When the train is attacked by Comanches, Franklin is blamed, though he bore little of the responsibility for the misfortune. The novel is not a story about pioneers "getting through"; it is a ship-of-fools journey that reveals much about the travellers who are making their way toward a promised land.

Despite his late start as a fiction writer, Reynolds is rapidly making a name for himself as a serious novelist. His books have been well received in this country and abroad. Both *The Vigil* and *Agatite* have sold well in Japanese versions and have been favorably noticed in Europe.

—James W. Lee

RHODES, Eugene Manlove. American. Born in Tecumseh, Nebraska, 19 January 1869. Attended University of the Pacific, San Jose, California 1889–90. Married May Davison Rhodes. Guide and government scout during Geronimo uprising, 1886; cowboy, miner and rancher in New Mexico; proprietor of Mutton Hill Farm, Apalachin, New York, 1906–26. *Died 27 June 1934.*

WESTERN PUBLICATIONS

Novels

Good Men and True. New York, Holt, 1910; with *Hit the Line Hard*, New York, Grosset and Dunlap, 1920; London, Hodder and Stoughton, 1923.

Bransford in Arcadia; or, The Little Eohippus. New York, Holt, 1914; as *Bransford of Rainbow Range*, New York, Grosset and Dunlap, 1920; London, Hodder and Stoughton, 1921.

The Desire of the Moth. New York, Holt, 1916; London, Hodder and Stoughton, 1922; with *The Come On*, New York, Grosset and Dunlap, 1920; London, Hodder and Stoughton, 1922.

West Is West. New York, Fly, 1917; London, Hodder and Stoughton, 1921; excerpt, as *Peñalosa*, Santa Fe, New Mexico, Writer's Editions, 1934.

Stepsons of Light. Boston, Houghton Mifflin, 1921; London, Hodder and Stoughton, 1922.

Copper Streak Trail. Boston, Houghton Mifflin, 1922; London, Hodder and Stoughton, 1923.

Once in the Saddle (includes *Pasó por Aquí*). Boston, Houghton Mifflin, 1927.

The Trusty Knaves. Boston, Houghton Mifflin, 1933; London, Wright and Brown, 1934.

Beyond the Desert. Boston, Houghton Mifflin, 1934; London, Wright and Brown, 1935.

The Proud Sheriff. Boston, Houghton Mifflin, and London, Wright and Brown 1935.

Short Stories

The Little World Waddies. El Paso, Texas, W.H. Hutchinson, 1946.

The Brave Adventure. Clarendon, Texas, Clarendon Press, 1971.

Uncollected Short Stories

"The Professor's Experiment," in *Argosy* (New York), December 1901.

"The Hour and the Man," in *Out West* (Los Angeles), January 1902.
"Lubly Ge-Ge and Gruffangrim," in *Out West* (Los Angeles), February 1902.
"Loved I Not Honor More," in *Out West* (Los Angeles), February 1902.
"The Bar Cross Liar," in *Out West* (Los Angeles), June 1902.
"His Father's Flag," in *McClure's* (New York), October 1902.
"The White Flyer," in *Argosy* (New York), December 1902.
"Slave of the Ring," in *Out West* (Los Angeles), June 1903.
"The Blunderer's Mark," in *Out West* (Los Angeles), November 1903.
"A Touch of Nature" (credited to Henry W. Phillips), in *McClure's* (New York), January 1905.
"Sons of the Soil," in *Out West* (Los Angeles), November 1905.
"Sealed Orders," in *Out West* (Los Angeles), July 1906.
"On Velvet," in *Argosy* (New York), September 1906.
"An Interlude," in *Argosy* (New York), October 1906.
"Sticky Pierce, Diplomat," in *Out West* (Los Angeles), October 1906.
"A Pink Trip Slip," in *Out West* (Los Angeles), January 1907.
"Neighbors," in *Argosy* (New York), February 1907.
"Wildcat Represents," in *Argosy* (New York), March 1907.
"Rule o' Thumb," in *Out West* (Los Angeles), June 1907.
"Extra Number," in *Saturday Evening Post* (Philadelphia), 1 June 1907.
"The End of a Story," in *Out West* (Los Angeles), July 1907.
"A Beggar on Horseback," in *Out West* (Los Angeles), November 1907.
"The Awaited Hour," in *Everybody's* (New York), May 1908.
"The Torch," in *Out West* (Los Angeles), August 1908.
"The God from the Machine," in *Redbook* (Chicago), October 1908.
"Check," with Henry W. Phillips, in *Saturday Evening Post* (Philadelphia), 3 October 1908.
"A Neighbor," in *Saturday Evening Post* (Philadelphia), 6 March 1909.
"The May with a Country," in *Saturday Evening Post* (Philadelphia), 3 July 1909.
"Lex Talionis," in *Pacific Monthly* (Seattle), February 1910.
"The House That Jack Built," in *Saturday Evening Post* (Philadelphia), 1 April 1911.
"Of the Lost Legion," in *Everybody's* (New York), April 1913.
"Reversion to Type," in *Sunset* (San Francisco), June 1913.
"A Ragtime Lady," with Lawrence Yates, in *Saturday Evening Post* (Philadelphia), 26 July 1913.
"When the Bills Come In," in *Harper's* (Boston), 13 June 1914.
"How the Dreams Came True," in *Out West* (Los Angeles), February 1916.
"The Ragged Twenty-Eighth," in *McClure's* (New York), June 1916.
"The Miracle," with Lawrence Yates, in *Redbook* (Chicago), July 1916.
"The Prodigal Calf," with Agnes Morley Cleaveland, in *The Silhouette* (Oakland, California), August 1916.
"Putting the Westerner into Fiction," in *Photodramatist* (Los Angeles), December 1922.
"The Civilized Minority," in *Southwest Review* (Dallas), October 1926.
"He'll Make a Hand," in *Sunset* (San Francisco), June 1927.
"The Star of Empire," in *Best Stories from the Southwest 1,* edited by Hilton G. Greer. Dallas, Southwest Press, 1928.
"Beer, Armed Thugs, and Civil War," in *Touring Topics* (Los Angeles), no.12, 1932.
"Geographical Inhumanities," in *Touring Topics* (Los Angeles), January 1933.
"The Hoi-Polloi and the Hoity-Toity," in *Touring Topics* (Los Angeles), February 1933.
"The Scorpion on the Hearth," in *Touring Topics* (Los Angeles), March 1933.
"The Great Tradition," in *Touring Topics* (Los Angeles), April–May 1933.
"Bunk Holidays," in *Touring Topics* (Los Angeles), June 1933.
"The Trouble Man," in *The Arbor House Treasury of Great Western Stories*, edited by Bill Pronzini and Martin H. Greenberg. New York, Arbor House, 1982.

OTHER PUBLICATIONS

Other

Say Now Shibboleth. Chicago, Bookfellows, 1921.
The Best Novels and Stories of Eugene Manlove Rhodes, edited by Frank V. Dearing. Boston, Houghton Mifflin, 1949; abridged edition, as *Sunset Land*, New York, Dell, 1955.
The Rhodes Reader: Stories of Virgins, Villains, and Varmints, edited by W.H. Hutchinson. Norman, University of Oklahoma Press, 1957; revised edition, 1975.
The Line of Least Resistance, edited by W.H. Hutchinson. Chicago, Hurst and Yount, 1958.

*

Bibliography: *A Bar Cross Liar: Bibliography of Eugene Manlove Rhodes Who Loved the West-That-Was When He Was Young* by W.H. Hutchinson, Stillwater, Oklahoma, Redlands Press, 1959.

Critical Studies: *The Hired Man on Horseback* by May D. Rhodes, Boston, Houghton Mifflin, 1938; *A Bar Cross Man: The Life and Personal Writings of Eugene Manlove Rhodes* by W.H. Hutchinson, Norman, University of Oklahoma Press, 1956; *Eugene Manlove Rhodes: Cowboy Chronicler* by Edwin W. Gaston, Jr., Austin, Texas, Steck Vaughn, 1967.

* * *

Eugene Manlove Rhodes's fiction did not conform to the patterned, formula "Western," a matter that perplexed critics and often readers. That they did not conform is because they were and remain hallmarked by fidelity to the times, places, people, and events of his stories. This fidelity came directly from the fact that Rhodes had lived the life he wrote about, lived it for 25 years, and put himself and those he had known into his stories, often not bothering to change names of the characters or places. His life in those years demanded many skills to survive, and Rhodes acquired them; hence he probably is the only one of all those who have written about the West-that-was who could perform the tasks he gave his characters to do. This is the strength of his fiction, that he photographed in color, recorded in faintest intonation, real people, real places, real events that he had known first-hand himself.

Rhodes's strength has concomitant weaknesses, chief among them being his inability to transcend the narrative he was spinning, to go very far beyond the external forces at work on his characters. It is quite true that his life and the life of his characters were dominated by externals, that the frontier parish in which he spent his best years was not the place for navel-gazing nor yet the chanting of mantras. It also is true that Rhodes limned in fiction the values that he held to be those held by the best of the humans he had known as well as by himself—truth, honor, valor, communion with God, fortitude, and magnanimity. The fact remains that while he wrote better, and more truthfully, than his contemporaries, as well as those who came later, about what he knew first-hand and had lived to the hilt, he stops short of greatness.

In Rhodes's frontier years and places, there were but two kinds of women, the good and the bad. He knew them both, but in his fiction you will find only the good woman for romantic interest and you never will find raw sex or the hint of it in his stories. His heroines resemble idealized maidens, genteelly skirting the whirlpools of life, and they have been described as "infrangibly virginal." Blunter criticism has called them "sawdust dolls," and women who "creaked when they moved."

Rhodes's villains, too, veered wildly from those who made the menace in the formula Western, in prose, on film, or fluttering out of the bat cave of television. His basic villains are those who operate inside the legalities to grow swollen and fat from the work and the misfortune of other men. They are distinguished by an appalling greed, and Rhodes uses them as Balzac used misers and Faulkner used the Snopes family to decry the corrosion of cherished values by the acid of cupidity. His villains caused him to be called a "Class Conscious Writer of Westerns," by the *Daily Worker*, perhaps the most egregious of all the critical asininities which Rhodes has suffered. In Rhodes's lexicon, as in his life, there was no such thing as "class" in the Marxist sense. His characters, and especially his protagonists, are existentialists in the best sense of that abused word, for they "stand out from" a society composed of rugged and often ragged individualists. Even as Rhodes, their credo is to be masters of no man and servants of none.

Contrary to the accepted wisdom about the vanished West, and quite contrary to the run-of-the-formula Western, Rhodes's stories are distinguished by their infrequent homicides and by their equally infrequent gun play. In Rhodes's most acclaimed piece of fiction, *Pasó por Aquí*, there are NO shots fired and NO deaths from any cause.

His land and his life had held outlaws, and he later remarked wryly that he had found outlaws better company than in-laws. He learned from Black Jack Ketchum and Bill Doolin, from cherokee Bill Kellum and Francisco Bojórquez, that there was no caste of lawfulness or pigmentation when it came down in life to what a man did when he was caught between a rock and a hard place. So, long before the Good Neighbor policy of the United States, Rhodes refused to type cast the Hispanic-American as the villain, a tradition that had its literary roots perhaps in Kingsley's *Westward Ho*.

As prickly with independence as a porcupine, Rhodes nonetheless knew his land's impositions for survival, and often his protagonist is not an individual but a group of individuals. This *group*, however, does not indulge in *groupthink* or *groupspeak*. When his groups coalesce, they do so because individual survival or true justice demand such banding together. When Rhodes's romanticism overcomes reality, as it sometimes did, his version of group activity bore a striking resemblance to the antics of Athos and friends. Even in these cases, each member of a Rhodesian group has enough iron in his bowels to remain his own whole man without needing to submerge another to retain his wholeness. In this again, Rhodes was true to the years that shaped him, and he once remarked that "The *Star* system never applied on the Open Range."

In his lifetime, Rhodes's fiction was lumped with the mass of formula fiction Westerns, which the literati dismissed then and now as a lamentable error of popular taste. For an added bar sinister, he wrote almost exclusively for *The Saturday Evening Post*, which every right-minded *littérateur* knew was damned beyond redemption by middle-class mores. He has had little more attention since his death, despite the brash pungency of Bernard De Voto's championing and the more careful acclaim bestowed by Walter Prescott Webb and Conrad Richter. Rhodes has been kept alive by those who belong to Arnold Bennett's "passionate few." They sense that Rhodes wrote truly about the life he had lived and loved; they relish his humor which he knew, as did Mark Twain, came from the fact that the frontier forgot to be joyless, and they agree with him that his planet is a good one upon which to spend a lifetime. In short, they say of Rhodes what once was said of De Maupassant: "He was almost irreproachable in a genre which was not."

—W.H. Hutchinson

RHODES, Leland. *See* **PAINE, Lauran.**

RICHARDSON, Gladwell (Grady). Also wrote as George Blacksnake; Ormand Clarkson; Buck Coleman; Laramie Colson; John Haines; Cary James; Calico Jones; Pete Kent; Maurice Kildare; Grant Maxwell; Charles McAdams; Warren O'Riley; Frank Warner; John Winslowe; John R. Winslowe. American. Born in Alvarado, Texas, 4 September 1904. Educated at Oklahoma Agricultural and Mechanical College (now Oklahoma State University), Oklahoma City; Northern Arizona Normal School (now Northern Arizona University), Flagstaff. Served in the United States Navy, 1920–24, and Naval Reserve; also served during World War II and Korean War. Married Millicent Green in 1925; two daughters. Trader at Houck Trading Post, Arizona, 1920, Tuba City Trading Post, Arizona, 1925, Inscription House Trading Post, Arizona; manager, 1935–39, and trader, 1943–45, Flagstaff Indian Pow Wow, Arizona; Reservation census taker, Bureau of Indian Affairs, 1940. Recipient: Western Writers of America Spur award, 1969. *Died 14 June 1980.*

WESTERN PUBLICATIONS

Novels

Two Guns for Arizona. N.p., F.M. Mowl, 1934.
Rio Colorado. London, Ward Lock, 1935.
The Gun Hand. London, Ward Lock, 1936.
Riders of the Long Rope. London, Ward Lock, 1936.
Sun in the West. London, Ward Lock, 1936.
The Black Vulture. London, Ward Lock, 1937.
The Land of Men Unhung. London, Ward Lock, 1937.
Desert Man. London, Ward Lock, 1938.
Roll On, Little Doggies. London, Ward Lock, 1938.
Utah. London, Ward Lock, 1938.
Dreary River. London, Ward Lock, 1939.
Night Riders. London, Ward Lock, 1939.
Spurs. London, Ward Lock, 1940.
Thunder on the Range. London, Ward Lock, 1940.
Range Dust. London, Ward Lock, 1941.
Riders Up. London, Ward Lock, 1941.
The Thin Gunman (as John Haines). London, Wright and Brown, 1941.
Six-Shooter Sheriff (as John Haines). London, Wright and Brown, 1942.
The Jinglebob Ranch. London, Ward Lock, 1942.
The Three Mavericks. London, Ward Lock, 1944.

The Killers of Strawberry Gap. London, Foulsham, 1945.
Eagle's Outlaws. London, Ward Lock, 1946.
Gun Tornado. London, Foulsham, 1946.
Kinky Jordan's Trail. London, Foulsham, 1946.
"Red" Moore on the Trail. London, Foulsham, 1946.
Silver Dollar Basin. London, Foulsham, 1946.
The Singing Sands. London, Wright and Brown, 1947.
Trigger Fingers. London, Wright and Brown, 1947.
Boots and Stirrups. London, Wright and Brown, 1948.
Incident at Pistol Creek. London, Foulsham, 1948.
Mountain Brood. London, Wright and Brown, 1948.
Arizona Ranger. London, Foulsham, 1949.
Death Rides the Little Horn. London, Foulsham, 1949.
The Gun Drifter. London, Coker, 1949.
Hacienda Gold. London, Coker, 1949.
Hangman's Bait. London, Coker, 1949.
The Killer Ghost. London, Wright and Brown, 1949.
The Last Stand. London, Foulsham, 1949.
Queer Trails to Doom. London, Background, 1949.
Short Rope for Rustlers. London, Coker, 1949.
Trail Town. London, Wright Brown, 1949.
Valley of the Powder. London, Coker, 1949.
El Vaquero. London, Coker, 1949.
The Bells of San Felice. London, Background, 1950.
Killer Outlaw. London, Foulsham, 1950.
Rustlers Moon. London, Boardman, 1950.
Shadow Creek. London, Foulsham, 1950.
Slick Ear. London, Foulsham, 1950.
Bad Men of Texico. London, Foulsham, 1951.
Hard Graze. London, Boardman, 1951.
Killers Ride Fast. London, Foulsham, 1951.
Riders of Moondance River. London, Partridge, 1951.
Riders of the Range. London, Partridge, 1951.
Robbery at Poker Bend. London, Gryphon, 1951.
Sagebrush Sal. London, Boardman, 1951.
Six-Horse Stage. London, Foulsham, 1951.
Texas Gun Law. London, Barker, 1951.
Cross Fire. London, Foulsham, 1952.
Mountain Grass. London, Wright and Brown, 1952.
Salt Hills Passage. London, Gryphon, 1952.
Cap Rock. London, Barker, 1953.
Getaway Trail. London, Wright and Brown, 1953.
My Gun Is Tired. London, Gryphon, 1953.
Paradise Range. London, Boardman, 1953.
Quick Trigger. London, Boardman, 1953.
Ranger Round Up. London, Mills and Boon, 1953.
Rider's Road. London, Foulsham, 1953.
Saddle Leather. London, Barker, 1953.
Tophand. London, Wright and Brown, 1953.
Bullet Puncher. London, Lane, 1954.
Horse Thief Trail. London, Jenkins, 1954.
Open Range. London, Mills and Boon, 1954.
Renegades' Den. London, Mills and Boon, 1954.
Spurtin' Lead. London, Foulsham, 1954.
X-Handed Gun. London, Mills and Boon, 1954.
Yesterday's Deadline. London, Barker, 1954.
Bandit Tamer. London, Wright and Brown, 1955.
Desperado's Range. London, W. H. Allen, 1955.
Iron Mountain. London, Barker, 1955.
Lightning Lomax. London, Mills and Boon, 1955.
Night Marshall. London, Foulsham, 1955.
No-Name Range. London, Barker, 1955.
Rattle Your Spurs (as Charles McAdams). London, Barker, 1955.
Gunslick Ramrod (as Cary James). London, Jenkins, 1955.
The .45 Kid (as Cary James). London, Jenkins, 1955.
Rider of Lost Places. London, Jenkins, 1955.
Sorry Cowtown. London, Mills and Boon, 1955.
Buffalo Head. London, Muller, 1956.
Action at Timberlane (as Grant Maxwell). London, Rich and Cowan, 1956.
Hang the Cowboy High. London, Mills and Boon, 1956.
The Jawbone Outfit. London, Wright and Brown, 1956.
Jeopardy Ranch. London, W.H. Allen, 1956.
Mud Walls. London, Barker, 1956.
The Rider of Montana. London, Macdonald, 1956.
Stagecoach 'Round the Bend. London, Barker, 1956.
Gun on the Chugwater. London, Mills and Boon, 1956.
Big Tracks (as Buck Coleman). London, Lane, 1956.
Me, Outlaw. London, Macdonald, 1956.
Cut-Throat Trail. London, Wright and Brown, 1957.
Ride Yonder. London, Mills and Boon, 1957.
Rider from Rifle Rock. London, Wright and Brown, 1957.
Greasewood Sink. London, Mills and Boon, 1957.
Texas Trouble (as Grant Maxwell). London, Long, 1957.
Western Justice. London, W.H. Allen, 1957.
Head of the Draw. London, Muller, 1958.
Lobo Country. London, Muller, 1958.
Cattle Anny. London, Wright and Brown, 1958.
Mesa Springs. London, Barker, 1958.
Monument Pass. London, W.H. Allen, 1958.
Off to Montan'. London, Barker, 1958.
Ride the Last Mile. London, Wright and Brown, 1958.
Rustler Vengeance. London, Mills and Boon, 1958.
Stoney Butte. London, Wright and Brown, 1958.
The Train Robber. London, Barker, 1958.
Two-Bit Puncher. London, Barker, 1958.
Dust Devils. London, Barker, 1959.
Gunfighter in Apache Land. London, Wright and Brown, 1959.
Footloose Cowboy. London, Mills and Boon, 1959.
Phantom Nester. London, Wright and Brown, 1959.
River Rascals. London, Barker, 1959.
Solitary Slim. London, Mills and Boon, 1959.
Tracks West. London, Mills and Boon, 1959.
Lasso. London, Barker, 1960.
Rondo Man. London, Brown Watson, 1960.
Fullhouse Dawson. London, Brown Watson, 1963.

Novels as George Blacksnake

Riders of the Chaparral. London, Clerke and Cockeran, 1950.
Showdown at Unitaw. London, Muller, 1955.
Squaw Trapper. London, Muller, 1955.
Sixgun Pass. London, Muller, 1956.
Wagon Boss. London, Muller, 1956.
Cross Kady. London, Muller, 1957.

Novels as Ormand Clarkson

The Boothill Kid. London, Ward Lock, 1936.
Arizona Guns. London, Ward Lock, 1937.
River of Lost Men. London, Ward Lock, 1937.
Dust on the Sage. London, Ward Lock, 1938.
Gun Thunder. London, Ward Lock, 1938.
River Rogues. London, Ward Lock, 1938.
The Haunted Corral. London, Ward Lock, 1938.
The Scorpion. London, Ward Lock, 1938.
The Kingdom of Mesquite. London, Ward Lock, 1940.
White Horse Mesa. London, Ward Lock, 1941.

Novels as Laramie Colson

The Marshall from Denver. London, Rich and Cowan, 1956.
Wild Cowboy. London, Rich and Cowan, 1956.

Raiders of the San Blas. London, Rich and Cowan, 1957.
Silver Dollar Mine. London, Long, 1958.

Novels as Calico Jones

Foxfire Creek. London, Boardman, 1951.
Prairie Wind. London, Foulsham, 1951.
A Ranger from Texas. London, Partridge, 1952.
Outlaws Two. London, Foulsham, 1953.
Vermilion Outlaw. London, Mills and Boon, 1953.
Bugles Before Dawn. London, Wright and Brown, 1954.
Dancing Rabbit Creek. London, Mills and Boon, 1955.
Six-Shooter Country. London, Mills and Boon, 1956.
Fighting Cowboy. London, Mills and Boon, 1957.
Bullet-Proof Cowboy. London, Mills and Boon, 1958.
Thief Killer. London, Mills and Boon, 1959.

Novels as Pete Kent

The Sunset Rider. London, Wright and Brown, 1937.
The Chief of Hells-Gap. London, Wright and Brown, 1938.
The Blue Hills. London, Wright and Brown, 1939.
Canyon of Hunted Men. London, Wright and Brown, 1939.
Rustler Basin. London, Barker, 1956.

Novels as Maurice Kildare

The Trail to Nowhere. London, Ward Lock, 1938.
Cowboy Joe. London, Ward Lock, 1939.
Rio Guns. London, Ward Lock, 1939.
Border Raider. London, Ward Lock, 1950.
Dude Scanlon. London, Ward Lock, 1950.
Pistol Packer. London, Ward Lock, 1953.
Stormy. London, Mills and Boon, 1955.
Emigrant Gap. London, Mills and Boon, 1955.
Lariat Law. London, Mills and Boon, 1955.

Novels as Warren O'Riley

Unfenced Meadows. London, Barker, 1951.
The Big Star. London, W. H. Allen, 1955.
Forbidding Canyons. London, W. H. Allen, 1955.
Mountain Ambush. London, W. H. Allen, 1957.
Wild Vermilion. London, W. H. Allen, 1958.

Novels as Frank Warner

The Branded Maverick. London, Wright and Brown, 1942.
The Outlaw Kid. London, Wright and Brown, 1942.
Sundown Land. London, Wright and Brown, 1943.
Outlaws of Jade Creek. London, Rich and Cowan, 1954.
Gunman's Town .London, Rich and Cowan, 1954.
Mountain Boss. London, Rich and Cowan, 1954.
Arizona Raider. London, Rich and Cowan, 1955.
Rustlers of Crooked River. London, Rich and Cowan, 1955.
Guns at Shadow Creek. London, Rich and Cowan, 1956.
Vengeance at Oak Springs. London, Rich and Cowan, 1956.
Reach for Your Guns .London, Long, 1957.
Red River Showdown. London, Long, 1959.

Novels as John Winslowe

Sundown. London, Ward Lock, 1939.
The Border Eagle. London, Ward Lock, 1941.
Bad Man. London, Ward Lock, 1950.
Zeb of Rustler Mountain. London, Ward Lock, 1950.
Ranger's Star. London, Ward Lock, 1951.
Marshal of Diablo. London, Ward Lock, 1953.
Red Rock of the YB Ranch. London, Ward Lock, 1953.

Novels as John R. Winslowe

The Marshal of Little Hell. London, Ward Lock, 1936.
The Killer of Kamerun. London, Ward Lock, 1937.
War Horse Range. London, Ward Lock, 1938.
The Rattlesnake Range. London, Ward Lock, 1938.
Thief River. London, Ward Lock, 1938.
Arizona. London, Ward Lock, 1939.
Whispering Mountain. London, Ward Lock, 1939.
Zero Range. London, Mills and Boon, 1954.
Tinhorn Gambler. London, Mills and Boon, 1955.
Dry Gulcher's Creek. London, Mills and Boon, 1956.

OTHER PUBLICATIONS

Short Stories

Strange Tales from Blackwood (as George Blacksnake). London, Blackwood, 1950.

Other

Two Guns, Arizona. Santa Fe, New Mexico, Press of the Territorian, 1968.
Navajo Trader (autobiography), edited by Philip Reed Rulon. Tucson, University of Arizona Press, 1986.

* * *

Texas born, Gladwell Grady "Toney" Richardson is reputed to have written close to 300 novels and almost 1,000 short stories and articles. These include range adventures, historicals, and treasure stories. So as not to saturate the market, Richardson employed various pseudonyms—Charles McAdams came from the use of his grandmother's maiden name, and John Winslowe from the town of Winslow on old route 66. From the outset of his writing career Richardson was helped by his wife, Millie, who would edit and type the manuscripts while he composed the storylines. This husband-and-wife team went on to produce books and articles until several years before Richardson's death in 1980. Much of his life was taken up in running trading posts, and he worked closely with various Indian tribes—the Richardson family were deeply involved with trading in Arizona—and this afforded him a unique position to write authentic nonfiction.

Richardson's first book appeared in serialised form in *Complete Novel* Magazine in 1929, then in hardback in 1934 as *Two Guns For Arizona*, published by F.M. Mowl. Richardson's agent managed to sell the hardback rights for future novels to Ward Lock in England. The books sold well overseas, and his work was soon translated in foreign languages, but he had to be content with the U.S. accepting his magazine works, not his novels.

The strength of Richardson's novels and his many magazine stories is his sense of the Old West. He knew, through his own experiences, the land and the people who inhabited it. His ability to transfer his thoughts into stories shows his understanding of what the reading public were to expect in a Richardson novel.

The action in *Lariat Law* is provided in the task set Lee Hite, the first sheriff of Chota County, in bringing the villainous Prid Esterbrook to justice. In *Emigrant Gap*, written as Maurice Kildare, Richardson relies on two opposing forces to tell his story. On one hand there is the greedy, ruthless cattle baron and on the other, the man who stands in his way.

Although much of Richardson's work is varied thematically, he does tend to rely on ranch settings. *Footloose Cowboy* is a murder mystery, where the foreman of the X 90 range is found knifed to death. *Thief Killer* has a retired law man trying to settle down on the Ten X spread, but rustlers are intent on spoiling his intentions. *The Rattlesnake Range* is another range mystery, with Bland Tonay called in to work out who the mysterious assassin is who leaves a headless rattlesnake as a calling card. Although he tries to create an atmosphere of suspense, Richardson fails to pull it off when he "reveals" the criminal three-quarters of the way into the book. Moreover he introduces a silencer into the story, a rifle with a telescopic sight, and to top that everyone is on the telephone to one another. It doesn't make for a bona-fide Western, more of an out-of-place detective story. *River Rascals* makes for a better read, as Richardson follows the more traditional form of Western. Two cattle barons wage a war of attrition on small cowmen who stand in their way. Two survivors decide to throw in their lot with the R Bar R, the remaining ranch that defies the aggressors. Through clever strategy, the two allies are thrown at each other's throats in open warfare. *Dancing Rabbit Creek* has fine suspense in a clichéd storyline of a determined man in Ted Pace, who fights off thieves intent on stealing his 6,000 head of cattle. They find to their chagrin that Pace is a man who would sooner shoot first, then ask questions.

Another theme Richardson was fond of using was that of outlaws and their gangs. One of the better examples of this is in *Bandit Tamer*, where Morgan Wyatt foils an attempt by bandits to rob the stage on his way into town. His mission is to find his uncle's killer, but he is dogged by the bandits. One by one he eliminates them, until finally he gets his uncle's killer and the leader of the gang. Other outlaw stories appear in *Guns on the Chugwater*, *Sorry Cowtown*, and *Dry Gulcher's Creek*, to name but a few.

Richardson's novels are well-paced adventures. Although his plots are formulaic, his characters keep the reader's attention throughout. He has the gift of manipulating people and showing them in their true light. A fine example of this is in *River Rascals*, when Sheriff Cooley finally realises that he has been supporting the wrong people and the honest, law-abiding citizens force him to do the job he was elected for. He does so with a new outlook on himself, but as usual, he is too late in changing and is killed.

Richardson's central characters are always portrayed as larger-than-life. They are the fastest on the draw, the quickest witted, and always get the woman in the end. The villains are blacker-than-black, more caricatures of evil rather than men with a single aim in mind. Writing at a time when the reader would not expect to see the antagonist outdo the good guy or even to have a greater personal or mental strength, Richardson delivered what was expected of him.

—Mike Stotter

RICHMOND, Roe (Roaldus Frederick Richmond). American. Born in Barton, Vermont, 19 January 1910. Educated at Barton Academy; Orleans High School, Vermont; Dean Academy, Franklin, Massachusetts; University of Michigan, Ann Arbor, B.A. 1933. Married Evelyn d'Este in 1930; one son. Sports editor, *Orleans County Monitor*, Barton, 1933–36; semi-professional baseball and basketball player, Barton, 1934–36; editor and state supervisor, Federal Writers Project, Montpelier, Vermont, 1936–42; inspector, Jones and Lamson Machine Company, Springfield, Vermont, 1942–47; freelance writer, Rutland, Vermont, 1947–55, and 1958–59; proofreader, Alan S. Browne Company, Brattleboro, Vermont, 1955–58; editor and proofreader, S.N.H. Typesetting, Concord, New Hampshire, 1959–72. Since 1972, freelance writer. Recipient: *College Life* prize, for short story, 1935. *Died.*

Western Publications

Novels (series: Lashtrow)

Conestoga Cowboy. New York, Phoenix Press, 1949; London, Clerke and Cockeran, 1951; as The *Utah Kid*, New York, Lion, 1953.
Maverick Heritage. New York, Phoenix Press, 1951; London, Boardman, 1952.
Riders of Red Butte. New York, Phoenix Press, 1951; London, Boardman, 1952; as *The Hard Men*, New York, Pyramid, 1958.
Mojave Guns. New York, Arcadia House, 1952; London, Boardman, 1953.
Death Rides the Dondrino. Boston, Little Brown, 1954; London, Barker, 1957.
Montana Bad Man. New York, Permabooks, 1957.
Wyoming Way. New York, Avalon, 1958.
Lash of Idaho. New York, Permabooks, 1958.
The Kansan. New York, Avalon, 1960; London, Wright and Brown, 1962.
The Deputy (novelization of tv series). New York, Dell, 1960; London, Consul, 1961.
The Wild Breed. New York, Avalon, 1961; as *Legacy of a Gunfighter*, New York, Nordon, 1980; Bath, Chivers, 1987.
War in the Panhandle. New York, Manor, 1979; London, Hale, 1980.
Showdown at Fire Hill. New York, Zebra, 1980.
Rio Grande Riptide (Lashtrow). New York, Nordon, 1980.
Crusade on the Chisholm (Lashtrow). New York, Nordon, 1980.
Hell on a Holiday (Lashtrow). New York, Nordon, 1980; *Carikee Crossfire*, New York, Dorchester, 1980.
Guns at Goliad (Lashtrow). New York, Nordon, 1980; London, Hale, 1983.
Nevada Queen High (Lashtrow). New York, Nordon, 1980.
Life-Line of Texas (Lashtrow). New York, Nordon, 1981.
Staked Plains Rendezvous (Lashtrow). New York, Nordon, 1981.
El Paso del Norte. New York, Ace, 1982.
Saga of Simon Fry. New York, Bantam, 1986.

Uncollected Short Stories

"Duel with Death," in *Five Novels* (New York), May-June 1947.
"The Girl from the East," in *Thrilling Ranch Stories* (London), April 1951.
"The Trap," in *Bar 1 Roundup of Best Western Stories*, edited by Scott Meredith. London, Dakers, 1952.
"Rimrock Revenge," in *Texas Rangers* (London), April 1953.
"Six Guns—Six Graves," in *Exciting Western* (London), November 1953.
"Ride the Wild Trail," in *Western Story* (London), February 1955.
"Pretty Devil," in *Exciting Western* (London), November 1955.
"Derelict's Choice," in *Exciting Western* (London), February 1956.

"There's Always a Chance," in *Thrilling Western* (London), December 1957.
"Roundup," in *Texas Rangers* (London), September 1960.
"The Badman," in *Texas Rangers* (London), January 1961.

OTHER PUBLICATIONS

Novels

Forced Gigolos. Chicago, Novel Books, 1960.
The Blazing Star. Chicago, Novel Books, 1963.
An End to Summer. New York, Nordon, 1980.
The Blaze of Autumn. New York, Nordon, 1980.
Kelleway's Luck. New York, Nordon, 1981.

Other

Island Fortress: The Story of Francis Marion. Philadelphia, Winston, 1952.

*

Manuscript Collection: Western History Research Center, University of Wyoming, Laramie.

Roe Richmond commented (1982):

I grew up with a love split almost evenly between books and sports (especially baseball). My folks were great readers, and wherever we lived the house was full of books. I was fascinated with them, even before I could read. I learned to read early and the enchantment grew, but I still spent plenty of time on the sports field.

The Depression gave me a chance to write and collect hundreds of rejections, because there were no jobs to be had. One year out of school I sold a fight story to a pulp mag, which vanished before I could hit them again. Two years out I won a $250 prize from *College Life*, which also disappeared almost instantly. Three years out I was selling to *Story* and other little quality markets, and one made the annual *Best Short Stories* (1936). Seemed I had a good quick start on a great career, but it didn't turn out that way. I wasn't ready to produce the novel that all the big publishers wanted to see *then.* I struck out with the bases loaded.

I started writing sport stories for the pulps, having a wife and son to support and the Depression still hanging on. Always liked to write action. Lacked the patience for more serious in-depth stuff. I wrote what I enjoyed writing, and that didn't lead to literary recognition and acclaim. On the strength of my experience in Wyoming, I switched to western stories and they became my mainstay. Was doing all right, my name blazoned on the cover of sport and western novels and pulp magazines.

Then television came along, wiping all the pulps and most of the slick mags out of existence, and I had to go back to work. The 1960's were a total loss, so far as writing went . . . I had sold my first book in 1949 (a big thrill), and sold 14 more in the 1950's, but never made much money from them. My agent never pushed them very hard for the better markets, or movie and TV sales. He did not realize what a good writer I actually was, and when I started a comeback in 1972 he wasn't interested in handling my novels.

So I went it on my own, and with the aid of two smart young editors from Yale, Greg Tobin and Sam Tanenhaus, who caught and liked my work at Tower Publications, I did make a comeback at age 70, and have had a dozen books published in the last two years, with more contracted for in the future. I live every novel I write, strive for excellence. There was a lot of solid satisfaction in that, for an old-timer who'd been written off and forgotten 10 years ago, or more. I had done what everyone (but myself) had thought impossible. I am grateful to "whatever gods may be."

* * *

Roe Richmond wrote in a traditional Texas setting but in a very modern idiom which requires plentiful sex and details of violence. The underlying theme of his novels is injustice to the small man and its redress. The history of the Texas Rangers and their role in the protection of homesteaders against local stockmen and rustlers forms an important background to the novels. As distinguished from the traditional sheriff, the Rangers have an important task from the governor to protect the small farmers and restore them to their rightful land.

Richmond wrote with extensive knowledge and a wide vocabulary of western technical words concerned with horse and cattle handling. The novels contain the conventional western stock towns and people, plus some unusual additions such as a wagon train of homesteaders in *War in the Panhandle* and rival freight shippers in *Guns at Goliad.*

The novels sometimes contain unusually deep character studies, such as the revealing portrait of the outcast Curt Metheny in *The Wild Breed* (*Legacy of a Gunfighter*) who is the victim of a broken home. These good studies are unfortunately too rare, and female characters are very slight. *The Wild Breed* also succeeds in its portrayal of the group psychology of the gang. Richmond spoils his success, however, by peopling his books with too many minor characters.

Descriptions of the Texas countryside are, surprisingly, not very vivid, although done with affection, while descriptions of the Texas sky and twilight are long and full of original phrases. Dialogue is effective and true to life, and does not contain the often silly exclamations found in some western dialogue. Plots are often cleverly contrived and skillfully worked up to a violent climax. The element of surprise in *The Wild Breed*, when the bank raid goes wrong and the gang shoot each other, is particularly successful.

Richmond's greatest expertise was in describing the physical effects of violence on the participants. Fist fights rather than gunfights are best done, and detail of the blood and gore is very convincing. He presented a good picture of a rough but slowly civilising territory.

—P.R. Meldrum

RICHTER, Conrad (Michael). American. Born in Pine Grove, Pennsylvania, 13 October 1890. Educated at the Susquehanna Academy and Tremont High School, Pennsylvania, graduated 1906. Married Harvena Achenbach in 1915; one daughter. Teamster, farm laborer, bank clerk, and journalist, in Pennsylvania, 1906–08; editor, *Weekly Courier*, Patton, Pennsylvania, 1909–10; reporter, Johnstown *Leader*, Pennsylvania, and Pittsburgh *Dispatch*, 1910–11; private secretary in Cleveland, 1911–13; freelance writer in Pennsylvania, 1914–27; settled in New Mexico, 1928. Recipient: New York University Society of Libraries Gold Medal, 1942; Pulitzer prize, 1951; American Academy grant, 1959; National Book award, 1960. Litt.D.: Susquehanna University, Selinsgrove, Pennsylvania, 1944; University of New Mexico, Albuquerque, 1958; Lafayette College, Easton, Pennsylvania, 1966; LL.D.: Temple University, Philadelphia, 1966; L.H.D.: Lebanon Valley College, Annville, Pennsylvania, 1966. Member, American Academy. *Died 30 October 1968.*

WESTERN PUBLICATIONS

Novels

The Sea of Grass. New York, Knopf, and London, Constable, 1937.
Tacey Cromwell. New York, Knopf, 1942; with *The Free Man*, London, Boardman, 1944.
The Lady. New York, Knopf, and London, Gollancz, 1957.

Short Stories

Early Americana and Other Stories. New York, Knopf, 1936.
Smoke over the Prairie and Other Stories. London, Boardman, 1947.

OTHER PUBLICATIONS

Novels

The Awakening Land. New York, Knopf, 1966.
The Trees. New York, Knopf, and London, Constable, 1940.
The Fields. New York, Knopf, 1946; London, Corgi, 1958.
The Town. New York, Knopf, 1950; London, Muller, 1951.
The Free Man. New York, Knopf, 1943; with *Tacey Cromwell*, London, Boardman, 1944.
Always Young and Fair. New York, Knopf, 1947.
The Light in the Forest. New York, Knopf, 1953; London, Gollancz, 1954.
The Waters of Kronos. New York, Knopf, and London, Gollancz, 1960.
A Simple Honorable Man. New York, Knopf, and London, Gollancz, 1962.
The Grandfathers. New York, Knopf, 1964.
A Country of Strangers. New York, Knopf, and London, Gollancz, 1966.
The Aristocrat. New York, Knopf, 1968.

Short Stories

Brothers of No Kin and Other Stories. New York, Hinds, 1924.
The Rawhide Knot and Other Short Stories. New York, Knopf, 1978.

Other

Human Vibration: The Mechanics of Life and Mind. New York, Dodd Mead, 1925.
Principles in Bio-Physics: The Underlying Process Controlling Life Phenomena and Inner Evolution. Harrisburg, Pennsylvania, Good Books, 1927.
The Mountain in the Desert: A Philosophical Journey. New York, Knopf, 1955.
Over the Blue Mountain (for children). New York, Knopf, 1967.
Writing to Survive: The Private Notebooks of Conrad Richter, edited by Harvena Richter. Albuquerque, University of New Mexico Press, 1988.

*

Critical Studies: *Conrad Richter* by Edwin W. Gaston, Jr., New York, Twayne, 1965; *Conrad Richter* by Robert J. Barnes, Austin, Texas, Steck Vaughn, 1968; *Richter's Ohio Trilogy: Its Ideas, Themes, and Relationship to Literary Tradition* by Clifford D. Edwards, Ann Arbor, University of Michigan Press, 1970; *Conrad Richter's America* by Marvin J. LaHood, The Hague, Mouton, 1975.

* * *

Conrad Richter has received too little critical attention despite the fact that he won a Pulitzer prize for *The Town* and a National Book award for *The Waters of Kronos*. Three of his 13 novels and a collection of short stories comprise his western fiction, although in Richter's case geography is artificially constricting. The so-called "Ohio trilogy," for example, deals with many of the same frontier problems faced by later pioneers. And *A Country of Strangers* is no less an authentic Indian tale for taking place near Pennsylvania settlements rather than Wyoming ones.

For Richter, oral history was as important as history in books, newspapers, and magazines; his interviews with the men and women who lived the daily life of the Old West provided the details ("those endless small authenticities," Richter called them) that give support to his quiet style. A sumptuous pattern of those details enriches the nine short stories collected as *Early Americana*.

Anthologizers have often been attracted to two of these stories: the title story, "Early Americana," and "Smoke over the Prairie." "Early Americana" concerns the entrance of Laban Oldham into manhood and the difficulty he has in choosing between the life of a farmer and that of a buffalo hunter. His internal conflict is framed by an external conflict between Kiowas and settlers; but the Indian uprising is descriptively muted with all violence suppressed, which rescues the story from the melodramatic.

"Smoke over the Prairie" shows the conflict of the Old West with the New East as symbolized by the characters of Frank Gant, an old-fashioned baronial sheepman, and Vance Rutherford, a construction engineer for the rapidly approaching railroad. Of course, Gant eventually loses the time-honored conflict as old must always yield to new; yet Richter avoids a hackneyed conventionality by being fair to both sides.

A third story, "As It Was in the Beginning," takes place in the Edenic high country between Bent's Fort in Colorado and Taos, New Mexico. A mountain man looking for a wife traces a legend—a white girl reared by the Comanches. He finds her and barters for her; but once restored to white civilization she forces him to court her in the Anglo way. He finally does so, and their marriage is celebrated with a mountain-style hoedown. The bartering scene is one of Richter's most finely executed; it generates narrative excitement at the same time it seems historically accurate and realistic.

The Sea of Grass, Richter's first novel, is thought by some readers to be his best. The narrator is a Westerner, but one who goes east to school, returning periodically to his uncle's ranch in New Mexico. The years and seasons are thus made to pass quickly with maximum contrasts, and at the end of a short narrative we have witnessed the disappearance of the great range. The fortunes of each character in the novel are controlled by the overriding metaphor of the title.

In *Tacey Cromwell* Richter centers his story on the mining town of Bisbee, Arizona. The title character, a former brothel madam turned dressmaker, has the strength of character, the will to succeed, and the human energy to live down her past. The novel contains a number of well-realized scenes: a miner's drilling contest, a school yard fight, a climactic canyon fire. Once again, too, Richter's gift for using authentic history is manifest.

The title character of *The Lady* is Ellen Sessions whose husband and son disappear mysteriously in the midst of a complicated New Mexican feud between cattlemen and sheepmen, between Anglos and Hispanics, and between members of the same family. More important than plot, however, are the beautifully written passages which deal with nature and man's responsible relationship to it, not just to the open grassland but to the desert graveyard and to the animals that inhabit both.

At the moment, Richter is best known for his Ohio trilogy: *The Trees, The Fields, The Town.* But his basic strengths and weaknesses are amply demonstrated in his earlier western fiction. His greatest contribution is his felicitous, graceful, but unpretentious style combined with an affinity for accurate history and a strong sense of detail.

—Robert J. Barnes

RICKARD, Cole. *See* **BARRETT, Geoffrey John.**

RIDER, Brett. *See* **GOODEN, Arthur Henry.**

RIFKIN, Shepard. Also writes as Jake Logan (house name); Dale Michaels. American. Born in New York City, 14 September 1918. Educated at City College (now City College of the City University of New York), 1936–38. Served with United States Merchant Marine, 1942–45. Worked in a variety of jobs, including cab-driver, ambulance driver, gardener, editor, cocktail lounge manager, cook, tugboatman, and manager of the first paperback bookstore in the United States. Full-time writer. Recipient: McDowell Colony fellowship, 1959, 1974; Yaddo fellowship 1972. Agent: Knox Burger Associates Ltd., 39½ Washington Square South, New York, New York 10012. Address: 105 Charles Street, New York, New York 10014, U.S.A.

WESTERN PUBLICATIONS

Novel

King Fisher's Road. New York, Fawcett, and London, Muller, 1963.

Novels as Jake Logan (series: Slocum in all books)

Across the Rio Grande. New York, Playboy Press, 1975.
Slocum's Woman. New York, Playboy Press, 1976.
Slocum's Rage. New York, Playboy Press, 1979.

OTHER PUBLICATIONS

Novels

Texas: Blood Red. New York, Dell, 1956.
Desire Island. New York, Ace, 1960.
What Ship? Where Bound? New York, Knopf, 1961.
The Warring Breed. New York, Fawcett, 1961; as Dale Michaels, London, Gold Lion, 1973.
Ladyfingers. Greenwich, Connecticut, Fawcett, and London, Coronet, 1969.
The Murderer Vine. New York, Dodd, 1970; London, Hale, 1973.
McQuaid. New York, Putnam, 1974; London, Hale, 1975.
The Snow Rattlers. New York, Putnam, 1977; London, Hale, 1978.
McQuaid in August. New York, Doubleday, 1979; London, Hale, 1980.

Other

The Savage Years: Authorized First Hand Accounts of the Bloody Conflicts Between the Whites and the Indians. Greenwich, Connecticut, Fawcett, 1967.

* * *

King Fisher's Road, Shepard Rifkin's best Western, is a book of staggering brutality. When Tom Carson waters his herd on King Fisher's land, he's confronted by one of Fisher's relatives bearing a shotgun. Carson realizes he's about to be killed. With his lightning draw, Carson kills the guard, but now he's on the run from King Fisher. Although Carson almost reaches freedom in Mexico, a Fisher posse captures him. The trip back to Fisher's ranch is one of the most gut-wrenching, horrendous journeys in western fiction. Carson survives—more dead than alive—and discovers he's about to be hung.

At this point in the novel, Rifkin throws the reader a curve: King Fisher—now bored by his ranching empire—sees in Carson the toughness he once had. Fisher spares Carson, helps heal him, and makes him a trusted lieutenant. Carson, his own financial fortunes in shambles, agrees to work for King Fisher. Carson becomes involved in a cattle-for-guns scheme with a Mexican revolutionary general. He meets the beautiful, sultry Luisa de Parral—a captive of the general—and falls in love. But the general takes Carson captive, and he almost dies in another round of beatings and torture, culminating in a scene where a branding iron is held so close to Carson's face he's temporarily blinded.

Fisher's men rescue Carson, who recovers quickly, and salvages the deal of cattle-for-guns with the general who nearly killed him. He manages to get Luisa de Parral away from the general, too. The final shootout is a bit pat, but there's not a dull moment on *King Fisher's Road.*

In Rifkin's Slocum books, written under the house name of "Jake Logan," similarities with *King Fisher's Road* abound. In *Across the Rio Grande*, brutality and sexual energy fuel the plot. Slocum's gang is ambushed by a sadistic sheriff and Slocum, wounded, manages to escape the hanging the rest of his band face. Slocum wakes from a three-week coma and finds himself among a band of Apaches; one of the Apache women lost a son and, when she found Slocum half-dead, decided to try to save him so he could be her son. Slocum stays with the Apaches until he's healed, but he longs for revenge on the sheriff who killed his men and nearly killed him. The rest of the story follows the typical revenge formula, including Slocum's seduction of the sheriff's new wife.

Slocum's Woman features a Mexican general named Ortega, who Slocum hopes to engage in a guns-and-horses deal. This leads to a bank robbery and a train robbery filled with action. But when the train is ambushed by Colonel Escalante, Slocum finds himself in the hands of a master torturer. Slocum's only hope of escape is the French whore, Ghislaine Marchand. The plotting is clever, and the final shootout provides a tidy ending.

Rifkin's Westerns specialize in clever schemes and brutality. These elements also appear in his excellent suspense novels.

—George Kelley

RIGSBY, (Vechel) Howard. Also wrote as Mark Howard; Vechel Howard. American. Born in Denver, Colorado, 11 November 1909. Educated at schools in Berkeley, California; San Mateo Junior College, California, 1928–29; San Jose State College, 1930; University of Nevada, Reno, 1930–31, B.A. 1931. Served in the United States Army Signal Corps, 1941–45: Captain; Army Commendation Ribbon. Married Margaret Eleanor Hunter in 1931 (divorced); two daughters. Freelance writer: reporter, *Nevada State Journal*, Reno, and *Herald Tribune*, Paris, in the 1930's; editor, *Argosy*, New York, 1938. Member of the Board of Directors, Mystery Writers of America, 1959. *Died 7 November 1975.*

WESTERN PUBLICATIONS

Novels

Rage in Texas. New York, Fawcett, 1953; London, Fawcett, 1956.
The Lone Gun. New York, Fawcett, 1956; London, Fawcett, 1957.
The Reluctant Gun. New York, Fawcett, 1957; London, Fawcett, 1958.

Novels as Vechel Howard

Sundown at Crazy Horse. New York, Fawcett, 1957; London, Fawcett, 1958; as *The Last Sunset*, London, Muller, 1961.
Tall in the West. New York, Fawcett, 1958; London, Fawcett, 1960.
Stage to Painted Creek. New York, Fawcett, 1959; London, Muller, 1961.

OTHER PUBLICATIONS

Novels

Kill and Tell. New York, Morrow, 1951; London, Muller, 1954.
Murder for the Holidays. New York, Morrow, 1951; London, Muller, 1952.
Lucinda. New York, Fawcett, 1954; London, Fawcett, 1955.
As a Man Falls. New York, Fawcett, 1954; London, Muller, 1960.
The Avenger. New York, Crowell, 1957; as *Naked to My Pride*, New York, Popular Library, 1958.
Clash of Shadows. Philadelphia, Lippincott, 1959; London, Hale, 1961.
Murder on Her Mind (as Vechel Howard). New York, Fawcett, 1959; London, Muller, 1960.
Murder with Love (as Vechel Howard). New York, Fawcett, 1959; London, Muller, 1960.
A Time for Passion (as Mark Howard). New York, Dell, 1960.
The Tulip Tree. New York, Doubleday, 1963.
Calliope Reef. New York, Doubleday, 1967.

Plays

South Pacific, with Dorothy Heyward (produced New York, 1943).

Television Plays: scripts for *Rawhide* series.

Other

Voyage to Leandro (for children). New York, Harper, 1939.

* * *

Howard Rigsby, better known for his mystery fiction—especially *Lucinda*, selected by the *New York Times* as one of the 10 best mysteries of 1954—produced a small number of western novels notable for their excellence.

Under his own name Rigsby wrote *Rage in Texas, The Lone Gun*, and *The Reluctant Gun.* The best of these is *The Lone Gun*, a powerful story of a man framed for murder and his attempts to clear himself. Brooks Cameron, jailed falsely, escapes with $1000 in gold bounty on his head; the true killer walks free with Cameron's girl, Mary Silk. The intensity of the action grows to the final court scene with its inevitable violent justice.
Rigsby wrote his best western work under the pseudonym of Vechel Howard—a name he constructed from his father's first name and his mother's maiden name. The first Vechel Howard Western is the best: *Sundown at Crazy Horse.* Two violent men, Cassidy and Stribbling, are brought together under an uneasy truce that leads to a deadly showdown in Crazy Horse. It was filmed as *The Last Sunset* with Rock Hudson, Kirk Douglas, and Dorothy Malone. *Tall in the West* is less successful. A bushwhacked cowboy is revived by buffalo hunters but has lost his memory because of the head wound. Much of the book is the story of the wandering of the memoryless hero, but suddenly the author supplies most of the missing pieces to the mystery and the story limps to a disappointing conclusion. *Stage to Painted Creek* packs suspense into every page. A United States Marshal is taking three vicious prisoners on the stage to Painted Creek. During the journey, they are attacked by outlaws, Indians, and Mexicans which forces the Marshal to choose whether to free his prisoners, arming them to fight, with the risk he might get a bullet in the back. This is taut storytelling at its best.

In addition to these fine western novels, Rigsby also wrote television scripts for the CBS Western *Rawhide.*

—George Kelley

RINGO, Johnny. *See* **ALLISON, Clay.**

RINGOLD, Clay. *See* **HOGAN, Ray.**

RIPLEY, Alvin. *See* **KING, Albert.**

RIVERA, Tomas. American. Born in Crystal City, Texas, 22 December 1935. Educated at Southwest Texas Junior College, Uvalde, A.A. 1956; Southwest Texas State College (now University), San Marcos, B.A. 1958, M.Ed. 1964; University of Oklahoma, Norman, M.A. 1969, Ph.D. 1969. Married Concepcion Garza in 1958; two daughters and one son. Teacher of English and Spanish, public schools, San Antonio, Texas, 1957–58, Crystal City, Texas, 1958–60, and League City, Texas, 1960–65; Instructor in English, French, and Spanish, Southwest Texas Junior College, Uvalde, 1965–66; Instructor in Spanish, University of Oklahoma, Norman, 1968–69; Associate Professor of Spanish, Sam Houston State University, Huntsville, Texas, 1969–71; from 1971 Professor of Spanish, University of Texas, San Antonio; associate dean of the College of Multidisciplinary Studies, 1973–76, vice-chancellor of administration, 1976, and vice-president of Academic Affairs, University of Texas, El Paso; Visiting Professor, Trinity University, San Antonio, Texas, 1973; chancellor, University of California, Riverside, 1979–84. Recipient: *Premio Quinto Sol* National Literary award, 1970. *Died in 1984.*

WESTERN PUBLICATIONS

Short Stories

. . . Y no se lo tragó la tierra . . . And the Earth Did Not Part (parallel Spanish and English texts). Berkeley, California, Quinto Sol, 1971.

Verse

Always and Other Poems. N.p., Sisterdale Press, 1973.
The Harvest. Houston, Texas, Arte Publico Press, 1989.

* * *

The achievement of Tomas Rivera does not reside in the number of books he wrote but in the timeliness (and timelessness) of his writing, and in his sensitive and authentic portrayals of mid-20th-century, Chicano migrant workers. Aside from miscellaneous essays and a collection of poetry entitled *Always and Other Poems*, most of Rivera's reputation as a Chicano author and a western writer centers around one book: *. . . Y no se lo tragó la tierra* (*. . . And the Earth Did Not Part*).

Because of that work, appearing as it did in 1971, Rivera's role as a writer helped establish modern Chicano literature on sound footing. Rivera, like Rudolfo A. Anaya, won the important Quinto Sol award and earned much praise both as a Chicano writer and as a Texas writer—for it is the life of the Mexican American living in and around San Antonio, Texas and traveling in the Anglo-American north, in "el norte", which affords Rivera his grand theme.

Critical consensus would claim Rivera as a Chicano novelist, first, classifying *. . . Y no se lo tragó la tierra* as a Mexican-American proletariat, "salt-of-the-earth" novel of the oppressed and downtrodden. Other critical views might choose to see Rivera as a writer of autobiography, an account of growing up "Tex-Mex," or as the teller of short narratives, clustering together around the age-old Hispanic theme of "la tristeza de la vida" (the sadness of life). Others would choose to see him as a poet. And still others would identify him as a Spanish professor at the University of Texas, San Antonio, or an administrator of higher education, for, as a member of the Hispanic minority he did succeed beyond all expectations in the dominantly Anglo-American world of higher education: first as a dean, then as a vice-president of Academic Affairs at the University of Texas, El Paso, and finally, for a few short years before his relatively early death in 1984, as chancellor of the University of California, Riverside.

Each of these "identities," however, is not separate and apart. He was all of these things, and each of them helped to empower him as a spokesperson for his heritage and his people, whose pride and self-worth came from their land, their Southwest, and from their continuing resistance to the debilitating attempts (both Anglo-American and Mexican-American) at exploitation and profiteering which jeopardized not just economic and physical well being but the solidarity of "la raza," of Rivera's people.

Whether one views *la tierra* as a novel, or as an autobiography, or as a grouping of short stories, or as narrative cries of protest, it is a provocative, tragically beautiful, but nevertheless uplifting work. Much of its compelling effect comes from its publication in bi-lingual editions, so that a reader in English can compare the lyricism and harmonies attendant to Spanish—the names, the syntax, the ambience of the indigenous language of the people. It is much to the credit of Rivera that the language itself, the style in either the translation to English, or to Spanish shines forth as testimonial to the linkage which a language provides to culture and geography. Whether for the Chicano or for the Anglo, Rivera's Texas and his characters' migrant routes north to the "promised land" (to beet fields and the melon fields of Utah, Kansas, Iowa, or Minnesota), the southwestern "experience," the feel and awareness of "la tierra," is infused with the Spanish language and with Hispanic/Indian assumptions and values.

La tierra takes its title most directly from a discovery, an epiphany, by the Chicano boy, who in several guises serves as the center of consciousness of all the chapters, all the stories. That discovery comes when, disheartened by all the evil in the world and oppression in his life, he questions the will and existence of God—and the earth does not open to devour him as superstition warned.

That recognition is both disturbing and liberating, and throws the boy back in his anguish on his own desperate isolation and aloneness. And yet it is a modern realization, one that allows him independence from misuse by the church, by capitalism, by all of institutionalized society. He is not at war with the earth, nor it with him; rather they are "part" of each other in reciprocal, inherent ways.

Such a realization is not the only one made by the youth and his counterparts in Rivera's story. In the final chapter, "Under the House," the chapter which integrates the previous, ostensibly disparate chapters, the boy, in hiding, realizes that his alienation is self-imposed; that he could participate in the connections which, if only perceived, exist among all the "parts" of life, all the many, separate people. Although alone, they are also united. He wishes only for the longest of arms so that he might hug, "un abrazo grande," all people at the same time, talk to them, listen to them, respect them simultaneously—all for one, one for all.

That wish, of course, is the wish and the result of Rivera's artistry, and his regard for his racial and cultural kinships represented in all the seemingly despairing, wounded, and lost souls (the maimed, the burned, the murdered, the exhausted, the fearful, the illiterate), restored and reanimated out of his memory into the "literature" and "love" of *. . . y no se lo tragó la tierra*.

It is the wish, also, of much of Rivera's poetry, expressed in the sonorities and cadences of his sobering but still hopeful lyricism: "Los cuentos contados/son los suenos sonados/de pasos contentos/de sienes repletas"—the contented stories, the sounding dreams, the contented steps, the temples repleat" of young and old, "De Nino, De Joven, De Viejo."

—Robert F. Gish

ROAN, Tom. Also wrote as Adam Rebel. American. Grew up in Alabama. Served in the United States Army in Hawaii and Far East. Married to Mollie Tannahill; one daughter. Worked with circus from age 14; company detective, San Francisco, California; deputy sheriff, Brannock County, Idaho. *Died in 1958.*

WESTERN PUBLICATIONS

Novels

Whispering Range. New York, King, 1934; London, Nicholson and Watson, 1935.
Montana Outlaw. New York, King, 1934; London, Nicholson and Watson, 1935.
The Rio Kid. New York, Godwin and London, Nicholson and Watson, 1935.
Smoky River. New York, Godwin, and London, Nicholson and Watson, 1935.
Roaring Frontier. London, Nicholson and Watson, 1937.
Riverboat Gambler. London, Nicholson and Watson, 1938.
Gun Lord of Silver River. London, Wright and Brown, 1943.
The Gun Ghost. London, Foulsham, 1952.
Gamblers in Gunsmoke. New York, Abelard Press, 1952; London, Abelard Schuman, 1960.
Lawless Old Wyoming. London, Foulsham, 1952; as *Wyoming Gun*, New York, Dell, 1955.
Outlaw in the Saddle. New York, Dodd Mead, and London, Wright and Brown, 1953.
Stable Boy (as Adam Rebel). New York, Beacon Publications, 1954.
Thunder in the Valley. London, Ward Lock, 1955.
Rawhiders. Rockville Centre, New York, Zenith, 1958.

Uncollected Short Stories

"Strictly Crooked," in *West* (New York), 24 September 1927.
"Untamed," in *Cowboy Story* (London), October 1927.
"Inferno Island," in *West* (New York), 1 October 1927.
"The Come-Back," in *North-West Stories* (London), Early December 1927.
"Gun Law," in *West* (New York), 10 December 1927.
"Black Mecca," in *West* (New York), 14 January 1928.
"Riders of the Night," in *West* (New York), 24 March 1928.
"Black Lightning," in *West* (New York), 26 May 1928.
"Accordin' to Law," in *West* (New York), 28 July 1928.
"Monkey Business,"in *West* (New York), 27 October 1928.
"Gun Fodder," in *West* (New York), 10 November 1928.
"Horsethief Pass," in *West* (New York), 2 October 1929.
"Wanted Men," in *West* (New York), 11 June 1930.
"Wolf Creek Crossing," in *West* (New York), 10 December 1930.
"The Texas Kid," in *West* (New York), 18 February 1931.
"Lonesome Range," in *Western Romances* (New York), May 1931.
"The Sheriff of Wolf River," in *West* (New York), 13 May 1931.
"Wyoming," in *West* (New York), 31 August–28 September 1932.
"Badmen," in *West* (New York), February 1933.
"Rawhide River," in *West* (New York), November 1933.
"Hangman's Rope," in *All Western* (New York), January 1934.
"Sheep Country," in *A Century of Western Stories*, edited by George Goodchild. London, Hutchinson, 1936.
"Danger River," in *All Western* (New York), July 1936.
"The Two-Gun Sheriff of Painted Rock," in *All Western* (New York), October 1936.
"Devil Mountain," in *All Western* (New York), December 1936.
"Hellaflyin' Hits Hoss Heaven," in *All Western* (New York), May 1938.
"Gun Raiders of Devil River," in *All Western* (New York), July 1938.
"Two-Gun Trouble-Shooter," in *All Western* (New York), August 1938.
"A Sheriff for Breakfast," in *Western Story* (New York), 17 September 1938.
"White Terror," in *Western Story* (New York), 1 October 1938.
"Buzzards Wait at Los Chinos," in *Western Story* (New York), 22 October 1938.
"The Gun Ghost of the Rio," in *Western Story* (New York), 5 November 1938.
"Boothill Pact," in *Western Story* (New York), 10 December 1938.
"Fang Law," in *Western Story* (New York), 7 January 1939.
"Tombstone Justice," in *Western Story* (New York), 28 January 1939.
"Funeral Mountain," in *Western Story* (New York), 18 February 1939.
"Caves of Damnation," in *Western Story* (New York), 11 March 1939.
"Red Gods Ride," in *Western Story* (New York), 25 March 1939.
"Breed of the Out-Trails," in *Western Story* (New York), 15 April 1939.
"Gunsmoke of the Dead," in *Western Story* (New York), 20 May 1939.
"Buzzards Never Crop Their Wings," in *Western Story* (New York), 27 May 1939.
"Boomtown Buckaroos," in *Western Story* (New York), 10 June 1939.
"Battle Monarch," in *Western Story* (New York), 8 July 1939.
"Gunsmoke Roundup," in *Western Story* (New York), 29 July 1939.
"Clan Call," in *Western Story* (New York), 19 August 1939.
"Rancho del Diablo," in *Western Story* (New York), 23 September 1939.
"Hangtown," in *Western Story* (New York), 4 November 1939.
"Death Song," in *Western Story* (New York), 18 November 1939.
"Indian Country," in *Western Story* (New York), 6 January 1940.
"The Bullwhip Man-Breaker," in *Star Western* (Chicago), February 1940.
"Bullwhip Bill's Blacksnake Tonic," in *Star Western* (Chicago), March 1940.
"Hell Served Hot for Bullwhip Bill," in *Star Western* (Chicago), April 1940.
"Gun Ghosts from Boothill," in *Western Story* (London), May 1940.
"Gunsmoke Gentlemen," in *Western Story* (London), August 1940.
"Common Ground," in *Adventure* (New York), September 1940.

"The Gringo Kid," in *Wild West* (New York), 28 September 1940.
"Grizzly on the Prod," in *Wild West* (New York), 18 January 1941.
"Reformation of the Two-Man Wild Bunch," in *Dime Western* (New York), March 1941.
"Squatters in Gunsmoke," in *Wild West* (New York), 15 March 1941.
"Fighting Frontier," in *Western Story* (London), April 1941.
"Bullet SOS to Heck Kilada," in *Star Western* (Chicago), May 1941.
"To Hell—or Hang!," in *Wild West* (New York), 10 May 1941.
"Sun God Valley," in *Wild West* (New York), 19–26 July 1941.
"Bullwhip Bill Returns!," in *Star Western* (Chicago), August 1941.
"Bullwhip Bill—Outlaw Buster," in *Star Western* (Chicago), September 1941.
"Bullwhip Bill's Skull Canyon Purgatory," in *Star Western* (Chicago), November 1941.
"Bullwhips for Purgatory," in *Star Western* (Chicago), February 1942.
"Black Drought—Red Guns!," in *Star Western* (Chicago), March 1942.
"Gun's Up—Here's Bullwhip Bill!," in *Star Western* (Chicago), April 1942.
"Smoky Salvation for Hang-Town Sinners," in *Star Western* (Chicago), May 1942.
"War-Song of the Bullwhip," in *Star Western* (Chicago), February 1943.
"Horned God of Battle," in *Dime Western*, March 1943.
"The Clean-Up at Gopher Flats," in *Star Western* (Chicago), April 1943.
"Gun-Gambler of the Big Muddy," in *Dime Western*, April 1943.
"Outcast in Buckskin," in *Star Western* (Chicago), May 1943.
"The Bullwhip Bonanza," in *Star Western* (Chicago), June 1943.
"The Devil's Mountaineers," in *Star Western* (Chicago), July 1943.
"Death-Song of the Flying J," in *Star Western* (Chicago), August 1943.
"The Gun-Gospel of Wolf Valley," in *West* (Kingswood, Surrey), August 1943.
"Guns Up for the Rafter Cross!," in *Star Western* (Chicago), September 1943.
"The Bullwhip Revolution," in *Star Western* (Chicago), October 1943.
"Death Song of the Bullwhip," in *West* (Kingswood, Surrey), October 1943.
"Lawless Law Hits San Gabriel," in *Star Western* (Chicago), November 1943.
"The Death Herd Legion Rides Tonight," in *Star Western* (Chicago), December 1943.
"Don Amadeo and the Devil," in *West* (Kingswood, Surrey), December 1943.
"Bullwhip Goes to Hell!," in *West* (Kingswood, Surrey), January 1944.
"The Town They Couldn't Tame," in *Star Western* (Chicago), March 1944.
"Wild Man in Buckskin," in *Star Western* (Chicago), April 1944.
"Bullwhip Hauls the Mail," in *West* (Kingswood, Surrey), April 1944.
"Roll 'em Through to Hellfire!," in *Star Western* (Chicago), May 1944.
"Rainbow River Runs Red," in *Star Western* (Chicago), June 1944.
"Blood and Bullets Build a Town," in *West* (Kingswood, Surrey), June 1944.
"Bullwhip Bill—Gunsmoke Judge-and-Jury," in *Star Western* (Chicago), August 1944.
"Satan Swings a Bullwhip," in *West* (Kingswood, Surrey), August 1944.
"No Law West of Funeral Bend," in *Star Western* (Chicago), September 1944.
"Jackass Whiskey Rebellion," in *West* (Kingswood, Surrey), October 1944.
"Hell's Loose in Pistol Pass!," in *Star Western* (Chicago), December 1944.
"Bullwhip Bill's Holiday in Hell," in *Star Western* (Chicago), January 1945.
"Bullwhip Bill's Hang-Tree Special," in *Star Western* (Chicago), February 1945.
"Head North to Wilderness Hell!," in *Star Western* (Chicago), March 1945.
"Outcast in Buckskin," in *West* (Kingswood, Surrey), March 1945.
"Outlaws Guard the Treasure Trail," in *Star Western* (Chicago), April 1945.
"Men That the Law Forgot!," in *Star Western* (Chicago), May 1945.
"Bullwhip Hell Hits Peace Pipe!," in *Star Western* (Chicago), June 1945.
"Dead Man's Canyon Lives Again," in *Big-Book Western*, June 1945.
"The Bullsnake Bend Rebellion," in *Star Western* (Chicago), July 1945.
"The Deadwood Kid's Last Fight," in *Star Western* (Chicago), August 1945.
"Doc Jaw's Owlhoot Pardner," in *Star Western* (Chicago), November 1945.
"Gun-Boss of Wipe-Out Range," in *Big-Book Western*, July 1947.
"Funeral Bend Greets the Devil," in *10 Story Western* (New York), August 1948.
"Hell's Trading Post Goes Mad," in *.44 Western*, January 1949.
"Hell-on-the-Law!," in *Big-Book Western*, February 1949.
"The Horsethief War," in *.44 Western*, March 1949.
"The Devil Rides the Death-Watch," in *Ace High Western Stories* (London), 1950(?).
"Forbidden Range," in *Western Story* (London), July 1950.
"Fight for Your Mate," in *Exciting Western* (London), August 1952.
"To Hell with Cow Pools," in *Exciting Western* (London), December 1952.
"Bully of the Town" and "Fighting Fool," in *Fifty Thrilling Wild West Stories*. London, Odhams Press, 1953.
"The Kid from Montana," in *Exciting Western* (London), June 1953.
"Hell Moves to Montana," in *Exciting Western* (London), September 1953.
"The Man from Calico Creek," in *Exciting Western* (London), November 1953.
"From Texas—to Hell," in *Exciting Western* (London), April 1954.
"Trail of the White Death," in *Western Story* (London), June 1955.
"Montana Showdown," in *Exciting Western* (London), April/May 1956.
"Fur Raiders of Hell's Frozen Pocket," in *Western Story* (London), August 1961.
"Bull of the Woods," in *Western Story* (London), September 1961.

"Trouble in the North," in *Texas Rangers* (London), December 1961.
"Gun-Devil of Red God Desert," in *Westerns of the 40's*, edited by Damon Knight. Indianapolis, Bobbs Merrill, 1977.

OTHER PUBLICATIONS

Novels

The Dragon Strikes Back. New York, Messner, and London, Melrose, 1936.
Slave Girl. New York, Falcon, 1952.
The Blue Dragon of Fan Wong. London, Mellifont Press, 1953.
Greedy Fingers. London, Mellifont Press, 1953.
Perils of the Barbary Coast. London, Mellifont Press, 1953.

* * *

A former peace officer who grew up in a lawless section of Alabama, where the towns had such names as Slick Lizard Ridge and Bloody Beat 22, Tom Roan was one of the more notorious pulp writers of the 1930's and 1940's. He had a reputation for being opinionated, tough-minded, flamboyant, and eccentric—in short, a character. (Damon Knight, a former editor with the Popular Publications line of pulps, has written that Roan made occasional visits to editorial offices wearing a ten-gallon hat and cussing like a mule-skinner.)

For close to 30 years, Roan produced hundreds of western stories for all the leading magazines in the field, as well as occasional mystery and adventure tales. In keeping with his personality, these stories are generally characterized by outrageous plot devices (e.g., a secret stronghold in the Sierra Nevadas, replete with subterranean passageways, built by a group of villainous Chinese bent on revenge against local ranchers and townspeople), wildly improbable situations, and some of the more lurid writing ever to appear in the western category.

Roan's novels are a bit more restrained, although *Smoky River*, *The Rio Kid*, *Outlaw in the Saddle* (starring the Apache Kid and Oregon Ike), and *Rawhiders*, among others, contain considerable amounts of the sensational and the improbable. Villainous and stereotypical Chinese, who seem to have been a source of endless fascination for Roan, also appear in such titles as *The Dragon Strikes Back*, *The Blue Dragon of Fan Wong*, and *Slave Girl*.

By today's standards, Roan's work is high camp. Nevertheless, it has tremendous energy and narrative drive, a fast and furious pace, and can be enjoyable to read if taken in carefully measured doses.

—Bill Pronzini

ROARK, Garland. *See* **GARLAND, George.**

ROBERTS, Dan. *See* **ROSS, W.E.D.**

ROBERTS, Elizabeth Madox. American. Born in Perryville, Kentucky, 30 October 1881. Educated at Covington Institute, Springfield, Kentucky; Covington High School, Kentucky, 1896–1900; State College of Kentucky (now University of Kentucky), Lexington, 1900–01, 1916; University of Chicago (McLaughlin prize; Fiske prize, 1921), 1917–21, Ph.B. in English 1921 (Phi Beta Kappa). Private tutor and teacher in public schools, Springfield, 1901–10. Recipient: O. Henry award, 1930. L.H.D.: Russell Sage College, Troy, New York, 1933. Member, American Academy, 1940. *Died 13 March 1941.*

WESTERN PUBLICATIONS

Novels

The Time of Man. New York, Viking Press, 1926; London, Cape, 1927.
My Heart and My Flesh. New York, Viking Press, 1927; London, Cape, 1928.
Jingling in the Wind. New York, Viking Press, 1928; London, Cape, 1929.
The Great Meadow. New York, Viking Press, and London, Cape, 1930.
A Buried Treasure. New York, Viking Press, 1931; London, Cape, 1932.
He Sent Forth a Raven. New York, Viking Press, and London, Cape, 1935.
Black Is My Truelove's Hair. New York, Viking Press, 1938; London, Hale, 1939.

Short Stories

The Haunted Mirror. New York, Viking Press, 1932; London, Cape, 1933.
Not by Strange Gods. New York, Viking Press, 1941.

Verse

In the Great Steep's Garden. Colorado Springs, Gowdy Simmons, 1915.
Under the Tree (for children) New York, Huebsch, 1922; London, Cape, 1928; revised edition, New York, Viking Press, 1930.
Song in the Meadow. New York, Viking Press, 1940.

*

Manuscript Collection: Library of Congress, Washington, D.C.

Critical Studies: *Elizabeth Madox Roberts: A Personal Note* by Glenway Wescott, New York, Viking Press, 1930; *Elizabeth Madox Roberts: An Appraisal* by J. Donald Adams and others, New York, Viking Press, 1938; *Elizabeth Madox Roberts, American Novelist* by Harry Modean Campbell and Ruel E. Foster, Norman, University of Oklahoma Press, 1956; *Herald to Chaos: The Novels of Elizabeth Madox Roberts* by Earl Rovit, Lexington, University Press of Kentucky, 1960; *Elizabeth Madox Roberts* by Frederick P.W. McDowell, New York, Twayne, 1963 (includes bibliography).

* * *

The philosophic idealism of Bishop Berkeley, the realistic conventions of regional fiction, and a poetic talent for rendering sensuous impressions are the unlikely ingredients that conjoin in the making of Elizabeth Madox Roberts's novels. Her characteristic way of harmonizing these disparate materials is through the focus of an introspective woman who serves as narrator–protagonist—a controlling consciousness that shapes the contours of her own growing personality and those of the outside world, interactively and simultaneously. Two of Roberts's novels, *The Time of Man* and *The Great Meadow*, attained considerable success when they were originally published. The first chronicles the sensibility of a Kentucky girl, Ellen Chesser, whose experience as a migrant farm wife is measured by the eternal cycles of poverty, labor, and the universal portions of grief, pain, joy, and love. Deliberately conceived on the model of the *Odyssey*, *The Time of Man* aims at a kind of epic quality in its unsentimental depiction of the struggle between creative life instincts and the implacable limitations of the human condition. *The Great Meadow* reworks this theme, but its heroine, Diony, is a more sophisticated consciousness; she is aware of herself and her role, and the journey motif does not comprise the 20-year wanderings of an impoverished farm family, but the great western trek from Virginia to the founding of Kentucky in the late 18th century. Both novels allowed Roberts to develop and display her strengths as a novelist: a supple, lyrical prose style, admirably suited to the particular feminine sensibility that she espoused; a sense of rhythmical narrative structure that moves in slow, undramatic accretions of episodic action; and an unforced, natural symbolism infusing the texture of events.

Although these two novels are regarded as Roberts's major achievements, *My Heart and My Flesh* and *He Sent Forth a Raven* are scarcely less accomplished. The first was meant to be an antithetical sequel to *The Time of Man*, the protagonist, in this case, being stripped of all buffers against adversity only to assert an indomitable will to live. The second is Roberts's most ambitious effort: *He Sent Forth a Raven* invokes the allegorical grandeur of the biblical story of Noah and of *Moby-Dick*, and, although the novel is not entirely able to control its materials, it is rich in meaning and strangely powerful. Roberts also wrote three other novels, two collections of short stories, and three volumes of poetry. Her poems—fresh, vivid, and marked by their capacity to record a direct sensuous immediacy—are frequently anthologized in collections of verse for children.

—Earl Rovit

ROBERTS, J.R. *See* **RANDISI, Robert J.**

ROBERTS, John. *See* **BINGLEY, David Ernest.**

ROBERTS, Wayne. *See* **OVERHOLSER, Wayne D.**

ROBERTSON, Frank C(hester). Also wrote as Robert Crane; Frank Chester Field. American. Born in Moscow, Idaho, 12 January 1890. Educated in elementary schools. Married Winnie Bowman in 1919; one son. Worked as ranchhand, sheepherder, construction worker, and homesteader; then freelance writer: columnist ("The Chopping Block"), Provo *Daily Herald*, Utah 1942–69. President, Western Writers of America. Recipient: Western Writers of America Spur award, for children's book, 1953; Headliners award, for nonfiction, 1956. *Died 29 July 1969.*

WESTERN PUBLICATIONS

Novels

The Foreman of the Forty-Bar. New York, Barse and Hopkins, 1925; London, Collins, 1927.
The Clean-Up on Deadman. New York, Garden City Publishing Company, 1926; as Robert Crane, London, Newnes, 1937.
The Outlaws of Flower-Pot Canyon. New York, Garden City Publishing Company, 1926.
The Boss of the Tumbling H. New York, Barse and Hopkins, 1927; London, Collins, 1928.
On the Trail of Chief Joseph. New York, Appleton, 1927.
The Fall of Buffalo Horn. New York, Appleton, 1928.
The Man Branders. New York, Barse, 1928; London, Collins, 1930.
The Boss of the Flying M. London, Collins, 1928.
The Boss of the Ten Mile Basin. London, Collins, 1928.
The Boss of the Double E. London, Collins, 1928.
Brand of the Open Hand. New York, Novel Selections, 1928; London, Collins, 1929.
The Far Horizon. London, Collins, 1929.
The Hidden Cabin. London, Collins, 1929.
The Silver Cow. New York, Barse, 1929; London, Collins, 1930.
Clawhammer Ranch. New York, Barse, 1930.
Riders of the Sunset Trail. London, Collins, 1930.
Wildhorse Henderson. London, Collins, 1930.
The Bandit of Bayhorse Basin. London, Collins, 1931.
Deadman's Grove. London, Collins, 1931.
The Mormon Trail. London, Collins, 1931.
The Range Defender. London, Collins, 1931.
We Want That Range. New York, Barse, 1931.
The Fight for River Range. New York, Barse, and London, Collins, 1932.
Outlaw's Trail. London, Collins, 1932.
Prairie Princess. London, Collins, 1932.
Red Rustlers. New York, Readers Choice, and London, Collins, 1932.
Shoot-Up! London, Collins, 1932.
The Powder Burner. London, Collins, 1932; New York, Washburn, 1935.
The Trouble Grabber. New York, Washburn, 1932.
Back to the West. London, Collins, 1933.
Cowboy Courage. London, Collins, 1933.
Freewater Range. New York, Washburn, and London, Collins, 1933.
Larruping Leather. New York, Washburn, 1933; as *Song of the Leather*, London, Collins, 1933.
Outlaw Ranch. New York, Washburn, 1934; as *Renegade Riders*, London, Collins, 1934.
Ex-Rustler. London, Collins, 1934.
Range Justice. London, Collins, 1934.
Wild Riding Hunt. New York, Washburn, 1934.
Brothers of the Range. London, Collins, 1935.
Forbidden Trails. New York, Washburn, 1935.
The Rocky Road to Jericho (as Frank Chester Field). New York, Curl, 1935; London, Allan, 1936.

Trail Boss. London, Collins, 1935.
Bandits of the Barrens. London, Collins, 1936; as *Feud at Blue Canyon*, New York, Belmont, 1963.
Branded Men. New York, Dodge, 1936.
Randy of Roaring River. London, Collins, 1936.
Silver Zone. New York, Greenberg, and London, Collins, 1936.
The Outlaw of Antler. New York, Dutton, and London, Collins, 1937.
Moose River Range. London, Collins, 1937; as *Thunder on the Range*, New York, Dutton, 1938.
The Pride of Pine Creek. New York, Dutton, 1938; as *Range Rebellion*, London, Collins, 1938.
Look Out for Outlaws. London, Collins, 1938.
Round Up and Trail. London, Collins, 1938; as *Fighting Jack Warbonnet*, New York, Dutton, 1939.
Rip Roarin' Rincon. New York, Dutton, 1939; as *Bullets for Silver*, London, Collins, 1939.
The Cabin in the Canyon. London, Collins, 1939; as *Cowboy Comes A-Fightin'*, New York, Dutton, 1940.
The Firebrand from Burnt Creek. New York, Dutton, and London, Collins, 1940.
Rifle Law. London, Collins, 1940.
Poison Valley. New York, Dutton, 1941; as *Pilgrims of Poison Valley*, London, Collins, 1941.
Snake River to Hell. New York, Dutton, 1941; as *Outlaw Country*, London, Collins, 1941.
Cowman's Jack-Pot. New York, Dutton, 1942; as *Greener Grows the Grass*, London, Collins, 1942.
Vigilante War in Buena Vista. New York, Dutton, 1942; as *The Roaring Sixties*, London, Collins, 1942.
Grizzly Meadows. New York, Dutton, 1943; as *Rustlers on the Loose*, London, Collins, 1943.
Kingdom for a Horse! London, Collins, 1943.
Getley's Gold. New York, Dutton, and London, Collins, 1944.
The Noose Hangs High. London, Collins, 1944; New York, Dutton, 1945.
Round-Up in the River. New York, Dutton, and London, Collins, 1945.
The Lost Range. New York, Dutton, 1946; as *Hoof-Beats in the Night*, London, Collins, 1946.
Boomerang Jail. New York, Dutton, and London, Collins, 1947.
Man Bait. London, Collins, 1948.
Rope Crazy. New York, Dutton, and London, Collins, 1948.
The Longhorns of Hate. New York, Dutton, 1949.
The Sheriff of Crow Country. London, Collins, 1949.
The Way of an Outlaw. London, Collins, 1949.
The Road to Paint Rock. London, Collins, 1950.
Wrangler on the Prod. New York, Dutton, 1950; as *Quicker on the Draw*, London, Collins, 1950.
Hangman of the Humbug. New York, Dutton, 1951.
Idaho Range. London, Collins, 1951.
Riders Against the Sky. London, Collins, 1951.
Reach for the Skies. London, Collins, 1952.
Saddle on a Cloud. New York, Dutton, and London, Collins, 1952.
Crooked Water. London, Collins, 1953.
Ride Out and Die. London, Collins, 1953.
The Cruel Winds of Winter. London, Collins, 1954.
The Double Brand. London, Collins, 1954.
Horn Silver. London, Collins, 1955.
Rock River Feud. London, Collins, 1955.
Squatter's Rights. London, Collins, 1956.
Boot Hill Bound. London, Collins, 1957.
Disaster Valley. New York, Ballantine, and London, Collins, 1957.
Lawman's Pay. New York, Ballantine, 1957.
The Young Nighthawk. London, Collins, 1957.
Deadhorse Mesa. London, Collins, 1958.
The Bandits of Crown Cliffs. London, Collins, 1959.
Wagon Trail to Danger. London, Collins, 1959.
The Poker Game. London, Collins, 1960.
Rawhide. New York, New American Library, 1961; London, Fontana, 1963.
Hornet Creek. London, Collins, 1962.
Cariboo. London, Collins, 1962.
A Man Called Paladin. New York, Macmillan, 1963.
Fugitives of Green Valley. London, Collins, 1963.
Showdown. London, Collins, 1963.
Hoodlums at Hogup. London, Collins, 1964.
Wayland's Law. London, Collins, 1964.
Sheriff's Deputy. London, Collins, 1965.
Windy Jake's Legacy. London, Collins, 1965.
Bullets on the Blackfoot. London, Collins, 1966.
The Bud Valley Bible. London, Collins, 1966.
Outlaw Sanctuary. London, Collins, 1967.
The Valley of Frightened Men. London, Collins, 1967.

Novels as Robert Crane

Thunder in the West. New York, Appleton, and London, Bles, 1934.
Wild Blood. New York, Godwin, and London, Newnes, 1935.
Stormy Range. London, Newnes, 1935; New York, Godwin, 1936.
Deadman's Canyon. London, Newnes, 1936.
Freedom of the Range. London, Newnes, 1936.
Squaw Pass War. London, Newnes, 1936.
Trigger Artist. London, Newnes, 1936.
Too Many Brands. London, Newnes, 1937.
Blocked Trails. London, Newnes, 1937.
Cache at Flower-Pot Canyon. London, Newnes, 1937.
The Fighting O'Farrells. London, Newnes, 1937.
He Built Himself a Loop. London, Newnes, 1937.
Diana of the Ophir Hills. London, Newnes, 1937.
The Man from Skull Valley. London, Newnes, 1937.
Desert Waters. London, Newnes, 1938.
Romance of Surprise Ranch. London, Newnes, 1939.
Six-Gun Challenge, and Bob Gates, Outlaw. London, Newnes, 1939.
Hero's Walk. New York, Ballantine, 1954; London, Cresset Press, 1955.
Bloody Ambush. New York, Pyramid, 1966.

Uncollected Short Stories

"The Hole in the Rock," in *Adventure* (New York), 30 June 1922.
"That Finer Fiber," in *Adventure* (New York), 20 August 1922.
"Silver Zone," in *Adventure* (New York), 20 November 1922.
"Denny," in *Adventure* (New York), 30 January 1923.
"The Mad Commanders," in *Adventure* (New York), 10 February 1923.
"Sportin' Blood," in *Adventure* (New York), 10 July 1923.
"Not Three of a Kind," in *Adventure* (New York), 20 August 1923.
"The Regeneration of Pesokie," in *Adventure* (New York), 30 September 1923.
"This Bandit Business Is the Bunk," in *Adventure* (New York), 30 November 1923.
"The Longstriker," in *Adventure* (New York), 10 April 1924.
"Desert Fame," in *Adventure* (New York), 10 June 1924.
"The Shrimp," in *Adventure* (New York), 10 August 1924.

"The Fence Builders," in *The Frontier* (New York), October 1924.
"The Valley of Desolation," in *The Frontier* (New York), November 1924.
"Lisbeth," in *Adventure* (New York), 20 June 1925.
"The Swamp Dwellers," in *West* (New York), 5 January 1926.
"The Cross F Case," in *West* (New York), 20 February 1926.
"Double Bitted Vengeance," in *West* (New York), 5 March 1926.
"The End of a Wrong Start," in *West* (New York), 20 May 1926.
"The Uncertain Stranger," in *West* (New York), 5 June 1926.
"Stub," in *West* (New York), 20 June 1926.
"The Man from Skull Valley," in *West* (New York), 5 August 1926.
"The Taming of Bill Leeds," in *West* (New York), 5 October 1926.
"When a Man's Vain," in *West* (New York), 20 November 1926.
"An Unwilling Meddler," in *West* (New York), 20 February 1927.
"The Man Branders," in *West* (New York), 5 March–20 April 1927.
"Cole of King Creek," in *West* (New York), 5 July–13 August 1927.
"In Sheep's Clothing," in *West* (New York), 21 April 1928.
"The Tie Down," in *West* (New York), 14 July 1928.
"Dirty Cards," in *West* (New York), 21 July 1928.
"Hammerhead," in *West* (New York), 15 September 1928.
"The Silver Cow," in *West* (New York), 29 September–3 November 1928.
"Blocked Trails," in *West* (New York), 9 January 1929.
"The Wrong Game," in *West* (New York), 6 February 1929.
"Kill Them Sheep!" in *West* (New York), 20 March 1929.
"Señor Collecto," in *West* (New York), 3 April 1929.
"Three Little Calves," in *West* (New York), 29 May 1929.
"The Show-Off Man," in *West* (New York), 26 June 1929.
"Hold That Range," in *West* (New York), 10 July 1929.
"Crazy Horse," in *West* (New York), 18 September 1929.
"The Phantom Passes," in *West* (New York), 20, August 1930.
"That Harmless Dutchman," in *West* (New York), 1 October 1930.
"Forbidden Valley," in *Argosy* (New York), 9 May–30 May 1931.
"The Destroying Horde," in *West* (New York), 10 June–24 June 1931.
"Explain Yourself," *Western Romances* (New York), July 1931.
"Snake Bite," in *West* (New York), 2 September 1931.
"The Wild-Riding Lashaways," in *West* (New York), 31 August 1932.
"The Hungry Rider," in *West* (New York), 28 September 1932.
"Renegade for Right," with O.A. Robertson, in *West* (New York), October 1934.
"The Toughness of Tex Cotton," with O.A. Robertson, in *West* (New York), March 1935.
"The Man the Gallows Didn't Get," with O.A. Robertson, in *West* (New York), December 1935.
"Hero of the Herd," with O.A. Robertson, in *Western Story* (New York), 28 March 1936.
"Dave of the Humbug Hills," with O.A. Robertson, in *Western Story* (New York), 20 June 1936.
"Outlaw Blood," in *Ranch Romances* (New York), 1 November 1936.
"Farewell to Sheep," with O.A. Robertson, in *Western Story* (New York), 16 January–13 February 1937.
"The Padlocked Valley," in *Ranch Romances* (New York), 2 May 1937.
"Ranchless Ranchers," with O.A. Robertson, in *Ranch Romances* (New York), 3 June 1937.
"Vagabond Vengeance," in *Sure-Fire Western* (Springfield, Massachusetts), July 1938.
"The Star-Faced Blacks," in *Zane Grey's Western* (New York), October 1947.
"Hot Saddle Bags," in *West* (Kingswood, Surrey), June 1948.
"The Humbug Mountain Murder," in *West* (Kingswood, Surrey), October 1950.
"The Courtship of Tireless Jones," in *West* (Kingswood, Surrey), December 1951.
"Lariats Make Cruel Lashes," in *Western Story* (London), May 1952.
"The Broken Rock," in *Thrilling Ranch Stories* (London), October 1952.
"The Smother Hole," in *West* (Kingswood, Surrey), February 1954.
"Hell in Hercules," in *Western Story* (London), June 1955.
"Boss of the Bottoms," in *They Won Their Spurs*, edited by Neljson Nye. New York, Avon 1962.

OTHER PUBLICATIONS

Play

Screenplay: *Blue Blazes*, with Frank Beresford, 1926.

Other

A Ram in the Thicket: An Autobiography. New York, Abelard Press, 1950.
Where Desert Blizzards Blow (for children). New York, Nelson, 1952; London, Collins, 1955.
Sagebrush Sorrel (for children). New York, Nelson, 1953; London, Collins, 1955.
Soapy Smith, King of the Frontier Con Men, with Mary Beth Harris. New York, Hastings House, 1961.
Boom Towns of the Great Basin, with Mary Beth Harris. Denver, Sage, 1962.
Fort Hall, Gateway to the Oregon Country. New York, Hastings House, 1963.

* * *

Without question, Frank C. Robertson was a fast gun in the writing trade. His productivity, style, and expertise were little short of amazing, although there were others of equal bent who could pace him during the decades when pulp and slick magazines were going strong, publishing an abundance of popular fiction and lots and lots of "Westerns."

These were grand and glorious years for writers of Robertson's generation. And like many others, he drew from his immediate surroundings and experiences of Idaho and Utah, where he was born, raised, and lived most of his life. These became rich veins of material for a lifetime of literary effort. His books and stories reveal an astounding versatility in subject, setting, and characterization, and a vast knowledge of the western world around him. One feels he is on sure ground when reading a Robertson novel. Robertson's experience filtered through his typewriter onto paper in some 220 western novels and more than a thousand articles. Of course he wrote to form; he needed to do so to sell his stories and survive as an author. But there was a flavor here; Robertson loved what he was doing, and believed in it, with a passionate endearment for the Old West.

Because of his life-long experience in western ranch life, Robertson never hungered for material. This also gained him high respect among his friends and colleagues who elected him President of Western Writers of America. He demonstrated, too, that he was an adaptable craftsman, for in later years he wrote books built around such television series as *Have Gun, Will Travel* and *Rawhide*. More and more Robertson turned to nonfiction in books such as *Fort Hall*, familiar ground, and a semi-fictional biography of Soapy Smith, Alaska's legendary con man. Like most all he did, Robertson's words provoked easy, relaxing reading. But probably his most lasting work was another nonfiction book, *A Ram in the Thicket*, an informal memory of his youth, a delightful tale about an equally delightful family. Reading this book, you can easily understand why Robertson succeeded as an author.

—Ellis Lucia

ROBSON, Lucia St. Clair. American. Born in Baltimore, Maryland, 24 September 1942. Educated at Palm Beach Community College, Palm Beach, Florida, A.A. 1962; University of Florida, Jacksonville, B.A. 1964; Florida State University, Tallahassee, Florida, M.L.S. 1974. Married Richard Charles Gauger in 1968 (divorced). Peace Corps volunteer worker in Caripito, Venezuela, 1964–66; teacher at public school, Brooklyn, New York, 1967–68; librarian, Hialeah Public Library, Florida, 1968–69; teacher of English in Japan, 1969–71; librarian, Fort Jackson Library, Columbia, South Carolina, 1971–72; librarian, Anne Arundel County Public Library, Annapolis, Maryland, 1975–81. Since 1981 full-time writer. Recipient: Western Writers of America Spur award, 1982. Agent: Virginia Barber, 353 West 21st Street, New York, New York 10011. Address: P.O. Box 327, Arnold, Maryland 21012, U.S.A.

WESTERN PUBLICATIONS

Novels

Ride the Wind: The Story of Cynthia Ann Parker, and the Last Days of the Comanche. New York, Ballantine, 1982.
Walk in My Soul. New York, Ballantine, 1985.
Light a Distant Fire. New York, Ballantine, 1988; London, Barrie and Jenkins, 1990.

OTHER PUBLICATIONS

Novel

The Tokaido Road. New York, Ballantine, and London, Barrie and Jenkins, 1991.

*

Manuscript Collection: University of Wyoming, Laramie.

Lucia St. Clair Robson comments:

I just want to tell a good story and treat my protagonists fairly.

* * *

In the 1980's, the publication of three historical novels about American Indians established Lucia St. Clair Robson as a first-rate storyteller. Focusing on historical Indian personalities and their tribes in each novel, Robson chronicled the steady erosion of the free way of life enjoyed by the Indian nations as the whites became increasingly hungry for land. Robson capably depicted the clash of two very diverse cultures and all three novels contain numerous carefully drawn white characters. Her view of the clash is a balanced one: not all whites are bad and not all Indians are good. Each book is also a love story.

Robson's first fictional account, *Ride the Wind*, became a national bestseller. Spanning the years 1836 to 1875, it tells the well-known story of Cynthia Ann Parker's capture by and assimilation into the Penateka Comanche tribe as daughter, wife, and mother with fresh eyes and meticulous detail (it's nearly 600 pages long). The daily lives of the Comanches at work, at play, and at war are richly and accurately recreated. There are scenes rarely, if ever, encountered in western fiction—in advance of an imminent raging grassfire, a Comanche camp is inundated with first the largest and fastest animals, then those smaller and slower, then reptiles and insects attempting to elude the flames. The tragic events following Cynthia's recapture by whites years later—the death of her five-year-old daughter who was also taken by the whites, her husband Wanderer's search for Cynthia, the advent of the buffalo hunters, and the defeat of her son Quanah Parker—are stunningly presented.

Walk in My Soul parallels the lives of Tiana Rogers, a mixed-blood Cherokee, and Sam Houston, white soldier and politician, who lived as husband and wife. Their story unfolds amid the the efforts of many of the members of the Cherokee nation to become desirable U.S. citizens, the political manipulations used to dispossess the Cherokees of their land, and the stuggles of the blacks to elude slavers. Roughly spanning the years 1810 to 1840, the book ends with the removal of the Cherokees and their trek on foot to the "Nightland" west of the Mississippi, known as the Nunna-da-ult-sun-yi, the Trail Where They Cried. The life of Tiana Rogers of which historically very little is known (she was the aunt of Will Rogers three generations removed), is so fascinating that some of the chapters devoted to Houston's political aspirations and wanderings seem extraneous.

The life of the Seminole leader Osceola and the Seminole Wars in Florida are the focus of *Light a Distant Fire*. The shortest of Robson's novels, it is also her most tightly written. It, too, contains many memorable scenes: alligator hunting, warfare in the swamps, Osceola and his family hiding in an alligator den during a white raid, and Osceola's incarceration. Blacks play a prominent role in the story because Florida was a refuge for runaway slaves and slaver activities. Although the book has fewer graphic scenes of violence than *Ride the Wind*, the carnage wrought by the seven years of war in the exotic Florida environment somehow seem far more vivid.

Robson's work is best characterized by her tenacious research. She makes use of innumerable human and printed resources in her writing and, having been a librarian, has an insider's familiarity with obscure materials. To her credit, this encyclopedic knowledge about tools, crafts, flora, fauna, diet, games, ceremonies, and clothing is not presented in a way so as to impress the reader but rather in fictional terms. The reader comes to know not only the people, but the places, the times, the smells, the tastes, the sounds. If there is a flaw in these books (and it is a common one among women writers of historical fiction), it is the desire and skill on the part of male characters to satisfy the female characters sexually. This small complaint aside, Robson has brought to her novels about American Indians integrity, a sense of humor, and an understanding that other writers of western fiction might wisely emulate.

—Vicki Piekarski

RODERUS, Frank. American. Born in Pittsburgh, Pennsylvania, 21 September 1942. Educated at Oxford Junior College, Georgia, 1958–60; St. Petersburg Junior College, Florida, 1964–65. Served in the United States Army, 1960–63. Married 1) Kay Marsh in 1965 (divorced 1977); 2) Betty Richardson in 1978; two daughters and two sons. Reporter, Tampa *Times*, 1965–66, Lakeland *Ledger*, 1966–68, and *Tampa Tribune*, 1968–72, all Florida; Waterloo *Courier*, Iowa, 1972–75; and Colorado Springs *Gazette Telegraph*, 1979–80. Since 1980 freelance writer. Recipient: Western Writers of America Golden Spur award, 1987. Address: c/o Bantam Doubleday Dell Publishing Group, 666 Fifth Avenue, New York, New York 10103, U.S.A.

WESTERN PUBLICATIONS

Novels (series: Harrison Wilke)

Journey to Utah. New York, Doubleday, 1977; London, Hale, 1978.
The 33 Brand. New York, Doubleday, 1977; London, Hale, 1979.
The Keystone Kid. New York, Doubleday, 1978; London, Hale, 1979.
Easy Money. New York, Doubleday, 1978; London, Hale, 1980.
Home to Texas. New York, Ace, 1978.
The Name Is Hart. New York, Ace, 1979.
Hell Creek Cabin. New York, Doubleday, 1979; London, Hale, 1981.
Sheepherding Man. New York, Doubleday, and London, Hale, 1980.
Jason Evers, His Own Story. New York, Doubleday, 1980; London, Hale, 1981.
Old Kyle's Boy. New York, Doubleday, and London, Hale, 1981.
Cowboy. New York, Doubleday, 1981; London, Hale, 1982.
The Ordeal of Hogue Bynell. New York, Doubleday, 1982; London, Hale, 1983.
Leaving Kansas (Wilke). New York, Doubleday, 1983; London, Hale, 1984.
Reaching Colorado (Wilke). New York, Doubleday, 1984; London, Hale, 1985.
Finding Nevada (Wilke). New York, Doubleday, 1985.
Stillwater Smith. New York, Doubleday, 1986.
Billy Ray and the Good News. New York, Doubleday, 1987.
The Ballad of Bryan Drayne. New York, Signet, 1987.
Charlie and the Sir. New York, Doubleday, 1988.
The Outsider. New York, Signet, 1988.
Billy Ray's Forty Days. New York, Doubleday, 1989.
J.A. Whitford and the Great California Gold Hunt. New York, Doubleday, 1990.

Uncollected Short Stories

"Ed," in *Roundup*, edited by Stephen Overholser. New York, Doubleday, 1982.

Fiction for children

Duster. Independence, Missouri, Independence Press, 1977.

OTHER PUBLICATIONS

Novels

The Oil Rig. New York, Bantam, 1984.
The Rain Rustlers. New York, Bantam, 1984.
The Video Vandals. New York, Bantam, 1984.
The Turn-Out Man. New York, Bantam, 1985.
The Coyote Crossing. New York, Bantam, 1985.

*

Manuscript Collection: University of Wyoming, Laramie.

* * *

Although he has been writing western fiction for little over a decade, Frank Roderus has produced a singularly admirable body of work. Following publication of a children's novel, *Duster*, Roderus turned to adult fiction with *Journey to Utah*. In this early novel, the formulary elements are more in evidence than would be the case later, but there are nonetheless some unusual aspects to the narrative. The story is told in the first person by its unlikely hero, Stumpy Williams, who considers himself homely. Unlike Louis L'Amour who used first-person narratives to provide some coherence to hopelessly picaresque and disparate plot ingredients (at least the narrator is there to keep some semblance of continuity), Roderus here, as well as in subsequent novels, used first-person narratives to probe depth of character in his protagonists. This is certainly the case with Tiny Spears in *The 33 Brand*, Bert Felloe in *Easy Money*, and Judas Priest in *Sheepherding Man*. All of these narrators are flawed men, and yet characters who become increasingly sympathetic as they reveal themselves and the reader comes to know them through reflection on their past experiences and as they describe their motivations and actions in the present. *Journey to Utah* is a pursuit story, after a fashion, insofar as the heroine is trying to escape from her greedy stepbrothers whose ambition is being fired by their mother, the widow Trask, who married Janet Cates's father and who successfully poisoned her brother, and who is now poisoning her father to gain control of his ranch. To make this scheme work, Janet has been declared feeble-minded. Stumpy sets out to rescue Janet and at one point is badly beaten, at another shot twice in the back, and finally charged with rape. *The 33 Brand* is even more of a pursuit story when Tiny adopts for a time three orphaned children, whose parents have been murdered by three men who have taken their older sister, Andy, prisoner to perform sexual favors for them. *Journey to Utah* has a conventional ranch romance ending. *The 33 Brand* does not, and in its final pages achieves the same bitter-sweet tone found in a novel such as Max Evans's *The Hi-Lo Country*.

From the beginning, Roderus frequently introduced a mystery element into his plots to maintain suspense, and in *Hell Creek Cabin* he made use of the confrontation between characters stranded in a snowed-in cabin to sustain tension. Also in this novel the villains are portrayed in such a fashion that what they do is comprehensible in terms more human than mere wickedness. In fact, as he has progressed as a novelist, Roderus has shown more and more, quite in the fashion of Eugene Manlove Rhodes, that the West is populated mostly by basically decent and even generous people. Added to this there is more than a little good humor, much of it growing organically from the characters and the situations in which they find themselves. The first time Tiny comes upon Andy in the villains' camp, chained to a tree, only one man is guarding her. He hits him so hard he breaks his jaw. Later, in a confrontation with all three men, a fight ensues and Tiny narrates how he "whipped a backhanded left across the jaw of the bandaged one. He screamed and fell down." However, it is the bandaged one who stops the fight by plugging Tiny, reversing the humor into desperate seriousness.

In Roderus's early books, there is the conventional gunplay and violence associated with the formulary Western. In his later books, this vanishes almost completely. In one of Roderus's finest achievements, the trilogy about the early manhood of Harrison Wilke, *Leaving Kansas*, *Reaching Colorado*, and *Finding Nevada*, Wilke starts out as a prig who detests ranching in all its aspects, and who is disconcerted by even the idea of firearms. There isn't a shot fired in any of the books in this trilogy. What there is instead is a subtle blending of coming of age through the interplay of appearance and reality, a mystery element in the first and third books (who is behind the rustling in *Leaving Kansas*, and who shot Harrison's best friend, John J. Trohoe, in *Finding Nevada*), and the hard-won wisdom which comes with experience and maturity. At the very outset, Harrison is told that "'opportunity, like success, comes from people, not from places.'" By the end of the trilogy, Harrison, now 35, has to choose between two lifestyles, that of a banker in Denver or of a miner in Goldfield, Nevada; but the Nevada that he finds at the end of his quest is Nevada Wiggin, a young girl who works with her mother in a tent eating house. Harrison changes in another significant way. When the murderer of his friend is lynched by a miners' court, he finds he is not made nauseous by the occurrence, recognizing that in some instances moral justice is above the law.

Although Roderus has moved farther and farther away from formulary conventions in his novels, there are still sufficient co-ordinates with traditional western fiction to permit his publishers to tout his books as if they were action-packed range thrillers when nothing could be further from the truth. The protagonist in *The Outsider*, one of his more recent novels and unquestionably one of his finest, is Leon Brown, a black man and a former corporal in the Tenth Cavalry. He purchases a ranch outside Kazumal, Arizona, with the intention of raising cattle, but when he shows up at the lawyer's office who handled the transaction by mail the lawyer insists he cannot be Leon Brown: "'You can't be,' Farr blurted . . . 'You're a nigger . . .'" In the course of the narrative Leon reveals his innate generosity of soul, and is rewarded in kind by the village priest (although Leon has been taught to distrust popists), by Manuela, a social outcast because she is half Apache, half Mexican, and a slut, and by a white man, his nearest neighbor. The theme of the two heroines, so much a standard ingredient in western fiction by Ernest Haycox and Luke Short and so many others following in the footsteps of Sir Walter Scott's *Waverley*, is present in novels such as *Finding Nevada* and *The Outsider*, but it is used so naturally and imaginatively that it is almost invisible: the characters are that well drawn and the conflicts that real.

Roderus has become a more capable novelist and storyteller with every book he has written, yet each of them—so consistent is the quality of his work—pays reading, and in some cases even rereading. What is most impressive about his fiction, and what raises it in significance above any attempt to classify it as strictly generic, is the humanity embodied in his perspective and in so many of his vividly realized characters. It is this spirit of humanity which illumines both a near satire such as *The Keystone Kid*, or a tense pursuit story such as *The Ballad of Bryan Drayne*, a humanity without sentimentality, but rather an affirmation of what is best in the human spirit, and an attempt to understand what is dark and sinister in the human condition. This is a quality as excellent as it is rare in fiction of any kind, and one deserving of the highest praise wherever it is found.

—Jon Tuska

RODGERS, Shirlaw Johnston. Address: c/o Robert Hale Ltd., Clerkenwell House, 45–47 Clerkenwell Green, London EC1R 0HT, England.

WESTERN PUBLICATIONS

Novels (series: Micah Truelove)

The Crooked Desert. London, Hale, 1978.
Oracle Springs. London, Hale, 1978.
Old Baldy's Map. London, Hale, 1982.
Silver and Lead (Truelove). London, Hale, 1982.
Boracho (Truelove). London, Hale, 1982.
Rough Diamonds (Truelove). London, Hale, 1983.

* * *

A relatively little-known writer whose lamentably few Westerns, published in the early 1980s, are now quite difficult to come by, Shirlaw Johnston Rodgers is nevertheless an author worth seeking out. His intelligent and witty Westerns can by turns be as intentionally funny as they are frequently compelling, and usually boast well-realised, difficult-to-predict plots. His work falls into two categories; his single, unrelated adventures, and those stories which feature his two incorrigible NCOs, Micah Truelove and Cornelius O'Hare.

Old Baldy's Map neatly exemplifies the Rodgers Western. On the surface, the action revolves around the search for a lost city of gold, initially discovered by the title character, who manages to send a map of its location to his estranged son before dying from a combination of old age and a weak heart. Underlying this plot, however, is the arrival of a mysterious stranger named Dan Fallon in the nearby town; an event which virtually coincides with the systematic murder of the town council—the mayor, sheriff, lawyer, doctor, and undertaker—who have, between them, been murdering lonely miners and stealing their gold for years.

Rodgers keeps both plots going at a rapid clip, succinctly expressing the frustration of the gold-seekers and the growing sense of paranoia among the surviving town councillors. Eventually both plots are resolved after a number of effective and well-executed twists, although the outcome is by no means an entirely happy one.

The quest for gold also forms the premise of *The Crooked Desert*, in which escaped outlaw Milo Scarman attempts to retrieve $50,000 worth of stolen gold from the place at which he buried it before being arrested. Of course, Scarman's plans grow increasingly complicated as Rodgers gradually introduces his customary subplots, which, like *Old Baldy's Map*, also feature a crooked New Mexico town and a considerable amount of double-dealing.

Rodgers normally writes in a series of short, sharp scenes, negating the need for chapters. He employs multiple viewpoints to good effect, and breaks up his prose with extensive passages of largely unattributed dialogue. Overall, his style is rather brief, and as a consequence his stories fairly gallop along. He seldom bothers much with "stage directions," prefering to allow characterisation, and a sense of his characters' movements, to impart itself through speech. Neither does he waste much space on physical description, although he frequently reveals a gift for creating atmosphere and a sense of "being there" in the shortest—and most telling—of sentences.

The humour in Rodgers's single Westerns is usually of the dry, perceptive kind. While it invariably brings a smile to the lips, and is certainly used more sparingly, the slightly broader humour of the Micah Truelove novels is more likely to elicit a full-blown chuckle.

Truelove and his sidekick, Cornelius O'Hare, are two cavalry sergeants with a talent for trouble, much to the unending dismay of their commanding officer, Colonel Kirkland. In size and demeanour, they conform entirely to the brawling Irish NCO stereotype so beloved of the old John Ford Westerns, and as may correctly be deduced, the stories in which they find themselves are largely lighthearted and undemanding.

Truelove and O'Hare do not so much get involved in adventures as *mis*-adventures, however. In *Silver and Lead*, for example, they are dispatched to find two deserters and return them to Fort Woodstock, their West Texas base, for trial. But no sooner do they achieve their aim than they lose their prisoners again, and unwittingly find themselves participating in a silver robbery. For *Boracho*, Truelove and O'Hare are sent to the Big Bend country to find a missing Government official, only to get caught up in a war between the Comanches and the Mexicans, and eventually tangle with a hostile Indian called Yolohani, or "Squint Eyes."

Squint Eyes makes a return appearance in the much-recommended *Rough Diamonds*, which displays Rodgers's skills as an entertainer to particularly good effect. A disgruntled New York insurance clerk, duped into stealing a quarter of a million dollars' worth of uncut diamonds, is subsequently cornered in a warehouse by the men who set him up. In desperation he secretes the gems in a crate bound for Colonel Kirkland, and Truelove and O'Hare become involved in the ensuing bid to retrieve them when they are sent to collect the crate from Laredo and transport it back to Fort Woodstock. The story grows more complicated still when the two sergeants become the prime suspects in a murder enquiry and are forced once again to trade shots with the vengeful Comanche, before finally managing to resolve the matter in their usual hamfisted but effective fashion.

At this late date, it is highly unlikely that a sudden and much deserved interest will be taken in the works of Shirlaw Johnston Rodgers—but it is quite possible that, in another place or at another time, his clever, observant, and well-written novels might easily have established him as one of the most popular exponents of light western fiction.

—David Whitehead

ROGERS, Floyd. *See* **BOWDEN, Jim.**

RØLVAAG, O(le) E(dvart). Also wrote as Paal Mörck. American. Born on Dönna Island, Helgeland, Norway, 22 April 1876; emigrated to the U.S., 1896; became citizen, 1908. Educated at Dönna schools to age 14; Augustana College, Canton, South Dakota, 1899–1901; St. Olaf College, Northfield, Minnesota, 1901–05, B.A. 1905, M.A. 1910; University of Oslo, 1905–06. Married Jennie Marie Berdahl in 1908; three sons and one daughter. Fisherman in Norway, 1891–95; worked on his uncle's farm in South Dakota, 1896–99; Professor of Norwegian language and literature, 1906–31, and Head of the Norwegian Department, 1916–31, St. Olaf College. Secretary, Norwegian-American Historical Association, 1925–31. Honorary degree: University of Wisconsin, Madison, 1929. Knight of the Order of St. Olaf, Norway, 1926. *Died 5 November 1931.*

Western Publications

Novels

Amerika-breve (Letters from America; as Paal Mörck). Minneapolis, Augsburg, 1912; translated by Ella Tweet and Solveig Zempel, as *The Third Life of Per Smevik*, Minneapolis, Dillon Press, 1971.

Paa Glemte Veie (On Forgotten Paths; as Paal Mörck). Minneapolis, Augsburg, 1914.

To Tullinger: Et Billede fra Idag (Two Fools: A Picture of Our Time). Minneapolis, Augsburg, 1920; revised edition, translated by Sivert Erdahl and Rølvaag, as *Pure Gold*, New York, Harper, 1930.

Laengselens Baat. Minneapolis, Augsburg, 1921; translated by Nora O. Solum, as *The Boat of Longing*, New York, Harper, 1933.

Giants in the Earth, translated by Lincoln Colcord and Rølvaag. New York, Harper, and London, Benn, 1927.

I de Dage: Fortaelling om Norske Nykommere i Amerika (In Those Days: A Story of Norwegian Pioneering in America). Christiania, Aeschehoug, 1924.

Ricket Grundlaegges (The Founding of the Kingdom). Christiania, Aeschehoug, 1925.

Peder Seier. Olso, Aeschehoug, 1928; translated by Rølvaag and Nora O. Solum, as *Peder Victorious*, New York, Harper, 1929.

Den Signede Dag (The Blessed Day). Oslo, Aeschehoug, 1931; translated by Trygve M. Ager, as *Their Fathers' God*, New York, Harper, 1931.

Other Publications

Other

Ordforklaring til Nordahl Rolfsens Laesebok for Folkeskolen II. Minneapolis, Augsburg, 1909.

Haanbok i Norsk Retskrivning og uttale til Skolebruk og Selvstudium, with P.J. Eikeland. Minneapolis, Augsburg, 1916.

Norsk Laesebok, with P.J. Eikeland. Minneapolis, Augsburg, 3 vols., 1919–25.

Omkring Faedrearven (essays). Northfield, Minnesota, St. Olaf College Press, 1922.

Editor, *Deklamationsboken*. Minneapolis, Augsburg, 1918.

*

Critical Studies: *Ole Edvart Rølvaag: A Biography* by Theodore Jorgenson and Nora O. Solum, New York, Harper, 1939; *O.E. Rølvaag: His Life and Art* by Paul Reigstad, Lincoln, University of Nebraska Press, 1972; *Ole Edvart Rølvaag og den norske Kulturen i Amerika*, Vinstra, Per Gynt nemuda, 1981; *Ole Edvart Røvaag* by Einar Haugen, Boston, Twayne, 1983; *Edvart Rølvaag* by Ann Moseley, Boise, Idaho, Boise State University, 1987; *Prairies Within: The Tragic Trilogy of Ole Rølvaag* by Harold P. Simonson, Seattle, University of Washington Press, 1987.

* * *

O.E. Rølvaag's *Giants in the Earth* may possibly be America's best and most popular novel about pioneering in the West, yet it was written in Norwegian by an immigrant. This paradox suggests the secret of Røvaag's success as a truly American novelist: he wrote about human experience which epitomizes one of the principal motifs of American history and shaped his story through the eyes and hearts of immigrants, who constitute the majority of the American people. Rølvaag believed that one could be most truly American by utilizing one's cultural heritage within the context of an evolving American culture, remaining true to one while contributing to the other. His own achievements demonstrate the validity of such a synthesis.

Giants in the Earth celebrates the pioneering challenge of the west in the character of Per Hansa, who thrives on hopes for a better future for his family: presumably an attainable goal for one who is willing to work. Per Hansa's epic struggle assumes tragic dimensions through awareness of counterforces: nature is indifferent to man's struggles (at times seemingly hostile, at others beneficent), and Beret (Per Hansa's wife) resists capitulation to a pioneering prairie environment which seems to demand denial of her cultural past and the adoption of ethics that are expedient and self-serving. Both characters are carefully rendered, winning our divided sympathies and thereby emphasizing the tragic dichotomies of the westward movement: gain vs. loss, materialism vs. idealism, epic conquest vs. exploitation, individualism vs. communal values.

Peder Victorious continues the story from the time of Per Hansa's death to his son Peder's marriage to an Irish Catholic girl. Beret seems stronger, more competent and vital in this novel, not simply because the narrative focus is no longer split between two major characters (as it is in *Giants*) but because she can most easily adapt and thrive when the pioneering scene evolves into a farming community. This novel and its sequel, *Their Fathers' God*, dramatize the hopes and problems facing those who participated in the full process of development from sod-breaking frontier to statehood. Peder (in *Their Fathers' God*) becomes involved in politics, attempting to promote the welfare of the farmers but reaping more frustration and disappointment than success. His father's struggle was against nature and against his wife's conservatism; Peder's struggle, less easily defined, is internal, for he finds that in pursuing ideological goals he has denied his cultural roots and is suffering from a spiritual drought as severe as the prairie drought with which the novel begins. Both Per Hansa and Peder have a vision of a better life they believe is possible on the western prairie; both face defeat that is epitomized in marital stress or rupture; both become exiles from the homes they sought to establish.

Rølvaag's *Pure Gold* portrays the corrupting power of materialism in the lives of a farming couple whose initially healthy desire for financial security evolves into an all-consuming greed which perverts their emotional lives, destroys their spiritual values, and hastens their deaths. *The Boat of Longing* is not so obviously western in conception; the focus is on the life of the artist and the plight of the immigrant who fails to adapt in ways that will nourish his creative soul. Rølvaag's first novel, *The Third Life of Per Smevik*, describes a young immigrant's experience in South Dakota. The narrative provides realistic depiction of farmlife from the point of view of a fisherman learning to be a farmer on the landlocked prairie.

A theme common to all of Rølvaag's fiction is the conviction that spiritual values must be preserved and nourished if one is to prevail in whatever struggle one faces: that of the pioneer, the prairie farmer, or the immigrant in an alien land. His fiction is starkly realistic, often tragic in conception, and brutally honest in portraying the pitfalls of human experience, yet imbued with a faith in the human spirit and a zest for life.

—Barbara Howard Meldrum

ROMNEY, Steve. *See* **BINGLEY, David Ernest.**

RORIPAUGH, Robert (Alan). American. Born in Oxnard, California, 26 August 1930. Educated at University of Texas, Austin, 1947–50; University of Wyoming, Laramie, B.A., 1952; M.A., 1953; graduate study, 1955–56; University of New Mexico, Albuquerque, graduate study, 1956–58. Served in United States Army, 1953–55; stationed in Japan. Married Yoshiko Horikoshi in 1956: one daughter. Worked as geological laboratory technician, oilfield roustabout, carpenter's helper, horse wrangler, clerk-typist, and ranch hand; University of Wyoming, Laramie, instructor, 1958–62, assistant professor 1962–67, associate professor 1967–72, and since 1972 professor of English. Member, Authors League of America, Western Literature Association (member of executive council, 1968–71), The Wilderness Society. Recipient: Western Heritage National Cowboy Hall of Fame award, for novel, 1963; Don D. Walker prize, for essay, 1982. Address: Department of English, University of Wyoming, Laramie, Wyoming 82071, U.S.A.

WESTERN PUBLICATIONS

Novel

Honor Thy Father. New York, Morrow, 1963.

Uncollected Short Stories

"The Peach Boy," in *Atlantic Monthly* (New York), September 1958.

"The Last Longhorn," in *Sage*, Spring 1966.

"The Legend of Billy Jenks," in *The Far Side of the Storm: New Ranges in Western Fiction*. Cerrillos, New Mexico, San Marcos Press, 1975.

"The Man Who Killed the Split-Toed Wolf," in *The Salt Cedar*, vol. 1, 1977.
"Winter Days Are Long: Themes Written By Virginia Shield in Freshman English," in *Quarterly West*, in Fall/Winter 1980–81.
"Leave's End," in *Writers' Forum*, Fall 1989.

Verse

Learn to Love the Haze. Vermillion, South Dakota, Spirit Mound Press, 1976.

Other Publications

Novel

A Fever for Living. New York, Morrow, 1961; London, Gollancz, 1962.

*

Robert Roripaugh comments:

Literature of the American West can exploit popular myths about the region's past and present . . . or present the material in ways that attempt to portray human experience in more universal and realistic terms. These two approaches often conflict with each other in the expectations or reactions of readers and critics, but also illustrate the West's literary richness—its surface appeal and deeper, less-accessible promise. My life has been spent in different parts of the West and Wyoming. Except for a novel set in Japan, almost all my writing involves this region. Whether working in fiction or poetry, I am interested in using western experience and background to explore character, interactions of different cultures and conflicting attitudes, the impact of history, land and its inhabitants—the natural and human dimensions of the country—in ways reflecting the West—but hopefully carrying meaning and concerns which reach beyond the region as well.

* * *

Robert Roripaugh has been an all-around hand in western literature, creating poetry, nonfiction, literary criticism, and fiction, all of top quality. His fiction is not formulaic and conventional; it is serious and artistic without being esoteric.

Roripaugh's award-winning novel *Honor Thy Father* is an historical novel, set in the Sweetwater country of Wyoming in 1889. It is the story of a range war, not as parallel to historical fact as Manfred's *Riders of Judgment*, but solidly fixed with historical detail and background. It gives the reader a good sense of ranching life in the political milieu of Wyoming on the verge of statehood. (Wyoming became a state in 1890; the Johnson County war took place in 1892.)

This novel's literary artistry qualifies it to rank above conventional historical fiction. The narrator is Martin Tyrrell, younger son of an old-guard rancher. The narrative voice is created and maintained as gracefully as in Conrad Richter's *The Sea of Grass*. Through Mart's perceptions the reader follows the events of the range war and its related conflicts: greed and political corruption in the struggle for land and power, character contrast between Mart and his older brother Ira, estrangement between Ira and the father, attraction of both brothers to the Indian girl Mary Lamar, contrast between the dark-haired heroine and the heroine with whiskey-colored hair, and Mart's own crossing the line into manhood with the help of the Mexican saloon girl. Mart's perceptions also provide frequent (and eloquent) evocations of the landscape and of the gritty details of daily ranch life.

Thematically, the novel presents a study of the passing of an old way of life and the beginning of a new one, from the era of open range to the era of fencing pastures and putting up hay. More significantly for some readers, it explores relationships among family members, between sexes, and between races. In its depiction of non-Anglo characters, the novel does not preach racial equality; the novel assumes such equality as a premise for the relationships presented. In its rejection of easy answers and of conventional character typing, *Honor Thy Father* is an enriching, mature western novel to read.

Roripaugh's short stories are, like his novel, of high literary quality. "The Peach Boy" is about a young man who comes home to the ranch country from a tour of duty in Japan, where he has left the woman he loves. The internal conflict of cross-cultural love finds a parallel in an Anglo-Indian romance in the story. Like *Honor Thy Father*, this is a delicately crafted work. The award-winning "The Legend of Billy Jenks," set in 1952 in the Wind River country of Wyoming, tells the story of a young man who grows up through a hard life, doesn't fit well into society, becomes something of a gunslinger, and, in the company of his Indian wife, comes to grief. This is a wistful, restrained, but sympathetic story of misfits in a small western town. "The Man Who Killed the Split-Toed Wolf" is a retrospective story, set in the Sweetwater country. Through the impressions of a narrator like Mart Tyrrell, it pieces together the story of a man, Slade Wilson, who, 30 years earlier, killed a legendary wolf, the last of the big ones. This is a graceful story about faded greatness and the mythic past, and the reader senses the power that such a past still holds on latter-day people such as the narrator and Charlie Six-Fingers, another of Roripaugh's realistic Indian characters. "Winter Days Are Long: Themes Written by Virginia Shield in Freshman English," also an award-winning story, is arranged as a series of essays written by a young Indian woman who has come to the university from, as she calls it, "the center of Wyoming," where the Wind River Indian Reservation is located. Through these essays, the reader gathers an understanding of contemporary life on the reservation and away from it. The speaking voice of Virginia Shield is an exquisite creation, and her story will become part of a reader's life.

Roripaugh's western fiction has not been abundant, but it has been steady and thoughtful. His work focuses on important issues of the American West: the passage of time from one era to the next, the importance of setting and place in human lives, and the inherent humanity of people perhaps unlike ourselves, with whom we share the earth.

—John D. Nesbitt

ROSCOE, Charles. *See* **ROWLAND, Donald S.**

ROSS, Sinclair. Canadian. Born in Shellbrook, Saskatchewan, 22 January 1908. Served in the Canadian Army, 1942–45. With the Royal Bank of Canada: in country branches, 1924–31, in Winnipeg, 1931–42, and in Montreal, 1946–68. Lived in Greece and Spain, 1968–80; now lives in Vancouver. Address: c/o McClelland and Stewart Ltd., 25 Hollinger Road, Toronto, Ontario M4B 3G2, Canada.

WESTERN PUBLICATIONS

Novels

As for Me and My House. New York, Reynal, 1941.
The Well. Toronto, Macmillan, 1958.
Whir of Gold. Toronto, McClelland and Stewart, 1970.
Sawbones Memorial. Toronto, McClelland and Stewart, 1974.

Short Stories

The Lamp at Noon and Other Stories. Toronto, McClelland and Stewart, 1968.
The Race and Other Stories, edited by Lorraine McMullen. Ottawa, University of Ottawa Press, 1982.

*

Bibliography: by David Latham, in *The Annotated Bibliography of Canada's Major Author 3* edited by Robert Lecker and Jack David, Downsview, Ontario, ECW Press, 1981.

Critical Studies: introduction by Roy Daniells to *As for Me and My House*, Toronto, McClelland and Stewart, 1957; "Wolf in the Snow" by Warren Tallman, in *A Choice of Critics* edited by George Woodcock, Toronto, Oxford University Press, 1966; introduction by Margaret Laurence to *The Lamp at Noon*, 1968; "Sinclair Ross's Ambivalent World" by W.H. New, in *Canadian Literature* (Vancouver), Spring 1969; "No Other Way: Sinclair Ross's Stories and Novels" by Sandra Djwa, in *Canadian Literature* (Vancouver), Winter 1971; *Patterns of Isolation in English—Canadian Fiction* by John G. Moss, Toronto, McClelland and Stewart, 1974; "The Mirror and the Lamp in Sinclair Ross's *As for Me and My House*" by David Stouck, in *Mosaic* (Winnipeg, Manitoba), Winter 1974; *Sinclair Ross and Ernest Buckler* by Robert D. Chambers, Vancouver, Copp Clark, 1975; introduction to *Sawbones Memorial*, Toronto, McClelland and Stewart, 1978, and *Sinclair Ross*, Boston, Twayne, 1979, both by Lorraine McMullen; *Sinclair Ross: A Reader's Guide* by Ken Mitchell, Regina, Saskatchewan, Thunder Creek, 1981; essay in *Canadian Literature* (Vancouver), Autumn 1984.

Sinclair Ross comments:

The setting for most of my stories is western Canada but they are not in the tradition of "Western." *No* cowboys or posses, but a great deal of frustration, gloom, and bad weather. I would say the world is "regional."

* * *

If Frederick Philip Grove wrote prolifically and monumentally about the early patriarch-settlers of the Canadian prairies, Sinclair Ross's compact chronicles of the prairies in the Depression 1930's excel in the artistry and insight with which they reveal the interaction of physical and psychological landscape in the lives of their survivor-victims. Like Grove's, Ross's characters must struggle not only with the harsh elements and desolate wilderness, but with spiritual alienation and emotional starvation as well. In Ross's fiction, however, Depression and dust bowl drought augment his characters' fears and insecurities which are projected onto the external environment, producing a mutual man-nature hostility. Many of Ross's themes and characters are regarded as typically Canadian, and his novel, *As for Me and My House* is now an established classic of Canadian literature.

The first of Ross's four novels of prairie realism, *As for Me and My House* is a taut, intense, and bitter record of repressed lives in Horizon, a small town in rural Saskatchewan, in the 1930's. The story is told in journal form by Mrs. Bentley, the minister's wife. An indictment of prairie puritanism and cultural sterility, the book is also bleakly pessimistic about the possibility of human communication, especially within a marriage. If the reader accepts the point of view of Mrs. Bentley's journal, she is a victim of the town's and her husband's failings; if he accepts Ross's implicit invitation to read between the lines, however, her elitist pride and belittling frigidity are the cause of her own and her husband's defeat. Outsiders by virtue of their social position and their parishioners' awareness that to them Horizon is merely another insignificant way station in a confining series of prairie pastorates, the Bentleys are estranged from the townsfolk as well as each other. With no real vocation as a minister of the gospel, Philip Bentley wants to believe he has some talent as a painter, though his daubing shows little evidence of this, partly because his creative imagination is frozen by self-lacerating guilt arising from his clerical charade. Honed to a fine precision in several previous short stories, the literary craftsmanship of this novel achieves a maturity and sophistication that Ross has never surpassed. His greatest accomplishment in this respect is the perfection of a lean but richly metaphorical prose style that relates the inner torment of his characters to the beauty and terror of the landscape.

The Well is again set in rural Saskatchewan, and deals with similar themes. Hardly a celebration of prairie life, the book does acknowledge its rewards, however, in treating the moral awakening of a young urban criminal, a quintessential outsider, who finds sanctuary on the prairies. Though weaker in structure and less penetrating than *As for Me and My House*, *The Well* is not without its finer qualities.

Whir of Gold takes place in Montreal, symbolic city of corruption. The young hero travels from prairie to city, reversing the pattern of *The Well*, and frequently recalls his prairie upbringing as an anchor of self and identity amid the violence and disorientation of his city sojourn. Thematically, the novel resembles its predecessors in its preoccupation with the guilt, entrapment, and alienation that govern the relationships among the three principal characters. Technically also, it recalls the careful structure, finely wrought style, and resonant language of Ross's first novel.

A collection of reminiscences in dialogue and monologue form by some 30 townspeople of Upward, Saskatchewan, *Sawbones Memorial* is a tribute to a retiring physician who has ministered to the little community through 45 years of pioneering, drought, Depression, and the effects of distant wars. Considerably more sprawling in form and conception than Ross's earlier novels, *Sawbones Memorial* nevertheless turns on two familiar themes: the failure of human communication and the small town's stultification of the human spirit. But the book also touches on such timeless human concerns as birth and death, youth and age, love and desire, courage and compassion. The mood of *Sawbones Memorial* is mellower, in fact, striking a better balance than earlier novels between bitterness and humorous detachment, rejection and grudging nostalgia. The fact that the book was written in Europe many years after the period it recreates may have provided the necessary distancing and perspective.

Early in his career Ross gained recognition as a writer of short stories, the best of which have been collected in *The Lamp at Noon and Other Stories*. The stories adumbrate many themes of the later novels, especially the human costs of prairie life in the 1930's, as revealed through mundane and apparently insignificant people and events. As in the novels, the style of Ross's short fiction combines economy and precision. Like the novels, too, the stories develop theme and narrative through the integration of mental and meteorological states, inner and outer landscape. Though he regards himself primarily as a novelist, some of Ross's stories can stand comparison with the best Canada has produced.

—John H. Ferres

ROSS, W(illiam) E(dward) D(aniel). Also writes as Leslie Ames; Rose Dana; Ruth Dorset; Ann Gilmer; Diane Randall; Ellen Randolph; Dan Roberts; Clarissa Ross; Dan Ross; Dana Ross; Marilyn Ross; Jane Rossiter; Tex Steel; Rose Williams. Canadian. Born in Saint John, New Brunswick, 16 November 1912. Educated at Provincetown Theatre School, New York, 1934; University of Chicago, Illinois; University of Oklahoma, Norman; Columbia University, New York; University of Michigan, Ann Arbor. Served in the British Entertainment Services during World War II. Married 1) Charlotte Edith MacCormack (died 1958); 2) Marilyn Ann Clark in 1960. Worked as a travelling actor and actor/manager with own touring company, 1930–48; film distributor, for own company, for Paramount, and for Monogram Films, 1948–57. Since 1957 full-time writer. Recipient: Dominion Drama Festival Prize, 1934; Queen Elizabeth Silver Jubilee Medal, 1978. Agent: Martha Millard, 357 West 19th Street, New York, New York 10011, U.S.A. Address: 80 Horton Road, East Riverside, Saint John, New Brunswick, Canada E2H IP8.

WESTERN PUBLICATIONS

Novels as Dan Roberts

The Wells Fargo Brand. New York, Arcadia House, 1964.
The Cheyenne Kid. New York, Arcadia House, 1965.
Durez City Bonanza. New York, Arcadia House, 1965.
Outlaw's Gold. New York, Arcadia House, 1965.
Stage to Link City. New York, Arcadia House, 1966.
Wyoming Range War. New York, Arcadia House, 1966.
Vengeance Rider. New York, Arcadia House, 1966.
Yuma Brand. New York, Arcadia House, 1967.
Lawman of Blue Rock. New York, Arcadia House, 1967.
The Dawn Riders. New York, Arcadia House, 1968.
Vengeance Spur. New York, Arcadia House, 1968.
Incident at Haddon City. New York, Arcadia House, 1968.
Wyoming Showdown. New York, Arcadia House, 1969.
The Sheriff of Mad River. New York, Arcadia House, 1970.

OTHER PUBLICATIONS

Novels

Alice in Love. New York, Popular Library, 1965.
Fog Island. New York, Paperback Library, 1965; as Marilyn Ross, New York, Popular Library, 1977.
The Ghost of Oaklands. New York, Arcadia House, 1967.
Journey to Love. New York, Bouregy, 1967.
The Third Spectre. New York, Arcadia House, 1967; as Dan Ross, New York, Macfadden-Bartell, 1969.
Love Must Not Waver. London, Hale, 1967.
Winslow's Daughter. New York, Bouregy, 1967.
Our Share of Love. London, Hale, 1967.
Dark Villa of Capri. New York, Arcadia House, 1968.
Let Your Heart Answer. New York, Bouregy, 1968.
The Twilight Web. New York, Arcadia House, 1968.
Behind Locked Shutters. New York, Arcadia House, 1968; as Dan Ross, New York, Manor, 1975.
Dark of the Moon. New York, Arcadia House, 1968.
Christopher's Mansion. New York, Bouregy, 1969.
Luxury Liner Nurse. London, Hale, 1969.
The Need to Love. New York, Avalon, 1969.
Sable in the Rain. New York, Lenox Hill, 1970.
The Web of Love. London, Hale, 1970.
An Act of Love. New York, Bouregy, 1970.
Magic Valley. London, Hale, 1970.
This Man I Love. London, Hale, 1970.
The Whispering Gallery. New York, Lenox Hill, 1970; as Dan Ross, New York, Manor, 1977.
Beauty Doctor's Nurse. New York, Lenox Hill, 1971.
The Yesteryear Phantom. New York, Lenox Hill, 1971.
King of Romance. London, Hale, 1971.
The Room Without a Key. New York, Lenox Hill, 1971.
Music Room. New York, Dell, 1971.
Wind over the Citadel. New York, Lenox Hill, 1971.
Rothhaven. New York, Avalon, 1972.
The House on Mount Vernon Street. New York, Lenox Hill, 1972.
Mansion on the Moors. New York, Dell, 1974.
An End of Summer. London, Hale, 1974.
Surgeon's Nurse. London, Hale, 1975.
Nightmare Abbey. New York, Berkeley, 1975.
One Louisburg Square. New York, Belmont Tower, 1975.
Witch of Goblin's Acres. New York, Belmont Tower, 1975.
Dark Is My Shadow. New York, Manor, 1976.
Summer's End. New York, Fawcett, 1976.
House on Lime Street. New York, Bouregy, 1976.
Pattern of Love. New York, Bouregy, 1977.
Shadows over Garden. New York, Belmont-Tower, 1978.
Return to Barton. New York, Avalon, 1978.
Queen's Stairway. New York, Arcadia House, 1978.
The Dark Lane. New York, Arcadia House, 1979.
Magic of Love. New York, Arcadia House, 1970.
Phantom of Edgewater Hall. New York, Arcadia House, 1980.
Nurse Ann's Secret. New York, Arcadia House, 1980.
Onstage for Love. New York, Arcadia House, 1981.
Nurse Grace's Dilemma. New York, Arcadia House, 1982.
This Uncertain Love. New York, Arcadia House, 1982.
Flight to Romance. New York, Arcadia House, 1983.
The Ghostly Jewels. New York, Arcadia House, 1983.
Rehearsal for Love. New York, Arcadia House, 1984.
A Love Discovered. New York, Arcadia House, 1984.
Nurse Janice's Dream. New York, Arcadia House, 1984.

Novels as Dan Ross

The Castle on the Cliff. New York, Bouregy, 1967.
Nurse in Crisis. New York, Avalon, 1971.
Nurse in Love. New York, Avalon, 1972.
Moscow Maze. New York, Dorchester, 1983.

Novels as Leslie Ames

Bride of Donnybrook. New York, Arcadia House, 1966.
The Hungry Sea. New York, Arcadia House, 1967.
The Hidden Chapel. New York, Arcadia House, 1967.
The Hill of Ashes. New York, Arcadia House, 1968.
King's Castle. New York, Lenox Hill, 1970.

Novels as Rose Dana

Citadel of Love. New York, Arcadia House, 1965.
Down East Nurse. New York, Arcadia House, 1967.

Nurse in Jeopardy. New York, Arcadia House, 1967.
Labrador Nurse. New York, Arcadia House, 1968.
Network Nurse. New York, Arcadia House, 1968.
Whitebridge Nurse. New York, Arcadia House, 1968.
Department Store Nurse. New York, Lenox Hill, 1970.

Novels as Ruth Dorset

Front Office Nurse. New York, Arcadia House, 1966.
Hotel Nurse. New York, Arcadia House, 1967.
Nurse in Waiting. New York, Arcadia House, 1967.

Novels as Ann Gilmer

The Fog and the Stars. New York, Avalon, 1963.
Winds of Change. New York, Bouregy, 1965.
Travelling with Sara. New York, Bouregy, 1965.
Private Nurse. New York, Bouregy, 1969.
Nurse on Emergency. New York, Bouregy, 1970.
Skyscraper Nurse. New York, Bouregy, 1976.
Nurse at Breakwater Hotel. New York, Arcadia House, 1982.

Novels as Diane Randall

The Secret of Graytowers. New York, Bouregy, 1968.
A Shadow on Capricorn. New York, Bouregy, 1970.
Psychiatric Nurse. New York, Bouregy, 1971.
Jennifer By Moonlight. New York and Toronto, Canada, Bantam, 1973.
Love Is a Riddle. New York, Bouregy, 1975.
Midhaven. New York, Bouregy, 1975.
Temple of Darkness. New York, Ballantine, 1976.
Pleasure's Daughter. New York, Popular Library, 1978.
Love in the Sun. New York, Avalon, 1978.

Novels as Ellen Randolph

Personal Secretary. New York, Avalon, 1963.
The Castle on the Hill. New York, Avalon, 1964.
Nurse Martha's Wish. New York, Arcadia House, 1983.

Novels as Clarissa Ross

Mistress of Ravenswood. New York, Arcadia House, 1966.
The Secret of Mallet Castle. New York, Arcadia House, 1966.
Fogbound. New York, Arcadia House, 1967; as Dan Ross, New York, Manor, 1976.
Let Your Heart Answer. New York, Valentine, 1968.
Secret of the Pale Lover. New York, Magnum, 1969.
Beware the Kindly Stranger. New York, Lancer, 1970.
Gemini in Darkness. New York, Magnum, 1970.
Glimpse into Terror. New York, Magnum, 1971.
The Spectral Mist. New York, Magnum, 1972.
Phantom of Glencourt. New York, Magnum, 1972.
Whispers in the Night. New York, Bantam, 1972.
China Shadow. New York, Avon, 1974.
Drafthaven. New York, Avon, 1974.
Ghost of Dark Harbor. New York, Avon, 1974.
A Hearse for Dark Harbor. New York, Avon, 1974.
Dark Harbor Haunting. New York, Avon, 1975.
Evil of Dark Harbor. New York, Avon, 1975.
Terror at Dark Harbor. New York, Avon, 1975.
Durrell Towers. New York, Pyramid, 1976.
Jade Princess. New York, Pyramid, 1977.
Moscow Mists. New York, Avon, 1977.
A Scandalous Affair. New York, Belmont Tower, 1978.
Kashmiri Passions. New York, Warner, 1978.
Istanbul Nights. New York, Jove, 1978.
Flame of Love. New York, Belmont Tower, 1978.
Wine of Passion. New York, Belmont Tower, 1978.
Casablanca Intrigue. New York, Warner, 1979.
So Perilous My Love. New York, Leisure Press, 1979.
Eternal Desire. New York, Jove, 1979.
Fan the Wanton Flame. New York, Pocket Books, 1980.
Only Make Believe. New York, Leisure Press, 1980.
Masquerade. New York, Pocket Books, 1980.
Venetian Affair. New York, Jove, 1980.
Beloved Scoundrel. New York, Belmont Tower, 1980.
Fortune's Mistress. New York, Popular Library, 1981.
Satan Whispers. New York, Leisure Press, 1981.
Summer of the Shaman. New York, Warner, 1982.
The Dancing Years. New York, Pinnacle, 1982.

Novels as Dana Ross

Demon of Darkness. New York, Paperback Library, 1975.
Lodge Sinister. New York, Paperback Library, 1975.
This Shrouded Night. New York, Paperback Library, 1975.
The Raven and the Phantom. New York, Paperback Library, 1976.

Novels as Marilyn Ross

The Locked Corridor. New York, Paperback Library, 1965.
Beware My Love! New York, Paperback Library, 1965.
Dark Shadows. New York, Paperback Library, 1968.
The Foe of Barnabas Collins. New York, Paperback Library, 1969.
Barnabas, Quentin, and Dr. Jekyll's Son. New York, Paperback Library, 1971.
Phantom of Fog Island. New York, Warner, 1971.
The Long Night of Fear. New York, Warner, 1972.
Dark Stars Over Seacrest. New York, Paperback Library, 1972.
Phantom of the Swamp. New York, Paperback Library, 1972.
Mistress of Moorwood Manor. New York, Warner, 1972.
Night of the Phantom. New York, Warner, 1972.
The Sinister Garden. New York, Warner, 1972.
Witch of Bralhaven. New York, Warner, 1972.
Behind the Purple Veil. New York, Warner, 1973.
Face in the Shadows. New York, Warner, 1973.
House of Ghosts. New York, Warner, 1973.
Don't Look Behind You. New York, Warner, 1973.
Marta. New York, Warner, 1973.
Step into Terror. New York, Warner, 1973.
The Amethyst Tears. New York, Ballantine, 1974.
The Vampire Contessa. New York, Pinnacle, 1974.
Witches' Cove. New York, Warner, 1974.
A Garden of Ghosts. New York, Popular Library, 1974.
Loch Sinister. New York, Popular Library, 1974.
Cameron Castle. New York, Warner, 1975.
The Ghost and the Garnet: Birthstone No. 1. New York, Ballantine, 1975.
Satan's Island. New York, Warner, 1975.
Shadow over Emerald Castle. New York, Ballantine, 1975.
Dark Towers of Fog Island. New York, Popular Library, 1975.
Fog Island Secret. New York, Popular Library, 1975.
Ghost Ship of Fog Island. New York, Popular Library, 1975.
Phantom of the Thirteenth Floor. New York, Popular Library, 1975.
Ravenhurst. New York, Popular Library, 1975.
Brides of Saturn. New York, Berkley, 1976.
Temple of Darkness. New York, Ballantine, 1976.
The Widow of Westwood. New York, Popular Library, 1976.

The Curse of Black Charlie. New York, Popular Library, 1976.
Haiti Circle. New York, Popular Library, 1976.
Phantom Wedding. New York, Popular Library, 1976.
Shadow over Denby. New York, Popular Library, 1976.
Stewards of Stormhaven: Cellars of the Dead. New York, Popular Library, 1976.
Waiting in the Shadows. New York, Popular Library, 1976.
Cauldron of Evil. New York, Popular Library, 1977.
Death's Dark Music. New York, Popular Library, 1977.
Mask of Evil. New York, Popular Library, 1977.
Phantom of the Snow. New York, Popular Library, 1977.
This Evil Village. New York, Popular Library, 1977.
Delta Flame. New York, Popular Library, 1978.
Rothby. New York, Popular Library, 1978.
Horror of Fog Island. New York, Popular Library, 1978.
The Twice Dead. New York, Fawcett, 1978.
Beloved Adversary. New York, Popular Library, 1981.
Forbidden Flame. New York, Popular Library, 1982.

Novels as Jane Rossiter

Backstage Nurse. New York, Avalon, 1963.
Love Is Forever. New York, Avalon, 1963.
Summer Star. New York, Avalon, 1964.

Novels as Rose Williams

Five Nurses. New York, Arcadia House, 1964.
Nurse in Doubt. New York, Arcadia House, 1965.
Nurse Diane. New York, Arcadia House, 1966.
Nurse in Spain. London, Hale, 1967.
Nurse in Nassau. New York, Arcadia House, 1967.
Airport Nurse. New York, Arcadia House, 1968.

Plays

Murder Game (as Dan Ross). New York, Playwrights Press, 1982.
This Frightened Lady (as Dan Ross). New York, Marginal, 1984.

*   *   *

In the late 1960's and early 1970's W.E.D. Ross established himself as one of the most accomplished exponents of the gothic genre. As Marilyn Ross—probably his most popular pseudonym—he penned numerous novels linked to the American TV soap operas *Dark Shadows* and *Strange Paradise*, and in many respects, his Westerns differ little in style and construction from these melodramas. Both are told in a somewhat naive or simplistic way, both rely upon plots that twist and turn at regular intervals to sustain reader-interest, romance and mystery form vital components in each story, and good always triumphs completely over evil at the conclusion of each frantic climax.

Regardless of genre, Ross writes about largely uncomplicated characters, employs little or no profanity, usually comes up with a surprise or two during the final scenes of his books, and seldom presents violence explicitly. Indeed, Ross's Westerns, like his gothics, may sometimes stretch credibility somewhat, or conveniently dispense with logic in order to prolong an otherwise easily-resolved situation, but for all their faults, there is something about his books which is at once both agreeable and endearing.

Ross has a preference for polite, trustworthy heroes—youngish men whose codes of conduct are beyond reproach. Even though some of them may be described as gunmen who care not so much about the rights and wrongs of a situation as how much the highest bidder will pay them for their involvement in it, as in *Incident at Haddon City*, for example, or *The Sheriff of Mad River*, they nevertheless eventually prove themselves to be men of high principles, who follow the dictates of a strong and clear conscience.

The author's women tend to fall into one of two categories—the domesticated, subservient type or, more common, quick-tempered women of spirit and courage. Rarely do Ross's female characters perform particularly active roles in his stories, however. As far as plots go, the author appears to enjoy recounting stories in which outlaw gangs terrorise the local inhabitants in order to clear the way for one land-grabbing scheme or another. Neither is Ross afraid to use coincidences, chance encounters, good twins, bad twins and lady sheriffs to propel his largely traditional stories along.

One of the better Westerns is *The Cheyenne Kid*, which displays the author's ability to sustain and finally gather together a number of plot-threads to form an amiable enough Western which is at once both patently improbable and strangely compelling. *The Cheyenne Kid* opens with the young hero recuperating from a beating which has left him with amnesia. At the suggestion of Rufe Tonner, the grizzled old prospector who found and nursed him, the young man takes the name of Ben Davis, Rufe's late partner, until he can discover his own identity. Almost at once, however, an attempt is made on "Ben's" life. He and Tonner are framed for the murder of the one man who could reveal "Ben's" true identity. Out on the trail they meet up with a mysterious artist from Boston who is evidently not what he seems. And, as the story wears on, events begin to suggest that "Ben" (who, as the archetypal Ross protagonist, is honest, well-mannered, and considerate of others) is in reality a notorious killer and thief known as the Cheyenne Kid.

How the author manages to resolve this situation certainly begs credibility, as indeed do nearly all his endings, and the final showdown, which occurs "off-screen," is far from satisfactory. Despite these faults, however, *The Cheyenne Kid* is a good, if undemanding, read.

Weak or rushed endings in which everything is tied up rather too neatly to be entirely convincing also typify both *The Dawn Riders* and *Wyoming Showdown*, two variations on the land-grabbing theme which also incorperate the traditional revenge motif. In the former, Chet Lane, a pistol-carrying lawyer, returns to Boise City after an absence of several years in order to get even with the men who were primarily responsible for his father's death at the hands of a lynch mob. Within a day of his arrival, however, Chet is hired by a number of small ranchers who have all received offers to buy their land from Bert Ketchel, the very man who was able to purchase the Lane spread for a fraction of its true value following Tom Lane's murder. The price of refusing Ketchel's offer is a visit from the Dawn Riders, a band of masked terrorists whose "calling card" is "a carved wooden skull with a capital D and R where the eye sockets would rightly be." Jim Mason, the hero of *Wyoming Showdown*, is a former sheriff who quits his job in order to track down the gang who shot and killed his brother during a bank robbery. Mason's only clue to the identity of his quarry are his brother's last words, "The Four Aces."

Subsequent enquiries lead Mason to Culver Valley, where a saloon of that name is located. Before he can reach his destination, however, he meets Gustav Bohn, the burly German owner of the Circle Z, and Bohn's beautiful but scarred daughter Erica. It soon becomes obvious that all the ranchers in the valley are having problems with Wilf Nestor, the owner of the Four Aces Saloon. To realise his dream of creating a haven for the lawless, Nestor needs to take control of the entire valley, and once again, employs intimidatory tactics to achieve his aims. Mason refuses to work for the ranchers, intending to check out Nestor alone. Nestor is a hard man to find, however, and his true identity (which is, sadly, all too obvious) is not revealed until the end of the book.

In spite of a tendency to create sometimes fantastic plots, write in a rather melodramatic manner (emphasising each new revelation with an exclamation mark) and handle romance or mystery in a contrived way, there can be no denying that Ross's Westerns offer entertainment that is both pleasant and untaxing.

—David Whitehead

ROSS, Zola (Helen, née Girdey). Also wrote as Helen Arre; Bert Iles; Z.H. Ross. American. Born in Dayton, Iowa, 9 May 1912. Educated at MacMurray College, Jacksonville, Illinois, B.A. 1932; University of Washington, Seattle, 1943–45. Married Frank William Ross in 1934. Associate Professor of creative writing, University of Washington, 1948–55. Adult education teacher, Lake Washington Schools, from 1956. *Died December 1989.*

WESTERN PUBLICATIONS

Novels

Bonanza Queen: A Novel of the Comstock Lode. Indianapolis, Bobbs Merrill, 1949.
Tonapah Lady. Indianapolis, Bobbs Merrill, 1950.
Reno Crescent. Indianapolis, Bobbs Merrill, 1951.
The Green Land. Indianapolis, Bobbs Merrill, 1952.
Cassy Scandal. Indianapolis, Bobbs Merrill, 1954; London, Redman, 1956.
The Golden Witch. Indianapolis, Bobbs Merrill, 1955; London, Redman, 1956.
A Land to Tame. Indianapolis, Bobbs Merrill, 1956; London, Redman, 1957.
Spokane Saga. Indianapolis, Bobbs Merrill, 1957; London, Redman, 1959.

Uncollected Short Story

"When Seattle Burned," in *This Land Around Us*, edited by Ellis Lucia. New York, Doubleday, 1969.

OTHER PUBLICATIONS

Novels as Z.H. Ross

Three Down Vulnerable. Indianapolis, Bobbs Merrill, 1946.
Overdue for Death. Indianapolis, Bobbs Merrill, 1947.
One Corpse Missing. Indianapolis, Bobbs Merrill, 1948.
Murder in Mink (as Bert Iles). New York, Arcadia House, 1956.

Novels as Helen Arre

The Corpse by the River. New York, Arcadia House, 1953.
No Tears at the Funeral. New York, Arcadia House, 1954.
Write It Murder. New York, Arcadia House, 1956.
The Golden Shroud. New York, Arcadia House, 1958.
Murder by the Book. New York, Arcadia House, 1960.

Other (for children) with Lucile McDonald

The Mystery of Catesby Island. New York, Nelson, 1950.
Stormy Year. New York, Nelson, 1952.
Friday's Child. New York, Nelson, 1954.
Mystery of the Long House. New York, Nelson, 1956.
Pigtail Pioneer. Philadelphia, Winston, 1956.
Wing Harbor. New York, Nelson, 1957.
The Courting of Ann Maria. New York, Nelson, 1958.
Assignment in Ankara. New York, Nelson, 1959; as *Stolen Letters*, New York, Pyramid, 1959.
Winter's Answer. New York, Nelson, 1961.
The Sunken Forest. New York, Weybright and Talley, 1968.
For Glory and the King. New York, Meredith Press, 1969.

* * *

Zola Ross wrote most of her books in the early 1950's. Her stories are set in the American Northwest or Great Basin area; she emphasizes the growth and development of such towns as Seattle, San Francisco, and Reno. Although the characters find themselves involved in land and mining speculation, early western businesses such as stores and newpapers, or Chinese or Indian race problems, Ross's genre is not really the Western but the historical romance with the West as background. Ross is also a mystery writer and an occasional "who-done-it" murder may also be a part of these western romances.

Unfortunately, the books tend to be formula writing, as over and over again the same general plot is replayed. If you happen to like romances, then there is nothing wrong with this, and hundreds of such books are selling in today's market. Those looking for a "man's Western" should look elsewhere. It is, however, refreshing to find a young woman as the leading character rather than the "tall, male stranger." The plots involve a young woman who is usually engaged or married to a man who unknown to her is involved in illegal or, at the least, immoral activities, such as owning saloons or brothels or using his public office to speculate on land. Somehow, this man conveniently dies either by illness, murder, or wounds in the Civil War. The heroine, who sees herself as a "Victorian lady," would much rather be taken care of by a husband. She is now forced into the business world. To her own surprise and to the surprise of her family and friends she finds she has strength and abilities. Fluttering around the new widow are several suitors. One is a man she despises who is a better businessman than she. He attempts to keep her from falling into the immoral activities or weak mistakes of her past love, but she is often too stubborn to listen to him. Another suitor is a man very much like her first suitor or husband, who is often involved in under-handed deals. She eventually becomes engaged to him. By the end of the book, she will, of course, realize her mistake and fall eagerly into the open arms of the man she has been "battling" with all along. The end of the book is always the final, romantic kiss.

These books are not the "hot" romances found on today's shelves. Still, the heroine, especially if she is widowed, has become an "experienced woman" and does admit her sexual desires.

In Ross's books men, except for the hero, tend to be weak. The father is often a dallier or drunkard, but likeable. It is the heroine who not only pulls herself together but supports her family, too. Her mother is often a powerful shrew whom the daughter wishes to evade to go on adventures, or if the mother is supportive, she is still very protective. The town "bad women"—madames, prostitutes, or saloon owners—are usually charitable and intelligent women whom the heroine is willing to befriend, much to her other young girl friends' chagrin. Minorities under attack by others are protected by the heroine, showing us again she can think for herself and that she is a kind person. Unfortunately, the Chinese or Indian characters are never really developed. They are not able to take care of themselves, and are relegated to the world of servants.

Ross's works are unusual because she sets her novels on the West Coast. Her settings of developing towns are interesting and indicative of this area in the mid-19th century. Some research has gone into the settings. The background is more interesting than the plot, although there is not enough development of it.

Her stories show young women growing up and learning to be responsible for their own lives and actions. Even when the heroine falls into the arms of her lover at the end of the book, it is obvious that the relationship will be a partnership. Women involved in business were unusual even in the 1950's when women were more involved in husband and children, so what might seem weak, romantic young women now were probably seen as more forceful characters then.

—Daryl Morrison

ROUNTREE, Owen. *See* **KITTREDGE, William; KRAUZER, Steven M.**

ROURKE, James. *See* **HECKELMANN, Charles N.**

ROWAN, M.M. Pseudonym for Marie Rowan. British. Born in Glasgow, 28 November 1943. Educated at Jordanhill College of Education, Glasgow, Primary Teacher's Diploma 1962–65, and Diploma in Special Education, 1968–69. Auxiliary, Royal Navy. Since 1965 Assistant Head Teacher, Strathclyde Regional Council, Glasgow. Address: 1 Leslie Avenue, Bishopton, Renfrewshire PA7 5EP, Scotland.

WESTERN PUBLICATIONS

Novels

No Long Farewell. London, Hale, 1985.
Beyond the High Mesas. London, Hale, 1986.
The Powder River Raid. London, Hale, 1988.
Absarokas. London, Hale, 1989.
Singing Wind Rise. London, Hale, 1991.

Uncollected Short Stories

"Hirta's Veil," in *Woman's Realm* (London), 1984.

*

M. M. Rowan comments:

The aim of my writing is to explore the relationships of ordinary people in the days of the pioneer, when the greed and corruption of their fellow-men were as much a hazard as the elements, to examine their hopes and frailties and to portray their amazing self-sufficiency and commitment in times of hardship.

* * *

Though in reality one of the most charming of Scotswomen, M.M. Rowan's Westerns reflect little of her gentility. Tough, intelligent, slick, and violent, her books are quite probably among the most interesting of their type presently being published in England, with intriguing plots which often confound expectation, and plausible, well-rounded characters who communicate their creator's keen understanding of human nature admirably.

Rowan's first book was the grim and rather convoluted *No Long Farewell*, an over-long but nonetheless interesting revenge Western which set the largely sober tone of the stories that follow. Possibly the weakest of the author's books, with a sometimes incoherent plot and a leaning towards the melodramatic ("And when Cole moved, somebody got very dead!") *No Long Farewell* is carried along by Rowan's enthusiasm—an enthusiasm and genuine care for plot and character which has communicated itself quite clearly in her work ever since.

Beyond the High Mesas is a much better Western, benefitting from a shorter word-count, a more intriguing plot, and more fully realised characters. Around the town of Salvation it is an open secret that a rancher named Hiram Gertz is responsible for a number of attacks on those neighbours of Indian blood or with Indian connections. The latest in a long line of outrages—the death of rancher Eyeler Pike—prompts Joel Creswell (whose son Reuben is half-Comanche) to find out why. Following a lead given him by Pike's daughter Sal, Creswell embarks upon a journey to Twin Peaks, a town which lies beyond the high mesas (hence the title). While he is away, however, Gertz's men attack the Creswell spread and kill Creswell's wife, and with no means of getting the news to his father, Reuben (who was absent from the ranch himself at the time of the attack) sets out on a quest of his own—to find his mother's killer. From this point on, Rowan tells the story from multiple viewpoints, reaching a rewarding conclusion only after some neat and well-executed plot-twists.

The twist is something Rowan uses to particularly good advantage in *The Powder River Raid.* Haunted by the memory of the Indian attack which gives the book its title (and which cost of the lives of his Cavalry patrol simply because he was too drunk to command them), Rad McLaurin is reunited with two of the survivors some years later. Now civilians like McLaurin, Gus Cameron and Toby Bernstein run a successful lumber business in Medicine Lodge, and discovering that McLaurin is about to join a wagon train on its way to Blackwater, they talk him into taking a box full of documents and jewellery with him for safekeeping. Although McLaurin is reluctant to get involved, he feels a certain obligation to Bernstein, who lost the use of his legs during the Powder River Raid. The journey is not without event, however; almost as soon as he joins the wagon train he is accidentally reunited with his ex-wife Mary, and as the column snakes slowly on towards its destination, attempts are made on McLaurin's life, presumably in order to gain access to the mysterious box. The reader is successfully kept off-balance as Rowan heaps one twist or surprise on top of another, handling each new revelation with consummate skill.

As satisfying as *The Powder River Raid* is, however, probably Rowan's best work is *Absarokas*, which once again blends the traditional Western with the most nagging of mysteries. The recent death of his brother Will finally brings gambler Dale Duggan home after an absence of 20 years. At last he believes the time is right to find out who was responsible for the deaths of his parents several years before, and more importantly, *why* they had to die. The most likely suspect is Tim Farrow, who certainly had a motive (to get control of the nearby river to power his mill). But as with nearly all of Rowan's work, all is not as it seems. In an atmosphere of mutual suspicion, Duggan searches to find the truth of the matter—a truth that everyone else appears to know, but will never reveal.

Rowan's strengths as a storyteller outweigh her weaknesses, though it would, of course, be foolish to pretend that her work is faultless. In particular, however, she handles her characters very well, presenting them as largely unglamorous, slightly cynical, and worn down by life on the frontier. Similarly, the love interest present in all her books is enacted with some originality. Although she has a tendency to refer to just about every male character as a "guy," her writing is generally spare and in period. She appears to have toned down the violence, which was quite graphic in her earlier books; in *Absarokas*, for example, nearly all of the beatings and shootings are somehow "shielded" from the reader. Another beating, which we are told about but never see, actually takes place between chapters. Her dialogue is also very slick, especially when stringing together sardonic comments and rejoinders.

A clever and accomplished western writer, Rowan normally produces one new book every 12 to 15 months, but in the future hopes to increase her output—no doubt much to the delight of her many admirers.

—David Whitehead

ROWLAND, Donald S(ydney). Also writes as Annette Adams; Jack Bassett; Hazel Baxter; Karla Benton; Helen Berry; Lewis Brant; Alison Bray; William Brayce; Fenton Brockley; Oliver Bronson; Chuck Buchanan; Rod Caley; Roger Carlton; Janita Cleve; Sharon Court; Vera Craig; Wesley Craille; John Delaney; John Dryden; Freda Fenton; Charles Field; Graham Garner; Burt Kroll; Helen Langley; Henry Lansing; Harvey Lant; Irene Lynn; Hank Madison; Chuck Mason; Stuart McHugh; G.J. Morgan; Glebe Morgan; Edna Murray; Lorna Page; Olive Patterson; Alvin Porter; Alex Random; Donna Rix; Matt Rockwell; Charles Roscoe; Minerva Rosetti; Norford Scott; Valerie Scott; Bart Segundo; Bart Shane; Frank Shaul; Clinton Spurr; Roland Starr; J.D. Stevens; Mark Suffling; Will Travers; Sarah Vine; Elaine Vinson; Rick Walters; Neil Webb. British. Born in Great Yarmouth, Suffolk, 23 September 1928. Educated to age 12. Served in the British Army, 1945–50: acting sergeant. Married Jessie Robinson in 1950; two daughters and one son. Worked in fish curing and exporting, fruit canning, and construction, 1950–53; film projectionist, 1953–57; clerk and local government officer, 1957–63; then full-time writer. Address: 1 Quay Angel, Gorleston-on-Sea, Great Yarmouth, Suffolk NR31 6TJ, England.

WESTERN PUBLICATIONS

Novels

The Battle Done. London, Brown Watson, 1958.
Vengeance for Water Valley. London, Wright and Brown, 1961.
Drygulch Valley. London, Wright and Brown, 1961.
Gunsmoke Pay-Off. London, Wright and Brown, 1961.
Murder Range. London, Wright and Brown, 1961.
Showdown at Singing Springs. London, Wright and Brown, 1962.
Rough Justice London, Hale, 1963; as *Bullets at Dry Creek*, New York, Arcadia House, 1965.
The Long Trail. London, Hale, 1963; as *Law of the Holster*, New York, Arcadia House, 1967.
Lonely Star. London, Hale, and New York, Arcadia House, 1964.
Empty Saddles. London, Hale, 1964.
Boss of Border Country (as Bart Segundo). London, Hale, 1964.
Raw Deal (as Oliver Bronson). London, Gresham, 1965.
Cattleman's Creed (as Oliver Bronson). London, Gresham, 1965.
Crossfire. London, Hale, 1966.
Range Hog (as William Brayce). London, Gresham, 1966.
Brave Star (as Chuck Buchanan). London, Hale, 1966.
Lonesome Valley (as Rod Caley). London, Gresham, 1966.
Hell-Bent (as Wesley Craille). London, Hale, 1966.
Bleak Range (as Henry Lansing). London, Gresham, 1966.
The Sidewinders (as W.J. Rimmer). London, Hale, 1966.
Trigger Help (as Matt Rockwell). London, Gresham, 1966.
Gunsmoke Pass (as Rick Walters). London, Gresham, 1966.
Gun Rogues. London, Hale, 1967; New York, Arcadia House, 1969.
Gun Wild. London, Hale, 1976.
The Rail Rogues (as Glebe Morgan). New York, Belmont, 1980; London, Hale, 1981.
Tough Country (as Rod Caley). London, Hale, 1982.
One-Way Trail. London, Hale, 1983.
Hanging Hill. London, Hale, 1983.
Gunsmoke Pass (as Rick Walters). London, Hale, 1983.
Violent Trail. London, Hale, 1984.

Novels as Charles Field

Kingdom of Grass. London, Hale, 1964.
Saddle Tramp. London, Hale, 1965.
Star Brand Killer. London, Hale, 1965.
Trail End. London, Hale, 1966.
Gunsmoke in the Air. London, Hale, 1984.

Novels as Charles Roscoe

Gunsmoke Law. London, Hale, 1964.
Cattleman's Country. London, Hale, 1965.
Gunswift Justice. London, Hale, 1965.
Draw or Die. London, Hale, 1966.
Trail of No Return. London, Hale, 1977.
Gun Boss. London, Hale, 1980.
Killer Trail. London, Hale, 1981.
Six-Gun Showdown. London, Hale, 1982.

Novels as Frank Shaul

Black Sundown. London, Hale, 1964.
Saddle Pard. London, Hale, 1966.
Lawman Courageous. London, Hale, 1968.
Sixgun Bart. London, Hale, 1981.
Uneasy Range. London, Hale, 1982.
Wild Country. London, Hale, 1983.

Novels as J.D. Stevens

Bitter Valley. London, Hale, 1964.
Twisted Trail. London, Hale, 1965.

Shoot First. London, Hale, 1965.
Heartbreak Range. London, Hale, 1965.

Novels as Will Travers

Rogue Rancher. London, Hale, 1964.
Gun Crazy. London, Hale, 1965.
Showdown. London, Hale, 1966.
Gold Fever. London, Hale, 1966.
Trail to Hell. London, Hale, 1983.
The Troublemakers. London, Hale, 1984.

Novels as Neil Webb

Danger Trail. London, Hale, 1964.
Rope Branded. London, Hale, 1965.
Thunder Canyon. London, Hale, 1965.
Trigger Law. London, Hale, 1966.
High Stakes. London, Hale, 1966.
Big Saddle. London, Hale, 1966.
Bullet Proof. London, Hale, 1966.
Bleak Valley. London, Hale, 1973.
Guns of Hate. London, Hale, 1973.
Gun Wolves. London, Hale, 1974.
Killer Law. London, Hale, 1975.
Hostile Range. London, Hale, 1976.
Gun Handy. London, Hale, 1977.
Hardcase Law. London, Hale, 1981.
Gun Hatred. London, Hale, 1981.
Short Cut to Hell. London, Hale, 1983.

Novels as Lewis Brant

Blood in the Dust. London, Hale, 1964.
Dark Prairie. London, Hale, 1964.
Hard to Kill. London, Hale, 1965.
Bitter Round-Up. London, Hale, 1966.
Gun Hand. London, Hale, 1966.
Gunshot Pay-Off. London, Hale, 1966.
The Back Shooter. London, Hale, 1967.
Gun Trail. London, Hale, 1967.
Gringo Basin. London, Hale, 1975.
Gunslick. London, Hale, 1975.
Shale Creek Showdown. London, Hale, 1976.
Bullets at Sunset. London, Hale, 1977.
Hair-Triggered. London, Hale, 1979.
Bloodthirsty Range. London, Hale, 1980.
Cowboy Law. London, Hale, 1982.
Lawless Gun. London, Hale, 1983.
Shoot First. London, Hale, 1983.

Novels as Clinton Spurr

Vengeance Gun. London, Hale, 1964.
The Hell Raisers. London, Hale, 1965.
Trail Fever. London, Hale, 1965.
Short Rope. London, Hale, 1966.
Shoot and Run. London, Hale, 1967.
Killer Brand. London, Hale, 1967.
Gun Fever. London, Hale, 1967.
Death Wore Spurs. London, Hale, 1969.
Trigger Fever. London, Hale, 1972.
Wyoming Wild. London, Hale, 1973.
The Loner. London, Hale, 1973.
The Ambusher. London, Hale, 1973.
Close Call. London, Hale, 1974.
Running Iron London, Hale, 1974.
Hell Tracks London, Hale, 1976.
Hell Town. London, Hale, 1978.
Railroad Marshal. London, Hale, 1980.
Hostile Hills. London, Hale, 1982.
Killer on the Range. London, Hale, 1982.

Novels as John Dryden

Quick on the Draw. London, Hale, 1965.
Wild Loop Range. London, Hale, 1965.
Hard Ridden. London, Hale, 1966.
Killer Streak. London, Hale, 1973.
Range Rights. London, Hale, 1973.
The Wildloopers London, Hale, 1974.
Crooked Brand. London, Hale, 1974.

Novels as Norford Scott

Roughshod. London, Hale, 1965.
Tight Rein. London, Hale, 1966.
Whip-Hand. London, Hale, 1966.
Vengeance of the Diamond M. London, Hale, 1967.
Saddled for Hell. London, Hale, 1967.
Kicking Horse Country. London, Hale, 1967.
Terror Law. London, Hale, 1969.
Smoke of the .45. London, Hale, 1977.
Border Bandit. London, Hale, 1980.
Hard Range. London, Hale, 1981.
Gun Wranglers. London, Hale, 1982.
Fighting Men. London, Hale, 1983.
Gunslick. London, Hale, 1987.

Novels as Jack Bassett

Shooting Trouble. London, Hale, 1966.
Forked Trail. London, Hale, 1966.
No Quarter. London, Hale, 1967.
Gunsmoke Creek. London, Hale, 1967.
Saddle Scum. London, Hale, 1967.
Big Tracks. London, Hale, 1968.
Texas Ranger. London, Hale, 1982.
Shooting Trail. London, Hale, 1987.

Novels as Burt Kroll

Water Rights. London, Gresham, 1966.
Greenhorn Gun. London, Gresham, 1966.
Hungry Guns. London, Hale, 1967.
Coyote Trail. London, Hale, 1968.
Snake Breed. London, Hale, 1968.
Gunsmoke Showdown. London, Hale, 1972.
Shoot on Sight. London, Hale, 1973.
Mocking Bird Creek. London, Hale, 1973.
Broken-Down Cowboy. London, Hale, 1974.
Lone-Wolf Lawman. London, Hale, 1974.
Trail to Boot Hill. London, Hale, 1977.
Gun Wages. London, Hale, 1980.
Flaming Range. London, Hale, 1981.
Ambush Range. London, Hale, 1981; as Harvey Lant, London, Hale, 1983.

Novels as Harvey Lant

Range Fury. London, Hale, 1966.
High, Wide, and Handsome. London, Hale, 1966.
Slaughter Trail. London, Hale, 1966.
Bad Medicine. London, Hale, 1967.
Gun Rage. London, Hale, 1967.
Angry Guns. London, Hale, 1972.

Pistol Range. London, Hale, 1973.
Fighting Marshal. London, Hale, 1973.
Gun Hell. London, Hale, 1973.
Range Grab. London, Hale, 1974.
The Sarbo Gang. London, Hale, 1976.
Hell on the Border. London, Hale, 1979.
Gunsmoke Marshal. London, Hale, 1980.
Gun Thunder. London, Hale, 1981.

Novels as Hank Madison

Riding High. London, Hale, 1966.
Wanted—Dead or Alive. London, Hale, 1966.
Fighting Mad. London, Hale, 1967.
Killer in the County. London, Hale, 1967.
Gunsmoke Legacy. London, Hale, 1967.
Arizona Pay-Off. London, Hale, 1972.
Man from Texas. London, Hale, 1973.
The Straightshooter. London, Hale, 1973.
Desperate Gun. London, Hale, 1974.
Frontier Law. London, Hale, 1976.
Blood on the Saddle. London, Hale, 1976.
Hell Rider. London, Hale, 1979.
Lawless Range. London, Hale, 1980.
Bullet Justice. London, Hale, 1982.
Hard Law. London, Hale, 1982.
Quicksilver Gun. London, Hale, 1984.

Novels as Stuart McHugh

Gun Shy. London, Hale, 1966.
Prairie Wolf. London, Hale, 1966.
Riding for a Fall. London, Hale, 1967.
Running Wild. London, Hale, 1967.
Coyote Breed. London, Hale, 1987.

Novels as Chuck Mason

Back Trail. London, Gresham, 1966.
The Law Dealer. London, Gresham, 1966.
Gunman Notorious. London, Hale, 1966.
Ride Hard—Shoot Fast. London, Hale, 1967.
Hell Branded. London, Hale, 1967.
Gun Lightning. London, Hale, 1967.
Undercover Law. London, Hale, 1968.
Hell Star. London, Hale, 1972.
Gun for Hire. London, Hale, 1973.
Hangrope Fever. London, Hale, 1973.
Quick Triggers. London, Hale, 1973.
Gun Trap. London, Hale, 1974.
Fast Draw Law. London, Hale, 1974.
Backlash. London, Hale, 1974.
Death in Oak Ridge. London, Hale, 1976.
Heller from Texas. London, Hale, 1977.
Hell on the Range. London, Hale, 1980.
Gunman's Law. London, Hale, 1981.

Novels as Alvin Porter

The Corpse Maker. London, Hale, 1966.
Bitter Feud. London, Hale, 1967.
Riding Through. London, Hale, 1967.
Crooked Spurs. London, Hale, 1967.
Die-Hard Lawman. London, Hale, 1977.
Devil's Brood. London, Hale, 1980.
Gunsmoke and Rawhide. London, Hale, 1981.
Range Justice. London, Hale, 1982.

Novels as G.J. Morgan

Hell on Wheels. London, Futura, 1975.
Border Fury. London, Futura, 1975.
Trail of Death. London, Futura, 1975.

Novels as John Delaney

The Deadly Stranger. London, Mews, 1976.
The Hard Bounty. London, Mews, 1976.
Oregon Outrage. London, New English Library, 1977.
Blood Brand. London, Mews, 1977.
Lawless Land. London, New English Library, 1978.

Novels as Bart Shane

Iron Rails. Ipswich, Magread, 1979.
Rails West. Ipswich, Magread, 1980.
Railhead. Ipswich, Magread, 1980.

OTHER PUBLICATIONS

Novels

12 Platoon. London, Brown Watson, 1962.
Both Feet in Hell. London, Brown Watson, 1962.
Not for Glory. London, Combat Library, 1962.
Where the Heart Lies (as Helen Langley). London, Gresham, 1968.
Overseas Nurse (as Sarah Vine). London, Wright and Brown, 1969.
Depot in Space. London, Hale, 1973.
Heiress to Crag Castle (as Minerva Rosetti). New York, Lenox Hill Press, 1973.
Master of Space. London, Hale, 1974.
Mansion to Menace. New York, Lenox Hill Press, 1974.
Star Quest (as Fenton Brockley). London, Hale, 1974.
Beyond Tomorrow (as Roger Carlton). London, Hale, 1975.
Star Arrow (as Roger Carlton). London, Hale, 1975.
Project Oceanus (as Mark Suffling). London, Hale, 1975.
Space Crusader (as Mark Suffling). London, Hale, 1975.
Space Venturer. London, Hale, 1976.
Nightmare Planet. London, Hale, 1976.

Novels as Annette Adams

Island of Decision. London, Gresham, 1968.
Doctor of the Heart. London, Gresham, 1968.
The Heart Healer. London, Gresham, 1968.

Novels as Hazel Baxter

Locum in Love. London, Gresham, 1968.
Surgeon's Help. London, Gresham, 1968.
Helicopter Nurse. London, Gresham, 1968.
Doctor in Doubt. London, Hale, 1969.
Night Sister. London, Hale, 1969.
Doctor's Endeavor. London, Gresham, 1970.

Novels as Helen Berry

Highland Love. London, Gresham, 1968.
Doctor Needs a Wife. London, Gresham, 1968.

Occupation: Nurse. London, Gresham, 1968.
Wayward Nurse. London, Gresham, 1968.
Highland Nurse. London, Gresham, 1969.
Winged Nurse. London, Gresham, 1970.

Novels as Alison Bray

Prescription for Love. London, Gresham, 1968.
Doctor's Destiny. London, Gresham, 1968.
Surgeon's Honour. London, Gresham, 1968.
Prescription for Nurse. London, Gresham, 1968.
Hospital Sister. London, Gresham, 1969.
Nurse at Crag House. London, Gresham, 1970.
Poor Little Rich Nurse. London, Gresham, 1970.
Impetuous Nurse. London, Hale, 1978.
Reluctant Doctor. London, Hale, 1979.

Novels as Freda Fenton

The Nurse Inherits. London, Gresham, 1968.
Nurse Hopeful. London, Gresham, 1968.
Doctor Abroad. London, Gresham, 1969.
Doctor's Inheritance. London, Gresham, 1969.
District Nurse. London, Gresham, 1969.
Impulsive Nurse. London, Gresham, 1969.

Novels as Irene Lynn

Romantic Doctor. London, Gresham, 1968.
Tropical Nurse. London, Gresham, 1969.
Doctor Duty. London, Gresham, 1970.
Doctor in Bondage. London, Gresham, 1970.
Duty Nurse. London, Hale, 1980.

Novels as Edna Murray

Patient Lover. London, Gresham, 1968.
Love Thy Doctor. London, Gresham, 1968.
Married to Medicine. London, Gresham, 1968.
Emergency Nurse. London, Gresham, 1968.
Ward Sister. London, Gresham, 1968.
Loving Nurse. London, Gresham, 1969.
Island Nurse. London, Gresham, 1970.
Faithful Nurse. London, Gresham, 1970.
Cruise Nurse. London, Gresham, 1970.
Nurse in Danger. London, Gresham, 1970.

Novels as Lorna Page

Love Is a Doctor. London, Gresham, 1968.
Doctor of Decision. London, Gresham, 1968.
Temporary Nurse. London, Gresham, 1969.
The Nurse Investigates. London, Gresham, 1969.
Fortunate Nurse. London, Gresham, 1970.
Doctor's Prescription. London, Gresham, 1970.
Nurse in Conflict. London, Hale, 1978.
Nurse in Charge. London, Hale, 1979.

Novels as Olive Patterson

Mystery Clinic. London, Gresham, 1968.
Runaway Doctor. London, Gresham, 1968.
Nurse Errant. London, Gresham, 1969.
Temptation Doctor. London, Gresham, 1970.
Nurse in Torment. London, Gresham, 1971.

Novels as Kay Talbot

Her Favourite Doctor. London, Gresham, 1968.
Doctor's Slave. London, Gresham, 1968.
Hospital Romance. London, Gresham, 1969.
Dental Nurse. London, Gresham, 1969.
Country Doctor. London, Gresham, 1969.
Passionate Nurse. London, Gresham, 1970.
Heartbreak Nurse. London, Gresham, 1970.

Novels as Vera Craig

Part-Time Nurse. London, Gresham, 1969; as *Now and Forever*, New York, Dell, 1973.
Enchanted Nurse. London, Gresham, 1969; as *Land of Enchantment*, New York, Dell, 1974.
Nurse in Jeopardy. London, Gresham, 1969; as *Path of Peril*, New York, Dell, 1974.
Unselfish Nurse. London, Gresham, 1970; as *The Love Barrier*, New York, Dell, 1974.
Case Nurse. London, Hale, 1970; as *Glen Hall*, New York, Dell, 1972.
Doctor's Orders. London, Hale, 1978.
Love in Ward Two. London, Hale, 1979.

Novels as Roland Starr

Operation Omina. New York, Lenox Hill Press, 1970; London, Hale, 1973.
Omina Uncharted. London, Hale, 1974.
Time Factor. London, Hale, 1975.
Return from Omina. London, Hale, 1976.

Novels as Karla Benton

Romantic Island. London, Hale, 1971.
Nurse on Loan. London, Hale, 1971.
Nurse Abroad. London, Hale, 1972.
Carefree Doctor. London, Hale, 1973.
Nurse in Love. London, Hale, 1973.

Novels as Janita Cleve

African Love Song. London, Hale, 1971.
For Love or Money. London, Hale, 1971.
Love Thy Neighbour. London, Hale, 1971.
Nurse at Pinewood. London, Hale, 1972.
Resident Nurse. London, Hale, 1973.

Novels as Sharon Court

Daughter of Destiny. London, Hale, 1971.
Pathway to Love. London, Hale, 1971.
Surgical Nurse. London, Hale, 1972.
Nurse in Need. London, Hale, 1972.
Dutiful Nurse. London, Hale, 1972.

Novels as Donna Rix

Doctor of the Isles. London, Hale, 1971.
Conflict of Love. London, Hale, 1971.
Career Nurse. London, Hale, 1972.
Nurse in Clover. London, Hale, 1973.
Heart of a Nurse. London, Hale, 1973.

Nurse Courageous. London, Hale, 1973.
Doctor from the Past. London, Hale, 1978.
Nurse in the Glen. London, Hale, 1979.

Novels as Valerie Scott

Ski Lift to Love. London, Hale, 1971.
Race to Love. London, Hale, 1971.
Doctor in Her Life. London, Hale, 1972.
Mysterious Nurse. London, Hale, 1973.
Secretive Nurse. London, Hale, 1973.
Dedicated Nurse. London, Hale, 1974.
Doctor in Her Heart. London, Hale, 1978.
Doctor's Dilemma. London, Hale, 1979.
Nurse in the Clouds. London, Hale, 1979.

Novels as Elaine Vinson

Lover's Quest. London, Hale, 1971.
Enchanted Isle. London, Hale, 1971.
Island of Desire. London, Hale, 1972.
Nurse on Skis. London, Hale, 1972.
Doubtful Nurse. London, Hale, 1973.

Novels as Graham Garner

Space Probe. London, Hale, 1974.
Starfall Muta. London, Hale, 1975.
Rifts of Time. London, Hale, 1976.

Novels as Alex Random

Star Cluster Seven. London, Hale, 1974.
Dark Constellation. London, Hale, 1975.
Cradle of Stars. London, Hale, 1975.

* * *

Donald S. Rowland has written Westerns, romances, and science fiction, all under a large number of pseudonyms as well as under his real name. He has written a very large number of Westerns in particular, and can write eight a year in addition to other work. The Westerns generally have simple two-word titles with obvious catchwords such as guns, trigger, killer, or hell which immediately suggest a western story to the prospective buyer or borrower. His novels are written primarily for the British western *aficionado* and are produced to a well-tried and modern formula. His books could only be produced in such quantities if a formula was ready to hand. One of his Westerns can, therefore, be said to be very much like another.

Rowland does have a preference for the lone man as hero who has to prove himself in the West. In *Drygulch Valley* it is an unfortunate meek bank clerk who has to triumph over tough Westerners. In *Empty Saddles* a man just out of jail is up against popular prejudice and has to fight for survival. In *Gun Wages* the hero wages a personal war, because the law is unable to, against hard-case gunmen.

The loneliness of the hero in Rowland's books is of sufficient importance that it is worthwhile to study one in detail. The main character, Nolan, in *Trail to Boot Hill* is a good example of a marginal member of society conditioned by a hard childhood. He is boastful and good with guns, knows hard men and how to handle them. He is a good specimen of western masculinity who "had to handle his own trouble and if he couldn't then he didn't deserve to win." Hard-bitten, this hero is very self-contained, and it is despite his usual unemotional self that he feels himself attracted to the young heroine. Nolan comes very close to being a caricature of a western hero, having many stock characteristics, but Rowland's great skill is an ability to give a psychological depth to his characters. We are told of the introspection and grim thoughts of Nolan and his callous mind. The hero, true to western tradition, is rather inarticulate himself, contenting himself with enigmatic but significant confessions such as "Never ask a man about his past, Beth." Whatever the misdeeds in his past, his character is improved, he is prepared to fight injustice, and he is even ready to die to save Miss Beth. In fact, he does die by gunfire, but his rather shady past is redeemed.

The hero's progress and end thus form the centerpiece of the typical Rowland novel. Around this drama we are given many stock features of the Western: the heroine, rather unapproachable, but romantic nevertheless; rustlers and crooked large ranchers persecuting small ranchers who are frequently the fathers of the heroine; sheriffs who are ineffective and have to be supplemented by lone gunmen or, as in *Flaming Range*, have to be forced to appoint effective deputies; a saloon which becomes a central arena for feuds to be fought out with the gun. Violence with gunfire is frequent and well illustrated with plenty of bloody detail, as in the shooting of the barman in *Gun Crazy*. The death throes of a gunman can occupy a whole paragraph as in *Gun Trap*. To give some local western colour, he frequently adds interesting bits of factual information about guns and cattle-handling.

Rowland's plots show their contrived nature with climaxes such as the shooting of a rustler or a hero coming right at the end. His style suits the modern idiom of Westerns, being factual and detailed where required but with rather clipped, short sentences and little western language dialogue.

—P.R. Meldrum

ROYAL, Dan. *See* **BARRETT, Geoffrey John.**

RUBEL, James L. *See* **MACRAE, Mason.**

RUSHING, Jane Gilmore. American. Born in Pyron, Texas, 15 November 1925. Educated at Texas Tech University, Lubbock, B.A. in journalism 1944, M.A. 1945, Ph.D. in English 1957. Married James A. Rushing in 1956; one son. Reporter, Abilene *Reporter-News*, Texas, 1946–47; English teacher, Ira High School, 1947–48, Snyder High School, 1948–52, and Level-land High School, 1953–54, all Texas; instructor, University of Tennessee, Knoxville, 1957–59; part-time teacher, Texas Tech University, 1959–79. Recipient: American Association of University Women Fellowship, 1956; Emily Clark Balch Award (*Virginia Quarterly Review*), for short story, 1961; LeBaron R. Barker, Jr. award, 1975; Texas Literary award, 1984. Address: 3809 39th Street, Lubbock, Texas 79413, U.S.A.

WESTERN PUBLICATIONS

Novels

Walnut Grove. New York, Doubleday, 1964.
Against the Moon. New York, Doubleday, 1968.
Tamzen. New York, Doubleday, 1972.
Mary Dove. New York, Doubleday, and London, Hodder and Stoughton, 1974.
The Raincrow. New York, Doubleday, 1977; London, Prior, 1978.
Winds of Blame. New York, Doubleday, 1983.

OTHER PUBLICATIONS

Novel

Covenant of Grace. New York, Doubleday, 1982.

Other

Evolution of a University: Texas Tech's First Fifty Years, with Kline A. Nall. Austin, Texas, Madrona Press, 1975.

*

Manuscript Collection: Texas Tech University, Lubbock.

Jane Gilmore Rushing comments:

I have never thought of myself as a western writer. I have written mainly about western Texas because that is where I have spent most of my life and Texans are the people I know best. I think their basic qualities are much the same as those of human beings everywhere, at least in countries shaped by a European heritage; and these qualities that transcend regional boundaries are primarily what I seek to portray in my fiction. Nevertheless, I try also to depict accurately the landscape, manners, morals, and customs of the region I write about; and since it is difficult to separate any of these aspects of an environment from the character of the people within it, I suppose my fiction is as throughly western as I am myself.

* * *

To date, Jane Gilmore Rushing has written six novels set in and around the mythical west Texas town of Walnut Grove (actually Pyron), located on the eastern edge of the Staked Plains, where the fertile tableland drops suddenly eastward into the broken terrain of canyons, mesas, and arroyos known as "the breaks" or the Rolling Plains. Spanning roughly a hundred years, the novels together paint a broad panorama of the land and its history; against this backdrop emerge vivid portraits of the people who shaped the land and who were in turn shaped by it. By dramatizing archetypal phases of human experience against the larger cycles of history and of nature, the novels assume individually and collectively the scope and resonance of myth.

Mary Dove, the fourth of Rushing's novels, is actually the earliest in terms of fictional chronology. Set on the Rolling Plains in the 1870's, the novel chronicles the struggle of moral innocents Christopher Columbus "Red" Jones, a cowboy, and Mary Dove, a mulatto girl reared beyond the bounds of society, to preserve the sanctity of their natural love as the edenic world they have known gives way to encroaching civilization, with its anti-miscegenation laws and its religious and racial bigotry. Unable to resist the forces of historical process, Red and Mary Dove are eventually cast out of Eden. In a scene of mixed sadness and promise, a scene at once suggestive of *Paradise Lost* and the New Testament Christmas story, the novel ends with Red and Mary Dove, the former on foot, the latter expecting a child and seated astride a gray mare, setting out on a journey farther west, in search of a place "where people's laws is the same as God's."

The cycles of nature and of history likewise provide a grand backdrop in *Tamzen.* Set in the 1890's, the novel epicts the confrontation between cattlemen and homesteaders for ownership of a disputed section of west Texas land known as Block 97. Representing two of the masculine forces which seek to preserve the land in its natural state are Turk Bascom, a powerful and sexually magnetic cattle baron, and Arthur Field, a genteel, small-scale rancher. Representing two of the feminine forces which seek to civilize and farm the land are Tamzen Greer, a strong-willed and passionate young woman, and her sister Lutie, a timid and pliant girl. Given this configuration of characters, the love relationships which develop as the plot unfolds come to represent the possible combinations of values and character attributes which will ultimately succeed in possessing the land and shaping its destiny. After relationships between Tamzen and Turk and between Lutie and Arthur prove untenable, the novel achieves romantic synthesis. With the marriage of Arthur and Tamzen, the best qualities of the male character and the female character, of the natural world and the civilized world, meet in fruitful union.

Walnut Grove, *Winds of Blame*, *Against the Moon*, and *The Raincrow* chronicle characters' attempts to come to terms with themselves and with the qualities and limitations of small-town life in west Texas. Set near the turn of the century, *Walnut Grove* is the story of John Carlile, whose maturation parallels the growth of the frontier community in which he lives. To realize his own potential, John learns, he must leave Walnut Grove and seek wider horizons. *Winds of Blame* reveals the dark underside of family life and the hypocrisy of small-town frontier values when well-intentioned neighbors conspire to cover up a "justifiable" patricide in the summer of 1916. The story's exploration of the problem of evil, the elusive nature of truth, and truth's relationship to moral law, civil law, and community standards places the novel squarely in the western genre. *Against the Moon*, set in the 1960's, focusses on three women, each in a different phase of life, who endure rites of passage and achieve new maturity as a result of events surrounding the death of the family matriarch. And *The Raincrow*, set in the 1970's, is the story of Gail Messenger, a middle-aged divorcée alienated from her west Texas origins. Returning to the dying town of Walnut Grove, Gail finds harmony with herself, her family, and the community which has shaped her character. Significantly, Gail's eastward return from the West Coast to West Texas brings the myth full circle, back to its point of origin and a new beginning.

—Daryl Jones

RUSSELL, Charles M(arion). American. Born in St. Louis, Missouri, 19 March 1865. Married Nancy Cooper in 1896. Illustrator and artist: exhibitions in many cities. Moved to Montana, 1880. LL.D.: Montana State Board of Education, 1925. *Died 24 October 1926.*

WESTERN PUBLICATIONS

Short Stories (series: Rawhide Rawlins in all books)

Rawhide Rawlins Stories. Great Falls, Montana Newspaper Association, 1921.
More Rawhides. Great Falls, Montana Newspaper Association, 1925.
Trails Plowed Under. New York, Doubleday, and London, Heinemann, 1927.
Rawhide Rawlins Rides Again; or, Behind the Swinging Doors: A Collection of Charlie Russell's Favorite Stories. Pasadena, California, Trail's End, 1948.

OTHER PUBLICATIONS

Other

Good Medicine: The Illustrated Letters of Charles M. Russell. New York, Doubleday, 1929; as *Good Medicine: Memories of the Real West*, New York, Garden City Publishing Company, 1936.
Forty Pen and Ink Drawings. Pasadena, California, Trail's End, 1947.
Paper Talk: Illustrated Letters, edited by Frederic G. Renner. Fort Worth, Texas, Amon Carter Museum of Western Art, 1962.
The CMR Book (illustrations), text by John Willard. Seattle, Superior, 1970.
Fifty CMR Paintings of the Old American West. New York, Crown, 1978.
Charles M. Russell: Paintings, Drawings and Sculpture, in the Collection of the R.W. Norton Art Gallery, Shreveport, Louisiana. Shreveport, The Gallery, 1979.

*

Bibliography: *A Bibliography of the Published Works of Charles M. Russell* by Karl Yost and Frederic G. Renner, Lincoln, University of Nebraska Press, 1971.

Critical Studies: *Charles M. Russell, The Cowboy Artist* by Ramon F. Adams and Homer E. Britzman, Pasadena, California, Trail's End, 1948; *The Charles M. Russell Book: The Life and Work of the Cowboy Artist* by Harold McCracken, New York, Doubleday, 1957; *Charles M. Russell, Cowboy Artist* by Austin Russell, New York, Twayne, 1957; *The Western Art of Charles M. Russell*, New York, Ballantine, 1975; *Charles M. Russell: American Artist, April 2nd–August 29th*, St. Louis, Museum of Westward Expansion, Gateway, 1982; *Recollections of Charley Russell* by Frank Bird Linderman, Norman, University of Oklahoma Press, 1988.

* * *

Charles Marion Russell was a brilliant painter, sculptor, and illustrator, but merely a competent writer. He spent 40 years in the West, as cowboy, itinerant artist, and studio celebrity. His art work depicts most phases of range life and many aspects of Indian life. As he grew older, he increasingly preferred semi-savage nature, Indian ways, and the good old days. His published writings and informal letters reflect these preferences.

Russell's *Rawhide Rawlins Stories* contains 17 pieces. *More Rawhides* offers 18 more, all new. A year after his death, his widow released *Trails Plowed Under*. This suggestively titled work contains 16 of the 17 items from the first collection (omitting a story about a Montanan in Europe during World War I), all 18 pieces from the second collection, one previously uncollected autobiographical sketch, and eight previously unpublished works. Thus, *Trails Plowed Under* contains Russell's 43 best prose pieces.

Russell the writer is sentimental, thrilling, informative, and funny. He provides apt illustrations as accompaniment to his prose. The narrators of the prose are sometimes Rawhide Rawlins, an old cowpuncher, and sometimes Russell himself. He clumsily adopts a uniform present tense. His tone varies from realistic to romantic, as he combines details and nostalgia. The pieces fall into four categories: humorous anecdotes, tales of Indians, informational essays, and serious yarns about white men.

Often the humor is situational, as when a cowboy to escape a wounded bear gallops off on a horse which is still tethered ("Lepley's Bear"), or when a snowed-in, starving prospector makes soup out of his faithful dog's tail and feeds the pet part ("Dog Eater"), or when a drunk is deposited by friends on a moving railroad flatbed loaded with tombstones and awakens to a puzzling hangover. Always the humor is heightened by Russell's wild verbal eccentricities. Thus, a narrator feels "wolfy," a rider "crawls his pony" and "busts the breeze" to "push the country behind him," and drinkers like their "wet goods" and "joy bringer."

Many tales extol Indians for their worship of the sun, love of nature, ability to read her secrets, inexplicable instincts, horses, and gratitude to friends. Several stories feature white men's bittersweet reminiscence of life among native Americans. Best are "Curley's Friend," "The Ghost Horse," and "How Lindsay Turned Indian."

Informational essays and stories about whites alone are few in number but significant. Through the essays we learn about whiskey, horses, ranches, range life, and the differences between California and Texas cowboys. The best of the all-white tales are "A Pair of Outlaws," in which an outlaw horse saves an outlaw by its fierce speed, and "Longrope's Last Guard," about a buddy's death during a Kansas stampede.

Well over a hundred of Russell's personal letters, often illustrated like medieval illuminated manuscripts, have been collected in *Good Medicine* and *Paper Talk*. Their spelling may be atrocious—in one, Russell identifies condensed milk as "som caned cow juce"—but these letters emphasize all elements in his philosophy of the West.

—Robert L. Gale

RUSSELL, John. *See* **FEARN, John Russell.**

RUSSELL Shane. *See* **NORWOOD, V.G.C.**

RYAN, Marah Ellis (née Martin). American. Born in Butler County, Pennsylvania, 27 February 1866. Married S. Erwan Ryan in 1883 (died). Actress, then freelance writer. *Died 11 July 1934.*

WESTERN PUBLICATIONS

Novels

In Love's Domains. Chicago, Rand McNally, 1890.
Told in the Hills. Chicago, Rand McNally, 1891.
Squaw Elouise. Chicago, Rand McNally, 1892.
The Bondwoman. Chicago, Rand McNally, and London, Unwin, 1899.
That Girl Montana. Chicago, Rand McNally, 1901.
Miss Moccasins. Chicago, Rand McNally, 1904.
For the Soul of Rafael. Chicago, McClurg, and London, Cazenove, 1906.
Indian Love Letters. Chicago, McClurg, 1907.
The Flute of the Gods. New York, Stokes, 1909.
The Woman of the Twilight. Chicago, McClurg, and London, Cazenove, 1913.
The House of the Dawn. Chicago, McClurg, 1914.
The Treasure Trail: A Romance of the Land of Gold and Sunshine. Chicago, McClurg, 1918.
The Dancer of Tuluum. Chicago, McClurg, 1924.

OTHER PUBLICATIONS

Novels

Merze: The Story of an Actress. Chicago, Rand McNally, 1889.
A Pagan of the Alleghenies. Chicago, Rand McNally, 1891.
A Flower of France: A Story of Old Louisiana. Chicago, Rand McNally, 1894.
My Quaker Maid. Chicago, Rand McNally, 1906.

Short Stories

A Chance Child, Comrades, Hendrex and Margotte, and Persephone. Chicago, Rand McNally, 1896.
The Druid Path. Chicago, McClurg, and London, Curtis Brown, 1917.

Play

Genesee of the Hills, with McPherson Turnbull, adaptation of novel *Told in the Hills* by Ryan (produced New York, 1907).

Other

Editor, *Pagan Prayers.* Chicago, McClurg, 1913.

* * *

A late 19th- and early 20th-century novelist, Marah Ellis Ryan was more or less ambivalent to the trends dominating western fiction during her writing career. Her stories often incorporated standard characters—Indian maidens, backwoodsmen, señoritas, Spanish lovers, and weak brothers—and common literary formulae—romantic intrigue, long-kept secrets, and concealed blood-ties—but Ryan adeptly manipulated these then conventional elements to come up with unusual and often unsuspected plot twists.

In much of Ryan's fiction her love of nature and admiration for people living on the frontier were combined with portraits of easterners as snobs. In *Told in the Hills* a woman from Kentucky, after numerous wilderness adventures, rejects "civilized life" forever and settles in the Northwest. In *That Girl Montana* a girl raised in the West and the daughter of a thief, having gone to live in New York City, finds the restrictions placed on her intolerable and returns to Idaho. In fact, in this story Ryan proposed that artists and westerners are the only truly free people. Her reservations about eastern society were summed up by the heroine in a conversation with an Easterner: "Your society is a very fine and very curious thing, and there is a great deal of false pretense about it. Individually, they would overlook the fact that I was accused of murder in Idaho—the gold mine would help some of them to do that! But if it should ever get in their papers here, they would collectively think it their duty to each other not to recognize me."

In books such as *Told in the Hills* and *Squaw Elouise*, Ryan's most thinly plotted novel, Ryan perceived Native Americans as essentially noble savages and children of nature. Throughout those of her books which incorporate Indians in their storylines, Ryan made the point that Indians would be best left alone and would survive much better without white man's education and whiskey. In *Squaw Élouise* the half-brother of Eloise, who as Eloise is of mixed-blood, leaves the white settlement after Eloise's death to return to a life with the Indians.

In one of her better novels, *Indian Love Letters*, Ryan structured the novel as a series of love letters written by a young Hopi Indian to a white woman. While decidedly sentimental in that the young Hopi is slowly dying in the course of his letter writing, it does nonetheless attain a lyrical poetry at times.

The Flute of the Gods upon publication was hailed as a classic of Indian lore and mysticism. Interestingly, Ryan had yet to meet an Indian, despite her many novels about them, but after *The Flute of the Gods* appeared, she went to Arizona and lived with the Navajos and became the first white woman ever admitted to the inner council of tribal chiefs. The central character is Tahnte, a fair-haired Tehua with mystical powers who believes the Spanish explorers represent a terrible threat to his people. The Spaniards are drawn as villains and among their crimes is a genocidal burning at the stake of two hundred Indians as part of a Christian crusade. Ryan employed extensively an abstract style in this book which sought to imitate as closely as possible the rhythms and character of the Indian language.

Ryan also wrote a number of books dealing with the Californios. These are her most romantic novels. The first was *For the Soul of Rafael.* As in Helen Hunt Jackson's *Romona* (1884), Ryan portrayed the Californios as being the best of Spanish blood. To a lesser extent this was also true in *Miss Moccasins*, a story in which a young Anglo woman attempts to correct the damage done by her weak brother in his exploitation of the land and of the Mexican peons. Ryan, however, did show that Mexicans were victims of an oppressive and unjust social order. Her later work, *The Treasure Trail*, made use of both Indian and Spanish-Mexican cultures and is a convoluted contemporary story set largely in Mexico dealing with the Yaqui slave trade, hidden gold, and German espionage.

Ultimately Ryan romanticized the Native American and the Californio. However, she did attempt to depict the religious practices and beliefs of the Indian at a time when it was not fashionable to do so. She saw the West as a free and invigorating land, particularly for women. Many of her novels may contain too many undeveloped characters, too much storyline, and emphasize romance too strongly for the modern reader. Yet her Indian novels set in the southwest, with their lyrical style and because of their historical significance, remain of interest.

—Vicki Piekarski

RYAN, Tex. *See* **FEARN, John Russell.**

S

SABIN, Mark. *See* **FOX, Norman A.**

SADLER, Amy. British. Born in Wensley, North Yorkshire, 17 November 1924. Educated at Wensley Church of England School, Yorkshire, until age of 14; some further education classes during army service; night schools in shorthand and typing, San Francisco, California. Served in the Women's Auxiliary Territorial Service, 1942–46; driver, attached to different regiments. Warrant officer, Control Commission, Germany, 1946–49; clerk, Shipping and Forwarding Section, JEIA US/UK, Frankfurt, Germany; clerk, American International Insurance Co., Frankfurt, 1949–52; travelled across Canada by train, lived in Vancouver and Montreal, 1952–54; worker with horses, Massachusetts, 1954; clerk, Indian Embassy, Washington, D.C., 1954; clerk, American International Insurance Co., San Francisco, California, from 1955; medical insurance adjuster, Union for Marine Engineers for West Coast Ports, San Francisco, 1955–58; secretary, Australian Trade Commission, Hong Kong, 1958; temporary secretary, London, 1959–60; secretary, United Engineers, Philadelphia, Pennsylvania, 1960–61; drove across United States via New Orleans and Route 66 to San Francisco; secretary, Southern Pacific Railroad, 1961–63; secretary in Australia, New Zealand, 1963–64; and Various Secretarial posts, London, 1964–75; secretary, 1976–78, and company secretary, 1979–85, Heating Engineering, Harrogate, Yorkshire. Since 1985 full-time writer. Address: 4 Hillside Crescent, Skipton, North Yorkshire BD23 2LE, England.

WESTERN PUBLICATIONS

Novels

California Their Aim. London, Hale, 1988.
Stop-Off at Wichita. London, Hale, 1989.
Showdown at Mesa Verde. London, Hale, 1990.
Striker Hits Pay-dirt. London, Hale, 1990.
Feuding at Dutchman's Creek. London, Hale, 1990.
Night of the Rope. London, Hale, 1991.
No Place to Die. London, Hale, 1991.
The Night Rider. London, Hale, 1992.

*

Amy Sadler comments:

I have always had a desire to write, but earning a living had to come first, and possibly I did not have the confidence one needs to have in oneself to keep trying. Working in an office all day makes it difficult to apply oneself to thought, and to the hours of writing out the story as it comes. Once one starts on a run of thought, one must go through with it.

To write a story is to be intensely involved with the characters, till they become almost real, and at times can take one over completely. To me it is a grand hobby (there being little monetary reward in Westerns unless getting into paperback).

As a teenager before the war, I loved Westerns and the western films. I wanted to be a cowboy. The wide open plains, and the horses, appealed to me. When I later drove across those plains and saw Indians in their blankets, it was as though one had become part of a giant movie screen.

I try to write about those pioneer days as it happened, with as much imagination to the truth as possible, and use places which are there, and at an earlier date may have had other names or been nothing but a few shacks near a water hole. In spite of the hardship of those days, I would like to have been part of it.

* * *

In general, Amy Sadler likes to recount the adventures of "decent" (or intrinsically "decent") young men whose lives have been turned upside-down because of events over which they have no control. In both her first novel, *California Their Aim* and *Showdown at Mesa Verde*, for example, her protagonists are thrust into a new and dangerous existence primarily because of the deaths of their parents. In *Stop-Off at Wichita*, Lee Boston comes home from the Civil War only to find that his mother is dead and his father and sister have moved on to places unknown, while in *Feuding at Dutchman's Creek*, young Bart Ariens is shanghaied at the age of 18 and put to work aboard a clipper, only managing to escape when the vessel finally docks in New Orleans.

Although her plots are somewhat convoluted, Sadler's heroes are just as clearly defined as her villains. More often than not her protagonists are sensitive, determined, and largely unsuited to the violence in which they must deal. They are respectful of women, pensive, not much given to displays of humour, and possessed of a curious (and incongruous) mixture of naivety and experience. Her villains, by contrast, are identified by their rougher speech (Sadler's heroes are also very polite), poor regard for women, and complete lack of morals. From these simplified characterisations, therefore, it may correctly be surmised that Sadler's Westerns lean toward the traditional, with the heroes always reaching the ultimately happy ending unscathed but triumphant.

This is particularly true of *Showdown at Mesa Verde*, which serves as a good example of the typical Sadler Western. A straightforward revenge story, the book opens with the rape of 14-year-old Joe Jones's mother, and Joe's subsequent abduction. Following a shoot-out Joe is rescued, but his father is fatally wounded in the process. Joe returns to the ranch just in time to see his mother (who has been considerably weakened by blood-loss following the rape) also die.

Three years later Joe is still after the men responsible, a father and son team known as Raifer and Lute Doyle. As the story wears on, Joe is joined in his hunt by an ageing miner (who falls neatly into the "crotchety old-timer" category) and an unusually sensitive bounty hunter. Quite early on in the story, Joe also encounters young Sally Drew, who becomes his love interest.

Although the outcome is never in doubt, Sadler makes sure that it is not accomplished too easily. Switching perspective to tell the story from the Doyles' point of view, and throwing in the odd subplot (Jones's hiring on with the local ranch to build up his stake, Lute's relationship with his new partner, the gunfast Newt Reeson), further stretches out the inevitable finale.

This tendency to complicate plots is also evident in the earlier *Stop-Off at Wichita*, where scar-faced Civil War veteran Lee Boston is sidetracked from his quest to locate his family by a saloon owner-cum-rancher named Amanda Savage, who employs him initially to patch up her somewhat ramshackle ranch-house. Later, however, Boston finds himself protecting her against the two men who would take possession of her land in order to gain access to the stretch of water that flows across it.

During the course of the story, the main villain, Cal Devereau, makes numerous attempts to succeed in his nefarious enterprise. The friction between him and Boston is further intensified by a high-class prostitute named Janet Hogan, upon whom they both have designs. But this is really just another subplot in a tale already heavy with such devices, which include arson, a plot to implicate the Indians in Devereau's schemes, and a healthy dose of cross and double-cross among the villains.

Although her stories tend to be a little predictable and her style occasionally melodramatic, Sadler is not a bad writer. She certainly has the ability to create and sustain characters and plots. Unfortunately, however, she also has a tendency to shatter an otherwise reasonable sense of place and period by littering her dialogue with words and phrases peculiar to the British; "chums" and "mates" for, say, the more American "buddies," and "bun in the oven" to denote a pregnancy. In Sadler's West, over-friendly townsmen who try to intrude upon another's privacy are more likely to be told to "sod off" than "get lost," while other particularly irritating characters may be described as "little sods" or "buggers." It should be pointed out, however, that the author is by no means alone in this practice (several British western writers fall into the same trap), although it can sometimes appear more intrusive in Sadler's work, and consequently more distracting.

Nevertheless, her work definitely seems to be growing increasingly slick and ambitious, boding well for her future in the western genre.

—David Whitehead

SADLER, Jeff (Geoffrey Willis Sadler). Also writes as Wes Calhoun; Geoff Sadler; Geoffrey Sadler. British. Born in Mansfield Woodhouse, Nottinghamshire, 7 October 1943. Educated at Oxclose Lane Junior School (later Robin Hood Junior School), Mansfield Woodhouse, 1950–54; Queen Elizabeth's Boys Grammar School, Mansfield, 1955–60; Manchester Library School, College of Commerce, A.L.A. 1966. Married Jennifer Watkinson in 1965; two sons. Library assistant, Mansfield Public Library, 1960–64; trainee librarian, Derbyshire County Library Service, Staveley, Derbyshire, 1966–68; branch librarian, Shirebrook, Derbyshire, 1968–80; team librarian, Bolsover, Derbyshire, 1981, and Staveley, Derbyshire, 1981–84. Assistant local studies librarian, 1985–90, and since 1990 acting local studies librarian, Chesterfield, Derbyshire. Address: 116 Langwith Road, Shirebrook, Near Mansfield, Nottinghamshire NG20 8TH, England.

WESTERN PUBLICATIONS

Novels (series: Anderson in all books)

Arizona Blood Trail. London, Hale, 1981.
Sonora Lode. London, Hale, 1982.
Tamaulipas Guns. London, Hale, 1982.
Severo Siege. London, Hale, 1983.
Lobo Moon. London, Hale, 1983.
Sierra Showdown. London, Hale, 1983.
Throw of a Rope. London, Hale, 1984.
Manhunt in Chihuahua. London, Hale, 1985.
Return of Amarillo. London, Hale, 1986.
Montana Mine. London, Hale, 1987.
Saltillo Road. London, Hale, 1987.
Long Gun War. London, Hale, 1988.
Palomino Stud. London, Hale, 1988.
Ghost Town Guns. London, Hale, 1990.

Novels as Wes Calhoun (series: Chulo in all books)

Chulo. London, Hale, 1988.
At Muerto Springs. London, Hale, 1989.
Texas Nighthawks. London, Hale, 1990.

OTHER PUBLICATIONS

Novels as Geoffrey Sadler

Justus Trilogy:
The Lash. London, New English Library, 1982.
Bloodwater. London, New English Library, 1982.
Black Vengeance. London, New English Library, 1982.

Other

Founding Fathers: Chesterfield Librarians, 1879–1944. Chesterfield, Derbyshire, Chesterfield Local Studies Department, 5 vols, 1986–88.
Queen's Park: The First Sixty Years, 1887–1947. Matlock, Derbyshire Library Service, 1989.
Journey to Freedom, with Antoni Snarski. Hollingwood, Derbyshire, Sadler/Castle Graphics, 1990.
The Rendezvous Dance Hall: A History. Matlock, Derbyshire Library Service, 1990.

Editor, *Twentieth-Century Western Writers,* 2nd edition. Chicago and London, St. James Press, 1991.

*

Manuscript Collection: Derbyshire Library Service, Matlock.

Jeff Sadler comments:

Like many of my generation, I was addicted to western films at an early age, and it is the western movie which must be counted the first and most abiding influence on my work. *Hondo*—the John Wayne film, I didn't read the book until much later—had a profound effect, and its evocation of the Apaches and their desert terrain has made this a favoured landscape for me. I don't try consciously for a visual effect, but if a reader "sees" the story, I'm happy. I see it myself in cinematic terms, the incidents visualized as scenes rather than chapters. All very un-literary, but hopefully it works.

There have been literary influences, of course—the grim realism of Noel Loomis, whose novels I read together with those of Henry Treece (another visual, almost tactile writer) during the 1950's, and the humour of Jack Borg. More recently, I have come to admire other writers in the genre—notably Matt Chisholm in his Blade series, William Rayner, and John L. Shelley—but cannot claim to have imitated them directly.

The Western is mythic territory, and one cannot pretend to be dealing in anything other than popular fantasy when writing about it from a distance. Hopefully, I make it credible and entertaining, and provide some factual basis for it all. Call it a formula if you will—so are most of the plots of "serious" contemporary literature, if it comes to that. At the moment I find my work very enjoyable and satisfying, and hope I'm making progress.

* * *

Jeff Sadler's output to date is marked by two characteristics: ethnic characters in leading roles, and ongoing western sagas with a whole repertory company of characters who interrelate book to book, within a setting of strong traditional-type tales where sex and graphic gore is at a minimum.

Central to his main series is Marshal Andrew Anderson, sometimes known as Apache Anderson, a flint-grey-eyed, long-haired half-breed, fathered by a Scottish Army scout. With a Shalako-like entry in the opening chapter, Anderson makes his debut in *Arizona Blood Trail*, a tale of revenge-seeking following the killing of his Apache mother. Characters who are to feature in later books also make their appearance here: his Indian half-brother Emilio, the fast-drawing Cole Valdez, and the woman of the series, Soledad. A large cast of characters walk, stalk, and ride through the pages with not only the virtuous but the villains reappearing throughout the series, allowing further development of relationships. A notable example of this is seen in *Palomino Stud* where, in the final confrontation, Valdez cannot bring himself to kill one of the villains as he had a yen for his sister in an earlier book.

Two distinctive features set the series apart. Firstly, the author locates the series base in Mexican Sonora, which allows him to build up his imagined world of San Severo with its own geography and complement of characters, and it is a tribute to this accomplished writer that one soon comes to believe it. Secondly, he often selects out-of-the-ordinary business on which to focus his action. For instance, in *Return of Amarillo*, the doings involve a shipment of marijuana which is a certain change from hackneyed greenbacks, gold, and rifles, and one senses an attempt to liven up the genre by cross-fertilising from others—almost a "Miami Vice" put back a hundred years. Similarly, in *Montana Mine* the villain's interest in the worked-out mine of the title is kept a mystery until it is revealed at the end that, having foreseen a boom in demand for the metal, he is in fact after mundane copper. On the other hand, *Saltillo Road* has the feel of a sweeping Roman epic, revolving as it does around a massive slavery operation in Chihuahua, a memorable sequence of the book being the enslavement of Anderson set against the unusual backdrop of Louisiana bayou country.

In counterbalance, Sadler can provide a simple tale. Set against the Arizona desert, the aptly-titled *Lobo Moon* (in which all the characters are simultaneously hunting and being hunted) is an archetypal story neatly bound together by the recurring motif of the full moon—that used by hunting wolves.

Different books give different emphasis to the regular characters. *Ghost Town Guns* sees Valdez making off with funds from the Severo bank. Even more exemplary is *Palomino Stud*, in which the heroine, Soledad, has a prize thoroughbred stolen from the ranch (which she has set up with money given to her by Anderson in an earlier book), the backbone of the story being her chase after the prize horse.

But Anderson is the mainspring of the series and is usually given centre stage. This is particularly so in those books (e.g., *Sonora Lode*, *Montana Mine*), where the series format is deliberately broken to take the form of adventures resulting from Anderson's services being loaned for out-of-bailiwick missions. However, in taking this path the author can sometimes lose the distinctive flavour of the series, with Anderson becoming virtually a nomadic soldier of fortune like so many other running heroes in the genre, and it must be said that Sadler is at his best in the Anderson series where he makes fuller use of the panoply of characters that he has built up. With successive books, there is a real sense of passing years as old friends meet up and old enemies are reencountered.

The Wes Calhoun nom-de-plume is used for a parallel series in which a notable entry is the first—*Chulo*—which has the simplicity of the traditional lone-man theme. With a minimum of characters, bleakness in the telling complements the bleakness of the locale, while the book offers well-crafted set-pieces of desert-crossing and man against the elements. Here again changes against type are wrought, with the central character being a negro, allowing for some exploration of prejudice within the context of a standard Western, an issue which is graphically exemplified by the third book in the series—*Texas Nighthawks*—where Chulo returns home to find romance and runs into precursors of the Ku Klux Klan.

The Western being the oldest of genres, the modern western writer needs to bring something new to his tale: new ideas, freshness in language. Sadler meets the bill with the novelty of his plots and the capability of encapsulating the essence of a scene in a single line, for instance where a character catches "the trapped expression of her face, and grinned around the cigar stub as he chewed."

With regard to style, Sadler tends to eschew mental introspection for his characters, rather letting the action tell the story, with action scenes which are crisp and in which the author displays a penchant for pitched battle denouements, as typified by *Long Gun War*. To open a book in the San Severo series is to meet up with old friends, and with its closing there is a sense of time having been well spent in good company.

—B.J. Holmes

ST. GEORGE, Harry. *See* **RATHBORNE, St. George.**

SANDERS, Brett. *See* **BARRETT, Geoffrey John.**

SANDERS, Charles (Wesley).

WESTERN PUBLICATIONS

Novels (series: Mournful Martin)

The Man from Michigan. New York, Chelsea House, 1923.
Ten Thousand Dollars Reward. New York, Garden City Publishing, 1924.

Troubled Range. New York, Watt, 1925.
Hill-Bred Barton's Code. New York, Chelsea House, 1925.
The Avenger. New York, Watt, 1926.
The Crimson Trail. New York, Grosset and Dunlap, 1927.
Young Lightning. New York, Chelsea House, 1927.
Outlaws of Chilberg's Valley. London, Collins, 1930.
Riders of the Oregon. New York, King, 1932.
Gunsmoke. New York, King, 1932.
Black Blood. London, Collins, 1932.
Desert Ranch. London, Collins, 1932.
Canyon Rims. London, Collins, 1933.
The Lone Fighter: Mournful Martin Makes His Bow. New York, King, 1933.
Blotted Brands. New York, Burt, 1933.
Killer's Code. New York, Burt, 1934.
Storm Riders. London, Collins, 1935.
The Roaring Rocketts. London, Collins, 1935.
Winged Bullets. London, Collins, 1935.
Moonlight Riders. London, Collins, 1937.
Mournful Martin. London, Collins, 1937.

* * *

Charles Sanders's writing career began in the mid 1920's and lasted to 1939 and in that short period he created his principal and most memorable character in Mournful Martin, a lean laconic cowboy with an unerring aim, reputed to be the best rider, roper, and shot in the cattle country. With his sombre expression giving rise to his moniker of "Mournful," he is the epitome of a hero, a fairly serious character and dependable to all who seek his help.

In *Mournful Martin* he agrees to take a sick friend to an associate's ranch in Arizona to recover and he soon becomes embroiled in a murder mystery, setting out to get the facts and producing the carbon from which all his adventures would be produced. Sanders's plots move along at a fair pace and cover a variety of troubles that befall Martin. In *Mournful Rides Again*, our hero is involved in breaking up a big cattle rustling outfit. There are no surprises and you know that Martin will triumph, as all literary heroes did at that time. As the series progressed, so did Martin's character and he began to help younger people in trouble. Whether Sanders meant this to be a social comment or not, it is a theme oft repeated. *Desert Ranch* deals with a set of twins; Bobby is a responsible, upright citizen, while his other half, Billy, is a drunkard, gambler, and spendthrift. The latter marries a dance hall girl and then suddenly disappears. Bobby turns to Martin for help and from here on in, Bobby sets Martin up as a surrogate father, looking to him for moral and emotional support—even perhaps seeing a little bit of the Mournful Martin character in himself.

Sanders knew from firsthand experience of life in the cattle country and was able to translate that invaluable source of reference into his works. His heroes try to justify the faith and trust people place in them, and are all of high moral standards. In *Storm Riders*, Martin sides with a gunman to protect a young girl and her brother from their tyrannical guardian, and in *The Roaring Rocketts*, he helps out Old Man Rockett when he is falsely accused of murdering a young cow puncher. In *The Lone Fighter*, tired of drifting from ranch to ranch, Martin is ready to settle down with the 3D Outfit, but trouble isn't far behind him and once again he is forced into action.

In his facination with the southwest cattle country, Sanders write some fine one-offs, not only dealing with range wars but with solitary men, standing for justice and their vigorous efforts in obtaining reparation from the villains. Thus Sanders writes traditional Westerns rather than historically-based fiction, but his descriptions of ranch life and countryside are exact and cannot be faulted. His ability to give attention to characters glosses over some of the more obvious plots he employed. *Outlaws of Chilberg's Valley* is a variation on the theme used for *Mournful Martin*; ranchers Nelson and Chilberg are opposed to one another and when Nelson is mysteriously murdered the finger of suspicion falls on Chilberg. This is atypical of Sanders's plotting: an argument, an unseen assassin, and the final unmasking of the killer. *Canyon Rims* and *Black Blood* use these keynotes to enhance their stories.

Sanders was able to produce tighter storylines in novels such as *Moonlight Riders* and *Winged Bullets*. *Moonlight Riders* concerns ex-deputy sheriff Tom Kane, a self-made man forced back into his old ways when he and his wife are kidnapped by Shartel—an evil blackguard who borders on the pychopathic.

Sanders's novels are a mixture of high adventure—often told at breakneck speed—astute character studies, and the love of the country which he so caringly describes.

—Mike Stotter

SANDON, J.D. *See* **HARVEY, John; WELLS, Angus.**

SANDOZ, Mari (Susette). American. Born in Sheridan Country, Nebraska, 11 May 1896. Educated at the University of Nebraska, Lincoln, intermittently 1922–31. Married for 5 years. School teacher in Nebraska, 5 years; worked in a drug laboratory and as a proofreader and researcher for Nebraska State Historical Society in the 1920's; associate editor, *School Executive*, Lincoln, 1927–29; proofreader, Lincoln *Star* and *Nebraska State Journal*; associate editor, *Nebraska History*, Lincoln 1934–35; freelance writer and lecturer from 1935. Recipient: *Atlantic Monthly* Press award, 1935, for non-fiction, 1935; Headliner award, 1957; Oppie award, for non-fiction, 1962, 1964; Western Heritage award, for non-fiction, 1962; Western Writers of America Spur award, for children's book. 1964. Litt.D.: University of Nebraska, 1950. *Died 10 March 1966.*

WESTERN PUBLICATIONS

Novels

Slogum House. Boston, Little Brown, 1937; London, Hutchinson, 1939.
Capital City. Boston, Little Brown, 1939.
The Tom-Walker. New York, Dial Press, 1947.
Winter Thunder. Philadelphia, Westminster Press, 1954.
Miss Morissa, Doctor of the Gold Trail. New York, McGraw Hill, 1955.
Son of the Gamblin' Man: The Youth of an Artist. New York, Potter, 1960.

Short Stories

Hostiles and Friendlies: Selected Short Writings. Lincoln, University of Nebraska Press, 1959.
The Great Council. Rushville, Nebraska, News Star, 1970.
Ossie and the Sea Monster and Other Stories, edited by Caroline Sandoz Pifer. Rushville, Nebraska, News Star, 1974.

The Cottonwood Chest and Other Stories, edited by Caroline Sandoz Pifer. Crawford, Nebraska, Cottonwood Press, 1980.

Uncollected Short Stories

"Sit Your Saddle Solid," in *Palomino and Other Stories*, edited by Wesley Dennis Cleveland, World, 1950.
"Lost School Bus," in *Saturday Evening Post Stories 1951*. New York, Random House, 1951.
"Girl in the Humbert," in *Out West*, edited by Jack Schaefer. Boston, Houghton Mifflin, 1955; London, Deutsch, 1959.
"Musky," in *Trails of Adventure*, edited by E.D. Mygatt. New York, Dodd Mead, 1961.
"The Spike-Eared Dog," in *Search for the Hidden Places*, edited by E.D. Mygatt. New York, McKay, 1963.

OTHER PUBLICATIONS

Other

Old Jules. Boston, Little Brown, 1935; London, Chapman and Hall, 1937.
Crazy Horse: The Strange Man of the Oglalas: A Biography. New York, Knopf, 1942.
Cheyenne Autumn. New York, McGraw Hill, 1953; London, Eyre and Spottiswoode, 1966.
The Buffalo Hunters: The Story of the Hide Men. New York, Hastings House, 1954; London, Eyre and Spottiswoode, 1960.
The Horsecatcher (for children). Philadelphia, Westminster Press, 1957; Leicester, Brockhampton Press, 1958.
The Cattlemen from the Rio Grande Across the Far Marias. New York, Hastings House, 1958; London, Eyre and Spottiswoode, 1961.
These Were the Sioux. New York, Hastings House, 1961.
Love Song to the Plains. New York, Harper, 1961.
The Far Looker. New York, Buffalo Head Press, 1962.
A New Introduction to "The Cheyenne Indians, Their History and Way of Life" by George Bird Grinnell. New York, Buffalo Head Press, 1962.
The Story Catcher (for children). Philadelphia, Westminister Press, 1963.
The Beaver Men: Spearheads of Empire. New York, Hastings House, 1964.
Old Jules Country: A Selection from Old Jules and Thirty Years of Writing since the Book Was Published. New York, Hastings House, 1965.
The Battle of the Little Bighorn. Philadelphia, Lippincott, 1966.
The Christmas of the Phonograph Records: A Recollection. Lincoln, University of Nebraska Press, 1966.
Sandhill Sundays and Other Recollections. Lincoln, University of Nebraska Press, 1970.

*

Manuscript Collection: University of Wyoming, Laramie.

* * *

Mari Sandoz's reputation rests most strongly on her nonfiction: her three fine biographies and her histories of the trans-Missouri region of her birth. Her fiction, while sometimes suffering from flaws not found in her nonfiction, is of considerable stature and worth consideration. A writer who enjoyed experimentation, she was particularly interested in allegory. Her strong sense of moral issues, particularly regarding the settling of the western frontier and the whites' treatment of the Indians, pervades her fiction as well as her nonfiction.

Her first novel, *Slogum House*, published two years after her award-winning biography of her father, *Old Jules*, is laid in the Niobrara River region of western Nebraska, the area she knew so well from her youth. (This landscape, however, is mythical, in the same sense as Faulkner's Yoknapatawpha County.) The story is that of the overweening ambition and will to power of one of the most villainous females in literature, Gulla Slogum, who uses every means, including murder and the prostitution of her daughters, to secure land and power in the newly developing region near the sand hills of Nebraska. Certainly one of the best of Sandoz's novels, it is also an allegory suggesting the results possible if a powerful, unscrupulous nation preys on less powerful neighbors. Sandoz had read Hitler's *Mein Kampf*, and was concerned that fascism was appearing in America. However, the book develops character and plot so successfully that hardly any one recognized it as allegory. Her next novel, *Capital City*, her only full-length book using a contemporary setting, dealt with political machinations of various families and groups just before election time in a mythical midwestern capital city having many characteristics of Lincoln, Nebraska. Sandoz declared that she did not intend her characters to imitate humans—they were to represent only certain facets of human characteristics. In this she succeeded too well. Readers have difficulty maintaining interest in any of the actors. However, the book is an interesting experiment: Sandoz was attempting to make the city itself the protagonist. It has much in common with other protest novels of the time. A third allegorical novel, which Sandoz felt should be considered a part of trilogy, *The Tom-Walker*, dealt with the effects of war on three generations of one family. The wounds suffered by the men in each successive war represented the wounds society suffered from those wars.

Many of Sandoz's published short stories fall into the category of light fiction, as does her novel *Miss Morissa*, about a frontier woman doctor living at a major crossing of the Platte River in western Nebraska in the 1870's. Local color, accurate portrayal of the time and place, fine details bringing the era to life, are admirable, but characterization is often weak. Sandoz's proclivities as a historian overpower her discipline as a fiction writer; she gives so much detail it distracts. Just the opposite is true in another experimental novel, *Son of the Gamblin' Man*, based on the early life of Robert Henri, famous artist of the early 1900's. Henri's real name was Cozad. His father had established the little town of Cozad, Nebraska. Later he fled with his family in order to avoid prosecution for killing a settler in a dispute. The family changed its name and disappeared. They had hidden their western life so well that even with years of intensive research Sandoz could not piece together some events. The result is a book with some gaping holes in it. Sandoz tried her hand at allegory as well, in the novel *Winter Thunder*, the story of a country school teacher and her pupils who must survive several days in the open country, after their school bus overturns during a blizzard. Based on the real blizzard of 1949, the story traces the behavior of the children during the emergency to their various home environments. The characters are so well-developed that once again readers missed the allegorical aspects. Two novels written for young readers, *The Horsecatcher* and *The Story Catcher*, both illustrate the problems a young Indian boy has integrating his own life and desires with those of his tribe. The setting for both is the mid-1800's; the tribes are the Cheyenne and the Sioux. Replete with intimate details of tribal life for books are well-written, taut, and interesting to both adult and young readers.

In Sandoz's nonfiction, she employs all the strategies and techniques of excellent fiction writing, and when she writes about actual characters her work is strong and compelling. Her three most outstanding "nonfiction novels" are actually biographies: *Old Jules*, the story of her father and a picture of home-steading on the northwestern Nebraska frontier, 1884–1928; *Crazy Horse*, the life and death of the famous Oglala Sioux War Chief who helped to defeat General Custer at the battle of the Little Big Horn, 1841–77; and *Cheyenne Autumn*, the account of Cheyenne Indian chiefs Dull Knife and Little Wolf, as they attempt to lead their small band away from a hated southern reservation, back to their old home in Montana, 1877–79. While based on prodigious research and considered to be nonfiction, they contain drama and conflict enough to satisfy any reader.

The imagination Sandoz could bring to her thoroughly researched histories and biographies was not the kind to work as well with creative fiction. She could make her real-life heroes come to life in a way that eludes her in most of her fiction, with some notable exceptions. Because of her didacticism, her fictional characters are often too plainly manipulated by the author's wishes, and her love of historical detail sometimes becomes too exuberant, leading readers away from the narrative. Her fiction is uneven, much of it flawed; nevertheless, it contains accurate portrayals of period and place.

Sandoz's love of the nature and the West, and her intimate understanding of the trans-Missouri region, particularly of the sandhills of western Nebraska, contribute beautiful and worthwhile passages in her words. She had a particularly fine grasp of western idiom and fought 11 eastern publishers to keep the western flavor in her books. Although her first book was published in 1935, her work is not dated; her distinctive style conveys much of her own personality as well as that of the West.

—Helen Stauffer

SANTEE, Ross. American. Born in Thornburg, Iowa, 16 August 1888. Educated at a high school in Moline, Illinios; Art Institute, Chicago, 1904. Married Eve Farrell in 1926 (died 1963). Lived in New York; miner and cowboy in Arizona from 1915; Arizona State supervisor, Federal Writers Project, 1936; lived in Delaware from the 1940's until 1963, and in Arizona, 1963–65. Freelance book illustrator and artist. *Died 28 June 1965.*

Western Publications

Novels

Cowboy. New York, Cosmopolitan, 1928.
The Bar X Golf Course. New York, Farrar and Rinehart, 1933.
The Bubbling Spring. New York, Scribner, 1949; revised edition (for children), as *Rusty: A Cowboy of the Old West*, 1950.
Hardrock and Silver Sage. New York, Scribner, 1951.

Short Stories

Men and Horses. New York, Century, 1926.
The Rummy Kid Goes Home and Other Stories of the Southwest. New York, Hastings House, 1965.

Other Publications

Other

The Pooch (for children). New York, Cosmopolitan, 1931; as *Spike: The Story of a Cowpuncher's Dog*, New York, Grosset and Dunlap, n.d.
Sleepy Black: The Story of a Horse (for children). New York, Farrar and Rinehart, 1933.
Apache Land. New York, Scribner, 1949.
Lost Pony Tracks. New York, Scribner, 1953.
Dog Days. New York, Scribner, 1955.

Editor, *Arizona: A State Guide.* New York, Hastings House, 1941.

*

Critical Studies: *The West of Ross Santee* by J.E. Reynolds, Van Nuys, California, Reynolds, 1961; *Ross Santee* by Neal B. Houston, Austin, Texas, Steck Vaughn, 1968.

* * *

J. Frank Dobie called Santee's *Cowboy* "the best story of the making of a cowboy yet written." It would be hard to dispute that judgment, though it is ironic that a midwesterner who never saw the real West until he was 26 should write with such authenticity and authority about western life. His eight fictional works compromise an indelible record of cowboy lore.

The first, *Men and Horses*, short fiction based on people and events he knew in Arizona, was published in 1926. Until 1933 others followed in quick succession. They include *Cowboy*, *The Pooch* (reprinted as *Spike: The Story of a Cowpuncher's Dog*), *The Bar X Golf Course*, and *Sleepy Black*. One of these is Santee's only humorous work based on the ultimately tedious joke of a million-acre golf course established to entrap dudes. Two others are tours de force told from the point of view of animals and aimed toward a juvenile audience. *Cowboy* is clearly the best of these earlier pieces, establishing patterns of plot and character that recur often. It follows the fortunes of Shorty, a runaway from East Texas, who makes his way to Arizona, where he begins the rigorous apprenticeship that leads to his acceptance as a cowpuncher. Without sentimentality, Santee reveals the dedication necessary to negotiate various rites of passage. For the initiate, compensation for the dust, grime, pain, and loneliness comes in the sense of accomplishment, camaraderie, and beauty of setting. Early tasks are menial, with inevitable mistakes and setbacks. By sheer determination the boy learns the necessary skills and jargon. The reader shares the quiet triumph reflected in statements like the following: "But once I got a dally round the post, he wasn't long in chokin' down . . . then . . . I wasn't long in slippin' on the hackamore . . ."

After a hiatus of several years, Santee returned to fiction in 1949 with the publication of *The Bubbling Spring* (reprinted as *Rusty: A Cowboy of the Old West*). This work and *Hardrock and Silver Sage* best represent Santee's late period, showing a craftsmanship lacking in the earlier fiction. They are fully plotted, structurally complex, and sophisticated in characterization. Like *Cowboy*, *The Bubbling Spring* focuses on the maturation of a young man, but his life has more variety, his emotions more complexity, and his values more subtlety. After a near-idyllic childhood in Illinois, he elects to spend his adolescent years in the wilderness with a peripatetic uncle. He abandons this life to submit himself to the regimen of ranching, settling eventually on his own ranch by the spring. He experiences the death of his mother early and his uncle late; he kills an enemy with cold calculation; he resigns himself to marrying the dancehall girl he first abandoned. By the end he is becoming Santee's archetypal cowboy. A few years later in *Hardrock and Silver Sage* Santee bifurcates his hero into two brothers, Tommie, another manifestation of the apprentice cowboy, and Robin, an idealist who gives himself over to art and medicine. From their mentor father each develops a social consciousness that had been lacking in the earlier protagonists.

Santee must have sensed that he had achieved his best work. His only remaining fiction is a collection of tales published posthumously in 1965. It does not extend the dimensions of his work.

—Sam H. Henderson

SANTEE, Walt. *See* **KING, Albert.**

SAUNDERS, John. *See* **NICKSON, Arthur.**

SAUNDERS, Mack. *See* **KETCHUM, Philip.**

SAVAGE, Les, Jr. Also wrote as Logan Stewart; Larabie Sutter. American. Born in Alhambra, California, 10 October 1922. Married Marian R. Savage in 1948; one son. Wrote short stories for *Action Stories*, *Frontier Stories*, and other magazines, 1943–1951, and novels, 1947–58. *Died 26 May 1958.*

WESTERN PUBLICATIONS

Novels

Treasure of the Brasada. New York, Simon and Schuster, 1947; New York, Editions for the Armed Services 1947; London, Earl, 1950.
The Doctor at Coffin Gap. New York, Doubleday, 1949; London, Barker, 1951.
The Wild Horse. New York, Fawcett; 1950; London, Fawcett, 1953; as *Black Horse Canyon*, New York, Fawcett, 1954.
The Hide Rustlers. New York, Doubleday, 1950; London, Barker, 1952.
Shadow Riders of the Yellowstone. New York, Doubleday, 1951; London, Barker, 1952.
Land of the Lawless. New York, Doubleday, 1951; London, Barker, 1953.
Outlaw Thickets. New York, Doubleday, 1952; London, Barker, 1954.
The White Squaw (as Larabie Sutter). New York, Fawcett, 1952.
Teresa. New York, Dell, 1954.
Last of the Breed. New York, Doubleday Dell, 1954; London, Viking, 1957.
Silver Street Woman. New York, Hanover House, 1954.
Return to Warbow. New York, Dell, 1955.
The Phantom Stallion (for children). New York, Dodd Mead, 1955.
Once a Fighter. New York, Pocket Books, 1956.
Hangtown. New York, Ballantine, 1956.
The Royal City. New York, Hanover House, 1956.
Beyond Wind River. New York, Doubleday, 1958.
Doniphan's Ride. New York, Doubleday, 1959.
Gun Shy. New York, Fawcett, 1959 (completed by Dudley Dean McGaughey).

Novels as Logan Stewart

War Bonnet Pass. New York, Fawcett, 1950.
They Died Healthy. New York, Fawcett, 1951; London, Fawcett, 1954.
The Trail. New York, Fawcett, 1951; London, Fawcett, 1954.
The Secret Rider. New York, Fawcett, 1952; London, Muller, 1953.
Savage Stronghold. New York, Fawcett, 1953; London, Fawcett, 1955.
Rails West. New York, Fawcett, 1954; London, Fawcett, 1955.

* * *

Les Savage died very young, at the age of 35, from complications arising out of hereditary diabetes and elevated cholesterol. He was a singularly gifted author who at the time of his demise was at work on his 25th western novel, *Gun Shy*, which his agent then engaged Dudley Dean McGaughey to complete. Savage's mother had been a silent screen actress and his father a Hollywood studio still photographer. Savage's first inclination was to be an artist, but at 17 he wrote his first short story and sold it. With that, his life changed permanently. Already by the end of 1943 his name was well-established in the western pulp magazines of the day, and over the next three years he could be relied upon whenever his name appeared on the contents page to tell a riveting, highly atmospheric and vividly evoked story. He was meticulous about plot and always had a detailed outline before him prior to setting the first word on paper. He was inventive, innovative, and he loved to experiment, all characteristics which got him in any number of battles with editors. He was painstaking in his research, and by 1944 had an amazing grasp of the terrain where he would set a story, an intimate knowledge of the flora of the region, specialized learning in a dozen disciplines including mining, geology, furnishing, dress, anthropology, and firearms. He might have been a poet because of the striking images he could evoke.

In a remarkable series of novelettes about Elegra Douglas, also known as Señorita Scorpion, and Chisos Owens, which he wrote for *Action Stories*, all of the fine qualities of his later historical fiction were clearly in evidence in embryonic form. In "The Brand of Señorita Scorpion," the second in this series, he generated a sinister mood when Elegra entered an area near a recently dead volcano. She "recognized cottonwoods and aspens and a scattering of juniper, but none of the trees had foliage. Their branches reached out naked and grey, like malignant clawing hands. When a slight wind sighed down from the rimrock, they rattled in hollow, mocking echo." It was rare to find this kind of writing in any pulp magazine. Savage could stun a reader sometimes with his inventiveness, as in "Lunatic Patrol," set in the far North and narrated in the first person, as is also his novelette, "The Man Who Tamed

Tombstone," in the latter by a former wild Apache who has lived as a civilized white man in the East and manager for a female vocalist for five years, before events transpire which take him back to live with his people.

The terrors engendered by snakes during the Hopi snake dance scene in "Trail of the Lonely Gun" clearly anticipate the use to which snakes are put in Savage's first novel, *Treasure of the Brasada*, published in 1947. The story is complexly and tensely plotted, set in the Southwest, and in it Savage demonstrated his idiomatic grasp of border Spanish and the kinds of characters to be found at the time around San Antonio. Almost from the beginning, Savage's protagonists were vulnerable men, forced to endure physical or mental anguish, and frequently flawed by a serious handicap, such as Glenn Crawford in this novel who, due to having been thrown from a horse, finds his body tensing into excruciating pain if he so much as tries to sit in a saddle.

Some of Savage's early novels were expansions of pulp novelettes, such as *The Doctor at Coffin Gap*, which had first appeared as "Doctor Gunswift," and *The Wild Horse*, which was previously published as a novelette titled "Lure of the Boot Hill Siren." Both of these novels were sold to film companies. Beginning with *The Hide Rustlers*, one of Savage's finest novels set near to the Texas Gulf and concerned with hide smuggling, he would publish what he considered his best western historical fiction first in hardbound editions with Doubleday. His expansions of pulp novelettes into western novels he would publish as original paperbacks under pseudonyms identifiable by his initials. Six of these appeared with the pseudonym Logan Stewart, and one of them, *The White Squaw*, as by Larabie Sutter. This last is remarkable in many ways and the titles given to it in previous pulp incarnations published by Fiction House—"Gun Witch of Wyoming" and "Mistress of Medicine Wheel"—are perhaps more indicative of the plot than the paperback title. It was, however, filmed under this title. Although the screenplay bore little resemblance to the original story, it brought Savage the first of his two screen credits. The plot of the novel is somewhat unusual in that a *femme fatale*, a rare bird in formulary western fiction, is given the role usually assigned to the traditional heroine. *The White Squaw* and all of the Logan Stewart titles richly repay reading. There is always something intriguing or out of the ordinary about them. In *War Bonnet Pass*, for example, it is shown that a psychological beating can be far more devastating than a physical one. The same quality is to be found in the original paperback novels Savage published under his own name, *Teresa*, *Last of the Breed*, *Once a Fighter* (which was an expansion of the novelette "Lone Star of the Camel Corps"), and the finest of them all, from which a film was also made, *Return to Warbow*. Indeed, if it is possible for formulary western fiction to ascend to the summit of literary artistry, this novel with its tensely etched scenes and unforgettable characters is surely a viable instance.

During the early 1950's Savage was a regular contributor to *Zane Grey's Western Magazine*, beginning with the award-winning story, "Saddlemates." Frequently, Savage novels would appear in condensed form or, as in the case of *Outlaw Thickets*, the entire story was carried in a single issue. Even one of Savage's finest historical reconstructions, *Silver Street Woman*, a story from the days of keelboats, was excerpted in the magazine and his short story, "Dangerous Orders," was also adapted as an episode for *Dick Powell's Zane Grey Theatre*. *The Royal City*, set in New Mexico during the Pueblo Revolt of 1680, is arguably Savage's best novel but, sadly, the only one still in print. Doubleday shied away from major historical fiction, especially from one of the brightest lights in its Double D series, but it did publish *Doniphan's Ride*, an historical novel set during the days of the Mexican War, a story filled with fascinating characters, both among the First Missouri Mounted Volunteers and the Mexican population in Santa Fe.

Had Savage lived longer and written more, or even if most of his novels had been kept in print, his reputation would be far more secure than it is now, and his extraordinary work, all of it, deserves to be reprinted. His was a talent combined with a masterful craftsmanship that was one of a kind. Lee E. Wells, a compadre of Savage's from their pulp days, quoting the old cowboy saying, "Success is the size of the hole a man leaves when he dies," was only one of many who was very "aware of the big hole that Les Savage left."

—Jon Tuska

SAVAGE, Thomas. American. Born in Salt Lake City, Utah, 25 April 1915. Raised on a ranch in southwestern Montana. Educated at the University of Montana, Missoula; Colby College, Waterville Maine, B.A. 1940, M.F.A. 1954. Worked in a variety of jobs, including horse wrangler on a dude ranch. Taught at Brandeis University, Waltham, Massachusetts; Visiting Professor, Vassar College, Poughkeepsie, New York, 1958–59; Guggenheim Fellow, 1980. Address: c/o William Morrow and Co., 105 Madison Avenue, New York, New York 10016, U.S.A.

WESTERN PUBLICATIONS

Novels

The Pass. New York, Doubleday, 1944.
Lona Hanson. New York, Simon and Schuster, 1948.
The Power of the Dog. Boston, Little Brown, 1967; London, Chatto and Windus, 1984.
The Liar. Boston, Little Brown, 1969.
I Heard My Sister Speak My Name. Boston, Little Brown, 1977.

OTHER PUBLICATIONS

Novels

A Bargain with God. New York, Simon and Schuster, 1953.
Trust in Chariots. New York, Random House, 1961.
Daddy's Girl. Boston, Little Brown, 1970.
A Strange God. Boston, Little Brown, 1974.
Midnight Line. Boston, Little Brown, 1976.
Her Side of It. Boston, Little Brown, 1981.
For Mary, With Love. Boston, Little Brown, 1983.
The Corner of Rife and Pacific. New York, Morrow, 1988.

* * *

With his first two novels, Thomas Savage made his escape from Montana. *The Pass* and *Lona Hanson* present closely observed local detail through a highly-controlled narrative omniscience, establishing both the writer's authority to describe the area of his upbringing and his acquired psychological distance from it. The success of this combination permitted Savage to leave Horse Prairie behind, to locate himself as a teacher and writer in New England, and to spend two decades in cultural and creative detachment from the West. He did not expect to return.

In his, fifties however, Savage learned he had an older sister, given up for adoption before his birth. It is difficult to overestimate the force of this crisis. The discovery collapsed the distance between Savage and his experience in Montana (and emphasized, perhaps, the fragility of his defense); if his perceptions of the West, an encapsulated past unchanged since he had left, were founded upon mistaken assumptions and received deceptions, then the narrative sense he had made of Montana was fundamentally delusional. Further, the discovery forced Savage to evaluate the technique of his remembering, since a claim to omniscience now seemed impossible. This movement is parallel to the theoretical acknowledgments of relativism, irresolution, and self-indicating antithesis associated with postmodernism; with Savage, however, these concepts indicate a plummet from an achieved detachment and from an assertion that studied distance is a source of creative actualization. That is, Savage had previously depicted Montana in order to demonstrate that he was no longer there, that he had grown into a larger perspective; after his discovery, he had to return to the narration of Montana in order to take up in ceaseless variation the topic of an individual's control over identity. This struggle informs Savage's work beginning with *The Power of the Dog*: consideration of the past must admit its reshaping in and of the present, and rationalization of the past must also analyze the process of narrative accommodation.

In actuality, Savage was not unprepared for the revision forced upon him. While *The Pass* is mainly a settlement tale, with particularly gripping images of sub-zero weather, its psychological concern is with the individual's recognition or assignment of causality. The opening image, of a strong wind blowing across the green shoots of new grass and the brown stubble of old grass, suggests not only naturalistic forces at work but a layered and even simultaneous recognition of complex influence. Further, the characters of *The Pass* are not newcomers to ranching, so that their struggles for survival will not be matters of acquiring technique but responses to relentless psychological battering. *Lona Hanson* reveals similar concerns underlying the plot of harsh ranch life, repression, and climactic homicide. Two stark facts of ranch life—low population and traditional taciturnity—ensure the protagonist's psychological deterioration by serving as both external cause and representative externalization of her isolation.

The slow, twisting build to violence in *Lona Hanson* likewise structures the plot of *The Power of the Dog*, Savage's first response to the discovery of his sister and his best work of sustained tension. Violence, in fact, is the opening note of the piece: "Phil always did the castrating . . ." Before the character is identified, before the action has a setting or an object or a context, before cause or intention is implied, the overarching theme is already placed. Eventually, the violence will be personally focused, as characters variously manipulate and abuse one another, but the opening movement of *The Power of the Dog* emphasizes the occupational and environmental inevitabilities of violence in isolated towns and on ranches. The relationship between Phil and the young protagonist, Peter, becomes the focus of whatever memory cannot rationalize. Phil is a brilliant sociopath, who so torments Peter's father that the weak, gentle doctor commits suicide, who then goes after the widow when she marries Phil's brother, and who seeks ultimate revenge by drawing Peter away from his mother and turning him into a "dog" like himself. Peter, having watched his parents destroyed by forces both impersonal and individual, takes up Phil's lessons in control as a means of withstanding the environment. Then he uses his new knowledge to arrange Phil's death.

Physical details are profusely noted in *The Power of the Dog*, almost forming a catalogue of available products and popular icons in the period between the world wars. Many of these details will be repeated in Savage's later works, so that the green leather armchairs in the town's good hotel, the Sugar Bowl Cafe, the Hambletonian carriage horses, and, always, the automobiles—Pierce Arrows, Stutzes, Auburns, Packards—compose a mnemonic of the author's childhood. This core of factuality, verifiable in newspapers and photographs, helps ground the reconstruction of action and intent which discovery has rendered so uncertain.

The sharp pain of discovery which is accommodated by violent action in *The Power of the Dog* lapses into patient sadness in *I Heard My Sister Speak My Name*, Savage's deepest development of the psychological responses to limitation and constraint. As with *Lona Hanson*, the isolation and small population of ranching communities—and the snobbishness of landholding families—are developed metaphorically as factors of impeded communication and conflicting intentions. These factors incapacitate or overwhelm the characters, but the first-person narrator concentrates upon forgiveness and recognition of effort: as in *The Liar* and *Midnight Line*, two earlier versions of Savage's adoption/discovery story, failure in *I Heard My Sister* occurs through circumstance or coincidence, not through viciousness or unwillingness to do good. Characters are basically humane but overwhelmed. Thus, Savage's visioning of the West after *The Power of the Dog* does not claim great difference from other regions, but emphasizes the existential placement of individuals as they bear the past and as they attempt to find interpretive order in distorted information. Savage's characters rarely face physical or extreme challenges, but the thoroughness of their isolation, their inability to locate sympathy and order, gives his Montana a faraway sweep and cold grandeur of its own.

—John Scheckter

SCARBOROUGH, Dorothy. American. Born in Mount Carmen, Texas, in 1877. Educated at Baylor University, Waco, Texas, B.A. and M.A.; University of Chicago; Oxford University, 1 year; Columbia University, New York, Ph.D. 1917. Member of the English Department, Baylor University, 1905–14, and Columbia University from 1917. Litt.D.: Baylor University, 1923. *Died 7 November 1935.*

Western Publications

Novels

In the Land of Cotton. New York, Macmillan, 1923.
The Wind, Anonymous. New York, Harper, 1925.
Can't Get a Red Bird. New York, Harper, 1929.
The Stretch-Berry Smile. Indianapolis, Bobbs Merrill, 1932.

Uncollected Short Story

"The Drought," in *Best Short Stories from the Southwest*, edited by Hilton R. Greer. Dallas, Southwest Press, 1928.

Other Publications

Novel

Impatient Griselda. New York, Harper, 1927.

Verse

Fugitive Verses. Waco, Texas, Baylor University Press, 1912.

Other

The Supernatural in Modern English Fiction. New York, Putnam, 1917.
From a Southern Porch. New York, Putnam, 1919.
Margaret Widdemer: A Biography. New York, Harcourt Brace, 1925.
On the Trail of Negro Folk-Songs. Cambridge, Massachusetts, Harvard University Press, 1925.
The Story of Cotton (for children). New York, Harper, 1933.
A Song Catcher in Southern Mountains: American Folk Songs of British Ancestry. New York, Columbia University Press, 1937.

Editor, *Famous Modern Ghost Stories.* New York, Putnam, 1921.
Editor, *Humorous Ghost Stories.* New York, Putnam, 1921.
Editor, *Selected Short Stories of Today.* New York, Farrar and Rinehart, 1935.

* * *

Although Dorothy Scarborough wrote various kinds of fiction, she is best known for her novel *The Wind, Anonymous,* set in west Texas during the 1880's. It is both a significant and unique contribution to western fiction because of Scarborough's unusual interpretation of the westering experience and the woman's side of pioneer life. *The Wind* was originally published anonymously as part of a publicity gimmick; but when sales did not attain Scarborough's expectations, she asked that her name appear on subsequent editions. The publication of the book brought hostile reactions from various civic groups in west Texas who felt Scarborough had deliberately maligned the area by exaggerating the arid climate. Enjoying the publicity created by the controversy, Scarborough, who believed herself to be a loyal Texan through and through, responded by stating she had been convicted of "realism in the first degree." Critics outside west Texas and throughout the United States responded favorably to the book.

The theme of *The Wind* was anticipated in Scarborough's short story, "The Drought." In the story a drought, intensified by incessant winds, brings about the ruin of a marriage between a young tenant farmer and his pregnant wife. At the request of a *Century* editor, the story was altered so as to end happily, a concession Scarborough would not make in the writing of *The Wind.* A study in defeat, the psychological drama is told from the point of view of Letty Mason, a recently orphaned 18-year-old from Virginia who travels to Texas to live with her cousin and his wife. Letty finds all aspects of pioneer life—the isolated environment, the impoverished living conditions, her hasty marriage, the people she meets, and the wind which takes on human dimensions through Scarborough's skillful writing—an alien world. Scarborough's interest in folk material is reflected throughout the story. These folk tales and ballads so adeptly woven into the storyline contribute to Letty's emotional and physical disintegration and final madness as do all aspects of her environment. Set in sharp contrast to Letty is Cora, her cousin's wife, a pioneer woman who accepts the challenges of frontier life but who, in Letty's view, resembles nature in that she was "contemptuous of weaklings, impatient and disregardful of others less capable." The story ends when Letty embraces death by running into the midst of a violent sandstorm.

The Wind is a naturalistic novel following a conventional plotline—easterner goes west—and peopled with standard western characters—cattlemen, cowboys, and isolated pioneer wives—which heads in a different direction, eschewing a hero (or in this case, a heroine) and heroic deeds. The West is represented as a cruel and indifferent land in which people are only victims. In direct contrast to such writers as Zane Grey, Willa Cather, and Eugene Manlove Rhodes who celebrated the triumph of the individual and the pioneering spirit, Scarborough opted for a more pessimistic interpretation of the pioneers' lot.

The unpopular view of the West was not reflected in three novels Scarborough wrote which are only marginally western, part of what might be called the sharecropper sub-genre. *In The Land of Cotton, Can't Get a Red Bird,* and *The Stretch-Berry Smile*—which Scarborough affectionately referred to as her cotton trilogy—are set in the post-frontier period and deal with the plight of the tenant farmers of Texas. Unlike *The Wind,* however, they emphasize the human triumphs in that the main characters rise above their repressive slum environments refusing to become victims. The weakest and most contrived is *The Stretch-Berry Smile* which traces the life of its heroine—the only book in the trilogy to feature a female—from a slave at age six in the cotton fields to an independent career woman in New York. Scarborough's trilogy represents the crusading period in sharecropper fiction and it vividly details all aspects of the tenant farmer's life and business. However, these books, as other Scarborough works, lack the power of *The Wind* which remains her literary tour de force as a regional novelist.

—Vicki Piekarski

SCHAEFER, Jack (Warner). American. Born in Cleveland, Ohio, 19 November 1907. Educated at Oberlin College, Ohio, A.B. in English 1929; Columbia University, New York, 1929–30. Married 1) Eugenia Hammond Ives in 1931 (divorced 1948), three sons and one daughter; 2) Louise Wilhide Deans in 1949, three daughters. Reporter, United Press, New Haven, Connecticut, 1930–31; assistant director of education, Connecticut State Reformatory, Cheshire, 1931–38; associate editor, 1932–39, and editor, 1939–42, New Haven *Journal Courier*; editorial writer, Baltimore *Sun*, 1942–44; associate editor, Norfolk *Virginian Pilot*, 1944–48; associate, Lindsay Advertising Company, 1949. Editor and publisher, *Theatre News*, 1935–40, *The Movies*, 1939–41, and *Shoreliner*, 1949, all New Haven. Recipient: Western Literature Association Distinguished Achievement award, 1975. *Died 24 January 1991.*

WESTERN PUBLICATIONS

Novels

Shane. Boston, Houghton Mifflin, 1949; London, Deutsch, 1954; edited by James C. Work, Lincoln, University of Nebraska Press, 1984.
First Blood. Boston, Houghton Mifflin, 1953; London, Deutsch, 1954.
The Canyon. Boston, Houghton Mifflin, 1953; augmented edition, as *The Canyon and Other Stories*, London, Deutsch, 1955.
The Pioneers. Boston, Houghton Mifflin, 1954; London, Deutsch, 1957.
Company of Cowards. Boston, Houghton Mifflin, 1957; London, Deutsch, 1958.

Old Ramon. Boston, Houghton Mifflin, 1960; London, Deutsch, 1962.
Monte Walsh. Boston, Houghton Mifflin, 1963; London, Deutsch, 1965.
The Short Novels of Jack Schaefer. Boston, Houghton Mifflin, 1967.

Short Stories

The Big Range. Boston, Houghton Mifflin, 1953; London, Deutsch, 1955.
The Kean Land and Other Stories. Boston, Houghton Mifflin, 1959; London, Deutsch, 1960.
Tales from the West. London, Hamish Hamilton, 1961.
Incident on the Trail. London, Corgi, 1962.
Collected Stories. Boston, Houghton Mifflin, 1966.
Jack Schaefer and the American West: Eight Stories, edited by C.E.J. Smith. London, Longman, 1978.
Conversations with a Pocket Gopher and Other Outspoken Neighbors. Santa Barbara, California, Capra Press, 1978.
The Collected Stories of Jack Schaefer. New York, Arbor House, 1985.

OTHER PUBLICATIONS

Play

Screenplay: *Advance to the Rear*, with Samuel A. Peeples and William Bowers, 1964.

Other

The Great Endurance Horse Race: 600 Miles on a Single Mount, 1908, from Evanston, Wyoming, to Denver. Santa Fe, New Mexico, Stagecoach Press, 1963.
The Plainsmen (for children). Boston, Houghton Mifflin, 1963.
Stubby Pringle's Christmas (for children). Boston, Houghton Mifflin, 1964.
Heroes Without Glory: Some Goodmen of the Old West. Boston, Houghton Mifflin, 1965; London, Deutsch, 1966.
Adolphe Francis Alphonse Bandelier. Santa Fe, New Mexico, Press of the Territorian, 1966.
Mavericks (for children). Boston, Houghton Mifflin, 1967; London, Deutsch, 1968.
New Mexico (for children). New York, Coward McCann, 1967.
Hal West: Western Gallery. Santa Fe, Museum of New Mexico Press, 1971.
An American Bestiary. Boston, Houghton Mifflin, 1975.

Editor, *Out West: An Anthology of Stories*. Boston, Houghton Mifflin, 1955; London, Deutsch, 1959.

*

Manuscript Collection: Western History Research Center, University of Wyoming, Laramie.

Critical Study: *Jack Schaefer* by Gerald W. Haslam, Boise, Idaho, Boise State University, 1975.

* * *

Although Jack Schaefer published a wide variety of short stories, accounts of western towns and cities, sketches of people and places in the West, other pieces in the *Saturday Evening Post*, *Collier's*, *Holiday*, and elsewhere, he is probably known best for his western novels, particularly for *Shane*. Like many other writers of popular Westerns, Schaefer was influenced by Frederick Jackson Turner's *The Significance of the Frontier in American History* (1894) and to some extent by Owen Wister's *The Virginian* (1902). Turner argued that the frontier, now closed, had evolved in six definable stages characterized by hunting, pathfinding and trading, ranches, farm communities, intensive culture and denser populations, and manufacturing and cities; Wister popularized the Western as an expression of social Darwinism and established many of the tenets of western romance. Schaefer's fiction draws on Turner to the extent that many of his stories portray conflicts arising during the transition from one stage to another, and he draws from Wister the natural inequality of men, a region characterized by risk, the genteel relations between the sexes, and many other paradigmatic themes. But while such influences place restraints on Schaefer's fiction and help to shape it, they are wrought into the shape of his own interests and often result in a fiction of startling though frequently deceptive power. A good impression of Schaefer's range can be found in *The Collected Stories* (1966), which includes Winfield Townley Scott's perceptive introduction. Containing stories published from 1948 through 1963, the collection displays Schaefer's blending of sentimental techniques and realistic detail to achieve a variety of effects ranging from humor to light irony.

Shane, his first novel, is often considered his best work. The novel evolved from a short story into a three part serial published in *Argosy* magazine entitled "Rider from Nowhere," which Schaefer further revised and expanded for the Houghton Mifflin edition. *Shane* is the story of a lone gunman's aid to homesteaders in danger of being driven from their land by a powerful rancher. From the opening paragraphs the novel has overtones of myth, but it can also be read as analytical psychology and as an expression of postwar ideology. Because the story is told in retrospect by a boy since grown to manhood, Schaefer is able to balance the tension of impending violence with the boy's growing awareness of the moral restraints which separate the violence of bad and good men. His father, Joe Starrett, is a man with a dream who worked every possible minute to wrest a home out of the earth; his mother, Marian, "knew she was still civilized and there was hope of getting ahead." In this context Shane becomes "a kind of symbol" to the homesteaders, who are painted as a mediocre collection of ex-cowhands and misfits, and the townspeople, who would rather remain neutral.

Shane "knows what will please a boy," trades fashion information with Marion, and is familiar with farm implements. A key passage, added for the book, involves the removal of a stump from Starrett's property. Angered by a shady merchant, Starrett and Shane attack the roots of the stump with axes in a ritual labor as familiar to the West as felling trees or driving spikes into railroad ties. Removal of the stump marks the last transition from nature to the garden, from the feudal style of the ranch to a community with a chance to be democratic. The stump episode not only serves several technical needs in the story, but serves as a moral exemplum: Shane "and the ax seemed to be partners in the work" in a way similar to his handling of a pistol. For Shane "a gun is just a tool" like "a shovel—or an ax or a saddle or a stove or anything," yet when he gripped "the gun, the hands seemed to have an intelligence all their own, a sure movement that needed no guidance of thought. . .like pointing a finger." *Shane* embodies a romantic view of weaponry and, by extension, of technology, based as it is on the belief that familiarity leads to wisdom, that man's wisdom can transcend his capacity for technological ingenuity. While *Shane* has probably been more appealing to readers than all the rest of Schaefer's fiction put together, the direction of his later fiction seems to suggest that Schaefer himself was more interested in the parameters of wisdom than of confrontation, and that he came to view the advance of civilization as an encroachment on human potentiality.

First Blood is a more conventional narrative related by a man of 20 who is impatient for more responsibility than is promised by driving a rickety old stagecoach on a spur off the main line. But he finds himself "bumping against the hard facts of living in an indifferent universe" where "the endless shading gradations between. . .black and white" replace the easy solutions of childhood. *Company of Cowards* is more a Civil War story than a Western, but it has to do with timeless problems of the Western—autonomy within a community, compromise without cowardice, freedom with restraint.

Schaefer's own favorite novel was *The Canyon*, which pits a lone Cheyenne against nature, the customs of his tribe, and himself. Little Bear leaves his tribe because he sees a basic difference between hunting food and carrying on inter-tribal skirmishes. In this most lyrical of Schaefer's novels, Little Bear comes to an understanding of the necessity of community after being trapped in a canyon alone for a winter and later returning with his bride. The small herd of buffalo trapped with him in this microcosm of the wilderness, where "all that has life must fight for that life," survives because, like Little Bear's tribe, instinct adapts to ecology. As usual Schaefer weaves several mythic strains into the story, including a mystical relationship between Little Bear and an ancient warrier. Schaefer's best touches in this short novel are the result of his naturalist's eye for the details of animal behavior, details that hint at motivation or a coherence among living things which share, while they compete for, their ecology. Mixed with Schaefer's tendency toward animism, such descriptions anticipate his fables in *An American Bestiary* and the *Audubon* pieces.

Monte Walsh carries on the tendencies toward realism and sentimental incident found in the short fiction and in *First Blood*. Monte is a "natural" cowboy, a drifter, an exceptional horseman, and a legendary representative of freedom and good will. In many ways Monte Walsh is the antithesis of Wister's Virginian. Walsh has all the skill and good spirits of the Virginian, but rather than settle down as foreman of someone else's ranch or become a rancher on his own, Walsh remains independent, generous, and free until his accidental death in middle age. Schaefer sketches him with a realism and good will that have a cumulative power. The episodic chapters of the novel are interspersed with brief anecdotes of Walsh told by an old newspaperman, giving the novel an aura of authenticity. Spanning the years from 1872 to 1913, the novel parallels Walsh's life to the rise and gradual decline of the cowboy as civilization and technology overtake the West.

In *Old Ramon* an old man and a boy are linked to an old dog and a young foolish dog as they herd sheep. The old man's role is to initiate the boy into wisdom by teaching him autonomy, tolerance, the survival of grief, holistic vision, and other verities. The old dog, like the old man and the boy, is born with the instincts necessary to his work, while the young dog dies because he lacks these and is foolish. The young boy is the owner's son—his heritage that of authority or management—the owner having decided that the boy needed experience as well as the knowledge of books. The subtle implications of this scheme are obvious, but also clear is Schaefer's larger purpose, which is to associate the old man with a wisdom of knowing himself: after getting drunk and allowing seven sheep to die, he had left sheepherding for several years, then seeing a flock, walks four days to return to the ranch.

The lowest of Westerners in Wister's *The Virginian* were the immigrants who brought filth, trash, and commercialization to the West, but we find little of this scapegoating in Schaefer's work. For Schaefer the encroachment of civilization is a burden shared by all creatures, since all share the fate of their ecology. From *Shane*, through *First Blood*, *The Canyon*, *Old Ramon*, and *Monte Walsh* to his *An American Bestiary* and the series of "conversations" with animals in *Audubon* magazine, Schaefer expressed a growing concern with the conflict between values endemic to holistic being-in-the-world and the careless limitations of technological exploitation.

—Larry N. Landrum

SCOTT, Cal. *See* **LAZENBY, Norman.**

SCOTT, Grover. *See* **KING, Albert.**

SCOTT, Norford. *See* **ROWLAND, Donald S.**

SEELYE, John (Douglas). American. Born in Hartford, Connecticut, 1 January 1931. Educated at Wesleyan University, Middletown, Connecticut, B.A. 1953; Claremont College, California, M.A. 1956, Ph.D. in English 1961. Served in the United States Naval Reserve, 1953–55: Lieutenant. Married 1) Catherine Maybury in 1968 (died 1982); 2) Alice Hunt Wilkerson in 1988. Associate Professor of English, University of California, Berkeley, 1960–65; Associate Professor, 1966–71, and Professor of English, 1971–74, University of Connecticut, Storrs; Professor of English, University of North Carolina, Chapel Hill, 1974–84. Since 1984 Graduate Research Professor, University of Florida, Gainesville. Contributing editor, *New Republic*, Washington, D.C., 1971–79; member of the editorial board, *American Literature*, Durham, North Carolina, 1974–78. Since 1979 consulting editor, Penguin Books, London. Recipient: National Endowment for the Arts fellowship, 1972, 1980, 1985; Guggenheim fellowship, 1973; Mellon fellowship, 1983. Address: 439 N.E. 9th Avenue, Gainesville, Florida 32601, U.S.A.

WESTERN PUBLICATIONS

Novels

The True Adventures of Huckleberry Finn, as Told by John Seelye. Evanston, Illinois, Northwestern University Press, 1970.

The Kid. New York, Viking Press, and London, Chatto and Windus, 1972.

OTHER PUBLICATIONS

Novel

Dirty Tricks; or, Nick Noxin's Natural Nobility. New York, Liveright, 1974.

Other

Melville: The Ironic Diagram. Evanston, Illinois, Northwestern University Press, 1970.
Prophetic Waters: The River in Early American Life and Literature. New York, Oxford University Press, 1977.
Mark Twain in the Movies: A Meditation with Pictures. New York, Viking Press, 1977.
Rational Exultation: Erie Canal Celebration. Worcester, Massachusetts, American Antiquarian Society, 1985.
If at First You Don't Secede, Try, Try Again: Southern Literature from Fenimore Cooper to Faulkner. Worcester, Massachusetts, American Antiquarian Society, 1989.

Editor, *Arthur Gordon Pym, Benito Cereno, and Related Writings.* Philadelphia, Lippincott, 1967.
Editor, *Etchings of a Whaling Cruise*, by J. Ross Browne. Cambridge, Massachusetts, Harvard University Press, 1968.
Editor, *The Adventures of Tom Sawyer*, by Mark Twain. New York, Penguin, 1985.
Editor, *The Adventures of Huckleberry Finn*, by Mark Twain. New York, Penguin, 1986.
Editor, *The Virginian*, by Owen Wister. New York, Penguin, 1986.
Editor, *Asa Sheldon, Yankee Drover.* Hanover, New Hampshire, University Press of New England, 1988.
Editor, *Life on the Mississippi*, by Mark Twain. Oxford, Oxford University Press, 1990.
Editor, *Tarzan of the Apes*, by Edgar Rice Burroughs. New York, Penguin, 1990.

* * *

Although John Seelye's western fiction consists of only two novels, his contributions are both singular and significant. Seelye's works examine the inter-relationships of classic American literature and the criticism which surrounds it. His unique method is to incorporate well-known literary characters, themes, and theories into works which have been labeled "revisionist novels" and "reactionary satires."

Seelye's first novel, *The True Adventures of Huckleberry Finn*, is a response to critics such as Leslie Fiedler who have pointed to Twain's novel as a cornerstone of American fiction. Only indirectly a "Western," the book nevertheless makes several observations about the conventions of the genre: the male bonding of a white and non-white in a wilderness setting; the recurring impulse to escape being "sivilized"; the inability to address sexual matters; the ultimate decision to head out for the Territory.

Seelye's novel "corrects" the flaws of Twain's book by rewriting it according to the demands of disputatious critics. As Huck says in the Introduction, "this time I told the story like it really happened, leaving in all the cuss words and the sex and the sadness." Seelye's version escapes the Victorian prudery which bound Twain and has continued to restrict writers of the popular Western. Huck's language is scatological and bawdy. He is preoccupied with sex (he French kisses and masturbates). He smokes hemp with Jim on the raft. Yet Seelye has retained Huck's essential moral sense. In a scene right out of Salinger, he rubs out a charcoaled "Fuk you" from a wall "because it didn't seem right, somehow."

Seelye's most important revision concerns the contrived and romantic conclusion of Twain's book, the flaw which most critics agree upon. (And, of course, the flaw common to western fiction.) In Seelye's version, Jim is drowned in the river and Huck is denied the hopeful resolution of lighting out for the Territory. Instead, he voices contemporary *angst* in the last lines, its allusion to *The Sun Also Rises* going Hemingway's existentialism one better: ". . . then all the miserableness come back, worse than before. But dark as it was and lonesome as it was, I didn't have no wish for daylight to come. In fact, I didn't much care if the goddamn sun never come up again."

In *The Kid* Seelye's range of literary manipulation is broadened even further and set firmly in the western genre with its frontier town, arriving strangers, saloon, villain, gunplay, and escalating violence. In this unique novel, the literary puzzle is more complex, juxtaposing major literary themes and theories from a number of classic American novels and playing them against the formula of the Western. In viewing Seelye's reordering of western myth and literary history, the reader is forced to construct multiple connections between literary and sub-literary works, Westerns and non-Westerns, literature and criticism.

From Cooper's *Jack Tier* Seelye borrows the assignment of male and female roles and the existence of unreformed evil. From *Huckleberry Finn* he examines the opposition of individual conscience and the dictates of society, as well as the merits of civilization and nature. From Melville's *Billy Budd* he extracts the clash of natural good vs. natural depravity and the dilemma of weighing natural law against the laws of man. From Van Tilburg Clark's *The Ox-Bow Incident* he focuses on the Western's preoccupation with violence, vengeance, and extra-legal justice. In the process, Seelye debunks such critical theories as the Garden of the West and the Western as morality play.

The Kid breaks new ground in western fiction by evaluating the genre against the serious novels and criticism which have helped to shape its development. The reader is forced to re-examine questions of literary interpretation and the easy expectations of the formula Western. Simultaneously, *The Kid* reads as an adventure, a tall tale, a parable, an allegory—and it manages to succeed on all levels. It is one of the most ingenious, ambitious, and important of the contemporary western novels.

—Michael Cleary

SELTZER, Charles Alden. Also wrote as Hiram Hopkins. American. Born in Janesville, Wisconsin, 15 August 1875. Educated at schools in Columbus, Ohio, and New Mexico. Married Ella Alberts in 1896; two daughters and three sons. Worked as a cowboy; carpenter and builder: building inspector for Cleveland, 4 years; tax consultant, 2 years. Mayor of North Olmsted, Ohio, 1926–32. *Died 9 February 1942.*

WESTERN PUBLICATIONS

Novels

The Council of Three. New York, Abbey Press, 1900.
The Two-Gun Man. New York, Outing, 1911; London, Nelson, 1923.
The Coming of the Law. New York, Outing, 1912; London, Nelson, 1924.

The Trail to Yesterday. New York, Outing, 1913; London, Nelson, 1924.
The Boss of the Lazy Y. Chicago, McClurg, and London, Casenove, 1915.
The Range Boss. Chicago, McClurg, 1916; London, Hodder and Stoughton, 1917.
The Vengeance of Jefferson Gawne. Chicago, McClurg, 1917; London, Hodder and Stoughton, 1921.
"Firebrand" Trevison. Chicago, McClurg, 1918; London, Methuen, 1920.
The Ranchman. Chicago, McClurg, 1919; London, Methuen, 1920.
The Trail Horde. Chicago, McClurg, 1920; London, Hodder and Stoughton, 1921; abridged edition, as *The Loner*, New York, Belmont, 1968.
"Beau" Rand. Chicago, McClurg, 1921; London, Hodder and Stoughton, 1922.
"Drag" Harlem. Chicago, McClurg, 1921; London, Hodder and Stoughton, 1922.
Square Deal Sanderson. Chicago, McClurg, and London, Hodder and Stoughton, 1922.
West! New York, Century, 1922; London, Hodder and Stoughton, 1923.
Brass Commandments. New York, Century, and London, Hodder and Stoughton, 1923.
Channing Comes Through. New York, Century, 1924; London, Hodder and Stoughton, 1926; abridged edition, as *Revenge Ambush*, New York, Belmont, 1967.
The Way of the Buffalo. New York, Century, and London, Hodder and Stoughton, 1924.
Lonesome Ranch. London, Hodder and Stoughton, 1924; New York, Grosset and Dunlap, 1931.
Last Hope Ranch. New York, Century, and London, Hodder and Stoughton, 1925.
Trailing Back. London, Hodder and Stoughton, 1925; as *Hellfire*, New York, Belmont, 1967.
The Valley of the Stars. New York, Century, and London, Hodder and Stoughton, 1926.
The Gentleman from Virginia. New York, Doubleday, and London, Hodder and Stoughton, 1926.
Slow Burgess. London, Hodder and Stoughton, 1926; New York, Belmont, 1963.
Land of the Free. New York, Doubleday, and London, Hodder and Stoughton, 1927; as *Sure Shot*, New York, Belmont, 1964.
The Mesa. New York, Doubleday, 1928.
Mystery Range. New York, Doubleday, and London, Hodder and Stoughton, 1928.
The Raider. New York, Doubleday, and London, Hodder and Stoughton, 1929.
The Red Brand. New York, Doubleday, 1929; London, Hodder and Stoughton, 1930.
Pedro the Magnificent. London, Hodder and Stoughton, 1929.
Gone North. New York, Doubleday, and London, Hodder and Stoughton, 1930; as *Gold Rock Ambush*, New York, Belmont, 1968.
A Son of Arizona. New York, Doubleday, and London, Hodder and Stoughton, 1931.
Double Cross Ranch. New York, Doubleday, and London, Hodder and Stoughton, 1932.
War on Wishbone Range. New York, Doubleday, 1932.
Breath of the Desert. London, Hodder and Stoughton, 1932.
Clear the Trail. New York, Doubleday, and London, Hodder and Stoughton, 1933.
West of Apache Pass. New York, Doubleday, and London, Hodder and Stoughton, 1934.
Silverspurs. New York, Doubleday, and London, Hodder and Stoughton, 1935; as *The Law of the Gun*, New York, Belmont, 1966.
Kingdom in the Cactus. New York, Doubleday, 1936; London, Hodder and Stoughton, 1937.
Arizona Jim. New York, Doubleday, and London, Hodder and Stoughton, 1939.
Treasure Ranch. New York, Doubleday, 1940; London, Hodder and Stoughton, 1941; as *Night of Vengeance*, New York, Belmont, 1968.
So Long, Sucker. New York, Doubleday, 1941; London, Hodder and Stoughton, 1942.
Gun-Law for Lavercombe. New York, Belmont, 1962.
Ferguson's Trail. New York, Belmont, 1964.
Desert Rider. New York, Belmont, 1968.

Short Stories

The Range Riders. New York, Outing, 1911.
The Triangle Cupid. New York, Outing, 1912.

Uncollected Short Stories

"Trouble—Plenty," in *Argosy* (New York), 14 September 1918.
"Forbidden Trails," in *Argosy* (New York), 18 January–22 February 1919.
"The Stray-Man," in *Argosy* (New York), 14 August–18 September 1920.
"Trailing Back," in *Argosy* (New York), 15 October–19 November 1921.
"Whoop-ee-e-e-e!," in *Western Story* (New York), 18 February 1922.
"Mystery Land," in *Argosy* (New York), 16 February–22 March 1922.
"Faro's Daughter," in *Argosy* (New York), 15 August–12 September 1925.
"Like a Gentleman," in *West* (New York), 20 January 1926.
"The Scar Man," in *West* (New York), 5 May 1927.
"Man-Hunt," in *Argosy* (New York), 20 April–25 May 1929.
"Breath of the Desert," in *Argosy* (New York), 18 June–23 July 1932.
"The Execution of Lanky," in *Thrilling Western* (London), Spring 1950.
"Set Me a Task," in *Thrilling Ranch Stories* (London), May 1950.
"Love's International," in *The Cattlemen*, edited by Bill Pronzini and Martin H. Greenberg. New York, Fawcett, 1986.
"The Horse Thief," in *More Wild Westerns*, edited by Bill Pronzini. New York, Walker, 1989.
"Seven-Up's Christmas," in *Christmas Out West*, edited by Bill Pronzini and Martin H. Greenberg. New York, Doubleday, 1990.

OTHER PUBLICATIONS

Novel

Parade of the Empty Boots. New York, Doubleday, 1937; London, Hodder and Stoughton, 1938.

Other

Sparks of Fun: A Series of Humorous Letters (as Hiram Hopkins). Cleveland, Sparks of Fun Publishing Company, 1901.

* * *

Charles Alden Seltzer was, in his day, a popular writer of Westerns. He wrote nearly 50 novels in a career that lasted for more than 40 years, from 1900 (when he published *The Council of Three*) to his death in 1942. For the modern reader, however, there is some difficulty in trying to account for so long and successful a career. Seltzer seems to have been a master of nothing so much as formula.

In *The Two-Gun Man* Ned Ferguson is hired to hunt down rustlers. Meanwhile a writer, Mary Radford, comes west for experience, and learns that her brother is suspected of being one of the rustlers. Ned solves the mystery, and along the way convinces Mary that life out west is more interesting than fiction (though a reviewer in the *New York Times* noted that this was a "West that never was."). In *The Coming of the Law* Kent Hollis goes west to claim his inheritance of—yes—ranch and newspaper: he encounters rustlers, he encounters love. In *The Range Boss* an eastern girl inherits a ranch and a good range boss. Her eastern fiancé, a villain-in-disguise, also comes west and allies himself with other villains. She learns where true worth is to be found. In *Brass Commandments* a rustler gang is confronted by a hero who is the very model of a "Romance" hero. In *Last Hope Ranch* an ex-outlaw helps a rancher and his daughter against adversities in the Mexican border country. *The Gentleman from Virginia* buys a large tract of Texas after the Civil War and reproduces his old Virginia home there; the romance centers on his disdainful daughter.

The list could go on and on. One is left with the impression that Seltzer was forever constructing his stories around East-West and good guy-rustler/villain dichotomies, that he got a little dull in the process. As well, he seems to have tried to enliven what had become a stale formula by importing elements of the Romance—haughty eastern beauty tamed by steadfast western knight of the wilderness.

Two of the novels deviate from the program and are much the better for doing so. *The Way of the Buffalo* involves the attempt by the hero Jim Cameron to bring the railroad, and progress, to the town of Ransome. His main enemy, Ballantine, is finally won over. The plot is hardly fresh, but Seltzer well conveys the days of the dying West. *Channing Comes Through* is even more interesting. It is a story of a "strong, silent" cowboy waiting for his little Eve to grow up. The characters are real, the incidents credible. Perhaps, because he was working to no common formula, and had to think through both his plot and the motivations of his characters, Seltzer produced a western novel that is unusual and interesting. It is still worth reading.

—George Walsh

SHANE, Bart. *See* **ROWLAND, Donald S.**

SHANE, John. *See* **DURST, Paul.**

SHANE, Mark. *See* **NORWOOD, V.G.C.**

SHANE, Rhondo. *See* **NORWOOD, V.G.C.**

SHANE, Steve. *See* **GRIBBLE, Leonard.**

SHANNON, Steve. *See* **BOUMA, J.L.**

SHAPPIRO, Herbert. *See* **ARTHUR, Burt.**

SHARPE, Jon. Pseudonym for Jon Messman. American. Address: c/o New American Library, 1633 Broadway, New York, New York 10019, U.S.A.

WESTERN PUBLICATIONS

Novels (series: Trailsman in all books)

1. *Seven Wagons West.* New York, New American Library, 1982.
2. *The Hanging Trail.* New York, New American Library, 1982.
3. *Mountain Man Kill.* New York, New American Library, 1982.
4. *The Sundown Searchers.* New York, New American Library, 1982.
5. *The River Raiders.* New York, New American Library, 1982.
6. *Dakota Wild.* New York, New American Library, 1982.
7. *Wolf Country.* New York, New American Library, 1982.
8. *Six Gun Drive.* New York, New American Library, 1982.
9. *Dead Man's Saddle.* New York, New American Library, 1982.
10. *Slave Hunter.* New York, New American Library, 1982.
11. *Montana Maiden.* New York, New American Library, 1982.
12. *Condor Pass.* New York, New American Library, 1982.
13. *Blood Chase.* New York, New American Library, 1983.
14. *Arrowhead Territory.* New York, New American Library, 1983.
15. *The Stalking Horse.* New York, New American Library, 1983.
16. *Savage Showdown.* New York, New American Library, 1983.
17. *Ride the Wild Shadow.* New York, New American Library, 1983.
18. *Cry the Cheyenne.* New York, New American Library, 1983.
19. *Spoon River Stud.* New York, New American Library, 1983.
20. *The Judas Killers.* New York, New American Library, 1983.

49. *The Swamp Slayers*. New York, New American Library, 1986.
51. *Sioux Captive*. New York, New American Library, 1986.
53. *Longhorn Guns*. New York, New American Library, 1986.
55. *Thief River Showdown*. New York, New American Library, 1986.
56. *Guns of Hungry Horse*. New York, New American Library, 1986.
57. *Fortune Riders*. New York, New American Library, 1986.
58. *Slaughter Express*. New York, New American Library, 1986.
59. *Thunderhawk*. New York, New American Library, 1986.
60. *The Wayward Lassie*. New York, New American Library, 1986.
61. *Bullet Caravan*. New York, New American Library, 1987.
62. *Horsethief Crossing*. New York, New American Library, 1987.
63. *Stagecoach to Hell*. New York, New American Library, 1987.
64. *Fargo's Woman*. New York, New American Library, 1987.
65. *River Kill*. New York, New American Library, 1987.
66. *Treachery Pass*. New York, New American Library, 1987.
67. *Manitoba Marauders*. New York, New American Library, 1987.
68. *Trapper Rampage*. New York, New American Library, 1987.
69. *Confederate Challenge*. New York, New American Library, 1987.
70. *Hostage Arrows*. New York, New American Library, 1987.
71. *Renegade Rebellion*. New York, New American Library, 1987.
72. *Calico Kill*. New York, New American Library, 1987.
73. *Santa Fe Slaughter*. New York, New American Library, 1988.
74. *White Hell*. New York, New American Library, 1988.
75. *Colorado Robber*. New York, New American Library, 1988.
76. *Wildcat Wagon*. New York, New American Library, 1988.
77. *Devil's Den*. New York, New American Library, 1988.
78. *Minnesota Massacre*. New York, New American Library, 1988.
79. *Smoky Hell Trail*. New York, New American Library, 1988.
80. *Blood Pass*. New York, New American Library, 1988.
81. *Twisted Trails*. New York, New American Library, 1988.
82. *Mescalero Mask*. New York, New American Library, 1988.
83. *Dead Man's Forest*. New York, New American Library, 1988.
84. *Utah Slaughter*. New York, New American Library, 1988.
85. *Call of the White Wolf*. New York, New American Library, 1989.
86. *Texas Hell Country*. New York, New American Library, 1989.
87. *Brothel Bullets*. New York, New American Library, 1989.
88. *Mexican Massacre*. New York, New American Library, 1989.
89. *Target Conestoga*. New York, New American Library, 1989.
90. *Mesabi Huntdown*. New York, New American Library, 1989.
91. *Cave of Death*. New York, New American Library, 1989.
92. *Death's Caravan*. New York, New American Library, 1989.
93. *The Texas Train*. New York, New American Library, 1989.
94. *Desperate Dispatch*. New York, New American Library, 1989.
95. *Cry Revenge*. New York, New American Library, 1989.
96. *Buzzard's Gap*. New York, New American Library, 1989.
97. *Queen's High Bid*. New York, New American Library, 1990.
98. *Desert Desperadoes*. New York, New American Library, 1990.
99. *Camp St. Lucifer*. New York, New American Library, 1990.
100. *Riverboat Gold*. New York, New American Library, 1990.
101. *Shoshoni Spirits*. New York, New American Library, 1990.
102. *The Coronado Killers*. New York, New American Library, 1990.
103. *Secret Sixguns*. New York, New American Library, 1990.
104. *Comanche Crossing*. New York, New American Library, 1990.
105. *Black Hills Blood*. New York, New American Library, 1990.
106. *Sierra Shootout*. New York, New American Library, 1990.
107. *Gunsmoke Gulch*. New York, New American Library, 1990.
108. *Pawnee Bargain*. New York, New American Library, 1990.
109. *Lone Star Lightning*. New York, New American Library, 1991.
110. *Counterfeit Cargo*. New York, New American Library, 1991.
111. *Blood Canyon*. New York, New American Library, 1991.
112. *Doomsday Warriors*. New York, New American Library, 1991.
113. *Southern Belles*. New York, New American Library, 1991.
114. *The Tamarind Trail*. New York, New American Library, 1991.

Novels (series: Canyon O'Grady in all books)

1. *Dead Men's Trails*. New York, New American Library, 1989.
2. *Silver Slaughter*. New York, New American Library, 1989.
3. *Machine Gun Madness*. New York, New American Library, 1989.
4. *Shadow Guns*. New York, New American Library, 1989.
5. *The Lincoln Assignment*. New York, New American Library, 1990.
6. *Comstock Crazy*. New York, New American Library, 1990.
7. *The King of Colorado*. New York, New American Library, 1990.

8. *Bleeding Kansas*. New York, New American Library, 1990.
9. *Counterfeit Madam*. New York, New American Library, 1990.
10. *The Great Land Swindle*. New York, New American Library, 1990.
11. *Soldier's Song*. New York, New American Library, 1991.
12. *Railroad Renegades*. New York, New American Library, 1991.
13. *Assassin's Trail*. New York, New American Library, 1991.

* * *

One of the most popular "adult" Western series to emerge in the wake of Jove Books' hugely successful *Longarm* sequence, Jon Sharpe's *Trailsman* novels (which have been appearing monthly since 1982) now number more than 100 titles. Furthermore, the introduction of a companion series in 1989, *Canyon O'Grady*, testifies not only to the *continuing* popularity of this author, but to his *growing* popularity as well.

Given the enormous pressures of producing 18 new Westerns each year, it is, of course, obvious that the pseudonym "Jon Sharpe" masks the identity of more than one writer. A number of *Trailsman* books, for example, are known to be the work of Will C. Knott. The creator of both these series, however, and the author of the vast majority of the novels which comprise them, is Jon Messman.

The hero of the *Trailsman* books is Skye Fargo, a searcher, scout, hunter and all-round ladies' man. At the age of 18, Fargo's life was completely shattered when he returned to the Wells Fargo way-station run by his parents and found them murdered. Adopting the name by which he is now best-known (the original is never revealed), he sets out on a vengeance quest, intending to track down the killers. At the time of this writing, he has yet to find and settle with the last two men who had a hand in his parents' deaths.

The vengeance angle, however, occupies little of the series, which is set before the Civil War and tends to concentrate more on the great expansion west. Rendered somewhat predictable in style and execution by the usual "adult" Western formula (Fargo nearly always manages to enjoy the charms of at least three willing young ladies before finally taking his main female "co-star" to bed), *The Trailsman* has nevertheless managed to maintain a certain level of originality. In *Devil's Den*, for example, Fargo is forced to get the most dangerous prisoners from the local jail to ride with him against a mentally unbalanced outlaw and his gang of cut-throats. In *Mescalero Mask*, Fargo is sent to evaluate plans for a campaign against the Apaches, only to find them little more than a blueprint for disaster. In *Dead Man's Forest*, he is forced to hunt down a bank robber when the citizens of the victimised town take his current lady-friend hostage, while *The Texas Train* finds the Trailsman in Mexico, rescuing the daughter of a wealthy businessman, only to discover that he has unwittingly been party to the biggest land-grab in American history. He is hired by another powerful millionaire in *Desperate Dispatch*, this time to help save the Pony Express from a series of raids and robberies.

Early on in the series, Fargo was frequently called upon to deal with outbreaks of Indian trouble. In later books, however, Sharpe has tended to pit his rather sober protagonist against outlaw gangs and criminal masterminds. Unlike other "adult" Western series, the Trailsman rarely leaves his usual stamping grounds, although he has been as far north as Canada (for *Manitoba Marauders*). A trail-wise loner "who could see where others only looked", Fargo is portrayed as very much a man of the West, and this is where Sharpe tends to keep him. Regular bursts of action constantly ensure that each new book has a "respectably" high body-count, although the violence is never too blood-thirsty. Neither does the author appear to have any preference for the type of female characters with whom he sprinkles his plots; they are by turns strong or weak, dominant or passive and so on. Due to the nature of the stories, they are seldom called upon to perform actively in any but the periodic sex scenes.

Because there is little or no continuity to link the books, the casual reader may begin at any point. A particularly good place to start, however, would be with the 100th title, *Riverboat Gold*, a special double-length adventure which teams Fargo with the second of Sharpe's continuing characters, Canyon O'Grady.

O'Grady is almost the complete opposite of Fargo. A flame-haired U.S. Federal Agent answerable only to President James Buchanan, he views himself as a poet, fighter, and lover. As sexually athletic as his counterpart, he is a much more gregarious and likeable figure, although in tone, style, and content the two series share few differences. In *Dead Men's Trails*, for example, O'Grady is called upon to solve a murder and track down a fortune in stolen gold. In *Silver Slaughter* he has to plug a hole through which the Government is losing a steady stream of silver bullion, and in *Machine Gun Madness* he has to keep a newly-invented machine gun from falling into the wrong hands.

Sharpe's Westerns are distinguished by adequate historical detail, good pacing, and a strong sense of period. They are at times quite original, though it must be said they are seldom inspired. Nonetheless, they are reasonable examples of their type, and constantly deliver exactly what they promise—fast and furious action—both out on the prairie and inside the bedroom.

—David Whitehead

SHARPE, Jon. *See* **KNOTT, Will C.**

SHAUL, Frank. *See* **ROWLAND, Donald S.**

SHEA, Cornelius. Born in 1863.

WESTERN PUBLICATIONS

Novel

Love and Lure; or, The Heart of a "Bad" Man: A Romance of Arizona. New York, Broadway, 1912.

Play

Look Out for Paint. Boston, Baker, 1912.

* * *

Proprietor of a Staten Island tobacco shop, a man who other dime novelists doubted "had ever seen the West," Cornelius Shea was the unlikely author of hundreds of dime novel Westerns. He was, in fact, responsible for the vast majority of titles in Frank Tousey's popular Wild West Weekly, a series which eventually ran to nearly 1300 numbers and included more than 1600 original stories.

Shea's reputation thus rests almost exclusively on the adventures of Young Wild West, the dashing plainsman hero of Wild West Weekly. Known by the epithets Prince of the Saddle and Champion Deadshot of the West, Young Wild West is a chestnut-haired youth of "medium height, handsome of face, and with the form of an Apollo." Garbed in a silk-fringed buckskin suit and mounted on his sorrel stallion Spitfire, Wild rides in company with his sweetheart Arietta Murdock, a crack shot and accomplished equestrian, and his faithful sidekicks. The latter include Cheyenne Charlie, a vociferous ex-Government scout and Indian fighter, Jim Dart, a laconic but able Westerner, and Hop Wah, a comic Chinaman whose clever sleight-of-hand tricks and feats with fireworks extricate Wild and his friends from more than one tight situation. Together these enforcers of law and order roam the "wildest parts of the great West," their exploits taking them anywhere from Old Mexico to Wild's ranch in Texas to the Black Hills town of Weston, named in Wild's honor. Much of their time they spend scouting for the U.S. Cavalry and fighting Indians, but their antagonists are just as likely to be rustlers, claim jumpers, road agents, or bank robbers. Wild himself is customarily at the center of the action, but frequently the stories feature one of his companions, most often Arietta.

Such is the case in *Young Wild West's Fight on the Plains; or, How Arietta Saved the Settlement*, a story which finds Wild and his friends pitted against Indians near Fort Bridger, Wyoming. Early chapters of the tale enable Wild to exhibit his matchless frontier skills. After defeating a cowboy and cavalry trooper in a horse race, Wild falls into the hands of villainous Chief Crow Foot and his warriors. But Wild knocks one rash brave senseless in a boxing match, slashes another's nose off in a knife fight, then makes his escape with the Indians in hot pursuit. At this point, however, the focus of the narrative shifts. While Wild is occupied with Crow Foot's warriors, another band of Indians prepares to attack the defenseless settlement of Bud Creek, where Arietta is temporarily staying with friends. Realizing that an attack is imminent, but undaunted by the Indians' proximity, Arietta mounts her cream-white broncho and gallops off in search of the cavalry. In her absence, Wild arrives in Bud Creek, and moments later the Indians attack. The situation, already critical, grows desperate when Wild suffers a blow to his head and drops to the ground, unconscious. An Indian "raises a club to strike the helpless form on the ground," when suddenly a shot rings out and a bullet speeds "through the red scoundrel's heart," signalling the arrival of the cavalry. With Arietta in the lead, the cavalry thunders into the fray, and within moments the Indians are soundly defeated. The story ends as Wild, regaining consciousness, beams proudly at his brave and adoring sweetheart, who has saved his life and rescued the settlement.

Stories such as this one, in which Shea revivifies a familiar formula by inverting the roles of the hero and the heroine, possess uncommon interest. Yet overall Shea's stories are mediocre, even when judged by dime novel standards, perhaps simply because he wrote them in such volume and so hastily. Their prose is scarcely readable, their dialogue stilted, their characterization superficial, and their plots predictable. The only surprise that they excite issues from their undeserved popularity.

—Daryl Jones

SHELBY, Cole. *See* **KING, Albert.**

SHELLEY, John L(ascola). American. Born in Turtle Creek, Pennsylvania, in 1907. Educated at schools in Pennsylvania and Monrovia, California. Married to Gertrude Cross; one daughter. Worked as truck driver, awning and upholstery fitter, for the California Division of Forestry, Southern Pacific Railroad, and at a fish hatchery in Oregon.

WESTERN PUBLICATIONS

Novels

Gunpoint! New York, Graphic, 1956; London, Hale, 1959.
The Avenging Gun. New York, Ace, 1959.
Cavalry Sergeant. New York, Ballantine, 1960; London, Consul, 1962.
The Rimlanders. New York, Ballantine, 1961; London, Jenkins, 1963.
The Dying Breed. New York, Berkley, 1962.
Hired Gun. New York, Berkley, 1963.
A Gun for Billy Hardin. New York, Paperback Library, 1965; London, Mayflower, 1969.
The Relentless Rider, with David Shelley. New York, Ace, 1965.
Saddle Tramp. New York, Berkley, 1965.
The Siege at Gunhammer. New York, Ace, 1967.
Hell-for-Leather Jones, with David Shelley. New York, Ace, 1968.
Ironhand. New York, Paperback Library, 1970.

Uncollected Short Stories

"Forbidden Range," in *Saturday Evening Post* (Philadelphia), 2 March 1957.
"Melody on the Range," in *The Pick of the Roundup*, edited by Stephen Payne. New York, Avon, 1963.

* * *

Though his reputation rests on a handful of works, John L. Shelley is more deserving of praise than many prolific western authors. The man who wrote *Gunpoint!* and *The Rimlanders* created in them two minor masterpieces worthy of comparison with the best. In these, his finest works, Shelley's vision fixes on the elemental situation. The actions of his characters are set respectively against a background of drought and flood, the catastrophes providing a natural echo to the smouldering violence of the novels themselves.

Gunpoint! centres on the efforts of Jim Rossiter, ex-sheriff and "retired" gunfighter, to build a canal in a drought-stricken valley, and the attempts of his enemy Hargrave to destroy him. Hargrave, a complex character who bears a grudge from years before when his rival won the woman they both loved, brings in a hired killer and tries to sabotage the work on the canal. The pattern of escalating violence rises to a climax when the thwarted Hargrave attacks Rossiter's wife, and the latter hunts him down in a relentless pursuit. The final confrontation is characteristic of Shelley, with the hero robbed of vengeance. Hargrave, his arm gangrenous from an untended wound, awakes Rossiter's pity, and is left to take his own life. Subsequently Rossiter shoots down the hired gunman Fraser, and is himself wounded, recovering as the first welcome rain falls on the land.

Gunpoint! is a masterly work, the dry simmering atmosphere established from the opening scene, and sustained to the end. Rossiter emerges as a compelling character, a short unhandsome, middle-aged man forced reluctantly to draw on the lessons of a violent past, and fight fire with fire. Against him Shelley sets the unstable figure of Hargrave, exploring ably and without comment the man's moody obsessional nature with its self-pity and murderous urges. Bad as he is, the horror of his death from the suppurating wound evokes pity as well as revulsion in the reader, a tribute rarely awarded to a villain. Secondary characters are strong and well-drawn without being intrusive, and the plot gains added depth from the conflicting interests of the towns Rossiter and Hargrave represent, Long Valley with its cattle herds and Crown Mesa with its businesses and gambling halls. Shelley sustains the unity of the novel with a strong spare prose that displays both descriptive skill and an excellent grasp of dialogue. The fact that *Gunpoint!* is no longer available in print can only be a source of regret to the western reader.

The Rimlanders, thought equally impressive, shares many of the themes of *Gunpoint!* Jess Langley, an ex-Union soldier, returns home to California to find his father murdered and their prosperous valley flooded, due to the dam built by a lumber syndicate backed by paid killers. Jess, another unspectacular but effective hero, organizes the local farmers into a vigilante group and uses military tactics to help break up the gang. Again, the main villains escape his retribution. Anderson, the company manager, shoots his hired gunman Davitt in a final quarrel, and is himself killed when an explosion breaches the dam and saves the valley. Once more Shelley's honed style carries the story well, the action unflagging and the imagery sustained to the final release of tension as the dam is blown. It is a considerable achievement.

Gunpoint! and *The Rimlanders* show Shelley at his best. *A Gun for Billy Hardin*, though capable enough, falls short of his own highest standards. The story of a nester's son who returns as an accomplished gunfighter to seek vengeance on the cattlemen who murdered his family, is fast-moving and exciting, with an authentic background of Wyoming in the 1880's. All the same, it lacks the depth and power of the other two novels, and the compelling atmosphere that distinguishes them is absent. Characters are thin, with Billy himself an athlete of improbable strength, whose final redemption is belied by his killing of his enemy at the end. A good average work for most, it is something of a disappointment.

At his best Shelley is a rare original. On the strength of *Gunpoint!* and *The Rimlanders* he merits a place apart.

—Jeff Sadler

SHIRREFFS, Gordon D(onald). Also writes as Gordon Donalds; Jackson Flynn; Stewart Gordon. American. Born in Chicago, Illinois, 15 January 1914. Educated at Northwestern University, Evanston, Illinois, 1946–49; California State University, Northridge, B.A. 1967; M.A. 1973. Served in United States Army, 1940–45, 1948: Captain. Married Alice Johanna Gutwein in 1941; one daughter and one son. Clerk, Union Tank Car Company, Chicago, 1935–40, 1946; salesman, Brown & Bigelow, Chicago, 1946–47; owner, Shirreffs Gadgets and Toys, Chicago, 1948–52. Since 1952 professional writer. Recipient: Commonwealth Club of California Silver Medal award, 1962. Address: c/o Fawcett, 201 East 50th Street, New York, New York 10022, U.S.A.

WESTERN PUBLICATIONS

Novels

Gunswift (as Stewart Gordon). New York, Avalon, 1956; London, Gold Lion, 1973.
Arizona Justice (as Gordon Donalds). New York, Avalon, 1956; Leicester, Ulverscroft, 1983.
Rio Bravo. New York, Fawcett, 1956; London, Fawcett, 1957.
Code of the Gun. New York, Avalon, 1956; London, Fawcett, 1958.
Range Rebel. New York, Pyramid, 1956; Bath, Chivers, 1985.
Top Gun (as Gordon Donalds). New York, Avalon, 1957.
Fort Vengeance. New York, Popular Library, 1957.
Bugles on the Prairie. New York, Fawcett, 1957; London, Fawcett, 1958.
Ambush on the Mesa. New York, Fawcett, 1957.
Massacre Creek. New York, Popular Library, 1958.
Shadow Valley. New York, Popular Library, 1958.
Last Train from Gun Hill (novelization of screenplay). New York, Signet, 1959.
The Brave Rifles. New York, Fawcett, 1959.
Trail's End. New York, Avalon, 1959.
The Lonely Gun. New York, Avon, 1959; London, Wright and Brown, 1960.
Renegade Lawman. New York, Avon, 1959.
Fort Suicide. New York, Avon, 1959; London, World, 1960.
Shadow of a Gunman. New York, Ace, 1959.
Apache Butte. New York, Ace, 1960.
The Proud Gun. New York, Ace, 1961.
Ride a Lone Trail. New York, Ace, 1961; Leicester, Linford, 1988.
The Valiant Bugles. New York, Signet, 1962.
The Border Guidon. New York, Signet, 1962.
Hangin' Pards. New York, Ace, 1962; Leicester, Ulverscroft, 1988.
Tumbleweed Trigger. New York, Ace, 1962.
Voice of the Gun. New York, Ace, 1962.
Rio Desperado. New York, Ace, 1962.
Slaughter at Broken Bow. New York, Avon, 1963.
Quicktrigger. New York, Ace, 1963.
The Nevada Gun. London, Consul, 1963; New York, Belmont Tower, 1977.
Gunslingers Three. London, Consul, 1963.
Last Man Alive. New York, Avon, 1964.
Too Tough to Die. New York, Avon, 1964; London, Gold Lion, 1973.
Blood Justice. New York, Signet, 1964.
The Hidden Rider of Dark Mountain. New York, Ace, 1964.
Judas Gun. New York, Fawcett, 1964.
Now He Is Legend. New York, Fawcett, 1965; Leicester, Linford, 1987.
The Lone Rifle. New York, Signet, 1965.
Barranca. New York, Signet, 1966.

Southwest Drifter. New York, Fawcett, 1967; London, Gold Lion, 1974.
The Godless Breed. New York, Fawcett, 1968; London, Barker, 1974.
Five Graves to Boothill. New York, Signet, 1968; revised edition, New York, Avon, 1970.
Showdown in Sonora. New York, Fawcett, 1969; London, Barker, 1974.
Jack of Spades. New York, Dell, 1970.
The Manhunter. New York, Fawcett, 1970; London, Barker, 1974.
Brasada. New York, Dell, 1972.
Bowman's Kid. New York, Fawcett, 1973.
Renegade's Trail. New York, Fawcett, 1974; Leicester, Ulverscroft, 1988.
The Apache Hunter. New York, Fawcett, 1976.
The Marauders. New York, Fawcett, 1977.
Rio Diablo. New York, Ace, 1977.
Legend of the Damned. New York, Fawcett, 1977.
The Untamed Breed. New York, Fawcett, 1981.
Bold Legend. New York, Fawcett, 1982.
Glorieta Pass. New York, Fawcett, 1984.
The Ghost Dancers. New York, Fawcett, 1986.
Hell's Forty Acres. New York, Fawcett, 1987.
Maximilian's Gold. New York, Fawcett, 1988.
The Walking Sands. New York, Fawcett, 1990.

Novels as Jackson Flynn

Shootout. New York, Award, and London, Universal Tandem, 1974.
Duel at Dodge City (novelization of television script). New York, Award, and London, Universal Tandem, 1974.
Cheyenne Vengeance (novelization of television script). New York, Award, and London, Universal Tandem, 1975.

Fiction for children

Son of the Thunder. Louisville, Kentucky, Westminster Press, 1957.
Swiftwagon. Louisville, Kentucky, Westminster Press, 1958.
The Haunted Treasure of the Espectros. Philadelphia, Chilton, 1962.
Mystery of Lost Canyon. Philadelphia, Chilton, 1963.
The Secret of the Spanish Desert. Philadelphia, Chilton, 1964.
Mystery of the Lost Cliff Dwelling. Englewood Cliffs, New Jersey, Prentice-Hall, 1968.

OTHER PUBLICATIONS

Novels

Captain Cutlass. Greenwich, Connecticut, Fawcett, 1978.
Calgaich the Swordsman. New York, Playboy Press, 1980.

Fiction for children

Roanoke Raiders. Louisville, Kentucky, Westminster Press, 1959.
The Rebel Trumpet. Louisville, Westminster Press, 1959.
The Mosquito Fleet. Philadelphia, Chilton, 1961.
The Gray Sea Raiders. Philadelphia, Chilton, 1961.
Powder Boy of the Monitor. Louisville, Kentucky, Westminster Press, 1961.
Action Front! Louisville, Kentucky, Westminster Press, 1962.
The Cold Seas Beyond. Louisville, Kentucky, Westminster Press, 1963.
The Hostile Beaches. Louisville, Kentucky, Westminster Press, 1964.
The Enemy Seas. Louisville, Kentucky, Westminster Press, 1965.
The Bolo Battalion. Louisville, Kentucky, Westminster Press, 1966.
Torpedoes Away! Louisville, Kentucky, Westminster Press, 1967.
The Killer Sea. Louisville, Kentucky, Westminster Press, 1968.

* * *

It was while stationed at Fort Bliss, Texas, in 1940 that Gordon D. Shirreffs became interested in the history of the U.S. Army in the West. After the war he contemplated becoming a professional military historian, but by 1952 he had discarded that idea in favor of writing fiction. He produced well over 100 articles, juvenile stories, and western fiction for the pulps. Many of his pulp stories focus on the Cavalry versus Indians plot, a notable example of which is "Till the Last Gun Cools" in the June 1954 issue of *Western Rangers Stories.* This plot is also the setting for his first novel, *Rio Bravo*, which was subsequently filmed. What distinguished Shirreffs's western fiction, even this early, was the recognition of sexuality as a drive in men and women alike, and rather unvarnished descriptions of violence and carnage, doubtless a consequence of having experienced the brutality of war firsthand. *Rio Bravo* is also impressive for its dialogue sections in the Apache language. Over the next two decades Shirreffs would continue to produce a number of Cavalry versus Indians original paperbacks, but the plots in these books tend to vary only slightly, even down to some aspects of furnishing, so that an Apache lance with a blade formed from a French cavalry sabre standing in a corner in *Rio Bravo* is hanging over a fireplace in *Fort Suicide.* The renegade Apache war chiefs—Asesino in *Rio Bravo*, Cuchillo Rojo in *Fort Suicide*, El Carnicero in *The Valiant Bugles*—are really the same character and are even identically attired, wearing a helmet of matted fur with two protruding horns. Because of his training as an historian and his interest in history, the details of these stories—from firearms to transportation to descriptions of terrain—are scrupulously accurate, and in all cases Shirreffs himself had been physically over the ground. What alone is distorted, primarily perhaps because of his early writing for the pulps, is the image of Indians, not only Apaches in the novels mentioned and others as well but other tribes, such as the Cheyennes in *Massacre Creek.* However, as he matured and developed as a writer, even this aspect of his work would change and his later portrayals of Indian nations lost this early harshness. Indeed, even in his second novel, *Code of the Gun*, the most memorable character is a half-breed Tonto Apache named Patched Clothes who can be counted upon when the protagonist desperately needs him. "I tried," Shirreffs once commented, "to avoid the so-called 'standard,' or 'adult,' type Western in favor of well-researched fiction, based as closely as possible on actual occurrences and characters. The Western, in most cases, is highly fictionalized, with standard plots and characters greatly overdrawn, and repeated *ad infinitum.* I have always been amazed at how these almost identical characters and situations are constantly published and republished."

There are, notwithstanding, some formulary elements in Shirreffs's Cavalry versus Indians novels, principally variations on the theme of the two heroines and a frequent use of the device whereby a trusted white scout is secretly in league with the war chief. On the other hand, Shirreffs, in contrast to James Warner Bellah, was no apologist for official arrogance or incompetence. The Army bureaucracy is at times insensitive and out of touch with the reality of frontier conditions, while personal considerations and prejudices often influence decisions in battle. When he did write a traditional ranch romance, such as *Code of the Gun*, the plot usually avoided the customary conventions. *Rio Desperado*, as another instance, is noteworthy for the remarkable friendship that develops between the protagonist and a younger man whose life he saves at the beginning of the story. Whether civilians or Cavalry officers, Shirreffs's protagonists are too ambiguous to be regarded as heroes, men who are not all good but also not all bad, rather prone to error, oversight, or miscalculation. Many of his non-Cavalry novels have an economic orientation and, as was actually the case, his villains are often land speculators and eastern investors who regard the West as a great Monopoly board which lax laws permit them to exploit and turn to their advantage.

Shirreffs published only three novels under pseudonyms and one of the best of all his early novels is *Gunswift*, published under the name Stewart Gordon. Shirreffs had been over every foot of the Yuma Penitentiary, and in it the protagonist Boone Shattuck comes to be confined there with vivid descriptions of the wretched conditions. *Showdown in Sonora* introduced Lee Kershaw, a manhunter whose adventures would come to fill an entire series of books. These novels are particularly notable for their poetic evocation of the arid regions of the Southwest and their variety of locations and diverse characters. No doubt the fiercely independent spirit of Shirreffs's wife, Alice, influenced the character of Shirreffs's heroines (she managed her own business for years), and particularly in the later novels the heroines frequently join the protagonists in the action and are generally quite capable of taking care of themselves.

It was as a result of the Lee Kershaw series that Shirreffs was inspired to go back into American history to write the saga which is his *magnum opus*, the trilogy concerned with the life of Quint Ker-Shaw, Lee's grandfather, and to produce the book which surely is his masterpiece: *The Untamed Breed*. It readily ranks as one of the finest mountain man novels, in a class with similar works by Guthrie, Gulick, Fisher, and Fergusson, and in its profoundly touching portrait of Quint's "winter squaw," Mountain Woman, it is an imposing literary achievement. It is also meticulously well defined in its presentation of diverse Indian characters and tribes—Crows, Shoshonis, Pawnees, Comanches, and Quint's Delaware friend, Moccasin. *Bold Legend* carries Quint's life through the Mexican War, and *Glorieta Pass* is concerned with the Civil War in New Mexico and the fate of Quint's two sons. *The Ghost Dancers* tells of Alec Kershaw, Quint's son from his night of passion with the Anglo-American, Jean Allen. While in more recent books such as *Hell's Forty Acres*, *Maximilian's Gold*, and *The Walking Sands*, Shirreffs returned to the conventional pursuit story, these are worth exploring for the interesting relationship between the two protagonists, Dave Hunter and Ash Mawson, and for the haunting desert imagery. Coincidentally, Jack Spade, the name given a villain in *The Walking Sands*, is the same as the name of the protagonist in *Jack of Spades*.

Shirreffs could not always make the historical backgrounds to his stories as fluid and natural as could, among others, Elmer Kelton and Les Savage, Jr., but he could generate mood as few others. Even in writing some 80 novels is less than 40 years, Shirreffs never fell into that trap of technical sloppiness so characteristic of Louis L'Amour or Walt Coburn. Above all, in his Quint Ker-Shaw saga he provided American literature with one of its highpoints and created a character far more interesting, and far more real and true to his time, than James Fenimore Cooper's Leatherstocking, and one which deserves to be as enduring.

—Jon Tuska

SHORT, Luke. Pseudonym for Frederick Dilley Glidden. Also wrote as F.D. Glidden; Fred Glidden. American. Born in Kewanee, Illinois, 19 November 1908; brother of Peter Dawson (i.e., Jonathan Glidden), *q.v.* Educated at the University of Illinois, Urbana; University of Missouri, Columbia, graduated 1930. Married Florence Elder in 1934; two sons and one daughter. Journalist, then a trapper; co-founder of a thorium corporation in Colorado, 1955. *Died 18 August 1975.*

Western Publications

Novels

The Feud at Single Shot. New York, Farrar and Rinehart, and London, Collins, 1936.

Guns of the Double Diamond. London, Collins, 1937; as *The Man on the Blue*, New York, Dell, 1954.

Bull-Foot Ambush. London, Collins, 1938; as *Marauder's Moon*, New York, Dell, 1955.

Misery Lode. London, Collins, 1938; as *King Colt*, New York, Dell, 1953.

Weary Range. London, Collins, 1939; as *The Branded Man*, New York, Dell, 1956.

The Gold Rustlers. London, Collins, 1939; as *Bold Rider*, New York, Dell, 1953.

Six Guns of San Jon. New York, Doubleday, and London, Collins, 1939; as *Savage Range*, New York, Bantam, 1952.

Flood-Water. London, Collins, 1939; as *Hard Money*, New York, Doubleday, 1940.

Bounty Guns. London, Collins, 1940; New York, Dell, 1953.

Brand of Empire. London, Collins, 1940; New York, Dell, 1954.

War on the Cimarron. New York, Doubleday, 1940; as *Hurricane Range*, London, Collins, 1940.

Dead Freight for Piute. New York, Doubleday, 1940; as *Western Freight*, London, Collins, 1941; as *Bull-Whip*, New York, Bantam, 1950.

Gunman's Chance. New York, Doubleday, 1941; as *Blood on the Moon*, London, Collins, 1943.

Hardcase. New York, Doubleday, 1942; as *Hard Case*, London, Collins, 1945.

Ride the Man Down. New York, Doubleday, 1942; London, Collins, 1943.

Sunset Graze. New York, Doubleday, 1942; as *The Rustlers*, New York, Bantam, 1949.

Ramrod. New York, Macmillan, 1943; London, Collins, 1945.

Bought with a Gun. London, Collins, 1943; New York, Dell, 1955.

Gauntlet of Fire. London, Collins, 1944; as *Raw Land*, New York, Bantam, 1952.

And the Wind Blows Free. New York, Macmillan, 1945; London, Collins, 1946.

Coroner Creek. New York, Macmillan, 1946; London, Collins, 1947.

Station West. Boston, Houghton Mifflin, and London, Collins, 1947.

High Vermilion. Boston, Houghton Mifflin, and London, Collins, 1948; as *Hands Off!*, New York, Bantam, 1949.
Fiddlefoot. Boston, Houghton Mifflin, and London, Collins, 1949.
Ambush. Boston, Houghton Mifflin, 1950; London, New English Library, 1960.
Vengeance Valley. Boston, Houghton Mifflin, 1950; London, Collins, 1951.
Trumpets West! (novella). New York, Dell, 1951.
Play a Lone Hand. Boston, Houghton Mifflin, 1951.
Barren Land Murders. New York, Fawcett, 1951; London, Muller, 1954; as *Barren Land Showdown*, New York, Fawcett, 1957.
Saddle by Starlight. Boston, Houghton Mifflin, 1952; London, Collins, 1953.
Silver Rock. Boston, Houghton Mifflin, 1953; London, Collins, 1954.
Rimrock. New York, Random House, 1955; London, Collins, 1956.
The Whip. New York, Bantam, 1957; London, Collins, 1958.
Summer of the Smoke. New York, Bantam, 1958; London, Hammond, 1959.
First Claim. New York, Bantam, and London, Hammond, 1960.
Desert Crossing. New York, Bantam, 1961; London, Hammond, 1963.
Last Hunt. New York, Bantam, 1962; London, Hammond, 1963.
The Some-Day Country. New York, Bantam, 1964; as *Trigger Country*, London, Hammond, 1965.
First Campaign. New York, Bantam, and London, Corgi, 1965.
Paper Sheriff. New York, Bantam, and London, Corgi, 1966.
Debt of Honor. New York, Bantam, 1967.
The Primrose Try. New York, Bantam, 1967; as *A Man Could Get Killed*, New York, Jove, 1980.
The Guns of Hanging Lake. New York, Bantam, 1968.
Donovan's Gun. New York, Bantam, 1968; London, Corgi, 1969.
The Deserters. New York, Bantam, 1969.
Three for the Money. New York, Bantam, 1970.
The Outrider. New York, Bantam, 1971.
Man from the Desert. New York, Bantam, 1971.
The Stalkers. New York, Bantam, 1973; Bath, Chivers, 1988.
The Man from Two Rivers. New York, Bantam, 1974.
Trouble Country. New York, Bantam, 1976.

Short Stories

Luke Short's Best of the West. New York, Arbor House, 1983.
The Marshal of Vengeance. New York, Carroll and Graf, 1985.

Uncollected Short Stories

"Six-Gun Lawyer" (as F.D. Glidden), in *Cowboy Stories* (New York), August 1935.
"Blood of His Enemies," in *Star Western*, October 1935.
"Gamblers Don't Quit," in *Star Western*, October 1935.
"Caribou Copper," in *Dynamic Adventures*, November 1935.
"Gambler's Glory," in *Dime Adventure*, December 1935.
"Gun Boss of Hell's Wells," in *Star Western*, December 1935.
"Border Rider," in *Dime Adventure*, January 1936.
"Guns for a Peacemaker," in *Star Western*, February 1936.
"Gun-Boss of Broken Men," in *Dime Western*, April 1936.
"Son of a Gun-Curse," in *Adventure*, April 1936.
"Tinhorn's Last Gamble," in *Star Western*, April 1936.
"Trigger Traitor," in *Cowboy Stories* (New York), April 1936.
"Long Rider Lawman," in *Cowboy Stories*, June 1936.
"Booze-Head Heritage," in *Top-Notch*, July 1936.
"Boothill Ride," in *10 Story Western*, August 1936.
"Doc Porter's Six-Gun Cure," in *Ace-High*, September 1936.
"Trial by Fury," in *Cowboy Stories* (New York), September 1936.
"Boothill Brotherhood," in *10 Story Western*, October 1936.
"Outlaws Make Good Neighbors," in *Star Western*, October 1936.
"The Buzzard Basin Gun Stampede," in *Star Western*, November 1936.
"Fighting Nesters of Sacaton," in *Ace-High Western*, November 1936.
"Gunhawks Die Hard!," in *Western Trails*, November 1936.
"Buckshot Freighter," in *Star Western*, December 1936.
"Buckskin-Popper's Last Ride," in *Dime Western*, January 1937.
"Bandit Lawman," in *Big-Book Western*, March 1937.
"Town-Tamer on the Dodge," in *Dime Western*, April 1937.
"Pattern," in *Daily News* (New York), 4 April 1937.
"The Ivory Butt-plate," in *Blue Book*, August 1937.
"Tough Enough," in *Argosy* (New York), 4 September 1937.
"The Right Kind of Tough," in *Blue Book*, October 1937.
"Lobo Quarantine," in *Argosy* (New York), 4 June 1938.
"Light the War Fires," in *Argosy* (New York), 24 September 1938.
"First Judgment," in *Argosy* (New York), 22 October 1938.
"Test Pit," in *Western Story* (New York), 7 January 1939.
"Brand of Justice," in *Country Home*, February 1939.
"Indian Scare," in *Argosy* (New York), 25 March 1939.
"Some Dogs Steal," in *Argosy* (New York), 10 June 1939.
"Belabor Day," in *Collier's* (Springfield, Ohio), 9 September 1939.
"The Fence," in *Adventure*, March 1940.
"Holy Show," in *Sunday News* (New York), August 1940.
"Smuggler's Bag," in *Short Stories*, 10 September 1940.
"Neutral Spirits," in *Blue Book*, January 1941.
"The Strange Affair at Seven Troughs," in *Blue Book*, June 1941.
"Brassguts," in *Argosy* (New York), 26 July 1941.
"Bitter Frontier," in *Argosy* (New York), 15 April 1942.
"The Drummer," in *The Fall Roundup*, edited by Harry E. Maule. New York, Random House, 1955.
"The Hangman," in *Iron Men and Silver Spurs*, edited by Donald Hamilton. New York, Fawcett, 1967.
"Danger Hole," in *Western Writers of America Silver Anniversary Anthology*, edited by August Lenniger. New York, Ace, 1969.

OTHER PUBLICATIONS

Plays

Retraction (as Fred Glidden). Columbia, University of Missouri, 1930.

Screenplays: *Blood on the Moon*, with Lillie Hayward and Harold Shumate, 1948; *The Hangman*, with Dudley Nichols, 1959.

Television Plays: *The Traveling Salesman*; *Bristol Meyers Stage 7*, 1955; four teleplays for *Zane Grey Theater*.

Other

Editor, *Cattle, Guns, and Men.* New York, Bantam, 1955.
Editor, *Frontier: 150 Years of the West.* New York, Bantam, 1955; London, Corgi, 1957.
Editor, *Colt's Law.* New York, Bantam, 1957.
Editor, *Rawhide and Bobwire.* New York, Bantam, 1958.

*

Critical Study: *Luke Short* by Robert Lee Gale, Boston, Twayne, 1981.

* * *

Luke Short's productive literary career spanned more than 40 years, from the mid-1930's until his death in 1975. During these four decades he wrote more than 50 novels and perhaps as many as 100 short stories known for their lively plots, skillful characterizations, and fast-paced narratives. Like Ernest Haycox and Louis L'Amour, the writers with whom he competed at the beginning and close of his career, Short gained a solid reputation as a notable author of popular Westerns.

Short's first stories and serials appeared in pulp magazines of the middle and late 1930's. Novels such as *The Feud at Single Shot*, *Bold Rider*, and *King Colt* illustrate his early tendency to create violence-prone heroes and villains. None of these Westerns contains memorable heroines or believable antagonists, but they do reveal Short's abundant narrative talents.

The best of the early works, *Flood-Water* (in U.S. As *Hard Money*), deals with a frontier mining town in the Mother Lode country. Emphasizing community and the ties that unite and the frictions that divide the town, Short provides a compelling portrait of the social life of a frontier hamlet. In addition, his revealing portraits of three heroines prove that, unlike many writers of Western, he can create believable fictional women. Finally, this Western avoids the excessive violence, action, and sentimentality that plague too much pulp fiction.

Another of Short's exceptional Westerns is *And the Wind Blows Free*, a novel dealing with the struggles of a beef contractor on the prairies and in Indian Territory in the 1880's. It is not the setting nor the historical backgrounds of the work—though they are both adequately treated—but the handling of the first-person narrator that is the outstanding quality of the book. Like Jack Schaefer's *Shane*, Short's *And the Wind Blows Free* is told from the perspective of a young man growing up, whose viewpoint magnifies the stature of the major characters, augments the magic of a well-formed plot, and enlarges the moral dilemmas of the narrative. Altogether this is an outstanding Western, rising above the general run of novels Short produced early in his career.

Most of Short's Westerns were set in the Old West of the late 19th century. On occasion, however, he drew on his experiences and knowledge of modern western mining for a novel set in the present century. Such is the case with *Rimrock*, which deals with a uranium boom in western Colorado and eastern Utah. Its plotting and characterizations are persuasively done; even the villains are believable. *Rimrock* is much stronger than other contemporary Westerns by Short, such as *Barren Land Showdown*, *Silver Rock*, and *Last Hunt*.

During the final years of his career, Short did not vary a great deal from the format he had used so successfully in slick magazines like *Collier's* and *Saturday Evening Post* in the 1940's and 1950's and original paperbacks in the late 1950's and early 1960's. But he did make small changes, some of which are notable. Beginning with *First Campaign*, Short set several of his Westerns in a small frontier town, Primrose, and its environs. *First Campaign* and subsequent novels like *Debt of Honor*, *The Guns of Hanging Lake*, *Man from the Desert*, and *The Primrose Try* draw upon familiar settings, characters, and events and thus provide readers with something of a Faulknerian Yoknapatawpha County as a community setting for nearly 10 of Short's later Westerns.

In addition, Short's treatment of women's roles and their sexual experiences in some of his final novels is refreshingly open for the Western. In *Paper Sheriff*, Jen Truro, a lawyer and the "good" woman, and Callie Hoad Branham, the hero's bitchy wife who was pregnant by him before their marriage, lock in competition for Reese Branham. Callie's vulgar insinuations about Jen and Reese and Jen's statements about Callie and her flawed marriage are extensive and pungent. In several of his other Westerns of the late 1960's and early 1970's, Short reflects the more open attitude of that era in his treatment of sex.

One can place too much emphasis, however, on the tinkering changes in Short's later Westerns. Instead, the typicalness of his novels should be stressed. Unlike Ernest Haycox and Alan LeMay, but like Max Brand and Zane Grey, Short chose to produce numerous Westerns noted more for their similarity and predictableness than for their innovations. This is not to berate Short as a writer but to clarify that he deserves his reputation as an author of more than 50 action-packed, well-crafted popular Westerns.

—Richard W. Etulain

SHRAKE, Edwin. Also writes as Bud Shrake; Budd Shrake. American. Born in Fort Worth, Texas, 6 September 1931. Educated at the University of Texas, Austin; Texas Christian University, Fort Worth. Served in the United States Army: Lieutenant. Married 1) Joyce Rogers in 1953; 2) Charlene Sedlmayr in 1966; two children. Reporter, Fort Worth *Press*, and Dallas *Times Herald*; columnist, Dallas *Morning News*; associate editor, *Sports Illustrated*, New York. Agent: Jim Wiatt, International Creative Management, 8899 Beverly Boulevard, Los Angeles, California 90048. Address: 1505 Wildcat Hollow, Austin, Texas 78746, U.S.A.

WESTERN PUBLICATIONS

Novels

Blood Reckoning. New York, Bantam, 1962.
But Not for Love. New York, Doubleday, and London, Joseph, 1964.
Blessed McGill. New York, Doubleday, 1968; London, Hodder and Stoughton, 1969.
Strange Peaches. New York, Harper's Magazine Press, 1972.
Peter Arbiter: The Adventures of a Young Man in Texas. Austin, Texas, Encino Press, 1973.
Limo, with Dan Jenkins. New York, Atheneum, 1976.
Night Never Falls. New York, Random House, 1987.

OTHER PUBLICATIONS

Plays

Screenplays: *J.W. Coop*, with Gary Cartwright, 1972; *Kid Blue*, 1973; *Nightwing* (as Budd Shrake), with Steve Shagan, 1978; *Tom Horn*, with Thomas McGuane, 1980.

Other

Willie Nelson: An Autobiography (as Bud Shrake), with Willie Nelson. New York, Simon and Schuster, 1988.

* * *

The novels of Edwin Shrake, who has also published under the name Bud Shrake, treat two different worlds, the contemporary or near-contemporary and the Old West. The contemporary novels, along with Shrake's journalism, screenplays, and collaboration with national celebrities in getting their stories before the public dwarf quantitatively the two Westerns, one of them Shrake's first published novel and the other, his third, now over two decades old.

Whether set in our time or in the days of the Old West, the novels feature stirring action, well-developed characters, and narrative skill. Some of the contemporary novels exploit current concerns of near-mythic notoriety: *But Not for Love* and *Strange Peaches* examine the world of the Texas Big Rich, for instance. The latter features a character bearing close resemblance to a fabulously wealthy Texas eccentric whose name 20 years ago would have been recognized across the nation. *Peter Arbiter* treats the drug subculture of urban Texas, and *Strange Peaches* devotes about one-third of its length to a monumental *Cinco de Mayo* celebration by a group of pleasure-bound sybarites. They travel to Mexico in the luxurious motor home of yet another Texas multimillionaire, there to drink heroically, fornicate, and, in one case, get shot during an abortive drug deal. Shrake's latest novel is set first in Dien Bien Phu during the final days of the French defense, then in Algeria, where another revolution is brewing. The violence and intrigue of these is vividly depicted.

The contemporary novels grow from Shrake's experiences, observation, and novelistic imagination, with no doubt some investigation through the printed word; this is certainly true of *Night Never Falls*. Although direct experience and observation were not available in conceiving and shaping the western novels, the printed word and creative imagination were. The novels are obviously well researched, and Shrake's creative imagination used to its fullest.

Blood Reckoning is set in post-Civil War Texas when the American cavalry was defending the frontier areas of the state against the frequent Indian raids on outlying settlements. West Texas was still Comanche country and Fort Griffin, on the edge of western settlement, was one of the mainstays of frontier defense. Shrake uses Fort Griffin as his locale for the action. The conflicts in the plot which initiate the action center around the bad feelings between the post Commander, Colonel Warren, and his son, Lieutenant Warren. These feelings are intensified in the Colonel when he begins to suspect that his son is having an affair with his wife, newly married to him and half his age.

A related conflict is the enmity between Colonel Warren and Crow Killer, a Comanche chief who has been proving a problem to both soldiers and settlers. The enmity is brought to a head when Crow Killer's son, Stumbling Bear, becomes a captive of the soldiers and is killed in an escape attempt. Colonel Warren knows that Crow Killer will not let his son's death go unavenged. Still brooding over his suspicions of betrayal by his wife and son, he sends the inexperienced Lieutenant upon a scouting party against Crow Killer which is almost certain to result in the son's death. When Ben is indeed captured—Crow Killer sends Colonel Warren a finger with Ben's West Point ring on it—Colonel Warren, repentant, mounts an expedition to the Comanches' remote hideaway. There he finds his son, still alive but staked out in such a way that he can view his father's death, for Crow Killer intends to kill the Colonel in hand-to-hand combat. Both fathers die in the duel and Ben, having escaped his bonds, sets off for Griffin with a new respect for his father.

What could be melodrama, and sounds like it in a bare summary, is transformed by Shrake's writing skill into a novel of action and psychological depth in character portrayal. Further, Shrake fills the novel with convincing details of time and place. He knows the flora, fauna, and geography of the vast area covered by the action, and shows them well. The details of soldiering on the frontier are vividly presented, and there is a penetrating portrait of cowardice and moral poverty in the depiction of Colonel Warren's second-in-command. *Blood Reckoning*, printed only in a paper edition and never reprinted, deserves resurrection.

Shrake's second western novel fulfils the promise of the first. *Blessed McGill* is in the form of a memoir discovered in an abandoned adobe house near Taos, New Mexico, many decades after it was written. The author is Peter Hermano McGill (1850–1883), a Texan and frontier adventurer who was beatified not long after his death. All this, however, is merely the machinery of the narration. What the narration proper does is to show us some major events of a life lived during the full flush of the Old West in American history. McGill comes of age after the Civil War, when what we understand as the Old West was coming into being, and experiences all that the frontier has to offer: cowboying, mining, buffalo hunting, close contact with Indians, some of them amicable and some deadly. He becomes an accomplished frontiersman. Despite all the action there is much thought in the novel, for it is narrated by a man waiting for death at the age of 33.

The early chapters of the novel bring in Peter's adopted brother, whose surrogate father—a Mr. Gerhardt—had been lynched by a band of Confederate sympathizers using that as a cover for looting. Jacob Gerhardt, as the boy is known, is one-half, perhaps more, Lipan Apache. After a fight with a sullen McGill slave in which he kills the man with an arrow—he and Peter had been playing Indian—Jacob leaves his adopted home and for the rest of his life lives as a Lipan Apache, becoming Octavio, one of the most formidable warriors of the wilds of West Texas, Mexico, and New Mexico. His association with McGill is not over, for in Mexico some years later, where McGill with a small party is searching for an old Spanish mine, the two meet again. It is a fatal encounter. One of McGill's party develops smallpox, which sweeps off Octavio's wife and young son who were in the camp with him. The resourceful McGill knows that Octavio will blame him for his loss, and through a trick manages to escape what would have been certain death. Having had enough of Mexico and the unpredictable Octavio, McGill returns to Texas and his wife of several years. The portion of the narrative dealing with his courtship of the lady, and retrieval of her from a Baltimore boarding school for young ladies, is one of the funniest episodes in a novel replete with humor.

Octavio's hatred drives him on, and he finally locates McGill living on a small ranch he owns near Taos, New Mexico. His wife is with him, and they now have a son. How Octavio attains his revenge and figures in the beatification of McGill is best left to the novel.

Blessed McGill presents many hilariously comic episodes, and has a fine sense for the ironic. It shows considerable research on the lives of the people, both Anglo and Indian, of the period. A.C. Greene, Texas man of letters and student of the West, was correct in including *Blessed McGill* in his work *The Fifty Best Books on Texas*.

—Don R. Swadley

SILKO, Leslie Marmon. American. Born in 1948. Educated at Board of Indian Affairs schools, Laguna, New Mexico, and a Catholic school in Albuquerque; University of New Mexico, Albuquerque, B.A. (summa cum laude) in English 1969; studied law briefly. Has two sons. Taught for two years at Navajo Community College, Tsaile, Arizona; lived in Ketchikan, Alaska, for two years; taught at University of New Mexico. Since 1978 Professor of English, University of Arizona, Tucson. Recipient: National Endowment for the Arts award, 1974; *Chicago Review* award, 1974; Pushcart prize, 1977; MacArthur Foundation grant, 1983. Address: Department of English, University of Arizona, Tucson, Arizona 85721, U.S.A.

WESTERN PUBLICATIONS

Novel

Ceremony. New York, Viking Press, 1977.

Uncollected Short Stories

"Bravura" and "Humaweepi, the Warrior Priest," in *The Man to Send Rain Clouds: Contemporary Stories by American Indians*, edited by Kenneth Rosen. New York, Viking Press, 1974.

"Laughing and Loving," in *Come to Power*, edited by Dick Lourie. Trumansburg, New York, Crossing Press, 1974.

OTHER PUBLICATIONS

Verse

Laguna Woman. Greenfield Center, New York, Greenfield Review Press, 1974.

Play

Lullaby, with Frank Chin, adaptation of the story by Silko (produced San Francisco, 1976).

Other

Storyteller. New York, Seaver, 1981.

The Delicacy and Strength of Lace: Letters Between Leslie Marmon Silko and James A. Wright, edited by Anne Wright. St. Paul, Minnesota, Graywolf Press, 1986.

*

Manuscript Collection: University of Arizona, Tucson.

Critical Studies: *Leslie Marmon Silko* by Per Seyersted, Boise, Idaho, Boise State University, 1980; *Four American Indian Literary Masters* by Alan R. Velie, Norman, University of Oklahoma Press, 1982.

* * *

Leslie Marmon Silko has become a major American novelist and short-story writer despite a relatively small body of work. Her single novel, *Ceremony*, appeared in 1977, and an idiosyncratic collection of stories/prose/poems/photographs, *Storyteller*, appeared in 1981.

The novel *Ceremony* weaves together many kinds of stories. Chief among them is that of Tayo, a mixed-blood Laguna who has returned mentally damaged from World War II in the Pacific, where he has survived the Bataan death march. Tayo has seen his cousin Rocky die, despite Tayo's promise to the family to bring Rocky home; he believes he has seen his uncle Josiah shot as a Japanese prisoner of war—and his uncle is indeed dead. Worst of all, during the long march of captives through the jungle's rainy season, he has prayed for a drought—and his homeland has suffered a drought ever since. Clearly, one theme of Tayo's story is the inter-connectedness of all things.

Other stories come from Tayo's childhood. He was raised by Rocky's mother—called Auntie throughout the book—after the death of his own mother who had left the Reservation, looking for a better life, but learned only shame. Auntie, in Pueblo tradition, became head of the family when Old Grandma became incapacitated; their extended household also includes Auntie's brother Josiah, who works on Auntie's ranch and plays the role of father and teacher to both his nephews and Auntie's husband Robert. What little Tayo knows of tribal traditions has come from Josiah; Auntie is a member of the church, much to Old Grandma's dismay: "Ah, Thelma, do you have to go *there* again?"

Yet Tayo and Auntie share one important bond: both seem connected to what Jung would call a tribal collective unconscious. For the Christianized Auntie, the connection is painful, serving mostly to make her aware of tribal disappointment over Tayo's mother and Josiah's affair with a Mexican woman. Auntie herself has been disappointed in Josiah's scheme to raise cattle of a Longhorn/Hereford mix that he hopes can survive in desert and near-desert conditions.

Running throughout the novel are another set of stories, told sometimes in prose but more often in narrative poetry, of how the people—including insects, animals, and birds—dealt with evil, especially in the form of witchcraft, in time immemorial. Included are stories which Silko invented about how Indian witchcraft created whites, effectively granting Indians a share in the many evils done to the land and the people, and perverted a natural rock formation which the reader later realizes is uranium. The desert Southwest, where Tayo's people live, is also the site of the first atomic bomb-making, the first tests. And the bomb, *Ceremony* eventually tells us, has made us all one people, no longer separate tribes.

Yet another set of stories are those told by Tayo's friends, his fellow Indian veterans: stories of how they passed for Italian in the beds of white women, of how well they were treated when they were in uniform. Frighteningly, some stories told by Emo, their leader, about taking teeth from dead Japanese sound oddly like the traditional stories of witchcraft.

All these stories are woven about Tayo, nearly incapacitated by guilt, battle fatigue, shell shock. The family seeks cures for Tayo: Auntie wishes him to pay attention to the doctors, to the psychiatrists; Old Grandma brings in a tribal healer. Neither hlps, but the tribal healer recommends a specialist: old Betonie, another mixed-blood (mostly Navaho, but with a little Mexican included—enough to make him suspect in the eyes of tribal purists). Finally, Tayo is desperate enough to travel to Betonie's, where his cure—and the great Ceremony of the title—begins.

Yet this Ceremony does not really begin with Tayo and Betonie; rather, it has gone on for centuries, as Betonie's people and others have struggled against the evil which would destroy all life, symbolized in the twin evils of witchcraft and the atomic bomb. Tayo achieves a successful vision quest under Betonie's guidance; but it simply confirms that he, too, is a part of the great Ceremony of healing, as were Josiah and his Mexican lover (most of the key characters are mixed-bloods, in further support of Silko's suggestion that we are now all one tribe). The vision will lead Tayo on a quest for Josiah's stolen cattle (healed people are able to make a living); but it will also lead him to the rain-mother, and an end to the drought, as well as to a final confrontation with Emo at an abandoned uranium mine with the world hanging in the balance. It is a measure of Silko's artistry that she is able to make this final confrontation believable. By the end of the novel Tayo the mixed-blood outcast has disappointed Auntie even more, by becoming the rain priest for his people.

But evil is never finally destroyed; in the poem which ends the book we learn only that

It is dead for now,
It is dead for now,
It is dead for now,
It is dead for now.

Silko's short stories, as collected in *Storyteller*, explore many of these same themes. Perhaps the best is "Yellow Woman," in which a young Pueblo woman becomes uncertain whether she is having an affair with a young Navaho kidnapper or a figure out of legend; whether she is herself or Yellow Woman of that legend. "Tony's Story" is based on an actual incident in which two young Indians became convinced that a violent and racist highway patrolman was a witch and took the appropriate Pueblo response: killing him and burning his body so that he could not return. "The Man to Bring Rain Clouds" weaves the story of an old man's traditional funeral with Pueblo belief that the dead join the spirit beings who bring rain clouds.

These and several other stories in *Storyteller* are told in traditional European prose style; others are told in narrative verse. Both narrative poetry and narrative prose are traditions in the Southwest; in all her work, Silko tends to combine Pueblo and European traditions (she has said, in conversation, that the most important European-American influences on her work are Marcel Proust and Henry James). Some of the narrative verse stories in *Storyteller* are actually excerpts from *Ceremony*, and there is one excerpt from *The Delicacy and the Strength of Lace: Letters Between Leslie Marmon Silko and James A. Wright* as well as several poems from her 1974 collection, *Laguna Woman*. *Storyteller* is a comprehensive sampling of Silko's practice as a storyteller.

If Silko were a less powerful artist, she would still be important as a technical innovator—or perhaps it would be better to say as a technical synthesizer. But added to that technical skill are a formidable sense of character, of language, of plot and structure, and an overpowering commitment to her themes. Were Silko not to write another word, she would remain not only a major western writer, but a major American writer to rank with Hawthorne, Melville, Twain, James, Faulkner, and Ellison.

—Wayne Ude

SILVER, Nicholas. *See* **BRAND, Max.**

SILVESTER, Frank. *See* **BINGLEY, David Ernest.**

SIMS, Lt. A.K. *See* **WHITSON, John H.**

SIMS, John. *See* **HOPSON, William.**

SKINNER, Mike (Michael Skinner). Also writes as Alix de Marquand; Cynthia Hyde; Nicholas Spain; Mark Swanson. American. Born in New York City, 28 April 1924. Educated at universities in New York, B.Sc. Served in the United States Army Air Force, 1943–45. Married Helga Skinner in 1956. Agent: Thomas Schlück Literary Agency, Hinter der Worth 12, 3008 Garbsen 9, Germany. Address: Jungfrauenthal 5, 2000 Hamburg 13, Germany.

Western Publications

Novels (series: Luke Wyatt in all books)

Remington .44. New York, Lancer, 1966.
Ride into Hell. London, Hale, 1982.
Raiders of Spanish Creek. London, Hale, 1982.
Rough Time in Dobie. London, Hale, 1983.

Other Publications

Novels

Wine, Women, and Bullets (as Nicholas Spain). N.p., Kozy, 1963.
House on Sombre Lake (as Alix de Marquand). New York, Lancer, 1968.
Fury (as Mark Swanson). New York, Paperback Library, 1969.
House of Sinister Shadows (as Cynthia Hyde). New York, Avon, 1972.
Among Those Hunted. London, Hale, 1978.
Somewhere in Hamburg. London, Hale, 1979.
When a Blonde Dies. London, Hale, 1983.

Monique la Magnifique. Hamburg, Rowohlt, 1987.
Misfortunes of Maurice. Hamburg, Rowohlt, 1988.
Memoirs of Montmorency. Hamburg, Rowohlt, 1989.
Nick. Hamburg, Rowohlt, 1990.

Other fiction published under pseudonyms.

*

Mike Skinner comments:

After dealing with skin-flint publishers, American agents—one of whom took a 60% fee—and having to write drivel to survive the last thing I would be is a writer if I had the chance to start all over again.

* * *

Although the majority of his work falls into the thriller and gothic categories, Mike Skinner also found time in the early 1980's to pen a handful of tough, effective Westerns which recount the adventures of a gambling gunman named Luke Wyatt.

On the surface, Wyatt is a typical western hero: good-looking, capable, irresistible to women, and a positive wizard with his matched Remington .44s. An Easterner of some breeding and taste, the trail-wise Wyatt is also possessed of a somewhat mercenary streak, although this ruthlessness is never quite so pronounced as that of the villains with whom he frequently locks horns. The West he inhabits is a dusty, inhospitable place clearly inspired by the spaghetti Western; a land where every town is just another ugly jumble of wood- or sod-built shacks; where townsfolk seldom offer a warm welcome to strangers; where the villains are completely amoral and the women invariably curvaceous and hot-blooded.

Wyatt makes his first appearance in *Ride into Hell*, a fast-moving revenge story which sets both the tone and pace for the adventures that follow. Probably the best of these (though really, it is difficult to judge since, in the final analysis, they are all equally satisfying) is *Raiders of Spanish Creek*, in which Wyatt, having narrowly escaped death at a roadside eaterie where the inhabitants specialise in murdering their customers (a sequence based on the real-life crimes of the notorious Bender family, right down to the crude but effective skull-bashing *modus operandi*) comes into possession of $8000 worth of stolen money. Deciding to hole up for a while in the town of the book's title, which is known to be a den of thieves in which the law can always be relied upon to turn a blind eye, Wyatt soon finds himself fighting off both marauding Apaches and Skinner's usual mixture of avaricious freebooters, all of whom are out for a share of the loot, before finally taking part in a devastating Indian attack which eventually wipes Spanish Creek off the map.

All the Wyatt books are linked by a vague thread of continuity, and Liz Birdwell, a beautiful but murderous redhead whose life Wyatt saves at the end of the book, returns for the interesting *Rough Time in Dobie*. In this title, Wyatt gets involved with a 16-year-old girl who stands to inherit a fortune in land and livestock so long as the villain of the piece (an arrogant young cowboy who supposedly married her widowed mother and then killed both her and her other heirs in order to qualify as sole beneficiary of the estate) doesn't get to her first. Once again Skinner injects an above-average number of double-crosses into the plot, along with the usual cast of crooked lawmen, scheming townsfolk, and man-hungry temptresses before bringing the story to a head with a violent gun-battle which, surprisingly, leaves Wyatt's fate in the balance.

Skinner's Westerns are nothing if not cynical in their outlook. During the climax of *Rough Time in Dobie*, when Wyatt is pitted against no fewer than 10 gunmen, the best the patrons of the "Let Loose" Saloon can do is place bets on the outcome of the fight. Not surprisingly, then, Wyatt comes across as an unusually friendless man, though quite charismatic in a rather predatory way. Similarly, the nearest Skinner comes to humour is in Wyatt's tendency to crack wise with overbearing lawmen, a trait which can sometimes be insufferable. For all that, however, Wyatt is a reasonably credible protagonist whose dialogue and motivations are handled consistently well.

Almost without exception, however, supporting characters are portrayed as greedy, self-centred, and cunning, while Skinner's women generally fall into two distinct categories: the young, who are always desirable and the old, often described as being fat or unwashed. There are repeated allusions to the female form in all the books—melon-shaped breasts, tight, spherical buttocks, trim calves, and so on—as well as erroneous references to lace brassieres (at least three decades before they were invented). Curiously, however, when the sexual act takes centre stage, Skinner always implies more than he actually shows.

There is little room for implication in his descriptions of violence, however, which are exceptionally graphic. Fist-fights, while rare, are nevertheless related in detail. The effects of bullet wounds (of which each book has a high complement) are invariably described with stomach-churning realism: "The boy had died as he tried to aim the Colt at Carter Ivers, taking a bullet through the mouth that shattered his teeth, severed his tongue and blew out the back of his neck," or "Merian turned before he fell, his hat, swiftly bloodied, falling off, an ear shot off, a cheekbone smashed, the back of his head exploding."

In general, Skinner allows his incident-filled stories to unfold at a fast clip, usually over 16 or so chapters. He is quite adept at painting effective word pictures, and maintains reader interest by frequent scene-switching. While there is something undeniably sad in the fact that so few of his secondary characters can ever be trusted or liked, Skinner's plots are inventive, different and, above all, hugely entertaining.

—David Whitehead

SLAUGHTER, Anson. *See* **ATHANAS, Verne.**

SLAUGHTER, Jim. *See* **PAINE, Lauran.**

SMEDLEY, Agnes. American. Born in Campground, Missouri, 23 February 1892. Educated at Knob Hill School, Osgood, Missouri, 1901–03; school in Trinidad, Colorado, 1904–06; County Teacher's Certificate, New Mexico, 1908; Temple Normal School, Arizona, 1911; San Diego Normal School, California, 1913–16. Married Ernest Thorberg in 1912 (divorced 1916). Teacher, Raton, Colfax County, New Mexico, 1908–10; secretary and magazine agent, Colorado and New Mexico, 1911; reporter, Fresno *Morning Republican*, Texas, 1916; political activist with Indian National Party, 1917–18; associate editor, *Birth Control Review* and *Call*, New York,

1919; co-founder, Friends of Freedom for India, 1919; political activist, visiting Berlin, Moscow, and Denmark, 1920–25; foreign correspondent in China, 1928–33, and Soviet Union, 1933–34; returned to China, including visit to Communist headquarters at Yan'an, 1936–37; member of writers' colony, Yaddo, New York, 1943–48; left to live in Wimbledon, England, 1949–50. *Died 6 May 1950.*

WESTERN PUBLICATIONS

Novel

Daughter of Earth. New York, Coward McCann, 1929; London, Virago Press, 1977.

OTHER PUBLICATIONS

Other

India and the Next War. Amritsar, Punjab, n.p., 1928.
Chinese Destinies: Sketches of Present-Day China. New York, Vanguard Press, 1933; London, Hurst and Blackett, 1934.
China's Red Army Marches. New York, Vanguard Press, 1934; London, Lawrence and Wishart, 1936.
China Fights Back: An American Woman with the Eighth Route Army. New York, Vanguard Press, and London, Gollancz, 1938.
Stories of the Wounded: An Appeal for the Orthopaedic Centres of the Chinese Red Cross. Hong Kong, Newspaper Enterprises, 1941.
Battle Hymn of China. New York, Knopf, 1943; London, Gollancz, 1944; as *China Correspondent*, London, Gollancz, 1943; Boston, Pandora Press, 1984.
The Great Road: The Life and Times of Chu Teh. New York, Monthly Review Press, 1956; London, Calder, 1958.
Portraits of Chinese Women in Revolution. New York, Feminist Press, 1976.

*

Critical Study: *Agnes Smedley: The Life and Times of an American Radical* by Janice R. and Stephen R. Mackinnon, London, Virago Press, 1988.

* * *

Unlike any of Agnes Smedley's other books, *Daughter of Earth* is an autobiographical novel. The story, told in retrospect, takes the reader from the Missouri of the 1890's through to the New York of the 1920's. Although she claims that this is not an autobiographical work, like her true autobiography Smedley's fictional heroine, *Battle Hymn of China*, Marie Rogers, is used to illustrate her own early years.

Rogers is born in poverty, although she is not at first aware of this fact, as all who surround her suffer the same rural deprivation. She is brought up in a family where any outward show of love and affection is suppressed by both parents, and her story centres on relationships—between parents, married couples, and lovers. She watches as her mother and father grow steadily apart, forced by circumstances to move from one area to another in search of work.

Marie's father dreams of becoming rich, and this obsession overshadows everything and everyone around him. It causes anger and distrust within the family, especially for Marie, who finds herself attracted to her Aunt Helen, who is a prostitute. She features largely in Marie's upbringing, the younger woman recognizing in Helen those qualities of strength, determination and independence that she herself strives for. It is Helen's ability to earn money which creates friction within the Rogers household, enabling her to subsidise Marie's education and feed her yearning "... to be somewhere else...".

Against her husband's wishes, Marie's mother agrees to send her to school, and she embarks on a phase which is to prove crucial to her future. Although her early life was lacking in outward affection, Marie remains indebted to her father for her love of the land. At one stage, as she watches him working, she reflects: "He was digging not just a hole in the ground, but uncovering marvellous things, all that lies in the earth. That I knew because I knew him, for I was my father's daughter."

As her life unfolds, we can see her development and what will be her future influences quite easily by the way the book is set out. By the age of 16, her mother has died, and she is forced to quit her education to care for her family. It is not long before she feels trapped, and finally, after a confrontation with her father, she returns to Helen. Marie is determined to continue with her studies, and for a while is employed as a stenographer. Here she first encounters sexual advances, and her response is one of revulsion. Her childhood memories have steeled her against the whole subject of sex, love, and men. She can understand why her Aunt Helen suffers men, but is unwilling to compromise herself.

From here on, Marie is unknowingly manipulated by a series of male characters, and undergoes a political awakening, which has only been hinted at earlier. From this emerges a different facet to her nature, and she devotes all her spare time to Indian nationalism. Through her involvement with the cause, she meets and marries an Indian, who has a profound effect on her beliefs. She is later jailed for these political activities, and Smedley was later to produce another book from her experiences (*Cell Mates*).

Marie remains fiercely independent in her marriage, much to her husband's consternation. Like her parents before her, their lives become separated by politics. Throughout the story her family seem to haunt her, and she is constantly reminded of the way she put her own wellbeing before theirs.

In writing this book, Smedley matches each section with part of Marie's life, thus allowing the reader to break off whenever the going becomes too heavy, but one is drawn on, wanting to know the final outcome. The reader is also left with the feeling that there should have been a sequel, to continue Marie's life outside America.

Smedley's story effectively re-creates periods, places, and people. The charm of this book lies in the fact that Marie Rogers was a pretty, ordinary young girl, who struggled through the heartbreak of rural poverty and a bleak home-life, to become her own woman by finding fulfilment in a political movement in which she truly believes.

Set at the close of the 19th century, Smedley's narrative paints a different picture of the West than that familiar to most readers. The characters in the early section of the book still cling to their beliefs that the land belongs to them, but in fact the big corporations have taken over, grinding them into conformity as manual workers. The days of the open range have gone, the ability to wander freely from job to job has vanished, and in its place a bureaucratic society dictates the limits of achievement, a theme which is repeated throughout the book.

Smedley comes out strongly on the side of women, and the men they come up against often get a rough deal. She presents Marie Rogers in a sympathetic light, often at emotional risk, or in attendance at illicit political gatherings. What Smedley has achieved with this highly individual story is a series of observations which are, at times, both sad and humorous.

—John L. Wolfe

SMITH, Charles. *See* **HECKELMANN, Charles N.**

SMITH, Ford. *See* **FRIEND, Oscar.**

SMITH, Lew. *See* **FLOREN, Lee.**

SMITH, Wade. *See* **SNOW, Charles H.**

SNOW, Charles H(orace). Also wrote as H.C. Averill; Charles Ballew; Robert Cole; James Dillard; Allen Forrest; Russ Hardy; John Harlow; Ranger Lee; Gary Marshall; Wade Smith; Dan Wardle; Chester Wills. American. Born in Lake County, California, in 1877. Full-time writer, 1922–67. *Died in 1967.*

WESTERN PUBLICATIONS

Novels (series: Tommy Thorne)

Dust of Gold. London, Methuen, 1928.
Rustlers and Ruby Silver. London, Long, 1930.
The Rider of San Felipe. Boston, Hale Cushman and Flint, 1930; London, Long, 1931.
Days of '50. London, Wright and Brown, 1930.
The Fighting Sheriff. London, Wright and Brown, 1931; as *The Sheriff of Chispa Loma*, Philadelphia, Macrae Smith, 1931.
Roaring Guns. London, Wright and Brown, 1931.
The Cowboy from Alamos. London, Long, 1932; Philadelphia, Macrae Smith, 1933.
Don Jim. London, Wright and Brown, and Philadelphia, Macrae Smith, 1932.
The Invisible Brand. London, Long, 1932; Philadelphia, Macrae Smith, 1933.
The Silent Shot. London, Wright and Brown, 1932.
The Lakeside Murder (Thorne). London, Wright and Brown, 1933.
Beyond Arizona. London, Wright and Brown, 1933.
The Gold-Pan Nugget. London, Wright and Brown, 1933.
The Nevadans. London, Long, 1933.
Pay Dirt Creek. London, Wright and Brown, 1933.
The Scorpion's Sting. London, Wright and Brown, 1933.
Tamer of Bad Men. London, Long, 1933.
The Black Riders of the Range. London, Wright and Brown, 1934.
The Bonanza Murder Case (Thorne). London, Wright and Brown, 1934.
The Gold of Alamito. London, Wright and Brown, 1934.
The Highgraders. London, Long, 1934.
Hollow Stump Mystery. London, Wright and Brown, 1934.
The Outlaws of Inspiration. London, Long, 1934.
Rubies and Red Blood. London, Wright and Brown, 1934.
Smugglers' Ranch. London, Wright and Brown, and Philadelphia, Macrae Smith, 1934.
Cactus Thorns. London, Wright and Brown, 1935.
Six-Guns of Sandoval. Philadelphia, Macrae Smith, 1935.
Cardigan—Cowboy. London, Wright and Brown, and Philadelphia, Macrae Smith, 1935.
The Gold Raiders. London, Wright and Brown, 1935.
The Iron-Nerved Maverick. London, Wright and Brown, 1935.
Murder on the Cattle Ranch. London, Wright and Brown, 1935.
The Sign of the Death Circle (Thorne). London, Wright and Brown, 1935.
Signal Smokes. London, Wright and Brown, 1935.
Argonaut Gold. London, Wright and Brown, and Philadelphia, Macrae Smith, 1936.
The Desert Castle Mystery. London, Wright and Brown, 1936.
Hidden Pay. London, Wright and Brown, 1936.
Law on the Mines. London, Wright and Brown, 1936.
Red Husky. London, Wright and Brown, 1936.
The Riders of Sunset Mesa. London, Wright and Brown, 1936.
The Seven Peaks. London, Wright and Brown, 1936.
Bandits of Bedrock. London, Wright and Brown, 1937.
The Brush Creek Murders. London, Wright and Brown, 1937.
The Fire Cloud, and Thoroughbreds. London, Wright and Brown, 1937.
Romance Rides a Red Horse, and Azalia Blossoms. London, Wright and Brown, 1937.
Sheriff of Olancha. London, Wright and Brown, 1937.
Steel of the North, and Mesquite's Loop. London, Wright and Brown, 1937.
Terry Orcutt's Guns. London, Wright and Brown, 1937.
The Trail to Abilene. London, Wright and Brown, and Philadelphia, Macrae Smith, 1937.
Trails of '56. London, Wright and Brown, 1937.
Big Strike. London, Wright and Brown, 1938.
Guns in the Chaparral. London, Wright and Brown, 1938.
Six Bars of Gold. London, Wright and Brown, 1938.
White Mountains. London, Wright and Brown, 1938.
Riders of the Range. Philadelphia, Macrae Smith, 1939.
The Bandit of Matagorda. London, Wright and Brown, 1939.
Irregular Ranger. London, Wright and Brown, 1939.
Roaring Range. London, Wright and Brown, 1939.
Three Rivers Range. London, Wright and Brown, 1939.
Outlaws of Red Canyon. Philadelphia, Macrae Smith, 1940.
Grizzly. London, Wright and Brown, 1940.
She Was Sheriff. London, Wright and Brown, 1940.
Top Hand. London, Wright and Brown, 1940.
War on the Penasco. London, Wright and Brown, 1940.
Sheriff of Yavisa. Philadelphia, Macrae Smith, 1941.
Dillard of Circle 22. London, Wright and Brown, 1941.
Fightin' Bob. London, Wright and Brown, 1941.
The Mystery of Devil's Canyon. London, Wright and Brown, 1942.
The Brand Stealer. Philadelphia, Macrae Smith, 1942.
Crowfoot Range. London, Wright and Brown, 1942.
Outlaws of Sugar Loaf. Philadelphia, Macrae Smith, 1942; London, Wright and Brown, 1944.

The Girl of the Bar D Bar. London, Wright and Brown, 1943.
Horsethief Pass. London, Wright and Brown, 1943; Philadelphia, Macrae Smith, 1944.
Rebel of Ronde Valley. Philadelphia, Macrae Smith, 1943; London, Wright and Brown, 1944.
Double-Cross Brand. London, Wright and Brown, 1944.
Rustlers of Lonesome Valley. London, Wright and Brown, 1945.
Ghost Camp. London, Wright and Brown, 1946.
The Rifle on the Rim. London, Wright and Brown, 1946.
Rustlers of Red Creek. London, Wright and Brown, 1946.
Lone Hand. London, Wright and Brown, 1947.
Valley of Lawless Men. London, Wright and Brown, 1947.
The Widow of Washoe. London, Wright and Brown, 1948.
Two Crimson Ropes. London, Wright and Brown, 1948.
Gunsmoke in Tombstone. London, Wright and Brown, 1948.
The Horsethief. London, Wright and Brown, 1949.
The Highgrade Murder. London, Wright and Brown, 1949.
Gold Dust and Bear Meat. London, Wright and Brown, 1950.
The Mysterious Missile. London, Wright and Brown, 1950.
Frontier Meetin' House. London, Wright and Brown, 1951.
The Mountain Murder Case. London, Wright and Brown, 1951.
Roaming Rider. London, Wright and Brown, 1951.
Under the Big Red Rim. London, Wright and Brown, 1951.
The Mesa Trial. London, Wright and Brown, 1952.
Snake Brand. London, Wright and Brown, 1952.
Feud at Carson's Ranch. London, Wright and Brown, 1953.
The Buckhorn Murder Case. London, Wright and Brown, 1953.
Saga of the Sierras. London, Wright and Brown, 1953.
The Forty-Niner. London, Wright and Brown, 1954.
Twice Murdered. London, Wright and Brown, 1954.
Battle of High Mesa. London, Wright and Brown, 1955.
Red Fire Stampede. London, Wright and Brown, 1955.
Shotgun. London, Wright and Brown, 1955.
Red Ring Dynamite. London, Wright and Brown, 1956.
Rustler Bait. London, Wright and Brown, 1956.
Vengeance Trail (as Robert Cole). London, Hale, 1956.
The Hangman's Tree (as Robert Cole). London, Hale, 1957.
Hell's Half Acre. London, Wright and Brown, 1957.
Last of an Outlaw Brand. London, Wright and Brown, 1957.
Rustlers of Moon River. London, Wright and Brown, 1957.
The Caves of Pinnacle Peak. London, Wright and Brown, 1958.
Gangster in the Desert. London, Wright and Brown, 1958.
Into the Gunsmoke. London, Wright and Brown, 1958.
Scars on the West. London, Wright and Brown, 1958.
Winter in the Ghost Camp. London, Wright and Brown, 1959.
Tenon's Task. London, Wright and Brown, 1959.
Horsethief of Carson Valley. London, Wright and Brown, 1960.
Last on the Outlaws' Trail. London, Wright and Brown, 1960.
Robbery in the Mountains. London, Wright and Brown, 1960.
Battle at Yellow Creek. London, Wright and Brown, 1961.
Guns and Black Gold. London, Wright and Brown, 1961.
Guns in the Sage. London, Wright and Brown, 1961.
Pay from the Grass Roots. London, Wright and Brown, 1961.
Death of a Rancher. London, Wright and Brown, 1962.
Gun Holds High Hand. London, Wright and Brown, 1962.
Jailbreak in Gold Horn. London, Wright and Brown, 1962.
Gun on the Mantel. London, Wright and Brown, 1963.
Riding the Back Trail. London, Wright and Brown, 1963.
Death in the Canyon. London, Wright and Brown, 1964.
Gold Beyond the Mountains. London, Wright and Brown, 1964.
Law on a Rampage. London, Wright and Brown, 1964.
The Dry Diggings Nugget. London, Wright and Brown, 1965.
Smoke Signals from Timberline. London, Wright and Brown, 1965.
Tangled Ropes. London, Wright and Brown, 1965.
Big Range Country. London, Wright and Brown, 1966.
Flame in the Storm. London, Wright and Brown, 1966.
Law Comes to Silver Blade. London, Wright and Brown, 1966.
Happy Ranch. London, Wright and Brown, 1967.

Novels as Charles Ballew (series: Rim-Fire)

Red Gold. London, Long, 1932.
The Gambler of Red Gulch. London, Long, 1933.
One Crazy Cowboy. London, Long, and New York, Morrow, 1933.
From Ragtown to Rugby. London, Long, 1934.
Sheriff Blood. London, Bles, 1934; as *Cowpuncher*, New York, Morrow, 1934.
The Bandit of Paloduro. New York, Morrow, 1934; London, Harrap, 1935.
Dogs of Discord. London, Wright and Brown, 1935.
Rim-Fire Rides. London, Wright and Brown, 1935.
Texas Spurs. New York, Loring and Mussey, 1935.
The Treasure of Aspen Canyon. London, Bles, and New York, Loring and Mussey, 1935.
Rim-Fire, Detective. London, Wright and Brown, 1936.
Rim-Fire on the Range. London, Wright and Brown, 1936.
Rim-Fire, Sheriff. London, Wright and Brown, 1936.
Rim-Fire Six Guns. London, Wright and Brown, 1936.
Rim-Fire Fights. London, Wright and Brown, 1937.
Rim-Fire Horns In. London, Wright and Brown, 1937.
Rim-Fire, Ranchero. London, Wright and Brown, 1937.
Rim-Fire Roams. London, Wright and Brown, 1937.
Rim-Fire on the Desert. London, Wright and Brown, 1938.
Rim-Fire Slips. London, Wright and Brown, 1938.
Rim-Fire and Slats. London, Wright and Brown, 1938.
Frontier Regiment. London, Wright and Brown, 1939.
Guns along the Border. London, Wright and Brown, 1939; as Charles H. Snow, Philadelphia, Macrae Smith, 1939.
Rim-Fire in Mexico. London, Wright and Brown, 1939.
Rim-Fire Presides. London, Wright and Brown, 1939.
Rouse River Range. London, Wright and Brown, 1939.
Blood Stain Trails. London, Wright and Brown, 1940.
Wolf of the Mesas. London, Wright and Brown, 1940; as Charles H. Snow, Philadelphia, Macrae Smith, 1941.
Rim-Fire Runs. London, Wright and Brown, 1941.
The New Sheriff. London, Wright and Brown, 1942.
Rim-Fire Gets 'em. London, Wright and Brown, 1942.
Wild Range. London, Wright and Brown, 1943.
Wolves of Grey Bluff. London, Wright and Brown, 1943.
Horse Thieves of Rock River. London, Wright and Brown, 1944.
Outlaw Town. London, Wright and Brown, 1944.
Rim-Fire on the Prod. London, Wright and Brown, 1944.
Rim-Fire Returns. London, Wright and Brown, 1944.
The Long Trail. London, Wright and Brown, 1946.
Rider of the High Country. London, Wright and Brown, 1946.
Rim-Fire Skunked. London, Wright and Brown, 1947.
Robbers' Rock. London, Wright and Brown, 1947.
Bandits of Jupiter Gulch. London, Wright and Brown, 1948.
Mystery of Limestone Mountain. London, Wright and Brown, 1949.
Robbers' Ranch. London, Wright and Brown, 1949.
Valley of Tumbling Waters. London, Wright and Brown, 1949.
Rim-Fire and the Bear. London, Wright and Brown, 1950.
Bandit of Mormon Mesa. London, Wright and Brown, 1951.

Rustlers and Powder Smoke. London, Wright and Brown, 1951.
Black Sage Range. London, Wright and Brown, 1953.
Rim-Fire Abstains. London, Wright and Brown, 1953.
The Slash K Ranch. London, Wright and Brown, 1953.
The Castle in the Sagebrush. London, Wright and Brown, 1954.
Sails in the Desert. London, Wright and Brown, 1954.
Mountain Valley. London, Wright and Brown, 1955.
Cattle on the Plains. London, Wright and Brown, 1956.
The Bushwhacker. London, Wright and Brown, 1956.
Kelly of the Badlands. London, Wright and Brown, 1957.
The Valley of Ten Thousand Horses. London, Wright and Brown, 1957.
The Fight for Monitor Mountain. London, Wright and Brown, 1958.
Fight for Pay Ground. London, Wright and Brown, 1958.
Range Beyond the Mountains. London, Wright and Brown, 1958.
Blood on the Saddle. London, Wright and Brown, 1959.
The Highwayman of Cedar Creek. London, Wright and Brown, 1959; as *Showdown at Cedar Creek*, 1963.
Frontier Wall of Fire. London, Wright and Brown, 1960.
Lawman of the Mountains. London, Wright and Brown, 1960.
Rifles at Cow Tail. London, Wright and Brown, 1960.
Cabin Fever. London, Wright and Brown, 1961.
The Gold of Poverty Flat. London, Wright and Brown, 1961.
The Trail-Blazer. London, Wright and Brown, 1961.
Danger Trail. London, Wright and Brown, 1962.
Gunslinger's Last Battle. London, Wright and Brown, 1962.
Ride That Buckskin. London, Wright and Brown, 1962.
Dead Men Ride. London, Wright and Brown, 1963.
Bushwhacker Bullet. London, Wright and Brown, 1963.
Monitor Mountain. London, Wright and Brown, 1963.
Mountain Trouble. London, Wright and Brown, 1963.
Sourdough Pay-Off. London, Wright and Brown, 1963.
Bad Medicine in Wyoming. London, Wright and Brown, 1964.
Gunsight Moon. London, Wright and Brown, 1964.
War on the Flying O. London, Wright and Brown, 1964.
Arizona Hunter. London, Wright and Brown, 1965.
Feud and Flood. London, Wright and Brown, 1965.
The Trail Together. London, Wright and Brown, 1965.
The Tenderfoot Called Rawhide. London, Wright and Brown, 1966.
Beyond the Rimrock. London, Wright and Brown, 1967.
Faro at Cottonwood Springs. London, Wright and Brown, 1967.

Novels as Gary Marshall

Flaming Six-Gun. London, Wright and Brown, 1934.
Runaway Horses. London, Wright and Brown, 1934.
The Scarlet Ace. London, Wright and Brown, 1934.
The Watchers of Gold Gulch. London, Wright and Brown, 1934; as *The Vigilantes of Gold Gulch* (as Charles H. Snow), Philadelphia, Macrae Smith, 1937.
Blood of the Sotone. London, Wright and Brown, 1935.
The Gallant Outlaw. London, Wright and Brown, 1935.
One Fightin' Cowboy. London, Wright and Brown, 1935; as *Raiders of the Tonto Rim*, New York, Hartney Press, 1935.
The Red Spider of Quartz Gulch. London, Wright and Brown, 1935.
The Saga of Sunny Jim. London, Wright and Brown, 1935.
The Sheriff's Daughter. London, Wright and Brown, 1935.
Border Blood. London, Wright and Brown, 1936; as *Border Feud* (as Charles H. Snow), Philadelphia, Macrae Smith, 1938.
The Fighting Tenderfoot. London, Wright and Brown, 1936.
Powder Smoke. London, Wright and Brown, 1936.
Raging River. London, Wright and Brown, 1936.
Rangeland Gold. London, Wright and Brown, 1936.
The Capture of the King. London, Wright and Brown, 1937.
The Feud of Lone Lake Valley. London, Wright and Brown, 1937.
Nesters of Chunk Valley. London, Wright and Brown, 1937.
Nevada Gold. London, Wright and Brown, 1937.
The Outlaw Chief. London, Wright and Brown, 1937.
Rough Ranges. London, Wright and Brown, 1937.
Empty Cartridges. London, Wright and Brown, 1938.
The Girl from Garrison's. London, Wright and Brown, 1938.
The Rider from Rincon. London, Wright and Brown, 1938.
Rimrock Range. London, Wright and Brown, 1938.
Copper Range. London, Wright and Brown, 1939.
Devils of Desolation. London, Wright and Brown, 1939.
Gun-Slinger. London, Wright and Brown, 1939.
Painted Hills. London, Wright and Brown, 1939.
Black Butte. London, Wright and Brown, 1940.
The New Range Boss. London, Collins, 1940.
Boots On. London, Collins, 1940.
The Girl of the Lazy L. London, Collins, 1941.
Six-Gun Smoke. London, Collins, 1941.
Barbed Wire. London, Collins, 1942.
Desperadoes of Diablo. London, Collins, 1942.
The Prospector of Signal Mountain. London, Collins, 1943.
Red Mesas. London, Collins, 1943.
Buckshot. London, Collins, 1944.
Big Smoke. London, Collins, 1945.
Guns of Arizona. London, Collins, 1945.
Cottonwood Creek. London, Collins, 1946.
Nevada Man. London, Collins, 1946.
The Outsider. London, Collins, 1947.
Riding for the Diamond S. London, Collins, 1947.
Copper Belt. London, Collins, 1948.
Rustlers of Sky Valley. London, Collins, 1948.
Buffalo Valley. London, Collins, 1949.
The Old Breed. London, Collins, 1950.
Old Panther-Foot. London, Collins, 1950.
Down Mexico Way. London, Collins, 1951.
Hair Trigger. London, Collins, 1951.
Mountain Gold. London, Collins, 1952.
Sagebrush Desert. London, Collins, 1953.
Cloudburst. London, Collins, 1953.
Sagebrush Empire. London, Collins, 1954.
Line Fence. London, Collins, 1954.
Bandits of the Brush Country. London, Collins, 1955.
Lost Loot. London, Collins, 1955.
Texan Sheriff. London, Collins, 1956.
Trouble in the Mountains. London, Collins, 1956.

Novels as Ranger Lee

Haunted Canyon. London, Hale, 1937.
Wild Riders. London, Hale, 1937.
Thundering Hoofs. New York, Greystone Press, 1937; London, Hale, 1938.
Rebel on the Range. New York, Greystone Press, 1938.
Marauders of the Mesas. London, Collins, 1939.
The Red Gash Outlaws. London, Collins, and New York, Greystone Press, 1939.
Outlaws of the Bad Lands. London, Collins, 1940.
Renegade Ranger. London, Collins, 1940; as Charles H. Snow, Philadelphia, Macrae Smith, 1943.
The Sixth Bandit. London, Collins, 1940.
The Man of the Bay. London, Collins, 1941.

Badland Bill. New York, Phoenix Press, 1941.
Free Range. London, Collins, 1942.
Rustler's Luck. London, Collins, 1942.
The Wide Loop. London, Collins, 1942.
The Bar D Boss. New York, Phoenix Press, 1943.
Red Shirt. London, Collins, 1943.
The Silver Train. London, Collins, 1943.
Just Dusty. London, Collins, 1944.
Outlaws of Ophir Creek. London, Collins, 1945.
Tangled Brands. London, Collins, 1945.
Short Grass Range. London, Collins, 1946.
The Valley Before Me. London, Collins, 1946.
Flames in the Forest. London, Collins, 1947.
Mountain Money. London, Collins, 1947.
Winding River Range. London, Collins, 1948.
Wolf of the Cactus. London, Collins, 1948.
Crimson Dust. London, Collins, 1949.
The Claim Jumpers. London, Collins, 1950.
The Ranch in the Canyon. London, Collins, 1950.
Brothers of the Sage. London, Collins, 1951.
Wild Range Country. London, Collins, 1951.
The New Marshal. London, Collins, 1952.
Wild Horse War. London, Collins, 1952.
Big Horse. London, Collins, 1953.
End of a Lawless Trail. London, Collins, 1953.
Big War for Little Ranch. London, Collins, 1954.
The Empty Scabbard. London, Collins, 1955.
Panther Canyon. London, Collins, 1955.
The Dagger of Wild Valley. London, Collins, 1956.
The Four Diamond Brand. London, Collins, 1956.
Boom Camp. London, Collins, 1957.
The Longhorns. London, Collins, 1957.
The Lost River Trail. London, Collins, 1958.
Outlaws at Bravo. London, Collins, 1959.
Bear Trap. London, Collins, 1959.
Justice Comes to Cactus City. London, Collins, 1960.
Skeletons in the Desert. London, Collins, 1961.
Quick Rifle. London, Collins, 1961.
Fighters of Ghost Camp. London, Collins, 1962.

Novels as H.C. Averill

Two Horizons. London, Wright and Brown, 1938.
Yukon Nights. London, Wright and Brown, 1946.
The Girls Go West. London, Wright and Brown, 1948.
Red Mountain. London, Wright and Brown, 1949.
Feud of the San Grigorio. London, Wright and Brown, 1950.
Yuba Diggings. London, Wright and Brown, 1950.
Brand of the Red Bird. London, Wright and Brown, 1952.
Feudin' in the Hills. London, Wright and Brown, 1954.
Bedrock Courage. London, Wright and Brown, 1955.
Trouble Country. London, Wright and Brown, 1956.
The Prisoner at Quartz Mountain. London, Wright and Brown, 1957.
Redistribution Bullet. London, Wright and Brown, 1957.
Wrong Man for Murder. London, Wright and Brown, 1958; as *The Wrong Man*, London, Digit, 1963.
Bunch Grass Range. London, Wright and Brown, 1959.
Guns at Sulpher Creek. London, Wright and Brown, 1959.
Long Trails. London, Wright and Brown, 1960.
Pay Ground and Powder Smoke. London, Wright and Brown, 1960.
Mustang Valley. London, Wright and Brown, 1961.
Trail's End. London, Wright and Brown, 1961.
War to the Last Man. London, Wright and Brown, 1961.
Law Arrives in Elkhorn. London, Wright and Brown, 1962.
Penning the Outlaw. London, Wright and Brown, 1962.
Guns in Arizona. London, Wright and Brown, 1963.
Rustlers on the Bar-S. London, Wright and Brown, 1963.
Sagebrush Gunsmoke. London, Wright and Brown, 1964.
Through Panther Pass. London, Wright and Brown, 1964.
California Trail. London, Wright and Brown, 1964.
Barred from the Range. London, Wright and Brown, 1965.
The Brand Was IXL. London, Wright and Brown, 1966.
The Shot in the Back. London, Wright and Brown, 1966.

Novels as Wade Smith

B Diamond Ranch. London, Collins, 1942.
The Red Steer. London, Collins, 1942.
Three Bar Cross. London, Collins, 1943.
Wild Country. London, Collins, 1944.
Battle at Black Mesa. London, Collins, 1945.
Bitter Range. London, Collins, 1945.
Rattlesnake. London, Collins, 1946.
Land Beyond the Law. London, Collins, 1947.
Three Masked Men. London, Collins, 1947.
Bound for Arizona. London, Collins, 1948.
Saddle Partners. London, Collins, 1948.
Boss of the Diamond Ranch. London, Collins, 1949.
Five Finger Valley. London, Collins, 1949.
Hidden River. London, Collins, 1950.
Montana Gunsmoke. London, Collins, 1950.
Montana Skies. London, Collins, 1951.
Below the Border. London, Collins, 1951.
Outlaws of Clover Valley. London, Collins, 1952.
The Trail of the Cimarron Kid. London, Collins, 1952.
The Outlaw Brothers. London, Collins, 1953.
Tough Tenderfoot. London, Collins, 1953.
The Bandit of Big Bend. London, Collins, 1954.
Dead Man's Saddle. London, Collins, 1955.
Tawny Men from Texas. London, Collins, 1955.
The Long Trail to Battle. London, Collins, 1956.
War for Water. London, Collins, 1956.
Big Cactus. London, Collins, 1957.
Wildcat Silver. London, Collins, 1957.
The Man Hunter. London, Collins, 1958.
The Fence Buster. London, Collins, 1959.
Marauder from Mexico. London, Collins, 1959.
Lone Mountain Gold. London, Collins, 1960.
Made of Sheriff's Stuff. London, Collins, 1960.
The Sheriff's Hunch. London, Collins, 1961.
The Taming of Wild River. London, Collins, 1961.
Baron of Big Cedar Basin. London, Collins, 1962.

Novels as Russ Hardy

Silver Hills. London, Hammond, 1946.
Riders of Apache Rim. London, Hammond, 1948.
The Saga of Gory Gold. London, Hammond, 1948.
Rustler King. London, Hammond, 1949.
Sycamore Canyon. London, Hammond, 1949.
Blizzard. London, Hammond, 1952.
The Notched Stick. London, Hammond, 1954.
The Hard Trail. London, Hammond, 1955.
Tiger of the West. London, Hammond, 1955.
The Red Trail. London, Hale, 1956.
Return of the Rancho. London, Hale, 1957.
Pack Train. London, Hale, 1957.
Hidden Gold. London, W.H. Allen, 1957.
Trouble Ranch. London, W.H. Allen, 1958.

Novels as Chester Wills

Loot. London, Collins, 1947.
Roaring Camp. London, Collins, 1948.
Silver on the Sage. London, Collins, 1949.
Treasure of the Pine Country. London, Collins, 1949.
Shoot-up at Two Rivers. London, Collins, 1950.
The Big Drive North. London, Collins, 1951.
The Devil's Trail. London, Collins, 1952.
Picture Rock. London, Collins, 1952.
Empty Guns. London, Collins, 1953.
The Long Rifle. London, Collins, 1953.
The Bandit of High Lonesome. London, Collins, 1954.
Call of the Mountains. London, Collins, 1954.
Coarse Gold. London, Collins, 1955.
Mountain Vengeance. London, Collins, 1955.
Bones of Amazing Valley. London, Collins, 1956.
The Man from Arizona. London, Collins, 1956.
The Fighting Doctor of Dobetown. London, Collins, 1957.
The Fighting Prospector. London, Collins, 1957.
Arizona Gold. London, Collin, 1958.
Raiders of Big Mesa. London, Collins, 1958.
Prospector from the Pine Mountain. London, Collins, 1959.
Stagecoach for Oro Grande. London, Collins, 1959.
The Back Trail. London, Collins, 1960.
Hair Trigger Country. London, Collins, 1961.
Sagebrush Funeral. London, Collins, 1961.
Smoking Them Out. London, Collins, 1962.
Powder Burns in Wyoming. London, Muller, 1962.
The Ghost of Tom Peck Canyon. London, Muller, 1963.
Ride to Red Rock. London, Muller, 1963.

Novels as Dan Wardle

The Twenty and One. London, Wright and Brown, 1954.
Five Bars of Gold. London, Wright and Brown, 1955.
Spear for a Tiger. London, Wright and Brown, 1956.

Novels as Allen Forrest

The Wheels Roll West. London, Corgi, 1956.
Apache Trail. London, Corgi, 1957.
Indian Fighter. London, Corgi, 1958.

Novels as James Dillard

From War to Longhorns. London, Muller, 1957.
Gold in the Canyon. London, Muller, 1957.
Prospector Trail. London, Muller, 1962.
The Gold of Oro Fino. London, Muller, 1962.
The Treasure of Eagle Peak. London, Muller, 1963.

Novels as John Harlow

Nevada Cowboy. London, Long, 1957.
Dead Man's Mine. London, Long, 1958.
Trail into Mexico. London, Long, 1958.

OTHER PUBLICATIONS

Fiction for children

Stocky of Lone Tree Ranch. Philadelphia, Macrae Smith, 1932; London, Wright and Brown, 1938.

* * *

If there is any single quality one associates with Charles H. Snow, it is surely his phenomenal stamina and appetite for writing. In a career spanning more than 30 years, he produced a mass of novels under his own name and at least a dozen aliases, to the extent that most of his pseudonyms rank as substantial "authors" in their own right. The sheer size of the output is staggering. It is fortunate, therefore, that the same basic characteristics are found in Snow's work under most of his names, enabling a considered judgement to be reached on his writing as a whole.

Snow the writer belongs to an earlier generation of western writers—Macrae and Tuttle are two other examples—whose novels tend to unfold at a more leisurely pace than that to which most modern readers are accustomed. Action in the Snow novel is usually sandwiched between long periods of lassitude, often rambling easily into more or less irrelevant subplots featuring minor characters. In this, it has to be said that Snow lacks Tuttle's directness, and Macrae's occasional skill with characterization. Few of his works stick to the storyline for long, and fewer still of his creations impress as living men and women. Under most names he tends to feature heroes who are unreal paragons, and villains either suspiciously personable, or downright stupid. Sometimes, as in *Pay from the Grass Roots*, digression sets in so much that the villains appear only briefly and to little purpose, a few pages from the end. The ponderous humour, too, tends to make for heavy going. On the other hand, it is perhaps unfair to mention the frequent examples of racial intolerance which—although distasteful—were probably commonly held at the time. The main strength which helps to counteract the flaws of his style is Snow's ability to set the scene for action, and to give his novels an authentic background. This is especially true of the books written as Ranger Lee and Chester Wills, where gold prospecting is a recurrent topic and California or Nevada the favoured location. At his best, Snow's use of his background knowledge in these areas helps one to suspend disbelief in the unlikely characters and the slow meanderings of the plot.

Wills and Lee apart, most of Snow's work under his pseudonyms tends to be predictably similar to that under his own name, and to each other. As Russ Hardy and Robert Cole, and occasionally as H.C. Averill, his novels are slightly shorter and more direct, and one notes a greater number of gruesome shooting incidents when he writes as Gary Marshall, but otherwise his writings are remarkably alike. The grisly details of some of the deaths—an aspect which often jars uncomfortably with the laboured humour in the same books—is more prevalent in the Marshall novels, but examples are found elsewhere. In *Blood on the Saddle* by Charles Ballew, the murder of a prospector for his quicksilver claim, and the discovery of his blood-stained horse by his wife, is probably the most striking scene. Another Ballew title, *The Castle in the Sagebrush*, features a villain who grows rich—again by murdering a prospector—and provides a gruesome touch whereby he is unmasked by the skull of his victim, recognizable by its gold teeth. Ballew is also "author" of the "Rim-Fire" sequence of novels. Examples of Snow's work as Gary Marshall include *Line Fence*, *Lost Loot*, and *Hair Trigger*, all of which feature death scenes quite as ugly as any modern "adult Western." Indeed, the combination of violence and contrived humour in some of the latter echoes Snow to a considerable degree.

The H.C. Averill novels tend to be less brutal in execution, and examples like *Mustang Valley*, with its theme of adventure on an emigrant train, are more compact than some. On the other hand action rambles, and the villain seems almost an afterthought. Other titles include *Bunch Grass Range*, *The Prisoner at Quartz Mountain*, and *War to the Last Man*. Work of a similar kind is produced as James Dillard, notable titles being *From War to Longhorns* and *The Treasure of Eagle Peak*. Dillard is a favoured name with Snow. A novel under his own name has the title *Dillard of Circle 22*, and a John Dillard is the hero of *End of a Lawless Trail* by Ranger Lee. Some of the better-known Wade Smith novels are *Lone Mountain Gold*, *The Trail of the Cimarron Kid*, *The Fence Buster*, and *Wildcat Silver*. Another example of the grisly element appears in Smith's *Rattlesnake*, whose prospector hero kills the sleek villain in graphic manner. As Russ Hardy and Robert Cole, Snow is at his briefest and most direct, and produces some of his most convincing work. *Vengeance Trail* by Cole, where the hero's hunt for a killer rarely digresses, and Hardy's *The Red Trail* are excellent instances of what Snow can achieve when he removes unnecessary subplots and sticks to the story.

Ranger Lee and Chester Wills deserve to be mentioned separately, as Snow's best background settings and much of his best work are produced under their names. *Prospector from the Pine Mountain*, by Wills, is among the author's finest. A story of a prospector wrongly suspected of theft, and his unmasking of the true robbers, it has well-sustained action and credible dialogue, and the accurate picture of the mining community helps to strengthen the characters. *Coarse Gold* is almost equally good, the plot shorn of superfluous elements with a constant focus on the main villains of the story, and some interesting background information on the deep dredging methods of gold mining current at the time. Other Wills titles, mostly featuring prospecting as a theme, are *Picture Rock*, *Treasure of the Pine Country*, *Silver on the Sage*, and *Bones of Amazing Valley*. Of the Ranger Lee titles, one of the best is *The Ranch in the Canyon*, where a son clears his father of murder and exposes a crooked rancher, and provides an authentic picture of Arizona life. *The Wide Loop* and *The Valley Before Me*, with their cattle rustling themes, and *Wild Range Country*, whose hero thwarts a plan to steal a ranch, are also good examples.

Snow's novels under his own name lack the background strength of Lee and Wills, but often contain the same basic elements. *Tenon's Task*, which describes the saving of an Indian's life by Texans, and his subsequent feud with another renegade, makes great play of maggot-infested wounds, and displays the usual humour. *Pay from the Grass Roots* has a hero who strikes it rich in California, and recovers money stolen from his father. *Winter in the Ghost Camp* also describes the fortunes of a young prospector. Other Snow novels include *Hell's Half Acre*, *The Fighting Sheriff*, and *Horsethief of Carson Valley*.

Snow was a prolific writer. He was not, one feels, a great one. All the same, his work as Wills, Lee, Hardy and Cole in particular produced several effective novels, not least in their settings.

—Jeff Sadler

SORENSEN, Virginia (née Eggertsen). American. Born in Provo, Utah, 17 February 1912. Educated at Brigham Young University, Provo, A.B. 1934; Stanford University, California. Married 1) Frederick C. Sorensen in 1933 (divorced), one daughter and one son; 2) the writer Alec Waugh in 1969 (died 1981). Writer-in-residence, State University of Oklahoma, Edmond, 1966–67. Recipient: Guggenheim fellowship, 1946, 1954; Child Study Committee award, 1956; American Library Association Newbery Medal, 1957. Fellow, Phi Beta Kappa. Agent: Curtis Brown, 10 Astor Place, New York, New York 10003. Address: 2521 Old Kanuga Road, Hendersonville, North Carolina 28739, U.S.A.

Western Publications

Novels

A Little Lower Than the Angels. New York, Knopf, 1942.
On This Star. New York, Reynal, 1946.
The Neighbors. New York, Reynal, 1947.
The Evening and the Morning. New York, Harcourt Brace, 1949.
The Proper Gods. New York, Harcourt Brace, 1951.
Many Heavens. New York, Harcourt Brace, 1954.
Kingdom Come. New York, Harcourt Brace, 1960.
The Man with the Key. New York, Harcourt Brace, 1974.

Short Stories

Where Nothing Is Long Ago: Memories of a Mormon Childhood. New York, Harcourt Brace, 1963.

Other Publications

Fiction (for children)

Curious Missie. New York, Harcourt Brace, 1953.
The House Next Door: Utah, 1896. New York, Scribner, 1954.
Plain Girl. New York, Harcourt Brace, 1955.
Miracles on Maple Hill. New York, Harcourt Brace, 1956; Leicester, Brockhampton Press, 1967.
Lotte's Locket. New York, Harcourt Brace, 1964.
Around the Corner. New York, Harcourt Brace, 1971.
Friends of the Road. New York, Atheneum, 1978.

*

Manuscript Collections: Special Collections, Boston University Library; Kerlan Collection, University of Minnesota, Minneapolis.

Critical Study: *Virginia Sorensen* by L.L. and Sylvia B. Lee, Boise, Idaho, Boise State University, 1978.

* * *

Although the landscape dominates most writing about the West, the focus of Virginia Sorensen's world is her people, a "peculiar" people to use their own term, the Mormons. This does not mean that landscape is meaningless to Sorensen; it is always present, usually as an awesome good. But she is an atypical western writer, offering a particular and sometimes more complex vision of western life than is usual. For the Mormons were and are the different Westerners, since they emphasize(d) the family, community, and order, as opposed to the received image of the Westerner as the lonely individual, in revolt against establishments and controls, outside of time and history.

Sorensen's thematic material, then, is multiple: the relationship, usually a conflict, between the individual and society to the land; and, because her central figure is usually a woman, the difficult life of women in a patriarchal world. But, too, she is continually concerned with time, with history, critically confronting that American dream of Eden, the natural and good world without history.

When the Mormons went west, they took their inescapable community past with them. But individuals also have inescapable pasts. In her best work, Sorensen, technically a rather traditional writer, will make good use of the flashback in order to juxtapose past and the present. Her emphasis on the past, from her first novel, *A Little Lower Than the Angels*, on, therefore, is an attempt not only to understand that past but also the present which has come from the past. The major subject in the novel is the conflict between the heroine and the society; she cannot accept, finally, polygamy. But polygamy was to shape Mormon society for most of the next hundred years.

The later *Many Heavens* also deals directly with polygamy, this time at a later moment, after the Mormon church had rejected the doctrine under pressure. But many good Mormons continued the practice. Here the heroine makes her accommodation, but nevertheless manages, within limits, to live her own life. This doubleness of acceptance and defiance is important in Sorensen's work. In *The Evening and the Morning*, probably her best novel, she not only enriches her portrayal of the difficult position of women in Mormonism but also of this doubleness. The protagonist, Kate Alexander, is the very type of the outsider, one betrayed and rejected by the insiders because she has attempted to live fully. Yet Kate is not simply a victim; she is strong, often headstrong, and she has been insensitive and selfish. The novel ends in an ambiguity: Kate has demonstrated her strength (and has helped her daughter and granddaughter to learn how better to live) but she is essentially alone.

And so Sorensen both asserts and criticizes individualism. *The Proper Gods*, a novel about the Yaqui Indians of Mexico rather than the Mormons, suggests this time that the hero is better for returning to, becoming a part of, his traditional community than in being separate. And that community is directly dependent upon the land. However, in *The Neighbors* the land is resistant. One can sum up Sorensen's work, then, by saying that in her world the dreams of community and the Garden of Eden are necessary for man, but that the actualities of life must be faced and accepted.

—L.L. Lee

SPEARMAN, Frank H(amilton). American. Born in Buffalo, New York, 6 September 1859. Educated in private and public schools; Lawrence College (now University), Appleton, Wisconsin. Married Eugenie A. Lonergan in 1884; five sons and one daughter. Salesman, then bank cashier and president. Recipient: Laetere Medal, 1935. LL.D.: University of Notre Dame, Indiana, 1917; Santa Clara University, California, 1924; Litt.D.: Loyola University, Los Angeles. *Died 29 December 1937.*

WESTERN PUBLICATIONS

Novels

Doctor Bryson. New York, Scribner, 1902.
The Daughter of a Magnate. New York, Scribner, 1903.
The Close of the Day. New York, Appleton, 1904.
Whispering Smith. New York, Scribner, 1906; London, Hodder and Stoughton, 1916.
Robert Kimberly. New York, Scribner, 1911.
The Mountain Divide. New York, Scribner, 1912.
Merrilie Dawes. New York, Scribner, 1913.
Nan of Music Mountain. New York, Scribner, and London, Hodder and Stoughton, 1916.
Laramie Holds the Range. New York, Scribner, and London, Hodder and Stoughton, 1921.
The Marriage Verdict. New York, Scribner, and London, Hodder and Stoughton, 1923.
Selwood of Sleepy Cat. New York, Scribner, and London, Hodder and Stoughton, 1925.
Flambeau Jim. New York, Scribner, 1927; London, Hodder and Stoughton, 1928.
Spanish Lover. New York, Scribner, 1930; London, Hodder and Stoughton, 1931.
Hell's Desert. New York, Doubleday, 1933; London, Hodder and Stoughton, 1934.
Gunlock Ranch. New York, Doubleday, and London, Hodder and Stoughton, 1935.
Carmen of the Rancho. New York, Doubleday, 1937; London, Hodder and Stoughton, 1938.

Short Stories

The Nerve of Foley and Other Railroad Stories. New York, Harper, 1900.
Held for Others, Being Stories of Railroad Life. New York, McClure, 1901.

Uncollected Short Story

"The Yellow Mail," in *The Railroaders* edited by Bill Pronzini and Martin H. Greenberg. New York, Fawcett, 1986.

OTHER PUBLICATIONS

Plays

Screenplays (serials): *The Girl and the Game*, 1915; *Whispering Smith Rides*, 1925.

Other

The Strategy of Great Railroads. New York, Scribner, 1904.
Divorce. New York, America Press, n.d.

* * *

Frank H. Spearman's Westerns are generally run-of-the-mill, hackneyed shoot-em-ups with very little to distinguish them from others of the genre. Spearman did have a feel for life in the open, was a student of the influence of the railroad on life in the

West, and was expert (for his time) in the ecology of the plains and American desert. But his western novels and stories, some 20 volumes of them, are generally plebeian. The one possible exception is his most successful novel, *Whispering Smith.* This novel has all the faults of his other works, but in the title character Spearman did create what has come to be the archetype of a certain kind of western hero. Whispering Smith is so quiet and soft-spoken that he earns the sibilant soubriquet of the novel's title. He is also a dead shot with his two revolvers and as quick on the draw as he is slow to anger and soft in speech. The character twanged a responsive chord in American readers, for the novel was often reprinted and became one of the most famous American Westerns of the 1920's—all this success in spite of the novel's rather obvious lack of any literary merit. Indeed, Spearman became identified with the one-character archetype and the movie version of it to such an extent that it dominated his later career as a scriptwriter for the movies. He rewrote the novel twice, once as a movie script in 1915 and again in 1926. He also wrote a sequel serial, *Whispering Smith Rides* in 1925 to cash in on the character's popularity. Alas, his readers may say Whispering Smith rides, he whispers, he shoots, but he does not, like Frodo, live.

—Herbert F. Smith

SPELLMAN, Roger G. *See* **COX, William R.**

SPURR, Clinton. *See* **ROWLAND, Donald S.**

STAFFORD, Jean. American. Born in Covina, California, 1 July 1915. Educated at the University of Colorado, Boulder, B.A. 1936, M.A. 1936; University of Heidelberg, 1936–37. Married 1) the poet Robert Lowell in 1940 (divorced 1948); 2) Oliver Jensen in 1950 (divorced 1953); 3) the writer A.J. Liebling in 1959 (died 1963). Instructor, Stephens College, Columbia, Missouri, 1937–38; secretary, *Southern Review*, Baton Rouge, Louisiana, 1940–41; Lecturer, Queens College, Flushing, New York, Spring 1945; Fellow, Center for Advanced Studies, Wesleyan University, Middletown, Connecticut, 1964–65; Adjunct Professor, Columbia University, New York, 1967–69. Recipient: American Academy grant, 1945; Guggenheim fellowship, 1945, 1948; National Press Club award, 1948; O. Henry award, 1955; Ingram-Merrill grant, 1969; Chapelbrook grant, 1969; Pulitzer prize, 1970. Member, American Academy, 1970. *Died 26 March 1979.*

Western Publications

Novel

The Mountain Lion. New York, Harcourt Brace, 1947; London, Faber, 1948.

Other Publications

Novels

Boston Adventure. New York, Harcourt Brace, 1944; London, Faber, 1946.
The Catherine Wheel. New York, Harcourt Brace, and London, Eyre and Spottiswoode, 1952.

Short Stories

Children Are Bored on Sunday. New York, Harcourt Brace, 1953; London, Gollancz, 1954.
New Short Novels, with others, edited by Mary Louise Aswell. New York, Ballantine, 1954; London, Gollancz, 1959.
Stories, with others. New York, Farrar Straus, 1956; as *A Book of Stories*, London, Gollancz, 1957.
Bad Characters. New York, Farrar Straus, 1964; London, Chatto and Windus, 1965.
Selected Stories. London, New English Library, 1966.
The Collected Stories of Jean Stafford. New York, Farrar Straus, 1969; London, Chatto and Windus, 1970.

Other

Elephi: The Cat with the High I.Q. (for children). New York, Farrar Straus, 1962.
The Lion and the Carpenter and Other Tales from the Arabian Nights Retold (for children). New York, Macmillan, and London, Macmillan, 1962.
A Mother in History (on Marguerite C. Oswald). New York, Farrar Straus, and London, Chatto and Windus, 1966.

*

Bibliography: *Jean Stafford: A Comprehensive Bibliography* by Wanda Avila, New York, Garland, 1983.

Manuscript Collection: University of Colorado, Boulder.

Critical Study: *Jean Stafford: A Biography* by David Roberts, London, Chatto and Windus, 1988.

* * *

In western fiction, violence is a requisite event. Authors often center a Western's plot around the showdown, the Indian raid, the cavalry, or they can select a marshal, a sheriff, or an outlaw as the main character. Jean Stafford's novel *The Mountain Lion* is refreshing as western fiction because it is one of the first in which the chaos and mystery of human existence are revealed not through the outlaws and gun-fights but through the perceptions and maturation of two children.

The novel juxtaposes the ease and artificiality of middle-class California with the rough, natural order of Colorado. Ralph at age 10 and his sister Molly at age eight are at the novel's opening bright, precocious, perceptive children. They quickly realise the artificiality of their mother's values in contrast with those of their grandfather, a "cowboy" from Colorado come to visit. When their mother finds it more convenient that they spend summers, then a year in Colorado, Ralph and Molly are transplanted into a world close to nature. Ralph thrives in this world, but Molly withdraws from it, preferring to retreat to a secret clearing to write arch, sarcastic stories destined, she fantasises, for greatness.

Stafford concentrates on the movement of the two children from innocence to maturity and parallels this movement with their knowledge of good and evil. She pursues this edenic motif by focusing on the psychology of children and on the necessity in maturation of coming to terms with the cycles of nature. Stafford shows the child's perceptions of nature and of the actions of adults as two aspects of the innocence of childhood. Drawing on folkloric elements, Stafford shows how children explain the world to themselves and how they learn to come to terms with the large crises of life. Ralph is initiated into adulthood by his father-priest figure, his uncle, who teaches him about nature and violence. Ralph witnesses the birth of a calf, for example, and finds it fascinating. Molly, on the other hand, tragically rejects these inevitable aspects of life. What she cannot ignore (she believes as late as age 12 that she can marry a dog or her brother), she rejects or finds disgusting. These differences in the children account for their reactions to their shared discovery of evil in the scene on the train when Ralph, flooded with adolescent fantasies, asks Molly to tell him all the dirty words she knows. This "evil" outrages Molly, but shows that Ralph has learned to accept these less-than-holy impulses as parts of himself.

In the stunning ending of the novel, Ralph and his uncle confront the female mountain lion who represents nature, sexuality, and maternity. As a prospective man, Ralph wants to kill her with "one clean shot," but the shot that kills her is his uncle's. Instead, Ralph has accidentally killed Molly. This tragic and enigmatic conclusion reveals the inadequacy of Ralph's male values, yet the scene also shows that nature favors the survival of the fittest; Ralph is fit, Molly is not. Thus the novel ends as a Western, the showdown between the boy who would be man, and nature which is female. Good and evil are not separated into marshal and outlaw; good and evil reside in the same person, in one gangling boy. Nature is not kind or unkind; life is not predictable or fair. These are the lessons children must learn, and according to Stafford, these are the lessons of the American West.

—Kathryn Lee Seidel

STAIRS, Gordon. *See* **AUSTIN, Mary.**

STANDISH, Buck. *See* **PAINE, Lauran.**

STANLEY, Chuck. *See* **STRONG, Charles S.**

STARK, Joshua. *See* **OLSEN, T.V.**

STARR, Henry. *See* **BINGLEY, David Ernest.**

STEAD, Robert J(ames) C(ampbell). Canadian. Born in Middleville, Ontario, 4 September 1880. Educated at schools in Cartwright, Manitoba; Winnipeg Business College, Manitoba. Married Nettie May Wallace in 1901; three sons. Founding publisher, Cartwright *Review*, circa 1898; publisher, Crystal City *Courier*, Manitoba, 1908; staff member, Calgary *Albertan*, 1912; assistant director of publicity for the colonization department, 1913–16, and publicity director, 1916–19, Canadian Pacific Railway, Calgary; publicity director, Department of Immigration and Colonization, Ottawa, 1919–36; superintendent of information and resources publicity, Department of Mines and Resources, Ottawa, 1936–46. Member of the Editorial Board, *Canadian Geographical Journal*, Ottawa, from 1942. President, Canadian Authors Association, 1923; Fellow, Royal Canadian Geographical Society, 1929. *Died 25 June 1959.*

Western Publications

Novels

The Bail Jumper. Toronto, Briggs, and London, Unwin, 1914.
The Homesteaders: A Novel of the Canadian West. Toronto, Musson, and London, Unwin, 1916.
The Cow Puncher. New York, Harper, 1918; London, Hodder and Stoughton, 1919.
Dennison Grant. Toronto, Musson, 1920; London, Hodder and Stoughton, 1921; revised edition, as *Zen of the Y.D.*, Hodder and Stoughton, 1925.
Neighbours. London, Hodder and Stoughton, 1922.
The Smoking Flax. New York, Doran, and London, Hodder and Stoughton, 1924.
Grain. New York, Doran, 1926.
The Copper Disc. New York, Doubleday, 1931.

Other Publications

Verse

The Empire Builders and Other Poems. Toronto, Briggs, 1908.
Prairie Born and Other Poems. Toronto, Briggs, 1911.
Songs of the Prairie. Toronto, Briggs, 1911; New York, Platt and Peck, and London, Gay and Hancock, 1912.
Kitchener and Other Poems. Toronto, Musson, 1917.
Why Don't They Cheer. London, Unwin, 1918.

Other

Words (essays). Winnipeg, Public Press, 1945.

Editor, *The Maple's Praise of Franklin Delano Roosevelt 1882–1945.* Ottawa, Tower, 1945.

* * *

Previously slighted by literary historians, Robert J.C. Stead is now regarded as an important figure in the evolution of western Canadian fiction from sentimental romance to realism. From the social historian's viewpoint, his work documents a time and place, the pre-World War I years and the 1920's in the prairie provinces, as obscure as any in Canada's past. Like those of Frederick Philip Grove, Martha Ostenso, and Sinclair Ross, Stead's subject is the settlement of the Canadian prairies, though limitations of technique and moral vision in Stead preclude the mind-stretching complexity and universal resonances found in the more problematic world of these successors.

The Bail Jumper, the first of Stead's western novels, concerns a clerk falsely accused of robbing his employer, the father of the girl he hopes to marry. Vitiated by the clichés of sentimental romance, the novel nevertheless holds interest today as the beginning of Stead's multi-volume chronicle of the settlement of Plainville, Manitoba. Another Plainville novel, *The Homesteaders*, is an initially idyllic account of the efforts of a young pioneering couple to develop a prosperous farm. Stead injects a realistic note into this Edenic myth, however, as the hero's success merely engenders a self-aggrandizing greed for more land, transforming a formerly gentle, sensitive nature into a brutalized workhorse and self-righteous prairie patriarch. The moral, increasingly insistent in Stead, is twofold: Mammon is a false god; and eastern culture must be blended with western vigor if there is to be a prairie civilization worthy of the name.

Despite its well-worn theme of rural innocence corrupted by urban values, *The Cow Puncher* makes imaginative use of landscape to symbolize the freedom and opportunity of life on the land, and reveals a new ambivalence toward eastern Canada as a necessary civilizing influence, but one whose adherence to traditions and institutions of the past inhibits the flowering of the western garden. Further signs of a maturing social and political vision are evident in *Dennison Grant*. Utopian theories of economic and social reform threaten to stop the novel in its tracks, but the new note of intellectuality, especially the foreshadowing of regional divisiveness between eastern and western Canada, frees it from the codified formulas of romance. Similarly, *Neighbours* sees the pioneers as rightful inheritors of the Promised Land, but acknowledges flaws in the myth. Describing homesteading in Saskatchewan with documentary thoroughness, Stead uses as *leitmotif* the settlers' yearning for a fulfillment of mind and spirit which the prairie cannot satisfy.

The Smoking Flax presages Stead's best novel, *Grain*, in the increasing ambivalence of its attitude toward the prairie experience and toward the second, more prosperous generation of settlers in Manitoba. *Grain* deals with the modern tension between traditional love of the land and the new enthrallment by machinery and technology. It implies that the future belongs not to those who live and work in harmony with the land, but to its exploiters. The machine in the western garden alienates man from the land, his fellows, and himself, guaranteeing financial profit but spiritual loss.

—John H. Ferres

STEELE, Harwood E(lmes Robert). Also writes as Howard Steele. Canadian. Born in Fort Macleod, Alberta, 5 May 1897. Educated privately and at Highfield School, Hamilton, Ontario. Served in the Canadian and British armies, 1914–18: Captain; mentioned in despatches; Military Cross; in the British Army, 1939–45: Lieutenant Colonel; mentioned in despatches. Assistant press representative, Canadian Pacific Railway, 1923–25; historian, Canadian Government Arctic Expedition, 1925; journalist and lecturer: military adviser, Canadian Broadcasting Commission, 1937–39. Fellow, Royal Geographical Society.

WESTERN PUBLICATIONS

Novels

Spirit-of-Iron (*Manitou-Pewabic*). New York, Doubleday, 1923; London, Hodder and Stoughton, 1924.
I Shall Arise. London, Hodder and Stoughton, 1926.
The Ninth Circle. London, Hodder and Stoughton, 1927; New York, Doubleday, 1928.
Ghosts Returning. Toronto, Ryerson Press, 1950.

Short Stories

To Effect an Arrest: Adventures of the Royal Canadian Mounted Police. Toronto Ryerson Press, and London, Jarrolds, 1947.

OTHER PUBLICATIONS

Verse

Cleared for Action (as Howard Steele). London, Unwin, 1914.
Lays of the Long, Long Trail. Privately printed, 1973.

Other

The Canadians in France 1915–1918. Toronto, Copp Clark, New York, Dutton, and London, Unwin, 1920.
The Long Ride: A Short History of the 17th Duke of York's Royal Canadian Hussars. Montreal, Gazette Printing, 1934.
Policing the Arctic: The Story of the Conquest of the Arctic by the Royal Canadian, Formerly North-West, Mounted Police. London, Jarrolds, 1936.
India: Friend or Foe? Toronto, Ryerson Press, 1947.
The Marching Call (for children). Toronto, Nelson, 1955.
The Red Serge: Stories of the Royal Canadian Mounted Police. Toronto, Ryerson Press, 1961.
The R.C.M.P.: Royal Canadian Mounted Police. London, Cape, 1969.

* * *

Harwood E. Steele has written history and poetry as well as novels, but in all media his favourite subject is the Royal Canadian Mounted Police. His aim is always educational accuracy. As he says in the preface to *Policing the Arctic*, he strictly avoids the "heroics of the 'two-gun, get your man' variety which, though well meant, often tend to make the Force ridiculous."

His main novels on the subject are *Spirit-of-Iron* and *The Ninth Circle*. He says, "*Spirit-of-Iron* is an attempt to present fact in the form of romantic fiction." He tells us that all the characters are types—for example, Hector Adair, the hero, whose career we follow from boyhood to enrolment in the new North-West Mounted Police in 1873 to high command, is intended to represent the ideal Mounted Police officer in particular and the ideal British officer generally. *The Ninth Circle* carries the typology a step further, making open and repeated connections with romance. It tells of Fate Westward, an English gentleman who, after a disappointment in love, assumes this alias and joins the RCMP. He is now in the Arctic as sergeant in charge of a detachment of natives. His face is described: "It seemed like a countenance of another age and clime. It was easy to picture it framed in a knightly helmet—the hood of his Arctic kooletal was distinctly like a helmet of that sort—and, at sight of it, scarred, weather-beaten, lonely, full of purpose, it was not difficult to picture its tall, broad-shouldered owner, from spur to plume a star of tournament, gracing the days of chivalry." When Fate is sent on a patrol to find a lost exploration team, his trials are compared to those of Christ, Christian, and Lancelot. It turns out that the one surviving member of the expedition is Fate's old enemy from England, who reveals that Fate's former fiancée has been searching for him for the last 12 years. In the end, Fate resumes his real name and marries his English love.

The conjunction of accurate details about the work of the RCMP with conventional and unconvincing romances is more interesting in principle than in practice, for Steele has a stiff, old-fashioned style and his fiction is not very exciting reading. Much more effective are his short stories, gathered together in *To Effect an Arrest*, which have less room for long-winded romance and, consequently, are more vigorous, accomplished vignettes about police working with animals, pursuing criminals, or struggling with Indians. Steele seems to try to do for the RCMP what Kipling did for the military in India, and, in the stories at least, he succeeds reasonably well.

—Christine Bold

STEELE, William O(wen). American. Born in Franklin, Tennessee, 22 December 1917. Educated at Cumberland University, Lebanon, Tennessee, 1936–40, B.A. 1940; University of Chattanooga, Tennessee, 1951. Served in the United States Army Air Corps during World War II. Married Mary Quintard Govan (i.e., the writer Mary Q. Steele) in 1943; two daughters and one son. Recipient: Women's International League for Peace and Freedom Jane Addams award, 1958. *Died 25 June 1979.*

Western Publications

Fiction (for children)

The Golden Root. New York, Aladdin, 1951.
The Buffalo Knife. New York, Harcourt Brace, 1952.
Over-Mountain Boy. New York, Aladdin, 1952.
Wilderness Journey. New York, Harcourt Brace, 1953.
Winter Danger. New York, Harcourt Brace, 1954; London, Macmillan, 1963.
Tomahawks and Trouble. New York, Harcourt Brace, 1955.
We Were There on the Oregon Trail. New York, Grosset and Dunlap, 1955.
David Crockett's Earthquake. New York, Harcourt Brace, 1956.
We Were There with the Pony Express. New York, Grosset and Dunlap, 1956.
The Lone Hunt. New York, Harcourt Brace, 1956; London, Macmillan, 1957.
Flaming Arrows. New York, Harcourt Brace, 1957; London, Macmillan, 1958.
Daniel Boone's Echo. New York, Harcourt Brace, 1957.
The Perilous Road. New York, Harcourt Brace, 1958; London, Macmillan, 1960.
Andy Jackson's Water Well. New York, Harcourt Brace, 1959.
The Far Frontier. New York, Harcourt Brace, 1959; London, Macmillan, 1960.
The Spooky Thing. New York, Harcourt Brace, 1960.
The Year of the Bloody Sevens. New York, Harcourt Brace, 1963.
Wayah of the Real People. Williamburg, Virginia, Colonial Williamburg Inc., 1964.
The No-Name Man of the Mountain. New York, Harcourt Brace, 1964.
Trail Through Danger. New York, Harcourt Brace, 1965.
Tomahawk Border. Williamburg, Virginia, Colonial Williamsburg Inc., 1966.
Hound Dog Zip to the Rescue. Champaign, Illinois, Garrard, 1970.
Triple Trouble for Hound Dog Zip. Champaign, Illinois, Garrard, 1972.
John's Secret Treasure. New York, Macmillan, 1975.
The Eye in the Forest, with Mary Q. Steele. New York, Dutton, 1975.
The Man with the Silver Eyes. New York, Harcourt Brace, 1976.
The War Party. New York, Harcourt Brace, 1978.
The Magic Amulet. New York, Harcourt Brace, 1979.

Other Publications

Other (for children)

John Sevier, Pioneer Boy. Indianapolis, Bobbs Merrill, 1953.
The Story of Daniel Boone. New York, Grosset and Dunlap, 1953; London, Muller, 1957.
Francis Marion: Young Swamp Fox. Indianapolis, Bobbs Merrill, 1954.
The Story of Leif Ericson. New York, Grosset and Dunlap, 1954; London, Sampson Low, 1960.
De Soto: Child of the Sun. New York, Aladdin, 1956.
Westward Adventure: The True Stories of Six Pioneers. New York, Harcourt Brace, 1962.
The Old Wilderness Road: An American Journey. New York, Harcourt Brace, 1968.
The Wilderness Tattoo: A Narrative of Juan Ortiz. New York, Harcourt Brace, 1972.
Henry Woodward of Carolina: Surgeon, Trader, Indian Chief. Columbia, South Carolina, Sandlapper Press, 1972.
The Cherokee Crown of Tannassy. Winston-Salem, North Carolina, Blair, 1977.
Talking Bones: Secrets of Indian Burial Mounds. New York, Harper, 1978.

*

Manuscript Collections: Kerlan Collection, University of Minnesota, Minneapolis; Special Collections, John Brister Library, Memphis State University, Tennessee.

* * *

Although William O. Steele's work was intended mainly for younger readers, the subjects on which he wrote have since been written for the adult market. Steele enjoyed writing for the 8-to-12 year-old age group with stories of pioneers of the old Southwest, usually in pre-Revolutionary times, and Indians of the Southeast. Not surprisingly, his heroes tended to be young men, with whom a child can identify, who fight adversity in whatever shape or form.

There's usually more to Steele's stories than the thrill of the frontier alone. There are deep insights into a character and his thinking, the contest between natural elements and human courage, and these are fully realized.

His pioneer stories have that backwoods flavor and excitement. *The Story of Daniel Boone* is a study of the famous frontiersman from boyhood through his career up until 1799.

Francis Marion: *Young Swamp Fox* gives a similar fictional portrait of another American hero, complete with alligators, rattlesnakes, and dark, mysterious swamps. *David Crockett's Earthquake* relates the adventures of Crockett in west Tennessee; it is a well-researched book, and Owen's tongue-in-cheek style adds well to the vigorous prose. With *Daniel Boone's Echo*, Boone is saddled with simple-minded travelling companion, Aaron Adamsale. The pair journey to Kentucky, and along the way Adamsale learns to conquer his fears. The story is absurd in places, with an excess of local dialect making for a heavy read, but nevertheless, it holds the interest of the reader.

Steele's descriptions of early America make it clear to his readers that everything was not simple in comparison to today's standards, and that the past had complexities of its own. The main thrust of his writing owes much to his unabashed love affair with frontier life. He is more than competent in his research, and his books are deceptively casual in their ability to relate life through childrens' eyes.

When he broke away from writing on established characters, Steele turned to vivid and intense stories such as *Flaming Arrows*. This book is a departure from earlier works, and is written in a much more consciously adult manner, dealing with cruelty and killings. The quality of Steele's writing is unaffected, and his delightful talent for crisp dialogue remains to the fore. He confines himself to exploring one particular moment in Chad Rabun's life, when a settlement fort is besieged by Chickamauga Indians, and describes the boy's growth to self-knowledge.

This theme of a boy's development from inexperience to self-knowledge is a device oft-repeated, but nowhere is it better achieved than in *The Year of the Bloody Sevens*. Set at a time of Indian massacres, the novel's hero, young Kel Bond, is among a band of travellers when they are ambushed, the men killed and Kel left alone to face capture by the Indians. The story is given strength through Steele's characterizations, fully exploring each person's weaknesses and strengths. Bond's own development comes through the realization that he may have been partly to blame for the death of his friends.

Children apart, Steele produced strong narrative-based works for an older readership. *The Old Wilderness Road* is an account of four men, Thomas Walker, Elisha Wallen, Daniel Boone, and John Filson, who explored the then western Virginian mountains and forests. It is a solidly written book of frontier history, replete with sections of "how-to-do-it-yourself" subjects—for example, how to preserve hides or make moccasins. Although these seem out of place at times, they help to lend authenticity to an already compelling story line.

His 1972 book, *The Wilderness Tattoo*, concerns 17-year-old Juan Ortiz and his experience with Spain's expedition to Florida in 1527. It echoes *The Year of The Bloody Sevens'* theme of the captured boy and his treatment at the hands of native Indians. The author's style is full of verve for his subject, but he limits himself to the most convincing of accounts.

Steele's descriptions of dangers and hardships are the mainstay of his historical fiction. The fact that he chose to write for the juvenile market in no way undermines his strength as a fine storyteller. Although his writing does stress the more flimsy make-up of his plots, where character treatment tends to be rather cursory, there is always plenty of action and excitement, and well-depicted scenes of historically accurate frontier life. His books are clearly and simply written, bringing color, warmth, and humour to a sparsely visited area in the western genre.

—John L. Wolfe

STEELMAN, Robert J(ames). American. Born in Columbus, Ohio, 7 March 1914. Educated at Ohio State University, Columbus, B.S. 1938. Served as a civilian electronics engineer in the United States Army Signal Corps, 1939–46, and in the United States Navy, 1946–69. Married Janet Eyler in 1941; one daughter and one son. Agent: Robert P. Mills Ltd., 333 Fifth Avenue, New York, New York 10016. Address: 875 Amiford Drive, San Diego, California 92107, U.S.A.

WESTERN PUBLICATIONS

Novels

Stages South. New York, Ace, 1956.
Apache Wells. New York, Ballantine, 1959.
Winter of the Sioux. New York, Ballantine, 1959.
Call of the Arctic. New York, Coward McCann, 1960.
Ambush at Three Rivers. New York, Ballantine, 1964.
Cheyenne Vengeance. New York, Doubleday, 1974.
Dakota Territory. New York, Ballantine, 1974.
The Fox Dancer. New York, Doubleday, 1975.
Sun Boy. New York, Doubleday, 1975.
Portrait of a Sioux. New York, Doubleday, 1976.
Lord Apache. New York, Doubleday, 1977.
The Galvanized Reb. New York, Doubleday, 1977.
White Medicine Man. New York, Ace, 1979.
Surgeon to the Sioux. New York, Doubleday, 1979.
The Great Yellowstone Steamboat Race. New York, Doubleday, 1980.
The Man They Hanged. New York, Doubleday, 1980.
The Prairie Baroness. New York, Doubleday, 1981.
The Santee Massacre. New York, Dell, 1982.
The Border Raiders. New York, Dorchester, 1982; Bath, Chivers, 1988.
Royal Charlie. New York, Ace, 1983.
The Holdout. New York, Walker, 1984; London, Hale, 1986.
Blood and Dust. New York, New American Library, 1987.

*

Manuscript Collection: University of Wyoming, Laramie.

Robert J. Steelman comments:

Editors have frequently classified my books as "falling between two stools"; i.e., not the classical western novel, nor yet the pure historical novel. While this has often made editorial acceptance difficult, I continue to write in my own way; that is to say, I write books, generally speaking, with a basis in an historical incident, and implement it with extensive research in an effort to make setting, character, and action true to the times. In addition, it is fair to say that I have been greatly influenced by the American authors Kenneth Roberts and Ernest Haycox, who did the same thing I attempt, but much better.

* * *

Robert J. Steelman's concern and sympathy for the American Indians are prominent in all his works. The arts, frequently in variety, and cleanliness, often raised to the level of symbol and ritual, are other constants.

Winter of the Sioux, a book tricked out with notes for a posthumous auction of paintings by the central character serving as chapter-head quotations, and *Cheyenne Vengeance* and *White Medicine Man*, both with bibliographies and the latter boasting a long historical anecdote (which quite gives away one of what should have been the book's better surprises) as prologue, are his most consciously belle lettristic works. *Apache Wells*, *Dakota Territory*, and *Cheyenne Vengeance*, the latter narrated in first person, are all sound novels of initiation, and the first two also cleverly combine the theme of the tenderfoot's discovery of the west.

The heroine of *Apache Wells* supports herself as an army laundress; that of *Winter of the Sioux* founds her business fortune with the opening of what is likely the first laundry in Deadwood. *Dakota Territory* opens in a Chinese laundry in the same town, and the hero is saved and sheltered by the laundryman and his fellow celestials when the community turns solidly against him. Sexual awakenings and seductions, forced or otherwise, in almost all the books center around bathing scenes.

Prominent characters in all the books exhibit taste and/or talent in various arts. Literature is prominently featured in *White Medicine Man* and *Cheyenne Vengeance*. The hero of *Dakota Territory* and his brother are theater entrepreneurs. In *Apache Wells* both the heroine and one prominent villain are accomplished musicians. In most of these books other characters exhibit aptitudes for other arts as well.

Steelman also shows occasional flashes of genius in construction of dramatic effects. This is particularly noticeable when heroes or their kind are awing credulous savages with "white man's magic." In one such case a deadly snakebite is invited; in another the hero actually sets himself on fire. On the negative side, there is considerably more overlap and cognate words between Indian languages, a subject the writer seems steadily to increase his emphasis upon, than is entirely credible. Furthermore the savages grow constantly more noble from book to book, reaching hardly believable heights of excellence in some of the later titles. Steelman's most recent works, however, display an altogether different trend, with humour well to the fore, and with essentially serious themes receiving an almost comic treatment. *The Holdout* exemplifies this latest development, with Steelman choosing the most unlikely of heroes, the draft-dodging gambler and former dentist Charlie Callaway, as the central voice of his novel. The reader follows Charlie in a series of lively and amusing adventures which include a narrow escape from a firing squad, the accidental "capture" of a Confederate raider, encounters with Sioux Indians and Chinese gangsters, and a final climactic card-game where in the guise of a Tennessee "colonel" he uses the holdout gadget of the title to win a fortune and save the mission of his pious girlfriend Lorna Bascomb. Charlie's innate dishonesty and his not-too-determined efforts at reform allow Steelman to exploit his talent for humour, including a number of surreal dream-sequences and some highly comic conversations with a disapproving God, referred to by Charlie as The Old Gentleman. Charlie Callaway would appear to be a character with a future, and Steelman, in novels like *The Holdout* and *Royal Charlie*, shows the true variety of his skills as a writer.

—R. Jeff Banks

STEGNER, Wallace (Earle). American. Born in Lake Mills, Iowa, 18 February 1909. Educated at the University of Utah, Salt Lake City, A.B. 1930; University of Iowa, Iowa City, A.M. 1932, Ph.D. 1935; University of California, Berkeley, 1932–33. Married Mary Stuart Page in 1934; one child. Instructor, Augustana College, Rock Island, Illinois, 1933–34, University of Utah, 1934–37, and University of Wisconsin, Madison, 1937–39; Faculty Instructor, Harvard University, Cambridge, Massachusetts, 1939–45. Professor of English, 1945–69, and Jackson Eli Reynolds Professor of humanities, 1969–71, Stanford University, California; Bissell Professor of Canadian–U.S. relations, University of Toronto, 1975; Tanner Lecturer, University of Utah, Salt Lake City, 1980; Montgomery Fellow, Dartmouth College, Hanover, New Hampshire, 1980. Writer-in-residence, American Academy in Rome, 1960; Phi Beta Kappa Visiting Scholar, 1960; West Coast editor, Houghton Mifflin Company publishers, Boston, 1945–53; Assistant to the United States Secretary of the Interior, Washington, D.C., 1961; member, 1962–66, and chair, 1965–66, National Parks Advisory Board, Washington, D.C.; editor-in-chief, *American West* magazine, Palo Alto, California, 1966–68. Recipient: Little Brown prize, 1937; O. Henry award, 1942, 1950, 1954; Houghton Mifflin Life-in-America award, 1945; Anisfield-Wolf award, 1945; Guggenheim fellowship, 1950–57, 1959; Rockefeller fellowship, 1950–51; Wenner-Gren grant, 1953; Center for Advanced Studies in the Behavioral Sciences fellowship, 1955; Blackhawk award, 1963; Commonwealth Club Gold Medal, 1968; National Endowment for the Humanities senior fellowship, 1972; Pulitzer prize, 1972; Western Literature Association award, 1974; National Book award, 1977; Los Angeles *Times* Kirsch award, 1980. D.Litt.: University of Utah, 1968; Utah State University, Logan, 1972; D.F.A.: University of California, 1969; D.L.: University of Saskatchewan, Regina, 1973; D.H.L.: University of Santa Clara, California, 1979; D.H.: University of Wisconsin, Madison, 1986; D.H.L.: University of Montana, Missoula, 1987. Member, American Academy, and American Academy of Arts and Sciences. Agent: Brandt and Brandt, 1501 Broadway, New York, New York 10036. Address: 13456 South Fork Lane, Los Altos Hills, California 94022, U.S.A.

WESTERN PUBLICATIONS

Novels

Remembering Laughter. Boston, Little Brown, and London, Heinemann, 1937.
The Potter's House. Muscatine, Iowa, Prairie Press, 1938.
On a Darkling Plain. New York, Harcourt Brace, 1940.
The Big Rock Candy Mountain. New York, Duell, 1943; London, Hammond, 1950.
The Preacher and the Slave. Boston, Houghton Mifflin, 1950; London, Hammond, 1951; as *Joe Hill: A Biographical Novel*, New York, Doubleday, 1969.
A Shooting Star. New York, Viking Press, and London, Heinemann, 1961.
All the Little Live Things. New York, Viking Press, 1967; London, Heinemann, 1968.
Angle of Repose. New York, Doubleday, and London, Heinemann, 1971.
The Spectator Bird. New York, Doubleday, 1976; London, Prior, 1977.
Recapitulation. New York, Doubleday, 1979.

Short Stories

The Women on the Wall. Boston, Houghton Mifflin, 1950; London, Hammond, 1952.
The City of the Living. Boston, Houghton Mifflin, 1956; London, Hammond, 1957.

New Short Novels 2, with others. New York, Ballantine, 1956.
Collected Stories. New York, Random House, 1990.

OTHER PUBLICATIONS

Novels

Fire and Ice. New York, Duell, 1941.
Second Growth. Boston, Houghton Mifflin, 1947; London, Hammond, 1948.
Crossing to Safety. New York, Random House, 1987.

Other

Mormon Country. New York, Duell, 1942.
One Nation, with editors of *Look*. Boston, Houghton Mifflin, 1945.
Look at America: The Central Northwest, with others. Boston, Houghton Mifflin, 1947.
The Writer in America (lectures). Tokyo, Hokuseido Press, 1952; South Pasadena, California, Perkins and Hutchins, 1953.
Beyond the Hundredth Meridian: John Wesley Powell and the Second Opening of the West. Boston, Houghton Mifflin, 1954.
Wolf Willow: A History, A Story, and A Memory of the Last Plains Frontier. New York, Viking Press, 1962; London, Heinemann, 1963.
Teaching the Short Story. Davis, University of California Press, 1965.
The Gathering of Zion: The Story of the Mormon Trail. New York, McGraw Hill, 1964; London, Eyre and Spottiswoode, 1966.
The Sound of Mountain Water: The Changing American West. New York, Doubleday, 1969.
Discovery: The Search for Arabian Oil. Beirut, Middle East Export Press, 1971.
Variations on a Theme of Discontent. Logan, Utah State University Press, 1972.
The Uneasy Chair: A Biography of Bernard DeVoto. New York, Doubleday, 1974.
Ansel Adams: Images 1923–1974. Greenwich, Connecticut, New York Graphic Society, 1974.
Robert Frost and Bernard DeVoto. Stanford, California, Association of Stanford University Librarians, 1974.
American Places, with Page Stegner, photographs by Eliot Porter. New York, Dutton, and London, Aurum Press, 1981.
One Way to Spell Man (essays). New York, Doubleday, 1982.
Conversations with Wallace Stegner on Western History and Literature, with Richard W. Etulain. Salt Lake City, University of Utah Press, 1983.
The American West as Living Space. Ann Arbor, University of Michigan Press, 1987.
On the Teaching of Creative Writing: Responses to a Series of Questions, edited by Edward Connory Lathen. Hanover, New Hampshire, University Press of New England, 1989.

Editor, with others, *An Exposition Workshop*. Boston, Little Brown, 1939.
Editor, with others, *Readings for Citizens at War*. New York, Harper, 1941.
Editor, with Richard Scowcroft, *Stanford Short Stories 1946*. Stanford, California, Stanford University Press, 1947 (and later volumes).
Editor, with Richard Scowcroft and Boris Llyin, *The Writer's Art: A Collection of Short Stories*. Boston, Heath, 1950.
Editor, *This Is Dinosaur: Echo Park Country and Its Magic Rivers*. New York, Knopf, 1955.
Editor, *The Exploration of the Colorado River of the West*, by J.W. Powell. Chicago, University of Chicago Press, 1957.
Editor, with Mary Stegner, *Great American Short Stories*. New York, Dell, 1957.
Editor, *Selected American Prose: The Realistic Movement*. New York, Rinehart, 1958; London, Owen, 1963.
Editor, *The Adventures of Huckleberry Finn*, by Mark Twain. New York, Dell, 1960.
Editor, *The Outcasts of Poker Flat*, by Bret Harte. New York, New American Library, 1961.
Editor, *Report on the Lands of the Arid Region of the United States*, by J.W. Powell. Cambridge, Massachusetts, Harvard University Press, and London, Oxford University Press, 1962.
Editor, with others, *Modern Composition*. New York, Holt Rinehart, 4 vols., 1964.
Editor, *The American Novel: From Cooper to Faulkner*. New York, Basic, 1965.
Editor, *The Big Sky*, by A.B. Guthrie, Jr. Boston, Houghton Mifflin, 1965.
Editor, with others, *Twenty Years of Stanford Short Stories*. Stanford, California, Stanford University Press, 1966.
Editor, *Twice-Told Tales*, by Nathaniel Hawthorne. New York, Heritage Press, 1967.
Editor, *The Letters of Bernard DeVoto*. New York, Doubleday, 1975.

*

Bibliography: *Wallace Stegner, A Descriptive Bibliography* by Nancy Colberg, Lewiston, Idaho, Confluence Press, 1990.

Manuscript Collections: University of Iowa, Iowa City; Stanford University, California.

Critical Studies: *Wallace Stegner* by Merrill and Lorene Lewis, Boise, Idaho, Boise State College, 1972; *Wallace Stegner* by Forrest G. and Margaret G. Robinson, Boston, Twayne, 1977; *Critical Essays on Wallace Stegner* edited by Anthony Arthur, Boston, G.K. Hall, 1982.

Wallace Stegner comments:

I have never considered myself a self-consciously "western" writer. I don't do horse opera, and I am not much interested in the mythic cowboy West. But since I grew up in Saskatchewan, Montana, Utah, Nevada, California, and some other western states, and since I necessarily write about what I know, I have written a good many stories that can be called "western," and whenever I have turned to history or biography I have found myself grappling with a western subject. I suppose, too, that my western upbringing shows even in stories that are laid in Denmark, Egypt, or the Côte d'Azur. I think I am a western writer, but I do not write "Westerns."

* * *

Wallace Stegner is one of America's distinguished writers, and he has managed to climax a continuing national recognition by winning a Pulitzer prize and then a National Book award. Western by training if not quite by his Iowa birth, Stegner has always had a keen interest in his region, but he has never been provincial in his dedication. For a time he tested his Westernness by living and working in the East, and while he chooses to make the West his permanent address, he continues to maintain a summer residence in Greensboro, Vermont. The West was not his inevitable subject or setting, but much of his best work is indeed set there. His writing, like his life, mirrors his experience across the continent.

When his interest in his region was not personal, it was scholarly. Suggestive of his bent is his 1935 Ph.D. dissertation on Clarence E. Dutton, the geologist who was a part of the U.S. geographical and geological survey of the Rocky Mountain region in the 1870's and 1880's. Stegner's highly successful nonfiction book *Beyond the Hundredth Meridian*, a study of the career of geologist-writer John Wesley Powell, is no anomaly in the Stegner canon. Throughout his career, Stegner has given thoughtful attention in books and essays to the problems of the West, problems that he sees also in a broad American framework. His 1945 book *One Nation* was a study of prejudice operating in America. His *Mormon Country* is a collection of tales, legends, and sketches that reflect the dominant Mormon culture of Utah; *The Gathering of Zion* recounts the migration of the Mormons from Nauvoo, Illinois, to the Great Salt Lake Basin. *Wolf Willow* is not only one of the most important autobiographies to come out of the American West, but in it Stegner also discusses the history of the region where Montana and Saskatchewan meet, and where he lived for several years when a boy. With his son Page Stegner, he has written *American Places*, which celebrates the beauty of the landscapes of Eliot Porter's photographs and pleads for more careful protection of the environment.

Stegner's greatest fame comes, however, from his substantial body of fiction. He launched his career as a writer of fiction with *Remembering Laughter*, a book that won the Little Brown novelette contest of 1937. The work bears certain resemblances to *Ethan Frome*, Edith Wharton's famous short novel, but in place of Wharton's New England, Stegner sets his story in rural Iowa. Stegner's protagonist, Alec Stuart, is—like Frome—a man of imagination who loses his essential vitality because of his wife's stern code. That vitality is momentarily heightened and realized when the wife's sister moves to the farm. Eventually Alec is trapped on the Iowa farm between these women even as Frome was trapped in New England. *Remembering Laughter*, like *Ethan Frome*, conveys a strong sense of place and shows how a narrow environment may strangle happiness.

Stegner followed *Remembering Laughter* with three other novels dealing with frustration and isolation. Set in California, *The Potter's House* recounts the struggles of a deaf-mute artisan to support himself and his family; the novel is the least known of Stegner's fiction. *On a Darkling Plain* features a protagonist disillusioned by World War I who seeks escape from all darkling plains by retreating to a Saskatchewan homestead. *Fire and Ice* has as its protagonist a young midwestern college student who is dedicated to the program of the Young Communist League, but who deceives himself greatly about his motivations.

Stegner's characters become more interesting for their own sakes in *The Big Rock Candy Mountain*, his first major novel. It is built on the experience of his own life, but the center of its vitality is the character based on his father. Bo Mason is a seeker after the Big Rock Candy Mountain, and he pursues it zealously over many years and in many parts of the West. His quest is complicated because he marries and has a family; Stegner's novel is pointedly a family chronicle. Like novels in that genre, Stegner's book is lengthy, but because Bo Mason moves his family so frequently, it has a scenic scope not usually part of the genre.

Unlike *The Big Rock Candy Mountain*, a panoramic novel portraying the vastness of the West, *Second Growth*, is set in New England (Stegner asserted that it could just as easily have been set in Carmel or Toas). Like his earlier novels, it warned against a provincialism that can too easily destroy human potential.

He returned to a western setting for his next novel, also his first historical novel. *The Preacher and the Slave* recreates the history of Joe Hill, the enigmatic Industrial Workers of the World leader who was executed in Utah for murder, and of the minister who befriended him. As Stegner presents him, Hill fits easily into the company of Stegner's other unfulfilled heroes, in sharp contrast to the likes of John Wesley Powell, whom he celebrated in nonfiction.

Stegner broke his stride as a novelist after *The Preacher and the Slave*, and 10 years passed before *A Shooting Star* was published. When the novel appeared in 1961, readers found it a very different kind of Stegner novel. For the first time, he focused on a woman's experience and a California setting, mainly suburban Hillsborough outside San Francisco. Previously Stegner had preferred an action in a somewhat distant past with attention on the have-nots. *A Shooting Star* accents a post-World War II milieu and portrays some of the very rich.

Stegner recognized that there was a "soap opera problem" with the novel, and he found a better voice for and approach to the contemporary in his next California novel. The protagonist and narrator of *All the Little Live Things* is Joe Allston, a retired literary agent with a sardonic view of modern life, especially in contemporary California, where he and his wife now live. As Joe thinks about the meaning of his past in the East, and worries about possible mistakes he made with his son Curtis, who died a possible suicide at 37, there is much in the present to concern him in the lives of his neighbors. Two especially receive his attention: Comus-like Jim Peck, a dropout from Berkeley, and Marian Catlin. Marian affirms the beauty of the natural order—a beauty that Joe has difficulty recognizing, the more so since Marian is dying of cancer.

Joe's search for understanding becomes more personal in *The Spectator Bird*. This novel is also told in first person, but the emphasis is more on Joe as the spectator bird than on an outer action. The story is partly a search for roots, and in it past and present play against each other continuously. Much of the narrative is the journal of the trip to Denmark that Joe and his wife Ruth had taken after Curtis's death 20 years before. Joe now shares his journal of that trip with Ruth, who had not known of its existence. In a double sense, Joe's narration is a confessional. In Denmark (from whence his mother had immigrated) Joe had fallen in love with a countess; Ruth had not known that either, for Joe had chosen to remain loyal to her and return to America. Her husband admits that "in every choice there is a component, maybe a big component of pain." But he has his reward, too, and the novel celebrates a married love that is unmatched in any of Stegner's previous novels.

Between the two novels about Joe Allston came Stegner's Pulitzer prize winner, *Angle of Repose*. It is also a novel that combines past and present, the past being both 19th-century America (especially the West) and 20th-century California. Like *The Preacher and the Slave*, it has its basis in actual history. Its narrative line owes much to the careers of Mary Hallock Foote, writer and illustrator, and Arthur DeWint Foote, her engineer husband, but Stegner chose a more complex way of portraying their history than he had taken in telling the story of Joe Hill. He presents the Wards through the imaginative recreation of their past by their grandson, Lyman Ward, a prize-winning professor of history forced into early retirement because of a bone disease. Seeking to understand his own failed marriage, Lyman researches the lives of his grandparents and writes about the tensions caused by his grandfather's commitment to the West and his grandmother's preference for the East. Although the bulk of the narrative is concerned with his grandparents, Lyman constantly reveals the present and his and its problems. He, too, is a spectator bird.

Recapitulation fits the mood of this late phase of Stegner's career. The backward look by a contemplative older man again shapes the narrative. The narrator, known to the readers of *The Big Rock Candy Mountain,* is Bruce Mason, Bo Mason's younger son. Bruce has proven to be a survivor and a successful man by the standards of the world and in part by his own. The stories that Bruce recapitulates (some of them known to readers of Stegner's short stories) at the time of his return to Salt Lake City after an absence of many years refocus the family saga of the earlier panoramic novel, allowing for the counterpointing across the years that characterizes the methods of Stegner's later fiction. In *Recapitulation* Stegner probes the nature of memory. Bruce's brief stay in the Mormon capital, where he had lived his adolescent and college years, calls up the ghosts of his past. Now a retired ambassador and lifelong bachelor, Bruce can also remind us of many of Stegner's heroes who have either avoided marriage or been defeated in it.

Crossing to Safety, Stegner's most recent novel, provides memorable stories of two marriages, both of which undergo extraordinary testing—caused in one case by nature (polio), in the other by human determination to control—and survive that testing. As the marriages prove strong, so does the friendship between the couples, whose history defines the book. Stegner's method is again in the mode of "recapitulation." Brought together at the Langs' Vermont summer place for a last reunion (Charity Lang is dying of cancer), their past is the present, and the couples define what they are—individually and collectively. The Langs are Easterners; the Morgans Westerners. Tellingly, Vermont serves as "the last good country."

Crossing to Safety belongs with Stegner's major accomplishments. It is now clear that his career differs from that of most major writers. He has done his best writing in the second half of a long career, in works that revisit the past at a crucial moment. *The Big Rock Candy Mountain* is his greatest achievement from the first half of his career, but his work from *All the Little Live Things* onward will likely be the novels we read most often. Although Stegner turned away from writing short stories in his late phase, publication of the *Collected Stories* in 1990 recalls his impressive contributions in that genre and calls appropriate attention to his place in American and western letters. Welcome also is *The American West as Living Space*, a 1987 publication comprising three lectures Stegner gave at the Law School of the University of Michigan in 1986. Those lectures encapsulate Stegner's understanding of western myth and realities, as well as his thoughtful concern for the continent Americans have so shortsightedly exploited. He noted in the first lecture, "I can't come to even tentative conclusions about the West without coming to some conclusions about myself."

Stegner's characters are usually seeking, very consciously, to define themselves, as Bruce is in *Recapitulation.* Often, too, they have made their search in a western setting, and it seems appropriate that Bruce's new definitions take place in the heart of the American West where his father pursued the American dream, however vainly. *Recapitulation* is an important contribution to the major vein of Stegner's later fiction, a vein which—along with *The Big Rock Candy Mountain*—will likely be his best remembered work. It is also his most western work.

—Joseph M. Flora

STEINBECK, John (Ernst). American. Born in Salinas, California, 27 February 1902. Educated at Salinas High School, graduated 1919; Stanford University, California, intermittently 1919–25. Married 1) Carol Henning in 1930 (divorced 1942); 2) Gwyn Conger (i.e., the actress Gwen Verdon) in 1943 (divorced 1948), two sons; 3) Elaine Scott in 1950. Worked at various jobs, including reporter for the New York *American*, apprentice hod-carrier, apprentice painter, chemist, caretaker of an estate at Lake Tahoe, surveyor, and fruit picker, 1925–35; full-time writer from 1935; settled in Monterey, California, 1930, later moved to New York City; special writer for the United States Army Air Force during World War II; correspondent in Europe for the New York *Herald Tribune*, 1943. Recipient: New York Drama Critics Circle award, 1938; Pulitzer prize, 1940; King Haakon Liberty Cross (Norway), 1946; O. Henry award, 1956; Nobel Prize for Literature, 1962; Presidential Medal of Freedom, 1964; United States Medal of Freedom, 1964. Member, American Academy, 1939. *Died 20 December 1968.*

Western Publications

Novels

The Pastures of Heaven. New York, Brewer Warren and Putnam, 1932; London, Philip Allan, 1933.
To a God Unknown. New York, Ballou, 1933; London, Heinemann, 1935.
Tortilla Flat. New York, Covici Friede, and London, Heinemann, 1935.
In Dubious Battle. New York, Covici Friede, and London, Heinemann, 1936.
Of Mice and Men. New York, Covici Friede, and London, Heinemann, 1937.
The Grapes of Wrath. New York, Viking Press, and London, Heinemann, 1939.
Cannery Row. New York, Viking Press, and London, Heinemann, 1945.
The Wayward Bus. New York, Viking Press, and London, Heinemann, 1947.
The Pearl. New York, Viking Press, 1947; London, Heinemann, 1948.
East of Eden. New York, Viking Press, and London, Heinemann, 1952.
Sweet Thursday. New York, Viking Press, and London, Heinemann, 1954.

Short Stories

Saint Katy the Virgin. New York, Covici Friede, 1936.
The Red Pony. New York, Covici Friede, 1937; London, Heinemann, 1949.
The Long Valley. New York, Viking Press, 1938; London, Heinemann, 1939.
The Short Novels. New York, Viking Press, 1953; London, Heinemann, 1954.

Uncollected Short Stories

"Fingers of Cloud," in *Stanford Writers 1891–1941*, edited by Violet L. Shue. Stanford, California, Dramatists Alliance, n.d.
"Tractored Off," in *America in Literature.* Madison, Wisconsin, Crofts, 1944.
"Nothing for Himself," in *Continent's End*, edited by Joseph Henry Jackson and others. New York, McGraw Hill, 1944.

"Over the Hill," in *Half-a-Hundred*, edited by C. Grayson. Toronto, Blakiston, 1945.
"The Hanging at San Quentin," in *Short Story Monthly 20*. New York, Avon, 1945.
"Death of Grampa," in *Taken at the Flood*, edited by Ann Watkins. New York, Harper, 1946.
"The Tractors," in *Our Lives: American Labor Stories*, edited by Joseph Gaer. New York, Boni and Gaer, 1948.
"Miracle at Tepayac," in *Collier's* (Springfield, Ohio), 25 December 1948.
"His Father," in *Reader's Digest* (Pleasantville, New York), September 1949.
"Sons of Cyrus Trask," in *Collier's* (Springfield, Ohio), 12 July 1952.
"The King Snake and the Rattles," in *Brief*, April 1953.
"A Snake of One's Own," in *The Bedside Esquire*, edited by Arnold Gingrich. New York, Tudor, 1954.
"How Mr. Hogan Robbed a Bank," in *Working with Prose*, edited by Otto Reinert. New York, Harcourt Brace, 1959.

OTHER PUBLICATIONS

Novels

Cup of Gold: A Life of Henry Morgan, Buccaneer, with Occasional Reference to History. New York, McBride, 1929; London, Heinemann, 1937.
The Moon Is Down. New York, Viking Press, and London, Heinemann, 1942.
Burning Bright: A Play in Story Form. New York, Viking Press, 1950; London, Heinemann, 1951.
The Short Reign of Pippin IV: A Fabrication. New York, Viking Press, and London, Heinemann, 1957.
The Winter of Our Discontent. New York, Viking Press, and London, Heinemann, 1961.

Plays

Of Mice and Men, adaptation of his own novel (produced San Francisco and New York, 1937). New York, Covici Friede, 1937.
The Forgotten Village (screenplay). New York, Viking Press, 1941.
The Moon Is Down, adaptation of his own novel (produced New York, 1942; London, 1943). New York, Viking Press, 1942; London, English Theatre Guild, 1943.
A Medal for Benny, with Jack Wagner and Frank Butler, in *Best Film Plays 1945*, edited by John Gassner and Dudley Nichols. New York, Crown, 1946.
Burning Bright, adaptation of his own novel (produced New York, 1950). New York, Dramatists Play Service, 1951.
Viva Zapata! The Original Screenplay, edited by Robert E. Morsberger. New York, Viking Press, 1975.

Screenplays: *The Forgotten Village* (documentary), 1941; *Lifeboat*, with Jo Swerling, 1944; *A Medal for Benny*, with Jack Wagner and Frank Butler, 1945; *The Pearl*, with Jack Wagner and Emilio Fernandez, 1947; *The Red Pony*, 1949; *Viva Zapata!*, 1952.

Other

Their Blood Is Strong. San Francisco, Lubin Society of California, 1938.
John Steinbeck Replies (letter). New York, Friends of Democracy, 1940.
Sea of Cortez: A Leisurely Journal of Travel and Research, with Edward F. Ricketts. New York, Viking Press, 1941.
Bombs Away: The Story of a Bomber Team. New York, Viking Press, 1942.
The Viking Portable Library Steinbeck, edited by Pascal Covici. New York, Viking Press, 1943; abridged edition as *The Steinbeck Pocket Book*, New York, Pocket Books, 1943; revised edition, as *The Portable Steinbeck*, Viking Press, 1946, 1958; revised edition, edited by Pascal Covici, Jr., Viking Press, 1971; London, Penguin, 1976; 1946 edition published as *The Indispensable Steinbeck*, New York, Book Society, 1950, and as *The Steinbeck Omnibus*, London, Heinemann, 1951.
The First Watch (letter). Los Angeles, Ward Ritchie Press, 1947.
Vanderbilt Clinic. New York, Presbyterian Hospital, 1947.
A Russian Journal, photographs by Robert Capa. New York, Viking Press, 1948; London, Heinemann, 1949.
The Log from the Sea of Cortez. New York, Viking Press, 1951; London, Heinemann, 1958.
Once There Was a War. New York, Viking Press, 1958; London, Heinemann, 1959.
Travels with Charley in Search of America. New York, Viking Press, and London, Heinemann, 1962.
Speech Accepting the Nobel Prize for Literature... New York, Viking Press, 1962(?).
America and Americans. New York, Viking Press, and London, Heinemann, 1966.
Journal of a Novel: The East of Eden Letters. New York, Viking Press, 1969; London, Heinemann, 1970.
Steinbeck: A Life in Letters, edited by Elaine Steinbeck and Robert Wallsten. New York, Viking Press, and London, Heinemann, 1975.
The Acts of King Arthur and His Noble Knights, From the Winchester Manuscripts of Malory and Other Sources, edited by Chase Horton. New York, Farrar Straus, and London, Heinemann, 1976.
Letters to Elizabeth: A Selection of Letters from John Steinbeck to Elizabeth Otis, edited by Florian J. Shasky and Susan F. Riggs. San Francisco, Book Club of California, 1978.
Conversations with John Steinbeck, edited by Thomas Fensch. Jackson, University Press of Mississippi, 1988.
Writing Days: The Journals of the Grapes of Wrath, edited by Robert DeMott. New York, Viking, 1989.

*

Bibliography: *A New Steinbeck Bibliography 1929–1971* and *1971–1981* by Tetsumaro Hayashi, Metuchen, New Jersey, Scarecrow Press, 2 vols., 1973; 1983; *John Steinbeck: A Bibliographical Catalogue of the Adrian H. Goldstone Collection* by Adrian H. Goldstone and John R. Payne, Austin, University of Texas Humanities Research Center, 1974; *Steinbeck Bibliographies: An Annotated Guide* by Robert B. Harmon, Metuchen, New Jersey, Scarecrow Press, 1987.

Critical Studies (selection): *The Novels of John Steinbeck: A First Critical Study* by Harry T. Moore, Chicago, Normandie House, 1939, as *John Steinbeck and His Novels*, London, Heinemann, 1939; *Steinbeck and His Critics: A Record of Twenty-Five Years* edited by E.W. Tedlock, Jr., and C.V. Wicker, Albuquerque, University of New Mexico Press, 1957; *The Wide World of John Steinbeck*, New Brunswick, New Jersey, Rutgers University Press, 1958, and *Steinbeck, Nature, and Myth*, New York, Crowell, 1978, both by Peter Lisca; *John*

Steinbeck by Warren French, New York, Twayne, 1961, revised edition, 1975; *John Steinbeck* by F.W. Watt, New York, Grove Press, and Edinburgh, Oliver and Boyd, 1962; *John Steinbeck: An Introduction and Interpretation* by Barry Fontenrose, New York, Barnes and Noble, 1964; Steinbeck Monograph series edited by Tetsumaro Hayashi, Muncie, Indiana, Ball State University English Department, from 1972; *Steinbeck: A Collection of Critical Essays* edited by Robert Murray Davis, Englewood Cliffs, New Jersey, Prentice Hall, 1972; *John Steinbeck and Edward F. Ricketts: The Shaping of a Novelist* by Richard Astro, Minneapolis, University of Minnesota Press, 1973; *The Novels of John Steinbeck: A Critical Study* by Howard Levant, Columbia, University of Missouri Press, 1974; *John Steinbeck: The Errant Knight: An Intimate Biography of His California Years* by Nelson Valjean, San Francisco, Chronicle Books, 1975; *The Intricate Music: A Biography of John Steinbeck* by Thomas Kiernan, Boston, Little Brown, 1979; *John Steinbeck* by Paul McCarthy, New York, Ungar, 1980; *The True Adventures of John Steinbeck: A Biography* by Jackson J. Benson, New York, Viking, 1983, London, Heinemann, 1984; *John Steinbeck: The California Years* by Brian St. Pierre, San Francisco, Chronicle, 1984; *Steinbeck's Reading: A Catalogue of Books Owned and Borrowed by John Steinbeck* by Robert J. DeMott, New York, Garland, 1984; *Steinbeck's New Vision of America* by Louis Owens, Athens, University of Georgia Press, 1985; *Steinbeck's Fiction: The Aesthetics of the Road Taken* by John H. Timmerman, Norman, University of Oklahoma Press, 1986; *Beyond the Red Pony: A Reader's Companion to Steinbeck's Complete Short Stories* by R.S. Hughes, Metuchen, New Jersey, Scarecrow Press, 1987; *Of Mice and Men: Guide* by John Mahoney and Stewart Martin, London, Letts, 1987; *Staging Steinbeck: Dramatising The Grapes of Wrath* by Peter Whitebrook, London, Cassell, 1988; *Looking for Steinbeck's Ghosts* by Jackson J. Benson, Norman, University of Oklahoma Press, 1988.

* * *

John Steinbeck's work cannot be neatly categorised; his wide-ranging imagination makes such a narrow judgment impossible. Variously—and mistakenly—described as a political writer, a proletarian, a regional writer, a sociological writer, a revolutionary and a communist, his work has been labelled "sentimental entertainment hooked up with heavyhanded symbolism" or "symbolism gone sentimental." Conservatives have criticised his writing as Communist, while Communists have damned him for not demanding the revolution. It has been said that his work lacks real thought, and is designed for readers who require the appearance of a novel for intellectuals, but not its content.

Such criticisms are more than countered by the small band of critics who refuse to accept Steinbeck as anything less than one of the greatest 20th-century American writers, and by the general public, who have continued to buy and read his novels in vast quantities.

It would be wrong to classify his work purely as that of a proletarian writer. His concern for poor people is evident, but, whatever his accusers may claim, he does little social probing. It is not the reasons for human behaviour that concern him so much as its actualities. He is in part a regional novelist, in that the area around the Salinas River is described frequently in his novels, but it is not the region alone that serves as the main source of his inspiration. It provides a background for the novels, but the foreground is occupied by people who are sufficiently universal to represent the human condition.

Having held a bewildering variety of part-time and temporary jobs while studying at Stanford University, Steinbeck gained the experience which is reflected in the humanity of the characters in his novels. Working as a ranch hand near King City gave him the knowledge which he later drew upon when writing *Of Mice and Men*, while a trip with migrant workers to California formed the basis of his best known work *The Grapes of Wrath*. Working with all kinds of people influenced the themes and concerns of his novels. In *The Grapes of Wrath*, a panoramic view of the land and people concentrates itself to become an intimate study of one family. The Joads *are* the "Okies", and their struggle symbolizes the greater struggle of the immigrant community.

Steinbeck's literary skills include the masterly use of colloquial speech and vernacular in his narratives, an ability to describe nature in simple but effective terms, a great sense of drama and climax, and a marked talent for describing the tensions and relationships existing within a group of people. One of his greatest gifts is an ability to create atmosphere, be it that of the bunk house, the migrant camp or the dawn over the Salinas River.

A deep interest in the workings of the natural world is reflected in his books, many of which contain minutely detailed descriptions of nature. In *The Grapes of Wrath* seed dispersal is described, along with the life cycle of turtles. In *Cannery Row* marine biology, starfish, shrimps, crabs, and octopus parallel human life. In *The Pearl* the undersea world appears again, along with the evil scorpion, and in *The Red Pony* nature takes two lives—Jody's pony, and the mother of the foal which replaces him.

Steinbeck had a great love of animals and outdoor pursuits, but what is equally obvious from his books is that beneath this lay an even deeper love of humanity, especially the plain working man, born out of a clear understanding of his strengths and weaknesses. Steinbeck was not a dispassionate observer, and could never limit himself to mere observation and description. In *The Log from The Sea of Cortez* (a collaboration with Ed Ricketts, a scientist friend), Steinbeck *was* able to show his "nonteleological" way of thinking, addressing the questions of 'what and how', instead of the usual 'why'. In *Tortilla Flat* and *Cannery Row* he offered observations on the drifters of Monterey which display an almost scientific accuracy. These latter works were conscious attempts at a nonteleological view of life and art, so the question of 'why' does not arise. But in novels like *The Grapes of Wrath*, and *The Pearl*, which describe racial and social injustice suffered by the poor, mere observation is not sufficient. Steinbeck also raised the issue of "what should be" or "could be", or "might be", because he was so aware of "what should not be". He worked hard to depict social problems in accurate detail, but also showed why they should stop.

The idea of going West to live and prosper in the "Promised Land" has formed the basis of the 'American Dream' for many generations. However, in his novels, Steinbeck shows that the realities often fall short of his characters' expectations. In *The Grapes of Wrath*, the west is seen as a 'Canaan' by the Joads, but their hopes are lost when they arrive there only to face more hardships. Lennie and George in *Of Mice and Men* have their dream of a perfect home shattered, and in *The Pearl* Kino's dream of giving his son an education is destroyed when his baby is killed. Written in straightforward prose, his books celebrate the sorrow and the joy of daily existence. They also give a dignity to the struggle for survival that is so often a part of human experience, especially for the poor.

This interest in ordinary men and women, which so typifies Steinbeck and his work, motivated *Travels with Charley in Search of America*, an account of a trip through America with his dog Charley. "The people I want to listen to", he said before going on the trip, "are . . . the man in a field who isn't likely to know my name even if he heard it".

—Ellie Brown

STERLING, Maria Sandra. *See* **FLOREN, Lee.**

STERLING, Sandra. *See* **FLOREN, Lee.**

STERN, Max. *See* **BARRETT, Geoffrey John.**

STEVENS, Dan J. *See* **OVERHOLSER, Wayne D.**

STEVENS, J.D. *See* **ROWLAND, Donald S.**

STEVENS, James (Floyd). American. Born in Albia, Iowa, 15 November 1892. Educated in public schools. Served in the United States Army in France, 1917–19: Sergeant. Married Theresa Seitz Fitzgerald in 1929. Public relations officer, West Coast Lumbermen's Association. Litt.D.: Pacific University, Forest Grove, Oregon, 1958. *Died 31 December 1971.*

WESTERN PUBLICATIONS

Novels

Brawny-Man. New York, Knopf, 1928.
Big Jim Turner. New York, Doubleday, 1948.

Short Stories

Homer in the Sagebrush. New York, Knopf, 1928.

Uncollected Short Stories

"The Dance Hall Fisherman," in *Adventure* (New York), 15 November 1927.
"Occidental's Prodigal," in *Adventure* (New York), 1 April 1928.
"Powder River," in *Adventure* (New York), 1 May 1928.
"The Old Warhouse," in *Adventure* (New York), 1 June 1928.
"Oleman Hattie," in *Adventure* (New York), 15 July 1928.
"The Grip of Life," in *Adventure* (New York), 15 September 1928.
"The Runt and the Roan," in *Adventure* (New York), 15 December 1928.
"Hellion," in *Collier's* (Springfield, Ohio), 29 December 1928.
"Slivers," in *Adventure* (New York), 1 January 1929.
"Stunt Night," in *Adventure* (New York), 15 February 1929.
"The Prodigious Delehanty," in *Adventure* (New York), 15 March 1929.
"The Bulldogger," in *Adventure* (New York), 1 April 1929.
"Fist and Boot," in *Adventure* (New York), 15 April 1929.
"Meals Make the Man," in *Adventure* (New York), 15 May 1930.
"The Son of Parson Joab," in *Adventure* (New York), 15 November 1930.
"Great Hunter of the Woods," in *Best Short Stories 1931*, edited by Edward J. O'Brien. Boston, Houghton Mifflin, 1931.
"When Rivers Were Young and Wild," in *Woman's Home Companion* (Springfield, Ohio), July 1931.
"King-Jack," in *Adventure* (New York), 1 November 1931.
"Downfall of Elder Barton," in *American Mercury* (New York), December 1931.
"Fightin' Mad," in *American Magazine* (Springfield, Ohio), December 1931.
"Rock-Candy Mountains," in *American Mercury* (New York), March 1932.
"The War of the Murphys," in *Argosy* (New York), 26 March 1932.
"Heartwood," in *Complete Stories* (New York), 1 April 1932.
"Trail Tamer," in *Complete Stories* (New York), 1 July 1932.
"Paddy the Devil," in *Adventure* (New York), 15 August 1932.
"Painted Ghosts," in *Complete Stories* (New York), 1 September 1932.
"Spiked Fists," in *American Magazine* (Springfield, Ohio), January 1933.
"Dynamite Straight," in *Adventure* (New York), 15 March 1933.
"Man and a Half," in *American Magazine* (Springfield, Ohio), May 1933.
"Yellow Hell," in *Argosy* (New York), 10 June 1933.
"Sawdust Savage," in *Argosy* (New York), 19 August 1933.
"Timber Trout," in *All Western* (New York), October 1933.
"Killer's Luck," in *Complete Stories* (New York), 1 October 1933.
"Big-Timber Getaway," in *Argosy* (New York), 6 January 1934.
"Luck Goes West," in *Complete Stories* (New York), 1 March 1934.
"Hobo's Sunset," in *Argosy* (New York), 3 March 1934.
"The Murder Twins," in *Complete Stories* (New York), 15 March 1934.
"White Murder," in *Complete Stories* (New York), 1 April 1934.
"Cap'n Dynamite," in *Adventure* (New York), May 1934.
"Rainbow Morning," in *Argosy* (New York), 3 November 1934.
"Sawdust Savage," in *Adventure* (Chicago), 15 November 1934.
"Wild Horses," in *Cowboy Stories* (New York), January 1936.
"Quaker Kid," in *Cowboy Stories* (New York), May 1936.
"Sons of Noah," in *Argosy* (New York), 3 October 1936.
"Two Pints of Dynamite," in *Argosy* (New York), 12 December 1936.
"Double David and Goliath," in *Argosy* (New York), 26 December 1936.
"When Twins Meet Twins," in *Argosy* (New York), 6 March 1936.
"Burnout," in *Argosy* (New York), 1 May 1936.

"Timber Fighter," in *Complete Stories* (New York), June 1937.
"Black Duck Dinner," in *America Is West*, edited by John T. Flanagan. Minneapolis, University of Minnesota Press, 1945.
"Jerkline," in *Zane Grey Western Award Stories*, edited by Don Ward. New York, Dell, 1951.
"C.P.R.," in *The Railroaders*, edited by Bill Pronzini and Martin H. Greenberg. New York, Fawcett, 1986.
"The River Smeller," in *The Steamboaters*, edited by Bill Pronzini and Martin H. Greenberg. New York, Fawcett, 1986.
"The Bullpuncher," in *Christmas Out West*, edited by Bill Pronzini and Martin H. Greenberg. New York, Doubleday, 1990.
"Ike the Diver's Friend," in *The Northwesterners*, edited by Bill Pronzini and Martin H. Greenberg. New York, Fawcett, 1990.

OTHER PUBLICATIONS

Novel

Mattock. New York, Knopf, 1927.

Other

Paul Bunyan. New York, Knopf, 1925.
Status Rerum: A Manifesto upon the Present Condition of Northwest Literature. . ., with H.L. Davis. Privately printed, 1927(?).
The Saginaw Paul Bunyan. New York, Knopf, 1932.
Timber! The Way of Life in the Lumber Camps (for children). Evanston, Illinois, Row Peterson, 1942.
Paul Bunyan's Bears (for children). Seattle, McCaffrey, 1947.
Tree Treasure: A Conservation Story (for children). Portland, Oregon, Binfords and Mort, 1950.
Green Power: The Story of Public Law 273. Seattle, Superior, 1958.
Lewis and Clark: Our National Epic of Exploration 1804–1806, with Robert Macfarlane. Tacoma, Washington State Historical Society, n.d.

* * *

James Stevens spent a lifetime writing about the Big Woods of the Pacific Northwest as an author of both novels and nonfiction works. Like logger-historian Stewart H. Holbrook, his friend and close contemporary, Stevens knew the woods and their people, the stories and legends, as did few others. He occupied a seat where he could observe the goings-on of the timberlands during the heyday when loggers were mining the big stuff of the Green Desert in unbelievable quantities. Stevens recorded these happenings with color and verve, and we are indeed enriched by his personal chronicles.

Yet much of Stevens's word-stringing energies went into his job as public relations chieftain for the old West Coast Lumbermen's Association, a trade organization which was among the most powerful and influential in the world. But he still found time to turn out books like *Big Jim Turner*, a rousing tale of the northwest woods. However, Stevens was more the nonfiction author than novelist and short story writer, and certainly wasn't of the traditional "Western" field, since his life and interests were deeply imbedded in logging and lumbering. His greatest contribution to the literature of his region, the nation, and the world combined both elements, the gathering together between hard covers of the legends and outlandish tales of Paul Bunyan and Babe, his great blue ox. Stevens had heard these yarns, arising out of Canada, for many years. Finally in 1925 he got them into print. His talent thus preserved a slice of the frontier, part fiction, part folklore, which might otherwise have been lost, for the lumberjacks had their god-like hero in Paul Bunyan as did the plainsmen in Pecos Bill.

Stevens might have done more of worth in fiction, but two things ran against him. He was bound to his typewriter as a publicist and promoter for big timber, and then, too, logging and lumbering have never been an accepted part of the frontier movement as have cowboys and cattle. Stevens surely had the talent and intimate knowledge of his field (for years he wrote a newspaper column called *Out of the Woods*), but at times his prose seems colorless and stilted, perhaps because he was simply too busy meeting deadlines.

—Ellis Lucia

STEWART, Dan. *See* **LINAKER, Mike.**

STEWART, Elinore Pruitt. American.

WESTERN PUBLICATIONS

Novels

Letters of a Woman Homesteader. Boston, Houghton, Mifflin, and London, Constable, 1914.
Letters on an Elk Hunt, by a Woman Homesteader. Boston, Houghton, Mifflin, 1915.

* * *

"The frontier myth," in Susan Armitage's words, "is a male myth." It is the white male hero who, from the time of the Leatherstocking saga onwards, has been primarily identified with the exploration and taming of the "virgin land" which lay before him. Such focus on the (male) encounter with the wilderness and its stress on physical bravery and camaraderie results in the denial of "full, authentic stature" to women. To marginalize them (as constraining "civilizers") because of the requirements of myth, or to fix their role on the frontier according to a set of stereotypical categorizations, is to deny the full range of female motivation and activity, fear, and desire in a new and strange environment. The fictions of such writers as Ellen Glasgow, Willa Cather, and Elizabeth Madox Roberts take strong issue with such formulaic representations.

Elinore Pruitt Stewart's *Letters of a Woman Homesteader* is a vital document in terms of the representation of the American West by a woman writer. Official versions of the frontier and what it meant were often expressed in the realm of public discourse (newspapers, political speech, etc.). The voice and views of the American woman are to be found more commonly in private documents: in letters and diaries. Such a voice is heard in the *Letters* written from Wyoming, between April 1909 and November 1913, by Stewart to Juliet Coney, her former employee in Denver. Hers is only one woman's view of frontier life and Stewart herself recognizes that it is her physical strength and temperament that contribute to her enthusiasm for it: "persons afraid of coyotes and work and loneliness had better let ranching alone." Other texts tell different stories. Stewart describes how that "beautiful [Wyoming] snow" can be "rather depressing" when it is everywhere. O.E. Rølvaag's fictional version of Norwegian settlement in the Dakotas, in *Giants in the Earth*, shows how it is exactly that all blanketing whiteness which drives Beret, the main female protagonist, to the point of madness.

Letters of a Woman Homesteader describes life in early 20th century Wyoming. The country, however, is far from settled, and Elinore's description of her homesteading is a vital element of her story. Here a woman takes centre stage in a narrative of the pioneer experience. We see exactly what it means to be female in this environment in these years, and get a detailed account Elinore's actions and perceptions as she lives out her version of the American dream. If any experience is marginalized here, it is the male one. Homesteading is to Elinore "the solution of all poverty's problems." The "troops of tired, worried women" from back East can raise plenty of food, have a comfortable home, independence, and success if they will take this option. She herself—though she soon marries Clyde Stewart, the rancher for whom she housekeeps—insists on meeting "all my land difficulties unaided." She homesteads on the plot adjacent to her husband, with her own house actually joining his. In this context traditional female roles are considerably modified. At first glance it seems otherwise, with Elinore busy "with three 'bairns' garden, chickens, cows, and housework." But the limits of these roles are considerably extended. The garden contains almost an acre of vegetables: enough for self-sufficiency. She asserts her ability to do the necessary ploughing herself. The butter she sells pays "for a year's supply of flour and gasoline." There is much more variety of, and flexible attitude to, gender role in this "sweet, free open" frontier space. The fact that she does homestead successfully, that she travels widely by herself (or with her daughter and/or other women), that she conducts herself socially with a great deal of freedom from conventional restraint, that she takes on roles normally denied to women (mowing the hay and doing "carpentry work"), and that Mrs. Louderer, her friend, actually runs her own ranch and "bosses" the men under her, all suggest as much.

There are, interestingly, two partial evasions contained in the *Letters*, which modify in their different ways the sense of the text given above. Elinore fails to reveal her marriage to Clyde until a year after the event, and her assertions "that a woman could ranch if she wanted to" and descriptions of homesteading generally are compromised to some degree by his presence in the background. The other evasion is perhaps more significant. In August, 1910, she tells how she conducts the funeral service of "a dear little child [who] has joined the angels." Over two years later she returns to this subject to say that "that was my own little Jamie, our first little son. For a long time my heart was crushed." Elinore, who knows that she is "extra strong," and whose confident and good-humoured voice sounds so strikingly in these letters leaves unsaid, or rather disguised, one of those personal tragedies which scarred the emotional lives of so many women in the West. Jeannie McKnight suggests that such suppressions, even in personal documents, signalled internal divisions in those women concerned. Here perhaps, the painful aspects of a woman's life in the West cannot be immediately reconciled with the more positive expectations and ambitions she had set for herself.

In *Heartland*, the recent film based on these letters, the death of the child becomes a central incident, and Elinore can only release her tears when Mrs. Louderer next visits. Though this latter detail may illustrate that need for womanly companionship which was felt so strongly by many frontier women, it is not taken from the original text. Neither is the conflict and lack of communication between husband and wife which the film also explores. *Heartland* makes gender conflict and gender roles its main concern. Though the latter subject is at the centre of the *Letters*, to convert Clyde into a stingy and taciturn oppositional figure, as the film does for its major part, is to ignore what is originally said by the author in order to make an ideological point about the nature of sexual politics.

—Peter Messent

STILWELL, Hart. American. Born in Texas, in 1902. Educated at the University of Texas, Austin, graduated 1924. Journalist and freelance writer: sports writer for *Field and Stream* and other magazines.

WESTERN PUBLICATIONS

Novels

Border City. New York, Doubleday, 1945; London, Hurst and Blackett, 1948.
Uncovered Wagon. New York, Doubleday, 1947; London, Hurst and Blackett, 1950.

OTHER PUBLICATIONS

Novel

Campus Town. New York, Doubleday, 1950.

Other

Hunting and Fishing in Texas. New York, Knopf, 1946.
Fishing in Mexico. New York, Knopf, 1948.
Old Soggy No. 1: The Uninhibited Story of Slats Rodgers, with Rodgers. New York, Messner, 1954.
Looking at Man's Past (for children). Austin, Texas, Steck Vaughn, 1965.
The Child Who Walks Alone: Case Studies of Rejection in Schools, with Anne Stilwell. Austin, University of Texas Press, 1972.

* * *

Hart Stilwell has written two above-average western novels, *Border City* and *Uncovered Wagon*. *Border City* is a novel of protest against the injustices to Mexicans in the Rio Grande Valley. The story relates an uneven conflict between Anglos and Mexicans in business, social life, and politics. Although a lesser work than some studies of Mexican-American relationships, Stilwell's novel joins those which show an appreciation for the qualities in the Mexican genius which can add to the variety and worth of life in America.

Uncovered Wagon is the story of a migratory family in the Rio Grande Valley (called "The Valley" by today's Texans) who are constantly on the move. The wife and children are dominated and terrorized by the father, known as "My Old Man," who rages at people and animals, but who has a way with things that grow from the soil. These people have a deep love for whatever soil they own, and their attempts to hold it and make it yield is to them the nourishment of life. Stilwell's characterization of Old Man Endicott was highly praised when the book appeared as the picture of a man who represented more than an individual, but almost an entire frame of mind.

—Dorys C. Grover

STOKOE, E(dward) G(eorge.) Has also written as Charles Clos; Paul Daner; Ross Dexter; Brian Peters; John Stark. British. Born in Wallsend, Northumberland, 15 April 1919. Educated at Dame Allan's School, Newcastle-upon-Tyne. Served in Royal Marines 43 Commando, 1939–45; discharged with war wounds. Widower; one son. Employee, 1936–84, and Welfare Officer 1960–84, North Eastern Electricity Board, Newcastle-upon-Tyne. Address: 474 Station Road North, Wallsend, Tyne and Wear NE28 8NF, England.

WESTERN PUBLICATIONS

Novels

Cade. London, Brown Watson, 1954.
End of the Trail (as Paul Daner). London, Brown Watson, 1954.
Carson's Killer (as Ross Dexter). London, Brown Watson, 1955.
Starbuck (as Brian Peters). London, Brown Watson, 1957.
Last of the Napiers. London, Brown Watson, 1960.
Death at Sundown. London, Brown Watson, 1961.
Once an Outlaw. London, Brown Watson, 1961.
Once a Marshal. London, Brown Watson, 1961.
Showdown at Mesa. London, New English Library, 1963.
Greed Is the Spur. London, Hale, 1988.
The Judas Trail. London, Hale, 1988.
A Nest of Rattlers. London, Hale, 1990.

OTHER PUBLICATIONS

Novels

Once a Marine. London, Brown Watson, 1957.
Call It Experience (as Charles Clos). London, Brown Watson, 1959.
Marine Commando (as John Stark). London, Brown Watson, 1959.

Other

Lower the Ramps: Autobiography. London, Brown Watson, 1955.

* * *

E.G. Stokoe began with standard "oaters," an early entrant being *Last of the Napiers* at the beginning of the 1960's, a unexceptional tale of gun-running. But in his later novels the author became more expansive, providing strong melodramas in western settings with long lists of characters. *Greed Is the Spur* is exemplary of this development, the story of a *femme fatale* who uses her sexuality to achieve her ends, bedding and killing when it suits her plans, against a sprawling tale which takes in rapings, hangings, a wagon trek, Indian attack, a bank robbery, a desert stake-out plus a bounty hunter thrown in for good measure. However, despite its convolutions, nothing is gratuitious, no detail is wasted and the loose ends are all neatly and satisfyingly tied together by the last page.

The Judas Trail has a similar construction, with ingredients including a nailing to a tree, a gang of stagecoach robbers on the run, family intrigue, and yet another woman central character who lies and uses her body to further her material interests. As in other books we get surprises. For example, the bounty hunter who has reappeared in this book and has looked set to continue in a series, hangs up his guns against type to marry and buy a spread.

Less satisfying of these later books is *A Nest of Rattlers*, in which a man searches for his brother only to find the man has been framed and hanged in a cover-up for incest and murder.

Generally Stokoe favours complex plots, especially in his later works, commonly deploying flashbacks, and sometimes several pages are needed at the end by way of explanation. There is often a psychological dimension to his characters where earlier traumatic events are referred to or—more graphically—illustrated by flashback, a technique used to structural advantage. With regard to content, lust and passion figure prominently in these later books—there is much sharing of blankets—which provides natural motivation for much of the action. Nor are we ever very far from a brothel and descriptions (albeit brief) of the activities therein. Mutilation occurs regularly in descriptive sections, but gore is never emphasised and the action scenes are presented with notable economy.

Although the author has a penchant for literary side references—the previously mentioned title *Greed Is the Spur* for example, and in the naming of sub-sections such as "Gun for Hire," his narrative style is straightforward and unpretentious, avoiding western folksiness, and with notably little use of figurative speech.

On the downside, he can be repetitive. Dancing girls in saloons are always doing "impossible things" with their bosoms—it wouldn't be so bad, but we are never told what! Moreover, he is prone to re-using material across books—from borrowing a couple of lines of description to one case where he virtually repeats a whole scene (the hanging of a woman) using the same dialogue for onlookers but putting the words into the mouths of different characters. Some self-plagiarism might be acceptable, but it runs the danger of breaking the suspension of disbelief in those who read more than one of an author's books.

However, in summary, good solid stories, plainly told.

—B.J. Holmes

STOTTER, Mike (Michael James Stotter). British. Born in London, 6 January 1957. Educated at Raine's Foundation Grammar School, London, 1967–74. Married Lorraine Desmond in 1980; two sons. Film and V.T. clerk, B.B.C. Television, Middlesex, 1974–78; bus conductor, London Transport, Barking, Essex, 1978–80; control clerk, Centre File, London, 1980–82; sales supervisor, Alpine Drinks, London, 1982–84. Bank messenger, 1986–87, and since 1988 assistant office manager, Morgan Grenfell stockbrokers, London. Editor, *The Westerner* magazine, 1978–80; co-originator and consultant, *The Western Magazine*, International Publishing Corporation, 1981–82. Address: 16 Roxwell Way, Woodford Green, Essex IG8 7JY, England.

WESTERN PUBLICATIONS

Novels

McKinney's Revenge. London, Hale, 1990.
Tombstone Showdown. London, Hale, 1991.

Uncollected Short Story

"Rimfire Revenge," in *The Westerner* (London), 1981.

*

Mike Stotter comments:

In my work I write stories about people. *McKinney's Revenge* could have easily been set on the streets of London or even New York. It was through my own interest in the West that determined the setting. I write for my own entertainment, which helps a great deal in creating those characters appearing in the books or stories. There are those of you out there who know what I mean. Because no man is an island, the knock-on effect of his actions aren't insular. It is that undercurrent that I have tried to capture in both the tragedy and the adventure of *McKinney's Revenge.*

* * *

McKinney's Revenge is Mike Stotter's first western novel, and marks an impressive debut for its author. Based on the familiar revenge theme, as its title implies, the action stems from a moment of adulterous passion, with the ranch-hand Thadius McKinney returning unexpectedly to discover his young wife and his boss—rancher Aaron Wyatt—in bed together. Enraged, McKinney maims Wyatt, and flees for his life. The story of his pursuit by Wyatt's cowhands, and his eventual return to exact a fearful retribution on the man who has wronged him, makes for compelling reading. The harshness of the wintry badlands terrain is superbly depicted, and much of the dialogue terse and effective. Stotter writes convincingly of his leading characters, McKinney and the scarred gunfighter Missouri Clay—a man with a score of his own to settle—and the friendship between these two hard-bitten, laconic men is one of the main strengths of the book. While Wyatt and his crew are shown as being tough and unscrupulous, Stotter stops short of presenting them as outright villains, instead viewing the action without undue moral comment through the eyes of both pursuers and pursued. This succeeds to the extent that one feels some sympathy for McKinney's enemies, as well as for the man himself. He also eschews the loving detail lavished on weapons by other western authors, with guns being referred to briefly by name and their power demonstrated in the ensuing action. Period and location are neatly achieved by—mostly unobtrusive—side references to past events from the Civil War, and the identification of such places as Adobe Walls and the Santa Fe Trail. There is perhaps a slight loss of pace midway through the novel, when McKinney and Clay encounter the legendary character "Uncle" Dick Wootten, and the story is sidetracked into secondary themes including a shootout with two cheating gambler-gunfighters. These and other scenes in the town of Dumas tend to detract from the gripping narrative of the pursuit, which occupies almost the opening half of the novel. This minor criticism aside, it must be said that Stotter quickly seizes the reins of his plot and builds the excitement to a powerful, cathartic climax in the last few pages. *McKinney's Revenge* is a very striking and individual first novel, whose central characters offer the definite promise of further development.

Tombstone Showdown has a more complicated plot than its predecessor, involving both robbery and the abduction of a Mexican woman, the wife of a rich diamond merchant. The main focus for the action is the town of Tombstone and the surrounding area of mountain and desert, and its chief protagonist the gun-toting gambler Jim Brandon, although the author varies this by intercutting chapters which feature secondary characters and their viewpoints. Brandon, who kills a Chinaman in self-defence, falls foul of Sheriff John Behan and his two crooked deputies, and is ordered out of Tombstone. On the stagecoach journey to the town of Contention, he becomes acquainted with the merchant's young wife, Maria Sanchez, and her attractive companion Karla Luz. The three of them are present when the stage is robbed by the outlaw gang of Clancy LeDuc, who are acting on information supplied by the two deputies, and Maria is kidnapped. Brandon then meets up with the mule-riding preacher and ex-soldier Joshua Slate, and the two of them set off to rescue Maria from the outlaws, an adventure which occupies the latter stages of the book. *Tombstone Showdown*, while more ambitious than *McKinney's Revenge*, is not quite as impressive. Unlike the excellent depictions of the earlier novel, the nature of the desert and mountain landscapes around Tombstone are captured only on occasion in descriptive passages, with dialogue perhaps a little over-emphasized in consequence. On the other hand, LeDuc and his henchmen are capably realised, and the action sequences are handled extremely well. The partnership of Brandon and Slate, although not quite as striking as the McKinney-Missouri Clay twosome, once more emerges as the core of this Stotter novel. Slate in particular shows potential for further exploration, and there seems little doubt that he and Brandon will be encountered in future novels, together with McKinney and Missouri Clay.

Stotter, in his first two works, shows considerable skill and storytelling ability, and has developed a definite voice of his own. It will be interesting to see what new directions he will take in future western novels, of which there will surely be many.

—Jeff Sadler

STRAIGHT, Michael (Whitney). American. Born in Southampton, Long Island, New York, 1 September 1916. Educated at the London School of Economics; Cambridge University, M.A. Served in the United States Army Air Force, 1943–45. Married 1) Belinda Crompton in 1939 (divorced 1969); two sons and three daughters; 2) Nina Auchincloss Steers in 1973. Economist, Department of State, Washington, D.C., 1937–38; ghost-writer, Department of the Interior, Washington, 1938–41; contributing editor, 1941–43, publisher, 1946–48, and editor, 1948–56, *The New Republic*, Washington, D.C. Secretary, Emergency Committee of Atomic Scientists, 1946–47; national chair, American Veterans Committee, 1950–52; president, Amnesty International, 1968–71; co-chair, legal and defense fund, National Association for the Advancement of Colored People; president, William C. Whitney Foundation; deputy chair, National Endowment for the Arts, 1969–77. Address: Box 89, Chilmark, Massachusetts 02535, U.S.A.

WESTERN PUBLICATIONS

Novels

Carrington: A Novel of the West. New York, Knopf, 1960; London, Cape, 1961.
A Very Small Remnant. New York, Knopf, and London, Cape, 1963.

OTHER PUBLICATIONS

Novel

Happy and Hopeless. Berkeley, California, Devon Press, 1979.

Play

Caravaggio. Berkeley, California, Devon Press, 1979.

Other

Make This the Last War: The Future of the United Nations. New York, Harcourt Brace, and London, Allen and Unwin, 1943.
Trial by Television (on the Army-McCarthy Hearings). Boston, Beacon Press, 1954; augmented edition, as *Trial by Television and Other Encounters*, Berkeley, California, Devon Press, 1979.
Three West: Conversations with Vardis Fisher, Max Evans, Michael Straight, by John R. Milton. Vermillion, South Dakota, Dakota Press, 1970.
Twigs for an Eagle's Nest: Reflections on the National Endowment for the Arts. Berkeley, California, Devon Press, 1979.
For Noah. Privately printed, 1980.
After Long Silence (autobiography). New York, Norton, and London, Collins, 1983.
Nancy Hanks: An Intimate Portrait. Durham, North Carolina, Duke University Press, 1989.

* * *

Michael Straight, one of America's most articulate liberals, has always written with the political and social realms in mind, whether the work was fiction or not. His model, he implies in one of the essays in *Twigs for an Eagle's Nest*, can be found in ancient Athens: literary artists "were not alienated intellectuals living by themselves in enclaves. They were active citizens . . . soldiers and statesmen." Straight, active as editor of *The New Republic* and for a decade deputy chair of the National Endowment for the Arts, was drawn to fiction when his own interest coincided with a reawakened national interest in the historical facts surrounding the last major clashes of white versus Indian civilization on the Great Plains. Both *Carrington* and *A Very Small Remnant* concern massacres during the Indian Wars of the 1860's, and in their presentation of human beings under the severe stress of clashing cultures, the novels can trace their tradition back to America's first best-sellers: the Indian captivity narratives of the late 17th and early 18th centuries. Although the constant references of that tradition of Calvinist orthodoxy are absent in Straight's fiction, his novels share with those early narratives a conviction of a universal oral truth which the art obligates itself to present.

Carrington and *A Very Small Remnant* share several basic qualities as historical novels. They convey the author's zealous research in western sources; each is minutely descriptive of the local geography, customs, and historical events. Straight's dedication to the model of Aristotelian drama ensures a clarity and simplicity of plot, and also a predictability, if not shallowness, of psychological portrayal. His attempt at total fidelity to historical fact was new in western fiction, and perhaps an inhibitor to the imaginative force of the novels.

Col. Henry B. Carrington, principal source for and protagonist of the first novel, is Straight's best and warmest characterization. By nature a contemplative man, sympathetic and aware of ambiguity, Col. Carrington finds himself in the remotest West breathing the uncongenial moral atmosphere of guerilla warfare. Two conflicting impulses—his own recognition of the tensions debilitating his men and his memory of Gen. William T. Sherman's admonition to him: "pity is the fault most to be feared in a commander"—give the novel its energy. That Carrington is perceived by his junior officers as weak, and that he is later victimized by perjurers in the Army bureaucracy, expresses the ironic vision so strong in Straight's fiction.

A Very Small Remnant conveys its sad vision in a similar way, not by investigating the psychology of evil, but by showing it at work. The zealot Chivington, the true fascination for Straight but "too dark, too destructive" to be at the center of the novel, is described through the senses of "simple, generous, innocent" Ned Wynkoop. Yet Wynkoop, unable to comprehend the evil phenomenon he faces, acts as a screen which eliminates any subtlety from Chivington, who emerges as a sort of Ahab without humanities. Later defeated by a corrupt Bureau of Indian Affairs, Wynkoop ends up a bitter man. Though the novel seeks to document this growth of character, he seems undone by the irrationality and mob violence and moralizers who live by death.

The "duty versus conscience" theme central to both novels is well served by Straight's method of fidelity to historical sources. His realism effectively counters America's myth-choked popular vision of the Indian wars period. His conception of the artist as a spokesman to his culture, responsible in part for its search for self-awareness, is not accompanied by naive optimism.

—Kerry Ahearn

STRANGE, (Thomas) Oliver. British. Born in Worcester in 1871. Married to Nora Strange (died 1948). Worked in the editorial department of George Newnes fiction and magazine publishers, London, for most of working life. Lived in Kew, London, until retirement, when moved to Twickenham, London, 1934–41; following bomb damage to house, moved to Kilmarnock, Scotland, in 1942. Badly injured when house destroyed by fire, April 1943; returned to Twickenham. *Died December 1952.*

WESTERN PUBLICATIONS

Novels (series: Sudden)

The Range Robbers. London, Newnes, 1930; New York, Dial Press, 1931.
The Law o' the Lariat. London, Newnes, 1931; New York, Dial Press, 1932.
The Marshal of Lawless. London, Newnes, 1933; as *Lawless, an Adventure of Sudden, the Outlaw*, New York, Dial Press, 1933.
Sudden. London, Newnes, 1934.

Outlaw Breed. New York, Doubleday, 1934.
Sudden, Outlawed. London, Newnes, 1935; as *Outlawed*, New York, Lothrop Lee, 1936.
Sudden, Goldseeker. London, Newnes, 1937.
Sudden Rides Again. London, Newnes, 1938; New York, Doubleday, 1939.
Sudden Takes the Trail. London, Newnes, 1940.
Sudden Takes Charge. New York, Doubleday, 1940.
Sudden Makes War. London, Newnes, 1942.
Sudden Plays a Hand. London, Newnes, 1950.

* * *

Oliver Strange was born in Worcester in 1871. Of his childhood and schooling nothing is known. He spent most, and perhaps all, of his working life in an editorial capacity in the periodicals department of George Newnes publishers (they ceased to exist around the middle 1970's) of illustrated books, popular and library fiction, and such journals as *John O'London's Weekly*, *Cassell's Weekly*, and *Pearson's Weekly*.

Up to the time of his retirement, Strange and his wife Nora, a former school teacher some 20 years younger than himself, lived in North Avenue, Kew. It was here that "Sudden" was born. A nephew, J.O. Harden, wrote that Strange was "obviously fascinated by the American scene and talked knowledgeably of it, but he certainly never visited the United States. When Sudden was conceived I never heard him say. *The Range Robbers* had been waiting to be written for a long time but I doubt whether he did any serious research until he left journalism. He told me [it] was the only Western he had intended to write and he meant to do something quite different after it."

As a result, the Sudden series reversed the usual formula: its hero ended his "legendary quest" in the first book. *The Range Robbers* tells how "Sudden" the outlaw gunfighter-knight errant pursues to a final confrontation Webb and Peterson, the two men he has been searching for. After he settles the hash of Webb—who was really the bad guy, not Peterson, who turns out to be his father—he falls in love and marries the spunky heroine, Noreen. Happy ending, fade to black.

To Strange's surprise, Sudden was an enormous success. Encouraged by publisher Sir Emsley Carr he embarked immediately upon a sequel, *The Law o'the Lariat*. It set the pattern for all the books which followed. Despite the fact that the ingredients are fairly predictable, and nearly every punch is telegraphed, the story has tremendous élan and is furiously readable.

The town of Hope Again is "owned" by Black Bart Bartholomew—all Strange's villains are black-hearted wretches straight out of Victorian melodrama—and Sudden's friend Philip Masters (he's the one who "sent for" Severn, and he has a spunky daughter named Phil) is in thrall to him. Until Sudden arrives, that is.

Masters decides to break Black Bart's hold on him by "disappearing." Black Bart lays claim to the orphaned Phil's heart. Offstage, there's a mysterious gang of bandits called The White Masks, who try to get rid of Sudden by tossing a rattlesnake into his room. Sudden's sidekick is Larry Barton, whose sunburned face earns him the nickname "Sunset" and who is, unknown to everyone else, the son of the man hanged by "Black Bart" in a pre-title sequence. Before the happy ending—Strange's denouements are like something out of Agatha Christie—there are set-piece fist fights, a kidnapping, a frame-up, a "forced" wedding that nearly comes off, and, of course, a final confrontation between Sudden and Black Bart. This takes place during a courtroom drama that ends when Bartholomew, trying to kill the unarmed Larry, is himself killed by a shot "Plumb atween the eyes, with a strange gun snaked from 'nother feller's belt."

When Compton Mackenzie, then at the height of his fame, said in a *Daily Mail* review "As one who considers himself something of a connoisseur of this kind of story I recommend *Sudden* with enthusiasm" Oliver Strange (who was also writing western short stories for the London *Evening News*) was prevailed upon by his publisher—and a clamouring public—to continue the saga. The books followed on a roughly annual basis: *The Marshal of Lawless*, *Sudden*, *Sudden, Outlawed*, *Sudden, Goldseeker*, and *Sudden Rides Again*.

In *Sudden, Outlawed*, we learn how the young boy, once "parentless, nameless, friendless, practically the property of an old Piute brave" was "bought" by rancher Bill Evesham, given the name Jim, and sent east to get an education. Two years later Jim comes home to find Evesham dying. "Peterson stole my li'l gal an' broke my heart," Evesham tells him. "An'... that houn' Webb stripped me ... I'm leavin' them two skunks to you."

So The Quest begins. Dubbing himself James Green of Texas, he heads for the town of Fourways, where he is immediately fitted up for a murder. "Allasame," remarks someone, "he put up the purtiest scrap against odds I ever see, and warn't he *sudden*?" After he escapes Jim learns he's now the outlaw "Sudden" with a price on his head. He joins a bandit gang, Rogue's Riders. Rogue is a philosophical sort of bandit leader ("Like a woman, a hoss any man can handle ain't no good") who is clearly better than the roughnecks who follow his flag. Sudden is befriended by a young fellow named Sandy and—inevitably—becomes involved in spunky Carol Eden's adoptive father Sam's difficulties with baddie Jethro Baudry, a professional gambler.

The plot of *Sudden, Outlawed*—which has some pretensions to being a trail-drive Western—revolves around Rogue's plans to steal the herd which is in turn part of Baudry's plan to ruin Eden, and features such staples as a flash flood, a stampede, and the kidnapping of Carol by Commanche [sic] chief Red Fox, who also captures Sandy and Sudden. They escape, are pursued by the "Injuns" and delivered by Rogue's Riders. The herd reaches Abilene, where Baudry teams up with Rogue's villainous lieutenant, Navajo, who robs Eden of the herd money and kidnaps Carol.

Rogue tries to rescue Carol, but in doing so he is fatally wounded by Baudry, who in turn is killed by Navajo when the gambler tries to cheat him as they cut cards for the girl. Sudden takes care of Navajo and rescues Carol. Sandy turns out to be none other than Eden's "scamp of a son" Andrew; cue a happy ending for everyone except Sudden, who must resume his quest.

By the time *Sudden, Outlawed* was published, the Stranges had moved to a new house in Tranmere Road, Whitton, near Twickenham, which they called "Fairways." Their next-door neighbours, the Coton family, recalled in 1966 that Strange was an avid reader who got through at least one and often two books a day, and that when he settled down to write a new "Sudden" he used to do so writing in longhand while sitting on a deckchair in the back garden of "Fairways."

The great strengths of Strange's stories were their complex plots and the tremendous verve and pace with which they were related. He wrote an odd mixture of formal English and mythical vernacular—"'Yo're a grateful cuss, ain't yu,' the rider apostrophised after one of these ebullitions" is an example—not untypical of the time.

Like some other practitioners of the genre, Strange offered a manufactured "western" lingo in which "you" became "yu", men were addressed not as "sir" but as "seh," and said things like "I'll blow you to hellamile" or "Roll yore tail"—picturesque, but hardly accurate reflections of frontier idiom. Too, the unconscious racism of the time—"greasers,"

"Chinks," and "niggers" abound—grates on the modern reader.

Next came *Sudden Rides Again*, in which Sudden cleaned up Hell City, Arizona and solved the mystery of the man who called himself "Satan". After another two years during which World War II had begun, Newnes published *Sudden Takes the Trail*. In 1941 the house at Whitton was severely bomb-damaged in an air raid, and the Stranges lost most of their personal possessions. Nevertheless, he managed to complete *Sudden Makes War* for publication in 1942.

Badly shaken by the experience of being "bombed out," the Stranges moved well out of harm's way—as they thought—to Kilmarnock, where they rented a house on Avenue Square. Ironically, Strange, now in his seventies, was severely injured in a fire which destroyed the house in April 1943. The following year they returned to Whitton, where their home had been rebuilt. Nora Strange died at a local hospital in 1948.

The last of the decalogue, *Sudden Plays a Hand* was published in 1950; it is open to doubt whether Strange actually wrote all of it. Featuring as Sudden's sidekick the New York urchin "Yorky" who had appeared in *Sudden Makes War*, and a final shootout on the brink of a chasm, it was a pale shadow of the muscular tales of yore. In addition, times and tastes had changed, and Sudden was no longer in vogue.

It was not until the early 1960's, when they were paper-backed by Corgi, that the Sudden stories found a new, multi-million copy lease of life which was to continue for well over a decade past the centenary of their creator's birth, and be continued in five more adventures written by Frederick H. Christian.

—Fred Nolan

STRONG, Charles S(tanley). Also wrote as Nancy Bartlett; William B. McClellan; Larry Regan; Chuck Stanley; Charles Stoddard; Carl Sturdy. American.

WESTERN PUBLICATIONS

Novels (series: Soapy Smith)

Doughgod Canyon. London, Ward Lock, 1950.
Riders of the Rio. London, Ward Lock, 1950.
Woolly War. London, Ward Lock, 1951.
Town Tamer (as William B. McLellan). Kingswood, Surrey, World's Work, 1952.
Comanche Crossing. London, Ward Lock, 1952.
The Trail of Soapy Smith. London, Foulsham, 1953.
Soapy Smith Heads North. London, Foulsham, 1953.
Tolliver on the Trail. London, Foulsham, 1954.
North to the Yukon. London, Foulsham, 1954.
The Ghost of Soapy Smith. London, Foulsham, 1955.
West to Denver. London, Foulsham, 1955.
Marshal Sloan of Fort Smith. London, Foulsham, 1956.
Horse Heaven. London, Foulsham, 1956.
Gold Town Gun Boss. London, Foulsham, 1957.
The Brand Rustlers. London, Foulsham, 1957.
Ray Bradley—Frontier Scout. London, Foulsham, 1958.
Prince of Gunfighters. London, Foulsham, 1958.
Wells Fargo Agent. London, Foulsham, 1960.
Dodge City Gun Boss. London, Foulsham, 1961.

Novels as Chuck Stanley

The Buckaroo Kid. New York, Gateway, 1940.
Ace of the Diamond Deuce. New York, Phoenix Press, 1943; London, Quality Press, 1946.
Buck Knight's Round-Up. London, Foulsham, 1945.
Wild Cayuses. New York, Phoenix Press, 1945.
Cherokee Fowler. New York, Phoenix Press, 1945; Redhill, Surrey, Wells Gardner Darton, 1947.
Six-Guns for Hire. London, Foulsham, 1945.
Delaney Rides Out. New York, Phoenix Press, 1946.
The Iron Cayuse. London, Foulsham, 1946.
The San Antonio Mail. London, Foulsham, 1946.
Quick Trigger. London and Melbourne, Australia, Ward Lock, 1946.
Trail to Timberline. New York, Phoenix Press, 1947.
Showdown Guns. Redhill, Surrey, Wells Gardner Darton, 1947.
The Short-Horn Trail. Redhill, Surrey, Wells Gardner Darton, 1947.
Top Hand. New York, Phoenix Press, 1948; Redhill, Surrey, Nicholson and Watson, 1949.
Larabee of Big Spring. Redhill, Surrey, Wells Gardner Darton, 1948.
Buckskin Pards. New York, Phoenix Press, 1949.
Kansas Marshal. Redhill, Surrey, Wells Gardner Darton, 1949.
The Buckskin Beau. New York, Phoenix Press, 1950; London, Foulsham, 1951.
Buffalo Brigade. New York, Phoenix Press, 1950; London, Foulsham, 1952.
Cayuse Courier. New York, Phoenix Press, 1950; London, Foulsham, 1951.
Wagon Boss. New York, Phoenix Press, 1950; London, Foulsham, 1951.
North of Santa Fe. London, Foulsham, 1950.
Trail Herd. New York, Phoenix Press, 1951; London, Foulsham, 1952.
Off to Laramie. London, Foulsham, 1951.
Apache Thunder. New York, Arcadia House, 1952.
Boss of Golden River. New York, Arcadia House, 1952; London, Foulsham, 1954.
Rio Patrol. London, Foulsham, 1953.
Stage Rider. New York, Arcadia House, 1953.
Frontier Scout. London, Foulsham, 1953.
Marshal Sam Clay. London, Foulsham, 1953.
Cattle King. New York, Arcadia House, 1954; as Larry Regan, London, Foulsham, 1955.
Mountain Showdown. London, Foulsham, 1954.
Bullwhacker. New York, Arcadia House, 1954; as Larry Regan, London, Foulsham, 1955.
Texas Kane. London, Foulsham, 1955.
High Country Tenderfoot. London, Foulsham, 1955.
Brand Blotter. New York, Arcadia House, 1956.
Red Arrows. New York, Arcadia House, 1956.
The Man from Elbow River. New York, Arcadia House, 1956; London, Foulsham, 1957.
Empty Saddles. New York, Arcadia House, 1956; London, Foulsham, 1957.
Deputy from Montana. London, Foulsham, 1956.
Frontier Renegade. London, Foulsham, 1956.
Frontier Medico. London, Foulsham, 1956; New York, Arcadia House, 1960.

Wagon Train. New York, Arcadia House, 1956; as *Arizona Jim*, London, Foulsham, 1957.
Cattle Camp. New York, Arcadia House, 1957; as *Kansas Kelly*, London, Foulsham, 1958.
Trigger Trouble. New York, Arcadia House, 1957; as *Gunfighter Gillen*, London, Foulsham, 1958.
Pistols at Potter's Ford. New York, Arcadia House, 1957; as Larry Regan, London, Foulsham, 1958.
Telegraph Trail. New York, Arcadia House, 1957; London, Foulsham, 1958.
Six Shooter Shelby. London, Foulsham, 1957.
Professor Colt. London, Foulsham, 1958.
Saddle Tramp. London, Foulsham, 1958.
Freight for Wells Fargo. London, Foulsham, 1958.
Cibolo Gold. New York, Arcadia House, 1958; as *Santa Fe Gold Trail*, London, Foulsham, 1959.
Supply Train. New York, Arcadia House, 1959.
Stage Station. New York, Arcadia House, 1959.
Wells Fargo Gunguard. London, Foulsham, 1959.
King of Cimarron Crossing. New York, Arcadia House, 1959.
Bullet Ballots. New York, Arcadia House, 1959; London, Foulsham, 1960.
Kansas Stage Coach. New York, Arcadia House, and London, Foulsham, 1960.
Border Bank. New York, Arcadia House, 1960.
The Lost Bugle. New York, Arcadia House, 1960.
Silver Lode. New York, Arcadia House, 1960; London, Ward Lock, 1965.
Wagon Train Colt. London, Foulsham, 1960.
Santa Fe Gold Rustlers. London, Foulsham, 1960.
Nebraska Wagon Train. London, Foulsham, 1961.
Trouble in Texas. London, Foulsham, 1961.
Wagon Train Hold-up. London, Foulsham, 1961.
Border Buckaroo. New York, Arcadia House, 1961.
Cowboy from Cowville. New York, Arcadia House, 1961; London, Wright and Brown, 1963.
Black Mountain Scout. New York, Arcadia House, 1961; London, Mayflower, 1963.
The Scarlet Riders. London, Wright and Brown, 1963.
Ghost City Gambler. London, Wright and Brown, 1964.
The Grey Buffalo. London, Wright and Brown, 1964.
Wagon Wheel Riders. London, Wright and Brown, 1964.
Night Hawk. London, Hammond, 1965.

Novels as Charles Stoddard (series: Malloy)

Trooper Maclean. New York, Caslon, 1936.
The Wilderness Patrol. New York, Dodge, 1938.
Devil's Portage. New York, Gateway, 1942.
Timber Beasts (Malloy). New York, Arcadia House, 1945.
The Trapper of Rat River (Malloy). New York, Phoenix Press, 1947.
Tundra Trail (Malloy). New York, Arcadia House, 1947.

Novels as Larry Regan

Frontier Trader. London, Foulsham, 1954.
Prairie Pioneer. London, Foulsham, 1956.
Wild Horse Raider. London, Foulsham, 1959.
Texas Outlaw. London, Foulsham, 1960.

Fiction (for children)

Ranger: Sea Dog of the Royal Mounted. Philadelphia, Winston, 1948.
South Pole Husky. New York, Longmans Green, 1950.
Ranger's Arctic Patrol. Philadelphia, Winston, 1952.
Seal Hunters: A Snow King Story. New York, Dodd Mead, 1958.

Other Publications

Novels

The Spectre of Masuria. Caldwell, Idaho, Caxton, 1932.
Betrayed. New York, Phoenix Press, 1935.
Beauty Racket. New York, Phoenix Press, 1936.
Embassy Ball (as Nancy Bartlett). New York, Gramercy, 1938.
Disorderly Conduct. New York, Phoenix Press, 1939.
Very Private Chauffeur. New York, Phoenix Press, 1941.
The King's Ram. New York, Day, 1961.

Novels as William McClellan

Waterfront Waitress. New York, Phoenix Press, 1937.
Call Girl. New York, Phoenix Press, 1939.
Dance Studio. New York, Phoenix Press, 1940.

Novels as Carl Sturdy

Doctor's Office. New York, Phoenix Press, 1937.
Company Nurse. New York, Phoenix Press, 1940.
Doctor De Luxe. New York, Phoenix Press, 1941.
Suburban Doctor. New York, Phoenix Press, 1941.
Doctor's Secretary. New York, Phoenix Press, 1943.

Other

We Were There with Byrd at the South Pole (for children). New York, Grosset and Dunlap, 1956.
The Young Traveller in Denmark. London, Phoenix House, 1957.
The Story of American Sailing Ships. New York, Grosset and Dunlap, 1957.
The Real Book About the Antarctic. New York, Garden City, 1959; London, Dobson, 1963.
The Lost Convoy: Adventures with the Norweigan Underground. Philadelphia, Chilton, 1960.

* * *

Whatever pseudonym Charles S. Strong chose to write under, he always prided himself on the authentic detail he put into his work. Strong makes subtle use of his fine technique of imparting information on American history and geography. A native New Yorker, he travelled extensively in the West to gather the material for his novels. His backgrounds are real places, and often the characters he writes on are actual people described in historically documented incidents. *Marshal Sam Clay*, *Ray Bradley—Frontier Scout*, *Gunfighter Gillen*, and *Marshal Sloan of Fort Smith* are some examples.

Strong is good at showing how hardship can create a stronger person. In *Texas Kane*, for instance, Arthur Kane is a young veteran fresh from the Civil War. He fought on the losing side, but is not unduly downcast about it, having other, more positive thoughts uppermost in his mind—to return home to his parents, the girl he is to marry, and the Texas he loves. But during his time away things have altered; his girl is promised to another man, his parents killed, and their ranch burnt to the ground. Kane makes an unlikely alliance with an old wrangler, and they, together with a mongrel dog and a swaybacked cayuse, set about planning retribution.

Frontier Renegade is an admirable book, which many readers will find a different kind of Western. There is only one criticism to be made, and this concerns the mechanics of the story rather than its substance. The author goes to painstaking lengths to disguise the identity of Ford Peterson in the first quarter of the book. Peterson has supposedly been thrown in the Missouri by outlaws, and when he learns that his twin brother is the outlaw's leader and that he, too, is a wanted man, he sets about clearing his name. Strong writes clearly and compactly, not content with a catalogue of subplots, but always keeping his eye on the pattern of the story. In *Frontier Renegade* he also leans towards his other main interest—that of the Canadian frontier. His many Westerns were produced under the Chuck Stanley by-name, while his works on Canada are usually written as Charles S. Strong. Several of these latter works are of interest to those seeking to read of a different wild frontier. *Ranger: Sea Dog of the Royal Mounted*, is the story of the crew of a Candian Royal Mounted police patrol boat, who discover a six-month-old puppy adrift in an Eskimo kayak. They rescue him and in time, after many adventures in the company of teenager Roger, Ranger proves his worth and becomes eligible for training. *Ranger* is no sentimental Lassie production, but an excellent adventure story with an Arctic setting. *South Pole Husky* is better written, and the thrill of ice-bound adventure is altogether memorable. It is a splendid story of both dogs and men, centred on the young Nils Paulsen, and on Amundsen's South Pole expedition in the "Fram".

Strong's characters are normally of a genial nature, with a smile or a nod for passersby, but when they are pushed into a corner they come out fighting. The author allows himself the time for all the elements in his plots to develop naturally, rather than forcing the pace unduly.

Strong is concerned about creating believable characters and letting them tell the story, rather than intrusive narration. To him, while plots are important, it is the characters who provide the solid central core of his novels. Strong is a good "people" writer, whose care for depth of human nature shows in his works. It is unfortunate that his books are infrequently found today, but those that do show up are well worth a closer look. His Westerns written under his other pseudonyms, such as *Prince of Gunfighters*, *Woolly War*, and *Mountain Showdown*, match the tone and pace of his other works. They seem to move along at a brisk pace, never faltering or sentimental, and not given to delving into too much western slang. As a result, they are still eminently readable today.

—Mike Stotter

STRONG, Zachary. *See* **MANN, E.B.**

STUART, Logan. *See* **SAVAGE, Les, Jr.**

STUART, Matt. *See* **HOLMES, L.P.**

SUBLETTE, C(lifford) M(acClellan). American. Born in Charleston, Illinois, 16 August 1887. Educated in schools in Indianapolis; Chicago Art Institute; Academy of Fine Arts, Chicago. Married Mary Shuler in 1913; one daughter. Art critic; worked for New York Central Railroad; journalist and newspaperman; in oil and vegetable businesses in Denver. Recipient: Atlantic Monthly Press prize, 1925. *Died in 1939.*

WESTERN PUBLICATIONS

Novels

The Golden Chimney. Boston, Little Brown, 1931.
Greenhorn's Hunt. Indianapolis, Bobbs Merrill, 1934.
Perilous Journey: A Tale of the Mississippi River and the Natchez Trace, completed by H.H. Kroll. Indianapolis, Bobbs Merrill, 1943; London, Boardman, 1944.

OTHER PUBLICATIONS

Fiction (for children)

The Scarlet Cockerel. Boston, Atlantic Monthly Press, 1925; London, Hodder and Stoughton, 1926.
The Bright Face of Danger. Boston, Little Brown, 1926; London, Hodder and Stoughton, 1927.

* * *

C.M. Sublette began writing relatively late, and he wrote only a small number of novels. His first novel, written for his young daughter, won a fiction prize in 1925 offered by the Atlantic Monthly Press for the best story in the manner of Charles Hawes. His entry, *The Scarlet Cockerel*, was an adventure story set in 16th-century France and America. It concerns a refugee from France at the time of the Huguenot colonization of the Carolinas and his many adventures with friendly Indians and unfriendly Spaniards in America. It is a hearty tale about a period of early America popular with Americans. Critics praised it for its freshness, dash, and colour. *The Bright Face of Danger*, also written for children, was set in Virginia during Bacon's Rebellion of 1676. Closely based on real events, the young hero has to deal with intrigue amongst the settlers as well as Indian and Negro trouble in the colony during a colourful period of Virginia history.

With *The Golden Chimney*, Sublette seems to have got into his stride as a writer. Set in Colorado, the novel concerns a rich silver mine and the success and eventual downfall of the man who owned it. An intimate knowledge of mining techniques and local topography is apparent in the book but, along with the realistic flavor, it also has a mildly romantic plot. With *Greenhorn's Hunt*, Sublette stayed in the states west of the Mississippi River with a hero who braves danger collecting furs in the mountains for the Missouri Fur Company. This adventure tale of early western times was well received as striking the right balance between daring action and good writing. The novel was planned as the first book of a trilogy, but the others were never completed. In *Perilous Journey* (finished by H.H. Kroll and published posthumously, Sublette's research into travellers' narratives of the early American frontier helped produce a convincing story about a journey down the Mississippi in 1821.

Sublette's style and his eye for historical detail improved with experience. His handling of local colour and adventure was tempered by an attractive style of writing that was clear, carefully written, and leisurely.

—P.R. Meldrum

SUCKOW, Ruth. American. Born in Hawarden, Iowa, 6 August 1892. Educated at Grinnell College, Iowa, 1910–13; Curry Dramatic School, Boston, 1914–15; University of Denver, 1915–18, B.A. 1917, M.A. 1918. Married Ferner Nuhn in 1929. Editorial assistant, *The Midland*, Iowa City, 1921–22; owner and manager, Orchard Apiary, Earlville, Iowa, 1920's; spent winters in New York, 1924–34; lived in Cedar Falls, Iowa, 1934–52, and Claremont, California, from 1952. M.A.: Grinnell College, 1931. *Died 23 January 1960.*

WESTERN PUBLICATIONS

Novels

Country People. New York, Knopf, 1924; London, Cape, 1926.
The Odyssey of a Nice Girl. New York, Knopf, 1925; London, Cape, 1926.
The Bonney Family. New York, Knopf, and London, Cape, 1928.
Cora. New York and London, Knopf, 1929.
The Kramer Girls. New York, Knopf, 1930.
The Folks. New York, Farrar and Rinehart, 1934.
New Hope. New York, Farrar and Rinehart, 1942.
The John Wood Case. New York, Viking, 1959.

Short Stories

Iowa Interiors. New York, Knopf, 1927; as *People and Houses*, London, Cape, 1927.
Children and Older People. New York, Knopf, 1931.
Carry-Over (includes *Country People*, *The Bonney Family*, and 16 stories). New York, Farrar and Rinehart, 1936.
Some Others and Myself: Seven Stories and a Memoir. New York, Rinehart, 1952.

OTHER PUBLICATIONS

Other

A Memoir. New York, Rinehart, 1952.
Modern Figures of Destiny: D.H. Lawrence and Frieda Lawrence. Fayetteville, University of Arkansas Press, 1970.

*

Manuscript Collections: University of Iowa, Iowa City; Earlville Public Library, Earlville, Iowa.

Critical Studies: *Ruth Suckow* by Leedice McAnelly Kissane, New York, Twayne, 1969; *Ruth Suckow: A Critical Study of Her Fiction* by Margaret Stewart Ormcanin, Philadelphia, Dorrance, 1972; *Ruth Suckow* by Abigail Ann Hamblen, Boise, Idaho, Boise State University, 1978.

* * *

Ruth Suckow immerses the reader in the landscape and the lives of early 20th-century farms and small towns in Iowa. Her prose carefully captures details of speech, daily life, and the environment. In *Country People*, the picnic ground grows green for the reader: "It was sprinkled with wild gooseberry bushes, bitter-smelling white yarrow, clumps of catnip filled with black-bodied wild bees. The creek was dry, a narrow stream bed filled with hot white sand."

Suckow's character descriptions are equally specific. Her readers come to know how these people dressed, how they wore their hair, where the tan line fell across a man's forehead. As readers gradually acquaint themselves with the intimate lives of these characters, the seeming tranquility of rural living dissolves. Beyond the literary resonance her detailed descriptions provide, her works are important for their historical realism.

Country People is a particularly interesting novel as a microcosm of rural Iowa. In about 200 pages, Suckow presents a family sage, beginning with German immigrants. English is not spoken; women don't sit at the same table as the men. By the end of the book, third- and fourth-generation people speak no German. Daughters have begun to run their own lives and move to the city to attend business college. Suckow even depicts the family reaction to war and the "change" in young men who must fight.

Change and movement are an intrinsic part of the era: people move off the farms, into town, back east, and even out west. Suckow doesn't, however, present the concept of leaving the land as always a healthy shift. Towns and cities represent a loss of innocence, a loss of family ties, a loss of inner satisfaction. Role-playing becomes increasingly predominant. Often characters away from the land become physically weak or ill, particularly farmers who retire into town.

In *Iowa Interiors*, several short stories depict town people inflicting their wills on others. In "Wanderers," townspeople throw out an old minister and his wife because they support a church member who is disliked by the powerful townspeople. In "Renters," town people display their power over the renters by treating them like servants, then by throwing them off the land once it is improved. It is also in town where role playing can be most devastating. A powerful story, "The Man of The Family" from *A Ruth Suckow Omnibus*, chills the reader. A widowed mother casts her little boy in the role of "man of the family." The boy accepts the role and the burden. He gives up activities with friends and settles into imitating his father: work, home to supper, sitting on the porch and having the final word on activities at home. When a man comes to call on his mother, the boy turns the man away:

> If his mother couldn't take care of herself, he'd do it for her. He was the man of the house now . . . She stood in the doorway looking at Gerald. The back of his red head was like his father's. So was the set of his sturdy shoulders. She looked at them with an unwilling respect that turned slowly to resentment . . . She turned . . . went back into the hot darkness of the empty house, and sat down there alone.

Suckow continually portrays role-playing, for men or women, as a game which everyone loses.

In town, innocence is often illusion. Suckow's last novel, *The John Wood Case*, focuses on that theme. The ideal young man in the ideal family in the lovely town must face the realization that his father has embezzled money. "Leading citizens" join in a cover-up to protect the church, the delicate wife, and their own idealism. The short story "What Have I?" from *A Ruth Suckow Omnibus* portrays a matron who has discovered that her position in town is based on the not-quite ethical business practices of her husband. Eventually she finds it difficult to even talk to the woman she hires to work in her home.

Town life can prove as debilitating for women as for men. In the short story, "The Little Girl From Town," the farm family is impressed with the beauty of the little girl, "as if . . . looking at a big doll in a store window." She is delicate, lovely to look at, and distant from life. She knows nothing of the animals or the land.

Some of Suckow's characters find satisfaction only by recognizing a tie to the land, even if they are a generation removed. In *The Odyssey of A Nice Girl* Marjorie grows up in town, unlike her parents who were raised on a farm. Her childhood dreams are of castles; later she imagines mysterious and sophisticated poets or artists. She manages to fight her way to Boston to go to school, convinced that eventually she will live her dreams. Eventually she is almost ready to give in to an unsatisfying life when impulse takes her on another search, this time west to Colorado. Ironically she settles with a fruit farmer in western Colorado, thereby taking a step back to the land.

In Suckow's long novel, *The Folks*, Carl is losing his marriage, his career, his happiness to a never-ending quest for something he can't identify. It isn't until he visits the old farmhouse that he begins to find some peace:

> He felt the wet heat of sweat . . . The sensual joy of life was all around him and yet he was apart from it . . . He was homesick for the summer heat of the hayfield—for hard, natural things, the ring of the axe in the woods on a smoky winter day, his old task of driving the big horses in from the field, even the stream of yellow animal urine beating down into the trampled muddy ground around the tank and sending up its sensual ammonia smell . . . He was jealous, like all people with a country background, of wholly urban experience for his children, of the thing that they would always have lost, not knowing they had lost it.

Carl is not able to return to the land, but in his visit to the farm he is able to return to himself.

In spite of persistent themes within a specific environment, Suckow's characters all develop strikingly different personalities. She handles equally well the perspectives of old age, childhood, male and female characters. Her prose is detailed and precise and carries the story smoothly.

Suckow's rare humor appears primarily in her short stories. *A Ruth Suckow Omnibus* presents an excellent selection of her short fiction.

Prolific and talented, Suckow has left us with a collection of work which deserves to be included in every anthology of American authors.

—Marian Blue

SULLIVAN, Reese. *See* **LUTZ, Giles A.**

SUMMERS, D.B. *See* **BARRETT, Geoffrey John.**

SUTTER, Larabie. *See* **SAVAGE, Les, Jr.**

SUTTON, Stack (Maurice Sutton). American. Born at Vero Beach, Florida, 9 February 1927. Educated at the University of Florida, Gainesville, 1948–50, 1961–64, B.A., M.Ed. Served in the United States Marine Corps, 1944–47; United States Marine Corps Reserve, 1950–52; United States Border Patrol, 1952–59. Married Kay W. Sutton in 1972: one daughter and three sons. Worked at various jobs including usher, bellhop, hotel desk clerk, life guard, and caddy. Freelance writer, 1959–61. Since 1964 College Professor, Polk Community College, Winter Haven, Florida. Address: 1225 Tangerine Parkway, Winter Haven, Florida 33881, U.S.A.

WESTERN PUBLICATIONS

Novels

Circle R Range. New York, Arcadia House, 1963.
Tumbleweed. New York, Avalon, 1964.
Leatherwood. N.p., Powell, 1972.
Marshall's Gun. Canoga Park, California, Major, 1978; London, Hale, 1980.
End of the Tracks. New York, Doubleday, 1981; London, Hale, 1982.
Buffalo Ground. London, Hale, 1990.

Uncollected Short Stories

"River Fury," in *Far West* (San Francisco), 1978.

OTHER PUBLICATIONS

Novel

The Last Eight Days. Nashville, Tennessee, Winston Dereck, 1985.

*

Stack Sutton comments:

I write Westerns because I love the classical Western. My heroes have always been the paladins of the West—Randolph Scott, John Wayne, Gary Cooper. I write the mythological Western, the West that never was or ever could be. They are morality plays. I am indebted to Ernest Haycox, Luke Short, and Max Brand, Haycox being my favorite writer. If I have a strong point in writing, it is dialogue; I am weak at narration and description. I write my own way, but always with the hope someone will read the book. If I have added anything to the Western, it is strong women characters—they don't just pour coffee, they play an important role.

I enjoy writing Westerns, and hope my readers finish the books satisfied.

* * *

Stack Sutton has written only a handful of western novels and magazine articles, but his works are well worth seeking out, if only for the strength of his characterizations. His earlier books offer fairly standard plots, but their outcomes are not always so predictable.

He likes to use older, established figures as his main characters, and whatever jobs they occupy are convincingly described. These protagonists always overcome whatever troubles are ailing them or their friends, bringing stability and order back to the town or ranch.

Conflict, is Sutton's main theme, and is explored in *Circle R Range*, perhaps his most predictable work in its range of characters and plotting. The stereotyped female ranch owner, Sara, turns to her jilted lover, Jim Wade, to help save her range. Adhering to the gentleman's Code of the West, he agrees, and is ready to put his life on the line for her, with the hope of winning her hand once again. Sutton's standard view of a lawless frontier, complete with corrupt figure-heads, is an overwhelming anthem which he explores in every one of his books. This is not a fault, but rather a view expressed by many, many writers who were influenced by pulp magazine writing in depicting the "Wild West."

His earlier works concentrate on US Marshal Creed Weatherall, a normally mild-mannered man who frequently finds himself in all sorts of trouble. In *The Marshal's Gun*, Weatherall is set the task of finding the murderer of the preceding two marshals of the small township of Benbow. He encounters antagonism from the townsfolk, and discovers that there are factions in town who want to fight the Civil War all over again, only this time with Weatherall in the middle, determined to uphold the rule of law.

The legend of a lawmen is an oft-used device for writers, who tend to saddle their characters with stereotyped quirks. In this regard, Sutton is no different, but he does allow the novel to create its own pace through the tension Weatherall experiences in being the middle-man. His main concern is that good will always triumph over evil. Accordingly, his antagonists are devious and throughly despicable, and his protagonists upright and, eventually, victorious.

Sutton continues with his marshal character in *End of the Tracks*. In this story, Weatherall believes that it is time to retire from being a marshal. He quits and moves on, and by the time he reaches the tracks of the Central Pacific Railroad he has mentally prepared himself to start a new life. Obviously, it will involve the use of a gun, and he becomes a trouble-shooter. His character is tested once again as he faces mysterious attackers out to destroy the railroad. Sutton's plot is filled with robbery, sabotage, and murder—everything that an action-packed Western required in the 1980's.

Violent confrontations pepper his works, and inevitably his characters die by the gun. But these passages do not appear to be key events within the story, more of a device to satisfy the blood-lust of the reader. Sutton says doesn't enjoy writing narration or description, but he excels in creating a sympathy for his characters, and this is where his strength lies.

His attempts to break away from traditional formulae have not been entirely successful, but in *Buffalo Ground* he further improves on his skilful character portrayals. Two old-timers—one a buffalo hunter, the other a skinner—are set up by an arrogant and self-centered gambler. Blackmailed into stealing buffalo hides from an Indian reservation they are aware of the consequences, and agree only reluctantly, due to their fear of being caged within four walls. On the whole, the four main characters (there's a good-time girl who blows hot and cold by degrees, and who can't be relied on to bring about any catastrophic changes, although she is integral to the plotting) are an odd bunch; sparking off each other at every given opportunity, and running the gamut of emotions, *Buffalo Ground* is a well researched book, its information skilfully imparted, and not thrust down the reader's throat. But it tends to be repetitive, thus losing much of the effect Sutton has so carefully built up.

Although Sutton is a sporadic writer of Westerns, his novels suffer from the routine nature of their plots. His characters are memorable even after the storyline is forgotten. One feels that if he could successfully match ideas to his portrayals, his work would stand head and shoulders above most of his fellow Western writers.

—John L. Wolfe

SWARTHOUT, Glendon (Fred). American. Born in Pinckney, Michigan, 8 April 1918. Educated at the University of Michigan, Ann Arbor, 1935–39, A.B. 1939, A.M. 1946; Michigan State University, East Lansing, 1952–55, Ph.D. 1955. Served in the United States Army Infantry, 1943–45: Sergeant: 2 battle stars. Married Kathryn Blair Vaughn in 1940; one son. Teaching Fellow, University of Michigan, 1946–48; Instructor, University of Maryland, College Park, 1948–51; Associate Professor of English, Michigan State University, 1951–59; Lecturer in English, Arizona State University, Tempe, 1959–62. Recipient: Theatre Guild award, in playwriting, 1947; Hopwood award, 1948; O. Henry award, 1960; National Society of Arts and Letters Gold Medal, 1972; Western Writers of America Spur award, 1975, 1988; Western Heritage Foundation Wrangler award, 1988. Agent: William Morris Agency, 1350 Avenue of the Americas, New York, New York 10019. Address: 4800 N. 68th Street, #115, Scottsdale, Arizona 85251, U.S.A.

WESTERN PUBLICATIONS

Novels

They Came to Cordura. New York, Random House, and London, Heinemann, 1958.
The Cadillac Cowboys. New York, Random House, 1964.
The Eagle and the Iron Cross. New York, New American Library, 1966; London, Heinemann, 1967.
Bless the Beasts and Children. New York, Doubleday, and London, Secker and Warburg, 1970.
The Tin Lizzie Troop. New York, Doubleday, and London, Secker and Warburg, 1972.
The Shootist. New York, Doubleday, and London, Secker and Warburg, 1975.
Skeletons. New York, Doubleday, and London, Secker and Warburg, 1979.
The Old Colts. New York, Fine, and London, Secker and Warburg, 1985.
The Homesman. New York, Weidenfeld and Nicolson, and London, Deutsch, 1988.

Uncollected Short Stories

"Pancho Villa's One-Man War," in *Cosmopolitan* (New York), February 1953.
"A Horse for Mrs. Custer," in *New World Writing 5.* New York, New American Library, 1954.
"A Glass of Blessings," in *Esquire* (New York), January 1959.
"Attack on the Mountain," in *Saturday Evening Post* (Philadelphia), 4 July 1959.
"Going to See George," in *Esquire* (New York), July 1965.
"The Ball Really Carries in the Cactus League Because the Air Is Dry," in *Esquire* (New York), March 1978.

OTHER PUBLICATIONS

Novels

Willow Run. New York, Crowell, 1943.
Where the Boys Are. New York, Random House, and London, Heinemann, 1960.
Welcome to Thebes. New York, Random House, 1962; London, Heinemann, 1963.
Loveland. New York, Doubleday, 1968.
Luck and Pluck. New York, Doubleday, and London, Secker and Warburg, 1973.
The Melodeon. New York, Doubleday, and London, Secker and Warburg, 1977.

Other (for children)

The Ghost and the Magic Saber, with Kathryn Swarthout. New York, Random House, 1963.
Whichaway, with Kathryn Swarthout. New York, Random House, 1966; London, Heinemann, 1967.
The Button Boat, with Kathryn Swarthout. New York, Doubleday, 1969; London, Heinemann, 1971.
TV Thompson, with Kathryn Swarthout. New York, Doubleday, 1972.
Whales to See the, with Kathryn Swarthout. New York, Doubleday, 1975.
Cadbury's Coffin, with Kathryn Swarthout. New York, Doubleday, 1982.

*

Manuscript Collection: Hayden Memorial Library, Arizona State University, Tempe.

* * *

Most of Glendon Swarthout's novels can be strongly recommended. *They Came to Cordura,* his second novel, but his first Western, is one of his best. The setting is the 1916 Mexican border, where troops of Pancho Villa are skirmishing with American soldiers. Major Thorne is responsible for seeing that five of them (plus a refugee woman from an over-run rancho) are taken out of the fighting to Cordura, where the soldiers will be honored as heroes for their valor in battle. In the six days of the hazardous trip, the men prove to be merely men—lustful, vulgar, boastful, querulous, even cowardly. Their battle heroics are shown to be largely self-serving and accidental. The only hero turns out to be the Major, whose courage and ability to lead men have already been questioned by the Army. This novel is exciting and absorbing; it was done small service by the weak film version, despite the central presence of Gary Cooper as the Major.

At the center of *The Eagle and the Iron Cross* are two German soldiers who escape from an Arizona prisoner-of-war camp in 1945. Although they cast their lot with Indians, their experience in an alien, forbidding world leads them ultimately to their deaths. Some readers may react negatively to the grim violence and sickening brutality of the novel, but these elements are balanced by the even-handed treatment of story, character, and theme.

Bless the Beasts and Children also involves an escape, this one from an exclusive summer camp in northern Arizona. Six young boys from varied, but moneyed, backgrounds have recently witnessed the first day of a buffalo kill, undertaken to thin the herd. Their concern for the animals still to be shot leads them to a forbidden night-time trek to set the buffalo free. Banded together in the first place because they are the goof-offs, the weak sisters, the ostracized of the camp, the six youngsters are, with this gesture of freedom, striking back at the society which has rejected them. In the process, they demonstrate individual courage, ingenuity, and sensitivity. Swarthout's theme is mature, his characterization is credible, and the narrative suspense is gripping.

Both *The Cadillac Cowboys* and *The Tin Lizzie Troop* are lesser efforts than the novels already mentioned. The first, set mostly in Scottsdale, Arizona, entangles an eastern protagonist in mock-adventures with a western cattle-buyer who has delusions of grandeur. The latter novel attempts to recapture the milieu so well rendered in *They Came to Cordura.* Here, however, the characters seem flat, and there is an uneasy blend of comedy and tragedy. *Skeletons* is a good, if unnecessarily complicated, mystery-thriller involving both past and present in a small New Mexico town.

The Shootist takes place in 1901 in El Paso. J.B. Brooks, an old gunman dying of cancer, prefers to choose both the time and the mode of his death. He expires in a bloody saloon gunfight, but not before his character, as well as that of his landlady, have been made both sympathetic and believable. *The Shootist* was the perfect vehicle for the last movie of John Wayne, assisted by a strong supporting cast.

Two elderly gunmen hold center stage in *The Old Colts.* What is more, Swarthout proves it is possible to revitalize the stories of Wyatt Earp and Bat Masterson. The ambiguity of the title, referring both to the ancient weapons the ex-lawmen employ and to the spectacle of two legends in their sixties cavorting like frisky young horses, is a pleasant introduction to a successful comedy-Western. The novel has two major settings in the year 1916: first, New York City where Bat, chronically in debt and threatened by bookies, writes sports for the New York *Telegraph.* Wyatt, tired of living off his wife Josie, arrives from California, to accompany Bat through various money-making schemes, all failures. Feeling the Old West owes them a little something, they decide to rob a bank in Dodge City. What happens in the old cowtown is enhanced by easy jokes, pungent satire, and gentle farce, in perfect cohesion.

In *The Homesman,* Swarthout creates his own memorable pair: Mary Lee Cuddy, a spinster homesteader in Nebraska Territory, and a claim jumper and Army deserter named Briggs. For very different reasons, this unlikely duo tackle the job of returning to eastern civilization four insane women, wives of homesteaders. The perils of the weird journey bring out the doggedness and the genuine humanity of the main characters. It is a powerful tragedy with a satisfying conclusion. A Book-of-the-Month Club selection, *The Homesman* is also a classic. Taken all in all, Swarthout is a fine craftsman of western novels.

—Robert J. Barnes

T

TAYLOR, Robert Lewis. American. Born in Carbondale, Illinois, 24 September 1912. Educated at Southern Illinois University, Carbondale, 1929; University of Illinois, Urbana, 1930–33, B.A. 1933. Served in the United States Navy, 1942–46: Lieutenant Commander. Married Judith Martin in 1945; one son and one daughter. Reporter, Carbondale, 1934; correspondent in the South Seas for *American Boy* magazine, 1935; reporter, St. Louis *Post-Dispatch*, 1936–39; profile writer, *New Yorker*, 1939–48. Recipient: Sigma Delta Chi award, for reporting, 1939; Pulitzer prize, 1959. Address: c/o Putman Berkley Group, 200 Madison Avenue, New York, New York 10016, U.S.A.

WESTERN PUBLICATIONS

Novels

The Travels of Jaimie McPheeters. New York, Doubleday, 1958; London, Macdonald, 1959.
A Journey to Matecumbe. New York, McGraw Hill, and London, Hutchinson, 1961; as *Treasure of Matecumbe*, New York, Pocket, 1976.
Two Roads to Guadalupé. New York, Doubleday, 1964; London, Deutsch, 1965.
A Roaring in the Wind, Being a History of Alder Gulch, Montana, in Its Great and Shameful Days. New York, Putnam, 1978.

OTHER PUBLICATIONS

Novels

Adrift in a Boneyard. New York, Doubleday, 1947.
Professor Fodorski: A Politico-Sporting Romance. New York, Doubleday, 1950.
The Bright Sands. New York, Doubleday, and London, Deutsch, 1954.
Niagara. New York, Putnam, 1980.
The Lost Sister. Chapel Hill, North Carolina, Algonquin, 1989.

Plays

Musical Plays: *All American* (based on his novel *Professor Fodorski*), 1961; *W.C.* (based on his book *W.C. Fields: His Follies and Fortunes*), 1971.

Screenplay: *The Silken Affair*, with John McCarton, 1956.

Television Play: *The Travels of Jaimie McPheeters* series, 1960.

Other

Doctor, Lawyer, Merchant, Chief. New York, Doubleday, 1948.
W.C. Fields: His Follies and Fortunes. New York, Doubleday, 1949; London, Cassell, 1950.
The Running Pianist. New York, Doubleday, 1950.
Winston Churchill: An Informal Study of Greatness. New York, Doubleday, 1952; as *The Amazing Mr. Churchill*, New York, McGraw Hill, 1962.
Center Ring: The People of the Circus. New York, Doubleday, 1956.
Vessel of Wrath: The Life and Times of Carry Nation. New York, New American Library, 1966.

* * *

After graduation from the University of Illinois, Robert Lewis Taylor worked for a year as a newspaper reporter in Carbondale, Illinois. He then spent more than a year traveling in Europe and in the South Pacific, returning to the United States in 1936. For the next three years he worked as a reporter on the St. Louis *Post-Dispatch*, leaving to become a staff writer with *The New Yorker*. He served in the Navy during World War II, and was discharged with rank of Lieutenant Commander. In addition to several dozen "Reporter-at-Large" and "Profile" pieces for *The New Yorker*, he wrote for the *Saturday Evening Post*, *Collier's*, *Life*, *Esquire*, *Redbook*, and other magazines.

His first book was *Adrift in a Boneyard*, a satirical novel of the adventures of a small band of survivors after a Great Storm has wiped out most of the world's population. A second novel, *Professor Fodorski*, subtitled "a politico-sporting romance," was the basis for an unsuccessful attempt at a musical play. *The Bright Sands*, his third novel, follows the activities of a weird and wonderful band of misfits through a summer on Cape Cod. The best of Taylor's prose sketches for *The New Yorker* were collected in two volumes, *Doctor, Lawyer, Merchant, Chief* and *The Running Pianist*. He has also written three highly regarded full-length biographies.

The book for which Taylor is best known, and for which he won the Pulitzer prize for fiction in 1959, is *The Travels of Jaimie McPheeters*. This is one of the enduring classics of western Americana: young Jaimie's narrative of his journey from Independence, Missouri, across the northern plains and deserts and over the Sierra Nevada range to California during the Gold Rush. Along with his father and a changing band of companions, Jaimie endures Indian attacks, captivity by the Mormons, brushes with outlaws, and finally the poverty of street life in San Francisco. Based on authentic letters and journals, the story is told with warmth and understanding, a clear-sighted lack of sentimentality, and a high, rollicking humor.

A Journey to Matecumbe is not set in the West, but is in the same style of joyous picaresque adventure as *Jaimie McPheeters*. The time is shortly after the Civil War. The narrator is David Burnie, who must flee with his swashbuckling uncle Jim from their home in Illinois down the Mississippi to New Orleans and through the Florida swamps to the Keys, pursued by a choice collection of villians—Ku Klux Klansmen, Indians, spies, and vengeful madmen.

In *Two Roads to Guadelupé* the Shelby brothers—14-year-old Sam and his older half-brother Blaine—join Col. Alexander Doniphan's Missouri Militia during the Mexican War of 1846. Their joint narrative is a series of epic misadventures with a wonderfully feckless, untidy army and its scores of camp-following "laundresses," leading up to an underplayed but stunning climax.

Taylor's most recent foray into western Americana is *A Roaring in the Wind*, "Being a History of Alder Gulch, Montana, in its great and shameful days," as seen through the eyes of Ross Mickerson, expelled from Harvard College in 1857 and seeking adventure in broader fields.

Taylor's novels of the West are based on meticulous research. Each has an Afterword and bibliography which tie the book firmly to historical sources. But out of authentic history the author carves sheer entertainment, filled with honest drama and with a humor reminiscent of Twain and Bret Harte. His books are compulsively readable, and re-readable.

—R.E. Briney

TEMPLE, Dan. *See* **NEWTON, D.B.**

TERRY, William. *See* **GILMAN, George G.**

TETLOW, L.D. Address: c/o Robert Hale Ltd., Clerkenwell House, 45–47 Clerkenwell Green, London EC1R 0HT, England.

WESTERN PUBLICATIONS

Novels (series: Brogan McNally)

The Ghost Riders (Brogan). London, Hale, 1986.
Brogan: Passing Through. London, Hale, 1987.
Brogan's Mexican Stand-Off. London, Hale, 1987.
Luther's Quest. London, Hale, 1988.
Brogan for Sheriff. London, Hale, 1988.
Brogan: Fool's Gold. London, Hale, 1989.
Brogan and the Bull. London, Hale, 1989.
Zeke and the Bounty Hunter. London, Hale, 1990.

* * *

In the main, L.D. Tetlow chronicles the adventures of Brogan McNally, an amiable drifter with a fast right hand and a talent for trouble. McNally—a burly six-footer originally from Seattle—speaks in a broad, largely uneducated fashion, as indeed do most of Tetlow's characters, has opinions on just about everything ("Ain't natural soakin' a body in all that hot soapy water, never know what it can lead to"), is rather immodest ("I guess I can outdraw an' outshoot most men") and sometimes downright insulting ("Lady . . . I like a woman just as much as the next man, but I'm particular. A dose of the pox is somethin' I can live without"). He frequently converses with his horse, occasionally reveals a stubborn or belligerent streak, is surprisingly gregarious for a loner and, by his own admission, is incurably work-shy. One is never quite able to believe in him completely, however, possibly because he tends to sail through each of his adventures in a rather cavalier manner, as if even the deadliest of situations is little more than irritating diversion to be tolerated rather than resolved.

This does not mean that Tetlow's Westerns are especially bad; they're not. But I suspect that reader enjoyment would be considerably heightened if his hero were not quite so boorish.

Brogan's first appearance, in 1986's *The Ghost Riders*, is probably his best. When heavy rains cause a young New Yorker named Greenberg to stop over in the sleepy little town of Pine Ridge, Arizona, the locals soon begin to speculate on the contents of the three boxes he guards to jealously. So valuable does his mysterious cargo appear to be, in fact, that the very next morning a gang known as the Ghost Riders turn up to steal the boxes from the vault of the local bank, where Greenberg had placed them for safekeeping.

It is purely by chance that Brogan, who is camped not far away, happens to see two gang-members hide their loot in a cave, and upon meeting Greenberg some hours later and learning of the robbery, he promptly offers to help the New Yorker retrieve his property. The Ghost Riders have no intention of losing out on the proceeds of their latest theft, however, and before long Brogan and Greenberg find themselves being pursued. The remainder of the book recounts Brogan's attempts to get the Easterner and his curious boxes safely to their destination, where their surprising contents are finally revealed.

Brogan: Passing Through sets the tone for Brogan's subsequent adventures. Befriending a widow named Cora Wiesnesky, Tetlow's straight-talking protagonist soon finds himself becoming increasingly involved in the woman's problems. Because she owns practically the only decent source of water for 30 miles around (and her land might just hold a fortune in gold) Cora's enemy, Phil Edmund, has made repeated attempts to buy it. Although she has so far refused to sell on principle, Cora suspects that Edmund will resort to more underhand methods before too long, and in that she is right. Fortunately, however, Brogan (together with a shell-shocked old soldier called "Last Post," who is probably the best-drawn character in the book) is on hand to thwart all of Edmund's subsequent attempts to seize the land.

Brogan's Mexican Stand-Off is little more than a rerun of the previous book. Yet again Brogan gets involved in the problems of a third party when he happens upon, and foils, the attempted rape of a Mexican girl and the general harassment of the Mexican men with her. Before long he learns that this is just one more attempt to scare the Mexicans into selling their land to the local big-wheel Nathaniel Coleman, who wants it for its considerable lead deposits. Inevitably Brogan sides with the underdogs, locks horns with Coleman and his men and gradually engineers a competently choreographed climax.

Although Tetlow tends to pit Brogan against rather standard, "textbook"-type villains who are rotten to the core, his plots occasionally show great promise, as in *Brogan: Fool's Gold*, where Brogan leads a group of nuns across the desert, or *Brogan and the Bull*, in which he locks horns with an outlaw called El Torro in order to rescue a young boy's abducted mother.

Generally, Tetlow's unconnected Westerns make for a more satisfying read, and the first of these, *Luther's Quest*, is a good example of just how well the author *can* handle the form. As with another single Western, *Zeke and the Bounty Hunter*, *Luther's Quest* is a revenge story in which the principal character sets out to get even with the men who killed his family. In this case, however, the hero is a black horse-breaker named Luther Marsh, who has fought long and hard to achieve acceptance in his predominantly white community. All prospect of a settled future is wiped out in one evening, however, when four hardcases (who are rather thoughtfully introduced at some length by their leader) ride in to terrorize, then kill Luther, his wife, son and daughter. Luther survives the attack, though, and in the best Western tradition, takes up his shotgun (the only weapon with which his hands, rendered almost useless during the attempt to kill him, can get to grips) and gradually tracks them down.

Though a little hackneyed, *Luther's Quest* does show Tetlow's ability to create and sustain believeable characters in a frequently tense but ultimately well-resolved story, the pace of which appears to be much more controlled than the sometimes helter-skelter tempo of the Brogan novels. Indeed, it is quite possible that the author's strength lies more in the one-off Western, and it is this side of his work in the genre that, in future, will bear the closest watching.

—David Whitehead

THOM, James Alexander. American. Born in Gosport, Indiana, 28 May 1933. Educated at Butler University, Indianapolis, Indiana, B.A. 1961. Served in the United States Marine Corps, 1953–56: Sergeant, Korean Service Medal. Married 1) Cody Sweet in 1975 (divorced 1980); 2) Claudia Dark Rain in 1990. Business editor, and columnist, Indianapolis *Star*, 1961–67; communications director, Insurance Institute of Indiana, 1971–73; Lecturer at Indiana University, Indianapolis, Indiana, 1977–81. Since 1967 editor, Saturday Evening Post Company, Indianapolis. Recipient: Western Writers of America Golden Spur award, 1989. Agent: International Creative Management, 40 West 57th Street, New York, New York 10019. Address: 10061 West Stogsdill Road, Bloomington, Indiana 47404, U.S.A.

WESTERN PUBLICATIONS

Novels

From Sea to Shining Sea. New York, Ballantine, 1984.
Panther in the Sky. New York, Ballantine, 1989.

OTHER PUBLICATIONS

Novels

Spectator Sport. New York, Avon, 1978.
Long Knife. New York, Avon, 1979.
Follow the River. New York, Ballantine, 1981.
Staying Out of Hell. New York, Ballantine, 1985.

*

James Alexander Thom comments:

Since my historical novels are about real people and real events, I spend an average of three years on research for each one. This includes not only archival research, but such field research as mastering period tools and weapons, following the routes of explorers, recreating battle plans, etc. No historical narrative takes place in a vacuum, so I seek to recreate the milieux in which these events took place, as well as the personalities of the characters—everything from their religious ceremonies and political beliefs to their economics and agriculture, medical practices and social customs.

* * *

After serving his time as a reporter, columnist, then senior editor, James Alexander Thom became a full-time, freelance writer. His works have appeared in *Reader's Digest*, *National Geographic*, and the Washington *Post*. His historical novels are noted for their accuracy, and are widely used in American high schools and college history and English courses.

Nobody matches Thom's skill for describing the great figures of early American history. His sympathies lie with those men and women, trying against all odds to find recognition through their ambitions and achievements. In his view, the Clark family has no equal for tenacity and capability. "I can't think of a single family in American history with such a history to it," he says.

He documented George Rogers Clark's efforts in *Long Knife*. This is an unforgettable story of a man's rise to power in the young revolutionary government, and his successful attempts in claiming the northwest territory between the Ohio and Mississippi rivers. With only a tiny army battling through winter to march from Kaskaskia to Vincennes, Clark won a resounding victory over the British. Thom's portrayal of this audacious, vigorous, and opinionated man reveals a rare ability to create atmosphere and pace from its opening sentences. This book is very readable and remarkably convincing. The colloquial style in which Thom writes conveys the rapidity and freedom of his source very well. He tells the story with feeling, judgement and taste.

His writings are based on facts, and he decries those authors who fictionalize incidents for commercial ends. Instead, he relies on actual accounts taken from Clark's own letters, and reports to those close to him. Thus, Thom is able to remain in touch with his character, and even when he has to re-create letters between Clark and Teresa de Leyba, they ring true. What this novel also captures is the sad fact that George Rogers Clark never lived to gain the reward for his tireless work for an ungrateful government. He died debt-ridden, disillusioned, and a drunkard. A bitter-sweet ending for such a commendable hero, while both English and Americans are shown as villains.

Follow the River is a powerful story of the endurance of a Virginian settler named Mary Ingles, who was captured by the Indians, and escaped to return home after a perilous 600-mile journey along the Ohio River in the company of an old Dutch woman. Whereas *Long Knife* had a large cast of characters to draw on, *Follow the River* deals with just two women traveling through the wilderness. Here, Thom reflects that to get the flavour and feeling of these characters, and their achievement he walked part of that route. He concluded that what would have frightened, intimidated and blocked Mary Ingles would have a similar effect on himself. This book presents women in a situation where they are shown to be equal, if not superior, to men, an idea that appeals to Thom. To give full scope and justice to this wonderful book is impossible. Based on what factual records exist, it must stand as the definitive work on its subject.

In *From Sea to Shining Sea*, the Clarks of Virginia are once again the subject for inspection. This time, Thom not only includes George Rogers Clark, but also his brothers and sisters, although the main interest lies in George and his younger brother, William. While George forges a career capturing British-held land, William joins forces with Meriwether Lewis and his expedition, to follow the uncharted Missouri River to its source in the Pacific. Thom successfully incorporates the remainder of the 10-strong family and their exploits—the sieges of Charles Town, Valley Forge, and Brandywine—all crucial events in the development of the country. He is most effective in his portrayal of Sacajawea, the young Shoshoni guide with Lewis and Clark, even to the extent of William's affections towards her.

Thom has the ability to bring people, events, and the country to life. His uncanny ear for dialogue aids the development of his characters from merely being names in a history book to living human beings, with all their complexities and failings. Having lived and travelled the land of which he writes, Thom can easily describe the way the sun touches the leaves in the trees at any point in the day, how the wind plays with the grass-tops, the smell of buffalo chips, and the heat and dust.

While writing *Follow the River*, Thom was drawn towards the challenge of writing on the frontier conflict, as seen from the Indian point of view. *Panther in the Sky* was the result, and led him to say, "I had never thought of myself as a 'Western Writer' until the Western Writers of America gave me their Spur Award. But as I remarked in my acceptance, the treatment of the Indians east of the Mississippi did create the conflicts that were finished in the far West, so *Panther* was in that sense pertinent to Western writing."

As with all of his novels to date, it is not a simple retelling of events. The story attempts to capture the spiritual movement of the Shawnee Indians through their leader, Tecumseh—the "Panther" of the story. It is he who attempts to unite the Indian nations after the whites break their many treaties, intending to drive his people from their land. Thom had the full co-operation of present day Shawnees, who are pleased with the outcome of the book, believing it to be the first time the story of Tecumseh has been told truthfully.

It is a moving story of a much-maligned race of Indians, seen through the eyes of their leader. Thom's study of Tecumseh is sympathetic in its insight of the man himself. Its exploration of one individual's ideas and spiritual beliefs is central to the unification of the Indian tribes against their oppressors. Together with Thom's powerful story-telling, this exploration is the core of the novel. In addition to its usefulness to the student of American history, it is a timely and thought-provoking condemnation of some contemporary attitudes.

Thom's words are chosen with care; they can make you laugh, and they can make you choke back the tears. He never compromises the truth, and brutalities on both sides are explored but never glamorized. What has turned this author into a bestseller is his magical quality of storytelling. He writes satisfying and engaging books, although his treatment of earlier periods of history is sometimes open to criticism. This fact he dismisses by explaining that he is not interested in writing scholarly works, and would rather see things from a different viewpoint to enhance his story.

—John L. Wolfe

THOMAS, Bruce. *See* **PAINE, Lauran.**

THOMAS, Lee. *See* **FLOREN, Lee.**

THOMASON, John W(illiam), Jr. American. Born in Huntsville, Texas, 28 February 1893. Educated at Southwestern University, Georgetown, Texas, 1909; Sam Houston Normal Institute (now State University), Huntsville, 1910–11; University of Texas, Austin (Honorary Phi Beta Kappa, 1935), 1912–13; Art Students League, New York, 1913–14. Married Leda Bass in 1917; one son. Staff member, Houston *Chronicle*, 1915–16; served in the United States Marine Corps, 1917–44: 2 years of sea duty, 7 years of foreign service, and 18 years of service in the United States; became 2nd Lieutenant, 1917, Lieutenant Colonel, 1937, and Colonel, 1941; member of the Army War College and Navy War College, Washington, D.C., 1938; chief of the American Republic Section, Department of the Navy, Washington, D.C., 1940–43; received Navy Cross, 1918, Silver Star (United States Army), 1918, and Air Medal (United States Army Air Corps). Also artist and illustrator: collections at Huntsville Museum and Library and Marine Corps Museum, Washington, D.C. Literary editor, *American Mercury*, New York, 1936–39. Recipient: O. Henry memorial award, 1930. Litt.D.: Southwestern University, 1938. Destroyer *U.S.S. John W. Thomason* named for him, 1944. *Died 12 March 1944.*

WESTERN PUBLICATIONS

Novel

Gone to Texas. New York, Scribner, 1937.

Short Stories

Lone Star Preacher, Being a Chronicle of the Acts of Praxiteles Swan. New York, Scribner, 1941; as *Texas Rebel*, New York, Berkley, 1961.

OTHER PUBLICATIONS

Short Stories

Red Pants and Other Stories. New York, Scribner, 1927.
Marines and Others. New York, Scribner, 1929.
Salt Winds and Gobi Dust. New York, Scribner, 1934.
—and a Few Marines. New York, Scribner, 1943.

Other

Fix Bayonets! With the U.S. Marine Corps in France, 1917–1918. New York, Scribner, 1926; London, Greenhill, 1989.
Jeb Stuart. New York, Scribner, 1930.
A Thomason Sketchbook: Drawings, edited by Arnold Rosenfeld. Austin, University of Texas Press, 1969.

Editor, *The Adventures of General Marbot, by Himself.* New York, Scribner, 1935.

*

Manuscript Collection: Sam Houston State University, Huntsville, Texas.

Critical Study: *Lone Star Marine: A Biography of the Late Colonel John W. Thomason, Jr., U.S.M.C.* by Roger Willock, Princeton, New Jersey, privately printed, 1961.

* * *

John W. Thomason, Jr., may be called a western writer only by defining the term "Western" in a very generous way. Thomason was born in the last decade of the 19th century in a part of southeast Texas that was steeped in the traditions and way of life of the Old South. And the South and the Civil War are subjects of much of his writing. During most of his 51 years he was a professional military man, an officer in the U.S. Marine Corps. And another large chunk of his work—particularly the formula stories published in the *Saturday Evening Post*—spring from his military experiences around the world.

The only fiction by Thomason that might, with some justification, be called "Western" are *Gone to Texas* and *Lone Star Preacher*. The first of these books, a novel, is a melodramatic tale of a young Army officer who comes to Texas immediately after the Civil War and finds himself soon involved in romance and international intrigue along the U.S.-Mexican border. The second book, *Lone Star Preacher*, is Thomason's best piece of writing. It is a collection of stories about the Reverend Praxiteles Swan, chaplain of Hood's Texas Brigade which fought for the Confederacy in the Civil War. Though the stories are set in Virginia, the central character is propelled by a kind of determined exuberance that makes him seem more western than southern. Perhaps we may call the work a Civil War "Western."

Thomason was a good enough writer to become a protegé of the famed editor of the 1920's and 1930's, Maxwell Perkins. Still, his fiction is not highly thought of today. It seems too sentimental, often too contrived. Perhaps Thomason's greatest artistic talent was an ability to draw. He illustrated all of his books, and reviewers often commented that those drawings were the most charming aspects of the works. *A Thomason Sketchbook*, published posthumously in 1969, collects some excellent samples by a truly gifted visual artist.

—William T. Pilkington

THOMPSON, Buck. *See* **PAINE, Lauran.**

THOMPSON, C(harles) Hall.

WESTERN PUBLICATIONS

Novels

Under the Badge. New York, Dell, 1957; London, Hale, 1958.
A Gun for Billy Reo. London, Hale, 1958.
Montana. London, Hale, 1960.

* * *

Although C. Hall Thompson only produced three Westerns, *A Gun for Billy Reo*, remains his best. The plot does not follow the well trod path of the formulaic Western, but concentrates on the development of its central character, the eponymous Billy Reo. In this young man we have an very impressionable 18-year-old, who has always idolized his older brother, Stuart—that is, until the latter returned from the Civil War a changed man. He is unable to cope with any emotional stress due to his treatment in a prison-of-war camp, and turns to the bottle for comfort, regularly beating his wife in the bargain. Billy is torn between his loyalty to his brother and the unwanted love from his sister-in-law. He discovers that Stuart has lost a section of the ranch as part of a gambling debt. Unable to stop his brother, Billy allows him to face Claiburne, the gambler, while drunk, as a result of which Stuart is gunned down. Then the taunts begin: Billy is goaded for being a spineless kid, unwilling to avenge his brother's death. In an attempt to prove himself, he faces Claiburne. The latter is killed but, much to everyone's surprise, the gambler is unarmed. Now the townsfolk turn against Billy, and he is thrown into utter emotional confusion when Stuart's wife rejects his advances. His one hope is to escape and to prove to all that he is not "just an 18-year-old kid."

The book strikes an equal balance of excitement and sentimentality, though the latter is not allowed to develop out of control. Thompson emerges as a clear-eyed and a keen-minded observer. It is through these differences to the normal run-of-the-mill stories that sets the book on a different level, and one which any discerning reader of the genre can enjoy.

Under the Badge, has a strong narrative, which forces its main character to face a personal dilemma. Deputy Virg Lewis brings in his prisoner, on whom he has pinned his hopes to destroy Lucas Temple and his gang in their iron rule of the town. There are many who stand in Lewis's way, but the closest to him is his wife, who constantly tries to persuade him to give up. The memory of his dead brother hangs around him like a spectre, as he too, was a lawman. Jessie, his wife, brings up the past at every given opportunity, and also uses the fact that she is pregnant. When the prisoner escapes he attacks Jessie, punching her in the stomach, and causes her to abort the child. Lewis kills him, and loses any chance of bringing Temple to justice. He is now ready to turn his back on the town and its people, who are too frightened to face Temple and support its law. Lewis takes up a previous offer made by cattleman John Rambo, and becomes sheriff of Cheyenne. Gradually, he realizes that this move was not offered for the best of motives, and Rambo is more kin to Temple than Lewis would like to admit.

Thompson writes well on personal struggles against insoluble problems. So much so, that these Westerns could be set in any particular time period and still work. The West is a timeless and unspecified area where Thompson's characters delve into self-examination. His only fault in his characterizations is their lack of humour, and their inability to take advice from those close to them. Unfortunately, *Montana* does not live up to the expectation of his previous books, and is a virtual re-working of *A Gun for Billy Reo*, even down to the facts that its central character loves his brother's wife, that his brother is killed by the villains who are running the valley, and that he was once a prisoner-of-war. Jace Highstreet, the protagonist, is a serious character, and one who dreams that the territory is worth fighting for. In this idealistic frame of mind he sets out to take over where his brother left off—in destroying the Pike brothers' grip on the valley.

Thompson is very good at handling his plot, sustaining the pace in a constant struggle through emotional and physical obstacles until the end. Unquestionably, the central character is a moralist, believing that whatever action he takes will be his only true course, and doggedly persists until all wrongs are righted. Violence is kept to a minimum, but when it does appear, it is short and sharp. The dialogue is written with great care, and is very effective in bringing his characters to life. Women, though, are never portrayed as strongly as their influence on their partners might suggest. They tend to be more of the "little lady at home" variety, and when called upon to further the plot they fall short, and are reduced to minor supporting roles. Nevertheless, if Thompson had only written *A Gun for Billy Reo*, it would have been a fine epitaph.

—Mike Stotter

THOMPSON, Gene. *See* **LUTZ, Giles A.**

THOMPSON, Russ. *See* **PAINE, Lauran.**

THOMPSON, Thomas. American. Born in Dixon, California, 24 February 1913. Educated at Visalia High School, California, graduated 1930; Heald Business College, San Francisco, graduated 1933. Married June Kentta in 1935; one daughter. Worked as sailor, nightclub entertainer, secretary, and furniture salesman. Since 1940 freelance writer. Story consultant, *Temple Houston* television series; associate producer, writer, and consultant, *Bonanza* television series, 10 years. Co-founder, and president, 1957 and 1966, Western Writers of America. Recipient: Western Writers of America Spur award, for short story, 1954, 1955; Levi Strauss Golden Saddleman award, 1971. Agent: Brandt and Brandt, 1501 Broadway, New York, New York 10036. Address: 207 Third Street, Newbury Park, California 91320, U.S.A.

WESTERN PUBLICATIONS

Novels

Range Drifter. New York, Doubleday, 1949; London, Hodder and Stoughton, 1950.
Broken Valley. New York, Doubleday, 1949; London, Hodder and Stoughton, 1951.
Sundown Riders. New York, Doubleday, 1950; London, Hodder and Stoughton, 1952.
Gunman Brand. New York, Doubleday, 1951; London, Hodder and Stoughton, 1952.
Shadow of the Butte. New York, Doubleday, 1952; London, Hodder and Stoughton, 1953.
The Steel Web. New York, Doubleday, 1953; London, Hodder and Stoughton, 1954.
King of Abilene. New York, Ballantine, 1953; London, Hodder and Stoughton, 1956.
Trouble Rider. New York, Ballantine, 1954; London, Hodder and Stoughton, 1956.
Forbidden Valley. New York, Popular Library, 1955; London, Hodder and Stoughton, 1957.
Born to Gunsmoke. New York, Popular Library, 1956.
Rawhide Rider. New York, Popular Library, 1957; as *Gun of the Stranger*, London, Ward Lock, 1960.
Brand of a Man. New York, Doubleday, 1958; London, Ward Lock, 1959.
Bitter Water. New York, Doubleday, and London, Ward Lock, 1960.
Bonanza: One Man with Courage (novelization of television series). New York, Media Books, 1966; London, Corgi, 1967.
Outlaw Valley. New York, Doubleday, 1987; Bath, Chivers, 1988.

Short Stories

They Brought Their Guns. New York, Ballantine, 1954.
Moment of Glory. New York, Doubleday, 1961.

Uncollected Short Stories

"Lynch Mob at Cimarron Crossing," in *Iron Men and Silver Spurs*, edited by Donald Hamilton. New York, Fawcett, 1967.
"The Hexer," in *Great Ghost Stories of the Old West*, edited by Betty Baker. New York, Four Winds Press, 1968.
"The Gunsmoke King Calls Quits," in *A Quintet of Sixes*, edited by Donald A. Wollheim. New York, Ace, 1969.
"Momento," in *With Guidons Flying*, edited by Charles N. Heckelmann. New York, Doubleday, 1970.
"Blood on the Sun," in *The Western Hall of Fame*, edited by Bill Pronzini and Martin H. Greenberg. New York, Morrow, 1984.
"Gun Job," in *The Lawmen*, edited by Bill Pronzini and Martin H. Greenberg. New York, Fawcett, 1984.
"A Wollopin' Good Chew," in *Wild Westerns*, edited by Bill Pronzini and Martin H. Greenberg. New York, Walker, 1986.
"The Silver Dollar," in *The Cattlemen*, edited by Bill Pronzini and Martin H. Greenberg. New York, Fawcett, 1986.
"Killer in Town," in *The Gunfighters*, edited by Bill Pronzini and Martin H. Greenberg. New York, Fawcett, 1987.

OTHER PUBLICATIONS

Plays

Screenplays: *Saddle the Wind*, with Rod Serling, 1958; *Cattle King*, 1963.

Television Plays: scripts for *Wagon Train*, *Restless Gun*, *Rifleman*, *Cimarron City*, *Empire*, *Bonanza*, *Gunsmoke*, and other series, 1957–78.

*

Manuscript Collection: University of Oregon Library, Eugene.

Thomas Thompson comments:

I have always felt that the Western was a true American art form. It is a morality tale, unique to the American dream. I am proud to have had a small part in keeping that dream alive.

* * *

Thomas Thompson has claimed that the Western is a genuine art form "unique to the American dream." His fiction, most of which has appeared in Doubleday's Double D series, brings to the popular Western not only some remarkably effective elements of style and narration but also moral concerns that really are expressions of the American dream.

Much of Thompson's writing resembles that of the hard-boiled detective school, particularly in his brief but exceedingly sharp descriptions of troubled characters. The woman who eventually admits her love for the hero in *The Steel Web* "was lithe and vividly alive and she never pretended. But she was hard. Not cynical or cruel, but hard. She wore a shell of pride around her emotions as if she had been hurt deeply and the wound had never quite healed." In *Bitter Water* the villain of the story, whose villainy is a product of his inability to change with the Texas Panhandle as that region develops from open range to small farms, is placed visually, geographically, and even morally before the reader in a single Thompson sentence: "Clovis was a big man, heavy through the chest and shoulders, and he looked as dirty as if he had not been born of woman but had sprung full grown from the abused earth of the Panhandle."

Thompson's literary range, however, is broad, stretching from a brooding sense of violence, of inexorable conflict, to humor of dialogue and situation. His *Moment of Glory*, a collection of stories written in the 1950's, is not only a fine sample of his work but also an example of the popular Western itself at the top of its form in its own decade of glory. It is hardly surprising that Thompson was not only a novelist but also an associate producer of *Bonanza*.

The morality of Thompson's stories is clear without being oversimplified. *The Steel Web*, for instance, involves a conflict between corrupt railroad officials and an equally corrupt radical. Neither the railroad nor the people it injures are wrong; it is corruption itself that Thompson's story condemns. His fiction always works towards a balance rather than towards the extremes of good and evil. Even the worst of characters have seeds of goodness in them; the germination of those seeds is often prevented, however, by a refusal to understand the views of others. The plaintive question of one character expresses the central message of Thompson's Westerns: "Has it got to the point where a man has to hear himself called a coward just because he tries to understand another man's way of thinking?" The answer is no, of course, and such understanding leads not to cowardice but to heroism.

Outlaw Valley, his most recent western novel, published after an interlude of 20 years, shows Thompson's continuing mastery of the form. His heroine—the self-reliant, recently widowed Opal Sprague—secures a government contract to take a pack of mules over the mountains, for a sale which she hopes will save her threatened ranch. Her decision coincides with the release of her ex-convict cousin, and the arrival of the mysterious drifter Larrabee Stone, both of whom decide to accompany her on the hazardous journey. Will Baker, the hard-bitten marshal in pursuit of Opal's escaped jailbird uncle, also tags along. Thompson assembles an intriguing cast of characters, and displays considerable skill in maintaining the interest of the reader as he pilots them through the dangerous mountain crossing, and into an eventual shootout with the Hoover family—more of Opal's unwanted relatives—in the Outlaw Valley of the title. Adroit dialogue and convincing character portrayal is matched by an assured but never overstressed knowledge of western daily routine, and by a story which unfolds to climax at a well-paced lope. The few criticisms that come to mind—one secondary figure drops out too early, the villains appear slightly late in the day—are minor, and count for little against the book's many virtues. *Outlaw Valley* is a memorable novel and a tribute to its author, who once again brings the Old West alive in its pages.

—William Bloodworth

TIPPETTE, Giles. Also writes as Wilson Young. American. Born in Texas, 25 August 1934. Educated at Sam Houston State University, Huntsville, Texas, B.S. 1959. Served as a pilot in the United States Air Force: 1st Lieutenant. Married 1) Mildred Ann Mebane in 1956 (divorced 1976), two daughters; 2) Betsyanne Wright Pool in 1981. Rodeo contestant, diamond courier, and gold miner in Mexico; then freelance writer. Agent: Owen Laster, William Morris Agency, 1350 Avenue of the Americans, New York, New York 10019, U.S.A.

WESTERN PUBLICATIONS

Novels (series: Justa Williams; Wilson Young)

The Bank Robber. New York, Macmillan, 1970; as *The Spikes Gang*, New York, Pocket Books, 1971.
The Trojan Cow. New York, Macmillan, 1971.
Austin Davis (as Wilson Young). New York, Dell, 1975.
The Sunshine Killers (as Wilson Young). New York, Dell, 1975.
Wilson's Gold. New York, Dell, 1980.
Wilson's Luck. New York, Dell, 1980.
Wilson's Choice. New York, Dell, 1981.
Wilson's Revenge. New York, Dell, 1981.
Wilson's Woman. New York, Dell, 1982.
The Texas Bank Robbing Company. New York, Dell, 1982.
Hard Luck Money (Wilson Young). New York, Dell, 1982.
Wilson Young on the Run. New York, Dell, 1983.
Bad News (Justa Williams). New York, Jove, 1989.
Cross Fire (Justa Williams). New York, Jove, 1990.

OTHER PUBLICATIONS

Novels

The Survivalist. New York, Macmillan, 1975.
The Mercenaries. New York, Delacorte Press, 1976; London, Sphere, 1977.
China Blue. New York, Dell, 1984.

Play

Television Play: *Man of Ice*, 1974.

Other

The Brave Men (on auto racing and rodeo). New York, Macmillan, 1972.
Saturday's Children (on college football). New York, Macmillan, 1973.
Donkey Baseball and Other Sporting Delights. Dallas, Taylor, 1989.

* * *

A life-long Texan, Giles Tippette has a varied and adventuresome background: a university degree in chemistry, a professional rodeo cowboy, a diamond courier, a "venture" pilot, a jewelry designer, a gold-mine operator in Mexico. He has been a full-time freelancer since 1963 and 14 of his 17 novels are Westerns.

"Mark Twain is the only writer I think has had much influence on me," Tippette says. "His influence causes me to write as simply as I can and to never forget that my main job as a writer is to entertain. His influence has also caused me to throw in a touch of humor in some of the most unlikely places."

Wilson Young, protagonist of several of Tippette's novels, is a successful bank robber and gunfighter and is an exemplar of

Tippette's approach to the western novel—have a strong central character and imbue that character with human faults and frailties as well as strengths, so that there is strong reader "identification" with the character. Wilson Young, Tippette explains, "doesn't overwhelm the reader . . . he can manage to foul up some of the simplest situations. . . Young's motto, that he never kicked a cripple, has many times nearly gotten him killed by a cripple with a shotgun taped to his crutch."

Tippette's attraction to the western novel he explains thusly: "Writing western fiction appeals to me because it is set in a time and a place and a mood that allows me to deal with very basic human motives and emotions. In other words, your action is not clouded by the complex issues of modern times. It can all be straightforward and direct. As a man, I very often wish I had lived in that time."

A facile writer whose talents enable him to write western and contemporary adventure novels as well as non-fiction periodical work, Tippette's Westerns are known for their taut characterization, simple but effective language, seemingly effortless but believable dialogue, and strong plots.

Tippette is a serious-minded writer of Westerns: "I think it is the only pure art form that is strictly American and, I hope, along with the efforts of other good western writers, to make the rest of the world take it as seriously as it is intended. We've come a long way from the pulp thrillers and I think we're going a lot further."

—Dale L. Walker

TOLBERT, Frank X(avier, Sr.). American. Born in Amarillo, Texas, 27 July 1912. Educated at Texas Tech University, Lubbock, 1929–33; University of Texas, Austin, 1934. Served in the United States Marine Corps during World War II: editor, 1942 and 1945, and combat correspondent, 1943–44, *The Leatherneck*: Lieutenant; four battle stars. Married Kathleen Hoover in 1943; one son and one daughter. Sports writer, Lubbock *Journal*, 1931–34; sports editor, Amarillo *Globe*, 1935, and Wichita Falls *Daily Times*, Texas, 1936; sports columnist, Fort Worth *Star-Telegram*, Texas, 1936–41; daily columnist, 1947–77, and weekly columnist, 1977–84, Dallas *News*. Chili expert and enthusiast; founded Texas Chili Parlor, Dallas, and helped organise the Terlingua World Chili Cookoff. Did television and radio food commercials for American Home Foods, 1973–84; president, Tolbert's Native Texas Foods, 1976–84. Recipient (for nonfiction): Summerfield Roberts award, 1960; Western Writers of America Spur award, 1960. *Died 9 January 1984.*

Western Publications

Novels

Bigamy Jones. New York, Holt, 1954.
The Staked Plain. New York, Harper, 1958.

Uncollected Short Stories

"Some Changes at Hell-to-Catch," in *Saturday Evening Post* (Philadelphia), 27 October 1945.
"The Horse That Made Rain," in *Collier's* (Springfield, Ohio), 22 February 1947.

Other Publications

Other

Nieman-Marcus: The Story of the Proud Dallas Store. New York, Holt, 1953.
The Day of San Jacinto. New York, McGraw Hill, 1959.
An Informal History of Texas: From Cabeza de Vaca to Temple Houston. New York, Harper, 1961.
Dick Dowling at Sabine Press. New York, McGraw Hill, 1962.
The Story of Lyne Taliaferro (Tol) Barret, Who Drilled Texas' First Oil Well. Dallas, Texas Mid-Continent Oil and Gas Association, 1966.
A Bowl of Red: Being the Natural History of Chili Con Carne. New York, Doubleday, 1966.
Tolbert's Texas. New York, Doubleday, 1983.

*

Critical Study: *Tolbert of Texas: The Man and His Work*, Fort Worth, Texas Christian Press, 1986.

Frank X. Tolbert commented (1982):

In my books on the West I try to use the language I heard as a child from old cowboys, including my grandfather, a Texas Panhandle rancher, and my grand-uncles. One of my relatives was an Oklahoma politician and he had a summer place at Medicine Park, in the middle of the Comanche Indian reservation. As a teenager in the 1920's I knew some very old Indians, including the one-time "hostiles" Hunting Horse and Big Tree. *The Staked Plain* is about the Comanches; it got good reviews in the *New Yorker*, *New York Times*, and other publications around the country, but I was most proud of a review written by a Comanche scholar who said that my writing on the wild Comanches depicted them pretty much as they were.

My best book is probably *The Day of San Jacinto*, a nonfiction work about that battle that separated Texas from Mexico. I did considerable research, particularly in Mexico City, and I found some strange new material. For instance, the Mexican soldiers referred to the Texas revolutionists as "Soldados God Dammes" because they were always cursing, and the leader of the revolt, General Sam Houston, was "General God Damn."

* * *

Frank X. Tolbert is today better remembered for his personality than for his writing. He was a successful and gregarious restauranteur in Dallas, Texas, and was organizer several years ago of the original World Championship Chili Cookoff in Terlingua, Texas. For several decades Tolbert contributed a breezy column on Texas history and Texas places to a Dallas newspaper. Sporadically he composed book-length works on Texas and western history; these are competently and popularly written narrative histories, but no one is likely to call them triumphs of the creative imagination.

Tolbert's most popular work of western fiction is *Bigamy Jones*. The title character of this rollicking tale lives up to his name with a vengeance. As a cowboy Bigamy rides and shoots superbly, is in fact impeccable in every way save one: he cannot resist getting married. He wanders around west Texas with a runty longhorn steer that has a taste for whiskey as fully developed as his master's taste for women. It turns out that Bigamy has been married 30 times—and never divorced. "It's all your fault, ma'am," he tells a prospective bride. "May God forgive you for lookin' so pretty this mornin'." The novel is, of course, a spoof of one of the hoariest of cowboy clichés—the western hero's traditional reticence around women.

Bigamy Jones features a light satirical touch and a fine sense of irony. It also offers a promise of more and better fiction from its author. But except for a novel about the wild Comanches, its author chose not to pursue fiction writing. Nearly three decades after the publication of *Bigamy Jones*, readers may lament that decision. Tolbert, however, found fulfillment and a modicum of fame in areas unrelated to literature.

—William T. Pilkington

TOMPKINS, Walker A(llison). American. Born in Prosser, Washington, 10 July 1909. Educated at Modesto Junior College, California; University of Washington, Seattle; Columbia University, New York; University of California, Berkeley; Oxford University. Served as a correspondent in the United States Army, 1942–45: Staff Sergeant. Married 1) Grace Spear in 1921 (divorced 1965), one son and two daughters; 2) Barbara Hathaway Wachner in 1975. Newspaper reporter, 1927–31; then freelance writer: wrote under house names for Street and Smith, Standard, and Popular magazine chains; columnist, and staff historian, 1966–76, Santa Barbara *News-Press*; staff historian, Santa Barbara Bank and Trust, from 1962; contributing editor, *Santa Barbara Magazine*, from 1975. *Died 1990(?)*.

WESTERN PUBLICATIONS

Novels

The Border Eagle. New York, Phoenix Press, 1939; London, Hutchinson, 1941.
Deadhorse Express. New York, Phoenix Press, 1940.
Wyoming Trail. New York, Phoenix Press, 1940; London, Hutchinson, 1941.
Señor Desperado: A Novel of Early California. London, Hutchinson, 1940.
The Phantom Sheriff. New York, Phoenix Press, 1941.
Thundergust Trail. New York, Phoenix Press, 1942.
The Wyoming Raiders. New York, Phoenix Press, 1942; London, Foulsham, 1943.
Border Bonanza. New York, Phoenix Press, 1943; London, Quality Press, 1945.
Ghost Mine Gold. New York, Modern Library, 1943.
Texas Tumbleweed. New York, Phoenix Press, 1943.
Six-Gun Legacy. London, Wells Gardner, 1943.
Trouble on Funeral Range. New York, Phoenix Press, 1944.
The Scout of Terror Trail. New York, Phoenix Press, 1944.
Texas Guns. London, Wells Gardner, 1945.
Lion of the Lavabeds. New York, Popular Library, 1947.
Flaming Canyon. Philadelphia, Macrae Smith, 1948; London, Ward Lock, 1949.
West of Texas Law. Philadelphia, Macrae Smith, 1948; as *West of the Law*, London, Ward Lock, 1948.
Manhunt West. Philadelphia, Macrae Smith, 1949; London, Ward Lock, 1950.
Rimrock Rider. Philadelphia, Macrae Smith, 1950; London, Ward Lock, 1951.
Border Ambush. Philadelphia, Macrae Smith, 1951; London, Ward Lock, 1952.
Prairie Marshal. Philadelphia, Macrae Smith, 1952; London, Wright and Brown, 1954.
Haunted Corral. London, Consul, 1952.
Pistol Empire. London, Consul, 1952.
Gold on the Hoof. Philadelphia, Macrae Smith, and London, Wright and Brown, 1953.
Guns of Massacre Gap. London, Wright and Brown, 1953.
One Against a Bullet Horde. New York, Ace, 1954.
Texas Renegade. Philadelphia, Macrae Smith, 1954; London, Ward Lock, 1956.
Deadwood. New York, Ace, 1954.

Short Stories

The Paintin' Pistoleer: Humorous Tales of the Old West. New York, Dell, 1949.

Uncollected Short Stories

"The Golden Lizard," in *Wild West Weekly* (New York), 23 January 1932.
"Terror in Snaketail Gorge," in *Wild West Weekly* (New York), 13 February 1932.
"Treasure of Juniper Mesa," in *Wild West Weekly* (New York), 30 April 1932.
"Lynch Law for Latigo," in *Wild West Weekly* (New York), 26 November 1932.
"The Desert Phantom," in *Wild West Weekly* (New York), 27 May 1933.
"Brand of the Phantom," in *Wild West Weekly* (New York), 10 June 1933.
"Phantom Justice," in *Wild West Weekly* (New York), 24 June 1933.
"Ghost Guns of the Phantom," in *Wild West Weekly* (New York), 8 July 1933.
"The Desert Phantom's Luck," in *Wild West Weekly* (New York), 22 July 1933.
"The Desert Phantom's Showdown," in *Wild West Weekly* (New York), 5 August 1933.
"The Sheriff Killer," in *Wild West Weekly* (New York), 9 September 1933.
"The Dynamite Kid," in *Wild West Weekly* (New York), 11 November 1933.
"Dead Man's Dinero," in *Wild West Weekly* (New York), 27 January 1934.
"Terror Trail," in *Wild West Weekly* (New York), 24 February 1934.
"Death Rides Terror Trail," in *Wild West Weekly* (New York), 10 March 1934.
"Terror Trail's Lost Cattle," in *Wild West Weekly* (New York), 24 March 1934.
"Ghost of Terror Trail Castle," in *Wild West Weekly* (New York), 7 April 1934.
"Terror Trail Treasure," in *Wild West Weekly* (New York), 21 April 1934.
"The End of Terror Trail," in *Wild West Weekly* (New York), 5 May 1934.
"Cougar Fang," in *Wild West Weekly* (New York), 16 February 1935.
"Death Trails Cougar Fang," in *Wild West Weekly* (New York), 2 March 1935.
"Torture for Cougar Fang," in *Wild West Weekly* (New York), 30 March 1935.
"Cougar Fang on the Warpath," in *Wild West Weekly* (New York), 13 April 1935.
"Cougar Fang's Show-down," in *Wild West Weekly* (New York), 27 April 1935.
"Skulls in Wrist Canyon," in *Wild West Weekly* (New York), 1 June 1935.

"The Desert Phantom Rides to Deathville," in *Wild West Weekly* (New York), 29 June 1935.
"Deputy Desert Phantom," in *Wild West Weekly* (New York), 6 July 1935.
"Phantom of the Flames," in *Wild West Weekly* (New York), 13 July 1935.
"Foes of the Phantom," in *Wild West Weekly* (New York), 20 July 1935.
"The Phantom's Forty-fives," in *Wild West Weekly* (New York), 27 July 1935.
"The Desert Phantom's Reward," in *Wild West Weekly* (New York), 3 August 1935.
"Guns and Gold Dust," in *Wild West Weekly* (New York), 17 August 1935.
"Bandit's Brand," in *Wild West Weekly* (New York), 21 September 1935.
"Gunman's Ghost," in *Wild West Weekly* (New York), 9 November 1935.
"Deputy Death," in *Wild West Weekly* (New York), 14 December 1935.
"Deputy Death's Night Ride," in *Wild West Weekly* (New York), 21 December 1935.
"A Trap for Deputy Death," in *Wild West Weekly* (New York), 28 December 1935.
"Deputy Death's Gold Strike," in *Wild West Weekly* (New York), 4 January 1936.
"Deputy Death Meets the Comanche Killer," in *Wild West Weekly* (New York), 18 January 1936.
"Tommy Rockford's Bullet Ballet," in *Wild West Weekly* (New York), 8 February 1936.
"Tommy Rockford's Stolen Handcuffs," in *Wild West Weekly* (New York), 14 March 1936.
"Tommy Rockford at Mystery Ranch," in *Wild West Weekly* (New York), 25 April 1936.
"Silver Six-Gun," in *Wild West Weekly* (New York), 2 May 1936.
"Tommy Rockford's Coffin Clew," in *Wild West Weekly* (New York), 18 July 1936.
"Trail of the Lizard," in *Wild West Weekly* (New York), 8 August 1936.
"Gold-Plated Six-Guns," in *Wild West Weekly* (New York), 24 October 1936.
"Texas Triggers," in *Wild West Weekly* (New York), 14 November 1936.
"Wanted, Dead—The Texas Triggers," in *Wild West Weekly* (New York), 21 November 1936.
"Texas Triggers Sling Lead," in *Wild West Weekly* (New York), 28 November 1936.
"Texas Triggers at Mystery Mountain," in *Wild West Weekly* (New York), 5 December 1936.
"Texas Triggers under Arrest," in *Wild West Weekly* (New York), 12 December 1936.
"Texas Triggers Clean Up Coyoteville," in *Wild West Weekly* (New York), 19 December 1936.
"Wanted for Murder—Tommy Rockford," in *Wild West Weekly* (New York), 26 December 1936.
"Bullet-Proof Dinero," in *Wild West Weekly* (New York), 16 January 1937.
"The Canyon of No Return," in *Wild West Weekly* (New York), 30 January 1937.
"Dead Man's Poker Chips," in *Wild West Weekly* (New York), 20 February 1937.
"Tommy Rockford's Suicide Stagecoach," in *Wild West Weekly* (New York), 6 March 1937.
"Tommy Rockford Ropes a Rattlesnake," in *Wild West Weekly* (New York), 27 March 1937.
"Tommy Rockford Trails a Ghost," in *Wild West Weekly* (New York), 22 May 1937.
"Alamo Kimber," in *Wild West Weekly* (New York), 12 June 1937.
"Alamo Kimber's Gold Strike," in *Wild West Weekly* (New York), 19 June 1937.
"A Stacked Deck for Alamo Kimber," in *Wild West Weekly* (New York), 26 June 1937.
"A Trap for Alamo Kimber," in *Wild West Weekly* (New York), 3 July 1937.
"Guilty of Murder—Alamo Kimber," in *Wild West Weekly* (New York), 10 July 1937.
"Alamo Kimber's Trail of Death," in *Wild West Weekly* (New York), 17 July 1937.
"Bait for a Man Trap," in *Wild West Weekly* (New York), 14 August 1937.
"Tommy Rockford Dodges the Gallows," in *Wild West Weekly* (New York), 28 August 1937.
"Golden Handcuffs and Guns," in *Wild West Weekly* (New York), 4 September 1937.
"The Haunted Bunk House," in *Wild West Weekly* (New York), 23 October 1937.
"The Ghost of Tommy Rockford," in *Wild West Weekly* (New York), 20 November 1937.
"Lone Star Buckaroo," in *Wild West Weekly* (New York), 27 November 1937.
"Buckaroo's Mustang Stampede," in *Wild West Weekly* (New York), 4 December 1937.
"Death Corrals the Buckaroo," in *Wild West Weekly* (New York), 11 December 1937.
"Buckaroo Trails a Sheriff," in *Wild West Weekly* (New York), 18 December 1937.
"Buckaroo's Outlaw Boss," in *Wild West Weekly* (New York), 25 December 1937.
"Lone Star Buckaroo's Last Fight," in *Wild West Weekly* (New York), 1 January 1938.
"Tommy Rockford Bucks the Nevada Wolves," in *Wild West Weekly* (New York), 8 January 1938.
"Tommy Rockford Arrests the Border Eagle," with Philip F. Deare, in *Wild West Weekly* (New York), 22 January 1938.
"Tommy Rockford's Owl Hoot Sign," in *Wild West Weekly* (New York), 5 March 1938.
"The Branded Skull," in *Wild West Weekly* (New York), 7 May 1938.
"Phantom Rancho," in *Wild West Weekly* (New York), 21 May 1938.
"Riders of Phantom Rancho," in *Wild West Weekly* (New York), 28 May 1938.
"Phantom Rancho Vengeance," in *Wild West Weekly* (New York), 4 June 1938.
"Phantom Rancho's Rustled Herd," in *Wild West Weekly* (New York), 11 June 1938.
"Bullets from Phantom Rancho," in *Wild West Weekly* (New York), 18 June 1938.
"Phantom Rancho Changes Brands," in *Wild West Weekly* (New York), 25 June 1938.
"Murder on Rainbow Butte," in *Wild West Weekly* (New York), 2 July 1938.
"Boot Hill Brotherhood," in *Wild West Weekly* (New York), 23 July 1938.
"Guns from the Grave," in *Wild West Weekly* (New York), 6 August 1938.
"Phantom Rustlers," in *Wild West Weekly* (New York), 17 September 1938.
"Dead Man's Handcuffs," in *Wild West Weekly* (New York), 8 October 1938.

"The Spider's Hang-Rope Web," in *Wild West Weekly* (New York), 22 October 1938.
"The Arizona Thunderbolt," in *Wild West Weekly* (New York), 5 November 1938.
"Thunderbolt's Trail Drive," in *Wild West Weekly* (New York), 12 November 1938.
"Mortgage Dinero for Thunderbolt," in *Wild West Weekly* (New York), 19 November 1938.
"Thunderbolt Bucks a Syndicate," in *Wild West Weekly* (New York), 26 November 1938.
"The Badge of Thunderbolt," in *Wild West Weekly* (New York), 3 December 1938.
"Thunderbolt Rides the Showdown Trail," in *Wild West Weekly* (New York), 10 December 1938.
"Tombstone Caboose," in *Wild West Weekly* (New York), 17 December 1938.
"The Hoodoo Herd of Mystery River," in *Wild West Weekly* (New York), 31 December 1938.
"Skull Ranch," in *Wild West Weekly* (New York), 28 January 1939.
"Firebrand of the Rio Grande," in *Wild West Weekly* (New York), 11 March 1939.
"Firebrand Leads the Legion," in *Wild West Weekly* (New York), 18 March 1939.
"Firebrand Captures a Sheriff," in *Wild West Weekly* (New York), 25 March 1939.
"Firebrand's Boothill Bounty," in *Wild West Weekly* (New York), 1 April 1939.
"Firebrand Fights the Legion," in *Wild West Weekly* (New York), 8 April 1939.
"Firebrand Wins His Heritage," in *Wild West Weekly* (New York), 15 April 1939.
"Bullion of Death," in *Wild West Weekly* (New York), 3 June 1939.
"Golden Handcuffs Mean Death," in *Wild West Weekly* (New York), 15 July 1939.
"Beef for Fort Bighorn," in *Wild West Weekly* (New York), 7 October 1939.
"Trail of the Iron Horse," in *Wild West Weekly* (New York), 2 December 1939–5 January 1940.
"Boothill Express," in *Wild West Weekly* (New York), 20 April–25 May 1940.
"Badge of Death," in *Wild West Weekly* (New York), 6 July 1940.
"Longhorn Desperado," in *Wild West Weekly* (New York), 21 September 1940.
"Ranger Law for Pecos Raiders," in *Wild West Weekly* (New York), 14 December 1940.
"Gun-Mad Masquerade," with Hal Dunning, in *Wild West Weekly* (New York), 15 March–22 March 1941.
"Gringo Gold," in *Wild West Weekly* (New York), 12 April–26 April 1941.
"The Haunted Saddle," in *Wild West Weekly* (New York), 24 May–7 June 1941.
"Gunhawk's Gamble," in *Wild West Weekly* (New York), 28 June–26 July 1941.
"Boothill on the Border," in *Wild West Weekly* (New York), 2 August 1941.
"Gunpowder Passport," in *Wild West Weekly* (New York), 13 September 1941.
"Fighting Caballero," in *Wild West Weekly* (New York), 4 October 1941.
"Golden Guns," in *Wild West Weekly* (New York), 1 November 1941.
"Renegades of Red Rim," in *Wild West Weekly* (New York), 13 December 1941.
"Phantom Pueblo," in *Wild West Weekly* (New York), 17 January 1942.
"Salty Six-Guns," in *Wild West Weekly* (New York), 21 February 1942.
"Boothill's for Bad Actors," in *Wild West Weekly* (New York), 6 June 1942.
"Buccaneer Bullets," in *Wild West Weekly* (New York), 20 June 1942.
"Hot Lead Legacy," in *Wild West Weekly* (New York), 4 July 1942.
"Lone Star Loot," in *Wild West Weekly* (New York), 8 August 1942.
"Border Buzzard," in *Wild West Weekly* (New York), 26 September 1942.
"Sheriff's Savvy," in *Wild West Weekly* (New York), 10 October 1942.
"Stagecoach to Boothill," in *Wild West Weekly* (New York), 21 November 1942.
"Salt-Water Waddy," in *Wild West Weekly* (New York), 2 January 1943.
"Murder Medico," in *Wild West Weekly* (New York), 6 February 1943.
"The Flaming Phantom," in *Wild West Weekly* (New York), 10 April 1943.
"Death Wears Golden Handcuffs," in *Wild West Weekly* (New York), 5 June 1943.
"Here's Mud in Yore Eye," in *Zane Grey's Western* (New York), July 1947.
"High-Water Doom for Lodeville," in *Thrilling Western* (London), Spring 1948.
"Hell-Bent for Election!," in *Zane Grey's Western* (New York), May 1948.
"The Horseless Head Man," in *Zane Grey's Western* (New York), July 1948.
"Go West, Young Woman!," in *Zane Grey's Western* (New York), September 1948.
"Rain, Rain, Come to Stay!," in *Zane Grey's Western* (New York), November 1948.
"Innocents Abroad in Los Scandalous," in *Zane Grey's Western* (New York), January 1949.
"Cupid Can Be Stupid," in *Zane Grey's Western* (New York), March 1949.
"The Bridegroom Wore Brass," in *Zane Grey's Western* (New York), September 1949.
"Gaunt with the Wind," in *Zane Grey's Western* (New York), March 1950.
"A Sense of Yuma," in *Zane Grey's Western* (New York), August 1950.
"Hoodoo State to Picche," in *Mammoth Western* (Chicago), December 1950.
"Rimfire Derides Again," in *Zane Grey's Western* (New York), February 1951.
"Britannia Waives the Rules," in *Zane Grey's Western* (New York), September 1951.
"Dead Men Tell Tales," in *Zane Grey's Western* (New York), March 1952.
"Sam's Son and Delighted," in *Zane Grey's Western* (New York), June 1952.
"Brand for a Maverick," in *Exciting Western* (London), August 1952.
"Saddle Gun," in *Exciting Western* (London), March 1953.
"Knife, Fork and Sixgun," in *Exciting Western* (London), January 1954.
"Frame-Up in Skunk Holler," in *Exciting Western* (London), April 1954.
"Guns Rule This Town!," in *Western Story* (London), June 1954.

"Winchester Law for Nesters," in *Thrilling Western* (London), September 1954.
"The Denver Dude," in *Thrilling Western* (London), October 1954.
"Last Job for a Lawman," in *Thrilling Western* (London), January 1958.
"Ambush!," in *Thrilling Western* (London), June 1958.

OTHER PUBLICATIONS

Novel

Ozar, The Aztec. London, Gramol, 1935.

Plays

Television Plays: scripts for *The Cisco Kid*, *The Lone Ranger*, *Death Valley Days*, and *Cheyenne* series.

Other

Red-Hot Holsters (for children). Akron, Ohio, Saalfield, 1938.
Roy Rogers and the Ghost of Mystery Rancho (for children). Racine, Wisconsin, Whitman, 1950; London, Adprint, 1953.
SOS at Midnight (for children). Philadelphia, Macrae Smith, 1957.
California Editor, with Thomas M. Storke. Los Angeles, Westernlore, 1958.
CQ Ghost Ship (for children). Philadelphia, Macrae Smith, 1960.
Santa Barbara's Royal Rancho. Berkeley, California, Howell North, 1960.
DX Brings Danger. Philadelphia, Macrae Smith, 1962.
California's Wonderful Corner (for children). Charlotte, North Carolina, McNally and Loftin, 1962.
Santa Barbara Yesterdays. Santa Barbara, California, McNally and Loftin, 1962.
Little Giant of Signal Hill: An Adventure in American Enterprise. Englewood Cliffs, New Jersey, Prentice Hall, 1964.
Fourteen at the Table. Privately printed, 1964.
Goleta: The Good Land. Goleta, California, Goleta Amvets Post 55, 1966.
Old Spanish Santa Barbara, From Cabrillo to Fremont. Santa Barbara, California, McNally and Loftin, 1967.
Historical High Lights of Santa Barbara. Santa Barbara, California, Santa Barbara National Bank, 1970.
Stearns Wharf Centennial. Santa Barbara, California, Stearns Wharf Company, 1972.
Mattel's Tavern: Where Road Met Rail. Santa Barbara, California, Charter House, 1974.
Santa Barbara, Past and and Present. Santa Barbara, California, Tecolote, 1975.
It Happened in Old Santa Barbara. Santa Barbara California, Santa Barbara National Bank, 1976.
Continuing Quest (biography of Dr. W.D. Sansum). Santa Barbara, California, Sansum Medical Research Foundation, 1977.
Santa Barbara Neighborhoods. Santa Barbara, California, Board of Realtors, 12 vols., 1977–79.
When Disaster Strikes. Santa Barbara, California, Santa Barbara County Red Cross, 1981.
Stagecoach Days in Santa Barbara County. Santa Barbara, California, McNally Loftin, 1982.
The Shepherd King (biography of Col. W.W. Hollister). Santa Barbara, California, McNally Loftin, 1982.
Santa Barbara History Makers. Santa Barbara, California, McNally Loftin, 1983.

* * *

"Here's adventure... Here's romance... Here's O. Henry's famous Robin Hood of the Old West, the Cisco Kid!"

If the Rio Kid, "on whom all oppressed could count for aid when the going was rough," seems to be the spittin' image of the "Cisco Kid" (a popular American television series of the 1950's), it is only natural. For Walker A. Tompkins did scripts for that series, as well as for others, including *The Lone Ranger*. And all the vivid life and times of the Old West—action, adventure, romance—depicted in these television programs are present again in Tompkins's Western novels.

The once and future Rio Kid—new Captain Bob Pryer of the U.S. Cavalry—heads for more than danger in *Lion of the Lavabeds*, where—with special orders from President Grant—he reports for duty to Brevet Major Tracy Williard. In dramatic style, Williard explains Pryor's mission: "Your mission sounds simple enough ... but I feel it only fair to warn you that President Grant has dispatched you out here on—a suicide assignment. You will read these orders, memorize them, and then I shall destroy them." "Yuh'll see me next," Pryor confidently promises, "after I've badgered the Lion of the Lavabeds [Medoc Chieftain "Captain Jack"] in his den." And he does, but only after *action* ("That's Darian Fishke yander... fashtest gun draw in Californy.") and *romance* ("The Rio Kid smiled down at the Indian girl ...") and *fame*—declined ("History books ... will give you the lion's share of the credit for ending the Medoc War ...").

Tompkins's experience as scriptwriter for *The Lone Ranger* shows in the tales of another Robin Hood of the Old West, Wayne Morgan, "The Masked Rider," an outlaw "whose wits and guns were pledged to the assistance of downtrodden and oppressed peoples." *Ghost Mine Gold* and others in the exciting "Masked Rider" series might well have been introduced by these (slightly revised) "Lone Ranger" lines:

> A fiery horse with the speed of light, a cloud of dust and a hearty hi-ye Midnight! The Masked Rider! With his faithful Yaqui companion, Blue Hawk, the daring and resourceful masked rider of the plains led the fight for law and order in the early West. Return with us now to those thrilling days of yesteryear: the Masked Rider rides again!

The Tompkins formula (good conquers evil) is plain by page 10—but *how*? That's the question that holds the reader to the end of The End and beyond. For his heroes ride off not into the sunset but into the sunrise. It's a cinch that few who pick up a Walker Tompkins story will ever put it down unfinished. He dispels the miasma of contemporary pulp fiction with welcome drafts of mountain, desert, prairie air.

—Marcia G. Fuchs

TRAVERS, Col. J.M. *See* **RATHBORNE, St. George.**

TRAVERS, Will. *See* **ROWLAND, Donald S.**

TRAVIS, Will. *See* **ALLISON, Clay.**

TRESSIDY, Jim. *See* **NORWOOD, V.G.C.**

TREVATHAN, Robert E(ugene). Also writes as Trev Roberts. American. Born in Detroit, Michigan, 21 February 1925. Educated at Trinity University, San Antonio, Texas, B.A. 1949, 1950–1951; University of Oklahoma, Norman, 1968–1971. Served in the United States Navy, 1943–46, in Alaska, Australia, and invasion of Okinawa; several battle stars. Married Velma Ward Gage in 1974; three sons and four daughters. Ranch and farm worker, Oran, Texas, 1932–43; teacher, Collier's Elementary School, San Antonio, Texas, 1949–51; United States Air Force, teacher at Dependent Children's School, Japan, 1951–52; sales correspondent, International Flour Milling Company, Detroit, Michigan, 1952–54; accounting supervisor, soldiers' deposits, United States Army, Fort Harrison, Indiana, 1954–55; position classifier, 1955–71, and Air Force chief historian, 1971–80, United States Air Force Civilian Personnel Office, Tinker Air Force Base, Oklahoma City, Oklahoma. Address: 7235 Janet, Lot 3, Oklahoma City, Oklahoma 73150, U.S.A.

WESTERN PUBLICATIONS

Novels

Longhorns for Fort Sill. New York, Criterion, 1962.
Badman's Roost. New York, Avon, 1963.
Showdown at Ringold. New York, Avalon, 1968.
Longhorn Gold. New York, Avalon, 1969; as *The Moonstone Bullet*, London, Hale, 1971.
Ballanger. New York, Manor, 1974.
Tracking the Bar-J Gold. New York, Avalon, 1979.
Rawhide Legacy. New York, Avalon, 1983.
Ransom Trail. New York, Avalon, 1984.
Ambush. New York, Avalon, 1984.
Plunder Trail. New York, Avalon, 1985.
Shootout. New York, Avalon, 1985.
Holdup. New York, Avalon, 1986.
Oklahoma Outrider. London, Hale, 1988.
Red River Bullets. London, Hale, 1990.

Novels as Trev Roberts

Dead in the Saddle. New York, Arcadia House, 1959; London, Gresham, 1960.
Stage to Laredo. New York, Arcadia House, 1961; London, Gresham, 1962.
Rawhide Trap. New York, Arcadia House, 1962; London, Hale, 1963.
Comanche Interlude. New York, Arcadia House, 1963.
The Hide Rustlers. New York, Arcadia House, 1967.
Cannon River. New York, Arcadia House, 1967.
Desert Campfires. New York, Arcadia House, 1967; as *Desert Flame*, London, Hale, 1970.

Uncollected Short Stories

"Last Crooked Mile," in *Texas Rangers*, 1956.
"A Practical Weapon," in *Texas Rangers*, 1957.
"Short Tally," in *Ranch Romances*, 1957.
"The Way of the Desert," in *Climax Magazine*, 1958.

*

Manuscript Collection: University of Wyoming, Laramie.

Robert E. Trevathan comments:

When I first began writing stories—30-odd years ago—as a hobby, I seemed to naturally turn to the western scene—possibly due to my background of ranching and farming in the West Cross Timber area there in north central Texas. I enjoyed reading early-day Texas and Oklahoma history involving cattle drives, Indians, "badmen," sheriffs, etc. Consequently, most of my short stories and novels about the West have been about these two states, as connected to the cattle industry, settlement, and related adventures. My stories are free of pornography, and suitable for young readers. The backgrounds have been closely researched; upon occasion, too, I have used *real* western characters interacting with my fictional ones, such as, for example, the famous "Hanging Judge" Isaac Parker, who appeared in my *Oklahoma Outrider*, just recently published. However, I seem to be getting away from the western story at present, leaning toward historical narratives such as *Reign of Discord* (as yet unpublished), and my current project concerning Old Testament history, and, specifically, Old Testament prophecy. My working title for this Old Testament narrative is *Messenger from Anathoth*, which implies that the story will be about Jeremiah, since he was a prophet (i.e., a messenger from God), and his hometown was Anathoth, a couple of miles or so northeast of Jerusalem.

* * *

Robert E. Trevathan is a very difficult writer to appraise. His Westerns run along fairly traditional lines, and appear not to have changed greatly in either style or execution over the years. His heroes are all cut from the same cloth, and are handsome, determined 30-year-olds. Frequently they are mustangers or cattlemen, and often they have partners, sometimes to provide a degree of comic relief (the overweight Cotton Johnson in *Ballanger*, say) or to handle such duties as tracking (Luke Dunworth in *Ambush*, or Randy Lockspur in *Ransom Trail*). They are nearly always gun-fast and attractive to women.

Trevathan's plots usually revolve around, or regularly feature, the staples of western fiction—rustling, murder, abduction, revenge, the establishing of stage lines, and so on. A favourite location appears to be Texas. There is little to set Trevathan's books apart from others of their type, however—but having said that, it should also be stressed that there is nothing particularly wrong with them; indeed, they generally make for a competent and entertaining light read.

Trevathan's heroes all seem to appear to share a similar fate; like it or not, they usually find themselves saddled with some sort of problem which soon thrusts them to centre stage. In *Ballanger*, for example, the title character has his plans to raise cattle disrupted when a mysterious fire wrecks the local courthouse, and later, while attempting to re-register his brand, discovers that someone else has already beaten him to it, effectively taking legal possession of his herd. In *Ambush*, Dave Banner finds himself attempting to track down the rustlers who killed his friends Scott and Andrea Farraday. Riding into the town of Limestone to attend the wedding of his sister to the town marshal in *Ransom Trail*, Dave Stoner soon becomes involved in a desperate manhunt when his sister is abducted. In *Oklahoma Outrider*, young Dan Earley becomes one of "Hanging Judge" Isaac Parker's deputies when he learns that some of the men rustling stock from his employer actually murdered his father during the Civil War, while Jory Levell almost bites off more than he can chew when he goes into the stage-line business with his girlfriend's uncle in *Red River Bullets*.

Trevathan usually splits his books down into between 17 and 20-plus fairly short chapters. In the main, he tells his stories from the hero's viewpoint only, and unfolds each plot in a logical if rather predictable sequence. He almost never "jump-cuts" ahead, and this sometimes dogged and conventional approach can slow down the action considerably (*Ambush* is an especially good example, where what should be a page-turning premise—the process of linking clues together in order to track down three murderers—instead becomes a somewhat plodding experience). The author usually maintains an acceptable balance between dialogue and prose, although his players do have a habit of constantly referring to each other by name. There is also a tendency to impart facts through dialogue ("And so you did get stuck in town with that bilious attack while your two other deputy friends went south to Perryville on other business, taking both your chuck-wagon and your prisoner-hauling vehicle"), and this often adds a clumsy feel to his books.

As Trevathan's heroes adhere to a certain type, so too do his villains, who are usually typified by some sort of physical disfigurement or remarkable characteristic—a scarred face, say, or a limp, a white eye, a gold tooth and so on. His females perform adequately, but seldom cross the line between decoration and domination, and his supporting characters are frequently drawn so broadly that they become caricatures. Similarly, Trevathan's admittedly limited use of humour is not always entirely successful. Sometimes—as with the eccentric old judge preparing for an imagined bandit raid by assembling an entire arsenal of weapons (including a Gatling gun) in his hotel suite—it is so far-fetched that it detracts from an otherwise credible story. Neither is there much action in Trevathan's books, although, as previously intimated, there is certainly conflict. As a consequence, there is little violence in his stories, and what there is is never portrayed explicitly. Generally there is an element of romance, however, and this is usually handled in a satisfactory manner.

A competent if largely uninspired writer, Trevathan's work is sometimes lifted by the odd surprise twist or flash of originality. Overall, his Westerns tend to unravel along familiar and long-established lines. For all of that, though, his is an amiable and enjoyable enough product, light, undemanding and entertaining, but it is one which I suspect probably finds more favour among staunch traditionalists than afficionados of the more modern Western.

—David Whitehead

TRIMBLE, Louis (Preston). Also wrote as Stuart Brock; Gerry Travis. American. Born in Seattle, Washington, 2 March 1917. Educated at Eastern Washington State College, Cheney, B.A. 1950, Ed.M. 1953; University of Washington, Seattle, 1952–53, 1955, 1956–57; University of Pennsylvania, Philadelphia, 1955–56. Served as an editor in the United States Army Corps of Engineers Architects Division. Married 1) Renee Eddy in 1938 (died 1951), one daughter; 2) Jacquelyn Whitney in 1952; 3) Mary Todd in 1974. English teacher, Bonners Ferry High School, Idaho, 1946–47; Instructor in Spanish and English, Eastern Washington State College, 1950–54; Instructor, 1956–59, Assistant Professor, 1959–65, Associate Professor, 1965–76, and Professor of humanities and social studies, 1976–80, now Emeritus, University of Washington. Participated in English as a Second Language seminars in Yugoslavia, 1972–74, 1976. Member of the Executive Board, Western Writers of America, 1963–64. Agent: Scott Meredith Literary Agency, 845 Third Avenue, New York, New York 10022, U.S.A. Address: 2 Radnor Terrace, Totnes, Devon TQ9 5JW, England.

Western Publications

Novels

Valley of Violence. Philadelphia, Macrae Smith, 1948; London, Corgi, 1951.
Gunsmoke Justice. Philadelphia, Macrae Smith, 1950; London, Corgi, 1951.
Gaptown Law. Philadelphia, Macrae Smith, 1950.
Fighting Cowman. New York, Popular 1952; London, Viking Press, 1956.
Crossfire. New York, Avalon, 1953.
Bullets on Bunchgrass. New York, Avalon, 1954.
Mountain Ambush. New York, Avalon, 1958.
Montana Gun. New York, Hillman, 1961; London, White Lion, 1972.
Deadman Canyon. New York, Ace, 1961.
Siege at High Meadow. New York, Ace, 1962.
The Man from Colorado. New York, Ace, 1963.
Wild Horse Range. New York, Ace, 1963.
Trouble at Gunsight. New York, Ace, 1964.
The Desperate Deputy of Cougar Hill. New York, Ace, 1965; London, Severn House, 1979.
Holdout in the Diablos. New York, Ace, 1965.
Showdown in the Cayuse. New York, Ace, 1966.
Standoff at Massacre Buttes. New York, Ace, 1967.
Marshal of Sangaree. New York, Ace, 1968.
West to the Pecos. New York, Ace, 1968.
The Hostile Peaks. New York, Ace, 1969; London, Severn House, 1979.
Trouble Valley. New York, Ace, 1970; London, Severn House 1979.
The Lonesome Mountains. New York, Ace, 1970.
The Ragbag Army. New York, Ace, 1971.

Novels as Stuart Brock

Railtown Sheriff. New York, Bouregy, 1949; London, Barker, 1959.
Double-Cross Ranch. New York, Avalon, 1954; London, Barker, 1957.
Action at Boundary Peak. New York, Avalon, 1955.
Whispering Canyon. New York, Avalon, 1955.
Forbidden Range. New York, Avalon, 1956.

Uncollected Short Story

"No Guns," in *Gunsmoke* (New York), August 1953.

Other Publications

Novels

Fit to Kill. New York, Phoenix Press, 1941.
Date for Murder. New York, Phoenix Press, 1942.
Tragedy in Turquoise. New York, Phoenix Press, 1942.
Design for Dying. New York, Phoenix Press, 1945.

Murder Trouble. New York, Phoenix Press, 1945; London, Wells Gardner, 1949.
Give Up the Body. Seattle, Superior, 1946.
You Can't Kill a Corpse. New York, Phoenix Press, 1946.
The Tide Can't Wait. New York, Bouregy, 1949; London, Wright and Brown, 1959.
The Case of the Blank Cartridge. New York, Phoenix Press, 1949.
Blondes Are Skin Deep. New York, Lion, 1950.
Stab in the Dark. New York, Ace, 1956.
The Virgin Victim. New York, Mercury, 1956.
Nothing to Lose But My Life. New York, Ace, 1957.
The Smell of Trouble. New York, Ace, 1958.
Cargo for the Styx. New York, Ace, 1959.
The Corpse Without a Country. New York, Ace, 1959.
Obit Deferred. New York, Ace, 1959.
Till Death Do Us Part. New York, Ace, 1959.
The Duchess of Skid Row. New York, Ace, 1960.
Girl on a Slay Ride. New York, Avon, 1960.
Love Me and Die. New York, Ace, 1960.
The Surfside Caper. New York, Ace, 1961.
The Dead and the Deadly. New York, Ace, 1963.
Anthropol. New York, Ace, 1968.
The Noblest Experiment in the Galaxy. New York, Ace, 1970.
Guardians of the Gate, with Jacqueline Trimble. New York, Ace, 1972.
The City Machine. New York, DAW, 1972.
The Wandering Variables. New York, DAW, 1972.
The Bodelan Way. New York, DAW, 1974.

Novels as Gerry Travis

Tarnished Love. New York, Phoenix Press, 1942.
A Lovely Mask for Murder. New York, Avalon, 1956.
The Big Bite. New York, Avalon, 1957.

Novels as Stuart Brock

Death Is My Lover. New York, Mill, 1948.
Just Around the Coroner. New York, Mill, 1948.
Bring Back Her Body. New York, Ace, 1953.
Killer's Choice. New York, Graphic, 1956.

Other

Sports of the World. Los Angeles, Golden West, 1939.
Working Papers in Scientific and Technical English, with Robert Bley-Vroman and Larry Selinker. Seattle, University of Washington, 1972.
New Horizons: A Reader in Scientific and Technical English, with others. Zagreb, Skolska Knjiga, 1975.
Course Materials for Non-Native Speakers Planning to Enter U.S. Universities to Study Science or Technology, with Mary Todd Trimble. San Francisco, Pacific American Institute, 1977.
English for Multinational Business, with Mary Todd Trimble. Washington, D.C., International Communication Agency, 1978.
English for Science and Technology: A Discourse Approach. New York and London, Cambridge University Press, 1986.

Editor, *Criteria for Highway Benefit Analysis.* Seattle, University of Washington-National Academy of Sciences, 3 vols., 1964–65; revised edition, with Robert G. Hennes, Washington, D.C., National Highway Research Board, 1966–67.
Editor, *Incorporation of Shelter into Apartments and Office Buildings.* Washington, D.C., Office of Civil Defense, 1965.
Editor, with Karl Drobnic and Mary Todd Trimble, *English for Specific Purposes: Scientific and Technical English.* Corvallis, Oregon State University Press, 1978.

*

Manuscript Collections: University of Oregon, Eugene; University of Wyoming, Laramie.

Critical Study: *English for Academic and Technical Purposes: Studies in Honor of Louis Trimble* edited by Larry Selinker and others, Rowley, Massachusetts, Newbury House, 1981.

Louis Trimble comments:

I began writing western fiction because of my interest in the history and physical character of the western United States and because the Western was (and is) a genre in which a writer could move with a good deal of freedom. Although, as with all popular fiction, there is a definite frame for the elements of the Western to fit into, this frame is large and very elastic compared to some other genres: thus, the Western can give a writer a good deal of flexibility in developing character, in treating locales, in handling historical elements, etc. Another characteristic that appealed to me was the opportunity to write stories ranging in scope from "historical narrative" to folktales; in fact, the folklore element is one of the strongest and most interesting elements in almost all well-written western fiction.

* * *

Louis Trimble wrote over 60 books, in science-fiction and mystery genres as well as Westerns. But his most enduring work seems to be his Westerns. Trimble's writing features strong characters in realistic situations confronting the savageness of western life. Many of Trimble's Westerns have an element of mystery to them that forces the hero to investigate.

A good example of this is *The Lonesome Mountains.* When Lee Cory's uncle is murdered, Cory vows to find the killers. An ex-sheriff, Cory uses some unorthodox methods to extract his vengeance. In *Siege at High Meadow*, Lieutenant Hart Cordell trails an outlaw for eight years. Just as he's closing in on the killer, Mont Lansford, Cordell finds himself teamed up with a spirited woman, Maudie Ellison, in a desperate fight among the snowy mountains. *Trouble Valley* is a one-on-one confrontation between Kirk Gannon and land-grabbing Lex Cowley over water rights in a valley too small for both men to live in peacebly. Ben Craig, the hero of *Marshal of Sangaree*, has sworn to kill the two men who murdered his friend Chalco. Craig has killed one of the murderers, but when he becomes the town marshal killing the second murderer presents problems. *The Man from Colorado* shares a similar vengeance theme. Jim Lane arrives in Mountain City to avenge the murder of his best friend, but must solve a mystery before justice can be done.

Trimble also wrote under the pseudonym of Stuart Brock. One of the best Brock books is *Action at Boundary Peak.* Captain Nat Dunn of the U.S. Cavalry had orders to stop the looting of the trains carrying gold from Canada. At Fort Kootenai, Dunn finds evidence that the raids and murders are controlled by someone inside the fort. His suspects are Will Burke, an ex-cavalry sergeant, and Will's sister, Leslie, who Dunn falls in love with. But when Will and Leslie disappear, Dunn takes to the trail vowing to discover who is guilty. Another exceptional Brock novel is *Whispering Canyon* where young lawyer Joel Lockhart arrives in Lace Curtain at the beginning of a range war that he has to stop in order to save the town and his career.

Trimble is a straightforward, unpretentious writer who did a professional job at providing quality entertainment in his Westerns as well as his mysteries and science fiction.

—George Kelley

TUBB, E(dwin) C(harles). British. Also writes as Chuck Adams; Stuart Allen; Anthony Armstrong; Ted Bain; Alice Beecham; Anthony Blake; L.T. Bronson; Raymond L. Burton; Morley Carpenter; Julian Carey; Jud Cary; Julian Cary; J.F. Clarkson; Norman Dale; Robert D. Ennis; James Evans; James S. Farrow; James R. Fenner; R.H. Godfrey; Charles S. Graham; Charles Grey; Volsted Gridban; Alan Guthrie; D.W R. Hill; George Holt; Gill Hunt; Alan (or Allan) Innes; E.F. Jackson; Gordon Kent; Gregory Kern; King Lang; Mike Lantry; P. Lawrence; Chet Lawson; Nigel Lloyd; Robert Lloyd; Frank T. Lomas; Ron Lowam; Arthur Maclean; Carl Maddox; Phillip Martyn; John Mason; Carl Moulton; L.C. Powers; M.L. Powers; Edward Richards; Paul Schofield; John Seabright; Brian Shaw; Roy Sheldon; John Stevens; Eric Storm; Andrew Sutton; Edward Thomson; Ken Wainwright; Frank Weight; Douglas West; Eric Wilding; Frank Winnard. British. Born in London, 15 October 1919. Married Iris Kathleen Smith in 1944; two daughters. Has worked as a welfare officer, catering manager, and printing machine salesman. Editor, *Authentic Science Fiction*, London, 1956–57, and *Eye and Vector*, 1958–60. Recipient: Cytricon award, 1955; Eurocon award, 1972. Guest of Honor World, World Science Fiction Convention, Heidelberg, 1970. Agent: Carnell Literary Agency, Rowneybury Bungalow, Sawbridgeworth, near Old Harlow, Essex CM20 2EX. Address: 67 Houston Road, London SE23 2RL, England.

WESTERN PUBLICATIONS

Novels

The Fighting Fury (as Paul Schofield). London, Spencer, 1955.
Comanche Capture (as E.F. Jackson). London, Spencer, 1955.
Men of the Long Rifle (as J.F. Clarson). London, Spencer, 1955.
Scourge of the South (as M.L. Powers). London, Spencer, 1956.
Vengeance Trail (as James S. Farrow). London, Spencer, 1956.
Quest for Quantrell (as John Stevens). London, Spencer, 1956.
Trail Blazers (as Chuck Adams). London, Spencer, 1956.
Drums of the Prairie (as P. Lawrence). London, Spencer, 1956.
Men of the West (as Chet Lawson). London, Spencer, 1956.
Wagon Trail (as Charles S. Graham). London, Spencer, 1957.
Colt Vengeance (as James R. Fenner). London, Spencer, 1957.

OTHER PUBLICATIONS

Novels

Saturn Patrol (as King Lang). London, Curtis, 1951.
Planetfall (as Gill Hunt). London, Curtis, 1951.
Argentis (as Brian Shaw). London, Curtis, 1952.
Alien Impact. London, Hamilton, 1952.
Atom War on Mars. London, Panther, 1952.
The Mutants Rebel. London, Panther, 1953.
Venusian Adventure. London, Comyns, 1953.
Alien Life. London, Paladin, 1954.
The Living World (as Carl Maddox). London, Pearson, 1954.
World at Bay. London, Panther, 1954.
The Metal Eater (as Roy Sheldon). London, Panther, 1954.
Journey to Mars. London, Scion, 1954.
Menace from the Past (as Carl Maddox). London, Pearson, 1954.
City of No Return. London, Scion, 1954.
The Stellar Legion. London, Scion, 1954.
The Hell Planet. London, Scion, 1954.
The Resurrected Man. London, Scion, 1954.
Alien Dust. London, Boardman, 1955; New York, Avalon, 1957.
Assignment New York (as Mike Lantry). London, Spencer, 1955.
Sands of Destiny (as Jud Cary). London, Spencer, 1955.
The Space-Born. New York, Ace, 1956; London, Digit, 1961.
Touch of Evil (as Arthur Maclean). London, Fleetway, 1959.
Moon Base. London, Jenkins, and New York, Ace, 1964.
Death Is a Dream. London, Hart Davis, and New York, Ace, 1967.
The Winds of Gath. New York, Ace, 1967; as *Gath*, London, Hart Davis, 1968.
C. O. D. Mars. New York, Ace, 1968.
Derai. New York, Ace, 1968; London, Arrow, 1973.
S. T. A. R. Flight. New York, Paperback Library, 1969; London, Hale, 1980.
Toyman. New York, Ace, 1969; London, Arrow, 1973.
Escape into Space. London, Sidgwick and Jackson, 1969.
Kalin. New York, Ace, 1969; London, Arrow, 1973.
The Jester at Scar. New York, Ace, 1970; London, Arrow, 1977.
Lallia. New York, Ace, 1971; London, Arrow, 1977.
Technos. New York, Ace, 1972; London, Arrow, 1977.
Century of the Manikin. New York, DAW, 1972; London, Millington, 1975.
Mayenne. New York, DAW, 1973; London, Arrow, 1977.
Veruchia. New York, Ace, 1973; London, Arrow, 1977.
Jondelle. New York, DAW, 1973; London, Arrow, 1977.
Zenya. New York, DAW, 1974; London, Arrow, 1978.
Breakaway (novelization of TV series). London, Futura, and New York, Pocket Books, 1975.
Eloise. New York, DAW, 1975; London, Arrow, 1978.
Eye of the Zodiac. New York, DAW, 1975; London, Arrow, 1978.
Collision Course (novelization of TV series). London, Futura, 1975; New York, Pocket Books, 1976.
Jack of Swords. New York, DAW, 1976; London, Arrow, 1979.
Alien Seed (novelization of TV series). New York, Pocket Books, and London, Barker, 1976.
Spectrum of a Forgotten Sun. New York, DAW, 1976; London, Arrow, 1980.
Rogue Planet (novelization of TV series). New York, Pocket Books, and London, Futura, 1976.
Earthfall (novelization of TV series). London, Futura, 1977.
Haven of Darkness. New York, DAW, 1977; London, Arrow, 1980.
Prison of Night. New York, DAW, 1977; London, Arrow, 1980.
The Primitive. London, Futura, 1977.
Incident on Ath. New York, DAW, 1978.
The Quillian Sector. New York, DAW, 1978; London, Arrow, 1982.
Stellar Assignment. London, Hale, 1979.

Web of Sand. New York, DAW, 1979; London, Arrow, 1983.
Death Wears a White Face. London, Hale, 1979.
Iduna's Universe. New York, DAW, 1979; London, Arrow, 1985.
The Luck Machine. London, Dobson, 1980.
The Terra Data. New York, DAW, 1980; London, Arrow, 1985.
Pawn of the Omphalos. New York, Fawcett, 1980.
The Coming Event. New York, DAW, 1982; London, Arrow, 1986.
Earth Is Heaven. New York, DAW, 1982; London, Arrow, 1986.
Stardeath. New York, Ballantine, 1983.
Melome. New York, DAW, 1983; with *Angado*, London, Legend, 1988.
Angado. New York, DAW, 1984; with *Melome*, London, Legend, 1988.
Symbol of Terra. New York, DAW, 1984.
The Temple of Truth. New York, DAW, 1985.

Novels as Volsted Gridban

Alien Universe. London, Scion, 1952.
Reverse Universe. London, Scion, 1952.
Planetoid Disposals Ltd. London, Milestone, 1953.
De Bracy's Drug. London, Scion, 1953.
Fugitive of Time. London, Milestone, 1953.

Novels as Charles Grey

The Wall. London, Milestone, 1953.
Dynasty of Doom. London, Milestone, 1953.
Tormented City. London, Milestone, 1953.
Space Hunger. London, Milestone, 1953.
I Fight for Mars. London, Milestone, 1953.
The Extra Man. London, Milestone, 1954.
The Hand of Havoc. London, Merit, 1954.
Enterprise 2115. London, Merit, 1954; as *The Mechanical Monarch* (as E.C. Tubb), New York, Ace, 1958.

Novels as Gregory Kern

Galaxy of the Lost. New York, DAW, 1973; London, Mews, 1976.
Slave Ship from Sergan. New York, DAW, 1973; London, Mews, 1976.
Monster of Metelaze. New York, DAW, 1973.
Enemy Within the Skull. New York, DAW, 1974.
Jewel of Jarhen. New York, DAW, 1974; London, Mews, 1976.
Seetee Alert! New York, DAW, 1974; London, Mews, 1976.
The Gholan Gate. New York, DAW, 1974.
The Eater of Worlds. New York, DAW, 1974.
Earth Enslaved. New York, DAW, 1974.
Planet of Dread. New York, DAW, 1974.
Spawn of Laban. New York, DAW, 1974.
The Genetic Buccaneer. New York, DAW, 1974.
A World Aflame. New York, DAW, 1974.
The Ghosts of Epidoris. New York, DAW, 1975.
Mimics of Dephene. New York, DAW, 1975.
Beyond the Galactic Lens. New York, DAW, 1975.
Das Kosmiche Duelle. Bergisch Gladbach, Germany, Bastei, 1976.
Galactiad. New York, DAW, 1983.

Novels as Edward Thomson

Atilus the Slave. London, Futura, 1975.
Atilus the Gladiator. London, Futura, 1975.
Gladiator. London, Futura, 1978.

Short Stories

Ten from Tomorrow. London, Hart Davis, 1966.
A Scatter of Stardust. New York, Ace, 1972; London, Dobson, 1976.

Other (comicbooks)

Target Death. London, Micron, 1961.
Lucky Strike. London, Fleetway, 1961.
Calculated Risk. London, Fleetway, 1961.
Too Tough to Handle. London, Fleetway, 1962.
The Dead Keep Faith. London, Fleetway, 1962.
The Spark of Anger. London, Fleetway, 1962.
Full Impact. London, Fleetway, 1962.
I Vow Vengeance. London, Fleetway, 1962.
Gunflash. London, Fleetway, 1962.
Hit Back. London, Fleetway, 1962.
One Must Die. London, Fleetway, 1962.
Suicide Squad. London, Fleetway, 1962.
Winged Commando. London, Fleetway, 1963.
No Higher Stakes. London, Fleetway, 1963.
Penalty of Fear. London, Fleetway, 1963.
Kalgan the Golden. London, Harrier, 1984.

*

Bibliography: in *Science Fiction Collector 7*, February 1980.

E.C. Tubb comments:

The West as most regard it was the period just after the Civil War and lasted about 20 years, from 1866 to 1888, when the advance of the railroads had put an end to the great cattle drives. It was a time of flux and expansion with many finding unexpected traits within themselves: William Bonney—Billy the Kid—being a prime example. In a sense it was something we would all like to experience and, now, never will outside the realms of fiction. To walk free, to be equal by the virtue of arms, to sense the wide open spaces, taste the thrill of danger, grasp a little of what it must have been like for primitive man who had no one to depend on but himself.

Stories about the West contain the basic elements of survival, of good and bad, of relentless disciplines and elementary justice. Things clearcut and sides sharply divided. The situations are basically simple. The cure for trouble the same. It is almost a microcosm of the development of civilisation itself. It is something we all feel we know, could belong to, and, often, wish we could.

As the essayist suspected, I had read a lot about the history of the West—usually via certain good novels of the period. Also it was a time when the film Western was in great demand and, like John Russell Fearn, I was a regular visitor to the cinema. So ideas stuck, were changed to fit the format, were produced fast because that was the only way to make them pay. Aside from that I enjoyed the chance to show something of the grim side—by assumption because, thank goodness, I've never yet been shot, penetrated by arrows, bitten by a snake, etc. The treatment for such wounds is a part of the western legend—for snake bite cut open the flesh as the point of bite, suck out poison, break open a cartridge, spill powder in the wound and set it alight so as to cauterise the wound. Arrows had their heads cut off and were shoved through. Bullets were dug out with a knife heated and cooled in whisky. Odd, really, because that would be to prevent infection and that type of hygene had yet to grab hold. Lister only used it first in 1865—antisepsis, I mean, and these things take time to spread.

All of the above elements were woven into my Westerns. I remember in one I wrote where I had my heroes use dynamite to blow up a bridge. It was during the Civil War and, just in time, I learned that the stuff hadn't been invented until 1866—after the war. So I had to change it to blasting powder! The same problems exist with weapons. Names and types had different times so your pre-war buffalo hunter using a Winchester would have been somewhat out of place. And so on . . . science fiction, with no such restrictions, was easier to write if less interesting. I should have liked to have written more Westerns, but they did not pay very well and when the science fiction field picked up again, with better rates, I returned to it.

* * *

E.C. Tubb is one of the most prolific British writers of science fiction to emerge after the war. His first short story appeared in 1950, in *New Worlds*, and within four years he was solidly established as a novelist, as well as a leading contributor to the science-fiction magazines on both sides of the Atlantic. His early novels were fast-moving action-adventure stories set against exotic backgrounds, a type of fiction demanded by the publishers. For the more selective magazines, he wrote a more thoughtful, psychological type of story, and it was the successful synthesis of both sides of his writing that brought him his greatest success with the Dumarest of Terra sf series, begun in 1969, and still continuing.

Although he has written crime thrillers and historical fiction, Tubb's writing talents would seem to be ideally suited to writing western fiction. Indeed, some of his early science-fiction novels can be seen as transplanted Westerns, substituting ray-guns for six-guns, bug eyed monsters for Indians, and fabulous metals ("urillium") for gold. However, his 11 western novels were all written over a short period for a single publisher, and seem to have come about through circumstances other than conscious choice.

In the mid-1950's, the British science-fiction market collapsed almost overnight, due to the collective failure of the publishing houses, resulting from complex social and economic factors. Of the few paperback publishers who survived, one was the firm of John Spencer & Co., a fact not without a certain irony, as they had published some of the poorest material. Perhaps the very fact that they had paid the lowest rates and had a healthy cost/profit ratio enabled them to weather the economic storm. Although they dropped their science fiction line, they continued to publish Westerns and other genre novels.

Tubb had been selling science fiction to Spencer, and he now switched to Westerns and other genres. Between 1955 and 1957, Spencer published 11 Westerns, each under a pseudonym of their choosing. The result of this was that none of Tubb's many followers were aware that he had written Westerns, and they remained totally unknown until 1976, when Mike Ashley and Philip Harbottle were commissioned to publish a comprehensive bibliography for a U.S. magazine, and Tubb was asked to confirm or add to the scores of pseudonyms they had identified. His listing of the Westerns came as a surprise, and the fact that they were completely out-of-print came as a bitter disappointment to his fans, most of whom were unable to find copies.

Approaching the Westerns for the first time today, we might reasonably be somewhat apprehensive, wondering why Tubb had declined to admit to their authorship much earlier than he did. Certainly, publication by Spencer in itself carried a certain opprobrium, because they had published some of the poorest writing in the early 1950's (paying the lowest rates in the field, they had received a commensurate standard of script). It comes as a surprise therefore that Tubb's Westerns turn out to be well-written and first-class entertainment.

But, on reflection, this should not have been surprising. By 1955, with 30 science-fiction novels and over 50 short stories published, Tubb had evolved a smooth writing style that was more than competent. He was also prolific, and had learned to write at high speed, while maintaining a reasonable prose quality. So while this group of Westerns may have the appearance of potboilers—and considering Spencer's reputed payment rates, were probably written at high speed—they are surprisingly readable. In fact, they were superior to much of his earlier science fiction.

The underpinnings of the novels have a firm basis in factual western history, which adds to their verisimiltude. Such details are never obtrusive, serving simply as the backdrop for stories of violent action and human nature. A characteristic of Tubb's fiction is that he deals unflinchingly with violence and death. He doesn't glory in it, and his prose is economical, but can be devastatingly effective. *Wagon Trail* opens with a harrowing tragedy when the Bowman family—husband, wife, their 12-year-old son Colin, and his Uncle—are the victims of a savage Indian attack on their homestead. Colin and his uncle are in the stables when the Indians fire the dwelling house. Colin sees his father, clothes alight, totter through the doorway, only to be bludgeoned and scalped. Then: 'Ma!' Colin strained against the hand holding him down. 'Where's Ma?' The wind brought his answer. A gust of it blew smoke and sparks towards them and, heavy on the odour of the burning wood was another, more terrible scent. It was the scent of roasting meat and charred bone."

Wagon Trail tells how Colin, hardened by his youthful experiences, enlists in the Civil War, and becomes a scout. After the war, he leads a poorly equipped party of homesteaders through Indian territory to find a land they can settle and farm. In the inevitable Indian attack, Colin relives the terror of the death of his parents, but his Civil War experiences enable him to fight off the attacks long enough for rescue to come. While unoriginal in theme, the novel is smoothly written, and the characters and events believable.

In *Trail Blazers*, some of the same background is explored in other directions. Again the hero, Gregg Halmar, is a veteran of the Civil War, which has created an anomaly over the price of cattle. In Texas, the numbers of cattle have increased during the war, as they were cut off from their markets. Hundreds of miles distant, in Kansas, cattle are at a premium, fetching high prices. In between are hostile Indians and jayhawkers, virtual outlaws who stop all travellers and demand tribute as reparations for the war. Gregg, one of Tubb's archetypal tough, capable heroes, uses his entire fortune to buy a herd and attempts to blaze a new trail into Wyoming. In a fiercely exciting narrative, hard man Halmar successfully completes his mission, fighting off outlaws and Indians alike, as well as coping with natural disasters.

A pleasing feature of this novel lies in the insights Tubb provides on the economic and social mores of the period. Gold mining camps suffered from the fact that the miners were so intent on getting gold, they neglected their food supplies. Professional hunters earned a good living supplying such camps with fresh meat, and entrepreneurs could make fortunes selling them various supplies. Gregg is successful in turning his $10,000 stake into an $80,000 fortune. He doesn't get the girl, but with the world at his feet, he should worry!

Tubb's heroes are not supermen, and their daring exploits invariably have a basis of hard logic and cunning. The climax of *Colt Vengeance* is a shoot-out. The hero notices as the villain walks towards him in the duelling mode that he is tensing to use the method of whipping over his other hand to fan the hammer of his Colt when drawn. But although achieving rapid fire, the method was inaccurate. Colts weighed over three pounds, and it was impossible to control recoil when hammering at the gun with the edge of the left palm. "A man who could force himself to take the time to aim accurately would have the advantage for his first shot would be the only one he needed." And so it proves!

Men of the West is especially notable for presenting the viewpoint of the Comanche Indians, with convincing detail of their philosophy and ways of life. This is skilfully interwoven with a satisfying tale of gold and human greed, and the rousing finale affects a reconciliation of disaffected captured Confederate soldiers with their Union captors: "Not as the North meeting the South, but as man to man, as soldiers, as men with a single purpose and a single country. Men of the West." Tubb's Westerns have much to commend them, and are well worth the effort of seeking.

—Philip J. Harbottle

TUCKER, Link. *See* **BINGLEY, David Ernest.**

TULLY, Paul. *See* **GARDNER, Jerome.**

TURNER, Clay. *See* **BALLARD, Willis Todhunter.**

TURNER, Len. *See* **FLOREN, Lee.**

TURNER, William O(liver). American. Born in Tacoma, Washington, 19 September 1914. Educated at high school, Evanston, Illinois; Knox College, Galesburg, Illinois, B.A. 1936. Served in the United States Army, 1942–46. Reporter, North Shore Publishing Company, Evanston, Illinois, 1937–40; editor, Stamats Publishing Company, Cedar Rapids, Iowa, 1950–55; full-time writer, 1955–80. President, Western Writers of America, 1963–64. *Died 26 February 1980.*

WESTERN PUBLICATIONS

Novels

The Proud Diggers. Boston, Houghton Mifflin, 1954; London, Ward Lock, 1956.
The Settler. Boston, Houghton Mifflin, 1956; London, Ward Lock, 1957.
War Country. Boston, Houghton Mifflin, 1957; London, Ward Lock, 1958.
The Long Rope. New York, Doubleday, and London, Ward Lock, 1959.
The Treasure of Fan Tan Flat. New York, Doubleday, and London, Ward Lock, 1961.
Throttle the Hawk. London, Ward Lock, 1960; New York, Berkley, 1966.
The High-Hander. New York, Ace, 1963; as *The Troublebuster*, London, Ward Lock, 1963.
Gunpoint. New York, Berkley, 1964; as *The Snare*, London, Ward Lock, 1964.
Destination Doubtful. London, Ward Lock, 1964; New York, Ballantine, 1965.
Five Days to Salt Lake. New York, Ballantine, and London, Ward Lock, 1966.
Blood Dance. New York, Berkley, 1967; London, Mayflower, 1969.
Thief Hunt. New York, Doubleday, 1968; London, Fontana, 1975.
Mayberly's Kill. New York, Doubleday, 1969; London, Hale, 1973.
Crucifixion Butte. London, Mayflower, 1969.
A Man Called Jeff. New York, Berkley, 1969.
Place of the Trap. New York, Doubleday, 1970; London, Hale, 1972.
Call the Beast Thy Brother. New York, Doubleday, 1973.
Medicine Creek. New York, Doubleday, 1974; London, Fontana, 1975.
Shortcut to Devil's Claw. New York, Berkley, 1977.

Uncollected Short Stories

"The Proud Diggers," in *Wild Streets*, edited by Don Ward. New York, Doubleday, 1958.
"Blackie Gordon's Corset," in *Frontiers West*, edited by S. Omar Barker. New York, Doubleday, 1959.
"The Tomato Can Kid," in *Western Roundup*, edited by Nelson Nye. New York, Macmillan, 1961.
"The Lobo Parker Legend," in *Western Writers of America Presents: Great Western Stories.* New York, Berkley, 1965.

OTHER PUBLICATIONS

Novel

The Man in the Yellow Mercedes. New York, Berkley, 1979.

Other

The Card Wizard: An Easy Course of Tricks. Philadelphia, McKay, 1949.
How to Do Tricks with Cards. New York, Collier, and London, Collier Macmillan, 1963.

*

Manuscript Collection: University of Oregon, Eugene.

* * *

William O. Turner was a student and promoter as well as a writer of western fiction. In a 1969 article on the western story for *Roundup*, the Western Writers of America bulletin, he wrote that it "survives as an art form (intellectuals are now beginning grudgingly to grant it that status) because it refuses to be shaped by and absorbed by other contemporary fiction. It is sometimes touched by fads and trends, but only touched. It goes its own way. It develops too slowly to suit many of us but it survives and it produces its share of fine books. It it produces more than its share of banality, at least this is its own banality. At its worst it is an imitation of itself and not an imitation of Dostoevsky, Joyce, Sartre, or Camus."

In another *Roundup* article published a year earlier, he stated: "The western story is an adventure story and its truth is the truth of action and open country and the possibility of a man rising above himself and acting heroically. Because of its roots in American history and tradition, it has an essential relationship to the American spirit and hence a potential that has not been fully realized. It sorely needs writers who see this relationship and can articulate it for the modern reader."

Turner himself was a writer who deftly articulated that relationship. His western novels are celebrations of the frontier spirit, solidly rooted in the western-story tradition without being conventional fare. They are historically accurate entertainments, honest and true in all aspects and marked by exuberant Twainlike storytelling, and as such rank with the best produced by his contemporaries.

Turner wrote both historical and traditional action Westerns with equal facility, though his novels of the former type represent his finest work. *The Proud Diggers* is only a cut below Ernest Haycox's *Alder Gulch* and Will Henry's *Reckoning at Yankee Flat* in its recreation of the hell-roaring days of Montana's gold boomtown, Virginia City. *War Country* is a powerful tale of Washington Territory in 1855, of a young missionary in love with an Indian girl who finds himself caught in the middle of a bloody clash between red and white cultures. *Call the Beast Thy Brother* is an excellent, offbeat story of two men captured and held as white slaves by the fierce Haida Indians of the Pacific Northwest. Other Turner historicals, notably *Blood Dance* and *Thief Hunt*, also reflect his interest in and understanding of the West Coast Indian tribes.

For the most part his traditional Westerns are set in Montana and feature lawmen on the trail of criminals of one sort or another, and either involved in a personal quest or—in the case of the younger protagonists—suffering growth pains. *The Long Rope*, *Gunpoint*, *Place of the Trap*, and *Mayberly's Kill* all have unusual elements of background, characterization, and/or plot that lift them well above the standard formulary Western of this type. Turner also found innovative ways to tell a story that stretched the rigid boundaries of the traditional Western. *Destination Doubtful* is narrated by the precocious 14-year-old sister of a Montana sheriff who is kidnapped by outlaws while trying to help her brother perform his duties, surely one of the very few, if not the only traditional Western told from the point of view of a young woman. "Catch Party," published posthumously—the account of a posse on the trail of a murderer who robbed a high-stakes poker game—begins and ends in the present and is otherwise told in alternating sections of third-person narration and first-person observations from the journal of the sheriff leading the "catch party."

All of Turner's novels are peopled by wholly believable individuals who live, love, and die in western landscapes that are evoked with care and in substantial detail. His ear for western speech patterns, and his scrupulous attention to correct word- and phrase-usage of the period, give his stories richness as well as verisimilitude. Other of his strong suits include dry, understated humor (especially evident in *The Place of the Trap* and "Catch Party") and liberal helpings of irony and pathos.

—Bill Pronzini

TUTTLE, W(ilbur) C(oleman). American. Born in Glendive, Montana Territory, 11 November 1883. Educated in local schools in Montana. Married Bertha M. Stutes in 1927; one son. Worked as a sheepherder, cowpuncher, salesman, railroader, and forest ranger; baseball player and manager: President, Pacific Coast Baseball League, 1935–43. Freelance writer from 1915: sold more than 1000 magazines stories. *Died.*

WESTERN PUBLICATIONS

Novels (series: Hashknife Hartley; Henry Sontag)

Reddy Brant, His Adventures. New York, Century, 1920.
The Medicine Man (Hartley). London, Collins, 1925; Boston, Houghton Mifflin, 1939.
Straight Shooting. New York, Garden City Publishing Company, 1926.
Sad Sontag Plays His Hunch. New York, Garden City Publishing Company, 1926.
Ghost Trails. London, Collins, 1926; Boston, Houghton Mifflin, 1940.
The Flood of Fate. London, Collins, 1926.
Sun Dog Loot. London, Collins, 1926.
The Devil's Payday. New York, Garden City Publishing Company, n.d.; Kingswood, Surrey, World's Work, 1929.
Law of the Range. New York, Garden City Publishing Company, n.d.
Powder Law. New York, Garden City Publishing Company, n.d.
Sontag of Sundown. New York, Garden City Publishing Company, n.d.; Kingswood, Surrey, World's Work, 1929.
Spawn of the Desert. New York, Garden City Publishing Company, n.d.; Kingswood, Surrey, World's Work, 1929.
Tramps of the Range. New York, Garden City Publishing Company, n.d.
Thicker Than Water (Hartley). Boston, Houghton Mifflin, 1927.
Hashknife of the Double Bar 8. London, Collins, 1927; Boston, Houghton Mifflin, 1936; as *Arizona Ways*, Collins, 1929.
The Dead-Line. London, Collins, 1927; Boston, Houghton Mifflin, 1941.
Rustlers' Roost. London, Collins, 1927.
Hashknife Lends a Hand. London, Collins, 1927.
The Morgan Trail (Hartley). Boston, Houghton Mifflin, 1928.
Hashknife of the Canyon Trail. London, Collins, 1928.
Lo Lo Valley. London, Collins, 1929.
Hidden Blood. London, Collins, 1929; Boston, Houghton Mifflin, 1943.
Tumbling River Range. London, Collins, 1929; Boston, Houghton Mifflin, 1935.
The Mystery of the Red Triangle. London, Collins, 1929; Boston, Houghton Mifflin, 1942.
The Keeper of Red Horse Pass. London, Collins, 1930; Boston, Houghton Mifflin, 1937.
Spooky Riders. London, Collins, 1930.
The Red Head from Sun Dog. Boston, Houghton Mifflin, and London, Collins, 1930.

Hashknife of Stormy River. London, Collins, 1931; Boston, Houghton Mifflin, 1935.
The Valley of Twisted Trails. Boston, Houghton Mifflin, 1931; London, Collins, 1932.
Singing River. London, Collins, 1931; Boston, Houghton Mifflin, 1939.
Mystery at JHC Ranch. Boston, Houghton Mifflin, 1932.
Bluffer's Luck. London, Collins, 1932; Boston, Houghton Mifflin, 1937.
The Silver Bar Mystery. London, Collins, 1932; Boston, Houghton Mifflin, 1933.
Loot of the Lazy F. London, Collins, 1933.
The Santa Dolores Stage (Hartley). Boston, Houghton Mifflin, 1934; London, Collins, 1935; as *Twisted Trails*, New York, Popular Library, 1950.
Rifled Gold (Hartley). Boston, Houghton Mifflin, and London, Collins, 1934.
Horse-Shoe Luck. London, Collins, 1934.
The Turquoise Trail. London, Collins, 1935.
Henry the Sheriff. Boston, Houghton Mifflin, 1936.
Rocky Rhodes. London, Collins, 1936.
Wild Horse Valley. (Sontag). Boston, Houghton Mifflin, 1938; London, Collins, 1939.
Wandering Dogies. Boston, Houghton Mifflin, 1938; London, Collins, 1939.
Shotgun Gold. Boston, Houghton Mifflin, 1940; London, Collins, 1941.
The Tin God of Twisted River. Boston, Houghton Mifflin, 1941; London, Collins, 1942.
The Valley of Vanishing Herds (Hartley). Boston, Houghton Mifflin, 1942.
The Wolf Pack of Lobo Butte. Boston, Houghton Mifflin, 1945; as *Wolf Creek Valley*, London, Collins, 1946.
The Trouble Trailer. Boston, Houghton Mifflin, and London, Collins, 1946.
Straws in the Wind. Boston, Houghton Mifflin, and London, Collins, 1948.
Gun Feud. New York, Popular Library, 1951.
The Trail of Deceit. Boston, Houghton Mifflin, 1951.
Salt for the Tiger. New York, Avalon, 1952; London, Collins, 1954.
Renegade Sheriff. New York, Avalon, 1953; London, Collins, 1954.
The Singing Kid. Kingswood Surrey, World's Work, 1953.
Thunderbird Range. New York, Avalon, 1954; London, Collins, 1955.
Mission River Justice. New York, Avalon, 1955; London, Collins, 1956.
The Shadow Shooter (Hartley). London, Collins, 1955.
Ghost Guns. London, Collins, 1957.
The Shame of Arizona. London, Collins, 1957.
Danger Trail. London, Collins, 1958.
The King of Dancing Valley. London, Collins, 1958.
The Rim Rider. London, Collins, 1959.
Silver Buckshot. London, Collins, 1959.
The Deputy. New York, Avalon, 1959.
Dynamite Days. London, Collins, 1960.
The Trail to Kingdom Come. London, Collins, 1960.
Outlaw Empire. New York, Avalon, 1960.
Galloping Gold (Sontag). London, Collins, 1961.
Gold at K-Bar-T. London, Collins, 1961.
Diamond Hitch. London, Collins, 1962.
Passengers for Painted Rock (Hartley). London, Collins, 1962.
The House of the Hawk. London, Collins, 1963.
West of the Aztec Pass. London, Collins, 1963.
Double Trouble. London, Collins, 1964.
Valley of Suspicion. London, Collins, 1964.
Arizona Drifters. London, Collins, 1964.
Double-Crossers of Ghost Tree. London, Collins, 1965.
Road to the Moon. London, Collins, 1965.
Stockade. London, Collins, 1965.
Buckshot Range. London, Collins, 1966.
The Payroll of Fate. London, Collins, 1966.
The Lone Wolf. London, Collins, 1967.
Lucky Pardners. London, Collins, 1967.
Medicine Maker. London, Collins, 1967.
The King of Blue Grass Valley. London, Fontana, 1977.
Vanishing Brands. London, Hale, 1977.
Red Trail of a .41 (Hartley). London, Hale, 1978.

Short Stories

Me and Rudolph. New York, Avalon, 1958.
Piperock Tales. New York, Avalon, 1963.

Uncollected Short Stories

"Magpie's Night-Bear," in *Adventure* (New York), March 1915.
"Derelicts of the Hills," in *Adventure* (New York), June 1916.
"When Oscar Went West," in *Adventure* (New York), July 1916.
"A Bull Movement in Yellow Horse," in *Adventure* (New York), September 1916.
"All Wool," in *Adventure* (New York), October 1916.
"For the Love of Annibel," in *Adventure* (New York), November 1916.
"A Man-Sized Pet," in *Adventure* (New York), December 1916.
"The Curse of Gold," in *Adventure* (New York), January 1917.
"In Self-Defense," in *Adventure* (New York), February 1917.
"Fate and a Fool," in *Adventure* (New York), March 1917.
"Fifty-Fifty with Bonnie," in *Adventure* (New York), April 1917.
"Sixteen to One on Friday," in *Adventure* (New York), May 1917.
"Magpie—Diplomat!," in *Adventure* (New York), July 1917.
"Bearly Reasonable," in *Adventure* (New York), August 1917.
"Honest to Doughgod," in *Adventure* (New York), 1 October 1917.
"Cows Is Cows," in *Adventure* (New York), Mid-November 1917.
"Nerves of Iron," in *Adventure* (New York), Mid-December 1917.
"A Tin Cup Trophy," in *Adventure* (New York), Mid-January 1918.
"Assisting Ananias," in *Adventure* (New York), 1 April 1920.
"Baa, Baa, Black Sheep," in *Short Stories* (New York), January 1921.
"The Devil's Dooryard," in *Adventure* (New York), 3 May 1921.
"The Law Rustlers," in *Adventure* (New York), 1 September 1921.
"Weaved by Warner," in *Adventure* (New York), 20 October 1921.
"Blame It on Brother Bill," in *Adventure* (New York), 20 November 1921.
"The Sheriff of Sun-Day," in *Adventure* (New York), 30 November 1921.
"Powder Law," in *Adventure* (New York), 20 January 1922.
"Wise Men and a Mule," in *Adventure* (New York), 20 February 1922.
"The Spark of Skeeter Bill," in *Adventure* (New York), 30 March 1922.
"Tangled Trails," in *Adventure* (New York), 20 May 1922.

"Ajax, for Example," in *Adventure* (New York), 10 July 1922.
"The Range-Boomer," in *Adventure* (New York), 30 July 1922.
"Flames of the Storm," in *Adventure* (New York), 30 November 1922.
"The Ranch of the Tombstones," in *Adventure* (New York), 30 December 1922.
"Tramps of the Range," in *Adventure* (New York), 28 February 1923.
"Sticky Ropes," in *Adventure* (New York), 20 April 1923.
"Peace Medicine," in *Adventure* (New York), 10 May 1923.
"The Misdeal," in *Adventure* (New York), 30 June 1923.
"Six Piegan Passes," in *Adventure* (New York), 10 August 1923.
"Reputation," in *Adventure* (New York), 30 August 1923.
"Blind Trails," in *Adventure* (New York), 10 November 1923.
"According to Ng Loy," in *Adventure* (New York), 20 December 1923.
"The Loom of Lies," in *Adventure* (New York), 10 January 1924.
"Hashknife and the Phantom Riders," in *Adventure* (New York), 29 February 1924.
"Out of the Flood," in *Adventure* (New York), 30 June 1924.
"Just for a Laugh," in *Adventure* (New York), 20 July 1924.
"The Trey of Spades," in *Adventure* (New York), 30 October 1924.
"Cinders," in *Adventure* (New York), 20 December 1924.
"The Yellow Seal," in *Liberty* (New York), 10 January 1925.
"The Lovable Liar," in *Adventure* (New York), 20 January 1925.
"When East Met West," in *Adventure* (New York), 10 June 1925.
"Fate of the Wolf," in *Short Stories* (New York), 25 June 1925.
"Hashknife of the Diamond H," in *Adventure* (New York), 30 August 1925.
"Silver .41," in *Adventure* (New York), 30 November 1925.
"Quien Sabe," in *World's Best Short Stories of 1926*, edited by H.E. Maule. New York, Doubleday, 1926.
"Alias Whispering White," in *Adventure's Best Stories 1926*, edited by Arthur Sullivant Hoffman. New York, Doran, 1926.
"Vanishing Brands," in *Adventure* (New York), 30 January 1926.
"The Swamper," in *Adventure* (New York), 28 February 1926.
"The Range of Restitution," in *Adventure* (New York), 8 July 1926.
"Gentle But Firm," in *West* (New York), 20 July 1926.
"Golden Silence," in *West* (New York), 5 August 1926.
"The Trouble Trailer," in *Adventure* (New York), 23 August 1926.
"Cause and Effect," in *Short Stories* (New York), 10 November 1926.
"Sudden Bud," in *West* (New York), 20 November 1926.
"The Buckaroo of Blue Wells," in *Adventure* (New York), 23 November 1926.
"Two Fares East," in *Adventure* (New York), 31 December 1926.
"Kingfisher's Roost," in *West* (New York), 5 January 1927.
"Desert Speed," in *Western Story* (New York), 8 January 1927.
"The Valley of Lost Herds," in *Adventure* (New York), 15 May 1927.
"Excused," in *West* (New York), 20 May 1927.
"Sealed Evidence," in *West* (New York), 20 June 1927.
"Dangling Doom," in *Western Story* (New York), 30 July 1927.
"Crooked Coin," in *Adventure* (New York), 1 September 1927.
"The Meddler," in *Adventure* (New York), 1 December 1927.
"Buzzards," in *Adventure* (New York), 15 April–1 May 1928.
"Bad and Mad," in *Western Story* (New York), 19 May 1928.
"By Order of Buck Brady," in *Adventure* (New York), 1 July 1928.
"Because He Listened In," in *Western Story* (New York), 25 August 1928.
"Me and Pewee Limited," in *Argosy* (New York), 27 October 1928.
"Monkey Business," in *West* (New York), 3 November–12 December 1928.
"Bucking Buck Brady," in *Adventure* (New York), 15 February 1929.
"The Red Devil from Sun Dog," in *Adventure* (New York), 1 March–1 April 1929.
"The Proof," in *Adventure* (New York), 1 July 1929.
"Injuneered," in *Adventure* (New York), 15 July 1929.
"The Luck of San Miguel," in *Adventure* (New York), 1 November 1929.
"A Scheme There Was," in *Adventure* (New York), 1 March 1930.
"White Shirt," in *Western Story* (New York), 12 April 1930.
"Bullet Crazy," in *Adventure* (New York), 1 June–1 July 1930.
"Passin' the Buck to Bronkville," in *West* (New York), 11 June 1930.
"Lead Language," in *West* (New York), 3 September–15 October 1930.
"I Buy Me Couple Horses," in *Adventure* (New York), 1 October 1930.
"Peaceful," in *Star* (New York), November 1930.
"Bronkville's Elephant Barbecue," in *West* (New York), 26 November 1930.
"Breakin' Even with Bronkville," in *West* (New York), 7 January 1931.
"Hard Pan Hawkins Busts the Veil," in *Star* (New York), February 1931.
"Sad Sontag Pays a Debt," in *West* (New York), 18 February 1931.
"In the Bunkhouse," in *Adventure* (New York), 1 March 1931.
"The Scar of Fate," in *Adventure* (New York), 15 March–15 April 1931.
"Joner of Ark," in *West* (New York), 18 March 1931.
"Six Months to Live," in *West* (New York), 1 April 1931.
"Outlaws," in *West* (New York), 22 July 1931.
"Backfired," in *Adventure* (New York), 1 August 1931.
"Horse Heaven's Elephant Hunt," in *West* (New York), 5 August 1931.
"Six-Gun Evidence," in *West* (New York), 19 August 1931.
"The Make-Believe Man," in *Adventure* (New York), 15 September–1 October 1931.
"Vinegaroon," in *West* (New York), 14 October–28 October 1931.
"Buzzard's Feast," in *Western Story* (New York), 19 December 1931.
"Wild Oats," in *Argosy* (New York), 26 December 1931–9 January 1932.
"Howdy Hepburn—Realtor," in *West* (New York), 6 January 1932.
"Sinners of Smoke Tree," in *West* (New York), 3 February 1932.
"Bluff on Burnt Fork," in *West* (New York), 2 March 1932.
"The Cross-in-a-Box Mystery," in *Adventure* (New York), 15 March 1932.
"Midnight Trial," in *Argosy* (New York), 23 April 1932.
"A Little Help from Howdy," in *West* (New York), 25 May 1932.
"Flimsy Evidence," in *Adventure* (New York), 15 July 1932.
"Fate and a .45," in *Western Story* (New York), 6 August 1932.
"Corn Juice and Justice," in *Western Story* (New York), 13 August 1932.

"Efficiency," in *Adventure* (New York), 15 August 1932.
"Buckboard Tracks," in *Argosy* (New York), 27 August–3 September 1932.
"The Heir to the Lazy H," in *West* (New York), 14 September 1932.
"The Ghost Riders," in *Adventure* (New York), 1 October–15 November 1932.
"The Shootin'est Dude," in *Western Story* (New York), 22 October 1932.
"The Storm of Fate," in *West* (New York), December 1932.
"Outlaw's Badge," in *Western Story* (New York), 24 December 1932.
"Christmas Ambush," in *Western Story* (New York), 31 December 1932.
"Traders," in *Adventure* (New York), 15 January 1933.
"Right Is Not Always Best," in *West* (New York), February 1933.
"Two Aces in a Hole," in *Argosy* (New York), 18 February 1933.
"The Showdown," in *Adventure* (New York), 1 April 1933.
"Ex-Outlaw Lawman," in *Western Story* (New York), 15 April 1933.
"Showdown," in *Argosy* (New York), 15 April 1933.
"Vanishing Herds," in *Western Story* (New York), 27 May 1933.
"Young Lochinvar Goes West," in *West* (New York), June 1933.
"Drifting's Tenderfoot Pard," in *Western Story* (New York), 12 August 1933.
"Unfinished Business," in *West* (New York), September 1933.
"Skeeter Bill Finds a Gun," in *All Western* (New York), October 1933.
"Hashknife Plays a Hunch," in *Argosy* (New York), 4 November 1933.
"Western Will," in *Western Story* (New York), 16 December 1933.
"The Santa Claus Trail," in *Argosy* (New York), 30 December 1933.
"Buzzards Know," in *Adventure* (New York), January 1934.
"Gunman's Spawn," in *All Western* (New York), January 1934.
"Alias Gunman," in *All Western* (New York), February 1934.
"Buckshot," in *Argosy* (New York), 17 February–10 March 1934.
"Where Ignorance Is Nerve," in *All Western* (New York), March 1934.
"The Fighting Kid," in *Western Story* (New York), 28 April 1934.
"Turkey Tracks," in *Adventure* (New York), May 1934.
"The Rawhide Tenderfoot," in *Western Story* (New York), 26 May 1934.
"Hashknife Throws a Diamond Hitch," in *Adventure* (New York), June 1934.
"Romance and Racehorses," in *Argosy* (New York), 16 June 1934.
"The Finger of Fate," in *Argosy* (New York), 30 June 1934.
"Gunmen of Sun Dance Valley," in *Western Story* (New York), 15 September 1934.
"Border Man," in *Adventure* (New York), 15 September 1934.
"Eggs-actly," in *West* (New York), November 1934.
"Deception Trail," in *Argosy* (New York), 15 December 1934.
"Hashknife Pays a Debt," in *Argosy* (New York), 2 February 1935.
"Henry Goes to Arizona," in *Argosy* (New York), 23 February 1935.
"The Power of Print," in *West* (New York), March 1935.
"Sundown of Ghost Dance," in *Western Story* (New York), 2 March 1935.
"With the Help of Henry," in *Argosy* (New York), 23 March 1935.
"The Sherlock of Sageland," in *Argosy* (New York), 27 April 1935.
"The Spirit of the Thing," in *Argosy* (New York), 4 May 1935.
"Powder-Smoke Canyon," in *All Western* (New York), June 1935.
"The Diplomacy of Henry," in *Argosy* (New York), 6 July 1935.
"The Tendon of Achilles," in *Argosy* (New York), 20 July 1935.
"The Sheriff of Tonto Town," in *Argosy* (New York), 14 September–19 October 1935.
"The Trail of Gold," in *Western Story* (New York), 5 October 1935.
"Suspected by Henry," in *Argosy* (New York), 7 December 1935.
"A Deal in Dogieville," in *Argosy* (New York), 4 January 1936.
"The Devil's Paint Pot," in *Argosy* (New York), 14 March 1936.
"The Revelation of Henry," in *Argosy* (New York), 25 April 1936.
"The Treasure of Peg-Leg Pete," in *Complete Story* (New York), May 1936.
"Henry Rides the Danger Trail," in *Argosy* (New York), 13 June–11 July 1936.
"When Hamlet Hit Dogieville," in *Argosy* (New York), 18 July 1936.
"Strike Three in Dogieville," in *Argosy* (New York), 15 August 1936.
"Hold' em, Dogieville," in *Argosy* (New York), 19 September 1936.
"No Law in Shadow Valley," in *Argosy* (New York), 26 September 1936.
"A Little Workup for Windy," in *Argosy* (New York), 14 November 1936.
"High Heels—and Henry," in *Argosy* (New York), 13 March–3 April 1937.
"Peaceful Peters," in *Western Story* (New York), 27 March 1937.
"A Horse of Two Different Colors," in *Western Story* (New York), 1 May 1937.
"Peaceful Peters' Fast Draw," in *Western Story* (New York), 3 July 1937.
"Henry Plays a Hunch," in *Argosy* (New York), 9 October–30 October 1937.
"Peaceful Peters Declares War," in *Western Story* (New York), 20 November 1937.
"Shotgun Justice," in *Western Story* (New York), 23 April 1938.
"Short Rope for Rustlers," in *Argosy* (New York), 14 May 1938.
"Chaps on Their Shoulders," in *Western Story* (New York), 21 May 1938.
"Peaceful Peters—Badman," in *Western Story* (New York), 2 July 1938.
"Lynch Law Holiday," in *Western Story* (New York), 3 September 1938.
"Henry Hits the Warpath," in *Argosy* (New York), 24 December 1938.
"Brand of Hate," in *Western Story* (New York), 13 May–3 June 1939.
"Thirsty Days for Henry," in *Argosy* (New York), 8 July–29 July 1939.
"Ramblin' Goes to Town," in *Western Story* (New York), 2 September 1939.
"Wolf Bait," in *Western Story* (New York), 7 October 1939.

"Three Guns for Tonto," in *Argosy* (New York), 28 June–12 July 1941.
"Sunset," in *Great Tales of the American West*, edited by H.E. Maule. New York, Modern Library, 1945.
"Thunder River Valley," in *Thrilling Western* (London), Autumn 1945.
"The Lobo Trail," in *West* (Kingswood, Surrey), February 1947.
"In Memory of Lobo Jones," in *West* (Kingswood, Surrey), May 1947.
"Tracks in the Sand," in *West* (Kingswood, Surrey), June 1947.
"The Wolves of Lobo Butte," in *West* (Kingswood, Surrey), August 1947.
"Blind Trails at Tonto," in *West* (Kingswood, Surrey), September 1947.
"Henry the Silent," in *West* (Kingswood, Surrey), October 1947.
"The Singing Kid," in *Thrilling Western* (London), Spring 1948.
"Law Rider," in *West* (Kingswood, Surrey), March 1948.
"The Luck of Arizona," in *West* (Kingswood, Surrey), April 1948.
"The Double-Crossers of Little Saguero," in *West* (Kingswood, Surrey), May 1948.
"To Save Cecil," in *West* (Kingswood, Surrey), August 1948.
"Seven Devils Gold," in *West* (Kingswood, Surrey), September 1948.
"Border Buzzards," in *West* (Kingswood, Surrey), October 1948.
"Hashknife Keeps a Faith," in *West* (Kingswood, Surrey), November 1948.
"By the Name of Smith," in *West* (Kingswood, Surrey), December 1948.
"Psychology and Copper," in *Selected Western Stories*, edited by Leo Margulies. New York, Popular Library, 1949.
"Fate and Some Fools," in *West* (Kingswood, Surrey), January 1949.
"Mr. Smith Comes Home," in *West* (Kingswood, Surrey), March 1949.
"Lightning Luck," in *West* (Kingswood, Surrey), April 1949.
"The Lobo of Saguero Bend," in *West* (Kingswood, Surrey), July 1949.
"Bullet-Proof," in *West* (Kingswood, Surrey), November 1949.
"Trouble in Tonto Town," in *West* (Kingswood, Surrey), January 1950.
"By Executive Appeal," in *West* (Kingswood, Surrey), February 1950.
"Death Trap at the Lazy M," in *West* (Kingswood, Surrey), May 1950.
"Crazy Moon Gold," in *West* (Kingswood, Surrey), July 1950.
"Terror Range," in *West* (Kingswood, Surrey), September 1950.
"The Case of Ripper Griggs," in *Thrilling Western* (London), September 1950.
"A Mixture of Mavericks," in *Exciting Western* (London), October 1950.
"When Peace Came to Tonto Town," in *West* (Kingswood, Surrey), November 1950.
"Horse-Shoe Luck," in *Exciting Western* (London), December 1950.
"Double Trouble at Willow Springs," in *Exciting Western* (London), February 1951.
"When Guns Went Wild," in *Thrilling Western* (London), March 1951.
"Two Loafers from Lynchville," in *Exciting Western* (London), April 1951.
"Six-Gun Law in Lazy Moon," in *West* (Kingswood, Surrey), April 1951.
"Forty-Eight Hours for Henry," in *West* (Kingswood, Surrey), May 1951.
"Blunder in Broken Wheel," in *Exciting Western* (London), June 1951.
"The Luck of Los Pintados," in *West* (Kingswood, Surrey), July 1951.
"Black Sheep's Trail," in *Exciting Western* (London), August 1951.
"The Menace of Spirit River," in *West* (Kingswood, Surrey), September 1951.
"Double Trouble at Circle C," in *Exciting Western* (London), October 1951.
"A Gun Debt Gathers Interest," in *West* (Kingswood, Surrey), October 1951.
"The Ghost of Angel Springs," in *Exciting Western* (London), December 1951.
"Whom the Gods Would Destroy," in *West* (Kingswood, Surrey), January 1952.
"Cowards," in *West* (Kingswood, Surrey), February 1952.
"Henry Goes Prehistoric," in *West* (Kingswood, Surrey), March 1952.
"Dead Men Don't Need to Talk," in *West* (Kingswood, Surrey), April 1952.
"Derelict City," in *Exciting Western* (London), June 1952.
"The Dumb Still Live," in *West* (Kingswood, Surrey), June 1952.
"Mr. Smith of the Ten Bar B," in *West* (Kingswood, Surrey), October 1952.
"The Deception Trail," in *West* (Kingswood, Surrey), January 1953.
"The Big Pay-Off," in *West* (Kingswood, Surrey), February 1953.
"The Lucky Mistake," in *West* (Kingswood, Surrey), March 1953.
"The Kingdom of Cole," in *West* (Kingswood, Surrey), May 1953.
"The Rattler of Fate," in *West* (Kingswood, Surrey), July 1953.
"Hellgate Valley," in *Thrilling Western* (London), November 1953.
"Lovable Liars," in *Exciting Western* (London), May 1954.
"Shadows on the Rafter R," in *Exciting Western* (London), June 1954.
"The Hunches of Tombstone Jones," in *Exciting Western* (London), July 1954.
"Trigger Trouble in Tejon," in *Exciting Western* (London), August 1954.
"Brains at Broken Fork," in *Exciting Western* (London), September 1954.
"Strangers in El Segundo," in *Exciting Western* (London), November 1954.
"Wise Men of Wisdom City," in *Exciting Western* (London), January 1955.
"Security in Silver River," in *Exciting Western* (London), February 1955.
"The Range Smugglers," in *Exciting Western* (London), March 1955.
"Blind Trails at Broken Butte," in *Thrilling Western* (London), April 1955.
"Heads I Win," in *Field and Stream* (New York), January 1956.
"It's a Tough Life," in *Gunpoint*, edited by Leo Margulies. New York, Pyramid, 1960.
"The Drifter," in *More Wild Westerns*, edited by Bill Pronzini. New York, Walker, 1989.
"The Code of Arizona," in *The Arizonans* edited by Bill Pronzini and Martin H. Greenberg. New York, Fawcett, 1989.

OTHER PUBLICATIONS

Plays

Screenplays: *Fools of Fortune*, 1922; *Sun Dog Trails*, with Daniel Whitcomb, 1923; *Western Pluck*, with Wyndham Gittens, 1926; *Man in the Rough*, with Frank Howard Clark and Randolph Bartlett, 1928.

Other

Montana Man (autobiography). New York, Avalon, 1966.

* * *

A long-lived author with first-hand experience of the West, W.C. Tuttle wrote prolifically in both the novel and short story forms. All of his works bear the unmistaken imprint of his personality, the action exciting but easy-paced, with periodic breaks for humour. At various times the scope of his writing has been broad enough to include comedy and apocalyptic destruction. *Straws in the Wind* features a battle between two rival towns which ends in the massacre of both population—this, ironically, described "offstage"—while the later *The Shame of Arizona* stars an inept sheriff and deputies more skilled in badinage than gunplay, W.C. Tuttle apparently paying tribute to W.C. Fields. More typical than these extremes are the mass of novels where humour and serious action are effectively harnessed, neither impairing the other.

The cattle detective is a familiar figure in Tuttle Westerns, and rustling the commonest crime, though often accompanied by blackmail and murder. Red Storm, in *The Rim Rider*, is a cattle detective tracking down rustlers, and rustling is also the problem in *Dynamite Days*. A similar theme obtains in *The Trail to Kingdom Come*, where a gang of cattle-thieves led by a crooked sheriff are unmasked—again by a cattle detective. Like Macrae or Charles Snow, Tuttle adopts a leisurely, unhurried style—perhaps reminding us that life in the west was not one continual gunfight—but unlike them he rarely allows himself to be sidetracked. Digressions are held on a tight rein, and action proceeds at a steady lope, untrammelled by subplots. The strong element of humour, present in almost all his books, is usually effective, leavening rather than blurring the course of events. Tuttle shows a fondness for two-man partnerships—no doubt an authentic touch—and in particular for comic sheriff-deputy teams, one of them grotesquely tall, to provide light relief. This is true of *The Rim Rider* and also *Gold at K-Bar-T*, where a group of cowhands prevent an heiress being cheated of her inheritance.

Tuttle is at his best in the series of novels which feature his cattle detective heroes Hashknife Hartley and Sleepy Stevens. Despite the comic names, and the laconic witticisms they exchange, these two come over as striking—and credible—individuals, among the finest heroes Tuttle ever created. Their adventures mingle tough action, an element of detection, humour, and occasional social comment within the confines of a straightforward but interesting plot. Over the years their author perfected his style, tightening up the structure of his plots, eliminating verbose passages and the more excessive touches of humour. The early *The Shadow Shooter* is an enjoyable read, but suffers a little from its slow opening. In later Hartely-Stevens novels like *Passengers for Painted Rock* or *Red Trail of a .41*, Tuttle presents an altogether more balanced story-line, with hardly a word out of place. Perhaps best of all is *Vanishing Brands*, where Hashknife and Sleepy investigate horse stealing in Wyoming. Terse and dramatic, flecked with wry touches of wit, the novel is an excellent example of the western form, and a credit to its author.

—Jeff Sadler

TYLER, Ellis. *See* **KING, Albert.**

U

UDE, Wayne (Richard). American. Born in Minneapolis, Minnesota, 23 March 1946. Educated at the University of Montana, Missoula, B.A. 1969; University of Massachusetts, Amherst, M.F.A., 1974. Married 1) Pattie Cowell in 1972 (divorced 1982); 2) Marian Blue in 1983, one son and one daughter. Community development specialist, Bear Paw Development Corporation, Havre, Montana, 1969–70; executive director, Community Action Program, Fort Belknap Indian Reservation, Montana, 1970–71, and Council on Aging, Amherst, 1974–76; Assistant Professor, 1976–82, and Associate Professor of English, 1982–84, Colorado State University, Fort Collins; fiction and managing editor, *Colorado State Review*, 1977–84; writer-in-residence and director of the Good Thunder Reading Series, Mankato State University, Minnesota, 1984–86; writer-in-residence, Lewis and Clark College, Portland, Oregon, 1986–87. Since 1987 Assistant Professor of English, and since 1989 director of creative writing, Old Dominion University, Norfolk, Virginia. Address: 527 Delaware Avenue, Norfolk, Virginia 23508, U.S.A.

WESTERN PUBLICATIONS

Novel

Becoming Coyote. Amherst, Massachusetts, Lynx House Press, 1981.

Short Stories

Buffalo and Other Stories. Amherst, Massachusetts, Lynx House Press, 1975; revised edition, 1991.

Three Coyote Tales. Petersham, Massachusetts, Lone Oak Press, 1989.

Uncollected Short Story

"Honoring the Mayor," in *North American Review* (Cedar Falls, Iowa), June 1987.

*

Wayne Ude comments:

My work tends—or attempts—to be magical realist in its approach (see my "Forging an American Style: The Romance-Novel and Magical Realism as Response to the Frontier and Wilderness Experiences" in *The Frontier Experience and the American Dream*, edited by Mogen, Busby, and Bryant, 1989). That is, I'm interested in the interweaving of various levels of metaphysical realities, and also interested in technique as a way to reshape realities, not merely to imitate. My first three books have centered on American Indian material; I'm currently at work on a western novel which will focus on other peoples who have moved into the part of the West I know best, which is northcentral Montana.

* * *

Wayne Ude, a professor of creative writing at Old Dominion University and author of *Becoming Coyote*, is a relatively new name to readers of western American fiction. From *Buffalo and Other Stories*, Ude protracts in his novel, with significant stylistic strength, unity, theme, and characterization to portray today's multi-ethnic reservation Indian, a subject heretofore largely ignored for literary treatment. From familiarization by attending school and playing with the Assiniboine and the Atsina (or Grosse Ventre of the Plains) of the Fort Belknap Reservation in eastern Montana, Ude convincingly voices as no non-Indian before him the contemporary complexities in the life of the Native American. Giving insight into the personal, metaphysical nature of man at variance with tribal police, the Bureau of Indian Affairs, the Bureau of Land Management, and 20th-century helicopters and communicative devices, Ude challenges the reader to comprehend the human condition of *being* a Native American today.

Becoming Coyote may be read at three levels. A deceptively simple plot may mislead the casual reader to believe that the story is an Indian hunt for Charley Many Rivers and Thunder Boy who steal clothing and artifacts from the Tribal Museum to hunt a buffalo the Indian Olaf Svenssen finds missing. Reading at a second level reveals the Indian as a person between what tribal tradition with its myths, legends, customs, and heritage as well as entrenched white stereotype perpetuate and what 20th-century changes and human self-awareness proffer. "Snook" Jones, the narrator-protagonist, himself a quarter-white, non-reservation Indian without a vision, authority figure for both the Tribal Museum board and the Tribal Police, experiences blurred vision, in part a fulfillment of his own search for a vision, as he tracks the perpetrators of the museum theft. The reader moves with Snook into both the legendry of Coyote and Coyote country—Coyote of the legends, Coyote the shape-changer, the rearranger, the crack-brain; "the fellow who showed up after the world was already here and fixed it up to suit himself." The perceptive reader travels with Snook, through the surrender of Thunder Boy and the episodes leading to the capitulation of Charley acquiescent to return to his wood-carving, aware that the subtlety of narration implies a third level of allegorical significance. From the beginning of the second chapter the reader finds a new level of interpretation incorporating Coyote of the Plains Indians; the theme of the novel becomes clear that latent in the maturation of the human animal rests accommodation of the inner being with external controls and demands. Slowly the reader yields, relating to the trickster with his feint, fantasy, curiosity, and downright inquisitiveness, power, and manipulation, to "becoming coyote."

The publisher of *Buffalo and Other Stories* selected for jacket commentary Frank Water's evaluation that

> . . . this collection compromises the best short stories of [plains Indians] I've ever read. In fact, these rank with the best short stories of Indians anywhere. Each one of them ends with a great surprise, a pure delight. And the characters are magnificently drawn—thinking, feeling, and actions all pure Indian as I know them. . . .

Eight of the nine stories in *Buffalo* present the contemporary Indian weighing a peculiarly individual insight into his (her) life; the ninth, "Four Coyote Tales," introduces Coyote. In "Enter Ramona, Laughing," a young woman recalls, for example, that her grandmother utilized every part of a deer for their survival while she reflects that she herself had not learned enough from her grandmother about being a woman. "Runner" relates the life of Frank Runs Far, who at great odds maintains a tribal existence for a small band dependent upon him. In "Joe Morris," a juvenile, who in running away from authorities leaves tracks for their pursuit, ironically yields to becoming a cop for the Indian Police, "to put his knowledge to work for the Tribe."

In depiction of character, subtlety of phraseology, structural excellence for a natural movement of action, description of the Montana landscape, and incarnation of Coyote lie Ude's fictional talent. Ude is able to show how the tribal past with its belief in visions and Coyote can blend with the fantasy-tomorrow-land innate in human dreams and the real world of reservation life. Ude's true artistry rests upon, paradoxical though the two may seem to be, his bringing the reservation Indian alive as a human being few outsiders know and using Snook's and Charley's relationship with Coyote to represent "magical realism." Explains Ude (in a conversation):

> Magical Realism is a kind of fiction which seeks to mingle present, historical past, and archetype (in the Jungian sense). It seems to me to be a perfect mode for Western American writers, since it allows for the "tall tale" and "larger than life" element, for Indian and Chicano metaphysics (without losing the European literary tradition), for a sense of the land as a living and sacred thing, and all this with some very contemporary techniques. Perhaps the best examples are Marquez' *One Hundred Years of Solitude* or, in the north, the work of Frank Waters and Leslie Silko.

Ude gives promise of becoming one of America's leading writers of the American West.

—Martha Scott Trimble

V

VANCE, William E. Also wrote as George Cassidy. American. Married to Elsie Vance. *Died 29 April 1986.*

WESTERN PUBLICATIONS

Novels

The Branded Lawman. New York, Ace, 1952.
Avenger from Nowhere. New York, Ace, 1953.
Hard-Rock Rancher. New York, Popular Library, 1953.
Apache War Cry. New York, Popular Library, 1955.
Way Station West. New York, Ace, 1955.
Outlaws Welcome! New York, Ace, 1958.
Day of Blood. Derby, Connecticut, Monarch, 1961.
Outlaw Brand. New York, Avalon, 1964.
Outlaw Country. New York, Avalon, 1964.
The Wolf Slayer. New York, Ace, 1964.
Tracker. New York, Avalon, 1964.
The Wild Riders of Savage Valley. New York, Ace, 1965.
Son of a Desperado. New York, Ace, 1966.
No Man's Brand. New York, Ace, 1967.
The Raid at Crazyhorse. New York, Ace, 1967.
Drifter's Gold. New York, Doubleday, 1979; London, Hale, 1980.
Death Stalks the Cheyenne Trail. New York, Doubleday, 1980; New York, 1981.
King of the Mountain (as George Cassidy). New York, Nordon, 1980.
Law and Outlaw. New York, Doubleday, 1982.

Uncollected Short Stories

"The Cowboy and the Lady," in *Exciting Western* (London), October 1952.
"Look over Your Shoulder," in *Best Western*, September 1955.
"Death on the Sweetwater," in *Zane Grey Western* (New York), March 1970.

OTHER PUBLICATIONS

Novels

Homicide Lost. New York, Graphic, 1956.

*   *   *

A prolific writer of radio plays, non-fiction articles, short stories, and novels, William E. Vance published some 20 full-length Westerns after 1952. The bulk of these were paperback originals, the most accomplished being *Apache War Cry*—a different sort of cavalry-versus-Indians story set in Arizona Territory in the 1880's—and *Hard-Rock Rancher*.

Vance's two strongest novels, are *Drifter's Gold* and *Death Stalks the Cheyenne Trail*. The former book, which also involves renegade Apaches, is the powerful account of two men who venture into the mountains of New Mexico to dig for a fortune in buried gold bars. The latter, even better, relates the perilous adventures of an undercover agent for the U.S. Secret Service who sets out to locate both a clever forger and a million dollars in stolen Treasury Notes.

Sound characterization, careful attention to historical background, and a fine story sense were Vance's strong points as a novelist. He also had a good ear for dialogue, although a penchant for elided words and old-fashioned phoenetic spellings such as "yore" and "shore" (for "your" and "sure") sometimes weakened the colloquies between his characters. Vance's untimely death cut short a promising career which seemed to improve with every book, and his works are well worth reading by anyone interested in the traditional western story.

—Bill Pronzini

VIZENOR, Gerald (Robert). American. Born in Minneapolis, Minnesota, 22 October 1934. Educated at New York University, 1955–56; University of Minnesota, Minneapolis, B.A., 1960, graduate study, 1962–65; additional graduate study, Harvard University, Cambridge, Massachusetts. Married 1) Judith Helen Horns in 1959 (divorced 1968), one son; 2) Laura Jane Hall in 1981. Served in Minnesota National Guard, 1950–51; United States Army, 1952–55; served in Japan. Group worker, Ramsey County Corrections Authority, St. Paul, Minnesota, 1957–58; roving group worker, Capital Community Center, St. Paul, 1958; corrections agent, Minnesota State Reformatory, St. Cloud, 1960–61; staff writer, Minneapolis *Tribune*, 1968–70; teacher trainer, Park Rapids Public Schools, Minnesota, 1971; instructor, Lake Forest College, Illinois, and Bemidji State University, Minnesota, 1971–73; lecturer, University of California, Berkeley, 1976–80; Professor of American Indian Studies, University of Minnesota, Minneapolis from 1980. Currently Professor of Native American Studies, University of California, Berkeley. Recipient: Fiction Collective Prize, 1986. Address: Native American Studies, 3415 Dwinelle Hall, University of California, Berkeley, California 94720, U.S.A.

WESTERN PUBLICATIONS

Novels

Darkness in Saint Louis Bearheart. St. Paul, Minnesota, Truck Press, 1973.
Crossblood Bone Courts Bingo. Minneapolis, University of Minnesota Press, 1990.

Short Stories

Wordarrows: Indians and Whites in the New Fur Trade. Minneapolis, University of Minnesota Press, 1978.

The Trickster of Liberty: Tribal Heirs to a Wild Baronage. Minneapolis, University of Minnesota Press, 1988.

OTHER PUBLICATIONS

Novel

Griever: An American Monkey King in China. New York, Fiction Collective, 1987.

Verse

Poems Born in the Wind. Minneapolis, Vizenor, 1960.
The Old Park Sleepers: A Poem. Minneapolis, Obercraft, 1961.
Two Wings the Butterfly: Haiku Poems in English. Minneapolis, Vizenor, 1962.
South of the Painted Stone. Minneapolis, Obercraft, 1963.
Raising the Moon Vines. Minneapolis, Callimachus, 1964.
17 Chirps. Minneapolis, Nodin, 1964.
Slight Abrasions: A Dialogue in Haiku (with Jerome Downes). Minneapolis, Nodin, 1966.
Empty Swings. Minneapolis, Nodin, 1967.
Matsushima: Pine Islands. Minneapolis, Nodin, 1984.

Other

A Selected Bibliography of the Dakota and Ojibway Indians of Minnesota, with a General Selection of References about the Indians of North America. Minneapolis, Grant Elementary School Curriculum Resource Center, 1967.
Thomas James White Hawk. Mound, Minnesota, Four Winds, 1968.
Tribal Scenes and Ceremonies. Minneapolis, Nodin, 1976.
Interior Landscapes: Autobiographical Myths and Metaphors. Minneapolis, University of Minnesota Press, 1990.

Editor and Translator, *Summer in the Spring: Lyric Poems of the Ojibway, Interpreted and Reexpressed.* Minneapolis, Nodin, 1965; as *Summer in the Spring: Ojibwa Songs and Stories,* 1981.
Editor, *Escorts to White Earth 1868–1968: 100 Year Reservation.* Mound, Minnesota, Four Winds, 1968.
Editor, *The Everlasting Sky: New Voices from the People Named the Chippewa.* New York, Crowell, 1972.
Editor, *Anishinabe Nagomon: Songs of the Ojibwa.* Minneapolis, Nodin, 1974.
Editor, *Anishinable Adisokan: Stories of the Ojibwa: Tales of the People.* Minneapolis, Nodin, 1970.
Editor, *Earthdivers: Tribal Narratives on Mixed Descent.* Minneapolis, University of Minnesota Press, 1981.
Editor, *The People Named the Chippewa: Narrative Histories.* Minneapolis, University of Minnesota Press, 1984.
Editor, *Touchwood: A Collection of Ojibway Prose.* St. Paul, Minnesota, New Rivers Press, 1987.
Narrative Chance: Postmodern Discourse on Native American Indian Literatures. Albuquerque, University of New Mexico Press, 1989.

*

Critical Studies: *Four American Indian Literary Masters* by Alan R. Velie, Norman, University of Oklahoma Press, 1982; *American Indian Quarterly* (Berkeley, California), Winter 1985.

* * *

Gerald Vizenor differs from many western writers in that, since he is Chippewa, he employs the perspective of the Indian rather than the cowboy. Both his fiction and nonfiction deal primarily with Indian mixed-bloods in the cities and on the reservation in Minnesota.

Vizenor began publishing poetry in the 1960's, and although he published a few stories and essays in the early 1970's, his breakthrough as a writer came in 1978 with *Wordarrows,* a collection of short pieces, and *Darkness in Saint Louis Bearheart,* a novel.

Wordarrows, subtitled *Indians and Whites in the New Fur Trade,* is about clashes and misunderstandings between whites and Indians. The book is a series of character studies of Indians and mixed-bloods as they try to cope with the problems of late 20th century life—alienation, alcoholism, unemployment—with the aid of bureaucratic institutions like the American Indian Employment and Guidance Center and the Bureau of Indian Affairs.

Many of Vizenor's sketches depict lost tribal souls. Roman Downwind was born in a station wagon in the Chippewa National Forest, and at 19 he still lives in a car in Minneapolis. Marlene American Horse, in despair and drunkenness, "gives herself to evil lust and hostilities of white men who loved to abuse tribal women." Laurel Hole in the Day abandons her dream of life in the cities, and returns to her tarpaper shack on the reservation.

Vizenor presents these people with love and irony, never romanticizing their characters or their plight. He transmutes their sordid lives into art through language, especially his imaginative use of metaphor. He is fond of catechresis, mixed metaphors that strain the limits of language, e.g., phrases like "tribal slipstreams and centerfold cultures."

Not all of Vizenor's characters are down and out; some are merely bizarre. Girlie Blahswomann is a "South Dakota born mixedblood prom queen turned Kundalini yogi" who abandons social work on the reservation to peddle fruit juice from a pushcart in Berkeley, California. Lilith Mae Farrier, a white woman who teaches on the White Earth Reservation, takes two boxers—dogs, not prize fighters—as lovers.

Lilith Mae Farrier appears as a character in *Darkness in Saint Louis Bearheart* as well. Vizenor's characters often turn up in subsequent books, giving his work as a whole the appearance of a literary mobius strip—a loop with no beginning or end that keeps passing the same points. Jimmy Carter and Scott Momaday also have bit parts in *Bearheart,* but as Vizenor points out in a preface, they are fictional characters with real names, whereas Lilith Mae and several others are real characters with fictional names.

Darkness in Saint Louis Bearheart centers around two trickster figures. The positive side of the trickster, the leader and hero, is Proude Cedarfair, a Chippewa from Red Cedar reservation in northern Minnesota. The United States has run out of oil, so the government has commandeered trees from the reservations. Proude recognizes that the Indians are no match for the "evil white treekillers," so he leads a small band of tribal refugees on a cross country odyssey, in which they have to escape from the Evil Gambler (a traditional opponent of the trickster in tribal myth), as well as the Fast Food Fascists of Ponca City, Oklahoma, and a paramilitary group from New Mexico.

The other facet of the trickster, the irresponsible, violent, oversexed scoundrel, is Benito Saint Saint Plumero, a mixed-blood freebooter, one of Proude's band. Proude becomes so serious in his leadership role that he neglects his wife Rosina. Bigfoot, the trickster/scoundrel, is killed while having sex with Rosina. *Bearheart* is a fair example of the postmodern novel. It departs from traditional realism, is both playful and violent, stretches language to its limits, and employs tribal myth and ritual.

Vizenor's most important trickster figure, his alter ego, is Griever de Hocus, who appears in *The Trickster of Liberty* and *Griever: A Monkey King in China*.

The Trickster of Liberty is a set of stories about the Browne family—Tulip, China, Slyboots, Father Mother *et al*—from the White Earth Reservation. The Brownes' enterprises include selling ginseng and microlight airplanes, establishing the Scapehouse, a refuge for "wounded reservation women," and The Last Lecture, a "tavern and sermon center" where people would deliver one last confession or speech of justification before assuming a new identity.

Griever, an adopted member of the Browne family, is a mixed-blood trickster who has disappeared while teaching English in China. China Browne goes to China to find him, but has no luck.

Griever, Vizenor's last novel, tells Griever's adventures in China in detail. Set it China, it is hardly western literature, so I will say only that we last see Griever, who has badly offended Chinese authorities, taking off for Macao in a reservation microlight.

—Alan R. Velie

WADE, Bill. *See* **BARRETT, Geoffrey John.**

WAGONER, David (Russell). American. Born in Massillon, Ohio, 5 June 1926. Educated at Pennsylvania State University, University Park, B.A. 1947; Indiana University, Bloomington, M.A. in English 1949. Served in the United States Navy, 1944–46. Married 1) Patricia Parrot in 1961 (divorced 1982); 2) Robin Heather Seyfried in 1982. Instructor, DePauw University, Greencastle, Indiana, 1949–50, and Pennsylvania State University, 1950–53. Assistant Professor, 1954–57, Associate Professor, 1958–66, and since 1966 Professor of English, University of Washington, Seattle. Elliston Professor of poetry, University of Cincinnati, 1968; editor, Princeton University Press Contemporary Poetry Series, 1977–81. Since 1966 editor, *Poetry Northwest*, Seattle; since 1983 poetry editor, University of Missouri Press, Columbia. Recipient: Guggenheim fellowship, 1956; Ford fellowship, for drama, 1964; American Academy grant, 1967; Morton Dauwen Zabel prize, 1967, Oscar Blumenthal prize, 1974, Eunice Tietjens memorial prize, 1977, and English-Speaking Union prize, 1980 (*Poetry*, Chicago); National Endowment for the Arts grant, 1969; Fels prize, 1975; Sherwood Anderson award, 1980. Chancellor, Academy of American Poets, 1978. Address: 1918-144th SE, Mill Creek, Washington 98102, U.S.A.

Western Publications

Novels

Where Is My Wandering Boy Tonight? New York, Farrar Straus, 1970.
The Road to Many a Wonder. New York, Farrar Straus, 1974.
Tracker. Boston, Little Brown, 1975.
Whole Hog. Boston, Little Brown, 1976.

Other Publications

Novels

The Man in the Middle. New York, Harcourt Brace, 1954; London, Gollancz, 1955.
Money, Money, Money. New York, Harcourt Brace, 1955.
Rock. New York, Viking Press, 1958.
The Escape Artist. New York, Farrar Straus, and London, Gollancz, 1965.
Baby, Come On Inside. New York, Farrar Straus, 1968.
The Hanging Garden. Boston, Little Brown, 1980; London, Hale, 1982.

Plays

An Eye for an Eye (produced Seattle, 1973).

Screenplay: *The Escape Artist*, 1981.

Verse

Dry Sun, Dry Wind. Bloomington, Indiana University Press, 1953.
A Place to Stand. Bloomington, Indiana University Press, 1958.
Poems. Portland, Oregon, Portland Art Museum, 1959.
The Nesting Ground. Bloomington, Indiana University Press, 1963.
Five Poets of the Pacific Northwest, with others edited by Robin Skelton. Seattle, University of Washington Press, 1964.
Staying Alive. Bloomington, Indiana University Press, 1966.
New and Selected Poems. Bloomington, Indiana University Press, 1969.
Working Against Time. London, Rapp and Whiting, 1970.
Riverbed. Bloomington, Indiana University Press, 1972.
Sleeping in the Woods. Bloomington, Indiana University Press, 1974.
A Guide to Dungeness Spit. Port Townsend, Washington, Graywolf Press, 1975.
Travelling Light. Port Townsend, Washington, Graywolf Press, 1976.
Collected Poems 1956–1976. Bloomington, Indiana University Press, 1976.
Who Shall Be the Sun? Poems Based on the Lore, Legends, and Myths of Northwest Coast and Plateau Indians. Bloomington, Indiana University Press, 1978.
In Broken Country. Boston, Little Brown, 1979.
Landfall. Boston, Little Brown, 1981.
First Light. Boston, Little Brown, 1983.
Through the Forest: New and Selected Poems, 1977–1987. New York, Atlantic Monthly Press, 1987.

Other

Editor, *Straw for the Fire: From the Notebooks of Theodore Roethke 1943–1963.* New York, Doubleday, 1972.

*

Manuscript Collections: Olin Library, Washington University, St. Louis; University of Washington, Seattle.

Critical Study: *David Wagoner* by Ron McFarland, Boise, Idaho, Boise State University, 1989.

* * *

In his four western novels, David Wagoner returns repeatedly to a number of themes and techniques which he treats with continuing success. Central to each of these works is a young protagonist's movement from innocence to experience as he journeys across the American frontier encountering an often debased and corrupted world. However, unlike those he meets, the hero retains his fundamental optimism and incorruptibility.

In Where Is My Wandering Boy Tonight? 17-year-old Jackson Holcomb and Fred Haskell learn that their outwardly respectable fathers are actually hyprocritical exploiters who initially control the town of Slope, Wyoming, but eventually lose their fortunes. As a result of this discovery, the boys reject the vocations of lawyer and clergyman to become apprentice cattle herders, and, in effect, repudiate their parents' middle-class ideals. 20-year-old Ike Bender in *The Road to Many a Wonder* also leaves his parents and sets out from Nebraska to Pikes Peak during the gold rush of 1859 with a jerry-built wheelbarrow. Following a picaresque pattern, Ike encounters numerous adversities but unlike the picaro refuses to alter his values in order to survive. Ironically, he achieves both survival and wealth when he accidentally claims a rich vein in an area ignored by more experienced prospectors.

In *Tracker* Eli, a 17-year-old stable boy, witnesses a back robbery and uses the incident as an excuse to persuade a drunken Tracker Byrd to teach him the intricacies of the man's profession. Although Eli is another of Wagoner's innocents, he learns by the novel's end that in order to survive he must compromise his principles and keep the stolen gold rather than return it and lose his life. Here, dishonesty becomes a means of survival and the protagonist must learn this above all else. In the last of the western novels, *Whole Hog*, Zeke Hunt is forced to witness the slaughter of most of his herd of hogs and suffer the loss of his parents as they travel from Nebraska to California. Like Jackson, Ike, and Eli before him, Zeke falls in with a hard-bitten, older man who teaches him the ways of the West and survival.

For each hero, his physical odyssey is a metaphor for the emotional, psychological, and ethical journey which leads eventually to a rite of passage. Each boy begins his trip questioning his identity and future occupation, and through his confrontations with the frontier encounters himself and the possibilities for personal and imaginative freedom. Each of them also moves from astonished wonder and a blanket acceptance of all he beholds to a position of mature discrimination that still allows for innocent rapture.

The device that makes all of this so effective and compelling is Wagoner's manipulation of a vernacular hero who narrates each tale. Theirs is the clipped, matter-of-fact, and frequently witty idiom of youth and the West, a language which not only makes perceptible the reality it describes but also perfectly captures the boys' attempts to grapple imaginatively with their lives. To identify personalities and their psychological dimensions, Wagoner also relies on an abundance of terse, carefully modulated dialogue. In choosing the western, Wagoner has found a fitting formula for examining isolated figures who approach the world and themselves with innocence, imagination, and quiet astonishment.

—David W. Madden

WALDO, Anna Lee. American. Born in Great Falls, Montana, 16 February 1925. Educated at Montana State College, Bozeman, B.S., 1946; University of Maryland, College Park, M.S., 1949. Married Willis H. Waldo in 1950; three daughters and two sons. Research chemist, Office of Naval Research, Washington, D.C., 1946–49, Central Research, Monsanto, Dayton, Ohio, 1949–51, and Kettering Institute and Miami Valley Hospital, Dayton, 1950–55; chemistry instructor, University of Dayton, Ohio, 1950–65, Mercy College, Frontenac, Missouri, 1965–75, and St. Louis Community College, Meramec, Missouri, 1975–85. Since 1985 chemistry instructor, California Polytechnic State University, San Luis Obispo. Recipient: Bausch and Lomb science award; Richardson award, 1946; L. White Quest award, 1981. Address: 3057, South Higuera, No. 211, San Luis Obispo, California 93401, U.S.A.

WESTERN PUBLICATIONS

Novels

Sacajawea. New York, Avon, 1979.
Prairie: The Legend of Charles Burton Irwin and the Y Ranch. New York, Berkley, 1986.

OTHER PUBLICATIONS

Other

Clinical Chemistry Methods: A Laboratory Manual. Dayton, Ohio, Miami Valley Hospital, 1952.

*

Anna Lee Waldo comments:

I was educated as a chemist, but have always written—I grew up with Blackfeet and Crow Indians, and used that material in my fiction writing to bind together the actual researched facts.

* * *

Anna Lee Waldo's first novel, *Sacajawea*, was born out of the author's early life in Montana, where she grew up among Blackfoot and Crow Indian children. She spent much of her time with her best friend, a Blackfoot girl, collecting spear points, hunted, fished, ate bear meat, and learned about medicinal plants. Sacajawea had always been been a heroine to American girls, and Waldo wondered what happened to her before and after the Lewis and Clark expedition. Her wondering grew into 10 years of research and writing the 1300-plus pages of this saga of a young Shoshoni girl, plucked from her adopted tribe to travel the 3000-mile Lewis and Clark Trail and into the history books.

The background to the novel is as authentic as possible, although Waldo does admit to making up part of the story where no facts exist. These fictional passages often enhance the sense of the main character's development from the age of 11 to almost 100 years old (a point of controversy, as several conflicting dates for her death exist). Waldo took her husband and five children across the Lewis and Clark Trail, gathering information which originally filled a 2000-page book.

This enormous volume re-creates a lifestyle long vanished, but living on in Indian "winter tales" and tribal tradition among the Comanche and Wind River Shoshoni. It is from this well of information that Waldo draws much of her material, to continue the story of Sacajawea beyond the Lewis and Clark Expedition.

The opening of the book deals with Sacajawea's capture from the Snake Indians, where she is brought back as a slave to the Arikaras. She is married off to a French trader, Toussaint Charbonneau, who is already married to several women. When Charbonneau meets up with Lewis and Clark at Fort Mandan, he explains the advantage of having a Shoshone-speaking member in their party. The explorers agree, even though Sacajawea is pregnant at the time.

Now, with the expedition underway, the novel is allowed to dwell on an exciting period of American history. Sacajawea (Bird Woman) is much appreciated by the other members of the expedition, and they turn to her often for advice or directions, her local knowledge proving a great asset. Unquestionably, it was her presence when leading the column, with her papoose strapped to her back, that indicated to hostile Indians hidden behind trees and rocks that this was no war party. Thus she ensured the expedition's success, and the survival of Lewis and Clark.

What emerges from this novel is a narrative which creates an enthusiasm within the reader. It has much to do with a way of life, attitudes, prejudices, and, above all, the holding on to a dream; Lewis and Clark's dream of mapping out the Missouri and Shining Mountains and beyond, and Sacajawea's early dream of being reunited with her family and friends, from whom she has been so violently wrested.

Waldo, in *Sacajawea*, is writing for a wider audience than critics and academics. She sticks to a chronological narrative style that does not allow her own views to colour the characters' actions. Obviously Waldo has read everything available on the subject, and has even interviewed one of Clark's descendants.

The Great American Dream is the theme explored in Waldo's second book, *Prairie*. This is the story of another strong individual, Charles Burton Irwin. Waldo's impeccable research again comes to the fore, bringing to a new generation of readers a stirring story of the Old West. She fleshes out C.B., from childhood in Missouri through to his final days in 1934. C.B., when we first meet him, is already a strong-willed, talented roper, with the flair of a showman. Indeed, in his meetings with medicine showman Colonel Johnson, C.B. reveals he is a natural. The reader is borne along by Waldo's effortless narrative, which once more allows the characters to speak for themselves. Some passages are gripping, others sentimental, but all are deftly explored.

C.B. Irwin's life was as large as the man himself. Not only was he a rancher, showman, trader, and breeder, he also gave his name to the Irwin Brothers' Wild West Show. Waldo shows considerable skill in characterization in presenting the personalities he encountered. His gregarious nature involved him with many of America's well-known characters—western painter Charles Russell, cowboy-showman Will Rogers, Baron de Rothschild, outlaw Tom Horn, President Teddy Roosevelt, and Buffalo Bill Cody, to name but a few.

The length of the book (1100 pages) does justice to C.B.'s capacious life, moving from his humble begining to the successful later years. There are few things in which he was not involved at sometime or another during his life among them horse racing, railroads, and his own Y6 ranch. As with *Sacajawea*, the book is distinguished by its careful research, and by the author's obvious love for writing on a subject that interests her.

Waldo has just completed her third novel, *America Has Been Discovered Before*, which at the time of writing is still awaiting publication. It is based on a story of the discovery of North America before Columbus, beginning in the British Isles in the 12th century, and ending with the Native Americans. If her track record is anything to go by, we can expect a fine, voluminous work, rich in detail and characters, weaving a story of early American myth and legend.

—John L. Wolfe

WALDO, Dale. Pseudonym for D(avid) Waldo Clarke. British. Born in Swansea, Wales, 13 August 1907. Educated at Swansea University College, B.A. 1929; Jesus College, Oxford, B.A. 1931, M.A. 1938. Married Gwen Williams in 1931; two daughters. English teacher, Egyptian Education Service, Cairo, 1931–38, and Derby School, 1939–43; Senior Lecturer in English, London Polytechnic, 1948–60; Head of English Department, West London College, from 1960. Literary adviser, Macmillan, publishers: general editor, Pattern Readers series. Address: 29 Broom Water, Teddington, Middlesex, England.

WESTERN PUBLICATIONS

Novels (series: Johnny Ross)

The Man from Thunder River. London, Boardman, 1951.
Warbonnet. London, Boardman, 1952.
Ride On, Stranger. London, Boardman, 1953.
The Long Riders. London, Mills and Boon, 1957.
Lariat. London, Mills and Boon, 1958.
Beat the Drum Slowly (Ross). London, Ward Lock, 1961.
Ride the High Hills. London, Ward Lock, 1961.
No Man Rides Alone (Ross). London, Ward Lock, 1965.
Once in the Saddle (Ross). London, Ward Lock, 1968.

OTHER PUBLICATIONS

Other

Modern English Writers. London, Longman, 1947.
William Shakespeare. London, Longman, 1950; New York, AMS Press, 1970.
Writers of Today. London, Longman, 1956.
Modern English Practice: Exercises in English for Foreign Students, with M.D. Mackenzie. London, Longman, 1957.
The Groundwork of English Sentence Structure, with M.D. Mackenzie. London, Macmillan, 1963.
Insight Through English. Edinburgh, Oliver and Boyd, 1968.
A Reference Book of English: A General Guide for Foreign Students of English, with Ronald Ridout. London, Macmillan, 1970.

* * *

Dale Waldo writes mainly about the New Mexico and Wyoming area with their lawless frontier towns near the great cattle trails. He sets his novels in the post-Civil War period, *Once in the Saddle* taking place as late as 1890.

The cattle trails appear in his books but they do not form the central theme, which is civilisation and respect for the law and how it was gradually being established in the west. The western town forms the main stabilizing force, showing the extent of law-abiding civilisation. The town of Warbonnet forms the setting in *Warbonnet* and the town of Gilburg Crossing does the same for *Beat the Drum Slowly*. The plot of *Beat the Drum Slowly* revolves around the important problem of a crooked sheriff and how the decent citizens can remove him.

Law and order is important in all of Waldo's novels, and we are given good explanations of how it is threatened by feuds between a big cattleman and homesteaders in *No Man Rides Alone*. Waldo returns to this theme in *Once in the Saddle*, which gives us a good deal of historical background to the situation in the west following the passing of the Maverick Bill. The consequences of this legislation were that, contrary to the old "law" of the open range, all unbranded cattle became the property of the Stockmen's Association. Small ranchers were therefore hounded by the big cattlemen and harried as though they were rustlers and outlaws. It is interesting that Waldo shows us the problems brought by the advance of civilisation.

The characters in Waldo's novels are quite deep. There is a good psychological study of Maffrey and his insanity in *Beat the Drum Slowly*. There are, however, many minor characters such as the girl Gail in *Warbonnet* or Jeannie in *Beat the Drum Slowly* whom Waldo does not have time to develop. Waldo's principal recurring character is Johnny Ross, who appears in *Beat the Drum Slowly*, *No Man Rides Alone*, and *Once in the Saddle*. Although Waldo takes the unusual course of using a first-person narrative in the series, Ross is a quiet type and we do not get to know much about his inner feelings. He is, however, quite capable of a fast draw with his gun to protect himself when the action demands it. Like most cowboys, he has stock strands in his make-up: a rather chequered past, a chivalric attitude to women, and a desire to see justice done for the small man.

Waldo's style makes his books very readable. He uses a minimum of western jargon or Spanish words. His powers of description are considerable, as is shown in the description of a western sunrise in *Beat the Drum Slowly* or the poker game in the same book. He builds plots well, and a notable feature is the suspense created at the end of each chapter. The books have conclusive and happy, even romantic, endings, and within these narrow limits Waldo succeeds in his task.

—P.R. Meldrum

WALKER, Reeve. *See* **HECKELMANN, Charles N.**

WARD, Brad. *See* **PEEPLES, Samuel Anthony.**

WARD, Jonas. Pseudonym for William (Thomas) Ard; also wrote as Ben Kerr; Mike Moran; Thomas Wills. American. Born in Brooklyn, New York, 7 July 1922. Educated at Dartmouth College, Hanover, New Hampshire, graduated 1944. Served in the United States Marine Corps 1944–45: medical discharge. Married Eileen Kovara in 1945; one daughter and one son. Copywriter. Buchanan Advertising Agency, New York, publicity writer, Warner Brothers New York office; freelance writer from 1950; lived in Clearwater, Florida, from 1953. *Died 12 March 1960.*

WESTERN PUBLICATIONS

Novels (series: Buchanan)

The Name's Buchanan. New York, Fawcett, 1956; London, Fawcett, 1958.
Buchanan Says No. New York, Fawcett, 1957; London, Fawcett, 1958.
One-Man Massacre (Buchanan). New York, Fawcett, 1958; London, Fawcett, 1959.
Buchanan Gets Mad. New York, Fawcett, 1958; London, Fawcett, 1960.
Buchanan's Revenge. New York, Fawcett, and London, Muller, 1960.
Buchanan on the Prod, completed by Robert Silverberg. New York, Fawcett, 1960; London, Muller, 1961.

OTHER PUBLICATIONS

Novels as William Ard

The Perfect Frame. New York, Mill, 1951; London, Hammond, 1953.
.38. New York, Rinehart, 1952; as *You Can't Stop Me*, New York, Popular Library, 1953; as *This Is Murder*, London, Hammond, 1954.
The Diary. New York, Rinehart, 1952; London, Hammond, 1954.
You'll Get Yours (as Thomas Wills). New York, Lion, 1952.
A Girl for Danny. New York, Popular Library, 1953.
A Private Party. Rinehart, 1953; as *Rogue's Murder*, London, Hammond, 1955.
Double Cross (as Mike Moran). New York, Popular Library, 1953.
Don't Come Crying to Me. New York, Rinehart, 1954.
No Angels for Me. New York, Popular Library, 1954.
Mr. Trouble. New York, Rinehart, 1954.
Hell Is a City. New York, Rinehart, 1955.
Mine to Avenge (as Thomas Wills). New York, Fawcett, 1955; London, Fawcett, 1956.
Cry Scandal. New York, Rinehart, 1956; London, Digit, 1960.
The Root of His Evil. New York, Rinehart, 1957; London, Boardman, 1958; as *Deadly Beloved*, New York, Dell, 1958.
All I Can Get. Derby, Connecticut, Monarch, 1959.
As Bad as I Am. New York, Rinehart, 1959; London, Boardman, 1960; as *Wanted: Danny Fontaine*, New York, Dell, 1960.
Like Ice She Was. Derby, Connecticut, Monarch, 1960.
When She was Bad. New York, Dell, 1960.
The Sins of Billy Serene. Derby, Connecticut, Monarch, 1960.
The Naked and the Innocent. London, Digit, 1960.

Novels as Ben Kerr

Shakedown. New York, Holt, 1952.
Down I Go. New York, Popular Library, 1955.
Damned If He Does. New York, Popular Library, 1956.
I Fear You Not. New York, Popular Library, 1956; London, Digit, 1960.
Club 17. New York, Popular Library, 1957.
The Blonde and Johnny Malloy. New York, Popular Library, 1958.

*

Bibliography: by Francis M. Nevins, Jr., in *Armchair Detective 15*, (New York), no. 2, 1982.

* * *

Jonas Ward, the byline on Fawcett Gold Medal's paperback series about the adventures of wandering Texas gunfighter Tom Buchanan, started out as the western-writing pseudonym of William Ard, one of the top private-eye novelists of the 1950's. Ard died of cancer in 1960 at age 37, but Buchanan survived in the hands of other writers commissioned by Gold

Medal to carry on the Ward byline. Some of these—science-fiction specialist Robert Silverberg who completed *Buchanan on the Prod* (1960) after Ard's death, pulp sports fiction veteran William R. Cox, best-selling thriller author Brian Garfield—are worth attention in their own right, but here our attention will be on Ard's half-dozen contributions to the saga.

Ard carried over into his westerns his habit of spicing books with references to his own life and earlier writing, even christening his cowboy hero with his own middle name plus that of the advertising agency he worked for in the 1940's. The first Jonas Ward novel, *The Name's Buchanan*, finds the protagonist saving a young Mexican who avenged his sister's rape by killing the son of the town despot, but basically it's a watered-down westernization of Ard's powerful *Hell Is a City* (1955) in which private eye Timothy Dane and a young Latino who killed the vice-cop rapist of his sister are hunted through a nightmarish New York by an army of corrupt police. Ard's stylistic traits and motifs—extreme economy of words, cimematic cross-cutting between scenes, anti-establishment stance, stress on violent factionalism and sexual rivalry within gangs, flashbacks to explore characters' social roots, interludes of recreational eroticism—figure in his Westerns no less than in his crime novels. And his inadvertent recycling of character names leads to some curious crossovers, like blackjack dealer Hal Harper of *Buchanan's Revenge* who shares his name with the tough cop in the early Timothy Dane books, and gunman Stix Larsen of *Buchanan of the Prod* who has the same handle as three separate and distinct gangsters in Ard's contemporary novels.

Internal consistency and historic accuracy were not Ard's long suits. Buchanan's first two adventures take place soon after the Mexican War and the rest a few years after the Civil War, but he himself remains unwaveringly 30 years old in all of them. Ard's half-dozen Buchanans have little connection with the genuine West but are essentially 1950's hardboiled novels in disguise, complete with an abundance of big-bosomed Good Time Girls of the sort no Mean Streets epic of the 1950's was without. None of them is a frontier classic, but they all confirm *New York Times* mystery critic Anthony Boucher's view that Ard "is just about unmatched for driving story movement and acute economy."

—Francis M. Nevins, Jr.

WARD, Jonas. *See* **COX, William R.; GARFIELD, Brian.**

WARDLE, Dan. *See* **SNOW, Charles H.**

WARNER, Frank. *See* **RICHARDSON, Gladwell.**

WARREN, Charles Marquis. American. Born in Baltimore, Maryland, 16 December 1912. Educated at McDonough School, Maryland; Baltimore City College, graduated. Served in the United States Naval Reserve, 1942–46: Commander; Purple Heart, Bronze Star; five battle stars. Married Anne Crawford Tootle in 1941; three daughters. Freelance writer, and film producer, director, and writer; created the television series *Gunsmoke*, 1955, *Rawhide*, 1958, and *The Virginian*, 1962; producer, *Iron Horse* series, 1966. President of Commander Films, 1951–90, CMW Productions, 1960–90, Emirau Productions, 1962–90, and MW Productions, 1987–90. Recipient: British Critics award, for film, 1956; Western Heritage award, 1959. *Died 15 August 1990.*

WESTERN PUBLICATIONS

Novels

Only the Valiant. New York, Macmillan, 1943; London, Corgi, 1953.
Valley of the Shadow. New York, Doubleday, 1948; London, Corgi, 1953.

Uncollected Short Stories

"Forward into Battle," in *Argosy* (New York), 7 June–26 July 1941.
"Lo, the Tattooed People!," in *Argosy* (New York), 1 November 1941.
"This Is Not Gettysburg," in *Saturday Evening Post* (Philadelphia), 24 April 1943.
"The Cowboy Quoted Keats," in *Saturday Evening Post* (Philadelphia), 26 July 1947.

OTHER PUBLICATIONS

Novel

Deadhead. New York, Coward McCann, 1949; London, Boardman, 1950.

Plays

Screenplays: *Beyond Glory*, with Jonathan Latimer and William Wister Haines, 1948; *Streets of Laredo*, with Louis Stevens and Elizabeth Hill, 1949; *The Redhead and the Cowboy*, with Jonathan Latimer and Liam O'Brien, 1951; *Fighting Coast Guard*, with Kenneth Gamet, 1951; *Oh Susanna*, 1951; *Little Big Horn*, with Harold Shumate, 1951; *Woman of the North Country*, with Norman Reilly Raine and Prescott Chaplin, 1952; *Springfield Rifle*, with Frank Davis and Sloan Nibley, 1952; *Hellgate*, with John C. Champion, 1952; *Pony Express*, with Frank Gruber, 1953; *Arrowhead*, 1953; *Flight to Tangier*, 1953; *Ride a Violent Mile*, with Eric Norden, 1958; *Desert Hell*, with Endre Bohem, 1958; *Day of the Evil Gun*, with Eric Bercovici, 1968; *Charro*, with Frederic Louis Fox, 1969; *Down to the Sea*, 1972; *Hunter*, 1978.

*

Theatrical Activities:
Director: **Films**—*Little Big Horn*, 1951; *Hellgate*, 1952; *Arrowhead*, 1952; *Flight to Tangier*, 1953; *Seven Angry Men*, 1955; *Tension at Table Rock*, 1956; *The Black Whip*, 1957; *Trooper Hook*, 1957; Back from the Dead, 1957; *The Violent Unknown*, 1957; *Copper Sky*, 1957; *Ride a Violent Mile*, 1957; *Desert Hell*, 1958; *Cattle Empire*, 1958; *Blood Arrow*, 1958; *Charro*, 1969.

* * *

Charles Marquis Warren's books are well written, fast moving and action filled, and can be recommended to the western enthusiast. Most of Warren's work has been writing and directing for movies, and such films as *Arrowhead*, *Little Big Horn*, *Day of the Evil Gun*, and others may be more familiar with his books. His books make good fodder for Hollywood and can easily be visualized in action form.

Warren's two books *Only the Valiant* and *Valley of the Shadow* are very similar, as the stories involve military excursions of the Indian-Fighting Army soon after the Civil War. The heroes in both books are the officers in charge of expeditions sent out to control or capture Indians. The hero is the "strong, silent type" who, in attempting to capture the Indian leader, sees himself as involved in a personal duel, not only with the Indians he is pursuing, but with the men he leads. The Indian is given respect as a cunning warrior who is equal if not more intelligent in his attempts to evade or attack the whites. Indians in general, however, are seen as cruel savages who torture, murder, and rape. Except for an occasional fleeting thought by the hero, there is little or no consideration given to the Indian's plight. There is no thought of a history of broken treaties, loss of lands, family and life-style, that has caused the Indian to turn attacker. This, however, is not atypical of 1940's and 1950's television, movie, and book plots. Warren may be severely criticized for his portrayal of the Indian, but the "only good Indian is a dead Indian" attitude where good and bad equals white and red was a common one at the time.

The women involved in the two books are mere side-line viewers, rather than real participants in the plot. They are only there to perceive how incredibly stalwart, honorable, and brave the hero has been. In *Only the Valiant* the heroine is the wife of another officer and except for glances between the two she remains distant and pure. Her husband, physically and mentally weak, stands between the two of them, but both remain honorable in that no real interaction between the hero and the wife occurs until the husband is safely dead. In *The Shadow of the Valley* the heroine is more involved in the action, but still is only an observer of the hero's actions. Although she is captured by the Apache along with the hero and a few other men, this beautiful woman is kept for ransom and is untouched by the Indians. This is hard to believe in view of the Indians' other actions, but somehow the hero's woman must remain pure and untouched. Her role is to watch the hero being tortured, which the Indians and the scout pretending to be Indian do with great skill. The relationship here is a little more interesting, as the hero is shy and unwilling to become totally involved with the woman until he has earned his commission by capturing the Indian leader, Deesohay.

The hero is usually misjudged by others who suspect him of being a coward or a failure in his methods of capturing Indians. The hero is aware of these attitudes, yet does nothing in his own defense. He remains aloof from all but his own mission. Misfits, drunkards, deserters, informers, and cowards, the men in his company are often more dangerous and loathsome than the Indians. Warren's books are interesting for the psychological sketches he draws of crazed, jealous, and/or incompetent men. The misfits surrounding the hero quickly break under the dangerous circumstances, though a few may actually rise to the occasion. In proving themselves they also come to realize the true value of their leader, and as they die heroically, they proclaim his worth.

Warren's books are typically western in their plots and attitudes regarding Indians and women. Where Warren differs and may be more interesting is in his psychological development of the men surrounding the hero. There is more to Warren's books than the immediate action; this is not often the case with other western writers.

—Daryl Morrison

WASHBURN, L(ivia) J(ane). Also writes as Livia James (with James M. Reasoner). American. Born in Lake Worth, Texas, 8 February 1957. Educated at Tarrant County Junior College, Fort Worth, Texas, 1975–77. Married James Morris Reasoner in 1976; two daughters. Recipient: Shamus award, 1987; American Mystery award, 1987. Agent: Barbara Puechner, Peekner Literary Agency, 3121 Portage Road, Bethlehem, Pennsylvania 18017. Address: Route 5, Box 392, Azle, Texas 76020, U.S.A.

Western Publications

Novels

The Emerald Land (with James M. Reasoner, as Livia James). New York, Fawcett, 1983.
Epitaph. New York, Evans, 1988.
Ghost River. New York, Evans, 1988.
Bandera Pass. New York, Evans, 1989.
Riders of the Monte. New York, Evans, 1990.
Red River Ruse. New York, Evans, 1990.

Uncollected Short Stories

"The Battle of Reno's Bend", in *Westeryear*. New York, Evans, 1988.

Other Publications

Novels

Wild Night. New York, Tor, 1987.
Dead-Stick. New York, Tor, 1989.
The Black Moon, with others. New York, Lynx, 1989.
Dog Heavies. New York, Tor, 1990.

*

L.J. Washburn comments:

I've always been interested in the West, its history and its people. My mystery novels and short stories featuring Lucas Hallam, a former gunfighter and Texas Ranger who works in Hollywood in the 1920's as a private detective, have strong western elements in them. As a reader, I like to be entertained, and I try to write the kind of stories that appeal to me as a reader—books with plenty of action, a good plot, humor, and characters that I care about. My western writing draws its inspiration from a variety of sources: history, western novels both old and new, films and television. I always try to tell a good story; that's the most important thing to me, as both writer and reader.

* * *

Strictly speaking, the best of L.J. Washburn's novels aren't really Westerns at all. Her continuing character, Lucas Hallam, is actually a private detective who boosts his income as a movie stuntman in 1920's Hollywood. There can be no denying the enormous influence the Old West plays in the Hallam books, however. The character himself was created following Washburn's discovery that the private eyes who first appeared in pulp magazines like *Black Mask* in the 1920's were, in effect, an out-growth of the earlier western dime novel heroes, and Hallam still remembers "the old days" himself (as a former U.S. Marshal, Texas Ranger, and Pinkerton operative, he was of course very much a part of that era). It is also significant that the first time we meet Hallam, in the short story of the same name, he is at work shooting scenes for a silent western movie, which firmly establishes a link between the past and the present that continues to run through the subsequent full-length novels.

In *Wild Night*, the first of the books, Hallam is hired to ride shotgun on Elton Forbes, the founder of an evangelical order known as the Holiness Temple of Faith. Forbes has a somewhat clandestine meeting to attend that same evening, and though he denies that anything sinister is involved, he does feel that he should have some sort of protection. The mysterious meeting goes disastrously wrong, however, and ends with Forbes standing over two dead bodies with a smoking revolver in his hand. The remainder of the book is taken up with Hallam's attempt to clear his client of the double murder, and as a whodunnit alone it is hard to beat (the book actually went on to win the Private Eye Writers of America's Shamus Award and the American Mystery Award for Best Paperback Original). What makes it especially worthy of comment here are its opening and closing chapters, which take place in a small California ghost town called Chuckwalla (and which Washburn describes as vividly as she does heyday Hollywood). Hallam is actually ambushed in Chuckwalla, and dispatches his two would-be killers in a bloody shoot-out on Main Street, further reinforcing the Old West feel that Washburn's big, dignified, and direct protagonist brings to the entire book. A very good "bunkhouse" atmosphere is also evoked in the cantina at which Hallam and his fellow stuntmen (mostly former cowboys themselves) congregate between pictures.

With the next book in the sequence, *Dead-Stick*, the author makes a conscious attempt to move Hallam away from his western origins by involving him in the making of a fictional aviation movie. He is planted very firmly back in the West for *Dog Heavies*, however, much of which takes place on or around a dude ranch in Texas, where Eliot Tremaine, a reluctant cowboy star, is sent to learn all the skills of the range. This time, Hallam is employed to tag along and ensure that Tremaine—who is something of a hellraiser—stays out of trouble. For Washburn's Colt-carrying private eye, however, Texas brings back memories of his past; of his lawman father, who died there; of Hallam's own hunt for the men who killed him; and of Liz Fletcher, the feisty redhead who came into his life in *Wild Night* and left it again in *Dead-Stick*. Soon, though, Hallam is too busy trying to solve a murder, foil a gang of rustlers and break a bootlegging ring for idle reflection, and as a consequence, there is a greater emphasis on the staples of western entertainment—gun-play and hard riding—which makes the book an entertaining, if somewhat over-long, read.

By any estimation, Lucas Hallam is a superbly drawn character, and to her credit Washburn displays as much care and attention to detail with her supporting cast. Her depiction of silent-movie Hollywood is excellent, clearly based on exhaustive research, the results of which she blends artfully with her fiction. Particularly in *Dog Heavies*, though, she displays a curious lack of imagination when describing Hallam's reactions to each new revelation, and as a consequence he appears to go through the whole book wearing just one expression, a "grimace." This is, of course, an admittedly minor criticism, but the author's otherwise-estimable command of the English language makes it all the more remarkable.

Washburn has also written more traditional Westerns, and the first of these, *Epitaph*, is fairly indicative of her approach to the genre. The story revolves around Hank Littleton, a naive but likeable 15 year-old, who lives with his grandfather Thomas in a sleepy little Texas town. They know little about the Civil War currently raging, until two Confederate spies, Reed and Ordway, come into their lives, requesting Thomas, who is an undertaker, to make them a coffin in which they can smuggle half a million dollars' worth of gold (to be used to buy arms for the South) out of the state. Upon completion of the task, however, Thomas is murdered and the "spies" are revealed to be displaced Georgians intent on heading for Mexico with the gold, which is stolen. What follows is essentially a manhunt story, in which Hank goes after his grandfather's killers, but as with all of Washburn's work, the story is much more involved than that, and moves along at a smooth and orderly pace.

Probably one of the most interesting American western writers to have emerged in the late 1980's, Washburn offers intriguing and imaginative plots that make her an author to watch.

—David Whitehead

WATERS, Frank (Joseph). American. Born in Colorado Springs, Colorado, 25 July 1902. Attended Colorado College, Colorado Springs, 1922–25. Served in the United States Army, 1941–43. Married 1) Lois Moseley in 1944 (divorced 1946); 2) Jane Somervell in 1947 (divorced, 1955); 3) Rose Marie Woodell in 1962 (divorced 1965); 4) Barbara Hayes in 1978. Engineer in Los Angeles, Riverside, and Imperial Valley, Southern California Telephone Company, 1926–35; propaganda analyst, Office of Inter-American Affairs, Washington, D.C., 1943–46; editor, *El Crepusculo* newspaper, Taos, New Mexico, 1949–51; information adviser, Los Alamos Scientific Laboratory, New Mexico, 1952–56, writer, C.O. Whitney Motion Picture Co., Los Angeles, 1957; writer-in-residence, Colorado State University, Fort Collins, 1966; director, New Mexico Arts Commission, Santa Fe, 1966–68: Book reviewer, *Saturday Review of Literature*, New York, 1950–56. Recipient: Commonwealth Club of California silver medal, 1942; Rockefeller grant, 1970; Western Heritage award, 1972; New Mexico Arts Commonwealth Literary award, 1975. Honorary doctorates: University of Albuquerque, New Mexico, 1973; Colorado State University, 1973; New Mexico State University, Las Cruces, 1976; University of New Mexico, Albuquerque, 1978; Colorado College, 1978; University of Nevada, Las Vegas, 1981, University of Colorado, Colorado Springs, 1982. Agent: Joan Daves, 21 West 26th Street, New York, New York 10010. Address: Box 1127, Taos, New Mexico 87571, U.S.A.

WESTERN PUBLICATIONS

Novels

Fever Pitch. New York, Liveright, 1930.

Pike's Peak: A Family Saga. Chicago, Swallow Press, 1971.

The Wild Earth's Nobility: A Novel of the Old West. New York, Liveright, 1935.

Below Grass Roots. New York, Liveright, 1937.

The Dust Within the Rock. New York, Liveright, 1940.

People of the Valley. New York, Farrar and Rinehart, 1941.
The Man Who Killed the Deer. New York, Farrar and Rinehart, 1942; London, Spearman, 1962.
River Lady, with Houston Branch. New York, Farrar and Rinehart, 1942; London, Cassell, 1948.
The Yogi of Cockroach Court. New York, Farrar and Rinehart, 1947.
Diamond Head, with Houston Branch. New York, Farrar and Rinehart, 1948; London, Boardman, 1950.
The Woman at Otowi Crossing. Denver, Swallow, 1966.
Flight from Fiesta. Santa Fe, Rydal, 1986.

Uncollected Short Story

"Easy Meat," in *North American Review* (New York), April 1931.

OTHER PUBLICATIONS

Other

Midas of the Rockies: The Story of Stratton and Cripple Creek. New York, Covici Friede, 1937.
The Colorado. New York, Farrar and Rinehart, 1946.
Masked Gods: Navajo and Pueblo Ceremonialism. Albuquerque, University of New Mexico Press, 1950.
The Earp Brothers of Tombstone: The Story of Mrs. Virgil Earp. New York, Potter, 1960; London, Spearman, 1962.
Book of the Hopi. New York, Viking Press, 1963; London, Penguin, 1977.
Leon Gaspard. Flagstaff, Arizona, Northland Press, 1964.
Pumpkin Seed Point. Chicago, Swallow Press, 1969.
Conversations with Frank Waters, by John R. Milton. Chicago, Swallow Press, 1971.
To Possess the Land: A Biography of Arthur Rochford Manby. Chicago, Swallow Press, 1974.
Mexico Mystique: The Coming Sixth World of Consciousness. Chicago, Swallow Press, 1975.
Mountain Dialogues. Athens and Chicago, Ohio University Press-Swallow Press, 1981.
Frank Waters: A Retrospective Anthology, edited by Charles L. Adams. Athens, Ohio Chicago, Ohio University Press-Swallow Press, 1985.

Editor, *Cuchama and Sacred Mountains*, by W.Y. Evans-Wentz. Athens and Chicago, Ohio University Press-Swallow Press, 1981.

*

Bibliography: *Frank Waters: A Bibliography* by Terence A. Tanner, Glenwood, Illinois, Meyer, 1983.

Manuscript Collection: University of New Mexico Library, Albuquerque.

Critical Studies: *Frank Waters* by Martin Bucco, Austin, Texas, Steck Vaughn, 1969; *Frank Waters* by Thomas J. Lyon, New York, Twayne, 1973.

* * *

Frank Waters rightly distinguishes between the popular Western and the novel of the West. His own novels of the West grow out of such polarities as technological-primitive, reason-intuition, conscious-unconscious, transient-eternal. Like his nonfiction, his fictions are variations on the theme: "Human history is the story of man's adaptation to his environment." His characters are Indians, Mexicans, and Anglos in conflict or in harmony with desert, plain, and mountain. Part Cheyenne, Waters sees the white man as a rapacious newcomer to ancient America, as one "not yet attuned to the deep rhythms of its wide and bitter earth, its immense and lonely skies, the thunder of its mountains, the tide-suck of its pelagic plains." To be attuned means to acquire an uncultish "Indian-ness," a *kachina* quality to counter imperialistic technology and to put oneself in harmony with natural forces.

Two Waters novels are western classics. The lyrical *People of the Valley* captures the patois and gestures of the pastoral folk who dwell in New Mexico's Sangre de Cristo Mountains. Fighting the irresistible *máquina* of "progress" is the sharp-tongued matriarch Doña Maria del Valle, Waters's finest character-creation. But regional gratuities, cliché similes, and aureate diction occasionally vitiate this compelling narrative. Even better known is *The Man Who Killed the Deer.* The Indian youth Martiniano, torn between the red world and the white, evolves to expansive awareness that his life has meaning only in relation to his pueblo. Waters's illusion of circular Indian time and tribal stream-of-consciousness (based on Jungian racial memory) is impressive. But, again, his didactic fervor and anthropological minutiae often obtrude on the "edgeless and phantasmal" flow he espouses.

Unlike the healthy landscapes in these novels, the Border is foul in *The Yogi of Cockroach Court*, a bit of revamped juvenilia. Southwest riffraff and half-breed lovers swirl around serene Tai Ling, a Chinese shopkeeper doing secret good and meditating Buddhist tenets. This overrated naturalist novel has forcible scenes. Unfortunately, the most memorable, Tai Ling's soul in the Zen afterlife, is preposterous. Bizarre also is Waters's much later *The Woman at Otowi Crossing.* The "explosive" vision of the heroine-mystic (who runs a little tearoom below the guarded mountain city of Los Alamos) attracts the FBI. To represent the One and the Many, the author resorts to multiple viewpoints, flashforwards, "documents," and the mingling of historical and invented characters. The beauty of Waters's effort rests less on his audacious *mélange*, however, than on his supposition that the novel is malleable enough to accommodate the absolute. Waters thrust the Red-White contrast even further in his next novel, published 20 years later. In *Flight from Fiesta* Elsie, a rich Anglo brat, manipulates an old drunken Indian, Inocencio, into "kidnapping" her. Semi-stereotypical and quasi-allegorical, the odd couple romp around like doodles in a 1930's bittersweet Hollywood melodrama.

The underrated *Pike's Peak*, however, is Waters's redaction of his epic Colorado mining trilogy: *The Wild Earth's Nobility, Below Grass Roots*, and *The Dust Within the Rock.* Joseph Rogier, the indomitable central figure in this long family chronicle, is based on Joseph Dozier, Water's grandfather. Despite repeated failure, Rogier holds that deep within the bowels of Pike's Peak lies a fabulous Bowl of Gold. His search profoundly influences his grandson, the introspective and divided March Cable (a thinly disguised Frank Waters). In the end, only March, brooding on his dead Indian father and the snowcapped peak, finds the true relationship to the land. Because Waters corrected such impediments as "underdistance," "nonselectivity," and "overwriting," his 743-page unity is marked advance over the 1511-page trilogy.

During the 1940's Frank Waters (with Houston Branch) kept the wolf from the door by manufacturing two bulky historical romances, actually mass-market "movie novels." Universal-International filmed *River Lady*—about amour, steamboating, and logging on the Upper Mississippi; later Columbia Pictures bought the title but not the film rights to *Diamond Head*—about amour, warfare, and whaling in the South Pacific. A decade earlier critics had also dismissed Waters's first published novel, *Fever Pitch.* Indeed, its scorching trek, weird killing, and purple prose smack of desert pulp; but its Conradian angles, Baja California symbology, and anguished mysticism suggest a gravely romantic imagination. Still, even Waters depreciates this bibliographical rarity, notwithstanding its early display of gold fever, mixed blood, landscape power, and cosmic consciousness.

Although esteemed as a novelist, as Charles L. Adams's collection *Frank Waters: A Retrospective Anthology* testifies, Frank Waters seems primarily interested in transcendence. Consequently, his medicine-man efforts to drum together the heartfelt *Hi-yah! Ai! Hi-yah!* and the heady $E=mc^2$ seem, by turns, weighty and banal. To be sure, Waters shapes his novels out of *both* inspiration and calculation, but as a professed intuitionist he disdains literary theory and criticism. His primitive assumption that literature emanates from the lofty cosmic life-force instead of from the individual aesthetic imagination obliges him to see language as magic and words as occult. Thus for Frank Waters the "sacred" novel of the west helps offset the "profane" popular Western.

—Martin Bucco

WATSON, Will. *See* **FLOREN, Lee.**

WAYNE, Joseph. *See* **OVERHOLSER, Wayne D.**

WEBB, Neil. *See* **ROWLAND, Donald S.**

WELCH, James. American. Born in Browning, Montana, in 1940. Educated at the University of Montana, Missoula, B.A.; Northern Montana University, Havre. Recipient: National Endowment for the Arts grant, 1969; Los Angeles *Times* prize, 1987. Address: Roseacres Farm, Route 6, Missoula, Montana 59801, U.S.A.

Western Publications

Novels

Winter in the Blood. New York, Harper, 1974; London, Bantam, 1975.
The Death of Jim Loney. New York, Harper, 1979; London, Gollancz, 1980.
Fools Crow. New York, Viking, 1986.
The Indian Lawyer. New York, Norton, 1990.

Other Publications

Verse

Riding the Earthboy 40. Cleveland, World, 1971; revised edition, New York, Harper, 1975.

Other

Editor, with Ripley S. Hugg and Lois M. Welch, *The Real West Marginal Way: A Poet's Autobiography* by Richard Hugo. New York, Norton, 1986.

*

Critical Studies: *Four American Indian Literary Masters* by Alan R. Velie, Norman, University of Oklahoma Press, 1982; *James Welch* by Peter Wild, Boise, Idaho, Boise State University, 1983; *James Welch* edited by Ron McFarland, Lewiston, Idaho, Confluence Press, 1986.

* * *

In some ways James Welch is a writer who just happens to be an American Indian. His themes and techniques are, admittedly, "universal" and much in the mainstream of modernism. He accomplishes this modernistic effect, however, by uniquely individualized ethnic and regional elements in his writing—fiction and poetry. So to read Welch's novels, *Winter in the Blood*, *The Death of Jim Loney*, *Fools Crow*, and *The Indian Lawyer*, and his early volume of verse, *Riding the Earthboy 40*, is to read about the geography and culture (in mythic past and the historical present, the old and new Wests) of Montana and of the Gros Ventre and Blackfeet peoples—to read, in other words, about the changing American Rocky Mountain West.

One of Welch's dominant themes is characteristic of the American West as place and idea. It is a theme which is also characteristic of much modernism too; but in Welch's writings it is complemented by the "spirit of place" associated with the "Big Sky" country of Montana. This is the theme of isolation, of loneliness, of what is now more commonly regarded as angst and alienation. Even when his heroes almost connect, almost succeed, as in Welch's two latest fictions, *Fools Crow* and *The Indian Lawyer*, they are catapulted into greater estrangement, ever in need of ancestral moorings and numina.

Lonesome cowboys have always roamed the landscape of the West, the pages of the Western, and the lyrics of western music. Seldom, as indigenous people, have Native Americans been lost. But the protagonists of Welch respective fictions, in varying degrees modernist anti-heroes in the vein of Camus's Mersault, are strangers not just to their own land and to the numerous non-Native Americans moving across it, but to their own blood relatives in the form of their immediate family and their more distant genealogical heritage.

The anonymous anti-hero in *Winter in the Blood*, and Jim Loney, whose death we see taking titular and inexorable shape during another winter, the Thanksgiving and Christmas times of Welch's second novel, are tragic *picaros* both in search of and living out the destiny of their names—parodic epic voyagers lost on a land sea of distance, marginality, and death. White Man's Dog, become Fools Crow, sees his future as a young brave and chosen shaman clouded by massacre and smallpox.

Sylvester Yellow Calf, a successful attorney in Helena, Montana must, as a new warrior in a new West, foil a blackmail plot, battle the spoiling influence of up-scale, 1980's professional and political success, and rediscover the special power of his great-grandfathers' war medicine. In *The Indian Lawyer*, Welch offers readers an especially interesting hybrid. To the conventions of the captivity narrative, the cowboy/Indian Western, the mountain-man saga, Indian love song and initiation story, he adds new elements of crime story and environmental advocacy.

Part of Welch's triumph as an artist is his ability to update the picaresque tradition and underscore the tragic straits of his characters by means of black comedy, melodrama, and mock mystery/intrigue. The specter of death's gaping skull-smile laughs throughout Welch's fiction—especially *Winter in the Blood*, still the most successful of his novels. Violence, loss (of material possessions, of relatives, lovers, titles, status, and of the capacity even to know emotion), poignant memories, meager hopes, drunkenness, grotesque nightmares and reveries, animals (dreamed and actual, killed and loved)—all of the many ideas, objects, persons, and happenings in Welch's narratives are masterfully unified by his comic, albeit ironic and absurdist, stance.

With *The Indian Lawyer* Welch moves more into the mainstream of popular, formula fiction—detective novel, among other modalities already mentioned, infusing the western novel. He does, however, maintain his continuing advocacy of Native American agendas, confirming that Welch's role as chronicler of the changing West has not been passive and simply entertaining. His novels have also helped foster the cultural and political causes that are now transforming the idea and the reality of the American West.

Certainly Welch's novels and book of poems are separate and distinct works, but they may also be viewed as a kind of mural, crowded with history and story, the themes of displacement and dispossession, and balanced by the noble and far from futile effort to make meaning out of words, out of attempting to connect and communicate with others in a world turned hostile and absurd, whether in success or in failure—even for the archetypally stolid, now modernized and marginalized, now "assimilated," American Indian.

—Robert F. Gish

WELLMAN, Paul I(selin). American. Born in Enid, Oklahoma, 14 October 1898; brother of the writer Manly Wade Wellman. Educated at the University of Wichita, Kansas, B.A. Served in the United States Army Signal Corps, 1918: Sergeant. Married Laura Bruner in 1923; one son. Cowhand; reporter, then city editor, Wichita *Beacon*, 1920–30; Sunday editor and news editor, Wichita *Eagle*, 1930–35; feature writer, Chicago *American*, 1935; editorial and feature writer, Kansas City *Star*; screenwriter in the 1940's; partner in a cattle ranch in Oregon, 7 years. President, Hollywood Authors Club. D.H.L.: University of California, Los Angeles, 1966. *Died 16 September 1966.*

Western Publications

Novels

Broncho Apache. New York and London, Macmillan, 1936.
Jubal Troop. New York, Carrick and Evans, and London, Cassell, 1939.
Angel with Spurs. Philadelphia, Lippincott, 1942; London, Cassell, 1948.
The Bowl of Brass. Philadelphia, Lippincott, 1942.
The Walls of Jericho. Philadelphia, Lippincott, 1947; London, Laurie, 1948.
The Chain. New York, Doubleday, 1949; London, Laurie, 1950.
The Iron Mistress. New York, Doubleday, 1951; London, Laurie, 1952.
The Comancheros. New York, Doubleday, 1952; London, Laurie, 1954.
Jericho's Daughters. New York, Doubleday, 1956; London, Muller, 1957.
Ride the Red Earth. New York, Doubleday, 1958; London, Muller, 1959.
Magnificent Destiny. New York, Doubleday, 1962.

Other Publications

Novels

The Female: A Novel of Another Time. New York, Doubleday, 1953; as *The Female City*, London, Laurie, 1954.
The Fiery Flower. New York, Doubleday, 1959.
The Buckstones. New York, Trident Press, 1967.

Play

Screenplay: *Cheyenne*, with Alan LeMay and Thames Williamson, 1947.

Other

Death on Horseback: Seventy Years of War for the American West. Philadelphia, Lippincott, 1947; as *The Indian Wars of the West*, New York, Doubleday, 1954.
  Death on the Prairie. New York, Macmillan, 1934; London, Foulsham, 1956.
  Death in the Desert. New York, Macmillan, 1935; London, Corgi, 1958.
The Trampling Herd: The Story of the Cattle Range in America. New York, Carrick and Evans, 1939; London, Foulsham, 1958.
The Callaghan, Yesterday and Today. Encinal, Texas, Callaghan Land and Pastoral Company, 1944(?).
Good Soldiers Do Die. Dallas, Times Herald, 1951.
Glory, God, and Gold. New York, Doubleday, 1954; London, Foulsham, 1959; as *The Blazing Southwest*, Foulsham, 1961.
Portage Bay. New York, Doubleday, and London, Museum Press, 1957.
Gold in California (for children). Boston, Houghton Mifflin, 1958.
Indian Wars and Warriors: East [and *West*] (for children). Boston, Houghton Mifflin, 2 vols., 1959.
Stuart Symington: Portrait of a Man with a Mission. New York, Doubleday, 1960.
Race to the Golden Spike (for children). Boston, Houghton Mifflin, 1961.
A Dynasty of Western Outlaws. New York, Doubleday, 1961; London, Museum Press, 1962.

The Greatest Cattle Drive (for children). Boston, Houston Mifflin, 1964.
Spawn of Evil. New York, Doubleday, and London, Foulsham, 1964.
The Devil's Disciples. London, Foulsham, 1965.
The House Divides: The Age of Jackson and Lincoln. New York, Doubleday, and London, Foulsham, 1966.

* * *

Born in Enid, Oklahoma, and a resident of California at the time of his death in 1966, Paul I. Wellman is known for his screenplays, children's fiction, and popular histories of the American West, as well as for his accomplished historical novels. In the novels, the West is best defined as the frontier of the historical period Wellman is examining, and much of his fiction concerns the transcontinental movement of that frontier with the increasing westward settlement of America. Wellman's serious interest in American history is clearly evident in these works which often investigate the vagaries of fortune, mischance, and circumstance which coalesce in the actual historical event. America as Manifest Destiny is a central theme in many of his western novels, and Wellman's characters are often more shaped by, than shapers of, the events of their stories.

Wellman best exemplifies this blend of the historian and the novelist in his biographical novels of Andrew Jackson and Sam Houston, *Magnificent Destiny*, and of Jim Bowie, *The Iron Mistress*. In these two novels, Wellman traces the American frontier as it moves westward to Texas. The contrast between East and West is particularly emphasized in *Magnificent Destiny* as Wellman alternates his story between the political and social subtleties of Jackson's presidency in Washington and the action-filled exploits of Sam Houston living with the Cherokee Indians and, finally, leading the Texas settlers against the Mexican armies at the Battle of San Jacinto. Though the plot is greatly romanticized, Wellman's account of the life of Jim Bowie is accomplished with unflagging fidelity to the actual historical events and personages that surround Bowie's career. Wellman's novels are distinguished by a richness of detail. He fills these stories with major and minor historical personalities—Stephen Austin, Jean Lafitte, John James Audubon—and depicts carefully the dress, manners, language, customs, and landscapes of his regions and cultures. Particularly interesting are his accounts of military strategies and maneuvers.

Angel with Spurs, a fictional account of Confederate General Joseph Shelby's military expedition into Mexico following the defeat of the South in the Civil War, is particularly worthy of note for its incorporation of historical documents and its examination of Mexican culture. The range of Wellman's literary methods and styles is clearly seen in the contrast between *Ride the Red Earth*, a cavalier romance of a French-Canadian chevalier and rake set in the Louisiana and Spanish territories, and the three realistic Jericho novels, *The Walls of Jericho*, *The Chain*, and *Jericho's Daughters*, which trace the growth of middle-border settlement Jericho, Kansas, into a 20th-century small city. Other western novels include *Bronco Apache* and *Jubal Troop*.

—David Marion Holman

WELLS, Angus. Also writes as William S. Brady; J.B. Dancer; Ian Evans; Charles C. Garrett; Matthew Kirk; James A. Muir; Charles R. Pike; J.D. Sandon. British. Born in England, 29 March 1943. Educated at a private school, 1947–54; Bromley Grammar School, Kent, 1954–61. Divorced twice. Junior executive, Roles and Parker, London; account executive, Harris and Hunter, and Hunter and Barney, both London; publicity manager, then editor, Sphere Books, London; publicity manager, Thomas Nelson, publishers, London. Since 1975 full-time writer. Agent: Blake Friedmann, 37–41 Gower Street, London WC1E 6HH. Address: 34 Cresta Gardens, Mapperley, Nottingham NG3 5GD, England.

WESTERN PUBLICATIONS

Novels as Charles R. Pike (series: Jubal Cade in all books)

Killer Silver. London, Mayflower, 1975.
Vengeance Hunt. London, Mayflower, 1976.
The Burning Man. London, Mayflower, 1976.
The Golden Dead. London, Mayflower, 1976.
Death Wears Grey. London, Mayflower, 1976.
Days of Blood. London, Mayflower, 1977.
The Killing Ground. London, Mayflower, 1977.
Brand of Vengeance. London, Mayflower, 1978.
Bounty Road. London, Mayflower, 1978.
Ashes and Blood. London, Mayflower, 1979.
The Death Pit. London, Mayflower, 1980.
Angel of Death. London, Mayflower, 1980.
Mourning Is Red. London, Granada, 1981.
Bloody Christmas. London, Granada, 1981.
Time of the Damned. London, Granada, 1982.
The Waiting Game. London, Granada, 1982.
Spoils of War. London, Granada, 1982.
The Violent Land. London, Granada, 1983.
Gallows Bait. London, Granada, 1983.

Novels as James A. Muir (series: Breed in all books)

The Lonely Hunt. London, Sphere, 1976.
The Silent Kill. London, Sphere, 1977.
Cry for Vengeance. London, Sphere, 1977.
Death Stage. London, Sphere, 1977.
The Gallows Tree. London, Sphere, 1978.
The Judas Goat. London, Sphere, 1978.
Time of the Wolf. London, Sphere, 1978.
Blood Debt. London, Sphere, 1979.
Blood Stock. London, Sphere, 1979.
Outlaw Road. London, Sphere, 1979.
The Dying and the Damned. London, Sphere, 1980.
Killer's Moon. London, Sphere, 1980.
Bounty Hunter. London, Sphere, 1980.
Spanish Gold. London, Sphere, 1981.
Slaughter Time. London, Sphere, 1981.
Bad Habits. London, Sphere, 1981.
The Day of the Gun. London, Sphere, 1982.
The Colour of Death. London, Sphere, 1982.
Blood Valley. London, Sphere, 1983.
Gundown. London, Sphere, 1983.
Blood Hunt. London, Sphere, 1984.
Apache Blood. London, Sphere, 1985.

Novels as J.B. Dancer (series: Lawmen in all books)

Kansas, Bloody Kansas. London, Coronet, 1977.
Vengeance Trail. London, Coronet, 1978.
One Way to Die. London, Coronet, 1980.

Novels as Charles C. Garrett (series: Gunslinger in all books)

Golden Gun. London, Sphere, Books, 1978.
Fifty Calibre Kill. London, Sphere, 1978.
Rebel Vengeance. London, Sphere, 1979.
Peacemaker. London, Sphere, 1980.
The Russian Lode. London, Sphere, 1980.

Novels as William S. Brady (series: Hawk in all books)

The Sudden Guns. London, Fontana, 1979.
Death's Bounty. London, Fontana, 1979.
Fool's Gold. London, Fontana, 1980.
The Gates of Death. London, Fontana, 1980.
The Widowmaker. London, Fontana, 1981.
Killer's Breed. London, Fontana, 1982.
Border War. London, Fontana, 1983.

Novels as J.D. Sandon (series: Gringos in all books)

Guns Across the River. London, Granada, 1979.
Fire in the Wind. London, Granada, 1979.
Easy Money. London, Granada, 1980.
One Too Many Mornings. London, Granada, 1981.
Survivors. London, Granada, 1982.

Novels as William S. Brady (series: Peacemaker in all books)

Comanche! London, Fontana, 1981.
Outlaws. London, Fontana, 1981.
Lynch Law. London, Fontana, 1981.
Blood Run. London, Fontana, 1982.
$1,000 Death. London, Fontana, 1984.
The Lost. London, Fontana, 1984.
Shootout! London, Fontana, 1984.

Novels as Matthew Kirk (series: Claw in all books)

Day of Fury. London, Granada, 1983.
Vengeance Road. London, Granada, 1983.
Yellow Stripe. London, Granada, 1983.
The Wild Hunt. London, Granada, 1983.
Blood for Blood. London, Granada, 1983.
Death in Red. London, Granada, 1984.

OTHER PUBLICATIONS

Novels

Return of a Man Called Horse (novelization of screenplay). London, Star, 1976.
Starmaidens (as Ian Evans; novelization of TV series). London, Corgi, 1977.
The Brothers Macgregor (novelization of TV series). London, Granada, 1984.
Big Deal (novelization of TV series). London, Futura, 1984.
Roll over Beethoven (novelization of TV series). London, Panther, 1985.

Books of the Kingdoms trilogy:
Wrath of Ashar. London, Orbit, 1988.
The Usurper. London, Orbit, 1989.
The Way Beneath. London, Orbit, 1990.

Other

Editor, *The Best of Arthur C. Clarke.* London, Sidgwick and Jackson, 1973.
Editor, *The Best of Isaac Asimov.* London, Sidgwick and Jackson, 1973.
Editor, *The Best of Robert Heinlein.* London, Sidgwick and Jackson, 1973.
Editor, *The Best of John Wyndham.* London, Sphere, 1973.
Editor, *The Best of A.E. Van Vogt.* London, Sphere, 1974.
Editor, *The Best of Fritz Leiber.* London, Sphere, 1974.
Editor, *The Best of Frank Herbert.* London, Sidgwick and Jackson, 1975.
Editor, *The Best of Clifford D. Simak.* London, Sidgwick and Jackson, 1975.

*

Angus Wells comments:

I began writing Westerns when I took over the *Jubal Cade* series from Terry Harknett, and between 1974 and 1983 wrote pretty exclusively in that genre. I had a good time doing it, and it's interesting to note that where copies are still available in libraries, Public Lending Right figures indicate that people still read them. That's a good feeling, even if the old horse has laid down and died.

* * *

Angus Wells belongs to the modern school of western writing. He was among the small band of English pulp western writers who tied up that scene from the early 1970's to the mid-1980's. This generation of writers ruled the "series western" for over a decade, and it was through his association with writers Terry Harknett and Laurence James that he was brought in to continue the Jubal Cade series from no.4, *Killer Silver*, onwards.

There was a ready-made market for the books and Wells adhered to the formula established by Harknett. The plots, each using the character of Dr. Jubal Cade, are dramatic, action-packed, and violent, with their roots firmly set in Cade's obsession with killing the scar-faced Lee Kincaid, his wife's murderer. This theme underlies the series to the very end. The unusual medical background serves as the basis of more than one plot. The humour in the series—typical Edge-like one one-liners—offsets the blood and guts oozing out of the pages. In *Vengeance Hunt*, Cade helps the Cheyenne against buffalo hunters and the cavalry. Bidding his farewell to Cade, an old chief says, "I have heard . . . of a white man raised by another Cheyenne village. They call him Little Big Man. I think we have our own Little Big Man now. We shall remember you, Jubal." "Thanks," smiles Jubal, "maybe someday someone will write a book about me." This is Wells tipping his hat to the film world and to Terry Harknett—both great influences on his works.

Wells has also contributed individual volumes to several multi-author series: *Lawmen*, *Hawk*, *Gringos*, and *Peacemaker* with John Harvey, and *Gunslinger* with Laurence James.

Peacemaker was conceived on unusual lines with the deliberate intention of producing a gentler Western, using the development of a town as the central theme. John T. McLain, the main character, is less violent than other Wells heroes; McLain is often balanced by strong women characters. The focal point of the town, Garrison, is used as the springboard for all the plots in the series.

Within *The Gringos* series Wells is able to use his talent for creating successful characters and descriptive narrative, something he prefers to writing dialogue. An older man, Cade Onslow, a disgraced soldier, and his black side-kick, Jonas Strong, head the team, while to offset their altruism there are two weaker links—a scar-faced drug addict, Jamie Durham, and an habitual rapist, Yates McCloud. This seemingly odd-ball team achieves a balance between action and personal conflict. The Mexican Revolution is the backdrop for the series.

The *Breed* series was Wells's own creation. The halfbreed Apache hero Matthew Gunn/Azul is destined to be the loner hero from the outset in *The Lonely Hunt*, seeking vengeance for his father's murder. Similar to the *Cade* stories, Azul's adventures stem from his determination to catch up with the killers. The running characters of Nolan and Christie establish themselves dramatically in the series. The Gunn/Azul/Breed persona is a complex one. Torn between the world of the *pinda-lick-oyi* (white man) and the Chiricahua Apache, he is detested by both. This is something over which troubles his conscience, and which drives him to the border of being a psychotic killer. Untypically, women are treated with respect rather than as casual sex/rape victims, even, as in *Bad Habits*, when they are not what they seem. To say that this character is somewhat flamboyant is an understatement. Throughout the books Wells experiments with the halfbreed, even to the point in *Blood Debt* where Breed's path intertwines with that of Nathan Allen, from the film *The Searchers*.

A rather specialised series was *Gunslinger*, in that each book revolves around a different weapon, a Sharps .50, a Gatling gun or a Peacemaker. There are pretty heavy sections of technical description which tend to divert the reader's attention from the story itself. Gunsmith John Ryker has to take a back seat in the books, but Wells still manages to entertain his readers.

Still working on the trusted pattern of the deadly loner as the hero, Wells created Jared Hawk, though not relying on the revenge syndrome this time. We have in Hawk a young gunslinger who is a vicious and savage. He even kills his own father: "Muzzle flash. One single blast of sound. A drift of powder smoke." Wells continues to experiment with character in these books. The idea for *Death's Bounty* came from the Santa Rita del Cobre massacre, and Wells's own fascination with bullfighting led to Hawk delivering a prized bull in *The Gates of Death*.

There are no standard plots in Wells's works. No ranchers versus nesters, no clearly defined villains. His heroes live in that shadowy world where personal retribution rules the heart and the gun rules the day. His background work is authentic, and his plotting is well paced. All of his works are written in a thoroughly entertaining style. The recession in the UK western market has brought Wells into the world of the fantasy novel. One can see that his new works could easily have originated as Westerns.

—Mike Stotter

WELLS, Hondo. *See* **WHITTINGTON, Harry.**

WEST, (Mary) Jessamyn. American. Born in North Vernon, Indiana, 18 July 1902. Educated at Union High School, Fullerton, California, graduated 1919; Whittier College, California, 1919, 1921–23, A.B. in English 1923; Fullerton Junior College, 1920–21; University of California, Berkeley, 1929–31. Married Harry Maxwell McPherson in 1923; two foster daughters. Teacher and secretary, Hemet, California, 1924–29; taught at Bread Loaf Writers Conference, Vermont, Indiana University, Bloomington, University of Notre Dame, Indiana, University of Utah, Salt Lake City, University of Washington, Seattle, Stanford University, California, and Wellesley College, Cambridge, Massachusetts. Recipient: Monsen award, 1958; Janet Kafka prize, 1976. Honorary degrees: Whittier College; Mills College, Oakland, California; Swarthmore College, Pennsylvania; Indiana University; Western College for Women, Oxford, Ohio. *Died 23 February 1984.*

WESTERN PUBLICATIONS

Novels

The Witch Diggers. New York, Harcourt Brace, 1951; London, Heinemann, 1952.
South of the Angels. New York, Harcourt Brace, 1960; London, Hodder and Stoughton, 1961.
A Matter of Time. New York, Harcourt Brace, 1966; London, Macmillan, 1967.
Leafy Rivers. New York, Harcourt Brace, 1967; London, Macmillan, 1968.
The Massacre at Fall Creek. New York, Harcourt Brace, and London, Macmillan, 1975.

Short Stories

The Friendly Persuasion. New York, Harcourt Brace, 1945; London, Hodder and Stoughton, 1946.
Cress Delahanty. New York, Harcourt Brace, 1953; London, Hodder and Stoughton, 1954.
Except for Me and Thee: A Companion to The Friendly Persuasion. New York, Harcourt Brace, and London, Macmillan, 1969.

OTHER PUBLICATIONS

Novels

Little Men, in *Star Short Novels*, edited by Frederik Pohl. New York, Ballantine, 1954; published separately, as *The Chile-kings*, 1967.
The Life I Really Lived. New York, Harcourt Brace, 1979.
The State of Stony Lonesome. New York, Harcourt Brace, 1984.

Short Stories

Love, Death, and the Ladies' Drill Team. New York, Harcourt Brace, 1955; as *Learn to Say Goodbye*, London, Hodder and Stoughton, 1957.
Crimson Ramblers of the World, Farewell. New York, Harcourt Brace, 1970; London, Macmillan, 1971.
The Story of a Story and Three Stories. Berkeley, University of California, 1982.

Collected Stories of Jessamyn West. San Diego, Harcourt Brace, 1986.

Plays

A Mirror for the Sky, music by Gail Kubik (produced Eugene, Oregon, 1958). New York, Harcourt Brace, 1948.

Screenplays: *Friendly Persuasion* (uncredited), with Michael Wilson, 1956; *The Big Country*, with others, 1958; *The Stolen Hours*, 1963.

Verse

The Secret Look. New York, Harcourt Brace, 1974.

Other

The Reading Public (address). New York, Harcourt Brace, 1952.
Friends and Violence. Philadelphia, Friends General Conference, n.d.
To See the Dream. New York, Harcourt Brace, 1957; London, Hodder and Stoughton, 1958.
Love Is Not What You Think. New York, Harcourt Brace, 1959; as *A Woman's Love*, London, Hodder and Stoughton, 1960.
Hide and Seek: A Continuing Journey. New York, Harcourt Brace, and London, Macmillan, 1973.
The Woman Said Yes: Encounters with Life and Death: Memoirs. New York, Harcourt Brace, 1976; as *Encounters with Death and Life*, London, Gollancz, 1977.
Double Discovery: A Journey. New York, Harcourt Brace, 1980.

Editor, *The Quaker Reader.* New York, Viking Press, 1962.

*

Manuscript Collection: Whittier College, California.

Critical Studies: *Jessamyn West* by Alfred S. Shivers, New York, Twayne, 1972; *Jessamyn West* by Ann Dahlstrom Farmer, Boise, Idaho, Boise State University, 1982.

* * *

Jessamyn West was a prolific writer, who left behind her an oeuvre of astonishing size and variety. History and romance combine in her novels and stories with a powerful talent for characterization and psychological motivation. The western frontier is central to her work, and most of her writings have pioneer settings, either in the Midwest of the 19th century, or the California of the early 20th. West, herself a native of Indiana, experienced the pioneer period in its latter stages, and much of her fiction examines the landscape of the western myth from a new and strikingly individual viewpoint.

In her first book, *The Friendly Persuasion*, West depicts the lives of midwestern Quakers during the American Civil War. Jess Birdwell, a market gardener, has a contented community life in what seems a veritable paradise beside the River Muscatatuck. His wife Eliza is a handsome and pious preacher in their Meeting House. They and a "houseful of children," provide the reader with separate yet interrelated episodes. There are solemn moments, exploring the religious restrictions and pacifist convictions of the sect, and there are moments of quiet humour as Jess longs for the "sin" of music and secretly buys a harmonium. The war itself intrudes upon them with the battle of Finney's Ford, but Jess and Eliza manage to endure this catastrophe with their pacifist convictions still intact, though severely tested. West's ability to convey a vivid scene, and to chose the perfect phrase make a lasting impression on the reader.

A companion volume, *Except for Me and Thee*, was published in 1969. At its opening, Jess and Eliza are looking back to the first five years of marriage before their journey west to Indiana to make a new home and establish fruit production. Here they prosper in harmony with the settlement. The book continues, relating domestic incidents, watching the progress of the four children, the tragic death of one daughter, social gatherings with neighbours, and the eventual signing of a peace treaty.

Also set in the late 19th century, *The Witch Diggers* features 22-year-old Christian Frazer, who has hopes of being an insurance salesman. After the death of his mother, Christie travels by train from Indianapolis to stay on his Uncle Wesley's farm. He forms a strong friendship with his cousin Sylvie in the opening chapters, but it is Cate Conboy who has the greater influence over the young man. West's style is broader and more introspective in this novel. The symbolism is not always easy to understand, but the sights and sounds and smells of the country are sharply drawn, and each character is colourfully portrayed. Yet there are disturbing elements behind the words. The "Diggers" of the title are the inmates of a poor house which Christie visits, who search for Truth in a futile turning of the soil. A complicated cycle of episodes ends in violent destruction by fire.

Cress Delahanty is the record of an adolescent girl growing up on a California ranch. Chapters are headed with a season, and divided into the five years of Crescent's early teens. Cress is a complex girl, given to dreaming and reading poetry one moment, lively and talkative the next. Her home family and schoolday friends all contribute to a story of remarkable imagery. Cress also has an odd notion of her future husband, and is fully aware of her own attractions. Yet her compassion for a boy called Edwin renders her likeable and human.

South of the Angels is a substantial novel whose action centres on Los Angeles around 1916. West provides the reader with an absorbing study of human emotions set against a dramatic background of real estate development, and her narrative forms a documentary on the customs and beliefs of an American settler community. Once more, the author shows her enviable gift for picturesque description, as well as that of profound psychological insight.

Written in the first person, *A Matter of Time* is the sensitive story of a woman in early middle age caring for a younger sister who has cancer. The mention of personalities, automobiles, and television, would suggest the time to be the early 1960's. Again we are shown the past in dialogue and description, with West delving back into the sisters' childhood near Los Angeles. Though this flashback technique is effective, its frequent use tends to become repetitive. Tasmania travels to the desert state to live in the home of her dying sister, Blix, who has been diagnosed as incurable. Here they spend the last months of Blix's life in companionship and courage, living on memories and making plans for the eventual manner of her death. Tassie also reveals her own private thoughts in eloquent passages throughout. Having herself attended a sister suffering from the same illness, West is able to translate her authentic knowledge into fiction, providing touches of humour and honesty between the women who refuse to allow themselves to sink into self-pity.

Leafy Rivers is the account of a young woman in her first years of marriage, living on the Ohio frontier in the 1880's. Daughter of Bass and Prill Converse, Mary (Leafy) is married to Reno Rivers, and as the novel begins she is awaiting her first child, in what proves a difficult birth. During this time, the reader is taken back to their meeting in school, where Leafy is a senior pupil and Reno a newly appointed teacher. Through her thoughts and those of her family, one shares the experiences leading up to the wedding preparations. When Reno applies for a new teaching post, the couple journey by wagon to begin their life near the school, but disaster prevents them reaching their destination as the wagon overturns at a river crossing, with the loss of one horse. Leafy, however, is a resourseful girl, and cheerfully takes up the offer of help from their rescuer, going on to occupy a wooden cabin and raise a herd of half wild pigs. Chapters deal with each of the principal characters in turn. The many transitions between present and past are often confusing, but make for compulsive reading, helped by West's memorably drawn landscapes. Owing to a serious injury to Reno's foot while tree logging, Leafy is obliged to make the pig drive overland to Cincinnati for money to pay land tax. The final chapter completes the cycle with the birth of a daughter in the parents' own home.

The short story collection, *Crimson Ramblers of the World, Farewell*, shows the same narrative skill within a briefer compass. Each story is in marked contrast to the rest, creating a variety of moods from sinister to romantic. There is a subtle sense of holding something back, to end on a question. In common with all West's books, it rewards a careful reading.

Massacre at Fall Creek has West developing a familiar western theme, namely the massacre of a group of friendly Indians by murderous whites, and the consequences of the atrocity. As might be expected, however, the author avoids drawing any obvious conclusions from her material, instead exploring the undercurrent of fear, suspicion and hatred that caused the murderers to act as they did. In the aftermath of the massacre, as the trial takes its course, West presents the horror of the past events in homely but convincing terms, through the eyes of the participants and the townsfolk who while not actively involved themselves, nevertheless condoned what took place. Subtly but compellingly, she investigates the depths and complexities of her characters, whose testimony is faithfully captured in accurate period dialogue. The psychology of the men who killed the friendly Senecas—a crime based on a factual incident in West's native Indiana in 1824—is presented with insight and understanding. The Indian-hating George Benson, who led the murderers, is shown to be a tragic figure, himself bearing the scars of past violence, rather than the "monster" so often encountered in western fiction. The sombre theme is relieved by the inevitable love story which virtually no West story is without, this time between the local girl Hannah Cape and the "imported" defence lawyer Charlie Fort, and it is the harmony of love, rather than racial hatred, which triumphs in the end.

West's explorations of the frontier experience, whether in its earlier phase, as with *Massacre at Fall Creek*, or in its latter days at the turn of the century, as in *South of the Angels*, shows an imaginative and original reworking of the age-old themes. Ultimately, however, her concern is for the people, the men and women of that time and our own, and her evocation of their dreams and hopes in her own writings is surely destined to survive a readership beyond our own century.

—Jo M. Hudman

WEST, Kingsley.

Western Publications

Novels

A Time for Vengeance. New York, Doubleday, 1961.
South to Gunsight Pass. London, Long, 1961.
Ride West to Pueblo. London, Long, 1962; New York, Doubleday, 1963.
Showdown at Gila Bend. New York, Berkley, 1963.
Killers' Kingdom. London, Long, 1963.
Latigo's Day. London, Long, 1963.
Comanche River. London, Long, and New York, Berkley, 1965.
Arroyo Hondo. New York, Berkley, 1966.
Arroyo West. New York, Berkley, 1976.
Cavalry Code. London, Hale, 1983.

* * *

The first thing a reader new to Kingsley West notices is his style. It is a sparse style, vastly understated in terms of action and violence, more often than not unadorned by descriptive ornaments; at times it could even be called eccentric. And yet it works. Western writers often rein their words so tightly that no life remains. What is missing is a voice, an attitude, which molds both the reader and the story. This is a dangerous road for a writer to tread, imposing his will so blatantly on his audience—some would even call it pretentious. At its worst, we throw the book down in disgust and walk away. At its best, we keep turning the pages as fast as we can.

West's style usually works, and works well: one imagines that if Hemingway and Jack London collaborated on Westerns the result would be similar. This approach works best during the frequent action sequences. In a West novel man resembles a predatory animal: he is remorseless, instinctive, and must act before thinking if he wants to stay alive. He is shaped by the savagery of the plains; he *feels*, rather than knows, when it is time for him to settle down or move on. Unfortunately, in more reflective sequences the style breaks down. In *South to Gunsight Pass*, in order to express a character's sexual longing, we are told that a minor woman character is "young and goodlooking. She had breasts." When the protagonist philosophizes about hearth and home, the results sound more like what we'd read in some teenager's guide to marriage than the ruminations of a weary, lone-wolf man.

West knows his strengths, however, and in later books like *Showdown at Gila Bend* these passages are kept to an absolute minimum. Scenes become almost episodic, as if in wild country there is no hindsight or foresight, no cause and effect, past or future, but simply the desperate scrabble to stay alive *now*. There is a fatal intensity to his writing at those points, and instead of merely looking on, safe within our spectators' shells, we become one with the character. We know the odds against survival, we sweat in fear with him, we feel his pain. We participate. And we realize afterwards that notwithstanding the few blunders, those stylistic chances were worth it, and that this author has accomplished his artistic goal.

—Joe Jackson

WEST, Tom. Pseudonym for Fred East. Also wrote as Roy Manning. British. Born in London in 1895. Served with the

British Army in France during World War I. Married; one son and one daughter. Lived in United States, working as choreman, teamster, cowhand in California, copywriter, reporter, country editor, and freelance writer. *Died c. 1980.*

Western Publications

Novels

Meddling Maverick. New York, Dutton, 1944; London, Ward Lock, 1946.
Bushwhack Basin. New York, Dutton, 1945; London, Ward Lock, 1946.
Trouble Trail. New York, Dutton, 1946.
Renegade Ranch. New York, Dutton, 1946; as *Renegade Range*, London, Ward Lock, 1947.
Six-Gun Showdown. New York, Dutton, 1947; London, Ward Lock, 1948.
Powdersmoke Pay-Off. New York, Dutton, 1948; London, Ward Lock, 1949.
Spectre Spread. New York, Dutton, 1948; London, Ward Lock, 1949.
Botched Brand. New York, Dutton, 1949; London, Ward Lock, 1950.
Ghost Gold. New York, Dutton, 1950; London, Wright and Brown, 1952.
Vulture Valley. New York, Dutton, 1951; London, Wright and Brown, 1953.
Flaming Feud. New York, Dutton, 1951; London, Wright and Brown, 1954.
Ghost Gun. New York, Dutton, 1952; London, Wright and Brown, 1954.
Gunsmoke Gold. New York, Dutton, 1952.
Lobo Legacy. New York, Ace, 1954.
Outlaw Brand. New York, Pyramid, 1956.
Torture Trail. New York, Ace, 1957.
Lead in His Fists. New York, Ace, 1958.
Slick on the Draw. New York, Ace, 1958.
Twisted Trail. New York, Ace, 1959.
The Cactus Kid. New York, Ace, 1959.
Nothing But My Gun. New York, Ace, 1960; London, Severn House, 1978.
The Gun from Nowhere. New York, Ace, 1961; London, Severn House, 1979.
Killer's Canyon. New York, Ace, 1961.
Battling Buckaroos. New York, Ace, 1962.
Triggering Texan. New York, Ace, 1963; London, Severn House, 1978.
Lobo Man. New York, Ace, 1963.
Sidewinder Showdown. New York, Ace, 1964; London, Severn House, 1978.
The Man at Rope's End. New York, Ace, 1964.
Lost Loot of Kittycat Ranch. New York, Ace, 1965.
Buchwhack Brand. New York, Ace, 1965.
The Toughest Town in the Territory. New York, Ace, 1965.
Bitter Brand. New York, Ace, 1966.
Rattlesnake Range. New York, Ace, 1966.
Hangrope Heritage. New York, Ace, 1966.
Crossfire at Barbed M. New York, Ace, 1967.
Showdown at Serano. New York, Ace, 1967; London, Sphere, 1970.
The Buzzard's Nest. London, Sphere, 1970.
Dead Man's Double Cross. London, Sphere, 1970.
Don't Cross My Line. London, Sphere, 1970.
Renegade Roundup. London, Sphere, 1970.
The Black Buzzards. London, Sphere, 1970.
Write His Name in Gunsmoke. New York, Ace, 1972.
Lone Gun. New York, Curtis, 1974.
Payoff at Piute. New York, Ace, 1977.
Battle at Rattlesnake Pass. New York, Ace, 1979.
Sagebrush Showdown. New York, Zebra, 1979.
Trigger Tyrant. New York, Zebra, 1979.
Hard Trail to Santa Fe. New York, Zebra, 1980.

Novels as Roy Manning

Trigger Trail. Philadelphia, Macrae Smith, 1945; London, Harrap, 1950.
Vengeance Valley. Philadelphia, Macrae Smith, 1946; as *The Marshal of Vengeance Valley*, London, Harrap, 1951.
Tangled Trail. Philadelphia, Macrae Smith, 1947; London, Ward Lock, 1948.
Six Gun Sheriff. Philadelphia, Macrae Smith, 1949; London, Foulsham, 1950.
Red Range. Philadelphia, Macrae Smith, 1950; London, Foulsham, 1951.
The Desperado Code. New York, Ace, 1953.
Beware of This Tenderfoot. New York, Ace, 1956.
Draw and Die! New York, Ace, 1958.

Other Publications

Other

Heroes on Horseback: The Story of the Pony Express. New York, Four Winds Press, 1969; London, Blackie, 1972.

* * *

Tom West was a prolific author whose love of alliteration extended both to the titles of his books—*Heroes on Horseback*, *Black Buzzards*, and *Triggering Texan* are three examples of many—and often to the names of his characters. His stories usually share a fairly standard format, featuring a hero wrongly suspected of some crime, who wins through in the end to clear his name and claim the heroine. Typical of his style are *Sweetgrass Valley Showdown* and *Sidewinder Showdown*, both of which also include an element of the detective story in their plots, with the hero unmasking the villain from a list of possible suspects. In the first, a good-natured drunkard unjustly accused of rustling emerges as a hero, while his respectable but mean brother-in-law is revealed as the actual leader of the outlaw gang. In the second, another wrongfully suspected hero brings a poisoner to justice, and marries an heiress. Description tends to be florid, and the characters mainly pasteboard, but the predictability of the plots are redeemed by odd touches of humour in the writing, and by West's skill in spinning out the detection of the villains.

The Gun from Nowhere, a fairly unremarked effort, probably deserves more praise than some. Its mysterious gunman hero, Butch, emerges as a credible character for once, and the plot is stronger. West's alliteration is given free rein with the three main villains—marshal Lanky Lakald, gambler Deuce Diamond, and Judge Jonathan Jenkins—but the prose is faster moving and far less cluttered than in most of his novels, and continuous action holds the attention of the reader. Better still is *Triggering Texan*, which must rank as one of West's finest achievements. Its story follows the adventures of Craig Carter, an ex-Confederate officer, who takes a trail herd north for Abilene in the period after the Civil War. West's account of his battles with outlaws, bad weather, and the crooked rancher Hobson is exciting, and moves at a rapid pace to its climax. Dialogue is good, and in Carter and his friend Pete Corrigan the author produces two of his most memorable—and believable—characters.

—Jeff Sadler

WEST, Ward. *See* **BORLAND, Hal.**

WESTLAND, Lynn. *See* **JOSCELYN, Archie.**

WESTON, Cole. *See* **RANDISI, Robert J.**

WESTWOOD, Perry. *See* **HOLMES, L.P.**

WETZEL, Lewis. *See* **KING, Albert.**

WHEELER, Richard S. American. Born in Milwaukee, Wisconsin, 12 March 1935. Educated at the University of Wisconsin, Madison, 1958–61. Married Rita Middleton in 1961 (divorced). Editorial writer, Phoenix *Gazette*, Arizona, 1961–62; page editor, Oakland *Tribune*, California, 1963–65; staff writer, *Reader's Digest*, Washington, D.C., 1966; reporter, Billings *Gazette*, Montana, 1968–69, and *Nevada Appeal*, Carson City, 1969–70; copy editor and city editor, Billings *Gazette*, 1970–72; book editor, Open Court Publishing Co., LaSalle, Illinois 1973–74, Icarus Press, South Bend, Indiana, 1980–81, Green Hill Publishers, Ottawa, Illinois, 1982–85, and Walker & Co., New York, 1985–87. Since 1988 full-time writer. Recipient: American Political Science Association award, for journalism, 1969; Western Writers of America Spur award, 1989. Agent: Barbara Puechner, P.O. Box 3308, Bethlehem, Pennsylvania 18017. Address: P.O. Box 1449, Big Timber, Montana 59011, U.S.A.

WESTERN PUBLICATIONS

Novels (series: Skye's West)

Bushwhack. New York, Doubleday, 1978; London, Hale, 1981.
Beneath the Blue Mountain. New York, Doubleday, 1979; London, Hale, 1980.
Winter Grass. New York, Walker, 1983.
Sam Hook. New York, Walker, 1986; London, Hale, 1987.
Richard Lamb. New York, Walker, 1987.
Dodging Red Cloud. New York, Evans, 1987.
Stop. New York, Evans, 1988; London, Hale, 1989.
Fool's Coach. New York, Evans, 1989.
Sun River (West). New York, Tor, 1989.
Bannack (West). New York, Tor, 1989.
Where the River Runs. New York, Evans, 1990.
The Far Tribes (West). New York, Tor, 1990.
Yellowstone (West). New York, Tor, 1990.
Montana Hitch. New York, Evans, 1990.
Incident at Fort Keogh. New York, Ballantine, 1990.
The Final Tally. New York, Fawcett, 1990.

*

Richard S. Wheeler comments:

I have tried to write Westerns that appeal to educated readers. They have deeper characterization and a richer vocabulary than one finds in most Westerns. They are largely offbeat stories: I've sought the borderline between serious literature and popular fiction, and admire those authors who work at that level, such as John le Carré. The 1840's and 1850's were the most colorful decades in the settlement of the West, and I am placing most of my stories in that period. I'm also moving away from the classic Western, the mythic Western, because the real, historical frontier is much better material. Among cultivated people, there's an intuitive hostility against Western fiction that I hope to shatter.

* * *

Among a number of prolific but solid western writers whose work has appeared only in the last decade or so—writers such as Loren D. Estleman, Jory Sherman, Robert J. Conley, Bryan Woolley, Terry Johnston, Dan Parkinson, Jack Cummings, Winfred Blevins, and Don Coldsmith—Richard S. Wheeler has an enviable record, recognized by his peers, as a consistently innovative writer of off-the-main-trail novels with a sound historical undergirding, a deceptively easy style, and a born-story-teller's knack for keeping his readers glued to his pages and guessing.

Winter Grass, his third novel, depicts a typical Wheeler approach to the Western—to distance himself from the stylized, rigid, arid, "formula" story and "to write a book that thumbed its nose at every cliché." Thus, *Winter Grass* has as its protagonist a Boston brahmin, John Quincy Putnam; in lieu of the customary gunfight, there is not a shot fired in anger in Wheeler's novel—indeed, *weather* is a critical factor; there are no heroes and villains, only protagonists and antagonists; there is a strong female character, an early woman lawyer, independent and strong-willed, and the novel deals with real-world issues such as public land policy, enclosure laws, and even presidential politics. Wheeler adds, "Western rarely had children, so I included one in *Winter Grass*; and Westerns were usually written in basic English, so I employed a full vocabulary and all the literary devices I could manage."

The novel was a success, receiving rave reviews, a nomination for a Golden Spur award from Western Writers of America, and a paperback reprint.

Wheeler, among the rare modern popular novelists who has written reflectively on his craft, says: "I really haven't varied much from my original wish to write a richer, more literate western story. Over the years I have been able to define what it is I love about good popular fiction. It's the storytelling quality.

A skilled category novelist knows how to tug at the heart, how to move people, horrify them, bring them to tears, plunge them into anguish or ecstasy . . . and how to hurry a story along to prevent boredom."

Even the briefest glimpses at some of Wheeler's novels give a sense of the richness and invention of this former newspaperman and editor. In *Beneath the Blue Mountain*, a stern New Englander stakes a homestead claim in Arizona Territory and comes into conflict with an equally stern Spaniard who refuses to recognize American claims to Arizona and who has a private army to enforce his beliefs. Sam Hook, in the book of that title, raises longhorns in Hereford and Angus cattle country in Montana and a reluctant sheriff has to stand between a determined stockmen's association and a courageous and determined old man. *Richard Lamb* is another novel about a fiercely independent frontiersman, this one a son of a classics professor and a Harvard alumnus who, for nearly 30 years has lived on the Upper Musselshell with a Blackfoot wife, running a small trading post, and now, in 1877, coming into conflict with "Bluebelly soldiers" and an Eastern newspaperman come West to cover the Army's Indian campaigns.

In *Dodging Red Cloud*, Wheeler's touch is serio-comic in a story about three travelers—a woman who has made a fortune in Virginia City, a horse-trader and confidence man, and a 12-year-old orphan—on the Bozeman Trail, a bloody traveler's route being defended to the death by the mighty Oglala war chief Red Cloud. *Stop*, perhaps a first in Western novels, has a banker as a hero in a story set in a Montana mining town in 1879. *Fool's Coach*, which earned the Spur award as the best Western novel, is a story set in Virginia City in the days of the infamous lawman-bandit Henry Plummer and concerns the plight of a miner, a gambler and a madame trying to get a stagecoach full of gold through Plummer's army of road agents.

And, in *Where the River Runs*, arguably his best novel, Wheeler reaches back to 1849 to tell a story of 12 men on a peaceful expedition to the Indian nations on the Upper Missouri River. A cholera epidemic wipes out the party, save for its leader, Capt. Jed Owens, whose fiancée hires a French guide, Jean Gallant, to find her betrothed and the fate of the exploring party. This book, above all of the author's repertoire, is a psychological study—Gallant is perhaps the deepest and most interesting character (with Richard Lamb a close runner-up) Wheeler has created—as well as a beautifully-told and moving story.

Wheeler's Skye's West series of paperback original novels are clearly a delight for both the writer and reader. Wheeler has a deft comic touch (especially in such books as *Dodging Red Cloud*, *Fool's Coach* and *Incident at Fort Keogh*, the latter concerning an Irish "remittance man" named Santiago Toole) but in the Skye books (*Sun River*, *Bannack*, *The Far Tribes*, *Yellow-stone*) he has created a character and milieu that are perfect for the Wheeleresque blend of character, story, history, and humor, and a particular theme the author loves—plunging eastern and European people into the Wild West well ahead of the frontier. ("The culture clash is marvelous," Wheeler says.)

Barnaby Skye is a deserter from the Royal Navy who has made his way from Fort Vancouver to the vastness of the Rockies, there for two decades ruling his domain with his belaying pin, his Sharps and Colt .44, his two Indian wives (one a Shoshoni, the other a Crow), and his ugly, vicious, battle-scarred horse Jawbone. Skye drinks prodigious amounts of corn whiskey, insists on being called *Mister* Skye, and takes occasional exploring or hunting parties of missionaries, would-be farmers, British sportsmen, scientists, and industrialists, into the wilderness.

The Skye novels are Wheeler's best pure storytelling with all the qualities he admires in reading the works of other writers: rich characterization, well-drawn female characters, unexpected elements, eccentricities, lore, and history that never slow the pace of the story.

—Dale L. Walker

WHITE, Harry. *See* **WHITTINGTON, Harry.**

WHITE, Stewart Edward. American. Born in Grand Rapids, Michigan, 12 March 1873. Educated at Grand Rapids High School; University of Michigan, Ann Arbor, Ph.B. 1895, M.A. 1903; Columbia University Law School, New York, 1896–97. Served in the 144th Field Artillery during World War I: Major. Married Elizabeth Grant in 1904 (died). Worked in a packing house, as a prospector, and in McClung's bookshop in Chicago; then freelance writer. *Died 18 September 1946.*

WESTERN PUBLICATIONS

Novels

The Claim Jumpers: A Romance. New York, Appleton, 1901; London, Hodder and Stoughton, 1905.

The Westerners. New York, McClure, and London, Constable, 1901.

The Blazed Trail. New York, McClure, and London, Constable, 1902.

Conjuror's House: A Romance of the Free Forest. New York, McClure, and London, Methuen, 1903; as *Call of the North*, New York, Triangle, 1941.

The Riverman. New York, McClure, and London, Hodder and Stoughton, 1908.

The Rules of the Game. New York, Doubleday, 1910; London, Nelson, 1911.

The Adventures of Bobby Orde. New York, Doubleday, 1911; London, Unwin, 1912; as *Bobby Orde*, London, Hodder and Stoughton, 1916.

The Story of California. New York, Doubleday, 1927.
- *Gold.* New York, Doubleday, 1913; London, Hodder and Stoughton, 1914.
- *The Gray Dawn.* New York, Doubleday, and London, Hodder and Stoughton, 1915.
- *The Rose Dawn.* New York, Doubleday, 1920; London, Hodder and Stoughton, 1921.

On Tiptoe: A Romance of the Redwoods. New York, Doran, and London, Hodder and Stoughton, 1922.

The Saga of Andy Burnett. New York, Doubleday, 1947.
- *The Long Rifle.* New York, Doubleday, and London, Hodder and Stoughton, 1932.
- *Ranchero.* New York, Doubleday, and London, Hodder and Stoughton, 1933.
- *Folded Hills.* New York, Doubleday, and London, Hodder and Stoughton, 1934.

Wild Geese Calling. New York, Doubleday, and London, Hodder and Stoughton, 1940.

Stampede. New York, Doubleday, 1942; London, Hale, 1952.

Short Stories

Blazed Trail Stories, and Stories of the Wild Life. New York, McClure, 1904; London, Hodder and Stoughton, 1906.

Arizona Nights. New York, Doubleday, and London, Hodder and Stoughton, 1907.
The Killer. New York, Doubleday, 1919; London, Hodder and Stoughton, 1920.
The Hold-Up. San Francisco, Book Club of California, 1937.

Uncollected Short Stories

"On the Clay Slab," in *Western Story* (New York), 11 February 1922.
"The Two-Gun Man," in *World's One Hundred Best Stories*, edited by Grant M. Overton. New York, Funk and Wagnalls, 10 vols., 1927.
"Free, Wide, and Handsome," in *World's Best Short Stories of 1928*, edited by William Johnston. New York, Minton, 1928.
"The Man with Nerve," in *West* (New York), September 1933.
"The Rawhider," in *West* (New York), October 1933.
"The Ole Virginia," in *West* (New York), November 1933.
"The Emigrants," in *West* (New York), December 1933.
"The Remittance Man," in *West* (New York), January 1934.
"The Cattle Rustlers," in *West* (New York), February 1934.
"A Corner in Horses," in *West* (New York), March 1934.
"Murder on the Beach," in *West* (New York), May 1934.
"Grampus and the Weasel," in *Post Stories of 1935*, edited by Wesley W. Stout. New York, Random House, 1935.
"The Honk-Honk Breed," in *Western Roundup*, edited by Arnold Hano. New York, Bantam, 1948.
"Guest's Gold," in *The Saturday Evening Post Reader of Western Stories*, edited by E.N. Brandt. New York, Doubleday, 1960.
"Buried Treasure," in *The Arizonans*, edited by Bill Pronzini and Martin H. Greenberg. New York, Fawcett, 1989.

OTHER PUBLICATIONS

Novels

The Silent Places. New York, McClure, and London, Hodder and Stoughton, 1904.
The Mystery, with Samuel Hopkins Adams. New York, McClure, and London, Hodder and Stoughton, 1907.
The Sign at Six. Indianapolis, Bobbs Merrill, and London, Hodder and Stoughton, 1912.
The Leopard Woman. New York, Doubleday, and London, Hodder and Stoughton, 1916.
The Glory Hole. New York, Doubleday, and London, Hodder and Stoughton, 1924.
Skookum Chuck. New York, Doubleday, and London, Heinemann, 1925.
Secret Harbor. New York, Doubleday, and London, Hodder and Stoughton, 1926.
Back of Beyond. New York, Doubleday, and London, Hodder and Stoughton, 1927.
Pole Star, with Harry DeVighne. New York, Doubleday, 1935; London, Hodder and Stoughton, 1936.

Short Stories

Simba. New York, Doubleday, 1918.
White Magic. London, Hodder and Stoughton, 1918.

Play

Call of the North, adaptation of his novel *Conjuror's House* (produced New York, 1908). New York, Doubleday, 1919.

Other

The Forest. New York, Outlook, 1903; London, Richards, 1904.
The Magic Forest: A Modern Fairy Story (for children). New York, Macmillan, 1903; London, Hodder and Stoughton, 1916.
The Mountains. New York, McClure, and London, Hodder and Stoughton, 1904.
The Pass. New York, Outing, and London, Hodder and Stoughton, 1906.
Camp and Trail. New York, Outing, 1907.
The Cabin. New York, Doubleday, 1911; London, Nelson, 1912.
The Land of Footprints. New York, Doubleday, 1912; London, Nelson, 1913.
African Camp Fires. New York, Doubleday, 1913; London, Nelson, 1914.
The Works of Stewart Edward White. New York, Doubleday, 8 vols., 1913; augmented edition, 10 vols., 1916.
The Rediscovered Country. New York, Doubleday, and London, Hodder and Stoughton, 1915.
The Forty-Niners: A Chronicle of the California Trail and El Dorado. New Haven, Connecticut, Yale University Press, 1918.
Daniel Boone, Wilderness Scout. New York, Doubleday, 1922; London, Hodder and Stoughton, 1923.
Credo. New York, Doubleday, and London, Heinemann, 1925.
Lions in the Path: A Book of Adventure on the High Veldt. New York, Doubleday, 1926.
Why Be a Mud Turtle? New York, Doubleday, 1928.
Dog Days, Other Times Other Dogs: The Autobiography of a Man and His Dog Friends Through Four Decades of Changing America. New York, Doubleday, 1930.
The Shepper-Newfounder (for children). New York, Doubleday, 1931.
Wild Animals (for children), drawings by Sydney Joseph. Burlingame, California, Workers' Shop for the Unemployed, 1932.
The Betty Book: Excursions into the World of Other-Consciousness, Made by Betty Between 1919 and 1936. New York, Dutton, 1937; London, Hale, 1945.
Old California in Picture and Story. New York, Doubleday, 1937.
Across the Unknown, with Harwood White. New York, Dutton, 1939.
The Unobstructed Universe. New York, Dutton, 1940; London, Hale, 1949.
The Road I Know. New York, Dutton, 1942; London, Hale, 1951.
Anchors to Windward: Stability and Personal Peace—Here and Now. New York, Dutton, 1943.

Speaking for Myself. New York, Doubleday, 1943.
The Stars Are Still There. New York, Dutton, 1946.
With Folded Wings. New York, Dutton, 1947; London, Hale, 1951.
The Job of Living. New York Dutton, 1948.

*

Critical Study: *Stewart Edward White* by Judy Alter, Boise, Idaho, Boise State University, 1975.

* * *

The strong autobiographical elements in Stewart Edward White's adventure stories, some of which are set in the West, give them authenticity and serve as a unifying element. His preference for history and historical fiction—particularly of the logging industry, the early years of the American fur trade, and the history of California—resulted in his careful attention to detail and historical fact. His descriptions of the outdoors have an imaginative and a lyrical quality which distinguishes them above mere accuracy because he was able to combine the experience of adventure with complexity of character. His habitual concern for fidelity to the life of the region was amplified by an awareness of the region's changing ways. While he was less given to nostalgia then some Western writers, he sensed and regretted the passing of an era as he explored the pioneer spirit, adventure, and experience on the edge of civilization. And at his best he wrote fiction that is carefully particularized without being limited by the anecdotalism of too faithful adherence to minutiae.

Often uneven as a writer he used pedantic nonfiction and predictable characters, substituted adventure for the complexity of human nature and for the regional or western experience, and resorted to formula for his western hero: he lives in the open air most of the year, he guards an athletic habit of body, and he proves himself in an adventure where finely controlled strength is required.

The heavily autobiographical logging novels about the Orde family—*The Riverman*, *The Adventures of Bobby Orde*, *The Rules of the Game*, and *The Blazed Trail*—glorify the hard perilous manual labor in the destruction of the last big corner of the immense primeval forest, stress that brutality stems more from nature than from man, and yield much technical information of the logging industry.

The Black Hills works, particularly *The Westerners* and *The Claim Jumpers*, brought White his first fame as a western writer. In a mock-heroic tone with bloody violence, these works rely heavily on coincidence to work out the structure and treat the time-honored theme of the West, where one goes to become a man.

The stories about Arizona—*Arizona Nights* and *The Killer*—closely relate to his Black Hills works in demonstrating the streak of cruelty and violence that comes from human perversion rather than from an onslaught by natural forces. In these short stories White makes the people lifelike and roots them in their environment. For example, in "Rawhide" Buck comes to a new awareness and a new capacity for human sympathy when he recognizes the stark and cruel fact of the desert where he once saw only beauty.

The 16 uneven California books roughly divide into historical narratives, a wilderness series, and a few miscellaneous works. The triology of *Gold*, *The Gray Dawn*, and *The Rose Dawn* covers the mining camps, period of lawlessness, and vigilante action on San Francisco. *The Saga of Andy Burnett*, another series, is his best work. The reader feels immersed in the study of growth of Andy Burnett, the settlement of California, 1832–55, and the blending of the Californian and Anglo cultures. Two works, not set in California, are an integral part of the Saga: *Daniel Boone*, the concept of pioneer, and *The Long Rifle*, the life of Burnett as mountain man and trapper. Beginning with *Ranchero* Burnett undergoes a transformation from mountain man to Californian. In *Folded Hills* Andy reaches the peak of his development against a background of class and cultural struggles and political events. *Stampede*, the weakest, uses coincidence to bring the saga to a resolution.

On Tiptoe, a slight novel in mock heroic vein, shows White's first interest in and use of spiritual phenomenon. Additional California works—*The Mountain, The Pass, Camp and Trail*, and *The Cabin*—mainly promote the cause of conservation.

Seven works comprise his African period, and four the Alaskan frontier, but none reaches the high mark of the Burnett saga.

—G. Dale Gleason

WHITEHEAD, David (Henry). Also writes as Ben Bridges; Matt Logan; Janet Whitehead. British. Born in London, 3 January 1958. Married Janet Ann Smith in 1981. Worked as a librarian, 1975; camera operator in an advertising department, 1976–79; administration assistant in a pest control firm, 1979–82; from 1981 senior clerk, later assistant in charge, BBC Books Registry. Address: c/o Robert Hale Ltd, 45–47 Clerkenwell Green, London EC1R 0HT, England.

Western Publications

Novels (series: Judge and Dury)

Hang 'em All (Judge and Dury). London, Hale 1989.
Heller. London, Hale, 1990.
Starpacker. London, Hale, 1990.
Riding for Justice (Judge and Dury). London, Hale, 1990.
Law of the Gun (Judge and Dury). London, Hale, 1991.
Tanner's Guns (as Matt Logan). London, Hale, 1991.

Novels as Ben Bridges (series: O'Brien; Wilde Boys)

The Silver Trail (O'Brien). London, Hale, 1986.
Hard as Nails (O'Brien). London, Hale, 1987.
Mexico Breakout (O'Brien). London, Hale, 1987.
Hangman's Noose (O'Brien). London, Hale, 1988.
The Wilde Boys. London, Hale, 1988.
The Deadly Dollars (O'Brien). London, Hale, 1988.
Wilde Fire. London, Hale, 1988.
Squaw Man (O'Brien). London, Hale, 1989.
Wilde's Law. London, Hale, 1990.
North of the Border (O'Brien). London, Hale, 1990.
Shoot to Kill (O'Brien). London, Hale, 1990.
Aces Wilde. London, Hale, 1991.
Stagecoach to Hell (O'Brien). London, Hale, 1991.

Other Publications

Novels as Janet Whitehead

Yours for Eternity. London, Hale, 1991.
Patterns in the Snow. London, Hale, 1991.

*

David Whitehead comments:

My goal as a writer of category fiction (a role to which I have aspired since primary school) is quite simply to entertain. In the grand scheme of things, of course, my Westerns are not "important"—they're not intended to be—but I see no reason why the quality of writing in *any* category should not be as fine or as interesting as the writer can make it. At the end of the day, however, there is no real message in any of my books except the one that says, "Read it and enjoy it, because it was written especially for *you.*"

So get reading!

* * *

From his first book onwards there is no sign of David Whitehead learning his craft or, indeed, having to learn it. His debut with *The Silver Trail* is a well-plotted page-turner which already demonstrates all of the qualities and competence that have come to mark his succeeding work: crisp action scenes, pounding narrative, well-realised characterisation, a hard-hitting racy style. Whitehead is one of those creatures that populate science fiction (but not all that common in the western field): the fanzine-writer-turned-novelist. The years of reading that makes an ardent fan, the writing required in compiling fanzines (reviewing books, articles analysing authors' styles, etc.), not to mention brushing shoulders with his idols, have clearly provided the necessary apprenticeship. Coupled with the fact that he is a superb, natural writer.

The Silver Trail introduces soldier of fortune Carter O'Brien whose exploits have become the mainstay of Whitehead's output. In these and all the other books, Whitehead's greatest strength is his style—snappy, crisp, vivid, and as appropriate to the Western as was Raymond Chandler's to the world of the private eye. It matters not whether he has actually caught the vernacular of the period (he will sometimes use modern words such as "teenager"), the *effect* is that he has. Words are employed for their vitality and he changes parts of speech to serve this purpose. Witness "Heller *hipped* around in the saddle to scan his backtrail" where he has verbalised a noun.

Whitehead chooses vivid metaphors. "When Tom finally went down, it was like watching a redwood topple." A hungry man aims "to wrap himself round some supper." A coffee-pot is "busy spewing smoke signals into the empty air." A character gets "all shook up like a San Francisco cocktail." A big man reaches "out a paw you could sit on." A busy town is "as active as a stomped-on ant hill." A deal struck with a dying man is "a bargain made with a corpse who was still awake." Maybe not all original but the thick-and-fast piling on gives vitality and colour to the writing akin to the effect of daubing on oil paint with a palette knife.

Further, Whitehead catches the attention with his juxtaposition of contrasting images, for instance where "the lazy flap-flap of washing drying in the breeze was replaced by a gun-blast." Elsewhere we get "snow-punctured darkness."

Taking these examples out of context does not do them justice. Whitehead does not so much succumb to cliché as grab it by the throat and subdue it to his purpose, which is to provide action entertainment at a gallop. Sounds corny? Far from it, because another of his tricks is to make us laugh: either out loud such as where his hero jumps on a farting horse—then rides like the wind, or with irony as where a man smiles "the kind of smile you reserve for the funeral of your worst enemy."

Whitehead enjoys word-play, a notable poetic example being the last lines of *Hang 'em All* which will not be repeated so as not to spoil the reader's enjoyment. When you least expect it he will come up with the unexpected. *Hangman's Noose* is a run-of-the-mill actioner until O'Brien, in need of help to take him across uncharted territory, after a long trek finally reaches the Indian guide to whom he has been recommended, only to find the man is blind. But as the succeeding adventures show the redman is not unduly handicapped by his disability.

Similarly the low-key start of *Hang 'em All* takes on bite when early in the plot, the lawman protagonist finds himself facing the guns of his long-lost son. Warmth exudes from the pages: warmth between friends, between family, between lovers, between people who find they owe each other something.

Whitehead has concentrated on writing series and the prime obstacles in the writing of this form are the maintenance of quality and the avoidance of staleness. While the author keeps his head up with distinction in the O'Brien series he is encumbered with the restrictions he imposes upon himself with the Wilde Boys format. This somewhat less successful series is a *Dirty Dozen* on horseback. Isaac Wilde, a retired judge decides to use outlaws to fight outlaws. The text tells us that it was an "outrageous new idea" and so it might have been at the time of the story, but at the time of writing, more than a little hackneyed along with their supposed advantages: the gang don't have to follow the letter of the law, they don't have to observe political boundaries, they are expendable, etc. We have heard it all before. The titles, all playing cleverly on the word Wilde, call to mind William Holden and his Wild Bunch. Presumably the intention was to evoke the hard imagery of Peckinpah's films but the snag is that idea is 20 years old and we know what to expect: the macho camaraderie, the conflict with regular law officers, and so on. Moreover, the device of having a regular gang of heroes has drawbacks in plotting: the stage will tend to be crowded (there are six in this bunch) and, as with all group series (the Doc Savage gang, for example), it is extremely difficult to give the protagonists any depth. One can't go much beyond cardboard cut-outs, with each member being characterised by some personality trait, together with a useful speciality. Further, to overcome the deadweight effect of the whole gang lumbering through all the action scenes, the device of splitting them up for encapsulated mini-adventures within the overall plot is often used but this does tend to lead to some fracturing of the structure.

But this is only one person's reaction and such a series might well be relished by A-Team enthusiasts. Their first adventure (*The Wilde Boys*) takes them south to Mexico to end the reign of terror of a vicious outlaw. The second (*Wilde Fire*), which to give it its due does link consecutively with the first, throws them into the assignment of protecting an attractive lady witness against a powerful senator due to be tried. The politician sends out a pack of killers to thwart them. As one expects from Whitehead, the verbal style is engrossing and action scenes are good.

There are, perhaps inevitably, a few minor irritations in Whitehead's style. When describing landscape Whitehead often goes overboard in merely listing flora: it is not unusual for him to list up to four varieties of vegetation that his characters may be be riding past. However, the fact that these occasional lapses stand out is a tribute to a colourful and vivid writer. In one less competent, such prosiness would go unnoticed. Secondly, there are some figures of speech of which he is overly fond. As an example, in almost every book there is some character who, when hit in the mouth, experiences a "worm of blood" from his lip. The first time you read that, it strikes as a good metaphor. But not the umpteenth time. Similarly, there are odd regularly-appearing nouns. "Star-packer" for a lawman, "she-male" for a female. These were refreshing when first seen, but appear much too frequently across the range of his books.

But these quibbles are minor, and do not detract from the overall impact. In his new books, including those under his new

Matt Logan pen-name, Whitehead continues to carry the standard of the new generation of western writing with pace, atmosphere, and momentum; he is well worth the time of lovers of the genre.

—B.J. Holmes

WHITSON, John H(arvey). Also wrote as Lt. A.K. Sims. American. Born in Seymour, Indiana, 28 December 1854. Married Flora Josselyn in 1900. Admitted to the Indiana bar, and practiced in Seymour, 1876–79; ordained a Baptist minister, 1898: head of the Department of Religious Education, Hardin College, Mexico, Missouri; teacher at Ward-Belmont, Nashville, 1920–23. *Died 2 May 1936.*

WESTERN PUBLICATIONS

Novels

Barbara, A Woman of the West. Boston, Little Brown, 1903.
The Rainbow Chasers. Boston, Little Brown, 1904; London, Ward Lock, 1905.
Justin Wingate, Ranchman. Boston, Little Brown, 1905.
The Castle of Doubt. Boston, Little Brown, 1907.

Novels as Lt. A.K. Sims

Captain Cactus. New York, Beadle and Adams, 1888.
Huckleberry, The Foot Hills Detective. New York, Beadle and Adams, 1888.
The Silver Sport. New York, Beadle and Adams, 1888.
Happy Hans, The Dutch Vidocq. New York, Beadle and Adams, 1889.
Prince Primrose. New York, Beadle and Adams, 1889.
Signal Sam. New York, Beadle and Adams, 1890.
Kansas Karl, The Detective King. New York, Beadle and Adams, 1890.
Stuttering Sam. New York, Beadle and Adams, 1891.
The River Rustlers. New York, Beadle and Adams, 1891.
Kent Kirby. New York, Beadle and Adams, 1892.
Lodestone Lem. New York, Beadle and Adams, 1892.
The Rustler of Rolling Stone. New York, Beadle and Adams, 1892.
Singer Sam. New York, Beadle and Adams, 1892.
Teamster Tom. New York, Beadle and Adams, 1892.
The Doctor Detective in Texas. New York, Beadle and Adams, 1893.
The King-Pin of the Leadville Lions. New York, Beadle and Adams, 1894.
The Crescent City. New York, Beadle and Adams, 1894.
The Six-Shot Spotter. New York, Beadle and Adams, 1895.
The Texan Detective. New York, Beadle and Adams, 1895.
The Texan Firebrand. New York, Beadle and Adams, 1895.
The Tramp's Trump-Trick. New York, Beadle and Adams, 1895.

OTHER PUBLICATIONS

Fiction (for children)

The Young Ditch Rider. Elgin, Illinois, Cook, 1899.
With Fremont the Pathfinder. Boston, Wilde, 1903.
Campaigning with Tippecanoe. New York, Federal, 1904.
A Courier of Empire. Boston, Wilde, 1904.

*

Bibliography: in *Dime Novel Round-up*, 15 May 1970 and 15 July 1972.

* * *

Born in an Indiana log cabin in 1854, ordained a Baptist minister in 1898, John H. Whitson based his numerous factual articles, adult novels, and dime novel Westerns on his travels in the West and his experiences as a homesteader and a cattleraiser near Garden City, Kansas. At its best, his fiction is well plotted, suspenseful, and rich with authentic descriptions of western life and scenery; at its worst, his fiction reads like a tourist's travelogue and guidebook.

Whitson's first cloth-bound adult novel, *Barbara, A Woman of the West*, typifies the best and worst features of his work. The novel opens on a homestead in Kansas, where husband and wife Roger and Barbara Timberly make a meager living writing stories. Their marriage is less than blissful, for Roger is self-centered and largely unappreciative of his beautiful and faithful wife. When a meeting with a hard-luck prospector results in the Timberly's acquiring claim to a Cripple Creek gold mine, Roger does not hesitate to leave Barbara behind and seek wealth and adventure in the West. Barbara, however, remains loyal, and spends the remainder of the novel engaged in a seemingly hopeless quest to find the husband who has so selfishly deserted her. The quest leads her first to the mining camps of Cripple Creek and then to San Diego, where she meets rich and manly Gilbert Bream, who immediately falls in love with her. Knowing, however, that Barbara will reject his attentions until she is convinced that her husband is dead, Gilbert sets out to find the missing man. When the effort proves fruitless, Barbara and Gilbert marry and move to Denver. Yet their happiness is short-lived, for the publication of a successful popular novel penned in Roger Timberly's characteristic style leads Barbara to the alarming conclusion that her former husband is still alive. She locates Roger in a Denver hospital, where he lies gravely injured, having been run down in the night by a cab. From his lips she learns that his travels had led him to Death Valley, where he had been found near death and crazed by thirst and subsequently confined in the Colorado Insane Asylum. Now, with his return to sanity and his arrival in Denver, Barbara faces the dilemma of having two husbands; but Roger dies, relieving her of the burden of choice and freeing her to remarry her true love and current husband Gilbert Bream. Relying on familiar conventions and fortuitous twists in plot, *Barbara, A Woman of the West* is redeemed only by its frequent passages describing authentic western scenes. In this regard the novel is similar to Whitson's other cloth-bound novels *The Rainbow Chasers*, a story of the Kansas land boom and the transition from a cattle to a farming country, and *Justin Wingate, Ranchman.*

Whitson also wrote a large number of stories for dime novels series such as Beadle's Half-Dime and Dime Libraries and Street & Smith's Diamond Dick Jr. Weekly, Rough Rider Weekly, and Buffalo Bill Stories. For the latter series Whitson penned 59 titles, including *Buffalo Bill's Clean-Sweep; or, Pawnee Bill's Race with the King-Pin Bandit*, a story which finds Buffalo Bill and his saddlemates on the trail of Mexican bandit Silvernail in the Rio Grande country, and *Buffalo Bill's Handful of Pearls; or, Pawnee Bill at Santa Fe*, a story in which an imposter's misdeeds while masquerading as Buffalo Bill lead Cody and his sidekicks into dangerous misunderstandings and a showdown with the Navajos. Making extensive use of doubles, mistaken identity and disguises, hidden caves and houses with secret closets and subterranean passages, Whitson's stories are indistinguishable from the usual dime novel fare, save that they display Whitson's distinctive trademark: authorial intrusions and digressions devoted to authentic scenic and geographical description.

—Daryl Jones

WHITTINGTON, Harry (Benjamin). Also wrote as Ashley Carter; Robert Hart Davis; Tabor Evans; Whit Harrison; Kel Holland; Harriet Kathryn Myers; Blaine Stevens; Clay Stuart; Hondo Wells; Harry White; Hallam Whitney. American. Born in Ocala, Florida, 4 February 1915. Educated in Florida public schools and extension and night classes. Served in the United States Navy, 1945–46; Petty Officer. Married Kathryn L. Lavinia Odom in 1936; one daughter and one son. Copywriter, Griffith Advertising Agency, St. Petersburg, Florida, 1932–33; assistant manager and advertising manager, Capitol Theatre, St. Petersburg, 1933–34; post office clerk, St. Petersburg, 1934–45; editor, *Advocate*, St. Petersburg, 1938–45; freelance writer, 1946–68; editor, U.S. Department of Agriculture, 1968–75; from 1975 freelance writer: author of many stories for King Features Syndicate, 1948–57, and *Man from U.N.C.L.E., Dime Detective, Manhunt, Bluebook, Mantrap. Died 11 June 1989.*

WESTERN PUBLICATIONS

Novels

Vengeance Valley. New York, Phoenix Press, 1945; London, Ward Lock, 1947.
Saddle the Storm. New York, Fawcett, 1954; London, Fawcett, 1955.
Shadow at Noon (as Harry White). New York, Pyramid, 1955; as Hondo Wells, London, New English Library, 1977.
Trouble Rides Tall. New York and London, Abelard Schuman, 1958.
Vengeance Is the Spur. New York and London, Abelard Schuman, 1960.
Desert Stake-Out. New York, Fawcett, 1961; London, Muller, 1963.
Searching Rider. New York, Ace, 1961.
A Trap for Sam Dodge. New York, Ace, 1962.
Dry Gulch Town. New York, Ace, 1963.
Prairie Raiders (as Hondo Wells). New York, Ace, 1963; London, New English Library, 1977.
High Fury. New York, Ballantine, 1964; London, Mews, 1976.
Hangrope Town. New York, Ballantine, 1964.
Wild Lonesome. New York, Ballantine, 1965.
Valley of the Savage Men. New York, Ace, 1965.
Treachery Trail. Racine, Wisconsin, Whitman, 1968.
Charro. New York, Fawcett, 1969.

Novels as Tabor Evans (series: Longarm in all books)

Longarm. New York, Jove, 1978; London, Magnum, 1979.
Longarm and the Avenging Angels. New York, Jove, 1978; London, Magnum, 1979.
Longarm on the Border. New York, Jove, 1978; London, Magnum, 1979.
Longarm and the Hatchett Men. New York, Jove, 1979; London, Methuem, 1981.
Longarm and the Highgraders. New York, Jove, 1979; London, Magnum, 1981.
Longarm and the Loggers. New York, Jove, 1979; London, Magnum, 1980.
Longarm and the Nesters. New York, Jove, 1979; London, Magnum, 1981.
Longarm and the Texas Rangers. New York, Jove, 1979; London, Magnum, 1982.
Longarm and the Wendigo. New York, Jove, and London, Magnum, 1979.
Longarm in the Indian Nation. New York, Jove, 1979; London, Magnum, 1980.
Longarm in Lincoln County. New York, Jove, 1979; London, Methuen, 1982.
Longarm on the Humboldt. New York, Jove, 1981.
Longarm and the Golden Lady. New York, Jove, 1981.
Longarm and the Blue Norther. New York, Jove, 1981.
Longarm in Silver City. New York, Jove, 1982.
Longarm in Boulder Canyon. New York, Jove, 1982.
Longarm in the Big Thicket. New York, Jove, 1982.
Longarm and the Lone Star Vengeance. New York, Jove, 1983.
Longarm and the Lone Star Rescue. New York, Jove, 1985.

OTHER PUBLICATIONS

Novels

Slay Ride for a Lady. Kingston, New York, Quinn, 1950.
The Brass Monkey. Kingston, New York, Quinn, 1951.
Call Me Killer. Hasbrouck Heights, New Jersey, Graphic, 1951.
Fires That Destroy. New York, Fawcett, 1951.
The Lady Was a Tramp. Kingston, New York, Quinn, 1951.
Married to Murder. New York, Paperback Library, 1951.
Murder Is My Mistress. Hasbrouck Heights, New Jersey, Graphic, 1951.
Satan's Widow. New York, Paperback Library, 1951.
Forever Evil. New York Paperback Library, 1951.
Drawn to Evil. New York, Ace, 1952.
Mourn the Hangman. Hasbrouck Heights, New Jersey, Graphic, 1952.
So Dead My Love! New York, Ace, 1953.
Vengeful Sinner. New York, Croydon, 1953; as *Die, Lover,* New York, Avon, 1960.
Cracker Girl. Beacon, New York, Beacon Signal, 1953.
Wild Oats. Beacon, New York, Beacon Signal, 1953.
Prime Sucker. Beacon, New York, Beacon Signal, 1953.
This Woman Is Mine. New York, Fawcett, 1953.
Naked Island. New York, Ace, 1954.
You'll Die Next! New York, Ace, 1954; London, Red Seal, 1959.
The Naked Jungle. New York, Ace, 1955.
One Got Away. New York, Ace, 1955.
Brute in Brass. New York, Fawcett, 1956; London, Red Seal, 1958.
Desire in the Dust. New York, Fawcett, 1956; London, Fawcett, 1957.
The Humming Box. New York, Ace, 1956.
Saturday Night Town. New York, Fawcett, 1956; London, Fawcett, 1958.
A Woman on the Place. New York, Ace, 1956; London, Red Seal, 1960.

Mink. Paris, Gallimard, 1956.
Across That River. New York, Ace, 1957.
Man in the Shadow (novelization of screenplay). New York, Avon, 1957.
One Deadly Dawn. New York, Ace, 1957.
Play for Keeps. New York and London, Abelard Schuman, 1957.
Temptations of Valerie (novelization of screenplay). New York, Avon, 1957.
Teen-Age Jungle. New York, Avon, 1958.
Web of Murder. New York, Fawcett, 1958; London, Fawcett, 1959.
Star Lust. N.p., B and B Library 1958.
Strictly for the Boys. N.p., Stanley, 1959.
Native Girl. New York, Berkley, 1959.
Shack Road Girl. New York, Berkley, 1959.
Backwoods Tramp. New York, Fawcett, 1959; London, Muller, 1961.
Halfway to Hell. New York, Avon, 1959.
Strange Bargain. New York, Avon, 1959.
Strangers on Friday. New York and London, Abelard Schuman 1959.
A Ticket to Hell. New York, Fawcett, 1959; London, Muller, 1960.
Connolly's Woman. New York, Fawcett, 1960; London, Muller, 1962.
The Devil Wears Wings. New York and London, Abelard Schuman, 1960.
Heat of Night. New York, Fawcett, 1960; London, Muller, 1961.
Hell Can Wait. New York, Fawcett, 1960; London, Muller, 1962.
A Night for Screaming. New York, Ace, 1960.
Nita's Place. New York, Pyramid, 1960.
Rebel Woman. New York, Avon, 1960.
Guerrilla Girls. New York, Pyramid, 1960; London, New English Library, 1970.
God's Back Was Turned. New York, Fawcett, 1961; London, Muller, 1962.
Journey into Violence. New York, Pyramid, 1961.
The Young Nurses. New York, Pyramid, 1961.
Wild Sky. New York, Ace, 1962.
Cross the Red Creek. New York, Avon, 1962.
Small Town Nurse (as Harriet Kathryn Myers). New York, Ace, 1962.
A Haven for the Damned. New York, Fawcett, 1962; London, Muller, 1963.
Hot as Fire, Cold as Ice. New York, Belmont, 1962.
69 Babylon Park. New York, Avon, 1962.
Don't Speak to Strange Girls. New York, Fawcett, and London, Muller, 1963.
Prodigal Nurse (as Harriet Kathryn Myers). New York, Ace, 1963.
The Fall of the Roman Empire (novelization of screenplay). New York, Fawcett, and London, Muller, 1964.
His Brother's Wife (as Clay Stuart). Beacon, New York, Beacon Signal, 1964.
The Tempted (as Kel Holland). Beacon, New York, Beacon Signal, 1964.
The Doomsday Affair (novelization of television play). New York, Ace, and London, New English Library, 1965.
Doomsday Mission. New York, Banner, 1967.
The Bitter Mission of Captain Burden. New York, Avon, 1968.
Smell of Jasmine. New York, Avon, 1968.
Mexican Connection. Whittier, California, Greenleaf, 1972.
Nightmare Alibi. Whittier, California, Greenleaf, 1973.
Rampago. New York, Fawcett, 1978.
Sicilian Woman. New York, Fawcett, 1979.
The Outlanders (as Blaine Stevens). New York, Jove, 1979; London, W.H. Allen, 1983.
Embrace the Wind (as Blaine Stevens). New York, Jove, 1982; London, W.H. Allen, 1985.
Forgive Me, Killer. Berkeley, California, Creative Arts, 1987.
A Moment to Prey. Berkeley, California, Creative Arts, 1988.

Novels as Whit Harrison

Swamp Kill. New York, Paperback Library, 1951.
Body and Passion. New York, Paperback Library, 1951.
Nature Girl. New York, Popular Library, 1952.
Sailor's Weekend. New York, Popular Library, 1952.
Army Girl. New York, Popular Library, 1952.
Girl on Parole. New York, Popular Library, 1952.
Rapture Alley. New York, Popular Library, 1952.
Violent Night. New York, Paperback Library, 1952.
Shanty Road. New York, Popular Library, 1953.
Strip the Town Naked. Beacon, New York, Beacon Signal, 1953.
Any Woman He Wanted. Beacon, New York, Beacon Signal, 1960.
A Woman Possessed. Beacon, New York, Beacon Signal, 1961.

Novels as Hallam Whitney

Backwoods Hussy. New York, Paperback Library, 1952; as *Lisa*, 1965.
Shack Road. New York, Paperback Library, 1953.
Sinners Club. New York, Paperback Library, 1953.
City Girl. New York, Paperback Library, 1953.
Backwoods Shack. New York, Paperback Library, 1954.
The Wild Seed. New York, Ace, 1956.

Novels as Ashley Carter

Golden Stud, with Lance Horner. New York, Fawcett, 1975.
Master of Black Oaks. New York, Fawcett, 1976; London, W.H. Allen, 1977.
The Sword of the Golden Stud. New York, Fawcett, 1977; London, W.H. Allen, 1978.
Secret of Blackoaks. New York, Fawcett, 1978; London, W.H. Allen, 1980.
Panama. New York, Fawcett, 1978; London, Pan, 1980.
Taproots of Falconhurst. New York, Fawcett, 1978; London, W.H. Allen, 1979.
Scandal of Falconhurst. New York, Fawcett, 1980; London, W.H. Allen, 1981.
Heritage of Blackoaks. New York, Fawcett, 1981; London, W.H. Allen, 1982.
Against All Gods. New York, Fawcett, and London, W.H. Allen, 1982.
Rogue of Falconhurst. New York, Fawcett, and New York, Fawcett, 1983.
Road to Falconhurst. New York, Fawcett, and London, W.H. Allen, 1983.
A Farewell to Blackoaks. New York, Fawcett, and London, W.H. Allen, 1984.
The Outlanders. London, W.H. Allen, 1983.
A Darkling Moon. London, W.H. Allen, 1985.
Embrace the Wind. London, W.H. Allen, 1985.
Falconhurst Fugitive. London, W.H. Allen, 1985.
Miz Lucretia of Falconhurst. London, W.H. Allen, 1985; New York, Fawcett, 1986.
Mondingo Mansa. London, W.H. Allen, 1986; New York, Fawcett, 1987.

Strange Harvest. New York, Fawcett, and London, W.H. Allen, 1986.

Plays

Screenplays: *Face of the Phantom*, 1960; *Pain and Pleasure*, 1965; *Strange Desires*, 1967; *Fireball Jungle*, 1968; *Island of Lost Women*, 1973.

Television Plays: *Lawman*, *The Alaskans*, and *The Dakotas* series.

*

Manuscript Collection: Florida State University, Tallahassee.

Theatrical Activities:
Director: **Film**—*Face of the Phantom*, 1960.

* * *

Harry Whittington has written successfully in virtually every genre of popular fiction, but his first book, *Vengeance Valley*, was a Western. In 1954 the Western Writers of America voted his *Saddle the Storm* the best paperback novel of the year. He continued to write Westerns, having published a number of books as Tabor Evans in Jove's Longarm series.

Saddle the Storm is typical of Whittington's strengths. The interest of the reader is invested much more in character than in action. Though the book is not without action and melodrama, these elements are underplayed. Instead, Whittington concentrates on the events of a July 4th weekend in a small western town and the effects of these events on the lives of several characters. The numerous story lines are all resolved in very satisfactory fashion.

Even in action-oriented books like *Shadow at Noon*, *High Fury*, and *Valley of the Savage Men*, Whittington never forgets the importance of character. But in these books he manages to provide at the same time emotion-charged plots in which his protagonists get tangled in more and more complicated webs of deceit and lies from which there appears to be no hope of escape. Whittington's picture of the aging "trouble marshal" Bry Shafter in *Trouble Rides Tall* is not only a tough and uncompromising portrait of a man whose reputation with a gun has determined the course of his life, but also an effective combination of the Western and the mystery story. Combined with this is a clear portrait of the hypocrisies of small-town politics and expediencies.

Whittington presents convincing stories of the frontier conflict between settlers and Indians in such novels as *Vengeance Is the Spur*, which is also concerned with the conflict between the desert-wise cavalry man and the by-the-book soldier sent to replace him. This fine work is continued in Whittington's contributions to the current Longarm series. These books are written by various hands, but Whittington's novels stand out as examples of good plotting and character development. In *Longarm and the Blue Norther*, for example, the weather itself becomes an important character, and the climactic scene is as effective in its portrayal of chilling cold as earlier books such as *Desert Stake-Out* are in the depiction of heat and dryness.

Harry Whittington's death in 1989 brought to a close a distinguished career in Western writing, but he left behind an impressive body of work that places him on a high plane in the ranks of chroniclers of the frontier.

—Bill Crider

WIGAN, Christopher. *See* **BINGLEY, David Ernest.**

WILDER, Laura (Elizabeth) Ingalls. American. Born in Pepin, Wisconsin, 7 February 1867. Educated at schools in Walnut Grove, Minnesota, Burr Oak, Iowa, and De Smet, Dakota Territory. Married Almanzo James Wilder in 1885 (died 1949); one daughter. Schoolteacher, De Smet, 1882–85; farmer in De Smet, 1885–90 and 1892–94, and from 1894 in Mansfield, Missouri; lived in Florida, 1890–92. Columnist, *Missouri Ruralist*, 1911–24; poultry editor, St. Louis *Star*; secretary-treasurer, Mansfield Farm Loan Association, 1919–27. Recipient: American Library Association Laura Ingalls Wilder award, 1954. *Died 10 February 1957.*

WESTERN PUBLICATIONS

Fiction (for children)

Little House in the Big Woods. New York, Harper, 1932; London, Methuen, 1956.
Farmer Boy. New York, Harper, 1933; London, Lutterworth Press, 1965.
Little House on the Prairie. New York, Harper, 1935; London, Methuen, 1957.
On the Banks of Plum Creek. New York, Harper, 1937; London, Methuen, 1958.
By the Shores of Silver Lake. New York, Harper, 1939; London, Lutterworth Press, 1961.
The Long Winter. New York, Harper, 1940; London, Lutterworth Press, 1962.
Little Town on the Prairie. New York, Harper, 1941; London, Lutterworth Press, 1963.
These Happy Golden Years. New York, Harper, 1943; London, Lutterworth Press, 1964.
The First Four Years. New York, Harper, 1971; Guildford, Surrey, Lutterworth Press, 1973.

OTHER PUBLICATIONS

Other

On the Way Home: The Diary of a Trip from South Dakota to Mansfield, Missouri, in 1894, with Rose Wilder Lane. New York, Harper, 1962.
West from Home: Letters from Laura Ingalls Wilder to Almanzo Wilder, San Francisco 1915, edited by Roger Lea MacBride. New York, Harper, 1974; Guildford, Surrey, Lutterworth Press, 1976.
A Little House Sampler, with Rose Wilder Lane, edited by William T. Anderson. Lincoln, University of Nebraska Press, 1988.

*

Bibliography: *Laura Ingalls Wilder: A Bibliography* by Mary J. Mooney-Getoff, Southold, New York, Wise Owl Press, 1980.

Manuscript Collections: Laura Ingalls Wilder Home and Museum, Mansfield, Missouri; Pomona Public Library, California; Detroit Public Library.

Critical Studies: *The Life of Laura Ingalls Wilder* by Donald Zochert, New York, Avon, 1977; *Laura Ingalls Wilder:*

American Authoress by Sheila Black, New York, Kipling Press, 1987; *The Plum Creek Story of Laura Ingalls Wilder* by William T. Anderson, Davison, Michigan, Anderson, 1987, and *The Horn Book's Laura Ingalls Wilder* edited by Anderson, Davison, Michigan, Anderson, 1987; *Laura Ingalls Wilder* by Janet Spaeth, Boston, Twayne, 1987.

* * *

Laura Ingalls Wilder's Little House series is a long-running phenomenon of American popular culture. These autobiographical novels trace a homesteading family's migration over the Great Plains, chronicling their efforts to transform a series of minimal Little Houses into a sustaining western home. Point of view is filtered through the lively sensibility of Laura, second of four Ingalls daughters, and the series extends from her fifth year (about 1870) until her marriage, at 18 when she takes possession of a Little House of her own. In her sixties, Wilder began to see the shape of western history in her own life:

> I realized that I had seen and lived it all—the successive phases of the frontier, first the frontiersman, then the pioneer, then the farmers, and the towns... I wanted the children now to understand more about the beginnings of things, to know what is behind the things they see—what it is that made America as they know it. Then I thought of writing the story of my childhood in several volumes ... covering every aspect of the American frontier.

Since their publication, Wilder's books have been much honored as children's literature and have stayed in print and sold steadily. A sprinkling of critical comment has emphasized Wilder's vision of western history and issues of place and displacement, and has explored matters of the books' authorship. However, a wider tribute is provided by the thousands of readers, of all ages, who yearly visit the small towns and rural sites where Wilder and her family lived in the Little House years. These visitors pore over the homeliest relics of the Ingalls family: quilt squares, tools, chipped crockery. For such pilgrims, Wilder's work obviously strikes a note of powerful immediacy, beyond simple historical recapitulation.

Much of this power comes from Wilder's acute handling of matters which seem especially pertinent in the critical climate of the 1890's: issues of gender and of material culture. For the fictionalized Laura Ingalls, her "Pa" epitomizes a spirit of westering adventure that is always ready to leave stability and things behind, and to make the adventure into a story or a song. As Wilder began to write, she thought of her father's tales as her main resource. The first book, *Little House in the Big Woods*, is punctuated with his tales, all recounting outdoor male adventures, usually solitary. Volatile, vocal Pa is the family storyteller and his daughter's model; she claimed that she wrote her first book "as a memorial to my father." Laura's quiet mother is not a storyteller. As a former teacher and an accomplished housekeeper, "Ma" introduces her pre-school daughters to processes—baking, buttermaking, quilting—and to things—a porcelain shepherdess, a treasured dress. Thus Ma inscribes for her daughters an unspoken tale, the story of women's traditional culture in the West. The conflict of the parents' stories is implied by the abrupt formal alternations of *Little House in the Big Woods*, as Pa's tales and his playful impersonation of a "mad dog" (Laura's favorite game) interrupt the predictable and supportive rhythms of domestic Wisconsin farm life. The book ends with five-year-old Laura's apprehension of a continuous present of blissful equilibrium: "Now is now," thinks the little girl. "It can never be a long time ago."

The next autobiographical novel, *Little House on the Prairie*, shatters that equilibrium, as the Ingalls family leaves the Big Woods to pioneer in unsettled Kansas. There Laura is plunged into her first apprehensions of history and of competing versions of time, inside and outside her family. Now Wilder is writing a more seamless narrative; young Laura seems to have internalized both her parents' agendas, as they begin to invent a small farm household on unbroken prairie. But Indians invade Ma's kitchen and their drums interrupt the Ingalls' sleep, while Congress finally decrees that Kansas will remain Indian territory and that non-Indian settlers like the Ingalls must leave. Ma speaks her regrets and her preservative sense of time's scarcity, mourning "a whole year gone." But Pa speaks for the abundance of western space and time: "We've got all the time in the world," he assures his wife and daughters. The novel ends with the family back in the moving, questing wagon.

On the Banks of Plum Creek chronicles a several years' stay in Minnesota. There the girls are introduced to the institutions which their parents (especially Ma) would have them value: church and school. And a series of agricultural disasters, including a plague of grasshoppers, necessitates long separations from Pa, who must work in the "East." When he is gone and she is living in an all-female western household, Laura must think more consciously of the gendered powers and limits of both her parents. At the same time, she measures herself constantly against older sister Mary, her rival and constant companion, a "good girl" who delights in female propriety.

In the last three novels, *By the Shores of Silver Lake*, *Little Town on the Prairie*, and *These Happy Golden Years*, the Ingalls leave behind the years of disastrous farming in Minnesota, where Mary was blinded in an epidemic, to take a homestead in South Dakota. With the added responsibility of "seeing" doubly, for her sightless but still relentlessly conventional sister and for herself, Laura plunges into adolescence and into new combat with her mother, who fears that Laura will become "wild" and be influenced by the "rough men" who are building the railroad. Just as Laura grows strong and large enough to help with her father's work, haying, the intensified gender strictures of adolescence gather force. In these last books, going against her own contradictory strengths and inclinations, Laura must confront a basic principle of gendered culture: men go out, women stay in.

At school, she becomes a passionate student of history, publicly reciting the entire first half of U.S. history (an account of male presidencies, movements, and legislation) and ending at the point where her own family's journeying began, as "the first wagons rolled into Kansas." This storytelling feat launches her career: at 15, she follows in Ma's footsteps as a rural schoolteacher. Now a prototypical woman, she is in position to perpetuate gendered history to her students. In *These Happy Golden Years* Laura learns, with Ma's help, how to "manage" this first school, and as her success as teacher propels her into marriage with a mobile young homesteader, Almanzo Wilder, she begins to invent an adult life which is informed and endowed by both her parents' stories. To the new Little House in which she begins her marriage, Laura takes the riches of her father's songs and tales, as well as the domestic and pedagogic resources of a "civilized" western woman, as taught by her mother.

Wilder's series is very much a product of the Depression, during which it was written. It shares with works by James Agee and with wide-ranging projects like the Farm Security Administration photographs and the Index of American Design an intense interest in the nature of *work*, as it becomes apparent to a lively girl. It is also part of the 1930's revival of traditional, preservative women's culture, such as quilting, which was promoted by the rural domestic magazines for which Wilder wrote. But while the books convey the mesmerizing power of American domestic myth, they also convey much about its consequences and costs, for women and for men. *The Long Winter*, perhaps the best of the novels, indicates this conflict most complexly. In this book, as the housebound family nearly starves in a seven-month blizzard, Laura must acknowledge the saving power of Ma's housekeeping skills, which keep them alive, and must begin to see that her father is weakened by the strains of staying put, as domestic homesteader, suppressing his impulses to venture farther West. As her parents' near-adult ally, Laura finds that she has, perhaps irrevocably, bought into the ongoing gendered history of the West.

Critical attention to Wilder as a western woman writer is just beginning to proliferate. The phenomenon of Wilder's late-blooming writing career, and her collaboration with her mentor-editor-daughter, the popular western novelist Rose Wilder Lane, is an instructive case study in female authorship, perhaps unique in American women's culture. Their correspondence, still largely unpublished, shows a protracted struggle to make honest and saleable fiction out of Wilder's insistent memories and her sense of the gendered rhythms of her prairie life. The novels they produced are among the most durably compelling versions of Great Plains pioneer experience. The Little House books both describe and deconstruct Western myth, in texts whose richness rewards rereading and invites critical attention.

—Ann Romines

WILLIAMS, Coe. *See* **HARRISON, C. William.**

WILLIAMS, (Dorothy) Jeanne (née Kreie). Also writes as Megan Castell; Jeanne Crecy; Jeanne Foster; Kristin Michaels; Deirdre Rowan; J.R. Williams. American. Born in Elkhart, Kansas, 10 April 1930. Attended elementary and secondary schools in Kansas, Oklahoma, and Missouri; University of Oklahoma, Norman, 1952–53. Married 1) Gene F. Williams in 1949 (divorced 1969), one daughter and one son; 2) the writer John Creasey in 1970 (divorced 1973); 3) Bob Morse in 1981. President, Western Writers of America, 1974–75. Recipient: Western Writers of America Spur award, for children's book, 1960, 1973, for adult novel, 1981; Levi Strauss Golden Saddleman award, 1962. Agent: Claire Smith, Harold Ober Associates, 40 East 49th Street, New York, New York 10017. Address: Box 105, Portal, Arizona 85632, U.S.A.

Western Publications

Novels

River Guns. London, Jenkins, 1963.
Beasts with Music. New York, Meredith Press, 1967; as Jeanne Crecy, London, Harrap, 1969.
A Lady Bought with Rifles. New York, Coward McCann, 1976; London, W.H. Allen, 1977.
Time of the Burning Mask (as Deirdre Rowan). New York, Fawcett, 1976.
A Woman Clothed in Sun. New York, Coward McCann, 1977; London, Wingate, 1978.
Bride of Thunder. New York, Pocket Books, 1978.
Daughter of the Sword. New York, Pocket Books, 1979.
Arizona Saga:
The Valiant Women. New York, Pocket Books, 1980.
Harvest of Fury. New York, Pocket Books, 1981.
A Mating of Hawks. New York, Pocket Books, 1982.
Texas Pride. New York, Avon, 1987.
Lady of No Man's Land. New York, St. Martin's Press, 1988.
No Roof but Heaven. New York, St. Martin's Press, 1990.
Home Mountain. New York, St. Martin's Press, 1990.

Novels as Kristin Michaels

To Begin with Love. New York, New American Library, 1975.
Make Believe Love. New York, New American Library, 1978.
Magic Side of the Moon. New York, New American Library, 1981.

Novels as Jeanne Foster

Frontier Women series:
Deborah Leigh. New York, Fawcett, 1981.
Wyoming Glory. New York, Fawcett, 1982.
Woman of Three Worlds. New York, Fawcett, 1984.

Uncollected Short Story

"Outlaw Horse," in *Search for the Hidden Places*, edited by E.D. Mygatt. New York, McKay, 1963.

Other Publications

Novels

The Cave Dreamers. New York, Avon, 1984.
The Heaven Sword. New York, Avon, 1985.
So Many Kingdoms. New York, Avon, 1986.

Novels as Jeanne Crecy

Hands of Terror. New York, Berkley, 1972; as *Lady Gift*, London, Hale, 1973.
The Lightning Tree. New York, Berkley, 1973.
The Night Hunters. New York, New American Library, 1975.
The Winter Keeper. New York, New American Library, 1975.
My Face Beneath the Stone. New York, New American Library, 1975.
The Evil among Us. New York, New American Library, 1975.
The Queen of a Lonely Country (as Megan Castell). New York, Pocket Books, 1980.

Novels as Deirdre Rowan

Dragon's Mount. New York, Fawcett, 1973; London, Coronet, 1975.
Silver Wood. New York, Fawcett, 1974; London, Coronet, 1975.
Shadow of the Volcano. New York, Fawcett, 1975.
Ravensgate. New York, Fawcett, 1976.

Novels as Kristin Michaels

Enchanted Twilight. New York, New American Library, 1976.

A Special Kind of Love. New York, New American Library, 1976.
Song of the Heart. New York, New American Library, 1977.
Enchanted Journey. New York, New American Library, 1977.
Voyage to Love. New York, New American Library, 1978.

Other (for children) as J.R. Williams

Tame the Wild Stallion. Englewood Cliffs, New Jersey, Prentice Hall, 1957; Kingswood, Surrey, World's Work, 1958.
Mission in Mexico. Englewood Cliffs, New Jersey, Prentice Hall, 1959.
The Horse Talker. Englewood Cliffs, New Jersey, Prentice Hall, 1961.
The Confederate Fiddle. Englewood Cliffs, New Jersey, Prentice Hall, 1962.
Oh, Susanna! New York, Putnam, 1963.

Other (for children)

To Buy a Dream. New York, Messner, 1958.
Promise of Tomorrow. New York, Messner, 1959.
Coyote Winter. New York, Norton, 1965.
Oil Patch Partners. New York, Meredith Press, 1968.
New Medicine. New York, Putnam, 1971.
Trails of Tears: American Indians Driven from Their Lands. New York, Putnam, 1972.
Freedom Trail. New York, Putnam, 1973.
Winter Wheat. New York, Putnam, 1975.

*

Manuscript Collection: Southwestern Collection Archives, Texas Tech University, Lubbock.

Critical Study: *Jeanne Williams* by Judy Alter, Boise, Idaho, Boise State University, 1990.

Jeanne Williams comments:

I have tried to show the western experience as it affected women, especially, and while telling the broader stories of wars, territorial struggles, and historical developments, I've shown details of daily life, homemaking, medicine, and what ordinary family living was like. A number of my books emphasize Indian lore and skills, from the Mayas of Yucatan to the Sioux of the Black Hills. I like to take little-known events and dramatize them so that readers will get a picture of the many influences that shaped the West, as in such diverse migrations as the forced, shameful Cherokee Trail of Tears and the apocalyptic fervor of the Mormon handcraft travelers who pushed and pulled their burdens across the plains to Utah. I try to develop my animal characters, too, and devote great effort to show the natural wonders and beauties of the land and man's responsibilities to other creatures and the earth that supports us all.

* * *

Jeanne Williams has written convincingly of England, medieval Wales, Russia, Norway, Mexico, Brazil, and the United States—especially the frontier in Kansas, Texas, New Mexico, and Arizona. In spite of the wide range of her subject matter, the American West and its history are an enduring interest, and she has written of Indians, Mennonites, Mormons, Basque sheepherders and Arizona miners, lumberjacks and bird watchers, army wives and cattle ranchers.

Williams's major contribution to western American fiction is her ability to combine women's history and women's fiction in novels that meet with commercial success. Having previously written young-adult novels and romances, Williams entered the field of historical romances in 1976 with *A Lady Bought with Rifles*. By 1990, her work has moved beyond the confines of historical romance and her most recent novels, published in hardback, may be classified as mainstream fiction.

Set in turn-of-the-century Mexico, *A Lady Bought with Rifles* features a strong and independent heroine, two men who love her, and a sister who hates her. It takes much killing, rape, and sex, all against a backdrop of the Yaqui war with the Mexican government, before the heroine triumphs in a happy conclusion. With this novel, Williams established her reputation for careful and accurate research, particularly through her portrayal of the little-known Yaqui culture.

Similar novels followed—*A Woman Clothed in Sun*, *Bride of Thunder*, *Daughter of the Sword*, and the massive Arizona trilogy—*The Valiant Women*, *Harvest of Fury*, and *A Mating of Hawks*. All published in mass market editions, these novels are page-turners, with fast, action-packed plots where complication piles upon complication. In many ways, they are formulaic, relying on stock situations and characters: the brother or lover turned outlaw, the protégé in love with her protector, the heroine who refuses to communicate with the good man who loves her and often allows herself to be involved with the villain. And the villains are frequently truly evil men, who use threats to a woman's loved ones to get their way—their way always including violent sexual possession. Clearly Williams mastered the necessary skills of the romance writer who would sell in the paperback market.

Reviewers often agreed that the plots of the early historical novels were secondary to the authenticity of setting and history. That authenticity distinguishes Williams's work, and makes her clearly more than a romance writer. For romance writers as a group, the love story is the most important ingredient in the novel; for Williams, it is the peg on which she can hang history, research, and women's concerns. Love and passion are time-honored elements for keeping the reader involved in fiction, Williams reminds us, suggesting that she merely reverses the roles of this traditional plot, telling an adventurous, lusty tale from a woman's point of view.

In later historical novels, Williams has chosen an episode in history around which to construct her novel—the Mormon handcart emigration in *Wyoming Glory*, the Texas oil boom in *Texas Pride*, Kansas' underground railway in *Daughter of the Sword*, the Cherokee Trail of Tears in *Deborah Leigh*—and then placed the heroine in that time and place, almost always in the role of starting a new life in difficult circumstances. It is a formula which Williams has used with much success and with increasing sophistication.

Williams takes strong, resourceful women and places them not only in tangled plots of romance and action and faces them with new beginnings, but centers them in the realities of everyday life in the American West. History comes alive in the details of daily life—how women cooked, cared for the sick, gave birth, fed and clothed their families. She pays particular attention to the way her characters live in relation to the land, because she is keenly interested in man's ability to live from the land and opposed to his greedy abuse of it. There are strong environmental themes in most of her novels.

Williams's work also reflects a deep interest in the many cultures which make up the American West, and in the way these cultures have interacted. The Arizona trilogy traces the history of a ranching empire whose descendants can claim heritage from the Mexican, Irish, German, and Papago cultures. The three novels in her Frontier Women series—

Deborah Leigh, *Wyoming Glory*, and *Woman of Three Worlds*—each explore a particular Indian culture—Cherokee, Sioux, and Apache. Interestingly, these novels, all published in the 1980's under the pseudonym of Jeanne Foster, contain less physical passion and violence and are, in a sense, steps towards the major novels of the late 1980's.

Lady of No Man's Land and *No Roof but Heaven* feature Williams's basic situation—a strong, independent heroine courted by two men, although neither of the men is villainous in the ways of characters from earlier novels. But the heroines of both of these books are 19th-century versions of career women—an interest that is also evident in some of Williams's lighter romances written under the Kristın Michaels pseudonym. *Lady of No Man's Land* is the story of an itinerant seamstress in the Oklahoma-Texas-Indian Territory neutral strip; *No Roof but Heaven* is the story of a schoolteacher in Kansas just after the Civil War, who is determined to establish a schoolhouse in a sod hut, and to unite the warring Northern and Southern sympathizers of the area. Both books are characterized by people more complex and situations more subtly drawn than earlier romances. There are still violence and villainy, for Williams never shirks the unpleasant realities of frontier life, but these elements are not what holds the reader's attention. Instead, the basic conflict which gives structure to the book is determined by the heroine, her dedication to her work and responsibilities, and her historical situation, not by the relationship between men and women.

In the ranks of women who write about the American West, a field once dominated by men, Williams must be classified as a pioneer. She was among the first to bring the woman's point of view to commercial western fiction, and she is today among the best and most successful of those writing western fiction for women.

—Judy Alter

WILLIAMS, John (Edward). American. Born in Clarksville, Texas, 29 August 1922. Educated at the University of Denver, B.A. 1949, M.A. 1950; University of Missouri, Columbia, Ph.D. 1954; Oxford University (English-Speaking Union Fellow), 1963. Served in the United States Army Air Force, 1942–45: Sergeant. Married 1) Avalon Smith in 1949, two daughters and one son; 2) Nancy Gardner in 1970, four step-children. Associate editor, Alan Swallow, publishers, Denver, 1948–50; Instructor, University of Missouri, 1950–54. Assistant Professor, 1954–60, Director of the Workshop for Writers, 1954–59, and of the Creative Writing Program, 1954–74, Associate Professor, 1960–64, since 1964 Professor of English, and Phipps Professor of Humanities, 1976–79, University of Denver. Writer-in-residence, Wisconsin State University, Whitewater, summers 1964–66, 1968–69; teacher at Bread Loaf Writers Conference, Vermont, 1966–72; writer-in-residence, Smith College, Northampton, Massachusetts, 1968; Hurst Professor of Creative Literature, Brandeis University, Waltham, Massachusetts, 1973. Editor, *Twentieth Century Literature*, Los Angeles, 1954–56, and *University of Denver Quarterly*, 1966–70. Recipient: Rockefeller grant, 1967; National Endowment for the Arts grant, 1969; National Book award, 1973; American Academy award, 1985; Guggenheim fellowship, 1985. Agent: Marie Rodell-Frances Collin Literary Agency, 110 West 40th Street, New York, New York 10018. Address: Department of English, University of Denver, Denver, Colorado 80210, U.S.A.

Western Publications

Novel

Butcher's Crossing. New York, Macmillan, and London, Gollancz, 1960.

Other Publications

Novels

Nothing But the Night. Denver, Swallow, 1948.
Stoner. New York, Viking Press, 1965; London, Allen Lane, 1973.
Augustus. New York, Viking Press, 1972; London, Allen Lane, 1973.

Verse

The Broken Landscape. Denver, Swallow, 1949.
The Necessary Lie. Denver, Verb, 1965.

Other

Editor, *English Renaissance Poetry: A Collection of Shorter Poems from Skelton to Jonson.* New York, Doubleday, 1963.

*   *   *

John Williams's one western novel, *Butcher's Crossing*, is precisely located in time and place. In fact, a strong underlying theme in the novel is the way people are bound by their vision of their immediate time and place—and the resultant ironies.

Specifically, the time is 1873, when the overwhelming demand for buffalo hides seems a constant economic fact of life, and has brought forth an entire economy based on hunters, traders, and transport to eastern buyers. The place, Butcher's Crossing, is a small prairie crossroads town near the Rockies, a growing center for hunters to sell their hides and spend the winter.

This expanding frontier provides the framework for Will Andrews's story. Andrews, after three years at Harvard College, listening and never talking, decides to go west for experience, and comes to Butcher's Crossing with a letter of introduction to a local trader, McDonald. McDonald is an emigrant from the East, a businessman with a growing investment in and control of the buffalo hide market; he is optimistic about the growth of the small settlement because he assumes the demand for hides will continue and that the railroad will be coming to the town. Andrew's other potential mentor is also firmly linked to a West that he wants to believe is the real West. He is the aging buffalo hunter Miller, who has resisted the "rationalized" hunting and marketing techniques of McDonald, and has long tried to organize a hunt to a secret valley in Colorado where he believes a huge buffalo herd still grazes.

Andrews does not want a desk job as McDonald's bookkeeper, so he decides to finance and accompany Miller on his hunt. They hire a skinner (Andrews will be the second skinner), and take along a fourth man as a general helper. Their trek to the mountain is successful: they find the valley, and Miller, in a blaze of gun-lust, proceeds to shoot the entire herd of some 3000 buffalo, even though they cannot carry back all the hides and have to cache half of them. Miller meticulously counts each day's shoot, almost as if building up his legend as the greatest buffalo hunter of all. His almost mindless determination to slaughter every animal means that they are delayed in the valley, and are snowed in for the winter.

They manage to survive, however, but the trip back begins to take on the quality of a nightmare. They have a ghastly accident crossing a river, and the skinner is accidentally killed and the hides lost; the helper grows increasingly senile or insane. On their arrival in Butcher's Crossing, after an absence of some six months, they find McDonald's huge holding of hides lying unguarded, the town almost deserted; even most of the saloon girls have left town. The demand for buffalo hides has completely dried up, and, moreover, the railroad is now being laid some 50 miles to the south. McDonald's hides are worthless, and he has become a cynical man, ready to return east. Miller's frustration is even more emphatic, involving not only the loss of the hides but also his image as a great hunter: in a second destructive rage, he sets fire to McDonald's bundles of useless hides.

Andrew's reaction is similar. Throughout the novel he is the young questing hero, a quiet observer rather than an active leader, searching for "the source and preserver of his world, a world which seemed to turn ever in fear away from its source, rather than search it out, as the prairie grass around him sent down its fibered roots into the rich dark dampness, the Wildness, and thereby renewed itself, year after year." To him Miller has been somewhat of a hero; even the young saloon girl, Francine, to whom he is obviously attracted before the hunt, carries an aura of confidence and identity that he can't tarnish by physical contact. Now, after his ordeal in the mountains and the deflating end of the adventure, in a daze he ruts with Francine for a week in a darkened room, as if to confirm that she too is part of a world that is brutal and destructive. Though the end of Andrew's quest has not been positive, it has been conclusive.

—George Walsh

WILLS, Chester. *See* **SNOW, Charles H.**

WILSON, Barbara (Ellen). American. Born in Long Beach, California, 17 October 1950. Publisher, Seal Press, Seattle, Washington. Address: c/o Seal Press, 3131 Western Avenue, Seattle, Washington 98121, U.S.A.

WESTERN PUBLICATIONS

Novels (series: Pam Nilsen; Cassandra Reilly)

Ambitious Woman. Seattle, Seal Press, 1982; London, Women's Press, 1983.
Murder in the Collective (Nilsen). Seattle, Seal Press, and London, Women's Press, 1984.
Sisters of the Road (Nilsen). Seattle, Seal Press, 1986; London, Women's Press, 1987.
Cows and Horses. Portland, Oregon, Eighth Mountain Press, 1988; London, Virago Press, 1989.
The Dog Collar Murders (Nilsen). Seattle, Seal Press, and London, Virago, 1989.
Gaudi Afternoon (Reilly). Seattle, Seal Press, 1990; London, Virago Press, 1991.

Short Stories

Talk and Contact. Seattle, Seal Press, 1978.
Thin Ice. Seattle, Seal Press, 1981.
Walking on the Moon. Seattle, Seal Press, 1983; London, Women's Press, 1986.
Miss Venezuela. Seattle, Seal Press, 1988.

Other

The Geography Lesson (for children). Seattle, Seal Press, 1977.

Editor, with Faith Conlon and Rachel de Silva, *The Things That Divide Us* (short stories). Seattle, Seal Press, 1985; London, Sheba, 1986.

Translator, *Cora Sandel: Collected Short Stories.* Seattle, Seal Press, 1985.
Translator *Nothing Happened*, by Ebba Haslund. Seattle, Seal Press, 1987.

* * *

Barbara Wilson, a Long Beach, California native, who has lived in Seattle since 1974, locates her fiction often on the Northwest coast of the U.S.—yet her women characters struggling for identity in a man's world, are of no country.

Wilson's heroines, like the author herself, are frequently sojourners, at times expatriates—women whose root systems are fragile. The West for them is not the place where the sun sets, the promised land at the end of the wagon train trail; rather; rather, it is a home from which they would prefer to escape, or a place for merely passing through. In "Miss Venezuela," the title story in Wilson's volume of collected stories, Long Beach—where young Rhonda has been born and finds herself stuck—will always only be a port of call for her glamorous idol, Dolores Maria Angelus Otero, a Miss Venezuela beauty queen; for Rhonda, the address, as much a state of mind as a place, is permanent. In "Take Louise Nevelson" Chris leaves Eugene, Oregon for Phoenix as a lesbian love affair falters; there, she sells encylopedias door-to-door, and suffers homophobic betrayal by the woman she had thought was her best friend; she does reconnect with her estranged lover—but not to come home. Instead, she urges them both to travel back to Barcelona, to complete the youthful journey she had once cut short. In "Phantom Limb Pain," one of Wilson's most memorable pieces, Cheryl, a nurse, studies Russian with Ivan Ivanovitch, an impassioned exile who opens the class with "Tonight ... we begin with memory." Her teacher helps her to understand that often all must be lost—in Cheryl's case it's time to leave her homebody partner, Edie, to seize her long-lost dream of working in a Latin American health clinic—before the self is found.

"Crater Lake" is one of several stories in which Wilson's character, Kate, a young woman whose early losses in life precede her restlessness and lack of focus, appears. In this piece Kate and her brother Kevin are children on the run from the emotional impact of their mother's recent death, and their father's impending remarriage, as he takes them on a driving vacation up the California coast from their home. When a fellow tourist drops his keys down Crater Lake ("... just like that, into a lake almost 2,000 feet deep"), it seems that only an image from the larger-than-life landscape of the West, beckoning yet dreadful, could have served to contain all that the children must accept.

Wilson's popular series of feminist mysteries—*Murder in the Collective*, *Sisters of the Road*, and *The Dog Collar Murders*—all featuring her amateur detective, Pam Nilsen, draw much of their appeal from their setting in the leftist/progressive/feminist/lesbian community of contemporary Seattle, alive with political, cultural, and ethnic diversity. Wilson's sense of place in the urban Northwest is strong. Nilsen identifies with the landscape of the city: "I returned to the houseboat on Portage Bay . . . sat out on the floating dock, drinking jasmine-scented tea and watching the lights of the bridge and the university opposite us on the dark water." She relates to Seattle, as well: "Seattle has become one of those trendy West Coast cities where every other person is from somewhere else. It's a little declassé, in fact, to admit that you were born here... But declassé or not, Penny and I were born and raised here and seem to have a continuity most other people we know seem to lack." The beauty of the watery city set on Puget Sound and around Lake Union and Lake Portage is never lost on Nilsen, yet she's also always very much a part of a more blighted terrain, one that humans have created. *Sisters of the Road* takes up the theme of a molested teenage runaway become prostitute; and begins in the red-light district of Seattle, against the emotional backdrop of the Green River Murders, a grim reminder of something else the city is known for.

Although many of Wilson's works are set abroad *Gaudi Afternoon*, a mystery featuring a new detective, Cassandra Reilly, in Barcelona, and *Walking on the Moon*, a novella, in Dusseldorf), the writer consistently returns, in her work, as in her real life, to her home on a continent's far edge. Here, the ocean's vastness informs the land's sense of itself, much as her characters must learn that more powerful forces often sweep away the frail human constructs they depend upon.

An example is *Cows and Horses*, the only one of Wilson's works not published by Seal Press, which she co-founded in 1986 and now runs with Faith Conlon. In this novel, Bet, still reeling from the break-up of a ten-year relationship which was also a business partnership, takes herself for healing to Anacortes Island north of Seattle in the Rosario Strait: "Soon the claustrophic terrarium around Puget Sound gave way to the lowering Dutch skies of the Skagit Valley, with its lonely farms and pastures, its single lines of windblown, leafless trees." Again, the sense of both the natural world and the particular kind of human community a certain place produces are central to the novel, developed to a somewhat deeper symbolic level than in the Nilsen mysteries.

A definitive summation of Wilson's own relationship to the themes of geographic location, the West, and cultural identity in her work can best be found in her story, "Looking for the Golden Gate," from *Miss Venezuela*. Edwin Kreutz, a German tourist, believes himself in San Francisco, while, really, having accidentally deplaned at the wrong airport, he's wandering around Bangor, Maine. Kreutz tries desperately to find the place he's come so far to find, the Golden Gate Bridge. The Golden Gate, Wilson seems to say, does not necessarily reside in the West; that gateway to an imagined land of bounty and freedom, could remain forever elusive, not unlike Gatsby's green light at the end of the dock, "You note the direction of her fingertip. [Kreutz thinks as waitress directs him] West. Good. Excellent... You can find the Golden Gate if someone only points the way."

As a contemporary American fiction writer living in and often writing about the West Coast, Wilson has travelled a long way from Fitzgerald's East Egg—perhaps only to discover a similar truth.

—Patricia Roth Schwartz

WILSON, Dave. *See* **FLOREN, Lee.**

WILSON, Harry Leon. American. Born in Oregon, Illinois, 1 May 1867. Married 1) Wilbertine Worders in 1899 (divorced); 2) Rose Latham in 1902 (separated 1907; divorced); 3) Helen Cooke in 1912 (divorced 1928), one son and one daughter. Worked in a furniture factory from age 15; stenographer, in Omaha, 1884, and Denver, 1885, 1889–92, for Union Pacific Railroad; secretary, Bancroft History Company, Denver, 1886–89; assistant to the editor, 1892, and editor, 1896–1902, *Puck*; then freelance writer. Lived in Carmel, California from 1910. *Died 19 June 1939.*

Western Publications

Novels

The Lions of the Lord: A Tale of the Old West. Boston, Lothrop, 1903; London, Richards, 1911.
Ruggles of Red Gap. New York, Doubleday, 1915; London, Lane, 1917.
Two Black Sheep. New York, Cosmopolitan, 1931.

Short Stories

Somewhere in Red Gap. New York, Doubleday, and London, Curtis Brown, 1916.
Ma Pettengill. New York, Doubleday, and London, Lane, 1919.
Ma Pettengill Talks. New York, Doubleday, 1925.

Other Publications

Novels

The Spenders: A Tale of the Third Generation. Boston, Lothrop, and London, Kelly, 1902.
The Seeker. New York, Doubleday, 1904; London, Heinemann, 1905.
The Boss of Little Arcady. Boston, Lothrop, and London, Kegan Paul, 1905.
Ewing's Lady. New York, Appleton, 1907.
Bunker Bean. New York, Doubleday, 1913; London, Lane, 1919.
The Man from Home (novelization of stage play). New York, Appleton, 1925.
The Wrong Twin. New York, Doubleday, and London, Lane, 1921.
Merton of the Movies. New York, Doubleday, and London, Lane, 1922.
Oh, Doctor! New York, Cosmopolitan, and London, Lane, 1923.

Professor How Could You! New York, Cosmopolitan, 1924; London, Lane, 1925.
Cousin Jane. New York, Cosmopolitan, 1925; London, Hodder and Stoughton, 1926.
Lone Tree. New York, Cosmopolitan, 1929.
When in the Course—. New York, Kinsey, 1940.

Short Stories

Zigzag Tales from the East to the West. New York, Keppler and Schwarzmann, 1894.

Plays (with Booth Tarkington)

The Man from Home (as *The Guardian*, produced Louisville, 1907; as *The Man from Home*, produced New York, 1908). New York, Harper, 1908; revised version, 1934.
Cameo Kirby (produced Columbus, Ohio, 1908; New York, 1909).
If I Had Money (produced Chicago, 1909).
Foreign Exchange (produced Chicago, 1909).
Springtime (produced New York, 1909).
Your Humble Servant (produced New York, 1910).
The Gibson Upright. New York, Doubleday, 1919.
Up from Nowhere (produced New York, 1919).
Life (by Wilson alone), music by Domenico Brescia (produced San Francisco, 1919). San Francisco, Bohemian Club, 1919.
Tweedles (produced Cleveland and New York, 1923). New York, French, 1924.
How's Your Health? (produced New York, 1929). New York, French, 1930.

Other

So This Is Golf! New York, Cosmopolitan, and London, Lane, 1923.

*

Critical Studies: *Harry Leon Wilson: Some Account of the Triumphs and Tribulations of an American Popular Writer* by George Kummer, Cleveland, Press of Western Reserve University, 1963.

* * *

Because of their similar backgrounds Harry Leon Wilson has been compared with Mark Twain, but Wilson's humorous fiction does not have the Pyrrhonism and strong sense of irony that are characteristic of Twain's. While making us laugh, Twain's humor simultaneously shows us that we are that "damned human race," whereas Wilson's work reveals his strong faith in the essential goodness of the common man.

Wilson's first books are serious historical fiction flawed by neo-romanticism, a defect diminished but still detectable in his best work: the five humorous novels of his middle period. Like Twain, Wilson used humor to attack class distinctions, but instead of switching the identities of two characters as Twain often did, Wilson gave a character of low rank a sudden rise into high social, economic, or artistic status. In attacking snobbery and elitism, Wilson depicted the West as a region of opportunity and comfortable democracy, whereas the culture of Europe and the east is exclusive and uncomfortable.

Unlike much western fiction, Wilson's does not focus much attention on the western land; but implicit in most of his novels is the view that the vast rich territory of the West presents the common man with boundless opportunities. Those Wilsonian rich who are not snobs maintain some tie with their humble beginnings; for example, the movie mogul in *Two Black Sheep* has furnished one room of his mansion to resemble the interior of a one-room log cabin. The resolution of the humorous clash between East and West is usually a combination of the best of both worlds, as when Ruggles settles in Red Gap, leaving behind his British sense of class distinctions but bringing with him a superior knowledge of cuisine.

Attracted to the opportunities of the West but not fully aware of the power of the land, Wilson occupies a transitional position between the first western novelists, who still saw with eastern eyes, and the writers of the 1920's and 1930's, for whom the land had become more than a treasure chest. *The Lions of the Lord* by Wilson marks the midpoint between the virulent anti-Mormon fiction of post-Civil War writers such as Joaquin Miller and the more balanced and better crafted *Children of God* by Vardis Fisher. In the tradition that begins with *Roughing It* and extends to Brautigan's *Trout Fishing in America*, *Ruggles of Red Gap* is Wilson's most widely known work, but its blatant sexism, tedious and inconsistent narrative voice, and unquestioned faith in the common man keep it from ranking with the best of Western humor. *Merton of the Movies*, however, does deserve to be placed with the finest Hollywood novels, for it has fewer flaws and greater irony, and it clearly anticipates *The Day of the Locust* by Nathanael West.

If Mark Twain is "the Lincoln of our literature," Wilson is the Norman Rockwell of the western novel, a writer who makes us laugh at pretense and snobbery but who shows us only the good side of the common man.

—James H. Maguire

WINSLOWE, John. *See* **RICHARDSON, Gladwell.**

WINSLOWE, John R. *See* **RICHARDSON, Gladwell.**

WINSTAN, Matt. *See* **NICKSON, Arthur.**

WINTERS, Logan. Pseudonym for Paul Joseph Lederer; also writes as Elizabeth Wolfe. American. Born in San Diego, California, 2 July 1944. Educated at San Diego State University. Married Sandra Katherine Trujillo in 1967; two daughters and two sons. Full-time writer. Agent: Richard Curtis Associates, 340 East 66th Street, New York, New York 10021. Address: c/o New American Library, 1633 Broadway, New York, New York 10019, U.S.A.

WESTERN PUBLICATIONS

Novels (series: Spectros in all books)

1. *Silverado.* New York, Dorchester, 1981.
2. *Hunt the Beast Down.* New York, Dorchester, 1981.

3. *Natchez.* New York, Dorchester, 1981.
4. *The Silver Canyon.* New York, Dorchester, 1981.

Novels as Paul J. Lederer (series: Indian Heritage)

Tecumseh. New York, New American Library, 1982.
Indian Heritage:
1. *Manitou's Daughter.* New York, New American Library, 1982.
2. *Shawnee Dawn.* New York, New American Library, 1982.
3. *Seminole Skies.* New York, New American Library, 1983.
4. *Cheyenne Dreams.* New York, New American Library, 1985.
5. *The Way of the Wind.* New York, New American Library, 1985.
6. *North Star.* New York, New American Library, 1987.
7. *The Far Dreamer.* New York, New American Library, 1987.

OTHER PUBLICATIONS

Novels as Elizabeth Wolfe

Boudicca. New York, Ace, 1980.
Ice Castle. New York, Leisure, 1982.

* * *

While it can be argued that all so-called "light" western fiction is really just another form of fantasy, true (and successful) combinations of the western and fantasy genres are quite rare. Joe Lansdale's *The Magic Wagon* is one example; the stories collected in Lansdale's anthology *Razored Saddles* serve as another. To be able to sustain such an uneasy mixture throughout five full-length novels, and make readers accept each incredible incident without question, requires a writer of considerable skill—and in the late 1970's and early 1980's, Logan Winters did exactly that with his underrated (and today, little-known) series Spectros.

Any attempt to condense the premise of the series into one paragraph, must inevitably dilute some of its impact. To appreciate fully the skill with which the author blends the fantastic with the traditional Western, Winters's books really need to be read, and not summarized.

When we first meet the elderly Doctor Spectros and his three companions (a gunman named Featherskill, a mute mountain man named Montak, and Inkada, the Moor) in "Showdown at Guyamas", they are travelling the West in search of a mysterious European named Blackschuster. As the plot develops, however, what initially appears to be just one more manhunt story soon takes on an entirely different aspect when Blackschuster is revealed to be a wizard, and that deep within the cave he is using as his present base he keeps a crystal coffin containing the body of a beautiful sleeping woman.

Winters slowly begins to expand upon these revelations as Spectros and his men become involved with Elisabeth Parker, whose ranch is under threat from a land-hungry despot who wants the property for its abundance of water and graze. In a series of flashbacks, we learn that many years before, Spectros—initially described as a trader from Boston, but in later books referred to as a cowboy who was shanghaied—is shipwrecked off the coast of India. Travelling to the Yahif's palace to request help, he meets the Yahif's beautiful daughter, Kirstina, and after a brief romance, a marriage is arranged. The court magician is against the union, however, and sells Kirstina to Blackschuster. Heartbroken, Spectros decides to learn something of the mystic arts himself before setting out in pursuit of the wizard. Blackschuster, meanwhile, facing the fact that he will never have Kirstina's love, puts her into a weird, trance-like sleep, keeping her that way by using a drug called Morphantis, the main component of which is silver. Consequently, Blackschuster's quest to obtain this precious metal is his primary motive in each book.

Although age has left the wizard and his unwilling bride untouched, it has taken a heavy toll on Spectros. Now an old man, he has to rely increasingly upon his three aides. There is a fourth member of the team, though, upon whom he relies even more than the others; the legendary Kid Soledad—because Soledad is in fact the younger, stronger gunfighter the old doctor is periodically able to become. As bizarre as this further twist may seem to Western purists, Soledad's appearances (usually made shortly after the Doctor has retreated into his black, windowless wagon, ostensibly to "rest," and nearly always at a time of crisis) rarely fail to evoke a genuine sense of veneration.

In such an unusual series, of course, the author constantly runs the risk of shattering credibility (as at the end of the first book, when Spectros transforms himself into a kestrel to do battle with Blackschuster's raven, a sequence which begs the indulgence of even the most flexible Western reader), but generally Winters manages this by playing down the magic and concentrating instead on telling a good western yarn. He usually employs multiple viewpoints, switching scenes at cliff-hanging moments, and has a preference for urbane, ambitious villains, whose underlings are vicious gunmen with curious codes of honour. Winters's women almost always play important roles (his women, in fact, are frequently less stereotypical than his men). Unusually, there is little or no profanity in the books.

It must also be said that the books rarely waver from the formula devised for "Showdown at Guyamas." Always scouring the West in search of Blackschuster, Spectros' three men (who form a likeable and well-drawn trio), are invariably separated by circumstances and become involved in the problems of a third party. Usually, these problems can only be solved by the emergence of Kid Soledad, who has to forsake the chance to finally settle matters with Blackschuster in order to help either his own men or the people they have befriended. Winters does manage to ring the changes from one adventure to the next, however. In *Hunt the Beast Down*, for example, Spectros tracks his arch-enemy to the Oregon coast, where Blackschuster has been lured by the wreck of a ship carrying a cargo of silver. There are some good, uneasy moments in this book, particularly when Winters introduces the legendary Bigfoot into the proceedings. *Natchez* is another particularly good example of an admittedly small sub-genre, with a number of evocative descriptions of the Mississippi swamplands, and the zombie-like creatures which inhabit them.

Obviously, the Spectros stories have a limited appeal for Western and fantasy fans alike, failing as they do to be one thing or the other. For all their spells and sorcery, however, these well-constructed and untaxing tales of frontier America are interesting departures from the traditional Western, and for a different kind of read, they take considerable beating.

—David Whitehead

WINTHER, Sophus K(eith). American. Born in Denmark, 24 June 1893. Educated at the University of Oregon, Eugene,

B.A. 1918, M.A. 1919; University of Washington, Seattle, Ph.D. 1925. Married in 1925. Member of the Department of English, University of Washington from 1922. Recipient: Liberation Medal of King Christian X of Denmark; Western Literature Association distinguished achievement award, 1980. *Died 10 May 1983.*

WESTERN PUBLICATIONS

Novels

Grimsen trilogy:
Take All to Nebraska. New York, Macmillan, 1935.
Mortgage Your Heart. New York, Macmillan, 1937.
This Passion Never Dies. New York, Macmillan, 1938.
Beyond the Garden Gate. New York, Macmillan, 1946.

OTHER PUBLICATIONS

Other

The Realistic War Novel. Seattle, University of Washington Book Store, 1930.
Eugene O'Neill: A Critical Study. New York, Random House, 1934; revised edition, New York, Russell and Russell, 1961.

*

Critical Study: *Sophus K. Winther* by Barbara Howard Meldrum, Boise, Idaho, Boise State University, 1983.

* * *

Sophus K. Winther is best known for his Grimsen trilogy about a Danish immigrant family. The story begins in the 1890's when the Grimsens arrive in Nebraska and rent a farm. Years of struggle follow; no matter how hard they work or how much they produce, economic prosperity evades them. Even their short tenure as landowners is doomed, for they are forced to buy at inflated prices to avoid eviction, then lose everything through foreclosure when prices fall after World War I. Like most immigrants, the Grimsens came to America, and specifically to western farmlands, hoping to achieve the financial security which would make possible a better way of life. The parents never achieve their dream, although some of the children may have more hopeful prospects. Shaping Winther's portrayal is a pervasive naturalism which emphasizes human limitations before forces (both economic and natural) which are greater than human aspiration and determination.

Winther's writing is especially vivid in descriptions of nature and in protraying the inner experience of boyhood and youth, schooltime traumas and adolescent romance. Young Hans, the third in a family of six boys, becomes the center of consciousness when the narrative is not focused on the parents. Peter Grimsen is a hardworking patriarch who expects his sons to work with the same dedication, not realizing their need for play or their inability to share his vision born of an adult's ambition to build a better life. Meta is a long-suffering mother, dedicated to meeting her husband's and her children's needs and disappointed in her lifelong desire for a daughter: one of the most poignant scenes of *Take All to Nebraska* is the illness and death of Meta's only daughter, a child whose place is never filled by the sons Meta subsequently bears. Winther's characterizations capture the emotional pain and loss endangered by the difficulties of immigrant farmlife during times of economic hardship.

Winther's trilogy is a fictionalized extension of his own experience as an immigrant boy in Nebraska. His later novel, *Beyond the Garden Gate*, is autobiographical only in the setting, Eugene, Oregon, where Winther's family moved in 1912 and where he attended the University of Oregon. This novel deals with "sin" in a secular age, values in a relativistic society, and responsibility from a scientific perspective. Winther's naturalistic philosophy shapes the narrative, not in the despairing tones so familiar to most naturalistic fiction, but in strains of hope and affirmation. Cause-effect means that people who are basically good and who have been trained in healthy, positive directions will make the "right" decisions. All of Winther's fiction emphasizes what it is to be human. In the trilogy affirmation is muted by the grinding force of indifferent fate. In *Beyond the Garden Gate* fate is still indifferent, but hope seems more realistically tenable.

—Barbara Howard Meldrum

WISLER, G(ary) Clifton. Also writes as Will McLennan. American. Born in Oklahoma City, Oklahoma, 15 May 1950. Educated at Southern Methodist University, Dallas, B.F.A., 1972, M.A., 1974. Recipient: Western Writers of America Spur award, 1984, 1990; Child Study Association Book of the Year award, 1986, 1988; International Reading Association award, for children's book, 1987; National Council for Social Studies award, for children's book, 1987. Agent: Barbara Puechner, 3121 Portage Road, Bethlehem, Pennsylvania 18017. Address: 1812 Savage Drive, Plano, Texas 75023, U.S.A.

WESTERN PUBLICATIONS

Novels (series: Delamer; Justiss Family; Darby Prescott)

My Brother, The Wind. New York, Doubleday, 1979.
A Cry of Angry Thunder. New York, Doubleday, 1980.
The Trident Brand (Delamer). New York, Doubleday, 1982; London, Hale, 1986.
West of the Cimarron. New York, Zebra, 1985.
Spirit Warrior. New York, Zebra, 1986.
High Plains Rider. New York, Zebra, 1986.
Antelope Springs. New York, Walker, 1986; London, Hale, 1987.
Starr's Showdown (Delamer). New York, Fawcett, 1986; London, Hale, 1989.
Purgatory (Delamer). New York, Fawcett, 1987; London, Hale, 1989.
Abrego Canyon (Delamer). New York, Fawcett, 1987; London, Hale, 1989.
Texas Brazos (Justiss Family). New York, Zebra, 1987.
Fortune Bend (Justiss Family). New York, Zebra, 1987.
Palo Pinto (Justiss Family). New York, Zebra, 1987.
Thompson's Mountain. New York, Zebra, 1987.
Comanche Crossing. New York, Paperjacks, 1987.
Comanche Summer. New York, Zebra, 1987.
The Return of Caulfield Blake. New York, Evans, 1987.
Illinois Prescott. New York, Zebra, 1987.
Caddo Creek (Justiss Family). New York, Zebra, 1988.
Avery's Law. New York, Paperjacks, 1988; London, Hale, 1989.
Ross's Gap. New York, Walker, 1988.

The Wayward Trail (Delamer). New York, Fawcett, and London, Hale, 1988.
South Pass Ambush (Delamer). New York, Fawcett, 1988.
Sweetwater Flats (Delamer). New York, Fawcett, 1989.
Among the Eagles (Delamer). New York, Fawcett, 1989.
Prescott's Trail. New York, Zebra, 1989.
Lakota. New York, Evans, 1989.
Esmeralda. New York, Walker, 1989.
Boswell's Luck. New York, Evans, 1990.
Pinto Lowery. New York, Evans, 1990.
Prescott's Law. New York, Zebra, 1990.
Prescott's Challenge. New York, Zebra, 1990.
Sam Delamer. New York, Fawcett, 1990.
Clear Fork (Delamer). New York, Fawcett, 1990.
North of Esperanza (Delamer). New York, Fawcett, 1991.

Novels as Will McLennan (series: the Ramseys in all books)

The Ramseys. New York, Jove, 1989.
Ramsey's Luck. New York, Jove, 1989.
Matt Ramsey. New York, Jove, 1989.

OTHER PUBLICATIONS

Novels

Sunrise. New York, Ace/Tempo, 1982.

Fiction (for children)

Winter of the Wolf. New York, Dutton, 1981.
The Chicken Must Have Died Laughing. Logan, Iowa, Perfection Form, 1983.
Thunder on the Tennessee. New York, Dutton, 1983.
A Special Gift. Grand Rapids, Michigan, Baker Book House, 1983.
Buffalo Moon. New York, Dutton, 1984.
The Raid. New York, Dutton, 1985.
The Antrian Messenger. New York, Dutton, 1986.
The Wolf's Tooth. New York, Dutton, 1987.
This New Land. New York, Walker, 1987.
The Seer. New York, Dutton, 1989.
Piper's Ferry: A Novel of the Texas Revolution. New York, Lodestar, 1990.
The Mind Trap. New York, Lodestar, 1990.
Red Cap. New York, Lodestar, 1991.

Other

"Writing the Young Adult Western," in *The Western Writer's Handbook*, edited by James L. Collins. Boulder, Colorado, Johnson, 1987.

* * *

G. Clifton Wisler is a prolific writer of western novels, his most popular novels being the Delamer series. Wisler chronicles Willie Delamer's life in 10 novels as the ex-Confederate soldier leaves his home in Texas and drifts west and then back again. In *Starr's Showdown*, Wisler shows his character's quick draw in Dodge City shootouts, and a tendency to wear out his welcome as the body count increases. Willie finds a home in *Abrego Canyon*, but doesn't find the peace he's looking for. Instead, he is drawn into gunplay again when he defends an immigrant family from the brutal Howton gang. After he rides *The Wayward Trail*, Willie finds himself back in Kansas in a little town called Edwards. Once again he's drawn into a battle, as powerful Rufus Macpherson plans to turn the sleepy town into a prime stop for Texas cattle drives by providing booze, gambling, and women to the eager cowboys. The ending is bittersweet as Willie finds himself on his black stallion Thunder, searching for peace westward. *South Pass Ambush* begins with Willie thinking he's found some stability as a guard for the supply wagons from Cheyenne to Sweetwater. But the outlaw gand led by the bloody Murphy brothers shatter the momentary peace. *Among the Eagles* won the Spur award for the best original paperback Western of 1989.

In two recent books in the Delamer series, *Sam Delamer* and *Clear Fork*, Wisler is deepening the series by exploring the character of Willie's powerful brother Sam, and Willie's attempt to come back to his real home after a decade of drifting. The series takes on an added dimension in these books, and promises more drama as the brothers struggle against each other.

Another Wisler series with solid writing and compelling characters is the Justiss Family series. In the first book, *Texas Brazos*, Wisler introduces us to Charlie Justiss and his wife Angela, who struggle to build the largest cattle ranch in Palo Pinto County. But the Kiowa and the Comanche are active; the winter storms and the searing summers test the will of the settlers. In *Fortune Bend*, Charlie Justiss discovers someone's rustling cattle, and has to expose some crooked lawmen to save his growing cattle empire. *Caddo Creek* focuses on Charlie's son Billy, now ranch manager, who must contend with a drought while Sheriff Bret Pruett tracks down a gang of land-grabbing bandits. Wisler convincingly captures the sense of constant challenge in the settlers' lives.

Wisler's career started with a flourish when his first novel, *My Brother, The Wind*, was nominated for an American Book Award in 1980. When Timothy Welles's father dies at Shiloh and his mother dies a few years afterward, he heads for Oregon to be with his sister. But on the way, his wagon is attacked by Cheyenne, and Timothy is taken captive. When Timothy is about to lose his life, he's rescued by a mountain man named Bear. The relationship between Bear and Timothy is heartfelt and moving.

Wisler went on to win a Spur award in 1983 for the best children's Western, *Thunder on the Tennessee*. A 16 year old Willie Delamer leaves Texas with his father to fight the Yankees in the Civil War. War seems like a big party to the young boy, but the ugly reality of war shows itself to Willie as a young Yankee drummer boy has his leg shattered by a cannonball fragment. *Thunder on the Tennessee* echoes *The Red Badge of Courage*, and shows war's effects on the innocence of a young man.

Winter of the Wolf was a Spur finalist in 1982. Told in the first person by Thomas Jefferson Clinton, this novel is the story of a boy coming of age while his father and brothers leave Texas to fight in the Civil War. T.J. keeps the homestead going, but is confronted by a deadly wolf who appears to be immune to bullets. One night T.J. shoots at the animal, but it escapes unharmed. When T.J. makes friends with a young Comanche, he's told the wolf is really a demon, and the two boys decide to kill the demon wolf together. *Winter of the Wolf* and *Thunder on the Tennessee* are two of the best children's Westerns ever written.

In "Writing the Young Adult Western" published in *The Western Writer's Handbook*, Wisler says, "I'm not sure there are any golden rules to writing for any audience. The best advice I ever received was simply, 'Tell a good story.' I think that works about as well as any . . ." G. Clifton Wisler's books certainly put that advice to good practice.

—George Kelley

WISTER, Owen. American. Born in Germantown, Philadelphia, Pennsylvania, 14 July 1860. Educated at schools in Hofwyl, Switzerland, 1870–71, and England, 1871–72; Germantown Academy, 1872; St. Paul's School, Concord, New Hampshire, 1873–78; Harvard University, Cambridge, Massachusetts, 1878–82, B.A. (summa cum laude) in music 1882; studied music in Paris, 1882–83; attended Harvard Law School, 1885–88, LL.B. 1888; admitted to Pennsylvania bar, 1889. Married his second cousin Mary Channing Wister in 1898 (died 1913); three sons and three daughters. Worked at Union Safe Deposit Vaults, Boston, 1884–85; lawyer in Philadelphia, 1889–91; thereafter a full-time writer; moved to Charleston, South Carolina, 1902. Overseer, Harvard University, 1912–18, 1919–25. Member, American Academy; honorary member, Society of Letters (Paris); honorary fellow, Royal Society of Literature (London). *Died 21 July 1938.*

WESTERN PUBLICATIONS

Novels

Lin McLean. New York, Harper, 1897.
The Virginian: A Horseman of the Plains. New York and London, Macmillan, 1902.

Short Stories

Red Men and White. New York, Harper, and London, Osgood, 1896.
The Jimmyjohn Boss and Other Stories. New York and London, Harper, 1900.
A Journey in Search of Christmas. New York and London, Harper, 1904.
Members of the Family. New York and London, Macmillan, 1911.
Padre Ignacio. New York, Harper, 1911.
When West Was West. New York and London, Macmillan, 1928.
The West of Owen Wister: Selected Short Stories, edited by Robert L. Hough. Lincoln, University of Nebraska Press, 1972.

OTHER PUBLICATIONS

Novels

The Dragon of Wantley: His Rise, His Voracity, and His Downfall. Philadelphia, Lippincott, 1892.
Philosophy 4: A Story of Harvard University. New York and London, Macmillan, 1903.
Lady Baltimore. New York and London, Macmillan, 1906.
How Doth the Simple Spelling Bee. New York and London, Macmillan, 1907.
Mother. New York, Dodd Mead, 1907.

Short Story

The New Swiss Family Robinson. Cambridge, Massachusetts, Sever, 1882.

Plays

Dido and Aeneas, music by Wister (produced Cambridge, Massachusetts, 1882).
Watch Your Thirst: A Dry Opera. New York, Macmillan, 1923; revised version, as *The Honeymoon Shiners,* in *Writings,* 1928.
The Vain, with Kirke La Shelle. Privately printed, 1958.

Verse

Done in the Open, illustrated by Frederic Remington. New York, Collier, 1903.
Indispensable Information for Infants; or, Easy Entrance to Education. New York, Macmillan, 1921.

Other

Ulysses S. Grant. Boston, Small Maynard, 1900.
Musk-Ox, Bison, Sheep, and Goat, with Caspar W. Whitney and George Bird Grinnell. New York, Macmillan, 1904.
The Seven Ages of Washington: A Biography. New York, Macmillan, 1907.
The Pentecost of Calamity. New York and London, Macmillan, 1915.
A Straight Deal; or, The Ancient Grudge. New York and London, Macmillan, 1920.
Neighbors Henceforth. New York and London, Macmillan, 1922.
The Writings of Owen Wister. New York, Macmillan, 11 vols., 1928.
Roosevelt: The Story of a Friendship 1880–1919. New York, Macmillan, 1930; as *Theodore Roosevelt,* London, Macmillan, 1930.
Two Appreciations of John Jay Chapman. New York, Wister, 1934.
My Father, Owen Wister, and Ten Letters . . . to His Mother During His First Trip to Wyoming in 1885, by Frances Kemble Wister Stokes. Laramie, University of Wyoming Library, 1952.
Owen Wister Out West: His Journals and Letters, edited by Fanny Kemble Wister. Chicago, University of Chicago Press, 1958.
My Dear Wister: The Frederic Remington-Owen Wister Letters, edited by Ben Vorpahl. Palo Alto, California, American West, 1972.
That I May Tell You: Journals and Letters of the Owen Wister Family, edited by Fanny Kemble Wister. Wayne, Pennsylvania, Haverford House, 1979.

*

Bibliography: "Owen Wister: An Annotated Bibliography" by Dean Sherman, in *Bulletin of Bibliography* (Boston), January–March 1971; "Owen Wister: An Annotated Bibliography of Secondary Material" by Sanford E. Morovitz, in *American Literary Realism* (Arlington, Texas), Winter 1974.

Manuscript Collection: Library of Congress, Washington, D.C.

Critical Studies: *The Eastern Establishment and the Western Experience: The West of Frederic Remington, Theodore Roosevelt, and Owen Wister* by G. Edward White, New Haven, Connecticut, Yale University Press, 1968; *Owen Wister* by Richard W. Etulain, Boise, Idaho, Boise State College, 1973; *Owen Wister* by John L. Cobbs, Boston, Twayne, 1984; *Owen Wister: Chronicler of the West, Gentleman of the East* by Darwin Payne, Dallas, Southern Methodist University Press, 1985.

* * *

Though he ultimately published six volumes of western fiction—four collections of short stories and two novels—Owen Wister's singular achievement was *The Virginian*, the novel which created the romantic cowboy hero and many of the stock themes of subsequent Westerns. As Cooper's Leatherstocking Tales shaped earlier frontier materials into an American tradition of romance, so *The Virginian* assimilated first-hand observation of the cowboy West into a new national frontier myth. Because *The Virginian*'s influence is so pervasive, the importance of Wister's contribution to western fiction can hardly be overstated. Yet, like Cooper, Wister is a myth-maker with an ambiguous literary reputation. This is partially because of the limitations of his own fiction, which does not always escape sentimental Victorian clichés. But Wister is also linked unfairly with a tradition of popular romance produced by such writers as Zane Grey and Max Brand, who simplified Wister's themes into the formulas of mass-market fiction. Actually, *The Virginian* has little in common stylistically or thematically with the countless pulp romances derivative of it, and it is scarcely fair to hold Wister himself accountable for the weaknesses of his imitators. Though he was not a major voice in American writing, Wister's achievement was original and significant: his best western fiction combines the virtues of good realist writing with the mythic symbolism of his central theme, the bitter-sweet drama of the conquest (or domestication) of America's last internal frontier, located most precisely in Wister's imagination as the "vanished world" of "Wyoming between 1874 and 1890" (Preface to *The Virginian*).

Like his friends Theodore Roosevelt and Frederic Remington, Wister was an Easterner who first discovered the invigorating effects of the West as a young man travelling for his health. Beginning with his first encounter with Wyoming in 1854, he avidly kept journals and notes (interesting documents in themselves, presented in edited form in *Wister Out West*) recording anecdotes, dialect, and impressions of western landscapes and western life. In 1891, after a conversation in which he and Roosevelt enthusiastically discussed the literary potentiality of such materials, Wister began writing his first western story, "Hank's Woman," which was subsequently published in *Harper's* and launched his career as a writer. By 1902 Wister had successfully transformed his western impressions into an enduring national myth: he had published two collections of short stories (*Red Men and White* and *The Jimmyjohn Boss and Other Stories*) as well as a first novel, *Lin McLean*; but it was the overwhelming success of *The Virginian* which firmly established the cowboy era in the nation's imagination as the last refuge of frontier romance. (Though he published two more collections of western stories in later years, neither *Members of the Family* nor *When West Was West* added significantly to Wister's achievement.) As *The Virginian* rose to the top of the bestseller list, the initial vision which Wister shared with Roosevelt—to "save the sagebrush for American literature"—was finally realized.

Though *The Virginian* is deservedly Wister's most renowned work, much of his other western fiction is of considerable interest, both as historical documentation about the period and as literature. His best stories have the journalistic virtues of good realist fiction: first-hand observation of western manners and dialect, colorful characters, exotic landscapes and incidents. Many of the stories remain merely anecdotal, some are clumsy humor, some lapse into melodrama, and many contain fine writing whose effects are ultimately dissipated. But they also exhibit the qualities which give subtlety and strength to *The Virginian* (and which elicited admiration from Henry James). At its best, Wister's fiction vividly dramatizes conflicts of manners and style, capturing the brash, irreverent spirit as well as the brutality of western life. Most of all, his best writing has wit, a quality that has all but disappeared in the popular romance formulas derived from *The Virginian*.

If Wister had written nothing but the western stories and *Lin McLean*, he would have remained a minor realist writer rather than the figure who shaped the cowboy legend. But in *The Virginian*, he created an image of the West that was heroic as well as exotic, that transformed local color into national myth. The differences between *Lin McLean* and *The Virginian* illustrate Wister's accomplishment in later novel, and the differences begin with the contrast between the heroes who give the novels their titles. Lin represents many of the qualities Wister valued in western character: he is independent, resourceful, witty, and free of spirit (until he falls in love). But, with all his western qualities, Lin remains boyish. He is essentially a pastoral hero, a cowboy shepherd whose identity is bound up with the free, open range. He serves admirably to depict the humor and spontaneity of western life, but as a romantic lead he is out of character and uncomfortable, like Huck scruffing around the Widow Watson's home in new clothes.

Like Lin, the image of the West in *Lin McLean* comes essentially from pastoral. The death of the West, the underlying theme of the novel, is the domestication of a glorious, still-unfenced playground, and *Lin McLean* is most successful when counterpointing western horseplay with elegy, lament for the vanishing world of boyish innocence which welcomes its own destruction in the good woman from the east. When Wister attempts to make Lin the romantic lead he descends into melodrama (the Dickensian scene in which Lin leaves his rowdy buddies to take Denver street waifs out for Christmas dinner) and sentimental cliché (the courtship of Jessamine Bunker).

Initially, the Virginian possesses Lin's carefree qualities, but he is also made of sterner stuff. We first see him indulging in horseplay, but the early confrontation with Trampas over a poker hand ("When ya' call me that, smile!") makes manifest the heroic theme Wister's imagery suggests from the opening scene—that there is more to this youthful spirit than meets the eye. The Virginian's true character is evoked by his name. Lin is merely a good-natured, untamed refugee from the conventional life of the eastern seaboard; but the Virginian is a southern gentleman, an American version of a standard European romance motif—the prince in disguise. By fusing the aristocratic myth of the South with his earlier democratic myth of the West, Wister created a hero who embodies Lin's youthful vitality yet also emerges as an instinctive nobleman. And as Wister's hero changed, so did the image he projected of the West. In the opening scenes in Medicine Bow, *The Virginian* evokes an Old West like that of *Lin McLean*, but the happy-go-lucky world of pastoral is already giving way to the more serious drama of "the game"—the testing of character that, like poker, separates the men from the "boys," the winners from the losers. In the end, the Virginian is a successful businessman and husband who rakes in the pot from his enemy, Trampas; but, more tragically, he also helps to string up his old buddy, Steve, a more sympathetically portrayed loser who refused to adapt to the rules of a new era, who finally cashed in his chips still adhering to an older western code of personal honor.

The poker metaphor structures *The Virginian*, symbolically fusing Wister's two major themes—the marriage plot, and the hero's emergence from the "equality" (the old, democratic west) to the "quality" (the new American aristocracy based on merit rather than privilege). If the game begins as uncomplicated fun, it finally is played for high stakes, for life and death. The Virginian's mastery of the game emanates from his mysterious reserve. The first American "cool" hero, he knows more than his countenance reveals. He knows when to call a bluff and when to spread his hand, whether in apparent horseplay (the Tulare Frog Story), in manly confrontation (the final shootout with Trampas), or in courtship. Wister uses the poker metaphor as a western symbol to reconcile fundamental conflicts in American values: for "the game" is ultimately a romantic image of American capitalism, in which a man's winnings are the external measure of his true merit, rather than a sign of inherited privilege. In the Virginian Wister created a new image of the American hero as nature's nobleman, representing the best in the nation's character, shaped by struggle and play in the game played out on our last frontier. An aura of mysterious potency and graceful ease has surrounded the cowboy hero in his vanishing sagebrush west ever since.

—David Mogen

WOOLLEY, Bryan. American. Born in Gorman, Texas, 22 August 1937. Educated at University of Texas, El Paso, B.A. 1958; Texas Christian University, Fort Worth, B.D. 1963; Harvard University, Cambridge, Massachusetts, Th. M., 1966. Married Isabel Nathaniel in 1979; two sons. Reporter, El Paso *Times*, 1955–58; teacher, Bel Air High School, El Paso, 1958–59; teller, Fort Davis State Bank, Texas, 1959–60; editor, Christian Board of Publication, St. Louis, 1966–67, and Associated Press, Tulsa, Oklahoma, 1967–68; editor, Anniston *Star*, Alabama, 1968–69; writer, Louisville *Courier-Journal*, Kentucky, 1969–76, and Dallas *Times Herald*, Dallas, Texas, 1976–89. Since 1989 writer, Dallas *Morning News*. Recipient: Western Writers of America Spur award, 1983. Agent: Nat Sobel, 146 East 19th Street, New York, New York 10003. Address: 18040 Midway Road, Apartment 215, Dallas, Texas 75287, U.S.A.

WESTERN PUBLICATIONS

Novels

Some Sweet Day. New York, Random House, 1974.
Time and Place. New York, Dutton, 1977.
Sam Bass. San Antonio, Texas, Corona, 1983.

Uncollected Short Stories

"Hard Country Friends" in *Redbook* (New York), December 1977.
"Generations" in *Redbook* (New York), July 1981.

OTHER PUBLICATIONS

Novel

November 22. New York, Seaview, 1981.

Other

We Be Here When the Morning Comes. Lexington, University Press of Kentucky, 1975.
The Time of My Life. Fredericksburg, Texas, Shearer, 1984.
Where Texas Meets the Sea. Dallas, Pressworks, 1985.
The Edge of the West and Other Texas Stories. El Paso, Texas Western Press, 1990.

*

Bryan Woolley comments:

Like Thomas Hardy, I have found that my native place is my source of inspiration and the proper setting for my work. Nearly all my fiction is set in rural Texas, where I was born and reared, and most of my characters are based on my ancestors and relatives and other people I have known. I grew up in a Texas that was barely past its frontier period, and I live now in a Texas that is across a narrow river from the Third World. There are many stories still to be written here.

* * *

Bryan Woolley's *Sam Bass* earned the Western Writers of America Spur award in 1983, winning the coveted award against formidable competition, including a Louis L'Amour novel. The Spur judges were impressed by Woolley's unique handling of the story of the ill-starred Texas stagecoach and train robber who was killed in 1878, telling it movingly and intricately by using six different first-person voices (none of them Bass's) and providing along the way a clear and meticuously accurate portrait of post-Civil War Texas.

Although it received the Spur award and uniformly laudatory reviews, and although the novel is (together with his *Some Sweet Day*) the author's choice as his best Western, *Sam Bass* has had a strangely difficult history. The book was originally under contract to E.P. Dutton (publishers of Woolley's 1977 novel, *Time and Place*), but when the manuscript was completed, Woolley says, "the editor had a 'brilliant' idea: By portraying Sam Bass and his pal Frank Jackson as homosexuals, he said, we could make a big splash in the publishing world with the first 'gay Western.' When I would not agree to do this, Dutton and I parted company." The novel was finally published by Corona Press, a small San Antonio firm, but has not yet been reprinted, a fact that disappoints the author. "The mass market paperback houses all said it was too 'Western' to be published as a 'mainstream' novel, and too 'mainstream' to be published as a 'Western,'" Woolley says. "I love *Sam Bass* for its cadence and the sense of the inevitable that begins to build in the reader after a while. I think *Sam* may be my best-written novel."

Woolley, a leading journalist in his home state of Texas, has published eight books since his first, *Some Sweet Day*, in 1974, four of them novels. When Woolley was growing up in the Davis Mountain country of West Texas, his grandmother, a schoolteacher, told him stories (and sang to him such songs as "The Ballad of Sam Bass") to try to get him to sleep and inculcated in him a love for books. "One of the most memorable days of my life was when my grandmother gave me 35 cents to buy a copy of *Treasure Island*," he says. "I was eight years old and still have that book and my 35-cent copy of *Tom*

Sawyer plus Jack O'Brien's *Silver Chief, Dog of the North* and copies of seven Will James books, some of which I bought on the installment plan at the Fort Davis Drug Store. Mark Twain and Will James were the first Western writers I read. I still consider Twain the greatest Western writer of us all."

Woolley also credits as important influences on his writing career the works of J. Frank Dobie ("who showed me that Texas is worth writing about and that Texans can write books"), Tom Lea ("the first novelist I ever met in person, while I was a reporter on the El Paso *Times*, and whose *The Wonderful Country* is one of the best Western novels ever written"), John Steinbeck ("especially *Of Mice and Men, Tortilla Flat*, and others of his shorter works"), and southwestern historian C.L. Sonnichsen ("whose college course, 'Life and Literature of the Southwest,' was one of those pivotal events in a young man's life: He taught me that the country and the people I had known all my life were not just interesting, but wonderful.")

He recalls: "When I was a small child, I would read an adventure story and ask my grandmother, 'Did it really happen?', hoping desperately that it had. Her reply always was, 'It *could* have happened.' This is still the best definition of good fiction that I know."

All of Woolley's fiction is set in Texas, with *Sam Bass* the only historical novel of his four published to date.

His first, *Some Sweet Day*, an autobiographical story about a boy and his father in World War II-era West Texas, is told in the voice of the boy, with the voice of the boy-turned-adult breaking in occasionally to interpret events. ("This is a balancing act that I don't think I could accomplish again," Woolley says.) This brief novel, published in 1974, still generates mail to Woolley from new readers of it. "There apparently is something in it that appeals to people on a very deep emotional level," he says.

Time and Place, also about growing up in a small Texas town, is a more complex novel than *Some Sweet Day*, involving, among other elements, a polio epidemic and racism in 1950's West Texas. In the Texas Christian University Press reprint of this novel, critic Tom Pilkington writes of it: "Some may see in *Time and Place* a southwestern *Catcher in the Rye*. A more appropriate predecessor to invoke would be Larry McMurtry's *The Last Picture Show*, which also sketches out some of the bleak contours of small-town Texas life. All three of these books, certainly, are notable examples of the initiation genre in American writing. I find *Time and Place*, however, more emotionally convincing than *Catcher in the Rye*. And it is simply a better novel, in both style and structure, than *The Last Picture Show*."

November 22 is as ambitious and innovative as any of Woolley's work, set on that single day, midnight to midnight, of the assassination of President John F. Kennedy in Dallas. The story involves some 30 characters, whose activities and states of mind give an uncanny sense of what it was like to be in Dallas and of Dallas on that infamous day of American history.

Character and dialogue Woolley cites as his greatest strengths as a novelist. "I think most of my characters are vivid, and my ear for the nuances of speech—especially Texas speech—is very sensitive," he says.

And, unusual among such contemporary Texas novelists, Woolley has no problem in being termed a "Western" writer. He says, "I think I'm good at creating a sense of place, not with long passages of description, but with a few details here and there. It is this sense of place, I believe, that makes me a Western writer and my novels Western novels (in the larger sense). And it's the reason Eastern reviewers, long ago, branded me a 'regional' writer, as opposed to the 'universal' writers who dwell in the East. Long ago, that branding used to bother me. It no longer does. Not very many writers are read by the whole country anymore, and if my readers happen to reside in the West and Southwest, that's fine with me. Most of the contemporary writers that I read myself reside in those same regions."

This willingness to be categorized as Texas, Western, or regional writer aside, Woolley is a gifted writer, deserving of a wide audience.

—Dale L. Walker

WORMSER, Richard (Edward). Also wrote as Ed Friend. American. Born in 1908. Recipient: Western Writers of America Spur award, for children's books, 1965, 1972; Western Heritage Award, for children's books, 1972; Mystery Writers of America Edgar Allan Poe award, 1973. *Died in 1977.*

WESTERN PUBLICATIONS

Novels

The Lonesome Quarter. New York, Mill, 1951; London, Corgi, 1953.
The Longhorn Trail, with Dan Gordon. New York, Ace, 1955.
Slattery's Range. London, Abelard Schuman, 1957; New York, New American Library, 1959.
Battalion of Saints. New York, McKay, 1961.
McLintock. New York, Fawcett, 1963; London, Muller, 1964.
The Wild Wild West. New York, New American Library, 1966.
The Ranch by the Sea. New York, Doubleday, 1970; as *Double Decker*, New York, Manor, 1974.
On the Prod. New York, Fawcett, 1978.

Uncollected Short Stories

"El Caballero," in *Argosy* (New York), 31 October–14 November 1936.
"Medals for McNally," in *Argosy* (New York), 20 August 1938.
"The Tattooed Sheep," in *Argosy* (New York), 17 December 1938.
"Little Horses, What Now?," in *Argosy* (New York), 5 July 1941.
"Camels on the Sage," in *Argosy* (New York), December 1942.
"Gunslick," in *Saturday Evening Post* (Philadelphia), 19 June 1954.
"The Hunter," in *Hoof Trails and Wagon Tracks*, edited by Don Ward. New York, Dodd Mead, 1957.
"Beat the Drums Slowly," in *The Pick of the Roundup*, edited by Stephen Payne. New York, Avon, 1963.

OTHER PUBLICATIONS

Novels

The Man with the Wax Face. New York, Smith and Haas, 1934.
The Communist's Corpse. New York, Smith and Haas, and London, Gollancz, 1935.
All's Fair . . . New York, Modern Age, 1937.
Pass Through Manhattan. New York, Morrow, 1940.

The Hanging Heiress. New York, Mill, 1949; as *The Widow Wore Red*, New York, Fawcett, 1958.
The Body Looks Familiar. New York, Dell, 1958.
The Late Mrs. Five. New York, Fawcett, 1960; London, Muller, 1962.
Drive East on 66. New York, Fawcett, 1961; London, Muller, 1962.
Thief of Baghdad. New York, Dell, 1961.
The Last Days of Sodom and Gomorrah. New York, Fawcett, and London, Muller, 1962.
Three Cornered War. New York, Avon, 1962.
Perfect Pigeon. New York, Fawcett, 1962; London, Coronet, 1972.
Pan Satyrus. New York, Avon, 1963.
A Nice Girl Like You. New York, Fawcett, and London, Muller, 1963.
Bedtime Story (novelization of screenplay). London, Muller, 1964.
Operation Crossbow. New York, Dell, 1965.
Torn Curtain (novelization of screenplay). New York, Dell, and London, Mayflower, 1966.
The Takeover. New York, Fawcett, 1971; London, Coronet, 1972.
The Invader. New York, Fawcett, 1972.

Novels as Ed Friend

Alvarez Kelly. New York, Fawcett, 1966.
The Infernal Light (novelization of TV play). New York, Dell, 1966.
The Scalphunters. New York, Fawcett, 1968; London, Gold Lion, 1974.
The Most Deadly Game (novelization of TV play). New York, Lancer, 1970.

Plays

Screenplays: *Start Cheering*, with Eugene Solow and Philip Rapp, 1937; *Let Them Live!*, with Bruce Manning and Lionel Houser, 1937; *Fugitives for a Night*, with Dalton Trumbo, 1938; *The Plainsman and the Lady* (*Drumbeats over Wyoming*), with Michael Uris and Ralph Spence, 1946; *The Phantom Thief*, with Richard Weil and G.A. Snow, 1946; *Perilous Waters*, with Francis Rosenwald, 1947; *Tulsa*, with others, 1949; *Powder River Rustlers*, 1950; *Vigilante Hideout*, 1950; *Rustlers on Horseback*, 1950; *Fort Dodge Stampede*, 1951; *Captive of Billy the Kid*, with Coates Webster, 1951; *The Half-Breed*, with others, 1952; *A Perilous Journey*, 1953; *Crime Wave*, with Crane Wilbur and Bernard Gordon, 1954; *The Outcast*, with John K. Butler, 1954.

Other

Trem McRae and the Golden Cinders (for children). Philadelphia, McKay, 1940.
Ride a Northbound Horse (for children). New York, Morrow, and London, Oxford University Press, 1964.
The Kidnapped Circus (for children). New York, Morrow, 1968.
Southwest Cookery; or, At Home on the Range. New York, Doubleday, 1969.
Gone to Texas (for children). New York, Morrow, 1970.
The Black Mustanger (for children). New York, Morrow, 1971.
Tubac. Tubac, Arizona, Tubac Historical Society, 1975.

* * *

Richard Wormser writes like a man who can drive a six-up and who has built a sage-root fire. Casual touches of authenticity lend credibility to his well-told stories, especially in a book like *The Ranch by the Sea* (*Double Decker*), where scientific methods of ranching come in conflict with not only the older ideas of how things should be done but with the problems of "nesters" as well. The resulting troubles can finally be solved only with guns, as much as Wormser's protagonist would like to avoid such a confrontation; but the violence is minimal and the new ideas win out on their own merits.

On the Prod is an unusual book, humorous in intent, in which a young man goes "fiddlefooting" around the West and getting into all sorts of difficulties with a truly odd assortment of characters. He also gets into numerous dangerous situations from which he is generally rescued at the last minute by a mule-riding half-wit. This book is probably unique among contemporary westerns.

Battalion of Saints was billed by the publishers as a "historical" novel, and *The Lonesome Quarter* was marketed as a "mainstream" book. Despite its contemporary setting, the latter is a good frontier story, and its central scene, the pursuit of a wild stallion, should appeal to any reader of western tales. *Battalion of Saints*, perhaps Wormser's finest novel, is set in 1846 and tells the story of a battalion of Mormons recruited to serve in the Mexican War. As they march from Iowa to Santa Fe, the Mormons seem inclined to fight the U.S. Army, their scout, and their doctor as much as the Mexicans, and Wormser keeps the colorful story moving along at a rapid pace, adding a Mormon/Gentile love story for spice.

Wormser has also written excellent and entertaining novels of the west for young readers, including *The Black Mustanger*, with a strong and positive message about race relations, and *Ride a Northbound Horse*, which won a Spur award.

—Bill Crider

WRIGHT, Harold Bell. American. Born in Rome, New York, 4 May 1872. Educated at local schools; two years in preparatory department, Hiram College, Ohio; left school after contracting tuberculosis and moved to the Ozark Mountains, Missouri, as a health cure. Married 1) Frances E. Long in 1899 (divorced), three sons; 2) Winifred Mary Potter Duncan in 1920. Minister, Church of the Disciples, 1897–1908: preached in Pierce City, Missouri, Pittsburg, Kansas, Kansas City, Lebanon, Missouri, and Redlands, California; full-time writer, 1908–44. *Died 24 May 1944.*

Western Publications

Novels

That Printer of Udell's: A Story of the Middle West. Chicago, Book Supply, 1903; London, Hodder and Stoughton, 1910.
The Shepherd of the Hills. Chicago, Book Supply, 1907; London, Hodder and Stoughton, 1909.
The Calling of Dan Matthews. Chicago, Book Supply, 1909; London, Hodder and Stoughton, 1910.
The Uncrowned King. Chicago, Book Supply, 1910.
The Winning of Barbara Worth. Chicago, Book Supply, 1911; London, Hodder and Stoughton, 1923.
Their Yesterdays. Chicago, Book Supply, 1912; London, Hodder and Stoughton, 1923.

The Eyes of the World. Chicago, Book Supply, 1914; London, Hodder and Stoughton, 1923.
When a Man's a Man. Chicago, Book Supply, and London, International News, 1916.
The Re-Creation of Brian Kent. Chicago, Book Supply, 1919; London, Hodder and Stoughton, 1923.
Helen of the Old House. New York, Appleton, 1921.
The Mine with the Iron Door: A Romance. New York, Appleton, 1923; London, Hodder and Stoughton, 1923.
A Son of His Father. New York, Appleton, 1925.
God and the Groceryman. New York, Appleton, 1927.
Exit. New York, Appleton, 1930.
Ma Cinderella. New York, Harper, 1932.
The Devil's Highway, with John Lebar. New York, Appleton, 1932.
The Man Who Went Away. New York, Harper, 1942.

OTHER PUBLICATIONS

Other

Long Ago Told/Huh-kew ah-tah: Legends of the Papago Indians. New York, Appleton, 1929.
To My Sons: Impressions and Experiences 1872–1932. New York, Harper, 1934.

*

Bibliography: *Kansas Authors of Best Sellers: A Bibliography of the Works of Martin and Osa Johnson, Margaret Hill McCarter, Charles M. Sheldon, and Harold Bell Wright* by Gene DeGruson, Pittsburg, Kansas, Kansas State College of Pittsburg, 1970.

Critical Study: *Harold Bell Wright: Storyteller to America* by Lawrence Tagg, Tucson, Westernlore Press, 1986.

* * *

The West of Harold Bell Wright is a ground for rediscovering virtues which, in his view, have been lost in a sophisticated and self-serving modern world. His settings vary from the Ozarks of southern Missouri (*The Shepherd of the Hills*), to Arizona (*A Son of His Father*), to southern California (*The Winning of Barbara Worth*). His plots are equally various, dealing with ranching (*When a Man's a Man*), or prospecting (*The Mine with the Iron Door*), or unemployed labourers (*That Printer of Udell's*). Despite their diversity, his plots tend to be little more than vehicles for his beliefs, and his settings have a similarly subservient role. Like the town of Westover in *God and the Groceryman*, they could be almost anywhere west of Kansas City.

The instrumental nature of Wright's West is well illustrated by his bestselling—and possibly also his finest—novel, *The Winning of Barbara Worth*. It deals with a land reclamation project in the Imperial Valley of California, and demonstrates the differences between malign and benign forms of capitalism. The bad capitalist is an Easterner called James Greenfield—with some irony, for all he touches turns first to gold dust, and then to dust. He manipulates everything and everyone in the search for greater profits and dividends. Of course, the inevitable happens. An irrigation system is built with shoddy materials, and when the Colorado River bursts its banks it floods hard-won farmland. The good capitalist is a Westerner called—this time without a trace of irony—Jefferson Worth. Inspired by the humanitarianism of his adopted daughter, the eponymous Barbara, he abandons banking in favour of projects which will help develop the new country, such as railroads and electricity supply. Poised between the two capitalists is another Easterner, Willard Holmes, the adopted son of Greenfield. Once again, the name is significant. The product of an elite background and education, Holmes lacks practical experience and is riddled with class prejudice. He gains the first and loses the second while working as an engineer in the desert. In this wilderness he is tested and not found wanting. He rejects malign capitalism, even though this means a temporary estrangement from his adopted father. He builds a dam, averts the flood, saves the Valley, and wins the hand of Barbara Worth.

Wright makes extensive use of cliché and stereotype. His heroes are self-reliant and courageous; his heroines wholesome and virtuous; his intellectuals are effete and pretentious; his villains would twirl moustaches if they were in style. It follows that his writing is racist and sexist, in common with much of the popular literature of his day. According to him, women exist only for marriage, Irishmen love to fight, and Mexicans are low and cunning. Native Americans are something of an exception. Only occasionally do they appear in his fiction and, as if in recompense, he devoted one of his later books to a single tribe. *Long Ago Told* relates the legends of the Papagos, whose reservation lay near his home town of Tucson. They had, he said, a "gentle, kindly, hospitable, industrious and home-loving character," which meant that "they have never figured in lurid Wild-West fiction."

In his autobiography, *To My Sons*, Wright remarked that he did not claim literary merit, but that he hoped he had touched the lives of a few people. He was not concerned, he added, about posthumous fame. This is a clear-eyed self-assessment. During Wright's lifetime, his 19 novels sold, in all, some 10 million copies. Small-town newspapers, always vehicles of popular sentiment, compared him with Shakespeare and Dickens. The Grand Rapids *Herald*, for instance, greeted *The Uncrowned King* as "the greatest story since Bunyan's *Pilgrim's Progress*." In one sense, this is an astute remark. Wright's novels appealed to a readership which would have the Bible and *Pilgrim's Progress* on its shelf, and little else. Inevitably, contemporary critics sneered at him, and today he is almost forgotten. He does not appear in most surveys of western writing.

Yet, reading Wright is still an interesting experience, for a number of reasons. First, he demonstrates the phenomenal persistence and popularity of Victorian values, even in the Jazz Age. The latter-day and partial prophet of Victorian values, Ronald Reagan, claims to have been deeply influenced by *That Printer of Udell's*. Second, Wright is a vivid opponent of Sunday religion. He believes in the practical, everyday applicability of Christianity. His novels may be regarded as illustrations of the religious beliefs of writers like Henry George and Walter Rauschenbusch, and of the work-ethics of Benjamin Franklin, Samuel Smiles, and Horatio Alger. It is no accident that his first novel was about a printer, that he admires engineers, and that he encourages anyone who struggles upwards from poverty. Third, his brand of Christianity is "muscular." It owes a lot to Thomas Hughes's *The Manliness of Christ* (1879) and Charles M. Sheldon's *In His Steps* (1897). Fourth, he believes that the manliness of Christianity can only be discovered in God's open spaces. His work may be seen as part of an old yet still potent belief, summed up by William Cowper's line, "God made the country, and man made the town," and to be found also in the strenuous life of Theodore Roosevelt and the fiction of Owen Wister.

Wister once described Wright's work as "a mess of mildewed pap." This is unkind. While it has few intellectual pretensions, it does contain some complexity. An example is the pair of orphans in *The Winning of Barbara Worth*, almost certainly developed from Dickens's *Great Expectations*, with its theme of the search for the proper parent. Finally, whether we like it or not, Wright's concerns are important ones in American culture. They can be traced in more sophisticated form in the films of John Ford, the novels of John Steinbeck (particularly *The Grapes of Wrath*), and the fishing trips of Ernest Hemingway.

—Robert Lawson-Peebles

WYLER, Richard. *See* **LINAKER, Mike.**

WYNNE, Brian. *See* **DEAN, Dudley; GARFIELD, Brian.**

WYNNE, Frank. *See* **GARFIELD, Brian.**

Y

YANCEY, Wes. *See* **LAZENBY, Norman.**

YARBO, Steve. *See* **KING, Albert.**

YORKE, Roger. *See* **BINGLEY, David Ernest.**

YOUNG, Carter Travis. Pseudonym for Louis (Henry) Charbonneau. American. Born in Detroit, Michigan, 20 January 1924. Educated at the University of Detroit, A.B. 1948, M.A. 1950. Served in the United States Army Air Force, 1943–46: Staff Sergeant. Married 1) Hilda Sweeney in 1945 (died 1984); 2) Diane Fries in 1984. Instructor in English, University of Detroit, 1948–52; copywriter, Mercury Advertising Agency, Los Angeles, 1952–56; staff writer, Los Angeles *Times*, 1956–71; freelance writer, 1971–74; Editor, Security World Publishing Company, Los Angeles, 1974–79. Since 1979 free-lance writer. Agent: Scott Meredith Literary Agency, 845 Third Avenue, New York, New York 10022, U.S.A.

WESTERN PUBLICATIONS

Novels (series: Cullom Blaine)

The Wild Breed. New York, Doubleday, 1960; as *The Sudden Gun*, London, Hammond, 1960.
The Savage Plain. New York, Doubleday, 1961; London, Hammond, 1963.
Shadow of a Gun. New York, Fawcett, 1961; London, Muller, 1962.
The Bitter Iron. New York, Doubleday, 1964; London, Ward Lock, 1965.
Long Boots, Hard Boots. New York, Doubleday, 1965; London, Ward Lock, 1966.
Why Did They Kill Charley? New York, Doubleday, and London, Ward Lock, 1967.
Winchester Quarantine. New York, Doubleday, 1970.
The Pocket Hunters. New York, Doubleday, 1972.
Winter of the Coup. New York, Doubleday, 1972.
The Captive. New York, Doubleday, 1973.
Guns of Darkness. New York, Doubleday, 1974.
Blaine's Law. New York, Doubleday, 1974.
Red Grass. (Blaine) New York, Doubleday, 1976.
Winter Drift. New York, Doubleday, 1980.
Smoking Hills. New York, Doubleday, 1988.

Uncollected Short Story

"Green Wounds," in *Iron Men and Silver Stars*, edited by Donald Hamilton. New York, Fawcett, 1967.

OTHER PUBLICATIONS

Novels as Louis Charbonneau

No Place on Earth. New York, Doubleday, 1958; London, Jenkins, 1966.
Night of Violence. New York, Torquil, and London, Digit, 1959; as *The Trapped Ones*, London, Barker, 1960.
Nor All Your Tears. New York, Torquil, 1959; as *The Time of Desire*, London, Digit, 1960.
Corpus Earthling. New York, Doubleday, 1960; London, Digit, 1963.
The Sentinel Stars. New York, Bantam, and London, Corgi, 1964.
Psychedelic-40. New York, Bantam, 1965; as *The Specials*, London, Jenkins, 1967.
Way Out. London, Barrie and Rockliff, 1966.
Down to Earth. New York, Bantam, 1967; as *Antic Earth*, London, Jenkins, 1967.
The Sensitives (novelization of screenplay). New York, Bantam, 1968.
Down from the Mountain. New York, Doubleday, 1969.
And Hope to Die. New York, Ace, 1970.
Barrier World. New York, Lancer, 1970.
From a Dark Place. New York, Dell, 1974.
Embryo (novelization of screenplay). New York, Warner, 1976.
Intruder. New York, Doubleday, 1979.
The Lair. New York, Fawcett, 1979.
The Brea File. New York, Doubleday, 1983.

Play

Television Play: *Cry of Silence* (*The Outer Limits* series), 1963–64.

Other

Trail: The Story of the Lewis and Clark Expedition. New York, Doubleday, 1989.

*

Manuscript Collection: University of Oregon, Eugene.

* * *

Clearly Carter Travis Young's novels are by a writer who is more than the hack producer of Westerns, for they display a facility of landscape description and dialogue more common to the general author. At the same time, however, the plots and images are those of the formulaic western.

The disjunction between Young's ability and his material is shown in subtle ways. For example, in *The Wild Breed* a father comes west to take home the body of his son, who has been lynched as a gunfighter. It is quite a familiar story, and the hero, Ben, obliquely acknowledges the presence of fictional convention: "It seemed a simple necessary thing to him, something Ellen would have wanted, something he must do. Then everything would be complete like a story ended." Yet Ben (and the reader) discover that this is not the world of absolute formula. He is given his son's gun and is surprised to find no notches on it: "Why should he have expected notches? Men talked of putting down a mark for each victim, but few men did it." All Young's novels tread this line between the familiar and the formulaic. Many scenes seem reminiscent of the cinema, and there are recurrent echoes from Owen Wister, Jack Schaefer, and Alan LeMay. His two favourite subjects are gun-fighters and settlers turned Indian-fighters, and he often introduces a strong element of mystery, giving the familiar story some depth and suspense. This, again, seems to be acknowledged by the hero of *The Wild Breed*: "He'd hoped without warrant that the mystery went deeper, that behind it was an answer that would change or soften the truth."

One of Young's most successful novels, *Why Did They Kill Charley?*, exploits the power of mystery. A small rancher, anticipating an Indian attack after his simple-witted helper, Charley, has molested and killed an Indian girl, sends away his wife and son without explanation. The action takes on a twist when two jailbirds trap the rancher in a cage and, under double attack, the rancher's escape becomes twice as difficult, especially as Charley is now completely confused by events. In the end, the rancher kills the outlaws, but Charley is executed by the Indians. Although the mystery has been gradually unfolded to the reader, there are characters, like Charley and the son, who never learn the truth. It is the son who, when he returns, asks the eponymous question.

The distinctions between these novels and the routine Western are quite subtle. In broader terms, Young's novels, set in a Texas without specific dates or places, seem above-average reenactments of familiar western adventure.

—Christine Bold

YOUNG, Gordon (Ray). Also wrote as Hugh Richmond. American. Born in Ray County, Missouri, 27 September 1886. Educated at public schools. *Died 10 February 1948.*

WESTERN PUBLICATIONS

Novels (series: Red Clark)

Days of '49. New York, Doran, 1925; London, Hodder and Stoughton, 1926.
Standish of the Star Y. London, Hodder and Stoughton, 1926.
La Rue of the Eighty-Eight. London, Hodder and Stoughton, 1927.
Treasure. London, Harrap, 1927; New York, Doubleday, 1928.
Fighting Blood. New York, Doubleday, 1932; as *The Fighting Fool*, London, Methuen, 1933.
Red Clark o'Tulluco. New York, Doubleday, and London, Methuen, 1933; as *Roaring Guns*, New York, Popular Library, 1949.
Red Clark Rides Alone. New York, Doubleday, 1933.
Red Clark of the Arrowhead. New York, Doubleday, and London, Methuen, 1935; as *Guns of the Arrowhead*, New York, Popular Library, 1950.
Huroc the Avenger. London, Methuen, 1936.
Red Clark on the Border. New York, Doubleday, and London, Methuen, 1937; as *Trouble on the Border*, New York, Popular Library, 1951.
Red Clark, Range Boss. New York, Doubleday, 1938; as *Red Clark, Boss!*, London, Methuen, 1938; as *Range Boss*, New York, Popular Library, 1951.
Red Clark, Two-Gun Man. New York, Doubleday, 1939; London, Hutchinson, 1940; as *Two-Gun Man*, New York, Popular Library, 1952.
Red Clark for Luck. New York, Doubleday, 1940; London, Hutchinson, 1941.
Red Clark Takes a Hand. New York, Doubleday, 1941; London, Hutchinson, 1942.
Iron Rainbow. New York, Doubleday, 1942.
Tall in the Saddle. New York, Doubleday, 1943; London, Wells Gardner, 1945.
Red Clark at the Showdown. New York, Doubleday, 1947; London, Hammond, 1949.
Red Clark in Paradise. New York, Doubleday, 1947; London, Hammond, 1951; as *Holster Law*, New York, Popular Library, n.d.
Gunman from Tulluco. New York, Popular Library, 1948.
Quarter Horse. New York, Doubleday, 1948; London, Hammond, 1952.
Red Clark to the Rescue. New York, Doubleday, 1948; London, Hammond, 1952.
Trouble Rides Double. London, Hutchinson, 1948.
Wanted—Dead or Alive! New York, Doubleday, 1949; London, Hammond, 1953.
Fast on the Draw. New York, Popular Library, 1950.
Hell on Hoofs. New York, Ace, 1953.

OTHER PUBLICATIONS

Novels

Savages. New York, Doubleday, 1921; London, Cape, 1922.
Wild Blood. Indianapolis, Bobbs Merrill, 1921; London, Unwin, 1923.
Tajola. London, Methuen, 1922.
Hurricane Williams. Indianapolis, Bobbs Merrill, 1922; London, Unwin, 1924.
Seibert of the Island. London, Unwin, 1924; New York, Doran, 1925.
Crooked Shadows. New York, Garden City Publishing Company, 1924.
Pearl-Hunger. London, Unwin, 1925; New York, Doran, 1927.
The Vengeance of Hurricane Williams. New York, Doran, and London, Unwin, 1925.
Mr. Beamish (as Hugh Richmond). New York, Coward McCann, 1940; London, Hale, 1941.

* * *

Gordon Ray Young had a long writing career spanning the 1920's to the late 1940's. His early novels are adventure stories rather than Westerns, with South Seas settings in several novels. Young was good at drawing picturesque settings popular with his readership, and chose California in the Gold Rush in *Days of '49*. He also wrote a melodramatic thriller, *Devil's Passport*, set in the Paris underworld.

While *Days of '49* was well-received critically, the adventure tales set outside America never had the success that Young's Westerns did, and he was able to find a profitable vein in literature as a writer of above average Westerns. Young had a considerable readership and even his early Westerns were reprinted many years after publication. (*The Fighting Fool* was well enough written to be reprinted in a school edition in the 1950's.) Young took time to perfect his technique; even by 1927 he had not yet done this. It is interesting to see the transition in Young's writing from the adventure story to the genre Western proper. *La Rue of the Eighty-Eight*, for instance, still has many of the attributes of the adventure story. In such a large book Young was unhurried and he drew a wide canvas of the West with many interesting factual details. The plot was, however, too, involved, though Young had a perceptive eye for faces and characters, especially female characters. By 1933 Young had settled on his technique of writing the genre Western. In *Red Clark Rides Alone* Young created a character who was to figure in most of his subsequent Westerns. A rather improbable character who once tried to ride a horse up a hotel stairs, Red Clark is, however, on the side of the law. As he shows in *Fighting Fool*, Clark is well able to handle a gun and deal with powerful lawbreakers. The character of Clark is curiously enigmatic and hard to assess in a psychological way. He undoubtedly inspired affection in his readers, perhaps because he was an amalgam of western characteristics. He was the archetypical singing cowboy. Young was very skilful in his characterisation. Minor characters such as alcoholics and saloon women are unusually well-portrayed.

Young was able to avoid the melodrama of his early adventure novels in his Westerns by striking the right balance between characterisation and action. Characterisation is just sufficient to give credibility, and the settings allow fighting and gunplay, the focus of the novels. Young's writing contains some very good prose with some memorable descriptions. The power of Young's language is such that the lack of a large number of technical western words and comic western dialogue is not missed. Young received considerable critical acclaim in America during his lifetime.

—P.R. Meldrum

YOUNG, Wilson. *See* **TIPPETTE, Giles.**

Z

ZIETLOW, Edward R. American. Born in Presho, South Dakota, 13 August 1932. Educated at Dakota Wesleyan University, Mitchell, South Dakota, B.A. 1954; Boston University, Massachusetts, M.A. 1959; University of Washington, Seattle, Ph.D. 1967. Served with United States Army, in Germany, 1954–57. Assistant Professor, 1965–77, and since 1977 Associate Professor of English, University of Victoria, British Columbia, Canada. Address: Department of English, University of Victoria, Victoria, British Columbia V8W 2Y2, Canada.

WESTERN PUBLICATIONS

Novels

These Same Hills. New York, Knopf, 1960.
The Indian Maiden's Captivity, and The Heart of the Country. Hermosa, South Dakota, Lame Johnny Press, 1978.

Short Stories

A Country for Old Men and Other Stories. Hermosa, South Dakota, Lame Johnny Press, 1977.

OTHER PUBLICATIONS

Other

Transhominal Criticism. New York, Philosophical Library, 1978.

* * *

Edward R. Zietlow's first published novel, *These Same Hills*, demonstrates his strengths and weaknesses as a western writer, and predicts the philosophy guiding his literary and critical writing.

This novel portrays an old man, representative of the West's pioneering past, and a young envoy from its future, struggling to make sense of their lives in the Badlands of South Dakota. Their relationship, its climax, and the characters woven into the story with them, set the tone for much of Zietlow's later writing. Women and other supporting characters are often caricatures of their type, used to demonstrate the author's moral lesson. Only in his short fiction, collected in the popular *A Country for Old Men and Other Stories*, does Zietlow's ability as a writer overshadow his philosophical tendencies.

Rudolph, in *These Same Hills*, dreams of what might have been; Jim dreams of what might be. Rudolph's life has been a failure in society's terms, but he still hopes for victory; what he is not what he expects. Jim is plagued by teenage problems of sex, education, and morality, as well as the community's economic and social tensions. Jim feels superior to his uneducated parents, even as he becomes aware of the difference between their actions and the Christian code of ethics to which they all give lip service. Their community is a microcosm of the West. Rudolph, the pioneer tough enough to survive the hardships of nature and necessity, is limited by his inability to learn the social skills and chicanery with which his neighbors operate. Jim, the community's hope for the future, misunderstands the important lessons of Rudolph's life and death; ironically, his future lies elsewhere. His success will make him an outcast.

Growing up in the Badlands, Zietlow observed firsthand how land and weather become active characters in western literature. Similarly, he contrasts past and present, urban and rural life, young and old, and shows his early awareness of a national tendency to regard physical labor as a lower class condition to be avoided by education, equated with both money and the elusive concept of "success."

Overall, though Zietlow portrays the West as a place of inspiration, honest toil, and strong moral values, he also shows its seamy and brutal side. This reality has caused some readers and critics to believe that plains residents are trapped in their lives, unhappy, longing for change and lacking in the intelligence to appreciate the higher beauties. While this value judgement may contain an element of truth, to accept it uncritically is to miss much of the beauty and strength of western writing.

Lonely, isolated, vacillating bachelors dominate nearly all Zietlow's fiction; often they have left the land for the city, and question their choice. Arthur Huseboe in *An Illustrated History of the Arts in South Dakota*, notes that the choice made by Jim in Zietlow's first novel is similar to that made by South Dakotans who have moved from rural to urban areas. It is "not unlike" the choice made by Zietlow, a man raised on a ranch who is now an "expatriate South Dakota writer" and English professor in British Columbia.

Introducing the single volume containing *The Indian Maiden's Captivity* and *The Heart of the Country*, Zietlow observes, "I can see that my thinking was then already moving in a direction I would only later articulate formally." The latter novel was written concurrently with his critical study *Transhominal Criticism*. He calls the novel in our time "largely pathological," and says "contemporary novelists have lied to us." He invented the term "transhominalism" to define the position he saw himself occupying in 20th-century literature, defining it as "a response to the *arrière-gardism* in which most contemporary writing is stuck . . ." By contrast, he suggests, "transhominalism restores art to man." Fiction, he believes, "must become holistic and healthy, with its values ultimately set beyond time."

In both novels, Zietlow seems less interested in his character's actions than in outlining his study of humanistic psychology and literature. Harold Kritze hesitates and fantasizes until he loses the opportunity for action to save the Indian girl from brutality and death in *Captivity*. Lon Byzick in *Heart* is nervous, without courage or convictions, so self-consciously absorbed in his interior monologues and indecision he is difficult to like.

The same isolated bachelors stalk Zietlow's short fiction, but are less distracting in the tighter plots. Len Schneider, middle-aged and divorced when he returns home after a long absence in "The Old Woman Who Read to Her House Plants," sneers at the other characters even while acting out his own failures. In "The Burial of the Bride," Claude Keefer is so torn by his conflicting feelings that he murders the first person who shares his lonely world; his own guilt creates a terrible retribution. Bud, the youth in "Winter Wheat," hears his father's lesson that one should not dream on the plains, but remains a dreamer, siding with his uncle. Zietlow's finest short story, "A Country for Old Men," the title story of his collection, revolves around a bachelor, again of German heritage, who has reaped mostly failure for his hard labor of farming, and his professor nephew. The story is told by the nephew, whose understanding of his uncle's life seems deeper and warmer than that shown by many of Zietlow's previous narrators; the prose becomes biblical, poetic, hinting finally at the dramas in the little lives of the plains. The reader wonders at the end which of the men is the real victor.

> From this angle," says the professor, "I can't tell where the distal turn should come. He seems to be steering for the sunset. The empyreal fire ignites the efflux of dust from his wheels: he is caught in a gyre of light.

—Linda M. Hasselstrom

TITLE INDEX

The following list includes the titles of all novels and short story collections (designated "s") cited as western publications. The name(s) in parentheses after the title is meant to direct the reader to the appropriate entry where full publication information is given. The term "series" indicates a recurring distinctive word or phrase (or name) in the titles of the entrant's books. Series characters (noted in the fiction lists) are also listed here, even if their names do not appear in specific titles of works.

Long Rope (Paine, as Harrison), 1982
Long Rope (Turner), 1959
Long-Rope Riders (Paine, as Beck), 1976
Long-Ropers (Borg), 1969
Long Run (Nye), 1959
Long S (Floren), 1945
Long Search (Lutz, as Ingram), 1969
Long Shadow (Bower), 1909
Long Shadow (Gilman), 1989
Long Siesta (Bingley, as Horsley), 1983
Long Sleep (Paine, as Benton), 1975
Long Storm (Haycox), 1946
Long Sword (Ballard, as D'Allard), 1962
Long Trail (Gooden), 1952
Long Trail (Rowland), 1963
Long Trail (Snow, as Ballew), 1946
Long Trail Back (Ballard), 1960
Long Trail Back (Paine, as Hayden), 1966
Long Trail North (Drago), 1961
Long Trail North (Grover), 1957
Long Trail North (Overholser), 1972
Long Trail to Battle (Snow, as Smith), 1956
Long Trail to Texas (K. Hamilton), n.d.
Long Trails (Snow, as Averill), 1960
Long Valley (s Steinbeck), 1938
Long Way to Texas (Kelton, as McElroy), 1976
Long West Trail (Arthur, as Shappiro), 1948
Long Wind (Overholser, as Wayne), 1953
Long Winter (Wilder), 1940
Long Winter Gone (Johnston), 1990
Long Wire (Cord), 1968
Long Years (Paine), 1956
Longarm series (Knott, as Evans), from 1978
Longbow Range (Paine, as Howard), 1978
Longhorn (M. Chisholm, as James), 1970
Longhorn Brand (Floren, as Hamilton), 1952
Longhorn Empire (Drago, as Ermine), 1933
Longhorn Feud (Brand), 1933
Longhorn Gold (Trevathan), 1969
Longhorn Guns (Sharpe), 1986
Longhorn Law (R. Hogan), 1957
Longhorn Legion (Fox), 1951
Longhorn Sisters (Randisi, as Weston), 1987
Longhorn Stampede (Ketchum), 1956
Longhorn Trail (Hobart), 1967
Longhorn Trail (Paine, as Glenn), 1966
Longhorn Trail (Wormser), 1955
Longhorn War (Randisi), 1982
Longhorns (Paine, as Beck), 1978
Longhorns (Snow, as Lee), 1957
Longhorns for Fort Sill (Trevathan), 1962
Longhorns North (Lawrence), 1962
Longhorns of Hate (Robertson), 1949
Longland Plain (Paine, as Armour), 1981
Longland Range (Paine, as Hartley), 1980
Longrider (Bouma), 1978
Longrider (Foreman), 1961
Lonigan (s L'Amour), 1988
Look Out for Outlaws (Robertson), 1938
Look to Your Guns (Ballard, as Bonner), 1969
Lookout Man (Bower), 1917
Loot (Snow, as Wills), 1947
Loot of the L & E (Donovan), 1954
Loot of the Lazy F (Tuttle), 1933
Loot of the Lone Wolf (Dexter), 1971
Lopez's Loot (Bingley, as Wigan), 1975
Lord Apache (Steelman), 1977
Lord Grizzly (Manfred), 1954
Lord of Lonely Valley (Kyne), 1932
Lord of Lost Valley (Paine), 1982
Lord of the Dawn (Anaya), 1987
Lord of the High Lonesome (Barrett, as Royal), 1970
Lord of the High Lonesome (Dailey), 1980
Lord of the South Plains (Paine), 1955
Lord Six-Gun (Fox), 1943
Lords of the Land (Braun), 1979
Lorenzo the Magnificent (Coolidge), 1925
Lorimer of the Northwest (Bindloss), 1909
Los Cerritos (Atherton), 1890
Los Olvidados (McCurtin), 1980
Loser (Paine, as Bosworth), 1967
Losers (Gilman), 1976
Lost (Wells, as Brady), 1984
Lost Borders (s Austin), 1909
Lost Buckaroo (Drago, as Lomax), 1949
Lost Bugle (Strong, as Stanley), 1960
Lost Cabin Mine (Niven), 1908
Lost Canyon (Cord, as Kane), 1964
Lost Expedition (Foster), 1905
Lost Face (s London), 1910
Lost Farm Camp (Knibbs), 1912
Lost Galleon of Doubloon Island (Foster), 1901
Lost Herd (Joscelyn), 1978
Lost in the Never Never and Silvermane (Grey), 1977
Lost Island (Rathborne, as Travers), 1882
Lost Lady (Cather), 1923
Lost Loot (Snow, as Marshall), 1955
Lost Loot of Kittycat Ranch (T. West), 1965
Lost Mine Named Salvation (Nye), 1968
Lost Mountain (Danvers, as Jordan), 1957
Lost Padre (Nye), 1988
Lost Patrol (Knott, as Sharpe), 1985
Lost Pueblo (Grey), 1954
Lost Range (Robertson), 1946
Lost River Buckaroos (Martin), 1937
Lost River Canyon (Joscelyn), 1976
Lost River Trail (Snow, as Lee), 1958
Lost Stage Valley (Bonham), 1948
Lost Trail (Paine, as Carter), 1977
Lost Valley (Ballard, as Hunter), 1971
Lost Valley (Booth), 1960
Lost Valley (Joscelyn, as Cody), 1954
Lost Wagon Train (Grey), 1936
Lost Wagons (Coolidge), 1923
Lost Wallowa 1869–1879 (Gulick), 1988
Lost Water (Nye, as Denver), 1942
Lost Wolf (Brand, as Morland), 1928
Lost Wolf River (D. Newton, as Bennett), 1952
Louly (Brink), 1974
Love Among the Cannibals (Morris), 1957
Love and Death (s Fisher), 1959
Love and Lure (Shea), 1912
Love Medicine (Erdrich), 1984
Love of Life (s London), 1907
Love Passed This Way (Ostenso), 1942
Lovely Lady (Austin), 1913
Luck (Brand), 1926
Luck of the Kid (Cullum), 1923
Luck of the Spindrift (Brand), 1972
Luck Rides with the Fastest Gun (Mann), 1965
Lucky Cowpoke (Gardner), 1973
Lucky Jake (Grover), 1982
Lucky Larribee (Brand), 1957
Lucky Pardners (Tuttle), 1967

Rough, Ready and Texan (Grover), 1991
Rough Rider (Cummings), 1988
Rough Route to Rodd County (Grover), 1986
Rough Time in Dobie (Skinner), 1983
Roughshod (Fox), 1951
Roughshod (Rowland, as Scott), 1965
Round Mountain Range (Paine, as Clark), 1976
Round Rock Range (Paine, as Brennan), 1986
Round-Up (Friend), 1924
Round-Up (Mulford), 1933
Round-Up (Paine, as Hill), 1981
Round Up and Trail (Robertson), 1938
Round-Up Guns (T. Curry), 1939
Round-Up in the River (Robertson), 1945
Rounders (M. Evans), 1960
Rounders Three (M. Evans), 1990
Roundup (Ballard), 1957
Roundup (Paine, as Hunt), 1976
Roundup at Wagonmound (Baldwin), 1960
Roundup on the Picketwire (Elston), 1952
Roundup on the Yellowstone (Elston), 1962
Rouse River Range (Snow, as Ballew), 1939
Routledge Rides Alone (Comfort), 1910
Roxie Raker (R. Hogan), 1975
Royal Charlie (Steelman), 1983
Royal City (L. Savage), 1956
Royal Gorge (Dawson), 1948
Royal Target (Grover), 1976
Rube Burrows' League (Rathborne, as Manly), 1891
Rubies and Red Blood (Snow), 1934
Ruckus at Gila Wells (Grover), 1991
Ruckus at Roaring Gap (Moore), 1941
Ruggles of Red Gap (H. Wilson), 1915
Ruler of the Range (Dawson), 1951
Rules of the Game (White), 1910
Rummy Kid Goes Home (s Santee), 1965
Run for Cover (Haas, as Benteen), 1976
Run for the Border (Edson), 1971
Run for the Border (Grover, as Murrell), 1960
Run from the Buzzards (Grover), 1978
Run of the Brush (Raine), 1936
Run River (Didion), 1963
Run to the Mountain (T.V. Olsen), 1974
Run with the Loot (Grover), 1985
Runaway (Gilman), 1983
Runaway (Rey), 1990
Runaway Horses (Snow, as Marshall), 1934
Runaway Ramsey (Grover), 1989
Runner (Connor), 1929
Running Gun (M. Chisholm, as James), 1966
Running Gun (MacLeod), 1979
Running Horses (F. Grove), 1980
Running Iron (Rowland, as Spurr), 1974
Running Iron Samaritans (Cord), 1973
Running Target (Frazee), 1957
Running Target (Grover, as Brennan), 1962
Running Wild (Rowland, as McHugh), 1967
Rushers (Edson), 1964
Russian Lode (Wells, as Garrett), 1980
Russian River (G. McCarthy), 1991
Rustler (McElrath), 1902
Rustler Bait (Snow), 1956
Rustler Basin (Richardson, as Kent), 1956
Rustler Guns (Borg, as Bexar), 1964
Rustler King (Snow, as Hardy), 1949
Rustler of Rolling Stone (Whitson, as Sims), 1892
Rustler Range (A. King, as Holland), 1989
Rustler Vengeance (Richardson), 1958
Rustlers (Short), 1949
Rustlers and Powder Smoke (Snow, as Ballew), 1951
Rustlers and Ruby Silver (Snow), 1930
Rustlers' Bend (Drago, as Ermine), 1949
Rustler's Brand (Langley), 1954
Rustler's Brand (Paine, as Ketchum), 1978
Rustlers Canyon (Fearn), 1948
Rustlers' Canyon (Halleran), 1948
Rustlers' Gap (Raine), 1949
Rustlers' Gulch (Gribble, as Grant), 1935
Rustler's Law (Paine, as Brennan), 1973
Rustler's Luck (Snow, as Lee), 1942
Rustlers' Moon (Bingley), 1972
Rustlers' Moon (Drago, as Ermine), 1939
Rustler's Moon (L. Holmes), 1971
Rustler's Moon (Paine, as Bradford), 1964
Rustlers Moon (Richardson), 1950
Rustlers of Beacon Creek (Brand), 1935
Rustlers of Crooked River (Richardson, as Warner), 1955
Rustlers of Cyclone Pass (Floren), 1968
Rustlers of Dry Range (Cord), 1956
Rustlers of K.C. Ranch (Nye), 1950
Rustlers of Lonesome Valley (Snow), 1945
Rustlers of Moon River (Snow), 1957
Rustlers of Pecos County (Grey), 1914
Rustlers of Red Creek (Snow), 1946
Rustlers of Sky Valley (Snow, as Marshall), 1948
Rustlers of the Rio Grande (Lehman), 1957
Rustlers of Yellow River (Chuck Adams), 1954
Rustlers on the Bar-S (Snow, as Averill), 1963
Rustlers on the Loose (Robertson), 1943
Rustlers on the Smoky Trail (Bardwell, as James), 1936
Rustlers' Paradise (MacDonald), 1932
Rustlers Ranch (Drago, as Ermine), 1935
Rustlers' Range (Borg), 1959
Rustlers' Range (Heuman), 1958
Rustler's Roost (Danvers, as Jordan), 1950
Rustlers' Roost (Nye, as Colt), 1943
Rustlers' Roost (Tuttle), 1927
Rustlers' Round-Up (Mann), 1935
Rustler's Trail (Borland, as West), 1948
Rustler's Trail (Floren), 1968
Rustler's Trail (Paine, as Slaughter), 1965
Rustlers' Valley (Mulford), 1924
Rustlin' Sheriff (Jenkins), 1934
Rusty (Brand, as Baxter), 1937
Rusty (Santee), 1950
Rusty Guns (Drago, as Lomax), 1944
Rusty Hines series (Nickson), from 1958
Rusty Irons (Cushman), 1984
Rusty Mallory (Joscelyn), 1945
Ruthless Breed (D. Newton, as Hardin), 1966
Ruthless Men (Patten), 1959
Ruthless Range (Hobart), 1957
Ruthless Range (Patten), 1963
Ruthless Renegades (Bingley, as Prescott), 1966
Rutledge Trails the Ace of Spades (Raine), 1930
Ryan Rides Back (Crider), 1988
Ryder series (Randisi, as Weston), 1987

Sabadilla (Jessup), 1960
Sabata (Ballard, as Fox), 1970
Sabers in the Sun (Heuman), 1958
Sabers West (Andrews), 1988
Sabrina (Chadwick), 1970
Sabrina Kane (Will Cook), 1956

Sweet Deadly Eden (McCaig), 1982
Sweet Grass (Bower), 1940
Sweet Thursday (Steinbeck), 1954
Sweetwater (Paine, as Bradshaw), 1984
Sweetwater Flats (Wisler), 1989
Sweetwater Ranch (Bindloss), 1935
Swept Out to Sea (Foster), n.d.
Swift Flows the River (N. Jones), 1940
Swift Jim Haywood (Donovan), 1990
Swift Lightning (Curwood), 1920
Swift Runner (O'Rourke), 1969
Swiftly to Evil (Arthur), 1961
Swiftwagon (Shirreffs), 1958
Sycamore Canyon (Snow, as Hardy), 1949
Sydney Carteret, Rancher (Bindloss), 1911
Syndicate Gun (D. Newton), 1972

Tabbart Brand (D. Newton), 1967
Tacey Cromwell (Richter), 1942
Taggart (L'Amour), 1959
Tago (Harvey), 1980
Tainted Range (Donovan), 1987
Take All to Nebraska (Winther), 1935
Takersville Shoot (Randisi), 1989
Tale of Three Bullets (Gardner, as Tully), 1990
Tale of Valor (Fisher), 1958
Tales from the Margin (s F. P. Grove), 1971
Tales from the West (s Schaefer), 1961
Tales of the Old-Timers (s Bechdolt), 1924
Tales of the Southwest (s Capps), 1991
Tales of Wells Fargo (s Gruber), 1958
Talk and Contact (s B. Wilson), 1978
Talking God (Hillerman), 1989
Tall for a Texan (Cox, as Spellman), 1965
Tall Hellion (Chuck Adams), 1959
Tall in the Saddle (Heuman), 1963
Tall in the Saddle (Martin), 1958
Tall in the Saddle (G. Young), 1943
Tall in the West (Rigsby, as Howard), 1958
Tall Ladder (Burt), 1932
Tall Man Riding (McCurtin), 1973
Tall Man Riding (Fox), 1951
Tall Man Riding (R. Hogan), 1977
Tall Man's Challenge (Grover), 1966
Tall Man's Mission (K. Hamilton), n.d.
Tall Men (H. Allen, as Fisher), 1954
Tall Riders (Grover), 1957
Tall Shadow (Grover), 1961
Tall Stranger (L'Amour), 1957
Tall Texan (Floren), 1967
Tall Texans (Paine, as O'Conner), 1964
Tall Timber Trollop (C. Cunningham, as Fletcher), 1989
Tall, Tough And Texan (Grover), 1959
Tall Trees Fall (Haig-Brown), 1943
Tall Wyoming (Cushman), 1957
Tallman, Ash series (Braun), from 1984
Talman's War (Linaker, as Stewart), 1976
Talons series (L'Amour), from 1975
Tamarind Trail (Sharpe), 1991
Tamaulipas Guns (J. Sadler), 1982
Tame a Wild Town (Grover), 1982
Tame the Tall Hombre (K. Hamilton), n.d.
Tamer of Bad Men (Snow), 1933
Tamer of the Wild (Brand), 1962
Taming of Wild River (Snow, as Smith), 1961
Tamzen (Rushing), 1972
Tandy's Legacy (Grover), 1984
Tang of Life (Knibbs), 1918
Tangled Brands (Snow, as Lee), 1945
Tangled Ropes (Snow), 1965
Tangled Trail (T. West, as Manning), 1947
Tangled Trails (Cord, as Kane), 1963
Tangled Trails (A. King), 1961
Tangled Trails (Raine), 1921
Tangled Web (Lutz), 1983
Tanglefoot (Grover), 1983
Tanner (Paine), 1984
Tanner's Guns (Whitehead, as Logan), 1991
Tanner's Last Chance (Bowers), 1990
Taps at Little Big Horn (Haas, as Benteen), 1973
Target: Charity Ross (Bickham), 1968
Target Conestoga (Sharpe), 1989
Target Is a Star (Dodge), n.d.
Tarnished Star (Gilman), 1979
Tarnished Star (A. King, as Harmon), 1990
Tarnished Star (Patten), 1963
Taste of Infamy (Locke), 1960
Taurus Gun (Paine), 1989
Tavern League (Rathborne, as Manly), 1881
Tawny Men from Texas (Snow, as Smith), 1955
Team Bells Woke Me (s Davis), 1953
Teamster Tom (Whitson, as Sims), 1892
Tears of Blood (L. James, as Marvin), 1980
Tecumseh (Winters, as Lederer), 1982
Teddy's Enchantress (Rathborne), n.d.
Tejano (K. Hamilton), n.d.
Tejas Country (Loomis, as Miller), 1953
Telegraph Trail (Strong, as Stanley), 1957
Temescal (Knibbs), 1925
Templeton Massacre (C. Cunningham, as Carrington), 1990
Temporary Duty (Will Cook, as Everett), 1964
Ten Fast Horses (Grover), 1984
Ten Grand (Gilman), 1972
Ten Pines Killer (Randisi), 1985
Ten Thousand Dollar Bounty (Giles), 1986
Ten Thousand Dollars, American (Gilman), 1972
Ten Thousand Dollars Reward (Sanders), 1924
Ten Tombstones (Gilman), 1976
Ten Tombstones to Texas (Gilman), 1975
Tenbow (Braun), 1991
Tenderfoot (Allan), 1939
Tenderfoot (Brand), 1953
Tenderfoot (Grey), 1977
Tenderfoot (McCulley), 1957
Tenderfoot Bill (Joscelyn), 1939
Tenderfoot Boss (Gooden), 1939
Tenderfoot Called Rawhide (Snow, as Ballew), 1966
Tenderfoot Kid (Drago, as Field), 1939
Tenderfoot Trail Boss (Bingley, as Chatham), 1983
Tenderfoot Veteran (Mack Bride), 1990
Tenino (Paine, as Ashby), 1983
Tennyson Rifle (Paine, as Durham), 1982
Tenon's Task (Snow), 1959
Teresa (L. Savage), 1954
Terror at Black Rock (Barrett, as Wade), 1972
Terror at Tres Alamos (Peeples), 1958
Terror for Sale (Grover), 1989
Terror in Eagle Basin (Farrell), 1974
Terror Law (Rowland, as Scott), 1969
Terror of Tombstone Trail (Mann), 1933
Terror Town (Gilman), 1988
Terror Trail to Tortosa (Grover), 1984
Terror Valley (Edson), 1967
Terror's Long Memory (Grover), 1985

NOTES
ON
ADVISERS
AND
CONTRIBUTORS

AHEARN, Kerry. Associate Professor of English, Oregon State University, Corvallis. **Essay:** Michael Straight.

ALMON, Bert. Professor of English, University of Alberta, Edmonton. Author of *Gary Snyder*, 1979. **Essays:** Linda Hogan; Tillie Olsen; Simon J. Ortiz.

ALMOND, Steven. Reporter, El Paso *Times*, Texas. **Essay:** Rick DeMarinis.

ALTER, Judy. Director, Texas Christian University Press, Fort Worth. Author of *Luke and the Van Zanat County War*, 1984, The Magpie Books (a trilogy for young adults), *Mattie Anouel*, 1988, and *Elmer Kelton and West Texas*, 1989. **Essays:** Dorothy M. Johnson; MacKinlay Kantor; Jeanne Williams.

ALY, Lucile F. Professor Emerita of English, University of Oregon, Eugene. Author of *A Rhetoric of Public Speaking* (with Bower Aly), 1973, *John G. Neihardt* (pamphlet), 1976, and *John G. Neihardt: A Critical Biography*, 1977. Editor, with Bower Aly, of two collections of speeches. **Essay:** John G. Neihardt.

AUSTIN, Wade. Instructor in film and popular music, Florida Institute of Technology, Melbourne. Author of "The Real Beverly Hillbillies," in *The South and Film*, 1981, and of an article on country music in *Southern Quarterly*, 1983. **Essays:** Niven Busch; Johnston McCulley.

BANKS, R. Jeff. Member of the Department of English, Stephen F. Austin State University, Nacogdoches, Texas. Author of several western short stories, and of articles in *Poisoned Pen*, *The Not-So-Private Eye*, *Mystery Fancier*, *Armchair Detective*, and *Journal of Popular Culture*. **Essays:** Burt Arthur; Brian Garfield; Charles N. Heckelmann; William Hopson; Paul Evan Lehman; William Colt MacDonald; Robert J. Steelman.

BARNES, Robert J. Regent's Professor Emeritus, Lamar University, Beaumont, Texas. Co-author of *Mechanics of English*, 1960, and *A Concordance to Byron's "Don Juan,"* 1967, and author of *Conrad Richter*, 1968. **Essays:** Bill Burchardt; Peggy Simson Curry; Edna Ferber; Oakley Hall; John Joseph Mathews; Conrad Richter; Glendon Swarthout.

BLOODWORTH, William. Provost and Professor of English, Central Missouri State University, Warrensburg. Author of *Upton Sinclair*, 1977, and "Varieties of American Indian Autobiography," in *Melus*, Fall 1978, "Mulford and Bower: Myth and History in the Early Western," in *Great Plains Quarterly*, Spring 1981, and of articles on the formula Western and Max Brand in *Western American Literature*. **Essays:** Hal Borland; B.M. Bower; Max Brand; Dee Brown; Dan Cushman; William Decker; Oliver La Farge; Thomas Thompson.

BLUE, Marian. Freelance writer. **Essays:** Robert J. Conley; Gretel Ehrlich; Jim Heynen; Ruth Suckow.

BOLD, Christine. Assistant Professor of English, University of Guelph, Ontario. Author of *Selling the Wild West: Popular Western Fiction, 1860 to 1960*, 1987, and of several essays and articles on popular culture of the American West. **Essays:** T.D. Allen; Clay Allison; Hoffman Birney; Michael Bonner; Frederick H. Christian; Van Cort; James R. Dowler; Hal G. Evarts, Jr.; Mary Hallock Foote; Edward Hoagland; George C. Jenks; Archie Joscelyn; Meridel Le Sueur; Milton Lott; Frances McElrath; Rutherford Montgomery; Bob Obets; Ed Earl Repp; Harwood E. Steele; Carter Travis Young.

BRINEY, R.E. Professor of computer science and former Department Chair, Salem State College, Massachusetts. Editor and publisher of *The Rohmer Review*. Co-author of *SF Bibliographies*, 1972. Contributor to *The Mystery Writer's Art*, 1971, *The Conan Grimoire*, 1971, *The Mystery Story*, 1976, *The Spell of Conan*, 1980, *Twentieth-Century Crime and Mystery Writers*, 1980, *Twentieth-Century Science-Fiction Writers*, 1981, and *1001 Midnights*, 1986. Editor of *Master of Villainy: A Biography of Sax Rohmer*, 1972, and co-editor of *Multiplying Villainies: Selected Mystery Criticism* by Anthony Boucher, 1973. Contributing editor of *Encyclopedia of Mystery and Detection*, 1976, and *Encyclopedia of Frontier and Western Fiction*, 1983. Contributor of introductions to works of John Dickson Carr, Sax Rohmer, Robert E. Howard, Christianna Brand, Frances and Richard Lockridge, Lewis B. Patten, and Bill Pronzini. Member of the editorial board of The Mystery Library, 1976–1981, and of the editorial board of The Collection of Classic Mysteries, Bantam Books. **Essays:** Jack M. Bickham; Will Cook; John H. Culp; Cliff Farrell; Norman A. Fox; Donald Hamilton; Philip Ketchum; Giles A. Lutz; John Myers Myers; Wayne D. Overholser; Robert Lewis Taylor.

BROWN, Ellie. Student of American studies, Derby College of Higher Education, Mickleover, Derbyshire. **Essay:** John Steinbeck.

BRYANT, Paul T. Dean of the Graduate School, Radford University, Virginia. Author of *H.L. Davis*, 1978. Editor, with Mark Busby and David Mogen, of *The Frontier Experience and the American Dream*, 1989. **Essays:** Mary Austin; H.L. Davis.

BUCCO, Martin. Professor of English, Colorado State University, Fort Collins. Author of *The Voluntary Tongue* (poetry), 1957, *The Age of Fable*, 1966, *Frank Waters*, 1969, *Wilbur Daniel Steele*, 1972, *E.W. Howe*, 1977, *René Wellek*, 1981, *Western American Literary Criticism*, 1984, and *Essays on Sinclair Lewis*, 1986, and of poetry, fiction, and criticism in periodicals. President, Western Literature Association, 1982. **Essay:** Frank Waters.

BUSBY, Mark. Associate Professor, Texas A and M University, College Station. Author of *Preston Jones*, 1983, *Lanford Wilson*, 1987, and *Ralph Ellison*, and of articles in *A Literary History of the American West*, *Western American Literature*, *MELUS*, *New Mexico Humanities Review*, and elsewhere. Editor, with Paul T. Bryant and David Mogen, of *The Frontier Experience and the American Dream*, 1989. Contributing editor of *Taking Stock: A Larry McMurtry Casebook*. **Essays:** Robert Flynn; Larry McMurtry.

CHEVALIER, Tracy. Editor and freelance writer in London. **Essay:** Katherine Anne Porter.

CLEARY, Michael. Professor of English, Broward Community College, Fort Lauderdale, Florida. Author of articles on Jack Schaefer, John Seelye, Thomas Berger, Flannery O'Connor, Richard Condon, Edward Albee, and Harold Pinter, in *Southwestern American Literature*, *Western American Literature*, *South Dakota Review*, *English Record*, *Theatre Annual*, and other periodicals. **Essays:** Charles Portis; John Seelye.

COCKS, J. Fraser, III. Curator of Special Collections, University of Oregon, Eugene. **Essays:** Frank Ramsay Adams; Willis Todhunter Ballard.

COHEN, Katharine Weston. Former Instructor in English and humanities, University of Arizona, Tucson, University of New Orleans, and Murray State University, Kentucky. Former author of *The Ibis*, newsletter of the New Orleans Audubon Society. Former editor of *Paw Prints*, newsletter of the Humane Society of Calloway County. **Essay:** Edgar Rice Burroughs.

CRIDER, Bill. See his own entry. **Essays:** Jack Ehrlich; Loren D. Estleman; Harry Whittington; Richard Wormser.

ETULAIN, Richard W. Professor of history and director, Center for the American West, University of New Mexico, Albuquerque. Author of *Western American Literature: A Bibliography*, 1972, *Owen Wister*, 1973, *The Frontier and the American West* (with Rodman W. Paul), 1977, *A Bibliographical Guide to the Study of Western American Literature*, 1982, *Conversations with Wallace Stegner: On Western History and Literature*, 1983, 1990, *Ernest Haycox*, 1988, and *The American West: A Twentieth-Century History* (with Michael P. Malone), 1989, and of many articles and bibliographies on aspects of western writing for *Journal of Popular Culture, Western American Literature, Western Historical Quarterly, Pacific Historical Review*, and other periodicals. Editor or co-editor of *The Popular Western*, 1974, *Jack London on the Road*, 1979, *The American Literary West*, 1980, *Fifty Western Writers*, 1982, *Western Films*, 1983, and *The Twentieth-Century West: Historical Interpretations*, 1989. Editor, Oklahoma Western Biographies Series. **Essays:** Don Berry; Jack London; Luke Short.

FEDRICK, Cassandra. Freelance writer. **Essays:** Ridgewell Cullum; Janet Dailey.

FERRES, John H. Professor of American thought and language, Michigan State University, East Lansing. Author of *Arthur Miller: A Reference Guide*, 1979. Editor of *Winesburg, Ohio* by Sherwood Anderson, 1966, *Twentieth-Century Interpretations of Arthur Miller's The Crucible*, 1972, and *Modern Commonwealth Literature*, 1977. **Essays:** Ralph Connor; Frederick Philip Grove; Sinclair Ross; Robert J.C. Stead.

FIEDLER, Leslie A. Samuel Clements Professor of English, State University of New York, Buffalo. Author of three novels, three collections of short stories, and several critical works, including *An End to Innocence*, 1955, *Love and Death in the American Novel*, 1960 (revised, 1966), *No! In Thunder*, 1960, *Waiting for the End*, 1964, *The Stranger in Shakespeare*, 1972, *Freaks*, 1978, and *The Inadvertent Epic*, 1979. Editor of several collections of essays.

FLANAGAN, John D. Freelance writer. **Essays:** Clifton Adams; Walt Coburn; Bernard De Voto; Robert Easton.

FLORA, Joseph M. Professor and Chair of the Department of English, University of North Carolina, Chapel Hill. President Elect, Western Literature Association, 1991. Author of *Vardis Fisher*, 1965, *William Ernest Henley*, 1970, *Frederick Manfred*, 1974, *Hemingway's Nick Adams*, 1982, and *Ernest Hemingway: A Study of the Short Fiction*, 1989. Editor of *The Cream of the Jest* by James Branch Cabell, 1975, *Southern Writers: A Biographical Dictionary* (with Robert Bain and Louis D. Rubin, Jr.), 1979, *Fifty Southern Writers Before 1900* (with Bain), 1987, and *Fifty Southern Writers After 1900* (with Bain), 1987. **Essay:** Wallace Stegner.

FOLSOM, James K. Former Chair of the Department of English, University of Colorado, Boulder. Author of *Man's Accidents and God's Purposes: Multiplicity in Hawthorne's Fiction*, 1963, *Timothy Flint*, 1965, *The American Western Novel*, 1966, and *Harvey Fergusson*, 1969. Editor of *The Western: A Collection of Critical Essays*, 1978. Died May 1988. **Essays:** Walter Van Tilburg Clark; Susan Ertz; Walter Gann; Will James; George Pattullo.

FOOTE, Cheryl J. Instructor, Albuquerque Technical Vocational Institute. Author of *Women of the New Mexico Frontier, 1846–1912*, 1990. **Essays:** Amelia Bean; Carol Ryrie Brink; Gwen Bristow; Douglas C. Jones.

FUCHS, Marcia G. Reference librarian and cataloguer, Guilford Free Library, Connecticut; reviewer for *Library Journal*. **Essays:** Paula Gunn Allen; Katharine Burt; Michael Dorris; Mary O'Hara; Walker A. Tompkins.

GALE, Robert L. Professor Emeritus of American literature, University of Pittsburgh. Author of *The Caught Image: Figurative Language in the Fiction of Henry James*, 1964, *Thomas Crawford, American Sculptor*, 1964, *Richard Henry Dana, Jr.*, 1969, *Francis Parkman*, 1973, *Plots and Characters in Works of Mark Twain*, 2 vols., 1973, *John Hay*, 1978, *Luke Short*, 1981, *Will Henry/Clay Fisher (Henry W. Allen)*, 1984, *Louis L'Amour*, 1985, and *A Henry James Encyclopedia*, 1989. **Essays:** Ernest Haycox; Louis L'Amour; Charles M. Russell.

GISH, Robert F. Professor of English, University of Northern Iowa, Cedar Falls. Author of *Hamlin Garland*, 1973, *Paul Horgan*, 1983, *Frontier's End: The Life and Literature of Harvey Fergusson*, 1988, *William Carlos Williams: The Short Fiction*, 1989, and *Songs of My Hunter Heart: A Family Kinship*, 1991. **Essays:** Rudolfo A. Anaya; Ray Hogan; Paul Horgan; Tomas Rivera; James Welch.

GLEASON, G. Dale. Member of the Department of Language and Literature, Hutchinson Community College, Kansas. **Essays:** Forrester Blake; Herbert Purdum; Stewart Edward White.

GROVER, Dorys C. Professor of English, East Texas State University, Commerce. Member of editorial advisory board, *Western American Literature* and *Yeats Eliot Review*; associate editor, *Kalki: Studies in James Branch Cabell* and *Journal of the American Studies Association of Texas*. President, American Studies Association of Texas. Author of three books, including *John Graves*, 1990, and of journal articles, short stories, and poetry. **Essays:** Frederick R. Bechdolt; Will Levington Comfort; Courtney Ryley Cooper; John Graves; Jackson Gregory; Frank Gruber; Elmer Kelton; Hart Stilwell.

HARBOTTLE, Philip J. Senior administrative assistant, Blyth Valley Borough Council. Part-time literary agent and bibliographer. Author of *The Multi-Man: A Bibliographic Study of John Russell Fearn*, 1968, and *Vultures of the Void: British Science-Fiction Paperbacks and Magazines, 1946–56*, 1991. Editor, *Vision of Tomorrow*, 1969–70. **Essays:** Norman Lazenby; E.C. Tubb.

HARVEY, John. Freelance author of novels and screenplays—western series, television adaptations, and television series (e.g., *Hard Cases, Hart the Regulator, Herne the Hunter, Hawk*). **Essay:** Jim Harrison.

HASSELSTROM, Linda M. Rancher and professional writer. Author of two books of poetry, and of *Windbreak: A Woman Rancher on the Northern Plains*, 1987, and *Going over East: Reflections of a Woman Rancher*, 1987. Editor of *James Clyman: Journal of a Mountain Man*, 1984. **Essay:** Edward R. Zietlow.

HENDERSON, Sam H. Former Professor of English, University of North Texas, Denton. Author of *Fred Gipson*, 1967, and of articles on English Renaissance literature. Editor of *Poetry: A Thematic Approach*, 1968, and former joint editor of the Southern Writers Series. **Essays:** George Sessions Perry; Ross Santee.

HERNDON, Jerry A. Professor of English, Murray State University, Kentucky. Author of articles on Emerson, Hawthorne, Melville, Whitman, Faulkner, Hemingway, Emily Dickinson, Robert Penn Warren, and Edward Abbey, in *American Literature*, *South Atlantic Quarterly*, *Christianity and Literature*, *Western American Literature*, *REAL: The Yearbook of Research in English and American Literature*, and other periodicals. **Essays:** E.B. Mann; Jack O'Connor.

HOLMAN, David Marion. Former Assistant Professor of English; Texas A and M University, College Station. Died May 1988. **Essays:** Howard Fast; Paul I. Wellman.

HOLMES, B.J. See his own entry. **Essays:** Ross Dexter; Jeff Sadler; E.G. Stokoe; David Whitehead.

HOLTZ, William V. Professor of English, University of Missouri, Columbia. Author of *Image and Immortality: A Study of "Tristam Shandy"*, 1970, and a forthcoming biography of Rose Wilder Lane, and of many articles and reviews. Editor of *Two Tales by Charlotte Brontë: "The Secret" and "Lily Hart"*, 1978, and *Travels with Zenobia: Paris to Albania by Model T Ford* by Rose Wilder Lane and Helen Boylston, 1983. **Essay:** Rose Wilder Lane.

HUDMAN, Jo M. Freelance writer; work included in anthologies of poetry and short stories. **Essay:** Jessamyn West.

HUTCHINSON, W.H. Freelance writer. Author of *A Bar Cross Man: The Life and Personal Writings of Eugene Manlove Rhodes*, 1956, and a bibliography of Rhodes. Editor of *The Rhodes Reader*, 1957. **Essays:** Eugene Cunningham; Hal G. Evarts, Sr.; Eugene Manlove Rhodes.

JACKSON, Joe. Freelance writer. **Essays:** Edwin Booth; Leslie Ernenwein; E.E. Halleran; Kingsley West.

JONES, Daryl. Professor of English and Dean, College of Arts and Sciences, Boise State University, Idaho. Author of *The Dime Novel Western*, 1978, and *Someone Going Home Late* (poetry), 1990, and of articles on Cooper, Poe, Twain, Fitzgerald, and poetry in *New Orleans Review*, *Sewanee Review*, *TriQuarterly*, and other periodicals. **Essays:** William Wallace Cook; W. Bert Foster; Frank Norris; St. George Rathborne; Jane Gilmore Rushing; Cornelius Shea; John H. Whitson.

KAYE, Frances W. Associate Professor of English, University of Nebraska, Lincoln. Editor, *Great Plains Quarterly*. Author of articles in *Alberta*, *Essays in Canadian Writing*, *Prairie Schooner*, *MOSAIC*, and other journals. Editor, with Frederick C. Luebke and Gary Moulton, of *Mapping the North American Plains*, 1987. **Essay:** Margaret Laurence.

KELLEY, George. Professor of business administration, Erie Community College, Buffalo, New York. Contributor to *Twentieth-Century Science-Fiction Writers*, *Twentieth-Century Crime and Mystery Writers*, *Mass Market Publishing in America*, and *Poisoned Pen*. **Essays:** Marvin H. Albert; Tim Champlin; Don Coldsmith; Bill Crider; Ron Hansen; John Jakes; Will F. Jenkins; Richard Jessup; Steven C. Lawrence; Thomas McGuane; Nelson Nye; Frank O'Rourke; James M. Reasoner; Shepard Rifkin; Howard Rigsby; Louis Trimble; G. Clifton Wisler.

LANDRUM, Larry N. Associate Professor of English, Michigan State University, East Lansing. Author of the chapter on detective fiction in *Handbook of American Popular Culture*, 1978. Co-editor of *Dimensions of Detective Fiction*, 1976. **Essay:** Jack Schaefer.

LANSDALE, Joe R. See his own entry. **Essays:** Forrest Carter; George Garland; Robert E. Howard; Elmore Leonard; T.V. Olsen.

LAWSON-PEEBLES, Robert. Lecturer in American and Commonwealth arts, University of Exeter. Review editor of *Landscape Research*. Author of *Landscape and Written Expression in Revolutionary America*, 1988. Co-editor of *Views of American Landscapes*, 1989. **Essay:** Harold Bell Wright.

LEE, James W. Professor of English, North Texas State University, Denton; former editor of *Studies in the Novel*. Author of *William Humphrey*, 1967, *Southwestern American Literature: A Bibliography* (with John Q. Anderson and Edwin W. Gaston, Jr.), 1980, *Classics of Texas Fiction*, 1987, and of several articles on western literature. Editor, *Benjamin Capps and the South Plains: A Literary Relationship* by Lawrence Clayton, 1990. **Essays:** Benjamin Capps; James Crumley; Al Dewlen; William Humphrey; David Lindsey; Clay Reynolds.

LEE, L.L. Professor of English, Western Washington University, Bellingham. Author of *Walter Van Tilburg Clark*, 1973, *Vladimir Nabokov*, 1976, and *Virginia Sorensen* (with Sylvia B. Lee), 1978. Co-editor of *The Westering Experience in American Literature*, 1977, *Women, Women Writers, and the West*, 1979, and *A Directory of Scholarly Journals in English Languages and Literature*, 1990. **Essay:** Virginia Sorensen.

LINAKER, Mike. See his own entry. **Essay:** B.J. Holmes.

LUCIA, Ellis. Freelance writer. Author of biographies and several books on the American West, including *The Saga of Ben Holladay*, 1959, *Tough Men, Tough Country*, 1963, *This Land Around Us*, 1969, *Owyhee Trail* (with Mike Hanley), 1974, *The Big Woods*, 1975, *Magic Valley*, 1976, *Seattle's Sisters of Providence*, 1978, and *Tillamook Burn Country: A Pictorial History*, 1983. Editor of *The Gunfighters*, 1971, and *Oregon's Golden Years*. 1976. **Essays:** Robert Ormond Case; Nard Jones; Peter B. Kyne; Frank C. Robertson; James Stevens.

LYON, Thomas J. Professor of English, Utah State University, Logan; editor of *Western American Literature*. Author of *John Muir*, 1972, and *Frank Waters*, 1973. Editor of *This Incomparable Land: A Book of American Nature Writing*, 1989.

MACDONALD, Andrew. Academic director of Intensive English Program, Loyola University, New Orleans. Author of articles on Jonson, Shakespeare, English as a second language, science fiction, and popular culture. **Essay:** E.L. Doctorow.

MACDONALD, Gina. Assistant Professor of English, Loyola University, New Orleans. Author of articles on southwestern writers, popular culture, science fiction, and Shakespearean influences. **Essays:** Rex Beach; W.F. Bragg; Dudley Dean; Donald Bayne Hobart; Alistair MacLean.

MADDEN, David W. Professor of American and Irish literatures, California State University, Sacramento. Author of articles on John Seelye, John Hawkes, Thomas Berger, John Barth, James M. Cain, and a bibliography of J.P. Donleavy, in *Western American Literature*, *South Dakota Review*, *Armchair Detective*, and other periodicals, and of a forthcoming book on Paul West. Guest editor of a special issue on Paul West in *Review of Contemporary Fiction*, Spring 1991. **Essay:** David Wagoner.

MAGUIRE, James H. Professor of English, Boise State University, Idaho; since 1971 co-editor of the Western Writers Series; member of the board of editors, *Literary History of the American West*. Author of *Mary Hallock Foote*, 1972. Editor of *My Seasons* by Daniel Long, 1977, and *The Literature of Idaho*, 1986; section editor of *A Literary History of the American West*, 1987. **Essay:** Harry Leon Wilson.

McCLURE, Charlotte S. Associate Professor of English and director of Honors Program, Georgia State University, Atlanta. Author of *Gertrude Atherton* (monograph), 1976, *Gertrude Atherton* (book), 1979, articles on Atherton and other American women writers, and a bibliography of autobiographies by American women. **Essays:** Gertrude Atherton; Janet Lewis.

McREYNOLDS, Douglas J. Provost, Upper Iowa University, Fayette. Author of articles on American literature and folklore in *Midwest Review*, *Denver Quarterly*, *Literature/Film Quarterly*, *Rocky Mountain Review*, *North Dakota Quarterly*, and other periodicals. **Essay:** Robert P. Day.

MELDRUM, Barbara Howard. Professor of English, University of Idaho, Moscow. President of Western Literature Association, 1989. Author and editor of books and articles on western literature. **Essays:** O.E. Rølvaag; Sophus K. Winther.

MELDRUM, P.R. Freelance writer. Worked with the Public Record Office, London, for 11 years. **Essays:** Luke Allan; Gordon C. Baldwin; David Ernest Bingley; Jim Bowden; A.M. Chisholm; Kenneth A. Fowler; Ray Gaulden; Arthur Henry Gooden; James B. Hendryx; Tex Houston; Amos Moore; William Byron Mowery; Frederick Niven; James Powell; John Prescott; Roe Richmond; Donald S. Rowland; C.M. Sublette; Dale Waldo; Gordon Young.

MERLOCK, Ray. Member of the Department of Language and Fine Arts, University of South Carolina, Spartanburg. **Essays:** J.T. Edson; Robert MacLeod.

MESSENT, Peter. Lecturer in American studies, University of Nottingham. Author of *New Readings of the American Novel*, 1990. Editor of *The Literature of the Occult: Twentieth-Century Views*, 1981; co-editor of *Henry James: Selected Tales*, 1982. **Essays:** Joan Didion; Susan Glaspell; Ishmael Reed; Elinore Pruitt Stewart.

METZ, Leon C. Historical consultant in private practice; also lectures on historical subjects, and leads historical tours. Author of many books on western history, most recently *Turning Points of El Paso, Texas*, 1985, *Desert Army: Fort Bliss on the Texas Border*, 1988, *Border: The U.S.–Mexico Line*, 1989, and *Southern New Mexico Empire: Frank O. Papen and the First National Bank of Dana Ana County*, 1991. **Essays:** Fred H. Grove; Robert McCaig.

MOGEN, David. Professor of English, Colorado State Univerity, Fort Collins. Author of *Wilderness Visions: Science Fiction Westerns*, 1982, *Ray Bradbury*, 1986, and articles on Owen Wister, Henry James, science fiction, and frontier writing in *Southwestern American Literature*, *American Literary Realism*, *Studies in Popular Culture*, *Genre*, and other periodicals. Editor, with Paul T. Bryant and Mark Busby, of *The Frontier Experience and the American Dream*, 1989. **Essay:** Owen Wister.

MORRISON, Daryl. Head of the Holt-Atherton Department for Special Collections, University of the Pacific Libraries, Stockton, California. Author of a chapter in *Women in Oklahoma* by Melvena Thurman, 1982, and "Discovery of the West," in *Pacific Historian*, Spring 1987. Compiler, with Cynthia Stevenson, of *The John Muir Papers*, 1990. **Essays:** Maxine Hong Kingston; Zola Ross: Charles Marquis Warren.

MURRAY, David. Lecturer in American studies, University of Nottingham. Author of *Forked Tongues: Speech, Writing and Representation in North American Indian Texts*. **Essay:** Louise Erdrich.

NAYLOR, Clarence. Farmer and freelance writer. Author of several articles and stories. **Essay:** Frank Fields.

NELSON, Nancy Owen. Instructor in English, Henry Ford Community College, Dearborn, Michigan. Co-editor of *The Selected Correspondence of Frederick Manfred: 1932–1954*, 1989. **Essay:** Frederick Manfred.

NESBITT, John D. Member of the Faculty, Eastern Wyoming College, Torrington. Author of articles on Louis L'Amour, the popular Western, Wyoming fiction, and of short stories, in *West Wind Review*, *Western American Literature*, *South Dakota Review*, and other periodicals. **Essays:** Zane Grey; A.B. Guthrie, Jr.; Dee Linford; Caroline Lockhart; Gray McCarthy; Robert Roripaugh.

NEVINS, Francis M., Jr. Professor of Law, St. Louis University School of Law, Missouri. Author of four mystery novels (*Publish and Perish*, 1975, *Corrupt and Ensnare*, 1978, *The 120-Hour Clock*, 1986, and *The Ninety Million Dollar Mouse*, 1987), two biographical-critical books about other crime writers (*Royal Bloodline: Ellery Queen, Author and Detective*, 1974, and *Cornell Woolrich: First You Dream, Then You Die*, 1988), and of about 40 mystery short stories and many articles about the genre; also author of *The Films of Hopalong Cassidy*, 1988. Editor of more than a dozen mystery anthologies and collections. **Essays:** Clarence E. Mulford; Jonas Ward.

NOLAN, Fred. See his own entry as Frederick H. Christian. **Essay:** Oliver Strange.

PAULSON, Kristoffer F. Associate Professor of English, Simon Fraser University, Burnaby, British Columbia. Author of articles on O.E. Rølvaag in *Melus*, *Norwegian-American Studies*, and other periodicals. **Essay:** Herbert Krause.

PETERSEN, Carol Miles. Author of a forthcoming biography of Bess Streeter Aldrich, and of several articles and poems. **Essay:** Bess Streeter Aldrich.

PEYER, Bernd C. Lecturer, Johann Wolfgang Goethe-Universität, Frankfurt. Editor of *The Singing Spirit: Early Short Stories by North American Indians*, 1989. **Essay:** Pauline Johnson.

PHILO, Simon. Post-graduate student, University of Nottingham. **Essay:** Raymond Carver.

PIEKARSKI, Vicki. Editor, with Jon Tuska, of *The American West in Fiction: An Anthology*, 1982, *Encyclopedia of Frontier and Western Fiction*, 1983, and *The Frontier Experience: A Reader's Guide to the Life and Literature of the American West*, 1984; editor of *Westward the Women: An Anthology of Western Stories by Women*, 1984. **Essays:** Jane Barry; P.A. Bechko; Ivan Doig; Marilyn Durham; Dorothy Gardiner; Lee Hoffman; Honoré Willsie Morrow; Lucia St. Clair Robson; Marah Ellis Ryan; Dorothy Scarborough.

PILKINGTON, William T. Member of the Department of English, Tarleton State University, Stephenville, Texas; member of the board of editors, *Literary History of the American West*. Author of *William A. Owens*, 1968, *My Blood's Country: Studies in Southwestern Literature*, 1973, *Harvey Fergusson*, 1975, and *Imagining Texas*, 1981. Editor of *Western Movies* (with Don Graham), 1979, and *Critical Essays on the Western American Novel*, 1980. **Essays:** Richard Bradford; Edwin Corle; Fred Gipson; O. Henry; Alan LeMay; John W. Thomason, Jr.; Frank X. Tolbert.

PRONZINI, Bill. See his own entry. **Essays:** J.O. Barnwell; J.L. Bouma; Will C. Brown; Joseph Chadwick; Giff Cheshire; Merle Constiner; H.A. De Rosso; Steve Frazee; C. William Harrison; Chuck Martin; Tom Roan; William O. Turner; William E. Vance.

PUTNAM, Ann L. Instructor of English, University of Puget Sound, Takoma, Washington. Author of essays in *South Dakota Review*, *Hemingway Review*, *Western American Literature Quarterly*, and in *Hemingway's Neglected Short Fiction*, edited by Susan Beegel. **Essay:** Lois Phillips Hudson.

ROMINES, Ann. Associate Professor of English, George Washington University, Washington, D.C. **Essay:** Laura Ingalls Wilder.

ROSOWSKI, Susan J. Professor of English, University of Nebraska, Lincoln. Author of *Voyage Perilous: Willa Cather's Romanticism*, 1987. Editor of *Women and Western American Literature* (with Helen W. Stauffer), 1982, and *Cather Studies, vol. 1*, 1990. **Essay:** Willa Cather.

ROVIT, Earl. Professor of English, City College of New York. Author of *Herald to Chaos: The Novels of Elizabeth Madox Roberts*, 1960, *Ernest Hemingway*, 1963, *Saul Bellow*, 1967, and three novels—*The Player King*, 1965, *A Far Cry*, 1967, and *Crossings*, 1973. Editor of *Saul Bellow: A Collection of Critical Essays*, 1975. **Essay:** Elizabeth Madox Roberts.

SADLER, Jeff. See his own entry. **Essays:** Jack Borg; Russ Brannigan; Matt Chisholm; Ross Dexter; Allan Vaughan Elston; Robert Eynon; Christopher Flood; John Langley; Noel M. Loomis; Mason Macrae; Joseph Millard; Arthur Nickson; John Prebble; Ron Pritchett; William Rayner; John L. Shelley; Charles H. Snow; Mike Stotter; W.C. Tuttle; Tom West.

SCHECKTER, John. Assistant Professor of English, Long Island University, Westchester, New York. Author of articles in *Western American Literature* and *Modern Fiction Studies*, and of the forthcoming *The Australian Novel: An Introduction for American Readers*. **Essay:** Thomas Savage.

SCHULTZ, Lee. Member of the Department of English, Stephen F. Austin State University, Nacogdoches, Texas; editor of *REAL: Re Arts & Letters* journal. **Essay:** Joe R. Lansdale.

SCHWARTZ, Patricia Roth. Writer and psychotherapist. Author of *Hungers* (poetry), 1978, and *The Names of the Moons of Mars* (short fiction), 1989. Women's poetry editor of *Bay Windows*. **Essay:** Barbara Wilson.

SEIDEL, Kathryn Lee. Associate Professor, University of Central Florida, Orlando. Author of *The Southern Belle in the American Novel*, 1985, and *Zora in Florida*, 1991. **Essay:** Jean Stafford.

SHAW, Walter. Freelance writer. Former chair of Chesterfield Writers' Group; editor of *A Better Mousetrap* (group anthology), 1989. **Essay:** Tony Hillerman.

SMITH, Herbert F. Professor of English, University of Victoria, British Columbia. Author of *John Muir*, 1969, and *The Popular Novel in America 1865–1920*, 1980. **Essays:** Andy Adams; Thomas Berger; Roger Pocock; Frank H. Spearman.

SONNICHSEN, C.L. Former Senior editor of the *Journal of Arizona History*, Tucson, and member of the staff of the Arizona Historical Society, Tucson. Author of 20 books on western history and writing, including *Cowboys and Cattle Kings*, 1950, *The Mescalero Apaches*, 1958, *Colonel Greene and the Copper Skyrocket*, 1974, *From Hopalong to Hud: Thoughts on Western Fiction*, 1978, *The Ambidextrous Historian*, 1981, *Tucson: The Life and Times of an American City* 1982, *Outlaw: On the Dodge with Baldy Russell*, 1984, and *Pioneer Heritage*, 1984. Editor of *The Southwest in Life and Literature*, 1962, *The Laughing West*, 1988, and *Texas Humoresque*, 1990. Died 1991. **Essays:** Max Evans; John Reese.

SPECK, Ernest B. Retired Professor of English, Sul Ross State University, Alpine, Texas. Author of *Mody C. Boatright*, 1971, *Benjamin Capps*, 1981, and of articles on folklore and the teaching of English. Editor of *Mody Boatright, Folklorist*, 1973. **Essay:** George Milburn.

STAUFFER, Helen. Emeritus Professor of English, Kearney State College, Nebraska. Author of *Mari Sandoz, Story Catcher of the Plains*, 1982, and of many articles. Editor, with Susan J. Rosowski, of *Woman and Western American Literature*, 1982, and of a forthcoming volume of Sandoz's letters. **Essays:** Wayne C. Lee; Martha Ostenso; Mari Sandoz.

STOTT, Jon C. Professor of English, University of Alberta, Edmonton. Founding director, Children's Literature Association. Author of *Children's Literature from A to Z*, 1984, and *A Guide to Authors and Illustrators* (with Raymond E. Jones), 1988. Editor, with Anita Moss, of *The Family of Stories: A Children's Literature Anthology*, 1986. **Essay:** Roderick Haig-Brown.

STOTTER, Mike. See his own entry. **Essays:** Denver Bardwell; Robert W. Broomall; Pete Danvers; Allan K. Echols; Wick Evans; John Russell Fearn; Oscar Friend; Ed Gorman; George G. Gilman; John Harvey; Laurence James; H. Paul Jeffers; Holt Madison; Cormac McCarthy; V.G.C. Norwood; Samuel Anthony Peeples; Hugh Pendexter; T.C.H. Pendower; Gladwell Richardson; Charles W. Sanders; Charles S. Strong; C. Hall Thompson; Angus Wells.

SWADLEY, Don R. Former member of the Department of English, University of Texas, Arlington. **Essays:** Loula Grace Erdman; Edwin Shrake.

TRIMBLE, Martha Scott. Professor Emeritus of English, Colorado State University, Fort Collins. Author of *N. Scott Momaday*, 1973, and the chapter on Momaday in *Fifty Western Writers*, 1982. **Essays:** N. Scott Momaday; Wayne Ude.

TUSKA, Jon. Author of *Philo Vance: The Life and Times of S.S. Van Dine* (with others), 1971, *The Films of Mae West*, 1973, *The Filming of the West*, 1976, *The Detective in Hollywood*, 1978, *Billy the Kid: A Handbook*, 1983, *The American West in Film: Critical Approaches to the Western*, 1985, *A Variable Harvest*, 1990, and *They Went Thataway: A History of Western Film Production*, 1992. Editor, with Piekarski, of *The American West in Fiction: An Anthology*, 1982, *Encyclopedia of Frontier and Western Fiction*, 1983, and *The Frontier Experience: A Reader's Guide to the Life and Literature of the American West*, 1984. **Essays:** Ann Ahlswede; Henry Wilson Allen; Verne Athanas; James Warner Bellah; Frank Bonham; Matt Braun; W.R. Burnett; Dane Coolidge; Tom Curry; Peter Dawson; Harvey Fergusson; Bill Gulick; William Heuman; L.P. Holmes; General Charles King; H.H. Knibbs; Frederic S. Remington; Frank Roderus; Les Savage, Jr; Gordon D. Shirreffs.

UDE, Wayne. See his own entry. **Essays:** Ralph Beer; Gerald Haslam; Norman Maclean; Leslie Marmon Silko.

ULPH, Owen. Taught at Reed College, Portland, Oregon, for 30 years. Author of two books on the cowboy, *The Fiddleback: Lore of the Line Camp*, 1981, and *The Leather Throne*, 1982. **Essay:** Borden Chase.

VELIE, Alan R. Member of the Department of English, University of Oklahoma, Norman. Author of *American Indian Literature*, 1979. **Essays:** N. Scott Momaday; Gerald Vizenor.

WALKER, Dale L. Director of Texas Western Press, University of Texas, El Paso. Author of books on John Reed, Jack London, C.L. Sonnichsen, Ted Parsons, and Januarius MacGahan. Editor of many anthologies including *In a Far Country: Jack London's Tales of the West*, 1987. "Westerns" book columnist for the *Rocky Mountain News*, Denver. **Essays:** Barry Cord; William R. Cox; Jack Cummings; James Oliver Curwood; Dan Parkinson; Giles Tippette; Richard S. Wheeler; Bryan Woolley.

WALSH, George. Publisher and freelance writer. **Essays:** S. Omar Barker; Harold Bindloss; Harry Sinclair Drago; Davis Dresser; Paul Durst; William Eastlake; T.T. Flynn; L.L. Foreman; Hamlin Garland; Alfred Henry Lewis; Charles L. McNichols; D'Arcy McNickle; James A. Michener; Lewis B. Patten; William MacLeod Raine; Charles Alden Seltzer; John Williams.

WEST, John O. Professor of English, University of Texas, El Paso. Author of *Tom Lea: Artist in Two Mediums*, 1967, *Mexican-American Folklore*, 1988, and *Cowboy Folk Humor*, 1990, and articles on western history, writing, and folklore in *Western Folklore, Journal of American Folklore*, and other periodicals. **Essays:** Elliott Arnold; Allan R. Bosworth; Walter Noble Burns; Vardis Fisher; Tom Lea.

WHITEHEAD, David. See his own entry. **Essays:** Chuck Adams; Patrick E. Andrews; Geoffrey John Barrett; Wayne Barton; Samuel P. Bishop; Terrell L. Bowers; Lou Cameron; Chet Cunningham; Emerson Dodge; Mark Donovan; Cyril Donson; Saran Essex; Mark Falcon; William Fieldhouse; Lee Floren; Jerome Gardner; Jack Giles; Lee F. Gregson; Leonard Gribble; Marshall Grover; Ben Haas; Kirk Hamilton; Vic J. Hanson; Terry C. Johnston; Hal Jons; Leo P. Kelley; J.D. Kincaid; Albert King; Will C. Knott; Mike Linaker; Elliot Long; Johnny Mack Bride; Paul McAfee; Peter McCurtin; Jim Miller; D.B. Newton; Mike Newton; Lauran Paine; Bernard Palmer; Gary Paulsen; Bill Pronzini; Robert J. Randisi; Bret Rey; Shirlaw Johnston Rodgers; W.E.D. Ross; M.M. Rowan; Amy Sadler; John Sharpe; Mike Skinner; L.D. Tetlow; Robert E. Trevathan; L.J. Washburn; Logan Winters.

WILD, Peter. Professor of English, University of Arizona, Tucson. Editorial positions on staffs of *Not Man Apart*, *Puerto Del Sol*, *U.S. Water News*, and other periodicals. Author of many books, most recently *The Peaceable Kingdom*, 1985, *John C. Van Dyke*, 1988, *The Brides of Christ*, 1990, and *The Desert Reader*, 1991. **Essays:** Edward Abbey; Myron Brinig; William Kittredge; John Nichols.

WOLFE, John L. Freelance writer and researcher. **Essays:** Chester Allen; Robert Vaughn Bell; Celeste De Blasis; Steven M. Krauzer; Charles O. Locke; David Nevin; Agnes Smedley; William O. Steele; Stack Sutton; James Alexander Thom; Anna Lee Waldo.

WYDEVEN, Joseph J. Professor of English and Chair of Humanities Division, Bellevue College, Nebraska. Author of several articles on Wright Morris in *Midwest Quarterly*, *Midamerica*, *Western American Literature*, and in *Women and Western American Literature*, edited by Helen W. Stauffer and Susan J. Rosowski, 1982, and *Under the Sun: Myth and Realism in Western American Literature*, edited by Barbara Meldrum, 1985, and of the forthcoming book *A Poetics of Vision: The Fiction and Photography of Wright Morris*. **Essay:** Wright Morris.

WYLDER, Delbert E. Professor of English, Murray State University, Kentucky. Author of *Hemingway's Heroes*, 1969, and two books on Emerson Hough. Associate editor, *Western American Literature*, 1966–68. **Essays:** J.P.S. Brown; Emerson Hough; Clair Huffaker.

YOUNG, Joseph A. Assistant Professor of English, University of Wisconsin, La Crosse. **Essay:** Oscar Micheaux.

WITHDRAWN FROM
JUNIATA COLLEGE LIBRARY

DO NOT REMOVE
THIS BOOK FROM
THE LIBRARY